# HARRAP'S

# French

## AND

# English

## POCKET

## DICTIONARY

Second Edition

D0002051

Mc Graw Hill Education

New York  Chicago  San Francisco  Athens  London  Madrid
Mexico City  Milan  New Delhi  Singapore  Sydney  Toronto

2 3 4 5 6 7 8 9 10   QLM/QLM   1 0 9 8 7 6 5

ISBN   978-0-07-181445-4
MHID       0-07-181445-0

Library of Congress Control Number:  2013950200

Words considered to be trademarks have been designated in this dictionary by the symbol ®. However, no judgment is implied concerning the legal status of any trademark by virtue of the presence or absence of such a symbol.

McGraw-Hill Education products are available at special quantity discounts to use as premiums and sales promotions or for use in corporate training programs. To contact a representative, please visit the Contact Us pages at www.mhprofessional.com.

# Contents

# Preface

This new edition of the Harrap's French and English Pocket Dictionary aims to provide all students of French at beginner and intermediate level with a reliable, comprehensive and user-friendly dictionary in a compact form. The clear, systematic layout of information makes it an easy-to-use tool and the extensive coverage of vocabulary should ensure that it becomes an invaluable resource.

This dictionary covers all essential words and phrases and packs a wealth of vocabulary into its pages. Colloquial and idiomatic language is well represented, as are words from a wide range of specialized fields, with particular emphasis on those where new coinages often appear, such as new technologies, the environment and the Internet.

Extra help is provided in the form of a supplement, which includes a complete list of irregular French verbs, a 29-page conversation guide with a feature on using the telephone, and a grammar section covering all the basics of French language, with helpful example sentences to illustrate usage.

# Abbreviations

| English | Abbr | Français |
|---|---|---|
| gloss | = | glose |
| [introduces an explanation] | | [introduit une explication] |
| cultural equivalent | ≃ | équivalent culturel |
| [introduces a translation | | [introduit une traduction |
| which has a roughly | | dont les connotations dans |
| equivalent status | | la langue cible sont |
| in the target language] | | comparables] |
| abbreviation | *abbr, abr* | abréviation |
| adjective | *adj* | adjectif |
| administration | *Admin* | administration |
| adverb | *adv* | adverbe |
| agriculture | *Agr* | agriculture |
| American English | *Am* | anglais américain |
| anatomy | *Anat* | anatomie |
| formerly | *Anc* | anciennement |
| architecture | *Archit* | architecture |
| art | *Bx-Arts* | beaux-arts |
| article | *art* | article |
| astronomy | *Astron* | astronomie |
| Australian English | *Austr* | anglais australien |
| cars | *Auto* | automobile |
| auxiliary | *aux* | auxiliaire |
| aviation | *Aviat* | aviation |
| Belgian French | *Belg* | belgicisme |
| biology | *Biol* | biologie |
| botany | *Bot* | botanique |
| British English | *Br* | anglais britannique |
| Canadian French | *Can* | canadianisme |
| chemistry | *Chem, Chim* | chimie |
| cinema | *Cin, Ciné* | cinéma |
| commerce | *Comm* | commerce |
| comparative | *compar* | comparatif |
| computing | *Comput* | informatique |
| conjunction | *conj* | conjonction |
| building industry | *Constr* | construction |
| cooking | *Culin* | cuisine |
| definite | *def, déf* | défini |
| demonstrative | dem, *dém* | démonstratif |
| ecology | *Ecol, Écol* | écologie |
| economics | *Econ, Écon* | économie |
| electricity, electronics | *Elec, Élec* | électricité, électronique |
| horseriding | *Équit* | équitation |
| especially | esp | surtout |
| euphemism | *Euph* | euphémisme |
| exclamation, exclamatory | *excl* | exclamation, exclamatif |
| feminine | *f* | féminin |

| | | |
|---|---|---|
| familiar | *Fam* | familier |
| figurative | *Fig* | figuré |
| finance | *Fin* | finance |
| football | *Ftbl, Foot* | football |
| generally | *gen, gén* | généralement |
| geography | *Geog, Géog* | géographie |
| geology | *Geol, Géol* | géologie |
| geometry | *Geom, Géom* | géométrie |
| grammar | *Gram* | grammaire |
| gymnastics | *Gym* | gymnastique |
| history | *Hist* | histoire |
| humorous | *Hum* | humoristique |
| impersonal | *impers* | impersonnel |
| industry | *Ind* | industrie |
| indefinite | *indef, indéf* | indéfini |
| interrogative | *interr* | interrogatif |
| invariable | *inv* | invariable |
| ironic | *Iron* | ironique |
| journalism | *Journ* | journalisme |
| law | *Jur* | droit |
| linguistics | *Ling* | linguistique |
| literary | *Liter, Litt* | littéraire |
| masculine | *m* | masculin |
| mathematics | *Math* | mathématique |
| medicine | *Med, Méd* | médecine |
| meteorology | *Met, Météo* | météorologie |
| military | *Mil* | militaire |
| music | *Mus* | musique |
| noun | *n* | nom |
| shipping | *Naut* | nautisme |
| feminine noun | *nf* | nom féminin |
| feminine plural noun | *nfpl* | nom féminin pluriel |
| masculine noun | *nm* | nom masculin |
| masculine and feminine noun | *nmf* | nom masculin et féminin |
| masculine plural noun | *nmpl* | nom masculin pluriel |
| plural noun | *npl* | nom pluriel |
| computing | *Ordinat* | ordinateurs, informatique |
| pejorative | *Pej, Péj* | péjoratif |
| personal | *pers* | personnel |
| philosophy | *Phil* | philosophie |
| photography | *Photo* | photographie |
| physics | *Phys* | physique |
| plural | *pl* | pluriel |
| politics | *Pol* | politique |
| possessive | *poss* | possessif |
| past participle | *pp* | participe passé |
| prefix | *pref, préf* | préfixe |
| preposition | *prep, prép* | préposition |
| present participle | *pres p* | participe présent |

| pronoun | *pron* | pronom |
| psychology | *Psych* | psychologie |
| past tense | *pt* | prétérit |
| something | *qch* | quelque chose |
| somebody | *qn* | quelqu'un |
| registered trademark | ® | marque déposée |
| radio | *Rad* | radio |
| rail | *Rail* | chemin de fer |
| relative | *rel* | relatif |
| religion | *Rel* | religion |
| somebody | *sb* | quelqu'un |
| school | *Sch, Scol* | domaine scolaire |
| Scottish English | *Scot* | anglais d'Écosse |
| singular | *sg* | singulier |
| something | *sth* | quelque chose |
| suffix | *suff* | suffixe |
| superlative | *superl* | superlatif |
| technology | *Tech* | technologie |
| telecommunications | *Tel, Tél* | télécommunications |
| very informal | *t Fam* | très familier |
| theatre | *Theat, Théât* | théâtre |
| television | *TV* | télévision |
| typography, printing | *Typ* | typographie, imprimerie |
| university | *Univ* | domaine universitaire |
| usually | *usu* | généralement |
| verb | *v* | verbe |
| very informal | *v Fam* | très familier |
| intransitive verb | *vi* | verbe intransitif |
| reflexive verb | *vpr* | verbe pronominal |
| transitive verb | *vt* | verbe transitif |
| inseparable transitive verb [eg: he **looks after** the children] | *vt insep* | verbe transitif à particule inséparable |
| separable transitive verb [eg: she **sent** the present **back** or she **sent back** the present] | *vt sep* | verbe transitif à particule séparable |
| vulgar | *vulg* | vulgaire |
| zoology | *Zool* | zoologie |

All other labels are written in full.

# French pronunciation

French pronunciation is shown in this dictionary using the symbols of the IPA (International Phonetic Alphabet). In the table below, examples of French words using these sounds are given, followed by English words which have a similar sound. Where there is no near-equivalent in English, an explanation is given.

| IPA symbol | French example | English example |
|---|---|---|
| **Consonants** | | |
| [b] | bébé | but |
| [d] | donner | door |
| [f] | forêt | fire |
| [g] | gare | get |
| [ʒ] | jour | pleasure |
| [k] | carte | kitten |
| [l] | lire | lonely |
| [m] | maman | mat |
| [n] | ni | now |
| [ŋ] | parking | singing |
| [ɲ] | campagne | canyon |
| [p] | patte | pat |
| [r] | rare | Like an English /r/ but pronounced at the back of the throat |
| [s] | soir | sit |
| [ʃ] | chose | sham |
| [t] | table | tap |
| [v] | valeur | value |
| [z] | zéro | zero |
| **Vowels** | | |
| [a] | chat | cat |
| [ɑ] | âge | gasp |
| [e] | été | bay |
| [ɛ] | père | bed |
| [ə] | le | amend |
| [ø] | deux | Does not exist in English : [e] pronounced with the lips rounded |
| [œ] | seul | curtain |
| [i] | vite | bee – not quite as long as the English [i:] |
| [ɔ] | donner | cot – slightly more open than the English /o/ |
| [o] | chaud | daughter – but higher than its English equivalent |

| IPA symbol | French example | English example |
|------------|----------------|-----------------|
| [u] | tout | **you** – but shorter than its English equivalent |
| [y] | voit**u**re | Does not exist in English: [i] with lips rounded |
| [ɑ̃] | enf**an**t | Nasal sound pronounced lower and further back in the mouth than [ɔ̃] |
| **Vowels** | | |
| [ɛ̃] | v**in** | Nasal sound: /a/ sound pronounced letting air pass through the nose |
| [ɔ̃] | b**on**jour | Nasal sound: closed /o/ sound pronounced letting air pass through the nose |
| [œ̃] | **un** | Nasal sound: like [ɛ̃] but with lips more rounded |
| **Semi-vowels** | | |
| [w] | v**oir** | **w**eek |
| [j] | **y**o**y**o, pa**ill**e | **y**ard |
| [ɥ] | n**ui**t | Does not exist in English: the vowel [y] elided with the following vowel |

# A

**A, a¹** [eɪ] *n* **a)** A, a *m inv*; **5A** [in address, street number] 5 bis; **to go from A to B** aller du point A au point B **b)** SCH [grade] **to get an A in French** avoir une très bonne note en français, ≃ avoir entre 16 et 20 en français **c)** [street atlas] **an A to Z of London** un plan de Londres

**a²** [ə] *(stressed* [eɪ]*)*

> a devient an [ən], stressed [æn] devant voyelle ou h muet.

*indef art* **a)** [in general] un, une; **a man** un homme; **an apple** une pomme; **an hour** une heure
**b)** [definite article in French] 60 pence **a kilo** 60 pence le kilo; **50 km an hour** 50 km à l'heure; **I have a broken arm** j'ai le bras cassé
**c)** [article omitted in French] **he's a doctor / a father** il est médecin / père; **Caen, a town in Normandy** Caen, ville de Normandie; **what a man!** quel homme!; **a hundred** cent
**d)** [a certain] **a Mr Smith** un certain M. Smith **e)** [time] **twice a month** deux fois par mois

**A3** **1.** *n* [paper size] format *m* A3 **2.** *adj* **A3 paper** papier *m* (format) A3

**A4** **1.** *n* Br [paper size] format *m* A4 **2.** *adj* **A4 paper** papier *m* (format) A4

**aback** [ə'bæk] *adv* **taken aback (by)** déconcerté (par)

**abandon** [ə'bændən] **1.** *n* abandon *m* **2.** *vt* abandonner; **to abandon ship** abandonner le navire

**abbey** ['æbɪ] *(pl -eys) n* abbaye *f*

**abbreviate** [ə'bri:vɪeɪt] *vt* abréger ■ **abbreviation** *n* abréviation *f*

**abdicate** ['æbdɪkeɪt] *vt & vi* abdiquer

**abdomen** ['æbdəmən] *n* abdomen *m*

**abduct** [æb'dʌkt] *vt* [kidnap] enlever ■ **abduction** *n* enlèvement *m*, rapt *m*

**ability** [ə'bɪlətɪ] *(pl -ies) n* capacité *f* **(to do** de faire); **to the best of my ability** de mon mieux

**ablaze** [ə'bleɪz] *adj* en feu; *Fig* **ablaze with** [light] resplendissant de

**able** ['eɪbəl] *adj* capable; **to be able to do sth** être capable de faire qch, pouvoir faire qch; **to be able to swim / drive** savoir nager / conduire ■ **able-bodied** *adj* robuste

**abnormal** [æb'nɔ:məl] *adj* anormal

**aboard** [ə'bɔ:d] **1.** *adv* [on ship, plane] à bord; **to go aboard** monter à bord **2.** *prep* **aboard the ship / plane** à bord du navire / de l'avion; **aboard the train** dans le train

**abolish** [ə'bɒlɪʃ] *vt* abolir ■ **abolition** [æbə'lɪʃən] *n* abolition *f*

**abominable** [ə'bɒmɪnəbəl] *adj* abominable

**Aborigine** [æbə'rɪdʒɪnɪ] *n* Aborigène *mf* (d'Australie)

**abort** [ə'bɔ:t] **1.** *vt* **a)** [space flight] avorter **b)** COMPUT abandonner **2.** *vi* MED faire une fausse couche ■ **abortion** *n* avortement *m*; **to have an abortion** se faire avorter

**about** [ə'baʊt] **1.** *adv* **a)** [approximately] à peu près, environ; **at about two o'clock** vers deux heures
**b)** [here and there] çà et là, ici et là; *Fig* **there's a lot of flu about at the moment** il y a beaucoup de cas de grippe en ce moment; **there's a rumour about (that...)** il y a une rumeur qui circule (selon laquelle...); **to look about** regarder autour de soi; **to follow someone about** suivre quelqu'un partout

**2.** *prep* **a)** [around] **about the garden** autour du jardin

**b)** [near to] **about here** par ici

**c)** [concerning] au sujet de ; **to talk about sth** parler de qch ; **a book about sth** un livre sur qch ; **what's it (all) about?** de quoi s'agit-il ?

**d)** [+ infinitive] **about to do** sur le point de faire ; **I was about to say…** j'étais sur le point de dire…

**above** [ə'bʌv] **1.** *adv* au-dessus ; [in book] ci-dessus ; **from above** d'en haut ; **the floor above** l'étage *m* du dessus **2.** *prep* **a)** [in height, hierarchy] au-dessus de ; **he's above me** [in rank] c'est mon supérieur ; **she's not above lying** elle n'est pas incapable de mentir ; **he's not above asking** il n'est pas trop fier pour demander ; **above all** surtout **b)** [with numbers] plus de ■ **above-board 1.** *adj* honnête **2.** *adv* sans tricherie ■ **above-mentioned** *adj* susmentionné

**abreast** [ə'brest] *adv* côte à côte, de front ; **four abreast** par rangs de quatre ; **to keep abreast of sth** se tenir au courant de qch

**abroad** [ə'brɔːd] *adv* à l'étranger ; **from abroad** de l'étranger

**abrupt** [ə'brʌpt] *adj* [sudden] brusque, soudain ; [rude] brusque, abrupt ; [slope, style] abrupt

**abs** [æbz] *npl Fam* [abdominal muscles] abdos *mpl*

**abscess** ['æbses] *n* abcès *m*

**absence** ['æbsəns] *n* absence *f* ; **in the absence of** [person] en l'absence de ; [thing] faute de

**absent 1.** ['æbsənt] *adj* absent **(from** de**) 2.** [æb'sent] *vt* **to absent oneself (from)** s'absenter (de) ■ **absent-minded** *adj* distrait

**absentee** [æbsən'tiː] *n* absent, -e *mf*

**absolute** ['æbsəluːt] *adj* absolu ; [proof] indiscutable ; **he's an absolute fool!** il est complètement idiot ! ; **it's an absolute disgrace!** c'est une honte ! ■ **absolutely** *adv* absolument ; **you're absolutely right** tu as tout à fait raison

**absorb** [əb'zɔːb] *vt* [liquid] absorber ; [shock] amortir ; **to be absorbed in sth** être plongé dans qch ■ **absorbent** *adj* absorbant

**abstain** [əb'steɪn] *vi* POL s'abstenir ; **to abstain from sth /from doing sth** s'abstenir de qch /de faire qch

**abstract** ['æbstrækt] **1.** *adj* abstrait **2.** *n* **a)** [notion] **the abstract** l'abstrait *m* **b)** [summary] résumé *m*

**absurd** [əb'sɜːd] *adj* absurde, ridicule

**abundant** [ə'bʌndənt] *adj* abondant ■ **abundantly** *adv* **abundantly clear** parfaitement clair

**abuse 1.** [ə'bjuːs] *n* [of power] abus *m* **(of** de**)** ; [of child] mauvais traitements *mpl* ; [insults] injures *fpl* **2.** [ə'bjuːz] *vt* [misuse] abuser de ; [ill-treat] maltraiter ; [insult] injurier ■ **abusive** [ə'bjuːsɪv] *adj* [person, language] grossier, -ère

**abysmal** [ə'bɪzməl] *adj Fam* [bad] exécrable

**AC** *n* **a)** *(abbr of* **alternating current***)* courant *m* alternatif **b)** = **air-conditioning**

**academic** [ækə'demɪk] **1.** *adj* **a)** [year, diploma - of school] scolaire ; [of university] universitaire **b)** [scholarly] intellectuel, -elle **c)** [theoretical] **the issue is of purely academic interest** cette question n'a d'intérêt que d'un point de vue théorique ; **this is academic now** cela n'a plus d'importance **2.** *n* [teacher] universitaire *mf*

**academy** [ə'kædəmɪ] *(pl* **-ies***) n* [society] académie *f* ; [military] école *f*

**accelerate** [ək'seləreɪt] **1.** *vt* accélérer **2.** *vi* [of pace] s'accélérer ; [of vehicle, driver] accélérer ■ **accelerator** *n* accélérateur *m*

**accent** ['æksənt] *n* accent *m*

**accept** [ək'sept] *vt* accepter ■ **acceptable** *adj* [worth accepting, tolerable] acceptable ; **to be acceptable to sb** convenir à qn

**access** ['ækses] **1.** *n* accès *m* **(to sth** à qch ; **to sb** auprès de qn**)** ; **access card** carte *f* d'accès ; COMPUT **access provider** fournisseur *m* d'accès ; **access**

**ramp** bretelle *f* d'accès ; **access road** route *f* d'accès **2.** *vt* COMPUT accéder à ■ **accessible** *adj* accessible

**accessories** [ək'sesəriz] *npl* [objects] accessoires *mpl*

**accessory** [ək'sesəri] *(pl* **-ies**) *n* JUR [accomplice] complice *mf* **(to** de)

**accident** ['æksɪdənt] *n* accident *m* ; **by accident** accidentellement ; [by chance] par hasard ■ **accidental** *adj* accidentel, -elle ■ **accidentally** *adv* accidentellement ; [by chance] par hasard

**acclaim** [ə'kleɪm] **1.** *n* **(critical) acclaim** éloges *mpl* **2.** *vt* [cheer] acclamer ; [praise] faire l'éloge de

**acclimatize** [ə'klaɪmətaɪz], *Am* **acclimate** ['ækləmeɪt] *vi* s'acclimater

**accommodate** [ə'kɒmədeɪt] *vt* **a)** [of house] loger **b)** [oblige] rendre service à ■ **accommodating** *adj* accommodant, obligeant

**accommodation** [əkɒmə'deɪʃən], *Am* **accommodations** *n* [lodging] logement *m* ; [rented room(s)] chambre(s) *f(pl)*

**accompany** [ə'kʌmpəni] *(pt & pp* **-ied**) *vt* accompagner

**accomplice** [ə'kʌmplɪs] *n* complice *mf*

**accomplish** [ə'kʌmplɪʃ] *vt* [task, duty] accomplir ; [aim] atteindre ■ **accomplishment** *n* [of task, duty] accomplissement *m* ; [thing achieved] réalisation *f*

**accord** [ə'kɔːd] **1.** *n* accord *m* ; **of my own accord** de mon plein gré **2.** *vt* [grant] accorder ■ **accordance** *n* **in accordance with** conformément à

**according** [ə'kɔːdɪŋ] ■ **according to** *prep* selon, d'après ■ **accordingly** *adv* en conséquence

**accordion** [ə'kɔːdɪən] *n* accordéon *m*

**accost** [ə'kɒst] *vt* accoster, aborder

**account** [ə'kaʊnt] **1.** *n* **a)** [with bank or company] compte *m* **b)** [report] compte rendu *m* ; [explanation] explication *f* **c)** [expressions] **by all accounts** au dire de tous ; **on account of** à cause de ; **on no account** en aucun cas ; **to**

**take sth into account** tenir compte de qch **2.** *vi* **to account for** [explain] expliquer ; [give reckoning of] rendre compte de ; [represent] représenter ■ **account executive** *n* responsable *mf* grands comptes ■ **account holder** *n* titulaire *mf* ■ **account number** *n* numéro *m* de compte ■ **accountable** *adj* responsable **(for** /**to** de /devant) ■ **accounts** *npl* [of business] comptabilité *f*, comptes *mpl*

**accountant** [ə'kaʊntənt] *n* comptable *mf*

**accounting** [ə'kaʊntɪŋ] *n* comptabilité *f*

**accumulate** [ə'kjuːmjʊleɪt] **1.** *vt* accumuler **2.** *vi* s'accumuler

**accuracy** ['ækjʊrəsɪ] *n* exactitude *f*, précision *f*

**accurate** ['ækjʊrət] *adj* exact, précis

**accuse** [ə'kjuːz] *vt* **to accuse sb (of sth /of doing sth)** accuser qn (de qch /de faire qch) ■ **accusation** *n* accusation *f* ; **to make an accusation against sb** lancer une accusation contre qn ■ **accused** *n* JUR **the accused** l'accusé, -e *mf*

**accustom** [ə'kʌstəm] *vt* habituer, accoutumer ■ **accustomed** *adj* **to be accustomed to sth /to doing sth** être habitué à qch /à faire qch ; **to get accustomed to sth /to doing sth** s'habituer à qch /à faire qch

**ace** [eɪs] *n* **a)** [card, person] as *m* **b)** [at tennis] ace *m*

**ache** [eɪk] **1.** *n* douleur *f* **2.** *vi* faire mal ; **my head aches** j'ai mal à la tête

**achieve** [ə'tʃiːv] *vt* [result] obtenir ; [aim] atteindre ; [ambition] réaliser ; [victory] remporter ; **to achieve success** réussir ■ **achievement** *n* [success] réussite *f* ; [of ambition] réalisation *f*

**aching** [eɪkɪŋ] *adj* douloureux, -euse

**acid** ['æsɪd] *adj & n* acide *(m)* ; **acid rain** pluies *fpl* acides

**acknowledge** [ək'nɒlɪdʒ] *vt* reconnaître **(as** pour) ; [greeting] répondre à ■ **acknowledg(e)ment** *n* [of letter] accusé *m* de réception ; [receipt] reçu *m* ; [confession] aveu *m* **(of** de)

**acne** ['æknɪ] n acné f

**acoustics** [ə'ku:stɪks] npl acoustique f

**acquaint** [ə'kweɪnt] vt **to be acquainted with** [person] connaître ; [fact] savoir ▪ **acquaintance** n [person, knowledge] connaissance f

**acquire** [ə'kwaɪə(r)] vt acquérir ; [taste] prendre (**for** à) ; [friends] se faire

**acquit** [ə'kwɪt] (pt & pp -tt-) vt a) JUR **to acquit sb (of a crime)** acquitter qn b) **to acquit oneself badly / well** mal / bien s'en tirer

**acre** ['eɪkə(r)] n ≃ demi-hectare m, acre f ; Fam **acres of space** plein de place

**acrimonious** [ækrɪ'məʊnɪəs] adj [person, remark] acrimonieux, -euse, hargneux, -euse ; [attack, dispute] virulent

**acrobat** ['ækrəbæt] n acrobate mf ▪ **acrobatics** npl acrobaties fpl

**acronym** ['ækrənɪm] n sigle m

**across** [ə'krɒs] **1.** prep [from side to side of] d'un côté à l'autre de ; [on the other side of] de l'autre côté de ; [crossways] en travers de ; **a bridge across the river** un pont sur la rivière ; **to walk** or **go across** [street, lawn] traverser ; **to run / swim across** traverser en courant / à la nage **2.** adv **to be a kilometre across** [wide] avoir un kilomètre de large ; **to get sth across to sb** faire comprendre qch à qn

**acrylic** [ə'krɪlɪk] adj [paint, fibre] acrylique ; [garment] en acrylique

**act** [ækt] **1.** n a) [deed] acte m ; **act (of parliament)** loi f ; **caught in the act** pris sur le fait b) THEAT [part of play] acte m ; [in circus, cabaret] numéro m ; Fig **to get one's act together** se secouer ; Fam **in on the act** dans le coup **2.** vt [part] jouer ; **to act the fool** faire l'idiot **3.** vi a) [take action, behave] agir ; **it's time to act** il est temps d'agir ; **to act as secretary / etc** faire office de secrétaire / etc ; **to act (up)on** [affect] agir

sur ; [advice] suivre ; **to act on behalf of sb** représenter qn ; Fam **to act up** [of person, machine] faire des siennes b) [in play, film] jouer ; [pretend] jouer la comédie ▪ **acting 1.** adj [temporary] intérimaire **2.** n [of play] représentation f ; [art] jeu m ; [career] théâtre m

**action** ['ækʃən] n action f ; [military] combats mpl ; [legal] procès m, action f ; **to take action** prendre des mesures ; **to put into action** [plan] exécuter ; **out of action** [machine] hors service ; [person] hors de combat

**active** ['æktɪv] **1.** adj actif, -ive ; [interest, dislike] vif (f vive) ; [volcano] en activité **2.** n GRAM actif m ▪ **activity** (pl -ies) n activité f ; [in street] animation f ; **activity centre** centre m d'activités ; [specifically for children] centre m aéré ou de loisirs

**activewear** ['æktɪvweə(r)] n vêtements mpl de sport

**actor** ['æktə(r)] n acteur m ▪ **actress** n actrice f

**actual** ['æktʃʊəl] adj réel (f réelle) ; [example] concret, -ète ; **the actual book** le livre même ; **in actual fact** en réalité ▪ **actually** adv [truly] réellement ; [in fact] en réalité, en fait

**acupuncture** ['ækjʊpʌŋktʃə(r)] n acuponcture f

**acute** [ə'kju:t] adj [pain, angle] aigu (f aiguë) ; [anxiety, emotion] vif (f vive) ; [mind, observer] perspicace ; [shortage] grave ▪ **acutely** adv [suffer, feel] profondément ; [painful] extrêmement

**ad** [æd] n Fam [on radio, TV] pub f ; [private, in newspaper] annonce f ; Br **small ad**, Am **want ad** petite annonce f

**AD** ['eɪ'di:] (abbr of anno Domini) apr. J.-C.

**adapt** [ə'dæpt] **1.** vt adapter (**to** à) ; **to adapt oneself to sth** s'adapter à qch **2.** vi s'adapter ▪ **adaptable** adj [person] souple ; [instrument] adaptable ▪ **adapter, adaptor** n [for use abroad] adaptateur m ; [for several plugs] prise f multiple

**add** [æd] **1.** *vt* ajouter (**to /that** à /que); **to add (up** *or* **together)** [numbers] additionner; **to add in** inclure **2.** *vi* **to add to** [increase] augmenter; **to add up to** [total] s'élever à ; [mean] signifier ; [represent] constituer ■ **add on** *vt sep* **to add sth on (to)** rajouter qch (à)

**adder** [ˈædə(r)] *n* vipère *f*

**addict** [ˈædɪkt] *n* **drug addict** toxicomane *mf*, drogué, -e *mf* ; **TV addict** fana(tique) *mf* de la télé ■ **addicted** *adj* **to be addicted to drugs** être toxicomane ; **to be addicted to alcohol** être alcoolique ; **to be addicted to cigarettes** ne pas pouvoir se passer de tabac ■ **addictive** *adj* [drug, TV] qui crée une dépendance

**addition** [əˈdɪʃən] *n* addition *f* ; [increase] augmentation *f* ; **in addition** de plus ; **in addition to** en plus de ■ **additional** *adj* supplémentaire

**additive** [ˈædɪtɪv] *n* additif *m*

**address** [*Br* əˈdres, *Am* ˈædres] **1.** *n* [on letter, parcel] adresse *f* ; [speech] allocution *f* **2.** [əˈdres] *vt* [person, audience] s'adresser à ; [words, speech] adresser (**to** à) ; [letter] mettre l'adresse sur

**adept** [əˈdept] *adj* expert (**in** *or* **at** à)

**adequate** [ˈædɪkwət] *adj* [enough] suffisant ; [acceptable] convenable ; [performance] acceptable ■ **adequately** *adv* [sufficiently] suffisamment ; [acceptably] convenablement

**adhere** [ədˈhɪə(r)] *vi* **to adhere to** adhérer à ; [decision, rule] s'en tenir à ■ **adhesive** [-ˈhiːsɪv] *adj & n* adhésif (*m*)

**adjacent** [əˈdʒeɪsənt] *adj* [house, angle] adjacent (**to** à)

**adjective** [ˈædʒɪktɪv] *n* adjectif *m*

**adjoin** [əˈdʒɔɪn] *vt* être attenant à ■ **adjoining** *adj* attenant

**adjourn** [əˈdʒɜːn] **1.** *vt* [postpone] ajourner ; [session] suspendre **2.** *vi* suspendre la séance

**adjust** [əˈdʒʌst] *vt* [machine] régler ; [machine part] ajuster, régler ; [salaries, prices] (r)ajuster ; [clothes] rajuster ; **to adjust to sth** s'adapter à qch ■ **adjustable** *adj* [seat] réglable

**ad-lib** [ædˈlɪb] *(pt & pp* -bb-*)* *vi* improviser

**administer** [ədˈmɪnɪstə(r)] *vt* administrer (**to** à) ■ **administration** *n* administration *f* ; [government] gouvernement *m* ■ **administrator** *n* administrateur, -trice *mf*

**administrative costs** *npl* frais *mpl* d'administration *ou* de gestion

**admiral** [ˈædmərəl] *n* amiral *m*

**admire** [ədˈmaɪə(r)] *vt* admirer (**for sth** pour qch; **for doing sth** de faire qch) ■ **admirable** *adj* admirable

**admit** [ədˈmɪt] *(pt & pp* -tt-*)* **1.** *vt* [let in] laisser entrer ; [to hospital, college] admettre ; [acknowledge] reconnaître, admettre (**that** que) **2.** *vi* **to admit to sth** avouer qch ; [mistake] reconnaître qch ■ **admission** *n* [to theatre] entrée *f* (**to** à *ou* de) ; [to club, school] admission *f* ; [acknowledgement] aveu *m* ; **admission (charge)** (prix *m* d')entrée *f* ■ **admittance** *n* entrée *f* ; 'no admittance' 'entrée interdite' ■ **admittedly** [-ɪdlɪ] *adv* de l'aveu général

**adolescent** [ædəˈlesənt] *n* adolescent, -e *mf*

**adopt** [əˈdɒpt] *vt* adopter ; POL [candidate] choisir ■ **adopted** *adj* [child] adopté ; [son, daughter] adoptif, -ive ; [country] d'adoption ■ **adoptive** *adj* [parent] adoptif, -ive

**adore** [əˈdɔː(r)] *vt* adorer (**doing** faire) ■ **adorable** *adj* adorable

**adrenalin(e)** [əˈdrenəlɪn] *n* adrénaline *f*

**Adriatic** [eɪdrɪˈætɪk] *n* **the Adriatic** l'Adriatique *f*

**adrift** [əˈdrɪft] **1.** *adj* à la dérive ; **to feel adrift** se sentir perdu **2.** *adv* Fig **to go adrift** aller à la dérive

**ADSL** *(abbr of* **Asymmetric Digital Subscriber Line)** *n* ADSL *m*

**adult** [ˈædʌlt, əˈdʌlt] **1.** *n* adulte *mf* **2.** *adj* [animal] adulte ; **adult class / film** classe *f* / film *m* pour adultes ■ **adulthood** [ˈædʌlthʊd] *n* âge *m* adulte ; **in adulthood** à l'âge adulte

**adultery** [əˈdʌltərɪ] *n* adultère *m* ; **to commit adultery** commettre l'adultère

**advance** [əd'vɑːns] **1.** n [movement, money] avance f; [of science] progrès mpl; [sexual] avances fpl; **in advance** [book, inform, apply] à l'avance; [pay] d'avance; [arrive] en avance

**2.** adj [payment] anticipé; **advance booking** réservation f

**3.** vt a) [put forward] faire avancer b) [science, one's work] faire progresser; [opinion] avancer

**4.** vi [go forward, progress] avancer; **to advance towards sb** s'avancer ou avancer vers qn

■ **advanced** adj avancé; [studies, level] supérieur; [course] de niveau supérieur; **advanced in years** âgé

**advantage** [əd'vɑːntɪʤ] n avantage m (**over** sur); **to take advantage of** [situation] profiter de; [person] exploiter; [woman] séduire; **advantage Hewitt** [in tennis] avantage Hewitt

**advent** ['ædvent] n arrivée f, avènement m; REL **Advent** l'Avent m

**adventure** [əd'ventʃə(r)] **1.** n aventure f **2.** adj [film, story] d'aventures ■ **adventurous** adj aventureux, -euse

**adverb** ['ædvɜːb] n adverbe m

**adverse** ['ædvɜːs] adj défavorable; [effect] négatif, -ive

**advert** ['ædvɜːt] n Br pub f; [private, in newspaper] annonce f

**advertise** ['ædvətaɪz] **1.** vt [commercially] faire de la publicité pour; [privately] passer une annonce pour vendre **2.** vi faire de la publicité; [privately] passer une annonce (**for** pour trouver) ■ **advertising** n publicité f; **advertising agency** agence f de publicité; **advertising campaign** campagne f de publicité

**advertisement** [Br əd'vɜːtɪsmənt, Am ædvər'taɪzmənt] n publicité f; [private or in newspaper] annonce f; [poster] affiche f; TV **the advertisements** la publicité

**advice** [əd'vaɪs] n conseil(s) m(pl); COMM [notification] avis m; **a piece of advice** un conseil; **to ask sb's advice**

demander conseil à qn; **to take sb's advice** suivre les conseils de qn; **advice slip** [from ATM] reçu m

**advise** [əd'vaɪz] vt a) [counsel] conseiller; [recommend] recommander; **to advise sb to do sth** conseiller à qn de faire qch; **to advise sb against doing sth** déconseiller à qn de faire qch b) [inform] **to advise sb that...** aviser qn que... ■ **advisable** adj [action] à conseiller; **it's advisable to wait /etc** il est plus prudent d'attendre /etc ■ **adviser, advisor** n conseiller, -ère mf

**advocate 1.** ['ædvəkət] n [of cause] défenseur m; [lawyer] avocat, -e mf **2.** ['ædvəkeɪt] vt préconiser

**aerial** ['eərɪəl] **1.** n Br antenne f **2.** adj [photo] aérien, -enne

**aerobics** [eə'rəʊbɪks] npl aérobic m

**aeroplane** ['eərəpleɪn] n Br avion m

**aerosol** ['eərəsɒl] n aérosol m

**aesthetic** [Br iːs'θetɪk, Am es'θetɪk] adj esthétique

**affair** ['əfeə(r)] n [matter, concern] affaire f; (**love**) **affair** liaison f; **state of affairs** situation f

**affect** [ə'fekt] vt [concern] concerner; [move, pretend to have] affecter; [harm] nuire à; [influence] influer sur; **to be deeply affected by sth** être très affecté par qch ■ **affected** adj [manner] affecté

**affection** [ə'fekʃən] n affection f (**for** pour) ■ **affectionate** adj affectueux, -euse

**affinity** [ə'fɪnɪtɪ] (pl **-ies**) n affinité f

**affirm** [ə'fɜːm] vt affirmer ■ **affirmative 1.** adj affirmatif, -ive **2.** n affirmative f; **to answer in the affirmative** répondre par l'affirmative

**affix** [ə'fɪks] vt [stamp, signature] apposer

**afflict** [ə'flɪkt] vt affliger (**with** de) ■ **affliction** n [misery] affliction f; [disability] infirmité f

**affluent** ['æfluənt] adj riche; **affluent society** société f d'abondance

**afford** [ə'fɔːd] vt [pay for] **I can't afford it /a new car** je n'ai pas les moyens de l'acheter /d'acheter une nouvelle voiture; **he can't afford the time (to read it)** il n'a pas le temps (de le lire); **I can afford to wait** je peux me permettre d'attendre ■ **affordable** *adj* [price] abordable

**Afghanistan** [æf'gænɪstɑːn] *n* l'Afghanistan *m*

**afield** [ə'fiːld] *adv* **further afield** plus loin

**afloat** [ə'fləʊt] *adv* [ship, swimmer, business] à flot; [awash] submergé; **to stay afloat** [of ship] rester à flot; [of business] se maintenir à flot

**afraid** [ə'freɪd] *adj* **to be afraid** avoir peur (**of** de); **to be afraid to do** *or* **of doing sth** avoir peur de faire qch; **I'm afraid (that) he'll fall** j'ai peur qu'il (ne) tombe; **I'm afraid he's out** je regrette, il est sorti

**afresh** [ə'freʃ] *adv* de nouveau; **to start afresh** recommencer

**Africa** ['æfrɪkə] *n* l'Afrique *f* ■ **African 1.** *adj* africain **2.** *n* Africain, -e *mf*

**African American** *n* Noir américain *m* (*f* Noire américaine) (*ressortissants américains d'origine africaine*) ■ **African(-)American** *adj* noir américain (*f* noire américaine)

**after** ['ɑːftə(r)] **1.** *adv* après; **soon / long after** peu / longtemps après; **the month after** le mois d'après; **the day after** le lendemain **2.** *prep* après; **after three days** au bout de trois jours; **the day after the battle** le lendemain de la bataille; **after eating** après avoir mangé; **day after day** jour après jour; **after all** après tout; **it's after five** il est cinq heures passées; *Am* **ten after four** quatre heures dix; **to be after sb /sth** [seek] chercher qn /qch **3.** *conj* après que; **after he saw you** après qu'il t'a vu ■ **after-effects** *npl* suites *fpl*, séquelles *fpl* ■ **afterlife** *n* vie *f* après la mort ■ **aftermath** *n* suites *fpl* ■ **after-sales service** *n* service *m* après-vente ■ **aftershave** *n* (lotion *f*) après-rasage *m*, after-shave *m inv* ■ **afterthought** *n* réflexion *f* après coup; **to add /say**

sth **as an afterthought** ajouter /dire qch après coup ■ **afterward(s)** *adv* après, plus tard

**afternoon** [ɑːftə'nuːn] *n* après-midi *m ou f inv*; **in the afternoon** l'après-midi; **at three in the afternoon** à trois heures de l'après-midi; **every Monday afternoon** tous les lundis après-midi; **good afternoon!** bonjour !

**again** [ə'gen] *adv* de nouveau, encore une fois; [furthermore] en outre; **to go down / up again** redescendre / remonter; **she won't do it again** elle ne le fera plus; **never again** plus jamais; **again and again** bien des fois; **what's his name again?** comment s'appelle-t-il déjà ?

**against** [ə'genst, ə'geɪnst] *prep* contre; **to lean against sth** s'appuyer contre qch; **to go** *or* **be against sth** s'opposer à qch; **against the law** illégal; *Br* **against the rules,** *Am* **against the rule** interdit, contraire aux règlements; **the pound rose against the dollar** la livre est en hausse par rapport au dollar

**age** [eɪdʒ] **1.** *n* âge *m*; (old) age vieillesse *f*; **what age are you?, what's your age?** quel âge as-tu ?; **five years of age** âgé de cinq ans; **under age** trop jeune, mineur; *Fam* **to wait (for) ages** attendre une éternité; **age gap** différence *f* d'âge; **age limit** limite *f* d'âge **2.** (*pres p* **ag(e)ing**) *vt & vi* vieillir ■ **aged** *adj* **a)** [eɪdʒd] **aged ten** âgé de dix ans **b)** ['eɪdʒɪd] vieux (*f* vieille), âgé; **the aged** les personnes *fpl* âgées

**agenda** [ə'dʒendə] *n* ordre *m* du jour

**agent** ['eɪdʒənt] *n* agent *m*; [car dealer] concessionnaire *mf* ■ **agency** *n* agence *f*

**aggravate** ['ægrəveɪt] *vt* [make worse] aggraver; *Fam* [annoy] exaspérer

**aggregate** ['ægrɪgət] **1.** *adj* global **2.** *n* [total] ensemble *m*; **on aggregate** au total

**aggressive** [ə'gresɪv] *adj* agressif, -ive

**aggrieved** [ə'griːvd] *adj* [offended] blessé, froissé; [tone] peiné

**aghast** [ə'gɑːst] *adj* horrifié (**at** par)

**agile** [*Br* 'ædʒaɪl, *Am* 'ædʒəl] *adj* agile

**agitated** ['ædʒɪteɪtɪd] *adj* agité

**agnostic** [æg'nɒstɪk] *adj* & *n* agnostique (*mf*)

**ago** [ə'gəʊ] *adv* **a year ago** il y a un an; **how long ago?** il y a combien de temps (de cela) ?; **long ago** il y a longtemps; **a short time ago** il y a peu de temps

**agonizing** ['ægənaɪzɪŋ] *adj* [pain] atroce; [situation] angoissant

**agony** ['ægənɪ] (*pl* -**ies**) *n* [pain] douleur *f* atroce; [anguish] angoisse *f*; **to be in agony** être au supplice; **agony column** [in newspaper] courrier *m* du cœur

**agree** [ə'griː] **1.** *vi* [come to an agreement] se mettre d'accord; [be in agreement] être d'accord (**with** avec); [of facts, dates] concorder; [of verb] s'accorder; **to agree (up)on** [decide] convenir de; **to agree to sth/to doing sth** consentir à qch / à faire qch **2.** *vt* [plan] se mettre d'accord sur; [date, price] convenir de; [approve] approuver; **to agree to do sth** accepter de faire qch; **to agree that...** admettre que... ■ **agreed** *adj* [time, place] convenu ■ **agreement** *n* [contract, assent & GRAM] accord *m* (**with** avec); **to be in agreement with sb** être d'accord avec qn; **to come to an agreement** se mettre d'accord

**agreeable** [ə'griːəbəl] *adj* [pleasant] agréable; **to be agreeable** [agree] être d'accord; **to be agreeable to sth** consentir à qch

**agriculture** ['ægrɪkʌltʃə(r)] *n* agriculture *f* ■ **agricultural** *adj* agricole

**agritourism** ['ægrɪtʊərɪzəm] *n* agritourisme *m*

**agro-industry** ['ægrəʊ-] *n* agro-industrie *f*

**aground** [ə'graʊnd] *adv* **to run aground** [of ship] (s')échouer

**ahead** [ə'hed] *adv* [in space] en avant; [leading] en tête; [in the future] à l'avenir; **ahead of** [in space] devant; [in time] avant; **one hour / etc ahead (of)** une heure / etc d'avance (sur); **to be ahead of schedule** être en avance; **to go on ahead** partir devant; **to go ahead** [advance] avancer; [continue]

continuer; [start] commencer; **go ahead!** allez-y !; **to think ahead** prévoir

**aid** [eɪd] **1.** *n* [help] aide *f*; [device] accessoire *m*; **with the aid of sb** avec l'aide de qn; **with the aid of sth** à l'aide de qch; **in aid of** [charity] au profit de **2.** *vt* aider (**sb to do** qn à faire)

**aide** [eɪd] *n* collaborateur, -trice *mf*

**AIDS** [eɪdz] (*abbr of* **Acquired Immune Deficiency Syndrome**) *n* SIDA *m*

**ailing** ['eɪlɪŋ] *adj* [ill] souffrant; [company] en difficulté ■ **ailment** *n* affection *f*

**aim** [eɪm] **1.** *n* but *m*; **to take aim (at)** viser; **with the aim of** dans le but de **2.** *vt* [gun] braquer (**at** sur); [stone] lancer (**at** *à ou* vers); [blow, remark] décocher (**at** à) **3.** *vi* viser; **to aim at sb** viser qn; **to aim to do sth** avoir l'intention de faire qch ■ **aimless** *adj* [existence] sans but

**air** [eə(r)] **1.** *n* **a)** [atmosphère] air *m*, aérienne; **in the open air** en plein air; **by air** [travel] en *ou* par avion; [send letter, goods] par avion; **to be** *or* **go on (the) air** [of person] passer à l'antenne; [of programme] être diffusé; **to throw sth in(to) the air** jeter qch en l'air; *Fig* **there's something in the air** il se prépare quelque chose; **air base** base *f*; **air bed** matelas *m* pneumatique; **air fare** prix *m* du billet d'avion; **air force** armée *f* de l'air; **air freshener** désodorisant *m* (*pour la maison*); **air mattress** matelas *m* pneumatique; **air steward** steward *m*

**b)** [appearance, tune] air *m*; **to put on airs** se donner des airs; **with an air of sadness** d'un air triste

**2.** *vt* [room] aérer; [views] exposer

**3.** *vi* **a)** [clothes] sécher

**b)** *Am* RADIO & TV **the movie airs next week** le film sera diffusé la semaine prochaine

■ **air-conditioning** *n* climatisation *f*

■ **aircraft** *n inv* avion *m*; **aircraft carrier** porte-avions *m inv*

■ **airfield** *n* terrain *m* d'aviation

■ **airgun** *n* carabine *f* à air comprimé

■ **airlift** *vt* transporter par avion

■ **airline** *n* compagnie *f* aérienne ; **airline ticket** billet *m* d'avion

■ **airmail** *n* poste *f* aérienne ; **by airmail** par avion

■ **airplane** *n Am* avion *m*

■ **airport** *n* aéroport *m*

■ **air-raid shelter** *n* abri *m* antiaérien

■ **airship** *n* dirigeable *m*

■ **airtight** *adj* hermétique

■ **air-traffic controller** *n* contrôleur *m* aérien, aiguilleur *m* du ciel

**airbag** ['eabæg] *n* AUTO Airbag® *m*

**airy** ['eərɪ] *(compar* -**ier***, superl* -**iest***) adj* [room] clair et spacieux, -euse ; *Fig* [manner] désinvolte

**aisle** [aɪl] *n* [in supermarket, cinema] allée *f* ; [in plane] couloir *m* ; [in church - on side] nef *f* latérale ; [central] allée *f* centrale

**ajar** [ə'dʒɑː(r)] *adj & adv* [door] entrouvert

**alarm** [ə'lɑːm] **1.** *n* [warning, fear, device] alarme *f* ; [mechanism] sonnerie *f* (d'alarme) ; **false alarm** fausse alerte *f* ; **alarm clock** réveil *m* **2.** *vt* [frighten] alarmer ; [worry] inquiéter ; **they were alarmed at the news** la nouvelle les a beaucoup inquiétés

**alas** [ə'læs] *excl* hélas !

**Albania** [æl'beɪnɪə] *n* l'Albanie *f* ■ **Albanian 1.** *adj* albanais **2.** *n* Albanais, -e *mf*

**album** ['ælbəm] *n* [book, record] album *m*

**alcohol** ['ælkəhɒl] *n* alcool *m* ; **alcohol level** taux *m* d'alcoolémie ■ **alcoholic 1.** *adj* [person] alcoolique ; **alcoholic drink** boisson *f* alcoolisée **2.** *n* [person] alcoolique *mf*

**alcove** ['ælkəʊv] *n* alcôve *f*

**ale** [eɪl] *n* bière *f*

**alert** [ə'lɜːt] **1.** *adj* [watchful] vigilant ; [lively - mind, baby] éveillé **2.** *n* alerte *f* ; **on the alert** sur le qui-vive **3.** *vt* alerter

**A-level** ['eɪlevəl] *(abbr of* **Advanced level***) n Br* [exam] ≃ baccalauréat *m*

**algebra** ['ældʒɪbrə] *n* algèbre *f*

**Algeria** [æl'dʒɪərɪə] *n* l'Algérie *f* ■ **Algerian 1.** *adj* algérien, -enne **2.** *n* Algérien, -enne *mf*

**alias** ['eɪlɪəs] **1.** *adv* alias **2.** *(pl* **aliases***) n* **a)** nom *m* d'emprunt **b)** COMPUT [in e-mail, on desktop] alias *m*

**alibi** ['ælɪbaɪ] *n* alibi *m*

**alien** ['eɪlɪən] **1.** *adj* étranger, -ère (**to** à) **2.** *n* [from outer space] extraterrestre *mf* ; *Formal* [foreigner] étranger, -ère *mf* ■ **alienate** *vt* [friend, supporters, readers] s'aliéner ; **to feel alienated** se sentir exclu

**alight¹** [ə'laɪt] *adj* [fire] allumé ; [building] en feu ; [face] éclairé ; **to set sth alight** mettre le feu à qch

**alight²** [ə'laɪt] *(pt & pp* **alighted** *or* **alit***) vi* **a)** *Formal* [from bus, train] descendre (**from** de) **b)** [of bird] se poser (**on** sur)

**align** [ə'laɪn] *vt* aligner

**alike** [ə'laɪk] **1.** *adj* [people, things] semblables, pareils, -eilles ; **to look** *or* **be alike** se ressembler **2.** *adv* de la même manière ; **summer and winter alike** été comme hiver

**alimony** [*Br* 'ælɪmənɪ, *Am* 'ælɪməʊnɪ] *n* JUR pension *f* alimentaire

**alit** [ə'lɪt] *pt & pp of* **alight**

**alive** [ə'laɪv] *adj* vivant, en vie ; **to stay alive** survivre ; **alive and well** bien portant ; *Fam* **alive and kicking** plein de vie

■■■ **all** [ɔːl] **1.** *adj* tout, toute, *pl* tous, toutes ; **all day** toute la journée ; **all men** tous les hommes ; **all the girls** toutes les filles ; **all four of them** tous les quatre ; **for all his wealth** malgré toute sa fortune **2.** *pron* [everyone] tous *mpl*, toutes *fpl* ; [everything] tout ; **my sisters are all here** toutes mes sœurs sont ici ; **he ate it all, he ate all of it** il a tout mangé ; **take all of it** prends (le) tout ; **all of us** nous tous ; **all together** tous ensemble ; **all (that) he has** tout ce qu'il a ; **all in all** à tout prendre ; **anything at all** quoi que ce soit ; **if there's any wind at all** s'il y a le moindre vent ; **nothing at all** rien du tout ; **not at all** pas du tout ; [after 'thank you'] il n'y a pas de quoi **3.** *adv* tout ; **all alone** tout seul ; **all bad** entièrement mauvais ; **all over**

[everywhere] partout ; [finished] fini ;
**all too soon** bien trop tôt ; SPORT **six
all** six partout ; *Fam* **not all there** un
peu fêlé

■ **all-night** *adj* [party] qui dure toute
la nuit ; [shop] ouvert toute la nuit

■ **all-out** *adj* [effort] acharné ; [war,
strike] tous azimuts

■ **all-purpose** *adj* [tool] universel,
-elle

■ **all-round** *adj* [knowledge] approfondi ; [athlete] complet, -ète

■ **all-time** *adj* [record] jamais battu ; **to
reach an all-time low / high** arriver à
son point le plus bas / le plus haut

**allegation** [ælɪ'geɪʃən] *n* accusation *f*

**allege** [ə'ledʒ] *vt* prétendre (**that** que)
■ **alleged** *adj* [so-called - crime, fact]
prétendu ; [author, culprit] présumé ; **he
is alleged to be...** on prétend qu'il est...

**allegiance** [ə'li:dʒəns] *n* [to party, cause]
fidélité *f* (**to** à)

**allergenic** [ælə'dʒenɪk] *adj* allergisant

**allergy** [ˈælədʒɪ] *(pl -ies)* *n* allergie *f* (**to** à)
■ **allergic** [ə'lɜːdʒɪk] *adj* allergique (**to** à)

**alleviate** [ə'li:vɪeɪt] *vt* [pain, suffering]
soulager ; [burden, task] alléger ; [prob-
lem] remédier à

**all-expenses-paid** *adj* tous frais
payés

**alley** [ˈælɪ] *(pl -eys)* *n* ruelle *f* ; *Fam* **that's
(right) up my alley** c'est mon rayon

**alliance** [ə'laɪəns] *n* alliance *f*

**allied** [ˈælaɪd] *adj* [country] allié ; [mat-
ters] lié

**alligator** [ˈælɪgeɪtə(r)] *n* alligator *m*

**allocate** [ˈæləkeɪt] *vt* [assign] affecter
(**to** à) ; [distribute] répartir

**allot** [ə'lɒt] *(pt & pp -tt-)* *vt* [assign] attribuer (**to** à) ; [distribute] répartir ; **in the
allotted time** dans le temps imparti
■ **allotment** *n Br* [land] jardin *m* ouvrier

**allow** [ə'laʊ] **1.** *vt* permettre (**sb sth** qch
à qn) ; [give, grant] accorder (**sb sth** qch
à qn) ; [request] accéder à ; **to allow sb to
do** permettre à qn de faire ; **to allow an
hour / a metre / etc** prévoir une heure /

un mètre / *etc* ; **it's not allowed** c'est
interdit ; **you're not allowed to go** on
vous interdit de partir **2.** *vi* **to allow for
sth** tenir compte de qch ■ **allowable**
*adj* [acceptable] admissible ; [expense]
déductible

**allowance** [ə'laʊəns] *n* allocation *f* ; [for
travel, housing, food] indemnité *f* ; [tax-
free amount] abattement *m* ; **to make
allowances for** [person] être indulgent
envers ; [thing] tenir compte de

**alloy** [ˈælɔɪ] *n* alliage *m*

**all right** [ɔːl'raɪt] **1.** *adj* [satisfactory]
bien *inv* ; [unharmed] sain et sauf ;
[undamaged] intact ; [without worries]
tranquille ; **it's all right** ça va ; **are you
all right?** ça va ? ; **I'm all right** [healthy]
je vais bien ; [financially] je m'en sors ;
**to be all right at maths** se débrouiller
en maths ; **the TV is all right now** [fixed]
la télé marche maintenant **2.** *adv* [well]
bien ; **all right!** [in agreement] d'accord ! ;
**is it all right if I smoke?** ça ne vous
dérange pas si je fume ?

**allude** [ə'lu:d] *vi* **to allude to** faire allusion à ■ **allusion** *n* allusion *f*

**ally 1.** [ˈælaɪ] *(pl -ies)* *n* allié, -e *mf* **2.** [ə'laɪ]
*(pt & pp -ied)* *vt* **to ally oneself with**
s'allier à *ou* avec

**almighty** [ɔːl'maɪtɪ] **1.** *adj* **a)** [power-
ful] tout-puissant (*f* toute-puissante)
**b)** *Fam* [enormous] terrible, formidable
**2.** *n* **the Almighty** le Tout-Puissant

**almond** [ˈɑːmənd] *n* amande *f*

**almost** [ˈɔːlməʊst] *adv* presque ; **he almost fell** il a failli tomber

**alone** [ə'ləʊn] *adj & adv* seul ; **an expert
alone can...** seul un expert peut... ;
**I did it (all) alone** je l'ai fait (tout) seul ;
**to leave** *or* **let alone** [person] laisser
tranquille ; [thing] ne pas toucher à ;
**I can't afford a bike, let alone a car!**
je n'ai pas les moyens de m'acheter un
vélo, encore moins une voiture

**along** [ə'lɒŋ] **1.** *prep* **(all) along** (tout) le
long de ; **to walk along the shore** mar-
cher le long du rivage ; **to walk along
the street** marcher dans la rue ; **along
here** par ici ; *Fig* **somewhere along the
way** à un moment donné **2.** *adv* **to**

**move along** avancer; **I'll be** or **come along shortly** je viendrai tout à l'heure; **come along!** venez donc !; **to bring sth along** apporter qch; **to bring sb along** amener qn; **all along** [all the time] dès le début; [all the way] d'un bout à l'autre; **along with** ainsi que

**alongside** [əlɒŋ'saɪd] *prep* & *adv* à côté (de); **alongside the kerb** le long du trottoir

**aloof** [ə'luːf] **1.** *adj* distant **2.** *adv* à distance

**aloud** [ə'laʊd] *adv* à haute voix

**alphabet** ['ælfəbet] *n* alphabet *m* ■ **alphabetical** *adj* alphabétique

**Alps** [ælps] *npl* **the Alps** les Alpes *fpl* ■ **Alpine** *adj* [club, range] alpin ; [scenery] alpestre

**already** [ɔːl'redɪ] *adv* déjà

**alright** [ɔːl'raɪt] *Fam adv* = **all right**

**Alsatian** [æl'seɪʃən] *n* [dog] berger *m* allemand

**also** ['ɔːlsəʊ] *adv* aussi, également ; [moreover] de plus

**altar** ['ɔːltə(r)] *n* autel *m*

**alter** ['ɔːltə(r)] **1.** *vt* changer ; [clothing] retoucher **2.** *vi* changer ■ **alteration** *n* changement *m* (**in** de); [of clothing] retouche *f*; **alterations** [to building] travaux *mpl*

**alternate 1.** [ɔːl'tɜːnət] *adj* alterné ; **on alternate days** tous les deux jours **2.** ['ɔːltəneɪt] *vt* faire alterner **3.** ['ɔːltəneɪt] *vi* alterner (**with** avec); ELEC **alternating current** courant *m* alternatif

**alternative** [ɔːl'tɜːnətɪv] **1.** *adj* [other] de remplacement; **an alternative way** une autre façon; **alternative medicine** médecine *f* douce **2.** *n* [choice] alternative *f*; **she had no alternative but to obey** elle n'a pas pu faire autrement que d'obéir ■ **alternatively** *adv* (**or**) **alternatively** ou alors, ou bien

**although** [ɔːl'ðəʊ] *adv* bien que (+ *subjunctive*)

**altitude** ['æltɪtjuːd] *n* altitude *f*

**altogether** [ɔːltə'geðə(r)] *adv* [completely] tout à fait ; [on the whole] somme toute ; **how much altogether?** combien en tout ?

**aluminium** [*Br* ælju'mɪnɪəm], *Am* **aluminum** [ə'luːmɪnəm] *n* aluminium *m*

**always** ['ɔːlweɪz] *adv* toujours ; **he's always criticizing** il est toujours à critiquer ; **as always** comme toujours

**Alwz** MESSAGING *written abbr of* **always**

**am** [æm] (*unstressed* [əm]) *see* **be**

**a.m.** [eɪ'em] *adv* du matin

**amalgamate** [ə'mælgəmeɪt] *vt* & *vi* fusionner

**amateur** ['æmətə(r)] **1.** *n* amateur *m* **2.** *adj* [interest, sports, performance] d'amateur; **amateur painter/actress** peintre *m*/actrice *f* amateur

**amaze** [ə'meɪz] *vt* stupéfier ■ **amazed** *adj* stupéfait (**at sth** de qch); [filled with wonder] émerveillé; **I was amazed by his courage** son courage m'a stupéfié ■ **amazing** *adj* [surprising] stupéfiant; [incredible] extraordinaire

**ambassador** [æm'bæsədə(r)] *n* ambassadeur, -drice *mf*

**amber** ['æmbə(r)] *n* ambre *m*; **amber (light)** [of traffic signal] (feu *m*) orange *m*

**ambiguous** [æm'bɪgjʊəs] *adj* ambigu (f ambiguë)

**ambition** [æm'bɪʃən] *n* ambition *f* ■ **ambitious** *adj* ambitieux, -euse

**ambivalent** [æm'bɪvələnt] *adj* ambivalent

**ambulance** ['æmbjʊləns] *n* ambulance *f*; **ambulance driver** ambulancier, -ère *mf*

**ambush** ['æmbʊʃ] **1.** *n* embuscade *f* **2.** *vt* tendre une embuscade à ; **to be ambushed** tomber dans une embuscade

**AMBW** MESSAGING *written abbr of* **all my best wishes**

**amend** [ə'mend] *vt* [text] modifier ; POL [law] amender

**amends** [ə'mendz] *npl* **to make amends** se racheter; **to make amends for sth** réparer qch

**amenities** [Br ə'mi:nɪtɪz, Am ə'menɪtɪz] npl [of town] aménagements mpl; [shops] commerces mpl

**America** [ə'merɪkə] n l'Amérique f; **North/South America** l'Amérique f du Nord/du Sud ▪ **American 1.** adj américain **2.** n Américain, -e mf

**amiable** ['eɪmɪəbəl] adj aimable

**amicable** ['æmɪkəbəl] adj amical

**amid(st)** [ə'mɪd(st)] prep au milieu de, parmi

**amiss** [ə'mɪs] adv & adj **something is amiss** [wrong] quelque chose ne va pas; **that wouldn't go amiss** ça ne ferait pas de mal

**AML** MESSAGING written abbr of **of all my love**

**ammunition** [æmju'nɪʃən] n munitions fpl

**among(st)** [ə'mʌŋ(st)] prep [amidst] parmi; [between] entre; **among(st) the crowd/books/others/etc** parmi la foule/les livres/les autres/etc; **among(st) friends** entre amis; **among(st) other things** entre autres (choses)

**amoral** [eɪ'mɒrəl] adj amoral

**amount** [ə'maʊnt] **1.** n quantité f; [sum of money] somme f; [total figure of invoice, debt] montant m; [scope, size] importance f **2.** vi **to amount to** [bill] s'élever à; Fig **it amounts to blackmail** ce n'est rien d'autre que du chantage; **it amounts to the same thing** ça revient au même

**amp** [æmp] n [unit of electricity] ampère m; Br **3-amp plug** prise f avec fusible de 3 ampères

**ample** ['æmpəl] adj **a)** [plentiful] abondant **b)** [large - woman, bosom] fort **c)** [roomy - garment] large

**amplify** ['æmplɪfaɪ] (pt & pp -ied) vt [essay, remarks] développer; [sound] amplifier ▪ **amplifier** n amplificateur m

**amputate** ['æmpjʊteɪt] vt amputer; **to amputate sb's hand/etc** amputer qn de la main/etc

**amuse** [ə'mju:z] vt amuser; **to keep sb amused** distraire qn ▪ **amusement** n amusement m, divertissement m; [pastime] distraction f; **amusements** [at fairground] attractions fpl; [gambling machines] machines fpl à sous; **amusement arcade** salle f de jeux; **amusement park** parc m d'attractions

**an** [æn] (unstressed [ən]) see **a**

**an(a)emic** [ə'ni:mɪk] adj anémique; **to become an(a)emic** faire de l'anémie

**an(a)esthetic** [ænəs'θetɪk] n [process] anesthésie f; [substance] anesthésique m; **under an(a)esthetic** sous anesthésie; **general/local an(a)esthetic** anesthésie f générale/locale

**analogy** [ə'nælədʒɪ] (pl -ies) n analogie f (**with** avec)

**analyse** ['ænəlaɪz] vt analyser ▪ **analysis** (pl -yses [-əsi:z]) n analyse f ▪ **analyst** n analyste mf

**anarchy** ['ænəkɪ] n anarchie f ▪ **anarchist** n anarchiste mf

**anatomy** [ə'nætəmɪ] n anatomie f

**ancestor** ['ænsestə(r)] n ancêtre m

**anchor** ['æŋkə(r)] **1.** n ancre f **2.** vt [ship] mettre à l'ancre **3.** vi jeter l'ancre, mouiller

**anchovy** [Br 'æntʃəvɪ, Am æn'tʃəʊvɪ] (pl -ies) n anchois m

**ancient** ['eɪnʃənt] adj ancien, -enne; [pre-medieval] antique

**and** [ænd] (unstressed [æn(d)]) conj et; **a knife and fork** un couteau et une fourchette; **my mother and father** mon père et ma mère; **two hundred and two** deux cent deux; **four and three quarters** quatre trois quarts; **nice and warm** bien chaud; **better and better** de mieux en mieux; **she can read and write** elle sait lire et écrire; **go and see** va voir; **I knocked and knocked** j'ai frappé pendant un bon moment

**anemic** [ə'ni:mɪk] adj = **anaemic**

**anesthetic** [ænɪs'θetɪk] n = **anaesthetic**

**angel** ['eɪndʒəl] n ange m ▪ **angelic** adj angélique

**anger** ['æŋgə(r)] **1.** n colère f; **in anger, out of anger** sous le coup de la colère **2.** vt mettre en colère

**angina** [æn'dʒaɪnə] *n* angine *f* de poitrine

**angle¹** ['æŋgəl] *n* angle *m*; **at an angle** en biais

**angle²** ['æŋgəl] *vi* [fish] pêcher à la ligne; *Fig* **to angle for** [compliments] quêter ■ **angler** *n* pêcheur, -euse *mf* à la ligne

**Anglican** ['æŋglɪkən] *adj* & *n* anglican, -e *(mf)*

**Anglo-** ['æŋgləʊ] *pref* anglo- ■ **Anglo-Saxon** *adj* & *n* anglo-saxon, -onne *(mf)*

**angry** ['æŋgrɪ] *(compar* -ier, *superl* -iest) *adj* [person] en colère, fâché; [look] furieux, -euse; **an angry letter** une lettre indignée; **angry words** des paroles indignées; **to get angry (with)** se fâcher (contre)

**anguish** ['æŋgwɪʃ] *n* angoisse *f*

**animal** ['ænɪməl] *n* animal *m*

**animated** ['ænɪmeɪtɪd] *adj* [lively] animé; **to become animated** s'animer

**animation** [ænɪ'meɪʃən] *n* [liveliness & CIN] animation *f*

**aniseed** ['ænɪsiːd] *n* [as flavouring] anis *m*

**ankle** ['æŋkəl] *n* cheville *f*; **ankle sock** socquette *f*

**annex¹** [ə'neks] *vt* annexer

**annex²**, *Br* **annexe** ['æneks] *n* [building] annexe *f*

**anniversary** [ænɪ'vɜːsərɪ] *(pl* -ies) *n* [of event] anniversaire *m*

**announce** [ə'naʊns] *vt* annoncer; [birth, marriage] faire part de ■ **announcement** *n* [statement] annonce *f*; [notice of birth, marriage, death - in newspaper] avis *m*; [private letter] faire-part *m inv* ■ **announcer** *n* [on TV] speaker, -ine *mf*

**annoy** [ə'nɔɪ] *vt* [inconvenience] ennuyer; [irritate] agacer ■ **annoyed** *adj* fâché; **to get annoyed (with)** se fâcher (contre) ■ **annoying** *adj* ennuyeux, -euse

**annual** ['ænjʊəl] **1.** *adj* annuel, -elle **2.** *n* [yearbook] annuaire *m*; [children's] album *m*; [plant] plante *f* annuelle ■ **annually** *adv* [every year] tous les ans; [per year] par an

**annul** [ə'nʌl] *(pt & pp* -ll-) *vt* [contract, marriage] annuler

**anoint** [ə'nɔɪnt] *vt* oindre **(with** de)

**anomalous** [ə'nɒmələs] *adj* anormal ■ **anomaly** *(pl* -ies) *n* anomalie *f*

**anonymous** [ə'nɒnɪməs] *adj* anonyme

**anorak** ['ænəræk] *n* anorak *m*

**anorexia** [ænə'reksɪə] *n* anorexie *f* ■ **anorexic** *adj* & *n* anorexique *(mf)*

**another** [ə'nʌðə(r)] *adj* & *pron* un(e) autre; **another man** [different] un autre homme; **another month** [additional] encore un mois; **another ten** encore dix; **one another** l'un(e) l'autre, *pl* les un(e)s les autres; **they love one another** ils s'aiment

**answer** ['ɑːnsə(r)] **1.** *n* réponse *f*; [to problem, riddle & MATH] solution *f* (**to** de); [reason] explication *f*; **in answer to your letter** en réponse à votre lettre **2.** *vt* [person, question, letter] répondre à; [prayer, wish] exaucer; **he answered yes** il a répondu oui; **to answer the door** ouvrir la porte; **to answer the phone** répondre au téléphone **3.** *vi* répondre ■ **answering machine** *n* répondeur *m*

**ant** [ænt] *n* fourmi *f*

**antagonize** [æn'tægənaɪz] *vt* provoquer (l'hostilité de)

**Antarctic** [æn'tɑːktɪk] **1.** *adj* antarctique **2.** *n* **the Antarctic** l'Antarctique *m*

**antenatal** [æntɪ'neɪtəl] *adj Br* prénatal; **antenatal classes** préparation *f* à l'accouchement

**antenna¹** [æn'tenə] *(pl* -ae [-iː]) *n* [of insect] antenne *f*

**antenna²** [æn'tenə] *(pl* -as) *n Am* [for TV, radio] antenne *f*

**anthem** ['ænθəm] *n* **national anthem** hymne *m* national

**anthology** [æn'θɒlədʒɪ] *(pl* -ies) *n* anthologie *f*

**anti-** [*Br* 'æntɪ, *Am* 'æntaɪ] *pref* anti- ■ **antibiotic** *adj* & *n* antibiotique *(m)* ■ **anticlimax** *n* déception *f* ■ **anticlockwise** *adv Br* dans le sens inverse des aiguilles d'une montre ■ **antidote** *n* antidote *m* ■ **antifreeze** *n* [for vehicle] antigel *m* ■ **antihistamine** *n* [drug] antihistaminique *m* ■ **antiperspirant** *n* déodorant *m* ■ **anti-Semitic** *adj* antisémite ■ **antiseptic** *adj & n* antiseptique *(m)* ■ **antisocial** *adj* [unsociable] peu sociable

**anticipate** [æn'tɪsɪpeɪt] *vt* [foresee] anticiper ; [expect] s'attendre à, prévoir ; [forestall] devancer ■ **anticipation** *n* [expectation] attente *f* ; [foresight] prévision *f* ; **in anticipation of** en prévision de ; **in anticipation** [thank, pay] d'avance

**antics** ['æntɪks] *npl* singeries *fpl* ; **he's up to his antics again** il a encore fait des siennes

**antiglobalization, antiglobalisation** [ˌæntɪɡləʊbəlaɪ'zeɪʃən] **1.** *n* POL antimondialisation *f* **2.** *adj* POL antimondialisation

**antiquated** ['æntɪkweɪtɪd] *adj* [expression, custom] vieillot, -otte ; [person] vieux jeu *inv* ; [object, machine] antédiluvien, -enne

**antique** [æn'tiːk] **1.** *adj* [furniture] ancien, -enne ; [of Greek or Roman antiquity] antique ; **antique dealer** antiquaire *mf* ; **antique shop** magasin *m* d'antiquités **2.** *n* antiquité *f*, objet *m* d'époque

**antivirus** ['æntɪvaɪrəs] *adj* antivirus ; **antivirus software** antivirus *m*

**Antwerp** ['æntwɜːp] *n* Anvers *m* ou *f*

**anxiety** [æŋ'zaɪətɪ] *(pl* **-ies)** *n* [worry] inquiétude *f* (**about** au sujet de) ; [fear] anxiété *f* ; [eagerness] désir *m* (**to do** de faire ; **for sth** de qch)

**anxious** ['æŋkʃəs] *adj* [worried] inquiet, -ète (**about** pour) ; [troubled] anxieux, -euse ; [causing worry] angoissant ; [eager] impatient (**to do** de faire)

**any** ['enɪ] **1.** *adj* **a)** [in questions] du, de la, des ; **have you any milk / tickets?** avez-vous du lait / des billets ? **b)** [in negatives] de ; [the slightest] aucun ; **he hasn't got any milk / tickets** il n'a pas de lait / de billets ; **there isn't any doubt / problem** il n'y a aucun doute / problème

**c)** [no matter which] n'importe quel ; **ask any doctor** demande à n'importe quel médecin **d)** [every] tout ; **at any moment** à tout moment ; **in any case, at any rate** de toute façon **2.** *pron* **a)** [no matter which one] n'importe lequel ; [somebody] quelqu'un ; **if any of you...** si l'un d'entre vous..., si quelqu'un parmi vous... **b)** [quantity] en ; **have you got any?** en as-tu ? ; **I don't see any** je n'en vois pas **3.** *adv* **not any further / happier** pas plus loin / plus heureux, -euse ; **I don't see him any more** je ne le vois plus ; **any more tea?** encore un peu de thé ? ; **I'm not any better** je ne vais pas mieux

**anybody** ['enɪbɒdɪ] *pron* **a)** [somebody] quelqu'un ; **do you see anybody?** tu vois quelqu'un ? ; **more than anybody** plus que tout autre **b)** [in negatives] personne ; **he doesn't know anybody** il ne connaît personne **c)** [no matter who] n'importe qui ; **anybody would think that...** on croirait que...

**anyhow** ['enɪhaʊ] *adv* [at any rate] de toute façon ; *Fam* [badly] n'importe comment

**anyone** ['enɪwʌn] *pron* = **anybody**

**ANY1** MESSAGING *written abbr of* **anyone**

**anyplace** ['enɪpleɪs] *Am adv* = **anywhere**

**anything** ['enɪθɪŋ] *pron* **a)** [something] quelque chose ; **can you see anything?** tu vois quelque chose ? **b)** [in negatives] rien ; **he doesn't do anything** il ne fait rien ; **without anything** sans rien **c)** [everything] tout ; **anything you like** tout ce que tu veux ; *Fam* **like anything** [work] comme un fou **d)** [no matter what] **anything (at all)** n'importe quoi

**anytime** ['enɪtaɪm] *adv* **a)** [at any time] n'importe quand, à n'importe quel moment ; **call me anytime** appelle-moi quand tu veux ; **they can flower anytime between May and September** ils peuvent fleurir à n'importe quel moment entre mai et septembre **b)** [you're welcome] je t'en prie, je vous en prie; **thanks for driving me to the airport — anytime!** merci de m'avoir conduit à l'aéroport — je t'en prie!

**anyway** ['enɪweɪ] *adv* [at any rate] de toute façon

**anywhere** ['enɪweə(r)] *adv* a) [no matter where] n'importe où b) [everywhere] partout; **anywhere you go** où que vous alliez, partout où vous allez; **anywhere you like** (là) où tu veux c) [somewhere] quelque part; **is he going anywhere?** va-t-il quelque part? d) [in negatives] nulle part; **he doesn't go anywhere** il ne va nulle part; **without anywhere to put it** sans un endroit où le/la mettre

**AP** ['eɪ'pi:] *(abbr of Advanced Placement)* *n Am* SCH *examen de niveau universitaire passé par les lycéens qui le souhaitent pour obtenir des crédits pour l'université*

**apart** [ə'pɑːt] *adv* a) [separated] **we kept them apart** nous les tenions séparés; **two years apart** à deux ans d'intervalle; **they are a metre apart** ils se trouvent à un mètre l'un de l'autre; **to come apart** [of two objects] se séparer; **to tell two things/people apart** distinguer deux choses/personnes (l'une de l'autre) b) [to pieces] **to tear apart** mettre en pièces; **to take apart** démonter c) [to one side] à part; **joking apart** sans blague; **apart from** [except for] à part

**apartment** [ə'pɑːtmənt] *n* appartement *m*; *Am* **apartment building, apartment house** immeuble *m* (d'habitation)

**apathy** ['æpəθɪ] *n* apathie *f*

**ape** [eɪp] **1.** *n* grand singe *m* **2.** *vt* [imitate] singer

**aperitif** [əperɪ'tiːf] *n* apéritif *m*

■ **aperture** ['æpətʃʊə(r)] *n* ouverture *f*

**apiece** [ə'piːs] *adv* chacun; **£ 2 apiece** 2 livres pièce *ou* chacun

**apologetic** [əpɒlə'dʒetɪk] *adj* [letter] plein d'excuses; [smile] d'excuse; **to be apologetic (about)** s'excuser (de)

**apology** [ə'pɒlədʒɪ] *(pl -ies)* *n* excuses *fpl* ■ **apologize** *vi* s'excuser (**for** de); **he**

**apologized for being late** il s'est excusé de son retard; **to apologize to sb (for)** faire ses excuses à qn (pour)

**apostle** [ə'pɒsəl] *n* apôtre *m*

**apostrophe** [ə'pɒstrəfɪ] *n* apostrophe *f*

**app** [æp] *(abbr of application)* *n* COMPUT application *f*, appli *f Fam*

**appal,** *Am* **appall** [ə'pɔːl] *(pt & pp -ll-)* *vt* consterner; **to be appalled (at)** être horrifié (par) ■ **appalling** *adj* épouvantable

**apparatus** [æpə'reɪtəs] *n* [equipment, organization] appareil *m*; *Br* [in gym] agrès *mpl*

**apparel** [ə'pærəl] *n* vêtements *mpl*

**apparent** [ə'pærənt] *adj* [seeming] apparent; [obvious] évident; **it's apparent that...** il est clair que... ■ **apparently** *adv* apparemment; **apparently she's going to Venice** il paraît qu'elle va à Venise

**appeal** [ə'piːl] **1.** *n* [charm] attrait *m*; [interest] intérêt *m*; [call] appel *m*; [pleading] supplication *f*; [to a court] appel *m* **2.** *vt* a) [in court] faire appel b) **to appeal to sb** [attract] plaire à qn; [interest] intéresser qn; [ask for help] faire appel à qn; **to appeal to sb's generosity** faire appel à la générosité de qn; **to appeal to sb for sth** demander qch à qn; **to appeal to sb to do sth** supplier qn de faire qch ■ **appealing** *adj* [attractive - offer, idea] séduisant; [begging - look] suppliant

**appear** [ə'pɪə(r)] *vi* [become visible] apparaître; [seem, be published] paraître; [on stage, in film] jouer; [in court] comparaître; **it appears that...** [it seems that] il semble que... (+ *subjunctive or indicative*); [it is rumoured that] il paraît que... (+ *indicative*) ■ **appearance** *n* [act] apparition *f*; [look] apparence *f*; [of book] parution *f*; **to put in an appearance** faire acte de présence; **to keep up appearances** sauver les apparences

**appendix** [ə'pendɪks] *(pl -ixes* [-ɪksɪz] *or -ices* [-ɪsiːz]*)* *n* [in book, body] appendice *m*; **to have one's appendix out** se faire opérer de l'appendicite ■ **appendicitis** *n* appendicite *f*

**appetite** ['æpɪtaɪt] *n* appétit *m* ■ **appetizer** *n* [drink] apéritif *m*; [food] amuse-gueule *m inv* ■ **appetizing** *adj* appétissant

**applaud** [ə'plɔːd] **1.** *vt* [clap] applaudir; [approve of] approuver, applaudir à **2.** *vi* applaudir ■ **applause** *n* applaudissements *mpl*

**apple** ['æpəl] *n* pomme *f*; *Br* **stewed apples** compote *f* de pommes; **cooking apple** pomme *f* à cuire; **eating apple** pomme *f* de dessert; **apple core** trognon *m* de pomme; **apple pie** tarte *f* aux pommes; **apple sauce** compote *f* de pommes; **apple tree** pommier *m*

**appliance** [ə'plaɪəns] *n* appareil *m*

**applicable** [ə'plɪkəbəl] *adj* [rule] applicable (**to** à); [relevant] pertinent (**to** à)

**applicant** ['æplɪkənt] *n* candidat, -e *mf* (**for** à)

**application** [æplɪ'keɪʃən] *n* **a)** [request] demande *f* (**for** de); [for job] candidature *f* (**for** de); [for membership] demande *f* d'inscription; **application (form)** [for job] formulaire *m* de candidature; [for club] formulaire *m* d'inscription; COMPUT **applications program** programme *m* d'application **b)** [diligence] application *f*

**apply** [ə'plaɪ] (*pt & pp* **-ied**) **1.** *vt* [put on, carry out] appliquer; [brake] appuyer sur; **to apply oneself (to)** s'appliquer (à) **2.** *vi* [be relevant] s'appliquer (**to** à); **to apply for** [job] poser sa candidature à; **to apply to sb (for)** [ask] s'adresser à qn (pour) ■ **applied** *adj* [maths, linguistics] appliqué

**appoint** [ə'pɔɪnt] *vt* [person] nommer (**to a post** à un poste; **to do** pour faire); [director, minister] nommer; [secretary, clerk] engager; [time, place] fixer; **at the appointed time** à l'heure dite ■ **appointment** *n* nomination *f*; [meeting] rendez-vous *m inv*; [post] situation *f*; **to make an appointment with** prendre rendez-vous avec

**appraise** [ə'preɪz] *vt* évaluer ■ **appraisal** *n* évaluation *f*

**appreciate** [ə'priːʃɪeɪt] **1.** *vt* [enjoy, value, assess] apprécier; [understand] comprendre; [be grateful for] être reconnaissant de **2.** *vi* [of goods] prendre de la valeur ■ **appreciation** *n* **a)** [gratitude] reconnaissance *f*; [judgement] appréciation *f* **b)** [rise in value] augmentation *f* (de la valeur) ■ **appreciative** *adj* [grateful] reconnaissant (**of** de); [favourable] élogieux, -euse; **to be appreciative of** [enjoy] apprécier

**apprehend** [æprɪ'hend] *vt* [seize, arrest] appréhender

**apprehensive** [æprɪ'hensɪv] *adj* inquiet, -ète (**about** de *ou* au sujet de); **to be apprehensive of** appréhender

**apprentice** [ə'prentɪs] *n* apprenti, -e *mf* ■ **apprenticeship** *n* apprentissage *m*

**approach** [ə'prəʊtʃ] **1.** *n* [method] façon *f* de s'y prendre; [path, route] voie *f* d'accès; [of winter, vehicle] approche *f* **2.** *vt* [draw near to] s'approcher de; [go up to, tackle] aborder; **to approach sb about sth** parler à qn de qch; **he's approaching forty** il va sur ses quarante ans **3.** *vi* [of person, vehicle] s'approcher; [of date] approcher ■ **approachable** *adj* [person] d'un abord facile

**appropriate 1.** [ə'prəʊprɪət] *adj* [place, clothes, means] approprié (**to** à); [remark, time] opportun; **appropriate to** *or* **for** qui convient à **2.** [ə'prəʊprɪeɪt] *vt* [steal] s'approprier; [set aside] affecter (**for** à)

**approve** [ə'pruːv] *vt* approuver; **to approve of** [conduct, decision, idea] approuver; **I don't approve of him** il ne me plaît pas ■ **approval** *n* approbation *f*; **on approval** [goods] à l'essai

**approving** [ə'pruːvɪŋ] *adj* [look] approbateur, -trice

**approximate 1.** [ə'prɒksɪmət] *adj* approximatif, -ive **2.** [ə'prɒksɪmeɪt] *vi* **to approximate to sth** se rapprocher de qch

**apricot** ['eɪprɪkɒt] *n* abricot *m* ■

**April** ['eɪprəl] *n* avril *m*; **April fool!** poisson d'avril !; **April Fools' Day** le 1ᵉʳ avril

**apron** ['eɪprən] *n* [garment] tablier *m*

**apt** [æpt] *adj* [remark, reply, means] qui convient ; [word, name] bien choisi; **to be apt to do sth** avoir tendance à faire qch ■ **aptly** *adv* [described] justement ; [chosen] bien

**aptitude** ['æptɪtjuːd] *n* aptitude *f* (**for** pour) ; [of student] don *m* (**for** pour)

**aquaculture** ['ækwəˌkʌltʃə(r)] *n* aquaculture *f*

**aquarium** [əˈkweərɪəm] *n* aquarium *m*

**Aquarius** [əˈkweərɪəs] *n* [sign] le Verseau

**aquatic** [əˈkwætɪk] *adj* [plant] aquatique ; [sport] nautique

**Arab** ['ærəb] **1.** *adj* arabe **2.** *n* Arabe *mf* ■ **Arabian** *adj* arabe ■ **Arabic** *adj* & *n* [language] arabe *(m)*; **Arabic numerals** chiffres *mpl* arabes

**arbitrary** ['ɑːbɪtrərɪ] *adj* arbitraire

**arbitration** [ɑːbɪˈtreɪʃən] *n* arbitrage *m*

**arc** [ɑːk] *n* [of circle] arc *m*

**arcade** [ɑːˈkeɪd] *n* [for shops - small] passage *m* couvert ; [large] galerie *f* marchande

**arch** [ɑːtʃ] **1.** *n* [of bridge] arche *f*; [of building] voûte *f*, arc *m* ; [of foot] cambrure *f* **2.** *vt* to arch one's back [inwards] se cambrer ; [outwards] se voûter

**arch-** [ɑːtʃ] *pref* **arch-enemy** ennemi *m* juré; **arch-rival** grand rival *m*

**archaeology** [ɑːkɪˈɒlədʒɪ] *n* archéologie *f* ■ **archaeologist** *n* archéologue *mf*

**archaic** [ɑːˈkeɪɪk] *adj* archaïque

**archbishop** [ɑːtʃˈbɪʃəp] *n* archevêque *m*

**archeologist** [ɑːkɪˈɒlədʒɪst] *n* = **archaeologist**

**archeology** [ɑːkɪˈɒlədʒɪ] *n* = **archaeology**

**archer** ['ɑːtʃə(r)] *n* archer *m*

**archetype** ['ɑːkɪtaɪp] *n* archétype *m*

**architect** ['ɑːkɪtekt] *n* architecte *mf* ■ **architecture** *n* architecture *f*

**archives** ['ɑːkaɪvz] *npl* archives *fpl*

**archway** ['ɑːtʃweɪ] *n* voûte *f*

**arctic** ['ɑːktɪk] **1.** *adj* arctique ; [weather] polaire, glacial **2.** *n* **the Arctic** l'Arctique *m*

**ardent** ['ɑːdənt] *adj* [supporter] ardent, chaud

**ardour** ['ɑːdə(r)] *n* ardeur *f*

**arduous** ['ɑːdjʊəs] *adj* pénible, ardu

**are** [ɑː(r)] *see* **be**

**area** ['eərɪə] *n* [of country] région *f*; [of town] quartier *m*; MIL zone *f*; [surface] superficie *f*; *Fig* [of knowledge] domaine *m*; **kitchen area** coin-cuisine *m*; **play area** aire *f* de jeux; *Am* **area code** [in phone number] indicatif *m*

**arena** [əˈriːnə] *n* [for sports] & *Fig* arène *f*

**aren't** [ɑːnt] = **are not**

**Argentina** [ɑːdʒənˈtiːnə] *n* l'Argentine *f*

**arguable** ['ɑːgjʊəbəl] *adj* discutable

**argue** ['ɑːgjuː] **1.** *vt* [matter] discuter (de) ; [position] défendre ; **to argue that...** soutenir que... **2.** *vi* [quarrel] se disputer (**with** / **about** avec / au sujet de) ; [reason] raisonner (**with** / **about** avec / sur)

**argument** ['ɑːgjʊmənt] *n* [quarrel] dispute *f*; [debate] discussion *f*; [point] argument *m*; **to have an argument with sb** [quarrel] se disputer avec qn ■ **argumentative** *adj* [person] querelleur, -euse

**Aries** ['eəriːz] *n* [sign] le Bélier; **to be Aries** être Bélier

**arise** [əˈraɪz] *(pt* **arose**, *pp* **arisen** [əˈrɪzən]*)* *vi* [of problem, opportunity] se présenter ; [of cry, objection] s'élever ; [result] provenir (**from** de)

**aristocracy** [ærɪˈstɒkrəsɪ] *n* aristocratie *f* ■ **aristocrat** [*Br* 'ærɪstəkræt, *Am* əˈrɪstəkræt] *n* aristocrate *mf*

**arithmetic** [əˈrɪθmətɪk] *n* arithmétique *f*

**ark** [ɑːk] *n* **Noah's ark** l'arche *f* de Noé

**arm¹** [ɑːm] *n* bras *m*; **arm in arm** bras dessus bras dessous; **with open arms** à bras ouverts ■ **armband** *n* brassard *m*

■ **armchair** n fauteuil m ■ **armpit** n aisselle f ■ **armrest** ['ɑːmrest] n accoudoir m

**arm²** [ɑːm] vt [with weapon] armer (**with** de) ■ **armaments** npl armements mpl

**armistice** ['ɑːmɪstɪs] n armistice m

**armour** ['ɑːmə(r)] n [of knight] armure f; [of tank] blindage m ■ **armoured**, **armour-plated** ['ɑːməpleɪtɪd] adj [car] blindé

**arms** [ɑːmz] npl [weapons] armes fpl; **the arms race** la course aux armements

**army** ['ɑːmɪ] 1. (pl -ies) n armée f; **to join the army** s'engager 2. adj [uniform] militaire

**A road** ['eɪrəʊd] n Br ≃ route f nationale

**aroma** [ə'rəʊmə] n arôme m ■ **aromatherapy** n aromathérapie f ■ **aromatic** [ærəʊ'mætɪk] adj aromatique

**arose** [ə'rəʊz] pp of **arise**

**around** [ə'raʊnd] 1. prep autour de ; [approximately] environ; **to travel around the world** faire le tour du monde 2. adv autour; **all around** tout autour; **around here** par ici; **to follow sb around** suivre qn partout; **to rush around** courir dans tous les sens; **is Jack around?** est-ce que Jack est dans le coin ?; **he's still around** il est encore là; **there's a lot of flu around** beaucoup de gens ont la grippe en ce moment

**arouse** [ə'raʊz] vt [suspicion, anger, curiosity] éveiller

**arrange** [ə'reɪndʒ] vt arranger ; [time, meeting] fixer; **to arrange to do sth** s'arranger pour faire qch ■ **arrangement** n [layout, agreement, for music] arrangement m; **arrangements** [preparations] préparatifs mpl; [plans] projets mpl; **to make arrangements to do sth** prendre des dispositions pour faire qch

**arrears** [ə'rɪəz] npl [payment] arriéré m; **to be in arrears** avoir du retard dans ses paiements

**arrest** [ə'rest] 1. vt [criminal, progress] arrêter 2. n [of criminal] arrestation f; **under arrest** en état d'arrestation

**arrive** [ə'raɪv] vi arriver; **to arrive at** [conclusion, decision] arriver à, parvenir à ■ **arrival** n arrivée f; **on my arrival** à mon arrivée; **new arrival** nouveau venu m, nouvelle venue f; [baby] nouveau-né, -e mf

**arrogant** ['ærəgənt] adj arrogant ■ **arrogance** n arrogance f

**arrow** ['ærəʊ] n flèche f

**arson** ['ɑːsən] n incendie m criminel

**art** [ɑːt] n art m; **faculty of arts, arts faculty** faculté f des lettres; **arts degree** ≃ licence f ès lettres; **art exhibition** exposition f d'œuvres d'art; **art gallery** [museum] musée m d'art ; [shop] galerie f d'art; **art school** école f des beaux-arts

**artery** ['ɑːtərɪ] (pl -ies) n artère f

**arthritis** [ɑː'θraɪtɪs] n arthrite f

**artichoke** ['ɑːtɪtʃəʊk] n (globe) artichoke artichaut m; **Jerusalem artichoke** topinambour m

**article** ['ɑːtɪkəl] n article m; **article of clothing** vêtement m; Br **articles** [of lawyer] contrat m de stage

**articulate** 1. [ɑː'tɪkjʊlət] adj [person] qui s'exprime clairement; [speech] clair 2. [ɑː'tɪkjʊleɪt] vt & vi [speak] articuler ■ **articulation** [-'leɪʃən] n articulation f

**artificial** [ɑːtɪ'fɪʃəl] adj artificiel, -elle

**artillery** [ɑː'tɪlərɪ] n artillerie f

**artist** ['ɑːtɪst] n artiste mf ■ **artiste** n [singer, dancer] artiste mf ■ **artistic** adj [pattern, treasure] artistique ; [person] artiste

**artless** ['ɑːtləs] adj naturel, -elle

**arty** ['ɑːtɪ] adj Pej du genre artiste

**as** [æz] (unstressed [əz]) 1. adv a) [with manner] comme ; **as promised / planned** comme promis / prévu; **as you like** comme tu veux ; **such as** comme, tel que; **as much as I can** (au) tant que je peux; **as it is** [this being the case] les choses étant ainsi; **to leave sth as it is** laisser qch comme ça ou tel quel; **it's late as it is** il est déjà tard; **as if, as though** comme si; **you look as if or as though you're tired** tu as l'air fatigué

**b)** [comparison] **as tall as you** aussi grand que vous; **as white as a sheet** blanc (*f* blanche) comme un linge; **as much as you** autant que vous; **as much money as** autant d'argent que; **as many people as** autant de gens que; **twice as big as** deux fois plus grand que; **the same as** le même que
**2.** *conj* **a)** [expressing time] **as always** comme toujours; **as I was leaving, as I left** comme je partais; **as one grows older** à mesure que l'on vieillit; **as he slept** pendant qu'il dormait; **one day as...** un jour que...; **as from, as of** [time] à partir de
**b)** [expressing reason] puisque, comme; **as it's late...** puisqu'il est tard..., comme il est tard...
**c)** [though] **(as) clever as he is...** si intelligent qu'il soit...
**d)** [concerning] **as for that** quant à cela
**e)** [+ infinitive] **so as to...** de manière à...; **so stupid as to...** assez bête pour...
**3.** *prep* comme; **she works as a cashier** elle est caissière, elle travaille comme caissière; **dressed up as a clown** déguisé en clown; **as a teacher** en tant que professeur

**asap, ASAP** *(abbr of* **as soon as possible***)* *adv* dès que possible, le plus tôt *ou* le plus vite possible, asap

**ascend** [ə'send] **1.** *vt* [throne] accéder à; [stairs, mountain] gravir **2.** *vi* monter ■ **ascent** *n* ascension *f* (**of** de); [slope] côte *f*

**ascertain** [æsə'teɪn] *vt* [discover] établir; [check] s'assurer de; **to ascertain that...** s'assurer que...

**ash** [æʃ] *n* **a)** [of cigarette, fire] cendre *f*; **Ash Wednesday** mercredi *m* des Cendres **b)** [tree] frêne *m* ■ **ashtray** *n* cendrier *m*

**ashamed** [ə'ʃeɪmd] *adj* **to be / feel ashamed (of sb / sth)** avoir honte (de qn / qch); **to be ashamed of oneself** avoir honte; **to make sb ashamed** faire honte à qn

**ashore** [ə'ʃɔː(r)] *adv* à terre; **to go ashore** débarquer

**Asia** ['eɪʃə, 'eɪʒə] *n* l'Asie *f* ■ **Asian 1.** *adj* asiatique; *Br* [from Indian sub-continent] du *sous-continent indien* **2.** *n* Asiatique *mf*; *Br* [from Indian sub-continent] *personne originaire du sous-continent indien*

**aside** [ə'saɪd] **1.** *adv* de côté; **to take** *or* **draw sb aside** prendre qn à part; **to step aside** s'écarter; *Am* **aside from** en dehors de **2.** *n* [in play, film] aparté *m*

**ask** [ɑːsk] **1.** *vt* [request, inquire about] demander; [invite] inviter (**to sth** à qch); **to ask sb sth** demander qch à qn; **to ask sb about sb / sth** interroger qn sur qn / qch; **to ask (sb) a question** poser une question (à qn); **to ask sb the time / way** demander l'heure / son chemin à qn; **to ask sb for sth** demander qch à qn; **to ask sb to do** [request] demander à qn de faire; [invite] inviter qn à faire; **to ask sb to leave / *etc*** demander à partir / *etc* **2.** *vi* [inquire] se renseigner (**about** sur); [request] demander; **to ask after** *or* **about sb** demander des nouvelles de qn; **to ask for sb / sth** demander qn / qch; **to ask for information** se renseigner; **to ask questions** poser des questions; **the asking price** le prix demandé

**askew** [ə'skjuː] *adv* de travers

**asleep** [ə'sliːp] *adj* endormi; [arm, leg] engourdi; **to be asleep** dormir; **to fall asleep** s'endormir

**AS level** *n Br* examen facultatif complétant les *A-levels*

**asparagus** [ə'spærəgəs] *n* [plant] asperge *f*; [food] asperges *fpl*

**aspect** ['æspekt] *n* aspect *m*; [of house] orientation *f*

**asphyxiate** [æs'fɪksɪeɪt] *vt* asphyxier

**aspire** [ə'spaɪə(r)] *vi* **to aspire to** aspirer à ■ **aspiration** [æspɪ'reɪʃən] *n* aspiration *f*

**aspirin** ['æsprɪn] *n* aspirine *f*

**ass** [æs] *n* âne *m*

**assailant** [ə'seɪlənt] *n* agresseur *m*

**assassin** [ə'sæsɪn] *n* assassin *m* ■ **assassinate** *vt* assassiner ■ **assassination** *n* assassinat *m*

**assault** [əˈsɔːlt] **1.** n [military] assaut m ; [crime] agression f **2.** vt [attack] agresser; **to be sexually assaulted** être victime d'une agression sexuelle

**assemble** [əˈsembəl] **1.** vt [objects, ideas] assembler ; [people] rassembler ; [machine] monter **2.** vi se rassembler ■ **assembly** n [meeting] assemblée f; [of machine] montage m, assemblage m ; [in school] rassemblement m (avant les cours); **assembly line** [in factory] chaîne f de montage

**assent** [əˈsent] **1.** n assentiment m **2.** vi consentir (**to** à)

**assert** [əˈsɜːt] vt affirmer (**that** que) ; [rights] faire valoir; **to assert oneself** s'affirmer ■ **assertion** n [statement] affirmation f ; [of rights] revendication f ■ **assertive** adj [forceful - tone, person] affirmatif, -ive ; [authoritarian] autoritaire

**assess** [əˈses] vt [value, damage] évaluer ; [situation] analyser ; [decide amount of] fixer le montant de ; [person] juger ■ **assessment** n [of value, damage] évaluation f ; [of situation] analyse f; [of person] jugement m

**asset** [ˈæset] n [advantage] atout m ; **assets** [of business] avoir m

**assign** [əˈsaɪn] vt [give] attribuer ; [day, time] fixer ; [appoint] nommer ; [send, move] affecter (**to** à) ■ **assignment** n [task] mission f ; [for student] devoir m

**assimilate** [əˈsɪmɪleɪt] **1.** vt [absorb] assimiler **2.** vi [of immigrants] s'assimiler

**assist** [əˈsɪst] vt & vi aider (**in doing** or **to do** à faire) ■ **assistance** n aide f; **to be of assistance to sb** aider qn ; **assistance dog** chien m guide ■ **assistant 1.** n assistant, -e mf; Br [in shop] vendeur, -euse mf **2.** adj adjoint ■ **assistant headmaster** [əˈsɪstənt ˌhedˈmɑːstə(r)], Am **assistant principal** [əˈsɪstənt ˌprɪnsəpl] n SCH principal m adjoint, principale f adjointe

**associate 1.** [əˈsəʊʃieɪt] vt associer (**with sth** à ou avec qch; **with sb** à qn) **2.** [əˈsəʊʃieɪt] vi **to associate with sb** [mix socially] fréquenter qn **3.** [əˈsəʊʃiət] n & adj associé, -e (mf) ■ **association** [-ˈeɪʃən] n association f

**assorted** [əˈsɔːtɪd] adj [different] variés ; [foods] assortis ■ **assortment** n assortiment m ; **an assortment of people** des gens de toutes sortes

**assume** [əˈsjuːm] vt a) [suppose] supposer (**that** que); **let us assume that...** supposons que... (+ subjunctive) b) [take on - power, control] prendre ; [responsibility, role] assumer ; [attitude, name] adopter ■ **assumed** adj [feigned] faux (f fausse) ; **assumed name** nom m d'emprunt ■ **assumption** [əˈsʌmpʃən] n [supposition] supposition f; **on the assumption that...** en supposant que... (+ subjunctive)

**assure** [əˈʃʊə(r)] vt assurer ■ **assurance** n a) [confidence, promise] assurance f b) Br [insurance] assurance f

**asterisk** [ˈæstərɪsk] n astérisque m

**asthma** [Br ˈæsmə, Am ˈæzmə] n asthme m

**astonish** [əˈstɒnɪʃ] vt étonner; **to be astonished (at sth)** s'étonner (de qch) ■ **astonishing** adj étonnant ■ **astonishment** n étonnement m

**astound** [əˈstaʊnd] vt stupéfier ■ **astounding** adj stupéfiant

**astray** [əˈstreɪ] adv **to go astray** s'égarer; **to lead astray** détourner du droit chemin

**astride** [əˈstraɪd] **1.** adv à califourchon **2.** prep à cheval sur

**astrology** [əˈstrɒlədʒɪ] n astrologie f

**astronaut** [ˈæstrənɔːt] n astronaute mf

**astronomy** [əˈstrɒnəmɪ] n astronomie f ■ **astronomer** n astronome mf

**astute** [əˈstjuːt] adj [crafty] rusé ; [clever] astucieux, -euse

**asylum** [əˈsaɪləm] n asile m ■ **asylumseeker** n demandeur, -euse mf d'asile

**at** [æt] (unstressed [ət]) prep a) à, ≈ 15 km; **at the end** à la fin; **at school** à l'école; **at work** au travail; **at six (o'clock)** à six heures ; **at Easter** à Pâques ; **to drive at 10 mph** rouler à; **to buy / sell at 10 euros a kilo** acheter / vendre (à) 10 euros le kilo b) chez; **at the doctor's** chez le médecin; **at home** chez soi, à la maison

**c)** en; **at sea** en mer; **at war** en guerre; **good at maths** fort en maths
**d)** contre; **angry at** fâché contre
**e)** sur; **to shoot at** tirer sur; **at my request** sur ma demande
**f)** de; **to laugh at sb/sth** rire de qn/qch; **surprised at sth** surpris de qch
**g)** (au)près de; **at the window** près de la fenêtre
**h)** par; **six at a time** six par six
**i)** [phrases] **at night** la nuit; **to look at** regarder; **while you're at it** tant que tu y es

**ate** [eɪt] *pt of* **eat**

**atheist** ['eɪθɪɪst] *n* athée *mf*

**Athens** ['æθənz] *n* Athènes *m ou f*

**athlete** ['æθliːt] *n* athlète *mf*; **athlete's foot** [disease] mycose *f* ■ **athletic** *adj* athlétique ■ **athletics** *npl Br* athlétisme *m*; *Am* sport *m*

**Atlantic** [ət'læntɪk] **1.** *adj* [coast, ocean] atlantique **2.** *n* **the Atlantic** l'Atlantique *m*

**atlas** ['ætləs] *n* atlas *m*

**ATM** *n* **a)** *Am* (*abbr of* **automatic** *or* **automated teller machine**) DAB **b)** (*abbr of* **at the moment**) maintenant

**atmosphere** ['ætməsfɪə(r)] *n* atmosphère *f* ■ **atmospheric** [-'ferɪk] *adj* atmosphérique

**atom** ['ætəm] *n* atome *m*; **atom bomb** bombe *f* atomique ■ **atomic** *adj* atomique

**atrocious** [ə'trəʊʃəs] *adj* atroce ■ **atrocity** *n* [cruel action] atrocité *f*

**at sign** *n* TYP & COMPUT arobase *f*

**attach** [ə'tætʃ] *vt* attacher (**to** à); [document] joindre (**to** à); **attached to sb** [fond of] attaché à qn ■ **attachment** *n* **a)** [affection] attachement *m* (**to sb** à qn) **b)** [tool] accessoire *m* **c)** COMPUT pièce *f* jointe

**attack** [ə'tæk] **1.** *n* [military] attaque *f* (**on** contre); [on someone's life] attentat *m*; [of illness] crise *f*; [of fever] accès *m*; **attack dog** chien *m* d'attaque **2.** *vt* attaquer; [problem, plan] s'attaquer à **3.** *vi* attaquer ■ **attacker** *n* agresseur *m*

**attain** [ə'teɪn] *vt* [aim] atteindre; [goal, ambition] réaliser; [rank] parvenir à

**attempt** [ə'tempt] **1.** *n* tentative *f*; **to make an attempt to do** tenter de faire **2.** *vt* tenter; [task] entreprendre; **to attempt to do** tenter de faire; **attempted murder** tentative *f* d'assassinat

**attend** [ə'tend] **1.** *vt* [meeting] assister à; [course] suivre; [school, church] aller à **2.** *vi* assister; **to attend to** [take care of] s'occuper de

**attendance** [ə'tendəns] *n* présence *f* (**at** à); [people] assistance *f*; (**school**) **attendance** scolarité *f*; **in attendance** de service ■ **attendant** *n* employé, -e *mf*; [in service station] pompiste *mf*; *Br* [in museum] gardien, -enne *mf*

**attention** [ə'tenʃən] *n* attention *f*; **to pay attention** faire *ou* prêter attention (**to** à); **for the attention of** à l'attention de ■ **attentive** *adj* [heedful] attentif, -ive (**to** à); [thoughtful] attentionné (**to** pour)

**attest** [ə'test] **1.** *vt* [certify, confirm] confirmer **2.** *vi* **to attest to** témoigner de

**attic** ['ætɪk] *n* grenier *m*

**attitude** ['ætɪtjuːd] *n* attitude *f*

**attorney** [ə'tɜːnɪ] (*pl* **-eys**) *n Am* [lawyer] avocat *m*

**attract** [ə'trækt] *vt* attirer ■ **attraction** *n* [charm, appeal] attrait *m*; [place, person] attraction *f*; [between people] attirance *f*; PHYS attraction *f* terrestre

**attractive** [ə'træktɪv] *adj* [house, room, person, car] beau (*f* belle); [price, offer] intéressant; [landscape] attrayant

**attribute 1.** ['ætrɪbjuːt] *n* [quality] attribut *m* **2.** [ə'trɪbjuːt] *vt* [ascribe] attribuer (**to** à)

**aubergine** ['əʊbəʒiːn] *n Br* aubergine *f*

**auburn** ['ɔːbən] *adj* [hair] auburn *inv*

**auction** ['ɔːkʃən] **1.** *n* vente *f* aux enchères **2.** *vt* **to auction (off)** vendre aux enchères ■ **auctioneer** *n* commissaire-priseur *m*

**audacity** [ɔː'dæsɪtɪ] *n* audace *f*

**audible** ['ɔːdɪbəl] *adj* [sound, words] audible

**audience** ['ɔːdɪəns] n a) [of speaker, musician, actor] public m ; [of radio broadcast] auditeurs mpl ; **TV audience** téléspectateurs mpl b) [interview] audience f (**with sb** avec qn)

**audio** ['ɔːdɪəʊ] adj [cassette, system] audio inv ; **audio tape** cassette f audio ; **audio tour** visite f guidée audio ■ **audiobook** ['ɔːdɪəʊbʊk] n livre m audio ■ **audiotypist** n audiotypiste mf ■ **audiovisual** adj audiovisuel, -elle

**audit** ['ɔːdɪt] 1. n audit m 2. vt [accounts] vérifier

**audition** [ɔː'dɪʃən] 1. n audition f 2. vt & vi auditionner

**auditorium** [ɔːdɪ'tɔːrɪəm] n [of theatre, concert hall] salle f

**August** ['ɔːgəst] n août m

**aunt** [ɑːnt] n tante f ■ **auntie, aunty** (pl -ies) n Fam tata f

**au pair** [əʊ'peə(r)] n au pair (**girl**) jeune fille f au pair

**aura** ['ɔːrə] n [of place] atmosphère f ; [of person] aura f

**austere** [ɔː'stɪə(r)] adj austère ■ **austerity** n austérité f

**Australia** [ɒ'streɪlɪə] n l'Australie f ■ **Australian** 1. adj australien, -enne 2. n Australien, -enne mf

**Austria** ['ɒstrɪə] n l'Autriche f ■ **Austrian** 1. adj autrichien, -enne 2. n Autrichien, -enne mf

**authentic** [ɔː'θentɪk] adj authentique ■ **authenticate** vt authentifier

**author** ['ɔːθə(r)] n auteur m

**authority** [ɔː'θɒrɪtɪ] (pl -ies) n autorité f ; [permission] autorisation f (**to do** de faire) ; **to be in authority** [in charge] être responsable ■ **authoritarian** adj & n autoritaire (mf) ■ **authoritative** adj [report, book] qui fait autorité ; [tone, person] autoritaire

**authorize** ['ɔːθəraɪz] vt autoriser (**to do** à faire) ■ **authorization** [-'zeɪʃən] n autorisation f (**to do** de faire)

**autistic** [ɔː'tɪstɪk] adj autiste

**auto** ['ɔːtəʊ] (pl -os) n Am auto f

**autobiography** [ɔːtəʊbaɪ'ɒgrəfɪ] (pl -ies) n autobiographie f

**autograph** ['ɔːtəgrɑːf] 1. n autographe m ; **autograph book** album m d'autographes 2. vt dédicacer (**for sb** à qn)

**automatic** [ɔːtə'mætɪk] adj automatique

**automobile** ['ɔːtəməbiːl] n Am automobile f

**autonomous** [ɔː'tɒnəməs] adj autonome ■ **autonomy** n autonomie f

**autopsy** ['ɔːtɒpsɪ] (pl -ies) n autopsie f

**autumn** ['ɔːtəm] n automne m ; **in autumn** en automne

**auxiliary** [ɔːg'zɪljərɪ] (pl -ies) adj & n auxiliaire (mf) ; **auxiliary (verb)** (verbe m) auxiliaire m

**avail** [ə'veɪl] 1. n **to no avail** en vain 2. vt **to avail oneself of** profiter de ■ **availability** n [of object] disponibilité f ; [of education] accessibilité f

**available** [ə'veɪləbəl] adj disponible ; **tickets are still available** il reste des tickets ; **this model is available in black or green** ce modèle existe en noir et en vert

**avalanche** ['ævəlɑːnʃ] n avalanche f

**Ave** (abbr of Avenue) av.

**avenge** [ə'vendʒ] vt venger ; **to avenge oneself (on)** se venger (de)

**avenue** ['ævənjuː] n avenue f ; Fig [possibility] possibilité f

**average** ['ævərɪdʒ] 1. n moyenne f ; **on average** en moyenne ; **above / below average** au-dessus / au-dessous de la moyenne 2. adj moyen, -enne 3. vt [do] faire en moyenne ; [reach] atteindre la moyenne de ; [figures] faire la moyenne de

**averse** [ə'vɜːs] adj **to be averse to doing** répugner à faire

**aversion** [ə'vɜːʃən] n [dislike] aversion f ; **to have an aversion to sth / to doing sth** avoir de la répugnance pour qch / à faire qch

**avert** [ə'vɜːt] vt [prevent] éviter ; **to avert one's eyes (from)** [turn away] détourner les yeux (de)

**aviation** [eɪvɪ'eɪʃən] n aviation f

**avid** ['ævɪd] adj avide (**for** de)

**avocado** [ævə'kɑːdəʊ] (pl **-os**) n avocat m

**avoid** [ə'vɔɪd] vt éviter; **to avoid doing** éviter de faire ■ **avoidable** adj évitable

**AWA** MESSAGING written abbr of **a while ago**

**await** [ə'weɪt] vt attendre

**awake** [ə'weɪk] **1.** adj réveillé, éveillé; **he's still awake** il ne dort pas encore **2.** (pt awoke, pp awoken) vi se réveiller **3.** vt réveiller ■ **awaken 1.** vi se réveiller **2.** vt réveiller

**award** [ə'wɔːd] **1.** n [prize] prix m, récompense f; [scholarship] bourse f **2.** vt [money] attribuer; [prize] décerner; **to award damages** [of judge] accorder des dommages-intérêts

**aware** [ə'weə(r)] adj **to be aware of** [conscious] être conscient de; [informed] être au courant de; [realize] se rendre compte de; **to become aware of/that** se rendre compte de /que ■ **awareness** n conscience f

**away** [ə'weɪ] adv **a)** [distant] loin; **5 km away** à 5 km (de distance) **b)** [in time] **ten days away** dans dix jours **c)** [absent, gone] absent; **to drive away** partir (en voiture); **to fade /melt away** disparaître /fondre complètement **d)** [to one side] **to look** or **turn away** détourner les yeux **e)** [continuously] **to work /talk away** travailler /parler sans arrêt **f)** Br **to play away** [of team] jouer à l'extérieur

**awe** [ɔː] n crainte f (mêlée de respect); **to be in awe of sb** éprouver pour qn une crainte mêlée de respect ■ **awesome** adj [impressive] impressionnant; [frightening] effrayant; Am Fam [excellent] super inv

**awful** ['ɔːfəl] adj affreux, -euse; [terrifying] effroyable; Fam **an awful lot (of)** énormément (de); **I feel awful (about it)** j'ai vraiment honte ■ **awfully** adv [suffer] affreusement; [very -good, pretty] extrêmement; [bad, late] affreusement

**awkward** ['ɔːkwəd] adj **a)** [clumsy - person, gesture] maladroit **b)** [difficult] difficile; [cumbersome] gênant; [tool] peu commode; [time] mal choisi; [silence] gêné ■ **awkwardly** adv [walk] maladroitement; [speak] d'un ton gêné; [placed, situated] à un endroit peu pratique

**awning** ['ɔːnɪŋ] n [of tent] auvent m; [over shop, window] store m; [canvas or glass canopy] marquise f

**awoke** [ə'wəʊk] pt of awake

**awoken** [ə'wəʊkən] pp of awake

**axe**, Am **ax** [æks] **1.** n hache f; Fig [reduction] coupe f sombre; **to get the axe** [of project] être abandonné; [of worker] être mis à la porte; Fig **to have an axe to grind** agir dans un but intéressé **2.** vt [costs] réduire; [job] supprimer; [project] abandonner

**axis** ['æksɪs] (pl **axes** ['æksiːz]) n axe m

**axle** ['æksəl] n essieu m

**B, b** [biː] *n* **a)** B, b *m inv*; **2B** [number] 2 ter **b)** MESSAGING *written abbr of* **be**

**BA** [biːˈeɪ] *n (abbr of* **Bachelor of Arts)** **to have a BA in history** ≃ avoir une licence en histoire

**babble** [ˈbæbəl] **1.** *vi* [mumble] bredouiller; [of baby, stream] gazouiller **2.** *n inv* [of voices] rumeur *f*; [of baby, stream] gazouillis *m*

**babe** [beɪb] *n* **a)** *Am Fam* [term of affection] chéri, -e *mf* **b) she's no babe in arms** elle n'est pas née de la dernière pluie

**baboon** [bəˈbuːn] *n* babouin *m*

**baby** [ˈbeɪbɪ] *(pl* **-ies)** *n* bébé *m*; **baby boy** petit garçon *m*; **baby girl** petite fille *f*; **baby tiger** */etc* bébé-tigre */etc m*; **baby clothes /toys /etc** vêtements *mpl* / jouets *mpl /etc* de bébé; *Am* **baby carriage** landau *m*; **baby sling** kangourou *m*, porte-bébé *m* ■ **baby-sit** *(pt & pp* **-sat,** *pres p* **-sitting)** *vi* faire du babysitting ■ **baby-sitter** *n* baby-sitter *mf*

**bachelor** [ˈbætʃələ(r)] *n* **a)** [not married] célibataire *m*; *Am* **bachelor party** enterrement *m* de vie de garçon; *Am* **to have a bachelor party** enterrer sa vie de garçon **b)** UNIV **Bachelor of Arts / of Science** [person] ≃ licencié, -e *mf* ès lettres /ès sciences; [qualification] ≃ licence *f* de lettres /de sciences; *Br* **bachelor's degree** ≃ licence *f*

**back** [bæk] **1.** *n* [of person, animal, hand] dos *m*; [of chair] dossier *m*; [of house, vehicle, train, head] arrière *m*; [of room] fond *m*; [of page] verso *m*; [of fabric] envers *m*; [in sport] arrière *m*; **at the back of the book** à la fin du livre; **at the back of the car** à l'arrière de la voiture; **at the back of one's mind** derrière la tête; **back to front** devant derrière, à l'envers; *Fam* **to get off sb's back** ficher la paix à qn; *Fam* **to get sb's back up** braquer qn

**2.** *adj* [wheel, seat] arrière *inv*; **back door** porte *f* de derrière; **back room** pièce *f* du fond; **back street** rue *f* écartée; **back tooth** molaire *f*

**3.** *adv* [behind] en arrière; **far back, a long way back** loin derrière; **a month back** il y a un mois; **to go back and forth** aller et venir; **to come back** revenir; **he's back** il est de retour, il est revenu; **the journey there and back** le voyage aller et retour

**4.** *vt* [with money] financer; [horse] parier sur; [vehicle] faire reculer; **to be backed with** [of curtain, picture] être renforcé de; **to back sb (up)** [support] appuyer qn; COMPUT **to back up** sauvegarder, faire une copie de sauvegarde de

**5.** *vi* [move backwards] reculer; **to back down** faire marche arrière; **to back out** [withdraw] se retirer; [of vehicle] sortir en marche arrière; **to back on to** [of house] donner par derrière sur; **to back up** [of vehicle] faire marche arrière

■ **backache** *n* mal *m* de dos

■ **backbencher** *n Br* POL député *m* de base

■ **backbone** *n* colonne *f* vertébrale; [of fish] grande arête *f*; *Fig* [main support] pivot *m*

■ **backpack** *n* sac *m* à dos

■ **backside** *n Fam* [buttocks] derrière *m*

■ **backslash** [ˈbækslæʃ] *n* COMPUT barre *f* oblique inversée

■ **backstage** *adv* dans les coulisses

■ **backstroke** *n* [in swimming] dos *m* crawlé

■ **backup 1.** *adj* [plan, team] de se-cours, de remplacement **2.** *n* appui *m* ; *Am* [tailback] embouteillage *m* ; COMPUT (copie *f* de) sauvegarde *f*

■ **backyard** *n Br* [enclosed area] arrière-cour *f* ; *Am* [garden] jardin *m* de derrière

**backer** ['bækə(r)] *n* [supporter] parti-san *m* ; [on horses] parieur, -euse *mf* ; [financial] commanditaire *m*

**backfire** [bæk'faɪə(r)] *vi* **a)** [of vehicle] pétarader **b)** *Fig* **to backfire on sb** [of plot] se retourner contre qn

**backgammon** ['bækgæmən] *n* backgammon *m*

**background** ['bækgraʊnd] *n* fond *m*, arrière-plan *m* ; [educational] forma-tion *f* ; [professional] expérience *f* ; [en-vironment] milieu *m* ; [circumstances] contexte *m* ; **background music / noise** musique *f* / bruit *m* de fond

**backlash** ['bæklæʃ] *n* retour *m* de bâton

**backlog** ['bæklɒg] *n* **a backlog of work** du travail en retard

**backstreet** ['bækstriːt] *adj* [under-handed] louche

**backward** ['bækwəd] **1.** *adj* [person, country] arriéré ; [glance] en arrière **2.** *adv* = **backwards** ■ **backwards** *adv* en arrière ; [walk] à reculons ; [fall] à la renverse ; **to go** *or* **move backwards** reculer

**bacon** ['beɪkən] *n* bacon *m* ; **bacon and eggs** œufs *mpl* au bacon

**bacteria** [bæk'tɪərɪə] *npl* bactéries *fpl*

**bad** [bæd] *(compar* **worse**, *superl* **worst)** *adj* mauvais ; [wicked] méchant ; [sad] triste ; [accident, wound] grave ; [tooth] carié ; [arm, leg] malade ; [pain] violent ; **bad language** gros mots *mpl* ; **bad cheque** chèque *m* sans provision ; **to feel bad** [ill] se sentir mal ; **to be bad at maths** être mauvais en maths ; **things are bad** ça va mal ; **it's not bad** ce n'est pas mal ; **to go bad** [of fruit, meat] se gâter ; [of milk] tourner ; **too bad!** tant pis ! ■ **bad-mannered** *adj* mal élevé ■ **bad-tempered** *adj* grincheux, -euse

**bade** [bæd] *pt of* **bid**

**badge** [bædʒ] *n* [of plastic, bearing slo-gan or joke] badge *m* ; [of metal, bearing logo] pin's *m* ; [of postman, policeman] plaque *f* ; [on school uniform] insigne *m*

**badger** ['bædʒə(r)] **1.** *n* [animal] blai-reau *m* **2.** *vt* importuner

**badly** ['bædlɪ] *adv* mal ; [hurt] griève-ment ; **to be badly mistaken** se trom-per lourdement ; **badly off** dans la gêne ; **to want sth badly** avoir grande envie de qch

**badminton** ['bædmɪntən] *n* badmin-ton *m*

**baffle** ['bæfəl] *vt* [person] laisser per-plexe

**bag** [bæg] *n* sac *m* ; **bags** [luggage] bagages *mpl* ; [under eyes] poches *fpl* ; *Fam & Pej* **an old bag** une vieille taupe ; *Fam* **in the bag** dans la poche ■ **bag-boy** ['bægbɔɪ] *n Am* commis *m* (qui aide à l'emballage des achats)

**baggage** ['bægɪdʒ] *n* bagages *mpl* ; *Am* **baggage car** fourgon *m* ; **baggage control** contrôle *m* des bagages ; **baggage handler** [in airport] baga-giste *mf* ; *Am* **baggage room** consigne *f*

**baggy** ['bægɪ] *(compar* -**ier**, *superl* -**iest**) *adj* [garment - out of shape] déformé ; [by design] large

**bagpipes** ['bægpaɪps] *npl* cornemuse *f*

**Bahamas** [bə'hɑːməz] *npl* **the Baha-mas** les Bahamas *fpl*

**bail** [beɪl] **1.** *n* JUR caution *f* ; **on bail** sous caution ; **to grant sb bail** libérer qn sous caution **2.** *vt* **to bail sb out** JUR se por-ter garant de qn ; *Fig* tirer qn d'affaire **3.** *vi* **to bail out** [from aircraft] s'éjecter

**bailiff** ['beɪlɪf] *n* [law officer] huissier *m* ; *Br* [of landowner] régisseur *m*

**bait** [beɪt] **1.** *n* appât *m* **2.** *vt* **a)** [fishing hook] amorcer **b)** [annoy] tourmenter

**bake** [beɪk] **1.** *vt* (faire) cuire au four **2.** *vi* [of person - make cakes] faire de la pâtisserie ; [make bread] faire du pain ; [of food] cuire (au four) ; *Fam* **it's bak-ing (hot)** on crève de chaleur ■ **baked** *adj* [potatoes, apples] au four ; **baked beans** haricots *mpl* blancs à la tomate

**baker** ['beɪkə(r)] n boulanger, -ère mf
■ **bakery** n boulangerie f

**baking** ['beɪkɪŋ] n cuisson f; **baking powder** levure f chimique; **baking tin** moule m à pâtisserie

**balaclava** [bælə'klɑːvə] n Br passe-montagne m

**balance** ['bæləns] **1.** n [equilibrium] équilibre m; [of account] solde m; [remainder] reste m; [in accounting] bilan m; [for weighing] balance f; **to lose one's balance** perdre l'équilibre; **to strike a balance** trouver le juste milieu; **on balance** à tout prendre; **balance of payments** balance f des paiements; **balance sheet** bilan m **2.** vt maintenir en équilibre (**on** sur); [budget, account] équilibrer; [compare] mettre en balance; **to balance (out)** [compensate for] compenser **3.** vi [of person] se tenir en équilibre; [of accounts] être en équilibre, s'équilibrer; **to balance (out)** [even out] s'équilibrer

**balcony** ['bælkənɪ] (pl -ies) n balcon m

**bald** [bɔːld] (compar -er, superl -est) adj chauve; [statement] brutal; [tyre] lisse; **bald patch** or **spot** tonsure f

**balk** [bɔːk] vi reculer (**at** devant)

**Balkans** ['bɔːlkənz] npl **the Balkans** les Balkans fpl

**ball**[1] [bɔːl] n balle f; [inflated, for football, rugby] ballon m; [for snooker, pool] bille f; [of string, wool] pelote f; [sphere] boule f; [of meat, fish] boulette f; Fam **to be on the ball** [alert] avoir de la présence d'esprit; [knowledgeable] connaître son affaire; **ball bearing** roulement m à billes; Am **ball game** match m de base-ball; Fig **it's a whole new ball game** c'est une tout autre affaire; **ball pit** piscine f à balles ■ **ballpark** n stade m de base-ball

**ball**[2] [bɔːl] n [dance] bal m (pl bals)

**ballad** ['bæləd] n [poem] ballade f; [song] romance f

**ballast** ['bæləst] **1.** n lest m **2.** vt lester

**ballet** ['bæleɪ] n ballet m ■ **ballerina** n ballerine f

**balloon** [bə'luːn] n [toy, airship] ballon m; [in cartoon] bulle f

**ballot** ['bælət] **1.** n [voting] scrutin m; **ballot paper** bulletin m de vote; **ballot box** urne f **2.** vt [members] consulter (par un scrutin)

**ballpoint (pen)** ['bɔːlpɔɪnt(pen)] n stylo m à bille

**ballroom** ['bɔːlruːm] n salle f de danse

**ballsy** ['bɔːlzɪ] adj Am v Fam culotté

**balsamic** [bɔːl'sæmɪk] adj **balsamic vinaigrette** vinaigrette f au vinaigre balsamique; **balsamic vinegar** vinaigre m balsamique

**Baltic** ['bɔːltɪk] n **the Baltic** la Baltique

**bamboo** [bæm'buː] n bambou m; **bamboo shoots** pousses fpl de bambou

**ban** [bæn] **1.** n interdiction f; **to impose a ban on sth** interdire qch **2.** (pt & pp -nn-) vt interdire; **to ban sb from doing sth** interdire à qn de faire qch; **to ban sb from** [club] exclure qn de

**banal** [bə'nɑːl] adj banal (mpl -als)

**banana** [bə'nɑːnə] n banane f

**band** [bænd] **1.** n a) [strip] bande f; [of hat] ruban m; **rubber** or **elastic band** élastique m b) [group of people] bande f; [of musicians] (petit) orchestre m; [pop group] groupe m **2.** vi **to band together** se (re)grouper

**bandage** ['bændɪdʒ] **1.** n [strip] bande f; [dressing] bandage m **2.** vt **to bandage (up)** [arm, leg] bander; [wound] mettre un bandage sur; **to bandage sb's arm** bander le bras à qn

**Band-Aid**® n Am pansement m adhésif

**B and B, B & B** [biːənd'biː] n (abbr of bed and breakfast) [service] ≃ chambre f avec petit déjeuner; **to stay at a B and B** ≃ prendre une chambre d'hôte

**bandit** ['bændɪt] n bandit m

**bandwagon** ['bændwægən] n Fig **to jump on the bandwagon** prendre le train en marche

**bandy**[1] ['bændɪ] (compar -ier, superl -iest) adj **to have bandy legs** avoir les jambes arquées

**bandy**[2] ['bændɪ] (pt & pp -ied) vt **to bandy about** [story, rumour] faire circuler

**bang¹** [bæŋ] **1.** n [blow, noise] coup m (violent) ; [of gun] détonation f; [of door] claquement m **2.** vt [hit] cogner, frapper ; [door] (faire) claquer ; **to bang one's head** se cogner la tête **3.** vi cogner, frapper ; [of door] claquer ; **to bang into sb/sth** heurter qn /qch **4.** excl vlan !, pan !; **to go bang** éclater

**bang²** [bæŋ] adv Br Fam [exactly] exactement; **bang in the middle** en plein milieu; **bang on six** à six heures tapantes

**banger** ['bæŋə(r)] n a) Br Fam [sausage] saucisse f b) [firecracker] pétard m c) Fam **old banger** [car] vieille guimbarde f

**bangle** ['bæŋgəl] n bracelet m

**bangs** [bæŋz] npl Am [of hair] frange f

**banish** ['bænɪʃ] vt bannir

**banister** ['bænɪstə(r)] n **banister(s)** rampe f (d'escalier)

**banjo** ['bændʒəʊ] (pl -os or -oes) n banjo m

**bank¹** [bæŋk] **1.** n [of river] bord m, rive f; [raised] berge f; [of earth] talus m ; [of sand] banc m; **the Left Bank** [in Paris] la Rive gauche **2.** vt **to bank (up)** [earth] amonceler ; [fire] couvrir **3.** vi [of aircraft] virer

**bank²** [bæŋk] **1.** n [for money] banque f; **bank account** compte m en banque; Br **bank balance** solde m bancaire; **bank card** carte f d'identité bancaire; **bank details** relevé m d'identité bancaire, RIB m; Br **bank holiday** jour m férié ; Br **bank note** billet m de banque **2.** vt [money] mettre à la banque **3.** vi avoir un compte en banque (**with** à) ■ **banker** n banquier, -ère mf; Br **banker's card** carte f d'identité bancaire ■ **banking 1.** adj [transaction] bancaire **2.** n [activity, profession] la banque

**bank³** [bæŋk] vi **to bank on sb/sth** [rely on] compter sur qn /qch

**bankrupt** ['bæŋkrʌpt] **1.** adj **to go bankrupt** faire faillite **2.** vt mettre en faillite

**banner** ['bænə(r)] n banderole f ; [military flag] & Fig bannière f; COMPUT bandeau m ; **banner ad** bannière f publicitaire

**banns** [bænz] npl bans mpl; **to put up the banns** publier les bans

**banquet** ['bæŋkwɪt] n banquet m

**banter** ['bæntə(r)] **1.** n plaisanteries fpl **2.** vi plaisanter

**baptism** ['bæptɪzəm] n baptême m
■ **Baptist** n & adj baptiste (mf)

**baptize** [bæp'taɪz] vt baptiser

---

**bar** [bɑ:(r)] **1.** n **a)** [of metal] barre f; [of gold] lingot m ; [of chocolate] tablette f; [on window] barreau m ; **bar of soap** savonnette f; **behind bars** [criminal] sous les verrous; JUR **the Bar** le barreau; **bar code** [on product] code-barres m **b)** [pub] bar m ; [counter] bar m, comptoir m **c)** [group of musical notes] mesure f **2.** (pt & pp -rr-) vt **a)** **to bar sb's way** barrer le passage à qn; **barred window** fenêtre f munie de barreaux **b)** [prohibit] interdire (**sb from doing** à qn de faire); [exclude] exclure (**from** à) **3.** prep [except] sauf; **bar none** sans exception
■ **barmaid** n Br serveuse f (de bar)
■ **barman** (pl -men) n Br barman m
■ **bartender** n Am barman m

**Barbados** [bɑ:'beɪdɒs] n la Barbade

**barbaric** [bɑ:'bærɪk] adj barbare

**barbecue** ['bɑ:bɪkju:] **1.** n barbecue m **2.** vt cuire au barbecue

**barbed wire** [bɑ:bd'waɪə(r)] n fil m de fer barbelé ; [fence] barbelés mpl

**barber** ['bɑ:bə(r)] n coiffeur m pour hommes ■ **barbershop** ['bɑ:bəʃɒp] n Am salon m de coiffure (pour hommes)

**bare** [beə(r)] **1.** (compar -er, superl -est) adj nu ; [tree, hill] dénudé ; [room, cupboard] vide ; [mere] simple ; **the bare necessities** le strict nécessaire; **with his bare hands** à mains nues **2.** vt [arm, wire] dénuder ■ **barefoot 1.** adv nu-pieds **2.** adj aux pieds nus

**barely** ['beəlɪ] adv [scarcely] à peine ; **barely enough** tout juste assez

**bargain** ['bɑ:gɪn] **1.** n [deal] marché m, affaire f; **a bargain** [good buy] une occasion, une bonne affaire; **to make a bar-**

**gain (with sb)** faire un marché (avec qn); **into the bargain** [in addition] par-dessus le marché; **bargain price** prix *m* exceptionnel **2.** *vi* [negotiate] négocier; [haggle] marchander; **to bargain for** or **on sth** [expect] s'attendre à qch

**barge** [bɑːdʒ] **1.** *n* péniche *f* **2.** *vi* **to barge in** [enter room] faire irruption; [interrupt] interrompre

**bark¹** [bɑːk] *n* [of tree] écorce *f*

**bark²** [bɑːk] **1.** *n* aboiement *m* **2.** *vi* aboyer

**barley** ['bɑːlɪ] *n* orge *f*; **barley sugar** sucre *m* d'orge

**barn** [bɑːn] *n* [for crops] grange *f*; [for horses] écurie *f*; [for cattle] étable *f* ▪ **barnyard** *n* cour *f* de ferme

**barometer** [bəˈrɒmɪtə(r)] *n* baro-mètre *m*

**baron** ['bærən] *n* baron *m*; *Fig* [indus-trialist] magnat *m*; **press/oil baron** magnat de la presse/du pétrole ▪ **bar-oness** *n* baronne *f*

**barracks** ['bærəks] *npl* caserne *f*

**barrage** [*Br* 'bærɑːʒ, *Am* bəˈrɑːʒ] *n* [across river] barrage *m*; *Fig* **a barrage of ques-tions** un feu roulant de questions

**barrel** ['bærəl] *n* **a)** [cask] tonneau *m*; [of oil] baril *m* **b)** [of gun] canon *m* **c)** **barrel organ** orgue *m* de Barbarie

**barren** ['bærən] *adj* [land, woman, ideas] stérile; [style] aride

**barricade** ['bærɪkeɪd] **1.** *n* barricade *f* **2.** *vt* barricader; **to barricade oneself (in)** se barricader (dans)

**barrier** ['bærɪə(r)] *n also Fig* barrière *f*; *Br* **(ticket) barrier** [of station] por-tillon *m*; **sound barrier** mur *m* du son

**barring** ['bɑːrɪŋ] *prep* sauf

**barrister** ['bærɪstə(r)] *n Br* ≃ avocat *m*

**barrow** ['bærəʊ] *n* [wheelbarrow] brouette *f*; [cart] charrette *f* ou voi-ture *f* à bras

**barter** ['bɑːtə(r)] **1.** *n* troc *m* **2.** *vt* troquer (**for** contre)

**base** [beɪs] **1.** *n* **a)** [bottom, main ingredi-ent] base *f*; [of tree, lamp] pied *m*; **base rate** [of bank] taux *m* de base **b)** [mili-tary] base *f* **2.** *adj* [dishonourable] bas (*f* basse). **3.** *vt* baser, fonder (**on** sur); **based in London** [person, company] basé à Londres

**baseball** ['beɪsbɔːl] *n* base-ball *m*

**base-jump** *vi* pratiquer le base-jump

**basement** ['beɪsmənt] *n* sous-sol *m*

**bash** [bæʃ] **1.** *n* [bang] coup *m*; *Br Fam* **to have a bash** [try] essayer un coup **2.** *vt* [hit] cogner; **to bash (about)** [ill-treat] malmener; **to bash in** or **down** [door, fence] défoncer

**bashful** ['bæʃfəl] *adj* timide

**basic** ['beɪsɪk] **1.** *adj* essentiel, -elle, de base; [elementary] élémentaire; [pay, food] de base; [room, house, meal] tout simple **2.** *n* **the basics** l'essentiel *m* ▪ **basically** *adv* [on the whole] en gros; [in fact] en fait; [fundamental-ly] au fond

**basil** [*Br* 'bæzəl, *Am* 'beɪzəl] *n* basilic *m*

**basin** [*Br* 'beɪsən, *Am* 'beɪzən] *n* **a)** [made of plastic] bassine *f*; [for soup, food] (grand) bol *m*; [portable washbasin] cuvette *f*; [sink] lavabo *m* **b)** [of river] bassin *m*

**basis** ['beɪsɪs] (*pl* -ses [-siːz]) *n* [for discus-sion] base *f*; [for opinion, accusation] fondement *m*; [of agreement] bases *fpl*; **on the basis of** d'après; **on a weekly basis** chaque semaine

**basket** ['bɑːskɪt] *n* panier *m*; [for bread, laundry, litter] corbeille *f* ▪ **basket-ball** *n* basket(-ball) *m*

**Basque** [bæsk] **1.** *adj* basque **2.** *n* Basque *mf*

**bass¹** [beɪs] **1.** *n* MUS basse *f* **2.** *adj* [note, voice, instrument] bas (*f* basse)

**bass²** [bæs] *n* [sea fish] bar *m*; [fresh-water fish] perche *f*

**bassoon** [bəˈsuːn] *n* basson *m*

**bat¹** [bæt] *n* [animal] chauve-souris *f*

**bat²** [bæt] **1.** *n* [for cricket, baseball] batte *f*; [for table-tennis] raquette *f*; **off my own bat** de ma propre initia-tive **2.** (*pt & pp* **-tt-**) *vt* **a)** [ball] frapper **b)** **she didn't bat an eyelid** elle n'a pas sourcillé

**batch** [bætʃ] n [of people] groupe m ; [of letters] paquet m ; [of books] lot m ; [of loaves] fournée f ; [of papers] liasse f

**bath** [bɑːθ] **1.** (pl **baths** [bɑːðz]) n bain m ; [tub] baignoire f ; **to have** or **take a bath** prendre un bain ; **bath towel** drap m de bain ; Br **swimming baths** piscine f **2.** vt Br baigner ■ **bathrobe** n Br peignoir m de bain ; Am robe f de chambre ■ **bathroom** n salle f de bain(s) ; Am [toilet] toilettes fpl ■ **bathtub** n baignoire f

**bathe** [beɪð] **1.** vt baigner ; [wound] laver **2.** vi [swim] se baigner ; Am [have bath] prendre un bain ■ **bathing** n baignades fpl ; **bathing suit**, Br **bathing costume** maillot m de bain

**baton** [Br 'bætən, Am bə'tɒn] n [of conductor] baguette f ; [of policeman] matraque f ; [of soldier, drum majorette] bâton m ; [in relay race] témoin m

**batshit** ['bætʃɪt] adj Fam taré, jeté

**battalion** [bə'tæljən] n bataillon m

**batter** ['bætə(r)] **1.** n pâte f à frire **2.** vt [strike] cogner sur ; [person] frapper ; [town] pilonner ; **to batter down** [door] défoncer ■ **battered** adj [car, hat] cabossé ; [house] délabré ; [face] meurtri ; **battered child** enfant m martyr ; **battered wife** femme f battue

**battery** ['bætərɪ] (pl -ies) n [in vehicle, of guns, for hens] batterie f ; [in radio, appliance] pile f ; **battery hen** poule f de batterie

**battle** ['bætəl] **1.** n bataille f ; [struggle] lutte f ; Fam **that's half the battle** la partie est à moitié gagnée **2.** vi se battre, lutter ■ **battlefield** n champ m de bataille ■ **battleship** n cuirassé m

**bawl** [bɔːl] vt & vi to **bawl (out)** brailler ; Fam **to bawl sb out** engueuler qn

**bay**¹ [beɪ] **1.** n a) [part of coastline] baie f b) [in room] renfoncement m ; **bay window** bow-window m, oriel m c) Br [for loading] aire f de chargement ; **loading bay** aire f de chargement d) **at bay** [animal, criminal] aux abois ; **to keep** or **hold at bay** [enemy, wild dog] tenir en respect ; [disease] juguler **2.** vi aboyer **3.** adj [horse] bai

**bay**² [beɪ] n [tree] laurier m ; **bay leaf** feuille f de laurier

**bayonet** ['beɪənɪt] n baïonnette f

**bazaar** [bə'zɑː(r)] n [market, shop] bazar m ; [charity sale] vente f de charité

**BBFN** MESSAGING written abbr of **bye bye for now**

**BBL** MESSAGING written abbr of **be back later**

**BC** [biː'siː] (abbr of **before Christ**) av. J.-C.

**Bcc** (abbr of **blind carbon copy**) n Cci m (copie conforme invisible)

**BCNU** (abbr of **be seeing you**) MESSAGING @+

**be** [biː] (present tense **am, are, is** ; past tense **was, were** ; pp **been** ; pres p **being**) **1.** vi a) [gen] être ; **it is green/small/etc** c'est vert/petit/etc ; **he's a doctor** il est médecin ; **he's an Englishman** c'est un Anglais ; **it's him** c'est lui ; **it's them** ce sont eux ; **it's three (o'clock)** il est trois heures ; **it's the sixth of May,** Am **it's May sixth** nous sommes le six mai ; **to be hot/right/lucky** avoir chaud / raison/de la chance ; **my feet are cold** j'ai froid aux pieds

b) [with age, height] avoir ; **to be twenty** [age] avoir vingt ans ; **to be 2 metres high** avoir 2 m de haut ; **to be 6 feet tall** ≃ mesurer 1,80 m

c) [with health] aller ; **how are you?** comment vas-tu ? ; **I'm well/not well** je vais bien/mal

d) [with place, situation] se trouver, être ; **she's in York** elle se trouve ou elle est à York

e) [exist] être ; **the best painter there is** le meilleur peintre qui soit

f) [go, come] **I've been to see her** je suis allé la voir ; **he's (already) been** il est (déjà) venu

g) [with weather, calculations] faire ; **it's nice** il fait beau ; **it's foggy** il y a du brouillard ; **2 and 2 are 4** 2 et 2 font 4

h) [cost] coûter, faire ; **it's 20 pence** ça coûte 20 pence ; **how much is it?** ça fait combien ?, c'est combien ?

**2.** v aux a) **I am going** je vais ; **I was going** j'allais ; **I'll be staying** je vais rester ; **I'm listening to the radio** je

suis en train d'écouter la radio; **what has she been doing?** qu'est-ce qu'elle a fait?; **she's been there some time** elle est là depuis un moment; **he was killed** il a été tué; **I've been waiting (for) two hours** j'attends depuis deux heures; **it is said** on dit
b) [in questions and answers] **isn't it?** / **aren't you?** / **etc** n'est-ce pas?, non?; **she's ill, is she?** [in surprise] alors, comme ça, elle est malade?; **he isn't English, is he?** il n'est pas anglais, si?
c) [+ infinitive] **he is to come at once** [must] il doit venir tout de suite
d) **there is** / **are** il y a; [pointing] voilà; **here is** / **are** voici; **there she is** la voilà; **here they are** les voici

---

**beach** [biːtʃ] n plage f; **beach umbrella** / **sunshade** parasol m

**beacon** ['biːkən] n [for ship, aircraft] balise f; [lighthouse] phare m

**bead** [biːd] n [small sphere] perle f; [of rosary] grain m; [of sweat] goutte f, gouttelette f; **(string of) beads** collier m

**beak** [biːk] n bec m

**beaker** ['biːkə(r)] n gobelet m

**beam** [biːm] **1.** n a) [of wood] poutre f b) [of light, sunlight] rayon m; [of headlight, flashlight] faisceau m (lumineux) **2.** vi [of light] rayonner; [of sun, moon] briller; [smile broadly] sourire largement; **to beam with pride** / **joy** rayonner de fierté / joie **3.** vt [signals, programme] transmettre (**to** à)

**bean** [biːn] n haricot m; [of coffee] grain m; Fam **to be full of beans** être plein d'énergie; **string bean** haricot m vert

**bear¹** [beə(r)] n [animal] ours m; **bear cub** ourson m

**bear²** [beə(r)] **1.** (pt **bore**, pp **borne**) vt [carry, show] porter; [endure] supporter; [resemblance] offrir; **I can't bear him** / **it** je ne peux pas le supporter / supporter ça; **to bear sth in mind** [remember] se souvenir de qch; [take into account] tenir compte de qch

**2.** vi **to bear left** / **right** [turn] tourner à gauche / droite; **to bear up** tenir le coup; **bear up!** courage!

**bearable** ['beərəbəl] adj supportable

**beard** [bɪəd] n barbe f; **to have a beard** porter la barbe

**bearing** ['beərɪŋ] n [relevance] rapport m (**on** avec); [posture, conduct] port m; [of ship, aircraft] position f; **to get one's bearings** s'orienter

**beast** [biːst] n bête f; Fam [person] brute f

**beat** [biːt] **1.** n [of heart, drum] battement m; [of policeman] ronde f; [in music] rythme m **2.** (pt **beat**, pp **beaten** [biːtən]) vt battre; Fam **it beats me** ça me dépasse; Fam **beat it!** fiche le camp!; **to beat sb to it** devancer qn; **to beat down** or **in** [door] défoncer; **to beat sb up** tabasser qn **3.** vi battre; [at door] frapper (**at** à); Fam **to beat about** or **around the bush** tourner autour du pot ■ **beating** n [blows, defeat] raclée f; [of heart, drums] battement m

**beater** ['biːtə(r)] n [whisk] fouet m

**beautician** [bjuːˈtɪʃən] n esthéticienne f

**beautiful** ['bjuːtɪfəl] adj (très) beau (f belle); [superb] merveilleux, -euse

**beauty** ['bjuːtɪ] (pl **-ies**) n [quality, woman] beauté f; Br [in countryside] endroit m pittoresque; **it's a beauty!** [car, house] c'est une merveille!; **beauty parlour** or **salon** institut m de beauté; **beauty spot** [on skin] grain m de beauté

**beaver** ['biːvə(r)] **1.** n castor m **2.** vi **to beaver away (at sth)** travailler dur (à qch)

**became** [bɪˈkeɪm] pt of **become**

**because** [bɪˈkɒz] conj parce que; **because of** à cause de

**beckon** ['bekən] vt & vi **to beckon (to) sb (to do sth)** faire signe à qn (de faire qch)

**become** [bɪˈkʌm] (pt **became**, pp **become**) vi devenir; **to become a paint-**

**er** devenir peintre ; **to become thin** maigrir ; **what has become of her?** qu'est-elle devenue ?

**becoming** [bɪ'kʌmɪŋ] *adj* [clothes] seyant ; [modesty] bienséant

**bed** [bed] *n* lit *m* ; [flowerbed] parterre *m* ; [of vegetables] carré *m* ; [of sea] fond *m* ; [of river] lit *m* ; [of rock] couche *f* ; **to go to bed** (aller) se coucher ; **to put sb to bed** coucher qn ; **in bed** couché ; **to get out of bed** se lever ; **to make the bed** faire le lit ; **bed and breakfast** [in hotel] chambre *f* avec petit déjeuner ; **to stay in a bed and breakfast** ≃ prendre une chambre d'hôte ; *Br* **bed settee** (canapé *m*) convertible *m* ■ **bedclothes** *npl* couvertures *fpl* et draps *mpl* ■ **bedding** *n* couvertures *fpl* et draps *mpl* ■ **bedridden** *adj* alité ■ **bedroom** *n* chambre *f* à coucher ■ **bedside** *n* chevet *m* ; **bedside lamp / book / table** lampe *f* / livre *m* / table *f* de chevet ■ **bedsit, bedsitter** ['bedsɪtə(r)] *n Br* chambre *f* meublée ■ **bedspread** *n* dessus-de-lit *m inv* ■ **bedtime** *n* heure *f* du coucher *(pour endormir les enfants)* ; **bedtime story** histoire *f*

**bedraggled** [bɪ'dræɡəld] *adj* [clothes, person] débraillé et tout trempé

**bee** [bi:] *n* abeille *f* ■ **beehive** *n* ruche *f*

**beech** [bi:tʃ] *n* [tree, wood] hêtre *m*

**beef** [bi:f] *n* bœuf *m* ■ **beefburger** *n* hamburger *m*

**been** [bi:n] *pp of* be

**beep** [bi:p] *Fam* **1.** *n* bip *m* **2.** *vi* faire bip ■ **beeper** ['bi:pə(r)] *n* récepteur *m* d'appels, bip *m*

**beer** [bɪə(r)] *n* bière *f* ; **beer glass** chope *f*

**beet** [bi:t] *n Am* betterave *f*

**beetle** ['bi:təl] *n* scarabée *m*

**beetroot** ['bi:tru:t] *n Br* betterave *f*

**before** [bɪ'fɔ:(r)] **1.** *adv* avant ; [already] déjà ; [in front] devant ; **the month before** le mois d'avant *ou* précédent ; **the day before** la veille ; **I've seen it before** je l'ai déjà vu ; **I've never done it before** je ne l'ai (encore) jamais fait **2.** *prep* [time] avant ; [place] devant ; **the year before last** il y a deux ans ; **before my very eyes** sous mes yeux

**3.** *conj* avant que (ne) (+ *subjunctive*), avant de (+ *infinitive*) ; **before he goes** avant qu'il (ne) parte ; **before going** avant de partir

**befriend** [bɪ'frend] *vt* **to befriend sb** se prendre d'amitié pour qn

**beg** [beg] **1.** *(pt & pp* -gg-*) vt* **to beg (for)** [favour, help] demander ; [bread, money] mendier ; **to beg sb to do sth** supplier qn de faire qch **2.** *vi* [in street] mendier ; [ask earnestly] supplier

**began** [bɪ'ɡæn] *pt of* begin

**beggar** ['beɡə(r)] *n* mendiant, -e *mf* ; *Br Fam* [person] type *m* ; **lucky beggar** veinard, -e *mf*

**begin** [bɪ'ɡɪn] **1.** *(pt* began, *pp* begun, *pres p* beginning*) vt* commencer ; [fashion, campaign] lancer ; [bottle, sandwich] entamer ; [conversation] engager ; **to begin doing** *or* **to do sth** commencer *ou* se mettre à faire qch ; **he began laughing** il s'est mis à rire **2.** *vi* commencer (**with** par ; **by doing** par faire) ; **beginning from** à partir de ; **to begin with** [first of all] d'abord ■ **beginner** *n* débutant, -e *mf* ■ **beginning** *n* commencement *m*, début *m* ; **in** *or* **at the beginning** au début, au commencement

**begrudge** [bɪ'ɡrʌdʒ] *vt* [envy] envier (**sb sth** qch à qn) ; [reproach] reprocher (**sb sth** qch à qn) ; [give unwillingly] donner à contrecœur ; **to begrudge doing sth** faire qch à contrecœur

**begun** [bɪ'ɡʌn] *pp of* begin

**behalf** [bɪ'hɑ:f] *n* **on behalf of sb, on sb's behalf** [representing] au nom de qn, de la part de qn ; [in the interests of] en faveur de qn

**behave** [bɪ'heɪv] *vi* se conduire ; **to behave (oneself)** se tenir bien ; [of child] être sage ■ **behaviour,** *Am* **behavior** *n* conduite *f*, comportement *m* ; **to be on one's best behaviour** se tenir particulièrement bien

**behind** [bɪ'haɪnd] **1.** *prep* derrière ; [in terms of progress] en retard sur **2.** *adv* derrière ; [late] en retard ; **to be behind with one's work** avoir du travail en retard **3.** *n Fam* [buttocks] derrière *m*

**beige** [beɪʒ] *adj* & *n* beige *(m)*

**Beijing** [beɪˈdʒɪŋ] *n* Beijing *m* ou *f*

**being** [ˈbiːɪŋ] *n* [person, soul] être *m*; **to come into being** naître

**belated** [bɪˈleɪtɪd] *adj* tardif, -ive

**belch** [beltʃ] **1.** *n* renvoi *m* **2.** *vi* [of person] roter **3.** *vt* **to belch (out)** [smoke] vomir

**Belgium** [ˈbeldʒəm] *n* la Belgique ■ **Belgian 1.** *adj* belge **2.** *n* Belge *mf*

**belief** [bɪˈliːf] *n* [believing, thing believed] croyance *f* (**in sb** en qn; **in sth** à ou en qch); [trust] confiance *f*, foi *f* (**in** en); [religious faith] foi *f*

**believe** [bɪˈliːv] **1.** *vt* croire; **I don't believe it** c'est pas possible; **I believe I'm right** je crois avoir raison, je crois que j'ai raison **2.** *vi* croire (**in sth** à qch); **to believe in God** croire en Dieu; **I believe so/not** je crois que oui/que non; **to believe in doing sth** croire qu'il faut faire qch ■ **believable** *adj* crédible ■ **believer** *n* [religious] croyant, -e *mf*; **to be a believer in sth** croire à qch

**belittle** [bɪˈlɪtəl] *vt* dénigrer

**bell** [bel] *n* [large - of church] cloche *f*; [small] clochette *f*; [in phone, mechanism, alarm] sonnerie *f*; [on door, bicycle] sonnette *f*; *Am* **bell pepper** poivron *m*; **bell tower** clocher *m* ■ **bellboy, bellhop** *n* *Am* groom *m*, chasseur *m* ■ **bell work** [ˈbel,wɜːk] *n* *Am* SCH travail affiché au tableau que les élèves doivent effectuer dès leur entrée en classe

**bellow** [ˈbeləʊ] *vi* beugler, mugir

**belly** [ˈbelɪ] *(pl* **-ies***) n* ventre *m*; *Fam* **belly button** nombril *m*; **belly dancing** danse *f* du ventre

**belong** [bɪˈlɒŋ] *vi* appartenir (**to** à); **to belong to a club** être membre d'un club; **that book belongs to me** ce livre m'appartient ou est à moi; **the cup belongs here** cette tasse se range ici ■ **belongings** *npl* affaires *fpl*

**beloved** [bɪˈlʌvɪd] *adj* & *n* Liter bien-aimé, -e *(mf)*

**below** [bɪˈləʊ] **1.** *prep* [lower than] au-dessous de; [under] sous; [with numbers] moins de; *Fig* [unworthy of] indigne de **2.** *adv* en dessous; [in text] ci-dessous; **on the floor below** à l'étage du dessous; **it's 10 degrees below** il fait moins 10 ■ **below-average** *adj* en dessous de la moyenne

**belt** [belt] **1.** *n* ceinture *f*; [in machine] courroie *f*; [area] zone *f*, région *f* **2.** *vi* **to belt up** [fasten seat belt] attacher sa ceinture; *Br Fam* **belt up!** [shut up] boucle-la ! **3.** *vt Fam* [hit - ball] cogner dans; [person] flanquer un gnon à

**beltway** [ˈbelt,weɪ] *n Am* route *f* périphérique

**bemused** [bɪˈmjuːzd] *adj* perplexe

**bench** [bentʃ] *n* [seat] banc *m*; [work table] établi *m*; JUR **the Bench** [magistrates] la magistrature (assise); [court] le tribunal; SPORT **to be on the bench** être remplaçant, -e

**benchmarking** [ˈbentʃmɑːkɪŋ] *n* benchmarking *m*, étalonnage *m* concurrentiel

**benchwarmer** [ˈbentʃwɔːmə(r)] *n Am Fam* SPORT joueur qui se trouve souvent sur le banc des remplaçants

**bend** [bend] **1.** *n* courbe *f*; [in river, pipe] coude *m*; [in road] virage *m*; *Fam* **round the bend** [mad] cinglé **2.** *(pt & pp bent) vt* courber; [leg, arm] plier; **to bend one's head** baisser la tête; **to bend the rules** faire une entorse au règlement **3.** *vi* [of branch] plier; [of road] tourner; [of river] faire un coude; **to bend (down)** [stoop] se courber; **to bend (over or forward)** se pencher

**bender** [ˈbendə(r)] *n Fam* [drinking binge] beuverie *f*; **to go on a bender** faire la noce

**bendy bus** *n Br* bus *m* à soufflet

**beneath** [bɪˈniːθ] **1.** *prep* sous; [unworthy of] indigne de **2.** *adv* (au-)dessous

**benefactor** [ˈbenɪfæktə(r)] *n* bienfaiteur *m* ■ **benefactress** *n* bienfaitrice *f*

**beneficial** [benɪˈfɪʃəl] *adj* bénéfique

**benefit** [ˈbenɪfɪt] **1.** *n* [advantage] avantage *m*; [money] allocation *f*; **benefits** [of science, education] bienfaits *mpl*; **to sb's benefit** dans l'intérêt de qn; **for**

**your (own) benefit** pour vous, pour votre bien ; **to be of benefit (to sb)** faire du bien (à qn) ; **benefit concert** concert *m* de bienfaisance **2.** *vt* faire du bien à ; [be useful to] profiter à **3.** *vi* to **benefit from doing sth** gagner à faire qch

**Benelux** [ˈbenɪlʌks] *n* Benelux *m*

**benevolent** [bɪˈnevələnt] *adj* bienveillant

**benign** [bɪˈnaɪn] *adj* [kind] bienveillant ; [climate] doux (*f* douce) ; **benign tumour** tumeur *f* bénigne

**bent** [bent] **1.** *adj* [nail, mind] tordu ; *Fam* [dishonest] pourri ; **bent on doing sth** résolu à faire qch **2.** *n* [talent] aptitude *f* (**for** pour) ; [inclination, liking] penchant *m*, goût *m* (**for** pour) **3.** *pt & pp of* **bend**

**bento** [ˈbentəʊ] *n* bento *m*

**bequeath** [bɪˈkwiːð] *vt Formal* léguer (**to** à)

**bereaved** [bɪˈriːvd] **1.** *adj* endeuillé **2.** *npl* **the bereaved** la famille du défunt / de la défunte ■ **bereavement** *n* deuil *m*

**beret** [*Br* ˈbereɪ, *Am* bəˈreɪ] *n* béret *m*

**Berlin** [bɜːˈlɪn] *n* Berlin *m ou f*

**Bermuda** [bəˈmjuːdə] *n* les Bermudes *fpl*

**berry** [ˈberɪ] (*pl* **-ies**) *n* baie *f*

**berserk** [bəˈzɜːk] *adj* **to go berserk** devenir fou furieux (*f* folle furieuse)

**berth** [bɜːθ] **1.** *n* **a)** [in ship, train] couchette *f* **b)** [anchorage] poste *m* à quai ; *Fig* **to give sb a wide berth** éviter qn comme la peste **2.** *vi* [of ship] aborder à quai

**beset** [bɪˈset] (*pt & pp* **beset**, *pres p* **besetting**) *vt* assaillir

**beside** [bɪˈsaɪd] *prep* **a)** à côté de ; **that's beside the point** ça n'a rien à voir **b)** to **be beside o.s. with joy** être fou (*f* folle) de joie

**besides** [bɪˈsaɪdz] **1.** *prep* [in addition to] en plus de ; [except] excepté ; **there are ten of us besides Paul** nous sommes dix sans compter Paul ; **what else can you do besides singing?**

que savez-vous faire à part chanter ? **2.** *adv* [in addition] en plus ; [moreover] d'ailleurs

**besiege** [bɪˈsiːdʒ] *vt* [of soldiers, crowd] assiéger ; *Fig* [annoy] assaillir (**with** de)

**besought** [bɪˈsɔːt] *pt & pp of* **beseech**

**best** [best] **1.** *adj* meilleur ; **my best dress** ma plus belle robe ; **the best part of** [most] la plus grande partie de ; **the best thing is to accept** le mieux c'est d'accepter ; **'best before…'** [on product] 'à consommer avant…' ; **best-before date** date *f* limite de consommation ; **best man** [at wedding] garçon *m* d'honneur **2.** *n* **the best (one)** le meilleur, la meilleure ; **it's for the best** c'est pour le mieux ; **at best** au mieux ; **to do one's best** faire de son mieux ; **to look one's best, to be at one's best** être à son avantage ; **to the best of my knowledge** autant que je sache ; **to make the best of sth** [accept] s'accommoder de qch ; **to get the best out of sth** tirer le meilleur parti de qch ; **in one's Sunday best** endimanché ; **all the best!** [when leaving] prends bien soin de toi ! ; [good luck] bonne chance ! ; [in letter] amicalement **3.** *adv* **(the) best** [play, sing] le mieux ; **to like sb/sth (the) best** aimer qn /qch le plus ; **I think it best to wait** je juge prudent d'attendre ■ **best-seller** *n* [book] best-seller *m*

**bet** [bet] **1.** *n* pari *m* **2.** (*pt & pp* **bet** or **betted**, *pres p* **betting**) *vt* parier (**on** sur ; **that** que) ; *Fam* **you bet!** tu parles ! ■ **betting** *n* paris *mpl* ; *Br* **betting shop** ≃ PMU® *m*

**betray** [bɪˈtreɪ] *vt* [person, secret] trahir ■ **betrayal** *n* [disloyalty] trahison *f* ; [disclosure - of secret] révélation *f*

**better** [ˈbetə(r)] **1.** *adj* meilleur (**than** que) ; **I need a better car** j'ai besoin d'une meilleure voiture ; **that's better** c'est mieux ; **she's (much) better** [in health] elle va (beaucoup) mieux ; **to get better** [recover] se remettre ; [improve] s'améliorer ; **it's better to go** il vaut mieux partir ; **the better part of** [most] la plus grande partie de **2.** *adv* mieux (**than** que) ; **better**

dressed / known / *etc* mieux habillé / connu / *etc*; **to look better** [of ill person] avoir meilleure mine; **better and better** de mieux en mieux; **so much the better, all the better** tant mieux (**for** pour); **I'd better go** il vaut mieux que je parte; **better off** [in better situation] mieux; **to be better off** [financially] être plus à l'aise **3.** *n* **to get the better of sb** l'emporter sur qn; **to change for the better** [of person] changer en bien; [of situation] s'améliorer; **one's betters** ses supérieurs *mpl* **4.** *vt* [improve] améliorer; [do better than] dépasser; **to better oneself** améliorer sa condition; **to better sb's results** / *etc* dépasser les résultats / *etc* de qn

**between** [bɪ'twiːn] **1.** *prep* entre; **in between** entre **2.** *adv* **in between** [space] au milieu; [time] dans l'intervalle

**beware** [bɪ'weə(r)] *vi* se méfier (**of** de); **beware!** attention !; **'beware of the dog!'** 'attention, chien méchant !'

**bewilder** [bɪ'wɪldə(r)] *vt* dérouter, laisser perplexe

**beyond** [bɪ'jɒnd] **1.** *prep* **a)** [further than] au-delà de; **beyond reach / doubt** hors de portée / de doute; **beyond belief** incroyable; **beyond my / our / *etc* means** au-dessus de mes / nos / *etc* moyens; **it's beyond me** ça me dépasse **b)** [except] sauf **2.** *adv* [further] au-delà

**BFN, B4N** MESSAGING *written abbr of* **bye for now**

**B4** MESSAGING *written abbr of* **before**

**BG** MESSAGING *written abbr of* **big grin**

**BHL8** MESSAGING *written abbr of* **(I'll) be home late**

**bias** ['baɪəs] **1.** *n* **a)** [inclination] penchant *m* (**towards** pour); [prejudice] préjugé *m*, parti pris *m* (**towards / against** en faveur de / contre) **b)** cut **on the bias** [fabric] coupé dans le biais **2.** (*pt & pp* **-ss-** *or* **-s-**) *vt* influencer (**towards / against** en faveur de / contre) ■ **bias(s)ed** *adj* partial; **to be bias(s)ed against** avoir des préjugés contre

**bib** [bɪb] *n* [for baby] bavoir *m*

**bible** ['baɪbəl] *n* bible *f*; **the Bible** la Bible ■ **biblical** *adj* biblique

**bibliography** [bɪblɪ'ɒɡrəfɪ] (*pl* **-ies**) *n* bibliographie *f*

**biceps** ['baɪseps] *n inv* [muscle] biceps *m*

**bicker** ['bɪkə(r)] *vi* se chamailler

**bicycle** ['baɪsɪkəl] *n* bicyclette *f*; **by bicycle** à bicyclette ■ **bicycler** ['baɪsɪklə(r)] *n Am* cycliste *mf*

**bid¹** [bɪd] **1.** *n* **a)** [offer] offre *f*; [at auction] enchère *f* (**for** pour) **b)** [attempt] tentative *f* **2.** (*pt & pp* **bid**, *pres p* **bidding**) *vt* [sum of money] offrir; [at auction] faire une enchère de **3.** *vi* faire une offre (**for** pour); [at auction] faire une enchère (**for** sur) ■ **bidder** *n* [at auction] enchérisseur, -euse *mf*; **to the highest bidder** au plus offrant

**bid²** [bɪd] (*pt* **bade**, *pp* **bidden** ['bɪdən] *or* **bid**, *pres p* **bidding**) *vt Liter* [command] commander (**sb to do** à qn de faire); [say, wish] dire, souhaiter

**bide** [baɪd] *vt* **to bide one's time** attendre le bon moment

**big** [bɪɡ] (*compar* **bigger**, *superl* **biggest**) *adj* [tall, large] grand; [fat] gros (*f* grosse); [drop, increase] fort; **to get big(ger)** [taller] grandir; [fatter] grossir; **my big brother** mon grand frère; *Fam* **big fish** huile *f*, gros bonnet *m*; *Fam* **big mouth** grande gueule *f*; **big toe** gros orteil *m* ■ **big-budget** *adj* à gros budget ■ **bighead** *n Fam* crâneur, -euse *mf* ■ **big money** *n Fam* **to earn big money** gagner gros; **you can earn big money selling carpets** on peut gagner beaucoup d'argent en vendant des tapis; **to make big money** se faire du pognon; **advertising is where the big money is** la publicité rapporte gros ■ **bigshot**, **bigwig** *n Fam* gros bonnet *m*

**Big Apple** *n* **the Big Apple** surnom de New York

**Big Easy** *n Am* surnom de La Nouvelle-Orléans

**bigot** ['bɪɡət] *n* sectaire *mf*; [religious] bigot, -e *mf* ■ **bigoted** *adj* sectaire; [religious] bigot

**bike** [baɪk] *n Fam* vélo *m*; [motorbike] moto *f*; **quad bike** (moto *f*) quad *m*; **bike lane** piste *f* cyclable; **bike shed** cabane *f* ou remise *f* à vélos ■ **bike-friendly, bicycle-friendly** *adj* [area, city] bien aménagé pour les cyclistes

**bikini** [bɪˈkiːnɪ] *n* Bikini® *m*; **bikini briefs** mini-slip *m*

**bilberry** [ˈbɪlbərɪ] *(pl -ies)* *n* myrtille *f*

**bilingual** [baɪˈlɪŋɡwəl] *adj* bilingue

**bill¹** [bɪl] **1.** *n* **a)** [invoice] facture *f*; [in restaurant] addition *f*; [in hotel] note *f* **b)** *Am* [banknote] billet *m* **c)** [bank draft] effet *m* **d)** [notice] affiche *f* **e)** POL projet *m* de loi; **Bill of Rights** *les dix premiers amendements de la Constitution américaine* **2.** *vt* **a) to bill sb** envoyer la facture à qn **b)** [publicize] annoncer ■ **billboard** *n* panneau *m* d'affichage

**bill²** [bɪl] *n* [of bird] bec *m*

**billiards** [ˈbɪljədz] *n* billard *m*

**billing** [ˈbɪlɪŋ] *n Am* [advertising] **to give sth advance billing** annoncer qch

**billion** [ˈbɪljən] *n* milliard *m* ■ **billionaire** *n* milliardaire *mf*

**billow** [ˈbɪləʊ] **1.** *n* [of smoke] volute *f* **2.** *vi* [of smoke] tourbillonner; [of sea] se soulever; [of sail] se gonfler

**bimonthly** [baɪˈmʌnθlɪ] *adj* [every two weeks] bimensuel, -elle; [every two months] bimestriel, -elle

**bin** [bɪn] **1.** *n* boîte *f*; [for litter] poubelle *f* **2.** *(pt & pp -nn-) vt Fam* mettre à la poubelle

**binary** [ˈbaɪnərɪ] *adj* binaire

**bind** [baɪnd] **1.** *(pt & pp bound) vt* [fasten] attacher; [book] relier; [fabric, hem] border; [unite] lier; **to bind sb hand and foot** ligoter qn; **to be bound by sth** être lié par qch **2.** *n Fam* [bore] plaie *f* ■ **binding 1.** *n* [of book] reliure *f* **2.** *adj* [contract] qui lie; **to be binding on sb** [legally] lier qn

**binder** [ˈbaɪndə(r)] *n* [for papers] classeur *m*

**binge** [bɪndʒ] *n Fam* **to go on a binge** [drinking] faire la bringue; [eating] se gaver; **binge drinking** *fait de boire de très grandes quantités d'alcool en une soirée, de façon régulière*; **binge eating** hyperphagie *f*, consommation *f* compulsive de nourriture

**bingo** [ˈbɪŋɡəʊ] *n* ≃ loto *m*

**binner** [ˈbɪnə(r)] *n Am* personne qui fait les poubelles

**binoculars** [bɪˈnɒkjʊləz] *npl* jumelles *fpl*

**bio** [ˈbaɪəʊ] *adj* bio *(inv)*

**biochemistry** [baɪəʊˈkemɪstrɪ] *n* biochimie *f*

**biodegradable** [baɪəʊdɪˈɡreɪdəbəl] *adj* biodégradable

**biofuel** [ˈbaɪəʊfjuːl] *n* biocarburant *m*

**biography** [baɪˈɒɡrəfɪ] *(pl -ies)* *n* biographie *f*

**biology** [baɪˈɒlədʒɪ] *n* biologie *f* ■ **biological** *adj* biologique; **biological warfare** guerre *f* bactériologique; **biological weapon** arme *f* biologique

**biometric** [ˌbaɪəʊˈmetrɪk] *adj* biométrique

**bioterrorism** [ˌbaɪəʊˈterərɪzm] *n* bioterrorisme *m*

**bioweapon** [ˈbaɪəʊwepən] *n* arme *f* biologique

**bird** [bɜːd] *n* **a)** [animal] oiseau *m*; [fowl] volaille *f*; **bird flu** grippe *f* aviaire; **bird of prey** oiseau *m* de proie; **bird's-eye view** perspective *f* à vol d'oiseau; *Fig* vue *f* d'ensemble **b)** *Br Fam* [girl] nana *f* ■ **birdseed** *n* graines *fpl* pour oiseaux

**birth** [bɜːθ] *n* naissance *f*; **to give birth to** donner naissance à; **from birth** [blind, deaf] de naissance; **birth certificate** acte *m* de naissance; **birth control** limitation *f* des naissances; **birth rate** (taux *m* de) natalité *f*; **birth sign** signe *m* du zodiaque; **what's your birth sign?** tu es de quel signe? ■ **birthday** *n* anniversaire *m*; **happy birthday!** joyeux anniversaire!; **birthday party** fête *f* d'anniversaire; *Fig* **in one's birthday suit** [man] en costume d'Adam; [woman] en costume d'Ève ∎ **birthmark** n tache f de naissance ∎ **birthparent** ['bɜːθpeərənt] n parent m biologique ∎ **birthplace** n lieu m de naissance ; [house] maison f natale

**biscuit** ['bɪskɪt] n Br biscuit m, petit gâteau m ; Am petit pain m au lait

**bishop** ['bɪʃəp] n évêque m ; [in chess] fou m

---

**bit¹** [bɪt] n **a)** [of string, time] bout m ; **a bit** [a little] un peu ; **not a bit** pas du tout ; **a bit of luck** une chance ; **bit by bit** petit à petit ; **in bits (and pieces)** en morceaux **b)** [coin] pièce f **c)** [of horse] mors m **d)** [of drill] mèche f **e)** COMPUT bit m

---

**bit²** [bɪt] pt of **bite**

**bitch** [bɪtʃ] **1.** n [dog] chienne f ; v Fam & Pej [woman] garce f **2.** vi Fam [complain] râler (**about** après)

**bite** [baɪt] **1.** n **a)** [wound] morsure f ; [from insect] piqûre f ; FISHING touche f **b)** [mouthful] bouchée f ; **to have a bite to eat** manger un morceau **2.** (pt bit, pp bitten ['bɪtən]) vt mordre ; [of insect] piquer ; **to bite one's nails** se ronger les ongles ; **to bite sth off** arracher qch d'un coup de dents **3.** vi mordre ; [of insect] piquer ; **to bite into sth** mordre dans qch ∎ **biting** adj [cold] mordant ; [wind] cinglant

**bitter** ['bɪtə(r)] **1.** n Br [beer] bière anglaise brune **2.** adj [person, taste, irony] amer, -ère ; [cold, wind] glacial ; [criticism] acerbe ; [shock, fate] cruel (f cruelle) ; [conflict] violent ; **to feel bitter (about sth)** être plein d'amertume (à cause de qch) ∎ **bitterly** adv **to cry/regret bitterly** pleurer /regretter amèrement ; **bitterly disappointed** cruellement déçu ; **it's bitterly cold** il fait un froid de canard ∎ **bittersweet** adj doux-amer (f douce-amère) ; Am **bittersweet chocolate** chocolat m noir

**bizarre** [bɪ'zɑː(r)] adj bizarre

**biz(z)arro** [bɪ'zɑːrəʊ] adj Am Fam bizarre, zarbi

**blab** [blæb] (pt & pp -bb-) vi jaser

**black** [blæk] **1.** (compar -er, superl -est) adj noir ; **black cab** taxi m londonien ; **black eye** œil m au beurre noir ; **black and blue** [bruised] couvert de bleus ; AVIAT **black box** boîte f noire ; Br **black ice** verglas m ; Br **black pudding** boudin m noir ; Fig **black sheep** brebis f galeuse **2.** n [colour] noir m ; [person] Noir, -e mf ∎ **blackberry** (pl -ies) n mûre f ∎ **blackbird** n merle m (noir) ∎ **blackboard** n tableau m (noir) ∎ **blackcurrant** n cassis m ∎ **blacken** vt & vi noircir ∎ **blacklist** **1.** n liste f noire **2.** vt mettre sur la liste noire ∎ **blackmail** **1.** n chantage m **2.** vt faire chanter ; **to blackmail sb into doing sth** faire chanter qn pour qu'il /elle fasse qch ∎ **blackout** n panne f d'électricité ; [during war] black-out m inv ; [fainting fit] évanouissement m ; **(news) blackout** black-out m inv ∎ **blacksmith** n forgeron m ; [working with horses] maréchal-ferrant m ∎ **black out** vi [faint] s'évanouir

**bladder** ['blædə(r)] n vessie f

**blade** [bleɪd] n lame f ; **blade of grass** brin m d'herbe

**blame** [bleɪm] **1.** n responsabilité f ; [criticism] blâme m ; **to lay the blame (for sth) on sb** faire porter à qn la responsabilité (de qch) ; **to take the blame for sth** endosser la responsabilité de qch **2.** vt rendre responsable, faire porter la responsabilité à (**for** de) ; **to blame sb for doing sth** reprocher à qn d'avoir fait qch ; **you're to blame** c'est de ta faute ∎ **blameless** adj irréprochable ∎ **blamestorm** ['bleɪmstɔː(r)m] **1.** n discussion destinée à déterminer à qui attribuer la responsabilité d'un échec **2.** vt **the group blamestormed to work out who was responsible for the failure of the product** le groupe s'est réuni pour déterminer à qui devait être attribué l'échec du produit

**blanch** [blɑːntʃ] **1.** vt [vegetables] blanchir **2.** vi [turn pale] blêmir

**bling**

**bland** [blænd] *(compar* -**er**, *superl* -**est)** *adj* [person] terne ; [food] insipide ; [remark, joke] quelconque

**blank** [blæŋk] **1.** *adj* [paper, page] blanc (*f* blanche), vierge ; [cheque] en blanc ; [look, mind] vide ; **blank tape** cassette *f* vierge **2.** *n* [space] blanc *m* ; [cartridge] cartouche *f* à blanc ; **to fire blanks** tirer à blanc ; **my mind's a blank** j'ai un trou

**blanket** ['blæŋkɪt] **1.** *n* [on bed] couverture *f* ; [of snow, leaves] couche *f* **2.** *adj* [term, remark] général

**blankly** ['blæŋklɪ] *adv* **to look blankly at sb/sth** [without expression] regarder qn/qch, le visage inexpressif ; [without understanding] regarder qn/qch sans comprendre

**blare** [bleə(r)] **1.** *n* [noise] beuglements *mpl* ; [of trumpet] sonnerie *f* **2.** *vi* **to blare (out)** [of radio] beugler ; [of music, car horn] retentir

**blasé** ['blɑːzeɪ] *adj* blasé

**blasphemous** ['blæsfəməs] *adj* [text] blasphématoire ; [person] blasphémateur, -trice

**blast** [blɑːst] **1.** *n* explosion *f* ; [air from explosion] souffle *m* ; [of wind] rafale *f* ; [of trumpet] sonnerie *f* ; **(at) full blast** [loud] à fond **2.** *vt* [hole, tunnel] creuser *(en dynamitant)* ; *Fam* [criticize] démolir **3.** *excl Br Fam* zut ! ■ **blasted** *adj Br Fam* fichu ■ **blast-off** *n* [of spacecraft] mise *f* à feu

**blatant** ['bleɪtənt] *adj* [obvious] flagrant ; [shameless] éhonté

**blaze** [bleɪz] **1.** *n* [fire] feu *m* ; [large] incendie *m* ; *Fig* [splendour] éclat *m* ; **a blaze of colour** une explosion de couleurs ; **blaze of light** torrent *m* de lumière **2.** *vi* [of fire, sun] flamboyer ; [of light, eyes] être éclatant **3.** *vt Fig* **to blaze a trail** ouvrir la voie ■ **blazing** *adj* [burning] en feu ; [sun] brûlant ; *Fig* [argument] violent

**blazer** ['bleɪzə(r)] *n* blazer *m*

**bleach** [bliːtʃ] **1.** *n* [household] (eau *f* de) Javel *f* ; [for hair] décolorant *m* **2.** *vt* [clothes] passer à l'eau de Javel ; [hair] décolorer

**bleak** [bliːk] *(compar* -**er**, *superl* -**est)** *adj* [appearance, countryside, weather] morne ; [outlook] lugubre ; [prospect] peu encourageant

**bleat** [bliːt] *vi* bêler

**bleed** [bliːd] *(pt & pp* bled [bled]) **1.** *vi* saigner ; **to bleed to death** saigner à mort ; **her nose is bleeding** elle saigne du nez **2.** *vt* [radiator] purger

**bleep** [bliːp] **1.** *n* bip *m* **2.** *vt* appeler au bip **3.** *vi* faire bip ■ **bleeper** ['bliːpə(r)] *n Br* bip *m*, biper *m*

**blemish** ['blemɪʃ] **1.** *n* [fault] défaut *m* ; [mark] marque *f* **2.** *vt Fig* [reputation] entacher

**blend** [blend] **1.** *n* mélange *m* **2.** *vt* mélanger **(with** à *ou* avec) **3.** *vi* se mélanger ; [of styles, colours] se marier **(with** avec) ■ **blender** *n* mixer *m*

**bless** [bles] *vt* bénir ; **to be blessed with sth** être doté de qch ; **bless you!** [when sneezing] à vos souhaits ! ■ **blessed** *adj* a) [holy] béni b) *Fam* [blasted] fichu ■ **blessing** *n REL* bénédiction *f* ; [benefit] bienfait *m* ; **it was a blessing in disguise** finalement, ça a été une bonne chose

**blew** [bluː] *pt of* **blow**

**blind**[1] [blaɪnd] **1.** *adj* aveugle ; **blind person** aveugle *mf* ; **blind in one eye** borgne ; *Fig* **to be blind to sth** ne pas voir qch ; **blind alley** impasse *f* ; **blind date** *rencontre arrangée avec quelqu'un qu'on ne connaît pas* ; *Br* AUTO **blind corner** virage *m* sans visibilité ; AUTO **blind side** angle *m* mort ; **blind testing** tests *mpl* aveugles **2.** *npl* **the blind** les aveugles *mpl* **3.** *adv* **blind drunk** ivre mort **4.** *vt* [dazzle, make blind] aveugler

**blind**[2] [blaɪnd] *n Br* [on window] store *m*

**blindfold** ['blaɪndfəʊld] **1.** *n* bandeau *m* **2.** *vt* bander les yeux à **3.** *adv* les yeux bandés

**blindly** ['blaɪndlɪ] *adv Fig* aveuglément

**bling** ['blɪŋ], **bling-bling** ['blɪŋ'blɪŋ] *Fam adj* a) [jewellery] clinquant b) [approach, attitude] bling(-)bling, tape-à-l'œil ; **the bling-bling generation** la génération bling-bling

**blink** [blɪŋk] **1.** *n* clignement *m*; *Br Fam* **on the blink** [machine] détraqué **2.** *vt* **to blink one's eyes** cligner des yeux **3.** *vi* [of person] cligner des yeux; [of eyes] cligner; [of light] clignoter

**blissful** ['blɪsfʊl] *adj* [wonderful] merveilleux, -euse; [very happy - person] aux anges ■ **blissfully** *adv* [happy] merveilleusement; **to be blissfully unaware that…** ne pas se douter le moins du monde que…

**blister** ['blɪstə(r)] **1.** *n* [on skin] ampoule *f* **2.** *vi* se couvrir d'ampoules

**blitz** [blɪts] **1.** *n* [air attack] raid *m* éclair; [bombing] bombardement *m* aérien; *Fam* [onslaught] offensive *f* **2.** *vt* bombarder

**blizzard** ['blɪzəd] *n* tempête *f* de neige

**bloated** ['bləʊtɪd] *adj* [swollen] gonflé

**blob** [blɒb] *n* [of ink, colour] tache *f*

**block** [blɒk] **1.** *n* [of stone] bloc *m*; [of buildings] pâté *m* de maisons; [in pipe] obstruction *f*; **block of flats** immeuble *m*; *Am* **a block away** une rue plus loin; **block booking** réservation *f* de groupe; **block capitals** *or* **letters** majuscules *fpl* **2.** *vt* [obstruct] bloquer; [pipe] boucher; [view] cacher; **to block up** [pipe, hole] boucher ■ **blockage** *n* obstruction *f* ■ **blockbuster** *n* [film] film *m* à grand spectacle

**blog** [blɒg] *(abbr of weblog) n* blog *m* ■ **blogger** ['blɒgə(r)] *n* bloggeur, -euse *mf*

**bloke** [bləʊk] *n Br Fam* type *m*

**blond** [blɒnd] *adj & n* blond *(m)* ■ **blonde** *adj & n* blonde *(f)*

**blood** [blʌd] *n* sang *m*; **blood bank** banque *f* du sang; **blood bath** bain *m* de sang; **blood donor** donneur, -euse *mf* de sang; **blood group** groupe *m* sanguin; **blood poisoning** empoisonnement *m* du sang; **blood pressure** tension *f* artérielle; **high blood pressure** hypertension *f*; **to have high blood pressure** avoir de la tension; *Am* **blood sausage** boudin *m*; **blood test** prise *f* de sang; **blood type** groupe *m* sanguin ■ **bloodshed** *n* effusion *f* de sang

■ **bloodshot** *adj* [eye] injecté de sang ■ **bloodstream** *n* sang *m* ■ **bloodthirsty** *adj* sanguinaire

**bloody** ['blʌdɪ] **1.** *(compar -ier, superl -iest) adj* **a)** [covered in blood] ensanglanté **b)** *Br v Fam* foutu; **a bloody liar** un sale menteur; **you bloody fool!** espèce de connard! **2.** *adv Br Fam* [very] vachement; **it's bloody hot!** il fait une putain de chaleur! ■ **bloody-minded** *adj* pas commode

**bloom** [bluːm] **1.** *n* fleur *f*; **in bloom** [tree] en fleur(s); [flower] éclos **2.** *vi* [of tree, flower] fleurir; *Fig* [of person] s'épanouir ■ **blooming** *adj* **a)** [in bloom] en fleur(s); [person] resplendissant; [thriving] florissant **b)** *Br Fam* [for emphasis] sacré; **you blooming idiot!** espèce d'idiot!

**blossom** ['blɒsəm] **1.** *n* fleurs *fpl* **2.** *vi* fleurir; **to blossom (out)** [of person] s'épanouir

**blot** [blɒt] **1.** *n* tache *f* **2.** *(pt & pp -tt-) vt* [stain] tacher; [dry] sécher; **to blot sth out** [obliterate] effacer qch ■ **blotting paper** *n* (papier *m*) buvard *m*

**blotch** [blɒtʃ] *n* tache *f* ■ **blotchy** *(compar -ier, superl -iest) adj* couvert de taches; [face, skin] marbré

**blouse** [blaʊz] *n* chemisier *m*

**blow¹** [bləʊ] *n* [hit, setback] coup *m*; **to come to blows** en venir aux mains

**blow²** [bləʊ] **1.** *(pt blew, pp blown) vt* [of wind] pousser; [of person - smoke, glass] souffler; [bubbles] faire; [trumpet] souffler dans; [kiss] envoyer (**to** à); *Br Fam* [money] claquer (**on sth** pour s'acheter qch); **to blow a fuse** faire sauter un plomb; **to blow one's nose** se moucher; **to blow a whistle** donner un coup de sifflet **2.** *vi* [of wind, person] souffler; [of fuse] sauter; [of papers - in wind] s'éparpiller ■ **blow away** *vt sep* **a)** [subj: wind] chasser, disperser **b)** *Am Fam* [impress] **it really blew me away!** j'ai trouvé ça génial! ■ **blow down 1.** *vt sep* [chimney, fence] faire tomber **2.** *vi* [fall] tomber ■ **blow off** *vt sep* [hat] emporter; [arm] arracher ■ **blow out 1.** *vt sep* [candle] souffler; [cheeks] gonfler **2.** *vi* [of light] s'éteindre **3.** *n*

crevaison *f* ∎ **blow over 1.** *vt* &
*vi* = **blow down 2.** *vi* [of quarrel] se
tasser ∎ **blow up 1.** *vt sep* [building]
faire sauter; [pump up] gonfler; [photo]
agrandir **2.** *vi* [explode] exploser

**blow-dry** ['bləʊdraɪ] **1.** *n* Brushing® *m*
**2.** *vt* to blow-dry sb's hair faire un
Brushing® à qn

**blown** [bləʊn] *pp of* **blow**

**blowout** ['bləʊaʊt] *n* a) [tyre] éclatement *m* b) Br Fam [meal] gueuleton *m*

**blowtorch** ['bləʊtɔːtʃ] *n* chalumeau *m*

**bludgeon** ['blʌdʒən] **1.** *n* gourdin *m* **2.** *vt*
matraquer

**blue** [bluː] **1.** (*compar* -er, *superl* -est) *adj*
bleu; *Fam* to feel blue avoir le cafard;
*Br* blue badge [for disabled drivers]
*carte de conducteur handicapé*; *Fam* blue
movie film *m* porno; *Am* blue state *État
qui vote traditionnellement démocrate*
**2.** *n* bleu *m*; **blues** [music] le blues;
*Fam* the blues [depression] le cafard;
**out of the blue** [unexpectedly] sans
crier gare ∎ **bluebell** *n* jacinthe *f* des
bois ∎ **blueberry** (*pl* -ies) *n* myrtille *f*
∎ **bluebottle** *n* mouche *f* de la viande
∎ **blueprint** *n* Fig plan *m*

**Bluetooth** ['bluːtuːθ] *n* TEL technologie *f*
Bluetooth

**bluff** [blʌf] **1.** *n* bluff *m* **2.** *vt* & *vi* bluffer

**blunder** ['blʌndə(r)] **1.** *n* [mistake]
gaffe *f* **2.** *vi* faire une gaffe

**blunt** [blʌnt] **1.** (*compar* -er, *superl* -est)
*adj* [edge] émoussé; [pencil] mal taillé;
[question, statement] direct; [person]
brusque **2.** *vt* [blade] émousser; [pen-
cil] épointer

**blur** [blɜː(r)] **1.** *n* tache *f* floue **2.** (*pt* & *pp*
-rr-) *vt* [outline] brouiller ∎ **blurred** *adj*
[image, outline] flou

**blurb** [blɜːb] *n* notice *f* publicitaire

**blurt** [blɜːt] *vt* to blurt (out) [secret]
laisser échapper; [excuse] bredouiller

**blush** [blʌʃ] **1.** *n* rougeur *f* **2.** *vi* rougir
(with de)

**blustery** ['blʌstərɪ] *adj* [weather] de
grand vent; [wind] violent

**boar** [bɔː(r)] *n* (wild) boar sanglier *m*

**board¹** [bɔːd] **1.** *n* [piece of wood]
planche *f*; [for notices] panneau *m*;
[for games] tableau *m*; [cardboard] carton *m*; on board (a ship /plane) à bord
(d'un navire /avion); **board sports**
sports *mpl* de glisse **2.** *vt* [ship, plane]
monter à bord de; [bus, train] monter
dans; **to board up** [door] condamner
**3.** *vi* flight Z001 is now boarding
vol Z001, embarquement immédiat
∎ **boarding** *n* [of passengers] embarquement *m*; **boarding pass** carte *f*
d'embarquement ∎ **boardwalk** *n*
*Am* [on beach] promenade *f*

**board²** [bɔːd] *n* [committee] conseil *m*;
**board (of directors)** conseil *m* d'administration; **board (of examiners)**
jury *m* (d'examen); **across the board**
[pay increase] global; [apply] globalement; **board room** salle *f* du conseil

**board³** [bɔːd] **1.** *n* [food] pension *f*;
**board and lodging**, *Br* full board pension *f* complète; *Br* half board demi-
pension *f* **2.** *vi* [lodge] être en pension
(with chez); **boarding house** pension *f*
de famille; **boarding school** pensionnat *m* ∎ **boarder** *n* pensionnaire *mf*

**boast** [bəʊst] **1.** *n* vantardise *f* **2.** *vt* se
glorifier de **3.** *vi* se vanter (**about** *or* **of**
de) ∎ **boastful** *adj* vantard

**boat** [bəʊt] *n* bateau *m*; [small] canot *m*;
[liner] paquebot *m*; by boat en bateau;
*Fig* in the same boat logé à la même
enseigne; **boat race** course *f* d'aviron;
**boat train** *train qui assure la correspondance avec un bateau*

**bode** [bəʊd] *vi* to bode well /ill (for) être
de bon /mauvais augure (pour)

**bodily** ['bɒdɪlɪ] **1.** *adj* [need] physique
**2.** *adv* [lift, seize] à bras-le-corps;
[carry] dans ses bras

**body** ['bɒdɪ] (*pl* -ies) *n* corps *m*; [of car]
carrosserie *f*; [quantity] masse *f*; [in-
stitution] organisme *m*; **(dead) body**
cadavre *m*; **body building** culturi-
risme *m*; **body warmer** gilet *m* matelassé ∎ **bodyguard** *n* garde *m* du corps
∎ **bodysurf** ['bɒdɪsɜːf] *vi* SPORT body-
surfer ∎ **bodywork** *n* carrosserie *f*

**bog** [bɒg] **1.** n [swamp] marécage m **2.** vt **to get bogged down in** [mud, work] s'enliser (dans) ; [details] se perdre (dans)

**bogus** ['bəʊgəs] adj faux (f fausse)

**boil¹** [bɔɪl] n [pimple] furoncle m

**boil²** [bɔɪl] **1.** n **to come to the boil** bouillir ; **to bring sth to the boil** amener qch à ébullition **2.** vt **to boil (up)** faire bouillir ; **to boil the kettle** mettre de l'eau à chauffer **3.** vi bouillir ; Fig **to boil down to** [of situation, question] revenir à ; **to boil over** [of milk] déborder ; Fig [of situation] empirer ▪ **boiled** adj bouilli ; **boiled egg** œuf m à la coque ▪ **boiling 1.** n ébullition f ; **to be at boiling point** [of liquid] bouillir **2.** adj **boiling (hot)** bouillant ; **it's boiling (hot)** [weather] il fait une chaleur infernale

**boiler** ['bɔɪlə(r)] n chaudière f ; Br **boiler suit** bleus mpl de chauffe

**boisterous** ['bɔɪstərəs] adj [noisy] bruyant ; [child] turbulent ; [meeting] houleux, -euse

**BOL** MESSAGING written abbr of **best of luck**

**bold** [bəʊld] (compar -er, superl -est) adj hardi

**bolster** ['bəʊlstə(r)] **1.** n [pillow] traversin m **2.** vt [confidence, pride] renforcer, consoler

**bolt** [bəʊlt] **1.** n a) [on door] verrou m ; [for nut] boulon m b) [dash] **to make a bolt for the door** se précipiter vers la porte c) **bolt of lightning** éclair m **2.** adv **bolt upright** tout droit **3.** vt a) [door] verrouiller b) [food] engloutir **4.** vi [dash] se précipiter ; [run away] détaler ; [of horse] s'emballer

**bomb** [bɒm] **1.** n bombe f ; **bomb scare** alerte f à la bombe **2.** vt [from the air] bombarder ; [of terrorist] faire sauter une bombe dans ou à ▪ **bombshell** n **to come as a bombshell** faire l'effet d'une bombe ▪ **bombsite** n zone f bombardée

**bombard** [bɒm'bɑːd] vt [with bombs, questions] bombarder (**with** de)

**bona fide** [bəʊnə'faɪdɪ] adj véritable

**bond** [bɒnd] **1.** n [link] lien m ; [agreement] engagement m ; FIN obligation f **2.** vt [of glue] coller (**to** à) **3.** vi [form attachment] créer des liens affectifs (**with** avec)

**bone** [bəʊn] **1.** n os m ; [of fish] arête f ; **bone china** porcelaine f tendre **2.** vt [meat] désosser ; [fish] ôter les arêtes de **3.** vi Fam **to bone up on** [subject] bûcher ▪ **bone-dry** adj complètement sec (f sèche) ▪ **bone-idle** adj Br paresseux, -euse

**bonfire** ['bɒnfaɪə(r)] n [for celebration] feu m de joie ; Br [for dead leaves] feu m (de jardin)

**bonkers** ['bɒŋkəz] adj Br Fam dingue

**bonnet** ['bɒnɪt] n [hat] bonnet m ; Br [of vehicle] capot m

**bonus** ['bəʊnəs] (pl -uses [-əsəz]) n prime f ; **no-claims bonus** [in motor insurance] bonus m

**boo** [buː] **1.** excl [to frighten] hou ! **2.** n boos huées fpl **3.** (pt & pp booed) vt & vi huer

**boob** [buːb], **boo-boo** [buːbuː] Br Fam **1.** n a) [mistake] gaffe f, bourde f b) Am [injury] bobo m **2.** vi gaffer ▪ **boobs** npl v Fam nichons mpl

**booby-trap** ['buːbɪtræp] **1.** n engin m piégé m **2.** (pt & pp -pp-) vt piéger

**book** [bʊk] **1.** n livre m ; [record] registre m ; [of tickets] carnet m ; [for exercises and notes] cahier m ; **books** [accounts] comptes mpl ; **book club** club m du livre **2.** vt [seat] réserver ; Br **to book sb** [for traffic offence] dresser une contravention à qn ; **fully booked** [hotel] complet, -ète ; [person] pris **3.** vi **to book (up)** réserver des places ; **to book in** [to hotel] signer le registre ; **to book into a hotel** prendre une chambre dans un hôtel ▪ **bookcase** n bibliothèque f ▪ **bookend** n serre-livres m inv ▪ **bookie** n Fam bookmaker m ▪ **booking** n réservation f ; **booking office** bureau m de location ▪ **bookkeeping** n comptabilité f ▪ **booklet** n brochure f ▪ **bookmaker** n bookmaker m ▪ **bookmark** n marque-page m ▪ **bookseller** n libraire mf ▪ **bookshelf** n étagère f ▪ **bookshop**, Am

**bookstore** n librairie f ▪ **bookstall** n kiosque m à journaux ▪ **bookworm** n passionné, -e mf de lecture

**boom** [bu:m] **1.** n a) [noise] grondement m b) [economic] boom m **2.** vi a) [of thunder, gun] gronder b) [of business, trade] être florissant

**boor** [buə(r)] n rustre m

**boost** [bu:st] **1.** n to give sb a boost remonter le moral à qn **2.** vt [increase] augmenter ; [economy] stimuler ; to boost sb's morale remonter le moral à qn ▪ **booster** n booster (injection) rappel m

**boot**[1] [bu:t] **1.** n a) [footwear] botte f; (ankle) boot bottillon m ; (knee) boot bottine f; to get the boot être mis à la porte ; hiking boots chaussures mpl de randonnée b) Br [of vehicle] coffre m c) to boot [in addition] en plus **2.** vt Fam [kick] donner un coup /des coups de pied à ; to boot sb out mettre qn à la porte

**boot**[2] [bu:t] **1.** vt COMPUT amorcer **2.** vi COMPUT s'amorcer

**booth** [bu:θ, bu:ð] n [for phone, in language lab] cabine f; [at fair] stand m ; [for voting] isoloir m

**booze** [bu:z] Fam **1.** n alcool m **2.** vi picoler ▪ **boozer** n Fam [person] poivrot, -e mf; Br [pub] pub m

**border** ['bɔ:də(r)] **1.** n [of country] & Fig frontière f; [edge] bord m ; [of garden] bordure f **2.** adj [town] frontière inv **3.** vt [street] border ; to border (on) [country] avoir une frontière commune avec ; [resemble, verge on] être voisin de

**bore**[1] [bɔ:(r)] **1.** vt [weary] ennuyer ; to be bored s'ennuyer **2.** n [person] raseur, -euse mf; it's a bore c'est ennuyeux ou rasoir ▪ **boredom** n ennui m ▪ **boring** adj ennuyeux, -euse

**bore**[2] [bɔ:(r)] **1.** n [of gun] calibre m **2.** vt [hole] percer ; [rock, well] forer, creuser **3.** vi forer

**bore**[3] [bɔ:(r)] pt of bear

**born** [bɔ:n] adj né ; to be born naître ; he was born in Paris / in 1980 il est né à Paris / en 1980

**borne** [bɔ:n] pp of bear

**borough** ['bʌrə] n circonscription f électorale urbaine

**borrow** ['bɒrəu] vt emprunter (from à)

**Bosnia** ['bɒznɪə] n la Bosnie

**bosom** ['buzəm] n [chest, breasts] poitrine f; [breast] sein m ; Fig [heart, soul] sein m

**boss** [bɒs] **1.** n patron, -onne mf **2.** vt to boss sb around or about donner des ordres à qn ▪ **bossy** (compar -ier, superl -iest) adj Fam autoritaire

**bot** [bɒt] n COMPUT bot m informatique

**botany** ['bɒtənɪ] n botanique f

**botch** [bɒtʃ] vt Fam to botch (up) [spoil] bâcler ; [repair badly] rafistoler

**both** [bəuθ] **1.** adj les deux ; both brothers les deux frères **2.** pron tous /toutes (les) deux ; both of the boys les deux garçons ; both of us tous les deux ; both of them died ils sont morts tous les deux **3.** adv [at the same time] à la fois ; both in England and in France en Angleterre comme en France ; both you and I know that... vous et moi, nous savons que...

**bother** ['bɒðə(r)] **1.** n [trouble] ennui m ; [effort] peine f; [inconvenience] dérangement m **2.** vt [annoy, worry] ennuyer ; [disturb] déranger ; [pester] importuner ; [hurt, itch - of foot, eye] gêner ; to bother doing or to do sth se donner la peine de faire qch ; I can't be bothered ça ne me dit rien **3.** vi to bother about [worry about] se préoccuper de ; [deal with] s'occuper de ; don't bother! ce n'est pas la peine !

**botnet** ['bɒtnet] n COMPUT botnet m, réseau m de robots IRC

**bottle** ['bɒtəl] **1.** n bouteille f; [for perfume] flacon m ; [for baby] biberon m ; bottle bank conteneur m pour verre usagé ; bottle opener ouvre-bouteilles m inv **2.** vt [milk, wine] mettre en bouteilles ; to bottle up [feeling] refouler ▪ **bottle-feed** (pt & pp -fed) vt nourrir au biberon ▪ **bottle-neck** n [in road] goulot m d'étranglement ; [in traffic] bouchon m

**bottom** ['bɒtəm] **1.** n [of sea, box] fond m ; [of page, hill] bas m ; [of table] bout *m* ; [buttocks] derrière *m* ; **to be (at the) bottom of the class** être le dernier / la dernière de la classe **2.** *adj* [shelf] inférieur, du bas ; **bottom floor** rez-de-chaussée *m* ; **bottom gear** première vitesse *f* ; **bottom part** *or* **half** partie *f* inférieure ; *Fig* **the bottom line is that…** le fait est que… ■ **bottomless** *adj* [funds] inépuisable ; **bottomless pit** gouffre *m* ■ **bottom-of-the-range** *adj* bas de gamme

**bought** [bɔːt] *pt & pp of* **buy**

**boulder** ['bəʊldə(r)] *n* rocher *m*

**bounce** [baʊns] **1.** *n* rebond *m* ; **bounce message** rapport *m* de non livraison (*d'un e-mail*) **2.** *vt* [ball] faire rebondir **3.** *vi* [of ball] rebondir (**off** contre) ; [of person] faire des bonds ; *Fam* [of cheque] être sans provision

**bouncer** ['baʊnsə(r)] *n Fam* [doorman] videur *m*

**bound¹** [baʊnd] *adj* **a)** **bound to do** [obliged] obligé de faire ; [certain] sûr de faire ; **it's bound to snow** il va sûrement neiger ; **to be bound for** [of person, ship] être en route pour ; [of train, plane] être à destination de **b)** **bound up with** [connected] lié à

**bound²** [baʊnd] **1.** *n* [leap] bond *m* **2.** *vi* bondir

**bound³** [baʊnd] *pt & pp of* **bind**

**boundary** ['baʊndərɪ] (*pl* -**ies**) *n* limite *f*

**bounds** [baʊndz] *npl* limites *fpl* ; **out of bounds** [place] interdit

**bouquet** [baʊ'keɪ] *n* [of flowers, wine] bouquet *m*

**bout** [baʊt] *n* [of fever, coughing, violence] accès *m* ; [of asthma, malaria] crise *f* ; [session] séance *f* ; [period] période *f* ; [in boxing] combat *m* ; **a bout of flu** une grippe

**boutique** [buːˈtiːk] *n* boutique *f* (de mode)

**bow¹** [bəʊ] *n* [weapon] arc *m* ; [of violin] archet *m* ; [knot] nœud *m* ; **bow tie** nœud *m* papillon ■ **bow-legged** *adj* aux jambes arquées

**bow²** [baʊ] **1.** *n* [with knees bent] révérence *f* ; [nod] salut *m* **2.** *vt* **to bow one's**

head incliner la tête **3.** *vi* s'incliner (**to** devant) ; [nod] incliner la tête (**to** devant) ; **to bow down (to)** [submit] s'incliner (devant)

**bow³** [baʊ] *n* [of ship] proue *f*

**bowels** ['baʊəlz] *npl* intestins *mpl*

**bowl¹** [bəʊl] *n* [small dish] bol *m* ; [for salad] saladier *m* ; [for soup] assiette *f* creuse ; [of toilet] cuvette *f*

**bowl²** [bəʊl] **1.** *n* **bowls** [game] boules *fpl* **2.** *vi* [in cricket] lancer la balle ■ **bowling** *n* **(tenpin) bowling** bowling *m* ; **bowling alley** bowling *m* ; **bowling ball** boule *f* de bowling ; **bowling green** terrain *m* de boules ■ **bowl over** *vt sep* [knock down] renverser ; *Fig* [astound] **to be bowled over by sth** être stupéfié par qch

**box** [bɒks] **1.** *n* boîte *f* ; [larger] caisse *f* ; [made of cardboard] carton *m* ; [in theatre] loge *f* ; [for horse, in stable] box *m* ; *BrFam* [television] télé *f* ; **box file** boîte *f* archive ; **box office** bureau *m* de location ; *Br* **box room** [for storage] débarras *m* ; [bedroom] petite chambre *f* **2.** *vt* **a)** **to box (up)** mettre en boîte / caisse ; **to box in** [enclose] enfermer **b)** **to box sb's ears** gifler qn **3.** *vi* boxer ■ **boxing** *n* **a)** [sport] boxe *f* ; **boxing gloves / match** gants *mpl* / combat *m* de boxe ; **boxing ring** ring *m* **b)** *Br* **Boxing Day** le lendemain de Noël

**boxer** ['bɒksə(r)] *n* [fighter] boxeur *m* ; [dog] boxer *m*

**boy** [bɔɪ] *n* garçon *m* ; **boy wonder** petit génie *m* ■ **boyfriend** *n* petit ami *m*

**boycott** ['bɔɪkɒt] **1.** *n* boycottage *m* **2.** *vt* boycotter

**bra** [brɑː] *n* soutien-gorge *m*

**brace** [breɪs] **1.** *n* [dental] appareil *m* dentaire ; [on leg, arm] appareil *m* orthopédique ; [for fastening] attache *f* ; *Br* **braces** [for trousers] bretelles *fpl* **2.** *vt* **to brace oneself for sth** [news, shock] se préparer à qch ■ **bracing** *adj* [air] vivifiant

**bracelet** ['breɪslɪt] *n* bracelet *m*

**bracket** ['brækɪt] **1.** *n* [for shelves] équerre *f* ; [in writing] parenthèse *f* ;

[group] groupe m ; [for tax] tranche f ; **in brackets** entre parenthèses **2.** vt mettre entre parenthèses

**brag** [bræg] (pt & pp **-gg-**) vi se vanter (**about** or **of** sth de qch ; **about doing sth** de faire qch)

**braid** [breɪd] **1.** n [of hair] tresse f ; [trimming] galon m **2.** vt [hair] tresser ; [trim] galonner

**Braille** [breɪl] n braille m ; **in Braille** en braille

**brain** [breɪn] **1.** n cerveau m ; [of animal, bird] cervelle f ; [of person] être intelligent ; Fam **to have sth on the brain** être obsédé par qch ; **brain death** mort f cérébrale ; **brain drain** fuite f des cerveaux **2.** vt Fam [hit] assommer ■ **brainchild** n trouvaille f ■ **brainstorm** n Am [brilliant idea] idée f géniale ; Br [mental confusion] aberration f ■ **brainwash** vt faire un lavage de cerveau à ■ **brainwave** n idée f géniale

**brainiac** [ˈbreɪnɪæk] n Am Fam intello mf

**brainy** [ˈbreɪnɪ] (compar **-ier**, superl **-iest**) adj Fam intelligent

**brake** [breɪk] **1.** n frein m ; **brake light** stop m **2.** vi freiner

**bran** [bræn] n son m

**branch** [brɑːntʃ] **1.** n branche f ; [of road] embranchement m ; [of river] bras m ; [of shop] succursale f ; [of bank] agence f ; **branch office** succursale f **2.** vi **to branch off** [of road] bifurquer ; **to branch out** [of company, person] étendre ses activités ; [of family, tree] se ramifier

**brand** [brænd] **1.** n [on product, on cattle] marque f ; [type] type m, style m ; **brand name** marque f **2.** vt [mark] marquer ; Fig **to be branded as a liar / coward** avoir une réputation de menteur / lâche

**brandish** [ˈbrændɪʃ] vt brandir

**brand-new** [brænd'njuː] adj tout neuf (f toute neuve)

**brandy** [ˈbrændɪ] (pl **-ies**) n cognac m ; [made with fruit] eau-de-vie f

**brash** [bræʃ] adj exubérant

**brass** [brɑːs] n cuivre m ; [instruments in orchestra] cuivres mpl ; Fam **brass band** fanfare f

**brat** [bræt] n Pej [child] morveux, -euse mf ; [badly behaved] sale gosse mf

**brave** [breɪv] **1.** (compar **-er**, superl **-est**) adj courageux, -euse **2.** n [native American] brave m **3.** vt [danger] braver ■ **bravery** n courage m

**brawl** [brɔːl] **1.** n [fight] bagarre f **2.** vi se bagarrer

**Brazil** [brə'zɪl] n le Brésil ■ **Brazilian 1.** adj brésilien, -enne **2.** n Brésilien, -enne mf

**BRB** MESSAGING written abbr of **be right back**

**breach** [briːtʃ] **1.** n [of rule] violation f (**of** de) ; **breach of contract** rupture f de contrat ; **breach of trust** abus m de confiance **2.** vt [law, code] enfreindre à ; [contract] rompre

**bread** [bred] n pain m ; Fam [money] blé m ; **loaf of bread** pain m ; **brown bread** pain m bis ; (**slice** or **piece of**) **bread and butter** pain m beurré ; **bread knife** couteau m à pain ■ **breadbin**, Am **breadbox** n boîte f à pain ■ **breadboard** n planche f à pain ■ **breadcrumb** n miette f de pain ; **breadcrumbs** [in cooking] chapelure f ■ **breaded** adj pané ■ **breadline** n **on the breadline** indigent ■ **breadwinner** n **to be the breadwinner** faire bouillir la marmite

**breadth** [bretθ] n largeur f

**break** [breɪk] **1.** n cassure f ; [in bone] fracture f ; [with person, group] rupture f ; [in journey] interruption f ; [rest] repos m ; [in activity] pause f ; [at school] récréation f ; [holidays] vacances fpl **2.** (pt **broke**, pp **broken**) vt casser ; [into pieces, with force] briser ; [silence, spell, vow] rompre ; [strike, will, ice] briser ; [agreement, promise] manquer à ; [law] violer ; [record] battre ; [journey] interrompre ; [news] annoncer (**to** à) ; [habit] se débarrasser de ; **to break one's arm** se casser le bras ; **to break sb's heart** briser le cœur à qn ; Fam **to break the sound barrier** franchir le mur du son ; **to break a fall** amortir une chute **3.** vi se casser ; [into pieces, of heart, of voice] se briser ; [of boy's voice] muer ; [of spell] se rompre ; [of weather] changer ; [of news] éclater ; [of day] se lever ; [stop work] faire la pause ; **to break in two** se casser en deux ; **to break free** se libérer ; **to break loose** se détacher ■ **breakable** adj fragile ■ **breakage** n **were there any breakages?** est-ce qu'il y a eu de la casse ? ■ **breakdown** n [of machine] panne f ; [of argument, figures] analyse f ; [of talks, negotiations] échec m ; [of person] dépression f ; Br **breakdown lorry** or **van** dépanneuse f ■ **break away 1.** vi se détacher **2.** vt sep détacher ■ **break down 1.** vt sep [door] enfoncer ; [resistance] briser ; [argument, figures] analyser **2.** vi [of machine] tomber en panne ; [of talks, negotiations] échouer ; [of person] [have nervous breakdown] craquer ; [start crying] éclater en sanglots ■ **break in 1.** vi [of burglar] entrer par effraction ; [interrupt] interrompre **2.** vt sep [door] enfoncer ; [horse] dresser ■ **break into** vt insep [house] entrer par effraction ; [safe] forcer ; **to break into song / a run** se mettre à chanter / courir ■ **break off 1.** vt sep [detach - twig, handle] détacher ; [relations] rompre **2.** vi [become detached] se casser ; [stop] s'arrêter ; **to break off with sb** rompre avec qn ■ **break out** vi [of war, fire] éclater ; [escape] s'échapper (**of** de) ; **to break out in a rash** se couvrir de boutons ■ **break through 1.** vi [of sun, army] percer **2.** vt insep [defences] percer ; [barrier] forcer ; [wall] faire une brèche dans ■ **break up 1.** vt sep [reduce to pieces] mettre en morceaux ; [marriage] briser ; [fight] mettre fin à **2.** vi [end] prendre fin ; [of group] se disperser ; [of marriage] se briser ; [from school] partir en vacances

**breakfast** ['brekfəst] n petit déjeuner m ; **to have breakfast** prendre le petit déjeuner ; **breakfast TV** émissions fpl (télévisées) du matin

**break-in** ['breɪkɪn] n cambriolage m

**breaking-point** ['breɪkɪŋpɔɪnt] n at **breaking-point** [person, patience] à bout ; [marriage] au bord de la rupture

**breakthrough** ['breɪkθruː] n [discovery] découverte f fondamentale, percée f

**breast** [brest] n [of woman] sein m ; [chest] poitrine f ; [of chicken] blanc m ■ **breastfeed** (pt & pp -fed) vt allaiter ■ **breaststroke** n [in swimming] brasse f

**breath** [breθ] n souffle m ; **bad breath** mauvaise haleine f ; **out of breath** à bout de souffle ; **to hold one's breath** retenir son souffle ; **under one's breath** tout bas ; **breath freshener** purificateur m d'haleine ; **breath test** Alcootest® m ■ **breathalyser**® n Alcootest® m ■ **breathless** adj hors d'haleine ■ **breathtaking** adj à couper le souffle

**breathe** [briːð] **1.** vi [of person, animal] respirer ; **to breathe in** inhaler ; **to breathe out** expirer **2.** vt respirer ; **to breathe a sigh of relief** pousser un soupir de soulagement ■ **breathing** n respiration f ; Fig **breathing space** moment m de repos

**bred** [bred] **1.** pt & pp of **breed 2.** adj **well-bred** bien élevé

**breed** [briːd] **1.** n race f **2.** (pt & pp **bred**) vt [animals] élever ; Fig [hatred, violence] engendrer **3.** vi [of animals] se reproduire ■ **breeding** n [of animals] élevage m ; Fig [manners] éducation f

**breeze** [briːz] n brise f ■ **breezy** (compar -ier, superl -iest) adj **a)** [weather, day] frais (f fraîche), venteux, -euse **b)** [cheerful] jovial ; [relaxed] décontracté

**brew** [bruː] **1.** n [drink] breuvage m ; [of tea] infusion f **2.** vt [beer] brasser ; Fig [trouble, plot] préparer **3.** vi [of beer] fermenter ; [of tea] infuser ; Fig [of storm] se préparer ■ **brewery** (pl -ies) n brasserie f

**bribe** [braɪb] **1.** n pot-de-vin m **2.** vt acheter, soudoyer ; **to bribe sb into doing sth** soudoyer qn pour qu'il fasse qch ■ **bribery** n corruption f

**brick** [brɪk] n brique f ; **brick wall** mur en briques ■ **bricklayer** n maçon m

**bridal** ['braɪdəl] *adj* [ceremony, bed] nuptial ; **bridal suite** [in hotel] suite *f* nuptiale

**bride** [braɪd] *n* mariée *f* ; **the bride and groom** les mariés *mpl* ■ **bridegroom** *n* marié *m* ■ **bridesmaid** *n* demoiselle *f* d'honneur

**bridge**[^1] [brɪdʒ] **1.** *n* pont *m* ; [on ship] passerelle *f* ; [of nose] arête *f* ; [on teeth] bridge *m* **2.** *vt* **to bridge a gap** combler une lacune

**bridge**[^2] [brɪdʒ] *n* [game] bridge *m*

**brief**[^1] [bri:f] *(compar* -er*, superl* -est*) adj* bref (*f* brève) ; **in brief** en résumé ■ **briefly** *adv* [say] brièvement ; [hesitate, smile] un court instant

**brief**[^2] [bri:f] **1.** *n* [instructions] instructions *fpl* ; [legal] dossier *m* ; *Fig* [task] tâche *f* **2.** *vt* donner des instructions à ; [inform] mettre au courant (**on** de) ■ **briefing** *n* [information] instructions *fpl* ; [meeting] briefing *m*

**briefcase** ['bri:fkeɪs] *n* serviette *f*

**briefs** [bri:fs] *npl* [underwear] slip *m*

**brigade** [brɪ'geɪd] *n* brigade *f*

**bright** [braɪt] **1.** *(compar* -er*, superl* -est*) adj* [star, eyes, situation] brillant ; [light, colour] vif (*f* vive) ; [weather, room] clair ; [clever] intelligent ; [happy] joyeux, -euse ; [future] prometteur, -euse ; [idea] génial **2.** *adv* **bright and early** de bon matin ■ **brightly** *adv* [shine] avec éclat

**brighten** ['braɪtən] **1.** *vt* **to brighten (up)** [room] égayer **2.** *vi* **to brighten (up)** [of weather] s'éclaircir ; [of face] s'éclairer ; [of person] s'égayer

**brilliant** ['brɪljənt] *adj* [light] éclatant ; [person, idea, career] brillant ; *Br Fam* [fantastic] super *inv*

**brim** [brɪm] **1.** *n* [of hat, cup] bord *m* **2.** *(pt & pp* -mm-*) vi* **to brim over (with)** déborder (de)

**bring** [brɪŋ] *(pt & pp* brought*) vt* [person, animal, car] amener ; [object] apporter ; [cause] provoquer ; **it has brought me great happiness** cela m'a procuré un grand bonheur ; **to bring sth to sb's attention** attirer l'attention de qn sur qch ; **to bring sth to an end** mettre

fin à qch ■ **bring about** *vt sep* provoquer ■ **bring along** *vt sep* [object] apporter ; [person] amener ■ **bring back** *vt sep* [person] ramener ; [object] rapporter ; [memories] rappeler ■ **bring down** *vt sep* [object] descendre ; [overthrow] faire tomber ; [reduce] réduire ; [shoot down - plane] abattre ■ **bring forward** *vt sep* [in time or space] avancer ; [witness] produire ■ **bring in** *vt sep* [object] rentrer ; [person] faire entrer ; [introduce] introduire ; [income] rapporter ■ **bring off** *vt sep* [task] mener à bien ■ **bring out** *vt sep* [object] sortir ; [person] faire sortir ; [meaning] faire ressortir ; [book] publier ; [product] lancer ■ **bring round** *vt sep* [revive] ranimer ; [convert] convaincre ; **she brought him round to her point of view** elle a su le convaincre ■ **bring to** *vt sep* **to bring sb to** ranimer qn ■ **bring together** *vt sep* [friends, members] réunir ; [reconcile] réconcilier ; [put in touch] mettre en contact ■ **bring up** *vt sep* [object] monter ; [child] élever ; [question] soulever ; [subject] mentionner ; [food] rendre

**brink** [brɪŋk] *n* bord *m* ; **on the brink of sth** au bord de qch

**brisk** [brɪsk] *(compar* -er*, superl* -est*) adj* [lively] vif (*f* vive) ; **at a brisk pace** vite ; **business is brisk** les affaires marchent bien

**bristle** ['brɪsəl] **1.** *n* poil *m* **2.** *vi* se hérisser

**Britain** ['brɪtən] *n* la Grande-Bretagne ■ **British 1.** *adj* britannique ; **the British Isles** les îles *fpl* Britanniques ; **British Summer Time** heure *f* d'été *(en Grande-Bretagne)* **2.** *npl* **the British** les Britanniques *mpl* ■ **Briton** *n* Britannique *mf*

**Brittany** ['brɪtənɪ] *n* la Bretagne

**brittle** ['brɪtəl] *adj* cassant

**broad** [brɔːd] *(compar* -er*, superl* -est*) adj* [wide] large ; [accent] prononcé ; **in broad daylight** en plein jour ; **the broad outline of** [plan] les grandes lignes de ; **broad bean** fève *f* ; *Am* SPORT **broad jump** saut *m* en longueur

■ **broad-minded** *adj* [person] à l'esprit large ■ **broad-shouldered** *adj* large d'épaules ■ **broaden 1.** *vt* élargir **2.** *vi* s'élargir ■ **broadly** *adv* broadly (speaking) en gros

**broadband** ['brɔ:dbænd] **1.** *adj* à larges bandes; **broadband Internet connection** connexion *f* à haut débit **2.** *n* COMPUT transmission *f* à larges bandes; **have you got broadband?** tu as (l')ADSL?

**broadcast** ['brɔ:dkɑ:st] **1.** *n* émission *f* **2.** (*pt & pp* broadcast) *vt* diffuser **3.** *vi* [of station] émettre; [of person] parler à la radio/à la télévision

**broccoli** ['brɒkəlɪ] *n inv* [plant] brocoli *m*; [food] brocolis *mpl*

**brochure** ['brəʊʃə(r)] *n* brochure *f*

**broil** [brɔɪl] *vt & vi* Am griller

**broke** [brəʊk] **1.** *pt of* break **2.** *adj* Fam [penniless] fauché ■ **broken 1.** *pp of* break **2.** *adj* [man, voice, line] brisé; [ground] accidenté; [spirit] abattu; **in broken English** en mauvais anglais; **broken home** famille *f* désunie ■ **brokenhearted** [,brəʊkn'hɑ:tɪd] *adj* au cœur brisé

**broker** ['brəʊkə(r)] *n* [for shares, currency] agent *m* de change; [for goods, insurance] courtier, -ère *mf*

**bromance** ['brəʊmæns] *n* Fam bromance *f* (amitié profonde entre hommes); **there's definitely nothing gay between Jack and Mike, it's more like just bromance** il n'y a vraiment rien entre Jack et Mike, ils sont tout simplement très amis

**bronchitis** [brɒŋ'kaɪtɪs] *n* bronchite *f*

**bronze** [brɒnz] *n* bronze *m*; **bronze statue** statue *f* en bronze

**brooch** [brəʊtʃ] *n* [ornament] broche *f*

**brood** [bru:d] **1.** *n* couvée *f* **2.** *vi* [of bird] couver; *Fig* **to brood over sth** [of person] ruminer qch ■ **broody** (*compar* -ier, *superl* -iest) *adj* [person - sulky] maussade; [dreamy] rêveur, -euse; *Br Fam* [woman] en mal d'enfant

**broom** [bru:m] *n* **a)** [for sweeping] balai *m* **b)** [plant] genêt *m*

**broth** [brɒθ] *n* [thin] bouillon *m*; [thick] potage *m*

**brothel** ['brɒθəl] *n* maison *f* close

**brother** ['brʌðə(r)] *n* frère *m* ■ **brother-in-law** (*pl* brothers-in-law) *n* beau-frère *m*

**brought** [brɔ:t] *pt & pp of* bring

**brow** [braʊ] *n* **a)** [forehead] front *m* **b)** [of hill] sommet *m*

**brown** [braʊn] **1.** (*compar* -er, *superl* -est) *adj* marron *inv*; [hair] châtain; [tanned] bronzé **2.** *n* marron *m* **3.** *vt* [food] faire dorer **4.** *vi* [of food] dorer

**brownie** ['braʊnɪ] *n* [cake] brownie *m*

**Brownie** ['braʊnɪ] *n* [girl scout] ≃ jeannette *f*

**browse** [braʊz] **1.** *vt* COMPUT **to browse the Web** naviguer sur le Web **2.** *vi* [in bookshop] feuilleter des livres; [in shop, supermarket] regarder; COMPUT naviguer; **to browse through** [book] feuilleter ■ **browser** ['braʊzə(r)] *n* COMPUT navigateur *m*, browser *m*

**BRT** MESSAGING *written abbr of* **be right there**

**bruise** [bru:z] **1.** *n* bleu *m*; [on fruit] meurtrissure *f* **2.** *vt* **to bruise one's knee/hand** se faire un bleu au genou/à la main ■ **bruised** *adj* [covered in bruises] couvert de bleus

**brunch** [brʌntʃ] *n* brunch *m*

**brunette** [bru:'net] *n* brunette *f*

**brunt** [brʌnt] *n* **to bear the brunt of** [attack, anger] subir le plus gros de; [expense] assumer la plus grosse part de

**brush** [brʌʃ] **1.** *n* [tool] brosse *f*; [for shaving] blaireau *m*; [for sweeping] balayette *f*; **to give sth a brush** donner un coup de brosse à qch **2.** *vt* [teeth, hair] brosser; [clothes] donner un coup de brosse à; **to brush sb/sth aside** écarter qn/qch; **to brush sth away** or **off** enlever qch; **to brush up (on) one's French** se remettre au français **3.** *vi* **to brush against sb/sth** effleurer qn/qch ■ **brush-off** *n* Fam **to give sb the brush-off** envoyer promener qn

**brusque** [bru:sk] *adj* brusque

**bulb**

**Brussels** ['brʌsəlz] n Bruxelles m ou f; **Brussels sprouts** choux mpl de Bruxelles

**brutal** ['bru:təl] adj brutal; [attack] sauvage

**brute** [bru:t] **1.** n [animal] bête f; [person] brute f **2.** adj **by brute force** par la force

**BSc** [bi:es'si:], Am **BS** [bi:'es] (abbr of **Bachelor of Science**) [person] ≃ licencié, -e mf ès sciences; [qualification] ≃ licence f de sciences

**BSE** [bi:es'i:] (abbr of **bovine spongiform encephalopathy**) n EBS f, maladie f de la vache folle

**BTWN** MESSAGING written abbr of **between**

**bubble** ['bʌbəl] **1.** n [of air, soap] bulle f; **bubble bath** bain m moussant; **bubble gum** chewing-gum m **2.** vi [of liquid] bouillonner; **to bubble over (with)** déborder (de)

**bubbly** ['bʌbli] **1.** adj [liquid] plein de bulles; [person, personality] débordant de vitalité **2.** n Fam champ m

**buck** [bʌk] **1.** n **a)** Am Fam dollar m **b)** [of rabbit] mâle m **2.** vt Fam **to buck sb up** remonter le moral à qn **3.** vi Fam **to buck up** [become livelier] reprendre du poil de la bête; [hurry] se grouiller

**bucket** ['bʌkɪt] n seau m

**buckle** ['bʌkəl] **1.** n boucle f **2.** vt **a)** [fasten] boucler **b)** [deform] déformer **3.** vi [deform] se déformer

**bud** [bʌd] **1.** n [on tree] bourgeon m; [on flower] bouton m **2.** (pt & pp -dd-) vi bourgeonner; [of flower] pousser des boutons ▪ **budding** adj [talent] naissant; [doctor] en herbe

**Buddhist** ['bʊdɪst] adj & n bouddhiste (mf)

**buddy** ['bʌdi] (pl -ies) n Am Fam pote m

**budge** [bʌdʒ] **1.** vi bouger **2.** vt faire bouger

**budgerigar** ['bʌdʒərɪgɑ:(r)] n Br perruche f

**budget** ['bʌdʒɪt] **1.** n budget m **2.** vi dresser un budget; **to budget for sth** inscrire qch au budget

**budgie** ['bʌdʒi] n Br Fam perruche f

**buff** [bʌf] **1.** adj **buff(-coloured)** chamois inv **2.** n Fam **jazz/film buff** fanatique mf de jazz/de cinéma

**buffalo** ['bʌfələʊ] (pl -oes or -o) n buffle m; **(American) buffalo** bison m

**buffer** ['bʌfə(r)] n [on train] tampon m; [at end of track] butoir m; Fig [safeguard] protection f (**against** contre); COMPUT mémoire f tampon

**buffet¹** ['bʊfeɪ] n [meal, café] buffet m; **cold buffet** viandes fpl froides; Br **buffet car** [on train] wagon-restaurant m

**buffet²** ['bʌfɪt] vt [of waves] secouer; [of wind, rain] cingler

**bug¹** [bʌg] **1.** n **a)** [insect] bestiole f; [bedbug] punaise f; Fam [germ] microbe m **b)** [in machine] défaut m; COMPUT bogue m, bug m **c)** [listening device] micro m **2.** (pt & pp -gg-) vt [room] installer des micros dans

**bug²** [bʌg] (pt & pp -gg-) vt Fam [nag] embêter

**buggy** ['bʌgi] (pl -ies) n Am [pram] landau m; Br **(baby) buggy** [pushchair] poussette f

**build** [bɪld] **1.** n [of person] carrure f **2.** (pt & pp built [bɪlt]) vt construire; **to build sth up** [increase] augmenter qch; [business] monter qch **3.** vi **to build up** [of tension, pressure] augmenter; [of dust, snow, interest] s'accumuler; [of traffic] devenir dense ▪ **builder** n [skilled] maçon m; [unskilled] ouvrier m; [contractor] entrepreneur m ▪ **building** n bâtiment m; [flats, offices] immeuble m; [action] construction f; **building site** chantier m; Br **building society** ≃ société f de crédit immobilier ▪ **build-up** n [increase] augmentation f; [of dust] accumulation f; [for author, book] publicité f

**built-in** [bɪlt'ɪn] adj [cupboard] encastré; [part of machine] incorporé; Fig [innate] inné

**built-up** ['bɪltʌp] adj urbanisé; **built-up area** agglomération f

**bulb** [bʌlb] n [of plant] bulbe m; [of lamp] ampoule f

**bulge** [bʌldʒ] **1.** *n* renflement *m* **2.** *vi* to bulge (out) bomber ; [of eyes] sortir de la tête ▪ **bulging** *adj* bombé ; [eyes] protubérant ; **to be bulging (with)** [of bag, pocket] être bourré (de)

**bulimia** [buˈlɪmɪə] *n* boulimie *f*

**bulk** [bʌlk] *n inv* [of building, parcel] volume *m* ; [of person] grosseur *f* ; **the bulk of sth** la majeure partie de qch ; **in bulk** [buy, sell] en gros ▪ **bulky** (*compar* -ier, *superl* -iest) *adj* volumineux, -euse

**bull** [bʊl] *n* **a)** [animal] taureau *m* **b)** *v Fam* [nonsense] conneries *fpl* ▪ **bullfight** *n* corrida *f*

**bulldozer** [ˈbʊldəʊzə(r)] *n* bulldozer *m*

**bullet** [ˈbʊlɪt] *n* balle *f* ▪ **bulletproof** *adj* [car] blindé ; **bulletproof glass** vitre *f* blindée ; *Br* **bulletproof jacket**, *Am* **bulletproof vest** gilet *m* pare-balles *inv*

**bulletin** [ˈbʊlətɪn] *n* bulletin *m* ; *Am* **bulletin board** panneau *m* d'affichage

**bullion** [ˈbʊljən] *n* **gold bullion** lingots *mpl* d'or

**bull's-eye** [ˈbʊlzaɪ] *n* [of target] centre *m* ; **to hit the bull's-eye** mettre dans le mille

**bully** [ˈbʊlɪ] **1.** (*pl* -ies) *n* terreur *f* **2.** (*pt & pp* -ied) *vt* [ill-treat] maltraiter

**bum** [bʌm] *Fam* **1.** *n* **a)** [loafer] clochard, -e *mf* ; [good-for-nothing] bon *m* à rien, bonne *f* à rien **b)** *Br* [buttocks] derrière *m* ; **bum bag** banane *f* **2.** (*pt & pp* -mm-) *vi* **to bum (around)** [be idle] glander ; [travel] vadrouiller **3.** *vt* **to bum sth off sb** taxer qch à qn

**bump** [bʌmp] **1.** *n* [impact] choc *m* ; [jerk] secousse *f* ; [on road, body] bosse *f* **2.** *vt* [of car] heurter ; **to bump one's head / knee** se cogner la tête / le genou ; **to bump into** [of person] se cogner contre ; [of car] rentrer dans ; [meet] tomber sur ▪ **bumper 1.** *n* [of car] pare-chocs *m inv* **2.** *adj* [crop, year] exceptionnel, -elle ; **bumper car** auto *f* tamponneuse

**bumpy** [ˈbʌmpɪ] (*compar* -ier, *superl* -iest) *adj* [road, ride] cahoteux, -euse

**bun** [bʌn] *n* **a)** [cake] petit pain *m* au lait **b)** [of hair] chignon *m*

**bunch** [bʌntʃ] *n* [of flowers] bouquet *m* ; [of keys] trousseau *m* ; [of bananas] régime *m* ; [of grapes] grappe *f* ; [of people] bande *f*

**bundle** [ˈbʌndəl] **1.** *n* paquet *m* ; [of papers] liasse *f* ; [of firewood] fagot *m* **2.** *vt* [put] fourrer (**into** dans) ; [push] pousser (**into** dans) ; **to bundle up** [newspapers, letters] mettre en paquet **3.** *vi* **to bundle (oneself) up** (bien) se couvrir

**bungalow** [ˈbʌŋgələʊ] *n* pavillon *m* de plain-pied

**bungee** [ˈbʌndʒiː] *n* **bungee jump(ing)** saut *m* à l'élastique

**bungle** [ˈbʌŋgəl] **1.** *vt* gâcher **2.** *vi* se tromper

**bunk** [bʌŋk] *n* [in ship, train] couchette *f* ; **bunk beds** lits *mpl* superposés

**bunker** [ˈbʌŋkə(r)] *n* MIL & GOLF bunker *m* ; [for coal] coffre *m* à charbon

**bunny** [ˈbʌnɪ] (*pl* -ies) *n Fam* **bunny (rabbit)** petit lapin *m*

**buoy** [bɔɪ] **1.** *n* bouée *f* **2.** *vt Fig* **to buoy up** [support] soutenir

**buoyant** [ˈbɔɪənt] *adj* [in water] qui flotte ; *Fig* [economy, prices] stable ; *Fig* [person, mood] plein d'allant

**burden** [ˈbɜːdən] **1.** *n* fardeau *m* **2.** *vt* charger (**with** de) ; *Fig* accabler (**with** de)

**bureau** [ˈbjʊərəʊ] (*pl* -eaux [-əʊz]) *n* [office] bureau *m* ; *Br* [desk] secrétaire *m* ; *Am* [chest of drawers] commode *f*

**bureaucracy** [bjʊəˈrɒkrəsɪ] *n* bureaucratie *f* ▪ **bureaucrat** *n* bureaucrate *mf*

**burger** [ˈbɜːgə(r)] *n* hamburger *m*

**burglar** [ˈbɜːglə(r)] *n* cambrioleur, -euse *mf* ; **burglar alarm** alarme *f* antivol ▪ **burglarize** *vt Am* cambrioler ▪ **burgle** *vt Br* cambrioler

**burial** [ˈberɪəl] **1.** *n* enterrement *m* **2.** *adj* [service] funèbre ; **burial ground** cimetière *m*

**burn** [bɜːn] **1.** *n* brûlure *f* **2.** (*pt & pp* burned *or* burnt) *vt* **a)** brûler ; **to burn sth down** incendier qch **b)** COMPUT graver ; **to burn a CD** graver un CD **3.** *vi* brûler ; **to burn down** [of house] être détruit par les flammes ; [of fuse] sauter ■ **burning 1.** *adj* en feu ; [fire] allumé ; *Fig* [fever] dévorant **2.** *n* **a smell of burning** une odeur de brûlé

**burner** ['bɜːnə(r)] *n* [on stove] brûleur *m* ; *Fig* **to put sth on the back burner** remettre qch à plus tard

**burp** [bɜːp] *Fam* **1.** *n* rot *m* **2.** *vi* roter

**burrow** ['bʌrəʊ] **1.** *n* [hole] terrier *m* **2.** *vt* & *vi* creuser

**burst** [bɜːst] **1.** *n* [of shell] éclatement *m*, explosion *f* ; [of laughter] éclat *m* ; [of applause] salve *f* ; [of thunder] coup *m* ; [surge] élan *m* **2.** (*pt* & *pp* burst) *vt* [bubble, balloon, boil] crever ; [tyre] faire éclater ; **to burst open** [door] ouvrir brusquement **3.** *vi* [of bubble, balloon, boil, tyre, cloud] crever ; [with force - of shell, boiler, tyre] éclater ; **to burst into a room** faire irruption dans une pièce ; **to burst into flames** prendre feu ; **to burst into tears** fondre en larmes ; **to burst out laughing** éclater de rire ; **to burst open** [of door] s'ouvrir brusquement

**bury** ['berɪ] (*pt* & *pp* -ied) *vt* [body] enterrer ; [hide] enfouir ; [plunge] plonger (**in** dans) ; **buried in one's work** plongé dans son travail

**bus** [bʌs] (*pl* buses *or* busses) *n* autobus *m*, bus *m* ; [long-distance] autocar *m*, car *m* ; **by bus** en bus /en car ; **bus driver** chauffeur *m* de bus /car ; *Br* **bus pass** carte *f* d'autobus pour le troisième âge ; *Fig* **I haven't got my bus pass yet!** ≃ je n'ai pas encore ma carte Vermeil ! ; **bus shelter** Abribus® *m* ; **bus station** gare *f* routière ; **bus stop** arrêt *m* de bus

**busboy** ['bʌsbɔɪ] *n Am* aide-serveur *m*

**bush** [bʊʃ] *n* buisson *m* ; **the bush** [land] la brousse ■ **bushy** (*compar* -ier, *superl* -iest) *adj* [hair, tail] touffu

**bushed** [bʊʃt] *adj Fam* [tired] crevé

**business** ['bɪznɪs] **1.** *n* affaires *fpl*, commerce *m* ; [shop] commerce *m* ; [company, task, concern, matter] affaire *f* ; **the textile /construction business** l'industrie *f* du textile /de la construction ; **big business** les grosses entreprises *fpl* ; **to go out of business** [stop trading] fermer ; **that's none of your business!, mind your own business!** ça ne vous regarde pas ! **2.** *adj* commercial ; [meeting, lunch] d'affaires ; **business card** carte *f* de visite ; **business hours** [office] heures *fpl* de bureau ; [shop] heures *fpl* d'ouverture ; **business school** école *f* de commerce ; **business angel** business angel *m*, investisseur *m* providentiel ; **business incubator** incubateur *m* d'entreprise, pépinière *f* d'entreprise ; **business model** modèle *m* économique, business model *m* ; **business park** zone *f* d'activités ; **business partner** associé, -e *mf* ■ **businessman** (*pl* -men) *n* homme *m* d'affaires ■ **businesswoman** (*pl* -women) *n* femme *f* d'affaires

**bust** [bʌst] **1.** *n* [statue] buste *m* ; [of woman] poitrine *f* **2.** *adj Fam* [broken] fichu ; **to go bust** [bankrupt] faire faillite **3.** (*pt* & *pp* bust *or* busted) *vt Fam* [break] bousiller ; [arrest] coffrer ■ **bust-up** *n Fam* [quarrel] engueulade *f* ; [break-up] rupture *f*

**buster** ['bʌstə(r)] *n Am Fam* [pal] **thanks, buster** merci, mon (petit) gars

**-buster** *suff Fam* **crime-busters** superflics *mpl*

**bustle** ['bʌsəl] **1.** *n* animation *f* **2.** *vi* to **bustle (about)** s'affairer

**busy** ['bɪzɪ] **1.** (*compar* -ier, *superl* -iest) *adj* occupé ; [active] actif, -ive ; [day] chargé ; [street] animé ; *Am* [phone, line] occupé ; **to be busy doing** [in the process of] être occupé à faire ; **to keep oneself busy** s'occuper ; **the shops were very busy** il y avait plein de monde dans les magasins ; *Am* **busy signal** sonnerie *f* occupé **2.** *vt* **to busy oneself** s'occuper (**with sth** à qch ; **doing sth** à faire qch) ■ **busybody** (*pl* -ies) *n Fam* fouineur, -euse *mf*

**but** [bʌt] (*unstressed* [bət]) **1.** *conj* mais **2.** *prep* [except] sauf ; **but for him** sans lui ; **no one but you** personne d'autre que toi ; **the last but one** l'avant-dernier, -ère *mf*

**butcher** ['butʃə(r)] **1.** *n* boucher *m* ;
**butcher's (shop)** boucherie *f* **2.** *vt*
[people] massacrer ; [animal] abattre

**butler** ['bʌtlə(r)] *n* maître *m* d'hôtel

**butt** [bʌt] **1.** *n* [of cigarette] mégot *m* ; [of
gun] crosse *f* ; *Am Fam* [buttocks] derrière *m* **2.** *vt* [with head] donner un
coup de tête à **3.** *vi* **to butt in** intervenir
■ **butt out** *vi insep Am Fam* **why don't
you just butt out?** fiche-moi la paix !

**butter** ['bʌtə(r)] **1.** *n* beurre *m* ; *Br* **butter bean** *gros haricot blanc* ; **butter
dish** beurrier *m* **2.** *vt* beurrer ; *Fam* **to
butter sb up** passer de la pommade à
qn ■ **butterscotch** *n* caramel *m* dur
au beurre

**butterfly** ['bʌtəflaɪ] (*pl* **-ies**) *n* papillon *m* ; *Fam* **to have butterflies** avoir
l'estomac noué ; **butterfly stroke** [in
swimming] brasse *f* papillon

**buttock** ['bʌtək] *n* fesse *f*

**button** ['bʌtən] **1.** *n* bouton *m* ; [of
phone] touche *f* ; *Am* [badge] badge *m*
**2.** *vt* **to button (up)** boutonner **3.** *vi*
**button (up)** [of garment] se boutonner
■ **buttonhole 1.** *n* boutonnière *f* **2.** *vt*
*Fam* [person] coincer

**buy** [baɪ] **1.** *n* **a good buy** une bonne affaire **2.** (*pt & pp* **bought**) *vt* **a)** [purchase]
acheter (**from sb** à qn ; **for sb** à *ou* pour
qn) **b)** *Am Fam* [believe] avaler ; **I'll buy
that!** je veux bien le croire ! ■ **buyer** *n*
acheteur, -euse *mf*

**buzz** [bʌz] **1.** *n* **a)** [noise] bourdonnement *m* **b)** *Fam* [phone call] **to give sb a
buzz** passer un coup de fil à qn **2.** *vt* **to
buzz sb** [using buzzer] appeler qn
**3.** *vi* bourdonner ; *Fam* **to buzz off** se
tirer ■ **buzzer** ['bʌzə(r)] *n* [for door]
sonnette *f* ; [on game show] buzzer *m* ;
[on microwave, radio alarm] sonnerie *f*

**by** [baɪ] **1.** *prep* **a)** [agent] par ; de ; **hit /
chosen by** frappé / choisi par ; **sur-
rounded / followed by** entouré / suivi
de ; **a book / painting by...** un livre /
tableau de...

**b)** [manner, means] par ; en ; à ; de ; **by
sea** par mer ; **by mistake** par erreur ; **by
car / train** en voiture / train ; **by bicycle**
à bicyclette ; **by moonlight** au clair de
lune ; **by doing** en faisant ; **one by one**
un à un ; **day by day** de jour en jour ; **by
sight / day** de vue / jour ; **(all) by oneself**
tout seul

**c)** [next to] à côté de ; [near] près de ; **by
the lake / sea** au bord du lac / de la mer ;
**to go** *or* **pass by the bank / school** passer devant la banque / l'école

**d)** [before in time] avant ; **by Monday**
avant lundi, d'ici lundi ; **by now** à cette
heure-ci ; **by yesterday** (dès) hier

**e)** [amount, measurement] à ; **by the kilo**
au kilo ; **taller by a metre** plus grand
d'un mètre ; **paid by the hour** payé à
l'heure

**f)** [according to] à, d'après ; **by my watch**
à ma montre ; **it's fine** *or* **OK** *or* **all right
by me** je n'y vois pas d'objection

**g)** [in arithmetic] par

**2.** *adv* **close by** tout près ; **to go** *or* **pass
by** passer ; **by and large** en gros ; *Liter* **by
and by** bientôt

**3.** *adj* **that's by the by** ça n'a pas d'importance

**bye(-bye)** ['baɪ('baɪ)] *excl Fam* salut !,
au revoir !

**by-law** ['baɪlɔː] *n* arrêté *m* (municipal)

**bypass** ['baɪpɑːs] **1.** *n* rocade *f* ; **(heart)
bypass operation** pontage *m* **2.** *vt*
[town] contourner ; *Fig* [ignore] court-
circuiter

**bystander** ['baɪstændə(r)] *n* passant, -e *mf*

**byte** [baɪt] *n* COMPUT octet *m*

**C, c¹** [siː] *n* C, c *m inv*

**c²** *(abbr of cent(s))* ct

**cab** [kæb] *n* taxi *m*; [of lorry] cabine *f*

**cabaret** [ˈkæbəreɪ] *n* cabaret *m*

**cabbage** [ˈkæbɪʤ] *n* chou *m (pl* choux)

**cabin** [ˈkæbɪn] *n* [on ship] cabine *f*; [hut] cabane *f*; AVIAT **cabin crew** équipage *m*

**cabinet¹** [ˈkæbɪnɪt] *n* [cupboard] armoire *f*; [for display] vitrine *f*; **(filing) cabinet** classeur *m (meuble)*

**cabinet²** [ˈkæbɪnɪt] *n* [government ministers] gouvernement *m*; **cabinet minister** ministre *m*

**cable** [ˈkeɪbəl] **1.** *n* câble *m*; **cable car** [with overhead cable] téléphérique *m*; **cable television** la télévision par câble **2.** *vt* [message] câbler (**to** à)

**cablecast** [ˈkeɪblkɑːst] *vt Am* TV transmettre par câble

**cache** [kæʃ] *n* COMPUT mémoire-cache *f*, antémémoire *f*; **cache memory** mémoire-cache *f*, antémémoire *f*

**cactus** [ˈkæktəs] *(pl* **-ti** [-taɪ] *or* **-tuses** [-təsɪz]*) n* cactus *m*

**caddie** [ˈkædɪ] *n* GOLF caddie *m*

**cadet** [kəˈdet] *n* élève *m* officier

**cadge** [kæʤ] *vt Fam* **to cadge money from** *or* **off sb** taper qn

**café** [ˈkæfeɪ] *n* café *m*

**caffeine** [ˈkæfiːn] *n* caféine *f*

**cage** [keɪʤ] **1.** *n* cage *f* **2.** *vt* **to cage (up)** mettre en cage

**cajole** [kəˈʤəʊl] *vt* enjôler

**cake** [keɪk] *n* gâteau *m*; [small] pâtisserie *f*

**calamity** [kəˈlæmɪtɪ] *(pl* **-ies**) *n* calamité *f*

**calculate** [ˈkælkjʊleɪt] *vti* calculer; **to calculate that...** [estimate] calculer

que... ▪ **calculated** *adj* [deliberate] délibéré; **a calculated risk** un risque calculé ▪ **calculation** [-ˈleɪʃən] *n* calcul *m* ▪ **calculator** *n* calculatrice *f*

**calendar** [ˈkælɪndə(r)] *n* calendrier *m*; *Am* [for engagements] agenda *m*; **calendar month** mois *m* civil

**calf** [kɑːf] *(pl* **calves**) *n* a) [animal] veau *m* b) [part of leg] mollet *m*

**calibre** [ˈkælɪbə(r)], *Am* **caliber** *n* calibre *m*

**call** [kɔːl] **1.** *n* [shout] cri *m*; [visit] visite *f*; **(telephone) call** appel *m* (téléphonique); **to make a call** téléphoner (**to** à); **to give sb a call** téléphoner à qn; *Br* **call box** cabine *f* téléphonique; **call centre**, *Am* **call center** centre *m* d'appels **2.** *vt* [phone] appeler; [shout to] crier; **he's called David** il s'appelle David; **to call sb a liar** traiter qn de menteur **3.** *vi* appeler; [cry out] crier; [visit] passer ▪ **call back 1.** *vt sep* rappeler **2.** *vi* rappeler ▪ **call by** *vi* [visit] passer ▪ **call for** *vt insep* [require] demander; [collect] passer prendre ▪ **call in 1.** *vt sep* [into room] faire entrer; [police] appeler **2.** *vi* **to call in (on sb)** [visit] passer (chez qn) ▪ **call off** *vt sep* [cancel] annuler; [strike] mettre fin à ▪ **call on** *vt insep* [visit] passer voir; **to call on sb to do** [urge] sommer qn de faire ▪ **call out 1.** *vt sep* [shout] crier; [doctor] appeler; [workers] donner une consigne de grève à **2.** *vi* [shout] crier; **to call out to sb** interpeller qn ▪ **call round** *vi* [visit] passer ▪ **call up** *vt sep* [phone] appeler; MIL [recruits] appeler (sous les drapeaux)

**caller** [ˈkɔːlə(r)] *n* visiteur, -euse *mf*; [on phone] correspondant, -e *mf*; TEL **caller ID display**, **caller display** présentation *f* du numéro

**calling card** n Am [visiting card] carte f de visite

**callous** ['kæləs] adj [cruel] insensible

**calm** [kɑːm] **1.** (compar -er, superl -est) adj calme, tranquille ; **keep calm!** restez calme ! **2.** n calme m **3.** vt **to calm (down)** calmer **4.** vi **to calm down** se calmer ■ **calmly** adv calmement

**calorie** ['kælərɪ] n calorie f ■ **calorie-conscious** adj **she's very calorie-conscious** elle fait très attention au nombre de calories qu'elle absorbe ■ **calorie-controlled** adj [diet] faible en calories ■ **calorie-free** adj sans calories

**calves** [kɑːvz] pl of calf

**camcorder** ['kæmkɔːdə(r)] n caméscope® m

**came** [keɪm] pt of come

**camel** ['kæməl] n chameau m

**camera** ['kæmrə] n appareil photo m ; [for film, video] caméra f ; **camera phone** téléphone m avec appareil photo

**camouflage** ['kæməflɑːʒ] **1.** n camouflage m **2.** vt also Fig camoufler

**camp¹** [kæmp] **1.** n camp m, campement m ; **camp bed** lit m de camp **2.** vi **to camp (out)** camper ■ **camper** n [person] campeur, -euse mf ; [vehicle] camping-car m ■ **camping** n camping m ; **camping site** (terrain m de) camping m ■ **campsite** n camping m

**camp²** [kæmp] adj [effeminate] efféminé

**campaign** [kæm'peɪn] **1.** n [political, military] campagne f ; **press/publicity campaign** campagne f de presse / publicité **2.** vi faire campagne (for / against pour / contre) ■ **campaigner** n militant, -e mf (for pour)

**camphone** ['kæmfəʊn] n téléphone m avec appareil photo

**campus** ['kæmpəs] n [of university] campus m

**can¹** [kæn] (unstressed [kən]) (pt could)

Le verbe **can** n'a ni infinitif, ni gérondif, ni participe. Pour exprimer l'infinitif ou le participe, on aura recours à la forme correspondante de **be able to** (he wanted to be able to speak English ; she has always been able to swim). La forme négative est **can't**, qui s'écrit **cannot** dans la langue soutenue.

v aux [be able to] pouvoir ; [know how to] savoir ; **he couldn't help me** il ne pouvait pas m'aider ; **she can swim** elle sait nager ; **he could do it tomorrow** il pourrait le faire demain ; **he could have done it** il aurait pu le faire ; **you could be wrong** [possibility] tu as peut-être tort ; **he can't be dead** [probability] il ne peut pas être mort ; **can I come in?** [permission] puis-je entrer ? ; **yes, you can!** oui !

**can²** [kæn] **1.** n [for food] boîte f ; [for beer] can(n)ette f **2.** (pt & pp -nn-) vt mettre en boîte ■ **canned** adj en boîte, en conserve ; **canned beer** bière f en can(n)ette ; **canned food** conserves fpl ■ **can-opener** n ouvre-boîtes m inv

**Canada** ['kænədə] n le Canada ■ **Canadian 1.** adj canadien, -enne **2.** n Canadien, -enne mf

**canal** [kə'næl] n canal m

**canary** [kə'neərɪ] (pl -ies) n canari m

**cancel** ['kænsəl] **1.** (Br -ll-, Am -l-) vt [flight, appointment] annuler ; [goods, taxi] décommander ; [train] supprimer **2.** vi se décommander ■ **cancellation** [-'leɪʃən] n annulation f ; [of train] suppression f

**cancer** ['kænsə(r)] n cancer m ; **stomach/skin cancer** cancer m de l'estomac / la peau

**candid** ['kændɪd] adj franc (f franche)

**candidate** ['kændɪdeɪt] n candidat, -e mf (for à)

**candle** ['kændəl] n [made of wax] bougie f ; [in church] cierge m ■ **candlelight** n **to have dinner by candlelight** dîner aux chandelles ■ **candlestick** n bougeoir m ; [taller] chandelier m

**candy** ['kændɪ] (pl -ies) n Am bonbon m ; [sweets] bonbons mpl ; Am **candy**

**apple** pomme *f* d'amour ; *Am* **candy bar** [chocolate] barre *f* de chocolat ; [muesli] barre *f* de céréales ; **candy store** confiserie *f* ■ **candyfloss** *n Br* barbe *f* à papa

**cane** [keɪn] **1.** *n* [stick] canne *f* ; [for punishment] baguette *f* **2.** *vt* [punish] frapper avec une baguette

**canine** ['keɪnaɪn] *adj* [tooth, race] canin

**canister** ['kænɪstə(r)] *n* boîte *f* (en métal)

**cannabis** ['kænəbɪs] *n* [drug] cannabis *m*

**cannon** ['kænən] *(pl* **-s** *or* **cannon)** *n* canon *m*

**cannot** ['kænɒt] = **can not**

**canoe** [kə'nu:] *n* canoë *m* ; [dugout] pirogue *f* ■ **canoeing** *n* to go canoeing faire du canoë-kayak

**canola** [kə'nəʊlə] *n* colza *m*

**canopy** ['kænəpɪ] *(pl* **-ies)** *n* [awning] auvent *m* ; [made of glass] marquise *f*

**can't** [kɑːnt] = **can not**

**canteen** [kæn'tiːn] *n* [in school, factory] cantine *f* ; *Br* **canteen of cutlery** ménagère *f*

**canvas** ['kænvəs] *n* **a)** [cloth] (grosse) toile *f* ; [for embroidery] canevas *m* **b)** [painting] toile *f*

**canvass** ['kænvəs] *vt* [opinions] sonder ; **to canvass sb** [seek votes] solliciter le suffrage de qn ; [seek orders] solliciter des commandes de qn ■ **canvassing** *n* [for orders] démarchage *m* ; [for votes] démarchage *m* électoral

**canyon** ['kænjən] *n* cañon *m*, canyon *m*

**cap¹** [kæp] *n* **a)** [hat] casquette *f* ; [for shower, of sailor] bonnet *m* ; [of soldier] képi *m* **b)** [of tube, valve] bouchon *m* ; [of bottle] capsule *f* ; [of pen] capuchon *m* **c)** [of child's gun] amorce *f*

**cap²** [kæp] *(pt & pp* **-pp-***)vt* **a)** [outdo] surpasser **b)** *Br* [spending] limiter

**capable** ['keɪpəbəl] *adj* [person] capable (**of sth** de qch ; **of doing sth** de faire qch) ■ **capability** *n* capacité *f*

**capacity** [kə'pæsətɪ] *(pl* **-ies)** *n* [of container] capacité *f* ; [ability] aptitude *f*, capacité *f* (**for sth** pour qch ; **for doing sth** à faire qch) ; [output] rendement *m* ; **in my capacity as a doctor** en ma qualité de médecin

**cape** [keɪp] *n* [cloak] cape *f* ; [of cyclist] pèlerine *f*

**capeesh** [kə'piːʃ] *vi Am Fam* [understand] comprendre ; **I'm not going, capeesh?** j'y vais pas, compris ?

**capital** ['kæpɪtəl] **1.** *adj* [letter, importance] capital ; **capital punishment** peine *f* capitale **2.** *n* **a)** **capital (city)** capitale *f* ; **capital (letter)** majuscule *f* **b)** [money] capital *m* ■ **capitalism** *n* capitalisme *m* ■ **capitalist** *adj &* *n* capitaliste *(mf)* ■ **capitalize** *vi* to **capitalize on** tirer parti de

**capris** [kə'priːz] *npl Am* pantacourt *m*

**capsize** [kæp'saɪz] **1.** *vt* faire chavirer **2.** *vi* chavirer

**capsule** [*Br* 'kæpsjuːl, *Am* 'kæpsəl] *n* [of medicine] gélule *f* ; **(space) capsule** capsule *f* spatiale

**captain** ['kæptɪn] **1.** *n* capitaine *m* **2.** *vt* [ship] commander ; [team] être le capitaine de

**caption** ['kæpʃən] *n* [of illustration] légende *f* ; [of film, article] sous-titre *m*

**captivate** ['kæptɪveɪt] *vt* captiver

**captive** ['kæptɪv] *n* captif, -ive *mf* ■ **captivity** *n* in **captivity** en captivité

**capture** ['kæptʃə(r)] **1.** *n* capture *f* ; [of town] prise *f* **2.** *vt* [person, animal] capturer ; [escaped prisoner or animal] reprendre ; [town] prendre ; *Fig* [mood] rendre ; COMPUT saisir

**car** [kɑː(r)] *n* voiture *f*, automobile *f* ; [train carriage] wagon *m*, voiture *f* ; AUTO **car alarm** alarme *f* de voiture ; **car insurance / industry** assurance *f* / industrie *f* automobile ; **the car door** la portière de la voiture ; **car crash** accident *m* de voiture ; **car ferry** ferry *m* ; *Br* **car hire** location *f* de voitures ; *Br* **car park** parking *m* ; **car phone** téléphone *m* de voiture ; **car radio** autoradio *m* ; **car rental** location *f* de voitures ; **car wash** [machine] *station de lavage* *automatique pour voitures* ■ **carpool** ['kɑːpuːl] *n* covoiturage *m* ■ **carport** *n* abri *m* pour voiture

**carafe** [kə'ræf] *n* carafe *f*

**caramel** ['kærəməl] *n* caramel *m*

**carat** ['kærət] *n* carat *m*; **18-carat gold** or *m* (à) 18 carats

**caravan** ['kærəvæn] *n* caravane *f*; [horse-drawn] roulotte *f*; **caravan site** camping *m* pour caravanes

**carbohydrates** [kɑːbəʊ'haɪdreɪts] *npl* hydrates *mpl* de carbone; [in food] glucides *mpl*

**carbon** ['kɑːbən] *n* carbone *m*; **carbon dioxide** dioxyde *m* de carbone, gaz *m* carbonique; **carbon footprint** empreinte *f* carbone; TYP **carbon paper** (papier *m*) carbone *m*

**card** [kɑːd] *n* [gen & COMPUT] carte *f*; [cardboard] carton *m*; **(index) card** fiche *f*; **to play cards** jouer aux cartes; **card game** jeu *m* de cartes ■ **cardboard** *n* carton *m*; **cardboard box** boîte *f* en carton, carton *m* ■ **cardphone** *n* téléphone *m* à carte

**cardigan** ['kɑːdɪgən] *n* cardigan *m*

**cardinal** ['kɑːdɪnl] *n* REL cardinal *m*

**care** [keə(r)] **1.** *n* [attention] soin *m*; [protection] soins *mpl*; [worry] souci *m*; **to take care to do** veiller à faire; **to take care not to do** faire attention à ne pas faire; **to take care of sb/sth** s'occuper de qn/qch; **to take care of oneself** [manage] savoir se débrouiller tout seul; [keep healthy] faire bien attention à soi; **take care!** [goodbye] au revoir!; **'care of'** [on envelope] 'chez' **2.** *vt* **I don't care what he says** peu m'importe ce qu'il en dit **3.** *vi* **I don't care** ça m'est égal; **who cares?** qu'est-ce que ça peut faire?; **to care about** [feel concern about] se soucier de; **to care about** or **for sb** [be fond of] avoir de la sympathie pour qn; **to care for sb** [look after] soigner qn ■ **care worker** *n* aide-soignant, aide-soignante *mf* ■ **caregiver** *n* [professional] aide *mf* à domicile; [relative] aidant *m* familial *(personne s'occupant d'un parent malade ou âgé)*

**career** [kə'rɪə(r)] **1.** *n* carrière *f* **2.** *vi* **to career along** aller à vive allure ■ **career-minded** *adj* ambitieux, -euse

**carefree** ['keəfriː] *adj* insouciant

**careful** ['keəfəl] *adj* [exact, thorough] soigneux, -euse (**about** de); [cautious] prudent; **to be careful of** or **with sth** faire attention à qch; **be careful!** (fais) attention! ■ **carefully** *adv* [thoroughly] avec soin; [cautiously] prudemment

**careless** ['keələs] *adj* négligent; [work] peu soigné; **careless mistake** faute *f* d'étourderie ■ **carelessness** *n* négligence *f*

**carer** ['keərə(r)] *n* [relative] personne s'occupant d'un parent malade ou âgé

**caress** [kə'res] **1.** *n* caresse *f* **2.** *vt* caresser

**caretaker** ['keəteɪkə(r)] *n* gardien, -enne *mf*, concierge *mf*

**cargo** ['kɑːgəʊ] *(pl* **-oes** *or* **-os)** *n* cargaison *f*; **cargo ship** cargo *m*

**Caribbean** [*Br* kærɪ'biːən, *Am* kə'rɪbɪən] **1.** *adj* caraïbe **2.** *n* **the Caribbean (islands)** les Antilles *fpl*

**caricature** ['kærɪkətʃʊə(r)] **1.** *n* caricature *f* **2.** *vt* caricaturer

**caring** ['keərɪŋ] *adj* [loving] aimant; [understanding] très humain

**carlot** ['kɑːlɒt] *n* *Am* parking *m* (*d'un garage automobile*)

**carnation** [kɑː'neɪʃən] *n* œillet *m*

**carnival** ['kɑːnɪvəl] *n* carnaval *m* (*pl* -als)

**carol** ['kærəl] *n* chant *m* de Noël

**carp** [kɑːp] **1.** *n inv* [fish] carpe *f* **2.** *vi* se plaindre (**at** de)

**carpenter** ['kɑːpɪntə(r)] *n* [for house building] charpentier *m*; [for light woodwork] menuisier *m* ■ **carpentry** *n* charpenterie *f*; [light woodwork] menuiserie *f*

**carpet** ['kɑːpɪt] **1.** *n* [rug] tapis *m*; [fitted] moquette *f* **2.** *vt* recouvrir d'un tapis/d'une moquette

**carriage** ['kærɪdʒ] *n* *Br* [of train] voiture *f*; [horse-drawn] voiture *f*, équipage *m*; *Br* [transport of goods] transport *m* ; [cost] frais *mpl* ; [of typewriter] chariot *m* ▪ **carriageway** *n* Br chaussée *f*

**carrier** [ˈkærɪə(r)] *n* [company, airline] transporteur *m* ; Br **carrier (bag)** sac *m* en plastique

**carrot** [ˈkærət] *n* carotte *f*

**carry** [ˈkærɪ] (*pt & pp* -**ied**) **1.** *vt* porter ; [goods, passengers] transporter ; [gun, money] avoir sur soi ; MATH [in calculation] retenir **2.** *vi* [of sound] porter ▪ **carry away** *vt sep* emporter ; **to be** *or* **get carried away** [excited] s'emballer ▪ **carry back** *vt sep* [thing] rapporter ; [person] ramener ▪ **carry forward** *vt sep* [in bookkeeping] reporter ▪ **carry off** *vt sep* [take away] emporter ▪ **carry on 1.** *vt sep* [continue] continuer (**doing** à faire) ; [negotiations] mener ; [conversation] poursuivre **2.** *vi* [continue] continuer ; *Pej* [behave badly] se conduire mal ; **to carry on with sth** continuer qch ▪ **carry out** *vt sep* [plan, promise] mettre à exécution ; [order] exécuter ; [repair, reform] effectuer ; [duty] accomplir ; *Am* [meal] emporter ▪ **carry through** *vt sep* [plan] mener à bien

**carrycot** [ˈkærɪkɒt] *n* Br porte-bébé *m* inv

**cart** [kɑːt] **1.** *n* **a)** [horse-drawn] charrette *f* ; [handcart] voiture *f* à bras **b)** *Am* [shopping cart] chariot *m*, Caddie® *m* **c)** [for online purchases] panier *m* **2.** *vt* *Fam* **to cart (around)** trimbaler

**carton** [ˈkɑːtən] *n* [box] carton *m* ; [of milk, fruit juice] brique *f* ; [of cigarettes] cartouche *f* ; [of cream] pot *m*

**cartoon** [kɑːˈtuːn] *n* [in newspaper] dessin *m* humoristique ; [film] dessin *m* animé ; **cartoon (strip)** bande *f* dessinée ; **cartoon character** personnage *m* de bande dessinée

**cartridge** [ˈkɑːtrɪdʒ] *n* **a)** [for gun, pen] cartouche *f* **b)** [for camera] chargeur *m*

**carve** [kɑːv] *vt* [cut] tailler (**out of** dans) ; [name] graver ; [sculpt] sculpter ; **to carve (up)** [meat] découper ▪ **carving 1.** *adj* **carving knife** couteau *m* à découper **2.** *n* (wood) **carving** sculpture *f* sur bois

**cascade** [kæsˈkeɪd] *vi* tomber en cascade

**case¹** [keɪs] *n* [instance, situation & MED] cas *m* ; JUR affaire *f* ; *Fig* [arguments] arguments *mpl* ; **in any case** en tout cas ; **in case it rains** au cas où il pleuvrait ; **in case of** en cas de

**case²** [keɪs] *n* [bag] valise *f* ; [crate] caisse *f* ; [for pen, glasses, camera, violin, cigarettes] étui *m* ; [for jewels] écrin *m* ; Br **trolley case** valise *f* à roulettes

**case-sensitive** *adj* **this password is case-sensitive** le respect des majuscules et des minuscules est nécessaire pour ce mot de passe

**cash** [kæʃ] **1.** *n* [coins, banknotes] liquide *m* ; *Fam* [money] sous *mpl* ; **to pay (in) cash** payer en liquide ; **cash box** caisse *f* ; **cash card** carte *f* de retrait ; Br **cash desk** caisse *f* ; **cash dispenser** *or* **machine** distributeur *m* de billets ; **cash price** prix *m* (au) comptant ; **cash register** caisse *f* enregistreuse **2.** *vt* **to cash a cheque** *or* *Am* **check** [of person] encaisser un chèque ; [of bank] payer un chèque ▪ **cashback** [ˈkæʃbæk] *n* Br [in supermarket] espèces retirées à la caisse d'un supermarché lors d'un paiement par carte

**cashew** [ˈkæʃuː] *n* **cashew (nut)** noix *f* de cajou

**cashier** [kæˈʃɪə(r)] *n* caissier, -ère *mf*

**cash point**, **cashpoint** [ˈkæʃpɔɪnt] *n* Br [cash dispenser] distributeur *m* (automatique de billets), DAB *m*

**casino** [kəˈsiːnəʊ] (*pl* -**os**) *n* casino *m*

**casket** [ˈkɑːskɪt] *n* [box] coffret *m* ; [coffin] cercueil *m*

**casserole** [ˈkæsərəʊl] *n* [covered dish] cocotte *f* ; [stew] ragoût *m*

**cassette** [kəˈset] *n* [audio, video] cassette *f* ; [for camera] cartouche *f* ; **cassette player** lecteur *m* de cassettes ; **cassette recorder** magnétophone *m* à cassettes

**cast** [kɑːst] **1.** *n* [actors] acteurs *mpl* ; [list of actors] distribution *f* ; MED **in a cast** dans le plâtre **2.** (*pt & pp* **cast**) *vt* **a)** [throw] jeter ; [light, shadow] projeter ; [glance] jeter (**at** à *ou* sur) ; **to cast**

doubt on sth jeter le doute sur qch ; **cast iron** fonte f b) CIN & THEAT donner un rôle à ■ **cast-iron** adj [pan] en fonte ; Fig [alibi, excuse] en béton ■ **cast aside** vt sep Fig écarter, rejeter ■ **cast off** vi NAUT larguer les amarres

**caster** ['kɑːstə(r)] n [wheel] roulette f ; Br **caster sugar** sucre m en poudre

**castle** ['kɑːsəl] n château m ; [in chess] tour f

**castoffs** ['kɑːstɒfs] npl vieux vêtements mpl

**castrate** [kæ'streɪt] vt châtrer

**casual** ['kæʒjʊəl] adj [offhand - remark, glance] en passant ; [relaxed, informal] décontracté ; [conversation] à bâtons rompus ; [clothes] sport inv ; [careless] désinvolte ; [employment, worker] temporaire ■ **casually** adv [remark, glance] en passant ; [informally] avec décontraction ; [dress] sport ; [carelessly] avec désinvolture

**casualty** ['kæʒjʊəltɪ] (pl -ies) n victime f ; Br **casualty (department)** [in hospital] (service m des) urgences fpl

**cat** [kæt] n chat m ; [female] chatte f ; **cat litter** litière f (pour chats)

**catalogue** ['kætəlɒg], Am **catalog 1.** n catalogue m **2.** vt cataloguer

**catalyst** ['kætəlɪst] n CHEM & Fig catalyseur m

**catapult** ['kætəpʌlt] **1.** n [toy] lance-pierres m inv **2.** vt catapulter

**catastrophe** [kə'tæstrəfɪ] n catastrophe f

**catch** [kætʃ] **1.** n [in fishing] prise f ; [of a whole day] pêche f ; [difficulty] piège m ; [on door] loquet m **2.** (pt & pp **caught**) vt [ball, thief, illness] attraper ; [fish, train, bus] prendre ; [grab] prendre, saisir ; [surprise] surprendre ; [understand] saisir ; [garment] accrocher (**on** à) ; **to catch sb's eye** or **attention** attirer l'attention de qn ; **to catch sight of sb/sth** apercevoir qn/qch ; **to catch fire** prendre feu ; **to catch sb doing** surprendre qn à faire ; **to catch sb out** prendre qn en défaut ; **to catch sb up** rattraper qn **3.** vi her skirt (got) caught in the door sa jupe s'est

prise dans la porte ; **to catch up with sb** rattraper qn ■ **catching** adj [illness] contagieux, -euse ■ **catch on** vi a) [become popular] prendre b) Fam [understand] **to catch on (to sth)** piger (qch)

**catchy** ['kætʃɪ] (compar -ier, superl -iest) adj [tune, slogan] facile à retenir

**category** ['kætɪgərɪ] (pl -ies) n catégorie f ■ **categorical** adj catégorique

**cater** ['keɪtə(r)] vi [provide food] s'occuper des repas (**for** pour) ; **to cater to,** Br **to cater for** [need, taste] satisfaire ■ **caterer** n traiteur m ■ **catering** n restauration f ; **to do the catering** s'occuper des repas

**caterpillar** ['kætəpɪlə(r)] n chenille f

**cathedral** [kə'θiːdrəl] n cathédrale f

**Catholic** ['kæθlɪk] adj & n catholique (mf)

**cattle** ['kætəl] npl bétail m ; **cattle grid,** Am **cattle guard** [sur une route] grille au sol destinée à empêcher le passage du bétail mais non celui des voitures

**caught** [kɔːt] pt & pp of **catch**

**cauliflower** ['kɒlɪflaʊə(r)] n chou-fleur m

**cause** [kɔːz] **1.** n [origin, ideal & JUR] cause f ; [reason] raison f, motif m (**of** de) **2.** vt causer, occasionner ; **to cause trouble for sb** créer ou causer des ennuis à qn

**caution** ['kɔːʃən] **1.** n [care] prudence f ; [warning] avertissement m **2.** vt [warn] avertir ; SPORT donner un avertissement à ■ **cautious** adj prudent

**cavalry** ['kævəlrɪ] n cavalerie f

**cave** [keɪv] **1.** n grotte f **2.** vi **to cave in** [of ceiling] s'effondrer ; [of floor] s'affaisser

**cavern** ['kævən] n caverne f

**cavity** ['kævɪtɪ] (pl -ies) n cavité f

**cc** n a) (abbr of **cubic centimetre**) $cm^3$ b) (abbr of **carbon copy**) pcc

**CD** [siː'diː] (abbr of **compact disc**) n CD m ; COMPUT **CD burner, CD writer** graveur m de CD ; **CD player** lecteur m de CD

**CD-ROM** [si:di:'rɒm] *(abbr of* **compact disc read-only memory)** *n* COMPUT CD-ROM *m inv*

**cease** [si:s] **1.** *vt* cesser **(doing** de faire) **2.** *vi* cesser ■ **cease-fire** *n* cessez-le-feu *m inv* ■ **ceaseless** *adj* incessant

**cedar** ['si:də(r)] *n* [tree, wood] cèdre *m*

**ceiling** ['si:lɪŋ] *n* [of room] & *Fig* [limit] plafond *m*

**celeb** [sɪ'leb] *n Fam* célébrité *f*, star *f*

**celebrate** ['selɪbreɪt] **1.** *vt* [event] célébrer, fêter ; [mass] célébrer **2.** *vi* faire la fête ■ **celebration** [-'breɪʃən] *n* [event] fête *f* ; **the celebrations** les festivités *fpl*

**celebrity** [sə'lebrɪtɪ] *(pl -ies)* *n* célébrité *f*

**celery** ['selərɪ] *n* céleri *m*

**celibate** ['selɪbət] *adj* **to be celibate** ne pas avoir de rapports sexuels ; [by choice] être chaste

**cell** [sel] *n* cellule *f* ; ELEC élément *m*

**cellar** ['selə(r)] *n* cave *f*

**cello** ['tʃeləʊ] *(pl -os)* *n* violoncelle *m*

**cellophane®** ['seləfeɪn] *n* Cellophane® *f*

**cellphone** ['selfəʊn] *n Am* (téléphone *m*) portable *m*

**cell tower, cell site** *n* antenne-relais *f*

**cellular** ['seljʊlə(r)] *adj* cellulaire ; **cellular phone** téléphone *m* cellulaire

**Celsius** ['selsɪəs] *adj* Celsius *inv*

**cement** [sɪ'ment] **1.** *n* ciment *m* ; **cement mixer** bétonnière *f* **2.** *vt also Fig* cimenter

**cemetery** ['semətrɪ] *(pl -ies)* *n* cimetière *m*

**censor** ['sensə(r)] **1.** *n* censeur *m* **2.** *vt* censurer ■ **censorship** *n* censure *f*

**census** ['sensəs] *n* recensement *m*

**cent** [sent] *n* [coin] cent *m*

**centenary** [Br sen'ti:nərɪ, Am sen'tenərɪ] *(pl -ies)* *n* centenaire *m*

**center** ['sentə(r)] *Am n* = **centre**

**center strip** *n Am* terre-plein *m* central

**centigrade** ['sentɪgreɪd] *adj* centigrade

**centimetre** ['sentɪmi:tə(r)] *n* centimètre *m*

**central** ['sentrəl] *adj* central ; **Central London** le centre de Londres ; **central heating** chauffage *m* central ■ **centralize** *vt* centraliser

**centre** ['sentə(r)], *Am* **center 1.** *n* centre *m* ; FTBL **centre forward** avant-centre *m* **2.** *vt* [attention, interest] concentrer (**on** sur)

**century** ['sentʃərɪ] *(pl -ies)* *n* siècle *m* ; **in the twenty-first century** au vingt et unième siècle

**ceramic** [sə'ræmɪk] *adj* [tile] en céramique

**cereal** ['sɪərɪəl] *n* céréale *f* ; **(breakfast) cereal** céréales *fpl* (*pour le petit déjeuner*)

**ceremony** ['serɪmənɪ] *(pl -ies)* *n* [event] cérémonie *f*

**certain** ['sɜ:tən] *adj* **a)** [sure] certain **(that** que) ; **she's certain to come, she'll come for certain** c'est certain qu'elle viendra ; **to be certain of sth** être certain *ou* sûr de qch ; **for certain** [say, know] avec certitude **b)** [particular, some] certain ; **certain people** certaines personnes ■ **certainly** *adv* [undoubtedly] certainement ; [yes] bien sûr ■ **certainty** *(pl -ies)* *n* certitude *f*

**certificate** [sə'tɪfɪkɪt] *n* certificat *m* ; [from university] diplôme *m*

**certify** ['sɜ:tɪfaɪ] *(pt & pp -ied)* *vt* [document, signature] certifier ; *Am* **certified letter** ≃ lettre *f* recommandée ; *Am* **certified public accountant** expert-comptable *m*

**chad** [tʃæd] *n Am* [residue from punched paper] confettis *mpl*

**chain** [tʃeɪn] **1.** *n* [of rings, mountains] chaîne *f* ; [of events] suite *f* ; [of lavatory] chasse *f* d'eau ; **chain reaction** réaction *f* en chaîne ; **chain saw** tronçonneuse *f* ; **chain store** magasin *m* à succursales multiples **2.** *vt* **to chain (up)** [dog] mettre à l'attache ■ **chain-smoker** *n* **to be a chain-smoker** fumer cigarette sur cigarette

**chair** 58

**chair** [tʃeə(r)] **1.** n chaise f; [armchair] fauteuil m; UNIV [of professor] chaire f; **the chair** [office of chairperson] la présidence; **chair lift** télésiège m **2.** vt [meeting] présider ■ **chairman** (pl **-men**), **chairperson** n président, -e mf

**chalet** ['ʃæleɪ] n chalet m

**chalk** [tʃɔːk] **1.** n craie f **2.** vt marquer à la craie

**challenge** ['tʃælɪndʒ] **1.** n défi m; [task] challenge m, gageure f **2.** vt défier (**sb to do** qn de faire); [question, dispute] contester ■ **challenger** n SPORT challenger m

**chamber** ['tʃeɪmbə(r)] n [room, assembly, of gun] chambre f; **chamber music / orchestra** musique f / orchestre m de chambre ■ **chambermaid** n femme f de chambre

**champagne** [ʃæm'peɪn] n champagne m

**champion** ['tʃæmpɪən] **1.** n champion, -onne mf; **champion skier, skiing champion** champion, -onne mf de ski **2.** vt [support] se faire le champion de ■ **championship** n championnat m

**chance** [tʃɑːns] **1.** n [luck] hasard m; [possibility] chance f; [opportunity] occasion f; [risk] risque m; **by chance** par hasard; **to have the chance to do sth** or **of doing sth** avoir l'occasion de faire qch; **to give sb a chance** donner une chance à qn; **to take a chance** tenter le coup **2.** adj [remark] fait au hasard **3.** vt **to chance it** risquer le coup

**chancellor** ['tʃɑːnsələ(r)] n POL chancelier m

**chandelier** [ʃændə'lɪə(r)] n lustre m

**change** [tʃeɪndʒ] **1.** n changement m; [money] monnaie f; **for a change** pour changer; **a change of clothes** des vêtements de rechange **2.** vt [modify] changer; [exchange] échanger (**for** pour ou contre); [money] changer (**into** en); [transform] changer, transformer (**into** en); **to change trains / colour / one's skirt** changer de train / de couleur / de jupe; **to change gear** [in vehicle] changer de vitesse; **to change the subject** changer de sujet; **to get changed** [put on other clothes] se changer **3.** vi [alter] changer; [change clothes] se changer; **to change into sth** [be transformed] se changer ou se transformer en qch; **she changed into a dress** elle a mis une robe; **to change over** passer (**from** de; **to** à) ■ **changeable** adj [weather, mood] changeant ■ **changeover** n passage m (**from** de; **to** à)

**changing** ['tʃeɪndʒɪŋ] n **changing room** vestiaire m; [in shop] cabine f d'essayage

**channel** ['tʃænəl] **1.** n [on television] chaîne f; [for boats] chenal m; [groove] rainure f; [of communication, distribution] canal m; GEOG **the Channel** la Manche; **the Channel Islands** les îles Anglo-Normandes; **the Channel Tunnel** le tunnel sous la Manche **2.** (Br **-ll-**, Am **-l-**) vt [energies, crowd, money] canaliser (**into** vers)

**chant** [tʃɑːnt] **1.** vt [slogan] scander **2.** vi [of demonstrators] scander des slogans

**chaos** ['keɪɒs] n chaos m ■ **chaotic** adj [situation, scene] chaotique

**chapel** ['tʃæpəl] n chapelle f; [nonconformist church] temple m

**chaplain** ['tʃæplɪn] n aumônier m

**chapped** ['tʃæpt] adj [hands, lips] gercé

**chapter** ['tʃæptə(r)] n chapitre m

**character** ['kærɪktə(r)] n a) [of person, place] caractère m; [in book, film] personnage m; [person] individu m; [unusual person] personnage m b) [letter] caractère m ■ **characteristic** adj & n caractéristique (f)

**char-broil** vt Am CULIN griller au charbon de bois

**charcoal** ['tʃɑːkəʊl] n ART fusain m

**charge¹** [tʃɑːdʒ] **1.** n [in battle] charge f; JUR chef m d'accusation; [care] garde f; **to take charge of sth** prendre qch en charge; **to be in charge of** être responsable de **2.** vt [battery, soldiers] charger; JUR [accuse] inculper (**with** de) **3.** vi [rush] se précipiter; [soldiers] charger ■ **charger** n [for battery] chargeur m

**charge²** [tʃɑːdʒ] **1.** n [cost] prix m; **charges** [expenses] frais mpl **2.** vt [amount] demander (**for** pour); **to charge sb** faire payer qn

**charity** [ˈtʃærɪtɪ] (pl -ies) n [kindness, alms] charité f; [society] œuvre f de charité

**charm** [tʃɑːm] **1.** n [attractiveness] charme m; [trinket] breloque f **2.** vt charmer ■ **charming** adj charmant

**chart** [tʃɑːt] n [map] carte f; [table] tableau m; [graph] graphique m; (**pop**) **charts** hit-parade m

**charter** [ˈtʃɑːtə(r)] n [aircraft] charter m; **charter flight** vol m charter ■ **chartered accountant** n Br expert-comptable m

**chase** [tʃeɪs] **1.** n poursuite f **2.** vt poursuivre; **to chase sb away** or **off** chasser qn **3.** vi **to chase after sb/sth** courir après qn/qch

**chasm** [ˈkæzəm] n also Fig abîme m, gouffre m

**chassis** [ˈʃæsɪ] n [of vehicle] châssis m

**chaste** [tʃeɪst] adj chaste

**chat** [tʃæt] **1.** n petite conversation f; INTERNET chat m; **to have a chat** causer (**with** avec) **2.** (pt & pp -tt-) vi causer (**with** avec); COMPUT bavarder **3.** vt Br Fam **to chat sb up** draguer qn ■ **chatroom** n INTERNET forum m de discussion, Can bavardoir m

**chatter** [ˈtʃætə(r)] **1.** n bavardage m **2.** vi [of person] bavarder; **his teeth were chattering** il claquait des dents

**chatty** [ˈtʃætɪ] (compar -ier, superl -iest) adj [person] bavard; [letter] plein de détails

**chauffeur** [ˈʃəʊfə(r)] n chauffeur m

**chauvinist** [ˈʃəʊvɪnɪst] n Pej (**male**) **chauvinist** macho m, phallocrate m

**cheap** [tʃiːp] **1.** (compar -er, superl -est) adj bon marché inv, pas cher (f pas chère); [rate, fare] réduit; [worthless] sans valeur; [vulgar] de mauvais goût; **cheaper** meilleur marché inv, moins cher (f moins chère) **2.** adv [buy] (à) bon marché, au rabais ■ **cheaply** adv (à) bon marché

**cheat** [tʃiːt] **1.** n [at games] tricheur, -euse mf; [crook] escroc m **2.** vt [deceive] tromper; [defraud] frauder; **to cheat sb out of sth** escroquer qch à qn **3.** vi [at games] tricher

**check¹** [tʃek] n check (**pattern**) carreaux mpl ■ **checked** adj [patterned] à carreaux

**check²** [tʃek] **1.** n vérification f (**on** de); [inspection] contrôle m; [in chess] échec m; Am [tick] ≃ croix f; Am [receipt] reçu m; Am [restaurant bill] addition f; Am [cheque] chèque m; **to keep a check on sth** contrôler qch **2.** vt [examine] vérifier; [inspect] contrôler; [mark off] cocher; Am [baggage] mettre à la consigne; **check box** case f (à cocher) **3.** vi vérifier; **to check on sth** vérifier qch; **to check on sb** surveiller qn ■ **checkbook** n Am carnet m de chèques ■ **check-in** n [at airport] enregistrement m (des bagages) ■ **checking account** n Am compte m courant ■ **checklist** n liste f de contrôle; AVIAT check-list f ■ **checkout** n [in supermarket] caisse f ■ **checkpoint** n poste m de contrôle ■ **checkroom** n Am vestiaire m; Am [left-luggage office] consigne f ■ **checkup** n [medical] bilan m de santé; **to have a checkup** faire un bilan de santé ■ **check in 1.** vt sep [luggage] enregistrer **2.** vi [arrive] arriver; [sign in] signer le registre; [at airport] se présenter à l'enregistrement ■ **check into** vt insep **to check into a hotel** descendre dans un hôtel ■ **check out 1.** vt sep a) [luggage, coat] retirer b) [investigate] vérifier **2.** vi [at hotel] régler sa note ■ **check up** vi vérifier

**checkers** [ˈtʃekərz] npl Am jeu m de dames

**cheddar** [ˈtʃedə(r)] n cheddar m (fromage)

**cheek** [tʃiːk] n joue f; Br [impudence] culot m ■ **cheeky** (compar -ier, superl -iest) adj Br [person, reply] insolent

**cheer** [tʃɪə(r)] **1.** n cheers [shouts] acclamations fpl; Fam cheers! [when drinking] à votre santé!; [thanks] merci! **2.** vt [applaud] acclamer; **to cheer sb**

up [comfort] remonter le moral à qn ; [amuse] faire sourire qn **3.** *vi* applaudir ; **cheer up!** (du) courage ! ■ **cheering** *n* [shouts] acclamations *fpl*

**cheerful** ['tʃɪəfəl] *adj* gai

**cheerio** [tʃɪərɪ'əʊ] *excl Br* salut !, au revoir !

**cheerleader** ['tʃɪə,liːdə(r)] *n majorette qui stimule l'enthousiasme des supporters des équipes sportives, surtout aux États-Unis*

**cheese** [tʃiːz] *n* fromage *m* ■ **cheeseburger** *n* cheeseburger *m* ■ **cheesecake** *n* cheesecake *m*, tarte *f* au fromage blanc ■ **cheesy** ['tʃiːzɪ] (compar -ier, superl -iest) adj a) [tasting of cheese] au goût de fromage b) *Fam* [song, TV programme] cucul, gnangnan, mièvre c) **a cheesy grin** un sourire toutes dents dehors

**chef** [ʃef] *n* chef *m* (cuisinier)

**chemical 1.** *adj* chimique **2.** *n* produit *m* chimique

**chemist** ['kemɪst] *n Br* [pharmacist] pharmacien, -enne *mf* ; [scientist] chimiste *mf* ; *Br* **chemist's (shop)** pharmacie *f* ■ **chemistry** *n* chimie *f*

**cheque** [tʃek] *n Br* chèque *m* ; **cheque card** carte *f* d'identité bancaire (*sans laquelle un chéquier n'est pas valable*) ■ **chequebook** *n Br* carnet *m* de chèques

**cherry** ['tʃerɪ] (pl -ies) *n* cerise *f*

**chess** [tʃes] *n* échecs *mpl* ■ **chessboard** *n* échiquier *m*

**chest** [tʃest] *n* a) [part of body] poitrine *f* ; *Fig* **to get it off one's chest** dire ce qu'on a sur le cœur b) [box] coffre *m* ; **chest of drawers** commode *f*

**chestnut** ['tʃestnʌt] **1.** *n* [nut] châtaigne *f* ; [cooked] marron *m* **2.** *adj* [hair] châtain

**chew** [tʃuː] **1.** *vt* **to chew (up)** mâcher **2.** *vi* mastiquer ; **chewing gum** chewing-gum *m*

**chewy** ['tʃuːɪ] *adj* [meat] caoutchouteux, -euse ; [sweet] mou (*f* molle)

**chick** [tʃɪk] *n* **a)** [chicken] poussin *m* **b)** *Fam* [woman] poupée *f*, nana *f* ; *Fam* **chick flick** *film qui cible les jeunes femmes* ; *Fam* **chick lit** *littérature populaire, en général écrite par des femmes, qui cible les jeunes femmes*

**chicken** ['tʃɪkɪn] **1.** *n* poulet *m* **2.** *vi Fam* **to chicken out** se dégonfler ■ **chickenpox** *n* varicelle *f*

**chickpea** ['tʃɪkpiː] *n* pois *m* chiche

**chief** [tʃiːf] **1.** *n* chef *m* ; *Fam* [boss] patron *m* **2.** *adj* [most important] principal ; COMM **chief executive** directeur *m* général ■ **chiefly** *adv* principalement, surtout

**chilblain** ['tʃɪlbleɪn] *n* engelure *f*

**child** [tʃaɪld] (pl children) *n* enfant *mf* ; **child abuse** mauvais traitements *mpl* à enfant, maltraitance *f* ; **child care** [for working parents] crèches *fpl* et garderies *fpl* ; *Br* **child minder** assistante *f* maternelle ■ **childhood** *n* enfance *f* ■ **childish** *adj* puéril ■ **childlike** *adj* enfantin ■ **childproof** *adj* [lock, bottle] que les enfants ne peuvent pas ouvrir

**children** ['tʃɪldrən] *pl of* child

**chill** [tʃɪl] **1.** *n* froid *m* ; [illness] refroidissement *m* ; **to catch a chill** prendre froid **2.** *vt* [wine, melon] mettre au frais ; [meat] réfrigérer **3.** *vi* [drink, food] rafraîchir ■ **chill out** *vi Fam* décompresser ; **chill out!** du calme !

**chillax** [tʃɪ'læks] *vi Fam & Hum* se poser ; **we're going to chillax at my place after the movie** on va aller se poser un peu chez moi après le cinéma

**chilli** ['tʃɪlɪ] (pl -is or -ies) *n* [vegetable] piment *m* ; [dish] chili *m* con carne ; **chilli powder** ≃ chili *m*

**chilly** ['tʃɪlɪ] (compar -ier, superl -iest) *adj* froid ; **it's chilly** il fait (un peu) froid

**chime** [tʃaɪm] *vi* [of bell] carillonner ; [of clock] sonner

**chimney** ['tʃɪmnɪ] (pl -eys) *n* cheminée *f*

**chimpanzee** [tʃɪmpæn'ziː] *n* chimpanzé *m*

**chin** [tʃɪn] *n* menton *m*

**china** ['tʃaɪnə] **1.** *n inv* porcelaine *f* **2.** *adj* en porcelaine

**China** ['tʃaɪnə] *n* la Chine ■ **Chinese 1.** *adj* chinois **2.** *n inv* [person] Chinois, -e *mf*; [language] chinois *m*

**chink** [tʃɪŋk] **1.** *n* [slit] fente *f* **2.** *vt* faire tinter

**chip** [tʃɪp] **1.** *n* [splinter] éclat *m*; [break] ébréchure *f*; [counter] jeton *m*; COMPUT puce *f*; **chips** Br [French fries] frites *fpl*; Am [crisps] chips *fpl*; Br **chip shop** boutique où l'on vend du poisson pané et des frites **2.** (*pt & pp* -pp-) *vt* [cup] ébrécher; [paint] écailler ■ **chip-and-pin** *n* Br paiement *m* par carte à puce

**chiropodist** [kɪ'rɒpədɪst] *n* Br pédicure *mf*

**chirp** [tʃɜːp] *vi* [of bird] pépier

**chisel** ['tʃɪzəl] **1.** *n* ciseau *m* **2.** (Br -ll-, Am -l-) *vt* ciseler

**chives** [tʃaɪvz] *npl* ciboulette *f*

**chlorine** ['klɔːriːn] *n* CHEM chlore *m*

**choc-ice** ['tʃɒkaɪs] *n* Br glace individuelle enrobée de chocolat

**chocoholic** ['tʃɒkəhɒlɪk] *n* Fam accro *mf* du chocolat, fondu *m* de chocolat

**chocolate** ['tʃɒklɪt] **1.** *n* chocolat *m*; **hot chocolate** chocolat *m* chaud; **plain chocolate** chocolat *m* à croquer **2.** *adj* [made of chocolate] en chocolat; [chocolate-flavoured] au chocolat

**choice** [tʃɔɪs] *n* choix *m*; **to make a choice** choisir

**choir** ['kwaɪə(r)] *n* chœur *m* ■ **choirboy** *n* jeune choriste *m*

**choke** [tʃəʊk] **1.** *n* [of car] starter *m* **2.** *vt* [strangle] étrangler; [clog] boucher **3.** *vi* **she choked on a fishbone** elle a failli s'étouffer avec une arête

**cholesterol** [kə'lestərɒl] *n* cholestérol *m*

**choose** [tʃuːz] **1.** (*pt* chose, *pp* chosen) *vt* choisir; **to choose to do sth** choisir de faire qch **2.** *vi* choisir ■ **choos(e)y** (*compar* choosier, *superl* choosiest) *adj* Fam difficile (**about** sur)

**chop** [tʃɒp] **1.** *n* [of lamb, pork] côtelette *f* **2.** (*pt & pp* -pp-) *vt* [wood] couper (à la hache); [food] couper en morceaux;

[finely] hacher; **to chop down** [tree] abattre; **to chop off** [branch, finger] couper; **to chop up** couper en morceaux ■ **chops** *npl* Fam babines *fpl*

**choppy** ['tʃɒpɪ] (*compar* -ier, *superl* -iest) *adj* [sea] agité

**chopsticks** ['tʃɒpstɪks] *npl* baguettes *fpl* (*pour manger*)

**choral** ['kɔːrəl] *adj* choral

**chord** [kɔːd] *n* MUS accord *m*

**chore** [tʃɔː(r)] *n* corvée *f*; **(household) chores** travaux *mpl* du ménage

**chorus** ['kɔːrəs] *n* [of song] refrain *m*; [singers] chœur *m*; [dancers] troupe *f*

**chose** [tʃəʊz] *pt of* choose

**chosen** ['tʃəʊzən] *pp of* choose

**Christ** [kraɪst] *n* le Christ ■ **Christian** *adj & n* chrétien, -enne (*mf*); **Christian name** prénom *m* ■ **Christianity** *n* christianisme *m*

**christen** ['krɪsən] *vt* [person, ship] baptiser ■ **christening** *n* baptême *m*

**Christmas** ['krɪsməs] **1.** *n* Noël *m*; **at Christmas (time)** à Noël; **Merry** or **Happy Christmas!** Joyeux Noël! **2.** *adj* [tree, card, Day, party] de Noël; **Christmas Eve** la veille de Noël

**chrome** [krəʊm], **chromium** ['krəʊmɪəm] *n* chrome *m*

**chronic** ['krɒnɪk] *adj* [disease, state] chronique

**chronological** [krɒnə'lɒdʒɪkəl] *adj* chronologique; **in chronological order** par ordre chronologique

**chubby** ['tʃʌbɪ] (*compar* -ier, *superl* -iest) *adj* [person, hands] potelé; [cheeks] rebondi

**chuck** [tʃʌk] *vt* Fam [throw] lancer; [boyfriend, girlfriend] plaquer; Br **to chuck (in** or **up)** [give up] laisser tomber; **to chuck out** [throw away] balancer; [from house, school, club] vider

**chuckle** ['tʃʌkəl] *vi* rire tout bas

**chug** [tʃʌg] (*pt & pp* -gg-) *vi* **to chug along** [of vehicle] avancer lentement; [of train] haleter

**chum** [tʃʌm] *n* Fam copain *m*, copine *f*

**chunk** [tʃʌŋk] *n* (gros) morceau *m*

**church** [tʃɜːtʃ] n église f; **to go to church** aller à l'église; **church hall** salle f paroissiale ■ **churchyard** n cimetière m

**churn** [tʃɜːn] vt Pej **to churn out** [books] pondre (en série); [goods] produire en série

**chute** [ʃuːt] n Br [in pool, playground] toboggan m; [for rubbish] vide-ordures m inv

**CID** [siːaɪˈdiː] (abbr of **Criminal Investigation Department**) n Br ≃ PJ f

**cider** [ˈsaɪdə(r)] n cidre m

**cigar** [sɪˈgɑː(r)] n cigare m

**cigarette** [sɪgəˈret] n cigarette f; **cigarette end** mégot m

**cinder** [ˈsɪndə(r)] n cendre f

**cinema** [ˈsɪnəmə] n [art] cinéma m; Br [place] cinéma; Br **to go to the cinema** aller au cinéma ■ **cinemagoer** n Br cinéphile mf

**cinnamon** [ˈsɪnəmən] n cannelle f

**circle** [ˈsɜːkəl] **1.** n [shape, group, range] cercle m; THEAT balcon m **2.** vt [move round] tourner autour de; [surround] entourer (**with** de) **3.** vi [of aircraft, bird] décrire des cercles

**circuit** [ˈsɜːkɪt] n [electrical path, journey, for motor racing] circuit m; ELEC **circuit breaker** disjoncteur m

**circular** [ˈsɜːkjʊlə(r)] **1.** adj circulaire **2.** n [letter] circulaire f; [advertisement] prospectus m

**circulate** [ˈsɜːkjʊleɪt] **1.** vt faire circuler **2.** vi circuler ■ **circulation** [-ˈleɪʃən] n [of air, blood, money] circulation f; [of newspaper] tirage m

**circumcised** [ˈsɜːkəmsaɪzd] adj circoncis

**circumference** [sɜːˈkʌmfərəns] n circonférence f

**circumstance** [ˈsɜːkəmstæns] n circonstance f; **circumstances** [financial] situation f financière; **in** or **under the circumstances** étant donné les circonstances; **in** or **under no circumstances** en aucun cas

**circus** [ˈsɜːkəs] n cirque m

**citizen** [ˈsɪtɪzən] n citoyen, -enne mf; [of city] habitant, -e mf

**citrus** [ˈsɪtrəs] adj **citrus fruit(s)** agrumes mpl

**city** [ˈsɪti] n ville f, cité f ■ **City** n Br the **City** la City (quartier financier de Londres; le nom est souvent employé pour désigner le monde britannique de la finance; la City est aussi connue sous le nom de 'Square Mile')

**civil** [ˈsɪvəl] adj **a)** [rights, war, marriage] civil; **civil partner** conjoint(e) m,f (par union civile); **civil partnership** loi britannique qui garantit aux couples homosexuels les mêmes droits qu'aux couples mariés en matière de succession, de retraite, et pour les questions de garde et d'éducation des enfants; **civil servant** fonctionnaire mf; **civil service** fonction f publique; **civil union** union f civile **b)** [polite] civil

**civilian** [sɪˈvɪljən] adj & n civil, -e (mf)

**civilize** [ˈsɪvɪlaɪz] vt civiliser ■ **civilization** [-ˈzeɪʃən] n civilisation f

**claim** [kleɪm] **1.** n [demand - for damages, compensation] demande f d'indemnisation; [as a right] revendication f; [statement] affirmation f; [right] droit m (**to** à); (**insurance**) **claim** demande f d'indemnité **2.** vt [as a right] réclamer, revendiquer; [payment, benefit, reduction] demander à bénéficier de; **to claim damages (from sb)** réclamer des dommages et intérêts (à qn); **to claim that...** [assert] prétendre que... ■ **claimant** n Br [for social benefits, insurance] demandeur, -euse mf

**clam** [klæm] n palourde f

**clamber** [ˈklæmbə(r)] vi **to clamber up** grimper

**clammy** [ˈklæmɪ] adj [skin] moite; [weather] lourd et humide

**clamour** [ˈklæmə(r)], Am **clamor 1.** n clameur f **2.** vi **to clamour for sth** demander qch à grands cris

**clamp** [klæmp] **1.** n [clip-like] pince f; (**wheel**) **clamp** [for vehicle] sabot m (de Denver) **2.** vt serrer; [vehicle] mettre un sabot à **3.** *vi* to clamp down on sévir contre ■ **clampdown** *n* coup *m* d'arrêt **(on** à)

**clan** [klæn] *n also Fig* clan *m*

**clang** [klæŋ] *n* son *m* métallique

**clap** [klæp] *(pt & pp* **-pp-***)* *vti* [applaud] applaudir; **to clap (one's hands)** applaudir; [once] frapper dans ses mains ■ **clapping** *n* applaudissements *mpl*

**claret** ['klærət] *n* [wine] bordeaux *m* rouge

**clarify** ['klærɪfaɪ] *(pt & pp* **-ied***)* *vt* clarifier ■ **clarification** [-ɪ'keɪʃən] *n* clarification *f*

**clarinet** [klærɪ'net] *n* clarinette *f*

**clarity** ['klærətɪ] *n* [of expression, argument] clarté *f*; [of sound] pureté *f*

**clash** [klæʃ] **1.** *n* [of interests] conflit *m*; [of events] coïncidence *f* **2.** *vi* [of objects] s'entrechoquer; [of interests, armies] s'affronter; [of colours] jurer **(with** avec); [coincide] tomber en même temps **(with** que)

**clasp** [klɑːsp] **1.** *n* [fastener] fermoir *m*; [of belt] boucle *f* **2.** *vt* [hold] serrer; **to clasp one's hands** joindre les mains

**class** [klɑːs] **1.** *n* classe *f*; [lesson] cours *m* **2.** *vt* classer **(as** comme) ■ **classmate** *n* camarade *mf* de classe ■ **classroom** *n* (salle *f* de) classe *f*

**classic** ['klæsɪk] **1.** *adj* classique **2.** *n* [writer, work] classique *m* ■ **classical** *adj* classique

**classify** ['klæsɪfaɪ] *(pt & pp* **-ied***)* *vt* classer ■ **classification** *n* classification *f* ■ **classified** *adj* [information, document] confidentiel, -elle; **classified advertisement** petite annonce *f*

**classy** ['klɑːsɪ] *(compar* **-ier,** *superl* **-iest***)* *adj Fam* chic *inv*

**clatter** ['klætə(r)] *n* fracas *m*

**clause** [klɔːz] *n* [in sentence] proposition *f*; [in legal document] clause *f*

**claustrophobic** [klɔːstrə'fəʊbɪk] *adj* [person] claustrophobe; [room, atmosphere] oppressant

**claw** [klɔː] **1.** *n* [of lobster] pince *f*; [of cat, sparrow] griffe *f*; [of eagle] serre *f* **2.** *vt* [scratch] griffer

**clay** [kleɪ] *n* argile *f*

**clean** [kliːn] **1.** *(compar* **-er,** *superl* **-est***)* *adj* propre; [clear-cut] net *(f* nette); [joke] pour toutes les oreilles; [game, fight] dans les règles; **to come clean** tout avouer **2.** *adv* [utterly] complètement **3.** *n* **to give sth a clean** nettoyer qch **4.** *vt* nettoyer; [wash] laver; **to clean one's teeth** se brosser *ou* se laver les dents; **to clean out** [room] nettoyer à fond; [empty] vider; **to clean up** [room] nettoyer; *Fig* [reform] épurer **5.** *vi* **to clean (up)** faire le nettoyage ■ **clean-burning** *adj* [fuel] brûlant sans résidu de combustible ■ **cleaner** *n* [in home] femme *f* de ménage; **(dry) cleaner** teinturier, -ère *mf* ■ **cleaning** *n* nettoyage *m*; [housework] ménage *m*; **cleaning woman** femme *f* de ménage ■ **cleanly** *adv* [break, cut] net ■ **clean-shaven** *adj* [with no beard or moustache] glabre; [closely shaven] rasé de près

**cleanse** [klenz] *vt* [wound] nettoyer; **cleansing cream** crème *f* démaquillante

**clear** [klɪə(r)] **1.** *(compar* **-er,** *superl* **-est***)* *adj* [sky, water, sound, thought] clair; [glass] transparent; [outline, photo, skin, majority] net *(f* nette); [road] libre; [winner] incontesté, clair; [certain] certain; **to make oneself clear** se faire comprendre; **it is clear that...** il est évident *ou* clair que... **2.** *adv* **to keep** *or* **steer clear of** se tenir à l'écart de; **to get clear of** [away from] s'éloigner de **3.** *vt* [table] débarrasser; [road, area] dégager; [accused person] disculper; [cheque] compenser; [debts] liquider; [through customs] dédouaner; [for security] autoriser; **to clear one's throat** s'éclaircir la gorge **4.** *vi* [of weather] s'éclaircir; [of fog] se dissiper ■ **clearing** *n* [in woods] clairière *f* ■ **clearly** *adv* [explain, write] clairement; [see, understand] bien; [obviously] évidemment ■ **clear away** *vt sep* [remove] enlever ■ **clear off** *vi Fam* [leave] filer ■ **clear out** *vt sep* [empty] vider ; [remove] enlever ■ **clear up 1.** *vt sep* [mystery] éclaircir ; [room] ranger **2.** *vi* [of weather] s'éclaircir ; [tidy] ranger

**clearance** ['klɪərəns] *n* [sale] liquidation *f* ; [space] dégagement *m* ; [permission] autorisation *f*

**clear-cut** [klɪə'kʌt] *adj* net (*f* nette)

**clef** [klef] *n* MUS clef *f*

**clench** [klentʃ] *vt* **to clench one's fist / teeth** serrer le poing / les dents

**clergy** ['klɜːdʒɪ] *n* clergé *m* ■ **clergyman** *(pl* -**men**) *n* ecclésiastique *m*

**clerical** ['klerɪkəl] *adj* [job] d'employé ; [work] de bureau

**clerk** [*Br* klɑːk, *Am* klɜːk] *n* employé, -e *mf* de bureau ; *Am* [in store] vendeur, -euse *mf*

**clever** ['klevə(r)] *(compar* -**er**, *superl* -**est**) *adj* intelligent ; [smart, shrewd] astucieux, -euse ; [skilful] habile (**at sth** à qch ; **at doing** à faire) ; [ingenious-machine, plan] ingénieux, -euse ; [gifted] doué ; **clever with one's hands** adroit de ses mains ■ **cleverly** *adv* intelligemment ; [ingeniously] astucieusement ; [skilfully] habilement

**cliché** ['kliːʃeɪ] *n* cliché *m*

**click** [klɪk] **1.** *n* **a)** [of lock] déclic *m* ; [of tongue, heels] claquement *m* **b)** COMPUT clic *m* **2.** *vt* **a)** faire claquer **b)** COMPUT cliquer ; **to click on** cliquer sur **3.** *vi* [heels] claquer ; [camera] faire un déclic ; *Fam* **it suddenly clicked** ça a fait tilt

**client** ['klaɪənt] *n* client, -e *mf* ■ **clientele** *n* clientèle *f*

**cliff** [klɪf] *n* falaise *f*

**climate** ['klaɪmɪt] *n* [weather] & *Fig* [conditions] climat *m* ; **climate change** changement *m* climatique

**climax** ['klaɪmæks] *n* point *m* culminant ; [sexual] orgasme *m*

**climb** [klaɪm] **1.** *n* montée *f* **2.** *vt* **to climb (up)** [steps, hill] gravir ; [mountain] faire l'ascension de ; [tree, ladder] grimper à ; **to climb (over)** [wall] escalader ; **to climb down (from)** [wall, tree]

descendre de ; [hill] descendre **3.** *vi* [of plant] grimper ; **to climb (up)** [steps, tree, hill] monter ; **to climb down** descendre ; *Fig* [back down] revenir sur sa décision ■ **climber** *n* [mountaineer] alpiniste *mf* ; [on rocks] varappeur, -euse *mf* ; [plant] plante *f* grimpante ■ **climbing** (mountain) **climbing** alpinisme *m* ; **(rock-)climbing** varappe *f*

**climb-down** ['klaɪmdaʊn] *n* reculade *f*

**clinch** [klɪntʃ] *vt* [deal] conclure

**cling** [klɪŋ] *(pt & pp* **clung**) *vi* s'accrocher (**to** à) ; [stick] adhérer (**to** à)

**clinic** ['klɪnɪk] *n Br* [private] clinique *f* ; [part of hospital] service *m* ■ **clinical** *adj* MED clinique

**clink** [klɪŋk] **1.** *vt* faire tinter **2.** *vi* tinter

**clip** [klɪp] **1.** *n* **a)** [for paper] trombone *m* ; [fastener] attache *f* ; [of brooch, of cyclist, for hair] pince *f* **b)** [of film] extrait *m* **2.** *(pt & pp* -**pp**-) *vt* [paper] attacher *(avec un trombone)* ; [cut] couper ; [hedge] tailler ; [ticket] poinçonner ; **to clip (on)** [attach] attacher (**to** à) **3.** *vi* **to clip together** s'emboîter ■ **clippers** *npl* [for hair] tondeuse *f* ; [for fingernails] coupe-ongles *m inv* ■ **clipping** *n Am* [from newspaper] coupure *f*

**clique** [kliːk] *n Pej* clique *f*

**cloak** [kləʊk] *n* cape *f* ■ **cloakroom** *n* vestiaire *m* ; *Br* [lavatory] toilettes *fpl*

**clock** [klɒk] *n* [large] horloge *f* ; [small] pendule *f* ; *Br Fam* [mileometer] compteur *m* ; **round the clock** vingt-quatre heures sur vingt-quatre ; **to put the clocks forward / back** [in spring, autumn] avancer / retarder les pendules ; **clock radio** radioréveil *m* ; **clock tower** clocher *m* ■ **clockface** ['klɒkfeɪs] *n* cadran *m* ■ **clockwise** *adv* dans le sens des aiguilles d'une montre ■ **clock-work 1.** *adj* [toy] mécanique **2.** *n* **to go like clockwork** marcher comme sur des roulettes

**clog** [klɒg] **1.** *n* [shoe] sabot *m* **2.** *(pt & pp* -**gg**-) *vt* **to clog (up)** [obstruct] boucher

**cloister** ['klɔɪstə(r)] *n* cloître *m*

**close**[1] ['kləʊs] **1.** *(compar* -**er**, *superl* -**est**) *adj* [in distance, time, relationship] proche ; [collaboration, resemblance, connection] étroit ; [friend] intime ; [contest] serré ; [study] rigoureux, -euse ; *Br* **it's close** [of weather] il fait lourd ; **that was a close shave** *or* **call** il s'en est fallu de peu ; **close on, close to** [almost] près de **2.** *adv* **close (by), close at hand** tout près ; **we stood/sat close together** nous étions debout / assis serrés les uns contre les autres ; **to follow close behind** suivre de près ▪ **close-fitting** *adj* [clothes] ajusté ▪ **closing 1.** *n* fermeture *f* **2.** *adj* [remarks] dernier, -ère ; **closing date** [for application] date *f* limite ; **closing time** heure *f* de fermeture ▪ **close-up** *n* gros plan *m*

**close²** [kləʊz] **1.** *n* [end] fin *f* **2.** *vt* [door, shop, account, book, eye] fermer ; [road] barrer ; [gap] réduire ; [deal] conclure ; **to close (a window)** fermer (une fenêtre) ; **to close (an application)** quitter (une application) **3.** *vi* [of door] se fermer ; [of shop] fermer ▪ **closed** *adj* [door, shop] fermé ; **closed-circuit television** télévision *f* en circuit fermé ▪ **closure** *n* [of business, factory] fermeture *f* (définitive) ▪ **close down 1.** *vt sep* [business, factory] fermer (définitivement) **2.** *vi* [of TV channel] terminer les émissions ; [of business, factory] fermer (définitivement) ▪ **close in** *vi* [approach] approcher ; **to close in on sb** se rapprocher de qn ▪ **close up 1.** *vt sep* fermer **2.** *vi* [of shopkeeper] fermer ; [of wound] se refermer ; [of line of people] se resserrer

**closet** ['klɒzɪt] *n Am* [cupboard] placard *m* ; [wardrobe] penderie *f*

**clot** [klɒt] **1.** *n* [of blood] caillot *m* **2.** *(pt & pp -tt-)vi* [of blood] (se) coaguler

**cloth** [klɒθ] *n* tissu *m* ; [for dusting] chiffon *m* ; [for dishes] torchon *m* ; [tablecloth] nappe *f* ▪ **clothing** *n* [clothes] vêtements *mpl*

**clothes** [kləʊðz] *npl* vêtements *mpl* ; **to put one's clothes on** s'habiller ; **to take one's clothes off** se déshabiller ; **clothes line** corde *f* à linge ; *Br* **clothes peg**, *Am* **clothes pin** pince *f* à linge ; **clothes shop** magasin *m* de vêtements

**cloud** [klaʊd] **1.** *n* nuage *m* **2.** *vi* **to cloud over** [of sky] se couvrir ▪ **cloudy** *(compar* -ier, *superl* -iest) *adj* [weather, sky] nuageux, -euse ; [liquid] trouble

**cloud computing** *n* cloud computing *m*

**clove** [kləʊv] *n* [spice] clou *m* de girofle ; **clove of garlic** gousse *f* d'ail

**clover** ['kləʊvə(r)] *n* trèfle *m*

**clown** [klaʊn] **1.** *n* clown *m* **2.** *vi* **to clown around** *or* **about** faire le clown

**club** [klʌb] **1.** *n* **a)** [society] club *m* **b)** [nightclub] boîte *f* de nuit **c)** [weapon] massue *f* ; [in golf] club *m* **d) clubs** [in cards] trèfle *m* **2.** *(pt & pp -bb-)vi Br* **to club together** se cotiser (**to buy sth** pour acheter qch) ▪ **clubbing** ['klʌbɪŋ] *n* sorties *fpl* en boîte, clubbing *m* ; **she loves clubbing** elle adore sortir en boîte ; **to go clubbing** sortir en boîte

**clue** [kluː] *n* indice *m* ; [of crossword] définition *f* ; *Fam* **I don't have a clue** je n'en ai pas la moindre idée

**clump** [klʌmp] *n* [of flowers, trees] massif *m*

**clumsy** ['klʌmzɪ] *(compar* -ier, *superl* -iest) *adj* maladroit

**clung** [klʌŋ] *pt & pp* of **cling**

**clunky** ['klʌŋkɪ] *adj* **a)** [shoes] gros (*f* grosse) **b)** [furniture] encombrant

**cluster** ['klʌstə(r)] **1.** *n* groupe *m* **2.** *vi* se grouper

**clusterfuck** ['klʌstəfʌk] *n Am vulg* **it was a complete clusterfuck** ça a complètement merdé ; **we're in the middle of an economic clusterfuck** on est en plein merdier *ou* bordel sur le plan économique

**clutch** [klʌtʃ] **1.** *n* [in car] embrayage *m* ; [pedal] pédale *f* d'embrayage **2.** *vt* tenir fermement **3.** *vi* **to clutch at** essayer de saisir

**clutter** ['klʌtə(r)] **1.** *n* [objects] désordre *m* **2.** *vt* **to clutter (up)** [room, table] encombrer (**with** de)

**cm** *(abbr of* **centimetre(s)**) cm

**CMON** MESSAGING *written abbr of* **come on**

**Co** *(abbr of* **company**) Cie

**co-** [kəʊ] *pref* co-

**c / o** *(abbr of* **care of)** [on envelope] chez

**coach** [kəʊtʃ] **1.** *n* a) *Br* [train carriage] voiture *f*, wagon *m* ; *Br* [bus] car *m* ; [horse-drawn] carrosse *m* **b)** [for sports] entraîneur, -euse *mf* **2.** *vt* [sportsman, team] entraîner

**coal** [kəʊl] **1.** *n* charbon *m* **2.** *adj* [fire] de charbon ; **coal industry** industrie *f* houillère ■ **coalmine** *n* mine *f* de charbon

**coalition** [kəʊə'lɪʃən] *n* coalition *f*

**coarse** [kɔːs] *(compar* -er, *superl* -est*) adj* [person, manners] grossier, -ère, vulgaire ; [surface, fabric] grossier, -ère

**coast** [kəʊst] *n* côte *f*

**coaster** ['kəʊstə(r)] *n* [for glass] dessous-de-verre *m inv*

**coat** [kəʊt] **1.** *n* manteau *m* ; [overcoat] pardessus *m* ; [jacket] veste *f* ; [of animal] pelage *m* ; [of paint] couche *f* ; **coat hanger** cintre *m* **2.** *vt* **to coat sth (with)** recouvrir qch (de) ; [with paint] enduire qch (de) ; [with flour, sugar] saupoudrer qch (de) ; [with chocolate] enrober qch (de) ■ **coating** *n* couche *f*

**-coated** [kəʊtɪd] *suff* **plastic-coated** plastifié ; **silver-coated** plaqué argent

**coax** [kəʊks] *vt* **to coax sb to do** *or* **into doing sth** amener qn à faire qch par des cajoleries

**cob** [kɒb] *n* [of corn] épi *m*

**cobbled** ['kɒbəld] *adj* [street] pavé

**cobweb** ['kɒbweb] *n* toile *f* d'araignée

**Coca-Cola®** [kəʊkə'kəʊlə] *n* Coca-Cola® *m*

**cocaine** [kəʊ'keɪn] *n* cocaïne *f*

**cock** [kɒk] *n* [rooster] coq *m*

**cockerel** ['kɒkərəl] *n* jeune coq *m*

**cockney** ['kɒknɪ] *adj & n* cockney *(mf)* (natif des quartiers est de Londres)

**cockpit** ['kɒkpɪt] *n* [of aircraft] poste *m* de pilotage

**cockroach** ['kɒkrəʊtʃ] *n* cafard *m*

**cocktail** ['kɒkteɪl] *n* cocktail *m* ; **fruit cocktail** macédoine *f* de fruits ; **cocktail party** cocktail *m*

**cocky** ['kɒkɪ] *(compar* -ier, *superl* -iest*) adj Fam* culotté

**cocoa** ['kəʊkəʊ] *n* cacao *m*

**coconut** ['kəʊkənʌt] *n* noix *f* de coco

**cod** [kɒd] *n* morue *f* ; [as food] cabillaud *m*

**COD** [siːəʊ'diː] *(abbr of* **cash on delivery)** *n Br* COMM paiement *m* à la livraison

**code** [kəʊd] *n* code *m* ; **in code** [letter, message] codé ; **code word** code

**coeducational** [kəʊedjʊ'keɪʃənəl] *adj* [school, teaching] mixte

**coerce** [kəʊ'ɜːs] *vt* contraindre **(sb into doing** qn à faire)

**coexist** [kəʊɪg'zɪst] *vi* coexister

**coffee** ['kɒfɪ] *n* café *m* ; **coffee with milk,** *Br* **white coffee** café *m* au lait ; **black coffee** café *m* noir ; *Br* **coffee bar, coffee house** café *m* ; **coffee break** pause-café *f* ; **coffee maker** cafetière *f* électrique ; **coffee pot** cafetière *f* ; **coffee table** table *f* basse

**coffin** ['kɒfɪn] *n* cercueil *m*

**cog** [kɒg] *n* dent *f*

**cognac** ['kɒnjæk] *n* cognac *m*

**cohabit** [kəʊ'hæbɪt] *vi* vivre en concubinage **(with** avec)

**coherent** [kəʊ'hɪərənt] *adj* [logical] cohérent ; [way of speaking] compréhensible, intelligible

**coil** [kɔɪl] *n* [of wire, rope] rouleau *m* ; [contraceptive] stérilet *m*

**coin** [kɔɪn] *n* pièce *f* (de monnaie)

**coincide** [kəʊɪn'saɪd] *vi* coïncider **(with** avec) ■ **coincidence** *n* coïncidence *f*

**coke** [kəʊk] *n* [fuel] coke *m* ; [boisson] Coca® *m inv*

**colander** ['kʌləndə(r)] *n* [for vegetables] passoire *f*

**cold** [kəʊld] **1.** *(compar* -er, *superl* -est*) adj* froid ; **to be** *or* **feel cold** [of person] avoir froid ; **my hands are cold** j'ai froid aux mains ; **it's cold** [of weather] il fait froid ; **to get cold** [of weather] se refroidir ; [of food] refroidir ; *Fam* **to get cold feet** se dégonfler ; **cold case** affaire *f* non élucidée *ou* résolue, cold case *m* ; *Br* **cold meats,** *Am* **cold cuts**

viandes *fpl* froides ; *Slang* **cold turkey** [drugs withdrawal] manque *m* ; **to go cold turkey** [stop taking drugs] arrêter de se droguer d'un seul coup ; [suffer withdrawal symptoms] être en manque **2.** *n* **a)** [temperature] froid *m* **b)** [illness] rhume *m* ; **to have a cold** être enrhumé ; **to catch a cold** attraper un rhume ; **to get a cold** s'enrhumer ■ **coldness** *n* froideur *f*

**coleslaw** ['kəʊlslɔː] *n* salade de chou cru à la mayonnaise

**collaborate** [kə'læbəreɪt] *vi* collaborer (on à) ■ **collaboration** [-'reɪʃən] *n* collaboration *f*

**collage** ['kɒlɑːʒ] *n* [picture] collage *m*

**collapse** [kə'læps] **1.** *n* effondrement *m* ; [of government] chute *f* **2.** *vi* [of person, building] s'effondrer ; [faint] se trouver mal ; [of government] tomber

**collar** ['kɒlə(r)] *n* [on garment] col *m* ; [of dog] collier *m*

**colleague** ['kɒliːg] *n* collègue *mf*

**collect** [kə'lekt] **1.** *vt* [pick up] ramasser ; [gather] rassembler ; [information] recueillir ; [stamps] collectionner ; **to collect money** [in street, church] quêter ; **to collect sb** [pick up] passer prendre qn **2.** *vi* [in street, church] quêter (**for** pour) **3.** *adv Am* **to call** *or* **phone sb collect** téléphoner à qn en PCV

**collection** [kə'lekʃən] *n* [of objects, stamps] collection *f* ; [of poems] recueil *m* ; [of money for church] quête *f* ; [of mail] levée *f*

**collector** [kə'lektə(r)] *n* [of stamps] collectionneur, -euse *mf*

**college** ['kɒlɪdʒ] *n Br* [of further education] établissement *m* d'enseignement supérieur ; *Am* [university] université *f* ; **to be at college** être étudiant

**collide** [kə'laɪd] *vi* entrer en collision (**with** avec) ■ **collision** *n* collision *f*

**colloquial** [kə'ləʊkwɪəl] *adj* familier, -ère

**colon** ['kəʊlən] *n* **a)** [punctuation mark] deux-points *m* **b)** ANAT côlon *m*

**colonel** ['kɜːnəl] *n* colonel *m*

**colonial** [kə'ləʊnɪəl] *adj* colonial

**colony** ['kɒlənɪ] (*pl* **-ies**) *n* colonie *f*

**colossal** [kə'lɒsəl] *adj* colosse

**colour** ['kʌlə(r)], *Am* **color 1.** *n* couleur *f* **2.** *adj* [photo, television] en couleurs ; [television set] couleur *inv* **3.** *vt* colorer ; **to colour (in)** [drawing] colorier ■ **coloured** *adj* [person, pencil] de couleur ; [glass] coloré ■ **colouring** *n* [in food] colorant *m* ; [shade, effect] coloris *m* ; **colouring book** album *m* de coloriages

**colour-blind** ['kʌləblaɪnd] *adj* daltonien, -enne

**colourful** ['kʌləfəl] *adj* [crowd, story] coloré ; [person] pittoresque

**column** ['kɒləm] *n* colonne *f* ; [newspaper feature] rubrique *f*

**.com** ['dɒtkɒm] COMPUT *abréviation désignant les entreprises commerciales dans les adresses électroniques*

**coma** ['kəʊmə] *n* **in a coma** dans le coma

**comb** [kəʊm] **1.** *n* peigne *m* **2.** *vt Fig* [search] ratisser, passer au peigne fin ; **to comb one's hair** se peigner

**combat** ['kɒmbæt] *n* combat *m* ; **combats, combat trousers** pantalon *m* treillis

**combination** [kɒmbɪ'neɪʃən] *n* combinaison *f* ; **in combination with** en association avec ; **combination lock** serrure *f* à combinaison

**combine** [kəm'baɪn] *vt* [activities, qualities, elements, sounds] combiner ; [efforts] joindre, unir ; **combine harvester** moissonneuse-batteuse *f*

**combustion** [kəm'bʌstʃən] *n* combustion *f*

**come** [kʌm] (*pt* **came**, *pp* **come**) *vi* venir (**from** de ; **to** à) ; **to come home** rentrer (à la maison) ; **to come first** [in race, exam] se classer premier ; **come and see me** viens me voir ; **to come near** *or* **close to doing sth** faillir faire qch ; **in the years to come** dans les années à venir

■ **come about** *vi* [happen] arriver

■ **come across 1.** *vi* **to come across well/badly** bien / mal passer **2.** *vt insep* [find] tomber sur

■ **come along** *vi* venir (**with** avec) ; [progress - of work] avancer ; [of student] progresser

■ **come apart** *vi* a) [fall to pieces] tomber en morceaux **b)** [come off] se détacher

■ **come at** *vt insep* [attack] attaquer

■ **come away** *vi* [leave, come off] partir (**from** de) ; **to come away from sb / sth** [step or move back from] s'écarter de qn / qch

■ **come back** *vi* revenir ; [return home] rentrer

■ **come by** *vt insep* [obtain] obtenir ; [find] trouver

■ **come down 1.** *vi* descendre ; [of rain, temperature, price] tomber ; [of building] être démoli **2.** *vt insep* [stairs, hill] descendre

■ **come down to** *vt insep* se résumer à, se réduire à

■ **come down with** *vt insep* [illness] attraper

■ **come for** *vt insep* venir chercher

■ **come forward** *vi* [make oneself known, volunteer] se présenter

■ **come from** *vt insep* venir de

■ **come in** *vi* [enter] entrer ; [of train] arriver ; [of money] rentrer ; **to come in useful** être bien utile

■ **come in for** *vt insep* **to come in for criticism** faire l'objet de critiques

■ **come into** *vt insep* [room] entrer dans ; [money] hériter de

■ **come off 1.** *vi* [of button] se détacher ; [succeed] réussir **2.** *vt insep* [fall from] tomber de ; [get down from] descendre de

■ **come on** *vi* [make progress - of work] avancer ; [of student] progresser ; **come on!** allez !

■ **come out** *vi* sortir ; [of sun, book] paraître ; [of stain] s'enlever, partir ; [of photo] réussir ; [of homosexual] révéler son homosexualité ; **to come out (on strike)** se mettre en grève

■ **come over** *vt insep* [subj : sensation, emotion] envahir ; **I don't know what's come over her** je ne sais pas ce qui lui a pris

■ **come round** *vi* [visit] passer (**to** chez) ; [regain consciousness] revenir à soi

■ **come through 1.** *vi* [survive] s'en tirer **2.** *vt insep* [crisis] sortir indemne de

■ **come to 1.** *vi* [regain consciousness] revenir à soi **2.** *vt insep* [amount to] revenir à ; **to come to a conclusion** arriver à une conclusion ; **to come to a decision** se décider

■ **come under** *vt insep* [heading] être classé sous

■ **come up 1.** *vi* [rise] monter ; [of question, job] se présenter **2.** *vt insep* [stairs] monter

■ **come up against** *vt insep* [problem] se heurter à

■ **come upon** *vt insep* [book, reference] tomber sur

■ **come up to** *vt insep* [reach] arriver jusqu'à ; [approach] s'approcher de

■ **come up with** *vt insep* [idea, money] trouver

---

**comeback** ['kʌmbæk] *n* **to make a comeback** [of actor, athlete] faire un come-back

**comedy** ['kɒmɪdɪ] *(pl* **-ies)** *n* comédie *f* ■ **comedian** *n* comique *mf*

**comet** ['kɒmɪt] *n* comète *f*

**comfort** ['kʌmfət] **1.** *n* [ease] confort *m* ; [consolation] réconfort *m*, consolation *f* **2.** *vt* consoler ■ **comfortable** *adj* [chair, house] confortable ; [rich] aisé

**comfortably** ['kʌmftəblɪ] *adv* [sit] confortablement ; [win] facilement ; **comfortably off** [rich] à l'aise financièrement

**comforter** ['kʌmfətə(r)] *n Am* [duvet] couette *f*

**comic** ['kɒmɪk] **1.** *adj* comique **2.** *n Br* [magazine] bande *f* dessinée, BD *f* ; **comic book** magazine *m* de bandes dessinées ; **comic strip** bande *f* dessinée ■ **comical** *adj* comique

**coming** ['kʌmɪŋ] **1.** *adj* [future - years, election] à venir ; **the coming days** les prochains jours **2.** *n* **comings and goings** allées *fpl* et venues *fpl*

**comma** ['kɒmə] *n* virgule *f*

**command** [kə'mɑːnd] **1.** *n* [order] ordre *m* ; [authority] commandement *m* ; [mastery] maîtrise *f* (**of** de) ; COMPUT commande *f* **2.** *vt* [order] commander (**sb to do** à qn de faire) ■ **commander** *n* MIL commandant *m* ■ **commanding** *adj* [authoritative] imposant ; [position] dominant ; **commanding officer** commandant *m*

**commandment** [kə'mɑːndmənt] *n* REL commandement *m*

**commemorate** [kə'meməreɪt] *vt* commémorer ■ **commemoration** [-'reɪʃən] *n* commémoration *f*

**commence** [kə'mens] *vti* Formal commencer (**doing** à faire)

**commend** [kə'mend] *vt* [praise] louer ■ **commendable** *adj* louable

**comment** ['kɒment] **1.** *n* commentaire *m* (**on** sur) **2.** *vi* faire des commentaires (**on** sur) ; **to comment on** [text, event, news item] commenter ; **to comment that...** remarquer que... ■ **commentary** *(pl* **-ies)** *n* commentaire *m* ; **live commentary** [on TV or radio] reportage *m* en direct ■ **commentator** *n* commentateur, -trice *mf* (**on** de)

**commerce** ['kɒmɜːs] *n* commerce *m* ■ **commercial** [kə'mɜːʃəl] **1.** *adj* commercial **2.** *n* [advertisement] publicité *f* ; **the commercials** la publicité

**commercialize** [kə'mɜːʃəlaɪz] *vt* Pej [event] transformer en une affaire de gros sous

**commiserate** [kə'mɪzəreɪt] *vi* **to commiserate with sb** être désolé pour qn

**commission** [kə'mɪʃən] **1.** *n* [fee, group] commission *f* ; [order for work] commande *f* **2.** *vt* [artist] passer une commande à ; [book] commander ; **to commission sb to do sth** charger qn de faire qch ■ **commissioner** *n Br* **(police) commissioner** commissaire *m* de police

**commit** [kə'mɪt] *(pt & pp* **-tt-)** *vt* [crime] commettre ; [bind] engager ; [devote] consacrer ; **to commit suicide** se suicider ; **to commit oneself** [make a promise] s'engager (**to** à) ■ **commitment** *n* [duty, responsibility] obligation *f* ; [promise] engagement *m* ; [devotion] dévouement *m* (**to** à)

**committee** [kə'mɪtɪ] *n* comité *m*

**commodity** [kə'mɒdɪtɪ] *(pl* **-ies)** *n* ECON marchandise *f*, produit *m*

**common** ['kɒmən] *(compar* **-er**, *superl* **-est)** *adj* [shared, vulgar] commun ; [frequent] courant, commun ; **in common** [shared] en commun (**with** avec) ; **to have nothing in common** n'avoir rien de commun (**with** avec) ; **common room** [for students] salle *f* commune ; [for teachers] salle *f* des professeurs ; **common sense** sens *m* commun, bon sens *m* ■ **commonly** *adv* communément

**commonplace** ['kɒmənpleɪs] *adj* courant

**Commonwealth** ['kɒmənwelθ] *n Br* **the Commonwealth** le Commonwealth

**commotion** [kə'məʊʃən] *n* [disruption] agitation *f*

**communal** [kə'mjuː-nəl] *adj* [shared - bathroom, kitchen] commun ; [of the community] communautaire

**commune** ['kɒmjuːn] *n* [district] commune *f* ; [group] communauté *f*

**communicate** [kə'mjuːnɪkeɪt] **1.** *vt* communiquer **2.** *vi* [of person] communiquer (**with** avec) ■ **communication** [-'keɪʃən] *n* communication *f* ; *Br* **communication cord** [on train] signal *m* d'alarme

**Communion** [kə'mjuːnjən] *n* **(Holy) Communion** communion ; **to take Communion** communier

**communism** ['kɒmjʊnɪzəm] *n* communisme *m* ■ **communist** *adj & n* communiste *(mf)*

**community** [kə'mjuːnɪtɪ] **1.** *(pl* **-ies)** *n* communauté *f* ; **the student community** les étudiants *mpl* **2.** *adj* [life, spirit] communautaire ; **community centre** centre *m* socioculturel

**commute** [kə'mjuːt] *vi* to commute
**(to work)** faire la navette entre son
domicile et son travail ■ **commuter**
*n* banlieusard, -e *mf*; **commuter train**
train *m* de banlieue

**compact¹** [kəm'pækt] *adj* **a)** [car,
crowd, substance] compact **b)** ['kɒm-
pækt] **compact disc** disque *m* compact

**compact²** ['kɒmpækt] *n* [for face
powder] poudrier *m*

**companion** [kəm'pænjən] *n* [person]
compagnon *m*, compagne *f*

**company** ['kʌmpənɪ] (*pl* **-ies**) *n* [com-
panionship] compagnie *f*; [guests]
invités *mpl*, -es *fpl*; [business] société *f*,
compagnie *f*; **(theatre) company** compagnie *f* (théâtrale); **to keep sb company** tenir compagnie à qn; **company
car** voiture *f* de société

**comparable** ['kɒmpərəbəl] *adj* comparable (**with** *or* **to** à)

**comparative** [kəm'pærətɪv] *adj*
[relative - costs, comfort] relatif, -ive
■ **comparatively** *adv* relativement

**compare** [kəm'peə(r)] **1.** *vt* comparer
(**with** *or* **to** à); **compared to** *or* **with** en
comparaison de **2.** *vi* être comparable
(**with** à) ■ **comparison** [kəm'pærɪsən]
*n* comparaison *f* (**between** entre; **with**
avec); **by** *or* **in comparison** en comparaison

**compartment** [kəm'pɑːtmənt] *n* compartiment *m*

**compass** ['kʌmpəs] *n* **a)** [for finding
direction] boussole *f* **b) (pair of) compasses** compas *m*

**compassion** [kəm'pæʃən] *n* compassion *f*

**compatible** [kəm'pætɪbəl] *adj* [gen &
COMPUT] compatible

**compatriot** [kəm'pætrɪət, kəm'peɪtrɪət]
*n* compatriote *mf*

**compel** [kəm'pel] (*pt & pp* **-ll-**) *vt* forcer,
obliger; **to compel sb to do sth** forcer
qn à faire qch ■ **compelling** *adj* [argu-
ment] convaincant

**compensate** ['kɒmpənseɪt] **1.** *vt* to
**compensate sb** [with payment,
reward] dédommager qn (**for** de) **2.** *vi*

compenser; **to compensate for sth**
[make up for] compenser qch ■ **compensation** [-'seɪʃən] *n* [financial]
dédommagement *m*; [consolation]
compensation *f*

**compère** ['kɒmpeə(r)] *n* animateur,
-trice *mf*

**compete** [kəm'piːt] *vi* [take part in race]
concourir (**in** à); **to compete (with sb)**
rivaliser (avec qn); [in business] faire
concurrence (à qn); **to compete for
sth** se disputer qch

**competent** ['kɒmpɪtənt] *adj* [capable]
compétent (**to do** pour faire) ■ **com-
petently** *adv* avec compétence

**competition** [kɒmpə'tɪʃən] *n* **a)** [ri-
valry] rivalité *f*; [between companies]
concurrence *f* **b)** [contest] concours *m*;
[in sport] compétition *f*

**competitive** [kəm'petɪtɪv] *adj* [price,
market] compétitif, -ive; [person] qui a
l'esprit de compétition ■ **competitor**
*n* concurrent, -e *mf*

**compile** [kəm'paɪl] *vt* [list, catalogue]
dresser; [documents] compiler

**complacent** [kəm'pleɪsənt] *adj* content
de soi

**complain** [kəm'pleɪn] *vi* se plaindre (**to**
sb à qn; **of** *or* **about sb/sth** de qn/qch;
**that** que) ■ **complaint** *n* plainte *f*; [in
shop] réclamation *f*; [illness] maladie *f*

**complement** ['kɒmplɪmənt] *vt* compléter

**complete** [kəm'pliːt] **1.** *adj* [whole]
complet, -ète; [utter] total; [finished]
achevé **2.** *vt* [finish] achever; [form]
compléter ■ **completely** *adv* complètement

**complex** ['kɒmpleks] **1.** *adj* complexe
**2.** *n* [feeling, buildings] complexe *m*
■ **complexion** [kəm'plekʃən] *n* [of
face] teint *m*

**compliant** [kəm'plaɪənt] *adj* **a)** [person]
docile; [document, object] conforme
**b)** [compatible] compatible

**complicate** ['kɒmplɪkeɪt] *vt* compliquer ■ **complication** *n* complication *f*

**compliment 1.** [ˈkɒmplɪmənt] *n* compliment *m*; **to pay sb a compliment** faire un compliment à qn **2.** [ˈkɒmplɪment] *vt* **to compliment sb on sth** [bravery] féliciter qn de qch ; [dress, haircut] faire des compliments à qn sur qch ■ **complimentary** [-ˈmentərɪ] *adj* **a)** [praising] élogieux, -euse **b)** [free] gratuit ; **complimentary ticket** billet *m* de faveur

**comply** [kəmˈplaɪ] *(pt & pp -ied) vi* **to comply with** [order] obéir à ; [request] accéder à

**component** [kəmˈpəʊnənt] *n* [of structure, furniture] élément *m* ; [of machine] pièce *f*

**compose** [kəmˈpəʊz] *vt* composer ; **to compose oneself** se calmer ■ **composed** *adj* calme ■ **composer** *n* [of music] compositeur, -trice *mf* ■ **composition** [kɒmpəˈzɪʃən] *n* [in music, art, chemistry] composition *f*

**compost** [ˈkɒmpɒst] *n* compost *m*

**composure** [kəmˈpəʊʒə(r)] *n* sang-froid *m*

**compound 1.** [ˈkɒmpaʊnd] *n* [word & CHEM] [substance] composé *m* ; [area] enclos *m* **2.** *adj* [word, substance & FIN] [interest] composé

**comprehend** [kɒmprɪˈhend] *vt* comprendre

**comprehensive** [kɒmprɪˈhensɪv] **1.** *adj* complet, -ète ; [study] exhaustif, -ive ; [knowledge] étendu ; [insurance] tous risques *inv* **2.** *adj & n Br* **comprehensive (school)** ≃ établissement *m* d'enseignement secondaire *(n'opérant pas de sélection à l'entrée)*

**compress** [kəmˈpres] *vt* [gas, air] comprimer

**comprise** [kəmˈpraɪz] *vt* [consist of] comprendre ; [make up] constituer

**compromise** [ˈkɒmprəmaɪz] **1.** *n* compromis *m* **2.** *vt* [person, security] compromettre **3.** *vi* transiger (**on** sur)

**compulsion** [kəmˈpʌlʃən] *n* [urge] besoin *m* ; [obligation] contrainte *f* ■ **compulsive** *adj* [smoker, gambler, liar] invétéré

**compulsory** [kəmˈpʌlsərɪ] *adj* obligatoire

**computer** [kəmˈpjuːtə(r)] **1.** *n* ordinateur *m* **2.** *adj* [program, system, network] informatique ; [course, firm] d'informatique ; **computer game** jeu *m* électronique; **computer science** informatique *f* ■ **computerized** *adj* informatisé

**computing** [kəmˈpjuːtɪŋ] *n* informatique *f*

**con** [kɒn] *Fam* **1.** *n* arnaque *f* ; **con man** arnaqueur *m* **2.** *(pt & pp -nn-) vt* arnaquer; **to be conned** se faire arnaquer

**conceal** [kənˈsiːl] *vt* [hide - object] dissimuler (**from sb** à qn) ; [plan, news] cacher (**from sb** à qn)

**concede** [kənˈsiːd] **1.** *vt* concéder (**to** à ; **that** que) **2.** *vi* s'incliner

**conceited** [kənˈsiːtɪd] *adj* vaniteux, -euse

**conceive** [kənˈsiːv] **1.** *vt* [idea, child] concevoir **2.** *vi* [of woman] concevoir ; **to conceive of sth** concevoir qch ■ **conceivable** *adj* concevable ; **it's conceivable that…** il est concevable que… (+ *subjunctive*))

**concentrate** [ˈkɒnsəntreɪt] **1.** *vt* concentrer (**on** sur) **2.** *vi* se concentrer (**on** sur); **to concentrate on doing sth** s'appliquer à faire qch ■ **concentration** [-ˈtreɪʃən] *n* concentration *f*; **concentration camp** camp *m* de concentration

**concept** [ˈkɒnsept] *n* concept *m*

**concern** [kənˈsɜːn] **1.** *n* [matter] affaire *f* ; [worry] inquiétude *f* ; **his concern for** son souci de ; **(business) concern** entreprise *f* **2.** *vt* concerner ; **to be concerned about** [be worried] s'inquiéter de ; **as far as I'm concerned…** en ce qui me concerne… ■ **concerned** *adj* [anxious] inquiet, -ète (**about/at** au sujet de); **the person concerned** [in question] la personne dont il s'agit ; [involved] la personne concernée ■ **concerning** *prep* en ce qui concerne

**concert** [ˈkɒnsət] *n* concert *m*; **concert hall** salle *f* de concert

**concerto** [kən'tʃɜːtəʊ] *(pl* **-os)** *n* concerto *m* ; **piano concerto** concerto *m* pour piano

**concession** [kən'seʃən] *n* concession *f* **(to** à)

**conciliatory** [kən'sɪlɪətərɪ, *Am* -tɔːrɪ] *adj* [tone, person] conciliant

**concise** [kən'saɪs] *adj* concis

**conclude** [kən'kluːd] **1.** *vt* [end, settle] conclure ; **to conclude that...** [infer] conclure que... **2.** *vi* [of event] se terminer **(with** par) ; [of speaker] conclure ■ **conclusion** *n* conclusion *f* ■ **conclusive** *adj* concluant

**concoct** [kən'kɒkt] *vt* [dish, scheme] concocter ■ **concoction** *n* [dish, drink] mixture *f*

**concourse** ['kɒŋkɔːs] *n* [in airport, train station] hall *m*

**concrete** ['kɒŋkriːt] **1.** *n* béton *m* ; **concrete wall** mur *m* en béton **2.** *adj* [ideas, example] concret, -ète

**concur** [kən'kɜː(r)] *(pt & pp* -**rr**-) *vi* [agree] être d'accord **(with** avec)

**concurrently** [kən'kʌrəntlɪ] *adv* simultanément

**concussion** [kən'kʌʃən] *n* [injury] commotion *f* cérébrale

**condemn** [kən'dem] *vt* condamner **(to** à) ; [building] déclarer inhabitable

**condense** [kən'dens] *vt* condenser ■ **condensation** [kɒnden'seɪʃən] *n* [mist] buée *f*

**condescend** [kɒndɪ'send] *vi* condescendre **(to do** à faire)

**condition** [kən'dɪʃən] *n* [stipulation, circumstance] condition *f* ; [state] état *m*, condition *f* ; [disease] maladie *f* ; **on the condition that...** à la condition que... (+ *subjunctive*) ; **in good condition** en bon état ; **in/out of condition** en bonne /mauvaise forme ■ **conditional** *adj* conditionnel, -elle

**conditioner** [kən'dɪʃənə(r)] *n* (hair) conditioner après-shampooing *m*

**condo** ['kɒndəʊ] *(pl* -**os)** *Am n* = **condominium**

**condolences** [kən'dəʊlənsɪz] *npl* condoléances *fpl*

**condom** ['kɒndɒm] *n* préservatif *m*

**condominium** [kɒndə'mɪnɪəm] *n Am* [building] immeuble *m* en copropriété ; [apartment] appartement *m* en copropriété

**condone** [kən'dəʊn] *vt* [overlook] fermer les yeux sur ; [forgive] excuser

**conducive** [kən'djuːsɪv] *adj* **to be conducive to** être favorable à

**conduct 1.** ['kɒndʌkt] *n* [behaviour, directing] conduite *f* **2.** [kən'dʌkt] *vt* [campaign, inquiry, experiment] mener ; [orchestra] diriger ; [electricity, heat] conduire ; **to conduct oneself** se conduire ; **conducted tour** [of building, region] visite *f* guidée

**conductor** [kən'dʌktə(r)] *n* [of orchestra] chef *m*, d'orchestre ; *Br* [on bus] receveur *m* ; *Am* [on train] chef *m* de train

**cone** [kəʊn] *n* cône *m* ; [for ice cream] cornet *m* ; **pine** *or* **fir cone** pomme *f* de pin ; *Br* **traffic cone** cône de chantier

**confectionery** [kən'fekʃənərɪ] *n* [sweets] confiserie *f* ; [cakes] pâtisserie *f*

**confederation** [kənfedə'reɪʃən] *n* confédération *f*

**confer** [kən'fɜː(r)] *(pt & pp* -**rr**-) **1.** *vt* [grant] octroyer **(on** à) **2.** *vi* [talk together] se consulter **(on** *or* **about** sur) ; **to confer with sb** consulter qn

**conference** ['kɒnfərəns] *n* conférence *f* ; [scientific, academic] congrès *m* ; **press** *or* **news conference** conférence *f* de presse

**confess** [kən'fes] **1.** *vt* avouer, confesser **(that** que ; **to sb** à qn) ; REL confesser **2.** *vi* avouer ; REL se confesser ; **to confess to sth** [crime] avouer *ou* confesser qch ■ **confession** *n* aveu *m*, confession *f* ; REL confession *f* ; **to go to confession** aller à confesse

**confetti** [kən'fetɪ] *n* confettis *mpl*

**confide** [kən'faɪd] **1.** *vt* confier **(to** à ; **that** que) **2.** *vi* **to confide in sb** se confier à qn

**confidence** ['kɒnfɪdəns] *n* [trust] confiance *f* **(in** en) ; **(self-)confidence** confiance *f* en soi ; **in confidence** en confidence ; **confidence trick** escroquerie f ■ **confident** *adj* [smile, exterior] confiant; **(self-)confident** sûr de soi ■ **confidently** *adv* avec confiance

**confidential** [kɒnfɪ'denʃəl] *adj* confidentiel, -elle ■ **confidentially** *adv* en confidence

**configure** [kən'fɪgə] *vt* [gen & COMPUT] configurer

**confine** [kən'faɪn] *vt* a) [limit] limiter **(to** à); **to confine oneself to doing sth** se limiter à faire qch b) [keep prisoner] enfermer **(to / in** dans) ■ **confined** *adj* [space] réduit; **confined to bed** alité; **confined to one's room** obligé de garder la chambre

**confirm** [kən'fɜ:m] *vt* confirmer **(that** que) ■ **confirmation** [kɒnfə'meɪʃən] *n* [gen & REL] confirmation f ■ **confirmed** *adj* [bachelor] endurci; [smoker] invétéré

**confiscate** ['kɒnfɪskeɪt] *vt* confisquer **(from** à)

**conflict 1.** ['kɒnflɪkt] *n* conflit *m* **2.** [kən'flɪkt] *vi* [of statement] être en contradiction **(with** avec); [of dates, events, programmes] tomber en même temps **(with** que) ■ **conflicting** *adj* [views, theories, evidence] contradictoire; [dates] incompatible

**conform** [kən'fɔ:m] *vi* [of person] se conformer **(to** or **with** à); [of ideas, actions] être en conformité **(to** with); [of product] être conforme **(to** or **with** à)

**confront** [kən'frʌnt] *vt* [danger] affronter; [problem] faire face à; **to confront sb** [be face to face with] se trouver en face de qn; [oppose] s'opposer à qn; **to confront sb with sth** mettre qn en face de qch ■ **confrontation** [kɒnfrʌn'teɪʃən] *n* confrontation f

**confuse** [kən'fju:z] *vt* [make unsure] embrouiller; **to confuse sb / sth with** [mistake for] confondre qn / qch avec; **to confuse matters** or **the issue** embrouiller la question ■ **confused** *adj* [situation, noises, idea] confus; **to get confused** s'embrouiller ■ **confusing** *adj* déroutant ■ **confusion** [-ʒən] *n* [bewilderment] perplexité f; [disorder, lack of clarity] confusion f

**congested** [kən'dʒestɪd] *adj* [street, town, lungs] congestionné; [nose] bouché ■ **congestion** [-tʃən] *n* [traffic] encombrements *mpl*; [overcrowding] surpeuplement *m*; Br **congestion zone** *zone du centre et autour du centre de Londres où la circulation est payante*

**congratulate** [kən'grætʃuleɪt] *vt* féliciter **(sb on sth** qn de qch; **sb on doing sth** qn d'avoir fait qch) ■ **congratulations** [-'leɪʃənz] *npl* félicitations *fpl* **(on** pour)

**congregate** ['kɒŋgrɪgeɪt] *vi* se rassembler ■ **congregation** [-'geɪʃən] *n* [worshippers] fidèles *mpl*

**Congress** ['kɒŋgres] *n* Am POL le Congrès *(assemblée législative américaine)*

**conifer** ['kɒnɪfə(r)] *n* conifère *m*

**conjunction** [kən'dʒʌŋkʃən] *n* in conjunction with conjointement avec

**connect** [kə'nekt] **1.** *vt* relier **(with** or to à); [telephone, washing machine] brancher; **to connect sb with sb** [on phone] mettre qn en communication avec qn; **to connect sth / sth with sth** établir un lien entre qn / qch et qn / qch **2.** *vi* to **connect with** [of train, bus] assurer la correspondance avec ■ **connected** *adj* [facts, events] lié; **to be connected with** [have to do with, relate to] avoir un lien avec

**connection** [kə'nekʃən] *n* [link] rapport *m*, lien *m* **(with** avec); [train, bus] correspondance f; [phone call] communication f; [between electrical wires] contact *m*; **connections** [contacts] relations *fpl*; **to have no connection with** n'avoir aucun rapport avec; **in connection with** à propos de

**connive** [kə'naɪv] *vi* **to connive with sb** être de connivence avec qn

**connoisseur** [kɒnə's3:(r)] *n* connaisseur *m*

**connotation** [kɒnə'teɪʃən] *n* connotation f

**conquer** ['kɒŋkə(r)] *vt* [country] conquérir; [enemy, habit, difficulty] vaincre ■ **conquest** *n* conquête f

**cons** [kɒnz] *npl* **the pros and (the) cons** le pour et le contre

**conscience** ['kɒnʃəns] *n* conscience *f*; **to have sth on one's conscience** avoir qch sur la conscience

**conscientious** [kɒnʃɪ'enʃəs] *adj* consciencieux, -euse; **conscientious objector** objecteur *m* de conscience

**conscious** ['kɒnʃəs] *adj* [awake] conscient; **to make a conscious effort to do sth** faire un effort particulier pour faire qch; **conscious of sth** [aware] conscient de qch ▪ **consciously** *adv* [knowingly] consciemment ▪ **consciousness** *n* **to lose / regain consciousness** perdre / reprendre connaissance

**conscript 1.** ['kɒnskrɪpt] *n* [soldier] conscrit *m* **2.** [kən'skrɪpt] *vt* enrôler ▪ **conscription** [kən'skrɪpʃən] *n* conscription *f*

**consecutive** [kən'sekjʊtɪv] *adj* consécutif, -ive

**consensus** [kən'sensəs] *n* consensus *m*

**consent** [kən'sent] **1.** *n* consentement *m* **2.** *vi* consentir (**to** à)

**consequence** ['kɒnsɪkwəns] *n* [result] conséquence *f* ▪ **consequently** *adv* par conséquent

**conservative** [kən'sɜːvətɪv] **1.** *adj* [estimate] modeste; [view, attitude] traditionnel, -elle; [person] traditionaliste; *Br* POL conservateur, -trice **2.** *n* *Br* POL conservateur, -trice *mf*

**conservatory** [kən'sɜːvətrɪ] (*pl* -ies) *n* *Br* [room] véranda *f*

**conserve** [kən'sɜːv] *vt* [energy, water, electricity] faire des économies de ▪ **conservation** [kɒnsə'veɪʃən] *n* [of energy] économies *fpl*; [of nature] protection *f* de l'environnement

**consider** [kən'sɪdə(r)] *vt* [think over] considérer; [take into account] tenir compte de; [an offer] étudier; **to consider doing sth** envisager de faire qch; **to consider that...** considérer que...; **I consider her (as) a friend** je la considère comme une amie; **all things considered** tout bien considéré

**considerable** [kən'sɪdərəbəl] *adj* [large] considérable; [much] beaucoup de ▪ **considerably** *adv* considérablement

**considerate** [kən'sɪdərət] *adj* attentionné (**to** à l'égard de)

**consideration** [kənsɪdə'reɪʃən] *n* considération *f*; **to take sth into consideration** prendre qch en considération

**considering** [kən'sɪdərɪŋ] **1.** *prep* étant donné **2.** *conj* **considering (that)** étant donné que

**consignment** [kən'saɪnmənt] *n* [goods] envoi *m*

**consist** [kən'sɪst] *vi* consister (**of** en; **in** en; **in doing** à faire)

**consistent** [kən'sɪstənt] *adj* [unchanging - quality, results] constant ▪ **consistency** *n* [of substance, liquid] consistance *f* ▪ **consistently** *adv* [always] constamment; [regularly] régulièrement

**console¹** [kən'səʊl] *vt* consoler ▪ **consolation** *n* consolation *f*; **consolation prize** lot *m* de consolation

**console²** ['kɒnsəʊl] *n* [control desk] console *f*

**consolidate** [kən'sɒlɪdeɪt] *vt* consolider

**consonant** ['kɒnsənənt] *n* consonne *f*

**conspicuous** [kən'spɪkjʊəs] *adj* [noticeable] bien visible; [striking] manifeste; [showy] voyant

**conspiracy** [kən'spɪrəsɪ] (*pl* -ies) *n* conspiration *f*

**conspire** [kən'spaɪə(r)] *vi* conspirer (**against** contre); **to conspire to do sth** comploter de faire qch

**constable** ['kʌnstəbəl] *n* *Br* **(police) constable** agent *m* de police

**constant** ['kɒnstənt] *adj* [frequent] incessant; [unchanging] constant ▪ **constantly** *adv* constamment, sans cesse

**constellation** [kɒnstə'leɪʃən] *n* constellation *f*

**constipated** ['kɒnstɪpeɪtɪd] *adj* constipé

**constituent** [kən'stɪtjuənt] n POL [voter] électeur, -trice mf ▪ **constituency** (pl -ies) n circonscription f électorale ; [voters] électeurs mpl

**constitute** ['kɒnstɪtjuːt] vt constituer ▪ **constitution** n constitution f

**constraint** [kən'streɪnt] n contrainte f

**construct** [kən'strʌkt] vt construire ▪ **construction** n [building, structure, in grammar] construction f ; **under construction** en construction ; **construction site** chantier m ▪ **constructive** adj constructif, -ive

**consul** ['kɒnsəl] n consul m ▪ **consulate** [-sjʊlət] n consulat m

**consult** [kən'sʌlt] 1. vt consulter 2. vi to consult with sb discuter avec qn ; **consulting fee** honoraires mpl d'expert ; Br **consulting room** [of doctor] cabinet m de consultation ▪ **consultation** [kɒnsəl'teɪʃən] n consultation f

**consultancy** [kən'sʌltənsɪ] (pl -ies) n **consultancy (firm)** cabinet-conseil m ▪ **consultant** n Br [doctor] spécialiste mf ; [adviser] consultant m

**consume** [kən'sjuːm] vt [food, supplies] consommer ; [of fire] consumer ; [of grief, hate] dévorer ▪ **consumer** n consommateur, -trice mf ▪ **consumption** [-'sʌmpʃən] n consommation f

**contact** ['kɒntækt] 1. n [act of touching] contact m ; [person] relation f ; **in contact with** en contact avec ; **contact lenses** lentilles fpl de contact 2. vt contacter

**contagious** [kən'teɪdʒəs] adj [disease] contagieux, -euse

**contain** [kən'teɪn] vt [enclose, hold back] contenir ▪ **container** n [box, jar] récipient m ; [for transporting goods] conteneur m

**contaminate** [kən'tæmɪneɪt] vt contaminer

**contemplate** ['kɒntəmpleɪt] vt [look at] contempler ; [consider] envisager (**doing** de faire)

**contemporary** [kən'tempərərɪ] 1. adj contemporain (**with** de) ; [style] moderne 2. (pl -ies) n [person] contemporain, -e mf

**contempt** [kən'tempt] n mépris m ; **to hold sb/sth in contempt** mépriser qn/qch ▪ **contemptible** adj méprisable ▪ **contemptuous** adj méprisant ; **to be contemptuous of sth** mépriser qch

**contend** [kən'tend] vi **to contend with** [problem] faire face à ▪ **contender** n [in sport] concurrent, -e mf ; [in election, for job] candidat, -e mf

**content¹** [kən'tent] adj [happy] satisfait (**with** de) ▪ **contented** adj satisfait ▪ **contentment** n contentement m

**content²** ['kɒntent] n [of book, text, film - subject matter] contenu m ; **contents** contenu m ; [in book] table f des matières ; **alcoholic/iron content** teneur f en alcool/fer

**contest 1.** ['kɒntest] n [competition] concours m ; [fight] lutte f ; [in boxing] combat m **2.** [kən'test] vt [dispute] contester ▪ **contestant** [kən'testənt] n concurrent, -e mf ; [in fight] adversaire mf

**context** ['kɒntekst] n contexte m ; **in/out of context** en/hors contexte ▪ **context-sensitive** adj COMPUT contextuel, -elle

**continent** ['kɒntɪnənt] n continent m ; **the Continent** l'Europe f continentale ; **on the Continent** en Europe ▪ **continental** [-'nentəl] adj [of Europe] européen, -enne ; **continental breakfast** petit déjeuner m à la française

**contingent** [kən'tɪndʒənt] n [group] contingent m ▪ **contingency** (pl -ies) n éventualité f ; **contingency plan** plan m d'urgence

**continual** [kən'tɪnjʊəl] adj continuel, -elle

**continue** [kən'tɪnjuː] 1. vt continuer (**to do** or **doing** à ou de faire) ; **to continue (with)** [work, speech] poursuivre ; [resume] reprendre 2. vi continuer ; [resume] reprendre

**continuous** [kən'tɪnjʊəs] adj continu ; SCH & UNIV **continuous assessment** contrôle m continu des connaissances ▪ **continuously** adv sans interruption

**contour** ['kɒntʊə(r)] n contour m
**contraception** [kɒntrə'sepʃən] n contraception f ■ **contraceptive** n contraceptif m
**contract**[1] ['kɒntrækt] **1.** n contrat m; **to be under contract** être sous contrat; **contract work** travail m en sous-traitance **2.** vt **to contract work out** sous-traiter du travail ■ **contractor** n entrepreneur m
**contract**[2] [kən'trækt] **1.** vt [illness] contracter **2.** vi [shrink] se contracter
**contradict** [kɒntrə'dɪkt] vt [person, statement] contredire; [deny] démentir; **to contradict oneself** se contredire ■ **contradictory** adj contradictoire
**contraption** [kən'træpʃən] n Fam machin m
**contrary** ['kɒntrərɪ] **1.** adj [opposite] contraire (**to** à) **2.** adv **contrary to** contrairement à **3.** n contraire m; **on the contrary** au contraire; **unless you/I/etc hear to the contrary** sauf avis contraire
**contrast 1.** ['kɒntrɑːst] n contraste m; **in contrast to** par opposition à **2.** [kən'trɑːst] vt mettre en contraste **3.** [kən'trɑːst] vi contraster (**with** avec)
**contravention** [kɒntrə'venʃən] n **in contravention of a treaty** en violation d'un traité
**contribute** [kən'trɪbjuːt] **1.** vt [time, clothes] donner (**to** à); [article] écrire (**to** pour); **to contribute money to** verser de l'argent à **2.** vi **to contribute to** contribuer à; [publication] collaborer à; [discussion] prendre part à; [charity] donner à ■ **contribution** [kɒntrɪ'bjuːʃən] n contribution f ■ **contributor** n [to newspaper] collaborateur, -trice mf; [of money] donateur, -trice mf
**contrive** [kən'traɪv] vt **to contrive to do sth** trouver moyen de faire qch
**contrived** [kən'traɪvd] adj qui manque de naturel
**control** [kən'trəʊl] **1.** n contrôle m; [authority] autorité f (**over** sur); (**self**)**control** la maîtrise (de soi); **the situation or everything is under control** je/il/etc contrôle la situation; **to lose control of** [situation, vehicle] perdre le contrôle de; **out of control** [situation, crowd] difficilement maîtrisable; COMPUT **control key** touche f de contrôle; **control panel** tableau m de bord **2.** (pt & pp -ll-)vt [business, organization] diriger; [prices, quality] contrôler; [emotion, reaction] maîtriser; [disease] enrayer; **to control oneself** se contrôler
**controversy** ['kɒntrəvɜːsɪ] (pl -ies) n controverse f ■ **controversial** [-'vɜːʃəl] adj controversé
**convalesce** [kɒnvə'les] vi [rest] être en convalescence
**convenience** [kən'viːnɪəns] n commodité f; Br (**public**) **conveniences** toilettes fpl; **convenience food(s)** plats mpl tout préparés; **convenience store** magasin m de proximité
**convenient** [kən'viːnɪənt] adj commode, pratique; **to be convenient (for)** [suit] convenir (à) ■ **conveniently** adv **conveniently situated** bien situé
**convention** [kən'venʃən] n [custom] usage m; [agreement] convention f; [conference] convention f, congrès m ■ **conventional** adj conventionnel, -elle
**converge** [kən'vɜːdʒ] vi converger (**on** sur)
**conversation** [kɒnvə'seɪʃən] n conversation f (**with** avec)
**convert 1.** [kən'vɜːt] [kɒnvɜːt] n converti, -e mf **2.** vt [change] convertir (**into** or **to** en); [building] aménager (**into, to** en); REL **to convert sb** convertir qn (**to** à) **3.** vi [change religion] se convertir (**to** à) ■ **conversion** n conversion f; [of building] aménagement m
**convertible** [kən'vɜːtəbəl] **1.** adj [sofa] convertible **2.** n [car] décapotable f
**convey** [kən'veɪ] vt [transport] transporter; [communicate] transmettre ■ **conveyor belt** n tapis m roulant
**convict 1.** ['kɒnvɪkt] n détenu m **2.** [kən'vɪkt] vt déclarer coupable (**of** de) ■ **conviction** [kən'vɪkʃən] n [for crime] condamnation f; [belief] conviction f (**that** que)

**convince** [kən'vɪns] *vt* convaincre (**of sth** de qch; **sb to do sth** qn de faire qch) ■ **convincing** *adj* [argument, person] convaincant

**convoy** ['kɒnvɔɪ] *n* convoi *m*

**cook** [kʊk] **1.** *n* [person] cuisinier, -ère *mf* **2.** *vt* [meal] préparer; [food] (faire) cuire **3.** *vi* [of food] cuire; [of person] faire la cuisine ■ **cookbook** *n* livre *m* de cuisine ■ **cooker** *n Br* [stove] cuisinière *f* ■ **cookery** *n* cuisine *f*; *Br* **cookery book** livre *m* de cuisine ■ **cooking** *n* [activity, food] cuisine *f*; [process] cuisson *f*; **to do the cooking** faire la cuisine; **cooking apple** pomme *f* à cuire

**cookie** ['kʊkɪ] *n* **a)** *Am* [biscuit] biscuit *m*, gâteau *m* sec **b)** COMPUT cookie *m*

**cool** [kuːl] **1.** *(compar* -er, *superl* -est) *adj* [weather, place, wind] frais (*f* fraîche); [tea, soup] tiède; [calm] calme; [unfriendly] froid; *Fam* [good] cool *inv*; *Fam* [fashionable] branché; **a (nice) cool drink** une boisson (bien) fraîche; **the weather is cool, it's cool** il fait frais; **to keep sth cool** tenir qch au frais **2.** *n* **to keep/lose one's cool** garder/perdre son sang-froid **3.** *vt* **to cool (down)** refroidir, rafraîchir **4.** *vi* **to cool (down** *or* **off)** [of hot liquid] refroidir; [of enthusiasm] se refroidir; [of angry person] se calmer; **to cool off** [by drinking, swimming] se rafraîchir ■ **cooler** *n* [for food] glacière *f*

**coop** [kuːp] *vt* **to coop up** [person, animal] enfermer

**co-op** ['kəʊɒp] *n* coopérative *f*

**cooperate** [kəʊ'ɒpəreɪt] *vi* coopérer (**in** à; **with** avec) ■ **cooperation** *n* coopération *f*

**coordinate** [kəʊ'ɔːdɪneɪt] *vt* coordonner ■ **coordination** [-'neɪʃən] *n* coordination *f*

**cop** [kɒp] *n Fam* [policeman] flic *m*

**coparenting** *n* coparentalité *f*

**cope** [kəʊp] *vi* **to cope with** [problem, demand] faire face à

**copier** ['kɒpɪə(r)] *n* [photocopier] photocopieuse *f*

**copper** ['kɒpə(r)] *n* [metal] cuivre *m*; *Br* **coppers** [coins] petite monnaie *f*

**copy** ['kɒpɪ] **1.** *(pl* -**ies**) *n* [of letter, document] copie *f*; [of book, magazine] exemplaire *m*; [of photo] épreuve *f* **2.** *(pt & pp* -**ied**) *vt* copier; **to copy out** *or* **down** [text, letter] copier **3.** *vi* copier

**coral** ['kɒrəl] *n* corail *m*

**cord** [kɔːd] *n* **a)** [of curtain, bell, pyjamas] cordon *m*; [electrical] cordon électrique **b) cords** [trousers] pantalon *m* en velours côtelé

**cordial** ['kɔːdɪəl] **1.** *adj* [friendly] cordial **2.** *n Br* **(fruit) cordial** sirop *m*

**cordless** ['kɔːdləs] *adj* **cordless phone** téléphone *m* sans fil

**cordon** ['kɔːdən] **1.** *n* cordon *m* **2.** *vt* **to cordon off** [road] barrer; [area] boucler

**corduroy** ['kɔːdərɔɪ] *n* velours *m* côtelé

**core** [kɔː(r)] *n* [of apple] trognon *m*; [of problem] cœur *m*; [group of people] noyau *m*

**cork** [kɔːk] **1.** *n* [material] liège *m*; [stopper] bouchon *m* **2.** *vt* [bottle] boucher ■ **corkscrew** *n* tire-bouchon *m*

**corn¹** [kɔːn] *n Br* [wheat] blé *m*; *Am* [maize] maïs *m*; **corn on the cob** maïs *m* en épi, *Can* blé *m* en Inde

**corn²** [kɔːn] *n* [on foot] cor *m*; *Am* **corn dog** saucisse enrobée de pâte à la farine de maïs et frite à l'huile

**cornbread** ['kɔːnbred] *n Am* pain *m* à la farine de maïs

**corner** ['kɔːnə(r)] **1.** *n* [of street, room, page, screen] coin *m*; [bend in road] virage *m*; [in football] corner *m*; **it's just round the corner** c'est juste au coin; **corner shop** épicerie *f* du coin **2.** *vt* [person, animal] acculer

**cornet** ['kɔːnɪt] *n Br* [of ice cream] cornet *m*

**cornfed** ['kɔːnfed] *adj Am Fam* rustre; **it's about a cornfed girl who makes it big in Manhattan** c'est l'histoire d'une fille de la campagne qui réussit à Manhattan

**cornflakes** ['kɔːnfleɪks] *npl* corn flakes *mpl*

**cornstarch** ['kɔːnstɑːʃ] *n* fécule *f* de maïs

**corny** ['kɔːnɪ] *(compar* -ier, *superl* -iest) *adj Fam* [joke] nul (*f* nulle) ; [film] tarte

**coronary** ['kɒrənərɪ] *(pl* -ies) *n* MED infarctus *m*

**coronation** [kɒrə'neɪʃən] *n* couronnement *m*

**corporal**[1] ['kɔːpərəl] *n* [in army] caporal-chef *m*

**corporal**[2] ['kɔːpərəl] *adj* **corporal punishment** châtiment *m* corporel

**corporate** ['kɔːpərət] *adj* [decision] collectif, -ive

**corporation** [kɔːpə'reɪʃən] *n* [business] société *f*

**corps** [kɔː(r)] *(pl* [kɔːz]) *n inv* MIL & POL corps *m* ; **the press corps** les journalistes *mpl*

**corpse** [kɔːps] *n* cadavre *m*

**correct** [kə'rekt] **1.** *adj* [accurate] exact ; [proper] correct ; **he's correct** il a raison ; **the correct time** l'heure exacte **2.** *vt* corriger ■ **correction** *n* correction *f*

**correspond** [kɒrɪ'spɒnd] *vi* correspondre ■ **corresponding** *adj* [matching] correspondant ; [similar] semblable

**correspondence** [kɒrɪ'spɒndəns] *n* correspondance *f* ; **correspondence course** cours *m* par correspondance

**corridor** ['kɒrɪdɔː(r)] *n* couloir *m*, corridor *m*

**corrosion** [kə'rəʊʒən] *n* corrosion *f*

**corrugated** ['kɒrəgeɪtɪd] *adj* ondulé

**corrupt** [kə'rʌpt] **1.** *adj* [gen & COMPUT] corrompu **2.** *vt* corrompre ■ **corruption** *n* corruption *f*

**Corsica** ['kɔːsɪkə] *n* la Corse

**cos** [kɒs] *n Br* **cos (lettuce)** (laitue *f*) romaine *f*

**cosmetic** [kɒz'metɪk] **1.** *adj* **cosmetic surgery** chirurgie *f* esthétique **2.** *n* produit *m* de beauté

**cosmopolitan** [kɒzmə'pɒlɪtən] *adj* cosmopolite

**cost** [kɒst] **1.** *n* coût *m* ; **the cost of living** le coût de la vie ; **at any cost, at all costs** à tout prix **2.** *(pt & pp cost) vti* a) coûter ; **how much does it cost?** ça coûte combien ? ; **it cost me £10** ça m'a coûté 10 livres b) *(pt & pp* -ed) COMM [estimate] évaluer le coût de ■ **costly** *(compar* -ier, *superl* -iest) *adj* [expensive - car, trip] coûteux, -euse

**costume** ['kɒstjuːm] *n* costume *m* ; *Br* **(swimming) costume** maillot *m* de bain

**cosy** ['kəʊzɪ] **1.** *(compar* -ier, *superl* -iest) *adj Br* [house] douillet, -ette ; [atmosphere] intime **2.** *n* **(tea) cosy** couvre-théière *m*

**cot** [kɒt] *n Br* [for child] lit *m* d'enfant ; *Am* [camp bed] lit *m* de camp

**cottage** ['kɒtɪdʒ] *n* petite maison *f* de campagne ; **(thatched) cottage** chaumière *f* ; **cottage cheese** fromage *m* blanc (maigre)

**cotton** ['kɒtən] *n* coton *m* ; [yarn] fil *m* de coton ; *Br* **cotton wool,** *Am* **absorbent cotton** coton *m* hydrophile, ouate *f* ; **cotton shirt** chemise *f* en coton ; *Am* **cotton candy** barbe *f* à papa

**couch** [kaʊtʃ] *n* [sofa] canapé *m* ; [for doctor's patient] lit *m*

**couchette** [kuː'ʃet] *n Br* [on train] couchette *f*

**cough** [kɒf] **1.** *n* toux *f* ; **cough syrup** *or* **medicine,** *Br* **cough mixture** sirop *m* pour la toux **2.** *vt* **to cough up** [blood] cracher **3.** *vi* tousser

**could** [kʊd] *(unstressed* [kəd]) *pt of* **can**

**couldn't** ['kʊdənt] = **could not**

**council** ['kaʊnsəl] *n* **(town /city) council** conseil *m* municipal ; *Br* **council flat / house** ≃ HLM *f* ; *Br* **council tax** *impôt regroupant taxe d'habitation et impôts locaux* ■ **councillor** *n* **(town) councillor** conseiller *m* municipal

**counselling,** *Am* **counseling** ['kaʊnsəlɪŋ] *n* assistance *f* psychosociale

**count**[1] [kaʊnt] **1.** *n* [calculation] compte *m* ; **to keep count of sth** tenir le compte de qch **2.** *vt* [find number of, include] compter ; [consider] considérer ; **count me in!** j'en suis ! ; **count me out!**

ne compte pas sur moi ! **3.** *vi* compter; **to count against sb** jouer contre qn; **to count on sb/sth** [rely on] compter sur qn/qch; **to count on doing sth** compter faire qch ■ **countdown** *n* compte *m* à rebours

**count²** [kaʊnt] *n* [title] comte *m*

**counter** ['kaʊntə(r)] **1.** *n* a) [in shop, bar] comptoir *m*; [in bank] guichet *m* b) [in games] jeton *m* c) [counting device] compteur *m* **2.** *adv* counter to contrairement à **3.** *vt* [threat] répondre à; [effects] neutraliser **4.** *vi* riposter (**with** par)

**counter-** ['kaʊntə(r)] *pref* contre-

**counterattack** ['kaʊntərətæk] **1.** *n* contre-attaque *f* **2.** *vti* contre-attaquer

**counterclockwise** [kaʊntə'klɒkwaɪz] *adj* & *adv* Am dans le sens inverse des aiguilles d'une montre

**counterfeit** ['kaʊntəfɪt] **1.** *adj* faux (*f* fausse) **2.** *vt* contrefaire

**counterpart** ['kaʊntəpɑːt] *n* [thing] équivalent *m*; [person] homologue *mf*

**countless** ['kaʊntlɪs] *adj* innombrable

**country** ['kʌntrɪ] (*pl* **-ies**) **1.** *n* pays *m*; [opposed to town] campagne *f*; **in the country** à la campagne **2.** *adj* [house, road] de campagne; **country and western music** country *f* ■ **countryman** (*pl* **-men**) *n* (fellow) **countryman** compatriote *m* ■ **countryside** *n* campagne *f*; **in the countryside** à la campagne

**county** ['kaʊntɪ] (*pl* **-ies**) *n* comté *m*

**coup** [kuː] (*pl* [kuːz]) *n* POL coup *m* d'État

**couple** ['kʌpəl] **1.** *n* [of people] couple *m*; **a couple of** deux ou trois; [a few] quelques **2.** *vt* [connect] accoupler

**coupon** ['kuːpɒn] *n* [for discount] bon *m*; [form] coupon *m*

**courage** ['kʌrɪdʒ] *n* courage *m* ■ **courageous** [kə'reɪdʒəs] *adj* courageux, -euse

**courgette** [kʊə'ʒet] *n* Br courgette *f*

**courier** ['kʊrɪə(r)] *n* [for tourists] guide *mf*; [messenger] messager *m*

**course** [kɔːs] **1.** *n* a) [of river, time, events] cours *m*; [of ship] route *f*;

**course of action** ligne *f* de conduite; **in the course of** au cours de; **in due course** en temps utile b) [lessons] cours *m* c) MED **course of treatment** traitement *m* d) [of meal] plat *m*; **first course** entrée *f* e) [for race] parcours *m*; [for horseracing] champ *m* de courses; [for golf] terrain *m* **2.** *adv* **of course!** bien sûr !; **of course not!** bien sûr que non !

**court¹** [kɔːt] *n* [of king] cour *f*; [for trials] cour *f*, tribunal *m*; [for tennis] court *m*; **to go to court** aller en justice; **to take sb to court** poursuivre qn en justice ■ **courthouse** *n* Am palais *m* de justice ■ **courtroom** *n* JUR salle *f* d'audience ■ **courtyard** *n* cour *f*

**court²** [kɔːt] **1.** *vt* [woman] faire la cour à; [danger] aller au-devant de **2.** *vi* to **be courting** [of couple] se fréquenter

**courteous** ['kɜːtɪəs] *adj* poli, courtois ■ **courtesy** [-təsɪ] (*pl* **-ies**) *n* politesse *f*, courtoisie *f*; **courtesy car** voiture mise à la disposition d'un client par un hôtel, un garage etc; **courtesy coach** navette *f* gratuite

**cousin** ['kʌzən] *n* cousin, -e *mf*

**cover** ['kʌvə(r)] **1.** *n* [lid] couvercle *m*; [of book] couverture *f*; [for furniture, typewriter] housse *f*; **to take cover** se mettre à l'abri; **under cover** [sheltered] à l'abri; **cover charge** [in restaurant] couvert *m* **2.** *vt* couvrir (**with** or **in** de); [include] englober; [treat] traiter; [distance] parcourir; [event - in newspaper, on TV] couvrir; [insure] assurer (**against** contre); **to cover up** recouvrir; [truth, tracks] dissimuler; [scandal] étouffer **3.** *vi* to **cover for sb** [of colleague] remplacer qn; **to cover up for sb** cacher la vérité pour protéger qn ■ **cover-up** *n* there was a cover-up on a étouffé l'affaire

**coverage** ['kʌvərɪdʒ] *n* [on TV, in newspaper] couverture *f* médiatique

**coveralls** ['kʌvərɔːlz] *n* bleu *m* de travail

**covering** ['kʌvərɪŋ] *n* [wrapping] enveloppe *f*; [layer] couche *f*; **covering letter** lettre *f* jointe

**cow** [kaʊ] *n* vache *f*; *v Fam* [nasty woman] peau *f* de vache ▪ **cowboy** *n* cowboy *m*; *BrFam & Pej* [workman] rigolo *m*

**coward** ['kaʊəd] *n* lâche *mf*

**cower** ['kaʊə(r)] *vi* [with fear] trembler

**COZ** MESSAGING *written abbr of* **because**

**cozy** ['kəʊzɪ] *Am adj* = **cosy**

**crab** [kræb] *n* [crustacean] crabe *m*

**crack**[1] [kræk] **1.** *n* [split] fente *f*; [in glass, china, bone] fêlure *f*; [noise] craquement *m* **2.** *vt* [glass, ice] fêler; [nut] casser; [whip] faire claquer; [problem] résoudre; [code] déchiffrer; *Fam* [joke] raconter **3.** *vi* se fêler; [of branch, wood] craquer; **to crack down on** prendre des mesures énergiques en matière de

**crack**[2] [kræk] *adj* [first-rate - driver, skier] d'élite; **crack shot** fin tireur *m*

**crack**[3] [kræk] *n* [drug] crack *m*

**cracker** ['krækə(r)] *n* **a)** [biscuit] biscuit *m* salé **b)** [firework] pétard *m*; **Christmas cracker** diablotin *m*

**crackle** ['krækəl] *vi* [of fire] crépiter; [of frying] grésiller; [of radio] crachoter

**cradle** ['kreɪdəl] **1.** *n* berceau *m* **2.** *vt* bercer

**craft** [krɑːft] **1.** *n* [skill] art *m*; [job] métier *m* **2.** *vt* façonner ▪ **craftsman** (*pl* **-men**) *n* artisan *m* ▪ **craftsmanship** *n* [skill] art *m*

**crafty** ['krɑːftɪ] (*compar* **-ier**, *superl* **-iest**) *adj* astucieux, -euse; *Pej* rusé

**cram** [kræm] (*pt & pp* **-mm-**) **1.** *vt* **to cram sth into** [force] fourrer qch dans; **to cram with** [fill] bourrer de **2.** *vi* **to cram into** [of people] s'entasser dans; **to cram (for an exam)** bûcher; *Am* SCH **cram school** école privée spécialisée dans le bachotage pour les examens

**cramp** [kræmp] *n* [pain] crampe *f* (**in** à)

**cramped** [kræmpt] *adj* [surroundings] exigu (*f* exiguë)

**crane** [kreɪn] **1.** *n* [machine, bird] grue *f* **2.** *vt* **to crane one's neck** tendre le cou

**crank**[1] [kræŋk] *n* [handle] manivelle *f*

**crank**[2] [kræŋk] *n Fam* [person] excentrique *mf*; [fanatic] fanatique *mf*

**crap** [kræp] *n v Fam* merde *f*; **it's a load of crap** tout ça, c'est des conneries

**crapfest** ['kræpfest] *n v Fam* fête, réunion ou événement très mal organisé; **it was a crapfest** c'était archinul

**crapware** ['kræpweə(r)] *n v Fam* logiciels *mpl* inutiles

**crash** [kræʃ] **1.** *n* [accident] accident *m*; [collapse of firm] faillite *f*; [noise] fracas *m*; COMPUT panne *f*; **crash course / diet** cours *m* / régime *m* intensif; **crash barrier** [on road] glissière *f* de sécurité; **crash helmet** casque *m*; **crash landing** atterrissage *m* en catastrophe **2.** *excl* [of fallen object] patatras! **3.** *vt* [car] avoir un accident avec; **to crash one's car into sth** rentrer dans qch (avec sa voiture) **4.** *vi* **a)** [of car, plane] s'écraser; **to crash into** rentrer dans **b)** COMPUT tomber en panne

**crate** [kreɪt] *n* [large] caisse *f*; [small] cageot *m*; [for bottles] casier *m*

**crater** ['kreɪtə(r)] *n* cratère *m*; **(bomb) crater** entonnoir *m*

**craving** ['kreɪvɪŋ] *n* envie *f* (**for** de)

**crawl** [krɔːl] **1.** *n* [swimming stroke] crawl *m* **2.** *vi* [of snake, animal] ramper; [of child] marcher à quatre pattes; [of vehicle] avancer au pas; **to be crawling with** grouiller de

**crayon** ['kreɪən] *n* [wax] crayon *m* gras

**craze** [kreɪz] *n* engouement *m* (**for** pour)

**crazy** ['kreɪzɪ] (*compar* **-ier**, *superl* **-iest**) *adj* fou (*f* folle) (**about** de); **to drive sb crazy** rendre qn fou; **to run / work like crazy** courir / travailler comme un fou

**creak** [kriːk] *vi* [of hinge] grincer; [of floor, timber] craquer

**cream** [kriːm] *n* [of milk, lotion] crème *f*; **cream of tomato soup** crème *f* de tomates; **cream cake** gâteau *m* à la crème; **cream cheese** fromage *m* à tartiner

**creamy** ['kriːmɪ] (*compar* **-ier**, *superl* **-iest**) *adj* crémeux, -euse

**crease** [kriːs] **1.** *n* pli *m* **2.** *vt* froisser **3.** *vi* se froisser

**crook**

**create** [kriː'eɪt] *vt* créer ■ **creation** *n* création *f* ■ **creative** *adj* [person, activity] créatif, -ive ■ **creator** *n* créateur, -trice *mf*

**creature** ['kriːtʃə(r)] *n* [animal] bête *f*; [person] créature *f*

**crèche** [kreʃ] *n Br* [nursery] crèche *f*

**credentials** [krɪ'denʃəlz] *npl* [proof of ability] références *fpl*

**credible** ['kredɪbəl] *adj* crédible ■ **credibility** *n* crédibilité *f*

**credit** ['kredɪt] **1.** *n* [financial] crédit *m*; [merit] mérite *m*; [from university] unité *f* de valeur; **credits** [of film] générique *m*; **to buy sth on credit** acheter qch à crédit; **to be in credit** [of account] être créditeur; [of person] avoir un solde positif; **to her credit, she refused** c'est tout à son honneur d'avoir refusé; **credit card** carte *f* de crédit; **credit crunch** crise *f* du crédit **2.** *vt* [of bank] créditer (**sb with sth** qn de qch); [believe] croire

**credulous** ['kredjʊləs] *adj* crédule

**creek** [kriːk] *n* [bay] crique *f*; *Am* [stream] ruisseau *m*

**creep** [kriːp] **1.** *n Fam* **it gives me the creeps** ça me fait froid dans le dos **2.** *(pt & pp* **crept)** *vi* ramper; [silently] se glisser (furtivement); [slowly] avancer lentement ■ **creepy** *(compar* **-ier,** *superl* **-iest)** *adj Fam* sinistre ■ **creepy-crawly** *n Fam* bestiole *f* qui rampe

**cremate** [krɪ'meɪt] *vt* incinérer ■ **cremation** *n* crémation *f*

**crematorium** [kremə'tɔːriəm] *(pl* **-ia** [-ɪə]*), Am* **crematory** ['kriːmətɔːrɪ] *n* crématorium *m*

**crept** [krept] *pt & pp of* **creep**

**crescent** ['kresənt] *n* [shape] croissant *m*; *Br Fig* [street] rue *f* en demi-lune

**crest** [krest] *n* [of wave, mountain, bird] crête *f*; [of hill] sommet *m*; [on seal, letters] armoiries *fpl*

**Crete** [kriːt] *n* la Crète

**crevice** ['krevɪs] *n* [crack] fente *f*

**crew** [kruː] *n* [of ship, plane] équipage *m*; *Fam* [gang] équipe *f*; **crew cut** coupe *f* en brosse

**crib** [krɪb] **1.** *n Am* [cot] lit *m* d'enfant; [cradle] berceau *m* **2.** *(pt & pp* **-bb-)** *vti Fam* pomper

**cricket¹** ['krɪkɪt] *n* [game] cricket *m*

**cricket²** ['krɪkɪt] *n* [insect] grillon *m*

**crime** [kraɪm] *n* crime *m*; JUR délit *m*; [criminal activity] criminalité *f*

**criminal** ['krɪmɪnəl] *adj & n* criminel, -elle *(mf)*; **criminal offence** [minor] délit *m*; [serious] crime *m*; **criminal record** casier *m* judiciaire

**crimson** ['krɪmzən] *adj & n* cramoisi *(m)*

**cringe** [krɪndʒ] *vi* [show fear] avoir un mouvement de recul; [be embarrassed] avoir envie de rentrer sous terre

**crinkle** ['krɪŋkəl] **1.** *n* [in paper, fabric] pli *m* **2.** *vt* [paper, fabric] froisser

**cripple** ['krɪpəl] **1.** *n* [lame] estropié, -e *mf*; [disabled] infirme *mf* **2.** *vt* [disable] rendre infirme; *Fig* [nation, system] paralyser

**crisis** ['kraɪsɪs] *(pl* **crises** ['kraɪsiːz]*) n* crise *f*

**crisp** [krɪsp] **1.** *(compar* **-er,** *superl* **-est)** *adj* [biscuit] croustillant; [apple, vegetables] croquant **2.** *npl Br* **(potato) crisps** chips *fpl* ■ **crispbread** *n* pain *m* suédois

**criterion** [kraɪ'tɪərɪən] *(pl* **-ia** [-ɪə]*) n* critère *m*

**critic** ['krɪtɪk] *n* [reviewer] critique *mf*; [opponent] détracteur, -trice *mf* ■ **critical** *adj* critique ■ **critically** *adv* [examine] en critique; **to be critically ill** être dans un état critique ■ **criticism** [-sɪzəm] *n* critique *f* ■ **criticize** [-saɪz] *vti* critiquer

**croak** [krəʊk] *vi* [of frog] croasser

**Croatia** [krəʊ'eɪʃə] *n* la Croatie

**crockery** ['krɒkərɪ] *n* vaisselle *f*

**crocodile** ['krɒkədaɪl] *n* crocodile *m*

**crocus** ['krəʊkəs] *(pl* **-uses** [-əsɪz]*) n* crocus *m*

**cromulent** ['krɒmjʊlənt] *adj Hum* **it's a perfectly cromulent word** c'est un mot tout ce qu'il y a de plus normal

**crook** [krʊk] *n* [thief] escroc *m*

**crooked** ['krʊkɪd] *adj* [hat, picture] de travers ; [deal, person] malhonnête

**crop** [krɒp] **1.** *n* [harvest] récolte *f* ; [produce] culture *f* **2.** *(pt & pp* -**pp**-*)vt* [hair] couper ras **3.** *vi* **to crop up** [of issue] survenir ; [of opportunity] se présenter ; [of name] être mentionné ■ **cropped** ['krɒpt] *adj* **cropped hair** cheveux coupés ras ; **cropped trousers** pantacourt *m*

**cross¹** [krɒs] **1.** *n* croix *f* ; **a cross between** [animal] un croisement entre ; *Fig* **it's a cross between a car and a van** c'est un compromis entre une voiture et une camionnette **2.** *vt* [street, room] traverser ; [barrier, threshold] franchir ; [legs, animals] croiser ; [cheque] barrer ; **to cross off** *or* **out** [word, name] rayer ; **to cross over** [road] traverser **3.** *vi* [of paths] se croiser ; **to cross over** traverser

**cross²** [krɒs] *adj* [angry] fâché (**with** contre) ; **to get cross** se fâcher (**with** contre) ■ **cross-country** *adj* **cross-country race** cross *m* ; **cross-country runner** coureur, -euse *mf* de fond ■ **cross-legged** *adj* & *adv* **to sit cross-legged** être assis en tailleur ■ **cross-platform** *adj* multiplateforme ■ **crossroads** *n* carrefour *m* ■ **cross-section** *n* coupe *f* transversale ; [sample] échantillon *m* représentatif ■ **crosstown street** *n* rue *f* transversale ■ **crossword (puzzle)** *n* mots *mpl* croisés

**crossing** ['krɒsɪŋ] *n* [of sea, river] traversée *f* ; *Br* **(pedestrian) crossing** passage *m* clouté ; *Am* **crossing guard** *employé municipal qui fait traverser les enfants*

**crotch** [krɒtʃ] *n* [of garment, person] entrejambe *m*

**crouch** [kraʊtʃ] *vi* **to crouch (down)** [of person] s'accroupir ; [of animal] se tapir

**crow** [krəʊ] **1.** *n* corbeau *m* ; **as the crow flies** à vol d'oiseau **2.** *vi* [of cock] chanter ; *Fig* [boast] se vanter (**about** de)

**crowbar** ['krəʊbɑː(r)] *n* levier *m*

**crowd** [kraʊd] **1.** *n* foule *f* ; *Fam* [group of people] bande *f* ; **there was quite a crowd** il y avait beaucoup de monde

**2.** *vt* [street] envahir ; **to crowd people /objects into** entasser des gens /des objets dans **3.** *vi* **to crowd into** [of people] s'entasser dans ; **to crowd round sb/sth** se presser autour de qn /qch ; **to crowd together** se serrer ■ **crowded** *adj* plein (**with** de) ; [train, room] bondé ; [city] surpeuplé ; **it's very crowded** il y a beaucoup de monde

**crown** [kraʊn] **1.** *n* [of king] couronne *f* ; [of head, hill] sommet *m* ; **the Crown** [monarchy] la Couronne **2.** *vt* couronner

**crucial** ['kruːʃəl] *adj* crucial

**crucify** ['kruːsɪfaɪ] *(pt & pp* -**ied**)*vt* crucifier ■ **crucifix** [-fɪks] *n* crucifix *m*

**crude** [kruːd] *(compar* -**er**, *superl* -**est**)*adj* [manners, person, language] grossier, -ère ; [painting, work] rudimentaire ; **crude oil** pétrole *m* brut

**cruel** [krʊəl] *(compar* **crueller**, *superl* **cruellest**) *adj* cruel, -elle ■ **cruelty** *n* cruauté *f*

**cruise** [kruːz] **1.** *n* croisière *f* ; **to go on a cruise** partir en croisière ; **cruise ship** bateau *m* de croisière **2.** *vi* [of ship] croiser ; [of vehicle] rouler ; [of taxi] marauder ; [of tourists] faire une croisière

**crumb** [krʌm] *n* miette *f*

**crumble** ['krʌmbəl] **1.** *vt* [bread] émietter **2.** *vi* [of bread] s'émietter ; [collapse - of resistance] s'effondrer ; **to crumble (away)** [in small pieces] s'effriter

**crummy** ['krʌmɪ] *(compar* -**ier**, *superl* -**iest**) *adj Fam* minable

**crumpet** ['krʌmpɪt] *n Br petite crêpe grillée servie beurrée*

**crumple** ['krʌmpəl] **1.** *vt* froisser **2.** *vi* se froisser

**crunch** [krʌntʃ] *vt* [food] croquer

**crusade** [kruː'seɪd] *n* HIST & *Fig* croisade *f*

**crush** [krʌʃ] **1.** *n* [crowd] foule *f* ; [rush] bousculade *f* ; *Fam* **to have a crush on sb** en pincer pour qn **2.** *vt* écraser ; [clothes] froisser ; [cram] entasser (**into** dans)

**crust** [krʌst] n croûte f ■ **crusty** (compar -ier, superl -iest) n [bread] croustillant

**crutch** [krʌtʃ] n a) [of invalid] béquille f b) [crotch] entrejambe m

**cry** [kraɪ] **1.** (pl **cries**) n [shout] cri m **2.** (pt & pp **cried**) vt **to cry (out)** [shout] crier **3.** vi [weep] pleurer; **to cry (out)** pousser un cri; **to cry for help** appeler au secours; **to cry over sb/sth** pleurer qn/ qch ■ **crying** n [weeping] pleurs mpl

**crypt** [krɪpt] n crypte f

**crystal** ['krɪstəl] n cristal m; **crystal vase** vase m en cristal

**CSR** (abbr of **Corporate Social Responsibility**) n RSE f (responsabilité sociale des entreprises)

**CTR** n abbr of **click-through rate**

**CU@** MESSAGING written abbr of **see you at**

**cub** [kʌb] n a) [of animal] petit m b) [scout] louveteau m

**Cuba** ['kju:bə] n Cuba f

**cube** [kju:b] n cube m; [of meat, vegetables] dé m; [of sugar] morceau m ■ **cubic** adj **cubic capacity** volume m; [of engine] cylindrée f; **cubic metre** mètre m cube

**cubicle** ['kju:bɪkəl] n [for changing clothes] cabine f

**cuckoo** ['kʊku:] (pl **-oos**) n [bird] coucou m

**cucumber** ['kju:kʌmbə(r)] n concombre m

**cuddle** ['kʌdəl] **1.** n câlin m; **to give sb a cuddle** faire un câlin à qn **2.** vt [hug] serrer dans ses bras; [caress] câliner **3.** vi [of lovers] se faire des câlins ■ **cuddly** (compar -ier, superl -iest) adj [person] mignon, -onne à croquer; **cuddly toy** peluche f

**cue¹** [kju:] n [in theatre] réplique f; [signal] signal m

**cue²** [kju:] n (billiard) **cue** queue f de billard

**cuff** [kʌf] n [of shirt] poignet m; Am [of trousers] revers m; **off the cuff** [remark] impromptu; **cuff link** bouton m de manchette

**CUL** (abbr of **see you later**) MESSAGING @+

**cul-de-sac** ['kʌldəsæk] n Br impasse f

**CUL8R** (abbr of **see you later**) MESSAGING @+

**culinary** ['kʌlɪnərɪ] adj culinaire

**culminate** ['kʌlmɪneɪt] vi **to culminate in** aboutir à

**culprit** ['kʌlprɪt] n coupable mf

**cult** [kʌlt] n culte m; **cult film** film m culte

**cultivate** ['kʌltɪveɪt] vt [land, mind] cultiver ■ **cultivated** adj cultivé

**culture** ['kʌltʃə(r)] n culture f ■ **cultural** adj culturel, -elle ■ **cultured** adj [person, mind] cultivé

**cumbersome** ['kʌmbəsəm] adj encombrant

**cunning** ['kʌnɪŋ] **1.** adj [ingenious] astucieux, -euse; [devious] rusé **2.** n astuce f; Pej ruse f

**cup** [kʌp] n tasse f; [prize] coupe f; **cup final** [in football] finale f de la coupe

**cupboard** ['kʌbəd] n Br armoire f; [built into wall] placard m

**cupcake** n a) Am [cake] petit gâteau m b) [term of affection] mon chou, ma puce

**curable** ['kjʊərəbəl] adj guérissable

**curate** ['kjʊərɪt] n vicaire m

**curb** [kɜ:b] **1.** n a) [limit] **to put a curb on** mettre un frein à b) Am [kerb] bord m du trottoir **2.** vt [feelings] refréner; [ambitions] modérer; [expenses] réduire

**cure** ['kjʊə(r)] **1.** n remède m (**for** contre) **2.** vt a) [person, illness] guérir; **to cure sb of** guérir qn de b) [meat, fish - smoke] fumer; [salt] saler; [dry] sécher

**curious** ['kjʊərɪəs] adj curieux, -euse (**about** de); **to be curious to know/see** être curieux de savoir/voir ■ **curiosity** (pl **-ies**) n curiosité f (**about** de)

**curl** [kɜ:l] **1.** n [in hair] boucle f **2.** vti [hair] boucler; [with small, tight curls] friser **3.** vi **to curl up** [shrivel] se racornir ■ **curler** n bigoudi m ■ **curly** (compar -ier, superl -iest) adj [hair] bouclé; [having many tight curls] frisé

**currant** ['kʌrənt] n [dried grape] raisin m de Corinthe

**currency** ['kʌrənsı] (pl -ies) n [money] monnaie f; **(foreign) currency** devises fpl (étrangères)

**current** ['kʌrənt] **1.** adj [fashion, trend] actuel, -elle; [opinion, use] courant; [year, month] en cours; **current account** [in bank] compte m courant; **current affairs** questions fpl d'actualité **2.** n [of river, air, electricity] courant m ■ **currently** adv actuellement

**curriculum** [kə'rɪkjʊləm] (pl -la [-lə]) n programme m scolaire; Br **curriculum vitae** curriculum vitae m inv

**curry** ['kʌrı] (pl -ies) n [dish] curry m, cari m; **curry powder** poudre f de curry

**curse** [kɜːs] **1.** n malédiction f; [swearword] juron m; [scourge] fléau m; Am **curse word** juron m **2.** vt maudire; **cursed with sth** affligé de qch **3.** vi [swear] jurer

**cursor** ['kɜːsə(r)] n COMPUT curseur m

**cursory** ['kɜːsərı] adj superficiel, -elle

**curt** [kɜːt] adj brusque

**curtail** [kɜː'teɪl] vt [visit] écourter

**curtain** ['kɜːtən] n rideau m; **to draw the curtains** [close] tirer les rideaux

**curts(e)y** ['kɜːtsı] **1.** (pl -ies or -eys) n révérence f **2.** (pt & pp -ied) vi faire une révérence (**to** à)

**curve** [kɜːv] **1.** n courbe f; [in road] virage m; Am SCH **curve grading** système de notation relative tenant compte des performances des élèves de la classe **2.** vt courber **3.** vi se courber; [of road] faire une courbe ■ **curved** adj [line] courbe

**cushion** ['kʊʃən] **1.** n coussin m **2.** vt [shock] amortir

**cushy** ['kʊʃı] (compar -ier, superl -iest) adj Fam [job, life] pépère

**custard** ['kʌstəd] n crème f anglaise; [when set] crème f renversée

**custody** ['kʌstədı] n [of child, important papers] garde f

**custom** ['kʌstəm] n coutume f; [of individual] habitude f; [customers] clientèle f ■ **customary** adj habituel, -elle; **it is customary to...** il est d'usage de...

**customer** ['kʌstəmə(r)] n client, -e mf; Pej [individual] individu m

**customs** ['kʌstəmz] npl **(the) customs** la douane; **to go through customs** passer la douane; **customs officer** douanier m

**cut** [kʌt] **1.** n [mark] coupure f; [stroke] coup m; [of clothes, hair] coupe f; [in salary, prices] réduction f; [of meat] morceau m **2.** (pt & pp cut, pres p cutting) vt couper; [meat, chicken] découper; [glass, diamond, tree] tailler; [salary, prices, profits] réduire; **to cut sb's hair** couper les cheveux à qn; **to cut sth open** ouvrir qch avec un couteau / des ciseaux / etc; **to cut sth short** [visit] écourter qch; Am **cutting board** planche f à découper **3.** vi [of knife, scissors] couper ■ **cut back 1.** vt sep **a)** [prune] tailler **b)** [reduce] réduire **2.** vi **to cut back on** réduire, diminuer ■ **cut down 1.** vt sep **a)** [tree] abattre **b)** [reduce] réduire **2.** vi réduire ■ **cut in** vi [interrupt] interrompre; [in vehicle] faire une queue de poisson (**on sb** à qn) ■ **cut off** vt sep [piece, limb, hair] couper; [isolate] isoler ■ **cut out 1.** vt sep [article] découper; [remove] enlever; [eliminate] supprimer; **to cut out drinking** s'arrêter de boire; Fam **cut it out!** ça suffit!; **cut out to be a doctor** fait pour être médecin **2.** vi [of car engine] caler ■ **cut up** vt sep couper en morceaux; [meat, chicken] découper; **to be very cut up about sth** [upset] être complètement chamboulé par qch

**cutback** n réduction f

**cute** [kjuːt] (compar -er, superl -est) adj Fam [pretty] mignon, -onne

**cutlery** ['kʌtlərı] n couverts mpl

**cutlet** ['kʌtlıt] n côtelette f

**cut-price** [kʌt'praɪs] adj à prix réduit

**cutting** ['kʌtıŋ] **1.** n [from newspaper] coupure f; [plant] bouture f **2.** adj [wind, remark] cinglant

**cutting-edge** adj [technology] de pointe

**CV** [siːˈviː] *(abbr of* **curriculum vitae***)* *n*
*Br* CV *m*

**CYA** *(abbr of* **see you around** *or* **see ya)**
MESSAGING @+

**cyberbully** [ˈsaɪbə(r)ˌbʊlɪ] *n* cyberinti-
midateur, -trice *m,f,* cyberharceleur,
-euse *m,f*

**cybercafé** [saɪbəˈkæfeɪ] *n* cybercafé *m*

**cybershop** *n* boutique *f* en ligne

**cybershopping** [ˈsaɪbəʃɒpɪŋ] *n*
achats *mpl* en ligne, cybershopping *m*

**cyberspace** [ˈsaɪbəspeɪs] *n* COMPUT
cyberespace *m*

**cyberstalk** [ˈsaɪbə(r)ˌstɔːk] *vt* cyber-
harceler

**cycle¹** [ˈsaɪkəl] **1.** *n* [bicycle] bicyclette *f;*
**cycle lane, cycle path** piste *f* cyclable
**2.** *vi* aller à bicyclette **(to** à) ; [as activ-
ity] faire de la bicyclette ■ **cycling** *n*
cyclisme *m* ■ **cyclist** *n* cycliste *mf*

**cycle²** [ˈsaɪkəl] *n* [series, period] cycle *m*

**cylinder** [ˈsɪlɪndə(r)] *n* cylindre *m*

**cymbal** [ˈsɪmbəl] *n* cymbale *f*

**cynical** [ˈsɪnɪkəl] *adj* cynique

**Cyprus** [ˈsaɪprəs] *n* Chypre *f*

**cyst** [sɪst] *n* MED kyste *m*

**Czech** [tʃek] **1.** *adj* tchèque; **the Czech
Republic** la République tchèque **2.** *n*
[person] Tchèque *mf*; [language]
tchèque *m*

# D

**D, d** [diː] *n* D, d *m inv*

**dab** [dæb] **1.** *n* a dab of un petit peu de **2.** *(pt & pp* -bb-*) vt* [wound, brow] tamponner ; **to dab sth on sth** appliquer qch (à petits coups) sur qch

**dabble** ['dæbəl] *vi* **to dabble in politics/journalism** faire vaguement de la politique/du journalisme

**dad** [dæd] *n Fam* papa *m* ■ **daddy** (*pl* -ies) *n Fam* papa *m*

**dadager** ['dædədʒə(r)] *n Am Fam* père qui gère la carrière de son enfant artiste ou sportif

**daffodil** ['dæfədɪl] *n* jonquille *f*

**daft** [dɑːft] *(compar* -er, *superl* -est*) adj Fam* bête

**dagger** ['dægə(r)] *n* dague *f*

**daily** ['deɪlɪ] **1.** *adj* quotidien, -enne ; [wage] journalier, -ère ; **daily paper** quotidien *m* **2.** *adv* chaque jour, quotidiennement ; **twice daily** deux fois par jour **3.** (*pl* -ies) *n* [newspaper] quotidien *m*

**dainty** ['deɪntɪ] *(compar* -ier, *superl* -iest*) adj* délicat

**dairy** ['deərɪ] **1.** (*pl* -ies) *n* [factory] laiterie *f* ; [shop] crémerie *f* **2.** *adj* laitier, -ère ; **dairy produce** produits *mpl* laitiers

**daisy** ['deɪzɪ] (*pl* -ies) *n* pâquerette *f* ; [bigger] marguerite *f*

**dam** [dæm] *n* [wall] barrage *m*

**damage** ['dæmɪdʒ] **1.** *n* dégâts *mpl* ; [harm] préjudice *m* ; **damages** [in court] dommages-intérêts *mpl* **2.** *vt* [object] endommager, abîmer ; [health] nuire à ; [eyesight] abîmer ; [plans, reputation] compromettre ■ **damaging** *adj* [harmful] préjudiciable (**to** à)

**damn** [dæm] **1.** *n Fam* **he doesn't care** *or* **give a damn** il s'en fiche pas mal **2.** *adj Fam* fichu **3.** *adv Fam* [very] vachement **4.** *vt* [condemn, doom] condamner ; [curse] maudire ; *Fam* **damn him!** qu'il aille se faire voir ! **5.** *excl Fam* **damn (it)!** mince ! ■ **damned** *Fam* **1.** *adj* [awful] fichu **2.** *adv* vachement

**damp** [dæmp] **1.** *(compar* -er, *superl* -est*) adj* humide ; [skin] moite **2.** *n* humidité *f* ■ **damp(en)** *vt* humecter ; **to damp(en) (down)** [enthusiasm, zeal] refroidir

**damson** ['dæmzən] *n* prune *f* de Damas

**dance** [dɑːns] **1.** *n* danse *f* ; [social event] bal *m* (*pl* bals) ; **dance hall** dancing *m* **2.** *vt* [waltz, tango] danser **3.** *vi* danser ■ **dancesport** ['dɑːnspɔːt] *n* danse *f* sportive ■ **dancing** *n* danse *f*

**dandelion** ['dændɪlaɪən] *n* pissenlit *m*

**dandruff** ['dændrʌf] *n* pellicules *fpl*

**Dane** [deɪn] *n* Danois, -e *mf*

**danger** ['deɪndʒə(r)] *n* danger *m* (**to** pour) ; **in danger** en danger ; **out of danger** hors de danger ; **to be in danger of doing sth** risquer de faire qch ■ **dangerous** *adj* dangereux, -euse (**to** pour)

**dangle** ['dæŋgəl] **1.** *vt* balancer **2.** *vi* [hang] pendre ; [swing] se balancer

**Danish** ['deɪnɪʃ] **1.** *adj* danois **2.** *n* [language] danois *m*

**dare** [deə(r)] **1.** *vt* **to dare (to) do sth** faire qch ; **I dare say he tried** il a essayé, c'est bien possible ; **to dare sb to do sth** défier qn de faire qch **2.** *vi* oser ; **how dare you!** comment osez-vous ! **3.** *n* défi *m* ■ **daring 1.** *adj* audacieux, -euse **2.** *n* audace *f*

**dark** [dɑːk] **1.** *(compar* -er, *superl* -est*) adj* [room, night] & *Fig* sombre ; [colour, skin, hair, eyes] foncé ; **it's dark at six** il fait nuit à six heures ; **dark glasses** lunettes *fpl* noires **2.** *n* obscurité *f* ;

**after dark** une fois la nuit tombée; *Fig* **to keep sb in the dark** laisser qn dans l'ignorance **(about** de) ▪ **dark-haired** *adj* aux cheveux bruns ▪ **dark-skinned** *adj* [person] à peau brune

**darken** ['dɑːkən] **1.** *vt* assombrir; [colour] foncer **2.** *vi* s'assombrir; [of colour] foncer

**darkness** ['dɑːknəs] *n* obscurité *f*

**darkroom** ['dɑːkruːm] *n* [for photography] chambre *f* noire

**darling** ['dɑːlɪŋ] *n* [favourite] chouchou, -oute *mf*; **(my) darling** (mon) chéri / (ma) chérie

**darn** [dɑːn] *vt* [mend] repriser

**dart** [dɑːt] **1.** *n* [in game] fléchette *f*; **darts** [game] fléchettes *fpl* **2.** *vi* [dash] se précipiter **(for** vers)

**dash** [dæʃ] **1.** *n* **a)** [run, rush] ruée *f*; **to make a dash for sth** se ruer vers qch **b) a dash of sth** un petit peu de qch **c)** [handwritten stroke] trait *m*; [punctuation sign] tiret *m* **2.** *vt* [throw] jeter; **to dash off** [letter] écrire en vitesse **3.** *vi* [rush] se précipiter; **to dash in / out** entrer / sortir en vitesse; **to dash off** *or* **away** filer ▪ **dashboard** *n* [of vehicle] tableau *m* de bord

**data** ['deɪtə] *npl* informations *fpl*; COMPUT données *fpl*; **data base** base *f* de données; TEL **data cap** plafond *m* d'échange de données *(sur téléphone mobile)*; **data processing** informatique *f*

**date¹** [deɪt] **1.** *n* [day] date *f*; *Fam* [meeting] rendez-vous *m inv*; *Fam* [person] ami, -e *mf*; **date of birth** date *f* de naissance; **up to date** [in fashion] à la mode; [information] à jour; [well-informed] au courant **(on** de); **out of date** [old-fashioned] démodé; [expired] périmé **2.** *vt* [letter] dater; *Fam* [girl, boy] sortir avec **3.** *vi* [go out of fashion] dater; **to date back to, to date from** dater de

**date²** [deɪt] *n* [fruit] datte *f*

**datebook** ['deɪtbʊk] *n Am* agenda *m*

**dated** ['deɪtɪd] *adj* démodé

**daughter** ['dɔːtə(r)] *n* fille *f* ▪ **daughter-in-law** *(pl* **daughters-in-law)** *n* belle-fille *f*

**dawdle** ['dɔːdəl] *vi* traîner

**dawn** [dɔːn] **1.** *n* aube *f*; **at dawn** à l'aube **2.** *vi* [of day] se lever; **it dawned on him that…** il s'est rendu compte que…

**day** [deɪ] *n* [period of daylight, 24 hours] jour *m*; [referring to duration] journée *f*; **all day (long)** toute la journée; **what day is it?** quel jour sommes-nous ?; **the following** *or* **next day** le lendemain; **the day before** la veille; **the day before yesterday** *or* **before last** avant-hier; **the day after tomorrow** après-demain; **in those days** en ce temps-là; **these days** de nos jours ▪ **daybreak** *n* point *m* du jour ▪ **daydream 1.** *n* rêverie *f* **2.** *vi* rêvasser ▪ **daylight** *n* (lumière *f* du) jour *m* ▪ **daypack** ['deɪpæk] *n* petit sac à dos *m (pour ses affaires de la journée)* ▪ **days** *adv* le jour ▪ **daytime** *n* journée *f*, jour *m*

**day care** *n* **a)** [for elderly, disabled] service *m* d'accueil de jour **b)** [for children] service *m* de garderie ▪ **day-care** *adj* **a)** [for elderly, disabled] d'accueil de jour **b)** [for children] de garderie

**daze** [deɪz] **1.** *n* **in a daze** étourdi; [because of drugs] hébété; [astonished] ahuri **2.** *vt* [by blow] étourdir

**dazzle** ['dæzəl] *vt* éblouir

**dead** [ded] **1.** *adj* mort; [numb - limb] engourdi; **the phone's dead** il n'y a pas de tonalité; **dead end** [street & Fig] impasse *f*; **a dead stop** un arrêt complet **2.** *npl* **the dead** les morts *mpl* **3.** *adv* [completely] totalement; *Fam* [very] très; **to stop dead** s'arrêter net

**deaden** ['dedən] *vt* [shock] amortir; [pain] calmer

**deadline** ['dedlaɪn] *n* date *f* limite; [hour] heure *f* limite

**deadlock** ['dedlɒk] *n Fig* impasse *f*

**deadly** ['dedlɪ] **1.** *(compar* -**ier**, *superl* -**iest)** *adj* [poison, blow, enemy] mortel, -elle; **deadly weapon** arme *f* meurtrière **2.** *adv* [pale, boring] mortellement

**dead tree edition** *n Fam* édition *f* papier, édition *f* imprimée

**dead tree media** *npl Fam* médias *mpl* imprimés

**deaf** [def] **1.** *adj* sourd ; **deaf and dumb** sourd-muet (*f* sourde-muette) **2.** *npl* **the deaf** les sourds *mpl* ■ **deafen** *vt* assourdir

**deal¹** [di:l] *n* **a good** *or* **great deal (of)** [a lot] beaucoup (de)

**deal²** [di:l] **1.** *n* [in business] marché *m*, affaire *f* ; [in card games] donne *f* ; **to make** *or* **do a deal (with sb)** conclure un marché (avec qn) ; **it's a deal!** d'accord ! ; *Iron* **big deal!** la belle affaire ! **2.** (*pt* & *pp* **dealt**) *vt* **to deal (out)** [cards, money] distribuer **3.** *vi* [trade] traiter **with sb** avec qn) ; **to deal in** faire le commerce de ; **to deal with** [take care of] s'occuper de ; [concern - of book] traiter de, parler de ■ **dealer** *n* marchand, -e *mf* (**in** de) ; [for cars] concessionnaire *mf* ; [in drugs] revendeur, -euse *mf* ; [in card games] donneur, -euse *mf* ■ **dealings** *npl* relations *fpl* (**with** avec) ; [in business] transactions *fpl*

**dealt** [delt] *pt* & *pp of* **deal**

**dean** [di:n] *n* **a)** doyen, enne *mf* d'université **b)** *Am* ≈ CPE *mf* (*membre de l'administration d'un lycée qui conseille les élèves et s'occupe des problèmes disciplinaires*)

**dear** [dɪə(r)] **1.** (*compar* **-er**, *superl* **-est**) *adj* [loved, precious, expensive] cher (*f* chère) ; **Dear Madam** [in letter] Madame ; **Dear Sir** Monsieur ; **Dear Jane** chère Jane ; **oh dear!** oh là là ! **2.** *n* (**my) dear** [darling] (mon) chéri /(ma) chérie ; [friend] mon cher /ma chère **3.** *adv* [cost, pay] cher

**dearly** [ˈdɪəlɪ] *adv* [love] tendrement ; [very much] beaucoup ; **to pay dearly for sth** payer qch cher

**death** [deθ] *n* mort *f* ; **to be bored to death** s'ennuyer à mourir ; **to be scared to death** être mort de peur ; **to be sick to death** en avoir vraiment marre (**of** de) ; **death certificate** acte *m* de décès ; **death penalty** peine *f* de mort ; **death sentence** condamnation *f* à mort ■ **deathly** *adj* [silence, paleness] de mort

**debate** [dɪˈbeɪt] **1.** *n* débat *m* **2.** *vti* discuter ■ **debatable** *adj* **it's debatable whether she will succeed** il est difficile de dire si elle réussira

**debit** [ˈdebɪt] **1.** *n* débit *m* ; **in debit** [account] débiteur **2.** *vt* débiter (**sb with sth** qn de qch)

**debris** [ˈdebri:] *n* [of building] décombres *mpl* ; [of plane, car] débris *mpl*

**debt** [det] *n* dette *f* ; **to be in debt** avoir des dettes ; **to run** *or* **get into debt** faire des dettes ■ **debtor** *n* débiteur, -trice *mf*

**debug** [ˌdi:ˈbʌg] *vt* COMPUT [program] déboguer, mettre au point

**debut** [ˈdebju:] *n* [on stage] début *m* ; **to make one's debut** faire ses débuts

**decade** [ˈdekeɪd] *n* décennie *f*

**decadent** [ˈdekədənt] *adj* décadent

**decaffeinated** [di:ˈkæfɪneɪtɪd] *adj* décaféiné

**decanter** [dɪˈkæntə(r)] *n* carafe *f*

**decay** [dɪˈkeɪ] **1.** *n* [rot] pourriture *f* ; [of tooth] carie *f* ; **to fall into decay** [of building] tomber en ruine **2.** *vi* [go bad] se gâter ; [rot] pourrir ; [of tooth] se carier

**deceased** [dɪˈsi:st] **1.** *adj* décédé **2.** *n* **the deceased** le défunt /la défunte

**deceit** [dɪˈsi:t] *n* tromperie *f* ■ **deceitful** *adj* [person] fourbe ; [behaviour] malhonnête

**deceive** [dɪˈsi:v] *vti* tromper ; **to deceive oneself** se faire des illusions

**December** [dɪˈsembə(r)] *n* décembre *m*

**decent** [ˈdi:sənt] *adj* [respectable] convenable ; [good] bon (*f* bonne) ; [kind] gentil, -ille ■ **decency** *n* décence *f* ; [kindness] gentillesse *f*

**deception** [dɪˈsepʃən] *n* tromperie *f* ■ **deceptive** *adj* trompeur, -euse

**decide** [dɪˈsaɪd] **1.** *vt* [outcome, future] décider de ; [question, matter] régler ; **to decide to do sth** décider de faire qch ; **to decide that...** décider que... **2.** *vi* [make decisions] décider ; [make up one's mind] se décider (**on doing** à faire); **to decide on sth** décider de qch; [choose] choisir qch

**decimal** ['desɪməl] **1.** *adj* décimal; **decimal point** virgule *f* **2.** *n* décimale *f*

**decipher** [dɪ'saɪfə(r)] *vt* déchiffrer

**decision** [dɪ'sɪʒən] *n* décision *f*

**decisive** [dɪ'saɪsɪv] *adj* [action, event, tone] décisif, -ive; [person] résolu

**deck** [dek] **1.** *n* a) [of ship] pont *m*; **top deck** [of bus] impériale *f* b) **deck of cards** jeu *m* de cartes c) [of record player] platine *f* **2.** *vt* **to deck (out)** [adorn] orner ■ **deckchair** *n* chaise *f* longue

**decking** ['dekɪŋ] *n* terrasse *f* en bois

**declare** [dɪ'kleə(r)] *vt* déclarer (**that** que); [result] proclamer ■ **declaration** *n* déclaration *f*

**decline** [dɪ'klaɪn] **1.** *n* déclin *m*; [fall] baisse *f* **2.** *vt* [offer] décliner; **to decline to do sth** refuser de faire qch **3.** *vi* [become less - of popularity, birthrate] être en baisse; [deteriorate - of health, strength] décliner; [refuse] refuser

**decode** [diː'kəʊd] *vt* [message] décoder ■ **decoder** *n* COMPUT & TV décodeur *m*

**decompose** [diːkəm'pəʊz] *vi* [rot] se décomposer

**decor** ['deɪkɔː(r)] *n* décor *m*

**decorate** ['dekəreɪt] *vt* [cake, house, soldier] décorer (**with** de); [hat, skirt] orner (**with** de); [paint] peindre; [wallpaper] tapisser ■ **decoration** *n* décoration *f* ■ **decorative** *adj* décoratif, -ive ■ **decorator** *n* Br [house painter] peintre *m* décorateur; (**interior**) **decorator** décorateur, -trice *mf*

**decrease 1.** ['diːkriːs] *n* diminution *f* (**in** de) **2.** [dɪ'kriːs] *vti* diminuer

**decree** [dɪ'kriː] **1.** *n* [by court] jugement *m*; [municipal] arrêté *m* **2.** (*pt & pp* **-eed**) *vt* décréter (**that** que)

**decrepit** [dɪ'krepɪt] *adj* [building] en ruine; [person] décrépit

**dedicate** ['dedɪkeɪt] *vt* [devote] consacrer (**to** à); [book] dédier (**to** à); **to dedicate oneself to sth** se consacrer à qch ■ **dedicated** *adj* a) [teacher]

consciencieux, -euse b) COMPUT spécialisé, -e ■ **dedication** *n* [in book] dédicace *f*; [devotion] dévouement *m*

**deduce** [dɪ'djuːs] *vt* [conclude] déduire (**from** de; **that** que)

**deduct** [dɪ'dʌkt] *vt* déduire (**from** de) ■ **deductible** *adj* [from income - expenses] déductible ■ **deduction** *n* [subtraction, conclusion] déduction *f*

**deed** [diːd] *n* action *f*, acte *m*; [feat] exploit *m*; [legal document] acte *m* notarié

**deep** [diːp] **1.** (*compar* **-er**, *superl* **-est**) *adj* profond; [snow] épais (*f* épaisse); [voice] grave; [musical note] bas (*f* basse); **to be 6 metres deep** avoir 6 mètres de profondeur; **deep in thought** plongé dans ses pensées; **deep red** rouge foncé **2.** *adv* profondément ■ **deeply** *adv* profondément

**deepen** ['diːpən] **1.** *vt* [increase] augmenter; [canal, knowledge] approfondir **2.** *vi* [of river] devenir plus profond; [of mystery] s'épaissir; [of voice] devenir plus grave

**deep-freeze** [diːp'friːz] **1.** *n* congélateur *m* **2.** *vt* surgeler

**deep-fry** *vt* faire frire

**Deep South** *n* **the Deep South** [in the US] *l'extrême Sud conservateur (Alabama, Floride, Géorgie, Louisiane, Mississippi, Caroline du Sud, partie orientale du Texas)*

**deer** [dɪə(r)] *n inv* cerf *m*

**deface** [dɪ'feɪs] *vt* [damage] dégrader; [daub] barbouiller

**default** [dɪ'fɔːlt] *n* a) COMPUT valeur *f* par défaut b) **by default** par défaut; **to win by default** gagner par forfait

**defeat** [dɪ'fiːt] **1.** *n* défaite *f*; **to admit defeat** s'avouer vaincu **2.** *vt* [opponent, army] vaincre; **that defeats the purpose** *or* **object** ça va à l'encontre du but recherché

**defect¹** ['diːfekt] *n* défaut *m*

**defect²** [dɪ'fekt] *vi* [of party member, soldier] déserter

**defective** [dɪ'fektɪv] *adj* [machine] défectueux, -euse

**defence**, *Am* **defense** [dɪ'fens] *n* défense *f* (**against** contre); **in his defence** à sa décharge

**defend** [dɪ'fend] *vti* défendre ■ **defendant** *n* [accused] prévenu, -e *mf* ■ **defender** *n* défenseur *m*; [of sports title] tenant, -e *mf*

**defense** [dɪ'fens] *Am n* = **defence**

**defensive** [dɪ'fensɪv] **1.** *adj* défensif, -ive; **to be defensive** être sur la défensive **2.** *n* **on the defensive** sur la défensive

**defer** [dɪ'fɜː(r)] *(pt & pp* -rr-*)vt* [postpone] différer

**defiant** [dɪ'faɪənt] *adj* [person] provocant ■ **defiance** *n* [resistance] défi *m* (**of** à)

**deficient** [dɪ'fɪʃənt] *adj* [not adequate] insuffisant; [faulty] défectueux, -euse; **to be deficient in** manquer de ■ **deficiency** *(pl* -ies*)n* [shortage] manque *m*; [in vitamins, minerals] carence *f* (**in** de); [flaw] défaut *m*

**deficit** ['defɪsɪt] *n* déficit *m*

**define** [dɪ'faɪn] *vt* définir

**definite** ['definɪt] *adj* [exact - date, plan, answer] précis; [clear - improvement, advantage] net (*f* nette); [firm - offer, order] ferme; [certain] certain; **he was quite definite** il a été tout à fait formel; **definite article** [in grammar] article *m* défini ■ **definitely** *adv* certainement; [improved, superior] nettement; [say] catégoriquement

**definition** [defɪ'nɪʃən] *n* définition *f*

**deflect** [dɪ'flekt] *vt* [bullet] faire dévier

**deformed** [dɪ'fɔːmd] *adj* [body] difforme

**defragment** [ˌdiːfræg'ment] *vt* COMPUT défragmenter

**defraud** [dɪ'frɔːd] *vt* [customs, State] frauder; **to defraud sb of sth** escroquer qch à qn

**defriend** [diː'frend] *vt Fam* virer (de mes, tes, ses *etc* amis)

**defrost** [diː'frɒst] *vt* [fridge] dégivrer; [food] décongeler

**defuse** [diː'fjuːz] *vt* [bomb, conflict] désamorcer

**defy** [dɪ'faɪ] *(pt & pp* -ied*)vt* [person, death, logic] défier; [efforts] résister à; **to defy sb to do sth** défier qn de faire qch

**degenerate 1.** [dɪ'dʒenərət] *adj & n* dégénéré, -e *(mf)* **2.** [dɪ'dʒenəreɪt] *vi* dégénérer (**into** en)

**degrading** [dɪ'greɪdɪŋ] *adj* dégradant

**degree** [dɪ'griː] *n* **a)** [of angle, temperature, extent] degré *m*; **it's 20 degrees** [temperature] il fait 20 degrés; **to some degree, to a certain degree** jusqu'à un certain point; **to such a degree** à tel point (**that** que) **b)** [from university] diplôme *m*; [Bachelor's] ≃ licence *f*; [Master's] ≃ maîtrise *f*; [PhD] ≃ doctorat *m*

**dehydrated** [diːhaɪ'dreɪtɪd] *adj* déshydraté; **to get dehydrated** se déshydrater

**de-ice** [diː'aɪs] *vt* [car window] dégivrer

**dejected** [dɪ'dʒektɪd] *adj* abattu

**delay** [dɪ'leɪ] **1.** *n* [lateness] retard *m*; [waiting period] délai *m*; **without delay** sans tarder **2.** *vt* retarder; [payment] différer; **to delay doing sth** tarder à faire qch; **to be delayed** avoir du retard **3.** *vi* [be slow] tarder (**in doing** à faire)

**delegate 1.** ['delɪgət] *n* délégué, -e *mf* **2.** ['delɪgeɪt] *vt* déléguer (**to** à) ■ **delegation** *n* délégation *f*

**delete** [dɪ'liːt] *vt* supprimer

**deliberate** [dɪ'lɪbərət] *adj* [intentional] délibéré; [slow] mesuré ■ **deliberately** *adv* [intentionally] délibérément

**delicate** ['delɪkət] *adj* délicat ■ **delicacy** *(pl* -ies*)n* [quality] délicatesse *f*; [food] mets *m* délicat

**delicatessen** [delɪkə'tesən] *n* [shop] épicerie *f* fine

**delicious** [dɪ'lɪʃəs] *adj* délicieux, -euse

**delight** [dɪ'laɪt] **1.** *n* [pleasure] plaisir *m*, joie *f* **2.** *vt* ravir **3.** *vi* **to delight in doing sth** prendre plaisir à faire qch ■ **delighted** *adj* ravi (**with sth** de qch; **to do** de faire; **that** que)

**delightful** [dɪ'laɪtfəl] *adj* charmant; [meal, perfume, sensation] délicieux, -euse

**delinquent** [dɪ'lɪŋkwənt] *adj & n* délinquant, -e *(mf)*

**delirious** [dɪ'lɪrɪəs] *adj* délirant ; **to be delirious** délirer

**deliver** [dɪ'lɪvə(r)] *vt* **a)** [goods] livrer ; [letters] distribuer ; [hand over] remettre (**to** à) **b)** [rescue] délivrer (**from** de) **c) to deliver a woman's baby** accoucher une femme **d)** [speech] prononcer ; [warning, ultimatum] lancer

**delivery** [dɪ'lɪvərɪ] *(pl -ies)* n **a)** [of goods] livraison *f* ; [of letters] distribution *f* ; **delivery vehicle** véhicule *m* de livraison **b)** [birth] accouchement *m* **c)** [speaking] débit *m*

**delude** [dɪ'lu:d] *vt* tromper ; **to delude oneself** se faire des illusions ■ **delusion** *n* illusion *f* ; [in mental illness] aberration *f* mentale

**deluxe** [dɪ'lʌks] *adj* de luxe

**demand** [dɪ'mɑ:nd] **1.** *n* exigence *f* ; [claim] revendication *f* ; [for goods] demande *f* (**for** pour) ; **to be in (great) demand** être très demandé ; **to make demands on sb** exiger beaucoup de qn **2.** *vt* exiger (**sth from sb** qch de qn) ; [rights, more pay] revendiquer ; **to demand that...** exiger que... ■ **demanding** *adj* exigeant

**demeaning** [dɪ'mi:nɪŋ] *adj* dégradant

**demeanour**, *Am* **demeanor** [dɪ'mi:nə(r)] *n* [behaviour] comportement *m*

**demo** ['deməʊ] *(pl -os)* n *Fam* [demonstration] manif *f*

**democracy** [dɪ'mɒkrəsɪ] *(pl -ies)* n démocratie *f* ■ **democratic** *adj* [institution] démocratique ; [person] démocrate

**demolish** [dɪ'mɒlɪʃ] *vt* démolir

**demon** ['di:mən] *n* démon *m*

**demonstrate** ['demənstreɪt] **1.** *vt* démontrer ; [machine] faire une démonstration de ; **to demonstrate how to do sth** montrer comment faire qch **2.** *vi* [protest] manifester ■ **demonstration** [-'streɪʃən] *n* démonstration *f* ; [protest] manifestation *f* ■ **demonstrator** *n* [protester] manifestant, -e *mf*

**demoralize** [dɪ'mɒrəlaɪz] *vt* démoraliser

**demote** [dɪ'məʊt] *vt* rétrograder

**den** [den] *n* [of lion, person] antre *m*

**denial** [dɪ'naɪəl] *n* [of rumour, allegation] démenti *m*

**denigrate** ['denɪgreɪt] *vt* dénigrer

**denim** ['denɪm] *n* denim *m* ; **denims** [jeans] jean *m*

**Denmark** ['denmɑ:k] *n* le Danemark

**denomination** [dɪnɒmɪ'neɪʃən] *n* [religion] confession *f* ; [of coin, banknote] valeur *f*

**denote** [dɪ'nəʊt] *vt* dénoter

**denounce** [dɪ'naʊns] *vt* [person, injustice] dénoncer (**to** à)

**dense** [dens] *(compar -er, superl -est)* adj dense ; *Fam* [stupid] lourd ■ **densely** *adv* **densely populated** très peuplé

**dent** [dent] **1.** *n* [in car, metal] bosse *f* **2.** *vt* cabosser

**dental** ['dentəl] *adj* dentaire ; **dental appointment** rendez-vous *m inv* chez le dentiste

**dentist** ['dentɪst] *n* dentiste *mf* ; **to go to the dentist** aller chez le dentiste

**dentures** ['dentʃəz] *npl* dentier *m*

**deny** [dɪ'naɪ] *(pt & pp -ied)* vt nier (**doing** avoir fait ; **that** que) ; [rumour] démentir ; **to deny sb sth** refuser qch à qn

**deodorant** [di:'əʊdərənt] *n* déodorant *m*

**deodorizer** [di:'əʊdəraɪzə(r)] *n* [for home] désodorisant *m*

**depart** [dɪ'pɑ:t] *vi* partir ; [deviate] s'écarter (**from** de)

**department** [dɪ'pɑ:tmənt] *n* département *m* ; [in office] service *m* ; [in shop] rayon *m* ; [of government] ministère *m* ; **department store** grand magasin *m*

**departure** [dɪ'pɑ:tʃə(r)] *n* départ *m* ; **departure lounge** [in airport] salle *f* d'embarquement

**depend** [dɪ'pend] *vi* dépendre (**on** *or* **upon** de) ; **to depend (up)on** [rely on] compter sur (**for sth** pour qch) ■ **dependant** *n* personne *f* à charge ■ **dependent** *adj* [relative, child] à charge ;

**to be dependent (up)on** dépendre de ; **to be dependent on sb** [financially] être à la charge de qn

**depict** [dɪ'pɪkt] *vt* [describe] décrire ; [in pictures] représenter

**deplorable** [dɪ'plɔːrəbəl] *adj* déplorable

**deploy** [dɪ'plɔɪ] *vt* [troops] déployer

**deport** [dɪ'pɔːt] *vt* [foreigner, criminal] expulser

**deposit** [dɪ'pɒzɪt] **1.** *n* **a)** [in bank] dépôt *m* ; [part payment] acompte *m* ; [returnable] caution *f* **b)** [sediment] dépôt *m* ; [of gold, oil] gisement *m* **2.** *vt* [object, money] déposer

**depot** [*Br* 'depəʊ, *Am* 'diːpəʊ] *n* [for goods] dépôt *m* ; *Am* [railroad station] gare *f* ; *Am* **(bus) depot** gare *f* routière

**depraved** [dɪ'preɪvd] *adj* dépravé

**depreciate** [dɪ'priːʃɪeɪt] *vi* [fall in value] se déprécier

**depress** [dɪ'pres] *vt* [discourage] déprimer ■ **depressed** *adj* [person, market] déprimé ; **to get depressed** se décourager ■ **depression** *n* dépression *f*

**deprive** [dɪ'praɪv] *vt* priver (**of** de) ■ **deprived** *adj* [child] défavorisé

**depth** [depθ] *n* profondeur *f* ; **in the depths of** [forest, despair] au plus profond de ; [winter] au cœur de ; **in depth** en profondeur

**deputy** ['depjʊtɪ] (*pl* **-ies**) *n* [replacement] remplaçant, -e *mf* ; [assistant] adjoint, -e *mf*

**derailed** [dɪ'reɪld] *adj* **to be derailed** [of train] dérailler

**derelict** ['derɪlɪkt] *adj* [building] abandonné

**derision** [dɪ'rɪʒən] *n* dérision *f*

**derisory** [dɪ'raɪsərɪ] *adj* [amount] dérisoire

**derive** [dɪ'raɪv] **1.** *vt* provenir (**from** de) ; **to be derived from** provenir de **2.** *vi* to derive from provenir de ■ **derivation** *n* LING dérivation *f*

**descend** [dɪ'send] **1.** *vt* [stairs, hill] descendre ; **to be descended from** descendre de **2.** *vi* descendre (**from** de) ;

**to descend upon** [of tourists] envahir ; [attack] faire une descente sur ; **in descending order** en ordre décroissant ■ **descendant** *n* descendant, -e *mf*

**descent** [dɪ'sent] *n* **a)** [of aircraft] descente *f* **b)** [ancestry] origine *f* ; **to be of Norman descent** être d'origine normande

**describe** [dɪ'skraɪb] *vt* décrire ■ **description** *n* description *f*

**desert¹** ['dezət] *n* désert *m* ; **desert island** île *f* déserte

**desert²** [dɪ'zɜːt] **1.** *vt* [person] abandonner ; [place, cause] déserter **2.** *vi* [of soldier] déserter ■ **deserted** *adj* désert

**deserve** [dɪ'zɜːv] *vt* mériter (**to do** de faire) ■ **deserving** *adj* [person] méritant ; [action, cause] méritoire

**design** [dɪ'zaɪn] **1.** *n* **a)** [pattern] motif *m* ; [sketch] plan *m* ; [of dress, car, furniture] modèle *m* **b)** [aim] dessein *m* ; **to have designs on** avoir des vues sur **2.** *vt* [car, building] concevoir ; [dress] créer ; **designed to do sth / for sth** conçu pour faire qch / pour qch ■ **designer** *n* [artistic] dessinateur, -trice *mf* ; [industrial] concepteur-dessinateur *m* ; [of clothes] styliste *mf* ; [well-known] couturier *m* ; **designer clothes** vêtements *mpl* de marque

**designate** ['dezɪgneɪt] *vt* désigner

**desire** [dɪ'zaɪə(r)] **1.** *n* désir *m* **2.** *vt* désirer (**to do** faire) ■ **desirable** *adj* désirable

**desk** [desk] *n* [in school] table *f* ; [in office] bureau *m* ; *Br* [in shop] caisse *f* ; **(reception) desk** [in hotel] réception *f* ; *Am* **desk clerk** [in hotel] réceptionniste *mf*

**desktop** ['desktɒp] *n* COMPUT bureau *m* ; **desktop computer** ordinateur *m* de bureau ; **desktop publishing** publication *f* assistée par ordinateur

**desolate** ['desələt] *adj* [deserted] désolé ; [dreary, bleak] morne, triste

**despair** [dɪ'speə(r)] **1.** *n* désespoir *m* ; **to be in despair** être au désespoir **2.** *vi* désespérer (**of sb** de qn ; **of doing** de faire)

**despatch** [dɪ'spætʃ] *n & vt* = **dispatch**

**device**

**desperate** ['despərət] *adj* désespéré;
**to be desperate for** [money, love] avoir
désespérément besoin de; [cigarette,
baby] mourir d'envie d'avoir ■ **des-**
**perately** *adv* [ill] gravement

**despicable** [dɪ'spɪkəbəl] *adj* méprisable

**despise** [dɪ'spaɪz] *vt* mépriser

**despite** [dɪ'spaɪt] *prep* malgré

**despondent** [dɪ'spɒndənt] *adj* abattu

**dessert** [dɪ'zɜ:t] *n* dessert *m* ■ **des-**
**sertspoon** *n Br* cuillère *f* à dessert

**destination** [destɪ'neɪʃən] *n* destination *f*

**destine** ['destɪn] *vt* destiner (**for** à; **to**
**do** à faire)

**destiny** ['destɪnɪ] (*pl* -**ies**) *n* destin *m*,
destinée *f*

**destitute** ['destɪtju:t] *adj* [poor] indigent

**destroy** [dɪ'strɔɪ] *vt* détruire; [cat, dog]
faire piquer

**destruction** [dɪ'strʌkʃən] *n* destruction *f* ■ **destructive** *adj* [person, war]
destructeur, -trice

**detach** [dɪ'tætʃ] *vt* détacher (**from** de)
■ **detached** *adj Br* **detached house**
maison *f* individuelle

**detachable** [dɪ'tætʃəbəl] *adj* amovible

**detail** ['di:teɪl] *n* [item of information]
détail *m*; **in detail** en détail; **to go into**
**detail** entrer dans les détails ■ **de-**
**tailed** *adj* [account] détaillé

**detailing** ['di:teɪlɪŋ] *n Am* [thorough
cleaning] nettoyage *m* complet

**detain** [dɪ'teɪn] *vt* [delay] retenir; [prisoner] placer en détention; [in hospital]
garder ■ **detention** *n* [at school] retenue *f*

**detect** [dɪ'tekt] *vt* détecter

**detective** [dɪ'tektɪv] *n* [police officer]
≃ inspecteur *m* de police; [private]
détective *m* privé; **detective film /**
**novel** film *m* / roman *m* policier

**detector** [dɪ'tektə(r)] *n* détecteur *m*

**deter** [dɪ'tɜ:(r)] (*pt & pp* -**rr**-) *vt* **to deter**
**sb** dissuader qn (**from doing** de faire)

**detergent** [dɪ'tɜːʤənt] *n* détergent *m*

**deteriorate** [dɪ'tɪərɪəreɪt] *vi* se détériorer

**determine** [dɪ'tɜ:mɪn] *vt* [cause, date]
déterminer; **to determine to do sth**
décider de faire qch ■ **determined** *adj*
[look, person] déterminé; **to be deter-**
**mined to do sth** être décidé à faire qch

**deterrent** [dɪ'terənt] *n* **to be a de-**
**terrent, to act as a deterrent** être
dissuasif, -ive

**detest** [dɪ'test] *vt* détester (**doing** faire)

**detonate** ['detəneɪt] **1.** *vt* faire exploser
**2.** *vi* exploser

**detour** ['di:tʊə(r)] *n* détour *m*; **to make**
**a detour** faire un détour

**detract** [dɪ'trækt] *vi* **to detract from**
[make less] diminuer

**detriment** ['detrɪmənt] *n* **to the detri-**
**ment of** au détriment de ■ **detrimen-**
**tal** *adj* préjudiciable (**to** à)

**devaluation** [di:væljʊ'eɪʃən] *n* [of
money] dévaluation *f*

**devastate** ['devəsteɪt] *vt* [crop, village]
dévaster; [person] anéantir ■ **devas-**
**tating** *adj* [news, results] accablant

**develop** [dɪ'veləp] **1.** *vt* [theory, argument] développer; [area, land] mettre
en valeur; [habit] contracter; [photo]
développer **2.** *vi* [grow] se développer;
[of event, crisis] se produire; [of talent,
illness] se manifester; **to develop into**
devenir ■ **developing** *adj* **develop-**
**ing country** pays *m* en voie de développement

**developer** [dɪ'veləpə(r)] *n* (**property**)
**developer** promoteur *m*

**development** [dɪ'veləpmənt] *n* [growth,
progress] développement *m*; (**hous-**
**ing**) **development** lotissement *m*;
[large] grand ensemble *m*; **a (new)**
**development** [in situation] un fait
nouveau

**deviate** ['di:vɪeɪt] *vi* dévier (**from** de)

**device** [dɪ'vaɪs] *n* [instrument, gadget]
dispositif *m*; [scheme] procédé *m*; **ex-**
**plosive device** engin *m* explosif; **left**
**to one's own devices** livré à soi-même

**devil** ['devəl] n diable m ; Fam **what / where / why the devil?** que /où /pourquoi diable... ?

**devious** ['di:vɪəs] adj [mind, behaviour] tortueux, -euse

**devise** [dɪ'vaɪz] vt imaginer ; [plot] ourdir

**devoid** [dɪ'vɔɪd] adj **devoid of** dénué ou dépourvu de

**devote** [dɪ'vəʊt] vt consacrer (**to** à) ▪ **devoted** adj dévoué ; [admirer] fervent

**devotion** [dɪ'vəʊʃən] n [to friend, family, cause] dévouement m (**to sb** à qn) ; [religious] dévotion f

**devour** [dɪ'vaʊə(r)] vt [eat, engulf, read] dévorer

**devout** [dɪ'vaʊt] adj [person] dévot

**dew** [dju:] n rosée f

**diabetes** [daɪə'bi:ti:z] n diabète m ▪ **diabetic** [-'betɪk] **1.** adj diabétique **2.** n diabétique mf

**diagnose** [daɪəg'nəʊz] vt diagnostiquer ▪ **diagnosis** [-'nəʊsɪs] (pl **-oses** [-əʊsi:z]) n diagnostic m

**diagonal** [daɪ'ægənəl] **1.** adj diagonal **2.** n diagonale f ▪ **diagonally** adv en diagonale

**diagram** ['daɪəgræm] n schéma m

**dial** ['daɪəl] **1.** n cadran m ; Am **dial tone** tonalité f **2.** (Br **-ll-**, Am **-l-**) vt [phone number] composer ; [person] appeler ▪ **dialling** n Br **dialling code** indicatif m ; Br **dialling tone** tonalité f

**dialect** ['daɪəlekt] n dialecte m

**dialogue**, Am **dialog** ['daɪəlɒg] n dialogue m

**diameter** [daɪ'æmɪtə(r)] n diamètre m

**diamond** ['daɪəmənd] n **a)** [stone] diamant m ; [shape] losange m ; **diamond necklace** rivière f de diamants **b)** **diamond(s)** [in card games] carreau m

**diaper** ['daɪpər] n Am couche f

**diarrh(o)ea** [daɪə'ri:ə] n diarrhée f ; **to have diarrh(o)ea** avoir la diarrhée

**diary** ['daɪərɪ] (pl **-ies**) n Br [for appointments] agenda m ; [private] journal m (intime)

**dice** [daɪs] n inv dé m

**dictate** [dɪk'teɪt] **1.** vt [letter, conditions] dicter (**to** à) **2.** vi dicter qn ▪ **dictation** n dictée f

**dictator** [dɪk'teɪtə(r)] n dictateur m

**dictionary** ['dɪkʃənərɪ] (pl **-ies**) n dictionnaire m

**did** [dɪd] pt of do

**die** [daɪ] (pt & pp died, pres p dying) vi mourir (**of** or **from** de) ; Fig **to be dying to do sth** mourir d'envie de faire qch ; **to be dying for sth** avoir une envie folle de qch ; **to die away** [of noise] mourir ; **to die down** [of storm] se calmer ; **to die out** [of custom] mourir

**diesel** ['di:zəl] adj & n diesel **(engine)** (moteur m) diesel m ; **diesel (oil)** gazole m

**diet** ['daɪət] **1.** n [usual food] alimentation f ; [restricted food] régime m ; **to go on a diet** faire un régime **2.** vi être au régime

**differ** ['dɪfə(r)] vi différer (**from** de) ; [disagree] ne pas être d'accord (**from** avec)

**difference** ['dɪfərəns] n différence f (**in** de) ; **difference of opinion** différend m ; **it makes no difference** ça n'a pas d'importance

**different** ['dɪfərənt] adj différent (**from** de) ; [another] autre ; [various] divers

**differentiate** [dɪfə'renʃɪeɪt] **1.** vt différencier (**from** de) **2.** vi faire la différence (**between** entre) ▪ **differently** adv différemment (**from** de)

**difficult** ['dɪfɪkəlt] adj difficile (**to do** à faire)

**difficulty** ['dɪfɪkəltɪ] (pl **-ies**) n difficulté f ; **to have difficulty doing sth** avoir du mal à faire qch

**dig** [dɪg] **1.** n [with elbow] coup de coude ; Fam [remark] pique f **2.** (pt & pp dug, pres p digging) vt [ground, garden] bêcher ; [hole, grave] creuser ; **to dig sth into sth** [push] planter qch dans qch ; **to dig out** [from ground] déterrer ; Fam [find] dénicher ; **to dig up** [from ground] déterrer ; [road] excaver **3.** vi [dig a hole] creuser

**digest** [daɪ'dʒest] *vti* digérer ■ **digestion** *n* digestion *f*

**digibox** ['dɪdʒɪbɒks] *n Br* TV décodeur *m* numérique

**digit** ['dɪdʒɪt] *n* [number] chiffre *m* ■ **digital** *adj* numérique ; [tape, recording] audionumérique ; **digital camcorder** Caméscope® *m* numérique ; **digital camera** appareil *m* photo numérique ; **digital divide, digital gap** fracture *f* numérique ; **digital radio** radio *f* numérique ; **digital signature** signature *f* électronique *ou* numérique

**dignified** ['dɪɡnɪfaɪd] *adj* digne ■ **dignity** *n* dignité *f*

**digress** [daɪ'gres] *vi* faire une digression

**digs** [dɪgz] *npl Br Fam* piaule *f*

**dilapidated** [dɪ'læpɪdeɪtɪd] *adj* [house] délabré

**dilemma** [daɪ'lemə] *n* dilemme *m*

**diligent** ['dɪlɪdʒənt] *adj* appliqué

**dilute** [daɪ'luːt] *vt* diluer

**dim** [dɪm] **1.** (*compar* dimmer, *superl* dimmest) *adj* [light] faible ; [room] sombre ; [memory] vague ; [person] stupide **2.** (*pt & pp* -mm-) *vt* [light] baisser ; *Am* **to dim one's headlights** se mettre en code

**dime** [daɪm] *n Am* (pièce *f* de) dix cents *mpl*

**dimension** [daɪ'menʃən] *n* dimension *f*

**diminish** [dɪ'mɪnɪʃ] *vti* diminuer

**dimple** ['dɪmpəl] *n* fossette *f*

**din** [dɪn] *n* [noise] vacarme *m*

**dine** [daɪn] *vi* dîner (**on** *or* **off** de) ; **to dine out** aller dîner au restaurant ■ **diner** *n* [person] dîneur, -euse *mf* ; *Am* [restaurant] petit restaurant *m* ■ **dining** *n* **dining car** [on train] wagon-restaurant *m* ; **dining room** salle *f* à manger

**dinghy** ['dɪŋgɪ] (*pl* -ies) *n* petit canot *m* ; (**rubber**) **dinghy** canot *m* pneumatique

**dingy** ['dɪndʒɪ] (*compar* -ier, *superl* -iest) *adj* [room] minable ; [colour] terne

**dinner** ['dɪnə(r)] *n* [evening meal] dîner *m* ; [lunch] déjeuner *m* ; **to have dinner** dîner ; **dinner jacket** smo-

king *m* ; **dinner party** dîner *m* ; **dinner plate** grande assiette *f* ; **dinner service, dinner set** service *m* de table

**dinosaur** ['daɪnəsɔː(r)] *n* dinosaure *m*

**dip** [dɪp] **1.** *n* [in road] petit creux *m* ; **to go for a dip** [swim] faire trempette **2.** (*pt & pp* -pp-) *vt* plonger ; *Br* **to dip one's headlights** se mettre en code **3.** *vi* [of road] plonger ; **to dip into** [pocket, savings] puiser dans ; [book] feuilleter

**diploma** [dɪ'pləʊmə] *n* diplôme *m*

**diplomat** ['dɪpləmæt] *n* diplomate *mf* ■ **diplomatic** *adj* diplomatique

**dire** ['daɪə(r)] *adj* [situation] affreux, -euse ; [consequences] tragique ; [poverty, need] extrême ; **to be in dire straits** être dans une mauvaise passe

**direct** [daɪ'rekt] **1.** *adj* [result, flight, person] direct ; *Br* **direct debit** prélèvement *m* automatique **2.** *adv* directement **3.** *vt* [gaze, light, attention] diriger (**at** sur) ; [traffic] régler ; [letter, remark] adresser (**to** à) ; [film] réaliser ; [play] mettre en scène ; **to direct sb to** [place] indiquer à qn le chemin de ; **to direct sb to do sth** charger qn de faire qch

**direction** [daɪ'rekʃən] *n* direction *f*, sens *m* ; **directions** [orders] indications *fpl* ; **directions (for use)** mode *m* d'emploi

**directly** [daɪ'rektlɪ] *adv* [without detour] directement ; [exactly] juste ; [at once] tout de suite ; **directly in front** juste devant

**director** [daɪ'rektə(r)] *n* directeur, -trice *mf* ; [board member] administrateur, -trice *mf* ; [of film] réalisateur, -trice *mf* ; [of play] metteur *m* en scène

**directory** [daɪ'rektərɪ] (*pl* -ies) *n* [phone book] annuaire *m* ; [of addresses & COMPUT] répertoire *m* ; **telephone directory** annuaire *m* du téléphone ; *Br* **directory enquiries** renseignements *mpl* téléphoniques

**dirt** [dɜːt] *n* saleté *f* ; [mud] boue *f* ; [earth] terre *f* ; *Fam* **dirt cheap** très bon marché

**dirty** ['dɜːtɪ] **1.** (*compar* -ier, *superl* -iest) *adj* sale ; [job] salissant ; [word] grossier, -ère ; **to get dirty** se salir ; **to get sth**

**dirty** salir qch; **a dirty joke** une histoire cochonne; **a dirty trick** un sale tour **2.** *vt* salir

**dis** [dɪs] *Am Fam vt* = **diss**

**disability** [dɪsə'bɪlɪtɪ] *(pl -ies) n* [injury] infirmité *f*; [condition] invalidité *f*; *Fig* désavantage *m*

**disabled** [dɪ'seɪbəld] **1.** *adj* handicapé **2.** *npl* **the disabled** les handicapés *mpl*

**disadvantage** [dɪsəd'vɑːntɪdʒ] **1.** *n* désavantage *m* **2.** *vt* désavantager

**disagree** [dɪsə'griː] *vi* ne pas être d'accord (**with** avec); **to disagree with sb** [of food, climate, medicine] ne pas réussir à qn ▪ **disagreement** *n* désaccord *m*; [quarrel] différend *m*

**disagreeable** [dɪsə'griːəbəl] *adj* désagréable

**disappear** [dɪsə'pɪə(r)] *vi* disparaître ▪ **disappearance** *n* disparition *f*

**disappoint** [dɪsə'pɔɪnt] *vt* décevoir ▪ **disappointing** *adj* décevant ▪ **disappointment** *n* déception *f*

**disapproval** [dɪsə'pruːvəl] *n* désapprobation *f*

**disapprove** [dɪsə'pruːv] *vi* **to disapprove of sb/sth** désapprouver qn/qch

**disarray** [dɪsə'reɪ] *n* **in disarray** [army, political party] en plein désarroi; [clothes, hair] en désordre

**disaster** [dɪ'zɑːstə(r)] *n* désastre *m*, catastrophe *f*; **disaster area** région *f* sinistrée ▪ **disastrous** *adj* désastreux, -euse

**disband** [dɪs'bænd] **1.** *vt* dissoudre **2.** *vi* se dissoudre

**disbelief** [dɪsbə'liːf] *n* incrédulité *f*

**disc, Am disk** [dɪsk] *n* disque *m*; **disc jockey** disc-jockey *m*

**discard** [dɪs'kɑːd] *vt* [get rid of] se débarrasser de; [plan] abandonner

**discern** [dɪ's3ːn] *vt* discerner ▪ **discerning** *adj* [person] averti

**discernible** [dɪ's3ːnəbəl] *adj* perceptible

**discharge 1.** ['dɪstʃɑːdʒ] *n* [of gun, electricity] décharge *f*; [dismissal] ren-

voi *m*; [freeing] libération *f* **2.** [dɪs'tʃɑːdʒ] *vt* [patient] laisser sortir; [employee] renvoyer; [soldier, prisoner] libérer; [gun] décharger

**disciple** [dɪ'saɪpəl] *n* disciple *m*

**discipline** ['dɪsɪplɪn] **1.** *n* [behaviour, subject] discipline *f* **2.** *vt* [control] discipliner; [punish] punir

**disclose** [dɪs'kləʊz] *vt* révéler ▪ **disclosure** [-ʒə(r)] *n* révélation *f*

**disco** ['dɪskəʊ] *(pl -os) n* discothèque *f*

**discolour, Am discolor** [dɪs'kʌlə(r)] *vt* décolorer; [teeth] jaunir

**discomfort** [dɪs'kʌmfət] *n* [physical] petite douleur *f*; [mental] malaise *m*

**disconcerting** [dɪskən's3ːtɪŋ] *adj* déconcertant

**disconnect** [dɪskə'nekt] *vt* [unfasten] détacher; [unplug] débrancher; [gas, telephone, electricity] couper

**discontented** [dɪskən'tentɪd] *adj* mécontent (**with** de)

**discord** ['dɪskɔːd] *n* [disagreement] discorde *f*

**discotheque** ['dɪskətek] *n* [club] discothèque *f*

**discount 1.** ['dɪskaʊnt] *n* [on article] réduction *f*; [on account paid early] escompte *m*; **discount store** solderie *f* **2.** [dɪs'kaʊnt] *vt* [story] ne pas tenir compte de

**discourage** [dɪs'kʌrɪdʒ] *vt* décourager (**sb from doing** qn de faire)

**discover** [dɪs'kʌvə(r)] *vt* découvrir (**that** que) ▪ **discovery** *(pl -ies) n* découverte *f*

**discredit** [dɪs'kredɪt] *vt* [cast slur on] discréditer

**discreet** [dɪ'skriːt] *adj* discret, -ète

**discrepancy** [dɪ'skrepənsɪ] *(pl -ies) n* décalage *m* (**between** entre)

**discretion** [dɪ'skreʃən] *n* [tact] discrétion *f*

**discriminate** [dɪ'skrɪmɪneɪt] *vi* **to discriminate against** faire de la discrimination envers; **to discriminate**

**between** distinguer entre ■ **discrimination** [-'neɪʃən] *n* [bias] discrimination *f*

**discus** ['dɪskəs] *n* SPORT disque *m*

**discuss** [dɪ'skʌs] *vt* discuter de ■ **discussion** *n* discussion *f*; INTERNET **discussion forum** forum *m* de discussion; INTERNET **discussion group** groupe *m* de discussion; INTERNET **discussion thread** fil *m* de discussion

**disdain** [dɪs'deɪn] *n* dédain *m*

**disease** [dɪ'ziːz] *n* maladie *f*

**disembark** [dɪsɪm'bɑːk] *vti* débarquer

**disenchanted** [dɪsɪn'tʃɑːntɪd] *adj* désenchanté

**disfigured** [dɪs'fɪɡə(r)] *adj* défiguré

**disgrace** [dɪs'ɡreɪs] **1.** *n* [shame] honte *f* (**to** à) **2.** *vt* déshonorer ■ **disgraceful** *adj* honteux, -euse

**disgruntled** [dɪs'ɡrʌntəld] *adj* mécontent

**disguise** [dɪs'ɡaɪz] **1.** *n* déguisement *m*; **in disguise** déguisé **2.** *vt* déguiser (**as** en)

**disgust** [dɪs'ɡʌst] **1.** *n* dégoût *m* (**for** or **at** or **with** de) **2.** *vt* dégoûter ■ **disgusted** *adj* dégoûté (**at** or **by** or **with** de); **to be disgusted with sb** [annoyed] être fâché contre qn ■ **disgusting** *adj* dégoûtant

**dish** [dɪʃ] **1.** *n* [container, food] plat *m*; **to do the dishes** faire la vaisselle; **dish rack** égouttoir *m* (à vaisselle) **2.** *vt* **to dish out** or **up** [food] servir ■ **dishcloth** *n* [for washing] lavette *f*; [for drying] torchon *m* ■ **dishtowel** *n* torchon *m* (à vaisselle) ■ **dishwasher** *n* [machine] lave-vaisselle *m* inv ■ **dishwashing liquid** *n* Am liquide *m* vaisselle

**dishevelled**, Am **disheveled** [dɪ'ʃevəld] *adj* [person, hair] ébouriffé

**dishonest** [dɪs'ɒnɪst] *adj* malhonnête ■ **dishonesty** *n* malhonnêteté *f*

**dishonourable**, Am **dishonorable** [dɪs'ɒnərəbəl] *adj* déshonorant

**disillusion** [dɪsɪ'luːʒən] *vt* décevoir; **to be disillusioned** être déçu (**with** de)

**disinclined** [dɪsɪn'klaɪnd] *adj* peu disposé (**to do** à faire)

**disinfect** [dɪsɪn'fekt] *vt* désinfecter ■ **disinfectant** *n* désinfectant *m*

**disinherit** [dɪsɪn'herɪt] *vt* déshériter

**disintegrate** [dɪs'ɪntɪɡreɪt] *vi* se désintégrer

**disinterested** [dɪs'ɪntrɪstɪd] *adj* [impartial] désintéressé

**disjointed** [dɪs'dʒɔɪntɪd] *adj* [words, style] décousu

**disk** [dɪsk] *n* **a)** Am = **disc b)** COMPUT disque *m*; **on disk** sur disque; **disk drive** unité *f* de disques; **disk space** espace *m* disque

**dislike** [dɪs'laɪk] **1.** *n* aversion *f* (**for** or **of** pour); **to take a dislike to sb/sth** prendre qn/qch en grippe **2.** *vt* ne pas aimer (**doing** faire)

**dislocate** ['dɪsləkeɪt] *vt* [limb] démettre; **to dislocate one's shoulder** se démettre l'épaule

**dislodge** [dɪs'lɒdʒ] *vt* faire bouger, déplacer; [enemy] déloger

**disloyal** [dɪs'lɔɪəl] *adj* déloyal

**dismal** ['dɪzməl] *adj* lugubre ■ **dismally** *adv* [fail, behave] lamentablement

**dismantle** [dɪs'mæntəl] *vt* [machine] démonter; [organization] démanteler

**dismay** [dɪs'meɪ] **1.** *n* consternation *f* **2.** *vt* consterner

**dismiss** [dɪs'mɪs] *vt* [from job] renvoyer (**from** de); [official] destituer; [thought, suggestion] écarter; **to dismiss a case** [of judge] classer une affaire ■ **dismissal** *n* renvoi *m*; [of official] destitution *f*

**dismount** [dɪs'maʊnt] *vi* [of person] descendre (**from** de)

**disobedient** [dɪsə'biːdɪənt] *adj* désobéissant

**disobey** [dɪsə'beɪ] **1.** *vt* désobéir à **2.** *vi* désobéir

**disorder** [dɪs'ɔːdə(r)] *n* [confusion] désordre *m*; [illness, riots] troubles *mpl* ■ **disorderly** *adj* [behaviour] désordonné; [meeting, crowd] houleux, -euse

**disorganized** [dɪs'ɔ:gənaɪzd] *adj* désorganisé

**disorientate** [dɪs'ɔ:rɪənteɪt], *Am* **disorient** [dɪs'ɔ:rɪənt] *vt* désorienter

**disown** [dɪs'əʊn] *vt* renier

**disparaging** [dɪs'pærɪdʒɪŋ] *adj* [remark] désobligeant

**dispatch** [dɪ'spætʃ] **1.** *n* [sending] expédition *f* (**of** de); [message] dépêche *f* **2.** *vt* [send, finish off] expédier; [troops, messenger] envoyer

**dispel** [dɪ'spel] (*pt & pp* -ll-) *vt* dissiper

**dispensary** [dɪ'spensərɪ] (*pl* -ies) *n* [in chemist's shop] officine *f*

**dispense** [dɪ'spens] **1.** *vt* [give out] distribuer; [medicine] préparer **2.** *vt* to **dispense with** [do without] se passer de ■ **dispenser** *n* [device] distributeur *m*

**disperse** [dɪ'spɜ:s] **1.** *vt* disperser **2.** *vi* se disperser

**displace** [dɪs'pleɪs] *vt* [shift] déplacer; [replace] supplanter

**display** [dɪ'spleɪ] **1.** *n* **a)** [in shop] étalage *m*; [of paintings, handicrafts] exposition *f*; **on display** exposé **b)** COMPUT [device] écran *m*; [information displayed] affichage *m*, visualisation *f*; **display (unit)** [of computer] moniteur *m* **2.** *vt* [goods] exposer; [sign, notice] afficher; [emotion] manifester; [talent, concern, ignorance] faire preuve de

**displeased** [dɪs'pli:zd] *adj* mécontent (**with** de)

**disposable** [dɪ'spəʊzəbəl] *adj Br* [plate, nappy] jetable; [income] disponible; **disposable camera** appareil *m* photo jetable

**disposal** [dɪ'spəʊzəl] *n* [of waste] évacuation *f*; **at sb's disposal** à la disposition de qn

**dispose¹** [dɪ'spəʊz] *vi* to **dispose of** [get rid of] se débarrasser de; [throw away] jeter; [matter, problem] régler

**dispose²** [dɪ'spəʊz] *vt* to **be disposed to do** être disposé à faire; **well-disposed towards** bien disposé envers

**disposition** [dɪspə'zɪʃən] *n* [character] tempérament *m*

**dispossess** [dɪspə'zes] *vt* déposséder (**of** de)

**disproportionate** [dɪsprə'pɔ:ʃənət] *adj* disproportionné

**disprove** [dɪs'pru:v] (*pp* **disproved**) (*pp Law* **disproven** [-'prəʊvən]) *vt* réfuter

**dispute** [dɪ'spju:t] **1.** *n* [quarrel] dispute *f*; [legal] litige *m*; **(industrial) dispute** conflit *m* social **2.** *vt* [claim, will] contester

**disqualify** [dɪs'kwɒlɪfaɪ] (*pt & pp* -ied) *vt* [make unfit] rendre inapte (**from** à); SPORT disqualifier; **to disqualify sb from driving** retirer son permis à qn ■ **disqualification** *n* SPORT disqualification *f*

**disregard** [dɪsrɪ'gɑ:d] **1.** *n* mépris *m* (**for** de) **2.** *vt* ne tenir aucun compte de

**disrepair** [dɪsrɪ'peə(r)] *n* **in (a state of) disrepair** délabré

**disreputable** [dɪs'repjʊtəbəl] *adj* peu recommandable; [behaviour] honteux, -euse

**disrepute** [dɪsrɪ'pju:t] *n* **to bring sb/ sth into disrepute** discréditer qn/qch

**disrespectful** [dɪsrɪ'spektfʊl] *adj* irrespectueux, -euse (**to** envers)

**disrupt** [dɪs'rʌpt] *vt* [traffic, class] perturber; [communications] interrompre; [plan] déranger ■ **disruption** *n* perturbation *f*

**disruptive** [dɪs'rʌptɪv] *adj* perturbateur, -trice

**diss** [dɪs] *vt* **a)** *Am Fam* faire semblant de ne pas voir, ignorer; **she dissed me** elle m'a même pas calculé **b)** (*abbr of* **disrespect**) insulter, offenser; **she dissed me** ≃ elle m'a traité

**dissatisfied** [dɪ'sætɪsfaɪd] *adj* mécontent (**with** de) ■ **dissatisfaction** [-'fækʃən] *n* mécontentement *m* (**with** devant)

**dissent** [dɪ'sent] **1.** *n* désaccord *m* **2.** *vi* être en désaccord (**from** avec)

**dissertation** [dɪsə'teɪʃn] *n* **a)** thèse *f* (*de doctorat*) **b)** exposé *m* **c)** UNIV mémoire *m*

**dissident** ['dɪsɪdənt] *adj & n* dissident, -e (*mf*)

**divine**

**dissimilar** [dɪ'sɪmɪlə(r)] *adj* différent (**to** de)

**dissipate** ['dɪsɪpeɪt] *vt* [fog, fears] dissiper ; [energy, fortune] gaspiller

**dissociate** [dɪ'səʊʃɪeɪt] *vt* dissocier (**from** de)

**dissolute** ['dɪsəluːt] *adj* dissolu

**dissolve** [dɪ'zɒlv] **1.** *vt* dissoudre **2.** *vi* se dissoudre

**dissuade** [dɪ'sweɪd] *vt* dissuader (**from doing** de faire)

**distance** ['dɪstəns] *n* distance *f* ; **in the distance** au loin ; **from a distance** de loin ; **to keep one's distance** garder ses distances

**distant** ['dɪstənt] *adj* lointain ; [relative] éloigné ; [reserved] distant

**distasteful** [dɪs'teɪstfʊl] *adj* déplaisant

**distil** [dɪ'stɪl] (*pt & pp* -ll-) *vt* distiller ; **distilled water** eau *f* déminéralisée

**distinct** [dɪ'stɪŋkt] *adj* **a)** [clear] clair ; [preference, improvement, difference] net (*f* nette) **b)** [different] distinct (**from** de) ■ **distinctly** *adv* [see, hear] distinctement ; [remember] très bien ; [better, easier] nettement

**distinction** [dɪ'stɪŋkʃən] *n* distinction *f* ; [in exam] mention *f* bien

**distinctive** [dɪ'stɪŋktɪv] *adj* distinctif, -ive

**distinguish** [dɪ'stɪŋgwɪʃ] *vti* distinguer (**from** de ; **between** entre) ; **to distinguish oneself** se distinguer (**as** en tant que)

**distinguished** [dɪs'tɪŋgwɪʃd] *adj* distingué

**distort** [dɪ'stɔːt] *vt* déformer ■ **distortion** *n* [of features, sound] distorsion *f* ; [of truth] déformation *f*

**distract** [dɪ'strækt] *vt* distraire (**from** de) ■ **distracted** *adj* préoccupé

**distraction** [dɪ'strækʃən] *n* distraction *f*

**distraught** [dɪ'strɔːt] *adj* éperdu

**distress** [dɪ'stres] **1.** *n* [mental] détresse *f* ; [physical] douleur *f* **2.** *vt* bouleverser ■ **distressing** *adj* bouleversant

**distribute** [dɪ'strɪbjuːt] *vt* [give out & COMM] [supply] distribuer ; [spread evenly] répartir ■ **distribution** [-'bjuːʃən] *n* distribution *f*

**distributor** [dɪs'trɪbjʊtə(r)] *n* [in car, of films] distributeur *m*

**district** ['dɪstrɪkt] *n* région *f* ; [of town] quartier *m* ; [administrative] district *m*

**distrust** [dɪs'trʌst] **1.** *n* méfiance *f* (**of** à l'égard de) **2.** *vt* se méfier de

**disturb** [dɪ'stɜːb] *vt* [sleep, water] troubler ; [papers, belongings] déranger ; **to disturb sb** [bother] déranger qn ; [worry, alarm] troubler qn ■ **disturbing** *adj* [worrying] inquiétant ; [annoying, irksome] gênant

**disturbance** [dɪ'stɜːbəns] *n* [noise] tapage *m* ; **disturbances** [riots] troubles *mpl*

**disunity** [dɪs'juːnɪtɪ] *n* désunion *f*

**disuse** [dɪs'juːs] *n* **to fall into disuse** tomber en désuétude ■ **disused** *adj* [building] désaffecté

**ditch** [dɪtʃ] **1.** *n* fossé *m* **2.** *vt* Fam [get rid of] se débarrasser de ; [plan] laisser tomber

**ditto** ['dɪtəʊ] *adv* idem

**dive** [daɪv] **1.** *n* [of swimmer, goalkeeper] plongeon *m* ; [of aircraft] piqué *m* **2.** (*pt* dived, Am *pt* dove) *vi* plonger ; [of plane] piquer ■ **diver** *n* plongeur, -euse *mf* ; [deep-sea] scaphandrier *m*

**diverge** [daɪ'vɜːdʒ] *vi* diverger (**from** de)

**diverse** [daɪ'vɜːs] *adj* divers ■ **diversity** *n* diversité *f* ■ **diversify** (*pt & pp* -ied) *vi* [of firm] se diversifier

**diversion** [daɪ'vɜːʃən] *n* Br [on road] déviation *f* ; [amusement] distraction *f* ; **to create a diversion** faire diversion

**divert** [daɪ'vɜːt] *vt* [attention, suspicions, river, plane] détourner ; Br [traffic] dévier ; [amuse] divertir

**divide** [dɪ'vaɪd] *vt* MATH diviser (**into** en ; **by** par) ; [food, money, time] partager (**between** *or* **among** entre) ; **to divide sth (off) (from sth)** séparer qch (de qch) ; **to divide sth up** [share out] partager qch

**divine** [dɪ'vaɪn] *adj* divin

**diving** ['daɪvɪŋ] n [underwater] plongée f sous-marine ; **diving board** plongeoir m

**division** [dɪ'vɪʒən] n division f ; [distribution] partage m ; SPORT **first division** première division

**divorce** [dɪ'vɔːs] **1.** n divorce m **2.** vt [husband, wife] divorcer de ; Fig [idea] séparer (**from** de) **3.** vi divorcer ■ **divorced** adj divorcé (**from** de) ; **to get divorced** divorcer ■ **divorcee** [dɪvɔː'siː, Am dɪvɔːr'seɪ] n divorcé, -e mf

**divulge** [dɪ'vʌldʒ] vt divulguer

**DIY** [diːaɪ'waɪ] (abbr of **do-it-yourself**) n Br bricolage m

**dizzy** ['dɪzɪ] (compar -ier, superl -iest) adj **to be** or **feel dizzy** avoir le vertige ; **to make sb (feel) dizzy** donner le vertige à qn

**DJ** ['diːdʒeɪ] (abbr of **disc-jockey**) n disc-jockey m

**Dk**, **DK** MESSAGING written abbr of **don't know**

**DNA** (abbr of **deoxyribonucleic acid**) n ADN m (acide désoxyribonucléique)

**DNS** [diːen'es] (abbr of **Domain Name System**) n COMPUT DNS m, système m de nom de domaine

**do** [duː] (3rd person sing present tense **does**) (pt **did**, pp **done**, pres p **doing**)

Les formes négatives sont **don't / doesn't** et **didn't**, qui deviennent **do not / does not** et **did not** dans un style plus soutenu.

**1.** v aux **do you know?** savez-vous ?, est-ce que vous savez ? ; **I do not** or **don't see** je ne vois pas ; **he did say so** [emphasis] il l'a bien dit ; **do stay** reste donc ; **you know him, don't you?** tu le connais, n'est-ce pas ? ; **better than I do** mieux que je ne le fais ; **so do I** moi aussi ; **don't!** non !

**2.** vt faire ; **what does she do?** [in general] qu'est-ce qu'elle fait ?, que fait-elle ? ; **what is she doing?** [now] qu'est-ce qu'elle fait ?, que fait-elle ? ; **what have you done (with...)?** qu'as-tu fait (de...) ? ; **well done** [congratulations] bravo ! ; [steak] bien cuit ; **it's over and done (with)** c'est fini ; **that'll**

**do me** [suit] ça m'ira ; Br Fam **I've been done** [cheated] je me suis fait avoir ; **to do sb out of sth** escroquer qch à qn ; Fam **I'm done (in)** [tired] je suis claqué ; **to do out** [clean] nettoyer ; **to do over** [redecorate] refaire ; **to do up** [coat, buttons] boutonner ; [zip] fermer ; [house] refaire ; [goods] emballer

**3.** vi **do as you're told** fais ce qu'on te dit ; **that will do** [be OK] ça ira ; [be enough] ça suffit ; **have you done?** vous avez fini ? ; **to do well / badly** [of person] bien / mal se débrouiller ; **business is doing well** les affaires marchent bien ; **how are you doing?** (comment) ça va ? ; **how do you do** [introduction] enchanté ; [greeting] bonjour ; **to make do** se débrouiller ; **to do away with sb / sth** supprimer qn / qch ; **I could do with a coffee** [need, want] je prendrais bien un café ; **it has to do with...** [relates to] cela a à voir avec... ; [concerns] cela concerne...

**4.** (pl **dos**) n Br Fam [party] fête f

■ **do without 1.** vt insep se passer de **2.** vi s'en passer

**docile** ['dəʊsaɪl] adj docile

**dock** [dɒk] **1.** n a) [for ship] dock m b) [in court] banc m des accusés **2.** vi [of ship at quayside] accoster ; [in port] relâcher

**doctor** ['dɒktə(r)] **1.** n [medical] médecin m, docteur m ; [having doctor's degree] docteur m **2.** vt [text, food] altérer ; Br [cat] châtrer ■ **doctorate** n doctorat m (in ès / en)

**document** ['dɒkjʊmənt] n document m ■ **documentary** [-'mentərɪ] (pl -ies) n [film] documentaire m

**dodge** [dɒdʒ] **1.** n [trick] truc m **2.** vt [question] esquiver ; [person] éviter ; [pursuer] échapper à ; [tax] éviter de payer **3.** vi [to one side] faire un saut de côté ; **to dodge through** [crowd] se faufiler dans

**Dodgems®** ['dɒdʒəmz] npl autos fpl tamponneuses

**dodgy** ['dɒdʒɪ] (compar -ier, superl -iest) adj Fam [suspect] louche ; [not working properly] en mauvais état ; [risky] risqué

**does** [dʌz] *see* **do**

**doesn't** ['dʌzənt] = **does not**

**dog**[1] [dɒg] *n* chien *m* ; [female] chienne *f* ; *Br***dog dirt** crottes *fpl* de chien ; *Br***dog mess** crottes *fpl* de chien ; [referred to in official notices] déjections *fpl* canines ; *Br***sniffer dog** chien *m* renifleur

**dog**[2] [dɒg] *(pt & pp -gg-) vt* [follow] suivre de près

**doggedly** ['dɒgɪdlɪ] *adv* obstinément

**doggone** ['dɑːgɑːn] *excl Am Fam* **doggone (it)!** zut !, nom d'une pipe !

**doing** ['duːɪŋ] *n* **that's your doing** c'est toi qui as fait ça

**do-it-yourself** [duːɪtjə'self] *n Br* bricolage *m* ; **do-it-yourself store / book** magasin *m* / livre *m* de bricolage

**dole** [dəʊl] *n Br* **dole (money)** allocation *f* de chômage ; **to go on the dole** s'inscrire au chômage

**doll** [dɒl] *n* poupée *f* ; *Br* **doll's house** maison *f* de poupée

**dollar** ['dɒlə(r)] *n* dollar *m*

**dollhouse** ['dɒlhaʊs] *n Am* maison *f* de poupée

**dollop** ['dɒləp] *n* [of cream, purée] grosse cuillerée *f*

**dolphin** ['dɒlfɪn] *n* dauphin *m*

**domain** [dəʊ'meɪn] *n* [land, sphere] domaine *m*

**dome** [dəʊm] *n* dôme *m*

**domestic** [də'mestɪk] *adj* [appliance, use, tasks] ménager, -ère ; [animal] domestique ; [policy, flight, affairs] intérieur

**dominant** ['dɒmɪnənt] *adj* dominant ; [person] dominateur, -trice

**dominate** ['dɒmɪneɪt] *vti* dominer

**domineering** [dɒmɪ'nɪərɪŋ] *adj* [person, character] dominateur, -trice

**domino** ['dɒmɪnəʊ] *(pl -oes) n* domino *m* ; **dominoes** [game] dominos *mpl*

**donate** [dəʊ'neɪt] **1.** *vt* faire don de ; [blood] donner **2.** *vi* donner ▪ **donation** *n* don *m*

**done** [dʌn] *pp of* **do**

**donkey** ['dɒŋkɪ] *(pl -eys) n* âne *m*

**donor** ['dəʊnə(r)] *n* donneur, -euse *mf*

**don't** [dəʊnt] = **do not**

**donut** ['dəʊnʌt] *n Am* beignet *m*

**doom** [duːm] **1.** *n* [fate] destin *m* **2.** *vt* condamner **(to** à) ; **to be doomed (to failure)** [of project] être voué à l'échec

**door** [dɔː(r)] *n* porte *f* ; [of vehicle, train] portière *f* ; **door handle** poignée *f* de porte ▪ **doorbell** *n* sonnette *f* ▪ **doorknob** *n* bouton *m* de porte ▪ **doorman** *(pl -men) n* [of hotel] portier *m* ▪ **doormat** *n* paillasson *m* ▪ **doorstep** *n* seuil *m* ▪ **door-to-door** *adj* **door-to-door salesman** démarcheur *m* ▪ **doorway** *n* **in the doorway** dans l'embrasure de la porte

**doozy** ['duːzɪ] *n Am Fam* **wow, that bruise is a real doozy!** eh ben, il est énorme ce bleu ! ; **I'm having a doozy of a problem with this camera** j'ai un sacré problème avec cet appareil ; **it's a doozy of a challenge** c'est un sacré défi

**dope** [dəʊp] *n Fam* **a)** [drugs] drogue *f* **b)** [idiot] andouille *f*

**dork** [dɔːk] *n Am Fam* [idiot] niais, -e *mf* ; [studious person] binoclard, -e *mf*

**dormitory** [*Br* 'dɔːmɪtrɪ, *Am* 'dɔːrmɪtɔːrɪ] *(pl -ies) n* dortoir *m* ; *Am* [university residence] résidence *f* universitaire

**dosage** ['dəʊsɪdʒ] *n* [amount] dose *f*

**dose** [dəʊs] *n* dose *f* ; **a dose of flu** une grippe

**dossier** ['dɒsɪeɪ] *n* [papers] dossier *m*

**dot** [dɒt] **1.** *n* point *m* ; *Fam* **on the dot** à l'heure pile **2.** *(pt & pp -tt-) vt* [letter] mettre un point sur ; **dotted with** parsemé de ; **dotted line** pointillé *m*

**dotcom** ['dɒtkɒm] *n* dot com *f*

**dote** [dəʊt] *vt* **to dote on** adorer

**dot-matrix** [dɒt'meɪtrɪks] *n* COMPUT **dot-matrix printer** imprimante *f* matricielle

**double** ['dʌbəl] **1.** *adj* double ; **a double bed** un grand lit ; **a double room** une chambre pour deux personnes ; **double 's'** deux 's' ; **double three four two** [phone number] trente-trois quarante-deux

**2.** *adv* [twice] deux fois ; [fold] en deux ; **he earns double what I do** il gagne le double de moi

**3.** *n* double *m* ; [person] double *m*, sosie *m* ; [stand-in in film] doublure *f*

**4.** *vt* doubler ; **to double sth back** or **over** [fold] replier qch ; **to be doubled up with pain /laughter** être plié (en deux) de douleur /rire

**5.** *vi* doubler ; **to double back** [of person] revenir en arrière

■ **double-bass** *n Br* [instrument] contrebasse *f*

■ **double-check** *vti* revérifier

■ **double-cross** *vt* doubler

■ **double-decker** *n* **double-decker (bus)** autobus *m* à impériale

■ **double figures** *npl Br* **to be in(to) double figures** être au-dessus de dix, dépasser la dizaine

■ **double-glazing** *n* [window] double vitrage *m*

---

**doubt** [daʊt] **1.** *n* doute *m* ; **I have no doubt about it** je n'en doute pas ; **no doubt** [probably] sans doute ; **in doubt** [result, career] dans la balance **2.** *vt* douter de ; **to doubt whether** or **that** or **if…** douter que… (+ *subjunctive*)

**doubtful** ['daʊtfəl] *adj* [person, future, success] incertain ; **to be doubtful (about sth)** avoir des doutes (sur qch) ; **it's doubtful whether** or **that** or **if…** il n'est pas certain que… (+ *subjunctive*)

■ **doubtless** *adv* sans doute

**dough** [dəʊ] *n* pâte *f* ; *Fam* [money] blé *m*

**doughnut** ['dəʊnʌt] *n* beignet *m*

**dove**[1] [dʌv] *n* colombe *f*

**dove**[2] [dəʊv] *Am* pt of **dive**

**Dover** ['dəʊvə(r)] *n* Douvres *m* ou *f*

**dowdy** ['daʊdɪ] *(compar* -**ier**, *superl* -**iest)** *adj* peu élégant

---

**down** [daʊn] **1.** *adj* **down payment** acompte *m*

**2.** *adv* en bas ; [to the ground] à terre ; **down there** or **here** en bas ; *Fam* **to feel down** [depressed] avoir le cafard ; **down to** [in series, numbers, dates] jusqu'à ; **down under** aux antipodes, en Australie

**3.** *prep* [at bottom of] en bas de ; [from top to bottom of] du haut en bas de ; [along] le long de ; **to go down** [hill, street, stairs] descendre ; **to live down the street** habiter plus loin dans la rue

**4.** *vt* **to down a drink** vider un verre

■ **down-and-out 1.** *adj* sur le pavé **2.** *n* clochard, -e *mf*

■ **downcast** *adj* découragé

■ **downfall** *n* chute *f*

■ **down-hearted** *adj* découragé

■ **downhill** *adv* en pente ; **to go downhill** descendre ; [of sick person, business] aller de plus en plus mal

■ **download** [,daʊn'ləʊd] *vt* COMPUT télécharger

■ **downloadable** [,daʊn'ləʊdəbl] *adj* COMPUT téléchargeable

■ **down-market** *adj Br* [car, furniture] bas de gamme *inv* ; [neighbourhood] populaire

■ **downpour** *n* averse *f*

■ **downright 1.** *adj* [rogue] véritable ; [refusal] catégorique **2.** *adv* [rude, disagreeable] franchement

■ **downstairs 1.** ['daʊnsteəz] *adj* [room, neighbours - below] d'en bas ; [on the ground floor] du rez-de-chaussée **2.** [daʊn'steəz] *adv* en bas ; [to the ground floor] au rez-de-chaussée ; **to come** or **go downstairs** descendre l'escalier

■ **downtime** ['daʊntaɪm] *n* **a)** temps *m* improductif **b)** *Am Fig* [time for relaxing] **on the weekends I need some downtime** j'ai besoin de faire une pause le week-end

■ **down-to-earth** *adj* terre-à-terre *inv*

■ **downtown** *adv* *Am* en ville ; **downtown Chicago** le centre de Chicago

■ **downward** *adj* vers le bas ; [path] qui descend ; [trend] à la baisse

■ **downward(s)** *adv* vers le bas

---

**Down's syndrome** *n* trisomie *f* 21

**doze** [dəʊz] **1.** *n* petit somme *m* **2.** *vi* sommeiller ; **to doze off** s'assoupir

**dozen** ['dʌzən] *n* douzaine *f* ; **a dozen books /eggs** une douzaine de livres /d'œufs ; *Fig* **dozens of** des dizaines de

**Dr** *(abbr of* **Doctor**) Docteur

**drab** [dræb] *adj* terne ; [weather] gris

**draft¹** [drɑːft] **1.** *n* **a)** [outline] ébauche *f* ; [of letter] brouillon *m* **b)** *Am* [military] conscription *f* **2.** *vt* **a) to draft (out)** [sketch out] faire le brouillon de ; [write out] rédiger **b)** *Am* [conscript] appeler sous les drapeaux

**draft²** [drɑːft] *Am n* = **draught**

**drafty** ['drɑːftɪ] *(compar* -ier, *superl* -iest) *Am adj* = **draughty**

**drag** [dræg] **1.** *n Fam* **it's a drag!** [boring] c'est la barbe ! **2.** *(pt & pp* -gg-) *vt* **a)** traîner ; **to drag sb/sth along** (en)traîner qn /qch ; **to drag sb away from** arracher qn à ; **to drag sb into** entraîner qn dans **b)** COMPUT faire glisser ; **to drag and drop** glisser-lâcher **3.** *vi* traîner ; **to drag on** *or* **out** [of film, day] traîner en longueur

**dragon** ['drægən] *n* dragon *m*

**dragonfly** ['drægənflaɪ] *(pl* -ies) *n* libellule *f*

**drain** [dreɪn] **1.** *n* [sewer] égout *m* ; [in street] bouche *f* d'égout **2.** *vt* [glass, tank] vider ; [vegetables] égoutter ; **to drain (off)** [liquid] faire écouler ; **to feel drained** être épuisé **3.** *vi* **to drain (off)** [of liquid] s'écouler ■ **draining** *n* **draining board** paillasse *f*

**drainpipe** ['dreɪnpaɪp] *n* tuyau *m* d'évacuation

**drama** ['drɑːmə] *n* [event] drame *m* ; [dramatic art] théâtre *m*

**dramatic** [drə'mætɪk] *adj* dramatique ; [very great, striking] spectaculaire

**dramatize** ['dræmətaɪz] *vt* [exaggerate] dramatiser ; [novel] adapter pour la scène /l'écran

**drank** [dræŋk] *pt of* **drink**

**drape** [dreɪp] *vt* [person, shoulders] draper (**with** de) ■ **drapes** *npl Am* [curtains] rideaux *mpl*

**drastic** ['dræstɪk] *adj* [change, measure] radical ; [remedy] puissant

**draught**, *Am* **draft** [drɑːft] *n* **a)** [wind] courant *m* d'air **b)** *Br* **draughts** [game] dames *fpl* **c) draught beer** bière *f* (à la) pression

**draughty**, *Am* **drafty** ['drɑːftɪ] *(compar* -ier, *superl* -iest) *adj* [room] plein de courants d'air

**draw¹** [drɔː] **1.** *n* SPORT match *m* nul ; [of lottery] tirage *m* au sort ; [attraction] attraction *f* **2.** *(pt* **drew,** *pp* **drawn)** *vt* **a)** [pull] tirer ; [pass, move] passer (**over** sur ; **into** dans) ; **to draw up** [chair] approcher ; [contract, list, plan] dresser, rédiger **b)** [extract] retirer ; [pistol, sword] dégainer ; *Fig* [strength, comfort] retirer, puiser (**from** de) **c)** [attract] attirer **3.** *vi* SPORT faire match nul ; **to draw near (to)** s'approcher (de) ; [of time] approcher (de) ; **to draw back** [go backwards] reculer ; **to draw up** [of vehicle] s'arrêter

**draw²** [drɔː] **1.** *(pt* **drew,** *pp* **drawn)** *vt* [picture] dessiner ; [circle] tracer ; *Fig* [parallel, distinction] faire (**between** entre) **2.** *vi* [as artist] dessiner

**drawback** ['drɔːbæk] *n* inconvénient *m*

**drawer** [drɔː(r)] *n* [in furniture] tiroir *m*

**drawing** ['drɔːɪŋ] *n* dessin *m* ; *Br* **drawing pin** punaise *f* ; **drawing room** salon *m*

**drawl** [drɔːl] *n* voix *f* traînante

**drawn** [drɔːn] **1.** *pp of* **draw 2.** *adj* **drawn match** *or* **game** match *m* nul

**dread** [dred] **1.** *n* terreur *f* **2.** *vt* [exam] appréhender ; **to dread doing sth** appréhender de faire qch

**dreadful** ['dredfəl] *adj* épouvantable ; [child] insupportable ; **I feel dreadful** [ill] je ne me sens vraiment pas bien ; **I feel dreadful about it** j'ai vraiment honte ■ **dreadfully** *adv* terriblement ; **to be dreadfully sorry** regretter infiniment

**dream** [driːm] **1.** *n* rêve *m* ; **to have a dream** faire un rêve (**about** de) ; **a dream world** un monde imaginaire **2.** *(pt & pp* **dreamed** *or* **dreamt** [dremt]) *vt* rêver (**that** que) ; **I never dreamt that...** [imagined] je n'aurais jamais songé que... ; **to dream sth up** imaginer qch **3.** *vi* rêver (*of* **about sb/sth** de qn / qch ; **of** *or* **about doing** de faire)

**dreary** ['drɪərɪ] *(compar* -ier, *superl* -iest) *adj* morne

**drench** [drentʃ] vt tremper; **to get drenched** se faire tremper (jusqu'aux os)

**dress** [dres] **1.** n [garment] robe f; [style of dressing] tenue f; Br **dress circle** [in theatre] premier balcon m; **dress rehearsal** [in theatre] (répétition f) générale f **2.** vt [person] habiller; [wound] panser; [salad] assaisonner; **to get dressed** s'habiller **3.** vi s'habiller; **to dress up** [smartly] bien s'habiller; [in disguise] se déguiser (**as** en)

**dressing** ['dresɪŋ] n [for wound] pansement m; [seasoning] assaisonnement m; Br **dressing gown** robe f de chambre; **dressing room** [in theatre] loge f; [in shop] cabine f d'essayage; **dressing table** coiffeuse f

**drew** [druː] pt of **draw**

**dribble** ['drɪbəl] vi a) [of baby] baver; [of liquid] tomber goutte à goutte b) [of footballer] dribbler

**dribs** [drɪbz] npl **in dribs and drabs** par petites quantités; [arrive] par petits groupes

**dried** [draɪd] adj [fruit] sec (f sèche); [milk, eggs] en poudre; [flowers] séché

**drier** ['draɪə(r)] n = **dryer**

**drift** [drɪft] **1.** n [movement] mouvement m; [of snow] congère f; [meaning] sens m général **2.** vi [through air] être emporté par le vent; [on water] être emporté par le courant; [of ship] dériver; Fig [of person, nation] aller à la dérive

**drill** [drɪl] **1.** n a) [tool] perceuse f; [bit] mèche f; [pneumatic] marteau m piqueur; [dentist's] roulette f b) [exercise] exercice m; [correct procedure] marche f à suivre **2.** vt [wood] percer; [tooth] fraiser **3.** vi **to drill for oil** faire de la recherche pétrolière ∎ **drilling** n **drilling platform** plate-forme f (de forage); **drilling rig** [on land] derrick m, tour f de forage; [at sea] plate-forme f (de forage)

**drily** ['draɪlɪ] adv [remark] sèchement, d'un ton sec

**drink** [drɪŋk] **1.** n boisson f; **to have a drink** boire quelque chose; [alcoholic] prendre un verre **2.** (pt **drank**, pp **drunk**) vt boire **3.** vi boire (**out of** dans); **to drink up** finir son verre ∎ **drink-driving** n Br conduite f en état d'ivresse ∎ **drinking** n **drinking chocolate** chocolat m en poudre; **drinking water** eau f potable

**drinkable** ['drɪŋkəbəl] adj [fit for drinking] potable; [not unpleasant] buvable

**drip** [drɪp] **1.** n [drop] goutte f; [sound] bruit m de l'eau qui goutte; MED **to be on a drip** être sous perfusion **2.** (pt & pp -pp-) vt [paint] laisser tomber goutte à goutte; **you're dripping water everywhere!** tu mets de l'eau partout! **3.** vi [of water, rain] goutter; [of tap] fuir

**drive** [draɪv] **1.** n [in car] promenade f en voiture; [road to private house] allée f; [energy] énergie f; [campaign] campagne f; COMPUT lecteur m; **an hour's drive** une heure de voiture **2.** (pt **drove**, pp **driven**) vt [vehicle, train, passenger] conduire (**to** à); [machine] actionner; **to drive sb to do sth** pousser qn à faire qch; **to drive sb mad** or **crazy** rendre qn fou/folle; **he drives a Ford** il a une Ford **3.** vi [drive a car] conduire; [go by car] rouler; **to drive on the left** rouler à gauche; **to drive to Paris** aller en voiture à Paris; **to drive to work** aller au travail en voiture; Fig **what are you driving at?** où veux-tu en venir? ∎ **drive along** vi [in car] rouler ∎ **drive away 1.** vt sep [chase away] chasser **2.** vi [in car] partir en voiture ∎ **drive back 1.** vt sep [passenger] ramener (en voiture); [enemy] repousser **2.** vi [in car] revenir (en voiture) ∎ **drive in** vt sep [nail] enfoncer ∎ **drive off** vi [in car] partir (en voiture) ∎ **drive on** vi [in car] continuer sa route ∎ **drive out** vt sep [chase away] chasser ∎ **drive up** vi [in car] arriver (en voiture)

**drive-in** ['draɪvɪn] adj Am **drive-in (movie theater)** drive-in m inv; **drive-in (restaurant)** restaurant où l'on est servi dans sa voiture

**drivel** ['drɪvəl] n idioties fpl

**driven** ['drɪvən] pp of **drive**

**driver** ['draɪvə(r)] n [of car] conducteur, -trice mf; [of taxi, truck] chauffeur m;

**(train** *or* **engine) driver** mécanicien *m*; **she's a good driver** elle conduit bien; *Am* **driver's license** permis *m* de conduire

**driveway** ['draɪweɪ] *n* [road to house] allée *f*

**driving** ['draɪvɪŋ] *n* [in car] conduite *f*; **driving instructor** moniteur, -trice *mf* d'auto-école; **driving lesson** leçon *f* de conduite; *Br* **driving licence** permis *m* de conduire; **driving school** auto-école *f*; **driving test** examen *m* du permis de conduire

**drizzle** ['drɪzəl] *vi* bruiner

**droop** [druːp] *vi* [of flower] se faner; [of head] pencher; [of eyelids, shoulders] tomber

**drop** [drɒp] **1.** *n* **a)** [of liquid] goutte *f*; **eye/nose drops** gouttes *fpl* pour les yeux / le nez **b)** [fall] baisse *f*, chute *f* (**in** de); [distance of fall] hauteur *f* de chute; [slope] descente *f* **2.** *(pt & pp* **-pp-)** *vt* laisser tomber; [price, voice] baisser; [bomb] larguer; [passenger, goods from vehicle] déposer; [leave out] faire sauter, omettre; [get rid of] supprimer; [team member] écarter; **to drop sb off** [from vehicle] déposer qn; **to drop sb a line** écrire un petit mot à qn; **to drop a hint that...** laisser entendre que... **3.** *vi* [fall] tomber; [of person] se laisser tomber; [of price] baisser; **to drop back** *or* **behind** rester en arrière; **to drop by** *or* **in** [visit sb] passer; **to drop off** [fall asleep] s'endormir; [fall off] tomber; [of interest, sales] diminuer; **to drop out** [fall out] tomber; [withdraw] se retirer; [of student] laisser tomber ses études; **to drop round** [visit sb] passer ■ **drop-off** *n* **a)** [decrease] baisse *f*, diminution *f*; **a drop-off in sales** une baisse des ventes **b)** *Am* [descent] à-pic *m inv*; **there's a sharp drop-off in the road** la rue descend en pente très raide

**dropout** ['drɒpaʊt] *n* marginal, -e *mf*; [student] étudiant, -e *mf* qui abandonne ses études

**droppings** ['drɒpɪŋz] *npl* [of animal] crottes *fpl*; [of bird] fiente *f*

**drought** [draʊt] *n* sécheresse *f*

**drove** [drəʊv] *pt of* **drive**

**drown** [draʊn] **1.** *vt* noyer; **to drown oneself, to be drowned** se noyer **2.** *vi* se noyer

**drowsy** ['draʊzɪ] *(compar* **-ier**, *superl* **-iest)** *adj* **to be** *or* **feel drowsy** avoir sommeil

**drudgery** ['drʌdʒərɪ] *n* corvée *f*

**drug** [drʌg] **1.** *n* [against illness] médicament *m*; [narcotic] drogue *f*; **drugs** [narcotics in general] la drogue; **to be on drugs, to take drugs** se droguer; **drug addict** drogué, -e *mf*; **drug dealer** [large-scale] trafiquant *m* de drogue; [small-scale] petit trafiquant *m* de drogue, dealer *m* **2.** *(pt & pp* **-gg-)** *vt* droguer

**druggist** ['drʌgɪst] *n Am* pharmacien, -enne *mf*

**drugstore** ['drʌgstɔːr] *n Am* drugstore *m*

**drum** [drʌm] **1.** *n* MUS tambour *m*; [for oil] bidon *m*; **the drums** [of rock group] la batterie **2.** *(pt & pp* **-mm-)** *vt* **to drum sth into sb** enfoncer qch dans la tête de qn; **to drum up** [support, interest] rechercher ■ **drummer** *n* tambour *m*; [in rock group] batteur *m* ■ **drumstick** *n* [for drum] baguette *f* de tambour; [of chicken] pilon *m*

**drunk** [drʌŋk] **1.** *pp of* **drink 2.** *adj* ivre; **to get drunk** s'enivrer **3.** *n* ivrogne *mf* ■ **drunkard** *n* ivrogne *mf* ■ **drunken** *adj* [person - regularly] ivrogne; [driver] ivre; [quarrel, brawl] d'ivrogne

**dry** [draɪ] **1.** *(compar* **drier**, *superl* **driest)** *adj* sec *(f* **sèche)**; [well, river] à sec; [day] sans pluie; [subject, book] aride; **to wipe sth dry** essuyer qch **2.** *vt* sécher; [by wiping] essuyer; [clothes] faire sécher; **to dry the dishes** essuyer la vaisselle; **to dry sth off** *or* **up** sécher qch **3.** *vi* sécher; **to dry off** sécher; **to dry up** sécher; [dry the dishes] essuyer la vaisselle; [of stream] se tarir ■ **dryer** *n* [for hair, clothes] séchoir *m*

**dry-clean** [draɪ'kliːn] *vt* nettoyer à sec ■ **dry-cleaner** *n* **the dry-cleaner's** [shop] le pressing, la teinturerie

**dual** ['djuːəl] *adj* double; *Br* **dual carriageway** route *f* à deux voies; **dual-core processor** processeur *m* à double cœur

**dub** [dʌb] *(pt & pp* **-bed,** *pres p* **-bing)** *vt* **a)** [nickname] surnommer **b)** CIN & TV [add soundtrack, voice] sonoriser ; [in foreign language] doubler

**dubious** ['dju:bɪəs] *adj* [offer, person] douteux, -euse ; **I'm dubious about going** *or* **about whether to go** je me demande si je dois y aller

**duchess** ['dʌtʃɪs] *n* duchesse *f*

**duck** [dʌk] **1.** *n* canard *m* **2.** *vt* [head] baisser subitement **3.** *vi* se baisser ■ **duckling** *n* caneton *m*

**due** [dju:] *adj* [money, sum] dû (*f* due) (**to** à) ; [rent, bill] à payer ; [fitting, proper] qui convient ; **he's due (to arrive)** il doit arriver d'un moment à l'autre ; **in due course** [when appropriate] en temps voulu ; [eventually] le moment venu ; **due to** par suite de, en raison de

**duel** ['dju:əl] **1.** *n* duel *m* **2.** (*Br* ll-, *Am* -l-) *vi* se battre en duel

**duet** [dju:'et] *n* duo *m*

**duffel, duffle** ['dʌfəl] *adj* **duffel coat** duffel-coat *m*

**dug** [dʌg] *pt & pp of* **dig**

**duke** [dju:k] *n* duc *m*

**dull** [dʌl] **1.** *(compar* **-er,** *superl* **-est)** *adj* [boring] ennuyeux, -euse ; [colour, character] terne ; [weather] maussade ; [sound, ache] sourd ; [edge, blade] émoussé **2.** *vt* [pain] endormir

**duly** ['dju:lɪ] *adv* [properly] dûment ; [as expected] comme prévu

**dumb** [dʌm] *(compar* **-er,** *superl* **-est)** *adj* muet (*f* muette) ; *Fam* [stupid] bête

**dumbfound** [dʌm'faʊnd] *vt* sidérer

**dummy** ['dʌmɪ] **1.** *(pl* **-ies)** *n Br* [of baby] tétine *f* ; [for displaying clothes] mannequin *m* ; [of ventriloquist] pantin *m* **2.** *adj* factice

**dump** [dʌmp] **1.** *n* [for refuse] décharge *f* ; *Fam & Pej* [town] trou *m* ; *Fam & Pej* [house] baraque *f* **2.** *vt* [rubbish] déposer ; *Fam* **to dump sb** plaquer qn

**dumpling** ['dʌmplɪŋ] *n* [in stew] boulette *f* de pâte

**dune** [dju:n] *n* (**sand**) **dune** dune *f*

**dung** [dʌŋ] *n* [of horse] crottin *m* ; [of cattle] bouse *f* ; [manure] fumier *m*

**dungarees** [dʌŋgə'ri:z] *npl* [of child, workman] salopette *f* ; *Am* [jeans] jean *m*

**dunk** [dʌŋk] *vt* tremper

**dupe** [dju:p] *vt* duper

**duplex** ['du:pleks] *n Am* [apartment] duplex *m*

**duplicate 1.** ['dju:plɪkət] *n* double *m* ; **in duplicate** en deux exemplaires **2.** ['dju:plɪkeɪt] *vt* [key, map] faire un double de ; [on machine] photocopier

**durable** ['djʊərəbəl] *adj* [material, shoes] résistant

**duration** [djʊə'reɪʃən] *n* durée *f*

**duress** [djʊ'res] *n* **under duress** sous la contrainte

**during** ['djʊərɪŋ] *prep* pendant, durant

**dusk** [dʌsk] *n* [twilight] crépuscule *m*

**dust** [dʌst] **1.** *n* poussière *f* ; **dust cover** *or* **sheet** [for furniture] housse *f* ; **dust cover** *or* **jacket** [for book] jaquette *f* **2.** *vt* [furniture] dépoussiérer **3.** *vi* faire la poussière ■ **dustbin** *n Br* poubelle *f* ■ **dustman** *(pl* **-men)** *n Br* éboueur *m* ■ **dustpan** *n* pelle *f* (à poussière) ■ **dusty** *(compar* **-ier,** *superl* **-iest)** *adj* poussiéreux, -euse

**duster** ['dʌstə(r)] *n* chiffon *m*

**Dutch** [dʌtʃ] **1.** *adj* hollandais **2.** *n* **a) the Dutch** [people] les Hollandais *mpl* **b)** [language] hollandais *m*

**duty** ['dju:tɪ] *(pl* **-ies)** *n* devoir *m* ; [tax] droit *m* ; **duties** [responsibilities] fonctions *fpl* ; **to be on /off duty** être /ne pas être de service

**duty-free** ['dju:tɪ'fri:] *adj* [goods, shop] hors taxe *inv*

**duvet** ['du:veɪ] *n Br* couette *f*

**DVD** [di:vi:'di:] *(abbr of* **Digital Versatile Disk, Digital Video Disk)** *n* COMPUT DVD *m inv*, disque *m* vidéo numérique ; **DVD burner** graveur *m* de DVD ; **DVD player** lecteur *m* de DVD

**DVR** *(abbr of* **digital video recorder)** *n* DVR *m*

**dwarf** [dwɔ:f] *n* nain, -e *mf*

**dwell** [dwel] *(pt & pp* **dwelt** [dwelt]*) vi* demeurer; **to dwell (up)on** [think about] penser sans cesse à; [speak about] parler sans cesse de

**dwindle** ['dwɪndəl] *vi* diminuer (peu à peu)

**dye** [daɪ] **1.** *n* teinture *f* **2.** *vt* teindre; **to dye sth green** teindre qch en vert

**dying** ['daɪɪŋ] **1.** *pres p see* **die 2.** *adj* [person, animal] mourant; [wish, words] dernier, -ère **3.** *n* [death] mort *f*

**dynamic** [daɪ'næmɪk] *adj* dynamique

**dynamite** ['daɪnəmaɪt] *n* dynamite *f*

**dynamo** ['daɪnəməʊ] *(pl* **-os***) n* dynamo *f*

**dyslexic** [dɪs'leksɪk] *adj & n* dyslexique *(mf)*

# E

**E, e** [iː] *n* [letter] E, e *m inv*

**each** [iːʃ] **1.** *adj* chaque; **each one** chacun, -e; **each one of us** chacun d'entre nous **2.** *pron* chacun, -e; **each other** l'un(e) l'autre, *pl* les un(e)s les autres; **to see/greet each other** se voir/se saluer; **each of us** chacun, -e d'entre nous

**eager** ['iːgə(r)] *adj* [impatient] impatient (**to do** de faire); [enthusiastic] plein d'enthousiasme ■ **eagerly** *adv* [work] avec enthousiasme; [await] avec impatience

**eagle** ['iːgəl] *n* aigle *m*

**ear** [ɪə(r)] *n* oreille *f*; **to play it by ear** improviser ■ **earache** *n* mal *m* d'oreille ■ **eardrum** ['ɪədrʌm] *n* tympan *m* ■ **earphones** *npl* écouteurs *mpl* ■ **earplug** *n* boule *f* Quiès® ■ **earring** *n* boucle *f* d'oreille ■ **earshot** *n* **within earshot** à portée de voix

**early** ['ɜːlɪ] **1.** (*compar* **-ier**, *superl* **-iest**) *adj* [first] premier, -ère; [death] prématuré; [age] jeune; [painting, work] de jeunesse; [retirement] anticipé; **it's early** [on clock] il est tôt; [referring to meeting, appointment] c'est tôt; **to be early** [ahead of time] être en avance; **in the early 1990s** au début des années 90; **to be in one's early fifties** avoir à peine plus de cinquante ans **2.** *adv* tôt, de bonne heure; [ahead of time] en avance; [die] prématurément; **earlier (on)** plus tôt; **at the earliest** au plus tôt ■ **early bird** *n* *Fam* **to be an early bird** être matinal

**earmark** ['ɪəmɑːk] *vt* [funds] assigner (**for** à)

**earn** [ɜːn] *vt* gagner; [interest] rapporter; **to earn one's living** gagner sa vie ■ **earnings** *npl* [wages] salaire *m*; [profits] bénéfices *mpl*

**earnest** ['ɜːnɪst] **1.** *adj* [serious] sérieux, -euse **2.** *n* **in earnest** sérieusement

**earth** [ɜːθ] *n* [ground] sol *m*; [soil] terre *f*; *Br* [electrical wire] terre *f*, masse *f*; **the Earth** [planet] la Terre; **where/what on earth?** où/que diable…? ■ **earthquake** *n* tremblement *m* de terre

**ease** [iːz] **1.** *n* [facility] facilité *f*; **with ease** facilement; **to be at ease/ill at ease** être à l'aise/mal à l'aise **2.** *vt* [pain] soulager; [mind] calmer; [tension] réduire; [restrictions] assouplir **3.** *vi* **to ease (off** *or* **up)** [of pressure] diminuer; [of demand] baisser; [of pain] se calmer

**easily** ['iːzɪlɪ] *adv* facilement; **easily the best** de loin le meilleur/la meilleure

**east** [iːst] **1.** *n* est *m*; **(to the) east of** à l'est de; **the East** [Eastern Europe] l'Est *m*; [the Orient] l'Orient *m* **2.** *adj* [coast] est *inv*; [wind] d'est; **East Africa** l'Afrique *f* orientale **3.** *adv* à l'est; [travel] vers l'est ■ **eastbound** *adj* [traffic] en direction de l'est; *Br* [carriageway] est *inv* ■ **easterly** *adj* [direction] de l'est ■ **eastern** *adj* [coast] est *inv*; **Eastern France** l'est *m* de la France; **Eastern Europe** l'Europe *f* de l'Est ■ **eastward(s)** *adj* & *adv* vers l'est

**Easter** ['iːstə(r)] *n* Pâques *fpl*; **Happy Easter!** joyeuses Pâques !; **Easter egg** œuf *m* de Pâques

**easy** ['iːzɪ] **1.** (*compar* **-ier**, *superl* **-iest**) *adj* [not difficult] facile; [solution] simple; [pace] modéré; **easy chair** fauteuil *m* **2.** *adv* doucement; **go easy on the salt** vas-y mollo avec le sel; **go easy on him** ne sois pas trop dur avec lui; **take it easy** [rest] repose-toi; [work less] ne te fatigue pas; [calm down] calme-toi;

[go slow] ne te presse pas ■ **easygoing** adj [carefree] insouciant ; [easy to get along with] facile à vivre

**eat** [i:t] (pt **ate** [Bret, eɪt, Ameɪt], pp **eaten** ['i:tən]) **1.** vt manger ; [meal] prendre ; **to eat sth up** [finish] finir qch **2.** vi manger ; **to eat into one's savings** entamer ses économies ; **to eat out** manger dehors ■ **eater** n **big eater** gros mangeur m, grosse mangeuse f ■ **eating** ['i:tɪŋ] adj **a)** [for eating] **eating apple / pear** pomme f / poire f à couteau ; **eating place** or **house** restaurant m **b)** [of eating] **eating disorder** trouble m du comportement alimentaire ; **eating habits** habitudes fpl alimentaires

**eaves** [i:vz] npl avant-toit m ■ **eavesdrop** (pt & pp -pp-) vti **to eavesdrop (on)** écouter avec indiscrétion

**ebb** [eb] **1.** n **the ebb and flow** le flux et le reflux ; Fig **to be at a low ebb** [of patient, spirits] être déprimé **2.** vi Fig **to ebb (away)** [of strength] décliner

**e-book** n livre m électronique, e-book m ; **e-book reader** liseuse f

**e-business** n **a)** [company] cyberentreprise f **b)** [trade] cybercommerce m, commerce m électronique

**EC** (abbr of **European Community**) n CE f (Communauté européenne)

**e-card** n COMPUT carte f électronique

**eccentric** [ɪk'sentrɪk] adj & n excentrique (mf)

**ecclesiastical** [ɪkli:zɪ'æstɪkəl] adj ecclésiastique

**echo** ['ekəʊ] **1.** (pl **-oes**) n écho m **2.** (pt & pp **echoed**) vt Fig [repeat] répéter **3.** vi résonner (**with** de)

**eclipse** [ɪ'klɪps] n [of sun, moon] éclipse f

**eco-house** n maison f écologique

**ecological** [i:kə'lɒdʒɪkəl] adj écologique

**e-commerce** n commerce m électronique, cybercommerce m

**economic** [i:kə'nɒmɪk] adj économique ; [profitable] rentable ■ **economical** adj économique ■ **economics 1.** n économie f **2.** npl [profitability] aspect m financier

**economize** [ɪ'kɒnəmaɪz] vti économiser (**on** sur)

**economy** [ɪ'kɒnəmɪ] (pl **-ies**) n économie f ; AVIAT **economy class** classe f économique

**ecorefill** [i:kəʊ'ri:fɪl] n écorecharge f

**ecotourism** ['i:kəʊˌtʊərɪzm] n écotourisme m, tourisme m vert

**eco-town** n ville f écologique

**ecstasy** ['ekstəsɪ] (pl **-ies**) n [state] extase f ; [drug] ecstasy f ■ **ecstatic** [ek'stætɪk] adj fou (f folle) de joie ; **to be ecstatic about** s'extasier sur

**edge** [edʒ] **1.** n bord m ; [of forest] lisière f ; [of town] abords mpl ; [of page] marge f ; [of knife, blade] tranchant m **2.** vt [clothing] border (**with** de) **3.** vi **to edge forward** avancer doucement

**edgeways** ['edʒweɪz], Am **edgewise** ['edʒwaɪz] adv de côté ; Fam **I can't get a word in edgeways** je ne peux pas en placer une

**edgy** ['edʒɪ] (compar **-ier**, superl **-iest**) adj énervé

**edible** ['edɪbəl] adj [safe to eat] comestible ; [fit to eat] mangeable

**edifice** ['edɪfɪs] n [building] édifice m

**Edinburgh** ['edɪnbərə] n Édimbourg m ou f

**edit** ['edɪt] vt [newspaper] diriger ; [article] corriger ; [prepare for publication] préparer pour la publication ; [film] monter

**edition** [ɪ'dɪʃən] n édition f

**editor** ['edɪtə(r)] n [of newspaper] rédacteur, -trice mf en chef ; [of film] monteur, -euse mf ; COMPUT [software] éditeur m

**educate** ['edjʊkeɪt] vt [bring up] éduquer ; [in school] instruire ■ **educated** adj (**well-)educated** [person] instruit

**education** [edjʊ'keɪʃən] n éducation f ; [teaching] enseignement m ; [training] formation f ; [university subject] pédagogie f ■ **educational** adj [qualification] d'enseignement ; [method, theory, content] pédagogique ; [game, film, system] éducatif, -ive ; [establishment] scolaire

**eel** [iːl] n anguille f

**eerie** ['ɪərɪ] (compar -ier, superl -iest) adj sinistre

**effect** [ɪ'fekt] **1.** n [result, impression] effet m (**on** sur); **in effect** en fait; **to come into effect, to take effect** [of law] entrer en vigueur **2.** vt [change, rescue] effectuer

**effective** [ɪ'fektɪv] adj [efficient] efficace; [actual] réel (réelle); **to become effective** [of law] prendre effet ∎ **effectively** adv [efficiently] efficacement; [in fact] effectivement

**efficient** [ɪ'fɪʃənt] adj efficace; [productive] performant ∎ **efficiently** adv efficacement

**effort** ['efət] n effort m; **to make an effort** faire un effort (**to** pour) ∎ **effortlessly** adv sans effort

**e.g.** [iːdʒiː] (abbr of **exempli gratia**) p. ex.

**egg¹** [eg] n œuf m; **egg timer** sablier m ∎ **eggplant** n Am aubergine f ∎ **eggy** ['egɪ] adj **an eggy taste / smell** un goût / une odeur d'œuf; **eggy bread** pain m perdu

**egg²** [eg] vt **to egg sb on** encourager qn (**to do** à faire)

**ego** ['iːgəʊ] (pl -os) n **to have an enormous ego** avoir une très haute opinion de soi-même

**egoistic(al)** [iːgəʊ'ɪstɪk(əl)] adj égoïste

**Egypt** ['iːdʒɪpt] n l'Égypte f ∎ **Egyptian** [ɪ'dʒɪpʃən] **1.** adj égyptien, -enne **2.** n Égyptien, -enne mf

**eight** [eɪt] adj & n huit (m) ∎ **eighth** adj & n huitième (mf); **an eighth** [fraction] un huitième

**eighteen** [eɪ'tiːn] adj & n dix-huit (m) ∎ **eighteenth** adj & n dix-huitième (mf)

**eighty** ['eɪtɪ] adj & n quatre-vingts (m); **eighty-one** quatre-vingt-un; **in the eighties** dans les années 80 ∎ **eightieth** adj & n quatre-vingtième (mf)

**Eire** ['eərə] n l'Eire f

**either** ['aɪðə(r), iː'ðə(r)] **1.** adj & pron [one or other] l'un(e) ou l'autre; [with negative] ni l'un(e) ni l'autre; [each] chaque; **on either side** des deux côtés **2.** adv **she can't swim either** elle ne sait pas nager non plus; **I don't either** (ni) moi non plus **3.** conj **either... or...** ou... ou..., soit... soit...; [with negative] ni... ni...

**eject** [ɪ'dʒekt] **1.** vt [troublemaker] expulser (**from** de); [from machine] éjecter **2.** vi [of pilot] s'éjecter

**elaborate¹** [ɪ'læbərət] adj [meal] élaboré; [scheme] compliqué; [description] détaillé; [style] recherché

**elaborate²** [ɪ'læbəreɪt] **1.** vt [theory] élaborer **2.** vi entrer dans les détails (**on** de)

**elapse** [ɪ'læps] vi s'écouler

**elastic** [ɪ'læstɪk] **1.** adj élastique; Br **elastic band** élastique m **2.** n [fabric] élastique m

**elated** [ɪ'leɪtɪd] adj transporté de joie

**elbow** ['elbəʊ] **1.** n coude m **2.** vt **to elbow one's way** se frayer un chemin en jouant des coudes (**through** à travers)

**elder** ['eldə(r)] adj & n [of two people] aîné, -e (mf) ∎ **eldest** adj & n aîné, -e (mf); **his / her eldest brother** l'aîné de ses frères

**elderly** ['eldəlɪ] **1.** adj âgé **2.** npl **the elderly** les personnes fpl âgées

**elect** [ɪ'lekt] vt [by voting] élire (**to** à)

**election** [ɪ'lekʃən] **1.** n élection f; **general election** élections fpl législatives **2.** adj [campaign] électoral; [day, results] des élections

**electoral** [ɪ'lektərəl] adj électoral ∎ **electorate** n électorat m

**electric** [ɪ'lektrɪk] adj électrique; **electric blanket** couverture f chauffante; Br **electric fire** radiateur m électrique; **electric shock** décharge f électrique ∎ **electrical** adj électrique

**electrician** [ɪlek'trɪʃən] n électricien m

**electricity** [ɪlek'trɪsɪtɪ] n électricité f

**electrify** [ɪ'lektrɪfaɪ] (pt & pp -ied) vt [excite] électriser

**electronic** [ɪlek'trɒnɪk] adj électronique; **electronic mail** courrier m électronique, messagerie f électronique ∎ **electronics** n [subject] électronique f

**elegant** ['elɪgənt] *adj* élégant ■ **elegantly** *adv* avec élégance

**element** ['eləmənt] *n* [component, chemical, person] élément *m*; [of heater, kettle] résistance *f*; **the elements** [bad weather] les éléments *mpl*; **to be in one's element** être dans son élément

**elementary** [elɪˈmentərɪ] *adj* élémentaire; *Am* [school] primaire

**elephant** ['elɪfənt] *n* éléphant *m*

**elevate** ['elɪveɪt] *vt* élever (**to** à)

**elevator** ['elɪveɪtə(r)] *n Am* ascenseur *m*

**eleven** [ɪˈlevən] *adj* & *n* onze (*m*) ■ **eleventh** *adj* & *n* onzième (*mf*)

**elicit** [ɪˈlɪsɪt] *vt* tirer (**from** de)

**eligible** ['elɪdʒəbəl] *adj* [for post] admissible (**for** à); **to be eligible for sth** [entitled to] avoir droit à qch

**eliminate** [ɪˈlɪmɪneɪt] *vt* éliminer

**elite** [eɪˈliːt] *n* élite *f* (**of** de)

**elongated** ['iːlɒŋgeɪtɪd] *adj* allongé

**elope** [ɪˈləʊp] *vi* [of lovers] s'enfuir (**with** avec)

**eloquent** ['eləkwənt] *adj* éloquent

**else** [els] *adv* d'autre; **somebody / anybody else** quelqu'un / n'importe qui d'autre; **everybody else** tous les autres; **something else** autre chose; **anything else?** [in shop] est-ce qu'il vous faut autre chose?; **somewhere else,** *Am* **someplace else** ailleurs, autre part; **nowhere else** nulle part ailleurs; **who else?** qui d'autre?; **or else** ou bien, sinon ■ **elsewhere** *adv* ailleurs

**elude** [ɪˈluːd] *vt* échapper à ■ **elusive** *adj* [person] insaisissable

**emaciated** [ɪˈmeɪsɪeɪtɪd] *adj* émacié

**e-mail** ['iːmeɪl] **1.** *n* courrier *m* électronique, mél *m*; **e-mail address** adresse *f* électronique **2.** *vt* envoyer un courrier électronique *ou* un mél à

**emanate** ['eməneɪt] *vi* émaner (**from** de)

**emancipation** [ɪmænsɪˈpeɪʃən] *n* émancipation *f*

**embankment** [ɪmˈbæŋkmənt] *n* [of path] talus *m*; [of river] berge *f*

**embargo** [ɪmˈbɑːgəʊ] (*pl* -**oes**) *n* embargo *m*

**embark** [ɪmˈbɑːk] *vi* (s')embarquer; **to embark on sth** s'embarquer dans qch

**embarrass** [ɪmˈbærəs] *vt* embarrasser ■ **embarrassing** *adj* embarrassant

**embassy** ['embəsɪ] (*pl* -**ies**) *n* ambassade *f*

**embellish** [ɪmˈbelɪʃ] *vt* embellir

**embers** ['embəz] *npl* braises *fpl*

**embezzle** [ɪmˈbezəl] *vt* [money] détourner

**emblem** ['embləm] *n* emblème *m*

**embody** [ɪmˈbɒdɪ] (*pt* & *pp* -**ied**) *vt* [express] exprimer; [represent] incarner

**embrace** [ɪmˈbreɪs] **1.** *n* étreinte *f* **2.** *vt* [person] étreindre; *Fig* [belief] embrasser **3.** *vi* s'étreindre

**embroider** [ɪmˈbrɔɪdə(r)] *vt* [cloth] broder; *Fig* [story, facts] enjoliver ■ **embroidery** *n* broderie *f*

**embryo** ['embrɪəʊ] (*pl* -**os**) *n* embryon *m*

**emerald** ['emərəld] *n* émeraude *f*

**emerge** [ɪˈmɜːdʒ] *vi* apparaître (**from** de); [from hole] sortir; [from water] émerger

**emergency** [ɪˈmɜːdʒənsɪ] **1.** (*pl* -**ies**) *n* [situation, case] urgence *f*; **in an emergency** en cas d'urgence **2.** *adj* [measure, operation, services] d'urgence; **emergency exit** sortie *f* de secours; **emergency landing** atterrissage *m* forcé

**emigrant** ['emɪgrənt] *n* émigrant, -e *mf* ■ **emigrate** [-greɪt] *vi* émigrer

**eminent** ['emɪnənt] *adj* éminent

**emission** [ɪˈmɪʃən] *n* [of gas, light] émission *f*

**emit** [ɪˈmɪt] (*pt* & *pp* -**tt**-) *vt* [light, heat] émettre

**e-money** *n* argent *m* électronique

**emotion** [ɪˈməʊʃən] *n* [strength of feeling] émotion *f*; [individual feeling] sentiment *m*

**emotional** [ɪˈməʊʃənəl] *adj* [person, reaction] émotif, -ive; [speech, plea] émouvant

**emotive** [ɪˈməʊtɪv] *adj* [word] affectif, -ive

**empathy** ['empəθɪ] *n* compassion *f*

**emperor** ['empərə(r)] *n* empereur *m*

**emphasis** ['emfəsɪs] *(pl* **-ases** [-əsiːz]*)* *n* [in word or phrase] accent *m* ; [insistence] insistance *f*

**emphasize** ['emfəsaɪz] *vt* [importance] souligner ; [word, fact] insister sur, souligner ; [syllable] appuyer sur ; **to emphasize that...** souligner que...

**emphatic** [em'fætɪk] *adj* [denial, refusal - clear] catégorique ; [forceful] énergique

**empire** ['empaɪə(r)] *n* empire *m*

**employ** [ɪm'plɔɪ] *vt* [person, means] employer ■ **employee** [em'plɔɪiː] *n* employé, -e *mf* ■ **employer** *n* patron, -onne *mf* ■ **employment** *n* emploi *m* ; **employment agency** bureau *m* de placement

**emptiness** ['emptɪnɪs] *n* vide *m*

**empty** ['emptɪ] **1.** *(compar* **-ier***, superl* **-iest***) adj* vide ; [threat, promise] vain ; **on an empty stomach** à jeun **2.** *npl* **empties** [bottles] bouteilles *fpl* vides **3.** *(pt & pp* **-ied***) vt* **to empty (out)** [box, pocket, liquid] vider ; [objects from box] sortir **(from** *or* **out of** *de)* **4.** *vi* [of building, tank] se vider ■ **empty-handed** *adv* **to return empty-handed** revenir les mains vides

**emulate** ['emjʊleɪt] *vt* imiter

**enable** [ɪ'neɪbəl] *vt* **to enable sb to do sth** permettre à qn de faire qch

**enamel** [ɪ'næməl] **1.** *n* émail *m* *(pl* émaux*)* **2.** *adj* en émail

**enamoured,** *Am* **enamored** [ɪ'næməd] *adj* **enamoured of** [thing] séduit par ; [person] amoureux, -euse de

**encapsulate** [ɪn'kæpsjʊleɪt] *vt* [ideas, views] résumer

**encase** [ɪn'keɪs] *vt* [cover] envelopper **(in** dans*)*

**enchanting** [ɪn'tʃɑːntɪŋ] *adj* enchanteur, -eresse

**encircle** [ɪn'sɜːkəl] *vt* entourer ; [of army, police] encercler

**encl** *(abbr of* **enclosure(s))** PJ

**enclose** [ɪn'kləʊz] *vt* [send with letter] joindre **(in** *or* **with** à*)* ; [fence off] clôturer ■ **enclosed** *adj* [receipt, document] ci-joint ; **please find enclosed** veuillez trouver ci-joint...

**enclosure** [ɪn'kləʊʒə(r)] *n* [in letter] pièce *f* jointe ; [place] enceinte *f*

**encompass** [ɪn'kʌmpəs] *vt* [include] inclure

**encore** ['ɒŋkɔː(r)] *excl & n* bis *(m)*

**encounter** [ɪn'kaʊntə(r)] **1.** *n* rencontre *f* **2.** *vt* [person, resistance] rencontrer

**encourage** [ɪn'kʌrɪdʒ] *vt* encourager **(to do** à faire*)* ■ **encouragement** *n* encouragement *m*

**encroach** [ɪn'krəʊtʃ] *vi* empiéter **(on** *or* **upon** sur*)*

**encryption** [en'krɪpʃn] *n* COMPUT cryptage *m*

**encyclop(a)edia** [ɪnsaɪkləˈpiːdɪə] *n* encyclopédie *f*

**end** [end] **1.** *n* [extremity] bout *m*, extrémité *f* ; [of month, meeting, book] fin *f* ; [purpose] but *m* ; **at an end** [discussion, war] fini ; [period of time] écoulé ; **end to end** [with ends adjacent] bout à bout ; d'un bout à l'autre ; **from end to end** d'un bout à l'autre ; **in the end** à la fin ; **to come to an end** prendre fin ; **for days on end** pendant des jours et des jours ; **to stand sth on end** mettre qch debout **2.** *adj* [row, house] dernier, -ère **3.** *vt* finir, terminer **(with** par*)* ; [rumour, speculation] mettre fin à **4.** *vi* finir, se terminer ; **to end up doing sth** finir par faire qch ; **he ended up in prison/a doctor** il a fini en prison /médecin

**endanger** [ɪn'deɪndʒə(r)] *vt* mettre en danger ; **endangered species** espèce *f* menacée

**endearing** [ɪn'dɪərɪŋ] *adj* [quality] qui inspire la sympathie

**endeavour,** *Am* **endeavor** [ɪn'devə(r)] **1.** *n* effort *m* **(to do** pour faire*)* **2.** *vi* s'efforcer **(to do** de faire*)*

**ending** ['endɪŋ] *n* fin *f* ; [of word] terminaison *f*

**endless** ['endləs] *adj* [speech, series, list] interminable ; [countless] innombrable

**endorse** [ɪn'dɔːs] *vt* [cheque] endosser ; [action, plan] approuver ■ **endorsement** *n Br* [on driving licence] *contravention inscrite sur le permis de conduire*

**endow** [ɪn'dau] *vt* **to be endowed with** [of person] être doté de ■ **endowment** *n* dotation *f*

**endurance** [ɪn'djuərəns] *n* endurance *f*

**endure** [ɪn'djuə(r)] **1.** *vt* [violence] endurer ; [person, insult] supporter **2.** *vi* [last] survivre

**enemy** ['enəmɪ] **1.** *(pl* **-ies)** *n* ennemi, -e *mf* **2.** *adj* [army, tank] ennemi

**energetic** [enə'dʒetɪk] *adj* énergique

**energy** ['enədʒɪ] **1.** *(pl* **-ies)** *n* énergie *f* **2.** *adj* [resources] énergétique ; **energy crisis** crise *f* de l'énergie ■ **energy-saving** *adj* [device] pour économiser l'énergie ; **energy-saving bulb** ampoule *f* à économie d'énergie

**enforce** [ɪn'fɔːs] *vt* [law] faire respecter ; [discipline] imposer **(on** à)

**engage** [ɪn'geɪdʒ] *vt* [take on] engager ■ **engaged** *adj* **a)** [occupied - person, toilet, phone] occupé **b) engaged (to be married)** fiancé ; **to get engaged** se fiancer

**engagement** [ɪn'geɪdʒmənt] *n* [to marry] fiançailles *fpl* ; [meeting] rendez-vous *m inv* ; **engagement ring** bague *f* de fiançailles

**engine** ['endʒɪn] *n* [of vehicle, aircraft] moteur *m* ; [of train] locomotive *f* ; [of ship] machine *f*

**engineer** [endʒɪ'nɪə(r)] **1.** *n* ingénieur *m* ; *Br* [repairer] dépanneur *m* ; **civil engineer** ingénieur *m* des travaux publics **2.** *vt* [arrange secretly] manigancer ■ **engineering** *n* ingénierie *f* ; **(civil) engineering** génie *m* civil

**England** ['ɪŋglənd] *n* l'Angleterre *f*

**English** ['ɪŋglɪʃ] **1.** *adj* anglais ; **English teacher** professeur *m* d'anglais ; **the English Channel** la Manche **2.** *n* [language] anglais *m* ; **the English** [people] les Anglais *mpl* ■ **English-**

**man** *(pl* **-men)** *n* Anglais *m* ■ **English-speaking** *adj* anglophone ■ **Englishwoman** *(pl* **-women)** *n* Anglaise *f*

**engraving** [ɪn'greɪvɪŋ] *n* gravure *f*

**engrossed** [ɪn'grəust] *adj* **engrossed in one's work/book** absorbé par son travail /dans sa lecture

**engulf** [ɪn'gʌlf] *vt* engloutir

**enhance** [ɪn'hɑːns] *vt* [beauty, prestige] rehausser ; [value] augmenter

**enigma** [ɪ'nɪgmə] *n* énigme *f*

**enjoy** [ɪn'dʒɔɪ] *vt* [like] aimer **(doing** faire) ; [meal] savourer ; [benefit from] jouir de ; **to enjoy oneself** s'amuser ■ **enjoyable** *adj* agréable ; [meal] excellent ■ **enjoyment** *n* plaisir *m*

**enlarge** [ɪn'lɑːdʒ] **1.** *vt* agrandir **2.** *vi* **to enlarge (up)on sth** s'étendre sur qch ■ **enlargement** *n* [increase & PHOTO] agrandissement *m*

**enlighten** [ɪn'laɪtən] *vt* éclairer **(sb on** *or* **about sth** qn sur qch) ■ **enlightening** *adj* instructif, -ive

**enlist** [ɪn'lɪst] **1.** *vt* [recruit] engager ; [supporter] recruter ; [support] s'assurer **2.** *vi* [in the army] s'engager

**enormous** [ɪ'nɔːməs] *adj* énorme ; [explosion, blow] terrible ; [patience, gratitude, success] immense ■ **enormously** *adv* [very much] énormément ; [very] extrêmement

**enough** [ɪ'nʌf] **1.** *adj* assez de ; **enough time /cups** assez de temps /de tasses **2.** *pron* assez ; **to have enough to live on** avoir de quoi vivre ; **to have had enough of sb /sth** en avoir assez de qn /qch ; **that's enough** ça suffit **3.** *adv* [work, sleep] assez ; **big /good enough** assez grand / bon **(to** pour)

**enquire** [ɪn'kwaɪə(r)] *vti* = **inquire**

**enquiry** [ɪn'kwaɪərɪ] *n* = **inquiry**

**enrage** [ɪn'reɪdʒ] *vt* mettre en rage

**enrich** [ɪn'rɪtʃ] *vt* enrichir ; [soil] fertiliser

**enrol**, *Am* **enroll** [ɪn'rəul] *(pt & pp* **-ll-)** **1.** *vt* inscrire **2.** *vi* s'inscrire **(on** *or* **for** à) ■ **enrolment**, *Am* **enrollment** *n* inscription *f*

**ensemble** [ɒn'sɒmbəl] n [musicians, clothes] ensemble m

**ensue** [ɪn'sjuː] vi s'ensuivre ■ **ensuing** adj [in the past] qui a suivi; [in the future] qui suivra

**ensure** [ɪn'ʃʊə(r)] vt assurer; **to ensure that...** s'assurer que...

**entail** [ɪn'teɪl] vt [involve] occasionner; **what does the job entail?** en quoi le travail consiste-t-il?

**entangle** [ɪn'tæŋgəl] vt **to get entangled in sth** [of person, animal] s'empêtrer dans qch

**enter** ['entə(r)] **1.** vt [room, army] entrer dans; [race, competition] participer à; [write down - on list] inscrire (**in** dans; **on** sur); [in accounts book] porter (**in** sur); COMPUT [data] entrer; **it didn't enter my head** or **mind** ça ne m'est pas venu à l'esprit (**that** que) **2.** vi entrer; **to enter for** [exam] se présenter à; [race] se faire inscrire à; **to enter into** [relations] entrer en; [negotiations] entamer; [agreement] conclure; [contract] passer (**with** avec)

**enterprise** ['entəpraɪz] n [undertaking, firm] entreprise f; [spirit, initiative] initiative f ■ **enterprising** adj [person] entreprenant

**entertain** [entə'teɪn] **1.** vt amuser, distraire; [guest] recevoir; [idea, possibility] envisager **2.** vi [receive guests] recevoir ■ **entertainer** n [comedian] comique mf; [singer, dancer] artiste mf de music-hall ■ **entertainment** n amusement m; [show] spectacle m

**enthusiasm** [ɪn'θjuːzɪæzəm] n enthousiasme m ■ **enthusiast** n enthousiaste mf; **jazz enthusiast** passionné, -e mf de jazz

**enthusiastic** [ɪnθjuːzɪ'æstɪk] adj enthousiaste; [golfer, photographer] passionné; **to get enthusiastic** s'emballer (**about** pour)

**entice** [ɪn'taɪs] vt attirer (**into** dans); **to entice sb to do sth** inciter qn à faire qch ■ **enticing** adj séduisant

**entire** [ɪn'taɪə(r)] adj entier, -ère ■ **entirely** adv entièrement

**entirety** [ɪn'taɪərətɪ] n intégralité f; **in its entirety** dans son intégralité

**entitle** [ɪn'taɪtəl] vt **to entitle sb to sth / to do sth** donner à qn le droit à qch /de faire qch ■ **entitled** adj **to be entitled to do sth** avoir le droit de faire qch; **to be entitled to sth** avoir droit à qch

**entrance** ['entrəns] n entrée f (**to** de); [to university, school] admission f (**to** à); **entrance fee** droit m d'entrée

**entrant** ['entrənt] n [in race] concurrent, -e mf; [for exam] candidat, -e mf

**entrée** ['ɒntreɪ] n CULIN [course before main dish] entrée f; Am [main dish] plat m principal

**entrepreneur** [ɒntrəprə'nɜː(r)] n entrepreneur m

**entrust** [ɪn'trʌst] vt confier (**to** à); **to entrust sb with sth** confier qch à qn

**entry** ['entrɪ] n entrée f; [in race] concurrent, -e mf; [to be judged in competition] objet m /œuvre f /projet m soumis(e) au jury; **entry form** feuille f d'inscription; **'no entry'** [on door] 'entrée interdite'; [road sign] 'sens interdit'

**enuf** MESSAGING written abbr of **enough**

**envelope** ['envələʊp] n enveloppe f

**enviable** ['envɪəbəl] adj enviable

**envious** ['envɪəs] adj envieux, -euse (**of** de); **to be envious of sb** envier qn

**environment** [ɪn'vaɪərənmənt] n [social, moral] milieu m; **the environment** [natural] l'environnement m ■ **environmental** [-'mentəl] adj [policy] de l'environnement; [environmental **disaster** catastrophe f écologique ■ **environmentally** adv **environmentally friendly product** produit m qui ne nuit pas à l'environnement

**envisage** [ɪn'vɪzɪʤ], Am **envision** [ɪn'vɪʒən] vt [imagine] envisager; [foresee] prévoir; **to envisage doing sth** envisager de faire qch

**envoy** ['envɔɪ] n [messenger] envoyé, -e mf; [diplomat] ministre m plénipotentiaire

**envy** ['envɪ] **1.** n envie f **2.** (pt & pp -ied) vt envier; **to envy sb sth** envier qch à qn

**ephemeral** [ɪ'femərəl] adj éphémère

**epic** ['epɪk] **1.** *adj* épique **2.** *n* [poem, novel] épopée *f*; [film] film *m* à grand spectacle

**epidemic** [epɪ'demɪk] *n* épidémie *f*

**epileptic** [epɪ'leptɪk] *adj* & *n* épileptique *(mf)*

**epilogue** ['epɪlɒg] *n* épilogue *m*

**episode** ['epɪsəʊd] *n* [part of story] épisode *m*; [incident] incident *m*

**epitaph** ['epɪtɑːf] *n* épitaphe *f*

**epitome** [ɪ'pɪtəmɪ] *n* **to be the epitome of sth** être l'exemple même de qch ■ **epitomize** *vt* incarner

**epoch** ['iːpɒk] *n* époque *f*

**equal** ['iːkwəl] **1.** *adj* égal **(to** à**)**; **to be equal to sth** [in quantity] égaler qch; [good enough] être à la hauteur de qch **2.** *n* [person] égal, -e *mf* **3.** *(Br-ll-, Am-l-)* *vt* égaler **(in** en**)**

**equality** [ɪ'kwɒlətɪ] *n* égalité *f*

**equalize** ['iːkwəlaɪz] *vi* [in sport] égaliser

**equally** ['iːkwəlɪ] *adv* [to an equal degree, also] également; [divide] en parts égales

**equals** ['iːkwəlz] *n* **equals sign** signe *m* d'égalité

**equation** [ɪ'kweɪʒən] *n* MATH équation *f*

**equator** [ɪ'kweɪtə(r)] *n* équateur *m*; **at** or **on the equator** sous l'équateur

**equilibrium** [iːkwɪ'lɪbrɪəm] *n* équilibre *m*

**equip** [ɪ'kwɪp] *(pt & pp -pp-)* *vt* [provide with equipment] équiper **(with** de**)**; [prepare] préparer **(for** pour**)**; **to be (well-)equipped to do sth** être compétent pour faire qch ■ **equipment** *n* équipement *m*; [in factory] matériel *m*

**equivalent** [ɪ'kwɪvələnt] *adj* & *n* équivalent *(m)*

**ER** *Am (abbr of* **Emergency Room***)* urgences *fpl*

**era** [*Br* 'ɪərə, *Am* 'erə] *n* époque *f*; [historical, geological] ère *f*

**eradicate** [ɪ'rædɪkeɪt] *vt* éradiquer

**erase** [*Br* 'reɪz, *Am* 'reɪs] *vt* effacer; [with eraser] gommer ■ **eraser** *n* gomme *f*

**ereader** ['iːriːdə(r)] *n* liseuse *f*

**erect** [ɪ'rekt] **1.** *adj* [upright] droit **2.** *vt* [building] construire; [statue, monument] ériger; [scaffolding] monter; [tent] dresser

**erode** [ɪ'rəʊd] *vt* [of sea] éroder; *Fig* [confidence] miner ■ **erosion** [-ʒən] *n* érosion *f*

**erotic** [ɪ'rɒtɪk] *adj* érotique

**errand** ['erənd] *n* commission *f*, course *f*; **to run errands for sb** faire des courses pour qn

**erratic** [ɪ'rætɪk] *adj* [unpredictable - behaviour] imprévisible; [service, machine] fantaisiste; [person] lunatique; [irregular - performance, results] irrégulier, -ère

**error** ['erə(r)] *n* [mistake] erreur *f*; **typing / printing error** faute *f* de frappe /d'impression

**erupt** [ɪ'rʌpt] *vi* [of volcano] entrer en éruption; [of war, violence] éclater ■ **eruption** *n* [of volcano] éruption *f*; [of violence] flambée *f*

**escalate** ['eskəleɪt] *vi* [of war, violence] s'intensifier; [of prices] monter en flèche

**escalator** ['eskəleɪtə(r)] *n* escalier *m* roulant

**escapade** ['eskəpeɪd] *n* frasque *f*

**escape** [ɪ'skeɪp] **1.** *n* [of gas, liquid] fuite *f*; [of person] évasion *f*; **escape lane** voie *f* de détresse; **he had a lucky** or **narrow escape** il l'a échappé belle **2.** *vt* [death, punishment] échapper à **3.** *vi* [of gas, animal] s'échapper **(from** de**)**; [of prisoner] s'évader **(from** de**)**

**escort 1.** ['eskɔːt] *n* [for convoy] escorte *f*; [of woman] cavalier *m* **2.** [ɪ'skɔːt] *vt* escorter; [prisoner] conduire sous escorte

**e-signature** *n* signature *f* électronique

**Eskimo** ['eskɪməʊ] *(pl -os)* *n* Esquimau, -aude *mf*

**ESOL** ['iːsɒl] *(abbr of* **English for Speakers of Other Languages***)* *n* *Am* SCH anglais *m* langue seconde

**especially** [ɪs'peʃəlɪ] *adv* [in particular] surtout; [more than normally] particulièrement ; [for a purpose] (tout) spécialement ; **especially as** d'autant plus que

**espresso** [e'spresəʊ] (pl **-os**) n expresso m

**Esq** (abbr of **Esquire**) Br **John Smith Esq** Monsieur John Smith

**essay** ['eseɪ] n [at school] rédaction f ; [at university] dissertation f (**on** sur)

**essence** ['esəns] n [distinctive quality] essence f ; CULIN [extract] extrait m ; **the essence of sth** [main point] l'essentiel m de qch ; **in essence** essentiellement

**essential** [ɪ'senʃəl] **1.** adj [principal] essentiel, -elle ; [necessary] indispensable, essentiel, -elle ; **it's essential that...** il est indispensable que... (+ subjunctive) **2.** npl **the essentials** l'essentiel m (**of** de)

**establish** [ɪ'stæblɪʃ] vt établir ; [state, society, company] fonder ; [post] créer ■ **established** adj (**well-)established** [company] solide ; [fact] reconnu ; [reputation] établi ■ **establishment** n [institution, company] établissement m ; **the Establishment** [dominant group] les classes fpl dirigeantes

**estate** [ɪ'steɪt] n [land] terres fpl, propriété f ; [possessions] biens mpl ; [property after death] succession f ; Br **estate agent** agent m immobilier ; Br **estate car** break m

**esteem** [ɪ'stiːm] **1.** n estime f ; **to hold sb in high esteem** avoir qn en haute estime **2.** vt estimer

**esthetic** [es'θetɪk] adj Am esthétique

**estimate 1.** ['estɪmət] n évaluation f ; COMM devis m **2.** ['estɪmeɪt] vt [value] estimer, évaluer ; [consider] estimer (**that** que)

**estranged** [ɪ'streɪndʒd] adj **her estranged husband** son mari, dont elle vit séparée

**estuary** ['estjʊərɪ] (pl **-ies**) n estuaire m

**etc** [et'setərə] (abbr of **et cetera**) adv etc

**etching** ['etʃɪŋ] n [picture] eau-forte f

**eternal** [ɪ'tɜːnəl] adj éternel, -elle ■ **eternity** n éternité f

**ethical** ['eθɪkəl] adj moral, éthique ; **ethical hacker** m fou hackeur, -euse m, f éthique

**ethics** ['eθɪks] n éthique f, morale f ; [of profession] déontologie f

**ethnic** ['eθnɪk] adj ethnique

**e-ticket** n e-billet m

**etiquette** ['etɪkət] n étiquette f

**e-trade** n cybercommerce m, commerce m électronique

**E2EG** MESSAGING written abbr of **ear to ear grin**

**etymology** [etɪ'mɒlədʒɪ] n étymologie f

**EU** [iː'juː] (abbr of **European Union**) n UE f

**euphemism** ['juːfəmɪzəm] n euphémisme m

**euphoria** [juː'fɔːrɪə] n euphorie f

**euro** ['jʊərəʊ] (pl **-os**) n [currency] euro m ; **euro cent** centime m, (euro) cent m

**Euro-** ['jʊərəʊ] pref euro- ; **Euro-MP** député m européen

**Europe** ['jʊərəp] n l'Europe f ■ **European** [-'piːən] **1.** adj européen, -enne ; **European Union** Union f européenne **2.** n Européen, -enne mf

**evacuate** [ɪ'vækjʊeɪt] vt évacuer

**evade** [ɪ'veɪd] vt éviter, esquiver ; [pursuer] échapper à ; [law, question] éluder ; **to evade tax** frauder le fisc

**evaluate** [ɪ'væljʊeɪt] vt évaluer (**at** à)

**evangelical** [iːvæn'dʒelɪkəl] adj évangélique

**evaporate** [ɪ'væpəreɪt] vi [of liquid] s'évaporer ; **evaporated milk** lait m condensé

**evasion** [ɪ'veɪʒən] n [of pursuer, responsibilities, question] dérobade f (**of** devant) ; **tax evasion** évasion f fiscale

**evasive** [ɪ'veɪsɪv] adj évasif, -ive

**eve** [iːv] n **on the eve of** à la veille de

**even** ['iːvən] **1.** adj [equal, flat] égal ; [smooth] uni ; [regular] régulier, -ère ; [temperature] constant ; [number] pair ; Fig **to get even with sb** prendre sa revanche sur qn ; **to break even** [financially] s'y retrouver **2.** adv même ; **even better / more** encore mieux / plus ; **even if** or **though...** bien que...

(+ *subjunctive*); **even so** quand même **3.** *vt* **to even sth (out** *or* **up)** égaliser qch ■ **evenly** *adv* [equally] de manière égale ; [regularly] régulièrement

**evening** ['iːvnɪŋ] *n* soir *m* ; [referring to duration, event] soirée *f*; **tomorrow / yesterday evening** demain / hier soir; **in the evening,** *Am* **evenings** le soir; **at seven in the evening** à sept heures du soir; **every Tuesday evening** tous les mardis soir; **evening meal /paper** repas *m* /journal *m* du soir; **evening class** cours *m* du soir; **evening dress** [of man] tenue *f* de soirée; [of woman] robe *f* du soir

**event** [ɪ'vent] *n* événement *m* ; [in sport] épreuve *f* ■ **eventful** *adj* [day, journey, life] mouvementé; [occasion] mémorable

**eventual** [ɪ'ventʃʊəl] *adj* [final] final, définitif, -ive ■ **eventuality** [-tjʊ'ælətɪ] *(pl* **-ies)** *n* éventualité *f* ■ **eventually** *adv* finalement; [some day] par la suite; **he'll get tired of it eventually** il s'en lassera à la longue, il finira par s'en lasser

**ever** ['evə(r)] *adv* jamais ; **have you ever been to Spain?** es-tu déjà allé en Espagne ?; **the first ever** le tout premier; **ever since (1990)** depuis (1990); **for ever** pour toujours; **ever so sorry** vraiment désolé; **she's ever so nice** elle est tellement gentille; **all she ever does is criticize** elle ne fait que critiquer

**evergreen** ['evəgriːn] *n* arbre *m* à feuilles persistantes

**everlasting** [evə'lɑːstɪŋ] *adj* éternel, -elle

**every** ['evrɪ] *adj* chaque ; **every time** chaque fois (**that**) ; **every one** chacun; **every second** *or* **other day** tous les deux jours; **every so often, every now and then** de temps en temps

**everybody** ['evrɪbɒdɪ] *pron* tout le monde ■ **everyday** *adj* [happening, life] de tous les jours ; [ordinary] banal (*mpl* -als) ; **in everyday use** d'usage courant ■ **everyone** *pron* = **everybody** ■ **everyplace** *adv Am* = **everywhere** ■ **everything**

*pron* tout; **everything (that) I have** tout ce que j'ai ■ **everywhere** *adv* partout; **everywhere she goes** où qu'elle aille

**evict** [ɪ'vɪkt] *vt* expulser (**from** de)

**evidence** ['evɪdəns] *n* [proof] preuve(s) *f(pl)* ; [testimony] témoignage *m*; **to give evidence** témoigner (**against** contre)

**evident** ['evɪdənt] *adj* évident (**that** que) ; **it is evident from...** il apparaît de... (**that** que) ■ **evidently** *adv* [clearly] manifestement; [apparently] apparemment

**evil** ['iːvəl] **1.** *adj* [spell, influence, person] malfaisant; [deed, system] mauvais **2.** *n* mal *m*

**evoke** [ɪ'vəʊk] *vt* [conjure up] évoquer ■ **evocative** [ɪ'vɒkətɪv] *adj* évocateur, -trice (**of** de)

**evolution** [iːvə'luːʃən] *n* évolution *f*

**evolve** [ɪ'vɒlv] **1.** *vt* [system] mettre au point **2.** *vi* [of society, idea] évoluer; [of plan] se développer

**EVRY1** MESSAGING *written abbr of* **everyone**

**e-wallet** *n* portefeuille *m* électronique

**ewe** [juː] *n* brebis *f*

**ex** [eks] *n Fam* [former spouse] ex *mf*

**ex-** [eks] *pref* ex- ; **ex-minister** ancien ministre *m*

**exact** [ɪg'zækt] **1.** *adj* exact **2.** *vt* [demand] exiger (**from** de) ; [money, promise] extorquer (**from** à) ■ **exactly** *adv* exactement

**exaggerate** [ɪg'zædʒəreɪt] *vti* exagérer

**exam** [ɪg'zæm] *(abbr of* **examination)** *n* examen *m*

**examine** [ɪg'zæmɪn] *vt* [evidence, patient, question] examiner; [accounts, luggage] vérifier; [passport] contrôler; [student] interroger ■ **examination** *n* examen *m*; [of accounts] vérification *f*; [of passport] contrôle *m*

**example** [ɪg'zɑːmpəl] *n* exemple *m* ; **for example** par exemple; **to set an example** *or* **a good example** donner l'exemple (**to** à); **to set a bad example** donner le mauvais exemple (**to** à)

**exasperate** [ɪgˈzɑːspəreɪt] *vt* exaspérer

**excavate** [ˈekskəveɪt] *vt* [dig] creuser; [archaeological site] faire des fouilles dans ▪ **excavation** [-ˈveɪʃən] *n* [archaeological] fouilles *fpl*

**exceed** [ɪkˈsiːd] *vt* dépasser; [one's powers] excéder

**exceedingly** [ɪkˈsiːdɪŋlɪ] *adv* extrêmement

**excel** [ɪkˈsel] (*pt & pp* -ll-) **1.** *vt* [be better than] surpasser **2.** *vi* **to excel in** *or* **at sth** exceller en qch

**excellent** [ˈeksələnt] *adj* excellent

**except** [ɪkˈsept] **1.** *prep* sauf, excepté; **except for** à part; **except that…** sauf que… **2.** *vt* excepter (**de** from)

**exception** [ɪkˈsepʃən] *n* exception *f*; **with the exception of…** à l'exception de…

**exceptional** [ɪkˈsepʃənəl] *adj* exceptionnel, -elle

**excerpt** [ˈeksɜːpt] *n* [from film, book] extrait *m*

**excess** [ˈekses] *n* excès *m*; [surplus] excédent *m*; **a sum in excess of…** une somme qui dépasse…; **excess luggage** excédent *m* de bagages

**excessive** [ɪkˈsesɪv] *adj* excessif, -ive ▪ **excessively** *adv* [too much] excessivement; [very] extrêmement

**exchange** [ɪksˈtʃeɪndʒ] **1.** *n* échange *m*; FIN [of currency] change *m*; (**telephone**) **exchange** central *m* téléphonique; **in exchange** en échange (**for** de); **exchange rate** taux *m* de change **2.** *vt* échanger (**for** contre)

**Exchequer** [ɪksˈtʃekə(r)] *n Br* **Chancellor of the Exchequer** ≃ ministre *m* des Finances

**excitable** [ɪkˈsaɪtəbəl] *adj* nerveux, -euse

**excite** [ɪkˈsaɪt] *vt* [get worked up] surexciter; [enthuse] passionner; [provoke, stimulate] exciter ▪ **excited** *adj* [happy] surexcité; [nervous] énervé; [enthusiastic] enthousiaste; **to get excited (about)** s'exciter (pour); [angry] s'énerver (contre) ▪ **exciting** *adj* [book, adventure] passionnant

**excitement** [ɪkˈsaɪtmənt] *n* agitation *f*; [enthusiasm] enthousiasme *m*

**exclaim** [ɪkˈskleɪm] *vti* s'écrier (**that** que) ▪ **exclamation** *n* exclamation *f*; *Br* **exclamation mark**, *Am* **exclamation point** point *m* d'exclamation

**exclude** [ɪkˈskluːd] *vt* exclure (**from** de); **excluding…** à l'exclusion de…

**exclusive** [ɪkˈskluːsɪv] *adj* [right, interview, design] exclusif, -ive; [club, group] fermé ▪ **exclusively** *adv* exclusivement

**excruciating** [ɪkˈskruːʃɪeɪtɪŋ] *adj* atroce

**excursion** [ɪkˈskɜːʃən] *n* excursion *f*

**excuse 1.** [ɪkˈskjuːs] *n* excuse *f*; **to make an excuse, to make excuses** se trouver une excuse **2.** [ɪkˈskjuːz] *vt* [forgive, justify] excuser; [exempt] dispenser (**from** de); **excuse me!** excusez-moi !, pardon !

**ex-directory** [eksdaɪˈrektərɪ] *adj Br* **to be ex-directory** être sur la liste rouge

**execute** [ˈeksɪkjuːt] *vt* [prisoner, order] exécuter; [plan] mettre à exécution

**execution** [eksɪˈkjuːʃən] *n* exécution *f*

**executive** [ɪgˈzekjʊtɪv] **1.** *adj* [job] de cadre; [car] de luxe **2.** *n* [person] cadre *m*

**exemplary** [ɪgˈzemplərɪ] *adj* exemplaire

**exemplify** [ɪgˈzemplɪfaɪ] (*pt & pp* -ied) *vt* illustrer

**exempt** [ɪgˈzempt] **1.** *adj* [person] dispensé (**from** de) **2.** *vt* dispenser (**from** de; **from doing** de faire)

**exemption** [ɪgˈzem(p)ʃən] *n* dispense *f* (**from** de)

**exercise** [ˈeksəsaɪz] **1.** *n* exercice *m*; **exercise book** cahier *m* **2.** *vt* exercer; [dog, horse] promener; [caution, restraint] user de **3.** *vi* faire de l'exercice

**exert** [ɪgˈzɜːt] *vt* exercer; [force] employer; **to exert oneself** se donner du mal ▪ **exertion** *n* effort *m*

**exhale** [eksˈheɪl] *vi* expirer

**exhaust** [ɪgˈzɔːst] **1.** *n* **exhaust (fumes)** gaz *mpl* d'échappement; **exhaust (pipe)** tuyau *m* d'échappement **2.** *vt*

**explicit**

[person, resources] épuiser ■ **exhausted** adj [person, resources] épuisé ■ **exhausting** adj épuisant

**exhaustive** [ɪg'zɔːstɪv] adj [list] exhaustif, -ive; [analysis] détaillé; [inquiry] approfondi

**exhibit** [ɪg'zɪbɪt] **1.** n objet m exposé; [in court] pièce f à conviction **2.** vt [put on display] exposer ■ **exhibition** [eksɪ'bɪʃən] n exposition f

**exhilarating** [ɪg'zɪləreɪtɪŋ] adj [experience] grisant

**exile** ['egzaɪl] **1.** n [banishment] exil m; [person] exilé, -e mf **2.** vt exiler

**exist** [ɪg'zɪst] vi exister; [live] survivre (**on** avec) ■ **existing** adj [situation, circumstances] actuel, -elle; [law] existant

**existence** [ɪg'zɪstəns] n existence f; **to come into existence** être créé; **to be in existence** exister

**exit** ['eksɪt, 'egzɪt] **1.** n sortie f **2.** vi [leave & COMPUT] sortir

**exodus** ['eksədəs] n inv exode m

**exorbitant** [ɪg'zɔːbɪtənt] adj exorbitant

**exotic** [ɪg'zɒtɪk] adj exotique

**expand** [ɪk'spænd] **1.** vt [production, influence] accroître; [knowledge] étendre; [trade, range, idea] développer **2.** vi [of knowledge] s'étendre; [of trade] se développer; [of production] augmenter; [of gas] se dilater; **to expand on** développer

**expanse** [ɪk'spæns] n étendue f

**expatriate** [Br eks'pætrɪət, Am eks'peɪtrɪət] adj & n expatrié, -e (mf)

**expect** [ɪk'spekt] vt [anticipate] s'attendre à; [think] penser (**that** que); [await] attendre; **to expect to do sth** compter faire qch; **to expect that...** [anticipate] s'attendre à ce que... (+ subjunctive); **to be expecting a baby** attendre un enfant; **as expected** comme prévu

**expectation** [ekspek'teɪʃən] n **to come up to expectations** se montrer à la hauteur

**expedient** [ɪks'piːdɪənt] **1.** adj opportun **2.** n expédient m

**expedition** [ekspɪ'dɪʃən] n expédition f

**expel** [ɪk'spel] (pt & pp -ll-) vt expulser (**from** de); [from school] renvoyer

**expend** [ɪk'spend] vt [energy, money] dépenser ■ **expendable** adj [person] qui n'est pas irremplaçable

**expenditure** [ɪk'spendɪtʃə(r)] n [of money, energy] dépense f

**expense** [ɪk'spens] n frais mpl, dépense f; COMM **expenses** frais mpl; **at the expense of sb/sth** aux dépens de qn/qch

**expensive** [ɪk'spensɪv] adj [goods, hotel, shop] cher (f chère) ■ **expensively** adv **expensively dressed/furnished** habillé/meublé luxueusement

**experience** [ɪk'spɪərɪəns] **1.** n expérience f; **from** or **by experience** par expérience **2.** vt [emotion] ressentir; [hunger, success] connaître; [difficulty] éprouver ■ **experienced** adj [person] expérimenté; **to be experienced in sth** s'y connaître en qch

**experiment 1.** [ɪk'sperɪmənt] n expérience f **2.** [ɪk'sperɪment] vi expérimenter (**on** sur); **to experiment with sth** [technique, drugs] essayer qch

**expert** ['ekspɜːt] **1.** n expert m (**on** or **in** en) **2.** adj expert (**in sth** en qch; **in** or **at doing** à faire) ■ **expertise** [-tiːz] n compétence f (**in** en)

**expiration** [ekspə'reɪʃən] Am n = **expiry**

**expire** [ɪk'spaɪə(r)] vi expirer ■ **expired** adj [ticket, passport] périmé

**expiry** [ɪk'spaɪərɪ], Am **expiration** [ekspə'reɪʃən] n expiration f; **expiry date** [on ticket] date f d'expiration; [on product] date f limite d'utilisation

**explain** [ɪk'spleɪn] vt expliquer (**to** à; **that** que); [reasons] exposer; [mystery] éclaircir

**explanation** [eksplə'neɪʃən] n explication f

**explanatory** [ɪk'splænətərɪ] adj explicatif, -ive

**expletive** [ɪk'spliːtɪv] n juron m

**explicit** [ɪk'splɪsɪt] adj explicite ■ **explicitly** adv explicitement

**explode** [ɪk'spləʊd] **1.** *vt* [bomb] faire exploser **2.** *vi* [of bomb] exploser

**exploit 1.** ['eksplɔɪt] *n* exploit *m* **2.** [ɪk'splɔɪt] *vt* [person, land] exploiter ■ **exploitation** [eksplɔɪ'teɪʃən] *n* exploitation *f*

**exploratory** [ɪk'splɒrətərɪ] *adj* [talks, surgery] exploratoire

**explore** [ɪk'splɔː(r)] *vt* explorer; [causes, possibilities] examiner

**explosion** [ɪk'spləʊʒən] *n* explosion *f*

**explosive** [ɪk'spləʊsɪv] **1.** *adj* [weapon, situation] explosif, -ive **2.** *n* explosif *m*

**export 1.** ['ekspɔːt] *n* [activity, product] exportation *f* **2.** [ɪk'spɔːt] *vt* exporter (**to** vers; **from** de) ■ **exporter** *n* exportateur, -trice *mf*; [country] pays *m* exportateur

**expose** [ɪk'spəʊz] *vt* [to air, cold, danger & PHOTO] exposer (**to** à); [plot, scandal] révéler; [criminal] démasquer

**exposure** [ɪk'spəʊʒə(r)] *n* exposition *f* (**to** à); PHOTO pose *f*; **to get a lot of exposure** [in the media] faire l'objet d'une importante couverture médiatique

**express**[1] [ɪk'spres] *vt* exprimer; **to express oneself** s'exprimer

**express**[2] [ɪk'spres] **1.** *adj* [letter, delivery] exprès *inv*; [train] rapide, express *inv* **2.** *adv* [send] en exprès **3.** *n* [train] rapide *m*, express *m inv*

**expression** [ɪk'spreʃən] *n* expression *f*

**expressive** [ɪk'spresɪv] *adj* expressif, -ive

**expressly** [ɪks'preslɪ] *adv* [forbid] expressément

**expressway** [ɪk'spresweɪ] *n Am* autoroute *f*

**expulsion** [ɪk'spʌlʃən] *n* expulsion *f*; [from school] renvoi *m*

**exquisite** [ɪk'skwɪzɪt] *adj* exquis

**extend** [ɪk'stend] **1.** *vt* [in space] étendre; [in time] prolonger (**by** de); [hand] tendre (**to sb** à qn); [house] agrandir; [knowledge] accroître; [thanks] offrir (**to** à) **2.** *vi* [in space] s'étendre (**to** jusqu'à); [in time] se prolonger

**extension** [ɪk'stenʃən] *n* [for table] rallonge *f*; [to building] annexe *f*; [for telephone] poste *m*; [for essay] délai *m* supplémentaire; **extension cable** rallonge *f*

**extensive** [ɪk'stensɪv] *adj* [powers, forests] vaste; [repairs, damage] important ■ **extensively** *adv* [very much] énormément

**extent** [ɪk'stent] *n* [scope] étendue *f*; [size] importance *f*; **to a large** *or* **great extent** dans une large mesure; **to some extent** *or* **a certain extent** dans une certaine mesure; **to such an extent that...** à tel point que...

**exterior** [ɪk'stɪərɪə(r)] *adj & n* extérieur *(m)*

**exterminate** [ɪk'stɜːmɪneɪt] *vt* exterminer

**external** [ɪk'stɜːnəl] *adj* [trade, event] extérieur; [wall] externe

**extinct** [ɪk'stɪŋkt] *adj* [volcano] éteint; [species, animal] disparu

**extinguish** [ɪk'stɪŋgwɪʃ] *vt* éteindre ■ **extinguisher** *n* (fire) extinguisher extincteur *m*

**extortionate** [ɪk'stɔːʃənət] *adj* exorbitant

**extra** ['ekstrə] **1.** *adj* [additional] supplémentaire; **to be extra** [spare] être en trop; [cost more] être en supplément; **extra charge** supplément *m*; **extra time** [in sport] prolongation *f* **2.** *adv* [more than usual] extrêmement; **to pay extra** payer un supplément; **wine costs** *or* **is £10 extra** il y a un supplément de 10 livres pour le vin **3.** *n* [perk] à-côté *m*; [actor in film] figurant, -e *mf*; [on bill] supplément *m*

**extra-** ['ekstrə] *pref* extra-

**extract 1.** ['ekstrækt] *n* extrait *m* **2.** [ɪk'strækt] *vt* extraire (**from** de); [information, money] soutirer (**from** à)

**extra-curricular** [ekstrəkə'rɪkjʊlə(r)] *adj* SCH extrascolaire

**extraordinary** [ɪk'strɔːdənərɪ] *adj* extraordinaire

**extravagant** [ɪk'strævəgənt] *adj* [behaviour, idea] extravagant; [wasteful] dépensier, -ère ; [tastes] dispendieux, -euse ■ **extravagance** *n* [of behaviour] extravagance *f* ; [wastefulness] gaspillage *m* ; [thing bought] folie *f*

**extreme** [ɪk'striːm] **1.** *adj* extrême **2.** *n* extrême *m* ; **to carry** *or* **take sth to extremes** pousser qch à l'extrême ; **extreme sport** sport *m* extrême ■ **extremely** *adv* extrêmement

**extremist** [ɪk'striːmɪst] *adj* & *n* extrémiste *(mf)*

**extremity** [ɪk'stremətɪ] *(pl* **-ies)** *n* extrémité *f*

**extrovert** ['ekstrəvɜːt] *n* extraverti, -e *mf*

**exuberant** [ɪg'zjuːbərənt] *adj* exubérant

**exude** [ɪg'zjuːd] *vt* [health, honesty] respirer

**eye** [aɪ] **1.** *n* œil *m* (*pl* yeux) ; **to have one's eye on sth** avoir qch en vue ; **to keep an eye on sb /sth** surveiller qn /qch ; *Am* **eye doctor** opticien, -enne *mf* **2.** *vt* regarder ■ **eyebrow** *n* sourcil *m* ■ **eyelash** *n* cil *m* ■ **eyelid** *n* paupière *f* ■ **eyeliner** *n* eye-liner *m* ■ **eye-opening** *adj Fam* qui ouvre les yeux, révélateur, -trice ■ **eyeshadow** *n* fard *m* à paupières ■ **eyesight** *n* vue *f* ■ **eyesore** *n* horreur *f* ■ **eyewitness** *n* témoin *m* oculaire ■ **eye up** *vt sep* reluquer

**EZ** MESSAGING *written abbr of* **easy**

**EZY** MESSAGING *written abbr of* **easy**

# F

**F, f** [ef] *n* [letter] F, f *m inv*

**fab** [fæb] *adj Fam* super

**fable** ['feɪbəl] *n* fable *f*

**fabric** ['fæbrɪk] *n* [cloth] tissu *m*, étoffe *f*

**fabricate** ['fæbrɪkeɪt] *vt* fabriquer

**fabulous** ['fæbjʊləs] *adj* [legendary, incredible] fabuleux, -euse

**face** [feɪs] **1.** *n* [of person] visage *m*, figure *f*; [expression] mine *f*; [of clock] cadran *m*; [of building] façade *f*; [of cube] face *f*; [of cliff] paroi *f*; **face down(wards)** [person] face contre terre; [thing] à l'envers; **face to face** face à face; **to save / lose face** sauver / perdre la face; *Br* **face cloth** gant *m* de toilette **2.** *vt* [danger, enemy, problem] faire face à; **to face, to be facing** [be opposite] être en face de; [of window, door, room] donner sur; **faced with** [prospect, problem] confronté à; [defeat] menacé par **3.** *vi* to face north [of building] être orienté au nord; **to face up to** [danger, problem] faire face à; [fact] accepter

**faceless** ['feɪsləs] *adj* anonyme

**face-lift** ['feɪslɪft] *n* [by surgeon] lifting *m*; [of building] ravalement *m*

**facepalm** ['feɪspɑːm] *Fam* **1.** *n* facepalm *m*; **it was a bit of a facepalm moment** ce fut un moment embarrassant où j'aurais voulu que la terre m'engloutisse **2.** *excl* la honte!

**facetious** [fə'siːʃəs] *adj* [person] facétieux, -euse

**facial** ['feɪʃəl] **1.** *adj* [expression] du visage **2.** *n* soin *m* du visage

**facilitate** [fə'sɪlɪteɪt] *vt* faciliter ■ **facilities** *npl* [for sports, cooking] équipements *mpl*; [in harbour, airport] installations *fpl*

**fact** [fækt] *n* fait *m*; **as a matter of fact, in fact** en fait

**faction** ['fækʃən] *n* faction *f*

**factor** ['fæktə(r)] *n* facteur *m*

**factory** ['fæktərɪ] *(pl* **-ies***) n* [large] usine *f*; [small] fabrique *f*

**factual** ['fæktʃʊəl] *adj* basé sur les faits

**faculty** ['fækltɪ] *(pl* **-ies***) n* [of mind, university] faculté *f*

**fad** [fæd] *n* [fashion] mode *f* (**for** de); [personal habit] marotte *f*

**fade** [feɪd] *vi* [of flower, material, colour] se faner; [of light] baisser; **to fade (away)** [of memory, smile] s'effacer; [of sound] s'affaiblir; [of person] dépérir

**fag** [fæg] *n Br Fam* [cigarette] clope *m* ou *f*

**fail** [feɪl] **1.** *n* **without fail** sans faute **2.** *vt* [exam] échouer à; [candidate] recaler; **to fail to do** [forget] manquer de faire; [not be able] ne pas arriver à faire **3.** *vi* [of person, plan] échouer; [of business] faire faillite; [of health, sight] baisser; [of memory, strength] défaillir; [of brakes] lâcher ■ **failed** *adj* [attempt, poet] raté ■ **failing 1.** *n* [fault] défaut *m* **2.** *prep* à défaut de; **failing this, failing that** à défaut

**failure** ['feɪljə(r)] *n* échec *m*; [of business] faillite *f*; [person] raté, -e *mf*

**faint** [feɪnt] **1.** *(compar* **-er***, superl* **-est***) adj* [weak - voice, trace, breeze, hope] faible; [colour] pâle; **to feel faint** se sentir mal **2.** *vi* s'évanouir (**with** or **from** de)

**fair**[1] [feə(r)] *n* [trade fair] foire *f*; *Br* [funfair] fête *f* foraine ■ **fairground** *n* parc *m* d'attractions

**fair**[2] [feə(r)] **1.** *(compar* **-er***, superl* **-est***) adj* **a)** [just] juste; [game, fight] loyal; **fair play** fair-play *m inv*; **fair trade** commerce *m* équitable **b)** [rather good] assez bon (*f* bonne); [price] raisonnable;

**a fair amount (of)** [a lot] pas mal (de) **c)** [wind] favorable ; [weather] beau (*f* belle) **2.** *adv* [fight] loyalement ; **to play fair** jouer franc jeu ■ **fairly** *adv* **a)** [treat] équitablement ; [act, fight, get] loyalement **b)** [rather] assez

**fair³** [feə(r)] *adj* [hair, person] blond ; [complexion, skin] clair ■ **fair-haired** *adj* blond

**fairy** ['feərɪ] (*pl* -**ies**) *n* fée *f* ■ **fairytale** *n* conte *m* de fées

**faith** [feɪθ] *n* foi *f* ; **to have faith in sb** avoir foi en qn ; **in good / bad faith** [act] de bonne /mauvaise foi

**faithful** ['feɪθfəl] *adj* fidèle ■ **faithfully** *adv* fidèlement ; *Br* **yours faithfully** [in letter] veuillez agréer l'expression de mes sentiments distingués

**fake** [feɪk] **1.** *adj* faux (*f* fausse) **2.** *n* [object] faux *m* ; [person] imposteur *m* **3.** *vt* [signature] contrefaire **4.** *vi* [pretend] faire semblant

**fall** [fɔːl] **1.** *n* [of person, snow, city] chute *f* ; [in price, demand] baisse *f* ; *Am* [season] automne *m* **2.** (*pt* fell, *pp* fallen) *vi* tomber ; [of price, temperature] baisser ; **the dollar is falling** le dollar est en baisse ; **to fall into** [hole, trap] tomber dans ; [habit] prendre ; **to fall off a bicycle / ladder** tomber d'une bicyclette /échelle ; **to fall out of a window** tomber d'une fenêtre ; **to fall over sth** tomber en butant contre qch ; **to fall asleep** s'endormir ; **to fall ill** tomber malade ■ **fall apart** *vi* [of book, machine] tomber en morceaux ; [of person] s'effondrer ■ **fall back on** *vt insep* [resort to] se rabattre sur ■ **fall behind** *vi* [in work, payments] prendre du retard ■ **fall down** *vi* tomber ; [of building] s'effondrer ■ **fall for** *vt insep* [person] tomber amoureux, -euse de ; [trick] se laisser prendre à ■ **fall in** *vi* [collapse] s'écrouler ■ **fall off** *vi* [come off] tomber ; [of numbers] diminuer ■ **fall out** *vi* [quarrel] se brouiller (**with** avec) ■ **fall over** *vi* tomber ; [of table, vase] se renverser ■ **fall through** *vi* [of plan] tomber à l'eau, échouer

**fallacy** ['fæləsɪ] (*pl* -**ies**) *n* erreur *f*

**fallen** ['fɔːlən] **1.** *pp of* **fall 2.** *adj* tombé ; **fallen leaves** feuilles *fpl* mortes

**fallible** ['fæləbəl] *adj* faillible

**false** [fɔːls] *adj* faux (*f* fausse) ; **false teeth** dentier *m*

**falsify** ['fɔːlsɪfaɪ] (*pt & pp* -**ied**) *vt* [forge] falsifier

**falter** ['fɔːltə(r)] *vi* [of voice, speaker] hésiter

**fame** [feɪm] *n* renommée *f* ■ **famed** *adj* renommé (**for** pour)

**familiar** [fə'mɪljə(r)] *adj* [well-known] familier, -ère (**to** à) ; **to be familiar with sb /sth** bien connaître qn /qch ; **he looks familiar** je l'ai déjà vu (quelque part)

**familiarize** [fə'mɪljəraɪz] *vt* **to familiarize oneself with sth** se familiariser avec qch

**family** ['fæmɪlɪ] **1.** (*pl* -**ies**) *n* famille *f* **2.** *adj* [name, doctor, jewels] de famille ; [planning, problems, business] familial ; **family leave** congé *m* parental ; **family man** homme *m* attaché à sa famille ; **family planning** planning *m* familial ■ **family-friendly** *adj* [pub, hotel, campsite] qui accueille volontiers les familles ; [policy, proposal] qui favorise la famille ; [show, entertainment] pour toute la famille ■ **family-size(d)** *adj* [jar, packet] familial

**famine** ['fæmɪn] *n* famine *f*

**famished** ['fæmɪʃt] *adj* affamé

**famous** ['feɪməs] *adj* célèbre (**for** pour)

**fan¹** [fæn] **1.** *n* [held in hand] éventail *m* (*pl* -ails) ; [mechanical] ventilateur *m* **2.** (*pt & pp* -**nn**-) *vt* [person] éventer

**fan²** [fæn] *n* [of person] fan *mf* ; [of team] supporter *m* ; **to be a jazz /sports fan** être passionné de jazz /de sport

**fanatic** [fə'nætɪk] *n* fanatique *mf* ■ **fanatical** *adj* fanatique

**fanciful** ['fænsɪfəl] *adj* fantaisiste

**fancy** ['fænsɪ] **1.** *n* **I took a fancy to it, it took my fancy** j'en ai eu envie **2.** *adj* [jewels, hat, button] fantaisie *inv* ; [car] de luxe ; [house, restaurant] chic *inv* ; *Br* **fancy dress** déguisement *m* ; *Br* **fancy dress party** soirée *f* déguisée **3.** (*pt &*

*pp* **-ied)** *vt* **a)** *Br Fam* [want] avoir envie de ; **he fancies her** elle lui plaît **b) to fancy that...** [imagine] se figurer que... ; [think] croire que...

**fanfare** ['fænfeə(r)] *n* fanfare *f*

**fantastic** [fæn'tæstɪk] *adj* fantastique ; [wealth, size] prodigieux, -euse ; *Fam* [excellent] formidable

**fantasy** ['fæntəsɪ] *(pl* **-ies)** *n* [imagination] fantaisie *f* ; [dream] chimère *f* ; [fanciful, sexual] fantasme *m* ▪ **fanta-size** *vi* fantasmer **(about** sur)

**FAQ** [fak, ˌfeɪˈkjuː] *n* COMPUT *(abbr of* frequently asked questions) foire *f* aux questions, FAQ *f*

**far** [fɑː(r)] **1.** *(compar* farther *or* further, *superl* farthest *or* furthest) *adj* **the far side/end** l'autre côté / bout ; **the Far East** l'Extrême-Orient *m* ; POL **the far left/right** l'extrême gauche *f* /droite *f* **2.** *adv* **a)** [in distance] loin **(from** de) ; **how far is it to Toulouse?** combien y a-t-il d'ici à Toulouse ? ; **is it far to...?** sommes-nous /suis-je /*etc* loin de... ? ; **how far has he got with his work?** où en est-il dans son travail ? ; **as far as** jusqu'à ; **as far** *or* **so far as I know** autant que je sache ; **as far** *or* **so far as I'm concerned** en ce qui me concerne ; **far from doing sth** loin de faire qch ; **far away** *or* **off** au loin ; **to be far away** être loin **(from** de)
**b)** [in time] **as far back as 1820** dès 1820 ; **far off** dans longtemps ; **so far** jusqu'ici
**c)** [much] **far bigger /more expensive** beaucoup plus grand /plus cher *(f* chère) **(than** que) ; **far more /better** beaucoup plus /mieux **(than** que) ; **by far** de loin
▪ **far-away** *adj* [country] lointain ; [look] perdu dans le vague
▪ **far-fetched** *adj* tiré par les cheveux
▪ **far-reaching** *adj* de grande portée
▪ **farsighted** *adj* clairvoyant

**farce** [fɑːs] *n* farce *f* ▪ **farcical** *adj* grotesque

**fare** [feə(r)] **1.** *n* [for journey - in train, bus] prix *m* du billet ; [in taxi] prix *m* de la course **2.** *vi* [manage] se débrouiller

**farewell** [feə'wel] **1.** *n & excl* adieu *(m)* **2.** *adj* [party, speech] d'adieu

**farm** [fɑːm] **1.** *n* ferme *f* **2.** *adj* [worker, produce] agricole **3.** *vt* cultiver **4.** *vi* être agriculteur, -trice ▪ **farmer** *n* fermier, -ère *mf*, agriculteur, -trice *mf* ▪ **farmhouse** *n* ferme *f* ▪ **farming** *n* agriculture *f* ; [breeding] élevage *m* ▪ **farmyard** *n* cour *f* de ferme

**fart** [fɑːt] *Fam* **1.** *n* pet *m* **2.** *vi* péter

**farther** ['fɑːðə(r)] **1.** *compar of* **far 2.** *adv* plus loin ; **farther forward** plus avancé ; **to get farther away** s'éloigner ▪ **farthest 1.** *superl of* **far 2.** *adj* le plus éloigné **3.** *adv* le plus loin

**fascinate** ['fæsɪneɪt] *vt* fasciner ▪ **fascinating** *adj* fascinant

**fascist** ['fæʃɪst] *adj & n* fasciste *(mf)*

**fashion** ['fæʃən] **1.** *n* **a)** [in clothes] mode *f* ; **in fashion** à la mode ; **out of fashion** démodé ; **fashion show** défilé *m* de mode **b)** [manner] façon *f* ; **after a fashion** tant bien que mal **2.** *vt* [form] façonner ; [make] confectionner ▪ **fashionable** *adj* à la mode ▪ **fashionably** *adv* [dressed] à la mode

**fast¹** [fɑːst] **1.** *(compar* **-er,** *superl* **-est)** *adj* rapide ; **to be fast** [of clock] avancer **(by** de) ; **fast food** restauration *f* rapide ; **fast food restaurant** fast-food *m* **2.** *adv* **a)** [quickly] vite ; **how fast?** à quelle vitesse ? **b) fast asleep** profondément endormi ▪ **fast-paced** [-'peɪst] *adj* [novel, film, TV show] au rythme trépidant

**fast²** [fɑːst] **1.** *n* jeûne *m* **2.** *vi* jeûner

**fasten** ['fɑːsən] **1.** *vt* attacher **(to** à) ; [door, window] fermer ; **to fasten sth down** attacher qch **2.** *vi* [of dress] s'attacher ; [of door, window] se fermer ▪ **fastener, fastening** *n* [clip] attache *f* ; [hook] agrafe *f* ; [press stud] bouton-pression *m* ; [of bag] fermoir *m*

**fat** [fæt] **1.** *(compar* **fatter,** *superl* **fattest)** *adj* gras *(f* grasse) ; [cheeks, salary, book] gros *(f* grosse) ; **to get fat** grossir **2.** *n* graisse *f* ; [on meat] gras *m*

**fatal** ['feɪtəl] *adj* mortel, -elle ▪ **fatally** *adv* **fatally wounded** mortellement blessé

**fatality** [fə'tælətɪ] *(pl* -ies*) n* [person] victime *f*

**fate** [feɪt] *n* destin *m*, sort *m* ■ **fateful** *adj* [words, day] fatidique

**father** ['fɑ:ðə(r)] **1.** *n* père *m*; **Father Christmas** le père Noël **2.** *vt* [child] engendrer ■ **father-in-law** *(pl* **fathers-in-law***) n* beau-père *m*

**fatherhood** ['fɑ:ðəhʊd] *n* paternité *f*

**fatherly** ['fɑ:ðəlɪ] *adj* paternel, -elle

**fatigue** [fə'ti:g] *n* [tiredness] fatigue *f*

**fatten** ['fætən] *vt* **to fatten (up)** engraisser ■ **fattening** *adj* [food] qui fait grossir

**fatty** ['fætɪ] *(compar* -ier, *superl* -iest*) adj* [food] gras *(f* grasse*)*

**faucet** ['fɔ:sɪt] *n Am* [tap] robinet *m*

**fault** [fɔ:lt] **1.** *n* [blame] faute *f*; [defect, failing] défaut *m*; GEOL faille *f*; **to find fault (with)** trouver à redire (à); **it's your fault** c'est (de) ta faute **2.** *vt* **to fault sb/sth** trouver des défauts chez qn/à qch

**faultless** ['fɔ:ltləs] *adj* irréprochable

**faulty** ['fɔ:ltɪ] *(compar* -ier, *superl* -iest*) adj* défectueux, -euse

**favour**, *Am* **favor** ['feɪvə(r)] **1.** *n* [act of kindness] service *m*; [approval] faveur *f*; **to do sb a favour** rendre service à qn; **in favour (with sb)** bien vu (de qn); **to be in favour of sth** être partisan de qch **2.** *vt* [encourage] favoriser; [support] être partisan de ■ **favourable**, *Am* **favorable** *adj* favorable **(to** à*)*

**favourite**, *Am* **favorite** ['feɪvərɪt] **1.** *adj* favori, -ite, préféré **2.** *n* favori, -ite *mf* ■ **favorites** *npl* COMPUT favoris *mpl*, signets *mpl* ■ **favouritism**, *Am* **favoritism** *n* favoritisme *m*

**fawn** [fɔ:n] **1.** *n* [deer] faon *m* **2.** *adj* & *n* [colour] fauve *(m)*

**fax** [fæks] **1.** *n* [message] télécopie *f*, fax *m*; **fax (machine)** télécopieur *m*, fax *m* **2.** *vt* [message] faxer; **to fax sb** envoyer un fax à qn

**fear** [fɪə(r)] **1.** *n* peur *f*; [worry] crainte *f*; **for fear of doing sth** de peur de faire qch; **for fear that...** de peur que... (+ *ne*

+ *subjunctive*) **2.** *vt* craindre; **I fear that he might leave** je crains qu'il ne parte **3.** *vi* **to fear for one's life** craindre pour sa vie ■ **fearful** *adj* [person] apeuré; [noise, pain, consequence] épouvantable ■ **fearless** *adj* intrépide

**feasible** ['fi:zəbəl] *adj* faisable

**feast** [fi:st] **1.** *n* festin *m*; [religious] fête *f* **2.** *vi* **to feast on sth** se régaler de qch

**feat** [fi:t] *n* exploit *m*

**feather** ['feðə(r)] *n* plume *f*

**feature** ['fi:tʃə(r)] **1.** *n* [of face, person] trait *m*; [of thing, place, machine] caractéristique *f*; **feature (article)** article *m* de fond; **feature (film)** long métrage *m* **2.** *vt* [of newspaper, exhibition, film - present] présenter; [portray] représenter; **a film featuring Nicole Kidman** un film ayant pour vedette Nicole Kidman **3.** *vi* [appear] figurer (**in** dans)

**February** ['februərɪ] *n* février *m*

**fed** [fed] **1.** *pt* & *pp of* **feed 2.** *adj Fam* **to be fed up** en avoir marre *ou* ras le bol (**with** de*)*

**federal** ['fedərəl] *adj* fédéral; *Am* **Federal Agent** agent *m* fédéral, agente *f* fédérale ■ **federation** [-'reɪʃən] *n* fédération *f*

**fee** [fi:] *n* **fee(s)** [of doctor, lawyer] honoraires *mpl*; [of artist] cachet *m*; [for registration, examination] droits *mpl*; [for membership] cotisation *f*; **school** *or* **tuition fees** frais *mpl* d'inscription

**feeble** ['fi:bəl] *(compar* -er, *superl* -est*) adj* faible; [excuse, smile] pauvre; [attempt] peu convaincant

**feed** [fi:d] **1.** *n* [animal food] nourriture *f*; [for baby - from breast] tétée *f*; [from bottle] biberon *m* **2.** *(pt* & *pp* **fed***) vt* donner à manger à; [baby - from breast] donner la tétée à; [from bottle] donner son biberon à; **to feed sb sth** faire manger qch à qn **3.** *vi* [eat] manger; **to feed on sth** se nourrir de qch

**feedback** ['fi:dbæk] *n* [response] réactions *fpl*

**feel** [fi:l] **1.** *n* [touch] toucher *m*; **to have a feel for sth** avoir qch dans la peau **2.** *(pt* & *pp* **felt***) vt* [be aware of] sentir; [experience] éprouver, ressentir;

[touch] tâter; **to feel that...** penser que...; **to feel one's way** avancer à tâtons **3.** *vi* **to feel (about)** [grope] tâtonner; [in pocket] fouiller (**for sth** pour trouver qch); **it feels hard** c'est dur au toucher; **to feel tired/old** se sentir fatigué/vieux (*f* vieille); **I feel hot/ sleepy/hungry** j'ai chaud/sommeil/ faim; **she feels better** elle va mieux; **to feel like sth** [want] avoir envie de qch; **it feels like cotton** on dirait du coton; **what do you feel about...?** que pensez-vous de...?; **I feel bad about it** ça m'ennuie

**feeling** ['fiːlɪŋ] *n* [emotion, impression] sentiment *m*; [physical] sensation *f*; **to have a feeling for** [music, painting] être sensible à

**feet** [fiːt] *pl of* **foot**

**feign** [feɪn] *vt* feindre

**feline** ['fiːlaɪn] *adj* félin

**fell** [fel] **1.** *pt of* **fall 2.** *vt* [tree] abattre; [opponent] terrasser

**fellow** ['feləʊ] *n* **a)** [man, boy] gars *m* **b)** [companion] **fellow countryman/ fellow countrywoman** compatriote *mf*; **fellow worker** collègue *mf* **c)** [of society] membre *m*

**fellowship** ['feləʊʃɪp] *n* [scholarship] bourse *f* de recherche

**felt¹** [felt] *pt & pp of* **feel**

**felt²** [felt] *n* feutre *m* ■ **felt-tip** *n* **felt-tip (pen)** crayon-feutre *m*

**female** ['fiːmeɪl] **1.** *adj* [person, name, voice] féminin; [animal] femelle **2.** *n* [woman] femme *f*; [girl] fille *f*; [animal, plant] femelle *f*

**femidom** *n* préservatif *m* féminin

**feminine** ['femɪnɪn] **1.** *adj* féminin **2.** *n* [in grammar] féminin *m* ■ **feminist** *adj & n* féministe (*mf*)

**fence** [fens] **1.** *n* [barrier] clôture *f*; [more solid] barrière *f*; [in race] obstacle *m* **2.** *vt* **to fence (in)** [land] clôturer **3.** *vi* [as sport] faire de l'escrime ■ **fencing** *n* [sport] escrime *f*

**fend** [fend] **1.** *vi* **to fend for oneself** se débrouiller **2.** *vt* **to fend off** [blow] parer

**fender** ['fendə(r)] *n Am* [of car] aile *f*

**ferment** [fə'ment] *vi* fermenter

**ferocious** [fə'rəʊʃəs] *adj* féroce

**ferret** ['ferɪt] **1.** *n* [animal] furet *m* **2.** *vt* **to ferret out** [object, information] dénicher

**Ferris wheel** ['ferɪs-] *n Am* grande roue *f*

**ferry** ['ferɪ] **1.** (*pl* **-ies**) *n* ferry-boat *m*; [small, for river] bac *m* **2.** (*pt & pp* **-ied**) *vt* transporter

**fertile** [*Br* 'fɜːtaɪl, *Am* 'fɜːrtəl] *adj* [land, imagination] fertile; [person, animal] fécond ■ **fertilizer** *n* engrais *m*

**fervent** ['fɜːvənt] *adj* fervent

**fest** [fest] *n Fam* **crazy shopping fest** folle virée shopping *f*

**festival** ['festɪvəl] *n* [of music, film] festival *m* (*pl* **-als**); [religious] fête *f*

**festive** ['festɪv] *adj* de fête; [mood] festif, -ive; **the festive season** les fêtes *fpl* de fin d'année ■ **festivities** *npl* festivités *fpl*

**fetch** [fetʃ] *vt* **a)** [bring] aller chercher **b)** [be sold for] rapporter

**fête** [feɪt] **1.** *n Br* fête *f* **2.** *vt* fêter

**fetus** ['fiːtəs] *Am n* = **foetus**

**feud** [fjuːd] *n* querelle *f*

**fever** ['fiːvə(r)] *n* fièvre *f*; **to have a fever** [temperature] avoir de la fièvre ■ **feverish** *adj* [person, activity] fiévreux, -euse

**few** [fjuː] **1.** *adj* **a)** [not many] peu de; **few towns** peu de villes; **every few days** tous les trois ou quatre jours; **one of the few books** l'un des rares livres; **few and far between** rarissime **b)** [some] **a few towns** quelques villes; **a few more books** encore quelques livres; **quite a few..., a good few...** bon nombre de.. **2.** *pron* peu; **few came** peu sont venus; **few of them** un petit nombre d'entre eux; **a few** quelques-un(e)s (**of** de); **a few of us** quelques-uns d'entre nous

**fewer** ['fjuːə(r)] **1.** *adj* moins de; **fewer houses** moins de maisons (**than** que);

**file**

**to be fewer (than)** être moins nombreux (que) **2.** *pron* moins ▪ **fewest 1.** *adj* le moins de **2.** *pron* le moins

**fiancé** [fɪˈɒnseɪ] *n* fiancé *m*

**fiancée** [fɪˈɒnseɪ] *n* fiancée *f*

**fiasco** [fɪˈæskəʊ] *(pl* -os, *Am pl* -oes*) n* fiasco *m*

**fib** [fɪb] *Fam* **1.** *n* bobard *m* **2.** *(pt & pp* -bb-*) vi* raconter des bobards

**fibre**, *Am* **fiber** [ˈfaɪbə(r)] *n* fibre *f*; [in diet] fibres *fpl*

**fickle** [ˈfɪkəl] *adj* inconstant

**fiction** [ˈfɪkʃən] *n* [invention] fiction *f*; **(works of) fiction** livres *mpl* de fiction ▪ **fictional** *adj* [character] fictif, -ive

**fictitious** [fɪkˈtɪʃəs] *adj* fictif, -ive

**fiddle** [ˈfɪdəl] **1.** *n* a) [violin] violon *m* b) *Br Fam* [dishonest act] combine *f* **2.** *vt Br Fam* [accounts] truquer **3.** *vi* **to fiddle about** [waste time] traînailler; **to fiddle (about) with sth** tripoter qch

**fiddly** [ˈfɪdlɪ] *(compar* -ier, *superl* -iest*) adj Fam* [task] minutieux, -euse

**fidget** [ˈfɪdʒɪt] **1.** *n* **to be a fidget** ne pas tenir en place **2.** *vi* **to fidget (about)** gigoter ▪ **fidgety** *adj* agité

**field** [fiːld] *n* [gen & COMPUT] champ *m*; [for sports] terrain *m*; [sphere] domaine *m*

**fierce** [fɪəs] *(compar* -er, *superl* -est*) adj* [animal, warrior, tone] féroce; [attack, wind] violent

**fiery** [ˈfaɪərɪ] *(compar* -ier, *superl* -iest*) adj* [person, speech] fougueux, -euse

**fifteen** [fɪfˈtiːn] *adj & n* quinze *(m)* ▪ **fifteenth** *adj & n* quinzième *(mf)*

**fifth** [fɪfθ] *adj & n* cinquième *(mf)*; **a fifth** [fraction] un cinquième; *Am SCH* **fifth grade** *classe de l'enseignement primaire correspondant au CM2 (9-10 ans)*

**fifty** [ˈfɪftɪ] *adj & n* cinquante *(m)* ▪ **fifty-fifty** *adj & adv* moitié-moitié, fifty-fifty; **a fifty-fifty chance** une chance sur deux; **to split the profits fifty-fifty** partager les bénéfices moitié-moitié ▪ **fiftieth** *adj & n* cinquantième *(mf)*

**fig** [fɪg] *n* figue *f*

**fight** [faɪt] **1.** *n* [between people] bagarre *f*; [between boxers, soldiers] combat *m*; [struggle] lutte *f* **(against/for** contre /pour); [quarrel] dispute *f* **2.** *(pt & pp* **fought*) vt* [person] se battre contre; [decision, enemy] combattre; [fire, temptation] lutter contre; **to fight a battle** livrer bataille; *POL* **to fight an election** se présenter à une élection; **to fight off** [attacker, attack] repousser **3.** *vi* se battre **(against** contre); [soldiers] combattre; [struggle] lutter **(against/for** contre/pour); [quarrel] se disputer; **to fight back** [retaliate] se défendre; **to fight over sth** se disputer qch ▪ **fight back 1.** *vt insep* refouler **2.** *vi* riposter

**fighter** [ˈfaɪtə(r)] *n* [determined person] battant, -e *mf*; [in brawl, battle] combattant, -e *mf*; [boxer] boxeur *m*; [aircraft] avion *m* de chasse

**fighting** [ˈfaɪtɪŋ] *n* [brawling] bagarres *fpl*; *MIL* combat *m*

**figment** [ˈfɪgmənt] *n* **it's a figment of your imagination** c'est le fruit de ton imagination

**figurative** [ˈfɪgjʊrətɪv] *adj* [meaning] figuré; [art] figuratif, -ive

**figure¹** [*Br* ˈfɪgə(r), *Am* ˈfɪgjə(r)] *n* a) [numeral] chiffre *m* b) [shape] forme *f*; [outline] silhouette *f*; **she has a nice figure** elle est bien faite c) [diagram] figure *f*; **figure skating** patinage *m* artistique d) [expression, word] **a figure of speech** une figure de rhétorique e) [important person] personnage *m*

**figure²** [*Br* ˈfɪgə(r), *Am* ˈfɪgjə(r)] **1.** *vt* **to figure that...** [think] penser que...; [estimate] supposer que...; **to figure out** [person, motive] arriver à comprendre; [answer] trouver; [amount] calculer **2.** *vi* [appear] figurer **(on** sur); **to figure on doing sth** compter faire qch

**file¹** [faɪl] **1.** *n* [tool] lime *f* **2.** *vt* **to file (down)** limer

**file²** [faɪl] **1.** *n* [folder] chemise *f*; [documents] dossier *m* **(on** sur); *COMPUT* fichier *m*; **to be on file** figurer au dossier **2.** *vt* [document] classer; [complaint, claim] déposer ▪ **filename** *n* nom *m* de fichier

**file³** [faɪl] **1.** n [line] file f; **in single file** en file indienne **2.** vi **to file in/out** entrer / sortir à la queue leu leu; **to file past sb/ sth** défiler devant qn /qch ■ **filing** adj **filing cabinet** classeur m (meuble)

**fill** [fɪl] **1.** n **to eat one's fill** manger à sa faim **2.** vt remplir (**with** de) ; [tooth] plomber; [time] occuper; **to fill in** [form] remplir ; [hole] combler; **to fill sb in on sth** mettre qn au courant de qch; **to fill out** [form] remplir; **to fill up** [container] remplir **3.** vi **to fill (up)** se remplir (**with** de); **to fill in for sb** remplacer qn; **to fill up** [with petrol] faire le plein

**fillet** [Br 'fɪlɪt, Am fɪ'leɪ] **1.** n [of fish, meat] filet m **2.** (Am pt & pp [fɪ'leɪd]) vt [fish] dé- couper en filets ; [meat] désosser

**filling** ['fɪlɪŋ] **1.** adj [meal] nourrissant **2.** n [in tooth] plombage m ; [in food] garniture f; **filling station** station- service f

**film** [fɪlm] **1.** n film m ; [for camera, layer] pellicule f; [for food] film m plastique **2.** adj [studio, technician, critic] de cinéma; **film star** vedette f de cinéma **3.** vt filmer **4.** vi [of film maker, actor] tourner

**Filofax®** ['faɪləfæks] n organiseur m

**filter** ['fɪltə(r)] **1.** n filtre m ; Br [traffic sign] flèche f de dégagement; **filter coffee** café m filtre **2.** vt filtrer **3.** vi to filter through filtrer ■ **filter-tipped** adj [cigarette] bout filtre inv

**filth** [fɪlθ] n saleté f; Fig [obscenities] saletés fpl ■ **filthy** (compar -ier, superl -iest) adj [hands, shoes] sale; [language] obscène; [habit] dégoûtant

**fin** [fɪn] n [of fish] nageoire f; [of shark] aileron m

**final** ['faɪnəl] **1.** adj [last] dernier, -ère ; [definite] définitif, -ive **2.** n [in sport] finale f; UNIV **finals** examens mpl de dernière année ■ **finalist** n fina- liste mf ■ **finalize** vt [plan] mettre au point ; [date] fixer définitivement ; [deal] conclure ■ **finally** adv [lastly] enfin; [eventually] finalement; [irrev- ocably] définitivement

**finale** [fɪ'nɑːlɪ] n [musical] finale m

**finance** ['faɪnæns] **1.** n finance f; **finances** [of person] finances fpl ; [of company] situation f financière **2.** vt financer

**financial** [faɪ'nænʃəl] adj financier, -ère; Br **financial year** exercice m comptable

**financier** [faɪ'nænsɪə(r)] n financier m

**find** [faɪnd] **1.** n [discovery] découverte f **2.** (pt & pp found) vt trouver; **I find that...** je trouve que... ■ **find out 1.** vt [secret, information] découvrir ; [person] prendre en défaut **2.** vi [inquire] se ren- seigner (**about** sur); **to find out about sth** [discover] apprendre qch

**findings** ['faɪndɪŋz] npl conclusions fpl

**fine¹** [faɪn] **1.** n [money] amende f; [for driving offence] contravention f **2.** vt to **fine sb £100** infliger une amende de 100 livres à qn

**fine²** [faɪn] **1.** (compar -er, superl -est) adj **a)** [thin, not coarse - hair, needle] fin; [gold, metal] pur ; [distinction] subtil **b)** [very good] excellent ; [beautiful - weather, statue] beau (f belle); **it's fine** [weather] il fait beau; **he's fine** [healthy] il va bien **2.** adv [very well] très bien ■ **finely** adv [dressed] magnifique- ment; [embroidered, ground] finement; **finely chopped** haché menu

**finger** ['fɪŋgə(r)] **1.** n doigt m ; **little fin- ger** petit doigt m, auriculaire m **2.** vt tâter ■ **fingernail** n ongle m ■ **finger- tip** n bout m du doigt

**fingerless glove** ['fɪŋgələs-] n mi- taine f

**finish** ['fɪnɪʃ] **1.** n [end] fin f; [of race] arrivée f; [of article, car] finition f **2.** vt **to finish sth (off** or **up)** finir qch; **to finish doing sth** finir de faire qch **3.** vi [of meeting, event] finir, se ter- miner ; [of person] finir, terminer; **to have finished with** [object] ne plus avoir besoin de ; [activity, person] en avoir fini avec; **to finish off** [of person] finir, terminer ■ **finishing** adj **finish- ing line** [of race] ligne f d'arrivée; **to put the finishing touches to sth** mettre la dernière main à qch ■ **finished** adj [ended, complete, ruined] fini

**finite** ['faɪnaɪt] adj fini

**fit**

**Finland** ['fɪnlənd] *n* la Finlande ■ **Finn** *n* Finlandais, -e *mf*, Finnois, -e *mf* ■ **Finnish 1.** *adj* finlandais, finnois **2.** *n* [language] finnois *m*

**fir** [fɜ:(r)] *n* sapin *m*

**fire** ['faɪə(r)] **1.** *n* feu *m*; [accidental] incendie *m*; *Br* [electric heater] radiateur *m*; **to light** *or* **make a fire** faire du feu; **to set fire to sth** mettre le feu à qch; **on fire** en feu; **fire!** [alarm] au feu !; **to open fire** ouvrir le feu; **fire alarm** sirène *f* d'incendie; *Br* **fire brigade**, *Am* **fire department** pompiers *mpl*; **fire engine** voiture *f* des pompiers; **fire escape** escalier *m* de secours; **fire station** caserne *f* des pompiers **2.** *vt* [cannon] tirer; [pottery] cuire; **to fire a gun** tirer un coup de fusil /de pistolet; **to fire questions at sb** bombarder qn de questions; **to fire sb** [dismiss] renvoyer qn **3.** *vi* tirer (**at** sur); **fire!** feu ! ■ **firearm** *n* arme *f* à feu ■ **fireguard** *n* garde-feu *m inv* ■ **fireman** *(pl* **-men)** *n* sapeur-pompier *m* ■ **fireplace** *n* cheminée *f* ■ **fireproof** *adj* [door] ignifugé ■ **fire-retardant** *adj* ignifuge ■ **fireside** *n* **by the fireside** au coin du feu ■ **firewall** ['faɪəwɔːl] *n* COMPUT pare-feu *m* ■ **firewood** *n* bois *m* de chauffage ■ **firework** *n* fusée *f*; [firecracker] pétard *m*; **fireworks**, *Br* **firework display** feu *m* d'artifice

**firm¹** [fɜ:m] *n* [company] entreprise *f*, firme *f*

**firm²** [fɜ:m] **1.** *(compar* **-er**, *superl* **-est**) *adj* [earth, decision] ferme; [foundations] solide **2.** *adv* **to stand firm** tenir bon *ou* ferme ■ **firmly** *adv* [believe] fermement; [shut] bien

**first** [fɜ:st] **1.** *adj* premier, -ère; **first aid** premiers secours *mpl*; *Am* SCH **first grade** *classe de l'école primaire correspondant au CP (5-6 ans)*; **first name** prénom *m* **2.** *adv* d'abord; [for the first time] pour la première fois; **first of all, first and foremost** tout d'abord; **at first** d'abord; **to come first** [in race] arriver premier; [in exam] être reçu premier **3.** *n* [person, thing] premier, -ère *mf*; **first (gear)** [of vehicle] première *f* ■ **first-class 1.** *adj* excellent; [ticket] de première

classe; [mail] ordinaire **2.** *adv* [travel] en première ■ **first-hand** *adj* **to have (had) first-hand experience of sth** avoir fait l'expérience personnelle de qch ■ **first-rate** *adj* excellent

**firstly** ['fɜ:stlɪ] *adv* premièrement

**fish** [fɪʃ] **1.** *(pl* inv *or* **-es** [-ɪz]) *n* poisson *m*; **fish bone** arête *f*; **fish factory** usine *f* piscicole; *Br* **fish fingers**, *Am* **fish sticks** bâtonnets *mpl* de poisson; **fish shop** poissonnerie *f*; **fish tank** aquarium *m* **2.** *vt* **to fish sth out** [from water] repêcher qch **3.** *vi* pêcher ■ **fish-and-chip** *adj* *Br* **fish-and-chip shop** *magasin où on vend du poisson frit et des frites* ■ **fishing** *n* pêche *f*; **to go fishing** aller à la pêche; **fishing boat** bateau *m* de pêche; **fishing net** filet *m* (de pêche); **fishing rod** canne à pêche

**fisherman** ['fɪʃəmən] *(pl* **-men)** *n* pêcheur *m*

**fishmonger** ['fɪʃmʌŋɡə(r)] *n* poissonnier, -ère *mf*

**fishy** ['fɪʃɪ] *(compar* **-ier**, *superl* **-iest)** *adj* [smell, taste] de poisson; *Fig* [suspicious] louche

**fist** [fɪst] *n* poing *m* ■ **fistful** *n* poignée *f* (**of** de)

**fit¹** [fɪt] **1.** *(compar* **fitter**, *superl* **fittest)** *adj* **a)** [healthy] en forme; **to keep fit** se maintenir en forme
**b)** [suitable] propre (**for** à; **to do** à faire); [worthy] digne (**for** de; **to do** de faire); [able] apte (**for** à; **to do** à faire)
**2.** *n* **a good fit** [clothes] à la bonne taille; **a tight fit** [clothes] ajusté
**3.** *(pt & pp* **-tt-**) *vt* [be the right size for] aller bien à; [match] correspondre à; [put in] poser; [go in] aller dans; [go on] aller sur; **to fit sth (on) to sth** [put] poser qch sur qch; [adjust] adapter qch à qch; [fix] fixer qch à qch; **to fit sth in** [install] poser qch; [insert] faire entrer qch
**4.** *vi* [of clothes, lid, key, plug] aller; **this shirt fits** [fits me] cette chemise me va; **to fit (in)** [go in] aller; [of facts, plans] cadrer (**with** avec); **he doesn't fit in** il n'est pas à sa place

**fit²** [fɪt] *n* [seizure] attaque *f*; **a fit of coughing** une quinte de toux; **in fits and starts** par à-coups

**FITB** MESSAGING *written abbr of* **fill in the blank**

**fitness** ['fɪtnɪs] *n* [health] santé *f*; [for job] aptitude *f* (**for** à)

**fitted** ['fɪtɪd] *adj Br* [cupboard] encastré; [garment] ajusté; **fitted carpet** moquette *f*; **fitted kitchen** cuisine *f* intégrée

**fitting** ['fɪtɪŋ] **1.** *adj* [suitable] approprié (**to** à) **2.** *n* **fitting room** cabine *f* d'essayage; **fittings** [in house] installations *fpl*

**five** [faɪv] *adj & n* cinq (*m*) ▪ **fiver** *n Br Fam* billet *m* de cinq livres

**fix** [fɪks] **1.** *vt* [make firm, decide] fixer (**to** à); [mend] réparer; [deal with] arranger; [prepare] préparer; *Fam* [election] truquer; **to fix sth on** [lid] mettre qch en place; **to fix sth up** [trip, meeting] arranger qch **2.** *n Fam* **in a fix** dans le pétrin

**fixed** [fɪkst] *adj* [price] fixe; [idea] bien arrêté

**fixture** ['fɪkstʃə(r)] *n* **a)** [in sport] rencontre *f* **b)** **fixtures** [in house] installations *fpl*

**fizz** [fɪz] *vi* [of champagne] pétiller ▪ **fizzy** (*compar* -ier, *superl* -iest) *adj* gazeux, -euse ▪ **fizzle out** ['fɪzəl] *vi* [of firework] rater; *Fam* [of plan] tomber à l'eau

**flabbergasted** ['flæbəɡɑːstɪd] *adj Fam* sidéré

**flabby** ['flæbɪ] (*compar* -ier, *superl* -iest) *adj* [person] bouffi; [skin] mou (*f* molle)

**flag** [flæɡ] **1.** *n* drapeau *m*; NAUT pavillon *m*; [for charity] insigne *m* **2.** (*pt & pp* -gg-) *vt* marquer; **to flag down a taxi** héler un taxi **3.** *vi* [of person, conversation] faiblir ▪ **flagpole** *n* mât *m*

**flagrant** ['fleɪɡrənt] *adj* flagrant

**flagstone** ['flæɡstəʊn] *n* dalle *f*

**flair** [fleə(r)] *n* [intuition] don *m* (**for** pour); **to have a flair for business** avoir le sens des affaires

**flake** [fleɪk] **1.** *n* [of snow] flocon *m*; [of paint] écaille *f*; [of soap] paillette *f* **2.** *vi* **to flake (off)** [of paint] s'écailler ▪ **flaky** *adj Br* **flaky pastry** pâte *f* feuilletée

**flamboyant** [flæm'bɔɪənt] *adj* [person] extraverti

**flame** [fleɪm] *n* flamme *f*; **to go up in flames** prendre feu

**flamingo** [flə'mɪŋɡəʊ] (*pl* -os *or* -oes) *n* flamant *m*

**flammable** ['flæməbəl] *adj* inflammable

**flan** [flæn] *n* tarte *f*

**flank** [flæŋk] **1.** *n* flanc *m* **2.** *vt* flanquer (**with** *or* **by** de)

**flannel** ['flænəl] *n Br* [face cloth] gant *m* de toilette

**flap** [flæp] **1.** *n* [of pocket, envelope] rabat *m*; [of table] abattant *m* **2.** (*pt & pp* -pp-) *vt* **to flap its wings** [of bird] battre des ailes **3.** *vi* [of wings, sail, shutter] battre

**flare** [fleə(r)] **1.** *n* **a)** [rocket] fusée *f* éclairante **b)** **(pair of) flares** [trousers] pantalon *m* pattes d'éléphant **2.** *vi* **to flare up** [of fire] s'embraser; [of violence, trouble] éclater

**flared** [fleəd] *adj* [skirt] évasé; [trousers] (à) pattes d'éléphant

**flash** [flæʃ] **1.** *n* [of light] éclair *m*; [for camera] flash *m*; **flash of lightning** éclair *m*; COMPUT **flash drive** clé *f* USB **2.** *vt* [light] projeter; [aim] diriger (**on** *or* **at** sur); [show] montrer rapidement; **to flash one's headlights** faire un appel de phares **3.** *vi* [shine] briller; [on and off] clignoter; **to flash past** *or* **by** [rush] passer comme un éclair ▪ **flashback** *n* retour *m* en arrière ▪ **flashlight** *n Am* [torch] lampe *f* électrique; [for camera] flash *m*

**flashy** ['flæʃɪ] (*compar* -ier, *superl* -iest) *adj Fam* [clothes, car] tape-à-l'œil *inv*

**flask** [flɑːsk] *n* [Thermos] Thermos® *f inv*; [for alcohol] flasque *f*

**flat¹** [flæt] **1.** (*compar* flatter, *superl* flattest) *adj* plat; [tyre, battery] à plat; [drink] éventé; [refusal] net (*f* nette);

**flat rate** tarif *m* unique ; **to put** *or* **lay sth (down) flat** mettre qch à plat **2.** *n* [puncture] crevaison *f* ; [of hand] plat *m* ; [in music] bémol *m* **3.** *adv* **to sing flat** chanter trop bas ; **to fall flat on one's face** tomber à plat ventre ; **to fall flat** [of joke, play] tomber à plat ; **flat out** [work] d'arrache-pied ; [run] à toute vitesse ■ **flatly** *adv* [deny, refuse] catégoriquement

**flat²** [flæt] *n Br* [in building] appartement *m*

**flatline** ['flætlaɪn] *vi Am Fam* [die] mourir

**flatmate** ['flætmeɪt] *n Br* colocataire *mf*

**flat-pack 1.** *n* meuble *m* en kit ; **it comes as a flat-pack** c'est livré en kit **2.** *adj* **flat-pack furniture** meubles *mpl* en kit

**flatten** ['flætən] *vt* aplatir ; [crops] coucher ; [town, buildings] raser

**flatter** ['flætə(r)] *vt* flatter ■ **flattering** *adj* [remark, words] flatteur, -euse

**flattery** ['flætərɪ] *n* flatterie *f*

**flaunt** [flɔːnt] *vt* [show off] faire étalage de

**flavour**, *Am* **flavor** ['fleɪvə(r)] **1.** *n* [taste] goût *m* ; [of ice cream] parfum *m* **2.** *vt* [food] relever (**with** de) ; **lemon-flavoured** (parfumé) au citron ■ **flavouring**, *Am* **flavoring** *n* [seasoning] assaisonnement *m* ; [in cake, ice cream] parfum *m*

**flaw** [flɔː] *n* défaut *m* ■ **flawed** *adj* qui a un défaut / des défauts ■ **flawless** *adj* parfait

**flea** [fliː] *n* puce *f* ; **flea market** marché *m* aux puces

**fleck** [flek] *n* [mark] petite tache *f*

**fled** [fled] *pt & pp of* **flee**

**flee** [fliː] **1.** *(pt & pp fled)vt* [place] s'enfuir de ; [danger] fuir **2.** *vi* s'enfuir, fuir

**fleece** [fliːs] **1.** *n* [of sheep] toison *f* ; [garment] fourrure *f* polaire **2.** *vt Fam* [overcharge] écorcher ■ **fleecy** *(compar -ier, superl -iest) adj* [gloves] molletonné

**fleet** [fliːt] *n* [of ships] flotte *f* ; [of taxis, buses] parc *m* ; **Fleet Street** *rue de la City de Londres dont le nom est utilisé pour désigner la presse britannique* ■ **fleeting** *adj* [visit, moment] bref (*f* brève)

**Flemish** ['flemɪʃ] **1.** *adj* flamand **2.** *n* [language] flamand *m*

**flesh** [fleʃ] *n* chair *f* ; **in the flesh** en chair et en os

**flew** [fluː] *pt of* **fly**

**flex** [fleks] **1.** *n* [wire] fil *m* ; [for telephone] cordon *m* **2.** *vt* [limb] fléchir ; [muscle] faire jouer

**flexible** ['fleksɪbəl] *adj* flexible

**flexitime** ['fleksɪtaɪm], *Am* **flextime** ['flekstaɪm] *n* horaire *m* à la carte *ou* flexible

**flick** [flɪk] **1.** *n* **a)** [with finger] chiquenaude *f* ; *Br* **flick knife** couteau *m* à cran d'arrêt **b)** *Fam* CIN film *m* **2.** *vt* [with finger] donner une chiquenaude à ; **to flick sth off** [remove] enlever qch d'une chiquenaude ; **to flick a switch** pousser un bouton **3.** *vi* **to flick through** [book, magazine] feuilleter

**flicker** ['flɪkə(r)] *vi* [of flame, light] vaciller

**flier** ['flaɪə(r)] *n* [leaflet] prospectus *m*

**flies** [flaɪz] *npl* [of trousers] braguette *f*

**flight** [flaɪt] *n* **a)** [of bird, aircraft] vol *m* ; **flight attendant** [man] steward *m* ; [woman] hôtesse *f* de l'air **b)** [floor] étage *m* ; **flight of stairs** escalier *m* **c)** [escape] fuite *f* (**from** de) ; **to take flight** prendre la fuite

**flimsy** ['flɪmzɪ] *(compar -ier, superl -iest) adj* [cloth, structure - light] (trop) léger, -ère ; [thin] (trop) mince ; [excuse] piètre

**flinch** [flɪntʃ] *vi* [with pain] tressaillir

**fling** [flɪŋ] **1.** *n* [affair] aventure *f* **2.** *(pt & pp flung)vt* jeter

**flint** [flɪnt] *n* [of lighter] pierre *f*

**flip** [flɪp] **1.** *(pt & pp -pp-)vt* [with finger] donner une chiquenaude à ; **to flip a coin** jouer à pile ou face ; **to flip sth over** retourner qch **2.** *vi* **to flip through a book** feuilleter un livre

**flip-flops** ['flɪpflɒps] *npl* tongs *fpl*

**flippant** ['flɪpənt] *adj* désinvolte

**flipper** ['flɪpə(r)] n [of swimmer] palme f; [of animal] nageoire f

**flip side** n Fig [disadvantage of] inconvénient m; **the flip side was that I felt lonely** le côté négatif était que je me sentais seul

**flirt** [flɜːt] **1.** n charmeur, -euse mf **2.** vi flirter (**with** avec)

**flit** [flɪt] (pt & pp -tt-) vi [fly] voltiger; Fig **to flit in and out** [of person] entrer et sortir rapidement

**float** [fləʊt] **1.** n [for fishing line] bouchon m; [for swimming] flotteur m; [in procession] char m **2.** vt [idea] lancer; [company] introduire en Bourse **3.** vi flotter (**on** sur); **to float down the river** descendre la rivière ■ **floating** adj [wood] flottant; **floating voters** électeurs mpl indécis ■ **floaty** ['fləʊtɪ] adj **floaty dress / skirt** robe f / jupe f vaporeuse ou flottante

**flock** [flɒk] **1.** n [of sheep] troupeau m; [of birds] volée f; [of people] foule f **2.** vi **people are flocking to the exhibition** les gens vont en foule voir l'exposition

**flood** [flʌd] **1.** n inondation f **2.** vt [land, bathroom, market] inonder (**with** de); **to flood (out)** [house] inonder **3.** vi [of river] déborder; **to flood in** [of people, money] affluer ■ **flooding** n inondation(s) f(pl)

**floodlight** ['flʌdlaɪt] **1.** n projecteur m **2.** (pt & pp -lit) vt illuminer

**floor** [flɔː(r)] **1.** n [of room] sol m; [wooden] plancher m; [storey] étage m; **on the floor** par terre; **on the first floor** Br au premier étage; Am [ground floor] au rez-de-chaussée **2.** vt [knock down] envoyer au tapis; [puzzle] stupéfier

**floorboard** ['flɔːbɔːd] n latte f (de plancher)

**flop** [flɒp] Fam **1.** n fiasco m; [play] four m **2.** (pt & pp -pp-) vi [fail - of business] échouer; [of play, film] faire un four; **to flop down** s'effondrer

**floppy** ['flɒpɪ] (compar -ier, superl -iest) adj [soft] mou (f molle); [clothes] (trop) large; COMPUT **floppy disk** disquette f

**floral** ['flɔːrəl] adj [material, pattern] à fleurs

**florist** ['flɒrɪst] n fleuriste mf

**floss** [flɒs] n **(dental) floss** fil m dentaire

**flouncy** ['flaʊnsɪ] adj [dress, skirt] froufroutant

**flour** ['flaʊə(r)] n farine f

**flourish** ['flʌrɪʃ] **1.** n [gesture] grand geste m; [decoration] fioriture f **2.** vt [wave] brandir **3.** vi [of person, plant] prospérer; [of arts, business] être florissant ■ **flourishing** adj [plant] qui prospère; [business] florissant

**flow** [fləʊ] **1.** n [of river] courant m; [of tide] flux m; [of current, information, blood] circulation f; [of liquid] écoulement m; **flow of traffic** circulation f; **flow chart** organigramme m **2.** vi couler; [of electric current] circuler; [of hair, clothes] flotter; [of traffic] s'écouler; **to flow in** [of money] affluer ■ **flowing** adj [movement, style] fluide; [hair, beard] flottant

**flower** ['flaʊə(r)] **1.** n fleur f; **in flower** en fleur(s); **flower bed** parterre m; **flower pot** pot m de fleurs; **flower shop** fleuriste mf **2.** vi fleurir ■ **flowering** adj [in bloom] en fleurs; [producing flowers - shrub] à fleurs

**flowery** ['flaʊərɪ] adj [style] fleuri; [material] à fleurs

**flown** [fləʊn] pp of **fly**

**flu** [fluː] n [influenza] grippe f

**fluctuate** ['flʌktʃʊeɪt] vi varier ■ **fluctuation** [-'eɪʃən] n variation f (**in** de)

**fluent** ['fluːənt] adj **he's fluent in Russian, his Russian is fluent** il parle couramment le russe; **to be a fluent speaker** s'exprimer avec facilité ■ **fluently** adv [write, express oneself] avec facilité; [speak language] couramment

**fluff** [flʌf] n peluche f ■ **fluffy** (compar -ier, superl -iest) adj [toy] en peluche

**fluid** ['fluːɪd] **1.** adj fluide; [plans] mal défini; **fluid ounce** 0,03 l **2.** n fluide m, liquide m

**fluke** [fluːk] n Fam coup m de chance; **by a fluke** par hasard

**flung** [flʌŋ] pt & pp of **fling**

**flunk** [flʌŋk] *Am Fam* **1.** *vt* [exam] être collé à ; [pupil] coller **2.** *vi* [in exam] être collé

**fluorescent** [fluəˈresənt] *adj* fluorescent

**fluoride** [ˈfluəraɪd] *n* fluorure *m* ; **fluoride toothpaste** dentifrice *m* au fluor

**flurry** [ˈflʌrɪ] *(pl* **-ies)** *n* [of snow] bourrasque *f* ; **a flurry of activity** une soudaine activité

**flush** [flʌʃ] **1.** *adj* [level] de niveau **(with** de) **2.** *n* **a)** [blush] rougeur *f* **b)** [in toilet] chasse *f* d'eau **3.** *vt* **to flush sth (out)** [clean] nettoyer qch à grande eau ; **to flush the toilet** tirer la chasse d'eau **4.** *vi* [blush] rougir **(with** de)

**fluster** [ˈflʌstə(r)] *vt* démonter ; **to get flustered** se démonter

**flute** [fluːt] *n* flûte *f*

**flutter** [ˈflʌtə(r)] **1.** *vt* **to flutter its wings** [of bird] battre des ailes **2.** *vi* [of bird, butterfly] voleter ; [of flag] flotter

**fly**[1] [flaɪ] *(pl* **-ies)** *n* [insect] mouche *f*

**fly**[2] [flaɪ] **1.** *(pt* **flew**, *pp* **flown)** *vt* [aircraft] piloter ; [passengers] transporter ; [flag] arborer ; [kite] faire voler ; **to fly the Atlantic** traverser l'Atlantique en avion **2.** *vi* [of bird, aircraft] voler ; [of passenger] aller en avion ; [of time] passer vite ; [of flag] flotter ; **to fly away** *or* **off** s'envoler ; **to fly across** *or* **over** [country, city] survoler ; **I must fly!** il faut que je file ! ▪ **flyer** *n* = **flier** ▪ **flying 1.** *n* [as passenger] voyage *m* en avion **2.** *adj* **to pass with flying colours** réussir haut la main ; **to get off to a flying start** prendre un très bon départ ; **flying saucer** soucoupe *f* volante ; **flying visit** visite *f* éclair *inv* ▪ **flyover** *n Br* [bridge] pont-route *m*

**fly**[3] [flaɪ] *n Br* [on trousers] braguette *f*

**foal** [fəʊl] *n* poulain *m*

**foam** [fəʊm] **1.** *n* [on sea, mouth] écume *f* ; [on beer] mousse *f* ; **foam bath** bain *m* moussant ; **foam rubber** caoutchouc *m* Mousse® **2.** *vi* [of beer, soap] mousser

**focal** [ˈfəʊkəl] *adj* focal

**focus** [ˈfəʊkəs] **1.** *(pl* **focuses** [ˈfəʊkəsəz] *or* **foci** [ˈfəʊkaɪ]*) n* [of attention, interest] centre *m* ; [optical] foyer *m* ; **the photo is in focus / out of focus** la photo est nette / floue **2.** *vt* [image, camera] mettre au point ; [attention, efforts] concentrer **(on** sur) **3.** *vi* **to focus on sb / sth** [with camera] faire la mise au point sur qn / qch **4.** *vti* **to focus (one's eyes) on sb / sth** fixer les yeux sur qn / qch ; **to focus (one's attention) on sb / sth** se tourner vers qn / qch

**fodder** [ˈfɒdə(r)] *n* fourrage *m*

**foe** [fəʊ] *n* ennemi, -e *mf*

**foetus**, *Am* **fetus** [ˈfiːtəs] *n* fœtus *m*

**fog** [fɒg] *n* brouillard *m* ▪ **foglamp**, **foglight** *n* [on vehicle] phare *m* anti-brouillard

**fogey** [ˈfəʊgɪ] *n* = **fogy**

**foggy** [ˈfɒgɪ] *(compar* **-ier**, *superl* **-iest)** *adj* brumeux, -euse ; **it's foggy** il y a du brouillard ; *Fam* **I haven't got the foggiest (idea)** je n'en ai pas la moindre idée

**fogy** [ˈfəʊgɪ] *n* **old fogy** vieux schnock *m*

**foil** [fɔɪl] **1.** *n* **a)** [for cooking] papier *m* alu **b)** [sword] fleuret *m* **2.** *vt* [plans] contrecarrer

**fold** [fəʊld] **1.** *n* [in paper, cloth] pli *m* **2.** *vt* plier ; **to fold away** *or* **down** *or* **up** [chair] plier ; **to fold back** *or* **over** [blanket] replier ; **to fold one's arms** croiser les bras **3.** *vi Fam* [of business] fermer ses portes ; **to fold (away** *or* **down** *or* **up)** [of chair] se plier ▪ **folding** *adj* [chair, bed] pliant

**-fold** [fəʊld] **1.** *adj* **tenfold** par dix **2.** *adv* **tenfold** dix fois

**folder** [ˈfəʊldə(r)] *n* [file holder] chemise *f* ; COMPUT répertoire *m*

**foliage** [ˈfəʊlɪdʒ] *n* feuillage *m*

**folk** [fəʊk] **1.** *(Am* **folks)** *npl* gens *mpl* ; *Fam* **my folks** [parents] mes parents *mpl* **2.** *adj* [dance, costume] folklorique ; **folk music** [contemporary] folk *m*

**follow** [ˈfɒləʊ] **1.** *vt* suivre ; [career] poursuivre ; [advantage] exploiter ; **to follow through** [plan, idea] mener à son terme ; **to follow up** [idea, story] creuser ; [clue, case] suivre ; [letter]

donner suite à ; [remark] faire suivre (**with** de) **2.** vi [of person, event] suivre ; **it follows that...** il s'ensuit que... ; **to follow on** [come after] suivre ■ **follow-up** n suite f

**follower** ['fɒləʊə(r)] n [of ideas, politician] partisan m

**following** ['fɒləʊɪŋ] **1.** adj suivant **2.** n [of politician] partisans mpl **3.** prep à la suite de

**folly** ['fɒlɪ] (pl -ies) n folie f

**FOMCL** (abbr of fell off my chair laughing) MESSAGING MDR

**fond** [fɒnd] (compar -er, superl -est) adj [loving] affectueux, -euse ; [memory, thought] doux (f douce) ; **to be (very) fond of sb/sth** aimer beaucoup qn / qch ■ **fondly** adv tendrement

**fondle** ['fɒndəl] vt caresser

**font** [fɒnt] n a) REL fonts mpl baptismaux b) TYP & COMPUT police f de caractères

**food** [fuːd] **1.** n nourriture f ; [particular substance] aliment m ; [cooking] cuisine f ; [for cats, dogs, pigs] pâtée f ; [for plants] engrais m **2.** adj [industry] alimentaire ; **food hall** rayon m alimentation ; **food mixer** mixer m ; **food poisoning** intoxication f alimentaire ; **food safety** sécurité f alimentaire

**foodstuffs** ['fuːdstʌfs] npl denrées fpl alimentaires

**fool** [fuːl] **1.** n imbécile mf ; **to make a fool of sb** [ridicule] ridiculiser qn ; [trick] rouler qn ; **to make a fool of oneself** se couvrir de ridicule **2.** vt [trick] duper **3.** vi **to fool about** or **around** faire l'imbécile ; [waste time] perdre son temps

**foolish** ['fuːlɪʃ] adj bête ■ **foolishly** adv bêtement

**foolproof** ['fuːlpruːf] adj [scheme] infaillible

**foot¹** [fʊt] (pl **feet**) n pied m ; [of animal] patte f ; [unit of measurement] pied m (30,48 cm) ; **at the foot of** [page, stairs] au bas de ; **on foot** à pied ■ **football** n [soccer] football m ; [American game] football m américain ; [ball] ballon m ; Am **football field** terrain m de football américain ■ **footballer** n

Br joueur, -euse mf de football ■ **footbridge** n passerelle f ■ **foothold** n prise f (de pied) ; **to gain a foothold** [of person] prendre pied (**in** dans) ■ **footnote** n note f de bas de page ; Fig [extra comment] post-scriptum m inv ■ **footpath** n sentier m ■ **footstep** n pas m ; **to follow in sb's footsteps** suivre les traces de qn ■ **footstool** n petit tabouret m ■ **footwear** n chaussures fpl

**foot²** [fʊt] vt [bill] payer

**footage** ['fʊtɪdʒ] n CIN séquences fpl

**footing** ['fʊtɪŋ] n a) [balance] **to lose one's footing** perdre l'équilibre b) [level] **to be on an equal footing** être sur un pied d'égalité (**with** avec)

**for** [fɔː(r)] (unstressed [fə(r)]) **1.** prep pour ; [for a distance or period of] pendant ; [in spite of] malgré ; **what's it for?** ça sert à quoi ? ; **I did it for love/pleasure** je l'ai fait par amour / par plaisir ; **to swim/rush for** [towards] nager / se précipiter vers ; **a train for** un train à destination de ; **the road for London** la route de Londres ; **it's time for breakfast** c'est l'heure du petit déjeuner ; **to come for dinner** venir dîner ; **to sell sth for 7 dollars** vendre qch 7 dollars ; **what's the French for 'book'?** comment dit-on 'book' en français ? ; **she walked for a kilometre** elle a marché pendant un kilomètre ; **he was away for a month** il a été absent pendant un mois ; **he's been here for a month** il est ici depuis un mois ; **I haven't seen him for ten years** ça fait dix ans que je ne l'ai pas vu, je ne l'ai pas vu depuis dix ans ; **it's easy for her to do it** il lui est facile de le faire ; **for that to be done** pour que ça soit fait **2.** conj [because] car

**forbad** [fəˈbæd] pt of **forbid**

**forbade** [fəˈbæd, fəˈbeɪd] pt of **forbid**

**forbid** [fəˈbɪd] (pt forbad(e), pp forbidden [fəˈbɪdən], pres p forbidding) vt interdire, défendre (**sb to do** à qn de faire) ; **to forbid sb sth** interdire qch à qn ; **she**

**form**

**is forbid to leave** il lui est interdit de partir ■ **forbidden 1.** *pp of* **forbid 2.** *adj* [fruit, region] défendu

**force** [fɔːs] **1.** *n* force *f*; **the (armed) forces** les forces *fpl* armées; **by force** de force; **in force** [rule] en vigueur; [in great numbers] en force **2.** *vt* forcer (**to do** à faire); [impose] imposer (**on** à); [door, lock] forcer; [confession] arracher (**from** à); **to force sth into sth** faire entrer qch de force dans qch ■ **forced** *adj* **forced to do** obligé *ou* forcé de faire; **a forced smile** un sourire forcé

**forceful** [ˈfɔːsfəl] *adj* énergique

**ford** [fɔːd] **1.** *n* gué *m* **2.** *vt* [river] passer à gué

**fore** [fɔː(r)] *n* **to come to the fore** [of issue] passer au premier plan

**forearm** [ˈfɔːrɑːm] *n* avant-bras *m inv*

**foreboding** [fɔːˈbəʊdɪŋ] *n* [feeling] pressentiment *m*

**forecast** [ˈfɔːkɑːst] **1.** *n* [of weather] prévisions *fpl*; [in racing] pronostic *m* **2.** (*pt & pp* **forecast(ed)**) *vt* prévoir; [in racing] pronostiquer

**forecourt** [ˈfɔːkɔːt] *n* [of hotel] avant-cour *f*; [of petrol station] devant *m*

**forefinger** [ˈfɔːfɪŋgə(r)] *n* index *m*

**forefront** [ˈfɔːfrʌnt] *n* **in the forefront of** au premier plan de

**forego** [fɔːˈgəʊ] (*pp* **-gone**) *vt* renoncer à

**foreground** [ˈfɔːgraʊnd] *n* premier plan *m*

**forehead** [ˈfɒrɪd, ˈfɔːhed] *n* front *m*

**foreign** [ˈfɒrɪn] *adj* [language, person, country] étranger, -ère; [trade] extérieur; [travel, correspondent] à l'étranger; **Foreign Minister,** *Br* **Foreign Secretary** ministre *m* des Affaires étrangères; *Br* **Foreign Office** ministère *m* des Affaires étrangères ■ **foreigner** *n* étranger, -ère *mf*

**foreman** [ˈfɔːmən] (*pl* **-men**) *n* [worker] contremaître *m*

**foremost** [ˈfɔːməʊst] *adj* principal

**forerunner** [ˈfɔːrʌnə(r)] *n* [person] précurseur *m*

**foresee** [fɔːˈsiː] (*pt* **-saw**, *pp* **-seen**) *vt* prévoir

**foreshadow** [fɔːˈʃædəʊ] *vt* annoncer

**foresight** [ˈfɔːsaɪt] *n* prévoyance *f*

**forest** [ˈfɒrɪst] *n* forêt *f*

**forestall** [fɔːˈstɔːl] *vt* devancer

**foretell** [fɔːˈtel] (*pt & pp* **-told**) *vt* prédire

**forever** [fəˈrevə(r)] *adv* [for always] pour toujours; [continually] sans cesse

**foreword** [ˈfɔːwɜːd] *n* avant-propos *m inv*

**forfeit** [ˈfɔːfɪt] **1.** *n* [in game] gage *m* **2.** *vt* [lose] perdre

**forge** [fɔːdʒ] **1.** *vt* [signature, money] contrefaire; **to forge a passport** faire un faux passeport **2.** *vi* **to forge ahead** [progress] aller de l'avant ■ **forged** *adj* faux (*f* fausse)

**forgery** [ˈfɔːdʒərɪ] (*pl* **-ies**) *n* contrefaçon *f*

**forget** [fəˈget] **1.** (*pt* **forgot**, *pp* **forgotten**, *pres p* **forgetting**) *vt* oublier (**to do** de faire); *Fam* **forget it!** [when thanked] pas de quoi!; [it doesn't matter] laisse tomber! **2.** *vi* oublier; **to forget about sb/sth** oublier qn/qch ■ **forgetful** *adj* **to be forgetful** avoir une mauvaise mémoire

**forgive** [fəˈgɪv] (*pt* **-gave**, *pp* **-given**) *vt* pardonner (**sb sth** qch à qn) ■ **forgiveness** *n* pardon *m*

**forgo** [fɔːˈgəʊ] (*pp* **-gone**) *vt* renoncer à

**forgot** [fəˈgɒt] *pt of* **forget**

**forgotten** [fəˈgɒtən] *pp of* **forget**

**fork** [fɔːk] **1.** *n* [for eating] fourchette *f*; [for gardening, in road] fourche *f* **2.** *vt Fam* **to fork out** [money] allonger **3.** *vi* [of road] bifurquer; *Fam* **to fork out** [pay] casquer (**for** *ou* **on** pour) ■ **forklift** *n* **forklift (truck)** chariot *m* élévateur

**forlorn** [fəˈlɔːn] *adj* [forsaken] abandonné; [unhappy] triste

**form** [fɔːm] **1.** *n* [shape, type, style] forme *f*; [document] formulaire *m*; *Br* SCH classe *f*; **in the form of** sous forme de; **on form, in good** *ou* **top form** en (pleine) forme **2.** *vt* [group, basis, character] former; [clay] façonner; [habit]

contracter ; [obstacle] constituer ; **to form part of sth** faire partie de qch **3.** *vi* [appear] se former

**formal** ['fɔ:məl] *adj* [person, tone] cérémonieux, -euse ; [announcement, dinner, invitation] officiel, -elle ; [agreement] en bonne et due forme ; [language] soutenu ; **formal dress** tenue *f* de soirée ■ **formality** [-'mælɪtɪ] *(pl -ies)* *n* [procedure] formalité *f* ■ **formally** *adv* [declare] officiellement ; **formally dressed** en tenue de soirée

**format** ['fɔ:mæt] **1.** *n* format *m* **2.** *(pt & pp -tt-)* *vt* COMPUT formater

**formation** [fɔ:'meɪʃən] *n* formation *f*

**former** ['fɔ:mə(r)] **1.** *adj* [previous - president, teacher, job, house] ancien, -enne *(before noun)* **2.** *pron* **the former** celui-là, celle-là ■ **formerly** *adv* autrefois

**formidable** ['fɔ:mɪdəbəl] *adj* effroyable

**formula** ['fɔ:mjʊlə] *n* a) *(pl* **-as** *or* **-ae** [-i:]) [rule, symbols] formule *f* b) *(pl* **-as**) [baby food] lait *m* en poudre ■ **formulate** [-leɪt] *vt* formuler

**fort** [fɔ:t] *n* MIL fort *m*

**forth** [fɔ:θ] *adv* en avant ; **and so forth** et ainsi de suite

**forthcoming** [fɔ:θ'kʌmɪŋ] *adj* a) [event] à venir b) [available] disponible c) [informative] expansif, -ive **(about** sur)

**forthright** ['fɔ:θraɪt] *adj* franc *(f* franche)

**fortieth** ['fɔ:tɪəθ] *adj & n* quarantième *(mf)*

**fortify** ['fɔ:tɪfaɪ] *(pt & pp* **-ied)** *vt* [strengthen] fortifier ; **to fortify sb** [of food, drink] réconforter qn, remonter qn ■ **fortification** [-fɪ'keɪʃən] *n* fortification *f*

**fortnight** ['fɔ:tnaɪt] *n* Br quinzaine *f* de jours

**fortress** ['fɔ:trɪs] *n* forteresse *f*

**fortunate** ['fɔ:tʃənət] *adj* heureux, -euse ; **to be fortunate** [of person] avoir de la chance ; **it's fortunate (for her) that...** c'est heureux (pour elle) que... (+ *subjunctive*) ■ **fortunately** *adv* heureusement

**fortune** ['fɔ:tʃu:n] *n* [wealth] fortune *f* ; [luck] chance *f* ■ **fortune-teller** *n* diseur, -euse *mf* de bonne aventure

**forty** ['fɔ:tɪ] *adj & n* quarante *(m)*

**forum** ['fɔ:rəm] *(pl* **-s**) *n* **a)** [gén] forum *m*, tribune *f* **b)** INTERNET forum *m*

**forward** ['fɔ:wəd] **1.** *adj* [position] avant *inv* ; [movement] en avant ; *Fig* [impudent] effronté ; COMPUT **forward slash** barre *f* oblique **2.** *n* [in sport] avant *m* **3.** *adv* en avant ; **to go forward** avancer **4.** *vt* [letter] faire suivre ; [goods] expédier

**forwards** ['fɔ:wədz] *adv* = **forward**

**fossil** ['fɒsəl] *n* fossile *m*

**foster** ['fɒstə(r)] *adj* **foster child** enfant placé dans une famille d'accueil ; **foster parents** parents *mpl* nourriciers

**fought** [fɔ:t] *pt & pp* of **fight**

**foul** [faʊl] **1.** *(compar* **-er**, *superl* **-est)** *adj* **a)** [smell, taste, weather, person] infect ; [breath] fétide ; [language] grossier, -ère ; [place] immonde **b)** **foul play** [in sport] jeu *m* irrégulier ; [in law] acte *m* criminel **2.** *n* [in sport] faute *f* **3.** *vt* Fam **to foul up** [ruin] gâcher

**found¹** [faʊnd] *pt & pp* of **find**

**found²** [faʊnd] *vt* [town, party] fonder ; [opinion, suspicions] fonder, baser **(on** sur) ■ **founder** *n* fondateur, -trice *mf*

**foundation** [faʊn'deɪʃən] *n* [basis] fondement *m* ; **the foundations** [of building] les fondations *fpl*

**fountain** ['faʊntɪn] *n* fontaine *f* ; **fountain pen** stylo-plume *m*

**four** [fɔ:(r)] *adj & n* quatre *(m)* ; **on all fours** à quatre pattes ■ **fourth** *adj & n* quatrième *(mf)* ; *Am* SCH **fourth grade** classe de l'école primaire correspondant au CM1 (8-9 ans) ; **the Fourth of July** Fête de l'Indépendance américaine, célébrée le 4 juillet ■ **four-letter** *adj* **four-letter word** gros mot *m* ■ **four-wheel drive** *n* with four-wheel drive à quatre roues motrices

**4** *(abbr of* for) MESSAGING pr

**4eva, 4E** *(abbr of* for ever) MESSAGING pr tjr

**4gv** MESSAGING *written abbr of* **forgive**

**freely**

**4gvn** MESSAGING *written abbr of* **forgiven**

**foursome** ['fɔ:səm] *n* groupe *m* de quatre personnes

**fourteen** [fɔ:'ti:n] *adj & n* quatorze (*m*)
■ **fourteenth** *adj & n* quatorzième (*mf*)

**fowl** [faʊl] *n inv* volaille *f*

**fox** [fɒks] **1.** *n* renard *m* **2.** *vt* [puzzle] laisser perplexe ; [deceive] duper

**foyer** ['fɔɪeɪ] *n* [in theatre] foyer *m* ; [in hotel] hall *m*

**fraction** ['frækʃən] *n* fraction *f*

**fracture** ['fræktʃə(r)] **1.** *n* fracture *f* **2.** *vt* fracturer ; **to fracture one's leg** se fracturer la jambe

**fragile** [*Br* 'frædʒaɪl, *Am* 'frædʒəl] *adj* fragile

**fragment** ['frægmənt] *n* fragment *m*

**fragrant** ['freɪgrənt] *adj* parfumé ; **fragrant rice** riz *m* parfumé ■ **fragrance** *n* parfum *m* ■ **fragrance-free** *adj* non parfumé, sans parfum

**frail** [freɪl] (*compar* -**er**, *superl* -**est**) *adj* [person] frêle ; [health] fragile

**frame** [freɪm] **1.** *n* [of picture, bicycle] cadre *m* ; [of door, window] encadrement *m* ; [of spectacles] monture *f* ; **frame of mind** état *m* d'esprit **2.** *vt* [picture] encadrer ; *Fig* [proposals, ideas] formuler ■ **framework** *n* structure *f* ; **(with)in the framework of** [context] dans le cadre de

**franc** [fræŋk] *n* franc *m*

**France** [frɑːns] *n* la France

**franchise** ['fræntʃaɪz] *n* [right to vote] droit *m* de vote ; [right to sell product] franchise *f*

**Franco-** ['fræŋkəʊ] *pref* franco-

**frank**[1] [fræŋk] (*compar* -**er**, *superl* -**est**) *adj* [honest] franc (*f* franche) ■ **frankly** *adv* franchement

**frank**[2] [fræŋk] *vt* [letter] affranchir

**frantic** ['fræntɪk] *adj* [activity, shouts, pace] frénétique ; [attempt, efforts] désespéré ■ **frantically** *adv* frénétiquement ; [run, search] comme un fou / une folle ; [work] avec frénésie

**frape** [freɪp] *vt Fam* poster, à l'insu de qqn, une information (fausse et désobligeante) sur sa page Facebook

**fraternize** ['frætənaɪz] *vi* fraterniser (**with** avec)

**fraud** [frɔːd] *n* **a)** [crime] fraude *f* **b)** [person] imposteur *m* ■ **fraudulent** *adj* frauduleux, -euse

**fraught** [frɔːt] *adj* [situation] tendu ; **fraught with** plein de

**fray** [freɪ] *vi* [of garment] s'effilocher ; [of rope] s'user ■ **frayed** *adj* [garment] élimé

**freak** [friːk] **1.** *adj* bizarre, insolite **2.** *n* **a)** [strange creature] monstre *m*, phénomène *m* **b)** [unusual event] accident *m* bizarre **c)** *Fam* [fanatic] fana *mf* ; [addict] accro *mf* ■ **freak out** *Fam* **1.** *vt sep* [shock, scare] faire flipper **2.** *vi* [panic] paniquer ; [get angry] piquer une crise

**freckle** ['frekəl] *n* tache *f* de rousseur ■ **freckled** *adj* couvert de taches de rousseur

**free** [friː] **1.** (*compar* **freer**, *superl* **freest**) *adj* [at liberty, not occupied] libre ; [without cost] gratuit ; [lavish] généreux, -euse (**with** de) ; **to get free** se libérer ; **to be free to do sth** être libre de faire qch ; **free of charge** gratuit ; **free gift** cadeau *m* ; **free hugs** câlins *mpl* gratuits ; **free kick** [in football] coup *m* franc ; *Br* **free paper** journal *m* gratuit ; **free trade** libre-échange *m* **2.** *adv* **free (of charge)** gratuitement **3.** (*pt & pp* **freed**) *vt* [prisoner, country] libérer ; [trapped person] dégager ; [untie] détacher ■ **Freefone®** *n Br* [phone number] ≃ numéro *m* vert ■ **freelance 1.** *adj* indépendant **2.** *n* travailleur, -euse *mf* indépendant(e) **3.** *adv* **to work freelance** travailler en indépendant ■ **Freepost®** *n Br* ≃ correspondance-réponse *f* ■ **free-range** *adj Br* **free-range egg** œuf *m* de ferme ■ **freestyle** *n* [in swimming] nage *f* libre ■ **freeway** *n Am* autoroute *f*

**freedom** ['friːdəm] *n* liberté *f*

**freely** ['friːlɪ] *adv* [speak, act, circulate] librement ; [give] sans compter

**freemium** ['fri:mɪəm] adj **a free-mium business model** un (modèle) freemium

**freeze** [fri:z] **1.** n [in weather] gel m ; [of prices, salaries] blocage m **2.** (pt **froze**, pp **frozen**) vt [food] congeler ; [credits, river] geler ; [prices, wages] bloquer ; **frozen food** surgelés mpl **3.** vi geler ; **to freeze to death** mourir de froid ; **to freeze up** or **over** [of lake] geler ■ **freezer** n [deep-freeze] congélateur m ; [ice-box] freezer m ■ **freezing 1.** adj [weather] glacial ; [hands, feet] gelée ; **it's freezing** il gèle **2.** n **it's 5 degrees below freezing** il fait 5 degrés au-dessous de zéro **3.** adv **freezing cold** très froid

**freight** [freɪt] n COMM [goods] cargaison f ; **freight train** train m de marchandises ■ **freighter** n [ship] cargo m

**French** [frentʃ] **1.** adj français ; [teacher] de français ; [embassy] de France ; **French fries** frites fpl ; Br **French stick** baguette f **2.** n [language] français m ; **the French** [people] les Français mpl ■ **Frenchman** (pl **-men**) n Français m ■ **French-speaking** adj francophone ■ **Frenchwoman** (pl **-women**) n Française f

**frenemy** ['frenəmɪ] n Fam **Emily and Susan are frenemies; they like each other but they're working on competing products** Emily et Susan sont meilleures ennemies ; elles s'aiment bien mais elles travaillent sur des produits concurrents

**frenzy** ['frenzɪ] (pl **-ies**) n frénésie f ■ **frenzied** adj [activity] frénétique ; [attack] violent

**frequency** ['fri:kwənsɪ] (pl **-ies**) n fréquence f

**frequent 1.** ['fri:kwənt] adj fréquent **2.** [frɪ'kwent] vt fréquenter ■ **frequently** adv fréquemment

**fresh** [freʃ] **1.** adj **a)** [gen] frais (f fraîche) ; **to get some fresh air** prendre l'air **b)** [not salty] doux (f douce) **c)** [new] [drink, piece of paper] autre ; [look, approach] nouveau, -elle **2.** adv **to be fresh from** [school, university] sortir tout juste de ■ **freshman** ['freʃmæn] (pl **-men**) n Am SCH bizut m, élève mf (en

première année) ; UNIV étudiant, -e mf (de première année) ■ **freshwater** ['freʃ.wɔ:tə(r)] adj d'eau douce

**fret** [fret] (pt & pp **-tt-**) vi [worry] se faire du souci

**friction** ['frɪkʃən] n friction f

**Friday** ['fraɪdeɪ] n vendredi m ; **Good Friday** le vendredi saint

**fridge** [frɪdʒ] n frigo m

**fried** [fraɪd] **1.** pt & pp of **fry 2.** adj frit ; **fried egg** œuf m sur le plat

**friend** [frend] n ami, -e mf ■ **friendly 1.** (compar **-ier**, superl **-iest**) adj amical **2.** n [match] match m amical ■ **friendship** n amitié f ■ **friendzone** ['frendzəʊn] Fam **1.** n **Alan really likes Emily but he's been stuck in the friendzone for way too long** Alan aime beaucoup Emily mais ça fait trop longtemps qu'il est coincé dans la friend zone ou qu'elle le considère simplement comme un ami **2.** vt **to friendzone sb** placer qqn dans la friend zone, faire comprendre à qqn que l'on souhaite avoir une relation purement amicale avec elle

**fright** [fraɪt] n peur f ; **to give sb a fright** faire peur à qn

**frighten** ['fraɪtən] vt effrayer, faire peur à ; **to frighten sb away** or **off** faire fuir qn ■ **frightened** adj effrayé ; **to be frightened** avoir peur (**of** de) ■ **frightening** adj effrayant

**frightful** ['fraɪtfəl] adj affreux, -euse

**frill** [frɪl] n volant m

**fringe** [frɪndʒ] n **a)** [of hair, on clothes] frange f **b)** [margin] **on the fringes of society** en marge de la société

**frisk** [frɪsk] vt [search] fouiller

**frisky** ['frɪskɪ] (compar **-ier**, superl **-iest**) adj [lively] vif (f vive)

**fritter** ['frɪtə(r)] **1.** n CULIN beignet m **2.** vt **to fritter away** gaspiller

**frivolous** ['frɪvələs] adj frivole

**frizzy** ['frɪzɪ] adj crépu

**fro** [frəʊ] adv **to go to and fro** aller et venir

**frock** [frɒk] n [dress] robe f

**frog** [frɒg] n grenouille f

**frolic** ['frɒlɪk] *(pt & pp* -ck-) *vi* to frolic (about) gambader

**from** [frɒm] *(unstressed* [frəm]) *prep*
a) [expressing origin] de; **a letter from sb** une lettre de qn; **to suffer from sth** souffrir de qch; **where are you from?** d'où êtes-vous ?; **a train from Paris** un train en provenance de Paris; **to be 10 m (away) from the house** être à 10 m de la maison
b) [expressing time] à partir de; **from today (on), as from today** à partir d'aujourd'hui; **from the beginning** dès le début
c) [expressing range] **from to...** de... à...; **from morning till night** du matin au soir; **they take children from the age of five** ils acceptent les enfants à partir de cinq ans
d) [expressing source] de; **to take / borrow sth from sb** prendre / emprunter qch à qn; **to drink from a cup** boire dans une tasse
e) [expressing removal] de; **to take sth from sb** prendre qch à qn; **to take sth from a box / from the table** prendre qch dans une boîte / sur la table
f) [according to] d'après; **from what I saw...** d'après ce que j'ai vu... g) [on behalf of] de la part de; **tell her from me** dis-lui de ma part

**front** [frʌnt] **1.** *n* devant *m*; [of boat, car] avant *m*; [of building] façade *f*; [of crowd] premier rang *m*; MIL, POL & MET front *m*; **in front of sb/sth** devant qn / qch; **in front** devant; [further ahead] en avant; [in race] en tête **2.** *adj* [tooth, garden] de devant; [car seat] avant *inv*; [row, page] premier, -ère; **front door** porte *f* d'entrée; *Am* **front yard** jardin *m* *(devant une maison)* **3.** *vt* [organization] être à la tête de; [TV programme] présenter ■ **frontrunner** *n Fig* favori, -ite *mf* ■ **front-wheel** *adj* AUTO **front-wheel drive** traction *f* avant

**frontier** ['frʌntɪə(r)] *n* frontière *f*

**frost** [frɒst] **1.** *n* gel *m* **2.** *vi* to frost up [of window] se couvrir de givre

**frostbite** ['frɒstbaɪt] *n* gelure *f* ■ **frostbitten** *adj* gelé

**frosting** ['frɒstɪŋ] *n Am* [on cake] glaçage *m*

**frosty** ['frɒstɪ] *(compar* -ier, *superl* -iest) *adj* [air, night] glacé; *Fig* [welcome] glacial; **it's frosty** il gèle

**froth** [frɒθ] **1.** *n* [on beer] mousse *f*; [on waves] écume *f* **2.** *vi* [liquid] mousser ■ **frothy** *(compar* -ier, *superl* -iest) *adj* [beer] mousseux, -euse

**frown** [fraʊn] **1.** *n* froncement *m* de sourcils **2.** *vi* froncer les sourcils; *Fig* **to frown (up)on** désapprouver

**froyo** ['frəʊˌjəʊ] *n Fam* yaourt *m* glacé

**froze** [frəʊz] *pt of* **freeze**

**frozen** ['frəʊzən] *pp of* **freeze**

**fructose** ['frʌktəʊs] *n* fructose *m*

**frugal** ['fruːgəl] *adj* frugal

**fruit** [fruːt] *n* fruit *m*; **some fruit** [one item] un fruit; [more than one] des fruits; **fruit bowl** compotier *m*; **fruit juice** jus *m* de fruits; **fruit salad** salade *f* de fruits; *Br* **fruit machine** [for gambling] machine *f* à sous ■ **fruitcake** *n* cake *m*

**fruitful** ['fruːtfəl] *adj* [meeting, discussion] fructueux, -euse ■ **fruitless** *adj* [attempt, search] infructueux, -euse

**frustrate** [frʌ'streɪt] *vt* [person] frustrer; [plans] contrarier ■ **frustrating** *adj* frustrant ■ **frustration** *n* frustration *f*

**fry** [fraɪ] *(pt & pp* fried) **1.** *vt* faire frire **2.** *vi* frire ■ **frying** *n* **frying pan** poêle *f* (à frire)

**ft** *(abbr of* **foot, feet)** pied(s) *m(pl)*

**F2F, FTF** MESSAGING *written abbr of* face to face

**fudge** [fʌdʒ] **1.** *n* [sweet] caramel *m* mou **2.** *vt* **to fudge the issue** éluder une question

**fuel** [fjʊəl] *n* combustible *m*; [for engine] carburant *m*; **fuel oil** mazout *m*; **fuel tank** [in vehicle] réservoir *m*

**fugitive** ['fjuːdʒɪtɪv] *n* fugitif, -ive *mf*

**fugly** ['fʌglɪ] *adj v Fam (abbr of* **fucking ugly)** à chier; **she's really fugly** c'est un vrai boudin *ou* cageot

**fulfil**, *Am* **fulfill** [fʊl'fɪl] *(pt & pp -ll-) vt* [ambition, dream] réaliser; [condition, duty] remplir; [desire, need] satisfaire ■ **fulfilling** *adj* satisfaisant ■ **fulfilment**, *Am* **fulfillment** *n* [of ambition] réalisation *f* (**of** de); [satisfaction] épanouissement *m*

**full** [fʊl] **1.** *(compar* -**er**, *superl* -**est**) *adj* plein (**of** de); [bus, theatre, hotel, examination] complet, -ète; [amount] intégral; [day, programme] chargé; [skirt] bouffant; **to be full (up)** [of person] n'avoir plus faim; [of hotel] être complet; **at full speed** à toute vitesse; **full name** nom et prénom; *Br* **full stop** point *m* **2.** *n* **in full** [pay] intégralement; [write] en toutes lettres **3.** *adv* **to know full well** savoir fort bien ■ **full-fat** *adj* entier, -ère ■ **full-length** *adj* [portrait] en pied; [dress] long (*f* longue); **full-length film** long métrage *m* ■ **full-scale** *adj* [model] grandeur nature *inv*; [operation] de grande envergure ■ **full-time** *adj & adv* [work] à plein temps

**fully** ['fʊlɪ] *adv* [completely] entièrement; [understand] parfaitement; [at least] au moins ■ **fully-equiped** *adj* totalement équipé ■ **fully-fitted** *adj* [kitchen] intégré ■ **fully-fledged**, *Am* **full-fledged** *adj* [engineer, teacher] diplômé; [member] à part entière ■ **fully-grown** *adj* adulte

**fumble** ['fʌmbəl] *vi* **to fumble (about)** [grope] tâtonner; [search] fouiller (**for** pour trouver)

**fume** [fjuːm] *vi* **to be fuming** [of person] rager ■ **fumes** *npl* émanations *fpl*; [from car] gaz *mpl* d'échappement

**fun** [fʌn] *n* plaisir *m*; **for fun, for the fun of it** pour le plaisir; **to be (good or great) fun** être (très) amusant; **to have (some) fun** s'amuser; **to make fun of sb/sth** se moquer de qn/qch ■ **fun-filled** *adj* divertissant ■ **fun-packed** *adj* divertissant

**function** ['fʌŋkʃən] **1.** *n* [role, duty & COMPUT] fonction *f*; [party] réception *f* **2.** *vi* fonctionner; **to function as** faire fonction de ■ **functional** *adj* fonctionnel, -elle

**fund** [fʌnd] **1.** *n* [of money] fonds *m*; **funds** fonds *mpl* **2.** *vt* financer

**fundamental** [fʌndə'mentəl] *adj* fondamental

**funeral** ['fjuːnərəl] *n* enterrement *m*; [grandiose] funérailles *fpl*; **funeral service** service *m* funèbre; *Br* **funeral parlour**, *Am* **funeral home** entreprise *f* de pompes funèbres

**funfair** ['fʌnfeə(r)] *n Br* fête *f* foraine

**fungus** ['fʌŋgəs] *(pl* -**gi** [-gaɪ]) *n* [plant] champignon *m*; [on walls] moisissure *f*

**funnel** ['fʌnəl] *n* **a)** [of ship] cheminée *f* **b)** [for filling] entonnoir *m*

**funny** ['fʌnɪ] *(compar* -**ier**, *superl* -**iest**) *adj* [amusing] drôle; [strange] bizarre; **a funny idea** une drôle d'idée ■ **funnily** *adv* **funnily enough, I was just about to...** bizarrement, j'étais sur le point de...

**fur** [fɜː(r)] **1.** *n* [of animal, for wearing] fourrure *f*; [of dog, cat] poil *m*; **fur coat** manteau *m* de fourrure **2.** *(pt & pp* -**rr**-*) vi Br* **to fur (up)** [of kettle] s'entartrer

**furious** ['fjʊərɪəs] *adj* [violent, angry] furieux, -euse (**with** *or* **at** contre); [efforts, struggle] violent

**furnace** ['fɜːnɪs] *n* [forge] fourneau *m*

**furnish** ['fɜːnɪʃ] *vt* **a)** [room, house] meubler **b)** [supply] fournir (**sb with sth** qch à qn) ■ **furnishings** *npl* ameublement *m*

**furniture** ['fɜːnɪtʃə(r)] *n* meubles *mpl*; **a piece of furniture** un meuble

**furrow** ['fʌrəʊ] *n* [in earth, on brow] sillon *m*

**furry** ['fɜːrɪ] *adj* [animal] à poil; [toy] en peluche

**further** ['fɜːðə(r)] **1.** *adv & adj* = **farther** **2.** *adj* [additional] supplémentaire; *Br* **further education** enseignement supérieur dispensé par un établissement autre qu'une université **3.** *adv* [more] davantage **4.** *vt* [cause, research, career] promouvoir ■ **furthermore** *adv* en outre ■ **furthest** *adj & adv* = **farthest**

**furtive** ['fɜːtɪv] *adj* sournois

**fury** ['fjʊərɪ] *n* [violence, anger] fureur *f*

**fuse** [fju:z] **1.** *n* [wire] fusible *m* ; [of bomb] amorce *f* **2.** *vt* [join] fusionner ; *Br* **to fuse the lights** faire sauter les plombs **3.** *vi Br* **the lights have fused** les plombs ont sauté

**fusion** ['fju:ʒən] *n* fusion *f*

**fuss** [fʌs] **1.** *n* histoires *fpl* ; **to kick up** *or* **make a fuss** faire des histoires ; **to make a fuss of sb** être aux petits soins pour qn **2.** *vi* faire des histoires ; **to fuss over sb** être aux petits soins pour qn ■ **fussy** *(compar* -ier, *superl* -iest) *adj* exigeant (**about** sur) ; **I'm not fussy** [I don't mind] ça m'est égal

**futile** [*Br* 'fju:taɪl, *Am* 'fju:təl] *adj* [remark] futile ; [attempt] vain

**futon** ['fu:tɒn] *n* futon *m*

**future** ['fju:tʃə(r)] **1.** *n* avenir *m* ; [in grammar] futur *m* ; **in (the) future** à l'avenir **2.** *adj* futur ; **my future wife** ma future épouse ; **the future tense** le futur

**fuze** [fju:z] *Am n* & *vti* = **fuse**

**fuzzy** ['fʌzɪ] *(compar* -ier, *superl* -iest) *adj* **a)** [unclear - picture, idea] flou **b)** [hair] crépu

**FWIW** *n* MESSAGING *written abbr of* **for what it's worth**

# G

**G, g** [dʒiː] n [letter] G, g m inv

**gabble** ['gæbəl] vi [chatter] jacasser ; [indistinctly] bredouiller

**gable** ['geɪbəl] n pignon m

**gadget** ['gædʒɪt] n gadget m

**gaffe** [gæf] n [blunder] gaffe f

**gag** [gæg] **1.** n a) [on mouth] bâillon m b) Fam [joke] blague f **2.** (pt & pp -gg-) vt [person] bâillonner ; Fig [press] museler **3.** vi [choke] s'étouffer (**on** avec)

**gaily** ['geɪlɪ] adv gaiement

**gain** [geɪn] **1.** n [increase] augmentation f (**in** de) ; [profit] gain m ; Fig [advantage] avantage m **2.** vt [obtain, win] gagner ; [experience, reputation] acquérir ; **to gain speed / weight** prendre de la vitesse / du poids **3.** vi [of clock] avancer ; **to gain on sb** gagner du terrain sur qn ; **to gain by sth** bénéficier de qch

**gala** [Br 'gɑːlə, Am 'geɪlə] n gala m ; Br **swimming gala** concours m de natation

**galaxy** ['gæləksɪ] (pl -ies) n galaxie f

**gale** [geɪl] n grand vent m

**gallant** ['gælənt] adj [brave] brave ; [polite] galant

**gallery** ['gælərɪ] (pl -ies) n [room] galerie f ; [museum] musée m ; [for public, press] tribune f

**Gallic** ['gælɪk] adj [French] français

**gallon** ['gælən] n gallon m (Br = 4,5 l, Am = 3,8 l)

**gallop** ['gæləp] **1.** n galop m **2.** vi galoper

**gamble** ['gæmbəl] **1.** n [risk] coup m risqué **2.** vt [bet] parier, jouer **3.** vi jouer (**on** sur ; **with** avec) ; **to gamble on sth** [count on] miser sur qch ▪ **gambler** n joueur, -euse mf ▪ **gambling** n jeu m

**game¹** [geɪm] n **a)** [activity] jeu m ; [of football, cricket] match m ; [of tennis, chess, cards] partie f ; **to have a game of football / tennis** faire un match de football / une partie de tennis ; Br **games** [in school] le sport ; COMPUT **games console** console f de jeux ; **game show** [on television] jeu m télévisé ; [on radio] jeu m radiophonique **b)** [animals, birds] gibier m ▪ **gamer** ['geɪmə(r)] n **a)** [who plays computer games] amateur de jeux vidéo **b)** Am [athlete, sportsperson] sportif très compétitif ▪ **gaming** ['geɪmɪŋ] n [video games] jeux mpl vidéo

**game²** [geɪm] adj [brave] courageux, -euse ; **to be game (to do sth)** être partant (pour faire qch)

**gammon** ['gæmən] n Br jambon m

**gang** [gæŋ] **1.** n [of children, friends] bande f ; [of workers] équipe f ; [of criminals] gang m **2.** vi **to gang up on** or **against** se mettre à plusieurs contre

**gangplank** ['gæŋplæŋk] n passerelle f

**gangsta** ['gæŋstə] n **a)** [music] **gangsta (rap)** gangsta rap m **b)** [rapper] rappeur, -euse mf gangsta **c)** Am [gang member] membre d'un gang

**gangster** ['gæŋstə(r)] n gangster m

**gangway** ['gæŋweɪ] n Br passage m ; [in train, plane] couloir m ; [on ship] passerelle f ; [in bus, cinema, theatre] allée f

**gaol** [dʒeɪl] Br n & vt = **jail**

**gap** [gæp] n [space] espace m (**between** entre) ; [in wall, fence] trou m ; [in time] intervalle m ; [in knowledge] lacune f ; SCH & UNIV **gap year** année d'interruption volontaire des études, avant l'entrée à l'université ; **I spent my gap year in Australia** j'ai passé un an en Australie avant d'aller à l'université

**gape** [geɪp] vi [stare] rester bouche bée ; **to gape at sb / sth** regarder qn / qch bouche bée ▪ **gaping** adj béant

**garage** [Br'gærɑ:(d)ʒ, 'gærɪdʒ, Am gə'rɑ:ʒ] n garage m; Am **garage sale** vente d'occasion chez un particulier, ≃ vide-grenier m

**garbage** ['gɑ:bɪdʒ] n Am ordures fpl; Am **garbage bag** sac-poubelle m; **garbage can** poubelle f; **garbage man** or **collector** éboueur m

**garbanzo** [gɑ:'bænzəʊ] n **garbanzo (bean)** pois m chiche

**garbled** ['gɑ:bəld] adj confus

**garden** ['gɑ:dən] 1. n jardin m; **gardens** [park] parc m; **garden centre** jardinerie f; **garden party** garden-party f 2. vi jardiner, faire du jardinage ■ **gardener** n jardinier, -ère mf ■ **gardening** n jardinage m

**gargle** ['gɑ:gəl] vi se gargariser

**garish** [Br'geərɪʃ, Am'gærɪʃ] adj [clothes] voyant; [colour] criard; [light] cru

**garland** ['gɑ:lənd] n guirlande f

**garlic** ['gɑ:lɪk] n ail m; **garlic bread** pain chaud au beurre d'ail

**garment** ['gɑ:mənt] n vêtement m

**garnish** ['gɑ:nɪʃ] 1. n garniture f 2. vt garnir (**with** de)

**garter** ['gɑ:tə(r)] n [round leg] jarretière f; [for socks] fixe-chaussette m; Am [attached to belt] jarretelle f

**gas** [gæs] 1. n gaz m inv; Am [gasoline] essence f; Br **gas cooker** cuisinière f à gaz; Br **gas heater, gas fire** radiateur m à gaz; **gas refill** recharge f de gaz; Am **gas station** station-service f; **gas stove** [large] cuisinière f à gaz; [portable] réchaud m à gaz; Am **gas tank** réservoir m à essence 2. (pt & pp -ss-) vt [person] asphyxier; [deliberately] gazer

**gash** [gæʃ] 1. n entaille f 2. vt to **gash one's knee** se faire une blessure profonde au genou

**gasoline** ['gæsəli:n] n Am essence f

**gasp** [gɑ:sp] 1. n halètement m; [of surprise] sursaut m 2. vi avoir le souffle coupé (**with** or **in** de); to **gasp for breath** haleter

**gassy** ['gæsɪ] (compar -ier, superl -iest) adj gazeux, -euse

**gastric** ['gæstrɪk] adj gastrique

**gate** [geɪt] n [in garden, field] barrière f; [made of metal] grille f; [of castle, at airport] porte f; [at stadium] entrée f

**gâteau** ['gætəʊ] (pl -eaux [-əʊz]) n Br [cake] gros gâteau m à la crème

**gatecrash** ['geɪtkræʃ] 1. vt to **gatecrash a party** s'inviter à une réception 2. vi Fam [at party] s'inviter, jouer les pique-assiette

**gateway** ['geɪtweɪ] n **a)** [entrance] entrée f **b)** [means of access] **gateway to** [generally] porte f de; Fig clé f de **c)** INTERNET portail m

**gather** ['gæðə(r)] 1. vt **a)** [people, objects] rassembler; [pick up] ramasser; [flowers, fruit] cueillir; [information] recueillir; to **gather speed** prendre de la vitesse; to **gather in** [crops, harvest] rentrer; to **gather one's strength** rassembler ses forces **b)** [understand] I **gather that...** je crois comprendre que... **c)** [sew pleats in] froncer 2. vi [of people] se rassembler; [of clouds] se former; [of dust] s'accumuler; to **gather round** [come closer] s'approcher; to **gather round sb** entourer qn

**gathering** ['gæðərɪŋ] n [group] rassemblement m

**gauge** [geɪdʒ] 1. n [instrument] jauge f; Fig to **be a gauge of sth** permettre de jauger qch 2. vt évaluer

**gaunt** [gɔ:nt] adj décharné

**gauze** [gɔ:z] n gaze f

**gave** [geɪv] pt of **give**

**gawk** [gɔ:k], **gawp** [gɔ:p] vi to **gawk at sb/sth** regarder qn/qch bouche bée

**gay** [geɪ] (compar -er, superl -est) 1. adj **a)** [homosexual] homosexuel, -elle **b)** Dated [cheerful] gai 2. n homosexuel, -elle mf

**gaze** [geɪz] 1. n regard m 2. vi to **gaze at sb/sth** regarder fixement qn/qch

**GB** [dʒi:'bi:] (abbr of **Great Britain**) n GB

**GCSE** [dʒi:si:es'i:] (abbr of **General Certificate of Secondary Education**) n Br diplôme de fin de premier cycle de l'enseignement secondaire, sanctionnant une matière déterminée

**gear** [gɪə(r)] **1.** *n a) Fam* [equipment] attirail *m* ; [belongings] affaires *fpl* ; [clothes] fringues *fpl* **b)** [on car, bicycle] vitesse *f* ; **in gear** [vehicle] en prise ; *Br* **gear lever**, *Am* **gear shift** levier *m* de (changement de) vitesse **2.** *vt* **to gear sth to sth** adapter qch à qch ; **to be geared up to do sth** être prêt à faire qch ■ **gearbox** *n* boîte *f* de vitesses

**geek** ['giːk] *n Fam* débile *mf* ; **a movie / computer geek** un dingue de cinéma / d'informatique

**geekazoid** ['giːkəzɔɪd] *Am Fam n* = **geek**

**geese** [giːs] *pl of* **goose**

**gel** [dʒel] *n* gel *m*

**gelatin(e)** [*Br* 'dʒelətiːn, *Am* -tən] *n* gélatine *f*

**gem** [dʒem] *n* [stone] pierre *f* précieuse ; *Fig* [person] perle *f* ; *Fig* [thing] bijou *m* (*pl* -oux)

**gen** [dʒen] *Br Fam* **1.** *n* [information] tuyaux *mpl* **2.** *(pt & pp* -nn-*) vi* **to gen up on sb / sth** se rancarder sur qn / qch

**gender** ['dʒendə(r)] *n* [in grammar] genre *m* ; [of person] sexe *m*

**gene** [dʒiːn] *n* BIOL gène *m*

**general** ['dʒenərəl] **1.** *adj* général ; **in general** en général ; **the general public** le grand public ; *Am* **general delivery** poste *f* restante **2.** *n* MIL général *m*

**generalize** ['dʒenərəlaɪz] *vi* généraliser ■ **generalization** [-'zeɪʃən] *n* généralisation *f*

**generally** ['dʒenərəlɪ] *adv* généralement ; **generally speaking** de manière générale

**generate** ['dʒenəreɪt] *vt* [fear, hope, unemployment] engendrer ; [heat, electricity] produire ; [interest, ideas] faire naître ; [jobs] créer

**generation** [dʒenə'reɪʃən] *n* [of people, products] génération *f* ; [of electricity] production *f* ; **generation gap** conflit *m* des générations

**generator** ['dʒenəreɪtə(r)] *n* générateur *m*

**generic** [dʒɪ'nerɪk] *adj* générique ; **generic brand / product** marque *f* / produit *m* générique

**generosity** ['dʒenə'rɒsɪtɪ] *n* générosité *f*

**generously** ['dʒenərəslɪ] *adv* généreusement

**genesis** ['dʒenəsɪs] *n* genèse *f*

**genetic** [dʒɪ'netɪk] *adj* génétique ; **genetic engineering** génie *m* génétique ■ **genetically** *adv* genetically modified génétiquement modifié ■ **genetics** *n* génétique *f*

**Geneva** [dʒɪ'niːvə] *n* Genève *m ou f*

**gengineering** [ˌdʒendʒɪ'nɪərɪŋ] *n* génie *m* génétique

**genitals** ['dʒenɪtəlz] *npl* organes *mpl* génitaux

**genius** ['dʒiːnɪəs] *n* [ability, person] génie *m*

**gent** [dʒent] *n Br Fam* monsieur *m* ; **gents' shoes** chaussures *fpl* pour hommes ; **the gents** [toilet] les toilettes *fpl* des hommes

**gentle** ['dʒentəl] *(compar* -er, *superl* -est*) adj* [person, sound, slope] doux (*f* douce) ; [hint] discret, -ète ; [exercise, speed] modéré ■ **gently** *adv* doucement ; [land] en douceur

**gentleman** ['dʒentəlmən] *(pl* -men*) n* monsieur *m* ; [well-bred] gentleman *m*

**genuine** ['dʒenjʊɪn] *adj* [leather, diamond] véritable ; [signature, work of art] authentique ; [sincere] sincère ■ **genuinely** *adv* [sincerely] sincèrement

**geography** [dʒɪ'ɒgrəfɪ] *n* géographie *f* ■ **geographical** [dʒɪə'græfɪkəl] *adj* géographique

**geology** [dʒɪ'ɒlədʒɪ] *n* géologie *f* ■ **geological** [dʒɪə'lɒdʒɪkəl] *adj* géologique

**geometry** [dʒɪ'ɒmɪtrɪ] *n* géométrie *f* ■ **geometric(al)** [dʒɪə'metrɪk(əl)] *adj* géométrique

**geotag** ['dʒiːəʊˌtæg] *n* [photo, video] géolocaliser, géomarquer

**geriatric** [dʒerɪ'ætrɪk] *adj* [hospital] gériatrique

**germ** [dʒɜːm] *n* [causing disease] microbe *m*

**German** ['dʒɜːmən] **1.** *adj* allemand ; **German teacher** professeur *m* d'allemand; **German measles** rubéole f 2. n [person] Allemand, -e mf; [language] allemand m

**Germany** ['dʒɜ:mənɪ] n l'Allemagne f

**germinate** ['dʒɜ:mɪneɪt] vi [of seed, idea] germer

**gesticulate** [dʒe'stɪkjʊleɪt] vi gesticuler

**gesture** ['dʒestʃə(r)] 1. n geste m 2. vi to **gesture to sb to do sth** faire signe à qn de faire qch

**get** [get] (Br pt & pp **got**, pres p **getting**, Am pt **got**, pp **gotten**, pres p **getting**) 1. vt [obtain] obtenir, avoir; [find] trouver; [buy] acheter; [receive] recevoir; [catch] attraper; [bus, train] prendre; [seize] prendre, saisir; [fetch] aller chercher; [put] mettre; [derive] tirer (**from** de); [prepare] préparer; [lead] mener; [hit with fist, stick] atteindre; [reputation] se faire; Fam [understand] piger; Fam [annoy] énerver; **to get sb to do sth** faire faire qch à qn; **to get sth done** faire faire qch; **to get sth clean/dirty** nettoyer/salir qch; **to get sth to sb** [send] faire parvenir qch à qn; **to get sb to the station** amener qn à la gare; **can I get you anything?** je te rapporte quelque chose?

2. vi [go] aller (**to** à); [arrive] arriver (**to** à); [become] devenir; **to get old** vieillir; **to get caught/run over** se faire prendre/écraser; **to get dressed/washed** s'habiller/se laver; **to get paid** être payé; **where have you got** or Am **gotten to?** où en es-tu?; **you've got to stay** [must] tu dois rester; **to get to do sth** [succeed in doing] parvenir à faire qch; **to get going** [leave] se mettre en route; [start working] se mettre au travail

▪ **getaway** n [escape] fuite f

▪ **get-together** n Fam réunion f

▪ **getup** n Fam [clothes] accoutrement m

▪ **get about** vi se déplacer; [of news] circuler

▪ **get across** 1. vt sep [message] faire passer 2. vi [succeed in crossing] traverser; **to get across to sb that...** faire comprendre à qn que...

▪ **get along** vi [manage] se débrouiller; [progress] avancer; [be on good terms] s'entendre (**with** avec); [leave] s'en aller

▪ **get around** vi = **get about**

▪ **get at** vt insep [reach] atteindre; **what is he getting at?** où veut-il en venir?

▪ **get away** vi [leave] s'en aller; [escape] se sauver; **to get away with a fine** s'en tirer avec une amende; **he got away with that crime** il n'a pas été inquiété pour ce crime

▪ **get back** 1. vt sep [recover] récupérer; **to get one's own back on sb** se venger de qn 2. vi [return] revenir; **to get back at sb** se venger de qn

▪ **get back to** vt insep **a)** [return to previous state, activity] revenir à; [after illness] reprendre son travail; **to get back to sleep** se rendormir; **to get back to work** [after pause] se remettre au travail **b)** Fam [phone back] rappeler; **I'll get back to you on that** je te reparlerai de ça plus tard

▪ **get by** vi [manage] se débrouiller

▪ **get down** 1. vi [go down] descendre (**from** de); **to get down to** [work] se mettre à 2. vt sep [bring down] descendre (**from** de); Fam **to get sb down** [depress] déprimer qn 3. vt insep **to get down the stairs/a ladder** descendre l'escalier/d'une échelle

▪ **get in** 1. vt sep [stock up with] faire provision de; **to get sb in** [call for] faire venir qn 2. vi [enter] entrer; [come home] rentrer; [enter vehicle or train] monter; [arrive] arriver; [be elected] être élu

▪ **get into** vt insep entrer dans; [vehicle, train] monter dans; [habit] prendre; **to get into bed/a rage** se mettre au lit/en colère

▪ **get off** 1. vt sep [remove] enlever; [send] expédier; [in court] faire acquitter; Fam **to get off doing sth** se dispenser de faire qch 2. vt insep **to get off a chair** se lever d'une chaise; **to get off a bus** descendre d'un bus 3. vi [leave] partir; [from vehicle or train] descendre (**from** de); [escape punishment] s'en tirer

■ **get on 1.** *vt sep* [shoes, clothes] mettre **2.** *vt insep* [bus, train] monter dans **3.** *vi* [enter bus or train] monter; [manage] se débrouiller; [succeed] réussir; [be on good terms] s'entendre (**with** avec); **how are you getting on?** comment ça va?; **how did you get on?** [in exam] comment ça s'est passé?; **to be getting on (in years)** se faire vieux (*f* vieille); **to get onto sb** [on phone] contacter qn; **to get on with** [task] continuer

■ **get out 1.** *vt sep* [remove] enlever; [bring out] sortir **2.** *vi* sortir; [from vehicle or train] descendre (**of** or **from** de); **to get out of** [obligation] échapper à; [danger] se tirer de; [habit] perdre

■ **get over 1.** *vt sep* [ideas] faire passer; **let's get it over with** finissons-en **2.** *vt insep* [illness] se remettre de; [shock] revenir de

■ **get round 1.** *vt insep* [obstacle] contourner **2.** *vi* [visit] passer; **to get round to doing sth** trouver le temps de faire qch

■ **get through 1.** *vt sep* [communicate] **to get sth through to sb** faire comprendre qch à qn **2.** *vt insep* [hole] passer par; [task] venir à bout de; [exam, interview] survivre à; [food] consommer **3.** *vi* [pass] passer; [pass exam] être reçu; **to get through to sb** [communicate with] se faire comprendre de qn; [on the phone] obtenir la communication avec qn

■ **get to** *vt insep Fam* [annoy] taper sur les nerfs à

■ **get together 1.** *vt sep* [organize - team, belongings] rassembler; [project, report] préparer **2.** *vi* se réunir

■ **get up 1.** *vt sep* **to get sb up** [out of bed] faire lever qn; **to get sth up** [bring up] monter qch **2.** *vt insep* [ladder, stairs] monter **3.** *vi* [rise, stand up] se lever (**from** de); **to get up to something** or **to mischief** faire des bêtises; **where have you got up to?** [in book] où en es-tu?

**GF** MESSAGING *written abbr of* **girlfriend**

**ghastly** ['gɑːstlɪ] *(compar* -**ier***, superl* -**iest***) adj* [horrible] épouvantable

**gherkin** ['gɜːkɪn] *n* cornichon *m*

**ghetto** ['getəʊ] *(pl* -**oes** *or* -**os***) n* ghetto *m*; *Fam* **ghetto blaster** radio-cassette *f*

**ghost** [gəʊst] *n* fantôme *m*; **ghost story** histoire *f* de fantômes ■ **ghostly** *adj* spectral

**giant** ['dʒaɪənt] **1.** *adj* [tree, packet] géant **2.** *n* géant *m*

**gibe** [dʒaɪb] **1.** *n* moquerie *f* **2.** *vi* **to gibe at sb** se moquer de qn

**giddy** ['gɪdɪ] *(compar* -**ier***, superl* -**iest***) adj* **to be** or **feel giddy** avoir le vertige; **to make sb giddy** donner le vertige à qn

**gift** [gɪft] *n* cadeau *m*; [talent, donation] don *m*; *Br* **gift voucher** or **token** chèque-cadeau *m* ■ **gifted** *adj* doué (**with** de; **for** pour)

**gift-wrapped** ['gɪftræpt] *adj* sous paquet-cadeau

**gig** [gɪg] *n Fam* [pop concert] concert *m*

**gigabyte** ['gaɪgəbaɪt] *n* COMPUT giga-octet *m*

**gigantic** [dʒaɪ'gæntɪk] *adj* gigantesque

**giggle** ['gɪgəl] **1.** *n* petit rire *m* bête **2.** *vi* rire (bêtement)

**gilt** [gɪlt] **1.** *adj* doré **2.** *n* dorure *f*

**gimmick** ['gɪmɪk] *n* [trick, object] truc *m*

**gimp** [gɪmp] *n Am Fam* **a)** *Pej* [person] gogol *v Fam mf* **b)** [object] scoubidou *m*

**gin** [dʒɪn] *n* [drink] gin *m*

**ginger** ['dʒɪndʒə(r)] **1.** *adj* [hair] roux (*f* rousse) **2.** *n* [spice] gingembre *m*; **ginger beer** limonade *f* au gingembre ■ **gingerbread** *n* pain *m* d'épice

**gipsy** ['dʒɪpsɪ] *(pl* -**ies***) n* bohémien, -enne *mf*; [Eastern European] tsigane *mf*; [Spanish] gitan, -e *mf*

**giraffe** [dʒɪ'ræf, *Br* dʒɪ'rɑːf] *n* girafe *f*

**girl** [gɜːl] *n* [child] (petite) fille *f*, fillette *f*; [young woman] jeune fille *f*; **English girl** jeune Anglaise *f*; **Girl Guide** éclai-

reuse f ■ **girlfriend** n [of girl] amie f;
[of boy] petite amie f ■ **girlish** adj de
(jeune) fille

**giro** ['ʤaɪrəʊ] (pl -os) n Br **bank giro**
virement m bancaire; **giro account**
compte m courant postal, CCP m

**gist** [ʤɪst] n to get the gist of sth saisir
l'essentiel de qch

**give** [gɪv] **1.** n [of fabric] élasticité f
**2.** (pt **gave**, pp **given**) vt donner; [as
present] offrir; [support] apporter;
[smile, gesture, pleasure] faire; [sigh]
pousser; [look] jeter; [blow] porter;
**to give sth to sb, to give sb sth** donner ou offrir qch à qn; **to give way** [of
branch, person] céder; [of roof] s'effondrer; [in vehicle] céder la priorité (**to** à)
**3.** vi a) [donate] donner
b) [of shoes] se faire; [of support] céder
■ **give away** vt sep [prize] distribuer;
[money] donner; [betray] trahir
■ **give back** vt sep [return] rendre
■ **give in 1.** vt sep [hand in] remettre
**2.** vi [surrender] céder (**to** à)
■ **give off** vt sep [smell, heat] dégager
■ **give out** vt sep [hand out] distribuer; [make known] annoncer
■ **give over** vi Br Fam **give over!** arrête!
■ **give up 1.** vt sep [possessions]
abandonner; [activity] renoncer à;
[seat] céder (**to** à); **to give up smoking**
cesser de fumer **2.** vi abandonner

**given** ['gɪvən] **1.** pp of **give 2.** adj [fixed]
donné; Am **given name** prénom m
**3.** conj [considering] étant donné;
**given that...** étant donné que...

**glacier** [Br 'glæsɪə(r), Am 'gleɪʃər] n glacier m

**glad** [glæd] adj [person] content (**of /
about** de; **that** que (+ subjunctive))
■ **gladly** adv volontiers

**glamorous** ['glæmərəs] adj [person,
dress] élégant; [job] prestigieux, -euse

**glance** [glɑːns] **1.** n coup m d'œil **2.** vi to
glance at sb/sth jeter un coup d'œil
à qn /qch

**gland** [glænd] n glande f

**glare** [gleə(r)] **1.** n [look] regard m
furieux **2.** vi to glare at sb foudroyer
qn (du regard) ■ **glaring** adj [light]
éblouissant; [eyes] furieux, -euse; **a
glaring mistake** une faute grossière

**glass** [glɑːs] **1.** n verre m **2.** adj [bottle]
de verre; **glass door** porte f vitrée
■ **glassful** n (plein) verre m

**glasses** ['glɑːsɪz] npl [spectacles]
lunettes fpl

**glaze** [gleɪz] **1.** n [on pottery] vernis m
**2.** vt [window] vitrer; [pottery] ver-
nisser

**gleam** [gliːm] **1.** n lueur f **2.** vi luire

**glean** [gliːn] vt [information] glaner

**glee** [gliː] n joie f

**glen** [glen] n Scot vallon m

**glide** [glaɪd] vi glisser; [of aircraft, bird]
planer ■ **glider** n [aircraft] planeur m
■ **gliding** n [sport] vol m à voile

**glimmer** ['glɪmə(r)] **1.** n [light, of hope]
faible lueur f **2.** vi luire (faiblement)

**glimpse** [glɪmps] **1.** n aperçu m; **to
catch** or **get a glimpse of sth** entrevoir qch **2.** vt entrevoir

**glint** [glɪnt] vi [of light, eye] briller

**glisten** ['glɪsən] vi [of wet surface] briller; [of water] miroiter

**glitter** ['glɪtə(r)] vi scintiller

**gloat** [gləʊt] vi jubiler (**over** à l'idée de)

**global** ['gləʊbəl] adj [universal] mondial; [comprehensive] global; **global
market** marché m mondial ou international; **global warming** réchauffement m de la planète ■ **globalization**
n ECON mondialisation f

**globe** [gləʊb] n globe m

**gloom** [gluːm] n [sadness] morosité f;
[darkness] obscurité f ■ **gloomy** (compar -ier, superl -iest) adj [sad] morose;
[dark, dismal] sombre

**glorious** ['glɔːrɪəs] adj [splendid] magnifique; [full of glory] glorieux, -euse

**glory** ['glɔːrɪ] **1.** n gloire f; [great beauty]
splendeur f **2.** vi to glory in sth se glorifier de qch

**gloss** [glɒs] **1.** n [shine] lustre m; **gloss
paint** peinture f brillante **2.** vt to gloss

**over sth** glisser sur qch ■ **glossy** *(compar* **-ier,** *superl* **-iest)** *adj* brillant ; [photo] glacé ; [magazine] de luxe

**glossary** ['glɒsərɪ] *(pl* **-ies)** *n* glossaire *m*

**glove** [glʌv] *n* gant *m* ; **glove compartment** [in car] boîte *f* à gants

**glow** [gləʊ] **1.** *n* [light] lueur *f* **2.** *vi* [of sky, fire] rougeoyer ; *Fig* [of eyes, person] rayonner (**with** de) ■ **glowing** *adj* [account, terms, reference] enthousiaste

**glue** [gluː] **1.** *n* colle *f* **2.** *vt* coller (**to/on** à)

**glug** [glʌg] *(pt & pp* **-ged,** *pres p* **-ging)** *Fam* **1.** *n* glug **(glug)** glouglou *m* ; **he took a long glug of lemonade** il prit une longue goulée de limonade **2.** *vi* faire glouglou

**glum** [glʌm] *(compar* **glummer,** *superl* **glummest)** *adj* triste

**glutton** ['glʌtən] *n* goinfre *mf*

**GM** [dʒiː'em] *(abbr of* **genetically modified)** *adj* génétiquement modifié

**GMT** [dʒiːem'tiː] *(abbr of* **Greenwich Mean Time)** *n* GMT *m*

**gnat** [næt] *n* moucheron *m*

**gnaw** [nɔː] *vti* **to gnaw (at) sth** ronger qch

**gnome** [nəʊm] *n* gnome *m*

**go** [gəʊ] **1.** *(pl* **goes)** *n* [turn] tour *m* ; [energy] dynamisme *m* ; **to have a go at (doing) sth** essayer (de faire) qch ; **at** *or* **in one go** d'un seul coup ; **on the go** en mouvement ; **to make a go of sth** réussir qch

**2.** *(3rd person sing present tense* **goes)** *(pt* **went,** *pp* **gone,** *pres p* **going)** *vt* [make sound] faire ; **to go it alone** se lancer en solo

**3.** *vi* aller (**to** à ; **from** de) ; [depart] partir, s'en aller ; [disappear] disparaître ; [be sold] se vendre ; [function] marcher ; [progress] aller ; [become] devenir ; [of time] passer ; [of hearing, strength] baisser ; [of fuse] sauter ; [of light bulb] griller ; **to go well/badly** [of event] se passer bien/mal ; **she's going to do sth** [is about to, intends to] elle va faire qch ; **it's going to rain** il va pleuvoir ; **it's all gone** [finished] il n'y en a plus ; **to go and get sb/sth** [fetch] aller chercher

qn/qch ; **to go and see** aller voir ; **to go riding/on a trip** faire du cheval/un voyage ; **to go to a doctor/lawyer** aller voir un médecin/un avocat ; **is there any beer going?** y a-t-il de la bière ? ; **two hours to go** encore deux heures

■ **to go** *adv* [remaining] **there are only three days to go** il ne reste que trois jours

■ **go about 1.** *vi* [of person] se promener ; [of rumour] circuler **2.** *vt* [get on with] s'occuper de ; [set about] se mettre à ; **how do you go about it?** comment est-ce qu'on procède ?

■ **go across 1.** *vt insep* traverser **2.** *vi* [cross] traverser ; [go] aller (**to** à) ; **to go across to sb('s)** faire un saut chez qn

■ **go after** *vt insep* [chase] poursuivre ; [job] essayer d'obtenir

■ **go against** *vt insep* [contradict] aller à l'encontre de ; [be unfavourable to] être défavorable à

■ **go ahead** *vi* [take place] avoir lieu ; [go in front] passer devant ; **to go ahead with sth** entreprendre qch ; **go ahead!** allez-y !

■ **go along** *vi* [proceed] se dérouler ; **to go along with sb/sth** être d'accord avec qn/qch ; **we'll see as we go along** nous verrons au fur et à mesure

■ **go around** *vi* = **go about**

■ **go away** *vi* partir, s'en aller

■ **go back** *vi* [return] revenir ; [step back, retreat] reculer ; **to go back to sleep** se rendormir ; **to go back to doing sth** se remettre à faire qch ; **to go back to** [in time] remonter à ; **to go back on one's promise** *or* **word** revenir sur sa promesse

■ **go by 1.** *vt insep* [act according to] se fonder sur ; [judge from] juger d'après ; **to go by the name of...** être connu sous le nom de... **2.** *vi* passer

■ **go down 1.** *vt insep* [stairs, street] descendre **2.** *vi* descendre ; [fall down] tomber ; [of ship] sombrer ; [of sun] se coucher ; [of temperature, price] baisser ; [of tyre, balloon] se dégonfler ; **to go down well/badly** être bien/mal reçu

■ **go for** *vt insep* [fetch] aller chercher; [attack] attaquer; **the same goes for you** ça vaut aussi pour toi

■ **go forward(s)** *vi* avancer

■ **go in** *vi* (r)entrer; [of sun] se cacher; *Br* **to go in for** [exam] s'inscrire à; **she doesn't go in for cooking** elle n'est pas très portée sur la cuisine

■ **go into** *vt insep* [enter] entrer dans; [examine] examiner

■ **go off 1.** *vt insep* [lose liking for] se lasser de **2.** *vi* [leave] partir; [go bad] se gâter; [of alarm] se déclencher; [of bomb] exploser

■ **go on** *vi* continuer (**doing** à faire); [travel] poursuivre sa route; [happen] se passer; [last] durer; **to go on to sth** passer à qch; *Fam* **to go on at sb** [nag] s'en prendre à qn; *Fam* **to go on about sb/sth** parler sans cesse de qn/qch

■ **go out** *vi* sortir; [of light, fire] s'éteindre; [of tide] descendre; [depart] partir; [date] sortir ensemble; **to go out for a meal** aller au restaurant; **to go out with sb** sortir avec qn; **to go out to work** travailler (hors de chez soi)

■ **go over 1.** *vt insep* **a)** [cross over] traverser; **the ball went over the wall** la balle est passée par-dessus le mur **b)** [examine] passer en revue; [speech] revoir **2.** *vi* [go] aller (**to** à); [to enemy] passer (**to** à); **to go over to sb** aller vers qn; **to go over to sb's** [visit] faire un saut chez qn

■ **go round 1.** *vt insep* **to go round a corner** tourner au coin; **to go round the shops** faire les magasins; **to go round the world** faire le tour du monde **2.** *vi* [turn] tourner; [make a detour] faire le tour; [of rumour] circuler; **to go round to sb's** faire un saut chez qn; **there is enough to go round** il y en a assez pour tout le monde

■ **go through 1.** *vt insep* [suffer, undergo] subir; [examine] passer en revue; [search] fouiller; [spend] dépenser; [wear out] user; [perform] accomplir; **to go through with sth** aller jusqu'au bout de qch **2.** *vi* passer; [of deal] être conclu

■ **go toward(s)** *vt insep* contribuer à

■ **go under** *vi* [of ship] couler; *Fig* [of firm] faire faillite

■ **go up 1.** *vt insep* monter **2.** *vi* monter; [explode] sauter; **to go up to sth** [approach] se diriger vers qch; [reach] aller jusqu'à qch

■ **go with** *vt insep* aller de pair avec; **the company car goes with the job** le poste donne droit à une voiture de fonction

■ **go without** *vt insep* se passer de

---

**goad** [gəʊd] *vt* **to goad sb (on)** aiguillonner qn

**go-ahead** ['gəʊəhed] **1.** *adj* dynamique **2.** *n* **to get the go-ahead** avoir le feu vert; **to give sb the go-ahead** donner le feu vert à qn

**goal** [gəʊl] *n* but *m* ■ **goalkeeper** *n* gardien *m* de but, goal *m* ■ **goalpost** *n* poteau *m* de but

**goat** [gəʊt] *n* chèvre *f*

**gobble** ['gɒbəl] *vt* **to gobble (up** or **down)** [food] engloutir

**go-between** ['gəʊbɪtwiːn] *n* intermédiaire *mf*

**goblet** ['gɒblɪt] *n* verre *m* à pied

**god** [gɒd] *n* dieu *m*; **God** Dieu; *Fam* **oh God!, my God!** mon Dieu! ■ **goddaughter** *n* filleule *f* ■ **godfather** *n* parrain *m* ■ **godforsaken** *adj* [place] perdu ■ **godmother** *n* marraine *f* ■ **godson** *n* filleul *m*

**goddammit** [ˌgɒdˈdæmɪt] *excl v Fam* bordel!

**goddam(n)** ['gɒdæm] *adj Am Fam* foutu

**goddess** ['gɒdɪs] *n* déesse *f*

**godsend** ['gɒdsend] *n* **to be a godsend** être un don du ciel

**goes** [gəʊz] *v & npl see* **go**

**go-getting** [-'getɪŋ] *adj Fam* [person] entreprenant

**goggles** ['gɒgəlz] *npl* lunettes *fpl* (*de protection, de plongée*)

**going** ['gəʊɪŋ] **1.** *n* **it's hard** or **heavy going** c'est difficile **2.** *adj* **the going rate** le tarif en vigueur; **a going concern** une affaire qui tourne ■ **going-away** *adj* [party, present] d'adieu

■ **going-over** (*pl* **goings-over**) *n Fam*
**a)** [checkup] révision *f*, vérification *f*;
[cleanup] nettoyage *m*; **the house
needs a good going-over** il faudrait
nettoyer la maison à fond **b) to give sb
a (good) going-over** [scolding] passer
un savon à qn; [beating] passer qn à
tabac ■ **goings-on** *npl Pej* activités *fpl*

**go-kart** ['gəʊkɑːt] *n* [for racing] kart *m*

**gold** [gəʊld] **1.** *n* or *m* **2.** *adj* [watch] en or;
[coin, dust] d'or; **gold medal** [in sport]
médaille *f* d'or ■ **golden** *adj* [of gold
colour] doré; **golden rule** règle *f* d'or
■ **goldmine** *n* mine *f* d'or ■ **gold-
plated** *adj* plaqué or ■ **goldsmith**
*n* orfèvre *m*

**goldfish** ['gəʊldfɪʃ] *n* poisson *m* rouge

**golf** [gɒlf] *n* golf *m*; **golf ball** balle *f*
de golf; **golf club** [stick, association]
club *m* de golf; **golf course** parcours *m*
de golf ■ **golfer** *n* golfeur, -euse *mf*

**gone** [gɒn] **1.** *pp* of **go 2.** *adj Br Fam* **it's
gone two** il est plus de deux heures

**gong** [gɒŋ] *n* gong *m*

**good** [gʊd] **1.** (*compar* **better**, *superl* **best**)
*adj* bon (*f* **bonne**); [kind] gentil, -ille;
[well-behaved] sage; **my good friend**
mon cher ami; **good!** bon !, bien !;
**very good!** [all right] très bien !; **that
isn't good enough** [bad] ça ne va
pas; [not sufficient] ça ne suffit pas;
**that's good of you** c'est gentil de ta
part; **to taste good** avoir bon goût;
**to feel good** se sentir bien; **to have
good weather** avoir beau temps; **to
be good at French** être bon en français; **to be good at swimming /tell-
ing jokes** savoir bien nager / raconter
des blagues; **to be good with children**
savoir s'y prendre avec les enfants; **a
good many, a good deal (of)** beaucoup
(de); **as good as** [almost] pratiquement; **good afternoon, good morning** bonjour; [on leaving someone] au
revoir; **good evening** bonsoir; **good
night** bonsoir; [before going to bed]
bonne nuit

**2.** *n* [advantage, virtue] bien *m*; **for her
(own) good** pour son bien; **for the
good of your family /career** pour ta
famille / carrière; **it will do you (some)**

**good** ça te fera du bien; **it's no good
crying /shouting** ça ne sert à rien de
pleurer / crier; **that's no good** [worth-
less] ça ne vaut rien; [bad] ça ne va pas;
**for good** [leave, give up] pour de bon
■ **good-for-nothing** *n* propre-à-
rien *mf*
■ **good-looking** *adj* beau (*f* belle)

**goodbye** [gʊd'baɪ] *excl* & *n* au revoir (*m inv*)

**goodness** ['gʊdnɪs] *n* bonté *f*; **my
goodness!** mon Dieu !

**goods** [gʊdz] *npl* marchandises *fpl*;
**goods train** train *m* de marchandises; **goods vehicle** poids lourd *m*,
véhicule *m* utilitaire

**goodwill** [gʊd'wɪl] *n* [willingness]
bonne volonté *f*; [benevolence] bienveillance *f*

**goof** [guːf] *Am Fam* **1.** *n* [mistake] gaffe *f*
**2.** *vi* faire une gaffe ■ **goof around** *vi*
*Am Fam* déconner

**Google®** ['guːgl] *vt* [look up using Goo-
gle] rechercher avec Google®; **I'll Google that** je vais chercher sur Google

**goose** [guːs] (*pl* **geese**) *n* oie *f*; **goose** *Br*
**pimples** *or Am* **bumps** chair *f* de poule
■ **gooseflesh** *n* chair *f* de poule

**gooseberry** ['gʊzbərɪ] (*pl* **-ies**) *n* groseille *f* à maquereau

**gorge** [gɔːdʒ] **1.** *n* [ravine] gorge *f* **2.** *vt*
**to gorge oneself** se gaver (**on** de)

**gorgeous** ['gɔːdʒəs] *adj* magnifique

**gorilla** [gə'rɪlə] *n* gorille *m*

**gormless** ['gɔːmləs] *adj Br Fam* balourd

**gory** ['gɔːrɪ] (*compar* **-ier**, *superl* **-iest**) *adj*
[bloody] sanglant

**gosh** [gɒʃ] *excl Fam* mince (alors) !

**go-slow** [gəʊ'sləʊ] *n Br* [strike] grève *f*
du zèle

**gospel** ['gɒspəl] *n* évangile *m*

**gossip** ['gɒsɪp] **1.** *n* [talk] bavardages *mpl*; [malicious] cancans *mpl*;
[person] commère *f*; **gossip column**
[in newspaper] échos *mpl* **2.** *vi* bavarder; [maliciously] colporter des commérages

**got** [gɒt] *Br* pt & pp of **get**

**Gothic** ['gɒθɪk] adj & n gothique (m)

**go-to** adj Am Fam he's your go-to guy c'est votre interlocuteur ou c'est à lui qu'il faut s'adresser en cas de problème

**gotten** ['gɒtən] Am pp of **get**

**gourmet** ['gʊəmeɪ] n gourmet m

**govern** ['gʌvən] **1.** vt [rule] gouverner; [city, province] administrer; [influence] déterminer **2.** vi [rule] gouverner

**government** ['gʌvənmənt] **1.** n gouvernement m; **local government** administration f locale **2.** adj [decision, policy] gouvernemental

**governor** ['gʌvənə(r)] n gouverneur m; [of school] administrateur, -trice mf; [of prison] directeur, -trice mf

**gown** [gaʊn] n [of woman] robe f; Br [of judge, lecturer] toge f

**GP** [dʒiː'piː] (abbr of **general practitioner**) n Br généraliste mf

**GPS** [ˌdʒiːpiː'es] (abbr of **Global Positioning System**) n GPS m

**grab** [græb] (pt & pp -bb-) vt to grab (hold of) **sb/sth** saisir qn /qch; **to grab sth from sb** arracher qch à qn

**grace** [greɪs] **1.** n [charm, goodwill, religious mercy] grâce f; REL **to say grace** dire le bénédicité; **ten days' grace** dix jours de grâce **2.** vt [adorn] orner; [honour] honorer (**with** de) ■ **graceful** adj [movement, person] gracieux, -euse

**gracious** ['greɪʃəs] adj [kind] aimable (**to** envers); Fam **good gracious!** bonté divine!

**grade** [greɪd] **1.** n a) [rank] grade m; [in profession] échelon m; [quality] qualité f; Am **grade crossing** passage m à niveau b) Am SCH [mark] note f; [year] classe f; Am **grade school** école f primaire **2.** vt [classify] classer; Am [exam] noter

**gradient** ['greɪdɪənt] n [slope] dénivellation f

**gradual** ['grædʒʊəl] adj progressif, -ive; [slope] doux (f douce) ■ **gradually** adv progressivement

**graduate 1.** ['grædʒʊət] n Br [from university] ≃ licencié, -e mf; Am [from high school] ≃ bachelier, -ère mf

**2.** ['grædʒʊeɪt] vi Br [from university] ≃ obtenir sa licence; Am [from high school] ≃ obtenir son baccalauréat; **to graduate from sth to sth** passer de qch à qch ■ **graduation** n UNIV remise f des diplômes

**graffiti** [grə'fiːtɪ] npl graffiti mpl

**graham cracker** ['greɪəm-] n Am biscuit légèrement sucré

**grain** [greɪn] n a) [seed, particle] grain m; [cereals] céréales fpl b) [in wood, leather] grain m

**gram** [græm] n gramme m

**grammar** ['græmə(r)] n grammaire f; Br **grammar school** ≃ lycée m ■ **grammatical** adj grammatical

**gramme** [græm] n gramme m

**grand** [grænd] **1.** (compar -er, superl -est) adj [splendid] grandiose; Fam [excellent] excellent; **grand piano** piano m à queue; **grand total** somme f totale **2.** n inv Br Fam mille livres fpl; Am Fam mille dollars mpl ■ **grandchild** (pl -children) n petit-fils m, petite-fille f; **grandchildren** petits-enfants mpl ■ **grand(d)ad** n Fam papi m ■ **granddaughter** n petite-fille f ■ **grandfather** n grand-père m ■ **grandma** n Fam mamie f ■ **grandmother** n grand-mère f ■ **grandpa** n Fam papi m ■ **grandparents** npl grands-parents mpl ■ **grandson** n petit-fils m

**grandstand** ['grændstænd] n tribune f

**granite** ['grænɪt] n granit m

**granny** ['grænɪ] (pl -ies) n Fam mamie f

**grant** [grɑːnt] **1.** n subvention f; [for student] bourse f **2.** vt accorder (**to** à); [request] accéder à; [prayer, wish] exaucer; [admit] admettre (**that** que); **to take sth for granted** considérer qch comme allant de soi; **to take sb for granted** ne pas avoir d'égard pour qn

**granule** ['grænjuːl] n granule m

**grape** [greɪp] n grain m de raisin; **some grapes** du raisin; **grape juice** jus m de raisin

**grapefruit** ['greɪpfruːt] n pamplemousse m

**graph** 152

**graph** [græf, grɑːf] n graphique m ;
**graph paper** papier m millimétré

**graphic** ['græfɪk] adj [description] très
détaillé ; **graphic artist** graphiste mf
■ **graphics** npl (computer) graphics
graphiques mpl

**grapple** ['græpəl] vi to grapple with
[problem] se débattre avec

**grasp** [grɑːsp] **1.** n [hold] prise f ;
[understanding] compréhension f ;
**within sb's grasp** à la portée de qn **2.** vt
[seize, understand] saisir ■ **grasping**
adj [mean] avide

**grass** [grɑːs] n herbe f ; [lawn] gazon m
■ **grasshopper** n sauterelle f
■ **grassy** adj herbeux, -euse

**grate** [greɪt] **1.** n [for fireplace] grille f
**2.** vt [cheese, carrot] râper **3.** vi [of
sound] grincer ■ **grater** n râpe f
■ **grating 1.** adj [sound] grinçant
**2.** n [bars] grille f

**grateful** ['greɪtfəl] adj reconnaissant
(**to** à ; **for** de) ; [words, letter] de remer-
ciement ■ **gratefully** adv avec reconnaissance

**gratified** ['grætɪfaɪd] adj [pleased]
satisfait (**by** or **with** de ; **to do** de faire)
■ **gratifying** adj très satisfaisant

**gratis** ['grætɪs, 'greɪtɪs] adv gratis

**gratitude** ['grætɪtjuːd] n gratitude f
(**for** de)

**gratuitous** [grə'tjuːɪtəs] adj [act] gratuit

**grave¹** [greɪv] n tombe f ■ **gravestone**
n pierre f tombale ■ **graveyard** n
cimetière m

**grave²** [grɑːv] (compar -er, superl -est)
adj [serious] grave ; [manner, voice]
solennel, -elle

**gravel** ['grævəl] n gravier m ; **gravel path**
allée f de gravier

**gravitate** ['grævɪteɪt] vi to gravitate towards sth [be drawn to] être attiré par
qch ; [move towards] se diriger vers qch

**gravity** ['grævɪtɪ] n a) PHYS [force] pesanteur f b) [seriousness] gravité f

**gravy** ['greɪvɪ] n sauce à base de jus de
viande

**gray** [greɪ] Am adj & n & vi = **grey**

**graze¹** [greɪz] **1.** n [wound] écorchure f
**2.** vt [scrape] écorcher

**graze²** [greɪz] vi [of cattle] paître

**grease** [griːs] **1.** n graisse f **2.** vt graisser ■ **greasy** (compar -ier, superl -iest)
adj graisseux, -euse ; [hair, skin, food]
gras (f grasse)

**great** [greɪt] (compar -er, superl -est) adj
grand ; [effort, heat] gros (f grosse),
grand ; Fam [very good] génial ; Fam **to
be great at tennis** être très doué pour
le tennis ; **a great deal** or **number (of)**,
**a great many** beaucoup (de) ; **Great
Britain** la Grande-Bretagne ; **Greater
London** le grand Londres ■ **great-
grandfather** n arrière-grand-père m
■ **great-grandmother** n arrière-
grand-mère f

**greatly** ['greɪtlɪ] adv très ; [much] beaucoup

**Greece** [griːs] n la Grèce

**greed** [griːd] n avidité f (**for** de) ; [for
food] gourmandise f ■ **greedy** (compar -ier, superl -iest) adj avide (**for** de) ;
[for food] gourmand

**Greek** [griːk] **1.** adj grec (f grecque) **2.** n
[person] Grec m, Grecque f ; [language]
grec m

**green** [griːn] **1.** (compar -er, superl -est) adj
vert ; Fig [immature] inexpérimenté ;
POL écologiste ; **to turn** or **go green**
[of traffic lights] passer au vert ; [of
person, garden, tree] verdir ; Am **green
card** ≃ permis m de travail ; **green tax**
taxe f verte **2.** n [colour] vert m ; [grassy
area] pelouse f ; **greens** [vegetables]
légumes mpl verts ; POL **the Greens**
les Verts mpl ■ **greenery** n verdure f
■ **greengrocer** n Br marchand, -e mf
de fruits et légumes ■ **greenhouse**
n serre f ; **the greenhouse effect** l'effet m de serre ■ **greenlight** ['griːnlaɪt]
vt donner le feu vert à

**greet** [griːt] vt [say hello to] saluer ;
[welcome] accueillir ■ **greeting** n
accueil m ; **greetings** [for birthday,
festival] vœux mpl ; **greetings card**,
Am **greeting card** carte f de vœux

**gregarious** [grɪ'geərɪəs] adj sociable

**GR8** MESSAGING written abbr of **great**

**ground**

**grenade** [grə'neɪd] n [bomb] grenade f

**grew** [gru:] pt of **grow**

**grey** [greɪ] **1.** adj (compar -er, superl -est) gris; **to be going grey** grisonner **2.** n gris m **3.** vi [of hair] grisonner ∎ **grey-haired** adj aux cheveux gris ∎ **greyhound** n lévrier m

**grid** [grɪd] n [bars] grille f; [on map] quadrillage m

**griddle** ['grɪdəl] n [for cooking] tôle f

**gridlock** ['grɪdlɒk] n [traffic jam] embouteillage m

**grief** [gri:f] n chagrin m; **to come to grief** échouer

**grievance** ['gri:vəns] n grief m; **grievances** [complaints] doléances fpl

**grieve** [gri:v] **1.** vt affliger **2.** vi **to grieve for sb/over sth** pleurer qn/qch

**grill** [grɪl] **1.** n [utensil] gril m; [dish] grillade f **2.** vt griller ∎ **grilling** ['grɪlɪŋ] n Br [of food] cuisson f sur le ou au gril

**grille** [grɪl] n [bars] grille f

**grim** [grɪm] (compar grimmer, superl grimmest) adj [stern] sinistre; Fam [bad] lamentable

**grimace** ['grɪməs] **1.** n grimace f **2.** vi grimacer

**grime** [graɪm] n crasse f ∎ **grimy** (compar -ier, superl -iest) adj crasseux, -euse

**grin** [grɪn] **1.** n large sourire m **2.** (pt & pp -nn-) vi avoir un large sourire

**grind** [graɪnd] **1.** n Fam [work] corvée f **2.** (pt & pp ground) vt [coffee, pepper] moudre; Am [meat] hacher **3.** vi **to grind to a halt** s'immobiliser ∎ **grinder** n **coffee grinder** moulin m à café

**grip** [grɪp] **1.** n [hold] prise f; [handle] poignée f; Fig **to get to grips with sth** s'attaquer à qch **2.** (pt & pp -pp-) vt [seize] saisir; [hold] empoigner; **the audience was gripped by the play** la pièce a captivé les spectateurs ∎ **gripping** adj passionnant

**grisly** ['grɪzlɪ] adj [gruesome] horrible

**gristle** ['grɪsəl] n [in meat] nerfs mpl

**grit** [grɪt] **1.** n [sand] sable m; [gravel] gravillons mpl **2.** (pt & pp -tt-) vt **a)** [road] sabler **b) to grit one's teeth** serrer les dents

**groan** [grəʊn] **1.** n [of pain] gémissement m; [of dissatisfaction] grognement m **2.** vi [with pain] gémir; [complain] grogner

**grocer** ['grəʊsə(r)] n épicier, -ère mf; **grocer's (shop)** épicerie f ∎ **groceries** npl [food] provisions fpl ∎ **grocery** (pl -ies) n Am [shop] épicerie f; **grocery shop**, Am **grocery store** épicerie f

**groin** [grɔɪn] n aine f

**groom** [gru:m] **1.** n **a)** [bridegroom] marié m **b)** [for horses] lad m **2.** vt [horse] panser; **to groom sb for sth** préparer qn pour qch

**groove** [gru:v] n [in wood, metal] rainure f; [in record] sillon m

**grope** [grəʊp] vi **to grope (about) for sth** chercher qch à tâtons

**gross** [grəʊs] **1.** adj **a)** [total - weight, income, profit] brut **b)** (compar -er, superl -est) [coarse] grossier, -ère; [injustice] flagrant **2.** n inv grosse f **3.** vt gagner brut ∎ **grossly** adv [negligent] extrêmement; [exaggerated] grossièrement; [unfair] vraiment

**grotesque** [grəʊ'tesk] adj grotesque

**grotto** ['grɒtəʊ] (pl -oes or -os) n grotte f

**grotty** ['grɒtɪ] (compar -ier, superl -iest) adj Br Fam minable

**ground**[1] [graʊnd] **1.** n [earth] terre f, sol m; [land] terrain m; [estate] terres fpl; **grounds** [gardens] parc m; Fig [reasons] motifs mpl; **on the ground** [lying, sitting] par terre; **to gain/lose ground** gagner/perdre du terrain; Br **ground floor** rez-de-chaussée m inv **2.** vt [aircraft] interdire de vol ∎ **grounded** ['graʊndɪd] adj **a) to be grounded** [emotionally stable] avoir les pieds sur terre **b)** être privé de sortie ∎ **grounding** n [basic knowledge] bases fpl (in de) ∎ **groundless** adj sans fondement ∎ **groundsheet** n tapis m de sol ∎ **groundwork** n travail m préparatoire

**ground²** [graʊnd] **1.** *pt & pp of* **grind 2.** *adj* [coffee] moulu ; *Am* **ground beef** steak *m* haché ; *Am* **ground meat** viande *f* hachée **3.** *npl* **(coffee) grounds** marc *m* (de café)

**group** [gruːp] **1.** *n* groupe *m* **2.** *vt to* **group (together)** grouper **3.** *vi* se grouper ■ **grouping** *n* [group] groupe *m*

**grovel** ['grɒvəl] (*Br* -ll-, *Am* -l-) *vi* [be humble] ramper, s'aplatir (**to** devant)

**grow** [grəʊ] **1.** (*pt* grew, *pp* grown) *vt* [vegetables] cultiver ; **to grow a beard** se laisser pousser la barbe **2.** *vi* [of person] grandir ; [of plant, hair] pousser ; [of economy, feeling] croître ; [of firm, town] se développer ; [of gap, family] s'agrandir ; **to grow to like sth** finir par aimer qch ; **when I grow up** quand je serai grand ; **it'll grow on you** [of music, book] tu finiras par t'y intéresser ■ **grower** *n* [person] cultivateur, -trice *mf* (**of** de) ■ **growing** *adj* [child] en pleine croissance ; [number, discontent] grandissant

**growl** [graʊl] **1.** *n* grognement *m* **2.** *vi* grogner (**at** contre)

**grown** [grəʊn] **1.** *pp of* **grow 2.** *adj* [man, woman] adulte

**grown-up** ['grəʊnʌp] **1.** *n* grande personne *f* **2.** *adj* [ideas, behaviour] d'adulte

**growth** [grəʊθ] *n* croissance *f* ; [increase] augmentation *f* (**in** de) ; [lump] grosseur *f* (**on** à)

**grub** [grʌb] *n* **a)** *Fam* [food] bouffe *f* **b)** [insect] larve *f*

**grubby** ['grʌbɪ] (*compar* -ier, *superl* -iest) *adj* sale

**grudge** [grʌdʒ] **1.** *n* rancune *f* ; **to have a grudge against sb** garder rancune à qn **2.** *vt* **to grudge sb sth** [give] donner qch à qn à contrecœur ■ **grudgingly** *adv* à contrecœur

**gruelling**, *Am* **grueling** ['grʊəlɪŋ] *adj* [journey, experience] épuisant

**gruesome** ['gruːsəm] *adj* horrible

**gruff** [grʌf] (*compar* -er, *superl* -est) *adj* bourru

**grumble** ['grʌmbəl] *vi* [complain] grommeler ; **to grumble about sth** rouspéter contre qch

**grumpy** ['grʌmpɪ] (*compar* -ier, *superl* -iest) *adj* grincheux, -euse

**grunt** [grʌnt] **1.** *n* grognement *m* **2.** *vti* grogner

**GTG, G2G** MESSAGING *written abbr of* **got to go**

**GTSY** MESSAGING *written abbr of* **glad to see you**

**guarantee** [gærən'tiː] **1.** *n* garantie *f* **2.** *vt* garantir (**against** contre) ; [vouch for] se porter garant de ; **to guarantee sb that…** garantir à qn que…

**guard** [gɑːd] **1.** *n* [supervision] garde *f* ; [sentry] garde *m* ; [on train] chef *m* de train ; **under guard** sous surveillance ; **on one's guard** sur ses gardes ; **on guard (duty)** de garde ; **to catch sb off (his/her) guard** prendre qn au dépourvu **2.** *vt* [protect] garder **3.** *vt insep* **to guard against** [protect oneself] se prémunir contre ; [prevent] empêcher ; **to guard against doing sth** se garder de faire qch

**guardian** ['gɑːdɪən] *n* [of child] tuteur, -trice *mf* ; [protector] gardien, -enne *mf*

**GUDLUK** MESSAGING *written abbr of* **good luck**

**guerilla, guerrilla** [gə'rɪlə] *n* [person] guérillero *m*

**guess** [ges] **1.** *n* [estimate] estimation *f* ; **to make** *or* **take a guess** deviner ; **at a guess** à vue de nez **2.** *vt* deviner (**that** que) ; [suppose] supposer, croire **3.** *vi* deviner ; **I guess (so)** je crois ■ **guesswork** *n* conjecture *f* ; **by guesswork** au jugé

**guest** [gest] *n* invité, -e *mf* ; [in hotel] client, -e *mf* ; [at meal] convive *mf* ; **guest room** chambre *f* d'amis ; **guest speaker** conférencier, -ère *mf* ■ **guesthouse** *n* pension *f* de famille

**guidance** ['gaɪdəns] *n* [advice] conseils *mpl*

**guide** [gaɪd] **1.** *n* [person] guide *m* ; [indication] indication *f* ; **guide (book)** guide *m* ; *Br* **(Girl) Guide** éclaireuse *f* ; **guide dog** chien *m* d'aveugle

**gyrate**

**2.** *vt* [lead] guider ■ **guided** *adj* [missile] guidé; **guided tour** visite *f* guidée ■ **guidelines** *npl* directives *fpl*

**guild** [gɪld] *n* association *f*

**guilt** [gɪlt] *n* culpabilité *f* ■ **guilty** *(compar -ier, superl -iest) adj* coupable; **to find sb guilty / not guilty** déclarer qn coupable / non coupable

**guinea** ['gɪnɪ] *n* **guinea pig** [animal & Fig] cobaye *m*

**guise** [gaɪz] *n* **under the guise of** sous l'apparence de

**guitar** [gɪ'tɑː(r)] *n* guitare *f* ■ **guitarist** *n* guitariste *mf*

**gulf** [gʌlf] *n* [in sea] golfe *m*; [chasm] gouffre *m* (**between** entre)

**gull** [gʌl] *n* mouette *f*

**gullible** ['gʌlɪbəl] *adj* crédule

**gulp** [gʌlp] **1.** *n* [of drink] gorgée *f*; **in** or **at one gulp** d'un coup **2.** *vt* **to gulp (down)** engloutir **3.** *vi* [with surprise] avoir la gorge serrée

**gum¹** [gʌm] *n* [in mouth] gencive *f*

**gum²** [gʌm] **1.** *n* **a)** [glue] colle *f* **b)** [for chewing] chewing-gum *m* **2.** *(pt & pp -mm-) vt* coller

**gun** [gʌn] **1.** *n* pistolet *m*; [rifle] fusil *m*; [firing shells] canon *m* **2.** *(pt & pp -nn-) vt sep* **to gun down** abattre ■ **gunfire** *n* coups *mpl* de feu; [in battle] tir *m* d'artillerie ■ **gunpowder** *n* poudre *f* à canon ■ **gunshot** *n* coup *m* de feu

**gurgle** ['gɜːgəl] *vi* [of water] gargouiller; [of baby] gazouiller

**gush** [gʌʃ] *vi* **to gush (out)** jaillir (**of** de)

**gust** [gʌst] **1.** *n* [of wind] rafale *f* **2.** *vi* [of wind] souffler par rafales

**gusto** ['gʌstəʊ] *n* **with gusto** avec entrain

**gut** [gʌt] **1.** *n* [inside body] intestin *m*; *Fam* **guts** [insides] entrailles *fpl*; [courage] cran *m* **2.** *(pt & pp -tt-) vt* [of fire] ravager

**gutter** ['gʌtə(r)] *n* [on roof] gouttière *f*; [in street] caniveau *m* ■ **guttering** *n* gouttières *fpl*

**guy** [gaɪ] *n Fam* [man] type *m*

**guzzle** ['gʌzəl] *vt* [eat] engloutir; [drink] siffler

**gym** [dʒɪm] *n* [activity] gym *f*; [gymnasium] gymnase *m*; **gym shoes** chaussures *fpl* de gym ■ **gymnasium** [-'neɪzɪəm] *n* gymnase *m* ■ **gymnastics** *n* gymnastique *f*

**gynaecologist**, *Am* **gynecologist** [gaɪnɪ'kɒlədʒɪst] *n* gynécologue *mf*

**gypsy** ['dʒɪpsɪ] *n* = **gipsy**

**gyrate** [dʒaɪ'reɪt] *vi* tournoyer

# H

**H, h** [eɪtʃ] *n* [letter] H, h *m inv*; **H bomb** bombe *f* H

**habit** ['hæbɪt] *n* **a)** [custom, practice] habitude *f*; **to be in /get into the habit of doing sth** avoir /prendre l'habitude de faire qch; **to make a habit of doing sth** avoir pour habitude de faire qch **b)** *Fam* [addiction] accoutumance *f* **c)** [of monk, nun] habit *m*

**habitat** ['hæbɪtæt] *n* [of animal, plant] habitat *m*

**habitual** [hə'bɪtʃʊəl] *adj* habituel, -elle; [smoker, drunk] invétéré

**hack** [hæk] *vt* [cut] tailler ■ **hack into** *vt insep* COMPUT pirater

**hacker** ['hækə(r)] *n* COMPUT pirate *m* informatique

**hackneyed** ['hæknɪd] *adj* [saying] rebattu

**hacktivism** ['hæktɪˌvɪzəm] *n* hacktivisme *m* ■ **hacktivist** ['hæktɪˌvɪst] *n* hacktiviste *mf*

**had** [hæd] *pt & pp of* **have**

**haemorrhage,** *Am* **hemorrhage** ['hemərɪdʒ] *n* hémorragie *f*

**haemorrhoids,** *Am* **hemorrhoids** ['hemərɔɪdz] *npl* MED hémorroïdes *fpl*

**hag** [hæg] *n Pej* **(old) hag** vieille taupe *f*

**haggard** ['hægəd] *adj* hâve

**haggle** ['hægəl] *vi* marchander; **to haggle over the price of sth** chicaner sur le prix de qch ■ **haggling** *n* marchandage *m*

**Hague** [heɪg] *n* **The Hague** La Haye

**hail¹** [heɪl] **1.** *n* grêle *f* **2.** *vi* **it's hailing** il grêle

**hail²** [heɪl] **1.** *vt* [greet] saluer (**as** comme); [taxi] héler **2.** *vt insep* **to hail from** [of person] être originaire de

**hair** [heə(r)] *n* [on head] cheveux *mpl*; [on body, of animal] poils *mpl*; **a hair** [on head] un cheveu; [on body, of animal] un poil; **by a hair's breadth** de justesse; **hair conditioner** après-shampooing *m*; **hair wax** cire *f* pour les cheveux ■ **hairbrush** *n* brosse *f* à cheveux ■ **haircut** *n* coupe *f* de cheveux; **to have a haircut** se faire couper les cheveux ■ **hairdo** *(pl* -*dos)* *n Fam* coiffure *f* ■ **hairdresser** *n* coiffeur, -euse *mf* ■ **hairdryer** *n* sèche-cheveux *m inv* ■ **hairgrip** *n* pince *f* à cheveux ■ **hairnet** *n* résille *f* ■ **hairpin** *n* épingle *f* à cheveux; **hairpin bend** [in road] virage *m* en épingle à cheveux ■ **hairspray** *n* laque *f* ■ **hairstyle** *n* coiffure *f*

**-haired** [heəd] *suff* **long- /red-haired** aux cheveux longs /roux

**hairy** ['heərɪ] *(compar* -**ier,** *superl* -**iest)** *adj* [person, animal, body] poilu

**HAK** *(abbr of* **hugs and kisses)** MESSAGING biz

**half** [hɑːf, *Am* hæf] **1.** *(pl* **halves** [*Br* hɑːvz, *Am* hævz]) *n* moitié *f*; [part of match] mi-temps *f*; *Br* [half fare] demi-tarif *m*; *Br* [beer] demi *m*; **half (of) the apple** la moitié de la pomme; **half past one** une heure et demie; **ten and a half** dix et demi; **half a dozen** une demi-douzaine; **to cut in half** couper en deux **2.** *adj* demi; **half board** demi-pension *f*; **half fare** demi-tarif *m*; **at half price** à moitié prix **3.** *adv* [dressed, full, asleep] à moitié; **half as much as** moitié moins que ■ **half-baked** [-'beɪkt] *adj Fam Fig* [idea] à la noix; [project] mal conçu; **they made a half-baked attempt to improve security** ils ont vaguement essayé d'améliorer la sécurité ■ **half-bottle** *n* demi-bouteille *f* ■ **half-brother** *n* demi-

frère *m* ■ **half-caste** *n* métis, -isse *mf*
■ **half-day** *n* demi-journée *f* ■ **half-hearted** *adj* [person, manner] peu enthousiaste ■ **half-hour** *n* demi-heure *f* ■ **half-light** *n* demi-jour *m* ■ **half-open** *adj* entrouvert ■ **half-price** *adj* & *adv* à moitié prix ■ **half-sister** *n* demi-sœur *f* ■ **half-term** *n* *Br* SCH congé *m* de milieu de trimestre ■ **half-time** *n* [in game] mi-temps *f* ■ **halfway** *adv* [between places] à mi-chemin (**between** entre)

**hall** [hɔ:l] *n* [room] salle *f* ; [entrance room] entrée *f* ; [of hotel] hall *m* ; [mansion] manoir *m* ; *Br* UNIV **hall of residence** résidence *f* universitaire

**hallelujah** [hælɪˈluːjə] *n* & *excl* alléluia *(m)*

**hallo** [həˈləʊ] *excl* = **hello**

**Hallowe'en** [hæləʊˈiːn] *n* veille de la Toussaint durant laquelle les enfants se déguisent en fantôme ou en sorcière

**hallucination** [həluːsɪˈneɪʃən] *n* hallucination *f*

**hallway** [ˈhɔ:lweɪ] *n* vestibule *m*, entrée *f*

**halo** [ˈheɪləʊ] *(pl* **-oes** *or* **-os)** *n* auréole *f*

**halt** [hɔ:lt] **1.** *n* halte *f* ; **to come to a halt** s'arrêter **2.** *excl* halte ! **3.** *vt* arrêter **4.** *vi* [of soldiers] faire halte ; [of production] s'arrêter

**halve** [hɑːv] *vt* [reduce by half] réduire de moitié ; [divide in two] diviser en deux

**ham** [hæm] *n* [meat] jambon *m* ; **ham and eggs** œufs *mpl* au jambon

**hamburger** [ˈhæmbɜːgə(r)] *n* hamburger *m*

**hammer** [ˈhæmə(r)] **1.** *n* marteau *m* **2.** *vt* [nail] enfoncer (**into** dans) ; [metal] marteler ; *Fam* [defeat] écraser ; **to hammer sth out** [agreement, plan] mettre au point qch

**hammock** [ˈhæmək] *n* hamac *m*

**hamper** [ˈhæmpə(r)] **1.** *n* *Br* [for food] panier *m* ; *Am* [laundry basket] panier *m* à linge **2.** *vt* [hinder] gêner

**hamster** [ˈhæmstə(r)] *n* hamster *m*

**hand¹** [hænd] **1.** *n* **a)** [part of the body] main *f* ; **to hold sth in one's hand** tenir qch à la main ; **to hold hands** se tenir par la main ; **by hand** [make, sew] à la main ; **on the one hand…** d'une part… ; **on the other hand…** d'autre part… ; **to lend sb a (helping) hand** donner un coup de main à qn ; **to get out of hand** [of child] devenir impossible ; [of situation] devenir incontrôlable ; **hand in hand** la main dans la main **b)** [of clock] aiguille *f* ; [in card game] jeu *m* ; [style of writing] écriture *f* **2.** *adj* [luggage, grenade] à main ; [cream, lotion] pour les mains ■ **handbag** *n* sac *m* à main ■ **handball** *n* handball *m* ■ **handbook** *n* [manual] manuel *m* ; [guide] guide *m* ■ **handbrake** *n* frein *m* à main ■ **handmade** *adj* fait à la main ■ **hands-free** [hænds-] *adj* [phone] mains libres ■ **handshake** *n* poignée *f* de main ■ **hands-on** *adj* [experience] pratique ■ **handwriting** *n* écriture *f* ■ **handwritten** *adj* écrit à la main

**hand²** [hænd] *vt* [give] donner (**to** à) ; **to hand sth in** remettre qch ; **to hand sth out** distribuer qch ; **to hand sth over** remettre qch ; **to hand sth round** faire circuler qch

**handful** [ˈhændfʊl] *n* [bunch, group] poignée *f*

**handicap** [ˈhændɪkæp] **1.** *n* [disadvantage, in sport] handicap *m* ; **handicap accessible** accessible aux handicapés **2.** *(pt* & *pp* **-pp-)** *vt* handicaper ■ **handicapped** *adj* [disabled] handicapé

**handicraft** [ˈhændɪkrɑːft] *n* [skill] artisanat *m*

**H&K** *(abbr of* **hugs and kisses)** MESSAGING biz

**handkerchief** [ˈhæŋkətʃɪf] *(pl* **-chiefs)** *n* mouchoir *m*

**handle** [ˈhændəl] **1.** *n* [of door] poignée *f* ; [of knife] manche *m* ; [of cup] anse *f* ; [of saucepan] queue *f* **2.** *vt* [manipulate] manier ; [touch] toucher à ; [deal with] s'occuper de ; [vehicle] manœuvrer ; [difficult child] s'y prendre avec

**handout** [ˈhændaʊt] *n* [leaflet] prospectus *m* ; [money] aumône *f*

**handsome** ['hænsəm] *adj* [person, building] beau (*f* belle) ; [profit, sum] considérable ∎ **handsomely** *adv* [generously] généreusement

**handy** ['hændɪ] *(compar* -ier, *superl* -iest) *adj* [convenient] commode ; [useful] pratique ; [skilful] habile (**at doing** à faire) ; **to come in handy** être utile ; **the flat is handy for the shops** l'appartement est près des commerces ∎ **handyman** *(pl* -men) *n* homme *m* à tout faire

**hang¹** [hæŋ] **1.** *n Fam* **to get the hang of sth** piger qch **2.** *(pt & pp* hung) *vt* suspendre (**on /from** à) ; [on hook] accrocher (**on or from** à) ; [wallpaper] poser **3.** *vi* [dangle] pendre ∎ **hanging** *adj* suspendu (**from** à) ; **hanging on the wall** accroché au mur ∎ **hang-up** *n Fam* complexe *m* ∎ **hang about, hang around** *vi* [loiter] traîner ; *Fam* [wait] poireauter ∎ **hang down** *vi* [dangle] pendre ∎ **hang on** *vi* [hold out] tenir le coup ; *Fam* [wait] patienter ; **to hang on to sth** garder qch ∎ **hang out 1.** *vt sep* [washing] étendre **2.** *vi* [from pocket, box] dépasser ; *Fam* [spend time] traîner ∎ **hang together** *vi* [of facts] se tenir ∎ **hang up 1.** *vt sep* [picture] accrocher **2.** *vi* [on phone] raccrocher

**hang²** [hæŋ] *(pt & pp* hanged) *vt* [criminal] pendre (**for** pour)

**hanger** ['hæŋə(r)] *n* (coat) hanger cintre *m*

**hang-glider** ['hæŋglaɪdə(r)] *n* Deltaplane *m* ∎ **hang-gliding** *n* vol *m* libre

**hangover** ['hæŋəʊvə(r)] *n Fam* gueule *f* de bois

**hankie, hanky** ['hæŋkɪ] *(pl* -ies) *n Fam* mouchoir *m*

**haphazard** [hæp'hæzəd] *adj* [choice, decision] pris au hasard

**happen** ['hæpən] *vi* arriver, se produire ; **to happen to sb** arriver à qn ; **do you happen to have…?** est-ce que par hasard vous avez… ?

**happily** ['hæpɪlɪ] *adv* joyeusement ; [contentedly] tranquillement ; [fortunately] heureusement

**happiness** ['hæpɪnəs] *n* bonheur *m*

**happy** ['hæpɪ] *(compar* -ier, *superl* -iest) *adj* heureux, -euse (**to do** de faire ; **about** de) ; **Happy New Year!** bonne année ! ; **Happy Christmas!** joyeux Noël ! ; **happy birthday!** joyeux anniversaire ! ∎ **happy-go-lucky** *adj* insouciant

**harass** [*Br* 'hærəs, *Am* hə'ræs] *vt* harceler ∎ **harassment** *n* harcèlement *m*

**harbour**, *Am* **harbor** ['hɑ:bə(r)] **1.** *n* port *m* **2.** *vt* [fugitive] cacher ; [hope, suspicion] nourrir

**hard** [hɑ:d] *(compar* -er, *superl* -est) **1.** *adj* [not soft, severe] dur ; [difficult] difficile, dur ; [water] calcaire ; **to be hard on sb** être dur avec qn ; **to be hard of hearing** être dur d'oreille ; *Fam* **hard up** [broke] fauché ; COMPUT **hard copy** sortie *f* papier ; COMPUT **hard disk** disque *m* dur ; **hard drugs** drogues *fpl* dures ; **hard shoulder** [on motorway] bande *f* d'arrêt d'urgence **2.** *adv* [work] dur ; [pull, push, hit] fort ; [study] assidûment ; [rain] à verse ; **to think hard** réfléchir bien ; **to try hard** faire de son mieux ; **hard at work** en plein travail ∎ **hardback** *n* livre *m* relié ∎ **hardball** *n* [game] base-ball *m* ; [ball] balle *f* de base-ball ∎ **hardboard** *n* aggloméré *m* ∎ **hard-boiled** *adj* [egg] dur ∎ **hardcover** ['hɑ:d,kʌvə(r)] *n* = **hardback** ∎ **hard-earned** *adj* [money] durement gagné ; [rest] bien mérité ∎ **hard-hit** *adj* gravement atteint *ou* touché ∎ **hard-wearing** *adj* résistant ∎ **hard-working** *adj* travailleur, -euse

**harden** ['hɑ:dən] **1.** *vt* endurcir ; **to become hardened to sth** s'endurcir à qch **2.** *vi* [of substance, attitude] durcir

**hardly** ['hɑ:dlɪ] *adv* à peine ; **I had hardly arrived when…** j'étais à peine arrivé que… ; **hardly anyone /anything** presque personne /rien ; **hardly ever** presque jamais

**hardware** ['hɑ:dweə(r)] *n inv* quincaillerie *f* ; COMPUT & MIL matériel *m* ; **hardware shop**, *Am* **hardware store** quincaillerie *f*

**hardy** ['hɑ:dɪ] *(compar* -ier, *superl* -iest) *adj* résistant

**hare** [heə(r)] *n* lièvre *m*

**harm** [hɑːm] **1.** *n* [hurt] mal *m*; [wrong] tort *m*; **to do sb harm** faire du mal à qn **2.** *vt* [physically] faire du mal à; [health, interests, cause] nuire à; [object] abîmer ■ **harmful** *adj* [influence] néfaste; [substance] nocif, -ive ■ **harmless** *adj* [person] inoffensif, -ive; [hobby, joke] innocent

**harmonica** [hɑːˈmɒnɪkə] *n* harmonica *m*

**harmonious** [hɑːˈməʊnɪəs] *adj* harmonieux, -euse

**harmonize** [ˈhɑːmənaɪz] **1.** *vt* harmoniser **2.** *vi* s'harmoniser

**harmony** [ˈhɑːmənɪ] *(pl* -**ies**) *n* harmonie *f*

**harness** [ˈhɑːnɪs] **1.** *n* [for horse, baby] harnais *m* **2.** *vt* [horse] harnacher; *Fig* [resources] exploiter

**harp** [hɑːp] **1.** *n* harpe *f* **2.** *vi Fam* **to harp on about sth** revenir sans arrêt sur qch

**harrowing** [ˈhærəʊɪŋ] *adj* [story] poignant; [experience] très éprouvant

**harsh** [hɑːʃ] *(compar* -**er**, *superl* -**est**) *adj* [person, treatment] dur; [winter, climate] rude; [sound, voice] strident; [light] cru; **to be harsh with sb** être dur envers qn

**harvest** [ˈhɑːvɪst] **1.** *n* moisson *f*; [of fruit] récolte *f* **2.** *vt* moissonner; [fruit] récolter

**has** [hæz] *see* **have**

**has-been** [ˈhæzbiːn] *n Fam & Pej* has-been *mf inv*

**hashish** [ˈhæʃiːʃ] *n* haschisch *m*

**hash key** *n* touche *f* dièse

**hashtag** [ˈhæʃtæg] *n* hashtag *m*

**hassle** [ˈhæsəl] *n Fam* embêtements *mpl*

**haste** [heɪst] *n* hâte *f*; **in haste** à la hâte; **to make haste** se hâter

**hasten** [ˈheɪsən] **1.** *vt* hâter **2.** *vi* se hâter **(to do** de faire)

**hasty** [ˈheɪstɪ] *(compar* -**ier**, *superl* -**iest**) *adj* [departure] précipité; [visit] rapide; [decision] hâtif, -ive ■ **hastily** *adv* [write, prepare] hâtivement; [say] précipitamment

**hat** [hæt] *n* chapeau *m*; [of child] bonnet *m*

**hatch** [hætʃ] **1.** *n Br* [in kitchen] passeplat *m* **2.** *vt* faire éclore; *Fig* [plot] tramer **3.** *vi* [of chick, egg] éclore

**hatchback** [ˈhætʃbæk] *n* [car - three-door] trois-portes *f inv*; [five-door] cinq-portes *f inv*

**hate** [heɪt] **1.** *n* haine *f* **2.** *vt* haïr, détester; **to hate doing** *or* **to do sth** détester faire qch ■ **hateful** *adj* odieux, -euse

**hatred** [ˈheɪtrɪd] *n* haine *f*

**haughty** [ˈhɔːtɪ] *(compar* -**ier**, *superl* -**iest**) *adj* hautain

**haul** [hɔːl] **1.** *n* [fish caught] prise *f*; [of thief] butin *m*; **a long haul** [trip] un long voyage **2.** *vt* [pull] tirer

**haunt** [hɔːnt] **1.** *n* [place] lieu *m* de rendez-vous; [of criminal] repaire *m* **2.** *vt* hanter ■ **haunted** *adj* [house] hanté

**have** [hæv] *(3rd person sing present tense* **has**) *(pt & pp* **had**, *pres p* **having**) **1.** *vt* avoir; [meal, bath, lesson] prendre; **he has (got) a big house** il a une grande maison; **she doesn't have** *or* **hasn't got a car** elle n'a pas de voiture; **to have a drink** prendre un verre; **to have a walk/dream** faire une promenade/un rêve; **to have a wash** se laver; **to have a pleasant holiday** passer d'agréables vacances; **to have flu** avoir la grippe; **will you have some tea?** est-ce que tu veux du thé?; **to let sb have sth** donner qch à qn; *Fam* **you've had it!** tu es fichu!; *Fam* **I've been had** [cheated] je me suis fait avoir; **to have gloves/a dress on** porter des gants/une robe; **to have sb over** *or* **round** inviter qn chez soi

**2.** *v aux* avoir; [with 'entrer', 'monter', 'sortir' etc & pronominal verbs] être; **to have decided** avoir décidé; **to have gone** être allé; **to have cut oneself** s'être coupé; **she has been punished** elle a été punie, on l'a punie; **I've got to go, I have to go** je dois partir, il faut que je parte; **I don't have to go** je ne suis pas obligé de partir; **to have sb do sth** faire faire qch à qn; **to have one's hair cut** se faire couper les cheveux; **he's had his**

suitcase brought up il a fait monter sa valise; **I've had my car stolen** on m'a volé mon auto; **I've been doing it for months** je le fais depuis des mois; **you have told him, haven't you?** tu le lui as dit, n'est-ce pas ?; **you've seen this film before — no I haven't!** tu as déjà vu ce film — mais non !; **you haven't done the dishes — yes I have!** tu n'as pas fait la vaisselle — mais si, je l'ai faite !; **after he had eaten** or **after having eaten, he left** après avoir mangé, il partit

■ **have on** vt sep a) [be wearing] porter b) Br Fam [fool] **to have sb on** faire marcher qn c) [have arranged] **to have a lot on** avoir beaucoup à faire; **to have nothing on** n'avoir rien de prévu
■ **have out** vt sep a) [have removed] **to have a tooth out** se faire arracher une dent b) [resolve] **to have it out with sb** s'expliquer avec qn

**haven** ['heɪvən] n refuge m

**haven't** ['hævənt] = have not

**havoc** ['hævək] n ravages mpl; **to wreak** or **cause havoc** faire des ravages

**hawk** [hɔːk] n faucon m

**hay** [heɪ] n foin m ■ **hayfever** n rhume m des foins ■ **haystack** n meule f de foin

**haywire** ['heɪwaɪə(r)] adj **to go haywire** [of machine] se détraquer; [of plan] mal tourner

**hazard** ['hæzəd] 1. n risque m; Br AUTO **hazard (warning) lights** feux mpl de détresse 2. vt [remark] risquer ■ **hazardous** adj dangereux, -euse

**haze** [heɪz] n brume f

**hazelnut** ['heɪzəlnʌt] n noisette f

**Hazmat** ['hæzmæt] n Am abbr of **hazardous material** ■ **Hazmat suit** n Am combinaison f de protection chimique

**hazy** ['heɪzɪ] (compar -ier, superl -iest) adj [weather] brumeux, -euse; [photo, idea] flou

**HD** adj a) COMPUT (abbr of **high density**) HD b) (abbr of **high definition**) HD ■ **HDTV** (abbr of **high-definition television**) n TVHD f ■ **HDV** (abbr of **high definition video**) n HDV m

**he** [hiː] 1. pron il; [stressed] lui; **he's a happy man** c'est un homme heureux; **he and I** lui et moi 2. n Fam **it's a he** [baby] c'est un garçon

**head** [hed] 1. n [of person, hammer] tête f; [leader] chef m; Br [of school] directeur, -trice mf; [of bed] chevet m, tête f; **head of hair** chevelure f; **head of state** chef m d'État; **head first** la tête la première; **at the head of** [in charge of] à la tête de; **it didn't enter my head** ça ne m'est pas venu à l'esprit (**that** que); **heads or tails?** pile ou face ?; **per head, a head** [each] par personne 2. adj **head office** siège m social; **head waiter** maître m d'hôtel 3. vt [group, firm] être à la tête de; [list, poll] être en tête de; **to head sb off** détourner qn de son chemin; **to head sth off** éviter qch 4. vi **to head for, to be heading for** [place] se diriger vers ■ **headache** n mal m de tête; Fig [problem] casse-tête m inv; **to have a headache** avoir mal à la tête ■ **head band, headband** ['hedbænd] n Am bandeau m ■ **headlamp, headlight** n [of vehicle] phare m ■ **headline** n [of newspaper, TV news] titre m ■ **headlong** adv [fall] la tête la première; [rush] tête baissée ■ **headmaster** n Br [of school] directeur m ■ **headmistress** n Br [of school] directrice f ■ **head-on** adv & adj de front ■ **headphones** npl écouteurs mpl; **headphone jack** prise f casque ■ **headquarters** npl [of company, political party] siège m (social); [of army, police] quartier m général, QG m ■ **headrest** n appuie-tête m inv ■ **headscarf** (pl -scarves) n foulard m ■ **headstrong** adj têtu

**headed** ['hedɪd] adj Br **headed (note) paper** papier m à en-tête

**header** ['hedə(r)] n [in football] (coup m de) tête f

**heading** ['hedɪŋ] n [of chapter, page] titre m; [of subject] rubrique f; [printed on letter] en-tête m

**heady** ['hedɪ] (compar -ier, superl -iest) adj [wine, perfume] capiteux, -euse; [atmosphere] enivrant

**heal** [hi:l] **1.** *vt* [wound] cicatriser **2.** *vi* to heal (up) [of wound] cicatriser

**health** [helθ] *n* santé *f*; **in good / bad health** en bonne / mauvaise santé; **health care** services *mpl* médicaux; **health club** club *m* de remise en forme; **health food shop** *or Am* **store** magasin *m* de produits biologiques; **health resort** station *f* climatique; *Br* **the (National) Health Service** ≃ la Sécurité sociale

**healthy** ['helθɪ] (compar -ier, superl -iest) *adj* [person] en bonne santé; [food, attitude] sain; [appetite] robuste

**heap** [hi:p] **1.** *n* tas *m*; *Fam* **heaps of** [money, people] des tas de **2.** *vt* entasser; **to heap sth on sb** [praise, gifts] couvrir qn de qch; [insults, work] accabler qn de qch

**hear** [hɪə(r)] (pt & pp heard [hɜ:d]) **1.** *vt* entendre; [listen to] écouter; [learn] apprendre (**that** que); **I heard him come** *or* **coming** je l'ai entendu venir; **have you heard the news?** connais-tu la nouvelle ?; **hear, hear!** bravo ! **2.** *vi* entendre; **to hear from sb** avoir des nouvelles de qn; **I've heard of him** j'ai entendu parler de lui

**hearing** ['hɪərɪŋ] *n* **a)** [sense] ouïe *f*; **hearing aid** audiophone *m* **b)** [of committee] séance *f*; [inquiry] audition *f*

**hearse** [hɜ:s] *n* corbillard *m*

**heart** [hɑ:t] *n* cœur *m*; **hearts** [in card games] cœur *m*; **(off) by heart** [know] par cœur; **at heart** au fond; **heart attack** crise *f* cardiaque; **heart disease** maladie *f* de cœur; **heart transplant** greffe *f* du cœur ■ **heartache** *n* chagrin *m* ■ **heartbeat** *n* battement *m* de cœur; *MED* pulsation *f* cardiaque ■ **heartbreaking** *adj* navrant ■ **heartbroken** *adj* inconsolable

**heartening** ['hɑ:tənɪŋ] *adj* encourageant

**hearth** [hɑ:θ] *n* foyer *m*

**hearty** ['hɑ:tɪ] (compar -ier, superl -iest) *adj* [appetite, meal] gros (*f* grosse)

**heat** [hi:t] **1.** *n* **a)** chaleur *f*; [heating] chauffage *m*; [of oven] température *f*; **on a low heat** [cook] à feu doux; **heat wave** vague *f* de chaleur **b)** [in competition] éliminatoire *f* **2.** *vti* to heat (up) chauffer ■ **heated** *adj* [swimming pool] chauffé; [argument] animé ■ **heating** *n* chauffage *m*

**heater** ['hi:tə(r)] *n* radiateur *m*

**heath** [hi:θ] *n* [land] lande *f*

**heather** ['heðə(r)] *n* bruyère *f*

**heave** [hi:v] *vt* [lift] soulever avec effort; [pull] tirer fort; *Fam* [throw] balancer

**heaven** ['hevən] *n* paradis *m*, ciel *m*; *Fam* **good heavens!** mon Dieu !

**heavily** ['hevɪlɪ] *adv* [walk, tax] lourdement; [breathe] bruyamment; [smoke, drink] beaucoup; **heavily in debt** lourdement endetté; **to rain heavily** pleuvoir à verse; **to be heavily defeated** subir une lourde défaite

**heavy** ['hevɪ] (compar -ier, superl -iest) *adj* lourd; [work, cold] gros (*f* grosse); [blow] violent; [rain] fort; [traffic] dense; [timetable, schedule] chargé; **to be a heavy drinker / smoker** boire / fumer beaucoup ■ **heavyweight** *n* [in boxing] poids *m* lourd; *Fig* personnage *m* important

**Hebrew** ['hi:bru:] *n* [language] hébreu *m*

**heck** [hek] *n* *Fam* zut !; **a heck of a lot** des masses (**of** de)

**heckle** ['hekəl] *vt* interpeller ■ **heckling** *n* chahut *m*

**hectic** ['hektɪk] *adj* [busy] agité; [eventful] mouvementé

**he'd** [hi:d] = he had, he would

**hedge** [hedʒ] **1.** *n* [in garden, field] haie *f* **2.** *vi* [answer evasively] ne pas se mouiller

**hedgehog** ['hedʒhɒg] *n* hérisson *m*

**hedgerow** ['hedʒrəʊ] *n* *Br* haie *f*

**heed** [hi:d] **1.** *n* **to pay heed to sth, to take heed of sth** tenir compte de qch **2.** *vt* tenir compte de

**heel** [hi:l] *n* [of foot, shoe] talon *m*

**hefty** ['heftɪ] (compar -ier, superl -iest) *adj* [large, heavy] gros (*f* grosse); [person] costaud

**height** [haɪt] *n* hauteur *f*; [of person] taille *f*; [of mountain, aircraft] altitude *f*; **the height of** [success, fame, glory] l'apogée *m* de; [folly] le comble de; **at the height of** [summer, storm] au cœur de

**H8** MESSAGING *written abbr of* **hate**

**heighten** ['haɪtən] *vt* [tension, interest] augmenter

**heir** [eə(r)] *n* héritier *m*; **to be heir to sth** être l'héritier de qch ◼ **heiress** *n* héritière *f* ◼ **heirloom** *n* **a family heirloom** un objet de famille

**held** [held] *pt & pp of* **hold**

**helicopter** ['helɪkɒptə(r)] *n* hélicoptère *m* ◼ **heliport** *n* héliport *m*

**hell** [hel] **1.** *n* **a)** *Lit & Fig* enfer *m* **b)** *Fam* [for emphasis] **he's a hell of a nice guy** c'est un type vachement sympa; **what/where/why the hell...?** que/où/pourquoi..., bon sang ?; *Fam* **it was a journey from hell!** ce voyage, c'était l'horreur ! **c)** *Fam* **to do sth for the hell of it** faire qch pour le plaisir, faire qch juste comme ça; *Fam* **to give sb hell** [verbally] engueuler qn; *v Fam* **go to hell!** va te faire foutre ! **2.** *excl Fam* merde !, zut !

**he'll** [hiːl] = **he will**

**hello** [hə'ləʊ] *excl* bonjour !; [answering phone] allô !

**helm** [helm] *n* [of ship] barre *f*

**helmet** ['helmɪt] *n* casque *m*

**help** [help] **1.** *n* aide *f*; *Br* [cleaning woman] femme *f* de ménage; [office or shop workers] employés, -es *mfpl*; **with the help of sth** à l'aide de qch; **help!** au secours !; COMPUT **help button** case *f* d'aide; COMPUT **help menu** menu *m* d'aide; **hired help** [for housework] aide *f* ménagère **2.** *vt* aider; **to help sb do** *or* **to do sth** aider qn à faire qch; **to help oneself (to sth)** se servir (de qch); **to help sb out** aider qn; **I can't help laughing** je ne peux pas m'empêcher de rire **3.** *vi* aider ◼ **helper** *n* assistant, -e *mf* ◼ **helping** *n* [serving] portion *f*

**helpful** ['helpfəl] *adj* [person] serviable; [useful] utile

**helpless** ['helpləs] *adj* [powerless] impuissant

**helpline** ['helplaɪn] *n* service *m* d'assistance téléphonique

**hem** [hem] **1.** *n* ourlet *m* **2.** *(pt & pp -mm-) vt* [garment] ourler; **to be hemmed in** [surrounded] être cerné (**by** de)

**hemisphere** ['hemɪsfɪə(r)] *n* hémisphère *m*

**hemorrhage** ['hemərɪdʒ] *Am n* = **haemorrhage**

**hemorrhoids** ['hemərɔɪdz] *Am npl* = **haemorrhoids**

**hen** [hen] *n* poule *f*; *Fam* **hen night, hen party** soirée *f* entre copines

**hence** [hens] *adv* **a)** [thus] d'où **b)** [from now] **ten years hence** d'ici dix ans

**her** [hɜː(r)] **1.** *pron* **a)** la, l'; [after prep, 'than', 'it is'] elle; **(to) her** [indirect] lui; **I saw her** je l'ai vue; **I gave it (to) her** je le lui ai donné **2.** *poss adj* son, sa, *pl* ses

**herb** [*Br* hɜːb, *Am* ɜːb] *n* herbe *f* aromatique ◼ **herbal** [*Br* 'hɜːbl, *Am* 'ɜːbl] *adj* à base de plantes; **herbal tea** tisane *f*

**herd** [hɜːd] **1.** *n* troupeau *m* **2.** *vt* [cattle, people] rassembler

**here** [hɪə(r)] **1.** *adv* ici; **here it/he is** le voici; **here she comes!** la voilà !; **here is a good example** voici un bon exemple; **I won't be here tomorrow** je ne serai pas là demain; **here and there** çà et là; **here you are!** [take this] tenez ! **2.** *excl* **here!** [giving sb sth] tenez ! ◼ **hereabouts** *adv* par ici

**hereditary** [hɪ'redɪtərɪ] *adj* héréditaire

**heritage** ['herɪtɪdʒ] *n* patrimoine *m*

**hero** ['hɪərəʊ] *(pl -oes) n* héros *m* ◼ **heroic** *adj* héroïque ◼ **heroine** *n* héroïne *f*

**heroin** ['herəʊɪn] *n* [drug] héroïne *f*

**heron** ['herən] *n* héron *m*

**herring** ['herɪŋ] *n* hareng *m*

**hers** [hɜːz] *poss pron* le sien, la sienne, *pl* les sien(ne)s; **this hat is hers** ce chapeau est à elle *ou* est le sien; **a friend of hers** un ami à elle

**herself** [hɜː'self] *pron* elle-même; [reflexive] se, s'; [after prep] elle; **she cut herself** elle s'est coupée

**hesitant** ['hezɪtənt] *adj* hésitant

**hesitate** ['hezɪteɪt] **1.** *vt* to hesitate to do sth hésiter à faire qch **2.** *vi* hésiter (**over** *or* **about** sur) ■ **hesitation** *n* hésitation *f*

**heterosexual** [hetərə'seksʃʊəl] *adj* & *n* hétérosexuel, -elle *(mf)*

**hexagon** ['heksəgən] *n* hexagone *m*

**hey** [heɪ] *excl* [calling sb] hé !, ohé ! ; [expressing surprise, annoyance] ho !

**hi** [haɪ] *excl Fam* salut !

**hibernate** ['haɪbəneɪt] *vi* hiberner

**hiccup, hiccough** ['hɪkʌp] **1.** *n* hoquet *m* ; *Fig* [in plan] accroc *m* ; **to have (the) hiccups** *or* **(the) hiccoughs** avoir le hoquet **2.** *vi* hoqueter

**hide**¹ [haɪd] *(pt* hid [hɪd], *pp* hidden [hɪdən]*)* **1.** *vt* cacher (**from** à) **2.** *vi* to hide (**away** *or* **out**) se cacher (**from** de)

**hide**² [haɪd] *n* [skin] peau *f* ■ **hide-and-seek** *n* to play hide-and-seek jouer à cache-cache

**hideaway** ['haɪdəweɪ] *n* cachette *f*

**hideous** ['hɪdɪəs] *adj* [ugly] hideux, -euse ; [horrific] horrible

**hide-out** ['haɪdaʊt] *n* cachette *f*

**hiding**¹ ['haɪdɪŋ] *n* to go into hiding se cacher ; **hiding place** cachette *f*

**hiding**² ['haɪdɪŋ] *n Fam* a good hiding [thrashing] une bonne raclée

**hierarchy** ['haɪərɑːkɪ] *(pl* -ies) *n* hiérarchie *f*

**hi-fi** ['haɪfaɪ] **1.** *n* [system, equipment] chaîne *f* hi-fi **2.** *adj* hi-fi *inv*

**high** [haɪ] **1.** *(compar* -er, *superl* -est) *adj* haut ; [speed] grand ; [price, standards] élevé ; [number, ideal] grand, élevé ; [voice, tone] aigu *(f* aiguë) ; *Fam* [on drugs] défoncé ; **to be 5 metres high** avoir 5 mètres de haut ; *Fam* **to get on one's high horse** monter sur ses grands chevaux ; **it is high time that you went** il est grand temps que tu y ailles ; **high jump** [sporting event] saut *m* en hauteur ; **high school** ≃ lycée *m* ; *Br* **high street** grand-rue *f* ; **high tide** marée *f* haute **2.** *adv* **high (up)** [fly, throw, aim] haut **3.** *n* **a new high, an all-time high** [peak] un nouveau record

■ **highchair** *n* chaise *f* haute ■ **high-class** *adj* [service] de premier ordre ; [person] raffiné ■ **high-definition** *adj* à haute définition ■ **high-fibre** *adj* [food, diet] riche en fibres ■ **high-powered** *adj* [engine, car] très puissant ; [job] à hautes responsabilités ■ **high-profile** *adj* [person] très en vue ; [campaign] de grande envergure ■ **high-res** [haɪrez] *adj Fam abbr of* **high-resolution** ■ **high-rise** *adj Br* **high-rise building** tour *f* ■ **high-speed** *adj* ultrarapide ; **high-speed train** train *m* à grande vitesse ■ **high-tech** *adj* [appliance] perfectionné ; [industry] de pointe

**highbrow** ['haɪbraʊ] *adj* & *n* intellectuel, -elle *(mf)*

**higher** ['haɪə(r)] **1.** *adj* [number, speed, quality] supérieur (**than** à) ; **higher education** enseignement *m* supérieur **2.** *adv* [fly, aim] plus haut (**than** que)

**highlands** ['haɪləndz] *npl* régions *fpl* montagneuses

**highlight** ['haɪlaɪt] **1.** *n* [of visit, day] point *m* culminant ; [of show] clou *m* ; [in hair] reflet *m* **2.** *vt* souligner ; [with marker & COMPUT] surligner

**highly** ['haɪlɪ] *adv* [very] très ; [recommend] chaudement ; **highly paid** très bien payé ; **to speak highly of sb** dire beaucoup de bien de qn ; *Br* **highly strung** hypersensible

**Highness** ['haɪnɪs] *n* His / Her Royal Highness Son Altesse *f*

**highway** ['haɪweɪ] *n Am* [motorway] autoroute *f* ; *Br* **Highway Code** code *m* de la route

**hijack** ['haɪdʒæk] **1.** *n* détournement *m* **2.** *vt* [plane] détourner ■ **hijacker** *n* [of plane] pirate *m* de l'air

**hike** [haɪk] **1.** *n* [walk] randonnée *f* **2.** *vi* faire de la randonnée ■ **hiker** *n* randonneur, -euse *mf*

**hilarious** [hɪ'leərɪəs] *adj* hilarant

**hill** [hɪl] *n* colline *f* ; [slope] pente *f* ■ **hillside** *n* on the hillside à flanc de coteau ■ **hilly** *(compar* -ier, *superl* -iest) *adj* vallonné

**him** [hɪm] *pron* le, l' ; [after prep, 'than', 'it is'] lui ; **(to) him** [indirect] lui ; **I saw him** je l'ai vu ; **I gave it (to) him** je le lui ai donné

**himself** [hɪm'self] *pron* lui-même ; [reflexive] se, s' ; [after prep] lui ; **he cut himself** il s'est coupé

**hind** [haɪnd] *adj* **hind legs** pattes *fpl* de derrière

**hinder** ['hɪndə(r)] *vt* [obstruct] gêner ; [delay] retarder ; **to hinder sb from doing sth** empêcher qn de faire qch ■ **hindrance** *n* obstacle *m*

**hindsight** ['haɪndsaɪt] *n* **with hindsight** avec le recul

**Hindu** ['hɪnduː] **1.** *adj* hindou **2.** *n* Hindou, -e *mf*

**hinge** [hɪndʒ] **1.** *n* gond *m*, charnière *f* **2.** *vt insep* **to hinge on** [depend on] dépendre de

**hint** [hɪnt] **1.** *n* [insinuation] allusion *f* ; [sign] signe *m* ; [clue] indice *m* **2.** *vt* laisser entendre **(that** que) **3.** *vt insep* **to hint at sb/sth** faire allusion à qn /qch

**hip** [hɪp] **1.** *n* hanche *f* **2.** *adj Fam* [fashionable] branché

**hippie** ['hɪpɪ] *n* hippie *mf*

**hippopotamus** [hɪpə'pɒtəməs] *n* hippopotame *m*

**hire** ['haɪə(r)] **1.** *n* location *f* ; *Br* [sign on taxi] 'libre' ; **for hire** à louer ; **on hire** en location ; *Br* **on hire purchase** à crédit **2.** *vt* [vehicle] louer ; [worker] engager ; **to hire sth out** louer qch

**his** [hɪz] **1.** *poss pron* le sien, la sienne, *pl* les sien(ne)s ; **this hat is his** ce chapeau est à lui ou est le sien ; **a friend of his** un ami à lui **2.** *poss adj* son, sa, *pl* ses

**Hispanic** [hɪ'spænɪk] *Am* **1.** *adj* hispano-américain **2.** *n* Hispano-Américain, -e *mf*

**hiss** [hɪs] **1.** *n* sifflement *m* ; **hisses** [booing] sifflets *mpl* **2.** *vti* siffler

**hissy fit** ['hɪsɪ-] *n Fam* **to have a hissy fit** piquer une crise

**history** ['hɪstərɪ] *(pl* **-ies)** *n* [study, events] histoire *f* ; COMPUT historique *f* ; **medical history** antécédents *mpl* médicaux

■ **historian** *n* historien, -enne *mf*
■ **historic(al)** [hɪ'stɒrɪk(əl)] *adj* historique

**hit** [hɪt] **1.** *n* [blow] coup *m* ; [in shooting] tir *m* réussi ; [success] succès *m* ; COMPUT [visit to website] hit *m*, contact *m* ; **hit (song)** hit *m* **2.** *(pt & pp* hit, *pres p* hitting*)* *vt* [beat] frapper ; [bump into] heurter ; [reach] atteindre ; [affect] toucher ; [problem, difficulty] rencontrer ; *Fam* **to hit it off** s'entendre bien **(with sb** avec qn) **3.** *vi* frapper ; **to hit back** riposter **(at** à) ; **to hit out at sb** [physically] frapper qn ; [verbally] s'en prendre à qn ; **to hit (up)on sth** [solution, idea] trouver qch ■ **hit-and-run** *n* **hit-and-run driver** chauffard *m* (qui prend la fuite) ■ **hit-or-miss** *adj* [chancy, random] aléatoire

**hitch** [hɪtʃ] **1.** *n* [difficulty] problème *m* **2.** *vt* [fasten] accrocher **(to** à) **3.** *vti* **to hitch (a ride)**, *Br* **to hitch a lift** faire du stop **(to** jusqu'à) ■ **hitchhike** *vi* faire du stop **(to** jusqu'à) ■ **hitchhiker** *n* autostoppeur, -euse *mf* ■ **hitchhiking** *n* auto-stop *m*

**HIV** [eɪtʃaɪ'viː] *(abbr of* **human immunodeficiency virus***)* *n* [virus] VIH *m* ; **HIV negative** séronégatif, -ive ; **HIV positive** séropositif, -ive

**hive** [haɪv] **1.** *n* ruche *f* **2.** *vt* **to hive off** [separate] séparer

**hoard** [hɔːd] **1.** *n* réserve *f* ; [of money] trésor *m* **2.** *vt* amasser

**hoarding** ['hɔːdɪŋ] *n Br* [for advertising] panneau *m* d'affichage

**hoarse** [hɔːs] *(compar* **-er**, *superl* **-est***)* *adj* enroué

**hoax** [həʊks] *n* canular *m*

**hob** [hɒb] *n* [on stove] plaque *f* chauffante

**hobby** ['hɒbɪ] *(pl* **-ies)** *n* passe-temps *m inv*

**hockey** ['hɒkɪ] *n* hockey *m* ; *Br* [field hockey] hockey *m* sur gazon ; *Am* [ice hockey] hockey *m* sur glace ; **hockey stick** crosse *f* de hockey ; *Am* **hockey mom** mère *f* au foyer dévouée à ses enfants

**hog** [hɒg] **1.** *n* **a)** *Am* [pig] cochon *m* **b)** *Fam* [greedy person] goinfre *m* **2.** *vt Fam* [monopolize] accaparer, monopoliser

**ho-hum** [həʊ'hʌm] *adj Am Fam* **a)** [mediocre] médiocre ; **it's a pretty ho-hum affair** ça ne casse pas des briques **b)** [unenthusiastic] peu enthousiaste ; **I was pretty ho-hum about it** ça ne m'a pas emballé

**hoist** [hɔɪst] **1.** *n* [machine] palan *m* **2.** *vt* hisser

**hold** [həʊld] **1.** *n* [grip] prise *f* ; [of ship] cale *f* ; [of plane] soute *f* ; **to get hold of** [grab] saisir ; [contact] joindre ; [find] trouver ; **to be on hold** [of project] être en suspens ; **to put sb on hold** [on phone] mettre qn en attente **2.** (*pt & pp* **held**) *vt* tenir ; [heat, attention] retenir ; [post] occuper ; [record] détenir ; [title, opinion] avoir ; [party, exhibition] organiser ; [ceremony] célébrer ; [contain] contenir ; [keep] garder ; **to hold sb prisoner** retenir qn prisonnier ; **to hold one's breath** retenir son souffle ; **hold the line!** [on phone] ne quittez pas ! ; **hold it!** [stay still] ne bouge pas ! ; **to be held** [of event] avoir lieu **3.** *vi* [of nail, rope] tenir ; [of weather] se maintenir

■ **hold-up** *n* [attack] hold-up *m inv* ; *Br* [traffic jam] ralentissement *m* ; [delay] retard *m*

■ **hold back** *vt sep* [restrain] retenir ; [hide] cacher (**from sb** à qn)

■ **hold down** *vt sep* [person on ground] maintenir au sol ; **to hold down a job** [keep] garder un emploi ; [occupy] avoir un emploi

■ **hold forth** *vi Pej* [talk] disserter

■ **hold off 1.** *vt sep* [enemy] tenir à distance **2.** *vi* **if the rain holds off** s'il ne pleut pas

■ **hold on 1.** *vt sep* [keep in place] tenir en place **2.** *vi* [wait] patienter ; [stand firm] tenir bon ; **hold on!** [on phone] ne quittez pas ! ; **hold on (tight)!** tenez bon !

■ **hold on to** *vt insep* [cling to] tenir bien ; [keep] garder

■ **hold out 1.** *vt sep* [offer] offrir ; [hand] tendre **2.** *vi* [resist] résister ; [last] durer

■ **hold over** *vt sep* [postpone] remettre

■ **hold together** *vt sep* [nation, group] assurer l'union de

■ **hold up** *vt sep* [raise] lever ; [support] soutenir ; [delay] retarder ; [rob] attaquer

**holdall** ['həʊldɔ:l] *n Br* fourre-tout *m inv*

**holder** ['həʊldə(r)] *n* **a)** [of passport, degree, post] titulaire *mf* ; [of record, card, ticket] détenteur, -trice *mf* **b)** [container] support *m*

**hole** [həʊl] *n* trou *m*

**holiday** ['hɒlɪdeɪ] **1.** *n Br* **holiday(s)** [from work, school] vacances *fpl* ; **a holiday** [day off] un congé ; **a (public** *or* **bank) holiday**, *Am* **a legal holiday** un jour férié ; **to be/go on holiday** être /partir en vacances **2.** *adj* [camp, clothes] de vacances ; **holiday let** location *f* saisonnière ■ **holidaymaker** *n Br* vacancier, -ère *mf*

**Holland** ['hɒlənd] *n* la Hollande

**hollow** ['hɒləʊ] **1.** *adj* creux (*f* creuse) ; [promise] vain **2.** *n* creux *m* **3.** *vt* **to hollow sth out** évider qch

**holly** ['hɒlɪ] *n* houx *m*

**holy** ['həʊlɪ] (*compar* -**ier**, *superl* -**iest**) *adj* saint ; [bread, water] bénit ; [ground] sacré

**homage** ['hɒmɪdʒ] *n* hommage *m* ; **to pay homage to sb** rendre hommage à qn

**home¹** [həʊm] **1.** *n* maison *f* ; [country] patrie *f* ; **at home** à la maison, chez soi ; **to feel at home** se sentir chez soi ; **make yourself at home** faites comme chez vous **2.** *adv* à la maison, chez soi ; **to go** *or* **come (back) home** rentrer chez soi **3.** *adj* [cooking] familial ; [visit, match] à domicile ; **home address** adresse *f* personnelle ; *Br* **home help** aide *f* ménagère ; *Br* **Home Office** ≃ ministère *m* de l'Intérieur ; **home owner** propriétaire *mf* ; COMPUT **home page** page *f* d'accueil ; *Br* **Home Secretary** ≃ ministre *m* de l'Intérieur ;

**home team** équipe *f* qui reçoit ; **home town** ville *f* natale ■ **homegrown** *adj* [fruit, vegetables] du jardin ; [not grown abroad] du pays ■ **homeland** *n* patrie *f* ■ **homemade** *adj* (fait) maison *inv* ■ **homeschooling** ['həʊm,sku:lɪŋ] *n Am* SCH instruction *f* à la maison ■ **homesick** *adj* **to be homesick** avoir le mal du pays ■ **homeware** *n* objets *mpl* pour la maison

**home²** [həʊm] ■ **home in on** *vt insep* viser, se diriger vers ; *Fig* [problem, solution] mettre l'accent sur ; [difficulty, question] viser, cerner

**homeless** ['həʊmlɪs] **1.** *adj* sans abri **2.** *npl* **the homeless** les sans-abri *mpl*

**homely** ['həʊmlɪ] *(compar* -**ier***, superl* -**iest***) adj* [comfortable] agréable et sans prétention ; *Am* [ugly] sans charme

**homeward** ['həʊmwəd] **1.** *adj* [trip] de retour **2.** *adv* **homeward bound** sur le chemin de retour

**homework** ['həʊmwɜːk] *n* SCH devoirs *mpl* ■ **homeworking** ['həʊm,wɜːkɪŋ] *n* travail *m* à domicile

**homicide** ['hɒmɪsaɪd] *n* homicide *m*

**homosexual** [həʊmə'sekʃʊəl] *adj & n* homosexuel, -elle *(mf)*

**honcho** ['hɒntʃəʊ] *n Am Fam* [boss] chef *m*

**honest** ['ɒnɪst] **1.** *adj* **a)** [trustworthy] honnête, probe **b)** [frank] franc *(f* franche), sincère ; **to be honest...** à dire vrai... **c)** [legal] légitime **2.** *adv Fam* = **honestly** ■ **honestly** *adv* honnêtement ■ **honesty** *n* honnêteté *f*

**honey** ['hʌnɪ] *n* miel *m* ■ **honeymoon** *n* voyage *m* de noces

**honk** [hɒŋk] *vi* [of driver] klaxonner

**honking** ['hɒŋkɪŋ] *adj Fam* **a)** [huge] énorme ; **he's bought a honking great plasma screen** il a acheté un énorme écran plasma **b)** [brilliant] génial ; **that's a honking great idea** c'est une idée géniale

**honorary** ['ɒnərərɪ] *adj* [member] honoraire ; [title] honorifique

**honour**, *Am* **honor** ['ɒnə(r)] **1.** *n* honneur *m* ; **in honour of** en l'honneur de ; *Br* UNIV **honours degree** diplôme *m* universitaire **2.** *vt* honorer (**with** de)

**honourable**, *Am* **honorable** ['ɒnərəbəl] *adj* honorable

**hood** [hʊd] *n* [of coat] capuche *f* ; [with eye-holes] cagoule *f* ; *Br* [of car, pram] capote *f* ; *Am* [car bonnet] capot *m*

**hoof** [hu:f] *(pl* **hoofs** [hu:fs] *or* **hooves** [hu:vz]) *n* sabot *m*

**hook** [hʊk] **1.** *n* crochet *m* ; [on clothes] agrafe *f* ; [for fishing] hameçon *m* ; **off the hook** [phone] décroché **2.** *vt* **to hook (on** *or* **up)** accrocher (**to** à) ■ **hooked** *adj* [nose] crochu ; *Fam* **to be hooked on sth** être accro à qch

**hook(e)y** ['hʊkɪ] *n Am Fam* **to play hook(e)y** sécher (les cours)

**hooligan** ['hu:lɪgən] *n* hooligan *m*

**hoot** [hu:t] *vi Br* [of vehicle] klaxonner ; [of owl] hululer ■ **hooter** *n Br* [of vehicle] Klaxon® *m*

**hoover®** ['hu:və(r)] *Br* **1.** *n* aspirateur *m* **2.** *vt* [room] passer l'aspirateur dans ; [carpet] passer l'aspirateur sur ; **to hoover® sth up** [dust, crumbs] enlever qch à l'aspirateur

**hop** [hɒp] **1.** *n* [leap] saut *m* **2.** *(pt & pp* -**pp**-*) vi* [jump] sautiller ; [on one leg] sauter à cloche-pied **3.** *vt Fam* **hop it!** fiche le camp !

**hope** [həʊp] **1.** *n* espoir *m* **2.** *vt* **to hope to do sth** espérer faire qch ; **to hope that...** espérer que... **3.** *vi* espérer ; **to hope for sth** espérer qch ; **I hope so / not** j'espère que oui / non ■ **hopeful** *adj* [person] optimiste ; [situation] encourageant ; **to be hopeful that...** avoir bon espoir que... ■ **hopefully** *adv* [with luck] avec un peu de chance ■ **hopeless** ['həʊplɪs] *adj* désespéré ; *Fam* [useless, bad] nul *(f* nulle) ■ **hopelessly** *adv* [lost] complètement ; [in love] éperdument

**horde** [hɔːd] *n* horde *f*

**horizon** [hə'raɪzən] *n* horizon *m* ; **on the horizon** à l'horizon ■ **horizontal** *adj* horizontal

**hormone** ['hɔːməʊn] *n* hormone *f*

**horn** [hɔːn] *n* [of animal] corne *f*; [on vehicle] Klaxon® *m*; [musical instrument] cor *m*

**hornet** [ˈhɔːnɪt] *n* frelon *m*

**horoscope** [ˈhɒrəskəʊp] *n* horoscope *m*

**horrendous** [hɒˈrendəs] *adj* horrible

**horrible** [ˈhɒrəbəl] *adj* horrible

**horrid** [ˈhɒrɪd] *adj* [unpleasant] affreux, -euse; [unkind] méchant

**horrific** [həˈrɪfɪk] *adj* horrible

**horrify** [ˈhɒrɪfaɪ] (*pt & pp* -ied) *vt* horrifier

**horror** [ˈhɒrə(r)] *n* horreur *f*; **horror film** film *m* d'horreur; **horror story** histoire *f* épouvantable

**hors d'œuvre** [ɔːˈdɜːv] (*pl inv or* **hors d'œuvres**) *n* hors-d'œuvre *m inv*

**horse** [hɔːs] *n* **a)** [animal] cheval *m*; **to go horse riding** faire du cheval; **horse racing** courses *fpl* **b)** [for exercise] cheval; **horse chestnut** [fruit] marron *m* ▪ **horseback** *n* **on horseback** à cheval; *Am* **to go horseback riding** faire du cheval ▪ **horsepower** *n* [unit] cheval-vapeur *m* ▪ **horseradish** *n* raifort *m*

**horticulture** [ˈhɔːtɪkʌltʃə(r)] *n* horticulture *f*

**hose** [həʊz] **1.** *n* [pipe] tuyau *m* **2.** *vt* arroser (au jet d'eau); **to hose sth down** [car] laver qch au jet ▪ **hosepipe** *n Br* tuyau *m* d'arrosage

**hospitable** [hɒˈspɪtəbəl] *adj* hospitalier, -ère (**to** envers) ▪ **hospitality** [-ˈtælɪtɪ] *n* hospitalité *f*

**hospital** [ˈhɒspɪtəl] *n* hôpital *m*; **in hospital**, *Am* **in the hospital** à l'hôpital; **hospital bed** lit *m* d'hôpital; **hospital staff** personnel *m* hospitalier ▪ **hospitalize** *vt* hospitaliser

**host¹** [həʊst] **1.** *n* [of guests] hôte *m*; [on TV or radio show] présentateur, -trice *mf*; **host country** pays *m* d'accueil **2.** *vt* [programme] présenter ▪ **hosting** *n* COMPUT [of web site] hébergement *m*; **hosting charge** frais *mpl* d'hébergement

**host²** [həʊst] *n* **a host of** [many] une foule de

**host³** [həʊst] *n* REL hostie *f*

**hostage** [ˈhɒstɪdʒ] *n* otage *m*; **to take sb hostage** prendre qn en otage; **to be held hostage** être retenu en otage

**hostel** [ˈhɒstəl] *n* foyer *m*; **(youth) hostel** auberge *f* de jeunesse

**hostess** [ˈhəʊstɪs] *n* [in house, nightclub] hôtesse *f*; **(air) hostess** hôtesse *f* (de l'air)

**hostile** [*Br* ˈhɒstaɪl, *Am* ˈhɒstəl] *adj* hostile (**to** *or* **towards** à)

**hostility** [hɒsˈtɪlɪtɪ] *n* hostilité *f* (**to** *or* **towards** envers); **hostilities** [in battle] hostilités *fpl*

**hot¹** [hɒt] (*compar* **hotter**, *superl* **hottest**) *adj* chaud; [spice] fort; *Fam* **to be a hot ticket** être très en demande; **to be** *or* **feel hot** avoir chaud; **it's hot** il fait chaud; **hot pink** rose fuchsia ▪ **hotcake** *n* crêpe *f* ▪ **hotdog** *n* hot dog *m* ▪ **hotheaded** *adj* exalté ▪ **hotly** *adv* passionnément ▪ **hotplate** *n* chauffe-plat *m*; [on stove] plaque *f* chauffante ▪ **hotspot** [ˈhɒtspɒt] *n* [dangerous area] point *m* chaud *ou* névralgique ▪ **hot-water** *n* **hot-water bottle** bouillotte *f*

**hot²** [hɒt] (*pt & pp* -tt-) *vi Fam* **to hot up** [increase] s'intensifier; [become dangerous or excited] s'envenimer

**hotchpotch** [ˈhɒtʃpɒtʃ] *n Fam* fatras *m*

**hotel** [həʊˈtel] *n* hôtel *m*; **hotel room/bed** chambre *f* / lit *m* d'hôtel; **three / four-star hotel** hôtel trois / quatre étoiles

**hound** [haʊnd] **1.** *n* [dog] chien *m* de chasse **2.** *vt* [pursue] traquer; [bother, worry] harceler

**hour** [ˈaʊə(r)] *n* heure *f*; **half an hour** une demi-heure; **a quarter of an hour** un quart d'heure; **in the small hours** au petit matin; **paid £10 an hour** payé 10 livres (de) l'heure; **10 miles an hour** 10 miles à l'heure; **hour hand** [of watch, clock] petite aiguille *f* ▪ **hours** *npl* [of business] heures *fpl* d'ouverture

**hourly** [ˈaʊəlɪ] **1.** *adj* [rate, pay] horaire **2.** *adv* toutes les heures; **hourly paid, paid hourly** payé à l'heure

**house 1.** [haʊs] (*pl* -**ses** [-zɪz]) *n* maison *f*; POL **the House of Commons / Lords** la Chambre des communes / lords; **the**

Houses of Parliament le Parlement; the House of Representatives la Chambre des représentants; **at/to my house** chez moi; **on the house** [free of charge] aux frais de la maison; **house plant** plante *f* d'intérieur; **house prices** prix *mpl* de l'immobilier; **house wine** vin *m* maison **2.** [hauz] *vt* loger; [of building] abriter ■ **houseboat** *n* péniche *f* aménagée ■ **housebound** *adj* confiné chez soi ■ **household** *n* ménage *m*; **household chores** tâches *fpl* ménagères ■ **householder** *n* [owner] propriétaire *mf* ■ **housekeeper** *n* [employee] gouvernante *f* ■ **housekeeping** *n* ménage *m* ■ **houseproud** *adj* qui s'occupe méticuleusement de sa maison ■ **house-sitter** *n* personne qui garde une maison en l'absence de ses occupants ■ **housetrained** *adj* Br [dog] propre ■ **housewarming** *n* & *adj* **to have a housewarming (party)** pendre la crémaillère ■ **housewife** (*pl* **-wives**) *n* ménagère *f* ■ **housework** *n* ménage *m*

**housing** [ˈhaʊzɪŋ] *n* logement *m*; [houses] logements *mpl*; *Am* **housing development** ensemble *m* immobilier; *Br* **housing estate** lotissement *m*; [council-owned] cité *f*

**hovel** [ˈhɒvəl] *n* taudis *m*

**hover** [ˈhɒvə(r)] *vi* [of bird, aircraft] planer; **to hover (around)** [of person] rôder

**hovercraft** [ˈhɒvəkrɑːft] *n* aéroglisseur *m*

**how** [haʊ] *adv* comment; **how kind!** comme c'est gentil !; **how long/high is...?** quelle est la longueur/hauteur de... ?; **how much?, how many?** combien ?; **how much time?** combien de temps ?; **how many apples?** combien de pommes ?; **how about some coffee?** (si on prenait) du café ?; **how do you do?** [greeting] enchanté; *Fam* **how's that?, how so?, how come?** comment ça ?

**however** [haʊˈevə(r)] **1.** *adv* **however big he may be** si grand soit-il; **however she may do it, however she does it** de quelque manière qu'elle le fasse;

however did she find out? comment a-t-elle bien pu l'apprendre ? **2.** *conj* cependant

**howl** [haʊl] **1.** *n* hurlement *m*; **howl of laughter** éclat *m* de rire **2.** *vi* hurler; [of wind] mugir

**hp** (abbr of **horsepower**) CV

**HP** [eɪtʃˈpiː] (abbr of **hire purchase**) *n Br* achat *m* à crédit

**HQ** [eɪtʃˈkjuː] (abbr of **headquarters**) *n* QG *m*

**HR** (abbr of **human resources**) *n* RH (ressources humaines)

**HRU** MESSAGING written abbr of **how are you**

**h2cus** MESSAGING written abbr of **hope to see you soon**

**hub** [hʌb] *n* [of wheel] moyeu *m*; *Fig* centre *m* ■ **hubcap** *n* [of wheel] enjoliveur *m*

**huddle** [ˈhʌdl] *vi* **to huddle (together)** se blottir (les uns contre les autres)

**huff** [hʌf] *n Fam* **in a huff** [offended] fâché

**hug** [hʌg] **1.** *n* **to give sb a hug** serrer qn (dans ses bras) **2.** (pt & pp -gg-) *vt* [person] serrer dans ses bras

**huge** [hjuːdʒ] *adj* énorme

**hull** [hʌl] *n* [of ship] coque *f*

**hullo** [hʌˈləʊ] *excl Br* bonjour !; [answering phone] allô !

**hum** [hʌm] **1.** *n* [of insect] bourdonnement *m* **2.** (pt & pp -mm-) *vt* [tune] fredonner **3.** *vi* [of insect] bourdonner; [of person] fredonner; [of engine] ronronner

**human** [ˈhjuːmən] **1.** *adj* humain; **the human race** la race humaine; **human being** être *m* humain; **human rights** droits *mpl* de l'homme; **human trafficking** trafic *m* ou traite *f* d'êtres humains **2.** *n* être *m* humain

**humane** [hjuːˈmeɪn] *adj* [kind] humain

**humanity** [hjuːˈmænətɪ] *n* [human beings, kindness] humanité *f*

**humble** [ˈhʌmbəl] **1.** *adj* humble **2.** *vt* humilier

**humid** [ˈhjuːmɪd] *adj* humide ■ **humidity** *n* humidité *f*

**humiliate** [hju:'mɪlɪeɪt] vt humilier
■ **humiliation** [-'eɪʃən] n humiliation f

**humility** [hju:'mɪlətɪ] n humilité f

**humongous** [hju:'mʌŋgəs] adj Am Fam énorme

**humorous** ['hju:mərəs] adj [book, writer] humoristique; [person, situation] drôle

**humour**, Am **humor** ['hju:mə(r)] 1. n [fun] humour m 2. vt **to humour sb** faire plaisir à qn

**hump** [hʌmp] n [lump, mound in road] bosse f

**hunch** [hʌntʃ] 1. n Fam [intuition] intuition f 2. vt **to hunch one's shoulders** rentrer les épaules ■ **hunchback** n bossu, -e mf

**hundred** ['hʌndrəd] adj & n cent (m); **a hundred pages** cent pages; **two hundred pages** deux cents pages; **hundreds of** des centaines de ■ **hundredth** adj & n centième (mf) ■ **hundredweight** n Br 50,8 kg, 112 livres; Am 45,3 kg, 100 livres

**hung** [hʌŋ] pt & pp of **hang**

**Hungary** ['hʌŋgərɪ] n la Hongrie ■ **Hungarian** [-'geərɪən] 1. adj hongrois 2. n [person] Hongrois, -e mf; [language] hongrois m

**hunger** ['hʌŋgə(r)] n faim f ■ **hungry** (compar -ier, superl -iest) adj **to be** or **feel hungry** avoir faim; **hungry for sth** avide de qch

**hunk** [hʌŋk] n [piece] gros morceau m

**hunt** [hʌnt] 1. n [search] recherche f (**for** de); [for animals] chasse f 2. vt [animals] chasser; [pursue] poursuivre; **to hunt down** [animal, fugitive] traquer 3. vi [kill animals] chasser; **to hunt for sth** rechercher qch ■ **hunter** n chasseur m ■ **hunting** n chasse f

**hurdle** ['hɜ:dəl] n [fence in race] haie f; Fig [problem] obstacle m

**hurl** [hɜ:l] vt [throw] jeter, lancer (**at** à); **to hurl insults** or **abuse at sb** lancer des insultes à qn

**hurray** [hʊ'reɪ] excl hourra !

**hurricane** [Br 'hʌrɪkən, Am 'hʌrɪkeɪn] n ouragan m

**hurried** ['hʌrɪd] adj [decision] précipité; [work] fait à la hâte; [visit] éclair inv

**hurry** ['hʌrɪ] 1. n hâte f; **in a hurry** à la hâte; **to be in a hurry** être pressé; **to be in a hurry to do sth** avoir hâte de faire qch; **there's no hurry** rien ne presse 2. (pt & pp -ied) vt [person] presser; [work] hâter 3. vi se dépêcher, se presser (**to do** de faire); **to hurry up** se dépêcher; **to hurry out** sortir à la hâte; **to hurry towards sb/sth** se précipiter vers qn /qch

**hurt** [hɜ:t] 1. adj [wounded, offended] blessé 2. n [emotional] blessure f 3. (pt & pp **hurt**) vt [physically] faire du mal à; [causing a wound] blesser; [emotionally] faire de la peine à; [reputation, chances] nuire à; **to hurt sb's feelings** blesser qn 4. vi faire mal; **his arm hurts** son bras lui fait mal ■ **hurtful** adj [remark] blessant

**hurtle** ['hɜ:təl] vi **to hurtle along** aller à toute vitesse

**husband** ['hʌzbənd] n mari m

**hush** [hʌʃ] 1. n silence m 2. excl chut ! 3. vt [person] faire taire; [baby] calmer; **to hush up** [scandal] étouffer ■ **hushed** adj [voice] étouffé; [silence] profond

**husky** ['hʌskɪ] (compar -ier, superl -iest) adj [voice] rauque

**hustle** ['hʌsəl] 1. n **hustle and bustle** effervescence f 2. vt [shove, push] **to hustle sb away** emmener qn de force ■ **hustler** ['hʌslə(r)] n Fam [swindler] arnaqueur, -euse mf

**hut** [hʌt] n cabane f; [dwelling] hutte f

**huzzah** [hə'zɑ:] excl hourrah !

**hybrid** ['haɪbrɪd] adj & n hybride (m)

**hydrogen** ['haɪdrədʒən] n CHEM hydrogène m

**hygiene** ['haɪdʒi:n] n hygiène f ■ **hygienic** adj hygiénique

**hymn** [hɪm] n cantique m

**hype** [haɪp] n Fam [publicity] battage m publicitaire

**hyper-** ['haɪpə(r)] pref hyper-

**hypermarket** ['haɪpəmɑ:kɪt] n hypermarché m

**hyphen** ['haɪfən] n trait m d'union ■ **hyphenated** adj [word] à trait d'union

**hypnotize** ['hɪpnətaɪz] vt hypnotiser

**hypochondriac** [haɪpə'kɒndrɪæk] n hypocondriaque mf

**hypocrisy** [hɪ'pɒkrɪsɪ] n hypocrisie f ■ **hypocrite** ['hɪpəkrɪt] n hypocrite mf ■ **hypocritical** [hɪpə'krɪtɪkəl] adj hypocrite

**hypothesis** [haɪ'pɒθɪsɪs] (pl -theses [-θɪsiːz]) n hypothèse f ■ **hypothetical** [haɪpə'θetɪkəl] adj hypothétique

**hysterical** [hɪs'terɪkəl] adj [very upset] qui a une crise de nerfs ; Fam [funny] tordant ■ **hysterics** npl [tears] crise f de nerfs ; **to be in hysterics** avoir une crise de nerfs ; [with laughter] être écroulé de rire

# I

**I¹, i** [aɪ] *n* [letter] I, i *m inv*

**I²** [aɪ] *pron* je, j' ; [stressed] moi

**ice¹** [aɪs] **1.** *n* glace *f* ; [on road] verglas *m* ; **ice cream** glace *f* ; **ice cube** glaçon *m* ; **ice hockey** hockey *m* sur glace **2.** *vi* to **ice over** *or* **up** [of lake] geler ; [of window] se givrer ■ **iceberg** *n* iceberg *m* ■ **icebox** *n Am* [fridge] réfrigérateur *m* ; *Br* [in fridge] freezer *m* ■ **iced** *adj* [tea, coffee] glacé ■ **ice-skating** *n* patinage *m* (sur glace)

**ice²** [aɪs] *vt Br* [cake] glacer ■ **icing** *n Br* [on cake] glaçage *m*

**Iceland** ['aɪslənd] *n* l'Islande *f* ■ **Icelandic** [-'lændɪk] *adj* islandais

**icicle** ['aɪsɪkəl] *n* glaçon *m (de gouttière etc)*

**icon** ['aɪkɒn] *n* [gen & COMPUT] icône *f*

**icy** ['aɪsɪ] *(compar* -**ier***, superl* -**iest***) adj* [road] verglacé ; [water, hands] glacé

**ID** [aɪ'diː] *n* pièce *f* d'identité

**I'd** [aɪd] = **I had, I would**

**idea** [aɪ'dɪə] *n* idée *f* ; **I have an idea that…** j'ai l'impression que…

**ideal** [aɪ'dɪəl] *adj & n* idéal *(m)*

**idealistic** [aɪdɪə'lɪstɪk] *adj* idéaliste

**ideally** [aɪ'dɪəlɪ] *adv* idéalement ; **ideally, we should stay** l'idéal, ce serait que nous restions

**identical** [aɪ'dentɪkəl] *adj* identique (**to** *or* **with** à)

**identify** [aɪ'dentɪfaɪ] *(pt & pp* -**ied***) vt* identifier ; **to identify (oneself) with** s'identifier avec ■ **identification** [-fɪ'keɪʃən] *n* identification *f* ; **to have (some) identification** [document] avoir une pièce d'identité

**identity** [aɪ'dentɪtɪ] *(pl* -**ies***) n* identité *f* ; **identity card** carte *f* d'identité ; **identity theft** vol *m* d'identité

**ideology** [aɪdɪ'ɒlədʒɪ] *(pl* -**ies***) n* idéologie *f*

**idiom** ['ɪdɪəm] *n* [phrase] expression *f* idiomatique

**idiosyncrasy** [ɪdɪə'sɪŋkrəsɪ] *(pl* -**ies***) n* particularité *f*

**idiot** ['ɪdɪət] *n* idiot, -e *mf* ■ **idiotic** [-'ɒtɪk] *adj* idiot, bête

**IDK** MESSAGING *written abbr of* **I don't know**

**idle** ['aɪdəl] **1.** *adj* [unoccupied] désœuvré ; [lazy] oisif, -ive ; [rumour] sans fondement ; **to lie idle** [of machine] être au repos **2.** *vt* **to idle away the** *or* **one's time** passer son temps à ne rien faire **3.** *vi* [of engine, machine] tourner au ralenti

**idol** ['aɪdəl] *n* idole *f* ■ **idolize** *vt* [adore] idolâtrer

**idyllic** [aɪ'dɪlɪk] *adj* idyllique

**i.e.** [aɪ'iː] *(abbr of* **id est***)* c'est-à-dire

**if** [ɪf] *conj* si ; **if he comes** s'il vient ; **if so** si c'est le cas ; **if not** sinon ; **as if** comme si ; **if necessary** s'il le faut

**ignite** [ɪg'naɪt] **1.** *vt* mettre le feu à **2.** *vi* prendre feu ■ **ignition** [-'nɪʃən] *n* [in vehicle] allumage *m* ; **to switch on/off the ignition** mettre/couper le contact ; **ignition key** clef *f* de contact

**ignorance** ['ɪgnərəns] *n* ignorance *f* (**of** de) ■ **ignorant** *adj* ignorant (**of** de)

**ignore** [ɪg'nɔː(r)] *vt* ignorer

**ill** [ɪl] **1.** *adj* [sick] malade ; [bad] mauvais ; **ill will** malveillance *f* **2.** *npl* **ills** maux *mpl* **3.** *adv* mal ■ **ill-advised** *adj* [person] malavisé ■ **ill-fitting** *adj* [garment, lid, window] mal ajusté ■ **ill-humoured,** *Am* **ill-humored** *adj* caractériel, -elle ■ **ill-informed** *adj* mal renseigné ■ **ill-intentioned**

[-ɪn'tenʃənd] *adj* malintentionné ■ **ill-mannered** *adj* mal élevé ■ **ill-matched** *adj* mal assorti

**I'll** [aɪl] = **I will, I shall**

**illegal** [ɪ'li:gəl] *adj* illégal

**illegible** [ɪ'ledʒəbəl] *adj* illisible

**illegitimate** [ɪlɪ'dʒɪtɪmət] *adj* illégitime

**illicit** [ɪ'lɪsɪt] *adj* illicite

**illiterate** [ɪ'lɪtərət] *adj* & *n* analphabète *(mf)*

**illness** [ˈɪlnɪs] *n* maladie *f*

**illogical** [ɪ'lɒdʒɪkəl] *adj* illogique

**illuminate** [ɪ'lu:mɪneɪt] *vt* [monument] illuminer ; [street, question] éclairer

**illusion** [ɪ'lu:ʒən] *n* illusion *f* (**about** sur)

**illustrate** [ˈɪləstreɪt] *vt* [with pictures, examples] illustrer (**with** de) ■ **illustration** *n* illustration *f*

**image** [ˈɪmɪdʒ] *n* image *f* ; **(public) image** [of company] image *f* de marque ; **he's the (living** *or* **spitting** *or* **very) image of his brother** c'est tout le portrait de son frère ■ **imagery** *n* imagerie *f*

**imaginary** [ɪ'mædʒɪnərɪ] *adj* imaginaire

**imagination** [ɪmædʒɪ'neɪʃən] *n* imagination *f*

**imaginative** [ɪ'mædʒɪnətɪv] *adj* [plan, novel] original ; [person] imaginatif, -ive

**imagine** [ɪ'mædʒɪn] *vt* imaginer (**that** que) ■ **imaginable** *adj* imaginable

**imitate** [ˈɪmɪteɪt] *vt* imiter ■ **imitation** *n* imitation *f* ; *Br* **imitation jewellery,** *Am* **imitation jewelry** faux bijoux *mpl*

**immaculate** [ɪ'mækjʊlət] *adj* impeccable

**immaterial** [ɪmə'tɪərɪəl] *adj* sans importance (**to** pour)

**immature** [ɪmə'tʃʊə(r)] *adj* [person] immature

**immediate** [ɪ'mi:dɪət] *adj* immédiat ■ **immediately 1.** *adv* [at once] tout de suite, immédiatement ; **it's immediately above / below** c'est juste au-dessus / en dessous **2.** *conj Br* [as soon as] dès que

**immense** [ɪ'mens] *adj* immense ■ **immensely** *adv* [rich] immensément ; **to enjoy oneself immensely** s'amuser énormément

**immerse** [ɪ'mɜ:s] *vt* [in liquid] plonger ; *Fig* **to immerse oneself in sth** se plonger dans qch ■ **immersion** *n Br* **immersion heater** chauffe-eau *m inv* électrique

**immigrate** [ˈɪmɪgreɪt] *vi* immigrer ■ **immigrant** *adj* & *n* immigré, -e *(mf)* ■ **immigration** *n* immigration *f*

**imminent** [ˈɪmɪnənt] *adj* imminent

**immobile** [*Br* ɪ'məʊbaɪl, *Am* ɪ'məʊbəl] *adj* immobile ■ **immobilize** *vt* immobiliser

**immoral** [ɪ'mɒrəl] *adj* immoral

**immortal** [ɪ'mɔ:təl] *adj* immortel, -elle

**immune** [ɪ'mju:n] *adj* MED [to disease] immunisé (**to** contre) ; *Fig* **immune to criticism** imperméable à la critique ; **immune system** système *m* immunitaire ■ **immunize** [ˈɪmjunaɪz] *vt* immuniser (**against** contre)

**IMO** MESSAGING *written abbr of* **in my opinion**

**impact** [ˈɪmpækt] *n* impact *m* ; **to make an impact on sb / sth** avoir un impact sur qn / qch

**impair** [ɪm'peə(r)] *vt* [sight, hearing] diminuer, affaiblir

**impartial** [ɪm'pɑ:ʃəl] *adj* impartial

**impassable** [ɪm'pɑ:səbəl] *adj* [road] impraticable ; [river] infranchissable

**impasse** [*Br* æm'pɑ:s, *Am* 'ɪmpæs] *n* [situation] impasse *f*

**impassive** [ɪm'pæsɪv] *adj* impassible

**impatient** [ɪm'peɪʃənt] *adj* impatient (**to do** de faire) ; **to get impatient (with sb)** s'impatienter (contre qn)

**impeccable** [ɪm'pekəbəl] *adj* [manners, person] impeccable

**impede** [ɪm'pi:d] *vt* gêner ; **to impede sb from doing** [prevent] empêcher qn de faire

**impediment** [ɪm'pedɪmənt] *n* obstacle *m* ; **speech impediment** défaut *m* d'élocution

**impending** [ɪm'pendɪŋ] *adj* imminent

**impenetrable** [ɪm'penɪtrəbəl] *adj* [forest, mystery] impénétrable

**imperative** [ɪm'perətɪv] **1.** *adj* it is imperative that he should come il faut impérativement qu'il vienne **2.** *n* [in grammar] impératif *m*

**imperceptible** [ɪmpə'septəbəl] *adj* imperceptible (**to** à)

**imperfect** [ɪm'pɜːfɪkt] **1.** *adj* imparfait ; [goods] défectueux, -euse **2.** *adj* & *n* imperfect (tense) [in grammar] imparfait (*m*) ■ **imperfection** [-pə'fekʃən] *n* imperfection *f*

**imperial** [ɪm'pɪərɪəl] *adj* impérial ; *Br* imperial measure *système de mesure anglo-saxon utilisant les miles, les pints etc*

**impersonal** [ɪm'pɜːsənəl] *adj* impersonnel, -elle

**impersonate** [ɪm'pɜːsəneɪt] *vt* [pretend to be] se faire passer pour ; [imitate] imiter

**impertinent** [ɪm'pɜːtɪnənt] *adj* impertinent (**to** envers)

**impervious** [ɪm'pɜːvɪəs] *adj also Fig* imperméable (**to** à)

**impetuous** [ɪm'petjʊəs] *adj* impétueux, -euse

**impetus** ['ɪmpɪtəs] *n* impulsion *f*

**impinge** [ɪm'pɪndʒ] *vi* to impinge on sth [affect] affecter qch ; [encroach on] empiéter sur qch

**implant 1.** ['ɪmplɑːnt] *n* MED implant *m* **2.** [ɪm'plɑːnt] *vt* MED implanter (**in** dans) ; [ideas] inculquer (**in** à)

**implement¹** ['ɪmplɪmənt] *n* [tool] instrument *m* ; [utensil] ustensile *m*

**implement²** ['ɪmplɪment] *vt* [carry out] mettre en œuvre

**implicate** ['ɪmplɪkeɪt] *vt* impliquer (**in** dans) ■ **implication** *n* [consequence] conséquence *f* ; [innuendo] insinuation *f* ; [impact] portée *f* ; by implication implicitement

**implicit** [ɪm'plɪsɪt] *adj* [implied] implicite ; [absolute] absolu

**implore** [ɪm'plɔː(r)] *vt* implorer (**sb to do** qn de faire)

**imply** [ɪm'plaɪ] *(pt & pp* -ied) *vt* [insinuate] insinuer (**that** que) ; [presuppose] supposer (**that** que) ; [involve] impliquer (**that** que) ■ **implied** *adj* implicite

**impolite** [ɪmpə'laɪt] *adj* impoli

**import 1.** ['ɪmpɔːt] *n* [item, activity] importation *f* **2.** [ɪm'pɔːt] *vt* [goods & COMPUT] importer (**from** de) ■ **importer** *n* importateur, -trice *mf*

**importance** [ɪm'pɔːtəns] *n* importance *f* ; to be of importance avoir de l'importance

**important** [ɪm'pɔːtənt] *adj* important (**to/for** pour) ; it's important that... il est important que... (+ *subjunctive*)

**impose** [ɪm'pəʊz] **1.** *vt* [conditions, silence] imposer (**on** à) ; [fine, punishment] infliger (**on sb** à qn) **2.** *vi* [take advantage] s'imposer ; to impose on sb abuser de la gentillesse de qn ■ **imposition** [-pə'zɪʃən] *n* [inconvenience] dérangement *m*

**imposing** [ɪm'pəʊzɪŋ] *adj* imposant

**impossible** [ɪm'pɒsəbəl] **1.** *adj* impossible (**to do** à faire) ; it is impossible (for us) to do it il (nous) est impossible de le faire **2.** *n* to do the impossible faire l'impossible ■ **impossibility** (*pl* -ies) *n* impossibilité *f*

**impostor** [ɪm'pɒstə(r)] *n* imposteur *m*

**impotent** ['ɪmpətənt] *adj* impuissant

**impound** [ɪm'paʊnd] *vt* [of police] saisir ; [vehicle] mettre à la fourrière

**impoverished** [ɪm'pɒvərɪʃd] *adj* appauvri

**impractical** [ɪm'præktɪkəl] *adj* peu réaliste

**imprecise** [ɪmprɪ'saɪs] *adj* imprécis

**impregnate** ['ɪmpregneɪt] *vt* [soak] imprégner (**with** de)

**impress** [ɪm'pres] *vt* [person] impressionner ; to be impressed with *or* by sb/sth être impressionné par qn/qch

**impression** [ɪm'preʃən] *n* impression *f* ; to be under *or* have the impression that... avoir l'impression que... ; to make a good/bad impression on sb faire une bonne / mauvaise impression à qn ∎ **impressionable** *adj* [person] impressionnable

**impressionist** [ɪmˈpreʃənɪst] *n* [mimic] imitateur, -trice *mf*

**impressive** [ɪmˈpresɪv] *adj* impressionnant

**imprint 1.** [ˈɪmprɪnt] *n* empreinte *f* **2.** [ɪmˈprɪnt] *vt* imprimer

**imprison** [ɪmˈprɪzən] *vt* emprisonner ∎ **imprisonment** *n* emprisonnement *m*; **life imprisonment** la prison à vie

**improbable** [ɪmˈprɒbəbəl] *adj* [unlikely] improbable; [unbelievable] invraisemblable

**impromptu** [ɪmˈprɒmptjuː] *adj* [speech, party] improvisé

**improper** [ɪmˈprɒpə(r)] *adj* **a)** [indecent] indécent **b)** [use, purpose] mauvais; [behaviour] déplacé

**improve** [ɪmˈpruːv] **1.** *vt* améliorer; [technique, invention] perfectionner; **to improve one's English** se perfectionner en anglais **2.** *vi* s'améliorer; [of business] reprendre ∎ **improvement** *n* amélioration *f* (**in** de); [progress] progrès *mpl*; **to be an improvement on sth** [be better than] être meilleur que qch

**improvise** [ˈɪmprəvaɪz] *vti* improviser ∎ **improvisation** *n* improvisation *f*

**impudent** [ˈɪmpjʊdənt] *adj* impudent

**impulse** [ˈɪmpʌls] *n* impulsion *f*; **on impulse** sur un coup de tête ∎ **impulsive** *adj* [person] impulsif, -ive

**impunity** [ɪmˈpjuːnɪtɪ] *n* **with impunity** impunément

**impurity** [ɪmˈpjʊərətɪ] *(pl* **-ies***) n* impureté *f*

**in** [ɪn] **1.** *prep* **a)** dans; **in the box / the school** dans la boîte / l'école; **in an hour('s time)** dans une heure; **in so far as** dans la mesure où

**b)** à; **in school** à l'école; **in Paris** à Paris; **in the USA** aux USA; **in pencil** au crayon; **in spring** au printemps; **the woman in the red dress** la femme à la robe rouge

**c)** en; **in summer / French** en été / français; **in Spain** en Espagne; **in May** en mai; **in 2001** en 2001; **in an hour** [during an hour] en une heure; **in doing sth** en faisant qch; **dressed in black** habillé en noir

**d)** de; **in a soft voice** d'une voix douce; **the best in the class** le meilleur / la meilleure de la classe; **an increase in salary** une augmentation de salaire; **at six in the evening** à six heures du soir

**e)** chez; **in children / animals** chez les enfants / les animaux; **in Shakespeare** chez Shakespeare

**f) in the morning** le matin; **he hasn't done it in months** ça fait des mois qu'il ne l'a pas fait; **one in ten** un sur dix; **in tens** dix par dix; **in hundreds / thousands** par centaines / milliers; **in here** ici; **in there** là-dedans

**2.** *adv* **to be in** [home] être là; [of train] être arrivé; [in fashion] être en vogue; [in power] être au pouvoir; **day in, day out** jour après jour; **in a sense** dans un sens; **in on a secret** au courant d'un secret; **we're in for some rain / trouble** on va avoir de la pluie / des ennuis **3.** *npl* **the ins and outs of** les moindres détails de

∎ **in all** *adv* en tout; **there are 30 in all** il y en a 30 en tout

∎ **in between 1.** *adv* **a)** [in intermediate position] **a row of bushes with little clumps of flowers in between** une rangée d'arbustes séparés par des petites touffes de fleurs; **she plays either very well or very badly, never in between** elle joue très bien ou très mal, jamais entre les deux **b)** [in time] entre-temps, dans l'intervalle **2.** *prep* entre ∎ **in kind** *adv* [with goods, services] en nature; **to pay sb in kind** payer qn en nature

**in-** [ɪn] *pref* in-

**inability** [ɪnəˈbɪlɪtɪ] *(pl* **-ies***) n* incapacité *f* (**to do** de faire)

**inaccessible** [ɪnəkˈsesəbəl] *adj* inaccessible

**inaccurate** [ɪnˈækjʊrət] *adj* inexact

**inadequate** [ɪnˈædɪkwət] *adj* [quantity] insuffisant; [person] pas à la hauteur; [work] médiocre

**inadmissible** [ɪnədˈmɪsəbəl] *adj* inadmissible

**inadvertently** [ɪnədˈvɜːtəntlɪ] *adv* par inadvertance

**inadvisable** [ɪnədˈvaɪzəbəl] *adj* **it is inadvisable to go out alone** il est déconseillé de sortir seul

**inanimate** [ɪnˈænɪmət] *adj* inanimé

**inappropriate** [ɪnəˈprəʊprɪət] *adj* [unsuitable - place, clothes] peu approprié; [remark, moment] inopportun

**inarticulate** [ɪnɑːˈtɪkjʊlət] *adj* [person] incapable de s'exprimer

**inasmuch as** [ɪnəzˈmʌtʃəz] *conj* [because] dans la mesure où; [to the extent that] en ce sens que

**inattentive** [ɪnəˈtentɪv] *adj* inattentif, -ive (**to** à)

**inaudible** [ɪnˈɔːdɪbəl] *adj* inaudible

**inauguration** [ɪnɔːgjʊˈreɪʃən] *n* inauguration *f*; [of official] investiture *f*

**inborn** [ɪnˈbɔːn] *adj* inné

**inbox** [ˈɪnbɒks] *n* COMPUT boîte *f* de réception

**Inc** (*abbr of* **Incorporated**) *Am* COMM ≃ SARL

**incalculable** [ɪnˈkælkjʊləbəl] *adj* incalculable

**incapable** [ɪnˈkeɪpəbəl] *adj* incapable (**of doing** de faire)

**incapacitate** [ɪnkəˈpæsɪteɪt] *vt* rendre infirme

**incense¹** [ˈɪnsens] *n* [substance] encens *m*

**incense²** [ɪnˈsens] *vt* rendre furieux, -euse

**incentive** [ɪnˈsentɪv] *n* motivation *f*; [payment] prime *f*; **to give sb an incentive to work** encourager qn à travailler ■ **incentive-based** *adj* reposant sur l'incitation

**incessant** [ɪnˈsesənt] *adj* incessant

**incestuous** [ɪnˈsestjʊəs] *adj* incestueux, -euse

**inch** [ɪntʃ] **1.** *n* pouce *m* (2,54 cm); **inch by inch** petit à petit **2.** *vti* **to inch (one's way) forward** avancer tout doucement

**incident** [ˈɪnsɪdənt] *n* incident *m*; [in book, film] épisode *m*

**incidental** [ɪnsɪˈdentəl] *adj* [additional] accessoire; **incidental music** [in film] musique *f* ■ **incidentally** *adv* [by the way] au fait

**incinerator** [ɪnˈsɪnəreɪtə(r)] *n* incinérateur *m*

**incision** [ɪnˈsɪʒən] *n* incision *f*

**incisive** [ɪnˈsaɪsɪv] *adj* incisif, -ive

**incite** [ɪnˈsaɪt] *vt* inciter (**to do** à faire)

**inclination** [ɪnklɪˈneɪʃən] *n* [liking] inclination *f*; [desire] envie *f* (**to do** de faire)

**incline 1.** [ˈɪnklaɪn] *n* [slope] pente *f* **2.** [ɪnˈklaɪn] *vt* [bend, tilt] incliner; **to be inclined to do sth** [feel desire to] avoir bien envie de faire qch; [tend to] avoir tendance à faire qch **3.** [ɪnˈklaɪn] *vi* **to incline to** *or* **towards sth** pencher pour qch

**include** [ɪnˈkluːd] *vt* [contain] comprendre, inclure; [in letter] joindre; **to be included** être compris; [on list] être inclus ■ **including** *prep* y compris; **not including** sans compter; **including service** service compris

**inclusive** [ɪnˈkluːsɪv] *adj* inclus; **from the fourth to the tenth of May inclusive** du quatre au dix mai inclus; **to be inclusive of** comprendre; **inclusive of tax** toutes taxes comprises

**incoherent** [ɪnkəʊˈhɪərənt] *adj* incohérent

**income** [ˈɪŋkʌm] *n* revenu *m* (**from** de); **private income** rentes *fpl*; **income tax** impôt *m* sur le revenu

**incoming** [ˈɪnkʌmɪŋ] *adj* [president] nouveau (*f* nouvelle); **incoming calls** [on telephone] appels *mpl* de l'extérieur; **incoming tide** marée *f* montante

**incomparable** [ɪnˈkɒmpərəbəl] *adj* incomparable

**incompatible** [ɪnkəmˈpætəbəl] *adj* incompatible (**with** avec)

**incompetent** [ɪn'kɒmpɪtənt] *adj* incompétent

**incomplete** [ɪnkəm'pliːt] *adj* incomplet, -ète

**incomprehensible** [ɪnkɒmprɪ'hensəbəl] *adj* incompréhensible

**inconceivable** [ɪnkən'siːvəbəl] *adj* inconcevable

**inconclusive** [ɪnkən'kluːsɪv] *adj* peu concluant

**inconsiderate** [ɪnkən'sɪdərət] *adj* [action, remark] inconsidéré ; [person] sans égards pour les autres

**inconsistent** [ɪnkən'sɪstənt] *adj* [person] incohérent ; [uneven] irrégulier, -ère

**inconspicuous** [ɪnkən'spɪkjʊəs] *adj* qui passe inaperçu

**inconvenient** [ɪnkən'viːnɪənt] *adj* [moment] mauvais ; [arrangement] peu commode ; **it's inconvenient (for me) to...** ça me dérange de... ▪ **inconvenience 1.** *n* [bother] dérangement *m* ; [disadvantage] inconvénient *m* **2.** *vt* déranger

**incorporate** [ɪn'kɔːpəreɪt] *vt* [contain] contenir ; [introduce] incorporer (**into** dans)

**incorrect** [ɪnkə'rekt] *adj* incorrect

**increase 1.** [ɪn'kriːs] **1.** ['ɪnkriːs] *n* augmentation *f* (**in** *or* **of** de) ; **on the increase** en hausse **2.** *vt* augmenter **3.** *vi* augmenter ; **to increase in price** augmenter ▪ **increasing** *adj* croissant ▪ **increasingly** *adv* de plus en plus

**incredible** [ɪn'kredəbəl] *adj* incroyable

**incredulous** [ɪn'kredjʊləs] *adj* incrédule

**increment** ['ɪŋkrəmənt] *n* augmentation *f*

**incriminate** [ɪn'krɪmɪneɪt] *vt* incriminer ▪ **incriminating** *adj* compromettant

**incubate** ['ɪŋkjʊbeɪt] *vt* [eggs] couver ▪ **incubator** *n* [for baby] couveuse *f*

**incur** [ɪn'kɜː(r)] (*pt & pp* **-rr-**) *vt* [expenses] encourir ; [debt] contracter ; [criticism, anger] s'attirer

**incurable** [ɪn'kjʊərəbəl] *adj* incurable

**indebted** [ɪn'detɪd] *adj* **indebted to sb for sth / for doing sth** redevable à qn de qch / d'avoir fait qch

**indecent** [ɪn'diːsənt] *adj* [obscene] indécent

**indecisive** [ɪndɪ'saɪsɪv] *adj* [person] indécis

**indeed** [ɪn'diːd] *adv* en effet ; **very good indeed** vraiment très bon ; **thank you very much indeed!** merci infiniment !

**indefensible** [ɪndɪ'fensəbəl] *adj* indéfendable

**indefinite** [ɪn'defɪnət] *adj* [duration, number] indéterminé ; [plan] mal défini ▪ **indefinitely** *adv* indéfiniment

**indented** [ɪn'dentɪd] *adj* [edge, coastline] découpé

**independence** [ɪndɪ'pendəns] *n* indépendance *f* ; **Independence Day** fête de l'indépendance américaine, le 4 juillet

**independent** [ɪndɪ'pendənt] *adj* indépendant (**of** de) ; [opinions, reports] de sources différentes ▪ **independently** *adv* de façon indépendante ; **independently of** indépendamment de

**indescribable** [ɪndɪ'skraɪbəbəl] *adj* indescriptible

**indestructible** [ɪndɪ'strʌktəbəl] *adj* indestructible

**indeterminate** [ɪndɪ'tɜːmɪnət] *adj* indéterminé

**index** ['ɪndeks] **1.** *n* [in book] index *m* ; [in library] fichier *m* ; [number, sign] indice *m* ; **index card** fiche *f* ; **index finger** index *m* **2.** *vt* [classify] classer

**India** ['ɪndɪə] *n* l'Inde *f* ▪ **Indian 1.** *adj* indien, -enne **2.** *n* Indien, -enne *mf*

**indicate** ['ɪndɪkeɪt] *vt* indiquer (**that** que) ; **I was indicating right** [in vehicle] j'avais mis mon clignotant droit ▪ **indication** *n* [sign] signe *m* ; [information] indication *f*

**indicative** [ɪn'dɪkətɪv] *adj* **to be indicative of** [symptomatic] être symptomatique de

**indicator** ['ɪndɪkeɪtə(r)] *n* [sign] indicateur *f* (**of** de) ; *Br* [in vehicle] clignotant *m*

**infect**

**indifferent** [ɪn'dɪfərənt] *adj* indifférent (**to** à) ; [mediocre] médiocre

**indigestion** [ɪndɪ'dʒestʃən] *n* troubles *mpl* digestifs ; **(an attack of) indigestion** une indigestion

**indignant** [ɪn'dɪgnənt] *adj* indigné (**at** *or* **about** de)

**indirect** [ɪndaɪ'rekt] *adj* indirect

**indiscreet** [ɪndɪ'skri:t] *adj* indiscret, -ète

**indiscriminately** [ɪndɪ'skrɪmɪnətlɪ] *adv* [at random] au hasard ; [without discrimination] sans discernement

**indispensable** [ɪndɪ'spensəbəl] *adj* indispensable (**to** à)

**indisputable** [ɪndɪ'spju:təbəl] *adj* incontestable

**indistinct** [ɪndɪ'stɪŋkt] *adj* indistinct

**indistinguishable** [ɪndɪ'stɪŋgwɪʃəbəl] *adj* indifférenciable (**from** de)

**individual** [ɪndɪ'vɪdʒʊəl] **1.** *adj* [separate, personal] individuel, -elle ; [specific] particulier, -ère **2.** *n* [person] individu *m* ■ **individually** *adv* [separately] individuellement

**indivisible** [ɪndɪ'vɪzəbəl] *adj* indivisible

**indoctrinate** [ɪn'dɒktrɪneɪt] *vt* endoctriner

**Indonesia** [ɪndəʊ'ni:zɪə] *n* l'Indonésie *f*

**indoor** ['ɪndɔ:(r)] *adj* [games, shoes] d'intérieur ; [swimming pool] couvert ■ **indoors** *adv* à l'intérieur ; **to go /come indoors** rentrer

**induce** [ɪn'dju:s] *vt* [persuade] persuader (**to do** de faire) ; [cause] provoquer

**induction hob** *n* plaque *f* de cuisson à induction

**indulge** [ɪn'dʌldʒ] **1.** *vt* [sb's wishes] satisfaire ; [child] gâter **2.** *vi* **to indulge in sth** [ice cream, cigar] s'offrir qch ; [hobby, vice] s'adonner à qch ■ **indulgent** *adj* indulgent (**to** envers)

**industrial** [ɪn'dʌstrɪəl] *adj* industriel, -elle ; *Br* **to take industrial action** se mettre en grève ; *Br* **industrial estate,** *Am* **industrial park** zone *f* industrielle ■ **industrialist** *n* industriel *m* ■ **industrialized** *adj* industrialisé

**industrious** [ɪn'dʌstrɪəs] *adj* travailleur, -euse

**industry** ['ɪndəstrɪ] (*pl* -ies) *n* [economic sector] industrie *f* ; [hard work] application *f*

**inedible** [ɪn'edəbəl] *adj* immangeable

**ineffective** [ɪnɪ'fektɪv] *adj* [measure] inefficace ; [person] incapable

**ineffectual** [ɪnɪ'fektʃʊəl] *adj* [measure] inefficace ; [person] incompétent

**inefficient** [ɪnɪ'fɪʃənt] *adj* [person, measure] inefficace ; [machine] peu performant

**ineligible** [ɪn'elɪdʒəbəl] *adj* [candidate] inéligible ; **to be ineligible for sth** [scholarship] ne pas avoir droit à qch

**inept** [ɪ'nept] *adj* [incompetent] incompétent ; [foolish] inepte

**inequality** [ɪnɪ'kwɒlətɪ] (*pl* -ies) *n* inégalité *f*

**inert** [ɪ'nɜ:t] *adj* inerte

**inescapable** [ɪnɪ'skeɪpəbəl] *adj* [outcome] inéluctable ; [conclusion] incontournable

**inevitable** [ɪn'evɪtəbəl] *adj* inévitable

**inexcusable** [ɪnɪk'skju:zəbəl] *adj* inexcusable

**inexpensive** [ɪnɪk'spensɪv] *adj* bon marché *inv*

**inexperienced** [ɪnɪks'pɪərɪənst] *adj* inexpérimenté

**inexplicable** [ɪnɪk'splɪkəbəl] *adj* inexplicable

**infallible** [ɪn'fæləbəl] *adj* infaillible

**infamous** ['ɪnfəməs] *adj* [well-known] tristement célèbre ; [crime] infâme

**infant** ['ɪnfənt] *n* bébé *m* ; *Br* **infant school** école *primaire pour enfants de cinq à sept ans*

**infantry** ['ɪnfəntrɪ] *n* infanterie *f*

**infatuated** [ɪn'fætʃʊeɪtɪd] *adj* entiché (**with** de)

**infect** [ɪn'fekt] *vt* [wound, person] infecter ; [water, food] contaminer ; **to get** *or* **become infected** s'infecter ■ **infection** *n* infection *f* ■ **infectious** [-ʃəs] *adj* [disease] infectieux, -euse

**infer** [ɪnˈfɜː(r)] *(pt & pp* **-rr-***) vt* déduire (**from** de; **that** que)

**inferior** [ɪnˈfɪərɪə(r)] **1.** *adj* inférieur (**to** à); [goods, work] de qualité inférieure **2.** *n* [person] inférieur, -e *mf* ▪ **inferiority** [-rɪˈɒrɪtɪ] *n* infériorité *f*

**infernal** [ɪnˈfɜːnəl] *adj* infernal

**inferno** [ɪnˈfɜːnəʊ] *(pl* **-os***) n* [blaze] brasier *m*

**infertile** [*Br* ɪnˈfɜːtaɪl, *Am* ɪnˈfɜːrtəl] *adj* [person, land] stérile

**infest** [ɪnˈfest] *vt* infester (**with** de)

**infidelity** [ɪnfɪˈdelɪtɪ] *(pl* **-ies***) n* infidélité *f*

**infiltrate** [ˈɪnfɪltreɪt] **1.** *vt* infiltrer **2.** *vi* s'infiltrer (**into** dans)

**infinite** [ˈɪnfɪnɪt] *adj* infini ▪ **infinitely** *adv* infiniment

**infinitive** [ɪnˈfɪnɪtɪv] *n* [in grammar] infinitif *m*

**infinity** [ɪnˈfɪnɪtɪ] *n* MATH & PHOTO infini *m*

**infirmary** [ɪnˈfɜːmərɪ] *(pl* **-ies***) n* [hospital] hôpital *m*

**inflamed** [ɪnˈfleɪmd] *adj* [throat, wound] enflammé; **to become inflamed** s'enflammer

**inflammable** [ɪnˈflæməbəl] *adj* inflammable ▪ **inflammation** [-fləˈmeɪʃən] *n* inflammation *f*

**inflate** [ɪnˈfleɪt] *vt* [balloon, prices] gonfler ▪ **inflatable** *adj* gonflable

**inflation** [ɪnˈfleɪʃən] *n* ECON inflation *f*

**inflexible** [ɪnˈfleksəbəl] *adj* inflexible

**inflict** [ɪnˈflɪkt] *vt* [punishment, defeat] infliger (**on** à); [wound, damage] occasionner (**on** à)

**influence** [ˈɪnfluəns] **1.** *n* influence *f* (**on** sur) **2.** *vt* influencer ▪ **influential** [-ˈenʃəl] *adj* influent

**influenza** [ɪnfluˈenzə] *n* grippe *f*

**influx** [ˈɪnflʌks] *n* afflux *m* (**of** de)

**info** [ˈɪnfəʊ] *n Fam* renseignements *mpl* (**on** sur)

**inform** [ɪnˈfɔːm] **1.** *vt* informer (**of** or **about** de; **that** que) **2.** *vi* **to inform on**

**sb** dénoncer qn ▪ **informed** *adj* **to keep sb informed of sth** tenir qn au courant de qch

**informal** [ɪnˈfɔːməl] *adj* [unaffected] simple; [casual] décontracté; [tone, language] familier, -ère; [unofficial] officieux, -euse ▪ **informally** *adv* [unaffectedly] avec simplicité; [casually] avec décontraction; [meet, discuss] officieusement

**information** [ɪnfəˈmeɪʃən] *n* [facts, news] renseignements *mpl* (**about** or **on** sur); COMPUT information *f*; **a piece of information** un renseignement, une information; **to get some information** se renseigner; **information technology** informatique *f*; **information desk** bureau *m* de(s) renseignements

**informative** [ɪnˈfɔːmətɪv] *adj* instructif, -ive

**infrequent** [ɪnˈfriːkwənt] *adj* peu fréquent

**infringe** [ɪnˈfrɪndʒ] **1.** *vt* [rule, law] enfreindre à **2.** *vt insep* **to infringe upon sth** empiéter sur qch

**infuriating** [ɪnˈfjʊərɪeɪtɪŋ] *adj* exaspérant

**infusion** [ɪnˈfjuːʒən] *n* [drink] infusion *f*

**ingenious** [ɪnˈdʒiːnɪəs] *adj* ingénieux, -euse

**ingrained** [ɪnˈɡreɪnd] *adj* [prejudice, attitude] enraciné; **ingrained dirt** crasse *f*

**ingredient** [ɪnˈɡriːdɪənt] *n* ingrédient *m*

**inhabit** [ɪnˈhæbɪt] *vt* habiter ▪ **inhabitant** *n* habitant, -e *mf*

**inhale** [ɪnˈheɪl] *vt* [gas, fumes] inhaler; [cigarette smoke] avaler

**inherent** [ɪnˈhɪərənt] *adj* inhérent (**in** à)

**inherit** [ɪnˈherɪt] *vt* hériter (**from** de); [title] accéder à ▪ **inheritance** *n* [legacy] héritage *m*

**inhibit** [ɪnˈhɪbɪt] *vt* [progress, growth] entraver; [of person] inhiber; **to inhibit sb from doing sth** empêcher qn de faire qch ▪ **inhibited** *adj* [person] inhibé ▪ **inhibition** *n* inhibition *f*

**inhospitable** [ɪnhɒˈspɪtəbəl] *adj* inhospitalier, -ère

**inhuman** [ɪn'hju:mən] *adj* inhumain
■ **inhumane** [-'meɪn] *adj* inhumain

**initial** [ɪ'nɪʃəl] **1.** *adj* initial **2.** *npl* **initials** [letters] initiales *fpl*; [signature] paraphe *m* **3.** *(Br* -**ll**-, *Am* -**l**-*) vt* parapher ■ **initially** *adv* au début, initialement

**initiate** [ɪ'nɪʃɪeɪt] *vt* [reform, negotiations] amorcer; [attack, rumour, project] lancer

**initiative** [ɪ'nɪʃɪtɪv] *n* initiative *f*

**inject** [ɪn'dʒekt] *vt* injecter (**into** dans); **to inject sth into sb, to inject sb with sth** faire une piqûre de qch à qn ■ **injection** *n* injection *f*, piqûre *f*; **to give sb an injection** faire une piqûre à qn

**injure** ['ɪndʒə(r)] *vt* [physically] blesser; [reputation] nuire à; **to injure one's foot** se blesser au pied ■ **injured 1.** *adj* blessé **2.** *npl* **the injured** les blessés *mpl*

**injury** ['ɪndʒərɪ] *(pl* -**ies***) n* [physical] blessure *f*; **injury time** [in sport] arrêts *mpl* de jeu

**injustice** [ɪn'dʒʌstɪs] *n* injustice *f*

**ink** [ɪŋk] *n* encre *f*

**inlaid** [ɪn'leɪd] *adj* [with jewels] incrusté (**with** de); [with wood] marqueté

**inland 1.** ['ɪnlənd, 'ɪnlænd] *adj* intérieur; *Br* **the Inland Revenue** ≃ le fisc **2.** [ɪn'lænd] *adv* [travel] vers l'intérieur

**in-laws** ['ɪnlɔ:z] *npl* belle-famille *f*

**inlet** ['ɪnlet] *n* [of sea] crique *f*

**inmate** ['ɪnmeɪt] *n* [of prison] détenu, -e *mf*; [of asylum] interné, -e *mf*

**inn** [ɪn] *n* auberge *f*

**innate** [ɪ'neɪt] *adj* inné

**inner** ['ɪnə(r)] *adj* intérieur; [feelings] intime; **inner circle** [of society] initiés *mpl*; **inner city** quartiers *mpl* déshérités du centre-ville; **inner tube** chambre *f* à air ■ **innermost** *adj* le plus profond (*f* la plus profonde); [thoughts] le plus secret (*f* la plus secrète)

**inning** ['ɪnɪŋ] *n* [in baseball] tour *m* de batte ■ **innings** *n inv* [in cricket] tour *m* de batte

**innocent** ['ɪnəsənt] *adj* innocent

**innovate** ['ɪnəveɪt] *vi & vt* innover

**innovation** [ɪnə'veɪʃən] *n* innovation *f*

**innumerable** [ɪ'nju:mərəbəl] *adj* innombrable

**inoculate** [ɪ'nɒkjʊleɪt] *vt* vacciner (**against** contre) ■ **inoculation** *n* inoculation *f*

**inoffensive** [ɪnə'fensɪv] *adj* inoffensif, -ive

**inopportune** [ɪn'ɒpətju:n] *adj* inopportun

**in-patient** ['ɪnpeɪʃənt] *n Br* malade *mf* hospitalisé(e)

**input** ['ɪnpʊt] **1.** *n* [contribution] contribution *f*; COMPUT [operation] entrée *f*; [data] données *fpl* **2.** *(pt & pp* -**put***) vt* COMPUT [data] entrer

**inquest** ['ɪnkwest] *n* [legal investigation] enquête *f*

**inquire** [ɪn'kwaɪə(r)] **1.** *vt* demander; **to inquire how to get to...** demander le chemin de... **2.** *vi* se renseigner (**about** sur); **to inquire after sb** demander des nouvelles de qn; **to inquire into sth** faire des recherches sur qch

**inquiry** [ɪn'kwaɪərɪ] *(pl* -**ies***) n* [request for information] demande *f* de renseignements; [official investigation] enquête *f*; **to make inquiries** demander des renseignements; [of police] enquêter; *Br* **inquiry desk** bureau *m* de(s) renseignements

**inquisitive** [ɪn'kwɪzɪtɪv] *adj* curieux, -euse

**insane** [ɪn'seɪn] *adj* dément, fou (*f* folle); **to go insane** perdre la raison

**insatiable** [ɪn'seɪʃəbəl] *adj* insatiable

**inscribe** [ɪn'skraɪb] *vt* inscrire; [book] dédicacer (**to** à) ■ **inscription** [-'skrɪpʃən] *n* inscription *f*; [in book] dédicace *f*

**insect** ['ɪnsekt] *n* insecte *m*; **insect repellent** anti-moustiques *m inv*

**insecure** [ɪnsɪ'kjʊə(r)] *adj* [unsafe] peu sûr; [job, future] précaire; [person] angoissé

**insemination** [ɪnsemɪ'neɪʃən] *n* **artificial insemination** insémination *f* artificielle

**insensitive** [ɪn'sensɪtɪv] *adj* [person] insensible (**to** à) ; [remark] indélicat

**inseparable** [ɪn'sepərəbəl] *adj* inséparable (**from** de)

**insert** [ɪn'sɜːt] *vt* insérer (**in** or **into** dans) ■ **insertion** *n* insertion *f*

**inside 1.** ['ɪnsaɪd] *adj* intérieur ; [information] obtenu à la source ; AUTO **the inside lane** [in Britain] la voie de gauche ; [in Europe, US] la voie de droite **2.** ['ɪn'saɪd] *n* intérieur *m* ; *Fam* **insides** [stomach] entrailles *fpl* ; **on the inside** à l'intérieur (**of** de) ; **inside out** [clothes] à l'envers ; [know, study] à fond **3.** [ɪn'saɪd] *adv* à l'intérieur **4.** [ɪn'saɪd] *prep* à l'intérieur de, dans ; [time] en moins de

**insider** [ɪn'saɪdə(r)] *n* initié, -e *mf*

**insidious** [ɪn'sɪdɪəs] *adj* insidieux, -euse

**insight** ['ɪnsaɪt] *n* perspicacité *f* ; [into question] aperçu *m*

**insignificant** [ɪnsɪg'nɪfɪkənt] *adj* insignifiant

**insincere** [ɪnsɪn'sɪə(r)] *adj* peu sincère

**insinuate** [ɪn'sɪnjʊeɪt] *vt* [suggest] insinuer (**that** que)

**insipid** [ɪn'sɪpɪd] *adj* insipide

**insist** [ɪn'sɪst] **1.** *vt* [maintain] soutenir (**that** que) ; **I insist that you come** or **on your coming** [I demand it] j'insiste pour que tu viennes **2.** *vi* insister ; **to insist on sth** [demand] exiger qch ; [assert] affirmer qch ; **to insist on doing sth** tenir à faire qch

**insistence** [ɪn'sɪstəns] *n* insistance *f* ■ **insistent** *adj* [person] pressant ; **to be insistent (that)** insister (pour que (+ *subjunctive*))

**insolent** ['ɪnsələnt] *adj* insolent

**insoluble** [ɪn'sɒljʊbəl] *adj* insoluble

**insolvent** [ɪn'sɒlvənt] *adj* [financially] insolvable

**insomnia** [ɪn'sɒmnɪə] *n* insomnie *f*

**insomuch as** [ɪnsəʊ'mʌtʃəz] *adv* = **inasmuch as**

**inspect** [ɪn'spekt] *vt* inspecter ; [tickets] contrôler ; [troops] passer en revue ■ **inspector** *n* inspecteur, -trice *mf* ; [on train] contrôleur, -euse *mf*

**inspire** [ɪn'spaɪə(r)] *vt* inspirer ; **to inspire sb to do sth** pousser qn à faire qch ■ **inspiration** [-spə'reɪʃən] *n* inspiration *f* ; [person] source *f* d'inspiration

**instability** [ɪnstə'bɪlɪtɪ] *n* instabilité *f*

**install**, *Am* **instal** [ɪn'stɔːl] *vt* [fit & COMPUT] installer

**instalment**, *Am* **installment** [ɪn'stɔːlmənt] *n* [part payment] versement *m* ; [of serial, story] épisode *m* ; [of publication] fascicule *m* ; **to pay by instalments** payer par versements échelonnés ; *Am* **to buy on the instalment plan** acheter à crédit

**instance** ['ɪnstəns] *n* [example] exemple *m* ; [case] cas *m* ; **for instance** par exemple ; **in this instance** dans le cas présent

**instant** ['ɪnstənt] **1.** *adj* immédiat ; **instant access** [bank account] à accès immédiat ; **instant coffee** café *m* instantané ; **instant messaging** messagerie *f* instantanée **2.** *n* [moment] instant *m* ; **this (very) instant** [at once] à l'instant ; **the instant that I saw her** dès que je l'ai vue ■ **instantly** *adv* immédiatement

**instantaneous** [ɪnstən'teɪnɪəs] *adj* instantané

**instead** [ɪn'sted] *adv* [in place of sth] à la place ; [in place of sb] à ma /ta /*etc* place ; **instead of sth** au lieu de qch ; **instead of doing sth** au lieu de faire qch ; **instead of him /her** à sa place

**instigate** ['ɪnstɪgeɪt] *vt* provoquer ■ **instigator** *n* instigateur, -trice *mf*

**instil**, *Am* **instill** [ɪn'stɪl] (*pt & pp* -ll-) *vt* [idea] inculquer (**into** à) ; [doubt] instiller (**in** à)

**instinct** ['ɪnstɪŋkt] *n* instinct *m* ; **by instinct** d'instinct ■ **instinctive** *adj* instinctif, -ive

**institute** ['ɪnstɪtjuːt] **1.** *n* institut *m* **2.** *vt* [rule, practice] instituer ; [legal inquiry] ordonner

**institution** [ɪnstɪ'tjuːʃən] *n* [organization, custom] institution *f* ; [public, financial, religious, psychiatric] établissement *m*

**instruct** [ɪn'strʌkt] *vt* [teach] enseigner (**sb in sth** qch à qn) ; **to instruct sb**

**interchange**

**about sth** [inform] instruire qn de qch; **to instruct sb to do** [order] charger qn de faire ■ **instruction** [-ʃən] n [teaching, order] instruction f; **instructions (for use)** mode m d'emploi ■ **instructor** n [for judo, dance] professeur m; [for skiing, swimming] moniteur, -trice mf; **driving instructor** moniteur, -trice mf d'auto-école

**instrument** ['ɪnstrəmənt] n instrument m

**instrumental** [ɪnstrə'mentəl] adj [music] instrumental; **to be instrumental in sth/in doing sth** contribuer à qch/à faire qch

**insubordinate** [ɪnsə'bɔːdɪnət] adj insubordonné

**insufferable** [ɪn'sʌfərəbəl] adj intolérable

**insufficient** [ɪnsə'fɪʃənt] adj insuffisant ■ **insufficiently** adv insuffisamment

**insulate** ['ɪnsjʊleɪt] vt [against cold & ELEC] isoler; [against sound] insonoriser ■ **insulation** n isolation f; [against sound] insonorisation f; [material] isolant m

**insulin** ['ɪnsjʊlɪn] n insuline f

**insult 1.** ['ɪnsʌlt] n insulte f (**to** à) **2.** [ɪn'sʌlt] vt insulter

**insure** [ɪn'ʃʊə(r)] vt **a)** [house, car, goods] assurer (**against** contre) **b)** Am = **ensure** ■ **insurance** n assurance f; **insurance policy** police f d'assurance

**insurmountable** [ɪnsə'maʊntəbəl] adj insurmontable

**intact** [ɪn'tækt] adj intact

**intake** ['ɪnteɪk] n [of food] consommation f; [of students, schoolchildren] admissions fpl

**intangible** [ɪn'tændʒəbəl] adj intangible

**integral** ['ɪntɪɡrəl] adj intégral; **to be an integral part of sth** faire partie intégrante de qch

**integrate** ['ɪntɪɡreɪt] **1.** vt intégrer (**into** dans) **2.** vi s'intégrer (**into** dans) ■ **integration** n intégration f; **(racial) integration** déségrégation f raciale

**integrity** [ɪn'teɡrətɪ] n intégrité f

**intellect** ['ɪntɪlekt] n intelligence f, intellect m ■ **intellectual** adj & n intellectuel, -elle (mf)

**intelligence** [ɪn'telɪdʒəns] n intelligence f

**intelligent** [ɪn'telɪdʒənt] adj intelligent

**intelligible** [ɪn'telɪdʒəbəl] adj intelligible

**intend** [ɪn'tend] vt [gift, remark] destiner (**for** à); **to be intended to do sth** être destiné à faire qch; **to intend to do sth** avoir l'intention de faire qch ■ **intended** adj [deliberate] voulu; [planned] prévu

**intense** [ɪn'tens] adj intense; [interest] vif (f vive); [person] passionné ■ **intensely** adv [look at] intensément; Fig [very] extrêmement

**intensify** [ɪn'tensɪfaɪ] (pt & pp -ied) **1.** vt intensifier **2.** vi s'intensifier

**intensity** [ɪn'tensətɪ] n intensité f

**intensive** [ɪn'tensɪv] adj intensif, -ive; **in intensive care** en réanimation; **intensive care unit** service m de réanimation, unité f de soins intensifs

**intent** [ɪn'tent] **1.** adj [look] intense; **to be intent on doing** être résolu à faire **2.** n intention f; **to all intents and purposes** quasiment

**intention** [ɪn'tenʃən] n intention f (**of doing** de faire)

**intentional** [ɪn'tenʃənəl] adj intentionnel, -elle; **it wasn't intentional** ce n'était pas fait exprès ■ **intentionally** adv intentionnellement, exprès

**inter** [ɪn'tɜː(r)] (pt & pp -rr-) vt enterrer

**inter-** [ɪntə(r)] pref inter-

**interact** [ɪntər'ækt] vi [of person] communiquer (**with** avec); [of several people] communiquer entre eux/elles; [of chemicals] réagir (**with** avec)

**interactive** [ɪntə'ræktɪv] adj COMPUT interactif, -ive; **interactive whiteboard** tableau m blanc interactif

**intercept** [ɪntə'sept] vt intercepter

**interchange** ['ɪntətʃeɪndʒ] n Br [on road] échangeur m

**interchangeable** [ɪntə'tʃeɪndʒəbəl] *adj* interchangeable

**inter-city** [ɪntə'sɪtɪ] *adj Br* inter-city **train** train *m* de grandes lignes

**intercom** ['ɪntəkɒm] *n* Interphone® *m*

**interconnected** [ɪntəkə'nektɪd] *adj* [facts] lié(e)s

**intercourse** ['ɪntəkɔːs] *n* [sexual] rapports *mpl* sexuels

**interdependent** [ɪntədɪ'pendənt] *adj* interdépendant ; [parts of machine] solidaire

**interest** ['ɪntərest, 'ɪntrɪst] **1.** *n* intérêt *m* ; [hobby] centre *m* d'intérêt ; [money] intérêts *mpl* ; **to take an interest in sb/sth** s'intéresser à qn/qch ; **to lose interest in sb/sth** se désintéresser de qn/qch ; **to be of interest to sb** intéresser qn **2.** *vt* intéresser ■ **interested** *adj* intéressé ; **to be interested in sb/sth** s'intéresser à qn/qch ; **are you interested?** ça vous intéresse ? ■ **interest-free** *adj* [loan] sans intérêts ; [credit] gratuit ■ **interesting** *adj* intéressant

**interface** ['ɪntəfeɪs] *n* COMPUT interface *f*

**interfere** [ɪntə'fɪə(r)] *vi* [meddle] se mêler **(in** de) ; **to interfere with sth** [hinder] gêner qch ; [touch] toucher à qch

**interference** [ɪntə'fɪərəns] *n* ingérence *f* ; [on television, radio] parasites *mpl*

**interim** ['ɪntərɪm] **1.** *n* **in the interim** entre-temps **2.** *adj* [measure] provisoire

**interior** [ɪn'tɪərɪə(r)] *adj & n* intérieur *(m)*

**interlock** [ɪntə'lɒk] *vi* [of machine parts] s'emboîter

**interlude** ['ɪntəluːd] *n* [on TV] interlude *m* ; [in theatre] intermède *m* ; [period of time] intervalle *m*

**intermediary** [ɪntə'miːdɪərɪ] *(pl* -ies*) n* intermédiaire *mf*

**intermediate** [ɪntə'miːdɪət] *adj* intermédiaire ; [course, student] de niveau moyen

**intermission** [ɪntə'mɪʃən] *n* entracte *m*

**intermittent** [ɪntə'mɪtənt] *adj* intermittent

**intern 1.** ['ɪntɜːn] *n Am* [gen] stagiaire *mf* ; *Am* MED interne *mf* **2.** [ɪn'tɜːn] *vt* [imprison] interner

**internal** [ɪn'tɜːnəl] *adj* interne ; [flight, policy] intérieur ; *Am* **the Internal Revenue Service** ≃ le fisc ■ **internally** *adv* intérieurement

**international** [ɪntə'næʃənəl] **1.** *adj* international **2.** *n* [match] rencontre *f* internationale ; [player] international *m*

**Internet** ['ɪntənet] *n* COMPUT **the Internet** l'Internet *m* ; **Internet access** accès *m* (à l')Internet ; **Internet address** adresse *f* Internet ; **Internet café** cybercafé *m* ; **Internet service provider** fournisseur *m* d'accès Internet ; **Internet user** internaute *mf*

**interpret** [ɪn'tɜːprɪt] **1.** *vt* interpréter **2.** *vi* [translate for people] faire l'interprète ■ **interpretation** *n* interprétation *f* ■ **interpreter** *n* interprète *mf*

**interrelated** [ɪntərɪ'leɪtɪd] *adj* lié

**interrogate** [ɪn'terəgeɪt] *vt* interroger ■ **interrogation** [-'geɪʃən] *n* interrogation *f* ; [by police] interrogatoire *m*

**interrupt** [ɪntə'rʌpt] **1.** *vt* interrompre **2.** *vi* **I'm sorry to interrupt** je suis désolé de vous interrompre ■ **interruption** *n* interruption *f*

**intersect** [ɪntə'sekt] **1.** *vt* couper **2.** *vi* se couper ■ **intersection** *n* intersection *f* ; [of roads] croisement *m*

**interstate** ['ɪntəsteɪt] *n* autoroute *f*

**interval** ['ɪntəvəl] *n* intervalle *m* ; *Br* [in theatre, cinema] entracte *m* ; **at intervals** [in time] de temps à autre ; [in space] par intervalles ; **at five-minute intervals** toutes les cinq minutes

**intervene** [ɪntə'viːn] *vi* [of person] intervenir **(in** dans) ; [of event] survenir ■ **intervention** [-'venʃən] *n* intervention *f*

**interview** ['ɪntəvjuː] **1.** *n* entretien *m* **(with** avec) ; TV & JOURN interview *m* ou *f* **2.** *vt* [for job] faire passer un entretien à ; TV & JOURN interviewer ■ **inter-**

**viewer** *n* TV intervieweur, -euse *mf*; [for research, in canvassing] enquêteur, -euse *mf*

**intestine** [ɪnˈtestɪn] *n* intestin *m*

**intimate** [ˈɪntɪmət] *adj* intime; [friendship] profond; [knowledge] approfondi ■ **intimately** *adv* intimement

**intimidate** [ɪnˈtɪmɪdeɪt] *vt* intimider

**into** [ˈɪntuː] (*unstressed* [ˈɪntə]) *prep* **a)** dans; **to put sth into sth** mettre qch dans qch; **to go into a room** entrer dans une pièce **b)** en; **to translate into French** traduire en français; **to change sb into sth** changer qn en qch; **to break sth into pieces** briser qch en morceaux; **to go into town** aller en ville **c)** MATH **three into six goes two** six divisé par trois fait deux **d)** *Fam* **to be into jazz** être branché jazz

**intolerable** [ɪnˈtɒlərəbəl] *adj* intolérable (**that** que (+ subjunctive))

**intolerance** [ɪnˈtɒlərəns] *n* intolérance *f* ■ **intolerant** *adj* intolérant

**intonation** [ɪntəˈneɪʃən] *n* intonation *f*

**intoxicated** [ɪnˈtɒksɪkeɪtɪd] *adj* ivre

**intransigent** [ɪnˈtrænsɪdʒənt] *adj* intransigeant

**intransitive** [ɪnˈtrænsɪtɪv] *adj* [in grammar] intransitif, -ive

**intricate** [ˈɪntrɪkət] *adj* compliqué

**intrigue 1.** [ˈɪntriːg] *n* [plot] intrigue *f* **2.** [ɪnˈtriːg] *vt* [interest] intriguer ■ **intriguing** *adj* [news, attitude] curieux, -euse

**introduce** [ɪntrəˈdjuːs] *vt* [bring in, insert] introduire (**into** dans); [programme, subject] présenter; **to introduce sb (to sb)** présenter qn (à qn)

**introduction** [ɪntrəˈdʌkʃən] *n* introduction *f*; [of person to person] présentation *f* ■ **introductory** *adj* [words, speech] d'introduction; [course] d'initiation

**introvert** [ˈɪntrəvɜːt] *n* introverti, -e *mf*

**intrude** [ɪnˈtruːd] *vi* [of person] déranger (**on sb** qn) ■ **intruder** *n* intrus, -e *mf* ■ **intrusion** *n* [bother] dérangement *m*; [interference] intrusion *f* (**into** dans)

**intuition** [ɪntjuːˈɪʃən] *n* intuition *f*

**inundate** [ˈɪnʌndeɪt] *vt* inonder (**with** de); **inundated with work / letters** submergé de travail / lettres

**invade** [ɪnˈveɪd] *vt* envahir ■ **invader** *n* envahisseur, -euse *mf*

**invalid**[1] [ˈɪnvəlɪd] *adj & n* malade (*mf*); [disabled person] infirme (*mf*)

**invalid**[2] [ɪnˈvælɪd] *adj* [ticket, passport] non valable ■ **invalidate** *vt* [ticket] annuler; [election, law] invalider; [theory] infirmer

**invaluable** [ɪnˈvæljʊəbəl] *adj* inestimable

**invariably** [ɪnˈveərɪəblɪ] *adv* invariablement

**invasion** [ɪnˈveɪʒən] *n* invasion *f*

**invent** [ɪnˈvent] *vt* inventer ■ **invention** *n* invention *f* ■ **inventor** *n* inventeur, -trice *mf*

**inventory** [ˈɪnvəntərɪ] (*pl* **-ies**) *n* inventaire *m*

**invert** [ɪnˈvɜːt] *vt* [order] intervertir; [turn upside down] renverser; *Br* **inverted commas** guillemets *mpl*

**invest** [ɪnˈvest] **1.** *vt* [money] investir (**in** dans); [time, effort] consacrer (**in à**) **2.** *vi* *Fig* [car] se payer; **to invest in** [company] investir dans ■ **investment** *n* investissement *m* ■ **investor** *n* [in shares] investisseur *m*

**investigate** [ɪnˈvestɪgeɪt] *vt* [examine] examiner; [crime] enquêter sur ■ **investigation** *n* examen *m*, étude *f*; [inquiry by journalist, police] enquête *f* (**of** *or* **into** sur) ■ **investigator** *n* [detective] enquêteur, -euse *mf*; [private] détective *m*

**invigilator** [ɪnˈvɪdʒɪleɪtə(r)] *n* *Br* surveillant, -e *mf* (à un examen)

**invigorating** [ɪnˈvɪgəreɪtɪŋ] *adj* vivifiant

**invincible** [ɪnˈvɪnsəbəl] *adj* invincible

**invisible** [ɪnˈvɪzəbəl] *adj* invisible

**invite 1.** [ɪn'vaɪt] *vt* inviter (**to do à** faire) ; [ask for] demander ; **to invite sb out** inviter qn (à sortir) **2.** ['ɪnvaɪt] *n Fam* invit' *f* ■ **invitation** [-vɪ'teɪʃən] *n* invitation *f*

**invoice** ['ɪnvɔɪs] **1.** *n* facture *f* **2.** *vt* [goods] facturer ; [person] envoyer la facture à

**invoke** [ɪn'vəʊk] *vt* invoquer

**involuntary** [ɪn'vɒləntərɪ] *adj* involontaire

**involve** [ɪn'vɒlv] *vt* [entail] entraîner ; **to involve sb in sth** impliquer qn dans qch ; [in project] associer qn à qch ; **the job involves going abroad** le poste nécessite des déplacements à l'étranger

**involved** [ɪn'vɒlvd] *adj* **a)** to be involved in an accident avoir un accident ; **fifty people were involved in the project** cinquante personnes ont pris part au projet ; **to be involved with sb** [emotionally] avoir une liaison avec qn ; **the factors involved** [at stake] les facteurs en jeu ; **the person involved** [concerned] la personne en question **b)** [complicated] compliqué

**involvement** [ɪn'vɒlvmənt] *n* participation *f* (**in** à) ; [commitment] engagement *m* (**in** dans)

**invulnerable** [ɪn'vʌlnərəbəl] *adj* invulnérable

**inward** ['ɪnwəd] **1.** *adj & adv* [movement, move] vers l'intérieur **2.** *adj* [inner-happiness] intérieur ; [thoughts] intime ■ **inwardly** *adv* [laugh, curse] intérieurement ■ **inwards** *adv* vers l'intérieur

**iodine** [*Br* 'aɪədiːn, *Am* 'aɪədaɪn] *n* [antiseptic] teinture *f* d'iode

**IOU** [aɪəʊ'juː] *(abbr of I owe you) n* reconnaissance *f* de dette

**IP** *(abbr of* **Internet Protocol***) n* IP **address** adresse *f* IP

**iPod**® ['aɪpɒd] *n* iPod® *m* ■ **iPodder** ['aɪpɒdə(r)] *n* utilisateur, -trice *m,f* d'iPod

**IQ** [aɪ'kjuː] *(abbr of* **intelligence quotient***) n* QI *m inv*

**Iran** [ɪ'rɑːn, ɪ'ræn] *n* l'Iran *m* ■ **Iranian** [ɪ'reɪnɪən, *Am* ɪ'rɑːnɪən] **1.** *adj* iranien, -enne **2.** *n* Iranien, -enne *mf*

**Iraq** [ɪ'rɑːk] *n* l'Irak *m* ■ **Iraqi 1.** *adj* irakien, -enne **2.** *n* Irakien, -enne *mf*

**irate** [aɪ'reɪt] *adj* furieux, -euse

**IRC** *(abbr of* **Internet Relay Chat***) n* IRC *m (dialogue en temps réel)*

**Ireland** ['aɪələnd] *n* l'Irlande *f* ■ **Irish** ['aɪrɪʃ] **1.** *adj* irlandais **2.** *n* [language] irlandais *m* ; **the Irish** [people] les Irlandais *mpl* ■ **Irishman** *(pl* **-men***) n* Irlandais *m* ■ **Irishwoman** *(pl* **-women***) n* Irlandaise *f*

**iris** ['aɪrɪs] *n* [plant, of eye] iris *m*

**iron** ['aɪən] **1.** *n* fer *m* ; [for clothes] fer *m* à repasser **2.** *vt* [clothes] repasser ; *Fig* **to iron out difficulties** aplanir les difficultés ■ **ironing** *n* repassage *m* ; **ironing board** planche *f* à repasser

**ironmonger** ['aɪənmʌŋgə(r)] *n* quincaillier, -ère *mf* ; **ironmonger's (shop)** quincaillerie *f*

**irony** ['aɪərənɪ] *n* ironie *f* ■ **ironic(al)** [aɪ'rɒnɪk(əl)] *adj* ironique

**irrational** [ɪ'ræʃənəl] *adj* irrationnel, -elle

**irrefutable** [ɪrɪ'fjuːtəbəl] *adj* [evidence] irréfutable

**irregular** [ɪ'regjʊlə(r)] *adj* irrégulier, -ère ■ **irregularity** [-'lærɪtɪ] *(pl* **-ies***) n* irrégularité *f*

**irrelevant** [ɪ'reləvənt] *adj* sans rapport (**to** avec) ; [remark] hors de propos ; **that's irrelevant** ça n'a rien à voir (avec la question)

**irreparable** [ɪ'repərəbəl] *adj* [harm, loss] irréparable

**irreplaceable** [ɪrɪ'pleɪsəbəl] *adj* irremplaçable

**irresistible** [ɪrɪ'zɪstəbəl] *adj* [person, charm] irrésistible

**irrespective** [ɪrɪ'spektɪv] *prep* **irrespective of** indépendamment de

**irresponsible** [ɪrɪ'spɒnsəbəl] *adj* [act] irréfléchi ; [person] irresponsable

**irreverent** [ɪ'revərənt] *adj* irrévérencieux, -euse

**irreversible** [ɪrɪ'vɜːsəbəl] *adj* [process] irréversible ; [decision] irrévocable

**irrigate** ['ɪrɪɡeɪt] *vt* irriguer

**irritable** ['ɪrɪtəbəl] *adj* [easily annoyed] irritable

**irritant** ['ɪrɪtənt] *n* [to eyes, skin] irritant *m*

**irritate** ['ɪrɪteɪt] *vt* [annoy, inflame] irriter ■ **irritating** *adj* irritant

**is** [ɪz] *see* **be**

**Islam** ['ɪzlɑːm] *n* l'Islam *m* ■ **Islamic** [ɪz'læmɪk] *adj* islamique

**island** ['aɪlənd] *n* île *f*; **(traffic) island** refuge *m* (pour piétons) ■ **islander** *n* insulaire *mf*

**isle** [aɪl] *n* île *f*

**isn't** ['ɪzənt] = **is not**

**isolate** ['aɪsəleɪt] *vt* isoler (**from** de) ■ **isolated** *adj* [remote, unique] isolé ■ **isolation** *n* isolement *m*; **in isolation** isolément

**ISP** [aɪes'piː] *(abbr of* **Internet Service Provider)** *n* COMPUT fournisseur *m* d'accès Internet

**Israel** ['ɪzreɪl] *n* Israël *m* ■ **Israeli 1.** *adj* israélien, -enne **2.** *n* Israélien, -enne *mf*

**ISS** ['aɪes'es] *(abbr of* **In School Suspension)** *n* Am SCH exclusion *f* interne

**issue** ['ɪʃuː] **1.** *n* [of newspaper, magazine] numéro *m*; [matter] question *f*; **at issue** [at stake] en cause ; **to make an issue** *or* **a big issue of sth** faire toute une affaire de qch **2.** *vt* [book] publier ; [tickets] distribuer ; [passport] délivrer ; [order] donner ; [warning] lancer ; [stamps, banknotes] émettre ; [supply] fournir (**with** de ; **to** à) ; **to issue a statement** faire une déclaration

**it** [ɪt] *pron* **a)** [subject] il, elle ; [object] le, la, l' ; **(to) it** [indirect object] lui ; **it bites** [dog] il mord ; **I've done it** je l'ai fait **b)** [impersonal] il ; **it's snowing** il neige ; **it's hot** il fait chaud

**c)** [non-specific] ce, cela, ça ; **it's good** c'est bon ; **who is it?** qui est-ce ? ; **to consider it wise to do sth** juger prudent de faire qch ; **it was Paul who...** c'est Paul qui... ; **to have it in for sb** en vouloir à qn **d)** of it, from it, about it en ; in it, to it, at it y ; on it dessus ; under it dessous

■ **it-girl** *n Fam* jeune femme fortement médiatisée ; **she's the it-girl** c'est la fille dont on parle

---

**IT** *(abbr of* **information technology)** *n* informatique *f*

**italics** [ɪ'tælɪks] *npl* italique *m* ; **in italics** en italique

**Italy** ['ɪtəlɪ] *n* l'Italie *f* ■ **Italian** [ɪ'tælɪən] **1.** *adj* italien, -enne **2.** *n* [person] Italien, -enne *mf* ; [language] italien *m*

**itch** [ɪtʃ] **1.** *n* démangeaison *f* **2.** *vi* [of person] avoir des démangeaisons ; **his arm itches** son bras le *ou* lui démange ; *Fig* **to be itching to do sth** brûler d'envie de faire qch ■ **itchy** ['ɪtʃɪ] *adj* qui démange

**item** ['aɪtəm] *n* [in collection, on list, in newspaper] article *m* ; [matter] question *f* ; **item of clothing** vêtement *m* ; **news item** information *f* ■ **itemize** *vt* [invoice] détailler

**itinerary** [aɪ'tɪnərərɪ] *(pl* **-ies)** *n* itinéraire *m*

**its** [ɪts] *poss adj* son, sa, *pl* ses ■ **itself** *pron* lui-même, elle-même ; [reflexive] se, s' ; **by itself** tout seul

**I've** [aɪv] = **I have**

**ivory** ['aɪvərɪ] *n* ivoire *m*

**ivy** ['aɪvɪ] *n* lierre *m*

**IWB** *n abbr of* **interactive whiteboard**

**IYD** MESSAGING *written abbr of* **in your dreams**

# J

**J, j** [dʒeɪ] n (letter) J, j m inv

**jab** [dʒæb] **1.** n coup m ; Br Fam [injection] piqûre f **2.** (pt & pp -bb-) vt [knife, stick] enfoncer (**into** dans) ; [prick] piquer (**with** du bout de)

**jack** [dʒæk] **1.** n a) [for vehicle] cric m b) [card] valet m **2.** vt to jack up [vehicle] soulever (avec un cric)

**jacket** ['dʒækɪt] n [coat] veste f ; [of book] jaquette f ; Br **jacket potato** pomme f de terre en robe des champs

**jackknife** ['dʒæknaɪf] **1.** (pl -knives) n couteau m de poche **2.** vi Br [of truck] se mettre en travers de la route

**jackpot** ['dʒækpɒt] n gros lot m

**Jacuzzi®** [dʒə'ku:zɪ] n Jacuzzi® m

**jagged** ['dʒægɪd] adj déchiqueté

**jail** [dʒeɪl] **1.** n prison f **2.** vt emprisonner (**for** pour)

**jam¹** [dʒæm] n [preserve] confiture f ; **strawberry jam** confiture f de fraises ▪ **jamjar** n pot m à confiture

**jam²** [dʒæm] **1.** n **(traffic) jam** embouteillage m **2.** (pt & pp -mm-) vt [squeeze, make stuck] coincer ; [street, corridor] encombrer ; **to jam sth into sth** entasser qch dans qch ; **to jam on the brakes** écraser la pédale de frein **3.** vi [get stuck] se coincer ▪ **jammed** adj [machine] coincé ; [street] encombré ▪ **jam-packed** adj [hall, train] bourré

**Jamaica** [dʒə'meɪkə] n la Jamaïque

**jammin'** ['dʒæmɪn] adj Am Fam [doing well] **we're jammin'** tout baigne

**jangle** ['dʒæŋgəl] vi cliqueter

**janitor** ['dʒænɪtə(r)] n Am Scot [caretaker] concierge m

**January** ['dʒænjʊərɪ] n janvier m

**Japan** [dʒə'pæn] n le Japon ▪ **Japanese** [dʒæpə'ni:z] **1.** adj japonais **2.** n [person] Japonais, -e mf ; [language] japonais m

**jar¹** [dʒɑ:(r)] n [container] pot m ; [large, glass] bocal m

**jar²** [dʒɑ:(r)] **1.** n [jolt] choc m **2.** (pt & pp -rr-) vt [shake] ébranler **3.** vi [of noise] grincer ; [of colours, words] jurer (**with** avec) ▪ **jarring** adj [noise, voice] discordant

**jargon** ['dʒɑ:gən] n jargon m

**jaunt** [dʒɔ:nt] n [journey] balade f

**javelin** ['dʒævlɪn] n javelot m

**jaw** [dʒɔ:] n ANAT mâchoire f

**jaywalking** ['dʒeɪwɔ:kɪŋ] n délit mineur qui consiste à traverser une rue en dehors des clous ou au feu vert

**jazz** [dʒæz] **1.** n jazz m **2.** vt Fam **to jazz sth up** [clothes, room, style] égayer qch ; [music] jazzifier qch

**jealous** ['dʒeləs] adj jaloux, -ouse (**of** de) ▪ **jealousy** n jalousie f

**jeans** [dʒi:nz] npl **(pair of) jeans** jean m

**Jeep®** [dʒi:p] n Jeep® f

**jeer** [dʒɪə(r)] **1.** n **jeers** [boos] huées fpl **2.** vt [boo] huer ; [mock] se moquer de **3.** vi **to jeer at sb/sth** [boo] huer qn / qch ; [mock] se moquer de qn /qch ▪ **jeering 1.** adj railleur, -euse **2.** n [mocking] railleries fpl ; [of crowd] huées fpl

**jeez** [dʒi:z] excl Am Fam purée !

**jell** [dʒel] vi Fam [of ideas] prendre tournure

**jello®** ['dʒeləʊ] n Am [dessert] gelée f

**jelly** ['dʒelɪ] (pl -ies) n [preserve, dessert] gelée f ▪ **jellyfish** n méduse f

**jeopardy** ['dʒepədɪ] n **in jeopardy** en péril ▪ **jeopardize** vt mettre en danger

**jerk** [dʒɜːk] **1.** n secousse f **2.** vt [pull] tirer brusquement

**jerky** [ˈdʒɜːkɪ] (compar -ier, superl -iest) adj [movement, voice] saccadé

**jersey** [ˈdʒɜːzɪ] (pl -eys) n [garment] tricot m ; [of footballer] maillot m

**Jersey** [ˈdʒɜːzɪ] n Jersey m ou f

**jest** [dʒest] **1.** n plaisanterie f ; **in jest** pour rire **2.** vi plaisanter

**Jesus** [ˈdʒiːzəs] n Jésus m ; **Jesus Christ** Jésus-Christ m

**jet** [dʒet] **1.** n **a)** [plane] avion m à réaction ; **jet engine** réacteur m, moteur m à réaction ; **jet lag** fatigue f due au décalage horaire **b)** [steam, liquid] jet m **2.** vi Fam **to jet off** s'envoler (**to** pour)

**jet-black** [dʒet'blæk] adj (noir) de jais

**jetfoil** [ˈdʒetfɔɪl] n hydroglisseur m

**jet-lagged** [ˈdʒetlægd] adj qui souffre du décalage horaire

**jetty** [ˈdʒetɪ] (pl -ies) n jetée f ; [landing place] embarcadère m

**Jew** [dʒuː] n [man] Juif m ; [woman] Juive f ■ **Jewish** adj juif (f juive)

**jewel** [ˈdʒuːəl] n bijou m (pl -oux) ; [in watch] rubis m ■ **jeweller**, Am **jeweler** n bijoutier, -ère mf ■ **jewellery**, Am **jewelry** n bijoux mpl

**jibe** [dʒaɪb] n & vi = **gibe**

**jiffy** [ˈdʒɪfɪ] n Fam instant m

**Jiffy** [ˈdʒɪfɪ] n **Jiffy bag**® enveloppe f matelassée

**jig** [dʒɪɡ] n [dance, music] gigue f

**jigsaw** [ˈdʒɪɡsɔː] n **jigsaw (puzzle)** puzzle m

**jilt** [dʒɪlt] vt [lover] laisser tomber

**jingle** [ˈdʒɪŋɡəl] **1.** vt faire tinter **2.** vi [of keys, bell] tinter

**jinx** [dʒɪŋks] n [spell, curse] mauvais sort m

**JIT** (abbr of **just in time**) adj juste à temps, JAT

**jittery** [ˈdʒɪtərɪ] adj Fam **to be jittery** être à cran

**JK** MESSAGING written abbr of **just kidding**

**job** [dʒɒb] n [employment, post] travail m, emploi m ; [task] tâche f ; **to have a (hard) job doing** or **to do sth** avoir du mal à faire qch ; **job offer** offre f d'emploi ■ **job-share 1.** n partage m du travail **2.** vi partager le travail

**Jobcentre** [ˈdʒɒbsentə(r)] n Br ≃ Pôle emploi m

**jobless** [ˈdʒɒbləs] adj au chômage

**jockey** [ˈdʒɒkɪ] (pl -eys) n jockey m

**jocular** [ˈdʒɒkjʊlə(r)] adj jovial

**jog** [dʒɒɡ] (pt & pp -gg-) **1.** vt [shake] secouer ; [push] pousser ; Fig [memory] rafraîchir **2.** vi [for fitness] faire du jogging ■ **jogging** n [for fitness] jogging m ; **to go jogging** aller faire un jogging

**john** [dʒɒn] n Am Fam **the john** [lavatory] le petit coin

**join** [dʒɔɪn] **1.** n raccord m **2.** vt **a)** [put together] joindre ; [wires, pipes] raccorder ; [words, towns] relier ; **to join two things together** relier une chose à une autre ; **to join sb** [catch up with, meet] rejoindre qn ; [associate oneself with, go with] se joindre à qn (**in doing** pour faire) **b)** [become a member of] s'inscrire à ; [army, police, company] entrer dans ; **to join the queue** or Am **line** prendre la queue **3.** vi **a)** [of roads, rivers] se rejoindre ; **to join (together** or **up)** [of objects] se joindre (**with** à) ; **to join in sth** prendre part à qch **b)** [become a member] devenir membre ; MIL **to join up** s'engager

**joiner** [ˈdʒɔɪnə(r)] n Br menuisier m

**joint** [dʒɔɪnt] **1.** n **a)** [in body] articulation f ; Br [meat] rôti m ; TECH joint m ; [in carpentry] assemblage m **b)** Fam [nightclub] boîte f **c)** Fam [cannabis cigarette] joint m **2.** adj [decision] commun ; **joint account** compte m joint ; **joint efforts** efforts mpl conjugués ■ **jointly** adv conjointement

**joke** [dʒəʊk] **1.** n plaisanterie f ; [trick] tour m **2.** vi plaisanter (**about** sur) ■ **joker** n plaisantin m ; [card] joker m ■ **jokingly** adv [say] en plaisantant

**jolly** [ˈdʒɒlɪ] (compar -ier, superl -iest) adj [happy] gai

**jolt** [dʒɒlt] **1.** *n* secousse *f* **2.** *vt* [shake] secouer

**jostle** ['dʒɒsəl] **1.** *vt* [push] bousculer **2.** *vi* [push each other] se bousculer (**for sth** pour obtenir qch)

**jot** [dʒɒt] (*pt & pp* -tt-) *vt* **to jot sth down** noter qch ■ **jotter** *n* [notepad] bloc-notes *m*

**journal** ['dʒɜːnəl] *n* [periodical] revue *f*; [diary] journal *m*; **to keep a journal** tenir un journal

**journalism** ['dʒɜːnəlɪzəm] *n* journalisme *m* ■ **journalist** *n* journaliste *mf*

**journey** ['dʒɜːnɪ] **1.** (*pl* -**eys**) *n* [trip] voyage *m*; [distance] trajet *m*; **to go on a journey** partir en voyage **2.** *vi* voyager

**jovial** ['dʒəʊvɪəl] *adj* jovial

**joy** [dʒɔɪ] *n* joie *f*; **the joys of** [countryside, motherhood] les plaisirs *mpl* de ■ **joyful** *adj* joyeux, -euse

**joyrider** ['dʒɔɪraɪdə(r)] *n* chauffard qui conduit une voiture volée

**joystick** ['dʒɔɪstɪk] *n* [of aircraft, computer] manche *m* à balai

**JPEG** (*abbr of* **joint picture expert group**) *n* COMPUT (format *m*) JPEG *m*

**jubilant** ['dʒuːbɪlənt] *adj* **to be jubilant** jubiler

**jubilee** ['dʒuːbɪliː] *n* **(golden) jubilee** jubilé *m*

**judder** ['dʒʌdə(r)] **1.** *n* vibration *f* **2.** *vi* [shake] vibrer

**judge** [dʒʌdʒ] **1.** *n* juge *m* **2.** *vti* juger; **to judge sb by** or **on sth** juger qn sur ou d'après qch; **judging by...** à en juger par... ■ **judg(e)ment** *n* jugement *m*

**judicial** [dʒuːˈdɪʃəl] *adj* judiciaire

**judo** ['dʒuːdəʊ] *n* judo *m*

**jug** [dʒʌg] *n* cruche *f*; [for milk] pot *m*

**juggle** ['dʒʌgəl] **1.** *vt* jongler avec **2.** *vi* jongler (**with** avec) ■ **juggler** *n* jongleur, -euse *mf*

**juice** [dʒuːs] *n* jus *m* ■ **juicy** (*compar* -**ier**, *superl* -**iest**) *adj* [fruit] juteux, -euse; [meat] succulent; *Fig* [story] savoureux, -euse

**jukebox** ['dʒuːkbɒks] *n* juke-box *m*

**July** [dʒuːˈlaɪ] *n* juillet *m*

**jumble** ['dʒʌmbəl] **1.** *n* [disorder] fouillis *m*; *Br* [unwanted articles] bric-à-brac *m inv*; *Br* **jumble sale** vente *f* de charité (*articles d'occasion uniquement*) **2.** *vt* **to jumble (up)** [objects, facts] mélanger

**jumbo** ['dʒʌmbəʊ] **1.** *adj* [packet] géant **2.** (*pl* -**os**) *adj & n* **jumbo (jet)** jumbo-jet (*m*)

**jump** [dʒʌmp] **1.** *n* [leap] saut *m*; [start] sursaut *m*; [increase] hausse *f* soudaine; *Am* **jump rope** corde *f* à sauter **2.** *vt* [ditch] sauter; *Br* **to jump the queue** passer avant son tour, resquiller **3.** *vi* sauter (**at** sur); [start] sursauter; [of price] faire un bond; **to jump across sth** traverser qch d'un bond; **to jump in** or **on** [train, vehicle, bus] sauter dans; **to jump off** or **out** sauter; [from bus] descendre; **to jump off sth, to jump out of sth** sauter de qch; **to jump out of the window** sauter par la fenêtre; **to jump up** se lever d'un bond ■ **jumpy** ['dʒʌmpɪ] (*compar* -**ier**, *superl* -**iest**) *adj* nerveux, -euse

**jumper** ['dʒʌmpə(r)] *n Br* pull(-over) *m*; *Am* [dress] robe *f* chasuble

**junction** ['dʒʌŋkʃən] *n* [crossroads] carrefour *m*; *Br* **junction 23** [on motorway-exit] la sortie 23; [entrance] l'entrée *f* 23

**June** [dʒuːn] *n* juin *m*

**jungle** ['dʒʌŋgəl] *n* jungle *f*

**junior** ['dʒuːnɪə(r)] **1.** *adj* [younger] plus jeune; [in rank, status] subalterne; [teacher, doctor] jeune; **to be sb's junior** être plus jeune que qn; [in rank, status] être au-dessous de qn; *Br* **junior school** école *f* primaire (*entre 7 et 11 ans*); *Am* **junior high school** ≃ collège *m* d'enseignement secondaire **2.** *n* cadet, -ette *mf*; [in school] petit, -e *mf*; [in sports] junior *mf*, cadet, -ette *mf*

**junk** [dʒʌŋk] **1.** *n* [unwanted objects] bric-à-brac *m inv*; [inferior goods] camelote *f*; [bad film, book] navet *m*; **junk e-mail** messages *mpl* publicitaires, spams *mpl*, pourriels *mpl*; **junk food** cochonneries *fpl*; **junk mail** [postal] publicité *f* (reçue par courrier); = **junk e-mail**; **junk shop** boutique *f* de brocanteur **2.** *vt Fam* [get rid of] balancer

**junkie** ['ʤʌŋkɪ] *n Fam* drogué, -e *mf*

**jury** ['ʤʊərɪ] *(pl* **-ies)** *n* [in competition, court] jury *m*

**just** [ʤʌst] **1.** *adv* [exactly, slightly] juste; [only] juste, seulement; [simply] (tout) simplement; **it's just as I thought** c'est bien ce que je pensais; **she has / had just left** elle vient / venait de partir; **he just missed it** il l'a manqué de peu; **just as big / light** tout aussi grand / léger (**as** que); **just a moment!** un instant!; **just one** un(e) seul(e) (**of** de); **just about** [approximately] à peu près; [almost] presque; **to be just about to do sth** être sur le point de faire qch **2.** *adj* [fair] juste (**to** envers)

**justice** ['ʤʌstɪs] *n* justice *f*; **it doesn't do you justice** [photo] cela ne vous avantage pas

**justify** ['ʤʌstɪfaɪ] *(pt & pp* **-ied)** *vt* justifier; **to be justified in doing sth** [have reason] être fondé à faire qch ■ **justifiable** *adj* justifiable ■ **justification** [-fɪ'keɪʃən] *n* justification *f*

**jut** [ʤʌt] *(pt & pp* **-tt-)** *vi* **to jut out** faire saillie

**juvenile** ['ʤu:vənaɪl, *Am* -ənəl] **1.** *n* [in law] mineur, -e *mf* **2.** *adj* [court] pour enfants; *Pej* [behaviour] puéril; **juvenile delinquent** jeune délinquant, -e *mf*

**juxtapose** [ʤʌkstə'pəʊz] *vt* juxtaposer

# K

**K, k** [keɪ] *n* (letter) K, k *m inv*

**kahuna** [kəˈhuːnə] *n Am Fam* **the big kahuna** le patron, le big boss

**kangaroo** [kæŋɡəˈruː] *n* kangourou *m*

**karate** [kəˈrɑːtɪ] *n* karaté *m*

**kB, KB** *(abbr of* **kilobyte(s))** *n* COMPUT Ko *m*

**kebab** [kəˈbæb] *n* brochette *f*

**keel** [kiːl] **1.** *n* [of boat] quille *f* **2.** *vi* to **keel over** [of boat] chavirer

**keen** [kiːn] *adj* **a)** *Br* [eager, enthusiastic] plein d'enthousiasme ; **to be keen on sth** [music, sport] être passionné de qch ; **he is keen on her / the idea** elle / l'idée lui plaît beaucoup **b)** [edge, appetite] aiguisé ; [interest] vif (*f* vive) ; [mind] pénétrant ; [wind] glacial

**keep** [kiːp] **1.** *(pt & pp* **kept)** *vt* garder ; [shop, car] avoir ; [diary, promise] tenir ; [family] entretenir ; [rule] respecter ; [delay, detain] retenir ; [put] mettre ; **to keep doing sth** continuer à faire qch ; **to keep sth clean** garder qch propre ; **to keep sth from sb** dissimuler qch à qn ; **to keep sb from doing sth** empêcher qn de faire qch ; **to keep sb waiting / working** faire attendre / travailler qn ; **to keep an appointment** se rendre à un rendez-vous
**2.** *vi* [remain] rester ; [continue] continuer ; [of food] se conserver ; **how is he keeping?** comment va-t-il ? ; **to keep still** rester immobile ; **to keep left** tenir sa gauche ; **to keep going** continuer ; **to keep at it** [keep doing it] persévérer
**3.** *n* [food] subsistance *f* ; *Fam* **for keeps** pour toujours

■ **keep away 1.** *vt* [person] éloigner (**from** de) **2.** *vi* ne pas s'approcher (**from** de)

■ **keep back 1.** *vt sep* [crowd] contenir ; [delay, withhold] retarder ; [hide] cacher (**from** à) **2.** *vi* ne pas s'approcher (**from** de)

■ **keep down** *vt sep* [restrict] limiter ; [price, costs] maintenir bas

■ **keep from** *vt insep* s'empêcher de, se retenir de ; **I couldn't keep from laughing** je n'ai pas pu m'empêcher de rire

■ **keep in** *vt sep* [not allow out] empêcher de sortir ; [as punishment in school] garder en retenue

■ **keep in with** *vt insep* **to keep in with sb** rester en bons termes avec qn

■ **keep off 1.** *vt sep* [person] éloigner ; **keep your hands off!** n'y touche pas ! **2.** *vt insep* '**keep off the grass**' 'défense de marcher sur les pelouses' **3.** *vi* [not go near] ne pas s'approcher

■ **keep on 1.** *vt sep* [hat, employee] garder ; **to keep on doing sth** continuer à faire qch **2.** *vi* **to keep on at sb** harceler qn

■ **keep out 1.** *vt sep* empêcher d'entrer **2.** *vi* rester en dehors (**of** de)

■ **keep to 1.** *vt insep* [subject, path] ne pas s'écarter de ; [room] garder **2.** *vi* **keep to the left** tenir la gauche ; **to keep to oneself** rester à l'écart

■ **keep up 1.** *vt sep* [continue, maintain] continuer ; [keep awake] empêcher de dormir ; **to keep up appearances** sauver les apparences **2.** *vi* [continue] continuer ; [follow] suivre ; **to keep up with sb** [follow] aller à la même allure que qn ; [in quality of work] se maintenir à la hauteur de qn

**keeper** [ˈkiːpə(r)] *n* [in park, in zoo, goalkeeper] gardien, -enne *mf*

**keeping** ['kiːpɪŋ] *n* in keeping with conformément à

**kennel** ['kenəl] *n* Br niche *f*

**Kenya** ['kiːnjə, 'kenjə] *n* le Kenya

**kept** [kept] **1.** *pt & pp of* keep **2.** *adj* well or nicely kept [house] bien tenu

**kerb** [kɜːb] *n* Br bord *m* du trottoir

**kernel** ['kɜːnəl] *n* [of nut] amande *f*

**kerosene** ['kerəsiːn] *n* [aircraft fuel] kérosène *m* ; *Am* [paraffin] pétrole *m* (lampant)

**ketchup** ['ketʃəp] *n* ketchup *m*

**kettle** ['ketəl] *n* bouilloire *f* ; the kettle is boiling l'eau bout ; to put the kettle on mettre l'eau à chauffer

**kewl** *adj* Am Fam cool

**key** [kiː] **1.** *n* clef *f*, clé *f* ; [of piano, typewriter, computer] touche *f* ; [of piano, typewriter, computer] touche *f* ; Fig the key to happiness / success la clé du bonheur / de la réussite ; SCH key skill compétence *f* de base ; COMPUT delete key touche *f* effacer ; COMPUT enter key (touche *f*) entrée *f* **2.** *adj* [industry, post] clef, clé **3.** *vt* to key in [data] saisir ■ keyboard *n* [of piano, computer] clavier *m* ■ keyguard ['kiːgɑːd] *n* [on mobile phone] verrouillage *m* du clavier ■ keyhole *n* trou *m* de serrure ■ keynote *n* [of speech] point *m* essentiel ■ keypad ['kiːpæd] *n* COMPUT pavé *m* numérique ■ keypal ['kiːpæl] *n* correspondant, -e *m,f* (avec qui l'on correspond via Internet) ■ keyring *n* porte-clefs *m inv*

**keyed** [kiːd] *adj* to be keyed up être surexcité

**khaki** ['kɑːki] *adj & n* kaki (*m*) *inv*

**kick** [kɪk] **1.** *n* coup *m* de pied ; [of horse] ruade *f* **2.** *vt* donner un coup de pied / des coups de pied à ; [of horse] lancer une ruade à **3.** *vi* donner des coups de pied ; [of horse] ruer ■ kickoff *n* [in football] coup *m* d'envoi ■ kick down, kick in *vt sep* [door] démolir à coups de pied ■ kick off *vi* [of footballer] donner le coup d'envoi ; Fam [start] démarrer ■ kick out *vt sep* Fam [throw out] flanquer dehors ■ kick up *vt sep* Br Fam to kick up a fuss faire des histoires

**kickboxing** ['kɪkbɒksɪŋ] *n* kickboxing *m*

**kid** [kɪd] **1.** *n* a) Fam [child] gosse *mf* ; Fam my kid brother mon petit frère b) [goat] chevreau *m* **2.** (*pt & pp* -dd-) *vti* Fam [joke, tease] faire marcher ; to be kidding plaisanter ; no kidding! sans blague !

**kidnap** ['kɪdnæp] (*pt & pp* -pp-, Am *pt & pp* -p-) *vt* kidnapper ■ kidnapper *n* ravisseur, -euse *mf* ■ kidnapping *n* enlèvement *m*

**kidney** ['kɪdnɪ] (*pl* -eys) *n* rein *m* ; [as food] rognon *m* ; kidney bean haricot *m* rouge

**kidult** *n* Fam jeune adulte *mf*

**kill** [kɪl] **1.** *vt* [person, animal, plant] tuer ; to kill oneself se tuer ; Fam my feet are killing me j'ai les pieds en compote ; to kill time tuer le temps **2.** *vi* tuer ■ killer *n* tueur, -euse *mf* ■ killing *n* [of person] meurtre *m* ; [of group] massacre *m* ; [of animal] mise *f* à mort

**killjoy** ['kɪldʒɔɪ] *n* rabat-joie *mf inv*

**kilo** ['kiːləʊ] (*pl* -os) *n* kilo *m* ■ kilogram(me) ['kɪləgræm] *n* kilogramme *m*

**kilobyte** ['kɪləbaɪt] *n* COMPUT kilooctet *m*

**kilometre**, Am **kilometer** [kɪ'lɒmɪtə(r)] *n* kilomètre *m*

**kilt** [kɪlt] *n* kilt *m*

**kin** [kɪn] *n* one's next of kin son plus proche parent

**kind**[1] [kaɪnd] *n* [sort, type] genre *m*, espèce *f* (of de) ; what kind of drink is it? qu'est-ce que c'est comme boisson ? ; Fam kind of worried / sad plutôt inquiet / triste

**kind**[2] [kaɪnd] (*compar* -er, *superl* -est) *adj* [helpful, pleasant] gentil, -ille (to avec) ; that's kind of you c'est gentil de votre part

**kindergarten** ['kɪndəgɑːtən] *n* jardin *m* d'enfants

**kindly** ['kaɪndlɪ] **1.** *adv* gentiment ; kindly wait ayez la bonté d'attendre **2.** *adj* [person] bienveillant

**kindness** ['kaɪndnɪs] *n* gentillesse *f*

**king** [kɪŋ] *n* roi *m* ■ **kingdom** *n* royaume *m*; **animal/plant kingdom** règne *m* animal/végétal ■ **king-size(d)** *adj* géant

**kiosk** ['ki:ɒsk] *n* kiosque *m*; *Br* **(telephone) kiosk** cabine *f* téléphonique

**kip** [kɪp] (*pt & pp* -pp-) *vi Br Fam* [sleep] roupiller

**kipper** ['kɪpə(r)] *n* hareng *m* salé et fumé

**kiss** [kɪs] **1.** *n* baiser *m*; **the kiss of life** [in first aid] le bouche-à-bouche **2.** *vt* [person] embrasser **3.** *vi* s'embrasser

**kit** [kɪt] **1.** *n* équipement *m*, matériel *m*; [set of articles] trousse *f*; *Br* [belongings] affaires *fpl*; *Br* [sports clothes] tenue *f*; **first-aid kit** trousse *f* de pharmacie; **(do-it-yourself) kit** kit *m* **2.** (*pt & pp* -tt-) *vt Br* **to kit sb out** équiper qn (**with** de)

**kitchen** ['kɪtʃɪn] *n* cuisine *f*; **kitchen sink** évier *m*; **kitchen units** éléments *mpl* de cuisine ■ **kitchenette** *n* coin-cuisine *m*

**kite** [kaɪt] *n* [toy] cerf-volant *m* ■ **kite-surfing** ['kaɪtsɜ:fɪŋ] *n* kitesurf *m*

**kitten** ['kɪtən] *n* chaton *m*

**kitty** ['kɪtɪ] (*pl* -ies) *n* [fund] cagnotte *f*

**kiwi** ['ki:wi:] *n* [bird, fruit] kiwi *m*

**KK** MESSAGING OK

**klutz** [klʌts] *n AmFam* balourd, -ourde *mf*

**km** (*abbr of* **kilometre(s)**) km

**knack** [næk] *n* [skill] talent *m*; **to have the knack of doing sth** avoir le don de faire qch

**knackered** ['nækəd] *adj Br Fam* [tired] vanné

**knapsack** ['næpsæk] *n* sac *m* à dos

**knead** [ni:d] *vt* [dough] pétrir

**knee** [ni:] *n* genou *m*; **to go down on one's knees** s'agenouiller ■ **kneecap** *n* rotule *f*

**kneel** [ni:l] (*pt & pp* knelt *or* kneeled) *vi* **to kneel (down)** s'agenouiller (**before** devant); **to be kneeling (down)** être à genoux

**knelt** [nelt] *pt & pp of* **kneel**

**knew** [nju:] *pt of* **know**

**knickers** ['nɪkəz] *npl Br* [underwear] culotte *f*

**knick-knack** ['nɪknæk] *n Fam* babiole *f*

**knife** [naɪf] **1.** (*pl* **knives**) *n* couteau *m*; [penknife] canif *m* **2.** *vt* poignarder

**knight** [naɪt] **1.** *n* chevalier *m*; [chess piece] cavalier *m* **2.** *vt Br* **to be knighted** être fait chevalier ■ **knighthood** *n Br* titre *m* de chevalier

**knit** [nɪt] (*pt & pp* -tt-) **1.** *vt* tricoter **2.** *vi* tricoter; **to knit (together)** [of bones] se ressouder ■ **knitting** *n* [activity, material] tricot *m*; **knitting needle** aiguille *f* à tricoter

**knob** [nɒb] *n* [on door] poignée *f*; [on radio] bouton *m*; **a knob of butter** une noix de beurre

**knock** [nɒk] **1.** *n* [blow] coup *m*; **there's a knock at the door** on frappe à la porte **2.** *vt* [strike] frapper; [collide with] heurter; **to knock one's head on sth** se cogner la tête contre qch **3.** *vi* [strike] frapper; **to knock against** *or* **into sth** heurter qch ■ **knocker** *n* [for door] marteau *m* ■ **knockout** *n* [in boxing] knock-out *m inv* ■ **knock about** *vt sep* [ill-treat] malmener ■ **knock back** *vt sep Br Fam* [drink, glass] s'envoyer (derrière la cravate) ■ **knock down** *vt sep* [object, pedestrian] renverser; [house, tree, wall] abattre; [price] baisser ■ **knock in** *vt sep* [nail] enfoncer ■ **knock off** **1.** *vt sep* [person, object] faire tomber (**from** de); *Fam* [do quickly] expédier; **to knock $50 off (the price)** baisser le prix de 50 dollars **2.** *vi Fam* [stop work] s'arrêter de travailler ■ **knock out** *vt sep* [make unconscious] assommer; [boxer] mettre K.-O.; [beat in competition] éliminer ■ **knock over** *vt sep* [pedestrian, object] renverser

**knot** [nɒt] **1.** *n* a) [in rope] nœud *m*; *Fig* **to tie the knot** se marier b) NAUT [unit of speed] nœud *m* **2.** (*pt & pp* -tt-) *vt* nouer

**know** [nəʊ] **1.** *n Fam* **to be in the know** être au courant
**2.** (*pt* knew, *pp* known) *vt* [facts, language] savoir; [person, place] connaître; [recognize] reconnaître

(by à); **to know that...** savoir que...; **to know how to do sth** savoir faire qch; **for all I know** que je sache; **I'll let you know** je vous le ferai savoir; **to know (a lot) about cars /sewing** s'y connaître en voitures /couture; **to get to know sb** apprendre à connaître qn **3.** *vi* savoir; **I know** je (le) sais; **I wouldn't know, I know nothing about it** je n'en sais rien; **to know about sth** être au courant de qch; **do you know of a good dentist?** connais-tu un bon dentiste?

■ **know-how** *n Fam* savoir-faire *m inv*

■ **know-it-all** *n Fam & Pej* je-sais-tout *mf*

■ **knowingly** *adv* [consciously] sciemment

---

**knowledge** ['nɒlɪdʒ] *n* [of fact] connaissance *f*; [learning] connaissances *fpl*, savoir *m*; **(not) to my knowledge** (pas) à ma connaissance; **general knowledge** culture *f* générale

■ **knowledgeable** *adj* savant; **to be knowledgeable about sth** bien s'y connaître en qch

**known** [nəʊn] **1.** *pp of* **know 2.** *adj* connu; **she is known to be...** on sait qu'elle est...

**knuckle** ['nʌkəl] *n* articulation *f* (du doigt) ■ **knuckle down** *vi Fam* se mettre au boulot; **to knuckle down to sth** se mettre à qch

**Koran** [kə'rɑːn] *n* **the Koran** le Coran

**Korea** [kə'rɪə] *n* la Corée

**kosher** ['kəʊʃə(r)] *adj* REL [food] kasher *inv*

**KOTC** *(abbr of* **hugs and kisses)** MESSAGING biz

**KOTL** MESSAGING *written abbr of* **kiss on the lips**

**kudos** ['kjuːdɒs] *n* [glory] gloire *f*; [prestige] prestige *m*

**Kuwait** [kʊ'weɪt] *n* le Koweït

**L, l** [el] *n* [letter] L, l *m inv*

**lab** [læb] *n Fam* labo *m* ■ **laboratory** [lə'bɒrətrı, *Am* 'læbrətɔːrı] *n* laboratoire *m*

**label** ['leıbəl] **1.** *n* étiquette *f*; [of record company] label *m* **2.** *(Br -ll-, Am -l-) vt* étiqueter; *Fig* **to label sb (as) a liar** qualifier qn de menteur

**Labor Day** *n* fête du travail américaine *(premier lundi de septembre, jour férié) marquant symboliquement la fin de l'été; fournit l'occasion de diverses activités de loisir: pique-niques et barbecues en famille, feux d'artifice, etc. Certaines villes organisent un défilé,* **Labor Day Parade.**

**laborious** [lə'bɔːrɪəs] *adj* laborieux, -euse

**labour**, *Am* **labor** ['leıbə(r)] **1.** *n* [work] travail *m*; [workers] main-d'œuvre *f*; *Br* **Labour** [political party] le parti travailliste; **in labour** [woman] en train d'accoucher **2.** *adj* [market] du travail; **labour force** effectifs *mpl*; *Am* **labour union** syndicat *m* **3.** *vi* [toil] peiner **(over** sur) ■ **labourer**, *Am* **laborer** *n* [on roads] manœuvre *m*; [on farm] ouvrier *m* agricole

**labyrinth** ['læbərɪnθ] *n* labyrinthe *m*

**lace** [leıs] **1.** *n* **a)** [cloth] dentelle *f* **b)** [of shoe] lacet *m* **2.** *vt* **to lace (up)** [tie up] lacer

**lack** [læk] **1.** *n* manque *m* **(of** de); **for lack of sth** à défaut de qch **2.** *vt* manquer de **3.** *vi* **to be lacking** manquer **(in** de)

**lad** [læd] *n Fam* [young man] jeune gars *m*; [child] garçon *m*

**ladder** ['lædə(r)] **1.** *n* échelle *f*; *Br* [in tights] maille *f* filée **2.** *vti Br* filer

**laddish** ['lædɪʃ] *adj Br* macho

**laden** ['leıdən] *adj* chargé **(with** de)

**lady** ['leıdı] *(pl* **-ies)** *n* dame *f*; **a young lady** une jeune fille; [married] une jeune dame; **Ladies and Gentlemen!** Mesdames, Mesdemoiselles, Messieurs!; **the ladies' room**, *Br* **the ladies** les toilettes *fpl* pour dames

**ladybird** ['leıdıbɜːd], *Am* **ladybug** ['leıdıbʌg] *n* coccinelle *f*

**ladyfinger** ['leıdıfɪŋgə(r)] *n Am* [biscuit] boudoir *m*

**lag** [læg] **1.** *n* **time lag** [between events] décalage *m*; [between countries] décalage *m* horaire **2.** *(pt & pp -gg-) vt* [pipe] isoler **3.** *vi* **to lag behind** [in progress, work] avoir du retard; [dawdle] être à la traîne

**lager** ['lɑːgə(r)] *n Br* bière *f* blonde

**lagoon** [lə'guːn] *n* lagune *f*; [of atoll] lagon *m*

**laid** [leıd] *pt & pp of* **lay** ■ **laid-back** *adj Fam* cool *inv*

**lain** [leın] *pp of* **lie**

**lair** [leə(r)] *n* tanière *f*

**lake** [leık] *n* lac *m*

**lamb** [læm] *n* agneau *m*

**lame** [leım] *(compar* **-er,** *superl* **-est)** *adj* [person, argument] boiteux, -euse; [excuse] piètre; **to be lame** [of person] boiter

**lament** [lə'ment] *vt* **to lament (over)** se lamenter sur

**laminated** ['læmıneıtıd] *adj* [glass] feuilleté; [wood, plastic] stratifié

**lamp** [læmp] *n* lampe *f* ■ **lamppost** *n* réverbère *m* ■ **lampshade** *n* abat-jour *m inv*

**lance** [lɑːns] **1.** *n* [weapon] lance *f* **2.** *vt* [abscess] inciser

**land** [lænd] **1.** *n* terre *f*; [country] pays *m*; **(plot of) land** terrain *m* **2.** *adj* [reform] agraire **3.** *vt* [passengers, cargo] débarquer ; [aircraft] poser ; [blow] flanquer (on à) ; *Fam* [job, prize] décrocher **4.** *vi* [of aircraft] atterrir ; [of passengers] débarquer ; [of bomb, missile] tomber ; **to land up in a ditch/in jail** se retrouver dans un fossé /en prison ■ **landing** n a) [of aircraft] atterrissage m ; [of cargo, troops] débarquement m ; **landing card** carte f de débarquement b) [of staircase] palier m ■ **landlady** *(pl -ies)* n propriétaire f ; [of pub] patronne f ■ **landlord** n propriétaire m ; [of pub] patron m ■ **landmark** n point m de repère ■ **landowner** n propriétaire m foncier ■ **landslide** n [falling rocks] glissement m de terrain ; [election victory] raz de marée m inv électoral

**landscape** ['lændskeɪp] n paysage m

**lane** [leɪn] n [in country] chemin m ; [in town] ruelle f ; [division of road] voie f ; [line of traffic] file f ; [for shipping, swimming] couloir m

**language** ['læŋwɪdʒ] **1.** n [of a people] langue f ; [faculty, style] langage m **2.** *adj* [laboratory] de langues ; [teacher, studies] de langue(s)

**languish** ['læŋgwɪʃ] vi languir (**for** or **after** après)

**lanky** ['læŋkɪ] *(compar -ier, superl -iest) adj* dégingandé

**lantern** ['læntən] n lanterne f

**lap** [læp] **1.** n a) [of person] genoux mpl b) [in race] tour m de piste **2.** *(pt & pp -pp-) vt* to lap up [drink] laper **3.** vi [of waves] clapoter

**lapel** [lə'pel] n revers m

**lapse** [læps] **1.** n a) [in concentration, standards] baisse f ; **a lapse of memory** un trou de mémoire b) [interval] laps m de temps ; **a lapse of time** un intervalle (**between** entre) **2.** vi a) [of concentration, standards] baisser b) [expire - of subscription] expirer

**laptop (computer)** ['læptɒp-(kəm'pju:tə(r))] n (ordinateur m) portable m

**larceny** ['lɑ:sənɪ] n Am vol m simple

**lard** [lɑ:d] n saindoux m

**larder** ['lɑ:də(r)] n garde-manger m inv

**large** [lɑ:dʒ] *(compar -er, superl -est) adj* [big] grand ; [fat, bulky] gros (f grosse) ; [quantity] grand, important ; **to become** or **grow** or **get large** s'agrandir ; [of person] grossir ; **at large** [of prisoner, animal] en liberté ; [as a whole] en général ■ **large-scale** *adj* [operation, reform] de grande envergure

**largely** ['lɑ:dʒlɪ] adv en grande partie

**lark¹** [lɑ:k] n [bird] alouette f

**lark²** [lɑ:k] *Fam* **1.** n [joke] rigolade f **2.** vi Br to lark about faire le fou /la folle

**larva** ['lɑ:və] *(pl -vae* [-vi:]*)* n larve f

**laryngitis** [lærɪn'dʒaɪtɪs] n MED laryngite f

**lasagne, lasagna** [lə'zænjə] n lasagnes fpl

**laser** ['leɪzə(r)] n laser m ; **laser beam /printer** rayon m /imprimante f laser ; **laser weapon** arme f laser

**lash¹** [læʃ] **1.** n [with whip] coup m de fouet **2.** vt [strike] fouetter ; [tie] attacher (**to** à) **3.** vi to lash out at sb [hit] donner des coups à qn ; [criticize] fustiger qn

**lash²** [læʃ] n [eyelash] cil m

**lass** [læs] n Br jeune fille f

**last¹** [lɑ:st] **1.** *adj* dernier, -ère ; **the last ten lines** les dix dernières lignes ; **last night** [evening] hier soir ; [night] la nuit dernière ; **last name** nom m de famille **2.** *adv* [lastly] en dernier lieu ; [on the last occasion] (pour) la dernière fois ; **to leave last** sortir le dernier **3.** n [person, object] dernier, -ère mf ; **last but one** avant-dernier m (f avant-dernière) ; **at (long) last** enfin ■ **last-minute** *adj* [decision] de dernière minute

**last²** [lɑ:st] **1.** *pron* **the Sunday before last** pas dimanche dernier, le dimanche d'avant ; **the year before last** il y a deux ans ; **the last but one** l'avant-dernier, l'avant-dernière mf ; **to leave sth till last** faire qch en dernier **2.** vi durer ; **to last (out)** [endure, resist] tenir (le coup) ; [of money, supplies] suffire ; **it lasted me ten years** ça m'a fait dix ans

**lasting** ['lɑ:stɪŋ] *adj* [impression, peace] durable

**lastly** [ˈlɑːstlɪ] *adv* en dernier lieu

**latch** [lætʃ] **1.** *n* loquet *m* ; **the door is on the latch** la porte n'est pas fermée à clef **2.** *vt insep Fam* **to latch onto** [understand] piger ; [adopt] adopter

**late¹** [leɪt] **1.** (*compar* -er, *superl* -est) *adj* [meal, season, hour] tardif, -ive ; [stage] avancé ; [edition] dernier, -ère ; **to be late (for sth)** être en retard (pour qch) ; **he's an hour late** il a une heure de retard ; **it's late** il est tard ; **in the late nineties** à la fin des années 90 ; **to be in one's late forties** approcher de la cinquantaine ; **at a later date** à une date ultérieure ; **at the latest** au plus tard **2.** *adv* [in the day, season] tard ; [not on time] en retard ; **it's getting late** il se fait tard ; **later (on)** plus tard ; **of late** récemment

**late²** [leɪt] *adj* **the late Mr Smith** feu Monsieur Smith

**latecomer** [ˈleɪtkʌmə(r)] *n* retardataire *mf*

**lately** [ˈleɪtlɪ] *adv* dernièrement

**latent** [ˈleɪtənt] *adj* [disease, tendency] latent

**lateral** [ˈlætərəl] *adj* latéral

**lather** [ˈlɑːðə(r)] **1.** *n* mousse *f* **2.** *vt* savonner

**Latin** [ˈlætɪn] *adj* latin ; **Latin America** l'Amérique *f* latine ■ **Latin American 1.** *adj* d'Amérique latine **2.** *n* Latino-Américain, -e *mf* **3.** *n* [language] latin *m*

**latitude** [ˈlætɪtjuːd] *n* [on map, freedom] latitude *f*

**latter** [ˈlætə(r)] **1.** *adj* [later, last-named] dernier, -ère ; [second] deuxième **2.** *n* **the latter** le dernier (*f* la dernière) ; [of two] le second (*f* la seconde)

**lattice** [ˈlætɪs] *n* treillis *m*

**laudable** [ˈlɔːdəbəl] *adj* louable

**laugh** [lɑːf] **1.** *n* rire *m* ; **to have a good laugh** bien rire ; **laugh lines** rides *fpl* du sourire **2.** *vt* **to laugh sth off** tourner qch en plaisanterie **3.** *vi* rire (**at/about** de) ■ **laughing** *adj* riant ; **it's no laughing matter** il n'y a pas de quoi rire ; **to be the laughing stock of** être la risée de

**laughable** [ˈlɑːfəbəl] *adj* ridicule

**laughter** [ˈlɑːftə(r)] *n* rire(s) *m(pl)*

**launch** [lɔːntʃ] **1.** *n* **a)** [motorboat] vedette *f* ; [pleasure boat] bateau *m* de plaisance **b)** [of ship, rocket, product] lancement *m* **2.** *vt* [ship, rocket, product] lancer **3.** *vi* **to launch (out) into** [begin] se lancer dans

**launder** [ˈlɔːndə(r)] *vt* [clothes, money] blanchir

**launderette** [lɔːndəˈret], *Am* **Laundromat®** [ˈlɔːndrəmæt] *n* laverie *f* automatique

**laundry** [ˈlɔːndrɪ] *n* [place] blanchisserie *f* ; [clothes] linge *m* ; **to do the laundry** faire la lessive

**lava** [ˈlɑːvə] *n* lave *f*

**lavatory** [ˈlævətərɪ] (*pl* -ies) *n* toilettes *fpl* ; *Br* **lavatory seat** abattant *m* de W-C

**lavender** [ˈlævɪndə(r)] *n* lavande *f*

**lavish** [ˈlævɪʃ] **1.** *adj* prodigue (**with** de) ; [meal, décor, gift] somptueux, -euse ; [expenditure] excessif, -ive **2.** *vt* **to lavish sth on sb** couvrir qn de qch

**law** [lɔː] *n* [rule, rules] loi *f* ; [study, profession, system] droit *m* ; **against the law** illégal ; **court of law, law court** cour *f* de justice ; **law and order** l'ordre *m* public

**lawful** [ˈlɔːfəl] *adj* [action] légal ; [claim] légitime

**lawless** [ˈlɔːləs] *adj* [country] anarchique

**lawn** [lɔːn] *n* pelouse *f*, gazon *m* ; **lawn mower** tondeuse *f* à gazon

**lawsuit** [ˈlɔːsuːt] *n* procès *m*

**lawyer** [ˈlɔːjə(r)] *n* [in court] avocat, -e *mf* ; [for wills, sales] notaire *m* ; [legal expert] juriste *mf*

**lax** [læks] *adj* [person] laxiste ; [discipline, behaviour] relâché

**laxative** [ˈlæksətɪv] *n* laxatif *m*

**lay¹** [leɪ] *pt of* **lie**

**lay²** [leɪ] *adj* [non-religious] laïque ; **lay person** profane *mf* ■ **layman** (*pl* -men) *n* [nonspecialist] profane *mf*

**lay³** [leɪ] (*pt & pp* **laid**) **1.** *vt* [put down, place] poser ; [blanket] étendre (**over**

sur); [trap] tendre; [egg] pondre; *Br* to **lay the table** mettre la table **2.** *vi* [of bird] pondre ■ **layabout** *n Fam* fainéant, -e *mf* ■ **lay-by** *(pl* **-bys)** *n Br* [for vehicles] aire *f* de stationnement ■ **lay-out** *n* disposition *f*; [of text] mise *f* en page ■ **lay down** *vt sep* [put down] poser; [arms] déposer; [principle, condition] établir; **to lay down the law** dicter sa loi (**to** à) ■ **lay into** *vt insep Fam* [physically] rosser; [verbally] voler dans les plumes à ■ **lay off** *vt sep* to **lay sb off** [worker] licencier qn ■ **lay on** *vt sep Br* [install] installer; [supply] fournir ■ **lay out** *vt sep* [garden] dessiner; [house] concevoir; [display] disposer; *Fam* [money] mettre (**on** dans)

**layer** [ˈleɪə(r)] *n* couche *f*

**laze** [leɪz] *vi* **to laze** (**about** or **around**) paresser

**lazy** [ˈleɪzɪ] (*compar* -**ier**, *superl* -**iest**) *adj* [person] paresseux, -euse ■ **lazybones** *n Fam* flemmard, -e *mf*

**lb** *(abbr* **libra)** **3lb** 3 livres (*unité de poids*)

**lead¹** [led] *n* [metal] plomb *m*; [of pencil] mine *f* ■ **leaded** *adj* [petrol] au plomb ■ **lead-free** *adj* [paint] sans plomb

**lead²** [liːd] **1.** *n* [distance or time ahead] avance *f* (**over** sur); [example] exemple *m*; [clue] indice *m*; [in film] rôle *m* principal; *Br* [for dog] laisse *f*; [electric wire] fil *m* électrique; **to take the lead** [in race] prendre la tête; **to be in the lead** [in race] être en tête; [in match] mener (à la marque) **2.** *(pt & pp* **led**) *vt* [guide, conduct, take] mener, conduire (**to** à); [team, government] diriger; [expedition, attack] commander; [procession] être en tête de; **to lead a happy life** mener une vie heureuse; **to lead sb in/out** faire entrer/sortir qn; **to lead sb to do sth** [cause, induce] amener qn à faire qch **3.** *vi* [of street, door] mener, conduire (**to** à); [in race] être en tête; [in match] mener (à la marque); [go ahead] aller devant; **to lead to sth** [result in] aboutir à qch; [cause] mener à qch; **to lead up to** [precede] précéder ■ **lead away** *vt sep*

emmener ■ **lead off** *vt sep* emmener ■ **lead on** *vt sep* [deceive] tromper, duper

**leader** [ˈliːdə(r)] *n* **a)** [person] chef *m*; [of country, party] dirigeant, -e *mf*; [of strike, riot] meneur, -euse *mf*; [guide] guide *m*; **to be the leader** [in race] être en tête **b)** *Br* [newspaper article] éditorial *m* ■ **leadership** *n* direction *f*; [qualities] qualités *fpl* de chef; [leaders of country, party] dirigeants *mpl*

**leading** [ˈliːdɪŋ] *adj* [best, most important] principal; **a leading figure, a leading light** un personnage marquant

**leaf** [liːf] **1.** *(pl* **leaves)** *n* feuille *f*; [of book] feuillet *m*; [of table] rallonge *f* **2.** *vi* **to leaf through** [book] feuilleter ■ **leafy** [ˈliːfɪ] (*compar* -**ier**, *superl* -**iest**) *adj* [tree] feuillu; [avenue] bordé d'arbres; [suburb] verdoyant

**leaflet** [ˈliːflɪt] *n* prospectus *m*; [containing instructions] notice *f*

**league** [liːg] *n* [alliance] ligue *f*; [in sport] championnat *m*; *Pej* **in league with** de connivence avec

**leak** [liːk] **1.** *n* [in pipe, information] fuite *f*; [in boat] voie *f* d'eau **2.** *vt Fig* [information] divulguer; **the pipe was leaking gas** du gaz fuyait du tuyau **3.** *vi* [of liquid, pipe, tap] fuir; [of ship] faire eau; *Fig* **to leak out** [of information] être divulgué

**leaky** [ˈliːkɪ] (*compar* -**ier**, *superl* -**iest**) *adj* [kettle, pipe, tap] qui fuit; [roof] qui a une fuite

**lean¹** [liːn] (*compar* -**er**, *superl* -**est**) *adj* [meat] maigre; [person] mince

**lean²** [liːn] *(pt & pp* **leaned** or **leant** [lent]*)* **1.** *vt* **to lean sth on/against sth** appuyer qch sur/contre qch **2.** *vi* [of object] pencher; [of person] se pencher; **to lean against/on sth** [of person] s'appuyer contre/sur qch; **to lean forward** [of person] se pencher (en avant); **to lean over** [of person] se pencher; [of object] pencher ■ **leaning** *adj* penché; **leaning against** [resting] appuyé contre ■ **leanings** *npl* tendances *fpl* (**towards** à)

**leap** [li:p] **1.** *n* [jump] bond *m*, saut *m* ; *Fig* [change, increase] bond *m* ; **leap year** année *f* bissextile **2.** *(pt & pp* **leaped** *or* **leapt)** *vi* bondir, sauter ; **to leap to one's feet, to leap up** se lever d'un bond

**leapt** [lept] *pt & pp of* **leap**

**learn** [lɜ:n] *(pt & pp* **learned** *or* **learnt** [lɜ:nt]*)* **1.** *vt* apprendre (**that** que) ; **to learn (how) to do sth** apprendre à faire qch **2.** *vi* apprendre ; **to learn about sth** [study] étudier qch ; [hear about] apprendre qch ■ **learned** [-ɪd] *adj* savant ■ **learner** *n* [beginner] débutant, -e *mf* ; [student] étudiant, -e *mf* ■ **learning** *n* [of language] apprentissage *m* (**of** de) ; [knowledge] savoir *m*

**lease** [li:s] **1.** *n* bail *m* (*pl* baux) **2.** *vt* [house] louer à bail (**from / to** à)

**leash** [li:ʃ] *n* [of dog] laisse *f* ; **on a leash** en laisse

**least** [li:st] **1.** *adj* **the least** [smallest amount of] le moins de ; **he has (the) least talent** il a le moins de talent (**of all** de tous) ; **the least effort / noise** le moindre effort / bruit **2.** *n* **the least** le moins ; **at least** du moins ; [with quantity] au moins ; **in the least** pas du tout **3.** *adv* [work, eat] le moins ; **the least difficult** le / la moins difficile ; **least of all** [especially not] surtout pas

**leather** [ˈleðə(r)] *n* cuir *m*

**leave** [li:v] **1.** *n* [holiday] congé *m* ; [of soldier, permission] permission *f* ; **to be on leave** être en congé ; [of soldier] être en permission ; **to take (one's) leave of sb** prendre congé de qn **2.** *(pt & pp* **left)** *vt* [allow to remain, forget] laisser ; [depart from] quitter ; **to leave sth with sb** [entrust, give] laisser qch à qn ; **to be left (over)** rester ; **there's no bread left** il ne reste plus de pain ; **I'll leave it (up) to you** je m'en remets à toi **3.** *vi* [go away] partir (**from** de ; **for** pour) ■ **leave aside** *vt sep* laisser de côté ; **leaving aside the question of cost** si on laisse de côté la question du coût ■ **leave behind** *vt sep* **to leave sth behind** [on purpose] laisser qch ; [accidentally] oublier qch ; **to leave sb behind** [not take] partir sans qn ; [surpass] dépasser qn ; [in race, at school]

distancer qn ■ **leave off** *vt sep* [lid] ne pas remettre ; *Fam* **to leave off doing sth** [stop] arrêter de faire qch ■ **leave on** *vt sep* [clothes] garder ■ **leave out** *vt sep* [forget to put] oublier de mettre ; [deliberately omit] décider de ne pas inclure ; [when reading] [word, line] sauter ; [exclude] exclure

**Lebanon** [ˈlebənən] *n* le Liban

**lecherous** [ˈletʃərəs] *adj* lubrique

**lecture** [ˈlektʃə(r)] **1.** *n* [public speech] conférence *f* ; [as part of series at university] cours *m* magistral ; [scolding] sermon *m* ; **lecture hall** amphithéâtre *m* **2.** *vt Fam* [scold] faire la morale à **3.** *vi* faire une conférence / un cours ■ **lecturer** *n* conférencier, -ère *mf* ; [at university] enseignant, -e *mf*

**led** [led] *pt & pp of* **lead**

**ledge** [ledʒ] *n* [on wall, window] rebord *m*

**ledger** [ˈledʒə(r)] *n* grand livre *m*

**leek** [li:k] *n* poireau *m*

**leer** [lɪə(r)] *vi* **to leer at sb** [lustfully] regarder qn d'un air lubrique

**leeway** [ˈli:weɪ] *n* marge *f* (de manœuvre)

**left¹** [left] *pt & pp of* **leave** ■ **left-luggage** *n Br* **left-luggage office** consigne *f*

**left²** [left] **1.** *adj* [side, hand] gauche **2.** *n* gauche *f* ; **on** *or* **to the left** à gauche (**of** de) **3.** *adv* à gauche ■ **left-hand** *adj* de gauche ; **on the left-hand side** à gauche (**of** de) ; **left-hand drive** conduite *f* à gauche ■ **left-handed** *adj* [person] gaucher, -ère ■ **left-wing** *adj* [views, government] de gauche

**left field** *n Am* SPORT **to play left field** être ailier gauche ; *Fam & Fig* **to be out in left field** être complètement à l'ouest

**leftovers** [ˈleftəʊvəz] *npl* restes *mpl*

**leg** [leg] *n* jambe *f* ; [of dog, bird] patte *f* ; [of table] pied *m* ; [of journey] étape *f* ; **leg of chicken, chicken leg** cuisse *f* de poulet ; **to pull sb's leg** [make fun of] mettre qn en boîte

**legacy** [ˈlegəsɪ] *(pl* **-ies***) n* [in a will] & *Fig* legs *m*

**legal** ['li:gəl] *adj* [lawful] légal ; [affairs, adviser] juridique ■ **legalize** *vt* légaliser ■ **legally** *adv* légalement

**legend** ['ledʒənd] *n* [story, inscription] légende f ■ **legendary** *adj* légendaire

**leggings** ['legɪŋz] *npl* [of woman] caleçon *m*

**legible** ['ledʒɪbəl] *adj* lisible

**legionella** [ˌliːdʒəˈnelə] *n* légionellose f

**legislation** [ledʒɪsˈleɪʃən] *n* [laws] législation f ; **(piece of) legislation** loi f

**legislative** ['ledʒɪslətɪv] *adj* législatif, -ive

**legislature** ['ledʒɪslətjə(r)] *n* (corps *m*) législatif *m*

**legitimate** [lɪˈdʒɪtɪmət] *adj* légitime

**legroom** ['legruːm] *n* place f pour les jambes

**L8r, L8R** MESSAGING *written abbr of* **later**

**leisure** [*Br* 'leʒə(r), *Am* 'liːʒər] *n* leisure **(time)** loisirs *mpl* ; **leisure centre** *or* **complex** centre *m* de loisirs ; **at (one's) leisure** à tête reposée ■ **leisurely** [*Br* 'leʒəlɪ, *Am* 'liːʒərlɪ] *adj* [walk, occupation] peu fatigant ; [meal, life] tranquille; **at a leisurely pace, in a leisurely way** sans se presser

**lemon** ['lemən] *n* citron *m* ; *Br* **lemon drink, lemon squash** citronnade f ; **lemon tea** thé *m* au citron ■ **lemonade** *n* [still] citronnade f ; *Br* [fizzy] limonade f

**lend** [lend] *(pt & pp* lent) *vt* prêter **(to** à) ; [support] apporter **(to** à) ; *Fig* [charm, colour] donner **(to** à) ■ **lender** *n* prêteur, -euse *mf*

**length** [leŋθ] *n* [in space] longueur f ; [section of road, string] tronçon *m* ; [of cloth] métrage *m* ; [duration] durée f ; **at length** [at last] enfin ; **at (great) length** [in detail] dans le détail ; **to go to great lengths** se donner beaucoup de mal **(to do** pour faire)

**lengthen** ['leŋθən] *vt* [garment] allonger ; [holiday, visit] prolonger ■ **lengthwise** *adv* dans le sens de la longueur ■ **lengthy** *(compar* -ier, *superl* -iest) *adj* long *(f* longue)

**lenient** ['liːnɪənt] *adj* indulgent **(to** envers) ■ **leniently** *adv* avec indulgence

**lens** [lenz] *(pl* **lenses** [-zɪz]) *n* lentille f ; [in spectacles] verre *m* ; [of camera] objectif *m*

**lent** [lent] *pt & pp of* **lend**

**Lent** [lent] *n* REL carême *m*

**lentil** ['lentəl] *n* lentille f

**leopard** ['lepəd] *n* léopard *m*

**leotard** ['liːətɑːd] *n* justaucorps *m*

**lesbian** ['lezbɪən] **1.** *adj* lesbien, -enne **2.** *n* lesbienne f

**less** [les] **1.** *adj & pron* moins (de) **(than** que) ; **less time** moins de temps ; **she has less (than you)** elle en a moins (que toi) ; **less than a kilo** moins d'un kilo **2.** *adv* moins **(than** que) ; **less (often)** moins souvent ; **one less** un(e) de moins **3.** *prep* moins

**-less** [ləs] *suff* sans ; **childless** sans enfants

**less-developed country** *n* pays *m* moins développé

**lessen** ['lesən] *vti* diminuer

**lesser** ['lesə(r)] **1.** *adj* moindre **2.** *n* **the lesser of** le /la moindre de

**lesson** ['lesən] *n* leçon f ; **an English lesson** une leçon d'anglais ; *Fig* **he has learnt his lesson** ça lui a servi de leçon

**lest** [lest] *conj* de peur que... (+ *ne* + *subjunctive*)

**let¹** [let] **1.** *(pt & pp* let, *pres p* letting) *vt* [allow] **to let sb do sth** laisser qn faire qch ; **to let sb have sth** donner qch à qn ; **to let go of sb/sth** lâcher qn /qch **2.** *v aux* **let's eat/go** mangeons /partons ; **let's go for a stroll** allons nous promener ; **let him come** qu'il vienne ■ **letdown** *n* déception f

■ **let down** *vt sep* [lower] baisser ; [hair] dénouer ; [tyre] dégonfler ; **to let sb down** [disappoint] décevoir qn ; **don't let me down** je compte sur toi

■ **let in** *vt sep* [person, dog] faire entrer ; [light] laisser entrer ; **to let sb in on sth** mettre qn au courant de qch ; **to let oneself in for trouble** s'attirer des ennuis

■ **let off** *vt sep* [firework] tirer ; [bomb] faire exploser ; [gun] faire partir ; **to let sb off** [allow to leave] laisser partir qn ; [not punish] ne pas punir qn ; **to be let off with a fine** s'en tirer avec une amende ; **to let sb off doing sth** dispenser qn de faire qch

■ **let on** *vi Fam* **to let on that...** [reveal] dire que...

■ **let out** *vt sep* [allow to leave] laisser sortir ; [prisoner] relâcher ; [cry, secret] laisser échapper ; [skirt] élargir

■ **let up** *vi* [of rain, person] s'arrêter

**let²** [let] *(pt & pp let, pres p letting) vt* **to let (out)** [house, room] louer

**lethal** ['li:θəl] *adj* [blow, dose] mortel, -elle ; [weapon] meurtrier, -ère

**lethargic** [lɪ'θɑːdʒɪk] *adj* léthargique

**letter** ['letə(r)] *n* [message, part of word] lettre *f* ; *Am* **letter carrier** facteur, -trice *mf* ; **letter opener** coupe-papier *m inv* ■ **letterbox** *n Br* boîte *f* aux lettres ■ **letterheaded** *adj* **letterheaded paper** papier *m* à en-tête ■ **lettering** *n* [letters] lettres *fpl*

**lettuce** ['letɪs] *n* laitue *f*

**letup** ['letʌp] *n* répit *m*

**leukaemia** [luːˈkiːmɪə] *n* leucémie *f*

**level** ['levəl] **1.** *n* **a)** [gen] niveau *m* ; **at eye level** à hauteur des yeux **b)** *Am* [spirit level] niveau *m* à bulle **2.** *adj* [surface] plat ; [equal in score] à égalité (**with** avec) ; [in height] à la même hauteur (**with** que) ; *Br* **level crossing** [for train] passage *m* à niveau **3.** *(Br -ll-, Am -l-) vt* [surface, differences] aplanir ; [building] raser ; [gun] braquer (**at** sur) ; [accusation] lancer (**at** contre) **4.** *vi* **to level off** *or* **out** [of prices] se stabiliser

■ **level-headed** *adj* équilibré

■ **level with** *vt insep Fam* être franc (*f* franche) *ou* honnête avec

**lever** [*Br* 'liːvə(r), *Am* 'levər] *n* levier *m*

**levy** ['levɪ] **1.** *(pl -ies) n* [tax] impôt *m* (**on** sur) **2.** *(pt & pp -ied) vt* [tax] lever

**lewd** [luːd] *(compar -er, superl -est) adj* obscène

**liability** [laɪəˈbɪlətɪ] *n* [legal responsibility] responsabilité *f* (**for** de) ; [disadvantage] handicap *m* ; FIN **liabilities** [debts] passif *m*

**liable** ['laɪəbəl] *adj* **liable to** [dizziness] sujet, -ette à ; [fine, tax] passible de ; **to be liable to do sth** risquer de faire qch ; **liable for sth** [responsible] responsable de qch

**liaise** [liːˈeɪz] *vi* travailler en liaison (**with** avec) ■ **liaison** [liːˈeɪzɒn] *n* [contact, love affair] liaison *f*

**liar** ['laɪə(r)] *n* menteur, -euse *mf*

**libel** ['laɪbəl] **1.** *n* [in law] diffamation *f* **2.** *(Br -ll-, Am -l-) vt* diffamer (par écrit)

**liberal** ['lɪbərəl] **1.** *adj* [open-minded & POL] libéral ; [generous] généreux, -euse (**with** de) **2.** *n* POL libéral, -e *mf*

**liberate** ['lɪbəreɪt] *vt* libérer ■ **liberation** *n* libération *f*

**liberty** ['lɪbətɪ] *(pl -ies) n* liberté *f* ; **to be at liberty to do sth** être libre de faire qch ; **to take liberties with sb / sth** prendre des libertés avec qn / qch

**library** ['laɪbrərɪ] *(pl -ies) n* bibliothèque *f* ■ **librarian** [-'breərɪən] *n* bibliothécaire *mf*

**libretto** [lɪˈbretəʊ] *(pl -os) n* MUS livret *m*

**Libya** ['lɪbɪə] *n* la Libye

**lice** [laɪs] *pl of* **louse**

**licence**, *Am* **license** ['laɪsəns] *n* [permit] permis *m* ; [for trading] licence *f* ; **(TV) licence** redevance *f* ; **licence plate / number** [of vehicle] plaque *f* / numéro *m* d'immatriculation

**license** ['laɪsəns] **1.** *n Am* = **licence 2.** *vt* accorder un permis / une licence à

**lick** [lɪk] *vt* lécher

**licorice** ['lɪkərɪʃ, 'lɪkərɪs] *n* réglisse *f*

**lid** [lɪd] *n* [of box, pan] couvercle *m*

**lie¹** [laɪ] **1.** *n* mensonge *m* **2.** *(pt & pp lied, pres p lying) vi* [tell lies] mentir

**lie²** [laɪ] *(pt lay, pp lain, pres p lying) vi* **a)** [of person, animal - be in a flat position] être allongé ; [get down] s'allonger ; **to be lying on the grass** être allongé sur l'herbe ; **he lay asleep** il dormait ; **here lies...** [on tomb] ci-gît... **b)** [of object] être, se trouver; **the problem lies in the fact that...** le problème réside dans le fait que... ■ **lie-down** n Br to have a lie-down faire une sieste ■ **lie-in** n Br to have a lie-in faire la grasse matinée ■ **lie about, lie around** vi [of objects, person] traîner ■ **lie down** vi s'allonger; **to be lying down** être allongé ■ **lie in** vi Br faire la grasse matinée

**lieu** [luː] n in lieu of sth au lieu de qch

**lieutenant** [luːˈtenənt, Br lefˈtenənt] n lieutenant m

**life** [laɪf] (pl lives) n vie f; [of battery, machine] durée f de vie; **to come to life** [of party, street] s'animer; **to take one's (own) life** se donner la mort; **life expectancy** espérance f de vie; **life insurance** assurance-vie f; **life jacket** gilet m de sauvetage; **life raft** canot m (pneumatique) de sauvetage ■ **lifebelt** n ceinture f de sauvetage ■ **lifeboat** n canot m de sauvetage ■ **lifebuoy** n bouée f de sauvetage ■ **lifeguard** n maître nageur m ■ **lifeless** adj sans vie ■ **lifelike** adj très ressemblant ■ **lifelong** adj de toute sa vie; [friend] de toujours ■ **life-saving** adj lifesaving apparatus appareils mpl de sauvetage; life-saving vaccine vaccin m qui sauve la vie ■ **lifesize(d)** adj grandeur nature inv ■ **lifestyle** n style m de vie ■ **lifetime** n vie f; Fig éternité f

**lift** [lɪft] **1.** n Br [elevator] ascenseur m; **to give sb a lift** emmener qn en voiture (**to** à) **2.** vt lever; [heavy object] soulever; Fig [ban] lever; Fig [steal] piquer (**from** à) **3.** vi [of fog] se lever ■ **lift-off** n [of space vehicle] décollage m ■ **lift down** vt sep [take down] descendre (**from** de) ■ **lift off 1.** vt sep [take down] descendre (**from** de) **2.** vi [of spacecraft] décoller ■ **lift out** vt sep [take out] sortir ■ **lift up** vt sep [arm, object, eyes] lever; [heavy object] soulever

**ligament** [ˈlɪɡəmənt] n ligament m

**light¹** [laɪt] **1.** n lumière f; [on vehicle] feu m; [vehicle headlight] phare m; **by the light of sth** à la clarté de qch; **in the light of...** [considering] à la lumière de...; **to bring sth to light** mettre qch en lumière; **to come to light** être découvert; **do you have a light?** [for cigarette] est-ce que vous avez du feu ?; **to set light to sth** mettre le feu à qch; **turn right at the lights** tournez à droite après les feux; **light bulb** ampoule f; **light switch** interrupteur m **2.** adj it will soon be light il fera bientôt jour **3.** (pt & pp lit or lighted) vt [fire, candle, gas] allumer; [match] allumer, gratter; **to light (up)** [room] éclairer; [cigarette] allumer; [face] s'éclairer **4.** vi to light up [of smoker] allumer une cigarette / un cigare / sa pipe ■ **lighting** n [act, system] éclairage m

**light²** [laɪt] adj [bright, not dark] clair; **a light green jacket** une veste vert clair

**light³** [laɪt] adj [in weight, quantity, strength] léger, -ère; [task] facile; **light rain** pluie f fine; **to travel light** voyager avec peu de bagages ■ **light-hearted** adj enjoué

**lighten** [ˈlaɪtən] vt [make less heavy] alléger

**lighter** [ˈlaɪtə(r)] n briquet m; [for cooker] allume-gaz m inv

**lighthouse** [ˈlaɪthaʊs] n phare m

**lightly** [ˈlaɪtlɪ] adv légèrement; **to get off lightly** s'en tirer à bon compte

**lightning** [ˈlaɪtnɪŋ] **1.** n éclairs mpl; **(flash of) lightning** éclair m **2.** adj [speed] foudroyant; [visit] éclair inv

**lightweight** [ˈlaɪtweɪt] **1.** adj [shoes, fabric] léger, -ère; Fig & Pej [person] pas sérieux, -euse **2.** n [in boxing] poids m léger

**like¹** [laɪk] **1.** prep comme; **like this** comme ça; **what's he like?** comment est-il ?; **to be** or **look like sb/sth** ressembler à qn /qch; **what was the book like?** comment as-tu trouvé le livre ? **2.** adv **nothing like as big** loin d'être aussi grand **3.** conj Fam [as] comme; **do like I do** fais comme moi **4.** n ...and the like ...et ainsi de suite; **the likes of you** des gens de ton acabit

**like²** [laɪk] **1.** vt aimer (bien) (**to do** or **doing** faire); **I like him** je l'aime bien; **I'd like to come** j'aimerais bien venir; **I'd like a kilo of apples** je voudrais un kilo de pommes ; **would you like an apple?** voulez-vous une pomme ? ; **if you like** si vous voulez **2.** *npl* **one's likes and dislikes** nos préférences *fpl* ▪ **liking** *n* **a liking for** [person] de la sympathie pour ; [thing] du goût pour ; **to my liking** à mon goût

**likeable** ['laɪkəbəl] *adj* sympathique

**likely** ['laɪklɪ] **1.** *(compar* -**ier***, superl* -**iest)** *adj* [result, event] probable ; [excuse] vraisemblable ; **it's likely (that) she'll come** il est probable qu'elle viendra **2.** *adv* **very likely** très probablement ▪ **likelihood** *n* probabilité *f*; **there isn't much likelihood that…** il y a peu de chances que… (+ *subjunctive*)

**liken** ['laɪkən] *vt* comparer (**to** à)

**likeness** ['laɪknɪs] *n* [similarity] ressemblance *f*; **it's a good likeness** c'est très ressemblant

**likewise** ['laɪkwaɪz] *adv* [similarly] de même

**lilac** ['laɪlək] **1.** *n* lilas *m* **2.** *adj* [colour] lilas *inv*

**Lilo**® ['laɪləʊ] *(pl* -**os)** *n Br* matelas *m* pneumatique

**lily** ['lɪlɪ] *(pl* -**ies)** *n* lis *m*

**limb** [lɪm] *n* [of body] membre *m*

**limber** ['lɪmbə(r)] *vi* **to limber up** s'échauffer

**lime** [laɪm] *n* [fruit] citron *m* vert

**limelight** ['laɪmlaɪt] *n* **to be in the limelight** occuper le devant de la scène

**limit** ['lɪmɪt] **1.** *n* limite *f*; [restriction] limitation *f* (**on** de) ; **off limits** interdit ; *Fam* **that's the limit!** c'est le comble ! ; **within limits** jusqu'à un certain point **2.** *vt* limiter (**to** à) ; **to limit oneself to sth / doing sth** se borner à qch / faire qch ▪ **limitation** *n* limitation *f*

**limited** ['lɪmɪtɪd] *adj* [restricted] limité ; [edition] à tirage limité ; *Br* **limited company** société *f* à responsabilité limitée ; *Br* **(public) limited company** [with shareholders] société *f* anonyme

**limousine** [lɪmə'ziːn] *n* [car] limousine *f*

**limp**[1] [lɪmp] **1.** *n* **to have a limp** boiter **2.** *vi* [of person] boiter

**limp**[2] [lɪmp] *(compar* -**er***, superl* -**est)** *adj* [soft] mou (*f* molle) ; [flabby - skin] flasque ; [person, hat] avachi

**line**[1] [laɪn] **1.** *n* ligne *f*; [stroke] trait *m*; [of poem] vers *m*; [wrinkle] ride *f*; [track] voie *f*; [rope] corde *f*; [row] rangée *f*; [of vehicles] file *f*; [queue of people] file *f*, queue *f*; COMM gamme *f*; *Fam* [work] **line of business** branche *f*; **to learn one's lines** [of actor] apprendre son texte ; **to be on the line** [at other end of phone line] être au bout du fil ; [at risk - of job] être menacé ; *Am* **to stand in line** faire la queue ; **in line with sth** conforme à qch ; **along the same lines** [work, think, act] de la même façon ; *Fam* **to drop sb a line** [send a letter] envoyer un mot à qn ; **line dancing** *danse de style country effectuée en rangs* **2.** *vt* **to line the street** [of trees] border la rue ; [of people] s'aligner le long du trottoir ; **to line up** [children, objects] aligner ; [organize] prévoir ; **lined paper** papier *m* réglé **3.** *vi Am* [queue up] faire la queue ; **to line up** s'aligner ▪ **line-up** *n* [row of people] file *f*; TV [of guests] plateau *m*

**line**[2] [laɪn] *vt* [clothes] doubler

**linen** ['lɪnɪn] *n* [sheets] linge *m*; [material] (toile *f* de) lin *m*

**liner** ['laɪnə(r)] *n* **a) (ocean) liner** paquebot *m* **b)** *Br* **(dust)bin liner***, Am* **garbage can liner** sac-poubelle *m*

**linesman** ['laɪnzmən] *(pl* -**men)** *n* [in football] juge *m* de touche

**linger** ['lɪŋgə(r)] *vi* **to linger (on)** [of person] s'attarder ; [of smell, memory] persister ; [of doubt] subsister

**linguist** ['lɪŋgwɪst] *n* [specialist] linguiste *mf* ▪ **linguistic** *adj* linguistique ▪ **linguistics** *n* linguistique *f*

**lining** ['laɪnɪŋ] *n* [of clothes] doublure *f*

**link** [lɪŋk] **1.** *n* [connection & COMPUT] lien *m*; [of chain] maillon *m*; [by road, rail] liaison *f* **2.** *vt* [connect] relier (**to** à) ; [relate, associate] lier (**to** à) ; **to link up** relier ; [computer] connecter **3.** *vi* COMPUT **to link to sth** mettre un lien avec qch ; **to link up** [of companies, countries] s'associer ; [of roads] se rejoindre

**livestock**

**lino** ['laɪnəʊ] (*pl* -os) *n* Br lino *m*

**lint** [lɪnt] *n* [bandage] tissu *m* ouaté ; [fluff] peluches *fpl*

**lion** ['laɪən] *n* lion *m* ; **lion cub** lionceau *m*

**lip** [lɪp] *n* [of person] lèvre *f* ; [of cup] bord *m* ■ **lip-read** (*pt & pp* -read [-red]) *vi* lire sur les lèvres ■ **lipstick** *n* rouge *m* à lèvres

**liqueur** [Br lɪ'kjʊə(r), Am lɪ'kɜ:r] *n* liqueur *f*

**liquid** ['lɪkwɪd] *n* & *adj* liquide (*m*)

**liquidate** ['lɪkwɪdeɪt] *vt* [debt] *Fam* [kill] liquider

**liquidizer, liquidiser** ['lɪkwɪdaɪzə(r)] *n* Br [for fruit juices, purées] mixeur *m* ■ **liquidize** *vt* Br passer au mixeur

**liquor** ['lɪkə(r)] *n* Am alcool *m* ; **liquor store** magasin *m* de vins et de spiritueux

**liquorice** ['lɪkərɪʃ, 'lɪkərɪs] *n* Br réglisse *f*

**lira** ['lɪərə] (*pl* lire ['lɪəreɪ]) *n* lire *f*

**lisp** [lɪsp] **1.** *n* to have a lisp zézayer **2.** *vi* zézayer

**list** [lɪst] **1.** *n* liste *f* **2.** *vt* [things] faire la liste de ; [names] mettre sur la liste ; [name one by one] énumérer ; Br **listed building** monument *m* classé

**listen** ['lɪsən] *vi* écouter ; **to listen to sb / sth** écouter qn / qch ; **to listen (out) for** [telephone, person] guetter ■ **listener** *n* [to radio] auditeur, -trice *mf*

**listless** ['lɪstləs] *adj* apathique

**lit** [lɪt] *pt & pp of* **light**

**liter** ['li:tə(r)] *n* Am litre *m*

**literal** ['lɪtərəl] *adj* littéral ; [not exaggerated] réel (*f* réelle)

**literally** ['lɪtərəlɪ] *adv* littéralement ; [really] réellement ■ **literary** *adj* littéraire

**literate** ['lɪtərət] *adj* qui sait lire et écrire

**literature** ['lɪtərətʃə(r)] *n* littérature *f* ; [pamphlets] documentation *f*

**lithe** [laɪð] *adj* agile

**litigation** [lɪtɪ'geɪʃən] *n* litige *m*

**litre, Am liter** ['li:tə(r)] *n* litre *m*

**litter** ['lɪtə(r)] **1.** *n* a) [rubbish] détritus *mpl* ; [papers] papiers *mpl* ; Br **litter bin** boîte *f* à ordures b) [young animals] portée *f* ; [for cat] litière *f* **2.** *vt* Br **to be littered with sth** être jonché de qch

**little** ['lɪtəl] **1.** *n* peu *m* ; **I've little left** il m'en reste peu ; **she eats little** elle mange peu ; **I have a little** j'en ai un peu **2.** *adj* a) [small] petit ; **a little bit** un (petit) peu ; **little finger** petit doigt *m*, auriculaire *m*

b) [not much] peu de ; **little time / money** peu de temps / d'argent ; **a little time / money** un peu de temps / d'argent

**3.** *adv* [somewhat, rather] peu ; **little by little** peu à peu ; **as little as possible** le moins possible ; **a little heavy / better** un peu lourd / mieux ; **to work a little** travailler un peu

**live¹** [laɪv] **1.** *adj* a) [electric wire] sous tension ; [plugged in - appliance] branché ; [ammunition] réel (*f* réelle), de combat b) [alive] vivant **2.** *adj & adv* [on radio, television] en direct ; **a live broadcast** une émission en direct ; **a live recording** un enregistrement public

**live²** [lɪv] **1.** *vt* [life] mener, vivre **2.** *vi* vivre ; **where do you live?** où habitez-vous ? ; **to live in Paris** habiter (à) Paris ■ **live down** *vt sep* faire oublier ■ **live off** *vt insep* [eat] vivre de ; [sponge off] vivre aux crochets de ■ **live on 1.** *vt sep* = **live off 2.** *vi* [of memory] survivre ■ **live through** *vt insep* [experience] vivre ■ **live up to** *vt insep* [sb's expectations] se montrer à la hauteur de

**livelihood** ['laɪvlɪhʊd] *n* my livelihood mon gagne-pain ; **to earn one's or a livelihood** gagner sa vie

**lively** ['laɪvlɪ] (*compar* -ier, *superl* -iest) *adj* [person, style] plein de vie ; [story] vivant ; [mind] vif (*f* vive) ; [discussion, conversation] animé ■ **liven up** ['laɪvən] **1.** *vt sep* [person] égayer ; [party] animer **2.** *vi* [of person, party] s'animer

**liver** ['lɪvə(r)] *n* foie *m*

**livestock** ['laɪvstɒk] *n* bétail *m*

**livestream** ['laɪvstriːm] *n* retransmission *f* en direct, diffusion *f* en direct, streaming *m* live

**livid** ['lɪvɪd] *adj* [angry] furieux, -euse

**living** ['lɪvɪŋ] **1.** *adj* [alive] vivant; **within living memory** de mémoire d'homme; **the living** les vivants *mpl* **2.** *n* [livelihood] vie *f*; **to make** *or* **earn a** *or* **one's living** gagner sa vie; **living room** salle *f* de séjour

**lizard** ['lɪzəd] *n* lézard *m*

**load** [ləʊd] **1.** *n* [object carried, burden] charge *f*; [freight] chargement *m*; [strain, weight] poids *m*; *Fam* **a load of, loads of** [people, money] un tas de **2.** *vt* [gen & COMPUT] charger; [DVD] mettre un DVD dans; **to load up** [car, ship] charger (**with** de) **3.** *vi* **a) to load (up)** prendre un chargement **b)** [computer program] se charger ■ **load down** *vt sep* charger (lourdement); **he was loaded down with packages** il avait des paquets plein les bras; **I'm loaded down with work** je suis surchargé de travail

**loaded** ['ləʊdɪd] *adj* [gun, vehicle] chargé; *Fam* [rich] plein aux as

**loaf** [ləʊf] **1.** (*pl* **loaves**) *n* pain *m* **2.** *vi* **to loaf (about)** fainéanter

**loan** [ləʊn] **1.** *n* [money lent] prêt *m*; [money borrowed] emprunt *m*; **on loan from** prêté par **2.** *vt* [lend] prêter (**to** à)

**loathe** [ləʊð] *vt* détester (**doing** faire)

**lobby** ['lɒbɪ] **1.** (*pl* **-ies**) *n* **a)** [of hotel] hall *m*; [of theatre] foyer *m* **b)** [in politics] groupe *m* de pression **2.** (*pt & pp* **-ied**) *vt* faire pression sur **3.** *vi* **to lobby for sth** faire pression pour obtenir qch

**lobster** ['lɒbstə(r)] *n* homard *m*; [spiny] langouste *f*

**local** ['ləʊkəl] **1.** *adj* local; [regional] régional; [of the neighbourhood] du quartier; **a local phone call** [within town] une communication urbaine **2.** *n* *Br Fam* [pub] bistrot *m* du coin; **the locals** [people] les gens *mpl* du coin

**locality** [ləʊ'kælətɪ] (*pl* **-ies**) *n* [neighbourhood] environs *mpl*

**localization**, *Br* **localisation** [ˌləʊkəlaɪ'zeɪʃn] *n* COMPUT localisation *f*

**locally** ['ləʊkəlɪ] *adv* dans le quartier

**locate** [ləʊ'keɪt] *vt* [find] repérer; [pain, noise, leak] localiser; [situate] situer; **to be located in Paris** être situé à Paris ■ **location** *n* [site] emplacement *m*; **on location** [shoot a film] en extérieur

**lock¹** [lɒk] *n* [of hair] mèche *f*

**lock²** [lɒk] **1.** *n* **a)** [on door, chest] serrure *f*; **(anti-theft) lock** [on vehicle] antivol *m* **b)** [on canal] écluse *f* **2.** *vt* [door, car] fermer à clef **3.** *vi* fermer à clef ■ **lock away** *vt sep* [prisoner] enfermer; [jewels] mettre sous clef ■ **lock in** *vt sep* [person] enfermer; **to lock sb in sth** enfermer qn dans qch ■ **lock out** *vt sep* [person] enfermer dehors ■ **lock up 1.** *vt sep* [house, car] fermer à clef; [prisoner] enfermer; [jewels] mettre sous clef, enfermer **2.** *vi* fermer à clef

**locker** ['lɒkə(r)] *n* [in school] casier *m*; [for luggage - at station, airport] casier *m* de consigne automatique; [for clothes] vestiaire *m* (métallique); *Am* SPORT **locker room** vestiaire *m*

**locket** ['lɒkɪt] *n* médaillon *m*

**locksmith** ['lɒksmɪθ] *n* serrurier *m*

**locomotive** [ləʊkə'məʊtɪv] *n* locomotive *f*

**locust** ['ləʊkəst] *n* sauterelle *f*

**lodge** [lɒdʒ] **1.** *n* [house] pavillon *m*; [of porter] loge *f* **2.** *vt* [person] loger **3.** *vi* [of bullet] se loger (**in** dans)

**lodger** ['lɒdʒə(r)] *n* [room and meals] pensionnaire *mf*; [room only] locataire *mf*

**lodgings** ['lɒdʒɪŋz] *n* [flat] logement *m*; [room] chambre *f*; **in lodgings** en meublé

**loft** [lɒft] *n* grenier *m*

**lofty** ['lɒftɪ] (*compar* **-ier**, *superl* **-iest**) *adj* [high, noble] élevé

**log** [lɒg] **1.** *n* [tree trunk] tronc *m* d'arbre; [for fire] bûche *f*; **log cabin** hutte *f* en rondin; **log fire** feu *m* de bois **2.** (*pt & pp* **-gg-**)*vt* [facts] noter **3.** *vi* COMPUT **log in, log on** ouvrir une session; COMPUT **log off, log out** fermer une session ■ **logbook** *n* [on ship] journal *m* de bord; [on plane] carnet *m* de vol

**logic** ['lɒdʒɪk] n logique f ■ **logical** adj logique ■ **logically** adv logiquement

**logistics** [lə'dʒɪstɪks] n logistique f

**logo** ['ləʊgəʊ] (pl -os) n logo m

**loiter** ['lɔɪtə(r)] vi traîner

**loll** [lɒl] vi [in armchair] se prélasser

**lollipop** ['lɒlɪpɒp] n sucette f; Br **lollipop man/lady** contractuel ou contractuelle qui aide les écoliers à traverser la rue ■ **lolly** (pl -ies) n Fam [lollipop] sucette f; (ice) lolly glace f à l'eau

**London** ['lʌndən] **1.** n Londres m ou f **2.** adj londonien, -enne

**lone** [ləʊn] adj solitaire

**loneliness** ['ləʊnlɪnəs] n solitude f ■ **lonely** (compar -ier, superl -iest) adj [road, house, life] solitaire; [person] seul

**loner** ['ləʊnə(r)] n solitaire mf

**long¹** [lɒŋ] **1.** (compar -er, superl -est) adj long (f longue); **to be 10 metres long** avoir 10 mètres de long; **to be six weeks long** durer six semaines; **how long is...?** quelle est la longueur de...?; [time] quelle est la durée de...?; **a long time** longtemps; **long jump** [sport] saut m en longueur

**2.** adv [a long time] longtemps; **has he been here long?** il y a longtemps qu'il est ici?; **how long?** [in time] combien de temps?; **not long** peu de temps; **before long** sous peu; **no longer** ne... plus; **a bit longer** [wait] encore un peu; **I won't be long** je n'en ai pas pour longtemps; **don't be long** dépêche-toi; **all summer/winter long** tout l'été/l'hiver; **long live the queen!** vive la reine!; **as long as, so long as** [provided that] pourvu que (+ subjunctive); **as long as I live** tant que je vivrai

■ **long-distance** adj [race] de fond; [phone call] interurbain

■ **long-haired** adj aux cheveux longs

■ **long-life** adj [battery] longue durée inv; [milk] longue conservation inv

■ **long-range** adj [forecast] à long terme

■ **longsighted** adj [person] presbyte

■ **longstanding** adj de longue date

■ **long-term** adj à long terme

■ **long-winded** adj [speech, speaker] verbeux, -euse

**long²** [lɒŋ] vi **to long for sth** avoir très envie de qch; **to long to do sth** avoir très envie de faire qch ■ **longing** n désir m

**longitude** ['lɒndʒɪtju:d] n longitude f

**loo** [lu:] (pl **loos**) n Br Fam **the loo** le petit coin

**look** [lʊk] **1.** n [glance] regard m; [appearance] air m, allure f; **to have a look (at sth)** jeter un coup d'œil (à qch); **to have a look (for sth)** chercher (qch); **to have a look (a)round** regarder; [walk] faire un tour; **let me have a look** fais voir **2.** vt **to look sb in the face** regarder qn dans les yeux **3.** vi regarder; **to look tired/happy** [seem] avoir l'air fatigué/heureux; **to look pretty/ugly** faire joli/laid; **you look like** or **as if** or **as though you're tired** tu as l'air fatigué; **to look like an apple** avoir l'air d'une pomme; **you look like my brother** tu ressembles à mon frère; **it looks like rain** on dirait qu'il va pleuvoir; **what does he look like?** comment est-il?; **to look well** or **good** [of person] avoir bonne mine; **you look good in that hat** ce chapeau te va très bien; **that looks bad** [action] ça fait mauvais effet ■ **looks** npl [attractiveness] beauté f ■ **look after** vt insep [take care of] s'occuper de; [keep safely] garder (**for sb** pour qn); **to look after oneself** [keep healthy] faire bien attention à soi; [manage, cope] se débrouiller ■ **look around 1.** vt insep [town, shops] faire un tour dans **2.** vi [have a look] regarder; [walk round] faire un tour ■ **look at** vt insep regarder; [consider] considérer ■ **look away** vi détourner les yeux ■ **look back** vi regarder derrière soi; [in time] regarder en arrière ■ **look down** vi baisser les yeux; [from a height] regarder en bas; **to look down on** [consider scornfully] regarder de haut ■ **look for** vt insep [seek] chercher ■ **look forward to** vt insep [event] attendre avec impatience; **to look forward to doing sth** avoir hâte de faire qch ■ **look in** vi regarder à l'intérieur ; **to look in on sb** passer voir qn ■ **look into** *vt insep* [examine] examiner ; [find out about] se renseigner sur ■ **look on 1.** *vt insep* [consider] considérer (**as** comme) **2.** *vi* [watch] regarder ; **to look on to** [of window, house] donner sur ■ **look out** *vi* [be careful] faire attention ; **to look out for sb/sth** [seek] chercher qn/qch ; [watch] guetter qn/qch ; **to look out on to** [of window, house] donner sur ■ **look over** *vt insep* [examine fully] examiner ; [briefly] parcourir ; [region, town] parcourir, visiter ■ **look round 1.** *vt insep* [visit] visiter **2.** *vi* [have a look] regarder ; [walk round] faire un tour ; [look back] se retourner ■ **look round for sb/sth** [seek] chercher qn/qch ■ **look through** *vt insep* [inspect] passer en revue ■ **look up 1.** *vt sep* [word] chercher ; **to look sb up** [visit] passer voir qn **2.** *vi* [of person] lever les yeux ; [into the air or sky] regarder en l'air ; [improve - of situation] s'améliorer ; *Fig* **to look up to sb** respecter qn

**-looking** ['lʊkɪŋ] *suff* **pleasant-/tired-looking** à l'air agréable/fatigué

**lookout** ['lʊkaʊt] *n* [soldier] guetteur *m* ; **lookout (post)** observatoire *m* ; **to be on the lookout for sb/sth** guetter qn/qch

**lookup** ['lʊkʌp] *n* COMPUT recherche *f*, consultation *f*

**loom** [luːm] **1.** *n* [weaving machine] métier *m* à tisser **2.** *vi* **to loom (up)** [of mountain] apparaître indistinctement ; [of event] paraître imminent

**loony** ['luːnɪ] *(pl* **-ies)** *n & adj Fam* dingue *(mf)*

**loop** [luːp] *n* [gen & COMPUT] boucle *f*

**loophole** ['luːphəʊl] *n* [in law] vide *m* juridique

**loose** [luːs] **1.** *(compar* **-er,** *superl* **-est)** *adj* [screw, belt, knot] desserré ; [tooth, stone] qui bouge ; [page] détaché ; [clothes] flottant ; [hair] dénoué ; [translation] vague ; [articles for sale] en vrac ; *Br* [cheese, tea] au poids ; **there's an animal/prisoner loose** [having escaped] il y a un animal échappé/un prisonnier évadé ; **loose change** petite monnaie *f* ; **to come loose** [of knot, screw] se desserrer ; [of page] se détacher ; [of tooth] se mettre à bouger ; **to get loose** [of dog] se détacher ; **to set** *or* **turn loose** [dog] lâcher **2.** *n* **on the loose** [prisoner] en cavale ; [animal] en liberté

**loosely** ['luːslɪ] *adv* [hang] lâchement ; [hold, tie] sans serrer ; [translate] de façon approximative

**loosen** ['luːsən] *vt* [knot, belt, screw] desserrer ; [rope] détendre ; **to loosen one's grip** relâcher son étreinte

**loot** [luːt] **1.** *n* butin *m* ; *Fam* [money] fric *m* **2.** *vt* piller ■ **looting** *n* pillage *m*

**lop** [lɒp] *(pt & pp* **-pp-**)*vt* **to lop (off)** couper

**lop-sided** [lɒp'saɪdɪd] *adj* [crooked] de travers

**lord** [lɔːd] *n* seigneur *m* ; [British title] lord *m* ; **the Lord** [God] le Seigneur ; *Fam* **good Lord!** bon sang !

**lorry** ['lɒrɪ] *(pl* **-ies)** *n Br* camion *m* ; [heavy] poids *m* lourd ; **lorry driver** camionneur *m* ; **(long-distance) lorry driver** routier *m*

**lose** [luːz] *(pt & pp* **lost**) **1.** *vt* perdre ; **to lose one's life** trouver la mort (**in** dans) ; **to lose one's way, to get lost** [of person] se perdre ; *Fam* **get lost!** fous le camp ! ; **that lost us the war/our jobs** cela nous a coûté la guerre/notre travail ; **the clock loses six minutes a day** la pendule retarde de six minutes par jour **2.** *vi* perdre ; **to lose out** être perdant ; **to lose to sb** [in contest] être battu par qn ■ **loser** *n* [in contest] perdant, -e *mf* ; *Fam* [failure in life] minable *mf* ■ **losing** *adj* [number, team, horse] perdant

**loss** [lɒs] *n* perte *f* ; **to be at a loss** être perplexe, être embarrassé, -e ; **to sell sth at a loss** vendre qch à perte ; **to make a loss** [financially] perdre de l'argent

**lost** [lɒst] **1.** *pt & pp of* **lose 2.** *adj* perdu ; *Br* **lost property,** *Am* **lost and found** objets *mpl* trouvés

**lot¹** [lɒt] *n* [destiny] sort *m* ; [batch] lot *m* ; **to draw lots** tirer au sort

**lot²** [lɒt] *n* **the lot** [everything] (le) tout; **the lot of you** vous tous; **a lot of, lots of** beaucoup de; **a lot** beaucoup; **quite a lot** pas mal (**of** de)

**lotion** ['ləʊʃən] *n* lotion *f*

**lottery** ['lɒtərɪ] (*pl* **-ies**) *n* loterie *f*; **lottery ticket** billet *m* de loterie

**loud** [laʊd] **1.** (*compar* **-er**, *superl* **-est**) *adj* [voice, music] fort; [noise, cry] grand; [laugh] gros (*f* grosse); [gaudy] voyant **2.** *adv* [shout] fort; **out loud** tout haut ■ **loudly** *adv* [speak, laugh, shout] fort ■ **loudspeaker** *n* haut-parleur *m*; [for speaking to crowd] porte-voix *m inv*; [of stereo system] enceinte *f*

**lounge** [laʊndʒ] **1.** *n* [in house, hotel] salon *m*; **airport lounge** salle *f* d'aéroport **2.** *vi* [loll in armchair] se prélasser; **to lounge about** [idle] paresser

**louse** [laʊs] (*pl* **lice**) *n* [insect] pou *m*

**lousy** ['laʊzɪ] (*compar* **-ier**, *superl* **-iest**) *adj Fam* [bad] nul (*f* nulle); [food, weather] dégueulasse; **to feel lousy** être mal fichu

**lout** [laʊt] *n* voyou *m*

**love** [lʌv] **1.** *n* **a)** [feeling] amour *m*; **in love** amoureux, -euse (**with** de); **they're in love** ils s'aiment; **give him/her my love** [greeting] dis-lui bien des choses de ma part; **love affair** liaison *f* **b)** [in tennis] rien *m*; **15 love** 15 à rien **2.** *vt* [person] aimer; [thing, activity] adorer (**to do** *or* **doing** faire) ■ **loving** *adj* affectueux, -euse

**lovely** ['lʌvlɪ] (*compar* **-ier**, *superl* **-iest**) *adj* [idea, smell] très bon (*f* bonne); [pretty] joli; [charming] charmant; [kind] gentil, -ille; **the weather's lovely, it's lovely** il fait beau; **(it's) lovely to see you!** je suis ravi de te voir!

**lover** ['lʌvə(r)] *n* [man] amant *m*; [woman] maîtresse *f*; **a lover of music/art** un amateur de musique/d'art

**low¹** [ləʊ] **1.** (*compar* **-er**, *superl* **-est**) *adj* bas (*f* basse); [speed, income, intelligence] faible; [opinion, quality] mauvais; **she's low on** [money] elle n'a plus beaucoup de; **to feel low** [depressed] être déprimé; **lower** inférieur; *Am* **low beams** [of vehicle] codes *mpl* **2.** (*compar*

-er, *superl* -est) *adv* bas; **to turn (down) low** mettre plus bas; **to run low** [of supplies] s'épuiser **3.** *n* **to reach a new low** *or* **an all-time low** [of prices] atteindre leur niveau le plus bas ■ **low-cut** *adj* décolleté ■ **lowdown** *n Fam* [facts] tuyaux *mpl* ■ **low-energy** *adj* à basse consommation; **low-energy light bulb** ampoule *f* basse consommation ■ **low-fat** *adj* [milk] écrémé; [cheese] allégé ■ **low-income** *adj* à faibles revenus ■ **low-interest** *adj* FIN [credit, loan] à taux réduit ■ **low-key** *adj* [discreet] discret, -ète ■ **low-maintenance** *adj* qui ne demande pas beaucoup d'entretien ■ **low-octane fuel** *n* carburant *m* à faible indice d'octane ■ **low-paid** *adj* mal payé ■ **low-resolution** *adj* à basse résolution ■ **low-risk** *adj* [investment, strategy] à faible risque ■ **low-voltage** *adj* à faible voltage

**low²** [ləʊ] *vi* [of cattle] meugler

**lower** ['ləʊə(r)] *vt* baisser; **to lower sb/sth** [by rope] descendre qn/qch; *Fig* **to lower oneself** s'abaisser ■ **lower-income group** *n* groupe *m* de contribuables à revenus moyens

**lowly** ['ləʊlɪ] (*compar* **-ier**, *superl* **-iest**) *adj* humble

**loyal** ['lɔɪəl] *adj* loyal (**to** envers) ■ **loyalty** *n* loyauté *f*; **loyalty card** carte *f* de fidélité

**lozenge** ['lɒzɪndʒ] *n* [tablet] pastille *f*; [shape] losange *m*

**LP** [el'piː] (*abbr of* **long-playing record**) *n* 33 tours *m inv*

**L-plate** ['elpleɪt] *n Br* plaque apposée sur une voiture pour signaler que le conducteur est en conduite accompagnée

**LPR** *n Am abbr of* **lawful permanent resident**

**Ltd** (*abbr of* **Limited**) *Br* COMM ≃ SARL

**lubricate** ['luːbrɪkeɪt] *vt* lubrifier; [machine, car wheels] graisser

**lucid** ['luːsɪd] *adj* lucide

**luck** [lʌk] *n* [chance] chance *f*; [good fortune] (bonne) chance *f*, bonheur *m*; **to be in luck** avoir de la chance; **to be out of luck** ne pas avoir de chance; **to**

wish sb luck souhaiter bonne chance à qn; **bad luck** malchance *f*; **hard luck!, tough luck!** pas de chance !

**luckily** ['lʌkɪlɪ] *adv* heureusement

**lucky** ['lʌkɪ] *(compar* **-ier***, superl* **-iest)** *adj* [person] chanceux, -euse; **to be lucky** [of person] avoir de la chance; **it's lucky that…** c'est une chance que… (+ *subjunctive*); **lucky number** chiffre *m* porte-bonheur

**lucrative** ['luːkrətɪv] *adj* lucratif, -ive

**ludicrous** ['luːdɪkrəs] *adj* ridicule

**luggage** ['lʌgɪdʒ] *n* bagages *mpl*; **a piece of luggage** un bagage; **hand luggage** bagages *mpl* à main; **luggage allowance** poids *m* maximal autorisé; **luggage compartment** compartiment *m* à bagages

**lukewarm** ['luːkwɔːm] *adj* [water, soup] tiède

**lull** [lʌl] **1.** *n* arrêt *m*; [in storm] accalmie *f* **2.** *vt* **to lull sb to sleep** endormir qn en le / la berçant

**lullaby** ['lʌləbaɪ] *(pl* **-ies***) n* berceuse *f*

**lumber¹** ['lʌmbə(r)] *n* [timber] bois *m* de charpente; *Br* [junk] bric-à-brac *m inv* ▪ **lumberyard** *n Am* dépôt *m* de bois

**lumber²** ['lʌmbə(r)] *vt Br Fam* **to lumber sb with sb / sth** coller qn / qch à qn

**luminous** ['luːmɪnəs] *adj* [colour, paper, ink] fluorescent; [dial, clock] lumineux, -euse

**lump** [lʌmp] **1.** *n* morceau *m*; [in soup] grumeau *m*; [bump] bosse *f*; [swelling] grosseur *f*; **lump sum** somme *f* forfaitaire **2.** *vt* **to lump together** réunir; *Fig & Pej* mettre dans le même sac ▪ **lumpy** *(compar* **-ier***, superl* **-iest)** *adj* [soup] grumeleux, -euse; [surface] bosselé

**lunar** ['luːnə(r)] *adj* lunaire; **lunar eclipse** éclipse *f* de lune

**lunatic** ['luːnətɪk] *n* fou *m*, folle *f*

**lunch** [lʌntʃ] **1.** *n* déjeuner *m*; **to have lunch** déjeuner; **lunch break, lunch hour, lunch time** heure *f* du déjeuner

**2.** *vi* déjeuner (**on** *or* **off** de) ▪ **lunchbox** *n* boîte *f* dans laquelle on transporte son déjeuner

**luncheon** ['lʌntʃən] *n* déjeuner *m*; *Br* **luncheon voucher** Chèque-Restaurant *m*

**lung** [lʌŋ] *n* poumon *m*

**lunge** [lʌndʒ] *vi* **to lunge at sb** se ruer sur qn

**lurch** [lɜːtʃ] **1.** *n Fam* **to leave sb in the lurch** laisser qn dans le pétrin **2.** *vi* [of person] tituber

**lure** [lʊə(r)] **1.** *n* [attraction] attrait *m* **2.** *vt* attirer (par la ruse) (**into** dans)

**lurid** ['lʊərɪd] *adj* [story, description] cru; [gaudy] voyant

**lurk** [lɜːk] *vi* [hide] être tapi (**in** dans); [prowl] rôder

**luscious** ['lʌʃəs] *adj* [food] appétissant

**lush** [lʌʃ] *adj* [vegetation] luxuriant; [wealthy-surroundings] luxueux, -euse

**lust** [lʌst] **1.** *n* [for person] désir *m*; [for object] convoitise *f* (**for** de); [for power, knowledge] soif *f* (**for** de) **2.** *vi* **to lust after** [object, person] convoiter; [power, knowledge] avoir soif de

**lustre**, *Am* **luster** ['lʌstə(r)] *n* [gloss] lustre *m*

**Luxembourg** ['lʌksəmbɜːg] *n* le Luxembourg

**luxury** ['lʌkʃərɪ] **1.** *n* luxe *m* **2.** *adj* [goods, car, home] de luxe; **luxury hotel** palace *m* ▪ **luxurious** [lʌg'ʒʊərɪəs] *adj* luxueux, -euse

**lying** ['laɪɪŋ] **1.** *pres p see* **lie 2.** *n* mensonges *mpl* **3.** *adj* [person] menteur, -euse

**lynch** [lɪntʃ] *vt* lyncher

**lyric** ['lɪrɪk] *adj* lyrique ▪ **lyrics** *npl* [of song] paroles *fpl*

# M

**M, m**[1] [em] *n* [letter] M, m *m inv*

**m**[2] **a)** *(abbr of* **metre)** mètre *m* **b)** *(abbr of* **mile)** mile *m*

**MA** *(abbr of* **Master of Arts)** *n* UNIV **to have an MA in French** ≃ avoir une maîtrise de français

**mac** [mæk] *n* **a)** *Br Fam* [raincoat] imper *m* **b)** *(abbr of* **Macintosh)** ordinateur personnel développé par Apple

**macabre** [mə'kɑːbrə] *adj* macabre

**machine** [mə'ʃiːn] **1.** *n Lit & Fig* machine *f*; **machine translation** traduction automatique **2.** *vt* **a)** SEWING coudre à la machine **b)** TECH usiner

**machinery** [mə'ʃiːnərɪ] *n* [machines] machines *fpl*; [works] mécanisme *m*

**mackerel** ['mækrəl] *n* maquereau *m*

**mackintosh** ['mækɪntɒʃ] *n Br* imperméable *m*

**macro** ['mækrəʊ] *(pl* **-os)** *n* COMPUT macrocommande *f*

**mad** [mæd] *(compar* **madder**, *superl* **maddest)** *adj* fou *(f* folle) ; **to be mad at sb** être furieux, -euse contre qn ■ **madly** *adv* [insanely, desperately] comme un fou / une folle ■ **madman** *(pl* **-men)** *n* fou *m* ■ **madness** *n* folie *f*

**madam** ['mædəm] *n* yes, madam oui, madame

**made** [meɪd] *pt & pp of* **make** ■ **made-to-measure** *adj Br* [garment] (fait) sur mesure

**madrasah, madrassa, madrasa** [mə'dræsə] *n* madrasa *f*, école *f* coranique

**magazine** [mægə'ziːn] *n* **a)** [periodical, TV or radio broadcast] magazine *m* **b)** [of gun, slide projector] magasin *m*

**magic** ['mædʒɪk] **1.** *adj* magique **2.** *n* magie *f* ■ **magician** [mə'dʒɪʃən] *n* magicien, -enne *mf*

**magistrate** ['mædʒɪstreɪt] *n* magistrat *m*

**magnet** ['mægnɪt] *n* aimant *m* ■ **magnetic** [-'netɪk] *adj* magnétique

**magnificent** [mæg'nɪfɪsənt] *adj* magnifique

**magnify** ['mægnɪfaɪ] *(pt & pp* **-ied)** *vt* [image] grossir ; **magnifying glass** loupe *f*

**mahogany** [mə'hɒgənɪ] *n* acajou *m*

**maid** [meɪd] *n* [servant] bonne *f*

**maiden** ['meɪdən] *adj* [flight, voyage] inaugural ; **maiden name** nom *m* de jeune fille

**mail** [meɪl] **1.** *n* [system] poste *f*; [letters] courrier *m* ; [e-mails] méls *mpl*, courrier *m* électronique **2.** *adj* [bag, train] postal ; **mail order** vente *f* par correspondance **3.** *vt* poster ; [send by e-mail] envoyer (par courrier électronique) ; **mailing list** liste *f* d'adresses ■ **mailbox** *n Am* & COMPUT boîte *f* aux lettres ■ **mailing** ['meɪlɪŋ] *n* **a)** [posting] expédition *f*, envoi *m* par la poste **b)** COMM & COMPUT mailing *m*, publipostage *m*

**maim** [meɪm] *vt* mutiler

**main**[1] [meɪn] *adj* principal ; **main course** plat *m* de résistance ; **main road** grande route *f*

**main**[2] [meɪn] *n* water / gas main conduite *f* d'eau / de gaz ; **the mains** [electricity] le secteur ■ **mainland** *n* continent *m* ■ **mainly** *adv* principalement ; **they were mainly Spanish** la plupart étaient espagnols

**mainstay** ['meɪnsteɪ] *n* [of organization, policy] pilier *m*

**maintain** [meɪn'teɪn] *vt* [continue] maintenir ; [machine, road] entretenir ; **to maintain that...** affirmer que...

■ **maintenance** ['meɪntənəns] n [of vehicle, road] entretien m; [alimony] pension f alimentaire

**maize** [meɪz] n Br maïs m

**majesty** ['mædʒəstɪ] n majesté f; **Your Majesty** Votre Majesté ■ **majestic** [mə'dʒestɪk] adj majestueux, -euse

**major** ['meɪdʒə(r)] **1.** adj [main, great & MUS] majeur **2.** n a) [officer] commandant m b) Am UNIV [subject] dominante f **3.** vi Am UNIV **to major in** se spécialiser en

**Majorca** [mə'jɔːkə] n Majorque f

**majority** [mə'dʒɒrətɪ] (pl -ies) n majorité f (**of** de); **the majority of people** la plupart des gens

**make** [meɪk] **1.** (pt & pp made) vt faire; [tool, vehicle] fabriquer; **to make a decision** prendre une décision; **to make sb happy / sad** rendre qn heureux / triste; **to make sb do sth** faire faire qch à qn; Fam **to make it** [succeed] réussir; **sorry I can't make it to the meeting** désolé, je ne pourrai pas assister à la réunion; **what time do you make it?** quelle heure avez-vous?; **what do you make of it?** qu'en penses-tu?; **he made 10 pounds on it** ça lui a rapporté 10 livres; **to be made of wood** être en bois; **made in France** fabriqué en France
**2.** vi **to make do** [manage] se débrouiller (**with** avec); **to make do with sb/sth** [be satisfied with] se contenter de qn / qch; **to make believe that one is…** faire semblant d'être…
**3.** n [brand] marque f; **of French make** de fabrication française

■ **make-up** n [for face] maquillage m; [of team, group] constitution f

■ **make for** vt insep [go towards] aller vers

■ **make off** vi Fam [leave] filer

■ **make out 1.** vt sep [see, hear] distinguer; [understand] comprendre; [decipher] déchiffrer; [cheque, list] faire; Fam **to make out that…** [claim] prétendre que… **2.** vi Fam [manage] se débrouiller

■ **make over** vt sep [transfer] céder (**to** à); [change, convert] transformer (**into** en)

■ **make up 1.** vt sep [story] inventer; [put together - list, collection, bed] faire; [prepare] préparer; [form] former, composer; [loss] compenser; [quantity] compléter; [quarrel] régler; **to make oneself up** se maquiller **2.** vi [of friends] se réconcilier; **to make up for** [loss, damage, fault] compenser; [lost time, mistake] rattraper

**makeshift** ['meɪkʃɪft] adj [arrangement, building] de fortune

**malaria** [mə'leərɪə] n MED paludisme m

**male** [meɪl] **1.** adj [child, animal] mâle; [sex] masculin; **male nurse** infirmier m **2.** n [person] homme m; [animal] mâle m

**malfunction** [mæl'fʌŋkʃən] vi fonctionner mal

**malice** ['mælɪs] n méchanceté f ■ **malicious** [mə'lɪʃəs] adj malveillant

**malignant** [mə'lɪgnənt] adj **malignant tumour** or **growth** tumeur f maligne

**mall** [mɔːl] n Am **(shopping) mall** centre m commercial ■ **mallrat** ['mɔːlræt] n Am adolescent qui traîne dans les centres commerciaux

**malnutrition** [mælnjuː'trɪʃən] n malnutrition f

**malt** [mɔːlt] n malt m

**Malta** ['mɔːltə] n Malte f

**malware** ['mælweə(r)] n logiciels mpl malveillants

**mammal** ['mæməl] n mammifère m

**man** [mæn] **1.** (pl men) n [adult male] homme m; [player in sports team] joueur m; [humanity] l'homme m; [chess piece] pièce f; Fam **my old man** [father] mon père; [husband] mon homme **2.** (pt & pp -nn-) vt [be on duty at] être de service à; [machine] assurer le fonctionnement de; [plane, ship] être membre de l'équipage de

**manage** ['mænɪdʒ] **1.** vt [company, project] diriger; [shop, hotel] être le gérant de; [economy, money, time, situation] gérer; **to manage to do sth** [succeed] réussir *ou* arriver à faire qch ; [by being smart] se débrouiller pour faire qch **2.** *vi* [succeed] y arriver ; [make do] se débrouiller (**with** avec) ; **to manage without sb/sth** se passer de qn /qch ; **managing director** directeur, -trice *mf* général, -e ■ **management** *n* [running, managers] direction *f* ; [of property, economy] gestion *f* ; [executive staff] cadres *mpl*

**manager** ['mænɪdʒə(r)] *n* [of company] directeur, -trice *mf* ; [of shop, café] gérant, -e *mf* ; (**business**) **manager** [of singer, boxer] manager *m* ■ **manageress** *n* directrice *f* ; [of shop, café] gérante *f*

**mandate** ['mændeɪt] *n* mandat *m*

**mane** [meɪn] *n* crinière *f*

**maneuver** [mə'nu:vər] *Am n & vti* = **manoeuvre**

**manga** ['mæŋɡə] *n* manga *m*

**mangle** ['mæŋɡəl] *vt* [body] mutiler

**mango** ['mæŋɡəʊ] *(pl* **-oes** *or* **-os)** *n* mangue *f*

**manhunt** ['mænhʌnt] *n* chasse *f* à l'homme

**mania** ['meɪnɪə] *n* [liking] passion *f* ; [psychological] manie *f*

**maniac** ['meɪnɪæk] *n* fou *m*, folle *f*

**manicure** ['mænɪkjʊə(r)] *n* manucure *f*

**manifesto** [mænɪ'festəʊ] *(pl* **-os** *or* **-oes)** *n* POL manifeste *m*

**manipulate** [mə'nɪpjʊleɪt] *vt* manipuler

**mankind** [mæn'kaɪnd] *n* l'humanité *f*

**man-made** ['mænmeɪd] *adj* [lake] artificiel, -elle ; [fibre] synthétique

**manner** ['mænə(r)] *n* [way] manière *f* ; [behaviour] comportement *m* ; **manners** [social habits] manières *fpl* ; **in this manner** [like this] de cette manière ; **to have good/bad manners** être bien / mal élevé

**mannerism** ['mænərɪzəm] *n Pej* tic *m*

**manoeuvre,** *Am* **maneuver** [mə'nu:və(r)] **1.** *n* manœuvre *f* **2.** *vti* manœuvrer

**manpower** ['mænpaʊə(r)] *n* [labour] main-d'œuvre *f*

**mansion** ['mænʃən] *n* [in town] hôtel *m* particulier ; [in country] manoir *m*

**manslaughter** ['mænslɔ:tə(r)] *n* [in law] homicide *m* involontaire

**mantelpiece** ['mæntəlpi:s] *n* dessus *m* de cheminée ; **on the mantelpiece** sur la cheminée

**manual** ['mænjʊəl] **1.** *adj* [work, worker] manuel, -elle **2.** *n* [book] manuel *m*

**manufacture** [mænjʊ'fæktʃə(r)] **1.** *n* fabrication *f* ; [of cars] construction *f* **2.** *vt* fabriquer ; [cars] construire ■ **manufacturer** *n* fabricant, -e *mf* ; [of cars] constructeur *m*

**manure** [mə'njʊə(r)] *n* fumier *m*

**manuscript** ['mænjʊskrɪpt] *n* manuscrit *m*

**many** ['menɪ] **1.** *adj* beaucoup de ; (**a good** *or* **great**) **many of** un (très) grand nombre de ; **how many?** combien (de) ? ; **too many** trop de **2.** *pron* beaucoup ; **too many** trop ; **many of them** beaucoup d'entre eux ; **as many as fifty** [up to] jusqu'à cinquante

**map** [mæp] **1.** *n* carte *f* ; [plan of town, underground] plan *m* **2.** *(pt & pp* **-pp-)** *vt* **to map out** [plan, programme] élaborer

**maple** ['meɪpəl] *n* [tree, wood] érable *m* ; **maple syrup** sirop *m* d'érable

**marathon** ['mærəθən] *n* marathon *m*

**marble** ['mɑ:bəl] *n* [substance] marbre *m* ; [toy ball] bille *f*

**march** [mɑ:tʃ] **1.** *n* marche *f* **2.** *vi* [of soldiers, demonstrators] défiler ; [walk in step] marcher au pas

**March** [mɑ:tʃ] *n* mars *m*

**mare** [meə(r)] *n* jument *f*

**margarine** [mɑ:dʒə'ri:n] *n* margarine *f*

**margin** ['mɑ:dʒɪn] *n* [on page] marge *f* ; **to win by a narrow margin** gagner de justesse ■ **marginally** *adv* très légèrement

**marijuana** [mærɪ'wɑ:nə] *n* marijuana *f*

**marinate** ['mærɪneɪt] *vti* CULIN (faire) mariner

**marine** [mə'ri:n] **1.** adj [life, flora] marin **2.** n [soldier] fusilier m marin ; Am marine m

**marital** ['mærɪtəl] adj conjugal ; **marital status** situation f de famille

**maritime** ['mærɪtaɪm] adj maritime

**mark** [mɑ:k] **1.** n [symbol] marque f ; [stain, trace] tache f, marque f ; [token, sign] signe m ; [in test, exam] note f **2.** vt marquer ; [exam] noter ; **to mark sth off** [separate] délimiter qch ; [on list] cocher qch ; **to mark sb out** distinguer qn

**marked** [mɑ:kt] adj [noticeable] marqué

**marker** ['mɑ:kə(r)] n a) [sign] repère m b) [pen] marqueur m

**market** ['mɑ:kɪt] **1.** n marché m ; **to put sth on the market** mettre qch en vente ; **on the black market** au marché noir ; **market price** prix m courant **2.** vt commercialiser ◼ **marketing** n marketing m, mercatique f ◼ **marketplace** n [in village, town] place f du marché

**markings** ['mɑ:kɪŋz] npl [on animal] taches fpl ; [on road] signalisation f horizontale

**marmalade** ['mɑ:məleɪd] n confiture f d'oranges

**marooned** [mə'ru:nd] adj abandonné

**marriage** ['mærɪdʒ] n mariage m ; **marriage certificate** extrait m d'acte de mariage

**marrow** ['mærəʊ] n Br [vegetable] courge f

**marry** ['mærɪ] **1.** (pt & pp -ied) vt épouser, se marier avec ; [of priest] marier **2.** vi se marier ◼ **married** adj marié ; **married life** vie f conjugale ; **married name** nom m de femme mariée ; **to get married** se marier

**marsh** [mɑ:ʃ] n marais m, marécage m

**marshal** ['mɑ:ʃəl] n [in army] maréchal m ; [district police officer] commissaire m ; [police chief] commissaire m de police ; [fire chief] capitaine m des pompiers

**martial** ['mɑ:ʃəl] adj martial

**martyr** ['mɑ:tə(r)] n martyr, -e mf

**marvel** ['mɑ:vəl] **1.** n [wonder] merveille f **2.** (Br -ll-, Am -l-) vi s'émerveiller (**at** de)

**marvellous**, Am **marvelous** ['mɑ:vələs] adj merveilleux, -euse

**Marxist** ['mɑ:ksɪst] adj & n marxiste (mf)

**marzipan** ['mɑ:zɪpæn] n pâte f d'amandes

**mascara** [mæ'skɑ:rə] n mascara m

**masculine** ['mæskjʊlɪn] adj masculin

**mash** [mæʃ] **1.** n Br [potatoes] purée f (de pommes de terre) **2.** vt **to mash (up)** [vegetables] écraser (en purée) ; **mashed potatoes** purée f de pommes de terre

**mask** [mɑ:sk] **1.** n masque m **2.** vt [cover, hide] masquer (**from** à)

**masochist** ['mæsəkɪst] n masochiste mf

**mason** ['meɪsən] n [stonemason, Freemason] maçon m ◼ **masonry** n maçonnerie f

**mass¹** [mæs] **1.** n [shapeless substance & PHYS] masse f ; **a mass of** [many] une multitude de ; POL **the masses** le peuple **2.** adj [demonstration, culture] de masse ; [protests] en masse ; [unemployment, destruction] massif, -ive ; **mass media** mass media mpl ; **mass production** production f en série **3.** vi [of troops, people] se masser ◼ **mass-produce** vt fabriquer en série

**mass²** [mæs] n [church service] messe f

**massacre** ['mæsəkə(r)] **1.** n massacre m **2.** vt massacrer

**massage** ['mæsɑ:ʒ] **1.** n massage m **2.** vt masser

**massive** ['mæsɪv] adj [increase, dose, vote] massif, -ive ; [amount, building] énorme

**mast** [mɑ:st] n [of ship] mât m ; [for TV, radio] pylône m

**master** ['mɑ:stə(r)] **1.** n maître m ; Br [teacher] professeur m ; **Master of Arts/Science** [qualification] ≃ maîtrise f ès lettres /sciences ; [person] ≃ maître mf ès lettres /sciences ; **master of ceremonies** [presenter] animateur, -trice *mf*; **master copy** original *m*; **master key** passe-partout *m inv*; **master plan** plan *m* d'action **2.** *vt* maîtriser; [subject, situation] dominer

**mastermind** ['mɑːstəmaɪnd] **1.** *n* [person] cerveau *m* **2.** *vt* organiser

**masterpiece** ['mɑːstəpiːs] *n* chef-d'œuvre *m*

**mastery** ['mɑːstərɪ] *n* maîtrise *f* (**of** de)

**masturbate** ['mæstəbeɪt] *vi* se masturber

**mat** [mæt] *n* tapis *m*; [of straw] natte *f*; [at door] paillasson *m*; **(table) mat** [for plates] set *m* de table; [for dishes] dessous-de-plat *m inv*

**match¹** [mætʃ] *n* [for lighting fire, cigarette] allumette *f* ■ **matchbox** *n* boîte *f* d'allumettes ■ **matchstick** *n* allumette *f*

**match²** [mætʃ] *n* [in sport] match *m*

**match³** [mætʃ] **1.** *n* [equal] égal, -e *mf*; [marriage] mariage *m*; **to be a good match** [of colours, people] aller bien ensemble; **to meet one's match** trouver son maître **2.** *vt* [of clothes, colour] être assorti à; [coordinate] assortir; [equal] égaler; **to match up** [colours, clothes, plates] assortir **3.** *vi* [of colours, clothes] être assortis, -es ■ **matching** *adj* assorti

**mate¹** [meɪt] **1.** *n* [of animal - male] mâle *m*; [female] femelle *f*; *Br* [friend] copain *m*, copine *f* **2.** *vi* [of animals] s'accoupler (**with** avec)

**mate²** [meɪt] **1.** *n* [in chess] mat *m* **2.** *vt* mettre mat

**material** [mə'tɪərɪəl] **1.** *adj* [needs, world] matériel, -elle; [important] essentiel, -elle **2.** *n* [substance] matière *f*; [cloth] tissu *m*; [for book] matériaux *mpl*; **material(s)** [equipment] matériel *m* ■ **materialistic** *adj* matérialiste

**materialize** [mə'tɪərɪəlaɪz] *vi* se matérialiser; [of hope, threat] se réaliser

**maternal** [mə't3ːnəl] *adj* maternel, -elle

**maternity** [mə't3ːnətɪ] *n* **maternity dress** robe *f* de grossesse; **maternity hospital, maternity unit** maternité *f*; **maternity leave** congé *m* de maternité

**mathematical** [mæθə'mætɪkəl] *adj* mathématique

**mathematics** [mæθə'mætɪks] *n* [subject] mathématiques *fpl* ■ **maths**, *Am* **math** *n Fam* maths *fpl*

**matinée** ['mætɪneɪ] *n* [of play, film] matinée *f*

**matrimony** ['mætrɪmənɪ] *n* mariage *m*

**matt**, *Am* **matte** [mæt] *adj* mat

**matter** ['mætə(r)] **1.** *n* [substance] matière *f*; [issue, affair] question *f*; **as a matter of fact** en fait; **no matter what she does** quoi qu'elle fasse; **no matter who you are** qui que vous soyez; **what's the matter?** qu'est-ce qu'il y a ?; **there's something the matter with my leg** j'ai quelque chose à la jambe **2.** *vi* [be important] importer (**to** à); **it doesn't matter if/when/who...** peu importe si/quand/qui...; **it doesn't matter** ça ne fait rien

**matter-of-fact** [mætərəv'fækt] *adj* [person, manner] terre à terre *inv*

**mattress** ['mætrəs] *n* matelas *m*

**mature** [mə'tʃʊə(r)] **1.** *adj* [person] mûr; [cheese] fort **2.** *vi* [person] mûrir

**maul** [mɔːl] *vt* [of animal] mutiler

**max** [mæks] *adv Fam* maximum ■ **max out** *vt sep Am* **I maxed out my credit card** j'ai atteint la limite sur ma carte de crédit

**maximize** ['mæksɪmaɪz] *vt* maximaliser

**maximum** ['mæksɪməm] **1.** *(pl* -**ima** [-ɪmə] *or* -**imums)** *n* maximum *m* **2.** *adj* maximal

**may** [meɪ] *(pt* **might** [maɪt]*)*

**May** et **might** peuvent s'utiliser indifféremment ou presque dans les expressions de la catégorie **(a)**.

*v aux* **a)** [expressing possibility] **he may come** il se peut qu'il vienne; **I may** *or* **might be wrong** je me trompe peut-être; **he may** *or* **might have lost it** il se peut qu'il l'ait perdu; **we may** *or* **might as well go** autant y aller; **she's afraid I may** *or* **might get lost** elle a peur que je ne me perde

b) *Formal* [for asking permission] **may I stay?** puis-je rester ? ; **you may go** tu peux partir c) *Formal* [expressing wish] **may you be happy** sois heureux ; **may the best man win!** que le meilleur gagne !

**May** [meɪ] *n* mai *m* ; **May Day** le Premier mai

**maybe** ['meɪbi:] *adv* peut-être

**mayhem** ['meɪhem] *n* [chaos] pagaille *f*

**mayonnaise** [meɪə'neɪz] *n* mayonnaise *f*

**mayor** [meə(r)] *n* maire *m*

**maze** [meɪz] *n* labyrinthe *m*

**MBA** *(abbr of* **Master of Business Administration)** *n* MBA *m*, maîtrise *f* de gestion

**me** [mi:] *pron* me, m' ; [after prep, 'than', 'it is'] moi ; **(to) me** [indirect] me, m' ; **he helps me** il m'aide ; **he gave it to me** il me l'a donné

**meadow** ['medəʊ] *n* pré *m*, prairie *f*

**meagre**, *Am* **meager** ['mi:gə(r)] *adj* maigre

**meal** [mi:l] *n* [food] repas *m*

**mean¹** [mi:n] *(pt & pp* meant) *vt* [of word, event] signifier ; [of person] vouloir dire ; [result in] entraîner ; [represent] représenter ; **to mean to do sth** avoir l'intention de faire qch ; **it means a lot to me** c'est très important pour moi ; **I didn't mean to!** je ne l'ai pas fait exprès !

**mean²** [mi:n] *(compar* -er, *superl* -est) *adj* [miserly] avare ; [nasty] méchant

**mean³** [mi:n] **1.** *adj* [average] moyen, -enne **2.** *n* MATH [average, mid-point] moyenne *f*

**meaning** ['mi:nɪŋ] *n* sens *m*, signification *f* ■ **meaningful** *adj* significatif, -ive ■ **meaningless** *adj* vide de sens

**means** [mi:nz] **1.** *n* [method] moyen *m* **(to do** *or* **of doing** de faire) ; **by means of...** au moyen de... ; **by no means** nullement **2.** *npl* [wealth] moyens *mpl*

**meant** [ment] *pt & pp of* **mean**

**meantime** ['mi:ntaɪm] *adv & n* **(in the) meantime** [at the same time] pendant ce temps ; [between two events] entre-temps

**meanwhile** ['mi:nwaɪl] *adv* [at the same time] pendant ce temps ; [between two events] entre-temps

**measles** ['mi:zəlz] *n* MED rougeole *f*

**measure** ['meʒə(r)] **1.** *n* mesure *f* ; [ruler] règle *f* **2.** *vt* mesurer ; **to measure sth out** [ingredient] mesurer qch **3.** *vi* **to measure up to** [task] être à la hauteur de

**measurement** ['meʒəmənt] *n* mesure *f* ; **hip / waist measurement(s)** tour *m* de hanches / de taille

**meat** [mi:t] *n* viande *f* ; [of crab, lobster] chair *f* ; *Fig* substance *f*

**Mecca** ['mekə] *n* La Mecque

**mechanic** [mɪ'kænɪk] *n* mécanicien, -enne *mf* ■ **mechanical** *adj* mécanique ■ **mechanics** *n* [science] mécanique *f* ; **the mechanics** [working parts] le mécanisme

**mechanism** ['mekənɪzəm] *n* mécanisme *m*

**medal** ['medəl] *n* médaille *f*

**medallion** [mə'dæljən] *n* médaillon *m*

**meddle** ['medəl] *vi* [interfere] se mêler **(in** de) ; [tamper] toucher **(with** à)

**media** ['mi:dɪə] *npl* a) **the media** les médias *mpl* ; **media player** lecteur *m* multimédia b) *pl of* **medium**

**mediaeval**, *Am* **medieval** [medɪ'i:vəl] *adj* médiéval

**mediate** ['mi:dɪeɪt] *vi* servir d'intermédiaire **(between** entre) ■ **mediator** *n* médiateur, -trice *mf*

**medical** ['medɪkəl] **1.** *adj* médical ; [school, studies] de médecine ; [student] en médecine ; **medical certificate** certificat *m* médical ; **medical insurance** assurance *f* maladie **2.** *n* [in school, army] visite *f* médicale ; [private] examen *m* médical

**medication** [medɪ'keɪʃən] *n* médicaments *mpl* ; **to be on medication** être en traitement

**medicine** ['medəsən] *n* [substance] médicament *m* ; [science] médecine *f* ; **medicine cabinet, medicine chest** (armoire *f* à) pharmacie *f*

**medieval** [medɪ'iːvəl] *adj* médiéval

**mediocre** [miːdɪ'əʊkə(r)] *adj* médiocre

**meditate** ['medɪteɪt] *vi* méditer (**on** sur) ■ **meditation** *n* méditation *f*

**Mediterranean** [medɪtə'reɪnɪən] **1.** *adj* méditerranéen, -enne **2.** *n* **the Mediterranean** la Méditerranée

**medium** ['miːdɪəm] **1.** *adj* [average, middle] moyen, -enne **2.** *n* **a)** (*pl* **media** ['miːdɪə]) [for conveying data or publicity] support *m* **b)** (*pl* **mediums**) [person] médium *m* ■ **medium-sized** *adj* de taille moyenne

**medley** ['medlɪ] (*pl* -**eys**) *n* mélange *m* ; [of songs, tunes] pot-pourri *m*

**meet** [miːt] **1.** *vt* (*pt & pp* **met**) [person, team] rencontrer ; [by arrangement] retrouver ; [pass in street, road] croiser ; [fetch] aller chercher ; [wait for] attendre ; [debt, enemy, danger] faire face à ; [need] combler ; **have you met my husband?** connaissez-vous mon mari ? **2.** *vi* [of people, teams] se rencontrer ; [by arrangement] se retrouver ; [of club, society] se réunir ; [of rivers] se rejoindre **3.** *n Am* [meeting] meeting *m* ■ **meet up** *vi* [by arrangement] se retrouver ; **to meet up with sb** retrouver qn ■ **meet with** *vt insep* [problem, refusal] se heurter à ; [accident] avoir ; *Am* **to meet with sb** rencontrer qn ; [as arranged] retrouver qn

**meeting** ['miːtɪŋ] *n* [for business] réunion *f* ; [large] assemblée *f* ; [by accident] rencontre *f* ; [by arrangement] rendez-vous *m inv* ; **to be in a meeting** être en réunion ; **meeting place** lieu *m* de rendez-vous

**megabucks** ['megəbʌks] *n Fam* un fric fou, une fortune ; **her job pays megabucks** elle gagne une fortune dans son travail

**megabyte** ['megəbaɪt] *n* COMPUT mégaoctet *m*

**megaphone** ['megəfəʊn] *n* porte-voix *m inv*

**megastore** ['megəstɔː(r)] *n* (très) grand magasin *m*

**mellow** ['meləʊ] (*compar* -**er**, *superl* -**est**) *adj* [wine] moelleux, -euse ; [flavour] suave ; [colour, voice] chaud

**melodic** [mɪ'lɒdɪk] *adj* mélodique

**melodrama** ['melədrɑːmə] *n* mélodrame *m* ■ **melodramatic** *adj* mélodramatique

**melody** ['melədɪ] (*pl* -**ies**) *n* mélodie *f*

**melon** ['melən] *n* melon *m*

**melt** [melt] **1.** *vt* faire fondre ; **to melt down** [metal object] fondre **2.** *vi* fondre

**member** ['membə(r)] *n* membre *m* ; *Br* **Member of Parliament**, *Am* **Member of Congress** ≃ député *m* ■ **membership** *n* [state] adhésion *f* (**of** à) ; [members] membres *mpl* ; **membership card** carte *f* de membre ; **membership fee** cotisation *f*

**memento** [mə'mentəʊ] (*pl* -**os** *or* -**oes**) *n* souvenir *m*

**memo** ['meməʊ] (*pl* -**os**) *n* note *f* de service

**memoirs** ['memwɑːz] *npl* [autobiography] mémoires *mpl*

**memorable** ['memərəbəl] *adj* mémorable

**memorial** [mə'mɔːrɪəl] **1.** *adj* commémoratif, -ive ; **memorial service** commémoration *f* **2.** *n* mémorial *m*

**memorize** ['meməraɪz] *vt* mémoriser

**memory** ['memərɪ] (*pl* -**ies**) *n* [faculty & COMPUT] mémoire *f* ; [recollection] souvenir *m* ; **to the** *or* **in memory of...** à la mémoire de... ; COMPUT **memory module** module *m* de mémoire ; **memory stick** carte *f* mémoire

**men** [men] *npl see* **man** ; **the men's room** les toilettes *fpl* pour hommes

**menace** ['menɪs] **1.** *n* [danger] danger *m* ; [threat] menace *f* **2.** *vt* menacer

**mend** [mend] *vt* [repair] réparer ; [clothes] raccommoder

**menial** ['miːnɪəl] *adj* [work] subalterne

**meningitis** [menɪn'dʒaɪtɪs] *n* MED méningite *f*

**menopause** ['menəpɔ:z] *n* ménopause *f*

**menstruation** [menstru'eɪʃən] *n* menstruation *f*

**menswear** ['menzweə(r)] *n* vêtements *mpl* pour hommes

**mental** ['mentəl] *adj* mental; **mental block** blocage *m*

**mentality** [men'tælətɪ] *(pl -ies)* *n* mentalité *f* ■ **mentally** *adv* mentalement; **he's mentally handicapped** c'est un handicapé mental; **she's mentally ill** c'est une malade mentale

**mention** ['menʃən] **1.** *n* mention *f* **2.** *vt* mentionner; **not to mention** sans parler de...; **don't mention it!** il n'y a pas de quoi!

**menu** ['menju:] *n* [in restaurant - for set meal] menu *m*; [list] carte *f*; COMPUT menu

**MEP** [emi:'pi:] *(abbr of Member of the European Parliament)* *n* député *m* du Parlement européen

**merchandise** ['mɜ:tʃəndaɪz] *n* marchandises *fpl*

**merchant** ['mɜ:tʃənt] *n* [trader] négociant, -e *mf*; [retailer] commerçant, -e *mf*

**merciless** ['mɜ:sɪləs] *adj* impitoyable

**mercury** ['mɜ:kjʊrɪ] *n* [metal] mercure *m*

**mercy** ['mɜ:sɪ] *(pl -ies)* *n* pitié *f*; [of God] miséricorde *f*; **at the mercy of** à la merci de

**mere** [mɪə(r)] *adj* simple; **she's a mere child** ce n'est qu'une enfant ■ **merely** *adv* simplement

**merge** [mɜ:dʒ] **1.** *vt* [companies & COMPUT] fusionner **2.** *vi* [blend] se mêler (**with** à); [of roads] se rejoindre; [of companies, banks] fusionner ■ **merger** *n* COMM fusion *f*

**merit** ['merɪt] **1.** *n* mérite *m* **2.** *vt* mériter

**merry** ['merɪ] *(compar -ier, superl -iest)* *adj* [happy, drunk] gai ■ **merry-go-round** *n* manège *m*

**mesh** [meʃ] *n* [of net, sieve] mailles *fpl*

**mesmerize** ['mezməraɪz] *vt* hypnotiser

**mess** [mes] **1.** *n* [confusion] désordre *m*; [muddle] gâchis *m*; [dirt] saletés *fpl*; **in a mess** en désordre; [in trouble] dans le pétrin; **to make a mess of sth** [do badly, get dirty] saloper qch **2.** *vt BrFam* **to mess sb about** [bother, treat badly] embêter qn; **to mess sth up** [plans] ficher qch en l'air; [hair, room, papers] mettre qch en désordre **3.** *vi* **to mess about** *or* **around** [waste time] traîner; [play the fool] faire l'imbécile; **to mess about** *or* **around with sth** [fiddle with] tripoter avec qch

**message** ['mesɪdʒ] *n* message *m* ■ **messaging** ['mesɪdʒɪŋ] *n* COMPUT messagerie *f*

**messenger** ['mesɪndʒə(r)] *n* messager, -ère *mf*; [in office, hotel] coursier, -ère *mf*; **messenger bag** sacoche *f*

**messy** ['mesɪ] *(compar -ier, superl -iest)* *adj* [untidy] en désordre; [dirty] sale; [job] salissant

**met** [met] *pt & pp of* **meet**

**metadata** ['metədeɪtə] *npl* métadonnées *fpl*

**metal** ['metəl] *n* métal *m*; **metal ladder** échelle *f* métallique ■ **metallic** [mɪ'tælɪk] *adj* [sound] métallique; [paint] métallisé ■ **metalwork** *n* [study, craft] travail *m* des métaux; [objects] ferronnerie *f*

**metaphor** ['metəfə(r)] *n* métaphore *f* ■ **metaphorical** [-'fɒrɪkəl] *adj* métaphorique

**meteor** ['mi:tɪə(r)] *n* météore *m*

**meteorological** [mi:tɪərə'lɒdʒɪkəl] *adj* météorologique

**meter¹** ['mi:tə(r)] *n* [device] compteur *m*; **(parking) meter** parcmètre *m*

**meter²** ['mi:tə(r)] **1.** *n Am* [measurement] mètre *m* **2.** *vt* [gas, electricity] établir la consommation de

**method** ['meθəd] *n* méthode *f* ■ **methodical** [mɪ'θɒdɪkəl] *adj* méthodique

**meticulous** [mɪ'tɪkjʊləs] *adj* méticuleux, -euse

**metre**, Am **meter** ['miːtə(r)] n mètre m ■ **metric** ['metrɪk] adj métrique

**metropolitan** [metrə'pɒlɪtən] adj métropolitain

**Mexico** ['meksɪkəʊ] n le Mexique ■ **Mexican 1.** adj mexicain **2.** n Mexicain, -e mf

**miaow** [miː'aʊ] **1.** excl miaou ! **2.** vi miauler

**mice** [maɪs] pl of **mouse**

**mickey** ['mɪkɪ] n Br Fam **to take the mickey out of sb** charrier qn

**microblog** ['maɪkrəʊˌblɒg] n microblog m ■ **microblogger** ['maɪkrəʊˌblɒgə(r)] n microblogeur, -euse m,f ■ **microblogging** ['maɪkrəʊˌblɒgɪŋ] n microblogging m

**microchip** ['maɪkrəʊtʃɪp] n COMPUT puce f

**microfilm** ['maɪkrəʊfɪlm] n microfilm m

**microphone** ['maɪkrəfəʊn] n micro m

**micropublishing** ['maɪkrəʊˌpʌblɪʃɪŋ] n microédition f

**microscope** ['maɪkrəskəʊp] n microscope m

**microwave** ['maɪkrəʊweɪv] n **microwave (oven)** (four m à) microondes m inv

**mid** [mɪd] adj **(in) mid June** (à) la mijuin ; **in mid air** en plein ciel ; **to be in one's mid-twenties** avoir environ vingt-cinq ans

**midday** [mɪd'deɪ] **1.** n **at midday** à midi **2.** adj [sun, meal] de midi

**middle** ['mɪdəl] **1.** n milieu m ; Fam [waist] taille f ; **(right) in the middle of sth** au (beau) milieu de qch **2.** adj [central] du milieu ; **the Middle Ages** le Moyen Âge ; **the Middle East** le Moyen-Orient ; **the middle class(es)** les classes moyennes ; **middle name** deuxième prénom m ; **middle school** Br ≃ premier cycle m du secondaire ; Am collège m d'enseignement secondaire ■ **middle-aged** adj d'âge mûr ■ **middle-class** adj bourgeois ■ **middle-of-the-road** adj [politics, views] modéré ; [music] grand public inv

**midge** [mɪdʒ] n moucheron m

**midget** ['mɪdʒɪt] n [small person] nain, -e mf

**midnight** ['mɪdnaɪt] n minuit m

**midst** [mɪdst] n **in the midst of** [middle] au milieu de

**midway** [mɪd'weɪ] adj & adv à mi-chemin

**midweek** [mɪd'wiːk] adv en milieu de semaine

**midwife** ['mɪdwaɪf] (pl **-wives**) n sage-femme f

**might**[1] [maɪt] (La forme **mightn't** s'écrit **might not** dans un style plus soutenu) v aux see **may**

**might**[2] [maɪt] n [strength] force f ■ **mighty** (compar **-ier**, superl **-iest**) **1.** adj puissant ; Fam [very great] sacré **2.** adv Am Fam [very] rudement

**migraine** ['miːgreɪn, 'maɪgreɪn] n migraine f

**migrate** [maɪ'greɪt] vi [of people] émigrer ; [of birds] migrer ■ **migrant** ['maɪgrənt] adj & n **migrant (worker)** (travailleur, -euse mf) immigré, -e

**mike** [maɪk] (abbr of **microphone**) n Fam micro m

**mild** [maɪld] (compar **-er**, superl **-est**) adj [weather, cheese, soap, person] doux (f douce) ; [punishment] léger, -ère ; [curry] peu épicé

**mile** [maɪl] n mile m ; **he lives miles away** il habite très loin d'ici ■ **mileage** n [distance] ≃ kilométrage m ; [rate of fuel consumption] consommation f ■ **mileometer** n Br ≃ compteur m kilométrique ■ **milestone** n [in history, career] étape f importante

**militant** ['mɪlɪtənt] adj & n militant, -e (mf)

**military** ['mɪlɪtərɪ] **1.** adj militaire **2.** n **the military** les militaires mpl

**milk** [mɪlk] **1.** n lait m ; **milk chocolate** chocolat m au lait ; **milk shake** milk-shake m **2.** vt [cow] traire ; Fig [exploit] exploiter ■ **milky** (compar **-ier**, superl **-iest**) adj [coffee, tea] au lait

**mill** [mɪl] **1.** n [for flour] moulin m ; [textile factory] filature f **2.** vi **to mill around** [of crowd] grouiller

**millennium** [mɪ'lenɪəm] (pl **-nia** [-nɪə]) n millénaire m

**milligram(me)** ['mɪlɪgræm] n milligramme m

**millimetre, Am millimeter** ['mɪlɪmiːtə(r)] n millimètre m

**million** ['mɪljən] n million m ; **a million men** un million d'hommes ; **two million** deux millions ■ **millionaire** n millionnaire mf

**milometer** [maɪ'lɒmɪtə(r)] n Br ≃ compteur m kilométrique

**mime** [maɪm] **1.** n [art] mime m **2.** vti mimer ; [of singer] chanter en play-back

**mimic** ['mɪmɪk] **1.** n imitateur, -trice mf **2.** (pt & pp **-ck-**) vt imiter

**mince** [mɪns] **1.** n [meat] viande f hachée ; **mince pie** [containing fruit] tartelette fourrée aux fruits secs et aux épices **2.** vt hacher ■ **mincemeat** n [dried fruit] mélange de fruits secs et d'épices utilisé en pâtisserie ■ **mincer** n [machine] hachoir m

**mind¹** [maɪnd] n esprit m ; [sanity] raison f ; Br **to my mind** à mon avis ; **to change one's mind** changer d'avis ; **to speak one's mind** dire ce que l'on pense ; Br **to be in two minds** [undecided] hésiter ; **to bear** or **keep sth in mind** garder qch à l'esprit ; **to have sb/sth in mind** avoir qn/qch en vue ; **to make up one's mind** se décider ; Fam **to be out of one's mind** avoir perdu la tête ; **it's on my mind** cela me préoccupe ; Br **to have a good mind to do sth** avoir bien envie de faire qch

**mind²** [maɪnd] **1.** vt Br [pay attention to] faire attention à ; [look after] garder ; Br **mind you don't fall** fais attention à ne pas tomber ; **I don't mind the cold/noise** le froid/bruit ne me gêne pas ; **if you don't mind my asking...** si je peux me permettre... ; **never mind the car** peu importe la voiture ; Br **mind you...** remarquez... ; **mind your own business!** occupe-toi de tes affaires !

**2.** vi **I don't mind** ça m'est égal ; **do you mind if I smoke?** ça vous gêne si je fume ? ; **never mind!** ça ne fait rien !, tant pis ! ; Br **mind (out)!** [watch out] attention !

**mind-boggling** ['maɪndbɒglɪŋ] adj stupéfiant

**minder** ['maɪndə(r)] n Fam [bodyguard] gorille m

**mindless** ['maɪndləs] adj [job, destruction] stupide

**mind-numbing** [-nʌmɪŋ] adj abrutissant

**mindset** ['maɪndset] n mentalité f ; **this is a dangerous mindset to be in** c'est une attitude dangereuse

**mine¹** [maɪn] poss pron le mien, la mienne, pl les mien(ne)s ; **this hat is mine** ce chapeau est à moi ou est le mien ; **a friend of mine** un ami à moi, un de mes amis

**mine²** [maɪn] **1.** n a) [for coal, gold] & Fig mine f b) [explosive] mine f **2.** vt [coal, gold] extraire ■ **mining** n exploitation f minière

**mineral** ['mɪnərəl] adj & n minéral (m) ; **mineral water** eau f minérale

**mingle** ['mɪŋgəl] vi [of things] se mêler (**with** à) ; [of people] parler un peu à tout le monde

**miniature** ['mɪnɪtʃə(r)] **1.** adj [train, model] miniature inv **2.** n miniature f ; **in miniature** en miniature

**mini-break** n mini-séjour m

**minicab** ['mɪnɪkæb] n Br radio-taxi m

**minigolf** ['mɪnɪgɒlf] n minigolf m

**minimal** ['mɪnɪməl] adj minimal

**minimize** ['mɪnɪmaɪz] vt minimiser

**minimum** ['mɪnɪməm] **1.** (pl **-ima** or **-imums**) n minimum m **2.** adj minimal ; **minimum charge** tarif m minimum ; **minimum wage** salaire m minimum

**mini-roundabout** [mɪnɪ'raʊndəbaʊt] n Br petit rond-point m

**miniskirt** ['mɪnɪskɜːt] n minijupe f

**minister** ['mɪnɪstə(r)] n Br [politician] ministre m; [of religion] pasteur m ■ **ministry** *(pl* -**ies**) n Br POL ministère m

**minor** ['maɪnə(r)] **1.** adj [unimportant & MUS] mineur; MED [operation] bénin, -igne; [road] secondaire **2.** n [in age] mineur, -e mf

**minority** [maɪ'nɒrətɪ] **1.** (pl -**ies**) n minorité f; **to be in the** or **a minority** être minoritaire **2.** adj minoritaire

**mint**[1] [mɪnt] **1.** n **the (Royal) Mint** ≃ l'hôtel m de la Monnaie **2.** vt [coins] frapper

**mint**[2] [mɪnt] n [herb] menthe f; [sweet] bonbon m à la menthe

**minus** ['maɪnəs] **1.** adj & n minus (sign) (signe m) moins m **2.** prep [with numbers] moins; Fam [without] sans; **it's minus 10 (degrees)** il fait moins 10

**minute**[1] ['mɪnɪt] n [of time] minute f; **this (very) minute** [now] tout de suite; **any minute (now)** d'une minute à l'autre ■ **minutes** npl [of meeting] procès-verbal m

**minute**[2] [maɪ'njuːt] adj [tiny] minuscule

**miracle** ['mɪrəkəl] n miracle m ■ **miraculous** [mɪ'rækjʊləs] adj miraculeux, -euse

**mirror** ['mɪrə(r)] n miroir m, glace f; **(rearview) mirror** [of vehicle] rétroviseur m; COMPUT **mirror site** site m miroir

**misbehave** [mɪsbɪ'heɪv] vi se conduire mal

**miscalculate** [mɪs'kælkjʊleɪt] vi faire une erreur de calcul; Fig faire un mauvais calcul

**miscarriage** [mɪs'kærɪdʒ] n MED **to have a miscarriage** faire une fausse couche; **miscarriage of justice** erreur f judiciaire

**miscellaneous** [mɪsə'leɪnɪəs] adj divers

**mischief** ['mɪstʃɪf] n espièglerie f; **to get into mischief** faire des bêtises ■ **mischievous** adj [naughty] espiègle; [malicious] méchant

**misconduct** [mɪs'kɒndʌkt] n [bad behaviour] inconduite f

**misdemeanor** [mɪsdɪ'miːnə(r)] n Am [crime] délit m

**miser** ['maɪzə(r)] n avare mf ■ **miserly** adj avare

**miserable** ['mɪzərəbəl] adj [wretched] misérable; [unhappy] malheureux, -euse; [awful] affreux, -euse

**misery** ['mɪzərɪ] (pl -**ies**) n [suffering] malheur m; [sadness] détresse f; Fam **misery guts** rabat-joie m

**misfire** [mɪs'faɪə(r)] vi [of plan] rater

**misfit** ['mɪsfɪt] n Pej inadapté, -e mf

**misfortune** [mɪs'fɔːtʃuːn] n malheur m

**misgivings** [mɪs'gɪvɪŋz] npl [doubts] doutes mpl (**about** sur); [fears] craintes fpl (**about** à propos de)

**misguided** [mɪs'gaɪdɪd] adj [attempt] malencontreux, -euse

**mishandle** [mɪs'hændəl] vt [situation] mal gérer; [person] malmener

**mishap** ['mɪshæp] n incident m

**misinform** [mɪsɪn'fɔːm] vt mal renseigner

**misinterpret** [mɪsɪn'tɜːprɪt] vt mal interpréter

**mislay** [mɪs'leɪ] (pt & pp -**laid**) vt égarer

**mislead** [mɪs'liːd] (pt & pp -**led**) vt tromper ■ **misleading** adj trompeur, -euse

**mismanage** [mɪs'mænɪdʒ] vt mal gérer

**misplace** [mɪs'pleɪs] vt [lose] égarer

**misprint** ['mɪsprɪnt] n faute f d'impression, coquille f

**mispronounce** [mɪsprə'naʊns] vt mal prononcer

**misrepresent** [mɪsreprɪ'zent] vt [theory] dénaturer; [person] présenter sous un faux jour

**miss** [mɪs] **1.** n coup m raté; **that was** or **we had a near miss** on l'a échappé belle; Fam **I'll give it a miss** [not go] je n'y irai pas **2.** vt [train, target, opportunity] manquer, rater; [not see] ne pas voir; [not understand] ne pas comprendre; [feel the lack of] regretter; **to miss sth out** [accidentally] oublier qch; [intentionally] omettre qch **3.** vi manquer ou rater son coup; **to miss out on sth** rater qch

**Miss** [mɪs] n Mademoiselle f

**missile** [Br'mɪsaɪl, Am'mɪsəl] n [rocket] missile m; [object thrown] projectile m

**missing** ['mɪsɪŋ] adj [absent] absent; [in war, after disaster] disparu; [object] manquant; **there are two cups/students missing** il manque deux tasses / étudiants; **to go missing** disparaître

**mission** ['mɪʃən] n mission f

**missionary** ['mɪʃənərɪ] (pl -ies) n REL missionnaire m

**misspell** [mɪs'spel] (pt & pp -ed or-spelt) vt mal écrire

**mist** [mɪst] 1. n [fog] brume f; [on glass] buée f 2. vi **to mist over** or **up** s'embuer

**mistake** [mɪ'steɪk] 1. n erreur f, faute f; **to make a mistake** faire une erreur; **by mistake** par erreur 2. (pt -took, pp -taken) vt [meaning, intention] se tromper sur; **to mistake sb for** prendre qn pour ■ **mistaken** adj [belief, impression] erroné; **to be mistaken** [of person] se tromper (**about** sur) ■ **mistakenly** adv par erreur

**Mister** ['mɪstə(r)] n Monsieur m

**mistletoe** ['mɪsltəʊ] n gui m

**mistreat** [mɪs'triːt] vt maltraiter

**mistress** ['mɪstrɪs] n maîtresse f; Br [in secondary school] professeur m

**mistrust** [mɪs'trʌst] 1. n méfiance f 2. vt se méfier de

**misty** ['mɪstɪ] (compar -ier, superl -iest) adj [foggy] brumeux, -euse

**misunderstand** [mɪsʌndə'stænd] (pt & pp -stood) vti mal comprendre ■ **misunderstanding** n [disagreement] mésentente f; [misconception] malentendu m

**misuse** 1. [mɪs'juːs] n [of equipment, resources] mauvais emploi m; [of power] abus m 2. [mɪs'juːz] vt [equipment, resources] mal employer; [power] abuser de

**mitt(en)** [mɪt, 'mɪtən] n [glove] moufle f

**mix** [mɪks] 1. n [mixture] mélange m 2. vt mélanger; [cement, drink, cake] préparer; **to mix up** [papers] mélanger; [mistake] confondre (**with** avec); **to be**

**mixed up in sth** être mêlé à qch 3. vi [blend] se mélanger; **to mix with sb** [socially] fréquenter qn

**mixed** [mɪkst] adj [school, marriage] mixte; [nuts, chocolates] assortis; **to be (all) mixed up** [of person] être désorienté; [of facts, account] être confus

**mixer** ['mɪksə(r)] n [for cooking] mixeur m

**mixture** ['mɪkstʃə(r)] n mélange m

**mix-up** ['mɪksʌp] n confusion f

**mm** (abbr of millimetre(s)) mm

**moan** [məʊn] 1. n [sound] gémissement m 2. vi [make sound] gémir; [complain] se plaindre (**to** à; **about** de; **that** que)

**mob** [mɒb] 1. n [crowd] foule f 2. (pt & pp -bb-) vt prendre d'assaut

**mobile** [Br'məʊbaɪl, Am'məʊbəl] 1. adj mobile; **mobile home** mobile home m; Br **mobile phone** téléphone m portable; **mobile phone mast** antenne-relais f (de téléphonie mobile) 2. n Br [phone] portable m

**mobilize** ['məʊbɪlaɪz] vti mobiliser

**mock** [mɒk] 1. adj [false] simulé; Br SCH **mock exam** examen m blanc 2. vt se moquer de; [mimic] singer ■ **mockery** n [act] moqueries fpl; [farce, parody] parodie f; **to make a mockery of sth** tourner qch en ridicule

**mod cons** [ˌmɒd-] (abbr of modern conveniences) npl Br Fam **all mod cons** tout confort

**mode** [məʊd] n [manner, way & COMPUT] mode m

**model** ['mɒdəl] 1. n [example, person] modèle m; [small version] maquette f; [in fashion show, magazine] mannequin m; **(scale) model** modèle m réduit 2. adj [behaviour, student] modèle; [car, plane] modèle réduit inv 3. (Br -ll-, Am -l-) vt [clay] modeler; [hats, dresses] présenter; **to model sth on** modeler qch sur 4. vi [for fashion] être mannequin; [pose for artist] poser

**modem** ['məʊdəm] n COMPUT modem m

**moderate** ['mɒdərət] **1.** adj modéré **2.** n POL modéré, -e mf ■ **moderately** adv [in moderation] modérément ; [averagely] moyennement

**moderation** [mɒdə'reɪʃən] n modération f; **in moderation** avec modération

**modern** ['mɒdən] adj moderne; **modern languages** langues fpl vivantes

**modernize** ['mɒdənaɪz] vt moderniser

**modest** ['mɒdɪst] adj [unassuming, moderate] modeste

**modify** ['mɒdɪfaɪ] (pt & pp -ied) vt modifier ■ **modification** n modification f (**to** à)

**module** ['mɒdjuːl] n module m

**moist** [mɔɪst] (compar -er, superl -est) adj humide ; [skin, hand] moite ■ **moisten** ['mɔɪsən] vt humecter

**moisture** ['mɔɪstʃə(r)] n humidité f; [on glass] buée f ■ **moisturizer** n crème f hydratante

**mojo** ['məʊdʒəʊ] n Am Fam [energy] peps m

**mold** [məʊld] Am n & vt = **mould**

**mole** [məʊl] n a) [on skin] grain m de beauté b) [animal, spy] taupe f

**molecule** ['mɒlɪkjuːl] n molécule f

**molest** [mə'lest] vt [child, woman] agresser (sexuellement)

**molt** [məʊlt] Am vi = **moult**

**mom** [mɒm] n Am Fam maman f

**moment** ['məʊmənt] n moment m, instant m; **at the moment** en ce moment ; **for the moment** pour le moment ; **in a moment** dans un instant ; **any moment (now)** d'un instant à l'autre

**momentary** ['məʊməntərɪ] adj momentané ■ **momentarily** [Br 'məʊməntərɪlɪ, Am məʊmən'terɪlɪ] adv [temporarily] momentanément ; Am [soon] tout de suite

**momentum** [məʊ'mentəm] n [speed] élan m; **to gather** or **gain momentum** [of campaign] prendre de l'ampleur

**mommy** ['mɒmɪ] n Am Fam maman f

**monarch** ['mɒnək] n monarque m ■ **monarchy** (pl -ies) n monarchie f

**monastery** ['mɒnəstərɪ] (pl -ies) n monastère m

**Monday** ['mʌndeɪ] n lundi m

**monetary** ['mʌnɪtərɪ] adj monétaire

**money** ['mʌnɪ] n argent m; **to make money** [of person] gagner de l'argent ; [of business] rapporter de l'argent ■ **moneybox** n tirelire f ■ **moneylender** n prêteur, -euse mf

**mongrel** ['mʌŋgrəl] n bâtard m

**monitor** ['mɒnɪtə(r)] **1.** n COMPUT, TV & TECH [screen, device] moniteur m **2.** vt [check] surveiller

**monk** [mʌŋk] n moine m

**monkey** ['mʌŋkɪ] (pl -eys) n singe m; Am **monkey bars** cage f d'écureuil

**monologue** ['mɒnəlɒg] n monologue m

**monopoly** [mə'nɒpəlɪ] n monopole m ■ **monopolize** vt monopoliser

**monotonous** [mə'nɒtənəs] adj monotone

**monster** ['mɒnstə(r)] n monstre m

**monstrosity** [mɒn'strɒsətɪ] (pl -ies) n monstruosité f

**monstrous** ['mɒnstrəs] adj monstrueux, -euse

**month** [mʌnθ] n mois m ■ **monthly 1.** adj mensuel, -elle **2.** (pl -ies) n [periodical] mensuel m **3.** adv tous les mois; **monthly payment** mensualité f

**Montreal** [mɒntrɪ'ɔːl] n Montréal m ou f

**monument** ['mɒnjʊmənt] n monument m

**moo** [muː] (pt & pp mooed) vi meugler

**mood** [muːd] n [of person] humeur f; [in grammar] mode m; **in a good / bad mood** de bonne / mauvaise humeur; **to be in the mood to do** or **for doing sth** être d'humeur à faire qch

**moody** ['muːdɪ] (compar -ier, superl -iest) adj [badtempered] maussade ; [changeable] lunatique

**moon** [muːn] n lune f ■ **moonlight** n by moonlight au clair de lune

**moor** [mʊə(r)] **1.** n [heath] lande f **2.** vt [ship] amarrer **3.** vi [of ship] mouiller

**moose** [muːs] n inv [animal] élan m

**mop** [mɒp] **1.** *n* [for floor] balai *m* à franges; [with sponge] balai-éponge *m* **2.** *(pt & pp* -pp-*)vt* **to mop sth up** [liquid] éponger qch

**mope** [məʊp] *vi* **to mope about** broyer du noir

**moped** ['məʊped] *n* Mobylette® *f*

**moral** ['mɒrəl] **1.** *adj* moral **2.** *n* [of story] morale *f*; **morals** [principles] moralité *f* ■ **morale** [mɒ'rɑːl] *n* moral *m* ■ **morality** [mə'rælətɪ] *n* moralité *f*

**morbid** ['mɔːbɪd] *adj* morbide

**more** [mɔː(r)] **1.** *adj* plus de; **more cars** plus de voitures; **he has more books than you** il a plus de livres que toi; **a few more months** quelques mois de plus; **(some) more tea** encore du thé; **(some) more details** d'autres détails; **more than a kilo/ten** plus d'un kilo/de dix **2.** *adv* [to form comparative of adjectives and adverbs] plus (**than** que); **more and more** de plus en plus; **more or less** plus ou moins **3.** *pron* plus; **have some more** reprenez-en; **she doesn't have any more** elle n'en a plus; **the more he shouts, the more hoarse he gets** plus il crie, plus il s'enroue; **what's more** qui plus est

**moreish** ['mɔːrɪʃ] *adj Br Fam* appétissant

**moreover** [mɔː'rəʊvə(r)] *adv* de plus

**morning** ['mɔːnɪŋ] **1.** *n* matin *m*; [referring to duration] matinée *f*; **in the morning** le matin; [during the course of the morning] pendant la matinée; [tomorrow] demain matin; **every Tuesday morning** tous les mardis matin **2.** *adj* [newspaper] du matin ■ **mornings** *adv Am* le matin

**Morocco** [mə'rɒkəʊ] *n* le Maroc ■ **Moroccan 1.** *adj* marocain **2.** *n* Marocain, -e *mf*

**moron** ['mɔːrɒn] *n* crétin, -e *mf*

**morph** [mɔːf] *vi* se transformer; **the car morphs into a robot** la voiture se transforme en robot

**mortal** ['mɔːtəl] *adj & n* mortel, -elle *(mf)*

**mortgage** ['mɔːgɪdʒ] **1.** *n* [money lent] prêt *m* immobilier; [money borrowed] emprunt *m* immobilier **2.** *vt* hypothéquer

**mortuary** ['mɔːtʃʊərɪ] *(pl* -ies*) n* morgue *f*

**mosaic** [məʊ'zeɪɪk] *n* mosaïque *f*

**Moscow** [*Br* 'mɒskəʊ, *Am* 'mɒskaʊ] *n* Moscou *m ou f*

**mosey** ['məʊzɪ] *vi Am Fam* [amble] marcher d'un pas tranquille; **to mosey along** aller *ou* se promener sans se presser; **let's mosey over to the pond** allons faire un petit tour jusqu'à l'étang

**Moslem** ['mɒzlɪm] *adj & n* musulman, -e *(mf)*

**mosque** [mɒsk] *n* mosquée *f*

**mosquito** [mɒ'skiːtəʊ] *(pl* -oes *or* -os*) n* moustique *m*

**moss** [mɒs] *n* mousse *f*

**most** [məʊst] **1.** *adj* **a)** [the majority of] la plupart de; **most women** la plupart des femmes **b)** [greatest amount of] **the most** le plus de; **I have the most books** j'ai le plus de livres **2.** *adv* **a)** [to form superlative of adjectives and adverbs] plus; **the most beautiful** le plus beau (*f* la plus belle) (**in/of** de); **to talk (the) most** parler le plus; **most of all** [especially] surtout **b)** [very] extrêmement **c)** *Am Fam* [almost] presque **3.** *pron* **a)** [the majority] la plupart; **most of the people/the time** la plupart des gens/du temps; **most of the cake** la plus grande partie du gâteau; **most of them** la plupart d'entre eux **b)** [greatest amount] le plus; **he earns the most** c'est lui qui gagne le plus; **to make the most of sth** [situation, talent] tirer le meilleur parti de qch; [holiday] profiter au maximum de qch; **at (the very) most** tout au plus ■ **mostly** *adv* [in the main] surtout; [most often] le plus souvent

**MOT** [eməʊ'tiː] *(abbr of* **Ministry of Transport***) n Br* contrôle obligatoire des véhicules de plus de trois ans

**motel** [məʊ'tel] *n* motel *m*

**moth** [mɒθ] n papillon m de nuit ; [in clothes] mite f

**mother** ['mʌðə(r)] n mère f; **Mother's Day** la fête des Mères ■ **motherhood** n maternité f ■ **mother-in-law** (pl **mothers-in-law**) n belle-mère f ■ **mother-to-be** (pl **mothers-to-be**) n future mère f ■ **mother tongue** n langue f maternelle

**motion** ['məʊʃən] **1.** n [of arm] mouvement m ; [in meeting] motion f; **to set sth in motion** mettre qch en mouvement; **motion picture** film m **2.** vti **to motion (to) sb to do sth** faire signe à qn de faire qch ■ **motionless** adj immobile

**motivate** ['məʊtɪveɪt] vt [person, decision] motiver ■ **motivation** n motivation f

**motive** ['məʊtɪv] n motif m (**for** de)

**motor** ['məʊtə(r)] **1.** n [engine] moteur m ; Br Fam [car] auto f **2.** adj [industry, insurance] automobile; **motor racing** courses fpl automobiles; **motor home** camping-car m ■ **motorbike** n moto f ■ **motorboat** n canot m à moteur ■ **motorcycle** n moto f, motocyclette f ■ **motorcyclist** n motocycliste f ■ **motorist** n Br automobiliste mf ■ **motorway** n Br autoroute f

**motto** ['mɒtəʊ] (pl **-oes** or **-os**) n devise f

**mould**[1], Am **mold** [məʊld] **1.** n [shape] moule m **2.** vt [clay, person's character] modeler

**mould**[2], Am **mold** [məʊld] n [fungus] moisissure f

**mouldy**, Am **moldy** ['məʊldɪ] (compar **-ier-**, superl **iest**) adj moisi; **to go mouldy** moisir

**moult**, Am **molt** [məʊlt] vi muer

**mound** [maʊnd] n [of earth] tertre m ; Fig [untidy pile] tas m

**mount** [maʊnt] **1.** n [frame for photo or slide] cadre m **2.** vt [horse, jewel, photo, demonstration] monter ; [ladder] monter à **3.** vi a) [on horse] se mettre en selle b) [increase, rise] monter ; **to mount up** [add up] monter, augmenter ; [accumulate - of debts, bills] s'accumuler

**mountain** ['maʊntɪn] n montagne f; **mountain bike** vélo m tout-terrain, VTT m ■ **mountaineer** n alpiniste mf ■ **mountaineering** n alpinisme m ■ **mountainous** adj montagneux, -euse

**mourn** [mɔːn] vti **to mourn (for) sb** pleurer qn ■ **mourner** n personne assistant aux obsèques ■ **mourning** n deuil m; **in mourning** en deuil

**mouse** [maʊs] (pl **mice** [maɪs]) n [animal & COMPUT] souris f

**mousse** [muːs] n mousse f

**moustache** [Br mə'stɑː], Am 'mʌstæʃ] n moustache f

**mouth** [maʊθ] (pl **-s** [maʊðz]) n [of person, horse] bouche f; [of other animals] gueule f; [of river] embouchure f; [of cave, harbour] entrée f ■ **mouthful** ['maʊθfʊl] n [of food] bouchée f; [of liquid] gorgée f ■ **mouth-organ** n harmonica m ■ **mouthpiece** n [of musical instrument] embouchure f; [spokesperson] porte-parole m inv ■ **mouthwash** n bain m de bouche ■ **mouth-watering** adj appétissant

**movable** ['muːvəbəl] adj mobile

**move** [muːv] **1.** n mouvement m ; [change of house] déménagement m ; [change of job] changement m d'emploi ; [in game] coup m; **to make a move** [leave] se préparer à partir ; [act] passer à l'action ; **it's your move** [turn] c'est à toi de jouer; Fam **to get a move on** se grouiller **2.** vt déplacer ; [arm, leg] remuer ; [employee] muter ; [piece in game] jouer; **to move sb** [emotionally] émouvoir qn; **to move house** déménager **3.** vi bouger ; [change position] se déplacer (**to** à) ; [leave] partir ; [act] agir ; [play] jouer ; [change house] déménager ; **to move to Paris** aller habiter Paris ■ **move about** vi se déplacer ; [fidget] remuer ■ **move along 1.** vt sep faire avancer **2.** vi avancer ■ **move around** vi = **move about** ■ **move away** vi [go away] s'éloigner ; [move house] déménager ■ **move back 1.** vt sep [chair] reculer ; [to its original position] remettre en place **2.** vi [withdraw] reculer ; [return] retourner (**to** à) ■ **move**

**down** *vt sep* [take down] descendre
■ **move forward** *vt sep* & *vi* avancer
■ **move in** *vi* [into house] emménager
■ **move off** *vi* [go away] s'éloigner ; [of vehicle] démarrer ■ **move on 1.** *vi* **a)** [after stopping] se remettre en route **b)** [progress] **can we move on to the second point?** pouvons-nous passer au deuxième point ? **c)** [in discussion] changer de sujet **2.** *vi Am* [in life] se tourner vers l'avenir ■ **move out** *vi* [out of house] déménager ■ **move over 1.** *vt sep* pousser **2.** *vi* [make room] se pousser ■ **move up** *vi* [on seats] se pousser

**movement** ['mu:vmənt] *n* mouvement *m*

**movie** ['mu:vɪ] *n* film *m* ; **the movies** [cinema] le cinéma ; **movie star** vedette *f* de cinéma ; *Am* **movie theater** cinéma *m*

**moving** ['mu:vɪŋ] *adj* en mouvement ; [vehicle] en marche ; [touching] émouvant

**mow** [məʊ] *(pp* **mown** [məʊn] *or* **mowed)** *vt* **to mow the lawn** tondre le gazon ■ **mower** *n* **(lawn) mower** tondeuse *f* (à gazon)

**MP** [em'pi:] *(abbr of* **Member of Parliament)** *n* député *m*

**MP3** [,empi:'θri:] *(abbr of* **moving picture experts group audio layer 3)** *n* COMPUT MP3 *m* ; **MP3 player** lecteur *m* (de) MP3

**MP4** *n* MP4

**mph** [empi:'eɪtʃ] *(abbr of* **miles per hour)** ≃ km / h

**Mr** ['mɪstə(r)] *n* **Mr Brown** M. Brown

**Mrs** ['mɪsɪz] *n* **Mrs Brown** Mme Brown

**Ms** [mɪz] *n* **Ms Brown** ≃ Mme Brown *(ne renseigne pas sur le statut de famille)*

**MS** [em'es] *(abbr of* **Master of Science)** *n Am* UNIV **to have an MS in chemistry** avoir une maîtrise de chimie

**MSc** [emes'si:] *(abbr of* **Master of Science)** *n* UNIV **to have an MSc in chemistry** avoir une maîtrise de chimie

---

**much** [mʌtʃ]

Hormis dans la langue soutenue et dans certaines expressions, ne s'utilise que dans des structures négatives ou interrogatives

**1.** *adj* beaucoup de ; **not much time / money** pas beaucoup de temps / d'argent ; **how much sugar do you want?** combien de sucre voulez-vous ? ; **twice as much traffic** deux fois plus de circulation ; **too much work** trop de travail **2.** *adv* beaucoup ; **very much** beaucoup ; **much better** bien meilleur ; **I love him so much** je l'aime tellement ; **she doesn't say very much** elle ne dit pas grand-chose

**3.** *pron* beaucoup ; **there isn't much left** il n'en reste pas beaucoup ; **it's not much of a garden** ce n'est pas terrible comme jardin ; **twice as much** deux fois plus ; **as much as you like** autant que tu veux ; *Fam* **that's a bit much!** c'est un peu fort !

**muck** [mʌk] **1.** *n* [manure] fumier *m* ; *Fig* [filth] saleté *f* **2.** *vt Br Fam* **to muck sth up** [task] bâcler qch ; [plans] chambouler qch **3.** *vi Br Fam* **to muck about** *or* **around** [waste time] traîner ; [play the fool] faire l'imbécile ■ **mucky** *(compar* **-ier,** *superl* **-iest)** *adj Fam* sale

**mud** [mʌd] *n* boue *f* ■ **muddy** *(compar* **-ier,** *superl* **-iest)** *adj* [water, road] boueux, -euse ; [hands] couvert de boue ■ **mudguard** *n* garde-boue *m inv*

**muddle** ['mʌdəl] **1.** *n* confusion *f* ; **to be in a muddle** [person] ne plus s'y retrouver ; [of things] être en désordre **2.** *vt* [facts] mélanger ; **to get muddled** [of person] s'embrouiller

**muesli** ['mju:zlɪ, 'mu:zlɪ] *n* muesli *m*

**muffin** ['mʌfɪn] *n* [cake] muffin *m*

**muffled** ['mʌfəld] *adj* [noise] sourd

**muffler** ['mʌflə(r)] *n Am* [on vehicle] silencieux *m*

**mug¹** [mʌg] *n* **a)** [for tea, coffee] grande tasse *f* ; **(beer) mug** chope *f* **b)** *Br Fam* [fool] poire *f*

**mug²** [mʌg] *(pt & pp* **-gg-)** *vt* [attack in street] agresser ■ **mugger** *n* agresseur *m*

**mutual**

**mule** [mju:l] *n* [male] mulet *m* ; [female] mule *f*

**multicoloured** ['mʌltɪkʌləd] *adj* multicolore

**multifunction** [ˌmʌltɪ'fʌŋkʃən] *adj* multifonction(s)

**multimedia** [mʌltɪ'mi:dɪə] *adj* multimédia

**multimillionaire** [mʌltɪmɪljə'neə(r)] *n* multimillionnaire *mf*

**multiple** ['mʌltɪpəl] **1.** *adj* multiple **2.** *n* MATH multiple *m*

**multiple-choice** [mʌltɪpəl'tʃɔɪs] *adj* à choix multiple ; SCH **multiple-choice examination** QCM *m*, questionnaire *m* à choix multiple

**multiplex** ['mʌltɪpleks] *n* [cinema] complexe *m* multisalles

**multiplication** [mʌltɪplɪ'keɪʃən] *n* multiplication *f*

**multiply** ['mʌltɪplaɪ] *(pt & pp -ied)* **1.** *vt* multiplier **2.** *vi* [of animals, insects] se multiplier

**multiracial** [mʌltɪ'reɪʃəl] *adj* multiracial

**multi-speed** *adj* à plusieurs vitesses

**multistorey**, *Am* **multistory** [mʌltɪ'stɔ:rɪ] *adj* [car park] à plusieurs niveaux

**multitask** ['mʌltɪˌtɑ:sk] *vi* mener plusieurs tâches de front

**multitude** ['mʌltɪtju:d] *n* multitude *f*

**mum** [mʌm] *n Br Fam* maman *f*

**mumble** ['mʌmbəl] *vti* marmotter

**mummy**[1] ['mʌmɪ] *(pl -ies) n Br Fam* [mother] maman *f*

**mummy**[2] ['mʌmɪ] *(pl -ies) n* [embalmed body] momie *f*

**mumps** [mʌmps] *n* MED oreillons *mpl*

**munch** [mʌntʃ] *vti* [chew] mâcher

**municipal** [mju:'nɪsɪpəl] *adj* municipal

**mural** ['mjʊərəl] *n* peinture *f* murale

**murder** ['mɜ:də(r)] **1.** *n* meurtre *m* **2.** *vt* [kill] assassiner ▪ **murderer** *n* meurtrier, -ère *mf*, assassin *m*

**murky** ['mɜ:kɪ] *(compar -ier, superl -iest) adj* [water, business, past] trouble

**murmur** ['mɜ:mə(r)] **1.** *n* murmure *m* **2.** *vti* murmurer

**muscle** ['mʌsəl] *n* muscle *m* ▪ **muscular** ['mʌskjʊlə(r)] *adj* [person, arm] musclé

**museum** [mju:'zɪəm] *n* musée *m*

**mush** [mʌʃ] *n* [pulp] bouillie *f* ▪ **mushy** *(compar -ier, superl -iest) adj* [food] en bouillie

**mushroom** ['mʌʃrʊm] *n* champignon *m*

**music** ['mju:zɪk] *n* musique *f* ▪ **musical** **1.** *adj* musical ; **musical instrument** instrument *m* de musique **2.** *n* [film, play] comédie *f* musicale ▪ **musician** [-'zɪʃən] *n* musicien, -enne *mf*

**Muslim** ['mʊzlɪm] *adj* & *n* musulman, -e *(mf)*

**mussel** ['mʌsəl] *n* moule *f*

---

**must** [mʌst] **1.** *n* **this is a must** c'est indispensable ; **this film is a must** il faut absolument voir ce film **2.** *v aux* **a)** [expressing necessity] **you must obey** tu dois obéir, il faut que tu obéisses

**b)** [expressing probability] **she must be clever** elle doit être intelligente ; **I must have seen it** j'ai dû le voir

▪ **must-have** *n* must *m*, indispensable *m*

▪ **must-see** *n* **that film is a must-see** il ne faut surtout pas manquer ce film

---

**mustache** ['mʌstæʃ] *n Am* moustache *f*

**mustard** ['mʌstəd] *n* moutarde *f*

**muster** ['mʌstə(r)] *vt* [gather] rassembler

**mustn't** ['mʌsənt] = **must not**

**musty** ['mʌstɪ] *(compar -ier, superl -iest) adj* [smell, taste] de moisi

**mute** [mju:t] *adj* [silent & LING] muet (*f* muette)

**mutiny** ['mju:tɪnɪ] **1.** *(pl -ies) n* mutinerie *f* **2.** *(pt & pp -ied) vi* se mutiner

**mutter** ['mʌtə(r)] *vti* marmonner

**mutton** ['mʌtən] *n* [meat] mouton *m*

**mutual** ['mju:tʃʊəl] *adj* [help, love] mutuel, -elle ; [friend] commun ▪ **mutually** *adv* mutuellement

**muzzle** ['mʌzəl] **1.** *n* [device for dog] muselière *f*; [snout] museau *m* **2.** *vt* [animal, the press] museler

**my** [maɪ] *poss adj* mon, ma, *pl* mes

**myself** [maɪ'self] *pron* moi-même ; [reflexive] me, m' ; [after prep] moi ; **I wash myself** je me lave

**mystery** ['mɪstərɪ] *(pl* **-ies***)n* mystère *m* ▪ **mysterious** [mɪs'tɪərɪəs] *adj* mysté-rieux, -euse

**mystical** ['mɪstɪkəl] *adj* mystique

**mystify** ['mɪstɪfaɪ] *(pt & pp* **-ied***) vt* [be-wilder] déconcerter

**myth** [mɪθ] *n* mythe *m* ▪ **mythology** *(pl* **-ies***)n* mythologie *f*

# N

**N, n** [en] *n* [letter] N, n *m inv*

**nab** [næb] *(pt & pp -bb-) vt Fam* [catch, arrest] coffrer

**nag** [næg] *(pt & pp -gg-) vti* **to nag (at) sb** [of person] être sur le dos de qn

**nail** [neɪl] **1.** *n* **a)** [of finger, toe] ongle *m*; **nail file** lime *f* à ongles; **nail polish,** *Br* **nail varnish** vernis *m* à ongles; **nail polish remover** dissolvant *m* **b)** [metal] clou *m* **2.** *vt* clouer; **to nail sth down** [lid] clouer qch

**naive** [naɪ'iːv] *adj* naïf (*f* naïve)

**naked** ['neɪkɪd] *adj* [person, flame] nu

**name** [neɪm] **1.** *n* nom *m*; [reputation] réputation *f*; [famous person] grand nom *m*, célébrité *f*; **my name is...** je m'appelle...; **in the name of** au nom de; **first name, given name** prénom *m* **2.** *vt* nommer; [ship, street] baptiser; [date, price] fixer

**namely** ['neɪmlɪ] *adv* à savoir

**nanny** ['nænɪ] *(pl -ies) n* nurse *f*; *Fam* [grandmother] mamie *f*

**nap** [næp] **1.** *n* [sleep] **to have** *or* **take a nap** faire un petit somme **2.** *(pt & pp -pp-) vi* faire un somme

**napkin** ['næpkɪn] *n* [at table] serviette *f*

**nappy** ['næpɪ] *(pl -ies) n Br* [for baby] couche *f*

**narcotic** [nɑː'kɒtɪk] *adj & n* narcotique *(m)*

**narrate** [nə'reɪt] *vt* raconter ■ **narrative** ['nærətɪv] *n* récit *m* ■ **narrator** *n* narrateur, -trice *mf*

**narrow** ['nærəʊ] **1.** *(compar* -er, *superl* -est) *adj* étroit **2.** *vt* **to narrow (down)** [choice, meaning] limiter **3.** *vi* [of path] se rétrécir ■ **narrowly** *adv* [only just] de peu; **he narrowly escaped being killed** il a bien failli être tué

**narrow-minded** [nærəʊ'maɪndɪd] *adj* borné

**nasty** ['nɑːstɪ] *(compar* -ier, *superl* -iest) *adj* [bad] mauvais; [spiteful] méchant (**to** *or* **towards** avec)

**nation** ['neɪʃən] *n* nation *f*

**national** ['næʃənəl] **1.** *adj* national; **national anthem** hymne *m* national; *Br* **National Health Service** ≃ Sécurité *f* sociale; *Br* **national insurance contributions** *fpl* sociales **2.** *n* [citizen] ressortissant, -e *mf*

**nationalist** ['næʃənəlɪst] *n* nationaliste *mf*

**nationality** [næʃə'nælətɪ] *(pl -ies) n* nationalité *f*

**nationalize** ['næʃənəlaɪz] *vt* nationaliser

**nationwide** ['neɪʃənwaɪd] *adj & adv* dans tout le pays

**native** ['neɪtɪv] **1.** *adj* [country] natal *(mpl -als)*; [tribe, plant] indigène; **to be an English native speaker** avoir l'anglais comme langue maternelle; **Native American** Indien, -enne *mf* d'Amérique, Amérindien, -enne *mf*; COMPUT **native file** fichier *m* natif **2.** *n* [person] indigène *mf*; **to be a native of** être originaire de

**NATO** ['neɪtəʊ] *(abbr of North Atlantic Treaty Organization) n* MIL OTAN *f*

**natter** ['nætə(r)] *vi Br Fam* bavarder

**natural** ['nætʃərəl] *adj* naturel, -elle; [talent] inné ■ **naturally** *adv* [unaffectedly, of course] naturellement; [by nature] de nature

**naturalized,** *Br* **naturalised** ['nætʃrəlaɪzd] *adj* [person] naturalisé

**nature** ['neɪtʃə(r)] *n* [world, character] nature *f*; **by nature** de nature; **nature reserve** réserve *f* naturelle

**naughty** ['nɔːtɪ] *(compar* -ier, *superl* -iest) *adj* [child] vilain

**nausea** ['nɔːzɪə] *n* nausée *f* ■ **nauseate** ['nɔːzɪeɪt] *vt* écœurer ■ **nauseous** ['nɔːʃəs] *adj Am* **to feel nauseous** [sick] avoir envie de vomir

**nautical** ['nɔːtɪkəl] *adj* nautique

**naval** ['neɪvəl] *adj* naval *(mpl* -als) ; [power] maritime ; [officer] de marine

**nave** [neɪv] *n* [of church] nef *f*

**navel** ['neɪvəl] *n* nombril *m*

**navigate** ['nævɪgeɪt] **1.** *vt* [boat] piloter ; [river] naviguer sur **2.** *vi* naviguer

**navy** ['neɪvɪ] **1.** *(pl* -ies*)* *n* marine *f* **2.** *adj* **navy (blue)** bleu marine *inv*

**Nazi** ['nɑːtsɪ] *adj* & *n* POL & HIST nazi, -e *(mf)*

**NB** [en'biː] *(abbr of nota bene)* NB

**NBD** MESSAGING *written abbr of* **no big deal**

**near** [nɪə(r)] **1.** *(compar* -er, *superl* -est*)* *prep* **near (to)** près de ; **near (to) the end** vers la fin **2.** *(compar* -er, *superl* -est*)* *adv* près ; **near to sth** près de qch ; **near enough** [more or less] plus ou moins **3.** *(compar* -er, *superl* -est*)adj* proche ; **in the near future** dans un avenir proche ; **to the nearest euro** [calculate] à un euro près ; AUTO **near side** *Br* côté *m* gauche ; *Am* côté *m* droit **4.** *vt* [approach] approcher de

**nearby 1.** [nɪə'baɪ] *adv* tout près **2.** ['nɪəbaɪ] *adj* proche

**nearly** ['nɪəlɪ] *adv* presque ; **she (very) nearly fell** elle a failli tomber

**nearsighted** [ˌnɪə'saɪtɪd] *adj Am* myope

**neat** [niːt] *(compar* -er, *superl* -est*)* *adj* [clothes, work] soigné ; [room] bien rangé ; *Am Fam* [good] super *inv* ■ **neatly** *adv* [carefully] avec soin ; [skilfully] habilement

**necessary** ['nesɪsərɪ] *adj* nécessaire ■ **necessarily** [-'serəlɪ] *adv* **not necessarily** pas forcément

**necessity** [nɪ'sesətɪ] *(pl* -ies*)* *n* [obligation, need] nécessité *f* ; **to be a necessity** être indispensable ■ **necessitate** *vt* nécessiter

**neck** [nek] *n* cou *m* ; [of dress] encolure *f* ; [of bottle] goulot *m*

**necklace** ['neklɪs] *n* collier *m* ■ **necktie** *n* cravate *f*

**nectarine** ['nektəriːn] *n* [fruit] nectarine *f*, brugnon *m*

**need** [niːd] **1.** *n* besoin *m* ; **to be in need of sth** avoir besoin de qch ; **there's no need (for you) to do that** tu n'as pas besoin de faire cela **2.** *vt* avoir besoin de ; **you need it** tu en as besoin ; **her hair needs cutting** il faut qu'elle se fasse couper les cheveux **3.** *v aux* **I needn't have rushed** ce n'était pas la peine de me presser ; **you needn't worry** inutile de t'inquiéter ■ **needs** *adv* **if needs must** s'il le faut

**needle** ['niːdəl] *n* aiguille *f* ; [of record player] saphir *m* ■ **needlework** *n* couture *f* ; [object] ouvrage *m*

**needlessly** ['niːdlɪslɪ] *adv* inutilement

**needy** ['niːdɪ] *(compar* -ier, *superl* -iest*)adj* nécessiteux, -euse

**negative** ['negətɪv] **1.** *adj* négatif, -ive **2.** *n* [of photo] négatif *m*

**negatory** [nɪ'geɪtərɪ] *adj Am Fam* négatif ; **I guess that's negatory** je suppose que ça veut dire non ; **did you fix it? — negatory** tu l'as réparé ? — négatif

**neglect** [nɪ'glekt] **1.** *n* [of person] négligence *f* **2.** *vt* [person, health, work] négliger ; [garden, car] ne pas s'occuper de ; [duty] manquer à ; **to neglect to do sth** négliger de faire qch ■ **neglected** *adj* [appearance] négligé ; [garden, house] mal tenu ; **to feel neglected** se sentir abandonné

**negligent** ['neglɪdʒənt] *adj* négligent

**negligible** ['neglɪdʒəbəl] *adj* négligeable

**negotiate** [nɪ'gəʊʃɪeɪt] *vti* [discuss] négocier ■ **negotiation** *n* négociation *f*

**neigh** [neɪ] *vi* hennir

**neighbour,** *Am* **neighbor** ['neɪbə(r)] *n* voisin, -e *m f*

**neighbourhood,** *Am* **neighborhood** ['neɪbəhʊd] *n* [district] quartier *m*, voisinage *m* ; [neighbours] voisinage *m* ; **in the neighbourhood of $10 / 10 kilos** dans les 10 dollars / 10 kilos

**neighbouring**, *Am* **neighboring** ['neɪbərɪŋ] *adj* voisin

**neither** [*Br* 'naɪðə(r), *Am* 'niːðə(r)] **1.** *conj* neither nor… ni… ni…; **he neither sings nor dances** il ne chante ni ne danse **2.** *adv* neither do I/neither can I (ni) moi non plus **3.** *adj* neither boy came aucun des deux garçons n'est venu **4.** *pron* neither (of them) aucun(e) (des deux)

**neon** ['niːɒn] *adj* neon sign enseigne *f* au néon

**NE1** MESSAGING *written abbr of* **anyone**

**nephew** ['nefjuː] *n* neveu *m*

**nerd** [nɜːd] *n Fam & Pej* débile *mf*; computer nerd accro *m* d'informatique

**nerve** [nɜːv] *n* nerf *m*; [courage] courage *m*; *Fam* [impudence] culot *m*; *Fam* he gets on my nerves il me tape sur les nerfs ■ **nerve-racking** *adj* éprouvant

**nervous** ['nɜːvəs] *adj* [apprehensive] nerveux, -euse; to be nervous about sth/doing sth être nerveux à l'idée de qch/de faire qch

**nest** [nest] **1.** *n* nid *m*; *Fig* nest egg pécule *m* **2.** *vi* [of bird] nicher

**nestle** ['nesəl] *vi* se pelotonner (up to contre)

**net¹** [net] *n* filet *m*

**net²** [net] **1.** *adj* [profit, weight] net (*f* nette) **2.** (*pt & pp* -tt-) *vt* [of person, company] gagner net

**Net** [net] *n* COMPUT the Net le Net; to surf the Net surfer sur le Net *ou* sur Internet

**Netherlands** ['neðələndz] *npl* the Netherlands les Pays-Bas *mpl*

**nettle** ['netəl] *n* ortie *f*

**network** ['netwɜːk] *n* réseau *m*

**neurotic** [njʊ'rɒtɪk] *adj & n* névrosé, -e (*mf*)

**neuter** ['njuːtə(r)] **1.** *adj & n* GRAM neutre (*m*) **2.** *vt* [cat] châtrer

**neutral** ['njuːtrəl] **1.** *adj* neutre; [policy] de neutralité **2.** *n* in neutral (gear) [vehicle] au point mort ■ **neutralize** *vt* neutraliser

**never** ['nevə(r)] *adv* [not ever] (ne…) jamais; **she never lies** elle ne ment jamais; **never again** plus jamais ■ **never-ending** *adj* interminable

**nevertheless** [nevəðə'les] *adv* néanmoins

**new** [njuː] *adj* a) (*compar* -er, *superl* -est) nouveau (*f* nouvelle); [brand-new] neuf (*f* neuve); **the new media** les nouveaux médias; to be new to [job] être nouveau dans; [city] être un nouveau-venu (*f* une nouvelle-venue) dans b) [different] a new glass/pen un autre verre/stylo ■ **newborn** *adj* a newborn baby un nouveau-né, une nouveau-née ■ **newcomer** [-kʌmə(r)] *n* nouveau-venu *m*, nouvelle-venue *f* (to dans) ■ **newly** *adv* nouvellement ■ **newlyweds** *n* jeunes mariés *mpl*

**NEway** MESSAGING *written abbr of* **anyway**

**newbie** ['njuːbɪ] *n Fam* a) néophyte *mf* b) COMPUT internaute *mf* novice, cyber-novice *mf*

**news** [njuːz] *n* nouvelles *fpl*; [in the media] informations *fpl*; a piece of news une nouvelle; sports news [newspaper column] rubrique *f* sportive ■ **newsagent** *n Br* marchand, -e *mf* de journaux ■ **newsdealer** *n Am* marchand, -e *mf* de journaux ■ **newsflash** *n* flash *m* d'informations ■ **newsletter** *n* [of club, group] bulletin *m* ■ **newspaper** *n* journal *m* ■ **newsreader** *n Br* présentateur, -trice *mf* de journal ■ **newsstand** ['njuːzstænd] *n* kiosque *m* à journaux

**New Zealand** [njuː'ziːlənd] *n* la Nouvelle-Zélande

**next** [nekst] **1.** *adj* prochain; [room, house] d'à côté; [following] suivant; **next month** [in the future] le mois prochain; **the next day** le lendemain; **within the next ten days** d'ici dix jours; **you're next** c'est ton tour; **the next size up** la taille au-dessus; to live next door habiter à côté (to de) **2.** *n* [in series] suivant, -e *mf* **3.** *adv* [afterwards] ensuite, après; [now] maintenant;

**when you come next** la prochaine fois que tu viendras ; **next to** [beside] à côté de

**next-door** ['nekstdɔ:(r)] *adj* **next-door neighbour/room** voisin *m* /pièce *f* d'à côté

**NHS** [eneɪʃˈes] (*abbr of* **National Health Service**) *n Br* ≃ Sécurité *f* sociale

**nibble** ['nɪbəl] *vti* grignoter

**nice** [naɪs] (*compar* -**er**, *superl* -**est**) *adj* [pleasant] agréable ; [tasty] bon (*f* bonne) ; [physically attractive] beau (*f* belle) ; [kind] gentil, -ille (**to** avec) ; **nice and warm** bien chaud ; **have a nice day!** bonne journée ! ■ **nicely** *adv* [well] bien

**niche** [ni:ʃ, nɪtʃ] *n* [recess] niche *f* ; (**market**) **niche** créneau *m*

**nick** [nɪk] **1.** *n* [on skin, wood] entaille *f* ; [in blade, crockery] brèche *f* ; **in the nick of time** juste à temps **2.** *vt Br Fam* [steal] piquer

**nickel** ['nɪkəl] *n Am* [coin] pièce *f* de cinq cents ■ **nickel-and-dime store** *n Am* ≃ magasin *m* à prix unique

**nickname** ['nɪkneɪm] **1.** *n* [informal] surnom *m* **2.** *vt* surnommer

**niece** [ni:s] *n* nièce *f*

**night** [naɪt] **1.** *n* nuit *f* ; [evening] soir *m* ; **at night** la nuit ; **last night** [evening] hier soir ; [night] cette nuit ; **to have an early/a late night** se coucher tôt /tard **2.** *adj* [work, flight] de nuit ; **night shift** [job] poste *m* de nuit ; [workers] équipe *f* de nuit ■ **nightcap** *n* [drink] boisson *f* alcoolisée ou chaude prise avant de se coucher ■ **nightclub** *n* boîte *f* de nuit ■ **nightdress** ['naɪtdres], **nightgown** ['naɪtgaʊn], **nightie** ['naɪtɪ] *Fam n* chemise *f* de nuit ■ **nightfall** *n* **at nightfall** à la tombée de la nuit ■ **nightlife** *n* vie *f* nocturne ■ **nights** *adv* **a)** *Am* [at night] la nuit **b)** *Br* [nightshift] **to work nights** travailler *ou* être de nuit ■ **night-time** *n* nuit *f*

**nightingale** ['naɪtɪŋgeɪl] *n* rossignol *m*

**nightly** ['naɪtlɪ] **1.** *adv* chaque nuit ; [every evening] chaque soir **2.** *adj* de chaque nuit /soir

**nightmare** ['naɪtmeə(r)] *n* cauchemar *m*

**nil** [nɪl] *n* [nothing] *Br* [score] zéro *m* ; **two nil** deux à zéro

**Nile** [naɪl] *n* **the Nile** le Nil

**nimble** ['nɪmbəl] (*compar* -**er**, *superl* -**est**) *adj* [person] souple

**nine** [naɪn] *adj & n* neuf (*m*)

**911 a)** *numéro de téléphone des urgences dans certains États des États-Unis* **b)** MESSAGING *signifie qu'il y a urgence ou que l'on souhaite être contacté rapidement*

**nineteen** [naɪn'ti:n] *adj & n* dix-neuf (*m*)

**ninety** ['naɪntɪ] *adj & n* quatre-vingt-dix (*m*)

**ninth** [naɪnθ] *adj & n* neuvième (*mf*) ; **a ninth** [fraction] un neuvième ; *Am* SCH **ninth grade** *classe de l'enseignement secondaire correspondant à la troisième* (*13-14 ans*)

**nip** [nɪp] **1.** (*pt & pp* -**pp**-) *vt* [pinch] pincer **2.** *vi Br Fam* **to nip round to sb's house** faire un saut chez qn ; **to nip out** sortir un instant

**nipple** ['nɪpəl] *n* mamelon *m* ; *Am* [on baby's bottle] tétine *f*

**NITING** MESSAGING *written abbr of* **anything**

**nitrogen** ['naɪtrədʒən] *n* azote *m*

**Njoy** MESSAGING *written abbr of* **enjoy**

**no** [nəʊ] **1.** (*pl* **noes** *or* **nos**) *n* non *m inv* **2.** *adj* [not any] pas de ; **there's no bread** il n'y a pas de pain ; **I have no idea** je n'ai aucune idée ; **no child came** aucun enfant n'est venu ; **of no importance** sans importance **3.** *adv* [interjection] non ; **no more time** plus de temps ; **no more/fewer than ten** pas plus /moins de dix

**noble** ['nəʊbəl] (*compar* -**er**, *superl* -**est**) *adj* noble ■ **nobility** *n* noblesse *f*

**nobody** ['nəʊbɒdɪ] **1.** *pron* (ne...) personne ; **nobody came** personne n'est venu ; **he knows nobody** il ne connaît personne **2.** *n* **a nobody** une nullité

**no-brainer** [nəʊ'breɪnə(r)] *n Am Fam* décision facile ; **it's a no-brainer!** la solution est claire !

**nod** [nɒd] **1.** *n* signe *m* de tête **2.** *(pt & pp* -dd-) *vti* **to nod (one's head)** faire un signe de tête **3.** *vi Fam* **to nod off** s'assoupir

**no-fault** *adj Am* JUR **no-fault divorce** divorce *m* par consentement mutuel; **no-fault insurance** assurance *f* à remboursement automatique

**no-frills** [-'frɪlz] *adj* [service] minimum (*inv*) ; [airline] à bas prix

**no-holds-barred** *adj* [report, documentary] sans fard

**noise** [nɔɪz] *n* bruit *m*; **to make a noise** faire du bruit

**noisy** ['nɔɪzɪ] *(compar* -ier, *superl* -iest) *adj* [person, street] bruyant ■ **noisily** *adv* bruyamment

**nominal** ['nɒmɪnəl] *adj* nominal; [rent, salary] symbolique

**nominate** ['nɒmɪneɪt] *vt* [appoint] nommer; [propose] proposer (**for** comme candidat à) ■ **nomination** *n* [appointment] nomination *f*; [proposal] candidature *f*

**nondescript** ['nɒndɪskrɪpt] *adj* très ordinaire

**none** [nʌn] **1.** *pron* aucun, -e *mf*; [in filling out a form] néant; **none of them** aucun d'eux; **she has none (at all)** elle n'en a pas (du tout); **none came** pas un(e) seul(e) n'est venu(e) **2.** *adv* **none too hot** pas très chaud; **he's none the wiser (for it)** il n'est pas plus avancé ■ **nonetheless** *adv* néanmoins

**nonentity** [nɒ'nentətɪ] *(pl* -ies) *n* [person] nullité *f*

**nonexistent** [nɒnɪg'zɪstənt] *adj* inexistant

**non-fiction** [nɒn'fɪkʃən] *n* ouvrages *mpl* généraux

**nonsense** ['nɒnsəns] *n* bêtises *fpl*; **that's nonsense** c'est absurde

**non-smoker** [nɒn'sməʊkə(r)] *n* [person] non-fumeur, -euse *mf*; [compartment on train] compartiment *m* nonfumeurs

**non-stop** [nɒn'stɒp] **1.** *adj* sans arrêt; [train, flight] sans escale **2.** *adv* [work] sans arrêt; [fly] sans escale

**noob** [nuːb] *n Fam* bleu *m*, *Slang* nioub *m*

**noodles** ['nuːdəlz] *npl* nouilles *fpl*; [in soup] vermicelles *mpl*

**noon** [nuːn] *n* midi *m*

**no-one** ['nəʊwʌn] *pron* = **nobody**

**noose** [nuːs] *n* nœud *m* coulant

**No1** MESSAGING *written abbr of* **no one**

**nor** [nɔː(r)] *conj* ni; **neither you nor me** ni toi ni moi; **she neither drinks nor smokes** elle ne fume ni ne boit; **nor do I /can I /etc** (ni) moi non plus

**norm** [nɔːm] *n* norme *f*

**normal** ['nɔːməl] **1.** *adj* normal **2.** *n* **above / below normal** au-dessus / au-dessous de la normale ■ **normally** *adv* normalement

**north** [nɔːθ] **1.** *n* nord *m*; **(to the) north of** au nord de **2.** *adj* [coast] nord *inv*; [wind] du nord; **North America / Africa** Amérique *f* /Afrique *f* du Nord; **North American** [adj] nord-américain; [n] Nord-Américain, -e *mf* **3.** *adv* au nord; [travel] vers le nord ■ **northbound** *adj* [traffic] en direction du nord; *Br* [carriageway] nord *inv* ■ **north-east** *n* & *adj* nord-est *(m)* ■ **northerly** ['nɔːðəlɪ] *adj* [direction] du nord ■ **northern** ['nɔːðən] *adj* [coast] nord *inv*; [town] du nord; **Northern France** le nord de la France; **Northern Ireland** l'Irlande *f* du Nord ■ **northerner** ['nɔːðənə(r)] *n* habitant, -e *mf* du Nord ■ **northward(s)** *adj* & *adv* vers le nord ■ **north-west** *n* & *adj* nord-ouest *(m)*

**Norway** ['nɔːweɪ] *n* la Norvège ■ **Norwegian 1.** *adj* norvégien, -enne **2.** *n* [person] Norvégien, -enne *mf*; [language] norvégien *m*

**nose** [nəʊz] *n* nez *m*; **her nose is bleeding** elle saigne du nez ■ **nosebleed** *n* saignement *m* de nez

**nosey** ['nəʊzɪ] *(compar* -ier, *superl* -iest) *adj Fam* indiscret, -ète

**no-smoking** [nəʊ'sməʊkɪŋ] *adj* [carriage, area] non-fumeurs ■ **no-smoking area** *n* zone *f* non-fumeurs

**nostalgic** [nɒsˈtældʒɪk] *adj* nostalgique

**nostril** [ˈnɒstrəl] *n* [of person] narine *f*

**no-strings** *adj* a) *Fam* [contract, agreement] sans pièges b) [relationship] sans lendemain; **looking for no-strings hookups** cherche rencontres sans lendemain

**nosy** [ˈnəʊzɪ] *adj* = **nosey**

**not** [nɒt]

À l'oral, et à l'écrit dans un style familier, on utilise généralement **not** à la forme contractée lors qu'il suit un modal ou un auxiliaire (**don't go!** ; **she wasn't there** ; **he couldn't see me**).

*adv* a) (ne…) pas; **he's not there, he isn't there** il n'est pas là; **not yet** pas encore; **not… any more** ne… plus; **we don't go there any more** nous n'y allons plus; **he still works here, doesn't he?** — **not any more (he doesn't)** il travaille encore ici, n'est-ce pas? — non, plus maintenant; **not at all** pas du tout; [after 'thank you'] je vous en prie b) non; **I think/hope not** je pense /j'espère que non; **not guilty** non coupable; **isn't she? /don't you? / etc** non?

**notable** [ˈnəʊtəbəl] *adj* notable ▪ **notably** *adv* [noticeably] notablement; [particularly] notamment

**notch** [nɒtʃ] **1.** *n* [in wood] encoche *f*; [in belt, wheel] cran *m* **2.** *vt* **to notch up** [points] marquer; [victory] remporter

**note** [nəʊt] **1.** *n* [information, reminder & MUS] note *f*; *Br* [banknote] billet *m*; [letter] mot *m*; **to take (a) note of sth, to make a note of sth** prendre note de qch **2.** *vt* [notice] remarquer, noter; **to note sth down** [word, remark] noter qch ▪ **notebook** *n* a) carnet *m*; [for school] cahier *m* b) COMPUT ordinateur *m* portable compact ▪ **notepad** *n* bloc-notes *m* ▪ **notepaper** *n* papier *m* à lettres

**noted** [ˈnəʊtɪd] *adj* éminent

**nothing** [ˈnʌθɪŋ] **1.** *pron* (ne…) rien; **he knows nothing** il ne sait rien; **nothing at all** rien du tout; **nothing much** pas grand-chose; **I've got nothing to do**

**with it** je n'y suis pour rien; **for nothing** [in vain, free of charge] pour rien **2.** *adv* **to look nothing like sb** ne ressembler nullement à qn **3.** *n* **to come to nothing** être anéanti

**notice** [ˈnəʊtɪs] **1.** *n* [notification] avis *m*; [sign] pancarte *f*, écriteau *m*; [poster] affiche *f*; **to give sb (advance) notice** [inform] avertir qn (**of** de); **notice (to quit), notice of dismissal** congé *m*; **to give in** *or* **hand in one's notice** [resign] donner sa démission; **to take notice** faire attention (**of** à); **until further notice** jusqu'à nouvel ordre; **at short notice** au dernier moment **2.** *vt* remarquer (**that** que) ▪ **noticeboard** *n Br* tableau *m* d'affichage

**noticeable** [ˈnəʊtɪsəbəl] *adj* perceptible

**notify** [ˈnəʊtɪfaɪ] (*pt & pp* -ied) *vt* [inform] avertir (**sb of sth** qn de qch); [announce] notifier (**to** à) ▪ **notification** [-fɪˈkeɪʃən] *n* avis *m*

**notion** [ˈnəʊʃən] *n* notion *f*

**notorious** [nəʊˈtɔːrɪəs] *adj* tristement célèbre; [criminal] notoire

**nought** [nɔːt] *n Br* MATH zéro *m*

**noun** [naʊn] *n* nom *m*

**nourish** [ˈnʌrɪʃ] *vt* nourrir ▪ **nourishment** *n* nourriture *f*

**novel** [ˈnɒvəl] **1.** *n* roman *m* **2.** *adj* [new] nouveau (*f* nouvelle), original ▪ **novelist** *n* romancier, -ère *mf* ▪ **novelty** *n* nouveauté *f*

**November** [nəʊˈvembə(r)] *n* novembre *m*

**novice** [ˈnɒvɪs] *n* [beginner] débutant, -e *mf* (**at** en)

**now** [naʊ] **1.** *adv* maintenant; **for now** pour le moment; **from now on** désormais; **until now, up to now** jusqu'ici, jusqu'à maintenant; **now and then** de temps à autre; **she ought to be here by now** elle devrait déjà être ici **2.** *conj* **now (that)**… maintenant que…

**nowadays** [ˈnaʊədeɪz] *adv* de nos jours

**nowhere** [ˈnəʊweə(r)], *Am* **noplace** [ˈnəʊpleɪs] *adv* nulle part; **nowhere else** nulle part ailleurs; **nowhere near** loin de; **nowhere near enough** loin d'être assez; **we're getting nowhere** on n'avance pas

**nozzle** ['nɒzəl] *n* embout *m*; [of hose] jet *m*

**nuance** ['njuːɑːns] *n* nuance *f*

**nuclear** ['njuːklɪə(r)] *adj* nucléaire

**nucleus** ['njuːklɪəs] *(pl* **-clei** [-klɪaɪ]*) n* noyau *m (pl* -aux)

**nude** [njuːd] **1.** *adj* nu **2.** *n* nu *m*; **in the nude** tout nu (*f* toute nue)

**nudge** [nʌdʒ] **1.** *n* coup *m* de coude **2.** *vt* pousser du coude

**nudist** ['njuːdɪst] **1.** *n* nudiste *mf* **2.** *adj* [camp] de nudistes

**nufn** *(abbr of* **nothing)** MESSAGING r1

**nuisance** ['njuːsəns] *n* **to be a nuisance** être embêtant

**nuke** [njuːk] *Fam* **1.** *n* bombe *f* nucléaire **2.** *vt* a) [bomb] lâcher une bombe atomique sur b) [microwave] cuire au micro-ondes

**null** [nʌl] *adj* **null (and void)** nul (et non avenu) (*f* nulle (et non avenue))

**numb** [nʌm] *adj* [stiff - hand] engourdi

**number** ['nʌmbə(r)] **1.** *n* nombre *m*; [of page, house, telephone] numéro *m*; [song] chanson *f*; **a/any number of** un certain /grand nombre de; TEL **number portability** portage *m* ou conservation *f* du numéro; *Am* **number shop** ≃ kiosque *m* de loterie **2.** *vt* [assign number to] numéroter ■ **numberplate** *n Br* plaque *f* d'immatriculation

**numeral** ['njuːmərəl] *n* chiffre *m*

**numerical** [njuː'merɪkəl] *adj* numérique

**numerous** ['njuːmərəs] *adj* nombreux, -euse

**nun** [nʌn] *n* religieuse *f*

**nurse** [nɜːs] **1.** *n* infirmière *f*; [for children] nurse *f* **2.** *vt* [look after] soigner; [suckle] allaiter ■ **nursing** *n* [care] soins *mpl*; [job] profession *f* d'infirmière; *Br* **nursing home** [for old people] maison *f* de retraite

**nursery** ['nɜːsərɪ] *(pl* **-ies)** *n* [children's room] chambre *f* d'enfants; [for plants, trees] pépinière *f*; **(day) nursery** [school] garderie *f*; **nursery rhyme** comptine *f*; **nursery school** école *f* maternelle

**nut**[1] [nʌt] **1.** *n* [fruit] noix, noisette ou autre fruit sec de cette nature; **Brazil nut** noix *f* du Brésil **2.** *excl Am Fam* zut ! ■ **nutcrackers** *npl* casse-noix *m inv* ■ **nutshell** *n Fig* **in a nutshell** en un mot

**nut**[2] [nʌt] *n* [for bolt] écrou *m*

**nut**[3] [nʌt] *n Fam* [crazy person] cinglé, -e *mf* ■ **nutcase** *n Fam* cinglé, -e *mf*

**nutmeg** ['nʌtmeg] *n* muscade *f*

**nutritious** [njuː'trɪʃəs] *adj* nutritif, -ive ■ **nutrition** [-ʃən] *n* nutrition *f*

**nuts** [nʌts] **1.** *adj Fam* [crazy] cinglé **2.** *excl Am Fam* zut ! ■ **nutty** ['nʌtɪ] *(compar* -**ier,** *superl* -**iest)** *adj* a) [tasting of or containing nuts] aux noix *(aux amandes, aux noisettes, etc.)*; **a nutty flavour** un goût de noix *(de noisette, etc.)* b) *Fam* [crazy] dingue, timbré c) **as nutty as a fruitcake** complètement dingue

**nylon** ['naɪlɒn] *n* Nylon® *m*; **nylon shirt** chemise *f* en Nylon®

**NYPD** [ˌenwaɪpiː'diː] *(abbr of* **New York Police Department)** *n* police *f* new-yorkaise

# O

**O**, **o** [əʊ] *n* [letter] O, o *m inv*

**oaf** [əʊf] *n* balourd *m*

**oak** [əʊk] *n* [tree, wood] chêne *m*

**OAP** [əʊeɪˈpiː] *(abbr of old-age pensioner)* *n Br* retraité, -e *mf*

**oar** [ɔː(r)] *n* aviron *m*, rame *f*

**oasis** [əʊˈeɪsɪs] *(pl oases* [əʊˈeɪsiːz]*) n* oasis *f*

**oath** [əʊθ] *(pl -s* [əʊðz]*) n* [promise] serment *m* ; [profanity] juron *m*

**oats** [əʊts] *npl* avoine *f* ; (porridge) oats flocons *mpl* d'avoine

**obedient** [əˈbiːdɪənt] *adj* obéissant ■ **obedience** *n* obéissance *f* (**to** à)

**obese** [əʊˈbiːs] *adj* obèse

**obey** [əˈbeɪ] **1.** *vt* obéir à **2.** *vi* obéir

**obituary** [əˈbɪtʃʊərɪ] *(pl -ies) n* nécrologie *f*

**object¹** [ˈɒbʤɪkt] *n* [thing] objet *m* ; [aim] but *m*, objet ; [in grammar] complément *m* d'objet

**object²** [əbˈʤekt] **1.** *vt* to object that... objecter que... **2.** *vi* émettre une objection ; **to object to sth / to doing sth** ne pas être d'accord avec qch / pour faire qch

**objection** [əbˈʤekʃən] *n* objection *f*

**objective** [əbˈʤektɪv] **1.** *adj* [impartial] objectif, -ive **2.** *n* [aim, target] objectif *m*

**obligation** [ɒblɪˈgeɪʃən] *n* obligation *f* ; **to be under an obligation to do sth** être dans l'obligation de faire qch

**obligatory** [əˈblɪgətərɪ] *adj* obligatoire

**oblige** [əˈblaɪʤ] *vt* a) [compel] **to oblige sb to do sth** obliger qn à faire qch b) [help] rendre service à ; **to be obliged to sb** être reconnaissant à qn (**for** de) ■ **obliging** *adj* serviable

**oblique** [əˈbliːk] *adj* [line, angle] oblique ; [reference] indirect

**oblivion** [əˈblɪvɪən] *n* oubli *m* ■ **oblivious** *adj* inconscient (**to** *or* **of** de)

**oblong** [ˈɒblɒŋ] **1.** *adj* [rectangular] rectangulaire **2.** *n* rectangle *m*

**obnoxious** [əbˈnɒkʃəs] *adj* [person, behaviour] odieux, -euse

**oboe** [ˈəʊbəʊ] *n* hautbois *m*

**obscene** [əbˈsiːn] *adj* obscène ■ **obscenity** [əbˈsenətɪ] *(pl -ies) n* obscénité *f*

**obscure** [əbˈskjʊə(r)] **1.** *adj* obscur **2.** *vt* [hide] cacher ; [confuse] obscurcir

**observant** [əbˈzɜːvənt] *adj* observateur, -trice

**observation** [ɒbzəˈveɪʃən] *n* [observing, remark] observation *f* ; **under observation** [hospital patient] en observation

**observe** [əbˈzɜːv] *vt* observer ; **to observe the speed limit** respecter la limitation de vitesse ■ **observer** *n* observateur, -trice *mf*

**obsess** [əbˈses] *vt* obséder ■ **obsession** *n* obsession *f* ■ **obsessive** *adj* [idea] obsédant ; [person] obsessionnel, -elle ; **to be obsessive about sth** être obsédé par qch

**obsolete** [ˈɒbsəliːt] *adj* obsolète ; [design, model] dépassé

**obstacle** [ˈɒbstəkəl] *n* obstacle *m*

**obstinate** [ˈɒbstɪnət] *adj* obstiné

**obstruct** [əbˈstrʌkt] *vt* [block - road, pipe] obstruer ; [view] cacher ; [hinder] gêner ■ **obstruction** *n* [action, in sport, MED & POL] obstruction *f* ; [obstacle] obstacle *m* ; [in pipe] bouchon *m*

**obtain** [əbˈteɪn] *vt* obtenir

**obvious** [ˈɒbvɪəs] *adj* évident (**that** que) ■ **obviously** *adv* [of course] évidemment ; [conspicuously] manifestement

**occasion** [ə'keɪʒən] n [time, opportunity] occasion f; [event] événement m; **on the occasion of...** à l'occasion de...; **on several occasions** à plusieurs reprises

**occasional** [ə'keɪʒənəl] adj occasionnel, -elle; **she drinks the occasional whisky** elle boit un whisky de temps en temps ■ **occasionally** adv de temps en temps

**occupant** ['ɒkjʊpənt] n [of house, car] occupant, -e mf

**occupation** [ɒkjʊ'peɪʃən] n **a)** [pastime] occupation f; [profession] métier m **b)** [of house, land] occupation f

**occupier** ['ɒkjʊpaɪə(r)] n [of house] occupant, -e mf; [of country] occupant m

**occupy** ['ɒkjʊpaɪ] (pt & pp -ied) vt [space, time, attention] occuper; **to keep oneself occupied** s'occuper (**doing** à faire)

**occur** [ə'kɜː(r)] (pt & pp -rr-) vi [happen] avoir lieu; [of opportunity] se présenter; [be found] se trouver; **it occurs to me that...** il me vient à l'esprit que...

**occurrence** [ə'kʌrəns] n [event] événement m

**OCD** (abbr of obsessive-compulsive disorder) n PSYCH TOC m

**ocean** ['əʊʃən] n océan m

**o'clock** [ə'klɒk] adv (**it's**) **three o'clock** (il est) trois heures

**octagonal** [ɒk'tægənəl] adj octogonal

**October** [ɒk'təʊbə(r)] n octobre m

**octopus** ['ɒktəpəs] n pieuvre f

**odd** [ɒd] adj **a)** [strange] bizarre, curieux, -euse **b)** [number] impair **c)** [left over] **sixty odd** soixante et quelques; **an odd glove / sock** un gant / une chaussette dépareillé(e) **d)** [occasional] **I smoke the odd cigarette** je fume une cigarette de temps en temps; **odd jobs** petits travaux mpl ■ **oddly** adv bizarrement; **oddly enough, he was elected** chose curieuse, il a été élu

**odds** [ɒdz] n **a)** [in betting] cote f; [chances] chances fpl; Fam **it makes no odds** ça n'a pas d'importance **b)** [expressions] **to be at odds (with sb)** être en désaccord (avec qn); Fam **odds and ends** des bricoles fpl

**odious** ['əʊdɪəs] adj odieux, -euse

**odometer** [əʊ'dɒmɪtə(r)] n Am compteur m kilométrique

**odour**, Am **odor** ['əʊdə(r)] n odeur f

**of** [əv] (stressed [ɒv]) prep de, d'; **of the boy** du garçon; **of the boys** des garçons; **of wood / paper** de ou en bois / papier; **she has a lot of it / of them** elle en a beaucoup; **there are ten of us** nous sommes dix; **a friend of his** un ami à lui, un de ses amis; **that's nice of you** c'est gentil de ta part; **of no value / interest** sans valeur / intérêt; Br **the fifth of June** le cinq juin

**off** [ɒf] **1.** adj [light, gas, radio] éteint; [tap] fermé; [switched off at mains] coupé; [removed] enlevé; [cancelled] annulé; [not fit to eat or drink] mauvais; [milk, meat] tourné; **I'm off today** j'ai congé aujourd'hui
**2.** adv **to be off** [leave] partir; **a day off** [holiday] un jour de congé; **I have today off** j'ai congé aujourd'hui; **five percent off** une réduction de cinq pour cent; **on and off, off and on** [sometimes] de temps à autre
**3.** prep [from] de; [distant] éloigné de; **to fall off the wall / ladder** tomber du mur / de l'échelle; **to take sth off the table** prendre qch sur la table; **she's off her food** elle ne mange plus rien
■ **off-air** adj hors-antenne
■ **off-chance** n **on the off-chance** à tout hasard
■ **off-colour**, Am **off-color** adj Br [ill] patraque; [indecent] d'un goût douteux
■ **offhand 1.** adj désinvolte **2.** adv [immediately] au pied levé
■ **off-licence** n Br ≃ magasin m de vins et de spiritueux
■ **offline** adj & adv COMPUT hors ligne
■ **off-peak** adj [rate, price] heures creuses inv
■ **off-putting** adj Br Fam peu engageant

■ **off-road** *adj* [driving] hors route (*inv*); **off-road vehicle** véhicule *m* tout-terrain

■ **offside** *adj* **to be offside** [of footballer] être hors jeu

■ **offspring** *n* progéniture *f*

■ **off-the-peg**, *Am* **off-the-rack** *adj* [clothes] de confection

**offence**, *Am* **offense** [əˈfens] *n* [against the law] infraction *f*; [more serious] délit *m*; **to take offence** s'offenser (**at** de); **to give offence** offenser

**offend** [əˈfend] *vt* offenser; **to be offended** s'offenser (**at** de) ■ **offender** *n* [criminal] délinquant, -e *mf*

**offense** [əˈfens] *Am n* = **offence**

**offensive** [əˈfensɪv] **1.** *adj* choquant **2.** *n* offensive *f*; **to be on the offensive** être passé à l'offensive

**offer** [ˈɒfə(r)] **1.** *n* offre *f*; **to make sb an offer** faire une offre à qn; **on (special) offer** en promotion **2.** *vt* offrir; [explanation] donner; [apologies] présenter; **to offer sb sth, to offer sth to sb** offrir qch à qn; **to offer to do sth** proposer *ou* offrir de faire qch ■ **offering** *n* [gift] offrande *f*

**office** [ˈɒfɪs] *n* **a)** [room] bureau *m*; *Am* [of doctor] cabinet *m*; **office hours** heures *fpl* de bureau; **office worker** employé, -e *mf* de bureau **b)** [position] fonctions *fpl*; **to be in office** être au pouvoir

**officer** [ˈɒfɪsə(r)] *n* [in the army, navy] officier *m*; **(police) officer** agent *m* de police

**official** [əˈfɪʃəl] **1.** *adj* officiel, -elle **2.** *n* responsable *mf*; [civil servant] fonctionnaire *mf* ■ **officially** *adv* officiellement

**offset** [ˈɒfset, ɒfˈset] *(pt & pp* **offset**, *pres p* **offsetting**) *vt* [compensate for] compenser

**often** [ˈɒf(ə)n] *adv* souvent; **how often?** combien de fois ?; **every so often** de temps en temps

**oh** [əʊ] *excl* oh !, ah !; [in pain] aïe !; **oh yes!** mais oui !

**OIC** MESSAGING *written abbr of* **oh, I see**

**oil** [ɔɪl] **1.** *n* [for machine, cooking] huile *f*; [petroleum] pétrole *m*; [fuel] mazout *m* **2.** *adj* [industry] pétrolier, -ère; [painting, paint] à l'huile; **oil lamp** lampe *f* à pétrole; **oil slick** marée *f* noire; **oil tanker** [ship] pétrolier *m*, tanker *m*; [lorry] camion-citerne *m*; **oil well** puits *m* de pétrole **3.** *vt* [machine] huiler ■ **oilcan** *n* burette *f* ■ **oil-dependent** *adj* pétrodépendant ■ **oilfield** *n* gisement *m* de pétrole ■ **oily** *(compar* -ier, *superl* -iest) *adj* [hands, rag] graisseux, -euse; [skin, hair] gras (*f* grasse)

**ointment** [ˈɔɪntmənt] *n* pommade *f*

**OK**, **okay** [əʊˈkeɪ] **1.** *adj & adv* see **all right 2.** *(pt & pp* **OKed** *or* **okayed**, *pres p* **OKing** *or* **okaying)** *vt* donner le feu vert à

**old** [əʊld] **1.** *(compar* -er, *superl* -est) *adj* vieux (*f* vieille); [former] ancien, -enne; **how old is he?** quel âge a-t-il ?; **he's ten years old** il a dix ans; **he's older than me** il est plus âgé que moi; **the oldest son** le fils aîné; **to get** *or* **grow old(er)** vieillir; **old age** vieillesse *f*; **old man** vieillard *m*, vieil homme *m*; **old people** les personnes *fpl* âgées; **old people's home** maison *f* de retraite; *Fam* **any old how** n'importe comment **2.** *npl* **the old** les personnes *fpl* âgées

**old-fashioned** [əʊldˈfæʃ(ə)nd] *adj* [out-of-date] démodé; [person] vieux jeu *inv*; [traditional] d'autrefois

**old-timer** *n* **a)** [veteran] vieux routier *m*, vétéran *m* **b)** *Am* [old man] vieillard *m*

**olive** [ˈɒlɪv] *n* [fruit] olive *f*; **olive oil** huile *f* d'olive

**Olympic** [əˈlɪmpɪk] *adj* **the Olympic Games** les jeux *mpl* Olympiques

**omelette**, *Am* **omelet** [ˈɒmlɪt] *n* omelette *f*; **mushroom omelette** omelette aux champignons

**omen** [ˈəʊmən] *n* augure *m*

**OMG** MESSAGING *written abbr of* **oh, my god**

**ominous** [ˈɒmɪnəs] *adj* inquiétant; [event] de mauvais augure

**omit** [əʊˈmɪt] *(pt & pp* -tt-*)* *vt* omettre (**to do** de faire) ■ **omission** *n* omission *f*

**on** [ɒn] **1.** *prep* **a)** [expressing position] sur; **on page 4** à la page 4; **on the right/left** à droite/gauche
**b)** [about] sur
**c)** [expressing manner or means] **on the train/plane** dans le train/l'avion; **to be on** [a course] suivre; [project] travailler à; [salary] toucher; [team, committee] faire partie de; *Fam* **it's on me!** [I'll pay] c'est pour moi!
**d)** [with time] **on Monday** lundi; **on Mondays** le lundi; **on (the evening of) May 3rd** le 3 mai (au soir); **on my arrival** à mon arrivée
**e)** [+ present participle] en; **on learning that...** en apprenant que...
**2.** *adv* [ahead] en avant; [in progress] en cours; [lid, brake] mis; [light, radio] allumé; [gas, tap] ouvert; [machine] en marche; **she has her hat on** elle a mis son chapeau; **I've got something on** [I'm busy] je suis pris; **the strike is on** la grève aura lieu; **what's on?** [on TV] qu'est-ce qu'il y a à la télé?; [in theatre, cinema] qu'est-ce qu'on joue?; **he went on and on about it** il n'en finissait pas; *Fam* **that's just not on!** c'est inadmissible!; **I've been on to him** [on phone] je l'ai eu au bout du fil; **on and off** de temps en temps
▪ **on-air** *adj* & *adv* TV & RADIO à l'antenne
▪ **on-camera** *adj* & *adv* TV à l'image
▪ **ongoing** *adj* [project, discussion] en cours
▪ **on-trend** *adj* dans le vent

**once** [wʌns] **1.** *adv* [on one occasion] une fois; [formerly] autrefois; **once a month** une fois par mois; **once again, once more** encore une fois; **at once** [immediately] tout de suite; **all at once** [suddenly] tout à coup; [at the same time] à la fois **2.** *conj* une fois que
▪ **once-only** *adj* **a once-only offer** une offre unique

**one** [wʌn] **1.** *adj* **a)** un, une; **page one** la page un; **twenty-one** vingt et un
**b)** [only] seul
**c)** [same] le même (*f* la même); **in the one bus** dans le même bus

**2.** *pron* **a)** un, une; **do you want one?** en veux-tu (un)?; **one of them** l'un d'eux, l'une d'elles; **a big/small one** un grand/petit; **this one** celui-ci, celle-ci; **that one** celui-là, celle-là; **the one who/which...** celui/celle qui...; **another one** un(e) autre; **I for one** pour ma part; **one after another, one after the other** l'un après l'autre, les uns après les autres
**b)** [impersonal] on; **one knows** on sait; **it helps one** ça vous aide; **one's family** sa famille
▪ **one-armed bandit** *n Fam* machine *f* à sous
▪ **one-off, one-of-a-kind** *adj Fam* unique
▪ **one-sided** *adj* [biased] partial; [contest] inégal
▪ **one-size** *adj* taille unique (*inv*)
▪ **one-time** *adj* [former] ancien, -enne
▪ **one-to-one,** *Am* **one-on-one** *adj* [discussion] en tête à tête
▪ **one-way** *adj* [street] à sens unique; **one-way ticket** billet *m* simple

**1DAY** MESSAGING *written abbr of* **one day**

**one-parent family** *n* famille *f* monoparentale

**oneself** [wʌn'self] *pron* soi-même; [reflexive] se, s'; **to cut oneself** se couper

**onion** ['ʌnjən] *n* oignon *m*

**online** ['ɒnlaɪn] *adj* & *adv* COMPUT en ligne; **online banking** banque *f* en ligne; **online community** communauté *f* en ligne; **online shopping** achats *mpl* par *ou* sur Internet

**onlooker** ['ɒnlʊkə(r)] *n* spectateur, -trice *mf*

**only** ['əʊnlɪ] **1.** *adj* seul; **the only one** le seul, la seule; **an only son** un fils unique **2.** *adv* seulement, ne... que; **I only have ten** je n'en ai que dix, j'en ai dix seulement; **if only** si seulement; **I have only just seen it** je viens tout juste de le voir; **only he knows** lui seul le sait **3.** *conj Fam* [but] mais

**onset** ['ɒnset] *n* [of disease, winter] début *m*

**onto** ['ɒntuː] (*unstressed* ['ɒntə]) *prep* = **on to**

**onward(s)** ['ɒnwəd(z)] *adv* en avant; **from that day onward(s)** à partir de ce jour-là

**opaque** [əʊ'peɪk] *adj* opaque

**open** ['əʊpən] **1.** *adj* ouvert; [view, road] dégagé; [post, job] vacant; [airline ticket] open *inv*; **in the open air** au grand air; **open to** [criticism, attack] exposé à; [ideas, suggestions] ouvert à; **to leave sth open** [date] ne pas préciser qch **2.** *n* **(out) in the open** [outside] dehors; **to sleep (out) in the open** dormir à la belle étoile **3.** *vt* ouvrir; [arms, legs] écarter; **to open sth out** [paper, map] ouvrir qch; **to open sth up** [bag, shop] ouvrir qch **4.** *vi* [of flower, door, eyes] s'ouvrir; [of shop, office] ouvrir; [of play] débuter; **to open on to sth** [of window] donner sur qch; **to open out** [widen] s'élargir; **to open up** [of flower, person] s'ouvrir; [of shopkeeper] ouvrir ■ **open-air** *adj* [pool] en plein air ■ **open-minded** *adj* à l'esprit ouvert ■ **open-plan** *adj* [office] paysager, -ère ■ **open-toe, open-toed** [-təʊd] *adj* [shoe] ouvert ■ **open-top** *adj* décapotable

**opening** ['əʊpənɪŋ] **1.** *n* ouverture *f*; [job, trade outlet] débouché *m*; [opportunity] occasion *f* favorable; **late-night opening** [of shops] nocturne *f* **2.** *adj* [time, hours, speech] d'ouverture; **opening night** [of play, musical] première *f*; *Br* **opening time** [of pub] heure *f* d'ouverture

**openly** ['əʊpənlɪ] *adv* ouvertement

**opera** ['ɒprə] *n* opéra *m*

**operate** ['ɒpəreɪt] **1.** *vt* [machine] faire fonctionner; [service] assurer **2.** *vi* **a)** to **operate on sb (for sth)** [of surgeon] opérer qn (de qch) **b)** [of machine] fonctionner; [of company] opérer ■ **operating** *adj Br* **operating theatre,** *Am* **operating room** salle *f* d'opération; COMPUT **operating system** système *m* d'exploitation

**operation** [ɒpə'reɪʃən] *n* MED, MIL & MATH opération *f*; [of machine] fonctionnement *m*; **in operation** [machine] en service; [plan] en vigueur; **to have an operation** se faire opérer

**operator** ['ɒpəreɪtə(r)] *n* [on phone, machine] opérateur, -trice *mf*

**opinion** [ə'pɪnjən] *n* opinion *f*; **in my opinion** à mon avis

**opponent** [ə'pəʊnənt] *n* adversaire *mf*

**opportune** ['ɒpətjuːn] *adj* opportun

**opportunity** [ɒpə'tjuːnətɪ] (*pl* **-ies**) *n* occasion *f* (**to do** *or* **of doing** de faire); **opportunities** [prospects] perspectives *fpl*; **to take the opportunity to do sth** profiter de l'occasion pour faire qch

**oppose** [ə'pəʊz] *vt* s'opposer à ■ **opposed** *adj* opposé (**to** à); **as opposed to...** par opposition à... ■ **opposing** *adj* [viewpoints] opposé; [team] adverse

**opposite** ['ɒpəzɪt] **1.** *adj* [side] opposé; [house, page] d'en face; **in the opposite direction** en sens inverse **2.** *adv* en face; **the house opposite** la maison d'en face **3.** *prep* **opposite (to)** en face de **4.** *n* **the opposite** le contraire

**opposition** [ɒpə'zɪʃən] *n* opposition *f* (**to** à); **the opposition** [rival camp] l'adversaire *m*; [in business] la concurrence

**oppress** [ə'pres] *vt* [treat cruelly] opprimer ■ **oppression** *n* oppression *f* ■ **oppressive** *adj* [heat] accablant, étouffant; [ruler, regime] oppressif, -ive

**opt** [ɒpt] *vi* **to opt for sth** opter pour qch; **to opt to do sth** choisir de faire qch; **to opt out** se désengager (**of** de)

**optical** ['ɒptɪkəl] *adj* optique; [instrument, illusion] d'optique

**optician** [ɒp'tɪʃən] *n* [dispensing] opticien, -enne *mf*

**optimism** ['ɒptɪmɪzəm] *n* optimisme *m* ■ **optimistic** *adj* optimiste (**about** quant à)

**optimum** ['ɒptɪməm] *adj* & *n* optimum (*m*)

**option** ['ɒpʃən] n [choice] choix m ;
[school subject] matière f à option ;
**she has no option** elle n'a pas le choix
■ **optional** adj facultatif, -ive

**or** [ɔː(r)] conj ou ; **he doesn't drink or
smoke** il ne boit ni ne fume ; **ten or so**
environ dix

**oral** ['ɔːrəl] **1.** adj oral **2.** n [exam] oral m

**orange** ['ɒrɪndʒ] **1.** n [fruit] orange f ;
**orange juice** jus m d'orange **2.** adj &
n [colour] orange (m) inv

**orbit** ['ɔːbɪt] **1.** n [of planet] orbite f **2.** vt
être en orbite autour de

**orchard** ['ɔːtʃəd] n verger m

**orchestra** ['ɔːkɪstrə] n orchestre m ; Am
**the orchestra** [in theatre] l'orchestre m

**orchid** ['ɔːkɪd] n orchidée f

**ordeal** [ɔːˈdiːl] n épreuve f

**order** ['ɔːdə(r)] **1.** n [instruction, arrangement & REL] ordre m ; [purchase] com-
mande f ; **in order** [passport] en règle ; **in
order of age** par ordre d'âge ; **in order
to do sth** afin de faire qch ; **in order
that...** afin que... (+ subjunctive) ; **in the
order of, on the order of** environ, de
l'ordre de ; **out of order** [machine] en
panne ; [telephone] en dérangement ;
**order form** bon m de commande **2.** vt
[meal, goods] commander ; [taxi] appeler ; **to order sb to do sth** ordonner à qn
de faire qch **3.** vi [in café] commander
■ **order about**, **order around** Br
vt sep commander

**orderly** ['ɔːdəlɪ] adj [room, life] ordonné ;
[crowd] discipliné

**ordinary** ['ɔːdənrɪ] adj ordinaire ; **it's
out of the ordinary** ça sort de l'ordinaire ; **she was just an ordinary
tourist** c'était une touriste comme
une autre

**organ** ['ɔːgən] n a) [part of body] organe m b) [musical instrument] orgue m

**organic** [ɔːˈgænɪk] adj organique ; [vege-
tables, farming] biologique

**organism** ['ɔːgənɪzəm] n organisme m

**organization** [ɔːgənaɪˈzeɪʃən] n organisation f

**organize** ['ɔːgənaɪz] vt organiser
■ **organizer** n [person] organisateur, -trice mf ; **(personal) organizer**
[diary] agenda m

**orgasm** ['ɔːgæzəm] n orgasme m

**oriental** [ɔːrɪˈentəl] adj oriental

**orientate** ['ɔːrɪənteɪt], Am **orient**
['ɔːrɪənt] vt orienter

**origin** ['ɒrɪdʒɪn] n origine f

**original** [əˈrɪdʒɪnəl] **1.** adj [novel,
innovative] original ; [first] d'origine
**2.** n [document, painting] original m
■ **originally** adv [at first] à l'origine

**originate** [əˈrɪdʒɪneɪt] **1.** vt être à l'origine de **2.** vi [begin] prendre naissance
(**in** dans) ; **to originate from** [of idea]
émaner de

**ornament** ['ɔːnəmənt] n ornement m
■ **ornamental** [-ˈmentəl] adj ornemental

**ornate** [ɔːˈneɪt] adj très orné

**orphan** ['ɔːfən] n orphelin, -e mf

**orthodox** ['ɔːθədɒks] adj orthodoxe

**Oscar** ['ɒskə(r)] n CIN oscar m

**ostentatious** [ɒstenˈteɪʃəs] adj prétentieux, -euse

**ostrich** ['ɒstrɪtʃ] n autruche f

**other** ['ʌðə(r)] **1.** adj autre ; **other doctors** d'autres médecins ; **the other one**
l'autre mf **2.** pron **the other** l'autre mf ;
**(some) others** d'autres ; **none other
than, no other than** nul autre que
**3.** adv **other than** autrement que
■ **otherwise** adv & conj autrement

**ouch** [aʊtʃ] excl aïe !

**ought** [ɔːt]

La forme négative **ought not** s'écrit
**oughtn't** en forme contractée.

v aux **a)** [expressing obligation, desir-
ability] **you ought to leave** tu devrais
partir ; **I ought to have done it** j'aurais
dû le faire **b)** [expressing probability] **it
ought to be ready** ça devrait être prêt

**ounce** [aʊns] n [unit of weight] once f
(28,35 g)

**our** [aʊə(r)] poss adj notre, pl nos

**ours** [aʊəz] *poss pron* le nôtre, la nôtre, *pl* les nôtres; **this book is ours** ce livre est à nous *ou* est le nôtre; **a friend of ours** un de nos amis

**ourselves** [aʊə'selvz] *pron* nous-mêmes; [reflexive and after prep] nous; **we wash ourselves** nous nous lavons

**oust** [aʊst] *vt* évincer (**from** de)

**out** [aʊt] **1.** *adv* [outside] dehors; [not at home] sorti; [light, fire] éteint; [flower] ouvert; [book] publié; **to have a day out** sortir pour la journée; **the sun's out** il fait soleil; **the tide's out** la marée est basse; **you're out** [wrong] tu t'es trompé; [in game] tu es éliminé (**of** de); **I was $10 out** [under] il me manquait 10 dollars; **before the week is out** avant la fin de la semaine; **the journey out** l'aller *m*; **out here** ici; **out there** là-bas **2.** *prep* **out of** [outside] hors de; **out of line** [remark, behaviour] déplacé; **to be out of the country** être à l'étranger; **she's out of town** elle n'est pas en ville; **to look/jump out of the window** regarder/sauter par la fenêtre; **to drink/take/copy sth out of sth** boire/prendre/copier qch dans qch; **made out of wood** fait en bois; **out of pity/love** par pitié/amour; **four out of five** quatre sur cinq

■ **out-of-date** *adj* [expired] périmé; [old-fashioned] démodé

■ **out-of-doors** *Br* **1.** *adv* = **outdoors** **2.** *adj* = **outdoor**

■ **out-of-hand** *adj Am Fam* [extraordinary] géant

■ **out-of-sync** *adj* désynchronisé

■ **out-of-the-box** [] *adj* dès sa sortie de l'emballage

■ **out-of-the-way** *adj* [place] isolé

■ **out-of-town** *adj* [shopping centre, retail park] situé à la périphérie d'une ville

**outbox** [aʊtbɒks] *n* [for e-mail] boîte *f* d'envoi

**outbreak** ['aʊtbreɪk] *n* [of war, epidemic] début *m*; [of violence] flambée *f*; [of hostilities] déclenchement *m*

**outburst** ['aʊtbɜːst] *n* [of anger, joy] explosion *f*; [of violence] flambée *f*

**outcast** ['aʊtkɑːst] *n* **(social) outcast** paria *m*

**outcome** ['aʊtkʌm] *n* résultat *m*, issue *f*

**outcry** ['aʊtkraɪ] *(pl* **-ies***) n* tollé *m*

**outdated** [aʊt'deɪtɪd] *adj* démodé

**outdo** [aʊt'duː] *(pt* **-did***, pp* **-done***) vt* surpasser (**in** en)

**outdoor** ['aʊtdɔː(r)] *adj* [pool, market] découvert ■ **outdoors** *adv* dehors

**outer** ['aʊtə(r)] *adj* extérieur; **outer space** l'espace *m* intersidéral

**outfit** ['aʊtfɪt] *n* [clothes] ensemble *m*; **sports/ski outfit** tenue *f* de sport/de ski

**outgoing** ['aʊtgəʊɪŋ] *adj* **a)** [minister] sortant; [mail] en partance; **outgoing calls** [on phone] appels *mpl* vers l'extérieur **b)** [sociable] liant ■ **outgoings** *npl* [expenses] dépenses *fpl*

**outgrow** [aʊt'grəʊ] *(pt* **-grew***, pp* **-grown***) vt* [habit] passer l'âge de; **she's outgrown her jacket** sa veste est devenue trop petite pour elle

**outing** ['aʊtɪŋ] *n* [excursion] sortie *f*

**outlast** [aʊt'lɑːst] *vt* [object] durer plus longtemps que; [person] survivre à

**outlaw** ['aʊtlɔː] **1.** *n* hors-la-loi *m inv* **2.** *vt* [ban] proscrire

**outlay** ['aʊtleɪ] *n* [expense] dépenses *fpl*

**outlet** ['aʊtlet] *n* [shop] point *m* de vente; [market for goods] débouché *m*; [for liquid] sortie *f*; [for feelings, energy] exutoire *m*

**outline** ['aʊtlaɪn] **1.** *n* [shape] contour *m*; [of play, novel] résumé *m*; **rough outline** [of article, plan] esquisse *f*; **the broad or general or main outline** [of plan, policy] les grandes lignes **2.** *vt* [plan, situation] esquisser

**outlive** [aʊt'lɪv] *vt* survivre à

**outlook** ['aʊtlʊk] *n* [for future] perspectives *fpl*; [point of view] façon *f* de voir les choses; [of weather] prévisions *fpl*

**outmoded** [aʊt'məʊdɪd] *adj* démodé

**outnumber** [aʊt'nʌmbə(r)] *vt* l'emporter en nombre sur

**outpatient** ['aʊtpeɪʃənt] *n* Br malade *mf* en consultation externe

**output** ['aʊtpʊt] *n* [of goods] production *f*; COMPUT sortie

**outrage** ['aʊtreɪdʒ] **1.** *n* [scandal] scandale *m*; [anger] indignation *f* (**at** face à); [crime] atrocité *f* **2.** *vt* [make indignant] scandaliser

**outrageous** [aʊt'reɪdʒəs] *adj* [shocking] scandaleux, -euse; [atrocious] atroce

**outright 1.** [aʊt'raɪt] *adv* [refuse] catégoriquement; [be killed] sur le coup **2.** ['aʊtraɪt] *adj* [failure] total; [refusal] catégorique; [winner] incontesté

**outset** ['aʊtset] *n* **at the outset** au début; **from the outset** dès le départ

**outside 1.** [aʊt'saɪd] *adv* dehors, à l'extérieur; **to go outside** sortir **2.** [aʊt'saɪd] *prep* à l'extérieur de, en dehors de; [in front of] devant; [apart from] en dehors de **3.** [aʊt'saɪd] *n* extérieur *m* **4.** ['aʊtsaɪd] *adj* extérieur; **the outside lane** [on road] Br la voie de droite; Am la voie de gauche; **an outside chance** une petite chance

**outsider** [aʊt'saɪdə(r)] *n* [stranger] étranger, -ère *mf*; [horse in race] outsider *m*

**outsize(d)** ['aʊtsaɪz(d)] *adj* **a)** [bigger than usual] énorme, colossal **b)** [clothes] grande taille (*inv*)

**outskirts** ['aʊtskɜːts] *npl* banlieue *f*

**outspoken** [aʊt'spəʊkən] *adj* [frank] franc (*f* franche)

**outstanding** [aʊt'stændɪŋ] *adj* exceptionnel, -elle; [problem, business] en suspens; [debt] impayé

**outstay** [aʊt'steɪ] *vt* **to outstay one's welcome** abuser de l'hospitalité de son hôte

**outstretched** [aʊt'stretʃt] *adj* [arm] tendu

**outward** ['aʊtwəd] *adj* [sign, appearance] extérieur; **outward journey** *or* **trip** aller *m* ■ **outward(s)** *adv* vers l'extérieur

**oval** ['əʊvəl] *adj* & *n* ovale (*m*)

**ovary** ['əʊvərɪ] (*pl* **-ies**) *n* ANAT ovaire *m*

**ovation** [əʊ'veɪʃən] *n* ovation *f*; **to give sb a standing ovation** se lever pour applaudir qn

**oven** ['ʌvən] *n* four *m*; **oven chips, oven fries** frites *fpl* au four

**over** ['əʊvə(r)] **1.** *prep* [on] sur; [above] au-dessus de; [on the other side of] par-dessus; **the bridge over the river** le pont qui traverse le fleuve; **to jump / look over sth** sauter / regarder par-dessus qch; **over it** [on] dessus; [above] au-dessus; **to fight over sth** se battre pour qch; **over the phone** au téléphone; Br **over the holidays** pendant les vacances; **over ten days** [more than] plus de dix jours; **men over sixty** les hommes de plus de soixante ans; **over and above** en plus de; **he's over his flu** il est remis de sa grippe
**2.** *adv* [above] par-dessus; **over here** ici; **over there** là-bas; **he's over in Italy** il est en Italie; **she's over from Paris** elle est venue de Paris; **to ask sb over** inviter qn; **to be (all) over** être terminé; **to start all over (again)** recommencer à zéro; **a kilo or over** [more] un kilo ou plus; **I have ten over** [left] il m'en reste dix; **over and over (again)** [often] à plusieurs reprises; **children of five and over** les enfants de cinq ans et plus

**overall 1.** ['əʊvərɔːl] *adj* [measurement, length] total; [result] global **2.** [əʊvər'ɔːl] *adv* dans l'ensemble **3.** ['əʊvərɔːl] *n* [protective coat] blouse *f*; Am [boiler suit] bleu *m* de travail ■ **overalls** *npl* Br [boiler suit] bleu *m* de travail; Am [dungarees] salopette *f*

**overbearing** [əʊvə'beərɪŋ] *adj* autoritaire

**overboard** ['əʊvəbɔːd] *adv* par-dessus bord

**overcast** [əʊvə'kɑːst] *adj* nuageux, -euse

**overcharge** [əʊvə'tʃɑːdʒ] *vt* **to overcharge sb for sth** faire payer qch trop cher à qn

**overcoat** ['əʊvəkəʊt] *n* pardessus *m*

**overcome** [əʊvə'kʌm] (*pt* **-came**, *pp* **-come**) *vt* [problem, disgust] surmonter ; [shyness, fear, enemy] vaincre ; **to be overcome by grief** être accablé de chagrin

**overcook** [əʊvə'kʊk] *vt* faire cuire trop

**overcrowded** [əʊvə'kraʊdɪd] *adj* [house, country] surpeuplé ; [bus, train] bondé

**overdo** [əʊvə'duː] *(pt* **-did***, pp* **-done)** *vt* exagérer ; [overcook] faire cuire trop ; **to overdo it** se surmener

**overdose** ['əʊvədəʊs] *n* overdose *f*

**overdraft** ['əʊvədrɑːft] *n* FIN découvert *m*

**overdrawn** [əʊvə'drɔːn] *adj* FIN [account] à découvert

**overdue** [əʊvə'djuː] *adj* [train, bus] en retard ; [bill] impayé ; [book] qui n'a pas été rendu

**overestimate** [əʊvər'estɪmeɪt] *vt* surestimer

**overexcited** [əʊvərɪk'saɪtɪd] *adj* surexcité

**overfish** [ˌəʊvə'fɪʃ] *vt* [fishing ground] surexploiter ▪ **overfishing** [ˌəʊvə(r)-'fɪʃɪŋ] *n* surpêche *f*

**overflow 1.** ['əʊvəfləʊ] *n* [outlet] trop-plein *m* **2.** [əʊvə'fləʊ] *vi* [of river, bath] déborder ; **to be overflowing with sth** [of town, shop, house] regorger de qch

**overgrown** [əʊvə'grəʊn] *adj* [garden, path] envahi par la végétation

**overhaul 1.** ['əʊvəhɔːl] *n* révision *f* **2.** [əʊvə'hɔːl] *vt* [vehicle, schedule, text] réviser

**overhead 1.** [əʊvə'hed] *adv* au-dessus **2.** ['əʊvəhed] *adj* [cable] aérien, -enne ; **overhead light** plafonnier *m* **3.** ['əʊvəhed] *n* Am = **overheads** ▪ **overheads** *npl* Br [expenses] frais *mpl* généraux

**overhear** [əʊvə'hɪə(r)] *(pt & pp* **-heard)** *vt* [conversation] surprendre ; [person] entendre

**overheat** [əʊvə'hiːt] *vi* [of engine] chauffer

**overjoyed** [əʊvə'dʒɔɪd] *adj* fou *(f* folle) de joie

**overland** ['əʊvəlænd] *adj & adv* par voie de terre

**overlap** [əʊvə'læp] **1.** *(pt & pp* **-pp-)** *vt* chevaucher **2.** *vi* se chevaucher

**overleaf** [əʊvə'liːf] *adv* au verso

**overload** [əʊvə'ləʊd] *vt* surcharger

**overlook** [əʊvə'lʊk] *vt* **a)** [not notice] ne pas remarquer ; [forget] oublier ; [disregard] fermer les yeux sur **b)** [of window, house] donner sur

**overnight 1.** [əʊvə'naɪt] *adv* [during the night] pendant la nuit ; *Fig* [suddenly] du jour au lendemain ; **to stay overnight** passer la nuit **2.** ['əʊvənaɪt] *adj* [train, flight] de nuit ; [stay] d'une nuit ; **overnight bag** (petit) sac *m* de voyage

**overpopulated** [əʊvə'pɒpjuleɪtɪd] *adj* surpeuplé

**overpower** [əʊvə'paʊə(r)] *vt* maîtriser ▪ **overpowering** *adj* [heat, smell] suffocant

**overpriced** [əʊvə'praɪst] *adj* trop cher *(f* trop chère)

**overrated** [əʊvə'reɪtɪd] *adj* surfait

**overreach** [əʊvə'riːtʃ] *vt* **to overreach oneself** trop présumer de ses forces

**overreact** [əʊvərɪ'ækt] *vi* réagir excessivement

**override** [əʊvə'raɪd] *(pt* **-rode***, pp* **-ridden)** *vt* [be more important than] l'emporter sur ; [invalidate] annuler ; [take no notice of] passer outre à ▪ **overriding** *adj* [importance] capital ; [factor] prédominant

**overrule** [əʊvə'ruːl] *vt* [decision] annuler ; [objection] rejeter

**overrun** [əʊvə'rʌn] *(pt* **-ran***, pp* **-run***, pres p* **-running)** *vt* [invade] envahir ; [go beyond] dépasser

**overseas 1.** ['əʊvəsiːz] *adj* d'outre-mer ; [trade] extérieur **2.** [əʊvə'siːz] *adv* à l'étranger

**oversee** [əʊvə'siː] *(pt* **-saw***, pp* **-seen)** *vt* [work] superviser

**overshadow** [əʊvə'ʃædəʊ] *vt* [make less important] éclipser ; [make gloomy] assombrir

**oversight** ['əʊvəsaɪt] *n* oubli *m*, omission *f*

**oversize(d)** [,əʊvə'saɪz(d)] *adj* [very big] énorme, démesuré

**oversleep** [əʊvə'sliːp] *(pt & pp -slept)* *vi* ne pas se réveiller à temps

**overspend** [əʊvə'spend] *(pt & pp -spent)* *vi* dépenser trop

**overstate** [əʊvə'steɪt] *vt* exagérer

**overstay** [əʊvə'steɪ] *vt* **to overstay one's welcome** abuser de l'hospitalité de son hôte

**overstep** [əʊvə'step] *(pt & pp -pp-)* *vt* outrepasser; *Fig* **to overstep the mark** dépasser les bornes

**overstretched** [əʊvə'stretʃt] *adj* [person] débordé; [budget] extrêmement serré

**overt** ['əʊvɜːt] *adj* manifeste

**overtake** [əʊvə'teɪk] *(pt -took, pp -taken)* **1.** *vt* dépasser **2.** *vi* [in vehicle] doubler, dépasser

**overthrow** [əʊvə'θrəʊ] *(pt -threw, pp -thrown)* *vt* renverser

**overtime** ['əʊvətaɪm] **1.** *n* heures *fpl* supplémentaires **2.** *adv* **to work overtime** faire des heures supplémentaires

**overturn** [əʊvə'tɜːn] **1.** *vt* [chair, table, car] renverser; [boat] faire chavirer; *Fig* [decision] annuler **2.** *vi* [of car] capoter; [of boat] chavirer

**overweight** [əʊvə'weɪt] *adj* trop gros (*f* trop grosse)

**overwhelm** [əʊvə'welm] *vt* [of feelings, heat] accabler; [enemy, opponent] écraser; [amaze] bouleverser ■ **overwhelmed** *adj* overwhelmed

with [work, offers] submergé de; **overwhelmed by** [kindness, gift] vivement touché par ■ **overwhelming** *adj* [heat, grief] accablant; [majority, defeat] écrasant; [desire] irrésistible

**overwork** [əʊvə'wɜːk] **1.** *n* surmenage *m* **2.** *vt* [person] surcharger de travail **3.** *vi* se surmener

**owe** [əʊ] *vt* devoir; **to owe sb sth, to owe sth to sb** devoir qch à qn ■ **owing 1.** *adj* **the money owing to me** l'argent que l'on me doit **2.** *prep* **owing to** à cause de

**owl** [aʊl] *n* hibou *m (pl* -oux)

**own** [əʊn] **1.** *adj* propre **2.** *pron* my own le mien, la mienne; **a house of his own** sa propre maison, sa maison à lui; **to do sth on one's own** faire qch tout seul; **to be (all) on one's own** être tout seul; **to get one's own back (on sb)** se venger (de qn) **3.** *vt* [possess] posséder; **who owns this ball?** à qui appartient cette balle? **4.** *vi* **to own up (to sth)** [confess] avouer (qch)

**ownage** ['əʊnɪdʒ] *n Fam* dérouillée *f*; **ownage!** ownage!, pownage!, je t'ai eu!

**owner** ['əʊnə(r)] *n* propriétaire *mf* ■ **ownership** *n* possession *f*

**ox** [ɒks] *(pl* **oxen** ['ɒksən]) *n* bœuf *m*

**oxygen** ['ɒksɪdʒən] *n* oxygène *m*; **oxygen mask** masque *m* à oxygène

**oyster** ['ɔɪstə(r)] *n* huître *f*

**oz** *(abbr of ounce)* once *f*

**ozone** ['əʊzəʊn] *n* CHEM ozone *m*; **ozone layer** couche *f* d'ozone

# P

**P, p¹** [piː] *n* [letter] P, p *m inv*

**p²** [piː] *(abbr of* **penny, pence)** *Br* penny *m* /pence *mpl*

**pa** [pɑː] *n Fam* [father] papa *m*

**pace** [peɪs] **1.** *n* [speed] allure *f*; [step, measure] pas *m*; **to keep pace with sb** [follow] suivre qn; [in quality of work] se maintenir à la hauteur de qn **2.** *vi* **to pace up and down** faire les cent pas

**pacemaker** [ˈpeɪsmeɪkə(r)] *n* [for heart] stimulateur *m* cardiaque

**Pacific** [pəˈsɪfɪk] *adj* **the Pacific (Ocean)** le Pacifique, l'océan *m* Pacifique

**pacifier** [ˈpæsɪfaɪə(r)] *n Am* [of baby] tétine *f*

**pacifist** [ˈpæsɪfɪst] *n* pacifiste *mf*

**pacify** [ˈpæsɪfaɪ] *(pt & pp* **-ied)** *vt* [crowd, person] calmer

**pack** [pæk] **1.** *n* **a)** [of cigarettes, washing powder] paquet *m*; [of beer] pack *m*; [of cards] jeu *m*; [of hounds, wolves] meute *f*; **a pack of lies** un tissu de mensonges **b)** [rucksack] sac *m* à dos **2.** *vt* [fill] remplir (**with** de); [object into box, suitcase] mettre; [make into package] empaqueter; [crush, compress] tasser; **to pack one's bags** faire ses valises **3.** *vi* [fill one's bags] faire sa valise /ses valises ■ **pack in 1.** *vi Br Fam* tomber en panne **2.** *vt sep Br Fam* [stop] arrêter; [give up] laisser tomber ■ **pack into 1.** *vt sep* [cram] entasser dans; [put] mettre dans **2.** *vt insep* [crowd into] s'entasser dans ■ **pack off** *vt sep Fam* [person] expédier ■ **pack up 1.** *vt sep* [put into box] emballer; *Fam* [give up] laisser tomber **2.** *vi Fam* [of machine, vehicle] tomber en panne

**package** [ˈpækɪdʒ] **1.** *n* paquet *m*; [contract] contrat *m* global; COMPUT progiciel *m*; *Br* **package deal** *or* **holiday** forfait *m (comprenant au moins transport et logement)* **2.** *vt* emballer ■ **packaging** *n* [material, action] emballage *m*

**packed** [pækt] *adj* [bus, room] bondé

**packet** [ˈpækɪt] *n* paquet *m*; *Fam* **to cost a packet** coûter les yeux de la tête

**packing** [ˈpækɪŋ] *n* [material, action] emballage *m*; **to do one's packing** faire sa valise /ses valises

**pact** [pækt] *n* pacte *m*

**pad** [pæd] **1.** *n* [of cotton wool] tampon *m*; [for writing] bloc *m*; **ink(ing) pad** tampon encreur **2.** *(pt & pp* **-dd-)** *vt* **to pad out** [speech, essay] étoffer ■ **padded** *adj* [jacket] matelassé ■ **padding** *n* [material] rembourrage *m*; [in speech, essay] remplissage *m*

**paddle** [ˈpædəl] **1.** *n* [for canoe] pagaie *f*; **to have a paddle** patauger **2.** *vt* **to paddle a canoe** pagayer **3.** *vi* [walk in water] patauger

**paddling** [ˈpædlɪŋ] *n Br* **paddling pool** [inflatable] piscine *f* gonflable; [in park] pataugeoire *f*

**padlock** [ˈpædlɒk] **1.** *n* cadenas *m* **2.** *vt* cadenasser

**paediatrician**, *Am* **pediatrician** [piːdɪəˈtrɪʃən] *n* pédiatre *mf*

**page¹** [peɪdʒ] *n* [of book] page *f*; **on page 6** à la page 6 ■ **page-turner** *n Fam* livre *m* captivant

**page²** [peɪdʒ] **1.** *n* **page (boy)** [in hotel] groom *m* **2.** *vt* **to page sb** faire appeler qn; [by electronic device] biper qn ■ **pager** *n* récepteur *m* d'appel

**paid** [peɪd] **1.** *pp of* **pay 2.** *adj* [person, work] rémunéré

**pain** [peɪn] *n* [physical] douleur *f*; [emotional] peine *f*; **to have a pain in one's arm** avoir une douleur au bras; **to go to** *or* **take (great) pains to do sth** se donner du mal pour faire qch ; *Fam* **to be a pain (in the neck)** être casse-pieds ■ **painful** *adj* [physically] douloureux, -euse ; [emotionally] pénible ■ **painless** *adj* [not painful] indolore

**painkiller** ['peɪnkɪlə(r)] *n* calmant *m*

**painstaking** ['peɪnzteɪkɪŋ] *adj* minutieux, -euse

**paint** [peɪnt] **1.** *n* peinture *f* **2.** *vt* peindre ; **to paint sth blue** peindre qch en bleu **3.** *vi* peindre ■ **painter** *n* peintre *m* ; *Br* **painter and decorator**, *Am* **(house) painter** peintre-tapissier *m* ■ **painting** *n* [activity] la peinture ; [picture] tableau *m*, peinture *f*

**paintball** ['peɪntbɔːl] *n* paintball *m*

**paintbrush** ['peɪntbrʌʃ] *n* pinceau *m*

**paintwork** ['peɪntwɜːk] *n* [of building, vehicle] peinture *f*

**pair** [peə(r)] *n* paire *f* ; **a pair of shorts / trousers** un short / pantalon

**pajamas** [pə'dʒɑːməz] *Am npl* = **pyjamas**

**Pakistan** [pɑːkɪ'stɑːn] *n* le Pakistan ■ **Pakistani 1.** *adj* pakistanais **2.** *n* Pakistanais, -e *mf*

**pal** [pæl] *n Fam* copain *m*, copine *f*

**palace** ['pælɪs] *n* palais *m*

**pale** [peɪl] **1.** *(compar* -er*, superl* -est*) adj* pâle **2.** *vi* pâlir ■ **pale-skinned** *adj* à la peau claire

**Palestine** ['pæləstaɪn] *n* la Palestine ■ **Palestinian** [-'stɪnɪən] **1.** *adj* palestinien, -enne **2.** *n* Palestinien, -enne *mf*

**palette** ['pælɪt] *n* [of artist] palette *f*

**palm**[1] [pɑːm] *n* [of hand] paume *f*

**palm**[2] [pɑːm] *n* **palm (tree)** palmier *m*

**palmtop** *n* COMPUT ordinateur *m* de poche

**pamper** ['pæmpə(r)] *vt* dorloter

**pamphlet** ['pæmflɪt] *n* brochure *f*

**pan** [pæn] *n* [saucepan] casserole *f* ; [for frying] poêle *f*

**Panama** ['pænəmɑː] *n* **the Panama Canal** le canal de Panama

**pancake** ['pænkeɪk] *n* crêpe *f* ; **Pancake Day** mardi *m* gras

**panda** ['pændə] *n* panda *m*

**pandemonium** [pændɪ'məʊnɪəm] *n* [confusion] chaos *m* ; [uproar] vacarme *m*

**pander** ['pændə(r)] *vi* **to pander to sb / sth** flatter qn /qch

**pane** [peɪn] *n* vitre *f*

**panel** ['pænəl] *n* **a)** [of door] panneau *m* ; **(instrument) panel** [in aircraft, vehicle] tableau *m* de bord **b)** [of judges] jury *m* ; [of experts] comité *m* ; [of TV or radio guests] invités *mpl*

**panic** ['pænɪk] **1.** *n* panique *f* **2.** *(pt & pp* -ck-*) vi* paniquer

**panorama** [pænə'rɑːmə] *n* panorama *m*

**pansy** ['pænzɪ] *(pl* -ies*) n* [flower] pensée *f*

**pant** [pænt] *vi* haleter

**pantomime** ['pæntəmaɪm] *n Br* [show] *spectacle de Noël*

**pantry** ['pæntrɪ] *(pl* -ies*) n* [larder] garde-manger *m inv*

**pants** [pænts] *npl* [underwear] slip *m* ; *Am* [trousers] pantalon *m*

**pantyhose** ['pæntɪhəʊz] *n Am* [tights] collant *m*

**paper** ['peɪpə(r)] **1.** *n* papier *m* ; [newspaper] journal *m* ; [wallpaper] papier *m* peint ; [exam] épreuve *f* écrite ; [student's exercise] copie *f* ; [scholarly study, report] article *m* ; **a piece of paper** un bout de papier ; **to put sth down on paper** mettre qch par écrit ; **papers** [documents] papiers **2.** *adj* [bag] en papier ; [cup, plate] en carton ; **paper lantern** lampion *m* ; *Br* **paper shop** marchand *m* de journaux ; **paper towel** essuie-tout *m inv* **3.** *vt* [room, wall] tapisser ■ **paperback** *n* livre *m* de poche ■ **paperclip** *n* trombone *m* ■ **paperweight** *n* presse-papiers *m inv* ■ **paperwork** *n* [in office] écritures *fpl* ; *Pej* [red tape] paperasserie *f*

**par** [pɑː(r)] *n* [in golf] par *m* ; **on a par** au même niveau **(with** que)

**paracetamol** [pærə'siːtəmɒl] *n* paracétamol *m*

**parachute** ['pærəʃuːt] *n* parachute *m* ; **parachute jump** saut *m* en parachute

**parade** [pə'reɪd] **1.** n a) [procession] défilé m b) Br [street] avenue f **2.** vt Fig [wealth, knowledge] faire étalage de **3.** vi [of troops] défiler; **to parade about** [of person] se pavaner

**paradise** ['pærədaɪs] n paradis m

**paradoxically** [pærə'dɒksɪklɪ] adv paradoxalement

**paraffin** ['pærəfɪn] n Br pétrole m lampant; Br **paraffin lamp** lampe f à pétrole

**paraglider** ['pærəglaɪdə(r)] n a) [person] parapentiste mf b) [parachute] parapente m ▪ **paragliding** ['pærəglaɪdɪŋ] n parapente m; **to go paragliding** faire du parapente

**paragraph** ['pærəgrɑːf] n paragraphe m

**paralegal** ['pærəliːgəl] n assistant, -e mf (d'un avocat)

**parallel** ['pærəlel] **1.** adj MATH parallèle (**with** or **to** à); Fig [comparable] semblable (**with** or **to** à) **2.** n MATH [line] parallèle f; Fig [comparison & GEOG] parallèle m

**Paralympics** [pærə'lɪmpɪks] npl the **Paralympics** les jeux mpl Paralympiques

**paralysis** [pə'ræləsɪs] (pl -yses [-əsiːz]) n paralysie f ▪ **paralyse**, Am **paralyze** ['pærəlaɪz] vt paralyser

**paramedic** [pærə'medɪk] n auxiliaire mf médical(e)

**paranoid** ['pærənɔɪd] adj paranoïaque

**paraphrase** ['pærəfreɪz] vt paraphraser

**parasite** ['pærəsaɪt] n [person, organism] parasite m

**parasol** ['pærəsɒl] n [over table, on beach] parasol m; [lady's] ombrelle f

**parcel** ['pɑːsəl] **1.** n colis m, paquet m **2.** (Br -ll-, Am -l-) vt **to parcel sth up** empaqueter

**parched** [pɑːʃt] adj **to be parched** [of person] être assoiffé

**pardon** ['pɑːdən] **1.** n [forgiveness] pardon m; [in law] grâce f; **I beg your pardon** [apologizing] je vous prie de m'excuser; **I beg your pardon?** [not hearing] pardon? **2.** vt [in law] gracier; **to pardon sb (for sth)** pardonner (qch) à qn; **pardon (me)!** [sorry] pardon!

**parent** ['peərənt] n [father] père m; [mother] mère f; **parents** parents mpl

**parental advisory** n Am TV avertissement m parental

**Paris** ['pærɪs] n Paris m ou f ▪ **Parisian** [pə'rɪzɪən, Am pə'riːʒən] **1.** adj parisien, -enne **2.** n Parisien, -enne mf

**parish** ['pærɪʃ] n [religious] paroisse f; [civil] ≃ commune f

**park¹** [pɑːk] n [garden] parc m

**park²** [pɑːk] **1.** vt [vehicle] garer **2.** vi [of vehicle] se garer; [remain parked] stationner ▪ **parking** n stationnement m; **'no parking'** 'défense de stationner'; Am **parking lot** parking m; **parking meter** parcmètre m; **parking place** or **space** place f de parking; **parking ticket** contravention f

**parliament** ['pɑːləmənt] n parlement m

**parody** ['pærədɪ] **1.** (pl -ies) n parodie f **2.** (pt & pp -ied) vt parodier

**parole** [pə'rəʊl] n **to be (out) on parole** être en liberté conditionnelle

**parrot** ['pærət] n perroquet m

**parsley** ['pɑːslɪ] n persil m

**parsnip** ['pɑːsnɪp] n panais m

**parson** ['pɑːsən] n pasteur m

**part¹** [pɑːt] **1.** n partie f; [quantity in mixture] mesure f; [of machine] pièce f; [of serial] épisode m; [role in play, film] rôle m; Am [in hair] raie f; **to take part** participer (**in** à); **to be a part of sth** faire partie de qch; **for the most part** dans l'ensemble; **on the part of...** de la part de...; **for my part** pour ma part **2.** adv [partly] en partie; **part silk, part cotton** soie et coton

**part²** [pɑːt] **1.** vt [separate] séparer; **to part one's hair** se faire une raie **2.** vi [of friends] se quitter; [of married couple] se séparer; **to part with sth** se défaire de qch

**partial** ['pɑːʃəl] adj [not total] partiel, -elle; [biased] partial (**towards** envers); **to be partial to sth** avoir un faible pour qch

**participate** [pɑːˈtɪsɪpeɪt] *vi* participer (**in** à) ■ **participant** *n* participant, -e *mf* ■ **participation** *n* participation *f*

**particular** [pəˈtɪkjʊlə(r)] **1.** *adj* [specific, special] particulier, -ère ; [exacting] méticuleux, -euse; **this particular book** ce livre en particulier; **to be particular about sth** faire très attention à qch **2.** *n* **in particular** en particulier ■ **particularly** *adv* particulièrement ■ **particulars** *npl* [details] détails *mpl*; **to take down sb's particulars** noter les coordonnées de qn

**parting** [ˈpɑːtɪŋ] *n Br* [in hair] raie *f*

**partition** [pɑːˈtɪʃən] **1.** *n* [of room] cloison *f* **2.** *vt* **to partition sth off** cloisonner qch

**partly** [ˈpɑːtlɪ] *adv* en partie ; **partly English, partly French** moitié anglais, moitié français

**partner** [ˈpɑːtnə(r)] *n* [in game] partenaire *mf*; [in business] associé, -e *mf*; [in relationship] compagnon *m*, compagne *f*; **(dancing) partner** cavalier, -ère *mf* ■ **partnership** *n* association *f*; [between companies] partenariat *m*; **in partnership with** en association avec

**partridge** [ˈpɑːtrɪdʒ] *n* perdrix *f*

**part-time** [ˈpɑːtˈtaɪm] *adj* & *adv* à temps partiel

**party** [ˈpɑːtɪ] (*pl* -**ies**) *n* **a)** [gathering] fête *f*; **to have** or **throw a party** donner une fête **b)** [group] groupe *m*; [political] parti *m*; [in contract, lawsuit] partie *f* ■ **partying** [ˈpɑːtɪŋ] *n Fam* **she's a great one for partying** elle adore faire la fête

**pass**[1] [pɑːs] *n* [over mountains] col *m*

**pass**[2] [pɑːs] *n* [entry permit] laissez-passer *m inv*; [for travel] carte *f* d'abonnement ; [in sport] passe *f*; **pass mark** [in exam] moyenne *f*

**pass**[3] [pɑːs] **1.** *vt* [move, give] passer (**to** à) ; [go past] passer devant ; [vehicle, runner] dépasser ; [exam] être reçu à ; [law] voter; **to pass sb** [in street] croiser qn; **to pass the time** passer le temps; **to pass sentence** [of judge] prononcer le verdict **2.** *vi* [vehicle] doubler ; [go past, go away] passer

(**to** à; **through** par) ; [in exam] avoir la moyenne ; [of time] passer ; SPORT faire une passe ■ **pass as** *vt insep* passer pour ■ **pass away** *vi* décéder ■ **pass by 1.** *vt insep* [building] passer devant; **to pass by sb** [in street] croiser qn **2.** *vi* passer à côté ■ **pass for** *vt insep* = **pass as** ■ **pass off** *vt sep* **to pass oneself off as sb** se faire passer pour qn ■ **pass on 1.** *vi* **a)** [move on] continuer son chemin **b)** *Euph* = **pass away 2.** *vt sep* [message, illness] transmettre (**to** à) ■ **pass out 1.** *vt sep* [hand out] distribuer **2.** *vi* [faint] s'évanouir ■ **pass over** *vt insep* [ignore] passer sur ■ **pass round** *vt sep* [cakes, document] faire passer ; [hand out] distribuer ■ **pass through** *vi* passer ■ **pass up** *vt sep* [opportunity] laisser passer

**passable** [ˈpɑːsəbəl] *adj* [not bad] passable

**passage** [ˈpæsɪdʒ] *n* **a)** [way through] passage *m*; [corridor] couloir *m*; **with the passage of time** avec le temps **b)** [of text] passage *m*

**passbook** [ˈpɑːsbʊk] *n* livret *m* de caisse d'épargne

**passenger** [ˈpæsɪndʒə(r)] *n* passager, -ère *mf*; [on train] voyageur, -euse *mf*; **passenger door** [of car] portière *f* avant côté passager

**passer-by** [pɑːsəˈbaɪ] (*pl* **passers-by**) *n* passant, -e *mf*

**passing** [ˈpɑːsɪŋ] **1.** *adj* [vehicle] qui passe **2.** *n* [of time] écoulement *m*; **in passing** en passant

**passion** [ˈpæʃən] *n* passion *f*; **to have a passion for sth** adorer qch ■ **passionate** *adj* passionné

**passive** [ˈpæsɪv] **1.** *adj* passif, -ive **2.** *n* [in grammar] passif *m*; **in the passive** au passif

**passport** [ˈpɑːspɔːt] *n* passeport *m*; **passport photo** photo *f* d'identité

**password** [ˈpɑːswɜːd] *n* mot *m* de passe

**past** [pɑːst] **1.** *n* passé *m*; **in the past** autrefois **2.** *adj* [gone by] passé ; [former] ancien, -enne **these past months** ces derniers mois; **in the past tense**

au passé **3.** *prep* [in front of] devant ;
[after] après ; [beyond] au-delà de ; **it's
past four o'clock** il est quatre heures
passées **4.** *adv* devant ; **to go past**
passer

**pasta** ['pæstə] *n* pâtes *fpl*

**paste** [peɪst] **1. n a)** [mixture] pâte *f* ; [of
meat] pâté *m* **b)** [glue] colle *f* **2.** *vt* coller ;
**to paste sth up** coller qch

**pastel** [*Br* 'pæstəl, *Am* pæ'stel] *n* pastel *m*

**pasteurized** ['pæstʃəraɪzd] *adj* **pasteurized milk** lait *m* pasteurisé

**pastille** [*Br* 'pæstɪl, *Am* pæ'stiːl] *n* pastille *f*

**pastime** ['pɑːstaɪm] *n* passe-temps *m*
*inv*

**pastor** ['pɑːstə(r)] *n* REL pasteur *m*

**pastry** ['peɪstrɪ] *(pl* -ies*)* *n* [dough] pâte *f* ;
[cake] pâtisserie *f*

**pasture** ['pɑːstʃə(r)] *n* pré *m*, pâture *f*

**pasty** ['pæstɪ] *(pl* -ies*)* *n* [pie] feuilleté *m*

**pat** [pæt] *(pt & pp* -tt-*)* *vt* [tap] tapoter ;
[animal] caresser

**patch** [pætʃ] **1.** *n* [for clothes] pièce *f* ;
[over eye] bandeau *m* ; [of colour]
tache *f* ; [of ice] plaque *f* ; *Fig* **to be going
through a bad patch** traverser une
mauvaise passe **2.** *vt* **to patch (up)**
[clothing] rapiécer ; **to patch things
up** [after argument] se raccommoder

**patchwork** ['pætʃwɜːk] *n* patchwork *m*

**patchy** ['pætʃɪ] *(compar* -ier, *superl* -iest*)*
*adj* inégal

**patent** ['peɪtənt, 'pætənt] **1.** *n* brevet *m*
d'invention **2.** *vt* (faire) breveter ▪ **pa-
tently** *adv* manifestement

**paternal** [pə'tɜːnəl] *adj* paternel, -elle

**path** [pɑːθ] *(pl* -s [pɑːðz]*)* *n* chemin *m* ;
[narrow] sentier *m* ; [in park] allée *f* ; [of
river] cours *m* ; [of bullet] trajectoire *f* ;
COMPUT chemin *m* (d'accès) ▪ **path-
breaking** *adj* révolutionnaire

**pathetic** [pə'θetɪk] *adj* pitoyable

**pathway** ['pɑːθweɪ] *n* sentier *m*

**patience** ['peɪʃəns] *n* **a)** [quality]
patience *f* ; **to lose patience** perdre

patience (**with sb** avec qn) **b)** *Br* [card
game] **to play patience** faire une
réussite

**patient** ['peɪʃənt] **1.** *adj* patient **2.** *n*
patient, -e *mf* ▪ **patiently** *adv* patiem-
ment

**patio** ['pætɪəʊ] *(pl* -os*)* *n* patio *m*

**patriot** ['pætrɪət, 'peɪtrɪət] *n* patriote *mf*
▪ **patriotic** [-rɪ'ɒtɪk, peɪtrɪ'ɒtɪk] *adj*
[views, speech] patriotique ; [person]
patriote

**patrol** [pə'trəʊl] **1.** *n* patrouille *f* ; **to be
on patrol** être de patrouille ; **patrol
car** voiture *f* de police **2.** *(pt & pp* -ll-*)* *vt*
patrouiller dans **3.** *vi* patrouiller ▪ **pa-
trolman** *(pl* -men*)* *n* *Am* [policeman]
agent *m* de police

**patron** ['peɪtrən] *n* [of arts] protecteur,
-trice *mf* ; [of charity] patron, -onne *mf* ;
[customer] client, -e *mf* ; REL **patron
saint** patron, -onne *mf*

**patronize** [*Br* 'pætrənaɪz, *Am* 'peɪtrənaɪz]
*vt* [be condescending towards] traiter
avec condescendance ▪ **patronizing**
*adj* condescendant

**patter** ['pætə(r)] *n* [of footsteps] petit
bruit *m* ; [of rain] crépitement *m*

**pattern** ['pætən] *n* [design] dessin *m*,
motif *m* ; [in sewing] patron *m* ; [in
knitting] & *Fig* [norm] modèle *m* ; [ten-
dency] tendance *f*

**paunch** [pɔːntʃ] *n* ventre *m*

**pause** [pɔːz] **1.** *n* pause *f* ; [in conver-
sation] silence *m* **2.** *vi* [stop] faire une
pause ; [hesitate] hésiter

**pave** [peɪv] *vt* [road] paver (**with** de) ; *Fig*
**to pave the way for sth** ouvrir la voie
à qch ▪ **paving** *n* **paving stone** pavé *m*

**pavement** ['peɪvmənt] *n* *Br* [beside road]
trottoir *m* ; *Am* [roadway] chaussée *f*

**pavilion** [pə'vɪljən] *n* pavillon *m*

**paw** [pɔː] *n* patte *f*

**pawn**[1] [pɔːn] *n* [chess piece] pion *m*

**pawn**[2] [pɔːn] *vt* mettre en gage ▪ **pawn-
broker** *n* prêteur, -euse *mf* sur gages
▪ **pawnshop** *n* mont-de-piété *m*

**pay** [peɪ] **1.** *n* paie *f*, salaire *m* ; [of sol-
dier] solde *f* ; **pay rise** augmentation *f*
de salaire ; *Br* **pay slip**, *Am* **pay stub**

fiche *f* de paie **2.** *(pt & pp* **paid)** *vt* [person, money, bill] payer ; [sum, deposit] verser ; [yield - of investment] rapporter ; **I paid £5 for it** je l'ai payé 5 livres ; **to pay sb to do sth** *or* **for doing sth** payer qn pour qu'il fasse qch ; **to pay sb for sth** payer qch à qn **3.** *vi* payer ; **pay channel** chaîne *f* payante ■ **payable** *adj* [due] payable ; **to make a cheque payable to sb** libeller un chèque à l'ordre de qn ■ **payment** *n* paiement *m* ; [of deposit] versement *m* ; **on payment of 20 euros** moyennant 20 euros ■ **payphone** *n* téléphone *m* public ■ **paywall** ['peɪwɔːl] *n* paywall *m* ; **the newspaper has put some of its best articles behind a paywall** le journal s'est doté d'un paywall et fait payer l'accès à certains de ses meilleurs articles ■ **pay back** *vt sep* [person, loan] rembourser ; *Fig* **I'll pay you back for this!** tu me le paieras ! ■ **pay for** *vt insep* payer ■ **pay in** *vt sep* [cheque, money] verser sur un compte ■ **pay off 1.** *vt sep* [debt] rembourser ; [in instalments] rembourser par acomptes **2.** *vi* [of work, effort] porter ses fruits ■ **pay out** *vt sep* [spend] dépenser ■ **pay up** *vi* payer

**PBJ** *n Am abbr of* **peanut butter and jelly**

**PC** [piː'siː] **a)** *(abbr of* **personal computer)** PC *m*, micro *m* ; **handheld PC** PC *m* de poche **b)** *(abbr of* **politically correct)** politiquement correct

**PDF** *(abbr of* **portable document format)** *n* COMPUT PDF *m*

**PE** [piː'iː] *(abbr of* **physical education)** *n* EPS *f*

**pea** [piː] *n* pois *m* ; **peas,** *Br* **garden** *or* **green peas** petits pois *mpl*

**peace** [piːs] *n* paix *f* ; **peace of mind** tranquillité *f* d'esprit ; **at peace** en paix **(with** avec) ; **I'd like some peace and quiet** j'aimerais un peu de silence

**peaceful** ['piːsfəl] *adj* [calm] paisible ; [non-violent] pacifique

**peach** [piːtʃ] *n* [fruit] pêche *f*

**peacock** ['piːkɒk] *n* paon *m*

**peak** [piːk] **1.** *n* [mountain top] sommet *m* ; [mountain] pic *m* ; [of cap] visière *f* ; *Fig* [of fame, success] apogée *m* **2.** *adj* [hours, period] de pointe

**peal** [piːl] **1.** *n* [of bells] sonnerie *f* ; **peals of laughter** éclats *mpl* de rire **2.** *vi* **to peal (out)** [of bells] sonner à toute volée

**peanut** ['piːnʌt] *n* cacah(o)uète *f* ; **peanut butter** beurre *m* de cacah(o)uètes

**pear** [peə(r)] *n* poire *f* ■ **pear-shaped** *adj* en forme de poire, piriforme ; **she's pear-shaped** elle a de fortes hanches ; *Fam* **to go pear-shaped** tourner mal ; **everything went pear-shaped** tout est parti en vrille

**pearl** [pɜːl] *n* perle *f* ; **pearl necklace** collier *m* de perles

**peasant** ['pezənt] *n & adj* paysan, -anne *(mf)*

**peat** [piːt] *n* tourbe *f*

**pebble** ['pebəl] *n* [stone] caillou *m* *(pl* -oux) ; [on beach] galet *m*

**pecan** ['piːkən] *n* [nut] noix *f* de pécan

**peck** [pek] *vti* **to peck (at)** [grain] picorer ; [person] donner un coup de bec à

**peckish** ['pekɪʃ] *adj Br* **to be peckish** avoir un petit creux

**peculiar** [pɪ'kjuːlɪə(r)] *adj* [strange] bizarre ; [special, characteristic] particulier, -ère **(to** à)

**pedal** ['pedəl] **1.** *n* pédale *f* ; **pedal bin** poubelle *f* à pédale **2.** *(Br* -ll-, *Am* -l-) *vt* **to pedal a bicycle** être à bicyclette **3.** *vi* pédaler

**pedantic** [pɪ'dæntɪk] *adj* pédant

**peddle** ['pedəl] *vt* [goods, ideas] colporter ; [drugs] faire du trafic de ■ **peddler** *n* [door-to-door] colporteur, -euse *mf* ; [in street] camelot *m* ; **(drug) peddler** trafiquant, -e *mf* de drogue

**pedestal** ['pedɪstəl] *n* piédestal *m*

**pedestrian** [pə'destrɪən] *n* piéton *m* ; *Br* **pedestrian crossing** passage *m* pour piétons ; *Br* **pedestrian precinct** zone *f* piétonnière

**pediatrician** [piːdɪə'trɪʃən] *Am n* = **paediatrician**

**pedigree** ['pedɪgriː] **1.** n [of animal] pedigree m; [of person] ascendance f **2.** adj [animal] de race

**pedlar** ['pedlə(r)] n [door-to-door] colporteur, -euse mf; [in street] camelot m

**pee** [piː] Fam **1.** n to go for a pee faire pipi **2.** vi faire pipi

**peek** [piːk] vi jeter un coup d'œil furtif (at à)

**peel** [piːl] **1.** n [of vegetable, fruit] peau f; [of orange, lemon] écorce f **2.** vt [vegetable] éplucher; [fruit] peler; **to peel sth off** [label] décoller qch **3.** vi [of skin, person] peler; [of paint] s'écailler ■ **peeler** n (potato) peeler épluche-légumes m inv ■ **peelings** npl épluchures fpl

**peep** [piːp] vi jeter un coup d'œil furtif (at à); **to peep out** se montrer

**peer** [pɪə(r)] **1.** n Br & [equal] [nobleman] pair m **2.** vi to peer at sb/sth scruter qn/qch du regard ■ **peer-to-peer** adj peer-to-peer

**peeved** [piːvd] adj en rogne

**peevish** ['piːvɪʃ] adj irritable

**peg** [peg] n [for coat, hat] patère f; [for drying clothes] pince à linge; [for tent] piquet m; [wooden pin] cheville f; Br **to buy sth off the peg** acheter qch en prêt-à-porter

**pejorative** [prˈdʒɒrətɪv] adj péjoratif, -ive

**pelican** ['pelɪkən] n pélican m; Br **pelican crossing** feux mpl à commande manuelle

**pelt** [pelt] **1.** vt bombarder (with de) **2.** vi Fam **it's pelting down** il pleut à verse

**pelvis** ['pelvɪs] n ANAT pelvis m

**pen¹** [pen] n [for writing] stylo m; **pen friend** or **pal** correspondant, -e mf

**pen²** [pen] n [for sheep, cattle] parc m

**penal** ['piːnəl] adj [code, law] pénal ■ **penalize** vt pénaliser

**penalty** ['penəltɪ] (pl -ies) n [prison sentence] peine f; [fine] amende f; [in football] penalty m; [in rugby] pénalité f

**pence** [pens] pl of penny

**pencil** ['pensəl] **1.** n crayon m; **in pencil** au crayon; **pencil sharpener** taille-crayon m **2.** (Br -ll-, Am -l-) vt Fig **to pencil sth in** fixer qch provisoirement

**pendant** ['pendənt] n [around neck] pendentif m

**pending** ['pendɪŋ] **1.** adj [matter, business] en attente **2.** prep [until] en attendant

**pendulum** ['pendjʊləm] n pendule m

**penetrate** ['penɪtreɪt] **1.** vt [substance] pénétrer; [mystery] percer **2.** vti **to penetrate (into)** [forest] pénétrer dans; [group] s'infiltrer dans ■ **penetrating** adj [mind, cold] pénétrant

**penguin** ['peŋgwɪn] n manchot m

**penicillin** [penɪˈsɪlɪn] n pénicilline f

**peninsula** [pəˈnɪnsjʊlə] n presqu'île f; [larger] péninsule f

**penis** ['piːnɪs] n pénis m

**penitentiary** [penɪˈtenʃərɪ] (pl -ies) Am prison f centrale

**penknife** ['pennaɪf] (pl -knives) n canif m

**penniless** ['penɪləs] adj sans le sou

**penny** ['penɪ] n a) (pl -ies) Br [coin] penny m; Am Can [cent] cent m; Fig **I don't have a penny** je n'ai pas un sou b) (pl pence) Br [value, currency] penny m

**pension** ['penʃən] **1.** n pension f; **(retirement) pension** retraite f; Br **old age pension** pension f de vieillesse **2.** vt **to pension sb off** mettre qn à la retraite ■ **pensioner** n retraité, -e mf; Br **old age pensioner** retraité, -e mf

**pentagon** ['pentəgən] n pentagone m ■ **Pentagon** n Am **the Pentagon** le Pentagone (siège du ministère américain de la Défense, à Washington; le terme désigne plus généralement les autorités militaires américaines)

**pent-up** ['pentʌp] adj [feelings] refoulé

**penultimate** [prˈnʌltɪmət] adj avant-dernier, -ère

**people** ['piːpəl] **1.** n [nation] peuple m **2.** npl [as group] gens mpl; [as individuals] personnes fpl; **the people** [citizens] le peuple; **two people**

deux personnes; **English people** les Anglais mpl; **people think that...** les gens pensent que...

**pepper** ['pepə(r)] n poivre m; [vegetable] poivron m; **pepper mill** moulin m à poivre; **pepper pot** poivrier m; Am **pepper shaker, pepperbox** = **pepper pot**

**peppermint** ['pepəmɪnt] n [flavour] menthe f; [sweet] bonbon m à la menthe

**per** [pɜː(r)] prep par; **per annum** par an; **50 pence per kilo** 50 pence le kilo; **40 km per hour** 40 km à l'heure

**perceive** [pə'siːv] vt [see, hear] percevoir; [notice] remarquer (**that** que)

**percentage** [pə'sentɪdʒ] n pourcentage m ▪ **percent** adv pour cent

**perception** [pə'sepʃən] n perception f (**of** de)

**perceptive** [pə'septɪv] adj [person] perspicace; [study, remark] pertinent

**perch** [pɜːtʃ] **1.** n [for bird] perchoir m **2.** vi se percher

**percolator** ['pɜːkəleɪtə(r)] n cafetière f à pression; [in café, restaurant] percolateur m

**perennial** [pə'renɪəl] **1.** adj [plant] vivace; [worry] perpétuel, -elle **2.** n plante f vivace

**perfect 1.** ['pɜːfɪkt] adj parfait; GRAM **perfect tense** parfait m **2.** ['pɜːfɪkt] n GRAM parfait m **3.** [pə'fekt] vt parfaire; **to perfect one's French** parfaire ses connaissances en français

**perfection** [pə'fekʃən] n [quality] perfection f ▪ **perfectly** adv parfaitement

**perforate** ['pɜːfəreɪt] vt perforer ▪ **perforation** n perforation f

**perform** [pə'fɔːm] **1.** vt [task, miracle] accomplir; [duty, function] remplir; [play, piece of music] jouer **2.** vi [act, play] jouer; [sing] chanter; [dance] danser; **to perform well/badly** [in job] bien/mal s'en tirer ▪ **performance** n **a)** [of play] représentation f **b)** [of actor, musician] interprétation f; [of

athlete] performance f; [of company] résultats mpl ▪ **performance-enhancing drug** n produit m dopant

**performer** [pə'fɔːmə(r)] n [entertainer] artiste mf; [in play, of music] interprète mf (**of** de)

**perfume** ['pɜːfjuːm] n parfum m

**perhaps** [pə'hæps] adv peut-être; **perhaps not/so** peut-être que non/que oui; **perhaps she'll come** peut-être qu'elle viendra, elle viendra peut-être

**peril** ['perɪl] n péril m, danger m

**period** ['pɪərɪəd] **1.** n **a)** [stretch of time] période f; [historical] époque f; [school lesson] heure f de cours; (**monthly**) **period(s)** [of woman] règles fpl **b)** Am [full stop] point m; **I refuse, period!** je refuse, un point c'est tout! **2.** adj [furniture, costume] d'époque ▪ **periodical** [-rɪ'ɒdɪkəl] n [magazine] périodique m ▪ **periodically** [-rɪ'ɒdɪklɪ] adv périodiquement

**peripheral** [pə'rɪfərəl] n COMPUT périphérique m

**perish** ['perɪʃ] vi [of person] périr

**perishable** ['perɪʃəbəl] adj [food] périssable

**perjury** ['pɜːdʒərɪ] n faux témoignage m

**perk** [pɜːk] **1.** n BrFam [in job] avantage m **2.** vt **to perk sb up** [revive] ragaillardir qn; [cheer up] remonter le moral à qn **3.** vi **to perk up** reprendre du poil de la bête

**perm** [pɜːm] **1.** n permanente f **2.** vt **to have one's hair permed** se faire faire une permanente

**permanent** ['pɜːmənənt] adj permanent; [address] fixe ▪ **permanently** adv à titre permanent

**permissible** [pə'mɪsəbəl] adj permis

**permission** [pə'mɪʃən] n permission f, autorisation f (**to do** de faire); **to give sb permission (to do sth)** donner la permission à qn (de faire qch)

**permissive** [pə'mɪsɪv] adj permissif, -ive

**permit 1.** ['pɜːmɪt] n permis m **2.** [pə'mɪt] (pt & pp -tt-) vt permettre (**sb to do** à qn de faire)

**perpendicular** [pɜ:pən'dɪkjʊlə(r)] *adj* & *n* perpendiculaire (*f*)

**perpetrate** ['pɜ:pɪtreɪt] *vt* [crime] perpétrer ■ **perpetrator** *n* auteur *m*

**perpetual** [pə'petʃʊəl] *adj* perpétuel, -elle ■ **perpetuate** [-veɪt] *vt* perpétuer

**perplexed** [pə'plekst] *adj* perplexe

**persecute** ['pɜ:sɪkju:t] *vt* persécuter ■ **persecution** *n* persécution *f*

**persevere** [pɜ:sɪ'vɪə(r)] *vi* persévérer (**with** dans) ■ **perseverance** *n* persévérance *f*

**Persian** ['pɜ:ʃən, 'pɜ:ʒən] **1.** *adj* [carpet, cat] persan; **the Persian Gulf** le golfe Persique **2.** *n* [language] persan *m*

**persist** [pə'sɪst] *vi* persister (**in doing** à faire; **in sth** dans qch) ■ **persistent** *adj* [person] tenace; [smell, rumours] persistant; [attempts] continuel, -elle

**person** ['pɜ:sən] *n* personne *f*; **in person** en personne

**personal** ['pɜ:sənəl] *adj* personnel, -elle; [friend] intime; [life] privé; [indiscreet] indiscret, -ète; **personal computer** ordinateur *m* individuel; **personal details** [name, address] coordonnées *fpl* personnelles; **personal organizer** agenda *m* électronique; **personal stereo** baladeur *m*

**personality** [pɜ:sə'nælɪtɪ] (*pl* -ies) *n* [character, famous person] personnalité *f*

**personally** ['pɜ:sənəlɪ] *adv* personnellement; [in person] en personne

**personify** [pə'sɒnɪfaɪ] (*pt & pp* -ied) *vt* personnifier

**personnel** [pɜ:sə'nel] *n* [staff] personnel *m*

**perspective** [pə'spektɪv] *n* perspective *f*; *Fig* **in perspective** sous son vrai jour

**perspire** [pə'spaɪə(r)] *vi* transpirer

**persuade** [pə'sweɪd] *vt* persuader (**sb to do** qn de faire) ■ **persuasion** *n* persuasion *f*; [creed] religion *f* ■ **persuasive** *adj* [person, argument] persuasif, -ive

**pertain** [pə'teɪn] *vi Formal* **to pertain to** [relate] se rapporter à

**pertinent** ['pɜ:tɪnənt] *adj* pertinent

**perturb** [pə'tɜ:b] *vt* troubler

**Peru** [pə'ru:] *n* le Pérou

**peruse** [pə'ru:z] *vt Formal* [read carefully] lire attentivement; [skim through] parcourir

**pervade** [pə'veɪd] *vt* imprégner ■ **pervasive** *adj* [feeling] général; [influence] omniprésent

**perverse** [pə'vɜ:s] *adj* [awkward] contrariant ■ **perversion** [-ʃən, *Am* -ʒən] *n* [sexual] perversion *f*

**pervert 1.** ['pɜ:vɜ:t] *n* [sexual deviant] pervers, -e *mf* **2.** [pə'vɜ:t] *vt* pervertir; [mind] corrompre

**pessimism** ['pesɪmɪzəm] *n* pessimisme *m* ■ **pessimistic** *adj* pessimiste

**pest** [pest] *n* [animal] animal *m* nuisible; [insect] insecte *m* nuisible; *Fam* [person] plaie *f*

**pester** ['pestə(r)] *vt* tourmenter; **to pester sb to do sth** harceler qn pour qu'il fasse qch

**pesticide** ['pestɪsaɪd] *n* pesticide *m*

**pet** [pet] **1.** *n* animal *m* domestique; [favourite person] chouchou, -oute *mf*; [term of address] petit chou *m* **2.** *adj* [dog, cat] domestique; [favourite] favori, -ite; **pet shop** animalerie *f* **3.** (*pt & pp* -tt-) *vt* [fondle] caresser **4.** *vi Fam* se peloter

**petal** ['petəl] *n* pétale *m*

**peter** ['pi:tə(r)] *vi* **to peter out** [of conversation] tarir; [of scheme] n'aboutir à rien; [of path, stream] disparaître

**petition** [pə'tɪʃən] *n* [signatures] pétition *f*; [request to court of law] requête *f*

**petrify** ['petrɪfaɪ] (*pt & pp* -ied) *vt* pétrifier

**petrol** ['petrəl] *n Br* essence *f*; **petrol station** station-service *f*; **petrol tank** réservoir *m* d'essence

**petticoat** ['petɪkəʊt] *n* jupon *m*

**petty** ['petɪ] (*compar* -ier, *superl* -iest) *adj* [trivial] insignifiant; [mean] mesquin; **petty cash** petite caisse *f*; **petty criminal** petit malfaiteur *m*

**pew** [pju:] *n* banc *m* d'église

**phantom** ['fæntəm] n fantôme m

**pharmacy** ['fɑːməsɪ] (pl -ies) n pharmacie f ■ **pharmacist** n pharmacien, -enne mf

**phase** [feɪz] **1.** n phase f **2.** vt **to phase sth in/out** introduire/supprimer qch progressivement

**PhD** [piːeɪtʃ'diː] (abbr of **Doctor of Philosophy**) n [degree] doctorat m (in de); [person] docteur m

**phenomenon** [fɪ'nɒmɪnən] (pl -ena [-ɪnə]) n phénomène m ■ **phenomenal** adj phénoménal

**Philippines** ['fɪlɪpiːnz] npl the Philippines les Philippines fpl

**philistine** ['fɪlɪstaɪn] n béotien, -enne mf, philistin m

**philosopher** [fɪ'lɒsəfə(r)] n philosophe mf

**philosophical** [fɪlə'sɒfɪkəl] adj philosophique; Fig [stoical, resigned] philosophe

**philosophy** [fɪ'lɒsəfɪ] (pl -ies) n philosophie f

**phishing** ['fɪʃɪŋ] n COMPUT phishing m

**phlegm** [flem] n [in throat] glaires fpl

**phobia** ['fəubɪə] n phobie f

**phone** [fəun] **1.** n téléphone m; **to be on the phone** [be talking] être au téléphone; [have a telephone] avoir le téléphone; **phone call** coup m de téléphone; **to make a phone call** téléphoner (**to** à); **phone book** annuaire m; **phone box**, Br **phone booth** cabine f téléphonique; **phone number** numéro m de téléphone **2.** vt téléphoner (**to** à); **to phone sb (up)** téléphoner à qn; **to phone sb back** rappeler qn **3.** vi to phone (up) téléphoner; **to phone back** rappeler ■ **phonecard** n Br carte f de téléphone

**phonetic** [fə'netɪk] adj phonétique

**phony, phoney** ['fəunɪ] Fam **1.** (compar -ier, superl -iest) adj [company, excuse] bidon inv **2.** n [impostor] imposteur m; [insincere person] faux jeton m

**photo** ['fəutəu] (pl -os) n photo f; **to take sb's photo** prendre qn en photo; **to have one's photo taken** se faire prendre en photo; **photo album** album m de photos; **photo frame** cadre m photo

**photocopy** ['fəutəukɒpɪ] **1.** (pl -ies) n photocopie f **2.** (pt & pp -ied) vt photocopier ■ **photocopier** n photocopieuse f

**photograph** ['fəutəgrɑːf] **1.** n photographie f **2.** vt photographier ■ **photographer** [fə'tɒgrəfə(r)] n photographe mf ■ **photography** [fə'tɒgrəfɪ] n [activity] photographie f

**phrase** [freɪz] **1.** n [saying] expression f; [idiom, in grammar] locution f; **phrase book** manuel m de conversation **2.** vt [verbally] exprimer; [in writing] rédiger

**physical** ['fɪzɪkəl] adj physique; **physical education** éducation f physique; **physical examination** visite f médicale

**physician** [fɪ'zɪʃən] n médecin m

**physics** ['fɪzɪks] n [science] physique f

**physiology** [fɪzɪ'ɒlədʒɪ] n physiologie f

**physiotherapy** [fɪzɪəu'θerəpɪ] n kinésithérapie f

**physique** [fɪ'ziːk] n physique m

**piano** [pɪ'ænəu] (pl -os) n piano m ■ **pianist** ['pɪənɪst] n pianiste mf

**pick¹** [pɪk] **1.** n [choice] choix m; **to take one's pick** choisir **2.** vt [choose] choisir; [flower, fruit] cueillir; [hole] faire (**in** dans); [lock] crocheter; **to pick a fight** chercher la bagarre (**with** avec) ■ **pick at** vt insep **to pick at one's food** picorer ■ **pick off** vt sep [remove] enlever ■ **pick on** vt insep [nag, blame] s'en prendre à ■ **pick out** vt sep [choose] choisir; [identify] repérer ■ **pick up 1.** vt sep [lift up] ramasser; [person into air, weight] soulever; [baby] prendre dans ses bras; [cold] attraper; [habit, accent, speed] prendre; [fetch, collect] passer prendre; [radio programme] capter; [arrest] arrêter; [learn] apprendre; **to pick up the phone** décrocher le téléphone **2.** vi [improve] s'améliorer; [of business] reprendre; **let's pick up where we left off** reprenons (là où nous en étions restés)

**pick²** [pɪk] n [tool] pic m; **ice pick** pic m à glace

**pickaxe**, Am **pickax** ['pɪkæks] n pioche f

**picket** ['pɪkɪt] n [in strike] **picket (line)** piquet m de grève

**pickle** ['pɪkəl] **1.** n **pickles** [vegetables] Br conserves fpl (au vinaigre); Am concombres mpl, cornichons mpl; Fam **to be in a pickle** être dans le pétrin **2.** vt conserver dans du vinaigre; **pickled onion** oignon m au vinaigre

**pickpocket** ['pɪkpɒkɪt] n pickpocket m

**pick-up** ['pɪkʌp] n **pick-up (truck)** pick-up m inv (petite camionnette à plateau); **pick-up point** [for goods, passengers] point m de ramassage

**picky** ['pɪkɪ] (compar -ier, superl -iest) adj Fam [choosy] difficile (about sur)

**picnic** ['pɪknɪk] **1.** n pique-nique m **2.** (pt & pp -ck-) vi pique-niquer

**picture** ['pɪktʃə(r)] **1.** n image f; [painting] tableau m; [drawing] dessin m; [photo] photo f; Fig [situation] situation f; Br Fam [film] film m; Br Fam **the pictures** le cinéma; **picture frame** cadre m **2.** vt **to picture sth (to oneself)** s'imaginer qch

**picturesque** [pɪktʃə'resk] adj pittoresque

**pie** [paɪ] n [open] tarte f; [with pastry on top] tourte f; **pie chart** camembert m

**piece** [piːs] **1.** n morceau m; [smaller] bout m; [in chess, puzzle] pièce f; **to take sth to pieces** démonter qch; **a piece of news / advice / luck** une nouvelle / un conseil / une chance; **in one piece** [object] intact **2.** vt **to piece together** [facts] reconstituer

**pier** [pɪə(r)] n [for walking, with entertainments] jetée f

**pierce** [pɪəs] vt percer; [of cold, bullet, sword] transpercer; **to have one's ears pierced** se faire percer les oreilles ■ **piercing 1.** adj [voice, look] perçant; [wind] vif (f vive) **2.** n (body) **piercing** piercing m

**pig** [pɪg] n [animal] cochon m, porc m; Fam [greedy person] goinfre m

**pigeon** ['pɪdʒɪn] n pigeon m

**pigeonhole** ['pɪdʒɪnhəʊl] **1.** n casier m **2.** vt [classify, label] classer; [person] étiqueter

**piggy** ['pɪgɪ] n **piggy bank** tirelire f (en forme de cochon)

**piggyback** ['pɪgɪbæk] n **to give sb a piggyback** porter qn sur son dos

**pigment** ['pɪgmənt] n pigment m

**pigtail** ['pɪgteɪl] n [hair] natte f

**pilchard** ['pɪltʃəd] n pilchard m

**pile** [paɪl] **1.** n [heap] tas m; [neat stack] pile f; Fam **to have piles of** or **a pile of things to do** avoir un tas de choses à faire **2.** vt entasser; [stack] empiler ■ **pile up 1.** vt sep entasser; [stack] empiler **2.** vi [accumulate] s'accumuler

**piles** [paɪlz] npl [illness] hémorroïdes fpl

**pile-up** ['paɪlʌp] n Fam [on road] carambolage m

**pilgrim** ['pɪlgrɪm] n pèlerin m ■ **pilgrimage** n pèlerinage m

**pill** [pɪl] n pilule f; **to be on the pill** [of woman] prendre la pilule

**pillage** ['pɪlɪdʒ] **1.** n pillage m **2.** vti piller

**pillar** ['pɪlə(r)] n pilier m; Br **pillar box** boîte f aux lettres

**pillow** ['pɪləʊ] n oreiller m ■ **pillowcase** n taie f d'oreiller

**pilot** ['paɪlət] **1.** n [of plane, ship] pilote m **2.** adj **pilot light** veilleuse f; **pilot scheme** projet m pilote **3.** vt [plane, ship] piloter

**pimple** ['pɪmpəl] n bouton m

**pin** [pɪn] **1.** n épingle f; Br [drawing pin] punaise f; [in machine] goupille f; Fam **pins and needles** fourmillements mpl; **I've got pins and needles in my arm** j'ai des fourmis dans le bras, je ne sens plus mon bras; Am **to be on pins and needles** trépigner d'impatience, ronger son frein **2.** (pt & pp -nn-) vt [attach] épingler (to à); [to wall] punaiser (to or on à); **to pin down** [immobilize] immobiliser; [fix] fixer; **to pin sth up** [notice] fixer qch au mur

**PIN** [pɪn] *(abbr of* **personal identification number***)n Br***PIN (number)** code *m* confidentiel

**pinball** ['pɪnbɔ:l] *n* flipper *m* ; **pinball machine** flipper *m*

**pincers** ['pɪnsəz] *npl* [tool] tenailles *fpl*

**pinch** [pɪntʃ] **1.** *n* [of salt] pincée *f* ; **to give sb a pinch** pincer qn ; *Br* **at a pinch,** *Am* **in a pinch** à la rigueur **2.** *vt* pincer ; *Br Fam* [steal] piquer **(from** à) **3.** *vi* [of shoes] serrer

**pine** [paɪn] **1.** *n* [tree, wood] pin *m* ; **pine forest** pinède *f* **2.** *vi* **to pine for sb/sth** se languir de qn /qch

**pineapple** ['paɪnæpəl] *n* ananas *m*

**pink** [pɪŋk] *adj & n* [colour] rose *(m)*

**pinnacle** ['pɪnəkəl] *n Fig* [of fame, career] apogée *m*

**pinpoint** ['pɪnpɔɪnt] *vt* [locate] repérer ; [identify] identifier

**pin-striped** [-ˌstraɪpt] *adj* à très fines rayures

**pint** [paɪnt] *n* pinte *f (Br = 0,57 l, Am = 0,47 l)* ; **a pint of beer** ≃ un demi-litre

**pioneer** [paɪə'nɪə(r)] **1.** *n* pionnier, -ère *mf* **2.** *vt* **to pioneer sth** être le premier /la première à mettre au point qch

**pious** ['paɪəs] *adj* [person, deed] pieux *(f* pieuse)

**pip** [pɪp] *n Br* [of fruit] pépin *m*

**pipe** [paɪp] **1.** *n* tuyau *m* ; [for smoking] pipe *f* ; [musical instrument] pipeau *m* ; **to smoke a pipe** fumer la pipe **2.** *vi Fam* **to pipe down** [shut up] se taire ■ **piping** *adv* **piping hot** très chaud

**pipeline** ['paɪplaɪn] *n* [for oil] pipeline *m* ; *Fig* **to be in the pipeline** être en préparation

**pirate** ['paɪərət] *n* pirate *m* ■ **pirated** *adj* [book, record, CD] pirate

**pissed** [pɪst] *adj v Fam* [drunk] bourré ; *Am* [angry] en rogne

**pistachio** [pɪ'stæʃɪəʊ] *(pl* **-os)** *n* [nut, flavour] pistache *f*

**pistol** ['pɪstəl] *n* pistolet *m*

**pit¹** [pɪt] *n* [hole] fosse *f* ; [mine] mine *f*

**pit²** [pɪt] *n Am* [stone of fruit] noyau *m* *(pl* -aux) ; [smaller] pépin *m*

**pit³** [pɪt] *(pt & pp* -tt-*) vt* **to pit oneself against sb** se mesurer à qn

**pitch** [pɪtʃ] **1.** *n* **a)** [for football] terrain *m* **b)** [of voice] hauteur *f* ; [musical] ton *m* **2.** *vt* [tent] dresser ; [ball] lancer **3.** *vi Fam* **to pitch in** [cooperate] mettre du sien ■ **pitch-black, pitch-dark** *adj* noir comme dans un four

**pitcher** ['pɪtʃə(r)] *n* cruche *f*

**pitfall** ['pɪtfɔ:l] *n* [trap] piège *m*

**pith** [pɪθ] *n* [of orange] peau *f* blanche

**pitiful** ['pɪtɪfəl] *adj* pitoyable ■ **pitiless** *adj* impitoyable

**pittance** ['pɪtəns] *n* [income] salaire *m* de misère

**pity** ['pɪtɪ] **1.** *n* pitié *f* ; **to take** *or* **have pity on sb** avoir pitié de qn ; **what a pity!** quel dommage ! ; **it's a pity that...** c'est dommage que... (+ *subjunctive*) **2.** *(pt & pp* -ied*) vt* plaindre

**pivot** ['pɪvət] **1.** *n* pivot *m* **2.** *vi* pivoter **(on** sur)

**pixel** ['pɪksl] *n* COMPUT pixel *m* ■ **pixelate** ['pɪksəleɪt], **pixelize** ['pɪksəlaɪz] *vt* pixéliser ■ **pixellated,** *Am* **pixelated** ['pɪksəleɪtɪd] *adj* COMPUT [image] pixellisé

**pizza** ['pi:tsə] *n* pizza *f*

**placard** ['plækɑ:d] *n* [on wall] affiche *f* ; [hand-held] pancarte *f*

**place** [pleɪs] **1.** *n* endroit *m*, lieu *m* ; [seat, position, rank] place *f* ; *Fam* **my place** chez moi ; **to lose one's place** [in queue] perdre sa place ; [in book] perdre sa page ; **to take the place of sb/sth** remplacer qn /qch ; **to take place** [happen] avoir lieu ; *Br* **to set** *or* **lay three places** [at the table] mettre trois couverts ; *Am* **some place** [somewhere] quelque part ; *Am* **no place** [nowhere] nulle part ; **all over the place** un peu partout ; **in the first place** [firstly] en premier lieu ; **in place of** à la place de ; **out of place** [remark] déplacé ; [object] pas à sa place ; **place of work** lieu *m* de travail **2.** *vt* [put, situate, invest, in sport] placer ; **to**

**be placed third** se classer troisième; **to place an order with sb** passer une commande à qn

**placement** ['pleɪsmənt] n stage m

**placid** ['plæsɪd] adj placide

**plague** [pleɪg] **1.** n [disease] peste f **2.** vt [of person] harceler (**with** de)

**plaice** [pleɪs] n [fish] carrelet m

**plain¹** [pleɪn] **1.** (compar -er, superl -est) adj [clear, obvious] clair; [simple] simple; [without a pattern] uni; [not beautiful] quelconque; **in plain clothes** en civil; **to make it plain to sb that...** faire comprendre à qn que...; **plain chocolate** chocolat m noir; **plain flour** farine f (sans levure) **2.** adv Fam [utterly] complètement ∎ **plainly** adv [clearly] clairement; [frankly] franchement

**plain²** [pleɪn] n [land] plaine f

**plait** [plæt] **1.** n tresse f, natte f **2.** vt tresser, natter

**plan** [plæn] **1.** n [proposal, intention] projet m; [of building, town, essay] plan m; **to go according to plan** se passer comme prévu **2.** (pt & pp -nn-) vt [arrange] projeter; [crime] comploter; [building, town] faire le plan de; **to plan to do** or **on doing sth** [intend] projeter de faire qch; **as planned** comme prévu **3.** vi faire des projets ∎ **planned** [plænd] adj [crime] prémédité; [economy] planifié, dirigé; [baby] désiré, voulu ∎ **plans** npl plans mpl, projets mpl; **have you any plans for tonight?** avez-vous prévu quelque chose pour ce soir?

**plane¹** [pleɪn] n [aircraft] avion m

**plane²** [pleɪn] **1.** n [tool] rabot m **2.** vt raboter

**plane³** [pleɪn] n [level, surface] & Fig plan m

**planet** ['plænɪt] n planète f

**plank** [plæŋk] n planche f

**planning** ['plænɪŋ] n conception f; **family planning** planning m familial

**plant** [plɑːnt] **1.** n a) [living thing] plante f b) [factory] usine f; [machin-

ery] matériel m **2.** vt [tree, flower] planter; [crops, seeds] semer; [field] ensemencer (**with** en); Fig [bomb] poser

**plantation** [plæn'teɪʃən] n [trees, land] plantation f

**plaque** [plæk] n [sign] plaque f; [on teeth] plaque f dentaire

**plasma screen** n TV écran m (à) plasma

**plasma TV** n télévision f (à) plasma

**plaster** ['plɑːstə(r)] **1.** n a) [on wall] plâtre m; **to put sb's leg in plaster** mettre la jambe de qn dans le plâtre; **plaster cast** [for broken bone] plâtre m b) Br **(sticking) plaster** pansement m adhésif **2.** vt [wall] plâtrer; **to plaster sth with** [cover] couvrir qch de

**plastic** ['plæstɪk] **1.** adj [object] en plastique; **plastic bag** sac m en plastique; **plastic surgery** [cosmetic] chirurgie f esthétique **2.** n plastique m

**plate** [pleɪt] n [dish] assiette f; [metal sheet] plaque f; [book illustration] gravure f

**plateau** ['plætəʊ] (pl -eaus [-əʊz] or -eaux) n [flat land] plateau m

**platform** ['plætfɔːm] n [raised surface] plate-forme f; [in train station] quai m; [for speaker] estrade f

**platinum** ['plætɪnəm] n [metal] platine m

**plausible** ['plɔːzəbəl] adj [argument, excuse] plausible

**play** [pleɪ] **1.** n [drama] pièce f (de théâtre); [amusement] jeu m; **to come into play** entrer en jeu; **a play on words** un jeu de mots **2.** vt [part, tune, card] jouer; [game] jouer à; [instrument] jouer de; [match] disputer (**with** avec); [team, opponent] jouer contre; [record, compact disc] passer; [radio, tape recorder] faire marcher; Fig **to play a part in doing/in sth** contribuer à faire / à qch **3.** vi jouer (**with** avec; **at** à); [of record player, tape recorder] marcher; Fam **what are you playing at?** à quoi tu joues? ∎ **playboy** n play-boy m ∎ **playground** n Br [in school] cour f de récréation; [in park] terrain m de jeux ∎ **playgroup** n garderie f ∎ **play-**

**mate** *n* camarade *mf* de jeu ■ **play-school** *n* garderie *f* ■ **playtime** *n* [in school] récréation *f* ■ **playwright** *n* dramaturge *mf* ■ **play about, play around** *vi* jouer, s'amuser ■ **play about with** *vt insep* a) [fiddle with, tamper with] **to play about with sth** jouer avec *ou* tripoter qch b) [juggle - statistics, figures] jouer avec ; [consider - possibilities, alternatives] envisager, considérer c) *Fam* [trifle with] **to play about with sb** faire marcher qn ■ **play along** *vi* **to play along (with sb)** entrer dans le jeu (de qn) ■ **play back** *vt sep* [tape] réécouter ■ **play down** *vt sep* minimiser ■ **play on** *vt insep* [feelings, fears] jouer sur ■ **play out** *vt sep* [scene, fantasy] jouer ■ **play up** **1.** *vt sep* [emphasize] insister sur **2.** *vi* *Fam* [of child, machine] faire des siennes

**player** ['pleɪə(r)] *n* [in game, of instrument] joueur *m*, joueuse *f* ; **clarinet player** joueur *m* / joueuse *f* de clarinette

**playful** ['pleɪfəl] *adj* [mood, tone] enjoué ; [child, animal] joueur (*f* joueuse)

**playing** ['pleɪɪŋ] *n* jeu *m* ; **playing card** carte *f* à jouer ; **playing field** terrain *m* de jeux

**plc** [pi:el'si:] *(abbr of* **public limited company)** *n* Br COMM ≃ SA *f*

**plea** [pli:] *n* [request] appel *m*

**plead** [pli:d] **1.** *vt* [argue] plaider ; [as excuse] alléguer **2.** *vi* **to plead with sb (to do sth)** implorer qn (de faire qch) ; **to plead guilty** plaider coupable

**pleasant** ['plezənt] *adj* agréable (**to** avec)

**please** [pli:z] **1.** *adv* s'il te / vous plaît ; **please sit down** asseyez-vous, je vous prie ; **please do!** bien sûr !, je vous en prie ! **2.** *vt* **to please sb** faire plaisir à qn ; [satisfy] contenter qn **3.** *vi* plaire ; **do as you please** fais comme tu veux ■ **pleased** *adj* content (**with** de) ; **pleased to meet you!** enchanté ! ■ **pleasing** *adj* agréable, plaisant

**pleasure** ['pleʒə(r)] *n* plaisir *m*

**pleat** [pli:t] *n* pli *m* ■ **pleated** *adj* plissé

**pledge** [pledʒ] **1.** *n* [promise] promesse *f* (**to do** de faire) **2.** *vt* promettre (**to do** de faire)

**plenty** ['plentɪ] *n* **plenty of** beaucoup de ; **that's plenty** [of food] merci, j'en ai assez ■ **plentiful** *adj* abondant

**pliers** ['plaɪəz] *npl* pince *f*

**plight** [plaɪt] *n* [crisis] situation *f* critique

**plimsolls** ['plɪmsəʊlz] *npl* Br tennis *mpl*

**plod** [plɒd] *(pt & pp* -dd-*)* *vi* **to plod (along)** [walk] avancer laborieusement ; [work] travailler laborieusement

**plonk¹** [plɒŋk] *vt* *Fam* **to plonk sth (down)** [drop] poser qch

**plonk²** [plɒŋk] *n* Br Fam [wine] pinard *m*

**plot** [plɒt] **1.** *n* [conspiracy] complot *m* ; [of novel, film] intrigue *f* ; **plot (of land)** parcelle *f* de terrain **2.** *(pt & pp* -tt-*)* *vti* comploter (**to do** de faire) **3.** *vt* **to plot (out)** [route] déterminer ; [graph] tracer

**plough**, *Am* **plow** [plaʊ] **1.** *n* charrue *f* **2.** *vt* [field] labourer **3.** *vi* labourer ■ **ploughman** *(pl* -men*)* *n* Br **ploughman's lunch** assiette de fromage ou jambon avec de la salade et des condiments

**PLS**, **PLZ** *(abbr of* **please)** MESSAGING stp, svp

**pluck** [plʌk] **1.** *n* courage *m* **2.** *vt* [hair, feathers] arracher ; [flower] cueillir ; [fowl] plumer ; [eyebrows] épiler ; [string of guitar] pincer ; **to pluck up the courage to do sth** trouver le courage de faire qch ■ **plucky** *(compar* -ier, *superl* -iest*)* *adj* courageux, -euse

**plug** [plʌg] **1.** *n* a) [of cotton wool, wood] tampon *m* ; [for sink, bath] bonde *f* b) [electrical - on device] fiche *f* ; [socket] prise *f* (de courant) ; AUTO **(spark) plug** bougie *f* **2.** *(pt & pp* -gg-*)* *vt* a) **to plug (up)** [gap, hole] boucher ; [appliance] brancher qch b) *Fam* [promote] faire de la pub pour ■ **plug-and-play** *adj* COMPUT plug-and-play ■ **plughole** *n* trou *m* d'écoulement

**plum** [plʌm] *n* prune *f*

**plumb** [plʌm] *adv* Am Fam [crazy] complètement ■ **plumb in** *vt sep* [washing machine] brancher

**plumber** [ˈplʌmə(r)] n plombier m ■ **plumbing** n [job, system] plomberie f

**plummet** [ˈplʌmɪt] vi [of prices] s'effondrer ; [of aircraft] plonger

**plump** [plʌmp] **1.** (compar -er, superl -est) adj [person, arm] potelé ; [chicken] dodu ; [cheek] rebondi **2.** vi Fam **to plump for sth** se décider pour qch

**plunder** [ˈplʌndə(r)] **1.** n [goods] butin m **2.** vt piller

**plunge** [plʌndʒ] **1.** n [dive] plongeon m ; Fig [decrease] chute f ; Fam **to take the plunge** [take on difficult task] se jeter à l'eau ; [get married] se marier **2.** vt [thrust] plonger (**into** dans) **3.** vi [dive] plonger (**into** dans) ; Fig [decrease] chuter

**plural** [ˈplʊərəl] **1.** adj [noun] au pluriel **2.** n pluriel m ; **in the plural** au pluriel

**plus** [plʌs] **1.** prep plus ; [as well as] en plus de **2.** adj [factor & ELEC] positif, -ive ; **twenty plus** plus de vingt **3.** (pl **plusses** [ˈplʌsɪz]) n **plus (sign)** (signe m) plus m ; **that's a plus** c'est un plus

**pluto** [pluːtəʊ] vt Am dévaluer (qn ou qch) ; **to be plutoed** se faire dévaluer

**ply** [plaɪ] (pt & pp **plied**) **1.** vt [trade] exercer ; **to ply sb with questions** bombarder qn de questions **2.** vi **to ply between** [travel] faire la navette entre

**p.m.** [piːˈem] adv [afternoon] de l'après-midi ; [evening] du soir

**pneumonia** [njuːˈməʊnɪə] n pneumonie f

**poach** [pəʊtʃ] **1.** vt [egg] pocher ; [employee] débaucher **2.** vi [hunt] braconner

**PO Box** [piːˈəʊbɒks] (abbr of **Post Office Box**) n boîte f postale, BP f

**pocket** [ˈpɒkɪt] **1.** n poche f ; **to be out of pocket** en être de sa poche ; **pocket calculator** calculette f ; **pocket money** argent m de poche **2.** vt [put in pocket] empocher ; Fam [steal] rafler ■ **pocketbook** n Am [handbag] sac m à main ■ **pocketful** n **a pocketful of** une pleine poche de

**podcast** [ˈpɒdkæst] n COMPUT podcast m

**podium** [ˈpəʊdɪəm] n podium m

**poem** [ˈpəʊɪm] n poème m ■ **poet** n poète m ■ **poetic** [pəʊˈetɪk] adj poétique ■ **poetry** n poésie f

**poignant** [ˈpɔɪnjənt] adj poignant

**point** [pɔɪnt] **1.** n **a)** [of knife, needle] pointe f ; Br **points** [for train] aiguillage m
**b)** [dot, score, degree, argument] point m ; [location] endroit m ; [importance] intérêt m ; **to make a point of doing sth** mettre un point d'honneur à faire qch ; **you have a point** tu as raison ; **there's no point (in) staying** ça ne sert à rien de rester ; **to get to the point** en arriver au fait ; **at this point in time** en ce moment ; **to be on the point of doing sth** être sur le point de faire qch ; **his good points** ses qualités fpl ; **point of view** point m de vue
**c)** MATH **three point five** trois virgule cinq
**2.** vt [aim] diriger ; [camera, gun] braquer (**at** sur) ; **to point one's finger at sb** montrer qn du doigt ; **to point sth out** [show] montrer qch ; [error, fact] signaler qch
**3.** vi **to point at** or **to sb/sth** [with finger] montrer qn /qch du doigt ; **to point north** [of arrow, compass] indiquer le nord

**point-blank** [pɔɪntˈblæŋk] **1.** adj [refusal] catégorique ; **at point-blank range** à bout portant **2.** adv [refuse] (tout) net

**pointed** [ˈpɔɪntɪd] adj pointu ; [beard] en pointe ; Fig [remark, criticism] pertinent

**pointer** [ˈpɔɪntə(r)] n [on dial] aiguille f ; [stick] baguette f ; [clue] indice m ; COMPUT pointeur m

**pointless** [ˈpɔɪntləs] adj inutile

**poise** [pɔɪz] n [composure] assurance f ; [grace] grâce f ■ **poised** adj [composed] calme ; [hanging] suspendu ; [balanced] en équilibre ; **to be poised to do sth** [ready] être prêt à faire qch

**poison** ['pɔɪzən] **1.** n poison m ; [of snake] venin m **2.** vt empoisonner ■ **poisonous** adj [fumes, substance] toxique ; [snake] venimeux, -euse ; [plant] vénéneux, -euse

**poke** [pəʊk] **1.** vt [person] donner un coup à ; [object] tâter ; [fire] attiser ; **to poke sth into sth** enfoncer qch dans qch ; **to poke one's finger at sb** pointer son doigt vers qn ; Fig **to poke one's nose into sth** mettre son nez dans qch **2.** vi **to poke at sth** [with finger, stick] tâter qch

**poker¹** ['pəʊkə(r)] n [for fire] tisonnier m

**poker²** ['pəʊkə(r)] n [card game] poker m

**Poland** ['pəʊlənd] n la Pologne ■ **Pole** n Polonais, -e mf ■ **Polish** ['pəʊlɪʃ] **1.** adj polonais **2.** n [language] polonais m

**polar** ['pəʊlə(r)] adj polaire ; **polar bear** ours m blanc ; **polar bread** pain m polaire

**Polaroid®** ['pəʊlərɔɪd] n [camera, photo] Polaroid® m

**pole¹** [pəʊl] n [rod] perche f ; [fixed] poteau m ; [for flag] hampe f ; **pole vault** or **vaulting** saut m à la perche

**pole²** [pəʊl] n GEOG pôle m ; **North/South Pole** pôle m Nord/Sud ; **pole dancing** danse f de poteau

**police** [pəˈliːs] **1.** n police f **2.** adj [inquiry, dog] policier, -ère ; **police car** voiture f de police ; Am **police department** service m de police ; **police station** poste m de police **3.** vt [city, area] maintenir l'ordre dans ■ **policeman** (pl -men) n agent m de police ■ **policewoman** (pl -women) n agent m de police

**policy** ['pɒlɪsɪ] (pl -ies) n **a)** [of government, organization] politique f **b)** (insurance) **policy** police f (d'assurance)

**polio** ['pəʊlɪəʊ] n polio f

**polish** ['pɒlɪʃ] **1.** n [for shoes] cirage m ; [for floor, furniture] cire f ; [for nails] vernis m ; Fig raffinement m ; **to give sth a polish** faire briller qch **2.** vt [floor, table, shoes] cirer ; [metal] astiquer ; Fig [style] polir ; Fam **to polish off** [food]

avaler ; [drink] descendre ; [work] expédier ; **to polish up one's French** travailler son français

**polite** [pəˈlaɪt] (compar -er, superl -est) adj poli (**to** or **with** avec) ■ **politely** adv poliment

**political** [pəˈlɪtɪkəl] adj politique ■ **politically** adv **politically correct** politiquement correct

**politician** [pɒlɪˈtɪʃən] n homme m / femme f politique

**politics** ['pɒlɪtɪks] n politique f

**poll** [pəʊl] **1.** n [voting] scrutin m ; **to go to the polls** aller aux urnes ; (opinion) **poll** sondage m (d'opinion) **2.** vt [votes] obtenir ; [people] sonder

**pollen** ['pɒlən] n pollen m

**polling** ['pəʊlɪŋ] n [election] élections fpl ; Br **polling station,** Am **polling place** bureau m de vote

**pollute** [pəˈluːt] vt polluer ■ **pollution** n pollution f

**polo** ['pəʊləʊ] n [sport] polo m ; **polo neck** [sweater, neckline] col m roulé

**polyester** [pɒlɪˈestə(r)] n polyester m ; **polyester shirt** chemise f en polyester

**polythene** ['pɒlɪθiːn] n Br polyéthylène m ; **polythene bag** sac m en plastique

**pompous** ['pɒmpəs] adj pompeux, -euse

**pond** [pɒnd] n étang m ; [smaller] mare f ; [artificial] bassin m

**ponder** ['pɒndə(r)] **1.** vt réfléchir à **2.** vi **to ponder (over sth)** réfléchir (à qch)

**pong** [pɒŋ] Br Fam **1.** n [smell] puanteur f **2.** vi puer

**pony** ['pəʊnɪ] (pl -ies) n poney m ■ **ponyride** ['pəʊnɪraɪd] n promenade f à dos de poney ■ **ponytail** n queue f de cheval

**poodle** ['puːdəl] n caniche m

**pool¹** [puːl] n [puddle] flaque f ; [of blood] mare f ; [for swimming] piscine f

**pool²** [puːl] **1.** n [of money, helpers] réserve f ; [of typists] pool m ; Br **the**

(football) **pools** concours de pronostics des matchs de football **2.** vt [share] mettre en commun

**pool³** [puːl] n [game] billard m américain

**poor** [pʊə(r)] **1.** (compar -er, superl -est) adj [not rich] pauvre ; [bad] mauvais ; [chances] maigre ; [harvest, reward] faible ; **to be in poor health** ne pas bien se porter **2.** npl **the poor** les pauvres mpl ■ **poorly 1.** adv mal ; [clothed, furnished] pauvrement **2.** adj Br Fam malade

**pop¹** [pɒp] **1.** excl pan !
**2.** n [noise] bruit m sec ; **to go pop** faire pan
**3.** (pt & pp -pp-) vt a) [balloon] crever ; [cork] faire sauter
**b)** Fam [put] mettre
**4.** vi a) [burst] éclater ; [of cork] sauter
**b)** Br Fam **to pop in** passer ; **to pop out** sortir (un instant) ; **to pop up** surgir
■ **pop-up 1.** adj a) [toaster] automatique **b)** [book] dont les images se déplient **2.** n COMPUT pop-up m

**pop²** [pɒp] **1.** n [music] pop f **2.** adj [concert, singer, group] pop inv

**pop³** [pɒp] n Am Fam [father] papa m

**pop⁴** [pɒp] n Am (soda) pop [drink] soda m

**popcorn** [ˈpɒpkɔːn] n pop-corn m inv

**pope** [pəʊp] n pape m

**poplar** [ˈpɒplə(r)] n [tree, wood] peuplier m

**poppy** [ˈpɒpɪ] (pl -ies) n [red, wild] coquelicot m ; [cultivated] pavot m

**Popsicle®** [ˈpɒpsɪkəl] n Am [ice lolly] ≃ Esquimau® m

**popular** [ˈpɒpjʊlə(r)] adj populaire ; [fashionable] à la mode ; [restaurant] qui a beaucoup de succès ■ **popularity** [-ˈlærətɪ] n popularité f (**with** auprès de)

**populated** [ˈpɒpjʊleɪtɪd] adj **densely / sparsely populated** très / peu peuplé

**population** [pɒpjʊˈleɪʃən] n population f

**porcelain** [ˈpɔːsəlɪn] n porcelaine f

**porch** [pɔːtʃ] n porche m ; Am [veranda] véranda f

**pore** [pɔː(r)] **1.** n [of skin] pore m **2.** vi **to pore over sth** [book, question] étudier qch de près

**pork** [pɔːk] n [meat] porc m ; **pork pie** ≃ pâté m en croûte ■ **porky** [ˈpɔːkɪ] (compar -ier, superl -iest) **1.** adj Fam & Pej [fat] gros (f grosse), gras (f grasse), adipeux, -euse Pej **2.** n Br Fam [lie] bobard m

**pornography** [pɔːˈnɒgrəfɪ] n pornographie f

**porridge** [ˈpɒrɪdʒ] n porridge m

**port¹** [pɔːt] n [harbour & COMPUT] port m ; **port of call** escale f

**port²** [pɔːt] n NAUT [left-hand side] bâbord m

**port³** [pɔːt] n [wine] porto m

**portable** [ˈpɔːtəbəl] adj portable

**porter** [ˈpɔːtə(r)] n [for luggage] porteur m ; [door attendant] chasseur m

**portfolio** [pɔːtˈfəʊlɪəʊ] (pl -os) n [for documents] porte-documents m inv ; [of shares, government minister] portefeuille m ; [of model, artist] book m

**porthole** [ˈpɔːthəʊl] n hublot m

**portion** [ˈpɔːʃən] n partie f ; [share, helping] portion f

**portrait** [ˈpɔːtreɪt, ˈpɔːtrɪt] n portrait m

**portray** [pɔːˈtreɪ] vt [describe] dépeindre ■ **portrayal** n [description] tableau m

**Portugal** [ˈpɔːtjʊgəl] n le Portugal ■ **Portuguese** [-ˈgiːz] **1.** adj portugais **2.** n [person] Portugais, -e mf ; [language] portugais m ; **the Portuguese** [people] les Portugais

**pose** [pəʊz] **1.** n [position] pose f **2.** vt [question] poser ; [threat] représenter **3.** vi poser (**for** pour) ; **to pose as a lawyer** se faire passer pour un avocat

**posh** [pɒʃ] adj Fam [smart] chic inv

**position** [pəˈzɪʃən] **1.** n [place, posture, opinion] position f ; [of building, town] emplacement m ; [job, circumstances] situation f ; **in a position to do sth** en mesure de faire qch ; **in position** en place **2.** vt [put] placer ; [troops] poster

**positive** [ˈpɒzɪtɪv] adj [person, answer, test] positif, -ive ; [progress, change] réel (f réelle) ; [certain] sûr, certain (**of** de ;

that que) ■ **positively** *adv* [identify] formellement; [think, react] de façon positive; [for emphasis] véritablement

**po$bl** MESSAGING *written abbr of* **possible**

**possess** [pə'zes] *vt* posséder ■ **possession** *n* [ownership] possession *f*; [thing possessed] bien *m*; **to be in possession of sth** être en possession de qch

**possessive** [pə'zesɪv] **1.** *adj* possessif, -ive **2.** *adj & n* [in grammar] possessif (*m*)

**possibility** [pɒsə'bɪlətɪ] *(pl* **-ies)** *n* possibilité *f*

**possible** ['pɒsəbəl] *adj* possible; **it is possible (for us) to do it** il (nous) est possible de le faire; **it is possible that...** il est possible que... (+ *subjunctive*); **as soon as possible** dès que possible

**possibly** ['pɒsəblɪ] *adv* **a)** [perhaps] peut-être **b)** [for emphasis] **to do all one possibly can** faire tout son possible (**to do** pour faire); **he cannot possibly stay** il ne peut absolument pas rester

**post¹** [pəʊst] **1.** *n Br* [postal system] poste *f*; [letters] courrier *m*; **by post** par la poste; **post office** (bureau *m* de) poste *f* **2.** *vt* [letter] poster; **to keep sb posted** tenir qn au courant ■ **postbox** *n Br* boîte *f* aux lettres ■ **postcard** *n* carte *f* postale ■ **postcode** *n Br* code *m* postal ■ **postdate** *vt* postdater ■ **postman** *(pl* **-men)** *n Br* facteur *m* ■ **postmark** *n* cachet *m* de la poste ■ **postwoman** ['pəʊst,wʊmən] *(pl* **-women)** *n* factrice *f*

**post²** [pəʊst] **1.** *n* [job, place] poste *m* **2.** *vt* [sentry, guard] poster; *Br* [employee] affecter (**to** à)

**post³** [pəʊst] *n* [pole] poteau *m*; [of door, bed] montant *m*; **finishing** *or* **winning post** [in race] poteau *m* d'arrivée

**post-** [pəʊst] *pref* post-; **post-1800** après 1800

**postage** ['pəʊstɪdʒ] *n* affranchissement *m* (**to** pour); **postage paid** port *m* payé; **postage stamp** timbre-poste *m*

**postal** ['pəʊstəl] *adj* [services] postal; [vote] par correspondance; *Br* **postal order** mandat *m* postal

**poster** ['pəʊstə(r)] *n* affiche *f*; [for decoration] poster *m*

**postgraduate** [pəʊst'grædjʊət] **1.** *adj* de troisième cycle **2.** *n* étudiant, -e *mf* de troisième cycle

**posthumous** ['pɒstjʊməs] *adj* posthume

**postmortem** [pəʊst'mɔːtəm] *adj & n* **postmortem (examination)** autopsie *f* (**on** de)

**postpone** [pəʊs'pəʊn] *vt* reporter

**posture** ['pɒstʃə(r)] *n* [of body] posture *f*; *Fig* attitude *f*

**postwar** ['pəʊstwɔː(r)] *adj* d'après-guerre

**posy** ['pəʊzɪ] *(pl* **-ies)** *n* petit bouquet *m*

**pot¹** [pɒt] *n* pot *m*; [for cooking] casserole *f*; *Fam* **to go to pot** aller à la ruine

**pot²** [pɒt] *n Fam* [drug] hasch *m*

**potato** [pə'teɪtəʊ] *(pl* **-oes)** *n* pomme *f* de terre; *Br* **potato crisps,** *Am* **potato chips** chips *fpl*

**potent** ['pəʊtənt] *adj* puissant; [drink] fort

**potential** [pə'tenʃəl] **1.** *adj* potentiel, -elle **2.** *n* potentiel *m*; **to have potential** avoir du potentiel

**pothole** ['pɒthəʊl] *n* [in road] nid-de-poule *m*; [cave] caverne *f*

**potion** ['pəʊʃən] *n* potion *f*

**potsticker** ['pɒtstɪkə(r)] *n Am* CULIN ravioli *m* chinois

**potter** ['pɒtə(r)] **1.** *n* [person] potier, -ère *mf* **2.** *vi Br* **to potter about** [do odd jobs] bricoler ■ **pottery** *n* [art] poterie *f*; [objects] poteries *fpl*; **a piece of pottery** une poterie

**potty¹** ['pɒtɪ] *n* [for baby] pot *m*

**potty²** ['pɒtɪ] *(compar* **-ier,** *superl* **-iest)** *adj Br Fam* [mad] dingue

**pouch** [paʊtʃ] *n* bourse *f*; [for tobacco] blague *f*

**poultry** ['pəʊltrɪ] *n* volaille *f*

**pounce** [paʊns] *vi* [of animal] bondir (**on** sur) ; [of person] se précipiter (**on** sur)

**pound¹** [paʊnd] *n* **a)** [weight] livre *f* (= 453,6 g) **b) pound (sterling)** livre *f* (sterling)

**pound²** [paʊnd] *n* [for cars, dogs] fourrière *f*

**pound³** [paʊnd] **1.** *vt* MIL [town] pilonner **2.** *vi* [of heart] battre à tout rompre

**pour** [pɔː(r)] **1.** *vt* verser ; **to pour sb a drink** verser à boire à qn **2.** *vi* it's pouring il pleut à verse ■ **pour down** *vi* it's pouring down il pleut à verse ■ **pour in 1.** *vt sep* [liquid] verser **2.** *vi* [of water, sunshine] entrer à flots ; *Fig* [of people, money] affluer ■ **pour off** *vt sep* [liquid] vider ■ **pour out 1.** *vt sep* [liquid] verser ; *Fig* [anger, grief] déverser **2.** *vi* [of liquid] se déverser ; *Fig* [of people] sortir en masse (**from** de)

**pout** [paʊt] *vi* faire la moue

**poverty** [ˈpɒvətɪ] *n* pauvreté *f*

**powder** [ˈpaʊdə(r)] **1.** *n* poudre *f* ; **powder puff** houppette *f* ; **powder room** toilettes *fpl* pour dames **2.** *vt* [body, skin] poudrer ; **to powder one's face** *or* **nose** se poudrer ■ **powdered** *adj* [milk, eggs] en poudre

**power** [ˈpaʊə(r)] **1.** *n* [ability, authority] pouvoir *m* ; [strength, nation] puissance *f* ; [energy] énergie *f* ; [electric current] courant *m* ; **to be in power** être au pouvoir ; **to have sb in one's power** tenir qn à sa merci ; *Br* **power failure** *or* **cut** coupure *f* de courant ; *Br* **power station**, *Am* **power plant** centrale *f* électrique ; AUTO **power steering** direction *f* assistée **2.** *vt* [provide with power] actionner

**powerful** [ˈpaʊəfəl] *adj* puissant ; [drug] fort ■ **powerless** *adj* impuissant (**to do** à faire)

**PPL** MESSAGING *written abbr of* people

**PR** [piːˈɑː(r)] *(abbr of* public relations) *n* RP *fpl*

**practical** [ˈpræktɪkəl] *adj* [tool, knowledge, solution] pratique ; **to be practical** [of person] avoir l'esprit pratique ; **practical joke** farce *f*

**practically** [ˈpræktɪkəlɪ] *adv* [almost] pratiquement

**practice** [ˈpræktɪs] **1.** *n* [action, exercise, custom] pratique *f* ; [in sport] entraînement *m* ; [surgery] centre *m* médical ; **in practice** [in reality] dans la *ou* en pratique ; **to put sth into practice** mettre qch en pratique ; **to be out of practice** avoir perdu l'habitude **2.** *vti* Am = **practise**

**practise**, *Am* **practice** [ˈpræktɪs] **1.** *vt* [sport, language, art, religion] pratiquer ; [medicine, law] exercer ; [musical instrument] travailler **2.** *vi* [of musician] s'exercer ; [of sportsperson] s'entraîner ; [of doctor, lawyer] exercer ■ **practising** *adj* [doctor, lawyer] en exercice ; REL pratiquant

**practitioner** [prækˈtɪʃənə(r)] *n* **general practitioner** (médecin *m*) généraliste *m*

**pragmatic** [prægˈmætɪk] *adj* pragmatique

**Prairie** [ˈpreərɪ] *n* **the Prairie** [in USA] la (Grande) Prairie ; [in Canada] les Prairies *fpl*

**praise** [preɪz] **1.** *n* éloges *mpl* **2.** *vt* faire l'éloge de ; [God] louer ; **to praise sb for doing** *or* **having done sth** louer qn d'avoir fait qch

**pram** [præm] *n Br* landau *m* (*pl* -aus)

**prank** [præŋk] *n* farce *f*

**prawn** [prɔːn] *n* crevette *f* rose ; **prawn crackers** chips *fpl* aux crevettes

**pray** [preɪ] **1.** *vt* **to pray that...** prier pour que... (+ *subjunctive*) **2.** *vi* prier ; *Fig* **to pray for good weather** prier pour qu'il fasse beau

**prayer** [preə(r)] *n* prière *f*

**pre-** [priː] *pref* **pre-1800** avant 1800

**preach** [priːtʃ] *vti* prêcher ; **to preach to sb** prêcher qn ; *Fig* faire la morale à qn ■ **preacher** *n* prédicateur, -trice *mf*

**prearrange** [priːəˈreɪndʒ] *vt* arranger à l'avance

**precarious** [prɪˈkeərɪəs] *adj* précaire

**precaution** [prɪˈkɔːʃən] *n* précaution *f* ; **as a precaution** par précaution

**precede** [prɪˈsiːd] *vti* précéder

**precedence** ['presɪdəns] n to take precedence over sb avoir la préséance sur qn; to take precedence over sth passer avant qch

**precedent** ['presɪdənt] n précédent m

**precinct** ['pri:sɪŋkt] n Br [for shopping] zone f commerçante piétonnière; Am [electoral district] circonscription f; Am [police district] secteur m

**precious** ['preʃəs] 1. adj précieux, -euse 2. adv precious little très peu (de)

**precipice** ['presɪpɪs] n précipice m

**precipitate** [prɪ'sɪpɪteɪt] vt [hasten, throw & CHEM] précipiter

**precise** [prɪ'saɪs] adj [exact] précis; [meticulous] méticuleux, -euse ■ **precisely** adv précisément; at three o'clock precisely à trois heures précises ■ **precision** [-'sɪʒən] n précision f

**preclude** [prɪ'klu:d] vt [prevent] empêcher (**from doing** de faire); [possibility] exclure

**precocious** [prɪ'kəʊʃəs] adj précoce

**preconception** [pri:kən'sepʃən] n idée f préconçue

**precondition** [pri:kən'dɪʃən] n condition f préalable

**predator** ['predətə(r)] n prédateur m

**predecessor** ['pri:dɪsesə(r)] n prédécesseur m

**predicament** [prɪ'dɪkəmənt] n situation f difficile

**predict** [prɪ'dɪkt] vt prédire ■ **predictable** adj prévisible ■ **prediction** n prédiction f ■ **predictive text(ing)** [prɪ'dɪktɪv-] n TEL écriture f prédictive, T9 m

**predispose** [pri:dɪs'pəʊz] vt prédisposer (**to do** à faire)

**predominant** [prɪ'dɒmɪnənt] adj prédominant ■ **predominate** vi prédominer (**over** sur)

**pre-empt** [pri:'empt] vt devancer

**preface** ['prefɪs] n [of book] préface f

**prefect** ['pri:fekt] n Br SCH élève chargé de la surveillance

**prefer** [prɪ'fɜ:(r)] (pt & pp -rr-) vt préférer (**to** à); to prefer to do sth préférer faire qch

**preferable** ['prefərəbəl] adj préférable (**to** à)

**preference** ['prefərəns] n préférence f (**for** pour); in preference to plutôt que

**prefix** ['pri:fɪks] n [before word] préfixe m

**pregnant** ['pregnənt] adj [woman] enceinte; [animal] pleine; five months pregnant enceinte de cinq mois ■ **pregnancy** (pl -ies) n grossesse f; pregnancy test test m de grossesse

**prehistoric** [pri:hɪ'stɒrɪk] adj préhistorique

**pre-installed** [pri:ɪn'stɔ:ld] adj [software] préinstallé

**prejudge** [pri:'dʒʌdʒ] vt [question] préjuger de; [person] juger sans connaître

**prejudice** ['predʒədɪs] 1. n [bias] préjugé m 2. vt [bias] prévenir (**against/in favour of** contre /en faveur de); [harm] nuire à ■ **prejudiced** adj to be prejudiced avoir des préjugés (**against/in favour of** contre /en faveur de)

**preliminary** [prɪ'lɪmɪnərɪ] adj préliminaire ■ **preliminaries** npl préliminaires mpl

**prelude** ['prelju:d] n prélude m (**to** à)

**premature** [Br 'premətʃʊə(r), Am pri:mə'tʃʊər] adj prématuré

**premeditate** [pri:'medɪteɪt] vt préméditer

**premier** [Br 'premɪə(r), Am prɪ'mɪər] n Premier ministre m

**première** [Br 'premɪeə(r), Am prɪ'mɪər] n [of play, film] première f

**premises** ['premɪsɪz] npl locaux mpl; on the premises sur place

**premium** ['pri:mɪəm] n FIN [for insurance] prime f; [additional sum] supplément m

**premonition** [Br premə'nɪʃən, Am pri:mə'nɪʃən] n prémonition f

**prenatal** [pri:'neɪtəl] adj Am prénatal

**preoccupy** [pri:'ɒkjʊpaɪ] (pt & pp -ied) vt préoccuper au plus haut point; to be

**preoccupied** être préoccupé (**with** par) ▪ **preoccupation** n préoccupation f (**with** pour)

**pre-owned** adj d'occasion

**prep** [prep] adj **prep school** Br école f primaire privée ; Am école f secondaire privée

**pre-packed** [priː'pækt] adj [meat, vegetables] préemballé

**prepaid** [priː'peɪd] adj prépayé

**preparation** [prepə'reɪʃən] n préparation f ; **preparations** préparatifs mpl (**for** de)

**preparatory** [prə'pærətərɪ] adj préparatoire ; **preparatory school** Br école f primaire privée ; Am école f secondaire privée

**prepare** [prɪ'peə(r)] **1.** vt préparer (**sth for** qch pour ; **sb for** qn à) **2.** vi se préparer pour ; **to prepare to do sth** se préparer à faire qch ▪ **prepared** adj [ready] prêt (**to do** à faire) ; **to be prepared for sth** s'attendre à qch

**preposition** [prepə'zɪʃən] n préposition f

**preposterous** [prɪ'pɒstərəs] adj ridicule

**preppie, preppy** ['prepɪ] (pl -ies) Am Fam **1.** n he's a preppie il est BCBG **2.** adj BCBG

**prerecorded** [priːrɪ'kɔːdɪd] adj préenregistré

**prerequisite** [priː'rekwɪzɪt] n (condition f) préalable m

**prerogative** [prɪ'rɒgətɪv] n prérogative f

**preschool** ['priːskuːl] **1.** adj préscolaire **2.** n Am école f maternelle

**prescribe** [prɪ'skraɪb] vt [of doctor] prescrire ▪ **prescribed** adj [textbook] (inscrit) au programme ▪ **prescription** n [for medicine] ordonnance f ; **on prescription** sur ordonnance

**presence** ['prezəns] n présence f ; **in the presence of** en présence de ; **presence of mind** présence f d'esprit

**present¹** ['prezənt] **1.** adj a) [in attendance] présent (**at** à ; **in** dans) b) [current] actuel, -elle ; **the present tense** le

présent **2.** n the present [time, tense] le présent ; **for the present** pour l'instant ; **at present** en ce moment ▪ **present-day** adj actuel, -elle ▪ **presently** adv [soon] bientôt ; Am [now] actuellement

**present²** **1.** ['prezənt] n [gift] cadeau m **2.** [prɪ'zent] vt [show, introduce] présenter (**to** à) ; [concert, film] donner ; **to present sb with** [gift] offrir à qn ; [prize] remettre à qn ▪ **presentable** [prɪ'zentəbəl] adj [person, appearance] présentable ▪ **presenter** [prɪ'zentə(r)] n présentateur, -trice mf

**presentation** [prezən'teɪʃən] n présentation f ; [of prize] remise f

**preservation** [prezə'veɪʃən] n [of building] conservation f ; [of species] protection f

**preservative** [prɪ'zɜːvətɪv] n conservateur m

**preserve** [prɪ'zɜːv] **1.** n [jam] confiture f **2.** vt [keep, maintain] conserver ; [fruit] mettre en conserve

**preside** [prɪ'zaɪd] vi présider ; **to preside over** or **at a meeting** présider une réunion

**presidency** ['prezɪdənsɪ] (pl -ies) n présidence f

**president** ['prezɪdənt] n [of country] président, -e mf ; **President's Day** jour férié aux États-Unis, le troisième lundi de février, en l'honneur des anniversaires des présidents Washington et Lincoln ▪ **presidential** [-'denʃəl] adj présidentiel, -elle

**press¹** [pres] n a) the press [newspapers] la presse ; **press conference** conférence f de presse ; **press release** communiqué m de presse b) [machine] presse f ; [for making wine] pressoir m ; (printing) press presse f

**press²** [pres] **1.** n to give sth a press [clothes] repasser qch ; **press stud** bouton-pression m **2.** vt [button, doorbell] appuyer sur ; [hand] serrer ; [clothes] repasser ; **to press sb to do sth** presser qn de faire qch **3.** vi [push] appuyer (**on** sur) ; [of weight] faire pression (**on** sur) ▪ **press-up** n [exercise] pompe *f* ■ **press down** *vt insep* [button] appuyer sur ■ **press for** *vt sep* [demand] exiger ■ **press on** *vi* [carry on] continuer

**pressed** [prest] *adj* **to be hard pressed** [in difficulties] être en difficulté ; **to be pressed for time** être pressé par le temps

**pressing** ['presɪŋ] *adj* [urgent] pressant

**pressure** ['preʃə(r)] **1.** *n* pression *f* ; **to be under pressure** être stressé ; **to put pressure on sb (to do sth)** faire pression sur qn (pour qu'il fasse qch) **2.** *vt* **to pressure sb to do sth** *or* **into doing sth** faire pression sur qn pour qu'il fasse qch

**pressurize** ['preʃəraɪz] *vt* **to pressurize sb (into doing sth)** faire pression sur qn (pour qu'il fasse qch)

**prestige** [pre'sti:ʒ] *n* prestige *m* ■ **prestigious** [pres'tɪdʒəs, *Am* pre'sti:dʒəs] *adj* prestigieux, -euse

**presume** [prɪ'zju:m] *vt* [suppose] présumer (**that** que) ■ **presumably** *adv* sans doute ■ **presumption** [-'zʌmpʃən] *n* présomption *f*

**presumptuous** [prɪ'zʌmptʃʊəs] *adj* présomptueux, -euse

**pretence**, *Am* **pretense** [prɪ'tens] *n* [sham] simulation *f* ; [claim, affectation] prétention *f* ; **to make a pretence of doing sth** feindre de faire qch ; **under false pretences** sous des prétextes fallacieux

**pretend** [prɪ'tend] **1.** *vt* [make believe] faire semblant (**to do** de faire) ; [claim, maintain] prétendre (**to do** faire ; **that** que) **2.** *vi* faire semblant

**pretense** [prɪ'tens] *Am n =* **pretence**

**pretentious** [prɪ'tenʃəs] *adj* prétentieux, -euse

**pretext** ['pri:tekst] *n* prétexte *m* ; **on the pretext of / that** sous prétexte de / que

**pretty** ['prɪtɪ] **1.** *(compar* **-ier**, *superl* **-iest)** *adj* joli **2.** *adv Fam* [rather, quite] assez ; **pretty well, pretty much** [almost] pratiquement

**prevail** [prɪ'veɪl] *vi* [predominate] prédominer ; [be successful] l'emporter (**over**

sur) ; **to prevail (up)on sb to do sth** persuader qn de faire qch ■ **prevailing** *adj* prédominant ; [wind] dominant

**prevalent** ['prevələnt] *adj* très répandu

**prevent** [prɪ'vent] *vt* empêcher (**from doing** de faire) ■ **prevention** *n* prévention *f*

**preview** ['pri:vju:] *n* [of film, play] avant-première *f*

**previous** ['pri:vɪəs] **1.** *adj* précédent ; **to have previous experience** avoir une expérience préalable **2.** *adv* **previous to** avant ■ **previously** *adv* auparavant

**prewar** ['pri:'wɔ:(r)] *adj* d'avant-guerre

**prey** [preɪ] **1.** *n* proie *f* ; *Fig* **to be (a) prey to** être en proie à **2.** *vi* **to prey on** [person] prendre pour cible ; [fears, doubts] exploiter ; **to prey on sb's mind** tourmenter qn

**price** [praɪs] **1.** *n* prix *m* ; **he wouldn't do it at any price** il ne le ferait à aucun prix **2.** *adj* [control, rise] des prix ; **price bracket** gamme *f* de prix ; **within my price bracket** dans mes prix ; **price bubble** bulle *f* des prix ; **price increase** hausse *f* ou augmentation *f* des prix ; **price list** tarif *m* **3.** *vt* **it's priced at £5** ça coûte 5 livres ■ **priceless** *adj* [invaluable] qui n'a pas de prix

**pricey** ['praɪsɪ] *(compar* **-ier**, *superl* **-iest)** *adj Fam* cher (*f* chère)

**prick** [prɪk] **1.** *n* [of needle] piqûre *f* **2.** *vt* [jab] piquer (**with** avec) ; [burst] crever ■ **prickly** *(compar* **-ier**, *superl* **-iest)** *adj* [plant] à épines ; [animal] couvert de piquants ; [beard] piquant

**pride** [praɪd] **1.** *n* [satisfaction] fierté *f* ; [self-esteem] amour-propre *m* ; *Pej* [vanity] orgueil *m* ; **to take pride in sth** mettre toute sa fierté dans qch **2.** *vt* **to pride oneself on sth / on doing sth** s'enorgueillir de qch / de faire qch

**priest** [pri:st] *n* prêtre *m*

**prim** [prɪm] *(compar* **primmer**, *superl* **primmest**) *adj* **prim (and proper)** [person] collet monté *inv* ; [manner] guindé

**primarily** [*Br* 'praɪmərəlɪ, *Am* praɪ'merəlɪ] *adv* essentiellement

**primary** ['praɪmərɪ] **1.** *adj* [main] principal; *Br* **primary school** école *f* primaire; **primary carer, primary caregiver** *personne qui s'occupe d'un proche dépendant* **2.** *(pl* **-ies)** *n Am* [election] primaire *f*

**prime** [praɪm] **1.** *adj* [principal] principal; [importance] capital; [excellent] excellent; **Prime Minister** Premier ministre *m*; MATH **prime number** nombre *m* premier **2.** *n* **in the prime of life** dans la fleur de l'âge **3.** *vt* [surface] apprêter ■ **primer** *n* **a)** [book] manuel *m* élémentaire **b)** [paint] apprêt *m*

**primitive** ['prɪmɪtɪv] *adj* [original] primitif, -ive; [basic] de base

**prince** [prɪns] *n* prince *m* ■ **princess** *n* princesse *f*

**principal** ['prɪnsɪpəl] **1.** *adj* [main] principal **2.** *n* [of school] proviseur *m*; [of university] ≃ président, -e *mf*

**principle** ['prɪnsɪpəl] *n* principe *m*; **in principle** en principe; **on principle** par principe

**print** [prɪnt] **1.** *n* [of finger, foot] empreinte *f*; [letters] caractères *mpl*; [engraving] estampe *f*; [photo] épreuve *f*; [fabric] imprimé *m*; **out of print** [book] épuisé **2.** *vt* [book, newspaper] imprimer; [photo] tirer; [write] écrire en script; COMPUT **to print out** imprimer ■ **printed** *adj* imprimé; **printed matter** imprimés *mpl* ■ **printing** *n* [technique, industry] imprimerie *f*; [action] tirage *m*; **printing error** faute *f* d'impression ■ **printout** *n* COMPUT sortie *f* papier

**printer** ['prɪntə(r)] *n* COMPUT imprimante *f*; **ink-jet printer** imprimante *f* à jet d'encre

**prior** ['praɪə(r)] **1.** *adj* antérieur; [experience] préalable **2.** *adv* **prior to sth** avant qch

**priority** [praɪ'ɒrɪtɪ] *(pl* **-ies)** *n* priorité *f* **(over** sur)

**prison** ['prɪzən] **1.** *n* prison *f*; **in prison** en prison **2.** *adj* [life, system] pénitentiaire; [camp] de prisonniers; **prison officer** gardien, -enne *mf* de prison

■ **prisoner** *n* prisonnier, -ère *mf*; **to take sb prisoner** faire qn prisonnier; **prisoner of war** prisonnier *m* de guerre

**privacy** ['praɪvəsɪ, *Br* 'prɪvəsɪ] *n* intimité *f*

**private** ['praɪvɪt] **1.** *adj* privé; [lesson] particulier, -ère; [letter] confidentiel, -elle; [personal] personnel, -elle; [dinner, wedding] intime; **private detective, private investigator,** *Fam* **private eye** détective *m* privé **2.** *n* **a) in private** [not publicly] en privé; [have dinner, get married] dans l'intimité **b)** [soldier] simple soldat *m*

**privately** ['praɪvɪtlɪ] *adv* [in private] en privé; [in one's heart of hearts] en son for intérieur; [personally] à titre personnel; **privately owned** [company] privé

**privatize** ['praɪvətaɪz] *vt* privatiser

**privilege** ['prɪvɪlɪdʒ] *n* privilège *m* ■ **privileged** *adj* privilégié; **to be privileged to do sth** avoir le privilège de faire qch

**prize**[1] [praɪz] *n* prix *m*; [in lottery] lot *m* ■ **prizegiving** *n* distribution *f* des prix ■ **prizewinner** *n* [in contest] lauréat, -e *mf*; [in lottery] gagnant, -e *mf*

**prize**[2] [praɪz] *vt* [value] attacher de la valeur à

**prize**[3] [praɪz] *Br vt* = **prise**

**pro** [prəʊ] *(pl* **pros)** *n Fam* [professional] pro *mf*

**probable** ['prɒbəbəl] *adj* probable **(that** que) ■ **probability** *(pl* **-ies)** *n* probabilité *f*; **in all probability** selon toute probabilité ■ **probably** *adv* probablement

**probation** [prə'beɪʃən] *n* **on probation** [criminal] en liberté surveillée; [in job] en période d'essai

**probe** [prəʊb] **1.** *n* [device] sonde *f*; [inquiry] enquête *f* **(into** dans) **2.** *vt* [prod] sonder; [inquire into] enquêter sur **3.** *vi* **to probe into sth** [past, private life] fouiller dans qch ■ **probing** *adj* [question] perspicace

**problem** ['prɒbləm] *n* problème *m*; *Fam* **no problem!** pas de problème ! ■ **problematic** *adj* problématique ■ **problem-free** *adj* sans problème

**project**

**procedure** [prə'si:dʒə(r)] n procédure f

**proceed** [prə'si:d] vi [go on] se poursuivre ; **to proceed with sth** poursuivre qch ; **to proceed to do sth** se mettre à faire qch

**proceedings** [prə'si:dɪŋz] npl [events] opérations fpl ; **to take (legal) proceedings** intenter un procès (**against** contre)

**proceeds** ['prəʊsi:dz] npl recette f

**process** ['prəʊses] **1.** n processus m ; [method] procédé m ; **in the process of doing sth** en train de faire qch **2.** vt [food, data] traiter ; [film] développer ; **processed food** aliments mpl conditionnés

**procession** [prə'seʃən] n défilé m

**processor** ['prəʊsesə(r)] n COMPUT processeur m ; **food processor** robot m de cuisine

**proclaim** [prə'kleɪm] vt proclamer (**that** que) ; **to proclaim sb king** proclamer qn roi

**prod** [prɒd] (pt & pp -dd-) vt [poke] donner un petit coup dans

**prodigy** ['prɒdɪdʒɪ] (pl -ies) n prodige m ; **child prodigy** enfant mf prodige

**produce¹** [prə'dju:s] vt [create] produire ; [machine] fabriquer ; [passport, ticket] présenter ; [documents] fournir ; [from bag, pocket] sortir ; [film, play, programme] produire ■ **producer** n producteur, -trice mf

**produce²** ['prɒdju:s] n [products] produits mpl

**product** ['prɒdʌkt] n [article, creation & MATH] produit m

**production** [prə'dʌkʃən] n production f ; [of play] mise f en scène ; **to work on a production line** travailler à la chaîne

**productive** [prə'dʌktɪv] adj productif, -ive ■ **productivity** [prɒdʌk'tɪvətɪ] n productivité f

**profession** [prə'feʃən] n profession f ; **by profession** de profession ■ **professional 1.** adj professionnel, -elle ; [man, woman] qui exerce une profession libérale ; [army] de métier ; [piece of work] de professionnel **2.** n professionnel, -elle mf

**professor** [prə'fesə(r)] n Br ≃ professeur m d'université ; Am enseignant d'université

**proficient** [prə'fɪʃənt] adj compétent (**in** en)

**profile** ['prəʊfaɪl] n [of person, object] profil m ; [description] portrait m ; **in profile** de profil ; Fig **to keep a low profile** garder un profil bas

**profit** ['prɒfɪt] **1.** n profit m, bénéfice m ; **to sell at a profit** vendre à profit **2.** vi **to profit by** or **from sth** tirer profit de qch ■ **profit-making** adj [aiming to make profit] à but lucratif ; [profitable] rentable

**profitable** ['prɒfɪtəbəl] adj [commercially] rentable ; Fig [worthwhile] profitable

**profound** [prə'faʊnd] adj profond ■ **profoundly** adv profondément

**profusely** [prə'fju:slɪ] adv [bleed] abondamment ; [thank] avec effusion ; **to apologize profusely** se confondre en excuses

**programme**, Am **program** ['prəʊgræm] **1.** n [for play, political party, computer] programme m ; [on TV, radio] émission f **2.** (pt & pp -mm-) vt [machine & COMPUT] programmer ■ **programmer** n (computer) programmeur programmeur, -euse mf ■ **programming** n (computer) programming programmation f

**progress 1.** ['prəʊgres] n progrès m ; **to make (good) progress** faire des progrès ; **in progress** en cours **2.** [prə'gres] vi [advance, improve] progresser ; [of story, meeting] se dérouler

**progressive** [prə'gresɪv] adj [gradual] progressif, -ive ; [company, ideas, political party] progressiste

**prohibit** [prə'hɪbɪt] vt interdire (**sb from doing** à qn de faire)

**prohibitive** [prə'hɪbɪtɪv] adj prohibitif, -ive

**project 1.** ['prɒdʒekt] n [plan, undertaking] projet m ; [at school] dossier m ;

*Am* **(housing) project** cité *f* HLM **2.** [prə'dʒekt] *vt* [propel, show] projeter **3.** [prə'dʒekt] *vi* [protrude] dépasser

**projector** [prə'dʒektə(r)] *n* projecteur *m*

**proliferate** [prə'lɪfəreɪt] *vi* proliférer

**prolific** [prə'lɪfɪk] *adj* prolifique

**prologue** ['prəʊlɒg] *n* prologue *m* **(to** de)

**prolong** [prə'lɒŋ] *vt* prolonger

**prom** [prɒm] *(abbr of* promenade*)* **a)** *Br* [at seaside] front *m* de mer **b)** *Am* [dance] bal *m* d'étudiants

**promenade** [prɒmə'nɑːd] *n Br* [at seaside] front *m* de mer

**prominent** ['prɒmɪnənt] *adj* [important] important ; [nose, chin] proéminent **■ prominently** *adv* bien en vue

**promiscuous** [prə'mɪskjʊəs] *adj* [person] qui a de multiples partenaires

**promise** ['prɒmɪs] **1.** *n* promesse *f* ; **to show promise** promettre **2.** *vt* promettre **(to do** de faire)**; to promise sth to sb, to promise sb sth** promettre qch à qn **3.** *vi* **I promise!** je te le promets ! **■ promising** *adj* prometteur, -euse

**promote** [prə'məʊt] *vt* [raise in rank, encourage] promouvoir ; [advertise] faire la promotion de **■ promotion** *n* promotion *f*

**prompt¹** [prɒmpt] **1.** *adj* [speedy] rapide ; [punctual] ponctuel, -elle **2.** *adv* **at eight o'clock prompt** à huit heures précises **■ promptly** *adv* [rapidly] rapidement ; [punctually] ponctuellement ; [immediately] immédiatement

**prompt²** [prɒmpt] *vt* **a)** [cause] provoquer ; **to prompt sb to do sth** pousser qn à faire qch **b)** [actor] souffler à

**prone** [prəʊn] *adj* **to be prone to sth** être sujet, -ette à qch ; **to be prone to do sth** avoir tendance à faire qch

**pronoun** ['prəʊnaʊn] *n* pronom *m*

**pronounce** [prə'naʊns] *vt* [say, articulate] prononcer **■ pronunciation** [-nʌnsɪ'eɪʃən] *n* prononciation *f*

**proof** [pruːf] *n* [evidence] preuve *f* ; [of book, photo] épreuve *f* ; **proof of identity** pièce *f* d'identité **■ proofreader** *n* correcteur, -trice *mf*

**prop** [prɒp] **1.** *n* [physical support] support *m* ; [in a play] accessoire *m* **2.** *(pt & pp* -pp-*)vt* **to prop sth (up) against sth** appuyer qch contre qch ; **to prop sth up** [building, tunnel] étayer qch ; *Fig* [economy, regime] soutenir qch

**propaganda** [prɒpə'gændə] *n* propagande *f*

**propel** [prə'pel] *(pt & pp* -ll-*)vt* propulser **■ propeller** *n* hélice *f*

**proper** ['prɒpə(r)] *adj* **a)** [correct] vrai ; [word] correct ; **the village proper** le village proprement dit **b)** [appropriate] bon (*f* bonne) ; [equipment] adéquat ; [behaviour] convenable **c)** *Br* [downright] véritable **■ properly** *adv* [suitably] convenablement ; [correctly] correctement

**property** ['prɒpətɪ] **1.** *(pl* -ies*) n* **a)** [land, house] propriété *f* ; [possessions] biens *mpl* **b)** [quality] propriété *f* **2.** *adj* [market] immobilier, -ère ; **property developer** promoteur *m* immobilier

**prophecy** ['prɒfɪsɪ] *(pl* -ies*) n* prophétie *f*

**prophet** ['prɒfɪt] *n* prophète *m*

**proportion** [prə'pɔːʃən] *n* [ratio, part] proportion *f* ; **proportions** [size] proportions *fpl* ; **in proportion** proportionné **(to** avec)**; out of proportion** disproportionné **(to** par rapport à) **■ proportional, proportionate** *adj* proportionnel, -elle **(to** à)

**proposal** [prə'pəʊzəl] *n* proposition *f* ; [plan] projet *m* ; [for marriage] demande *f* en mariage **■ proposition** [prɒpə'zɪʃən] *n* proposition *f*

**propose** [prə'pəʊz] **1.** *vt* proposer ; **to propose to do sth, to propose doing sth** [suggest] proposer de faire qch ; [intend] se proposer de faire qch **2.** *vi* **to propose to sb** demander qn en mariage

**proprietor** [prə'praɪətə(r)] *n* propriétaire *mf*

**pros** [prəʊz] *npl* **the pros and cons** le pour et le contre

**prose** [prəʊz] *n* prose *f* ; *Br* [translation] thème *m*

**prosecute** ['prɒsɪkju:t] *vt* [in law court] poursuivre (en justice) ▪ **prosecution** *n* [in law court] poursuites *fpl* judiciaires; **the prosecution** [lawyers] ≃ le ministère public

**prospect¹** ['prɒspekt] *n* [expectation, thought] perspective *f*; [chance, likelihood] perspectives *fpl*; **(future) prospects** perspectives *fpl* d'avenir ▪ **prospective** [prə'spektɪv] *adj* [potential] potentiel, -elle; [future] futur

**prospect²** [prə'spekt] *vi* to prospect for gold chercher de l'or

**prospectus** [prə'spektəs] *n* [publicity leaflet] prospectus *m*; *Br* [for university] guide *m* (de l'étudiant)

**prosper** ['prɒspə(r)] *vi* prospérer ▪ **prosperity** [-'sperətɪ] *n* prospérité *f* ▪ **prosperous** *adj* prospère

**prostitute** ['prɒstɪtju:t] *n* [woman] prostituée *f*; **male prostitute** prostitué *m* ▪ **prostitution** *n* prostitution *f*

**prostrate** ['prɒstreɪt] *adj* [lying flat] sur le ventre

**protagonist** [prəʊ'tægənɪst] *n* protagoniste *mf*

**protect** [prə'tekt] *vt* protéger (**from** *or* **against** de) ▪ **protection** *n* protection *f* ▪ **protective** *adj* [clothes, screen] de protection; [person, attitude] protecteur, -trice (**to** *or* **towards** envers)

**protein** ['prəʊti:n] *n* protéine *f*

**protest** [prə'test] **1.** ['prəʊtest] *n* protestation *f* (**against** contre); **in protest** en signe de protestation (**at** contre) **2.** *vt* protester contre; [one's innocence] protester de; **to protest that…** protester en disant que… **3.** *vi* protester (**against** contre) ▪ **protester** *n* contestataire *mf*

**Protestant** ['prɒtɪstənt] *adj* & *n* protestant, -e *(mf)*

**protracted** [prə'træktɪd] *adj* prolongé

**protrude** [prə'tru:d] *vi* dépasser (**from** de); [of tooth] avancer ▪ **protruding** *adj* [chin, veins, eyes] saillant

**proud** [praʊd] *(compar* -er, *superl* -est*) adj* [person] fier (*f* fière) (**of** de) ▪ **proudly** *adv* fièrement

**prove** [pru:v] **1.** *vt* prouver (**that** que); **to prove sb wrong** prouver que qn a tort **2.** *vi* to prove (**to be) difficult** s'avérer difficile ▪ **proven** *adj* [method] éprouvé

**proverb** ['prɒvɜ:b] *n* proverbe *m*

**provide** [prə'vaɪd] **1.** *vt* [supply] fournir; [service] offrir (**to** à); **to provide sb with sth** fournir qch à qn **2.** *vi* to provide for **sb** [sb's needs] pourvoir aux besoins de qn; [sb's future] assurer l'avenir de qn; **to provide for sth** [make allowance for] prévoir qch ▪ **provided, providing** *conj* **provided (that)…** pourvu que… (+ *subjunctive*) ▪ **provider** [prə'vaɪdə(r)] *n* [gen] fournisseur, -euse *mf*; COMPUT fournisseur *m* (d'accès), provider *m*; **she's the family's sole provider** elle subvient seule aux besoins de la famille

**province** ['prɒvɪns] *n* province *f*; **in the provinces** en province ▪ **provincial** [prə'vɪnʃəl] *adj* & *n* provincial, -e *(mf)*

**provision** [prə'vɪʒən] *n* [clause] disposition *f*; **provisions** [supplies] provisions *fpl*

**provisional** [prə'vɪʒənəl] *adj* provisoire

**provocation** [prɒvə'keɪʃən] *n* provocation *f*

**provocative** [prə'vɒkətɪv] *adj* provocateur, -trice

**provoke** [prə'vəʊk] *vt* provoquer; **to provoke sb into doing sth** pousser qn à faire qch

**prowl** [praʊl] **1.** *n* to be on the prowl rôder **2.** *vi* to prowl (**around)** rôder

**proxy** ['prɒksɪ] *(pl* -ies) *n* by proxy par procuration

**PRT** MESSAGING *written abbr of* **party**

**prudent** ['pru:dənt] *adj* prudent

**prudish** ['pru:dɪʃ] *adj* pudibond

**prune¹** [pru:n] *n* [dried plum] pruneau *m*

**prune²** [pru:n] *vt* [tree, bush] tailler

**pry** [praɪ] **1.** *(pt & pp pried) vt Am* to pry open forcer (avec un levier) **2.** *vi* être indiscret, -ète ; **to pry into sth** [meddle] mettre son nez dans qch ; [sb's reasons] chercher à découvrir qch

**PS** [piː'es] *(abbr of postscript)* n PS *m*

**psalm** [sɑːm] n psaume *m*

**pseudonym** ['sjuːdənɪm] n pseudonyme *m*

**psychiatry** [saɪ'kaɪətrɪ] n psychiatrie *f* ■ **psychiatric** [-kɪ'ætrɪk] *adj* psychiatrique ■ **psychiatrist** n psychiatre *mf*

**psychic** ['saɪkɪk] *adj* [paranormal] paranormal

**psycho-** ['saɪkəʊ] *pref* psycho- ■ **psychoanalyst** n psychanalyste *mf*

**psychology** [saɪ'kɒlədʒɪ] n psychologie *f* ■ **psychological** [-kə'lɒdʒɪkəl] *adj* psychologique ■ **psychologist** n psychologue *mf*

**psychopath** ['saɪkəʊpæθ] n psychopathe *mf*

**PTB** MESSAGING *written abbr of* **please text back**

**PTO** *(abbr of* **please turn over**) TSVP

**pub** [pʌb] n *Br* pub *m*

**puberty** ['pjuːbətɪ] n puberté *f*

**public** ['pʌblɪk] **1.** *adj* public, -ique ; [library, swimming pool] municipal ; **public holiday** jour *m* férié ; **public property** [land, *etc*] bien *m* public ; **public relations** relations *fpl* publiques ; **public school** *Br* école *f* privée ; *Am* école *f* publique ; **public transport** transports *mpl* en commun **2.** n public *m* ; **in public** en public

**publication** [pʌblɪ'keɪʃən] n publication *f*

**publicity** [pʌ'blɪsətɪ] n publicité *f*

**publicize** ['pʌblɪsaɪz] *vt* faire connaître au public

**publicly** ['pʌblɪklɪ] *adv* publiquement ; **publicly owned** à capitaux publics

**publish** ['pʌblɪʃ] *vt* publier ■ **publisher** n [person] éditeur, -trice *mf* ; [company] maison *f* d'édition

**pudding** ['pʊdɪŋ] n [dish] pudding *m* ; *Br* [dessert] dessert *m*

**puddle** ['pʌdəl] n flaque *f* (d'eau)

**puff** [pʌf] **1.** n [of smoke] bouffée *f* ; [of wind, air] souffle *m* ; **puff pastry,** *Am* **puff paste** pâte *f* feuilletée **2.** *vt* **to puff sth out** [cheeks, chest] gonfler qch **3.** *vi* [of person] souffler ; **to puff at a cigar** tirer sur un cigare

**puke** [pjuːk] *vi Fam* dégueuler

**pull** [pʊl] **1.** n [attraction] attraction *f* ; **to give sth a pull** tirer qch **2.** *vt* [draw, tug] tirer ; [tooth] arracher ; [trigger] appuyer sur ; [muscle] se froisser ; *Fig* **to pull sth apart** *or* **to bits** *or* **to pieces** démolir qch **3.** *vi* [tug] tirer (**on** sur) ■ **pull along** *vt sep* [drag] traîner (**to** jusqu'à) ■ **pull away 1.** *vt sep* [move] éloigner ; [snatch] arracher (**from** à) **2.** *vi* [in vehicle] démarrer ■ **pull back 1.** *vt sep* retirer ; [curtains] ouvrir **2.** *vi* [withdraw] se retirer ■ **pull down** *vt sep* [lower] baisser ; [knock down] faire tomber ; [demolish] démolir ■ **pull in 1.** *vt sep* [drag into room] faire entrer (de force) ; [rope] ramener ; [stomach] rentrer **2.** *vi* [arrive] arriver ; [stop in vehicle] s'arrêter ■ **pull off** *vt sep* [remove] enlever ; *Fig* [plan, deal] réaliser ■ **pull on** *vt sep* [boots, clothes] mettre ■ **pull out 1.** *vt sep* [tooth, hair] arracher ; [cork, pin] enlever (**from** de) ; [from pocket, bag] sortir (**from** de) **2.** *vi* [of car] déboîter ; [of train] partir ; [withdraw] se retirer (**of** de) ■ **pull over 1.** *vt sep* [drag] traîner (**to** jusqu'à) ; [knock down] faire tomber **2.** *vi* [in vehicle] s'arrêter ■ **pull through** *vi* [recover] s'en tirer ■ **pull together** *vt sep* **to pull oneself together** se ressaisir ■ **pull up 1.** *vt sep* [socks, blinds] remonter ; [haul up] hisser ; [plant, tree] arracher ; [stop] arrêter **2.** *vi* [of car] s'arrêter

**pullover** ['pʊləʊvə(r)] n pull-over *m*

**pulp** [pʌlp] n [of fruit] pulpe *f*

**pulse** [pʌls] n MED pouls *m*

**pump**[1] [pʌmp] **1.** n [machine] pompe *f* ; *Br* **petrol pump,** *Am* **gas pump** pompe *f* à essence ; **pump prices** [of petrol] prix *mpl* à la pompe **2.** *vt* pomper ; **to pump sth up** [mattress] gonfler qch ■ **pumped** [pʌmpt] *adj Am Fam* excité

**pump²** [pʌmp] n [flat shoe] escarpin m ; [for sports] tennis f

**pumpkin** ['pʌmpkɪn] n potiron m

**pun** [pʌn] n jeu m de mots

**punch¹** [pʌntʃ] **1.** n [blow] coup m de poing ; **punch line** [of joke, story] chute f **2.** vt [person] donner un coup de poing à ; [sb's nose] donner un coup de poing sur ■ **punch-up** n Br Fam bagarre f

**punch²** [pʌntʃ] **1.** n [for paper] perforeuse f ; [for tickets] poinçonneuse f **2.** vt [ticket] poinçonner ; [with date] composter ; [paper, card] perforer ; **to punch a hole in sth** faire un trou dans qch

**punch³** [pʌntʃ] n [drink] punch m

**punctual** ['pʌŋktʃʊəl] adj ponctuel, -elle ■ **punctually** adv à l'heure

**punctuation** [pʌŋktjʊ'eɪʃən] n ponctuation f ; **punctuation mark** signe m de ponctuation

**puncture** ['pʌŋktʃə(r)] **1.** n [in tyre] crevaison f ; **to have a puncture** crever **2.** vt [tyre] crever **3.** vi [of tyre] crever

**pungent** ['pʌndʒənt] adj âcre

**punish** ['pʌnɪʃ] vt punir (**for** de) ; **to punish sb for doing sth** punir qn pour avoir fait qch

**punishment** ['pʌnɪʃmənt] n punition f ; [in law] peine f

**punk** [pʌŋk] n punk mf ; **punk (rock)** le punk

**punter** ['pʌntə(r)] n Br [gambler] parieur, -euse mf ; Fam [customer] client, -e m

**puny** ['pju:nɪ] (compar -ier, superl -iest) adj chétif, -ive

**pup** [pʌp] n [young dog] chiot m

**pupil¹** ['pju:pəl] n [student] élève mf

**pupil²** ['pju:pəl] n [of eye] pupille f

**puppet** ['pʌpɪt] n marionnette f ; **puppet show** spectacle m de marionnettes

**puppy** ['pʌpɪ] (pl -ies) n [dog] chiot m

**purchase** ['pɜ:tʃɪs] **1.** n [action, thing bought] achat m **2.** vt acheter (**from** à) ■ **purchaser** n acheteur, -euse mf

**pure** [pjʊə(r)] (compar -er, superl -est) adj pur

**purée** ['pjʊəreɪ] n purée f

**purely** ['pjʊəlɪ] adv purement

**purge** [pɜ:dʒ] **1.** n purge f **2.** vt purger (**of** de)

**purify** ['pjʊərɪfaɪ] (pt & pp -ied) vt purifier

**puritanical** [pjʊərɪ'tænɪkəl] adj puritain

**purity** ['pjʊərətɪ] n pureté f

**purple** ['pɜ:pəl] **1.** adj violet, -ette **2.** n violet m

**purpose** ['pɜ:pəs] n a) [aim] but m ; **on purpose** exprès ; **for the purposes of** pour les besoins de b) [determination] résolution f

**purposely** ['pɜ:pəslɪ] adv exprès

**purr** [pɜ:(r)] vi ronronner

**purse** [pɜ:s] **1.** n [for coins] porte-monnaie m inv ; Am [handbag] sac m à main **2.** vt **to purse one's lips** pincer les lèvres

**pursue** [pə'sju:] vt poursuivre ; [fame, pleasure] rechercher ■ **pursuit** n [of person] poursuite f ; [of pleasure, glory] quête f ; [activity] occupation f

**push** [pʊʃ] **1.** n [act of pushing, attack] poussée f ; **to give sb / sth a push** pousser qn / qch ; **at a push** à la rigueur **2.** vt pousser (**to** or **as far as** jusqu'à) ; [button] appuyer sur ; [lever] abaisser ; [product] faire la promotion de ; Fam [drugs] vendre ; **to push sth into / between** enfoncer qch dans / entre ; Fig **to push sb into doing sth** pousser qn à faire qch ; **to push sth off the table** faire tomber qch de la table (en le poussant) **3.** vi pousser ; [on button] appuyer (**on** sur) ■ **push about, push around** vt sep Fam **to push sb about** or **around** faire de qn ce que l'on veut ■ **push aside** vt sep écarter ■ **push down** vt sep [button] appuyer sur ; [lever] abaisser ■ **push in** vi Br [in queue] resquiller ■ **push off** vi Fam ficher le camp ■ **push on** vi [go on] continuer ; **to push on with sth** continuer qch ■ **push over** vt sep faire tomber ■ **push up** vt sep [lever, collar] relever ; [sleeves] remonter ;

[increase] augmenter ■ **push-button** *n* bouton *m* ; [of phone] touche *f* ; **push-button phone** *n Br* poussette *f* ■ **push-up** *n Am* [exercise] pompe *f*

**pushed** [puʃt] *adj* **to be pushed for time** être très pressé

**pushy** ['puʃi] *(compar* -**ier**, *superl* -**iest**) *adj Fam* batailleur, -euse

**puss, pussy** ['pus, 'pusi] *(pl* -**ies**) *n Fam* [cat] minou *m*

**put** [put] *(pt & pp* put, *pres p* putting) *vt* mettre ; [on flat surface] poser ; [problem, argument] présenter (**to** à) ; [question] poser (**to** à) ; [say] dire ; [estimate] évaluer (**at** à) ; **to put money on a horse** parier sur un cheval ; **to put a lot of work into sth** beaucoup travailler à qch ; **to put it bluntly** pour parler franc

■ **put across** *vt sep* [message, idea] faire comprendre (**to** à)

■ **put aside** *vt sep* [money, object] mettre de côté

■ **put away** *vt sep* [tidy away] ranger ; **to put sb away** [criminal] mettre qn en prison

■ **put back** *vt sep* [replace, postpone] remettre ; [telephone receiver] raccrocher ; [clock] retarder

■ **put by** *vt sep* [money] mettre de côté

■ **put down** *vt sep* [on floor, table] poser ; [a deposit] verser ; [revolt] réprimer ; [write down] inscrire ; [attribute] attribuer (**to** à) ; [kill] faire piquer ; **to put oneself down** se rabaisser

■ **put forward** *vt sep* [clock, meeting, argument] avancer ; [candidate] proposer (**for** à)

■ **put in 1.** *vt sep* [into box] mettre dedans ; [insert] introduire ; [add] ajouter ; [install] installer ; [claim, application] soumettre ; [time] passer (**doing** à faire) **2.** *vi* **to put in for sth** [new job, transfer] faire une demande de qch

■ **put off** *vt sep* [postpone] remettre (à plus tard) ; [dismay] déconcerter ; **to**

**put off doing sth** retarder le moment de faire qch ; **to put sb off sth** dégoûter qn de qch

■ **put on** *vt sep* [clothes, shoe, record] mettre ; [accent] prendre ; [play, show] monter ; [gas, radio] allumer ; [clock] avancer ; **to put on weight** prendre du poids ; **she put me on to you** elle m'a donné votre adresse ; **put me on to him!** [on phone] passez-le-moi !

■ **put out** *vt sep* [take outside] sortir ; [arm, leg, hand] tendre ; [gas, light] éteindre ; [inconvenience] déranger ; [upset] vexer ; [report, statement] publier ; **to put one's shoulder out** se démettre l'épaule

■ **put through** *vt sep* **to put sb through (to sb)** [on phone] passer qn (à qn)

■ **put together** *vt sep* [assemble] assembler ; [meal, team] composer ; [file, report] préparer ; [collection] rassembler

■ **put up** *vt sep* [lift] lever ; [tent, fence] monter ; [statue, ladder] dresser ; [flag] hisser ; [building] construire ; [umbrella] ouvrir ; [picture, poster] mettre ; [price, numbers] augmenter ; [resistance] offrir ; [candidate] présenter (**for** à) ; [guest] loger ; **to put sth up for sale** mettre qch en vente

■ **put up with** *vt insep* supporter

**putting** ['putiŋ] *n* [in golf] putting *m* ; **putting green** green *m*

**puzzle** ['puzəl] **1.** *n* [jigsaw] puzzle *m* ; [game] casse-tête *m inv* ; [mystery] mystère *m* **2.** *vt* laisser perplexe **3.** *vi* **to puzzle over sth** essayer de comprendre qch ■ **puzzled** *adj* perplexe

**PVC** [piː.viː.ˈsiː] *n* PVC *m*

**pwn** [pəʊn] *v Fam* vaincre *(qn au cours d'un jeu vidéo sur Internet)*

**pyjamas** [pəˈdʒɑːməz] *npl Br* pyjama *m* ; **a pair of pyjamas** un pyjama

**pylon** ['paɪlən] *n* pylône *m*

**pyramid** ['pɪrəmɪd] *n* pyramide *f*

**Pyrex®** ['paɪreks] *n* Pyrex® *m* ; **Pyrex® dish** plat *m* en Pyrex®

# Q

**Q, q** [kju:] *n* [letter] Q, q *m inv*

**QPSA?** *(abbr of* **qué pasa?)** MESSAGING *qu'est-ce qui se passe ?*

**quack** [kwæk] *n* [of duck] coin-coin *m inv*

**quadruple** [kwɒ'dru:pəl] *vti* quadrupler

**quaint** [kweɪnt] *(compar* -er, *superl* -est) *adj* [picturesque] pittoresque ; [old-fashioned] vieillot, -otte ; [odd] bizarre

**quake** [kweɪk] **1.** *n Fam* tremblement *m* de terre **2.** *vi* trembler (**with** de)

**Quaker** ['kweɪkə(r)] *n* REL quaker, -eresse *mf*

**qualification** [kwɒlɪfɪ'keɪʃən] *n* [diploma] diplôme *m* ; [skill] compétence *f* ; [modification] précision *f*

**qualify** ['kwɒlɪfaɪ] *(pt & pp* -ied) **1.** *vt* **a)** [make competent, in sport] qualifier (**for sth** pour qch) **b)** [modify] nuancer **2.** *vi* [of sportsperson] se qualifier (**for** pour) ; **to qualify as a doctor** obtenir son diplôme de médecin ; **to qualify for sth** [be eligible] avoir droit à qch ▪ **qualified** *adj* [competent] compétent ; [having diploma] diplômé ; [support] mitigé

**quality** ['kwɒlətɪ] *(pl* -ies) *n* qualité *f*

**qualm** [kwɑːm] *n* **a)** [scruple] scrupule *m* **b)** [pang of nausea] haut-le-cœur *m inv*

**quantity** ['kwɒntətɪ] *(pl* -ies) *n* quantité *f*

**quarantine** ['kwɒrənti:n] *n* quarantaine *f*

**quarrel** ['kwɒrəl] **1.** *n* dispute *f*, querelle *f* **2.** *(Br* -ll-, *Am* -l-) *vi* se disputer (**with** avec) ; **to quarrel with sth** ne pas être d'accord avec qch

**quarry** ['kwɒrɪ] *(pl* -ies) *n* [for stone] carrière *f*

**quart** [kwɔːt] *n* [liquid measurement] *Br* 1,14 l ; *Am* 0,95 l

**quarter¹** ['kwɔːtə(r)] *n* quart *m* ; [of fruit, moon] quartier *m* ; [division of year] trimestre *m* ; *Am Can* [money] pièce *f* de 25 cents ; **quarter (of a) pound** quart *m* de livre ; *Br* **a quarter past nine,** *Am* **a quarter after nine** neuf heures et quart ; **a quarter to nine** neuf heures moins le quart

**quarter²** ['kwɔːtə(r)] *n* [district] quartier *m* ; **(living) quarters** logements *mpl* ; [of soldier] quartiers *mpl*

**quarterback** ['kwɔːtəbæk] *n* quarterback *m*

**quarterfinal** [kwɔːtə'faɪnəl] *n* quart *m* de finale

**quarterly** ['kwɔːtəlɪ] **1.** *adj* [magazine, payment] trimestriel, -elle **2.** *adv* tous les trimestres

**quartet(te)** [kwɔː'tet] *n* [music, players] quatuor *m* ; **(jazz) quartet(te)** quartette *m*

**quartz** [kwɔːts] **1.** *n* quartz *m* **2.** *adj* [watch] à quartz

**quash** [kwɒʃ] *vt* [rebellion] réprimer ; [sentence] annuler

**quasi-** ['kweɪzaɪ] *pref* quasi-

**quay** [ki:] *n* quai *m*

**queasy** ['kwi:zɪ] *(compar* -ier, *superl* -iest) *adj* **to feel** *or* **be queasy** avoir mal au cœur

**Quebec** [kwɪ'bek] *n* le Québec

**queen** [kwi:n] *n* reine *f*

**queer** ['kwɪə(r)] *(compar* -er, *superl* -est) *adj* [strange] bizarre

**quench** [kwentʃ] *vt* [thirst] étancher

**query** ['kwɪərɪ] **1.** *(pl* -ies) *n* question *f* **2.** *(pt & pp* -ied) *vt* mettre en question

**quest** [kwest] *n* quête *f* (**for** de)

**question** ['kwestʃən] **1.** *n* question *f* ; **there's no question of it, it's out of the**

**question** c'est hors de question; **the matter/person in question** l'affaire / la personne en question; **question mark** point *m* d'interrogation **2.** *vt* interroger (**about** sur); [doubt] mettre en question

**questionable** ['kwestʃənəbəl] *adj* discutable

**questionnaire** [kwestʃə'neə(r)] *n* questionnaire *m*

**queue** [kjuː] *Br* **1.** *n* [of people] queue *f*; [of cars] file *f*; **to form a queue, to stand in a queue** faire la queue **2.** *vi* to **queue (up)** faire la queue

**quiche** [kiːʃ] *n* quiche *f*

**quick** [kwɪk] **1.** (*compar* -er, *superl* -est) *adj* [rapid] rapide; [clever] vif (*f* vive); **be quick!** fais vite!; **to have a quick shower/meal** se doucher /manger en vitesse **2.** (*compar* -er, *superl* -est) *adv Fam* vite ■ **quick-drying** *adj* [paint, concrete] qui sèche rapidement ■ **quick-setting** *adj* [cement] à prise rapide; [jelly] qui prend rapidement

**quicken** ['kwɪkən] **1.** *vt* accélérer **2.** *vi* s'accélérer

**quickfire** ['kwɪkfaɪə(r)] *adj* **he directed quickfire questions at me** il m'a mitraillé de questions; **a series of quickfire questions** un feu roulant de questions

**quickie** ['kwɪkɪ] *n Fam* [gen] truc *m* vite fait

**quickly** ['kwɪklɪ] *adv* vite

**quicksand** ['kwɪksænd] *n* sables *mpl* mouvants

**quid** [kwɪd] *n inv Br Fam* [pound] livre *f*

**quiet** ['kwaɪət] **1.** (*compar* -er, *superl* -est) *adj* [silent, still, peaceful] tranquille, calme; [machine, vehicle] silencieux, -euse; [person, voice, music] doux (*f* douce); **to be** *or* **keep quiet** [say nothing] se taire; [make no noise] ne pas faire de bruit; **to keep quiet about sth, to keep sth quiet** ne rien dire au sujet de qch; **quiet!** silence! **2.** *n Fam* **on**

**the quiet** [secretly] en cachette **3.** *vt Am* calmer, apaiser ■ **quiet down 1.** *vt sep* calmer, apaiser **2.** *vi* se calmer

**quieten** ['kwaɪətən] *Br* **1.** *vt* to **quieten (down)** calmer **2.** *vi* to **quieten down** se calmer

**quietly** ['kwaɪətlɪ] *adv* tranquillement; [gently, not loudly] doucement; [silently] silencieusement; [secretly] en cachette; [discreetly] discrètement

**quilt** [kwɪlt] *n* édredon *m*; *Br* (**continental**) **quilt** [duvet] couette *f*

**quip** [kwɪp] **1.** *n* boutade *f* **2.** (*pt & pp* -pp-) *vti* plaisanter

**quirk** [kwɜːk] *n* [of character] particularité *f* ■ **quirky** (*compar* -ier, *superl* -iest) *adj* bizarre

**quit** [kwɪt] (*pt & pp* quit *or* quitted, *pres p* quitting) **1.** *vt* [leave] quitter; COMPUT sortir de; **to quit doing sth** arrêter de faire qch **2.** *vi* [give up] abandonner; [resign] démissionner; COMPUT sortir

**quite** [kwaɪt] *adv* [entirely] tout à fait; [really] vraiment; [fairly] assez; **quite good** [not bad] pas mal du tout; **quite (so)!** exactement!; **quite a lot** pas mal (**of** de)

**quits** [kwɪts] *adj* quitte (**with** envers); **to call it quits** en rester là

**quiver** ['kwɪvə(r)] *vi* [of voice] trembler

**quiz** [kwɪz] **1.** (*pl* -zz-) *n* [on radio] jeu *m* radiophonique; [on TV] jeu *m* télévisé; [in magazine] questionnaire *m* **2.** (*pt & pp* -zz-) *vt* interroger

**quota** ['kwəʊtə] *n* quota *m*

**quotation** [kwəʊ'teɪʃən] *n* [from author] citation *f*; [estimate] devis *m*; **in quotation marks** entre guillemets

**quote** [kwəʊt] **1.** *n* [from author] citation *f*; [estimate] devis *m*; **in quotes** entre guillemets **2.** *vt* [author, passage] citer; [reference number] rappeler; [price] indiquer **3.** *vi* to **quote from** [author, book] citer

# R

**R, r** [ɑː(r)] *n* [lettre] R, r *m inv*

**rabbi** ['ræbaɪ] *n* rabbin *m*

**rabbit** ['ræbɪt] *n* lapin *m*

**rabies** ['reɪbiːz] *n* rage *f*

**raccoon** [rə'kuːn] *n* raton *m* laveur

**race¹** [reɪs] **1.** *n* [contest] course *f*; **race
bike** moto *f* de course **2.** *vt* **to race
(against** *or* **with) sb** faire une course
avec qn **3.** *vi* [run] courir ■ **racecourse** *n* champ *m* de courses ■ **racehorse** *n* cheval *m* de course ■ **racetrack** *n* Am [for horses] champ *m* de
courses ; Br [for cars, bicycles] piste *f*
■ **racing** *n* courses *fpl*; **racing car**
voiture *f* de course ; **racing driver**
coureur *m* automobile

**race²** [reɪs] *n* [group] race *f*; **race relations** relations *fpl* interraciales
■ **racial** ['reɪʃəl] *adj* racial ■ **racism** *n*
racisme *m* ■ **racist** *adj & n* raciste (*mf*)

**rack** [ræk] **1.** *n* [for bottles, letters,
records] casier *m*; [for plates] égouttoir *m*; **(luggage) rack** porte-ba-
gages *m inv*; **(roof) rack** [of car] galerie *f*
**2.** *vt* **to rack one's brains** se creuser
la cervelle

**racket¹** ['rækɪt] *n* [for tennis] raquette *f*

**racket²** ['rækɪt] Fam *n* **a)** [din] vacarme *m*
**b)** [criminal activity] racket *m*

**radar** ['reɪdɑː(r)] *n* radar *m*; **radar speed
check** contrôle *m* de radar

**radiant** ['reɪdɪənt] *adj* [person, face]
resplendissant (**with** de)

**radiate** ['reɪdɪeɪt] **1.** *vt* [heat, light] dégager ; Fig [joy, health] être rayonnant de
**2.** *vi* rayonner (**from** de) ■ **radiation**
*n* [radioactivity] radiation *f*

**radiator** ['reɪdɪeɪtə(r)] *n* [heater] radiateur *m*

**radical** ['rædɪkəl] *adj & n* radical, -e (*mf*)

**radio** ['reɪdɪəʊ] **1.** *(pl* **-os)** *n* radio *f*; **on
the radio** à la radio ; **radio cassette
(player)** radiocassette *f* **2.** *(pt & pp* **-oed)**
*vt* [message] transmettre par radio (**to**
à) ; **to radio sb** contacter qn par radio
■ **radio-controlled** *adj* radioguidé

**radioactivity** [reɪdɪəʊæk'tɪvətɪ] *n*
radioactivité *f*

**radish** ['rædɪʃ] *n* radis *m*

**radius** ['reɪdɪəs] *(pl* **-dii)** *n* rayon *m*; **within a radius of 10 km** dans un rayon de
10 km

**RAF** [ɑːreɪ'ef] *(abbr of* **Royal Air Force)** *n*
armée de l'air britannique

**raffle** ['ræfəl] *n* tombola *f*

**raft** [rɑːft] *n* radeau *m*

**rag** [ræg] *n* **a)** [piece of old clothing]
chiffon *m*; **in rags** [clothes] en loques ;
[person] en haillons **b)** Fam & Pej
[newspaper] torchon *m*

**rage** [reɪdʒ] **1.** *n* [of person] rage *f*; **to fly
into a rage** entrer dans une rage folle ;
Fam **to be all the rage** [of fashion] faire
fureur **2.** *vi* [be angry] être furieux,
-euse ; [of storm, battle] faire rage
■ **raging** *adj* [storm, fever, fire] violent

**ragged** ['rægɪd] *adj* [clothes] en loques ;
[person] en haillons ; [edge] irrégulier,
-ère

**ragtop** ['rægtɒp] *n* Am Fam AUTO décapotable *f*

**raid** [reɪd] **1.** *n* [military] raid *m*; [by
police] descente *f*; [by thieves] hold-
up *m inv*; **air raid** raid *m* aérien **2.** *vt*
faire un raid / une descente / un hold-
up dans

**rail** [reɪl] **1.** *n* **a)** [for train] rail *m*; **by rail**
par le train **b)** [rod on balcony] balus-
trade *f*; [on stairs] rampe *f*; [curtain rod]

tringle f **2.** adj [ticket] de chemin de fer ; [strike] des cheminots ■ **railcard** n carte f d'abonnement de train

**railings** ['reɪlɪŋz] npl grille f

**railroad** ['reɪlrəud] n Am [system] chemin m de fer ; [track] voie f ferrée

**railway** ['reɪlweɪ] Br **1.** n [system] chemin m de fer ; [track] voie f ferrée **2.** adj [ticket] de chemin de fer ; [timetable] des chemins de fer ; [network, company] ferroviaire ; **railway line** ligne f de chemin de fer ; **railway station** gare f

**rain** [reɪn] **1.** n pluie f ; **in the rain** sous la pluie **2.** vi pleuvoir ; **it's raining** il pleut ■ **rainbow** n arc-en-ciel m ■ **raincoat** n imperméable m ■ **rainfall** n [amount] précipitations fpl ■ **rainforest** n forêt f tropicale humide ■ **rainwater** n eau f de pluie ■ **rainy** (compar -ier, superl -iest) adj pluvieux, -euse ; [day] de pluie ; **the rainy season** la saison des pluies

**raise** [reɪz] **1.** vt [lift] lever ; [child, family, voice] élever ; [salary, price] augmenter ; [temperature] faire monter ; [question, protest] soulever ; [taxes] lever ; **to raise money** réunir des fonds ; **to raise the alarm** donner l'alarme **2.** n Am [pay rise] augmentation f (de salaire)

**raisin** ['reɪzən] n raisin m sec

**rake** [reɪk] **1.** n râteau m **2.** vt [soil] ratisser ; **to rake (up)** [leaves] ratisser

**rally** ['rælɪ] **1.** (pl -ies) n [political] rassemblement m ; [car race] rallye m **2.** (pt & pp -ied) vt [unite, win over] rallier (**to** à) **3.** vi se rallier (**to** à) ; [recover] reprendre ses forces ; **to rally round sb** venir en aide à qn

**ram** [ræm] **1.** n [animal] bélier m **2.** (pt & pp -mm-) vt [vehicle] emboutir ; [ship] aborder ; **to ram sth into sth** enfoncer qch dans qch

**RAM** [ræm] (abbr of **random access memory**) n COMPUT mémoire f vive

**ramble** ['ræmbəl] **1.** n [hike] randonnée f **2.** vi [hike] faire une randonnée ; **to ramble on** [talk] divaguer ■ **rambler** n randonneur, -euse mf

**rambling** ['ræmblɪŋ] adj a) [house] plein de coins et de recoins ; [spread out] vaste b) [speech] décousu

**ramp** [ræmp] n [for wheelchair] rampe f d'accès ; [in garage] pont m (de graissage) ; [on road] petit dos m d'âne

**rampant** ['ræmpənt] adj endémique

**ran** [ræn] pt of **run**

**ranch** [rɑːntʃ] n ranch m

**rancid** ['rænsɪd] adj rance

**random** ['rændəm] **1.** n **at random** au hasard **2.** adj [choice] (fait) au hasard ; [sample] prélevé au hasard

**rang** [ræŋ] pt of **ring**

**range** [reɪndʒ] **1.** n a) [of gun, voice] portée f ; [of singer's voice] registre m ; [of aircraft, ship] rayon m d'action ; [of colours, prices, products] gamme f ; [of sizes] choix m b) [of mountains] chaîne f c) [stove] fourneau m d) **(shooting) range** champ m de tir **2.** vi [vary] varier (**from** de ; **to** à) ; [extend] s'étendre

**ranger** ['reɪndʒə(r)] n **(forest) ranger** garde m forestier

**rank¹** [ræŋk] **1.** n [position, class] rang m ; [military grade] grade m ; [row] rangée f ; [for taxis] station f **2.** vt placer (**among** parmi) **3.** vi compter (**among** parmi)

**rank²** [ræŋk] (compar -er, superl -est) adj [smell] fétide

**-ranking** suff high-ranking de haut rang ou grade ; low-ranking à petit grade

**ransack** ['rænsæk] vt [house] mettre sens dessus dessous ; [shop, town] piller

**ransom** ['rænsəm] **1.** n rançon f ; **to hold sb to ransom** rançonner qn **2.** vt rançonner

**rant** [rænt] vi Fam **to rant and rave** tempêter (**at** contre)

**rap** [ræp] **1.** n a) [blow] coup m sec b) **rap (music)** rap m **2.** vi [hit] frapper (**on** à)

**rape** [reɪp] **1.** n viol m **2.** vt violer ■ **rapist** n violeur m

**rapid** ['ræpɪd] adj rapide ■ **rapidly** adv rapidement

**rapids** ['ræpɪdz] npl [of river] rapides mpl

**rare** [reə(r)] adj a) (compar -er, superl -est) [uncommon] rare b) [meat] saignant ■ **rarely** adv rarement ■ **rarity** (pl -ies) n [quality, object] rareté f

**raring** ['reərɪŋ] *adj* **raring to do sth** impatient de faire qch

**rascal** ['rɑːskəl] *n* coquin, -e *mf*

**rash**[1] [ræʃ] *n* [on skin - red patches] rougeurs *fpl* ; [spots] (éruption *f* de) boutons *mpl*

**rash**[2] [ræʃ] *(compar* -er, *superl* -est) *adj* [imprudent] irréfléchi ▪ **rashly** *adv* sans réfléchir

**rasher** ['ræʃə(r)] *n* Br tranche *f* (de bacon)

**raspberry** ['rɑːzbərɪ] *(pl* -ies) *n* [fruit] framboise *f*

**rat** [ræt] *n* rat *m* ; Fig **rat race** foire *f* d'empoigne

**rate** [reɪt] **1.** *n* [level, percentage] taux *m* ; [speed] rythme *m* ; [price] tarif *m* ; **interest rate** taux *m* d'intérêt ; **at the rate of** au rythme de ; [amount] à raison de ; **at this rate** [slow speed] à ce train-là ; **at any rate** en tout cas **2.** *vt* [regard] considérer (**as** comme) ; [deserve] mériter ; **to rate sb/sth highly** tenir qn/qch en haute estime

**rather** ['rɑːðə(r)] *adv* [preferably, quite] plutôt ; **I'd rather stay** j'aimerais mieux rester (**than** que) ; **I rather liked it** j'ai bien aimé

**ratify** ['rætɪfaɪ] *(pt & pp* -ied) *vt* ratifier

**rating** ['reɪtɪŋ] *n* [classification] classement *m*

**ratio** ['reɪʃɪəʊ] *(pl* -os) *n* rapport *m*

**ration** ['ræʃən] **1.** *n* ration *f* ; **rations** [food] vivres *mpl* **2.** *vt* rationner ▪ **rationing** *n* rationnement *m*

**rational** ['ræʃənəl] *adj* [sensible] raisonnable ; [sane] rationnel, -elle ▪ **rationalize** *vt* [organize] rationaliser ; [explain] justifier ▪ **rationally** *adv* [behave] raisonnablement

**rattle** ['rætəl] **1.** *n* [for baby] hochet *m* **2.** *vt* [window] faire vibrer ; [keys, chains] faire cliqueter ; Fam **to rattle sth off** [speech, list] débiter qch **3.** *vi* [of window] vibrer

**raucous** ['rɔːkəs] *adj* [noisy, rowdy] bruyant

**rave** [reɪv] **1.** *n* [party] rave *f* **2.** *vi* [talk nonsense] délirer ; **to rave about sb/**

sth [enthuse] ne pas tarir d'éloges sur qn/qch ▪ **raving** *adj* **to be raving mad** être complètement fou (*f* folle)

**raven** ['reɪvən] *n* corbeau *m*

**ravenous** ['rævənəs] *adj* **I'm ravenous** j'ai une faim de loup

**ravine** [rə'viːn] *n* ravin *m*

**ravioli** [rævɪ'əʊlɪ] *n* ravioli(s) *mpl*

**raw** [rɔː] *(compar* -er, *superl* -est) *adj* [vegetable] cru ; [data] brut ; **raw material** matière *f* première

**ray** [reɪ] *n* [of light, sun] rayon *m* ; Fig [of hope] lueur *f*

**rayon** ['reɪɒn] *n* rayonne *f*

**razor** ['reɪzə(r)] *n* rasoir *m* ; **razor blade** lame *f* de rasoir

**Rd** *(abbr of* road) rue

**re** [riː] *prep* COMM en référence à ; **re your letter** suite à votre lettre

**reach** [riːtʃ] **1.** *n* portée *f* ; **within reach of** à portée de ; [near] à proximité de ; **within (easy) reach** [object] à portée de main ; [shops] tout proche **2.** *vt* [place, aim, distant object] atteindre, arriver à ; [decision] prendre ; [agreement] aboutir à ; [contact] joindre ; **to reach a conclusion** arriver à une conclusion ; **to reach out one's arm** tendre le bras **3.** *vi* [extend] s'étendre (**to** jusqu'à) ; **to reach (out) for sth** tendre le bras pour prendre qch

**react** [rɪ'ækt] *vi* réagir (**against** contre ; **to** à) ▪ **reaction** *n* réaction *f*

**reactionary** [rɪ'ækʃənərɪ] *(pl* -ies) *adj* & *n* réactionnaire (*mf*)

**reactor** [rɪ'æktə(r)] *n* réacteur *m*

**read** [riːd] **1.** *(pt & pp* read [red]) *vt* lire ; [meter] relever ; [of instrument] indiquer ; Br UNIV [study] étudier **2.** *vi* [of person] lire (**about** sur) ; **to read to sb** faire la lecture à qn **3.** *n* **to be a good read** être agréable à lire ▪ **readable** *adj* [handwriting] lisible ; [book] facile à lire ▪ **read back** *vt sep* relire ▪ **read out** *vt sep* lire (à haute voix) ▪ **read over** *vt sep* relire ▪ **read through** *vt sep* [skim] parcourir ▪ **read up (on)** *vt insep* [study] étudier

**reader** [ˈriːdə(r)] n lecteur, -trice mf; [book] livre m de lecture

**readily** [ˈredɪlɪ] adv [willingly] volontiers; [easily] facilement

**reading** [ˈriːdɪŋ] n lecture f; [of meter] relevé m; **reading glasses** lunettes fpl de lecture; **reading lamp** [on desk] lampe f de bureau; [at bedside] lampe f de chevet; **reading light** liseuse f; **reading matter** de quoi lire

**readjust** [riːəˈdʒʌst] 1. vt [instrument] régler 2. vi [of person] se réadapter (**to** à)

**ready** [ˈredɪ] 1. (compar -ier, superl -iest) adj prêt (**to do** à faire; **for sth** pour qch); **to get sb/sth ready** préparer qn/qch; **to get ready** se préparer (**for sth** pour qch; **to do** à faire); **ready cash, ready money** argent m liquide 2. n **to be at the ready** être tout prêt (f toute prête) ■ **ready-made** adj [food] tout prêt (f toute prête); **ready-made clothes** le prêt-à-porter ■ **ready-to-wear** adj **ready-to-wear clothes** le prêt-à-porter

**real** [rɪəl] 1. adj vrai; [leather] véritable; [world, danger] réel (f réelle); **in real life** dans la réalité; Am **real estate** immobilier m 2. adv Fam vraiment 3. n Fam **for real** pour de vrai

**realistic** [rɪəˈlɪstɪk] adj réaliste

**reality** [rɪˈælətɪ] (pl -ies) n réalité f; **in reality** en réalité; **reality TV** télévision/TV f réalité

**realization** [rɪəlaɪˈzeɪʃən] n [awareness] prise f de conscience

**realize** [ˈrɪəlaɪz] vt a) [become aware of] se rendre compte de; **to realize that...** se rendre compte que... b) [carry out] réaliser

**really** [ˈrɪəlɪ] adv vraiment

**Realtor®** [ˈrɪəltɔː(r)] n Am agent m immobilier

**ream** [riːm] n [of paper] rame f

**reap** [riːp] vt [crop] moissonner; Fig [profits] récolter

**reappear** [riːəˈpɪə(r)] vi réapparaître

**rear¹** [rɪə(r)] 1. n [back part] arrière m; **in** or **at the rear** à l'arrière (**of** de) 2. adj [entrance, legs] de derrière; [lights, window] arrière inv

**rear²** [rɪə(r)] 1. vt [child, animals] élever; [one's head] relever 2. vi **to rear (up)** [of horse] se cabrer

**rearrange** [riːəˈreɪndʒ] vt [hair, room] réarranger; [plans] changer

**rearview** [ˈrɪəvjuː] n **rearview mirror** rétroviseur m

**reason** [ˈriːzən] 1. n [cause, sense] raison f; **the reason for/why** la raison de/pour laquelle; **for no reason** sans raison; **it stands to reason** cela va de soi; **within reason** dans les limites raisonnables 2. vt **to reason that...** estimer que... 3. vi raisonner (**about** sur); **to reason with sb** raisonner qn ■ **reasoning** n raisonnement m

**reasonable** [ˈriːzənəbəl] adj [fair] raisonnable; [quite good] passable ■ **reasonably** adv [behave, act] raisonnablement; [quite] plutôt

**reassure** [riːəˈʃʊə(r)] vt rassurer ■ **reassuring** adj rassurant

**rebate** [ˈriːbeɪt] n [discount] rabais m; [refund] remboursement m

**rebel** 1. [ˈrebəl] n rebelle mf 2. [ˈrebəl] adj [camp, chief, attack] des rebelles 3. [rɪˈbel] (pt & pp -ll-) vi se rebeller (**against** contre) ■ **rebellion** [rɪˈbeljən] n rébellion f

**reboot** [ˌriːˈbuːt] vi COMPUT redémarrer

**rebound** 1. [ˈriːbaʊnd] n [of ball] rebond m 2. [rɪˈbaʊnd] vi [of ball] rebondir; Fig [of lies, action] se retourner (**on** contre)

**rebuild** [riːˈbɪld] (pt & pp -built) vt reconstruire

**rebuke** [rɪˈbjuːk] 1. n réprimande f 2. vt réprimander

**recall** [rɪˈkɔːl] 1. n [calling back] rappel m 2. vt [remember] se rappeler (**that** que; **doing** avoir fait); [call back] rappeler; **to recall sth to sb** rappeler qch à qn

**recap** [ˈriːkæp] 1. n récapitulation f 2. (pt & pp -pp-) vi récapituler

**recapitulate** [riːkəˈpɪtjʊleɪt] *vti* récapituler

**recede** [rɪˈsiːd] *vi* [into the distance] s'éloigner ; [of floods] baisser ■ **receding** *adj* **his hairline is receding, he has a receding hairline** son front se dégarnit

**receipt** [rɪˈsiːt] *n* [for payment, object] reçu *m* (**for** de) ; [for letter, parcel] récépissé *m* ; **receipts** [at box office] recette *f* ; **on receipt of sth** dès réception de qch

**receive** [rɪˈsiːv] *vt* recevoir ; [stolen goods] receler

**receiver** [rɪˈsiːvə(r)] *n* [of phone] combiné *m* ; [radio] récepteur *m* ; **to pick up** *or* **lift the receiver** [of phone] décrocher

**recent** [ˈriːsənt] *adj* récent ; [development] dernier, -ère ; **in recent months** au cours des derniers mois ■ **recently** *adv* récemment

**reception** [rɪˈsepʃən] *n* [party, of radio] réception *f* ; [welcome] accueil *m* ; **reception (desk)** réception *f* ■ **receptionist** *n* réceptionniste *mf*

**receptive** [rɪˈseptɪv] *adj* réceptif, -ive (**to** à)

**recess** [*Br* rɪˈses, *Am* ˈriːses] *n* **a)** [holiday] vacances *fpl* ; *Am* [between classes] récréation *f* **b)** [in wall] renfoncement *m* ; [smaller] recoin *m*

**recession** [rɪˈseʃən] *n* ECON récession *f*

**recharge** [riːˈtʃɑːdʒ] *vt* [battery, mobile phone] recharger ■ **rechargeable** *adj* [battery] rechargeable

**recipe** [ˈresɪpɪ] *n* [for food] & *Fig* recette *f* (**for sth** de qch)

**recipient** [rɪˈsɪpɪənt] *n* [of gift, letter] destinataire *mf* ; [of award] lauréat, -e *mf*

**reciprocal** [rɪˈsɪprəkəl] *adj* réciproque ■ **reciprocate** **1.** *vt* retourner **2.** *vi* rendre la pareille

**recital** [rɪˈsaɪtəl] *n* [of music] récital *m* (*pl* -als)

**recite** [rɪˈsaɪt] *vt* [poem] réciter ; [list] énumérer

**reckless** [ˈrekləs] *adj* [rash] imprudent

**reckon** [ˈrekən] **1.** *vt* [calculate] calculer ; [consider] considérer ; *Fam* [think] penser (**that** que) **2.** *vi* calculer, compter ; **to reckon with** [take into account] compter avec ; [deal with] avoir affaire à ; **to reckon on sb/sth** [rely on] compter sur qn/qch ■ **reckoning** *n* [calculation] calcul *m*

**reclaim** [rɪˈkleɪm] *vt* [lost property, luggage] récupérer ; [expenses] se faire rembourser

**recline** [rɪˈklaɪn] *vi* [be stretched out] être allongé ■ **recliner** [rɪˈklaɪnə(r)] *n* [for sunbathing] chaise *f* longue ; [armchair] fauteuil *m* à dossier inclinable, fauteuil *m* relax ■ **reclining** *adj* **reclining seat** siège *m* à dossier inclinable

**recluse** [rɪˈkluːs] *n* reclus, -e *mf*

**recognition** [rekəgˈnɪʃən] *n* reconnaissance *f* ; **to gain recognition** être reconnu

**recognize** [ˈrekəgnaɪz] *vt* reconnaître ■ **recognizable** *adj* reconnaissable

**recoil** [rɪˈkɔɪl] *vi* [of person] avoir un mouvement de recul

**recollect** [rekəˈlekt] *vt* se souvenir de ■ **recollection** *n* souvenir *m*

**recommend** [rekəˈmend] *vt* [praise, support, advise] recommander (**to** à ; **for** pour) ; **to recommend sb to do sth** recommander à qn de faire qch ■ **recommendation** *n* recommandation *f*

**recommended daily allowance** *or* **intake** *n* [food] apport *m* quotidien recommandé

**recompense** [ˈrekəmpens] **1.** *n* récompense *f* **2.** *vt* [reward] récompenser

**reconcile** [ˈrekənsaɪl] *vt* [person] réconcilier (**with** *or* **to** avec) ; [opinions, facts] concilier ; **to reconcile oneself to sth** se résigner à qch

**reconditioned** [riːkənˈdɪʃənd] *adj* [engine, machine] remis à neuf

**reconsider** [riːkənˈsɪdə(r)] **1.** *vt* réexaminer **2.** *vi* réfléchir

**reconstruct** [riːkənˈstrʌkt] *vt* [crime] reconstituer

**record 1.** ['rekɔːd] *n* **a)** [disc] disque *m*;
**record player** électrophone *m*
**b)** [best sporting performance] record *m*
**c)** [report] rapport *m*; [background] antécédents *mpl*; [file] dossier *m*; **to make** *or* **keep a record of sth** garder une trace écrite de qch; **on record** [fact, event] attesté; **(police) record** casier *m* judiciaire; **(public) records** archives *fpl*
**2.** ['rekɔːd] *adj* record *inv*; **to be at a record high / low** être à son taux le plus haut / bas
**3.** [rɪ'kɔːd] *vt* [on tape, in register] enregistrer; [in diary] noter
**4.** [rɪ'kɔːd] *vi* [on tape, of tape recorder] enregistrer

**recorded** [rɪ'kɔːdɪd] *adj* enregistré; [fact] attesté; [TV broadcast] en différé; *Br* **to send sth (by) recorded delivery** ≃ envoyer qch en recommandé avec accusé de réception

**recorder** [rɪ'kɔːdə(r)] *n* [musical instrument] flûte *f* à bec

**recording** [rɪ'kɔːdɪŋ] *n* enregistrement *m*

**recount** [rɪ'kaʊnt] *vt* [relate] raconter

**recoup** [rɪ'kuːp] *vt* récupérer

**recourse** [rɪ'kɔːs] *n* recours *m*; **to have recourse to** avoir recours à

**recover** [rɪ'kʌvə(r)] **1.** *vt* [get back] récupérer; [one's appetite, balance] retrouver **2.** *vi* [from illness, shock, surprise] se remettre **(from** de); [of economy, country] se redresser; [of sales] reprendre ■ **recovery** (*pl* **-ies**) *n* **a)** [from illness] rétablissement *m*; [of economy] redressement *m* **b)** *Br* **recovery vehicle** dépanneuse *f*

**re-create** [riːkrɪ'eɪt] *vt* recréer

**recreation** [rekrɪ'eɪʃən] *n* SCH [break] récréation *f*

**recrimination** [rɪkrɪmɪ'neɪʃən] *n* récrimination *f*

**recruit** [rɪ'kruːt] **1.** *n* recrue *f* **2.** *vt* recruter

**rectangle** ['rektæŋgəl] *n* rectangle *m*
■ **rectangular** *adj* rectangulaire

**rectify** ['rektɪfaɪ] (*pt & pp* **-ied**) *vt* rectifier

**rector** ['rektə(r)] *n* [priest] pasteur *m* anglican

**recuperate** [rɪ'kuːpəreɪt] *vi* [from illness] récupérer

**recur** [rɪ'kɜː(r)] (*pt & pp* **-rr-**) *vi* [of event, problem] se reproduire; [of illness] réapparaître; [of theme] revenir

**recycle** [riː'saɪkəl] *vt* recycler; COMPUT **recycle bin** poubelle *f*, corbeille *f*

**red** [red] **1.** (*compar* **redder**, *superl* **reddest**) *adj* rouge; [hair] roux (*f* rousse); **to turn** *or* **go red** rougir; **the Red Cross** la Croix-Rouge; **red light** [traffic light] feu *m* rouge; *Am* **red state** *État qui vote traditionnellement républicain*; *Fig* **red tape** paperasserie *f* **2.** *n* [colour] rouge *m*; **in the red** [in debt] dans le rouge ■ **red-handed** *adv* **to be caught red-handed** être pris la main dans le sac ■ **redhead** *n* roux *m*, rousse *f* ■ **red-hot** *adj* brûlant

**redcurrant** [red'kʌrənt] *n* groseille *f*

**redecorate** [riː'dekəreɪt] *vt* [repaint] refaire la peinture de

**redeem** [rɪ'diːm] *vt* [restore to favour, buy back, free] racheter; [gift token, coupon] échanger; **his one redeeming feature is...** la seule chose qui le rachète, c'est...

**redirect** [riːdaɪ'rekt] *vt* [mail] faire suivre

**redo** [riː'duː] (*pt* **-did**, *pp* **-done**) *vt* refaire

**reduce** [rɪ'djuːs] *vt* réduire **(to** à; **by** de); [temperature, price] baisser; **at a reduced price** à prix réduit; **to be reduced to doing sth** en être réduit à faire qch ■ **reduction** [-'dʌkʃən] *n* [of temperature, price] baisse *f*; [discount] réduction *f* **(in** / **on** de / **sur**)

**redundant** [rɪ'dʌndənt] *adj* [not needed] superflu; *Br* **to make sb redundant** licencier qn ■ **redundancy** (*pl* **-ies**) *n* *Br* [of worker] licenciement *m*; **redundancy pay** *or* **payment** *etc* **money** prime *f* de licenciement

**reed** [riːd] *n* [plant] roseau *m*

**reef** [riːf] *n* récif *m*

**reek** [riːk] *vi* **to reek (of sth)** puer (qch)

**reel** [riːl] **1.** n [of thread, film] bobine f; [for fishing line] moulinet m **2.** vt sep **to reel off** [names, statistics] débiter

**re-elect** [riːɪˈlekt] vt réélire

**re-establish** [riːɪˈstæblɪʃ] vt rétablir

**ref** [ref] (abbr of referee) n Fam arbitre m

**refectory** [rɪˈfektəri] (pl **-ies**) n réfectoire m

**refer** [rɪˈfɜː(r)] (pt & pp **-rr-**) **1.** vt **to refer sth to sb** [submit] soumettre qch à qn; **to refer sb to a specialist** envoyer qn voir un spécialiste **2.** vt insep **to refer to** [allude to] faire allusion à; [mention] parler de; [apply to] s'appliquer à; [consult] consulter

**referee** [refəˈriː] **1.** n [in sport] arbitre m; **to give the names of two referees** [for job] fournir deux références **2.** vti arbitrer

**reference** [ˈrefərəns] n [source, consultation] référence f; [allusion] allusion f (**to** à); [mention] mention f (**to** de); [for employer] lettre f de référence; **with** or **in reference to** concernant; **reference book** ouvrage m de référence

**referendum** [refəˈrendəm] n référendum m

**refill 1.** [ˈriːfɪl] n [for pen] cartouche f; [for lighter] recharge f; **would you like a refill?** [of drink] je te ressers ? **2.** [riːˈfɪl] vt [glass] remplir à nouveau; [lighter, pen] recharger

**refine** [rɪˈfaɪn] vt [oil, sugar, manners] raffiner; [technique, machine] perfectionner ■ **refined** adj [person, manners] raffiné ■ **refinement** n [of person, manners] raffinement m; **refinements** [technical improvements] améliorations fpl

**reflect** [rɪˈflekt] **1.** vt a) [light, image] refléter, réfléchir; Fig [portray] refléter; **to be reflected (in)** [of light] se refléter (dans) b) **to reflect that...** se dire que... **2.** vi a) **to reflect on sb** [of prestige, honour] rejaillir sur qn; **to reflect badly on sb** faire du tort à qn b) [think] réfléchir (**on** à)

**reflection** [rɪˈflekʃən] n a) [image] & Fig reflet m b) [thought, criticism] réflexion (**on** sur); **on reflection** tout bien réfléchi

**reflector** [rɪˈflektə(r)] n [on bicycle, vehicle] catadioptre m

**reflex** [ˈriːfleks] n & adj réflexe (m); **reflex action** réflexe m

**reflexive** [rɪˈfleksɪv] adj [verb] réfléchi

**reform** [rɪˈfɔːm] **1.** n réforme f **2.** vt réformer; [person, conduct] corriger **3.** vi [of person] se réformer

**refrain** [rɪˈfreɪn] **1.** n [of song] & Fig refrain m **2.** vi s'abstenir (**from sth** de qch; **from doing** de faire)

**refresh** [rɪˈfreʃ] vt [of drink] rafraîchir; [of bath] revigorer; [of sleep, rest] reposer; **to refresh one's memory** se rafraîchir la mémoire ■ **refreshing** adj [drink] rafraîchissant; [bath] revigorant; [original] nouveau (f nouvelle)

**refreshments** [rɪˈfreʃmənts] npl rafraîchissements mpl

**refrigerate** [rɪˈfrɪdʒəreɪt] vt réfrigérer ■ **refrigerator** n [domestic] réfrigérateur m

**refuel** [riːˈfjʊəl] **1.** (Br **-ll-**, Am **-l-**) vt [aircraft] ravitailler en carburant **2.** vi [of aircraft] se ravitailler en carburant

**refuge** [ˈrefjuːdʒ] n refuge m; **to take refuge** se réfugier (**in** dans)

**refugee** [refjʊˈdʒiː] n réfugié, -e mf

**refund 1.** [ˈriːfʌnd] n remboursement m **2.** [rɪˈfʌnd] vt rembourser

**refurbish** [riːˈfɜːbɪʃ] vt rénover

**refusal** [rɪˈfjuːzəl] n refus m

**refuse¹** [rɪˈfjuːz] **1.** vt refuser; **to refuse to do sth** refuser de faire qch; **to refuse sb sth** refuser qch à qn **2.** vi refuser

**refuse²** [ˈrefjuːs] n Br [rubbish] ordures fpl; **refuse collection** ramassage m des ordures

**refute** [rɪˈfjuːt] vt réfuter

**regain** [rɪˈgeɪn] vt [lost ground, favour] regagner; [health, sight] retrouver; **to regain consciousness** reprendre connaissance

**regal** [ˈriːgəl] adj royal

**regard** [rɪ'gɑːd] **1.** n [admiration] respect m ; [consideration] égard m ; **to hold sb in high regard** tenir qn en haute estime; **with regard to** en ce qui concerne; **to give** or **send one's regards to sb** transmettre son meilleur souvenir à qn **2.** vt [admire, respect] estimer; **to regard sb/sth as...** considérer qn /qch comme... ■ **regarding** prep en ce qui concerne

**regardless** [rɪ'gɑːdləs] **1.** adj **regardless of...** [without considering] sans tenir compte de... **2.** adv [all the same] quand même

**regenerate** [rɪ'dʒenəreɪt] vt régénérer

**reggae** ['regeɪ] n [music] reggae m

**régime** [reɪ'ʒiːm] n régime m

**regiment** ['redʒɪmənt] n régiment m

**region** ['riːdʒən] n région f; Fig **in the region of** [about] environ ■ **regional** adj régional

**register** ['redʒɪstə(r)] **1.** n registre m ; [in school] cahier m d'appel; **electoral register** liste f électorale; **to take the register** [of teacher] faire l'appel **2.** vt [birth, death] déclarer ; [record, note] enregistrer ; [vehicle] immatriculer ; [complaint] déposer **3.** vi [enrol] s'inscrire (for à) ; [at hotel] signer le registre ; [of voter] s'inscrire sur les listes électorales ■ **registered** adj [member] inscrit ; [letter, package] recommandé; **to send sth by registered post** or Am **mail** envoyer qch en recommandé

**registration** [redʒɪ'streɪʃən] n [enrolment] inscription f; Br **registration (number)** [of vehicle] numéro m d'immatriculation; Br **registration document** [of vehicle] ≃ carte f grise

**registry** ['redʒɪstrɪ] adj & n Br **registry (office)** bureau m de l'état civil; **to get married in a registry office** se marier à la mairie

**regret** [rɪ'gret] **1.** n regret m **2.** (pt & pp -tt-) vt regretter (**to do** de faire; **that** que (+ subjunctive)); **to regret doing sth** regretter d'avoir fait qch

**regrettable** [rɪ'gretəbəl] adj regrettable (**that** que (+ subjunctive))

**regroup** [riː'gruːp] vi se regrouper

**regular** ['regjʊlə(r)] **1.** adj [steady, even, in grammar] régulier, -ère ; [usual] habituel, -elle ; [price] normal ; [size] moyen, -enne ; [listener, reader] fidèle ; Am Fam **a regular guy** un chic type **2.** n [in bar] habitué, -e mf ■ **regularly** adv régulièrement

**regulate** ['regjʊleɪt] vt [adjust] régler ; [control] réglementer ■ **regulations** npl [rules] règlement m

**rehabilitate** [riːə'bɪlɪteɪt] vt réhabiliter

**rehearse** [rɪ'hɜːs] vti répéter ■ **rehearsal** n répétition f

**reign** [reɪn] **1.** n règne m; **in** or **during the reign of** sous le règne de **2.** vi régner (**over** sur)

**reimburse** [riːɪm'bɜːs] vt rembourser (**for** de)

**reindeer** ['reɪndɪə(r)] n inv renne m

**reinforce** [riːɪn'fɔːs] vt renforcer (**with** de) ; **reinforced concrete** béton m armé ■ **reinforcements** npl [troops] renforts mpl

**reinstall** [riːɪn'stɔːl] vt COMPUT réinstaller

**reinstate** [riːɪn'steɪt] vt réintégrer

**reissue** [riː'ɪʃuː] **1.** n [of book] réédition f; [of film] rediffusion f **2.** vt [book] rééditer ; [film, CD] ressortir

**reiterate** [riː'ɪtəreɪt] vt réitérer

**reject 1.** ['riːdʒekt] n [object] rebus m **2.** [rɪ'dʒekt] vt rejeter ; [candidate, goods, offer] refuser ■ **rejection** [rɪ'dʒekʃən] n rejet m ; [of candidate, goods, offer] refus m

**rejoice** [rɪ'dʒɔɪs] vi se réjouir (**over** or **at** de) ■ **rejoicing** n réjouissance f

**rejoin** [rɪ'dʒɔɪn] vt [join up with] rejoindre

**rejuvenate** [rɪ'dʒuːvəneɪt] vt rajeunir

**relapse** ['riːlæps] n rechute f

**relate** [rɪ'leɪt] **1.** vt **a)** [narrate] raconter (**that** que) ; [report] rapporter (**that** que) **b)** [connect] mettre en rapport (**to** avec) **2.** vi **to relate to** [apply to] avoir rapport à ; [person] avoir des affinités avec ■ **related** adj [linked] lié (**to** à) ; [languages, styles] apparenté; **to be related to sb** [by family] être parent de qn

**relation** [rɪ'leɪʃən] n **a)** [relative] parent, -e mf **b)** [relationship] rapport m; **international relations** relations fpl internationales

**relationship** [rɪ'leɪʃənʃɪp] n [within family] lien m de parenté; [between people] relation f; [between countries] relations fpl; [connection] rapport m

**relative** ['relətɪv] **1.** n parent, -e mf **2.** adj [comparative] relatif, -ive; [respective] respectif, -ive; **relative to** [compared to] relativement à ■ **relatively** adv relativement

**relax** [rɪ'læks] **1.** vt [person, mind] détendre; [grip, pressure] relâcher; [law, control] assouplir **2.** vi [of person] se détendre; **relax!** [calm down] du calme! ■ **relaxed** adj [person, atmosphere] détendu ■ **relaxing** adj délassant

**relaxation** [ri:læk'seɪʃən] n [of person] détente f

**relay 1.** ['ri:leɪ] n **relay (race)** (course f de) relais m **2.** [ri:'leɪ] vt [information] transmettre (**to** à)

**release** [rɪ'li:s] **1.** n [of prisoner] libération f; [of film] sortie f (**of** de); [film] nouveau film m; [record] nouveau disque m **2.** vt [person] libérer (**from** de); [brake] desserrer; [film, record] sortir; [news] communiquer; **to release sb's hand** lâcher la main de qn

**relegate** ['relɪɡeɪt] vt reléguer (**to** à); Br **to be relegated** [of team] descendre en division inférieure

**relent** [rɪ'lent] vi [of person] céder

**relentless** [rɪ'lentləs] adj implacable

**relevant** ['reləvənt] adj **a)** [apt] pertinent; **to be relevant to sth** avoir rapport à qch; **that's not relevant** ça n'a rien à voir **b)** [appropriate - chapter] correspondant; [authorities] compétent; [qualifications] requis **c)** [topical] d'actualité ■ **relevance** n pertinence f (**to** à); [connection] rapport m (**to** avec)

**reliable** [rɪ'laɪəbəl] adj [person, machine] fiable; [information] sûr ■ **reliability** n [of person] sérieux m; [of machine] fiabilité f

**relic** ['relɪk] n relique f; Fig **relics** vestiges mpl

**relief** [rɪ'li:f] **1.** n [comfort] soulagement m; [help] secours m; [in art] relief m **2.** adj [train, bus] supplémentaire; [work] de secours; **relief map** carte f en relief; Br **relief road** route f de délestage

**relieve** [rɪ'li:v] vt [alleviate] soulager; [boredom] tromper; [replace] remplacer; [free] libérer; **to relieve sb of sth** débarrasser qn de qch; Hum **to relieve oneself** se soulager

**religion** [rɪ'lɪdʒən] n religion f ■ **religious** adj religieux, -euse

**relinquish** [rɪ'lɪŋkwɪʃ] vt [hope, habit, thought] abandonner; [share, claim] renoncer à

**relish** ['relɪʃ] **1.** n [pickle] condiments mpl; [pleasure] goût m (**for** pour); **to do sth with relish** faire qch avec délectation **2.** vt savourer

**reload** [ri:'ləʊd] vt [gun, camera] recharger

**relocate** [Br ri:ləʊ'keɪt, Am ri:'ləʊkeɪt] vi [of company] être transféré; [of person] se déplacer

**reluctant** [rɪ'lʌktənt] adj [greeting, promise] accordé à contrecœur; **to be reluctant (to do sth)** être réticent (à faire qch) ■ **reluctantly** adv à contrecœur

**rely** [rɪ'laɪ] (pt & pp -ied) vi **to rely (up)on** [count on] compter sur; [be dependent on] dépendre de

**remain** [rɪ'meɪn] vi [stay behind, continue to be] rester; [be left] subsister ■ **remaining** adj restant ■ **remains** npl restes mpl

**remainder** [rɪ'meɪndə(r)] n reste m; [book] invendu m soldé

**remark** [rɪ'mɑ:k] **1.** n remarque f **2.** vt faire remarquer **3.** vi **to remark on sth** [comment] faire un commentaire sur qch ■ **remarkable** adj remarquable ■ **remarkably** adv remarquablement

**remarry** [ri:'mærɪ] (pt & pp -ied) vi se remarier

**remedy** ['remɪdɪ] **1.** (pl -ies) n remède m **2.** (pt & pp -ied) vt remédier à

**remember** [rɪ'membə(r)] **1.** *vt* se souvenir de, se rappeler ; [commemorate] commémorer ; **to remember that / doing** se rappeler que /d'avoir fait ; **to remember to do sth** penser à faire qch ; **to remember sb to sb** rappeler qn au bon souvenir de qn **2.** *vi* se souvenir, se rappeler

**Remembrance Day, Remembrance Sunday** *Br* n l'Armistice *m*

**remind** [rɪ'maɪnd] *vt* **to remind sb of sth** rappeler qch à qn ; **to remind sb to do sth** rappeler à qn de faire qch ■ **reminder** *n* [letter, of event] rappel *m*

**reminisce** [remɪ'nɪs] *vi* évoquer des souvenirs ; **to reminisce about sth** évoquer qch ■ **reminiscence** *n* souvenir *m*

**reminiscent** [remɪ'nɪsənt] *adj* **reminiscent of** qui rappelle

**remittance** [rɪ'mɪtəns] *n* [sum] paiement *m*

**remorse** [rɪ'mɔːs] *n* remords *m* ; **to feel remorse** avoir du ou des remords ■ **remorseless** *adj* impitoyable

**remote** [rɪ'məʊt] *(compar* -er, *superl* -est) *adj* **a)** [far-off] éloigné (**from** de) ; **remote control** télécommande *f* **b)** [slight] vague ■ **remotely** *adv* [slightly] vaguement

**removable** [rɪ'muːvəbəl] *adj* [lining] amovible

**removal** [rɪ'muːvəl] *n* **a)** [of control, threat] suppression *f* ; [of politician] renvoi *m* **b)** *Br* **removal van** camion *m* de déménagement

**remove** [rɪ'muːv] *vt* [clothes, stain, object] enlever (**from sb** à qn; **from sth** de qch) ; [obstacle, threat, word] supprimer ; [fear, doubt] dissiper ; [politician] renvoyer

**remover** [rɪ'muːvə(r)] *n* [for nail polish] dissolvant *m* ; [for paint] décapant *m* ; [for stains] détachant *m*

**remunerate** [rɪ'mjuːnəreɪt] *vt* rémunérer

**rename** [riː'neɪm] *vt* rebaptiser ; COMPUT [file] renommer

**rendezvous** ['rɒndɪvuː] (*pl* [-vuːz]) *n inv* rendez-vous *m inv*

**renew** [rɪ'njuː] *vt* renouveler ; [resume] reprendre ; [library book] renouveler le prêt de ■ **renewed** *adj* [efforts] renouvelé ; [attempt] nouveau (*f* nouvelle)

**renounce** [rɪ'naʊns] *vt* [give up] renoncer à ; [disown] renier

**renovate** ['renəveɪt] *vt* [house] rénover ; [painting] restaurer

**renowned** [rɪ'naʊnd] *adj* renommé (**for** pour)

**rent** [rent] **1.** *n* [for house, flat] loyer *m* **2.** *vt* louer ; **to rent out** louer ; **rented car** voiture *f* de location

**rental** ['rentəl] *n* [of television, car] location *f* ; [of telephone] abonnement *m*

**reopen** [riː'əʊpən] *vti* rouvrir

**reorganize** [riː'ɔːɡənaɪz] *vt* réorganiser

**rep** [rep] (*abbr of* **representative**) *n Fam* VRP *m*

**repair** [rɪ'peə(r)] **1.** *n* réparation *f* ; **under repair** en travaux **2.** *vt* réparer

**repay** [riː'peɪ] (*pt & pp* -**paid**) *vt* [pay back] rembourser ; [reward] remercier (**for** de) ■ **repayment** *n* remboursement *m*

**repeal** [rɪ'piːl] *vt* abroger

**repeat** [rɪ'piːt] **1.** *n* [of event] répétition *f* ; [on TV, radio] rediffusion *f* **2.** *vt* répéter (**that** que) ; [promise, threat] réitérer ; [class] redoubler ; [TV programme] rediffuser ; **to repeat oneself** se répéter **3.** *vi* répéter ■ **repeated** *adj* [attempts] répété ; [efforts] renouvelé ■ **repeatedly** *adv* à maintes reprises

**repel** [rɪ'pel] (*pt & pp* -**ll**-) *vt* repousser ■ **repellent 1.** *adj* [disgusting] repoussant **2.** *n* **insect repellent** antimoustiques *m inv* ; **water-repellent** imperméabilisant

**repent** [rɪ'pent] *vi* se repentir (**of** de) ■ **repentant** *adj* repentant

**repercussions** [riːpə'kʌʃənz] *npl* répercussions *fpl* (**on** sur)

**repertoire** ['repətwɑː(r)] *n* THEAT & *Fig* répertoire *m* ■ **repertory** [-tərɪ] (*pl* -**ies**) *n* THEAT & *Fig* répertoire *m* ; **repertory theatre** théâtre *m* de répertoire

**repetition** [repɪ'tɪʃən] n répétition f
■ **repetitious, repetitive** [repə'tɪʃəs, rɪ'petɪtɪv] adj répétitif, -ive

**rephrase** [riː'freɪz] vt reformuler

**replace** [rɪ'pleɪs] vt [take the place of] remplacer (**by** or **with** par) ; [put back] remettre (à sa place) ; **to replace the receiver** [on phone] raccrocher ■ **replacement** n [substitution] remplacement m (**of** de) ; [person] remplaçant, -e mf ; [machine part] pièce f de rechange

**replay 1.** ['riːpleɪ] n [match] nouvelle rencontre f ; **(instant** or **action) replay** [on TV] répétition d'une séquence précédente **2.** [riː'pleɪ] vt [match] rejouer

**replica** ['replɪkə] n réplique f

**reply** [rɪ'plaɪ] **1.** (pl **-ies**) n réponse f ; **in reply** en réponse (**to** à) **2.** (pt & pp **-ied**) vti répondre (**to** à ; **that** que)

**report** [rɪ'pɔːt] **1.** n [analysis] rapport m ; [account] compte rendu m ; [in media] reportage m ; Br **(school) report,** Am **report card** bulletin m scolaire **2.** vt [information] rapporter ; [accident, theft] signaler (**to** à) ; **to report sb to the police** dénoncer qn à la police **3.** vi [give account] faire un rapport (**on** sur) ; [of journalist] faire un reportage (**on** sur) ; [go] se présenter (**to** à) ■ **reported** adj **reported speech** [in grammar] discours m indirect ; **it is reported that...** on dit que... ; **to be reported missing** être porté disparu ■ **reporter** n reporter m

**repossess** [riːpə'zes] vt saisir

**represent** [reprɪ'zent] vt représenter ■ **representation** n représentation f

**representative** [reprɪ'zentətɪv] **1.** adj représentatif, -ive (**of** de) **2.** n représentant, -e mf ; Am POL ≃ député m

**repress** [rɪ'pres] vt réprimer ; [memory, feeling] refouler ; **to be repressed** [of person] être un(e) refoulé(e) ■ **repressive** adj [régime] répressif, -ive ; [measures] de répression

**reprieve** [rɪ'priːv] n [cancellation of sentence] commutation f de la peine capitale ; [temporary] & Fig sursis m

**reprimand** ['reprɪmɑːnd] **1.** n réprimande f **2.** vt réprimander

**reprint 1.** ['riːprɪnt] n réimpression f **2.** [riː'prɪnt] vt réimprimer

**reprisal** [rɪ'praɪzəl] n représailles fpl ; **as a reprisal for, in reprisal for** en représailles de

**reproach** [rɪ'prəʊtʃ] **1.** n [blame] reproche m **2.** vt faire des reproches à ; **to reproach sb with sth** reprocher qch à qn

**reproduce** [riːprə'djuːs] **1.** vt reproduire **2.** vi se reproduire ■ **reproduction** [-'dʌkʃən] n reproduction f

**reptile** ['reptaɪl] n reptile m

**republic** [rɪ'pʌblɪk] n république f ■ **republican** adj & n républicain, -e (mf)

**repugnant** [rɪ'pʌɡnənt] adj répugnant

**repulsive** [rɪ'pʌlsɪv] adj repoussant

**reputable** ['repjʊtəbəl] adj de bonne réputation ■ **reputed** adj **she's reputed to be wealthy** on la dit riche

**reputation** [repjʊ'teɪʃən] n réputation f

**request** [rɪ'kwest] **1.** n demande f (**for** de) ; **on request** sur demande ; **at sb's request** à la demande de qn ; Br **request stop** [for bus] arrêt m facultatif **2.** vt demander ; **to request sb to do sth** prier qn de faire qch

**require** [rɪ'kwaɪə(r)] vt [of task, problem, situation] requérir ; [of person] avoir besoin de ; **to be required to do sth** être tenu de faire qch ; **the required qualities** les qualités fpl requises ■ **requirement** n [need] exigence f ; [condition] condition f (requise)

**requisite** ['rekwɪzɪt] adj requis

**reschedule** [Br riː'ʃedjuːl, Am riː-'skedʒʊəl] vt changer la date / l'heure de

**rescue** ['reskjuː] **1.** n [action] sauvetage m (**of** de) ; **to go / come to sb's rescue** aller / venir au secours de qn **2.** adj [team, operation, attempt] de sauvetage **3.** vt [save] sauver ; [set free] délivrer (**from** de)

**research** [rɪ'sɜːtʃ] **1.** n recherches fpl (**on** or **into** sur) **2.** vi faire des recherches (**on** or **into** sur) ■ **researcher** n chercheur, -euse mf

**resemble** [rɪ'zembəl] *vt* ressembler à ■ **resemblance** *n* ressemblance *f* (**to** avec)

**resent** [rɪ'zent] *vt* ne pas aimer ■ **resentment** *n* ressentiment *m*

**reservation** [rezə'veɪʃən] *n* a) [booking] réservation *f*; **to make a reservation** réserver b) [doubt] réserve *f* c) [land for Indians, animals] réserve *f*

**reserve** [rɪ'zɜːv] **1.** *n* a) [reticence] réserve *f* b) [stock, land] réserve *f*; **reserve (player)** [in team] remplaçant, -e *mf*; MIL **the reserves** les réservistes *mpl*; **in reserve** en réserve; **reserve tank** [of vehicle, aircraft] réservoir *m* de secours **2.** *vt* [room, decision] réserver; [right] se réserver ■ **reserved** *adj* [person, room] réservé

**reservoir** ['rezəvwɑː(r)] *n* [of water] réservoir *m*

**reset** [riː'set] *vt* [counter] remettre à zéro; COMPUT ré-initialiser

**reshuffle** [riː'ʃʌfəl] *n* (**cabinet**) **reshuffle** remaniement *m* (ministériel)

**reside** [rɪ'zaɪd] *vi* résider

**residence** ['rezɪdəns] *n* [home] résidence *f*; [of students] foyer *m*; Br **residence permit** permis *m* de séjour

**resident** ['rezɪdənt] **1.** *n* [of country, street] habitant, -e *mf*; [of hotel] pensionnaire *mf*; [foreigner] résident, -e *mf* **2.** *adj* **to be resident in London** résider à Londres

**residential** [rezɪ'denʃəl] *adj* [neighbourhood] résidentiel, -elle

**resign** [rɪ'zaɪn] **1.** *vt* [job] démissionner de; **to resign oneself to sth / to doing sth** se résigner à qch / à faire qch **2.** *vi* démissionner (**from** de) ■ **resigned** *adj* résigné

**resignation** [rezɪg'neɪʃən] *n* [from job] démission *f*; [attitude] résignation *f*

**resilient** [rɪ'zɪlɪənt] *adj* élastique; Fig [person] résistant

**resist** [rɪ'zɪst] **1.** *vt* résister à; **to resist doing sth** s'empêcher de faire qch **2.** *vi* résister ■ **resistance** *n* résistance *f* (**to** à) ■ **resistant** *adj* résistant (**to** à)

**resit** [riː'sɪt] (*pt & pp* -sat, *pres p* -sitting) *vt* Br [exam] repasser

**resolute** ['rezəluːt] *adj* résolu ■ **resolution** *n* résolution *f*

**resolve** [rɪ'zɒlv] **1.** *n* résolution *f* **2.** *vt* [problem] résoudre; **to resolve to do sth** [of person] se résoudre à faire qch

**resort** [rɪ'zɔːt] **1.** *n* a) [holiday place] lieu *m* de villégiature; Br **seaside resort**, Am **beach resort** station *f* balnéaire b) [recourse] **as a last resort**, **in the last resort** en dernier ressort **2.** *vi* **to resort to sth** avoir recours à qch; **to resort to doing sth** finir par faire qch

**resounding** [rɪ'zaʊndɪŋ] *adj* [failure] retentissant; [success] éclatant

**resource** [rɪ'sɔːs, rɪ'zɔːs] *n* ressource *f* ■ **resourceful** *adj* ingénieux, -euse ■ **resources** [rɪ'sɔːsɪz] *npl* ressources *fpl*

**respect** [rɪ'spekt] **1.** *n* respect *m* (**for** pour); [aspect] égard *m*; **in many respects** à bien des égards; **with respect to**, **in respect of** en ce qui concerne **2.** *vt* respecter

**respectable** [rɪ'spektəbəl] *adj* [decent, fairly large] respectable; [fairly good] honorable

**respective** [rɪ'spektɪv] *adj* respectif, -ive ■ **respectively** *adv* respectivement

**respond** [rɪ'spɒnd] *vi* [answer] répondre (**to** à); [react] réagir (**to** à); **to respond to treatment** bien réagir (au traitement) ■ **response** *n* [answer] réponse *f*; [reaction] réaction *f*; **in response to** en réponse à

**responsible** [rɪ'spɒnsəbəl] *adj* responsable (**for** de); [job] à responsabilités ■ **responsibility** (*pl* -ies) *n* responsabilité *f* (**for** de) ■ **responsibly** *adv* de façon responsable

**responsive** [rɪ'spɒnsɪv] *adj* [reacting] qui réagit bien; [alert] éveillé; **responsive to** [suggestion] réceptif, -ive à

**rest¹** [rest] **1.** *n* [relaxation] repos *m*; [support] support *m*; **to have** *or* **take a rest** se reposer; **to set** *or* **put sb's mind at rest** tranquilliser qn; Am **rest room**

toilettes *fpl* **2.** *vt* [lean] poser (**on** sur) ; [horse] laisser reposer **3.** *vi* [relax] se reposer ; [lean] être posé (**on** sur) ; **to rest on** [of argument, roof] reposer sur ; **a resting place** un lieu de repos

**rest²** [rest] **1.** *n* [remainder] reste *m* (**of** de) ; **the rest** [others] les autres *mfpl* **2.** *vi* **to rest with sb** [of decision, responsibility] incomber à qn

**restaurant** ['restərɒnt] *n* restaurant *m* ; *Br* **restaurant car** [on train] wagon-restaurant *m*

**restful** ['restfəl] *adj* reposant

**restless** ['restləs] *adj* agité

**restore** [rɪ'stɔː(r)] *vt* [give back] rendre (**to** à) ; [order, peace, rights] rétablir ; [building, painting, monarchy] restaurer

**restrain** [rɪ'streɪn] *vt* [person, dog] maîtriser ; [crowd, anger] contenir ; **to restrain sb from doing sth** retenir qn pour qu'il ne fasse pas qch ■ **restrained** *adj* [manner] réservé ■ **restraint** *n* [moderation] mesure *f* ; [restriction] restriction *f*

**restrict** [rɪ'strɪkt] *vt* restreindre ; **to restrict oneself to sth/doing sth** se limiter à qch/à faire qch ■ **restricted** *adj* restreint ■ **restriction** *n* restriction *f* (**on** à)

**result** [rɪ'zʌlt] **1.** *n* [outcome, success] résultat *m* ; **as a result** en conséquence ; **as a result of** à la suite de **2.** *vi* résulter (**from** de) ; **to result in sth** aboutir à qch

**resume** [rɪ'zjuːm] *vti* reprendre ; **to resume doing sth** se remettre à faire qch ■ **resumption** [-'zʌmpʃən] *n* reprise *f*

**résumé** ['rezjʊmeɪ] *n* [summary] résumé *m* ; *Am* [CV] curriculum vitae *m inv*

**resurgence** [rɪ'sɜːdʒəns] *n* réapparition *f*

**resurrect** [rezə'rekt] *vt* *Fig* [fashion] remettre au goût du jour ■ **resurrection** *n* REL résurrection *f*

**resuscitate** [rɪ'sʌsɪteɪt] *vt* MED ranimer

**retail** ['riːteɪl] **1.** *n* (vente *f* au) détail *m* ; *Br* **retail park** centre *m* commercial ; *Fam* **retail therapy** faire du shopping pour

se remonter le moral **2.** *adj* [price] de détail **3.** *vi* se vendre (au détail) (**at** à) ■ **retailer** *n* détaillant *m*

**retain** [rɪ'teɪn] *vt* [keep] conserver ; [hold in place] retenir

**retaliate** [rɪ'tælɪeɪt] *vi* riposter ■ **retaliation** *n* représailles *fpl* ; **in retaliation for** en représailles à

**retch** [retʃ] *vi* avoir des haut-le-cœur

**rethink** [riː'θɪŋk] (*pt & pp* **-thought**) *vt* repenser

**reticent** ['retɪsənt] *adj* peu communicatif, -ive

**retire** [rɪ'taɪə(r)] *vi* **a)** [from work] prendre sa retraite **b)** [withdraw] se retirer (**from** de ; **to** à) ; [go to bed] aller se coucher ■ **retired** *adj* [no longer working] retraité

**retirement** [rɪ'taɪəmənt] *n* retraite *f* ; **retirement age** l'âge *m* de la retraite

**retrace** [riː'treɪs] *vt* **to retrace one's steps** revenir sur ses pas

**retract** [rɪ'trækt] **1.** *vt* **a)** [statement] revenir sur **b)** [claws] rentrer **2.** *vi* [of person] se rétracter

**retrain** [riː'treɪn] **1.** *vt* recycler **2.** *vi* se recycler ■ **retraining** *n* recyclage *m*

**retreat** [rɪ'triːt] **1.** *n* [withdrawal] retraite *f* ; [place] refuge *m* **2.** *vi* se réfugier ; [of troops] battre en retraite

**retribution** [retrɪ'bjuːʃən] *n* châtiment *m*

**retrieve** [rɪ'triːv] *vt* [recover] récupérer ; COMPUT rechercher et extraire

**retrospect** ['retrəspekt] *n* **in retrospect** rétrospectivement

**retrospective** [retrə'spektɪv] *adj* rétrospectif, -ive ; [law] à effet rétroactif

**return** [rɪ'tɜːn] **1.** *n* retour *m* ; FIN [on investment] rapport *m* ; **returns** [profits] bénéfices *mpl* ; *Br* **return (ticket)** (billet *m*) aller et retour *m* ; **many happy returns!** bon anniversaire ! ; **in return** en échange (**for** de) ; **by return of post** retour du courrier **2.** *adj* [trip, flight] (de) retour ; **return match** match *m* retour **3.** *vt* [give back] rendre ; [put back] remettre ; [bring back] rapporter ; [send back] renvoyer ; **to return sb's**

**call** [on phone] rappeler qn **4.** vi [come back] revenir ; [go back] retourner ; [go back home] rentrer ; **to return to** [subject] revenir à

**retweet** ['ri:twi:t] **1.** vi retweeter **2.** n retweet m

**reunion** [ri:'ju:njən] n réunion f ■ **reunite** vt réconcilier ; **to be reunited with sb** retrouver qn

**reuse** [ri:'ju:z] vt réutiliser

**revamp** [,ri:'væmp] vt Fam rénover

**reveal** [rɪ'vi:l] vt [make known] révéler (**that** que) ; [make visible] laisser voir ■ **revealing** adj [sign, comment] révélateur, -trice

**revel** ['revəl] (Br -ll-, Am -l-) vi faire la fête ; **to revel in sth** savourer qch

**revelation** [revə'leɪʃən] n révélation f

**revenge** [rɪ'vendʒ] **1.** n vengeance f ; **to have** or **get one's revenge (on sb)** se venger (de qn) ; **in revenge** pour se venger **2.** vt venger

**revenue** ['revənju:] n [income] revenu m ; [from sales] recettes fpl

**reverence** ['revərəns] n révérence f

**reversal** [rɪ'vɜ:səl] n [of situation, roles] renversement m ; [of policy, opinion] revirement m ; **reversal (of fortune)** revers m (de fortune)

**reverse** [rɪ'vɜ:s] **1.** adj [opposite] contraire ; [image] inverse ; **in reverse order** dans l'ordre inverse **2.** n contraire m ; [of coin] revers m ; [of fabric] envers m ; [of paper] verso m ; **in reverse (gear)** [when driving] en marche arrière **3.** vt [situation] renverser ; [order, policy] inverser ; [decision] revenir sur ; **to reverse the car** faire marche arrière ; Br **to reverse the charges** [when phoning] téléphoner en PCV **4.** vi Br [in car] faire marche arrière ; **to reverse in /out** rentrer / sortir en marche arrière

**revert** [rɪ'vɜ:t] vi **to revert to** revenir à

**review** [rɪ'vju:] **1.** n **a)** [of book, film] critique f ; **to be under review** faire l'objet d'une révision **b)** [magazine] revue f **2.** vt [book, film] faire la critique de ;

[troops] passer en revue ; [situation] faire le point sur ; [salary] réviser ■ **reviewer** n critique m

**revise** [rɪ'vaɪz] **1.** vt [opinion, notes, text] réviser **2.** vi [for exam] réviser (**for** pour) ■ **revision** n révision f

**revival** [rɪ'vaɪvəl] n [of custom, business, play] reprise f ; [of fashion] renouveau m

**revive** [rɪ'vaɪv] **1.** vt [person] ranimer ; [custom, industry] faire renaître ; [fashion] relancer **2.** vi [of person] reprendre connaissance ; [of industry] connaître un renouveau ; [of interest] renaître

**revolt** [rɪ'vəʊlt] **1.** n révolte f **2.** vt [disgust] révolter **3.** vi [rebel] se révolter (**against** contre) ■ **revolting** adj dégoûtant

**revolution** [revə'lu:ʃən] n révolution f ■ **revolutionary** (pl -ies) adj & n révolutionnaire (mf)

**revolve** [rɪ'vɒlv] vi tourner (**around** autour de) ■ **revolving** adj revolving **door(s)** porte f à tambour

**revolver** [rɪ'vɒlvə(r)] n revolver m

**revulsion** [rɪ'vʌlʃən] n [disgust] dégoût m

**reward** [rɪ'wɔ:d] **1.** n récompense f (**for** de) **2.** vt récompenser (**for** de ou pour) ■ **rewarding** adj intéressant

**rewind** [ri:'waɪnd] (pt & pp -wound) vt [tape, film] rembobiner

**rewrite** [ri:'raɪt] (pt -wrote, pp -written) vt réécrire

**RGDS** MESSAGING written abbr of **regards**

**rhetoric** ['retərɪk] n rhétorique f ■ **rhetorical** [rɪ'tɒrɪkəl] adj rhetorical **question** question f de pure forme

**rheumatism** ['ru:mətɪzəm] n rhumatisme m ; **to have rheumatism** avoir des rhumatismes

**rhinoceros** [raɪ'nɒsərəs] n rhinocéros m

**rhubarb** ['ru:bɑ:b] n rhubarbe f

**rhyme** [raɪm] **1.** n rime f ; [poem] vers mpl **2.** vi rimer (**with** avec)

**rhythm** ['rɪðəm] *n* rythme *m*
■ **rhythmic(al)** ['rɪðmɪk(əl)] *adj* rythmé

**rib** [rɪb] *n* [bone] côte *f*

**ribbon** ['rɪbən] *n* ruban *m*

**rice** [raɪs] *n* riz *m* ; **rice pudding** riz *m*
au lait

**rich** [rɪtʃ] **1.** *(compar* -er, *superl* -est) *adj*
[person, food] riche ; **to be rich in sth**
être riche en qch **2.** *npl* **the rich** les
riches *mpl* ■ **riches** *npl* richesses *fpl*

**rid** [rɪd] *(pt & pp* rid, *pres p* ridding) *vt* débarrasser (**of** de) ; **to get rid of, to rid
oneself of** se débarrasser de ■ **riddance** ['rɪdəns] *n Fam* **good riddance!**
bon débarras !

**ridden** ['rɪdən] *pp of* ride

**riddle** ['rɪdəl] **1.** *n* [puzzle] devinette *f* ;
[mystery] énigme *f* **2.** *vt* cribler (**with**
de) ; **riddled with mistakes** truffé de
fautes

**ride** [raɪd] **1.** *n* [on horse] promenade *f* ;
[on bicycle, in car] tour *m* ; [in taxi]
course *f* ; **to go for a ride** aller faire un
tour ; **to give sb a ride** [in car] emmener qn en voiture ; *Fam* **to take sb for a
ride** mener qn en bateau **2.** *(pt* rode, *pp*
ridden) *vt* [horse, bicycle] monter à ; [a
particular horse] monter ; **to know how
to ride a bicycle** savoir faire de la bicyclette **3.** *vi* [on horse] faire du cheval ;
[on bicycle] faire de la bicyclette ; **to go
riding** [on horse] faire du cheval ; **I ride
to work** [on bicycle] je vais travailler
à bicyclette

**rider** ['raɪdə(r)] *n* [on horse] cavalier,
-ère *mf* ; [cyclist] cycliste *mf*

**ridge** [rɪdʒ] *n* [of mountain] crête *f*

**ridicule** ['rɪdɪkjuːl] **1.** *n* ridicule *m* ; **to
hold sb/sth up to ridicule** tourner
qn/qch en ridicule **2.** *vt* tourner en
ridicule, ridiculiser

**ridiculous** [rɪ'dɪkjʊləs] *adj* ridicule

**riding** ['raɪdɪŋ] *n* **(horse) riding** équitation *f*

**rife** [raɪf] *adj* [widespread] répandu

**riffraff** ['rɪfræf] *n* racaille *f*

**rifle** ['raɪfəl] *n* fusil *m*

**rift** [rɪft] *n* [in political party] scission *f* ;
[disagreement] désaccord *m*

**rig** [rɪg] **1.** *n* (oil) **rig** derrick *m* ; [at sea]
plate-forme *f* pétrolière **2.** *(pt & pp* -gg-)
*vt Fam* [result, election] truquer ; **to rig
up** [equipment] installer

**right¹** [raɪt] **1.** *adj* **a)** [correct] bon
(*f* bonne), exact ; [word] juste ; **to be
right** [of person] avoir raison (**to do**
faire) ; **it's the right time** c'est l'heure
exacte ; **that's right** c'est ça ; **right!** bon !
**b)** [appropriate] bon (*f* bonne) ; **he's
the right man** c'est l'homme qu'il faut
**c)** [morally good] bien *inv* ; **to do the
right thing** faire ce qu'il faut
**d)** *Fam* [for emphasis] véritable ; **I felt
a right fool** je me suis vraiment senti
stupide
**e)** MATH **right angle** angle *m* droit
**2.** *adv* [straight] (tout) droit ; [complete-
ly] tout à fait ; [correctly] correctement ; **to put sth right** [rectify] corriger qch ;
[fix] arranger qch ; **to put sb right** détromper qn ; **right round** tout autour
(**sth** de qch) ; **right behind** juste derrière ; **right here** ici même ; **right away,
right now** tout de suite
**3.** *n* **to be in the right** avoir raison ; **right
and wrong** le bien et le mal
**4.** *vt* [error, wrong, boat, car] redresser

**right²** [raɪt] **1.** *adj* [not left-hand, side]
droit **2.** *adv* à droite **3.** *n* droite *f* ; **on
or to the right** à droite (**of** de) ■ **right-
click 1.** *vt* COMPUT cliquer avec le bouton droit de la souris sur **2.** *vi* COMPUT
cliquer avec le bouton droit de la souris ■ **right-hand** *adj* de droite ; **on
the right-hand side** à droite (**of** de)
■ **right-handed** *adj* [person] droitier,
-ère ■ **right-wing** *adj* POL de droite

**right³** [raɪt] *n* [entitlement] droit *m* (**to
do** de faire) ; **to have a right to sth** avoir
droit à qch ; **to have (the) right of way**
[on road] avoir la priorité

**rightful** ['raɪtfəl] *adj* légitime

**rightly** ['raɪtlɪ] *adv* [correctly] bien ; [jus-
tifiably] à juste titre

**rigid** ['rɪdʒɪd] *adj* rigide

**rigorous** ['rɪgərəs] *adj* rigoureux, -euse

**rim** [rɪm] *n* [of cup] bord *m* ; [of wheel]
jante *f*

**rind** [raɪnd] n [of cheese] croûte f ; [of bacon] couenne f

**ring**¹ [rɪŋ] n [for finger, curtain] anneau m ; [for finger, with stone] bague f ; [on stove] brûleur m ; [of people, chairs] cercle m ; [of criminals] bande f ; [at circus] piste f ; [for boxing] ring m ; **to have rings under one's eyes** avoir les yeux cernés ; Br **ring road** périphérique m

**ring**² [rɪŋ] **1.** n [sound] **there's a ring at the door** on sonne à la porte ; Fam **to give sb a ring** passer un coup de fil à qn **2.** (pt **rang**, pp **rung**) vt [bell] sonner ; [alarm] déclencher ; **to ring sb** [on phone] téléphoner à qn ; **to ring the doorbell** sonner à la porte ; Fam **that rings a bell** ça me dit quelque chose **3.** vi [of bell, phone, person] sonner ; [of sound, words] retentir ; [of ears] bourdonner ; [make a phone call] téléphoner ■ **ringing** adj Br **ringing tone** [on phone] sonnerie f ■ **ring back 1.** vt sep **to ring sb back** rappeler qn **2.** vi rappeler ■ **ring off** vi [on phone] raccrocher ■ **ring out** vi [of bell] sonner ; [of voice, shout] retentir ■ **ring up 1.** vt sep **to ring sb up** téléphoner à qn **2.** vi téléphoner

**ringleader** ['rɪŋliːdə(r)] n Pej [of rebellion, strike] meneur, -euse mf

**rink** [rɪŋk] n [for ice-skating] patinoire f ; [for roller-skating] piste f

**rinse** [rɪns] **1.** n rinçage m ; **to give sth a rinse** rincer qch **2.** vt rincer ; **to rinse one's hands** se rincer les mains ; **to rinse out** rincer

**riot** ['raɪət] **1.** n [uprising] émeute f ; **to run riot** se déchaîner **2.** vi [rise up] faire une émeute ; [of prisoners] se mutiner ■ **rioter** n émeutier, -ère mf ; [vandal] casseur m ■ **rioting** n émeutes fpl

**rip** [rɪp] **1.** n déchirure f **2.** (pt & pp -pp-) vt déchirer ; **to rip sth off** arracher qch (**from** de) ; Fam [steal] faucher qch ; Fam **to rip sb off** [deceive] rouler qn ; **to rip sth up** déchirer qch **3.** vi [of fabric] se déchirer ■ **rip-off** n Fam arnaque f

**ripe** [raɪp] (compar -er, superl -est) adj [fruit] mûr ; [cheese] fait ■ **ripen** vti mûrir

**ripped** [rɪpt] adj Am Fam **to be ripped, to have a ripped body** être super musclé

**rise** [raɪz] **1.** n [in price, pressure] hausse f (**in** de) ; [slope in ground] montée f ; [of leader, party] ascension f ; Br **(pay) rise** augmentation f (de salaire) ; **to give rise to sth** donner lieu à qch **2.** (pt **rose**, pp **risen** ['rɪzən]) vi [of temperature, balloon, price] monter ; [in society] s'élever ; [of sun, theatre curtain] se lever ; [of dough] lever ; [get up from chair or bed] se lever ; **to rise (up)** [rebel] se soulever (**against** contre)

**rising** ['raɪzɪŋ] adj [sun] levant ; [number] croissant ; [prices] en hausse

**risk** [rɪsk] **1.** n risque m ; **at risk** [person] en danger ; [job] menacé ; **to run the risk of doing sth** courir le risque de faire qch **2.** vt [life, reputation] risquer ; **I can't risk going** je ne peux pas prendre le risque d'y aller ■ **risky** (compar -ier, superl -iest) adj risqué

**rite** [raɪt] n rite m ; REL **the last rites** les derniers sacrements mpl ■ **ritual** ['rɪtjʊəl] **1.** adj rituel, -elle **2.** n rituel m

**rival** ['raɪvəl] **1.** adj rival **2.** n rival, -e mf **3.** (Br -ll-, Am -l-) vt [equal] égaler (**in** en) ■ **rivalry** (pl -ies) n rivalité f (**between** entre)

**river** ['rɪvə(r)] **1.** n [small] rivière f ; [flowing into sea] fleuve m **2.** adj **river bank** rive f ■ **riverside 1.** n bord m de l'eau **2.** adj au bord de l'eau

**riveting** ['rɪvɪtɪŋ] adj Fig fascinant

**Riviera** [rɪvɪ'eərə] n **the (French) Riviera** la Côte d'Azur

**RLR** MESSAGING written abbr of **earlier**

**rly** MESSAGING written abbr of **really**

**RMB** (abbr of **ring my bell**) MESSAGING ça veut dire quoi ?

**road** [rəʊd] **1.** n route f ; [small] chemin m ; [in town] rue f ; [roadway] chaussée f ; **the Paris road** la route de Paris ; **by road** par la route ; **to live across** or **over the road** habiter en face **2.** adj [map, safety] routier, -ère ; [accident] de la route ; **road sign** panneau m de signalisation ; Am **road trip** [short] promenade f en voiture ; [longer] voyage m en voiture ; Br **road**

works, Am **road work** travaux mpl de voirie ▪ **roadblock** n barrage m routier ▪ **roadside** n bord m de la route

**roam** [rəʊm] **1.** vt parcourir; **to roam the streets** traîner dans les rues **2.** vi errer

**roar** [rɔː(r)] **1.** n [of lion] rugissement m; [of person] hurlement m **2.** vt **to roar sth (out)** hurler qch **3.** vi [of lion, wind, engine] rugir; [of person, crowd] hurler; **to roar with laughter** hurler de rire ▪ **roaring** adj **a roaring fire** une belle flambée; **to do a roaring trade** faire des affaires en or

**roast** [rəʊst] **1.** n [meat] rôti m **2.** adj rôti; **roast beef** rosbif m **3.** vt [meat, potatoes] faire rôtir **4.** vi [of meat] rôtir

**rob** [rɒb] (pt & pp -bb-) vt [person] voler; [shop, bank] dévaliser; **to rob sb of sth** voler qch à qn; Fig [deprive] priver qn de qch ▪ **robber** n voleur, -euse mf ▪ **robbery** (pl -ies) n vol m; **it's daylight robbery!** c'est du vol pur et simple!

**robe** [rəʊb] n [of priest, judge] robe f

**robin** [ˈrɒbɪn] n [bird] rouge-gorge m

**robot** [ˈrəʊbɒt] n robot m

**robust** [rəʊˈbʌst] adj robuste

**rock¹** [rɒk] **1.** n [music] rock m **2.** vt [boat] balancer; [building] secouer **3.** vi [sway] se balancer; [of building, ground] trembler ▪ **rocking** adj **rocking chair** fauteuil m à bascule

**rock²** [rɒk] n [substance] roche f; [boulder, rock face] rocher m; Am [stone] pierre f; Br [sweet] sucrerie en forme de bâton parfumée à la menthe; **on the rocks** [whisky] avec des glaçons; [marriage] en pleine débâcle; **rock climbing** varappe f; **rock face** paroi f rocheuse

**rocket** [ˈrɒkɪt] **1.** n fusée f **2.** vi [of prices, unemployment] monter en flèche

**rocky** [ˈrɒkɪ] (compar -ier, superl -iest) adj [road] rocailleux, -euse; Fig [relationship] instable

**rod** [rɒd] n [wooden] baguette f; [metal] tige f; [of curtain] tringle f; [for fishing] canne f à pêche

**rode** [rəʊd] pt of **ride**

**rodent** [ˈrəʊdənt] n rongeur m

**rodeo** [Br ˈrəʊdɪəʊ, Am rəʊˈdeɪəʊ] (pl -os) n Am rodéo m

**ROFL** (abbr of **rolling on the floor laughing**) MESSAGING MDR

**ROFLOL** (abbr of **rolling on the floor laughing out loud**) MESSAGING MDR

**rogue** [rəʊg] n [dishonest] crapule f; [mischievous] coquin, -e mf

**role** [rəʊl] n rôle m; **role model** modèle m

**roll** [rəʊl] **1.** n [of paper] rouleau m; [of drum, thunder] roulement m; [bread] petit pain m; [list] liste f; **roll of film** pellicule f; **to have a roll call** faire l'appel; **roll neck** col m roulé **2.** vt [cigarette] rouler; [ball] faire rouler **3.** vi [of ball] rouler; [of camera] tourner ▪ **rolling** adj [hills] ondulant; **rolling pin** rouleau m à pâtisserie ▪ **roll around, roll about** Br vi [person] se rouler; [object] rouler çà et là ▪ **roll down** vt sep [car window] baisser; [sleeves] redescendre ▪ **roll in** vi Fam [flow in] affluer; [of person] s'amener ▪ **roll on** vi Fam **roll on tonight!** vivement ce soir! ▪ **roll out 1.** vi insep sortir; **to roll out of bed** [person] sortir du lit **2.** vt sep **a)** [ball] rouler (dehors); [pastry] étendre (au rouleau) **b)** [produce - goods, speech] débiter **c)** [product, offer] introduire ▪ **roll over 1.** vt sep retourner **2.** vi [many times] se rouler; [once] se retourner ▪ **roll up 1.** vt sep [map, cloth] rouler; [sleeve] retrousser **2.** vi Fam [arrive] s'amener

**roller** [ˈrəʊlə(r)] n [for hair, painting] rouleau m; **roller coaster** montagnes fpl russes; **roller skates** patins mpl à roulettes ▪ **roller-skate** vi faire du patin à roulettes

**rollerblades** [ˈrəʊləbleɪdz] npl patins mpl en ligne

**ROM** [rɒm] (abbr of **read only memory**) n COMPUT mémoire f morte

**Roman** [ˈrəʊmən] **1.** adj romain **2.** n Romain, -e mf **3.** adj & n **Roman Catholic** catholique (mf)

**romance** [rəʊˈmæns] n [love] amour m; [affair] aventure f amoureuse; [story] histoire f d'amour; [charm] poésie f

**Romania** [rəʊˈmeɪnɪə] n la Roumanie ■ **Romanian 1.** adj roumain **2.** n [person] Roumain, -e mf; [language] roumain m

**romantic** [rəʊˈmæntɪk] **1.** adj [of love, tenderness] romantique; [fanciful, imaginary] romanesque **2.** n romantique mf

**romp** [rɒmp] vi s'ébattre

**rompers** [ˈrɒmpəz] npl [for baby] barboteuse f

**roof** [ruːf] n [of building, vehicle] toit m; [of tunnel, cave] plafond m; **roof rack** [of car] galerie f ■ **rooftop** n toit m

**room** [ruːm, rʊm] n a) [in house] pièce f; [bedroom] chambre f; [large, public] salle f; **room fragrance** parfum m pour la maison b) [space] place f; **to make room** faire de la place (**for** pour) ■ **roomie** [ˈruːmɪ] n Am Fam colocataire mf ■ **roommate** n camarade mf de chambre ■ **roomy** (compar -ier, superl -iest) adj spacieux, -euse

**roost** [ruːst] vi se percher

**rooster** [ˈruːstə(r)] n coq m

**root** [ruːt] **1.** n [of plant, tooth, hair & MATH] racine f; Fig [origin] origine f; [cause] cause f; **to take root** [of plant, person] prendre racine **2.** vt **to root sth out** supprimer qch

**rooted** [ˈruːtɪd] adj deeply rooted bien enraciné (**in** dans); **rooted to the spot** [immobile] cloué sur place

**rope** [rəʊp] **1.** n corde f; [on ship] cordage m; Fam **to know the ropes** connaître son affaire **2.** vt Fam **to rope sb in** recruter qn

**rop(e)y** [ˈrəʊpɪ] (compar -ier, superl -iest) adj Br Fam [thing] minable; [person] patraque

**rosary** [ˈrəʊzərɪ] (pl -ies) n REL chapelet m

**rose¹** [rəʊz] n [flower] rose f

**rose²** [rəʊz] pt of **rise**

**rosette** [rəʊˈzet] n rosette f

**roster** [ˈrɒstə(r)] n (**duty) roster** liste f de service

**rostrum** [ˈrɒstrəm] n tribune f; [for prizewinner] podium m

**rosy** [ˈrəʊzɪ] (compar -ier, superl -iest) adj [pink] rose; Fig [future] prometteur, -euse

**rot** [rɒt] **1.** n pourriture f; Br Fam [nonsense] inepties fpl **2.** (pt & pp -tt-) vti pourrir

**rota** [ˈrəʊtə] n roulement m

**rotary** [ˈrəʊtərɪ] **1.** adj rotatif, -ive **2.** (pl -ies) n Am [for traffic] rond-point m

**rotate** [rəʊˈteɪt] **1.** vt faire tourner **2.** vi tourner

**rotation** [rəʊˈteɪʃən] n **in rotation** à tour de rôle

**rotten** [ˈrɒtən] adj [fruit, egg, wood] pourri; Fam [bad] nul (f nulle); Fam [weather] pourri; Fam **to feel rotten** [ill] être mal fichu

**rough¹** [rʌf] **1.** (compar -er, superl -est) adj [surface] rugueux, -euse; [ground] accidenté; [life] rude; [wine] âpre; [neighbourhood] dur; [sea] agité; [brutal] brutal **2.** adv Br **to sleep / live rough** coucher / vivre à la dure **3.** vt Fam **to rough it** vivre à la dure ■ **rough up** vt sep Fam [person] tabasser, passer à tabac

**rough²** [rʌf] **1.** n a) GOLF rough m b) [undetailed form] **in rough** au brouillon **2.** (compar -er, superl -est) adj [approximate] approximatif, -ive; **rough guess, rough estimate** approximation f; **rough copy, rough draft** brouillon m; **rough paper** papier m brouillon **3.** vt **to rough sth out** [plan] ébaucher

**rough-and-ready** [rʌfənˈredɪ] adj [solution] rudimentaire; [accommodation] sommaire

**roughen** [ˈrʌfən] vt rendre rugueux, -euse

**roughly¹** [ˈrʌflɪ] adv [brutally] brutalement

**roughly²** [ˈrʌflɪ] adv [approximately] à peu près

**round** [raʊnd] **1.** (compar -er, superl -est) adj rond; Am **round trip** aller et retour m **2.** adv autour; **all round, right round** tout autour; **all year round** toute l'année; **the wrong way round** à l'envers

**3.** *prep* autour de ; **round here** par ici ; **round about** [approximately] environ
**4.** *n Br* [slice] tranche *f* ; [in competition] manche *f* ; [of golf] partie *f* ; [in boxing] round *m* ; [of talks] série *f* ; [of drinks] tournée *f*
**5.** *vt* **to round sth off** [meal, speech] terminer qch (**with** par) ; **to round up** [gather] rassembler ; [price] arrondir au chiffre supérieur

**roundabout** ['raʊndəbaʊt] **1.** *adj* [method, route] indirect **2.** *n Br* [at funfair] manège *m* ; [road junction] rond-point *m*

**rounders** ['raʊndəz] *npl* jeu similaire au base-ball

**rouse** [raʊz] *vt* [awaken] éveiller ; **roused (to anger)** en colère

**rousing** ['raʊzɪŋ] *adj* [speech] vibrant

**route** [ruːt] *n* itinéraire *m* ; [of aircraft, ship] route *f* ; **bus route** ligne *f* d'autobus

**router** ['ruːtə, *Am* 'raʊtə(r)] *n* COMPUT routeur *m*

**routine** [ruːˈtiːn] **1.** *n* [habit] routine *f* ; **the daily routine** le train-train quotidien **2.** *adj* [inquiry, work] de routine ; *Pej* routinier, -ère

**row**[1] [rəʊ] *n* [line] rangée *f* ; **two days in a row** deux jours d'affilée

**row**[2] [rəʊ] **1.** *n Am* **row boat** bateau *m* à rames **2.** *vt* [boat] faire aller à la rame ; [person] transporter en canot **3.** *vi* [in boat] ramer

**row**[3] [raʊ] **1.** *n* [noise] vacarme *m* ; [quarrel] dispute *f* **2.** *vi* se disputer (**with** avec)

**rowdy** ['raʊdɪ] *(compar* -ier, *superl* -iest) *adj* chahuteur, -euse

**rowing** ['rəʊɪŋ] *n* [as sport] aviron *m* ; *Br* **rowing boat** bateau *m* à rames

**royal** ['rɔɪəl] *adj* royal ; **the Royal Air Force** l'armée de l'air britannique

**royalty** ['rɔɪəltɪ] **1.** *n* [rank, position] royauté *f* **2.** *npl* **royalties** [from book] droits *mpl* d'auteur

**rub** [rʌb] **1.** *n* [massage] friction *f* ; **to give sth a rub** frotter qch **2.** *(pt & pp* -bb-) *vti* frotter ■ **rub down** *vt sep* [person]

frictionner ; [wood, with sandpaper] poncer ■ **rub in** *vt sep* [cream] faire pénétrer (en massant) ; *Fam* **to rub it in** retourner le couteau dans la plaie ■ **rub off** *vt sep* [mark] effacer ■ **rub out** *vt sep* [mark, writing] effacer

**rubber** ['rʌbə(r)] *n* [substance] caoutchouc *m* ; *Br* [eraser] gomme *f* ; *Am Fam* [contraceptive] capote *f* ; **rubber band** élastique *m* ; **rubber stamp** tampon *m*

**rubbish** ['rʌbɪʃ] *n Br* [waste] ordures *fpl* ; *Fig* [nonsense] idioties *fpl* ; *Fam* **that's rubbish** [absurd] c'est absurde ; [worthless] ça ne vaut rien ; **rubbish bin** poubelle *f*

**rubbishy** ['rʌbɪʃɪ] *adj* [book, film] nul (*f* nulle) ; [goods] de mauvaise qualité

**rubble** ['rʌbəl] *n* décombres *mpl*

**ruby** ['ruːbɪ] *(pl* -ies) *n* [gem] rubis *m*

**rucksack** ['rʌksæk] *n* sac *m* à dos

**rudder** ['rʌdə(r)] *n* gouvernail *m*

**ruddy** ['rʌdɪ] *(compar* -ier, *superl* -iest) *adj* [complexion] rose ; *Br Fam* [bloody] fichu

**rude** [ruːd] *(compar* -er, *superl* -est) *adj* [impolite] impoli (**to** envers) ; [indecent] obscène

**rudiments** ['ruːdɪmənts] *npl* rudiments *mpl*

**ruffian** ['rʌfɪən] *n* voyou *m* (*pl* -ous)

**rug** [rʌg] *n* tapis *m* ; [over knees] plaid *m*

**rugby** ['rʌgbɪ] *n* **rugby (football)** rugby *m*

**rugged** ['rʌgɪd] *adj* [terrain, coast] accidenté ; [features] rude

**rugrat** ['rʌgræt] *n Am Fam* [child] mioche *mf*

**ruin** ['ruːɪn] **1.** *n* [destruction, rubble, building] ruine *f* ; **in ruins** [building] en ruine **2.** *vt* [health, country, person] ruiner ; [clothes] abîmer ; [effect, meal, party] gâcher ■ **ruined** *adj* [person, country] ruiné ; [building] en ruine

**rule** [ruːl] **1.** *n* **a)** [principle] règle *f* ; [regulation] règlement *m* ; [government] autorité *f* ; *Br* **against the rules** *or Am* **rule** contraire au règlement ; **as a rule** en règle générale **b)** [for measuring] règle *f* **2.** *vt* [country] gouverner ; [decide - of judge, referee] décider (**that** que) ; **to rule sth out** [exclude] exclure

qch **3.** *vi* [of king] régner (**over** sur) ; [of judge] statuer (**against** contre ; **on** sur)
■ **ruling 1.** *adj* POL **the ruling party** le parti au pouvoir **2.** *n* [of judge, referee] décision *f*

**ruler** ['ruːlə(r)] *n* **a)** [for measuring] règle *f* **b)** [king, queen] souverain, -e *mf* ; [political leader] dirigeant, -e *mf*

**rum** [rʌm] *n* rhum *m*

**Rumania** [ruːˈmeɪnɪə] *see* **Romania**

**rumble** ['rʌmbəl] *vi* [of train, thunder] gronder ; [of stomach] gargouiller

**rummage** ['rʌmɪdʒ] *vi* **to rummage (about)** farfouiller ; Am **rummage sale** vente *f* de charité (*articles d'occasion uniquement*)

**rumour**, Am **rumor** ['ruːmə(r)] *n* rumeur *f* ■ **rumoured**, Am **rumored** *adj* **it is rumoured that...** on dit que...

**rump** [rʌmp] *n* [of horse] croupe *f* ; **rump steak** romsteck *m*

**run** [rʌn] **1.** *n* [series] série *f* ; [running] course *f* ; [outing] tour *m* ; [for skiing] piste *f* ; [in cricket, baseball] point *m* ; [in stocking] maille *f* filée ; **to go for a run** aller courir ; **on the run** [prisoner] en fuite ; **in the long / short run** à long / court terme
**2.** (*pt* ran, *pp* run, *pres p* running) *vt* [distance, race] courir ; [machine] faire fonctionner ; [business, country] diriger ; [courses, events] organiser ; COMPUT [program] exécuter ; [bath] faire couler ; **to run one's hand over** passer la main sur ; **to run sb to the airport** conduire qn à l'aéroport
**3.** *vi* courir ; [flee] fuir ; [of river, nose, tap] couler ; [of colour in washing] déteindre ; [of ink] baver ; [function - of machine] marcher ; [idle - of engine] tourner ; **to run down / in / out** descendre / entrer / sortir en courant ; **to go running** faire du jogging ; **to run for president** être candidat à la présidence ; **it runs in the family** c'est de famille
■ **run about** *vi* courir çà et là
■ **run across** *vt insep* [meet] tomber sur
■ **run along** *vi* **run along!** filez !

■ **run around** *vi* = **run about**
■ **run away** *vi* [flee] s'enfuir (**from** de)
■ **run down** *vt sep* [pedestrian] renverser ; [knock over and kill] écraser ; *Fig* [belittle] dénigrer ; [restrict] limiter peu à peu
■ **run into** *vt insep* [meet] tomber sur ; [crash into - of vehicle] percuter
■ **run off 1.** *vt sep* [print] tirer **2.** *vi* [flee] s'enfuir (**with** avec)
■ **run out** *vi* [of stocks] s'épuiser ; [of lease] expirer ; [of time] manquer ; **to run out of time / money** manquer de temps / d'argent ; **we've run out of coffee** on n'a plus de café ; **I ran out of petrol** *or* Am **gas** je suis tombé en panne d'essence
■ **run over 1.** *vt sep* [kill] écraser ; [knock down] renverser **2.** *vt insep* [notes, text] revoir **3.** *vi* [of liquid] déborder
■ **run round** *vt insep* [surround] entourer
■ **run through** *vt insep* [recap] revoir
■ **run up** *vt sep* [debts, bill] laisser s'accumuler

**runaway** ['rʌnəweɪ] **1.** *n* fugitif, -ive *mf* **2.** *adj* [car, horse] fou (*f* folle) ; [inflation] galopant

**rundown** ['rʌndaʊn] *n* [report] bref résumé *m* ■ **run-down** [rʌnˈdaʊn] *adj* [weak, tired] fatigué ; [district] délabré

**rung¹** [rʌŋ] *n* [of ladder] barreau *m*

**rung²** [rʌŋ] *pp of* **ring**

**runner** ['rʌnə(r)] *n* [athlete] coureur *m* ; Br **runner bean** haricot *m* d'Espagne

**runner-up** [rʌnərˈʌp] *n* [in race] second, -e *mf*

**running** ['rʌnɪŋ] **1.** *n* course *f* ; [of business, country] gestion *f* ; **to be in / out of the running** être / ne plus être dans la course **2.** *adj* **six days running** six jours de suite ; **running water** eau *f* courante ; **running costs** [of factory] frais *mpl* d'exploitation ; [of car] dépenses *fpl* courantes

**runny** ['rʌnɪ] (*compar* -ier, *superl* -iest) *adj* [cream, sauce] liquide ; [nose] qui coule

**run-up** ['rʌnʌp] *n* in the run-up to [elections, Christmas] dans la période qui précède

**runway** ['rʌnweɪ] *n* [for aircraft] piste *f* (d'envol)

**RUOK?** MESSAGING *written abbr of* are you OK?

**rupture** ['rʌptʃə(r)] **1.** *n* [hernia] hernie *f* **2.** *vt* rompre

**rural** ['rʊərəl] *adj* rural

**ruse** [ru:z] *n* ruse *f*

**rush¹** [rʌʃ] **1.** *n* [demand] ruée *f* (for vers; on sur) ; [confusion] bousculade *f*; to be in a rush être pressé (to do de faire) ; rush hour heures *fpl* de pointe **2.** *vt* to rush sb [hurry] bousculer qn; to rush sb to hospital *or Am* the hospital transporter qn d'urgence à l'hôpital ; to rush sth [job] faire qch en vitesse ; [decision] prendre qch à la hâte **3.** *vi* [move fast, throw oneself] se ruer (at sur; towards vers) ; [hurry] se dépêcher (to do de faire) ; [of vehicle] foncer; to rush out sortir précipitamment

**rush²** [rʌʃ] *n* [plant] jonc *m*

**rusk** [rʌsk] *n* Br biscotte *f*

**Russia** ['rʌʃə] *n* la Russie ■ **Russian 1.** *adj* russe **2.** *n* [person] Russe *mf*; [language] russe *m*

**rust** [rʌst] **1.** *n* rouille *f* **2.** *vi* rouiller

**rustic** ['rʌstɪk] *adj* rustique

**rustle** ['rʌsəl] **1.** *vt Fam* to rustle sth up [meal, snack] improviser qch **2.** *vi* [of leaves] bruire

**rustproof** ['rʌstpru:f] *adj* inoxydable

**rusty** ['rʌstɪ] *(compar* -ier, *superl* -iest) *adj* rouillé

**rut** [rʌt] *n* ornière *f; Fig* to be in a rut être encroûté

**ruthless** ['ru:θləs] *adj* impitoyable

**RV** [ɑ:'vi:] *(abbr of* recreational vehicle) *n Am* camping-car *m*

**rye** [raɪ] *n* seigle *m*; rye bread pain *m* de seigle

**S, s** [es] *n* [letter] S, s *m inv*

**Sabbath** ['sæbəθ] *n* **the Sabbath** le sabbat

**sabotage** ['sæbətɑːʒ] **1.** *n* sabotage *m* **2.** *vt* saboter

**sachet** ['sæʃeɪ] *n* sachet *m*

**sack** [sæk] **1.** *n* [bag] sac *m*; *Fam* **to get the sack** se faire virer **2.** *vt Fam* [dismiss] virer

**sacred** ['seɪkrɪd] *adj* sacré

**sacrifice** ['sækrɪfaɪs] **1.** *n* sacrifice *m* **2.** *vt* sacrifier (**to** à)

**sad** [sæd] *(compar* **sadder,** *superl* **saddest)** *adj* triste ■ **sadden** *vt* attrister ■ **sadly** *adv* [unhappily] tristement; [unfortunately] malheureusement ■ **sadness** *n* tristesse *f*

**saddle** ['sædəl] **1.** *n* selle *f* **2.** *vt* [horse] seller

**sadistic** [sə'dɪstɪk] *adj* sadique

**sae** [eseɪ'iː] *(abbr of* **(Br)** stamped addressed envelope, **(Am)** self-addressed envelope*) n* enveloppe *f* timbrée

**safari** [sə'fɑːrɪ] *n* safari *m*

**safe** [seɪf] **1.** *(compar* **-er,** *superl* **-est)** *adj* [person] en sécurité; [equipment, animal] sans danger; [place, investment, method] sûr; **to be on the safe side** par précaution, pour plus de sûreté; **safe (and sound)** sain et sauf (*f* saine et sauve) **2.** *n* [for money] coffre-fort *m* ■ **safely** *adv* [without risk] en toute sécurité; [drive] prudemment; [with certainty] avec certitude

**safeguard** ['seɪfgɑːd] **1.** *n* garantie *f* (**against** contre) **2.** *vt* sauvegarder

**safety** ['seɪftɪ] **1.** *n* sécurité *f* **2.** *adj* [belt, device, margin] de sécurité; [pin, chain, valve] de sûreté; **safety lock** serrure *f* de sécurité

**sag** [sæg] *(pt & pp* **-gg-)** *vi* [of roof, bed] s'affaisser

**saga** ['sɑːgə] *n* saga *f*

**Sahara** [sə'hɑːrə] *n* **the Sahara (desert)** le Sahara

**sail** [seɪl] **1.** *n* [on boat] voile *f*; **to set sail** prendre la mer **2.** *vt* [boat] commander **3.** *vi* [of person, ship] naviguer; [leave] prendre la mer ■ **sailing** *n* [sport] voile *f*; **to go sailing** faire de la voile; *Br* **sailing boat** voilier *m* ■ **sailboat** *n Am* voilier *m*

**sailor** ['seɪlə(r)] *n* marin *m*

**saint** [seɪnt] *n* saint *m*, sainte *f*

**sake** [seɪk] *n* **for my / your / his sake** pour moi / toi / lui; **for heaven's** *or* **God's sake!** pour l'amour de Dieu!; **(just) for the sake of eating** simplement pour manger

**salad** ['sæləd] *n* salade *f*; *Br* **salad cream** sorte de mayonnaise; **salad dressing** sauce pour salade

**salami** [sə'lɑːmɪ] *n* salami *m*

**salary** ['sælərɪ] *(pl* **-ies)** *n* salaire *m*

**sale** [seɪl] *n* [action, event] vente *f*; [at reduced price] solde *m*; **on sale** en vente; **in the sales** en solde; **(up) for sale** à vendre; *Am* **sales check** *or* **slip** [receipt] ticket *m* de caisse, reçu *m*; *Am* **sales tax** ≃ TVA *f* ■ **salesclerk** *n Am* vendeur, -euse *mf* ■ **salesman** *(pl* **-men)** *n* [in shop] vendeur *m*; [for company] représentant *m* ■ **saleswoman** *(pl* **-women)** *n* [in shop] vendeuse *f*; [for company] représentante *f*

**salmon** ['sæmən] *n inv* saumon *m*

**salon** ['sælɒn] *n* **beauty salon** institut *m* de beauté; **hairdressing salon** salon *m* de coiffure

**saloon** [sə'lu:n] *n Am* [bar] bar *m*; *Br* **saloon car** berline *f*

**salt** [sɔ:lt] **1.** *n* sel *m* **2.** *vt* saler ∎ **saltcellar** *n Br* salière *f* ∎ **salt-shaker** *n Am* salière *f* ∎ **saltwater** *adj* [lake] salé; [fish] de mer ∎ **salty** (*compar* -**ier**, *superl* -**iest**) *adj* salé

**salute** [sə'lu:t] **1.** *n* salut *m* **2.** *vt* [greet & MIL] saluer **3.** *vi* faire un salut

**salvage** ['sælvɪdʒ] *vt* [ship] sauver; [waste material] récupérer

**salvation** [sæl'veɪʃən] *n* salut *m*

**same** [seɪm] **1.** *adj* même; **the (very) same house as...** (exactement) la même maison que...
**2.** *pron* **the same** le même, la même, *pl* les mêmes; **I would have done the same** j'aurais fait la même chose; **it's all the same to me** ça m'est égal **3.** *adv* **to look the same** [of two things] sembler pareils; **all the same** [nevertheless] tout de même

**sample** ['sɑ:mpəl] **1.** *n* échantillon *m*; [of blood] prélèvement *m* **2.** *vt* [wine, cheese] goûter

**sanatorium**, *Am* **sanitorium** (*pl* -**iums** *or* -**ia**) [ˌsænə'tɔ:rɪəm] *n* sanatorium *m*

**sanction** ['sæŋkʃən] *n* [penalty] sanction *f*

**sanctuary** [*Br* 'sæŋktʃʊərɪ, *Am* -erɪ] (*pl* -**ies**) *n* [for fugitive, refugee] refuge *m*; [for wildlife] réserve *f*

**sand** [sænd] **1.** *n* sable *m*; **sand castle** château *m* de sable **2.** *vt* **to sand (down)** [wood] poncer ∎ **sandpit** ['sændpɪt], *Am* **sandbox** ['sændbɒks] *n* bac *m* à sable

**sandal** ['sændəl] *n* sandale *f*

**sandwich** ['sænwɪdʒ] **1.** *n* sandwich *m*; **cheese sandwich** sandwich *m* au fromage **2.** *vt* **to be sandwiched between** [of person, building] être coincé entre

**sandy** ['sændɪ] (*compar* -**ier**, *superl* -**iest**) *adj* **a)** [beach] de sable; [ground] sablonneux, -euse **b)** [hair] blond roux *inv*

**sane** [seɪn] (*compar* -**er**, *superl* -**est**) *adj* [person] sain d'esprit

**sang** [sæŋ] *pt of* **sing**

**sanitary** [*Br* 'sænɪtərɪ, *Am* -erɪ] *adj* [fittings] sanitaire; *Br* **sanitary towel,** *Am* **sanitary napkin** serviette *f* hygiénique

**sanitation** [sænɪ'teɪʃən] *n* hygiène *f* publique; [plumbing] installations *fpl* sanitaires

**sanity** ['sænətɪ] *n* santé *f* mentale

**sank** [sæŋk] *pt of* **sink**

**Santa Claus** ['sæntəklɔ:z] *n* le Père Noël

**sap** [sæp] **1.** *n* [of tree, plant] sève *f* **2.** (*pt & pp* -**pp**-) *vt* [weaken] saper

**sapphire** ['sæfaɪə(r)] *n* saphir *m*

**sarcastic** [sɑ:'kæstɪk] *adj* sarcastique

**sardine** [sɑ:'di:n] *n* sardine *f*

**Sardinia** [sɑ:'dɪnɪə] *n* la Sardaigne

**SARS** ['sɑ:z] (*abbr of* **severe acute respiratory syndrome**) *n* SRAS *m* (*syndrome respiratoire aigu sévère*)

**sat** [sæt] *pt & pp of* **sit**

**SAT** [sæt] *n* **a)** (*abbr of* **Standard Assessment Test**) *examen national en Grande-Bretagne pour les élèves de 7 ans, 11 ans et 14 ans* **b)** (*abbr of* **SAT Reasoning Test**) *examen d'entrée à l'université aux États-Unis*

**Satan** ['seɪtən] *n* Satan *m*

**satchel** ['sætʃəl] *n* cartable *m*

**satellite** ['sætəlaɪt] *n* satellite *m*; **satellite dish** antenne *f* parabolique; **satellite television** télévision *f* par satellite

**satin** ['sætɪn] *n* satin *m*

**satire** ['sætaɪə(r)] *n* satire *f* (**on** contre) ∎ **satirical** *adj* satirique

**satisfaction** [sætɪs'fækʃən] *n* satisfaction *f* ∎ **satisfactory** *adj* satisfaisant

**satisfy** ['sætɪsfaɪ] (*pt & pp* -**ied**) *vt* satisfaire; [convince] persuader (**that** que); [condition] remplir; **to be satisfied (with)** être satisfait (de) ∎ **satisfying** *adj* satisfaisant; [meal, food] substantiel, -elle

**satnav** ['sætnæv] *n* GPS *m*

**satsuma** [sæt'su:mə] *n Br* mandarine *f*

**saturate** ['sætʃəreɪt] *vt* saturer (**with** de)

**Saturday** ['sætədeɪ] n samedi m; **Saturday girl** vendeuse f (travaillant le samedi)

**sauce** [sɔ:s] n sauce f; **mint sauce** sauce à la menthe

**saucepan** ['sɔ:spən] n casserole f

**saucer** ['sɔ:sə(r)] n soucoupe f

**Saudi Arabia** [saʊdɪə'reɪbɪə] n l'Arabie f saoudite

**sauna** ['sɔ:nə] n sauna m

**saunter** ['sɔ:ntə(r)] vi flâner

**sausage** ['sɒsɪdʒ] n saucisse f; Br **sausage roll** feuilleté m à la viande

**savage** ['sævɪdʒ] **1.** adj [animal, person] féroce; [attack, criticism] violent **2.** vt [physically] attaquer

**save¹** [seɪv] **1.** vt [rescue] sauver (**from** de); [keep] garder; [money] économiser; [time] gagner; COMPUT sauvegarder; **to save sb's life** sauver la vie de qn; **to save sb from doing sth** empêcher qn de faire qch **2.** vi **to save (up)** faire des économies (**for/on** pour /sur) **3.** n [by goalkeeper] arrêt m

**save²** [seɪv] prep Formal [except] hormis

**saving** ['seɪvɪŋ] n [of time, money] économie f; **savings** [money saved] économies fpl; **savings account** compte m d'épargne

**saviour**, Am **savior** ['seɪvjə(r)] n sauveur m

**savour**, Am **savor** ['seɪvə(r)] vt savourer ▪ **savoury**, Am **savory** adj [not sweet] salé

**saw¹** [sɔ:] **1.** n scie f **2.** (pt sawed, pp sawn or sawed) vt scier; **to saw sth off** scier qch ▪ **sawdust** n sciure f

**saw²** [sɔ:] pt of **see**

**sawn** [sɔ:n] pp of **saw**

**saxophone** ['sæksəfəʊn] n saxophone m

**say** [seɪ] **1.** (pt & pp said) vt dire (**to** à; **that** que); [of dial, watch] indiquer; **to say again** répéter; **that is to say** c'est-à-dire **2.** vi dire; Am Fam **say!** dis donc !; **that goes without saying** ça va sans dire

**3.** n to have one's say avoir son mot à dire; **to have no say** ne pas avoir voix au chapitre (**in** concernant)

**saying** ['seɪɪŋ] n maxime f

**scab** [skæb] n [of wound] croûte f

**scaffolding** ['skæfəldɪŋ] n échafaudage m

**scald** [skɔ:ld] vt ébouillanter

**scale¹** [skeɪl] **1.** n [of instrument, map] échelle f; [of salaries] barème m; Fig [of problem] étendue f; **on a small /large scale** sur une petite /grande échelle **2.** vt **to scale sth down** revoir qch à la baisse

**scale²** [skeɪl] n [on fish] écaille f; [in kettle] dépôt m calcaire

**scales** [skeɪlz] npl [for weighing] balance f; **(bathroom) scales** pèse-personne m

**scalp** [skælp] n cuir m chevelu

**scamper** ['skæmpə(r)] vi **to scamper off** or **away** détaler

**scampi** ['skæmpɪ] n scampi mpl

**scan** [skæn] **1.** n to have a scan passer une échographie **2.** (pt & pp -nn-) vt [look at briefly] parcourir; [scrutinize] scruter; COMPUT passer au scanner

**scandal** ['skændəl] n [outrage] scandale m; [gossip] ragots mpl ▪ **scandalous** adj scandaleux, -euse

**Scandinavia** [skændɪ'neɪvɪə] n la Scandinavie ▪ **Scandinavian 1.** adj scandinave **2.** n Scandinave mf

**scanner** ['skænə(r)] n MED & COMPUT scanner m

**scant** [skænt] adj insuffisant ▪ **scanty** (compar-ier, superl-iest) adj insuffisant; [bikini] minuscule

**scapegoat** ['skeɪpgəʊt] n bouc m émissaire

**scar** [skɑ:(r)] **1.** n cicatrice f **2.** (pt & pp -rr-) vt marquer d'une cicatrice; Fig [of experience] marquer

**scarce** [skeəs] (compar-er, superl-est) adj rare ▪ **scarcely** adv à peine; **scarcely anything** presque rien

**scare** [skeə(r)] **1.** n to give sb a scare faire peur à qn; **scare story** histoire f pour faire peur **2.** *vt* faire peur à; **to scare sb off** faire fuir qn ■ **scared** *adj* effrayé; **to be scared of sb/sth** avoir peur de qn/qch

**scarf** [skɑːf] *(pl* **scarves)** *n* [long] écharpe *f*; [square] foulard *m*

**scarlet** ['skɑːlət] *adj* écarlate; **scarlet fever** scarlatine *f*

**scary** ['skeərɪ] *(compar* **-ier,** *superl* **-iest)** *adj Fam* effrayant

**scathing** ['skeɪðɪŋ] *adj* [remark] acerbe; **to be scathing about sb/sth** faire des remarques acerbes sur qn/qch

**scatter** ['skætə(r)] **1.** *vt* [demonstrators] disperser; [corn, seed] jeter à la volée; [papers] laisser traîner **2.** *vi* [of crowd] se disperser

**scatterbrain** ['skætəbreɪn] *n* tête *f* de linotte

**scavenge** ['skævɪndʒ] *vi* **to scavenge for sth** fouiller pour trouver qch

**scenario** [sɪ'nɑːrɪəʊ] *(pl* **-os)** *n* [of film] scénario *m*

**scene** [siːn] *n* [in book, film, play] scène *f*; [of event, crime, accident] lieu *m*; *also Fig* **behind the scenes** dans les coulisses; **on the scene** sur les lieux; **to make a scene** faire un scandale

**scenery** ['siːnərɪ] *(pl* **-ies)** *n* [landscape] paysage *m*; [in play, film] décors *mpl*

**scenic** ['siːnɪk] *adj* pittoresque; **scenic route** route *f* touristique

**scent** [sent] *n* [smell] odeur *f*; [perfume] parfum *m*; [in hunting] fumet *m*

**sceptical,** *Am* **skeptical** ['skeptɪkəl] *adj* sceptique

**schedule** [*Br* 'ʃedjuːl, *Am* 'skedjʊl] **1.** *n* [plan] programme *m*; [for trains, buses] horaire *m*; [list] liste *f*; **according to schedule** comme prévu **2.** *vt* prévoir; [event] fixer la date/l'heure de ■ **scheduled** [*Br* 'ʃedjuːld, *Am* 'skedjuːld] *adj* [planned] prévu; [service, flight, train] régulier, -ère

**scheme** [skiːm] **1.** *n* [plan] plan *m* (**to do** pour faire); [plot] complot *m*; [arrange-

ment] arrangement *m* **2.** *vi Pej* comploter ■ **scheming** *Pej* **1.** *adj* intrigant **2.** *n* machinations *fpl*

**schizophrenic** [skɪtsəʊ'frenɪk] *adj* & *n* schizophrène (*mf*)

**schmuck** [ʃmʌk] *n Am Fam* andouille *f*

**scholar** ['skɒlə(r)] *n* érudit, -e *mf* ■ **scholarly** *adj* érudit ■ **scholarship** *n* [learning] érudition *f*; [grant] bourse *f* d'études

**school** [skuːl] **1.** *n* école *f*; [within university] département *m*; *Am Fam* [college] université *f*; *Br* **secondary school,** *Am* **high school** établissement *m* d'enseignement secondaire **2.** *adj* [year, book, equipment] scolaire; **school bag** cartable *m*; **school fees** frais *mpl* de scolarité; *Am* **school yard** cour *f* de récréation ■ **schoolboy** *n* écolier *m* ■ **schoolchildren** *npl* écoliers *mpl* ■ **schoolfriend** *n* camarade *mf* de classe ■ **schoolgirl** *n* écolière *f* ■ **schoolteacher** *n* [primary] instituteur, -trice *mf*; [secondary] professeur *m*

**schtum** [ʃtʊm] *adj Br Fam* **to keep schtum** ne pas piper mot

**science** ['saɪəns] *n* science *f*; **to study science** étudier les sciences; **science fiction** science-fiction *f* ■ **scientific** *adj* scientifique ■ **scientist** *n* scientifique *mf*

**sci-fi** [,saɪ'faɪ] *(abbr of* **science fiction)** *n Fam* science-fiction *f*, S.F. *f*

**scissors** ['sɪzəz] *npl* ciseaux *mpl*

**scoff** [skɒf] **1.** *vt* **to scoff at sb/sth** se moquer de qn/qch **2.** *vti Br Fam* [eat] bouffer

**scold** [skəʊld] *vt* gronder (**for doing** pour avoir fait)

**scone** [skəʊn, skɒn] *n Br* scone *m*

**scoop** [skuːp] **1.** *n* [for flour, sugar] pelle *f*; [for ice cream] cuillère *f*; [amount - of ice cream] boule *f* **2.** *vt* **to scoop sth out** [hollow out] évider qch; **to scoop sth up** ramasser qch

**scooter** ['skuːtə(r)] *n* [for child] trottinette *f*; [motorcycle] scooter *m*

**scope** [skəʊp] n [range] étendue f ; [of action] possibilité f

**scorch** [skɔːtʃ] **1.** n **scorch (mark)** brûlure f **2.** vt roussir ▪ **scorching** adj [day] torride ; [sun, sand] brûlant

**score¹** [skɔː(r)] **1.** n [in sport] score m ; [in music] partition f ; [of film] musique f **2.** vt [point, goal] marquer ; [exam mark] avoir ; [piece of music] adapter (**for** pour) **3.** vi [score a goal] marquer ; [count points] marquer les points ▪ **scoreboard** n tableau m d'affichage ▪ **scorer** n marqueur m

**score²** [skɔː(r)] n **a score** [twenty] vingt ; Fam **scores of** des tas de

**scorn** [skɔːn] **1.** n mépris m **2.** vt mépriser ▪ **scornful** adj méprisant

**scorpion** ['skɔːpɪən] n scorpion m

**Scot** [skɒt] n Écossais, -e mf ▪ **Scotland** n l'Écosse f ▪ **Scotsman** (pl -men) n Écossais m ▪ **Scotswoman** (pl -women) n Écossaise f ▪ **Scottish** adj écossais

**Scotch** [skɒtʃ] **1.** n [whisky] scotch m **2.** adj Am **Scotch tape**® Scotch® m

**scoundrel** ['skaʊndrəl] n crapule f

**scour** ['skaʊə(r)] vt [pan] récurer ; Fig [streets, house] ratisser (**for** à la recherche de) ▪ **scourer** n tampon m à récurer

**scout** [skaʊt] n (boy) scout m, éclaireur m ; Am (girl) scout éclaireuse f

**scowl** [skaʊl] vi lancer des regards noirs (**at** à)

**scram** [skræm] (pt & pp -mm-) vi Fam se tirer

**scramble** ['skræmbəl] **1.** vt **scrambled eggs** œufs mpl brouillés **2.** vi to **scramble up a hill** gravir une colline en s'aidant des mains

**scrap** [skræp] **1.** n **a)** [piece] bout m (**of** de) ; [of information] bribe f ; **scraps** [food] restes mpl ; **scrap paper** papier m brouillon **b)** **scrap (metal)** ferraille f ; **scrap heap** tas m de ferraille ; **scrap dealer, scrap merchant** ferrailleur m ; **scrap yard** casse f **2.** (pt & pp -pp-) vt [get rid of] se débarrasser de ; [car] envoyer

à la casse ; Fig [plan, idea] abandonner ▪ **scrapbook** n album m (de coupures de presse etc)

**scrape** [skreɪp] **1.** vt gratter ; [skin] érafler ; **to scrape a living** arriver tout juste à vivre **2.** vi **to scrape against sth** frotter contre qch ▪ **scrape away, scrape off** vt sep racler ▪ **scrape through** vt insep & vi **to scrape through (an exam)** passer de justesse (à un examen) ▪ **scrape together** vt sep [money, people] parvenir à rassembler

**scratch** [skrætʃ] **1.** n [mark, injury] éraflure f ; [on glass, wood] rayure f ; Fam **to start from scratch** repartir de zéro ; **it isn't up to scratch** ce n'est pas au niveau **2.** vt [to relieve itching] gratter ; [by accident] érafler ; [glass] rayer ; [with claw] griffer ; [write, draw] griffonner (**on** sur) **3.** vi [of person] se gratter ; [of pen, new clothes] gratter ▪ **scratchcard** n [lottery card] carte f à gratter

**scrawl** [skrɔːl] **1.** n gribouillis m **2.** vt gribouiller

**scream** [skriːm] **1.** n hurlement m **2.** vt hurler **3.** vi hurler ; **to scream at sb** crier après qn

**screech** [skriːtʃ] vti hurler

**screen** [skriːn] **1.** n [of TV set, computer, cinema] écran m ; COMPUT **screen saver** économiseur m d'écran **2.** vt [hide] cacher (**from sb** à qn) ; [protect] protéger (**from** de) ; [film] projeter ; [visitors, calls] filtrer ; [for disease] faire subir un test de dépistage à ▪ **screenager** ['skriːneɪdʒə(r)] n jeunes mpl adeptes de l'ordinateur et d'Internet, ≃ la génération TIC ▪ **screening** n [of film] projection f ; [selection] tri m ; [for disease] dépistage m ▪ **screenplay** n [of film] scénario m

**screw** [skruː] **1.** n vis f **2.** vt visser (**to** à) ; **to screw sth down** or **on** visser qch ; **to screw sth off** dévisser qch ; **to screw sth up** [paper] chiffonner qch **3.** vi [bolt, lid] se visser ▪ **screwdriver** n tournevis m ▪ **screw up** vt sep

**a)** [crumple up] froisser, chiffonner **b)** [eyes] plisser ; [face] tordre **c)** v Fam [ruin] gâcher, bousiller

**scribble** ['skrɪbəl] **1.** n griffonnage m **2.** vti griffonner

**script** [skrɪpt] n **a)** [of film] script m ; [of play] texte m ; [in exam] copie f **b)** [handwriting] script m

**Scripture(s)** ['skrɪptʃə(z)] n REL les saintes Écritures fpl

**scroll** [skrəʊl] **1.** n rouleau m ; [manuscript] manuscrit m **2.** vt COMPUT faire défiler **3.** vi COMPUT défiler ; **to scroll down / up** défiler vers le bas / haut

**scrounge** [skraʊndʒ] vt Fam [meal] se faire payer (**off** or **from sb** par qn) ; [steal] taper (**off** or **from sb** à qn) ; **to scrounge money off** or **from sb** taper qn ■ **scrounger** n Fam parasite m

**scrub** [skrʌb] **1.** n **a) to give sth a scrub** bien frotter qch ; Am **scrub brush** brosse f dure **b)** [land] broussailles fpl **2.** (pt & pp -bb-) vt [surface] frotter ; [pan] récurer ; **to scrub sth off** [remove] enlever qch (à la brosse ou en frottant)

**scrubbing** ['skrʌbɪŋ] n **scrubbing brush** brosse f dure

**scruff** [skrʌf] n **by the scruff of the neck** par la peau du cou

**scruffy** ['skrʌfɪ] (compar -ier, superl -iest) adj [person] peu soigné

**scrum** [skrʌm] n [in rugby] mêlée f

**scrupulous** ['skru:pjʊləs] adj scrupuleux, -euse

**scrutinize** ['skru:tɪnaɪz] vt [document] éplucher

**scuba** ['sku:bə] n **scuba diving** la plongée sous-marine

**scuff** [skʌf] vt **to scuff sth (up)** [shoe] érafler qch

**scuffle** ['skʌfəl] n bagarre f

**sculpt** [skʌlpt] vti sculpter ■ **sculptor** n sculpteur m ■ **sculpture** n [art, object] sculpture f

**scum** [skʌm] n **a)** [froth] écume f **b)** Fam & Pej [people] racaille f ; [person] ordure f

**scurry** ['skʌrɪ] vi [rush] courir ; **to scurry off** se sauver

**sea** [si:] **1.** n mer f ; **(out) at sea** en mer ; **by sea** par mer ; **by** or **beside the sea** au bord de la mer **2.** adj [level, breeze] de la mer ; [water, fish, salt] de mer ; [air] marin ; [battle] naval (mpl -als) ; [route] maritime ; **sea bed, sea floor** fond m de la mer ■ **seafood** n fruits mpl de mer ■ **seafront** n Br front m de mer ■ **seagull** n mouette f ■ **seashell** n coquillage m ■ **seaside** n Br bord m de la mer ; **seaside resort** station f balnéaire ■ **seashore** n rivage m ■ **seasick** adj **to be seasick** avoir le mal de mer ■ **seaweed** n algues fpl

**seal¹** [si:l] n [animal] phoque m

**seal²** [si:l] **1.** n [stamp] sceau m ; [device for sealing] joint m d'étanchéité **2.** vt [document, container] sceller ; [stick down] cacheter ; [make airtight] fermer hermétiquement ; **to seal off an area** boucler un quartier ■ **sealable** ['si:ləbl] adj qui peut être fermé hermétiquement

**seam** [si:m] n [in cloth] couture f ■ **seamless** ['si:mlɪs] adj sans couture ; Fig homogène, cohérent

**search** [sɜ:tʃ] **1.** n recherches fpl (**for** de) ; [of place] fouille f ; **in search of** à la recherche de ; COMPUT **to do a search for sth** rechercher qch ; COMPUT **search engine** moteur m de recherche ; **search result** résultat m (d'une recherche sur Internet) **2.** vt [person, place] fouiller (**for** pour trouver) **3.** vi chercher ; **to search for sth** chercher qch ■ **searchlight** n projecteur m

**season¹** ['si:zən] n saison f ; [of films] cycle m ; **in the peak season, in (the) high season** en haute saison ; **in the low** or **off season** en basse saison ; **season ticket** abonnement m

**season²** ['si:zən] vt [food] assaisonner ■ **seasoning** n CULIN assaisonnement m

**seasonal** ['si:zənəl] adj [work, change] saisonnier, -ère

**seat** [si:t] **1.** n siège m ; [of trousers] fond m ; **to take** or **have a seat** s'asseoir ; **seat belt** ceinture f de sécurité **2.** vt [at table] placer ; [on one's lap] asseoir ■ **seated** *adj* [sitting] assis ■ **seating** *n* [seats] places *fpl* assises

**-seater** ['si:tə(r)] *suff* **two-seater (car)** voiture *f* à deux places

**secluded** [sɪ'klu:dɪd] *adj* [remote] isolé ■ **seclusion** *n* solitude *f*

**second**[1] ['sekənd] **1.** *adj* deuxième, second ; **every second week** une semaine sur deux ; AUTO **in second (gear)** *Am* SCH **second grade** classe de l'enseignement primaire correspondant au CE1 (6-7 ans) **2.** *adv* [say] deuxièmement ; **to come second** [in competition] se classer deuxième ; **the second biggest** le deuxième en ordre de grandeur **3.** *n* [in series] deuxième *mf*, second, -e *mf* ; [in month] deux *m* ; **Louis the Second** Louis Deux ; **seconds** [goods] articles *mpl* défectueux **4.** *vt* [motion, proposal] appuyer ■ **second-class** *adj* [ticket on train] de seconde (classe) ; [mail] non urgent ; [product] de qualité inférieure ■ **secondly** *adv* deuxièmement ■ **second-rate** *adj* médiocre

**second**[2] ['sekənd] *n* [part of minute] seconde *f* ; **second hand** [of clock, watch] trotteuse *f*

**secondary** ['sekəndərɪ] *adj* secondaire ; *Br* **secondary school** établissement *m* secondaire

**second-hand** [sekənd'hænd] **1.** *adj* & *adv* [not new] d'occasion **2.** *adj* [report, news] de seconde main

**secrecy** ['si:krəsɪ] *n* [discretion, silence] secret *m*

**secret** ['si:krɪt] **1.** *adj* secret, -ète **2.** *n* secret *m* ; **in secret** en secret ■ **secretly** *adv* secrètement

**secretary** [*Br* 'sekrətərɪ, *Am* -erɪ] *(pl* -ies) *n* secrétaire *mf* ; *Br* **Foreign Secretary**, *Am* **Secretary of State** ≃ ministre *m* des Affaires étrangères ■ **secretarial** [-'teərɪəl] *adj* [work] administratif, -ive ; [job, course] de secrétariat

**secretive** ['si:krətɪv] *adj* [person] secret, -ète ; **to be secretive about sth** faire des cachotteries à propos de qch

**sect** [sekt] *n* secte *f*

**section** ['sekʃən] *n* partie *f* ; [of road] tronçon *m* ; [of machine] élément *m* ; [of organization] département *m* ; **the sports section** [of newspaper] la page des sports

**sector** ['sektə(r)] *n* secteur *m*

**secular** ['sekjʊlə(r)] *adj* [music, art] profane

**secure** [sɪ'kjʊə(r)] **1.** *adj* [person] en sécurité ; [investment, place] sûr ; [door, window] bien fermé **2.** *vt* [fasten] attacher ; [window, door] bien fermer ; [position, future] assurer ; [support, promise] procurer ; **to secure sth (for oneself)** se procurer qch ■ **securely** *adv* [firmly] solidement ; [safely] en sûreté

**security** [sɪ'kjʊərətɪ] *(pl* -ies) *n* sécurité *f* ; FIN [for loan, debt] garantie *f* ; **securities** [stocks, bonds] titres *mpl* ; **security check(point)** contrôle *m* de sécurité ; **security gate** [at airport] portique *m*

**sedan** [sɪ'dæn] *n* *Am* [saloon] berline *f*

**sedate** [sɪ'deɪt] **1.** *adj* calme **2.** *vt* mettre sous calmants

**sedative** ['sedətɪv] *n* calmant *m*

**seduce** [sɪ'dju:s] *vt* séduire ■ **seductive** [-'dʌktɪv] *adj* [person, offer] séduisant

**see** [si:] *(pt* saw, *pp* seen) *vti* voir ; **we'll see** on verra ; **I can see a hill** je vois une colline ; **I saw him run(ning)** je l'ai vu courir ; **to see reason** entendre raison ; **see you (later)!** à tout à l'heure ! ; **to see that...** [make sure that] faire en sorte que... (+ *subjunctive*) ; [check] s'assurer que... (+ *indicative*) ; **to see sb to the door** accompagner qn jusqu'à la porte

■ **see about** *vt insep* [deal with] s'occuper de ; [consider] songer à

■ **see off** *vt sep* [say goodbye to] dire au revoir à

■ **see out** *vt sep* accompagner jusqu'à la porte

■ **see through 1.** *vt sep* [task] mener à bien **2.** *vt insep* **to see through sb** percer qn à jour

■ **see to** *vt insep* [deal with] s'occuper de ; [mend] réparer ; **to see to it that...** [make sure that] faire en sorte que... (+ *subjunctive*) ; [check] s'assurer que... (+ *indicative*)

**seed** [siːd] *n* graine *f* ; [of fruit] pépin *m* ; *Fig* [source] germe *m*

**seedy** ['siːdɪ] (*compar* -ier, *superl* -iest) *adj* miteux, -euse

**seeing** ['siːɪŋ] *conj* **seeing (that)** vu que

**seek** [siːk] (*pt & pp* sought) *vt* chercher (**to do** à faire) ; [ask for] demander (**from** à) ; **to seek sb out** dénicher qn

**seem** [siːm] *vi* sembler (**to do** faire) ; **it seems that...** [impression] il semble que... (+ *subjunctive*) ; **it seems to me that...** il me semble que... (+ *indicative*)

**seemingly** ['siːmɪŋlɪ] *adv* apparemment

**seemly** ['siːmlɪ] *adj Formal* bienséant

**seen** [siːn] *pp of* **see**

**seep** [siːp] *vi* suinter ; **to seep into sth** s'infiltrer dans qch

**seesaw** ['siːsɔː] *n* balançoire *f* à bascule

**see-through** ['siːθruː] *adj* transparent

**segment** ['segmənt] *n* segment *m* ; [of orange] quartier *m*

**segregate** ['segrɪgeɪt] *vt* séparer (**from** de) ■ **segregation** *n* ségrégation *f*

**seize** [siːz] **1.** *vt* saisir ; [power, land] s'emparer de **2.** *vi* **to seize (up)on** [offer] sauter sur ; **to seize up** [of engine] se bloquer

**seizure** ['siːʒə(r)] *n* [of goods, property] saisie *f* ; *MED* crise *f*

**seldom** ['seldəm] *adv* rarement

**select** [sɪ'lekt] **1.** *vt* sélectionner **2.** *adj* [exclusive] sélect ■ **selection** *n* sélection *f*

**selective** [sɪ'lektɪv] *adj* sélectif, -ive

**self** [self] (*pl* **selves** [selvz]) *n* **he's back to his old self** il est redevenu comme avant ■ **self-addressed** *n* **self-addressed envelope** enveloppe *f* libellée à ses nom et adresse ■ **self-assured** *adj* sûr de soi ■ **self-belief** *n* confiance *f* en soi ; **to have self-belief** croire en soi-même ■ **self-catering**

*adj Br* [holiday] en appartement meublé ; [accommodation] meublé ■ **self-centred**, *Am* **-centered** *adj* égocentrique ■ **self-checkout** *n* caisse *f* sans caissière ■ **self-confidence** *n* confiance *f* en soi ■ **self-confident** *adj* sûr de soi ■ **self-conscious** *adj* gêné ■ **self-contained** *adj* [flat] indépendant ■ **self-control** *n* maîtrise *f* de soi ■ **self-defence**, *Am* **-defense** *n* [in law] légitime défense *f* ; **in self-defence** en état de légitime défense ■ **self-discipline** *n* autodiscipline *f* ■ **self-employed** *adj* indépendant ■ **self-esteem** *n* confiance *f* en soi ■ **self-evident** *adj* évident ■ **self-important** *adj* suffisant ■ **self-indulgent** *adj* complaisant ■ **self-injury** *n* automutilation *f* ■ **self-interest** *n* intérêt *m* personnel ■ **self-loathing** *n* dégoût *m* de soi-même ■ **self-obsessed** *adj* obsédé par soi-même ■ **self-pity** *n* **to be full of self-pity** s'apitoyer sur son propre sort ■ **self-portrait** *n* autoportrait *m* ■ **self-raising**, *Am* **-rising** *n* **self-raising flour** farine contenant de la levure chimique ■ **self-respect** *n* amour-propre *m* ■ **self-righteous** *adj* suffisant ■ **self-sacrifice** *n* abnégation *f* ■ **self-satisfied** *adj* content de soi ■ **self-service** *n & adj* libre-service (*m inv*) ■ **self-sufficient** *adj* indépendant ■ **self-taught** *adj* autodidacte

**selfish** ['selfɪʃ] *adj* égoïste ; [motive] intéressé ■ **selfishness** *n* égoïsme *m* ■ **selfless** *adj* désintéressé

**sell** [sel] **1.** (*pt & pp* sold) *vt* vendre ; *Fig* [idea] faire accepter ; **to sell sb sth, to sell sth to sb** vendre qch à qn ; **she sold it to me for $100** elle me l'a vendu 100 dollars **2.** *vi* [of product] se vendre ; [of person] vendre ■ **sell-by** *adj* **sell-by date** date *f* limite de vente ■ **sell off** *vt sep* liquider ■ **sell out** *vt insep* **to have** *or* **be sold out of sth** n'avoir plus de qch ; **to be sold out** [of book, item] être épuisé ; [of show, concert] afficher complet ■ **sell up** *vi* [sell home, business] tout vendre

**seller** ['selə(r)] *n* vendeur, -euse *mf*

**Sellotape®** ['seləteɪp] n Br Scotch® m

**semblance** ['sembləns] n semblant m

**semen** ['si:mən] n sperme m

**semester** [sɪ'mestə(r)] n semestre m

**semi-** ['semɪ] pref semi-, demi- ▪ **semicircle** n demi-cercle m ▪ **semicolon** n point-virgule m ▪ **semi-detached** adj Br semi-detached house maison f jumelée ▪ **semi-final** n demi-finale f ▪ **semi-skimmed** adj [milk] demi-écrémé

**seminar** ['semɪnɑ:(r)] n séminaire m

**semolina** [semə'li:nə] n semoule f

**senate** ['senɪt] n the Senate le Sénat ▪ **senator** [-nətə(r)] n sénateur m

**send** [send] (pt & pp sent) vt envoyer (to à); to send sth to sb, to send sb sth envoyer qch à qn; to send sb home renvoyer qn chez soi; Fam to send sb packing envoyer promener qn ▪ **sender** n expéditeur, -trice mf ▪ **send away 1.** vt sep [person] renvoyer **2.** vi to send away for sth se faire envoyer qch ▪ **send back** vt sep renvoyer ▪ **send for** vt insep envoyer chercher; [doctor] faire venir; [send away for] se faire envoyer ▪ **send in** vt sep [form, invoice, troops] envoyer; [person] faire entrer ▪ **send off 1.** vt sep [letter] envoyer (to à); [player] expulser **2.** vi to send off for sth se faire envoyer qch ▪ **send on** vt sep [letter] faire suivre ▪ **send out 1.** vt sep envoyer **2.** vi to send out for sth envoyer chercher qch ▪ **send up** vt sep Br Fam [parody] se moquer de

**senile** ['si:naɪl] adj sénile

**senior** ['si:nɪə(r)] **1.** adj a) [in age] aîné; [in position, rank] supérieur; to be sb's senior, to be senior to sb être l'aîné de qn; [in rank, status] être le supérieur de qn; Brown senior Brown père; senior citizen personne f âgée b) Am SCH senior year [in school, college] dernière année f; Am SCH senior high school ≃ lycée m **2.** n aîné, -e mf; Am [in last year of school or college] étudiant, -e mf de dernière année; [in sport] senior mf

**sensation** [sen'seɪʃən] n sensation f ▪ **sensational** adj sensationnel, -elle

**sense** [sens] **1.** n [faculty, awareness, meaning] sens m; **sense of smell** odorat m; **a sense of shame** un sentiment de honte; **sense of direction** sens de l'orientation; **to have a sense of humour** avoir le sens de l'humour; **to have the sense to do sth** avoir l'intelligence de faire qch; **to bring sb to his/her senses** ramener qn à la raison; **to make sense** être logique; **to make sense of sth** comprendre qch **2.** vt sentir (that que)

**senseless** ['sensləs] adj [pointless] absurde

**sensibility** [sensɪ'bɪlətɪ] n sensibilité f

**sensible** ['sensəbəl] adj [wise] sensé; [clothes, shoes] pratique

**sensitive** ['sensɪtɪv] adj [person] sensible (to à); [skin, question] délicat; [information] confidentiel, -elle ▪ **sensitivity** n sensibilité f; [touchiness] susceptibilité f

**sensor** ['sensə(r)] n détecteur m

**sensual** ['senʃʊəl] adj sensuel, -elle ▪ **sensuous** adj sensuel, -elle

**sent** [sent] pt & pp of send

**sentence** ['sentəns] **1.** n a) [words] phrase f b) [in prison] peine f **2.** vt [criminal] condamner; **to sentence sb to three years (in prison)/to death** condamner qn à trois ans de prison/à mort

**sentiment** ['sentɪmənt] n sentiment m ▪ **sentimental** [-'mentəl] adj sentimental

**separate 1.** ['sepərət] adj [distinct] séparé; [organization] indépendant; [occasion, entrance] différent; [room] à part **2.** ['sepəreɪt] vt séparer (from de) **3.** ['sepəreɪt] vi se séparer (from de) ▪ **separately** ['sepərətlɪ] adv séparément ▪ **separation** n séparation f

**September** [sep'tembə(r)] n septembre m

**septic** ['septɪk] adj [wound] infecté; **to go** or **turn septic** s'infecter

**sequel** ['si:kwəl] n [book, film] suite f

**sequence** ['si:kwəns] *n* [order] ordre *m* ; [series] succession *f* ; [in film, COMPUT, MUS & CARDS] séquence *f* ; **in sequence** dans l'ordre

**sequin** ['si:kwɪn] *n* paillette *f*

**Serbia** ['sɜːbɪə] *n* la Serbie

**serenade** [serə'neɪd] **1.** *n* sérénade *f* **2.** *vt* chanter la sérénade à

**serene** [sə'riːn] *adj* serein

**sergeant** ['sɑːdʒənt] *n* MIL sergent *m* ; [in police] brigadier *m*

**serial** ['sɪərɪəl] *n* [story, film] feuilleton *m* ; **serial killer** tueur *m* en série ; **serial number** numéro *m* de série ■ **serialize** *vt* [in newspaper] publier en feuilleton ; [on television or radio] adapter en feuilleton

**series** ['sɪəriːz] *n inv* série *f*

**serious** ['sɪərɪəs] *adj* [person] sérieux, -euse ; [illness, mistake, tone] grave ; [damage] important ; **to be serious about doing sth** envisager sérieusement de faire qch ■ **seriously** *adv* sérieusement ; [ill, damaged] gravement ; **to take sb/sth seriously** prendre qn / qch au sérieux

**sermon** ['sɜːmən] *n* sermon *m*

**servant** ['sɜːvənt] *n* domestique *mf*

**serve** [sɜːv] **1.** *n* [in tennis] service *m* **2.** *vt* [country, cause, meal, customer] servir ; [prison sentence] purger ; [apprenticeship] faire ; *Fam* **(it) serves you right!** ça t'apprendra ! **3.** *vi* servir (**as** de) ; **to serve on** [committee, jury] être membre de ■ **server** *n* [in tennis] serveur, -euse *mf* ; COMPUT serveur *m* ■ **serve out, serve up** *vt sep* [food] servir

**service** ['sɜːvɪs] **1.** *n* [with army, firm, in restaurant, in tennis & REL] service *m* ; [of machine] entretien *m* ; [of car] révision *f* ; **to be at sb's service** être au service de qn ; **the (armed) services** les forces *fpl* armées ; **service charge** service *m* ; *Br* **service area** [on motorway] aire *f* de service ; COMPUT **service provider** fournisseur *m* d'accès Internet ; **service station** station-service *f* **2.** *vt* [machine] entretenir ; [car] réviser

**serviceman** ['sɜːvɪsmən] *(pl* **-men)** *n* militaire *m*

**serviette** [sɜːvɪ'et] *n Br* serviette *f* de table

**servile** ['sɜːvaɪl] *adj* servile

**serving** ['sɜːvɪŋ] *n* [of food] portion *f* ; **serving dish** plat *m*

**session** ['seʃən] *n* [meeting, period] séance *f* ; [university term] trimestre *m* ; [university year] année *f* universitaire

**set** [set] **1.** *n* [of keys, tools] jeu *m* ; [of stamps, numbers] série *f* ; [of people] groupe *m* ; [of facts, laws & MATH] ensemble *m* ; [of books] collection *f* ; [of dishes] service *m* ; [kit] trousse *f* ; [in theatre] décor *m* ; [for film] plateau *m* ; [in tennis] set *m* ; **chess set** jeu *m* d'échecs ; **tea set** service *m* à thé ; **television set, TV set** téléviseur *m*
**2.** *adj* [time, price] fixe ; [lunch] à prix fixe ; [school book] au programme ; [ideas, purpose] déterminé ; **to be set on doing sth** être résolu à faire qch ; **to be dead set against sth** être formellement opposé à qch ; **to be all set** être prêt (**to do** pour faire) ; **set menu** menu *m* ; **set phrase** expression *f* figée
**3.** *(pt & pp* **set,** *pres p* **setting)** *vt* [put] mettre, poser ; [date, limit, task] fixer ; [homework] donner (**for sb** à qn) ; [jewel] sertir ; [watch] régler ; [alarm clock] mettre (**for** pour) ; [bone fracture] réduire ; [trap] tendre (**for** à) ; **to set a record** établir un record ; **to set a precedent** créer un précédent ; **to set sb free** libérer qn
**4.** *vi* [of sun] se coucher ; [of jelly] prendre ; [of bone] se ressouder ■ **set about** *vt insep* [begin] se mettre à ; **to set about doing sth** se mettre à faire qch

■ **set back** *vt sep* [in time] retarder ; *Fam* [cost] coûter à ■ **set down** *vt sep* [object] poser

■ **set off 1.** *vt sep* [bomb] faire exploser ; [mechanism] déclencher ; *Fig* [beauty] rehausser ; **to set sb off (crying)** faire pleurer qn **2.** *vi* [leave] partir ■ **set out 1.** *vt sep* [display, ex-

plain] exposer ; [arrange] disposer **2.** *vi*
[leave] partir ; **to set out to do sth** avoir
l'intention de faire qch

■ **set up 1.** *vt sep* [tent, statue] dresser ; [roadblock] mettre en place ; [company] créer ; [meeting] organiser ; [inquiry] ouvrir **2.** *vi* **to set up in business** s'installer (**as** comme)

**setback** ['setbæk] *n* revers *m*

**SETE** MESSAGING *written abbr of* **smiling ear to ear**

**settee** [se'tiː] *n* canapé *m*

**setting** ['setɪŋ] *n* [surroundings] cadre *m* ; [of sun] coucher *m* ; [on machine] réglage *m*

**settle** ['setəl] **1.** *vt* [put in place] installer ; [decide, arrange, pay] régler ; [date] fixer ; [nerves] calmer ; [land] coloniser ; **that settles it!** c'est décidé ! **2.** *vi* [of person, family] s'installer ; [of dust] se déposer ; [of bird] se poser ■ **settled** *adj* [weather, period] stable ; [life] rangé

■ **settle down** *vi* [in chair, house] s'installer ; [become quieter] s'assagir ; [of situation] se calmer ; **to settle down with sb** mener une vie stable avec qn ; **to settle down to work** se mettre au travail ■ **settle for** *vt insep* se contenter de ■ **settle in** *vi* [in new home] s'installer ■ **settle up** *vi* [pay] régler ; **to settle up with sb** régler qn

**settlement** ['setəlmənt] *n* [agreement] accord *m* ; [payment] règlement *m* ; [colony] colonie *f*

**settler** ['setlə(r)] *n* colon *m*

**setup** ['setʌp] *n* *Fam* [arrangement] système *m*

**seven** ['sevən] *adj* & *n* sept (*m*) ■ **seventh** *adj* & *n* septième (*mf*) ; *Am* SCH **seventh grade** classe de l'enseignement secondaire correspondant à la cinquième (11-12 ans)

**7K** MESSAGING *written abbr of* **sick**

**seventeen** [sevən'tiːn] *adj* & *n* dix-sept (*m*) ■ **seventeenth** *adj* & *n* dix-septième (*mf*)

**seventy** ['sevəntɪ] *adj* & *n* soixante-dix (*m*) ; **seventy-one** soixante et onze ■ **seventieth** *adj* & *n* soixante-dixième (*mf*)

**sever** ['sevə(r)] *vt* couper ; *Fig* [relations] rompre

**several** ['sevərəl] *adj* & *pron* plusieurs (**of** d'entre)

**severe** [sə'vɪə(r)] *adj* [person, punishment, tone] sévère ; [winter] rigoureux, -euse ; [illness, injury] grave ; [blow, pain] violent ; [cold, frost] intense ■ **severely** *adv* [criticize, punish] sévèrement ; [damaged, wounded] gravement

**sew** [səʊ] (*pt* sewed, *pp* sewn *or* sewed) *vt* coudre ; **to sew a button on a shirt** coudre un bouton à une chemise ; **to sew sth up** recoudre qch ■ **sewing** *n* couture *f* ; **sewing machine** machine *f* à coudre

**sewage** ['suːɪdʒ] *n* eaux *fpl* d'égout ■ **sewer** *n* égout *m*

**sewn** [səʊn] *pp of* sew

**sex** [seks] **1.** *n* sexe *m* ; **to have sex with sb** coucher avec qn **2.** *adj* [education, life, act] sexuel, -elle ; **sex offender** auteur *m* d'un délit sexuel ■ **sexist** *adj* & *n* sexiste (*mf*)

**sexting** ['sekstɪŋ] *n* *Am* envoi de SMS à caractère sexuel

**sexual** ['sekʃʊəl] *adj* sexuel, -elle ; **sexual harassment** harcèlement *m* sexuel ■ **sexuality** [seksjʊ'ælətɪ] *n* sexualité *f* ■ **sexy** ['seksɪ] (*compar* -ier, *superl* -iest) *adj* *Fam* sexy *inv*

**sh** [ʃ] *excl* chut !

**shabby** ['ʃæbɪ] (*compar* -ier, *superl* -iest) *adj* miteux, -euse ; [behaviour, treatment] mesquin

**shack** [ʃæk] *n* cabane *f*

**shade** [ʃeɪd] **1.** *n* ombre *f* ; [of colour, meaning, opinion] nuance *f* ; [for lamp] abat-jour *m inv* ; **in the shade** à l'ombre ; **a shade faster / taller** un rien plus vite / plus grand **2.** *vt* [of tree] ombrager ■ **shady** (*compar* -ier, *superl* -iest) *adj* [place] ombragé ; *Fig* [person, business] louche

**shadow** ['ʃædəʊ] **1.** *n* ombre *f* **2.** *adj* Br POL **shadow cabinet** cabinet *m* fantôme **3.** *vt* **to shadow sb** [follow] filer qn

**shaft** [ʃɑːft] *n* a) [of tool] manche *m*; **shaft of light** rayon *m* de lumière b) [of mine] puits *m*; [of lift] cage *f*

**shaggy** ['ʃægɪ] *(compar* -ier, *superl* -iest) *adj* [hairy] hirsute

**shake** [ʃeɪk] **1.** *n* secousse *f*; **to give sth a shake** secouer qch **2.** *(pt* shook, *pp* shaken)*vt* [move up and down] secouer; [bottle, fist] agiter; [building] faire trembler; *Fig* [belief, resolution] ébranler; **to shake one's head** faire non de la tête; **to shake hands with sb** serrer la main à qn; **to shake off** [dust] secouer; *Fig* [illness, pursuer] se débarrasser de; **to shake up** [reorganize] réorganiser de fond en comble **3.** *vi* [of person, windows, voice] trembler (**with** de)

**shaken** ['ʃeɪkən] *pp of* **shake**

**shaky** ['ʃeɪkɪ] *(compar* -ier, *superl* -iest) *adj* [voice] tremblant; [table, chair] branlant; [handwriting] tremblé; [health] précaire; [argument, start] incertain

---

**shall** [ʃæl] *(unstressed* [ʃəl])

On trouve généralement **I**/**you**/**he**/*etc* **shall** sous leurs formes contractées **I'll**/ **you'll**/**he'll**/*etc*. La forme négative correspondante est **shan't**, que l'on écrira **shall not** dans des contextes formels.

*v aux* a) [expressing future tense] **I shall come, I'll come** je viendrai; **we shall not come, we shan't come** nous ne viendrons pas
b) [making suggestion] **shall I leave?** veux-tu que je parte ?; **let's go in, shall we?** entrons, tu veux bien ? c) *Formal* [expressing order] **he shall do it if I order it** il le fera si je l'ordonne

---

**shallow** ['ʃæləʊ] *(compar* -er, *superl* -est) *adj* [water, river] peu profond; *Fig & Pej* [argument, person] superficiel, -elle

**sham** [ʃæm] **1.** *n* [pretence] comédie *f* **2.** *adj* [false] faux (*f* fausse); [illness, emotion] feint **3.** *(pt & pp* -mm-) *vt* feindre **4.** *vi* faire semblant

**shambles** ['ʃæmbəlz] *n* pagaille *f*

**shame** [ʃeɪm] **1.** *n* [guilt, disgrace] honte *f*; **it's a shame** c'est dommage (**to do** de faire); **it's a shame (that)…** c'est dommage que… (+ *subjunctive*); **what a shame!** quel dommage ! **2.** *vt* [make ashamed] faire honte à

**shameful** ['ʃeɪmfəl] *adj* honteux, -euse

**shameless** ['ʃeɪmləs] *adj* impudique

**shampoo** [ʃæm'puː] **1.** *n* shampooing *m* **2.** *vt* [carpet] shampouiner

**shandy** ['ʃændɪ] *n* Br panaché *m*

**shan't** [ʃɑːnt] = **shall not**

**shape** [ʃeɪp] **1.** *n* forme *f*; **what shape is it?** quelle forme cela a-t-il ?; **to take shape** [of plan] prendre forme; **to be in good/bad shape** [of person] être en bonne/mauvaise forme; [of business] marcher bien/mal; **to keep in shape** garder la forme **2.** *vt* [clay] modeler; [wood] façonner (**into** en); *Fig* [events, future] influencer **3.** *vi* **to shape up** [of person] progresser; [of teams, plans] prendre forme ■ **-shaped** *suff* **pear-shaped** en forme de poire ■ **shapeless** *adj* informe ■ **shapely** *(compar* -ier, *superl* -iest) *adj* bien fait

**share** [ʃeə(r)] **1.** *n* part *f* (**of** *or* **in** de); FIN [in company] action *f*; **to do one's (fair) share** mettre la main à la pâte **2.** *vt* partager; [characteristic] avoir en commun; **to share sth out** partager qch **3.** *vi* partager; **to share in sth** avoir sa part de qch ■ **shareholder** *n* FIN actionnaire *mf*

**shark** [ʃɑːk] *n* [fish, crook] requin *m*

**sharp** [ʃɑːp] **1.** *(compar* -er, *superl* -est) *adj* [knife] bien aiguisé; [pencil] bien taillé; [point] aigu (*f* aiguë); [claws] acéré; [rise, fall] brusque; [focus] net (*f* nette); [contrast] marqué; [eyesight] perçant; [taste] acide; [intelligent] vif (*f* vive) **2.** *adv* **five o'clock sharp** cinq heures pile; **to turn sharp right/left** tourner tout de suite à droite/à gauche **3.** *n* MUS dièse *m*

**sharpen** ['ʃɑːpən] *vt* [knife] aiguiser; [pencil] tailler

**Sharpie**® ['ʃɑːpɪ] *n Am* marqueur *m* permanent

**sharply** ['ʃɑːplɪ] *adv* [rise, fall] brusquement ; [contrast] nettement

**shatter** ['ʃætə(r)] **1.** *vt* [glass] faire voler en éclats ; [health, hopes] briser **2.** *vi* [of glass] voler en éclats ■ **shattered** *adj Fam* [exhausted] crevé ■ **shattering** *adj* [news, experience] bouleversant

**shave** [ʃeɪv] **1.** *n* to have a shave se raser **2.** *vt* [person, head] raser **3.** *vi* se raser ■ **shaver** *n* rasoir *m* électrique ■ **shaving** *n* [strip of wood] copeau *m* ; **shaving cream, shaving foam** mousse *f* à raser

**shawl** [ʃɔːl] *n* châle *m*

**she** [ʃiː] **1.** *pron* elle ; **she's a happy woman** c'est une femme heureuse **2.** *n Fam* **it's a she** [of baby] c'est une fille

**sheaf** [ʃiːf] (*pl* **sheaves** [ʃiːvz]) *n* [of corn] gerbe *f* ; [of paper] liasse *f*

**shear** [ʃɪə(r)] **1.** *vt* tondre **2.** *npl* **shears** cisaille *f*

**sheath** [ʃiːθ] (*pl* **-s** [ʃiːðz]) *n* [for sword] fourreau *m* ; [contraceptive] préservatif *m*

**shed**[1] [ʃed] *n* [in garden] abri *m*

**shed**[2] [ʃed] (*pt & pp* **shed**, *pres p* **shedding**) *vt* [leaves] perdre ; [tears, blood] verser ; *Fig* **to shed light on sth** éclairer qch

**she'd** [ʃiːd] = **she had, she would**

**sheep** [ʃiːp] *n inv* mouton *m* ■ **sheepdog** *n* chien *m* de berger ■ **sheepskin** *n* peau *f* de mouton

**sheepish** ['ʃiːpɪʃ] *adj* penaud

**sheer** [ʃɪə(r)] *adj* [pure] pur ; [stockings] très fin ; [cliff] à pic ; **by sheer chance** tout à fait par hasard

**sheet** [ʃiːt] *n* [on bed] drap *m* ; [of paper] feuille *f* ; [of glass, ice] plaque *f*

**shelf** [ʃelf] (*pl* **shelves** [ʃelvz]) *n* étagère *f* ; [in shop] rayon *m*

**shell** [ʃel] **1.** *n* **a)** [of egg, snail, nut] coquille *f* ; [of tortoise, lobster] carapace *f* ; [on beach] coquillage *m* ; [of peas] cosse *f* **b)** [explosive] obus *m* **2.** *vt* **a)** [peas] écosser ; [nut] décortiquer **b)** [town] bombarder

**she'll** [ʃiːl] = **she will, she shall**

**shellfish** ['ʃelfɪʃ] *npl* fruits *mpl* de mer

**shelter** ['ʃeltə(r)] **1.** *n* [place, protection] abri *m* ; **to take shelter** se mettre à l'abri (**from** de) **2.** *vt* abriter (**from** de) ; [criminal] accueillir **3.** *vi* s'abriter (**from** de) ■ **sheltered** *adj* [place] abrité

**shelve** [ʃelv] *vt* [postpone] mettre au placard

**shelving** ['ʃelvɪŋ] *n* rayonnages *mpl*

**shepherd** ['ʃepəd] *n* berger *m* ; *Br* **shepherd's pie** ≃ hachis *m* Parmentier

**sherbet** ['ʃɜːbət] *n Br* [powder] poudre *f* acidulée ; *Am* [sorbet] sorbet *m*

**sheriff** ['ʃerɪf] *n Am* shérif *m*

**sherry** ['ʃerɪ] *n* sherry *m*, xérès *m*

**shield** [ʃiːld] **1.** *n* [of warrior] bouclier *m* **2.** *vt* protéger (**from** de)

**shift** [ʃɪft] **1.** *n* [change] changement *m* (**of** *or* **in** de) ; [period of work] poste *m* ; [workers] équipe *f* ; **shift key** [on computer, typewriter] touche *f* des majuscules **2.** *vt* [move] déplacer ; [stain] enlever ; *Am* **to shift gear(s)** [in vehicle] changer de vitesse **3.** *vi* [move] bouger ■ **shiftwork** *n* travail *m* posté

**shifty** ['ʃɪftɪ] (*compar* **-ier**, *superl* **-iest**) *adj* [person] louche

**shimmer** ['ʃɪmə(r)] *vi* [of silk] chatoyer ; [of water] miroiter

**shin** [ʃɪn] *n* tibia *m* ; **shin pad** [of hockey player] jambière *f*

**shine** [ʃaɪn] **1.** *n* brillant *m* ; [on metal] éclat *m* **2.** (*pt & pp* **shone**) *vt* [polish] faire briller ; [light, torch] braquer **3.** *vi* briller

**shiny** ['ʃaɪnɪ] (*compar* **-ier**, *superl* **-iest**) *adj* brillant

**ship** [ʃɪp] **1.** *n* navire *m* **2.** (*pt & pp* **-pp-**) *vt* [send] expédier ; [transport] transporter ■ **shipment** *n* cargaison *f* ■ **shipping** *n* [traffic] navigation *f* ; [ships] navires *mpl* ■ **shipwreck** *n* naufrage *m* ■ **shipwrecked** *adj* naufragé ; **to be shipwrecked** faire naufrage ■ **shipyard** *n* chantier *m* naval

**shirk** [ʃɜːk] **1.** *vt* [duty] se dérober à ; [work] éviter de faire **2.** *vi* tirer au flanc

**shirt** [ʃɜːt] *n* chemise *f* ; [of woman] chemisier *m* ; [of sportsman] maillot *m*

**shiver** ['ʃivə(r)] **1.** n frisson m **2.** vi frissonner (**with** de)

**shoal** [ʃəʊl] n [of fish] banc m

**shock** [ʃɒk] **1.** n [impact, emotional blow] choc m; (**electric**) **shock** décharge f (électrique) **2.** adj [wave, tactics, troops] de choc; AUTO **shock absorber** amortisseur m; **shock resistant** résistant aux chocs **3.** vt [offend] choquer; [surprise] stupéfier ▪ **shock-horror** adj Fam [story, headline] à sensation ▪ **shocking** adj [outrageous] choquant; [very bad] atroce

**shoddy** ['ʃɒdɪ] (compar -ier, superl -iest) adj [goods] de mauvaise qualité

**shoe** [ʃuː] n chaussure f; [for horse] fer m à cheval; **shoe polish** cirage m; **shoe shop** magasin m de chaussures ▪ **shoelace** n lacet m

**shone** [Br ʃɒn, Am ʃəʊn] pt & pp of **shine**

**shoo** [ʃuː] **1.** (pt & pp shooed) vt to **shoo** (**away**) chasser **2.** excl ouste!

**shook** [ʃʊk] pt of **shake**

**shoot** [ʃuːt] **1.** n [of plant] pousse f **2.** (pt & pp shot) vt [bullet] tirer; [arrow] lancer; [film, scene] tourner; **to shoot sb** [kill] tuer qn par balle; [wound] blesser qn par balle; [execute] fusiller qn **3.** vi [with gun] tirer (**at** sur); [of footballer] shooter ▪ **shoot-em-up** n jeu m vidéo violent ▪ **shooting** n [shots] coups mpl de feu; [incident] fusillade f; [of film, scene] tournage m ▪ **shoot down** vt sep [plane] abattre ▪ **shoot off** vi [leave quickly] filer ▪ **shoot up** vi [of price] monter en flèche; [of plant, child] pousser vite; [of rocket] s'élever

**shop** [ʃɒp] **1.** n magasin m; [small] boutique f; [workshop] atelier m; **at the baker's shop** à la boulangerie, chez le boulanger; Br **shop assistant** vendeur, -euse mf; **shop window** vitrine f **2.** (pt & pp -pp-) vi faire ses courses (**at** chez); **to shop around** comparer les prix ▪ **shopkeeper** n commerçant, -e mf ▪ **shoplifter** n voleur, -euse mf à l'étalage ▪ **shoplifting** ['ʃɒp,lɪftɪŋ] n vol m à l'étalage ▪ **shopper** n [customer] client, -e mf ▪ **shopping 1.** n [goods] achats mpl; **to go shopping** faire des courses; **to do one's shopping** faire ses courses **2.** adj [street, district] commerçant; **shopping bag** sac m à provisions; **shopping basket** panier m (à provisions); **shopping centre, shopping plaza** centre m commercial; TV **shopping channel** chaîne f de télé-achat; **shopping list** liste f des commissions; **shopping trolley,** Am **shopping cart** chariot m, Caddie® m; **to go on a shopping spree** aller faire du shopping

**shopsoiled** ['ʃɒpsɔɪld], Am **shopworn** ['ʃɒpwɔːn] adj qui a fait l'étalage, abîmé (en magasin)

**shore** [ʃɔː(r)] n [of sea] rivage m; [of lake] bord m; **on shore** à terre

**short** [ʃɔːt] **1.** (compar -er, superl -est) adj court; [person, distance] petit; [impatient, curt] brusque; **to be short of sth** être à court de qch; **money/time is short** l'argent / le temps manque; **a short time** or **while ago** il y a peu de temps; **Tony is short for Anthony** Tony est le diminutif d'Anthony; **in short** bref; **short cut** raccourci m; **short story** nouvelle f **2.** adv **to cut short** [hair] couper court; [visit] abréger; [person] couper la parole à; **to stop short of doing sth** se retenir tout juste de faire qch; **to be running short of sth** n'avoir presque plus de qch ▪ **shortbread** n sablé m ▪ **short-circuit 1.** n court-circuit m **2.** vt court-circuiter **3.** vi se mettre en court-circuit ▪ **shortcoming** n défaut m ▪ **shorthand** sténo f; **shorthand typist** sténodactylo m ▪ **short-lived** adj de courte durée ▪ **short-sighted** adj myope; Fig [in one's judgements] imprévoyant ▪ **short-sleeved** adj à manches courtes ▪ **short-staffed** adj à court de personnel; **to be short-staffed** manquer de personnel ▪ **short-term** adj à court terme

**shortage** ['ʃɔːtɪdʒ] n pénurie f

**shorten** ['ʃɔːtən] vt raccourcir

**shortly** ['ʃɔːtlɪ] adv [soon] bientôt; **shortly before/after** peu avant /après

**shorts** [ʃɔːts] npl (pair of) **shorts** short m; **boxer shorts** caleçon m

**shot** [ʃɒt] **1.** pp of **shoot 2.** n [from gun] coup m ; [with camera] prise f de vue ; [in football] coup m de pied ; Fam [injection] piqûre f ; **to fire a shot** tirer ; **to be a good shot** [of person] être bon tireur ; **to have a shot at sth/doing sth** essayer qch/de faire qch ▪ **shotgun** n fusil m de chasse

**should** [ʃʊd] (unstressed [ʃəd])

La forme négative **should not** s'écrit **shouldn't** en forme contractée.

v aux **a)** [expressing obligation] **you should do it** vous devriez le faire ; **I should have stayed** j'aurais dû rester **b)** [expressing possibility] **the weather should improve** le temps devrait s'améliorer ; **she should have arrived by now** elle devrait être arrivée à l'heure qu'il est **c)** [expressing preferences] **I should like to stay** j'aimerais bien rester ; **I should like to** j'aimerais bien ; **I should hope so** j'espère bien **d)** [in subordinate clauses] **it's strange (that) she should say no** il est étrange qu'elle dise non ; **he insisted that she should meet her parents** il a insisté pour qu'elle rencontre ses parents **e)** [in conditional clauses] **if he should come, should he come** s'il vient **f)** [in rhetorical questions] **why should you suspect me?** pourquoi me soupçonnez-vous ? ; **who should I meet but Martin!** et qui a-t-il fallu que je rencontre ? Martin !

**shoulder** [ˈʃəʊldə(r)] **1.** n épaule f ; **shoulder bag** sac m besace ; **shoulder pad** épaulette f ; **shoulder strap** [of garment] bretelle f **2.** vt [responsibility] endosser

**shout** [ʃaʊt] **1.** n cri m ; **to give sb a shout** appeler qn **2.** vt **to shout sth (out)** crier qch **3.** vi **to shout (out)** crier ; **to shout to sb to do sth** crier à qn de faire qch ; **to shout at sb** crier après qn ▪ **shouting** n [shouts] cris mpl

**shove** [ʃʌv] **1.** n poussée f ; **to give sb/sth a shove** pousser qn/qch **2.** vt pous-

ser ; Fam **to shove sth into sth** fourrer qch dans qch **3.** vi pousser ; Fam **to shove over** [move over] se pousser

**shovel** [ˈʃʌvəl] **1.** n pelle f **2.** (Br -ll-, Am -l-) vt pelleter ; **to shovel leaves up** ramasser des feuilles à la pelle

**show** [ʃəʊ] **1.** n [concert, play] spectacle m ; [on TV] émission f ; [exhibition] exposition f ; [of force, friendship] démonstration f ; [pretence] semblant m (of de) ; **to be on show** être exposé ; **to put sth on show** exposer qch ; **show business** le monde du spectacle ; Br **show flat** appartement m témoin ; **show jumping** jumping m **2.** (pt showed, pp shown) vt montrer (**to** à ; **that** que) ; [in exhibition] exposer ; [film] passer ; [indicate] indiquer ; **to show sb sth, to show sth to sb** montrer qch à qn ; **to show sb to the door** reconduire qn à la porte **3.** vi [be visible] se voir ; [of film] passer ▪ **showcase** [ˈʃəʊkeɪs] n vitrine f ▪ **showdown** n confrontation f ▪ **show-off** n Pej crâneur, -euse mf ▪ **showroom** n magasin m d'exposition ▪ **show-stopping** adj sensationnel, -elle ▪ **show around** vt sep **to show sb around the town/the house** faire visiter la ville/la maison à qn ▪ **show in** vt sep [visitor] faire entrer ▪ **show off 1.** vt sep Pej [display] étaler ; [highlight] faire valoir **2.** vi Pej crâner ▪ **show out** vt sep [visitor] reconduire ▪ **show round** vt sep = **show around** ▪ **show up 1.** vt sep [embarrass] faire honte à ; [reveal] faire ressortir **2.** vi [stand out] ressortir (**against** contre) ; Fam [of person] se présenter

**shower** [ˈʃaʊə(r)] **1.** n [bathing, device] douche f ; [of rain] averse f ; **to have** or **take a shower** prendre une douche ; **shower curtain** rideau m de douche ; **shower gel** gel m de douche ; **shower room** salle f d'eau **2.** vt **to shower sb with** [gifts, abuse] couvrir qn de ▪ **showery** adj pluvieux, -euse

**shown** [ʃəʊn] pp of **show**

**showy** [ˈʃəʊɪ] (compar -ier, superl -iest) adj voyant

**shrank** [ʃræŋk] pt of **shrink**

**shred** [ʃred] **1.** *n* lambeau *m*; **to tear sth to shreds** mettre qch en lambeaux; *Fig* **not a shred of truth** pas une once de vérité **2.** *(pt & pp -dd-) vt* mettre en lambeaux; [documents] déchiqueter; [food] couper grossièrement

**shrewd** [ʃruːd] *(compar -er, superl -est) adj* [person, plan] astucieux, -euse

**shriek** [ʃriːk] **1.** *n* cri *m* strident **2.** *vi* pousser un cri strident; **to shriek with pain / laughter** hurler de douleur / de rire

**shrill** [ʃril] *(compar -er, superl -est) adj* aigu (*f* aiguë)

**shrimp** [ʃrimp] *n* crevette *f*

**shrine** [ʃrain] *n* [place of worship] lieu *m* saint; [tomb] tombeau *m*

**shrink** [ʃriŋk] **1.** *(pt* shrank *or (Am)* shrunk, *pp* shrunk *or* shrunken) *vt* [of clothes] faire rétrécir **2.** *vi* rétrécir

**shrivel** [ʃrivəl] *(Br -ll-, Am -l-)* **1.** *vt* **to shrivel (up)** dessécher **2.** *vi* **to shrivel (up)** se dessécher

**shroud** [ʃraud] **1.** *n* linceul *m* **2.** *vt* **to be shrouded in sth** être enveloppé de qch

**Shrove** [ʃrəʊv] *adj* **Shrove Tuesday** mardi *m* gras

**shrub** [ʃrʌb] *n* arbuste *m*

**shrug** [ʃrʌg] **1.** *n* haussement *m* d'épaules **2.** *(pt & pp -gg-) vt* **to shrug one's shoulders** hausser les épaules; **to shrug sth off** dédaigner qch

**shrunk(en)** [ʃrʌŋk(ən)] *pp of* **shrink**

**shudder** [ʃʌdə(r)] *vi* [of person] frémir (**with** de); [of machine] vibrer

**shuffle** [ʃʌfəl] **1.** *vt* [cards] battre **2.** *vti* **to shuffle (one's feet)** traîner les pieds

**shun** [ʃʌn] *(pt & pp -nn-) vt* fuir, éviter

**shush** [ʃʊʃ] *excl* chut !

**shut** [ʃʌt] **1.** *(pt & pp* shut, *pres p* shutting) *vt* fermer **2.** *vi* [of door] se fermer; [of shop, museum] fermer ■ **shut away** *vt sep* [lock away] enfermer ■ **shut down 1.** *vt sep* fermer (définitivement); COMPUT éteindre **2.** *vi* fermer (définitivement); COMPUT éteindre ■ **shut in** *vt sep* [lock in] enfermer ■ **shut off** *vt sep* [gas, electricity]

couper; [engine] arrêter; [road] fermer; [isolate] isoler ■ **shut out** *vt sep* [keep outside] empêcher d'entrer; [exclude] exclure (**of** *or* **from** de); **to shut sb out** enfermer qn dehors ■ **shut up 1.** *vt sep* [close] fermer; [confine] enfermer; *Fam* [silence] faire taire **2.** *vi Fam* [be quiet] se taire

**shutter** [ʃʌtə(r)] *n* [on window] volet *m*; [of shop] store *m*; [of camera] obturateur *m*

**shuttle** [ʃʌtəl] **1.** *n* [bus, train, plane] navette *f*; **shuttle service** navette *f* **2.** *vi* faire la navette

**shy** [ʃai] **1.** *(compar -er, superl -est) adj* timide **2.** *vi* **to shy away from doing sth** éviter de faire qch

**sibling** [siblɪŋ] *n* [brother] frère *m*; [sister] sœur *f*

**Sicily** [sisili] *n* la Sicile

**sick** [sik] **1.** *(compar -er, superl -est) adj* [ill] malade; **to be sick** [be ill] être malade; [vomit] vomir; **to feel sick** avoir mal au cœur; **to be off sick, to be on sick leave** être en congé de maladie; **to be sick of sb / sth** en avoir assez de qn / qch; *Fig* **he makes me sick** il m'écœure **2.** *n Br Fam* [vomit] vomi *m* **3.** *npl* **the sick** [sick people] les malades *mpl*

**sicken** [sikən] **1.** *vt* écœurer **2.** *vi Br* **to be sickening for something** couver quelque chose ■ **sickening** *adj* écœurant

**sickly** [sikli] *(compar -ier, superl -iest) adj* maladif, -ive; [pale, faint] pâle; [taste] écœurant

**sickness** [siknis] *n* [illness] maladie *f*

**side** [said] **1.** *n* côté *m*; [of hill, animal] flanc *m*; [of road, river] bord *m*; [of question, character] aspect *m*; [team] équipe *f*; **at** *or* **by the side of** [nearby] à côté de; **at** *or* **by my side** à côté de moi, à mes côtés; **side by side** l'un à côté de l'autre; **to move to one side** s'écarter; **on this side of** de ce côté; **to take sides with sb** se ranger du côté de qn; **she's on our side** elle est de notre côté **2.** *adj* [lateral] latéral; [view, glance] de côté; [street] transversal; [effect, issue] secondaire **3.** *vi* **to side with sb**

se ranger du côté de qn ■ **sideboard** *n* buffet *m* ■ **sideburns** *npl* [hair] pattes *fpl* ■ **-sided** *suff* **ten-sided** à dix côtés ■ **sidelight** *n Br* [on vehicle] feu *m* de position ■ **sideline** *n* [activity] activité *f* secondaire ; [around playing field] ligne *f* de touche ■ **sidestep** *(pt & pp* -pp-*)* *vt* éviter ■ **sidetrack** *vt* distraire ; **to get sidetracked** s'écarter du sujet ■ **sidewalk** *n Am* trottoir *m* ■ **sideways** *adv* [look, walk] de côté

**siege** [siːdʒ] *n* [by soldiers, police] siège *m* ; **under siege** assiégé

**siesta** [sɪ'estə] *n* sieste *f* ; **to take** *or* **have a siesta** faire la sieste

**sieve** [sɪv] *n* tamis *m* ; [for liquids] passoire *f*

**sift** [sɪft] **1.** *vt* [flour] tamiser **2.** *vt* **to sift through** [papers] examiner (à la loupe)

**sigh** [saɪ] **1.** *n* soupir *m* **2.** *vti* soupirer

**sight** [saɪt] **1.** *n* [faculty] vue *f* ; [thing seen] spectacle *m* ; [on gun] viseur *m* ; **to lose sight of sb/sth** perdre qn / qch de vue ; **to catch sight of sb/sth** apercevoir qn/qch ; **at first sight** à première vue ; **by sight** de vue ; **in sight** [target, end, date] en vue ; **out of sight** [hidden] caché ; [no longer visible] disparu ; **he hates the sight of me** il ne peut pas me voir ; **the (tourist) sights** les attractions *fpl* touristiques ; **to set one's sights on** [job] viser **2.** *vt* [land] apercevoir

**sightseer** ['saɪtsiːə(r)] *n* touriste *mf* ■ **sightseeing** *n* **to go sightseeing, to do some sightseeing** faire du tourisme

**sign** [saɪn] **1.** *n* signe *m* ; [notice] panneau *m* ; [over shop, pub] enseigne *f* ; **no sign of** aucune trace de ; **sign language** langage *m* des signes **2.** *vt* [put signature to] signer ; **to sign on** *or* **up** [worker, soldier] engager **3.** *vi* signer ; **to sign for** [letter] signer le reçu de ; *Br* **to sign on** [on the dole] s'inscrire au chômage ; **to sign on** *or* **up** [of soldier, worker] s'engager ; [for course] s'inscrire ■ **sign off** *vi insep* **a)** RADIO & TV terminer l'émission **b)** [in letter] **I'll sign off now** je vais conclure ici

**signal** ['sɪgnəl] **1.** *n* signal *m* ; RAIL *Br* **signal box,** *Am* **signal tower** poste *m* d'aiguillage **2.** *(Br* -ll-, *Am* -l-*)* *vt* [be a sign of] indiquer ; [make gesture to] faire signe à **3.** *vi* [make gesture] faire signe **(to)** ; [of driver] mettre son clignotant ; **to signal (to) sb to do sth** faire signe à qn de faire qch

**signature** ['sɪgnətʃə(r)] *n* signature *f* ; **signature tune** indicatif *m*

**significance** [sɪg'nɪfɪkəns] *n* [meaning] signification *f* ; [importance] importance *f*

**significant** [sɪg'nɪfɪkənt] *adj* [important, large] important ; [meaningful] significatif, -ive ■ **significantly** *adv* [appreciably] sensiblement

**signify** ['sɪgnɪfaɪ] *(pt & pp* -ied*)* *vt* [mean, make known] signifier **(that** que)

**signpost** ['saɪnpəʊst] **1.** *n* poteau *m* indicateur **2.** *vt* signaliser

**silence** ['saɪləns] **1.** *n* silence *m* ; **in silence** en silence **2.** *vt* faire taire

**silent** ['saɪlənt] *adj* silencieux, -euse ; [film, anger] muet (*f* muette) ; **to keep** *or* **be silent** garder le silence **(about** sur) ■ **silently** *adv* silencieusement

**silhouette** [sɪluː'et] *n* silhouette *f*

**silicon** ['sɪlɪkən] *n* silicium *m* ; **silicon chip** puce *f* électronique

**silk** [sɪlk] *n* soie *f* ■ **silky** *(compar* -ier, *superl* -iest*)* *adj* soyeux, -euse

**sill** [sɪl] *n* [of window] rebord *m*

**silly** ['sɪlɪ] *(compar* -ier, *superl* -iest*)* *adj* bête, idiot ; **to do something silly** faire une bêtise ; **to look silly** avoir l'air ridicule

**silver** ['sɪlvə(r)] **1.** *n* argent *m* ; [plates] argenterie *f* **2.** *adj* [spoon] en argent, d'argent ; [colour] argenté ; **silver jubilee** vingt-cinquième anniversaire *m* ; *Br* **silver paper** papier *m* d'argent ■ **silver-plated** *adj* plaqué argent

**similar** ['sɪmɪlə(r)] *adj* semblable **(to** à) ■ **similarity** [-'lærətɪ] *(pl* -ies*)* *n* ressemblance *f* **(between** entre ; **to** avec) ■ **similarly** *adv* de la même façon ; [likewise] de même

**simile** ['sɪmɪlɪ] *n* comparaison *f*

**simmer** ['sɪmə(r)] **1.** *vt* [vegetables] mijoter **2.** *vi* [of vegetables] mijoter ; [of water] frémir ; *Fig* [of revolt, hatred] couver

**simple** ['sɪmpəl] *(compar* -**er**, *superl* -**est**) *adj* [easy] simple ▪ **simple-minded** *adj* simple d'esprit ▪ **simplicity** *n* simplicité *f*

**simplify** ['sɪmplɪfaɪ] *(pt & pp* -**ied**) *vt* simplifier

**simply** ['sɪmplɪ] *adv* [plainly, merely] simplement ; [absolutely] absolument

**simulate** ['sɪmjʊleɪt] *vt* simuler

**simultaneous** [*Br* sɪməl'teɪnɪəs, *Am* saɪməl'teɪnɪəs] *adj* simultané ▪ **simultaneously** [*Br* sɪməl'teɪnɪəslɪ, *Am* saɪməl'teɪnɪəslɪ] *adv* simultanément

**sin** [sɪn] **1.** *n* péché *m* **2.** *(pt & pp* -**nn**-) *vi* pécher

**since** [sɪns] **1.** *prep* [in time] depuis ; **since then** depuis **2.** *conj* [in time] depuis que ; [because] puisque ; **it's a year since I saw him** ça fait un an que je ne l'ai pas vu **3.** *adv* (ever) since depuis

**sincere** [sɪn'sɪə(r)] *adj* sincère ▪ **sincerely** *adv* sincèrement ; *Br* **yours sincerely**, *Am* **sincerely** [in letter] veuillez agréer, Madame / Monsieur, mes salutations distinguées ▪ **sincerity** [-'serətɪ] *n* sincérité *f*

**sinful** ['sɪnfəl] *adj* [act] coupable ; [waste] scandaleux, -euse

**sing** [sɪŋ] *(pt* **sang**, *pp* **sung**) *vti* chanter ▪ **singer** *n* chanteur, -euse *mf* ▪ **singing 1.** *n* [of bird, musical technique] chant *m* **2.** *adj* **singing lesson / teacher** leçon *f* / professeur *m* de chant

**singe** [sɪndʒ] *vt* [cloth] roussir ; [hair] brûler

**single** ['sɪŋgəl] **1.** *adj* [only one] seul ; [room, bed] pour une personne ; [unmarried] célibataire ; **not a single book** pas un seul livre ; **every single day** tous les jours sans exception ; **single mother, single mum** mère *f* célibataire ; *Br* **single ticket** aller *m* simple ; **single parent** père *m* / mère *f* célibataire **2.** *n Br* [ticket] aller *m* simple ; [record] single *m*; **singles** [in tennis] simples *mpl* **3.** *vt* **to single sb out** sélectionner qn ▪ **single-handedly** *adv* tout seul (*f* toute seule) ▪ **single-minded** *adj* [person] résolu ; [determination] farouche ▪ **single-sex** *adj Br* **single-sex school** école *f* non mixte ▪ **single-use** *adj* à usage unique

**singly** ['sɪŋglɪ] *adv* [one by one] un à un

**singular** ['sɪŋgjʊlə(r)] **1.** *adj* [in grammar] singulier, -ère ; [remarkable] remarquable **2.** *n* singulier *m*; **in the singular** au singulier

**sinister** ['sɪnɪstə(r)] *adj* sinistre

**sink¹** [sɪŋk] *n* [in kitchen] évier *m* ; [in bathroom] lavabo *m*

**sink²** [sɪŋk] *(pt* **sank**, *pp* **sunk**) **1.** *vt* [ship] couler **2.** *vi* [of ship, person] couler ; [of water level, sun, price] baisser ; [collapse] s'affaisser; **my heart sank** j'ai eu un pincement de cœur; **to sink (down) into** [mud] s'enfoncer dans ; [armchair] s'affaler dans; *Fam* **it hasn't sunk in yet** je n'ai / il n'a / *etc* pas encore digéré la nouvelle

**sinner** ['sɪnə(r)] *n* pécheur(eresse) *mf*

**sinus** ['saɪnəs] *n* ANAT sinus *m*

**sip** [sɪp] **1.** *n* petite gorgée *f* **2.** *(pt & pp* -**pp**-) *vt* siroter

**siphon** ['saɪfən] **1.** *n* siphon *m* **2.** *vt* **to siphon sth off** [liquid] siphonner qch ; [money] détourner qch

**sir** [sɜː(r)] *n* monsieur *m*; **Sir Walter Raleigh** [title] sir Walter Raleigh

**siren** ['saɪərən] *n* sirène *f*

**sister** ['sɪstə(r)] *n* sœur *f*; [nurse] infirmière-chef *f* ▪ **sister-in-law** *(pl* **sisters-in-law***)* belle-sœur *f*

**sit** [sɪt] *(pt & pp* **sat**, *pres p* **sitting**) **1.** *vt* [child on chair] asseoir ; *Br* [exam] se présenter à **2.** *vi* [of person] s'asseoir ; [for artist] poser (**for** pour) ; [of assembly] siéger; **to be sitting** [of person, cat] être assis; **she was sitting reading, she sat reading** elle était assise à lire ▪ **sit around** *vi* rester assis à ne rien faire ▪ **sit back** *vi* [in chair] se caler ; [rest] se détendre ; [do nothing] ne rien faire ▪ **sit down 1.** *vt* **to sit sb down** asseoir qn **2.** *vi* s'asseoir; **to be sitting down**

être assis ■ **sit for** *vt insep Br* [exam] se présenter à ■ **sit in on** *vt insep* [lecture] assister à ■ **sit on** *vt insep* [jury] être membre de ■ **sit out** *vt sep* [dance] ne pas prendre part à ■ **sit through** *vt insep* [film] rester jusqu'au bout de ■ **sit up** *vi* to sit up (**straight**) s'asseoir (bien droit); **to sit up waiting for sb** veiller jusqu'au retour de qn

**sitcom** ['sɪtkɒm] *n* sitcom *m* ou *f*

**site** [saɪt] **1.** *n* [position] emplacement *m*; [archaeological, on Internet] site *m*; (**building**) **site** chantier *m* (de construction) **2.** *vt* situer, placer

**sitting** ['sɪtɪŋ] *n* séance *f*; [in restaurant] service *m*; **sitting room** salon *m*

**situate** ['sɪtʃueɪt] *vt* situer; **to be situated** être situé ■ **situation** *n* situation *f*

**six** [sɪks] *adj* & *n* six (*m*) ■ **sixth** *adj* & *n* sixième (*mf*); **a sixth** [fraction] un sixième; *Br* SCH (**lower**) **sixth form** ≃ classe *f* de première; *Br* SCH (**upper**) **sixth form** ≃ classe *f* terminale; *Am* SCH **sixth grade** *classe du primaire pour les 10-11 ans*

**sixteen** [sɪk'stiːn] *adj* & *n* seize (*m*) ■ **sixteenth** *adj* & *n* seizième (*mf*)

**sixty** ['sɪkstɪ] *adj* & *n* soixante (*m*) ■ **sixtieth** *adj* & *n* soixantième (*mf*)

**size** [saɪz] **1.** *n* [of person, animal, clothes] taille *f*; [of shoes, gloves] pointure *f*; [of shirt] encolure *f*; [measurements] dimensions *fpl*; [of packet] grosseur *f*; [of town, damage, problem] étendue *f*; [of sum] montant *m*; **hip / chest size** tour *m* de hanches / de poitrine **2.** *vt* **to size up** [person] jauger; [situation] évaluer ■ **sizeable** *adj* non négligeable

**sizzle** ['sɪzəl] *vi* grésiller

**skanky** ['skæŋkɪ] *adj Am Fam* moche

**skate** [skeɪt] **1.** *n* [on foot] patin *m* **2.** *vi* [on ice-skates] faire du patin à glace; [on roller-skates] faire du roller ■ **skateboard** *n* planche *f* à roulettes ■ **skater** *n* patineur, -euse *mf* ■ **skating** *n* patinage *m*; **to go skating** faire du patinage

**skeleton** ['skelɪtən] *n* squelette *m*; **skeleton staff** personnel *m* minimum

**skeptical** ['skeptɪkəl] *adj Am* sceptique

**sketch** [sketʃ] **1.** *n* [drawing] croquis *m*; [comic play] sketch *m* **2.** *vt* **to sketch (out)** [idea, view] exposer brièvement **3.** *vi* faire un / des croquis ■ **sketchy** (*compar* -ier, *superl* -iest) *adj* vague

**skewer** ['skjuːə(r)] *n* [for meat] broche *f*; [for kebab] brochette *f*

**ski** [skiː] **1.** (*pl* **skis**) *n* ski *m*; **ski boot** chaussure *f* de ski; **ski lift** remonte-pente *m*; **ski mask** cagoule *f*, passe-montagne *m*; **ski pants** fuseau *m*; **ski resort** station *f* de ski; **ski run** or **slope** piste *f* de ski **2.** (*pt* **skied** [skiːd], *pres p* **skiing**) *vi* skier, faire du ski ■ **skier** *n* skieur, -euse *mf* ■ **skiing 1.** *n* [sport] ski *m* **2.** *adj* [clothes] de ski

**skid** [skɪd] **1.** *n* dérapage *m* **2.** (*pt & pp* -**dd**-) *vi* déraper; **to skid into sth** déraper et heurter qch

**skill** [skɪl] *n* [ability] qualités *fpl*; [technique] compétence *f* ■ **skilful**, *Am* **skillful** *adj* habile (**at doing** à faire; **at sth** en qch) ■ **skilled** *adj* habile (**at doing** à faire; **at sth** en qch); [worker] qualifié; [work] de spécialiste

**skim** [skɪm] (*pt & pp* -**mm**-) **1.** *vt* [milk] écrémer; [soup] écumer; **to skim (over)** **sth** [surface] effleurer qch; **skimmed milk** lait *m* écrémé **2.** *vt insep* **to skim through** [book] parcourir

**skimp** [skɪmp] *vi* [on food, fabric] lésiner (**on** sur) ■ **skimpy** (*compar* -ier, *superl* -iest) *adj* [clothes] étriqué; [meal] maigre

**skin** [skɪn] **1.** *n* peau *f*; **skin diving** plongée *f* sous-marine **2.** (*pt & pp* -**nn**-) *vt* [fruit] peler; [animal] écorcher ■ **skin-tight** *adj* moulant

**skinflint** ['skɪnflɪnt] *n* avare *mf*

**skinhead** ['skɪnhed] *n Br* skinhead *mf*

**skinny** ['skɪnɪ] (*compar* -ier, *superl* -iest) *adj* maigre

**skint** [skɪnt] *adj Br Fam* [penniless] fauché

**skip¹** [skɪp] **1.** (*pt & pp* -**pp**-) *vt* [miss, omit] sauter; **to skip classes** sécher les cours **2.** *vi* [hop about] sautiller ; *Br* [with rope] sauter à la corde ; *Br* **skipping rope** corde *f* à sauter

**skip²** [skɪp] *n Br* [for rubbish] benne *f*

**skipper** [ˈskɪpə(r)] *n* [of ship, team] capitaine *m*

**skirt** [skɜːt] *n* jupe *f*

**skittle** [ˈskɪtəl] *n Br* quille *f* ; **to play skittles** jouer aux quilles

**skulk** [skʌlk] *vi* rôder

**skull** [skʌl] *n* crâne *m*

**skunk** [skʌŋk] *n* [animal] moufette *f*

**sky** [skaɪ] *n* ciel *m* ▪ **skydiving** *n* parachutisme *m* en chute libre ▪ **skylight** *n* lucarne *f* ▪ **skyline** *n* [horizon] horizon *m* ▪ **skyscraper** *n* gratte-ciel *m inv*

**slack** [slæk] **1.** *(compar* -**er**, *superl* -**est)** *adj* [not tight] mou *(f* molle) ; [careless] négligent ; **to be slack** [of rope] avoir du mou ; **business is slack** les affaires vont mal **2.** *vi* **to slack off** [in effort] se relâcher

**slacken** [ˈslækən] **1.** *vt* **to slacken (off)** [rope] relâcher ; [pace, effort] ralentir **2.** *vi* **to slacken (off)** [in effort] se relâcher ; [of production, demand, speed, enthusiasm] diminuer

**slacker** [ˈslækə(r)] *n Fam* fainéant, -e *mf*

**slam** [slæm] **1.** *(pt & pp* -**mm**-*)* *vt* [door, lid] claquer ; [hit] frapper violemment ; **to slam sth (down)** [put down] poser qch violemment ; **to slam on the brakes** écraser la pédale de frein **2.** *vi* [of door] claquer

**slander** [ˈslɑːndə(r)] **1.** *n* calomnie *f* **2.** *vt* calomnier

**slang** [slæŋ] **1.** *n* argot *m* **2.** *adj* [word] d'argot, argotique

**slant** [slɑːnt] **1.** *n* pente *f* ; *Fig* [point of view] perspective *f* ; *Fig* [bias] parti *m* pris **2.** *vi* [of roof, handwriting] être incliné ▪ **slanted**, **slanting** *adj* penché ; [roof] en pente

**slap** [slæp] **1.** *n* [with hand] claque *f* ; **a slap in the face** une gifle **2.** *(pt & pp* -**pp**-*)* *vt* [person] donner une claque à ; **to slap sb's face** gifler qn ; **to slap sb's bottom** donner une fessée à qn

**slapdash** [ˈslæpdæʃ] *adj* [person] négligent ; [work] fait à la va-vite

**slapstick** [ˈslæpstɪk] *adj & n* **slapstick (comedy)** grosse farce *f*

**slash** [slæʃ] **1.** *n* entaille *f* **2.** *vt* [cut] taillader ; [reduce] réduire considérablement

**slat** [slæt] *n* latte *f*

**slate** [sleɪt] *n* ardoise *f*

**slaughter** [ˈslɔːtə(r)] **1.** *n* [of people] massacre *m* ; [of animal] abattage *m* **2.** *vt* [people] massacrer ; [animal] abattre ; *Fam* [defeat] massacrer

**slave** [sleɪv] **1.** *n* esclave *mf* **2.** *vi* **to slave (away)** trimer ▪ **slavery** *n* esclavage *m*

**sleazebag** [ˈsliːzbæg], **sleazeball** [ˈsliːzbɔːl] *n Fam* [despicable person] raclure *f*

**sleazy** [ˈsliːzɪ] *(compar* -**ier**, *superl* -**iest)** *adj Fam* sordide

**sledge** [sledʒ], *Am* **sled** [sled] *n Br* luge *f*

**sledgehammer** [ˈsledʒhæmə(r)] *n* masse *f*

**sleek** [sliːk] *(compar* -**er**, *superl* -**est)** *adj* [smooth] lisse et brillant ; *Pej* [manner] mielleux, -euse

**sleep** [sliːp] **1.** *n* sommeil *m* ; **to have a sleep, to get some sleep** dormir ; **to go to sleep** [of person] s'endormir ; **to put an animal to sleep** [kill] faire piquer un animal **2.** *(pt & pp* **slept***)* *vi* dormir ; *Euph* **to sleep with sb** coucher avec qn **3.** *vt* **this flat sleeps six** on peut dormir à six dans cet appartement ▪ **sleeping** *adj* [asleep] endormi ; **sleeping bag** sac *m* de couchage ; **sleeping car** wagon-lit *m* ; **sleeping pill** somnifère *m*

**sleeper** [ˈsliːpə(r)] *n* **a)** **to be a light / sound sleeper** avoir le sommeil léger / lourd **b)** *Br* RAIL [on track] traverse *f* ; [bed in train] couchette *f* ; [train] train-couchettes *m* ▪ **sleepless** *adj* [night] d'insomnie

**sleepy** [ˈsliːpɪ] *(compar* -**ier**, *superl* -**iest)** *adj* [town, voice] endormi ; **to be sleepy** [of person] avoir sommeil

**sleet** [sliːt] **1.** *n* neige *f* fondue **2.** *vi* **it's sleeting** il tombe de la neige fondue

**sleeve** [sli:v] n [of shirt, jacket] manche f; [of record] pochette f; **long-/short-sleeved** à manches longues / courtes

**sleigh** [sleɪ] n traîneau m

**slender** ['slendə(r)] adj [person] svelte; [neck, hand, waist] fin; Fig [small, feeble] faible

**slept** [slept] pt & pp of **sleep**

**slice** [slaɪs] **1.** n tranche f; Fig [portion] part f **2.** vt **to slice sth (up)** couper qch en tranches; **to slice sth off** couper qch

**slick** [slɪk] **1.** (compar -er, superl -est) adj [campaign] bien mené; [reply, person] habile **2.** n [on beach] marée f noire

**slide** [slaɪd] **1.** n [in playground] toboggan m; [for hair] barrette f; PHOTO diapositive f; [in prices, popularity] baisse f **2.** (pt & pp slid [slɪd]) vt glisser (**into** dans); [table, chair] faire glisser **3.** vi glisser ■ **sliding** adj [door, panel] coulissant

**slight** [slaɪt] **1.** (compar -er, superl -est) adj [small, unimportant] léger, -ère; [chance] faible; **the slightest thing** la moindre chose; **not in the slightest** pas le moins du monde **2.** n affront m (**on** à) **3.** vt [offend] offenser; [ignore] bouder

**slightly** ['slaɪtlɪ] adv légèrement

**slim** [slɪm] **1.** (compar slimmer, superl slimmest) adj mince **2.** (pt & pp -mm-) vi Br suivre un régime

**slime** [slaɪm] n vase f; [of snail] bave f ■ **slimy** (compar -ier, superl -iest) adj [muddy] boueux (f boueuse); Fig [sticky, smarmy] visqueux, -euse

**slimeball** ['slaɪmbɔ:l] Am v Fam n = **sleazebag**

**sling** [slɪŋ] **1.** n [weapon] fronde f; [for injured arm] écharpe f; **in a sling** en écharpe **2.** (pt & pp slung) vt [throw] lancer

**slip** [slɪp] **1.** n [mistake] erreur f; [garment] combinaison f; [fall] chute f; **a slip of paper** un bout de papier; [printed] un bordereau; **a slip of the tongue** un lapsus; Br **slip road** bretelle f **2.** (pt & pp -pp-) vt [slide] glisser (**to** à; **into** dans); **it slipped my mind** ça m'est sorti de l'esprit **3.** vi glisser; Fam [of popularity, ratings] baisser; **to let sth slip** [chance, secret] laisser échapper qch ■ **slip away** vi [escape] s'éclipser ■ **slip into** vt insep [room] se glisser dans; [bathrobe] passer ■ **slip off** vt sep [coat] enlever ■ **slip on** vt sep [coat] mettre ■ **slip out** vi [leave] sortir furtivement; [for a moment] sortir (un instant); [of secret] s'éventer ■ **slip up** vi Fam se planter

**slipper** ['slɪpə(r)] n pantoufle f

**slippery** ['slɪpərɪ] adj glissant

**slippy** ['slɪpɪ] (compar -ier, superl -iest) adj [slippery] glissant

**slit** [slɪt] **1.** n fente f **2.** (pt & pp slit, pres p slitting) vt [cut] couper; **to slit open** [sack] éventrer

**slither** ['slɪðə(r)] vi glisser; [of snake] se couler

**slob** [slɒb] n Fam [lazy person] gros fainéant m; [dirty person] porc m

**slobber** ['slɒbə(r)] vi [of dog, baby] baver

**slog** [slɒg] Br Fam **1.** n **a (hard) slog** [effort] un gros effort **2.** (pt & pp -gg-) vi **to slog (away)** trimer

**slogan** ['sləʊgən] n slogan m

**slop** [slɒp] **1.** (pt & pp -pp-) vt renverser **2.** vi **to slop (over)** se renverser

**slope** [sləʊp] **1.** n pente f; [of mountain] versant m; [for skiing] piste f **2.** vi [of ground, roof] être en pente ■ **sloping** adj [roof] en pente

**sloppy** ['slɒpɪ] (compar -ier, superl -iest) adj [work, appearance] négligé; [person] négligent; [sentimental] sentimental

**slot** [slɒt] **1.** n [slit] fente f; [in schedule, list] créneau m; **slot machine** [for vending] distributeur m automatique; [for gambling] machine f à sous **2.** (pt & pp -tt-) vt [insert] insérer (**into** dans) **3.** vi s'insérer (**into** dans)

**slouch** [slaʊtʃ] vi ne pas se tenir droit; [in chair] être avachi

**slovenly** ['slʌvənlɪ] adj négligé

**slow** [sləʊ] **1.** (compar -er, superl -est) adj lent; **in slow motion** au ralenti; **to be slow** [of clock, watch] retarder; **business is slow** les affaires tournent au ralenti **2.** adv lentement **3.** vt **to slow sth down** or **up** ralentir qch; [delay]

retarder qch **4.** *vi* **to slow down** *or* **up** ralentir ■ **slowcoach** *n Br Fam* lambin, -e *mf* ■ **slow-cook** *vt* mitonner, mijoter ■ **slowly** *adv* lentement ; [bit by bit] peu à peu

**sludge** [slʌdʒ] *n* gadoue *f*

**slug** [slʌg] **1.** *n* **a)** [mollusc] limace *f* **b)** *Am Fam* [bullet] pruneau *m* **2.** *(pt & pp* -**gg**-*) vt Am Fam* [hit] frapper

**sluggish** ['slʌgɪʃ] *adj* [person] amorphe ; **business is sluggish** les affaires ne marchent pas très bien

**slum** [slʌm] *n* [house] taudis *m* ; **the slums** les quartiers *mpl* délabrés

**slump** [slʌmp] **1.** *n* baisse *f* soudaine (**in** de) ; [in prices] effondrement *m* ; [economic depression] crise *f* **2.** *vi* [of person, prices] s'effondrer

**slung** [slʌŋ] *pt & pp of* **sling**

**slur** [slɜː(r)] **1.** *n* [insult] insulte *f* **2.** *(pt & pp* -**rr**-*) vt* mal articuler ■ **slurred** *adj* [speech] indistinct

**slush** [slʌʃ] *n* [snow] neige *f* fondue

**slut** [slʌt] *n Pej* [promiscuous woman] salope *f* ; [untidy woman] souillon *f*

**sly** [slaɪ] **1.** *(compar* -**er***, superl* -**est***) adj* [deceitful] sournois ; [cunning, crafty] rusé **2.** *n* **on the sly** en douce

**smack** [smæk] **1.** *n* [blow] claque *f* ; [on bottom] fessée *f* **2.** *vt* [person] donner une claque à ; **to smack sb's face** gifler qn ; **to smack sb('s bottom)** donner une fessée à qn **3.** *vi* **to smack of** [be suggestive of] avoir des relents de

**small** [smɔːl] **1.** *(compar* -**er***, superl* -**est***) adj* petit ; *Br* **small ads** petites annonces *fpl* ; **small change** petite monnaie *f* ; **small talk** banalités *fpl* **2.** *adv* [cut, chop] menu ; [write] petit **3.** *n* **the small of the back** la chute des reins ■ **small-minded** *adj* à l'esprit étroit ■ **small-scale** *adj* [model] réduit ; [research] à petite échelle

**smallpox** ['smɔːlpɒks] *n* variole *f*

**smarmy** ['smɑːmɪ] *(compar* -**ier***, superl* -**iest***) adj Fam & Pej* obséquieux, -euse

**smart¹** [smɑːt] *(compar* -**er***, superl* -**est***) adj* [in appearance] élégant ; [clever] intelligent ; [astute] astucieux, -euse ; [quick] rapide ; **smart card** carte *f* à puce

**smart²** [smɑːt] *vi* [sting] brûler

**smarten** ['smɑːtən] **1.** *vt* **to smarten sth up** égayer qch **2.** *vti* **to smarten (oneself) up** se faire beau (*f* belle)

**smartly** ['smɑːtlɪ] *adv* [dressed] avec élégance

**smartphone** ['smɑːtfəʊn] *n* smartphone *m* ; **the smartphone market** le marché des smartphones

**smash** [smæʃ] **1.** *n* [accident] collision *f* ; [in tennis] smash *m* **2.** *vt* [break] briser ; [shatter] fracasser ; [record] pulvériser **3.** *vi* **to smash into sth** [of vehicle] entrer dans qch ; **to smash into pieces** éclater en mille morceaux ■ **smash-up** *n* collision *f* ■ **smash down**, **smash in** *vt sep* [door] enfoncer ■ **smash up** *vt sep* [vehicle] esquinter

**smashing** ['smæʃɪŋ] *adj Br Fam* [wonderful] génial

**smattering** ['smætərɪŋ] *n* **a smattering of French** quelques notions *fpl* de français

**smear** [smɪə(r)] **1.** *n* [mark] trace *f* **2.** *vt* [coat] enduire (**with** de) ; [stain] tacher (**with** de) ; [smudge] faire une trace sur ; **to smear sb** calomnier qn

**smell** [smel] **1.** *n* odeur *f* ; (sense of) **smell** odorat *m* **2.** *(pt & pp* **smelled** *or* **smelt***) vt* sentir ; [of animal] flairer **3.** *vi* [stink] sentir mauvais ; [have a smell] sentir ; **to smell of smoke** sentir la fumée ■ **smelly** *(compar* -**ier***, superl* -**iest***) adj* **to be smelly** sentir mauvais

**smelt** [smelt] *pt & pp of* **smell**

**smile** [smaɪl] **1.** *n* sourire *m* **2.** *vi* sourire (**at sb** à qn ; **at sth** de qch)

**smirk** [smɜːk] *n* [smug] sourire *m* suffisant ; [scornful] sourire *m* goguenard

**smog** [smɒg] *n* smog *m*

**smoke** [sməʊk] **1.** *n* fumée *f* ; **to have a smoke** fumer ; **smoke detector** *or* **alarm** détecteur *m* de fumée **2.** *vt* [cigarette] fumer ; **smoked salmon** saumon *m* fumé **3.** *vi* fumer ; '**no**

**smoking'** 'défense de fumer'; **smoking compartment** [on train] compartiment *m* fumeurs ■ **smoker** *n* fumeur, -euse *mf* ■ **smoky** *(compar* -ier, *superl* -iest) *adj* [room, air] enfumé

**smooth** [smuːð] **1.** *(compar* -er, *superl* -est) *adj* [surface, skin] lisse; [cream, sauce] onctueux, -euse; [sea, flight] calme; *Pej* [person, manners] doucereux, -euse; **the smooth running of** [machine, service, business] la bonne marche de **2.** *vt* **to smooth sth down** [hair, sheet, paper] lisser qch; **to smooth sth out** [paper, sheet, dress] lisser qch; [crease] faire disparaître qch ■ **smoothly** *adv* [without problems] sans problèmes

**smoothie** ['smuːðɪ] *n* CULIN smoothie *m* *(boisson glacée aux fruits)*

**smother** ['smʌðə(r)] *vt* [stifle] étouffer; **to smother sth in sth** recouvrir qch de qch

**smoulder,** *Am* **smolder** ['sməʊldə(r)] *vi* [of fire, passion] couver

**SMS** [ˌesem'es] *(abbr of* **short message service)** *n* sms *m*, texto *m*, minimessage *m*

**smudge** [smʌdʒ] **1.** *n* tache *f* **2.** *vt* [paper] faire des taches sur; [ink] étaler

**smug** [smʌg] *(compar* smugger, *superl* smuggest) *adj* [person] content de soi

**smuggle** ['smʌgəl] *vt* passer en fraude; **smuggled goods** contrebande *f* ■ **smuggler** *n* contrebandier, -ère *mf*; [of drugs] trafiquant, -e *mf* ■ **smuggling** *n* contrebande *f*

**smut** [smʌt] *n inv* [obscenity] cochonneries *fpl* ■ **smutty** *(compar* -ier, *superl* -iest) *adj* [joke] cochon, -onne

**snack** [snæk] *n* [meal] casse-croûte *m inv*; **snack bar** snack-bar *m* ■ **snacking** ['snækɪŋ] *n fait de manger entre les repas*; **is snacking healthy?** est-ce qu'il est sain de grignoter entre les repas?

**snag** [snæg] *n* [hitch] problème *m*

**snail** [sneɪl] *n* escargot *m*; *Fam* COMPUT **snail mail** poste *f*

**snake** [sneɪk] *n* serpent *m*

**snap** [snæp] **1.** *n Fam* [photo] photo *f*; **snap fastener** pression *f*; **cold snap** coup *m* de froid **2.** *adj* [judgement, decision] hâtif, -ive **3.** *(pt & pp* -pp-) *vt* [break] casser net; [fingers] faire claquer; **to snap up a bargain** sauter sur une occasion **4.** *vi* se casser net; *Fig* [of person] parler sèchement (at à); **to snap off** se casser net; *Fam* **snap out of it!** secoue-toi!

**snare** [sneə(r)] *n* piège *m*

**snarky** ['snɑːkɪ] *adj Fam* hargneux, -euse *m,f*

**snarl** [snɑːl] *vi* grogner (en montrant les dents)

**snatch** [snætʃ] *vt* [grab] saisir; [steal] arracher; **to snatch sth from sb** arracher qch à qn

**sneak** [sniːk] **1.** *n Br Fam* [telltale] mouchard, -e *mf* **2.** *(pt & pp* sneaked, *Am pt & pp* snuck) *vi Br Fam* [tell tales] rapporter; **to sneak in/out** entrer/sortir furtivement; **to sneak off** s'esquiver

**sneaker** ['sniːkə(r)] *n Am* [shoe] chaussure *f* de sport

**sneer** [snɪə(r)] *vi* ricaner; **to sneer at sb/sth** se moquer de qn/qch

**sneeze** [sniːz] *vi* éternuer

**snicker** ['snɪkə(r)] *Am vi* = **snigger**

**snickerdoodle** ['snɪkəduːdl] *n Am* CULIN *cookie à la cannelle*

**snide** [snaɪd] *adj* méprisant

**sniff** [snɪf] **1.** *vt* renifler; **to sniff glue** sniffer de la colle **2.** *vi* renifler

**sniffle** ['snɪfəl] **1.** *n Fam* **to have the sniffles** avoir un petit rhume **2.** *vi* renifler

**snigger** ['snɪgə(r)] *vi* ricaner

**snip** [snɪp] **1.** *n* [cut] petite entaille *f*; *Br Fam* [bargain] bonne affaire *f* **2.** *(pt & pp* -pp-) *vt* **to snip sth (off)** couper qch

**snivel** ['snɪvəl] *(Br* -ll-, *Am* -l-) *vi* pleurnicher

**snob** [snɒb] *n* snob *mf* ■ **snobbish** *adj* snob *inv*

**snooker** ['snuːkə(r)] *n* [game] *billard qui se joue avec vingt-deux billes*

**snoop** [snuːp] *vi* fouiner; **to snoop on sb** espionner qn

**snooze** [snu:z] **1.** *n* petit somme *m*; **to have a snooze** faire un petit somme **2.** *vi* faire un petit somme

**snore** [snɔ:(r)] *vi* ronfler ■ **snoring** *n* ronflements *mpl*

**snorkel** ['snɔ:kəl] **1.** *n* tuba *m* **2.** *(Br-ll-, Am-l-)vi* nager sous l'eau avec un tuba

**snort** [snɔ:t] *vi* [of person] grogner; [of horse] s'ébrouer

**snot** [snɒt] *n Fam* morve *f*

**snout** [snaʊt] *n* museau *m*

**snow** [snəʊ] **1.** *n* neige *f* **2.** *vi* it's snowing il neige **3.** *vt* to be snowed in être bloqué par la neige; *Fig* to be snowed under with work être submergé de travail ■ **snowball 1.** *n* boule *f* de neige **2.** *vi* [increase] faire boule de neige ■ **snowdrop** *n* [flower] perce-neige *m ou f inv* ■ **snowflake** *n* flocon *m* de neige ■ **snowman** *(pl* -men*) n* bonhomme *m* de neige ■ **snowplough,** *Am* **snowplow** *n* chasse-neige *m inv* ■ **snowshoe** *n* raquette *f* ■ **snowstorm** *n* tempête *f* de neige

**snub** [snʌb] **1.** *n* rebuffade *f* **2.** *(pt & pp* -bb-*) vt* [offer] rejeter; **to snub sb** snober qn **3.** *adj* **snub nose** nez *m* retroussé

**snuck** [snʌk] *Am pt & pp of* **sneak**

**snuff** [snʌf] **1.** *n* tabac *m* à priser **2.** *vt* to **snuff (out)** [candle] moucher

**snug** [snʌg] *(compar* snugger*, superl* snuggest*) adj* [house] douillet, -ette; [garment] bien ajusté

**snuggle** ['snʌgəl] *vi* to snuggle up to sb se blottir contre qn

**so** [səʊ] **1.** *adv* [to such a degree] si, tellement (**that** que); [thus] ainsi, comme ça; **to work/drink so much that...** travailler/boire tellement que...; **so much courage** tellement de courage (**that** que); **so many books** tant de livres (**that** que); **and so on** et ainsi de suite; **I think so** je crois que oui; **is that so?** c'est vrai?; **so am I** moi aussi; **I told you so** je vous l'avais bien dit; *Fam* **so long!** au revoir! **2.** *conj* [therefore] donc; [in that case] alors; **so what?** et alors?; **so that...** pour que... (+ *subjunctive*); **so as to do sth** pour faire qch ■ **So-and-So** *n* **Mr So-and-so** Monsieur Untel ■ **so-called** *adj* soi-disant *inv* ■ **so-so** *adj & adv Fam* comme ci comme ça

**soak** [səʊk] **1.** *vt* [drench] tremper; [washing, food] faire tremper; **to be soaked (through** *or* **to the skin)** être trempé (jusqu'aux os); **to soak sth up** absorber qch **2.** *vi* [of washing] tremper ■ **soaking** *adj & adv* **soaking (wet)** trempé

**soap** [səʊp] *n* savon *m*; **soap opera** feuilleton *m* populaire; **soap powder** lessive *f* ■ **soapsuds** *npl* mousse *f* de savon

**soar** [sɔ:(r)] *vi* [of bird] s'élever; [of price] monter en flèche

**sob** [sɒb] **1.** *n* sanglot *m* **2.** *(pt & pp* -bb-*) vi* sangloter

**sober** ['səʊbə(r)] **1.** *adj* [sensible] sobre; **he's sober** [not drunk] il n'est pas ivre **2.** *vti* to sober up dessoûler

**soccer** ['sɒkə(r)] *n* football *m*

**sociable** ['səʊʃəbəl] *adj* [person] sociable; [evening] amical

**social** ['səʊʃəl] *adj* social; **to have a good social life** sortir beaucoup; **social media** médias *mpl* sociaux; **social network** réseau *m* social; **social networking** réseautage *m* social; **Social Security** ≃ la Sécurité sociale; **social security** [aid] aide *f* sociale; *Am* [retirement pension] pension *f* de retraite; **the social services** les services *mpl* sociaux; **social welfare** protection *f* sociale; **social worker** assistant, -e *mf* social(e)

**socialist** ['səʊʃəlɪst] *adj & n* socialiste *(mf)*

**socialize** ['səʊʃəlaɪz] *vi* fréquenter des gens; **to socialize with sb** fréquenter qn

**socially** ['səʊʃəlɪ] *adv* socialement; [meet] en société; **socially responsible** socialement responsable; **socially responsible investment** *(SRI)* investissement socialement responsable *(ISR)*

**society** [sə'saɪətɪ] *(pl* -ies*) n* [community, club, companionship] société *f*; [school/university club] club *m*; **(high) society** haute société *f*

**sociology** [səʊsɪˈɒlədʒɪ] *n* sociologie *f*

**sock** [sɒk] *n* chaussette *f*

**socket** ['sɒkɪt] *n Br* [of electric plug] prise *f* de courant; *Br* [of lamp] douille *f*

**soda** ['səʊdə] *n Am* **soda (pop)** boisson *f* gazeuse; **soda (water)** eau *f* de Seltz

**sofa** ['səʊfə] *n* canapé *m*; **sofa bed** canapé-lit *m*

**soft** [sɒft] *(compar* -er, *superl* -est) *adj* [gentle, not stiff] doux (*f* douce); [butter, ground, paste, snow] mou (*f* molle); [wood, heart, colour] tendre; [indulgent] indulgent; **soft drink** boisson *f* non alcoolisée; **soft drugs** drogues *fpl* douces; **soft toy** peluche *f* ▪ **soft-boiled** *adj* [egg] à la coque

**softball** ['sɒftbɔːl] *n* sorte de base-ball

**soften** ['sɒfən] **1.** *vt* [object] ramollir; [colour, light, voice, skin] adoucir **2.** *vi* ramollir ▪ **softener** *n* adoucissant *m*

**softly** ['sɒftlɪ] *adv* doucement

**software** ['sɒftweə(r)] *n inv* COMPUT logiciel *m*; **software licence** licence *f* logicielle; **software package** progiciel *m*

**soggy** ['sɒgɪ] *(compar* -ier, *superl* -iest) *adj* trempé

**soil** [sɔɪl] **1.** *n* [earth] terre *f* **2.** *vt* [dirty] salir

**solar** ['səʊlə(r)] *adj* solaire; **solar power** énergie *f* solaire; **solar system** système *m* solaire

**sold** [səʊld] *pt & pp of* **sell**

**soldier** ['səʊldʒə(r)] *n* soldat *m*

**sole¹** [səʊl] **1.** *n* [of shoe] semelle *f*; [of foot] plante *f* **2.** *vt* [shoe] ressemeler

**sole²** [səʊl] *adj* [only] unique; [rights, representative, responsibility] exclusif, -ive ▪ **solely** *adv* uniquement

**solemn** ['sɒləm] *adj* solennel, -elle

**solicit** [səˈlɪsɪt] **1.** *vt* [seek] solliciter **2.** *vi* [of prostitute] racoler

**solicitor** [səˈlɪsɪtə(r)] *n Br* [for wills] notaire *m*

**solid** ['sɒlɪd] **1.** *adj* [not liquid] solide; [not hollow] plein; [gold, silver] massif, -ive **2.** *adv* **frozen solid** complètement gelé; **ten days solid** dix jours

d'affilée **3.** *n* solide *m*; **solids** [food] aliments *mpl* solides ▪ **solidly** *adv* [built] solidement; [work] sans interruption

**solidarity** [sɒlɪˈdærətɪ] *n* solidarité *f* (**with** avec)

**solitary** ['sɒlɪtərɪ] *adj* [lonely, alone] solitaire; [only] seul ▪ **solitude** *n* solitude *f*

**solo** ['səʊləʊ] **1.** *(pl* -os) *n* MUS solo *m*; **solo parent** [father] père *m* célibataire; [mother] mère *f* célibataire **2.** *adj* [guitar, violin] solo *inv* **3.** *adv* [play, sing] en solo; [fly] en solitaire ▪ **soloist** *n* MUS soliste *mf*

**soluble** ['sɒljʊbəl] *adj* [substance, problem] soluble

**solution** [səˈluːʃən] *n* **a)** [to problem] solution *f* (**to** de) **b)** [liquid] solution *f*

**solve** [sɒlv] *vt* [problem] résoudre

**solvent** ['sɒlvənt] **1.** *adj* [financially] solvable **2.** *n* CHEM solvant *m*

**sombre**, *Am* **somber** ['sɒmbə(r)] *adj* sombre

**some** [sʌm] **1.** *adj* **a)** [a quantity of] du, de la, des; **some wine** du vin; **some water** de l'eau; **some dogs** des chiens; **some pretty flowers** de jolies fleurs **b)** [unspecified] un, une; **some man (or other)** un homme (quelconque); **for some reason or other** pour une raison ou pour une autre; **I have been waiting some time** ça fait un moment que j'attends **c)** [a few] quelques; [in contrast to others] certains; **some days ago** il y a quelques jours; **some people think that...** certains pensent que... **2.** *pron* **a)** [a certain quantity] en; **I want some** j'en veux; **some of my wine** un peu de mon vin; **some of the time** une partie du temps **b)** [as opposed to others] certain(e)s; **some say...** certains disent...; **some of the guests** certains invités **3.** *adv* [about] environ; **some ten years** environ dix ans

▪ **somebody** *pron* quelqu'un; **somebody small** quelqu'un de petit

▪ **someday** *adv* un jour

■ **somehow** *adv* [in some way] d'une manière ou d'une autre ; [for some reason] on ne sait pourquoi

■ **someone** *pron* quelqu'un ; **someone small** quelqu'un de petit

■ **someplace** *adv* *Am* quelque part

■ **something 1.** *pron* quelque chose ; **something awful** quelque chose d'affreux **2.** *adv* **she plays something like...** elle joue un peu comme...

■ **sometime** *adv* un jour ; **sometime in May** au mois de mai

■ **sometimes** *adv* quelquefois, parfois

■ **somewhat** *adv* quelque peu, assez

■ **somewhere** *adv* quelque part ; **somewhere about fifteen** [approximately] environ quinze

**somersault** ['sʌməsɔːlt] *n* [on ground] roulade *f* ; [in air] saut *m* périlleux

**son** [sʌn] *n* fils *m* ■ **son-in-law** (*pl* **sons-in-law**) *n* gendre *m*

**sonata** [sə'nɑːtə] *n* sonate *f*

**song** [sɒŋ] *n* chanson *f* ; [of bird] chant *m*

**soon** [suːn] (*compar* **-er**, *superl* **-est**) *adv* [in a short time] bientôt ; [quickly] vite ; [early] tôt ; **soon after** peu après ; **as soon as...** aussitôt que... ; **no sooner had he spoken than...** à peine avait-il parlé que... ; **I'd sooner leave** je préférerais partir ; **sooner or later** tôt ou tard

**soot** [sʊt] *n* suie *f*

**soothe** [suːð] *vt* calmer

**sophisticated** [sə'fɪstɪkeɪtɪd] *adj* [person, taste] raffiné ; [machine, method] sophistiqué

**sophomore** ['sɒfəmɔː(r)] *n* *Am* étudiant, -e *mf* de deuxième année

**sopping** ['sɒpɪŋ] *adj* & *adv* **sopping (wet)** trempé

**soppy** ['sɒpɪ] (*compar* **-ier**, *superl* **-iest**) *adj* *Br Fam* [sentimental] sentimental

**soprano** [sə'prɑːnəʊ] (*pl* **-os**) *n* [singer] soprano *mf*

**sordid** ['sɔːdɪd] *adj* sordide

**sore** [sɔː(r)] **1.** (*compar* **-er**, *superl* **-est**) *adj* [painful] douloureux, -euse ; *Am* [angry] fâché (**at** contre) ; **to have a sore throat** avoir mal à la gorge **2.** *n* [wound] plaie *f*

**sorrow** ['sɒrəʊ] *n* chagrin *m*

**sorry** ['sɒrɪ] (*compar* **-ier**, *superl* **-iest**) *adj* [sight, state] triste ; **to be sorry (about sth)** [regret] être désolé (de qch) ; **to feel** *or* **be sorry for sb** plaindre qn ; **I'm sorry she can't come** je regrette qu'elle ne puisse pas venir ; **sorry!** pardon ! ; **to say sorry** demander pardon (**to** à)

**sort¹** [sɔːt] *n* sorte *f* ; **a sort of** une sorte de ; **all sorts of** toutes sortes de ; **what sort of drink is it?** qu'est-ce que c'est comme boisson ? ; **sort of sad** [somewhat] plutôt triste

**sort²** [sɔːt] **1.** *vt* [papers] trier ; **to sort out** [classify, select] trier ; [separate] séparer (**from** de) ; [organize] ranger ; [problem] régler **2.** *vi* **to sort through letters/magazines** trier des lettres / magazines

**sought** [sɔːt] *pt* & *pp of* **seek**

**soul** [səʊl] *n* âme *f*

**sound¹** [saʊnd] **1.** *n* son *m* ; [noise] bruit *m* ; **sound effects** bruitage *m* **2.** *vt* [bell, alarm] sonner ; [bugle] sonner de ; **to sound one's horn** [in vehicle] klaxonner **3.** *vi* [seem] sembler ; **to sound like** sembler être ; [resemble] ressembler à ; **it sounds like** *or* **as if...** il semble que... (+ *subjunctive or indicative*)

**sound²** [saʊnd] **1.** (*compar* **-er**, *superl* **-est**) *adj* [healthy] sain ; [in good condition] en bon état ; [basis] solide ; [argument] valable ; [advice] bon (*f* bonne) ; [investment] sûr **2.** *adv* **sound asleep** profondément endormi ■ **soundly** *adv* [asleep, sleep] profondément

**sound³** [saʊnd] *vt* [test, measure] sonder ■ **sound out** *vt sep* **to sound sb out (on** *or* **about)** sonder qn (sur)

**soundproof** ['saʊndpruːf] **1.** *adj* insonorisé **2.** *vt* insonoriser

**soundtrack** ['saʊndtræk] *n* [of film] bande *f* sonore

**soup** [suːp] *n* soupe *f* ; **soup dish** *or* **plate** assiette *f* creuse

**sour** ['saʊə(r)] *(compar* -er, *superl* -est)
*adj* aigre ; [milk] tourné ; **to turn sour**
[of milk] tourner ; [of friendship] se
détériorer

**source** [sɔːs] *n* [origin] source *f*

**south** [saʊθ] **1.** *n* sud *m* ; **(to the) south
of** au sud de **2.** *adj* [coast] sud *inv* ;
[wind] du sud ; **South America/Africa**
l'Amérique *f*/l'Afrique *f* du Sud ; **South
American** [adj] sud-américain ; [n]
Sud-Américain, -e *mf* ; **South African**
[adj] sudafricain ; [n] Sud-Africain,
-e *mf* **3.** *adv* au sud ; [travel] vers le sud
■ **southbound** *adj* [traffic] en direction du sud ; *Br* [carriageway] le sud de
■ **south-east** *n* & *adj* sud-est *(m)*
■ **southerly** *adj* [direction] du sud
■ **southern** ['sʌðən] *adj* [town] du sud ;
[coast] sud *inv* ; **Southern Italy** le sud de
l'Italie ■ **southerner** ['sʌðənə(r)] *n* habitant, -e *mf* du sud ■ **southward(s)**
*adj* & *adv* vers le sud ■ **south-west** *n*
& *adj* sud-ouest *(m)*

**souvenir** [suːvə'nɪə(r)] *n* souvenir *m*

**sovereign** ['sɒvrɪn] *n* [monarch] souverain, -e *mf* ■ **sovereignty** [-rəntɪ] *n*
souveraineté *f*

**sow**[1] [saʊ] *n* [pig] truie *f*

**sow**[2] [səʊ] *(pt* sowed, *pp* sowed *or* sown
[səʊn]) *vt* [seeds, doubt] semer ; [land]
ensemencer (**with** de)

**soya** ['sɔɪə] *n* *Br* soja *m* ; **soya bean**
graine *f* de soja ■ **soybean** *n* *Am*
graine *f* de soja

**spa** [spɑː] *n* [town] station *f* thermale

**space** [speɪs] **1.** *n* [gap, emptiness,
atmosphere] espace *m* ; [for parking]
place *f* ; **to take up space** prendre de la
place ; **blank space** espace *m*, blanc *m* ;
**space bar** [on keyboard] barre *f* d'espacement **2.** *adj* [voyage, capsule] spatial
**3.** *vt* **to space out** espacer ■ **spaceship** *n* vaisseau *m* spatial ■ **spacing**
*n* TYP **in double/single spacing** à
double/simple interligne

**spacious** ['speɪʃəs] *adj* spacieux, -euse

**spade** [speɪd] *n* **a)** [for garden] bêche *f*
**b)** CARDS **spade(s)** pique *m*

**spaghetti** [spə'ɡetɪ] *n* spaghettis *mpl*

**Spain** [speɪn] *n* l'Espagne *f*

**span** [spæn] *(pt & pp* -nn-) *vt* [of bridge]
enjamber ; *Fig* [in time] couvrir

**Spaniard** ['spænjəd] *n* Espagnol, -e *mf*
■ **Spanish 1.** *adj* espagnol **2.** *n* [lan-
guage] espagnol *m*

**spank** [spæŋk] *vt* donner une tape sur
les fesses à ■ **spanking** *n* fessée *f*

**spanner** ['spænə(r)] *n* *Br* [tool] clef *f*

**spare** [speə(r)] **1.** *adj* [extra, surplus]
de *ou* en trop ; [reserve] de rechange ;
[wheel] de secours ; [available] disponible ; **spare room** chambre *f* d'ami ;
**spare time** loisirs *mpl* **2.** *n* **spare (part)**
[for vehicle, machine] pièce *f* détachée
**3.** *vt* [do without] se passer de ; [efforts,
sb's feelings] ménager ; **to spare sb sth**
[grief, details] épargner qch à qn ; **I can't
spare the time** je n'ai pas le temps ;
**with five minutes to spare** avec cinq
minutes d'avance

**sparingly** ['speərɪŋlɪ] *adv* en petite
quantité

**spark** [spɑːk] **1.** *n* étincelle *f* ; AUTO **spark
plug** bougie *f* **2.** *vt* **to spark off** [cause]
provoquer

**sparkle** ['spɑːkəl] *vi* briller ; [of diamond,
star] scintiller ■ **sparkling** *adj* [wine,
water] pétillant

**sparrow** ['spærəʊ] *n* moineau *m*

**sparse** [spɑːs] *adj* clairsemé ■ **sparsely** *adv* [populated] peu ; **sparsely furnished** à peine meublé

**spasm** ['spæzəm] *n* [of muscle] spasme *m*

**spat** [spæt] *pt & pp of* spit

**spate** [speɪt] *n* **a spate of sth** [of letters,
calls] une avalanche de qch ; [of crimes]
une vague de qch

**spatter** ['spætə(r)] *vt* [clothes, person]
éclabousser (**with** de)

**speak** [spiːk] **1.** *(pt* spoke, *pp* spoken) *vt*
[language] parler ; [say] dire ; **to speak
one's mind** dire ce que l'on pense **2.** *vi*
parler (**about** *or* **of** de) ; [formally, in as-
sembly] prendre la parole ; **so to speak**
pour ainsi dire ; **that speaks for itself**
c'est évident ; **Jayne speaking!** [on
the telephone] Jayne à l'appareil ! ; **to
speak out** *or* **up** [boldly] parler (franchement) ; **to speak up** [more loudly]

parler plus fort ■ **speak for** *vt insep* [represent] parler pour, parler au nom de; **she's already spoken for** elle est déjà prise ■ **speak up** *vi* **a)** [support] **to speak up for sb/sth** parler en faveur de qn/qch, soutenir qn/qch **b)** [speak louder] parler plus fort

**speaker** ['spiːkə(r)] *n* [at meeting] intervenant, -e *mf*; [at conference] conférencier, -ère *mf*; [loudspeaker] enceinte *f*; **to be a Spanish speaker** parler espagnol

**spear** [spɪə(r)] *n* lance *f*

**spearmint** ['spɪəmɪnt] *adj* [sweet] à la menthe; [chewing gum] mentholé

**spec** [spek] *n Br Fam* **on spec** à tout hasard

**special** ['speʃəl] **1.** *adj* spécial; [care, attention] particulier, -ère; *Br* **by special delivery** en exprès; **special effects** effets *mpl* spéciaux; *Br* **special needs children** enfants ayant des difficultés scolaires **2.** *n* **today's special** [in restaurant] le plat du jour

**specialist** ['speʃəlɪst] **1.** *n* spécialiste *mf* (**in** de) **2.** *adj* [dictionary, knowledge] spécialisé; [equipment] de spécialiste ■ **speciality** [-ʃɪ'ælɪtɪ] *(pl* **-ies**) *n Br* spécialité *f*

**specialize** ['speʃəlaɪz] *vi* se spécialiser (**in** dans)

**specially** ['speʃəlɪ] *adv* [specifically] spécialement; [particularly] particulièrement

**specialty** ['speʃəltɪ] *(pl* **-ies**) *n Am* spécialité *f*

**species** ['spiːʃiːz] *n inv* espèce *f*

**specific** [spə'sɪfɪk] *adj* précis ■ **specifically** *adv* [explicitly] expressément; [exactly] précisément; [specially] spécialement

**specify** ['spesɪfaɪ] *(pt & pp* **-ied**) *vt* [state exactly] préciser; [stipulate] stipuler ■ **specification** [-fɪ'keɪʃən] *n* spécification *f*

**specimen** ['spesɪmɪn] *n* [individual example] spécimen *m*; [of urine, blood] échantillon *m*

**speck** [spek] *n* [stain] petite tache *f*; [of dust] grain *m*; [dot] point *m*

**speckled** ['spekəld] *adj* tacheté

**specs** [speks] *npl Fam* lunettes *fpl*

**spectacle** ['spektəkəl] *n* [sight] spectacle *m* ■ **spectacles** *npl* [glasses] lunettes *fpl*

**spectacular** [spek'tækjʊlə(r)] *adj* spectaculaire

**spectator** [spek'teɪtə(r)] *n* spectateur, -trice *mf*

**spectre** ['spektə(r)] *n* spectre *m* (**of** de)

**spectrum** ['spektrəm] *(pl* **-tra** [-trə]) *n* spectre *m*; *Fig* [range] gamme *f*

**speculate** ['spekjʊleɪt] **1.** *vt* **to speculate that...** [guess] conjecturer que... **2.** *vi* FIN spéculer; **to speculate about** [make guesses] faire des suppositions sur ■ **speculation** *n* suppositions *fpl*; FIN spéculation *f*

**sped** [sped] *pt & pp of* **speed**

**speech** [spiːtʃ] *n* [talk, lecture] discours *m* (**on** *or* **about** sur); [faculty] parole *f*; [diction] élocution *f*; **to make a speech** faire un discours ■ **speechless** *adj* muet (*f* muette) (**with** de)

**speed** [spiːd] **1.** *n* [rapidity, gear] vitesse *f*; **at top** *or* **full speed** à toute vitesse; **speed bump** dos-d'âne *m inv*; **speed camera** radar *m*; **speed dating** *rencontre organisée entre plusieurs partenaires potentiels ayant quelques minutes pour décider s'ils veulent se revoir*; **speed limit** [on road] limitation *f* de vitesse **2.** *(pt & pp* **sped**) *vt* **to speed sth up** accélérer qch **3.** *vi* **a)** **to speed up** [of person] aller plus vite; **to speed past sth** passer à toute vitesse devant qch **b)** *(pt & pp* **speeded**) [exceed speed limit] faire un excès de vitesse ■ **speedboat** *n* vedette *f* ■ **speeding** *n* [in vehicle] excès *m* de vitesse ■ **speedometer** *n Br* [in vehicle] compteur *m* de vitesse

**speedy** ['spiːdɪ] *(compar* **-ier**, *superl* **-iest)** *adj* rapide

**spell¹** [spel] *n* [magic words] formule *f* magique; **to cast a spell on sb** jeter un sort à qn ■ **spellbound** *adj* fasciné

**spell²** [spel] *n* [period] période *f*; **cold spell** vague *f* de froid

**spell³** [spel] (*pt & pp* spelled *or* spelt [spelt]) *vt* [write] écrire; [say aloud] épeler; [of letters] former; *Fig* [mean] signifier; **how do you spell it?** comment ça s'écrit?; **to spell sth out** [word] épeler qch; *Fig* [explain] expliquer clairement qch ■ **spell-checker** *n* COMPUT correcteur *m* d'orthographe ■ **spelling** *n* orthographe *f*; **spelling mistake** faute *f* d'orthographe

**spend** [spend] (*pt & pp* spent) *vt* [money] dépenser (**on** pour /en); [time] passer (**on sth** sur qch; **doing** à faire); [energy] consacrer (**on sth** à qch; **doing** à faire) ■ **spending** *n* dépenses *fpl*; **spending money** argent *m* de poche ■ **spendthrift** *n* **to be a spendthrift** être dépensier, -ère

**spent** [spent] *pt & pp of* spend

**sperm** [spɜːm] *n* sperme *m*

**spew** [spjuː] *vt* vomir

**sphere** [sfɪə(r)] *n* [of influence, action, MATH & POL] sphère *f* ■ **spherical** [ˈsferɪkəl] *adj* sphérique

**spice** [spaɪs] **1.** *n* épice *f*; *Fig* [interest] piquant *m* **2.** *vt* [food] épicer; **to spice sth (up)** [add interest to] ajouter du piquant à qch ■ **spicy** (*compar* -ier, *superl* -iest) *adj* épicé

**spider** [ˈspaɪdə(r)] *n* araignée *f*

**spike** [spaɪk] *n* [of metal] pointe *f* ■ **spiky** (*compar* -ier, *superl* -iest) *adj* [hair] tout hérissé

**spill** [spɪl] (*pt & pp* spilled *or* spilt [spɪlt]) **1.** *vt* [liquid] renverser ■ *vi* se répandre ■ **spill out** *vt sep* [empty] vider ■ **spill over** *vi* [of liquid] déborder

**spin** [spɪn] **1.** *n* [motion] tournoiement *m*; [on ball] effet *m*; *Fam* **to go for a spin** [in car] aller faire un tour **2.** (*pt & pp* spun, *pres p* spinning) *vt* [wool, cotton] filer; [wheel, top] faire tourner; [spin-dry] essorer; **to spin sth out** [speech] faire durer qch **3.** *vi* tourner; **to spin round** [of dancer, wheel, top, planet] tourner; **my head's spinning** j'ai la tête qui tourne

**spinach** [ˈspɪnɪdʒ] *n* épinards *mpl*

**spin-dry** [ˈspɪndraɪ] *vt* essorer ■ **spin-dryer** *n* essoreuse *f*

**spine** [spaɪn] *n* [backbone] colonne *f* vertébrale; [of book] dos *m*

**spinster** [ˈspɪnstə(r)] *n* vieille fille *f*

**spiral** [ˈspaɪərəl] **1.** *n* spirale *f* **2.** *adj* en spirale; [staircase] en colimaçon **3.** (*Br* -ll-, *Am* -l-) *vi* [of prices] s'envoler

**spire** [ˈspaɪə(r)] *n* [of church] flèche *f*

**spirit** [ˈspɪrɪt] **1.** *n* [soul, ghost, mood] esprit *m*; *Fig* [determination] courage *m*; **spirits** [drink] spiritueux *mpl*; **in good spirits** de bonne humeur **2.** *adj* [lamp] à alcool; **spirit level** niveau *m* (à bulle) ■ **spirited** *adj* [campaign, attack] vigoureux, -euse; [person, remark] énergique

**spiritual** [ˈspɪrɪtʃʊəl] *adj* spirituel, -elle

**spit¹** [spɪt] **1.** *n* [on ground] crachat *m*; [in mouth] salive *f* **2.** (*pt & pp* spat *or* spit, *pres p* spitting) *vt* cracher; **to spit sth out** cracher qch; **to be the spitting image of sb** être le portrait (tout craché) de qn **3.** *vi* cracher

**spit²** [spɪt] *n* [for meat] broche *f*

**spite** [spaɪt] **1.** *n* [dislike] dépit *m*; **in spite of sb /sth** malgré qn /qch; **in spite of the fact that...** bien que... (+ *subjunctive*) **2.** *vt* vexer ■ **spiteful** *adj* vexant

**splash** [splæʃ] **1.** *n* [of liquid] éclaboussure *f*; *Fig* [of colour] tache *f* **2.** *vt* [spatter] éclabousser (**with** de) **3.** *vi* [of mud] faire des éclaboussures; [of waves] clapoter; **to splash (about)** [in river, mud] patauger; [in bath] barboter; *Fam* **to splash out** [spend money] claquer des ronds

**splendid** [ˈsplendɪd] *adj* splendide ■ **splendour**, *Am* **splendor** *n* splendeur *f*

**splint** [splɪnt] *n* attelle *f*

**splinter** [ˈsplɪntə(r)] *n* [of wood, glass] éclat *m*; [in finger] écharde *f*

**split** [splɪt] **1.** *n* fente *f*; [tear] déchirure *f*; [in political party] scission *f* **2.** *adj* **in a split second** en une fraction de seconde **3.** (*pt & pp* split, *pres p* splitting) *vt* [break apart] fendre; [tear]

déchirer; **to split (up)** [group] diviser; [money, work] partager (**between** entre) **4.** *vi* se fendre; [tear] se déchirer; **to split (up)** [of group] se diviser (**into** en); **to split up** [because of disagreement - of couple, friends] se séparer; [of crowd] se disperser; **to split up with sb** rompre avec qn

**spoil** [spɔɪl] *(pt & pp spoilt or spoiled) vt* [ruin] gâcher; [indulge] gâter ▪ **spoilsport** *n* rabat-joie *mf inv*

**spoilt** [spɔɪlt] *pt & pp of* spoil

**spoke**[^1] [spəʊk] *n* [of wheel] rayon *m*

**spoke**[^2] [spəʊk] *pt of* speak ▪ **spoken 1.** *pp of* **speak 2.** *adj* [language] parlé ▪ **spokesman** *(pl -men)*, **spokesperson**, **spokeswoman** *(pl -women) n* porte-parole *mf inv* (**for** or **of** de)

**sponge** [spʌndʒ] **1.** *n* éponge *f*; *Br* **sponge bag** trousse *f* de toilette; **sponge cake** génoise *f* **2.** *vt* **to sponge sth down/off** laver /enlever qch avec une éponge **3.** *vi Fam* **to sponge off** or **on sb** vivre aux crochets de qn ▪ **sponger** *n Fam* parasite *m*

**sponsor** ['spɒnsə(r)] **1.** *n* sponsor *m* **2.** *vt* sponsoriser ▪ **sponsorship** *n* sponsoring *m*

**spontaneous** [spɒn'teɪnɪəs] *adj* spontané

**spooky** ['spuːkɪ] *(compar -ier, superl -iest) adj Fam* qui donne le frisson

**spoon** [spuːn] *n* cuillère *f* ▪ **spoonful** *n* cuillerée *f*

**sporadic** [spə'rædɪk] *adj* sporadique

**sport**[^1] [spɔːt] *n* sport *m*; **to play** *Br* **sport** or *Am* **sports** faire du sport; **sports club** club *m* de sport; **sports car/ground** voiture *f* /terrain *m* de sport ▪ **sporting** *adj* [attitude, person] sportif, -ive ▪ **sportsman** *(pl -men) n* sportif *m* ▪ **sportswoman** *(pl -women) n* sportive *f* ▪ **sporty** *(compar -ier, superl -iest) adj* sportif, -ive

**sport**[^2] [spɔːt] *vt* [wear] arborer

**sportswear** ['spɔːtsweə(r)] *n* vêtements *mpl* de sport

**spot**[^1] [spɒt] *n* [stain, mark] tache *f*; [dot] point *m*; [polka dot] pois *m*; [drop] goutte *f*; [pimple] bouton *m*; [place] endroit *m*; **on the spot** sur place; [at once] sur le coup; **to be in a tight spot** [difficulty] être dans le pétrin

**spot**[^2] [spɒt] *(pt & pp -tt-) vt* [notice] apercevoir

**spotless** ['spɒtləs] *adj* [clean] impeccable

**spotlight** ['spɒtlaɪt] *n* projecteur *m*; [for photography] spot *m*

**spotty** ['spɒtɪ] *(compar -ier, superl -iest) adj* [face, person] boutonneux, -euse

**spouse** [spaʊs, spaʊz] *n* époux *m*, épouse *f*

**spout** [spaʊt] **1.** *n* [of teapot, jug] bec *m* **2.** *vt Pej* [say] débiter

**sprain** [spreɪn] **1.** *n* entorse *f* **2.** *vt* **to sprain one's ankle/wrist** se fouler la cheville /le poignet

**sprang** [spræŋ] *pt of* spring

**spray** [spreɪ] **1.** *n* [can, device] vaporisateur *m*; [water drops] gouttelettes *fpl*; [from sea] embruns *mpl* **2.** *vt* [liquid, surface] vaporiser; [plant, crops] pulvériser; [car] peindre à la bombe

**spread** [spred] **1.** *n* [of idea, religion, language] diffusion *f*; [of disease] propagation *f*; *Fam* [meal] festin *m*; **cheese spread** fromage *m* à tartiner **2.** *(pt & pp* **spread***) vt* [stretch, open out] étendre; [legs, fingers] écarter; [paint, payment, visits, cards] étaler; [sand, fear] répandre; [news, illness] propager; **to spread out** [map, payments, visits] étaler; [fingers] écarter **3.** *vi* [of fog] s'étendre; [of fire, epidemic] se propager; [of news, fear] se répandre; **to spread out** [of people] se disperser ▪ **spreadsheet** *n* COMPUT tableur *m*

**spree** [spriː] *n* **to go on a spending spree** faire des folies dans les magasins

**sprightly** ['spraɪtlɪ] *(compar -ier, superl -iest) adj* alerte

**spring**[^1] [sprɪŋ] **1.** *n* [device] ressort *m*; [leap] bond *m* **2.** *(pt* **sprang***, pp* **sprung***) vt* [surprise] faire (**on** à) **3.** *vi* [leap] bondir; **to spring to mind** venir à l'esprit; **to spring from** [stem from] provenir de; **to spring up** [appear] surgir ▪ **springboard** *n* tremplin *m*

**spring²** [sprɪŋ] n [season] printemps m; **in (the) spring** au printemps; Br **spring onion** petit oignon m ■ **spring-cleaning** n nettoyage m de printemps ■ **springtime** n printemps m

**spring³** [sprɪŋ] n [of water] source f; **spring water** eau f de source

**sprinkle** ['sprɪŋkəl] vt [sand] répandre (**on** or **over** sur); **to sprinkle sth with water, to sprinkle water on sth** arroser qch; **to sprinkle sth with sth** [sugar, salt, flour] saupoudrer qch de qch

**sprint** [sprɪnt] vi [run] sprinter

**sprout** [spraʊt] **1.** n (Brussels) sprout chou m de Bruxelles **2.** vt [leaves] pousser **3.** vi [of seed, bulb] pousser

**spruce** [spruːs] **1.** (compar **-er**, superl **-est**) adj [neat] impeccable **2.** vt **to spruce oneself up** se faire beau (f belle)

**sprung** [sprʌŋ] pp of **spring**

**spud** [spʌd] n Fam [potato] patate f

**spun** [spʌn] pt & pp of **spin**

**spur** [spɜː(r)] **1.** n [of horse rider] éperon m; Fig [stimulus] aiguillon m; **to do sth on the spur of the moment** faire qch sur un coup de tête **2.** (pt & pp **-rr-**) vt **to spur sb on** [urge on] aiguillonner qn

**spurn** [spɜːn] vt rejeter

**spurt** [spɜːt] **1.** n [of energy] regain m; **to put on a spurt** foncer **2.** vi **to spurt (out)** [of liquid] gicler

**spy** [spaɪ] **1.** (pl **-ies**) n espion, -onne mf **2.** adj [story, film] d'espionnage **3.** (pt & pp **-ied**) vt [notice] repérer **4.** vi espionner; **to spy on sb** espionner qn ■ **spying** n espionnage m

**squabble** ['skwɒbəl] **1.** n querelle f **2.** vi se quereller (**over** à propos de)

**squad** [skwɒd] n [of workmen, footballers] équipe f; [of soldiers] section f; [of police] brigade f

**squalid** ['skwɒlɪd] adj sordide ■ **squalor** n [poverty] misère f

**squander** ['skwɒndə(r)] vt [money, resources] gaspiller; [time] perdre

**square** ['skweə(r)] **1.** n carré m; [on chessboard, map] case f; [in town] place f **2.** adj carré; MATH **square root**

racine f carrée **3.** vt [settle] régler; MATH [number] élever au carré **4.** vi [tally] cadrer (**with** avec)

**squash** [skwɒʃ] **1.** n [game] squash m; [vegetable] courge f; Br **lemon / orange squash** ≃ sirop m de citron / d'orange **2.** vt écraser

**squat** [skwɒt] **1.** adj [person, object, building] trapu **2.** (pt & pp **-tt-**) vi squatter; **to squat (down)** s'accroupir; **to be squatting (down)** être accroupi

**squawk** [skwɔːk] vi pousser un cri rauque

**squeak** [skwiːk] vi [of person] pousser un cri aigu; [of door] grincer

**squeal** [skwiːl] vi pousser un cri perçant

**squeamish** ['skwiːmɪʃ] adj de nature délicate

**squeeze** [skwiːz] **1.** n **to give sth a squeeze** presser qch; **to give sb's hand / arm a squeeze** serrer la main / le bras à qn **2.** vt [press] presser; **to squeeze sb's hand** serrer la main à qn; **to squeeze sth into sth** faire rentrer qch dans qch; **to squeeze the juice (out)** faire sortir le jus (**of** de) **3.** vi **to squeeze through / into sth** [force oneself] se glisser par / dans qch; **to squeeze in** trouver de la place; **to squeeze up** se serrer (**against** contre)

**squelch** [skweltʃ] vi patauger

**squid** [skwɪd] n inv calmar m

**squint** [skwɪnt] **1.** n **to have a squint** loucher **2.** vi loucher; [in the sunlight] plisser les yeux

**squirm** [skwɜːm] vi [wriggle] se tortiller

**squirrel** [Br 'skwɪrəl, Am 'skwɜːrəl] n écureuil m

**squirt** [skwɜːt] **1.** vt [liquid] faire gicler **2.** vi [of liquid] gicler

**Sry** (abbr of **sorry**) MESSAGING dsl

**Sta)** (abbr of **Street**) rue **b)** (abbr of **Saint**) St, Ste

**stab** [stæb] **1.** n **stab (wound)** coup m de couteau **2.** (pt & pp **-bb-**) vt [with knife] poignarder

**stability** [stə'bɪlətɪ] n stabilité f

**stand**

**stabilize** ['steɪbəlaɪz] **1.** *vt* stabiliser **2.** *vi* se stabiliser

**stable¹** ['steɪbəl] *(compar* -**er**, *superl* -**est)** *adj* stable

**stable²** ['steɪbəl] *n* écurie *f*

**stack** [stæk] **1.** *n* [heap] tas *m*; *Fam* **stacks of** [lots of] des tas de **2.** *vt to* **stack (up)** entasser ■ **stackable** ['stækəbl] *adj* empilable

**stadium** ['steɪdɪəm] *n* stade *m*

**staff** [stɑːf] *n* personnel *m*; [of school, university] professeurs *mpl*; *Br* **staff room** [in school] salle *f* des professeurs

**stag** [stæɡ] *n* cerf *m*; **stag night** *or* **party** enterrement *m* de la vie de garçon

**stage¹** [steɪʤ] **1.** *n* [platform] scène *f*; **on stage** sur scène **2.** *vt* [play] monter; *Fig* organiser

**stage²** [steɪʤ] *n* [phase] stade *m*

**stagger** ['stæɡə(r)] **1.** *vt* [holidays] échelonner; [astound] stupéfier **2.** *vi* [reel] chanceler ■ **staggering** *adj* stupéfiant

**stagnant** ['stæɡnənt] *adj* stagnant ■ **stagnate** *vi* stagner

**staid** [steɪd] *adj* collet monté *inv*

**stain** [steɪn] **1.** *n* [mark] tache *f* **2.** *vt* [mark] tacher (**with** de); [dye] teinter ■ **stained-glass** *adj* **stained-glass window** vitrail *m* (*pl* -aux) ■ **stainless** *adj* **stainless steel** acier *m* inoxydable, Inox® *m*

**stair** [steə(r)] *n* **a stair** [step] une marche; **the stairs** [staircase] l'escalier *m* ■ **staircase**, **stairway** *n* escalier *m*

**stake** [steɪk] **1.** *n* **a)** [post] pieu *m*; [for plant] tuteur *m* **b)** [in betting] enjeu *m*; **to have a stake in sth** [share] avoir des intérêts dans qch; **at stake** en jeu **2.** *vt* [bet] jouer (**on** sur)

**stale** [steɪl] *(compar* -**er**, *superl* -**est)** *adj* [bread] rassis; [air] vicié; [joke] éculé

**stalemate** ['steɪlmeɪt] *n* [in chess] pat *m*; *Fig* impasse *f*

**stalk** [stɔːk] **1.** *n* [of plant] tige *f*; [of fruit] queue *f* **2.** *vt* [animal, criminal] traquer; [celebrity] harceler **3.** *vi to* **stalk out** [walk angrily] sortir d'un air furieux mais digne ■ **stalker** ['stɔːkə(r)] *n* harceleur, -euse *mf (qui suit sa victime obsessionnellement)*

**stall** [stɔːl] **1.** *n* [in market] étal *m*; [for newspapers, flowers] kiosque *m*; [in stable] stalle *f*; *Br* **the stalls** [in cinema, theatre] l'orchestre *m* **2.** *vt* [engine, car] caler **3.** *vi* [of car] caler; **to stall** **(for time)** chercher à gagner du temps

**stamina** ['stæmɪnə] *n* résistance *f* physique

**stammer** ['stæmə(r)] **1.** *n* **to have a stammer** être bègue **2.** *vi* bégayer

**stamp** [stæmp] **1.** *n* [for letter] timbre *m*; [mark] cachet *m*; [device] tampon *m*; **stamp collector** philatéliste *mf* **2.** *vt* [document] tamponner; [letter] timbrer; [metal] estamper; **to stamp** **one's foot** taper du pied; *Br* **stamped** **addressed envelope**, *Am* **stamped** **self-addressed envelope** enveloppe *f* timbrée libellée à ses noms et adresse **3.** *vi to* **stamp on sth** écraser qch

**stampede** [stæm'piːd] **1.** *n* débandade *f* **2.** *vi* se ruer

**stamping ground** ['stæmpɪŋ-] *n Fam* lieu *m* favori

**stance** [stɑːns] *n* position *f*

**stand** [stænd] **1.** *n* [opinion] position *f*; [support] support *m*; [stall] étal *m*; [at exhibition] stand *m*; [at sports ground] tribune *f*; **to take a stand** prendre position **2.** *(pt & pp* **stood)** *vt* [pain, journey] supporter; [put straight] mettre debout; **to stand a chance** avoir des chances; **I can't stand him** je ne peux pas le supporter **3.** *vi* [be upright] se tenir debout; [get up] se mettre debout; [remain] rester debout; [of building] se trouver; [of object] être

■ **stand about**, **stand around** *vi* [in street] traîner

■ **stand aside** *vi* s'écarter

■ **stand back** *vi* reculer

■ **stand by 1.** *vt insep* [opinion] s'en tenir à; [person] soutenir **2.** *vi* [do nothing] rester sans rien faire; [be ready] être prêt

■ **stand down** *vi* [withdraw] se retirer

■ **stand for** *vt insep* [mean] signifier ; [represent] représenter ; *Br* [be candidate for] être candidat à ; [tolerate] supporter

■ **stand in for** *vt insep* [replace] remplacer

■ **stand out** *vi* [be visible] ressortir (**against** sur)

■ **stand over** *vt insep* [watch closely] surveiller

■ **stand up 1.** *vt sep* mettre debout ; *Fam* **to stand sb up** poser un lapin à qn **2.** *vi* [get up] se lever

■ **stand up for** *vt insep* [defend] défendre

■ **stand up to** *vt insep* [resist] résister à ; [defend oneself against] tenir tête à

**standard** ['stændəd] **1.** *n* [norm] norme *f* ; [level] niveau *m* ; **standards** [principles] principes *mpl* moraux ; **standard of living, living standards** niveau *m* de vie **2.** *adj* [average] ordinaire ; [model, size] standard *inv*
■ **standardize** *vt* standardiser

**stand-by** ['stændbaɪ] **1.** (*pl* **-bys**) *n* **on stand-by** [troops, emergency services] prêt à intervenir **2.** *adj* [plane ticket] en stand-by

**stand-in** ['stændɪn] *n* remplaçant, -e *mf* (**for** de) ; [actor] doublure *f* (**for** de)

**standing** ['stændɪŋ] **1.** *adj* [upright] debout ; [permanent] permanent ; *Br* **standing order** virement *m* automatique ; **standing charges** [on bill] frais *mpl* d'abonnement **2.** *n* [reputation] réputation *f* ; [social, professional] rang *m* ; **of long standing** de longue date

**stand-offish** [stænd'ɒfɪʃ] *adj* distant

**standpoint** ['stændpɔɪnt] *n* point *m* de vue

**standstill** ['stændstɪl] *n* **to bring sth to a standstill** immobiliser qch ; **to come to a standstill** s'immobiliser ; **at a standstill** immobile ; [negotiations, industry] paralysé

**stank** [stæŋk] *pt of* **stink**

**stanza** ['stænzə] *n* strophe *f*

**staple¹** ['steɪpəl] *adj* [basic] de base ; **staple food** *or* **diet** nourriture *f* de base

**staple²** ['steɪpəl] **1.** *n* [for paper] agrafe *f* **2.** *vt* agrafer ■ **stapler** *n* [for paper] agrafeuse *f*

**star** [stɑː(r)] **1.** *n* étoile *f* ; [famous person] star *f* ; *Br* **four-star (petrol)** du super **2.** (*pt & pp* **-rr-**) *vt* [of film] avoir pour vedette **3.** *vi* [of actor, actress] être la vedette (**in** de)

**starboard** ['stɑːbəd] *n* NAUT tribord *m*

**starch** [stɑːtʃ] *n* amidon *m*

**stare** [steə(r)] **1.** *n* regard *m* fixe **2.** *vi* **to stare at sb/sth** fixer qn/qch (du regard)

**stark** [stɑːk] **1.** (*compar* **-er**, *superl* **-est**) *adj* [place] désolé ; [fact, reality] brutal ; **to be in stark contrast to** contraster nettement avec **2.** *adv* **stark naked** complètement nu

**start¹** [stɑːt] **1.** *n* [beginning] début *m* ; [of race] départ *m* ; **for a start** pour commencer ; **from the start** dès le début ; **to make a start** commencer **2.** *vt* commencer ; [packet, conversation] entamer ; [fashion, campaign, offensive] lancer ; [engine, vehicle] mettre en marche ; [business, family] fonder ; **to start doing** *or* **to do sth** commencer à faire qch **3.** *vi* commencer (**with sth** par qch ; **by doing** par faire) ; [of vehicle] démarrer ; [leave] partir (**for** pour) ; [in job] débuter ; **to start with** [firstly] pour commencer ; **starting from now/10 euros** à partir de maintenant/10 euros ■ **starting** *adj* [point, line, salary] de départ ; **starting post** [in race] ligne *f* de départ ■ **start off** *vi* [leave] partir (**for** pour) ; [in job] débuter ■ **start out** *vi* [begin] débuter ; [on journey] se mettre en route ■ **start up 1.** *vt sep* [engine, vehicle] mettre en marche ; [business] fonder **2.** *vi* [of engine, vehicle] démarrer

**start²** [stɑːt] **1.** *n* [movement] sursaut *m* ; **to give sb a start** faire sursauter qn **2.** *vi* sursauter

**starter** ['stɑːtə(r)] *n* [in vehicle] démarreur *m* ; [in meal] entrée *f* ; [runner] partant, -e *mf* ; *Fam* **for starters** [firstly] pour commencer

**steam**

**startle** ['stɑːtəl] *vt* faire sursauter

**starvation** [stɑːˈveɪʃən] **1.** *n* faim *f* **2.** *adj* [wage, ration] de misère

**starve** [stɑːv] **1.** *vt* [make suffer] faire souffrir de la faim ; *Fig* [deprive] priver (**of** de) **2.** *vi* [suffer] souffrir de la faim ; **to starve to death** mourir de faim ; *Fam* **I'm starving!** je meurs de faim !

**state¹** [steɪt] **1.** *n* **a)** [condition] état *m* ; [situation] situation *f* ; **not in a (fit) state to...**, **in no (fit) state to...** hors d'état de... ; **state of mind** état *m* d'esprit, humeur *f* **b)** State [nation] État *m* ; *Fam* **the States** les États-Unis *mpl* **2.** *adj* [secret] d'État ; *Br* [school, education] public, -ique ; **state visit** voyage *m* officiel ; **state pension** pension *f* de l'État ■ **state-run** *adj* d'état ■ **state-owned** *adj* étatisé

**state²** [steɪt] *vt* déclarer (**that** que) ; [opinion] formuler ; [problem] exposer

**statement** ['steɪtmənt] *n* déclaration *f* ; [in court] déposition *f* ; **(bank) statement** relevé *m* de compte

**statesman** ['steɪtsmən] *(pl* -**men**) *n* homme *m* d'État

**static** ['stætɪk] *adj* statique

**station** ['steɪʃən] **1.** *n* [for trains] gare *f* ; [underground] station *f* ; [social] rang *m* ; **bus station** gare *f* routière ; **docking station** station *f* d'accueil *(d'un appareil électronique)* ; **radio station** station *f* de radio ; *Am* **station wagon** break *m* **2.** *vt* [position] placer ; **to be stationed at/in** [of troops] être en garnison à /en

**stationary** ['steɪʃənərɪ] *adj* [vehicle] à l'arrêt

**stationer** ['steɪʃənə(r)] *n* papetier, -ère *mf* ; **stationer's (shop)** papeterie *f* ■ **stationery** *n* [articles] articles *mpl* de bureau ; [paper] papier *m*

**statistic** [stəˈtɪstɪk] *n* [fact] statistique *f* ; **statistics** [science] la statistique

**statue** ['stætʃuː] *n* statue *f*

**stature** ['stætʃə(r)] *n* [importance] envergure *f*

**status** ['steɪtəs] *n* [position] situation *f* ; [legal, official] statut *m* ; [prestige] prestige *m* ; COMPUT **status bar** barre *f* d'état ; **status symbol** marque *f* de prestige

**staunch** [stɔːntʃ] *(compar* -**er**, *superl* -**est**) *adj* [resolute] convaincu ; [supporter] ardent

**stave** [steɪv] *vt* **to stave sth off** [disaster, danger] conjurer qch ; **to stave off hunger** tromper la faim

**stay** [steɪ] **1.** *n* [visit] séjour *m* **2.** *vi* [remain] rester ; [reside] loger ; [visit] séjourner ; **to stay put** ne pas bouger ■ **stay away** *vi* ne pas s'approcher (**from** de) ; **to stay away from school** ne pas aller à l'école ■ **stay behind** *vi* rester en arrière ■ **stay in** *vi* [at home] rester à la maison ; [of nail, screw, tooth] tenir ■ **stay out** *vi* [outside] rester dehors ; [not come home] ne pas rentrer ; **to stay out of sth** [not interfere in] ne pas se mêler de qch ; [avoid] éviter qch ■ **stay up** *vi* [at night] ne pas se coucher ; [of fence] tenir ; **to stay up late** se coucher tard

**stead** [sted] *n* **to stand sb in good stead** être bien utile à qn ; **in sb's stead** à la place de qn

**steadfast** ['stedfɑːst] *adj* dévoué ; [opponent] constant

**steady** ['stedɪ] **1.** *(compar* -**ier**, *superl* -**iest**) *adj* [firm, stable] stable ; [hand, voice] assuré ; [progress, speed, demand] constant ; **to be steady on one's feet** être solide sur ses jambes **2.** *vt* faire tenir ; **to steady one's nerves** se calmer ; **to steady oneself** retrouver son équilibre ■ **steadily** *adv* [gradually] progressivement ; [regularly] régulièrement ; [continuously] sans arrêt ; [walk] d'un pas assuré

**steak** [steɪk] *n* [beef] steak *m*

**steal¹** [stiːl] *(pt* stole, *pp* stolen) *vti* voler (**from sb** à qn)

**steal²** [stiːl] *(pt* stole, *pp* stolen) *vi* **to steal in /out** entrer /sortir furtivement

**stealthy** ['stelθɪ] *(compar* -**ier**, *superl* -**iest**) *adj* furtif, -ive

**steam** [stiːm] **1.** *n* vapeur *f* ; [on glass] buée *f* ; *Fam* **to let off steam** se défouler ; **steam engine /iron** locomotive *f* /

fer *m* à vapeur **2.** *vt* [food] cuire à la vapeur; **to get steamed up** [of glass] se couvrir de buée **3.** *vi* **to steam up** [of glass] s'embuer ■ **steamer** *n* bateau *m* à vapeur; [for food] panier *m* pour cuisson à la vapeur

**steel** [sti:l] **1.** *n* acier *m* **2.** *vt* **to steel oneself** s'armer de courage

**steep** [sti:p] **1.** *(compar* -**er***, superl* -**est***) adj* [stairs, slope] raide; [hill, path] escarpé; *Fig* [price] excessif, -ive **2.** *vt* [soak] tremper (**in** dans) ■ **steeply** *adv* [rise] en pente raide; *Fig* [of prices] excessivement

**steeple** ['sti:pəl] *n* clocher *m*

**steer** [stɪə(r)] **1.** *vt* diriger **2.** *vi* [of person] conduire; [of ship] se diriger (**for** vers); **to steer clear of sb/sth** éviter qn/qch ■ **steering** *n* [in vehicle] direction *f*; **steering wheel** volant *m*

**stem** [stem] **1.** *n* [of plant] tige *f*; [of glass] pied *m* **2.** *(pt & pp* -**mm**-*) vt* [stop] arrêter **3.** *vi* **to stem from sth** provenir de qch

**stench** [stentʃ] *n* puanteur *f*

**step** [step] **1.** *n* [movement, sound] pas *m*; [of stairs] marche *f*; [on train, bus] marchepied *m*; [doorstep] pas de la porte; *Fig* [action] mesure *f*; **(flight of) steps** [indoors] escalier *m*; [outdoors] perron *m*; *Br* **(pair of) steps** [ladder] escabeau *m*; **step by step** pas à pas **2.** *(pt & pp* -**pp**-*) vi* [walk] marcher (**on** sur) ■ **stepdaughter** *n* belle-fille *f* ■ **stepfather** *n* beau-père *m* ■ **stepladder** *n* escabeau *m* ■ **stepmother** *n* belle-mère *f* ■ **stepson** *n* beau-fils *m* ■ **step aside** *vi* s'écarter ■ **step back** *vi* reculer ■ **step down** *vi* descendre (**from** de); *Fig* [withdraw] se retirer ■ **step forward** *vi* faire un pas en avant ■ **step in** *vi* [intervene] intervenir ■ **step off** *vt insep* [chair] descendre de ■ **step over** *vt insep* [obstacle] enjamber ■ **step up** *vt sep* [increase] augmenter; [speed up] accélérer

**stereo** ['sterɪəʊ] **1.** *(pl* -**os***) n* [hi-fi, record player] chaîne *f* stéréo; **in stereo** en stéréo **2.** *adj* [record] stéréo *inv*; [broadcast] en stéréo

**stereotype** ['sterɪətaɪp] *n* stéréotype *m*

**sterile** [*Br* 'sterail, *Am* 'sterəl] *adj* stérile

**sterilize** ['sterəlaɪz] *vt* stériliser

**sterling** ['stɜ:lɪŋ] *n Br* [currency] livre *f* sterling

**stern¹** [stɜ:n] *(compar* -**er***, superl* -**est***) adj* sévère

**stern²** [stɜ:n] *n* [of ship] arrière *m*

**steroid** ['stɪərɔɪd] *n* stéroïde *m*

**stethoscope** ['steθəskəʊp] *n* stéthoscope *m*

**stew** [stju:] **1.** *n* ragoût *m* **2.** *vt* [meat] faire cuire en ragoût; [fruit] faire de la compote de; **stewed fruit** compote *f* **3.** *vi* cuire

**steward** ['stju:əd] *n* [on plane, ship] steward *m* ■ **stewardess** *n* [on plane] hôtesse *f*

**stick¹** [stɪk] *n* [piece of wood, chalk, dynamite] bâton *m*; [for walking] canne *f*

**stick²** [stɪk] **1.** *(pt & pp* stuck*) vt* [glue] coller; *Fam* [put] fourrer; *Fam* [tolerate] supporter; **to stick sth into sth** fourrer qch dans qch **2.** *vi* coller (**to** à); [of food in pan] attacher (**to** dans); [of drawer] se coincer ■ **stick by** *vt insep* rester fidèle à ■ **stick down** *vt sep* [envelope, stamp] coller ■ **stick on** *vt sep* [stamp, label] coller ■ **stick out 1.** *vt sep* [tongue] tirer; *Fam* [head or arm from window] sortir **2.** *vi* [of shirt] dépasser; [of tooth] avancer ■ **stick up** *vt sep* [notice] coller; *Fam* [hand] lever ■ **stick up for** *vt insep* défendre

**sticker** ['stɪkə(r)] *n* autocollant *m*

**sticky** ['stɪkɪ] *(compar* -**ier***, superl* -**iest***) adj* collant; [label] adhésif, -ive

**stiff** [stɪf] *(compar* -**er***, superl* -**est***) adj* raide; [joint] ankylosé; [brush, paste] dur; *Fig* [person] guindé; **to have a stiff neck** avoir un torticolis; *Fam* **to be bored stiff** s'ennuyer à mourir; *Fam* **frozen stiff** complètement gelé

**stiffen** ['stɪfən] **1.** *vt* raidir **2.** *vi* se raidir

**stifle** ['staɪfəl] **1.** *vt* [feeling, person] étouffer **2.** *vi* **it's stifling** on étouffe

**stigma** ['stɪgmə] *n* [moral stain] flétrissure *f*

**stiletto** [stɪ'letəʊ] n a) [heel] talon m aiguille b) [knife] stylet m ▪ **stilettos** npl (chaussures fpl à) talons mpl aiguilles

**still¹** [stɪl] adv encore, toujours ; [even] encore ; [nevertheless] tout de même ; **better still, still better** encore mieux

**still²** [stɪl] (compar -er, superl -est) adj [not moving] immobile ; [calm] calme ; Br [drink] non gazeux, -euse ; **to stand still** rester immobile ; **still life** nature f morte

**stilt** [stɪlt] n a) [for walking] échasse f b) [in architecture] pilotis m

**stilted** ['stɪltɪd] adj [speech, person] guindé

**stimulate** ['stɪmjʊleɪt] vt stimuler ▪ **stimulant** n stimulant m ▪ **stimulus** (pl -li [-laɪ]) n [encouragement] stimulant m ; [physiological] stimulus m inv

**sting** [stɪŋ] 1. n piqûre f 2. (pt & pp **stung**) vt [of insect, ointment, wind] piquer 3. vi piquer

**stingy** ['stɪndʒɪ] (compar -ier, superl -iest) adj avare

**stink** [stɪŋk] 1. n puanteur f 2. (pt & pp **stank** or **stunk**, pp **stunk**) vi puer ; Fam [of book, film] être infect 3. vt **to stink out** [room] empester

**stint** [stɪnt] 1. n [period] période f de travail ; [share] part f de travail 2. vi **to stint on sth** lésiner sur qch

**stipulate** ['stɪpjʊleɪt] vt stipuler (**that** que) ▪ **stipulation** n stipulation f

**stir** [stɜː(r)] 1. n **to give sth a stir** remuer qch ; Fig **to cause a stir** faire du bruit 2. (pt & pp -rr-) vt [coffee, leaves] remuer ; Fig [excite] exciter ; [incite] inciter (**sb to do** qn à faire) ; **to stir up trouble** semer la zizanie ; **to stir things up** envenimer les choses 3. vi [move] remuer, bouger ▪ **stirring** adj [speech] émouvant

**stirrup** ['stɪrəp] n étrier m

**stitch** [stɪtʃ] 1. n point m ; [in knitting] maille f ; [in wound] point m de suture ; [sharp pain] point m de côté ; Fam **to be in stitches** être plié (de rire) 2. vt **to stitch (up)** [sew up] coudre ; MED recoudre

**stock** [stɒk] 1. n [supply] provisions fpl ; COMM stock m ; FIN valeurs fpl ; [soup] bouillon m ; Br **stock cube** bouillon-cube m ; FIN **stocks and shares** valeurs fpl mobilières ; **in stock** [goods] en stock ; **out of stock** [goods] épuisé ; Fig **to take stock** faire le point (**of** de) ; **the Stock Exchange** or **Market** la Bourse 2. adj classique 3. vt [sell] vendre ; [keep in store] stocker ; **to stock (up)** [shop] approvisionner ; [fridge, cupboard] remplir 4. vi **to stock up** s'approvisionner (**with** en) ▪ **stockbroker** n agent m de change ▪ **stockholder** ['stɒk,həʊldə(r)] n Am actionnaire mf ▪ **stockpile** vt faire des réserves de ▪ **stocktaking** n Br COMM inventaire m

**stocking** ['stɒkɪŋ] n [for woman] bas m

**stocky** ['stɒkɪ] (compar -ier, superl -iest) adj trapu

**stodgy** ['stɒdʒɪ] (compar -ier, superl -iest) adj Fam [food] bourratif, -ive ; Fig [book] indigeste

**stoked** [stəkd] adj Am Fam **to be stoked about sth** [excited] être tout excité à cause de qch

**stole¹** [stəʊl] n [shawl] étole f

**stole²** [stəʊl] pt of **steal**

**stolen** ['stəʊlən] pp of **steal**

**stomach** ['stʌmək] 1. n ventre m ; [organ] estomac m 2. vt [put up with] supporter ▪ **stomachache** n mal m de ventre ; **to have (a) stomachache** avoir mal au ventre

**stone** [stəʊn] n pierre f ; [pebble] caillou m ; [in fruit] noyau m ; Br [unit of weight] 6,348 kg ▪ **stone-cold** adj glacé ▪ **stone-deaf** adj sourd comme un pot

**stoned** [stəʊnd] adj Fam [on drugs] défoncé (**on** à)

**stony** ['stəʊnɪ] (compar -ier, superl -iest) adj [path] caillouteux, -euse ; Br Fam **stony broke** [penniless] fauché

**stood** [stʊd] pt & pp of **stand**

**stool** [stuːl] n tabouret m

**stoop** [stuːp] vi se baisser ; Fig **to stoop to doing sth** s'abaisser à faire qch

**stop** [stɒp] **1.** n [place, halt] arrêt m; [for plane, ship] escale f; **to put a stop to sth** mettre fin à qch; **to come to a stop** s'arrêter; **stop sign** [on road] stop **2.** (pt & pp -pp-) vt arrêter; [end] mettre fin à; [cheque] faire opposition à; **to stop sb/sth from doing sth** empêcher qn /qch de faire qch **3.** vi s'arrêter; [of pain, bleeding] cesser; [stay] rester; **to stop snowing** cesser de neiger ■ **stop-and-search** n fouilles fpl dans la rue ■ **stopgap** n bouche-trou m ■ **sto-poff** n halte f; [in plane journey] escale f ■ **stopover** n arrêt m; [in plane journey] escale f ■ **stopwatch** n chrono-mètre m ■ **stop by** vi [visit] passer (sb's chez qn) ■ **stop off, stop over** vi [on journey] s'arrêter ■ **stop up** vt sep [sink, pipe, leak] boucher

**stoppage** [ˈstɒpɪdʒ] n [strike] dé-brayage m; Br [in pay] retenue f; **stop-page time** [in sport] arrêts mpl de jeu

**stopper** [ˈstɒpə(r)] n bouchon m

**store** [stɔː(r)] **1.** n [supply] provision f; Fig [of knowledge] fonds m; [warehouse] entrepôt m; [shop] Br grand maga-sin m; Am magasin m; **to have sth in store for sb** réserver qch à qn **2.** vt [in warehouse] stocker; [furniture] entre-poser; [food] ranger; COMPUT [in mem-ory] mettre en mémoire ■ **storage** n emmagasinage m; COMPUT stockage m, mémorisation f; **storage room** [small] cagibi m; [larger] débarras m; **storage space** espace m de rangement; COMPUT **storage capacity** capacité f de mémoire ■ **store away** vt sep [put away, file away] ranger; [furniture] en-treposer ■ **store up** vt sep accumuler

**storekeeper** [ˈstɔːkiːpə(r)] n Am [shop-keeper] commerçant, -e mf

**storeroom** [ˈstɔːruːm] n [in house] débarras m; [in office, shop] réserve f

**storey** [ˈstɔːrɪ] (pl -eys) n Br [of building] étage m

**stork** [stɔːk] n cigogne f

**storm** [stɔːm] **1.** n [bad weather] tem-pête f; [thunderstorm] orage m **2.** vt [of soldiers, police] prendre d'assaut **3.** vi to

**storm out** [angrily] sortir comme une furie ■ **stormy** (compar -ier, superl -iest) adj [weather, meeting] orageux, -euse

**story¹** [ˈstɔːrɪ] (pl -ies) n histoire f; [newspaper article] article m ■ **sto-rytelling** [ˈstɔːrɪˌtelɪŋ] n **a)** [art] art m de conter; **to be good at storytelling** avoir l'art de raconter des histoires **b)** Euph [telling lies] mensonges mpl

**story²** [ˈstɔːrɪ] (pl -ies) n Am [of building] étage m

**stout** [staʊt] **1.** (compar -er, superl -est) adj [person] corpulent; [shoes] solide **2.** n Br [beer] bière f brune

**stove** [stəʊv] n [for cooking] cuisinière f; [for heating] poêle m

**stow** [stəʊ] **1.** vt [cargo] arrimer; **to stow sth away** [put away] ranger qch **2.** vi **to stow away** [on ship] voyager clandestinement ■ **stowaway** n [on ship] passager, -ère mf clandestin(e)

**straddle** [ˈstrædəl] vt [chair, fence] se mettre à califourchon sur; [step over, span] enjamber

**straggle** [ˈstrægəl] vi [lag behind] être à la traîne ■ **straggler** n retardataire mf

**straight** [streɪt] **1.** (compar -er, superl -est) adj droit; [hair] raide; [honest] honnête; [answer] clair; [consecutive] consécutif, -ive; [conventional] confor-miste; Fam [heterosexual] hétéro **2.** adv [in straight line] droit; [directly] direc-tement; [immediately] tout de suite; **straight away** [at once] tout de suite; Br **straight ahead** or **on** [walk] tout droit; **to look straight ahead** regar-der droit devant soi; **straight off** tout de suite, sur-le-champ; **straight out** sans mâcher ses mots

**straightaway** [streɪtəˈweɪ] adv tout de suite

**straighten** [ˈstreɪtən] vt **to straighten (out)** [wire] redresser; **to straighten (up)** [tie, hair, room] arranger

**straight-faced** adj qui garde son sérieux, impassible

**straightforward** [streɪtˈfɔːwəd] adj [easy, clear] simple; [frank] franc (f franche)

**stretch**

**strain** [streɪn] **1.** *n* tension *f*; [mental stress] stress *m* **2.** *vt* **a)** [rope, wire] tendre excessivement; [muscle] se froisser; [ankle, wrist] se fouler; [eyes] fatiguer; [voice] forcer; *Fig* [patience, friendship] mettre à l'épreuve; **to strain oneself** [hurt oneself] se faire mal; [tire oneself] se fatiguer **b)** [soup] passer; [vegetables] égoutter **3.** *vi* faire un effort (**to do** pour faire)

**strained** [streɪnd] *adj* [muscle] froissé; [ankle, wrist] foulé; [relations] tendu

**strainer** ['streɪnə(r)] *n* passoire *f*

**strait** [streɪt] *n* GEOG **strait(s)** détroit *m*; **in financial straits** dans l'embarras

**strand** [strænd] *n* [of wool] brin *m*; [of hair] mèche *f*; *Fig* [of story] fil *m*

**stranded** ['strændɪd] *adj* [person, vehicle] en rade

**strange** [streɪndʒ] *(compar* **-er**, *superl* **-est)** *adj* [odd] bizarre; [unknown] inconnu ■ **strangely** *adv* étrangement; **strangely (enough), she…** chose étrange, elle…

**stranger** ['streɪndʒə(r)] *n* [unknown] inconnu, -e *mf*; [outsider] étranger, -ère *mf*

**strangle** ['stræŋɡəl] *vt* étrangler

**strap** [stræp] **1.** *n* sangle *f*; [on dress] bretelle *f*; [on watch] bracelet *m*; [on sandal] lanière *f* **2.** *(pt & pp* **-pp-)** *vt* **to strap (down** *or* **in)** attacher *(avec une sangle)*; **to strap sb in** attacher qn avec une ceinture de sécurité

**strapping** ['stræpɪŋ] *adj* robuste

**strategy** ['strætədʒɪ] *(pl* **-ies)** *n* stratégie *f* ■ **strategic** [strə'tiːdʒɪk] *adj* stratégique

**straw** [strɔː] *n* [from wheat, for drinking] paille *f*

**strawberry** ['strɔːbərɪ] **1.** *(pl* **-ies)** *n* fraise *f* **2.** *adj* [flavour, ice cream] à la fraise; [jam] de fraises; [tart] aux fraises

**stray** [streɪ] **1.** *adj* [animal, bullet] perdu; **a few stray cars** quelques rares voitures **2.** *n* [dog] chien *m* errant; [cat] chat *m* égaré **3.** *vi* s'égarer; **to stray from** [subject, path] s'écarter de

**streak** [striːk] *n* [of paint, dirt] traînée *f*; [of light] rai *m*; [in hair] mèche *f* ■ **streaked** *adj* [marked] strié; [stained] taché (**with** de)

**stream** [striːm] **1.** *n* [brook] ruisseau *m*; [of light, blood] jet *m*; [of people] flot *m* **2.** *vi* ruisseler (**with** de); **to stream in** [of sunlight, people] entrer à flots **3.** *vt* **a)** COMPUT [music, news] télécharger en streaming **b)** *Br* SCH répartir par niveau

**streamer** ['striːmə(r)] *n* [banner] banderole *f*

**streaming** ['striːmɪŋ] **1.** *n* **a)** *Br* SCH répartition *f* en classes de niveau **b)** COMPUT streaming *m* **2.** *adj* [surface, window] ruisselant; *Br* **I've got a streaming cold** j'ai attrapé un gros rhume

**streamline** ['striːmlaɪn] *vt* [work, method] rationaliser ■ **streamlined** *adj* [shape] aérodynamique; [industry, production] rationalisé

**street** [striːt] *n* rue *f*; **street lamp, street light** lampadaire *m*; **street map** plan *m* des rues ■ **streetcar** *n Am* [tram] tramway *m*

**strength** [streŋθ] *n* force *f*; [of wood, fabric] solidité *f* ■ **strengthen** *vt* [building, position] renforcer; [body, limb] fortifier

**strenuous** ['strenjʊəs] *adj* [effort] vigoureux, -euse; [work] fatigant

**stress** [stres] **1.** *n* [physical] tension *f*; [mental] stress *m*; [emphasis, in grammar] accent *m*; **under stress** [person] stressé, sous pression; [relationship] tendu **2.** *vt* insister sur; [word] accentuer; **to stress that…** souligner que… ■ **stress-buster** *n Fam* éliminateur *m* de stress ■ **stress-related** *adj* dû (*f* due) au stress ■ **stressful** *adj* stressant

**stretch** [stretʃ] **1.** *n* [area] étendue *f*; [period of time] période *f*; [of road] tronçon *m* **2.** *vt* [rope, neck] tendre; [shoe, rubber] étirer; *Fig* [income, supplies] faire durer; **to stretch (out)** [arm, leg] tendre; *Fig* **to stretch one's legs** se dégourdir les jambes; *Fig* **to stretch sb** pousser qn à son maximum **3.** *vi* [of person, elastic] s'étirer ; [of influence] s'étendre ; **to stretch (out)** [of rope, plain] s'étendre

**stretcher** ['strɛtʃə(r)] n brancard m

**strew** [struː] (pt **strewed**, pp **strewed** or **strewn** [struːn]) vt [scatter] éparpiller ; **strewn with** [covered] jonché de

**stricken** ['strɪkən] adj [town, region] sinistré

**strict** [strɪkt] (compar **-er**, superl **-est**) adj [severe, absolute] strict ■ **strictly** adv strictement ; **strictly forbidden** formellement interdit

**stride** [straɪd] **1.** n pas m ; Fig **to make great strides** faire de grands progrès **2.** (pt **strode**) vi **to stride across** or **over** [fields] traverser à grandes enjambées ; **to stride along / out** avancer / sortir à grands pas

**strike** [straɪk] **1.** n [of workers] grève f ; MIL raid m ; **to go on strike** se mettre en grève **2.** (pt & pp **struck**) vt [hit, impress] frapper ; [collide with] heurter ; [gold, oil] trouver ; [match] craquer ; **it strikes me that…** il me semble que… (+ indicative) **3.** vi [of workers] faire grève ; [attack] attaquer ■ **strike at** vt insep [attack] attaquer ■ **strike back** vi [retaliate] riposter ■ **strike down** vt sep [of illness] terrasser ■ **strike off** vt sep [from list] rayer (**from** de) ; **to be struck off** [of doctor] être radié ■ **strike out** vi **to strike out at sb** essayer de frapper qn ■ **strike up** vt sep **to strike up a friendship** se lier amitié (**with sb** avec qn)

**striker** ['straɪkə(r)] n [worker] gréviste mf ; [footballer] buteur m

**striking** ['straɪkɪŋ] adj [impressive] frappant

**string** [strɪŋ] **1.** n ficelle f ; [of apron] cordon m ; [of violin, racket] corde f ; [of questions] série f ; Fig **to pull strings** faire jouer ses relations **2.** adj [instrument, quartet] à cordes **3.** (pt & pp **strung**) vt [beads] enfiler ■ **stringed** adj [instrument] à cordes

**stringent** ['strɪndʒənt] adj rigoureux, -euse

**strip** [strɪp] **1.** n [piece] bande f ; [of metal] lame f ; [of sports team] tenue f ; **strip cartoon** bande f dessinée ; Am **strip mall** centre commercial qui longe une route **2.** (pt & pp **-pp-**) vt [undress] déshabiller ; [deprive] dépouiller (**of** de) ; **to strip off** [remove] enlever **3.** vi **to strip (off)** [get undressed] se déshabiller ■ **stripper** n [woman] strip-teaseuse f ; [paint] stripper [substance] décapant m ■ **striptease** n strip-tease m

**stripe** [straɪp] n rayure f ; [indicating rank] galon m ■ **striped** adj rayé (**with** de)

**strive** [straɪv] (pt **strove**, pp **striven** ['strɪvən]) vi s'efforcer (**to do** de faire ; **for** d'obtenir)

**strode** [strəʊd] pt of **stride**

**stroke** [strəʊk] **1.** n [movement] coup m ; [of pen] trait m ; [of brush] touche f ; [caress] caresse f ; MED [illness] attaque f ; **at a stroke** d'un coup ; **stroke of luck** coup m de chance **2.** vt [caress] caresser

**stroll** [strəʊl] **1.** n promenade f **2.** vi se promener ; **to stroll in** entrer sans se presser

**stroller** ['strəʊlə(r)] n Am [for baby] poussette f

**strong** [strɒŋ] **1.** (compar **-er**, superl **-est**) adj fort ; [shoes, chair, nerves] solide ; [interest] vif (f vive) ; [measures] énergique ; [supporter] ardent **2.** adv **to be going strong** aller toujours bien ■ **strong-box** n coffre-fort m ■ **stronghold** n bastion m ■ **strongly** adv [protest, defend] énergiquement ; [advise, remind, desire] fortement

**strove** [strəʊv] pt of **strive**

**struck** [strʌk] pt & pp of **strike**

**structure** ['strʌktʃə(r)] n structure f ; [building] édifice m ■ **structural** adj structural ; [building defect] de construction

**struggle** ['strʌɡəl] **1.** n [fight] lutte f (**to do** pour faire) ; **to have a struggle doing** or **to do sth** avoir du mal à faire qch **2.** vi [fight] lutter (**with** avec) ; **to**

**be struggling** [financially] avoir du mal; **to struggle to do sth** s'efforcer de faire qch

**strung** [strʌŋ] pt & pp of **string**

**strut¹** [strʌt] (pt & pp -tt-) vi to strut (about or around) se pavaner

**strut²** [strʌt] n [for frame] étai m

**stub** [stʌb] **1.** n [of pencil, cigarette] bout m; [of cheque] talon m **2.** (pt & pp -bb-) vt **to stub one's toe** se cogner l'orteil (on or against contre); **to stub out** [cigarette] écraser

**stubble** ['stʌbəl] n [on face] barbe f de plusieurs jours

**stubborn** ['stʌbən] adj [person] têtu

**stuck** [stʌk] **1.** pt & pp of **stick 2.** adj [caught, jammed] coincé; **stuck in bed/indoors** cloué au lit/chez soi; **to get stuck** être coincé; **to be stuck with sb/sth** se farcir qn/qch

**stuck-up** [stʌˈkʌp] adj Fam snob

**stud¹** [stʌd] n [on football boot] crampon m; [earring] clou m d'oreille ■ **studded** adj **studded with** [covered] constellé de

**stud²** [stʌd] n [farm] haras m; [stallion] étalon m

**student** ['stjuːdənt] **1.** n [at university] étudiant, -e mf; [at school] élève mf; **music student** étudiant, -e mf en musique **2.** adj [life, protest] étudiant; [restaurant, residence, grant] universitaire

**studio** ['stjuːdɪəʊ] (pl -os) n studio m; [of artist] atelier m; Br **studio flat**, Am **studio apartment** studio m

**studious** ['stjuːdɪəs] adj [person] studieux, -euse

**study** ['stʌdɪ] **1.** (pl -ies) n étude f; [office] bureau m **2.** (pt & pp -ied) vt [learn, observe] étudier **3.** vi étudier; **to study to be a doctor** faire des études de médecine; **to study for an exam** préparer un examen

**stuff** [stʌf] **1.** n [possessions] affaires fpl; Fam **some stuff** [substance] un truc; [things] des trucs; Fam **this stuff's good, it's good stuff** c'est bien **2.** vt [pocket] remplir (with de); [cushion] rembourrer (with avec); [animal]

empailler; [chicken, tomatoes] farcir; **to stuff sth into sth** fourrer qch dans qch ■ **stuffing** n [padding] bourre f; [for chicken, tomatoes] farce f

**stuffed shirt** n prétentieux, -euse mf; **he's a real stuffed shirt** il est vraiment suffisant

**stuffy** ['stʌfɪ] (compar -ier, superl -iest) adj [room] qui sent le renfermé; [person] vieux jeu inv

**stumble** ['stʌmbəl] vi trébucher; **to stumble across or on** [find] tomber sur

**stump** [stʌmp] n [of tree] souche f; [of limb] moignon m; [in cricket] piquet m

**stumpy** ['stʌmpɪ] (compar -ier, superl -iest) adj [person] courtaud

**stun** [stʌn] (pt & pp -nn-) vt [make unconscious] assommer; Fig [amaze] stupéfier ■ **stunned** adj [amazed] stupéfait (by par) ■ **stunning** adj Fam [excellent] excellent; Fam [beautiful] superbe

**stung** [stʌŋ] pt & pp of **sting**

**stunk** [stʌŋk] pt & pp of **stink**

**stunt¹** [stʌnt] n [in film] cascade f; [for publicity] coup m de pub; **stunt man** cascadeur m

**stunt²** [stʌnt] vt [growth] retarder ■ **stunted** adj [person] rabougri

**stupid** ['stjuːpɪd] adj stupide; **to do/say a stupid thing** faire/dire une stupidité ■ **stupidity** n stupidité f ■ **stupidly** adv bêtement

**sturdy** ['stɜːdɪ] (compar -ier, superl -iest) adj [person, shoe] robuste

**stutter** ['stʌtə(r)] **1.** n to have a stutter être bègue **2.** vi bégayer

**sty¹** [staɪ] n [for pigs] porcherie f

**sty²**, **stye** [staɪ] n [on eye] orgelet m

**style** [staɪl] **1.** n style m; [sophistication] classe f **2.** vt [design] créer; **to style sb's hair** coiffer qn

**stylish** ['staɪlɪʃ] adj chic inv

**stylist** ['staɪlɪst] n (hair) stylist coiffeur, -euse mf

**sub-** [sʌb] pref sous-, sub-

**subconscious** [sʌbˈkɒnʃəs] adj & n subconscient (m) ■ **subconsciously** adv inconsciemment

**subcontract** [sʌbkən'trækt] *vt* sous-traiter

**subdivide** [sʌbdɪ'vaɪd] *vt* subdiviser (**into** en)

**subdue** [səb'dju:] *vt* [country, people] soumettre ; [feelings] maîtriser ∎ **subdued** *adj* [light] tamisé ; [voice, tone] bas (*f* basse) ; [person] inhabituellement calme

**subject¹** ['sʌbdʒɪkt] *n* **a)** [matter, in grammar] sujet *m* ; [at school, university] matière *f* ; **subject matter** [topic] sujet *m* ; [content] contenu *m* **b)** [of monarch] sujet, -ette *mf*

**subject²** 1. ['sʌbdʒekt] *adj* **to be subject to depression / jealousy** avoir tendance à la dépression / à la jalousie ; **it's subject to my agreement** c'est sous réserve de mon accord 2. [səb'dʒekt] *vt* soumettre (**to** à)

**subjective** [səb'dʒektɪv] *adj* subjectif, -ive ∎ **subjectively** *adv* subjectivement

**subjunctive** [səb'dʒʌŋktɪv] *n* subjonctif *m*

**sublet** [sʌb'let] (*pt & pp* -let, *pres p* -letting) *vt* sous-louer

**sublime** [sə'blaɪm] *adj* sublime ; [utter] suprême

**submarine** ['sʌbməri:n] *n* sous-marin *m*

**submerge** [səb'mɜːdʒ] *vt* [flood, overwhelm] submerger ; [immerse] immerger (**in** dans)

**submit** [səb'mɪt] 1. (*pt & pp* -tt-) *vt* soumettre (**to** à) 2. *vi* se soumettre (**to** à) ∎ **submissive** *adj* [person] soumis ; [attitude] de soumission

**subordinate** [sə'bɔːdɪnət] 1. *adj* subalterne ; **subordinate to** subordonné à 2. *n* subordonné, -e *mf*

**subprime** ['sʌbpraɪm] *n* *Am* FIN **subprime (loan** *or* **mortgage)** subprime *m* (*type de crédit immobilier à risque*)

**subscribe** [səb'skraɪb] *vi* [pay money] cotiser (**to** à) ; **to subscribe to a newspaper** s'abonner à un journal ∎ **subscriber** *n* [to newspaper,

telephone] abonné, -e *mf* ∎ **subscription** [səb'skrɪpʃən] *n* [to newspaper] abonnement *m* ; [to club] cotisation *f*

**subsequent** ['sʌbsɪkwənt] *adj* ultérieur (**to** à) ; **our subsequent problems** les problèmes que nous avons eus par la suite ∎ **subsequently** *adv* par la suite

**subside** [səb'saɪd] *vi* [of ground, building] s'affaisser ; [of wind, flood, fever] baisser ∎ **subsidence** *n* [of ground] affaissement *m*

**subsidiary** [*Br* səb'sɪdɪərɪ, *Am* -dɪerɪ] 1. *adj* subsidiaire 2. (*pl* -**ies**) *n* [company] filiale *f*

**subsidize** ['sʌbsɪdaɪz] *vt* subventionner ∎ **subsidy** (*pl* -**ies**) *n* subvention *f*

**substance** ['sʌbstəns] *n* substance *f* ; [solidity, worth] fondement *m*

**substantial** [səb'stænʃəl] *adj* important ; [meal] substantiel, -elle ∎ **substantially** *adv* considérablement

**substitute** ['sʌbstɪtju:t] 1. *n* [thing] produit *m* de remplacement ; [person] remplaçant, -e *mf* (**for** de) 2. *vt* **to substitute sb / sth for** substituer qn / qch à 3. *vi* **to substitute for sb** remplacer qn ∎ **substitution** *n* substitution *f*

**subtext** ['sʌbˌtekst] *n* message *m* sous-jacent (*de livre, de film*)

**subtitle** ['sʌbtaɪtəl] 1. *n* [of film] sous-titre *m* 2. *vt* [film] sous-titrer

**subtle** ['sʌtəl] (*compar* -er, *superl* -est) *adj* subtil

**subtotal** [sʌb'təʊtəl] *n* sous-total *m*

**subtract** [səb'trækt] *vt* soustraire (**from** de) ∎ **subtraction** *n* soustraction *f*

**suburb** ['sʌbɜːb] *n* banlieue *f* ; **the suburbs** la banlieue ∎ **suburban** [sə'bɜːbən] *adj* [train, house] de banlieue ∎ **suburbia** [sə'bɜːbɪə] *n* la banlieue ; **in suburbia** en banlieue

**subversive** [səb'vɜːsɪv] *adj* subversif, -ive

**subway** ['sʌbweɪ] *n* *Br* [under road] passage *m* souterrain ; *Am* [railroad] métro *m*

**succeed** [sək'si:d] 1. *vt* **to succeed sb** succéder à qn 2. *vi* réussir (**in doing** à faire ; **in sth** dans qch) ; **to succeed**

to the throne monter sur le trône ■ **succeeding** adj [in past] suivant ; [in future] futur ; [consecutive] consécutif, -ive

**success** [sək'ses] n succès m, réussite f ; **he was a success** il a eu du succès ; **it was a success** c'était réussi

**successful** [sək'sesfəl] adj [effort, venture] couronné de succès ; [outcome] heureux, -euse ; [company, businessman] prospère ; [candidate in exam] admis, reçu ; [candidate in election] élu ; [writer, film] à succès ; **to be successful** réussir ; **to be successful in doing sth** réussir à faire qch ■ **successfully** adv avec succès

**succession** [sək'seʃən] n succession f ; **ten days in succession** dix jours consécutifs ■ **successive** adj successif, -ive ; **ten successive days** dix jours consécutifs ■ **successor** n successeur m (**to** de)

**succinct** [sək'sɪŋkt] adj succinct

**succumb** [sə'kʌm] vi succomber (**to** à)

**such** [sʌtʃ] **1.** adj [of this or that kind] tel (f telle) ; **such a car** une telle voiture ; **such happiness/noise** tant de bonheur/bruit ; **there's no such thing** ça n'existe pas ; **such as** comme, tel que **2.** adv [so very] si ; [in comparisons] aussi ; **such long trips** de si longs voyages **3.** pron **happiness as such** le bonheur en tant que tel ■ **suchlike** pron & adj ...**and suchlike** ...et autres

**suck** [sʌk] **1.** vt sucer ; [of baby] téter ; **to suck (up)** [with straw, pump] aspirer ; **to suck up** or **in** [absorb] absorber **2.** vi [of baby] téter

**suckle** ['sʌkəl] **1.** vt [of woman] allaiter **2.** vi [of baby] téter

**suction** ['sʌkʃən] n succion f

**sudden** ['sʌdən] adj soudain ; **all of a sudden** tout à coup ■ **suddenly** adv tout à coup, soudain ; [die] subitement

**suds** [sʌdz] npl mousse f de savon

**sue** [su:] **1.** vt poursuivre (en justice) **2.** vi engager des poursuites judiciaires

**suede** [sweɪd] n daim m

**suffer** ['sʌfə(r)] **1.** vt [loss, damage, defeat] subir ; [pain] ressentir ; [tolerate] supporter **2.** vi souffrir (**from** de) ; **your work will suffer** ton travail s'en ressentira ■ **sufferer** n [from misfortune] victime f ; **AIDS sufferer** malade mf du SIDA ■ **suffering** n souffrance f

**suffice** [sə'faɪs] vi suffire

**sufficient** [sə'fɪʃənt] adj suffisant ; **sufficient money** [enough] suffisamment d'argent ; **to be sufficient** suffire ■ **sufficiently** adv suffisamment

**suffix** ['sʌfɪks] n suffixe m

**suffocate** ['sʌfəkeɪt] **1.** vt étouffer **2.** vi suffoquer

**sugar** ['ʃʊgə(r)] **1.** n sucre m ; **sugar bowl** sucrier m ; **sugar lump** morceau m de sucre **2.** vt [tea] sucrer

**suggest** [sə'dʒest] vt [propose] suggérer ; [imply] indiquer ■ **suggestion** n suggestion f ■ **suggestive** adj suggestif, -ive ; **to be suggestive of** évoquer

**suicide** ['su:ɪsaɪd] n suicide m ; **to commit suicide** se suicider

**suit¹** [su:t] **n a)** [man's] costume m ; [woman's] tailleur m ; **flying/diving/ ski suit** combinaison f de vol/plongée/ ski **b)** [in card games] couleur f ; Fig **to follow suit** faire de même **c)** [lawsuit] procès m

**suit²** [su:t] **1.** vt [please, be acceptable to] convenir à ; [of dress, colour] aller (bien) à ; [adapt] adapter (**to** à) ; **suited to** [job, activity] fait pour ; [appropriate to] qui convient à ; **to be well suited** [of couple] être bien assorti **2.** vi convenir, aller

**suitable** ['su:təbəl] adj convenable (**for** à) ; [candidate, date] adéquat ; [example] approprié ; **this film is not suitable for children** ce film n'est pas pour les enfants

**suitcase** ['su:tkeɪs] n valise f

**suite** [swi:t] n [rooms] suite f

**sulk** [sʌlk] vi bouder

**sullen** ['sʌlən] adj maussade

**sultana** [sʌl'tɑ:nə] n [raisin] raisin m de Smyrne

**sum** [sʌm] **1.** n [amount of money] somme f; [mathematical problem] problème m; **sum total** somme f totale **2.** (pt & pp -mm-) vt **to sum up** [summarize] résumer; [assess] évaluer **3.** vi **to sum up** résumer

**summarize** ['sʌməraɪz] vt résumer ■ **summary** (pl -ies) n résumé m

**summer** ['sʌmə(r)] **1.** n été m; **in (the) summer** en été **2.** adj d'été; Am **summer camp** colonie f de vacances; Br **summer holidays**, Am **summer vacation** grandes vacances fpl ■ **summertime** n été m; **in (the) summertime** en été

**summit** ['sʌmɪt] n sommet m

**summon** ['sʌmən] vt [call] appeler; [meeting, person] convoquer (**to** à); **to summon up one's courage/strength** rassembler son courage/ses forces

**summons** ['sʌmənz] **1.** n [in law] assignation f à comparaître **2.** vt assigner à comparaître

**SUM1** (abbr of **someone**) MESSAGING kelk1

**sumptuous** ['sʌmptʃʊəs] adj somptueux, -euse

**sun** [sʌn] **1.** n soleil m; **in the sun** au soleil; **the sun is shining** il fait soleil; **sun cream** crème f solaire **2.** (pt & pp -nn-) vt **to sun oneself** prendre le soleil ■ **sunbathe** vi prendre un bain de soleil ■ **sunbed** n lit m à ultraviolets ■ **sunblock** n [cream] écran m total ■ **sunburn** n coup m de soleil ■ **sunburnt** adj brûlé par le soleil ■ **sundial** n cadran m solaire ■ **sunflower** n tournesol m ■ **sunglasses** npl lunettes fpl de soleil ■ **sunhat** n chapeau m de soleil ■ **sunlamp** n lampe f à bronzer ■ **sunlight** n lumière f du soleil ■ **sunrise** n lever m du soleil ■ **sunroof** n [in car] toit m ouvrant ■ **sunset** n coucher m du soleil ■ **sunshade** n [on table] parasol m; [portable] ombrelle f ■ **sunshine** n soleil m ■ **sunstroke** n insolation f ■ **suntan** n bronzage m; **suntan lotion/oil** crème f/huile f solaire ■ **suntanned** adj bronzé

**Sunday** ['sʌndeɪ] n dimanche m; **Sunday school** ≃ catéchisme m

**sundry** ['sʌndrɪ] **1.** adj divers **2.** n **all and sundry** tout le monde

**sung** [sʌŋ] pp of **sing**

**sunk** [sʌŋk] pp of **sink**

**sunken** adj [rock, treasure] submergé

**sunny** ['sʌnɪ] (compar -ier, superl -iest) adj [day] ensoleillé; **it's sunny** il fait soleil; **sunny periods** or **intervals** éclaircies fpl

**sup** [sʌp] excl Am Fam (abbr of **what's up?**) salut! Ça roule ou ça boume?

**super** ['su:pə(r)] adj Fam super inv

**super-** ['su:pə(r)] pref super-

**superb** [su:'pɜ:b] adj superbe

**superficial** [su:pə'fɪʃəl] adj superficiel, -elle

**superfluous** [su:'pɜ:flʊəs] adj superflu

**superglue** ['su:pəglu:] n colle f extraforte

**superintendent** [su:pərɪn'tendənt] n Am [of apartment building] gardien, -enne mf; **(police) superintendent** ≃ commissaire mf de police

**superior** [su:'pɪərɪə(r)] **1.** adj supérieur (**to** à) **2.** n [person] supérieur, -eure mf ■ **superiority** [-rɪ'ɒrətɪ] n supériorité f

**superlative** [su:'pɜ:lətɪv] **1.** adj sans pareil **2.** adj & n GRAM superlatif (m)

**supermarket** ['su:pəmɑ:kɪt] n supermarché m

**supermodel** ['su:pəmɒdl] n top model m

**supernatural** [su:pə'nætʃərəl] adj & n surnaturel, -elle (m)

**superpower** ['su:pəpaʊə(r)] n POL superpuissance f

**supersede** [su:pə'si:d] vt supplanter

**supersize** ['su:pəsaɪz] **1.** adj géant **2.** vt augmenter la taille de; **the company has supersized itself** la société a augmenté sa taille

**supersonic** [su:pə'sɒnɪk] adj supersonique

**superstition** [su:pə'stɪʃən] n superstition f ■ **superstitious** adj superstitieux, -euse

**superstore** ['su:pəstɔ:r] n hypermarché m

**supervise** ['su:pəvaɪz] vt [person, work] surveiller ; [research] superviser ■ **supervisor** n surveillant, -e mf ; [in office] chef m de service ; [in store] chef m de rayon

**supper** ['sʌpə(r)] n [meal] dîner m ; [snack] casse-croûte pris avant d'aller se coucher

**supple** ['sʌpəl] adj souple

**supplement 1.** ['sʌplɪmənt] n supplément m (**to** à) **2.** ['sʌplɪment] vt compléter ; **to supplement one's income** arrondir ses fins de mois ■ **supplementary** [-'mentərɪ] adj supplémentaire

**supplier** [sə'plaɪə(r)] n COMM fournisseur m

**supply** [sə'plaɪ] **1.** (pl -ies) n [stock] provision f ; **supply and demand** l'offre f et la demande ; Br **supply teacher** suppléant, -e mf **2.** (pt & pp -ied) vt [provide] fournir ; [with gas, electricity, water] alimenter (**with** en) ; [equip] équiper (**with** de) ; **to supply sb with sth, to supply sth to sb** fournir qch à qn

**support** [sə'pɔ:t] **1.** n [backing, person supporting] soutien m ; [thing supporting] support m ; **in support of** [person] en faveur de ; [evidence, theory] à l'appui de **2.** vt [bear weight of] supporter ; [help, encourage] soutenir ; [theory, idea] appuyer ; [family, wife, husband] subvenir aux besoins de

**supporter** [sə'pɔ:tə(r)] n partisan m ; [of football team] supporter m

**supportive** [sə'pɔ:tɪv] adj **to be supportive of sb** être d'un grand soutien à qn

**suppose** [sə'pəʊz] vti supposer (**that** que) ; **I'm supposed to be working** je suis censé travailler ; **he's supposed to be rich** on le dit riche ; **I suppose (so)** je pense ; **suppose** or **supposing (that) you're right** supposons que tu aies raison

**suppress** [sə'pres] vt [revolt, feelings, smile] réprimer ; [fact, evidence] faire disparaître

**supreme** [su:'pri:m] adj suprême

**surcharge** ['sɜ:tʃɑ:dʒ] n [extra charge] supplément m

**sure** [ʃʊə(r)] (compar -er, superl -est) **1.** adj sûr (**of** de ; **that** que) ; **she's sure to accept** c'est sûr qu'elle acceptera ; **to make sure of sth** s'assurer de qch ; **for sure** à coup sûr ; **sure enough** en effet, effectivement ; Fam **sure!, sure thing!** bien sûr ! **2.** adv a) Fam [yes] bien sûr b) Am [really] vraiment ■ **surely** adv [certainly] sûrement ; **surely he didn't refuse?** il n'a quand même pas refusé ?

**surf** [sɜ:f] **1.** n [waves] ressac m **2.** vt COMPUT **to surf the Net** naviguer sur l'Internet ■ **surfboard** n planche f de surf ■ **surfing** n [sport] surf m ; **to go surfing** faire du surf

**surface** ['sɜ:fɪs] **1.** n surface f ; **surface area** superficie f ; **on the surface** [of water] à la surface ; Fig [to all appearances] en apparence **2.** vi [of swimmer] remonter à la surface ; Fam [of person, thing] réapparaître

**surge** ['sɜ:dʒ] **1.** n [of enthusiasm] vague f ; [of anger, pride] accès m **2.** vi [of crowd] déferler ; [of prices] monter (soudainement) ; **to surge forward** [of person] se lancer en avant

**surgeon** ['sɜ:dʒən] n chirurgien, -enne mf ■ **surgery** ['sɜ:dʒərɪ] n Br [doctor's office] cabinet m ; [period, sitting] consultation f ; [science] chirurgie f ; **to have heart surgery** se faire opérer du cœur ■ **surgical** adj chirurgical

**surly** ['sɜ:lɪ] (compar -ier, superl -iest) adj revêche

**surmount** [sə'maʊnt] vt surmonter

**surname** ['sɜ:neɪm] n nom m de famille

**surpass** [sə'pɑ:s] vt surpasser (**in** en)

**surplus** ['sɜ:pləs] **1.** n surplus m **2.** adj [goods] en surplus

**surprise** [sə'praɪz] **1.** n surprise f ; **to give sb a surprise** faire une surprise à qn ; **surprise visit/result** visite f / résultat m inattendu(e) **2.** vt étonner, surprendre ■ **surprised** adj surpris (that que (+ subjunctive); at sth de qch; at seeing de voir) ■ **surprising** adj surprenant

**surrender** [sə'rendə(r)] **1.** n [of soldiers] reddition f **2.** vt [town] livrer; [right, claim] renoncer à **3.** vi [give oneself up] se rendre (to à)

**surrogate** ['sʌrəgət] n substitut m; **surrogate mother** mère f porteuse

**surround** [sə'raund] vt entourer (with de); [of army, police] cerner; **surrounded by** entouré de ■ **surrounding** adj environnant ■ **surroundings** npl [of town] environs mpl; [setting] cadre m

**surveillance** [sɜː'veɪləns] n surveillance f

**survey 1.** ['sɜːveɪ] n [investigation] enquête f; [of opinion] sondage m; [of house] inspection f **2.** [sə'veɪ] vt [look at] regarder; [review] passer en revue; [house] inspecter; [land] faire un relevé de ■ **surveyor** n [of land] géomètre m; [of house] expert m

**survive** [sə'vaɪv] **1.** vt survivre à **2.** vi survivre ■ **survival** n [act] survie f; [relic] vestige m ■ **survivor** n survivant, -e mf

**susceptible** [sə'septəbəl] adj [sensitive] sensible (to à)

**suspect 1.** ['sʌspekt] n & adj suspect, -ecte (mf) **2.** [sə'spekt] vt soupçonner (sb of sth qn de qch; sb of doing qn d'avoir fait); [have intuition of] se douter de

**suspend** [sə'spend] vt **a)** [hang] suspendre (from à) **b)** [service, employee, player] suspendre; [pupil] renvoyer temporairement

**suspenders** [sə'spendəz] npl **a)** Br [for stockings] jarretelles fpl **b)** Am [for trousers] bretelles fpl

**suspense** [sə'spens] n [uncertainty] incertitude f; [in film, book] suspense m; **to keep sb in suspense** tenir qn en haleine

**suspicion** [sə'spɪʃən] n soupçon m; **to be under suspicion** être soupçonné

**suspicious** [sə'spɪʃəs] adj [person] soupçonneux, -euse; [behaviour] suspect; **to be suspicious of** or **about sth** se méfier de qch

**sustain** [sə'steɪn] vt [effort, theory] soutenir; [weight] supporter; [life] maintenir; [damage, loss, attack] subir; **to sustain an injury** être blessé

**sustainability** [sə,steɪnə'bɪlɪtɪ] n durabilité f ■ **sustainable** [səs'teɪnəbl] adj [development, agriculture, politics, housing] durable; **sustainable resources** ressources fpl renouvelables

**SUV** (abbr of **sport utility vehicle**) n AUTO 4 x 4 m

**swagger** ['swægə(r)] vi [walk] se pavaner

**swallow¹** ['swɒləʊ] **1.** vt avaler; **to swallow sth down** avaler qch **2.** vi avaler

**swallow²** ['swɒləʊ] n [bird] hirondelle f

**swam** [swæm] pt of **swim**

**swamp** [swɒmp] **1.** n marais m **2.** vt [flood, overwhelm] submerger (with de)

**swan** [swɒn] n cygne m

**swanky** ['swæŋkɪ] (compar -ier, superl -iest) adj Fam chic

**swap** [swɒp] **1.** n échange m **2.** (pt & pp -pp-) vt échanger (for contre); **to swap seats** or **places** changer de place **3.** vi échanger

**swarm** [swɔːm] **1.** n [of bees, people] essaim m **2.** vi [of streets, insects, people] fourmiller (with de)

**swat** [swɒt] (pt & pp -tt-) vt écraser

**sway** [sweɪ] **1.** vt balancer; Fig [person, public opinion] influencer **2.** vi se balancer

**swear** [sweə(r)] **1.** (pt swore, pp sworn) vt [promise] jurer (to do de faire; that que); **to swear an oath** prêter serment **2.** vi [take an oath] jurer (to sth de qch); **to swear at sb** injurier qn ■ **swearing** ['sweərɪŋ] n [use of swear words] jurons mpl, gros mots mpl ■ **swearword** n juron m

**sweat** [swet] **1.** n sueur f **2.** vi suer ■ **sweatshirt** n sweat-shirt m

**sweater** ['swetə(r)] n pull m

**sweaty** ['swetɪ] *(compar* -ier, *superl* -iest) *adj* [shirt] plein de sueur ; [hand] moite ; [person] en sueur

**Swede** [swiːd] *n* Suédois, -e *mf* ■ **Sweden** *n* la Suède ■ **Swedish 1.** *adj* suédois **2.** *n* [language] suédois *m*

**sweep** [swiːp] **1.** *(pt & pp* **swept)** *vt* [with broom] balayer ; [chimney] ramoner **2.** *vi* balayer ■ **sweep aside** *vt sep* [opposition, criticism] écarter ■ **sweep away** *vt sep* [leaves] balayer ; [carry off] emporter ■ **sweep out** *vt sep* [room] balayer ■ **sweep through** *vt insep* [of fear] saisir ; [of disease] ravager ■ **sweep up** *vt sep &* *vi* balayer

**sweeping** ['swiːpɪŋ] *adj* [gesture] large ; [change] radical ; [statement] trop général

**sweet** [swiːt] **1.** *(compar* -est, *superl* -est) *adj* doux *(f* douce) ; [tea, coffee, cake] sucré ; [pretty, kind] adorable ; **to have a sweet tooth** aimer les sucreries **2.** *n Br* [piece of confectionery] bonbon *m* ; *Br* [dessert] dessert *m* ; *Br* **sweet shop** confiserie *f* ■ **sweetcorn** *n Br* maïs *m* ■ **sweetie** ['swiːtɪ] *n Fam* **a)** [darling] chéri, -e *mf*, chou *m* ; **he's a real sweetie** il est vraiment adorable **b)** *Br* (baby talk) [sweet] bonbon *m* ■ **sweet-tempered** *adj* doux *(f* douce), agréable

**sweeten** ['swiːtən] *vt* [food] sucrer ; *Fig* [person] amadouer

**sweetheart** ['swiːthɑːt] *n* petit, -e ami, -e *mf*

**swell**[1] [swel] **1.** *(pt* **swelled**, *pp* **swollen** *or* **swelled)** *vt* [river, numbers] grossir **2.** *vi* [of hand, leg] enfler ; [of wood] gonfler ; [of river, numbers] grossir ; **to swell up** [of body part] enfler ■ **swelling** *n* [on body] enflure *f*

**swell**[2] [swel] *adj Am Fam* [excellent] super *inv*

**swelter** ['sweltə(r)] *vi* étouffer ■ **sweltering** *adj* étouffant ; **it's sweltering** on étouffe

**swept** [swept] *pt & pp of* **sweep**

**swerve** [swɜːv] *vi* [of vehicle] faire une embardée ; [of player] faire un écart

**swift** [swɪft] **1.** *(compar* -er, *superl* -est) *adj* rapide **2.** *n* [bird] martinet *m* ■ **swiftly** *adv* rapidement

**swill** [swɪl] *vt Fam* [drink] écluser ; **to swill (out** *or* **down)** rincer à grande eau

**swim** [swɪm] **1.** *n* to go for a swim aller nager ; **swim briefs** maillot *m* de bain *(masculin)* **2.** *(pt* **swam**, *pp* **swum**, *pres p* **swimming)** *vt* [river] traverser à la nage ; [length, crawl] nager **3.** *vi* nager ; [as sport] faire de la natation ; **to go swimming** aller nager ; **to swim away** s'éloigner à la nage ■ **swimmer** *n* nageur, -euse *mf* ■ **swimming** *n* natation *f* ; **swimming cap** bonnet *m* de bain ; *Br* **swimming costume** maillot *m* de bain ; *Br* **swimming pool** piscine *f* ; **swimming trunks** slip *m* de bain

**swindle** ['swɪndəl] **1.** *n* escroquerie *f* **2.** *vt* escroquer ■ **swindler** *n* escroc *m*

**swine** [swaɪn] *n inv Pej* [person] salaud *m*

**swing** [swɪŋ] **1.** *n* [in playground] balançoire *f* ; [movement] balancement *m* ; [in opinion] revirement *m* ; [of golfer] swing *m* **2.** *(pt & pp* **swung)** *vt* [arms, legs] balancer ; [axe] brandir **3.** *vi* [sway] se balancer ; [turn] virer ; **to swing round** [turn suddenly] se retourner

**swipe** [swaɪp] *vt* [card] passer dans un lecteur de cartes ; *Fam* **to swipe sth** [steal] faucher qch **(from sb** à qn) ; **swipe card** carte *f* magnétique

**swirl** [swɜːl] *vi* tourbillonner

**Swiss** [swɪs] **1.** *adj* suisse ; *Br* **Swiss roll** roulé *m* **2.** *n inv* Suisse *m*, Suissesse *f* ; **the Swiss** les Suisses *mpl*

**switch** [swɪtʃ] **1.** *n* [electrical] interrupteur *m* ; [change] changement *m* (**in** de) ; [reversal] revirement *m* (**in** de) ; **toggle switch** ELEC interrupteur *m* à bascule ; COMPUT bascule *f* ou interrupteur *m* de changement de mode **2.** *vt* [money, employee] transférer (**to** à) ; [support, affection] reporter (**to** sur) ; [exchange] échanger (**for** contre) **3.** *vi* **to switch to** [change to] passer à ■ **switchboard** *n* TEL standard *m* ; **switchboard operator** standardiste *mf* ■ **switch off** **1.** *vt sep* [lamp, gas, radio] éteindre ; [engine] arrêter ; [electricity] couper

**2.** *vi* [of appliance] s'éteindre ■ **switch on 1.** *vt sep* [lamp, gas, radio] allumer ; [engine] mettre en marche **2.** *vi* (of appliance) s'allumer ■ **switch over** *vi* [change TV channels] changer de chaîne ; **to switch over to** [change to] passer à

**Switzerland** ['swɪtsələnd] *n* la Suisse

**swivel** ['swɪvəl] **1.** (*Br* -ll-, *Am* -l-) *vi* to **swivel (round)** [of chair] pivoter **2.** *adj* **swivel chair** chaise *f* pivotante

**swollen** ['swəʊlən] **1.** *pp of* **swell 2.** *adj* [leg] enflé ; [stomach] gonflé

**swoop** [swuːp] *vi* faire une descente (on dans) ; **to swoop (down) on** [of bird] fondre sur

**swop** [swɒp] *n & vti* = **swap**

**sword** [sɔːd] *n* épée *f*

**swore** [swɔː(r)] *pt of* **swear**

**sworn** [swɔːn] *pp of* **swear**

**swot** [swɒt] *Br Fam & Pej* **1.** *n* bûcheur, -euse *mf* **2.** (*pt & pp* -tt-) *vti* to **swot (up)** bûcher ; **to swot up on sth** bûcher qch

**swum** [swʌm] *pp of* **swim**

**swung** [swʌŋ] *pt & pp of* **swing**

**sycamore** ['sɪkəmɔː(r)] *n* [maple] sycomore *m* ; *Am* [plane tree] platane *m*

**syllable** ['sɪləbəl] *n* syllabe *f*

**syllabus** ['sɪləbəs] *n* programme *m*

**symbol** ['sɪmbəl] *n* symbole *m* ■ **symbolic** [-'bɒlɪk] *adj* symbolique ■ **symbolize** *vt* symboliser

**symmetrical** [sɪ'metrɪkəl] *adj* symétrique

**sympathetic** [sɪmpə'θetɪk] *adj* [showing pity] compatissant ; [understanding] compréhensif, -ive ; **sympathetic to sb/sth** [favourable] bien disposé à l'égard de qn /qch

**sympathize** ['sɪmpəθaɪz] *vi* **I sympathize with you** [pity] je suis désolé (pour vous) ; [understanding] je vous comprends

**sympathy** ['sɪmpəθɪ] *n* [pity] compassion *f* ; [understanding] compréhension *f* ; **to have sympathy for sb** éprouver de la compassion pour qn

**symphony** ['sɪmfənɪ] **1.** (*pl* -ies) *n* symphonie *f* **2.** *adj* [orchestra, concert] symphonique

**symptom** ['sɪmptəm] *n* MED & *Fig* symptôme *m*

**synagogue** ['sɪnəgɒg] *n* synagogue *f*

**synchronize** ['sɪŋkrənaɪz] *vt* synchroniser

**syndicate** ['sɪndɪkət] *n* syndicat *m*

**syndrome** ['sɪndrəʊm] *n* MED & *Fig* syndrome *m*

**synonym** ['sɪnənɪm] *n* synonyme *m* ■ **synonymous** [-'nɒnɪməs] *adj* synonyme (**with** de)

**synopsis** [sɪ'nɒpsɪs] (*pl* -opses [-ɒpsiːz]) *n* résumé *m* ; [of film] synopsis *m*

**synthetic** [sɪn'θetɪk] *adj* synthétique

**syphon** ['saɪfən] *n & vt* = **siphon**

**syringe** [sə'rɪndʒ] *n* seringue *f*

**syrup** ['sɪrəp] *n* sirop *m* ; *Br* (**golden**) **syrup** mélasse *f* raffinée

**SYS** MESSAGING *written abbr of* **see you soon**

**system** ['sɪstəm] *n* [structure & COMPUT] système *m* ; [human body] organisme *m* ; [method] méthode *f* ; **the digestive system** l'appareil *m* digestif ; COMPUT **systems analyst** analyste *m* programmeur

**systematic** [sɪstə'mætɪk] *adj* systématique

# T

**T, t** [tiː] *n* [letter] T, t *m inv*

**T+** MESSAGING *written abbr of* **think positive**

**ta** [tɑː] *excl Br Fam* merci !

**tab** [tæb] *n* **a)** [label] étiquette *f* **b)** *Am Fam* [bill] addition *f* **c)** [on computer, typewriter] tabulateur *m* ; **tab key** touche *f* de tabulation

**table¹** ['teɪbəl] *n* **a)** [furniture] table *f* ; *Br* **to set** *or* **lay/clear the table** mettre / débarrasser la table ; **(sitting) at the table** à table ; **table tennis** tennis *m* de table ; **table wine** vin *m* de table **b)** [list] table *f* ; **table of contents** table *f* des matières ■ **tablecloth** *n* nappe *f* ■ **tablespoon** *n* ≃ cuillère *f* à soupe ■ **tablespoonful** *n* ≃ cuillerée *f* à soupe

**table²** ['teɪbəl] *vt Br* [motion] présenter ; *Am* [postpone] ajourner

**tablet** ['tæblɪt] *n* **a)** [pill] comprimé *m* **b)** [of chocolate] tablette *f* **c)** COMPUT = **tablet (computer)**

**tablet (computer)** *n* tablette *f*, tablette *f* tactile

**tabloid** ['tæblɔɪd] *n* [newspaper] tabloïd *m*

**taboo** [təˈbuː] *(pl -oos) adj & n* tabou *(m)*

**tack** [tæk] **1.** *n* [nail] clou *m* ; *Am* [thumbtack] punaise *f* **2.** *vt* **to tack (down)** clouer

**tackle** ['tækəl] **1.** *n* [gear] matériel *m* ; [in rugby] placage *m* ; [in football] tacle *m* **2.** *vt* [task, problem] s'attaquer à ; [subject] aborder ; [rugby player] plaquer ; [football player] tacler

**tacky** ['tækɪ] *(compar -ier, superl -iest) adj* [sticky] collant ; *Fam* [shoddy] minable, moche

**tact** [tækt] *n* tact *m* ■ **tactful** *adj* [remark] diplomatique ; **to be tactful** [of person] avoir du tact ■ **tactless** *adj* [person, remark] qui manque de tact

**tactic** ['tæktɪk] *n* **a tactic** une tactique ; **tactics** la tactique ■ **tactical** *adj* tactique

**TAFN** MESSAGING *written abbr of* **that's all for now**

**tag** [tæg] **1.** *n* [label] étiquette *f* **2.** *vi* **to tag along with sb** venir avec qn

**tail** [teɪl] **1.** *n* [of animal] queue *f* ; **tails, tail coat** queue-de-pie *f* ; **the tail end** la fin (**of** de) **2.** *vt Fam* [follow] filer **3.** *vi* **to tail off** [lessen] diminuer ■ **tailback** *n Br* [of traffic] bouchon *m* ■ **taillight** *n Am* [of vehicle] feu *m* arrière *inv*

**tailor** ['teɪlə(r)] **1.** *n* [person] tailleur *m* **2.** *vt* [garment] faire ; *Fig* [adjust] adapter (**to** à) ■ **tailor-made** *adj Fig* sur mesure

**tainted** ['teɪntɪd] *adj* [air] pollué ; [food] gâté ; *Fig* [reputation, system] souillé

**take** [teɪk] *(pt* took, *pp* taken) *vt* prendre ; [bring] amener (**to** à) ; [by car] conduire (**to** à) ; [escort] accompagner (**to** à) ; [lead away] emmener (**to** à) ; [exam] passer ; [credit card] accepter ; [contain] avoir une capacité de ; [tolerate] supporter ; MATH [subtract] soustraire (**from** de) ; **to take sth to sb** apporter qch à qn ; **to take sth with one** emporter qch ; **it takes an army/courage** il faut une armée /du courage (**to do** pour faire) ; **I took an hour to do it** j'ai mis une heure à le faire ; **I take it that...** je présume que...

■ **takeaway** *Br* **1.** *adj* [meal] à emporter **2.** *n* [shop] restaurant *m* qui fait des plats à emporter ; [meal] plat *m* à emporter

■ **takeoff** *n* [of plane] décollage *m*

■ **take-out** *adj* & *n Am* = **takeaway**

■ **takeover** *n* [of company] rachat *m*

■ **take after** *vt insep* **to take after sb** ressembler à qn

■ **take along** *vt sep* [object] emporter ; [person] emmener

■ **take apart** *vt sep* [machine] démonter

■ **take away** *vt sep* [thing] emporter ; [person] emmener ; [remove] enlever **(from** à) ; MATH [subtract] soustraire **(from** de)

■ **take back** *vt sep* reprendre ; [return] rapporter ; [statement] retirer ; [accompany] ramener **(to** à)

■ **take down** *vt sep* [object] descendre ; [notes] prendre

■ **take in** *vt sep* [chair, car] rentrer ; [skirt] reprendre ; [include] inclure ; [understand] saisir ; *Fam* [deceive] rouler

■ **take off 1.** *vt sep* [remove] enlever ; [lead away] emmener ; [mimic] imiter ; MATH [deduct] déduire **(from** de) **2.** *vi* [of aircraft] décoller

■ **take on** *vt sep* [work, staff, passenger, shape] prendre

■ **take out** *vt sep* [from pocket] sortir ; [tooth] arracher ; [insurance policy, patent] prendre ; *Fam* **to take it out on sb** passer sa colère sur qn

■ **take over 1.** *vt sep* [become responsible for] reprendre ; [buy out] racheter ; [overrun] envahir ; **to take over sb's job** remplacer qn **2.** *vi* [relieve] prendre la relève **(from** de) ; [succeed] prendre la succession **(from** de)

■ **take round** *vt sep* [bring] apporter **(to** à) ; [distribute] distribuer ; [visitor] faire visiter

■ **take to** *vt insep* **to take to doing sth** se mettre à faire qch ; **I didn't take to him/it** il /ça ne m'a pas plu

■ **take up 1.** *vt sep* [carry up] monter ; [continue] reprendre ; [space, time] prendre ; [offer] accepter ; [hobby] se mettre à **2.** *vi* **to take up with sb** se lier avec qn

■ **take up on** *vt sep* [accept] **to take sb up on an offer** accepter l'offre de qn

**taken** ['teɪkən] *adj* [seat] pris ; [impressed] impressionné **(with** or **by** par) ; **to be taken ill** tomber malade

**taking** ['teɪkɪŋ] **1.** *adj* engageant, séduisant **2.** *n* [of city, power] prise *f* ; [of criminal] arrestation *f* ; [of blood, sample] prélèvement *m*

**takings** ['teɪkɪŋz] *n* [money] recette *f*

**talc** [tælk], **talcum powder** ['tælkəm paʊdə(r)] *n* talc *m*

**tale** [teɪl] *n* [story] histoire *f* ; [lie] salades *fpl* ; **to tell tales** rapporter **(on sb** sur qn)

**talent** ['tælənt] *n* talent *m* ■ **talented** *adj* talentueux, -euse

**talk** [tɔːk] **1.** *n* [conversation] conversation *f* **(about** à propos de) ; [lecture] exposé *m* **(on** sur) ; **talk radio** radio *f* parlée ; **talks** [negotiations] pourparlers *mpl* ; **to have a talk with sb** parler avec qn **2.** *vt* [nonsense] dire ; **to talk politics** parler politique ; **to talk sb into doing/out of doing sth** persuader qn de faire /de ne pas faire qch ; **to talk sth over** discuter (de) qch **3.** *vi* parler **(to / about** à /de) ; [gossip] jaser

**talkative** ['tɔːkətɪv] *adj* bavard

**tall** [tɔːl] *(compar* **-er,** *superl* **-est)** *adj* [person] grand ; [tree, house] haut ; *Fig* **a tall story** une histoire invraisemblable

**tally** ['tælɪ] *(pt* & *pp* **-ied)** *vi* correspondre **(with** à)

**tambourine** [tæmbə'riːn] *n* tambourin *m*

**tame** [teɪm] **1.** *(compar* **-er,** *superl* **-est)** *adj* [animal] apprivoisé ; *Fig* [book, play] fade **2.** *vt* [animal] apprivoiser

**tamper** ['tæmpə(r)] *vt insep* **to tamper with** [lock, car] essayer de forcer ; [machine] toucher à ; [documents] trafiquer

**tampon** ['tæmpɒn] *n* tampon *m* (hygiénique)

**tan** [tæn] **1.** *n* [suntan] bronzage *m* **2.** *adj* [colour] marron clair *inv* **3.** *(pt* & *pp* **-nn-)** *vt* [skin] hâler ; [leather] tanner **4.** *vi* [of person, skin] bronzer

**tangerine** [tændʒə'riːn] *n* mandarine *f*

**tangible** ['tændʒəbəl] *adj* tangible

**tangle** ['tæŋgəl] *n Fig* [of person] s'embrouiller ; **to get into a tangle** [of rope] s'enchevêtrer ; [of hair] s'emmêler ■ **tangled** *adj* enchevêtré ; [hair] emmêlé

**tango** ['tæŋgəʊ] *(pl* **-os)** *n* tango *m*

**tangy** ['tæŋi] *(compar* **-ier,** *superl* **-iest)** *adj* acidulé

**tank** [tæŋk] *n* [container] réservoir *m* ; [military vehicle] tank *m* ; **(fish) tank** aquarium *m*

**tanker** ['tæŋkə(r)] *n* [lorry] camion-citerne *m* ; **(oil) tanker** [ship] pétrolier *m*

**Tannoy®** ['tænɔɪ] *n Br* **over the Tannoy®** au haut-parleur

**tantalizing** ['tæntəlaɪzɪŋ] *adj* alléchant

**tantrum** ['tæntrəm] *n* caprice *m*

**tap¹** [tæp] **1.** *n Br* [for water] robinet *m* ; **tap water** eau *f* du robinet **2.** *(pt & pp* **-pp-)** *vt* [resources] puiser dans ; [phone] placer sur écoute

**tap²** [tæp] **1.** *n* [blow] petit coup *m* ; **tap dancing** claquettes *fpl* **2.** *(pt & pp* **-pp-)** *vt* [hit] tapoter

**tape** [teɪp] **1.** *n* **a)** [ribbon] ruban *m* ; **(sticky** *or* **adhesive) tape** ruban *m* adhésif ; **tape measure** mètre *m* (à) ruban **b)** [for recording] bande *f* ; [cassette] cassette *f* ; **tape deck** platine *f* cassette ; **tape recorder** magnétophone *m* **2.** *vt* **a)** [stick] scotcher **b)** [record] enregistrer

**taper** ['teɪpə(r)] **1.** *n* [candle] bougie *f* filée **2.** *vi* s'effiler ; *Fig* **to taper off** diminuer

**tapestry** ['tæpəstrɪ] *n* tapisserie *f*

**tar** [tɑː(r)] *n* goudron *m*

**tardy** ['tɑːdɪ] *(compar* **-ier,** *superl* **-iest)** **1.** *adj Am* SCH en retard **2.** *n Am* SCH élève *mf* retardataire

**target** ['tɑːgɪt] **1.** *n* cible *f* ; [objective] objectif *m* **2.** *vt* [campaign, product] destiner **(at** à) ; [age group] viser

**tariff** ['tærɪf] *n* [tax] tarif *m* douanier ; *Br* [price list] tarif *m*

**tarmac** ['tɑːmæk] *n Br* [on road] macadam *m* ; [runway] piste *f*

**tarnish** ['tɑːnɪʃ] *vt* ternir

**tart** [tɑːt] **1.** *(compar* **-er,** *superl* **-est)** *adj* [sour] aigre **2.** *n* [pie - large] tarte *f* ; [small] tartelette *f*

**tartan** ['tɑːtən] **1.** *n* tartan *m* **2.** *adj* [skirt, tie] écossais

**tase** [teɪz] *vt* **to tase sb** utiliser un pistolet à impulsion électronique *ou* un Taser® contre qn

**taser** ['teɪzə(r)] *n* pistolet *m* à impulsion électronique, Taser® *m*

**task** [tɑːsk] *n* tâche *f*

**tassel** ['tæsəl] *n* gland *m*

**taste** [teɪst] **1.** *n* goût *m* ; **in good / bad taste** de bon / mauvais goût ; **to have a taste of sth** goûter à qch **2.** *vt* [detect flavour of] sentir ; [sample] goûter ; *Fig* [experience] goûter à **3.** *vi* **to taste of** *or* **like sth** avoir un goût de qch ; **to taste good** être bon (*f* bonne)

**tasteful** ['teɪstfəl] *adj* de bon goût ■ **tasteless** *adj* [food] insipide ; *Fig* [joke] de mauvais goût ■ **tasty** *(compar* **-ier,** *superl* **-iest)** *adj* savoureux, -euse

**tatters** ['tætəz] *npl* **in tatters** [clothes] en lambeaux

**tattoo** [tæ'tuː] **1.** *(pl* **-oos)** *n* [design] tatouage *m* **2.** *(pt & pp* **-ooed)** *vt* tatouer

**tatty** ['tætɪ] *(compar* **-ier,** *superl* **-iest)** *adj Br Fam* minable

**taught** [tɔːt] *pt & pp of* **teach**

**taunt** [tɔːnt] **1.** *n* raillerie *f* **2.** *vt* railler

**taut** [tɔːt] *adj* tendu

**tax¹** [tæks] **1.** *n* [on goods] taxe *f*, impôt *m* ; [on income] impôts *mpl* ; *Br* **road tax** ≃ vignette *f* automobile **2.** *adj* fiscal ; **tax collector** percepteur *m* ; *Br* **(road) tax disc** ≃ vignette *f* automobile **3.** *vt* [person] imposer ; [goods] taxer ■ **taxable** *adj* imposable ■ **taxation** *n* [taxes] impôts *mpl* ; [act] imposition *f* ■ **tax-free** *adj* exempt d'impôts ■ **taxpayer** *n* contribuable *mf*

**tax²** [tæks] *vt* [put under strain] mettre à l'épreuve

**taxi** ['tæksɪ] *n* taxi *m* ; *Br* **taxi rank,** *Am* **taxi stand** station *f* de taxis

**TB** *n* **a)** = **tuberculosis b)** = **text back**

**tea** [tiː] n [plant, drink] thé m ; Br [snack] goûter m ; Br **high tea** dîner m (pris tôt dans la soirée) ; Br **tea break** ≃ pause-café f ; **tea leaves** feuilles fpl de thé ; **tea set** service m à thé ; Br **tea towel** torchon m ■ **teabag** n sachet m de thé ■ **teacup** n tasse f à thé ■ **teapot** n théière f ■ **tearoom** n salon m de thé ■ **teaspoon** n petite cuillère f ■ **teaspoonful** n cuillerée f à café ■ **teatime** n l'heure f du thé

**teach** [tiːtʃ] **1.** (pt & pp taught) vt apprendre (**sb sth** qch à qn ; **that** que) ; [in school, at university] enseigner (**sb sth** qch à qn) ; **to teach sb (how) to do sth** apprendre à qn à faire qch **2.** vi enseigner ■ **teaching 1.** n enseignement m **2.** adj [staff] enseignant ; [method, material] pédagogique

**teacher** ['tiːtʃə(r)] n professeur m ; [in primary school] instituteur, -trice mf

**team** [tiːm] **1.** n équipe f ; [of horses, oxen] attelage m ; **team mate** coéquipier, -ère mf **2.** vi **to team up** faire équipe (**with sb** avec qn) ■ **teamwork** n travail m d'équipe

**tear¹** [teə(r)] **1.** n déchirure f **2.** (pt tore, pp torn) vt [rip] déchirer ; [snatch] arracher (**from** à) ; **to tear off** or **out** arracher ; **to tear up** déchirer **3.** vi **to tear along / past** aller / passer à toute vitesse

**tear²** [tɪə(r)] n larme f ; **in tears** en larmes ; **tear gas** gaz m lacrymogène

**tease** [tiːz] **1.** n [person] taquin, -e mf **2.** vt taquiner

**technical** ['teknɪkəl] adj technique

**technician** ['teknɪʃən] n technicien, -enne mf

**technique** [tek'niːk] n technique f

**technology** [tek'nɒlədʒɪ] (pl -ies) n technologie f ■ **technological** [-nə'lɒdʒɪkəl] adj technologique

**tedious** ['tiːdɪəs] adj fastidieux, -euse

**teem** [tiːm] vi [swarm] grouiller (**with** de) ; **to teem (with rain)** pleuvoir à torrents

**teen** [tiːn] adj Fam [fashion] pour ados ; [music, problems] d'ados ■ **teens** npl **to be in one's teens** être adolescent

**teenage** ['tiːneɪdʒ] adj [boy, girl, behaviour] adolescent ; [fashion, magazine] pour adolescents ■ **teenager** n adolescent, -e mf

**tee-shirt** ['tiːʃɜːt] n tee-shirt m

**teeth** [tiːθ] pl of **tooth**

**teethe** [tiːð] vi faire ses dents

**teetotaller**, Am **teetotaler** [tiː-'təʊtələ(r)] n personne qui ne boit jamais d'alcool

**TEFL** ['tefl] (abbr of teaching English as a foreign language) n enseignement de l'anglais langue étrangère

**telecommunications** [telɪkəmjuːnɪ'keɪʃənz] npl télécommunications fpl

**telegram** ['telɪgræm] n télégramme m

**telegraph** ['telɪgrɑːf] adj **telegraph pole / wire** poteau m / fil m télégraphique

**telephone** ['telɪfəʊn] **1.** n téléphone m ; **to be on the telephone** [speaking] être au téléphone **2.** adj [call, line, message] téléphonique ; Br **telephone booth**, **telephone box** cabine f téléphonique ; **telephone directory** annuaire m du téléphone ; **telephone number** numéro m de téléphone **3.** vt [message] téléphoner (**to** à) ; **to telephone sb** téléphoner à qn **4.** vi téléphoner ■ **telephonist** n Br téléphoniste mf

**telescope** ['telɪskəʊp] n télescope m

**teletext** ['telɪtekst] n télétexte m

**televise** ['telɪvaɪz] vt téléviser

**television** [telɪ'vɪʒən] **1.** n télévision f ; **on (the) television** à la télévision **2.** adj [programme, screen] de télévision ; [interview, report] télévisé

**telex** ['teleks] **1.** n [service, message] télex m **2.** vt [message] télexer

**tell** [tel] **1.** (pt & pp told) vt dire (**sb sth** qch à qn ; **that** que) ; [story] raconter ; [distinguish] distinguer (**from** de) ; **to tell sb to do sth** dire à qn de faire qch ; **to tell the difference** voir la différence (**between** entre) ; **I could tell she was lying** je savais qu'elle mentait ; Fam **to tell sb off** disputer qn **2.** vi dire ; [have an effect] se faire sentir ; **to tell of** or **about sb / sth** parler de qn / qch ;

**you can never tell** on ne sait jamais ; *Fam* **to tell on sb** dénoncer qn ■ **tell apart** *vt sep* distinguer

**telling-off** *(pl* **tellings-off)** *n* réprimande *f*

**telltale** ['telteɪl] **1.** *adj* révélateur, -trice **2.** *n* rapporteur, -euse *mf*

**telly** ['telɪ] *n Br Fam* télé *f* ; **on the telly** à la télé

**temp** [temp] *Br Fam* **1.** *n* intérimaire *mf* **2.** *vi* faire de l'intérim

**temper** ['tempə(r)] **1.** *n* [mood, nature] humeur *f* ; [bad mood] mauvaise humeur *f* ; **in a bad temper** de mauvaise humeur ; **to lose one's temper** se mettre en colère **2.** *vt* [moderate] tempérer

**temperament** ['tempərəmənt] *n* tempérament *m* ■ **temperamental** [-'mentəl] *adj* [person, machine] capricieux, -euse

**temperate** ['tempərət] *adj* [climate] tempéré

**temperature** ['tempərətʃə(r)] *n* température *f*

**template** ['templət, -pleɪt] *n* gabarit *m* ; COMPUT modèle *m*

**temple¹** ['tempəl] *n* [religious building] temple *m*

**temple²** ['tempəl] *n* ANAT tempe *f*

**tempo** ['tempəʊ] *(pl* **-os)** *n* [of life, work] rythme *m* ; MUS tempo *m*

**temporary** [Br 'tempərərɪ, Am -erɪ] *adj* temporaire ; [secretary] intérimaire ■ **temporarily** [Br tempə'reərəlɪ, Am tempə'reərəlɪ] *adv* temporairement

**tempt** [tempt] *vt* tenter ; **tempted to do sth** tenté de faire qch ■ **temptation** *n* tentation *f* ■ **tempting** *adj* tentant

**ten** [ten] *adj & n* dix *(m)*

**tenable** ['tenəbəl] *adj* [argument, position] défendable

**tenacious** [tə'neɪʃəs] *adj* tenace

**tenant** ['tenənt] *n* locataire *mf* ■ **tenancy** *n* [lease] location *f* ; [period] occupation *f*

**tend¹** [tend] *vi* **to tend to do sth** avoir tendance à faire qch ; **to tend towards** incliner vers ■ **tendency** *(pl* **-ies)** *n* tendance *f* (**to do** à faire)

**tend²** [tend] *vt* [look after] s'occuper de

**tender¹** ['tendə(r)] *adj* [soft, delicate, loving] tendre ; [painful] sensible

**tender²** ['tendə(r)] **1.** *n* **to be legal tender** [of money] avoir cours **2.** *vt* [offer] offrir

**tenement** ['tenəmənt] *n* immeuble *m*

**tenner** ['tenə(r)] *n Br Fam* billet *m* de 10 livres

**tennis** ['tenɪs] *n* tennis *m* ; **tennis court** court *m* de tennis

**tenor** ['tenə(r)] *n* MUS ténor *m*

**tenpin** ['tenpɪn] *adj Br* **tenpin bowling** bowling *m*

**10Q** MESSAGING *written abbr of* **thank you**

**tense¹** [tens] **1.** *(compar* **-er**, *superl* **-est)** *adj* [person, muscle, situation] tendu **2.** *vt* tendre ; [muscle] contracter **3.** *vi* **tense (up)** [of person, face] se crisper ■ **tension** *n* tension *f*

**tense²** [tens] *n* [in grammar] temps *m*

**tent** [tent] *n* tente *f* ; *Br* **tent peg** piquet *m* de tente ; *Br* **tent pole**, *Am* **tent stake** mât *m* de tente

**tentative** ['tentətɪv] *adj* [not definite] provisoire ; [hesitant] timide

**tenth** [tenθ] *adj & n* dixième *(mf)* ; **a tenth** [fraction] un dixième ; *Am* SCH **tenth grade** *classe de l'enseignement secondaire correspondant à la seconde (14-15 ans)*

**tenuous** ['tenjʊəs] *adj* [link] ténu

**tepid** ['tepɪd] *adj* [liquid] & *Fig* tiède

**term** [tɜːm] **1.** *n* [word] terme *m* ; [period] période *f* ; *Br* [of school or university year] trimestre *m* ; *Am* [semester] semestre *m* ; **terms** [conditions] conditions *fpl* ; [of contract] termes *mpl* ; **to be on good / bad terms** être en bons / mauvais termes (**with sb** avec qn) ; **in terms of** [speaking of] sur le plan de ; **to come to terms with sth**

se résigner à qch ; **in the long / short / medium term** à long / court / moyen terme **2.** *vt* appeler

**terminal** ['tɜːmɪnəl] **1.** *n* [electronic & COMPUT] terminal *m* ; [of battery] borne *f* ; **(air) terminal** aérogare *f* **2.** *adj* [patient, illness] en phase terminale

**terminate** ['tɜːmɪneɪt] **1.** *vt* mettre fin à ; [contract] résilier ; [pregnancy] interrompre **2.** *vi* se terminer

**terminus** ['tɜːmɪnəs] *n* terminus *m*

**terrace** ['terɪs] *n* [next to house, on hill] terrasse *f* ; Br [houses] *rangée de maisons attenante* ; Br **the terraces** [at football ground] les gradins *mpl* ■ **terraced** *n* Br **terraced house** *maison située dans une rangée d'habitations attenantes*

**terrain** [tə'reɪn] *n* MIL & GEOL terrain *m*

**terrestrial** [tə'restrɪəl] *adj* terrestre

**terrible** ['terəbəl] *adj* terrible ■ **terribly** *adv* Fam [extremely] terriblement ; [badly] affreusement mal

**terrier** ['terɪə(r)] *n* [dog] terrier *m*

**terrific** [tə'rɪfɪk] *adj* Fam [excellent] super *inv* ■ **terrifically** *adv* Fam [extremely] terriblement ; [extremely well] terriblement bien

**terrify** ['terɪfaɪ] (*pt & pp* -**ied**) *vt* terrifier ; **to be terrified of sb / sth** avoir une peur bleue de qn / qch ■ **terrifying** *adj* terrifiant

**territory** ['terɪtərɪ] (*pl* -**ies**) *n* territoire *m*

**terror** ['terə(r)] *n* terreur *f* ; **terror attack** attentat *m* terroriste ■ **terrorism** *n* terrorisme *m* ■ **terrorist** *n* & *adj* terroriste (*mf*) ■ **terrorize** *vt* terroriser

**test** [test] **1.** *n* [trial] essai *m* ; [of product] test *m* ; SCH & UNIV interrogation *f* ; [by doctor] examen *m* ; [of blood] analyse *f* **2.** *adj* **test drive** essai *m* sur route ; **test tube** éprouvette *f* ; **test tube baby** bébé-éprouvette *m* **3.** *vt* [try] essayer ; [product, machine] tester ; [pupil] interroger ; [of doctor] examiner ; [blood] analyser ; Fig [try out] mettre à l'épreuve ; **to test sb for AIDS** faire subir à qn un test de dépistage du SIDA **4.** *vi* **to test positive** [for drugs] être positif, -ive

**testament** ['testəmənt] *n* [will] testament *m* ; [tribute] preuve *f* ; REL **the Old / New Testament** l'Ancien / le Nouveau Testament

**testicle** ['testɪkəl] *n* ANAT testicule *m*

**testify** ['testɪfaɪ] (*pt & pp* -**ied**) **1.** *vt* **to testify that…** témoigner que… **2.** *vi* [in law] témoigner (**against** contre) ; **to testify to sth** [be proof of] témoigner de qch ■ **testimony** ['testɪmənɪ] (*pl* -**ies**) *n* témoignage *m*

**tetanus** ['tetənəs] *n* MED tétanos *m*

**tether** ['teðə(r)] *n* **at the end of one's tether** à bout

**text** [tekst] *n* texte *m* ; **text message** message *m* texte, mini-message *m* ■ **textbook** *n* manuel *m* ■ **texting** ['tekstɪŋ] *n* [telephone & COMPUT] envoi *m* de textos *ou* de SMS

**textile** ['tekstaɪl] *adj* & *n* textile (*m*)

**texture** ['tekstʃə(r)] *n* [of fabric, cake] texture *f* ; [of paper, wood] grain *m*

**Thames** [temz] *n* **the (River) Thames** la Tamise

**than** [ðən] (*stressed* [ðæn]) *conj* que ; **happier than me** plus heureux que moi ; **he has more / less than you** il en a plus / moins que toi ; **more than six** plus de six

**thank** [θæŋk] *vt* remercier (**for sth** de qch ; **for doing** d'avoir fait) ; **thank you** merci ; **no, thank you** (non) merci ; **thank God!, thank heavens!, thank goodness!** Dieu merci ! ■ **thanks** *npl* remerciements *mpl* ; **(many) thanks!** merci (beaucoup) ! ; **thanks to** [because of] grâce à

**thankful** ['θæŋkfəl] *adj* reconnaissant (**for** de) ; **to be thankful that…** être heureux, -euse que… (+ *subjunctive*) ■ **thankless** *adj* ingrat

**Thanksgiving** [θæŋks'gɪvɪŋ] *n* Am **Thanksgiving (Day)** *quatrième jeudi de novembre, commémorant la première action de grâce des colons anglais*

**that** [ðət] (*stressed* [ðæt]) **1.** *conj* (*souvent omise*) que ; **she said that she would come** elle a dit qu'elle viendrait

**2.** *rel pron* (*On peut omettre le pronom relatif* **that** *sauf s'il est en position sujet*) [subject] qui ; [object] que ; [with preposition] lequel, laquelle, *pl* lesquel(le)s ; **the boy that left** le garçon qui est parti ; **the book that I read** le livre que j'ai lu ; **the house that she told me about** la maison dont elle m'a parlé ; **the day / morning that she arrived** le jour / matin où elle est arrivée

**3.** (*pl* **those**) *dem adj* ce, cet (*before vowel or mute h*), cette ; [opposed to 'this'] ce... -là (*f* cette...-là) ; **that woman** cette femme(-là) ; **that day** ce jour-là ; **that one** celui-là *m*, celle-là *f*

**4.** (*pl* **those**) *dem pron* cela ; *Fam* ça ; **give me that** donne-moi ça ; **that's right** c'est exact ; **who's that?** qui est-ce ? ; **that's the house** voilà la maison ; **what do you mean by that?** qu'entends-tu par là ? ; **that is (to say)...** c'est-à-dire...

**5.** *adv Fam* [so] si ; **not that good** pas si bon que ça ; **it cost that much** ça a coûté tant que ça

**thatched** [θætʃt] *adj* [roof] de chaume ; **thatched cottage** chaumière *f*

**thaw** [θɔː] **1.** *n* dégel *m* **2.** *vt* [snow, ice] faire fondre ; **to thaw (out)** [food] se décongeler **3.** *vi* dégeler ; [of snow, ice] fondre ; [of food] décongeler

**the** [ðə] (*before vowel* [ðɪ], *stressed* [ðiː]) *def art* le, l', la, *pl* les ; **of the, from the** du, de l', de la, *pl* des ; **to the, at the** au, à l', à la, *pl* aux ; **Elizabeth the Second** Élisabeth Deux

**theatre**, *Am* **theater** [ˈθɪətə(r)] *n* [place, art] théâtre *m* ; *Br* **(operating) theatre** [in hospital] salle *f* d'opération ■ **theatrical** [θɪˈætrɪkəl] *adj also Fig* théâtral

**theft** [θeft] *n* vol *m*

**their** [ðeə(r)] *poss adj* leur, *pl* leurs ■ **theirs** *poss pron* le leur, la leur, *pl* les leurs ; **this book is theirs** ce livre est à eux *ou* est le leur ; **a friend of theirs** un ami à eux

**them** [ðəm] (*stressed* [ðem]) *pron* les ; [after prep, 'than', 'it is'] eux *mpl*, elles *fpl* ; **(to) them** [indirect] leur ; **I see them** je les vois ; **I gave it (to) them** je le leur ai donné ; **ten of them** dix d'entre

eux / elles ; **all of them came** tous sont venus, toutes sont venues ; **I like all of them** je les aime tous / toutes

**theme** [θiːm] *n* thème *m* ; **theme tune** [of TV, radio programme] indicatif *m* ; **theme park** parc *m* à thème

**themselves** [ðəmˈselvz] (*stressed* [ðemˈselvz]) *pron* eux-mêmes *mpl*, elles-mêmes *fpl* ; [reflexive] se, s' ; [after prep] eux *mpl*, elles *fpl* ; **they cut themselves** ils / elles se sont coupé(e)s

**then** [ðen] **1.** *adv* [at that time] à cette époque-là, alors ; [just a moment ago] à ce moment-là ; [next] ensuite, puis ; [therefore] donc, alors ; **from then on** dès lors ; **before then** avant cela ; **until then** jusque-là, jusqu'alors **2.** *adj* **the then mayor** le maire d'alors

**theory** [ˈθɪərɪ] (*pl* **-ies**) *n* théorie *f* ; **in theory** en théorie ■ **theoretical** *adj* théorique

**therapy** [ˈθerəpɪ] (*pl* **-ies**) *n* thérapeutique *f* ; **seawater therapy** thalassothérapie *f* ■ **therapeutic** [-ˈpjuːtɪk] *adj* thérapeutique

**there** [ðeə(r)] **1.** *adv* là ; **(down / over) there** là-bas ; **on there** là-dessus ; **she'll be there** elle y sera ; **there is, there are** il y a ; [pointing] voilà ; **there he is** le voilà ; **that man there** cet homme-là ; **there (you are)!** [take this] tenez ! **2.** *excl* **there, I knew he'd turn up** tiens *ou* voilà, je savais bien qu'il s'amènerait ; **there, there** allons, allons ■ **thereabouts** *adv* dans les environs ; [in amount] à peu près ■ **there again** *adv* après tout ; **but there again, no one really knows** mais après tout, personne ne sait vraiment ■ **there and then, then and there** *adv* immédiatement, sur-le-champ ; **I liked the bike so much when I saw it in the shop, that I bought it there and then** *or* **then and there** j'ai tellement aimé le vélo quand je l'ai vu dans le magasin, que je l'ai acheté immédiatement *ou* sur-le-champ ■ **thereby** *adv Formal* ainsi ■ **therefore** *adv* donc

**thermometer** [θəˈmɒmɪtə(r)] *n* thermomètre *m*

**Thermos®** [ˈθɜːməs] (pl **-moses** [-məsəz]) n Thermos® (flask) Thermos® f

**thermostat** [ˈθɜːməstæt] n thermostat m

**these** [ðiːz] (sing **this**) **1.** dem adj ces ; [opposed to 'those'] ces...-ci ; **these men** ces hommes(-ci) ; **these ones** ceux-ci mpl, celles-ci fpl **2.** dem pron ceux-ci mpl, celles-ci fpl ; **these are my friends** ce sont mes amis

**thesis** [ˈθiːsɪs] (pl **theses** [ˈθiːsiːz]) n thèse f

**they** [ðeɪ] pron a) [subject] ils mpl, elles fpl ; [stressed] eux mpl, elles fpl ; **they are doctors** ce sont des médecins b) [people in general] on ■ **they'd** = **they had, they would** ■ **they'll** = **they will**

**thick** [θɪk] **1.** (compar **-er**, superl **-est**) adj épais (f épaisse) ; Fam [stupid] lourd **2.** adv [spread] en couche épaisse ■ **thickly** adv [spread] en couche épaisse

**thicken** [ˈθɪkən] **1.** vt épaissir **2.** vi [of fog] s'épaissir ; [of cream, sauce] épaissir ■ **thickness** n épaisseur f

**thick-skinned** [θɪkˈskɪnd] adj [person] peu susceptible

**thief** [θiːf] (pl **thieves**) n voleur, -euse mf ■ **thieving 1.** adj voleur, -euse **2.** n vol m

**thigh** [θaɪ] n cuisse f

**thimble** [ˈθɪmbəl] n dé m à coudre

**thin** [θɪn] **1.** (compar **thinner**, superl **thinnest**) adj [person, slice, paper] mince ; [soup] peu épais (f peu épaisse) ; [crowd, hair] clairsemé **2.** adv [spread] en couche mince ; [cut] en tranches minces **3.** (pt & pp **-nn-**) vt **to thin (down)** [paint] diluer **4.** vi **to thin out** [of crowd, mist] s'éclaircir ■ **thinly** adv [spread] en couche mince ; [cut] en tranches minces

**thing** [θɪŋ] n chose f ; **things** [belongings, clothes] affaires fpl ; **poor little thing!** pauvre petit ! ; **how are things?**, Fam **how's things?** comment ça va ? ; **for one thing... and for another thing...** d'abord... et ensuite...

**think** [θɪŋk] **1.** (pt & pp **thought**) vt penser (**that** que) ; **I think so** je pense ou crois que oui ; **what do you think of him?** que penses-tu de lui ? ; **to think out** [plan, method] élaborer ; [reply] réfléchir sérieusement à ; **to think sth over** réfléchir à qch ; **to think sth up** [invent] inventer qch **2.** vi penser (**about/of** à) ; **to think (carefully)** réfléchir (**about/of** à) ; **to think of doing sth** penser à faire qch ; **to think highly of sb** penser beaucoup de bien de qn **3.** n Fam **to have a think** réfléchir (**about** à)

**third** [θɜːd] **1.** adj troisième ) **the Third World** le tiers-monde ; Am SCH **third grade** classe de l'enseignement primaire correspondant au CE2 (7-8 ans) **2.** n troisième mf ; **a third** [fraction] un tiers **3.** adv **to come third** [in race] se classer troisième ■ **third-generation** adj COMPUT & TEL de troisième génération, 3G ■ **thirdly** adv troisièmement

**third-party** [θɜːdˈpɑːtɪ] adj **third-party insurance** assurance f au tiers

**third-rate** [θɜːdˈreɪt] adj très inférieur

**thirst** [θɜːst] n soif f (**for** de) ■ **thirst-quenching** [-kwentʃɪŋ] adj désaltérant ■ **thirsty** (compar **-ier**, superl **-iest**) adj **to be** or **feel thirsty** avoir soif ; **to make sb thirsty** donner soif à qn

**thirteen** [θɜːˈtiːn] adj & n treize (m) ■ **thirteenth** adj & n treizième (mf)

**thirty** [ˈθɜːtɪ] adj & n trente (m) ■ **thirtieth** adj & n trentième (mf)

**this** [ðɪs] **1.** (pl **these**) dem adj ce, cet (before vowel or mute h), cette ; [opposed to 'that'] ce...-ci ; **this man** cet homme(-ci) ; **this one** celui-ci m, celle-ci f **2.** (pl **these**) dem pron [subject] ce, ceci ; [object] ceci ; **I prefer this** je préfère celui-ci ; **who's this?** qui est-ce ? ; **this is Paul** c'est Paul ; [pointing] voici Paul **3.** adv [so] **this high** [pointing] haut comme ceci ; **this far** [until now] jusqu'ici

**thistle** [ˈθɪsəl] n chardon m

**thorn** [θɔːn] n épine f

**thorough** [ˈθʌrə] adj [search, cleaning, preparation] minutieux, -euse ; [knowledge, examination] approfondi ■ **thoroughly** adv [completely] tout à fait ; [carefully] avec minutie ; [know, clean, wash] à fond

**thoroughfare** ['θʌrəfeə(r)] *n Br* 'no thoroughfare' 'passage interdit'

**those** [ðəʊz] **1.** (*sing* **that**) *dem adj* ces ; [opposed to 'these'] ces...-là ; **those men** ces hommes(-là) ; **those ones** ceux-là *mpl*, celles-là *fpl* **2.** (*sing* **that**) *dem pron* ceux-là *mpl*, celles-là *fpl* ; **those are my friends** ce sont mes amis

**though** [ðəʊ] **1.** *conj* bien que (+ *subjunctive*) ; **(even) though** même si ; **as though** comme si ; **strange though it may seem** si étrange que cela puisse paraître **2.** *adv* [however] pourtant

**thought** [θɔːt] **1.** *pt & pp of* **think 2.** *n* pensée *f* ; **(careful) thought** réflexion *f* ; **to have second thoughts** changer d'avis ; *Br* **on second thoughts**, *Am* **on second thought** à la réflexion

**thoughtful** ['θɔːtfəl] *adj* [considerate, kind] attentionné ; [pensive] pensif, -ive

**thoughtless** ['θɔːtləs] *adj* irréfléchi

**thousand** ['θaʊzənd] *adj & n* mille (*m*) *inv* ; **a thousand pages** mille pages ; **two thousand pages** deux mille pages ; **thousands of** des milliers de

**thrash** [θræʃ] **1.** *vt* **to thrash sb** donner une correction à qn ; [defeat] écraser qn **2.** *vi* **to thrash around** *or* **about** [struggle] se débattre ■ **thrashing** *n* [beating] correction *f*

**thread** [θred] **1.** *n* [yarn] & *Fig* fil *m* ; [of screw] filetage *m* **2.** *vt* [needle, beads] enfiler

**threat** [θret] *n* menace *f* ■ **threaten 1.** *vt* menacer (**to do** de faire ; **with sth** de qch) **2.** *vi* menacer ■ **threatening** *adj* menaçant

**three** [θriː] *adj & n* trois (*m*) ■ **three-course** *adj* [meal] complet (*f* complète) (*entrée, plat, dessert*) ■ **three-dimensional** *adj* à trois dimensions ■ **threefold 1.** *adj* triple **2.** *adv* **to increase threefold** tripler ■ **three-piece** *adj Br* **three-piece suite** canapé *m* et deux fauteuils assortis ■ **three-quarters 1.** *n* **three-quarters (of)** les trois quarts *mpl* (de) **2.** *adv* **it's three-quarters full** c'est aux trois quarts plein

**threshold** ['θreʃhəʊld] *n* seuil *m*

**threw** [θruː] *pt of* **throw**

**thrifty** ['θrɪftɪ] (*compar* **-ier**, *superl* **-iest**) *adj* économe

**thrill** [θrɪl] **1.** *n* frisson *m* ; **to get a thrill out of doing sth** prendre plaisir à faire qch **2.** *vt* [delight] réjouir ; [excite] faire frissonner ■ **thrilled** *adj* ravi (**with sth** de qch ; **to do** de faire) ■ **thriller** *n* thriller *m* ■ **thrilling** *adj* passionnant

**thrive** [θraɪv] *vi* [of business, person, plant] prospérer ; **to thrive on sth** avoir besoin de qch pour s'épanouir ■ **thriving** *adj* [business] prospère

**throat** [θrəʊt] *n* gorge *f*

**throb** [θrɒb] (*pt & pp* **-bb-**) *vi* [of heart] palpiter ; **my head is throbbing** j'ai une douleur lancinante dans la tête

**throes** [θrəʊz] *npl* **in the throes of** au milieu de ; [illness, crisis] en proie à ; **in the throes of doing sth** en train de faire qch

**throne** [θrəʊn] *n* trône *m*

**throttle** ['θrɒtəl] **1.** *n* [accelerator] manette *f* des gaz **2.** *vt* [strangle] étrangler

**through** [θruː] **1.** *prep* [place] à travers ; [by means of] par ; [because of] à cause de ; **through the window/door** par la fenêtre / porte ; **through ignorance** par ignorance ; *Am* **Tuesday through Saturday** de mardi à samedi **2.** *adv* à travers ; **to go through** [of bullet, nail] traverser ; **to let sb through** laisser passer qn ; **to be through with sb / sth** [finished] en avoir fini avec qn / qch ; **through to** *or* **till** jusqu'à ; **I'll put you through (to him)** [on telephone] je vous le passe **3.** *adj* [train, ticket] direct ; *Br* **'no through road'** [no exit] 'voie sans issue'

**throughout** [θruː'aʊt] **1.** *prep* **throughout the neighbourhood** dans tout le quartier ; **throughout the day** pendant toute la journée **2.** *adv* [everywhere] partout ; [all the time] tout le temps

**throw** [θrəʊ] **1.** *n* [in sport] lancer *m* ; [of dice] coup *m* **2.** (*pt* **threw**, *pp* **thrown**) *vt* jeter (**to / at** à) ; [javelin, discus] lancer ; [image, shadow] projeter ; [of horse] désarçonner ; [party] donner ; *Fam* [baffle] déconcerter ■ **throw away** *vt sep* [discard] jeter ; *Fig* [life, chance] gâcher ■ **throw back** *vt sep* [ball] renvoyer (**to** à) ; [one's head] rejeter en arrière ■ **throw in** *vt sep Fam* [include as extra] donner en prime ■ **throw out** *vt sep* [unwanted object] jeter ; [suggestion] repousser ; [expel] mettre à la porte ■ **throw up** *vi Fam* [vomit] vomir

**thrown** [θrəʊn] *pp of* **throw**

**thrush** [θrʌʃ] *n* [bird] grive *f*

**thrust** [θrʌst] **1.** *n* [movement] mouvement *m* en avant ; [of argument] idée *f* principale **2.** *(pt & pp* **thrust***) vt* to thrust sth into sth enfoncer qch dans qch ; **to thrust sb/sth aside** écarter qn/qch

**thud** [θʌd] *n* bruit *m* sourd

**thug** [θʌɡ] *n* voyou *m* (*pl* -ous)

**thumb** [θʌm] **1.** *n* pouce *m* **2.** *vt Fam* **to thumb a lift** *or* **a ride** faire du stop **3.** *vi* **to thumb through a book** feuilleter un livre

**thump** [θʌmp] **1.** *n* [blow] coup *m* ; [noise] bruit *m* sourd **2.** *vt* [hit] frapper ; **to thump one's head** se cogner la tête (**on** contre) **3.** *vi* frapper, cogner (**on** sur) ; [of heart] battre la chamade

**thunder** [ˈθʌndə(r)] **1.** *n* tonnerre *m* **2.** *vi* tonner ; **to thunder past** [of train, truck] passer dans un bruit de tonnerre ■ **thunderstorm** *n* orage *m*

**Thursday** [ˈθɜːzdeɪ] *n* jeudi *m*

**thus** [ðʌs] *adv* ainsi

**Thx, THX, Thnx** MESSAGING *written abbr of* **thanks**

**thyme** [taɪm] *n* thym *m*

**tic** [tɪk] *n* tic *m*

**tick** [tɪk] **1.** *n* [of clock] tic-tac *m inv* ; [mark] ≃ croix *f* ; *Fam* [moment] instant *m* ; **tick box** case *f* à cocher **2.** *vt* **to tick sth (off)** [on list] cocher qch **3.** *vi* faire tic-tac ; *Br* **to tick over** [of engine, factory] tourner au ralenti ■ **ticking** *n* [of clock] tic-tac *m inv*

**ticket** [ˈtɪkɪt] *n* billet *m* ; [for bus, metro] ticket *m* ; *Fam* [for parking, speeding] contravention *f* ; **(price) ticket** étiquette *f* ; **ticket collector** contrôleur, -euse *mf* ; **ticket office** guichet *m*

**tickle** [ˈtɪkəl] *vt* chatouiller ; *Fig* [amuse] amuser ■ **ticklish** *adj* [person] chatouilleux, -euse

**tic-tac-toe** [tɪktækˈtəʊ] *n Am* morpion *m* (*jeu*)

**tidbit** [ˈtɪdbɪt] *n Am* [food] bon morceau *m*

**tide** [taɪd] **1.** *n* marée *f* **2.** *vt* **to tide sb over** dépanner qn

**tidy** [ˈtaɪdɪ] **1.** *(compar* -ier, *superl* -iest) *adj* [place, toys] bien rangé ; [clothes, hair] soigné ; [person - methodical] ordonné ; [in appearance] soigné **2.** *vt* **to tidy sth (up** *or* **away)** ranger qch ; **to tidy sth out** mettre de l'ordre dans qch ; **to tidy oneself up** s'arranger **3.** *vi* **to tidy up** ranger ■ **tidily** *adv* [put away] soigneusement, avec soin

**tie** [taɪ] **1.** *n* [garment] cravate *f* ; [link] lien *m* ; [draw] égalité *f* ; [drawn match] match *m* nul **2.** *vt* [fasten] attacher (**to** à) ; [knot] faire (**in** à) ; [shoe] lacer **3.** *vi* [draw] être à égalité ; [at end of match] faire match nul ; [in race] être ex aequo ■ **tie down** *vt sep* attacher ■ **tie in** *vi* [of facts] concorder ■ **tie up** *vt sep* [animal] attacher ; [parcel] ficeler ; [money] immobiliser ; *Fig* **to be tied up** [busy] être occupé

**tier** [tɪə(r)] *n* [of seats] gradin *m* ; [of cake] étage *m*

**tiger** [ˈtaɪɡə(r)] *n* tigre *m*

**tight** [taɪt] **1.** *(compar* -er, *superl* -est) *adj* [clothes, knot, race, bend] serré ; [control] strict ; *Fam* [mean] radin **2.** *adv* [hold, shut] bien ; [squeeze] fort ; **to sit tight** ne pas bouger ■ **tight-fitting** *adj* [garment] ajusté ■ **tightly** *adv* [hold] bien ; [squeeze] fort ■ **tightrope** *n* corde *f* raide

**tighten** [ˈtaɪtən] *vt Fig* [security] renforcer ; **to tighten (up)** [bolt] serrer ; [rope] tendre

**tights** [taɪts] *npl Br* [garment] collant *m*

**tile** [taɪl] **1.** *n* [on roof] tuile *f* ; [on wall, floor] carreau *m* **2.** *vt* [wall, floor] carreler ■ **tiled** *adj* [roof] de tuiles ; [wall, floor] carrelé

**till¹** [tɪl] *prep & conj* = **until**

**till²** [tɪl] *n Br* [for money] caisse *f* enregistreuse

**tilt** [tɪlt] **1.** *n* inclinaison *f* **2.** *vti* pencher

**timber** ['tɪmbə(r)] *n Br* [wood] bois *m* (de construction)

**time** [taɪm] **1.** *n* temps *m* ; [period, moment] moment *m* ; [age] époque *f* ; [on clock] heure *f* ; [occasion] fois *f* ; MUS mesure *f* ; [simultaneously] à la fois ; **about time too!** ce n'est pas trop tôt ! ; **in time, with time** avec le temps ; **it's about time (that)...** il est grand temps que... ; **it's time to do sth** il est temps de faire qch ; **some of the time** [not always] une partie du temps ; **most of the time** la plupart du temps ; **all (of) the time** tout le temps ; **in a year's time** dans un an ; **a long time** longtemps ; **a short time** peu de temps ; **to have a good** *or* **a nice time** s'amuser (bien) ; **to have time off** avoir du temps libre ; **in no time (at all)** en un rien de temps ; **(just) in time** [arrive] à temps (**for sth** pour qch ; **to do** pour faire) ; **from time to time** de temps en temps ; **what time is it?** quelle heure est-il ? ; **the right** *or* **exact time** l'heure *f* exacte ; **on time** à l'heure ; **at the same time** en même temps (**as** que) ; **for the time being** pour le moment ; **at the** *or* **that time** à ce moment-là ; **at times** parfois ; **(the) next time you come** la prochaine fois que tu viendras ; **(the) last time** la dernière fois ; **one at a time** un à un ; **ten times ten** dix fois dix ; **time difference** décalage *m* horaire ; **time limit** délai *m* ; **time zone** fuseau *m* horaire ; **time waster** fainéant, -e *mf* ; **no time wasters please** [in advertisement] pas sérieux s'abstenir **2.** *vt* [sportsman, worker] chronométrer ; [activity, programme] minuter ; [choose the time of] choisir le moment de ; [plan] prévoir ■ **time-consuming** *adj* qui prend du temps ■ **timeline** ['taɪm,laɪn] *n* frise *f* chronologique ■ **timespan** ['taɪmspæn] *n* intervalle *m* de temps

**timely** ['taɪmlɪ] *adj* à propos

**timer** ['taɪmə(r)] *n* [device] minuteur *m* ; [sand-filled] sablier *m* ; [built into appliance] programmateur *m* ; [plugged into socket] prise *f* programmable

**timeshare** *n* logement *m* en multipropriété

**timetable** ['taɪmteɪbəl] *n* horaire *m* ; [in school] emploi *m* du temps

**timid** ['tɪmɪd] *adj* timide

**timing** ['taɪmɪŋ] *n* [of election] moment *m* choisi ; [of musician] sens *m* du rythme

**tin** [tɪn] *n* [metal] étain *m* ; *Br* [can] boîte *f* ; **cake tin** moule *m* à gâteaux ; **tin opener** ouvre-boîtes *m inv* ■ **tinfoil** *n* papier *m* aluminium

**tinge** [tɪndʒ] *n* pointe *f* ■ **tinged** *adj* **tinged with sth** teinté de qch

**tingle** ['tɪŋgəl] *vi* picoter

**tinker** ['tɪŋkə(r)] *vi* **to tinker (about** *or* **around) with sth** bricoler qch

**tinkle** ['tɪŋkəl] *vi* tinter

**tinned** [tɪnd] *adj Br* **tinned pears / salmon** poires *fpl* / saumon *m* en boîte ; **tinned food** conserves *fpl*

**tinsel** ['tɪnsəl] *n* guirlandes *fpl* de Noël

**tint** [tɪnt] *n* teinte *f* ; [for hair] rinçage *m* ■ **tinted** *adj* [paper, glass] teinté

**tiny** ['taɪnɪ] *(compar* **-ier,** *superl* **-iest)** *adj* minuscule

**tip¹** [tɪp] *n* [end] bout *m* ; [pointed] pointe *f*

**tip²** [tɪp] **1.** *n Br* [rubbish dump] décharge *f* **2.** *(pt & pp* **-pp-)** *vt* [pour] déverser ; **to tip sth up** *or* **over** renverser qch ; **to tip sth out** [liquid, load] déverser qch (**into** dans) **3.** *vi* **to tip (up** *or* **over)** [tilt] se renverser ; [overturn] basculer

**tip³** [tɪp] **1.** *n* [money] pourboire *m* ; [advice] conseil *m* ; [information] tuyau *m* **2.** *(pt & pp* **-pp-)** *vt* [waiter] donner un pourboire à ; **to tip off** [police] prévenir

**tipsy** ['tɪpsɪ] *(compar* **-ier,** *superl* **-iest)** *adj* [drunk] éméché, gai

**tiptoe** ['tɪptəʊ] **1.** *n* **on tiptoe** sur la pointe des pieds **2.** *vi* marcher sur la pointe des pieds ; **to tiptoe into / out of a room** entrer dans une pièce / sortir d'une pièce sur la pointe des pieds

**tire¹** ['taɪə(r)] **1.** *vt* fatiguer ; **to tire sb out** épuiser qn **2.** *vi* se fatiguer ■ **tired** *adj* fatigué ; **to be tired of sth / doing sth** en avoir assez de qch / de faire qch

■ **tiredness** n fatigue f ■ **tireless** adj infatigable ■ **tiresome** adj ennuyeux, -euse ■ **tiring** adj fatigant

**tire²** ['taɪə(r)] n Am pneu m (pl pneus)

**tissue** ['tɪʃuː] n [handkerchief] mouchoir m en papier ; BIOL tissu m ; **tissue paper** papier m de soie

**titbit** ['tɪtbɪt] n Br [food] bon morceau m

**titillate** ['tɪtɪleɪt] vt exciter

**title** ['taɪtəl] **1.** n [name, claim, in sport] titre m ; **title role** [in film, play] rôle-titre m **2.** vt intituler

**titter** ['tɪtə(r)] vi rire bêtement

**Tks** MESSAGING written abbr of **thanks**

**TMB** MESSAGING written abbr of **text me back**

**to** [tə] (stressed [tuː]) **1.** prep **a)** [towards] à ; [until] jusqu'à ; **give it to him / her** donne-le-lui ; **to go to town** aller en ville ; **to go to France / Portugal** aller en France / au Portugal ; **to go to the butcher's** aller chez le boucher ; **the road to London** la route de Londres ; **the train to Paris** le train pour Paris ; **kind / cruel to sb** gentil / cruel envers qn ; **to my surprise** à ma grande surprise ; **it's ten (minutes) to one** il est une heure moins dix ; **ten to one** [proportion] dix contre un ; **one person to a room** une personne par chambre **b)** [with infinitive] **to say / jump** dire / sauter ; **(in order) to do sth** pour faire qch ; **she tried to** elle a essayé **c)** [with adjective] **I'd be happy to do it** je serais heureux de le faire ; **it's easy to do** c'est facile à faire

**2.** adv **to push the door to** fermer la porte ; **to go** or **walk to and fro** aller et venir

**toad** [təʊd] n crapaud m

**toadstool** ['təʊdstuːl] n champignon m vénéneux

**toast¹** [təʊst] **1.** n [bread] pain m grillé **2.** vt [bread] faire griller ■ **toaster** n grille-pain m inv ■ **toastie** ['təʊstɪ] n Fam sandwich m grillé ■ **toasty** ['təʊstɪ] Fam **1.** adj Am [warm] **it's toasty in here** il fait bon ici **2.** n [sandwich] = **toastie**

**toast²** [təʊst] **1.** n [drink] toast m **2.** vt [person] porter un toast à ; [success, event] arroser

**tobacco** [tə'bækəʊ] (pl -os) n tabac m ; Am **tobacco store** (bureau m de) tabac ■ **tobacconist** [-kənɪst] n buraliste mf ; Br **tobacconist's (shop)** (bureau m de) tabac m

**toboggan** [tə'bɒgən] n luge f

**today** [tə'deɪ] adv aujourd'hui

**toddler** ['tɒdlə(r)] n enfant mf (en bas âge)

**toe** [təʊ] **1.** n orteil m **2.** vt **to toe the line** bien se tenir

**TOEFL** ['təʊfl] (abbr of **Test of English as a Foreign Language**) n test évaluant le niveau d'anglais universitaire reconnu internationalement

**toffee** ['tɒfɪ] n Br caramel m (dur) ; **toffee apple** pomme f d'amour

**together** [tə'geðə(r)] adv ensemble ; [at the same time] en même temps

**toil** [tɔɪl] **1.** n labeur m **2.** vi travailler dur

**toilet** ['tɔɪlɪt] n Br [room] toilettes fpl ; [bowl, seat] cuvette f des toilettes ; Br **to go to the toilet** aller aux toilettes ; **toilet facilities** toilettes fpl ; **toilet paper** papier m hygiénique ; **toilet roll** rouleau m de papier hygiénique ; [paper] papier m hygiénique ■ **toiletries** npl articles mpl de toilette

**token** ['təʊkən] **1.** n [for vending machine] jeton m ; [symbol] signe m ; Br **book token** chèque-livre m **2.** adj symbolique

**told** [təʊld] **1.** pt & pp of **tell 2.** adv **all told** [taken together] en tout

**tolerable** ['tɒlərəbəl] adj [bearable] tolérable ; [fairly good] acceptable

**tolerant** ['tɒlərənt] adj tolérant (**of** à l'égard de) ■ **tolerance** n tolérance f

**tolerate** ['tɒləreɪt] vt tolérer

**toll** [təʊl] **1.** n **a)** [fee] péage m ; **toll road / bridge** route f / pont m à péage **b)** **the death toll** le nombre de morts ; Fig **to take its toll** faire des dégâts **2.** vi [of bell] sonner ■ **toll-free** Am **1.** adj **toll-free number** ≃ numéro m vert **2.** adv [call] gratuitement

**tomato** [Br təˈmɑːtəʊ, Am təˈmeɪtəʊ] *(pl -oes)* *n* tomate *f*; **tomato sauce** sauce *f* tomate

**tomb** [tuːm] *n* tombeau *m* ▪ **tombstone** *n* pierre *f* tombale

**tomorrow** [təˈmɒrəʊ] *adv* & *n* demain *(m)*; **tomorrow morning/evening** demain matin/soir; **the day after tomorrow** après-demain

**ton** [tʌn] *n* tonne *f*; *Fam* **tons of** [lots of] des tonnes de

**tone** [təʊn] **1.** *n* ton *m*; [of telephone, radio] tonalité *f*; [of answering machine] signal *m* sonore; *Br* **the engaged tone** [on telephone] la sonnerie 'occupé' **2.** *vt* **to tone sth down** atténuer qch; **to tone up** [muscles, skin] tonifier

**tongs** [tɒŋz] *npl* pinces *fpl*; **sugar tongs** pince *f* à sucre; **curling tongs** fer *m* à friser

**tongue** [tʌŋ] *n* [in mouth, language] langue *f*

**tonic** [ˈtɒnɪk] *n* [medicine] fortifiant *m*; **tonic (water)** Schweppes® *m*; **gin and tonic** gin-tonic *m*

**tonight** [təˈnaɪt] *adv* & *n* [this evening] ce soir *(m)*; [during the night] cette nuit *(f)*

**tonne** [tʌn] *n* [metric] tonne *f*

**tonsil** [ˈtɒnsəl] *n* amygdale *f* ▪ **tonsillitis** [-ˈlaɪtɪs] *n* **to have tonsillitis** avoir une angine

**too** [tuː] *adv* a) [excessively] trop; **too tired to play** trop fatigué pour jouer; **too much, too many** trop; **too much salt** trop de sel; **too many people** trop de gens; **one too many** un de trop b) [also] aussi; [moreover] en plus

**took** [tʊk] *pt of* **take**

**tool** [tuːl] *n* outil *m*; **tool bag, tool kit** trousse *f* à outils; **tool box** boîte *f* à outils

**tooth** [tuːθ] *(pl* **teeth***)* *n* dent *f*; **tooth decay** carie *f* dentaire ▪ **toothache** *n* mal *m* de dents; **to have toothache** avoir mal aux dents ▪ **toothbrush** *n* brosse *f* à dents ▪ **toothpaste** *n* dentifrice *m*

**top¹** [tɒp] **1.** *n* [of mountain, tower, tree] sommet *m*; [of wall, ladder, page] haut *m*; [of table, box, surface] dessus *m*; [of list] tête *f*; [of bottle, tube] bouchon *m*; [crown cap] capsule *f*; [of pen] capuchon *m*; [garment] haut *m*; **(at the) top of the class** le premier / la première de la classe; **on top** dessus; [in bus] en haut; **on top of** sur; *Fig* [in addition to] en plus de; **from top to bottom** de fond en comble; *Fam* **over the top** [excessive] exagéré **2.** *adj* [drawer, shelf] du haut; [step, layer] dernier, -ère; [upper] supérieur; [in rank, exam] premier, -ère; [chief] principal; [best] meilleur; **on the top floor** au dernier étage; **at top speed** à toute vitesse; **top copy** original *m*; **top hat** haut-de-forme *m* ▪ **top-quality** *adj* de qualité supérieure ▪ **top-secret** *adj* top secret *inv* ▪ **topsy-turvy** *adj* & *adv* sens dessus dessous [sɑ̃dsydsu]

**top²** [tɒp] *(pt* & *pp* -**pp**-*)* *vt* [exceed] dépasser; **topped with cream** nappé de crème ▪ **topping** *n* [of pizza] garniture *f* ▪ **top up**, *Am* **top off** *vt sep* [glass] remplir (de nouveau)

**top³** [tɒp] *n* **(spinning) top** toupie *f*

**top dollar** *n* **to pay top dollar for sth** payer qch au prix fort

**topic** [ˈtɒpɪk] *n* sujet *m* ▪ **topical** *adj* d'actualité

**topple** [ˈtɒpəl] *vi* **to topple (over)** tomber

**top-up card** *n* recharge *f* de téléphone mobile

**torch** [tɔːtʃ] *n Br* [electric] lampe *f* de poche; [flame] torche *f*

**tore** [tɔː(r)] *pt of* **tear**

**torment 1.** [ˈtɔːment] *n* supplice *m* **2.** [tɔːˈment] *vt* tourmenter

**torn** [tɔːn] *pp of* **tear**

**tornado** [tɔːˈneɪdəʊ] *(pl -oes)* *n* tornade *f*

**torpedo** [tɔːˈpiːdəʊ] **1.** *(pl -oes)* *n* torpille *f* **2.** *vt* torpiller

**torrent** [ˈtɒrənt] *n* torrent *m* ▪ **torrential** [tɒˈrenʃəl] *adj* **torrential rain** pluie *f* torrentielle

**tortoise** [ˈtɔːtəs] *n* tortue *f*

**tortuous** ['tɔːtʃʊəs] *adj* tortueux, -euse

**torture** ['tɔːtʃə(r)] **1.** *n* torture *f*; *Fig* **it's (sheer) torture!** quel supplice ! **2.** *vt* torturer

**Tory** ['tɔːrɪ] **1.** *n* POL tory *m* **2.** *adj* POL tory *inv*

**toss** [tɒs] **1.** *vt* [throw] lancer (**to** à); [pancake] faire sauter; **to toss sb (about)** [of boat, vehicle] ballotter qn; **to toss a coin** jouer à pile ou face **2.** *vi* to **toss (about), to toss and turn** [in bed] se tourner et se retourner; **let's toss up, let's toss (up) for it** jouons-le à pile ou face

**tot** [tɒt] **1.** *n* (tiny) tot tout-petit *m* **2.** *(pt & pp -tt-) vt Fam* **to tot up** [total] additionner

**total** ['təʊtəl] **1.** *adj* total; **the total sales** le total des ventes **2.** *n* total *m*; **in total** au total **3.** *(Br -ll-, Am -l-) vt* [of sum] s'élever à; **to total (up)** [find the total of] totaliser; **that totals $9** ça fait 9 dollars en tout ■ **totally** *adv* totalement

**totter** ['tɒtə(r)] *vi* chanceler

**touch** [tʌtʃ] **1.** *n* [contact] contact *m*; [sense] toucher *m*; [of painter] touche *f*; **a touch of** [small amount] une pointe de; **to have a touch of flu** être un peu grippé; **to be/get in touch with sb** être/se mettre en contact avec qn **2.** *vt* toucher; [interfere with, eat] toucher à **3.** *vi* [of lines, hands, ends] se toucher; **don't touch!** ne touche pas ! ■ **touchdown** *n* [of aircraft] atterrissage *m*; [in American football] essai *m* ■ **touched** *adj* [emotionally] touché (**by** de) ■ **touching** *adj* [moving] touchant ■ **touchline** *n* ligne *f* de touche ■ **touchpad** *n* pavé *m* tactile, touchpad *m*; **touchpad mouse** souris *f* tactile ■ **touch-sensitive** *adj* [screen] tactile; [key, switch] à effleurement ■ **touch down** *vi* [of plane] atterrir ■ **touch on** *vt insep* aborder ■ **touch up** *vt sep* [photo] retoucher

**touchy** ['tʌtʃɪ] *(compar -ier, superl -iest) adj* [sensitive] susceptible (**about** à propos de)

**tough** [tʌf] *(compar -er, superl -est) adj* [strict, hard] dur; [sturdy] solide ■ **toughen** *vt* [body, person] endurcir

**toupee** ['tuːpeɪ] *n* postiche *m*

**tour** [tʊə(r)] **1.** *n* [journey] voyage *m*; [visit] visite *f*; [by artiste, team] tournée *f*; [on bicycle, on foot] randonnée *f*; **to go on tour** [of artiste, team] être en tournée; **(package) tour** voyage *m* organisé; **tour guide** guide *mf*; **tour operator** voyagiste *m* **2.** *vt* visiter; [of artiste, team] être en tournée en /dans

**tourism** ['tʊərɪzəm] *n* tourisme *m* ■ **tourist 1.** *n* touriste *mf* **2.** *adj* [region] touristique; **tourist attraction** attraction *f* touristique; **tourist office** syndicat *m* d'initiative

**tournament** ['tʊənəmənt] *n* [in sport & HIST] tournoi *m*

**tout** [taʊt] **1.** *n* racoleur, -euse *mf* **2.** *vi* **to tout for trade** racoler des clients

**tow** [təʊ] *vt* remorquer; **to tow a car away** [of police] mettre une voiture à la fourrière

**toward(s)** [tə'wɔːd(z)] *prep* vers; [of feelings] envers; **cruel toward(s) sb** cruel envers qn

**towel** ['taʊəl] *n* serviette *f* (de toilette); **(kitchen) towel** [paper] essuie-tout *m inv*

**tower** ['taʊə(r)] **1.** *n* tour *f*; *Br* **tower block** tour **2.** *vi* **to tower over sb/sth** dominer qn /qch

**town** [taʊn] *n* ville *f*; **to go into town** aller en ville; **town centre** centre-ville *m*; *Br* **town council** conseil *m* municipal; *Br* **town hall** mairie *f*; **town house** maison *f* de ville; *Br* **town planning** urbanisme *m*

**toxic** ['tɒksɪk] *adj* toxique; **toxic waste** déchets *mpl* toxiques

**toy** [tɔɪ] **1.** *n* jouet *m*; **toy shop** magasin *m* de jouets **2.** *adj* [gun] d'enfant; [car, train] miniature **3.** *vi* **to toy with an idea** caresser une idée

**trace** [treɪs] **1.** *n* trace *f*; **without trace** sans laisser de traces **2.** *vt* [diagram, picture] tracer; [person] retrouver la trace de; **to trace sth back to...** faire remonter qch à... ■ **tracing** *n* [drawing] calque *m*; **tracing paper** papier-calque *m*

**track** [træk] n [mark] trace f; [trail] piste f; [path] chemin m, piste f; [for trains] voie f; [of record, CD, tape] morceau m; Am [racetrack] champ m de courses; **to keep track of sth** surveiller qch; **to lose track of** [friend] perdre de vue; **to be on the right track** être sur la bonne voie; **track event** [in athletics] épreuve f sur piste; Fig **track record** passé m ■ **tracksuit** n survêtement m ■ **track down** vt sep [criminal, animal] dépister; [object, address] retrouver

**tractor** ['træktə(r)] n tracteur m

**trade** [treɪd] **1.** n commerce m; [job] métier m; [exchange] échange f **2.** adj [fair, balance, route] commercial; [price] de (demi-)gros; [secret] de fabrication; [barrier] douanier, -ère; Br **trade union** syndicat m **3.** vt [exchange] échanger (**for** contre); **to trade in** [old article] faire reprendre qch **4.** vi faire du commerce (**with** avec); **to trade in** [sugar] faire le commerce de ■ **trademark** n marque f de fabrique ■ **trader** n Br [shopkeeper] commerçant, -e mf; [on Stock Exchange] opérateur, -trice mf; Br **street trader** vendeur, -euse mf de rue ■ **tradesman** (pl -**men**) n Br commerçant m

**trading** ['treɪdɪŋ] **1.** n commerce m; **trading hours** heures fpl d'ouverture **2.** adj [port, debts, activity] commercial

**tradition** [trə'dɪʃən] n tradition f ■ **traditional** adj traditionnel, -elle

**traffic** ['træfɪk] **1.** n **a)** [on road] circulation f; [air, sea, rail] trafic m; Am **traffic circle** rond-point m; **traffic island** refuge m (pour piétons); **traffic jam** embouteillage m; **traffic lights** feux mpl (de signalisation); **traffic warden** contractuel, -elle mf **b)** Pej [trade] trafic m (**in** de) **2.** (pt & pp -**ck**-) vi trafiquer (**in** de) ■ **trafficker** n Pej trafiquant, -e mf

**tragedy** ['trædʒədɪ] (pl -**ies**) n tragédie f ■ **tragic** adj tragique

**trail** [treɪl] **1.** n [of smoke, blood, powder] traînée f; [path] piste f, sentier m **2.** vt [drag] traîner; [follow] suivre **3.** vi [drag] traîner; [of plant] ramper;

[move slowly] se traîner; **to be trailing (behind)** [in sporting contest] être mené ■ **trailer** n **a)** [for car] remorque f; Am [caravan] caravane f; Am [camper] camping-car m **b)** [advertisement for film] bande-annonce f

**train** [treɪn] **1.** n **a)** [engine, transport] train m; [underground] rame f; **train set** [toy] petit train m; Am **train station** gare f **b)** [procession] file f; [of events] suite f; [of dress] traîne f; **my train of thought** le fil de ma pensée **2.** vt [person] former (**to do** à faire); [sportsman] entraîner; [animal] dresser (**to do** à faire); **to train oneself to do sth** s'entraîner à faire qch; **to train sth on sb/sth** [aim] braquer qch sur qn/qch **3.** vi [of sportsman] s'entraîner; **to train as a nurse** faire une formation d'infirmière ■ **trained** adj [skilled] qualifié; [nurse, engineer] diplômé ■ **training** n formation f; [in sport] entraînement m; [of animal] dressage m; **to be in training** [of sportsman] s'entraîner; **training course** cours m ou stage m de formation

**trainee** [treɪ'niː] n & adj stagiaire (mf)

**trainer** ['treɪnə(r)] n [of athlete, racehorse] entraîneur m; [of animals] dresseur m; Br **trainers** [shoes] chaussures fpl de sport

**traipse** [treɪps] vi Fam **to traipse around** [tiredly] traîner les pieds; [wander] se balader

**trait** [treɪt] n trait m (de caractère)

**traitor** ['treɪtə(r)] n traître m, traîtresse f

**tram** [træm] n tram(way) m

**tramp** [træmp] **1.** n Br [vagrant] clochard, -e mf **2.** vi marcher d'un pas lourd

**trample** ['træmpəl] vti **to trample sth (underfoot), to trample on sth** piétiner qch

**trampoline** [træmpə'liːn] n trampoline m

**trance** [trɑːns] n **to be in a trance** être en transe

**tranquillizer**, Am **tranquilizer** ['træŋkwɪlaɪzə(r)] n tranquillisant m

**transaction** [træn'zækʃən] n opération f, transaction f

**transatlantic** [trænzət'læntɪk] adj transatlantique

**transcend** [træn'send] vt transcender

**transcript** ['trænskrɪpt] n a) transcription f b) Am SCH livret m scolaire

**transfer 1.** ['trænsfɜː(r)] n transfert m (to à); [of political power] passation f; Br [picture, design] décalcomanie f; **credit transfer** virement m bancaire **2.** [træns'fɜː(r)] (pt & pp -rr-) vt transférer (to à); [political power] faire passer (to à) **3.** [træns'fɜː(r)] vi être transféré (to à)

**transform** [træns'fɔːm] vt transformer (into en) ■ **transformation** [-fə'meɪʃən] n transformation f ■ **transformer** n ELEC transformateur m

**transfusion** [træns'fjuːʒən] n (blood) transfusion transfusion f (sanguine)

**transit** ['trænzɪt] n in transit en transit

**transition** [træn'zɪʃən] n transition f

**transitional** [træn'zɪʃənəl] adj de transition

**transitive** ['trænsɪtɪv] adj [verb] transitif

**translate** [trænz'leɪt] vt traduire (**from** de; **into** en) ■ **translation** n traduction f ■ **translator** n traducteur, -trice mf

**transmit** [trænz'mɪt] **1.** (pt & pp -tt-) vt transmettre **2.** vti [broadcast] émettre ■ **transmission** n transmission f; [broadcast] émission f ■ **transmitter** n [for radio, TV] émetteur m

**transparent** [træn'spærənt] adj transparent

**transpire** [træn'spaɪə(r)] vi Fam [happen] arriver; **it transpired that...** il s'est avéré que...

**transplant 1.** ['trænsplɑːnt] n [surgical] greffe f, transplantation f **2.** [træns'plɑːnt] vt transplanter

**transport 1.** ['trænspɔːt] n transport m (of de); Br **transport café** routier m (restaurant) **2.** [træns'pɔːt] vt transporter

**transpose** [træn'spəʊz] vt transposer

**transvestite** [trænz'vestaɪt] n travesti m

**trap** [træp] **1.** n piège m **2.** (pt & pp -pp-) vt prendre au piège; **to trap one's finger** se coincer le doigt (in dans) ■ **trapdoor** n trappe f

**trappings** ['træpɪŋz] npl signes mpl extérieurs

**trash** [træʃ] n [nonsense] bêtises fpl; [junk] bric-à-brac m inv; Am [waste] ordures fpl; [riffraff] racaille f; Am **trash can** poubelle f; Am **trash collector** éboueur, -euse m,f ■ **trashy** (compar -ier, superl -iest) adj Fam à la noix

**trashed** [træʃt] adj Am Fam [drunk] bourré; **to get trashed** se bourrer la gueule

**trauma** ['trɔːmə] n traumatisme m ■ **traumatic** [-'mætɪk] adj traumatisant ■ **traumatize** vt traumatiser

**travel** ['trævəl] **1.** n voyage m; **travel agent** agent m de voyages; **travel documents** titres mpl de voyage; **travel insurance** assurance f voyage; **travel sickness** [in car] mal m de la route; [in aircraft] mal m de l'air **2.** (Br -ll-, Am -l-) vt [country, distance, road] parcourir **3.** vi [of person] voyager; [of vehicle, light, sound] se déplacer ■ **travelling**, Am **traveling 1.** n voyages mpl **2.** adj [bag, clothes] de voyage; [expenses] de déplacement; [musician, circus] ambulant ■ **travel-size(d)** adj [shampoo, etc] de voyage

**traveller**, Am **traveler** ['trævələ(r)] n voyageur, -euse mf; **traveller's cheque** chèque m de voyage

**travesty** ['trævəstɪ] (pl -ies) n parodie f; **a travesty of justice** un simulacre de justice

**tray** [treɪ] n plateau m; [in office] corbeille f; **baking tray** plaque f de four

**treacherous** ['tretʃərəs] adj [road, conditions] très dangereux, -euse; [person, action] traître ■ **treachery** (pl -ies) n traîtrise f

**treacle** ['triːkəl] n Br mélasse f

**tread** [tred] **1.** n [footstep] pas m; [step of stairs] marche f; [of tyre] chape f **2.** (pt trod, pp trodden) vt **to tread sth into**

**a carpet** étaler qch sur un tapis (avec ses chaussures) **3.** *vi* [walk] marcher (**on** sur)

**treadmill** ['tredmɪl] *n* **a)** [fitness] tapis *m* de course **b)** *Fig* [dull routine] routine *f*, train-train *m*

**treason** ['tri:zən] *n* trahison *f*

**treasure** ['treʒə(r)] **1.** *n* trésor *m*; **treasure hunt** chasse *f* au trésor **2.** *vt* [value] tenir beaucoup à ■ **treasurer** *n* trésorier, -ère *mf*

**treat** [tri:t] **1.** *n* [pleasure] plaisir *m*; [gift] cadeau *m*; **it's my treat** c'est moi qui régale **2.** *vt* [person, illness, product] traiter; **to treat sb to sth** offrir qch à qn

**treatment** ['tri:tmənt] *n* traitement *m*

**treaty** ['tri:tɪ] *(pl* -ies*)* [international] traité *m*

**treble** ['trebəl] **1.** *adj* triple **2.** *n* le triple; **it's treble the price** c'est le triple du prix **3.** *vti* tripler

**tree** [tri:] *n* **a)** arbre *m*; **tree trunk** tronc *m* d'arbre **b)** COMPUT arbre *m*, arborescence *f*

**trek** [trek] **1.** *n* [long walk] randonnée *f* **2.** *(pt & pp* -kk-*)vi* faire de la randonnée ■ **trekking** ['trekɪŋ] *n* randonnée *f*, trekking *m*

**tremble** ['trembəl] *vi* trembler (**with** de)

**tremendous** [trə'mendəs] *adj* [huge] énorme; [dreadful] terrible; [wonderful] formidable

**trench** [trentʃ] *n* tranchée *f*

**trend** [trend] *n* tendance *f* (**towards** à); [fashion] mode *f* ■ **trendy** *(compar* -ier, *superl* -iest*) adj Br Fam* branché

**trespass** ['trespəs] *vi* s'introduire illégalement dans une propriété privée; **'no trespassing'** entrée interdite'

**trial** ['traɪəl] **1.** *n* [in law] procès *m*; [test] essai *m*; [ordeal] épreuve *f*; **to go** *or* **be on trial, to stand trial** passer en jugement; **by trial and error** par tâtonnements **2.** *adj* [period, flight, offer] d'essai

**triangle** ['traɪæŋgəl] *n* triangle *m* ■ **triangular** [-'æŋgjʊlə(r)] *adj* triangulaire

**tribe** [traɪb] *n* tribu *f*

**tribunal** [traɪ'bju:nəl] *n* tribunal *m*

**tribute** ['trɪbju:t] *n* hommage *m*; **to pay tribute to** rendre hommage à

**trick** [trɪk] **1.** *n* [joke, deception, of conjurer] tour *m*; [clever method] astuce *f*; [in card game] pli *m*; **to play a trick on sb** jouer un tour à qn **2.** *vt* [deceive] duper; **to trick sb into doing sth** amener qn à faire qch par la ruse ■ **trickery** *n* ruse *f*

**trickle** ['trɪkəl] **1.** *n* [of liquid] filet *m* **2.** *vi* [of liquid] couler goutte à goutte; *Fig* **to trickle in** [of letters, people] arriver en petit nombre

**tricky** ['trɪkɪ] *(compar* -ier, *superl* -iest*) adj* [problem] délicat

**tricycle** ['traɪsɪkəl] *n* tricycle *m*

**trifle** ['traɪfəl] **1.** *n* [insignificant thing] bagatelle *f*; *Br* [dessert] dessert où alternent génoise, fruits en gelée et crème anglaise **2.** *adv* **a trifle wide** un tantinet trop large **3.** *vi* **to trifle with** plaisanter avec ■ **trifling** *adj* insignifiant

**trigger** ['trɪgə(r)] **1.** *n* [of gun] détente *f* **2.** *vt* **to trigger sth (off)** déclencher qch

**trilogy** ['trɪlədʒɪ] *(pl* -ies*)* *n* trilogie *f*

**trim** [trɪm] **1.** *(compar* trimmer, *superl* trimmest*) adj* [neat] soigné; [slim] svelte **2.** *n* **to give sb's hair a trim** faire une coupe d'entretien à qn **3.** *(pt & pp* -mm-*) vt* couper (un peu); **to trim sth with sth** orner qch de qch ■ **trimmings** *npl* [on clothes] garniture *f*; [of meal] accompagnements *mpl* traditionnels

**trinket** ['trɪŋkɪt] *n* babiole *f*

**trio** ['tri:əʊ] *(pl* -os*)* *n* trio *m*

**trip** [trɪp] **1.** *n* [journey] voyage *m*; [outing] excursion *f* **2.** *(pt & pp* -pp-*) vt* **to trip sb up** faire trébucher qn **3.** *vi* **to trip (over** *or* **up)** trébucher; **to trip over sth** trébucher sur qch

**triple** ['trɪpəl] **1.** *adj* triple **2.** *vti* tripler ■ **triplets** *npl* [children] triplés, -es *mfpl*

**triplicate** ['trɪplɪkət] *n* **in triplicate** en trois exemplaires

**tripod** ['traɪpɒd] *n* trépied *m*

**triumph** ['traɪəmf] **1.** *n* triomphe *m* (**over** sur) **2.** *vi* triompher (**over** de)

■ **triumphant** [traɪˈʌmfənt] *adj* triomphant ; [success, welcome, return] triomphal

**trivial** [ˈtrɪvɪəl] *adj* [unimportant] insignifiant ; [trite] banal (*mpl* -als)

**trod** [trɒd] *pt of* **tread**

**trodden** [ˈtrɒdən] *pp of* **tread**

**trolley** [ˈtrɒlɪ] (*pl* -eys) *n* Br chariot *m* ; Br (tea) trolley table *f* roulante ; Am trolley (car) tramway *m*

**trombone** [trɒmˈbəʊn] *n* trombone *m*

**troop** [tru:p] **1.** *n* bande *f* ; [of soldiers] troupe *f* ; **the troops** [soldiers] les troupes *fpl* **2.** *vi* **to troop in / out** entrer / sortir en groupe

**trophy** [ˈtrəʊfɪ] (*pl* -ies) *n* trophée *m*

**tropics** [ˈtrɒpɪks] *n* **in the tropics** sous les tropiques ■ **tropical** *adj* tropical

**trot** [trɒt] **1.** *n* trot *m* ; Fam **on the trot** [consecutively] de suite **2.** (*pt & pp* -tt-) *vt* Fam **to trot sth out** débiter qch **3.** *vi* [of horse] trotter

**trouble** [ˈtrʌbəl] **1.** *n* [difficulty] ennui *m* ; [inconvenience] problème *m* ; [social unrest, illness] trouble *m* ; **to be in trouble** avoir des ennuis ; **to get into trouble** s'attirer des ennuis ; **to have trouble doing sth** avoir du mal à faire qch ; **to go to the trouble of doing sth** se donner la peine de faire qch ; **it's no trouble** pas de problème **2.** *vt* [inconvenience] déranger ; [worry] inquiéter

**troublemaker** [ˈtrʌbəlmeɪkə(r)] *n* [in school] élément *m* perturbateur ; [political] fauteur *m* de troubles

**troublesome** [ˈtrʌbəlsəm] *adj* pénible

**trough** [trɒf] *n* [for drinking] abreuvoir *m* ; [for feeding] auge *f*

**troupe** [tru:p] *n* [of actors] troupe *f*

**trousers** [ˈtraʊzəz] *npl* Br pantalon *m* ; **a pair of trousers, some trousers** un pantalon ; **short trousers** culottes *fpl* courtes

**trout** [traʊt] *n inv* truite *f*

**trowel** [ˈtraʊəl] *n* [for cement or plaster] truelle *f* ; [for plants] déplantoir *m*

**truant** [ˈtru:ənt] *n* **to play truant** faire l'école buissonnière

**truce** [tru:s] *n* MIL trêve *f*

**truck** [trʌk] *n* [lorry] camion *m* ; **truck driver** camionneur *m* ; Am **truck stop** [restaurant] routier *m* ■ **trucker** *n* Am camionneur *m*

**trudge** [trʌdʒ] *vi* marcher péniblement

**true** [tru:] (*compar* -er, *superl* -est) *adj* vrai ; [genuine] véritable ; [accurate] exact ; [faithful] fidèle (**to** à) ■ **truly** *adv* vraiment ; **well and truly** bel et bien

**trump** [trʌmp] *n* atout *m*

**trumpet** [ˈtrʌmpɪt] *n* trompette *f*

**truncheon** [ˈtrʌntʃən] *n* Br matraque *f*

**trundle** [ˈtrʌndəl] *vti* **to trundle along** rouler bruyamment

**trunk** [trʌŋk] *n* [of tree, body] tronc *m* ; [of elephant] trompe *f* ; [case] malle *f* ; Am [of vehicle] coffre *m* ; **trunks** [for swimming] slip *m* de bain

**trust** [trʌst] **1.** *n* [faith] confiance *f* (**in** en) **2.** *vt* [believe in] faire confiance à ; **to trust sb with sth, to trust sth to sb** confier qch à qn ; **I trust that...** j'espère que... **3.** *vi* **to trust in sb** faire confiance à qn ■ **trusted** *adj* [method] éprouvé

**trustworthy** [ˈtrʌstwɜːðɪ] *adj* digne de confiance

**truth** [tru:θ] (*pl* -s [tru:ðz]) *n* vérité *f* ; **there's some truth in...** il y a du vrai dans... ■ **truthful** *adj* [story] véridique ; [person] sincère

**try** [traɪ] **1.** (*pl* -ies) *n* [attempt, in rugby] essai *m* ; **to have a try at doing sth** essayer de faire qch ; **it's worth a try** ça vaut la peine d'essayer **2.** (*pt & pp* -ied) *vt* [attempt, sample] essayer ; [food, drink] goûter à ; [in law court] juger (**for** pour) ; **to try doing** *or* **to do sth** essayer de faire qch **3.** *vi* essayer ■ **trying** *adj* difficile ■ **try on** *vt sep* [clothes, shoes] essayer ■ **try out** *vt sep* [car, method, recipe] essayer ; [person] mettre à l'essai

**T-shirt** [ˈtiːʃɜːt] *n* tee-shirt *m*

**T2Go** MESSAGING *written abbr of* **time to go**

**T2ul** (*abbr of* **talk to you later**) MESSAGING @+

**TTYL, TTYL8R** (*abbr of* **talk to you later**) MESSAGING @+

**tub** [tʌb] n [basin] baquet m ; [bath] baignoire f ; Br [for ice cream] pot m ; Br [for flower, bush] bac m

**tuba** ['tjuːbə] n MUS tuba m

**tube** [tjuːb] n tube m ; [of tyre] chambre f à air ; Br Fam **the tube** [underground railway] le métro

**tuberculosis** [tjuːbɜːkjuˈləʊsɪs] n MED tuberculose f

**tuck** [tʌk] **1.** vt [put] mettre ; **to tuck sth away** [put] ranger qch ; [hide] cacher qch ; **to tuck in** [shirt, blanket] rentrer ; [child] border **2.** vi Br Fam **to tuck in** [start eating] attaquer

**Tuesday** ['tjuːzdeɪ] n mardi m

**tuft** [tʌft] n touffe f

**tug** [tʌg] **1.** n **to give sth a tug** tirer sur qch **2.** (pt & pp -gg-) vt [pull] tirer sur **3.** vi tirer (**at** or **on** sur)

**tuition** [tjuːˈɪʃən] n [lessons] cours mpl ; [fee] frais mpl de scolarité

**TUL** MESSAGING written abbr of **tell you later**

**tulip** ['tjuːlɪp] n tulipe f

**tumble** ['tʌmbəl] **1.** n [fall] chute f ; Br **tumble dryer** or **drier** sèche-linge m inv **2.** vi [of person] faire une chute ; Fig [of prices] chuter

**tumbler** ['tʌmblə(r)] n [glass] verre m droit

**tummy** ['tʌmɪ] n Fam ventre m

**tumour**, Am **tumor** ['tjuːmə(r)] n tumeur f

**tuna** ['tjuːnə] n tuna (**fish**) thon m

**tune** [tjuːn] **1.** n [melody] air m ; **in tune** [instrument] accordé ; **out of tune** [instrument] désaccordé ; **to be** or **sing in tune/out of tune** chanter juste/faux ; Fig **to be in tune with sb/sth** être en harmonie avec qn/qch **2.** vt **to tune (up)** [instrument] accorder ; [engine] régler **3.** vi **to tune in** brancher son poste (**to** sur)

**tuner** ['tjuːnə(r)] n [on TV, radio] tuner m

**tunic** ['tjuːnɪk] n tunique f

**Tunisia** [tjuːˈnɪzɪə] n la Tunisie

**tunnel** ['tʌnəl] **1.** n tunnel m **2.** (Br -ll-, Am -l-) vi creuser un tunnel (**into** dans)

**turban** ['tɜːbən] n turban m

**turbulence** ['tɜːbjʊləns] n turbulence f

**turf** [tɜːf] n [grass] gazon m

**turkey** ['tɜːkɪ] (pl -eys) n [bird] dinde f

**Turkey** ['tɜːkɪ] n la Turquie ▪ **Turk** n Turc m, Turque f ▪ **Turkish 1.** adj turc (f turque) ; **Turkish delight** des loukoums mpl **2.** n [language] turc m

**turmoil** ['tɜːmɔɪl] n **to be in turmoil** [of person] être dans tous ses états ; [of country] être en ébullition

**turn** [tɜːn] **1.** n [of wheel, in game, queue] tour m ; [in road] tournant m ; [of events] tournure f ; Br Fam [fit] crise f ; **to take turns** se relayer ; **in turn** à tour de rôle ; **it's your turn (to play)** c'est à toi (de jouer) ; **the turn of the century** le tournant du siècle ; **turn of phrase** tournure de phrase **2.** vt tourner ; [mechanically] faire tourner ; [mattress, pancake] retourner ; **to turn sb/sth into sb/sth** changer qn/qch en qn/qch ; **to turn sth red/black** rougir/noircir qch ; **to turn sth on sb** [aim] braquer qch sur qn ; **she has turned twenty** elle a vingt ans passés **3.** vi [of wheel, driver] tourner ; [of person] se retourner ; **to turn red/black** rougir/noircir ; **to turn nasty** [of person] devenir méchant ; [of situation] mal tourner ; **to turn to sb** se tourner vers qn ; **to turn into sb/sth** devenir qn/qch ; **to turn against sb** se retourner contre qn ▪ **turned** [tɜːnd] adj [milk] tourné ▪ **turn-off** n [on road] sortie f ▪ **turnout** n [people] assistance f ; [at polls] participation f ▪ **turnover** n COMM [sales] chiffre m d'affaires ; [of stock] rotation f ; [of staff] renouvellement m ▪ **turnup** n Br [on trousers] revers m ▪ **turn around** vi [of person] se retourner ▪ **turn away 1.** vt sep [eyes] détourner (**from** de) ; [person] refuser **2.** vi se détourner ▪ **turn back 1.** vt sep [sheets] rabattre ; [clock] retarder **2.** vi [return] faire demi-tour ▪ **turn down** vt sep [gas, radio] baisser ; [fold down] rabattre ; [refuse] rejeter ▪ **turn in 1.** vt sep [person] livrer à la police **2.** vi Fam [go to bed] aller au pieu ▪ **turn off 1.** vt sep [light, radio] éteindre ;

[tap] fermer ; [machine] arrêter ; *Fam* **to turn sb off** dégoûter qn **2.** *vi* [leave road] sortir ■ **turn on 1.** *vt sep* [light, radio] allumer ; [tap] ouvrir ; [machine] mettre en marche ; *Fam* **to turn sb on** [sexually] exciter qn **2.** *vi* **to turn on sb** [attack] attaquer qn ■ **turn out 1.** *vt sep* [light] éteindre ; [pocket, box] vider ; [produce] produire **2.** *vi* [appear, attend] se déplacer ; **it turns out that...** il s'avère que... ; **she turned out to be...** elle s'est révélée être... ■ **turn over 1.** *vt sep* [page] tourner **2.** *vi* [of person] se retourner ; [of car] faire un tonneau ■ **turn round 1.** *vt sep* [head] tourner ; [object] retourner ; [situation] renverser **2.** *vi* [of person] se retourner ; [in vehicle] faire demi-tour ■ **turn up 1.** *vt sep* [radio, heat] mettre plus fort ; [collar] remonter **2.** *vi* [arrive] arriver ; [be found] être retrouvé

**turning** ['tɜːnɪŋ] *n Br* [street] petite rue *f* ; [bend in road] tournant *m* ; *Fig* **turning point** tournant *m*

**turnip** ['tɜːnɪp] *n* navet *m*

**turnpike** ['tɜːnpaɪk] *n Am* autoroute *f* à péage

**turnstile** ['tɜːnstaɪl] *n* tourniquet *m*

**turntable** ['tɜːnteɪbəl] *n* platine *f*

**turquoise** ['tɜːkwɔɪz] *adj* turquoise *inv*

**turret** ['tʌrɪt] *n* tourelle *f*

**turtle** ['tɜːtəl] *n Br* tortue *f* de mer ; *Am* tortue *f*

**tusk** [tʌsk] *n* défense *f* ((dent))

**tussle** ['tʌsəl] *n* bagarre *f*

**tutor** ['tjuːtə(r)] **1.** *n* professeur *m* particulier ; [in British university] directeur, -trice *mf* d'études **2.** *vt* donner des cours particuliers à ■ **tutorial** [-'tɔːrɪəl] *n* UNIV ≃ travaux *mpl* dirigés

**tuxedo** [tʌk'siːdəʊ] *(pl -os)* *n Am* smoking *m*

**TV** [tiː'viː] *n* télé *f* ; **on TV** à la télé

**tweed** [twiːd] *n* tweed *m* ; **tweed jacket** veste *f* en tweed

**tweeps** [twiːps] *npl Fam* **my tweeps** mes potes *mpl* sur Twitter®, ceux qui me suivent (sur Twitter®)

**Tweet**® [twiːt] *n* Tweet®

**tweezers** ['twiːzəz] *npl* pince *f* à épiler

**twelve** [twelv] *adj & n* douze *(m)* ■ **twelfth** *adj & n* douzième *(mf)* ; *Am* SCH **twelfth grade** classe de l'enseignement secondaire correspondant à la terminale (17-18 ans)

**twenty** ['twentɪ] *adj & n* vingt *(m)* ■ **twentieth** *adj & n* vingtième *(mf)* ■ **twenty-four seven** *adv* vingt-quatre heures sur vingt-quatre, sept jours sur sept

**twice** [twaɪs] *adv* deux fois ; **twice as heavy (as)** deux fois plus lourd (que) ; **twice a month, twice monthly** deux fois par mois

**twiddle** ['twɪdəl] *vti* **to twiddle (with) sth** tripoter qch ; **to twiddle one's thumbs** se tourner les pouces

**twig**[1] [twɪg] *n* [of branch] brindille *f*

**twig**[2] [twɪg] *(pt & pp -gg-)* *vti Br Fam* piger

**twilight** ['twaɪlaɪt] *n* crépuscule *m*

**twin** [twɪn] **1.** *n* jumeau *m*, jumelle *f* ; **twin brother** frère *m* jumeau ; **twin pack** paquet *m* double ; **twin sister** sœur *f* jumelle ; **twin beds** lits *mpl* jumeaux ; **twin town** ville *f* jumelée **2.** *(pt & pp -nn-)* *vt* [town] jumeler

**twine** [twaɪn] **1.** *n* [string] ficelle *f* **2.** *vi* [twist] s'enrouler (**round** autour de)

**twinge** [twɪndʒ] *n* **a twinge (of pain)** un élancement ; **a twinge of remorse** un peu de remords

**twinkle** ['twɪŋkəl] *vi* [of star] scintiller ; [of eye] pétiller

**twirl** [twɜːl] **1.** *vt* faire tournoyer ; [moustache] tortiller **2.** *vi* tournoyer

**twist** [twɪst] **1.** *n* [action] tour *m* ; [bend] tortillement *m* ; *Fig* [in story] tour *m* inattendu **2.** *vt* [wire, arm] tordre ; [roll] enrouler (**round** autour de) ; **to twist one's ankle** se tordre la cheville ; *Fig* **to twist sb's arm** forcer la main à qn ; **to twist sth off** [lid] dévisser qch **3.** *vi* [wind] s'entortiller (**round sth** autour de qch) ; [of road, river] serpenter ■ **twisted** *adj* [person, mind, logic] tordu

**twit** [twɪt] *n Br Fam* andouille *f*

**twitch** [twɪtʃ] **1.** *n* [nervous] tic *m* **2.** *vi* [of person] avoir un tic ; [of muscle] se contracter nerveusement

**twitter** ['twɪtə(r)] *vi* [of bird] pépier

**two** [tu:] *adj & n* deux *(m)* ▪ **two-dimensional** *adj* à deux dimensions ▪ **two-faced** *adj Fig* hypocrite ▪ **two-piece** *adj* [suit, swimsuit] deux-pièces ▪ **two-seater** *n* [car] voiture *f* à deux places

**2** MESSAGING **a)** *written abbr of* **to b)** *written abbr of* **too**

**2DAY** MESSAGING *written abbr of* **today**

**2d4** MESSAGING *written abbr of* **to die for**

**twofold** ['tu:fəʊld] **1.** *adj* double **2.** *adv* **to increase twofold** doubler

**2L8** MESSAGING *written abbr of* **too late**

**2MORO** *(abbr of* **tomorrow***)* MESSAGING **2m1**

**2NITE** MESSAGING *written abbr of* **tonight**

**twosome** ['tu:səm] *n* couple *m*

**tycoon** [taɪ'ku:n] *n* magnat *m*

**type¹** [taɪp] *n* **a)** [sort] genre *m*, type *m* **b)** [print] caractères *mpl* ; **in large type** en gros caractères

**type²** [taɪp] **1.** *vti* [write] taper (à la machine) **2.** *vt* **to type sth in** [on computer] entrer qch au clavier ; **to type sth out** [letter] taper qch ▪ **typewriter** *n* machine *f* à écrire ▪ **typewritten** *adj* dactylographié ▪ **typing** *n* dactylographie *f* ; **typing error** faute *f* de frappe ▪ **typist** *n* dactylo *mf*

**typhoid** ['taɪfɔɪd] *n* MED typhoïde *f*

**typhoon** [taɪ'fu:n] *n* typhon *m*

**typical** ['tɪpɪkəl] *adj* typique (**of** de)

**tyrant** ['taɪrənt] *n* tyran *m*

**tyre** ['taɪə(r)] *n Br* pneu *m* (*pl* pneus)

**TYVM** MESSAGING *written abbr of* **thank you very much**

# U

**U, u** [juː] n [letter] U, u m inv

**ugh** [ʌʊ] excl berk !

**ugly** [ˈʌglɪ] (compar -ier, superl -iest) adj laid

**UHF** (abbr of **ultra high frequency**) n UHF

**UK** [juːˈkeɪ] (abbr of **United Kingdom**) n the UK le Royaume-Uni

**ulcer** [ˈʌlsə(r)] n ulcère m

**ulterior** [ʌlˈtɪərɪə(r)] adj **ulterior motive** arrière-pensée f

**ultimate** [ˈʌltɪmət] adj [last] final ; [supreme, best] absolu ■ **ultimately** adv [finally] finalement ; [basically] en fin de compte

**ultimatum** [ʌltɪˈmeɪtəm] n ultimatum m

**ultra-** [ˈʌltrə] pref ultra-

**ultramodern** [ˌʌltrəˈmɒdən] adj ultramoderne

**ultraviolet** [ʌltrəˈvaɪələt] adj ultraviolet, -ette

**umbrella** [ʌmˈbrelə] n parapluie m

**umpire** [ˈʌmpaɪə(r)] n arbitre m

**umpteen** [ʌmpˈtiːn] adj Fam **umpteen times** je ne sais combien de fois ■ **umpteenth** adj Fam énième

**UN** [juːˈen] (abbr of **United Nations**) n the UN les Nations fpl unies

**unable** [ʌnˈeɪbəl] adj **to be unable to do sth** être incapable de faire qch

**unabridged** [ʌnəˈbrɪdʒd] adj intégral

**unacceptable** [ʌnəkˈseptəbəl] adj inacceptable

**unaccompanied** [ʌnəˈkʌmpənɪd] adj [person] non accompagné ; [singing] sans accompagnement

**unaccustomed** [ʌnəˈkʌstəmd] adj inaccoutumé ; **to be unaccustomed to sth/to doing sth** ne pas être habitué à qch/à faire qch

**unaided** [ʌnˈeɪdɪd] adv sans aide

**unanimous** [juːˈnænɪməs] adj unanime ■ **unanimously** adv à l'unanimité

**unappetizing** [ʌnˈæpɪtaɪzɪŋ] adj peu appétissant

**unarmed** [ʌnˈɑːmd] adj non armé

**unashamedly** [ʌnəˈʃeɪmədlɪ] adv sans aucune honte

**unassuming** [ʌnəˈsjuːmɪŋ] adj sans prétention

**unattached** [ʌnəˈtætʃt] adj [without partner] sans attaches

**unattainable** [ʌnəˈteɪnəbəl] adj inaccessible

**unattended** [ʌnəˈtendɪd] adj **to leave sb/sth unattended** laisser qn/qch sans surveillance

**unattractive** [ʌnəˈtræktɪv] adj peu attrayant

**unauthorized** [ʌnˈɔːθəraɪzd] adj non autorisé

**unavailable** [ʌnəˈveɪləbəl] adj **to be unavailable** ne pas être disponible

**unavoidable** [ʌnəˈvɔɪdəbəl] adj inévitable

**unaware** [ʌnəˈweə(r)] adj **to be unaware of sth** ignorer qch ; **to be unaware that...** ignorer que... ■ **unawares** adv **to catch sb unawares** prendre qn au dépourvu

**unbalanced** [ʌnˈbælənst] adj [mind, person] instable

**unbearable** [ʌnˈbeərəbəl] adj insupportable

**unbeatable** [ʌnˈbiːtəbəl] adj imbattable

**unbeaten** [ʌn'biːtən] *adj* [player] invaincu ; [record] jamais battu

**unbelievable** [ʌnbɪ'liːvəbəl] *adj* incroyable

**unbias(s)ed** [ʌn'baɪəst] *adj* impartial

**unblock** [ʌn'blɒk] *vt* [sink, pipe] déboucher

**unbolt** [ʌn'bəʊlt] *vt* [door] déverrouiller

**unborn** [ʌn'bɔːn] *adj* **unborn child** enfant *mf* à naître

**unbreakable** [ʌn'breɪkəbəl] *adj* incassable ■ **unbroken** *adj* [intact] intact ; [continuous] continu ; [record] jamais battu

**unbutton** [ʌn'bʌtən] *vt* déboutonner

**uncalled-for** [ʌn'kɔːldfɔː(r)] *adj* déplacé

**uncanny** [ʌn'kænɪ] *(compar* -ier, *superl* -iest) *adj* étrange

**uncertain** [ʌn'sɜːtən] *adj* incertain ; **to be uncertain about sth** ne pas être certain de qch ; **it's uncertain whether** *or* **that...** il n'est pas certain que... (+ *subjunctive*) ■ **uncertainty** *(pl* -ies) *n* incertitude *f*

**unchanged** [ʌn'tʃeɪndʒd] *adj* inchangé ■ **unchanging** *adj* immuable

**uncheck** [ʌn'tʃek] *vt* [box] décocher

**unclaimed** [ʌn'kleɪmd] *adj* [luggage] non réclamé

**uncle** [ʌŋkəl] *n* oncle *m*

**unclear** [ʌn'klɪə(r)] *adj* vague ; [result] incertain ; **it's unclear whether...** on ne sait pas très bien si...

**uncomfortable** [ʌn'kʌmftəbəl] *adj* inconfortable ; [heat, experience] désagréable ; **to feel uncomfortable** [physically] ne pas être à l'aise ; [ill at ease] être mal à l'aise

**uncommon** [ʌn'kɒmən] *adj* peu commun

**uncompromising** [ʌn'kɒmprəmaɪzɪŋ] *adj* intransigeant

**unconditional** [ʌnkən'dɪʃənəl] *adj* sans condition

**unconfirmed** [ʌnkən'fɜːmd] *adj* non confirmé

**unconnected** [ʌnkə'nektɪd] *adj* sans lien

**unconscious** [ʌn'kɒnʃəs] **1.** *adj* [person] sans connaissance ; [desire] inconscient ; **to be unconscious of sth** ne pas avoir conscience de qch **2.** *n* **the unconscious** l'inconscient *m* ■ **unconsciously** *adv* inconsciemment

**uncontrollable** [ʌnkən'trəʊləbəl] *adj* incontrôlable

**unconventional** [ʌnkən'venʃənəl] *adj* non conformiste

**unconvinced** [ʌnkən'vɪnst] *adj* **to be** *or* **remain unconvinced** ne pas être convaincu (**of** de) ■ **unconvincing** *adj* peu convaincant

**uncooked** [ʌn'kʊkt] *adj* cru

**uncooperative** [ʌnkəʊ'ɒpərətɪv] *adj* peu coopératif, -ive

**uncouth** [ʌn'kuːθ] *adj* fruste

**uncover** [ʌn'kʌvə(r)] *vt* découvrir

**undaunted** [ʌn'dɔːntɪd] *adj* nullement impressionné

**undecided** [ʌndɪ'saɪdɪd] *adj* [person] indécis (**about** sur) ; **I'm undecided whether to do it or not** je n'ai pas décidé si je le ferai ou non

**undeniable** [ʌndɪ'naɪəbəl] *adj* indéniable

**under** [ʌndə(r)] **1.** *prep* sous ; [less than] moins de ; **children under nine** les enfants de moins de neuf ans ; **under it** dessous ; **under (the command of)** sb sous les ordres de qn ; **under the circumstances** dans ces circonstances ; **to be under discussion / repair** être en discussion / réparation ; **to be under way** [in progress] être en cours ; [on the way] être en route ; **to get under way** [of campaign] démarrer **2.** *adv* au-dessous

**undercharge** [ʌndə'tʃɑːdʒ] *vt* **I undercharged him (for it)** je ne (le) lui ai pas fait payer assez

**underclothes** [ʌndəkləʊðz] *npl* sous-vêtements *mpl*

**undercooked** [ʌndə'kʊkt] *adj* pas assez cuit

**undercover** [ˈʌndəkʌvə(r)] *adj* secret, -ète

**undercut** [ʌndəˈkʌt] *(pt & pp* -cut, *pres p* -cutting) *vt* vendre moins cher que

**underdeveloped** [ʌndədɪˈveləpt] *adj* [country, region] sous-développé

**underdog** [ˈʌndədɒg] *n* [politically, socially] opprimé, -e *mf*; [likely loser] outsider *m*

**underdone** [ʌndəˈdʌn] *adj* [food] pas assez cuit; [steak] saignant

**underestimate** [ʌndərˈestɪmeɪt] *vt* sous-estimer

**underfoot** [ʌndəˈfʊt] *adv* sous les pieds

**undergo** [ʌndəˈgəʊ] *(pt* -went, *pp* -gone) *vt* subir; **to undergo surgery** être opéré

**undergraduate** [ʌndəˈgrædʒʊət] *n* étudiant, -e *mf* de licence

**underground 1.** [ˈʌndəgraʊnd] *adj* [subterranean] souterrain **2.** [ˈʌndəgraʊnd] *n Br* [railway] métro *m* **3.** [ʌndəˈgraʊnd] *adv* sous terre; *Fig* **to go underground** [of fugitive] passer dans la clandestinité

**undergrowth** [ˈʌndəgrəʊθ] *n* broussailles *fpl*

**underhand** [ʌndəˈhænd] *adj* sournois

**underline** [ʌndəˈlaɪn] *vt* souligner

**underlying** [ʌndəˈlaɪɪŋ] *adj* sous-jacent

**undermine** [ʌndəˈmaɪn] *vt* [weaken] saper

**underneath** [ʌndəˈniːθ] **1.** *prep* sous **2.** *adv* (en) dessous; **the book underneath** le livre d'en dessous **3.** *n* **the underneath (of)** le dessous (de)

**underpaid** [ʌndəˈpeɪd] *adj* sous-payé

**underpants** [ˈʌndəpænts] *npl* [male underwear] slip *m*

**underpass** [ˈʌndəpɑːs] *n* [for pedestrians] passage *m* souterrain; [for vehicles] passage *m* inférieur

**underprivileged** [ʌndəˈprɪvɪlɪdʒd] *adj* défavorisé

**underrate** [ʌndəˈreɪt] *vt* sous-estimer

**underside** [ˈʌndəsaɪd] *n* **the underside (of)** le dessous (de)

**understaffed** [ʌndəˈstɑːft] *adj* **to be understaffed** manquer de personnel

**understand** [ʌndəˈstænd] *(pt & pp* -stood) *vti* comprendre; **I understand that…** je crois comprendre que… ■ **understanding 1.** *n* [act, faculty] compréhension *f*; [agreement] accord *m*, entente *f*; [sympathy] entente *f*; **on the understanding that…** à condition que… (+ *subjunctive*) **2.** *adj* [person] compréhensif, -ive ■ **understood** *adj* [agreed] entendu; [implied] sous-entendu

**understandable** [ʌndəˈstændəbəl] *adj* compréhensible

**understatement** [ˈʌndəsteɪtmənt] *n* euphémisme *m*

**undertake** [ʌndəˈteɪk] *(pt* -took, *pp* -taken) *vt* [task] entreprendre; **to undertake to do sth** entreprendre de faire qch

**undertaker** [ˈʌndəteɪkə(r)] *n* entrepreneur *m* de pompes funèbres

**undertaking** [ʌndəˈteɪkɪŋ] *n* [task] entreprise *f*; [promise] promesse *f*

**undertone** [ˈʌndətəʊn] *n* **in an undertone** à mi-voix

**underwater** [ʌndəˈwɔːtə(r)] *adv* sous l'eau

**underwear** [ˈʌndəweə(r)] *n* sous-vêtements *mpl*

**undesirable** [ʌndɪˈzaɪərəbəl] *adj & n* indésirable (*mf*)

**undignified** [ʌnˈdɪgnɪfaɪd] *adj* indigne

**undisciplined** [ʌnˈdɪsɪplɪnd] *adj* indiscipliné

**undisclosed** [ˌʌndɪsˈkləʊzd] *adj* non divulgué

**undiscovered** [ʌndɪˈskʌvəd] *adj* **to remain undiscovered** [of crime, body] ne pas être découvert

**undisputed** [ʌndɪˈspjuːtɪd] *adj* incontesté

**undistinguished** [ʌndɪˈstɪŋgwɪʃt] *adj* médiocre

**undo** [ʌnˈduː] *(pt* -did, *pp* -done) *vt* défaire; [bound person] détacher; [parcel] ouvrir; [mistake, damage] réparer; COMPUT [command] annuler ■ **undo-**

**ing** *n* ruine *f* ■ **undone** *adj* to come undone [of knot] se défaire ; **to leave sth undone** [work] ne pas faire qch

**undoubtedly** [ʌn'dautɪdlɪ] *adv* indubitablement

**undress** [ʌn'dres] **1.** *vt* déshabiller ; **to get undressed** se déshabiller **2.** *vi* se déshabiller

**undrinkable** [ʌn'drɪnkəbəl] *adj* imbuvable

**undue** [ʌn'djuː] *adj* excessif, -ive ■ **unduly** *adv* excessivement

**unearth** [ʌn'ɜːθ] *vt* [from ground] déterrer ; *Fig* [discover] mettre à jour

**unearthly** [ʌn'ɜːθlɪ] *adj Fam* **at an unearthly hour** à une heure impossible

**uneasy** [ʌn'iːzɪ] *adj* [person] mal à l'aise ; [silence] gêné

**uneconomic(al)** [ʌniːkə'nɒmɪk(əl)] *adj* peu économique

**uneducated** [ʌn'edjʊkeɪtɪd] *adj* [person] sans éducation

**unemployed** [ʌnɪm'plɔɪd] **1.** *adj* au chômage **2.** *npl* **the unemployed** les chômeurs *mpl* ■ **unemployment** *n* chômage *m*; *Br* **unemployment benefit** allocation *f* chômage

**unenthusiastic** [ʌnɪnθjuːzɪ'æstɪk] *adj* peu enthousiaste

**unenviable** [ʌn'envɪəbəl] *adj* peu enviable

**unequal** [ʌn'iːkwəl] *adj* inégal

**unequivocal** [ʌnɪ'kwɪvəkəl] *adj* sans équivoque

**uneven** [ʌn'iːvən] *adj* inégal

**uneventful** [ʌnɪ'ventfəl] *adj* sans histoires

**unexpected** [ʌnɪk'spektɪd] *adj* inattendu ■ **unexpectedly** *adv* [arrive] à l'improviste ; [fail, succeed] contre toute attente

**unexplained** [ʌnɪk'spleɪnd] *adj* inexpliqué

**unexplored** [ʌnɪk'splɔːd] *adj* inexploré

**unfailing** [ʌn'feɪlɪŋ] *adj* [optimism, courage] à toute épreuve

**unfair** [ʌn'feə(r)] *adj* injuste (**to sb** envers qn) ; [competition] déloyal ■ **unfairly** *adv* injustement

**unfaithful** [ʌn'feɪθfəl] *adj* infidèle (**to** à)

**unfamiliar** [ʌnfə'mɪlɪə(r)] *adj* inconnu ; **to be unfamiliar with sth** ne pas connaître qch

**unfashionable** [ʌn'fæʃənəbəl] *adj* démodé

**unfasten** [ʌn'fɑːsən] *vt* défaire

**unfavourable**, *Am* **unfavorable** [ʌn'feɪvərəbəl] *adj* défavorable

**unfilled** [ʌn'fɪld] *adj* [post, vacancy] à pourvoir

**unfinished** [ʌn'fɪnɪʃt] *adj* inachevé

**unfit** [ʌn'fɪt] *adj* [unsuitable] inapte ; [in bad shape] pas en forme ; **to be unfit to do sth** être incapable de faire qch

**unflattering** [ʌn'flætərɪŋ] *adj* peu flatteur, -euse

**unfold** [ʌn'fəʊld] **1.** *vt* déplier ; [wings] déployer **2.** *vi* [of story] se dérouler

**unforeseeable** [ʌnfɔː'siːəbəl] *adj* imprévisible ■ **unforeseen** *adj* imprévu

**unforgettable** [ʌnfə'getəbəl] *adj* inoubliable

**unforgivable** [ʌnfə'gɪvəbəl] *adj* impardonnable

**unfortunate** [ʌn'fɔːtʃənət] *adj* malchanceux, -euse ; [event] fâcheux, -euse ; **you were unfortunate** tu n'as pas eu de chance ■ **unfortunately** *adv* malheureusement

**unfounded** [ʌn'faʊndɪd] *adj* [rumour] sans fondement

**unfriend** [ʌn'frend] *vt* **to unfriend sb** supprimer qqn de la liste de ses amis *(sur Facebook, etc)*

**unfriendly** [ʌn'frendlɪ] *adj* peu aimable (**to** avec)

**unfulfilled** [ʌnfʊl'fɪld] *adj* [plan, dream] non réalisé

**unfurnished** [ʌn'fɜːnɪʃt] *adj* non meublé

**ungainly** [ʌn'geɪnlɪ] *adj* [clumsy] gauche

**ungrateful** [ʌn'greɪtfəl] *adj* ingrat

**unhappy** [ʌn'hæpɪ] *(compar* **-ier**, *superl* **-iest)** *adj* [sad, unfortunate] malheureux, -euse ; [not pleased] mécontent ; **to be unhappy about doing sth** ne pas vouloir faire qch

**unharmed** [ʌn'hɑːmd] *adj* indemne

**unhealthy** [ʌn'helθɪ] *(compar* **-ier,** *superl* **-iest)** *adj* [person] maladif, -ive ; [climate, place, job] malsain

**unheard-of** [ʌn'hɜːdɒv] *adj* [unprecedented] inouï

**unhelpful** [ʌn'helpfəl] *adj* [person] peu serviable ; [advice] peu utile

**unhurt** [ʌn'hɜːt] *adj* indemne

**unhygienic** [ʌnhaɪ'dʒiːnɪk, *Am* -'dʒenɪk] *adj* contraire à l'hygiène

**uniform** ['juːnɪfɔːm] **1.** *n* uniforme *m* **2.** *adj* [regular] uniforme ; [temperature] constant

**unify** ['juːnɪfaɪ] *(pt & pp* **-ied)** *vt* unifier

**unilateral** [juːnɪ'lætərəl] *adj* unilatéral

**unimaginable** [ʌnɪ'mædʒɪnəbəl] *adj* inimaginable ■ **unimaginative** *adj* [person, plan] qui manque d'imagination

**unimportant** [ʌnɪm'pɔːtənt] *adj* sans importance

**uninhabitable** [ʌnɪn'hæbɪtəbəl] *adj* inhabitable ■ **uninhabited** *adj* inhabité

**uninhibited** [ʌnɪn'hɪbɪtɪd] *adj* [person] sans complexes

**uninjured** [ʌn'ɪndʒəd] *adj* indemne

**uninspiring** [ʌnɪn'spaɪərɪŋ] *adj* [subject] pas très inspirant

**unintelligible** [ʌnɪn'telɪdʒəbəl] *adj* inintelligible

**unintended** [ˌʌnɪn'tendɪd] *adj* non intentionnel, -elle, accidentel, -elle, fortuit

**unintentional** [ʌnɪn'tenʃənəl] *adj* involontaire

**uninterested** [ʌn'ɪntrɪstɪd] *adj* indifférent (**in** à) ■ **uninteresting** *adj* inintéressant

**uninterrupted** [ʌnɪntə'rʌptɪd] *adj* ininterrompu

**uninvited** [ʌnɪn'vaɪtɪd] *adv* [arrive] sans invitation ■ **uninviting** *adj* peu attrayant

**union** ['juːnɪən] **1.** *n* union *f* ; [trade union] syndicat *m* **2.** *adj* syndical ; **the Union Jack** *le drapeau britannique*

**unique** [juː'niːk] *adj* unique

**unisex** ['juːnɪseks] *adj* [clothes] unisexe

**unison** ['juːnɪsən] *n* **in unison** à l'unisson (**with** de)

**unit** ['juːnɪt] *n* unité *f* ; [of furniture] élément *m* ; [system] bloc *m* ; [group, team] groupe *m* ; **psychiatric / heart unit** [of hospital] service *m* de psychiatrie / cardiologie

**unite** [juː'naɪt] **1.** *vt* unir ; [country, party] unifier ; **the United Kingdom** *le Royaume-Uni* ; **the United Nations** *les Nations fpl unies* ; **the United States (of America)** *les États-Unis mpl* (d'Amérique) **2.** *vi* s'unir

**unity** ['juːnətɪ] *n* [cohesion] unité *f* ; *Fig* [harmony] harmonie *f*

**universal** [juːnɪ'vɜːsəl] *adj* universel, -elle

**universe** ['juːnɪvɜːs] *n* univers *m*

**university** [juːnɪ'vɜːsətɪ] **1.** *(pl* **-ies)** *n* université *f* ; **to go to university** aller à l'université ; *Br* **at university** à l'université **2.** *adj* [teaching, town, restaurant] universitaire ; [student, teacher] d'université

**unjust** [ʌn'dʒʌst] *adj* injuste

**unjustified** [ʌn'dʒʌstɪfaɪd] *adj* injustifié

**unkind** [ʌn'kaɪnd] *adj* pas gentil (*f* pas gentille) (**to sb** avec qn)

**unknowingly** [ʌn'nəʊɪŋlɪ] *adv* inconsciemment

**unknown** [ʌn'nəʊn] **1.** *adj* inconnu **2.** *n* [person] inconnu, -e *mf* ; *MATH & Fig* **unknown (quantity)** inconnue *f*

**unlawful** [ʌn'lɔːfəl] *adj* illégal

**unleaded** [ʌn'ledɪd] **1.** *adj* **unleaded petrol** essence *f* sans plomb, sans plomb *m inv* **2.** *n* *Fam* [petrol] sans-plomb *m inv*

**unleash** [ʌn'liːʃ] *vt* [emotion] susciter

**unless** [ʌn'les] *conj* à moins que (+ *subjunctive*) ; **unless she comes**

à moins qu'elle ne vienne; **unless you work harder, you'll fail** à moins de travailler plus dur, vous échouerez

**unlike** [ʌn'laɪk] *prep* **to be unlike sb/ sth** ne pas être comme qn/qch; **unlike her brother, she…** à la différence de son frère, elle…; **it's very unlike him to…** ça ne lui ressemble pas du tout de…

**unlikely** [ʌn'laɪklɪ] *adj* improbable; [unbelievable] invraisemblable; **she's unlikely to win** il est peu probable qu'elle gagne

**unlimited** [ʌn'lɪmɪtɪd] *adj* illimité

**unlisted** [ʌn'lɪstɪd] *adj Am* [phone number] sur liste rouge

**unload** [ʌn'ləʊd] *vti* décharger

**unlock** [ʌn'lɒk] *vt* ouvrir

**unlucky** [ʌn'lʌkɪ] *(compar* -**ier***, superl* -**iest**) *adj* [person] malchanceux, -euse; [number, colour] qui porte malheur ■ **unluckily** *adv* malheureusement

**unmade** [ʌn'meɪd] *adj* [bed] défait

**unmanageable** [ʌn'mænɪdʒəbəl] *adj* [child] difficile; [hair] difficile à coiffer

**unmarried** [ʌn'mærɪd] *adj* non marié

**unmistakable** [ʌnmɪ'steɪkəbəl] *adj* [obvious] indubitable; [face, voice] caractéristique

**unmoved** [ʌn'muːvd] *adj* **to be unmoved by sth** rester insensible à qch

**unnatural** [ʌn'nætʃərəl] *adj* [abnormal] anormal; [affected] affecté

**unnecessary** [ʌn'nesəsərɪ] *adj* inutile; [superfluous] superflu

**unnerve** [ʌn'nɜːv] *vt* troubler

**unnoticed** [ʌn'nəʊtɪst] *adv* **to go unnoticed** passer inaperçu

**UNO** *(abbr of* **United Nations Organization**)*n* ONU *m*, Onu *m (Organisation des Nations unies)*

**unobtainable** [ʌnəb'teɪnəbəl] *adj* impossible à obtenir

**unoccupied** [ʌn'ɒkjʊpaɪd] *adj* [house] inoccupé; [seat] libre

**unofficial** [ʌnə'fɪʃəl] *adj* officieux, -euse; [visit] privé; [strike] sauvage

**unorthodox** [ʌn'ɔːθədɒks] *adj* peu orthodoxe

**unpack** [ʌn'pæk] **1.** *vt* [suitcase] défaire; [contents] déballer **2.** *vi* défaire sa valise

**unpaid** [ʌn'peɪd] *adj* [bill, sum] impayé; [work, worker] bénévole; [leave] non payé

**unparalleled** [ʌn'pærəleld] *adj* sans égal

**unplanned** [ʌn'plænd] *adj* imprévu

**unpleasant** [ʌn'plezənt] *adj* désagréable (**to sb** avec qn)

**unplug** [ʌn'plʌg] *(pt & pp* -**gg**-*) vt* [appliance] débrancher

**unpopular** [ʌn'pɒpjʊlə(r)] *adj* impopulaire; **to be unpopular with sb** ne pas plaire à qn

**unprecedented** [ʌn'presɪdentɪd] *adj* sans précédent

**unpredictable** [ʌnprɪ'dɪktəbəl] *adj* imprévisible; [weather] indécis

**unprepared** [ʌnprɪ'peəd] *adj* **to be unprepared for sth** [not expect] ne pas s'attendre à qch

**unprofessional** [ʌnprə'feʃənəl] *adj* [person, behaviour] pas très professionnel, -elle

**unprovoked** [ʌnprə'vəʊkt] *adj* gratuit

**unpublished** [ʌn'pʌblɪʃt] *adj* [text, writer] inédit

**unqualified** [ʌn'kwɒlɪfaɪd] *adj* [teacher] non diplômé; [support] sans réserve; [success] parfait; **to be unqualified to do sth** ne pas être qualifié pour faire qch

**unquestionable** [ʌn'kwestʃənəbəl] *adj* incontestable

**unravel** [ʌn'rævəl] *(Br* -**ll**-*, Am* -**l**-*) vt* [threads] démêler; *Fig* [mystery] éclaircir

**unreal** [ʌn'rɪəl] *adj* irréel, -elle

**unrealistic** [ʌn'rɪəlɪstɪk] *adj* irréaliste

**unreasonable** [ʌn'riːzənəbəl] *adj* [person, attitude] déraisonnable

**unrecognizable** [ʌn'rekəgnaɪzəbəl] *adj* méconnaissable

**unrelated** [ʌnrɪ'leɪtɪd] *adj* [facts] sans rapport (**to** avec); **we're unrelated** il n'y a aucun lien de parenté entre nous

**unrelenting** [ʌnrɪˈlentɪŋ] *adj* incessant; [person] tenace

**unreliable** [ʌnrɪˈlaɪəbəl] *adj* peu fiable

**unremarkable** [ʌnrɪˈmɑːkəbəl] *adj* quelconque

**unrepentant** [ʌnrɪˈpentənt] *adj* impénitent

**unreservedly** [ʌnrɪˈzɜːvɪdlɪ] *adv* sans réserve

**unrest** [ʌnˈrest] *n* agitation *f*, troubles *mpl*

**unrestricted** [ʌnrɪˈstrɪktɪd] *adj* illimité

**unrewarding** [ʌnrɪˈwɔːdɪŋ] *adj* ingrat; [financially] peu rémunérateur, -trice

**unrivalled**, *Am* **unrivaled** [ʌnˈraɪvəld] *adj* hors pair *inv*

**unroll** [ʌnˈrəʊl] **1.** *vt* dérouler **2.** *vi* se dérouler

**unruly** [ʌnˈruːlɪ] (*compar* -ier, *superl* -iest) *adj* indiscipliné

**unsafe** [ʌnˈseɪf] *adj* [place, machine] dangereux, -euse

**unsaid** [ʌnˈsed] *adj* **to leave sth unsaid** passer qch sous silence

**unsatisfactory** [ʌnsætɪsˈfæktərɪ] *adj* peu satisfaisant ■ **unsatisfied** *adj* insatisfait; **unsatisfied with sb/sth** peu satisfait de qn/qch

**unscheduled** [*Br* ʌnˈʃeduːld, *Am* ʌnˈskedjʊld] *adj* imprévu

**unscrew** [ʌnˈskruː] *vt* dévisser

**unscrupulous** [ʌnˈskruːpjʊləs] *adj* [person] peu scrupuleux, -euse

**unseemly** [ʌnˈsiːmlɪ] *adj* inconvenant

**unseen** [ʌnˈsiːn] *adv* **to do sth unseen** faire qch sans qu'on vous voie

**unselfish** [ʌnˈselfɪʃ] *adj* [person, motive] désintéressé

**unsettle** [ʌnˈsetəl] *vt* [person] troubler ■ **unsettled** *adj* [weather, situation] instable

**unshak(e)able** [ʌnˈʃeɪkəbəl] *adj* inébranlable

**unshaven** [ʌnˈʃeɪvən] *adj* pas rasé

**unsightly** [ʌnˈsaɪtlɪ] *adj* laid

**unskilled** [ʌnˈskɪld] *adj* non qualifié

**unsociable** [ʌnˈsəʊʃəbəl] *adj* peu sociable

**unsolved** [ʌnˈsɒlvd] *adj* [mystery] inexpliqué; [crime] dont l'auteur n'est pas connu

**unsophisticated** [ʌnsəˈfɪstɪkeɪtɪd] *adj* simple

**unsound** [ʌnˈsaʊnd] *adj* [construction] peu solide; [method] peu sûr; [decision] peu judicieux, -euse

**unspeakable** [ʌnˈspiːkəbəl] *adj* indescriptible

**unspecified** [ʌnˈspesɪfaɪd] *adj* non spécifié

**unspent** [ʌnˈspent] **1.** *adj* non dépensé, restant **2.** *adv* **the money went unspent** l'argent n'a pas été dépensé

**unsporting** [ʌnˈspɔːtɪŋ] *adj* qui n'est pas fair-play

**unstable** [ʌnˈsteɪbəl] *adj* instable

**unsteady** [ʌnˈstedɪ] *adj* [hand, voice, step] mal assuré; [table, ladder] bancal (*mpl* -als) ■ **unsteadily** *adv* [walk] d'un pas mal assuré

**unstuck** [ʌnˈstʌk] *adj Br Fam* [of person, plan] se casser la figure; **to come unstuck** [of stamp] se décoller

**unsuccessful** [ʌnsəkˈsesfəl] *adj* [attempt] infructueux, -euse; [outcome, candidate] malheureux, -euse; [application] non retenu; [of book, film, artist] ne pas avoir de succès; **to be unsuccessful** ne pas réussir (**in doing** à faire) ■ **unsuccessfully** *adv* en vain, sans succès

**unsuitable** [ʌnˈsuːtəbəl] *adj* qui ne convient pas (**for** à); [manners, clothes] peu convenable; **to be unsuitable for sth** ne pas convenir à qch ■ **unsuited** *adj* **to be unsuited to sth** ne pas être fait pour qch; **they're unsuited (to each other)** ils ne sont pas compatibles

**unsupervised** [ʌnˈsuːpəvaɪzd] *adv* [play] sans surveillance

**unsure** [ʌnˈʃʊə(r)] *adj* incertain (**of** *or* **about** de)

**unsustainable** [ʌnsəˈsteɪnəbl] *adj* non viable

**unsympathetic** [ˌʌnsɪmpə'θetɪk] *adj* peu compatissant (**to** à); **unsympathetic to a cause / request** insensible à une cause / requête

**untangle** [ʌn'tæŋgəl] *vt* [rope, hair] démêler

**unthinkable** [ʌn'θɪŋkəbəl] *adj* impensable, inconcevable

**untidy** [ʌn'taɪdɪ] (*compar* -ier, *superl* -iest) *adj* [clothes, hair] peu soigné; [room] en désordre; [person] désordonné

**untie** [ʌn'taɪ] *vt* [person, hands] détacher; [knot, parcel] défaire

**until** [ʌn'tɪl] **1.** *prep* jusqu'à; **until now** jusqu'à présent; **until then** jusque-là; **not until tomorrow** pas avant demain; **I didn't see her until Monday** c'est seulement lundi que je l'ai vue **2.** *conj* jusqu'à ce que (+ *subjunctive*); **until she comes** jusqu'à ce qu'elle vienne; **do nothing until I come** ne fais rien avant que j'arrive

**untimely** [ʌn'taɪmlɪ] *adj* [remark, question] inopportun; [death] prématuré

**untold** [ʌn'təʊld] *adj* [wealth, quantity] incalculable

**untoward** [ʌntə'wɔːd] *adj* fâcheux, -euse

**untrue** [ʌn'truː] *adj* faux (*f* fausse) **■ untruthful** *adj* [person] menteur, -euse; [statement] mensonger, -ère

**unusable** [ʌn'juːzəbəl] *adj* inutilisable

**unused¹** [ʌn'juːzd] *adj* [new] neuf (*f* neuve); [not in use] inutilisé

**unused²** [ʌn'juːst] *adj* **unused to sth / to doing sth** peu habitué à qch / à faire qch

**unusual** [ʌn'juːʒəl] *adj* [not common] inhabituel, -elle; [strange] étrange **■ unusually** *adv* exceptionnellement

**unveil** [ʌn'veɪl] *vt* dévoiler

**unwanted** [ʌn'wɒntɪd] *adj* non désiré

**unwarranted** [ʌn'wɒrəntɪd] *adj* injustifié

**unwelcome** [ʌn'welkəm] *adj* [news] fâcheux, -euse; [gift, visit] inopportun; [person] importun

**unwell** [ʌn'wel] *adj* souffrant

**unwieldy** [ʌn'wiːldɪ] *adj* [package] encombrant; [system] lourd

**unwilling** [ʌn'wɪlɪŋ] *adj* **to be unwilling to do sth** être réticent à faire qch **■ unwillingly** *adv* à contrecœur

**unwind** [ʌn'waɪnd] (*pt & pp* -wound-) **1.** *vt* [thread] dérouler **2.** *vi* se dérouler; *Fam* [relax] décompresser

**unwise** [ʌn'waɪz] *adj* imprudent

**unwittingly** [ʌn'wɪtɪŋlɪ] *adv* involontairement

**unworthy** [ʌn'wɜːðɪ] *adj* indigne (**of** de)

**unwrap** [ʌn'ræp] (*pt & pp* -pp-) *vt* déballer

**unwritten** [ʌn'rɪtən] *adj* [agreement] verbal

**unzip** [ʌn'zɪp] (*pt & pp* -pp-) *vt* ouvrir (la fermeture Éclair® de)

---

**up** [ʌp] **1.** *adv* en haut; **to come / go up** monter; **to walk up and down** marcher de long en large; **up there** là-haut; **up above** au-dessus; **further** *or* **higher up** plus haut; **up to** [as far as] jusqu'à; **up to a point** jusqu'à un certain point, dans une certaine mesure; **to be up to doing sth** [capable of] être de taille à faire qch; **to feel up to doing sth** [well enough] être assez bien pour faire qch; **it's up to you to do it** c'est à toi de le faire; **it's up to you** [you decide] c'est à toi de décider; **where are you up to?** [in book] où en es-tu?; *Fam* **what are you up to?** que fais-tu?; *Fam* **to be well up in** [versed in] s'y connaître en **2.** *prep* **up a hill** en haut d'une colline; **up a tree** dans un arbre; **up a ladder** sur une échelle; **to live up the street** habiter plus loin dans la rue **3.** *adj* [out of bed] levé; **we were up all night** nous sommes restés debout toute la nuit; **the two weeks were up** les deux semaines étaient terminées; *Fam* **what's up?** qu'est-ce qu'il y a? **4.** *npl* **ups and downs** des hauts et des bas *mpl* **5.** (*pt & pp* -pp-) *vt Fam* [price, offer] augmenter

**■ up-and-coming** *adj* qui monte

**■ upbeat** *adj Fam* optimiste

**■ upbringing** *n* éducation *f*

■ **upcoming** [ˈʌpˌkʌmɪŋ] adj [event] à venir, prochain ; [book] à paraître, qui va paraître ; [film] qui va sortir ; **'upcoming attractions'** 'prochainement'

■ **update** vt mettre à jour

■ **upgrade** [ʌpˈgreɪd] **1.** n **a)** [of system] extention f **b)** [of software] mise à jour, actualisation f **2.** vt [job] revaloriser ; [person] promouvoir ; COMPUT [hardware] augmenter la puissance de

■ **uphill 1.** [ʌpˈhɪl] adv **to go uphill** monter **2.** [ˈʌphɪl] adj Fig [struggle, task] pénible

■ **uphold** (pt & pp -held) vt [decision] maintenir

■ **upkeep** n entretien m

■ **upload** [ˈʌpləʊd] **1.** n COMPUT téléchargement m (vers le serveur) **2.** vt & vi COMPUT télécharger (vers le serveur)

■ **up-market** adj Br [car, product] haut de gamme inv ; [area, place] chic inv

■ **upright 1.** adv [straight] droit **2.** adj [vertical, honest] droit

■ **uprising** n insurrection f

■ **uproot** vt [plant, person] déraciner

■ **upside** adv **upside down** à l'envers ; **to turn sth upside down** retourner qch ; Fig mettre qch sens dessus dessous

■ **upstairs 1.** [ʌpˈsteəz] adv en haut **2.** [ˈʌpsteəz] adj [people, room] du dessus ; **to go upstairs** monter

■ **upstream** adv en amont

■ **uptight** adj Fam [tense] crispé ; [inhibited] coincé

■ **up-to-date** adj moderne ; [information] à jour ; [well-informed] au courant **(on** de)

■ **upturn** n [improvement] amélioration f **(in** de)

■ **upward** adj [movement] ascendant ; [path] qui monte ; [trend] à la hausse

■ **upwards** adv vers le haut ; **from 5 euros upwards** à partir de 5 euros ; **upwards of fifty** cinquante et plus

**upheaval** [ʌpˈhiːvəl] n bouleversement m

**upholstery** [ʌpˈhəʊlstəri] n [padding] rembourrage m ; [covering] revêtement m ; [in car] sièges mpl

**upon** [əˈpɒn] prep sur

**upper** [ˈʌpə(r)] **1.** adj supérieur ; **upper class** aristocratie f ; **to have / get the upper hand** avoir / prendre le dessus **2.** n [of shoe] empeigne f ■ **upper-class** adj aristocratique ■ **uppermost** adj le plus haut (f la plus haute)

**uproar** [ˈʌprɔː(r)] n tumulte m

**upset 1.** [ʌpˈset] (pt & pp -set, pres p -setting) vt [knock over, spill] renverser ; [person, plans, schedule] bouleverser **2.** [ʌpˈset] adj [unhappy] bouleversé **(about** par) ; **to have an upset stomach** avoir l'estomac dérangé **3.** [ˈʌpset] n [disturbance] bouleversement m ; [surprise] défaite f ; **to have a stomach upset** avoir l'estomac dérangé ■ **upsetting** adj bouleversant

**upshot** [ˈʌpʃɒt] n résultat m

**uptown** [ˌʌpˈtaʊn] Am **1.** adj [area] résidentiel, -elle **2.** n quartier résidentiel

**urban** [ˈɜːbən] adj urbain

**urge** [ɜːdʒ] **1.** n forte envie f ; **to have an urge to do sth** avoir très envie de faire qch **2.** vt **to urge sb to do sth** presser qn de faire qch

**urgency** [ˈɜːdʒənsɪ] n urgence f ; **it's a matter of urgency** il y a urgence

**urgent** [ˈɜːdʒənt] adj urgent ■ **urgently** adv d'urgence

**urine** [ˈjʊərɪn] n urine f ■ **urinate** vi uriner

**urn** [ɜːn] n urne f ; [for coffee or tea] fontaine f

**us** [əs] (stressed [ʌs]) pron nous ; **(to) us** [indirect] nous ; **she saw us** elle nous a vus ; **he gave it (to) us** il nous l'a donné

**US** [juːˈes] (abbr of **United States**) n **the US** les USA mpl

**USA** [juːesˈeɪ] (abbr of **United States of America**) n **the USA** les USA mpl

**usage** [ˈjuːsɪdʒ] n usage m

**USB key, USB pen** n clé f USB

**use 1.** [juːs] n [utilization] emploi m, usage m ; [ability, permission to use] emploi m ; **to have the use of sth** avoir l'usage de qch ; **to make (good) use of sth** faire (bon) usage de qch ; **to be of use to sb** être utile à qn ; **in use**

en usage; **not in use, out of use** hors d'usage; **it's no use crying** ça ne sert à rien de pleurer; **what's the use of worrying?** à quoi bon s'inquiéter? **2.** [ju:z] *vt* [utilize] utiliser, se servir de; [force, diplomacy] avoir recours à; [electricity] consommer; **it's used to do** *or* **for doing sth** ça sert à faire qch; **it's used as…** ça sert de…; **to use sth up** [food, fuel] finir; [money] dépenser ■ **use-by** ['ju:zbaɪ] *adj* **use-by date** date *f* limite de consommation

**used 1.** *adj* **a)** [ju:zd] [second-hand] d'occasion; [stamp] oblitéré **b)** [ju:st] **to be used to sth/to doing sth** être habitué à qch/à faire qch; **to get used to sb/ sth** s'habituer à qn/qch **2.** [ju:st] *v aux* **I used to sing** avant, je chantais; **she used to jog every Sunday** elle faisait du jogging tous les dimanches

**useful** ['ju:sfəl] *adj* utile (**to** à); **to come in useful** être utile; **to make oneself useful** se rendre utile ■ **useless** *adj* inutile; [person] nul (*f* nulle) (**at** en)

**user** ['ju:zə(r)] *n* [of train, telephone] usager *m*; [of road, machine] utilisateur, -trice *mf*; **user ID** = **user name**; COMPUT **user name** nom *m* d'utilisateur; **user profile** profil *m* utilisateur ■ **user-friendly** *adj* convivial

**usher** ['ʌʃə(r)] **1.** *n* [in church, theatre] ouvreur *m* **2.** *vt* **to usher sb in** faire entrer qn ■ **usherette** *n* ouvreuse *f*

**USPS** *(abbr of* **United States Postal Service)** *n* ≃ la Poste

**usual** ['ju:ʒʋəl] **1.** *adj* habituel, -elle; **as usual** comme d'habitude **2.** *n Fam* **the usual** [food, excuse] la même chose que d'habitude ■ **usually** *adv* d'habitude

**usurp** [ju:'zɜ:p] *vt* usurper

**utensil** [ju:'tensəl] *n* ustensile *m*

**uterus** ['ju:tərəs] *(pl* **-i** *or* **-uses)** *n* utérus *m*

**utility** [ju:'tɪlətɪ] *n* **a)** (**public**) **utility** service *m* public **b)** COMPUT utilitaire *m*

**utilize** ['ju:tɪlaɪz] *vt* utiliser

**utmost** ['ʌtməʊst] **1.** *adj* **the utmost ease** [greatest] la plus grande facilité; **it is of the utmost importance that…** il est de la plus haute importance que… (+ *subjunctive*) **2.** *n* **to do one's utmost** faire de son mieux (**to do** pour faire)

**utter¹** ['ʌtə(r)] *adj* total; [folly, lie] pur; **it's utter nonsense** c'est complètement absurde ■ **utterly** *adv* complètement

**utter²** ['ʌtə(r)] *vt* [cry, sigh] pousser; [word] prononcer; [threat] proférer

**U-turn** ['ju:tɜ:n] *n* [in vehicle] demi-tour *m*; *Fig* [change of policy] virage *m* à 180°

**U2** MESSAGING *written abbr of* **you too**

**V, v** [viː] *n* **a)** [letter] V, v *m inv* **b)** MESSAGING = **very**

**vacant** ['veɪkənt] *adj* [room, seat] libre ; [post] vacant ■ **vacancy** *(pl -ies)n* [post] poste *m* vacant ; [room] chambre *f* libre

**vacate** [Brvə'keɪt, Am'veɪkeɪt] *vt* quitter

**vacation** [veɪ'keɪʃən] *n Am* vacances *fpl* ; **to take a vacation** prendre des vacances

**vaccinate** ['væksɪneɪt] *vt* vacciner ■ **vaccination** *n* vaccination *f* ■ **vaccine** [-'siːn] *n* vaccin *m*

**vacuum** ['vækjuəm] **1.** *n* vide *m* ; **vacuum cleaner** aspirateur *m* ; *Br* **vacuum flask** Thermos® *f* **2.** *vt* [room] passer l'aspirateur dans ; [carpet] passer l'aspirateur sur

**vagabond** ['vægəbɒnd] *n* vagabond, -e *mf*

**vagina** [və'dʒaɪnə] *n* ANAT vagin *m*

**vague** [veɪg] *(compar -er, superl -est) adj* vague ; [outline] flou ; **he was vague (about it)** il est resté vague ■ **vaguely** *adv* vaguement

**vain** [veɪn] *(compar -er, superl -est) adj* **a)** [attempt, hope] vain ; **in vain** en vain ; **her efforts were in vain** ses efforts ont été inutiles **b)** [conceited] vaniteux, -euse

**valentine** ['væləntaɪn] *n* [card] carte *f* de la Saint-Valentin ; **(Saint) Valentine's Day** la Saint-Valentin

**valid** ['vælɪd] *adj* valable ■ **validate** *vt* valider

**valley** ['vælɪ] *(pl -eys) n* vallée *f*

**valuable** ['væljuəbəl] **1.** *adj* [object] de valeur ; *Fig* [help, time] précieux, -euse **2.** *npl* **valuables** objets *mpl* de valeur

**value** ['væljuː] **1.** *n* valeur *f* ; **to be of value** avoir de la valeur ; **to be good**

**value (for money)** être d'un bon rapport qualité-prix **2.** *vt* [appreciate] apprécier ; [assess] évaluer ■ **valuation** [-jʊ'eɪʃən] *n* [by expert] expertise *f*

**valve** [vælv] *n* [of machine, car] soupape *f* ; [of pipe, tube] valve *f*

**van** [væn] *n* [vehicle] camionnette *f*, fourgonnette *f*

**vandal** ['vændəl] *n* vandale *mf* ■ **vandalism** *n* vandalisme *m* ■ **vandalize** *vt* saccager

**vanilla** [və'nɪlə] **1.** *n* vanille *f* **2.** *adj* [ice cream] à la vanille

**vanish** ['vænɪʃ] *vi* disparaître

**vanity** ['vænɪtɪ] *n* vanité *f*

**vapour**, *Am* **vapor** ['veɪpə(r)] *n* vapeur *f*

**variable** ['veərɪəbəl] *adj & n* variable (*f*)

**variant** ['veərɪənt] *n* variante *f*

**variation** [veərɪ'eɪʃən] *n* variation *f*

**varicose** ['værɪkəus] *adj* **varicose veins** varices *fpl*

**varied** ['veərɪd] *adj* varié

**variety** [və'raɪətɪ] *n* **a)** [diversity] variété *f* ; **a variety of** toutes sortes de **b)** **variety show** spectacle *m* de variétés

**various** ['veərɪəs] *adj* divers

**varnish** ['vɑːnɪʃ] **1.** *n* vernis *m* **2.** *vt* vernir

**vary** ['veərɪ] *(pt & pp -ied) vti* varier (**in / with** en / selon) ■ **varying** *adj* variable

**vase** [Br vɑːz, Am veɪs] *n* vase *m*

**vast** [vɑːst] *adj* immense

**vat** [væt] *n* cuve *f*

**VAT** [viːeɪ'tiː, væt] *(abbr of* **value added tax)** *n Br* TVA *f*

**Vatican** ['vætɪkən] *n* **the Vatican** le Vatican

**vault¹** [vɔːlt] *n* [roof] voûte *f* ; [tomb] caveau *m* ; [cellar] cave *f* ; [in bank] salle *f* des coffres

**vault²** [vɔːlt] *vti* [jump] sauter

**VBG** MESSAGING *written abbr of* **very big grin**

**VCR** [viːsiːˈɑː(r)] *(abbr of* **video cassette recorder***) n* magnétoscope *m*

**VDU** [viːdiːˈjuː] *(abbr of* **visual display unit***) n* COMPUT moniteur *m*

**veal** [viːl] *n* veau *m*

**veer** [vɪə(r)] *vi* [of car] virer ; **to veer off the road** quitter la route

**vegan** [ˈviːɡən] *n* végétalien, -enne *mf*

**vegetable** [ˈvedʒtəbəl] *n* légume *m* ■ **vegetarian** [vedʒɪˈteərɪən] *adj & n* végétarien, -enne *(mf)* ■ **vegetation** [vedʒɪˈteɪʃən] *n* végétation *f*

**vehicle** [ˈviːɪkəl] *n* véhicule *m*

**veil** [veɪl] *n* [covering] & *Fig* voile *m* ■ **veiled** *adj* voilé

**vein** [veɪn] *n* [in body] veine *f*

**Velcro®** [ˈvelkrəʊ] *n* Velcro® *m*

**velvet** [ˈvelvɪt] **1.** *n* velours *m* **2.** *adj* de velours

**vending** [ˈvendɪŋ] *n* **vending machine** distributeur *m* automatique

**vendor** [ˈvendɔː(r)] *n* vendeur, -euse *mf*

**veneer** [vəˈnɪə(r)] *n* [wood] placage *m* ; *Fig* [appearance] vernis *m*

**vengeance** [ˈvendʒəns] *n* vengeance *f* ; **to take vengeance on sb** se venger de qn ; *Fig* **with a vengeance** de plus belle

**venison** [ˈvenɪsən] *n* venaison *f*

**venom** [ˈvenəm] *n* [poison] & *Fig* venin *m*

**vent** [vent] *n* conduit *m*

**ventilate** [ˈventɪleɪt] *vt* ventiler, aérer ■ **ventilation** *n* ventilation *f*, aération *f*

**ventriloquist** [venˈtrɪləkwɪst] *n* ventriloque *mf*

**venture** [ˈventʃə(r)] **1.** *n* entreprise *f* (hasardeuse) **2.** *vt* risquer ; **to venture to do sth** se risquer à faire qch **3.** *vi* s'aventurer (**into** dans)

**venue** [ˈvenjuː] *n* [for meeting, concert] salle *f* ; [for football match] stade *m*

**veranda(h)** [vəˈrændə] *n* véranda *f*

**verb** [vɜːb] *n* verbe *m* ■ **verbal** *adj* verbal

**verdict** [ˈvɜːdɪkt] *n* verdict *m*

**verge** [vɜːdʒ] **1.** *n Br* [of road] bord *m* ; **on the verge of ruin / tears** au bord de la ruine / des larmes ; **to be on the verge of doing sth** être sur le point de faire qch **2.** *vi* **to verge on** friser ; [of colour] tirer sur

**verify** [ˈverɪfaɪ] *(pt & pp -ied) vt* vérifier

**vermin** [ˈvɜːmɪn] *n* [animals] animaux *mpl* nuisibles ; [insects, people] vermine *f*

**versatile** [Br ˈvɜːsətaɪl, Am ˈvɜːrsətəl] *adj* polyvalent

**verse** [vɜːs] *n* [poetry] vers *mpl* ; [stanza] strophe *f* ; [of Bible] verset *m*

**versed** [vɜːst] *adj* **(well) versed in sth** versé dans qch

**version** [Br ˈvɜːʃən, Am ˈvɜːʒən] *n* version *f*

**versus** [ˈvɜːsəs] *prep* [in sport, law] contre ; [compared to] comparé à

**vertical** [ˈvɜːtɪkəl] *adj* vertical

**very** [ˈveri] **1.** *adv* très ; **very much** beaucoup ; **the very first** le tout premier (*f* la toute première) ; **the very next day** le lendemain même ; **at the very least / most** tout au moins / plus ; **at the very latest** au plus tard **2.** *adj* [emphatic use] **this very house** cette maison même ; **at the very end** tout à la fin

**vessel** [ˈvesəl] *n* [ship] vaisseau *m* ; [container] récipient *m*

**vest** [vest] *n* maillot *m* de corps ; *Am* [waistcoat] gilet *m*

**vested** [ˈvestɪd] *adj* **to have a vested interest in sth** avoir un intérêt personnel dans qch

**vestige** [ˈvestɪdʒ] *n* vestige *m*

**vet¹** [vet] *n* vétérinaire *mf*

**vet²** [vet] *(pt & pp -tt-) vt Br* faire une enquête sur

**veteran** [ˈvetərən] *n* MIL ancien combattant *m* ; *Fig* vétéran *m*

**veto** [ˈviːtəʊ] **1.** *(pl -oes) n* veto *m inv* **2.** *(pt & pp -oed) vt* mettre son veto à

**VGA** *(abbr of* **video graphics array / adapter***) n* COMPUT VGA *m*

**via** ['vaɪə, 'vɪə] *prep* via, par

**viable** ['vaɪəbəl] *adj* viable

**viaduct** ['vaɪədʌkt] *n* viaduc *m*

**vibrant** ['vaɪbrənt] *adj* [colour] vif (*f* vive)

**vibrate** [vaɪ'breɪt] *vi* vibrer ■ **vibration** *n* vibration *f*

**vicar** ['vɪkə(r)] *n* [in Church of England] pasteur *m* ■ **vicarage** [-rɪdʒ] *n* presbytère *m*

**vice** [vaɪs] *n* [depravity, fault] vice *m*; *Br* [tool] étau *m*

**vice-** [vaɪs] *pref* vice-

**vice versa** [vaɪs(ɪ)'vɜːsə] *adv* vice versa

**vicinity** [və'sɪnətɪ] *n* environs *mpl*; **in the vicinity of** aux environs de

**vicious** ['vɪʃəs] *adj* [malicious] méchant; [violent] brutal; **vicious circle** cercle *m* vicieux

**victim** ['vɪktɪm] *n* victime *f*; **to be the victim of** être victime de

**victimize** ['vɪktɪmaɪz] *vt* persécuter

**Victorian** [vɪk'tɔːrɪən] **1.** *adj* victorien, -enne **2.** *n* Victorien, -enne *mf*

**victory** ['vɪktərɪ] (*pl* **-ies**) *n* victoire *f* ■ **victorious** [-'tɔːrɪəs] *adj* victorieux, -euse

**vidcast** ['vɪdkɑːst] *n* vidcast *m*

**video** ['vɪdɪəʊ] **1.** (*pl* **-os**) *n* [medium] vidéo *f*; [cassette] cassette *f* vidéo; [recorder] magnétoscope *m*; **on video** sur cassette vidéo; **viral video** vidéo *f* virale **2.** *adj* [camera, cassette, game] vidéo *inv*; TEL **video call** appel *m* vidéo; **video projector** vidéoprojecteur *m*; **video recorder** magnétoscope *m* **3.** (*pt & pp* **-oed**) *vt* [on camcorder] filmer en vidéo; [on video recorder] enregistrer (sur magnétoscope) ■ **videocast** ['vɪdɪəʊkɑːst] *n* vidéocast *m*, émission *f* vidéo téléchargeable ■ **videotape** *n* bande *f* vidéo

**vie** [vaɪ] (*pres p* **vying**) *vi* **to vie with sb (for sth / to do sth)** rivaliser avec qn (pour qch / pour faire qch)

**Vietnam** [*Br* vjet'næm, *Am* -'nɑːm] *n* le Viêt Nam

**view** [vjuː] **1.** *n* vue *f*; [opinion] opinion *f*; **in my view** [opinion] à mon avis; **in view of** [considering] étant donné; **on view** [exhibit] exposé; **with a view to doing sth** dans l'intention de faire qch **2.** *vt* [regard] considérer; [look at] voir; [house] visiter ■ **viewer** *n* **a)** TV téléspectateur, -trice *mf* **b)** [for slides] visionneuse *f* ■ **viewfinder** *n* [in camera] viseur *m* ■ **viewpoint** *n* point *m* de vue

**vigilant** ['vɪdʒɪlənt] *adj* vigilant

**vigorous** ['vɪgərəs] *adj* vigoureux, -euse

**vile** [vaɪl] (*compar* **-er**, *superl* **-est**) *adj* [unpleasant] abominable; [food, drink] infect

**villa** ['vɪlə] *n* villa *f*

**village** ['vɪlɪdʒ] *n* village *m* ■ **villager** *n* villageois, -e *mf*

**villain** ['vɪlən] *n* [scoundrel] scélérat *m*; [in story, play] méchant *m*

**vindicate** ['vɪndɪkeɪt] *vt* justifier

**vindictive** [vɪn'dɪktɪv] *adj* vindicatif, -ive

**vine** [vaɪn] *n* vigne *f* ■ **vineyard** ['vɪnjəd] *n* vigne *f*

**vinegar** ['vɪnɪgə(r)] *n* vinaigre *m*

**vintage** ['vɪntɪdʒ] **1.** *n* [year] année *f*; [wine] cru *m* **2.** *adj* [wine] de cru; [car] de collection (*(datant généralement des années 1920)*)

**vinyl** ['vaɪnəl] *n* vinyle *m*

**viola** [vɪ'əʊlə] *n* MUS alto *m*

**violate** ['vaɪəleɪt] *vt* [agreement] violer

**violence** ['vaɪələns] *n* violence *f* ■ **violent** *adj* violent ■ **violently** *adv* violemment

**violet** ['vaɪələt] **1.** *adj* [colour] violet, -ette **2.** *n* [colour] violet *m*; [plant] violette *f*

**violin** [vaɪə'lɪn] *n* violon *m* ■ **violinist** *n* violoniste *mf*

**VIP** [viːaɪ'piː] (*abbr of* **very important person**) *n* VIP *mf*

**viper** ['vaɪpə(r)] *n* vipère *f*

**virgin** ['vɜːdʒɪn] *n* vierge *f*

**virile** [*Br* 'vɪraɪl, *Am* 'vɪrəl] *adj* viril

**virtual** ['vɜːtʃʊəl] *adj* quasi ; COMPUT virtuel, -elle ■ **virtually** *adv* [almost] quasiment

**virtue** ['vɜːtʃuː] *n* [goodness, chastity] vertu *f* ; [advantage] mérite *m* ■ **virtuous** [-tjʊəs] *adj* vertueux, -euse

**virus** ['vaɪərəs] *n* MED & COMPUT virus *m* ■ **virus-free** *adj* COMPUT dépourvu de virus

**Visa**® ['viːzə] *n* **Visa**® **(card)** carte *f* Visa®

**visa** ['viːzə] *n* visa *m*

**visible** ['vɪzəbəl] *adj* visible ■ **visibility** *n* visibilité *f*

**vision** ['vɪʒən] *n* [eyesight] vue *f* ; [foresight] clairvoyance *f* ; [apparition] vision *f*

**visit** ['vɪzɪt] **1.** *n* visite *f* ; **to pay sb a visit** rendre visite à qn **2.** *vt* [place] visiter ; [person] rendre visite à **3.** *vi* **to be visiting** être de passage ; *Br* **visit hours / card** heures *fpl* / carte *f* de visite ■ **visitor** *n* visiteur, -euse *mf* ; [guest] invité, -e *mf*

**visor** ['vaɪzə(r)] *n* visière *f*

**visual** ['vɪʒʊəl] *adj* visuel, -elle ; **visual aid** support *m* visuel ; **visual arts** arts *mpl* plastiques ■ **visualize** *vt* [imagine] visualiser ; [foresee] envisager

**vital** ['vaɪtəl] *adj* vital ; **it's vital that...** il est vital que... (+ *subjunctive*)

**vitality** [vaɪ'tælətɪ] *n* vitalité *f*

**vitamin** [*Br* 'vɪtəmɪn, *Am* 'vaɪtəmɪn] *n* vitamine *f*

**vivacious** [vɪ'veɪʃəs] *adj* enjoué

**vivid** ['vɪvɪd] *adj* vif (*f* vive) ; [description] vivant ; [memory] clair

**V-neck** ['viːnek] *adj* à col en V

**vocabulary** [*Br* və'kæbjʊlərɪ, *Am* -erɪ] *n* vocabulaire *m*

**vocal** ['vəʊkəl] *adj* [cords, music] vocal ; [noisy, critical] qui se fait entendre

**vocation** [vəʊ'keɪʃən] *n* vocation *f* ■ **vocational** *adj* professionnel, -elle

**vociferous** [və'sɪfərəs] *adj* bruyant

**vodka** ['vɒdkə] *n* vodka *f*

**vogue** [vəʊg] *n* vogue *f* ; **in vogue** en vogue

**voice** [vɔɪs] **1.** *n* voix *f* ; **at the top of one's voice** à tue-tête ; TEL **voice dialling** numérotation *f* vocale ; COMPUT **voice mail** messagerie *f* vocale **2.** *vt* [opinion, feelings] exprimer

**void** [vɔɪd] **1.** *n* vide *m* **2.** *adj* [deed, contract] nul (*f* nulle)

**volatile** [*Br* 'vɒlətaɪl, *Am* 'vɒlətəl] *adj* [person] inconstant ; [situation] explosif, -ive

**volcano** [vɒl'keɪnəʊ] *(pl -oes)* *n* volcan *m*

**volley** ['vɒlɪ] *n* [in tennis] volée ■ **volleyball** *n* volley(-ball) *m*

**volt** [vəʊlt] *n* volt *m* ■ **voltage** [-tɪdʒ] *n* voltage *m*

**volume** ['vɒljuːm] *n* [book, capacity, loudness] volume *m*

**voluntary** [*Br* 'vɒləntərɪ, *Am* -erɪ] *adj* volontaire ; [unpaid] bénévole ■ **voluntarily** *adv* volontairement ; [on an unpaid basis] bénévolement

**volunteer** [vɒlən'tɪə(r)] **1.** *n* volontaire *mf* ; [for charity] bénévole *mf* **2.** *vt* [information] donner spontanément **3.** *vi* se porter volontaire (**for sth** pour qch ; **to do** pour faire)

**vomit** ['vɒmɪt] **1.** *n* vomi *m* **2.** *vti* vomir

**vote** [vəʊt] **1.** *n* [choice] vote *m* ; [election] scrutin *m* ; [paper] voix *f* ; **to take a vote on sth** voter sur qch ; **to have the vote** avoir le droit de vote **2.** *vt* [funds, bill] voter **3.** *vi* voter ; **to vote Labour** voter travailliste ■ **voter** *n* [elector] électeur, -trice *mf* ■ **voting** *n* [polling] scrutin *m*

**vouch** [vaʊtʃ] *vi* **to vouch for sb / sth** répondre de qn / qch

**voucher** ['vaʊtʃə(r)] *n* coupon *m*, bon *m* ; **(gift-)voucher** chèque-cadeau *m*

**vow** [vaʊ] **1.** *n* vœu *m* **2.** *vt* jurer (**to** à) ; **to vow to do sth** jurer de faire qch

**vowel** ['vaʊəl] *n* voyelle *f*

**voyage** ['vɔɪɪdʒ] *n* voyage *m*

**vulgar** ['vʌlgə(r)] *adj* vulgaire

**vulnerable** ['vʌlnərəbəl] *adj* vulnérable

**vulture** ['vʌltʃə(r)] *n* vautour *m*

# W

**W, w** [ˈdʌbəljuː] *n* **a)** [letter] W, w *m inv* **b)** MESSAGING = **with**

**W@** *(abbr of* **what***)* MESSAGING koi, koa, kwa

**WABOL** MESSAGING *written abbr of* **with a bit of luck**

**wacko** [ˈwækəʊ] *(pl* **-s***) n & adj Fam* cinglé, dingue ∎ **wacky** [ˈwækɪ] *(compar* **-ier***, superl* **-iest***) adj Fam* farfelu

**wad** [wɒd] *n* [of papers, banknotes] liasse *f*; [of cotton wool] morceau *m*

**waddle** [ˈwɒdəl] *vi Fig* [of duck, person] se dandiner

**wade** [weɪd] *vi Fig* [book] venir péniblement à bout de; **to wade through** [mud, water] patauger dans

**wafer** [ˈweɪfə(r)] *n* [biscuit] gaufrette *f*; REL hostie *f*

**waffle¹** [ˈwɒfəl] *n* [cake] gaufre *f*

**waffle²** [ˈwɒfəl] *Br Fam* **1.** *n* remplissage *m* **2.** *vi* faire du remplissage

**waft** [wɒft] *vi* [of smell, sound] parvenir

**wag** [wæg] *(pt & pp* **-gg-***) vt* remuer, agiter; **to wag one's finger at sb** menacer qn du doigt

**wage** [weɪdʒ] **1.** *n* **wage(s)** salaire *m*, paie *f*; **wage earner** salarié, -e *mf*; *Br* **wage packet** [money] paie **2.** *vt* **to wage war** faire la guerre (**on** à)

**wager** [ˈweɪdʒə(r)] **1.** *n* pari *m* **2.** *vt* parier (**that** que)

**waggle** [ˈwægəl] *vti* remuer

**wag(g)on** [ˈwægən] *n Br* [of train] wagon *m* (découvert); [horse-drawn] charrette *f*

**wail** [weɪl] *vi* [of person] gémir; [of siren] hurler

**waist** [weɪst] *n* taille *f* ∎ **waistcoat** *n Br* gilet *m* ∎ **waistline** *n* taille *f*

**wait** [weɪt] **1.** *n* attente *f*; **to lie in wait for sb** guetter qn **2.** *vt* **to wait one's turn** attendre son tour **3.** *vi* **a)** attendre; **to wait for sb/sth** attendre qn/qch; **to keep sb waiting** faire attendre qn; **wait till** *or* **until I've gone, wait for me to go** attends que je sois parti; **I can't wait to see her** j'ai vraiment hâte de la voir **b) to wait on sb** servir qn ∎ **waiting 1.** *n* attente *f*; *Br* **'no waiting'** arrêt interdit **2.** *adj* **waiting list/room** liste *f*/salle *f* d'attente ∎ **waitlist** [ˈweɪtlɪst] *vt Am* mettre sur la liste d'attente; **I'm waitlisted for the next flight** je suis sur la liste d'attente pour le prochain vol ∎ **wait about, wait around** *vi* attendre ∎ **wait behind** *vi* rester ∎ **wait up** *vi* veiller; **to wait up for sb** attendre le retour de qn pour aller se coucher

**waiter** [ˈweɪtə(r)] *n* serveur *m* ∎ **waitress** *n* serveuse *f*

**wake¹** [weɪk] *(pt* **woke***, pp* **woken***) 1.** *vt* **to wake sb (up)** réveiller qn **2.** *vi* **to wake (up)** se réveiller; **to wake up to sth** prendre conscience de qch ∎ **wake-up call** *n* réveil *m* téléphonique

**wake²** [weɪk] *n* [of ship] sillage *m*; *Fig* **in the wake of sth** à la suite de qch

**Wales** [weɪlz] *n* le pays de Galles

**walk** [wɔːk] **1.** *n* [short] promenade *f*; [long] marche *f*; [gait] démarche *f*; [path] avenue *f*; **to go for a walk, to take a walk** aller se promener; **to take the dog for a walk** promener le chien; **five minutes' walk (away)** à cinq minutes à pied **2.** *vt* **to walk the dog** promener le chien; **to walk sb home** raccompagner qn; **I walked 3 miles** ≃ j'ai fait presque 5 km à pied **3.** *vi* marcher; [as opposed to cycling, driving] aller à pied; [for exercise, pleasure] se promener; **to walk home** rentrer à pied

■ **walker** n marcheur, -euse mf; [for pleasure] promeneur, -euse mf ■ **walking** n marche f (à pied); **walking stick** canne f ■ **walk-up** Am **1.** adj [apartment] situé dans un immeuble sans ascenseur; [building] sans ascenseur **2.** n [apartment, office] appartement ou bureau situé dans un immeuble sans ascenseur; [building] immeuble sans ascenseur ■ **walkway** n passage m couvert; **moving walkway** trottoir m roulant ■ **walk away** vi s'en aller (**from** de) ■ **walk in** vi entrer ■ **walk off** vi s'en aller; **to walk off with sth** [steal] partir avec qch ■ **walk out** vi [leave] sortir; Br [of workers] se mettre en grève; **to walk out on sb** quitter qn ■ **walk over** vi **to walk over to** [go up to] s'approcher de

**Walkman®** ['wɔːkmən] (pl **-mans**) n baladeur m, Walkman® m

**wall** [wɔːl] **1.** n mur m; [of cabin, tunnel, stomach] paroi f **2.** adj [map, hanging] mural ■ **wallpaper 1.** n papier m peint **2.** vt tapisser ■ **wall-to-wall** adj **wall-to-wall carpet(ing)** moquette f

**wallet** ['wɒlɪt] n portefeuille m

**wallow** ['wɒləʊ] vi se vautrer

**walnut** ['wɔːlnʌt] n [nut] noix f; [tree, wood] noyer m

**walrus** ['wɔːlrəs] (pl **-ruses** [-rəsəz]) n morse m

**waltz** [Br wɔːls, Am wɒlts] **1.** n valse f **2.** vi valser

**wan** [wɒn] adj pâle, blême

**wand** [wɒnd] n (**magic**) **wand** baguette f magique

**wander** ['wɒndə(r)] **1.** vt **to wander the streets** errer dans les rues **2.** vi [of thoughts] vagabonder; [of person] errer, vagabonder; **to wander from** [path, subject] s'écarter de ■ **wander about, wander around** vi [roam] errer, vagabonder; [stroll] flâner ■ **wander off** vi [go away] s'éloigner

**wangle** ['wæŋgəl] vt Br Fam [obtain] se débrouiller pour avoir

**want** [wɒnt] **1.** n [lack] manque m (**of** de); **for want of** par manque de; **for want of money / time** faute d'argent / de temps

**2.** vt vouloir (**to do** faire); **I want him to go** je veux qu'il parte; **the lawn wants cutting** la pelouse a besoin d'être tondue; **you're wanted on the phone** on vous demande au téléphone ■ **wanted** adj [criminal] recherché par la police

**wanton** ['wɒntən] adj [gratuitous] gratuit

**WAN2** MESSAGING written abbr of **want to**

**war** [wɔː(r)] **1.** n guerre f; **at war** en guerre (**with** avec); **to declare war** déclarer la guerre (**on** à). **2.** adj [wound, crime] de guerre; **war memorial** monument m aux morts

**ward¹** [wɔːd] n [in hospital] salle f

**ward²** [wɔːd] vt **to ward off** [blow] éviter; [danger] chasser

**warden** ['wɔːdən] n [of institution, hostel] directeur, -trice mf

**warder** ['wɔːdə(r)] n Br gardien m (de prison)

**wardrobe** ['wɔːdrəʊb] n [cupboard] penderie f; [clothes] garde-robe f

**warehouse** ['weəhaʊs] (pl **-ses** [-zɪz]) n entrepôt m

**wares** [weəz] npl marchandises fpl

**warfare** ['wɔːfeə(r)] n guerre f

**warm** [wɔːm] **1.** (compar **-er**, superl **-est**) adj chaud; Fig [welcome] chaleureux, -euse; **to be** or **feel warm** avoir chaud; **to get warm** [of person, room] se réchauffer; **it's warm** [of weather] il fait chaud **2.** vt **to warm (up)** [person, food] réchauffer **3.** vi **to warm up** [of person, room] se réchauffer; [of athlete] s'échauffer ■ **warmly** adv [dress] chaudement; Fig [welcome, thank] chaleureusement ■ **warmth** n chaleur f

**warn** [wɔːn] vt avertir, prévenir (**that** que); **to warn sb against** or **of sth** mettre qn en garde contre qch ■ **warning** n [caution] avertissement m; [advance notice] avis m; **without warning** sans prévenir; **warning light** [on appliance] voyant m lumineux; Br (**hazard**) **warning lights** feux mpl de détresse

**warp** [wɔːp] **1.** vt [wood] gauchir; Fig [judgement, person] pervertir **2.** vi [of door] gauchir

**warrant** ['wɒrənt] *n* [in law] mandat *m*
■ **warranty** *(pl -ies)* *n* COMM garantie *f*

**warren** ['wɒrən] *n* **(rabbit)** warren garenne *f*

**warrior** ['wɒrɪə(r)] *n* guerrier, -ère *mf*

**wart** [wɔːt] *n* verrue *f*

**wartime** ['wɔːtaɪm] *n* **in wartime** en temps de guerre

**wary** ['weərɪ] *(compar -ier, superl -iest) adj* prudent; **to be wary of sb/sth** se méfier de qn/qch; **to be wary of doing sth** hésiter beaucoup à faire qch

**was** [wəz] *(stressed* [wɒz]) *pt of* **be**

**wash** [wɒʃ] **1.** *n* to have a wash se laver; **to give sth a wash** laver qch **2.** *vt* laver; **to wash one's hands** se laver les mains **(of sth** de qch) **3.** *vi* [have a wash] se laver ■ **washbasin** *n Br* lavabo *m* ■ **washcloth** *n Am* gant *m* de toilette ■ **washing-up** *n Br* vaisselle *f*; **to do the washing-up** faire la vaisselle; **washing-up liquid** liquide *m* vaisselle ■ **washroom** *n Am* toilettes *fpl* ■ **wash down** *vt sep* [car, deck] laver à grande eau; [food] arroser **(with** de) ■ **wash off 1.** *vt sep* enlever **2.** *vi* partir ■ **wash out 1.** *vt sep* [bowl, cup] rincer; [stain] faire partir (en lavant) **2.** *vi* [of stain] partir (au lavage) ■ **wash up 1.** *vt sep Br* [dishes, forks] laver **2.** *vi Br* [do the dishes] faire la vaisselle; *Am* [have a wash] se débarbouiller

**washable** ['wɒʃəbəl] *adj* lavable

**washer** ['wɒʃə(r)] *n* [ring] joint *m*

**washing** ['wɒʃɪŋ] *n* [action] lavage *m*; [clothes] linge *m*; **to do the washing** faire la lessive; **washing machine** machine *f* à laver; *Br* **washing powder** lessive *f*

**wasp** [wɒsp] *n* guêpe *f*

**waste** [weɪst] **1.** *n* gaspillage *m*; [of time] perte *f*; [rubbish] déchets *mpl*; **waste carrier** transporteur *m* de déchets; **waste management** gestion *f* des déchets; **waste material** *or* **products** déchets *mpl*; *Br* **waste ground** [in town] terrain *m* vague; **waste land** [unculti-vated] terres *fpl* incultes; [in town] terrain *m* vague; **waste pipe** tuyau *m* d'évacuation **2.** *vt* [money, food] gas-

piller; [time] perdre; [opportunity] gâcher; **to waste no time doing sth** ne pas perdre de temps pour faire qch **3.** *vi* to waste away dépérir ■ **wasted** *adj* [effort] inutile

**wastebin** ['weɪstbɪn] *n* [in kitchen] poubelle *f*

**wasteful** ['weɪstfəl] *adj* [person] gaspil-leur, -euse; [process] peu économique

**watch** [wɒtʃ] **1.** *n* **a)** [timepiece] montre *f* **b)** to keep a close watch on sb/sth surveiller qn/qch de près **2.** *vt* regar-der; [observe] observer; [suspect, baby, luggage] surveiller; [be careful of] faire attention à; **watch it!** attention! **3.** *vi* regarder; **to watch out for sb/sth** guetter qn/qch; **to watch out** [take care] faire attention **(for** à); **watch out!** attention!; **to watch over** sur-veiller ■ **watchdog** *n* chien *m* de garde ■ **watchstrap** *n* bracelet *m* de montre

**watchful** ['wɒtʃfəl] *adj* vigilant

**water** ['wɔːtə(r)] **1.** *n* eau *f*; **under water** [road, field] inondé; [swim] sous l'eau; **water heater** chauffe-eau *m inv*; **water pistol** pistolet *m* à eau; **water polo** water-polo *m*; **water skiing** ski *m* nautique; **water wings** brassards *mpl* de natation **2.** *vt* [plant] arroser; **to water sth down** [wine] diluer qch; [text] édulcorer qch **3.** *vi* [of eyes] lar-moyer; **it makes my mouth water** ça me met l'eau à la bouche ■ **waterco-lour,** *Am* **-color** *n* aquarelle *f* ■ **wa-tercress** *n* cresson *m* (de fontaine) ■ **waterfall** *n* cascade *f* ■ **watering** *n* watering can arrosoir *m* ■ **water-mark** *n* filigrane *m* ■ **watermelon** *n* pastèque *f* ■ **waterpark** ['wɔːtəpɑːk] *n* parc *m* aquatique ■ **waterproof** *adj* imperméable; [watch] étanche ■ **wa-terside** ['wɔːtəsaɪd] **1.** *adj* au bord de l'eau **2.** *n* **the waterside** le bord de l'eau ■ **watertight** *adj* [container] étanche

**water ski** *n* ski *m* nautique ■ **water-ski** *vi* faire du ski nautique

**watery** ['wɔːtərɪ] *adj* [soup] trop liquide; [coffee, tea] insipide; [colour] délavé

**watt** [wɒt] *n* watt *m*

**wave** [weɪv] **1.** *n* [of water, crime] vague *f*; [in hair] ondulation *f*; PHYS onde f; **wave farm** ferme f hydrolienne; **wave pool** bassin m ou piscine f à vagues **2.** vt [arm, flag] agiter; [stick] brandir **3.** vi [of person] faire signe (de la main); **to wave to sb** [signal] faire signe de la main à qn; [greet] saluer qn de la main ■ **waveband** n bande f de fréquences ■ **wavefile** ['weɪvfaɪl] n COMPUT fichier m son ■ **wavelength** n longueur f d'onde; Fig **on the same wavelength** sur la même longueur d'onde

**waver** ['weɪvə(r)] vi [of person, flame] vaciller

**wavy** ['weɪvɪ] (compar -ier, superl -iest) adj [line] qui ondule; [hair] ondulé

**wax** [wæks] **1.** n cire f; [for ski] fart m **2.** adj [candle, doll] de cire; Am **wax paper** [for wrapping] papier m paraffiné **3.** vt cirer; [ski] farter; [car] lustrer

**way** [weɪ] **1.** n a) [path, road] chemin m (to de); [direction] sens m, direction f; **the way in** l'entrée f; **the way out** la sortie; **the way to the station** le chemin pour aller à la gare; **to ask sb the way** demander son chemin à qn; **to show sb the way** montrer le chemin à qn; **to lose one's way** se perdre; **I'm on my way** [coming] j'arrive; [going] je pars; **to make way for sb** faire de la place à qn; **out of the way** [isolated] isolé; **to get out of the way** s'écarter; **to go all the way** aller jusqu'au bout; **to give way** céder; Br [in vehicle] céder le passage (**to** à); **it's a long way away** or **off** c'est très loin; **it's the wrong way up** c'est dans le mauvais sens; **this way** par ici; **that way** par là; **which way?** par où? **b)** [manner] manière f; **in this way** de cette manière; **by way of** [via] par; Fig [as] comme; Fig **by the way** à propos; Fam **no way!** [certainly not] pas question!; **way of life** mode m de vie **2.** adv Fam **way behind** très en arrière; **way ahead** très en avance (**of** sur)

**wayward** ['weɪwəd] adj difficile

**WB** MESSAGING a) written abbr of **welcome back** b) written abbr of **write back**

**WBS** MESSAGING written abbr of **write back soon**

**WC** [dʌbəlju:'si:] n W.-C. mpl

**WDYT** MESSAGING written abbr of **what do you think?**

**we** [wi:] pron nous; [indefinite] on; **we teachers** nous autres professeurs; **we all make mistakes** tout le monde peut se tromper

**weak** [wi:k] (compar -er, superl -est) adj faible; [tea, coffee] léger, -ère; **to have a weak heart** avoir le cœur fragile ■ **weakling** n [in body] mauviette f; [in character] faible mf ■ **weakness** n faiblesse f; [fault] point m faible; **to have a weakness for sb/sth** avoir un faible pour qn /qch

**weaken** ['wi:kən] **1.** vt affaiblir **2.** vi s'affaiblir

**wealth** [welθ] n richesse f; Fig **a wealth of sth** une abondance de qch ■ **wealthy 1.** (compar -ier, superl -iest) adj riche **2.** npl **the wealthy** les riches mpl

**weapon** ['wepən] n arme f

**wear** [weə(r)] **1.** n a) men's wear vêtements mpl pour hommes; **evening wear** tenue f de soirée b) [use] **wear and tear** usure f naturelle **2.** (pt wore, pp worn) vt [garment, glasses] porter; **to wear black** porter du noir **3.** vi to wear thin [of clothing] s'user; **to wear well** [of clothing] bien vieillir ■ **wear down 1.** vt sep user; **to wear sb down** avoir qn à l'usure **2.** vi s'user ■ **wear off** vi [of colour, pain] disparaître ■ **wear out 1.** vt sep [clothes] user; **to wear sb out** épuiser qn **2.** vi [of clothes] s'user; Fig [of patience] s'épuiser

**weary** ['wɪərɪ] **1.** (compar -ier, superl -iest) adj las (f lasse) (**of doing** de faire) **2.** vi se lasser (**of** de)

**weather** ['weðə(r)] **1.** n temps m; **what's the weather like?** quel temps fait-il?; **in hot weather** par temps chaud; **under the weather** [ill] patraque **2.** adj **weather forecast** prévisions fpl météorologiques; **weather report** (bulletin m) météo f **3.** vt [storm] essuyer; Fig [crisis] surmonter ■ **weather girl** n [on TV, radio] présentatrice *f* de la météo ■ **weather man** *n* [on TV, radio] présentateur *m* météo

**weave** [wi:v] **1.** *(pt* wove, *pp* woven) *vt* [cloth, plot] tisser ; [basket, garland] tresser **2.** *vi* tisser ; *Fig* **to weave in and out of** [crowd, cars] se faufiler entre

**web** [web] *n* [of spider] toile *f*; *Fig* [of lies] tissu *m*; COMPUT **the Web** le Web; **web access** accès *m* à Internet ; **web address** adresse *f* Web ; **web administrator** administrateur, -trice *m,f* Web ; **web browser** navigateur *m* ; **web designer** concepteur *m* de site web ; **web developer** développeur, -euse *m,f* de sites Web ; **web host** hébergeur *m* Web ; **web hosting** hébergement *m* de sites Web ; **web page** page *f* Web ; **web site, website** site *m* Web ; **web space** espace *m* Web ; **web user** internaute *mf* ■ **webcam** ['webkæm] *n* webcam *f* ■ **webcast** ['webkɑːst] **1.** *n* COMPUT webcast *m* **2.** *vt* COMPUT diffuser sur le Web ■ **webcasting** ['webkɑːstɪŋ] *n* COMPUT webcasting *m* ■ **weblog** ['weblɒg] *n* COMPUT weblog *m* ■ **webphone** ['webfəʊn] *n* téléphone *m* compatible Web ■ **webzine** ['webziːn] *n* COMPUT webzine *m*

**wed** [wed] *(pt & pp* -dd-) **1.** *vt* [marry] épouser **2.** *vi* se marier

**we'd** [wiːd] = **we had, we would**

**wedding** ['wedɪŋ] **1.** *n* mariage *m* ; **golden / silver wedding** noces *fpl* d'or / d'argent **2.** *adj* [anniversary, present, cake] de mariage ; [dress] de mariée ; **his / her wedding day** le jour de son mariage ; *Br* **wedding ring**, *Am* **wedding band** alliance *f*

**wedge** [wedʒ] **1.** *n* [of wheel, table] cale *f* **2.** *vt* [wheel, table] caler ; [push] enfoncer (**into** dans) ; **to wedge a door open** maintenir une porte ouverte avec une cale ; **wedged (in) between** coincé entre

**Wednesday** ['wenzdeɪ] *n* mercredi *m*

**wee**[1] [wiː] *adj Scot Fam* [tiny] tout petit (*f* toute petite)

**wee**[2] [wiː] *vi Br Fam* faire pipi

**weed** [wiːd] **1.** *n* [plant] mauvaise herbe *f* **2.** *vti* désherber ; *Fig* **to weed sth out** éliminer qch (**from** de) ■ **weed-killer** *n* désherbant *m* ■ **weedy** *(compar* -ier, *superl* -iest) *adj Fam* [person] malingre

**week** [wiːk] *n* semaine *f*; **tomorrow week, a week tomorrow** demain en huit ■ **weekday** *n* jour *m* de semaine

**weekend** [wiːkˈend] *n* week-end *m*; **at** *or* **on** *or* **over the weekend** ce week-end ; [every weekend] le week-end

**weekly** ['wiːklɪ] **1.** *adj* hebdomadaire **2.** *adv* toutes les semaines **3.** *n* [magazine] hebdomadaire *m*

**weep** [wiːp] *(pt & pp* wept) *vi* pleurer

**weigh** [weɪ] **1.** *vt* peser ; **to weigh sb / sth down** [with load] surcharger qn / qch (**with** de) ; **to weigh up** [chances] peser **2.** *vi* peser ; **it's weighing on my mind** ça me tracasse ■ **weighing-machine** *n* balance *f*

**weight** [weɪt] **1.** *n* poids *m* ; **to put on weight** grossir ; **to lose weight** maigrir ; *Fig* **to carry weight** [of argument] avoir du poids **2.** *vt* **to weight sth (down)** [hold down] faire tenir qch avec un poids ■ **weightlifter** *n* haltérophile *mf* ■ **weightlifting** *n* haltérophilie *f*

**W8** MESSAGING *written abbr of* **wait**

**W84M** MESSAGING *written abbr of* **wait for me**

**W8N** MESSAGING *written abbr of* **waiting**

**weighty** ['weɪtɪ] *(compar* -ier, *superl* -iest) *adj* [serious, important] grave

**weir** [wɪə(r)] *n* barrage *m*

**weird** [wɪəd] *(compar* -er, *superl* -est) *adj* bizarre

**welcome** ['welkəm] **1.** *adj* [person, news, change] bienvenu ; **to make sb welcome** faire un bon accueil à qn ; **welcome!** bienvenue ! ; **you're welcome!** [after 'thank you'] il n'y a pas de quoi ! ; **you're welcome to use my bike** mon vélo est à ta disposition **2.** *n* accueil *m* ; **to give sb a warm welcome** faire un accueil chaleureux à qn **3.** *vt* [person] souhaiter la bienvenue à ;

[news, change] accueillir favorablement ■ **welcoming** adj accueillant; [speech, words] de bienvenue

**welfare** ['welfeə(r)] n [wellbeing] bien-être m; Am Fam **to be on welfare** recevoir l'aide sociale; Br **the Welfare State** l'État m providence

**well¹** [wel] n [for water, oil] puits m

**well²** [wel] **1.** (compar **better**, superl **best**) adj bien; **to be well** aller bien; **to get well** se remettre; **it's just as well** heureusement que… **2.** adv bien; **you'd do well to refuse** tu ferais bien de refuser; **she might (just) as well have stayed at home** elle aurait mieux fait de rester chez elle; **as well** [also] aussi; **as well as** aussi bien que; **as well as two cats, he has…** en plus de deux chats, il a… **3.** excl eh bien!; **well, well!** [surprise] tiens, tiens!; **huge, well quite big** énorme, enfin, assez grand ■ **well-behaved** adj sage ■ **well-being** n bien-être m ■ **well-built** adj [person, car] solide ■ **well-dressed** adj bien habillé ■ **well-informed** adj bien informé ■ **well-known** adj (bien) connu ■ **well-meaning** adj bien intentionné ■ **wellness** ['welnɪs] n bien-être m; **wellness centre** centre m de bien-être ■ **well-off** adj riche ■ **well-paid** adj bien payé ■ **well-prepared** adj bien préparé ■ **well-read** adj instruit ■ **well-respected** adj respecté ■ **well-stocked** [-stɒkt] adj [shop] bien approvisionné ■ **well-timed** adj opportun ■ **well-to-do** adj aisé ■ **wellwisher** n sympathisant, -e mf ■ **well-worn** adj [clothes, carpet] très usé

**we'll** [wi:l] = **we will**, **we shall**

**wellington** ['welɪŋtən], **welly** [welɪ] (pl **-ies**) Fam n Br **wellington (boot)** botte f de caoutchouc

**Welsh** [welʃ] **1.** adj gallois **2.** n [language] gallois m; **the Welsh** [people] les Gallois mpl ■ **Welshman** (pl -**men**) n Gallois m ■ **Welshwoman** (pl -**women**) n Galloise f

**went** [went] pt of **go**

**wept** [wept] pt & pp of **weep**

**were** [wə(r)] (stressed [wɜ:(r)]) pt of **be**

**we're** [wɪə(r)] = **we are**

**west** [west] **1.** n ouest m; **(to the) west of** à l'ouest de; POL **the West** l'Occident m **2.** adj [coast] ouest inv; [wind] d'ouest; **West Africa** l'Afrique f occidentale; **West Indian** [adj] antillais; [n] Antillais, -e mf; **the West Indies** les Antilles fpl **3.** adv à l'ouest; [travel] vers l'ouest ■ **westbound** adj [traffic] en direction de l'ouest; Br [carriageway] ouest inv ■ **westerly** adj [direction] de l'ouest ■ **western 1.** adj [coast] ouest inv; POL [culture] occidental; **Western Europe** l'Europe f de l'Ouest **2.** n [film] western m ■ **westerner** n POL occidental, -e mf ■ **westward** adj & adv vers l'ouest ■ **westwards** adv vers l'ouest

**wet** [wet] **1.** (compar **wetter**, superl **wettest**) adj mouillé; [weather] pluvieux, -euse; [day] de pluie; **to get wet** se mouiller; **to be wet through** être trempé; **it's wet** [raining] il pleut; **'wet paint'** 'peinture fraîche'; **wet suit** combinaison f de plongée **2.** n **the wet** [rain] la pluie; [damp] l'humidité f **3.** (pt & pp -**tt**-) vt mouiller

**we've** [wi:v] = **we have**

**W4u** MESSAGING written abbr of **waiting for you**

**whack** [wæk] vt Fam donner un grand coup à

**whale** [weɪl] n baleine f

**whassup** [wɒˈsʌp] excl Am Fam [hello] salut; [what's going on] qu'est-ce qui se passe?

**what** [wɒt] **1.** adj quel, quelle, pl quel(le)s; **what book?** quel livre?; **what a fool!** quel idiot!; **what little she has** le peu qu'elle a **2.** pron **a)** [in questions - subject] qu'est-ce qui; [object] (qu'est-ce) que; [after prep] quoi; **what's happening?** qu'est-ce qui se passe?; **what does he do?** qu'est-ce qu'il fait?, que fait-il?; **what is it?** qu'est-ce que c'est?; **what's that book?** c'est quoi, ce livre?; **what!** [surprise] quoi!, comment!; **what's it called?** comment ça s'appelle?; **what for?** pourquoi?; **what about going**

**out for lunch?** si on allait déjeuner ?
**b)** [in relative construction - subject] ce
qui ; [object] ce que ; **I know what will
happen / what she'll do** je sais ce qui
arrivera / ce qu'elle fera ; **what I need...**
ce dont j'ai besoin...

**whatever** [wɒt'evə(r)] **1.** *adj* **whatever
(the) mistake** quelle que soit l'erreur ;
**of whatever size** de n'importe quelle
taille ; **no chance whatever** pas la
moindre chance ; **nothing whatever**
rien du tout **2.** *pron* [no matter what]
quoi que (+ *subjunctive*) ; **whatever you
do** quoi que tu fasses ; **do whatever you
want** fais tout ce que tu veux

**whatsit** ['wɒtsɪt] *n* Fam machin *m*

**whatsoever** [wɒtsəʊ'evə(r)] *adj* **for no
reason whatsoever** sans aucune raison ; **none whatsoever** aucun

**wheat** [wi:t] *n* blé *m*

**wheedle** ['wi:dəl] *vt* **to wheedle sb**
enjôler qn (**into doing** pour qu'il / elle
fasse) ; **to wheedle sth out of sb** obtenir qch de qn par la flatterie

**wheel** [wi:l] **1.** *n* roue *f* ; **to be at the
wheel** être au volant **2.** *vt* [push]
pousser ■ **wheelbarrow** *n* brouette *f*
■ **wheelchair** *n* fauteuil *m* roulant
■ **wheelclamp** *n* sabot *m* de Denver

**wheeze** [wi:z] *vi* respirer bruyamment
■ **wheezy** (compar *-ier*, superl *-iest*) *adj*
poussif, -ive

**when** [wen] **1.** *adv* quand **2.** *conj* [with
time] quand, lorsque ; **when I finish,
when I've finished** quand j'aurai
fini ; **the day / moment when** le jour /
moment où

**whenever** [wen'evə(r)] *conj* [at whatever
time] quand ; [each time that] chaque
fois que

**where** [weə(r)] **1.** *adv* où ; **where are
you from?** d'où êtes-vous ? **2.** *conj*
où ; **I found it where she'd left it** je
l'ai trouvé là où elle l'avait laissé ; **the
place / house where I live** l'endroit /
la maison où j'habite ■ **whereabouts
1.** *adv* où **2.** ['weərəbaʊts] *n* his whereabouts l'endroit *m* où il est ■ **whereas**
*conj* alors que ■ **whereby** *adv* Formal al
par quoi

**wherever** [weər'evə(r)] *conj* **wherever
you go** [everywhere] partout où tu iras,
où que tu ailles ; **I'll go wherever you
like** j'irai (là) où vous voudrez

**whet** [wet] *(pt & pp -tt-)* *vt* [appetite,
desire] aiguiser

**whether** ['weðə(r)] *conj* si ; **I don't know
whether to leave** je ne sais pas si je dois
partir ; **whether she does it or not**
qu'elle le fasse ou non ; **it's doubtful
whether** il est douteux que... (+ *subjunctive*)

**which** [wɪtʃ] **1.** *adj* [in questions] quel,
quelle, *pl* quel(le)s ; **which book?** quel
livre ? ; **which one?** lequel / laquelle ? ;
**in which case** auquel cas
**2.** *rel pron* [subject] qui ; [object]
que ; [after prep] lequel, laquelle, *pl*
lesquel(le)s ; [referring to a whole clause
- subject] ce qui ; [object] ce que ; **the
house, which is old...** la maison, qui
est vieille... ; **the book which I like...** le
livre que j'aime... ; **the table which I put
it on...** la table sur laquelle je l'ai mis... ;
**the film of which she was speaking** le
film dont *ou* duquel elle parlait ; **she's
ill, which is sad** elle est malade, ce qui
est triste ; **he lies, which I don't like** il
ment, ce que je n'aime pas ; **after which**
[whereupon] après quoi
**3.** *interrogative pron* [in questions]
lequel, laquelle, *pl* lesquel(le)s ; **which
of us?** lequel / laquelle d'entre nous ? ;
**which are the best of the books?**
quels sont les meilleurs de ces livres ?
**4.** *pron* **which (one)** [the one that -
subject] celui qui, celle qui, *pl* ceux
qui, celles qui ; [object] celui que, celle
que, *pl* ceux que, celles que ; **I know
which (ones) you want** je sais ceux /
celles que vous désirez

**whichever** [wɪtʃ'evə(r)] **1.** *adj* [no matter
which] **take whichever books inter-
est you** prenez les livres qui vous inté-
ressent ; **take whichever one you like**
prends celui / celle que tu veux **2.** *pron*
[no matter which] quel que soit celui qui
(*f* quelle que soit celle qui) ; **whichever
you choose...** quel que soit celui que tu
choisiras... ; **take whichever you want**
prends celui / celle que tu veux

**while** [waɪl] **1.** *conj* [when] pendant que; [although] bien que (+ *subjunctive*); [as long as] tant que; [whereas] tandis que; **while eating** en mangeant **2.** *n* **a while** un moment; **all the while** tout le temps **3.** *vt* **to while away the time** passer le temps (**doing sth** à faire qch) ■ **whilst** *conj Br* = **while**

**whim** [wɪm] *n* caprice *m*; **on a whim** sur un coup de tête

**whimper** ['wɪmpə(r)] *vi* gémir

**whine** [waɪn] *vi* gémir

**whip** [wɪp] **1.** *n* fouet *m* **2.** (*pt & pp* -**pp**-) *vt* fouetter; **whipped cream** crème *f* fouettée ■ **whip off** *vt sep Fam* [clothes] enlever rapidement ■ **whip out** *vt sep Fam* sortir brusquement (**from** de) ■ **whip up** *vt sep* [interest] susciter; *Fam* [meal] préparer rapidement

**whirl** [wɜːl] **1.** *vt* to whirl sb/sth (round) faire tourbillonner qn/qch **2.** *vi* to whirl (round) tourbillonner ■ **whirlpool** *n* tourbillon *m* ■ **whirlwind** *n* tourbillon *m*

**whirr** [wɜː(r)] *vi* ronfler

**whisk** [wɪsk] **1.** *n* [for eggs] fouet *m* **2.** *vt* battre; **to whisk away** or **off** [object] enlever rapidement; [person] emmener rapidement

**whiskers** ['wɪskəz] *npl* [of cat] moustaches *fpl*; [of man] favoris *mpl*

**whisky**, *Am* **whiskey** ['wɪskɪ] *n* whisky *m*

**whisper** ['wɪspə(r)] **1.** *n* chuchotement *m* **2.** *vti* chuchoter; **to whisper sth to sb** chuchoter qch à l'oreille de qn

**whistle** ['wɪsəl] **1.** *n* sifflement *m*; [object] sifflet *m* **2.** *vti* siffler

**white** [waɪt] **1.** (*compar* -**er**, *superl* -**est**) *adj* blanc (*f* blanche); **to go** or **turn white** blanchir; *Br* **white coffee** café *m* au lait; **white lie** pieux mensonge *m*; **white man** Blanc *m*; **white woman** Blanche *f* **2.** *n* [colour, of egg, eye] blanc *m* ■ **whitewash 1.** *n* [paint] badigeon *m* à la chaux **2.** *vt* [paint] badigeonner à la chaux; *Fig* [person] blanchir

**Whitsun** ['wɪtsən] *n Br* la Pentecôte

**whizz** [wɪz] **1.** *vi* [rush] aller à toute vitesse; **to whizz past** or **by** passer à toute vitesse **2.** *adj Fam* **whizz kid** petit prodige *m*

**who** [huː] *pron* qui; **who did it?** qui (est-ce qui) a fait ça?; **the woman who came** la femme qui est venue; **who were you talking to?** à qui est-ce que tu parlais?

**whodun(n)it** [huː'dʌnɪt] *n Fam* polar *m*

**whoever** [huː'evə(r)] *pron* [no matter who - subject] qui que ce soit qui; [object] qui que ce soit que; **whoever has seen this** [anyone who] quiconque a vu cela; **whoever you are** qui que vous soyez; **this man, whoever he is** cet homme, quel qu'il soit

**whole** [həʊl] **1.** *adj* entier, -ère; **the whole time** tout le temps; **the whole apple** toute la pomme, la pomme tout entière; **the whole world** le monde entier **2.** *n* totalité *f*; **the whole of the village** le village tout entier, tout le village; **on the whole, as a whole** dans l'ensemble ■ **wholefood** *n* aliment *m* complet ■ **whole grain** ['həʊlgreɪn] *adj* [bread, flour] complet (*f* complète) ■ **whole-hearted** *adj* sans réserve ■ **wholemeal**, *Am* **wholewheat** *adj* [bread] complet, -ète ■ **wholesome** *adj* [food, climate] sain

**wholesale** ['həʊlseɪl] **1.** *adj* [price] de gros; **wholesale business** or **trade** commerce *m* de gros **2.** *adv* [buy, sell] au prix de gros

**wholly** ['həʊlɪ] *adv* entièrement

**whom** [huːm] *pron Formal* [object] que; [in questions and after prep] qui; **whom did she see?** qui a-t-elle vu?; **the man whom you know** l'homme que tu connais; **the man of whom we were speaking** l'homme dont nous parlions

**whooping** ['huːpɪŋ] *adj* **whooping cough** coqueluche *f*

**whoops** [wʊps] *excl* houp-là!

**whopping** ['wɒpɪŋ] *adj Fam* [big] énorme

**whore** [hɔː(r)] *n Fam* putain *f*

**whose** [huːz] *poss pron & adj* à qui, de qui; **whose book is this?, whose is this book?** à qui est ce livre ?; **whose daughter are you?** de qui es-tu la fille ?; **the woman whose book I have** la femme dont j'ai le livre; **the man whose mother I spoke to** l'homme à la mère de qui j'ai parlé

**why** [waɪ] **1.** *adv* pourquoi; **why not?** pourquoi pas ? **2.** *conj* **the reason why they...** la raison pour laquelle ils... **3.** *excl* [surprise] tiens !

**wick** [wɪk] *n* [of candle, lighter, oil lamp] mèche *f*

**wicked** ['wɪkɪd] *adj* [evil] méchant

**wicker** ['wɪkə(r)] *n* osier *m*

**wicket** ['wɪkɪt] *n* [cricket stumps] guichet *m*

**wide** [waɪd] **1.** *(compar* -er, *superl* -est) *adj* large; [choice, variety, knowledge] grand; **to be 3 metres wide** avoir 3 mètres de large **2.** *adv* [fall, shoot] loin du but; **wide open** [eyes, mouth, door] grand ouvert; **wide awake** complètement réveillé ■ **widely** *adv* [travel] beaucoup; [spread] largement; **it's widely thought that...** on pense généralement que... ■ **widen 1.** *vt* élargir **2.** *vi* s'élargir

**widespread** ['waɪdspred] *adj* répandu

**widow** ['wɪdəʊ] *n* veuve *f* ■ **widower** *n* veuf *m*

**width** [wɪdθ] *n* largeur *f*

**wield** [wiːld] *vt* [brandish] brandir; *Fig* **to wield power** exercer le pouvoir

**wife** [waɪf] *(pl* **wives**) *n* femme *f*, épouse *f*

**Wifi** ['waɪfaɪ] *(abbr of* **wireless fidelity**) *n* COMPUT WiFi *m*; **Wifi hotspot** point *m* d'accès WiFi

**wig** [wɪg] *n* perruque *f*

**wiggle** ['wɪgəl] **1.** *vt* remuer **2.** *vi* [of worm] se tortiller; [of tail] remuer

**wild** [waɪld] **1.** *(compar* -er, *superl* -est) *adj* [animal, flower, region] sauvage; [idea] fou *(f* folle); **wild with joy /anger** fou de joie /colère; **to be wild** [of person] mener une vie agitée; *Fam* **I'm not wild about it** ça ne m'emballe pas; **the Wild West** le Far West **2.** *adv* **to grow wild** [of plant] pousser à l'état sauvage; **to run wild** [of animals] courir en liberté; [of crowd] se déchaîner **3.** *n* **in the wild** à l'état sauvage; **in the wilds** en pleine brousse ■ **wildlife** *n* nature *f*

**wilderness** ['wɪldənəs] *n* région *f* sauvage

**wildly** ['waɪldlɪ] *adv* [cheer] frénétiquement; [guess] au hasard

**wilful,** *Am* **willful** ['wɪlfəl] *adj* [intentional, obstinate] volontaire

**will¹** [wɪl]

On trouve généralement **I /you /he /etc will** sous leurs formes contractées **I'll / you'll /he'll /etc.** La forme négative correspondante est **won't,** que l'on écrira **will not** dans des contextes formels.

*v aux* [expressing future tense] **he will come, he'll come** il viendra; **you will not come, you won't come** tu ne viendras pas; **will you have some tea?** veux-tu du thé ?; **will you be quiet!** veux-tu te taire !; **it won't open** ça ne s'ouvre pas

**will²** [wɪl] *n* [resolve, determination] volonté *f*; [legal document] testament *m*; **free will** libre arbitre *m*; **against one's will** à contrecœur; **at will** à volonté; [cry] à la demande

**willing** ['wɪlɪŋ] *adj* [helper, worker] plein de bonne volonté; **to be willing to do sth** bien vouloir faire qch ■ **willingly** *adv* [with pleasure] volontiers; [voluntarily] de son plein gré ■ **willingness** *n* bonne volonté *f*; **her willingness to do sth** [enthusiasm] son empressement à faire qch

**willow (tree)** ['wɪləʊ-] *n* saule *m*; **weeping willow** saule *m* pleureur

**willpower** ['wɪlpaʊə(r)] *n* volonté *f*

**wilt** [wɪlt] *vi* [of plant] dépérir

**wily** ['waɪlɪ] *(compar* -ier, *superl* -iest) *adj* rusé

**wimp** [wɪmp] *n* *Fam* [weakling] mauviette *f*

**win** [wɪn] **1.** *n* [victory] victoire *f* **2.** *(pt & pp* **won**, *pres p* **winning**) *vt* [money, race, prize] gagner; [victory] remporter; [fame] acquérir; [friends] se faire; *Br*

**to win sb over** or **round** gagner qn (**to** à) **3.** vi gagner ■ **winning 1.** adj [number, horse] gagnant ; [team] victorieux, -euse ; [goal] décisif, -ive **2.** npl **winnings** gains mpl ■ **win-win** adj **it's a win-win situation** on ne peut que gagner, c'est une situation gagnant-gagnant

**wince** [wɪns] vi faire une grimace

**winch** [wɪntʃ] **1.** n treuil m **2.** vt **to winch (up)** hisser

**wind**[1] [wɪnd] **1.** n vent m ; [breath] souffle m ; **to have wind** [in stomach] avoir des gaz ; **to get wind of sth** avoir vent de qch ; MUS **wind instrument** instrument m à vent **2.** vt **to wind sb** [of blow] couper le souffle à qn ■ **windcheater**, Am **windbreaker** n coupe-vent m inv ■ **windfall** n [unexpected money] aubaine f ■ **windmill** n moulin m à vent ■ **windscreen**, Am **windshield** n [of vehicle] pare-brise m inv; **windscreen wiper** essuie-glace m ■ **windsurfer** n [person] véliplanchiste mf ■ **windsurfing** n **to go windsurfing** faire de la planche à voile ■ **windy** (compar -ier, superl -iest) adj **it's windy** [of weather] il y a du vent; **windy day** jour m de grand vent

**wind**[2] [waɪnd] **1.** (pt & pp **wound**) vt [roll] enrouler (**round** autour de) ; [clock] remonter ; **to wind a cassette back** rembobiner une cassette **2.** vi [of river, road] serpenter ■ **winding** adj [road] sinueux, -euse ; [staircase] en colimaçon ■ **wind down 1.** vt sep [car] baisser **2.** vi Fam [relax] se détendre ■ **wind up 1.** vt sep [clock] remonter ; [meeting, speech] terminer; Br Fam **to wind sb up** faire marcher qn **2.** vi [end up] finir (**doing sth** par faire qch) ; **to wind up with sb/sth** se retrouver avec qn /qch

**window** [ˈwɪndəʊ] n [gen & COMPUT] fenêtre f ; [pane] vitre f ; [of shop] vitrine f ; [counter] guichet m ; Br **French window** porte-fenêtre f; **window box** jardinière f ; Br **window cleaner**, Am **window washer** laveur, -euse mf de vitres ; Br **window ledge** rebord m de fenêtre ■ **windowpane** n vitre f, carreau m ■ **window-shopping** n to

go **window-shopping** faire du lèche-vitrines ■ **windowsill** n rebord m de fenêtre

**wine** [waɪn] n vin m; **wine bar /bottle** bar m / bouteille f à vin; **wine cellar** cave f à vin; **wine list** carte f des vins; **wine tasting** dégustation f; **wine waiter** sommelier m ■ **wineglass** n verre m à vin

**wing** [wɪŋ] n aile f; **the wings** [in theatre] les coulisses fpl; **wing mirror** rétroviseur m extérieur

**wink** [wɪŋk] vi faire un clin d'œil (**at** à)

**winner** [ˈwɪnə(r)] n gagnant, -e mf

**winter** [ˈwɪntə(r)] **1.** n hiver m; **in (the) winter** en hiver **2.** adj d'hiver ■ **wintertime** n hiver m ■ **wintry** adj hivernal; **wintry day** jour m d'hiver

**wipe** [waɪp] **1.** n **to give sth a wipe** essuyer qch **2.** vt essuyer; **to wipe one's feet /hands** s'essuyer les pieds / les mains; **to wipe sth away** or **off** or **up** [liquid] essuyer qch; **to wipe sth out** [clean] essuyer qch ; [destroy] anéantir qch ■ **wiper** n essuie-glace m

**wire** [ˈwaɪə(r)] **1.** n fil m ; **wire mesh** or **netting** toile f métallique **2.** vt **to wire (up)** [house] faire l'installation électrique de ; **to wire sth (up) to sth** [connect electrically] relier qch à qch ■ **wiring** n [system] installation f électrique

**wisdom** [ˈwɪzdəm] n sagesse f

**wise** [waɪz] (compar -er, superl -est) adj [in knowledge] sage ; [advisable] prudent; **to be none the wiser** ne pas être plus avancé ■ **wisely** adv sagement

**-wise** [waɪz] suff [with regard to] **money-wise** question argent

**wish** [wɪʃ] **1.** n [specific] souhait m, vœu m ; [general] désir m; **to do sth against sb's wishes** faire qch contre le souhait de qn; **best wishes, all good wishes** [in letter] amitiés fpl; **send him my best wishes** fais-lui mes amitiés **2.** vt souhaiter (**to do** faire); **I wish (that) you could help me** je voudrais que vous m'aidiez; **I wish she could come** j'aurais bien aimé qu'elle vienne; **I wish you (a) happy birthday /(good)**

**luck** je vous souhaite bon anniversaire / bonne chance; **I wish I could** si seulement je pouvais **3.** *vi* **to wish for sth** souhaiter qch; **as you wish** comme vous voudrez ■ **wishful** *adj* **it's wishful thinking (on your part)** tu prends tes désirs pour des réalités

**wisp** [wɪsp] *n* [of smoke] traînée *f*; [of hair] mèche *f*

**wistful** [ˈwɪstfəl] *adj* nostalgique

**wit** [wɪt] *n* [humour] esprit *m*; [person] homme *m* /femme *f* d'esprit; **wits** [intelligence] intelligence *f*; **to be at one's wits'** *or* **wit's end** ne plus savoir que faire

**witch** [wɪtʃ] *n* sorcière *f*

**with** [wɪð] *prep* **a)** [expressing accompaniment] avec; **come with me** viens avec moi; **with no hat /gloves** sans chapeau /gants; **I'll be right with you** je suis à vous dans une seconde; *Fam* **I'm with you** [I understand] je te suis; *Fam* **to be with it** [up-to-date] être dans le vent

**b)** [at the house, flat of] chez; **she's staying with me** elle loge chez moi

**c)** [expressing cause] de; **to tremble with fear** trembler de peur; **to be ill with measles** être malade de la rougeole

**d)** [expressing instrument, means] **to write with a pen** écrire avec un stylo; **to fill with sth** remplir de qch; **satisfied with sb /sth** satisfait de qn /qch; **with my own eyes** de mes propres yeux

**e)** [in description] à; **a woman with blue eyes** une femme aux yeux bleus

**f)** [despite] malgré; **with all his faults** malgré tous ses défauts

**withdraw** [wɪðˈdrɔː] **1.** (*pt* -drew, *pp* -drawn) *vt* retirer (**from** de) **2.** *vi* se retirer (**from** de) ■ **withdrawal** *n* retrait *m* ■ **withdrawn** *adj* [person] renfermé

**withhold** [wɪðˈhəʊld] (*pt & pp* -held) *vt* [permission, help] refuser (**from** à); [decision] différer; [money] retenir (**from** de); [information] cacher (**from** à)

**within** [wɪðˈɪn] **1.** *prep* [inside] à l'intérieur de; **within 10 km (of)** [less than] à moins de 10 km (de); [inside an area of] dans un rayon de 10 km (de); **within a month** [return] avant un mois; [finish] en moins d'un mois; **within sight** en vue **2.** *adv* à l'intérieur

**without** [wɪðˈaʊt] **1.** *prep* sans; **without a tie** sans cravate; **without doing sth** sans faire qch; **to do without sb /sth** se passer de qn /qch **2.** *adv* **to do without** se priver

**withstand** [wɪðˈstænd] (*pt & pp* -stood) *vt* résister à

**witness** [ˈwɪtnɪs] **1.** *n* [person] témoin *m* **2.** *vt* [accident] être témoin de; [document] signer (pour attester l'authenticité de)

**wittily** [ˈwɪtɪlɪ] *adv* avec beaucoup d'esprit

**witty** [ˈwɪtɪ] (*compar* -ier, *superl* -iest) *adj* spirituel, -elle

**wives** [waɪvz] *pl of* **wife**

**wizard** [ˈwɪzəd] *n* magicien *m*; *Fig* [genius] as *m*

**WKND** (*abbr of* **weekend**) MESSAGING we

**WMD** (*abbr of* **weapons of mass destruction**) *npl* ADM *fpl*

**wobble** [ˈwɒbəl] *vi* [of chair] branler; [of jelly, leg] trembler; [of wheel] tourner de façon irrégulière; [of person] chanceler ■ **wobbly** *adj* [table, chair] branlant

**woe** [wəʊ] *n* malheur *m*

**wok** [wɒk] *n* poêle *f* chinoise

**woke** [wəʊk] *pt of* **wake**

**woken** [ˈwəʊkən] *pp of* **wake**

**wolf** [wʊlf] **1.** (*pl* **wolves**) *n* loup *m* **2.** *vt* **to wolf (down)** [food] engloutir

**woman** [ˈwʊmən] (*pl* **women**) *n* femme *f*; **women's** [clothes, attitudes, magazine] féminin; **women's rights** droits *mpl* des femmes

**womb** [wuːm] *n* ANAT utérus *m*

**women** [ˈwɪmɪn] *pl of* **woman**

**won** [wʌn] *pt & pp of* **win**

**wonder** [ˈwʌndə(r)] **1.** *n* [marvel] merveille *f*; [feeling] émerveillement *m*; **it's no wonder** ce n'est pas étonnant (**that** que (+ subjunctive)); **it's a wonder she wasn't killed** c'est un miracle qu'elle n'ait pas été tuée **2.** *vt* [ask oneself] se demander (**if** si; **why** pourquoi) **3.** *vi* [ask oneself questions] s'interroger (**about** au sujet de *ou* sur); **I was just wondering** je réfléchissais

**wonderful** ['wʌndəfəl] *adj* merveilleux, -euse

**wonky** ['wɒŋkɪ] *(compar* -ier, *superl* -iest) *adj Br Fam* [table] déglingué; [hat, picture] de travers

**won't** [wəʊnt] = **will not**

**woo** [wuː] *(pt & pp* wooed) *vt* [voters] chercher à plaire à

**wood** [wʊd] *n* [material, forest] bois *m* ■ **wooded** *adj* boisé ■ **wooden** *adj* en bois; *Fig* [manner, dancer, actor] raide ■ **woodland** *n* région *f* boisée ■ **woodwind** *n* **the woodwind** [musical instruments] les bois *mpl* ■ **woodwork** *n* [school subject] menuiserie *f* ■ **woodworm** *n* it has woodworm c'est vermoulu

**wool** [wʊl] *n* laine *f* ■ **woollen**, *Am* **woolen 1.** *adj* [dress] en laine **2.** *npl* **woollens**, *Am* **woolens** [garments] lainages *mpl* ■ **woolly** *(compar* -ier, *superl* -iest) **1.** *adj* en laine; *Fig* [unclear] nébuleux, -euse **2.** *n Br Fam* [garment] lainage *m*

**word** [wɜːd] **1.** *n* mot *m*; [promise] parole *f*; **words** [of song] paroles *fpl*; **to have a word with sb** parler à qn; **to keep one's word** tenir sa promesse; **in other words** autrement dit; **word for word** [report] mot pour mot; [translate] mot à mot; **word processing** traitement *m* de texte; **word processor** machine *f* à traitement de texte **2.** *vt* [express] formuler ■ **wording** *n* termes *mpl* ■ **wordy** *(compar* -ier, *superl* -iest) *adj* prolixe

**wore** [wɔː(r)] *pt of* **wear**

**work** [wɜːk] **1.** *n* travail *m*; [literary, artistic] œuvre *f*; **to be at work** travailler; **it's hard work (doing that)** ça demande beaucoup de travail (de faire ça); **to be out of work** être sans travail; **a day off work** un jour de congé; **work permit** permis *m* de travail; COMPUT **work station**, **workstation** poste *m* de travail; **work of**

art œuvre *f* d'art **2.** *vt* [person] faire travailler; [machine] faire marcher; [metal, wood] travailler **3.** *vi* [of person] travailler; [of machine] marcher, fonctionner; [of drug] agir; **to work loose** [of knot, screw] se desserrer; **to work towards** [result, agreement, aim] travailler à ■ **workaholic** [-ə'hɒlɪk] *n Fam* bourreau *m* de travail ■ **workforce** *n* main-d'œuvre *f* ■ **workload** *n* charge *f* de travail ■ **workman** *(pl* -men) *n* ouvrier *m* ■ **workmanship** *n* travail *m* ■ **workmate** *n Br* camarade *mf* de travail ■ **workout** *n* [sports training] séance *f* d'entraînement ■ **works 1.** *n* [factory] usine *f* **2.** *npl* **a)** [mechanism] mécanisme *m* **b)** [digging, building] travaux *mpl* ■ **workshop** *n* [place, study course] atelier *m* ■ **work at** *vt insep* [improve] travailler ■ **work off** *vt sep* [debt] payer en travaillant; [excess fat] se débarrasser de (par l'exercice) ■ **work on** *vt insep* [book, problem] travailler à; [French] travailler ■ **work out 1.** *vt sep* [calculate] calculer; [problem] résoudre; [plan] préparer; [understand] comprendre **2.** *vi* [succeed] marcher; [do exercises] s'entraîner; **it works out at 50 euros** ça fait 50 euros ■ **work up 1.** *vt sep* **to work up enthusiasm** s'enthousiasmer (**for** pour); **I worked up an appetite** ça m'a ouvert l'appétit; **to get worked up** s'énerver **2.** *vi* **to work up to sth** se préparer à qch

**worker** ['wɜːkə(r)] *n* travailleur, -euse *mf*; [manual] ouvrier, -ère *mf*; **(office) worker** employé, -e *mf* (de bureau)

**working** ['wɜːkɪŋ] **1.** *adj* [day, clothes] de travail; **in working order** en état de marche; **working class** classe *f* ouvrière; **working conditions** conditions *fpl* de travail; *Br* **working week** semaine *f* de travail **2.** *npl* **the workings of** [clock] le mécanisme de ■ **working-class** *adj* ouvrier, -ère

**workplace** ['wɜːkpleɪs] *n* lieu *m* de travail

**workspace** ['wɜːkspeɪs] *n* COMPUT bureau *m*

**worktop** ['wɜːktɒp] *n Br* plan *m* de travail

**workweek** *Am n* = **working week**

**world** [wɜːld] **1.** *n* monde *m*; **all over the world** dans le monde entier **2.** *adj* [war, production] mondial; [champion, record] du monde; **the World Cup** [in football] la Coupe du Monde ■ **worldly** *adj* [person] qui a l'expérience du monde ■ **worldwide 1.** *adj* mondial **2.** *adv* dans le monde entier

**worm** [wɜːm] **1.** *n* [animal & COMPUT] ver *m* **2.** *vt* **to worm one's way into** s'insinuer dans; **to worm sth out of sb** soutirer qch à qn

**worn** [wɔːn] **1.** *pp of* **wear 2.** *adj* [clothes, tyre] usé ■ **worn-out** *adj* [object] complètement usé; [person] épuisé

**worry** ['wʌrɪ] **1.** *(pl -ies)* *n* souci *m*; **it's a worry** ça me cause du souci **2.** *(pt & pp -ied)* *vt* inquiéter **3.** *vi* s'inquiéter **(about sth** de qch; **about sb** pour qn) ■ **worried** *adj* inquiet, -ète **(about** au sujet de**)** ■ **worrying** *adj* inquiétant

**worse** [wɜːs] **1.** *adj* pire **(than** que**)**; **to get worse** se détériorer; **he's getting worse** [in health] il va de plus en plus mal; [in behaviour] il se conduit de plus en plus mal **2.** *adv* plus mal **(than** que**)**; **I could do worse** j'aurais pu tomber plus mal; **she's worse off (than before)** sa situation est pire (qu'avant); [financially] elle est encore plus pauvre (qu'avant) **3.** *n* **there's worse to come** le pire reste à venir; **a change for the worse** une détérioration

**worsen** ['wɜːsən] **1.** *vt* aggraver **2.** *vi* empirer

**worship** ['wɜːʃɪp] **1.** *n* culte *m* **2.** *(pt & pp -pp-)* *vt* [person, god] adorer; *Pej* [money] avoir le culte de

**worst** [wɜːst] **1.** *adj* pire; **the worst book I've ever read** le plus mauvais livre que j'aie jamais lu **2.** *adv* **(the) worst** le plus mal **3.** *n* **the worst (one)** [object, person] le /la pire, le /la plus mauvais(e); **the worst (thing) is that...** le pire, c'est que...; **at (the) worst** au pire

**worth** [wɜːθ] **1.** *adj* **to be worth sth** valoir qch; **how much** *or* **what is it worth?** ça vaut combien ?; **the film's (well) worth seeing** le film vaut la peine d'être vu **2.** *n* valeur *f*; **to buy**

**50 pence worth of chocolates** acheter pour 50 pence de chocolats; **to get one's money's worth** en avoir pour son argent ■ **worthless** *adj* qui ne vaut rien

**worthwhile** ['wɜːθ'waɪl] *adj* [book, film] qui vaut la peine d'être lu /vu; [activity] qui vaut la peine; [plan, contribution] valable; [cause] louable; [satisfying] qui donne des satisfactions

**worthy** ['wɜːðɪ] *(compar -ier, superl -iest)* *adj* [person] digne; [cause, act] louable; **to be worthy of sb /sth** être digne de qn /qch

**would** [wʊd] *(unstressed* [wəd]**)**

On trouve généralement **I /you /he /etc would** sous leurs formes contractées **I'd /you'd /he'd /etc**. La forme négative correspondante est **wouldn't**, que l'on écrira **would not** dans des contextes formels.

*v aux* **a)** [expressing conditional tense] **I would stay if I could** je resterais si je le pouvais; **he would have done it** il l'aurait fait; **I said she'd come** j'ai dit qu'elle viendrait

**b)** [willingness, ability] **would you help me, please?** veux-tu bien m'aider ?; **she wouldn't help me** elle n'a pas voulu m'aider; **would you like some tea?** prendrez-vous du thé ?; **the car wouldn't start** la voiture ne démarrait pas **c)** [expressing past habit] **I would see her every day** je la voyais chaque jour

**wound¹** [wuːnd] **1.** *n* blessure *f* **2.** *vt* [hurt] blesser; **the wounded** les blessés *mpl*

**wound²** [waʊnd] *pt & pp of* **wind**

**wove** [wəʊv] *pt of* **weave**

**woven** ['wəʊvən] *pp of* **weave**

**wow** [waʊ] *excl Fam* oh là là !

**wrap** [ræp] **1.** *n Am* **plastic wrap** film *m* plastique **2.** *(pt & pp -pp-)* *vt* **to wrap (up)** envelopper; [parcel] emballer; *Fig* **wrapped up in** [engrossed] absorbé par **3.** *vti* **to wrap (oneself) up** [dress warmly] s'emmitoufler ■ **wrapped** [ræpt] *adj* [bread, cheese] préemballé ■ **wrapper** *n* [of sweet] papier *m*

■ **wrapping** n [action, material] emballage m; **wrapping paper** papier m d'emballage

**wreath** [riːθ] (pl **-s** [riːðz]) n couronne f

**wreck** [rek] **1.** n [ship] épave f; [train] train m accidenté; [person] épave f (humaine); **to be a nervous wreck** être à bout de nerfs **2.** vt [break, destroy] détruire; Fig [spoil] gâcher; [career, hopes] briser ■ **wreckage** [-ɪdʒ] n [of plane, train] débris mpl

**wrench** [rentʃ] **1.** n Am [tool] clef f (à écrous) **2.** vt **to wrench sth from sb** arracher qch à qn

**wrestle** ['resəl] vi lutter (**with sb** avec qn); Fig **to wrestle with a problem** se débattre avec un problème ■ **wrestler** n lutteur, -euse mf; [in all-in wrestling] catcheur, -euse mf ■ **wrestling** n lutte f; **(all-in) wrestling** [with relaxed rules] catch m

**wretch** [retʃ] n [unfortunate person] malheureux, -euse mf; [rascal] misérable mf ■ **wretched** [-ɪd] adj [poor, pitiful] misérable; [dreadful] affreux, -euse; Fam [annoying] maudit

**wriggle** ['rɪgəl] **1.** vt [toes, fingers] tortiller **2.** vi to wriggle **(about)** se tortiller; [of fish] frétiller; **to wriggle out of sth** couper à qch

**wring** [rɪŋ] (pt & pp wrung) vt **to wring (out)** [clothes] essorer; **to wring one's hands** se tordre les mains

**wrinkle** ['rɪŋkəl] **1.** n [on skin] ride f; [in cloth, paper] pli m **2.** vi [of skin] se rider; [of cloth] faire des plis ■ **wrinkled** adj [skin] ridé; [cloth] froissé

**wrist** [rɪst] n poignet m ■ **wristwatch** n montre-bracelet f

**write** [raɪt] (pt wrote, pp written) vti écrire; **to write to sb** écrire à qn ■ **write-off** n Br **to be a (complete) write-off** [of vehicle] être bon pour la casse ■ **write away for** vt insep [details] écrire pour demander ■ **write back** vi répondre ■ **write down** vt sep noter ■ **write in 1.** vt sep [insert] inscrire **2.** vi [send letter] écrire ■ **write off** vt sep [debt] annuler

■ **write out** vt sep [list, recipe] noter; [cheque] faire ■ **write up** vt sep [notes] rédiger

**writer** ['raɪtə(r)] n auteur m (**of** de); [literary] écrivain m

**writing** ['raɪtɪŋ] n [handwriting, action, profession] écriture f; **to put sth (down) in writing** mettre qch par écrit; **writing pad** bloc-notes m; **writing paper** papier m à lettres

**written** ['rɪtən] pp of **write**

**wrong** [rɒŋ] **1.** adj [sum, idea] faux (f fausse); [direction, time] mauvais; [unfair] injuste; **to be wrong** [of person] avoir tort (**to do** de faire); **it's the wrong road** ce n'est pas la bonne route; **the clock's wrong** la pendule n'est pas à l'heure; **to get the wrong number** [on phone] se tromper de numéro; **something's wrong with the phone** le téléphone ne marche pas bien; **something's wrong with her leg** elle a quelque chose à la jambe; **what's wrong with you?** qu'est-ce que tu as?; **the wrong way round** or **up** à l'envers **2.** adv mal; **to go wrong** [of plan] mal tourner; [of vehicle, machine] tomber en panne; [of person] se tromper **3.** n [injustice] injustice f; **to be in the wrong** être dans son tort; **right and wrong** le bien et le mal **4.** vt faire du tort à ■ **wrongful** adj **wrongful arrest** arrestation f arbitraire ■ **wrongly** adv [inform, translate] mal; [accuse, condemn, claim] à tort

**wrote** [rəʊt] pt of **write**

**wrung** [rʌŋ] pt & pp of **wring**

**wry** [raɪ] (compar wryer, superl wryest) adj ironique

**WTG** MESSAGING written abbr of **way to go**

**WTH** MESSAGING written abbr of **what the hell**

**wuss** [wʌs] n Am Fam mauviette f

**WUWH** MESSAGING written abbr of **wish you were here**

**WWW** (abbr of World Wide Web) n WWW m

**X, x** [eks] *n* [letter] X, x *m inv*

**xenophobia** [*Br* zenə'fəʊbɪə, *Am* zi:nəʊ-] *n* xénophobie *f*

**Xerox®** ['zɪərɒks] **1.** *n* [copy] photocopie *f* **2.** *vt* photocopier

**XLNT** MESSAGING *written abbr of* **excellent**

**Xmas** ['krɪsməs] *n Fam* Noël *m*

**XML** [,eksem'el] *(abbr of* **Extensible Markup Language***)n* COMPUT XML *m*

**XO** MESSAGING *written abbr of* **kiss and a hug**

**X-ray** ['eksreɪ] **1.** *n* [picture] radio *f*; **to have an X-ray** passer une radio **2.** *vt* radiographier

**xylophone** ['zaɪləfəʊn] *n* xylophone *m*

# Y

**Y, y** [waɪ] *n* [letter] Y, y *m inv*

**yacht** [jɒt] *n* [sailing boat] voilier *m* ; [large private boat] yacht *m* ■ **yachting** *n* voile *f*

**yap** [jæp] *(pt & pp* **-pp-***) vi* [of dog] japper

**yard¹** [jɑːd] *n* [of house, farm, school, prison] cour *f* ; [for working] chantier *m* ; [for storage] dépôt *m* de marchandises ; *Am* [garden] jardin *m* ■ **yardman** [ˈjɑːdmæn] *n Am* jardinier *m*

**yard²** [jɑːd] *n* [measure] yard *m* (= 91,44 cm)

**yarn** [jɑːn] *n* [thread] fil *m* ; *Fam* [tale] histoire *f* à dormir debout

**yawn** [jɔːn] *vi* bâiller

**year** [jɪə(r)] *n* an *m*, année *f* ; [of wine] année *f* ; **school /tax year** année *f* scolaire /fiscale ; **in the year 2004** en (l'an) 2004 ; **he's ten years old** il a dix ans ; **New Year** Nouvel An *m* ; **New Year's Day** le jour de l'An ; **New Year's Eve** la Saint-Sylvestre ■ **yearly 1.** *adj* annuel, -elle **2.** *adv* annuellement ; **twice yearly** deux fois par an

**yearn** [jɜːn] *vi* **to yearn for sb** languir après qn ; **to yearn for sth** désirer ardemment qch ; **to yearn to do sth** brûler de faire qch

**yeast** [jiːst] *n* levure *f*

**yell** [jel] *vti* **to yell (out)** hurler ; **to yell at sb** [scold] crier après qn

**yellow** [ˈjeləʊ] **1.** *adj* [in colour] jaune ; **yellow card** [in football] carton *m* jaune **2.** *n* jaune *m*

**yenta** [ˈjentə] *n Am Fam* [gossip] commère *f* ; **she's a yenta** c'est une vraie concierge

**yes** [jes] **1.** *adv* oui ; [after negative question] si **2.** *n* oui *m inv*

**yesterday** [ˈjestədeɪ] **1.** *adv* hier **2.** *n* hier *m* ; **yesterday morning /evening** hier matin /soir ; **the day before yesterday** avant-hier

**yet** [jet] **1.** *adv* **a)** [still] encore ; [already] déjà ; **she hasn't arrived (as) yet** elle n'est pas encore arrivée ; **the best yet** le meilleur jusqu'ici ; **yet another mistake** encore une erreur ; **not (just) yet** pas pour l'instant **b)** [in questions] **has he come yet?** est-il arrivé ? **2.** *conj* [nevertheless] pourtant

**yew** [juː] *n* [tree, wood] if *m*

**yield** [jiːld] **1.** *n* [of field, shares] rendement *m* **2.** *vt* [result] donner ; [interest] rapporter ; [territory, right] céder ; **to yield a profit** rapporter **3.** *vi* [surrender] se rendre ; *Am* '**yield**' [road sign] 'cédez le passage'

**yikes** [jaɪks] *excl* mince !

**yob** [jɒb], **yobbo** [ˈjɒbəʊ] *(pl* **yob(bo)s***) n Br Fam* loubard *m*

**yoga** [ˈjəʊgə] *n* yoga *m*

**yog(h)urt** [*Br* ˈjɒgət, *Am* ˈjəʊgərt] *n* yaourt *m*

**yolk** [jəʊk] *n* jaune *m* (d'œuf)

**yolo** [ˈjəʊləʊ] *excl Fam* (*abbr of* **you only live once***)* on ne vit qu'une fois

**yonks** [jɒŋks] *n Br Fam* **I haven't been there for yonks** il y a une paie *ou* ça fait un bail que je n'y suis pas allé

**you** [juː] *pron* **a)** [subject - pl, polite form sing] vous ; [familiar form sing] tu ; [object] vous, te, t', *pl* vous ; [after prep, 'than', 'it is'] vous, toi, *pl* vous ; **(to) you** [indirect] vous, te, t', *pl* vous ; **I gave it (to) you** je vous /te l'ai donné ; **you teachers** vous autres professeurs ; **you idiot!** espèce d'imbécile ! **b)** [indefinite] on ; [object] vous, te, t', *pl* vous ;

**you never know** on ne sait jamais
■ **you'd** = you had, you would
■ **you'll** = you will

**young** [jʌŋ] **1.** *(compar* -er, *superl* -est*)* *adj* jeune; **she's two years younger than me** elle a deux ans de moins que moi; **my young(er) brother** mon (frère) cadet; **my youngest sister** la cadette de mes sœurs; **young people** les jeunes *mpl* **2.** *n* [of animals] petits *mpl*; **the young** [people] les jeunes *mpl*; **she's my youngest** [daughter] c'est ma petite dernière ■ **youngster** *n* jeune *mf*

**your** [jɔː(r)] *poss adj* [polite form sing, polite and familiar form pl] votre, *pl* vos; [familiar form sing] ton, ta, *pl* tes; [one's] son, sa, *pl* ses

**yours** [jɔːz] *poss pron* le vôtre, la vôtre, *pl* les vôtres; [familiar form sing] le tien, la tienne, *pl* les tien(ne)s; **this book is yours** ce livre est à vous *ou* est le vôtre / ce livre est à toi *ou* est le tien; **a friend of yours** un ami à vous / toi

**yourself** [jɔːˈself] *pron* [polite form] vous-même; [familiar form] toi-même; [reflexive] vous, te, t'; [after prep] vous, toi; **you wash yourself** vous vous lavez / tu te laves ■ **yourselves** *pron pl* vous-mêmes; [reflexive and after prep] vous; **did you cut yourselves?** est-ce que vous vous êtes coupés?

**youth** [juːθ] *(pl* -s [juːθz]*)* *n* [age] jeunesse *f*; [young man] jeune *m*; **youth club** centre *m* de loisirs pour les jeunes; **youth hostel** auberge *f* de jeunesse ■ **youthful** *adj* [person] jeune

**YouTube®** [ˈjuːˌtjuːb] *vi* COMPUT aller sur le site internet YouTube, poster une vidéo

**you've** [juːv] = **you have**

**yo-yo** [ˈjəʊjəʊ] *(pl* **yo-yos**) *n* Yo-Yo® *m inv*

**Yugoslavia** [ˌjuːɡəˈslɑːvɪə] *n* Yougoslavie *f*; **the former Yugoslavia** l'ex-Yougoslavie

**yuppie** [ˈjʌpɪ] *n* yuppie *mf*

**Z, z** [Br zed, Am ziː] n [letter] Z, z m inv

**zany** ['zeɪnɪ] (compar -ier, superl -iest) adj loufoque

**zap** [zæp] (pt & pp -pp-) vt Fam COMPUT effacer

**zeal** [ziːl] n zèle m ▪ **zealous** ['zeləs] adj zélé

**zebra** ['ziːbrə, Br 'zebrə] n zèbre m; Br **zebra crossing** passage m pour piétons

**zero** ['zɪərəʊ] (pl -os) n zéro m ▪ **zerocarbon** adj zéro-carbone

**zest** [zest] n [enthusiasm] enthousiasme m; [of lemon, orange] zeste m

**zigzag** ['zɪgzæg] 1. n zigzag m 2. adj & adv en zigzag 3. (pt & pp -gg-) vi zigzaguer

**zinc** [zɪŋk] n zinc m

**zinger** ['zɪŋə(r)] n Am Fam a) [pointed remark] pique f b) [impressive thing] **it was a real zinger** c'était impressionnant; **a real zinger of a black eye** un œil au beurre noir pas croyable

**zip** [zɪp] 1. n Br **zip (fastener)** fermeture Éclair® f 2. adj Am **zip code** code m postal 3. (pt & pp -pp-) vt **to zip sth (up)** remonter la fermeture Éclair® de qch 4. vi **to zip past** [of car] passer en trombe ▪ **zipper** n Am fermeture Éclair® f

**zit** [zɪt] n Fam [pimple] bouton m

**zodiac** ['zəʊdɪæk] n zodiaque m

**zone** [zəʊn] n zone f

**zoo** [zuː] (pl zoos) n zoo m

**zoom** [zuːm] 1. n **zoom lens** zoom m 2. vi **to zoom in** [of camera] faire un zoom avant (**on** sur); Fam **to zoom past** passer comme une flèche

**zucchini** [zuːˈkiːnɪ] (pl -ni or -nis) n Am courgette f

# Supplements

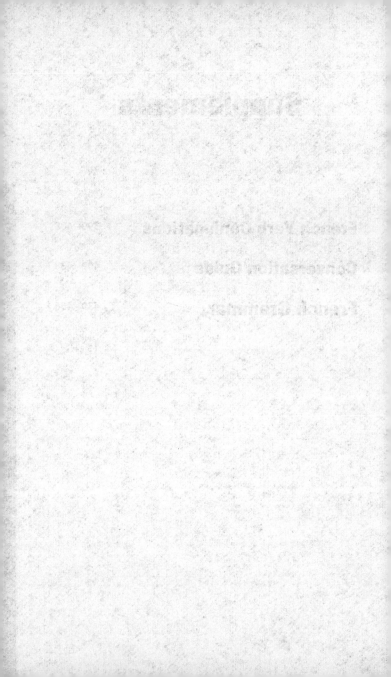

# French Verb Conjugations

## Regular verbs

|  | -ER verbs | -IR verbs | -RE verbs |
|---|---|---|---|
| *Infinitive* | *donn/er* | *fin/ir* | *vend/re* |
| **1** Present | je donne | je finis | je vends |
|  | tu donnes | tu finis | tu vends |
|  | il donne | il finit | il vend |
|  | nous donnons | nous finissons | nous vendons |
|  | vous donnez | vous finissez | vous vendez |
|  | ils donnent | ils finissent | ils vendent |
| **2** Imperfect | je donnais | je finissais | je vendais |
|  | tu donnais | tu finissais | tu vendais |
|  | il donnait | il finissait | il vendait |
|  | nous donnions | nous finissions | nous vendions |
|  | vous donniez | vous finissiez | vous vendiez |
|  | ils donnaient | ils finissaient | ils vendaient |
| **3** Past historic | je donnai | je finis | je vendis |
|  | tu donnas | tu finis | tu vendis |
|  | il donna | il finit | il vendit |
|  | nous donnâmes | nous finîmes | nous vendîmes |
|  | vous donnâtes | vous finîtes | vous vendîtes |
|  | ils donnèrent | ils finirent | ils vendirent |
| **4** Future | je donnerai | je finirai | je vendrai |
|  | tu donneras | tu finiras | tu vendras |
|  | il donnera | il finira | il vendra |
|  | nous donnerons | nous finirons | nous vendrons |
|  | vous donnerez | vous finirez | vous vendrez |
|  | ils donneront | ils finiront | ils vendront |
| **5** Subjunctive | je donne | je finisse | je vende |
|  | tu donnes | tu finisses | tu vendes |
|  | il donne | il finisse | il vende |
|  | nous donnions | nous finissions | nous vendions |
|  | vous donniez | vous finissiez | vous vendiez |
|  | ils donnent | ils finissent | ils vendent |
| **6** Imperative | donne | finis | vends |
|  | donnons | finissons | vendons |
|  | donnez | finissez | vendez |
| **7** Present participle | donnant | finissant | vendant |
| **8** Past participle | donné | fini | vendu |

**!** The conditional is formed by adding the following endings to the infinitive: **-ais**, **-ais**, **-ait**, **-ions**, **-iez**, **-aient**. The final **e** is dropped in infinitives ending **-re**.

## Irregular French verbs

Listed below are those verbs considered to be the most useful. Forms and tenses not given fully derivable, such as the third person singular of the present tense which is normally formed by substituting 't' for the final 's' of the first person singular, eg 'crois' becomes 'croit', 'dis' becomes 'dit'. Note that the endings of the past historic fall into three categories, the 'a' and 'i' categories shown at *donner*, and at *finir* and *vendre*, and the 'u' category which has the following endings: -us, -ut, -ûmes, -ûtes, -urent. Most of the verbs listed below form their past historic with 'u'. The imperfect may usually be formed by adding -ais, -ait, -ions, -iez, -aient to the stem of the first person plural of the present tense, eg 'je buvais' etc may be derived from 'nous buvons' (stem 'buv-' and ending '-ons'); similarly, the present participle may generally be formed by substituting -ant for -ons (eg buvant). The future may usually be formed by adding -ai, -as, -a, -ons, -ez, -ont to the infinitive or to an infinitive without final 'e' where the ending is -re (eg *conduire*). The imperative usually has the same forms as the second persons singular and plural and first person plural of the present tense.

**1** = Present    **2** = Imperfect    **3** = Past historic    **4** = Future    **5** = Subjunctive
**6** = Imperative    **7** = Present participle    **8** = Past participle    n = nous    v = vous
**\*** verbs conjugated with **être** only

| | | |
|---|---|---|
| abattre | *like* | **battre** |
| absoudre | **1** j'absous, n absolvons    **2** j'absolvais    **3** j'absolus (*rarely used*)    **5** j'absolve    **7** absolvant    **8** absous, absoute | |
| s'abstenir\* | *like* | **tenir** |
| abstraire | **1** j'abstrais, n abstrayons    **2** j'abstrayais    **3** none    **5** j'abstraie    **7** abstrayant    **8** abstrait | |
| accourir | *like* | **courir** |
| accroître | *like* | **croître** *except* **8** accru |
| accueillir | *like* | **cueillir** |
| acquérir | **1** j'acquiers, n acquérons    **2** j'acquérais    **3** j'acquis    **4** j'acquerrai    **5** j'acquière    **7** acquérant    **8** acquis | |
| adjoindre | *like* | **joindre** |
| admettre | *like* | **mettre** |
| advenir | *like* | **venir** (*third person only*) |
| aller\* | **1** je vais, tu vas, il va, n allons, v allez, ils vont    **4** j'irai    **5** j'aille, n allions, ils aillent    **6** va, allons, allez (*but note* vas-y) | |
| apercevoir | *like* | **recevoir** |
| apparaître | *like* | **connaître** |
| appartenir | *like* | **tenir** |
| apprendre | *like* | **prendre** |
| asseoir | **1** j'assieds, il assied, n asseyons, ils asseyent    **2** j'asseyais    **3** j'assis    **4** j'assiérai    **5** j'asseye    **7** asseyant    **8** assis | |

| | | |
|---|---|---|
| **astreindre** | *like* | **atteindre** |
| **atteindre** | | **1** j'atteins, n atteignons, ils atteignent  **2** j'atteignais  **3** j'atteignis  **4** j'atteindrai  **5** j'atteigne  **7** atteignant  **8** atteint |
| **avoir** | | **1** j'ai, tu as, il a, n avons, v avez, ils ont  **2** j'avais  **3** j'eus  **4** j'aurai  **5** j'aie, il ait, n ayons, ils aient  **6** aie, ayons, ayez  **7** ayant  **8** eu |
| **battre** | | **1** je bats, il bat, n battons  **5** je batte |
| **boire** | | **1** je bois, n buvons, ils boivent  **2** je buvais  **3** je bus  **5** je boive, n buvions  **7** buvant  **8** bu |
| **bouillir** | | **1** je bous, n bouillons, ils bouillent  **2** je bouillais  **3** je bouillis  **5** je bouille  **7** bouillant |
| **braire** | | (*defective*) **1** il brait, ils braient  **4** il braira, ils brairont |
| **circonscrire** | *like* | **écrire** |
| **circonvenir** | *like* | **tenir** |
| **clore** | *like* | **éclore** |
| **combattre** | *like* | **battre** |
| **commettre** | *like* | **mettre** |
| **comparaître** | *like* | **connaître** |
| **complaire** | *like* | **plaire** |
| **comprendre** | *like* | **prendre** |
| **compromettre** | *like* | **mettre** |
| **concevoir** | *like* | **recevoir** |
| **conclure** | | **1** je conclus, n concluons, ils concluent  **5** je conclue |
| **concourir** | *like* | **courir** |
| **conduire** | | **1** je conduis, n conduisons  **3** je conduisis  **5** je conduise  **8** conduit |
| **confire** | *like* | **suffire** |
| **connaître** | | **1** je connais, il connaît, n connaissons  **3** je connus  **5** je connaisse  **7** connaissant  **8** connu |
| **conquérir** | *like* | **acquérir** |
| **consentir** | *like* | **mentir** |
| **construire** | *like* | **conduire** |
| **contenir** | *like* | **tenir** |
| **contraindre** | *like* | **craindre** |
| **contredire** | *like* | **dire** *except* **1** v contredisez |
| **convaincre** | *like* | **vaincre** |
| **convenir** | *like* | **tenir** |
| **corrompre** | *like* | **rompre** |

| | |
|---|---|
| **coudre** | **1** je couds, ils coud, n cousons, ils cousent **3** je cousis **5** je couse **7** cousant **8** cousu |
| **courir** | **1** je cours, n courons **3** je courus **4** je courrai **5** je coure **8** couru |
| **couvrir** | **1** je couvre, n couvrons **2** je couvrais **5** je couvre **8** couvert |
| **craindre** | **1** je crains, n craignons, ils craignent **2** je craignais **3** je craignis **4** je craindrai **5** je craigne **7** craignant **8** craint |
| **croire** | **1** je crois, n croyons, ils croient **2** je croyais **3** je crus **5** je croie, n croyions **7** croyant **8** cru |
| **croître** | **1** je crois, il croît, n croissons **2** je croissais **3** je crûs **5** je croisse **7** croissant **8** crû, crue |
| **cueillir** | **1** je cueille, n cueillons **2** je cueillais **4** je cueillerai **5** je cueille **7** cueillant |
| **cuire** | **1** je cuis, n cuisons **2** je cuisais **3** je cuisis **5** je cuise **7** cuisant **8** cuit |
| **débattre** | *like* **battre** |
| **décevoir** | *like* **recevoir** |
| **déchoir** | (*defective*) **1** je déchois **2** *none* **3** je déchus **4** je déchoirai **6** *none* **7** *none* **8** déchu |
| **découdre** | *like* **coudre** |
| **découvrir** | *like* **couvrir** |
| **décrire** | *like* **écrire** |
| **décroître** | *like* **croître** *except* **8** décru |
| **se dédire·** | *like* **dire** |
| **déduire** | *like* **conduire** |
| **défaillir** | **1** je défaille, n défaillons **2** je défaillais **3** je défaillis **5** je défaille **7** défaillant **8** défailli |
| **défaire** | *like* **faire** |
| **démentir** | *like* **mentir** |
| **démettre** | *like* **mettre** |
| **se départir·** | *like* **mentir** |
| **dépeindre** | *like* **atteindre** |
| **déplaire** | *like* **plaire** |
| **déteindre** | *like* **atteindre** |
| **détenir** | *like* **tenir** |
| **détruire** | *like* **conduire** |
| **devenir·** | *like* **tenir** |
| **se dévêtir·** | *like* **vêtir** |

| devoir | **1** je dois, n devons, ils doivent  **2** je devais  **3** je dus<br>**4** je devrai  **5** je doive, n devions  **6** *not used*  **7** devant<br>**8** dû, due, *pl* dus, dues |
|---|---|
| dire | **1** je dis, n disons, v dites  **2** je disais  **3** je dis  **5** je dise<br>**7** disant  **8** dit |
| disconvenir | *like* **tenir** |
| disjoindre | *like* **joindre** |
| disparaître | *like* **connaître** |
| dissoudre | *like* **absoudre** |
| distraire | *like* **abstraire** |
| dormir | *like* **mentir** |
| échoir* | (*defective*) **1** il échoit  **2** *none*  **3** il échut, ils échurent<br>**4** il échoira  **6** *none*  **7** échéant  **8** échu |
| éclore | **1** il éclôt, ils éclosent  **8** éclos |
| éconduire | *like* **conduire** |
| écrire | **1** j'écris, n écrivons  **2** j'écrivais  **3** j'écrivis  **5** j'écrive<br>**7** écrivant  **8** écrit |
| élire | *like* **lire** |
| émettre | *like* **mettre** |
| émouvoir | *like* **mouvoir** *except* **8** ému |
| enclore | *like* **éclore** |
| encourir | *like* **courir** |
| endormir | *like* **mentir** |
| enduire | *like* **conduire** |
| enfreindre | *like* **atteindre** |
| s'enfuir* | *like* **fuir** |
| enjoindre | *like* **joindre** |
| s'enquérir* | *like* **acquérir** |
| s'ensuivre* | *like* **suivre** (*third person only*) |
| entreprendre | *like* **prendre** |
| entretenir | *like* **tenir** |
| entrevoir | *like* **voir** |
| entrouvrir | *like* **couvrir** |
| envoyer | **4** j'enverrai |
| s'éprendre* | *like* **prendre** |
| équivaloir | *like* **valoir** |
| éteindre | *like* **atteindre** |
| être | **1** je suis, tu es, il est, n sommes, v êtes, ils sont  **2** j'étais<br>**3** je fus  **4** je serai  **5** je sois, n soyons, ils soient<br>**6** sois, soyons, soyez  **7** étant  **8** été |

| | | |
|---|---|---|
| étreindre | *like* | **atteindre** |
| exclure | *like* | **conclure** |
| extraire | *like* | **abstraire** |
| faillir | (*defective*) **3** je faillis   **4** je faillirai   **8** failli | |
| faire | **1** je fais, n faisons, v faites, ils font   **2** je faisais   **3** je fis   **4** je ferai   **5** je fasse   **7** faisant   **8** fait | |
| falloir | (*impersonal*) **1** il faut   **2** il fallait   **3** il fallut   **4** il faudra   **5** il faille   **6** *none*   **7** *none*   **8** fallu | |
| feindre | *like* | **atteindre** |
| foutre | **1** je fous, n foutons   **2** je foutais   **3** *none*   **5** je foute   **7** foutant   **8** foutu | |
| frire | (*defective*) **1** je fris, tu fris, il frit   **4** je frirai   **6** fris   **8** frit (*for other persons and tenses use* faire frire) | |
| fuir | **1** je fuis, n fuyons, ils fuient   **2** je fuyais   **3** je fuis   **5** je fuie   **7** fuyant   **8** fui | |
| geindre | *like* | **atteindre** |
| haïr | **1** je hais, il hait, n haïssons | |
| inclure | *like* | **conclure** |
| induire | *like* | **conduire** |
| inscrire | *like* | **écrire** |
| instruire | *like* | **conduire** |
| interdire | *like* | **dire** *except* **1** v interdisez |
| interrompre | *like* | **rompre** |
| intervenir | *like* | **tenir** |
| introduire | *like* | **conduire** |
| joindre | **1** je joins, n joignons, ils joignent   **2** je joignais   **3** je joignis   **4** je joindrai   **5** je joigne   **7** joignant   **8** joint | |
| lire | **1** je lis, n lisons   **2** je lisais   **3** je lus   **5** je lise   **7** lisant   **8** lu | |
| luire | *like* | **nuire** |
| maintenir | *like* | **tenir** |
| maudire | **1** je maudis, n maudissons   **2** je maudissais   **3** je maudis   **4** je maudirai   **5** je maudisse   **7** maudissant   **8** maudit | |
| méconnaître | *like* | **connaître** |
| médire | *like* | **dire** *except* **1** v médisez |
| mentir | **1** je mens, n mentons   **2** je mentais   **5** je mente   **7** mentant | |
| mettre | **1** je mets, n mettons   **2** je mettais   **3** je mis   **5** je mette   **7** mettant   **8** mis | |
| moudre | **1** je mouds, il moud, n moulons   **2** je moulais   **3** je moulus   **5** je moule   **7** moulant   **8** moulu | |

| | |
|---|---|
| **mourir**<sup>*</sup> | **1** je meurs, n mourons, ils meurent **2** je mourais **3** je mourus **4** je mourrai **5** je meure, n mourions **7** mourant **8** mort |
| **mouvoir** | **1** je meus, n mouvons, ils meuvent **2** je mouvais **3** je mus **4** je mouvrai **5** je meuve, n mouvions **8** mû, mue, *pl* mus, mues |
| **naître**<sup>*</sup> | **1** je nais, il naît, n naissons **2** je naissais **3** je naquis **4** je naîtrai **5** je naisse **7** naissant **8** né |
| **nuire** | **1** je nuis, n nuisons **2** je nuisais **3** je nuisis **5** je nuise **7** nuisant **8** nui |
| **obtenir** | *like* **tenir** |
| **offrir** | *like* **couvrir** |
| **omettre** | *like* **mettre** |
| **ouvrir** | *like* **couvrir** |
| **paître** | (*defective*) **1** il paît **2** ils paissait **3** *none* **4** il paîtra **5** il paisse **7** paissant **8** *none* |
| **paraître** | *like* **connaître** |
| **parcourir** | *like* **courir** |
| **parfaire** | *like* **faire** (*present tense, infinitive and past participle only*) |
| **partir**<sup>*</sup> | *like* **mentir** |
| **parvenir**<sup>*</sup> | *like* **tenir** |
| **peindre** | *like* **atteindre** |
| **percevoir** | *like* **recevoir** |
| **permettre** | *like* **mettre** |
| **plaindre** | *like* **craindre** |
| **plaire** | **1** je plais, il plaît, n plaisons **2** je plaisais **3** je plus **5** je plaise **7** plaisant **8** plu |
| **pleuvoir** | (*impersonal*) **1** il pleut **2** il pleuvait **3** il plut **4** il pleuvra **5** il pleuve **6** *none* **7** pleuvant **8** plu |
| **poindre** | (*defective*) **1** il point **4** il poindra **8** point |
| **poursuivre** | *like* **suivre** |
| **pourvoir** | *like* **voir** *except* **3** je pourvus *and* **4** je pourvoirai |
| **pouvoir** | **1** je peux *or* je puis, tu peux, il peut, n pouvons, ils peuvent **2** je pouvais **3** je pus **4** je pourrai **5** je puisse **6** *not* used **7** pouvant **8** pu |
| **prédire** | *like* **dire** *except* v prédisez |
| **prendre** | **1** je prends, il prend, n prenons, ils prennent **2** je prenais **3** je pris **5** je prenne **7** prenant **8** pris |
| **prescrire** | *like* **écrire** |
| **pressentir** | *like* **mentir** |
| **prévaloir** | *like* **valoir** *except* **5** je prévale |
| **prévenir** | *like* **tenir** |

| | | |
|---|---|---|
| prévoir | *like* | **voir** *except* **4** je prévoirai |
| produire | *like* | **conduire** |
| promettre | *like* | **mettre** |
| promouvoir | *like* | **mouvoir** *except* **8** promu |
| proscrire | *like* | **écrire** |
| provenir* | *like* | **tenir** |
| rabattre | *like* | **battre** |
| rasseoir | *like* | **asseoir** |
| réapparaître | *like* | **connaître** |
| recevoir | | **1** je reçois, n recevons, ils reçoivent  **2** je recevais  **3** je reçus  **4** je recevrai  **5** je reçoive, n recevions, ils reçoivent  **7** recevant  **8** reçu |
| reconduire | *like* | **conduire** |
| reconnaître | *like* | **connaître** |
| reconquérir | *like* | **acquérir** |
| reconstruire | *like* | **conduire** |
| recoudre | *like* | **coudre** |
| recourir | *like* | **courir** |
| recouvrir | *like* | **couvrir** |
| récrire | *like* | **écrire** |
| recueillir | *like* | **cueillir** |
| redevenir* | *like* | **tenir** |
| redire | *like* | **dire** |
| réduire | *like* | **conduire** |
| réécrire | *like* | **écrire** |
| réélire | *like* | **lire** |
| refaire | *like* | **faire** |
| rejoindre | *like* | **joindre** |
| relire | *like* | **lire** |
| reluire | *like* | **nuire** |
| remettre | *like* | **mettre** |
| renaître | *like* | **naître** |
| rendormir | *like* | **mentir** |
| renvoyer | *like* | **envoyer** |
| se repaître* | *like* | **paître** |
| reparaître | *like* | **connaître** |
| repartir* | *like* | **mentir** |
| repeindre | *like* | **atteindre** |
| repentir | *like* | **mentir** |

| | | |
|---|---|---|
| reprendre | *like* | **prendre** |
| reproduire | *like* | **conduire** |
| résoudre | **1** je résous, n résolvons    **2** je résolvais    **3** je résolus    **5** je résolve    **7** résolvant    **8** résolu | |
| ressentir | *like* | **mentir** |
| resservir | *like* | **mentir** |
| ressortir | *like* | **mentir** |
| restreindre | *like* | **atteindre** |
| retenir | *like* | **tenir** |
| retransmettre | *like* | **mettre** |
| revenir | *like* | **tenir** |
| revêtir | *like* | **vêtir** |
| revivre | *like* | **vivre** |
| revoir | *like* | **voir** |
| rire | **1** je ris, n rions    **2** je riais    **3** je ris    **5** je rie, n riions    **7** riant    **8** ri | |
| rompre | *regular except* **1** il rompt | |
| rouvrir | *like* | **couvrir** |
| satisfaire | *like* | **faire** |
| savoir | **1** je sais, n savons, il savent    **2** je savais    **3** je sus    **4** je saurai    **5** je sache    **6** sache, sachons, sachez    **7** sachant    **8** su | |
| séduire | *like* | **conduire** |
| sentir | *like* | **mentir** |
| servir | *like* | **mentir** |
| sortir | *like* | **mentir** |
| souffrir | *like* | **couvrir** |
| soumettre | *like* | **mettre** |
| sourire | *like* | **rire** |
| souscrire | *like* | **écrire** |
| soustraire | *like* | **abstraire** |
| soutenir | *like* | **tenir** |
| se souvenir* | *like* | **tenir** |
| subvenir | *like* | **tenir** |
| suffire | **1** je suffis, n suffisons    **2** je suffisais    **3** je suffis    **5** je suffise    **7** suffisant    **8** suffi | |
| suivre | **1** je suis, n suivons    **2** je suivais    **3** je suivis    **5** je suive    **7** suivant    **8** suivi | |
| surprendre | *like* | **prendre** |
| survenir | *like* | **tenir** |

| | | |
|---|---|---|
| survivre | *like* **vivre** | |
| taire | **1** je tais, n taisons  **2** je taisais  **3** je tus  **5** je taise  **7** taisant<br>**8** tu | |
| teindre | *like* **atteindre** | |
| tenir | **1** je tiens, ne tenons, ils tiennent  **2** je tenais<br>**3** je tins, tu tins, il tint, n tînmes, v tîntes, ils tinrent<br>**4** je tiendrai  **5** je tienne  **7** tenant  **8** tenu | |
| traduire | *like* **conduire** | |
| traire | *like* **abstraire** | |
| transcrire | *like* **écrire** | |
| transmettre | *like* **mettre** | |
| transparaître | *like* **connaître** | |
| tressaillir | *like* **défaillir** | |
| vaincre | **1** je vaincs, il vainc, n vainquons  **2** je vainquais  **3** je vainquis<br>**5** je vainque  **7** vainquant  **8** vaincu | |
| valoir | **1** je vaux, il vaut, n valons  **2** je valais  **3** je valus  **4** je vaudrai<br>**5** je vaille  **6** *not used*  **7** valant  **8** valu | |
| venir* | *like* **tenir** | |
| vêtir | **1** je vêts, n vêtons  **2** je vêtais  **5** je vête  **7** vêtant  **8** vêtu | |
| vivre | **1** je vis, n vivons  **2** je vivais  **3** je vécus  **5** je vive  **7** vivant<br>**8** vécu | |
| voir | **1** je vois, n voyons  **2** je voyais  **3** je vis  **4** je verrai<br>**5** je voie, n voyions  **7** voyant  **8** vu | |
| vouloir | **1** je veux, il veut, n voulons, ils veulent  **2** je voulais<br>**3** je voulus  **4** je voudrai  **5** je veuille<br>**6** veuille, veuillons, veuillez  **7** voulant  **8** voulu | |

# I. The Basics

French has two separate sets of words to translate "you", "your", "yours" and "yourself". **Tu**, **te**, **t'**, **ton/ta/tes**, and **le tien** etc. all correspond to the **tu** form of the verb, used when speaking to one person you know well (such as a friend or relative) or to someone younger. **Vous**, **votre/vos**, and **le vôtre** etc. correspond to the **vous** form of the verb and are used when speaking to more than one person, even if you know them well, or when speaking to one person you do not know well. If in doubt as to whether to call someone **tu** or **vous**, it is always safer to use the polite **vous** form. A French person may invite you to use the less formal **tu** form by saying, "Vous pouvez me tutoyer."

| | |
|---|---|
| **good evening** bonsoir | **see you later** à toute à l'heure, à plus tard, or (Fam) à plus, à la prochaine |
| **good morning/afternoon** bonjour | |
| **good night** bonne nuit | **see you on Monday** à lundi |
| **goodbye** au revoir | **see you soon** à bientôt |
| **hello** bonjour | **see you tomorrow** à demain |
| **hi** salut | **thank you** merci |
| **no** non | **yes** oui (*when answering an affirmative question*), si (*when contradicting a negative question*) |
| **no, thank you** non merci | |
| **OK** d'accord | |
| **please** s'il vous/te plaît | **yes, please** oui, s'il vous/te plaît |

## 1) Meeting someone you know

**How are you?**
Comment allez-vous ?

**Very good, thank you. And you?**
Très bien, merci. Et vous(-même) ?

**Hi, how are you doing?**
Salut, ça va ?

**Fine, and you?**
Ça va, et toi ?

**Good evening, how are you?**
Bonsoir, vous allez bien ?

**Not too bad.**
Pas trop mal.

**Not very well, I have the flu.**
Pas très bien, j'ai la grippe.

**How are your parents/children?**
Comment vont vos parents/enfants ?

**They're doing well, thanks.**
Ils vont très bien, merci.

# 2) Introducing yourself and meeting people you don't know

- **Name:**

| | |
|---|---|
| **What's your name?** | **My name is John.** |
| Comment vous appelez-vous ? | Je m'appelle John. |

**Let me introduce you to my brother Steve. And this is my cousin Rachel.**
Je vous présente mon frère Steve. Et voici Rachel, ma cousine.

**Hi, I'm Peter, Anna's colleague.**
Bonjour, je suis Peter, le collègue d'Anna.

**I'm sorry, I've forgotten your name.**
Excusez-moi, je n'ai pas retenu votre prénom.

**Pleased to meet you.**
Enchanté./Ravi de faire votre connaissance.

- **Age:**

| | |
|---|---|
| **How old are you?** | **I'm 12/24/45 years old.** |
| Quel âge avez-vous ? | J'ai douze/vingt-quatre/quarante-cinq ans. |
| **What's your date of birth?** | **I was born in 1967** |
| Quelle est votre date de naissance ? | Je suis né en mille neuf cent soixante-sept |

- **Nationality:**

| | |
|---|---|
| **What country are you from?** | **I'm from the United States.** |
| De quel pays venez-vous ? | Je viens des États-Unis. |
| **What's your nationality?** | **I'm American.** |
| De quelle nationalité êtes-vous ? | Je suis américain. |
| **Where do you live?** | **I live in New York.** |
| Où habitez-vous ? | J'habite à New York. |

**I come from a little rural town in Montana.**
Je viens d'une petite ville de campagne dans le Montana.

- **Occupation:**

| | |
|---|---|
| **What do you do?** | **I'm still in high school.** |
| Que faites-vous dans la vie ? | Je suis encore au lycée. |
| **I'm a student/a teacher/a doctor.** | **I'm retired.** |
| Je suis étudiant/professeur/médecin. | Je suis à la retraite. |

**I work in a bank.**
Je travaille dans une banque.

**I work in the export department of a computer hardware company.**
Je travaille dans le service export d'une entreprise de matériel informatique.

- **Family:**

| | |
|---|---|
| **Do you have any brothers and sisters?** | **I have two brothers and one sister.** |
| Est-ce que tu as des frères et sœurs ? | J'ai deux frères et une sœur. |
| **I'm an only child.** | **I have an older brother.** |
| Je suis fils/fille unique. | J'ai un frère aîné. |
| **I have a younger sister.** | **I have two little sisters.** |
| J'ai une sœur plus jeune que moi. | J'ai deux petites sœurs. |
| **Are you married?** | **I'm single/separated/divorced.** |
| Êtes-vous marié ? | Je suis célibataire/séparé/divorcé. |
| **Do you have any children?** | **I have one son/daughter.** |
| Vous avez des enfants ? | J'ai un fils/une fille. |

## 3) Likes and dislikes

| | |
|---|---|
| **I like skiing/swimming/playing basketball.** | **I'm fond of classical music.** |
| J'aime le ski/la natation/le basket. | J'aime bien la musique classique. |
| **I love movies.** | **I like/love playing chess/pool.** |
| J'adore le cinéma. | J'aime/j'adore jouer aux échecs/au billard. |
| **What's your favorite band/ movie/actor?** | **I prefer reading/shopping.** |
| Quel est ton groupe/film/acteur préféré ? | Je préfère lire/faire les magasins. |
| **I prefer coffee to tea.** | **I prefer football to basketball.** |
| J'aime mieux le café que le thé. | Je préfère le football américain au basket. |
| **Did you enjoy the movie?** | **I really liked it/didn't like it.** |
| Est-ce que le film t'a plu ? | Il m'a beaucoup plu/ne m'a pas plu. |
| **I liked/didn't like the ending.** | **I don't like going to the opera.** |
| J'ai bien aimé/je n'ai pas aimé la fin. | Je n'aime pas aller à l'opéra. |
| **I don't like that at all.** | **I hate cheese.** |
| Je n'aime pas ça du tout. | Je déteste le fromage. |
| **I can't stand this kind of music.** | **This book is (really) awful.** |
| Je ne supporte pas ce genre de musique. | Ce livre est (vraiment) nul. |

## 4) Expressing surprise and interest

**No, you're kidding! Are you sure?**
Non ! C'est pas vrai ! Tu en es sûr ?

**Really?**
Ah bon ?

**You're kidding?**
Tu plaisantes ?

**Are you pulling my leg?**
Tu me fais marcher ?

**What a coincidence/a surprise!**
Quelle coïncidence/surprise !

**Really? I'm a doctor too!**
C'est vrai ? Moi aussi je suis médecin !

**That's strange.**
C'est bizarre/étrange/curieux.

**It's really interesting/fascinating/ amazing.**
C'est vraiment intéressant/ passionnant/étonnant.

## 5) Expressing disappointment

**What a shame!**
Quel dommage !

**It's too bad it's raining.**
C'est dommage qu'il pleuve. (*subjunctive*)

**What a pity he couldn't come!**
Quel dommage qu'il n'ait pas pu venir. (*subjunctive*)

**The concert has been canceled, how disappointing!**
Le concert a été annulé, c'est vraiment dommage !

## 6) Saying thank you and expressing gratitude

**Thank you.**
Merci (bien).

**Thank you very much.**
Merci beaucoup.

**Thank you, that's really nice.**
Je vous remercie, c'est très gentil.

**Thank you, but you shouldn't have!**
Merci, mais vous n'auriez pas dû !

**It's very kind of you.**
C'est très gentil de votre part.

**I'd like that very much.**
Ça me ferait très plaisir.

**Thanks for your help/for helping me.**
Merci pour votre aide/de m'avoir aidé.

• **To which the other person may reply:**

De rien./Il n'y a pas de quoi.
**You're welcome.**

Je vous en prie.
**Please, don't mention it.**

## 7) Apologizing

**Sorry, it was an accident!**
Pardon, je ne l'ai pas fait exprès !

**I'm (really) sorry.**
Je suis (vraiment) désolé.

**I'm sorry I'm late.**
Je suis désolé d'être en retard.

**I'm sorry to bother you, but …**
Je m'excuse de vous déranger, mais …

**I apologize.**
Je suis désolé./Je m'excuse.

**Excuse me.**
Excusez-moi.

**Sorry for interrupting the conversation.**
Désolé d'avoir interrompu la conversation.

**Sorry, it's my fault.**
Désolé, c'est ma faute.

**I'm sorry but it's not my fault.**
Je suis désolé mais ce n'est pas
de ma faute.

**I'm afraid I won't be able to come.**
Je suis désolé mais je ne pourrai pas venir.

**That's very kind of you but unfortunately I'm not free that day.**
C'est très gentil mais malheureusement je ne suis pas libre ce jour-là.

- **To which the other person may reply:**

  Ce n'est rien./Ce n'est pas grave./Cela n'a pas d'importance.
  **It doesn't matter.**

  Ne vous inquiétez pas/tracassez pas pour ça.
  **Don't worry about it.**

# 8) Congratulations and compliments

**Congratulations!**
Félicitations !/Toutes mes félicitations !/Je vous félicite !

**I'm very happy for you!**
Je suis très heureux pour vous !

**I wish you lots of happiness.**
Je vous souhaite beaucoup de
bonheur.

**It was very good/delicious.**
C'était très bon.

**It's great/wonderful/beautiful!**
C'est génial/merveilleux/beau !

**The party was a big success.**
La soirée était très réussie.

**I had a great time.**
Je me suis bien amusé.

# 9) Making suggestions and expressing desires

**Do you want to go?**
Est-ce que tu veux y aller ?

**Would you like to go to the restaurant?**
Ça te plairait d'aller au restaurant ?

**How about going to the museum?**
Et si on allait au musée ?

**How about a pizza?**
Ça te dit une pizza ?

**I think we should meet at seven.**
Je propose qu'on se retrouve à sept heures.

**Let's meet outside the restaurant.**
On se retrouve devant le restaurant ?

| | |
|---|---|
| **I want to go back to the apartment.**<br>Je veux rentrer à l'appartement. | **I don't want to go to the swimming pool.**<br>Je ne veux pas aller à la piscine. |
| **I feel like going to the movies.**<br>J'ai envie d'aller au cinéma. | **I don't feel like watching TV.**<br>Je n'ai pas envie de regarder la télévision. |
| **I wouldn't mind going to the theater.**<br>J'aimerais bien aller/ça me plairait d'aller au théâtre. | **I'd rather stay at home/do something else.**<br>Je préfèrerais rester à la maison/faire autre chose. |
| **I'd like to go to Spain next year.**<br>J'aimerais aller en Espagne l'année prochaine. | **I wish I was on vacation.**<br>Je voudrais être en vacances. |
| **I don't mind.**<br>Ça m'est égal./Peu importe. | **I have no preference.**<br>Je n'ai pas de préférence. |

## 10) Making requests

**Can we have more bread, please?**
Est-ce qu'on peut avoir plus de pain, s'il vous plaît ?

| | |
|---|---|
| **Could I have a glass of water?**<br>Est-ce que je pourrais avoir un verre d'eau ? | **Could you please make a little less noise?**<br>Pourriez-vous faire un peu moins de bruit ? |
| **Can I open the window?**<br>Est-ce que je peux ouvrir la fenêtre ? | **Could I make a phone call?**<br>Est-ce que je pourrais téléphoner ? |
| **Can I borrow …?**<br>Est-ce que je peux emprunter … ? | **Could you lend me …?**<br>Est-ce que vous pourriez me prêter … ? |
| **Do you mind if I smoke?**<br>Ça vous dérange si je fume ? | **Would it be possible to go?**<br>Est-ce qu'il serait possible d'y aller ? |

**Would you be able to give me a ride?**
Est-ce qu'il vous serait possible de m'emmener ?

## 11) Expressing an opinion

| | |
|---|---|
| **What do you think?**<br>Qu'en penses-tu ? | **What's your opinion?**<br>Quel est ton avis ? |

**I think/I don't think that's a very good idea.**
Je crois que c'est/je ne crois pas que ce soit une très bonne idée.

| | |
|---|---|
| **I think we should go.**<br>Je pense qu'on devrait y aller. | **I think she's very pretty.**<br>Je la trouve très jolie. |

**In my opinion, he shouldn't have said that.**
À mon avis, il n'aurait pas dû dire ça.

**I'm sure they'll win.**
Je suis sûr qu'ils vont gagner.

**I've changed my mind.**
J'ai changé d'avis.

**I agree/don't agree with you.**
Je suis/ne suis pas d'accord avec vous.

**I totally agree with him.**
Je suis tout à fait d'accord avec lui.

**I disagree.**
Je ne suis pas d'accord.

**You're (absolutely) right.**
Vous avez (entièrement) raison

**No, not at all/absolutely not.**
Non, pas du tout/absolument pas.

**Of course not!**
Bien sûr que non !

**You're mistaken.**
Tu te trompes.

**You're wrong.**
Tu as tort.

**That's true/not true.**
C'est vrai/ce n'est pas vrai.

**Nonsense!**
N'importe quoi !

---

# 12) Having problems understanding French

**Could you speak more slowly?**
Est-ce que vous pourriez parler plus lentement ?

**Can you repeat that, please?**
Vous pouvez répéter ?

**I don't understand this expression.**
Je ne comprends pas cette expression.

**I understand a little.**
Je comprends un petit peu.

**I don't understand a word of that.**
Je ne comprends rien.

**I didn't understand.**
Je n'ai pas compris.

**I can understand French but I can't speak it.**
J'arrive à comprendre le français mais je ne peux pas le parler.

**I speak hardly any French.**
Je parle à peine français.

**I have trouble understanding/ speaking.**
J'ai du mal à comprendre/parler.

**Do you speak English?**
Est-ce que vous parlez anglais ?

**Pardon?/What?/Eh?**
Pardon ?/Quoi ?/Hein ?

**What's it called?**
Comment on appelle ça ?

**How do you say... in French?**
Comment est-ce qu'on dit ... en français ?

**How do you spell/pronounce it?**
Comment ça s'écrit/se prononce ?

**Could you write it down?**
Est-ce que vous pourriez l'écrire ?

**What does it mean?**
Qu'est-ce que ça veut dire ?

**What's that?**
Qu'est-ce que c'est ?

# II. Vacations in France

## 1) Traveling and using public transportation

- Traveling by plane:

**Where is the Air France check-in desk?**
Où est l'enregistrement des bagages pour Air France ?

**What time does boarding start?**
À quelle heure embarque-t-on ?

**I'd like to confirm my return flight.**
Je voudrais confirmer mon vol de retour.

**I'd like a window seat/an aisle seat.**
Je voudrais une place côté hublot/côté couloir.

**One of my suitcases is missing.**
Il me manque une valise.

**I'd like to report the loss of my luggage/my hand luggage.**
Je voudrais faire une déclaration de perte pour mes bagages/ mon bagage à main.

**The plane was two hours late and I've missed my connection.**
L'avion a eu deux heures de retard et j'ai raté ma correspondance.

- Traveling by train:

**I'd like to reserve a ticket, please.**
Je voudrais réserver un billet, s'il vous plaît.

**What are the reduced fares?**
Quels sont les tarifs réduits ?

**How much is a ticket to …?**
Combien coûte un billet pour … ?

**Are there any tickets left for …?**
Est-ce qu'il vous reste des places pour … ?

**No smoking (section), please.**
(Voiture) non fumeur, s'il vous plaît.

**Do you have a timetable, please?**
Auriez-vous un dépliant avec les horaires ?

**When is the next train to Nantes?**
À quelle heure est le prochain train pour Nantes ?

**Is there an earlier/a later one?**
Il n'y en a pas plus tôt/tard ?

**What platform does the train for … leave from?**
De quel quai part le train pour … ?

**I've missed the last train.**
J'ai raté le dernier train.

- **On the subway or on the RER (= Paris metropolitan and regional rail system):**

**Where can I buy tickets?**
Où est-ce que je peux acheter des billets ?

**A book of ten (tickets), please.**
Un carnet de dix (tickets), s'il vous plaît.

**Can I have a map of the subway?**
Est-ce que je peux avoir un plan du métro ?

**Does this RER stop at Versailles?**
Est-ce que ce RER s'arrête à Versailles ?

**Which line do I take to get to …?**
Quelle ligne dois-je prendre pour aller à … ?

**What time is the last subway train?**
Vers quelle heure passe le dernier métro ?

- **Traveling by bus:**

**Where can I get a bus to …?**
Où est-ce que je peux prendre un bus pour … ?

**Is this the right stop for …?**
C'est bien l'arrêt pour … ?

**Does the bus for Charles de Gaulle airport leave from here?**
C'est bien d'ici que part le car pour l'aéroport Charles de Gaulle/Roissy ?

**Where is the bus station?**
Où se trouve la gare routière ?

- **Renting a car:**

**I'd like to rent a car for a week.**
Je voudrais louer une voiture pour une semaine.

**How much is the deposit?**
À combien s'élève la caution ?

**I'd like to take out comprehensive insurance.**
Je voudrais prendre une assurance tous risques.

**I'd like an automatic/a stickshift.**
Je voudrais une voiture à boîte de vitesse automatique/à boîte de vitesse classique.

- **On the road:**

**Where can I find a gas station/a garage?**
Où est-ce que je peux trouver une station-service/un garage ?

**I have a flat tire. Where can I park?**
J'ai un pneu à plat.
Où puis-je me garer ?

**I've broken down.**
Je suis (tombé) en panne.

**It won't start; the battery's dead.**
Elle ne veut pas démarrer ; la batterie est morte.

**I have a problem with the brakes/the light indicators.**
J'ai un problème avec les freins/les clignotants.

• **Taking a cab:**

**I'd like to reserve a taxi for 8 o'clock.**
Je voudrais un taxi pour huit heures.

**Is this cab for hire?**
Est-ce que ce taxi est libre ?

**How much will it cost to go to the airport?**
Combien ça va me coûter pour aller à l'aéroport ?

**I'd like to go to the train station.**
Je voudrais aller à la gare.

**Could you take me to this address, please?**
Pouvez-vous me conduire/m'emmener à cette adresse, s'il vous plaît ?

**You can drop me off here, thanks.**
Vous pouvez m'arrêter/me déposer/ me laisser ici, merci.

• **Asking for directions:**

**Excuse me, where is …, please?**
Excusez-moi, où est/où se trouve …, s'il vous plaît ?

**I'm looking for …**
Je cherche …

**Could you tell me how to get to …?**
Est-ce que vous pouvez me dire/m'indiquer comment aller à … ?

**Which way is it to …?**
Quelle est la route pour … ?

**Is it far/near?**
C'est loin/près ?

**How do I get to the station?**
Comment fait-on pour se rendre à la gare ?

**Can you show me the way?**
Pouvez-vous m'indiquer le chemin ?

**Could you show me on the map?**
Est-ce que vous pourriez me montrer sur le plan ?

**I'm lost.**
Je suis perdu.

• **Understanding the person you asked for help:**

C'est la deuxième rue à droite/à gauche.
**It's the second street on the right/on the left.**

Prenez la prochaine sortie.
**Take the next exit.**

Continuez tout droit jusqu'au feu.
**Keep going straight on until you get to the (traffic) lights.**

# 2) Renting accommodations

- **Staying in a hotel or a B&B:**

**Do you have any rooms available?**
Est-ce qu'il vous reste des chambres de libres ?

**It's for a couple and two children.**
C'est pour un couple et deux enfants.

**I'd like to reserve a room for tomorrow night, please.**
Je voudrais réserver une chambre pour demain soir, s'il vous plaît.

**I've reserved three single/double rooms over the phone, in the name of ...**
J'ai réservé par téléphone trois chambres pour une personne/deux personnes, au nom de ...

**Would it be possible to stay another night/to add an extra bed?**
Est-ce qu'il serait possible de rester une autre nuit/d'ajouter un lit supplémentaire ?

**Can I see the room?**
Est-ce que je peux voir la chambre ?

**Do you take credit cards?**
Vous acceptez les cartes de crédit ?

**How much is a room with its own bathroom?**
Combien coûte une chambre avec salle de bains ?

**Is breakfast included?**
Est-ce que le petit déjeuner est inclus ?

**The key for room 12, please.**
La clé de la 12, s'il vous plaît.

**We're planning to stay for two nights.**
Nous pensons rester deux nuits.

**Could you wake me up at seven o'clock?**
Pouvez-vous me réveiller à sept heures ?

**The outlet for razors isn't working.**
La prise pour rasoir ne marche pas.

**We don't have towels/toilet paper.**
Nous n'avons pas de serviettes (de toilette)/de papier toilette.

- **Understanding the receptionist:**

Non, je regrette, nous sommes complets.
**No, I'm sorry, we're full.**

Est-ce que vous pouvez remplir cette fiche ?
**Could you fill out this form?**

Les chambres doivent être libérées avant midi.
**Check-out time is noon.**

Le petit déjeuner est servi entre 7h30 et 9h.
**Breakfast is served between 7:30 and 9.**

- **Renting an apartment or a gîte:**

**I'm looking for something to rent close to the center of town.**
Je cherche quelque chose en location près du centre.

**Is it completely furnished?**
Est-ce que c'est entièrement
meublé ?

**Is there a washing machine?**
Est-ce qu'il y a une machine à laver ?

**Where do I pick up/leave the keys?**
Où dois-je prendre/laisser les clés ?

**Where is the electricity meter?**
Où est le compteur électrique ?

**Where do I take the garbage out?**
Où dois-je sortir les poubelles ?

**Are there any spare ...?**
Est-ce qu'il y a des ... de rechange ?

**I'm sorry, I can't find/I've broken the ...**
Je suis désolé, je ne trouve pas/j'ai cassé le/la ...

**There's no hot water.**
Il n'y a pas d'eau chaude.

- Camping:

**Is there a campsite near here?**
Y a-t-il un camping près d'ici ?

**I'd like a space for one tent for two days.**
Je voudrais un emplacement pour une tente pour deux jours.

**We want to rent a camper/ trailer.**
Nous voulons louer une caravane/
un mobil-home.

**Where are the showers?**
Où sont les douches ?

**Is there a swimming pool/a night club/a tennis court on the campsite?**
Est-ce qu'il y a une piscine/une boîte de nuit/un court de tennis dans le camping ?

**How much is it a day/per person/per tent?**
C'est combien par jour/par personne/par tente ?

# 3) Visiting

**I'd like some information on ...**
Je voudrais des renseignements/
informations sur ...

**What is there to see/visit in the area?**
Qu'est-ce qu'il y a à voir/visiter dans la région ?

**Is it open on Sundays?**
Est-ce que c'est ouvert le dimanche ?

**Is it free?**
C'est gratuit ?

**How much does it cost to get in?**
Combien coûte l'entrée ?

**Are there any discounts for young people?**
Est-ce qu'il y a des réductions pour les jeunes ?

**Is this ticket valid for the exhibition too?**
Le ticket est valable aussi pour l'exposition ?

**When is the next guided tour?**
À quelle heure est la prochaine visite guidée ?

**How long does the tour last?**
Combien de temps dure la visite ?

**Are there many hiking paths/ski slopes here?**
Est-ce qu'il y a beaucoup de sentiers de randonnée/de pistes de ski ici ?

---

## 4) Inquiring about the weather

**Do you know what the weather's going to be like this weekend?**
Est-ce que vous savez quel temps il va faire ce week-end ?

**What's the weather forecast for tomorrow?**
Quelle est le temps prévu/la météo pour demain ?

- **Understanding the answer:**

Ils annoncent de la pluie/des orages.
**They've forecast rain/storms.**

Il va faire froid/chaud/une chaleur étouffante.
**It's going to be cold/hot/ stiflingly hot.**

Malheureusement ils prévoient du mauvais temps.
**I'm afraid they're forecasting bad weather.**

On va avoir du soleil, comme aujourd'hui.
**It will be sunny, like today.**

Il va faire 30° C à l'ombre/moins deux.
**It's going to be 86° F in the shade/minus 2.**

Il va pleuvoir/neiger.
**It's going to rain/to snow.**

Normalement il doit faire beau demain.
**The weather should be good tomorrow.**

Il va y avoir du brouillard/du verglas.
**It's going to be foggy/icy.**

Il va y avoir du vent/beaucoup de vent.
**It's going to be windy/very windy.**

Ça va se rafraîchir/se réchauffer.
**It's going to get colder/warmer.**

# III. Going Out

## 1) Going for a drink

**Do you want to go for a drink?**
On va boire/prendre un verre ?

**Let's go for a coffee.**
Allons prendre un café.

**Excuse me, please!** (*to call the waiter*) S'il vous plaît !

**What are you having?**
Qu'est-ce que tu prends ?

**I'll buy you a drink. What would you like?**
Je t'offre un verre. Qu'est-ce que tu veux ?

**It's on me!**
C'est moi qui invite !

**Could I have a beer?**
Je pourrais avoir une bière/une pression ?

**I'd like a glass of dry white wine.**
Je voudrais un verre de vin blanc sec.

**I'll have a Coke⁺ with/without ice, please.**
Je vais prendre un Coca⁺ avec des glaçons/sans glaçons, s'il vous plaît.

**A coffee and a glass of water, please.**
Un café et un verre d'eau, s'il vous plaît.

**Something non-alcoholic.**
Quelque chose de non alcoolisé.

**I'll have the same.**
La même chose pour moi.

**I'll have the same again.**
J'en reprendrai un autre./La même chose.

**To your health!**
À ta santé !/À la tienne !/ Tchin-tchin !

**We can go to a club afterwards.**
EOn peut aller en boîte après.

---

# 2) Going to the restaurant

• **Reserving a table:**

**Hello, I'd like to reserve a table for two for tomorrow night, around 8 o'clock.**
Allô, bonjour, je voudrais réserver une table pour deux pour demain soir, vers huit heures.

**I've reserved a table in the name of …**
J'ai réservé une table au nom de …

**A table for four, please.**
Une table pour quatre, s'il vous plaît.

**You don't have a table available before then?**
Vous n'avez pas de table libre plus tôt ?

• **Understanding the waiter:**

Pour quelle heure ?
**For what time?**

Huit heures trente, ça vous va ?
**Would 8:30 suit you?**

Bonjour, c'est pour manger ?
**Hello, will you be eating?**

Vous êtes combien ?
**For how many people?**

Est-ce que vous avez réservé ? C'est à quel nom ?
**Have you reserved a table? What's the name?**

- **Ordering food:**

  **Could you bring me the menu/the wine list/the dessert menu, please?**
  Pourriez-vous m'apporter la carte/la carte des vins/la carte des desserts, s'il vous plaît ?

  **What do you recommend?**
  Qu'est-ce que vous nous conseillez ?

  **Do you have vegetarian dishes?**
  Est-ce que vous avez des plats végétariens ?

  **What's today's special?**
  Quel est le plat du jour ?

  **I'll take that, then.**
  Je vais prendre ça alors.

  **We'll both have the set menu.**
  On va prendre deux menus.

  **Where is the restroom, please?**
  Où sont les toilettes, s'il vous plaît ?

  **This isn't what I ordered, I asked for …**
  Ce n'est pas ce que j'ai commandé, j'avais demandé …

  **Could we have another jug of water/some more bread, please?**
  Est-ce qu'on peut avoir une autre carafe d'eau/encore du pain ?

- **Understanding the waiter:**

  Vous avez choisi ?
  **Are you ready to order?**

  Et comme boisson ?
  **And what would you like to drink?**

  Désirez-vous un dessert ?
  **Would you like a dessert?**

  Bon appétit !
  **Enjoy your meal!**

- **Commenting on the food:**

  **It's delicious.**
  C'est délicieux.

  **It was really good.**
  C'était très bon.

  **It's very greasy/too spicy.**
  C'est très gras/trop épicé.

  **It doesn't have enough salt.**
  Ce n'est pas assez salé.

- **Asking for the check:**

  **Could I have the check, please?**
  L'addition, s'il vous plaît.

  **I think there's a mistake in the check.**
  Je crois qu'il y a une erreur dans l'addition.

  **Is the tip included?**
  Le service est-il compris ?

  **We're all paying together.**
  Nous réglons tout ensemble.

## 3) Arranging to meet someone

**What are you doing tonight?**
Qu'est-ce que tu fais ce soir ?

**Do you have anything planned?**
Tu as quelque chose de prévu ?

**How about going to the movies?**
Ça te dit d'aller au cinéma ?

**When do you want to meet? And where?**
On se retrouve à quelle heure ? Et où ?

**We can meet in front of the movie theater.**
On peut se retrouver/se donner rendez-vous devant le cinéma.

**I'll meet you later, I need to stop by the hotel first.**
Je vous rejoindrai plus tard, il faut que je passe à l'hôtel d'abord.

## 4) Going to see movies, shows, and concerts

**I'd like three tickets for ...**
Je voudrais trois places pour ...

**Are there any discounts for students?**
Il y a des réductions pour les étudiants ?

**What time does the program/ movie start?**
À quelle heure est la séance/le film ?

**How long is the movie?**
Combien de temps dure le film ?

**Is the movie in the original language?**
Est-ce que le film est en version originale ?

**It's out next week.**
Ça sort la semaine prochaine.

**I'd like to go to a show.**
J'aimerais aller voir un spectacle.

**Do we have to reserve in advance?**
Est-ce qu'il faut réserver à l'avance ?

**Do we have good seats?**
Sommes-nous bien placés ?

**Will we be able to see the stage?**
Est-ce qu'on verra bien la scène ?

**Are there any free/open-air concerts?**
Est-ce qu'il y a des concerts gratuits/ en plein air ?

**What kind of music is it?**
C'est quel genre de musique ?

• **Understanding the clerk in the box office:**

Il n'y a plus de places pour cette séance.
**This showing is sold out.**

C'est complet jusqu'au ...
**It's sold out until ...**

La pièce (de théâtre)/représentation dure une heure et demie, en comptant l'entracte.
**The play/performance lasts for an hour and a half, including the intermission.**

# IV. Stores, Banks, and Post Offices

## 1) Buying food

**Is there a supermarket/market nearby?**
Est-ce qu'il y a un supermarché/marché dans le quartier ?

**Where can I find a grocery store that stays open late?**
Où est-ce que je peux trouver une épicerie qui ouvre tard le soir ?

**I'm looking for the frozen foods/dairy products aisle.**
Je cherche le rayon des surgelés/produits laitiers.

**I'd like five slices of ham/a little piece of that cheese.**
Je voudrais/je vais prendre cinq tranches de jambon/un petit morceau
de ce fromage.

**It's for four people.**
C'est pour quatre personnes.

**A kilo of potatoes, please.**
Un kilo de pommes de terre, s'il vous plaît.

**A little more/less, please.**
Un peu plus/moins, s'il vous plaît.

**Could I taste it?**
C'est possible de goûter ?

**That's everything, thanks.**
Ce sera tout, merci.

**Could I have a (plastic) bag?**
Est-ce que je peux avoir un sac
(plastique) ?

• **Paying:**

**Where can I pay?**
Où est-ce qu'on paye ?

**How much do I owe you?**
Combien je vous dois ?

**Can I pay by Visa˚?**
Est-ce que je peux payer par carte
Visa˚ ?

**I'll pay cash.**
Je vais payer en liquide.

**You've made a mistake with my change.**
Vous vous êtes trompé en me
rendant la monnaie.

**Sorry, I don't have any change.**
Désolé, je n'ai pas de monnaie.

**Could you give me change, please?**
Est-ce vous pouvez me faire de la
monnaie ?

**Could I have a receipt?**
Je peux avoir un reçu ?

- **Understanding the clerk:**

Et avec ceci ?
**Is there anything else?**

Vous réglez comment ?
**How would you like to pay?**

Vous n'avez pas du tout de monnaie ?
**Don't you have any change?**

Vous pouvez composer votre code.
**You can type in your number.**

---

## 2) Buying clothes

**No thanks, I'm only looking.**
Non merci, je regarde, c'est tout.

**I'd like a jacket/a pair of pants/a shirt.**
Je voudrais une veste/un pantalon/
une chemise.

**I'm looking for the men's/
children's department.**
Je cherche le rayon hommes/enfants.

**Where are the dressing rooms?**
Où sont les cabines d'essayage ?

**I'd like to try on the one in the
window.**
Je voudrais essayer celui/celle qui
est en vitrine.

**Can I try it on?**
Je peux l'essayer ?

**I take a size 8 (shoe).**
Je chausse du 39.

**It's too small/large.**
C'est trop petit/grand.

**Do you have it in another color/in red?**
Vous ne l'avez pas dans une autre couleur/en rouge ?

**I need a bigger/smaller size.**
Il me faut la taille au-dessus/
en-dessous.

**The skirt is too short/long.**
La jupe est trop courte/longue.

**Yes, that's fine, I'll take them.**
Oui, ça va, je les prends.

**I'll think about it.**
Je vais réfléchir.

- **Understanding the clerk:**

Bonjour, je peux vous aider ?
**Hello, can I help you?**

Vous cherchez quelque chose ?
**Are you looking for something?**

Vous faites quelle taille ?
**What's your size?**

Il ne nous en reste que en bleu ou en noir.
**We only have it in blue or black.**

Il ne nous en reste plus dans cette taille.
**We don't have any left in this size.**

Ça vous va bien.
**It really suits/fits you.**

Nous pouvons le/la commander/faire des retouches.
**We can order it/do alterations.**

## 3) Buying presents and souvenirs

**I'm looking for a present to take back.**
Je cherche un cadeau à ramener.

**It's for a little four-year-old girl.**
C'est pour une petite fille de quatre ans.

**I'd like something easy to transport.**
Je voudrais quelque chose de facile à transporter.

**Does it keep well?**
Ça se conserve bien ?

**It's a present; can you gift-wrap it for me?**
C'est pour offrir ; vous pouvez me faire un paquet-cadeau ?

## 4) Going to the bank

**Are banks open on Saturdays?**
Les banques sont-elles ouvertes le samedi ?

**I'm looking for an ATM.**
Je cherche un distributeur automatique.

**Where can I change money?**
Où est-ce qu'il y a un bureau de change ?

**I'd like to change $80.**
Je voudrais changer 80 dollars.

**What commission do you charge?**
Qu'est-ce que vous prenez comme commission ?

**Can I have €300 in cash?**
Je peux avoir 300 euros en espèces/en liquide ?

**I'd like to transfer some money.**
Je voudrais faire un virement.

**I'm waiting for a money order.**
J'attends un mandat.

**The ATM has swallowed my card.**
Le distributeur de billets a avalé ma carte.

**I'd like to report the loss of my credit cards.**
Je voudrais signaler la perte de mes cartes de crédit.

## 5) Going to the post office

**Is there a mailbox near here?**
Y a-t-il une boîte aux lettres par ici ?

**Where can I find a post office?**
Où est-ce que je peux trouver un bureau de poste ?

**Is the post office open on Saturdays?**
Est-ce que la poste est ouverte le samedi ?

**What time does the post office close?**
À quelle heure ferme la poste ?

**I'd like five stamps for the United States.**
Je voudrais cinq timbres pour les États-Unis.

**How much is a stamp for Canada?**
Combien coûte un timbre pour le Canada ?

**I'd like to send it by registered mail.**
Je voudrais l'envoyer en recommandé.

**I'd like to send this letter/postcard/package to New York.**
Je voudrais envoyer cette lettre/cette carte postale/ce colis à New York.

**How long will it take to get there?**

Ça va prendre/mettre combien de temps ?

**Where can I buy envelopes?**
Où est-ce que je peux acheter des enveloppes ?

**Is there any mail for me?**
Y a-t-il du courrier pour moi ?

**Did I receive any mail?**
Est-ce que j'ai reçu du courrier ?

# V. Expressions of Time

## 1) The date

| | |
|---|---|
| **Monday** | lundi |
| **Tuesday** | mardi |
| **Wednesday** | mercredi |
| **Thursday** | jeudi |
| **Friday** | vendredi |
| **Saturday** | samedi |
| **Sunday** | dimanche |
| | |
| **January** | janvier |
| **February** | février |
| **March** | mars |
| **April** | avril |
| **May** | mai |
| **June** | juin |
| **July** | juillet |
| **August** | août |
| **September** | septembre |
| **October** | octobre |
| **November** | novembre |
| **December** | décembre |

*i* Note that in French, months and days are masculine and do not have a capital letter. Cardinals (e.g. *deux*, *trois*, etc.) are used for the dates of the month except the first. French write either *mil* or *mille* (a **thousand**) in dates from 1001. *Année*, *journée*, *matinée*, *soirée* (the feminine forms of *an*, *jour*, *matin*, and *soir*) are usually found when duration is implied: *toute la journée*, *dans la matinée*, etc.

**What's today's date?**
On est le combien aujourd'hui ?

**What day is it today?**
On est quel jour aujourd'hui ?

**It's Tuesday, May first.**
On est le mardi premier (1er) mai.

**It's November second/third, 2004.**
On est le deux/trois novembre deux mille quatre.

**Today is July fourteenth.**
C'est le quatorze juillet aujourd'hui.

**Tomorrow is Tuesday.**
Demain c'est mardi.

**I wrote to you on March twenty-second.**
Je vous ai écrit le vingt-deux mars.

**He arrives on Monday.**
Il arrive lundi.

**See you on Monday!**
À lundi !

**I'm arriving on the tenth/on May tenth.**
J'arrive le dix/le dix mai.

**I'm going on vacation two weeks from Monday.**
Je pars en vacances lundi en quinze.

**This store is open on Sunday mornings.**
Ce magasin est ouvert le dimanche matin.

**I was born in 1962/1975/1985.**
Je suis né en mille neuf cent soixante-deux/mille neuf cent soixante-quinze/mille neuf cent quatre-vingt-cinq.

**I've been there before, several years ago. I think it was in 1996.**
Je suis déjà venu il y a plusieurs années. Je crois que c'était en mille neuf cent quatre-vingt-seize.

**I spent a month in France a few years ago.**
J'ai passé un mois en France il y a quelques années.

**I came last year at the same time/in 2002.**
Je suis venu l'année dernière à la même époque/en deux mille deux.

• **Understanding:**

Ça a été construit au milieu du dix-septième (XVII$^e$)/dix-neuvième (XIX$^e$) siècle.
**It was built in the middle of the 17th/19th century.**

Ça sort une fois toutes les deux semaines/deux fois par mois.
**It comes out once every two weeks/twice a month.**

Prenez-le trois fois par jour/heure.
**Take it three times a day/an hour.**

Les gens sortent surtout le week-end, très peu en semaine.
**People go out mainly on the weekend, but very rarely during the week.**

Vous restez jusqu'à quand ?
**How long are you staying?**

Vous repartez dans deux jours ?
**Are you leaving in two days?**

## 2) The time

*i* The 24-hour clock is commonly used in French (e.g. 2:35 p.m. = 14h35 = *deux heures trente-cinq* or *quatorze heures trente-cinq*).

**I'm on time/early/late.**
Je suis à l'heure/en avance/en retard.

**It's very early/late.**
Il est très tôt/tard.

**Excuse me, do you have the time, please?**
Excusez-moi, vous auriez l'heure, s'il vous plaît ?

**What time is it?**
Quelle heure est-il ?

**It's three o'clock exactly.**
Il est trois/quinze heures pile.

**It's almost one o'clock.**
Il est presque une heure/treize heures.

**It's ten after one/ten to one.**
Il est une heure dix/une heure moins dix.

**It's a quarter after one/to one.**
Il est une heure et quart/une heure moins le quart.

**It's one-thirty.**
Il est une heure et demie/une heure trente.

**It's noon/midnight.**
Il est midi/minuit.

**It's eleven-forty.**
Il est midi/minuit moins vingt/onze heures quarante.

**It's twenty after twelve.**
Il est midi/minuit vingt.

**It was eight (o'clock) in the morning/in the evening.**
Il était huit heures du matin/du soir.

**It's two (o'clock) in the afternoon.**
Il est deux heures de l'après-midi.

**I have an appointment at 8 a.m./8 p.m.**
J'ai rendez-vous à huit heures/à vingt heures.

**I arrived around two o'clock.**
Je suis arrivé vers deux/quatorze heures.

**Are you free in the morning? Does 10:30 suit you?**
Êtes-vous libre le matin ? Est-ce que 10h30 vous conviendrait ?

| | |
|---|---|
| **I've been waiting for two hours/ since 3 p.m.**<br>Ça fait deux heures que j'attends./ J'attends depuis trois heures de l'après-midi. | **I waited for twenty minutes.**<br>J'ai attendu vingt minutes. |
| **The train was fifteen minutes late.**<br>Le train a eu quinze minutes de retard. | **I got home an hour ago.**<br>Je suis rentré il y a une heure. |
| **Do you want to meet in half an hour?**<br>On se retrouve dans une demi-heure ? | **I'll be back in a quarter of an hour.**<br>Je serai de retour d'ici un quart d'heure. |

**It lasts for around three quarters of an hour/an hour and a half.**
Ça dure environ trois quarts d'heure/une heure et demie.

**There's a three-hour time difference between … and …**
Il y a trois heures de décalage entre … et …

| | |
|---|---|
| **I don't have time to take a nap in the afternoon.**<br>Je n'ai pas le temps de faire la sieste l'après-midi. | **I'm in a hurry, come on, hurry up!**<br>Je suis pressé, allez, dépêche-toi ! |

# VI. Using the Telephone

| | |
|---|---|
| **answering machine** un répondeur | **phone book** un annuaire |
| **area code** un indicatif | **phone booth** une cabine téléphonique |
| **cell phone** un (téléphone) portable | |
| **charger** un chargeur | **phone card** une carte de téléphone |
| **collect call** un appel en PCV | **phone number** un numéro de téléphone |
| **dial tone** une tonalité | |
| **handset** un combiné | **receiver** un combiné |
| **information** les renseignements | **receptionist** un(e) réceptionniste |
| **international/national/local call** un appel international/national/local | **ringtone** une sonnerie |
| | **telephone** un téléphone |
| **landline** une ligne terrestre/fixe | **text (message)** un (message) SMS |
| **message** un message | **voicemail** une messagerie vocale, un répondeur |
| **network** un réseau | |
| **operator** (*company*) un opérateur, (*person*) un(e) standardiste | **Yellow Pages®** les Pages Jaunes® |
| **payphone** un téléphone public/ à pièces | |

| | |
|---|---|
| **to answer the phone** répondre au téléphone | **to hang up** raccrocher |
| **to be on the phone** être au téléphone | **to phone** téléphoner |
| **to call someone** appeler quelqu'un | **to pick up the phone** décrocher |
| **to call someone back** rappeler quelqu'un | **to put one's phone on silent/vibrate** mettre son portable en mode silencieux/vibreur |
| **to dial a number** composer un numéro | **to put someone on hold** mettre quelqu'un en attente |
| **to dial a wrong number** se tromper de numéro | **to text someone** envoyer un SMS/un message à quelqu'un |
| **to give someone a call** passer un coup de téléphone/de fil à quelqu'un | **to turn one's cell phone on/off** allumer/éteindre son portable |

When giving their telephone numbers, French people say them two by two: 01 45 67 44 32: *zéro un, quarante-cinq, soixante-sept, quarante-quatre, trente-deux*. The first two numbers will be one of the five main regional codes existing in France: 01= Paris area, 02 = North West, 03 = North East, 04 = South East, 05 =South West. A number starting with 06 is a cell phone number.
When calling from abroad, you need to dial the country code and then delete the 0 of the regional code: 0033 1 45 67 44 32.

## 1) Calling from a pay phone

**Where can I buy a phone card?**
Où est-ce que je peux acheter une carte de téléphone ?

**Do you know if there's a card-/coin-operated pay phone near here?**
Est-ce que vous savez s'il y a une cabine téléphonique à pièces/à carte près d'ici ?

**Could you give me change of … to make a phone call?**
Pourriez-vous me faire la monnaie de …, c'est pour téléphoner ?

**I'd like to make a collect call.**
Je voudrais appeler en PCV.

## 2) Asking for information from the operator or switchboard

**Could you put me through to information, please?**
Est-ce que vous pouvez me passer les renseignements, s'il vous plaît ?

**I'm trying to get a number in Marseilles.**
J'essaie d'obtenir un numéro à Marseille.

**Could you give me the number for …, please?**
Vous pouvez me donner le numéro de …, s'il vous plaît ?

| What's the country code for Morocco? | How do I get an outside line? |
|---|---|
| Quel est l'indicatif pour le Maroc ? | Comment fait-on pour appeler à l'extérieur ? |

## 3) Answering the telephone

- **When the phone is ringing:**

| **I'll get it!** | **Can you get it, please?** |
|---|---|
| J'y vais !/Je réponds ! | Tu peux répondre, s'il te plaît ? |

- **When you pick up the phone:**

| **Hello?** | **Hello, Helen Smith speaking.** |
|---|---|
| Allô ? | Allô, Helen Smith à l'appareil. |

## 4) Confirming you are the person to whom the caller wishes to speak

| **Yes, it's me.** | **This is he/she.** |
|---|---|
| Oui, c'est moi. | C'est lui-même/elle-même. |
| **How can I help you?** | **What can I do for you?** |
| En quoi puis-je vous être utile ? | Que puis-je faire pour vous ? |

## 5) Asking to speak to someone

**Hi Marie. This is Sharon here. Is Pierre there?**
Bonjour Marie. C'est Sharon (à l'appareil). Est-ce que Pierre est là ?

**Can/could I speak to Stéphane, please? It's David.**
Est-ce que je peux/pourrais parler à Stéphane, s'il vous plaît ? C'est de la part de David.

- **To which the other person may reply:**

Un instant, s'il vous plaît. Je vais le chercher.
**Just a moment, please. I'll get him for you.**

Ne quittez pas, je vous le passe.
**Hold on, I'll just hand you over to him.**

Je suis désolé mais il n'est pas là pour le moment.
**I'm sorry, but he's not in right now.**

Il est sorti. Il sera de retour dans une demi-heure.
**He's gone out. He'll be back in half an hour.**

# 6) Asking to speak to someone in a company or institution

**Hello, I'd like to speak to Mr. Dupont, this is Tim Clark.**
Allô, bonjour, je voudrais parler à Monsieur Dupont, de la part de Tim Clark.

**Could you put me through to the sales manager, please?**
Pouvez-vous me passer le responsable du service des ventes, s'il vous plaît ?

**Could you put me through to extension 321, please?**
Pouvez-vous me passer le poste 321, s'il vous plaît ? (*pronounced trois cent vingt-et-un*)

- **Phrases used by a receptionist or secretary taking a call:**

Déménagements Leclerc, bonjour.
Déménagements Leclerc, je vous écoute.
**Good morning/afternoon, Déménagements Leclerc.**

| | |
|---|---|
| C'est de la part de qui ?/Qui est à l'appareil ? **Who's calling?** | Qui dois-je annoncer ? **Who should I say is calling?** |
| Ça ne répond pas. **There's no answer.** | C'est occupé./Ça sonne occupé. **The line's busy.** |
| Ne quittez pas, je vous le passe. **One moment, I'll put you through.** | Je regrette, il est en réunion/en vacances. **I'm sorry, he's in a meeting/on vacation.** |
| Il est en communication, voulez-vous patienter ? **He's on another call, would you like to hold?** | Je lui dirai que vous avez appelé. **I'll tell him you called.** |
| Voulez-vous que je lui transmette un message ? **Would you like me to give him a message?** | Voulez-vous laisser un message ? **Would you like to leave a message?** |

# 7) Leaving a message for someone

**Just tell him I called, thanks. I'll try again later.**
Dites-lui simplement que j'ai appelé, merci. Je réessaierai plus tard.

**Could you tell her that I called? Thank you.**
Vous pouvez lui dire que j'ai appelé ? Je vous remercie.

**Could you tell him I'll call back later? Do you know when I'll be able to reach him/when he'll be back?**
Vous pouvez lui dire que je rappellerai plus tard ? Est-ce que vous savez quand je pourrai le joindre/quand il sera de retour ?

**Could you ask her to call me back today? She can reach me at …**
Pouvez-vous lui demander de me rappeler dans la journée ? Elle peut me joindre au …

**Do you have a pen and paper?**
Vous avez de quoi écrire ?

**My  name is … and my phone number is …**
Mon nom est … et mon numéro est le …

# 8) Stating the reason for one's call

**Hi Georges, it's James. I just wanted to know if you had any plans for this evening.**
Salut, Georges, c'est James. Je voulais juste savoir si tu avais quelque chose de prévu ce soir.

**Hello, Lucie? It's me, Peter. Are you free to go to the movies on Saturday?**
Allô, Lucie ? C'est moi, Peter. Est-ce que tu es libre pour aller au ciné samedi ?

**Hello, is this Mr. Moreau? … Hi. This is Frank Simpson. I'm calling about the ad in …**
Allô, est-ce que je suis bien chez Monsieur Moreau ? … Bonjour. Je m'appelle/je suis Frank Simpson. Je vous appelle au sujet de l'annonce qui est parue dans …

**I'm calling to inform you that I still haven't received my itemized phone bill.**
J'appelle pour vous signaler que je n'ai toujours pas reçu ma facture (de téléphone) détaillée.

**I'm just calling to let you know I'll be a bit late.**
J'appelle pour vous dire que je serai un peu en retard.

**I'd like to make an appointment for next Monday.**
J'aurais voulu prendre un rendez-vous pour lundi prochain.

# 9) Understanding recorded messages

• **On someone's answering machine:**

Bonjour. Vous êtes bien chez Laurent et Stéphanie. Nous ne sommes pas là pour le moment mais vous pouvez laisser un message et nous vous rappellerons dès notre retour.
**Hello, you've reached Laurent and Stéphanie. We're not available right now, but please leave us a message and we'll return your call as soon as we can.**

Veuillez laisser un message après le bip.
**Please leave a message after the tone.**

- **When you are asked to follow instructions:**

  Appuyez sur la touche dièse/étoile.
  **Press the hash/star key.**

- **If you are put through to an answering machine, the usual recorded message while waiting is:**

  Nous vous demandons de bien vouloir patienter quelques instants. Nous allons donner suite à votre appel.
  **Please hold while we connect your call.**

- **If you have to leave a message, you will hear the following standard set of sentences:**

  Vous êtes bien en communication avec … Nous ne pouvons répondre à votre appel. Veuillez nous laisser votre nom et numéro de téléphone après le signal sonore et nous vous rappellerons dès que possible. Merci.
  **You've reached … We're unable to take your call right now. Please leave your name and number after the beep and we'll get back to you as soon as we can. Thank you.**

- **If you have dialed a number that doesn't exist, you will hear:**

  Le numéro que vous avez demandé n'est pas attribué.
  **The number you have dialed has not been recognized.**

## 10) Leaving a message on an answering machine

**Hi, it's Kate. I see you're not at home. Oh well … I'll call back later. Bye!**
Salut, c'est Kate. Je vois que tu n'es pas chez toi. Bon, eh bien … je rappellerai plus tard. Salut !

**Hello, it's me again. It's just to tell you there are some traffic delays, but I see you've already left. Too bad.**
Bonjour, c'est encore moi. C'est juste pour te dire qu'il y a des embouteillages sur la route. Mais je vois que tu es déjà parti. Tant pis.

**Hello, it's David McLean here. Can you contact me on my cell phone whenever you get this message? The number's 07712 745 792. Thank you.**
Bonjour, c'est David McLean. Est-ce que vous pouvez me contacter sur mon portable quand vous aurez ce message ? C'est le 07712 745 792. Merci.

**Hello, this is Kim Thomas from Double Page bookstore. I'm calling to tell you that the book you ordered has arrived.**
Bonjour, Kim Thomas de la librairie Double Page. J'appelle pour vous dire que le livre que vous avez commandé est arrivé.

# 11) Ending the conversation

**Thank you, goodbye.**
Je vous remercie, au revoir.

**Thanks a lot. Bye.**
Merci bien. Salut.

**Thanks for your help, bye.**
Merci pour votre aide, au revoir.

**Thank you for calling.**
Merci d'avoir appelé.

**Sorry, but I've got to hang up. My mom needs the phone. Can I call you back later?**
Désolé mais je dois raccrocher. Ma mère a besoin du téléphone. Je peux te rappeler plus tard ?

**I've got to go.**
Il faut que j'y aille.

**We'll talk soon, OK?**
On s'appelle bientôt ?

**We'll talk again, OK?**
On se rappelle, ok ?

# 12) Cell phones

**Do you have a cell phone number?**
Vous avez un numéro de portable ?

**I've run out of minutes.**
Je n'ai plus d'argent sur mon portable.

**The signal's very bad.**
Il y a une très mauvaise réception.

**I can't get any reception here.**
Je ne capte pas ici.

**Do you know where I can get a new phone card for my cell phone?**
Vous savez où je peux acheter une carte pour mon téléphone portable ?

**Can I plug my cell phone in here to recharge it? The battery's dead.**
Est-ce que je peux brancher mon portable ici pour le recharger ? Je n'ai plus de batterie.

**Is there an outlet so that I can recharge my cell phone?**
Est-ce qu'il y a une prise pour que je recharge mon portable ?

**Did you get my text message?**
Tu as eu mon message/mon SMS ?

**I forgot my charger.**
J'ai oublié mon chargeur.

# 13) Problems

**I'm sorry, I must have dialed the wrong number.**
Excusez-moi, j'ai dû faire un faux numéro.

**Sorry to have bothered you.**
Je suis désolé de vous avoir dérangé.

**You've dialed the wrong number.**
Vous avez fait un faux numéro.

**You've got the wrong number.**
Vous vous êtes trompé de numéro.

**Could you say that again more slowly?**
Est-ce que vous pouvez répéter plus lentement ?

**I can barely hear you. Could you speak up?**
Je vous entends très mal. Est-ce que vous pouvez parler plus fort ?

**I'm sorry, I didn't quite understand. Could you spell it?**
Je suis désolé, je n'ai pas très bien compris. Est-ce que vous pouvez l'épeler ?

| **Hello, can you hear me?** | **We got cut off.** |
|---|---|
| Allô, vous m'entendez ? | On a été coupés. |

**Hold on, we're going to be cut off, I need to put some more change in.**
Attends, ça va couper, il faut que je rajoute de la monnaie.

| **I can't reach him.** | **I keep getting a busy signal.** |
|---|---|
| Je n'arrive pas à le joindre. | C'est toujours occupé. |

**I don't have many minutes left on my card.**
Il ne me reste plus beaucoup d'unités sur ma carte.

# ▪ articles

## Use of the definite article

**le**, **la**, **les** *(the)*

- for a particular person or thing
  **Les** amis dont je t'ai parlés.

- for a noun used in a general sense
  **Le** sucre est mauvais pour les dents.

- for geographical names, seasons, languages, subjects and parts of the body
  **la** France, **l'**automne, **le** français, **les** maths, ouvrez **la** bouche

- for names following an adjective and titles
  **le** petit Pierre, **le** docteur Coste

- for days of the week (to describe regular occurrences)
  Que fais-tu **le** samedi ?

- for prices and quantities
  C'est combien **le** kilo/**la** douzaine/**la** bouteille ?

> **!** Note that **le** and **la** become **l'** before a word beginning with a vowel or silent **h**: **l'**enfant, **l'**histoire

## Use of the indefinite article

**un**, **une**, **des** *(a/an/one/some/any)*

- for a general person or thing
  **un** homme, **une** femme, **des** livres

- for abstract nouns followed by an adjective
  avec **une** patience remarquable

> **!** In negative sentences, **de** or **d'** is used instead of **un**, **une**, **des**:
> Je n'ai pas **d'**amis.
> Je n'ai plus **de** voiture.

## When to omit the article

- for professions
  Elle est ⊘ médecin.

> **!** Note that the article *is* used after **c'est**, **c'était** etc:
> C'est **un** acteur célèbre.

- after **quel** in exclamations
  Quelle ⊘ surprise !

- for abstract nouns with no adjective
  Avec ⊘ plaisir.

## Use of the partitive article
**du**, **de la**, **des** *(some/any)*

- to mean *some/any*
  As-tu **du** vin ? *Do you have any wine?*
  Il a **de la** glace. *He's got some ice-cream.*

- the partitive article is not always translated in English
  Tu veux **de la** soupe ? *Do you want (any) soup?*

> Note that the partitive article is replaced by **de** or **d'**:
> - after negative expressions:
>   Il n'y a plus **de** café.
> - after expressions of quantity:
>   Il gagne assez **d'**argent.
> - after **avoir besoin de**:
>   Tu as besoin **de** timbres ?
> - when an adjective precedes a plural noun:
>   **de** petites villes

---

### *partitive or definite article?*
When no article is used in English, it is not always clear which article to use in French. If *some/any* can be inserted before the English noun, use the partitive article:
Tu as acheté **du** poisson ?
*Did you buy fish? (= any fish)*
J'aime **le** poisson.
*I like fish. (= fish in general)*

---

# ■ nouns

## Typical masculine endings
There are some typical masculine noun endings for words of more than one syllable:
le chauff**age**, le trav**ail**, le bat**eau**, le nav**et**, le commun**isme**, le coll**ège**, le probl**ème**, le vêt**ement**

## Typical feminine endings
la tend**ance**, la d**anse**, la nat**ion**, la cuis**ine**, la car**otte**, la nourrit**ure**

## Feminine of nouns

There is often a separate word for the feminine form of a noun:

frère → **sœur**, fils → **fille**

When there is no separate word, most feminine nouns are formed by adding **-e** to the masculine noun: **ami → amie**. In certain cases this alters the masculine form:

| masculine ending | feminine ending | examples |
|---|---|---|
| -t | -te | chat → chat**te** |
| -n | -ne | chien → chien**ne** |
| -er | -ère | ouvrier → ouv**rière** |
| -eur | -euse/-eresse | vendeur → vend**euse** <br> pécheur → péch**eresse** |
| -teur | -teuse/-trice | chanteur → chant**euse** <br> lecteur → lec**trice** |
| -f | -ve | veuf → veu**ve** |
| -x | -se | époux → épou**se** |
| -eau | -elle | jumeau → jum**elle** |

> *i* Note that there are also several irregular feminine forms, for example:
> hôte → **hôtesse**, Grec → **Grecque**, héros → **héroïne**

## Plural of nouns

As in English, the plural form of a noun is usually formed by adding **-s**: chanson → chanson**s**. Note that the final **-s** is not pronounced.

| exceptions | examples |
|---|---|
| **Plural form -x** <br> nouns ending in –au, -eau, eu <br> some nouns ending in -ou | tuyau → tuyau**x** <br> bateau → bateau**x** <br> neveu → neveu**x** <br> genou → genou**x** <br> (*but:* landaus, pneus, clous…) |
| **Plural form -aux** <br> nouns ending in -al <br> nouns ending in -ail | journal → journ**aux** <br> travail → trav**aux** <br> (*but:* festivals, détails…) |
| **Plural form unchanged** <br> nouns ending is –s, -z, -x | radis <br> nez <br> prix |
| **Some irregular plurals** | œil → **yeux** <br> ciel → **cieux** |

> *!* Note that family names are invariable:
> J'ai recontré **les Leblanc**.

# ■ adjectives

## Noun + adjective

In French, adjectives agree with nouns in number and gender and usually go after the noun:

J'aime le vin **blanc**.

Ce sont des rues **étroites**.

## Adjective + noun

A few very common adjectives always go before the noun:

bon/bonne → un **bon** repas

beau/belle → une **belle** maison

mauvais(e) → du **mauvais** temps

grand(e) → un **grand** bâtiment

gros/grosse → une **grosse** somme

petit(e) → un **petit** garçon

## Feminine of adjectives

The feminine of adjectives is usually formed by adding **-e**: froid → froide. There are some common patterns of exceptions:

| masculine ending | feminine ending | examples |
|---|---|---|
| -c | -che | blanc → blan**che** |
| -x | -se | heureux → heureu**se** |
| -er | -ère | léger → lég**ère** |
| -eau | -elle | beau → b**elle** |
| -ou | -olle | fou → f**olle** |

## Plural of adjectives

The plural of adjectives is formed by adding **-s** in the same way as for nouns: **des gants verts**

# ■ comparison

## Regular comparatives and superlatives

| comparative | more … (than); …er (than) | plus … (que)<br>plus long (que) |
|---|---|---|
| | less … (than); not as … (as) | moins … (que)<br>moins récent (que) |
| | as … (as) | aussi … (que)<br>aussi important (que) |
| superlative | the most …; the …est | le/la/les plus …<br>le plus grand |
| | the least … | le/la/les moins …<br>la moins difficile |

## Irregular comparatives and superlatives

bon → **meilleur, le meilleur**
mauvais → **pire, le pire** → **plus mauvais, le plus mauvais**
petit → **moindre, le moindre** → **plus petit, le plus petit**

> *i* **Pire** and **le pire** are used to mean *the worst*, while **plus mauvais** and **le plus mauvais** indicate comparison:
> C'est **la pire** chose qui pouvait lui arriver.
> *It's the worst thing that could happen to him.*
> Ma note est **plus mauvaise** que la tienne.
> *My mark is worse than yours.*
>
> **Moindre** and **le moindre** are used to mean 'less in importance', whereas **plus petit** and **le plus petit** mean 'less in size':
> Le **moindre** de mes soucis.
> *The least of my worries.*
> Elle est **plus petite** que moi.
> *She is smaller than me.*

# ■ personal pronouns

## Subject pronouns

**je** *(I)*                                    **nous** *(we)*
**tu** *(you)*                                  **vous** *(you)*
**il** *(he, it)*, **elle** *(she, it)*        **ils/elles** *(they)*

> *i* **Tu** is used informally when speaking to one person only. **Vous** can be singular or plural; it is used when speaking to more than one person (plural) or to one person you do not know well (formal singular).

> *!* **Il/ils** and **elle/elles** may refer to people or things and must be the same gender as the noun they replace:
> Ton stylo ? **Il** est là.
> Ta montre ? **Elle** est là.

## Object pronouns

Object pronouns replace a noun which directly follows the verb.

| | |
|---|---|
| **me** *(I)* | **nous** *(us)* |
| **te** *(you)* | **vous** *(you)* |
| **le** *(him, it)*, **la** *(her, it)* | **les** *(them)* |

Je **les** ai trouvés. *I found them.*

> *!* When the verb takes a preposition, the 3rd person object pronouns become **lui** *(him, her, it)* and **leur** *(them)*.

## Order of object pronouns

· before the verb

**me te nous vous**
**la la les**
**lui leur**

  Il **me l'**a donné.
  Ne **la leur** vends pas.

· after the verb

**le la les**
**moi toi nous vous**
**lui leur**

  Apporte-**les-moi** !
  Rends-**la-leur** !

> *!* **Moi** and **toi** are used instead of **me** and **te** with the imperative.

# ■ *en* and *y*

## The pronoun *en*

En replaces **de** + noun and can be used:

· to mean *of it/them, with it/them, about it/them, from it/them, out of it/them*
  Tu es sûr **du prix** ? – J'**en** suis sûr.
  *Are you sure of the price? – I'm sure of it.*

- with verbal constructions

**Il a envie de ce livre. Il en a envie.**
*He wants this book. He wants it.*

**Tu as besoin de ces papiers ? Tu en as besoin ?**
*Do you need these papers? Do you need them?*

- to replace the partitive article (**du**, **de la**, **des**)

**Tu veux du café ? – Non, je n'en veux pas.**
*Do you want (any) coffee? – No, I don't want any.*

- to replace expressions of quantity not followed by a noun

**Vous avez combien de frères ? – J'en ai deux.**
*How many brothers do you have? – I've got two.*

## The pronoun y

The pronoun **y** replaces **à** + noun but never when referring to a person. It can be used:

- to replace the indirect object of a verb

**Tu joues au tennis ? – Non j'y joue rarement.**
*Do you play tennis? – No, I seldom play (it).*

> *i* Since the preposition **à** can be translated many different ways in English, **y** may also have a variety of meanings:
> **J'y pense souvent.** *I often think about it.*
> **Il s'y intéresse.** *He's interested in it.*

- to mean *there*

**Il est allé en Grèce. Il y est allé.**
*He went to Greece. He went there.*

> *!* Note that **y** must always be used with the verb **aller** when the place is not mentioned. It is often not translated in English:
> **Comment vas-tu à l'école? – J'y vais en bus.**
> *How do you get to school? – I go (there) by bus.*

- to replace **en**, **dans**, **sur** + noun to mean *there, in it/them, on it/them*

**Sur la table ? – Non je ne l'y vois pas.**
*On the table? – No , I don't see it there.*

# ■ possessives

## Possessive adjectives

Possessive adjectives agree with the noun that follows, unlike in English where they agree with the possessor.

**mon**, **ma**, **mes** *(my)*
**ton**, **ta**, **tes** *(your)*
**son**, **sa**, **ses** *(his, her, its)*

**notre**, **nos** (our)
**votre**, **vos** (your)
**leur**, **leurs** (their)

> Il a perdu **son** agenda. *He's lost his diary.*
> **Notre** rue est assez calme. *Our street is fairly quiet.*

## Possessive pronouns

Possessive pronouns replace a possessive adjective + noun.

**le mien/la mienne**, **les miens/les miennes** (mine)
**le tien/la tienne**, **les tiens/les tiennes** (yours)
**le sien/la sienne**, **les siens/les siennes** (his, hers, its)
**le/la nôtre**, **les nôtres** (ours)
**le/la vôtre**, **les vôtres** (yours)
**le/la leur**, **les leurs** (theirs)

> J'aime bien ton appartement, mais je préfère **le mien**.
> *I like your flat, but I prefer mine.*

# ■ relative pronouns

### *Qui*

**Qui** (that, who, which) replaces the subject in a relative clause:

> Ce n'est pas lui **qui** a menti. *He's not the one who lied.*

### *Que*

**Que** (that, who, which) replaces the object in a relative clause:

> La fille **que** j'aime ne m'aime pas. *The girl (that) I love doesn't love me.*

### *Lequel*

**lequel**, **laquelle**, **lesquels**, **lesquelles** (which)

The relative pronoun **lequel** combines with the prepositions **à** and **de** as follows:

| | |
|---|---|
| à + lequel → **auquel** | de + lequel → **duquel** |
| à + lesquels → **auxquels** | de + lesquels → **desquels** |
| à + lesquelles → **auxquelles** | de + lesquelles → **desquelles** |

> Quels sont les sports **auxquels** tu t'intéresses ?
> *What sports are you interested in?*
> Voilà le village auprès **duquel** on campait.
> *Here's the village which we camped near.*

> ### *qui or lequel?*
> **Qui** is generally used after a preposition when referring to people:
> **La fille avec qui** j'ai dansé.
> *The girl (who) I danced with.*
> **Lequel** is often used after a preposition when referring to objects, or when referring to people after the prepositions **entre** and **parmi**:
> **L'immeuble dans lequel** j'habite est très moderne.
> *The building (which) I live in is very modern.*
> Il y avait deux candidates, entre **lesquels** nous avons dû choisir.
> *There were two candidates, between whom we had to choose.*

## Dont

- = *of which/of whom*
Un métier **dont** il est fier.  *A job (which) he is proud of.*

> *i* Note that **dont** is not always translated in English:
> **Voilà les choses dont** j'ai besoin.
> *Here are the things ⊘ I need.*

- = *whose*
Mon copain, **dont** le père a eu un accident.
*My friend, whose father had an accident.*

- **dont** replaces **que** when the verb takes the preposition **de**
C'est ce **dont** j'avais peur. (avoir peur de)
*That's what I was afraid of.*

## Other relative pronouns

- **où** = *where* or *when*
L'hôtel **où** on a logé était très confortable.
*The hotel where we stayed was very comfortable.*
Le jour **où** j'ai eu mon permis de conduire.
*The day (when) I got my driving licence.*

- **ce** + **qui/que** = *what* (when there is no specific noun)
Fais **ce que** tu veux. *Do what you want.*
**Ce qui** s'est passé ne vous regarde pas.  *What happened is none of your business.*

- **quoi** replaces **que** when the verb takes a preposition:
C'est **ce à quoi** je pensais. *That's what I was thinking about.*
Voici **ce sur quoi** il devra s'éxpliquer. *This is what he'll have to explain.*

# ■ reflexive verbs

Reflexive verbs reflect the action back onto the subject and always have a reflexive pronoun. Compare:

**Je lave la voiture.**     **Je me lave.**
*I'm washing the car.*     *I'm washing (myself).*

## Reflexive pronouns

| | |
|---|---|
| **me** *(myself)* | **nous** *(ourselves)* |
| **te** *(yourself)* | **vous** *(yourselves)* |
| **se** *(himself, herself, itself)* | **se** *(themselves)* |

- French reflexive pronouns are not always translated in English:
  **Je me demande si ...** *I wonder if ...*

- reflexive pronouns can be translated by *each other* or *one another*:
  **Nous nous détestons.** *We hate each other.*

- **se** can mean *ourselves* or *each other* when used with the pronoun **on**:
  **On s'est perdu.** *We got lost.*
  **On se connaît.** *We know each other.*

## Use

- reflexive verbs are conjugated with the auxiliary verb **être** in compound tenses (see 410):
  **Il s'est trompé.** *He made a mistake.*

- the past participle agrees with the reflexive pronoun when it is a direct object
  **Elle s'est endormie.** *She fell asleep.*
  **Ils se sont excusés.** *They apologized.*

> **!** The past participle is unchanged when:
>
> - the reflexive pronoun is an indirect object:
>   **Elle se l'est acheté.** *She bought it for herself.*
>
> - the reflexive verb has a direct object that is not the reflexive pronoun:
>   **Vous vous êtes lavé les mains, les filles ?**
>   *Did you wash your hands, girls?*

# ■ present tense

## Regular verbs in the present tense

Regular verbs in the present tense are conjugated by taking the stem of the infinitive + the present tense endings:

| -ER verbs | -IR verbs | -RE verbs |
|---|---|---|
| parler | finir | attendre |
| je parl-**e** | je fin-**is** | j'attend-**s** |
| tu parl-**es** | tu fin-**is** | tu attend-**s** |
| il/elle parl-**e** | il/elle fin-**it** | il/elle attend |
| nous parl-**ons** | nous fin-**issons** | nous attend-**ons** |
| vous parl-**ez** | vous fin-**issez** | vous attend-**ez** |
| ils/elles parl-**ent** | ils/elles fin-**issent** | ils/elles attend-**ent** |

## Irregular verbs in the present tense

For irregular verbs in the present tense see the verb tables on p. 400.

## Use of the present tense

- for general truths
  **La vie est dure.** *Life is hard.*
- for regular actions
  **Il travaille dans un bureau.** *He works in an office.*
- for continuous actions
  **Ne le dérangez pas, il travaille.** *Don't disturb him, he's working.*

> ! Note that there is no present continuous tense in French:
> **Je mange.** = *I eat/I am eating.*
> A continuous action can also be expressed by **être en train de**:
> **Je suis en train de cuisiner.** *I'm (busy) cooking.*

- to express the immediate future
  **Je pars demain.** *I'm leaving tomorrow.*

# ■ future tense

## Regular verbs in the future tense

Regular verbs in the future tense are conjugated with the infinitive + the future endings:
**-ai, -as, -a, -ons, -ez, -ont**

> ! For -**re** verbs, the final -**e** is omitted.

## Irregular verbs in the future tense

Some verbs have an irregular stem but still take the future endings, for example:
**être → je serai**, tu **seras**, il/elle **sera**, nous **serons**, vous **serez**, ils/elles **seront**
**avoir → j'aurai**, tu **auras**, il/elle **aura**, nous **aurons**, vous **aurez**, ils/elles **auront**
For other irregular verbs in the future tense see the verb tables on p. 400.

## Use of the future tense

The future tense is used to describe what someone will do/be doing or something that will happen/be happening

Je **ferai** la vaisselle demain. *I'll do the dishes tomorrow.*

Il **arrivera** tard. *He'll be arriving late.*

> *!* The verb **aller** + infinitive can be used to express the immediate future:
> Il **va déménager** la semaine prochaine. *He's moving house next week.*

# ■ imperfect tense

## Regular verbs in the imperfect tense

Regular verbs are conjugated in the imperfect tense by taking the stem of the first person plural present tense (**nous** minus the ending -**ons**) + the imperfect endings:
-**ais**, -**ais**, -**ait**, -**ions**, -**iez**, -**aient**

## Irregular verbs in the imperfect tense

Only one verb is irregular in the imperfect tense:

**être → j'étais**, tu **étais**, il/elle **était**, nous **étions**, vous **étiez**, ils/elles **étaient**

## Use of the imperfect tense

- to describe continuous actions in the past
  Il **prenait** un bain quand le téléphone a sonné.
  *He was having a bath when the phone rang.*

- to describe regular actions in the past
  Quand il était jeune, il **voyageait** beaucoup.
  *When he was younger he used to travel a lot.*

- for description in the past
  C'**était** formidable ! *It was great!*

# ■ present perfect tense

The present perfect tense is formed with an auxiliary verb (**avoir** or **être**) + a past participle.

## Auxiliary verbs

- **avoir** is the auxiliary for most verbs:
  J'**ai marqué** un but. *I scored a goal.*

- **être** is the auxiliary for verbs of motion and change of state:

**aller, arriver, descendre, entrer, monter, mourir, naître, partir, passer, rester, retourner, sortir, tomber, venir**

When a verb forms the present perfect tense with **être**, the past participle agrees with the subject of the verb:

Les élèves sont **sortis** à midi. *The pupils came out at midday.*

Elle n'est pas encore **descendue**.  *She hasn't come down yet*

> **!** Note that **être** takes the auxiliary verb **avoir** in the present perfect tense.

## Past participle of regular verbs

The past participle of regular verbs is formed by taking the stem of the infinitive + the following endings:

| -ER verbs | -IR verbs | -RE verbs |
|---|---|---|
| parl(er) + **é** | fin(ir) + **i** | attend(re) + **u** |
| parl**é** | fin**i** | attend**u** |

## Past participle of irregular verbs

Some of the most common verbs have an irregular past participle, for example:

**avoir** → **eu**     **devoir** → **dû**     **être** → **été**

For other irregular past participles see the verb tables on p. 400.

## Use of the present perfect tense

The present perfect tense is used for single completed actions in the past:

J'**ai lu** toute la journée.  *I've been reading all day.*

Tu **as** déjà **mangé** ?  *Have you eaten?*

# ■ pluperfect tense

The pluperfect tense is formed by taking the imperfect of the auxiliary verb (**avoir** or **être**) + a past participle:

**aimer** → j'**avais aimé** etc     **devenir** → j'étais **devenu(e)** etc

## Use of the pluperfect tense

The pluperfect tense is used to describe what someone had done/had been doing or something that had happened/had been happening:

Il **n'avait pas voulu** aller avec eux.  *He hadn't wanted to go with them.*

> **!** The verb **venir** + **de** + infinitive can be used in the present or imperfect to describe something that has/had just happened:
> L'avion **vient d'arriver**.  *The plane has just arrived.*
> Le film **venait de commencer**.  *The film had just started.*

# ■ subjunctive mood

## Regular verbs in the subjunctive mood

The subjunctive mood is formed by taking the stem of the first person plural present tense (**nous** minus the ending **-ons**) + the subjunctive endings:

**-e**, **-es**, **-e**, **-ions**, **-iez**, **-ent**

## Irregular verbs in the subjunctive mood

For irregular verbs in the subjunctive mood, see the verb tables on p. 400.

## Perfect subjunctive mood

The perfect subjunctive mood is formed by taking the present subjunctive of **avoir** or **être** + past participle.

Le meilleur choix que j'**aie fait**. *The best choice I've made.*

Je ne crois pas qu'il **soit venu**. *I don't think he came.*

## Use of the subjunctive mood

The subjunctive always follows **que** in subordinate clauses where the subject is different from the subject of the main verb:

- after verbs of emotion, wishing and willing
  Je serais très étonné **qu'il mente**. *I would be very surprised if he was lying.*
- after impersonal constructions expressing necessity, possibility, doubt or preference
  Il semble **qu'elle ait raison**. *She appears to be right.*
- after some verbs and impersonal constructions expressing uncertainty
  Je doute **qu'il veuille t'aider**. *I doubt he'll want to help you.*
- after **attendre que**
  Attendons **qu'il revienne**. *Let's wait until he comes back.*
- after some subordinating conjunctions
  Il est allé travailler **bien qu'il soit malade**. *He went to work even though he was ill.*
- after superlatives and adjectives such as **premier**, **dernier**, **seul**
  C'était le coureur **le plus rapide que j'aie jamais vu**.
  *He was the fastest runner I ever saw.*
- after negative and indefinite pronouns
  Ils cherchent quelqu'un **qui puisse garder le bébé**.
  *They're looking for someone who can look after the baby.*

# ■ conditional mood

## Conditional present

The conditional present is formed with the infinitive + conditional endings:
**-ais**, **-ais**, **-ait**, **-ions**, **-iez**, **-aient**

> **!**
> - For -**re** verbs, the final -**e** is omitted.
> - Irregular verbs in the conditional present have the same stems as irregular verbs in the future tense.

## Use of the conditional present

The conditional present is used to describe what someone would do/would be doing or what would happen (if something else were to happen):

Si j'avais de l'argent, je **ferais** le tour du monde.

*If I had money, I would travel around the world.*

## Conditional perfect

The conditional perfect is formed with the conditional present of an auxiliary verb (**avoir** or **être**) + past participle:

> finir → j'**aurais fini** etc

## Use of the conditional perfect

The conditional perfect is used to describe what someone would have done or would have been doing or what would have happened (if something else had happened):

> Si j'avais su, je **n'aurais rien dit**.
>
> *If I had known, I wouldn't have said anything.*

---

> #### Si + imperfect or pluperfect?
> Conditional present + **si** + imperfect
> **Je te le dirais, si je le savais.**
> *I would tell you if I knew.*
> Conditional perfect + **si** + pluperfect
> **Je te l'aurais dit, si je l'avais su.**
> *I would have told you, if I had known.*

---

# ■ use of tenses with *il y a, depuis, pendant*

## *Il y a*

- present perfect tense + **il y a** + period of time = *ago*
  J'ai vu le film **il y a** trois semaines. *I saw the film three weeks ago.*
- **il y a ... que** + present tense = *for*
  **Il y a** dix minutes **que** ça sonne. *It's been ringing for ten minutes.*

> ! **Voilà que** can also be used to express *for* :
> **Voilà** dix minutes **que** ça sonne. *It's been ringing for ten minutes.*

- **il y avait ... que** + imperfect tense = *for*
  **Il y avait** longtemps **qu'**elle habitait seule.
  *She'd been living alone for a long time.*

## *Depuis*

- **depuis** + present tense = *for* or *since* (when an action is ongoing)
  Il habite ici **depuis** trois ans. *He's been living here for three years.*
  Elle t'attende **depuis** ce matin. *She's been waiting for you since this morning*

> ! **Depuis** must be used with the present perfect tense when the clause is
> negative or the action is complete:
> **Il n'a pas pris de vacances depuis longtemps.**
> *He hasn't taken any holidays for a long time.*

- **depuis** + imperfect tense = *for* or *since* (when an action started in the past and was still ongoing at a certain time)

Elle le connaissait **depuis** son enfance.
*She had known him since her childhood.*

Il attendait **depuis** trois heures quand on est arrivé.
*He had been waiting for three hours when we arrived.*

>  **Depuis** must be used with the pluperfect tense when the clause is negative or the action is complete:
> Je n'étais pas allé au cinéma **depuis** des années.
> *I hadn't been to the cinema for years.*
> Il était parti **depuis** peu.  *He had been gone for a short while.*

- **depuis que** + present tense = *since* (when a clause is introduced by *since*)

Elle dort **depuis que** vous êtes parties.
*She's been sleeping since you left.*

- **depuis que** + imperfect tense = *since*

Il pleuvait **depuis que** nous étions en vacances.
*It had been raining since we'd been on holiday.*

>  **Depuis que** must be used with the pluperfect tense when the action is complete:
> Il pleuvait **depuis** que nous étions arrivés.
> *It had been raining since we arrived.*

## Pendant

- **pendant** + noun = *during*

J'ai vu un film **pendant** mon séjour.
*I saw a film during my stay.*

- **pendant** + period of time = *for* (in any tense)

Il a vécu ici **pendant** deux mois.
*He lived here for two months.*

J'y avais travaillé **pendant** un an.
*I had worked there for a year.*

Je vais habiter en France **pendant** deux ans.
*I'm going to live in France for two months.*

>  **Pour** can also be used to express *for* in the future tense:
> Je vais habiter en France **pour** deux ans.

---

### *Depuis or pendant?*

**Depuis** is used to refer to the starting point of an action in the past and **pendant** is used to refer to the duration of an action in the past or future.

# ■ modal auxiliary verbs

The five modal auxiliary verbs **devoir**, **pouvoir**, **savoir**, **vouloir** and **falloir** are always followed by a verb in the infinitive.

## Devoir

**Devoir** can be used to express obligation, probability, intention or expectation.

> Nous **devons** arriver à temps.   *We must arrive in time.*
>
> Il **doit** être en train de dormir.   *He must be sleeping. (He's probably sleeping).*
>
> Je **dois** aller chez le dentiste.   *I am supposed to go to the dentist.*

In the conditional, **devoir** can be used to give advice:

> Tu **n'aurais pas dû** manger ces champignons.   *You shouldn't have eaten those mushrooms.*

> **!** Note that the French infinitive is translated by a past participle in English:
> **manger** = eaten

## Pouvoir

**Pouvoir** can be used to express ability, permission or probability.

> Il **ne pouvait pas** sortir de son lit.   *He couldn't get out of bed.*
>
> **Puis**-je entrer ?   *May I come in?*
>
> Cela **peut** arriver.   *It can happen.*

In the conditional, **pouvoir** expresses something that could or might be/have been:

> Tu **pourrais** t'excuser.   *You might apologize.*

> **!** With verbs of perception (**entendre**, **sentir**, **voir** etc) **pouvoir** is often omitted:
> J'entendais le bruit des vagues.   *I could hear the sound of the waves.*

## Savoir

**Savoir** can be used to express 'know how to'.

> Je **sais/savais** conduire une moto.   *I can/used to be able to ride a motorbike.*

> **!** Note that **savoir** is often translated as *can* in English.

## Vouloir

**Vouloir** can be used to express desire, wish or intention.

> Je **veux** partir.   *I want to go.*
>
> Je **voudrais** trouver un travail intéressant.   *I'd like to find an interesting job.*
>
> Il **a voulu** sauter par la fenêtre.   *He tried to jump out of the window.*

## Falloir

Falloir can be used to express necessity.

> Il **faudrait** y aller tout de suite.   *We should go right away.*

> *i* **Falloir** can also be followed by a noun or the subjunctive mood:
> Il **faut** deux heures pour aller à Paris. *It takes two hours to get to Paris.*
> Il **faut** que tu parles à Papa. *You have to speak to Dad.*

# ■ present participle

The present participle is formed with the first person plural present tense (**nous** minus the ending -**ons**) + -**ant** (similar to the English –*ing*):

Three verbs have irregular present participles:

avoir → **ayant**      être → **étant**          savoir → **sachant**

## Use as an adjective

The present participle agrees with its noun or pronoun:

Ils sont très **exigeants**. *They're very demanding.*

## Use as a verb

- to mean –*ing*

 **Pensant** bien faire, j'ai insisté. *Thinking I was doing the right thing, I insisted.*

- **en** + present participle to express simultaneous actions or manner

 Il est tombé **en descendant** l'escalier. *He fell as he was going downstairs.*

 J'ai trouvé du travail **en lisant** les petites annonces. *I found a job by reading the classified ads.*

- **en** + present participle to express phrasal verbs of motion

 Il est sorti du magasin **en courant**. *He ran out of the shop. (to run out)*

- **ayant/étant** + past participle to express that one action occurred before another

 **Ayant fini**, je suis parti. *Having finished, I left.*

 **Étant arrivé** en retard, il a manqué le train. *Having arrived late, he missed the train.*

> *!* Both **ayant** and **étant** translate as *having* in English.

# A

**A, a¹** [a] *nm inv* A, a; **A1** [autoroute] *Br* ≃ M1, *Am* ≃ I1

**a²** [a] *voir* **avoir**

## à [a]

**à + le = au** [o], **à + les = aux** [o]

*prép* **a)** [indique la direction] to; **aller à Paris** to go to Paris; **partir au Venezuela** to leave for Venezuela; **de Paris à Lyon** from Paris to Lyons
**b)** [indique la position] at; **être au bureau / à la ferme / à Paris** to be at or in the office / on or at the farm / in Paris; **à la maison** at home
**c)** [dans l'expression du temps] **à 8 heures** at 8 o'clock; **du lundi au vendredi** from Monday to Friday, *Am* Monday through Friday; **au vingt-et-unième siècle** in the twenty-first century; **à mon arrivée** on (my) arrival; **à lundi!** see you (on) Monday!
**d)** [dans les descriptions] **l'homme à la barbe** the man with the beard; **verre à vin** wine glass
**e)** [introduit le complément d'objet indirect] **donner qch à qn** to give sth to sb, to give sb sth; **penser à qn / qch** to think about or of sb / sth
**f)** [devant infinitif] **apprendre à lire** to learn to read; **avoir du travail à faire** to have work to do; **maison à vendre** house for sale; **prêt à partir** ready to leave
**g)** [indique l'appartenance] **un ami à moi** a friend of mine; **c'est à lui** it's his; **c'est à vous de...** [il vous incombe de] it's up to you to...; [c'est votre tour] it's your turn to...
**h)** [indique le moyen, la manière] **à bicyclette** by bicycle; **à pied** on foot; **à la main** by hand; **au crayon** in pencil; **deux à deux** two by two
**i)** [prix] **pain à 1 euro** loaf for 1 euro
**j)** [poids] **vendre au kilo** to sell by the kilo
**k)** [vitesse] **100 km à l'heure** 100 km an or per hour
**l)** [pour appeler] **au voleur!** (stop) thief!; **au feu!** (there's a) fire!

**abaisser** [abese] **1.** *vt* [levier, pont-levis] to lower; [store] to pull down **2. s'abaisser** *vpr* **a)** [barrière] to lower **b)** [être en pente] to slope down

**abandon** [abɑ̃dɔ̃] *nm* [d'enfant, de projet] abandonment; [de lieu] neglect; [de sportif] withdrawal; ORDINAT abort ∎ **abandonner 1.** *vt* [personne, animal, lieu] to desert, to abandon; [pouvoir, combat] to give up; [projet] to abandon; **abandonner ses études** to drop out (of school) **2.** *vi* [renoncer] to give up; [sportif] to withdraw

**abasourdi, -e** [abazurdi] *adj* stunned

**abat-jour** [abaʒur] *nm inv* lampshade

**abats** [aba] *nmpl* offal; [de volaille] giblets

**abattement** [abatmɑ̃] *nm* [mental] dejection; [physique] exhaustion; **abattement fiscal** tax allowance

**abattoir** [abatwar] *nm* slaughterhouse

**abattre** [abatr] **1.** *vt* [arbre] to cut down; [personne] to kill; [animal de boucherie] to slaughter; [animal blessé ou malade] to destroy; [avion] to shoot down; *Fig* [déprimer] to demoralize **2. s'abattre** *vpr* [tomber] to crash down (**sur** on); [pluie] to pour down (**sur** on)

**abattu, -e** [abaty] *adj* [mentalement] dejected; [physiquement] exhausted

**abbaye** [abei] *nf* abbey

**abcès** [apsɛ] *nm* abscess

**abdomen** [abdɔmɛn] *nm* abdomen ∎ **abdominal, -e, -aux** *adj* abdominal ∎ **abdominaux** *nmpl* **a)** [muscles] abdominal *or* stomach muscles **b)** [exercices] **faire des abdominaux** to do stomach exercises ■ **abdos** *nmpl* **a)** [muscles] abs, stomach muscles **b)** [exercices] stomach exercises, abs (exercises); **faire des abdos** to do abs *or* stomach exercises

**abeille** [abɛj] *nf* bee

**aberrant, -e** [aberɑ̃, -ɑ̃t] *adj* absurd

**abîme** [abim] *nm* abyss

**abîmer** [abime] **1.** *vt* to spoil, to damage **2. s'abîmer** *vpr* [gén] to be damaged; [fruits] to go bad ■ **abîmé, e** *adj* [vêtement] ruined; [livre, meuble] damaged

**abject, -e** [abʒɛkt] *adj* despicable

**abolir** [abɔlir] *vt* to abolish ■ **abolition** *nf* abolition

**abominable** [abɔminabl] *adj* appalling

**abondant, -e** [abɔ̃dɑ̃, -ɑ̃t] *adj* plentiful, abundant ■ **abondance** *nf* abundance (**de** of) ■ **abonder** *vi* to be plentiful

**abonné, -e** [abɔne] *nmf* [d'un journal, du téléphone] subscriber; [du gaz] consumer ■ **abonnement** *nm* [de journal] subscription; [de téléphone] line rental ■ **s'abonner** *vpr* [à un journal] to subscribe (**à** to)

**abord** [abɔr] *nm* **a)** [accès] **d'un abord facile** easy to approach; **abords** [d'un bâtiment] surroundings; [d'une ville] outskirts **b)** [expressions] **au premier abord, de prime abord** at first sight; **d'abord, tout d'abord** [pour commencer] at first, to begin with; [première ment] first (and foremost)

**abordable** [abɔrdabl] *adj* [prix, marchandises] affordable

**aborder** [abɔrde] **1.** *vt* [personne, lieu, virage] to approach; [problème] to tackle **2.** *vi* to land

**aborigène** [abɔriʒɛn] *nm* [d'un pays] native; **les Aborigènes d'Australie** the (Australian) Aborigines

**aboutir** [abutir] *vi* [réussir] to be successful; **aboutir à qch** [avoir pour résultat] to result in sth ■ **aboutissement** *nm* [succès] success; [résultat] outcome

**aboyer** [abwaje] *vi* to bark

**abréger** [abreʒe] *vt* [texte] to shorten; [visite] to cut short; [mot] to abbreviate ■ **abrégé** *nm* [d'un texte] summary; [livre] abstract; **en abrégé** [mot] in abbreviated form

**abréviation** [abrevjasjɔ̃] *nf* abbreviation

**abri** [abri] *nm* shelter; **mettre qn /qch à l'abri** to shelter sb /sth; **se mettre à l'abri** to take shelter; **être à l'abri de qch** to be sheltered from sth; **sans abri** homeless ■ **abriter 1.** *vt* [protéger] to shelter (**de** from); [loger] to house **2. s'abriter** *vpr* to (take) shelter (**de** from)

**abricot** [abriko] *nm* apricot

**abrier** [abrije] **1.** *vt Can Fig* [cacher, dissimuler] to hide **2. s'abrier** *vpr* [couvrir pour protéger] to cover; **s'abrier sous une couverture** to tuck in (bed)

**abroger** [abrɔʒe] *vt* to repeal

**abrupt, -e** [abrypt] *adj* [pente] steep

**abrutir** [abrytir] *vt* [hébéter] to daze ■ **abrutissant, -e** *adj* mind-numbing

**absence** [apsɑ̃s] *nf* [d'une personne] absence; [manque] lack ■ **absent, -e 1.** *adj* [personne] absent (**de** from); [chose] missing **2.** *nmf* absentee ■ **s'absenter** *vpr* to go away

**absolu, -e** [apsɔly] *adj* absolute ■ **absolument** *adv* absolutely

**absorber** [apsɔrbe] *vt* [liquid] to absorb; [nourriture] to eat; [boisson] to drink; [médicament] to take ■ **absorbant, -e** *adj* [papier] absorbent; [travail] absorbing ■ **absorption** *nf* [de liquide] absorption; [de nourriture] eating; [de boisson] drinking; [de médicament] taking

**abstenir** [apstənir] ■ **s'abstenir** *vpr* [ne pas voter] to abstain; **s'abstenir de qch /de faire qch** to refrain from sth /from doing sth ■ **abstention** *nf* *POL* abstention

**abstrait, -e** [apstrɛ, -ɛt] *adj* abstract ■ **abstraction** *nf* abstraction

**absurde** [apsyrd] *adj* absurd ■ **absurdité** *nf* absurdity ; **dire des absurdités** to talk nonsense

**ab1to** *(abr de* à bientôt*)* SMS CU

**abus** [aby] *nm* [excès] overindulgence (**de** in) ; [pratique] abuse (**de** of) ; **abus de pouvoir** abuse of power ; **abus d'alcool** alcohol abuse ; **abus de confiance** breach of trust ■ **abuser 1.** *vi* to go too far ; **abuser de** [situation, personne] to take unfair advantage of ; [autorité] to abuse ; [nourriture] to overindulge in **2. s'abuser** *vpr* **si je ne m'abuse** if I am not mistaken

**abusif, -ive** [abyzif, -iv] *adj* excessive ; [mère] possessive

**académie** [akademi] *nf* academy ; [administration scolaire] ≃ school district ; **l'Académie française** *learned society responsible for promoting the French language and imposing standards*

**acajou** [akaʒu] *nm* mahogany

**accabler** [akable] *vt* to overwhelm (**de** with) ; **accablé de dettes** (over) burdened with debt ■ **accablant, -e** *adj* [chaleur] oppressive ; [témoignage] damning

**accalmie** [akalmi] *nf* lull

**accaparer** [akapare] *vt* [personne] to monopolize

**accéder** [aksede] *vi* ORDINAT [programme] to access ; **accéder à** [lieu] to reach ; [rang] to gain ; [requête] to comply with ; **accéder au trône** to accede to the throne

**accélérer** [akselere] **1.** *vt* [allure, pas] to quicken **2.** *vi* [en voiture] to accelerate **3. s'accélérer** *vpr* to speed up ■ **accélérateur** *nm* [de voiture, d'ordinateur] accelerator ■ **accélération** *nf* acceleration

**accent** [aksɑ̃] *nm* [prononciation] accent ; [sur une syllabe] stress ; *Fig* **mettre l'accent sur qch** to stress sth ; **accent aigu / circonflexe / grave** acute / circumflex / grave (accent) ■ **accentuation** *nf* [sur lettre] accentuation ; [de phénomène] intensification ■ **accentuer 1.** *vt* [syllabe] to

stress ; [lettre] to put an accent on ; *Fig* [renforcer] to emphasize **2. s'accentuer** *vpr* to become more pronounced

**accepter** [aksepte] *vt* to accept ; **accepter de faire qch** to agree to do sth ■ **acceptable** *adj* [recevable] acceptable ■ **acceptation** *nf* acceptance

**acception** [aksepsjɔ̃] *nf* [de mot] meaning

**accès** [aksɛ] *nm* **a)** [approche & ORDINAT] access (**à** to) ; **avoir accès à qch** to have access to sth ; **'accès interdit'** 'no entry' ; **'accès aux quais'** to the trains ; **accès à distance** remote access **b)** [de folie, de colère] fit ; [de fièvre] bout ■ **accessible** *adj* [lieu, livre] accessible

**accession** [aksesjɔ̃] *nf* accession (**à** to) ; **accession à la propriété** home ownership

**accessoire** [akseswar] *adj* minor ■ **accessoires** *nmpl* [de théâtre] props ; [de mode, de voiture] accessories ; **accessoires de toilette** toilet accessories

**accident** [aksidɑ̃] *nm* accident ; **accident de chemin de fer** train crash ; **accident de la route** road accident ; **accident du travail** industrial accident ; **accident de parcours** hitch ; **par accident** by accident, by chance ■ **accidenté, -e 1.** *adj* [terrain] uneven ; [voiture] damaged **2.** *nmf* accident victim ■ **accidentel, -elle** *adj* accidental

**acclamer** [aklame] *vt* to cheer ■ **acclamations** *nfpl* cheers

**acclimater** [aklimate] **1.** *vt* Br to acclimatize, Am to acclimate (**à** to) **2. s'acclimater** *vpr* to become Br acclimatized *or* Am acclimated (**à** to) ■ **acclimatation** *nf* Br acclimatization, Am acclimation (**à** to)

**accolade** [akɔlad] *nf* [embrassade] embrace ; [signe] curly bracket

**accommoder** [akɔmɔde] **1.** *vt* [nourriture] to prepare ; [restes] to use up **2.** *vi* [œil] to focus

**3. s'accommoder** *vpr* **s'accommoder de qch** to put up with sth ▪ **accommodant, -e** *adj* accommodating

**accompagner** [akɔ̃paɲe] *vt* [personne] to accompany; **accompagner qn à la gare** [en voiture] to take sb to the station ▪ **accompagnateur, -trice** *nmf* [musical] accompanist; [de touristes] guide; [d'enfants] group leader ▪ **accompagnement** *nm* [de musique] accompaniment; [légumes] accompaniment

**accomplir** [akɔ̃plir] *vt* [tache] to carry out; [formalités] to go through ▪ **accompli, -e** *adj* [parfait] accomplished

**accord** [akɔr] *nm* [traité, entente & GRAM] agreement; [autorisation] consent; [musical] chord; **être d'accord** to agree (**avec** with); **d'accord !** all right! ▪ **accorder 1.** *vt* [instrument] to tune; **accorder qch à qn** [faveur] to grant sb sth; [prêt] to authorize sth to sb **2. s'accorder** *vpr* [se mettre d'accord] to agree (**avec/sur** with/on); GRAM [mots] to agree (**avec** with); **s'accorder qch** to allow oneself sth

**accordéon** [akɔrdeɔ̃] *nm* accordion

**accoster** [akɔste] **1.** *vt* [personne] to approach **2.** *vi* NAUT to dock

**accotement** [akɔtmɑ̃] *nm* [de route] verge; [de voie ferrée] shoulder

**accoucher** [akuʃe] *vi* to give birth (**de** to) ▪ **accouchement** *nm* delivery

**accouder** [akude] ▪ **s'accouder** *vpr* **s'accouder à** *ou* **sur qch** to lean one's elbows on sth ▪ **accoudoir** *nm* armrest

**accoupler** [akuple] ▪ **s'accoupler** *vpr* [animaux] to mate

**accourir** [akurir] *vi* to run up

**accoutrement** [akutrəmɑ̃] *nm* Péj rig-out

**accoutumer** [akutyme] **1.** *vt* **accoutumer qn à qch** to get sb accustomed to sth **2. s'accoutumer** *vpr* to get accustomed (**à** to) ▪ **accoutumance** *nf* [adaptation] familiarization (**à** with); MÉD [dépendance] addiction ▪ **accoutumé, -e** *adj* usual; **comme à l'accoutumée** as usual

**accro** [akro] Fam **1.** *adj* hooked; **être accro à qch** [drogue] to be hooked on sth; Fig to be hooked on *or* really into sth **2.** *nmf* fanatic; **c'est un accro du football** he's really mad on football

**Accrobranche®** [akrobrɑ̃ʃ] *nm* treetop walking

**accroc** [akro] *nm* [déchirure] tear; [difficulté] hitch; **sans accroc** without a hitch

**accrocher** [akrɔʃe] **1.** *vt* [déchirer] to catch; [fixer] to hook (**à** onto); [suspendre] to hang up (**à** on) **2.** *vi* [achopper] to hit a stumbling block; [se remarquer] to grab one's attention **3. s'accrocher** *vpr* [se fixer] to fasten; Fam [persévérer] to stick at it; **s'accrocher à qn/qch** [s'agripper] to cling to sb/sth ▪ **accrochage** *nm* [de véhicules] minor accident ▪ **accrocheur, -euse** *adj* [personne] tenacious; [titre, slogan] catchy

**accroître** [akrwatr] **1.** *vt* to increase **2. s'accroître** *vpr* to increase ▪ **accroissement** *nm* increase (**de** in)

**accroupir** [akrupir] ▪ **s'accroupir** *vpr* to squat (down)

**accueil** [akœj] *nm* [bureau] reception; [manière] welcome; **faire un bon accueil à qn** to give sb a warm welcome ▪ **accueillant, -e** *adj* welcoming ▪ **accueillir** *vt* [personne, proposition] to greet; [sujet : hôtel] to accommodate

**acculer** [akyle] *vt* **acculer qn à qch** to drive sb to sth

**accumuler** [akymyle] **1.** *vt* to accumulate **2. s'accumuler** *vpr* to accumulate ▪ **accumulation** *nf* accumulation

**accuser** [akyze] *vt* [dénoncer] to accuse; [accentuer] to bring out; [baisse] to show; **accuser qn de qch/de faire qch** to accuse sb of sth/of doing sth ▪ **accusateur, -trice 1.** *adj* [regard] accusing **2.** *nmf* accuser ▪ **accusation** *nf* accusation ▪ **accusé, -e** *nmf* **l'accusé** the accused; [au tribunal] the defendant

**achalandé, -e** [aʃalɑ̃de] *adj* **bien achalandé** [magasin] well-stocked

**achaler** [aʃale] *vt Can* to bother, to bug, to embarrass, to annoy ■ **achalant, e** **1.** *adj Can* annoying **2.** *nmf* [personne] pest, nuisance

**acharner** [aʃarne] ■ **s'acharner** *vpr* **s'acharner sur** *ou* **contre qn** [persécuter] to persecute sb; **s'acharner à faire qch** to try very hard to do sth ■ **acharné, e** *adj* [effort, travail] relentless; [combat] fierce ■ **acharnement** *nm* relentlessness; [dans un combat] fury

**achat** [aʃa] *nm* purchase; **faire l'achat de qch** to buy sth; **achats** [paquets] shopping

**acheter** [aʃte] **1.** *vt* to buy; **acheter qch à qn** [faire une transaction] to buy sth from sb; [faire un cadeau] to buy sth for sb **2.** *vi* to buy **3. s'acheter** *vpr* **je vais m'acheter une glace** I'm going to buy (myself) an ice cream ■ **acheteur, -euse** *nmf* buyer; [dans un magasin] shopper

**achever** [aʃve] **1.** *vt a* **a)** [finir] to end; [travail] to complete; **achever de faire qch** to finish doing sth **b)** [tuer - animal malade] to put out of its misery; **achever qn** to finish sb off **2. s'achever** *vpr* to end ■ **achèvement** *nm* completion

**acide** [asid] **1.** *adj* acid(ic); [au goût] sour **2.** *nm* acid ■ **acidité** *nf* acidity; [au goût] sourness

**acier** [asje] *nm* steel; **acier inoxydable** stainless steel ■ **aciérie** *nf* steelworks

**acné** [akne] *nf* acne

**acompte** [akɔ̃t] *nm* down payment; **verser un acompte** to make a down payment

**à-coup** [aku] *(pl* **à-coups)** *nm* jolt; **sans à-coups** smoothly; **par à-coups** [avancer] in fits and starts

**acoustique** [akustik] *nf* [qualité] acoustics *(pl)*

**acquérir** [akerir] *vt* [acheter] to purchase; [obtenir] to acquire; **acquérir de la valeur** to increase in value; **tenir qch pour acquis** to take sth for granted ■ **acquéreur** *nm* purchaser ■ **acquis** *nm* [expérience] experience;

**les acquis sociaux** social benefits ■ **acquisition** *nf* [action] acquisition; [bien acheté] purchase

**acquitter** [akite] **1.** *vt* [accusé] to acquit; [dette] to pay **2. s'acquitter** *vpr* **s'acquitter d'un devoir** to fulfil a duty ■ **acquittement** *nm* [d'un accusé] acquittal; [d'une dette] payment

**âcre** [akr] *adj* [goût] bitter; [odeur] acrid

**acrobate** [akrɔbat] *nmf* acrobat ■ **acrobatie** *nf* acrobatics *(sg)*; **acrobaties aériennes** aerobatics *(sg)*

**acrylique** [akrilik] *nm* acrylic

**acte** [akt] *nm* [action & THÉÂT] act; **faire acte de candidature** to apply; **prendre acte de qch** to take note of sth; **acte terroriste** terrorist act; **acte unique européen** Single European Act; **acte de naissance** birth certificate

**acteur** [aktœr] *nm* actor

**actif, -ive** [aktif, -iv] **1.** *adj* active **2.** *nm* GRAM active; COMM [d'une entreprise] assets

**action** [aksjɔ̃] *nf* [acte] action; [en Bourse] share; **bonne action** good deed; **passer à l'action** to take action ■ **actionnaire** *nmf* shareholder ■ **actionner** *vt* [mettre en marche] to start up

**activer** [aktive] **1.** *vt* [accélérer] to speed up; ORDINAT [option] to select **2. s'activer** *vpr* [être actif] to be busy

**activité** [aktivite] *nf* activity; **en activité** [personne] working; [volcan] active

**actrice** [aktris] *nf* actress

**actu** [akty] *(abr de* **actualité***) nf* **l'actu** the (latest) news

**actualisation** [aktyalizasjɔ̃] *nf* [de texte] updating

**actualité** [aktyalite] *nf* [d'un problème] topicality; **l'actualité** current affairs; **les actualités** [à la radio, à la télévision] the news; **d'actualité** topical

**actuel, -elle** [aktyɛl] *adj* [présent] present; [d'actualité] topical ■ **actuellement** *adv* at present

**acupuncture** [akypɔ̃ktyr] *nf* acupuncture ■ **acupuncteur, -trice** *nmf* acupuncturist

**adapter** [adapte] **1.** *vt* to adapt (à to) **2. s'adapter** *vpr* [s'acclimater] to adapt (à to) ; **s'adapter à qn/qch** to get used to sb/sth ■ **adaptateur** *nm* adapter ■ **adaptation** *nf* adaptation ; **faculté d'adaptation** adaptability

**addiction** [adiksjɔ̃] *nf* (drug) addiction

**additif** [aditif] *nm* [substance] additive

**addition** [adisjɔ̃] *nf* addition (à to) ; [de restaurant] *Br* bill, *Am* check ■ **additionner** *vt* to add (up) (à to)

**adepte** [adept] *nmf* follower

**adéquat, -e** [adekwa, -at] *adj* appropriate ; [quantité] adequate

**a2m1** SMS *abr écrite de* à demain

**adhérer** [adere] *vi* **adhérer à qch** [coller] to stick to sth ; [s'inscrire] to join sth ■ **adhérent, -e** *nmf* member

**adhésif, -ive** [adezif, -iv] *adj* adhesive ■ **adhésion** *nf* [inscription] joining (à of)

**adieu, -x** [adjø] **1.** *excl* farewell **2.** *nm* farewell ; **faire ses adieux** to say one's goodbyes

**adjacent, -e** [adʒasɑ̃, -ɑ̃t] *adj* adjacent (à to)

**adjectif** [adʒɛktif] *nm* adjective

**adjoint, -e** [adʒwɛ̃, -ɛ̃t] *nmf* assistant ; **adjoint au maire** deputy mayor

**adjuger** [adʒyʒe] **1.** *vt* **adjuger qch à qn** [prix, contrat] to award sth to sb ; [aux enchères] to knock sth down to sb **2. s'adjuger** *vpr* **s'adjuger qch** to appropriate sth

**admettre** [admɛtr] *vt* [accueillir, reconnaître] to admit ; [autoriser] to allow ; **être admis à un examen** to pass an exam

**administratif, ive** [administratif, iv] *adj* administrative

**administrer** [administre] *vt* [gérer] to administer ■ **administrateur, -trice** *nmf* [de société] director ; **administrateur de site (Web)** webmaster ■ **administration** *nf* administration ; **l'Administration** [service public] ≃ the Civil Service ; [fonctionnaires] civil servants

**admirer** [admire] *vt* to admire ■ **admirable** *adj* admirable ■ **admirateur, -trice** *nmf* admirer ■ **admiratif, -ive** *adj* admiring ■ **admiration** *nf* admiration ; **être en admiration devant qn/qch** to be filled with admiration for sb/sth

**admissible** [admisibl] *adj* [tolérable] acceptable, admissible ; SCOL & UNIV **candidats admissibles** candidates who have qualified for the oral examination ■ **admission** *nf* admission (à/dans to)

**ADN** *(abr de* **acide désoxyribonucléique)** *nm* DNA *(deoxyribonucleic acid)*

**ado** [ado] *(abr de* **adolescent)** *nmf Fam* teen, teenager

**adolescent, -e** [adolesɑ̃, -ɑ̃t] *nmf* adolescent, teenager ■ **adolescence** *nf* adolescence

**adonner** [adone] ■ **s'adonner** *vpr* **s'adonner à qch** to devote oneself to sth ; **s'adonner à la boisson** to be an alcoholic

**adopter** [adopte] *vt* to adopt ■ **adoptif, -ive** *adj* [enfant, patrie] adopted ; [parents] adoptive ■ **adoption** *nf* adoption

**adorer** [adore] *vt* [dieu] to worship ; [chose, personne] to adore ; **adorer faire qch** to adore doing sth **2. s'adorer** *vpr* **ils s'adorent** they adore each other ■ **adorable** *adj* adorable

**adosser** [adose] ■ **s'adosser** *vpr* **s'adosser à qch** to lean (back) against sth

**adoucir** [adusir] **1.** *vt* [traits, peau] to soften ; [caractère] to take the edge off **2. s'adoucir** *vpr* [temps] to turn milder ; [voix] to soften ; [caractère] to mellow

**adresse** [adrɛs] *nf* **a)** [domicile] address ; **adresse électronique** *ou* **e-mail** e-mail address **b)** [habileté] skill ■ **adresser 1.** *vt* [lettre, remarque] to address (à to) ; **adresser qch à qn** [lettre] to send sb sth ; **adresser la parole à qn** to speak to sb **2. s'adresser** *vpr* **s'adresser à qn**

[parler] to speak to sb ; [aller trouver] to go and see sb ; [être destiné à] to be aimed at sb

**Adriatique** [adriatik] *nf* **l'Adriatique** the Adriatic

**adroit, -e** [adrwa, -at] *adj* [habile] skilful

**ADSL** (*abr de* **asymmetric digital subscriber line**) *nm* ADSL ; **passer à l'ADSL** to switch or upgrade or go over to ADSL

**adulte** [adylt] **1.** *adj* [personne, animal] adult **2.** *nmf* adult

**adultère** [adylter] *nm* adultery

**advenir** [advənir] (*aux être*) *v impers* **a)** to happen **b) advenir de qn** [devenir] to become of sb

**adverbe** [adverb] *nm* adverb

**adversaire** [adverser] *nmf* opponent ■ **adverse** *adj* opposing

**aérer** [aere] **1.** *vt* [pièce, lit] to air **2. s'aérer** *vpr* to get some fresh air ■ **aération** *nf* ventilation ■ **aéré, e** *adj* **a)** [chambre] well-ventilated, airy ; **bien aéré** well-ventilated, airy ; **mal aéré** poorly-ventilated, stuffy **b)** [présentation, texte] well-spaced

**aérien, -enne** [aerjɛ̃, -ɛn] *adj* [transport, attaque, défense] air ; [photo] aerial ; [câble] overhead

**aérobic** [aerɔbik] *nm* aerobics (*sg*) ■ **aérodynamique** *adj* aerodynamic ■ **aérogare** *nf* air terminal ■ **aéroglisseur** *nm* hovercraft ■ **aérogramme** *nm* airmail letter ■ **aéroport** *nm* airport ■ **aérosol** *nm* aerosol

**aéro-club** (*pl* **aéro-clubs**) [aerɔklœb] *nm* flying club

**affable** [afabl] *adj* affable

**affaiblir** [afeblir] **1.** *vt* to weaken **2. s'affaiblir** *vpr* to weaken ■ **affaiblissement** *nm* weakening

**affaire** [afer] *nf* [question] matter, affair ; [marché] deal ; [firme] business ; [scandale] affair ; [procès] case ; **affaires** [commerce] business (*sg*) ; [effets personnels] belongings ; **les Affaires étrangères** *Br* ≃ the Foreign Office, *Am* ≃ the State Department ; **avoir affaire à qn/qch** to have to deal with

sb /sth ; **faire une bonne affaire** to get a bargain ; **c'est mon affaire** that's my business ; **ça fera l'affaire** that will do nicely ; **affaire de cœur** love affair

**affairer** [afere] ■ **s'affairer** *vpr* to busy oneself ■ **affairé, -e** *adj* busy

**affaisser** [afese] ■ **s'affaisser** *vpr* [personne, bâtiment] to collapse ; [sol] to subside

**affaler** [afale] ■ **s'affaler** *vpr* to collapse ; **affalé dans un fauteuil** slumped in an armchair

**affamé, -e** [afame] *adj* starving

**affecter** [afɛkte] *vt* **a)** [employé] to appoint (**à** to) ; [soldat] to post (**à** to) ; [fonds] to assign (**à** to) **b)** [feindre, émouvoir] to affect ■ **affectation** *nf* [d'employé] appointment (**à** to) ; [de soldat] posting (**à** to) ; [de fonds] assignment (**à** to) ; *Péj* [pose] affectation ■ **affecté, -e** *adj Péj* [manières, personne] affected

**affection** [afɛksjɔ̃] *nf* [attachement] affection ; [maladie] ailment ; **avoir de l'affection pour qn** to be fond of sb ■ **affectionner** *vt* to be fond of ■ **affectueux, -euse** *adj* affectionate

**affiche** [afiʃ] *nf* notice ; [publicitaire] poster ; **être à l'affiche** [spectacle] to be on ■ **afficher** *vt* [avis] to put up ; [prix, horaire, résultat & ORDINAT] [message] to display ; *Péj* [sentiment] to show ; **afficher complet** [sujet : spectacle] to be sold out ■ **affichage** *nm* bill-posting ; ORDINAT display

**affiliation** [afiljɑsjɔ̃] *nf* affiliation ■ **affilié, -e** *adj* affiliated ■ **s'affilier** *vpr* (*emploi réfléchi*) **s'affilier à** to affiliate o.s. or to become affiliated to

**affiner** [afine] **1.** *vt* [métal, goût] to refine **2. s'affiner** *vpr* [goût] to become more refined ; [visage] to get thinner

**affinité** [afinite] *nf* affinity

**affirmatif, -ive** [afirmatif, -iv] *adj* [réponse & GRAM] affirmative ■ **affirmative** *nf* **nous aimerions savoir si vous serez libre mercredi ; dans l'affirmative, nous vous prions de…** we'd like to know if you are free on

Wednesday; if you are or if so, please...; **répondre par l'affirmative** to reply in the affirmative

**affirmer** [afirme] **1.** *vt* [manifester] to assert ; [soutenir] to maintain **2. s'affirmer** *vpr* [personne] to assert oneself ; [tendance] to be confirmed ■ **affirmation** *nf* assertion

**affliger** [afliʒe] *vt* [peiner] to distress ; [atteindre] to afflict (**de** with)

**affluence** [aflyɑ̃s] *nf* [de personnes] crowd ; [de marchandises] abundance

**affluer** [aflye] *vi* [sang] to rush (**à** to) ; [gens] to flock (**vers** to)

**afflux** [afly] *nm* [de sang] rush ; [de visiteurs] flood ; [de capitaux] influx

**affoler** [afɔle] **1.** *vt* to throw into a panic **2. s'affoler** *vpr* to panic ■ **affolant, -e** *adj* terrifying ■ **affolement** *nm* panic

**affranchir** [afrɑ̃ʃir] *vt* [timbrer] to put a stamp on ; [émanciper] to free ■ **affranchissement** *nm* [tarif] postage

**affréter** [afrete] *vt* to charter

**affreux, -euse** [afrø, -øz] *adj* [laid] hideous ; [atroce] dreadful

**affront** [afrɔ̃] *nm* insult ; **faire un affront à qn** to insult sb

**affronter** [afrɔ̃te] **1.** *vt* to confront ; [mauvais temps] to brave **2. s'affronter** *vpr* [ennemis, équipes] to clash ■ **affrontement** *nm* confrontation

**affût** [afy] *nm Fig* **à l'affût de** on the lookout for

**affûter** [afyte] *vt* to sharpen

**Afghanistan** [afganistɑ̃] *nm* **l'Afghanistan** Afghanistan ■ **afghan, -e 1.** *adj* Afghan **2.** *nmf* **Afghan, Afghane** Afghan

**afin** [afɛ̃] **1.** *prép* **afin de faire qch** in order to do sth **2.** *conj* **afin que...** (+ *subjunctive*) so that...

**Afrique** [afrik] *nf* **l'Afrique** Africa ■ **africain, -e 1.** *adj* African **2.** *nmf* **Africain, Africaine** African

**agacer** [agase] *vt* [personne] to irritate ■ **agaçant, -e** *adj* irritating

**âge** [ɑʒ] *nm* age ; **quel âge as-tu ?** how old are you? ; **d'un certain âge** middle-aged ■ **âgé, -e** *adj* old ; **être âgé de six ans** to be six years old ; **un enfant âgé de six ans** a six-year-old child

**agence** [aʒɑ̃s] *nf* agency ; [de banque] branch ; **agence de voyage** travel agent's ; **agence immobilière** *Br* estate agent's, *Am* real estate office

**agencer** [aʒɑ̃se] *vt* to arrange ; **bien agencé** [maison] well laid-out

**agenda** [aʒɛ̃da] *nm Br* diary, *Am* datebook

**agenouiller** [aʒənuje] ■ **s'agenouiller** *vpr* to kneel (down) ; **être agenouillé** to be kneeling (down)

**agent** [aʒɑ̃] *nmf* [employé, espion] agent ; **agent de police** police officer ; **agent de change** stockbroker ; **agent immobilier** *Br* estate agent, *Am* real estate agent ; **agent secret** secret agent

**agglomérer** [aglɔmere, aglɔmɛre] *vt* to mix together ■ **agglomération** *nf* [ville] built-up area, town ; **l'agglomération parisienne** Paris and its suburbs

**aggraver** [agrave] **1.** *vt* [situation, maladie] to make worse ; [difficultés] to increase **2. s'aggraver** *vpr* [situation, maladie] to get worse ; [état de santé] to deteriorate ; [difficultés] to increase ■ **aggravation** *nf* [de maladie] aggravation ; [de conflit] worsening

**agile** [aʒil] *adj* agile, nimble ■ **agilité** *nf* agility, nimbleness

**agios** [aʒjo] *nmpl* FIN bank charges

**agir** [aʒir] **1.** *vi* to act **2. s'agir** *v impers* **de quoi s'agit-il ?** what is it about? ; **il s'agit de se dépêcher** we have to hurry

**agitateur, -trice** [aʒitatœr, -tris] *nmf* agitator

**agitation** [aʒitɑsjɔ̃] *nf* [fébrilité] restlessness ; [troubles] unrest

**agiter** [aʒite] **1.** *vt* [remuer] to stir ; [secouer] to shake ; [brandir] to wave ; [troubler] to agitate **2. s'agiter** *vpr* [enfant] to fidget ■ **agité, -e** *adj* [mer] rough ; [personne] restless ; [enfant] fidgety ; [period] unsettled

**agneau, -x** [aɲo] *nm* lamb

**agonie** [agɔni] *nf* death throes; **être à l'agonie** to be at death's door ■ **agoniser** *vi* to be dying

**agrafe** [agraf] *nf* [pour vêtement] hook; [pour papiers] staple ■ **agrafer** *vt* [vêtement] to fasten; [papiers] to staple ■ **agrafeuse** *nf* stapler

**agrandir** [agrɑ̃dir] **1.** *vt* [rendre plus grand] to enlarge; [grossir] to magnify **2. s'agrandir** *vpr* [entreprise] to expand; [ville] to grow ■ **agrandissement** *nm* [d'entreprise] expansion; [de ville] growth; [de maison] extension; [de photo] enlargement

**agréable** [agreabl] *adj* pleasant

**agréer** [agree] *vt* [fournisseur] to approve; **veuillez agréer l'expression de mes salutations distinguées** [dans une lettre - à quelqu'un dont on ne connaît pas le nom] *Br* yours faithfully, *Am* sincerely; [à quelqu'un dont on connaît le nom] *Br* yours sincerely, *Am* sincerely ■ **agréé, -e** *adj* [fournisseur, centre] approved

**agrégation** [agregasjɔ̃] *nf* **(le concours de) l'agrégation** *competitive examination for posts on the teaching staff of lycées and universities*

**agrémenter** [agremɑ̃te] *vt* to adorn (de with)

**agrès** [agrɛ] *nmpl* [de voilier] tackle; GYM *Br* apparatus, *Am* equipment

**agresser** [agrese] *vt* to attack; **se faire agresser** to be attacked; [pour son argent] to be mugged ■ **agresseur** *nm* attacker; [dans un conflit] aggressor ■ **agression** *nf* attack; [pour de l'argent] mugging; [d'un État] aggression; **être victime d'une agression** to be attacked; [pour son argent] to be mugged

**agressif, -ive** [agresif, -iv] *adj* aggressive ■ **agressivité** *nf* aggressiveness

**agricole** [agrikɔl] *adj* agricultural; [ouvrier, machine] farm; **travaux agricoles** farm work

**agriculteur, -trice** [agrikyltœr, -tris] *nmf* farmer ■ **agriculture** *nf* farming, agriculture; **agriculture biologique** organic farming

**agripper** [agripe] ■ **s'agripper** *vpr* **s'agripper à qn/qch** to cling on to sb/sth

**agritourisme** [agrituism] *nm* agritourism

**agroalimentaire** [agroalimɑ̃tɛr] **1.** *adj* **industrie agroalimentaire** food-processing industry; **les produits agroalimentaires** processed foods *or* foodstuffs **2.** *nm* **l'agroalimentaire** the food-processing industry

**agrotourisme** [agrotuism] *nm* agrotourism

**agrume** [agrym] *nm* citrus fruit

**aguerri, -e** [ageri] *adj* seasoned, hardened

**aguets** [agɛ] ■ **aux aguets** *adv* on the lookout

**aguichant, -e** [agiʃɑ̃, -ɑ̃t] *adj* seductive

**ahurir** [ayrir] *vt* [étonner] to astound

**ai** [ɛ] *voir* **avoir**

**aide** [ɛd] **1.** *nf* help, assistance; **à l'aide de qch** with the aid of sth; **appeler à l'aide** to call for help; **aide humanitaire** aid **2.** *nmf* [personne] assistant; **aide de camp** aide-de-camp ■ **aide-éducateur, -trice** [ɛdedykatœr, tris] *nmf* SCOL teaching assistant ■ **aide-mémoire** *nm inv* notes ■ **aide-soignante** (*pl* **aides-soignantes**) *nf* *Br* nursing auxiliary, *Am* nurse's aid

**aider** [ede] **1.** *vt* to help; **aider qn à faire qch** to help sb to do sth **2. s'aider** *vpr* **s'aider de qch** to use sth

**aïe** [aj] *excl* ouch!

**aie(s), aient** [ɛ] *voir* **avoir**

**aigle** [ɛgl] *nm* eagle

**aigre** [ɛgr] *adj* [acide] sour; [parole] cutting; **d'un ton aigre** sharply ■ **aigreur** *nf* [de goût] sourness; [de ton] sharpness; **aigreurs d'estomac** heartburn

**aigri, -e** [ɛgri] *adj* [personne] embittered

**aigu**

**aigu, -ë** [egy] *adj* [douleur, crise, accent] acute ; [son] high-pitched

**aiguille** [egɥij] *nf* [à coudre] needle ; [de montre] hand ; [de balance] pointer ; **aiguille (rocheuse)** peak ; **aiguille de pin** pine needle

**aiguiller** [egɥije] *vt* [train] *Br* to shunt, *Am* to switch ; *Fig* [personne] to steer (**vers** towards) ■ **aiguillage** *nm* [appareil] *Br* points, *Am* switches ■ **aiguilleur** *nm* [de trains] signalman ; **aiguilleur du ciel** air-traffic controller

**aiguiser** [egize] *vt* [outil] to sharpen ; *Fig* [appétit] to whet ■ **aiguise-crayon** [egizkrɛjɔ̃] *(pl* **aiguise-crayons**) *nm* *Can* pencil sharpener

**ail** [aj] *nm* garlic

**aile** [ɛl] *nf* wing ; [de moulin] sail ; [de voiture] *Br* wing, *Am* fender ■ **ailé, -e** *adj* winged ■ **aileron** *nm* [de requin] fin ; [d'avion] aileron ■ **ailier** *nm* [au football] winger ; [au rugby] wing

**aille(s), aillent** [aj] *voir* **aller**

**ailleurs** [ajœr] *adv* somewhere else, elsewhere ; **d'ailleurs** [du reste] besides, anyway ; **par ailleurs** [en outre] moreover ; [par d'autres côtés] in other respects

**aimable** [ɛmabl] *adj* [gentil] kind

**aimant¹** [ɛmɑ̃] *nm* magnet ■ **aimanter** *vt* to magnetize

**aimant², -e** [ɛmɑ̃, -ɑ̃t] *adj* loving

**aimer** [eme] **1.** *vt* to love ; **aimer bien qn / qch** to like sb /sth ; **aimer faire qch** to like doing sth ; **j'aimerais qu'il vienne** I would like him to come ; **aimer mieux qch** to prefer sth **2. s'aimer** *vpr* **ils s'aiment** they're in love

**aine** [ɛn] *nf* groin

**aîné, -e** [ene] **1.** *adj* [de deux enfants] elder ; [de plus de deux] eldest **2.** *nmf* [de deux enfants] elder ; [de plus de deux] eldest

**ainsi** [ɛ̃si] *adv* [de cette façon] in this way ; [alors] so ; **ainsi que...** as well as... ; **et ainsi de suite** and so on ; **pour ainsi dire** so to speak ; **ainsi soit-il !** amen!

**air** [ɛr] *nm* a) [gaz] air ; **prendre l'air** to get some fresh air ; **au grand air** in the fresh air ; **en plein air** outside ; **en l'air** [jeter] (up) in the air ; [paroles, menaces] empty ; **regarder en l'air** to look up b) [expression] look, appearance ; **avoir l'air content** to look happy ; **avoir l'air de s'ennuyer** to look bored ; **air de famille** family likeness c) [mélodie] tune

**airbag** [ɛrbag] *nm* airbag

**aire** [ɛr] *nf* [surface & MATH] area ; [d'oiseau] eyrie ; **aire de jeux** (children's) play area ; **aire de lancement** launch pad ; **aire de repos** [sur autoroute] rest area ; **aire de stationnement** lay-by

**aisance** [ɛzɑ̃s] *nf* [facilité] ease ; [prospérité] affluence

**aise** [ɛz] *nf* **à l'aise** [dans un vêtement] comfortable ; [dans une situation] at ease ; [fortuné] comfortably off ; **mal à l'aise** uncomfortable, ill at ease ■ **aisé, -e** [eze] *adj* [fortuné] comfortably off ; [facile] easy ■ **aisément** *adv* easily

**aisselle** [ɛsɛl] *nf* armpit

**ait** [ɛ] *voir* **avoir**

**ajourner** [aʒurne] *vt* to postpone ; [après le début de la séance] to adjourn

**ajout** [aʒu] *nm* addition (**à** to) ■ **ajouter 1.** *vt & vi* to add (**à** to) **2. s'ajouter** *vpr* **s'ajouter à qch** to add to sth

**ajuster** [aʒyste] *vt* [appareil, outil] to adjust ; [vêtement] to alter ■ **ajustable** *adj* adjustable

**alarme** [alarm] *nf* alarm ; **donner l'alarme** to raise the alarm ; **alarme antivol / d'incendie** burglar / fire alarm ■ **alarmer 1.** *vt* to alarm **2. s'alarmer** *vpr* **s'alarmer de qch** to become alarmed at sth

**Albanie** *nf* **l'Albanie** Albania ■ **Albanais, -e 1.** *adj* Albanian **2.** *nmf* **Albanais, Albanaise** Albanian

**album** [albɔm] *nm* album ; **album de bandes dessinées** comic book ; **album de photos** photo album

**alcool** [alkɔl] *nm* CHIM alcohol ; [spiritueux] spirits ; **alcool à 90°** *Br* surgical spirit, *Am* rubbing alcohol ; **alcool à brûler** *Br* methylated spirits, *Am* wood alcohol ■ **alcoolémie** [alkɔlemi] *nf* **taux d'alcoolémie** blood alcohol level ■ **alcoolique** *adj & nmf* alcoholic

■ **alcoolisée** *adj f* **boisson alcoolisée** alcoholic drink; **boisson non alcoolisée** soft drink ■ **alcoolisme** *nm* alcoholism ■ **Alcootest®** *nm* [test] breath test; [appareil] Breathalyzer®

**alcôve** [alkov] *nf* alcove

**aléas** [alea] *nmpl* hazards ■ **aléatoire** *adj* [résultat] uncertain; [nombre & ORDINAT] random

**alentour** [alɑ̃tur] *adv* round about; **les villages alentour** the surrounding villages ■ **alentours** *nmpl* surroundings; **aux alentours de la ville** in the vicinity of the town

**alerte** [alɛrt] **1.** *adj* [leste] sprightly; [éveillé] alert **2.** *nf* alarm; **en état d'alerte** on the alert; **donner l'alerte** to give the alarm; **alerte à la bombe** bomb scare; **fausse alerte** false alarm ■ **alerter** *vt* to alert (**de** to)

**alezan, -e** [alzɑ̃, -an] *adj & nmf* [cheval] chestnut

**algèbre** [alʒɛbr] *nf* algebra

**Algérie** [alʒeri] *nf* **l'Algérie** Algeria ■ **algérien, -enne 1.** *adj* Algerian **2.** *nmf* **Algérien, Algérienne** Algerian

**algues** [alg] *nfpl* seaweed

**alias** [aljɑs] **1.** *adv* alias **2.** *nm* ORDINAT [dans un mail, sur le bureau] alias

**alibi** [alibi] *nm* alibi

**aliéner** [aljene] **1.** *vt* to alienate **2. s'aliéner** *vpr* **s'aliéner qn** to alienate sb

**aligner** [aliɲe] **1.** *vt* to line up; [politique] to align (**sur** with) **2. s'aligner** *vpr* [personnes] to line up; [pays] to align oneself (**sur** with) ■ **alignement** *nm* alignment

**aliment** [alimɑ̃] *nm* food ■ **alimentaire** *adj* [ration, industrie] food; **produits alimentaires** foods ■ **alimentation** *nf* [action] feeding; [en eau, en électricité] supply(ing); [régime] diet; [nourriture] food; **avoir une alimentation saine** to have a healthy diet; **magasin d'alimentation** grocer's, grocery store ■ **alimenter** *vt* [nourrir] to feed; [fournir] to supply (**en** with); [débat, feu] to fuel

**alité, -e** [alite] *adj* bedridden

**allaiter** [alete] *vt* [femme] to breast-feed

**allécher** [aleʃe] *vt* to tempt

**allée** [ale] *nf* [de parc] path; [de ville] avenue; [de cinéma, de supermarché] aisle; [devant une maison] driveway; **allées et venues** comings and goings

**allégation** [alegasjɔ̃] *nf* allegation

**alléger** [aleʒe] *vt* [impôt] to reduce; [fardeau] to lighten ■ **allégé, -e** *adj* [fromage] low-fat

**allégorie** [alegɔri] *nf* allegory

**allègre** [alɛgr] *adj* lively, cheerful

**allégresse** [alegrɛs] *nf* joy

**Allemagne** [alman] *nf* **l'Allemagne** Germany ■ **allemand, -ande 1.** *adj* German **2.** *nmf* **Allemand, Allemande** German **3.** *nm* [langue] German

---

**aller¹** [ale] **1.** (*aux* **être**) *vi* to go; **aller à Paris** to go to Paris; **aller à la pêche** to go fishing; **aller faire qch** to go and do sth; **aller à qn** [convenir à] to suit sb; **aller avec** [vêtement] to go with; **aller bien/mieux** [personne] to be well/better; **comment vas-tu ?, (comment) ça va ?** how are you?; **ça va !** all right!, fine!; **allez-y** go ahead **2.** *v aux* [futur proche] **aller faire qch** to be going to do sth; **il va venir** he'll come; **il va partir** he's about to leave **3. s'en aller** [sɑ̃nale] *vpr* [personne] to go away; [tache] to come out

---

**aller²** [ale] *nm* outward journey; **aller (simple)** *Br* single (ticket), *Am* one-way (ticket); **aller (et) retour** *Br* return (ticket), *Am* round-trip (ticket)

**allergénique** [alɛrʒenik] *adj* allergenic

**allergie** [alɛrʒi] *nf* allergy ■ **allergique** *adj* allergic (**à** to)

**alliage** [aljaʒ] *nm* alloy

**alliance** [aljɑ̃s] *nf* [anneau] wedding ring; [mariage] marriage; [de pays] alliance

**allier** [alje] **1.** *vt* [associer] to combine (**à** with); [pays] to ally (**à** with); [famille] to unite by marriage **2. s'allier** *vpr* [couleurs] to combine; [pays] to become allied (à with); **s'allier à contre** qn/qch to unite against sb/sth ∎ **allié, -e** nmf ally

**allô** [alo] excl hello!

**allocation** [alɔkasjɔ̃] nf [somme] allowance; **allocation (de) chômage** unemployment benefit; **allocation (de) logement** housing benefit; **allocations familiales** child benefit

**allocution** [alɔkysjɔ̃] nf address

**allonger** [alɔ̃ʒe] 1. vt [bras] to stretch out; [sauce] to thin; **allonger le pas** to quicken one's pace 2. vi [jours] to get longer 3. **s'allonger** vpr [jours] to get longer; [personne] to lie down ∎ **allongé, -e** adj [étiré] elongated; **être allongé** [personne] to be lying down

**allouer** [alwe] vt **allouer** qch **à** qn [ration] to allocate sb sth; [indemnité] to grant sb sth

**allumer** [alyme] 1. vt [feu, pipe] to light; [électricité, radio] to switch on; [incendie] to start 2. **s'allumer** vpr [lumière, lampe] to come on ∎ **allumage** nm [de feu] lighting; [de moteur] ignition ∎ **allumé, -e** Fam 1. adj crazy; **son frère est complètement allumé !** his brother's a complete nutter! 2. nmf nutter Fam; **il traîne avec une bande d'allumés** he hangs around with a load of nutters ∎ **allume-cigare(s)** [alymsigar] (pl **allume-cigares**) nm cigarette lighter

**allumette** [alymɛt] nf match

**allure** [alyr] nf [vitesse] speed; [démarche] gait, walk; [maintien] bearing; **à toute allure** at top speed; **avoir de l'allure** to look stylish

**allusion** [alyzjɔ̃] nf [référence] allusion (à to); [voilée] hint; **faire allusion à** qch to allude to sth; [en termes voilés] to hint at sth

**aloi** [alwa] nm **de bon aloi** [plaisanterie] in good taste

**alors** [alɔr] adv [donc] so; [à ce moment-là] then; [dans ce cas] in that case; **alors que...** [lorsque] when...; [tandis que] whereas...; **et alors ?** so what?

**alouette** [alwɛt] nf lark

**alourdir** [alurdir] 1. vt [chose] to make heavier 2. **s'alourdir** vpr to get heavy

**ALP** SMS abr écrite de **à la prochaine**

**alpage** [alpaʒ] nm mountain pasture ∎ **Alpes** nfpl **les Alpes** the Alps ∎ **alpestre, alpin, -e** [alpɛ̃, -in] adj alpine

**alphabet** [alfabɛ] nm alphabet ∎ **alphabétique** adj alphabetical

**alphanumérique** [alfanymerik] adj alphanumeric

**alpinisme** [alpinism] nm mountaineering; **faire de l'alpinisme** to go mountaineering ∎ **alpiniste** nmf mountaineer

**altérer** [altere] 1. vt a) [viande, vin] to spoil b) [changer] to affect 2. **s'altérer** vpr [relations] to deteriorate

**altermondialisation** [altɛrmɔ̃djalizasjɔ̃] nf alterglobalisation ∎ **altermondialisme** nm alterglobalism ∎ **altermondialiste** adj & nmf alterglobalist

**alternatif, -ive** [altɛrnatif, -iv] adj [successif] alternating; [de remplacement] alternative ∎ **alternative** nf alternative ∎ **alternativement** adv alternately

**alterner** [altɛrne] 1. vt [crops] to rotate 2. vi [se succéder] to alternate (**avec** with); [personnes] to take turns (**avec** with) ∎ **alternance** nf alternation; **en alternance** alternately

**Altesse** [altɛs] nf **son Altesse royale** His/Her Royal Highness

**altier, -ère** [altje, -ɛr] adj haughty

**altitude** [altityd] nf altitude; **prendre de l'altitude** to climb

**aluminium** [alyminjɔm] nm Br aluminium, Am aluminum; **papier (d') aluminium** tinfoil

**Alzheimer** [alzajmɛr] nom **la maladie d'Alzheimer** Alzheimer's disease

**amabilité** [amabilite] nf kindness

**amaigrir** [amegrir] vt to make thin or thinner ∎ **amaigri, -e** adj gaunt

**amande** [amɑ̃d] nf almond

**amant** [amɑ̃] nm lover

**amoral**

**amarre** [amar] *nf* (mooring) rope ; **amarres** moorings

**amas** [amɑ] *nm* heap, pile ▪ **amasser 1.** *vt* to amass **2. s'amasser** *vpr* [preuves, foule] to build up ; [neige] to pile up

**amateur** [amatœr] **1.** *nm* [non professionnel] amateur ; **amateur de tennis** tennis enthusiast ; **faire de la photo en amateur** to be an amateur photographer **2.** *adj* **une équipe amateur** an amateur team

**amazone** [amazɔn] *nf* horsewoman ; **monter en amazone** to ride sidesaddle

**ambages** [ɑ̃baʒ] ▪ **sans ambages** *adv* without beating about the bush

**ambassade** [ɑ̃basad] *nf* embassy ▪ **ambassadeur, -drice** *nmf* ambassador

**ambiance** [ɑ̃bjɑ̃s] *nf* atmosphere ▪ **ambiant, -e** *adj* surrounding ; **température ambiante** room temperature

**ambidextre** [ɑ̃bidɛkstr] *adj* ambidextrous

**ambigu, -ë** [ɑ̃bigy] *adj* ambiguous ▪ **ambiguïté** *nf* ambiguity

**ambitieux, -euse** [ɑ̃bisjø, -øz] *adj* ambitious ▪ **ambition** *nf* ambition ▪ **ambitionner** *vt* to aspire to

**ambre** [ɑ̃br] *nm* [résine] amber

**ambulance** [ɑ̃bylɑ̃s] *nf* ambulance

**ambulant, -e** [ɑ̃bylɑ̃, -ɑ̃t] *adj* travelling, itinerant ; **marchand ambulant** (street) hawker

**âme** [ɑm] *nf* soul ; **rendre l'âme** to give up the ghost ; **âme sœur** soul mate

**améliorer** [ameljɔre] **1.** *vt* to improve **2. s'améliorer** *vpr* to improve ▪ **amélioration** *nf* improvement

**amen** [amɛn] *adv* amen

**aménager** *vt* [changer] to adjust ; [maison] to convert (**en** into) ▪ **aménagement** *nm* [changement] adjustment ; [de pièce] conversion (**en** into) ; **aménagement du temps de travail** flexibility of working hours

**amende** [amɑ̃d] *nf* fine ; **infliger une amende à qn** to impose a fine on sb

**amender** [amɑ̃de] *vt* [texte de loi] to amend

**amener** [amne] **1.** *vt* [apporter] to bring ; [causer] to bring about ; [tirer à soi] to pull in ; **amener qn à faire qch** [sujet : personne] to get sb to do sth ; **ce qui nous amène à parler de...** which brings us to the issue of... **2. s'amener** *vpr Fam* to turn up

**amenuiser** [amənɥize] ▪ **s'amenuiser** *vpr* to dwindle ; [écart] to get smaller

**amer, -ère** [amɛr] *adj* bitter

**Amérique** [amerik] *nf* **l'Amérique** America ; **l'Amérique du Nord / du Sud** North / South America ; **l'Amérique latine** Latin America ▪ **américain, -e 1.** *adj* American **2.** *nmf* **Américain, Américaine** American

**amertume** [amɛrtym] *nf* bitterness

**ameublement** [amœbləmɑ̃] *nm* [meubles] furniture

**ami, -e** [ami] **1.** *nmf* friend ; **petit ami** boyfriend ; **petite amie** girlfriend **2.** *adj* friendly ; **être ami avec qn** to be friends with sb

**amiable** [amjabl] ▪ **à l'amiable 1.** *adj* amicable **2.** *adv* amicably

**amical, -e, -aux** [amikal, -o] *adj* friendly ▪ **amicale** *nf* association

**amincir** [amɛ̃sir] *vt* to make thin *or* thinner ; **cette robe t'amincit** that dress makes you look thinner

**amiral, -aux** [amiral, -o] *nm* admiral

**amitié** [amitje] *nf* friendship ; **mes amitiés à votre mère** give my best wishes to your mother

**amnésie** [amnezi] *nf* amnesia

**amnistie** [amnisti] *nf* amnesty

**amoindrir** [amwɛ̃drir] **1.** *vt* to diminish **2. s'amoindrir** *vpr* to diminish

**amonceler** [amɔ̃sle] **1.** *vt* to pile up **2. s'amonceler** *vpr* to pile up ▪ **amoncellement** *nm* heap, pile

**amont** [amɔ̃] ▪ **en amont** *adv* upstream (**de** from)

**amoral, -e, -aux** [amɔral, -o] *adj* amoral

**amorce** [amɔrs] *nf* [début] start ; [de pêcheur] bait ; [détonateur] detonator ; [de pistolet d'enfant] cap ■ **amorcer 1.** *vt* [commencer] to start ; [hameçon] to bait ; [bombe] to arm ; ORDINAT to boot up **2. s'amorcer** *vpr* to start

**amortir** [amɔrtir] *vt* [coup] to absorb ; [bruit] to deaden ; [chute] to break ; [achat] to recoup the costs of ; FIN [dette] to pay off ■ **amortissement** *nm* [d'un emprunt] redemption ■ **amortisseur** *nm* [de véhicule] shock absorber

**amour** [amur] *nm* [sentiment, liaison] love ; **faire l'amour avec qn** to make love with or to sb ; **pour l'amour du ciel !** for heaven's sake! ; **mon amour** my darling, my love ■ **amour-propre** *nm* self-respect ■ **amoureux, -euse 1.** *adj* **être amoureux de qn** to be in love with sb ; **tomber amoureux de qn** to fall in love with sb **2.** *nm* boyfriend ; **un couple d'amoureux** a pair of lovers ■ **amours** *nmpl* [vie sentimentale] love-life

**amovible** [amɔvibl] *adj* removable, detachable

**amphétamine** [ɑ̃fetamin] *nf* amphetamine

**amphithéâtre** [ɑ̃fiteatr] *nm* [romain] amphitheatre ; [à l'université] lecture hall

**ample** [ɑ̃pl] *adj* [vêtement] full ; [geste] sweeping ; **de plus amples renseignements** more detailed information ■ **amplement** *adv* amply, fully ; **c'est amplement suffisant** it is more than enough ■ **ampleur** *nf* [de vêtement] fullness ; [importance] scale, extent ; **prendre de l'ampleur** to grow in size

**amplifier** [ɑ̃plifje] **1.** *vt* [son] to amplify ; [phénomène] to intensify **2. s'amplifier** *vpr* [son] to increase ; [phénomène] to intensify ■ **amplificateur** *nm* amplifier ■ **amplification** *nf* [de son] amplification ; [de phénomène] intensification

**amplitude** [ɑ̃plityd] *nf* [de désastre] magnitude ; [variation] range

**ampoule** [ɑ̃pul] *nf* [électrique] (light) bulb ; [sur la peau] blister ; [de médicament] phial ; **ampoule basse consommation** low-energy light bulb ; **ampoule à économie d'énergie** energy saving bulb

**amputer** [ɑ̃pyte] *vt* [membre] to amputate ; **amputer qn de la jambe** to amputate sb's leg ■ **amputation** *nf* [de membre] amputation

**amuser** [amyze] **1.** *vt* to amuse **2. s'amuser** *vpr* to amuse oneself ; **s'amuser avec qn/qch** to play with sb/sth ; **s'amuser à faire qch** to amuse oneself doing sth ; **bien s'amuser** to have a good time ■ **amusant, -e** *adj* amusing ■ **amusement** *nm* amusement

**amygdales** [amidal] *nfpl* tonsils

**an** [ɑ̃] *nm* year ; **il a dix ans** he's ten (years old) ; **par an** per year ; **en l'an 2005** in the year 2005 ; **bon an, mal an** on average over the years

**anabolisant, e** [anabɔlizɑ̃, ɑ̃t] **1.** *adj* anabolic **2.** *nm* anabolic steroid

**anachronisme** [anakrɔnism] *nm* anachronism

**anagramme** [anagram] *nf* anagram

**analogie** [analɔʒi] *nf* analogy

**analogue** [analɔg] *adj* similar (**à** to)

**analphabète** [analfabɛt] *adj* & *nmf* illiterate

**analyse** [analiz] *nf* analysis ; **analyse de sang/d'urine** blood/urine test ■ **analyser** *vt* to analyse

**ananas** [anana(s)] *nm* pineapple

**anarchie** [anarʃi] *nf* anarchy ■ **anarchiste 1.** *adj* anarchistic **2.** *nmf* anarchist

**anatomie** [anatɔmi] *nf* anatomy ■ **anatomique** *adj* anatomical

**ancestral, -e, -aux** [ɑ̃sɛstral, -o] *adj* ancestral

**ancêtre** [ɑ̃sɛtr] *nm* ancestor

**anchois** [ɑ̃ʃwa] *nm* anchovy

**ancien, -enne** [ɑ̃sjɛ̃, -ɛn] **1.** *adj* [vieux] old ; [meuble] antique ; [qui n'est plus] former, old ; **dans l'ancien temps** in the old days ; **ancien combattant** *Br* ex-serviceman, *Am* veteran **2.** *nmf* [par l'âge] elder ■ **anciennement** *adv* formerly ■ **ancienneté** *nf* [âge] age ; [expérience] seniority

**ancre** [ɑ̃kr] *nf* anchor ■ **ancrer** *vt* [navire] to anchor

**Andorre** [ɑ̃dɔr] *nf* Andorra

**andouille** [ɑ̃duj] *nf* **a)** [charcuterie] *sausage made from pigs' intestines* **b)** *Fam* [idiot] fool

**âne** [ɑn] *nm* [animal] donkey

**anéantir** [aneɑ̃tir] *vt* [ville] to destroy ; [armée] to crush ; [espoirs] to shatter ■ **anéanti, -e** *adj* [épuisé] exhausted ; [accablé] overwhelmed ■ **anéantissement** *nm* [de ville] destruction

**anecdote** [anɛkdɔt] *nf* anecdote ■ **anecdotique** *adj* anecdotal

**anémie** [anemi] *nf* an(a)emia ■ **anémique** *adj* an(a)emic

**anémone** [anemɔn] *nf* anemone

**ânerie** [ɑnri] *nf* [parole] stupid remark ; [action] stupid act

**anesthésie** [anɛstezi] *nf* an(a)esthesia ; **être sous anesthésie** to be under ana(e)sthetic ; **anesthésie générale / locale** general / local an(a)esthetic ■ **anesthésier** *vt* to an(a)esthetize ■ **anesthésiste** *nmf Br* an(a)esthetist, *Am* anesthesiologist

**aneth** [anɛt] *nm* dill

**anévrysme, anévrisme** [anevrism] *nm* MÉD aneurism ; **rupture d'anévrysme** aneurysmal rupture

**ange** [ɑ̃ʒ] *nm* angel ; **être aux anges** to be in seventh heaven ; **ange gardien** guardian angel ■ **angélique 1.** *adj* angelic **2.** *nf* CULIN angelica

**angine** [ɑ̃ʒin] *nf* sore throat ; **angine de poitrine** angina (pectoris)

**anglais, -e** [ɑ̃glɛ, -ɛz] **1.** *adj* English **2.** *nmf* **Anglais, Anglaise** Englishman, Englishwoman ; **les Anglais** the English **3.** *nm* [langue] English **4.** *nf Fam* **filer à l'anglaise** to slip away

**angle** [ɑ̃gl] *nm* [point de vue & MATH] angle ; [coin de rue] corner ; **la maison qui fait l'angle** the house on the corner ; AUTO **angle mort** blind spot

**Angleterre** [ɑ̃glətɛr] *nf* l'**Angleterre** England

**anglican, -e** [ɑ̃glikɑ̃, -an] *adj* & *nmf* Anglican

**anglo-normand, -e** [ɑ̃glonɔrmɑ̃, -ɑ̃d] *adj* **les îles anglo-normandes** the Channel Islands

**anglophone** [ɑ̃glofɔn] **1.** *adj* English-speaking **2.** *nmf* English speaker

**anglo-saxon, -onne** [ɑ̃glosaksɔ̃, -ɔn] *(mpl* **anglo-saxons,** *fpl* **anglo-saxonnes)** *adj* & *nmf* Anglo-Saxon

**angoisse** [ɑ̃gwas] *nf* anguish ; **une crise d'angoisse** an anxiety attack ■ **angoissant, -e** *adj* [nouvelle] distressing ; [attente] agonizing ; [livre] frightening ■ **angoissé, -e** *adj* [personne] anxious ; [cri, regard] anguished ■ **angoisser 1.** *vt* **angoisser qn** to make sb anxious **2. s'angoisser** *vpr* to get anxious

**angora** [ɑ̃gɔra] *nm* [laine] angora ; **pull en angora** angora sweater

**anguille** [ɑ̃gij] *nf* eel

**anguleux, -euse** [ɑ̃gylø, -øz] *adj* [visage] angular

**anicroche** [anikrɔʃ] *nf* hitch, snag

**animal, -aux** [animal, -o] **1.** *nm* animal ; **animal domestique** pet **2.** *adj* [règne, graisse] animal ■ **animalerie** [animalri] *nf* pet shop ■ **animalier, ère** [animalje, ɛr] *adj* **parc animalier** wildlife park

**animateur, -trice** [animatœr, -tris] *nmf* [de télévision, de radio] presenter ; [de club] leader

**animer** [anime] **1.** *vt* [débat] to lead ; [jeu télévisé] to present ; [inspirer] to prompt **2. s'animer** *vpr* [rue] to come to life ; [visage] to light up ; [conversation] to get more lively ■ **animation** *nf* [vie] life ; [divertissement] event ; CINÉ animation ; **mettre de l'animation dans une soirée** to liven up a party ■ **animé, -e** *adj* [personne, conversation] lively ; [rue, quartier] busy

**animosité** [animozite] *nf* animosity

**anis** [ani(s)] *nm* aniseed

**ankylosé, -e** [ɑ̃kiloze] *adj* stiff

**annales** [anal] *nfpl* annals

**anneau, -x** [ano] *nm* [bague] ring; [de chaîne] link; GYM **les anneaux** the rings

**année** [ane] *nf* year; **les années 90** the nineties; **année bissextile** leap year; **année civile** calendar year; **année scolaire** school year; **souhaiter la bonne année à qn** to wish sb a happy New Year

**annexe** [anɛks] **1.** *nf* [bâtiment] annexe; [de lettre] enclosure; [de livre] appendix; **document en annexe** enclosed document **2.** *adj* [pièces] enclosed; [revenus] supplementary; **bâtiment annexe** annex(e) ■ **annexer** *vt* [pays] to annex; [document] to append

**annihiler** [aniile] *vt* [ville, armée] to annihilate

**anniversaire** [anivɛrsɛr] **1.** *nm* [d'événement] anniversary; [de naissance] birthday **2.** *adj* **date anniversaire** anniversary

**annonce** [anɔ̃s] *nf* [déclaration] announcement; [publicitaire] advertisement; [indice] sign; **passer une annonce dans un journal** to put an ad(vertisement) in a newspaper; **petites annonces** classified advertisements, *Br* small ads ■ **annoncer 1.** *vt* [déclarer] to announce; [dans la presse - soldes, exposition] to advertise; [indiquer] to herald; **annoncer qn** [visiteur] to show sb in **2. s'annoncer** *vpr* **ça s'annonce bien /mal** things aren't looking too bad /good ■ **annonceur** *nm* [publicitaire] advertiser

**annuaire** [anɥɛr] *nm* [d'organisme] yearbook; [liste d'adresses] directory; **être dans l'a** to be in the phone book; **annuaire téléphonique** telephone directory; **annuaire électronique** *telephone directory available on Minitel®*

**annuel, -elle** [anɥɛl] *adj* annual, yearly

**annuité** [anɥite] *nf* [d'emprunt] annual repayment

**annulaire** [anɥlɛr] *nm* ring finger

**annuler** [anɥle] **1.** *vt* [commande, rendez-vous] to cancel; [dette] to write off; [mariage] to annul; [jugement] to quash; ORDINAT to undo **2. s'annuler** *vpr* to cancel each other out ■ **annulation** *nf* [de commande, de rendez-vous] cancellation; [de dette] writing off; [de mariage] annulment; [de jugement] quashing; ORDINAT deletion

**anodin, -e** [anɔdɛ̃, -in] *adj* [remarque] harmless; [personne] insignificant

**anomalie** [anɔmali] *nf* [bizarrerie] anomaly

**anonymat** [anɔnima] *nm* anonymity; **garder l'anonymat** to remain anonymous ■ **anonyme** *adj* & *nmf* anonymous

**anorak** [anɔrak] *nm* anorak

**anorexie** [anɔrɛksi] *nf* MÉD anorexia ■ **anorexique** *adj* & *nmf* MÉD anorexic

**anormal, -e, -aux** [anɔrmal, -o] *adj* [non conforme] abnormal; [mentalement] educationally subnormal; [injuste] unfair

**anse** [ɑ̃s] *nf* [de tasse, de panier] handle

**antagonisme** [ɑ̃tagɔnism] *nm* antagonism

**antan** [ɑ̃tɑ̃] ■ **d'antan** *adj Litt* of yesteryear

**antarctique** [ɑ̃tarktik] *nm* **l'Antarctique** the Antarctic, Antarctica

**antécédent** [ɑ̃tesedɑ̃] *nm* GRAM antecedent; **antécédents** [de personne] past record; **antécédents médicaux** medical history

**antenne** [ɑ̃tɛn] *nf* [de radio, de satellite] aerial, antenna; [d'insecte] antenna, feeler; [société] branch; **être à l'antenne** to be on the air; **antenne parabolique** satellite dish ■ **antenne-relais** (*pl* **antennes-relais**) [ɑ̃tɛnrəlɛ] *nf* TÉL *Br* mobile phone mast

**antérieur, -e** [ɑ̃terjœr] *adj* [période] former; [année] previous; [date] earlier; [placé devant] front; **antérieur à qch** prior to sth

**anthologie** [ɑ̃tɔlɔʒi] *nf* anthology

**anthropologie** [ɑ̃trɔpɔlɔʒi] *nf* anthropology

**anti-** [ɑ̃ti] *préf* [contre] anti-

**antiacarien** [ɑ̃tiakarjɛ̃, ɛ] **1.** *adj* antimite ; **traitement** *ou* **shampooing antiacarien** antimite treatment *or* shampoo **2.** *nm* antimite treatment

**antiaérien, -enne** [ɑ̃tiaerjɛ̃, -ɛn] *adj* abri **antiaérien** air-raid shelter

**anti-âge** [ɑ̃tiaʒ] *adj* **crème anti-âge** *Br* antiageing *or* *Am* antiaging cream

**antiatomique** [ɑ̃tiatɔmik] *adj* abri **antiatomique** fallout shelter

**antiavortement** [ɑ̃tiavɔrtəmɑ̃] *adj inv* antiabortion, pro-life

**antibiotique** [ɑ̃tibjɔtik] *nm* antibiotic

**antibrouillard** [ɑ̃tibrujar] *adj* & *nm* **(phare) antibrouillard** fog lamp

**anticancéreux, euse** [ɑ̃tikɑ̃serø, øz] *adj* **a)** [centre, laboratoire] cancer **b)** [médicament] anticancer ■ **anticancéreux** *nm* cancer treatment

**antichambre** [ɑ̃tiʃɑ̃br] *nf* antechamber

**antichoc** [ɑ̃tiʃɔk] *adj inv* shock-proof

**anticipation** [ɑ̃tisipasjɔ̃] *nf* anticipation ; **d'anticipation** [roman, film] futuristic ■ **anticipé, -e** *adj* [retraite, retour] early ; [paiement] advance

**anticommuniste** [ɑ̃tikɔmynist] *adj* anti-communist

**anticonformiste** [ɑ̃tikɔ̃fɔrmist] *adj* & *nmf* nonconformist

**anticonstitutionnel, -elle** [ɑ̃tikɔ̃stitysjɔnɛl] *adj* unconstitutional

**anticorps** [ɑ̃tikɔr] *nm* antibody

**anticyclone** [ɑ̃tisiklon] *nm* anticyclone

**antidépresseur** [ɑ̃tidepresœr] *nm* antidepressant

**antidérapant, -e** [ɑ̃tiderapɑ̃, -ɑ̃t] *adj* [surface, pneu] non-skid ; [semelle] non-slip

**antidopage** [ɑ̃tidɔpaʒ] *adj* **contrôle antidopage** drug detection test

**antidote** [ɑ̃tidɔt] *nm* antidote

**antidouleur** [ɑ̃tidulœr] **1.** *adj inv* [médicament] painkilling ; **centre antidouleur** pain control unit **2.** *nm* painkiller

**antiémeutes** [ɑ̃tiemøt] *adj* riot ; **brigade antiémeutes** riot squad

**antieuropéen, enne** [ɑ̃tiørɔpeɛ̃, ɛn] *adj* & *nmf* anti-European

**antigel** [ɑ̃tiʒɛl] *nm* antifreeze

**antihistaminique** [ɑ̃tiistaminik] *adj* MÉD antihistamine

**anti-inflammatoire** [ɑ̃tiɛ̃flamatwar] *(pl* **anti-inflammatoires)** **1.** *adj* anti-inflammatory **2.** *nm* anti-inflammatory agent

**Antilles** [ɑ̃tij] *nfpl* **les Antilles** the West Indies ■ **antillais, -e 1.** *adj* West Indian **2.** *nmf* **Antillais, Antillaise** West Indian

**antilope** [ɑ̃tilɔp] *nf* antelope

**antimite** [ɑ̃timit] *nm* **de l'antimite** mothballs

**antimondialisation** [ɑ̃timɔ̃djalizasjɔ̃] *nf* & *adj inv* POL antiglobalization ■ **antimondialiste** *adj* antiglobalization

**antinucléaire** [ɑ̃tinykleɛr] *adj* anti-nuclear

**antipathique** [ɑ̃tipatik] *adj* unpleasant ; **elle m'est antipathique** I find her unpleasant

**antipelliculaire** [ɑ̃tipelikylɛr] *adj* **shampooing antipelliculaire** antidandruff shampoo

**antiperspirant, e** [ɑ̃tiperspirɑ̃, ɑ̃t] *adj* antiperspirant ■ **antiperspirant** *nm* antiperspirant

**antipodes** [ɑ̃tipɔd] *nmpl* antipodes ; **être aux antipodes de** to be on the other side of the world from ; *Fig* to be the exact opposite of

**antique** [ɑ̃tik] *adj* [de l'Antiquité] ancient ■ **antiquaire** *nmf* antique dealer ■ **antiquité** *nf* [objet ancien] antique ; **l'antiquité grecque/romaine** ancient Greece / Rome ; **antiquités** [de musée] antiquities

**antirabique** [ɑ̃tirabik] *adj* MÉD antirabies

**antiradiation** [ɑ̃tiradjasjɔ̃] *adj* **bouclier antiradiation** radiation shield ; **étui antiradiation** [pour téléphone portable] anti-radiation case

**antireflet** [ɑ̃tirəflɛ] *adj inv* non-reflecting

**antisèche** [ɑ̃tisɛʃ] *nf* [argot scolaire] crib (sheet), *Am* cheat sheet, *Am* pony

**antisémite** [ɑ̃tisemit] **1.** *nmf* anti-Semite **2.** *adj* anti-Semitic

**antiseptique** [ɑ̃tisɛptik] *adj & nm* antiseptic

**antislash** [ɑ̃tislaʃ] *nm* ORDINAT back-slash

**antisocial, -e, -aux** [ɑ̃tisɔsjal, -o] *adj* antisocial

**antitabac** [ɑ̃titaba] *adj inv* **lutte anti-tabac** anti-smoking campaign

**antiterrorisme** [ɑ̃titerɔrism] *nm* antiterrorism ■ **antiterroriste** *adj* anti-terrorist

**antithèse** [ɑ̃titɛz] *nf* antithesis

**antitranspirant, e** [ɑ̃titrɑ̃spirɑ̃, ɑ̃t] *adj* antiperspirant

**antivirus** [ɑ̃tivirys] *nm* ORDINAT antivirus software

**antivol** [ɑ̃tivɔl] *nm* anti-theft device

**Anvers** [ɑ̃vɛr(s)] *nm ou f* Antwerp

**anxiété** [ɑ̃ksjete] *nf* anxiety ■ **anxieux, -euse** *adj* anxious ■ **anxiolytique** [ɑ̃ksjɔlitik] *nm Br* tranquillizer, *Am* tranquilizer

**août** [u(t)] *nm* August

**aoûtat** [auta] *nm* harvest mite, *Am* chigger, *Am* redbug

**apaiser** [apeze] **1.** *vt* [personne] to calm (down); [douleur] to soothe; [craintes] to allay **2. s'apaiser** *vpr* [personne, colère] to calm down; [tempête, douleur] to subside ■ **apaisant, -e** *adj* soothing

**apanage** [apanaʒ] *nm* prerogative

**aparté** [aparte] *nm* THÉÂT aside; [dans une réunion] private exchange; **en aparté** in private

**apathique** [apatik] *adj* apathetic

**Apec** [apɛk] *(abr de* **Association pour l'emploi des cadres)** *nf* employment agency for executives and managers

**apercevoir** [apɛrsəvwar] **1.** *vt* to see; [brièvement] to catch a glimpse of **2. s'apercevoir** *vpr* **s'apercevoir de qch** to realize sth; **s'apercevoir que...** to realize that... ■ **aperçu** *nm* [idea] general idea

**apéritif** [aperitif] *nm* aperitif; **prendre un apéritif** to have a drink before lunch/dinner

**à-peu-près** [apøprɛ] *nm inv* vague approximation

**apeuré, -e** [apœre] *adj* frightened, scared

**aphone** [afɔn] *adj* voiceless; **je suis complètement aphone** I've lost my voice

**aphrodisiaque** [afrɔdizjak] *nm* aphrodisiac

**aphte** [aft] *nm* mouth ulcer

**aphteuse** [aftøz] *adj f* **fièvre aphteuse** foot-and-mouth disease

**apiculture** [apikyltyr] *nf* beekeeping ■ **apiculteur, -trice** *nmf* beekeeper

**apitoyer** [apitwaje] **1.** *vt* **apitoyer qn** to move sb to pity **2. s'apitoyer** *vpr* **s'apitoyer sur qn** to feel sorry for sb; **s'a sur son sort** to feel sorry for oneself

**aplanir** [aplanir] *vt* [terrain] to level; [difficulté] to iron out

**aplatir** [aplatir] **1.** *vt* to flatten **2. s'aplatir** *vpr* [être plat] to be flat; [devenir plat] to go flat; **s'aplatir contre qch** to flatten oneself against sth ■ **aplati, -e** *adj* flat

**aplomb** [aplɔ̃] *nm* [assurance] self-confidence; *Péj* cheek; **mettre qch d'aplomb** to stand sth up straight

**A+** *(abr de* **à plus tard)** SMS CUL

**apocalypse** [apɔkalips] *nf* apocalypse; **d'apocalypse** [vision] apocalyptic

**apogée** [apɔʒe] *nm* [d'orbite] apogee; *Fig* **être à l'apogée de sa carrière** to be at the height of one's career

**apostrophe** [apɔstrɔf] *nf* [signe] apostrophe ■ **apostropher** *vt* [pour attirer l'attention] to shout at

**apothéose** [apɔteoz] *nf* [consécration] crowning glory

**apparaître** [aparɛtr] *(aux être)* *vi* [se montrer, sembler] to appear; **il m'ap-**

**paraît comme le seul capable d'y parvenir** he seems to me to be the only person capable of doing it

**appareil** [apaʀɛj] *nm* [instrument, machine] apparatus ; [téléphone] telephone ; [avion] aircraft ; **qui est à l'appareil ?** [au téléphone] who's speaking? ; **appareil (dentaire)** [correctif] brace ; **appareil photo** camera ; **appareils ménagers** household appliances

**apparence** [apaʀɑ̃s] *nf* appearance ; **en apparence** outwardly ; **sauver les apparences** to keep up appearances ■ **apparemment** *adv* apparently ■ **apparent, -e** *adj* apparent

**apparenter** [apaʀɑ̃te] ■ **s'apparenter** *vpr* [ressembler] to be akin (**à** to)

**apparition** [apaʀisjɔ̃] *nf* [manifestation] appearance ; [fantôme] apparition ; **faire son apparition** [personne] to make one's appearance

**appartement** [apaʀtəmɑ̃] *nm Br* flat, *Am* apartment ■ **appart hôtel** [apaʀtotɛl] *nm* apartment hotel

**appartenance** [apaʀtənɑ̃s] *nf* [de groupe] belonging (**à** to) ; [de parti] membership (**à** of)

**appartenir** [apaʀtəniʀ] **1.** *vi* to belong (**à** to) **2.** *v impers* **il vous appartient de prendre la décision** it's up to you to decide

**appât** [apa] *nm* [amorce] bait ; *Fig* [attrait] lure ■ **appâter** *vt* [hameçon] to bait ; [animal] to lure ; *Fig* [personne] to entice

**appauvrir** [apovʀiʀ] **1.** *vt* to impoverish **2.** **s'appauvrir** *vpr* to become impoverished ■ **appauvrissement** *nm* impoverishment

**appel** [apɛl] *nm* [cri, attrait] call ; [invitation & JUR] appeal ; MIL [recrutement] call-up ; [pour sauter] take-off ; **faire l'appel** [à l'école] to take the register ; MIL to have a roll call ; **faire appel à qn** to appeal to sb ; [plombier, médecin] to send for sb ; **appel au secours** call for help ; **appel gratuit** *Br* freefone call, *Am* toll-free call ; **appel téléphonique** telephone call ■ **appeler 1.** *vt* [personne, nom] to call ; [en criant] to

call out to ; MIL [recruter] to call up ; [nécessiter] to call for ; **appeler qn à l'aide** to call to sb for help ; **appeler qn au téléphone** to call sb **2.** **s'appeler** *vpr* to be called ; **comment vous appelez-vous ?** what's your name? ; **je m'appelle David** my name is David ■ **appellation** *nf* [nom] term ; **appellation contrôlée** [de vin] guaranteed vintage ■ **appelé** *nm* MIL conscript

**appendice** [apɛ̃dis] *nm* [du corps, de livre] appendix ; [d'animal] appendage ■ **appendicite** *nf* appendicitis

**appesantir** [apəzɑ̃tiʀ] ■ **s'appesantir** *vpr* to become heavier ; **s'appesantir sur** [sujet] to dwell upon

**appétit** [apeti] *nm* appetite (**de** for) ; **couper l'appétit à qn** to spoil sb's appetite ; **manger de bon appétit** to tuck in ; **bon appétit !** enjoy your meal! ■ **appétissant, -e** *adj* appetizing

**applaudir** [aplodiʀ] *vt & vi* to applaud ■ **applaudissements** *nmpl* applause

**applicable** [aplikabl] *adj* applicable (**à** to) ■ **application** *nf* [action, soin & ORDINAT] application ; [de loi] enforcement ; **entrer en application** to come into force

**applique** [aplik] *nf* wall light

**appliquer** [aplike] **1.** *vt* to apply (**à / sur** to) ; [loi, décision] to enforce **2.** **s'appliquer** *vpr* [se concentrer] to apply oneself (**à** to) ; **s'appliquer à faire qch** to take pains to do sth ; **cette décision s'applique à...** [concerne] this decision applies to... ■ **appliqué, -e** *adj* [personne] hard-working ; [écriture] careful ; [sciences] applied

**appoint** [apwɛ̃] *nm* **a)** **faire l'appoint** to give the exact money **b)** **d'appoint** extra

**apport** [apɔʀ] *nm* contribution (**à** to) ; **apport nutritionnel** [d'un aliment] nutritional value

**apporter** [apɔʀte] *vt* to bring (**à** to) ; [preuve] to provide ; [modification] to bring about

**apposer** [apoze] *vt* [sceau, signature] to affix (**à** to) ; [affiche] to put up

**apprécier** [apresje] *vt* [aimer, percevoir] to appreciate ; [évaluer] to estimate ■ **appréciable** *adj* a) [notable] appreciable b) [précieux] **un grand jardin, c'est appréciable !** I / we really appreciate having a big garden ■ **appréciation** *nf* [opinion de professeur] comment (**sur** on) ; [évaluation] valuation ; [augmentation de valeur] appreciation

**appréhender** [apreɑ̃de] *vt* [craindre] to dread (**de faire qch** doing sth) ; [arrêter] to arrest ; [comprendre] to grasp ■ **appréhension** *nf* [crainte] apprehension (**de** about)

**apprenant, e** [aprənɑ̃, ɑ̃t] *nmf* learner

**apprendre** [aprɑ̃dr] *vt & vi* [étudier] to learn ; [nouvelle] to hear ; [mariage, mort] to hear of; **apprendre à faire qch** to learn to do sth; **apprendre qch à qn** [enseigner] to teach sb sth ; [informer] to tell sb sth; **apprendre à qn à faire qch** to teach sb to do sth; **apprendre que...** to learn that... ; [être informé] to hear that...

**apprenti, -e** [aprɑ̃ti] *nmf* apprentice ■ **apprentissage** *nm* [professionnel] training ; [chez un artisan] apprenticeship ; [d'une langue] learning (**de** of); **faire l'apprentissage de qch** to learn about sth

**apprivoiser** [aprivwaze] **1.** *vt* to tame **2. s'apprivoiser** *vpr* to become tame

**approbation** [aprɔbasjɔ̃] *nf* approval ■ **approbateur, -trice** *adj* approving

**approche** [aprɔʃ] *nf* approach ; **approches** [de ville] outskirts

**approcher** [aprɔʃe] **1.** *vt* [objet] to bring up ; [personne] to approach, to get close to; **approcher qch de qn** to bring sth near to sb **2.** *vi* to approach, to get closer; **approcher de qn / qch** to approach sb / sth **3. s'approcher** *vpr* to approach, to get closer; **s'approcher de qn / qch** to approach sb / sth; **il s'est approché de moi** he came up to me

**approfondir** [aprɔfɔ̃dir] *vt* [question, idée] to go thoroughly into ■ **approfondi, -e** *adj* [étude, examen] thorough

**approprié, -e** [aprɔprije] *adj* appropriate (**à** for)

**approprier** [aprɔprije] ■ **s'approprier** *vpr* **s'approprier qch** to appropriate sth

**approuver** [apruve] *vt* [facture, contrat] to approve ; [décision] to approve of

**approvisionner** [aprɔvizjɔne] **1.** *vt* [ville, armée] to supply (**en** with) ; [magasin] to stock (**en** with) ; [compte bancaire] to pay money into **2. s'approvisionner** *vpr* to get supplies (**en** of) ■ **approvisionnement** *nm* [d'une ville, d'une armée] supplying (**en** with) ; [d'un magasin] stocking (**en** with)

**approximatif, -ive** [aprɔksimatif, -iv] *adj* approximate ■ **approximation** *nf* approximation

**appui** [apɥi] *nm* support; **prendre appui sur qch** to lean on sth; **à l'appui de qch** in support of sth; **appui de fenêtre** windowsill ■ **appui-tête** (*pl* **appuis-tête**) *nm* headrest

**appuyer** [apɥije] **1.** *vt* [poser] to lean, to rest ; *Fig* [proposition] to second ; **appuyer qch sur qch** [poser] to rest sth on sth; [presser] to press sth on sth **2.** *vi* [presser] to press; **appuyer sur un bouton** to press a button **3. s'appuyer** *vpr* *Fig* [être basé sur] to be based on sth ; **s'appuyer sur qch** to lean on sth, to rest on sth

**âpre** [ɑpr] *adj* sour ; *Fig* [lutte] fierce

**après** [aprɛ] **1.** *prép* [dans le temps] after ; [dans l'espace] beyond ; **après tout** after all ; **après avoir mangé** after eating; **après qu'il t'a vu** after he saw you; **d'après** [selon] according to **2.** *adv* after(wards) ; **l'année d'après** the following year; **et après ?** [et ensuite] and then what ? ; [et alors] so what ? ■ **après-demain** *adv* the day after tomorrow ■ **après-guerre** *nm* postwar period; **d'après-guerre** post-war ■ **après-midi** *nm ou f inv* afternoon; **trois heures de l'après-midi** three o'clock in the afternoon ■ **après-rasage** (*pl* **après-rasages**) *nm* aftershave ■ **après-shampooing** *nm inv* conditioner ■ **après-ski**

*(pl* **après-skis)** *nm* snowboot ■ **après-soleil** [apʀesɔlɛj] **1.** *adj inv* after-sun **2.** *(pl* **après-soleils)** *nm* after sun cream ■ **après-vente** *adj inv* COMM service après-vente after-sales service

**âpreté** [ɑpʀəte] *nf* sourness ; *Fig* [lutte] fierceness

**à-propos** [apʀɔpo] *nm* aptness ; **avoir l'esprit d'à-propos** to have presence of mind

**apte** [apt] *adj* **apte à qch / à faire qch** fit for sth / for doing sth ■ **aptitude** *nf* aptitude (**à** *ou* **pour** for) ; **avoir des aptitudes pour qch** to have an aptitude for sth

**Aquagym®** [akwaʒim] *nf* aquarobics *(sg)*

**aquarelle** [akwaʀɛl] *nf* watercolour

**aquarium** [akwaʀjɔm] *nm* aquarium

**aquatique** [akwatik] *adj* aquatic

**arabe 1.** *adj* [peuple, littérature] Arab ; [langue] Arabic **2.** *nmf* **Arabe** Arab **3.** *nm* [langue] Arabic ■ **Arabie** *nf* **l'Arabie** Arabia ; **l'Arabie Saoudite** Saudi Arabia

**arable** [aʀabl] *adj* arable

**arachide** [aʀaʃid] *nf* peanut

**araignée** [aʀeɲe] *nf* spider

**arbitraire** [aʀbitʀɛʀ] *adj* arbitrary

**arbitre** [aʀbitʀ] *nm* [de football] referee ; [de tennis] umpire ■ **arbitrage** *nm* [de football] refereeing ; [de tennis] umpiring

**arborer** [aʀbɔʀe] *vt* [insigne] to sport

**arbre** [aʀbʀ] *nm* [végétal] tree ; TECH shaft ; **arbre fruitier** fruit tree ; **arbre de transmission** transmission shaft ■ **arbuste** *nm* shrub

**arc** [aʀk] *nm* [arme] bow ; [voûte] arch ; [de cercle] arc ■ **arcade** *nf* archway ; **arcades** [de place] arcade

**arc-boutant** [aʀkbutɑ̃] *(pl* **arcs-boutants)** *nm* flying buttress

**arc-en-ciel** [aʀkɑ̃sjɛl] *(pl* **arcs-en-ciel)** *nm* rainbow

**archaïque** [aʀkaik] *adj* archaic

**arche** [aʀʃ] *nf* [voûte] arch ; **l'arche de Noé** Noah's ark

**archéologie** [aʀkeɔlɔʒi] *nf* archaeology ■ **archéologique** *adj* archaeological ■ **archéologue** *nmf* archaeologist

**archet** [aʀʃɛ] *nm* [de violon] bow

**architecte** [aʀʃitɛkt] *nm* architect ■ **architecture** *nf* architecture

**archives** [aʀʃiv] *nfpl* archives, records

**arctique** [aʀktik] **1.** *adj* arctic **2.** *nm* **l'Arctique** the Arctic

**ardent, -e** [aʀdɑ̃, -ɑ̃t] *adj* [désir] burning ; [soleil] scorching ■ **ardeur** *nf* [passion] fervour, ardour ; [du soleil] intense heat

**ardoise** [aʀdwaz] *nf* slate

**ardu, -e** [aʀdy] *adj* arduous

**aréna** [aʀena] *nm* Can Am arena *(sports centre with skating rink)*

**arène** [aʀɛn] *nf* [pour taureaux] bullring ; [romaine] arena ; **arènes** bullring ; [romaines] amphitheatre

**arête** [aʀɛt] *nf* [de poisson] bone ; [de cube] edge ; [de montagne] ridge

**argent** [aʀʒɑ̃] **1.** *nm* [métal] silver ; [monnaie] money ; **argent liquide** cash ; **argent de poche** pocket money **2.** *adj* [couleur] silver ■ **argenté, -e** *adj* [plaqué] silver-plated ; [couleur] silvery ■ **argenterie** *nf* silverware

**Argentine** [aʀʒɑ̃tin] *nf* **l'Argentine** Argentina ■ **argentin, -e 1.** *adj* Argentinian **2.** *nmf* **Argentin, Argentine** Argentinian

**argile** [aʀʒil] *nf* clay

**argot** [aʀgo] *nm* slang ■ **argotique** *adj* [terme] slang

**argument** [aʀgymɑ̃] *nm* argument

**argumenter** [aʀgymɑ̃te] *vi* to argue ; **argumenter en faveur de / contre qch** to argue for / against sth

**aride** [aʀid] *adj* [terre] arid, barren ; [sujet] dry

**aristocrate** [aʀistɔkʀat] *nmf* aristocrat ■ **aristocratie** [-asi] *nf* aristocracy ■ **aristocratique** *adj* aristocratic

**arithmétique** [aʀitmetik] *nf* arithmetic

**armature** [armatyr] *nf* [charpente] framework ; [de lunettes, de tente] frame

**arme** [arm] *nf* weapon ; **prendre les armes** to take up arms ; *Fig* **à armes égales** on equal terms ; **arme à feu** firearm ; **arme blanche** knife ■ **armes** *nfpl* [blason] (coat of) arms

**armée** [arme] *nf* army ; **être à l'armée** to be doing one's military service ; **armée de l'air** air force ; **armée de terre** army ; **armée active /de métier** regular /professional army

**armer** [arme] **1.** *vt* [personne] to arm (**de** with) ; [fusil] to cock ; [appareil photo] to set **2. s'armer** *vpr* to arm oneself (**de** with) ; **s'armer de patience** to summon up one's patience ■ **armements** *nmpl* [armes] armaments

**armistice** [armistis] *nm* armistice

**armoire** [armwar] *nf* [penderie] *Br* wardrobe, *Am* closet ; **armoire à pharmacie** medicine cabinet

**armure** [armyr] *nf* armour

**arnaquer** [arnake] *vt Fam* to rip off ; **se faire arnaquer** to be had

**arobase** [arɔbaz] *nf* ORDINAT at, @ ; **l'arobase** the "at" symbol *or* sign

**aromate** [arɔmat] *nm* [herbe] herb ; [épice] spice

**aromathérapie** [arɔmaterapi] *nf* aromatherapy

**aromatique** [arɔmatik] *adj* aromatic

**arôme** [arom] *nm* [goût] flavour ; [odeur] aroma

**arpenter** [arpɑ̃te] *vt* [parcourir] to pace up and down

**arqué, -e** [arke] *adj* [jambes] bandy

**arraché** [araʃe] *nm* **gagner à l'arraché** to snatch victory

**arrache-pied** [araʃpje] ■ **d'arrache-pied** *adv* relentlessly

**arracher** [araʃe] *vt* [plante] to uproot ; [clou, dent, mauvaise herbe] to pull out ; [page] to tear out ; **arracher qch à qn** [objet] to snatch sth from sb ; [promesse] to force sth out of sb ; **se faire arracher une dent** to have a tooth out

**arrangement** [arɑ̃ʒmɑ̃] *nm* [disposition & MUS] arrangement ; [accord] agreement

**arranger** [arɑ̃ʒe] **1.** *vt* [fleurs] to arrange ; [col] to straighten ; [réparer] to repair ; **ça m'arrange** that suits me (fine) **2. s'arranger** *vpr* [se mettre d'accord] to come to an agreement ; [finir bien] to turn out fine ; [s'organiser] to manage

**arrestation** [arɛstasjɔ̃] *nf* arrest

**arrêt** [arɛ] *nm* [halte, endroit] stop ; [action] stopping ; JUR judgment ; **temps d'arrêt** pause ; **à l'arrêt** stationary ; **sans arrêt** continuously ; **arrêt du cœur** cardiac arrest ; SPORT **arrêt de jeu** stoppage ; **arrêt de mort** death sentence ; **arrêt de travail** [congé] sick leave ■ **arrêt-maladie** *nm* sick leave

**arrêté¹** [arete] *nm* [décret] order, decree

**arrêté², -e** [arete] *adj* [idées] fixed

**arrêter** [arete] **1.** *vt* [personne, animal, véhicule] to stop ; [criminel] to arrest ; [moteur] to turn off ; [date] to fix ; [études] to give up ; ORDINAT [ordinateur] to shut down **2.** *vi* to stop ; **arrêter de faire qch** to stop doing sth **3. s'arrêter** *vpr* to stop ; **s'arrêter de faire qch** to stop doing sth

**arrière** [arjɛr] **1.** *nm* [de maison] back, rear ; [de bâteau] stern ; [au football] full back ; **à l'arrière** in /at the back **2.** *adj inv* [siège] back, rear ; **feu arrière** rear light **3.** *adv* **en arrière** [marcher, tomber] backwards ; [rester] behind ; [regarder] back, behind ; **en arrière de qn /qch** behind sb /sth ■ **arrière-goût** [arjɛrgu] *(pl* **arrière-goûts)** *nm* aftertaste ■ **arrière-grand-mère** *(pl* **arrière-grands-mères)** *nf* great-grandmother ■ **arrière-grand-père** *(pl* **arrière-grands-pères)** *nm* great-grandfather ■ **arrière-grands-parents** *nmpl* great-grandparents ■ **arrière-pays** *nm inv* hinterland ■ **arrière-pensée** *(pl* **arrière-pensées)** *nf* ulterior motive ■ **arrière-petits-enfants** *nmpl* great-grandchildren ■ **arrière-plan** *nm* background ; **à l'arrière-plan** in the background ■ **arrière-saison** (pl **arrière-saisons**) nf late autumn, Am late fall

**arriéré, -e** [arjere] **1.** adj [pays, idées, enfant] backward **2.** nm [dette] arrears

**arriver** [arive] **1.** (aux **être**) vi [venir] to arrive ; **arriver à** [lieu] to reach ; [résultat] to achieve ; **arriver à faire qch** to manage to do sth **2.** v impers [survenir] to happen ; **arriver à qn** to happen to sb ; **qu'est-ce qu'il t'arrive ?** what's wrong with you ? ■ **arrivage** nm consignment ■ **arrivée** nf arrival ; [ligne, poteau] winning post ■ **arriviste** nmf Péj social climber

**arrogant, -e** [arɔgɑ̃, -ɑ̃t] adj arrogant ■ **arrogance** nf arrogance

**arroger** [arɔʒe] ■ **s'arroger** vpr [droit] to claim

**arrondir** [arɔ̃dir] vt [chiffre, angle] to round off ; **arrondir qch** to make sth round ; **arrondir à l'euro supérieur / inférieur** to round up / down to the nearest euro ; Fam **arrondir ses fins de mois** to supplement one's income ■ **arrondi, -e** adj round

**arrondissement** [arɔ̃dismɑ̃] nm administrative subdivision of Paris, Lyons and Marseilles

**arroser** [aroze] vt [plante] to water ; [pelouse] to sprinkle ; Fam [succès] to drink to ■ **arrosage** nm [de plante] watering ; [de pelouse] sprinkling ■ **arrosoir** nm watering can

**arsenal, -aux** [arsənal, -o] nm MIL arsenal

**arsenic** [arsənik] nm arsenic

**art** [ar] nm art ; **critique d'art** art critic ; **arts martiaux** martial arts ; **arts ménagers** home economics ; **arts plastiques** fine arts

**artère** [arter] nf [veine] artery ; [rue] main road

**artichaut** [artiʃo] nm artichoke ; **fond d'artichaut** artichoke heart

**article** [artikl] nm [de presse, de contrat & GRAM] article ; COMM item ; **articles de toilette** toiletries ; **articles de voyage** travel goods

**articuler** [artikyle] **1.** vt [mot] to articulate **2.** s'articuler vpr [membre] to articulate ; **s'articuler autour de qch** [théorie] to centre on ■ **articulation** nf [de membre] joint ; [prononciation] articulation

**artifice** [artifis] nm trick

**artificiel, -elle** [artifisjɛl] adj artificial

**artillerie** [artijri] nf artillery ■ **artilleur** nm artilleryman

**artisan** [artizɑ̃] nm craftsman, artisan ■ **artisanal, -e, -aux** adj **objet artisanal** object made by craftsmen ; **bombe artisanale** homemade bomb ■ **artisanat** nm craft industry

**artiste** [artist] nmf artist ; [acteur, musicien] performer, artiste ■ **artistique** adj artistic

**as** [ɑs] nm [carte, champion] ace

**ascendant** [asɑ̃dɑ̃] **1.** adj ascending ; [mouvement] upward **2.** nm [influence] influence ; **ascendants** ancestors ■ **ascendance** nf [ancêtres] ancestry

**ascenseur** [asɑ̃sœr] nm **a)** Br lift, Am elevator **b)** ORDINAT scroll bar

**ascension** [asɑ̃sjɔ̃] nf [escalade] ascent ; REL **l'Ascension** Ascension Day

**Asie** [azi] nf **l'Asie** Asia ■ **asiatique 1.** adj Asian **2.** nmf **Asiatique** Asian

**asile** [azil] nm [abri] refuge, shelter ; [pour vieillards] home ; Péj **asile (d'aliénés)** (lunatic) asylum ; **asile politique** (political) asylum

**aspartam(e)** [aspartam] nm aspartame

**aspect** [aspɛ] nm [air] appearance ; [perspective] aspect

**asperger** [asperʒe] **1.** vt [par jeu ou accident] to splash (**de** with) ; **se faire asperger** to get splashed **2.** s'asperger vpr **s'asperger de parfum** to splash oneself with perfume

**asperges** [aspɛrʒ] nfpl asparagus

**asphalte** [asfalt] nm asphalt

**asphyxie** [asfiksi] nf asphyxiation ■ **asphyxier 1.** vt to suffocate **2.** s'asphyxier vpr to suffocate

**aspirateur** [aspiratœr] *nm* vacuum cleaner; **passer l'aspirateur dans la maison** to vacuum the house

**aspirer** [aspire] **1.** *vt* [liquide] to suck up; [air] to breathe in, to inhale **2.** *vi* **aspirer à qch** [bonheur, gloire] to aspire to sth ■ **aspiration** *nf* [inhalation] inhalation; [ambition] aspiration (à for)

**aspirine** [aspirin] *nf* aspirin

**assaillir** [asajir] *vt* to attack ■ **assaillant** *nm* attacker, assailant

**assainir** [asenir] *vt* [purifier] to clean up; [marché, économie] to stabilize

**assaisonner** [asezone] *vt* to season ■ **assaisonnement** *nm* seasoning

**assassin** [asasɛ̃] *nm* murderer; [de politicien] assassin ■ **assassinat** *nm* murder; [de politicien] assassination ■ **assassiner** *vt* to murder; [politicien] to assassinate

**assaut** [aso] *nm* attack, assault; MIL charge

**assécher** [asefe] **1.** *vt* to drain **2. s'assécher** *vpr* to dry up

**assemblée** [asɑ̃ble] *nf* [personnes réunies] gathering; [réunion] meeting; **assemblée générale** [de compagnie] annual general meeting; **l'Assemblée nationale** *Br* ≃ the House of Commons, *Am* ≃ the House of Representatives

**assembler** [asɑ̃ble] **1.** *vt* to put together, to assemble **2. s'assembler** *vpr* to gather ■ **assemblage** *nm* [montage] assembly; [réunion d'objets] collection

**asséner, assener** [asene] *vt* **asséner un coup à qn** to deliver a blow to sb

**asseoir** [aswar] **1.** *vt* [personne] to seat (**sur** on); *Fig* [autorité] to establish **2.** *vi* **faire asseoir qn** to ask sb to sit down **3. s'asseoir** *vpr* to sit (down)

**assermenté, -e** [asɛrmɑ̃te] *adj* sworn; [témoin] under oath

**asservir** [asɛrvir] *vt* to enslave

**assez** [ase] *adv* **a)** [suffisament] enough; **assez de pain /de gens** enough bread /people; **j'en ai assez (de)** I've had enough (of); **assez grand /intelligent (pour faire qch)** big /clever enough (to do sth) **b)** [plutôt] quite, rather

**assidu, -e** [asidy] *adj* [toujours présent] regular; [appliqué] diligent; **assidu auprès de qn** attentive to sb ■ **assiduité** *nf* [d'élève] regularity

**assiéger** [asjeʒe] *vt* [ville, magasin] to besiege

**assiette** [asjɛt] *nf* [récipient] plate; CULIN **assiette anglaise** *Br* (assorted) cold meats, *Am* cold cuts

**assigner** [asiɲe] *vt* [attribuer] to assign (à to); [en justice] to summon ■ **assignation** *nf* JUR summons

**assimiler** [asimile] *vt* [aliments, savoir, immigrés] to assimilate

**assis, -e¹** [asi, -iz] **1.** *pp de* **asseoir 2.** *adj* sitting (down), seated; **rester assis** to remain seated; **place assise** seat

**assise²** [asiz] *nf* [base] foundation; **assises** [d'un parti] congress; JUR **les assises** the assizes

**assistance** [asistɑ̃s] *nf* **a)** [public] audience **b)** [aide] assistance

**assister** [asiste] **1.** *vt* [aider] to assist **2.** *vi* **assister à** [réunion, cours] to attend; [accident] to witness ■ **assistant, -e** *nmf* assistant; **assistante maternelle** *Br* child minder, *Am* baby-sitter; **assistante sociale** social worker ■ **assisté, -e** *adj* **assisté par ordinateur** computer-aided

**association** [asɔsjɑsjɔ̃] *nf* association; COMM partnership; **association de parents d'élèves** parent-teacher association; **association sportive** sports club

**associer** [asɔsje] **1.** *vt* to associate (à with); **associer qn à** [travaux] to involve sb in **2. s'associer** *vpr* to join forces (à *ou* avec with); COMM **s'associer avec qn** to enter into partnership with sb ■ **associé, -e** *nmf* partner, associate

**assoiffé, -e** [aswafe] *adj* thirsty (de for)

**assombrir** [asɔ̃brir] **1.** *vt* [obscurcir] to darken; [attrister] to cast a shadow over **2. s'assombrir** *vpr* [ciel, visage] to cloud over ; [personne] to become gloomy

**assommer** [asɔme] *vt Fig* [ennuyer] to bore sb to death ; **assommer qn** to knock sb unconscious ■ **assommant, -e** *adj* very boring

**Assomption** [asɔ̃psjɔ̃] *nf* REL **l'Assomption** the Assumption

**assortir** [asɔrtir] *vt* [harmoniser] to match ■ **assorti, -e** *adj* [objet semblable] matching ; [bonbons] assorted ; **assorti de** accompanied by ■ **assortiment** *nm* assortment

**assoupir** [asupir] ■ **s'assoupir** *vpr* to doze off

**assouplir** [asuplir] **1.** *vt* [cuir, muscles] to make supple ; [corps] to limber up ; *Fig* [réglementation] to relax **2. s'assouplir** *vpr* [personne, cuir] to get supple ■ **assouplissement** *nm* **exercices d'assouplissement** warm-up exercises

**assourdissant, -e** [asurdisɑ̃, -ɑ̃t] *adj* deafening

**assouvir** [asuvir] *vt* to satisfy

**assujettir** [asyʒetir] *vt* [soumettre] to subject (**à** to) ; [peuple] to subjugate ; [objet] to fix (**à** to)

**assumer** [asyme] **1.** *vt* [tâche, rôle] to assume, to take on ; [risque] to take **2. s'assumer** *vpr* to come to terms with oneself

**assurance** [asyrɑ̃s] *nf* [confiance] (self-)assurance ; [promesse] assurance ; [contrat] insurance ; **prendre une assurance** to take out insurance ; **assurance au tiers / tous risques** third-party / comprehensive insurance ; **assurance maladie / vie** health / life insurance

**assurer** [asyre] **1.** *vt* [garantir] *Br* to ensure, *Am* to insure ; [par contrat] to insure ; **assurer qn de qch, assurer qch à qn** to assure sb of sth ; **un service régulier est assuré** there is a regular service **2. s'assurer** *vpr* [par contrat] to insure oneself ; **s'assurer de qch / que...** to make sure of sth / that... ■ **assuré, -e 1.** *adj* [succès]

guaranteed ; [air, personne] confident **2.** *nmf* policyholder ■ **assurément** *adv* certainly ■ **assureur** *nm* insurer, underwriter

**asthme** [asm] *nm* asthma ■ **asthmatique** *adj & nmf* asthmatic

**asticot** [astiko] *nm Br* maggot, *Am* worm

**astiquer** [astike] *vt* to polish

**astre** [astr] *nm* star

**astreindre** [astrɛ̃dr] **1.** *vt* **astreindre qn à faire qch** to compel sb to do sth **2. s'astreindre** *vpr* **s'astreindre à faire qch** to force oneself to do sth ■ **astreignant, -e** *adj* exacting ■ **astreinte** *nf* constraint

**astrologie** [astrɔlɔʒi] *nf* astrology

**astrologue** [astrɔlɔg] *nm* astrologer

**astronaute** [astrɔnot] *nmf* astronaut ■ **astronautique** *nf* space travel

**astronomie** [astrɔnɔmi] *nf* astronomy ■ **astronome** *nm* astronomer

**astuce** [astys] *nf* [truc] trick ; [plaisanterie] witticism ■ **astucieux, -euse** *adj* clever

**atelier** [atəlje] *nm* [d'ouvrier] workshop ; [de peintre] studio ; [personnel] workshop staff ; **atelier de montage** assembly shop ; **atelier de réparation** repair shop

**athée** [ate] **1.** *adj* atheistic **2.** *nmf* atheist

**Athènes** [atɛn] *nm ou f* Athens

**athlète** [atlɛt] *nmf* athlete ■ **athlétique** *adj* athletic ■ **athlétisme** *nm* athletics *(sg)*

**atlantique** [atlɑ̃tik] **1.** *adj* Atlantic **2.** *nm* **l'Atlantique** the Atlantic

**atlas** [atlɑs] *nm* atlas

**atmosphère** [atmɔsfɛr] *nf* atmosphere ■ **atmosphérique** *adj* atmospheric

**atome** [atom] *nm* atom ■ **atomique** *adj* atomic

**atomiser** [atɔmize] *vt* [liquide] to spray ; [région] to destroy with nuclear weapons ■ **atomiseur** *nm* spray

**atout** [atu] *nm* trump ; *Fig* [avantage] asset

**âtre** [ɑtr] *nm* [foyer] hearth

**atroce** [atʀɔs] *adj* atrocious ; [douleur] excruciating ■ **atrocité** *nf* [cruauté] atrociousness ; **les atrocités de la guerre** the atrocities committed in wartime

**attabler** [atable] ■ **s'attabler** *vpr* to sit down at a /the table

**attache** [ataʃ] *nf* [lien] fastener ■ **attaches** *nfpl Fig* links, connections

**attaché, -e** [ataʃe] **1.** *adj* [fixé] fastened ; [chien] chained up ; **être attaché à qn** to be attached to sb **2.** *nmf* attaché ; **attaché de presse** press officer

**attaché-case** [ataʃekɛz] *(pl* **attachés-cases)** *nm* attaché case

**attacher** [ataʃe] **1.** *vt* **attacher qch à qch** to fasten sth to sth ; [avec de la ficelle] to tie sth to sth ; [avec une chaîne] to chain sth to sth ; **attacher de l'importance à qch** to attach great importance to sth **2.** *vi* [en cuisant] to stick (to the pan) **3.** **s'attacher** *vpr* [se fixer] to be fastened ; **s'attacher à qn** to get attached to sb ■ **attachant, -e** *adj* engaging ■ **attachement** *nm* [affection] attachment (**à** to)

**attaque** [atak] *nf* attack ; **attaque aérienne** air raid ; **attaque à main armée** holdup, armed attack ■ **attaquer 1.** *vt* [physiquement, verbalement] to attack **2.** *vi* to attack **3.** **s'attaquer** *vpr* **s'attaquer à** [adversaire] to attack ; [problème] to tackle ■ **attaquant, -e** *nmf* attacker

**attarder** [atarde] ■ **s'attarder** *vpr* to linger ■ **attardé, -e** *adj* [enfant] mentally retarded

**atteindre** [atɛ̃dʀ] *vt* [parvenir à] to reach ; [cible] to hit ; **être atteint d'une maladie** to be suffering from a disease

**atteinte** [atɛ̃t] *nf* attack (**à** on) ; **porter atteinte à** to undermine ; **hors d'atteinte** [objet, personne] out of reach

**atteler** [atle] **1.** *vt* [bêtes] to harness **2.** **s'atteler** *vpr* **s'atteler à une tâche** to apply oneself to a task

**attenant, -e** [atnɑ̃, -ɑ̃t] *adj* **attenant (à)** adjoining

**attendre** [atɑ̃dʀ] **1.** *vt* [personne, train] to wait for ; **attendre son tour** to wait one's turn ; **elle attend un bébé** she's expecting a baby ; **attendre que qn fasse qch** to wait for sb to do sth ; **attendre qch de qn** to expect sth from sb **2.** *vi* to wait ; **faire attendre qn** to keep sb waiting ; **en attendant** meanwhile ; **en attendant que...** (+ *subjunctive*) until... **3.** **s'attendre** *vpr* **s'attendre à qch** to expect sth ; **s'attendre à ce que qn fasse qch** to expect sb to do sth ■ **attendu, -e 1.** *adj* [prévu] expected **2.** *prép Formel* considering

**attendrir** [atɑ̃dʀir] **1.** *vt* [émouvoir] to move **2.** **s'attendrir** *vpr* to be moved (**sur** by) ■ **attendri, -e** *adj* compassionate ■ **attendrissant, -e** *adj* moving

**attentat** [atɑ̃ta] *nm* attack ; **attentat à la bombe** bombing ; **attentat à la pudeur** indecent assault ■ **attentat-suicide** [atɑ̃tasɥisid] *(pl* **attentats-suicides)** *nm* suicide attack ; [à la bombe] suicide bombing

**attente** [atɑ̃t] *nf* [fait d'attendre] waiting ; [période] wait ; **en attente** [au téléphone] on hold ; **contre toute attente** against all expectations

**attentif, -ive** [atɑ̃tif, -iv] *adj* attentive ; **attentif à qch** to pay attention to sth

**attention** [atɑ̃sjɔ̃] *nf* [soin, amabilité] attention ; **faire attention à qch** to pay attention to sth ; **faire attention (à ce) que...** (+ *subjunctive*) to be careful that... ; **attention !** watch out! ; **attention à la voiture !** watch out for the car! ; **à l'attention de qn** [sur lettre] for the attention of sb ■ **attentionné, -e** *adj* considerate

**atténuer** [atenɥe] **1.** *vt* [effet, douleur] to reduce **2.** **s'atténuer** *vpr* [douleur] to ease

**atterrir** [aterir] *vi* to land ; **atterrir en catastrophe** to make an emergency landing ■ **atterrissage** *nm* landing ; **atterrissage forcé** forced landing

**attester** [atɛste] *vt* to testify to ; **attester que...** to testify that... ■ **attestation** *nf* [document] certificate

**attirail** [atiraj] *nm* equipment ; *Fam & Péj* gear

**attirance** [atirɑ̃s] *nf* attraction (**pour** for)

**attirer** [atire] **1.** *vt* [sujet : aimant, personne] to attract ; [sujet : matière, pays] to appeal to ; **attirer l'attention de qn** to catch sb's attention ; **attirer qn dans un piège** to lure sb into a trap **2. s'attirer** *vpr* [mutuellement] to be attracted to each other ; **s'attirer des ennuis** to get oneself into trouble ▪ **attirant, -e** *adj* attractive

**attitré, -e** [atitre] *adj* [représentant] appointed

**attitude** [atityd] *nf* [conduite, position] attitude

**attraction** [atraksjɔ̃] *nf* [force, centre d'intérêt] attraction ; **attraction touristique** tourist attraction

**attrait** [atrɛ] *nm* attraction

**attraper** [atrape] *vt* [ballon, maladie, voleur] to catch ; **attraper froid** to catch cold

**attrayant, -e** [atrejɑ̃, -ɑ̃t] *adj* attractive

**attribuer** [atribɥe] *vt* [allouer] to assign (**à** to) ; [prix, bourse] to award (**à** to) ; [œuvre] to attribute (**à** to) ; **attribuer de l'importance à qch** to attach importance to sth ▪ **attribution** *nf* [allocation] assigning (**à** to) ; [de prix] awarding (**à** to) ; [d'une œuvre] attribution (**à** to) ; **attributions** [fonctions] duties

**attribut** [atriby] *nm* [caractéristique] attribute

**attrister** [atriste] *vt* to sadden

**attrouper** [atrupe] ▪ **s'attrouper** *vpr* to gather ▪ **attroupement** *nm* crowd

**au** [o] *voir* **à**

**aubaine** [obɛn] *nf* piece of good fortune ; **quelle aubaine !** what a godsend!

**aube** [ob] *nf* dawn ; **dès l'aube** at the crack of dawn

**auberge** [oberʒ] *nf* inn ; **auberge de jeunesse** youth hostel

**aubergine** [oberʒin] *nf Br* aubergine, *Am* eggplant

**aucun, -e** [okœ̃, -yn] **1.** *adj* no, not any ; **il n'a aucun talent** he has no talent ; **au-cun professeur n'est venu** no teacher came **2.** *pron* none ; **il n'en a aucun** he has none (at all) ; **aucun d'entre nous** none of us ; **aucun des deux** neither of the two

**audace** [odas] *nf* [courage] daring, boldness ; [impudence] audacity ▪ **audacieux, -euse** *adj* [courageux] daring, bold

**au-dehors** [odǝor] *adv* outside

**au-delà** [odǝla] **1.** *adv* beyond ; **100 euros mais pas au-delà** 100 euros but no more **2.** *prép* **au-delà de** beyond **3.** *nm* **l'au-delà** the next world

**au-dessous** [odǝsu] **1.** *adv* [à l'étage inférieur] downstairs ; [moins, dessous] below, under **2.** *prép* **au-dessous de** [dans l'espace] below, under, beneath ; [âge, prix] under ; [température] below

**au-dessus** [odǝsy] **1.** *adv* above ; [à l'étage supérieur] upstairs **2.** *prép* **au-dessus de** above ; [âge, température, prix] over ; [posé sur] on top of

**au-devant** [odǝvɑ̃] *prép* **aller au-devant de** [personne] to go to meet ; [danger] to court ; [désirs de qn] to anticipate

**audible** [odibl] *adj* audible

**audience** [odjɑ̃s] *nf* [entretien] audience ; [de tribunal] hearing ; JUR **l'audience est suspendue** the case is adjourned

**Audimat®** [odimat] *nm* audience rating, *Am* ≃ Nielsen® ratings

**audio** [odjo] *adj inv* [matériel, fichier, livre] audio ▪ **audioguide** [odjɔgid] *nm* audio guide, headset

**audiovisuel, -elle** [odjɔvizɥɛl] **1.** *adj* [méthodes] audiovisual ; [de radio, de télévision] radio and television **2.** *nm* **l'audiovisuel** radio and television

**auditeur, -trice** [oditœr, -tris] *nmf* [de radio] listener ▪ **audition** *nf* [ouïe] hearing ; [d'acteurs] audition ; **passer une audition** to have an audition ▪ **auditionner** *vt & vi* to audition ▪ **auditoire** *nm* audience ▪ **auditorium** *nm* concert hall

**auditif, ive** [oditif, iv] *adj* **a)** [appareil] hearing **b)** [mémoire] auditory

**augmenter** [ɔgmɑ̃te] **1.** *vt* to increase (**de** by); **augmenter qn** to give sb a *Br* rise *or Am* raise **2.** *vi* to increase (**de** by); [prix, population] to rise ■ **augmentation** *nf* increase (**de** in, of); **augmentation de salaire** *Br* (pay) rise, *Am* raise; **être en augmentation** to be on the increase

**augure** [ɔgyr] *nm* [présage] omen; **être de bon/mauvais augure** to be a good / bad omen

**aujourd'hui** [oʒurdɥi] *adv* today; [de nos jours] nowadays, today; **aujourd'hui en quinze** two weeks from today

**auparavant** [oparavɑ̃] *adv* [avant] before(-hand); [d'abord] first

**auprès** [oprɛ] ■ **auprès de** *prép* [près de] by, next to; **se renseigner auprès de qn** to ask sb

**auquel** [okɛl] *voir* **lequel**

**aura, aurait** [ora, ore] *voir* **avoir**

**auréole** [ɔreɔl] *nf* [de saint] halo; [tache] ring

**auriculaire** [ɔrikylɛr] *nm* little finger

**aurore** [ɔrɔr] *nf* dawn, daybreak; **à l'aurore** at dawn

**auspices** [ɔspis] *nmpl* **sous les auspices de** under the auspices of

**aussi** [osi] **1.** *adv* **a)** [comparaison] as; **aussi lourd que...** as heavy as... **b)** [également] too, as well; **moi aussi** so do/can/am/*etc* I; **aussi bien que...** as well as...; **(tout) aussi bien** just as easily, just as well; **j'aurais pu (tout) aussi bien refuser** I could just as easily have said no **c)** [tellement] so; **un repas aussi délicieux** such a delicious meal **d)** [quelque] **aussi bizarre que cela paraisse** however odd this may seem **2.** *conj* [donc] therefore

**aussitôt** [osito] *adv* immediately, straight away; **aussitôt que...** as soon as...; **aussitôt dit, aussitôt fait** no sooner said than done

**austère** [ɔstɛr] *adj* [vie, style] austere; [vêtement] severe ■ **austérité** *nf* [de vie, de style] austerity; [de vêtement] severity; **mesure d'austérité** austerity measures

**austral, -e, -als** [ɔstral] *adj* southern

**Australie** [ɔstrali] *nf* **l'Australie** Australia ■ **australien, -enne 1.** *adj* Australian **2.** *nmf* **Australien, Australienne** Australian

**autant** [otɑ̃] *adv* **a)** **autant de... que** [quantité] as much... as; [nombre] as many... as; **il a autant d'argent/de pommes que vous** he has as much money/as many apples as you **b)** **autant de** [tant de] so much; [nombre] so many; **je n'ai jamais vu autant d'argent/de pommes** I've never seen so much money/so many apples; **pourquoi manges-tu autant?** why are you eating so much? **c)** **autant que** [quantité] as much as; [nombre] as many as; **il lit autant que vous/que possible** he reads as much as you/as possible; **il n'a jamais souffert autant** he's never suffered as *or* so much **d)** [expressions] **autant l'histoire la passionne, autant la géographie l'ennuie** she is as passionate about history as she is bored by geography; **d'autant** accordingly, in proportion; **d'autant mieux (que)** all the better (since); **d'autant (plus) que...** all the more (so) since...; **en faire autant** to do the same; **j'aimerais autant aller au musée** I'd just as soon go to the museum; **pour autant** for all that; **(pour) autant que je sache, il n'est pas encore arrivé** as far as I know he hasn't arrived yet

**autel** [otɛl] *nm* altar

**auteur, e** [otœr] *nmf* **a)** [d'œuvre] author **b)** [responsable] perpetrator ■ **auteur-compositeur** [otœrkɔ̃pozitœr] (*pl* **auteurs-compositeurs**) *nm* composer and lyricist; **auteur-compositeur-interprète** singer-songwriter; **je suis auteur-compositeur-interprète** I write and sing my own material

**authenticité** [otɑ̃tisite] *nf* authenticity ■ **authentique** *adj* genuine, authentic

**autiste** [otist] *adj* autistic

**autobiographie** [otobjɔgrafi] *nf* autobiography ■ **autobiographique** *adj* autobiographical

**autobronzant, e** [otobrɔ̃zɑ̃, ɑ̃t] **1.** *adj* self-tanning **2.** *nm* [crème] tanning cream

**autobus** [otobys] *nm* **a)** bus **b)** *Can* SCOL school bus

**autocar** [otokar] *nm* bus, *Br* coach

**autocollant, -e** [otokɔlɑ̃, -ɑ̃t] **1.** *adj* self-adhesive ; [enveloppe, timbre] self-seal **2.** *nm* sticker

**autodéfense** [otodefɑ̃s] *nf Br* self-defence, *Am* self-defense

**autodidacte** [otodidakt] *nmf* self-taught person

**auto-école** [otoekɔl] *(pl* **auto-écoles)** *nf* driving school

**autoentrepreneur, euse** [otoɑ̃trəprənœr, øz] *nom* self-employed businessman (*f* businesswoman)

**autographe** [otograf] *nm* autograph

**automatique** [ɔtɔmatik] *adj* automatic ■ **automatiquement** *adv* automatically

**automatiser** *vt* to automate

**automédication** [otomedikasjɔ̃] *nf* self-medication

**automne** [otɔn] *nm* autumn, *Am* fall

**automobile** [otɔmɔbil] *nf* car, *Br* motorcar, *Am* torcar; **l'automobile** [industrie] the car industry ■ **automobiliste** *nmf* motorist

**autonettoyant, -e** [otonetwajɑ̃, -ɑ̃t] *adj* **four autonettoyant** self-cleaning oven

**autonome** [otonɔm] *adj* [région] autonomous, self-governing; [personne] self-sufficient ■ **autonomie** *nf* [de région] autonomy; [de personne] self-sufficiency

**autopartage** [otopartaʒ] *nm* an urban rent-a-car service which allows short-term car hire

**autopsie** [ɔtɔpsi] *nf* autopsy, post-mortem

**autoradio** [otoradjo] *nm* car radio

**autoriser** [otorize] *vt* **autoriser qn à faire qch** to authorize *or* permit sb to do sth ■ **autorisation** *nf* [permission] permission, authorization; [document] authorization; **demander à qn l'autorisation de faire qch** to ask sb permission to do sth; **donner à qn l'autorisation de faire qch** to give sb permission to do sth ■ **autorisé, -e** *adj* [qualifié] authoritative; [permis] permitted, allowed

**autorité** [otorite] *nf* [fermeté, domination] authority; **faire qch d'autorité** to do sth on one's own authority

**autoroute** [otorut] *nf Br* motorway, *Am* highway, *Am* freeway; **autoroute à péage** *Br* toll motorway, *Am* turnpike (road); ORDINAT **autoroute de l'information** information superhighway ■ **autoritaire** *adj* authoritarian

**autosatisfaction** [otosatisfaksjɔ̃] *nf* self-satisfaction

**auto-stop** [otostɔp] *nm* hitchhiking; **faire de l'auto-stop** to hitchhike ■ **auto-stoppeur, -euse** *nmf* hitchhiker

**autour** [otur] **1.** *adv* around; **tout autour** all around **2.** *prép* **autour de** around, round; [environ] around, round about

**autre** [otr] *adj & pron* other; **un autre livre** another book; **un autre** another (one); **d'autres** others; **d'autres livres** other books; **quelqu'un d'autre** somebody else; **personne / rien d'autre** no one / nothing else; **autre chose** something else; **autre part** somewhere *or Am* someplace else; **qui / quoi d'autre ?** who / what else?; **l'un ou l'autre** either (of them); **ni l'un ni l'autre** neither (of them)

**autrefois** [otrəfwa] *adv* in the past, once

**autrement** [otrəmɑ̃] *adv* [différemment] differently; [sinon] otherwise; [plus] far more (**que** than)

**Autriche** [otriʃ] *nf* **l'Autriche** Austria ■ **autrichien, -enne 1.** *adj* Austrian **2.** *nmf* **Autrichien, Autrichienne** Austrian

**autruche** [otryʃ] *nf* ostrich

**autrui** [otrɥi] *pron* others, other people

**auvent** [ovã] *nm* [toit] porch roof ; [de tente, de magasin] awning, canopy

**aux** [o] *voir* à

**auxiliaire** [ɔksiljɛr] **1.** *adj* [machine, troupes] auxiliary **2.** *nm* [verbe] auxiliary **3.** *nmf* [aide] assistant ; [d'hôpital] auxiliary ; [dans l'administration] temporary worker

**auxquels, -elles** [okɛl] *voir* lequel

**av.** *(abr de* **avenue)** Ave

**avait** [avɛ] *voir* avoir

**aval** [aval] *nm* downstream section ; **en aval (de)** downstream (from)

**avalanche** [avalɑ̃ʃ] *nf* avalanche

**avaler** [avale] *vt & vi* to swallow

**avance** [avɑ̃s] *nf* [progression, acompte] advance ; [avantage] lead ; **faire une avance à qn** [donner de l'argent] to give sb an advance ; **avoir de l'avance sur qn** to be ahead of sb ; **à l'avance, d'avance, par avance** in advance ; **en avance** early ; **avoir une heure d'avance** to be an hour early

**avancé, e** [avɑ̃se] *adj* **a)** [dans le temps] late ; **à une heure avancée** late at night ; **te voilà bien avancé !** [par dérision] a (fat) lot of good that's done you! **b)** [développé : intelligence, économie] advanced

**avancée** [avɑ̃se] *nf* [saillie] projection ; [progression, découverte] advance

**avancement** [avɑ̃smɑ̃] *nm* [de personne] promotion ; [de travail] progress

**avancer** [avɑ̃se] **1.** *vt* [dans le temps] to bring forward ; [dans l'espace] to move forward ; [pion, thèse] to advance ; [montre] to put forward ; **avancer de l'argent à qn** to lend sb money **2.** *vi* [aller de l'avant] to move forward ; [armée] to advance ; [faire des progrès] to progress ; [faire saillie] to jut out (**sur** over) ; **avancer (de cinq minutes)** [montre] to

be (five minutes) fast **3. s'avancer** *vpr* to move forward ; **s'avancer vers qch** to head towards sth

**avant** [avɑ̃] **1.** *prép* before ; **avant de faire qch** before doing sth ; **je vous verrai avant de partir / que vous (ne) partiez** I'll see you before I / you leave ; **avant peu** soon, before long ; **avant tout** above all

**2.** *adv* [auparavant] before ; [d'abord] beforehand ; **avant j'avais les cheveux longs** I used to have long hair ; **en avant** [mouvement] forward ; [en tête] ahead ; **en avant de** in front of ; **la nuit d'avant** the night before

**3.** *nm* [de navire, de voiture] front ; [joueur de football] forward ; **à l'avant** in (the) front ; **aller de l'avant** to get on with it

**4.** *adj inv* [pneu, roue] front

■ **avant-bras** *nm inv* forearm

■ **avant-centre** *(pl* **avants-centres)** *nm* [au football] centre-forward

■ **avant-dernier, -ère** *(mpl* **avant-derniers,** *fpl* **avant-dernières)** *adj & nmf* second last

■ **avant-hier** *adv* the day before yesterday

■ **avant-première** *(pl* **avant-premières)** *nf* preview

■ **avant-propos** *nm inv* foreword

**avantage** [avɑ̃taʒ] *nm* advantage ; **être / tourner à l'avantage de qn** to be / turn to sb's advantage ; **avantages sociaux** social security benefits ■ **avantager** *vt* **avantager qn** [favoriser] to give sb an advantage over ; [faire valoir] to show sb off to advantage ■ **avantageux, -euse** *adj* [offre] attractive ; [prix] reasonable

**avare** [avar] **1.** *adj* miserly **2.** *nmf* miser ■ **avarice** *nf* miserliness, avarice

**avaries** [avari] *nf* damage ; **subir une avaries** to be damaged ■ **avarié, -e** *adj* [aliment] rotten

**avatar** [avatar] *nm* **a)** [transformation] metamorphosis **b)** ORDINAT avatar ■ **avatars** *nmpl Fam* [mésaventures] misfortunes

**avec** [avɛk] **1.** *prép* with; **méchant/aimable avec qn** nasty / kind to sb; **avec enthousiasme** with enthusiasm, enthusiastically; *Fam* **et avec ça ?** [dans un magasin] anything else? **2.** *adv Fam* with it / him *etc*; **tiens mon sac, je ne peux pas courir avec !** hold my bag: I can't run with it!

**avenant, -e** [avnɑ̃, -ɑ̃t] **1.** *adj* [personne, manières] pleasing **2.** *nm* **à l'avenant (de)** in keeping (with)

**avènement** [avɛnmɑ̃] *nm* [d'une ère] advent; [d'un roi] accession

**avenir** [avnir] *nm* future; **à l'avenir** [désormais] in future; **d'avenir** [métier] with good prospects

**aventure** [avɑ̃tyr] *nf* adventure; [en amour] affair; **dire la bonne aventure à qn** to tell sb's fortune ■ **aventurer 1.** *vpr* to venture (**dans** into) **2. s'aventurer** *vpr* to venture (**dans** into) ■ **aventureux, euse** *adj* [personne, vie] adventurous ■ **aventurier, -ère** *nmf* adventurer

**avenue** [avny] *nf* avenue

**avérer** [avere] ■ **s'avérer** *vpr* [se révéler] to prove to be; **il s'avère que...** it turns out that... ■ **avéré, -e** *adj* [fait] established

**averse** [avɛrs] *nf* shower

**aversion** [avɛrsjɔ̃] *nf* aversion (**pour** to)

**avertir** [avɛrtir] *vt* **avertir qn de qch** [informer] to inform sb of sth; [danger] to warn sb of sth ■ **avertissement** *nm* warning; [de livre] foreword ■ **avertisseur** *nm* [klaxon] horn

**aveu, -x** [avø] *nm* confession

**aveugle** [avœgl] **1.** *adj* blind; **devenir aveugle** to go blind; **avoir une confiance aveugle en qn** to trust sb implicitly **2.** *nmf* blind man, *f* blind woman; **les aveugles** the blind ■ **aveuglement** *nm* [moral, mental] blindness ■ **aveuglément** *adv* blindly ■ **aveugler** *vt* [éblouir] & *Fig* to blind; **aveuglé par la colère** blind with rage

**aveuglette** [avœglɛt] ■ **à l'aveuglette** *adv* blindly; **chercher qch à l'aveuglette** to grope for sth

**aviateur, -trice** [avjatœr, -tris] *nmf* aviator ■ **aviation** *nf* [secteur] aviation; [armée de l'air] air force; **l'aviation** [activité] flying

**avide** [avid] *adj* [cupide] greedy; [passionné] eager (**de** for) ■ **avidité** *nf* [voracité, cupidité] greed; [passion] eagerness

**avilir** [avilir] *vt* to degrade

**avion** [avjɔ̃] *nm* plane, *Br* aeroplane, *Am* airplane; **par avion** [sur lettre] airmail; **en avion, par avion** [voyager] by plane, by air; **avion à réaction** jet; **avion de tourisme** private plane

**aviron** [avirɔ̃] *nm* oar; **l'aviron** [sport] rowing; **faire de l'aviron** to row

**avis** [avi] *nm* opinion; [communiqué] notice; [conseil] advice; **à mon avis** in my opinion, to my mind; **être de l'avis de qn** to be of the same opinion as sb; **changer d'avis** to change one's mind; **sauf avis contraire** unless I / you /*etc* hear to the contrary

**aviser** [avize] **1.** *vt* **aviser qn de qch / que...** to inform sb of sth / that... **2. s'aviser** *vpr* **s'aviser de qch** to become aware of sth; **s'aviser que...** to notice that... ■ **avisé, -e** *adj* wise (**de faire** to do); **bien / mal avisé** well- / ill-advised

**avocat¹, -e** [avɔka, -at] *nmf* JUR lawyer; *Fig* advocate

**avocat²** [avɔka] *nm* [fruit] avocado

**avoine** [avwan] *nf* oats

**avoir** [avwar] **1.** *v aux* to have; **je l'ai vu** I have *or* I've seen him **2.** *vt* [posséder] to have; [obtenir] to get; [porter] to wear; *Fam* [tromper] to take for a ride; **qu'est-ce que tu as ?** what's the matter with you?; **j'ai à faire** I have things to do; **il n'a qu'à essayer** he only has to try; **avoir faim/chaud** to be *or* feel hungry / hot; **avoir cinq ans** to be five (years old); **avoir du diabète** to be diabetic **3.** *v impers* **il y a** there is, *pl* there are; **il y a six ans** six years ago; **il n'y a pas de quoi !** [en réponse à 'merci'] don't mention it!; **qu'est-ce qu'il y a ?** what's the matter?

**4.** *nm* assets, property ; [d'un compte] credit

---

**avoisiner** [avwazine] *vt* [dans l'espace] to border on ; [en valeur] to be close to ■ **avoisinant, -e** *adj* neighbouring, nearby

**avorter** [avɔrte] *vi* [subir une IVG] to have an abortion ; *Fig* [projet] to fall through ; **se faire avorter** to have an abortion ■ **avortement** *nm* abortion

**avouer** [avwe] **1.** *vt* [crime] to confess to ; **il faut avouer que...** it must be admitted that... **2. s'avouer** *vpr* **s'avouer vaincu** to acknowledge defeat

**avril** [avril] *nm* April

**axe** [aks] *nm* [géométrique] axis ; [essieu] axle ; **les grands axes** [routes] the main roads ■ **axer** *vt* to centre (**sur** on)

**ayant** [ɛjɑ̃], **ayez** [ɛje], **ayons** [ɛjɔ̃] *voir* **avoir**

**ayé** SMS *abr écrite de* **ça y est**

**azote** [azɔt] *nm* nitrogen

# B

**B, b** [be] *nm inv* B, b

**b.a.-ba** [beaba] *nm* ABCs, rudiments; **apprendre le b.a.-ba du métier** to learn the ABCs *or* basics of the trade

**babillard** [babijar] *nm Can* bulletin board

**babiller** [babije] *vi* [enfant] to babble

**babines** [babin] *nfpl* [lèvres] chops

**bâbord** [babɔr] *nm* port (side) ; **à bâbord** to port

**baby-foot** [babifut] *nm inv* table football

**baby-sitting** [babisitiŋ] *nm* baby-sitting; **faire du baby-sitting** to baby-sit ■ **baby-sitter** (*pl* **baby-sitters**) *nmf* baby-sitter

**bac¹** [bak] *nm* [bateau] ferry (boat) ; [cuve] tank; **bac à glace** ice tray

**bac²** [bak] *(abr de* **baccalauréat***) nm Fam secondary school examination qualifying for entry to university, Br* ≃ A-levels, *Am* ≃ high school diploma

**BAC** [bak] *(abr de* **brigade anticriminalité***) nf police squad specializing in patrols to combat crime*

**baccalauréat** [bakalɔrea] *nm* secondary school examination qualifying for entry to university, Br ≃ A-levels, Am ≃ high school diploma

**bâche** [baʃ] *nf* [de toile] tarpaulin ; [de plastique] plastic sheet ■ **bâcher** *vt* to cover (*with a tarpaulin or plastic sheet*)

**bachelier, -ère** [baʃəlje, -ɛr] *nmf* student who has passed the 'baccalauréat'

**bâcler** [bakle] *vt Fam* to botch (up)

**bactérie** [bakteri] *nf* bacterium

**badaud, -aude** [bado, -od] *nmf* [promeneur] stroller ; [curieux] onlooker

**badge** [badʒ] *nm Br* badge, *Am* button ■ **badgeuse** [badʒøz] *nf* swipe card reader

**badigeonner** [badiʒɔne] *vt* [surface] to daub (**de** with) ; [mur] to whitewash ; CULIN to brush (**de** with) ; [plaie] to paint (**de** with)

**badinage** [badinaʒ] *nm* banter

**badine** [badin] *nf* switch

**badiner** [badine] *vi* to jest

**baffle** [bafl] *nm* speaker

**bafouer** [bafwe] *vt* [person] to jeer at ; [autorité] to flout

**bafouiller** [bafuje] *vt & vi* to stammer

**bagages** [bagaʒ] *nmpl* [valises] luggage, baggage; **faire ses bagages** to pack (one's bags)

**bagarre** [bagar] *nf* fight, brawl ■ **se bagarrer** *vpr* to fight ■ **bagarreur, -euse** *adj* [personne, caractère] aggressive

**bagatelle** [bagatɛl] *nf* **a)** [objet] trinket **b)** [somme d'argent] **acheter qch pour une bagatelle** to buy sth for next to nothing; *Iron* **la bagatelle de X euros** a mere X euros **c)** [chose futile] trifle

**baggy** [bagi] *nm* baggy pants *pl*

**bague** [bag] *nf* [anneau] ring ; [de cigare] band ■ **baguer** *vt* [oiseau, arbre] to ring

**baguette** [bagɛt] *nf* [canne] stick ; [de chef d'orchestre] baton ; [pain] baguette; **baguettes** [de tambour] drumsticks ; [pour manger] chopsticks

**Bahamas** [baamas] *nfpl* **les Bahamas** the Bahamas

**bahut** [bay] *nm* [buffet] sideboard

**baie¹** [be] *nf* GÉOG bay

**baie²** [be] *nf* [fruit] berry

**baie³** [be] *nf* **baie vitrée** picture window

**baignade** [bɛɲad] *nf* [activité] swimming; **'baignade interdite'** 'no swimming'

**baigner** [beɲe] **1.** *vt* [pied, blessure] to bathe; [enfant] *Br* to bath, *Am* to bathe; [sujet : mer] to wash **2.** *vi* [tremper] to soak (**dans** in) **3. se baigner** *vpr* [nager] to have a swim ■ **baigneur, -euse 1.** *nmf* swimmer **2.** *nm* [poupée] baby doll ■ **baignoire** *nf* bath (tub)

**bail** [baj] *(pl* **baux** [bo]) *nm* lease; *Fam* **ça fait un bail que je ne l'ai pas vu** I haven't seen him for ages ■ **bailleur** *nm* **bailleur de fonds** financial backer

**bâiller** [baje] *vi* to yawn; [col] to gape; [porte] to be ajar

**bâillon** [bajɔ̃] *nm* gag; **mettre un bâillon à qn** to gag sb ■ **bâillonner** *vt* [victime, presse] to gag

**bain** [bɛ̃] *nm* bath; **prendre un bain** to have *or* take a bath; **prendre un bain de soleil** to sunbathe; **petit / grand bain** [de piscine] small / large pool

**baiser** [beze] *nm* kiss

**baisse** [bes] *nf* fall, drop (**de** in); **en baisse** [température] falling; [popularité] declining

**baisser** [bese] **1.** *vt* [rideau, vitre, prix] to lower; [radio, chauffage] to turn down; **baisser la tête** to lower one's head; **baisser les yeux** to look down **2.** *vi* [prix, niveau, température] to fall; [vue, mémoire] to fail; [popularité, qualité] to decline **3. se baisser** *vpr* to bend down; [pour éviter quelque chose] to duck

**baissier** [besje] *adj m* FIN **marché baissier** bear market

**bal** [bal] *(pl* **bals**) *nm* [élégant] ball; [populaire] dance; **bal costumé, bal masqué** fancy dress ball; **bal populaire** *dance, usually outdoors, open to the public*

**balade** [balad] *nf Fam* [à pied] walk; [en voiture] drive; **faire une balade** [à pied] to go for a walk; [en voiture] to go for a drive ■ **balader** *Fam* **1.** *vi* **envoyer qn balader** to send sb packing **2. se balader** *vpr* [à pied] to go for a walk; [en voi-

ture] to go for a drive ■ **baladeur** *nm* personal stereo ■ **baladodiffusion** [baladodifyzjɔ̃] *nf Can* podcasting

**balafre** [balafr] *nf* [cicatrice] scar; [coupure] gash ■ **balafrer** *vt* to gash

**balai** [balɛ] *nm* broom; **donner un coup de balai** to give the floor a sweep

**balance** [balɑ̃s] *nf* **a)** [instrument] (pair of) scales **b) la Balance** [signe] Libra

**balancer** [balɑ̃se] **1.** *vt* [bras, jambe] to swing **2. se balancer** *vpr* [arbre, bateau] to sway; [sur une balançoire] to swing; [sur une chaise] to rock ■ **balancement** *nm* swaying

**balancier** [balɑ̃sje] *nm* [d'horloge] pendulum

**balançoire** [balɑ̃swar] *nf* [suspendue] swing; [bascule] see-saw

**balayer** [baleje] *vt* [pièce] to sweep; [feuilles, saletés] to sweep up ■ **balayage** *nm* [nettoyage] sweeping; [coiffure] highlighting

**balayeur, -euse** [balɛjœr, -øz] *nmf* [personne] road-sweeper

**balbutier** [balbysje] *vt & vi* to stammer ■ **balbutiement** *nm* **balbutiement(s)** stammering

**balcon** [balkɔ̃] *nm* balcony; [de théâtre] circle, *Am* mezzanine; **premier / deuxième balcon** dress / upper circle

**Baléares** [balear] *nfpl* **les Baléares** the Balearic Islands

**baleine** [balɛn] *nf* [animal] whale; [de corset] whalebone; [de parapluie] rib

**balèze** [balɛz] *adj Fam* [grand et fort] hefty; [intelligent] brainy

**balise** [baliz] *nf* NAUT beacon; AVIAT light; [de piste de ski] marker; ORDINAT tag ■ **balisage** *nm* [signaux & NAUT] beacons; AVIAT lights ■ **baliser** *vt* [chenal] to beacon; [aéroport] to equip with lights; [route] to mark out with beacons; [piste de ski] to mark out; ORDINAT to tag

**balivernes** [balivɛrn] *nfpl* twaddle

**Balkans** [balkɑ̃] *nmpl* **les Balkans** the Balkans

**ballant, -e** [balɑ̃, -ɑ̃t] *adj* [bras, jambes] dangling

**ballast** [balast] *nm* [de route, de voie ferrée] ballast

**balle** [bal] *nf* [pour jouer] ball ; [d'arme] bullet ; **balle de tennis** tennis ball ; **balle perdue** stray bullet ■ **balle(-)molle** [balmɔl] (*pl* **balles(-)molles**) *nf* *Can* SPORT softball

**ballet** [balɛ] *nm* ballet ■ **ballerine** *nf* [danseuse] ballerina ; [chaussure] pump

**ballon** [balɔ̃] *nm* [balle, dirigeable] balloon ; [verre] round wine glass ; **jouer au ballon** to play with a ball ; **ballon de football** *Br* football, *Am* soccer ball

**ballonné** [balɔne] *adj m* [ventre, personne] bloated

**ballottage** [balɔtaʒ] *nm* POL **il y a ballottage** there will be a second ballot

**ballotter** [balɔte] *vt* [bateau] to toss about ; [passagers] to shake about

**balluchon** [balyʃɔ̃] *nm* bundle ; **faire son balluchon** to pack one's bags

**balnéaire** [balneɛr] *adj* **station balnéaire** *Br* seaside resort, *Am* beach resort

**balourd, -e** [balur, -urd] *adj* oafish

**balsamique** [balzamik] *adj* BOT & MÉD balsamic ; **vinaigre balsamique** balsamic vinegar

**balte** [balt] *adj* **les États baltes** the Baltic states

**Baltique** [baltik] *nf* **la (mer) Baltique** the Baltic (Sea)

**baluchon** [balyʃɔ̃] *nm* = **balluchon**

**balustrade** [balystrad] *nf* [de pont] railing ; [de balcon] balustrade

**bambou** [bɑ̃bu] *nm* bamboo

**ban** [bɑ̃] *nm* [applaudissements] round of applause ; **bans** [de mariage] banns

**banal, -e, -als** [banal] *adj* [objet, gens] ordinary ; [idée] trite, banal ; **pas banal** unusual ■ **banalité** *nf* [d'objet, de gens] ordinariness ; [d'idée] triteness

**banalisé, e** [banalize] *adj* [véhicule] unmarked ; ORDINAT general-purpose

**banaliser** [banalize] *vt* [rendre commun] to trivialize

**banane** [banan] *nf* [fruit] banana ; [coiffure] quiff ■ **bananier** *nm* [arbre] banana tree

**banc** [bɑ̃] *nm* [siège] bench ; [établi] (work-)bench ; [de poissons] shoal ; **banc des accusés** dock ; **banc d'essai** IND test bed ; *Fig* testing ground ; **banc de sable** sandbank

**bancaire** [bɑ̃kɛr] *adj* [opération] banking ; [chèque, compte] bank

**bancal, -e, -als** [bɑ̃kal] *adj* [meuble] wobbly ; *Fig* [raisonnement] unsound

**bandage** [bɑ̃daʒ] *nm* [pansement] bandage

**bande** [bɑ̃d] *nf* **a)** [de tissu, de papier, de terre] strip ; [pansement] bandage ; [pellicule] film ; **bande magnétique** tape ; AUTO **bande d'arrêt d'urgence** *Br* hard shoulder, *Am* shoulder ; **bande dessinée** comic strip ; **bande sonore** soundtrack **b)** [de personnes] band, group ; [de voleurs] gang ; [de loups] pack ; **faire bande à part** [agir seul] to do one's own thing ■ **bande-annonce** (*pl* **bandes-annonces**) *nf* trailer (de for) ■ **bande-son** (*pl* **bandes-son**) *nf* soundtrack

**bandeau, -x** [bɑ̃do] *nm* [pour cheveux] headband ; [sur les yeux] blindfold

**bander** [bɑ̃de] *vt* [blessure, main] to bandage ; [arc] to bend ; **bander les yeux à qn** to blindfold sb

**banderole** [bɑ̃drɔl] *nf* [de manifestants] banner ; [publicitaire] streamer

**bandit** [bɑ̃di] *nm* [escroc] crook

**bandoulière** [bɑ̃duljɛr] *nf* [de sac] shoulder strap ; **en bandoulière** slung across the shoulder

**banlieue** [bɑ̃ljø] *nf* suburbs ; **la banlieue parisienne** the suburbs of Paris ; **de banlieue** [maison, magasin] suburban ; **train de banlieue** commuter train ■ **banlieusard, -e** *nmf* [habitant] suburbanite ; [voyageur] commuter

**bannière** [banjɛr] *nf* banner ; **la bannière étoilée** the Star-Spangled Banner

**bannir** [banir] *vt* [personne, idée] to banish (**de** from)

**banque** [bɑ̃k] *nf* [établissement] bank; **la banque** [activité] banking; **employé de banque** bank clerk; ORDINAT **banque de données** data bank

**banqueroute** [bɑ̃krut] *nf* bankruptcy; **faire banqueroute** to go bankrupt

**banquet** [bɑ̃kɛ] *nm* banquet

**banquette** [bɑ̃kɛt] *nf* [siège] (bench) seat

**banquier, -ère** [bɑ̃kje, -ɛr] *nmf* banker

**banquise** [bɑ̃kiz] *nf* ice floe

**baptême** [batɛm] *nm* christening, baptism ▪ **baptiser** *vt* to christen, to baptize

**baquet** [bakɛ] *nm* [cuve] tub

**bar¹** [bar] *nm* [café, comptoir] bar; Can **bar laitier** milk bar, ice cream parlour

**bar²** [bar] *nm* [poisson] bass

**baraque** [barak] *nf* [cabane] hut, shack; [de foire] stall ▪ **baraquement** *nm* shacks; MIL camp

**baraqué, e** [barake] *adj Fam* well-built

**baratin** [baratɛ̃] *nm Fam* [verbiage] waffle; [de séducteur] sweet talk; [de vendeur] sales talk ▪ **baratiner** *vt Fam* to chatter; [sujet : séducteur] *Br* to chat up, *Am* to hit on

**barbare** [barbar] **1.** *adj* [cruel, sauvage] barbaric **2.** *nmf* barbarian ▪ **barbarie** *nf* [cruauté] barbarity

**barbe** [barb] *nf* beard; **barbe à papa** *Br* candyfloss, *Am* cotton candy

**barbecue** [barbəkju] *nm* barbecue

**barbelés** [barbəle] *nmpl* barbed wire

**barber** [barbe] *Fam* **1.** *vt* **barber qn** to bore sb stiff **2. se barber** *vpr* to be bored stiff ▪ **barbant, e** *adj Fam* deadly dull *or* boring

**barbiche** [barbiʃ] *nf* goatee

**barbiturique** [barbityrik] *nm* barbiturate

**barboter** [barbɔte] *vi* to splash about ▪ **barboteuse** *nf* rompers

**barbouiller** [barbuje] *vt* [salir] to smear (**de** with)

**barbu, -e** [barby] **1.** *adj* bearded **2.** *nm* bearded man

**barder¹** [barde] *vt* CULIN to bard; *Fig* **bardé de décorations** covered with decorations

**barder²** [barde] *v impers Fam* **ça va barder !** there's going to be trouble!

**barème** [barɛm] *nm* [de notes, de salaires, de prix] scale; [pour calculer] ready reckoner

**baril** [baril] *nm* [de pétrole, de vin] barrel; [de lessive] drum

**bariolé, -e** [barjɔle] *adj Br* multicoloured, *Am* multi-colored

**barjo(t)** [barʒo] *adj inv Fam* [fou] crazy

**barman** [barman] *(pl* **-men** [-men] *ou* **-mans)** *nm Br* barman, *Am* bartender

**baromètre** [barɔmɛtr] *nm* barometer

**baron** [barɔ̃] *nm* baron; *Fig* **baron de la finance** financial tycoon ▪ **baronne** *nf* baroness

**baroque** [barɔk] **1.** *adj* [édifice, style, musique] baroque **2.** *nm* ARCHIT & MUS **le baroque** the baroque

**baroudeur** [barudœr] *nm Fam* [combattant] fighter; [voyageur] keen traveller

**barque** [bark] *nf* (small) boat ▪ **barquette** [barkɛt] *nf* **a)** [tartelette] pastry boat **b)** [récipient] container; [de fruits] basket, *Br* punnet

**barrage** [baraʒ] *nm* [sur l'eau] dam; **barrage de police** police roadblock; **barrage routier** roadblock

**barre** [bar] *nf* [de fer, de bois] bar; [de danse] barre; [trait] line, stroke; NAUT [volant] helm; **barre chocolatée** chocolate bar; MUS **barre de mesure** bar (line); JUR **barre des témoins** *Br* witness box, *Am* witness stand; **barre d'appui** [de fenêtre] rail; ORDINAT **barre de défilement** scroll bar; ORDINAT **barre d'espacement** [de clavier] space bar; ORDINAT **barre d'état** status bar; ORDINAT **barre d'outils** tool bar; ORDINAT **barre de sélection** menu bar

**barré, e** [bare] *adj* **a)** [chèque] crossed **b) on est bien barré(s) !** *Iron*, **on est mal barré(s) !** (that's) great! *Iron*, (that's) marvellous! *Iron*; *Fam* **c'est mal barré** it's got off to a bad start; **on est mal barré pour y être à 8 h** we haven't got a hope in hell of being there at 8; **entre eux deux c'est mal barré** they started off on the wrong foot with each other

**barreau, -x** [baro] *nm* [de fenêtre, de cage] bar; [d'échelle] rung; JUR **le barreau** the bar; **être derrière les barreaux** [en prison] to be behind bars

**barrer** [bare] **1.** *vt* [voie] to block off; [porte] to bar; [chèque] to cross; [mot] to cross out; NAUT [bateau] to steer; **barrer le passage** *ou* **la route à qn** to bar sb's way; **'route barrée'** 'road closed' **2. se barrer** *vpr Fam* to beat it

**barrette** [barɛt] *nf* [pour cheveux] *Br* (hair) slide, *Am* barrette

**barricade** [barikad] *nf* barricade ■ **barricader 1.** *vt* [rue, porte] to barricade **2. se barricader** *vpr* to barricade oneself (**dans** in)

**barrière** [barjɛr] *nf* [obstacle] barrier; [de passage à niveau] gate; [clôture] fence

**barrique** [barik] *nf* (large) barrel

**barrir** [barir] *vi* [éléphant] to trumpet

**baryton** [baritɔ̃] *nm* MUS baritone

**bas¹, basse¹** [bɑ, bɑs] **1.** *adj* [dans l'espace, en quantité, en intensité & MUS] low; [origine] lowly; *Péj* [acte] mean, low; **à bas prix** cheaply; **enfant en bas âge** young child; **avoir la vue basse** to be short-sighted **2.** *adv* [dans l'espace] low (down); [dans une hiérarchie] low; [parler] quietly; **plus bas** further *or* lower down; **voir plus bas** [sur document] see below; **en bas** at the bottom; [dans une maison] downstairs; **en bas de** at the bottom of; **à bas les dictateurs !** down with dictators! **3.** *nm* [partie inférieure] bottom; **l'étagère du bas** the bottom shelf; **au bas de** at the bottom of; **de bas en haut** upwards ■ **bas de gamme 1.** *adj* downmarket **2.** *nm* bottom of the range

**bas²** [bɑ] *nm* [chaussette] stocking; *Fig* **bas de laine** [économies] nest egg

**basané, -e** [bazane] *adj* [bronzé] tanned

**bas-côté** [bakote] (*pl* **bas-côtés**) *nm* [de route] verge; [d'église] (side) aisle

**bascule** [baskyl] *nf* [balançoire] see-saw; [balance] weighing machine; **fauteuil à bascule** rocking chair ■ **basculer 1.** *vt* [chargement] to tip over; [benne] to tip up **2.** *vi* [tomber] to topple over; **faire basculer** [personne] to knock over; [chargement] to tip over

**base** [bɑz] *nf* [partie inférieure, CHIM, MATH & MIL] base; [de parti politique] rank and file; [principe] basis; **avoir de bonnes bases en anglais** to have a good grounding in English; **de base** basic; **salaire de base** basic pay; ORDINAT **base de données** database ■ **baser 1.** *vt* to base (**sur** on) **2. se baser** *vpr* **se baser sur qch** to base oneself on sth

**bas-fond** [bafɔ̃] (*pl* **bas-fonds**) *nm* [de mer, de rivière] shallow; *Péj* **les bas-fonds** [de ville] the rough areas

**basic** [bazik] *nm* ORDINAT BASIC

**basilic** [bazilik] *nm* [plante, aromate] basil

**basilique** [bazilik] *nf* basilica

**basket-ball** [basketbol] *nm* basketball

**baskets** [baskɛt] *nmpl ou* nfpl [chaussures] baseball boots

**basque¹** [bask] **1.** *adj* Basque **2.** *nmf* **Basque** Basque

**basque²** [bask] *nfpl* [de veste] tail; *Fig* **être toujours pendu aux basques de qn** to be always at sb's heels

**basse²** [bɑs] **1.** *voir* **bas 2.** *nf* MUS [contrebasse] (double) bass; [guitare] bass (guitar)

**basse-cour** [baskur] (*pl* **basses-cours**) *nf Br* farmyard, *Am* barnyard

**bassesse** [basɛs] *nf* [d'action] lowness; [action] low act

**bassin** [basɛ̃] *nm* **a)** [pièce d'eau] ornamental lake; [de fontaine] basin; [récipient] bowl, basin; **petit bassin** [de piscine] children's pool; **grand bassin** [de piscine] large pool **b)** [du corps] pelvis **c)** [région] basin; **le bassin parisien** the Paris Basin ■ **bassine** nf bowl

**basson** [basɔ̃] nm [instrument] bassoon; [musicien] bassoonist

**basta** [basta] excl Fam (that's) enough; **je termine la page 14 et basta !** I'll finish page 14 and then that's it!

**bastion** [bastjɔ̃] nm aussi Fig bastion

**bas-ventre** [bavɑ̃tr] nm lower abdomen

**bat** [ba] voir **battre**

**bataille** [bataj] nf [lutte] battle; [jeu de cartes] ≃ beggar-my-neighbour ■ **batailleur, -euse** adj aggressive

**bataillon** [batajɔ̃] nm MIL batallion

**bâtard, -e** [bɑtar, -ard] **1.** adj [enfant] illegitimate; [solution] hybrid **2.** nmf [enfant] illegitimate child; Péj bastard; [chien] mongrel; [pain] small, thick baguette

**bateau, -x** [bato] **1.** nm [embarcation] boat; [grand] ship; **faire du bateau** to go boating; **bateau à moteur** motorboat; **bateau à voiles** Br sailing boat, Am sailboat; **bateau de plaisance** pleasure boat **2.** adj inv Fam [sujet] hackneyed; **col bateau** boat neck ■ **bateau-bus** [batobys] (pl **bateaux-bus**) nm riverbus; **prendre le bateau-bus** to take the riverbus ■ **bateau-mouche** (pl **bateaux-mouches**) nm river boat (on the Seine)

**bâtiment** [bɑtimɑ̃] nm [édifice] building; [navire] vessel; **le bâtiment, l'industrie du bâtiment** the building trade

**bâtir** [bɑtir] vt [construire] to build; COUTURE to tack; **terrain à bâtir** building plot ■ **bâti, -e 1.** adj **bien bâti** [personne] well-built **2.** nm [charpente] frame; COUTURE tacking ■ **bâtisse** nf Péj ugly building

**bâton** [bɑtɔ̃] nm [canne] stick; [de maréchal] baton; [d'agent de police] Br truncheon, Am nightstick; [trait] vertical line; **donner des coups de bâton à qn** to beat sb (with a stick); **bâton de rouge** lipstick; **bâtons de ski** ski sticks ■ **bâtonnet** nm stick

**battage** [bataʒ] nm **battage (publicitaire** ou **médiatique)** (media) hype, Am ballyhoo

**battant¹** [batɑ̃] nm **a)** [de porte, de volet] leaf; **porte à deux battants** double door **b)** [personne] fighter

**battant², -e** [batɑ̃, -ɑ̃t] adj **pluie battante** driving rain; **porte battant** Br swing door, Am swinging door

**battement** [batmɑ̃] nm **a)** [de tambour] beat(ing); [de porte] banging; [de paupières] blink(ing); [d'ailes] flapping **b)** [délai] gap

**batterie** [batri] nf [d'orchestre] drums; [ensemble, MIL & ÉLEC] battery; [de questions] series; **être à la batterie** [sujet: musicien] to be on drums; **élevage en batterie** battery farming; **batterie de cuisine** kitchen utensils

**batteur** [batœr] nm [musicien] drummer; [de cuisine] mixer

**battre** [batr] **1.** vt [frapper, vaincre] to beat; [œufs] to whisk; [beurre] to churn; [record] to break; [cartes] to shuffle; MUS **battre la mesure** to beat time **2.** vi [cœur] to beat; [porte, volet] to bang; **battre des mains** to clap one's hands; **battre des ailes** to flap its wings **3. se battre** vpr to fight; **se battre au couteau** to fight with a knife; **se battre contre qn** to fight sb

**battu, -e¹** [baty] **1.** pp de **battre 2.** adj [femme, enfant] battered

**battue²** [baty] nf [à la chasse] beat; [recherche] search

**baume** [bom] nm aussi Fig balm

**baux** [bo] voir **bail**

**bavard, -e** [bavar, -ard] **1.** adj [qui parle beaucoup] chatty **2.** nmf [qui parle beaucoup] chatterbox ■ **bavardage** nm [action] chatting; [commérage] gossiping; **bavardages** [paroles] chats ■ **bavarder** vi [parler] to chat; [commérer] to gossip

**bave** [bav] nf [de personne] dribble; [de chien] slaver; [de chien enragé] froth ■ **baver** vi [personne] to dribble; [chien] to slaver; [chien enragé] to foam at the mouth; [stylo] to leak; Fam **en baver** to have a hard time of it

**bêche**

**bavette** [bavɛt] *nf* [de bébé] bib ; [de bœuf] skirt (of beef)

**baveux, -euse** [bavø, -øz] *adj* [omelette] runny

**bavoir** [bavwar] *nm* bib

**bavure** [bavyr] *nf* [tache] smudge ; [erreur] slip-up

**bayer** [baje] *vi* **bayer aux corneilles** to stare into space

**bazar** [bazar] *nm* [marché] bazaar ; [magasin] general store ; *Fam* [désordre] shambles (*sg*) ; *Fam* [affaires] gear ; *Fam* **mettre du bazar dans qch** to make a shambles of sth

**BCBG** (*abr de* **bon chic bon genre**) **1.** *nmf Br* ≃ Sloane (Ranger), ≃ preppie *Am* **2.** *adj Br* ≃ Sloaney, *Am* ≃ preppie

**BCG** [beseʒe] *nm MÉD* BCG

**bd** = **boulevard**

**BD** [bede] (*abr de* **bande dessinée**) *nf* comic strip

**beach-volley** [bitʃvɔlɛ] (*pl* **beach-volleys**) *nm* beach volleyball ; **jouer au beach-volley** to play beach volleyball

**béant, -e** [beɑ̃, -ɑ̃t] *adj* [gouffre] yawning

**béat, -e** [bea, -at] *adj Hum* [heureux] blissful ; *Péj* [niais] inane ; **être béat d'admiration** to be open-mouthed in admiration ■ **béatement** *adv* [sourire] inanely

**beau, belle** [bo, bɛl] (*pl* **beaux, belles**)

**bel** is used before masculine singular nouns beginning with a vowel or h mute.

**1.** *adj* **a)** [femme, enfant, fleur, histoire] beautiful ; [homme] handsome, good-looking ; [spectacle, discours] fine ; [maison, voyage, temps] lovely ; **une belle somme** a tidy sum ; **se faire beau** to smarten oneself up ; **c'est trop beau pour être vrai** it's too good to be true ; **c'est le plus beau jour de ma vie !** it's the best day of my life! **b)** [expressions] **au beau milieu de** right in the middle of ; **bel et bien** [complètement] well and truly **2.** *adv* **il fait beau** the weather's nice ; **j'ai beau crier…** it's no use (my) shouting…

**3.** *nm* **le beau** [la beauté] beauty **4.** *nf* **belle** [jeu, partie] decider

■ **beau-fils** (*pl* **beaux-fils**) *nm* [gendre] son-in-law ; [après remariage] stepson

■ **beau-frère** (*pl* **beaux-frères**) *nm* brother-in-law

■ **beau-père** (*pl* **beaux-pères**) *nm* [père du conjoint] father-in-law ; [après remariage] stepfather

■ **beaux-arts** *nmpl* fine arts ; **école des beaux-arts, les Beaux-arts** art school

■ **beaux-enfants** *nmpl* [conjoint des enfants] children-in-law ; [après remariage] stepchildren

■ **beaux-parents** *nmpl* parents-in-law

**beaucoup** [boku] *adv* [intensément, en grande quantité] a lot ; **de beaucoup** by far ; **aimer beaucoup qch** to like sth very much ; **s'intéresser beaucoup à qch** to be very interested in sth ; **beaucoup d'entre nous** many of us ; **beaucoup de** [quantité] a lot of ; [nombre] many, a lot of ; **pas beaucoup d'argent** not much money ; **pas beaucoup de gens** not many people ; **j'en ai beaucoup** [quantité] I have a lot ; [nombre] I have lots ; **beaucoup plus / moins (que)** much more / less (than), a lot more / less (than) ; [nombre] many or a lot more / a lot fewer (than)

**beauté** [bote] *nf* [qualité, femme] beauty

**bébé** [bebe] *nm* baby ■ **bébé-bulle** [bebebyl] (*pl* **bébés-bulles**) *nm* bubble baby ■ **bébé-éprouvette** (*pl* **bébés-éprouvette**) *nm* test-tube baby

**bébelle** [bebɛl] *nf Can Fam* **a)** [jouet] toy **b)** [objet quelconque, gadget] knick-knack

**bébête** [bebɛt] *adj Fam* silly

**bec** [bɛk] *nm* [d'oiseau] beak, bill ; [de pot] lip ; [de flûte] mouthpiece ; *Fam* [bouche] mouth ; *Fam* **clouer le bec à qn** to shut sb up ; **bec verseur** spout ■ **bec-de-lièvre** (*pl* **becs-de-lièvre**) *nm* harelip

**bêche** [bɛʃ] *nf* spade ■ **bêcher** *vt* to dig

**bedonnant, -e** [bədɔnɑ̃, -ɑ̃t] *adj* pot-bellied, paunchy

**bée** [be] *adj* fj'en suis resté bouche bée I was speechless

**beffroi** [befrwa] *nm* belfry

**bégayer** [begeje] *vi* to stutter, to stammer

**bègue** [bɛg] **1.** *adj* être bègue to stutter, to stammer **2.** *nmf* stutterer, stammerer

**beige** [bɛʒ] *adj & nm* beige

**beigne** [bɛɲ] *nf* Can [pâtisserie] donut

**beignet** [beɲe] *nm* fritter; [au sucre, à la confiture] doughnut

**Beijing** [beidʒiŋ] *nm ou f* Beijing

**bel** [bel] *voir* beau

**bêler** [bele] *vi* to bleat

**belette** [bəlɛt] *nf* weasel

**Belgique** [bɛlʒik] *nf* la Belgique Belgium ■ **belge 1.** *adj* Belgian **2.** *nmf* Belge Belgian

**bélier** [belje] *nm* [animal, machine] ram; **le Bélier** [signe] Aries

**belle** [bɛl] *voir* beau ■ **belle-famille** *(pl* **belles-familles)** *nf* in-laws ■ **belle-fille** *(pl* **belles-filles)** *nf* [épouse du fils] daughter-in-law; [après remariage] stepdaughter ■ **belle-mère** *(pl* **belles-mères)** *nf* [mère du conjoint] mother-in-law; [après remariage] stepmother ■ **belle-sœur** *(pl* **belles-sœurs)** *nf* sister-in-law

**belvédère** [belvedɛr] *nm* [construction] gazebo; [sur site naturel] viewpoint

**bémol** [bemɔl] *nm* MUS flat

**ben** [bɛ̃] *adv* Fam **a)** [pour renforcer] **ben quoi ?** so what?; **ben non** well, no; **ben voyons (donc) !** what next! **b)** [bien] **pt'êt ben qu'oui, pt'êt ben qu'non** maybe yes, maybe no

**bénédiction** [benediksjɔ̃] *nf* REL & *Fig* blessing

**bénéfice** [benefis] *nm* [financier] profit; [avantage] benefit; **accorder le bénéfice du doute à qn** to give sb the benefit of the doubt

**bénéficiaire** [benefisjɛr] **1.** *nmf* [de chèque] payee; JUR beneficiary **2.** *adj* [entreprise] profit-making; [compte] in credit

**bénéficier** [benefisje] *vi* **bénéficier de qch** [profiter de] to benefit from sth; [avoir] to have sth

**bénéfique** [benefik] *adj* beneficial (à to)

**Benelux** [benelyks] *nm* **le Bénélux** the Benelux

**bénévolat** [benevola] *nm* voluntary work

**bénévole** [benevɔl] **1.** *adj* [travail, infirmière] voluntary **2.** *nmf* volunteer, voluntary worker

**bénin, -igne** [benɛ̃, -iɲ] *adj* [accident, opération] minor; [tumeur] benign

**bénir** [benir] *vt* to bless; **que Dieu te bénisse !** God bless you! ■ **bénit, -e** *adj* eau bénite holy water

**benjamin, e** [bɛ̃ʒamɛ̃, in] *nmf* [de famille] youngest child; [de groupe] youngest member

**benne** [bɛn] *nf* [de camion] tipping body; [de téléphérique] cable car; **benne à ordures** bin lorry

**BEP** [beəpe] *(abr de* **brevet d'études professionnelles)** *nm* SCOL *vocational diploma taken at 18*

**BEPC** [beəpese] *(abr de* **brevet d'études du premier cycle)** *nm* SCOL *former school leaving certificate taken at 15*

**béquille** [bekij] *nf* [canne] crutch; [de moto] stand

**berceau, -x** [berso] *nm* [de bébé] cradle; *Fig* [de civilisation] birthplace

**bercer** [berse] **1.** *vt* [bébé] to rock **2. se bercer** *vpr* **se bercer d'illusions** to delude oneself ■ **berceuse** *nf* **a)** [chanson] lullaby **b)** Can [fauteuil] rocking chair

**béret** [berɛ] *nm* beret

**berge** [bɛrʒ] *nf* [rive] bank

**berger** [berʒe] *nm* shepherd; **berger allemand** German shepherd, *Br* Alsatian ■ **bergère** *nf* shepherdess

**berline** [bɛrlin] *nf* [voiture] *Br* (four-door) saloon, *Am* sedan

**berlingot** [bɛrlɛ̃go] *nm* [bonbon] *Br* boiled sweet, *Am* hard candy ; [de lait] carton

**bermuda** [bɛrmyda] *nm* Bermuda shorts

**Bermudes** [bɛrmyd] *nfpl* **les Bermudes** Bermuda

**berner** [bɛrne] *vt* to fool

**besogne** [bəzɔɲ] *nf* job, task ; *Fig* **aller vite en besogne** to jump the gun

**besoin** [bəzwɛ̃] *nm* need ; **avoir besoin de qn/qch** to need sb /sth ; **avoir besoin de faire qch** to need to do sth ; **au besoin, si besoin est** if necessary, if need be ■ **besoins** *nmpl* a) [exigences] needs b) **faire ses besoins** to relieve o.s.

**bestial, -e, -aux** [bɛstjal, -o] *adj* bestial ■ **bestiaux** *nmpl* livestock

**bestiole** [bɛstjɔl] *nf* [insecte] *Br* creepy-crawly, *Am* creepy-crawler

**best of** [bɛstɔf] *nm inv* **un best of de Serge Gainsbourg** a selection of Serge Gainsbourg's most popular songs ; **le best of du championnat** selected highlights from the championship

**bétail** [betaj] *nm* livestock

**bête¹** [bɛt] *adj* stupid, silly

**bête²** [bɛt] *nf* animal ; [insecte] bug ; **bête féroce** wild animal ; **bête noire** *Br* pet hate, *Am* pet peeve ■ **bêtement** *adv* stupidly ; **tout bêtement** quite simply ■ **bêtise** *nf* [manque d'intelligence] stupidity ; [action, parole] stupid thing ; **faire une bêtise** to do something stupid ; **dire des bêtises** to talk nonsense

**béton** [betɔ̃] *nm* [matériau] concrete ; **mur en béton** concrete wall

**bette** [bɛt] *nf* Swiss chard

**betterave** [bɛtrav] *nf* [plante] *Br* beetroot, *Am* beet ; **betterave sucrière** sugar beet

**beur** [bœr] **1.** *nmf Fam* person born in France of North African immigrant parents **2.** *adj* pertaining to a person born in France of North African immigrant parents

**beurre** [bœr] *nm* butter ; *Can* **beurre d'érable** maple butter ■ **beurrer** *vt* to butter ■ **beurrier** [bœrje] *nm* butter dish

**bévue** [bevy] *nf* slip-up

**biais** [bjɛ] *nm* [de mur] slant ; [moyen] way ; [aspect] angle ; **regarder qn de biais** to look sideways at sb ; **par le biais de** through

**biaiser** [bjeze] *vi* (ruser) to dodge the issue

**bibande** [bibɑ̃d] *adj* dual-band

**bibelot** [biblo] *nm* small ornament

**biberon** [bibrɔ̃] *nm* (feeding) bottle ; **nourrir un bébé au biberon** to bottle-feed a baby

**bibit(t)e** [bibit] *nf Can Fam* insect, bug

**bible** [bibl] *nf* bible ; **la Bible** the Bible ■ **biblique** *adj* biblical

**bibliographie** [biblijɔgrafi] *nf* bibliography

**bibliothèque** [biblijɔtɛk] *nf* [bâtiment, salle] library ; [meuble] bookcase ; **bibliothèque municipale** public library ■ **bibliothécaire** *nmf* librarian

**Bic®** [bik] *nm* ballpoint, *Br* biro®

**bicarbonate** [bikarbɔnat] *nm* CHIM bicarbonate ; **bicarbonate de soude** bicarbonate of soda

**biceps** [bisɛps] *nm* biceps

**biche** [biʃ] *nf* [animal] doe, hind

**bicolore** [bikɔlɔr] *adj* two-coloured

**bicyclette** [bisiklɛt] *nf* bicycle ; **faire de la bicyclette** to go cycling

**bidet** [bidɛ] *nm* [cuvette] bidet

**bidon** [bidɔ̃] **1.** *nm* [d'essence, d'huile] can ; [de lait] churn ; **bidon d'essence** petrol can, jerry can **2.** *adj inv Fam* [simulé] phoney, fake

**bidonville** [bidɔ̃vil] *nf* shantytown

**bidouiller** [biduje] *vt* [logiciel] to fiddle around with, to tamper with ; [appareil] to fix

**bidule** [bidyl] *nm Fam* [chose] whatsit ; **Bidule** [personne] what's-his-name, *f* what's-her-name

**Biélorussie** [bjelɔrysi] *nf* **la Biélorussie** Belarussia, Byelorussia

**bien** [bjɛ̃] **1.** *adv* **a)** [convenablement] well; **il joue bien** he plays well; **je vais bien** I'm fine *or* well; **écoutez-moi bien !** listen carefully

**b)** [moralement] right; **bien se conduire** to behave (well); **vous avez bien fait** you did the right thing; **tu ferais bien de te méfier** you would be wise to behave

**c)** [très] very

**d)** [beaucoup] a lot, a great deal; **bien plus / moins** much more / less; **bien des gens** a lot of people; **bien des fois** many times; **tu as bien de la chance** you're really lucky!; **merci bien !** thanks very much!

**e)** [en intensif] **regarder qn bien en face** to look sb right in the face; **je sais bien** I'm well aware of it; **je vous l'avais bien dit** I told you so!; **nous verrons bien !** we'll see!; **c'est bien fait pour lui** it serves him right; **c'est bien ce que je pensais** that's what I thought

**f)** [locutions] **bien que...** (+ *subjunctive*) although, though; **bien entendu, bien sûr** of course; **bien sûr que non !** of course, not!; **bien sûr que je viendrai !** of course, I'll come!

**2.** *adj inv* [satisfaisant] good; [à l'aise] comfortable; [en forme] well; [moral] decent; [beau] attractive; **être bien avec qn** [en bons termes] to be on good terms with sb; **on est bien ici** it's nice here; **ce n'est pas bien de mentir** it's not nice to lie; **elle est bien sur cette photo** she looks good on this photo

**3.** *excl* fine!, right!; **eh bien !** well!

**4.** *nm* PHIL & REL good; [chose, capital] possession; JUR asset; **le bien et le mal** good and evil; JUR **biens** property; **faire le bien** to do good; **ça te fera du bien** it will do you good; **dire du bien de qn** to speak well of sb; **c'est pour ton bien** it's for your own good; **biens de consommation** consumer goods; **biens immobiliers** real estate *or* property

■ **bien-aimé, -e** (*mpl* **bien-aimés**, *fpl* **bien-aimées**) *adj* & *nmf* beloved

■ **bien-être** *nm* well-being

**bienfaisance** [bjɛ̃fəzɑ̃s] *nf* **œuvre de bienfaisance** charity

**bienfaisant, -e** [bjɛ̃fəzɑ̃, -ɑ̃t] *adj* [remède] beneficial; [personne] charitable

**bienfait** [bjɛ̃fɛ] *nm* [acte] kindness; [avantage] benefit

**bienfaiteur, -trice** [bjɛ̃fɛtœr, -tris] *nmf* benefactor, *f* benefactress

**bien-fondé** [bjɛ̃fɔ̃de] *nm* validity

**bienheureux, -euse** [bjɛ̃nœrø, -øz] *adj* blissful; REL blessed

**bienséance** [bjɛ̃seɑ̃s] *nf* propriety

**bientôt** [bjɛ̃to] *adv* soon; **à bientôt !** see you soon!

**bienveillant, -e** [bjɛ̃vɛjɑ̃, -ɑ̃t] *adj* kind ■ **bienveillance** *nf* kindness

**bienvenu, -e¹** [bjɛ̃vny] **1.** *adj* [repos, explication] welcome **2.** *nmf* **soyez le bienvenu !** welcome!

**bienvenue²** [bjɛ̃vny] *nf* welcome; **souhaiter la bienvenue à qn** to welcome sb

**bière¹** [bjɛr] *nf* [boisson] beer; **bière blonde** lager; **bière brune** *Br* brown ale, *Am* dark beer; **bière pression** *Br* draught beer, *Am* draft beer

**bière²** [bjɛr] *nf* [cercueil] coffin

**biffer** [bife] *vt* to cross out

**bifteck** [biftɛk] *nm* steak; **bifteck haché** *Br* mince, *Am* mincemeat

**bifurquer** [bifyrke] *vi* [route, chemin] to fork; [automobiliste] to turn off ■ **bifurcation** *nf* fork

**bigamie** [bigami] *nf* bigamy

**bigarré, -e** [bigare] *adj* [étoffe] multicoloured; [foule] motley

**bigorneau, -x** [bigɔrno] *nm* winkle

**bigoudi** [bigudi] *nm* (hair) curler *or* roller

**bijou, -x** [biʒu] *nm* jewel; *Fig* gem ■ **bijouterie** *nf* [boutique] *Br* jeweller's shop, *Am* jewelry shop; [commerce, fabrication] jeweller's trade ■ **bijoutier, -ère** *nmf* *Br* jeweller, *Am* jeweler

**bilan** [bilɑ̃] *nm* [de situation] assessment; [résultats] results; [d'un accident] toll; COMM **déposer son bilan** to file for bankruptcy; FIN **bilan (comptable)** balance sheet; **bilan de santé** complete check-up

**bilatéral, -e, -aux** [bilateral, -o] *adj* bilateral

**bile** [bil] *nf* bile

**bilingue** [bilɛ̃g] *adj* bilingual

**billard** [bijar] *nm* [jeu] billiards ; [table] billiard table ; **billard américain** pool ; **billard électrique** pinball

**bille** [bij] *nf* [de verre] marble ; [de billard] billiard ball

**billet** [bijɛ] *nm* ticket ; **billet (de banque)** *Br* (bank) note, *Am* bill ; **billet d'avion / de train** plane / train ticket ; **billet de première / seconde** first-class / second-class ticket ; **billet simple** single ticket, *Am* one-way ticket ; **billet aller retour** return ticket, *Am* round trip ticket

**billetterie** [bijɛtri] *nf* [lieu] ticket office ; **billetterie automatique** [de billet de transport] ticket machine

**billion** [biljɔ̃] *nm* trillion

**bimensuel, -elle** [bimɑ̃sɥɛl] *adj* bimonthly, *Br* fortnightly

**bimode** [bimɔd] *adj* dual-use

**bimoteur** [bimɔtœr] *adj* twin-engined

**binaire** [binɛr] *adj* MATH binary

**biner** [bine] *vt* to hoe

**bingo** [bingo] *nm & excl* bingo

**binocle** [binɔkl] *nm* pince-nez

**bio** [bjo] *adj inv* organic ; **aliments bio** organic food ; **produits bio** organic products

**biochimie** [bjoʃimi] *nf* biochemistry

**biocombustible** [bjokɔ̃bystibl] *nm* biofuel

**biodégradable** [bjodegradabl] *adj* biodegradable

**biodiversité** [bjodiversite] *nf* biodiversity

**biographie** [bjɔgrafi] *nf* biography ■ **biographique** *adj* biographical

**bio-industrie** [bjoɛ̃dystri] *(pl* **bio-industries)** *nf* biotechnology industry

**biologie** [bjɔlɔʒi] *nf* biology ■ **biologique** *adj* biological ; [sans engrais chimiques] organic ; **les produits biologiques** organic products ■ **biologiste** *nmf* biologist

**biométrique** [bjɔmetrik] *adj* biometric

**biotechnologie** [bjotɛknolɔʒi] *nf* biotechnology

**bioterrorisme** [bjɔtɛrorism] *nm* bioterrorism

**bip** [bip] *nm* [son] beep ; [appareil] beeper

**bipède** [bipɛd] *nm* biped

**Birmanie** [birmani] *nf* **la Birmanie** Burma ■ **birman, -e 1.** *adj* Burmese **2.** *nmf* **Birman, Birmane** Burmese

**bis¹** [bis] *adv* [au théâtre] encore ; [en musique] repeat ; **4 bis** [adresse] ≃ 4A

**bis², bise¹** [bi, biz] *adj Br* greyish-brown, *Am* grayish-brown

**biscornu, -e** [biskɔrny] *adj* [objet] oddly shaped ; *Fam* [idée] cranky

**biscotte** [biskɔt] *nf* rusk

**biscuit** [biskɥi] *nm Br* biscuit, *Am* cookie

**bise²** [biz] *nf* [vent] north wind

**bise³** [biz] *nf Fam* [baiser] kiss ; **faire la bise à qn** to kiss sb on both cheeks

**bisexuel, -elle** [bisɛksɥel] *adj* bisexual

**bison** [bizɔ̃] *nm* bison

**bisou** [bizu] *nm Fam* kiss

**bissextile** [bisɛkstil] *adj f* **année bissextile** leap year

**bistro(t)** [bistro] *nm Fam* bar

**bit** [bit] *nm* ORDINAT bit

**bitume** [bitym] *nm* [revêtement] asphalt

**biz** *(abr de* **bises)** SMS KOTC, HAK

**bizarre** [bizar] *adj* odd ■ **bizarroïde** [bizarɔid] *adj Fam* odd, weird

**bjr** SMS *abr écrite de* **bonjour**

**black** [blak] *adj Fam* black ■ **Black** *nmf Fam* Black

**blafard, -e** [blafar, -ard] *adj* pallid

**blague** [blag] *nf* [plaisanterie] joke ; **faire une blague à qn** to play a joke on sb

**blaguer** [blage] *vi Fam* to joke ■ **blagueur, -euse** *nmf Fam* joker

**blaireau, -x** [blɛro] *nm* [animal] badger ; [brosse] shaving brush

**blâme** [blɑm] nm [reproche] blame ; [sanction] reprimand ■ **blâmer** vt [désapprouver] to blame ; [sanctionner] to reprimand

**blanc, blanche** [blɑ̃, blɑ̃ʃ] **1.** adj white ; [peau] pale ; [page] blank **2.** nm [couleur] white ; [espace] blank ; [vin] white wine ; **(article de) blanc** [linge] linen ; **en blanc** [chèque] blank ; **tirer à blanc** to fire blanks ; **blanc d'œuf** egg white ; **blanc de poulet** chicken breast **3.** nf [note de musique] Br minim, Am half-note **4.** nmf **Blanc** [personne] White man, f White woman ; **les Blanc** the Whites ■ **blanchâtre** adj whitish ■ **blancheur** nf whiteness

**blanchiment** [blɑ̃ʃimɑ̃] nm [d'argent] laundering

**blanchir** [blɑ̃ʃir] **1.** vt to whiten ; [mur] to whitewash ; [linge] to launder ; CULIN to blanch ; Fig [argent] to launder ; **blanchir qn** [disculper] to clear sb **2.** vi to turn white ■ **blanchisserie** nf [lieu] laundry ■ **blanchisseur, -euse** nmf laundryman, f laundrywoman

**blanquette** [blɑ̃kɛt] nf **blanquette de veau** blanquette of veal ; **blanquette de Limoux** sparkling white wine from Limoux

**blasé, -e** [blɑze] adj blasé

**blason** [blazɔ̃] nm coat of arms

**blasphème** [blasfɛm] nm blasphemy ■ **blasphémer** vi to blaspheme

**blatte** [blat] nf cockroach

**blazer** [blazœr] nm blazer

**bld** (abr de **boulevard**) Blvd

**blé** [ble] nm wheat, Br corn

**blême** [blɛm] adj sickly pale ; **blême de colère** livid ■ **blêmir** vi to turn pale

**blesser** [blese] **1.** vt [dans un accident] to injure, to hurt ; [par arme] to wound ; [offenser] to hurt **2. se blesser** vpr [par accident] to hurt or injure oneself ; [avec une arme] to wound oneself ; **se blesser au bras** to hurt one's arm ■ **blessant, -e** adj hurtful ■ **blessé, -e** nmf [victime d'accident] injured person ; [victime d'aggression] wounded person ; **les blessés** the injured / wounded ■ **blessure** nf [dans un accident] injury ; [par arme] wound

**blette** [blɛt] nf = **bette**

**bleu, -e** [blø] (mpl **-s**) **1.** adj blue ; [steak] very rare **2.** nom [couleur] blue ; [ecchymose] bruise ; [fromage] blue cheese ; Fam [novice] novice ; **bleu de travail** Br overalls, Am overall ; **bleu ciel** sky blue ; **bleu marine** navy blue ; **bleu roi** royal blue **3.** nmf Fam [novice - généralement] newcomer ; [à l'armée] raw recruit ; [à l'université] Br fresher, Am freshman

**bleuet** [bløɛ] nm [plante] cornflower ; Can [fruit] blueberry

**blinder** [blɛ̃de] vt [véhicule] Br to armour-plate, Am to armor-plate ■ **blindé, -e 1.** adj MIL Br armoured, armour-plated, Am armored, armor-plated ; [voiture] bulletproof **2.** nm MIL Br armoured or Am armored vehicle

**bling-bling** [blingbling] **1.** adj Fam bling-bling, bling ; **la génération bling-bling** the bling-bling generation **2.** nm **le bling-bling** bling-bling, bling ; **il fait dans le bling-bling maintenant** he's gone all bling-bling

**bloc** [blɔk] nm [de pierre, de bois] block ; [de papier] pad ; [de maison & POL] bloc ; **en bloc** [démissionner] all together ; **à bloc** [visser, serrer] as tightly as possible ; **bloc opératoire** operating theatre ■ **bloc-notes** (pl **blocs-notes**) nm notepad

**blocage** [blɔkaʒ] nm [de mécanisme] jamming ; [de freins, de roues] locking

**blocus** [blɔkys] nm blockade ; **lever le blocus** to raise the blockade

**blog** [blɔg] nm blog ■ **bloguer** [blɔge] vt to blog ■ **blogueur, euse** [blɔgœr, øz] nmf blogger

**blond, -e** [blɔ̃, -ɔ̃d] **1.** adj [cheveux, personne] blond ; [sable] golden **2.** nm [homme] fair-haired or blond man ; [couleur] blond ; **blond cendré** ash blond ; **blond vénitien** strawberry blond **3.** nf [femme] fair-haired woman, blonde ■ **blondeur** nf fairness, blondness

**bloquer** [bloke] **1.** *vt* [route, ballon, compte] to block ; [porte, mécanisme] to jam ; [roue] to lock ; [salaires, prix, crédits] to freeze ; [grouper] to group together; **bloquer le passage à qn** to block sb's way; **bloqué par la neige** snowbound **2. se bloquer** *vpr* [machine] to get stuck

**blottir** [blɔtir] ■ **se blottir** *vpr* to snuggle up; **se blottir contre qn** to snuggle up to sb

**blouse** [bluz] *nf* [tablier] overall ; [corsage] blouse ; **blouse blanche** [de médecin, de biologiste] white coat ■ **blouson** *nm* short jacket; **blouson en cuir** leather jacket; **blouson d'aviateur** bomber jacket

**blue-jean(s)** [bludʒin] *(pl* **blue-jeans** [bludʒins]*) nm* jeans *pl*

**bluff** [blœf] *nm* bluff ■ **bluffer** *vi* [aux cartes & Fam] to bluff

**BO** *(abr de* **bande originale***) nf* soundtrack

**boa** [bɔa] *nm* [serpent, tour de cou] boa

**bobard** [bɔbar] *nm Fam* tall story

**bobettes** [bɔbɛt] *nfpl Can Fam* shorts, panties, underwear

**bobine** [bɔbin] *nf* [de ruban, de fil] reel ; [de machine à coudre] bobbin ; [de film, de papier] roll ; ÉLEC coil

**bobo** [bɔbo] *(abr de* **bourgeois bohème***) nmf Fam* left-leaning yuppie

**bocal, -aux** [bɔkal, -o] *nm* jar ; [aquarium] bowl

**body** *(pl* **bodys** *ou* **bodies)** [bɔdi] *nm* body(suit)

**bœuf** [bœf] *(pl* **bœufs** [bø]*) nm* [animal] bullock; [de trait] ox *(pl* oxen) ; [viande] beef

**bogue** [bɔg] *nm* ORDINAT bug

**bohème** [bɔɛm] *adj & nmf* bohemian ■ **bohémien, -enne** *adj & nmf* gypsy

**boire** [bwar] **1.** *vt* [sujet : personne] to drink ; [sujet : plante] to soak up **2.** *vi* [sujet : personne] to drink ; [sujet : plante] to soak in ; *Fam* **boire un coup** to have a drink **3. se boire** *vpr* to be drunk **4.** *nm* **le boire et le manger** food and drink

**bois** [bwa] *nm* [matériau, forêt] wood ; [de raquette] frame; **en** *ou* **de bois** wooden; **les bois** [d'un cerf] the antlers ; [d'un orchestre] woodwind instruments; **bois de chauffage** firewood ; **bois de construction** timber ■ **boisé, -e** *adj* wooded ■ **boiseries** *nfpl Br* panelling, *Am* paneling

**boisson** [bwasɔ̃] *nf* drink

**boit** [bwa] *voir* **boire**

**boîte** [bwat] *nf* **a)** [récipient] box; **boîte d'allumettes** [pleine] box of matches ; [vide] matchbox ; **des haricots en boîte** canned *or Br* tinned beans; **boîte à bijoux** jewel box; **boîte à gants** glove compartment; **boîte à** *ou* **aux lettres** *Br* postbox, *Am* mailbox; ORDINAT **boîte à lettres électronique** mailbox; **boîte de conserve** can, *Br* tin ; AUTO **boîte de vitesses** gearbox; **boîte postale** Post Office Box ; ORDINAT **boîte de réception** inbox; **boîte vocale** voice mail **b)** *Fam* [entreprise] firm ; **boîte de nuit** nightclub ■ **boîtier** *nm* [de montre] case

**boiter** [bwate] *vi* to limp ■ **boiteux, -euse** *adj* [personne] lame ; *Fig* [raisonnement] shaky

**boive** [bwav] *subj voir* **boire**

**bol** [bɔl] *nm* [récipient, contenu] bowl

**bolide** [bɔlid] *nm* [voiture] racing car

**Bolivie** [bɔlivi] *nf* **la Bolivie** Bolivia ■ **bolivien, -enne 1.** *adj* Bolivian **2.** *nmf* **Bolivien, Bolivienne** Bolivian

**bombardement** [bɔ̃bardəmɑ̃] *nm* [avec des bombes] bombing ; [avec des obus] shelling

**bombarder** [bɔ̃barde] *vt* [avec des bombes] to bomb ; [avec des obus] to shell; **bombarder qn de questions** to bombard sb with questions ■ **bombardier** *nm* [avion] bomber

**bombe** [bɔ̃b] *nf* **a)** [explosif] bomb ; *Fig* **faire l'effet d'une bombe** to be a bombshell **b)** [atomiseur] spray (can) **c)** [chapeau] riding hat

**bomber** [bɔ̃be] **1.** *vt* **bomber le torse** to throw out one's chest **2.** *vi* [mur] to bulge ; [planche] to warp

**bon¹, bonne¹** [bɔ̃, bɔn] **1.** adj **a)** [satisfaisant] good ; **c'est bon** [d'accord] that's fine

**b)** [agréable] nice, good ; **passer une bonne soirée** to spend a pleasant evening ; **bon anniversaire !** happy birthday! ; **bonne année !** Happy New Year!

**c)** [charitable] kind, good (**avec qn** to sb)

**d)** [correct] right

**e)** [apte] fit ; **bon à manger** fit to eat ; **elle n'est bonne à rien** she's useless

**f)** [prudent] wise, good ; **juger bon de partir** to think it wise to leave

**g)** [compétent] good ; **bon en français** good at French

**h)** [profitable - investissement, conseil, idée] good ; **c'est bon à savoir** it's worth knowing

**i)** [valable] valid

**j)** [en intensif] **un bon rhume** a bad cold ; **dix bonnes minutes** a good ten minutes ; **j'ai mis un bon moment à comprendre** it took me a while to understand

**k)** [locutions] **à quoi bon ?** what's the point? ; **quand bon vous semble** whenever you like ; **pour de bon** [partir, revenir] for good ; **tenir bon** [personne] to hold out ; **elle est bien bonne !** that's a good one!

**2.** nm avoir du bon to have some good points ; **un bon à rien** a good-for-nothing ; **les bons et les méchants** the goodies and the baddies

**3.** adv **sentir bon** to smell good ; **il fait bon** it's nice and warm

**4.** excl **bon ! on y va ?** right, shall we go? ; **ah bon, je ne le savais pas** really? I didn't know ; **ah bon ?** is that so?

**bon²** [bɔ̃] nm [papier] coupon, Br voucher ; FIN [titre] bond ; **bon d'achat** gift voucher ; **bon de réduction** money-off coupon

**bonbon** [bɔ̃bɔ̃] nm Br sweet, Am candy

**bonbonne** [bɔ̃bɔn] nf [bouteille] demijohn ; [de gaz] cylinder

**bond** [bɔ̃] nm leap, jump ; [de balle] bounce ; **faire un bond** to leap up ; **se**

lever d'un bond [du lit] to jump out of bed ; [d'une chaise] to leap up ; **faire faux bond à qn** to leave sb in the lurch

**bonde** [bɔ̃d] nf [bouchon] plug ; [trou] plughole

**bondé, -e** [bɔ̃de] adj packed, crammed

**bondir** [bɔ̃dir] vi to leap, to jump ; **bondir sur qn/qch** to pounce on sb/sth

**bonheur** [bɔnœr] nm [bien-être] happiness ; [chance] good fortune ; **porter bonheur à qn** to bring sb luck ; **par bonheur** luckily

**bonhomie** [bɔnɔmi] nf good-naturedness

**bonhomme** [bɔnɔm] (pl **bonshommes** [bɔ̃zɔm]) nm fellow, guy ; **bonhomme de neige** snowman

**bonjour** [bɔ̃ʒur] nm & excl [le matin] hello, good morning ; [l'après-midi] hello, good afternoon

**bonne²** [bɔn] voir **bon**

**bonne³** [bɔn] nf [domestique] maid ; **bonne d'enfants** nanny

**bonnement** [bɔnmɑ̃] adv **tout bonnement** simply

**bonnet** [bɔnɛ] nm [coiffure] hat ; [de soutien-gorge] cup ; Fam **gros bonnet** bigshot ; **bonnet de bain** bathing cap ■ **bonneterie** nf [bas] hosiery

**bonniche** [bɔniʃ] nf = **boniche**

**bonsoir** [bɔ̃swar] nm & excl [en rencontrant quelqu'un] hello, good evening ; [en partant] goodbye ; [au coucher] goodnight

**bonté** [bɔ̃te] nf kindness, goodness

**bonus** [bɔnys] nm [de salaire] bonus ; [d'assurance] no-claims bonus

**bookmaker** [bukmɛkœr] nm bookmaker

**booster** [buste] vt to boost

**bord** [bɔr] nm [limite] edge ; [de chapeau] brim ; [de verre] rim ; **le bord du trottoir** Br the kerb, Am the curb ; **au bord de la route** at the side of the road ; **au bord de la rivière** beside the river ; **au bord de la mer** at the seaside ; **au bord des larmes** on the verge of tears ; **à bord**

d'un bateau /d'un avion on board a boat /a plane; **monter à bord** to go on board; **par-dessus bord** overboard

**bordeaux** [bɔrdo] **1.** nm [vin] Bordeaux (wine); [rouge] claret **2.** adj inv burgundy

**bordée** [bɔrde] nf NAUT [salve] broadside; Fig [d'injures] torrent

**bordel** [bɔrdɛl] nm **a)** Vulg [maison close] brothel **b)** t Fam [désordre] shambles sg

**border** [bɔrde] vt [lit] to tuck in; [sujet : arbres] to line

**bordereau, -x** [bɔrdəro] nm FIN & COMM note

**bordure** [bɔrdyr] nf [bord] edge; [de vêtement] border; **en bordure de route** by the roadside

**borgne** [bɔrɲ] adj [personne] one-eyed

**borne** [bɔrn] nf [limite] boundary marker; [pierre] boundary stone; ÉLEC terminal; Fam [kilomètre] kilometer; Fig **sans bornes** boundless; Fig **dépasser les bornes** to go too far

**borné, -e** [bɔrne] adj [personne] narrow-minded; [esprit] narrow

**borner** [bɔrne] **1.** vt [terrain] to mark out **2. se borner** vpr **se borner à qch /à faire qch** [personne] to restrict oneself to sth /to doing sth; **se borner à qch** [chose] to be limited to sth

**Bosnie-Herzégovine** [bɔsnierzegɔvin] nom **(la) Bosnie-Herzégovine** Bosnia-Herzegovina ■ **bosniaque** [bɔsnjak] adj & nm Bosnian ■ **Bosniaque** nmf Bosnian

**bosquet** [bɔske] nm grove

**bosse** [bɔs] nf [de bossu, de chameau] hump; [enflure] bump, lump; [de terrain] bump

**bosseler** [bɔsle] vt [déformer] to dent

**bosser** [bɔse] vi Fam to work

**bosseur, -euse** [bɔsœr, -øz] nmf Fam hard-worker

**bossu, -e** [bɔsy] **1.** adj [personne] hunchbacked **2.** nmf hunchback

**botanique** [bɔtanik] **1.** adj botanical **2.** nf botany

**botte** [bɔt] nf [chaussure] boot; [de fleurs, de radis] bunch; **bottes en caoutchouc** rubber boots ■ **botter** vt **botté de cuir** wearing leather boots; Fam **botter le derrière à qn** to boot sb up the backside ■ **bottillon** nm ankle boot ■ **bottine** nf ankle boot

**Bottin®** [bɔtɛ̃] nm phone book

**bouc** [buk] nm [animal] billy goat; [barbe] goatee; **bouc émissaire** scapegoat

**boucan** [bukɑ̃] nm Fam din, row; **faire du boucan** to kick up a row

**boucane** [bukan] nf Can Fam smoke

**bouche** [buʃ] nf mouth; **de bouche à oreille** by word of mouth; **bouche d'égout** manhole; **bouche d'incendie** Br fire hydrant, Am fireplug ■ **bouchée** nf mouthful ■ **bouche-à-bouche** nm mouth-to-mouth resuscitation

**boucher¹** [buʃe] **1.** vt [fente, trou] to fill in; [conduite, fenêtre] to block up; [vue, rue, artère] to block; [bouteille] to cork **2. se boucher** vpr [conduite] to get blocked up; **se boucher le nez** to hold one's nose ■ **bouché, -e** adj [conduite] blocked; Fam [personne] dense; **j'ai le nez bouché** my nose is stuffed up ■ **bouche-trou** (pl **bouche-trous**) nm Fam stopgap

**boucher², ère** [buʃe, -ɛr] nmf butcher ■ **boucherie** nf butcher's (shop); Fig [carnage] butchery

**bouchon** [buʃɔ̃] nm **a)** [à vis] cap, top; [de tonneau] stopper; [de liège] cork; [de canne à pêche] float **b)** [embouteillage] traffic jam ■ **bouchonner** vt Fam **ça bouchonne** [sur la route] there's congestion

**boucle** [bukl] nf [de ceinture] buckle; [de cheveu] curl; [méandre & ORDINAT] loop; **boucle d'oreille** earring

**boucler** [bukle] **1.** vt [ceinture, valise] to buckle; [quartier] to seal off; **boucler ses valises** [se préparer à partir] to pack one's bags **2.** vi [cheveux] to be curly ■ **bouclé, -e** adj [cheveux] curly

**bouclier** [buklije] nm shield

**bouddhisme** [budism] nm Buddhism ■ **bouddhiste** adj & nmf Buddhist

**bouder** [bude] **1.** *vi* to sulk **2.** *vt* [personne] to refuse to talk to; **bouder une élection** to refuse to vote ▪ **boudeur, -euse** *adj* sulky

**boudin** [budɛ̃] *nm* **boudin noir** *Br* black pudding, *Am* blood sausage; **boudin blanc** white pudding

**boue** [bu] *nf* mud ▪ **boueux, -euse** *adj* muddy

**bouée** [bwe] *nf* NAUT buoy; **bouée de sauvetage** lifebelt; **bouée (gonflable)** [d'enfant] (inflatable) rubber ring

**bouffe** [buf] *nf Fam* [nourriture] grub

**bouffée** [bufe] *nf* [de fumée] puff; [de parfum] whiff; *Fig* [de colère] outburst; MÉD **bouffée de chaleur** *Br* hot flush, *Am* hot flash

**bouffer¹** [bufe] *vt & vi Fam* [manger] to eat

**bouffer²** [bufe] *vi* [manche, jupe] to puff out ▪ **bouffi, -e** *adj* [yeux, visage] puffy

**bouffon, -onne** [bufɔ̃, -ɔn] **1.** *adj* farcical **2.** *nm* buffoon ▪ **bouffonneries** *nfpl* [actes] antics

**bougeoir** [buʒwar] *nm* candlestick

**bougeotte** [buʒɔt] *nf Fam* **avoir la bougeotte** to be fidgety

**bouger** [buʒe] **1.** *vt & vi* to move; **rester sans bouger** to keep still **2. se bouger** *vpr Fam* [se déplacer] to move; [s'activer] to get a move on

**bougie** [buʒi] *nf* [en cire] candle; [de moteur] spark plug

**bougonner** [bugɔne] *vi Fam* to grumble

**bouillabaisse** [bujabɛs] *nf* bouillabaisse (*Provençal fish soup*)

**bouilli, -e¹** [buji] *adj* boiled

**bouillie²** [buji] *nf* [pour bébé] baby food; [à base de céréales] baby cereal

**bouillir** [bujir] *vi* to boil; **faire bouillir qch** to boil sth; **bouillir de colère** to be seething (with anger) ▪ **bouillant, -e** *adj* [qui bout] boiling; [très chaud] boiling hot

**bouilloire** [bujwar] *nf* kettle

**bouillon** [bujɔ̃] *nm* [aliment] stock; [bulles] bubbles ▪ **bouillonner** *vi* to bubble

**bouillotte** [bujɔt] *nf* hot-water bottle

**boulanger, -ère** [bulɑ̃ʒe, -ɛr] *nmf* baker ▪ **boulangerie** *nf* baker's (shop)

**boule** [bul] *nf* [sphère] ball; **boules** [jeu] boules (*game played on bare ground with steel bowls*); *tFam* **avoir les boules** [être effrayé] to be scared stiff; [être furieux] to be pissed off *tFam*; [être déprimé] to be feeling down; **boule de neige** snowball; *Fig* **faire boule de neige** to snowball; **boules Quiès®** earplugs

**bouledogue** [buldɔg] *nm* bulldog

**boulet** [bulɛ] *nm* [de forçat] ball and chain; **boulet de canon** cannonball

**boulette** [bulɛt] *nf* [de papier] ball; [de viande] meatball

**boulevard** [bulvar] *nm* boulevard

**bouleverser** [bulvɛrse] *vt* [émouvoir] to move deeply; [perturber] to distress; [projets, habitudes] to disrupt; [vie] to turn upside down ▪ **bouleversant, -e** *adj* [émouvant] deeply moving; [perturbant] distressing

**boulgour** [bulgur] *nm* bulgar *or* bulgur wheat

**boulimie** [bulimi] *nf* MÉD bulimia ▪ **boulimique** *adj* **être boulimique** to have bulimia

**boulon** [bulɔ̃] *nm* bolt

**boulot¹** [bulo] *nm Fam* [emploi] job; [travail] work

**boulot², -otte** [bulo, -ɔt] *adj Fam* tubby

**bouquet** [bukɛ] *nm* [fleurs] bunch of flowers; [d'arbres] clump; [de vin] bouquet; *Fig* **c'est le bouquet!** that takes the *Br* biscuit *or Am* cake!; **bouquet de programmes** channel package; **bouquet numérique** digital channel package

**bouquin** [bukɛ̃] *nm Fam* book ▪ **bouquiner** *vt & vi Fam* to read ▪ **bouquiniste** *nmf* second-hand bookseller

**bourbier** [burbje] *nm* [lieu, situation] quagmire

**bourde** [burd] *nf Fam* [gaffe] blunder; **faire une bourde** to put one's foot in it

**bourdon** [burdɔ̃] *nm* [insecte] bumblebee ■ **bourdonnement** *nm* [d'insecte] buzz(ing) ■ **bourdonner** *vi* [insecte, oreilles] to buzz

**bourg** [bur] *nm* market town ■ **bourgade** *nf* village

**bourgeois, -e** [burʒwa, -waz] **1.** *adj* middle-class **2.** *nmf* middle-class person ■ **bourgeoisie** *nf* middle class

**bourgeon** [burʒɔ̃] *nm* bud ■ **bourgeonner** *vi* to bud

**bourgogne** [burgɔɲ] *nm* [vin] Burgundy

**bourrage** [buraʒ] *nm Fam* **bourrage de crâne** brainwashing

**bourrasque** [burask] *nf* squall, gust of wind

**bourratif, -ive** [buratif, -iv] *adj Fam* stodgy

**bourre** [bur] *nf* [pour rembourrer] stuffing

**bourreau, -x** [buro] *nm* executioner; **bourreau de travail** workaholic

**bourrelet** [burlɛ] *nm* [contre les courants d'air] weather strip; **bourrelet de graisse** spare *Br* tyre *or Am* tire

**bourrer** [bure] **1.** *vt* [coussin] to stuff (**de** with); [sac] to cram (**de** with); [pipe] to fill; **bourrer qn de qch** [gaver] to fill sb up with sth **2. se bourrer** *vpr* **se bourrer de qch** [se gaver] to stuff oneself up with ■ **bourré, -e** *adj* **a)** [plein] **bourré à craquer** full to bursting **b)** *Fam* [ivre] plastered

**bourrique** [burik] *nf* she-ass; *Fam* **faire tourner qn en bourrique** to drive sb crazy

**bourru, -e** [bury] *adj* surly

**bourse** [burs] *nf* [sac] purse; *SCOL & UNIV* **bourse (d'étude)** grant; **la Bourse** the Stock Exchange ■ **boursier, -ère 1.** *adj* **opération boursière** Stock Exchange transaction **2.** *nmf* [élève, étudiant] grant holder

**boursouflé, -e** [bursufle] *adj* [visage, yeux] puffy

**bous** [bu] *voir* **bouillir**

**bousculer** [buskyle] **1.** *vt* [pousser] to jostle; [presser] to rush; *Fig* [habitudes] to disrupt **2. se bousculer** *vpr* [foule] to push and shove ■ **bousculade** *nf* [agitation] pushing and shoving

**bousiller** [buzije] *vt Fam* to wreck

**boussole** [busɔl] *nf* compass

**bout¹** [bu] *voir* **bouillir**

**bout²** [bu] *nm* [extrémité] end; [de langue, de doigt] tip; [morceau] bit; **faire un bout de chemin** to go part of the way; **d'un bout à l'autre** from one end to the other; **au bout de la rue** at the end of the street; **au bout d'un moment** after a while; *Fam* **au bout du fil** [au téléphone] on the other end; **jusqu'au bout** [lire, rester] (right) to the end; **à bout de forces** exhausted; **à bout de souffle** out of breath; **pousser qn à bout** to push sb too far

**boutade** [butad] *nf* [plaisanterie] quip

**boute-en-train** [butɑ̃trɛ̃] *nm inv* [personne] live wire

**bouteille** [butɛj] *nf* bottle; [de gaz] cylinder

**boutique** [butik] *nf Br* shop, *Am* store; [de couturier] boutique; **fermer boutique** to shut up shop ■ **boutiquier, -ère** *nmf Br* shopkeeper, *Am* storekeeper

**bouton** [butɔ̃] *nm* [bourgeon] bud; [au visage] spot; [de vêtement] button; [de porte, de télévision] knob; **bouton de manchette** cufflink ■ **bouton-d'or** (*pl* **boutons-d'or**) *nm* buttercup ■ **boutonner 1.** *vt* [vêtement] to button (up) **2. se boutonner** *vpr* [vêtement] to button (up) ■ **boutonnière** *nf* buttonhole ■ **bouton-pression** [butɔ̃presjɔ̃] (*pl* **boutons-pression**) *nm Br* press-stud, *Am* snap fastener

**bouture** [butyr] *nf* cutting

**bovins** [bɔvɛ̃] *nmpl* cattle

**bowling** [boliŋ] *nm* [jeu] *Br* tenpin bowling, *Am* tenpins; [lieu] bowling alley

**box** [bɔks] (*pl* **boxes**) *nm* [d'écurie] stall; [de dortoir] cubicle; [garage] lock-up garage; *JUR* **box des accusés** dock

**boxe** [bɔks] *nf* boxing ■ **boxer** *vi* to box ■ **boxeur** *nm* boxer

**boyau, -x** [bwajo] *nm* [intestin] gut; [corde] catgut; [de vélo] tubular *Br* tyre *or Am* tire; [de mine] narrow gallery

**boycotter** [bɔjkɔte] *vt* to boycott ■ **boycottage** *nm* boycott

**BP** [bepe] *(abr de* **boîte postale)** *nf* PO Box

**bracelet** [braslɛ] *nm* [bijou] bracelet; [rigide] bangle; [de montre] *Br* strap, *Am* band ■ **bracelet-montre** *(pl* **bracelets-montres)** *nm* wristwatch

**braconner** [brakɔne] *vi* to poach ■ **braconnier** *nm* poacher

**brader** [brade] *vt* to sell off cheaply ■ **braderie** *nf* clearance sale

**braguette** [bragɛt] *nf* [de pantalon] fly, *Br* flies

**braille** [brɑj] *nm* Braille; **en braille** in Braille

**brailler** [brɑje] *vt & vi* to yell

**braire** [brɛr] *vi* [âne] to bray

**braises** [brɛz] *nfpl* embers ■ **braiser** *vt* CULIN to braise

**brancard** [brɑ̃kar] *nm* [civière] stretcher; [de charrette] shaft

**branche** [brɑ̃ʃ] *nf* [d'arbre, de science] branch; [de lunettes] side piece ■ **branchages** *nmpl* [des arbres] branches; [coupés] cut branches

**brancher** [brɑ̃ʃe] **1.** *vt* [à une prise] to plug in; [à un réseau & ORDINAT] to connect **2. se brancher** *vpr* se **brancher sur** [station de radio] to tune in to ■ **branché, e** *adj* **a)** [électricité] plugged in, connected **b)** *Fam* [à la mode] trendy ■ **branchement** *nm* [fils] connection

**brandir** [brɑ̃dir] *vt* to brandish

**branle** [brɑ̃l] *nm* **mettre qch en branle** [mécanisme, procédure] to set sth in motion ■ **branlant, -e** *adj* [chaise, escalier] rickety ■ **branler** *vi* [chaise, escalier] to be rickety

**braquer** [brake] **1.** *vt* [diriger] to point (**sur** at); [regard] to fix (**sur** on); *Fam* [banque] to hold up; **braquer qn contre qn/qch** to turn sb against sb/sth **2.** *vi* AUTO to turn the steering wheel

**braquet** [brakɛ] *nm* gear ratio

**bras** [brɑ] *nm* arm; **bras dessus bras dessous** arm in arm; **les bras croisés** with one's arms folded; *Fig* **bras droit** [assistant] right-hand man

**brasier** [brɑzje] *nm* blaze, inferno

**brassard** [brasar] *nm* armband

**brasse** [bras] *nf* [nage] breaststroke; [mouvement] stroke; **brasse papillon** butterfly stroke

**brassée** [brase] *nf* armful

**brasser** [brase] *vt* [mélanger] to mix; [bière] to brew ■ **brassage** *nm* [mélange] mixing; [de la bière] brewing

**brasserie** [brasri] *nf* [usine] brewery; [café] brasserie

**brassière** [brasjɛr] *nf* **a)** [de bébé] *Br* vest, *Am* undershirt **b)** *Can* [soutiengorge] bra

**bravade** [bravad] *nf* bravado

**brave** [brav] **1.** *adj* [courageux] brave; [bon] good **2.** *nm* [héros] brave man

**braver** [brave] *vt* [personne] to defy; [danger] to brave

**bravo** [bravo] *excl* bravo!

**bravoure** [bravur] *nf* bravery

**break** [brɛk] *nm* [voiture] *Br* estate car, *Am* station wagon

**breakdance** [brɛkdɛns] *nf* breakdancing

**brebis** [brəbi] *nf* ewe; *Fig* **brebis galeuse** black sheep

**brèche** [brɛʃ] *nf* gap; [dans la coque d'un bateau] hole

**bréchet** [breʃɛ] *nm* breastbone

**bredouille** [brəduj] *adj* empty-handed

**bredouiller** [brəduje] *vt & vi* to mumble

**bref, brève** [brɛf, brɛv] **1.** *adj* brief, short **2.** *adv* in short; **enfin bref** in a word...

**Brésil** [brezil] *nm* le Brésil Brazil ■ **brésilien, -enne 1.** *adj* Brazilian **2.** *nmf* Brésilien, Brésilienne Brazilian

**Bretagne** [brətaɲ] *nf* la Bretagne Brittany ■ **breton, -onne 1.** *adj* Breton **2.** *nmf* Breton, Bretonne Breton

**bretelle** [brətɛl] *nf* strap; **bretelles** [de pantalon] *Br* braces, *Am* suspenders; **bretelle (d'accès)** [route] access road

**breuvage** [brœvaʒ] *nm* potion

**brève** [brɛv] *voir* bref

**brevet** [brəvɛ] *nm* [certificat] certificate; [diplôme] diploma; SCOL **brevet des collèges** *exam taken at 14*; **brevet de technicien supérieur** *advanced vocational training certificate*; **brevet (d'invention)** patent ■ **breveter** *vt* to patent

**bric-à-brac** [brikabrak] *nm inv* [vieux objets] odds and ends

**bricole** [brikɔl] *nf* [objet, futilité] trifle

**bricoler** [brikɔle] **1.** *vt* [construire] to put together; [réparer] to fix **2.** *vi* to do-it-yourself ■ **bricolage** *nm* [travail] DIY, do-it-yourself; **faire du bricolage** to do some DIY ■ **bricoleur, -euse 1.** *adj* être bricoleur to be good with one's hands **2.** *nmf* handyman, *f* handywoman

**bride** [brid] *nf* [de cheval] bridle ■ **brider** *vt* [cheval] to bridle; [personne, désir] to curb; **avoir les yeux bridés** to have slanting eyes

**bridge** [bridʒ] *nm* [jeu, prothèse] bridge

**brièvement** [brijɛvmɑ̃] *adv* briefly ■ **brièveté** *nf* brevity

**brigade** [brigad] *nf* [de gendarmerie] squad; MIL brigade ■ **brigadier** *nm* [de police] police sergeant; MIL corporal

**brigand** [brigɑ̃] *nm* [bandit] brigand

**briguer** [brige] *vt* [honneur, poste] to solicit

**brillant, -e** [brijɑ̃, -ɑ̃t] **1.** *adj* [luisant] shining; [couleur] bright; [cheveux, cuir] shiny; *Fig* [remarquable] brilliant **2.** *nm* [éclat] shine; [diamant] diamond; **brillant à lèvres** lip gloss ■ **brillamment** [-amɑ̃] *adv* brilliantly

**briller** [brije] *vi* to shine; **le soleil brille** the sun's shining; **faire briller qch** to polish sth

**brimer** [brime] *vt* to bully ■ **brimades** *nfpl* [vexations] bullying

**brin** [brɛ̃] *nm* [d'herbe] blade; [de muguet] spray; [de fil] strand; *Fig* **un brin de qch** a bit of sth; **faire un brin de toilette** to have a quick wash

**brindille** [brɛ̃dij] *nf* twig

**bringue¹** [brɛ̃g] *nf Fam* **faire la bringue** to go on a binge

**bringue²** [brɛ̃g] *nf Fam* **grande bringue** [fille] beanpole

**brio** [brijo] *nm* brilliance

**brioche** [brijɔʃ] *nf* brioche ■ **brioché** *adj* **pain brioché** milk bread

**brique** [brik] *nf* [de construction] brick; **mur de briques** brick wall

**briquer** [brike] *vt* [nettoyer] to scrub down

**briquet** [brikɛ] *nm* (cigarette) lighter

**bris** [bri] *nm* [de verre] breaking; **bris de glaces** broken windows

**brise** [briz] *nf* breeze

**briser** [brize] **1.** *vt* to break; [opposition, résistance] to crush; [espoir, carrière] to wreck; [fatiguer] to exhaust **2. se briser** *vpr* to break ■ **brise-glace** *nm inv* [navire] ice breaker ■ **brise-lames** *nm inv* breakwater

**britannique** [britanik] **1.** *adj* British **2.** *nmf* Britannique Briton; **les Britanniques** the British

**broc** [bro] *nm* pitcher, jug

**brocante** [brɔkɑ̃t] *nf* [commerce] second-hand trade ■ **brocanteur** *nm* second-hand dealer

**broche** [brɔʃ] *nf* [pour rôtir] spit; [bijou] brooch; [pour fracture] pin; *Can* [fil de fer] iron wire; **faire cuire qch à la broche** to spit-roast sth ■ **brochette** *nf* [tige] skewer; [plat] kebab

**broché, -e** [brɔʃe] *adj* **livre broché** paperback

**brochet** [brɔʃɛ] *nm* pike

**brochure** [brɔʃyr] *nf* brochure, pamphlet

**brocolis** [brɔkɔli] *nmpl* broccoli

**broder** [brɔde] *vt* to embroider (**de** with) ▪ **broderie** *nf* [activité] embroidery

**broncher** [brɔ̃ʃe] *vi* **il n'a pas bronché** he didn't bat an eyelid

**bronches** [brɔ̃ʃ] *nfpl* bronchial tubes ▪ **bronchite** *nf* bronchitis; **avoir une bronchite** to have bronchitis

**bronze** [brɔ̃z] *nm* bronze

**bronzer** [brɔ̃ze] *vi* to tan ▪ **bronzage** *nm* (sun)tan ▪ **bronzé, e** *adj* *Br* tanned, *Am* tan, suntanned

**brosse** [brɔs] *nf* brush; **donner un coup de brosse à qch** to give sth a brush; **cheveux en brosse** crew cut; **brosse à dents** toothbrush ▪ **brosser** **1.** *vt* [tapis, cheveux] to brush; **brosser un tableau de qch** to give an outline of sth **2. se brosser** *vpr* **se brosser les dents / les cheveux** to brush one's teeth / one's hair

**brouette** [brwɛt] *nf* wheelbarrow

**brouhaha** [bruaa] *nm* hubbub

**brouillard** [brujar] *nm* fog; **il y a du brouillard** it's foggy

**brouiller** [bruje] **1.** *vt* [idées] to muddle up; [vue] to blur; [émission] to jam **2. se brouiller** *vpr* [vue] to get blurred; [se disputer] to fall out (**avec** with) ▪ **brouillé, -e** *adj* [teint] blotchy; **être brouillé avec qn** to have fallen out with sb

**brouillon, -onne** [brujɔ̃, -ɔn] **1.** *adj* [mal organisé] disorganized; [mal présenté] untidy **2.** *nm* rough draft; **(papier) brouillon** *Br* scrap paper, *Am* scratch paper

**broussailles** [brusaj] *nfpl* scrub

**brousse** [brus] *nf* **la brousse** the bush

**brouter** [brute] *vt & vi* to graze

**broyer** [brwaje] *vt* to grind; [doigt, bras] to crush

**bru** [bry] *nf* daughter-in-law

**brugnon** [bryɲɔ̃] *nm* nectarine

**bruine** [brɥin] *nf* drizzle ▪ **bruiner** *v impers* to drizzle; **il bruine** it's drizzling

**bruissement** [brɥismɑ̃] *nm* [de feuilles] rustle, rustling

**bruit** [brɥi] *nm* noise, sound; [nouvelle] rumour; **faire du bruit** to make a noise ▪ **bruitage** *nm* CINÉ sound effects

**brûlant, -e** [brylɑ̃, -ɑ̃t] *adj* [objet, soupe] burning hot; [soleil] scorching; *Fig* [sujet] burning

**brûlé, -e** [bryle] **1.** *adj* [calciné] burnt **2.** *nm* **odeur de brûlé** burnt smell; **sentir le brûlé** to smell burnt

**brûle-pourpoint** [brylpurpwɛ̃] ▪ **à brûle-pourpoint** *adv* point-blank

**brûler** [bryle] **1.** *vt* [sujet : flamme, acide] to burn; [feu rouge] to go through **2.** *vi* to burn **3. se brûler** *vpr* to burn oneself; **se brûler la langue** to burn one's tongue

**brûlure** [brylyr] *nf* burn

**brume** [brym] *nf* mist, haze ▪ **brumeux, -euse** *adj* misty, hazy

**brun, -e** [brœ̃, bryn] **1.** *adj* [cheveux] dark, brown; [personne] dark-haired; **être brun de peau** to be dark-skinned **2.** *nm* [couleur] brown **3.** *nmf* dark-haired man, *f* dark-haired woman ▪ **brunette** *nf* brunette ▪ **brunir** *vi* [personne, peau] to tan; [cheveux] to darken

**bruncher** [brœ̃ʃe] *vi* to have brunch

**Brushing®** [brœʃiŋ] *nm* blow-dry; **faire un Brushing®** à qn to blow-dry sb's hair

**brusque** [brysk] *adj* abrupt ▪ **brusquement** [-əmɑ̃] *adv* abruptly ▪ **brusquer** *vt* [décision] to rush ▪ **brusquerie** *nf* abruptness

**brut, -e** [bryt] *adj* [pétrole] crude; [diamant] rough; [poids, salaire] gross; [champagne] extra-dry; **à l'état brut** in its raw state

**brutal, -e, -aux** [brytal, -o] *adj* [personnes, manières, paroles] brutal; [franchise, réponse] crude, blunt; [changement] abrupt; **être brutal avec qn** to be rough with sb ▪ **brutalement** *adv* [violemment] brutally; [avec brusquerie] bluntly; [soudainement] abruptly

■ **brutaliser** *vt* to ill-treat ■ **brutalité** *nf* [violence, acte] brutality ; [soudaineté] abruptness ■ **brute** *nf* brute

**Bruxelles** [brysɛl] *nom* Brussels

**bruyant, -e** [brɥijɑ̃, -ɑ̃t] *adj* noisy ■ **bruyamment** [-amɑ̃] *adv* noisily

**bruyère** [brɥijɛr] *nf* [plante] heather ; [terrain] heath

**bsr** SMS *abr écrite de* **bonsoir**

**BTS** [beteɛs] *(abr de* brevet de technicien supérieur*) nm advanced vocational training certificate*

**bu, -e** [by] *pp de* **boire**

**buanderie** [bɥɑ̃dri] *nf* [lieu] laundry

**bûche** [byʃ] *nf* log ; **bûche de Noël** Yule log ■ **bûcher** *nm* [à bois] woodshed ; [de supplice] stake

**bûcheron** [byʃrɔ̃] *nm* woodcutter

**bûcheur, -euse** [byʃœr, -øz] *nmf Br* swot, *Am* grind

**budget** [bydʒɛ] *nm* budget ■ **budgétaire** *adj* budgetary ; [année] financial ■ **budgéter** [bydʒete] *vt* to budget for

**buée** [bɥe] *nf* [sur vitre] condensation ; [sur miroir] mist

**buffet** [byfɛ] *nm* [meuble bas] sideboard ; [meuble haut] dresser ; [repas] buffet

**buffle** [byfl] *nm* buffalo

**bug** [bœg], *Can* **bogue** [bɔg] *nm* ORDINAT bug

**buisson** [bɥisɔ̃] *nm* bush

**buissonnière** [bɥisɔnjɛr] *adj f* **faire l'école buissonnière** *Br* to play truant, *Am* to play hookey

**bulbe** [bylb] *nm* bulb

**Bulgarie** [bylgari] *nf* **la Bulgarie** Bulgaria ■ **bulgare 1.** *adj* Bulgarian **2.** *nmf* **Bulgare** Bulgarian

**bulldozer** [byldozœr] *nm* bulldozer

**bulle** [byl] *nf* [d'air, de savon] bubble ; [de bande dessinée] balloon ; **faire des bulles** to blow bubbles ; ORDINAT **bulle d'aide** pop-up text, tooltip

**bulletin** [byltɛ̃] *nm* [communiqué, revue] bulletin ; **bulletin d'informations** news bulletin ; **bulletin de paie** *ou* de **salaire** *Br* pay slip, *Am* pay stub ; **bulletin de santé** medical bulletin ; **bulletin de vote** ballot paper ; **bulletin météo** weather report ; **bulletin scolaire** *Br* school report, *Am* report card

**b1sur** SMS *abr écrite de* **bien sûr**

**bureau, -x** [byro] *nm* [table] desk ; [lieu] office ; [comité] committee ; ORDINAT desktop ; **bureau de change** bureau de change ; **bureau de poste** post office ; **bureau de tabac** *Br* tobacconist's (shop), *Am* tobacco store

**bureaucratie** [byrokrasi] *nf* bureaucracy ■ **bureaucratique** *adj* bureaucratic

**Bureautique®** [byrotik] *nf* office automation

**burette** [byrɛt] *nf* [pour huile] oilcan ; [de chimiste] burette

**burin** [byrɛ̃] *nm* [de graveur] burin ; [pour découper] (cold) chisel

**buriné, -e** [byrine] *adj* [visage] lined

**burlesque** [byrlɛsk] *adj* [idée] ludicrous ; [genre] burlesque

**burqa, burka** [burka] *nm ou f* burqa

**bus¹** [bys] *nm* bus

**bus²** [by] *v voir* **boire**

**buste** [byst] *nm* [torse] chest ; [sculpture] bust ■ **bustier** *nm* [corsage] bustier

**but¹** [by(t)] *nm* [objectif] aim, goal ; [intention] purpose ; SPORT goal

**but²** [by] *v voir* **boire**

**butane** [bytan] *nm* butane

**buter** [byte] **1.** *vt* **buter qn** to put sb's back up **2.** *vi Fig* [difficulté] to come up against sth ; **buter contre qch** [cogner] to bump into sth ; [trébucher] to stumble over sth **3.** **se buter** *vpr* [s'entêter] to dig one's heels in ■ **buté, -e** *adj* obstinate

**butin** [bytɛ̃] *nm* [de voleur] loot ; [de pillards] spoils ; [d'armée] booty

**butoir** [bytwar] *nm* [pour train] buffer ; [de porte] stopper, *Br* stop

**buvard** [byvar] *nm* blotting paper

**buvette** [byvɛt] *nf* refreshment bar

**buveur, -euse** [byvœr, -øz] *nmf* drinker ; **un grand buveur** a heavy drinker

**buviez** [byvje] *voir* **boire**

**buzz** [bœz] *nm* buzz; **le film a fait un énorme buzz** the film created a huge buzz ■ **buzzer** [bœze] *vi* to be all the rage; **un clip qui fait buzzer la Toile** a clip which is all the rage on the Internet

# C

**C, c** [se] *nm inv* [letter] C, c ■ **C** *(abr de* **Celsius***)* C

**c'** [s] *voir* **ce**

**ça** [sa] *(abr de* **cela***) pron dém* [pour désigner] that ; [plus près] this ; [sujet indéfini] it, that ; **où/quand ça ?** where? / when? ; **ça dépend** it depends ; **ça va ?** how are things? ; **ça va !** fine!, OK! ; **c'est ça** that's right

**çà** [sa] ■ **çà et là** *adv* here and there

**cabane** [kaban] *nf* [baraque] hut ; [en rondin] cabin ; [de jardin] shed ; **cabane à outils** tool shed ; *Can* **cabane à sucre** sugarhouse

**cabaret** [kabarɛ] *nm* cabaret

**cabillaud** [kabijo] *nm* (fresh) cod

**cabine** [kabin] *nf* [de bateau] cabin ; **cabine d'essayage** fitting room ; **cabine de pilotage** cockpit ; **cabine téléphonique** phone box

**cabinet** [kabinɛ] *nm* [de médecin] *Br* surgery, *Am* office ; [d'avocat] firm ; [de ministre] departmental staff ; **cabinet de toilette** (small) bathroom ; *Fam* **les cabinets** *Br* the loo, *Am* the john

**câble** [kɑbl] *nm* cable ; TV **le câble** cable ■ **câbler** *vt* TV [ville, quartier] to install cable television in

**cabrer** [kabre] ■ **se cabrer** *vpr* [cheval] to rear (up)

**cabriole** [kabriɔl] *nf* [saut] caper ; **faire des cabrioles** to caper about

**cabriolet** [kabriɔlɛ] *nm* [auto] convertible

**cacah(o)uète** [kakawɛt] *nf* peanut

**cacao** [kakao] *nm* [poudre] cocoa

**cache** [kaʃ] *nf* hiding place ■ **cache-cache** *nm inv* **jouer à cache-cache** to play hide and seek ■ **cache-nez** *nm inv* scarf

**cachemire** [kaʃmir] *nm* [laine] cashmere

**cacher** [kaʃe] **1.** *vt* to hide (**à** from) **2. se cacher** *vpr* to hide

**cachet** [kaʃɛ] *nm* [sceau] seal ; [de fabrication] stamp ; [comprimé] tablet ; [d'acteur] fee ; [originalité] character ; **cachet de la poste** postmark ■ **cacheter** *vt* to seal

**cachette** [kaʃɛt] *nf* hiding place ; **en cachette** in secret

**cachot** [kaʃo] *nm* dungeon

**cachotteries** [kaʃɔtri] *nfpl* **faire des cachotteries** to be secretive

**cactus** [kaktys] *nm* cactus

**cadavre** [kadavr] *nm* corpse ■ **cadavérique** *adj* [teint] deathly pale

**Caddie®** [kadi] *nm Br* trolley, *Am* cart

**cadeau, -x** [kado] **1.** *nm* present, gift ; **faire un cadeau à qn** to give sb a present **2.** *adj* **idée cadeau** gift idea

**cadenas** [kadnɑ] *nm* padlock

**cadence** [kadɑ̃s] *nf* [taux, vitesse] rate ; [de chanson] rhythm

**cadet, -ette** [kade, -ɛt] **1.** *adj* [de deux] younger ; [de plus de deux] youngest **2.** *nmf* [de deux] younger (one) ; [de plus de deux] youngest (one) ; SPORT junior

**cadran** [kadrɑ̃] *nm* [de téléphone] dial ; [de montre] face ; **cadran solaire** sundial

**cadre** [kadr] *nm* **a)** [de photo, de vélo] frame ; [décor] setting ; **dans le cadre de** within the framework of **b)** [d'entreprise] executive ; **les cadres** the management ; MIL the officers

**cadrer** [kadre] **1.** *vt* [photo] to centre **2.** *vi* [correspondre] to tally (**avec** with)

**caduc, caduque** [kadyk] *adj* [feuille] deciduous

**cafard** [kafar] nm [insecte] cockroach

**café** [kafe] nm [produit, boisson] coffee ; [bar] café ; **café au lait, café crème** Br white coffee, Am coffee with milk ; **café noir** black coffee ; **café soluble** ou **instantané** instant coffee ■ **caféine** nf caffeine ■ **cafétéria** nf cafeteria ■ **cafetier** nm café owner ■ **cafetière** nf [récipient] coffeepot ; [électrique] coffee machine

**cafter** [kafte] vi Fam to sneak

**cage** [kaʒ] nf [d'oiseau, de zoo] cage ; [d'ascenseur] shaft ; SPORT goal ; **cage d'escalier** stairwell

**cageot** [kaʒo] nm crate

**cagneux** [kaɲø] adj **avoir les genous cagneux** to have knock-knees

**cagnotte** [kaɲɔt] nf [caisse commune] kitty ; [de jeux] pool

**cagoule** [kagul] nf [de bandit] hood ; [d'enfant] Br balaclava, Am ski mask

**cahier** [kaje] nm notebook ; [d'écolier] exercise book ; **cahier de brouillon** Br rough book, Am ≈ scratch pad ; SCOL **cahier d'appel** register

**cahin-caha** [kaɛ̃ kaa] adv Fam **aller cahin-caha** [se déplacer] to struggle along

**caille** [kɑj] nf [oiseau] quail

**cailler** [kaje] vi [lait] to curdle ■ **caillot** nm [de sang] clot

**caillou, -x** [kaju] nm stone ; [sur la plage] pebble

**Caire** [kɛr] nm **le Caire** Cairo

**caisse** [kɛs] nf **a)** [boîte] case ; [d'outils] box ; [cageot] crate **b)** [de magasin] cash desk ; [de supermarché] checkout ; **caisse d'épargne** savings bank ; **caisse enregistreuse** cash register

**caissier, -ère** [kesje, -ɛr] nmf cashier ; [de supermarché] checkout operator

**cajoler** [kaʒɔle] vt to cuddle

**cajou** [kaʒu] nm **noix de cajou** cashew nut

**calamité** [kalamite] nf [fléau] calamity ; [malheur] great misfortune

**calcaire** [kalkɛr] **1.** adj [eau] hard ; [terrain] chalky **2.** nm GÉOL limestone ; [dépôt] fur

**calciné, -e** [kalsine] adj burnt to a cinder

**calcium** [kalsjɔm] nm calcium

**calcul** [kalkyl] nm **a)** [opérations, estimation] calculation ; SCOL **le calcul** arithmetic ; **faire un calcul** to make a calculation **b)** MÉD stone ; **calcul rénal** kidney stone

**calculatrice** [kalkylatris] nf **calculatrice (de poche)** (pocket) calculator

**calculer** [kalkyle] vt [prix, superficie] to calculate ; [chances, conséquences] to weigh (up)

**calculette** [kalkylɛt] nf (pocket) calculator

**cale** [kal] nf **a)** [de meuble, de porte] wedge **b)** [de navire] hold

**caleçon** [kalsɔ̃] nm boxer shorts

**calembour** [kalɑ̃bur] nm pun, play on words

**calendrier** [kalɑ̃drije] nm [mois et jours] calendar ; [programme] timetable

**calepin** [kalpɛ̃] nm notebook

**caler** [kale] **1.** vt [meuble, porte] to wedge ; [chargement] to secure **2.** vi **a)** [moteur] to stall **b)** Can [s'enfoncer, s'enliser] to punch through, to get deeper, to sink **3. se caler** vpr [dans un fauteuil] to settle oneself comfortably

**calfeutrer** [kalføtre] vt [brèches] to block up

**calibre** [kalibr] nm [diamètre] Br calibre, Am caliber ; [d'œuf, de fruit] grade ; [outil] gauge

**Californie** [kaliforni] nf **la Californie** California

**califourchon** [kalifurʃɔ̃] ■ **à califourchon** adv astride ; **se mettre à califourchon sur qch** to sit astride sth

**câlin, -e** [kalɛ̃, -in] **1.** adj affectionate **2.** nm cuddle ; **faire un câlin à qn** to give sb a cuddle

**calmant** [kalmɑ̃] nm [pour les nerfs] sedative

**calmar** [kalmar] *nm* squid

**calme** [kalm] **1.** *adj* [flegmatique] calm, cool ; [tranquille] quiet ; [mer] calm **2.** *nm* calm(ness) ; **garder / perdre son calme** to keep / lose one's calm ; **du calme !** [taisez-vous] keep quiet! ; [pas de panique] keep calm!

**calmer** [kalme] **1.** *vt* [douleur] to soothe ; [inquiétude] to calm ; [faim] to appease ; **calmer qn** to calm sb down **2. se calmer** *vpr* [personne] to calm down ; [vent] to die down ; [mer] to become calm ; [douleur] to subside

**calomnie** [kalɔmni] *nf* [en paroles] slander ; [par écrit] libel **calomnier** *vt* [en paroles] to slander ; [par écrit] to libel **calomnieux, -euse** *adj* [paroles] slanderous ; [écrits] libellous

**calorie** [kalɔri] *nf* calorie

**calorifère** [kalɔrifɛr] *nm Can* radiator

**calotte** [kalɔt] *nf* **a)** [chapeau rond] skullcap **b)** *Can* [casquette] cap **c)** GÉOG **calotte glaciaire** ice cap

**calque** [kalk] *nm* [copie] tracing ; **(papier-)calque** tracing paper

**calvaire** [kalvɛr] *nm* REL calvary ; *Fig* ordeal

**calvitie** [kalvisi] *nf* baldness

**camarade** [kamarad] *nmf* friend ; **camarade de classe** classmate ; **camarade d'école** school friend ; **camarade de jeu** playmate **camaraderie** *nf* camaraderie

**Cambodge** [kɑ̃bɔdʒ] *nm* **le Cambodge** Cambodia

**cambouis** [kɑ̃bwi] *nm* dirty oil

**cambrer** [kɑ̃bre] **1.** *vt* to arch **2. se cambrer** *vpr* to arch one's back **cambrure** *nf* [du pied, du dos] arch

**cambrioler** [kɑ̃brijɔle] *vt Br* to burgle, *Am* to burglarize **cambriolage** *nm* burglary **cambrioleur, -euse** *nmf* burglar

**camée** [kame] *nm* cameo

**caméléon** [kameleɔ̃] *nm* chameleon

**camelot** [kamlo] *nm* street peddler *or Br* hawker, *Am* huckster **camelote** *nf* [pacotille] junk ; [marchandise] stuff

**camembert** [kamɑ̃bɛr] *nm* [fromage] Camembert (cheese)

**caméra** [kamera] *nf* camera **cameraman** *(pl* **-mans** *ou* **-men)** *nm* cameraman

**Caméscope®** [kameskɔp] *nm* camcorder

**camion** [kamjɔ̃] *nm Br* lorry, *Am* truck ; **camion de déménagement** *Br* removal van, *Am* moving van **camion-citerne** *(pl* **camions-citernes)** *nm Br* tanker, *Am* tank truck **camionnette** *nf* van **camionneur** *nm* [conducteur] *Br* lorry driver, *Am* truck driver ; [entrepreneur] *Br* haulier, *Am* trucker **camion-poubelle** *(pl* **camions-poubelles** [kamjɔ̃pubɛl])*nm Br* dustcart, *Br* (dust)bin lorry, *Am* garbage truck

**camomille** [kamɔmij] *nf* [plante] camomile ; [tisane] camomile tea

**camoufler** [kamufle] *vt* MIL to camouflage **camouflage** *nm* MIL camouflage

**camp** [kɑ̃] *nm* [campement] camp ; [de parti, de jeu] side ; **camp de concentration** concentration camp ; **camp de prisonniers** prison camp

**campagne** [kɑ̃paɲ] *nf* **a)** [par opposition à la ville] country ; [paysage] countryside ; **à la campagne** in the country ; **en pleine campagne** deep in the countryside **b)** MIL, COMM & POL campaign ; **campagne de presse / publicité** press / publicity campaign **campagnard, -e** *adj* country

**camper** [kɑ̃pe] **1.** *vi* to camp **2.** *vt* [chapeau] to plant **3. se camper** *vpr* to plant oneself (**devant** in front of) **campeur, -euse** *nmf* camper

**camping** [kɑ̃piŋ] *nm* [activité] camping ; [terrain] camp(ing) site ; **faire du camping** to go camping ; **camping sauvage** unauthorized camping **camping-car** *(pl* **camping-cars)** *nm* camper ; **partir en camping-car** to go on a camper holiday

**campus** [kɑ̃pys] *nm* campus

**Canada** [kanada] *nm* le Canada Canada ▪ **canadien, -enne 1.** *adj* Canadian **2.** *nmf* Canadien, Canadienne Canadian

**canal, -aux** [kanal, -o] *nm* [cours d'eau] canal ; [conduite] conduit ; *Fig* channel

**canaliser** [kanalize] *vt* [rivière, fleuve] to canalize ; *Fig* [foule, énergie] to channel ▪ **canalisation** *nf* [conduite] pipe

**canapé** [kanape] *nm* **a)** [siège] sofa, couch **b)** [pour l'apéritif] canapé ▪ **canapé-lit** *(pl* **canapés-lits***) nm* sofa bed

**canard** [kanar] *nm* duck ; [mâle] drake ; *Fam* [journal] rag

**canari** [kanari] *nm* canary

**cancaner** [kɑ̃kane] *vi* to gossip ▪ **cancan** [kɑ̃kɑ̃] *nm* **a)** *Fam* [ragot] piece of gossip **b)** [danse] cancan ▪ **cancans** [kɑ̃kɑ̃] *nmpl* gossip

**cancer** [kɑ̃sɛr] *nm* [maladie] cancer ; **cancer de l'estomac** stomach cancer ; **avoir un cancer** to have cancer ; **le Cancer** [signe] Cancer ▪ **cancéreux, -euse 1.** *adj* cancerous **2.** *nmf* cancer patient ▪ **cancérigène** *adj* carcinogenic

**candeur** [kɑ̃dœr] *nf* guilelessness

**candi** [kɑ̃di] *adj* **sucre candi** candy

**candidat, -e** [kɑ̃dida, -at] *nmf* [d'examen, d'élection] candidate (**à** for) ; [de poste] applicant (**à** for) ; **être candidat aux élections** to stand for election ▪ **candidature** *nf* [à un poste] application (**à** for) ; [aux élections] candidature (**à** for) ; **poser** *ou* **envoyer sa candidature** to apply (**à** for) ; **candidature spontanée** unsolicited application

**candide** [kɑ̃did] *adj* guileless

**cane** [kan] *nf* (female) duck ▪ **caneton** *nm* duckling

**canette** [kanɛt] *nf* [boîte] can

**canevas** [kanva] *nm* [toile] canvas

**caniche** [kaniʃ] *nm* poodle

**canicule** [kanikyl] *nf* heatwave

**canif** [kanif] *nm* penknife

**canin, e** [kanɛ̃, in] **1.** *adj* canine ; **exposition canine** dog show **2.** *nf* [dent] canine (tooth)

**caniveau, -x** [kanivo] *nm* gutter

**cannabis** [kanabis] *nm* cannabis

**canne** [kan] *nf* [tige] cane ; [pour marcher] (walking) stick ; **canne à pêche** fishing rod ; **canne à sucre** sugar cane

**cannelle** [kanɛl] *nf* cinnamon

**cannette** [kanɛt] *nf* = **canette**

**cannibale** [kanibal] *nmf* cannibal

**canoë-kayak** [kanɔekajak] *nm* canoeing

**canon¹** [kanɔ̃] *nm* gun ; [ancien, à boulets] cannon ; [de fusil] barrel

**canon²** [kanɔ̃] *nm* REL & *Fig* [règle] canon

**canot** [kano] *nm* boat ; **canot de sauvetage** lifeboat ; **canot pneumatique** rubber dinghy

**cantatrice** [kɑ̃tatris] *nf* opera singer

**cantine** [kɑ̃tin] *nf* **a)** [réfectoire] canteen ; [d'école] dining hall **b)** [coffre] trunk

**cantique** [kɑ̃tik] *nm* hymn ; **cantique de Noël** Christmas carol

**canton** [kɑ̃tɔ̃] *nm* [en France] canton *(division of a department)* ; [en Suisse] canton *(semi-autonomous region)*

**cantonade** [kɑ̃tɔnad] ▪ **à la cantonade** *adv* to everyone present

**cantonner** [kɑ̃tɔne] **1.** *vt* [troupes] to quarter ; **cantonner qn dans /à** to confine sb to **2. se cantonner** *vpr* **se cantonner dans /à** to confine oneself to ▪ **cantonnement** *nm* [lieu] quarters

**canular** [kanylar] *nm Fam* hoax

**canyoning** [kanjɔniŋ], **canyonisme** [kanjɔnism] *nm* canyoning

**CAO** [seao] *(abr de* **conception assistée par ordinateur***) nf* ORDINAT CAD

**caoutchouc** [kautʃu] *nm* rubber ; [élastique] rubber band ▪ **caoutchouteux, euse** [kautʃutø, øz] *adj* [viande] rubbery

**cap** [kap] *nm* GÉOG cape, headland ; NAUT [direction] course

**CAP** [seape] *(abr de* **certificat d'aptitude professionnelle***) nm* SCOL *vocational training certificate*

**capable** [kapabl] *adj* capable, able; **capable de qch** capable of sth; **capable de faire qch** able to do sth, capable of doing sth ■ **capacité** *nf* capacity; [aptitude] ability

**CAPES** [kapɛs] *(abr de* **certificat d'aptitude professionnelle à l'enseignement secondaire)** *nm postgraduate teaching certificate*

**capillaire** [kapilɛr] *adj* **huile / lotion capillaire** hair oil / lotion

**capitaine** [kapitɛn] *nm* captain

**capital, -e, -aux** [kapital, -o] **1.** *adj* [essentiel] major **2.** *adj f* **lettre capitale** capital letter **3.** *nm* FIN capital ■ **capitale** *nf* [lettre, ville] capital

**capitalisme** [kapitalism] *nm* capitalism ■ **capitaliste** *adj & nmf* capitalist

**capiteux, -euse** [kapitø, -øz] *adj* [parfum] heady

**capitonné, -e** [kapitɔne] *adj* padded

**capituler** [kapityle] *vi* to surrender ■ **capitulation** *nf* surrender

**caporal, -e, -aux** [kapɔral, -o] *nmf* MIL corporal

**capot** [kapo] *nm* AUTO Br bonnet, Am hood

**capote** [kapɔt] *nf* AUTO [de décapotable] top, Br hood

**capoter** [kapɔte] *vi* [véhicule] to overturn

**câpre** [kɑpr] *nf* caper

**caprice** [kapris] *nm* whim; **faire un caprice** to throw a tantrum ■ **capricieux, -euse** *adj* [personne] capricious

**Capricorne** [kaprikɔrn] *nm* **le Capricorne** [signe] Capricorn

**capsule** [kapsyl] *nf* [spatiale, de médicament] capsule; [de bouteille] cap

**capter** [kapte] *vt* [signal, radio] to pick up; [attention] to capture

**captif, -ive** [kaptif, -iv] *adj & nmf* captive ■ **captivité** *nf* captivity; **en captivité** in captivity

**captiver** [kaptive] *vt* to captivate ■ **captivant, -e** *adj* captivating

**capture** [kaptyr] *nf* capture; **capture d'écran** [image] screenshot; [action] screen capture ■ **capturer** *vt* to capture

**capuche** [kapyʃ] *nf* hood ■ **capuchon** *nm* [de manteau] hood; [de stylo, de tube] cap, top

**caqueter** [kakte] *vi* [poule] to cackle

**car¹** [kar] *conj* because, for

**car²** [kar] *nm* bus, Br coach; **car de police** police van ■ **car-ferry** *nm* car-ferry

**carabine** [karabin] *nf* rifle; **carabine à air comprimé** air gun

**caractère¹** [karaktɛr] *nm* [lettre] character; **en caractères gras** in bold characters; **caractères d'imprimerie** block letters

**caractère²** [karaktɛr] *nm* [tempérament, nature] character, nature; **avoir bon caractère** to be good-natured; **avoir mauvais caractère** to be bad-tempered

**caractériser** [karakterize] **1.** *vt* to characterize **2. se caractériser** *vpr* **se caractériser par** to be characterized by

**caractéristique** [karakteristik] *adj & nf* characteristic

**carafe** [karaf] *nf* [pour l'eau, le vin] carafe

**carambolage** [karɑ̃bɔlaʒ] *nm* pile-up

**caramel** [karamɛl] *nm* caramel ■ **caraméliser** *vt & vi* to caramelize

**carapace** [karapas] *nf* [de tortue] & Fig shell

**carat** [kara] *nm* carat; **or à 18 carats** 18-carat gold

**caravane** [karavan] *nf* [pour camper] Br caravan, Am trailer; [dans le désert] caravan; **des vacances en caravane** a caravanning holiday ■ **caravaning** *nm* caravanning; **faire du caravaning** to go caravanning

**carbone** [karbɔn] *nm* carbon; **(papier) carbone** carbon (paper) ■ **carbonique** *adj* **gaz carbonique** carbon dioxide; **neige carbonique** dry ice

**carbonisé, -e** [karbɔnize] *adj* [nourriture] burnt to a cinder

**carburant** [karbyrɑ̃] *nm* fuel ▪ **carburateur** *nm* AUTO Br carburettor, Am carburetor

**carcasse** [karkas] *nf* [os] carcass; [d'immeuble] shell

**carcéral, -e, -aux** [karseral, -o] *adj* prison

**cardiaque** [kardjak] **1.** *adj* [arrêt, massage] cardiac; **être cardiaque** to have a heart condition **2.** *nmf* heart patient

**cardigan** [kardigɑ̃] *nm* cardigan

**cardinal, -e, -aux** [kardinal, -o] **1.** *adj* [nombre, point, vertu] cardinal **2.** *nm* REL cardinal

**cardiologie** [kardjɔlɔʒi] *nf* cardiology

**carême** [karɛm] *nm* REL **le carême** Lent; **faire carême** to fast

**carence** [karɑ̃s] *nf* [manque] deficiency

**caresse** [karɛs] *nf* caress; **faire des caresses à qn** to caress sb

**caresser** [karese] *vt* [personne] to caress; [animal] to stroke; *Fig* [espoir] to cherish

**cargaison** [kargɛzɔ̃] *nf* cargo

**caricature** [karikatyr] *nf* caricature

**carie** [kari] *nf* **carie (dentaire)** tooth decay; **avoir une carie** to have a cavity

**carillon** [karijɔ̃] *nm* [sonnerie] chimes; [horloge] chiming clock; [de porte] door chime

**caritatif, -ive** [karitatif, -iv] *adj* charitable

**carlingue** [karlɛ̃g] *nf* [d'avion] cabin

**carnage** [karnaʒ] *nm* carnage

**carnassier, -ère** [karnasje, -ɛr] **1.** *adj* flesh-eating **2.** *nm* carnivore

**carnaval, -als** [karnaval] *nm* carnival

**carnet** [karnɛ] *nm* [carnet] notebook; [de tickets] *book of tickets*; **carnet d'adresses** address book; **carnet de chèques** Br cheque book, Am check book; **carnet de notes** Br school report, Am report card; **carnet de santé** health record

**carnivore** [karnivɔr] **1.** *adj* carnivorous **2.** *nm* carnivore

**carotte** [karɔt] *nf* carrot

**carpette** [karpɛt] *nf* rug

**carré, -e** [kare] **1.** *adj* square; [épaules] square, broad; **mètre carré** square metre **2.** *nm* square; **avoir une coupe au carré** to have (one's hair in) a bob; CULIN **carré d'agneau** rack of lamb

**carreau, -x** [karo] *nm* [motif] square; [sur tissu] check; [de céramique] tile; [vitre] (window) pane; CARTES [couleur] diamonds; **tissu à carreaux** check(ed) material

**carrefour** [karfur] *nm* crossroads (*sg*)

**carrelage** [karlaʒ] *nm* [sol] tiled floor; [carreaux] tiles

**carrelet** [karlɛ] *nm* Br plaice, Am flounder

**carrément** [karemɑ̃] *adv* Fam [franchement] straight out; [très] really

**carrière** [karjɛr] *nf* **a)** [lieu] quarry **b)** [métier] career; **faire carrière dans** to make a career in

**carriole** [karjɔl] *nf* **a)** [petite charrette] cart **b)** Can [traîneau] sleigh

**carrosse** [karɔs] *nm* HIST (horse-drawn) carriage ▪ **carrosserie** *nf* [de véhicule] bodywork

**carrure** [karyr] *nf* [de personne] build; [de vêtement] width across the shoulders

**cartable** [kartabl] *nm* **a)** schoolbag **b)** Can [reliure] ringbinder

**carte** [kart] *nf* **a)** [carton, document officiel, informatisé & ORDINAT] card; [géographique] map; [marine, météo] chart; [professionnelle] business card; *Fig* **avoir carte blanche** to have a free hand; **carte (à jouer)** (playing) card; **jouer aux cartes** to play cards; ORDINAT **carte à puce** smart card; **carte de crédit** credit card; **carte d'identité** identity card; **carte de séjour** residence permit; **carte de téléphone** phonecard; **carte de visite** Br visiting card, Am calling card; **carte de vœux** greetings card; ORDINAT **carte mémoire** memory card; **carte postale** postcard; **carte routière** road map; ORDINAT **carte graphique** graphics card; ORDINAT **carte son** soundcard **b)** [de restaurant] menu; **manger à la carte** to eat à la carte; **carte des vins** wine list ■ **carte-cadeau** *(pl* **cartes-cadeaux)** *nf* gift card

**cartel** [kartɛl] *nm* ÉCON cartel

**cartomancien, -enne** [kartɔmɑ̃sjɛ̃, -ɛn] *nmf* fortune-teller *(who uses cards)*

**carton** [kartɔ̃] *nm* [matière] cardboard; [boîte] cardboard box; **carton à dessin** portfolio; **carton jaune/rouge** [au football] yellow/red card ■ **cartonné** *adj* livre **cartonné** hardback

**cartonner** [kartɔne] *vi Fam* [film, musique] to be a hit; [livre] to be a best-seller; **j'ai cartonné en maths** I did brilliantly in maths

**cartouche** [kartuʃ] *nf* [gén & ORDINAT] cartridge; [de cigarettes] carton

**cas** [kɑ] *nm* case; **en tout cas** in any case; **en cas de besoin** if need be; **en cas d'accident** in the event of an accident; **en cas d'urgence** in an emergency; **au cas où elle tomberait** if she should fall

**casanier, -ère** [kazanje, -ɛr] *adj* stay-at-home

**cascade** [kaskad] *nf* **a)** [d'eau] waterfall; **en cascade** in succession **b)** [de cinéma] stunt ■ **cascadeur, -euse** *nmf* stunt man, *f* stunt woman

**case** [kɑz] *nf* **a)** [de tiroir] compartment; [d'échiquier] square; [de formulaire] box **b)** [hutte] hut

**caser** [kaze] *Fam* **1.** *vt* [placer] to fit in **2. se caser** *vpr* [se marier] to get married and settle down

**caserne** [kazɛrn] *nf* barracks; **caserne de pompiers** fire station

**casier** [kazje] *nm* compartment; [pour courrier] pigeonhole; [pour vêtements] locker; **casier à bouteilles** bottle rack; JUR **casier judiciaire** criminal *or* police record

**casino** [kazino] *nm* casino

**casque** [kask] *nm* helmet; **casque (à écouteurs)** headphones

**casquette** [kaskɛt] *nf* cap

**cassation** [kasasjɔ̃] *nf* JUR annulment

**casse** [kɑs] **1.** *nf* [objets cassés] breakages; **aller à la casse** to go for scrap **2.** *nm Fam* [cambriolage] break-in

**casse-gueule** [kasɡœl] *(pl* **casse-gueule** *ou* **casse-gueules)** *adj Fam* [chemin] treacherous; [projet] risky; **c'est casse-gueule, ton projet !** this plan of yours is going to be a complete disaster!; **dis donc, il est casse-gueule ton escalier !** hey, this staircase of yours is dangerous!

**casser** [kɑse] **1.** *vt* **a)** [briser] to break; [noix] to crack; [voix] to strain; *Fam* **casser les pieds à qn** to get on sb's nerves **b)** JUR [verdict] to quash; [mariage] to annul **2.** *vi* to break **3. se casser** *vpr* to break; **se casser la jambe** to break one's leg; *Fam* **se casser la figure** [tomber] to fall flat on one's face ■ **cassant, -e** *adj* [fragile] brittle; [brusque] curt, abrupt ■ **casse-cou** *nmf inv* [personne] daredevil ■ **casse-croûte** *nm inv* **a)** *Fam* snack **b)** *Can* [snack-bar] snack-bar ■ **casse-noisettes, casse-noix** [kɑswa] *nm inv* nutcrackers ■ **casse-pieds** *nmf inv Fam* [personne] pain (in the neck) ■ **casse-tête** *nm inv* [problème] headache; *Can* [jeu] puzzle ■ **casseur** *nm* [manifestant] rioter

**casserole** [kasrɔl] *nf* (sauce)pan

**cassette** [kasɛt] *nf* [magnétique] cassette, tape; **enregistrer qch sur cassette** to tape sth; **cassette vidéo** video cassette

**cassis** [kasis] *nm* [fruit] blackcurrant; [boisson] blackcurrant liqueur

**cassoulet** [kasulɛ] *nm* cassoulet, *stew of beans, pork and goose*

**cassure** [kasyr] *nf* break

**castagnettes** [kastaɲɛt] *nfpl* castanets

**caste** [kast] *nf* caste

**castor** [kastɔr] *nm* beaver

**castrer** [kastre] *vt* to castrate; [chat, chien] to neuter

**cata** [kata] *nf Fam* **c'est la cata !** it's a disaster

**catalogue** [katalɔg] *nm Br* catalogue, *Am* catalog ▪ **cataloguer** *vt Br* to catalogue, *Am* to catalog; *Fig & Péj* to label

**catalyseur** [katalizœr] *nm* CHIM & *Fig* catalyst

**catalytique** [katalitik] *adj* AUTO **pot catalytique** catalytic converter

**catapulte** [katapylt] *nf* catapult

**catastrophe** [katastrɔf] *nf* disaster, catastrophe ▪ **catastrophique** *adj* disastrous, catastrophic

**catch** [katʃ] *nm* wrestling ▪ **catcheur, -euse** *nmf* wrestler

**catéchisme** [kateʃism] *nm* REL catechism

**catégorie** [kategɔri] *nf* category; [d'hôtel] grade

**catégorique** [kategɔrik] *adj* categorical; **c'est lui, je suis catégorique** I'm positive it's him

**cathédrale** [katedral] *nf* cathedral

**catho** [kato] *adj & nmf Fam* Catholic

**catholicisme** [katɔlisism] *nm* Catholicism ▪ **catholique** *adj & nmf* (Roman) Catholic

**catimini** [katimini] ▪ **en catimini** *adv* on the sly

**cauchemar** [koʃmar] *nm aussi Fig* nightmare; **faire un cauchemar** to have a nightmare

**cause** [koz] *nf* [origine] cause; [procès, parti] case; **à cause de qn/qch** because of sb/sth

**causer¹** [koze] *vt* [provoquer] to cause

**causer²** [koze] *vi* [bavarder] to chat (**de** about); [cancaner] to talk ▪ **causerie** *nf* talk

**caustique** [kostik] *adj* [substance, esprit] caustic

**caution** [kosjɔ̃] *nf* [d'appartement] deposit; JUR bail; [personne] guarantor; *Fig* [appui] backing; JUR **sous caution** on bail ▪ **cautionner** *vt Fig* [approuver] to back

**cavalier, -ère** [kavalje, -ɛr] **1.** *nmf* [à cheval] rider; ÉCHECS knight; [de bal]
partner, escort; *Fig* **faire cavalier seul** to go it alone **2.** *adj* [manière, personne] cavalier

**cave** [kav] *nf* cellar ▪ **caveau, -x** *nm* [sépulture] burial vault

**caverne** [kavɛrn] *nf* cave, cavern; **homme des cavernes** caveman

**caviar** [kavjar] *nm* caviar

**cavité** [kavite] *nf* hollow, cavity

**Cb1** SMS *abr écrite de* **c'est bien**

**CCP** [sesepe] *(abr de* **compte chèque postal)** *nm Br* ≈ PO Giro account, *Am* ≈ Post Office checking account

**CD** [sede] *(abr de* **disque compact)** *nm* CD

**CDI** [sedei] *nm inv* **a)** *(abr de* **contrat à durée indéterminée)** permanent contract **b)** *(abr de* **centre de documentation et d'information)** school library *(with special resources on how to find information)*

**CD-Rom** [sederɔm] *nm inv* ORDINAT CD-ROM

---

**ce¹, cette, ces** [sə, sɛt, se]

**cet** is used before a masculine singular adjective beginning with a vowel or mute h.

*adj dém* this, that, *pl* these, those; **cet homme** this/that man; **cet homme-ci** this man; **cet homme-là** that man

---

**ce²** [sə]

**ce** becomes **c'** before a vowel.

*pron dém* **a)** [pour désigner, pour qualifier] it, that; **c'est facile** it's easy; **c'est exact** that's right; **c'est mon père** that's my father; [au téléphone] it's my father; **ce sont eux qui...** they are the people who...; **qui est-ce?** [en général] who is it?; [en désignant] who is that?; **ce faisant** in so doing; **sur ce** thereupon **b)** [après une proposition] **ce que..., ce qui...** what...; **je sais ce qui est bon/ce que tu veux** I know what is good/what you want; **ce que c'est beau!** it's so beautiful!

**CE** [sea] **1.** nm (abr de **cours élémentaire**) SCOL **CE1** second year of primary school; **CE2** third year of primary school **2.** nf (abr de **Communauté européenne**) EC

**ceci** [səsi] pron dém this; **ceci étant dit** having said this

**cécité** [sesite] nf blindness

**céder** [sede] **1.** vt [donner] to give up (**à** to); [par testament] to leave (**à** to); '**cédez le passage**' Br 'give way', Am 'yield'; '**à céder**' 'for sale' **2.** vi [personne] to give in (**à/devant** to); [branche, chaise] to give way

**cédérom** [sederɔm] nm ORDINAT CD-ROM

**CEDEX, Cedex** [sedɛks] (abr de **courrier d'entreprise à distribution exceptionnelle**) nm accelerated postal service for bulk users

**cèdre** [sɛdr] nm **a)** [arbre, bois] cedar **b)** Can [thuya] white cedar

**CEI** (abr de **Communauté des États indépendants**) nf CIS

**ceinture** [sɛ̃tyr] nf [accessoire] belt; [taille] waist; **ceinture de sécurité** [de véhicule] seatbelt

**cela** [s(ə)la] pron dém [pour désigner] that; [sujet indéfini] it, that; **cela dit** having said that; **cela m'attriste que...** it saddens me that...; **quand/comment cela?** when?/how?

**célèbre** [selɛbr] adj famous ■ **célébrité** nf fame; [personne] celebrity

**célébrer** [selebre] vt to celebrate ■ **célébration** nf celebration (**de** of)

**céleri** [selri] nm celery

**céleste** [selɛst] adj celestial, heavenly

**célibat** [seliba] nm [de prêtre] celibacy ■ **célibataire 1.** adj [non marié] single, unmarried **2.** nmf bachelor, f single woman

**celle** voir **celui**

**cellier** [selje] nm storeroom

**Cellophane®** [selɔfan] nf cellophane®; **sous Cellophane®** cellophane-wrapped

**cellule** [selyl] nf [de prison & BIOL] cell ■ **cellulaire** adj BIOL cell; **téléphone cellulaire** cellular phone

**celte** [sɛlt] adj Celtic

**celui, celle, ceux** [səlɥi, sɛl, sø, sɛl] pron dém the one, pl those, the ones; **celui de Jean** Jean's (one); **ceux de Jean** Jean's (ones), those of Jean; **celui qui appartient à Jean** the one that belongs to Jean; **celui-ci** this one; [le dernier] the latter; **celui-là** that one; [le premier] the former

**cendre** [sɑ̃dr] nf ash

**cendrier** [sɑ̃drije] nm ashtray

**censé, -e** [sɑ̃se] adj **être censé faire qch** to be supposed to do sth

**censeur** [sɑ̃sœr] nm [de films, de journaux] censor; [de lycée] Br deputy head, Am assistant principal ■ **censure** nf [activité] censorship; [comité] board of censors ■ **censurer** vt [film] to censor

**cent** [sɑ̃] adj & nm a hundred; **cent pages** a or one hundred pages; **deux cents pages** two hundred pages; **cinq pour cent** five per cent ■ **centaine** nf **une centaine (de)** about a hundred; **des centaines de** hundreds of ■ **centenaire 1.** adj hundred-year-old; **être centenaire** to be a hundred **2.** nmf centenarian **3.** nm [anniversaire] centenary ■ **centième** adj & nmf hundredth

**centigrade** [sɑ̃tigrad] adj centigrade

**centilitre** [sɑ̃tilitr] nm Br centilitre, Am centiliter

**centimètre** [sɑ̃timɛtr] nm centimetre; [ruban] tape measure

**central, -e, -aux** [sɑ̃tral, -o] **1.** adj central **2.** nm **central téléphonique** telephone exchange ■ **centrale** nf **centrale électrique** Br power station, Am power plant; **centrale nucléaire** nuclear Br power station or Am power plant ■ **centraliser** vt to centralize

**centre** [sɑ̃tr] nm centre; **centre aéré** outdoor activity centre; **centre commercial** Br shopping centre, Am (shopping) mall; **centre hospitalo-universitaire** ≃ teaching hospital; **centre médicale** clinic; **centre de sport**

sports centre; **centre de vacances** holiday centre or complex ■ **centre-ville** (pl **centres-villes**) nm town centre; [de grande ville] Br city centre, Am downtown ■ **centrer** vt to centre

**centuple** [sãtypl] nm x est le centuple de y x is a hundred times y; **au centuple** a hundredfold

**cependant** [səpãdã] conj however, yet

**céramique** [seramik] nf [matière] ceramic; [art] ceramics (sg); **de** ou **en céramique** ceramic

**cercle** [sɛrkl] nm [forme, groupe] circle; **le cercle polaire arctique** the Arctic Circle; **cercle vicieux** vicious circle

**cercueil** [sɛrkœj] nm coffin

**céréale** [sereal] nf cereal

**cérébral, -e, -aux** [serebral, -o] adj cerebral

**cérémonie** [seremɔni] nf ceremony

**cerf** [sɛr] nm stag ■ **cerf-volant** (pl **cerfs-volants**) nm [jeu] kite

**cerise** [səriz] nf cherry ■ **cerisier** nm cherry tree

**cerne** [sɛrn] nm ring ■ **cerner** vt to surround; [problème] to define; **avoir les yeux cernés** to have rings under one's eyes

**certain, -e** [sɛrtɛ̃, -ɛn] **1.** adj [sûr] certain; **il est certain que tu réussiras** you're certain to succeed; **je suis certain de réussir** I'm certain I'll be successful or of being successful; **être certain de qch** to be certain of sth **2.** adj indéf [avant nom] certain; **un certain temps** a while **3.** pron indéf **certains pensent que...** some people think that...; **certains d'entre nous** some of us ■ **certainement** adv most probably

**certificat** [sɛrtifika] nm certificate

**certifier** [sɛrtifje] vt to certify; **je te certifie que...** I assure you that...

**certitude** [sɛrtityd] nf certainty; **avoir la certitude que...** to be certain that...

**cerveau, -x** [sɛrvo] nm [organe] brain; [intelligence] mind, brain(s); Fam [de projet] mastermind

**cervelle** [sɛrvɛl] nf [substance] brain; [plat] brains

**ces** voir **ce**

**CES** [seəɛs] (abr de **collège d'enseignement secondaire**) nm Anc secondary school for pupils aged 12 to 15

**César** [sezar] nm CINÉ French cinema award

**césarienne** [sezarjɛn] nf MÉD Caesarean (section)

**cesse** [sɛs] nf **sans cesse** constantly

**cesser** [sese] vt & vi to stop; **faire cesser qch** to put a stop to sth; **cesser de faire qch** to stop doing sth ■ **cessez-le-feu** nm inv cease-fire

**c'est-à-dire** [setadir] conj that is (to say)

**cet, cette** voir **ce**

**ceux** voir **celui**

**CFC** (abr de **chlorofluorocarbure**) nm CFC

**chacal, als** [ʃakal] nm ZOOL jackal

**chacun, -e** [ʃakœ̃, -yn] pron indéf each (one), every one; [tout le monde] everyone; **(à) chacun son tour !** wait your turn!

**chagrin** [ʃagrɛ̃] nm grief, sorrow; **avoir du chagrin** to be upset ■ **chagriner** vt [peiner] to grieve; [contrarier] to bother

**chahut** [ʃay] nm Fam racket ■ **chahuter** Fam **1.** vi to make a racket **2.** vt [professeur] to bait

**chaîne** [ʃɛn] nf [attache, décoration, série] chain; [de montagnes] chain, range; **réaction en chaîne** chain reaction; **travailler à la chaîne** to work on the assembly line; AUTO **chaînes** (snow) chains; **chaîne de montage** assembly line; **chaîne de télévision** television channel; **chaîne privée** private channel; **chaîne publique** public or state-owned channel; **chaîne (hi-fi)** hi-fi (system) ■ **chaînette** nf (small) chain ■ **chaînon** nm link

**chair** [ʃɛr] nf flesh; **(couleur) chair** fleshcoloured; **en chair et en os** in the flesh; **avoir la chair de poule** to have Br goose pimples or Am goose bumps

**chaire** [ʃɛr] nf [d'université] chair ; [d'église] pulpit

**chaise** [ʃɛz] nf chair ; **chaise longue** deckchair ; **chaise roulante** wheelchair

**châle** [ʃal] nm shawl

**chalet** [ʃalɛ] nm **a)** chalet **b)** Can [maison de campagne] Br (holiday) cottage, Am (vacation) cottage

**chaleur** [ʃalœr] nf heat ; [de personne, de couleur, de voix] warmth ; **coup de chaleur** heatstroke ■ **chaleureux, -euse** adj warm

**challenge** [ʃalɑ̃ʒ] nm SPORT tournament ; [défi] challenge

**chaloupe** [ʃalup] nf launch

**chalumeau, -x** [ʃalymo] nm blowtorch, Br blowlamp

**chalutier** [ʃalytje] nm trawler

**chamailler** [ʃamaje] ■ **se chamailler** vpr to squabble

**chambre** [ʃɑ̃br] nf bedroom ; [de tribunal] division ; **chambre (d'hôtel)** (hotel) room ; **chambre à coucher** [pièce] bedroom ; [mobilier] bedroom suite ; **chambre à un lit/deux lits** single/twin room ; **chambre d'ami** spare room ; **chambre d'hôte** ≃ guesthouse ; **Chambre de commerce** Chamber of Commerce ; POL **Chambre des députés** lower chamber of Parliament ■ **chambrer** vt [vin] to bring to room temperature

**chameau, -x** [ʃamo] nm camel

**champ** [ʃɑ̃] nm [étendue, ÉLEC & ORDINAT] field ; Fig [portée] scope ; Fig **laisser le champ libre à qn** to leave the field free for sb ; **champ de bataille** battlefield ; **champ de courses** Br racecourse, Am racetrack

**champagne** [ʃɑ̃paɲ] nm champagne

**champêtre** [ʃɑ̃pɛtr] adj rustic

**champignon** [ʃɑ̃piɲɔ̃] nm [végétal] mushroom ; MÉD fungus ; **champignon de Paris** button mushroom ; **champignon vénéneux** toadstool, poisonous mushroom

**champion, -onne** [ʃɑ̃pjɔ̃, -ɔn] **1.** nmf champion ; **le champion olympique** the Olympic champion **2.** adj **l'équipe**

**championne du monde** the world champions ■ **championnat** nm championship

**chance** [ʃɑ̃s] nf [sort favorable] luck ; [possibilité] chance ; **avoir de la chance** to be lucky ; **ne pas avoir de chance** to be unlucky ; **par chance** luckily ■ **chanceux, -euse** adj lucky

**chanceler** [ʃɑ̃sle] vi to stagger

**chancelier** [ʃɑ̃səlje] nm POL chancellor

**chandail** [ʃɑ̃daj] nm sweater

**Chandeleur** [ʃɑ̃dlœr] nf **la Chandeleur** Candlemas

**chandelier** [ʃɑ̃dəlje] nm [à une branche] candlestick ; [à plusieurs branches] candelabra

**chandelle** [ʃɑ̃dɛl] nf candle

**change** [ʃɑ̃ʒ] nm FIN exchange

**changer** [ʃɑ̃ʒe] **1.** vt [modifier, remplacer, convertir] to change ; **changer qch de place** to move sth **2.** vi to change ; **changer de voiture/d'adresse** to change one's car/address ; **changer de vitesse/de couleur** to change gear/colour **3.** **se changer** vpr to change (one's clothes) ; **se changer en qch** to change into sth ■ **changeant, -e** adj [temps] unsettled ■ **changement** nm change ; AUTO **changement de vitesse** [levier] Br gear lever, Am gear shift

**chanson** [ʃɑ̃sɔ̃] nf song ■ **chant** nm [art] singing ; [chanson] song ; **chant de Noël** Christmas carol

**chanter** [ʃɑ̃te] **1.** vt [chanson] to sing ; [exploits] to sing of **2.** vi [personne, oiseau] to sing ; [coq] to crow ; **faire chanter qn** to blackmail sb ■ **chantage** nm blackmail ■ **chanteur, -euse** nmf singer

**chantier** [ʃɑ̃tje] nm (building) site ; [sur route] roadworks ; **mettre qch en chantier** to get sth under way ; **chantier naval** shipyard

**chantilly** [ʃɑ̃tiji] nf whipped cream

**chantonner** [ʃɑ̃tɔne] vt & vi to hum

**chaos** [kao] nm chaos ■ **chaotique** adj chaotic

**chapeau, -x** [ʃapo] *nm* hat; **chapeau de paille** straw hat; **chapeau melon** bowler hat

**chapelle** [ʃapɛl] *nf* chapel; **chapelle ardente** chapel of rest

**chapelure** [ʃaplyr] *nf* breadcrumbs

**chapiteau, -x** [ʃapito] *nm* [de cirque] big top; [pour expositions] tent, *Br* marquee

**chapitre** [ʃapitr] *nm* chapter

**chaque** [ʃak] *adj* each, every

**char** [ʃar] *nm* [romain] chariot; [de carnaval] float; *Can* [voiture] car; MIL **char (d'assaut)** tank

**charabia** [ʃarabja] *nm Fam* gibberish

**charbon** [ʃarbɔ̃] *nm* coal; **charbon de bois** charcoal

**charcuterie** [ʃarkytri] *nf* [magasin] pork butcher's shop; [aliments cooked (pork) meats ■ **charcutier, -ère** *nmf* pork butcher

**chardon** [ʃardɔ̃] *nm* [plante] thistle

**charge** [ʃarʒ] *nf* [poids] load; [responsabilité] responsibility; [d'une arme, ÉLEC & MIL] charge; [fonction] office; **être en charge de qch** to be in charge of sth; **prendre qn/qch en charge** to take charge of sb/sth; **être à la charge de qn** [personne] to be dependent on sb; [frais] to be payable by sb; **charges sociales** *Br* national insurance contributions, *Am* Social Security contributions ■ **charges** *nfpl* **a)** [d'appartement] service charge **b)** ÉCON expenses, costs; **charges patronales** employer's contributions; **charges sociales** *Br* national insurance contributions, *Am* Social Security contributions

**charger** [ʃarʒe] **1.** *vt* [véhicule, marchandises, arme & ORDINAT] to load; [batterie & MIL] to charge; **charger qn de qch** to entrust sb with; **charger qn de faire qch** to give sb the responsibility of doing sth **2.** *vi* ORDINAT to load up; MIL to charge **3. se charger** *vpr* [s'encombrer] to weigh oneself down; **se charger de qn/qch** to take care of sb/sth; **se charger de faire qch** to undertake to do sth ■ **chargé, -e 1.** *adj* [véhicule] loaded (**de** with);

[arme] loaded; [journée, programme] busy; **être chargé de faire qch** to be responsible for doing sth **2.** *nmf* UNIV **chargé de cours** part-time lecturer ■ **chargement** *nm* [action] loading; [marchandises] load; [de bateau] cargo

**charia** [ʃarja] *nf* REL sharia, sheria

**chariot** [ʃarjo] *nm* [de supermarché] *Br* trolley, *Am* cart; [de ferme] waggon; [de machine à écrire] carriage; **chariot à bagages** luggage trolley

**charisme** [karism] *nm* charisma

**charitable** [ʃaritabl] *adj* charitable (**envers** towards)

**charité** [ʃarite] *nf* [vertu] charity; **faire la charité** to give to charity

**charme** [ʃarm] *nm* [attrait] charm; [magie] spell

**charmer** [ʃarme] *vt* to charm ■ **charmant, -e** *adj* charming ■ **charmeur, -euse 1.** *adj* [sourire, air] charming **2.** *nmf* charmer

**charnel, -elle** [ʃarnɛl] *adj* carnal

**charnier** [ʃarnje] *nm* mass grave

**charnière** [ʃarnjɛr] *nf* hinge

**charnu, -e** [ʃarny] *adj* fleshy

**charpente** [ʃarpɑ̃t] *nf* framework; [de personne] build ■ **charpentier** *nm* carpenter

**charpie** [ʃarpi] *nf* **mettre qch en charpie** to tear sth to shreds

**charrette** [ʃarɛt] *nf* cart

**charrier** [ʃarje] *vt* [transporter] to cart; [rivière] to carry along

**charrue** [ʃary] *nf Br* plough, *Am* plow

**charter** [ʃarter] *nm* [vol] charter (flight); [avion] charter plane

**chasse¹** [ʃas] *nf* [activité] hunting; [événement] hunt; [poursuite] chase; **aller à la chasse** to go hunting; **chasse à courre** hunting; **chasse au trésor** treasure hunt; **chasse gardée** private hunting ground

**chasse²** [ʃas] *nf* **chasse d'eau** flush; **tirer la chasse** to flush the toilet

**chassé-croisé** [ʃasekrwaze] (*pl* **chassés-croisés**) *nm* [de personnes] comings and goings

**chasser** [ʃase] **1.** *vt* [animal] to hunt; [faisan, perdrix] to shoot; **chasser qn** [expulser] to chase sb away; [employé] to dismiss sb **2.** *vi* to hunt ■ **chasse-neige** *nm inv* *Br* snowplough, *Am* snowplow ■ **chasseur, -euse 1.** *nmf* hunter; **chasseur de têtes** headhunter **2.** *nm* [d'hôtel] *Br* pageboy, *Am* bellboy; [avion] fighter

**châssis** [ʃasi] *nm* frame; [d'automobile] chassis

**chat¹** [ʃa] *nm* cat; **chat sauvage** wildcat

**chat²** [tʃat] *nm* ORDINAT chat

**châtaigne** [ʃatɛɲ] *nf* chestnut ■ **châtaignier** *nm* chestnut tree ■ **châtain** *adj* [cheveux] (chestnut) brown; [personne] brown-haired

**château, -x** [ʃato] *nm* [forteresse] castle; [manoir] mansion

**châtiment** [ʃatimã] *nm* punishment; **châtiment corporel** corporal punishment

**chaton** [ʃatɔ̃] *nm* **a)** [chat] kitten **b)** [de bague] bezel **c)** [d'arbre] catkin

**chatouiller** [ʃatuje] *vt* to tickle ■ **chatouilleux, -euse** *adj* ticklish

**chatoyer** [ʃatwaje] *vi* to shimmer; [pierre] to sparkle

**châtrer** [ʃatre] *vt* to castrate

**chatte** [ʃat] *nf* (female) cat

**chatter, tchatter** [tʃate] *vi* ORDINAT to chat ■ **chatteur, euse, tchatteur, euse** [tʃatœr, øz] *nmf* ORDINAT chatter

**chaud, -e** [ʃo, ʃod] **1.** *adj* **a)** [modérément] warm; [intensément] hot **b)** *Fig* [couleur] warm; [voix] sultry **2.** *nm* **avoir chaud** to be hot; **il fait chaud** it's hot ■ **chaudement** *adv* [s'habiller, féliciter] warmly

**chaudière** [ʃodjɛr] *nf* boiler

**chauffage** [ʃofaʒ] *nm* heating; [de voiture] heater

**chauffard** [ʃofar] *nm* **a)** reckless driver **b)** [qui s'enfuit] hit-and-run driver

**chauffer** [ʃofe] **1.** *vt* to heat (up); [moteur] to warm up **2.** *vi* to heat (up); [s'échauffer - moteur] to overheat; **faire chauffer qch** to heat sth up

**3. se chauffer** *vpr* to warm oneself ■ **chauffant, -e** *adj* **couverture chauffante** electric blanket; **plaque chauffante** hot plate ■ **chauffé, -e** *adj* [piscine] heated ■ **chauffe-eau** *nm inv* water heater; **chauffe-eau électrique** immersion heater ■ **chauffe-plat** *(pl* **chauffe-plats)** *nm* hotplate ■ **chaufferie** *nf* boiler room

**chauffeur** [ʃofœr] *nm* [de véhicule] driver; [employé] chauffeur; **chauffeur de taxi** taxi driver

**chaume** [ʃom] *nm* [pour toits] thatch; **toit de chaume** thatched roof ■ **chaumière** *nf* [à toit de chaume] thatched cottage; [maison pauvre] cottage

**chaussée** [ʃose] *nf* road(way)

**chausser** [ʃose] **1.** *vt* [chaussures, lunettes, skis] to put on; **chausser qn** to put shoes on sb; **chausser du 40** to take a size 40 shoe **2. se chausser** *vpr* to put one's shoes on

**chaussette** [ʃosɛt] *nf* sock

**chausson** [ʃosɔ̃] *nm* [pantoufle] slipper; [de danse] ballet shoe; [de bébé] bootee; CULIN **chausson aux pommes** apple turnover

**chaussure** [ʃosyr] *nf* shoe; **chaussures de ski** ski boots

**chauve** [ʃov] **1.** *adj* bald **2.** *nm* bald (-headed) man

**chauve-souris** [ʃovsuri] *(pl* **chauves-souris)** *nf* bat

**chauvin, -e** [ʃovɛ̃, -in] **1.** *adj* chauvinistic **2.** *nmf* chauvinist

**chaux** [ʃo] *nf* lime; **blanchir qch à la chaux** to whitewash sth

**chavirer** [ʃavire] *vt & vi* [bateau] to capsize

**chef** [ʃɛf] *nm* **a)** [de parti, de bande] leader; [de tribu] chief; **rédacteur en chef** editor in chief; **le chef du gouvernement** the head of government; **chef d'entreprise** company head; **chef d'État** head of state; **chef d'orchestre** conductor **b)** [cuisinier] chef

**chef-d'œuvre** [ʃɛdœvr] *(pl* **chefs-d'œuvre)** *nm* masterpiece

**chef-lieu** [ʃɛfljø] *(pl* **chefs-lieux**) *nm* administrative centre of a 'département'

**chemin** [ʃəmɛ̃] *nm* [route étroite] path, track; [itinéraire] way **(de** to); **à mi-chemin** half-way; **en chemin, chemin faisant** on the way; **chemin de grande randonnée** hiking trail; **chemin de terre** track ■ **chemin de fer** *(pl* **chemins de fer**) *nm Br* railway, *Am* railroad

**cheminée** [ʃəmine] *nf* [âtre] fireplace; [encadrement] mantelpiece; [sur le toit] chimney

**cheminot** [ʃəmino] *nm Br* railwayman, *Am* railroader

**chemise** [ʃəmiz] *nf* [vêtement] shirt; [classeur] folder; **chemise de nuit** [de femme] nightdress ■ **chemisier** *nm* [corsage] blouse

**chenal, -aux** [ʃənal, -o] *nm* channel

**chêne** [ʃɛn] *nm* [arbre, bois] oak

**chenil** [ʃəni(l)] *nm Br* kennels, *Am* kennel

**chenille** [ʃənij] *nf* [insecte] caterpillar; [de char] caterpillar track

**chèque** [ʃɛk] *nm Br* cheque, *Am* check; **faire un chèque à qn** to write sb a cheque; **payer qch par chèque** to pay sth by cheque; **chèque de voyage** *Br* traveller's cheque, *Am* traveler's check ■ **chèque-cadeau** [ʃɛkkado] *nm Br* gift token, *Br* gift voucher, *Am* gift certificate ■ **chèque-repas** *(pl* **chèques-repas**), **chèque-restaurant** *(pl* **chèques-restaurants**) *nm Br* luncheon voucher, *Am* meal ticket ■ **Chèque-Vacances®** *(pl* **Chèques-Vacances**) [ʃɛkvakɑ̃s] *nm* voucher that can be used to pay for holiday accommodation, activities, meals, etc. ■ **chéquier** *nm Br* cheque book, *Am* checkbook

**cher, chère** [ʃɛr] **1.** *adj* **a)** [aimé] dear (à to); **Cher Monsieur** [dans une lettre] Dear Mr X; [officiel] Dear Sir **b)** [coûteux] expensive, dear **2.** *adv* **coûter cher** to be expensive **3.** *nmf* **mon cher, ma chère** my dear ■ **chèrement** *adv* [à un prix élevé] dearly

**chercher** [ʃɛrʃe] **1.** *vt* to look for; [dans ses souvenirs] to try to think of; [dans un dictionnaire] to look up; **aller cher-cher qn/qch** to (go and) fetch sb/sth; **chercher à faire qch** to try to do sth **2. se chercher** *vpr* [chercher son identité] to try to find oneself ■ **chercheur, -euse** *nmf* [scientifique] researcher; **chercheur d'or** gold digger

**chérir** [ʃerir] *vt* to cherish ■ **chéri, -e** *adj* dear

**cherté** [ʃɛrte] *nf* high cost

**chétif, -ive** [ʃetif, -iv] *adj* [personne] puny

**cheval, -aux** [ʃəval, -o] *nm* horse; **à cheval** on horseback; **faire du cheval** *Br* to go horse riding, *Am* to go horseback riding; **cheval de course** racehorse; AUTO **cheval (-vapeur)** horsepower

**chevalet** [ʃəvalɛ] *nm* [de peintre] easel

**chevalier** [ʃəvalje] *nm* knight

**chevalière** [ʃəvaljɛr] *nf* signet ring

**chevaline** [ʃəvalin] *adj f* **boucherie chevaline** horse butcher's (shop)

**chevaucher** [ʃəvoʃe] **1.** *vt* to straddle **2.** *vi* to overlap **3. se chevaucher** *vpr* to overlap

**chevelu, -e** [ʃəvly] *adj* long-haired ■ **chevelure** *nf* (head of) hair

**chevet** [ʃəvɛ] *nm* bedhead; **rester au chevet de qn** to stay at sb's bedside

**cheveu, -x** [ʃəvø] *nm* **un cheveu** a hair; **cheveux** hair; **avoir les cheveux noirs** to have black hair

**cheville** [ʃəvij] *nf* [partie du corps] ankle

**chèvre** [ʃɛvr] **1.** *nf* goat **2.** *nm* goat's cheese

**chevreau, -x** [ʃəvro] *nm* kid

**chèvrefeuille** [ʃɛvrəfœj] *nm* honeysuckle

**chevreuil** [ʃəvrœj] *nm* roe deer; [viande] venison

**chevronné, -e** [ʃəvrɔne] *adj* experienced

**chez** [ʃe] *prép* **chez qn** at sb's house; **il n'est pas chez lui** he isn't at home; **elle est rentrée chez elle** she's gone home; **chez Mme Dupont** [adresse] c/o Mme Dupont ■ **chez-soi** *nm inv* **son petit chez-soi** one's own little home

**chiadé, e** [ʃjade] *adj Fam* [élaboré] top-notch

**chic** [ʃik] **1.** *adj inv* smart, stylish ; *Fam* [gentil] decent **2.** *nm* [élégance] style ; **avoir le chic pour faire qch** to have the knack of doing sth

**chicaner** [ʃikane] *vi* **chicaner sur qch** to quibble over sth

**chiche-kebab** *(pl* **chiches-kebabs)** [ʃiʃkebab] *nm* kebab, shish kebab

**chicorée** [ʃikɔre] *nf* [en poudre] chicory

**chicos** [ʃikɔs] *adj Fam* classy, smart

**chien, chienne** [ʃjɛ̃, ʃjɛn] *nmf* dog, *f* bitch ; *Fam* **quel temps de chien !** what foul weather! ; **chien d'aveugle** guide dog ; **chien de berger** sheepdog ; **chien de garde** guard dog ; **chien policier** police dog

**chiendent** [ʃjɛ̃dɑ̃] *nm* [plante] couch grass

**chiffon** [ʃifɔ̃] *nm* rag ; **passer un coup de chiffon sur qch** to give sth a dust ; **chiffon (de poussière)** *Br* duster, *Am* dustcloth

**chiffonner** [ʃifɔne] *vt* to crumple ; *Fig* [ennuyer] to bother

**chiffre** [ʃifr] *nm* [nombre] figure, number ; [total] total ; **chiffres romains / arabes** Roman / Arabic numerals ; **chiffre d'affaires** turnover ■ **chiffrer 1.** *vt* [montant] to work out ; [réparations] to assess **2. se chiffrer** *vpr* **se chiffrer à** to amount to

**chignon** [ʃiɲɔ̃] *nm* bun, chignon

**Chili** [ʃili] *nm* **le Chili** Chile ■ **chilien, -enne 1.** *adj* Chilean **2.** *nmf* **Chilien, Chilienne** Chilean

**chimie** [ʃimi] *nf* chemistry ■ **chimique** *adj* chemical ■ **chimiste** *nmf* (research) chemist

**chimio** [ʃimjo] *(abr de* **chimiothérapie)** *nf Fam* chemo

**chimiothérapie** [ʃimjoterapi] *nf* MÉD chemotherapy

**chimpanzé** [ʃɛ̃pɑ̃ze] *nm* chimpanzee

**Chine** [ʃin] *nf* **la Chine** China ■ **chinois, -e 1.** *adj* Chinese **2.** *nmf*

**Chinois, Chinoise** Chinese ; **les Chinois** the Chinese **3.** *nm* [langue] Chinese

**chiot** [ʃjo] *nm* puppy, pup

**chipoter** [ʃipɔte] *vi* [contester] to quibble (**sur** about)

**chips** [ʃips] *nf Br* (potato) crisp, *Am* (potato) chip

**chiromancien, -enne** [kirɔmɑ̃sjɛ̃, -ɛn] *nmf* palmist

**chirurgie** [ʃiryrʒi] *nf* surgery ; *Can* **chirurgie d'un jour** outpatient surgery, one-day surgery ; **chirurgie esthétique** plastic surgery ■ **chirurgical, -e, -aux** *adj* surgical ■ **chirurgien, -enne** *nmf* surgeon ■ **chirurgien-dentiste** *(pl* **chirurgiens-dentistes)** *nm* dental surgeon

**chlem** [ʃlɛm] *nm* SPORT **le grand chlem** the grand slam

**chlore** [klɔr] *nm* chlorine

**choc** [ʃɔk] **1.** *nm* [coup] impact ; [forte émotion] shock ; *Fig* [conflit] clash ; **faire un choc à qn** to give sb a shock ; **choc pétrolier** oil crisis **2.** *adj* **image-choc** shocking image ; **'prix-chocs'** 'drastic reductions'

**chocolat** [ʃɔkɔla] **1.** *nm* chocolate ; **gâteau au chocolat** chocolate cake ; **chocolat à croquer** *Br* plain chocolate, *Am* bittersweet chocolate ; **chocolat au lait** milk chocolate **2.** *adj inv Br* chocolate(-coloured), *Am* chocolate (-colored) ■ **chocolaté, -e** *adj* chocolate

**chœur** [kœr] *nm* [chanteurs, nef] choir ; [d'opéra] chorus ; **en chœur** [chanter] in chorus ; [répéter] (all) together

**choisir** [ʃwazir] *vt* to choose, to pick ; **choisir de faire qch** to choose to do sth ■ **choisi, -e** *adj* [œuvres] selected ; [langage] careful

**choix** [ʃwa] *nm* choice ; [assortiment] selection ; **avoir le choix** to have a choice

**cholestérol** [kɔlɛsterɔl] *nm* MÉD cholesterol

**chômer** [ʃome] *vi* **vous n'avez pas chômé !** you've not been idle! ; **jour chômé** (public) holiday ■ **chômage** *nm* unemployment; **être au chômage** to be unemployed ■ **chômeur, -euse** *nmf* unemployed person; **les chômeurs** the unemployed

**choquer** [ʃɔke] *vt* [scandaliser] to shock ■ **choquant, -e** *adj* shocking

**choral, -e, -aux** *ou* **-als** [kɔral] *adj* choral ■ **chorale** *nf* [club] choral society; [chanteurs] choir ■ **choriste** *nmf* chorister

**chorégraphe** [kɔregraf] *nmf* choreographer

**chose** [ʃoz] *nf* thing; **avant toute chose** first of all

**chou, -x** [ʃu] *nm* cabbage; **choux de Bruxelles** Brussels sprouts; **chou à la crème** cream puff ■ **chou-fleur** (*pl* **choux-fleurs**) *nm* cauliflower

**chouchou, oute** [ʃuʃu, ut] *nmf Fam Br* favourite, *Am* favorite; [élève] teacher's pet

**choucroute** [ʃukrut] *nf* sauerkraut

**chouette** [ʃwɛt] 1. *nf* [oiseau] owl 2. *adj Fam* [chic] great 3. *excl* great!

**choyer** [ʃwaje] *vt* to pamper

**chrétien, -enne** [kretjɛ̃, -ɛn] *adj & nmf* Christian ■ **Christ** [krist] *nm* **le Christ** Christ ■ **christianisme** *nm* Christianity

**chrome** [krom] *nm* chromium; **chromes** [de voitures] chrome

**chronique¹** [krɔnik] *adj* [malade, chômage] chronic

**chronique²** [krɔnik] *nf* [de journal] column; [annales] chronicle

**chronologie** [krɔnɔlɔʒi] *nf* chronology ■ **chronologique** *adj* chronological

**chronomètre** [krɔnɔmɛtr] *nm* chronometer; [pour le sport] stopwatch ■ **chronométrer** *vt* to time

**chrysanthème** [krizɑ̃tɛm] *nm* chrysanthemum

**CHU** (*abr de* **centre hospitalo-universitaire**) *nm* teaching hospital

**chuchoter** [ʃyʃɔte] *vt & vi* to whisper ■ **chuchotement** *nm* whisper

**chuinter** [ʃwɛ̃te] *vi* [siffler] to hiss

**chut** [ʃyt] *excl* sh!, shush!

**chute** [ʃyt] *nf* fall; [d'histoire drôle] punchline; [de tissu] scrap; **chute de neige** snowfall; **chute libre** free fall ■ **chuter** *vi* [diminuer] to fall, to drop; *Fam* [tomber] to fall

**Chypre** [ʃipr] *nm ou f* Cyprus ■ **chypriote** 1. *adj* Cypriot 2. *nmf* **Chypriote** Cypriot

**ci** [si] *pron dém* **comme ci comme ça** so so

**-ci** [si] *adv* a) **par-ci, par-là** here and there b) *voir* **ce, celui** ■ **ci-après** *adv* below ■ **ci-contre** *adv* opposite ■ **ci-dessous** *adv* below ■ **ci-dessus** *adv* above ■ **ci-gît** *adv* here lies... (*on gravestones*) ■ **ci-joint, -e** (*mpl* **ci-joints**, *fpl* **ci-jointes**) 1. *adj* **le document ci-joint** the enclosed document 2. *adv* **vous trouverez ci-joint copie de...** please find enclosed a copy of...

**cible** [sibl] *nf* target

**ciboulette** [sibulɛt] *nf* chives

**cicatrice** [sikatris] *nf* scar

**cicatriser** [sikatrize] 1. *vt & vi* to heal 2. **se cicatriser** *vpr* to heal ■ **cicatrisation** *nf* healing

**cidre** [sidr] *nm* cider

**Cie** (*abr de* **compagnie**) Co

**ciel** [sjɛl] *nm* a) (*pl* **ciels**) sky; **à ciel ouvert** open-air b) (*pl* **cieux** [sjø]) [paradis] heaven

**cierge** [sjɛrʒ] *nm* REL candle

**cigale** [sigal] *nf* cicada

**cigare** [sigar] *nm* cigar ■ **cigarette** *nf* cigarette

**cigogne** [sigɔɲ] *nf* stork

**cil** [sil] *nm* eyelash

**cime** [sim] *nf* [d'arbre] top; [de montagne] peak

**ciment** [simɑ̃] *nm* cement

**cimetière** [simtjɛr] *nm* cemetery; [d'église] graveyard

**cinéaste** [sineast] *nm* film maker ■ **ciné-club** (*pl* **ciné-clubs**) *nm* film club ■ **cinéphile** *nmf Br* film or *Am* movie enthusiast

**cinéma** [sinema] *nm* [art, industrie] *Br* cinema, *Am* movies; [salle] *Br* cinema,

*Am* movie theater; *Can* **cinéma maison** home *Br* theatre *or Am* theater; **cinéma d'art et d'essai** [art, industrie] arthouse (movies); [salle] arthouse, *Br* cinema *or Am* movie theater; **faire du cinéma** to be a movie actor /actress; **aller au cinéma** to go to the *Br* cinema *or Am* movies ▪ **cinématographique** *adj* film; **industrie cinématographique** film industry

**cinglé, -e** [sɛ̃gle] *adj Fam* crazy

**cingler** [sɛ̃gle] *vt* to lash ▪ **cinglant, -e** *adj* [pluie] lashing; [remarque] cutting

**cinq** [sɛ̃k] **1.** *adj inv* five **2.** *nm inv* five ▪ **cinquième** *adj & nmf* fifth; **un cinquième** a fifth

**cinquante** [sɛ̃kɑ̃t] *adj & nm inv* fifty ▪ **cinquantaine** *nf* **une cinquantaine (de)** about fifty; **avoir la cinquantaine** to be about fifty ▪ **cinquantenaire** *nm* [anniversaire] fiftieth anniversary ▪ **cinquantième** *adj & nmf* fiftieth

**cintre** [sɛ̃tr] *nm* coathanger

**cirage** [siraʒ] *nm* (shoe) polish

**circonscription** [sirkɔ̃skripsjɔ̃] *nf* division, district; **circonscription (électorale)** *Br* constituency, *Am* district

**circonscrire** [sirkɔ̃skrir] *vt* [encercler] to encircle; [incendie] to contain

**circonspect, -e** [sirkɔ̃spɛ, -ɛkt] *adj* cautious, circumspect

**circonstance** [sirkɔ̃stɑ̃s] *nf* circumstance; **en pareilles circonstances** under such circumstances

**circuit** [sirkɥi] *nm* ÉLEC & SPORT circuit; [chemin] way; **circuit automobile** racing circuit; **circuit touristique** (organized) tour

**circulaire** [sirkyler] **1.** *adj* circular **2.** *nf* [lettre] circular

**circulation** [sirkylasjɔ̃] *nf* [du sang, de l'information, de billets] circulation; [d'autos] traffic; **circulation routière / aérienne** road /air traffic ▪ **circuler** *vi* [sang, air, information] to circulate; [voyageur] to travel; [train, bus] to run

**cire** [sir] *nf* wax; [pour meubles] polish ▪ **ciré** *nm* [vêtement] oilskin(s) ▪ **cirer** *vt* to polish ▪ **cireux, -euse** *adj* waxy

**cirque** [sirk] *nm* [spectacle] circus

**cisailles** [sizaj] *nfpl* (garden) shears ▪ **ciseau, -x** *nm* [de menuisier] chisel; **(une paire de) ciseaux** (a pair of) scissors

**ciseler** [sizle] *vt* to chisel; [or, argent] to chase

**citadelle** [sitadɛl] *nf* citadel ▪ **citadin, -e 1.** *adj* city **2.** *nmf* city dweller

**cité** [site] *nf* [ville] city; [immeubles] *Br* housing estate, *Am* housing development; **cité universitaire** *Br* (students') halls of residence, *Am* university dormitory complex

**citer** [site] *vt* [auteur, texte] to quote; [énumérer] to name ▪ **citation** *nf* quotation

**citerne** [sitɛrn] *nf* tank

**citoyen, -enne** [sitwajɛ̃, -ɛn] *nmf* citizen ▪ **citoyenneté** *nf* citizenship

**citron** [sitrɔ̃] *nm* **a)** lemon; **citron pressé** freshly squeezed lemon juice served with water and sugar; **citron vert** lime **b)** *Can* AUTO lemon, dud ▪ **citronnade** *nf Br* lemon squash, *Am* lemonade

**citrouille** [sitruj] *nf* pumpkin

**civet** [sive] *nm* stew

**civière** [sivjɛr] *nf* stretcher

**civil, -e** [sivil] **1.** *adj* [guerre, mariage, droits] civil; [non militaire] civilian; [courtois] civil; **année civile** calendar year **2.** *nmf* civilian; **dans le civil** in civilian life; **en civil** [policier] in plain clothes ▪ **civilité** *nf* civility

**civilisation** [sivilizasjɔ̃] *nf* civilization ▪ **civilisé, -e** *adj* civilized

**civique** [sivik] *adj* civic; SCOL **instruction civique** civics

**clair, -e** [klɛr] **1.** *adj* [net, limpide, évident] clear; [éclairé, pâle] light; **bleu / vert clair** light blue /green **2.** *adv* [voir] clearly; **il fait clair** it's light **3.** *nm* **en clair** in plain language; **clair de lune** moonlight

**clairière** [klɛrjɛr] *nf* clearing

**clairon** [klɛrɔ̃] *nm* bugle ; [soldat] bugler

**clairsemé, -e** [klɛrsəme] *adj* [auditoire, population] sparse

**clairvoyant, -e** [klɛrvwajɑ̃, -ɑ̃t] *adj* perceptive

**clameur** [klamœr] *nf* clamour

**clan** [klɑ̃] *nm* [tribu] clan ; *Péj* [groupe] clique

**clandestin, -e** [klɑ̃dɛstɛ̃, -in] *adj* [rencontre] clandestine ; [mouvement] underground ; [travailleur] illegal

**clapier** [klapje] *nm* (rabbit) hutch

**clapoter** [klapɔte] *vi* [vagues] to lap

**claque** [klak] *nf Fam* slap

**claquer** [klake] **1.** *vt* [porte] to slam **2.** *vi* [porte] to slam ; [drapeau] to flap ; [talons] to click ; [coup de feu] to ring out ; **elle claque des dents** her teeth are chattering **3. se claquer** *vpr* **se claquer un muscle** to pull a muscle ■ **claquement** *nm* [de porte] slam(ming)

**claquettes** [klakɛt] *nfpl* tap dancing ; **faire des claquettes** to do tap dancing

**clarifier** [klarifje] *vt* to clarify ■ **clarification** *nf* clarification

**clarinette** [klarinɛt] *nf* clarinet

**clarté** [klarte] *nf* [lumière] light ; [transparence] clearness ; *Fig* [d'explications] clarity ; **avec clarté** clearly

**classe** [klɑs] *nf* [catégorie, leçon, élèves] class ; **en classe de sixième** *Br* in the first year, *Am* in fifth grade ; **aller en classe** to go to school ; **avoir de la classe** [personne] to have class ; **(salle de) classe** classroom ; **de première classe** [billet, compartiment] first-class ; **classe ouvrière/moyenne** working / middle class ; **classes préparatoires** *school preparing students for "grandes écoles" entrance exams* ; **classe sociale** social class

**classer** [klɑse] **1.** *vt* [objets] to classify ; [papiers] to file ; **classer une affaire** to consider a matter closed **2. se classer** *vpr* **se classer parmi les meilleurs** to rank among the best ; *SPORT* **se classer troisième** to be placed third ■ **classé, -e** *adj* [monument] listed ;

[au tennis] seeded ■ **classement** *nm* classification ; [de papiers] filing ; [rang] place ; *SPORT* table ■ **classeur** *nm* [meuble] filing cabinet ; [portefeuille] ring binder

**classifier** [klasifje] *vt* to classify ■ **classification** *nf* classification

**classique** [klasik] **1.** *adj* [période] classical ; [typique, conventionnel] classic **2.** *nm* [œuvre] classic ; [auteur] classical author

**claustrophobe** [klostrofob] *adj* claustrophobic

**clavecin** [klavsɛ̃] *nm* harpsichord

**clavicule** [klavikyl] *nf* collarbone

**clavier** [klavje] *nm* keyboard

**clé, clef** [kle] **1.** *nf* [de porte] key ; [outil] *Br* spanner, *Am* wrench ; **fermer qch à clé** to lock sth ; **clé de contact** ignition key ; *MUS* **clé de sol** treble clef ; *Fig* **clé de voûte** cornerstone **2.** *adj* key ; **poste clé** key post

**clément, -e** [klemɑ̃, -ɑ̃t] *adj* [juge] clement ; [temps] mild ■ **clémence** *nf* [de juge] clemency ; [de temps] mildness

**clémentine** [klemɑ̃tin] *nf* clementine

**clerc** [klɛr] *nm REL* cleric ; **clerc de notaire** ≃ solicitor's clerk ■ **clergé** *nm* clergy ■ **clérical, -e, -aux** *adj* clerical

**clic** [klik] *nm ORDINAT* click ; **clic droit** right-click ; **clic gauche** left-click ; **d'un clic de souris** at the click of a mouse

**Clic-Clac®** [klikklak] *nm* pull-out sofa bed

**cliché** [kliʃe] *nm* [photo] photo ; [negative] negative ; [idée] cliché

**client, -e** [klijɑ̃, -ɑ̃t] *nmf* [de magasin] customer ; [d'avocat] client ; [d'hôtel] guest ; [de taxi] fare ■ **clientèle** *nf* [de magasin] customers ; [d'avocat] practice

**cligner** [kliɲe] *vi* **cligner des yeux** to blink ; **cligner de l'œil** to wink

**clignoter** [kliɲɔte] *vi* [lumière, voyant] to flash ■ **clignotant** *nm* [de voiture] *Br* indicator, *Am* flasher ; **mettre son clignotant** to indicate

**clim** [klim] *(abr de* **climatisation***) nf Fam* air conditioning, AC

**climat** [klima] *nm* [de région] & *Fig* climate ■ **climatique** *adj* climatic

**climatisation** [klimatizɑsjɔ̃] *nf* air-conditioning ■ **climatisé, -e** *adj* air-conditioned

**clin d'œil** [klɛ̃dœj] *(pl* **clins d'œil)** *nm* wink; **faire un clin d'œil à qn** to wink at sb; **en un clin d'œil** in a flash

**clinique** [klinik] *nf* [hôpital] clinic

**clinquant, -e** [klɛ̃kɑ̃, -ɑ̃t] *adj* flashy

**clip** [klip] *nm* [vidéo] (music) video

**cliquer** [klike] *vi* ORDINAT to click ■ **cliquable** [klikabl] *adj* clickable; **plan cliquable** sensitive map

**cliqueter** [klikte] *vi* [monnaie, clefs] to jingle ■ **cliquetis** *nm* [de monnaie, de clefs] jingling

**clivage** [klivaʒ] *nm* [de société] divide; [de parti] split

**clochard, -e** [klɔʃar, -ard] *nmf* tramp

**cloche** [klɔʃ] **1.** *nf* [d'église] bell; **cloche à fromage** covered cheese dish **2.** *adj* *Fam* **ce qu'il peut être cloche, celui-là !** he can be such an idiot! ■ **clocher 1.** *nm* [d'église] bell tower, steeple **2.** *vi* *Fam* **il y a quelque chose qui cloche** there's something wrong somewhere

**cloche-pied** [klɔʃpje] ■ **à cloche-pied** *adv* **sauter à cloche-pied** to hop

**clodo** [klɔdo] *nmf* *Fam* tramp, *Am* bum

**cloison** [klwazɔ̃] *nf* [entre pièces] partition

**cloître** [klwatr] *nm* [de monastère] cloister; [pour moines] monastery; [pour religieuses] convent

**clonage** [klɔnaʒ] *nm* cloning; **clonage thérapeutique** therapeutic cloning ■ **clone** [klon] *nm* clone ■ **cloner** *vt* to clone

**clopin-clopant** [klɔpɛ̃klɔpɑ̃] *adv* **aller clopin-clopant** to hobble along

**cloque** [klɔk] *nf* [au pied] blister

**clore** [klɔr] *vt* [réunion] to conclude; [débat] to close; ORDINAT **clore une session** to log off

**clos, -e** [klo, kloz] **1.** *adj* [porte, volets] closed; **l'incident est clos** the matter is closed; **espace clos** enclosed space **2.** *nm* enclosure

**clôture** [klotyr] *nf* [barrière] fence; [de réunion] conclusion; [de débat] closing; [de Bourse] close ■ **clôturer** *vt* [terrain] to enclose

**clou** [klu] *nm* [pointe] nail; [de spectacle] main attraction; **les clous** [passage] *Br* the pedestrian crossing, *Am* the crosswalk; **clou de girofle** clove ■ **clouer** *vt* [au mur] to nail up; [ensemble] to nail together; **cloué au lit** confined to (one's) bed

**clown** [klun] *nm* clown; **faire le clown** to clown around

**club** [klœb] *nm* club

**cm** *(abr de* **centimètre)** cm

**CM** *(abr de* **cours moyen)** *nm* **CM1** *fourth year of primary school;* **CM2** *fifth year of primary school*

**coacher** [kotʃe] *vt* **a)** [entraîner] to coach **b)** [conseiller] to advise ■ **coaching** [kotʃiŋ] *nm* coaching

**coalition** [kɔalisjɔ̃] *nf* coalition

**cobaye** [kɔbaj] *nm* [animal] & *Fig* guinea pig

**cocaïne** [kɔkain] *nf* cocaine

**coccinelle** [kɔksinɛl] *nf* [insecte] *Br* ladybird, *Am* ladybug; [voiture] Beetle

**cocher** [kɔʃe] *vt* *Br* to tick, *Am* to check

**cochon, -onne** [kɔʃɔ̃, -ɔn] **1.** *nm* [animal] pig; [viande] pork; **cochon d'Inde** guinea pig **2.** *nmf* [personne sale] pig **3.** *adj* [histoire, film] dirty ■ **cochonnerie** *nf* [chose sans valeur] trash, *Br* rubbish; [obscénité] smutty remark; **manger des cochonneries** to eat junk food

**cocktail** [kɔktɛl] *nm* [boisson] cocktail; [réunion] cocktail party; **cocktail de fruits** fruit cocktail

**coco** [koko] *nm* **noix de coco** coconut

**cocon** [kokɔ̃] *nm* *pr* & *Fig* cocoon

**cocu, -e** [kɔky] **1.** *adj* **il est cocu** his wife's cheating on him **2.** *nm* cuckold

**code** [kɔd] nm [symboles, lois & ORDI-NAT] code; **passer le code** [du permis de conduire] to sit the written part of one's driving test; **codes** Br dipped head-lights, Am low beams; **le Code de la route** Br the Highway Code, Am the traf-fic regulations; JUR **code civil/pénal** civil/penal code; **code confidentiel** security code; [de carte bancaire] PIN; **code postal** Br postcode, Am zip code ■ **code-barres** (pl **codes-barres**) nm bar code ■ **coder** vt to code

**coéquipier, -ère** [kɔekipje, -ɛr] nmf team-mate

**cœur** [kœr] nm heart; CARTES [couleur] hearts; **avoir mal au cœur** to feel sick; **par cœur** (off) by heart; **de bon cœur** [volontiers] willingly; [rire] heartily

**coexister** [kɔɛgziste] vi to coexist

**coffre** [kɔr] nm [meuble] chest; [pour objets de valeur] safe; [de voiture] Br boot, Am trunk; **coffre à bagages** [d'avion] baggage compartment; **coffre à jouets** toy box ■ **coffre-fort** (pl **coffres-forts**) nm safe ■ **coffret** nm [petit coffre] box; **coffret à bijoux** Br jewellery or Am jewelry box

**cogner** [kɔɲe] 1. vt [heurter] to knock 2. vi [buter] to bang (**sur/contre** on) 3. **se cogner** vpr to bang oneself; **se cogner la tête contre qch** to bang one's head on sth; **se cogner à qch** to bang into sth

**cohabiter** [kɔabite] vi to live together; **cohabiter avec qn** to live with sb

**cohérent, -e** [kɔerɑ̃, -ɑ̃t] adj [discours] coherent; [attitude] consistent ■ **co-hérence** nf [de discours] coherence; [d'attitude] consistency ■ **cohésion** nf cohesion

**cohue** [kɔy] nf crowd

**coiffe** [kwaf] nf headdress

**coiffer** [kwafe] 1. vt Fig [surmonter] to cap; [service] to head; **coiffer qn de qch** to put sth on sb's head; **elle est bien coiffée** her hair is lovely 2. **se coiffer** vpr to do one's hair; **se coif-fer de qch** to put sth on ■ **coiffant, e** adj **gel coiffant** styling gel

**coiffeur, -euse** [kwafœr, -øz] nmf hairdresser ■ **coiffeuse** nf [meuble] dressing table ■ **coiffure** nf [chapeau] headgear; [coupe de cheveux] hairstyle

**coin** [kwɛ̃] nm [angle] corner; [endroit] spot; [cale] wedge; **faire le coin** to be on the corner; **dans le coin** in the area; Fam **le petit coin** [toilettes] the smallest room in the house

**coincer** [kwɛ̃se] 1. vt [mécanisme, tiroir] to jam; [caler] to wedge 2. vi [mé-canisme, tiroir] to jam 3. **se coincer** vpr [mécanisme] to jam; **se coincer le doigt dans la porte** to catch one's finger in the door ■ **coincé, -e** adj **a)** [mécanisme, tiroir] stuck, jammed **b)** Fam [personne] hung up

**coïncider** [kɔɛ̃side] vi to coincide (**avec** with) ■ **coïncidence** nf coincidence

**col** [kɔl] nm [de chemise] collar; GÉOG col; **col en V** V-neck; **col roulé** Br polo neck, Am turtleneck

**colère** [kɔlɛr] nf anger; **être en colère** (**contre qn**) to be angry (with sb); **se mettre en colère** to get angry (**contre** with) ■ **coléreux, -euse** adj [per-sonne] quick-tempered

**colimaçon** [kɔlimasɔ̃] ■ **en colima-çon** adv **escalier en colimaçon** spiral staircase

**colin** [kɔlɛ̃] nm [merlu] hake; [lieu noir] coley

**colique** [kɔlik] nf Br diarrhoea, Am diarrhea

**colis** [kɔli] nm parcel

**collaborer** [kɔlabɔre] vi collaborate (**avec** with); **collaborer à qch** [projet] to take part in sth ■ **collaborateur, -trice** nmf [aide] assistant ■ **collabo-ration** nf [aide] collaboration

**collage** [kɔlaʒ] nm [œuvre, jeu] collage

**collant, -e** [kɔlɑ̃, -ɑ̃t] 1. adj [papier] sticky; [vêtement] skin-tight 2. nm Br tights, Am pantihose

**colle** [kɔl] nf [transparente] glue; [blanche] paste; Fam [question] poser; Fam [retenue] detention

**collecte** [kɔlɛkt] nf collection ■ **col-lecter** vt to collect

**collectif, -ive** [kɔlɛktif, -iv] *adj* collective ▪ **collectivité** *nf* [groupe] community

**collection** [kɔlɛksjɔ̃] *nf* [ensemble] collection; **faire la collection de qch** to collect sth ▪ **collectionner** *vt* to collect ▪ **collectionneur, -euse** *nmf* collector

**collector** [kɔlɛktɔr] *nm* collector's edition; **coffret collector** boxed collector's set

**collège** [kɔlɛʒ] *nm* [école] school ▪ **collégien** *nm* schoolboy ▪ **collégienne** *nf* schoolgirl

**collègue** [kɔlɛg] *nmf* colleague

**coller** [kɔle] **1.** *vt* [timbre] to stick; [à la colle transparente] to glue; [à la colle blanche & ORDINAT] to paste; [enveloppe] to stick (down); [deux objets] to stick together; [affiche] to stick up; *Fam* **coller un élève** [en punition] to keep a pupil in; *Fam* **être collé** [à un examen] to fail **2.** *vi* a) [adhérer] to stick b) [être adapté] **coller à qch** [vêtement] to cling to sth; *Fig* to fit in with sth, to adhere to sth **3. se coller** *vpr* **se coller contre un mur** to flatten oneself against a wall

**collier** [kɔlje] *nm* [bijou] necklace; [de chien] collar

**colline** [kɔlin] *nf* hill

**collision** [kɔlizjɔ̃] *nf* [de véhicules] collision; **entrer en collision avec qch** to collide with sth

**colloque** [kɔlɔk] *nm* [conférence] seminar

**colmater** [kɔlmate] *vt* to fill in

**coloc** [kɔlɔk] *Fam* **1.** *nmf* [colocataire - dans une maison] *Br* housemate, *Am* roommate; [dans un appartement] *Br* flat-mate, *Am* roommate **2.** *nf* [colocation] shared accommodation; **habiter en coloc** to live in shared accommodation

**colocataire** [kɔlɔkatɛr] *nmf* ADMIN co-tenant; [gén] *Br* flatmate, *Am* roommate ▪ **colocation** [kɔlɔkasjɔ̃] *nf* joint tenancy, joint occupancy

**colombe** [kɔlɔ̃b] *nf* dove

**Colombie** [kɔlɔ̃bi] *nf* **la Colombie** Columbia ▪ **colombien, -enne 1.** *adj* Columbian **2.** *nmf* **Colombien, Colombienne** Columbian

**colon** [kɔlɔ̃] *nm* [pionnier] settler, colonist

**colonel** [kɔlɔnɛl] *nm* [d'infanterie] colonel

**colonial, -e, -aux** [kɔlɔnjal, -jo] *adj* colonial

**colonie** [kɔlɔni] *nf* colony; **colonie de vacances** *Br* (children's) holiday camp, *Am* summer camp

**coloniser** [kɔlɔnize] *vt* to colonize

**colonne** [kɔlɔn] *nf* column; ANAT **colonne vertébrale** spine

**colorer** [kɔlɔre] *vt* to colour; **colorer qch en vert** to colour sth green ▪ **colorant, -e** *nm* [pour teindre] colorant; [alimentaire] colouring ▪ **colorier** *vt* [dessin] to colour (in) ▪ **coloris** *nm* [nuance] shade ▪ **coloriser** [kɔlɔrize] *vt* CINÉ *Br* to colourize, *Am* to colorize

**colosse** [kɔlɔs] *nm* giant ▪ **colossal, -e, -aux** *adj* colossal

**colporter** [kɔlpɔrte] *vt* [marchandises] to hawk; [rumeur] to spread

**colza** [kɔlza] *nm* rape

**COM** [kɔm] *(abr de* **collectivités d'outre-mer)** *nm* overseas territories of France that have the status of "collectivities" but not of full departments

**coma** [kɔma] *nm* coma; **être dans le coma** to be in a coma

**combat** [kɔ̃ba] *nm* [bataille] & *Fig* fight; **combat de boxe** boxing match ▪ **combatif, -ive** *adj* combative ▪ **combattant, e** *nmf* [en guerre] combatant; [dans bagarre] fighter

**combattre** [kɔ̃batr] **1.** *vt* [personne, incendie] to fight (against); [maladie] to fight **2.** *vi* to fight ▪ **combattant, -e 1.** *adj* [troupes] fighting **2.** *nmf* combattant; **anciens combattants** veterans

**combien** [kɔ̃bjɛ̃] **1.** *adv* a) [en quantité] how much; [en nombre] how many; **combien d'argent** how much money; **combien de temps** how long; **combien de gens** how many people;

**combien y a-t-il d'ici à... ?** how far is it to...? **b)** [comme] how; **tu verras combien il est bête** you'll see how silly he is **2.** *nm inv Fam* **le combien sommes-nous ?** what's the date?

**combinaison** [kɔ̃binɛzɔ̃] *nf* [assemblage] combination ; [vêtement de travail] *Br* boiler suit, *Am* coveralls ; **combinaison de ski** ski suit

**combiner** [kɔbine] **1.** *vt* [unir] to combine **2. se combiner** *vpr* to combine ■ **combiné** *nm* [de téléphone] receiver

**comble** [kɔ̃bl] **1.** *adj* [salle, bus] packed; THÉÂT **faire salle comble** to have a full house **2.** *nm* **le comble du bonheur** the height of happiness; **c'est un** *ou* **le comble !** that's the last straw!

**combler** [kɔ̃ble] *vt* [trou] to fill in ; [lacune] to fill; [désir] to satisfy

**combustible** [kɔ̃bystibl] **1.** *adj* combustible **2.** *nm* fuel ■ **combustion** *nf* combustion

**comédie** [kɔmedi] *nf* comedy; **jouer la comédie** to act; **comédie musicale** musical ■ **comédien** *nm* actor ■ **comédienne** *nf* actress

**comestible** [kɔmɛstibl] *adj* edible

**comète** [kɔmɛt] *nf* comet

**coming out** [kɔmiŋawt] *nm inv* **faire son coming out** to come out; **son coming out remonte à 2010** he came out in 2010

**comique** [kɔmik] **1.** *adj* [amusant] funny, comical ; [acteur, rôle] comedy **2.** *nm* [genre] comedy ; [acteur] comic actor

**comité** [kɔmite] *nm* committee; **comité d'entreprise** works council

**commandant** [kɔmɑ̃dɑ̃] *nm* [de navire] captain; [grade - dans l'infanterie] major ; [dans l'aviation] squadron leader; AVIAT **commandant de bord** captain

**commande** [kɔmɑ̃d] *nf* **a)** [achat] order; **sur commande** to order; **passer une commande** to place an order **b)** TECH [action, manette] control ; ORDINAT

command; **commande à distance** remote control; **à commande vocale** voice-activated

**commandement** [kɔmɑ̃dmɑ̃] *nm* [ordre, autorité] command; REL Commandment

**commander** [kɔmɑ̃de] **1.** *vt* [diriger, exiger] to command; [marchandises] to order (**à** from) **2.** *vi* **commander à qn de faire qch** to command sb to do sth

**commando** [kɔmɑ̃do] *nm* commando

**comme** [kɔm] **1.** *adv* **a)** [devant nom, pronom] like ; **comme moi / elle** like me / her; **comme cela** like that; **qu'as-tu comme diplômes ?** what do you have in the way of certificates?; **les femmes comme les hommes** men and women alike; **P comme pomme** p as in 'pomme' **b)** [devant proposition] as ; **il écrit comme il parle** he writes as he speaks; **comme si** as if; **comme pour faire qch** as if to do sth **2.** *adv* [exclamatif] **regarde comme il pleut !** look how it's raining!; **comme c'est petit !** isn't it small! **3.** *conj* [cause] as, since ; **comme tu es mon ami...** as *or* since you're my friend...; **comme elle entrait** (just) as she was coming in

**commémorer** [kɔmemɔre] *vt* to commemorate ■ **commémoration** *nf* commemoration

**commencer** [kɔmɑ̃se] *vt & vi* to begin, to start (**à faire** to do, doing ; **par qch** with sth ; **par faire** by doing); **pour commencer** to begin with ■ **commencement** *nm* beginning, start; **au commencement** at the beginning *or* start

**comment** [kɔmɑ̃] *adv* how; **comment le sais-tu ?** how do you know?; **comment t'appelles-tu ?** what's your name?; **comment est-il ?** what is he like?; **comment va-t-il ?** how is he?; **comment faire ?** what's to be done?; **comment ?** [pour faire répéter] pardon?

**commentaire** [kɔmɑ̃tɛr] *nm* [remarque] comment; [de radio, de télévision] commentary ■ **commentateur, -trice** *nmf* commentator ■ **commenter** *vt* to comment (up)on

**commérages** [kɔmeraʒ] *nmpl* gossip

**commerçant, -e** [kɔmɛrsɑ̃, -ɑ̃t] **1.** *nmf* trader ; [de magasin] shopkeeper **2.** *adj* **rue commerçante** shopping street

**commerce** [kɔmɛrs] *nm* [activité, secteur] trade ; [affaires, magasin] business ; **commerce de proximité** *Br* local shop, *Am* local store ■ **commercial, -e, -aux** *adj* commercial ■ **commercialisation** *nf* marketing ■ **commercialiser** *vt* to market

**commère** [kɔmɛr] *nf* gossip

**commettre** [kɔmɛtr] *vt* [meurtre] to commit ; [erreur] to make

**commis** [kɔmi] *nm* [de magasin] shop assistant ; [de bureau] clerk

**commissaire** [kɔmisɛr] *nm* [de course] steward ; **commissaire (de police)** *Br* ≃ police superintendent, *Am* ≃ police captain ■ **commissariat** *nm* **commissariat (de police)** (central) police station

**commission** [kɔmisjɔ̃] *nf* [course] errand ; [message] message ; [comité] commission, committee ; COMM [pourcentage] commission (**sur** on) ; **faire les commissions** to go shopping

**commode** [kɔmɔd] **1.** *adj* [pratique] handy ; **pas commode** [pas aimable] awkward ; [difficile] tricky **2.** *nf Br* chest of drawers, *Am* dresser ■ **commodité** *nf* convenience

**commotion** [kɔmosjɔ̃] *nf* MÉD shock ; **commotion cérébrale** concussion

**commun, -e** [kɔmœ̃, -yn] **1.** *adj* [non exclusif, répandu, vulgaire] common ; [cuisine] shared ; [démarche] joint ; **peu commun** uncommon ; **ami commun** mutual friend ; **en commun** in common ; **mettre qch en commun** to share sth **2.** *nm* **hors du commun** out of the ordinary

**communauté** [kɔmynote] *nf* [collectivité] community ; **la Communauté (économique) européenne** the European (Economic) Community ; **la**

**Communauté d'États indépendants** the Commonwealth of Independent States ■ **communautaire** *adj* [de la CE] Community ; **vie communautaire** community life

**commune** [kɔmyn] *nf* [municipalité] commune ■ **communal, -e, -aux** *adj Br* ≃ council, *Am* ≃ district ; **école communale** ≃ local *Br* primary or *Am* grade school

**communicant, e** [kɔmynikɑ̃, ɑ̃t] **1.** *adj* communicating ; **deux chambres communicantes** two *Br* connecting or *Am* adjoining rooms **2.** *nm* communicator

**communicatif, -ive** [kɔmynikatif, -iv] *adj* [personne] communicative ; [rire] infectious

**communication** [kɔmynikɑsjɔ̃] *nf* communication ; **communication téléphonique** telephone call ; **je vous passe la communication** I'll put you through ; **la communication est mauvaise** the line is bad

**communion** [kɔmynjɔ̃] *nf* communion ; REL (Holy) Communion

**communiquer** [kɔmynike] **1.** *vt* to communicate (**à** to) ; [maladie] to pass on (**à** to) **2.** *vi* [personne, pièces] to communicate (**avec** with) **3. se communiquer** *vpr* to spread (**à** to) ■ **communiqué** *nm* [avis] communiqué ; **communiqué de presse** press release

**communisme** [kɔmynism] *nm* communism ■ **communiste** *adj* & *nmf* communist

**commutateur** [kɔmytatœr] *nm* [bouton] switch

**compact, -e** [kɔ̃pakt] **1.** *adj* [foule, amas] dense ; [appareil] compact **2.** *nm* [CD] compact disc

**compacter** [kɔ̃pakte] *vt* [gén] to compact ; ORDINAT [données] to compress

**compagne** [kɔ̃paɲ] *nf* [camarade] companion ; [concubine] partner

**compagnie** [kɔ̃paɲi] *nf* [présence, société, soldats] company ; **tenir compagnie à qn** to keep sb company

**compagnon** [kɔ̃paɲɔ̃] nm companion; [concubin] partner; **compagnon de jeu** playmate; **compagnon de route** travelling companion

**comparaître** [kɔ̃parɛtr] vi [devant tribunal] to appear (in court) (**devant** before)

**comparer** [kɔ̃pare] vt to compare (**à** to, with) ■ **comparable** adj comparable (**à** to, with) ■ **comparaison** nf comparison (**avec** with); **en comparaison de…** in comparison with…

**compartiment** [kɔ̃partimɑ̃] nm compartment; **compartiment à bagages** [de car] luggage compartment; **compartiment fumeurs** smoking compartment

**compas** [kɔ̃pa] nm MATH Br (pair of) compasses, Am compass; NAUT compass

**compassion** [kɔ̃pasjɔ̃] nf compassion

**compatible** [kɔ̃patibl] adj [gén & ORDINAT] compatible (**avec** with) ■ **compatibilité** nf compatibility

**compatir** [kɔ̃patir] vi to sympathize ■ **compatissant, -e** adj compassionate, sympathetic

**compatriote** [kɔ̃patrijɔt] nmf compatriot

**compenser** [kɔ̃pɑ̃se] **1.** vt [perte, défaut] to make up for, to compensate for **2.** vi to compensate ■ **compensation** nf [de perte] compensation; **en compensation** in compensation (**de** for)

**compétent, -e** [kɔ̃petɑ̃, -ɑ̃t] adj competent ■ **compétence** nf competence; **compétences** [connaissances] skills, abilities

**compétition** [kɔ̃petisjɔ̃] nf [rivalité] competition; [épreuve sportive] event; **être en compétition avec qn** to compete with sb; **sport de compétition** competitive sport ■ **compétitif, -ive** adj competitive

**compiler** [kɔ̃pile] vt to compile

**complaire** [kɔ̃plɛr] ■ **se complaire** vpr **se complaire dans qch/à faire qch** to delight in sth/in doing sth

**complaisant, -e** [kɔ̃plɛzɑ̃, -ɑ̃t] adj [bienveillant] kind, obliging; [satisfait] complacent ■ **complaisance** nf [bienveillance] kindness; [vanité] complacency

**complément** [kɔ̃plemɑ̃] nm [reste] rest; GRAM complement; **un complément d'information** additional information; **complément d'objet direct/indirect** direct/indirect object ■ **complémentaire** adj complementary; [détails] additional

**complet, -ète** [kɔ̃plɛ, -ɛt] **1.** adj [entier, absolu] complete; [train, hôtel, théâtre] full; [pain] wholemeal **2.** nm [costume] suit

**compléter** [kɔ̃plete] **1.** vt [collection, formation] to complete; [formulaire] to fill in; [somme] to make up **2. se compléter** vpr to complement each other

**complexe** [kɔ̃plɛks] **1.** adj complex **2.** nm [sentiment, construction] complex; **avoir des complexes** to have a hang-up ■ **complexé, -e** adj Fam hung up (**par** about) ■ **complexer** vt [personne] **arrête, tu vas le complexer** stop, you'll give him a complex ■ **complexité** nf complexity

**complication** [kɔ̃plikasjɔ̃] nf [ennui & MÉD] complication; [complexité] complexity

**complice** [kɔ̃plis] **1.** nm accomplice **2.** adj [regard] knowing; [silence] conniving; **être complice de qch** to be a party to sth ■ **complicité** nf complicity

**compliment** [kɔ̃plimɑ̃] nm compliment; **faire des compliments à qn** to pay sb compliments ■ **complimenter** vt to compliment (**sur** on)

**compliquer** [kɔ̃plike] **1.** vt to complicate **2. se compliquer** vpr [situation] to get complicated; **se compliquer la vie** to make life complicated for oneself ■ **compliqué, -e** adj complicated

**complot** [kɔ̃plo] nm conspiracy (**contre** against)

**comporter** [kɔ̃pɔrte] **1.** vt [contenir] to contain; [être constitué de] to consist of **2. se comporter** *vpr* [personne] to behave ■ **comportement** [-əmɑ̃] *nm* *Br* behaviour, *Am* behavior

**composer** [kɔ̃poze] **1.** *vt* [faire partie de] to make up ; [musique, poème] to compose ; [numéro de téléphone] to dial ; TYP to set ; **être composé de qch** to be made up *or* composed of sth **2.** *vi* [étudiant] to take a test **3. se composer** *vpr* **se composer de qch** to be made up *or* composed of sth ■ **composant** *nm* component ■ **composante** *nf* component

**compositeur, -trice** [kɔ̃pozitœr, -tris] *nmf* [musicien] composer ; [typographe] typesetter

**composition** [kɔ̃pozisjɔ̃] *nf* [de musique, de poème] composing ; TYP typesetting ; [éléments] composition ; [d'aliment] ingredients ; [examen] test

**composter** [kɔ̃pɔste] *vt* [billet] to cancel

**compote** [kɔ̃pɔt] *nf Br* stewed fruit, *Am* sauce ; **compote de pommes** *Br* stewed apples, *Am* applesauce

**compréhensible** [kɔ̃preɑ̃sibl] *adj* [justifié] understandable ; [clair] comprehensible ■ **compréhensif, -ive** *adj* understanding ■ **compréhension** *nf* understanding

**comprendre** [kɔ̃prɑ̃dr] **1.** *vt* [par l'esprit, par les sentiments] to understand ; [être composé de] to consist of ; [comporter] to include ; **mal comprendre qch** to misunderstand sth ; **je n'y comprends rien** I can't make head or tail of it **2. se comprendre** *vpr* **ça se comprend** that's understandable

**compresse** [kɔ̃prɛs] *nf* compress

**compresser** [kɔ̃prese] *vt* ORDINAT to compress

**comprimé** [kɔ̃prime] *nm* [médicament] tablet

**comprimer** [kɔ̃prime] *vt* [gaz, artère] to compress

**compris, -e** [kɔ̃pri, -iz] **1.** *pp de* **comprendre 2.** *adj* [inclus] included (**dans** in) ; **y compris** including

**compromettre** [kɔ̃prɔmɛtr] *vt* [personne] to compromise ; [sécurité] to jeopardize ■ **compromis** *nm* compromise

**comptabiliser** [kɔ̃tabilize] *vt* [compter] to count

**comptabilité** [kɔ̃tabilite] *nf* [comptes] accounts ; [science] book-keeping, accounting ; [service] accounts department ■ **comptable** *nmf* accountant

**comptant** [kɔ̃tɑ̃] **1.** *adv* **payer comptant** to pay (in) cash **2.** *nm* **acheter au comptant** to buy for cash

**compte** [kɔ̃t] *nm* **a)** [de banque, de commerçant, ORDINAT & INTERNET] account ; [calcul] calculation ; **avoir un compte en banque** to have a bank account ; **faire ses comptes** to do one's accounts ; **compte chèque** *Br* current account, *Am* checking account ; **compte à rebours** countdown

**b)** [expressions] **en fin de compte** all things considered ; **tenir compte de qch** to take sth into account ; **compte tenu de qch** considering sth ; **se rendre compte de qch** to realize sth ; **rendre compte de qch** [exposer] to report on sth ; [justifier] to account for sth ; **travailler à son compte** to be self-employed ; *Fig* **être loin du compte** to be wide of the mark

■ **compte-gouttes** *nm inv* dropper ; *Fig* **au compte-gouttes** in dribs and drabs

**compter** [kɔ̃te] **1.** *vt* [calculer] to count ; [prévoir] to allow ; [include] to include ; **compter faire qch** [espérer] to expect to do sth ; [avoir l'intention de] to intend to do sth ; **compter qch à qn** [facturer] to charge sb for sth ; **sans compter** [sans parler de] not to mention... **2.** *vi* [calculer, être important] to count ; **compter sur qn/qch** to count *or* rely on sb/sth ; **à compter de demain** as from tomorrow **3. se compter** *vpr* **ses membres se comptent par milliers** it has thousands of members ■ **compteur** *nm* meter ; **compteur de gaz** gas meter; AUTO **compteur kilométrique** *Br* milometer, *Am* odometer ; AUTO **compteur de vitesse** speedometer

**compte rendu** [kɔ̃trɑ̃dy] *(pl* **comptes rendus)** *nm* report ; [de livre, de film] review

**comptoir** [kɔ̃twar] *nm* [de magasin] counter ; [de café] bar

**comte** [kɔ̃t] *nm* [noble] count ; [en Grande-Bretagne] earl ■ **comtesse** *nf* countess

**concéder** [kɔ̃sede] *vt* [victoire, but] to concede; **concéder qch à qn** to grant sb sth

**concentrer** [kɔ̃sɑ̃tre] **1.** *vt* to concentrate ; [attention] to focus **2. se concentrer** *vpr* [réfléchir] to concentrate ■ **concentration** *nf* concentration ■ **concentré, -e 1.** *adj* [lait] condensed ; [attentif] concentrating (hard) **2.** *nm* **concentré de tomates** tomato purée

**concept** [kɔ̃sept] *nm* concept ■ **conception** *nf* [d'idée] conception ; [création] design; **conception assistée par ordinateur** computer-aided design

**concerner** [kɔ̃serne] *vt* to concern; **en ce qui concerne** concerning, as regards; **en ce qui me concerne** as far as I'm concerned ■ **concernant** *prép* concerning

**concert** [kɔ̃ser] *nm* [de musique] concert

**concerter** [kɔ̃serte] ■ **se concerter** *vpr* to consult together ■ **concertation** *nf* consultation

**concession** [kɔ̃sesjɔ̃] *nf* [compromis] concession (**à** to) ; [terrain] plot ■ **concessionnaire** *nmf* dealer

**concevoir** [kɔ̃səvwar] **1.** *vt* [enfant, plan, idée] to conceive ; [produit] to design ; [comprendre] to understand **2. se concevoir** *vpr* ça se conçoit that's understandable ■ **concevable** *adj* conceivable

**concierge** [kɔ̃sjerʒ] *nmf* caretaker, *Am* janitor

**concilier** [kɔ̃silje] *vt* [choses] to reconcile

**concis, -e** [kɔ̃si, -is] *adj* concise

**conclure** [kɔ̃klyr] *vt* [terminer] to conclude ; [accord] to finalize ; [marché] to clinch ■ **concluant, -e** *adj* conclusive ■ **conclusion** *nf* conclusion; **tirer une conclusion de qch** to draw a conclusion from sth

**concombre** [kɔ̃kɔ̃br] *nm* cucumber

**concorder** [kɔ̃kɔrde] *vi* [preuves, dates, témoignages] to tally (**avec** with)

**concourir** [kɔ̃kurir] *vi* SPORT to compete (**pour** for) ; [converger] to converge; **concourir à qch / faire qch** to contribute to sth / to do sth

**concours** [kɔ̃kur] *nm* [examen] competitive examination ; [jeu] competition ; [aide] assistance; **concours de beauté** beauty contest

**concret, -ète** [kɔ̃kre, -et] *adj* concrete ■ **concrétiser 1.** *vt* [rêve] to realize ; [projet] to carry out **2. se concrétiser** *vpr* to materialize

**conçu, -e** [kɔ̃sy] **1.** *pp de* **concevoir** **2.** *adj* **conçu pour faire qch** designed to do sth

**concubine** [kɔ̃kybin] *nf* JUR cohabitant ■ **concubinage** *nm* cohabitation; **vivre en concubinage** to cohabit

**concurrent, -e** [kɔ̃kyrɑ̃, -ɑ̃t] *nmf* competitor ■ **concurrence** *nf* competition ; **faire concurrence à** to compete with ; **jusqu'à concurrence de 100 euros** up to the amount of 100 euros ■ **concurrencer** *vt* to compete with

**condamnation** [kɔ̃danɑsjɔ̃] *nf* JUR [jugement] conviction (**pour** for) ; [peine] sentence (**à** to) ; [critique] condemnation; **condamnation à mort** death sentence

**condamner** [kɔ̃dane] *vt* [blâmer] to condemn ; JUR to sentence (**à** to) ; [porte] to block up ; **condamner qn à une amende** to fine sb ; **condamner qn à qch** [forcer à] to force sb into sth ■ **condamné, -e 1.** *adj* [malade] terminally ill **2.** *nmf* [prisonnier] convicted person

**condensation** [kɔ̃dɑ̃sasjɔ̃] *nf* condensation

**condescendant, -e** [kɔ̃desɑ̃dɑ̃, -ɑ̃t] *adj* condescending

**condition** [kɔ̃disjɔ̃] *nf* [état, stipulation, sort] condition ; [classe sociale] station ; **conditions** [circonstances] conditions ; [de contrat] terms ; **conditions de vie** living conditions ; **conditions météo** weather conditions ; **à condition de faire qch, à condition que l'on fasse qch** providing or provided (that) one does sth ■ **conditionnel, -elle 1.** *adj* conditional **2.** *nm* GRAM conditional ■ **sans condition 1.** *adj* unconditional **2.** *adv* unconditionally

**conditionner** [kɔ̃disjɔne] *vt* [être la condition de] to govern ; [emballer] to package ; [personne] to condition ■ **conditionnement** *nm* [emballage] packaging ; [de personne] conditioning

**condoléances** [kɔ̃dɔleɑ̃s] *nfpl* condolences

**conducteur, -trice** [kɔ̃dyktœr, -tris] **1.** *nmf* [de véhicule, de train] driver **2.** *adj* ÉLEC **fil conducteur** lead (wire)

**conduire** [kɔ̃dɥir] **1.** *vt* [troupeau] to lead ; [voiture] to drive ; [moto] to ride ; [électricité] to conduct ; **conduire qn à** [accompagner] to take sb to **2.** *vi* [en voiture] to drive ; **conduire à** [lieu] to lead to **3. se conduire** *vpr* to behave

**conduit** [kɔ̃dɥi] *nm* [tuyau] pipe

**conduite** [kɔ̃dɥit] *nf* [de véhicule] driving (**de** of) ; [d'entreprise] management ; [tuyau] pipe ; [comportement] conduct, behaviour ; **conduite à gauche / droite** [volant] left-hand / right-hand drive ; **conduite de gaz** gas main

**cône** [kon] *nm* cone

**confection** [kɔ̃fɛksjɔ̃] *nf* [réalisation] making (**de** of) ; [industrie] clothing industry ; **vêtements de confection** ready-to-wear clothes ■ **confectionner** *vt* to make

**confédération** [kɔ̃federasjɔ̃] *nf* confederation

**conférence** [kɔ̃ferɑ̃s] *nf* [réunion] conference ; [exposé] lecture ; **conférence de presse** press conference

**conférer** [kɔ̃fere] *vt* [titre] to confer (**à** on)

**confesser** [kɔ̃fese] **1.** *vt* REL to confess **2. se confesser** *vpr* REL to confess (**à** to) ■ **confession** *nf* REL confession

**confettis** [kɔ̃feti] *nmpl* confetti

**confiance** [kɔ̃fjɑ̃s] *nf* confidence ; **faire confiance à qn, avoir confiance en qn** to trust sb ; **de confiance** [mission] of trust ; [personne] trustworthy ; **confiance en soi** self-confidence ; **avoir confiance en soi** to be self-confident ■ **confiant, -e** *adj* [qui fait confiance] trusting ; [optimiste] confident ; [qui a confiance en soi] self-confident

**confidence** [kɔ̃fidɑ̃s] *nf* confidence ; **faire une confidence à qn** to confide in sb ■ **confident, -e** *nmf* confidant, *f* confidante ■ **confidentiel, -elle** *adj* confidential

**confier** [kɔ̃fje] **1.** *vt* **confier qch à qn** [laisser] to entrust sb with sth ; [dire] to confide sth to sb **2. se confier** *vpr* **se confier à qn** to confide in sb

**configuration** [kɔ̃figyrasjɔ̃] *nf* [disposition] layout ; ORDINAT configuration ; ORDINAT **configuration par défaut** default setting ■ **configurer** *vt* ORDINAT to configure

**confiner** [kɔ̃fine] **1.** *vt* to confine **2.** *vi* **confiner à** to border on **3. se confiner** *vpr* **se confiner chez soi** to shut oneself up indoors

**confins** [kɔ̃fɛ̃] *nmpl* confines ; **aux confins de** on the edge of

**confirmation** [kɔ̃firmasjɔ̃] *nf* confirmation

**confirmer** [kɔ̃firme] **1.** *vt* to confirm (**que** that) **2. se confirmer** *vpr* [nouvelle] to be confirmed ; [tendance] to continue

**confiserie** [kɔ̃fizri] *nf* [magasin] *Br* sweetshop, *Am* candy store ; **confiseries** [bonbons] *Br* sweets, *Am* candy ■ **confiseur** *nm* confectioner

**confisquer** [kɔ̃fiske] *vt* to confiscate (**à qn** from sb)

**confit, -e** [kɔ̃fi] **1.** *adj* [fruits] candied **2.** *nm* **confit d'oie** potted goose

**confiture** [kɔ̃fityr] *nf* jam; **confiture de fraises** strawberry jam

**conflit** [kɔ̃fli] *nm* conflict; **conflits sociaux** industrial disputes ■ **conflictuel, -elle** *adj* [intérêts] conflicting

**confondre** [kɔ̃fɔ̃dr] **1.** *vt* [choses, personnes] to mix up, to confuse; [consterner] to astound; [démasquer] to confound; **confondre qn/qch avec qn/qch** to mistake sb/sth for sb/sth **2. se confondre** *vpr* [couleurs, intérêts] to merge; **se confondre en excuses** to apologize profusely

**conforme** [kɔ̃fɔrm] *adj* **conforme à** in accordance with; [modèle] true to ■ **conformément** *adv* **conformément à** in accordance with

**conformer** [kɔ̃fɔrme] **1.** *vt* to model **2. se conformer** *vpr* to conform (**à** to)

**conformiste** [kɔ̃fɔrmist] *adj* & *nmf* conformist

**conformité** [kɔ̃fɔrmite] *nf* conformity (**à** with)

**confort** [kɔ̃fɔr] *nm* comfort ■ **confortable** *adj* comfortable

**confrère** [kɔ̃frɛr] *nm* [de profession] colleague

**confronter** [kɔ̃frɔ̃te] *vt* [personnes] to confront; [expériences, résultats] to compare; **confronté à** [difficulté] confronted with ■ **confrontation** *nf* [face-à-face] confrontation; [comparaison] comparison

**confus, -e** [kɔ̃fy, -yz] *adj* [esprit, situation, explication] confused; [gêné] embarrassed ■ **confusion** *nf* [désordre, méprise] confusion; [gêne] embarrassment

**congé** [kɔ̃ʒe] *nm* [vacances] *Br* holiday, *Am* vacation; [arrêt de travail] leave; [avis de renvoi] notice; **donner son congé à qn** [employé, locataire] to give notice to sb; **être en congé** to be on holiday *or* off work; **congé de maladie** sick leave; **congé de maternité** maternity leave; **congé de paternité** paternity leave; **congés payés** *Br* paid holidays, *Am* paid vacation

**congédier** [kɔ̃ʒedje] *vt* to dismiss

**congeler** [kɔ̃ʒle] *vt* to freeze ■ **congelé, -e** *adj* frozen; **les produits congelés** frozen food ■ **congélateur** *nm* freezer ■ **congélo** [kɔ̃ʒelo] *nm Fam* freezer

**congère** [kɔ̃ʒɛr] *nf* snowdrift

**Congo** [kɔ̃go] *nm* **le Congo** Congo ■ **congolais, -e 1.** *adj* Congolese **2.** *nmf* **Congolais, Congolaise** Congolese

**congratuler** [kɔ̃gratyle] *vt* to congratulate (**sur** on)

**congrès** [kɔ̃grɛ] *nm* conference; **le Congrès** [aux États-Unis] the Congress

**conique** [kɔnik] *adj* conical

**conjoint, -e** [kɔ̃ʒwɛ̃, -wɛ̃t] **1.** *adj* joint **2.** *nm* spouse; **conjoints** husband and wife

**conjonction** [kɔ̃ʒɔ̃ksjɔ̃] *nf* [union] union; GRAM conjunction

**conjonctivite** [kɔ̃ʒɔ̃ktivit] *nf* MÉD conjunctivitis

**conjoncture** [kɔ̃ʒɔ̃ktyr] *nf* circumstances

**conjugal, -e, -aux** [kɔ̃ʒygal, -o] *adj* [bonheur] marital; [vie] married; [devoir] conjugal

**conjuguer** [kɔ̃ʒyge] **1.** *vt* [verbe] to conjugate; [efforts] to combine **2. se conjuguer** *vpr* [verbe] to be conjugated ■ **conjugaison** *nf* GRAM conjugation

**conjurer** [kɔ̃ʒyre] *vt* [danger] to avert; [mauvais sort] to ward off; **conjurer qn de faire qch** to beg sb to do sth ■ **conjuré, -e** *nmf* conspirator

**connaissance** [kɔnɛsɑ̃s] *nf* [savoir] knowledge; [personne] acquaintance; **à ma connaissance** to my knowledge; **avoir connaissance de qch** to be aware of sth; **faire connaissance avec qn** to get to know sb; **perdre/reprendre connaissance** to lose/

regain consciousness; **sans connaissance** unconscious ■ **connaisseur** *nm* connoisseur

**connaître** [kɔnɛtr] **1.** *vt* [personne, endroit, faits] to know; [rencontrer] to meet; [famine, guerre] to experience; **faire connaître qch** to make sth known; **faire connaître qn** [présenter] to introduce sb; [rendre célèbre] to make sb known **2. se connaître** *vpr* **nous nous connaissons déjà** we've met before; **s'y connaître en qch** to know all about sth

**connecter** [kɔnɛkte] *vt* [appareil électrique] to connect; ORDINAT **connecté** online ■ **connexion** *nf* connection

**connu, -e** [kɔny] **1.** *pp de* **connaître 2.** *adj* [célèbre] well-known

**conquérir** [kɔ̃kerir] *vt* [pays, sommet] to conquer; [marché] to capture ■ **conquérant, -e** *nmf* conqueror ■ **conquête** *nf* conquest

**consacrer** [kɔ̃sakre] **1.** *vt* [temps] to devote (**à** to); [église] to consecrate; [entériner] to establish **2. se consacrer** *vpr* **se consacrer à** to devote oneself to

**consciemment** [kɔ̃sjamɑ̃] *adv* consciously

**conscience** [kɔ̃sjɑ̃s] *nf* **a)** [esprit] consciousness; **avoir / prendre conscience de qch** to be / become aware of sth; **perdre conscience** to lose consciousness **b)** [morale] conscience; **avoir bonne / mauvaise conscience** to have a clear / guilty conscience ■ **consciencieux, -euse** *adj* conscientious

**conscient, -e** [kɔ̃sjɑ̃, -ɑ̃t] *adj* [lucide] conscious; **conscient de qch** aware or conscious of sth

**conscrit** [kɔ̃skri] *nm* conscript

**consécutif, -ive** [kɔ̃sekytif, -iv] *adj* consecutive; **consécutif à** following upon

**conseil** [kɔ̃sɛj] *nm* **a) un conseil** [recommandation] a piece of advice; **des conseils** advice **b)** [assemblée] council, committee; **conseil d'administration** board of directors; SCOL **conseil de classe** *staff meeting with participation of class representatives*; POL **conseil des ministres** cabinet meeting

**conseiller¹** [kɔ̃seje] *vt* [guider] to advise; **conseiller qch à qn** to recommend sth to sb; **conseiller à qn de faire qch** to advise sb to do sth

**conseiller², -ère** [kɔ̃seje, -ɛr] *nmf* [expert] consultant, adviser; **conseiller d'orientation** careers adviser

**consentir** [kɔ̃sɑ̃tir] **1.** *vi* **consentir à qch / à faire qch** to consent to sth / to do sth **2.** *vt* [prêt] to grant (**à** to) ■ **consentement** *nm* consent

**conséquence** [kɔ̃sekɑ̃s] *nf* consequence; **en conséquence** accordingly; **sans conséquence** [sans importance] of no importance

**conservateur, -trice** [kɔ̃sɛrvatœr, -tris] **1.** *adj* & *nmf* POL Conservative **2.** *nmf* [de musée] curator; [de bibliothèque] librarian **3.** *nm* [alimentaire] preservative

**conservatoire** [kɔ̃sɛrvatwar] *nm* school, academy

**conserve** [kɔ̃sɛrv] *nf* **conserves** canned *or Br* tinned food; **en conserve** canned, *Br* tinned

**conserver** [kɔ̃sɛrve] **1.** *vt* to keep; [fruits, tradition] to preserve **2. se conserver** *vpr* [aliment] to keep

**considérable** [kɔ̃siderabl] *adj* considerable

**considérer** [kɔ̃sidere] *vt* to consider (**que** that); **tout bien considéré** all things considered ■ **considération** *nf* [respect] regard, esteem; **prendre qch en considération** to take sth into consideration

**consigne** [kɔ̃siɲ] *nf* [instructions] orders; [de bouteille] deposit; **consigne (à bagages)** *Br* left-luggage office, *Am* checkroom; **consigne automatique** lockers ■ **consigner** *vt* [bouteille] to charge a deposit on; [bagages] *Br* to deposit in the left-luggage office, *Am* to check; [écrire] to record; [punir - soldat] to confine to barracks

**consistant, -e** [kɔ̃sistɑ̃, -ɑ̃t] *adj* [sauce, bouillie] thick ; [repas] substantial ■ **consistance** *nf* consistency

**consister** [kɔ̃siste] *vi* **consister en qch** to consist of sth; **consister à faire qch** to consist in doing sth

**consœur** [kɔ̃sœr] *nf* female colleague

**console** [kɔ̃sɔl] *nf* [d'ordinateur, de jeux] console ; ORDINAT **console de jeux** games console

**consoler** [kɔ̃sɔle] **1.** *vt* to comfort, to console **2. se consoler** *vpr* **se consoler de qch** to get over sth ■ **consolation** *nf* comfort, consolation

**consolider** [kɔ̃sɔlide] *vt* [mur, position] to strengthen ■ **consolidation** *nf* strengthening

**consommateur, -trice** [kɔ̃sɔmatœr, -tris] *nmf* consumer ; [au café] customer ■ **consommation** *nf* [de nourriture, d'électricité] consumption ; [de voiture] fuel consumption ; [boisson] drink

**consommer** [kɔ̃sɔme] **1.** *vt* [aliment, carburant] to consume ; [mariage] to consummate **2.** *vi* [au café] to drink

**consonne** [kɔ̃sɔn] *nf* consonant

**consortium** [kɔ̃sɔrsjɔm] *nm* [entreprises] consortium

**conspirer** [kɔ̃spire] *vi* [comploter] to conspire (**contre** against); **conspirer à faire qch** [concourir] to conspire to do sth ■ **conspirateur, -trice** *nmf* conspirator ■ **conspiration** *nf* conspiracy

**constant, -e** [kɔ̃stɑ̃, -ɑ̃t] **1.** *adj* constant **2.** *nf* MATH **constante** constant ■ **constamment** [-amɑ̃] *adv* constantly ■ **constance** *nf* constancy

**constat** [kɔ̃sta] *nm* (official) report

**constater** [kɔ̃state] *vt* [observer] to note (**que** that) ; JUR [enregistrer] to record ; [décès] to certify ■ **constatation** *nf* [remarque] observation

**constellation** [kɔ̃stɛlasjɔ̃] *nf* constellation

**consterner** [kɔ̃sterne] *vt* to dismay

**constipation** [kɔ̃stipasjɔ̃] *nf* constipation

**constituer** [kɔ̃stitɥe] **1.** *vt* [composer] to make up ; [équivaloir à] to constitute ; [former] to form ; **constitué de** made up of **2. se constituer** *vpr* **se constituer prisonnier** to give oneself up

**constitution** [kɔ̃stitysjɔ̃] *nf* [santé, lois] constitution ; [de gouvernement] formation ■ **constitutionnel, -elle** *adj* constitutional

**constructeur** [kɔ̃stryktœr] *nm* [bâtisseur] builder ; [fabricant] maker (**de** of) ; **constructeur automobile** car manufacturer ■ **constructif, -ive** *adj* constructive ■ **construction** *nf* [de pont, de route, de maison] building, construction (**de** of) ; [édifice] building ; **en construction** under construction

**construire** [kɔ̃strɥir] *vt* [maison, route] to build

**consul** [kɔ̃syl] *nmf* consul ■ **consulat** *nm* consulate

**consultant, e** [kɔ̃syltɑ̃, ɑ̃t] *nmf* consultant ; **consultant en gestion** management consultant

**consulter** [kɔ̃sylte] **1.** *vt* to consult **2.** *vi* [médecin] to see patients, *Br* to take surgery **3. se consulter** *vpr* [discuter] to confer ■ **consultation** *nf* consultation

**consumer** [kɔ̃syme] *vt* [brûler] to consume

**contact** [kɔ̃takt] *nm* contact ; **être en contact avec qn** to be in contact with sb ; **prendre contact** to get in touch (**avec** with) ; AUTO **mettre / couper le contact** to switch on / off ■ **contacter** *vt* to contact

**contagieux, -euse** [kɔ̃taʒjø, -øz] *adj* [maladie, personne] contagious

**contaminer** [kɔ̃tamine] *vt* to contaminate ■ **contamination** *nf* contamination

**conte** [kɔ̃t] *nm* tale ; **conte de fées** fairy tale

**contempler** [kɔ̃tɑ̃ple] *vt* to gaze at, to contemplate

**contemporain, -e** [kɔ̃tɑ̃pɔrɛ̃, -ɛn] *adj* & *nmf* contemporary

**contenance** [kɔ̃tnɑ̃s] *nf* **a)** [de récipient] capacity **b)** [allure] bearing

**contenir** [kɔ̃tnir] *vt* [renfermer] to contain ; [contrôler] to hold back, to contain ■ **conteneur** *nm* container

**content, -e** [kɔ̃tɑ̃, -ɑ̃t] **1.** *adj* pleased, happy (**de** with ; **de faire** to do) ; **être content de soi** to be pleased with oneself **2.** *nm* **avoir son content** to have had one's fill (**de** of)

**contenter** [kɔ̃tɑ̃te] **1.** *vt* [satisfaire] to satisfy ; [faire plaisir à] to please **2. se contenter** *vpr* **se contenter de qch** to content oneself with sth ■ **contentement** *nm* contentment, satisfaction

**contentieux** [kɔ̃tɑ̃sjø] *nm* [querelles] dispute ; JUR litigation ; [service] legal department

**contenu** [kɔ̃tny] *nm* [de paquet, de bouteille] contents ; [de lettre, de film] content

**conter** [kɔ̃te] *vt* to tell (**à** to) ■ **conteur, -euse** *nmf* storyteller

**contestable** [kɔ̃tɛstabl] *adj* debatable

**contestation** [kɔ̃tɛstasjɔ̃] *nf* protest

**conteste** [kɔ̃tɛst] ■ **sans conteste** *adv* indisputably

**contester** [kɔ̃tɛste] **1.** *vt* to dispute **2.** *vi* **faire qch sans contester** to do sth without protest ■ **contesté, -e** *adj* [théorie, dirigeant] controversial

**contexte** [kɔ̃tɛkst] *nm* context

**contigu, -ë** [kɔ̃tigy] *adj* [maisons] adjoining ; **contigu à qch** adjoining sth

**continent** [kɔ̃tinɑ̃] *nm* continent ; [opposé à une île] mainland ■ **continental, -e, -aux** *adj* [climat, plateau] continental

**contingent** [kɔ̃tɛ̃ʒɑ̃] *nm* MIL contingent ; [quota] quota

**continu, -e** [kɔ̃tiny] *adj* continuous ■ **continuel, -elle** *adj* [ininterrompu] continuous ; [qui se répète] continual ■ **continuellement** *adv* [de façon ininterrompue] continuously ; [de façon répétitive] continually

**continuer** [kɔ̃tinɥe] **1.** *vt* [études, efforts, politique] to continue, to carry on with ; **continuer à** *ou* **de faire qch** to continue *or* carry on doing sth **2.** *vi* to continue, to go on ■ **continuation** *nf* continuation

**continuité** [kɔ̃tinɥite] *nf* continuity

**contour** [kɔ̃tur] *nm* outline

**contourner** [kɔ̃turne] *vt* to go round ; *Fig* [difficulté, loi] to get round

**contraceptif, -ive** [kɔ̃trasɛptif, -iv] *adj & nm* contraceptive

**contracter** [kɔ̃trakte] **1.** *vt* [muscle, habitude, dette] to contract **2. se contracter** *vpr* [muscle] to contract ; [personne] to tense up ■ **contraction** *nf* contraction

**contractuel, -elle** [kɔ̃traktɥɛl] **1.** *adj* [politique] contractual **2.** *nmf* Br ≈ traffic warden, Am ≈ traffic policeman, f traffic policewoman

**contradiction** [kɔ̃tradiksjɔ̃] *nf* contradiction ; **être en contradiction avec qch** to contradict sth ■ **contradictoire** *adj* contradictory

**contraindre** [kɔ̃trɛ̃dr] **1.** *vt* to compel, to force (**à faire** to do) **2. se contraindre** *vpr* to compel *or* force oneself (**à faire** to do) ■ **contraignant, -e** *adj* restricting ■ **contrainte** *nf* [obligation, limitation] constraint ; **sous la contrainte** under duress

**contraire** [kɔ̃trɛr] **1.** *adj* [opposé] conflicting ; **contraire à qch** contrary to sth ; **en sens contraire** in the opposite direction **2.** *nm* opposite ; **(bien) au contraire** on the contrary ■ **contrairement** *adv* **contrairement à** contrary to ; **contrairement à qn** unlike sb

**contrarier** [kɔ̃trarje] *vt* [projet, action] to thwart ; [personne] to annoy ■ **contrariant, -e** *adj* [situation] annoying ; [personne] contrary ■ **contrariété** *nf* annoyance

**contraste** [kɔ̃trast] *nm* contrast ■ **contraster** *vi* to contrast (**avec** with)

**contrat** [kɔ̃tra] *nm* contract

**contravention** [kɔ̃travɑ̃sjɔ̃] *nf* [amende] fine ; [pour stationnement interdit] (parking) ticket

**contre** [kɔ̃tr] **1.** *prép* against ; [en échange de] (in exchange) for ; **échanger qch contre qch** to exchange sth for sth ; **fâché contre qn** angry with sb ; **six voix contre deux** six votes to two ; **Nîmes contre Arras** [match] Nîmes versus *or* against Arras ; **sirop contre la toux** cough mixture ; *Fam* **par contre** on the other hand **2.** *nm* [au volley, au basket] block **3.** *adv* [juxtaposition] **prends la rampe et appuie-toi contre** take hold of the rail and lean against it ■ **contre-attaque** *nf* counter-attack ■ **contre-attaquer** *vt* to counter-attack

**contrebalancer** [kɔ̃trəbalɑ̃se] *vt* to counterbalance ; *Fig* [compenser] to offset

**contrebande** [kɔ̃trəbɑ̃d] *nf* [activité] smuggling ; [marchandises] contraband ; **tabac de contrebande** smuggled tobacco ; **faire de la contrebande** to smuggle goods ■ **contrebandier, -ère** *nmf* smuggler

**contrebas** [kɔ̃trəba] ■ **en contrebas** *adv* & *prép* (down) below ; **en contrebas de** below

**contrebasse** [kɔ̃trəbas] *nf* [instrument] double-bass

**contrecarrer** [kɔ̃trəkare] *vt* to thwart

**contrecœur** [kɔ̃trəkœr] ■ **à contrecœur** *adv* reluctantly

**contrecoup** [kɔ̃trəku] *nm* repercussions

**contre-courant** [kɔ̃trəkurɑ̃] ■ **à contre-courant** *adv* [nager] against the current

**contredire** [kɔ̃trədir] **1.** *vt* to contradict **2. se contredire** *vpr* [soi-même] to contradict oneself ; [l'un l'autre] to contradict each other

**contrée** [kɔ̃tre] *nf Litt* [region] region ; [pays] land

**contre-espionnage** [kɔ̃trεspjɔnaʒ] *nm* counter-espionage

**contrefaçon** [kɔ̃trəfasɔ̃] *nf* [pratique] counterfeiting ; [produit] fake ■ **contrefaire** *vt* [écriture] to disguise ; [argent] to counterfeit ; [signature] to forge

**contre-indiqué, e** *(mpl* **contre-indiqués**, *fpl* **contre-indiquées)** [kɔ̃trɛ̃dike] *adj* MÉD contraindicated

**contre-jour** [kɔ̃trəʒur] ■ **à contre-jour** *adv* against the light

**contremaître** [kɔ̃trəmεtr] *nm* foreman

**contremarque** [kɔ̃trəmark] *nf* [pour sortir d'un spectacle] *Br* pass-out ticket

**contre-offensive** [kɔ̃trɔfɑ̃siv] *(pl* **contre-offensives)** *nf* counter-offensive

**contrepartie** [kɔ̃trəparti] *nf* compensation ; **en contrepartie** in return (de for)

**contre-pied** [kɔ̃trəpje] *nm* SPORT **prendre son adversaire à contre-pied** to wrongfoot one's opponent

**contreplaqué** [kɔ̃trəplake] *nm* plywood

**contrepoids** [kɔ̃trəpwa] *nm* counterbalance

**contrepoison** [kɔ̃trəpwazɔ̃] *nm* antidote

**contrer** [kɔ̃tre] *vt* [personne, attaque] to counter

**contresens** [kɔ̃trəsɑ̃s] *nm* misinterpretation ; [en traduisant] mistranslation ; **prendre une rue à contresens** to go down / up a street the wrong way

**contresigner** [kɔ̃trəsiɲe] *vt* to countersign

**contretemps** [kɔ̃trətɑ̃] *nm* hitch, mishap

**contrevenir** [kɔ̃trəvnir] *vi* **contrevenir à** to contravene

**contribuable** [kɔ̃tribɥabl] *nmf* taxpayer

**contribuer** [kɔ̃tribɥe] *vi* to contribute (à to) ; **contribuer à faire qch** to help (to) do sth

**contributif, ive** [kɔ̃tribytif, iv] *adj* ORDINAT **logiciel contributif** shareware ; **encyclopédie contributive** collaborative encyclopedia

**contribution** [kɔ̃tribysjɔ̃] *nf* contribution (à to) ; [impôt] tax ; **contributions** [administration] tax office

**contrôle** [kɔ̃trol] nm [vérification] checking (**de** of) ; [surveillance] monitoring ; [maîtrise] control ; SCOL test ; **avoir le contrôle de qch** to have control of sth ; **le contrôle des naissances** birth control ; **contrôle de soi** self-control ; **contrôle fiscal** tax inspection

**contrôler** [kɔ̃trole] **1.** vt [vérifier] to check ; [surveiller] to monitor ; [maîtriser] to control **2. se contrôler** vpr to control oneself ■ **contrôleur, -euse** nmf [de train] Br (ticket) inspector ; [de bus] conductor, f conductress ; **contrôleur aérien** air-traffic controller

**contrordre** [kɔ̃trɔrdr] nm countermand ; **sauf contrordre** unless otherwise instructed

**controverse** [kɔ̃trɔvɛrs] nf controversy ■ **controversé, -e** adj controversial

**contumace** [kɔ̃tymas] ■ **par contumace** adv JUR in absentia

**contusion** [kɔ̃tyzjɔ̃] nf bruise

**convaincre** [kɔ̃vɛ̃kr] vt to convince (**de** of) ; **convaincre qn de faire qch** to persuade sb to do sth ■ **convaincant, -e** adj convincing ■ **convaincu, -e** adj convinced (**de** of ; **que** that) ; [partisan] committed

**convalescent, -e** [kɔ̃valɛsɑ̃, -ɑ̃t] adj & nmf convalescent ■ **convalescence** nf convalescence ; **être en convalescence** to be convalescing

**convenable** [kɔ̃vnabl] adj [approprié] suitable ; [acceptable, décent] decent

**convenance** [kɔ̃vnɑ̃s] nf **faire qch à sa convenance** to do sth at one's own convenience

**convenir** [kɔ̃vnir] **1.** vi **convenir à** [être fait pour] to be suitable for ; [plaire à, aller à] to suit ; **convenir de qch** [lieu, prix] to agree upon sth ; **convenir de faire qch** to agree to do sth ; **convenir que...** to admit that... **2.** v impers **il convient de...** it is advisable to... ; [selon les usages] it is proper to... ; **il fut convenu que...** [décidé] it was agreed that... ■ **convenu, -e** adj [décidé] agreed

**convention** [kɔ̃vɑ̃sjɔ̃] nf [accord] agreement ; [règle] convention ; **convention collective** collective agreement

**conventionné, -e** [kɔ̃vɑ̃sjone] adj [médecin, clinique] attached to the health system, Br ≃ NHS ; **médecin non conventionné** private doctor

**conventionnel, -elle** [kɔ̃vɑ̃sjonɛl] adj conventional

**convergence** [kɔ̃vɛrʒɑ̃s] nf convergence ■ **converger** vi to converge (**vers** on)

**conversation** [kɔ̃vɛrsasjɔ̃] nf conversation

**conversion** [kɔ̃vɛrsjɔ̃] nf [changement] conversion (**en** into) ; [à une doctrine] conversion (**à** to) ■ **convertible 1.** adj convertible (**en** into) **2.** nm sofa bed ■ **convertir 1.** vt [changer] to convert (**en** into) ; [à une doctrine] to convert (**à** to) **2. se convertir** vpr [à une doctrine] to be converted (**à** to) ■ **convertisseur** [kɔ̃vɛrtisœr] nm ORDINAT & TV **convertisseur d'images** image converter

**conviction** [kɔ̃viksjɔ̃] nf [certitude, croyance] conviction ; **avoir la conviction que...** to be convinced that...

**convier** [kɔ̃vje] vt Formel to invite (**à** to ; **à faire** to do)

**convive** [kɔ̃viv] nmf guest

**convivial, -e, -aux** [kɔ̃vivjal, -jo] adj convivial ; ORDINAT user-friendly

**convoi** [kɔ̃vwa] nm [véhicules, personnes] convoy ; [train] train ; **convoi funèbre** funeral procession

**convoiter** [kɔ̃vwate] vt [poste, richesses] to covet

**convoquer** [kɔ̃vɔke] vt [employé, postulant] to call in ; **convoquer qn à un examen** to notify sb of an examination ■ **convocation** nf [lettre] notice to attend ; **convocation à un examen** notification of an examination

**convoyer** [kɔ̃vwaje] vt [troupes] to convoy ; [fonds] to transport under armed guard

**convulsion** [kɔ̃vylsjɔ̃] nf convulsion

**cookie** [kuki] *nm* **a)** [petit gâteau] *Br* biscuit, *Am* cookie **b)** ORDINAT cookie

**coopérer** [kɔɔpere] *vi* to cooperate (**à** in, **avec** with) ■ **coopératif, -ive** *adj* & *nf* cooperative ■ **coopération** *nf* cooperation (**entre** between) ; POL overseas development

**coordonner** [kɔɔrdɔne] *vt* to coordinate (**à** *ou* **avec** with) ■ **coordination** *nf* coordination ■ **coordonnées** *nfpl* [adresse, téléphone] address and telephone number

**copain** [kɔpɛ̃] *nm Fam* [camarade] pal ; [petit ami] boyfriend

**copeau, -x** [kɔpo] *nm* [de bois] shaving

**copie** [kɔpi] *nf* [manuscrit, double] copy ; SCOL [devoir, examen] paper ; **copie d'écran** screen dump

**copier** [kɔpje] *vt* [texte, musique, document & SCOL] to copy (**sur** from) ■ **copier-coller** [kɔpjekɔle] *nm inv* ORDINAT copy and paste ■ **copieur, -euse 1.** *nmf* [élève] copier **2.** *nm* [machine] photocopier

**copieux, -euse** [kɔpjø, -øz] *adj* [repas] copious ; [portion] generous

**copine** [kɔpin] *nf Fam* [camarade] pal ; [petite amie] girlfriend

**copropriété** [kɔprɔprijete] *nf* joint ownership

**coq** [kɔk] *nm* cock, *Am* rooster

**coque** [kɔk] *nf* [de noix] shell ; [de navire] hull ; [fruit de mer] cockle

**coquelet** [kɔklɛ] *nm* cockerel

**coquelicot** [kɔkliko] *nm* poppy

**coqueluche** [kɔklyʃ] *nf* [maladie] whooping cough

**coquet, -ette** [kɔkɛ, -ɛt] *adj* [intérieur] charming ; *Fam* [somme] tidy

**coquetier** [kɔktje] *nm* egg-cup

**coquille** [kɔkij] *nf* shell ; [faute d'imprimerie] misprint ; CULIN **coquille Saint-Jacques** scallop ■ **coquillage** *nm* [mollusque] shellfish *inv* ; [coquille] shell

**coquin, -e** [kɔkɛ̃, -in] **1.** *adj* [sourire, air] mischievous ; [sous-vêtements] naughty **2.** *nmf* rascal

**cor** [kɔr] *nm* [instrument] horn ; [du-rillon] corn

**corail, -aux** [kɔraj, -o] *nm* coral

**Coran** [kɔrɑ̃] *nm* **le Coran** the Koran

**corbeau, -x** [kɔrbo] *nm* [oiseau] crow

**corbeille** [kɔrbɛj] *nf* **a)** [panier] basket ; **corbeille à linge** washing basket, *Am* hamper ; **corbeille à pain** breadbasket ; **corbeille à papier** wastepaper basket **b)** [à la Bourse] trading floor **c)** THÉÂT dress circle **d)** ORDINAT trash (can)

**corbillard** [kɔrbijar] *nm* hearse

**corde** [kɔrd] *nf* [lien] rope ; [de raquette, de violon] string ; **corde à linge** washing *or* clothes line ; **corde à sauter** *Br* skipping rope, *Am* jump-rope ; **cordes vocales** vocal cords ■ **cordée** *nf* roped party ■ **corder** *vt* [raquette] to string

**cordial, -e, -aux** [kɔrdjal, -o] **1.** *adj* [accueil, personne] cordial **2.** *nm* [remontant] tonic ■ **cordialement** *adv* [saluer] warmly, cordially ; [en fin de lettre] kind regards

**cordon** [kɔrdɔ̃] *nm* [de tablier, de sac] string ; [de rideau] cord ; [de policiers] cordon ; ANAT **cordon ombilical** umbilical cord ■ **cordon-bleu** *(pl* **cordons-bleus)** *nm Fam* gourmet cook

**cordonnier** [kɔrdɔnje] *nm* shoe repairer ■ **cordonnerie** *nf* [boutique] shoe repairer's shop

**Corée** [kɔre] *nf* **la Corée** Korea ■ **coréen, -enne 1.** *adj* Korean **2.** *nmf* **Coréen, Coréenne** Korean

**coriace** [kɔrjas] *adj* [viande, personne] tough

**corne** [kɔrn] *nf* [d'animal, matière, instrument] horn ; [au pied, à la main] hard skin ; **corne de brume** foghorn

**corneille** [kɔrnɛj] *nf* crow

**cornemuse** [kɔrnəmyz] *nf* bagpipes

**corner¹** [kɔrne] *vt* [page] to turn down the corner of ; [abîmer] to make dog-eared

**corner²** [kɔrner] *nm* [au football] corner ; **tirer un corner** to take a corner

**cornet** [kɔrnɛ] *nm* [glace] cone, *Br* cornet

**corniche** [kɔrniʃ] *nf* [de rocher] ledge ; [route] coast road ; [en haut d'un mur] cornice

**cornichon** [kɔrniʃɔ̃] *nm* gherkin

**cornu, -e** [kɔrny] *adj* [diable, animal] horned

**corporation** [kɔrpɔrasjɔ̃] *nf* corporate body

**corporel, -elle** [kɔrpɔrɛl] *adj* [besoin] bodily ; [hygiène] personal

**corps** [kɔr] *nm* [organisme, cadavre & CHIM] body ; [partie principale] main part ; **corps et âme** body and soul ; **corps d'armée/diplomatique** army / diplomatic corps ; **corps enseignant** teaching profession ; **corps gras** fat

**corpulent, -e** [kɔrpylɑ̃, -ɑ̃t] *adj* stout, corpulent

**correct, -e** [kɔrɛkt] *adj* [exact, courtois] correct ; *Fam* [acceptable] reasonable ■ **correctement** *adv* [sans faire de fautes, décemment] correctly ; *Fam* [de façon acceptable] reasonably

**correcteur, -trice** [kɔrɛktœr, -tris] **1.** *adj* **verres correcteurs** corrective lenses **2.** *nmf* [d'examen] examiner ; [en typographie] proofreader **3.** *nm* ORDINAT **correcteur d'orthographe** spellchecker

**correction** [kɔrɛksjɔ̃] *nf* [rectification] correction ; [punition] beating ; [décence, courtoisie] correctness ; SCOL [de devoirs, d'examens] marking

**correctionnel, -elle** [kɔrɛksjɔnɛl] **1.** *adj* **tribunal correctionnel** criminal court **2.** *nf* **correctionnelle** criminal court ; **passer en correctionnel** to go before a criminal court

**correspondance** [kɔrɛspɔ̃dɑ̃s] *nf* [relation, lettres] correspondence ; [de train, d'autocar] *Br* connection, *Am* transfer

**correspondre** [kɔrɛspɔ̃dr] *vi* **correspondre à qch** to correspond to sth ; **correspondre avec qn** [par lettres] to correspond with sb ■ **correspondant, -e 1.** *adj* corresponding (à to) **2.** *nmf* [reporter] correspondent ;

[par lettres] pen friend, pen pal ; [au téléphone] caller ; **correspondant de guerre** war correspondent

**corrida** [kɔrida] *nf* bullfight

**corridor** [kɔridɔr] *nm* corridor

**corriger** [kɔriʒe] **1.** *vt* [texte, erreur, myopie, injustice] to correct ; [exercice, devoir] to mark ; **corriger qn** to give sb a beating ; **corriger qn de qch** to cure sb of sth **2. se corriger** *vpr* to mend one's ways ; **se corriger de qch** to cure oneself of sth ■ **corrigé** *nm* [d'exercice] correct answers (**de** to)

**corrompre** [kɔrɔ̃pr] *vt* [personne, goût] to corrupt ; [soudoyer] to bribe ■ **corrompu, -e** *adj* corrupt ■ **corruption** *nf* corruption

**corrosion** [kɔrozjɔ̃] *nf* corrosion ■ **corrosif, -ive** *adj* corrosive

**corsage** [kɔrsaʒ] *nm* blouse

**Corse** [kɔrs] *nf* **la Corse** Corsica ■ **corse 1.** *adj* Corsican **2.** *nmf* **Corse** Corsican

**corser** [kɔrse] **1.** *vt* [plat] to spice up ; *Fig* [récit] to liven up **2. se corser** *vpr* **ça se corse** things are getting complicated ■ **corsé, -e** *adj* [café] *Br* full-flavoured, *Am* full-flavored ; *Fig* [histoire] spicy

**corset** [kɔrse] *nm* corset

**cortège** [kɔrtɛʒ] *nm* [défilé] procession

**corvée** [kɔrve] *nf* chore ; MIL fatigue duty

**cosmétique** [kɔsmetik] *adj* & *nm* cosmetic

**cosmique** [kɔsmik] *adj* cosmic ■ **cosmonaute** *nmf* cosmonaut

**cosmopolite** [kɔsmɔpɔlit] *adj* cosmopolitan

**cossu, -e** [kɔsy] *adj* [personne] well-to-do ; [maison, intérieur] opulent

**Costa Rica** [kɔstarika] *nm* **le Costa Rica** Costa Rica

**costaud** [kɔsto] *adj* sturdy

**costume** [kɔstym] *nm* [habit] costume ; [complet] suit

**costumé, e** [kɔstyme] *adj* **bal costumé** fancy-dress ball

**cotation** [kɔtasjɔ̃] *nf* **cotation (en Bourse)** quotation (on the Stock Market)

**cote** [kɔt] *nf* [marque de classement] classification mark; [valeur] quotation; [liste] share index; [de cheval] odds; [altitude] altitude

**côte** [kot] *nf* **a)** [os] rib; **à côtes** [étoffe] ribbed; **côte à côte** side by side; **côte d'agneau/de porc** lamb/pork chop; **côte de bœuf** rib of beef **b)** [de montagne] slope **c)** [littoral] coast; **la Côte d'Azur** the French Riviera

**coté, -e** [kɔte] *adj* **bien coté** highly rated; **coté en Bourse** quoted on the Stock Market

**côté** [kote] *nm* side; **de l'autre côté** on the other side (**de** of); [partir] the other way; **de ce côté** [passer] this way; **du côté de** [près de] near; **à côté** close by, nearby; [pièce] in the other room; [maison] next door; **la maison d'à côté** the house next door; **à côté de qn/qch** next to sb/sth; [en comparaison de] compared to sb/sth; **passer à côté** [balle] to fall wide (**de** of); **mettre qch de côté** to put sth aside

**coteau, -x** [kɔto] *nm* hill; [versant] hillside

**côtelé, -e** [kotle] *adj* **velours côtelé** corduroy

**côtelette** [kotlɛt] *nf* [d'agneau, de porc] chop

**coter** [kɔte] *vt* [prix, action] to quote

**côtier, -ère** [kotje, -ɛr] *adj* coastal; [pêche] inshore

**cotiser** [kɔtize] **1.** *vi* [à un cadeau, pour la retraite] to contribute (**à** to; **pour** towards) **2. se cotiser** *vpr Br* to club together, *Am* to club in ▪ **cotisation** *nf* [de club] dues, subscription; [de retraite, de chômage] contribution

**coton** [kɔtɔ̃] *nm* cotton; **coton hydrophile** *Br* cotton wool, *Am* absorbent cotton ▪ **Coton-Tige®** [kɔtɔ̃tiʒ] *(pl* **Coton-Tiges)** *nm Br* cotton bud, *Am* Q-tip®

**côtoyer** [kotwaje] *vt* [personnes] to mix with

**cou** [ku] *nm* neck

**couchage** [kuʃaʒ] *nm* **sac de couchage** sleeping bag

**couchant** [kuʃɑ̃, -ɑ̃t] **1.** *adj m* **soleil couchant** setting sun **2.** *nm* **le couchant** [ouest] the west

**couche** [kuʃ] *nf* **a)** [épaisseur] layer; [de peinture] coat; **la couche d'ozone** the ozone layer **b)** [linge de bébé] *Br* nappy, *Am* diaper ▪ **couche-culotte** *(pl* **couches-culottes)** *nf Br* disposable nappy, *Am* disposable diaper

**coucher** [kuʃe] **1.** *nm* [moment] bedtime; **l'heure du coucher** bedtime; **au coucher** at bedtime; **coucher de soleil** sunset **2.** *vt* [allonger] to lay down; **coucher qn** to put sb to bed **3.** *vi* to sleep (**avec** with) **4. se coucher** *vpr* [personne] to go to bed; [s'allonger] to lie down; [soleil] to set, to go down; **aller se coucher** to go to bed ▪ **couché, -e** *adj* **être couché** to be in bed; [étendu] to be lying (down)

**couchette** [kuʃɛt] *nf* [de train] couchette; [de bateau] bunk

**coude** [kud] *nm* elbow; [tournant] bend; **donner un coup de coude à qn** to nudge sb

**cou-de-pied** [kudpje] *(pl* **cous-de-pied)** *nm* instep

**coudre** [kudr] *vt & vi* to sew

**couette¹** [kwɛt] *nf* [édredon] duvet

**couette²** [kwɛt] *nf Fam* [coiffure] bunch

**couffin** [kufɛ̃] *nm* [de bébé] *Br* Moses basket, *Am* bassinet

**coulée** [kule] *nf* **coulée de lave** lava flow

**couler** [kule] **1.** *vt* **a)** [métal, statue] to cast; [liquide, ciment] to pour **b)** [navire] to sink **2.** *vi* **a)** [eau, rivière] to flow; [nez, sueur] to run; [robinet] to leak **b)** [bateau, nageur] to sink

**couleur** [kulœr] **1.** *nf* [teinte] *Br* colour, *Am* color; [colorant] paint; [pour cheveux] dye; CARTES suit; **de quelle couleur est... ?** what colour is...?; *Fam* **en faire voir de toutes les couleurs à qn** to give sb a hard time; **télévision cou-**

**leur** *ou* **en couleurs** colour television (set) **2.** *adj inv* [télévision, pellicule] *Br* colour, *Am* color

**couleuvre** [kulœvr] *nf* grass snake

**coulisse** [kulis] *nf* [de porte] runner; **porte à coulisse** sliding door; THÉÂT **les coulisses** the wings ■ **coulissant, -e** *adj* sliding

**couloir** [kulwar] *nm* [de maison, de train] corridor; [en natation, en athlétisme] lane; **couloir de bus** bus lane

**coup** [ku] *nm* **a)** [choc] blow; [essai] attempt, go; **donner un coup à qn** to hit sb; **se donner un coup contre qch** to knock against sth; **donner un coup de couteau à qn** to knife sb; **coup de pied** kick; **donner un coup de pied à qn** to kick sb; **coup de poing** punch; **donner un coup de poing à qn** to punch sb; **coup de tête** header; *Fam* AUTO **coup du lapin** whiplash

**b)** [action soudaine, événement soudain] *Fam* **coup de fil** phone call; **coup de téléphone** telephone *or* phone call; **donner** *ou* **passer un coup de téléphone à qn** to telephone *or* phone sb; **coup de vent** gust of wind; **donner un coup de frein** to brake; **coup de soleil** sunburn; **prendre un coup de soleil** to get sunburned; *Fig* **coup de foudre** love at first sight; *Fig* **ça a été le coup de foudre** it was love at first sight; **coup d'État** coup; **coup de théâtre** coup de théâtre

**c)** [bruit] **coup de feu** shot; **coup de fusil** shot; **coup de sifflet** whistle; **coup de tonnerre** clap of thunder; **l'horloge sonna deux coups** the clock struck two **d)** [expressions] **à coup sûr** definitely; **après coup** after the event; **coup sur coup** one after the other; **sur le coup** [alors] at the time; **tué sur le coup** killed outright; **tout à coup, tout d'un coup** suddenly; **du coup** as a result; **d'un seul coup** [avaler] in one go; [soudain] all of a sudden; **du premier coup** at the first attempt; **sous le coup de la colère** in a fit of anger; **tenir le coup** to hold out; **tomber sous le coup de la loi** to be an offence; **coup d'envoi** [au football, au rugby] kickoff; **coup de**

**maître** masterstroke; **coup droit** [au tennis] forehand; **coup franc** [au football] free kick; **coup monté** put-up job

**coupable** [kupabl] **1.** *adj* guilty (**de** of); [négligence] culpable; **se sentir coupable** to feel guilty **2.** *nmf* culprit

**coupant, -e** [kupɑ̃, -ɑ̃t] *adj* sharp

**coupe¹** [kup] *nf* [trophée] cup; [récipient] bowl; **la Coupe du monde** the World Cup; **coupe à champagne** champagne glass

**coupe²** [kup] *nf* [de vêtement] cut; [plan] section; **coupe de cheveux** haircut ■ **coupe-ongles** [kupɔ̃gl] *nm inv* nail clippers *pl* ■ **coupe-papier** *nm inv* paper knife ■ **coupe-vent** *nm inv* [blouson] *Br* windcheater, *Am* Windbreaker®

**couper** [kupe] **1.** *vt* [trancher, supprimer & ORDINAT] to cut; [arbre] to cut down; **couper la parole à qn** to interrupt sb; **nous avons été coupés** [au téléphone] we were cut off **2.** *vi* [être tranchant] to be sharp; [aux cartes] to cut; [prendre un raccourci] to take a short cut; **ne coupez pas !** [au téléphone] hold the line! **3. se couper** *vpr* **a)** [se blesser] to cut o.s. **b)** [se croiser] to cross **c)** [s'isoler] **se couper de** to cut o.s. off from ■ **coupé** *nm* [voiture] coupé ■ **couper-coller** [kupekɔle] *nm inv* ORDINAT **faire un couper-coller** to cut and paste

**couperet** [kuprɛ] *nm* [de boucher] cleaver; [de guillotine] blade

**couple** [kupl] *nm* couple

**couplet** [kuplɛ] *nm* verse

**coupole** [kupɔl] *nf* dome

**coupon** [kupɔ̃] *nm* [tissu] remnant; **coupon de réduction** money-off coupon; **coupon-réponse** reply coupon

**coupure** [kupyr] *nf* [blessure] cut; **5 000 euros en petites coupures** 5,000 euros in small notes; **coupure**

d'électricité *ou* de courant blackout, *Br* power cut ; **coupure de presse** newspaper cutting

**cour** [kur] *nf* **a)** [de maison, de ferme] yard ; **cour de récréation** *Br* playground, *Am* schoolyard **b)** [de roi, tribunal] court ; **cour d'appel** court of appeal **c)** **faire la cour à qn** to court sb

**courage** [kuraʒ] *nm* courage ; **bon courage !** good luck! ▪ **courageux, -euse** *adj* [brave] courageous ; [énergique] spirited

**couramment** [kuramɑ̃] *adv* [parler] fluently ; [généralement] commonly

**courant, -e** [kurɑ̃, -ɑ̃t] **1.** *adj* [commun] common ; [en cours] current **2.** *nm* [de rivière] current ; **être au courant de qch** to know about sth ; **mettre qn au courant de qch** to tell sb about sth ; **courant d'air** *Br* draught, *Am* draft ; **courant électrique** electric current

**courbature** [kurbatyr] *nf* ache ; **avoir des courbatures** to be aching (all over)

**courbe** [kurb] **1.** *adj* curved **2.** *nf* curve ; **courbe de niveau** contour line ▪ **courber 1.** *vt* to bend **2. se courber** *vpr* [personne] to bend down ; **se courber en deux** to bend double

**courge** [kurʒ] *nf Br* marrow, *Am* squash

**courgette** [kurʒɛt] *nf Br* courgette, *Am* zucchini

**courir** [kurir] **1.** *vi* to run ; [à une course automobile] to race ; **courir après qn / qch** to run after sb /sth ; **descendre une colline en courant** to run down a hill ; **le bruit court que...** rumour has it that... **2.** *vt* **courir un risque** to run a risk ; **courir le 100 mètres** to run the 100 metres ▪ **coureur, -euse** *nmf* [sportif] runner ; [cycliste] cyclist ; **coureur automobile** racing driver ; **coureur de jupons** womanizer

**couronne** [kurɔn] *nf* [de roi, de reine] crown ; [pour enterrement] wreath ; [de dent] crown ▪ **couronnement** *nm* [de roi] coronation ; *Fig* [réussite] crowning achievement ▪ **couronner** *vt* [roi] to crown ; [auteur, ouvrage] to award a prize to ; **et pour couronner le tout...** and to crown it all...

**courriel** [kurjɛl] *nm* email

**courrier** [kurje] *nm* [lettres] mail, *Br* post ; **par retour du courrier** *Br* by return of post, *Am* by return mail ; **recevoir du courrier** to receive mail *or Br* post ; JOURN **courrier du cœur** problem page ; **courrier électronique** e-mail

**courroie** [kurwa] *nf* [attache] strap

**cours** [kur] *nm* **a)** [de rivière, d'astre] course ; [de monnaie] currency ; FIN [d'action] price ; **suivre son cours** to run its course ; **avoir cours** [monnaie] to be legal tender ; [pratique] to be current ; **en cours** [travail] in progress ; [année] current ; [affaires] outstanding ; **au cours de qch** in the course of sth ; **cours d'eau** river, stream **b)** [leçon] class ; [série de leçons] course ; [conférence] lecture ; [établissement] school ; **suivre un cours** to take a course ; **cours particulier** private lesson **c)** [allée] avenue

**course¹** [kurs] *nf* [action de courir] running ; SPORT [épreuve] race ; [discipline] racing ; [trajet en taxi] journey ; [de projectile, de planète] course ; **les courses de chevaux** the races ; **faire la course avec qn** to race sb ; **course automobile** motor race ; **course cycliste** cycle race

**course²** [kurs] *nf* [commission] errand ; **courses** [achats] shopping ; **faire une course** to get something from the shops ; **faire les courses** to do the shopping

**coursier, -ère** [kursje, -ɛr] *nmf* messenger

**court, -e** [kur, kurt] **1.** *adj* short **2.** *adv* short ; **à court d'argent** short of money **3.** *nm* court (de tennis /de squash) tennis /squash court ▪ **court-circuit** *(pl* **courts-circuits***) nm* short-circuit

**courtier, -ère** [kurtje, -ɛr] *nmf* broker

**courtisan** [kurtizɑ̃] *nm* HIST courtier ▪ **courtiser** *vt* [femme] to court

**courtois, -e** [kurtwa, -az] *adj* courteous ▪ **courtoisie** *nf* courtesy

**couru, -e** [kury] *adj* [spectacle, lieu] popular

**couscous** [kuskus] nm couscous (traditional North African dish of semolina served with a spicy stew of meat and vegetables)

**cousin, -e** [kuzɛ̃, -in] **1.** nmf cousin; **cousin germain** first cousin **2.** nm [insecte] mosquito

**coussin** [kusɛ̃] nm cushion

**cousu, -e** [kuzy] adj sewn; **cousu main** hand-sewn

**coût** [ku] nm cost; **le coût de la vie** the cost of living ■ **coûter** vi a) [valoir] to cost; **ça coûte combien ?** how much is it?; **coûter cher** to be expensive, to cost a lot; Fig to be costly b) Fig [être pénible] to be difficult; **coûte que coûte** at all costs, whatever the cost, no matter what

**couteau, -x** [kuto] nm knife; **couteau à pain** breadknife; **couteau-scie** serrated knife

**coûteux, -euse** [kutø, -øz] adj costly, expensive

**coutume** [kutym] nf [habitude, tradition] custom; **avoir coutume de faire qch** to be accustomed to doing sth; **comme de coutume** as usual

**couture** [kutyr] nf [activité] sewing, needlework; [raccord] seam; **faire de la couture** to sew ■ **couturier** nm fashion designer ■ **couturière** nf dressmaker

**couvent** [kuvɑ̃] nm [de religieuses] convent; [de moines] monastery; [pensionnat] convent school

**couver** [kuve] **1.** vt [œufs] to sit on; [maladie] to be coming down with **2.** vi [poule] to brood; [feu] Br to smoulder, Am to smolder ■ **couveuse** nf [pour nouveaux-nés] incubator

**couvercle** [kuvɛrkl] nm lid; [vissé] cap

**couvert¹** [kuvɛr] nm a) **mettre le couvert** to set or Br lay the table; **table de cinq couverts** table set or Br laid for five; **couverts** [ustensiles] cutlery b) **sous le couvert de** [sous l'apparence de] under cover of; **se mettre à couvert** to take cover

**couvert², -e** [kuvɛr, -ɛrt] **1.** pp de **couvrir 2.** adj covered (**de** with or in); [ciel] overcast; **être bien couvert** [habillé chaudement] to be warmly dressed

**couverture** [kuvɛrtyr] nf [de lit] blanket; [de livre, de magazine] cover; [de bâtiment] roofing; JOURN coverage; **couverture chauffante** electric blanket; **couverture sociale** social security cover

**couvrir** [kuvrir] **1.** vt to cover (**de** with); [bruit] to drown **2.** se **couvrir** vpr [s'habiller] to wrap up; [se coiffer] to cover one's head; [ciel] to cloud over ■ **couvre-feu** (pl **couvre-feux**) nm curfew ■ **couvre-lit** (pl **couvre-lits**) nm bedspread

**cow-boy** [kɔbɔj] (pl **cow-boys**) nm cowboy

**CP** [sepe] (abr de **cours préparatoire**) nm first year of primary school

**CPE** [sepeə] (abr de **conseiller principal d'éducation**) nm inv school administrator

**crabe** [krab] nm crab

**crachat** [kraʃa] nm gob of spit; **crachats** spit

**cracher** [kraʃe] **1.** vt to spit out **2.** vi [personne] to spit; [stylo] to splutter; [radio] to crackle

**crachin** [kraʃɛ̃] nm (fine) drizzle

**crack** [krak] nm a) [cheval] top horse b) Fam [as] star (performer); **c'est un crack en mathématiques** he's a whiz at Br maths or Am math c) [drogue] crack

**crade** [krad] adj inv Fam [personne, objet] filthy

**craie** [krɛ] nf [matière] chalk; [bâton] stick of chalk

**craindre** [krɛ̃dr] vt [redouter] to be afraid of, to fear; [chaleur, froid] to be sensitive to; **craindre de faire qch** to be afraid of doing sth; **je crains qu'elle ne soit partie** I'm afraid she's left; **ne craignez rien** [n'ayez pas peur] don't be afraid; [ne vous inquiétez pas] don't worry

**crainte** [krɛ̃t] nf fear; **de crainte de faire qch** for fear of doing sth

**craintif, -ive** [krɛ̃tif, -iv] *adj* timid

**cramé, e** [krame] *adj Fam* [brûlé] burnt, charred ; [tissu] burnt, scorched ; **la tarte est complètement cramée** the tart is burnt to a cinder ■ **cramé** *nm Fam* **ça sent le cramé** there's a smell of burning

**crampe** [krɑ̃p] *nf* cramp

**crampon** [krɑ̃põ] *nm* [de chaussure] stud ; [pour l'alpinisme] crampon

**cramponner** [krɑ̃pɔne] ■ **se cramponner** *vpr* to hold on ; **se cramponner à qn/qch** to hold on to sb /sth

**cran** [krɑ̃] *nm* **a)** [entaille] notch ; [de ceinture] hole ; **cran d'arrêt** *ou* **de sûreté** safety catch **b)** [de cheveux] wave **c)** *Fam* [courage] guts ; **avoir du cran** to have guts **d)** *Fam* **être à cran** [excédé] to be wound up

**crâne** [krɑn] *nm* skull

**crapaud** [krapo] *nm* toad

**crapule** [krapyl] *nf* villain, scoundrel

**craquer** [krake] **1.** *vt* [allumette] to strike **2.** *vi* [branche] to crack ; [escalier] to creak ; [se casser] to snap ; [se déchirer] to rip ■ **craquements** *nmpl* [de branches] cracking ; [d'escalier] creaking

**crasse** [kras] *nf* filth ■ **crasseux, -euse** *adj* filthy

**cratère** [krater] *nm* crater

**cravate** [kravat] *nf* tie

**crawlé** [krole] *adj m* **dos crawlé** backstroke

**crayon** [krɛjõ] *nm* [en bois] pencil ; [en cire] crayon ; *Can* **crayon de plomb** lead pencil

**créancier, -ère** [kreɑ̃sje, -ɛr] *nmf* debtor

**créateur, -trice** [kreatœr, -tris] **1.** *adj* creative **2.** *nmf* creator ■ **création** *nf* creation ; **1000 créations d'emplois** 1,000 new jobs

**créature** [kreatyr] *nf* [être vivant] creature

**crèche** [krɛʃ] *nf* [de Noël] manger, *Br* crib ; [garderie] (day) nursery, *Br* crèche

**crédible** [kredibl] *adj* credible

**crédit** [kredi] *nm* [prêt, influence] credit ; **crédits** [somme d'argent] funds ; **à crédit** on credit ■ **créditer** *vt* [compte] to credit (**de** with) ; *Fig* **créditer qn de qch** to give sb credit for sth ■ **créditeur, -trice** *adj* **solde créditeur** credit balance ; **être créditeur** to be in credit

**crédule** [kredyl] *adj* credulous ■ **crédulité** *nf* credulity

**créer** [kree] *vt* to create

**crémaillère** [kremajɛr] *nf* **pendre la crémaillère** to have a housewarming (party)

**crématorium** [krematɔrjɔm] *nm Br* crematorium, *Am* crematory

**crème** [krɛm] **1.** *nf* [de lait, dessert, cosmétique] cream ; **crème Chantilly** whipped cream ; **crème glacée** ice cream ; **crème à raser** shaving cream **2.** *adj inv* cream(-coloured) **3.** *nm Fam* coffee with milk, *Br* white coffee ■ **crémerie** *nf* [magasin] dairy ■ **crémeux, -euse** *adj* creamy

**créneau, -x** [kreno] *nm* COMM niche ; TV & RADIO slot

**créole** [kreɔl] **1.** *adj* creole **2.** *nmf* Creole **3.** *nm* [langue] Creole

**crêpe** [krɛp] **1.** *nf* pancake, crêpe **2.** *nm* [tissu] crepe ■ **crêperie** *nf* pancake restaurant

**crépiter** [krepite] *vi* [feu] to crackle ■ **crépitement** *nm* [du feu] crackling

**crépu, -e** [krepy] *adj* frizzy

**crépuscule** [krepyskyl] *nm* twilight

**cresson** [kresõ] *nm* watercress

**Crète** [krɛt] *nf* **la Crète** Crete

**crête** [krɛt] *nf* [de montagne, d'oiseau, de vague] crest

**creuser** [krøze] **1.** *vt* [trou, puits] to dig ; [évider] to hollow (out) ; *Fig* [idée] to look into **2.** *vi* to dig **3. se creuser** *vpr* [joues] to become hollow ; *Fam* **se creuser la tête** *ou* **la cervelle** to rack one's brains

**creux, -euse** [krø, -øz] **1.** *adj* [tube, joues, arbre, paroles] hollow ; [sans activité] slack ; **assiette creuse** soup plate **2.** *nm* hollow ; [moment] slack period

**croître**

**crevaison** [krəvɛzɔ̃] *nf* [de pneu] flat, *Br* puncture

**crevasse** [krəvas] *nf* [trou] crack ; [de glacier] crevasse

**crever** [krəve] **1.** *vt* [ballon, bulle] to burst ; *Fam* [épuiser] to wear out **2.** *vi* [bulle, ballon, pneu] to burst ■ **crevé, -e** *adj* [ballon, pneu] burst ; *Fam* [épuisé] worn out

**crevette** [krəvɛt] *nf* [grise] shrimp ; [rose] prawn

**cri** [kri] *nm* [de personne] cry, shout ; [perçant] scream ; [d'animal] cry ■ **criard, -e** *adj* [son] shrill ; [couleur] loud

**cribler** [krible] *vt* a) [trouer de] **cribler de** to riddle sth with holes ; **la façade est criblée d'impacts de balles** the facade is riddled with bullet holes b) *Fig* **être criblé de dettes** to be crippled with debt, to be up to one's eyes in debt

**crier** [krije] **1.** *vt* [injure, ordre] to shout (**à** to) **2.** *vi* [personne] to shout, to cry out ; [fort] to scream ; [parler très fort] to shout ; **crier au secours** to shout for help

**crime** [krim] *nm* crime ; [assassinat] murder ■ **criminalité** *nf* crime ■ **criminel, -elle 1.** *adj* criminal **2.** *nmf* criminal ; [assassin] murderer

**crinière** [krinjɛr] *nf* mane

**crique** [krik] *nf* creek

**criquet** [krikɛ] *nm* locust ; [sauterelle] grasshopper

**crise** [kriz] *nf* crisis ; [de maladie] attack ; **crise de nerfs** fit of hysteria

**crisper** [krispe] **1.** *vt* [poing] to clench ; [muscle] to tense **2. se crisper** *vpr* [visage] to tense ; [personne] to get tense ■ **crispé, -e** *adj* [personne] tense

**crisser** [krise] *vi* [pneu, roue] to squeal ; [neige] to crunch

**cristal, -aux** [kristal, -o] *nm* crystal ; TECH **cristaux liquides** liquid crystal ■ **cristallin, -e** *adj* [eau, son] crystal-clear

**critère** [kritɛr] *nm* criterion

**critique** [kritik] **1.** *adj* [situation, phase] critical **2.** *nf* [reproche] criticism ; [de film, de livre] review ; **faire la critique de** [film] to review **3.** *nm* critic ■ **critiquer** *vt* to criticize

**croasser** [krɔase] *vi* to caw

**Croatie** [krɔasi] *nf* **la Croatie** Croatia

**croc** [krɔ] *nm* [crochet] hook ; [dent] fang

**croche** [krɔʃ] **1.** *nf* MUS *Br* quaver, *Am* eighth (note) **2.** *adj* Can Fam **a)** [courbe, crochu] crooked, bent **b)** *Fig* [malhonnête] dishonest **3.** *adv* Can [de travers] sham

**croche-pied** [krɔʃpje] *nm* trip ; **faire un croche-pied à qn** to trip sb up

**crochet** [krɔʃɛ] *nm* [pour accrocher, en boxe] hook ; [aiguille] crochet hook ; [parenthèse] square bracket ; **faire du crochet** to crochet ; **faire un crochet** [détour] to make a detour ; [route] to make a sudden turn ■ **crocheter** *vt* [serrure] to pick

**crochu, -e** [krɔʃy] *adj* [nez] hooked ; [doigts] claw-like

**crocodile** [krɔkɔdil] *nm* crocodile

**croire** [krwar] **1.** *vt* to believe ; [penser] to think (**que** that) ; **j'ai cru la voir** I thought I saw her ; **je crois que oui** I think or believe so **2.** *vi* to believe (**à** *ou* **en** in) **3. se croire** *vpr* **il se croit malin** he thinks he's smart

**croisé¹** [krwaze] *nm* HIST crusader ■ **croisade** *nf* HIST crusade

**croiser** [krwaze] **1.** *vt* [passer] to pass ; [ligne] to cross ; [espèce] to crossbreed ; **croiser les jambes** to cross one's legs ; **croiser les bras** to fold one's arms ; *Fig* **croiser les doigts** to keep one's fingers crossed **2.** *vi* [navire] to cruise **3. se croiser** *vpr* [voitures] to pass each other ; [lignes, routes] to cross, to intersect ; [lettres] to cross ; [regards] to meet ■ **croisé², -e** *adj* [bras] folded ; [veston] double-breasted ■ **croisement** *nm* [de routes] crossroads (*sg*), intersection ; [d'animaux] crossing

**croisière** [krwazjɛr] *nf* cruise

**croître** [krwatr] *vi* [plante] to grow ; [augmenter] to grow, to increase (de by); [lune] to wax ■ **croissance** *nf* growth ■ **croissant, -e 1.** *adj* [nombre] growing **2.** *nm* crescent; [pâtisserie] croissant

**croix** [krwa] *nf* cross; **la Croix-Rouge** the Red Cross

**croquer** [krɔke] **1.** *vt* [manger] to crunch **2.** *vi* [fruit] to be crunchy; **croquer dans qch** to bite into sth ■ **croquant, -e** *adj* crunchy ■ **croque-monsieur** *nm inv* toasted cheese and ham sandwich

**croquis** [krɔki] *nm* sketch

**crosse** [krɔs] *nf* [de fusil] butt; [de hockey] stick; [d'évêque] crook; *Can* SPORT lacrosse

**crotte** [krɔt] *nf* [de mouton, de lapin] droppings; **crotte de chien** dog dirt ■ **crottin** *nm* dung

**crouler** [krule] *vi* [édifice] to crumble; **crouler sous le travail** to be snowed under with work ■ **croulant, -e** *adj* [mur] crumbling

**croupe** [krup] *nf* rump

**croupier** [krupje] *nm* croupier

**croupir** [krupir] *vi* [eau] to stagnate

**croustiller** [krustije] *vi* to be crunchy; [pain] to be crusty ■ **croustillant, -e** *adj* crunchy; [pain] crusty; *Fig* [histoire] spicy

**croûte** [krut] *nf* [de pain] crust; [de fromage] rind; [de plaie] scab; *Fam* **casser la croûte** to have a snack ■ **croûton** *nm* [de pain] end; **croûtons** [pour la soupe] croûtons

**croyable** [krwajabl] *adj* credible, believable ■ **croyance** *nf* belief (**en** in) ■ **croyant, -e 1.** *adj* **être croyant** to be a believer **2.** *nmf* believer

**CRS** [seɛrɛs] (*abr de* **compagnie républicaine de sécurité**) **1.** *nf* riot and security police **2.** *nm* French riot policeman

**cru¹, -e¹** [kry] *pp de* **croire**

**cru², -e²** [kry] **1.** *adj* [aliment] raw; [lait] unpasteurized; [lumière] garish; [propos] crude; **monter à cru** to ride bareback **2.** *nm* [vignoble] vineyard; **un grand cru** [vin] a vintage wine; **vin du cru** local wine

**cruauté** [kryote] *nf* cruelty (**envers** to)

**cruche** [kryʃ] *nf* pitcher, jug

**crucial, -e, -aux** [krysjal, -o] *adj* crucial

**crucifier** [krysifje] *vt* to crucify ■ **crucifix** *nm* crucifix ■ **crucifixion** *nf* crucifixion

**crudités** [krydite] *nfpl* [légumes] assorted raw vegetables

**crue³** [kry] *nf* [montée] swelling; [inondation] flood; **en crue** [rivière, fleuve] in spate

**cruel, -elle** [kryɛl] *adj* cruel (**envers** *ou* **avec** to) ■ **cruellement** *adv* cruelly

**crûment** [krymɑ̃] *adv* [sans détour] bluntly; [grossièrement] crudely

**crustacés** [krystase] *nmpl* CULIN shellfish *inv*

**crypte** [kript] *nf* crypt

**crypter** [kripte] *vt* to encrypt ■ **crypté, -e** *adj* [message & TV] coded

**Cuba** [kyba] *nom* Cuba ■ **cubain, -e 1.** *adj* Cuban **2.** *nmf* **Cubain, Cubaine** Cuban

**cube** [kyb] **1.** *nm* cube; [de jeu] building block **2.** *adj* **mètre cube** cubic metre ■ **cubique** *adj* cubic

**cueillir** [kœjir] *vt* to pick, to gather

**cuiller, cuillère** [kɥijɛr] *nf* spoon; [mesure] spoonful; **cuiller à café, petite cuiller** teaspoon; **cuiller à soupe** tablespoon ■ **cuillerée** *nf* spoonful; **cuillerée à café** teaspoonful; **cuillerée à soupe** tablespoonful

**cuir** [kɥir] *nm* leather; [d'éléphant] hide; **pantalon en cuir** leather trousers; **cuir chevelu** scalp

**cuirassé** [kɥirase] *nm* NAUT battleship

**cuire** [kɥir] **1.** *vt* [aliment, plat] to cook; **cuire qch à l'eau** to boil sth; **cuire qch au four** to bake sth; [viande] to roast sth **2.** *vi* [aliment] to cook; **faire cuire qch** to cook sth

**cuisant, -e** [kɥizɑ̃, -ɑ̃t] *adj* [douleur] burning; [affront] stinging

**cuiseur** [kɥizœr] *nm* cooker; **cuiseur (vapeur)** steam cooker

**cyanure**

**cuisine** [kɥizin] *nf* [pièce] kitchen ; [art] cookery, cooking ; **faire la cuisine** to do the cooking ; **cuisine américaine** open-plan kitchen ; **cuisiner** *vt & vi* to cook ▪ **cuisiné, e** *adj* **plat cuisiné** ready-cooked *or* ready-made meal

**cuisinier, -ère**[1] [kɥizinje, -ɛr] *nmf* cook

**cuisinière**[2] [kɥizinjɛr] *nf* [appareil] stove, *Br* cooker

**cuisse** [kɥis] *nf* thigh ; **cuisse de poulet** chicken leg ; **cuisses de grenouilles** frogs' legs

**cuisson** [kɥisɔ̃] *nm* [d'aliments] cooking ; [de pain] baking

**cuit, -e** [kɥi, kɥit] **1.** *pp de* **cuire 2.** *adj* cooked ; **bien cuit** well done

**cuit-vapeur** [kɥivapœr] *nm inv* steamer, steam-cooker

**cuivre** [kɥivr] *nm* [rouge] copper ; [jaune] brass ; MUS **les cuivres** the brass (section) ▪ **cuivré, -e** *adj Br* copper-coloured, *Am* copper-colored

**culbuter** [kylbyte] *vi* [personne] to take a tumble

**cul-de-sac** [kydsak] *(pl* **culs-de-sac)** *nm* dead end, *Br* cul-de-sac

**culinaire** [kylinɛr] *adj* culinary

**culminer** [kylmine] *vi* [tension, crise] to peak ; **la montagne culmine à 3 000 mètres** the mountain is 3,000 metres at its highest point ▪ **culminant** *adj* **point culminant** [de montagne] highest point

**culot** [kylo] *nm* [d'ampoule, de lampe] base ; *Fam* [audace] nerve, *Br* cheek ▪ **culotté, e** *adj* [effronté] *Fam* **elle est culottée** she's got a nerve

**culotte** [kylɔt] *nf* [de femme] knickers, *Am* panties ; [d'enfant] pants ; **culottes courtes** *Br* short trousers, *Am* short pants

**culpabiliser** [kylpabilize] **1.** *vt* **culpabiliser qn** to make sb feel guilty **2. se culpabiliser** *vpr* to feel guilty ▪ **culpabilité** *nf* guilt

**culte** [kylt] **1.** *nm* [de dieu] worship ; [religion] religion **2.** *adj* **film culte** cult film

**cultiver** [kyltive] **1.** *vt* [terre, amitié] to cultivate ; [plantes] to grow **2. se cultiver** *vpr* to improve one's mind ▪ **cultivateur, -trice** *nmf* farmer ▪ **cultivé, -e** *adj* [terre] cultivated ; [esprit, personne] cultured, cultivated

**culture** [kyltyr] *nf* **a)** [action] farming, cultivation ; [de plantes] growing ; **cultures** [terres] fields under cultivation ; [plantes] crops **b)** [éducation, civilisation & BIOL] culture ; **culture générale** general knowledge ; **culture physique** physical training ▪ **culturel, -elle** *adj* cultural

**culturisme** [kyltyrism] *nm* body-building

**cumulatif, -ive** *adj* cumulative ▪ **cumuler** *vt* **cumuler deux fonctions** to hold two offices

**cupide** [kypid] *adj* avaricious

**cure** [kyr] *nf* (course of) treatment ; **cure de désintoxication** [d'alcool] drying-out treatment ; [de drogue] detoxification treatment ; **faire une cure thermale** to undergo treatment at a spa

**curé** [kyre] *nm* parish priest

**curer** [kyre] **1.** *vt* to clean out **2. se curer** *vpr* **se curer les dents** to clean one's teeth ▪ **cure-dents** *nm inv* toothpick

**curieux, -euse** [kyrjø, -øz] **1.** *adj* [bizarre] curious ; [indiscret] inquisitive, curious (**de** about) **2.** *nmf* inquisitive person ; [badaud] onlooker ▪ **curiosité** *nf* curiosity ; [chose] curio

**curriculum vitae** [kyrikylɔmvite] *nm inv Br* curriculum vitae, *Am* résumé

**curseur** [kyrsœr] *nm* ORDINAT cursor

**cutané, -e** [kytane] *adj* **maladie cutanée** skin condition

**cuti** [kyti] *nf* skin test

**cuve** [kyv] *nf* tank ; [de fermentation] vat ▪ **cuvée** *nf* [récolte] vintage ▪ **cuvette** *nf* [récipient & GÉOG] basin ; [des cabinets] bowl

**CV** [seve] *(abr de* **curriculum vitae)** *nm Br* CV, *Am* résumé

**cyanure** [sjanyr] *nm* cyanide

**cybercafé** [siberkafe] *nm* cybercafé

**cybercrime** [siberkrim] *nm* ORDINAT e-crime ■ **cybercriminalité** *nf* cybercrime

**cycle** [sikl] *nm* **a)** [série, movement] cycle **b) premier / second cycle** SCOL *lower / upper classes in secondary school;* UNIV *first / last two years of a degree course* **c)** [bicyclette] cycle ■ **cyclable** *adj* **piste cyclable** cycle path

**cyclisme** [siklism] *nm* cycling ■ **cycliste 1.** *nmf* cyclist **2.** *adj* **course cycliste** cycle race

**cyclomoteur** [siklɔmɔtœr] *nm* moped

**cyclone** [siklon] *nm* cyclone

**cygne** [siɲ] *nm* swan

**cylindre** [silɛ̃dr] *nm* cylinder; [rouleau] roller ■ **cylindrée** *nf* (cubic) capacity ■ **cylindrique** *adj* cylindrical

**cymbale** [sɛ̃bal] *nf* cymbal

**cynique** [sinik] **1.** *adj* cynical **2.** *nmf* cynic

**cyprès** [sipre] *nm* cypress

**cypriote** [siprijɔt] **1.** *adj* Cypriot **2.** *nmf* **Cypriote** Cypriot

# D

**D, d** [de] **1.** *nm inv* D, d **2.** *(abr de* **route départementale***) designation of a secondary road*

**dactylo** [daktilo] *nf* [personne] typist ; [action] typing

**daigner** [deɲe] *vt* **daigner faire qch** to deign to do sth

**daim** [dɛ̃] *nm* [animal] fallow deer ; [mâle] buck ; [cuir] suede

**dalle** [dal] *nf* [de pierre] paving stone ; [de marbre] slab

**daltonien, -enne** [daltɔnjɛ̃, -ɛn] *adj* colour-blind

**dame** [dam] *nf* [femme] lady ; CARTES queen ; [au jeu de dames] king ; **dames** [jeu] *Br* draughts, *Am* checkers

**damner** [dane] *vt* to damn

**Danemark** [danmark] *nm* **le Danemark** Denmark ▪ **danois, -e 1.** *adj* Danish **2.** *nmf* **Danois, Danoise** Dane **3.** *nm* [langue] Danish

**danger** [dɑ̃ʒe] *nm* danger ; **en danger** in danger ▪ **dangereux, -euse** *adj* dangerous (**pour** to)

**dans** [dɑ̃] *prép* **a)** in ; [changement de lieu] into ; [à l'intérieur de] inside **b)** [provenance] from, out of ; **boire dans un verre** to drink out of a glass **c)** [exprime la temporalité] in ; **dans deux jours** in two days' time **d)** [exprime une approximation] **dans les dix euros** about ten euros

**danse** [dɑ̃s] *nf* dance ; **la danse** [art] dancing ; **danse classique** ballet ▪ **danser** *vt & vi* to dance ▪ **danseur, -euse** *nmf* dancer

**dard** [dar] *nm* [d'insecte] sting

**date** [dat] *nf* date ; **date de naissance** date of birth ; **date limite** deadline ; **date limite de vente** sell-by date ▪ **dater 1.** *vt* to date **2.** *vi* **à dater du 15** as from the 15th

**datte** [dat] *nf* date

**daube** [dob] *nf* **bœuf en daube** braised beef stew

**dauphin** [dofɛ̃] *nm* [animal] dolphin

**davantage** [davɑ̃taʒ] *adv* more ; **davantage de temps / d'argent** more time / money

---

## de¹ [də]

> **de** becomes **d'** before vowel and h mute ; de + le = **du**, de + les = **des**.

*prép* **a)** [complément de nom] of ; **le livre de Paul** Paul's book ; **un livre de Flaubert** a book by Flaubert ; **le train de Londres** the London train ; **une augmentation de salaire** an increase in salary

**b)** [complément d'adjectif] **digne de qn** worthy of sb ; **content de qn / qch** pleased with sb / sth ; **heureux de partir** happy to leave

**c)** [complément de verbe] **parler de qn / qch** to speak of sb / sth ; **se souvenir de qn / qch** to remember sb / sth ; **décider de faire qch** to decide to do sth ; **empêcher qn de faire qch** to stop sb from doing sth

**d)** [indique la provenance] from ; **venir de...** to come from... ; **sortir de qch** to come out of sth ; **le train de Londres** the train from London

**e)** [introduit l'agent] **accompagné de qn** accompanied by sb ; **entouré de qch** surrounded by *or* with sth

**f)** [introduit le moyen] **armé de qch** armed with sth

**g)** [introduit la manière] **d'une voix douce** in a gentle voice

**h)** [introduit la cause] **puni de son impatience** punished for his / her impatience; **mourir de faim** to die of hunger **i)** [introduit le temps] **travailler de nuit** to work by night; **six heures du matin** six o'clock in the morning **j)** [mesure] **avoir six mètres de haut, être haut de six mètres** to be six metres high; **homme de trente ans** thirty-year-old man; **gagner cent francs de l'heure** to earn a hundred francs an hour

**de²** [də] *art part* some; **elle boit du vin** she drinks (some) wine; **il ne boit pas de vin** he doesn't drink (any) wine; **est-ce que vous buvez du vin ?** do you drink (any) wine?

**de³** [də] *art indéf* de, des some; **des fleurs** (some) flowers; **de jolies fleurs** (some) pretty flowers; **d'agréables soirées** (some) pleasant evenings

**dé** [de] *nm* [à jouer] dice; [à coudre] thimble

**dealer, euse** [dikɛr, øz] *nmf Fam* dealer

**déballer** [debale] *vt* to unpack

**débarbouiller** [debarbuje] ▪ **se débarbouiller** *vpr* to wash one's face

**débarcadère** [debarkadɛr] *nm* **a)** NAUT landing stage **b)** *Can* [zone réservée] unloading dock

**débardeur** [debardœr] *nm* [vêtement] vest

**débarquer** [debarke] **1.** *vt* [passagers] to land; [marchandises] to unload **2.** *vi* [passagers] to disembark ▪ **débarquement** *nm* [de passagers, de troupes] landing; [de marchandises] unloading

**débarras** [debara] *nm* storeroom ▪ **débarrasser 1.** *vt* [chambre, table] to clear (**de** of); **débarrasser qn de qch** to relieve sb of sth **2. se débarrasser** *vpr* **se débarrasser de qn / qch** to get rid of sb / sth

**débat** [deba] *nm* debate

**débattre** [debatr] **1.** *vt* to discuss, to debate; **débattre de qch** to discuss sth **2. se débattre** *vpr* to struggle

**débaucher** [deboʃe] *vt* **débaucher qn** [licencier] to lay sb off; [inciter à la débauche] to corrupt sb

**débile** [debil] *adj Fam* stupid

**débit** [debi] *nm* FIN debit; [de fleuve] flow; [de personne] delivery; **débit de tabac** *Br* tobacconist's (shop), *Am* tobacco store

**débiter** [debite] *vt* [découper] to cut up (**en** into); [compte] to debit; *Péj* [dire] to spout ▪ **débiteur** *adj m* **solde débiteur** debit balance; **mon compte est débiteur** my account is in debit

**débloquer** [debloke] *vt* [mécanisme] to unjam; [compte, prix] to unfreeze

**déboiser** [debwaze] *vt* [terrain] to clear of trees

**déboîter** [debwate] **1.** *vt* [tuyau] to disconnect **2.** *vi* [véhicule] to pull out **3. se déboîter** *vpr* **se déboîter l'épaule** to dislocate one's shoulder

**déborder** [deborde] **1.** *vi* [fleuve, liquide] to overflow; [en bouillant] to boil over **2.** *vt* [dépasser] to stick out from; **débordé de travail** snowed under with work

**débouché** [debuʃe] *nm* [carrière] opening; [de produit] outlet

**déboucher** [debuʃe] **1.** *vt* [bouteille] to uncork; [bouchon vissé] to uncap; [lavabo, tuyau] to unblock **2.** *vi* [surgir] to emerge (**de** from); **déboucher sur** [rue] to lead out onto / into

**debout** [dəbu] *adv* [personne] standing; [objet] upright; **se mettre debout** to stand up; **rester debout** to stand; **être debout** [hors du lit] to be up

**déboutonner** [debutone] **1.** *vt* to unbutton **2. se déboutonner** *vpr* [personne] to undo one's coat / jacket / *etc*

**débraillé, -e** [debraje] *adj* slovenly

**débrancher** [debrãʃe] *vt* to unplug

**débrayer** [debʀeje] *vi* **a)** AUTO to release the clutch **b)** [se mettre en grève] to stop work ■ **débrayage** *nm* **a)** AUTO declutching **b)** [grève] stoppage

**débriefer** [debʀife] *vt* to debrief ■ **débriefing** [debʀifiŋ] *nm* debrief; **faire un débriefing** to debrief

**débris** [debʀi] *nmpl* [de voiture, d'avion] debris

**débrouiller** [debʀuje] **1.** *vt* [fil, mystère] to unravel **2. se débrouiller** *vpr Fam* to manage; **se débrouiller pour faire qch** to manage to do sth ■ **débrouillard, -e** *adj Fam* resourceful

**débuguer** [debyge] *vt* = **déboguer**

**début** [deby] *nm* beginning, start; **au début (de)** at the beginning (of); **dès le début** (right) from the start or beginning

**débuter** [debyte] *vi* to start, to begin (**par** with); [dans une carrière] to start out ■ **débutant, -e** *nmf* beginner

**deçà** [dəsa] ■ **en deçà 1.** *adv* (on) this side **2.** *prép* **en deçà de** (on) this side of

**décadent, -e** [dekadã, -ãt] *adj* decadent

**décaféiné, -e** [dekafeine] *adj* decaffeinated

**décalcomanie** [dekalkɔmani] *nf Br* transfer (*adhesive*), *Am* decal

**décalé, e** [dekale] *adj* **a)** [style, humour] off-beat, quirky **b)** [personne] quirky

**décaler** [dekale] **1.** *vt* [dans le temps] to change the time of; [dans l'espace] to shift, to move **2. se décaler** *vpr* to move, to shift ■ **décalage** *nm* [écart] gap (**entre** between); **décalage horaire** time difference; **souffrir du décalage horaire** to have jet lag

**décalquer** [dekalke] *vt* to trace

**décaper** [dekape] *vt* [avec un produit] to strip; [au papier de verre] to sand (down); [four] to clean

**décapiter** [dekapite] *vt* [personne] to decapitate

**décapotable** [dekapɔtabl] *adj & nf* convertible

**décapsuleur** [dekapsylœʀ] *nm* bottle opener

**décédé, -e** [desede] *adj* deceased

**déceler** [desle] *vt* [trouver] to detect

**décembre** [desɑ̃bʀ] *nm* December

**décence** [desɑ̃s] *nf* [de comportement] propriety; [d'habillement] decency

**décennie** [deseni] *nf* decade

**décent, -e** [desɑ̃, -ɑ̃t] *adj* [comportement] proper; [vêtements] decent

**décentralisation** [desɑ̃tʀalizɑsjɔ̃] *nf* decentralization

**déception** [desɛpsjɔ̃] *nf* disappointment

**décerner** [desɛʀne] *vt* [prix] to award (**à** to)

**décès** [desɛ] *nm* death

**décevant, -e** [desvɑ̃, -ɑ̃t] *adj* disappointing

**décevoir** [desvwaʀ] *vt* to disappoint

**déchaîner** [deʃene] **1.** *vt* [colère, violence] to unleash **2. se déchaîner** *vpr* [tempête] to rage; [personne] to fly into a rage (**contre** with)

**décharge** [deʃaʀʒ] *nf* **décharge (électrique)** (electric) shock; **décharge (publique)** *Br* (rubbish) dump, *Am* (garbage) dump

**décharger** [deʃaʀʒe] **1.** *vt* [camion, navire, cargaison] to unload; **décharger qn de qch** [tâche, responsabilité] to relieve sb of **2. se décharger** *vpr* [batterie] to go flat

**déchausser** [deʃose] **1.** *vt* **déchausser qn** to take sb's shoes off **2. se déchausser** *vpr* [personne] to take one's shoes off

**déchéance** [deʃeɑ̃s] *nf* [déclin] decline

**déchets** [deʃɛ] *nmpl* scraps; **déchets radioactifs** radioactive waste

**Déchetterie®** [deʃetʀi] *nf* recycling *Br* centre or *Am* center

**déchiffrer** [deʃifʀe] *vt* [message, écriture] to decipher

**déchiqueté, -e** [deʃikte] *adj* [tissu] torn to shreds

**déchirer** [deʃire] **1.** *vt* [accidentellement] to tear; [volontairement] to tear up **2. se déchirer** *vpr* [tissu, papier] to tear

**déchirure** [deʃiryr] *nf* tear

**déchoir** [deʃwar] *vi* [personne] to demean oneself

**déchu, -e** [deʃy] *adj* **être déchu de qch** to be stripped of sth

**décidé, -e** [deside] *adj* [personne, air] determined; [fixé] settled; **être décidé à faire qch** to be determined to do sth

**décidément** [desidemɑ̃] *adv* really

**décider** [deside] **1.** *vt* **décider quand / que...** to decide when / that... **2.** *vi* **décider de qch** to decide on sth; **décider de faire qch** to decide to do sth **3. se décider** *vpr* **se décider (à faire qch)** to make up one's mind (to do sth)

**décilitre** [desilitr] *nm Br* decilitre, *Am* deciliter

**décimal, -e, -aux** [desimal, -o] *adj* decimal

**décimer** [desime] *vt* to decimate

**décimètre** [desimɛtr] *nm* decimetre

**décisif, -ive** [desizif, -iv] *adj* [bataille] decisive; [moment] critical ■ **décision** *nf* decision (**de faire** to do); **prendre une décision** to make a decision

**déclaration** [deklarɑsjɔ̃] *nf* [annonce] statement; [de naissance, de décès] registration; [à la police] report; **déclaration d'impôts** income tax return

**déclarer** [deklare] **1.** *vt* [annoncer] to declare (**que** that); [naissance, décès] to register; **déclarer qn coupable** to find sb guilty (**de** of); **déclarer la guerre** to declare war (**à** on); **rien à déclarer** [en douane] nothing to declare **2. se déclarer** *vpr* [incendie, maladie] to break out

**déclencher** [deklɑ̃ʃe] **1.** *vt* [appareil] to start; [mécanisme] to activate; [sonnerie] to set off; [révolte] to trigger off; [attaque] to launch **2. se déclencher** *vpr* [alarme, sonnerie] to go off; [incendie] to start

**déclic** [deklik] *nm* [bruit] click

**déclin** [deklɛ̃] *nm* decline; **être en déclin** to be in decline

**décliner** [dekline] **1.** *vi* [forces] to decline; [jour] to draw to a close **2.** *vt* [refuser] to decline

**décocher** [dekɔʃe] *vt* [flèche] to shoot

**décoder** [dekɔde] *vt* to decode ■ **décodeur** *nm* TV decoder

**décoiffer** [dekwafe] **1.** *vt* **décoiffer qn** to mess up sb's hair **2. se décoiffer** *vpr* [se dépeigner] to mess up one's hair; [ôter son chapeau] to remove one's hat

**décoincer** [dekwɛ̃se] **1.** *vt* [tiroir, mécanisme] to loosen **2. se décoincer** *vpr* [tiroir, mécanisme] to loosen

**décollage** [dekɔlaʒ] *nm* [d'avion] takeoff

**décoller** [dekɔle] **1.** *vt* [enlever] to peel off **2.** *vi* [avion] to take off **3. se décoller** *vpr* to peel off

**décolleté, -e** [dekɔlte] **1.** *adj* [robe] low-cut **2.** *nm* [de robe] low neckline

**décolorer** [dekɔlɔre] **1.** *vt* [cheveux] to bleach **2. se décolorer** *vpr* [tissu] to fade; **se décolorer les cheveux** to bleach one's hair ■ **décoloré, e** *adj* **a)** [fané] faded **b)** [blondi] bleached; **une femme décolorée** a peroxide *or* bleached blonde

**décombres** [dekɔ̃br] *nmpl* ruins, debris

**décommander** [dekɔmɑ̃de] **1.** *vt* [marchandises, invitation] to cancel; [invité] to put off **2. se décommander** *vpr* to cancel

**décomposer** [dekɔ̃poze] **1.** *vt* CHIM to decompose **2. se décomposer** *vpr* [pourrir] to decompose ■ **décomposition** *nf* decomposition

**décompression** [dekɔ̃prɛsjɔ̃] *nf* decompression

**décompte** [dekɔ̃t] *nm* [soustraction] deduction; [détail] breakdown ■ **décompter** *vt* to deduct (**de** from)

**déconcentrer** [dekɔ̃sɑ̃tre] ■ **se déconcentrer** *vpr* to lose concentration

**déconcerter** [dekɔ̃sɛrte] *vt* to disconcert

**décongeler** [dekɔ̃ʒle] *vt* to thaw, to defrost

**décongestionner** [dekɔ̃ʒɛstjɔne] *vt* [rue, poumons] to relieve congestion in

**déconnecter** [dekɔnɛkte] **1.** *vt* to disconnect; *Fam* **être déconnecté** to be out of touch **2. se déconnecter** *vpr* ORDINAT to disconnect, to log off ■ **déconnexion** [dekɔnɛksjɔ̃] *nf* ORDINAT logging off

**déconseiller** [dekɔ̃seje] *vt* **déconseiller qch à qn** to advise sb against sth; **déconseiller à qn de faire qch** to advise sb against doing sth

**déconsidérer** [dekɔ̃sidere] *vt* to discredit

**décontaminer** [dekɔ̃tamine] *vt* to decontaminate

**décontracter** [dekɔ̃trakte] **1.** *vt* [muscle] to relax **2. se décontracter** *vpr* to relax ■ **décontracté, -e** *adj* [ambiance, personne] relaxed; [vêtement] casual

**décor** [dekɔr] *nm* [de maison] decor; [paysage] surroundings; THÉÂT **décors** scenery, set

**décorer** [dekɔre] *vt* [maison, soldat] to decorate (**de** with) ■ **décorateur, -trice** *nmf* (interior) decorator; THÉÂT stage designer ■ **décoratif, -ive** *adj* decorative ■ **décoration** *nf* [action, ornement, médaille] decoration; [d'une maison] decoration; **faire de la décoration** to decorate; **décoration d'intérieur** interior decorating; **décorations de Noël** Christmas decorations

**décortiquer** [dekɔrtike] *vt* [riz, orge] to hull; [crevette, noisette] to shell

**découdre** [dekudr] **1.** *vt* [ourlet, vêtement] to unstitch; [bouton] to take off **2. se découdre** *vpr* [ourlet, vêtement] to come unstitched; [bouton] to come off

**découler** [dekule] *vi* **découler de qch** to follow from sth

**découper** [dekupe] *vt* [viande] to carve; [gâteau, papier] to cut up ■ **découpé, -e** *adj* [irrégulier] jagged

**décourager** [dekuraʒe] **1.** *vt* [dissuader] to discourage (**de faire** from doing); [démoraliser] to dishearten, to discourage **2. se décourager** *vpr* to get discouraged *or* disheartened ■ **découragement** *nm* discouragement

**décousu, -e** [dekuzy] *adj* [ourlet, vêtement] unstitched; *Fig* [propos] disjointed

**découvert, -e** [dekuvɛr, -ɛrt] **1.** *adj* [terrain] open; [tête, épaule] bare **2.** *nm* [de compte] overdraft

**découverte** [dekuvɛrt] *nf* discovery; **faire une découverte** to make a discovery

**découvrir** [dekuvrir] **1.** *vt* [trouver, apprendre à connaître] to discover; [secret] to uncover; **faire découvrir qch à qn** to introduce sb to sth **2. se découvrir** *vpr* [ciel] to clear

**décrire** [dekrir] *vt* [représenter] to describe

**décrocher** [dekrɔʃe] **1.** *vt* [détacher] to unhook; [tableau, rideau] to take down; **décrocher (le téléphone)** [pour répondre] to pick up the phone; [pour ne pas être dérangé] to take the phone off the hook **2. se décrocher** *vpr* [tableau, rideau] to come unhooked

**décroître** [dekrwatr] *vi* [forces, nombre] to decrease; [jours] to get shorter

**décrypter** [dekripte] *vt* to decipher

**déçu, -e** [desy] **1.** *pp de* **décevoir 2.** *adj* disappointed

**décupler** [dekyple] *vt* & *vi* to increase tenfold

**dédaigner** [dedeɲe] *vt* [offre, richesses] to scorn; [conseil] to disregard ■ **dédaigneux, -euse** *adj* scornful, disdainful (**de** of)

**dédain** [dedɛ̃] *nm* scorn, disdain (**pour/de** for)

**dedans** [dədɑ̃] *adv* inside; **de dedans** from (the) inside; **en dedans** on the inside; **tomber dedans** [trou] to fall in (it)

**dédicace** [dedikas] *nf* dedication ■ **dédicacer** *vt* [signer] to sign (**à** for)

**dédier** [dedje] *vt* to dedicate (**à** to)

**dédommager** [dedɔmaʒe] *vt* to compensate (**de** for) ∎ **dédommagement** *nm* compensation

**dédouaner** [dedwane] *vt* [marchandises] to clear through customs

**déduire** [dedɥir] *vt* [retirer] to deduct (**de** from); [conclure] to deduce (**de** from) ∎ **déductible** *adj* deductible ∎ **déduction** *nf* [raisonnement, décompte] deduction

**déesse** [deɛs] *nf* goddess

**défaillir** [defajir] *vi* [s'évanouir] to faint; [faiblir] to fail ∎ **défaillance** *nf* [évanouissement] fainting fit; [faiblesse] weakness; [panne] failure; **avoir une défaillance** [s'évanouir] to faint; [faiblir] to feel weak

**défaire** [defɛr] **1.** *vt* [nœud] to undo; [valises] to unpack **2. se défaire** *vpr* [nœud] to come undone

**défait, -e¹** [defɛ, -ɛt] *adj* [lit] unmade; [visage] haggard

**défaite²** [defɛt] *nf* defeat

**défaut** [defo] *nm* [de personne] fault, shortcoming; [de machine] defect; [de diamant, de raisonnement] flaw; **à défaut de qch** for lack of sth; **ou, à défaut...** or, failing that...; **défaut de fabrication** manufacturing fault; **défaut de prononciation** speech impediment

**défavorable** [defavɔrabl] *adj* unfavourable (**à** to) ∎ **défavorisé, -e** *adj* [milieu] underprivileged ∎ **défavoriser** *vt* to put at a disadvantage

**défection** [defɛksjɔ̃] *nf* [de soldat, d'espion] defection; **faire défection** [soldat, espion] to defect

**défectueux, -euse** [defɛktɥø, -øz] *adj* faulty, defective

**défendre** [defɑ̃dr] **1.** *vt* [protéger, soutenir] to defend (**contre** against); **défendre à qn de faire qch** to forbid sb to do sth; **défendre qch à qn** to forbid sb sth **2. se défendre** *vpr* to defend oneself

**défense¹** [defɑ̃s] *nf* [protection] *Br* defence, *Am* defense; **sans défense** *Br* defenceless, *Am* defenseless; **'défense de fumer'** 'no smoking'

**défense²** [defɑ̃s] *nf* [d'éléphant] tusk

**défenseur** [defɑ̃sœr] *nm* defender

**défensif, -ive** [defɑ̃sif, -iv] **1.** *adj* defensive **2.** *nf* **sur la défensive** on the defensive

**déferler** [defɛrle] *vi* [vagues] to break

**défi** [defi] *nm* challenge (**à** to); **lancer un défi à qn** to challenge sb; **mettre qn au défi de faire qch** to defy sb to do sth

**défiance** [defjɑ̃s] *nf* mistrust

**déficience** [defisjɑ̃s] *nf* deficiency

**déficit** [defisit] *nm* deficit; **être en déficit** to be in deficit; **déficit commercial** trade deficit ∎ **déficitaire** *adj* [budget] in deficit; [entreprise] loss-making; [compte] in debit

**défier** [defje] *vt* [provoquer] to challenge; [danger, mort] to defy; **défier qn de faire qch** to defy sb to do sth

**défiguré, -e** [defigyre] *adj* [personne] disfigured

**défilé** [defile] *nm* [cortège] procession; [de manifestants] march; MIL parade; GÉOG pass; **défilé de mode** fashion show

**définir** [definir] *vt* to define ∎ **défini, -e** *adj* definite ∎ **définition** *nf* definition; [de mots croisés] clue

**définitif, -ive** [definitif, -iv] **1.** *adj* [version] final; [fermeture] permanent **2.** *nf* **en définitive** in the final analysis ∎ **définitivement** *adv* [partir, exclure] for good

**déflagration** [deflagrasjɔ̃] *nf* explosion

**défoncer** [defɔ̃se] *vt* [porte, mur] to smash in; [trottoir] to break up ∎ **défoncé, -e** *adj* [route] bumpy

**déformation** [defɔrmasjɔ̃] *nf* [de membre] deformation; [de fait] distortion

**déformer** [defɔrme] **1.** *vt* [membre] to deform; [vêtement, chaussures] to put out of shape; [image] to distort;

[propos] to twist **2. se déformer** *vpr* to lose its shape ▪ **déformé, -e** *adj* [objet] misshapen ; [corps] deformed

**défricher** [defriʃe] *vt* [terrain] to clear

**défriser** [defrize] *vt* [cheveux] to straighten

**défroisser** [defrwase] *vt* to smooth out

**défunt, -e** [defœ̃, -œ̃t] **1.** *adj* [mort] departed ; **mon défunt mari** my late husband **2.** *nmf* **le défunt, la défunte** the deceased

**dégager** [degaʒe] **1.** *vt* [passage, voie] to clear (**de** of) ; [odeur, chaleur] to emit ; **dégager qn de** [décombres] to free sb from **2. se dégager** *vpr* [odeur] to be given off ; [ciel] to clear ; **se dégager de qch** [personne] to free oneself from sth ▪ **dégagé, -e** *adj* [ciel] clear ; [ton] casual ; [vue] open ▪ **dégagement** *nm* [action] clearing ; [de chaleur] emission

**dégainer** [degene] *vt & vi* to draw

**dégarnir** [degarnir] ▪ **se dégarnir** *vpr* [personne] to go bald

**dégâts** [dega] *nmpl* damage

**dégel** [deʒɛl] *nm* thaw ▪ **dégeler 1.** *vt* to thaw ; [surgelé] to defrost ; [crédits] to unfreeze **2.** *vi* to thaw ; **faire dégeler qch** [surgelé] to defrost sth **3.** *v impers* **il dégèle** it's thawing **4. se dégeler** *vpr Fig* [atmosphère] to become less chilly

**dégénérer** [deʒenere] *vi* to degenerate (**en** into)

**dégonfler** [degɔ̃fle] **1.** *vt* [pneu] to let the air out of **2. se dégonfler** *vpr* [pneu] to go flat ▪ **dégonflé, -e 1.** *adj* [pneu] flat **2.** *nmf Fam* [personne] chicken, yellow-belly

**dégouliner** [deguline] *vi* to trickle

**dégourdir** [degurdir] ▪ **se dégourdir** *vpr* **se dégourdir les jambes** to stretch one's legs ▪ **dégourdi, -e** *adj* [malin] smart

**dégoût** [degu] *nm* disgust

**dégoûter** [degute] *vt* [moralement] to disgust ; [physiquement] to turn sb's stomach ; **dégoûter qn de qch** to put

sb off sth ▪ **dégoûtant, -e** *adj* disgusting ▪ **dégoûté, -e** *adj* disgusted ; **être dégoûté de qch** to be sick of sth

**dégradation** [degradɑsjɔ̃] *nf* [de matériel] damage (**de** to)

**dégrader** [degrade] **1.** *vt* [matériel] to damage **2. se dégrader** *vpr* [situation] to deteriorate ▪ **dégradant, -e** *adj* degrading

**dégrafer** [degrafe] **1.** *vt* [vêtement] to undo **2. se dégrader** *vpr* [vêtement] to come undone

**degré** [dəgre] *nm* [d'angle, de température] degree ; [d'alcool] proof ; [d'échelle] rung ; **au plus haut degré** in the extreme ; **degré Celsius / Fahrenheit** degree Celsius / Fahrenheit

**dégressif, ive** [degresif, iv] *adj* **tarif dégressif** decreasing price rate

**dégrèvement** [degrɛvmɑ̃] *nm* **dégrèvement fiscal** tax relief

**dégriffé, e** [degrife] **1.** *adj* ex-designer label **2.** *nm* ex-designer label garment

**dégringoler** [degrɛ̃gɔle] *vi Fam* [tomber] to tumble ; *Fig* to crash

**dégrossir** [degrosir] *vt* [travail] to rough out

**déguiser** [degize] **1.** *vt* [pour tromper] to disguise ; **déguiser qn en qch** [costumer] to dress sb up as sth **2. se déguiser** *vpr* [pour s'amuser] to dress oneself up (**en** as) ▪ **déguisement** *nm* disguise ; [de bal costumé] fancy dress

**déguster** [degyste] *vt* [savourer] to savour ▪ **dégustation** *nf* tasting

**dehors** [dəɔr] **1.** *adv* outside ; [pas chez soi] out ; [en plein air] out of doors ; **en dehors de la ville** out of town ; *Fig* **en dehors de** [excepté] apart from **2.** *nm* [extérieur] outside ; **au dehors** on the outside ; [se pencher] out

**déjà** [deʒa] *adv* already ; **est-il déjà parti ?** has he left yet *or* already? ; **elle l'a déjà vu** she's seen it before, she's already seen it

**déjeuner** [deʒœne] **1.** *nm* **a)** lunch ; **petit déjeuner** breakfast **b)** *Can* [dîner] dinner **2.** *vi* [à midi] to have lunch ; [le matin] to have breakfast

**déjouer** [deʒwe] vt [intrigue] to foil

**délabré, -e** [delabre] adj [bâtiment] dilapidated

**délacer** [delase] **1.** vt [chaussure] to untie **2. se délacer** vpr [chaussure] to come untied

**délai** [delɛ] nm [laps de temps] time allowed; [sursis] extension; **dans les plus brefs délais** as soon as possible; **dernier délai** final date

**délaisser** [delese] vt [négliger] to neglect

**délasser** [delase] **1.** vt to relax **2. se délasser** vpr to relax

**délavé, -e** [delave] adj [tissu, jean] faded; [couleur, ciel] watery

**délayer** [deleje] vt [poudre] to add water to; [liquide] to water down

**délecter** [delɛkte] ■ **se délecter** vpr **se délecter de qch** to take delight in sth

**déléguer** [delege] vt to delegate (**à** to) ■ **délégation** nf delegation ■ **délégué, -e** nmf delegate; SCOL **délégué de classe** pupil elected to represent his or her class at class meetings

**délibération** [deliberasjɔ̃] nf deliberation

**délibéré, -e** [delibere] adj [intentionnel] deliberate

**délicat, -e** [delika, -at] adj [santé, travail] delicate; [question] tricky, delicate; [peau] sensitive; [geste] tactful ■ **délicatesse** nf [tact] tact

**délice** [delis] nm delight ■ **délicieux, -euse** adj [mets] delicious; [parfum] delightful

**délier** [delje] vt to untie

**délimiter** [delimite] vt [terrain] to mark off; [sujet] to define

**délinquant, -e** [delɛ̃kɑ̃, -ɑ̃t] nmf delinquent ■ **délinquance** nf delinquency

**délirant, e** [delirɑ̃, ɑ̃t] adj **a)** MÉD delirious **b)** [excité, exalté] frenzied **c)** Fam [extravagant] crazy ■ **délire** [delir] nm MÉD delirium; [exaltation] frenzy

**délit** [deli] nm Br offence, Am offense

**délivrer** [delivre] vt **a)** [captif] to rescue; **délivrer qn de qch** to rid sb of sth **b)** [marchandises] to deliver; [passeport] to issue (**à** to) ■ **délivrance** nf [soulagement] relief; [de passeport] issue

**délocaliser** [delɔkalize] vt to relocate

**déloger** [delɔʒe] vt [envahisseur] to drive out (**de** from)

**déloyal, -e, -aux** [delwajal, -o] adj [personne] disloyal; [concurrence] unfair

**deltaplane** [deltaplan] nm hang-glider; **faire du deltaplane** to go hang-gliding

**déluge** [delyʒ] nm [de pluie] downpour; [de paroles] flood; [d'insultes] torrent

**démago** [demago] Fam adj **il est démago** he's a demagogue

**demain** [dəmɛ̃] adv tomorrow; **demain soir** tomorrow evening; **à demain !** see you tomorrow!

**demande** [dəmɑ̃d] nf [requête] request (**de** for); ÉCON demand; **faire une demande de qch** [prêt, permis] to apply for sth; **demandes d'emploi** [dans le journal] jobs wanted, Br situations wanted

**demander** [dəmɑ̃de] **1.** vt [conseil] to ask for; [prix, raison] to ask; [nécessiter] to require; **demander son chemin / l'heure** to ask the way / the time; **demander qch à qn** to ask sb for sth; **demander à qn de faire qch** to ask sb to do sth; **demander qn en mariage** to propose (marriage) to sb **2.** vi **a)** [réclamer] **demander à qn de faire qch** to ask sb to do sth; **ne demander qu'à...** to be ready to... **b)** [nécessiter] **ce projet demande à être étudié** this project requires investigation or needs investigating **3. se demander** vpr to wonder, to ask oneself (**pourquoi** why; **si** if) ■ **demandeur, euse** nmf [solliciteur] **demandeur d'asile** asylum seeker, Am asylee; **demandeur d'emploi** job-seeker

**démanger** [demɑ̃ʒe] vt & vi to itch ■ **démangeaisons** nfpl **avoir des démangeaisons** to be itching

**démanteler** [demɑ̃tle] vt to break up

**démaquiller** [demakije] ■ **se démaquiller** vpr to remove one's make-up ■ **démaquillant** nm cleanser

**démarcation** [demarkasjɔ̃] nf demarcation

**démarche** [demarʃ] nf [allure] walk, gait ; [requête] step ; **faire les démarches nécessaires pour...** to take the necessary steps to...

**démarcheur, -euse** [demarʃœr, -øz] nmf [vendeur] door-to-door salesman, f saleswoman

**démarquer** [demarke] vt [marchandises] to mark down

**démarrer** [demare] 1. vi [moteur] to start ; [voiture] to move off ; [ordinateur] to start (up) ; Fig [entreprise] to get off the ground 2. vt to start ; ORDINAT to start up, to boot up ■ **démarrage** nm [de moteur] starting ; **au démarrage** when moving off ; **démarrage en côte** hill start ■ **démarreur** nm AUTO starter ; Can **démarreur à distance** remote starter

**démasquer** [demaske] vt to unmask

**démêlant, e** [demɛlɑ̃, ɑ̃t] adj conditioning ■ **démêlant** nm conditioner

**démêler** [demele] vt to untangle

**déménager** [demenaʒe] 1. vi to move 2. vt [meubles] to move ■ **déménagement** nm move ■ **déménageur** nm Br removal man, Am (furniture) mover

**démener** [demne] ■ **se démener** vpr [s'agiter] to thrash about

**dément, -e** [demɑ̃, -ɑ̃t] adj insane ■ **démentiel, -elle** adj insane

**démentir** [demɑ̃tir] vt [nouvelle, fait] to deny ■ **démenti** nm denial

**démesuré, -e** [demzyre] adj excessive

**démettre** [demɛtr] 1. vt **démettre qn de ses fonctions** to remove sb from his / her post 2. **se démettre** vpr **se démettre l'épaule** to dislocate one's shoulder

**demeurant** [dəmœrɑ̃] ■ **au demeurant** adv [malgré tout] for all that

**demeure** [dəmœr] nf [belle maison] mansion

**demeurer** [dəmœre] vi a) (aux **être**) [rester] to remain b) (aux **avoir**) Formel [habiter] to reside

**demi, -e** [dəmi] **1.** adj half ; **une heure et demie** [90 minutes] an hour and a half ; [à l'horloge] half past one, one-thirty
**2.** adv **(à) demi** plein half-full ; **à demi nu** half-naked
**3.** nmf [moitié] half
**4.** nm [au football] midfielder ; **un demi** [bière] a beer, Br a half(-pint) ; **demi de mêlée** [au rugby] scrum half
**5.** nf **à la demie** [à l'horloge] at half-past
■ **demi-bouteille** [dəmibutɛj] (pl **demi-bouteilles**) nf half-bottle
■ **demi-cercle** (pl **demi-cercles**) nm semicircle
■ **demi-douzaine** (pl **demi-douzaines**) nf **une demi-douzaine (de)** half a dozen
■ **demi-écrémé** adj semi-skimmed
■ **demi-finale** (pl **demi-finales**) nf SPORT semi-final
■ **demi-frère** (pl **demi-frères**) nm half brother
■ **demi-heure** (pl **demi-heures**) nf **une demi-heure** half an hour
■ **demi-journée** (pl **demi-journées**) nf half-day
■ **demi-litre** [dəmilitr] (pl **demi-litres**) nm half a Br litre or Am liter, Br half-litre, Am half-liter
■ **demi-pension** nf Br half-board, Am breakfast and one meal
■ **demi-pensionnaire** (pl **demi-pensionnaires**) nmf pupil who has school dinners (Br)
■ **demi-sœur** (pl **demi-sœurs**) nf half sister
■ **demi-tarif** (pl **demi-tarifs**) nm half-price
■ **demi-tour** (pl **demi-tours**) nm Br about turn, Am about face ; [en voiture] U-turn ; **faire demi-tour** [à pied] to turn back ; [en voiture] to do a U-turn

**démission** [demisjɔ̃] *nf* resignation ; **donner sa démission** to hand in one's resignation ▪ **démissionner** *vi* to resign

**démocrate** [demɔkrat] **1.** *adj* democratic **2.** *nmf* democrat ▪ **démocratie** [-asi] *nf* democracy ▪ **démocratique** *adj* democratic

**démodé, -e** [demode] *adj* old-fashioned

**démographie** [demɔgrafi] *nf* demography

**demoiselle** [dəmwazɛl] *nf* [jeune fille] young lady ; **demoiselle d'honneur** bridesmaid

**démolir** [demɔlir] *vt* [bâtiment] to pull down, to demolish ▪ **démolition** *nf* demolition

**démon** [demɔ̃] *nm* demon ; **le démon** the Devil

**démonstratif, -ive** [demɔ̃stratif, -iv] *adj* demonstrative

**démonstration** [demɔ̃strasjɔ̃] *nf* demonstration

**démonter** [demɔ̃te] **1.** *vt* [mécanisme, tente] to dismantle **2. se démonter** *vpr* to be put out

**démontrer** [demɔ̃tre] *vt* to demonstrate

**démoraliser** [demɔralize] **1.** *vt* to demoralize **2. se démoraliser** *vpr* to become demoralized

**démordre** [demɔrdr] *vi* **ne pas démordre de qch** to stick to sth

**démotivé, e** [demɔtive] *adj* demotivated

**démouler** [demule] *vt* [gâteau] to turn out

**démuni, e** [demyni] *adj* **a)** [pauvre] destitute **b)** [sans défense] powerless, resourceless

**démunir** [demynir] ▪ **se démunir** *vpr* **se démunir de qch** to part with sth

**démystifier** [demistifje] *vt* to demystify

**dénicher** [denife] *vt Fig* **a)** [personne] to flush out **b)** [objet] to unearth

**dénier** [denje] *vt* [responsabilité] to deny ; **dénier qch à qn** to deny sb sth

**dénigrer** [denigre] *vt* to denigrate

**dénivellation** [denivelasjɔ̃] *nf* difference in level ; **dénivellations** [relief] bumps

**dénombrer** [denɔ̃bre] *vt* to count

**dénommer** [denɔme] *vt* to name

**dénoncer** [denɔ̃se] **1.** *vt* [injustice, abus, malfaiteur] to denounce (**à** to) ; [élève] to tell on (**à** to) **2. se dénoncer** *vpr* [malfaiteur] to give oneself up (**à** to) ; [élève] to own up (**à** to)

**dénoter** [denɔte] *vt* to denote

**dénouement** [denumɑ̃] *nm* [de livre] ending ; [de pièce de théâtre] dénouement ; [d'affaire] outcome

**dénouer** [denwe] **1.** *vt* [nœud, corde] to undo, to untie ; [cheveux] to let down, to undo ; *Fig* [intrigue] to unravel **2. se dénouer** *vpr* [nœud] to come undone ; [cheveux] to come down

**denrée** [dɑ̃re] *nf* foodstuff ; **denrées alimentaires** foodstuffs ; **denrées périssables** perishable goods

**dense** [dɑ̃s] *adj* dense ▪ **densité** *nf* density

**dent** [dɑ̃] *nf* tooth (*pl* teeth) ; [de roue] cog ; [de fourchette] prong ; **dent de lait / sagesse** milk / wisdom tooth ; **faire ses dents** [enfant] to be teething ; **en dents de scie** serrated ; *Fig* [résultats] uneven ▪ **dentaire** *adj* dental

**dentelé, -e** [dɑ̃tle] *adj* [côte, feuille] jagged

**dentelle** [dɑ̃tɛl] *nf* lace

**dentier** [dɑ̃tje] *nm* (set of) false teeth, dentures

**dentifrice** [dɑ̃tifris] *nm* toothpaste

**dentiste** [dɑ̃tist] *nmf* dentist

**dénuder** [denyde] *vt* to (lay) bare ▪ **dénudé, -e** *adj* bare

**dénué, -e** [denɥe] *adj* **dénué d'intérêt** devoid of interest

**dénuement** [denymɑ̃] *nm* destitution ; **dans le dénuement** poverty-stricken, destitute

**déodorant** [deɔdɔrɑ̃] *nm* deodorant

**dépanner** [depane] vt [machine] to repair ■ **dépannage** nm (emergency) repairs; **voiture / service de dépannage** breakdown vehicle / service ■ **dépanneur** nm [de télévision] repairman; [de voiture] breakdown mechanic ■ **dépanneuse** nf [voiture] Br breakdown lorry, Am wrecker

**dépareillé, -e** [depareje] adj [chaussure] odd

**déparler** [deparle] vi Can [dire n'importe quoi] to babble away, to babble on, to babbling

**départ** [depar] nm departure; [de course] start; **les grands départs** the mass exodus of people from major cities at the beginning of the holiday period; **point / ligne de départ** starting point / post; **au départ** at the outset, at the start; **au départ de Paris** [excursion] leaving from Paris

**départager** [departaʒe] vt to decide between

**département** [departəmɑ̃] nm department (division of local government) ■ **départemental, -e, -aux** adj departmental; **route départementale** secondary road, Br ≃ B road

**départir** [departir] ■ **se départir** vpr il ne s'est jamais départi de son calme his calm never deserted him

**dépasser** [depɑse] **1.** vt [véhicule] Br to overtake, Am to pass; [endroit] to go past; [vitesse] to exceed; **dépasser qn** [en hauteur] to be taller than sb **2.** vi [clou] to stick out ■ **dépassé, -e** adj [démodé] outdated; [incapable] unable to cope

**dépayser** [depeize] vt Br to disorientate, Am to disorient ■ **dépaysant, e** adj **un voyage dépaysant** a trip that gives you a complete change of scene

**dépêche** [depɛʃ] nf dispatch ■ **dépêcher 1.** vt to dispatch **2.** se **dépêcher** vpr to hurry (up); se **dépêcher de faire qch** to hurry to do sth

**dépendant, -e** [depɑ̃dɑ̃, -ɑ̃t] adj dependent (de on) ■ **dépendance** nf dependence; **sous la dépendance de qn** under sb's domination ■ **dépendances** nfpl [bâtiments] outbuildings

**dépendre** [depɑ̃dr] vi to depend (de on or upon); **dépendre de** [appartenir à] to belong to; [être soumis à] to be dependent on

**dépens** [depɑ̃] nmpl apprendre qch à ses dépens to learn sth to one's cost

**dépense** [depɑ̃s] nf [frais] expense, expenditure; **faire des dépenses** to spend money ■ **dépenser 1.** vt [argent] to spend; [forces] to exert **2.** se **dépenser** vpr to burn up energy

**dépensier, -ère** [depɑ̃sje, -ɛr] adj extravagant

**dépérir** [deperir] vi [personne] to waste away; [plante] to wither

**dépeupler** [depœple] **1.** vt to depopulate **2.** se **dépeupler** vpr to become depopulated

**dépilatoire** [depilatwar] nm hairremover

**dépister** [depiste] vt [maladie] to detect ■ **dépistage** nm [de maladie] screening; **dépistage du SIDA** AIDS testing

**dépit** [depi] nm spite; **en dépit de qn / qch** in spite of sb / sth

**dépité, -e** [depite] adj annoyed

**déplacement** [deplasmɑ̃] nm [voyage] trip; **être en déplacement** [homme d'affaires] to be on a business trip; **frais de déplacement** Br travelling or Am traveling expenses

**déplacer** [deplase] **1.** vt [objet] to move **2.** se **déplacer** vpr [aiguille de montre] to move; [personne, animal] to move (about); [marcher] to walk (around); [voyager] to travel ■ **déplacé, -e** adj [mal à propos] out of place; **personne déplacée** [réfugié] displaced person

**déplaire** [deplɛr] **1.** vi **déplaire à qn** to displease sb; **ça me déplaît** I don't like it **2.** se **déplaire** vpr il se déplaît **à Paris** he doesn't like it in Paris ■ **déplaisant, -e** adj unpleasant

**déplier**

**déplier** [deplije] *vt* to open out, to unfold ■ **dépliant** *nm* [prospectus] leaflet

**déplorer** [deplɔre] *vt* [regretter] to deplore; **déplorer que...** (+ *subjunctive*) to deplore the fact that...; **déplorer la mort de qn** to mourn sb's death

**déployer** [deplwaje] *vt* [ailes] to spread; [journal, carte] to unfold; [troupes] to deploy ■ **déploiement** *nm* [démonstration] display; [d'une armée] deployment

**dépoli, -e** [depɔli] *adj* **verre dépoli** frosted glass

**dépolluant, e** [depɔlɥɑ̃, ɑ̃t] **1.** *adj* depolluting, anti-pollutant **2.** *nm* depollutant, anti-pollutant

**déporter** [depɔrte] *vt* **déporter qn** to send sb to a concentration camp

**déposer** [depoze] **1.** *vt* [poser] to put down; [gerbe] to lay; [projet de loi] to introduce; [souverain] to depose; **déposer qn** [en voiture] to drop sb off; **déposer de l'argent sur un compte** to deposit money in an account; **déposer une plainte contre qn** to lodge a complaint against sb **2.** *vi* JUR to testify; [liquide] to leave a deposit **3. se déposer** *vpr* to settle

**dépositaire** [depoziter] *nmf* [vendeur] agent

**déposséder** [deposede] *vt* to deprive, to dispossess (**de** of)

**dépôt** [depo] *nm* [de vin] deposit, sediment; [entrepôt] depot; [prison] jail; **faire un dépôt** [d'argent] to make a deposit; **dépôt de munitions** munitions depot

**dépouille** [depuj] *nf* [d'animal] hide, skin; **dépouille mortelle** [de personne] mortal remains

**dépouiller** [depuje] **1.** *vt* [animal] to skin; [analyser] to go through; **dépouiller qn de qch** to deprive sb of sth; **dépouiller un scrutin** to count the votes **2. se dépouiller** *vpr* **se dépouiller de qch** to rid oneself of sth ■ **dépouillé, -e** *adj* [style] austere ■ **dépouillement** *nm* [de documents] analysis; [privation] deprivation; [sobriété] austerity; **dépouillement du scrutin** counting of the votes

**dépourvu, -e** [depurvy] *adj* **dépourvu de qch** devoid of sth; **prendre qn au dépourvu** to catch sb off guard or unawares

**dépoussiérer** [depusjere] *vt* to dust

**dépraver** [deprave] *vt* to deprave

**déprécier** [depresje] ■ **se déprécier** *vpr* [valeurs, marchandises] to depreciate

**dépression** [depresjɔ̃] *nf* [creux, maladie] depression; **dépression atmosphérique** low, trough; **dépression économique** slump; **dépression nerveuse** nervous breakdown; **faire de la dépression** to be suffering from depression ■ **dépressif, -ive** *adj* depressive

**déprimer** [deprime] *vt* to depress ■ **déprimant, e** *adj* depressing ■ **déprimé, -e** *adj* depressed

**depuis** [dəpɥi] **1.** *prép* since; **depuis lundi / 2014** since Monday / 2014; **j'habite ici depuis un mois** I've been living here for a month; **depuis quand êtes-vous là ?, depuis combien de temps êtes-vous là ?** how long have you been here?; **depuis longtemps** for a long time; **depuis peu** recently **2.** *adv* since (then), ever since **3.** *conj* **depuis que** since

**député** [depyte] *nm* POL deputy, *Br* ≃ MP, *Am* ≃ representative; **député du Parlement européen** Member of the European Parliament

**déraciner** [derasine] *vt* [arbre, personne] to uproot ■ **déraciné, e** *adj* *Fig* uprooted; **ils se sentent déracinés** they feel cut off from their roots

**dérailler** [deraje] *vi* [train] to leave the rails; **faire dérailler un train** to derail a train

**déranger** [derɑ̃ʒe] **1.** *vt* [affaires] to disturb; **je viendrai si ça ne te dérange pas** I'll come if that's all right with you; **ça vous dérange si je fume ?** do you mind if I smoke? **2. se déranger** *vpr* to put oneself to a lot of trouble (**pour faire** to do); [se déplacer] to move; **ne te dérange pas!** don't bother! ■ **dérangement** nm [gêne] trouble; **en dérangement** [téléphone] out of order

**déraper** [derape] vi [véhicule] to skid; [personne] to slip

**dérégler** [deregle] **1.** vt [mécanisme] to cause to malfunction **2. se dérégler** vpr [mécanisme] to go wrong

**dérider** [deride] **1.** vt to cheer up **2. se dérider** vpr to cheer up

**dérision** [derizjɔ̃] nf derision; **tourner qch en dérision** to deride sth ■ **dérisoire** adj [somme] derisory

**dérive** [deriv] nf NAUT drift; **à la dérive** adrift

**dérivé** [derive] nm **produit dérivé** by-product

**dériver** [derive] **1.** vt [cours d'eau] to divert **2.** vi NAUT to drift

**dermato** [dɛrmato] nmf Fam dermatologist

**dermatologue** [dɛrmatɔlɔg] nmf dermatologist ■ **dermatologique** [dɛrmatɔlɔʒik] adj skin, dermatological

**dernier, -ère** [dɛrnje, -ɛr] **1.** adj [ultime] last; [marquant la fin] final; [nouvelles, mode] latest; [étage] top; [degré] highest; **le dernier rang** the back or last row; **ces derniers mois** these past few months; **les dix dernières minutes** the last ten minutes; **en dernier** last **2.** nmf last; **ce dernier** [de deux] the latter; [de plusieurs] the last-mentioned

**dérober** [derobe] **1.** vt [voler] to steal (**à** from); [cacher] to hide (**à** from) **2. se dérober** vpr [s'esquiver] to slip away; [éviter de répondre] to dodge the issue

**dérogation** [derɔgasjɔ̃] nf exemption (**à** from)

**déroger** [derɔʒe] vi **déroger à une règle** to depart from a rule

**dérouler** [derule] **1.** vt [tapis] to unroll; [fil] to unwind **2. se dérouler** vpr [tapis] to unroll; [fil] to unwind; [avoir lieu] to take place

**déroute** [derut] nf [d'armée] rout

**dérouter** [derute] vt [avion, navire] to divert, to reroute; [poursuivant] to throw off the scent; Fig [étonner] to throw

**derrière** [dɛrjɛr] **1.** prép & adv behind; **derrière moi** behind me; **assis derrière** [dans une voiture] sitting in the back; **par derrière** [attaquer] from behind, from the rear **2.** nm [de maison] back, rear; [fesses] behind; **roue de derrière** back or rear wheel

**des** [dɛ] voir **de, un**

**dès** [dɛ] prép from; **dès le début** (right) from the start; **dès maintenant** from now on; **dès le VIᵉ siècle** as early as or as far back as the sixth century; **dès lors** [dans le temps] from then on; [en conséquence] consequently; **dès leur arrivée** as soon as they arrive / arrived; **dès qu'elle viendra** as soon as she comes

**désabusé, -e** [dezabyze] adj disillusioned

**désaccord** [dezakɔr] nm disagreement; **être en désaccord avec qn** to disagree with sb

**désaffecté, -e** [dezafɛkte] adj disused

**désaffection** [dezafɛksjɔ̃] nf disaffection (**à l'égard de** with)

**désagréable** [dezagreabl] adj unpleasant

**désagrément** [dezagremɑ̃] nm [gêne] trouble; [souci, aspect négatif] problem

**désaltérer** [dezaltere] **1.** vt **désaltérer qn** to quench sb's thirst **2. se désaltérer** vpr to quench one's thirst

**désamorcer** [dezamɔrse] vt [bombe, conflit] to defuse

**désapprouver** [dezapruve] **1.** vt to disapprove of **2.** vi to disapprove ■ **désapprobateur, -trice** adj disapproving ■ **désapprobation** nf disapproval

**désarmer** [dezarme] **1.** vt [soldat, nation] to disarm; Fig **désarmer qn** [franchise, attitude] to disarm sb **2.** vi [pays] to disarm ■ **désarmement** nm [de nation] disarmament

**désarroi** [dezarwa] nm confusion

**désastre** [dezastr] *nm* disaster
■ **désastreux, -euse** *adj* disastrous

**désavantage** [dezavɑ̃taʒ] *nm* disadvantage ■ **désavantager** *vt* to put at a disadvantage

**désavouer** [dezavwe] *vt* [renier] to disown

**désaxé, -e** [dezakse] *nmf* unbalanced person

**desceller** [desele] **1.** *vt* [pierre] to loosen **2. se desceller** *vpr* to come loose

**descendant, -e** [desɑ̃dɑ̃, -ɑ̃t] *nmf* descendant ■ **descendance** *nf* [enfants] descendants; [origine] descent

**descendre** [desɑ̃dr] **1.** (*aux* **être**) *vi* to come / go down (**de** from); [d'un train] to get off (**de** from); [d'un arbre] to climb down (**de** from); [marée] to go out; **descendre à l'hôtel** to put up at a hotel; **descendre de** [être issu de] to be descended from **2.** (*aux* **avoir**) *vt* [escalier] to come / go down; [objet] to bring / take down

**descente** [desɑ̃t] *nf* [d'avion] descent; [en parachute] drop; [pente] slope; [de police] raid (**dans** upon); **descente de lit** bedside rug

**descriptif, -ive** [deskriptif, -iv] *adj* descriptive ■ **description** *nf* description

**désemparé, -e** [dezɑ̃pare] *adj* [personne] at a loss

**désemplir** [dezɑ̃plir] *vi* **ce magasin ne désemplit pas** this shop is always crowded

**désenchanté, -e** [dezɑ̃ʃɑ̃te] *adj* disillusioned ■ **désenchantement** *nm* disenchantment

**déséquilibre** [dezekilibr] *nm* imbalance; **en déséquilibre** unsteady ■ **déséquilibré, -e 1.** *adj* unbalanced **2.** *nmf* unbalanced person ■ **déséquilibrer** *vt* to throw off balance

**désert, -e** [dezɛr, -ɛrt] **1.** *adj* [lieu] deserted; [région] uninhabited; **île déserte** desert island **2.** *nm* desert ■ **désertique** *adj* **région désertique** desert region

**déserter** [dezɛrte] *vt & vi* to desert ■ **désertion** *nf* desertion

**désespérer** [dezɛspere] **1.** *vt* to drive to despair **2.** *vi* to despair (**de** of) **3. se désespérer** *vpr* to despair ■ **désespérant, -e** *adj* [situation, personne] hopeless ■ **désespéré, -e** *adj* [personne] in despair; [cas, situation, efforts] desperate ■ **désespérément** *adv* desperately

**désespoir** [dezɛspwar] *nm* despair; **en désespoir de cause** in desperation

**déshabiller** [dezabije] **1.** *vt* to undress **2. se déshabiller** *vpr* to undress

**désherber** [dezɛrbe] *vt & vi* to weed

**déshériter** [dezerite] *vt* to disinherit

**déshonneur** [dezɔnœr] *nm* dishonour

**déshonorer** [dezɔnɔre] *vt* to disgrace ■ **déshonorant, -e** *adj* dishonourable

**déshydrater** [dezidrate] **1.** *vt* to dehydrate **2. se déshydrater** *vpr* to become dehydrated

**désigner** [dezine] *vt* [montrer] to point to; [choisir] to choose; [nommer] to appoint; **désigner qn par son nom** to refer to sb by name ■ **désignation** *nf* designation

**désillusion** [dezilyzjɔ̃] *nf* disillusion ■ **désillusionner** *vt* to disillusion

**désinfecter** [dezɛ̃fɛkte] *vt* to disinfect ■ **désinfectant** *nm* disinfectant

**désinformation** [dezɛ̃fɔrmasjɔ̃] *nf* disinformation

**désinstallation** [dezɛ̃stalasjɔ̃] *nf* ORDINAT uninstalling, deinstalling ■ **désinstaller** *vt* ORDINAT to uninstall

**désintégrer** [dezɛ̃tegre] ■ **se désintégrer** *vpr* to disintegrate

**désintéresser** [dezɛ̃terese] ■ **se désintéresser** *vpr* **se désintéresser de qch** to lose interest in sth ■ **désintéressé, -e** *adj* [altruiste] disinterested ■ **désintérêt** *nm* lack of interest

**désintoxiquer** [dezɛ̃tɔksike] **1.** *vt* [alcoolique, drogué] to treat for alco-

**détermination** [detɛrminɑsjɔ̃] *nf* [fermeté] determination

**déterminer** [detɛrmine] *vt* [préciser] to determine ; [causer] to bring about
■ **déterminant, -e** *adj* decisive
■ **déterminé, -e** *adj* [précis] specific ; [résolu] determined

**déterrer** [detere] *vt* to dig up

**détester** [detɛste] *vt* to hate, to detest ; **détester faire qch** to hate doing *or* to do sth ■ **détestable** *adj* foul

**détonation** [detɔnɑsjɔ̃] *nf* explosion ; [d'arme] bang

**détonner** [detɔne] *vi* [contraster] to clash

**détour** [detur] *nm* [crochet] detour ; [de route] bend, curve

**détourner** [deturne] **1.** *vt* [dévier] to divert ; [avion] to hijack ; [conversation, sens] to change ; [fonds] to embezzle ; [coup] to ward off ; **détourner la tête** to turn one's head away ; **détourner les yeux** to look away ; **détourner qn de** [son devoir] to take sb away from ; [sa route] to lead sb away from **2. se détourner** *vpr* to turn away ■ **détourné, -e** *adj* [chemin, moyen] roundabout, indirect ■ **détournement** [-əmɑ̃] *nm* [de cours d'eau] diversion ; **détournement d'avion** hijack(ing) ; **détournement de fonds** embezzlement

**détracteur, -trice** [detraktœr, -tris] *nmf* detractor

**détraquer** [detrake] **1.** *vt* [mécanisme] to put out of order **2. se détraquer** *vpr* [machine] to go wrong

**détresse** [detrɛs] *nf* distress ; **en détresse** [navire] in distress

**détriment** [detrimɑ̃] ■ **au détriment de** *prép* to the detriment of

**détritus** [detritys] *nmpl Br* rubbish, *Am* garbage

**détroit** [detrwa] *nm* strait

**détromper** [detrɔ̃pe] **1.** *vt* **détromper qn** to put sb right **2. se détromper** *vpr* **détrompez-vous !** don't you believe it!

**détrôner** [detrone] *vt* [souverain] to dethrone ; [supplanter] to supersede

**détruire** [detrɥir] *vt* [ravager] to destroy ; [tuer] to kill

**dette** [dɛt] *nf* debt ; **avoir des dettes** to be in debt ; **faire des dettes** to run into debt

**DEUG** [dœg] *(abr de* **diplôme d'études universitaires générales***) nm Anc degree gained after two years' study at university*

**deuil** [dœj] *nm* [affliction, vêtements] mourning ; [décès] bereavement ; **être en deuil** to be in mourning

**deux** [dø] *adj inv & nm inv* two ; **deux fois** twice ; **mes deux sœurs** both my sisters, my two sisters ; **tous (les) deux** both ■ **deux-pièces** *nm inv* [maillot de bain] bikini ; [appartement] two-roomed *Br* flat *or Am* apartment ■ **deux-roues** *nm inv* two-wheeled vehicle

**deuxième** [døzjɛm] *adj & nmf* second ■ **deuxièmement** *adv* secondly

**dévaler** [devale] *vt* [escalier] to hurtle down

**dévaliser** [devalize] *vt* [personne, banque] to rob

**dévaloriser** [devalɔrize] **1.** *vt* [monnaie, diplôme] to devalue **2. se dévaloriser** *vpr* [monnaie] to depreciate ■ **dévalorisation** *nf* [de diplôme] loss of value

**dévaluer** [devalɥe] *vt* [monnaie] to devalue ■ **dévaluation** *nf* FIN devaluation

**devancer** [dəvɑ̃se] *vt* [concurrent] to be ahead of ; [arriver avant] to arrive before

**devant** [dəvɑ̃] **1.** *prép & adv* in front (of) ; **passer devant une église** to go past a church ; **marcher devant qn** to walk in front of sb ; **assis devant** [dans une voiture] sitting in the front **2.** *nm* front ; **roue /porte de devant** front wheel /door ; **prendre les devants** [action] to take the initiative

**devanture** [dəvɑ̃tyr] *nf* [vitrine] window ; [façade] front

**dévaster** [devaste] *vt* to devastate ■ **dévastation** *nf* devastation

**développer** [devlɔpe] **1.** *vt* to develop **2. se développer** *vpr* to develop ■ **développement** *nm* development; [de photo] developing; **en plein développement** [entreprise, pays] growing fast ■ **développeur** *nm* ORDINAT [entreprise] software development *or* design company; [personne] software developer *or* designer

**devenir** [dəvnir] (*aux* être) *vi* to become; **devenir médecin** to become a doctor; **devenir vieux** to get *or* grow old; **devenir tout rouge** to go all red; **qu'est-elle devenue ?** what's become of her?

**dévergondé, -e** [devergɔ̃de] *adj* shameless

**déverser** [deverse] **1.** *vt* [liquide] to pour out; [ordures] to dump **2. se déverser** *vpr* [liquide, rivière] to empty (**dans** into)

**dévêtir** [devetir] **1.** *vt* to undress **2. se dévêtir** *vpr* to undress

**dévier** [devje] **1.** *vt* [circulation] to divert; [coup, rayons] to deflect **2.** *vi* [balle] to deflect; [véhicule] to veer; **dévier de sa route** to veer off course ■ **déviation** *nf* [itinéraire] *Br* diversion, *Am* detour

**devin** [dəvɛ̃] *nm* soothsayer

**deviner** [dəvine] *vt* to guess (**que** that) ■ **devinette** *nf* riddle

**devis** [dəvi] *nm* estimate

**dévisager** [devizaʒe] *vt* **dévisager qn** to stare at sb

**devise** [dəviz] *nf* [légende] motto; [monnaie] currency; **devises étrangères** foreign currency

**dévisser** [devise] **1.** *vt* to unscrew **2. se dévisser** *vpr* [bouchon] to unscrew; [par accident] to come unscrewed

**dévoiler** [devwale] **1.** *vt* [statue] to unveil; *Fig* [secret] to disclose **2. se dévoiler** *vpr* [mystère] to come to light

**devoir¹** [dəvwar] *v aux* **a)** [indique la nécessité] **je dois refuser** I must refuse, I have (got) to refuse; **j'ai dû refuser** I had to refuse

**b)** [indique une forte probabilité] **il doit être tard** it must be late; **elle a dû oublier** she must have forgotten; **cela devait arriver** it had to happen **c)** [indique l'obligation] **tu dois apprendre tes leçons** you must learn your lessons; **vous devriez rester** you should stay, you ought to stay; **il aurait dû venir** he should have come, he ought to have come **d)** [indique l'intention] **elle doit venir** she's supposed to be coming, she's due to come; **le train devait arriver à midi** the train was due (to arrive) at noon; **je devais le voir** I was (due) to see him

**devoir²** [dəvwar] **1.** *vt* to owe; **devoir qch à qn** to owe sb sth, to owe sth to sb **2. se devoir** *vpr* **comme il se doit** as is proper **3.** *nm* [obligation] duty; **présenter ses devoirs à qn** to pay one's respects to sb; SCOL **devoirs** homework; **faire ses devoirs** to do one's homework; **devoir sur table** test

**dévorer** [devɔre] *vt* [manger] to devour

**dévotion** [devosjɔ̃] *nf* [adoration] devotion

**dévouer** [devwe] ■ **se dévouer** *vpr* [se sacrifier] to volunteer; [se consacrer] to devote oneself (**à** to) ■ **dévoué, -e** *adj* [ami, femme] devoted (**à** to) ■ **dévouement** [-umɑ̃] *nm* devotion; [de héros] devotion to duty

**dextérité** [dɛksterite] *nf* dexterity, skill

**dézipper** [dezipe] *vt* ORDINAT [fichier] to unzip

**diabète** [djabɛt] *nm* MÉD diabetes ■ **diabétique** *adj* & *nmf* diabetic

**diable** [djɑbl] *nm* devil; **le diable** the Devil ■ **diabolique** *adj* diabolical

**diadème** [djadɛm] *nm* tiara

**diagnostic** [djagnɔstik] *nm* diagnosis ■ **diagnostiquer** *vt* to diagnose

**diagonal, -e, -aux** [djagɔnal, -o] *adj* diagonal ■ **diagonale** *nf* diagonal (line); **en diagonale** diagonally

**diagramme** [djagram] *nm* graph

**dialecte** [djalɛkt] *nm* dialect

**dialogue** [djalɔg] *nm Br* dialogue, *Am* dialog ; [conversation] conversation ■ **dialoguer** *vi* to communicate ; ORDINAT to interact

**diamant** [djamɑ̃] *nm* diamond

**diamètre** [djamɛtr] *nm* diameter

**diapason** [djapazɔ̃] *nm* MUS [appareil] tuning fork

**diapositive** [djapozitiv] *nf* slide

**diarrhée** [djare] *nf* diarrhoea

**dictateur** [diktatœr] *nm* dictator ■ **dictatorial, -e, -aux** *adj* dictatorial ■ **dictature** *nf* dictatorship

**dicter** [dikte] *vt* to dictate (**à** to) ■ **dictée** *nf* dictation

**diction** [diksjɔ̃] *nf* diction

**dictionnaire** [diksjɔnɛr] *nm* dictionary

**dièse** [djɛz] *adj & nm* MUS sharp

**diesel** [djezɛl] *adj & nm* (**moteur**) **diesel** diesel (engine)

**diète** [djɛt] *nf* [partielle] diet ; [totale] fast ; **être à la diète** to be on a diet /to be fasting

**diététicien, -enne** [djetetisjɛ̃, -ɛn] *nmf* dietician ■ **diététique 1.** *nf* dietetics (*sg*) **2.** *adj* **aliment** *ou* **produit diététique** health food ; **magasin diététique** health-food shop

**dieu, -x** [djø] *nm* god ; **Dieu** God ; **le bon Dieu** God

**diffamation** [difamasjɔ̃] *nf* [en paroles] slander ; [par écrit] libel ■ **diffamatoire** *adj* [paroles] slanderous ; [écrit] libellous

**différé** [difere] *nm* **en différé** [émission] prerecorded

**différence** [diferɑ̃s] *nf* difference (**de** in) ; **à la différence de qn /qch** unlike sb /sth ; **faire la différence entre** to make a distinction between ; **différences culturelles** cultural differences

**différencier** [diferɑ̃sje] **1.** *vt* to differentiate (**de** from) **2. se différencier** *vpr* to differ (**de** from)

**différend** [diferɑ̃] *nm* difference of opinion

**différent, -e** [diferɑ̃, -ɑ̃t] *adj* different ; **différents** [divers] different, various ; **différent de** different from ■ **différemment** [-amɑ̃] *adv* differently (**de** from)

**différer** [difere] **1.** *vt* [remettre] to postpone ; [paiement] to defer **2.** *vi* to differ (**de** from)

**difficile** [difisil] *adj* difficult ; [exigeant] fussy ; **c'est difficile à faire** it's hard *or* difficult to do ■ **difficilement** *adv* with difficulty

**difficulté** [difikylte] *nf* difficulty (**à faire** in doing) ; **en difficulté** in a difficult situation ; **avoir de la difficulté à faire qch** to have difficulty (in) doing sth

**difforme** [difɔrm] *adj* deformed, misshapen ■ **difformité** *nf* deformity

**diffus, -e** [dify, -yz] *adj* [lumière] diffuse ; [impression] vague

**diffuser** [difyze] *vt* [émission] to broadcast ; [nouvelle] to spread ; [lumière, chaleur] to diffuse ■ **diffusion** *nf* [d'émission] broadcasting ; [de lumière, de chaleur] diffusion

**digérer** [diʒere] **1.** *vt* to digest **2.** *vi* to digest

**digestif, -ive** [diʒɛstif, -iv] **1.** *adj* [tube, sucs] digestive **2.** *nmf* after-dinner liqueur

**digestion** [diʒɛstjɔ̃] *nf* digestion

**Digicode®** [diʒikɔd] *nm* door code (*for entrance to building*)

**digne** [diɲ] *adj* [air, attitude] dignified ; **digne de qn /qch** worthy of sb /sth ; **digne d'admiration** worthy of *or* deserving of admiration ■ **dignement** [-əmɑ̃] *adv* with dignity

**dignitaire** [diɲitɛr] *nm* dignitary

**dignité** [diɲite] *nf* dignity

**digue** [dig] *nf* dike, dyke ; [en bord de mer] sea wall

**dilapider** [dilapide] *vt* to squander

**dilater** [dilate] **1.** *vt* [pupille] to dilate **2. se dilater** *vpr* [pupille] to dilate

**dilemme** [dilɛm] *nm* dilemma

**diluer** [dilɥe] *vt* [liquide, substance] to dilute (**dans** in)

**dimanche** [dimãʃ] *nm* Sunday

**dimension** [dimãsjɔ̃] *nf* [mesure, aspect] dimension ; [taille] size ; **à deux dimensions** two-dimensional ; **prendre les dimensions de qch** to measure sth up

**diminuer** [diminɥe] **1.** *vt* [réduire] to reduce, to decrease ; [affaiblir] to affect **2.** *vi* [réserves, nombre] to decrease, to diminish ; [jours] to get shorter ; [prix, profits] to decrease, to drop ■ **diminution** *nf* reduction, decrease (**de** in)

**diminutif** [diminytif] *nm* [nom] diminutive

**dinde** [dɛ̃d] *nf* [volaille, viande] turkey ■ **dindon** *nm* turkey (cock)

**dîner** [dine] **1.** *nm* [repas du soir] dinner ; [repas de midi] lunch ; [soirée] dinner party **2.** *vi* to have dinner ; *Belg Can* to (have) lunch

**dinosaure** [dinozɔr] *nm* dinosaur

**diplomate** [diplɔmat] **1.** *adj* diplomatic **2.** *nmf* diplomat ■ **diplomatie** [-asi] *nf* [tact] diplomacy ; [carrière] diplomatic service ■ **diplomatique** *adj* diplomatic

**diplôme** [diplom] *nm* diploma ; [d'université] degree ■ **diplômé, -e 1.** *adj* qualified ; UNIV **être diplômé (de)** to be a graduate (of) **2.** *nmf* holder of a diploma ; UNIV graduate

**dire** [dir] **1.** *nm* **au dire de** according to ; **selon ses dires** according to him/her **2.** *vt* [mot] to say ; [vérité, secret] to tell ; **dire des bêtises** to talk nonsense ; **dire qch à qn** to tell sb sth, to say sth to sb ; **dire à qn que...** to tell sb that..., to say to sb that... ; **dire à qn de faire qch** to tell sb to do sth ; **dire du mal/du bien de qn** to speak ill/well of sb ; *Fam* **dis donc** so ; [au fait] by the way ; [à qn qui exagère] look here ! ; **on dirait un château** it looks like a castle ; **on dirait du cabillaud** it tastes like cod ; **autrement dit** in other words ; **à vrai dire** to tell the truth

**3. se dire** *vpr* **a)** [s'employer] **ça ne se dit pas** [par décence] you mustn't say that ; [par usage] people don't say that, nobody says that **b)** [se traduire] **"chat" se dit "gato" en espagnol** the Spanish for "cat" is "gato" ; **comment ça se dit en anglais ?** how do you say that in English ? **c)** [se présenter comme] **il se dit malade** he says he's ill

**direct, -e** [dirɛkt] **1.** *adj* direct **2.** *nm* RADIO & TV live broadcasting ; **en direct (de)** live (from) ■ **directement** [-əmã] *adv* [sans intermédiaire] directly ; [sans détour] straight

**directeur, -trice** [dirɛktœr, -tris] **1.** *nmf* director ; [de magasin, de service] manager ; [de journal] editor ; [d'école] *Br* headmaster, *f* headmistress, *Am* principal **2.** *adj* [principe] guiding ; [idées] main ; [équipe] management

**direction** [dirɛksjɔ̃] *nf* **a)** [sens] direction ; **train en direction de Lille** train to Lille **b)** [de société, de club] running, management ; [de parti] leadership ; AUTO steering ; **sous la direction de** under the supervision of ; [orchestre] conducted by ; **un poste de direction** a management post ; **direction du personnel** personnel department

**dirigeant, -e** [diriʒã, -ãt] **1.** *adj* [classe] ruling **2.** *nm* [de pays] leader ; [d'entreprise, de club] manager

**diriger** [diriʒe] **1.** *vt* [entreprise, club] to run, to manage ; [pays, parti] to lead ; [orchestre] to conduct ; [travaux] to supervise ; [acteur] to direct ; [orienter] to turn (**vers** to) ; [arme, lumière] to point (**sur** at) ; [véhicule] to steer **2.** **se diriger** *vpr* **se diriger vers** [lieu, objet] to head for ; [personne] to go up to ; [dans une carrière] to go into

**dis, disant** [di, dizã] *voir* **dire**

**discerner** [disɛrne] *vt* [voir] to make out ; [différencier] to distinguish (**de** from) ■ **discernement** [-əmã] *nm* discernment

**disciple** [disipl] *nm* disciple

**discipline** [disiplin] *nf* [règle, matière] discipline

**discipliner** [disipline] **1.** *vt* [enfant] to control **2. se discipliner** *vpr* to discipline oneself ■ **discipliné, -e** *adj* well-disciplined

**discompte** [diskɔ̃t] *nm* discount

**discontinu, -e** [diskɔ̃tiny] *adj* [ligne] broken ; [bruit] intermittent ■ **discontinuer** *vi* **sans discontinuer** without stopping

**discorde** [diskɔrd] *nf* discord

**discothèque** [diskɔtɛk] *nf* [organisme] record library ; [club] disco

**discours** [diskur] *nm* speech ; [écrit littéraire] discourse ; **faire un discours** to make a speech

**discréditer** [diskredite] **1.** *vt* to discredit **2. se discréditer** *vpr* [personne] to discredit oneself

**discret, -ète** [diskrɛ, -ɛt] *adj* [personne, manière] discreet ; [vêtement] simple ■ **discrètement** *adv* [avec retenue] discreetly ; [sobrement] simply

**discrétion** [diskresjɔ̃] *nf* discretion ; **laisser qch à la discrétion de qn** to leave sth to sb's discretion

**discrimination** [diskriminasjɔ̃] *nf* discrimination

**disculper** [diskylpe] *vt* to exonerate (**de** from)

**discussion** [diskysjɔ̃] *nf* discussion ; **avoir une discussion** to have a discussion (**sur** about)

**discutable** [diskytabl] *adj* questionable

**discuter** [diskyte] **1.** *vt* to discuss ; [contester] to question **2.** *vi* to discuss ; [protester] to argue ; **discuter de qch avec qn** to discuss sth with sb **3. se discuter** *vpr* **ça se discute** that's debatable

**dise, disent** [diz] *voir* **dire**

**disgrace** [disgras] *nf* **tomber en disgrace** to fall into disfavour ■ **disgracier** *vt* to disgrace ■ **disgracieux, -euse** *adj* ungainly

**disjoint, -e** [disʒwɛ̃, -ɛt] *adj* separated

**disjoncter** [disʒɔ̃kte] *vi* [circuit électrique] to fuse ■ **disjoncteur** *nm* circuit breaker

**dislocation** [dislɔkasjɔ̃] *nf* [de membre] dislocation

**disloquer** [dislɔke] **1.** *vt* [membre] to dislocate **2. se disloquer** *vpr* **se disloquer le bras** to dislocate one's arm

**disons** [dizɔ̃] *voir* **dire**

**disparaître** [disparɛtr] *vi* to disappear ; [être porté manquant] to go missing ; [mourir] to die ; [coutume] to die out ; **faire disparaître qch** to get rid of sth ■ **disparition** *nf* disappearance ; [mort] death ■ **disparu, -e 1.** *adj* [personne] missing ; **être porté disparu** to be reported missing **2.** *nmf* [absent] missing person ; [mort] departed

**disparité** [disparite] *nf* disparity (**entre** *ou* **de** between)

**dispensaire** [dispɑ̃sɛr] *nm* community health centre

**dispense** [dispɑ̃s] *nf* [d'obligation] exemption ■ **dispenser 1.** *vt* [soins, bienfaits] to dispense ; **dispenser qn de qch** to exempt sb from sth ; **dispenser qn de faire qch** to exempt sb from doing sth **2.** *vpr* **se dispenser de qch** to get out of sth ; **se dispenser de faire qch** to get out of doing sth

**disperser** [dispɛrse] **1.** *vt* [papiers, foule] to scatter ; [brouillard] to disperse ; [collection] to break up **2. se disperser** *vpr* [foule] to scatter, to disperse ■ **dispersion** *nf* [d'armée, de manifestants, de brouillard] dispersal

**disponible** [dispɔnibl] *adj* [article, place, personne] available ■ **disponibilité** *nf* availability ; **disponibilités** [fonds] available funds

**dispos** [dispo] *adj m* **frais et dispos** hale and hearty

**disposé, -e** [dispoze] *adj* **bien / mal disposé** in a good / bad mood ; **disposé à faire qch** disposed to do sth

**disposer** [dispoze] **1.** *vt* [objets] to arrange ; **disposer qn à (faire) qch** to dispose sb to (do) sth **2.** *vi* **disposer de**

qch to have sth at one's disposal **3. se disposer** *vpr* se disposer à faire qch to prepare to do sth

**dispositif** [dispozitif] *nm* [mécanisme] device

**disposition** [dispozisjɔ̃] *nf* arrangement ; [tendance] tendency (**à** to) ; [de maison, de page] layout ; **être** *ou* **rester** *ou* **se tenir à la disposition de qn** to be *or* remain at sb's disposal ; **dispositions** [aptitudes] ability, aptitude (**pour** for)

**disproportionné, -e** [disproporsjone] *adj* disproportionate

**dispute** [dispyt] *nf* quarrel ■ **disputer 1.** *vt* [match] to play ; [rallye] to compete in ; [combat de boxe] to fight ; [droit] to contest ; **disputer qch à qn** [prix, première place] to fight with sb for *or* over sth **2. se disputer** *vpr* to quarrel (**avec** with) ; [match] to take place ; **se disputer qch** to fight over sth

**disqualifier** [diskalifje] *vt* [équipe, athlète] to disqualify ■ **disqualification** *nf* disqualification

**disque** [disk] *nm* [de musique] record ; [cercle] *Br* disc, *Am* disk ; ORDINAT disk ; SPORT discus ; **disque compact** compact *Br* disc *or Am* disk ; **disque dur** hard disk ■ **disquaire** *nmf* record dealer ■ **disquette** *nf* ORDINAT floppy (disk), diskette

**disséminer** [disemine] *vt* [graines, mines] to scatter

**disséquer** [diseke] *vt* to dissect

**dissert'** [disert] *(abr de* **dissertation)** *nf Arg* essay

**dissertation** [disertasjɔ̃] *nf* essay

**dissident, -e** [disidɑ̃, -ɑ̃t] *nmf* dissident

**dissimuler** [disimyle] **1.** *vt* [cacher] to conceal (**à** from) **2. se dissimuler** *vpr* to be hidden ■ **dissimulation** *nf* concealment ; [duplicité] deceit

**dissiper** [disipe] **1.** *vt* [nuages] to disperse ; [brouillard] to clear ; [malentendu] to clear up ; [craintes] to dispel ; **dissiper qn** to lead sb astray **2. se dissiper** *vpr* [nuage] to disperse ; [brume]

to clear ; [craintes] to vanish ; [élève] to misbehave ■ **dissipé, -e** *adj* [élève] unruly

**dissocier** [disosje] *vt* to dissociate (**de** from)

**dissolu, -e** [disoly] *adj* [vie] dissolute

**dissolution** [disolysjɔ̃] *nf* dissolution

**dissolvant** [disolvɑ̃] *nm* solvent ; [pour vernis à ongles] nail polish remover

**dissoudre** [disudr] **1.** *vt* to dissolve **2. se dissoudre** *vpr* to dissolve

**dissuader** [disɥade] *vt* to dissuade (**de qch** from sth ; **de faire** from doing) ■ **dissuasif, -ive** *adj* deterrent ; **avoir un effet dissuasif** to be a deterrent ■ **dissuasion** *nf* dissuasion ; MIL **force de dissuasion** deterrent

**distance** [distɑ̃s] *nf* distance ; **à deux mètres de distance** two metres apart ; **à distance** at *or* from a distance ; **garder ses distances** to keep one's distance (**vis-à-vis de** from) ; **commandé à distance** remote-controlled

**distancer** [distɑ̃se] *vt* to outstrip ; **se laisser distancer** to fall behind

**distant, -e** [distɑ̃, -ɑ̃t] *adj* distant ; [personne] aloof, distant ; **distant de dix kilomètres** [éloigné] ten kilometres away ; [à intervalles] ten kilometres apart

**distendre** [distɑ̃dr] **1.** *vt* to stretch **2. se distendre** *vpr* to stretch

**distiller** [distile] *vt* to distil ■ **distillerie** *nf* [lieu] distillery

**distinct, -e** [distɛ̃, -ɛ̃kt] *adj* [différent] distinct, separate (**de** from) ; [net] clear, distinct ■ **distinctif, -ive** *adj* distinctive ■ **distinction** *nf* [différence, raffinement] distinction

**distinguer** [distɛ̃ge] **1.** *vt* [différencier] to distinguish ; [voir] to make out ; [choisir] to single out ; **distinguer le bien du mal** to tell good from evil **2. se distinguer** *vpr* [s'illustrer] to distinguish oneself ; **se distinguer de qn / qch (par)** to be distinguishable from sb / sth (by) ■ **distingué, -e** *adj* [bien élevé, éminent] distinguished

**distorsion** [distorsjɔ̃] *nf* distortion

**distraction** [distraksjɔ̃] *nf* [étourderie] absent-mindedness ▪ **distraire 1.** *vt* [divertir] to entertain; **distraire qn** to distract sb (**de** from) **2. se distraire** *vpr* to amuse oneself ▪ **distrait, -e** *adj* [gén] absent-minded; [élève] inattentive; **excusez-moi, j'étais distrait** sorry, I wasn't paying attention ▪ **distrayant, -e** *adj* entertaining

**distribuer** [distribɥe] *vt* [donner & COMM] to distribute; [courrier] to deliver; [cartes] to deal; [tâches] to allocate; [eau] to supply

**distributeur** [distribytœr] *nm* COMM distributor; **distributeur automatique** vending machine; **distributeur de billets** [de train] ticket machine; [de billets de banque] cash machine

**distribution** [distribysjɔ̃] *nf* distribution; [du courrier] delivery; [de l'eau] supply; [acteurs de cinéma] cast; **distribution des prix** prizegiving

**district** [distrikt] *nm* district

**dit¹, dite** [di, dit] **1.** *pp de* **dire 2.** *adj* [convenu] agreed; [surnommé] called

**dit², dites** [di, dit] *voir* **dire**

**divaguer** [divage] *vi* [dérailler] to rave

**divan** [divɑ̃] *nm* divan, couch

**divergent, -e** [diverʒɑ̃, -ɑ̃t] *adj* [lignes] divergent; [opinions] differing ▪ **divergence** *nf* [de lignes] divergence; [d'opinions] difference ▪ **diverger** *vi* to diverge (**de** from)

**divers, -e** [diver, -ɛrs] *adj* [varié] varied; **divers(es)** [plusieurs] various

**diversifier** [diversifje] **1.** *vt* to diversify **2. se diversifier** *vpr* to diversify

**diversion** [diversjɔ̃] *nf* diversion; **faire diversion** to create a diversion

**diversité** [diversite] *nf* diversity

**divertir** [divertir] **1.** *vt* to entertain **2. se divertir** *vpr* to enjoy oneself ▪ **divertissement** *nm* entertainment, amusement

**divin, -e** [divɛ̃, -in] *adj* divine ▪ **divinité** *nf* divinity

**diviser** [divize] **1.** *vt* to divide (**en** into) **2. se diviser** *vpr* to divide (**en** into) ▪ **divisé, e** *adj* **a)** [fragmenté] divided

**b)** [en désaccord] divided; **être divisé sur** to be divided on (the question of) ▪ **division** *nf* division

**divorce** [divɔrs] *nm* divorce ▪ **divorcer** *vi* to get divorced; **divorcer d'avec qn** to divorce sb ▪ **divorcé, -e 1.** *adj* divorced (**d'avec** from) **2.** *nmf* divorcee

**divulguer** [divylge] *vt* to divulge

**dix** [dis] ( [di] *before consonant,* [diz] *before vowel*) *adj & nm* ten ▪ **dix-huit** *adj & nm* eighteen ▪ **dixième** *adj & nmf* tenth; **un dixième** a tenth ▪ **dix-neuf** *adj & nm* nineteen ▪ **dix-sept** *adj & nm* seventeen

**dizaine** [dizen] *nf* **une dizaine (de)** about ten

**do** [do] *nm inv* [note] C

**doc** [dɔk] *(abr de* **documentation)** *nf* Fam literature, brochures *pl*

**docile** [dɔsil] *adj* docile

**docteur** [dɔktœr] *nm* [en médecine, d'université] doctor (**ès /en** of) ▪ **doctorat** *nm* doctorate, ≃ PhD (**ès /en** in)

**doctrine** [dɔktrin] *nf* doctrine

**document** [dɔkymɑ̃] *nm* document ▪ **documentaire** *adj & nm* documentary ▪ **documentaliste** *nmf* archivist; [à l'école] (school) librarian

**documentation** [dɔkymɑ̃tasjɔ̃] *nf* [documents] documentation; [brochures] literature ▪ **se documenter** *vpr* to gather information or material (**sur** on)

**dodu, -e** [dɔdy] *adj* chubby, plump

**doigt** [dwa] *nm* finger; **doigt de pied** toe; **petit doigt** little finger, *Am Scot* pinkie; **un doigt de vin** a drop of wine; **montrer qn du doigt** to point at sb

**doigté** [dwate] *nm* MUS fingering; [savoir-faire] tact

**dois, doit** [dwa] *voir* **devoir**

**doléances** [dɔleɑ̃s] *nfpl* [plaintes] grievances

**dollar** [dɔlar] *nm* dollar

**domaine** [dɔmen] *nm* [terres] estate, domain; [matière] field, domain; **être du domaine public** to be in the public domain

**dôme** [dom] *nm* dome

**domestique** [dɔmɛstik] **1.** *adj* [vie, marché, produit] domestic ; **travaux domestiques** housework **2.** *nmf* servant ▪ **domestiquer** *vt* to domesticate

**domicile** [dɔmisil] *nm* home ; [demeure légale] abode ; **sans domicile fixe** of no fixed abode ; JUR **domicile conjugal** marital home

**dominateur, -trice** [dɔminatœr, -tris] *adj* domineering ▪ **domination** *nf* domination

**dominer** [dɔmine] **1.** *vt* to dominate ; [situation, sentiment] to master ; [être supérieur à] to surpass **2.** *vi* [être le plus fort] to be dominant ; [être le plus important] to predominate **3. se dominer** *vpr* to control oneself ▪ **dominant, -e** *adj* dominant

**dommage** [dɔmaʒ] *nm* [tort] harm ; **dommages** [dégâts] damage ; **quel dommage !** what a pity, what a shame! ; **c'est (bien) dommage qu'elle ne soit pas venue** it's a (great) pity *or* shame she didn't come ; **dommages-intérêts** damages

**dompter** [dɔ̃te] *vt* [animal] to tame

**DOM-TOM** [dɔmtɔm] *(abr de **départements et territoires d'outre-mer**) nmpl Anc French overseas departments and territories*

**don** [dɔ̃] *nm* [cadeau, aptitude] gift ; [à un musée, à une œuvre] donation ; **faire don de qch** to give sth ; **don du sang** blood donation

**donateur, -trice** [dɔnatœr, -tris] *nmf* donor ▪ **donation** *nf* donation

**donc** [dɔ̃(k)] *conj* so, then ; [par conséquent] so, therefore ; **asseyez-vous donc !** [intensif] do sit down!

**donjon** [dɔ̃ʒɔ̃] *nm* keep

**donné, e** [dɔne] *adj* given ; **à cet instant donné** at this (very) moment ; **c'est donné** it's a gift ; **c'est pas donné** it's not exactly cheap ▪ **donnée** *nf* **a)** ORDINAT & MATH datum, piece of data ; **données numériques** numerical data **b)** [élément] fact, particular

**donner** [dɔne] **1.** *vt* to give ; [récolte, résultat] to produce ; [cartes] to deal ; [pièce, film] to put on ; **pourriez-vous me donner l'heure ?** could you tell me the time? ; **donner un coup à qn** to hit sb ; **donner à manger à qn** [animal, enfant] to feed sb ; **elle m'a donné de ses nouvelles** she told me how she was doing ; **ça donne soif / faim** it makes you thirsty / hungry ; **étant donné considering..., in view of... ; **étant donné que...** seeing (that), considering (that)... ; **à un moment donné** at some stage **2.** *vi* **donner sur** [fenêtre] to overlook, to look out onto ; [porte] to open onto **3. se donner** *vpr* [se consacrer] to devote oneself (**à** to) ; **se donner du mal** to go to a lot of trouble (**pour faire** to do)

**donneur, -euse** [dɔnœr, -øz] *nmf* [de sang, d'organe] donor

**dont** [dɔ̃] (= de qui, duquel, de quoi) *pron rel* [exprime la partie d'un tout] [personne] of whom ; [chose] of which ; [exprime l'appartenance - personne] whose, of whom ; [chose] of which, whose ; **une mère dont le fils est malade** a mother whose son is ill ; **la fille dont il est fier** the daughter he is proud of *or* of whom he is proud ; **les outils dont j'ai besoin** the tools I need ; **la façon dont elle joue** the way (in which) she plays ; **cinq enfants dont deux filles** five children two of whom are daughters, five children including two daughters ; **voici ce dont il s'agit** here's what it's about

**doper** [dɔpe] **1.** *vt* to dope **2. se doper** *vpr* to take drugs ▪ **dopage** *nm* [action] doping ; [de sportif] drug-taking

**dorénavant** [dɔrenavɑ̃] *adv* from now on

**dorer** [dɔre] **1.** *vt* [objet] to gild **2.** *vi* [à la cuisson] to brown **3. se dorer** *vpr* **se dorer au soleil** to sunbathe ▪ **doré, -e** *adj* [objet] gilt, gold ; [couleur] golden

**dorloter** [dɔrlɔte] *vt* to pamper

**dormir** [dɔrmir] *vi* to sleep ; [être endormi] to be asleep ; *Fig* [argent] to lie idle

**dortoir** [dɔrtwar] *nm* dormitory

**dorure** [dɔryr] *nf* **a)** [couche d'or] gilt ; [artificielle] gold-effect finish ; **un bureau couvert de dorures** a desk covered in gilding **b)** [ce qui est doré] golden *or* gilt decoration

**dos** [do] *nm* [de personne, d'animal] back ; [de livre] spine ; **'voir au dos'** [verso] 'see over'

**dose** [doz] *nf* dose ; [dans un mélange] proportion ▪ **doser** *vt* [médicament, ingrédients] to measure out

**dosette** [dozɛt] *nf* capsule ; **café en dosette** coffee capsule

**dossard** [dosar] *nm* [de sportif] number *(worn by player or competitor)*

**dossier** [dosje] *nm* [de siège] back ; [documents] file ; ORDINAT folder

**dot** [dɔt] *nf* dowry

**doter** [dɔte] *vt* [équiper] to equip (**de** with) ; **doté d'une grande intelligence** endowed with great intelligence

**douane** [dwan] *nf* customs ; **passer la douane** to go through customs ▪ **douanier, -ère** *nmf* customs officer

**doublage** [dublaʒ] *nm* [de film] dubbing

**double** [dubl] **1.** *adj* double ; [rôle, avantage] twofold, double ; **en double exemplaire** in duplicate **2.** *adv* double **3.** *nm* [de personne] double ; [copie] copy, duplicate ; **le double (de)** [quantité] twice as much (as) ; **je l'ai en double** I have two of them

**double-clic** [dubləklik] *(pl* **doubles-clics)** *nm* ORDINAT double-click ▪ **double-cliquer** *vt* ORDINAT to double-click on ; **double-cliquer sur l'image** to double-click on the picture

**doubler** [duble] **1.** *vt* [augmenter] to double ; [vêtement] to line ; [film] to dub ; [acteur] to dub the voice of ; [classe à l'école] to repeat **2.** *vi* [augmenter] to double **3.** *vt & vi* [en voiture] *Br* to overtake, *Am* to pass **4. se doubler** *vpr* **se doubler de** to be coupled with

**doublure** [dublyr] *nf* [étoffe] lining ; [au théâtre] understudy ; [au cinéma] stand-in

**douce** [dus] *voir* **doux** ▪ **doucement** *adv* [délicatement] gently ; [bas] softly ; [lentement] slowly ; [sans bruit] quietly ▪ **douceur** *nf* [de miel] sweetness ; [de peau] softness ; [de temps] mildness ; [de personne] gentleness

**douche** [duʃ] *nf* shower ; **prendre une douche** to have *or* take a shower ▪ **se doucher** *vpr* to have *or* take a shower

**doudou** [dudu] *nm* Fam [langage enfantin] security blanket

**doué, -e** [dwe] *adj* gifted, talented (**en** at) ; **être doué pour qch** to have a gift for sth

**douille** [duj] *nf* [d'ampoule] socket ; [de cartouche] case

**douillet, -ette** [duje, -ɛt] *adj* [lit] *Br* cosy, *Am* cozy

**douleur** [dulœr] *nf* [mal] pain ; [chagrin] sorrow, grief ▪ **douloureux, -euse** *adj* painful

**doute** [dut] *nm* doubt ; **sans doute** no doubt, probably ; **sans aucun doute** without (any) doubt ; **mettre qch en doute** to cast doubt on sth

**douter** [dute] **1.** *vi* to doubt ; **douter de qn / qch** to doubt sb / sth **2.** *vt* **je doute qu'il soit assez fort** I doubt whether he's strong enough **3. se douter** *vpr* **se douter de quelque chose** to suspect something

**douteux, -euse** [dutø, -øz] *adj* [peu certain] doubtful ; [louche, médiocre] dubious

**Douvres** [duvr] *nm ou f* Dover

**doux, douce** [du, dus] *adj* [miel, son] sweet ; [peau, lumière] soft ; [temps, climat] mild ; [personne, pente] gentle

**douze** [duz] *adj & nm* twelve ▪ **douzaine** *nf* [douze] dozen ; [environ] about twelve ; **une douzaine d'œufs** a dozen eggs

**dragée** [draʒe] *nf* sugared almond

**dragon** [dragɔ̃] *nm* [animal, personne acariâtre] dragon

**drainer** [drene] *vt* to drain

**drame** [dram] *nm* [genre littéraire] drama ; [catastrophe] tragedy ▪ **dra-**

**matique 1.** *adj* dramatic ; **auteur dramatique** playwright, dramatist **2.** *nf* drama

**drap** [dra] *nm* [de lit] sheet ; [tissu] cloth ; **drap-housse** fitted sheet ; **drap de bain** bath towel

**drapeau, -x** [drapo] *nm* flag

**dresser** [drese] **1.** *vt* [échelle, statue] to put up, to erect ; [liste] to draw up ; [piège] to set, to lay ; [animal] to train ; **dresser les oreilles** to prick up one's ears **2. se dresser** *vpr* [personne] to stand up ; [statue, montagne] to rise up **■ dressage** *nm* training **■ dresseur, -euse** *nmf* trainer

**driver** [drajvœr] *nm* ÉQUIT, GOLF & ORDINAT driver

**drogue** [drɔg] *nf* [stupéfiant] & *Péj* [médicament] drug ; **drogue dure / douce** hard / soft drug **■ drogué, -e** *nmf* drug addict **■ droguer 1.** *vt* [victime] to drug ; [malade] to dose up **2. se droguer** *vpr* to take drugs

**droguerie** [drɔgri] *nf* hardware *Br* shop or *Am* store **■ droguiste** *nmf* hardware dealer

**droit¹** [drwa] *nm* [privilège] right ; [d'inscription] fee(s) ; **le droit** [science juridique] law ; **avoir droit à qch** to be entitled to sth ; **avoir le droit de faire qch** to be entitled to do sth, to have the right to do sth ; **droits de douane** (customs) duty ; **droits de l'homme** human rights

**droit², droite¹** [drwa, drwat] **1.** *adj* [route, ligne] straight ; [angle] right ; *Fig* [honnête] upright **2.** *adv* straight ; **tout droit** straight or right ahead ; **aller droit au but** to go straight to the point

**droit³, droite²** [drwa, drwat] *adj* [côté, bras] right

**droite³** [drwat] *nf* [ligne] straight line

**droite⁴** [drwat] *nf* **la droite** [côté] the right (side) ; POL the right (wing) ; **à droite** [tourner] (to the) right ; [rouler, se tenir] on the right, on the right (-hand) side ; **de droite** [fenêtre] right-hand ; [candidat] right-wing ; **à droite de** on or to the right of

**droitier, -ère** [drwatje, -ɛr] **1.** *adj* right-handed **2.** *nmf* right-handed person

**droiture** [drwatyr] *nf* rectitude

**drôle** [drol] *adj* funny **■ drôlement** *adv* funnily ; *Fam* [extrêmement] terribly, dreadfully

**DROM** [drɔm] *(abr de* **Département et Région d'outre-mer)** *nmpl Overseas territories of France that have the status of departments*

**dromadaire** [drɔmadɛr] *nm* dromedary

**drone** [drɔn] *nm* MIL drone

**dru, drue** [dry] **1.** *adj* [herbe] thick, dense **2.** *adv* **tomber dru** [pluie] to pour down heavily ; **pousser dru** to grow thickly

**du** [dy] *voir* **de**

**dû, due** [dy] **1.** *adj* **dû à qch** due to sth ; **en bonne et due forme** in due form **2.** *nm* due

**duc** [dyk] *nm* duke **■ duchesse** *nf* duchess

**duel** [dɥɛl] *nm* duel

**dûment** [dymɑ̃] *adv* duly

**dune** [dyn] *nf* (sand) dune

**duo** [dɥo] *nm* MUS duet

**dupe** [dyp] **1.** *adj* **être dupe de** to be taken in by ; **il n'est pas dupe** he's well aware of it **2.** *nf* dupe **■ duper** *vt* to fool, to dupe

**duplex** [dypleks] *nm Br* maisonette, *Am* duplex

**duplicata** [dyplikata] *nm inv* duplicate

**duquel** [dykɛl] *voir* **lequel**

**dur, dure** [dyr] **1.** *adj* [substance] hard ; [difficile] hard, tough ; [viande] tough ; [hiver, ton] harsh ; [personne] hard, harsh ; **dur d'oreille** hard of hearing **2.** *adv* [travailler] hard **■ durement** *adv* harshly **■ dureté** *nf* [de substance] hardness ; [d'hiver, de ton] harshness ; [de viande] toughness

**durable** [dyrabl] *adj* lasting

**durant** [dyrɑ̃] *prép* during ; **durant l'hiver** during the winter ; **des heures durant** for hours and hours

**durcir** [dyrsir] **1.** *vt* & *vi* to harden **2. se durcir** *vpr* to harden

**durée** [dyre] *nf* [de film, d'événement] length ; [période] duration ; **de longue durée** [bonheur] lasting ; **de courte durée** [attente] short ; [bonheur] short-lived

**durer** [dyre] *vi* to last

**duvet** [dyvɛ] *nm* [d'oiseau] down ; [sac] sleeping bag

**DVD** *(abr de* digital video ou versatile disc) *nm inv* DVD

**dynamique** [dinamik] *adj* dynamic

**dynamite** [dinamit] *nf* dynamite

**dynamo** [dinamo] *nf* dynamo

**dynastie** [dinasti] *nf* dynasty

**dyslexique** [dislɛksik] *adj* dyslexic

# E

**E, e** [ə] *nm inv* E, e

**EAO** [əao] *(abr de* enseignement assisté par ordinateur) *nm inv* CAL

**eau, -x** [o] *nf* water; **sports d'eau vive** whitewater sports; **eau courante** running water; **eau de toilette** eau de toilette; **eau du robinet** tap water; **eau douce** fresh water ▪ **eau-de-vie** *(pl* **eaux-de-vie)** *nf* brandy

**ébahir** [ebair] *vt* to astound

**ébattre** [ebatr] ▪ **s'ébattre** *vpr* to frolic

**ébaucher** [eboʃe] *vt* [tableau, roman] to rough out

**ébéniste** [ebenist] *nm* cabinetmaker

**éblouir** [ebluir] *vt* to dazzle

**e-book** [ibuk] *(pl* **e-books)** *nm* e-book

**éboueur** [ebwœr] *nm Br* dustman, *Am* garbage collector

**ébouillanter** [ebujɑ̃te] **1.** *vt* to scald **2. s'ébouillanter** *vpr* to scald oneself

**ébouler** [ebule] ▪ **s'ébouler** *vpr* [falaise] to collapse; [tunnel] to cave in ▪ **éboulement** *nm* [écroulement] collapse; [de mine] cave-in

**ébouriffé, -e** [eburife] *adj* dishevelled

**ébranler** [ebrɑ̃le] **1.** *vt* [mur, confiance, personne] to shake **2. s'ébranler** *vpr* [train, cortège] to move off

**ébrécher** [ebreʃe] *vt* [assiette] to chip; [lame] to nick

**ébriété** [ebrijete] *nf* **en état d'ébriété** under the influence of drink

**ébrouer** [ebrue] ▪ **s'ébrouer** *vpr* [chien] to shake itself; [cheval] to snort

**ébruiter** [ebrɥite] *vt* [nouvelle] to spread

**EBS** [øbeɛs] *(abr de* encéphalite bovine spongiforme) *nf* BSE

**ébullition** [ebylisjɔ̃] *nf* boiling; **être en ébullition** [eau] to be boiling; **porter qch à ébullition** to bring sth to the boil

**écaille** [ekaj] *nf* [de poisson] scale ▪ **écailler 1.** *vt* [poisson] to scale **2. s'écailler** *vpr* [peinture] to peel (off)

**écarquiller** [ekarkije] *vt* **écarquiller les yeux** to open one's eyes wide

**écart** [ekar] *nm* [intervalle] gap, distance; [différence] difference (**de** in; **entre** between); **faire le grand écart** to do the splits; **à l'écart** out of the way; **à l'écart de qch** away from sth

**écartelé, -e** [ekartəle] *adj* **écartelé entre** [tiraillé] torn between

**écartement** [ekartəmɑ̃] *nm* [espace] gap, distance (**de** between)

**écarter** [ekarte] **1.** *vt* [objets, personnes] to move apart; [jambes, doigts] to spread; [rideaux] to draw (back); [idée] to brush aside; [proposition] to turn down; **écarter qch de qch** to move sth away from sth **2. s'écarter** *vpr* **a)** [se séparer - personnes] to move apart (**de** from); [foule] to part **b)** [piéton] to move away (**de** from); **s'écarter du sujet** to wander from the subject ▪ **écarté, -e** *adj* **les jambes écartées** with his / her legs (wide) apart

**ecclésiastique** [eklezjastik] *nm* clergyman

**écervelé, -e** [esɛrvəle] **1.** *adj* scatterbrained **2.** *nmf* scatterbrain

**échafaudage** [eʃafodaʒ] *nm* scaffolding; **des échafaudages** scaffolding

**échalote** [eʃalɔt] *nf* **a)** shallot **b)** *Can Fam* [personne grande et maigre] skinny person, bony person

**échancré, -e** [eʃɑ̃kre] *adj* low-cut ▪ **échancrure** *nf* low neckline

**échange** [eʃɑ̃ʒ] *nm* exchange ; **en échange** in exchange (**de** for) ; **échange scolaire** (school) exchange ; **participer à un échange scolaire** to go on a school exchange ■ **échanger** *vt* to exchange (**contre** for)

**échangeur** [eʃɑ̃ʒœʀ] *nm* interchange

**échantillon** [eʃɑ̃tijɔ̃] *nm* sample

**échapper** [eʃape] **1.** *vi* **échapper à qn** to escape from sb ; **son nom m'échappe** his / her name escapes me ; **ça lui a échappé des mains** it slipped out of his / her hands **2.** *vt* **il l'a échappé belle** he had a narrow escape **3. s'échapper** *vpr* [personne, gaz, eau] to escape (**de** from) ■ **échappée** *nf* [de cyclistes] breakaway

**écharde** [eʃaʀd] *nf* splinter

**écharpe** [eʃaʀp] *nf* scarf ; [de maire] sash ; **avoir le bras en écharpe** to have one's arm in a sling

**échasse** [eʃas] *nf* [bâton] stilt

**échauffer** [eʃofe] **1.** *vt* [moteur] to overheat **2. s'échauffer** *vpr* [sportif] to warm up ■ **échauffement** *nm* [de moteur] overheating ; [d'athlète] warm-up

**échauffourée** [eʃofuʀe] *nf* clash, brawl, skirmish

**échéance** [eʃeɑ̃s] *nf* [de facture, de dette] date of payment ; **à brève / longue échéance** [projet, emprunt] short- / long-term

**échéant** [eʃeɑ̃] ■ **le cas échéant** *adv* if need be

**échec** [eʃɛk] *nm* failure ; **faire échec à qch** to hold sth in check ; **les échecs** [jeu] chess ; **échec !** check! ; **échec et mat !** checkmate!

**échelle** [eʃɛl] *nf* **a)** [marches] ladder **b)** [de carte] scale ; **à l'échelle nationale** on a national scale

**échelon** [eʃlɔ̃] *nm* [d'échelle] rung ; [d'employé] grade ; [d'organisation] echelon ; **à l'échelon régional** on a regional level

**échelonner** [eʃlɔne] **1.** *vt* [paiements] to spread **2. s'échelonner** *vpr* to be spread out

**échevelé, -e** [eʃəvle] *adj* [ébouriffé] dishevelled

**échiquier** [eʃikje] *nm* [plateau] chessboard

**écho** [eko] *nm* [de son] echo ; **échos** [de presse] gossip column

**échographie** [ekɔgʀafi] *nf* (ultra-sound) scan ; **passer une échographie** to have a scan

**échoir** [eʃwaʀ] *vi* **échoir à qn** to fall to sb

**échouer** [eʃwe] **1.** *vi* to fail ; **échouer à** [examen] to fail **2.** *vi* [navire] to run aground **3. s'échouer** *vpr* [navire] to run aground

**éclabousser** [eklabuse] *vt* to splash, to spatter (**avec** with) ■ **éclabous-sure** *nf* splash

**éclair** [eklɛʀ] **1.** *nm* **a)** [lumière] flash ; [d'orage] flash of lightning **b)** [gâteau] éclair **2.** *adj inv* **visite éclair** lightning visit

**éclairage** [eklɛʀaʒ] *nm* lighting

**éclaircie** [eklɛʀsi] *nf* sunny spell

**éclaircir** [eklɛʀsiʀ] **1.** *vt* [couleur] to lighten ; [mystère] to clear up **2. s'éclaircir** *vpr* [ciel] to clear ; [mystère] to be cleared up ; **s'éclaircir la voix** to clear one's throat ■ **éclaircisse-ment** *nm* [explication] explanation

**éclairer** [eklere] **1.** *vt* [pièce] to light (up) ; **éclairer qn** [avec une lampe] to give sb some light ; [informer] to enlighten sb (**sur** about) **2.** *vi* [lampe] to give light ; **éclairer bien / mal** to give good / poor light **3. s'éclairer** *vpr* [visage] to light up ; **s'éclairer à la bougie** to use candlelight ; **s'éclairer à l'électricité** to have electric lighting ■ **éclairé, -e** *adj* [averti] enlightened ; **bien / mal éclairé** [illuminé] well- / badly lit

**éclaireur, -euse** [eklɛʀœʀ, -øz] **1.** *nmf* (boy) scout, (girl) guide **2.** *nm* [soldat] scout

**éclat** [ekla] *nm* **a)** [de lumière] bright-ness ; [de phare] glare ; [de diamant] flash **b)** [de verre] splinter ; **éclat de rire** burst of laughter

**éclatant, -e** [eklatɑ̃, -ɑ̃t] *adj* [lumière, succès] brilliant ; **être éclatant de santé** to be glowing with health

**éclater** [eklate] *vi* [pneu] to burst ; [bombe] to go off, to explode ; [verre] to shatter ; [guerre] to break out ; [orage, scandale] to break ; [parti] to break up ; **éclater de rire** to burst out laughing ; **éclater en sanglots** to burst into tears ■ **éclatement** *nm* [de pneu] bursting ; [de bombe] explosion ; [de parti] break-up

**éclectique** [eklɛktik] *adj* eclectic

**éclipse** [eklips] *nf* eclipse ■ **éclipser** *vt* to eclipse

**éclore** [eklɔr] *vi* [œuf] to hatch ; [fleur] to open (out), to blossom

**écluse** [eklyz] *nf* [de canal] lock

**écocitoyen, enne** [ekɔsitwajɛ̃, ɛn] *adj* eco-responsible ; **ayez des gestes écocitoyens** behave like eco-citizens

**écœurer** [ekœre] *vt* **écœurer qn** [aliment] to make sb feel sick ; [moralement] to sicken sb ■ **écœurant, -e** *adj* disgusting, sickening ■ **écœurement** *nm* [nausée] nausea ; [indignation] disgust

**écolabel** [ekɔlabɛl] *nm* eco-label

**école** [ekɔl] *nf* school ; **à l'école** at school ; **faire école** to gain a following ; **les grandes écoles** *university-level colleges specializing in professional training* ; **école de dessin** art school ; **école privée** private school, *Br* public school ; **école publique** *Br* state school, *Am* public school ■ **écolier, -ère** *nmf* schoolboy, *f* schoolgirl

**écologie** [ekɔlɔʒi] *nf* ecology ■ **écologique** *adj* ecological ■ **écologiste** *adj & nmf* environmentalist

**économe** [ekɔnɔm] **1.** *adj* thrifty, economical **2.** *nm* [couteau] (vegetable) peeler

**économie** [ekɔnɔmi] *nf* [activité, vertu] economy ; **économies** [argent] savings ; **faire des économies** to save (up) ■ **économique** *adj* **a)** [relatif à l'économie] economic ; **science économique** economics (*sg*) **b)** [avantageux] economical

**économiser** [ekɔnɔmize] **1.** *vt* [forces, argent, énergie] to save **2.** *vi* to economize (**sur** on)

**écoper** [ekɔpe] *vi Fam* **écoper de qch** [punition, amende] to get sth

**écoproduit** [ekɔprɔdɥi] *nm* green product

**écoquartier** [ekɔkartje] *nm* environmentally friendly area

**écorce** [ekɔrs] *nf* [d'arbre] bark ; [de fruit] peel ; **l'écorce terrestre** the earth's crust

**écorcher** [ekɔrʃe] **1.** *vt* [érafler] to graze ; *Fig* [mot] to mispronounce **2. s'écorcher** *vpr* to graze oneself ; **s'écorcher le genou** to graze one's knee

**Écosse** [ekɔs] *nf* **l'Écosse** Scotland ■ **écossais, -e 1.** *adj* Scottish ; [tissu] tartan **2.** *nmf* **Écossais, Écossaise** Scot

**écotourisme** [ekɔturism] *nm* ecotourism

**écouler** [ekule] **1.** *vt* [se débarrasser de] to dispose of **2. s'écouler** *vpr* [eau] to flow out, to run out ; [temps] to pass ■ **écoulé, -e** *adj* [passé] past ■ **écoulement** *nm* [de liquide] flow ; [de marchandises] sale

**écourter** [ekurte] *vt* [séjour] to cut short ; [texte, tige] to shorten

**écoute** [ekut] *nf* listening ; **être à l'écoute** to be listening in (**de** to) ; **écoutes téléphoniques** phone tapping

**écouter** [ekute] **1.** *vt* to listen to ; **faire écouter qch à qn** [disque] to play sb sth **2. s'écouter** *vpr* **si je m'écoutais** if I did what I wanted ■ **écouteur** *nm* [de téléphone] earpiece ; **écouteurs** [casque] headphones

**écran** [ekrɑ̃] *nm* screen ; **à l'écran** on screen ; **le petit écran** television ; **écran plat** flat screen ; **écran publicitaire** commercial break ; **écran tactile** touch screen ; **écran total** sun block

**écraser** [ekraze] **1.** *vt* [broyer, vaincre] to crush ; [fruit, insecte] to squash ; [cigarette] to put out ; [piéton] to run over ; **se faire écraser par une voiture**

to get run over by a car **2. s'écra-ser** *vpr* [avion] to crash (**contre** into) ■ **écrasant, -e** *adj* [victoire, chaleur] overwhelming

**écrémer** [ekreme] *vt* [lait] to skim

**écrevisse** [ekrəvis] *nf* crayfish *inv*

**écrier** [ekrije] ■ **s'écrier** *vpr* to exclaim, to cry out (**que** that)

**écrin** [ekrɛ̃] *nm* (jewel) case

**écrire** [ekrir] **1.** *vt* to write ; [noter] to write down **2.** *vi* to write **3. s'écrire** *vpr* [mot] to be spelt ; **comment ça s'écrit ?** how do you spell it? ■ **écrit** *nm* [document] written document ; [examen] written examination ; **par écrit** in writing

**écriteau, -x** [ekrito] *nm* notice, sign

**écriture** [ekrityr] *nf* [système] writing ; [calligraphie] (hand)writing ; COMM **écritures** accounts ; **les Écritures** [la Bible] the Scriptures

**écrivain** [ekrivɛ̃] *nm* writer

**écrou** [ekru] *nm* [de boulon] nut

**écrouer** [ekrue] *vt* to imprison

**écrouler** [ekrule] ■ **s'écrouler** *vpr* [édifice, personne] to collapse ■ **écroulement** *nm* collapse

**écru, -e** [ekry] *adj* [beige] écru ; [naturel] unbleached

**ecsta** [ɛksta] *(abr de* ecstasy) *nm* E, ecstasy

**écueil** [ekœj] *nm* [rocher] reef ; *Fig* [obstacle] pitfall

**écuelle** [ekɥɛl] *nf* bowl

**écume** [ekym] *nf* [de mer] foam ■ **écumer 1.** *vt* [piller] to plunder **2.** *vi* to foam (**de rage** with anger)

**écureuil** [ekyrœj] *nm* squirrel

**écurie** [ekyri] *nf* stable

**écusson** [ekysɔ̃] *nm* [en étoffe] badge

**écuyer, -ère** [ekɥije, -ɛr] *nmf* [cavalier] rider

**édifice** [edifis] *nm* edifice ■ **édifier** *vt* [bâtiment] to erect ; [théorie] to construct

**Édimbourg** [edɛ̃bur] *nm ou f* Edinburgh

**éditer** [edite] *vt* [publier] to publish ; ORDINAT to edit ■ **éditeur, -trice** *nmf* [dans l'édition] publisher ■ **édition** *nf* [livre, journal] edition ; [métier, diffusion] publishing

**éditorial, -aux** [editɔrjal, -o] **1.** *nm* [article] editorial, *Br* leader **2.** *adj* editorial ■ **éditorialiste** *nmf* editorial or *Br* leader writer

**éducateur, -trice** [edykatœr, -tris] *nmf* educator

**éducatif, -ive** [edykatif, -iv] *adj* educational

**éducation** [edykasjɔ̃] *nf* [enseignement] education ; [des parents] upbringing ; **avoir de l'éducation** to have good manners ; **l'Éducation nationale** ≃ the Department of Education ; **éducation physique** physical education or training ■ **éduquer** *vt* [à l'école] to educate ; [à la maison] to bring up

**édulcorant** [edylkɔrɑ̃] *nm* sweetener

**EEE** [əəə] *(abr de* **Espace économique européen**) *nm* EEA

**effacé, -e** [efase] *adj* [modeste] self-effacing

**effacer** [efase] **1.** *vt* [avec une gomme] to rub out, to erase ; [avec un chiffon] to wipe away ; *Fig* [souvenir] to blot out, to erase ; ORDINAT to delete **2. s'effacer** *vpr* [souvenir] to fade ; [se placer en retrait] to step aside ■ **efface** [efas] *nf Can* [gomme à effacer] eraser ■ **effaceur** [efasœr] *nm* **effaceur (d'encre)** ink *Br* rubber or *Am* eraser

**effarant, -e** [efarɑ̃, -ɑ̃t] *adj* astounding

**effaroucher** [efaruʃe] **1.** *vt* to scare away **2. s'effaroucher** *vpr* to take fright

**effectif, -ive** [efɛktif, -iv] **1.** *adj* [réel] effective **2.** *nm* [de classe] size ; [employés] staff ■ **effectivement** *adv* [en effet] actually

**effectuer** [efɛktɥe] *vt* [expérience, geste difficile] to carry out, to perform ; [paiement, trajet] to make

**efféminé, -e** [efemine] *adj* effeminate

**effervescence** [efɛrvesɑ̃s] nf [agitation] turmoil; **en effervescence** bubbling or buzzing with excitement

**effervescent, -e** [efɛrvesɑ̃, -ɑ̃t] adj [médicament] effervescent

**effet** [efɛ] nm [résultat] effect; [impression] impression (**sur** on); **en effet** indeed, in fact; **effet de serre** greenhouse effect; **effet secondaire** side effect; CINÉ **effets spéciaux** special effects

**efficace** [efikas] adj [mesure] effective; [personne] efficient ■ **efficacité** nf [de mesure] effectiveness; [de personne] efficiency

**effilocher** [efilɔʃe] ■ **s'effilocher** vpr to fray

**effleurer** [eflœre] vt [frôler] to touch lightly; **effleurer qn** [pensée] to cross sb's mind

**effondrer** [efɔ̃dre] ■ **s'effondrer** vpr [tomber, chuter] to collapse; [plan] to fall through; Fig [perdre ses forces] to go to pieces; **s'effondrer en larmes** to break down and cry ■ **effondrement** nm [chute] collapse; [sentiment] dejection

**efforcer** [efɔrse] ■ **s'efforcer** vpr **s'efforcer de faire qch** to try hard to do sth

**effort** [efɔr] nm effort; **faire des efforts** to make an effort

**effraction** [efraksjɔ̃] nf **entrer par effraction** to break in; **vol avec effraction** housebreaking

**effrayer** [efreje] **1.** vt to frighten, to scare **2. s'effrayer** vpr to be frightened or scared ■ **effrayant, -e** adj frightening, scary

**effriter** [efrite] ■ **s'effriter** vpr to crumble

**effronté, -e** [efrɔ̃te] adj [personne] impudent

**effroyable** [efrwajabl] adj dreadful

**effusion** [efyzjɔ̃] nf **effusion de sang** bloodshed

**égal, -e, -aux** [egal, -o] **1.** adj equal (**à** to); [régulier] even; **ça m'est égal** it's all the same to me **2.** nmf [personne] equal

■ **également** adv [au même degré] equally; [aussi] also, as well ■ **égaler** vt to equal, to match (**en** in); **3 plus 4 égale(nt) 7** 3 plus 4 equals 7

**égaliser** [egalize] vi SPORT to equalize

**égalité** [egalite] nf equality; [régularité] evenness; [au tennis] deuce; SPORT **à égalité** even, equal (in points) ■ **égalitaire** adj egalitarian

**égard** [egar] nm **à l'égard de** [envers] towards; **à cet égard** in this respect; **par égard pour qn** out of consideration for sb

**égarer** [egare] **1.** vt [objet] to mislay; [personne] to mislead **2. s'égarer** vpr [personne, lettre] to get lost; [objet] to go astray

**égayer** [egeje] **1.** vt [pièce] to brighten up; **égayer qn** to cheer sb up **2. s'égayer** vpr [s'animer] to cheer up

**église** [egliz] nf church

**égoïste** [egɔist] **1.** adj selfish **2.** nmf selfish person

**égorger** [egɔrʒe] vt to cut or slit the throat of

**égout** [egu] nm sewer

**égoutter** [egute] **1.** vt to drain **2.** vi to drain **3. s'égoutter** vpr to drain ■ **égouttoir** nm [panier] drainer

**égratigner** [egratiɲe] **1.** vt to scratch **2. s'égratigner** vpr to scratch oneself ■ **égratignure** nf scratch

**Égypte** [eʒipt] nf **l'Égypte** Egypt ■ **égyptien, -enne 1.** adj Egyptian **2.** nmf **Égyptien, Égyptienne** Egyptian

**éjecter** [eʒɛkte] vt to eject

**élaborer** [elabɔre] vt [plan, idée] to develop ■ **élaboration** nf [de plan, d'idée] development

**élan** [elɑ̃] nm **a)** [vitesse] momentum; [course] run-up; **prendre son élan** to take a run-up **b)** Can [golf] swing

**élancé, -e** [elɑ̃se] adj [personne] slender

**élancer** [elɑ̃se] **1.** vi [abcès] to give shooting pains **2. s'élancer** vpr [bondir] to rush forward; SPORT to take a run-up ■ **élancement** nm [douleur] shooting pain

**élargir** [elaʀʒiʀ] **1.** vt [chemin] to widen; [vêtement] to let out **2. s'élargir** vpr [sentier] to widen out; [vêtement] to stretch

**élasthanne** [elastan] nm Spandex®

**élastique** [elastik] **1.** adj [tissu] elastic **2.** nm [lien] rubber band, Br elastic band; [pour la couture] elastic

**e-learning** [ilœʀniŋ] nm e-learning

**élection** [elɛksjɔ̃] nf election; **élection partielle** by-election ■ **électeur, -trice** nmf voter, elector ■ **électoral, -e, -aux** adj **campagne électorale** election campaign; **liste électorale** electoral roll ■ **électorat** nm [électeurs] electorate, voters

**électricien, -enne** [elɛktʀisjɛ̃, -ɛn] nmf electrician ■ **électricité** nf electricity ■ **électrifier** vt [voie ferrée] to electrify ■ **électrique** adj [pendule, décharge] & Fig electric; [courant, fil] electric(al)

**électrocuter** [elɛktʀɔkyte] vt to electrocute

**électroménager** [elɛktʀɔmenaʒe] **1.** adj m **appareil électroménager** household electrical appliance **2.** nm household appliances

**électronique** [elɛktʀɔnik] **1.** adj electronic **2.** nf electronics (sg)

**élégant, -e** [elegã, -ãt] adj [bien habillé] smart, elegant ■ **élégance** nf elegance

**élément** [elemã] nm [de meuble] unit ■ **éléments** nmpl [notions] elements, basic principles

**élémentaire** [elemãtɛʀ] adj basic

**éléphant** [elefã] nm elephant

**élevage** [elvaʒ] nm [production] breeding (**de** of); [ferme] farm

**élève** [elɛv] nmf [à l'école] pupil

**élevé, -e** [elve] adj [haut] high; [noble] noble; **bien / mal élevé** well- / bad-mannered

**élever** [elve] **1.** vt [objection] to raise; [enfant] to bring up; [animal] to breed

**2. s'élever** vpr [montagne] to rise; [monument] to stand; **s'élever à** [prix] to amount to; **s'élever contre** to rise up against

**éleveur, -euse** [elvœʀ, -øz] nmf breeder

**éliminer** [elimine] vt to eliminate ■ **élimination** nf elimination ■ **éliminatoire** adj **épreuve éliminatoire** SPORT qualifying round, heat; SCOL qualifying exam; SCOL **note éliminatoire** disqualifying mark ■ **éliminatoires** nfpl SPORT qualifying rounds

**élire** [eliʀ] vt to elect (**à** to)

**élite** [elit] nf elite (**de** of)

**elle** [ɛl] pron pers **a)** [sujet] she; [chose, animal] it; **elles** they **b)** [complément] her; [chose, animal] it; **elles** them ■ **elle-même** pron [personne] herself; [chose, animal] itself; **elles-mêmes** themselves

**éloge** [elɔʒ] nm [compliment] praise ■ **élogieux, -euse** adj laudatory

**éloigné, -e** [elwaɲe] adj [lieu] far away, remote; **éloigné de** [village, maison] far (away) from; [très différent] far removed from

**éloignement** [elwaɲəmã] nm [distance] remoteness, distance; [absence] separation (**de** from)

**éloigner** [elwaɲe] **1.** vt [chose, personne] to move away (**de** from); [malade] to keep away; **éloigner qn de qch** [sujet, but] to take sb away from sth **2. s'éloigner** vpr [partir] to move away (**de** from); [dans le passé] to become (more) remote; **s'éloigner de qch** [sujet, but] to wander from sth

**éloquent, -e** [elɔkã, -ãt] adj eloquent

**élu, -e** [ely] **1.** pp de **élire 2.** nmf POL elected member or representative

**élucider** [elyside] vt to elucidate

**Élysée** [elize] nm **(le palais de) l'Élysée** the Élysée palace (French President's residence)

**e-mail** [imɛl] nm e-mail; **envoyer un e-mail** to send an e-mail (**à** to); **rece-**

**voir un e-mail** to receive an e-mail (**de from**); **vérifier son e-mail** to check one's e-mail

**émail, -aux** [emaj, -o] *nm* enamel

**émanations** [emanɑsjɔ̃] *nfpl* **des émanations** [odeurs] smells; [vapeurs] fumes

**émanciper** [emɑ̃sipe] **1.** *vt* [femmes] to emancipate **2. s'émanciper** *vpr* to become emancipated

**émaner** [emane] *vt* **émaner de qch** to emanate from sth

**emballer** [ɑ̃bale] **1.** *vt* [dans une boîte] to pack; [dans du papier] to wrap (up) **2. s'emballer** *vpr* [cheval] to bolt; [moteur] to race ▪ **emballage** *nm* [action] packing; [dans du papier] wrapping; [boîte] packaging; **papier d'emballage** wrapping paper; **emballage recyclable** recyclable container

**embarcadère** [ɑ̃barkadɛr] *nm* landing stage

**embarcation** [ɑ̃barkɑsjɔ̃] *nf* (small) boat

**embarquer** [ɑ̃barke] **1.** *vt* [passagers] to take on board; [marchandises] to load **2.** *vi* to (go on) board **3. s'embarquer** *vpr* to (go on) board ▪ **embarquement** *nm* [de passagers] boarding

**embarras** [ɑ̃bara] *nm* [gêne] embarrassment; **dans l'embarras** in an awkward situation; [financièrement] in financial difficulties

**embarrasser** [ɑ̃barase] **1.** *vt* [encombrer] to clutter up; [mettre mal à l'aise] to embarrass **2. s'embarrasser** *vpr* **s'embarrasser de qch** to burden oneself with sth ▪ **embarrassant, -e** *adj* [paquet] cumbersome; [question] embarrassing ▪ **embarrassé, e** *adj* [gêné] embarrassed

**embauche** [ɑ̃boʃ] *nf* [action] hiring; [travail] work ▪ **embaucher** *vt* [ouvrier] to hire, to take on

**embaumer** [ɑ̃bome] **1.** *vt* [parfumer] to give a sweet smell to **2.** *vi* to smell sweet

**embellir** [ɑ̃belir] **1.** *vt* [pièce, personne] to make more attractive **2.** *vi* [personne] to grow more attractive

**embêter** [ɑ̃bete] *Fam* **1.** *vt* [agacer] to annoy; [ennuyer] to bore **2. s'embêter** *vpr* [s'ennuyer] to get bored ▪ **embêtant, -e** *adj Fam* annoying

**emblée** [ɑ̃ble] ▪ **d'emblée** *adv* right away

**emblème** [ɑ̃blɛm] *nm* emblem

**emboîter** [ɑ̃bwate] **1.** *vt* to fit together **2. s'emboîter** *vpr* to fit together

**embouchure** [ɑ̃buʃyr] *nf* [de fleuve] mouth

**embourber** [ɑ̃burbe] ▪ **s'embourber** *vpr* [véhicule] to get bogged down

**embouteillage** [ɑ̃butɛjaʒ] *nm* traffic jam

**emboutir** [ɑ̃butir] *vt* [voiture] to crash into

**embranchement** [ɑ̃brɑ̃ʃmɑ̃] *nm* [de voie] junction

**embraser** [ɑ̃braze] **1.** *vt* to set ablaze **2. s'embraser** *vpr* [prendre feu] to flare up

**embrasser** [ɑ̃brase] **1.** *vt* **embrasser qn** [donner un baiser à] to kiss sb; [serrer contre soi] to embrace *or* hug sb **2. s'embrasser** *vpr* to kiss (each other)

**embrasure** [ɑ̃brazyr] *nf* [de fenêtre, de porte] aperture; **dans l'embrasure de la porte** in the doorway

**embrayer** [ɑ̃breje] *vi* AUTO to engage the clutch ▪ **embrayage** *nm* [mécanisme, pédale] clutch

**embrouiller** [ɑ̃bruje] **1.** *vt* [fils] to tangle (up); **embrouiller qn** to confuse sb, to get sb muddled **2. s'embrouiller** *vpr* to get confused *or* muddled (**dans** in *or* with)

**embroussaillé, -e** [ɑ̃brusaje] *adj* [barbe, chemin] bushy

**embûches** [ɑ̃byʃ] *nfpl* [difficultés] traps, pitfalls

**embuer** [ɑ̃bɥe] *vt* [vitre] to mist up

**embusquer** [ɑ̃byske] ▪ **s'embusquer** *vpr* to lie in ambush ▪ **embuscade** *nf* ambush

**émeraude** [emrod] *nf* & *adj inv* emerald

**émerger** [emɛrʒe] *vi* to emerge (**de** from)

**émerveiller** [emɛrveje] **1.** *vt* to amaze, to fill with wonder **2. s'émerveiller** *vpr* to marvel, to be filled with wonder (**de** at)

**émettre** [emɛtr] *vt* [lumière, son] to give out, to emit ; [message radio] to broadcast ; [monnaie] to issue ; [vœu] to express ; [chèque] to draw ; [emprunt] to float ■ **émetteur** *nm* RADIO transmitter

**émeute** [emøt] *nf* riot

**émietter** [emjete] **1.** *vt* [pain] to crumble **2. s'émietter** *vpr* [pain] to crumble

**émigrer** [emigre] *vi* [personne] to emigrate ■ **émigrant, -e** *nmf* emigrant ■ **émigration** *nf* emigration ■ **émigré, e 1.** *adj* migrant **2.** *nmf* emigrant

**émincer** [emɛ̃se] *vt* CULIN to slice thinly, to cut into thin strips

**éminent, -e** [eminɑ̃, -ɑ̃t] *adj* eminent ■ **éminence** *nf* [colline] hill ; **son Éminence** [cardinal] his Eminence

**émissaire** [emisɛr] *nm* emissary

**émission** [emisjɔ̃] *nf* [de radio] programme ; [diffusion] transmission ; [de lumière, de son] emission (**de** of)

**emmanchure** [ɑ̃mɑ̃ʃyr] *nf* armhole

**emmêler** [ɑ̃mele] **1.** *vt* [fil, cheveux] to tangle (up) **2. s'emmêler** *vpr* to get tangled

**emménager** [ɑ̃menaʒe] *vi* to move in ; **emménager dans** to move into ■ **emménagement** [-əmɑ̃] *nm* moving in

**emmener** [ɑ̃mne] *vt* to take (**à** to) ; [prisonnier] to take away ; **emmener qn faire une promenade** to take sb for a walk ; **emmener qn en voiture** to give sb a *Br* lift or *Am* ride

**emmitoufler** [ɑ̃mitufle] ■ **s'emmitoufler** *vpr* to wrap (oneself) up (**dans** in)

**émoticon** [emotikɔ̃] *nm* ORDINAT emoticon, smiley

**émotion** [emosjɔ̃] *nf* [sentiment] emotion ■ **émotif, -ive** *adj* emotional

**émoussé, -e** [emuse] *adj* [pointe] blunt

**émouvoir** [emuvwar] **1.** *vt* [affecter] to move, to touch **2. s'émouvoir** *vpr* to be moved *or* touched ■ **émouvant, -e** *adj* moving, touching

**empailler** [ɑ̃paje] *vt* [animal] to stuff

**empaqueter** [ɑ̃pakte] *vt* to pack

**emparer** [ɑ̃pare] ■ **s'emparer** *vpr* **s'emparer de** [lieu, personne, objet] to seize ; [sujet : émotion] to take hold of

**empathie** [ɑ̃pati] *nf* Sout empathy

**empêcher** [ɑ̃peʃe] *vt* to prevent, to stop ; **empêcher qn de faire qch** to prevent *or* stop sb from doing sth ■ **empêchement** [-ɛʃmɑ̃] *nm* hitch ; **il a /j'ai eu un empêchement** something came up

**empereur** [ɑ̃prœr] *nm* emperor

**empester** [ɑ̃pɛste] **1.** *vt* [tabac] to stink of ; [pièce] to stink out **2.** *vi* to stink

**empêtrer** [ɑ̃petre] ■ **s'empêtrer** *vpr* to get entangled (**dans** in)

**empiéter** [ɑ̃pjete] *vi* **empiéter sur** to encroach (**up**)on

**empiler** [ɑ̃pile] **1.** *vt* to pile up (**sur** on) **2. s'empiler** *vpr* to pile up (**sur** on) ; **s'empiler dans** [passagers] to cram into

**empire** [ɑ̃pir] *nm* [territoires] empire ; [autorité] hold, influence

**empirer** [ɑ̃pire] *vi* to worsen, to get worse

**emplacement** [ɑ̃plasmɑ̃] *nm* [de construction] site, location ; [de stationnement] place

**emplettes** [ɑ̃plɛt] *nfpl* **faire des emplettes** to do some shopping

**emplir** [ɑ̃plir] **1.** *vt* to fill (**de** with) **2. s'emplir** *vpr* to fill (**de** with)

**emploi** [ɑ̃plwa] *nm* **a)** [usage] use ; **emploi du temps** timetable **b)** [travail] job ; **sans emploi** unemployed

**employer** [ɑ̃plwaje] **1.** *vt* [utiliser] to use ; [personne] to employ **2. s'employer** *vpr* [expression] to be used ■ **employé, -e** *nmf* employee ; **em-**

**ploy**é **de banque** bank clerk ; **em-ployé de bureau** office worker ■ **employeur, -euse** *nmf* employer

**empocher** [ɑ̃pɔʃe] *vt* to pocket

**empoigner** [ɑ̃pwaɲe] *vt* [saisir] to grab

**empoisonner** [ɑ̃pwazɔne] **1.** *vt* [personne, aliment] to poison **2. s'empoisonner** *vpr* [par accident] to be poisoned ; [volontairement] to poison oneself ■ **empoisonnement** *nm* poisoning

**emporter** [ɑ̃pɔrte] **1.** *vt* [prendre] to take (**avec soi** with one) ; [transporter] to take away ; [entraîner] to carry along or away ; [par le vent] to blow off or away ; [par les vagues] to sweep away ; **pizza à emporter** takeaway pizza ; **l'emporter sur qn** to get the upper hand over sb **2. s'emporter** *vpr* to lose one's temper (**contre** with)

**empreinte** [ɑ̃prɛ̃t] *nf* mark ; **empreinte digitale** fingerprint

**empresser** [ɑ̃prese] ■ **s'empresser** *vpr* **s'empresser de faire qch** to hasten to do sth

**emprise** [ɑ̃priz] *nf* hold (**sur** over)

**emprisonner** [ɑ̃prizɔne] *vt* to imprison ■ **emprisonnement** *nm* imprisonment

**emprunt** [ɑ̃prœ̃] *nm* [argent] loan ; **faire un emprunt** [auprès d'une banque] to take out a loan ■ **emprunter** *vt* [argent, objet] to borrow (**à qn** from sb) ; [route] to take

**ému, -e** [emy] **1.** *pp de* **émouvoir 2.** *adj* [attendri] moved ; [attristé] upset ; [apeuré] nervous ; **une voix émue** a voice charged with emotion

**en¹** [ɑ̃] *prép* **a)** [indique le lieu] in ; [indique la direction] to **b)** [indique le temps] in **c)** [indique le moyen] by ; [indique l'état] in ; **en avion** by plane ; **en fleur** in flower ; **en congé** on leave **d)** [indique la matière] in ; **en bois** made of wood, wooden ; **chemise en Nylon®** nylon shirt ; **c'est en or** it's (made of) gold

**e)** [domaine] **étudiant en anglais** English student ; **docteur en médecine** doctor of medicine **f)** [comme] **en cadeau** as a present ; **en ami** as a friend **g)** [+ participe présent] **en souriant** smiling, with a smile ; **en chantant** while singing ; **en apprenant que** en on hearing that… ; **sortir en courant** to run out **h)** [transformation] into ; **traduire en français** to translate into French

**en²** [ɑ̃] *pron* **a)** [indique la provenance] from there ; **j'en viens** I've just come from there **b)** [remplace les compléments introduits par 'de'] **en parler** to talk about it ; **il en est content** he's pleased with it / him / them ; **il s'en souviendra** he'll remember it **c)** [partitif] some ; **j'en ai** I have some ; **en veux-tu ?** do you want some ? ; **donne-m'en** give some to me

**ENA** [ena] *(abr de* **École nationale d'administration)** *nf university-level college preparing students for senior positions in law and economics*

**encadrer** [ɑ̃kadre] *vt* [tableau] to frame ; [mot] to circle ; [personnel] to manage ; [prisonnier] to flank ■ **encadrement** *nm* [de porte, de photo] frame

**encaisser** [ɑ̃kese] *vt* [argent] to collect ; [chèque] to cash

**encart** [ɑ̃kar] *nm* **encart publicitaire** insert

**en-cas, encas** [ɑ̃ka] *nm inv* snack

**encastré, -e** [ɑ̃kastre] *adj* [cuisinière, lave-linge] built-in

**enceinte¹** [ɑ̃sɛ̃t] *adj f* [femme] pregnant

**enceinte²** [ɑ̃sɛ̃t] *nf* [muraille] (surrounding) wall ; [espace] enclosure ; **dans l'enceinte de** within, inside ; **enceinte (acoustique)** speaker

**encercler** [ɑ̃serkle] *vt* [lieu, ennemi] to surround, to encircle ; [mot] to circle

**enchaîner** [ɑ̃ʃene] **1.** *vt* [animal, prisonnier] to chain up ; [idées] to link (up) **2.** *vi* [continuer à parler] to continue **3. s'enchaîner** *vpr* [idées] to be linked (up) ■ **enchaînement** [-ɑ̃nmɑ̃] *nm* [succession] chain, series ; [liaison] link(ing) (**de** between or of)

**enchanter** [ɑ̃ʃɑ̃te] *vt* [ravir] to delight, to enchant ; [ensorceler] to bewitch ■ **enchanté, -e** *adj* [ravi] delighted (**de** with ; **que** (+ subjunctive) that) ; [magique] enchanted ; **enchanté de faire votre connaissance !** pleased to meet you! ■ **enchantement** *nm* [ravissement] delight ; [sortilège] magic spell

**enchère** [ɑ̃ʃɛr] *nf* [offre] bid ; **vente aux enchères** auction ; **mettre qch aux enchères** to put sth up for auction, to auction sth

**enchérir** [ɑ̃ʃerir] *vi* to make a higher bid ; **enchérir sur qn** to outbid sb

**enchevêtrer** [ɑ̃ʃvetre] ■ **s'enchevêtrer** *vpr* to get entangled (**dans** in)

**enclencher** [ɑ̃klɑ̃ʃe] *vt* to engage

**enclin, -e** [ɑ̃klɛ̃, -in] *adj* **enclin à** inclined to

**enclos** [ɑ̃klo] *nm* [terrain, clôture] enclosure

**encoche** [ɑ̃kɔʃ] *nf* notch (**à** in)

**encolure** [ɑ̃kɔlyr] *nf* [de cheval, de vêtement] neck ; [tour du cou] collar (size)

**encombre** [ɑ̃kɔ̃br] ■ **sans encombre** *adv* without a hitch

**encombrer** [ɑ̃kɔ̃bre] **1.** *vt* [pièce, couloir] to clutter up (**de** with) ; [rue, passage] to block ; **encombrer qn** to hamper sb **2. s'encombrer** *vpr* **s'encombrer de qch** to load oneself down with sth ■ **encombrant, -e** *adj* [paquet] bulky, cumbersome ■ **encombré, -e** *adj* [lignes téléphoniques, route] jammed ■ **encombrement** [-əmɑ̃] *nm* [d'objets] clutter ; [embouteillage] traffic jam ; [volume] bulk(iness)

**encontre** [ɑ̃kɔ̃tr] ■ **à l'encontre de** *prép* against

**encore** [ɑ̃kɔr] *adv* **a)** [toujours] still **b)** [avec négation] **pas encore** not yet ; **je ne suis pas encore prêt** I'm not ready yet **c)** [de nouveau] again **d)** [de plus, en plus] **encore un café** another coffee ; **encore une fois** (once) again, once more ; **encore un autre (one)**, one more ; **encore du pain** (some) more bread ; **quoi encore ?** what else? **e)** [avec comparatif] even, still ; **encore mieux** even better, better still **f)** [aussi] **mais encore** but also **g) et encore** [à peine] if that, only just **h) encore que...** (+ *subjunctive*) although...

**encourager** [ɑ̃kuraʒe] *vt* to encourage (**à faire** to do) ■ **encourageant, -e** *adj* encouraging ■ **encouragement** *nm* encouragement ; [parole] (word of) encouragement

**encrasser** [ɑ̃krase] **1.** *vt* to clog up (with dirt) **2. s'encrasser** *vpr* to get clogged up

**encre** [ɑ̃kr] *nf* ink

**encyclopédie** [ɑ̃siklɔpedi] *nf* encyclopedia

**endetter** [ɑ̃dete] ■ **s'endetter** *vpr* to get into debt ■ **endetté, e** *adj* indebted ■ **endettement** *nm* debts

**endimanché, -e** [ɑ̃dimɑ̃ʃe] *adj* in one's Sunday best

**endive** [ɑ̃div] *nf* chicory *inv*, endive

**endoctriner** [ɑ̃dɔktrine] *vt* to indoctrinate

**endolori, -e** [ɑ̃dɔlɔri] *adj* painful

**endommager** [ɑ̃dɔmaʒe] *vt* to damage

**endormir** [ɑ̃dɔrmir] **1.** *vt* [enfant] to put to sleep ; [ennuyer] to send to sleep **2. s'endormir** *vpr* to fall asleep, to go to sleep ■ **endormi, -e** *adj* asleep, sleeping

**endosser** [ɑ̃dose] *vt* [vêtement] to put on ; [chèque] to endorse

**endroit** [ɑ̃drwa] *nm* **a)** [lieu] place, spot ; **par endroits** in places **b)** [de tissu] right side ; **à l'endroit** [vêtement] the right way round

**enduire** [ɑ̃dɥir] *vt* to smear, to coat (**de** with) ■ **enduit** *nm* coating ; [de mur] plaster

**endurant, -e** [ɑ̃dyrɑ̃, -ɑ̃t] *adj* hardy, tough ■ **endurance** *nf* stamina; **course d'endurance** endurance race

**endurcir** [ɑ̃dyrsir] **1.** *vt* **endurcir qn à** [douleur] to harden sb to **2. s'endurcir** *vpr* [moralement] to become hard; [physiquement] to toughen up

**endurer** [ɑ̃dyre] *vt* to endure, to bear

**énergie** [enɛrʒi] *nf* energy ■ **énergétique** [enɛrʒetik] *adj* **a)** [ressource] energy **b)** [aliment] energy-giving ■ **énergique** *adj* [personne] energetic; [mesure, ton] forceful

**énerver** [enɛrve] **1.** *vt* **énerver qn** [irriter] to get on sb's nerves; [rendre nerveux] to make sb nervous **2. s'énerver** *vpr* to get worked up ■ **énervant, e** [enɛrvɑ̃, ɑ̃t] *adj* annoying, irritating ■ **énervé, -e** *adj* [agacé] irritated; [excité] on edge, agitated

**enfance** [ɑ̃fɑ̃s] *nf* childhood ■ **enfantillages** *nmpl* childish behaviour ■ **enfantin, -e** *adj* [voix, joie] childlike; [langage] children's; [simple] easy

**enfant** [ɑ̃fɑ̃] *nmf* child (*pl* children); **attendre un enfant** to be expecting a baby; **enfant unique** only child

**enfarger** [ɑ̃farʒe] *vt Can* [faire trébucher] to trip ■ **s'enfarger** *vpr* [s'empêtrer] to trip up

**enfer** [ɑ̃fɛr] *nm* hell

**enfermer** [ɑ̃fɛrme] **1.** *vt* [personne, chose] to shut up; **enfermer qn/qch à clef** to lock sb/sth up **2. s'enfermer** *vpr* **s'enfermer dans** [chambre] to shut oneself (up) in; **s'enfermer à clef** to lock oneself in

**enfiler** [ɑ̃file] *vt* [aiguille] to thread; [perles] to string; *Fam* [vêtement] to slip on

**enfin** [ɑ̃fɛ̃] *adv* [à la fin] finally, at last; [en dernier lieu] lastly; [en somme] in a word; [de résignation] well; *Fam* **enfin bref...** [en somme] in a word...; **(mais) enfin!** for heaven's sake!

**enflammer** [ɑ̃flame] **1.** *vt* to set fire to; [allumette] to light **2. s'enflammer** *vpr* to catch fire

**enfler** [ɑ̃fle] *vi* [membre] to swell (up) ■ **enflé, e** *adj* [gonflé] swollen ■ **enflure** *nf* swelling

**enfoncer** [ɑ̃fɔ̃se] **1.** *vt* [clou] to bang in; [porte] to smash in; **enfoncer dans qch** [couteau, mains] to plunge into sth **2. s'enfoncer** *vpr* [s'enliser] to sink (**dans** into); [couteau] to go in; **s'enfoncer dans** [pénétrer] to disappear into

**enfouir** [ɑ̃fwir] *vt* to bury

**enfourner** [ɑ̃furne] *vt* to put in the oven

**enfreindre** [ɑ̃frɛ̃dr] *vt* to infringe

**enfuir** [ɑ̃fɥir] ■ **s'enfuir** *vpr* to run away (**de** from)

**engager** [ɑ̃gaʒe] **1.** *vt* [discussion, combat] to start; [bijou] to pawn; [clef] to insert (**dans** into); **engager qn** [embaucher] to hire sb **2. s'engager** *vpr* [dans l'armée] to enlist; [prendre position] to commit oneself; [partie] to start; **s'engager à faire qch** to undertake to do sth; **s'engager dans** [voie] to enter; [affaire] to get involved in ■ **engagé, -e** *adj* [écrivain] committed ■ **engageant, -e** *adj* engaging ■ **engagement** *nm* [promesse] commitment; [de soldats] enlistment; [au football] kick-off; **prendre l'engagement de faire qch** to undertake to do sth

**engelure** [ɑ̃ʒlyr] *nf* chilblain

**engendrer** [ɑ̃ʒɑ̃dre] *vt* [causer] to generate, to engender; [procréer] to father

**engin** [ɑ̃ʒɛ̃] *nm* [machine] machine; [outil] device; **engin explosif** explosive device; **engin spatial** spacecraft

**englober** [ɑ̃glɔbe] *vt* to include

**engloutir** [ɑ̃glutir] *vt* [nourriture] to wolf down; [bateau, village] to submerge

**engorger** [ɑ̃gɔrʒe] **1.** *vt* to block up, to clog **2. s'engorger** *vpr* **a)** [tuyau] to become blocked **b)** [route] to get congested

**engouement** [ɑ̃gumɑ̃] *nm* craze (**pour** for)

**engouffrer** [ɑ̃gufre] ■ **s'engouffrer** *vpr* **s'engouffrer dans** to rush into

**engourdir** [ɑ̃gurdir] ■ **s'engourdir**
*vpr* [membre] to go numb

**engrais** [ɑ̃grɛ] *nm* fertilizer

**engraisser** [ɑ̃grese] *vt* [animal, personne] to fatten up

**engrenage** [ɑ̃grənaʒ] *nm* TECH gears; *Fig* chain; *Fig* **pris dans l'engrenage** caught in a trap

**engueuler** [ɑ̃gœle] **1.** *vt Fam* **engueuler qn** to bawl sb out **2. s'engueuler** *vpr Fam* to have a row, *Br* to have a slanging match

**énigme** [enigm] *nf* [devinette] riddle; [mystère] enigma ■ **énigmatique** *adj* enigmatic

**enivrer** [ɑ̃nivre] **1.** *vt* to get drunk **2. s'enivrer** *vpr* [devenir ivre] to get drunk

**enjamber** [ɑ̃ʒɑ̃be] *vt* to step over; [sujet : pont-rivière] to span ■ **enjambée** *nf* stride

**enjeu, -x** [ɑ̃ʒø] *nm* [mise] stake; *Fig* [de pari, de guerre] stakes

**enjoliver** [ɑ̃ʒɔlive] *vt* to embellish

**enjoué, -e** [ɑ̃ʒwe] *adj* playful

**enlacer** [ɑ̃lase] *vt* [mêler] to entwine; [embrasser] to clasp

**enlaidir** [ɑ̃ledir] **1.** *vt* to make ugly **2.** *vi* to grow ugly

**enlevé, -e** [ɑ̃lve] *adj* [style, danse] lively

**enlever** [ɑ̃l(ə)ve] **1.** *vt* to remove; [meubles] to take away, to remove; [vêtement, couvercle] to take off, to remove; [tapis] to take up; [rideau] to take down; [enfant] to kidnap, to abduct; [ordures] to collect **2. s'enlever** *vpr* [tache] to come out; [vernis] to come off ■ **enlèvement** [-ɛvmɑ̃] *nm* [d'enfant] kidnapping, abduction; [d'objet] removal

**enliser** [ɑ̃lize] ■ **s'enliser** *vpr* [véhicule] & *Fig* to get bogged down (**dans** in)

**enneigé, -e** [ɑ̃neʒe] *adj* snow-covered

**ennemi, -e** [ɛnmi] **1.** *nmf* enemy **2.** *adj* [personne] hostile (**de** to)

**ennui** [ɑ̃nɥi] *nm* [lassitude] boredom; [souci] problem; **avoir des ennuis** [soucis] to be worried; [problèmes] to have problems

**ennuyer** [ɑ̃nɥije] **1.** *vt* [agacer] to annoy; [préoccuper] to bother; [lasser] to bore **2. s'ennuyer** *vpr* to get bored ■ **ennuyant, e** *adj Belg, Can* boring ■ **ennuyé, -e** *adj* [air] bored ■ **ennuyeux, -euse** *adj* [contrariant] annoying; [lassant] boring

**énoncer** [enɔ̃se] *vt* to state

**énorme** [enɔrm] *adj* enormous, huge ■ **énormément** *adv* [travailler, pleurer] an awful lot; **je le regrette énormément** I'm awfully sorry about it; **il n'a pas énormément d'argent** he hasn't got a huge amount of money ■ **énormité** *nf* [de demande, de crime, de somme] enormity; [faute] glaring mistake

**enquête** [ɑ̃kɛt] *nf* [de policiers, de journalistes] investigation; [judiciaire, administrative] inquiry; [sondage] survey ■ **enquêter** *vi* [policier, journaliste] to investigate; **enquêter sur qch** to investigate sth

**enraciner** [ɑ̃rasine] ■ **s'enraciner** *vpr* to take root; **enraciné dans** [personne, souvenir] rooted in

**enrager** [ɑ̃raʒe] *vi* to be furious (**de faire** about doing); **faire enrager qn** to get on sb's nerves ■ **enragé, -e** *adj* [chien] rabid

**enrayer** [ɑ̃reje] **1.** *vt* [maladie] to check **2. s'enrayer** *vpr* [fusil] to jam

**enregistrer** [ɑ̃r(ə)ʒistre] *vt* [par écrit, sur bande] to record; [afficher] to register; ORDINAT to save; **faire enregistrer ses bagages** [à l'aéroport] to check in, to check one's baggage in ■ **enregistré, -e** *adj* recorded; **émission enregistrée** recorded *Br* programme *or Am* program ■ **enregistrement** [-əmɑ̃] *nm* [sur bande] recording; **l'enregistrement des bagages** [à l'aéroport] (baggage) check-in; **se présenter à l'enregistrement** to check in

**enrhumer** [ɑ̃ryme] ■ **s'enrhumer** *vpr* to catch a cold; **être enrhumé** to have a cold

**enrichir** [ɑ̃riʃir] **1.** vt to enrich (**de** with) **2. s'enrichir** vpr [personne] to get rich

**enrober** [ɑ̃rɔbe] vt to coat (**de** in)

**enrouer** [ɑ̃rwe] ▪ **s'enrouer** vpr to get hoarse

**enrouler** [ɑ̃rule] **1.** vt [fil] to wind **2. s'enrouler** vpr **s'enrouler dans qch** [couvertures] to wrap oneself up in sth; **s'enrouler sur** ou **autour de qch** to wind round sth

**ensabler** [ɑ̃sable] ▪ **s'ensabler** vpr [port] to silt up

**ensanglanté, -e** [ɑ̃sɑ̃glɑ̃te] adj blood-stained

**enseignant, -e** [ɑ̃sɛɲɑ̃, -ɑ̃t] **1.** nmf teacher **2.** adj **corps enseignant** teaching profession

**enseigne** [ɑ̃sɛɲ] **1.** nf [de magasin] sign; **enseigne lumineuse** neon sign **2.** nm **enseigne de vaisseau** Br lieutenant, Am ensign

**enseigner** [ɑ̃seɲe] **1.** vt to teach; **enseigner qch à qn** to teach sb sth **2.** vi to teach ▪ **enseignement** [-ɛɲmɑ̃] nm education; [action, métier] teaching; **enseignement assisté par ordinateur** computer-assisted learning; **enseignement par correspondance** distance learning; **enseignement privé** private education; **enseignement public** Br state ou Am public education

**ensemble** [ɑ̃sɑ̃bl] **1.** adv together; **aller (bien) ensemble** [couleurs] to go (well) together; [personnes] to be well-matched **2.** nm [d'objets] group, set; MATH set; [vêtement] outfit; [harmonie] unity; **l'ensemble du personnel** [totalité] the whole (of the) staff; **l'ensemble des enseignants** all (of) the teachers; **dans l'ensemble** on the whole

**ensevelir** [ɑ̃səvlir] vt to bury

**ensoleillé, -e** [ɑ̃sɔleje] adj [endroit, journée] sunny

**ensoleillement** [ɑ̃sɔlɛjmɑ̃] nm sun(shine); **cinq heures d'ensoleillement par jour** five hours of sunshine a day

**ensommeillé, -e** [ɑ̃sɔmeje] adj sleepy

**ensorceler** [ɑ̃sɔrsəle] vt [envoûter, séduire] to bewitch

**ensuite** [ɑ̃sɥit] adv [puis] next, then; [plus tard] afterwards

**ensuivre** [ɑ̃sɥivr] ▪ **s'ensuivre** v impers **il s'ensuit que...** it follows that...

**entailler** [ɑ̃taje] vt [fendre] to notch; [blesser] to gash, to slash

**entamer** [ɑ̃tame] vt [pain] to cut into; [bouteille, boîte] to open; [négociations] to enter into

**entartrer** [ɑ̃tartre] **1.** vt [chaudière] Br to fur up, Am to scale **2. s'entartrer** vpr [chaudière] Br to fur up, Am to scale

**entasser** [ɑ̃tase] **1.** vt [objets] to pile up, to heap up **2. s'entasser** vpr [objets] to pile up, to heap up

**entendre** [ɑ̃tɑ̃dr] **1.** vt to hear; [comprendre] to understand; **entendre parler de qn/qch** to hear of sb/sth; **entendre dire que...** to hear (it said) that... **2. s'entendre** vpr [être entendu] to be heard; [être compris] to be understood; **s'entendre** [être d'accord] to agree (**sur** on); **(bien) s'entendre avec qn** to get along ou Br on with sb

**entendu, -e** [ɑ̃tɑ̃dy] adj [convenu] agreed; [sourire, air] knowing; **entendu !** all right!; **bien entendu** of course

**entente** [ɑ̃tɑ̃t] nf [accord] agreement, understanding; **(bonne) entente** [amitié] harmony

**entériner** [ɑ̃terine] vt to ratify

**enterrer** [ɑ̃tere] vt [défunt] to bury; Fig [projet] to scrap ▪ **enterrement** [-ɛrmɑ̃] nm [ensevelissement] burial; [funérailles] funeral

**en-tête** [ɑ̃tɛt] (pl **en-têtes**) nm [de papier] heading; **papier à en-tête** headed paper, letterhead

**entêter** [ɑ̃tete] ▪ **s'entêter** vpr to persist (**à faire** in doing) ▪ **entêté, -e** adj stubborn

**enthousiasme** [ɑ̃tuzjasm] nm enthusiasm ▪ **enthousiaste** adj enthusiastic

**enticher** [ɑ̃tiʃe] ▪ **s'enticher** vpr **s'enticher de qn/qch** to become infatuated with sb/sth

**entier, -ère** [ɑ̃tje, -ɛr] **1.** *adj* [total] whole, entire ; [intact] intact ; [absolu] absolute, complete ; [caractère] uncompromising ; **le pays tout entier** the whole *or* entire country **2.** *nm* **en entier** in its entirety, completely

**entonner** [ɑ̃tɔne] *vt* [air] to start singing

**entonnoir** [ɑ̃tɔnwar] *nm* funnel

**entorse** [ɑ̃tɔrs] *nf* MÉD sprain ; **se faire une entorse à la cheville** to sprain one's ankle

**entortiller** [ɑ̃tɔrtije] **1.** *vt* to wrap (**dans** in) **2. s'entortiller** *vpr* [lierre] to coil (**autour de** round)

**entourage** [ɑ̃turaʒ] *nm* [proches] circle of family and friends

**entourer** [ɑ̃ture] **1.** *vt* to surround (**de** with) ; [envelopper] to wrap (**de** in) ; **entouré de** surrounded by **2. s'entourer** *vpr* **s'entourer de** to surround oneself with

**entracte** [ɑ̃trakt] *nm* Br interval, Am intermission

**entraide** [ɑ̃trɛd] *nf* mutual aid ■ **s'entraider** *vpr* to help each other

**entraînant, -e** [ɑ̃trɛnɑ̃, -ɑ̃t] *adj* [musique] lively

**entraîner** [ɑ̃trene] **1.** *vt* **a)** [charrier] to carry away ; [causer] to bring about ; [dépenses] to entail ; **entraîner qn** [emmener] to lead sb away ; [de force] to drag sb away ; [attirer] to lure sb ; **se laisser entraîner** to allow oneself to be led astray **b)** [athlète, cheval] to train (**à** for) **2. s'entraîner** *vpr* to train oneself (**à faire qch** to do sth) ; SPORT to train ■ **entraînement** [-ɛnmɑ̃] *nm* SPORT training ; [élan] impulse ■ **entraîneur** [-ɛnœr] *nm* [d'athlète] coach ; [de cheval] trainer

**entraver** [ɑ̃trave] *vt* to hinder, to hamper

**entre** [ɑ̃tr] *prép* between ; [parmi] among(st) ; **l'un d'entre vous** one of you ; **se dévorer entre eux** [réciprocité] to devour each other

**entrebâiller** [ɑ̃trəbɑje] *vt* [porte] to open slightly

**entrecôte** [ɑ̃trəkot] *nf* rib steak

**entrecouper** [ɑ̃trəkupe] *vt* [entremêler] to punctuate (**de** with)

**entrée** [ɑ̃tre] *nf* [action] entry, entrance ; [porte] entrance ; [vestibule] entrance hall, entry ; [accès] admission, entry (**de** to) ; ORDINAT input ; [plat] starter ; **faire son entrée** to make one's entrance ; **'entrée interdite'** 'no entry', 'no admittance' ; **'entrée libre'** 'admission free' ; **entrée de service** service *or* Br tradesmen's entrance ; **entrée des artistes** stage door

**entrejambe** [ɑ̃trəʒɑ̃b] *nm* crotch

**entrelacer** [ɑ̃trəlase] **1.** *vt* to intertwine **2. s'entrelacer** *vpr* to intertwine

**entremêler** [ɑ̃trəmele] **1.** *vt* to intermingle **2. s'entremêler** *vpr* to intermingle

**entremets** [ɑ̃trəmɛ] *nm* [plat] dessert, Br sweet

**entreposer** [ɑ̃trəpoze] *vt* to store ■ **entrepôt** *nm* warehouse

**entreprendre** [ɑ̃trəprɑ̃dr] *vt* [travail, voyage] to undertake ; **entreprendre de faire qch** to undertake to do sth ■ **entreprenant, -e** [-ɑ̃nɑ̃, -ɑ̃t] *adj* [dynamique] enterprising ; [galant] forward

**entrepreneur** [ɑ̃trəprənœr] *nm* [en bâtiment] contractor ; [chef d'entreprise] entrepreneur

**entreprise** [ɑ̃trəpriz] *nf* [firme] company, firm

**entrer** [ɑ̃tre] **1.** *(aux être)* *vi* [aller] to go in, to enter ; [venir] to come in, to enter ; **entrer dans** to go into ; [pièce] to come / go into, to enter ; **entrer à l'université** to start university ; **entrer dans les détails** to go into detail ; **entrez !** come in ! **2.** *(aux avoir)* *vt* ORDINAT to enter, to input ; ORDINAT **entrer des données** to enter data (**dans** into)

**entresol** [ɑ̃trəsɔl] *nm* mezzanine floor

**entre-temps** [ɑ̃trətɑ̃] *adv* meanwhile

**entretenir** [ɑ̃trətnir] **1.** *vt* [voiture, maison, famille] to maintain ; [relations] to keep ; **entretenir qn de qch** to talk to sb about sth **2. s'entretenir** *vpr* **s'entretenir de qch** to talk about sth (**avec** with) ▪ **entretenu, -e** *adj* **bien / mal entretenu** [maison] well-kept / badly kept

**entretien** [ɑ̃trətjɛ̃] *nm* [de route, de maison] maintenance, upkeep; [dialogue] conversation; [entrevue] interview

**entrevoir** [ɑ̃trəvwar] *vt* [rapidement] to catch a glimpse of; [pressentir] to foresee

**entrevue** [ɑ̃trəvy] *nf* interview

**entrouvrir** [ɑ̃truvrir] **1.** *vt* to half-open **2. s'entrouvrir** *vpr* to half-open ▪ **entrouvert, -e** *adj* [porte, fenêtre] half-open

**énumérer** [enymere] *vt* to list ▪ **énumération** *nf* listing

**envahir** [ɑ̃vair] *vt* [pays] to invade; [marché] to flood; **envahir qn** [doute, peur] to overcome sb ▪ **envahissant, -e** *adj* [personne] intrusive ▪ **envahisseur** *nm* invader

**enveloppant, -e** [ɑ̃vlɔpɑ̃, -ɑ̃t] *adj* [séduisant] captivating

**enveloppe** [ɑ̃vlɔp] *nf* [pour lettre] envelope

**enveloppé, e** [ɑ̃vlɔpe] *adj Fam* (un peu) **enveloppé** [personne] (a bit) chubby

**envelopper** [ɑ̃vlɔpe] **1.** *vt* to wrap (up) (**dans** in) **2. s'envelopper** *vpr* to wrap oneself (up) (**dans** in)

**envenimer** [ɑ̃vnime] ▪ **s'envenimer** *vpr* [plaie] to turn septic; *Fig* to become acrimonious

**envergure** [ɑ̃vɛrgyr] *nf* [d'avion, d'oiseau] wingspan; [de personne] calibre; [ampleur] scope

**envers** [ɑ̃vɛr] **1.** *prép Br* towards, *Am* toward(s), to **2.** *nm* [de tissu] wrong side; **à l'envers** [chaussette] inside out; [pantalon] back to front; [la tête en bas] upside down

**envie** [ɑ̃vi] *nf* [jalousie] envy; [désir] desire; **avoir envie de qch** to want sth; **avoir envie de faire qch** to feel like doing sth ▪ **envier** *vt* to envy (**qch à qn** sb sth) ▪ **envieux, -euse** *adj* envious

**environ** [ɑ̃virɔ̃] *adv* [à peu près] about ▪ **environs** *nmpl* outskirts, surroundings; **aux environs de qch** around sth, in the vicinity of sth

**environnant, -e** [ɑ̃virɔnɑ̃, -ɑ̃t] *adj* surrounding

**environnement** [ɑ̃virɔnmɑ̃] *nm* [gén & ORDINAT] environment

**envisager** [ɑ̃vizaʒe] *vt* [considérer] to consider; [projeter] *Br* to envisage, *Am* to envision; **envisager de faire qch** to consider doing sth

**envoi** [ɑ̃vwa] *nm* [action] sending; [paquet] package; [marchandises] consignment

**envoler** [ɑ̃vɔle] ▪ **s'envoler** *vpr* [oiseau] to fly away; [avion] to take off; [chapeau, papier] to blow away; *Fig* [espoir] to vanish

**envoûter** [ɑ̃vute] *vt* to bewitch

**envoyer** [ɑ̃vwaje] *vt* to send; [lancer] to throw; **envoyer chercher qn** to send for sb ▪ **envoyé, -e** *nmf* envoy; **envoyé spécial** [reporter] special correspondent ▪ **envoyeur** *nm* sender; **retour à l'envoyeur** 'return to sender'

**éolien, enne** [eɔljɛ̃, ɛn] *adj* wind ▪ **éolien** *nm* **l'éolien** wind power ▪ **éolienne** *nf* windmill *(for generating power)*, wind turbine

**épais, -aisse** [epɛ, -ɛs] *adj* thick ▪ **épaisseur** *nf* thickness; **avoir 1 mètre d'épaisseur** to be 1 metre thick ▪ **épaissir** [epesir] **1.** *vt* to thicken **2.** *vi* to thicken; [grossir] to fill out; **le mystère s'épaissit** the mystery is deepening **3. s'épaissir** *vpr* = **épaissir** *vi*

**épanouir** [epanwir] ▪ **s'épanouir** *vpr* [fleur] to bloom; *Fig* [personne] to blossom; [visage] to beam ▪ **épanoui, -e** *adj* [fleur, personne] in full bloom; [visage] beaming ▪ **épanouissant, e** [epanwisɑ̃, ɑ̃t] *adj* fulfilling ▪ **épanouissement** *nm* [de fleur] full bloom; [de personne] blossoming

**épargne** [eparɲ] *nf* [action, vertu] saving; [sommes] savings ▪ **épargnant, -e** *nmf* saver ▪ **épargner** *vt* [argent, provisions] to save; [ennemi] to spare; **épargner qch à qn** [ennuis, chagrin] to spare sb sth

**éparpiller** [eparpije] **1.** *vt* to scatter; [efforts] to dissipate **2. s'éparpiller** *vpr* to scatter; [efforts] to dissipate

**épaule** [epol] *nf* shoulder ■ **épauler 1.** *vt* [fusil] to raise (to one's shoulder); **épauler qn** [aider] to back sb up **2.** *vi* to take aim ■ **épaulette** *nf* [de veste] shoulder pad

**épave** [epav] *nf* [bateau, personne] wreck

**épeautre** [epotr] *nm* spelt *(wheat)*

**épée** [epe] *nf* sword

**épeler** [eple] *vt* to spell

**éperon** [eprɔ̃] *nm* [de cavalier, de coq] spur

**épeurer** [epœre] *vt Can* to scare, to frighten ■ **épeurant, e** *adj Can* scary

**épi** [epi] *nm* [de blé] ear; [de cheveux] tuft of hair

**épice** [epis] *nf* spice ■ **épicé, -e** *adj* [plat, récit] spicy ■ **épicer** *vt* to spice

**épicier, -ère** [episje, -εr] *nmf* grocer ■ **épicerie** *nf* [magasin] *Br* grocer's (shop), *Am* grocery (store); **épicerie fine** delicatessen

**épidémie** [epidemi] *nf* epidemic

**épier** [epje] *vt* [observer] to watch closely; [occasion] to watch out for; **épier qn** to spy on sb

**épiler** [epile] ■ **s'épiler** *vpr* to remove unwanted hair; **s'épiler les jambes à la cire** to wax one's legs ■ **épilateur** [epilatœr] *nm* hair remover; **épilateur à cire** wax hair remover; **épilateur électrique** electric hair remover ■ **épilatoire** [epilatwar] *adj* hair-removing, depilatory

**épilogue** [epilɔg] *nm* epilogue

**épinards** [epinar] *nmpl* spinach

**épine** [epin] *nf* [de plante] thorn; [d'animal] spine, prickle ■ **épineux, -euse** *adj* [tige, question] thorny; [poisson] spiny

**épinette** [epinɛt] *nf Can* [épicéa] spruce

**épingle** [epɛ̃gl] *nf* pin; **épingle à nourrice** safety pin; **épingle à linge** *Br* clothes peg, *Am* clothes pin ■ **épingler** *vt* to pin

**Épiphanie** [epifani] *nf* **l'Épiphanie** Epiphany

**épique** [epik] *adj* epic

**épiscopal, -e, -aux** [episkɔpal, -o] *adj* episcopal

**épisode** [epizɔd] *nm* episode ■ **épisodique** *adj* [intermittent] occasional

**épitaphe** [epitaf] *nf* epitaph

**éplucher** [eplyʃe] *vt* [carotte, pomme] to peel ■ **épluchure** *nf* peeling

**éponge** [epɔ̃ʒ] *nf* sponge; *Fig* **jeter l'éponge** to throw in the towel ■ **éponger 1.** *vt* [liquide] to mop up; [dette] to absorb **2. s'éponger** *vpr* **s'éponger le front** to mop one's brow

**époque** [epɔk] *nf* [date] time, period; [historique] age; **meubles d'époque** period furniture; **à l'époque** at the *or* that time

**épouse** [epuz] *nf* wife

**épouser** [epuze] *vt* to marry

**épousseter** [epuste] *vt* to dust

**épouvantable** [epuvɑ̃tabl] *adj* appalling

**épouvantail** [epuvɑ̃taj] *nm* [de jardin] scarecrow

**épouvante** [epuvɑ̃t] *nf* terror ■ **épouvanter** *vt* to terrify

**époux** [epu] *nm* husband; **les époux** the husband and wife

**éprendre** [eprɑ̃dr] ■ **s'éprendre** *vpr* **s'éprendre de qn** to fall in love with sb

**épreuve** [eprœv] *nf* [essai, examen] test; [sportive] event; [malheur] ordeal, trial; [photo] print; **mettre qn à l'épreuve** to put sb to the test; **à toute épreuve** [patience] unfailing; [nerfs] rock-solid; **à l'épreuve du feu** fireproof

**éprouver** [epruve] *vt* [méthode, personne] to test; [sentiment] to feel; [difficultés] to meet with ■ **éprouvant, -e** *adj* [pénible] trying

**éprouvette** [epɾuvɛt] *nf* test tube

**EPS** [əpeɛs] *(abr de* **éducation physique et sportive)** *nf* PE

**épuiser** [epɥize] **1.** *vt* [personne, provisions, sujet] to exhaust **2.** **s'épuiser** *vpr* [réserves, patience] to run out; **s'épuiser à faire qch** to exhaust oneself doing sth ▪ **épuisant, -e** *adj* exhausting ▪ **épuisé, -e** *adj* exhausted; [marchandise] sold out; [édition] out of print

**épuisette** [epɥizɛt] *nf* landing net

**épurer** [epyre] *vt* [eau, gaz] to purify; [minerai] to refine ▪ **épuration** *nf* purification; [de minerai] refining

**équateur** [ekwatœr] *nm* equator; **sous l'équateur** at the equator

**Équateur** [ekwatœr] *nm* **(la république de) l'Équateur** (the Republic of) Ecuador

**équation** [ekwɑsjɔ̃] *nf* MATH equation

**équerre** [ekɛr] *nf* **équerre (à dessin)** *Br* set square, *Am* triangle

**équestre** [ekɛstr] *adj* [statue, sports] equestrian

**équilibre** [ekilibr] *nm* balance; **garder/perdre l'équilibre** to keep/lose one's balance

**équilibrer** [ekilibre] **1.** *vt* [charge, composition, budget] to balance **2.** **s'équilibrer** *vpr* to balance each other out

**équinoxe** [ekinɔks] *nm* equinox

**équipage** [ekipaʒ] *nm* [de navire, d'avion] crew

**équipe** [ekip] *nf* team; [d'ouvriers] gang; **faire équipe avec qn** to team up with sb; **travailler en** *ou* **par équipe** to work as a team; **équipe de nuit** night shift; **équipe de secours** rescue team ▪ **équipier, -ère** *nmf* team member

**équiper** [ekipe] **1.** *vt* to equip (**de** with) **2.** **s'équiper** *vpr* to equip oneself (**de** with) ▪ **équipé, e** *adj* **cuisine équipée** fitted kitchen ▪ **équipement** *nm* equipment

**équitable** [ekitabl] *adj* fair, equitable

**équitation** [ekitɑsjɔ̃] *nf Br* (horse) riding, *Am* (horseback) riding; **faire de l'équitation** to go riding

**équivalent, -e** [ekivalɑ̃, -ɑ̃t] *adj & nm* equivalent ▪ **équivalence** *nf* equivalence ▪ **équivaloir** *vi* **équivaloir à qch** to be equivalent to sth

**équivoque** [ekivɔk] **1.** *adj* [ambigu] equivocal; [douteux] dubious **2.** *nf* ambiguity

**érable** [erabl] *nm* [arbre, bois] maple

**érafler** [erafle] *vt* to graze, to scratch ▪ **éraflure** *nf* graze, scratch

**ère** [ɛr] *nf* era; **avant notre ère** BC; **en l'an 800 de notre ère** in the year 800 AD

**éreinter** [erɛ̃te] **1.** *vt* [fatiguer] to exhaust **2.** **s'éreinter** *vpr* **s'éreinter à faire qch** to wear oneself out doing sth

**ériger** [eriʒe] **1.** *vt* to erect **2.** **s'ériger** *vpr* **s'ériger en qch** to set oneself up as sth

**érosion** [erozjɔ̃] *nf* erosion ▪ **éroder** *vt* to erode

**errer** [ɛre] *vi* to wander ▪ **errant** *adj m* **chien/chat errant** stray dog/cat

**erreur** [erœr] *nf* [faute] mistake, error; **par erreur** by mistake; **erreur judiciaire** miscarriage of justice

**erroné, e** [ɛrɔne] *adj* wrong

**érudit, -e** [erydi, -it] **1.** *adj* scholarly, erudite **2.** *nmf* scholar ▪ **érudition** *nf* scholarship, erudition

**éruption** [erypsjɔ̃] *nf* [de volcan] eruption; [de boutons] rash

**es** [ɛ] *voir* **être**

**ès** [ɛs] *prép* of; **licencié ès lettres** ≃ BA; **docteur ès lettres** ≃ PhD

**escabeau, -x** [ɛskabo] *nm* [marchepied] stepladder, *Br* (pair of) steps; [tabouret] stool

**escadrille** [ɛskadrij] *nf* AVIAT [unité] flight

**escadron** [ɛskadrɔ̃] *nm* squadron

**escalade** [ɛskalad] *nf* climbing; [de prix, de violence] escalation ▪ **escalader** *vt* to climb, to scale

**escale** [ɛskal] *nf* AVIAT stopover; NAUT [lieu] port of call; **faire escale à** [avion] to stop (over) at; [navire] to put in at; **vol sans escale** non-stop flight

**escalier** [ɛskalje] *nm* [marches] stairs ; [cage] staircase ; **l'escalier, les escaliers** the stairs ; **escalier mécanique** *ou* **roulant** escalator ; **escalier de secours** fire escape

**escalope** [ɛskalɔp] *nf* escalope

**escamoter** [ɛskamɔte] *vt* [faire disparaître] to make vanish ; [esquiver] to dodge

**escapade** [ɛskapad] *nf* [voyage] outing

**escargot** [ɛskargo] *nm* snail

**escarpé, -e** [ɛskarpe] *adj* steep ■ **escarpement** [-əmɑ̃] *nm* [côte] steep slope

**escarpin** [ɛskarpɛ̃] *nm* [soulier] pump, *Br* court shoe

**esclandre** [ɛsklɑ̃dr] *nm* scene

**esclave** [ɛsklav] *nmf* slave ■ **esclavage** *nm* slavery

**escompte** [ɛskɔ̃t] *nm* discount ; **taux d'escompte** bank discount rate ■ **escompter** *vt* [espérer] to anticipate (**faire** doing), to expect (**faire** to do)

**escorte** [ɛskɔrt] *nf* escort ■ **escorter** *vt* to escort

**escrime** [ɛskrim] *nf* fencing ; **faire de l'escrime** to fence ■ **escrimeur, -euse** *nmf* fencer

**escrimer** [ɛskrime] ■ **s'escrimer** *vpr* s'escrimer à faire qch to struggle to do sth

**escroc** [ɛskro] *nm* crook, swindler ■ **escroquer** *vt* escroquer qn to swindle sb ; **escroquer qch à qn** to swindle sb out of sth ■ **escroquerie** *nf* [action] swindling ; [résultat] swindle

**espace** [ɛspas] *nm* space ; **espace aérien** air space ; **espace vert** garden, park

**espacer** [ɛspase] **1.** *vt* to space out ; **espacés d'un mètre** one metre apart **2. s'espacer** *vpr* [maisons, visites] to become less frequent

**espadrille** [ɛspadrij] *nf* espadrille, *rope-soled sandal*

**Espagne** [ɛspaɲ] *nf* l'Espagne Spain ■ **espagnol, -e 1.** *adj* Spanish **2.** *nmf* **Espagnol, Espagnole** Spaniard **3.** *nm* [langue] Spanish

**espèce** [ɛspɛs] *nf* [race] species ; [genre] kind, sort ■ **espèces** *nfpl* [argent] cash ; **en espèces** in cash

**espérance** [ɛsperɑ̃s] *nf* hope ; **espérance de vie** life expectancy

**espérer** [ɛspere] **1.** *vt* to hope for ; **espérer que...** to hope that... ; **espérer faire qch** to hope to do sth **2.** *vi* to hope ; **j'espère (bien) !** I hope so!

**espiègle** [ɛspjɛgl] *adj* mischievous

**espion, -onne** [ɛspjɔ̃, -ɔn] *nmf* spy ■ **espionnage** *nm* spying, espionage ■ **espionner 1.** *vt* to spy on **2.** *vi* to spy

**espoir** [ɛspwar] *nm* hope ; **avoir l'espoir de faire qch** to have hopes of doing sth

**esprit** [ɛspri] *nm* [attitude, fantôme] spirit ; [intellect] mind ; [humour] wit ; **venir à l'esprit de qn** to cross sb's mind ; **avoir de l'esprit** to be witty ; **avoir l'esprit large /étroit** to be broad- /narrow-minded

**esquimau, -aude, -aux** [ɛskimo, -od] **1.** *adj* Eskimo, *Am* Inuit **2.** *nmf* **Esquimau, Esquimaude** Eskimo, *Am* Inuit **3.** *nm* **Esquimau®** [glace] *Br* ≈ choc-ice *(on a stick)*, *Am* ≈ ice-cream bar

**esquisse** [ɛskis] *nf* [croquis, plan] sketch ■ **esquisser** *vt* to sketch ; **esquisser un geste** to make a (slight) gesture

**esquiver** [ɛskive] **1.** *vt* [coup, problème] to dodge **2. s'esquiver** *vpr* to slip away

**essai** [ese] *nm* [test] test, trial ; [tentative, au rugby] try ; [ouvrage] essay ; **à l'essai** [objet] on a trial basis

**essaim** [esɛ̃] *nm* swarm

**essayer** [eseje] *vt* to try (**de faire** to do) ; [vêtement] to try on ; [méthode] to try out ■ **essayage** [-ɛjaʒ] *nm* [de vêtement] fitting

**essence** [esɑ̃s] *nf* [carburant] *Br* petrol, *Am* gas ; [extrait & PHIL] essence ;

**essence sans plomb** unleaded; **essence ordinaire** Br two-star petrol, Am regular gas

**essentiel, -elle** [esɑ̃sjɛl] **1.** adj essential (**à / pour** for) **2.** nm **l'essentiel** [le plus important] the main thing; [le minimum] the essentials

**essor** [esɔr] nm [d'oiseau] flight; [de pays, d'entreprise] rapid growth; **en plein essor** booming; **prendre son essor** to take off

**essorer** [esɔre] vt [dans une essoreuse] to spin-dry; [dans une machine à laver] to spin

**essouffler** [esufle] **1.** vt to make out of breath **2.** s'**essouffler** vpr to be breathless or out of breath; Fig to run out of steam

**essuyer** [esɥije] **1.** vt [objet, surface] to wipe; [liquide] to wipe up; [larmes] to wipe away; [défaite] to suffer; [refus] to meet with; **essuyer la vaisselle** to dry the dishes **2.** s'**essuyer** vpr to wipe oneself; s'**essuyer les yeux** to wipe one's eyes ■ **essuie-glace** (pl **essuie-glaces**) nm Br windscreen wiper, Am windshield wiper

**est¹** [ɛ] voir **être**

**est²** [ɛst] **1.** nm east; **à l'est** in the east; [direction] (to the) east (**de** of); **d'est** [vent] east(erly); **de l'est** eastern **2.** adj inv [côte] east(ern)

**estampe** [ɛstɑ̃p] nf print

**estampille** [ɛstɑ̃pij] nf [de produit] mark; [de document] stamp

**esthéticienne** [ɛstetisjɛn] nf beautician

**estime** [ɛstim] nf esteem, regard

**estimer** [ɛstime] **1.** vt [tableau] to value (**à** at); [prix, distance, poids] to estimate; [dommages, besoins] to assess; [juger] to consider (**que** that); **estimer qn** to esteem sb **2.** s'**estimer** vpr s'**estimer heureux** to consider oneself happy ■ **estimable** adj respectable ■ **estimation** nf [de mobilier] valuation; [de prix, de distance, de poids] estimation; [de dommages, de besoins] assessment

**estival, -e, -aux** [ɛstival, -o] adj température; **température estivale** summer temperature ■ **estivant, -e** nmf Br holidaymaker, Am vacationer

**estomac** [ɛstɔma] nm stomach

**estomper** [ɛstɔ̃pe] **1.** vt [rendre flou] to blur **2.** s'**estomper** vpr to become blurred

**Estonie** [ɛstɔni] nf **l'Estonie** Estonia

**estrade** [ɛstrad] nf platform

**estragon** [ɛstragɔ̃] nm tarragon

**esturgeon** [ɛstyrʒɔ̃] nm sturgeon

**et** [e] conj and; **vingt et un** twenty-one; **et moi ?** what about me?

**établi** [etabli] nm workbench

**établir** [etablir] **1.** vt [paix, relations, principe] to establish; [liste] to draw up; [record] to set; [démontrer] to establish, to prove **2.** s'**établir** vpr [pour habiter] to settle; [pour exercer un métier] to set up in business ■ **établissement** nm [de paix, de relations, de principe] establishment; [entreprise] business, firm; **établissement scolaire** school

**étage** [etaʒ] nm [d'immeuble] floor, Br storey, Am story; [de fusée] stage; **à l'étage** upstairs; **au premier étage** on the Br first or Am second floor; **maison à deux étages** Br two-storeyed or Am two-storied house

**étagère** [etaʒɛr] nf shelf; [meuble] shelving unit

**étain** [etɛ̃] nm [métal] tin; [de gobelet] pewter

**étais, était** [etɛ] voir **être**

**étal** [etal] (pl **étals**) nm [au marché] stall

**étalage** [etalaʒ] nm display; [vitrine] display window

**étaler** [etale] **1.** vt [disposer] to lay out; [en vitrine] to display; [beurre] to spread; [vacances, paiements] to stagger **2.** s'**étaler** vpr s'**étaler sur** [congés, paiements] to be spread over ■ **étalement** nm [de vacances, de paiements] staggering

**étanche** [etɑ̃ʃ] adj watertight; [montre] waterproof

**étancher** [etɑ̃ʃe] *vt* [sang] to stop the flow of ; [soif] to quench

**étang** [etɑ̃] *nm* pond

**étant** [etɑ̃] *p prés voir* **être**

**étape** [etap] *nf* [de voyage] stage ; [lieu] stop(over) ; **faire étape à** to stop off or over at ; **par étapes** in stages

**état** [eta] *nm* a) [condition, manière d'être] state ; **à l'état neuf** as new ; **en bon état** in good condition ; **état d'esprit** state or frame of mind ; **état des lieux** inventory of fixtures ; **état civil** register office b) [autorité centrale] **État** [nation] State

**état-major** [etamaʒɔr] (*pl* **états-majors**) *nm* MIL (general) staff ; [de parti] senior staff

**États-Unis** [etazyni] *nmpl* **les États-Unis** the United States ; **les États-Unis d'Amérique** the United States of America

**étau, -x** [eto] *nm* [instrument] *Br* vice, *Am* vise

**été¹** [ete] *nm* summer

**été²** [ete] *pp de* **être**

**éteindre** [etɛ̃dr] **1.** *vt* [feu, cigarette] to put out, to extinguish ; [lampe] to switch off ; [gaz] to turn off ; ORDINAT to shut down **2.** *vi* to switch off **3. s'éteindre** *vpr* [feu] to go out ; [personne] to pass away ■ **éteint, -e** *adj* [feu, bougie] out ; [lampe, lumière] off ; [volcan] extinct

**étendre** [etɑ̃dr] **1.** *vt* [linge] to hang out ; [agrandir] to extend ; **étendre le bras** to stretch out one's arm ; **étendre qn** to stretch sb out **2. s'étendre** *vpr* [personne] to lie down ; [plaine] to stretch ; [feu] to spread ; **s'étendre sur qch** [sujet] to dwell on sth

**étendu, -e¹** [etɑ̃dy] *adj* [forêt, vocabulaire] extensive ; [personne] lying

**étendue²** [etɑ̃dy] *nf* [importance] extent ; [surface] area

**éternel, -elle** [etɛrnɛl] *adj* eternal ■ **s'éterniser** *vpr* [débat] to drag on endlessly ; *Fam* [visiteur] to stay for ever ■ **éternité** *nf* eternity

**éternuer** [etɛrnɥe] *vi* to sneeze

**êtes** [ɛt] *voir* **être**

**Éthiopie** [etjɔpi] *nf* **l'Éthiopie** Ethiopia ■ **éthiopien, -enne 1.** *adj* Ethiopian **2.** *nmf* **Éthiopien, Éthiopienne** Ethiopian

**ethnie** [ɛtni] *nf* ethnic group ■ **ethnique** *adj* ethnic

**étinceler** [etɛ̃sle] *vi* to sparkle ■ **étincelle** *nf* spark

**étiqueter** [etikte] *vt* to label ■ **étiquette** *nf* [marque] label ; [protocole] (diplomatic or court) etiquette

**étirer** [etire] **1.** *vt* to stretch **2. s'étirer** *vpr* to stretch (oneself)

**étoffe** [etɔf] *nf* material, fabric

**étoffer** [etɔfe] **1.** *vt* to fill out ; [texte] to make more meaty **2. s'étoffer** *vpr* [personne] to fill out

**étoile** [etwal] *nf* star ; **à la belle étoile** in the open ; **étoile de mer** starfish ; **étoile filante** shooting star

**étoilé, e** [etwale] *adj* a) [ciel, nuit] starry ; **la bannière étoilée** the Star-Spangled Banner b) [vitre, pare-brise] shattered

**étonner** [etɔne] **1.** *vt* to surprise **2. s'étonner** *vpr* to be surprised (**de** qch at sth ; **que** (+ subjunctive) that) ■ **étonnant, -e** *adj* [ahurissant] surprising ; [remarquable] amazing ■ **étonnement** *nm* surprise

**étouffant, -e** [etufɑ̃, -ɑ̃t] *adj* [air] stifling

**étouffer** [etufe] **1.** *vt* [tuer] to suffocate ; *Fig* [révolte] to stifle ; *Fig* [scandale] to hush up **2.** *vi* to suffocate **3. s'étouffer** *vpr* [en mangeant] to choke (**avec** on) ; [mourir] to suffocate

**étourdi, -e** [eturdi] **1.** *adj* scatter-brained **2.** *nmf* scatterbrain ■ **étourderie** *nf* absent-mindedness ; **une étourderie** a thoughtless blunder

**étourdissant, -e** [eturdisɑ̃, -ɑ̃t] *adj* [bruit] deafening ; [beauté] stunning

**étourdissement** [eturdismɑ̃] *nm* [malaise] dizzy spell

**étrange** [etrɑ̃ʒ] *adj* strange, odd ■ **étranger, -ère 1.** *adj* [d'un autre pays] foreign ; [non familier] strange (**à** to) **2.** *nmf* [d'un autre pays] foreigner ; [inconnu] stranger ; **à l'étranger** abroad ; **aller à l'étranger** to go abroad

**étrangler** [etrɑ̃gle] **1.** *vt* **étrangler qn** [tuer] to strangle sb **2. s'étrangler** *vpr* [de colère, en mangeant] to choke ■ **étranglé, -e** *adj* [voix] choking

**être** [etr] **1.** *vi* to be ; **il est professeur** he's a teacher ; **est-ce qu'elle vient ?** is she coming? ; **il vient, n'est-ce pas ?** he's coming, isn't he? ; **est-ce qu'il aime le thé ?** does he like tea? ; **nous sommes dix** there are ten of us ; **nous sommes le dix** today is the tenth ; **il a été à Paris** [il y est allé] he has been to Paris ; **elle est de Paris** she's from Paris ; **il est cinq heures** it's five (o'clock) ; **c'est à lire pour demain** this has to be read for tomorrow ; **c'est à lui** it's his

**2.** *v aux* [avec 'venir', 'partir', etc] to have / to be ; **elle est arrivée** she has arrived ; **elle est née en 1999** she was born in 1999

**3.** *nm* [personne] being ; **les êtres chers** the loved ones ; **êêtre humain** human being ; **êêtre vivant** living being

**étreindre** [etrɛ̃dr] *vt* to grip ; [avec amour] to embrace

**étrennes** [etrɛn] *nfpl* New Year gift ; [gratification] ≃ Christmas tip

**étrier** [etrije] *nm* stirrup

**étroit, -e** [etrwa, -at] *adj* narrow ; [vêtement] tight ; [lien, collaboration] close ; **être à l'étroit** to be cramped

**étude** [etyd] *nf* [action, ouvrage] study ; [de notaire] office ; SCOL [pièce] study room ; [période] study period ; **à l'étude** [projet] under consideration ; **faire des études de français** to study French ; **faire une étude de marché** to do market research

**étudiant, -e** [etydjɑ̃, -ɑ̃t] **1.** *nmf* student ; **étudiant en médecine / en droit** medical / law student ; **é participant à un échange** exchange student **2.** *adj* [vie] student

**étudier** [etydje] *vt & vi* to study

**étui** [etɥi] *nm* [à lunettes, à cigarettes] case ; [de revolver] holster

**eu, eue** [y] *pp de* **avoir**

**eurent** [yr] *voir* **avoir**

**euro** [øro] *nm* [monnaie] Euro

**euro-** [øro] *préf* Euro-

**eurodéputé** [ørodepyte] *nm* Euro MP

**Europe** [ørɔp] *nf* **l'Europe** Europe ; **l'Europe verte** European Union agriculture ■ **européen, -enne 1.** *adj* European **2.** *nmf* **Européen, Européenne** European

**eut** [y] *voir* **avoir**

**euthanasie** [øtanazi] *nf* euthanasia ■ **euthanasier** [øtanazje] *vt* [animal] to put down, to put to sleep ; [personne] to *Br* practise *or Am* practice euthanasia on, to help to die

**eux** [ø] *pron pers* [sujet] they ; [complément] them ; [réfléchi, emphase] themselves ■ **eux-mêmes** *pron* themselves

**évacuer** [evakɥe] *vt* [bâtiment] to evacuate ; [liquide] to drain off ■ **évacuation** *nf* evacuation

**évader** [evade] ■ **s'évader** *vpr* to escape (**de** from) ■ **évadé, -e** *nmf* escaped prisoner

**évaluer** [evalɥe] *vt* [fortune] to estimate ; [bien] to value ■ **évaluation** *nf* estimation ; [de bien] valuation

**évangile** [evɑ̃ʒil] *nm* gospel ; **l'Évangile** the Gospel

**évanouir** [evanwir] ■ **s'évanouir** *vpr* [personne] to faint ; *Fig* [espoir, crainte] to vanish ■ **évanoui, -e** *adj* unconscious ■ **évanouissement** *nm* [syncope] fainting fit

**évaporer** [evapɔre] ■ **s'évaporer** *vpr* to evaporate ; *Fig* [disparaître] to vanish into thin air

**évasé, -e** [evaze] *adj* [jupe] flared

**évasif, -ive** [evazif, -iv] *adj* evasive

**évasion** [evazjɔ̃] *nf* escape (**de** from) ; [de la réalité] escapism ; **évasion fiscale** tax evasion

**éveil** [evɛj] *nm* awakening ; **être en éveil** to be alert

**éveiller** [eveje] **1.** *vt* [susciter] to arouse **2. s'éveiller** *vpr* to awaken (à to) ■ **éveillé, -e** *adj* awake ; [vif] alert

**événement, évènement** [evenmɑ̃] *nm* event

**éventail** [evɑ̃taj] *nm* [instrument] fan ; [choix] range

**éventuel, -elle** [evɑ̃tɥɛl] *adj* possible ■ **éventualité** *nf* possibility ■ **éventuellement** *adv* possibly

**évêque** [evɛk] *nm* bishop

**évertuer** [evɛrtɥe] ■ **s'évertuer** *vpr* **s'évertuer à faire qch** to *Br* endeavour *or Am* endeavor to do sth

**éviction** [eviksjɔ̃] *nf* [de concurrent, de président] ousting ; [de locataire] eviction

**évident, -e** [evidɑ̃, -ɑ̃t] *adj* obvious (que that) ■ **évidemment** [-amɑ̃] *adv* obviously ■ **évidence** *nf* obviousness ; **une évidence** an obvious fact ; **en évidence** in a prominent position

**évier** [evje] *nm* (kitchen) sink

**évincer** [evɛ̃se] *vt* [concurrent] to oust (de from)

**éviter** [evite] *vt* to avoid (**de faire** doing) ; **éviter qch à qn** to spare *or* save sb sth

**évoluer** [evɔlɥe] *vi* [changer] to develop ; [société, situation] to evolve ; [se déplacer] to move around ■ **évolué, -e** *adj* [pays] advanced ; [personne] enlightened ■ **évolution** *nf* [changement] development ; BIOL evolution

**évoquer** [evɔke] *vt* to evoke

**ex** [ɛks] *nmf* ex

**exact, -e** [ɛgzakt] *adj* [quantité, poids, nombre] exact, precise ; [rapport, description] exact, accurate ; [mot] right, correct ; [ponctuel] punctual ■ **exactement** [-əmɑ̃] *adv* exactly ■ **exactitude** *nf* [précision, fidélité] exactness ; [justesse] correctness ; [ponctualité] punctuality

**ex æquo** [ɛgzeko] **1.** *adj inv* SPORT **être classés ex æquo** to tie, to be equally placed **2.** *adv* SPORT **être troisième ex æquo** to tie for third place

**exagérer** [ɛgzaʒere] **1.** *vt* to exaggerate **2.** *vi* [parler] to exaggerate ; [agir] to go too far ■ **exagération** *nf* exaggeration ■ **exagéré, -e** *adj* excessive

**exalter** [ɛgzalte] *vt* [passionner] to stir ■ **exaltant, -e** *adj* stirring ■ **exalté, -e** *adj* [sentiment] impassioned

**examen** [ɛgzamɛ̃] *nm* examination ; **examen blanc** mock exam ; **examen médical** medical examination ; **examen de la vue** eye test ■ **examinateur, -trice** *nmf* examiner ■ **examiner** *vt* [considérer, regarder] to examine

**exaspérer** [ɛgzaspere] *vt* [personne] to exasperate

**exaucer** [ɛgzose] *vt* [désir] to grant

**excavation** [ɛkskavasjɔ̃] *nf* [trou, action] excavation

**excéder** [ɛksede] *vt* [dépasser] to exceed ; **excéder qn** [énerver] to exasperate sb ■ **excédent** *nm* surplus, excess ■ **excédentaire** *adj* **poids excédentaire** excess weight

**excellent, -e** [ɛkselɑ̃, -ɑ̃t] *adj* excellent ■ **excellence** *nf* excellence ■ **exceller** *vi* to excel (**en** at)

**excentrique** [ɛksɑ̃trik] *adj & nmf* eccentric

**excepté¹** [ɛksɛpte] *prép* except

**excepté², -e** *adj* except (for)

**exception** [ɛksɛpsjɔ̃] *nf* exception ; **à l'exception de** except (for), with the exception of ■ **exceptionnel, -elle** *adj* exceptional

**excès** [ɛksɛ] *nm* excess ; **excès de vitesse** speeding ■ **excessif, -ive** *adj* excessive

**exciter** [ɛksite] **1.** *vt* [faire naître] to arouse ; **exciter qn** [énerver] to excite sb **2. s'exciter** *vpr* [devenir nerveux] to get excited ■ **excitant, -e** *nm* stimulant ■ **excitation** *nf* [agitation] excitement ■ **excité, -e** *adj* excited

**exclamer** [ɛksklame] ■ **s'exclamer** *vpr* to exclaim ■ **exclamation** *nf* exclamation

**exclure** [ɛksklyr] *vt* [écarter] to exclude (**de** from) ; [chasser] to expel (**de** from) ■ **exclu, -e** *adj* [solution] out of the question ; [avec une date] exclusive

**exclusif, -ive** [ɛksklyzif, -iv] *adj* [droit, modèle] exclusive ■ **exclusivité** *nf* COMM exclusive rights ; [dans la presse] scoop ; **en exclusivité** [film] having an exclusive showing (**à** at)

**exclusion** [ɛksklyzjɔ̃] *nf* exclusion ; **à l'exclusion de** with the exception of

**excursion** [ɛkskyrsjɔ̃] *nf* trip, excursion ; [de plusieurs jours] tour ; **faire une excursion** to go on a trip / tour

**excuse** [ɛkskyz] *nf* [prétexte] excuse ; **excuses** [regrets] apology ; **faire des excuses** to apologize (**à** to) ■ **excuser** **1.** *vt* [justifier, pardonner] to excuse (**qn d'avoir fait** / **qn de faire** sb for doing) **2. s'excuser** *vpr* to apologize (**de** for ; **auprès de** to) ; **excusez-moi !, je m'excuse !** excuse me!

**exécrer** [ɛgzekre] *vt* to loathe ■ **exécrable** *adj* atrocious

**exécuter** [ɛgzekyte] **1.** *vt* [tâche] to carry out ; [jouer] to perform ; **exécuter qn** to execute sb **2. s'exécuter** *vpr* to comply ■ **exécutable** *adj* OR-DINAT executable ■ **exécutant, -e** *nmf* [ouvrier, employé] subordinate ■ **exécution** *nf* [de tâche] carrying out ; [de musique] performance ; [de condamné] execution

**exécutif** [ɛgzekytif] **1.** *adj m* **pouvoir exécutif** executive power **2.** *nm* **l'exécutif** the executive

**exemplaire** [ɛgzɑ̃plɛr] **1.** *adj* exemplary **2.** *nm* [livre] copy

**exemple** [ɛgzɑ̃pl] *nm* example ; **par exemple** for example, for instance ; **donner l'exemple** to set an example (**à** to)

**exempt, -e** [ɛgzɑ̃, -ɑ̃t] *adj* **exempt de** [dispensé de] exempt from ; [sans] free from ■ **exempter** [ɛgzɑ̃te] *vt* to exempt (**de** from) ■ **exemption** *nf* exemption

**exercer** [ɛgzɛrse] **1.** *vt* [voix, droits] to exercise ; [autorité, influence] to exert (**sur** on) ; [profession] *Br* to practise, *Am* to practice ; **exercer qn à qch** to train sb in sth **2.** *vi* [médecin] *Br* to practise, *Am* to practice **3. s'exercer** *vpr* [s'entraîner] to train ; **s'exercer à** *Br* practise *or Am* practice sth ; **s'exercer à faire qch** to *Br* practise *or Am* practice doing sth

**exercice** [ɛgzɛrsis] *nm* [physique & SCOL] exercise ; MIL drill ; **en exercice** [fonctionnaire] in office ; [médecin] in practice ; **faire** *ou* **prendre de l'exercice** to exercise, to take exercise

**exhiber** [ɛgzibe] *vt* [documents, passeport] to produce ; *Péj* [savoir, richesses] to show off, to flaunt

**exiger** [ɛgziʒe] *vt* [exiger] to demand (**de** from) ; [nécessiter] to require ■ **exigeant, -e** *adj* demanding, exacting ■ **exigence** *nf* [caractère] exacting nature ; [condition] demand

**exigu, -ë** [ɛgzigy] *adj* cramped, tiny

**exil** [ɛgzil] *nm* exile ■ **exilé, -e** *nmf* [personne] exile ■ **exiler 1.** *vt* to exile **2. s'exiler** *vpr* to go into exile

**existence** [ɛgzistɑ̃s] *nf* [fait d'exister] existence ; [vie] life ; **moyen d'existence** means of existence ■ **existant, -e** *adj* existing ■ **exister 1.** *vi* to exist **2.** *v impers* **il existe…** there is / are…

**exode** [ɛgzɔd] *nm* exodus

**exonérer** [ɛgzɔnere] *vt* to exempt (**de** from) ■ **exonération** *nf* exemption

**exorbitant, -e** [ɛgzɔrbitɑ̃, -ɑ̃t] *adj* exorbitant

**exotique** [ɛgzɔtik] *adj* exotic

**expansif, -ive** [ɛkspɑ̃sif, -iv] *adj* expansive

**expansion** [ɛkspɑ̃sjɔ̃] *nf* [de commerce, de pays, de gaz] expansion ; **en (pleine) expansion** (fast *or* rapidly) expanding

**expatrier** [ɛkspatrije] ■ **s'expatrier** *vpr* to leave one's country

**expédier** [ɛkspedje] *vt* [envoyer] to send, to dispatch ; [affaires, client] to deal promptly with ■ **expéditeur, -trice** *nmf* sender ■ **expéditif, -ive** *adj* hasty ■ **expédition** *nf* [envoi] dispatch ; [voyage] expedition

**expérience** [ɛksperjɑ̃s] nf [connaissance] experience ; [scientifique] experiment ; **faire l'expérience de qch** to experience sth ; **avoir de l'expérience** to have experience ■ **expérimental, -e, -aux** adj experimental

**expérimenter** [ɛksperimɑ̃te] vt [remède, vaccin] to try out (**sur** on) ■ **expérimenté, -e** adj experienced

**expert, -e** [ɛksper, -ert] **1.** adj expert, skilled (**en** in) **2.** nmf expert (**en** on or in) ; [d'assurances] valuer ■ **expert-comptable** (pl **experts-comptables**) nmf Br ≃ chartered accountant, Am ≃ certified public accountant

**expertise** [ɛkspertiz] nf [évaluation] valuation ; [rapport] expert's report ; [compétence] expertise

**expier** [ɛkspje] vt [péchés] to expiate, to atone for

**expirer** [ɛkspire] **1.** vt & vi to breathe out **2.** vi [mourir] to pass away ; [finir, cesser] to expire ■ **expiration** [ɛkspirasjɔ̃] nf **a)** [d'air] exhalation **b)** [de contrat] Br expiry, Am expiration ; **arriver à expiration** to expire ; **date d'expiration** Br expiry or Am expiration date

**explication** [ɛksplikasjɔ̃] nf explanation ; [mise au point] discussion

**explicite** [ɛksplisit] adj explicit

**expliquer** [ɛksplike] **1.** vt to explain (**à** to ; **que** that) **2. s'expliquer** vpr to explain oneself ; [discuter] to talk things over (**avec** with) ; **s'expliquer qch** [comprendre] to understand sth ■ **explicatif, -ive** adj explanatory

**exploit** [ɛksplwa] nm feat

**exploiter** [ɛksplwate] vt [champs] to farm ; [ferme] to run ; [mine] to work ; Fig & Péj [personne, situation] to exploit ■ **exploitant, -e** nmf **exploitant agricole** farmer ■ **exploitation** nf [de champs] farming ; [de ferme] running ; [de mine] working ; Péj exploitation ; **exploitation agricole** farm

**explorer** [ɛksplɔre] vt to explore ■ **explorateur, -trice** nmf explorer

**exploser** [ɛksploze] vi [gaz, bombe] to explode ; **faire exploser qch**

to explode sth ■ **explosif, -ive** adj & nm explosive ■ **explosion** nf explosion ; [de colère] outburst

**expo** [ɛkspo] nf Fam exhibition

**exporter** [ɛkspɔrte] vt to export (**vers** to ; **de** from) ■ **exportateur, -trice** **1.** nmf exporter **2.** adj exporting ■ **exportation** nf [produit] export ; [action] export(ation)

**exposer** [ɛkspoze] **1.** vt [tableau] to exhibit ; [marchandises] to display ; [théorie] to set out ; PHOTO [film] to expose **2. s'exposer** vpr **s'exposer au danger** to put oneself in danger ; **s'exposer à la critique** to lay oneself open to criticism ■ **exposé, -e 1.** adj **exposé au sud** facing south **2.** nm [compte rendu] account (**de** of) ; [présentation] talk ; SCOL paper

**exposition** [ɛkspozisjɔ̃] nf [d'objets d'art] exhibition ; [de marchandises] display ; PHOTO exposure (**à** to) ; [de maison] aspect

**exprès¹** [ɛksprɛ] adv on purpose, intentionally ; [spécialement] specially

**exprès², -esse** [ɛksprɛs] adj [ordre, condition] express ■ **expressément** adv expressly

**exprès³** [ɛksprɛs] adj inv **lettre exprès** express delivery letter

**express** [ɛksprɛs] adj & nm inv [train] express ; [café] espresso

**expressif, -ive** [ɛkspresif, -iv] adj expressive ■ **expression** nf [phrase, mine] expression ■ **exprimer 1.** vt to express **2. s'exprimer** vpr to express oneself

**expulser** [ɛkspylse] vt to expel (**de** from) ; [joueur] to send off ; **se faire expulser** to be thrown out ■ **expulsion** nf expulsion ; [de joueur] sending off

**exquis, -e** [ɛkski, -iz] adj [nourriture] exquisite

**extase** [ɛkstaz] nf ecstasy ■ **s'extasier** vpr to be in raptures (**sur** over or about)

**extensible** [ɛkstɑ̃sibl] adj [métal] tensile ; [tissu] stretch ■ **extension** nf [de muscle] stretching ; [de durée, de contrat] extension

**exténué, -e** [ɛkstenɥe] *adj* exhausted

**extérieur, -e** [ɛksterjœr] **1.** *adj* [monde] outside ; [surface] outer, external ; [signe] outward, external ; [politique] foreign **2.** *nm* outside, exterior ; **à l'extérieur (de)** outside ; **à l'extérieur** [match] away ▪ **extérieurement** *adv* [dehors] externally ; [en apparence] outwardly ▪ **extérioriser** *vt* to express

**exterminer** [ɛkstɛrmine] *vt* to exterminate

**externaliser** [ɛkstɛrnalize] *vt* to outsource

**externat** [ɛkstɛrna] *nm* [école] day school

**externe** [ɛkstɛrn] **1.** *adj* external **2.** *nmf* [élève] day pupil ; MÉD *non-resident hospital medical student*, Am extern

**extincteur** [ɛkstɛ̃ktœr] *nm* fire extinguisher ▪ **extinction** *nf* [de feu] extinguishing ; [de race] extinction ; **extinction de voix** loss of voice

**extorquer** [ɛkstɔrke] *vt* to extort (**à** from) ▪ **extorsion** *nf* extortion ; **extorsion de fonds** extortion

**extraconjugal, e, aux** [ɛkstrakɔ̃ʒygal, o] *adj* extramarital

**extradition** [ɛkstradisjɔ̃] *nf* extradition ▪ **extrader** *vt* to extradite

**extrafin, e** [ɛkstrafɛ̃, in] *adj* [haricots] extra(-)fine ; [collants] sheer ; [chocolats] superfine

**extraire** [ɛkstrɛr] *vt* to extract (**de** from) ; [charbon] to mine ▪ **extrait** *nm* extract ; **extrait de naissance** birth certificate

**extralucide** [ɛkstralysid] *adj* & *nmf* clairvoyant

**extraordinaire** [ɛkstraɔrdinɛr] *adj* extraordinary

**extrascolaire** [ɛkstraskɔlɛr] *adj* out-of-school

**extraterrestre** [ɛkstraterɛstr] *adj* & *nmf* extraterrestrial

**extravagant, -e** [ɛkstravagɑ̃, -ɑ̃t] *adj* [idée, comportement] extravagant

**extraverti, -e** [ɛkstravɛrti] *nmf* & *adj* extrovert

**extrême** [ɛkstrɛm] **1.** *adj* extreme ; POL **l'extrême droite /gauche** the far *or* extreme right / left **2.** *nm* extreme ▪ **Extrême-Orient** *nm* **l'Extrême-Orient** the Far East ▪ **extrémiste** *adj* & *nmf* extremist ▪ **extrémité** *nf* [bout] extremity, end ; **extrémités** [pieds et mains] extremities

**exulter** [ɛgzylte] *vi* to exult, to rejoice

# F

**F, f** [ɛf] *nm inv* F, f

**fa** [fa] *nm* [note] F

**fabricant, -e** [fabrikɑ̃, -ɑ̃t] *nmf* manufacturer ■ **fabrication** *nf* manufacture

**fabrique** [fabrik] *nf* factory

**fabriquer** [fabrike] *vt* [objet] to make; [en usine] to manufacture

**fabuleux, -euse** [fabylø, -øz] *adj* [légendaire, incroyable] fabulous

**façade** [fasad] *nf* façade

**face** [fas] *nf* [visage] face; [de cube, de montagne] side; [de pièce de monnaie] head; **en face** opposite; **en face de** opposite, facing; [en présence de] in front of; **face à** [vis-à-vis] facing; **face à face** face to face; **faire face à qch** to face up to sth; **sauver/perdre la face** to save / lose face

**facette** [fasɛt] *nf* [de diamant, de problème] facet

**fâcher** [faʃe] ■ **se fâcher** *vpr* to get angry (**contre** with); **se fâcher avec qn** to fall out with sb ■ **fâché, -e** *adj* [air] angry; [personnes] on bad terms; **fâché contre qn** angry with sb

**facile** [fasil] *adj* easy; **facile à vivre** easy to get along with ■ **facilité** *nf* [simplicité] easiness; [aisance] ease ■ **faciliter** *vt* to make easier, to facilitate

**façon** [fasɔ̃] *nf* [manière] way; **la façon dont elle parle** the way (in which) she talks; **de quelle façon ?** how?; **de toute façon** anyway, anyhow; **de façon à** so as to; **de façon générale** generally speaking; **d'une façon ou d'une autre** one way or another; **à ma façon** my way, (in) my own way

**façonner** [fasɔne] *vt* [former] to shape; [fabriquer] to make

**facteur** [faktœr] *nm* **a)** [employé] *Br* postman, *Am* mailman **b)** [élément] factor

**facture** [faktyr] *nf* COMM bill, invoice ■ **facturer** *vt* to bill, to invoice

**facultatif, -ive** [fakyltatif, -iv] *adj* [travail] optional; SCOL **matière facultative** optional subject

**faculté** [fakylte] *nf* **a)** [aptitude] faculty **b)** [d'université] faculty; **à la faculté** *Br* at university, *Am* at school

**fade** [fad] *adj* insipid

**fader** [fade] ■ **se fader** *vpr Fam* to get stuck with, to get lumbered with; **on s'est fadé trois heures de queue** we got lumbered with a three hour-long queue

**faible** [fɛbl] **1.** *adj* weak, feeble; [voix] faint; [chances] slight; [revenus] small **2.** *nm* weakling; **faible d'esprit** feeble-minded person ■ **faiblesse** *nf* [physique, morale] weakness

**faiblir** [feblir] *vi* [forces] to weaken; [courage, vue] to fail; [vent] to drop

**faïence** [fajɑ̃s] *nf* [matière] earthenware; **faïences** [objets] earthenware

**faille¹** [faj] *nf* GÉOL fault; *Fig* flaw

**faille²** [faj] *voir* **falloir**

**faillir** [fajir] *vi* **il a failli tomber** he almost *or* nearly fell

**faillite** [fajit] *nf* COMM bankruptcy; **faire faillite** to go bankrupt

**faim** [fɛ̃] *nf* hunger; **avoir faim** to be hungry

**fainéant, e** [feneɑ̃, ɑ̃t], **feignant, e** [fɛɲɑ̃, ɑ̃t] *Fam*, **faignant, e** [fɛɲɑ̃, ɑ̃t] *Fam* **1.** *adj* lazy, idle **2.** *nmf* lazybones

**faire** [fɛr] **1.** *vt* [faute, gâteau, voyage, repas] to make; [devoir, ménage] to do ; [rêve, chute] to have ; [sourire] to give ; [promenade, sieste] to have, to take ; [guerre] to wage, to make ; **ça fait 10 mètres de large** it's 10 metres wide ; **ça fait 10 euros** it's or that's 10 euros ; **2 et 2 font 4** 2 and 2 are 4 ; **que faire ?** what's to be done? ; **faire du tennis/du piano** to play tennis /the piano ; **faire du droit** to study law ; **faire du bien à qn** to do sb good ; **faire du mal à qn** to hurt or harm sb ; **ça ne fait rien** that doesn't matter ; **comment as-tu fait pour... ?** how did you manage to...? ; **'oui', fit-elle** 'yes',' she said

**2.** vi [agir] to do ; [paraître] to look ; **faire comme chez soi** to make oneself at home ; **elle ferait bien de partir** she'd do well to leave

**3.** v impers **il fait beau/froid** it's fine / cold ; **il fait du vent** it's windy ; **quel temps fait-il ?** what's the weather like? ; **ça fait deux ans que je ne l'ai pas vu** I haven't seen him for two years, it's (been) two years since I saw him

**4.** v aux [+ infinitive] **faire construire une maison** to have a house built (**à qn** for sb ; **par qn** by sb) ; **faire souffrir qn** to make sb suffer

**5. se faire** vpr [fabrication] to be made ; [activité] to be done ; **se faire couper les cheveux** to have one's hair cut ; **se faire renverser** to get knocked down ; **se faire des amis** to make friends ; **il se fait tard** it's getting late ; **comment se fait-il que... ?** how is it that...? ; **ça se fait beaucoup** people do that a lot ; **se faire à qch** to get used to sth ; **ne t'en fais pas !** don't worry!

■ **faire-part** nm inv announcement

**fais, fait** [fɛ] voir **faire**

**faisable** [fəzabl] adj feasible

**faisan** [fəzɑ̃] nm pheasant

**faisceau, -x** [fɛso] nm [rayons] beam

**fait, -e** [fɛ, fɛt] **1.** pp de **faire 2.** adj [fromage] ripe ; [ongles] polished ; **tout fait** ready made **3.** nm [événement] event ; [donnée, réalité] fact ; **du fait de** on account of ; **au fait** [à propos] by the way ; **en fait** in fact ; **en fait de** by way

of ; **prendre qn sur le fait** to catch sb red-handed or in the act ; JOURN **faits divers** ≃ news in brief

**faîte** [fɛt] nm [haut] top ; Fig [apogée] height

**faites** [fɛt] voir **faire**

**falaise** [falɛz] nf cliff

**falloir** [falwar] **1.** v impers **il faut qn/ qch** I /you /we /etc need sb /sth ; **il te faut un stylo** you need a pen ; **il faut partir** I /you /we /etc have to go ; **il faut que je parte** I have to go ; **il faudrait qu'elle reste** she ought to stay ; **il faut un jour** it takes a day (**pour faire** to do) ; **comme il faut** [adjectif] proper ; [adverbe] properly ; **s'il le faut** if need be **2. s'en falloir** vpr **il s'en est fallu de peu qu'il ne pleure** he almost cried ; **tant s'en faut** far from it

**famé, e** [fame] adj **mal famé** ou **malfamé** with a (bad) reputation

**fameux, -euse** [famø, -øz] adj [célèbre] famous

**familial, -e, -aux** [familjal, -o] adj [atmosphère, ennuis] family ; [entreprise] family-run

**familier, -ère** [familje, -ɛr] adj [connu] familiar (**à** to) ; [désinvolte] informal (**avec** with) ; [locution] colloquial ■ **familiariser 1.** vt to familiarize (**avec** with) **2. se familiariser** vpr to familiarize oneself (**avec** with)

**famille** [famij] nf family ; **famille d'accueil** host family ; **famille monoparentale** single-parent family ; **famille nucléaire** nuclear family

**famine** [famin] nf famine

**fana** [fana] Fam **1.** adj crazy **2.** nmf fan ; **c'est une fana de cinéma** she loves the cinema ; **il est fana de sport** he is crazy about sport

**fanatique** [fanatik] **1.** adj fanatical **2.** nmf fanatic

**faner** [fane] ■ **se faner** vpr [fleur, beauté] to fade ■ **fané, -e** adj faded

**fanfare** [fɑ̃far] nf [orchestre] brass band

**fantaisie** [fɑ̃tezi] *nf* [imagination] imagination; **bijoux fantaisie** costume jewellery

**fantastique** [fɑ̃tastik] *adj* [imaginaire, excellent] fantastic

**fantôme** [fɑ̃tom] **1.** *nm* ghost, phantom **2.** *adj* **ville/train fantôme** ghost town/train

**faon** [fɑ̃] *nm* fawn

**farce¹** [fars] *nf* [tour] practical joke, prank; **faire une farce à qn** to play a practical joke *or* a prank on sb ■ **farceur, -euse** *nmf* [blagueur] practical joker

**farce²** [fars] *nf* CULIN stuffing ■ **farcir** *vt* [poulet] to stuff

**fardeau, -x** [fardo] *nm* burden, load

**farder** [farde] **1.** *vt* [maquiller] to make up **2. se farder** *vpr* [se maquiller] to put on one's make-up; **se farder les yeux** to put eyeshadow on

**farine** [farin] *nf* [de blé] flour

**farouche** [faruʃ] *adj* [personne] shy; [animal] timid; [haine] fierce

**fart** [far] *nm* wax

**fascicule** [fasikyl] *nm* [de publication] instalment; [brochure] brochure

**fasciner** [fasine] *vt* to fascinate ■ **fascination** *nf* fascination

**fascisme** [faʃism] *nm* fascism ■ **fasciste** *adj* & *nmf* fascist

**fasse(s), fassent** [fas] *voir* **faire**

**faste** [fast] **1.** *nm* splendour **2.** *adj* **jour faste** lucky day

**fastidieux, -euse** [fastidjø, -øz] *adj* tedious

**fatal, -e, -als** [fatal] *adj* [mortel] fatal; [inévitable] inevitable; [moment] fateful ■ **fataliste** *adj* fatalistic ■ **fatalité** *nf* [destin] fate ■ **fatidique** *adj* [jour, date] fateful

**fatigant, -e** [fatigɑ̃, -ɑ̃t] *adj* [épuisant] tiring; [ennuyeux] tiresome

**fatigue** [fatig] *nf* tiredness

**fatiguer** [fatige] **1.** *vt* [épuiser] to tire; [yeux] to strain; [ennuyer] to bore **2.** *vi* [personne] to get tired; [moteur] to labour **3. se fatiguer** *vpr* [s'épuiser, se lasser] to get tired (**de** of); **se fatiguer à faire qch** to tire oneself out doing sth; **se fatiguer les yeux** to strain one's eyes ■ **fatigué, -e** *adj* tired (**de** of)

**fauché, e** [foʃe] *adj* Fam broke, hard-up

**faucher** [foʃe] *vt* [herbe] to mow; [blé] to reap

**faucon** [fokɔ̃] *nm* hawk, falcon

**faudra, faudrait** [fodra, fodrɛ] *voir* **falloir**

**faufiler** [fofile] ■ **se faufiler** *vpr* to work one's way (**dans** through or into; **entre** between)

**faune** [fon] *nf* wildlife, fauna

**faussaire** [fosɛr] *nm* forger

**fausse** [fos] *voir* **faux**

**fausser** [fose] *vt* [réalité] to distort

**fausseté** [foste] *nf* [hypocrisie] duplicity

**faut** [fo] *voir* **falloir**

**faute** [fot] *nf* [erreur] mistake; [responsabilité & au tennis] fault; [au football] foul; **c'est de ta faute** it's your fault; **faute de mieux** for want of anything better; **faire une faute** to make a mistake; **faute professionnelle** professional misconduct

**fauteuil** [fotœj] *nm* armchair; [de président] chair; **fauteuil roulant** wheelchair

**fautif, -ive** [fotif, -iv] *adj* [personne] at fault; [erroné] faulty

**fauve** [fov] *nm* big cat

**faux, fausse** [fo, fos] **1.** *adj* [pas vrai] false, untrue; [inexact] wrong; [inauthentique] false; [monnaie] forged; [tableau] fake; **faire une fausse couche** to have a miscarriage; **faux départ** false start **2.** *adv* [chanter] out of tune **3.** *nm* [tableau] fake; [document] forgery ■ **faux-filet** *(pl* **faux-filets)** *nm* sirloin ■ **faux-monnayeur** *(pl* **faux-monnayeurs)** *nm* counterfeiter

**faveur** [favœr] *nf* Br favour, Am favor; **en faveur de** [au profit de] in aid of; **être**

**en faveur de qch** to be in *Br* favour or *Am* favor of sth ▪ **favorable** *adj Br* favourable (**à** to) ; *Am* favorable (**à** to) ▪ **favori, -e** *adj* & *nmf Br* favourite, *Am* favorite ▪ **favoriser** *vt* to *Br* favour or *Am* favor

**fax** [faks] *nm* [appareil, message] fax ; **envoyer un fax** to send a fax (**à** to) ; **envoyer qch par fax** to send sth by fax ; **recevoir un fax** to receive a fax (**de** from) ▪ **faxer** *vt* [message] to fax

**fayot, otte** [fajo, ɔt] **1.** *nmf Fam Péj* [employé] toady, bootlicker ; [élève] *Br* swot, *Am* apple-polisher **2.** *nm* [haricot] bean ▪ **fayotage** *nm Fam* bootlicking

**fécond, -e** [fekɔ̃, -ɔ̃d] *adj* [femme, idée] fertile ▪ **fécondité** *nf* fertility

**féculent** [fekylɑ̃] *nm* starchy food

**fédéral, -e, -aux** [federal, -o] *adj* federal ▪ **fédération** *nf* federation

**fée** [fe] *nf* fairy ▪ **féerique** *adj* [personnage, monde] fairy ; [vision] enchanting

**feeling** [filiŋ] *nm Fam* **on va y aller au feeling** we'll play it by ear ; **j'ai un bon feeling** I have a good feeling about it

**feindre** [fɛ̃dr] *vt* to feign ; **feindre de faire qch** to pretend to do sth ▪ **feint, -e** *adj* feigned ▪ **feinte** *nf* [ruse] ruse

**fêler** [fele] **1.** *vt* to crack **2. se fêler** *vpr* to crack

**féliciter** [felisite] *vt* to congratulate (**de** *ou* **sur** on) ▪ **félicitations** *nfpl* congratulations (**pour** on)

**félin** [felɛ̃] *nm* feline

**fêlure** [felyr] *nf* crack

**femelle** [fəmɛl] *adj* & *nf* female

**féminin, -e** [feminɛ̃, -in] *adj* [prénom, hormone] female ; [trait, intuition, pronom] feminine ; [mode] women's ▪ **féministe** *adj* & *nmf* feminist ▪ **féminité** *nf* femininity

**femme** [fam] *nf* woman (*pl* women) ; [épouse] wife ; **femme de ménage** cleaning lady, maid ; **femme au foyer** housewife

**fendiller** [fɑ̃dije] ▪ **se fendiller** *vpr* to crack

**fendre** [fɑ̃dr] **1.** *vt* [bois, lèvre] to split ; *Fig* [cœur] to break **2. se fendre** *vpr* [se fissurer] to crack

**fenêtre** [fənɛtr] *nf* window

**fenouil** [fənuj] *nm* fennel

**fente** [fɑ̃t] *nf* [de tirelire, de palissade] slit ; [de rocher] split, crack

**féodal, -e, -aux** [feɔdal, -o] *adj* feudal

**fer** [fɛr] *nm* iron ; [partie métallique] metal (part) ; **fer à cheval** horseshoe ; **fer forgé** wrought iron ; **fer à repasser** iron bar ; **fer à cheval** horseshoe ; **fer forgé** wrought iron ; **fer à repasser** iron

**fera, ferait** [fəra, fərɛ] *voir* **faire**

**férié** [ferje] *adj m* **jour férié** (public) holiday

**ferme¹** [fɛrm] *nf* farm ; [maison] farm(house)

**ferme²** [fɛrm] **1.** *adj* [fruit, beurre, décision] firm ; [autoritaire] firm (**avec** with) **2.** *adv* [travailler] hard ; **s'ennuyer ferme** to be bored stiff

**fermenter** [fɛrmɑ̃te] *vi* to ferment

**fermer** [fɛrme] **1.** *vt* to close, to shut ; [gaz, radio] to turn *or* switch off ; [passage] to block ; **fermer qch à clef** to lock sth ; **fermer un magasin** [définitivement] to close *or* shut (down) a shop **2.** *vi* to close, to shut **3. se fermer** *vpr* **a)** [porte, partie du corps] to close, to shut **b)** [plaie] to close up **c)** [vêtement] to do up ▪ **fermé, -e** *adj* [porte, magasin] closed, shut ; [route, circuit] closed ; [gaz] off

**fermeté** [fɛrməte] *nf* firmness

**fermeture** [fɛrmətyr] *nf* closing, closure ; [heure] closing time ; [mécanisme] catch ; **fermeture annuelle** annual closing ; **fermeture Éclair®** *Br* zip (fastener), *Am* zipper

**fermier, -ère** [fɛrmje, -ɛr] *nmf* farmer

**fermoir** [fɛrmwar] *nm* clasp

**féroce** [ferɔs] *adj* ferocious ▪ **férocité** *nf* ferocity

**feront** [fərɔ̃] *voir* **faire**

**ferraille** [fɛrɑj] *nf* scrap iron ; **mettre qch à la ferraille** to scrap sth

**ferronnerie** [fɛrɔnri] *nf* ironwork

**ferroviaire** [fɛrɔvjɛr] *adj* **compagnie ferroviaire** *Br* railway company, *Am* railroad company

**ferry** [fɛri] *(pl* **ferrys** *ou* **ferries)** *nm* ferry

**fertile** [fɛrtil] *adj* [terre, imagination] fertile ■ **fertiliser** *vt* to fertilize ■ **fertilité** *nf* fertility

**ferveur** [fɛrvœr] *nf* fervour

**fesse** [fɛs] *nf* buttock ; **fesses** *Br* bottom, *Am* butt ■ **fessée** *nf* spanking

**festif, ive** [fɛstif, iv] *adj* festive

**festin** [fɛstɛ̃] *nm* feast

**festival, -als** [fɛstival] *nm* festival

**festivités** [fɛstivite] *nfpl* festivities

**fêtard, e** [fɛtar, ard] *nmf Fam* fun-loving person

**fête** [fɛt] *nf* [civile] holiday ; [religieuse] festival, feast ; [entre amis] party ; **jour de fête** (public) holiday ; **les fêtes (de Noël et du nouvel an)** the Christmas holidays ; **faire la fête** to have a good time ; **c'est sa fête** it's his / her saint's day ; **la fête des Mères /des Pères** Mother's / Father's Day ; **la fête du Travail** Labour Day ■ **fêter** *vt* [événement] to celebrate

**feu, -x** [fø] *nm* **a)** fire ; [de réchaud] burner ; *AUTO, NAUT & AVIAT* [lumière] light ; **en feu** on fire, ablaze ; **faire du feu** to light *or* make a fire ; **mettre le feu à qch** to set fire to sth ; **prendre feu** to catch fire ; **donner du feu à qn** to give sb a light ; **avez-vous du feu ?** have you got a light ? ; **faire cuire qch à feu doux** to cook sth on a low heat ; **au feu !** (there's a) fire ! ; **feu d'artifice** firework ; *AUTO* **feu rouge** [lumière] red light ; [objet] traffic lights **b)** *Can* MÉD **feu sauvage** cold sore

**feuille** [fœj] *nf* leaf ; [de papier] sheet ; [de journal] newssheet ; **feuille de garde** [d'un fax] cover sheet ; **feuille de maladie** *form given by doctor to patient for* claiming reimbursement from the Social Security ; **feuille de paie** *Br* pay slip, *Am* pay stub ■ **feuillage** *nm* leaves, foliage

**feuilleté** [fœjte] *nm* **feuilleté au fromage** cheese pastry

**feuilleter** [fœjte] *vt* [livre] to flip through

**feuilleton** [fœjtɔ̃] *nm* [roman, film] serial ; **feuilleton télévisé** television serial

**feutre** [føtr] *nm* felt ; **(crayon) feutre** felt-tip(ped) pen

**fève** [fɛv] *nf* (broad) bean

**février** [fevrije] *nm* February

**fiable** [fjabl] *adj* reliable

**fiancer** [fjɑ̃se] ■ **se fiancer** *vpr* to become engaged (**avec to**) ■ **fiabilité** *nf* reliability ■ **fiançailles** *nfpl* engagement ■ **fiancé** *nm* fiancé ; **fiancés** engaged couple ■ **fiancée** *nf* fiancée

**fibre** [fibr] *nf* fibre ; **fibre de verre** fibreglass ; **fibres optiques** optical fibres

**ficelle** [fisɛl] *nf* [de corde] string ; [pain] *long thin loaf* ■ **ficeler** *vt* to tie up

**fiche** [fiʃ] *nf* **a)** [carte] index card ; [papier] form ; **fiche de paie** *Br* pay slip, *Am* pay stub **b)** ÉLEC [broche] pin ; [prise] plug ■ **fichier** *nm* card index, file ; ORDINAT file

**ficher** [fiʃe] **1.** *vt* [enfoncer] to drive in ; [mettre sur fiche] to put on file **2. se ficher** *vpr Fam* **a)** [s'enfoncer] **se ficher dans** to go into **b)** [se moquer] **se ficher de** to make fun of **c)** [ne pas tenir compte] **se ficher de** not to give a damn about

**fichu¹** *nm* scarf

**fichu², e** [fiʃy] *adj Fam* **a)** [cassé, fini] done for **b)** [désagréable] nasty **c)** **être mal fichu** [personne] to feel rotten ; [objet] to be badly made ; **il n'est même pas fichu de faire son lit** he can't even make his own bed

**fictif, -ive** [fiktif, -iv] *adj* fictitious ■ **fiction** *nf* fiction

**fidèle** [fidɛl] **1.** *adj* faithful (**à** to) **2.** *nmf* faithful supporter ; **les fidèles**

[croyants] the faithful; [à l'église] the congregation ■ **fidélité** *nf* fidelity, faithfulness

**fier¹** [fje] ■ **se fier** *vpr* se fier à qn /qch to trust sb /sth

**fier²**, **fière** [fjɛr] *adj* proud (**de** of) ■ **fierté** *nf* pride

**fièvre** [fjɛvr] *nf* [maladie] fever; **avoir de la fièvre** to have a temperature or a fever ■ **fiévreux**, **-euse** *adj* feverish

**figer** [fiʒe] **1.** *vt* [liquide] to congeal **2.** **se figer** *vpr* [liquide] to congeal; *Fig* [sourire, personne] to freeze

**figue** [fig] *nf* fig

**figurant**, **-e** [figyrã, -ãt] *nmf* [de film] extra

**figure** [figyr] *nf* [visage] face; [personnage] figure

**figurer** [figyre] **1.** *vt* to represent **2.** *vi* to appear **3.** **se figurer** *vpr* to imagine; **figure-toi que... ?** would you believe that...?

**fil** [fil] *nm* **a)** [de coton, de pensée] thread; [lin] linen; **fil dentaire** dental floss **b)** [métallique] wire; **fil de fer** wire **c)** [expressions] **au fil de l'eau** with the current; **au bout du fil** [au téléphone] on the line

**file** [fil] *nf* line; AUTO [couloir] lane; **file d'attente** *Br* queue, *Am* line; **être en double file** to be double-parked

**filer** [file] **1.** *vt* [coton] to spin; **filer qn** to shadow sb **2.** *vi* [partir] to rush off; [aller vite] to speed along; [collant] to run, *Br* to ladder

**filet** [file] *nm* **a)** [en maille] net; **filet à provisions** string bag **b)** [d'eau] trickle **c)** [de poisson, de viande] fillet

**filial**, **-e**, **-aux** [filjal, -o] *adj* filial ■ **filiale** *nf* subsidiary (company)

**filière** [filjɛr] *nf* [voie obligée] channels; [domaine d'études] field of study; [organisation clandestine] network; **suivre la filière normale** to go through the official channels

**fille** [fij] *nf* [enfant] girl; [descendante] daughter; **petite fille** (little or young) girl; **jeune fille** girl, young lady ■ **fillette** *nf* little girl

**film** [film] *nm* [œuvre] film, movie; [pour photo] film; **voir un film** to see a film or movie; **film muet** silent film or movie; **film policier** thriller ■ **filmer** *vt* [personne, scène] to film

**fils** [fis] *nm* son

**filtre** [filtr] *nm* filter; **bout filtre** filter tip; ORDINAT **filtre parental** parental filter, internet filter ■ **filtrer 1.** *vt* [liquide, lumière] to filter; [personne, nouvelles] to screen **2.** *vi* [liquide] to filter (through); [nouvelle] to leak out

**fin¹** [fɛ̃] *nf* **a)** [conclusion] end; **mettre fin à qch** to put an end to sth; **prendre fin** to come to an end; **à la fin** in the end; **à la fin de** at the end of; **fin de série** oddment; **fin mai** at the end of May **b)** [but] end, aim ■ **sans fin** *adj* endless

**fin²**, **fine** [fɛ̃, fin] **1.** *adj* [pointe, tissu] fine; [couche] thin; [visage, mets] delicate; [oreille] sharp; [intelligent] subtle **2.** *adv* [couper, moudre] finely

**final**, **-e**, **-aux** *ou* **-als** [final, -o] *adj* final ■ **finale** *nf* SPORT final ■ **finaliste** *nmf* SPORT finalist

**finance** [finãs] *nf* finance ■ **financement** *nm* financing ■ **financer** *vt* to finance

**financier**, **-ère** [finãsje, -ɛr] **1.** *adj* financial **2.** *nm* financier

**finesse** [fines] *nf* [de pointe] fineness; [de taille] thinness; [de visage] delicacy; [intelligence] subtlety

**finir** [finir] **1.** *vt* to finish; [discours, vie] to end, to finish **2.** *vi* to finish, to end; **finir de faire qch** to finish doing sth; **finir par faire qch** to end up doing sth; **finir par qch** to finish (up) or end (up) with sth ■ **fini**, **-e** *adj* [produit] finished; [univers & MATH] finite

**finissant**, **e** [finisã, ãt] *nmf* *Can* UNIV graduating student

**Finlande** [fɛ̃lãd] *nf* **la Finlande** Finland ■ **finlandais**, **-e 1.** *adj* Finnish **2.** *nmf* **Finlandais**, **Finlandaise** Finn

**firme** [firm] *nf* firm

**fisc** [fisk] *nm Br* ≈ Inland Revenue, *Am* ≈ Internal Revenue ■ **fiscal, -e, -aux** *adj* **charges fiscales** taxes; **fraude fiscale** tax fraud *or* evasion ■ **fiscalité** *nf* tax system

**fissure** [fisyr] *nf* crack ■ **se fissurer** *vpr* to crack

**fivete** [fivɛt] *(abr de* **fécondation in vitro et transfert d'embryon)** *nf* GIFT; **une fivete** a test-tube baby

**fixation** [fiksasjɔ̃] *nf* [action] fixing; [dispositif] fastening, binding; [idée fixe] fixation; **faire une fixation sur qn/qch** to be fixated on sb/sth

**fixe** [fiks] **1.** *adj* **a)** [gén] fixed **b)** TÉL [ligne] fixed; [poste] landline **2.** *nm* **a)** [salaire] fixed salary **b)** TÉL [poste fixe] landline phone, fixed phone ■ **fixement** [-əmɑ̃] *adv* **regarder qn/qch fixement** to stare at sb/sth

**fixer** [fikse] **1.** *vt* [attacher] to fix (**à** to); [date, règle] to decide, to fix; **fixer qn/qch du regard** to stare at sb/sth; **être fixé** [décidé] to be decided **2. se fixer** *vpr* [regard] to become fixed; [s'établir] to settle

**flacon** [flakɔ̃] *nm* small bottle

**flageolet** [flaʒɔlɛ] *nm* [haricot] flageolet bean

**flagrant, -e** [flagrɑ̃, -ɑ̃t] *adj* [injustice] flagrant, blatant; **pris en flagrant délit** caught in the act *or* red-handed

**flair** [flɛr] *nm* [de chien] (sense of) smell, scent; [de personne] intuition, flair ■ **flairer** *vt* to smell, to sniff at

**flamand, -e** [flamɑ̃, -ɑ̃d] **1.** *adj* Flemish **2.** *nmf* **Flamand, Flamande** Fleming **3.** *nm* [langue] Flemish

**flamant** [flamɑ̃] *nm* **flamant rose** flamingo

**flambant** [flɑ̃bɑ̃] *adv* **flambant neuf** brand new

**flambeau, -x** [flɑ̃bo] *nm* torch

**flamber** [flɑ̃be] *vi* to blaze

**flamboyer** [flɑ̃bwaje] *vi* to blaze

**flamme** [flam] *nf* flame; **en flammes** on fire

**flan** [flɑ̃] *nm* baked custard

**flânage** [flanaʒ] *nm Can* loitering

**flanc** [flɑ̃] *nm* side; [d'armée, d'animal] flank

**Flandre** [flɑ̃dr] *nf* **la Flandre, les Flandres** Flanders

**flâner** [flane] *vi* to stroll

**flanquer** [flɑ̃ke] *vt* to flank (**de** with)

**flaque** [flak] *nf* [d'eau] puddle

**flash** [flaʃ] *(pl* **flashes)** *nm* PHOTO flashlight; RADIO & TV **flash d'informations** (news) flash

**flasher** [flaʃe] *vi Fam* **flasher sur** to go crazy over

**flatter** [flate] *vt* to flatter ■ **flatterie** *nf* flattery ■ **flatteur, -euse** *adj* flattering

**fléau, -x** [fleo] *nm* [catastrophe] scourge

**flèche** [flɛʃ] *nf* [projectile] arrow; [d'église] spire; **monter en flèche** [prix] to shoot up ■ **fléchette** *nf* dart; **fléchettes** [jeu] darts

**fléchir** [fleʃir] **1.** *vt* [ployer] to bend **2.** *vi* [ployer] to bend; [faiblir] to give way; [baisser] to fall

**flétrir** [fletrir] **1.** *vt* to wither **2. se flétrir** *vpr* to wither

**fleur** [flœr] *nf* flower; [d'arbre, d'arbuste] blossom; **en fleur(s)** in flower, in bloom; [arbre] in blossom

**fleurir** [flœrir] **1.** *vt* [table] to decorate with flowers; [tombe] to lay flowers on **2.** *vi* [plante] to flower, to bloom; [arbre] to blossom; *Fig* [prospérer] to flourish ■ **fleuri, -e** *adj* [fleur, jardin] in bloom; [tissu] floral

**fleuriste** [flœrist] *nmf* florist

**fleuve** [flœv] *nm* river

**flexible** [fleksibl] *adj* flexible ■ **flexibilité** *nf* flexibility

**flippant, e** [flipɑ̃, ɑ̃t] *adj Fam* [déprimant] depressing; [inquiétant] worrying ■ **flipper** *vi Fam* **a)** [être déprimé] to feel down **b)** [planer] to freak out

**fliquer** [flike] *vt Fam* to keep under surveillance; **son chef n'arrête pas de le fliquer** his boss is always keeping tabs on him

**flocon** [flɔkɔ̃] *nm* flake; **flocon de neige** snowflake

**floraison** [flɔrɛzɔ̃] *nf* flowering; **en pleine floraison** in full bloom ■ **floral, -e, -aux** *adj* floral

**flore** [flɔr] *nf* flora

**florissant, -e** [flɔrisɑ̃, -ɑ̃t] *adj* flourishing

**flot** [flo] *nm* [de larmes] flood, stream; **les flots** [la mer] the waves; **à flot** [bateau] afloat; *Fig* **couler à flots** [argent, vin] to flow freely

**flotte** [flɔt] *nf* [de bateaux, d'avions] fleet

**flotter** [flɔte] *vi* [bateau] to float; [drapeau] to fly ■ **flotteur** *nm* float

**flou, -e** [flu] *adj* [image] fuzzy, blurred; [idée] vague

**fluet, -ette** [flyɛ, -ɛt] *adj* thin, slender

**fluide** [flɥid] *adj & nm* [liquide] fluid

**fluorescent, -e** [flyɔresɑ̃, -ɑ̃t] *adj* fluorescent

**flûte** [flyt] *nf* [instrument] flute; [verre] champagne glass ■ **flûtiste** *nmf Br* flautist, *Am* flutist

**flux** [fly] *nm* [abondance] flow; **flux et reflux** ebb and flow

**foi** [fwa] *nf* faith; **être de bonne / mauvaise foi** to be sincere / insincere

**foie** [fwa] *nm* liver; **foie gras** foie gras; **crise de foie** bout of indigestion

**foin** [fwɛ̃] *nm* hay

**foire** [fwar] *nf* fair

**fois** [fwa] *nf* time; **une fois** once; **deux fois** twice; **trois fois** three times; **deux fois trois** two times three; **chaque fois que...** whenever..., each time (that)...; **une fois qu'il sera arrivé** once he has arrived; **à la fois** at the same time, at once; **il était une fois...** once upon a time there was...

**foisonner** [fwazɔne] *vi* to abound (**de** *ou* **en** in)

**fol** [fɔl] *voir* **fou**

**folie** [fɔli] *nf* madness; **aimer qn à la folie** to be madly in love with sb

**folklo** [fɔlklo] *adj inv Fam* weird; **c'est un type plutôt folklo** he's a bit of a weirdo

**folklore** [fɔlklɔr] *nm* folklore ■ **folklorique** *adj* [costume] traditional; [musique, danse] folk

**folle** [fɔl] *voir* **fou**

**foncé, -e** [fɔ̃se] *adj* dark

**foncer** [fɔ̃se] **1.** *vi* [aller vite] to tear *or* charge along; **foncer sur qn / qch** to swoop on sb / sth **2.** *vt & vi* [couleur] to darken

**foncier, -ère** [fɔ̃sje, -ɛr] *adj* [taxe] land

**fonction** [fɔ̃ksjɔ̃] *nf* function; [emploi] office; **appartement** *ou* **logement de fonction** *Br* tied accommodation, *Am* accommodations that go with the job; **voiture de fonction** company car; **en fonction de** according to; **faire fonction de** [personne] to act as; [objet] to serve *or* act as; **prendre ses fonctions** to take up one's duties; **la fonction publique** the civil service ■ **fonctionnaire** *nmf* civil servant; **haut fonctionnaire** high-ranking civil servant ■ **fonctionnel, -elle** *adj* functional

**fonctionner** [fɔ̃ksjɔne] *vi* [machine] to work, to function; **faire fonctionner qch** to operate sth ■ **fonctionnement** *nm* [de machine] working; **en état de fonctionnement** in working order

**fond** [fɔ̃] *nm* [de boîte, de jardin, de vallée] bottom; [de salle, d'armoire] back; [arrière-plan] background; **au fond de** [boîte, jardin] at the bottom of; [salle] at the back of; *Fig* **au fond, dans le fond** basically; **à fond** [connaître] thoroughly; **de fond en comble** from top to bottom; **course de fond** long-distance race; **ski de fond** cross-country skiing; **bruits de fond** background noise; **fond sonore** background music

**fondamental, -e, -aux** [fɔ̃damɑ̃tal, -o] *adj* fundamental, basic

**fonder** [fɔ̃de] **1.** *vt* [ville] to found; [commerce] to set up; [famille] to start; **fonder qch sur qch** to base sth on sth **2. se fonder** *vpr* **se fonder sur qch** [sujet : théorie] to be based on sth ▪ **fondateur, -trice** *nmf* founder ▪ **fondation** *nf* [création, œuvre] foundation (**de** of); **fondations** [de bâtiment] foundations ▪ **fondement** *nm* foundation

**fondre** [fɔ̃dr] **1.** *vt* [métal] to melt down; [neige] to melt; **faites fondre le chocolat** melt the chocolate **2.** *vi* [se liquéfier] to melt; **fondre en larmes** to burst into tears; **fondre sur qch** to swoop on sth **3. se fondre** *vpr* **se fondre dans qch** [disparaître] to merge into sth ▪ **fondant, -e** *adj* [aliment] which melts in the mouth

**fonds** [fɔ̃] **1.** *nm* [organisme] fund; [de bibliothèque] collection; **fonds de commerce** business; **Fonds monétaire international** International Monetary Fund **2.** *nmpl* [argent] funds; **être en fonds** to be in funds

**font** [fɔ̃] *voir* **faire**

**fontaine** [fɔ̃tɛn] *nf* [construction] fountain; [source] spring

**fonte** [fɔ̃t] *nf* **a)** [de neige] melting; [d'acier] smelting **b)** [alliage] cast iron; **en fonte** [poêle] cast-iron **c)** TYP font

**football** [futbol] *nm* Br football, Am soccer ▪ **footballeur, -euse** *nmf* Br footballer, Am soccer player

**footing** [futiŋ] *nm* jogging

**forage** [fɔraʒ] *nm* drilling, boring

**forain** [fɔrɛ̃] *nm* fairground stallholder

**force** [fɔrs] *nf* [violence & PHYS] force; [vigueur] strength; **de toutes ses forces** with all one's strength; **de force** by force, forcibly; **à force de faire qch** through doing sth; **les forces armées** the armed forces ▪ **forcément** *adv* inevitably; **pas forcément** not necessarily

**forcer** [fɔrse] **1.** *vt* [obliger] to force; [porte] to force open; [voix] to strain; **forcer qn à faire qch** to force sb to do

sth **2.** *vi* [appuyer, tirer] to force it; [se surmener] to overdo it **3. se forcer** *vpr* to force oneself (**à faire** to do)

**forer** [fɔre] *vt* to drill, to bore

**forêt** [fɔrɛ] *nf* forest

**forfait** [fɔrfɛ] *nm* **a)** [prix] all-in price; [de ski] pass; **forfait week-end** week-end package **b)** [crime] heinous crime ▪ **forfaitaire** *adj* [indemnités] basic; **prix forfaitaire** all-in price

**forge** [fɔrʒ] *nf* forge ▪ **forger** *vt* [métal, liens] to forge; *Fig* [caractère] to form ▪ **forgeron** [-ərɔ̃] *nm* (black)smith

**formaliser** [fɔrmalize] ▪ **se formaliser** *vpr* to take offence (**de** at)

**formalité** [fɔrmalite] *nf* formality

**format** [fɔrma] *nm* format

**formater** [fɔrmate] *vt* ORDINAT to format ▪ **formatage** [fɔrmataʒ] *nm* ORDINAT formatting

**formation** [fɔrmasjɔ̃] *nf* [de roche, de mot] formation; [éducation] education; **formation permanente** continuing education; **formation professionnelle** vocational training ▪ **formateur, -trice 1.** *adj* formative **2.** *nmf* trainer

**forme** [fɔrm] *nf* [contour] shape, form; [manière, bonne santé] form; **en forme de qch** in the shape of sth; **en forme de poire** pear-shaped; **sous forme de qch** in the form of sth; **en (pleine) forme** [en bonne santé] on (top) form

**formel, -elle** [fɔrmɛl] *adj* [structure] formal; [personne, preuve] positive; [interdiction] strict

**former** [fɔrme] **1.** *vt* [groupe, caractère] to form; [apprenti] to train **2. se former** *vpr* [apparaître] to form; [association, liens] to be formed; [apprendre son métier] to train oneself

**formidable** [fɔrmidabl] *adj* [fantastique] great; [gigantesque] tremendous

**formulaire** [fɔrmylɛr] *nm* form

**formule** [fɔrmyl] *nf* MATH formula; [phrase] expression; [solution] method; **nouvelle formule** [menu] new-style; **formule magique** magic formula ■ **formulation** *nf* formulation ■ **formuler** *vt* to formulate

**fort¹, -e** [fɔr, fɔrt] **1.** *adj* [vigoureux] strong; [gros, important] large; [pluie, mer, chute de neige] heavy; [voix] loud; [fièvre] high; [pente] steep; **être fort en qch** [doué] to be good at sth **2.** *adv* [frapper, pleuvoir] hard; [parler] loud(ly); [serrer] tight; **sentir fort** to have a strong smell; **respirer fort** to breathe heavily **3.** *nm* [spécialité] strong point ■ **fortiche** [fɔrtiʃ] *adj Fam* **elle est fortiche en anglais!** she's *Br* dead *or Am* real good at English!

**fort²** [fɔr] *nm* HIST & MIL fort ■ **forteresse** *nf* fortress

**fortifié, -e** [fɔrtifje] *adj* [ville, camp] fortified ■ **fortification** *nf* fortification

**fortifier** [fɔrtifje] *vt* [mur, ville] to fortify; [corps] to strengthen ■ **fortifiant** *nm* tonic

**fortune** [fɔrtyn] *nf* [richesse, hasard] fortune; **faire fortune** to make one's fortune

**fosse** [fos] *nf* [trou] pit; **fosse d'orchestre** orchestra pit

**fossé** [fose] *nm* ditch; [de château] moat; *Fig* [désaccord] gulf

**fossette** [fɔsɛt] *nf* dimple

**fossoyeur** [foswajœr] *nm* gravedigger

**fou, folle** [fu, fɔl]

fol is used before masculine singular nouns beginning with a vowel or h mute.

**1.** *adj* [personne, projet] mad, insane; [succès, temps] tremendous; [envie] wild, mad; [espoir] foolish; **fou de qch** [musique, personne] mad about sth; **fou de joie** beside oneself with joy **2.** *nmf* madman, *f* madwoman **3.** *nm* [bouffon] jester; ÉCHECS bishop

**foudre** [fudr] *nf* **la foudre** lightning ■ **foudroyant, -e** *adj* [succès, vitesse] staggering ■ **foudroyer** *vt* to strike; **foudroyer qn du regard** to give sb a withering look

**fouet** [fwɛ] *nm* whip; CULIN whisk; **coup de fouet** lash (with a whip); **de plein fouet** head-on ■ **fouetter** *vt* to whip; [sujet : pluie] to lash (against); **crème fouettée** whipped cream

**fougère** [fuʒɛr] *nf* fern

**fougue** [fug] *nf* fire, spirit ■ **fougueux, -euse** *adj* fiery, ardent

**fouille** [fuj] **1.** *nf* [de personne, de bagages] search **2.** *nfpl* **fouilles archéologiques** excavations, dig ■ **fouiller 1.** *vt* [personne, maison] to search **2.** *vi* **fouiller dans qch** [tiroir] to search through sth **3.** *vt & vi* [creuser] to dig

**fouillis** [fuji] *nm* jumble

**fouiner** [fwine] *vi Fam* to ferret around

**foulard** [fular] *nm* (head)scarf

**foule** [ful] *nf* crowd; **une foule de** [objets] a mass of

**foulée** [fule] *nf* [de coureur, de cheval] stride

**fouler** [fule] **1.** *vt* [sol] to tread; **fouler qch aux pieds** to trample sth underfoot **2. se fouler** *vpr* **se fouler la cheville** to sprain one's ankle ■ **foulure** *nf* sprain

**four** [fur] *nm* [de cuisine] oven; [de potier] kiln; **petit four** [gâteau] (small) fancy cake

**fourche** [furʃ] *nf* [outil, embranchement] fork; **faire une fourche** to fork ■ **fourcher** *vi* [arbre] to fork ■ **fourchette** *nf* [pour manger] fork; [salaires] bracket ■ **fourchu, -e** *adj* forked

**fourgon** [furgɔ̃] *nm* [camion] van; **fourgon cellulaire** *Br* prison van, *Am* patrol wagon

**fourmi** [furmi] *nf* [insecte] ant; **avoir des fourmis dans les jambes** to have pins and needles in one's legs ■ **fourmiller** *vi* to teem, to swarm (**de** with)

**fourneau, -x** [furno] *nm* [de cuisine] stove

**fournir** [furnir] *vt* [approvisionner] to supply (**en** with); [alibi, preuve, document] to provide; [effort] to make; **fournir qch à qn** to provide sb with sth;

**pièces à fournir** required documents ■ **fourni, -e** adj [barbe] bushy; **bien fourni** [boutique] well-stocked ■ **fournisseur** nm [commerçant] supplier; ORDINAT **fournisseur d'accès** access provider ■ **fournitures** nfpl **fournitures de bureau** office supplies; **fournitures scolaires** school stationery

**fourrage** [fuʀaʒ] nm fodder

**fourré, -e** [fuʀe] **1.** adj [vêtement] fur-lined; [gâteau] jam- / cream-filled **2.** nm BOT thicket

**fourreau, -x** [fuʀo] nm [gaine] sheath

**fourrer** [fuʀe] **1.** vt [vêtement] to fur-line; [gâteau] to fill ■ **se fourrer** vpr Fam to put oneself (**dans** in); **où est-il allé se fourrer ?** where's he got to? ■ **fourre-tout** nm inv [sac] Br holdall, Am carryall

**fourrière** [fuʀjɛʀ] nf [lieu] pound; **mettre à la fourrière** [voiture] to impound; [chien] to put in the pound

**fourrure** [fuʀyʀ] nf fur

**foyer** [fwaje] nm [maison] home; [d'étudiants] residence; [de travailleurs] hostel; [de théâtre] foyer; [de lunettes] focus; [de chaleur, d'infection] source; [d'incendie] seat; [âtre] hearth; [famille] family

**fracas** [fʀaka] nm crash ■ **fracassant, -e** adj [nouvelle, révélation] shattering ■ **fracasser 1.** vt to smash **2. se fracasser** vpr to smash

**fraction** [fʀaksjɔ̃] nf fraction; [partie] part ■ **fractionner 1.** vt to split (up) **2. se fractionner** vpr to split (up)

**fracture** [fʀaktyʀ] nf fracture ■ **fracturer 1.** vt [porte] to break open; [os] to fracture **2. se fracturer** vpr **se fracturer la jambe** to fracture one's leg

**fragile** [fʀaʒil] adj [objet, matériau] fragile; [santé, équilibre] delicate; [personne - physiquement] frail; [mentalement] sensitive ■ **fragilité** nf [d'objet, de matériau] fragility; [de personne - physique] frailty; [mentale] sensitivity

**fragment** [fʀagmɑ̃] nm fragment

**fraîcheur** [fʀɛʃœʀ] nf [d'aliments] freshness; [de température] coolness

**frais¹, fraîche** [fʀɛ, fʀɛʃ] **1.** adj [aliment, fleurs] fresh; [vent, air] cool, fresh; [nouvelles] recent; [peinture] wet **2.** adv servir **frais** [vin] to serve chilled **3.** nm **mettre qch au frais** to put sth in a cool place; [au réfrigérateur] to refrigerate sth; **il fait frais** it's cool ■ **fraîchir** vi [temps] to freshen

**frais²** [fʀɛ] nmpl expenses; **à mes frais** at my (own) expense; **faire des frais** to go to great expense; **frais d'envoi** ou **d'expédition** postage; **frais de scolarité** school fees

**fraise** [fʀɛz] nf [fruit] strawberry; [de dentiste] drill ■ **fraisier** nm [plante] strawberry plant; [gâteau] strawberry cream cake

**framboise** [fʀɑ̃bwaz] nf raspberry ■ **framboisier** nm raspberry bush

**franc¹, franche** [fʀɑ̃, fʀɑ̃ʃ] adj **a)** [sincère] frank; [visage] open **b)** [net - couleur] pure **c)** [zone, ville, port] free ■ **franchement** adv [sincèrement] frankly; [vraiment] really; [sans ambiguïté] clearly

**franc²** [fʀɑ̃] nm Anc [monnaie] franc

**France** nf la France France ■ **français, -e 1.** adj French **2.** nmf **Français** Frenchman; **Française** Frenchwoman; **les Français** the French **3.** nm [langue] French

**franchir** [fʀɑ̃ʃiʀ] vt [obstacle] to get over; [fossé] to jump over; [frontière, ligne d'arrivée] to cross; [porte] to go through; [distance] to cover

**franchise** [fʀɑ̃ʃiz] nf [sincérité] frankness; [exonération] exemption; COMM franchise; **franchise postale** ≃ postage paid

**francilien, enne** [fʀɑ̃siljɛ̃, ɛn] adj of / from the Île-de-France ■ **Francilien, enne** nmf person from the Île-de-France

**franc-maçon** [fʀɑ̃masɔ̃] (pl **francs-maçons**) nm freemason

**francophone** [frãkɔfɔn] **1.** *adj* French-speaking **2.** *nmf* French speaker

**franc-parler** [frãparle] *nm* avoir son franc-parler to speak one's mind

**frange** [frãʒ] *nf* [de cheveux] *Br* fringe, *Am* bangs; [de vêtement] fringe

**frappe** [frap] *nf* [sur machine à écrire] typing; [sur ordinateur] keying; **faute de frappe** typing error

**frapper** [frape] **1.** *vt* [battre] to strike, to hit; [monnaie] to mint; **frapper qn** [impressionner] to strike sb; [impôt, mesure] to hit sb **2.** *vi* [donner un coup] to strike, to hit; **frapper du pied** to stamp (one's foot); **frapper du poing sur la table** to bang (on) the table; **frapper à une porte** to knock on a door; **'entrez sans frapper'** 'go straight in' ▪ **frappant, -e** *adj* striking ▪ **frappé, -e** *adj* [boisson] chilled

**fraternel, -elle** [fraternel] *adj* fraternal, brotherly ▪ **fraternité** *nf* fraternity, brotherhood

**fraude** [frod] *nf* fraud; **passer qch en fraude** to smuggle sth in; **fraude fiscale** tax evasion ▪ **frauder 1.** *vt* **frauder le fisc** to evade tax **2.** *vi* to cheat (**sur** on) ▪ **fraudeur, -euse** *nmf* defrauder ▪ **frauduleux, -euse** *adj* fraudulent

**frayer** [freje] ▪ **se frayer** *vpr* **se frayer un chemin** to clear a way (**à travers / dans** through)

**frayeur** [frejœr] *nf* fright

**fredonner** [frədɔne] *vt & vi* to hum

**frein** [frɛ̃] *nm* brake; **donner un coup de frein** to put on the brakes; **frein à main** handbrake ▪ **freiner 1.** *vt* [véhicule] to slow down; [chute] to break; *Fig* [inflation] to curb **2.** *vi* to brake

**frelaté, -e** [frəlate] *adj* [vin] & *Fig* adulterated

**frêle** [frɛl] *adj* frail

**frémir** [fremir] *vi* [personne] to tremble (**de** with); [feuilles] to rustle; [eau chaude] to simmer ▪ **frémissement** *nm* [de peur] shudder; [de plaisir] thrill; [de colère] quiver; [de feuilles] rustle; [d'eau chaude] simmering

**frénétique** [frenetik] *adj* frenzied

**fréquent, -e** [frekã, -ãt] *adj* frequent ▪ **fréquence** *nf* frequency

**fréquenter** [frekãte] **1.** *vt* [lieu] to frequent; **fréquenter qn** to see sb regularly **2.** **se fréquenter** *vpr* [se voir régulièrement] to see each other socially ▪ **fréquentation** *nf* [de lieu] frequenting; **fréquentations** [relations] company ▪ **fréquenté, -e** *adj* **très fréquenté** busy; **c'est très bien / mal fréquenté** the right / wrong sort of people go there

**frère** [frɛr] *nm* brother

**friable** [frijabl] *adj* crumbly

**friand, -e** [frijã, -ãd] **1.** *adj* **friand de qch** fond of sth **2.** *nm* [salé] small savoury pastry ▪ **friandise** *nf Br* titbit, *Am* tidbit

**friction** [friksjɔ̃] *nf* [massage] rubdown; [de cuir chevelu] scalp massage; [désaccord] friction ▪ **frictionner** *vt* [partie du corps] to rub; [personne] to rub down

**Frigidaire®** [friʒider] *nm* fridge

**frileux, -euse** [frilø, -øz] *adj* être frileux to feel the cold

**friper** [fripe] **1.** *vt* to crumple **2.** **se friper** *vpr* to get crumpled ▪ **fripé, -e** *adj* crumpled

**friperie** [fripri] *nf* [boutique] second-hand clothes *Br* shop *or Am* store

**friqué, -e** [frike] *adj Fam* [personne] loaded; [quartier] rich; **ils sont très friqués** they're rolling in it

**frire** [frir] **1.** *vt* to fry **2.** *vi* to fry; **faire frire qch** to fry sth

**friser** [frize] **1.** *vt* [cheveux] to curl; [effleurer] to skim; **friser la catastrophe** to come within an inch of disaster **2.** *vi* [cheveux] to curl; [personne] to have curly hair ▪ **frisé, -e** *adj* [cheveux] curly; [personne] curly-haired

**frisquet, -ette** [friske] *adj Fam* **il fait frisquet** it's chilly

**fur**

**frisson** [frisɔ̃] *nm* [de froid, de peur] shiver; [de plaisir] thrill ■ **frissonner** *vi* [de froid, de peur] to shiver

**frit, -e** [fri, -it] **1.** *pp de* **frire 2.** *adj* fried ■ **frites** *nfpl Br* chips, *Am* (French) fries ■ **friture** *nf* [mode de cuisson] frying; [aliment] fried food

**frivole** [frivɔl] *adj* frivolous

**froid, -e** [frwa, frwad] **1.** *adj* cold **2.** *nm* cold; **avoir froid** to be/catch cold; **il fait froid** it's cold

**froisser** [frwase] **1.** *vt* [tissu] to crumple, to crease **2. se froisser** *vpr* [tissu] to crease, to crumple; **se froisser un muscle** to strain a muscle

**frôler** [frole] *vt* [effleurer] to brush against, to touch lightly; *Fig* [catastrophe] to come close to

**fromage** [frɔmaʒ] *nm* cheese; **fromage de chèvre** goat's cheese; **fromage blanc** soft cheese; **fromage frais** fromage frais; *Can* **fromage en grains** curd cheese ■ **fromager, -ère** *nmf* [fabricant] cheesemaker; [commerçant] cheese seller ■ **fromagerie** *nf* [magasin] cheese shop

**froment** [frɔmɑ̃] *nm* wheat

**froncer** [frɔ̃se] *vt* [tissu] to gather; **froncer les sourcils** to frown

**front** [frɔ̃] *nm* [du visage] forehead; [avant, MIL & POL] front; **de front** [heurter] head-on; [côte à côte] abreast; [à la fois] (all) at once; **faire front à qn/qch** to face up to sb/sth; **front de mer** sea front ■ **frontal, -e, -aux** *adj* [collision] head-on

**frontière** [frɔ̃tjɛr] **1.** *nf* [de pays] border **2.** *adj inv* **ville frontière** border town ■ **frontalier, -ère** *adj* **ville frontalière** border *or* frontier town

**frotter** [frɔte] **1.** *vt* to rub; [plancher] to scrub; [allumette] to strike **2.** *vi* to rub (**contre** against) **3. se frotter** *vpr* to rub oneself; **se frotter le dos** to scrub one's back

**fructifier** [fryktifje] *vi* [arbre, capital] to bear fruit ■ **fructueux, -euse** *adj* fruitful

**frugal, -e, -aux** [frygal, -o] *adj* frugal

**fruit** [frɥi] *nm* fruit; **des fruits** fruit; **un fruit** a piece of fruit; **fruits de mer** seafood; **fruits secs** dried fruit ■ **fruité, -e** *adj* fruity ■ **fruitier** *adj m* **arbre fruitier** fruit tree

**frustrer** [frystre] *vt* **frustrer qn** to frustrate sb; **frustrer qn de qch** to deprive sb of sth ■ **frustration** *nf* frustration ■ **frustré, -e** *adj* frustrated

**FTP** (*abr de* **file transfer protocol**) *nm* FTP; **un serveur FTP** an FTP server

**fuel** [fjul] *nm* fuel oil

**fugitif, -ive** [fyʒitif, -iv] **1.** *adj* [passager] fleeting **2.** *nmf* runaway, fugitive

**fugue** [fyg] *nf* **faire une fugue** [enfant] to run away ■ **fuguer** *vi Fam* to run away

**fuir** [fɥir] **1.** *vt* [pays] to flee; [personne] to run away from; [guerre] to escape **2.** *vi* [s'échapper] to run away (**devant** from); [gaz, robinet, stylo] to leak ■ **fuite** *nf* [évasion] flight (**devant** from); [de gaz] leak; **en fuite** on the run; **prendre la fuite** to take flight

**fulgurant, -e** [fylgyrɑ̃, -ɑ̃t] *adj* [progrès] spectacular; [douleur] shooting

**fumer** [fyme] **1.** *vt* [cigarette, poisson] to smoke; **fumer la pipe** to smoke a pipe **2.** *vi* [fumeur, moteur] to smoke; [liquide brûlant] to steam ■ **fumé, -e** *adj* [poisson, verre] smoked ■ **fumée** *nf* smoke; [vapeur] steam ■ **fumeur, -euse** *nmf* smoker

**fumeux, -euse** [fymø, -øz] *adj Fig* [idée] hazy

**fumier** [fymje] *nm* [engrais] manure, dung

**funambule** [fynɑ̃byl] *nmf* tightrope walker

**funèbre** [fynɛbr] *adj* [lugubre] gloomy; **marche funèbre** funeral march ■ **funérailles** *nfpl* funeral ■ **funéraire** *adj* funeral

**funiculaire** [fynikylɛr] *nm* funicular

**fur** [fyr] ■ **au fur et à mesure** *adv* as one goes along, progressively; **au fur et à mesure que...** as...

**furent** [fyr] *voir* **être**

**furie** [fyri] *nf* [colère] fury ■ **furieux, -euse** *adj* [en colère] furious (**contre** with)

**fuseau, -x** [fyzo] *nm* [pantalon] ski pants ; [bobine] spindle ; **fuseau horaire** time zone

**fusée** [fyze] *nf* rocket

**fuselage** [fyzlaʒ] *nm* [d'avion] fuselage

**fusible** [fyzibl] *nm* Br fuse, Am fuze

**fusil** [fyzi] *nm* rifle, gun ; [de chasse] shotgun ■ **fusillade** *nf* [tirs] gunfire ■ **fusiller** *vt* [exécuter] to shoot

**fusion** [fyzjɔ̃] *nf* **a)** [de métal] melting ; PHYS fusion ; **métal en fusion** molten metal **b)** [de sociétés] merger ■ **fusionner** *vt & vi* to merge

**fut** [fy] *voir* **être**

**fute-fute** [fytfyt] *adj Fam* bright, smart ; **il n'est pas très fute-fute** he's a bit thick, he's not very bright

**futile** [fytil] *adj* [personne] frivolous ; [prétexte] trivial

**futur, -ure** [fytyr] **1.** *adj* future ; **future mère** mother-to-be **2.** *nmf* **mon futur / ma future** my intended **3.** *nm* [avenir] future

**fuyant** [fɥijɑ̃] **fuir** ■ **fuyant, -e** *adj* [front] receding ; [personne] evasive ■ **fuyard, -e** *nmf* runaway

**G**

**G, g** [ʒe] *nm inv* G, g

**gabarit** [gabari] *nm* [dimension] size

**gâcher** [gɑʃe] *vt* [gâter] to spoil; [gaspiller] to waste ■ **gâchis** *nm* waste

**gâchette** [gɑʃɛt] *nf* trigger

**gadget** [gadʒɛt] *nm* gadget

**gadoue** [gadu] *nf* mud

**gag** [gag] *nm* gag

**gage** [gaʒ] *nm* [garantie] guarantee; [au jeu] forfeit; [preuve] token

**gagnant, -e** [gaɲɑ̃, -ɑ̃t] **1.** *adj* [billet, cheval] winning **2.** *nmf* winner

**gagner** [gaɲe] **1.** *vt* [par le travail] to earn; [par le jeu] to win; [obtenir] to gain; [atteindre] to reach; [sujet: feu, épidémie] to spread to; **gagner sa vie** to earn one's living; **gagner du temps** [aller plus vite] to save time; [temporiser] to gain time; **gagner du terrain** to gain ground; **gagner de la place** to save space **2.** *vi* [être vainqueur] to win ■ **gagne-pain** *nm inv* livelihood

**gai, -e** [ɡɛ] *adj* cheerful ■ **gaieté** *nf* cheerfulness

**gaillard** [gajar] *nm* [homme] fellow; **un grand gaillard** a strapping man

**gain** [ɡɛ̃] *nm* [profit] gain, profit; [succès] winning; **gains** [à la Bourse] profits; [au jeu] winnings

**gaine** [ɡɛn] *nf* [étui] sheath

**gala** [gala] *nm* gala

**galant, -e** [galɑ̃, -ɑ̃t] *adj* [homme] gallant; [rendez-vous] romantic ■ **galanterie** *nf* gallantry

**galaxie** [galaksi] *nf* galaxy

**gale** [gal] *nf* **a)** MÉD scabies **b)** *Can* [croûte] scab

**galère** [galɛr] *nf* NAUT galley; *Fam & Fig* **quelle galère !** what a hassle!, what a drag!

**galérer** [galere] *vi Fam* to have a hard time

**galerie** [galri] *nf* [passage, salle] gallery; [de taupe] tunnel; **galerie d'art** art gallery; **galerie marchande** (shopping) mall

**galet** [galɛ] *nm* pebble; **plage de galets** shingle beach

**galette** [galɛt] *nf* [gâteau] butter cookie; [crêpe] buckwheat pancake; **galette des Rois** *Twelfth Night cake*

**Galles** [gal] *nm* **pays de Galles** Wales ■ **gallois, -e 1.** *adj* Welsh **2.** *nmf* **Gallois** Welshman; **Galloise** Welshwoman **3.** *nm* [langue] Welsh

**galon** [galɔ̃] *nm* [ruban] braid; [de soldat] stripe

**galop** [galo] *nm* gallop; **aller au galop** to gallop ■ **galoper** *vi* [cheval] to gallop

**gambader** [gɑ̃bade] *vi* to leap *or* frisk about

**Gambie** [gɑ̃bi] *nf* **la Gambie** the Gambia

**gamelle** [gamɛl] *nf* [de chien] bowl; [d'ouvrier] billy(can); [de soldat] mess tin

**gamin, e** [gamɛ̃, in] *Fam* **1.** *adj* [puéril] childish **2.** *nmf* [enfant] kid

**gamme** [gam] *nf* MUS scale; [éventail] range; **téléviseur haut / bas de gamme** top-of-the-range / bottom-of-the-range television

**gang** [gɑ̃g] *nm* gang

**gant** [gɑ̃] *nm* glove; **gant de toilette** ≃ facecloth

**garage** [garaʒ] *nm* [de voitures] garage ■ **garagiste** *nmf* [mécanicien] garage mechanic; [propriétaire] garage owner

**garant, -e** [garɑ̃, -ɑ̃t] *nmf* JUR [personne] guarantor; **se porter garant de qn** to stand guarantor for sb; **se porter garant de qch** to vouch for sth

**garantie** [garɑ̃ti] *nf* guarantee; *Fig* [précaution] safeguard; **sous garantie** under guarantee ■ **garantir** *vt* to guarantee; [emprunt] to secure; **garantir à qn que...** to guarantee sb that...

**garçon** [garsɔ̃] *nm* boy; [jeune homme] young man; [serveur] waiter; **garçon de café** waiter; **garçon d'honneur** best man; **garçon manqué** tomboy

**garde** [gard] **1.** *nm* [gardien] guard; [soldat] guardsman; **garde du corps** bodyguard **2.** *nf* **a)** [d'enfants, de bagages] care, custody (**de** of); **avoir la garde de** to be in charge of; **prendre garde** to pay attention (**à qch** to sth); **être de garde** to be on duty; [soldat] to be on guard duty; **médecin de garde** duty doctor **b)** [escorte, soldats] guard **3.** *nm* **garde de nuit** [de malade] night nurse ■ **garde-à-vous** *nm inv* MIL (position of) attention; **se mettre au garde-à-vous** to stand to attention ■ **garde-chasse** *(pl gardes-chasses)* *nm* gamekeeper ■ **garde-côte(s)** [gardəkot] *(pl garde-côtes)* *nm* [bateau] coastguard ship; [personne] coastguard ■ **garde-manger** *nm inv* [armoire] food safe; [pièce] pantry, *Br* larder ■ **garde-meuble** [gardəmœbl] *(pl garde-meubles)* *nm* warehouse ■ **garde-robe** *(pl garde-robes)* *nf* wardrobe

**garder** [garde] **1.** *vt* [conserver] to keep; [vêtement] to keep on; [habitude] to keep up; [surveiller] to look after; [défendre] to protect **2. se garder** *vpr* [aliment] to keep; **se garder de qch** to beware of sth; **se garder de faire qch** to take care not to do sth

**garderie** [gardəri] *nf Br* (day) nursery, *Am* daycare center

**gardien, -enne** [gardjɛ̃, -ɛn] *nmf* [d'immeuble, d'hôtel] caretaker, *Am* janitor; [de prison] (prison) guard, *Br* warder; [de zoo] keeper; [de musée] *Br* attendant, *Am* guard; *Can* [d'enfants] baby-sitter; **gardien de but** [au football] goalkeeper; **gardienne d'enfants** childminder, baby-sitter; **gardien de nuit** night watchman; **gardien de la paix** policeman

**gare** [gar] *nf* [pour trains] station; **gare routière** bus *or Br* coach station

**garer** [gare] **1.** *vt* [voiture] to park **2. se garer** *vpr* [automobiliste] to park

**gargariser** [gargarize] ■ **se gargariser** *vpr* to gargle

**gargouiller** [garguje] *vi* [fontaine, eau] to gurgle; [ventre] to rumble

**garnir** [garnir] *vt* [décorer] to trim (**de** with); [équiper] to fit out (**de** with); [couvrir] to cover; [remplir] to fill ■ **garniture** *nf* CULIN garnish

**garnison** [garnizɔ̃] *nf* garrison

**gaspiller** [gaspije] *vt* to waste ■ **gaspillage** *nm* waste

**gastronomie** [gastronomi] *nf* gastronomy

**gâté, -e** [gate] *adj* [dent, fruit] bad; **enfant gâté** spoilt child

**gâteau, -x** [gato] *nm* cake; **gâteau sec** *Br* biscuit, *Am* cookie

**gâter** [gate] **1.** *vt* to spoil **2. se gâter** *vpr* [aliment, dent] to go bad; [temps] to take a turn for the worst

**gâteux, -euse** [gatø, -øz] *adj* senile

**gauche¹** [goʃ] **1.** *adj* [côté, main] left **2.** *nf* **la gauche** [côté] the left (side); POL the left (wing); **à gauche** [tourner] (to the) left; [marcher] on the left, on the left(-hand) side; **de gauche** [fenêtre, colonne] left-hand; [parti, politique] left-wing; **à gauche de** on *or* to the left of ■ **gaucher, -ère 1.** *adj* left-handed **2.** *nmf* left-hander ■ **gauchiste** *adj & nmf* POL (extreme) leftist

**gauche²** [goʃ] *adj* [maladroit] awkward

**gaufre** [gofr] *nf* waffle ■ **gaufrette** *nf* wafer (biscuit)

**gaver** [gave] **1.** *vt* [animal] to force-feed; *Fig* [personne] to stuff (**de** with) **2. se gaver** *vpr* to stuff oneself (**de** with)

**gay** [gɛ] *adj inv & nm* gay

**gaz** [gɑz] nm inv gas; **masque à gaz** gas mask; **gaz carbonique** carbon dioxide; **gaz d'échappement** exhaust fumes; **gaz de schiste** shale gas ▪ **gazeux, -euse** adj [état] gaseous; [boisson] fizzy, carbonated; [eau] sparkling

**gazole** [gɑzɔl] nm diesel oil

**gazon** [gɑzɔ̃] nm [herbe] grass; [surface] lawn

**gazouiller** [gazuje] vi [oiseau] to chirp; [bébé, ruisseau] to babble

**géant, -e** [ʒeɑ̃, -ɑ̃t] adj & nmf giant

**geindre** [ʒɛ̃dr] vi [gémir] to moan

**gel** [ʒɛl] nm a) [temps, glace] frost b) [pour cheveux] gel ▪ **gelé, -e** adj frozen; MÉD frostbitten ▪ **gelée** nf a) frost; **gelée blanche** ground frost b) [de fruits, de viande] jelly ▪ **geler 1.** vt to freeze **2.** vi to freeze; **on gèle ici** it's freezing here **3.** v impers **il gèle** it's freezing

**Gémeaux** [ʒemo] nmpl **les Gémeaux** [signe] Gemini

**gémir** [ʒemir] vi to groan, to moan ▪ **gémissement** nm groan, moan

**gênant, -e** [ʒenɑ̃, -ɑ̃t] adj [objet] cumbersome; [présence, situation] awkward; [bruit, personne] annoying

**gencive** [ʒɑ̃siv] nf gum

**gendarme** [ʒɑ̃darm] nm gendarme, policeman ▪ **gendarmerie** nf [corps] police force; [local] police headquarters

**gendre** [ʒɑ̃dr] nm son-in-law

**gène** [ʒɛn] nm BIOL gene

**gêne** [ʒɛn] nf [trouble physique] discomfort; [confusion] embarrassment; [dérangement] inconvenience; Can [timidité] shyness

**gêné, -e** [ʒene] adj a) [physiquement] **être gêné pour marcher** to have difficulty walking b) [intimidé] embarrassed; [silence, sourire] awkward

**généalogie** [ʒenealɔʒi] nf genealogy ▪ **généalogique** adj genealogical; **arbre généalogique** family tree

**gêner** [ʒene] **1.** vt [déranger, irriter] to bother; [troubler] to embarrass; [mouvement] to hamper; [circulation] to hold up; Can [intimider] to intimidate;

**ça ne me gêne pas** I don't mind (**si** if) **2. se gêner** vpr [se déranger] to put oneself out

**général, -e, -aux** [ʒeneral, -o] **1.** adj general; **en général** in general **2.** nmf MIL general ▪ **généralité** nf generality

**généralisation** [ʒeneralizasjɔ̃] nf generalization ▪ **généraliser 1.** vt & vi to generalize **2. se généraliser** vpr to become widespread ▪ **généraliste** nmf [médecin] Br general practitioner, GP, Am family doctor

**générateur** [ʒeneratœr] nm ÉLEC generator

**génération** [ʒenerasjɔ̃] nf generation

**génératrice** [ʒeneratris] nf ÉLEC generator

**générer** [ʒenere] vt to generate

**généreux, -euse** [ʒenerø, -øz] adj generous (**de** with)

**générique** [ʒenerik] **1.** nm [de film] credits **2.** adj **produit générique** generic product

**générosité** [ʒenerozite] nf generosity

**génétique** [ʒenetik] **1.** nf genetics (sg) **2.** adj genetic; **manipulation génétique** genetic engineering ▪ **génétiquement** adv **génétiquement modifié** genetically modified

**Genève** [ʒənɛv] nm ou f Geneva

**génial, -e, -aux** [ʒenjal, -jo] adj [personne, invention] brilliant

**génie** [ʒeni] nm a) [aptitude, personne] genius; **avoir le génie pour faire qch** to have a genius for doing sth b) **génie civil** civil engineering; **génie génétique** genetic engineering c) [esprit] genie, spirit

**genou, -x** [ʒ(ə)nu] nm knee; **être à genoux** to be kneeling (down); **se mettre à genoux** to kneel (down)

**genre** [ʒɑ̃r] nm [espèce] kind, sort; [attitude] manner; ART genre; GRAM gender; **le genre humain** mankind

**gens** [ʒɑ̃] nmpl people

**gentil, -ille** [ʒɑ̃ti, -ij] adj [aimable] nice (**avec** to); [sage] good ▪ **gentillesse** nf kindness; **avoir la gentillesse de**

faire qch to be kind enough to do sth
■ **gentiment** *adv* [aimablement] kindly ; [sagement] nicely

**géo** [ʒeo] *nf Arg* geography

**géographie** [ʒeɔgrafi] *nf* geography
■ **géographique** *adj* geographical

**geôlier, -ère** [ʒolje, -jɛr] *nmf* jailer

**géologie** [ʒeɔlɔʒi] *nf* geology ■ **géologique** *adj* geological

**géomètre** [ʒeɔmɛtr] *nm* surveyor

**géométrie** [ʒeɔmetri] *nf* geometry
■ **géométrique** *adj* geometric(al)

**gérant, -e** [ʒerã, -ãt] *nmf* manager, *f* manageress

**gerbe** [ʒɛrb] *nf* [de blé] sheaf ; [de fleurs] bunch ; [d'eau] spray

**gercer** [ʒɛrse] **1.** *vi* [peau, lèvres] to chap **2. se gercer** *vpr* [peau, lèvres] to chap ■ **gerçure** *nf* chap, crack

**gérer** [ʒere] *vt* to manage

**germe** [ʒɛrm] *nm* [microbe] germ ; [de plante] shoot ■ **germer** *vi* [graine] to start to grow ; [pomme de terre] to sprout

**geste** [ʒɛst] *nm* gesture ; **faire un geste** [bouger, agir] to make a gesture ; **ne pas faire un geste** [ne pas bouger] not to make a move

**gestion** [ʒɛstjɔ̃] *nf* [action] management ; ORDINAT **gestion de fichiers** file management ■ **gestionnaire** *nmf* administrator ; ORDINAT **gestionnaire de données** data manager

**Ghana** [gana] *nm* **le Ghana** Ghana

**gibier** [ʒibje] *nm* game

**giboulée** [ʒibule] *nf* sudden shower ; **giboulées de mars** ≃ April showers

**gicler** [ʒikle] *vi* [liquide] to spurt out ; [boue] to splash up

**gifle** [ʒifl] *nf* slap in the face ■ **gifler** *vt* **gifler qn** to slap sb in the face

**gigantesque** [ʒigɑ̃tɛsk] *adj* gigantic

**gigaoctet** [ʒigaɔktɛ] *nm* ORDINAT gigabyte

**gigot** [ʒigo] *nm* leg of mutton / lamb

**gilet** [ʒilɛ] *nm* [cardigan] cardigan ; [de costume] *Br* waistcoat, *Am* vest ; **gilet pare-balles** bulletproof vest ; **gilet de sauvetage** life jacket

**gingembre** [ʒɛ̃ʒɑ̃br] *nm* ginger

**girafe** [ʒiraf] *nf* giraffe

**giratoire** [ʒiratwar] *adj* AUTO **sens giratoire** *Br* roundabout, *Am* traffic circle

**girofle** [ʒirɔfl] *nm* **clou de girofle** clove

**gisement** [ʒizmɑ̃] *nm* [de minerai] deposit ; **gisement de pétrole** oilfield

**gitan, -e** [ʒitɑ̃, -an] *nmf* gipsy

**gîte** [ʒit] *nm* [abri] resting place ; **gîte rural** gîte, *self-catering holiday cottage or apartment* ; *Can* **gîte touristique** bed and breakfast, guest-house

**givre** [ʒivr] *nm* frost ■ **givré, -e** *adj* frost-covered

**glace** [glas] *nf* **a)** [eau gelée] ice ; [crème glacée] ice cream **b)** [vitre] window ; [miroir] mirror

**glacer** [glase] *vt* [durcir] to freeze ; [gâteau] *Br* to ice, *Am* to frost ■ **glaçage** *nm* [de gâteau] *Br* icing, *Am* frosting ■ **glacé, -e** *adj* [eau, pièce] ice-cold, icy ; [vent] freezing, icy ; [thé, café] iced ; [papier] glazed

**glacial, -e, -aux** [glasjal, -o] *adj* icy

**glacier** [glasje] *nm* **a)** GÉOL glacier **b)** [vendeur] ice-cream seller

**glacière** [glasjɛr] *nf* [boîte] icebox

**glaçon** [glasɔ̃] *nm* CULIN ice cube ; GÉOL block of ice ; [sur toit] icicle

**glande** [glɑ̃d] *nf* gland

**glaner** [glane] *vt* [blé, renseignement] to glean

**glisse** [glis] *nf* **sports de glisse** *sports involving sliding and gliding motion, such as skiing, surfing etc*

**glisser** [glise] **1.** *vt* [introduire] to slip (**dans** into) ; [murmurer] to whisper **2.** *vi* [involontairement] to slip ; [volontairement - sur glace] to slide ; [sur l'eau] to glide ; ORDINAT to drag ; **ça glisse** it's slippery **3. se glisser** *vpr* **se glisser dans / sous qch** to slip into / under sth ■ **glissade** *nf* [involontaire] slip ;

[volontaire] slide ■ **glissant, -e** *adj* slippery ■ **glissement** *nm* glissement de terrain landslide

**glissière** [glisjɛr] *nf* TECH runner, slide; **porte à glissière** sliding door

**global, -e, -aux** [glɔbal, -o] *adj* total, global ■ **globalement** *adv* overall

**globe** [glɔb] *nm* globe; **globe terrestre** [mappemonde] globe ■ **globe-trotter** *(pl* **globe-trotters)**, **globe-trotter, euse** [glɔbtrɔtœr, øz] *nmf* globetrotter

**globuleux, -euse** [glɔbylø, -øz] *adj* **yeux globuleux** protruding eyes

**gloire** [glwar] *nf* [renom] glory; [personne célèbre] celebrity ■ **glorieux, -euse** *adj* glorious ■ **glorifier 1.** *vt* to glorify **2. se glorifier** *vpr* **se glorifier de qch** to glory in sth

**gloss** [glɔs] *nm* lipgloss

**glousser** [gluse] *vi* [poule] to cluck; [personne] to chuckle

**glouton, -onne** [glutɔ̃, -ɔn] **1.** *adj* greedy, gluttonous **2.** *nmf* glutton

**gluant, -e** [glyɑ̃, -ɑ̃t] *adj* sticky

**glucide** [glysid] *nm* carbohydrate

**goal** [gol] *nm* [au football] goalkeeper

**gobelet** [gɔblɛ] *nm* tumbler; [de plastique, de papier] cup

**goéland** [gɔelɑ̃] *nm* (sea)gull

**golf** [gɔlf] *nm* golf; [terrain] golf course ■ **golfeur, -euse** *nmf* golfer

**golfe** [gɔlf] *nm* gulf, bay

**gomme** [gɔm] *nf* [pour effacer] eraser, *Br* rubber; *Can* **gomme à mâcher** chewing-gum ■ **gommer** *vt* [effacer] to rub out, to erase

**gond** [gɔ̃] *nm* [de porte] hinge

**gondoler** [gɔ̃dɔle] **1.** *vi* [planche] to warp; [papier] to crinkle **2. se gondoler** *vpr* [planche] to warp; [papier] to crinkle

**gonflable** [gɔ̃flabl] *adj* inflatable

**gonfler** [gɔ̃fle] **1.** *vt* to swell; [pneu] to inflate **2.** *vi* to swell ■ **gonflé, -e** *adj* swollen ■ **gonflement** *nm* swelling

**gore** [gɔr] **1.** *(pl* **gore)** *adj* gory **2.** *nm* le **gore** gore; **il aime le gore** he likes gore

**gorge** [gɔrʒ] *nf* throat; GÉOG gorge; **avoir la gorge serrée** to have a lump in one's throat

**gorgé, -e** [gɔrʒe] *adj* **gorgé de qch** [saturé] gorged with sth

**gorgée** [gɔrʒe] *nf* mouthful; **petite gorgée** sip

**gorger** [gɔrʒe] **1.** *vt* [remplir] to stuff (**de** with) **2. se gorger** *vpr* **se gorger de qch** to gorge oneself with sth

**gorille** [gɔrij] *nm* [animal] gorilla

**gothique** [gɔtik] *adj & nm* Gothic

**goudron** [gudrɔ̃] *nm* tar

**gouffre** [gufr] *nm* abyss

**goulot** [gulo] *nm* [de bouteille] neck; **boire au goulot** to drink from the bottle

**goulu, -e** [guly] *adj* greedy

**goupille** [gupij] *nf* [de grenade] pin

**gourde** [gurd] *nf* [à eau] water bottle, flask

**gourmand, -e** [gurmɑ̃, -ɑ̃d] **1.** *adj* fond of eating; **gourmand de qch** fond of sth **2.** *nmf* hearty eater ■ **gourmandise** *nf* fondness for food; **gourmandises** [mets] delicacies

**gourmet** [gurmɛ] *nm* gourmet; **fin gourmet** gourmet

**gousse** [gus] *nf* **gousse d'ail** clove of garlic

**goût** [gu] *nm* taste; **de bon goût** in good taste; **par goût** by choice; **avoir du goût** [personne] to have (good) taste; **avoir un goût de noisette** to taste of hazelnut

**goûter** [gute] **1.** *vt* [aliment] to taste; [apprécier] to enjoy; **goûter à qch** to taste (a little of) sth **2.** *vi* to have an afternoon snack, *Br* to have tea **3.** *nm* afternoon snack, *Br* tea

**goutte** [gut] *nf* [de liquide] drop; **couler goutte à goutte** to drip ■ **goutte-à-goutte** *nm inv* MÉD *Br* drip, *Am* IV ■ **gouttelette** *nf* droplet ■ **goutter** *vi* to drip

**gouttière** [gutjɛr] *nf* [le long du toit] gutter; [le long du mur] drainpipe

**gouvernail** [guvɛrnaj] *nm* [pale] rudder ; [barre] helm

**gouvernant, e** [guvɛrnɑ̃, ɑ̃t] **1.** *adj* ruling ; **les classes gouvernantes** the ruling classes **2.** *nm f* man (*f* woman) in power ; **les gouvernants** the people in power, the Government ■ **gouvernante** *nf* a) [d'enfants] governess b) [de maison] housekeeper

**gouvernants** [guvɛrnɑ̃] *nmpl* rulers

**gouvernement** [guvɛrnəmɑ̃] *nm* government ■ **gouvernemental, -e, -aux** *adj* **politique gouvernementale** government policy

**gouverner** [guvɛrne] *vt & vi* POL & *Fig* to govern, to rule ■ **gouverneur** *nm* governor

**goyave** [gɔjav] *nf* guava

**GPS** *(abr de global positioning system)* *nm* GPS

**grâce** [grɑs] **1.** *nf* [charme & REL] grace ; [acquittement] pardon ; **de bonne / mauvaise grâce** with good / bad grace ; **délai de grâce** period of grace **2.** *prép* **grâce à** thanks to

**gracier** [grasje] *vt* [condamné] to pardon

**gracieux, -euse** [grasjø, -øz] *adj* [élégant] graceful ; [aimable] gracious ; [gratuit] gratuitous ; **à titre gracieux** free (of charge) ■ **gracieusement** *adv* [avec élégance] gracefully ; [aimablement] graciously ; [gratuitement] free (of charge)

**grade** [grad] *nm* [militaire] rank ; **monter en grade** to be promoted ■ **gradé** *nm* MIL non-commissioned officer

**gradins** [gradɛ̃] *nmpl* [d'amphithéâtre] rows of seats ; [de stade] *Br* terraces, *Am* bleachers

**graduel, -elle** [graduɛl] *adj* gradual

**graduer** [gradue] *vt* [règle] to graduate ; [augmenter] to increase gradually

**graffiti** [grafiti] *nmpl* graffiti

**grain** [grɛ̃] *nm* a) [de blé] & *Fig* grain ; [de café] bean ; [de poussière] speck ; **grain de beauté** mole ; [sur le visage] beauty spot ; **grain de raisin** grape b) [averse] shower

**graine** [grɛn] *nf* seed

**graisse** [grɛs] *nf* fat ; [lubrifiant] grease ■ **graisser** *vt* to grease ■ **graisseux, -euse** *adj* [vêtement] greasy, oily ; [tissu] fatty

**grammaire** [gramɛr] *nf* grammar ■ **grammatical, -e, -aux** *adj* grammatical

**gramme** [gram] *nm* gram(me)

**grand, -e** [grɑ̃, grɑ̃d] **1.** *adj* big, large ; [en hauteur] tall ; [chaleur, découverte, âge, mérite, ami] great ; [bruit] loud ; [différence] big, great ; [adulte] grown-up, big ; [illustre] great ; **grand frère** [plus âgé] big brother ; **le grand air** the open air ; **il est grand temps que je parte** it's high time that I left ; **il n'y avait pas grand monde** there were not many people **2.** *adv* **grand ouvert** [yeux, fenêtre] wide open ; **ouvrir grand** to open wide ; **en grand** on a grand *or* large scale **3.** *(gén pl) nm f* a) [adulte] grown-up ; [personnage] great man (*f* woman) ; **les grands de ce monde** the people in (positions of) power *or* in high places b) [enfant] older *or* bigger boy (*f* girl) ■ **grande école** *nf* competitive-entrance higher education establishment ■ **grandement** *adv* [beaucoup] greatly ; [généreusement] grandly ■ **grand-mère** *(pl* **grands-mères)** *nf* grandmother ■ **grand-père** *(pl* **grands-pères)** *nm* grandfather ■ **grands-parents** *nmpl* grandparents

**grand-chose** [grɑ̃ʃoz] *pron* **pas grand-chose** not much

**Grande-Bretagne** [grɑ̃dbrətaɲ] *nf* **la Grande-Bretagne** Great Britain

**grandeur** [grɑ̃dœr] *nf* [importance, gloire] greatness ; [dimension] size ; [majesté, splendeur] grandeur ; **grandeur nature** life-size

**grandiose** [grɑ̃djoz] *adj* imposing

**grandir** [grɑ̃dir] **1.** *vi* [en taille] to grow ; [en âge] to grow up ; **grandir de 2 cm** to grow 2 cm **2.** *vt* **grandir qn** [faire paraître plus grand] to make sb look taller

**grange** [grɑ̃ʒ] *nf* barn

**granit(e)** [granit] *nm* granite

**graphique** [grafik] **1.** *adj* [signe, art] graphic **2.** *nm* graph ; ORDINAT graphic

**grappe** [grap] *nf* [de fruits] cluster ; **grappe de raisin** bunch of grapes

**gras, grasse** [grɑ, grɑs] **1.** *adj* [personne, ventre] fat ; [aliment] fatty ; [graisseux] greasy, oily ; [toux] loose ; **faire la grasse matinée** to have a lie-in **2.** *nm* [de viande] fat **■ grassement** *adv* **grassement payé** handsomely paid **■ grassouillet, -ette** *adj* plump

**gratifier** [gratifje] *vt* **gratifier qn de qch** to present sb with sth **■ gratification** *nf* [prime] bonus

**gratin** [gratɛ̃] *nm* [plat] *baked dish with a cheese topping* ; **chou-fleur au gratin** cauliflower cheese

**gratis** [gratis] *adv* free (of charge)

**gratitude** [gratityd] *nf* gratitude

**gratte-ciel** [gratsjɛl] *nm inv* skyscraper

**gratter** [grate] **1.** *vt* [avec un outil] to scrape ; [avec les ongles, les griffes] to scratch ; [effacer] to scratch out ; *Fam* **ça me gratte** it's itchy **2.** *vi* [tissu] to be scratchy **3. se gratter** *vpr* to scratch oneself

**gratuit, -e** [gratɥi, -it] **1.** *adj* [billet, entrée] free ; [acte] gratuitous **2.** *nm* free magazine **■ gratuité** *nf* **la gratuité de l'enseignement** free education **■ gratuitement** *adv* [sans payer] free (of charge) ; [sans motif] gratuitously

**gravats** [grava] *nmpl* rubble, debris

**grave** [grav] *adj* [maladie, faute] serious ; [visage] grave ; [voix] deep, low ; **ce n'est pas grave !** it's not important ! **■ gravement** *adv* [malade] seriously ; [dignement] gravely

**graver** [grave] *vt* [sur métal] to engrave ; [sur bois] to carve ; [disque] to cut ; ORDINAT to burn **■ graveur** *nm* **a)** en-

graver **b)** ORDINAT CD-RW drive, (CD-) burner ; **graveur de CD** CD writer *or* burner

**gravier** [gravje] *nm* gravel **■ gravillon** *nm* piece of gravel ; **gravillons** gravel, *Br* (loose) chippings

**gravir** [gravir] *vt* to climb

**gravité** [gravite] *nf* [de situation] seriousness ; [solennité & PHYS] gravity ; PHYS **centre de gravité** centre of gravity

**graviter** [gravite] *vi* to revolve (**autour** around)

**gravure** [gravyr] *nf* [image] print ; [action, art] engraving ; **gravure sur bois** [action] woodcarving ; [objet] woodcut

**gré** [gre] *nm* **de son plein gré** of one's own free will ; **de bon gré** willingly ; **contre le gré de qn** against sb's will ; **bon gré mal gré** whether we / you / *etc* like it or not ; **de gré ou de force** one way or another

**Grèce** [grɛs] *nf* **la Grèce** Greece **■ grec, grecque 1.** *adj* Greek **2.** *nmf* **Grec, Grecque** Greek **3.** *nm* [langue] Greek

**greffe** [grɛf] **1.** *nf* [de peau, d'arbre] graft ; [d'organe] transplant **2.** *nm* JUR record office **■ greffer** *vt* [peau & BOT] to graft (**à** on to) ; [organe] to transplant **■ greffier** *nm* JUR clerk (of the court)

**grêle**[1] [grɛl] *nf* hail **■ grêler** *v impers* to hail ; **il grêle** it's hailing **■ grêlon** *nm* hailstone

**grêle**[2] [grɛl] *adj* [jambes] skinny ; [voix] shrill

**grelot** [grəlo] *nm* (small) bell

**grelotter** [grəlɔte] *vi* to shiver (**de** with)

**grenade** [grənad] *nf* [fruit] pomegranate ; [projectile] grenade

**grenier** [grənje] *nm* [de maison] attic ; [pour le fourrage] granary

**grenouille** [grənuj] *nf* frog

**grès** [grɛ] *nm* [roche] sandstone ; [poterie] stoneware

**grésiller** [grezije] *vi* [huile] to sizzle

**grève**[1] [grɛv] *nf* [arrêt du travail] strike ; **faire grève** to be on strike ; **grève de la**

**faim** hunger strike; **grève du zèle** *Br* work-to-rule, *Am* rule-book slow-down ■ **gréviste** *nmf* striker

**grève²** [grɛv] *nf* [de mer] shore; [de rivière] bank

**gribouiller** [gribuje] *vt & vi* to scribble

**grief** [grijɛf] *nm* [plainte] grievance; **faire grief de qch à qn** to hold sth against sb

**grièvement** [grijɛvmɑ̃] *adv* seriously, badly

**griffe** [grif] *nf* [ongle] claw; [de couturier] (designer) label; *Fig* [style] stamp ■ **griffer** *vt* to scratch

**griffonner** [grifɔne] *vt* to scribble, to scrawl

**grignoter** [griɲɔte] *vt & vi* to nibble; **grignoter entre les repas** to snack between meals

**gril** [gril] *nm* [ustensile] *Br* grill, *Am* broiler ■ **grillade** *nf* [viande] *Br* grilled meat, *Am* broiled meat ■ **grille-pain** *nm inv* toaster ■ **griller 1.** *vt* [viande] *Br* to grill, *Am* to broil; [pain] to toast; [ampoule électrique] to blow; *Fam* **griller un feu rouge** to jump the lights **2.** *vi* [viande] to grill; [pain] to toast

**grille** [grij] *nf* [clôture] railings; [porte] gate; [de foyer] grate; *Fig* [de salaires] scale ■ **grillage** *nm* wire mesh *or* netting

**grillon** [grijɔ̃] *nm* cricket

**grimace** [grimas] *nf* [pour faire rire] (funny) face; [de douleur] grimace; **faire la grimace** to pull a face ■ **grimacer** *vi* to make a face; [de douleur] to wince (**de** with)

**grimer** [grime] ■ **se grimer** *vpr* to put one's make-up on

**grimper** [grɛ̃pe] **1.** *vi* to climb (**à qch** up sth) **2.** *vt* [escalier] to climb

**grincer** [grɛ̃se] *vi* to creak; **grincer des dents** to grind one's teeth ■ **grincement** *nm* creaking

**grincheux, -euse** [grɛ̃ʃø, -øz] *adj* grumpy

**grippe** [grip] *nf* [maladie] flu, influenza; **prendre qn en grippe** to take a strong dislike to sb ■ **grippé, -e** *adj* **être grippé** to have (the) flu

**gripper** [gripe] ■ **se gripper** *vpr* [moteur] to seize up

**gris, -e** [gri, griz] **1.** *adj Br* grey, *Am* gray; [temps] dull; [ivre] merry **2.** *nm Br* grey, *Am* gray ■ **grisaille** [grizaj] *nf* [de ciel] *Br* greyness, *Am* grayness

**grisonner** [grizɔne] *vi* [cheveux, personne] to go *Br* grey *or Am* gray

**grivois, -e** [grivwa, -waz] *adj* bawdy

**Groenland** [grɔɛnlɑ̃d] *nm* **le Groenland** Greenland

**grog** [grɔg] *nm* hot toddy

**grogner** [grɔɲe] *vi* [personne] to grumble (**contre** at); [cochon] to grunt ■ **grognement** *nm* [de personne] growl; [de cochon] grunt ■ **grognon, -onne** *adj* grumpy

**grommeler** [grɔm(ə)le] *vt & vi* to mutter

**gronder** [grɔ̃de] **1.** *vt* [réprimander] to scold, to tell off **2.** *vi* [chien] to growl; [tonnerre] to rumble

**gros, grosse** [gro, gros] **1.** *adj* [corpulent, important] big; [gras] fat; [épais] thick; [effort, progrès] great; [somme, fortune] large; [rhume, mer] heavy; [faute] serious, gross; [traits, laine] coarse; **gros mot** swearword **2.** *adv* **risquer gros** to take a big risk; **écrire gros** to write big; **en gros** [globalement] roughly; [écrire] in big letters; [vendre] in bulk, wholesale **3.** *nmf* [personne] fat man, *f* fat woman **4.** *nm* **le gros de** the bulk of; **prix de gros** wholesale prices

**groseille** [grozɛj] *nf* redcurrant

**grossesse** [grosɛs] *nf* pregnancy

**grosseur** [grosœr] *nf* [volume] size; [tumeur] lump

**grossier, -ère** [grosje, -ɛr] *adj* [tissu, traits] rough, coarse; [personne, manières] rude, coarse; [erreur] gross; [ruse, instrument] crude ■ **grossièrement** *adv* [calculer] roughly;

[répondre] coarsely, rudely ; [se tromper] grossly ■ **grossièreté** *nf* [incorrection, vulgarité] coarseness ; [mot] rude word

**grossir** [grosir] **1.** *vt* [sujet : verre, loupe] to magnify **2.** *vi* [personne] to put on weight ; [fleuve] to swell ; [bosse, foule] to get bigger ■ **grossissement** *nm* [augmentation de taille] increase in size ; [de microscope] magnification

**grossiste** [grosist] *nmf* COMM wholesaler

**grosso modo** [grosomɔdo] *adv* [en gros] roughly

**grotesque** [grɔtɛsk] *adj* ludicrous

**grotte** [grɔt] *nf* cave

**grouiller** [gruje] *vi* [se presser] to swarm around ; **grouiller de qch** to swarm with sth

**groupe** [grup] *nm* group ; **groupe sanguin** blood group ■ **groupement** *nm* [action] grouping ; [groupe] group ■ **grouper 1.** *vt* to group (together) **2. se grouper** *vpr* [en association] to form a group

**gruau** [gryo] *nm* Can CULIN porridge, oatmeal

**grue** [gry] *nf* [machine, oiseau] crane

**grumeau, -x** [grymo] *nm* [dans une sauce] lump

**Guadeloupe** [gwadlup] *nf* **la Guadeloupe** Guadeloupe

**Guatemala** [gwatemala] *nm* **le Guatemala** Guatemala

**gué** [ge] *nm* ford

**guenon** [gənɔ̃] *nf* female monkey

**guépard** [gepar] *nm* cheetah

**guêpe** [gɛp] *nf* wasp

**guère** [gɛr] *adv* **(ne...) guère** [pas beaucoup] not much ; [pas longtemps] hardly, scarcely ; **il n'a guère d'amis** he hasn't got many friends

**guéri, -e** [geri] *adj* cured

**guérilla** [gerija] *nf* guerrilla warfare

**guérir** [gerir] **1.** *vt* [personne, maladie] to cure (**de** of) ; [blessure] to heal **2.** *vi* [personne] to get better, to recover ; [blessure] to heal ; [rhume] to get bet-

ter **3. se guérir** *vpr* to get better ■ **guérison** *nf* [rétablissement] recovery ■ **guérisseur, -euse** *nmf* faith healer

**Guernesey** [gɛrnzɛ] *nf* Guernsey

**guerre** [gɛr] *nf* war ; [technique] warfare ; **en guerre** at war (**avec** with) ; **faire la guerre** to wage *or* make war (**à** on *or* against) ; [soldat] to fight ; **crime de guerre** war crime ; **guerre d'usure** war of attrition ■ **guerrier, -ère 1.** *adj* **danse guerrière** war dance ; **chant guerrier** battle song **2.** *nmf* warrior

**guet** [gɛ] *nm* **faire le guet** to be on the lookout ■ **guetter** *vt* [occasion] to watch out for ; [gibier] to lie in wait for

**guet-apens** [gɛtapɑ̃] (*pl* **guets-apens**) *nm* ambush

**gueule** [gœl] *nf* [d'animal, de canon] mouth

**gui** [gi] *nm* mistletoe

**guichet** [giʃɛ] *nm* [de gare, de banque] window ; **guichet automatique** [de banque] cash dispenser ■ **guichetier, -ère** *nmf* [de banque] *Br* counter clerk, *Am* teller ; [de gare] ticket clerk

**guide** [gid] *nm* [personne, livre] guide ; **guide touristique** tourist guide ■ **guider** *vt* to guide

**guidon** [gidɔ̃] *nm* handlebars

**guignol** [ginɔl] *nm* [spectacle] ≃ Punch and Judy show

**guillemets** [gijmɛ] *nmpl* TYP inverted commas, quotation marks ; **entre guillemets** in inverted commas, in quotation marks

**guillotine** [gijɔtin] *nf* guillotine ■ **guillotiner** *vt* to guillotine

**guimauve** [gimov] *nf* **a)** [confiserie, plante] marshmallow **b)** *Fam* [sentimentalité] mush

**guindé, -e** [gɛ̃de] *adj* [peu naturel] stiff ; [style] stilted

**Guinée** [gine] *nf* **la Guinée** Guinea

**guirlande** [girlɑ̃d] *nf* garland ; **guirlande de Noël** piece of tinsel

**guise** [giz] *nf* n'en faire qu'à sa guise to do just as one pleases ; **en guise de** by way of

**guitare** [gitar] *nf* guitar ▪ **guitariste** *nmf* guitarist

**Guyane** [gɥijan] *nf* la Guyane Guiana

**gym** [ʒim] *nf* gym

**gymnase** [ʒimnɑz] *nm* gymnasium ▪ **gymnaste** *nmf* gymnast ▪ **gymnastique** *nf* gymnastics (*sg*)

**gynécologue** [ʒinekɔlɔg] *nmf Br* gynaecologist, *Am* gynecologist

**H, h** [aʃ] *nm inv* H, h

**habile** [abil] *adj* skilful, *Am* skillful (**à qch** at sth); **habile de ses mains** good with one's hands ■ **habileté** *nf* skill

**habilité, -e** [abilite] *adj* (legally) authorized (**à faire** to do)

**habillé, -e** [abije] *adj* dressed (**de** in; **en** as); [costume, robe] smart

**habiller** [abije] **1.** *vt* [vêtir] to dress (**de** in); [fournir en vêtements] to clothe **2. s'habiller** *vpr* to dress, to get dressed; [avec élégance] to dress up ■ **habillement** *nm* [vêtements] clothes

**habit** [abi] *nm* [tenue de soirée] evening dress, tails; **habits** [vêtements] clothes; *Can* **habit de neige** snowsuit

**habitable** [abitabl] *adj* (in)habitable; [maison] fit to live in

**habitat** [abita] *nm* [d'animal, de plante] habitat; [conditions] housing conditions

**habitation** [abitɑsjɔ̃] *nf* [lieu] dwelling; [fait de résider] living

**habiter** [abite] **1.** *vt* [maison, région] to live in **2.** *vi* to live (**à/en** in) ■ **habitant, -e** *nmf* [de pays] inhabitant; [de maison] occupant; *Can* [paysan] farmer; **loger chez l'habitant** [en voyage] to stay with local people ■ **habité, -e** *adj* [région] inhabited; [maison] occupied

**habitude** [abityd] *nf* habit; **avoir l'habitude de qch** to be used to sth; **avoir l'habitude de faire qch** to be used to doing sth; **prendre l'habitude de faire qch** to get into the habit of doing sth; **d'habitude** usually; **comme d'habitude** as usual

**habituel, -elle** [abityɛl] *adj* usual, customary

**habituer** [abitɥe] **1.** *vt* **habituer qn à qch** to accustom sb to sth; **être habitué à qch / à faire qch** to be used to sth / to doing sth **2. s'habituer** *vpr* **s'habituer à qn / qch** to get used to sb / sth ■ **habitué, -e** *nmf* regular

**hache** ['aʃ] *nf* axe, *Am* ax ■ **hache-légumes** *(pl* **hache-légumes)** [aʃlegym] *nm* vegetable chopper

**hacher** ['aʃe] *vt* [au couteau] to chop up; [avec un appareil] *Br* to mince, *Am* to grind ■ **haché, -e** *adj* [viande] *Br* minced, *Am* ground ■ **hachis** *nm* **hachis Parmentier** ≃ cottage pie

**hachurer** ['aʃyre] *vt* to hatch

**hackeur, euse** [akœr, øz], **hacker** [akœr] *nom Fam* hacker

**haie** ['ɛ] *nf* [clôture] hedge; [en équitation] fence; **400 mètres haies** [épreuve d'athlétisme] *Br* 400-metre or *Am* 400-meter hurdles; **haie d'honneur** guard of *Br* honour or *Am* honor

**haine** ['ɛn] *nf* hatred, hate ■ **haineux, -euse** *adj* full of hatred

**haïr** ['air] *vt* to hate ■ **haïssable** *adj* hateful

**hâle** ['ɑl] *nm* suntan ■ **hâlé, -e** *adj* suntanned

**haleine** [alɛn] *nf* breath; **reprendre haleine** to get one's breath back

**haleter** ['alte] *vi* to pant, to gasp ■ **haletant, -e** *adj* panting, gasping

**hall** ['ol] *nm* [de maison] entrance hall; [d'hôtel] lobby; **hall de gare** station concourse

**halle** ['al] *nf* (covered) market; **les halles** the central food market

**hallucination** [alysinɑsjɔ̃] *nf* hallucination ■ **hallucinant, -e** *adj* extraordinary

**halluciner** [alysine] *vi Fam & Fig* **mais j'hallucine ou quoi ?** I don't believe it!

**halogène** [alɔʒɛn] *nm* [lampe] halogen lamp

**halte** ['alt] *nf* [arrêt] stop ; MIL halt ; [lieu] stopping place ; MIL halting place ; **faire halte** to stop

**haltère** [altɛr] *nm* dumbbell ▪ **haltérophile** *nmf* weightlifter ▪ **haltérophilie** *nf* weightlifting

**hamac** ['amak] *nm* hammock

**hamburger** ['ɑ̃bœrgœr] *nm* (ham) burger

**hameau, -x** ['amo] *nm* hamlet

**hameçon** [amsɔ̃] *nm* (fish-)hook

**hameçonnage** [amsɔnaʒ] *nm Can* phishing

**hamster** ['amstɛr] *nm* hamster

**hanche** ['ɑ̃ʃ] *nf* hip

**handball** ['ɑ̃dbal] *nm* SPORT handball

**handicap** ['ɑ̃dikap] *nm* [physique, mental] disability ; *Fig* handicap ▪ **handicapé, -e 1.** *adj* disabled **2.** *nmf* disabled person ; **handicapé physique / mental** physically / mentally handicapped person

**handisport** [ɑ̃dispɔr] *adj* **activité handisport** sport for the disabled

**hangar** ['ɑ̃gar] *nm* [entrepôt] shed

**hanter** ['ɑ̃te] *vt* [sujet : fantôme, souvenir] to haunt ▪ **hantise** *nf* **avoir la hantise de qch** to really dread sth

**harasser** ['arase] *vt* to exhaust

**harceler** ['arsəle] *vt* [importuner] to harass ; [insister auprès de] to pester ▪ **harcèlement** *nm* harassment ; **harcèlement moral** bullying *(in the workplace)* ; **harcèlement sexuel** sexual harassment

**hardi, -e** ['ardi] *adj* bold

**hardware** [ardwɛr] *nm* ORDINAT hardware

**hargneux, -euse** ['arɲø, -øz] *adj* bad-tempered

**haricot** ['ariko] *nm* bean ; CULIN **haricot de mouton** mutton stew ; **haricot rouge** kidney bean ; **haricot vert** green bean, *Br* French bean

**harmonica** [armɔnika] *nm* harmonica, mouthorgan

**harmonie** [armɔni] *nf* harmony ▪ **harmonieux, -euse** *adj* harmonious ▪ **harmoniser 1.** *vt* MUS to harmonize ; *Fig* [salaires] to bring into line **2. s'harmoniser** *vpr* to harmonize

**harnais** ['arnɛ] *nm* [de cheval, de bébé] harness

**harpe** ['arp] *nf* harp

**harpon** ['arpɔ̃] *nm* harpoon

**hasard** ['azar] *nm* **le hasard** chance ; **un hasard** a coincidence ; **par hasard** by chance ; **au hasard** [choisir, répondre] at random ; [marcher] aimlessly ; **à tout hasard** [par précaution] just in case ; [pour voir] on the off chance ▪ **hasarder 1.** *vt* [remarque] to venture **2. se hasarder** *vpr* **se hasarder dans** to venture into ; **se hasarder à faire qch** to risk doing sth ▪ **hasardeux, -euse** *adj* risky, hazardous

**hâte** ['at] *nf* haste ; **à la hâte** hastily ; **en (toute) hâte** hurriedly ; **avoir hâte de faire qch** to be eager to do sth ▪ **hâter 1.** *vt* [pas, départ] to hasten **2. se hâter** *vpr* to hurry **(de faire** to do**)** ▪ **hâtif, -ive** *adj* [trop rapide] hasty

**hausse** ['os] *nf* rise **(de** in**)** ; **en hausse** rising ▪ **hausser 1.** *vt* [prix, voix] to raise ; [épaules] to shrug **2. se hausser** *vpr* **se hausser sur la pointe des pieds** to stand on tiptoe

**haut, -e** ['o, 'ot] **1.** *adj* high ; [en taille] tall ; **haut de 5 mètres** 5 metres high *or* tall ; **à haute voix, à voix haute** aloud ; **en haute mer** out at sea ; **la mer est haute** it's high tide ; **la haute couture** designer fashion ; **un instrument de haute précision** a precision instrument ; **un renseignement de la plus haute importance** news of the utmost importance ; ORDINAT & TÉL **haut débit** broadband ; **haute trahison** high treason

**2.** *adv* [dans l'espace & MUS] high ; [dans une hiérarchie] highly ; [parler] loud, loudly ; **de haut** [avec dédain] haughtily ; **le prendre de haut** to react haughtily ; **de haut en bas** from top to bottom ; **du**

**haut** de from the top of; **tout haut** [lire, penser] out loud; **haut placé** [personne] in a high position; **plus haut** [dans un texte] above

**3.** *nm* [partie haute] top; **en haut de** at the top of; **en haut** [loger] upstairs; [regarder] up; [mettre] on (the) top; **d'en haut** [de la partie haute, du ciel] from high up, from up above; **avoir 5 mètres de haut** to be 5 metres high *or* tall; *Fig* **des hauts et des bas** ups and downs

■ **haut-parleur** *(pl* **haut-parleurs)** *nm* loudspeaker

**hautain, -e** [otɛ̃, -ɛn] *adj* haughty

**hautbois** ['obwa] *nm* oboe

**haut-de-forme** ['odfɔrm] *(pl* **hauts-de-forme)** *nm* top hat

**hautement** ['otmɑ̃] *adv* [très] highly ■ **hauteur** *nf* height; [colline] hill; *Péj* [orgueil] haughtiness; **à la hauteur de** [objet] level with; [rue] opposite; **arriver à la hauteur de qch** [mesurer] to reach (the level of) sth; **il n'est pas à la hauteur** he isn't up to it

**Haye** ['ɛ] *nf* **La Haye** The Hague

**hebdomadaire** [ɛbdɔmadɛr] *adj* & *nm* weekly

**héberger** [ebɛrʒe] *vt* to put up ■ **hébergement** *nm* putting up

**hébreu, -x** [ebrø] **1.** *adj m* Hebrew **2.** *nm* [langue] Hebrew

**hectare** [ɛktar] *nm* hectare (= 2.47 acres)

**hélas** ['elɑs] *excl* unfortunately

**héler** ['ele] *vt* [taxi] to hail

**hélice** [elis] *nf* [d'avion, de navire] propeller

**hélico** [eliko] *nm Fam* chopper

**hélicoptère** [elikɔptɛr] *nm* helicopter

**helvétique** [ɛlvetik] *adj* Swiss

**hémisphère** [emisfɛr] *nm* hemisphere

**hémophilie** [emɔfili] *nf* MÉD haemophilia

**hémorragie** [emɔraʒi] *nf* MÉD haemorrhage; *Fig* [de capitaux] drain; **faire une hémorragie** to haemorrhage; **hémorragie cérébrale** stroke

**hémorroïdes** [emɔrɔid] *nfpl* piles, haemorrhoids

**hennir** ['enir] *vi* [cheval] to neigh

**herbe** [ɛrb] *nf* grass; **mauvaise herbe** weed; CULIN **fines herbes** herbs

**herbivore** [ɛrbivɔr] *adj* herbivorous

**hérédité** [eredite] *nf* heredity ■ **héréditaire** *adj* hereditary

**hérésie** [erezi] *nf* heresy ■ **hérétique 1.** *adj* heretical **2.** *nmf* heretic

**hérisser** ['erise] **1.** *vt* [poils] to bristle up; *Fig* **hérisser qn** [irriter] to get sb's back up **2. se hérisser** *vpr* [animal, personne] to bristle; [poils, cheveux] to stand on end ■ **hérissé, -e** *adj* [cheveux] bristly; **hérissé de** bristling with

**hérisson** ['erisɔ̃] *nm* hedgehog

**hériter** [erite] **1.** *vt* to inherit (**qch de qn** sth from sb) **2.** *vi* **hériter de qch** to inherit sth ■ **héritage** *nm* [biens] inheritance; *Fig* [culturel] heritage; **faire un héritage** to come into an inheritance ■ **héritier** *nm* heir (**de** to) ■ **héritière** *nf* heiress (**de** to)

**hermétique** [ɛrmetik] *adj* hermetically sealed; *Fig* [obscur] impenetrable

**héros** ['ero] *nm* hero ■ **héroïne** *nf* [femme] heroine; [drogue] heroin ■ **héroïque** *adj* heroic ■ **héroïsme** *nm* heroism

**hésiter** [ezite] *vi* to hesitate (**sur** over *or* about; **entre** between; **à faire** to do) ■ **hésitant, -e** *adj* hesitant ■ **hésitation** *nf* hesitation; **avec hésitation** hesitatingly

**hétérogène** [eterɔʒɛn] *adj* mixed

**hétérosexuel, elle** [eterɔsɛksɥɛl] *adj* & *nmf* heterosexual

**hêtre** ['ɛtr] *nm* [arbre, bois] beech

**heure** [œr] *nf* [mesure] hour; [moment] time; **quelle heure est-il ?** what time is it?; **il est six heures** it's six (o'clock); **six heures moins cinq** five to six; **six heures cinq** *Br* five past six, *Am* five after six; **à l'heure** [arriver] on time; [être payé] by the hour; **100 km à l'heure** 100 km an hour; **de bonne heure** early; **nouvelle de dernière heure** latest *or* last-minute news; **tout**

**à l'heure** [futur] in a few moments, later ; [passé] a moment ago; **à tout à l'heure !** [au revoir] see you soon!; **à toute heure** [continuellement] at all hours ; **24 heures sur 24** 24 hours a day; **d'heure en heure** hourly, hour by hour; **faire des heures supplémentaires** to work or do overtime; **heures d'affluence, heures de pointe** [circulation] rush hour ; [dans les magasins] peak period ; **heures creuses** off-peak or slack periods; **heure d'été** Br summer time, Am daylight-saving time; **heure de grande écoute** [à la radio] prime time

**heureux, -euse** [œrø, -øz] **1.** adj happy (**de** with) ; [chanceux] lucky, fortunate ; [issue] successful **2.** adv [vivre, mourir] happily ■ **heureusement** adv [par chance] fortunately, luckily (**pour** for) ; [avec succès] successfully

**heurter** ['œrte] **1.** vt [cogner] to hit (**contre** against) ; [entrer en collision avec] to collide with; **heurter qn** [choquer] to offend sb **2. se heurter** vpr to collide (**à** ou **contre** against) ; Fig **se heurter à qch** to meet with sth

**hexagone** [egzagon] nm hexagon; Fig **l'Hexagone** France

**hiberner** [iberne] vi to hibernate

**hibou, -x** ['ibu] nm owl

**hier** [ijer] adv yesterday; **hier soir** yesterday evening

**hiérarchie** ['jerarʃi] nf hierarchy

**hi-fi** ['ifi] adj inv & nf inv hi-fi

**hilare** [ilar] adj grinning ■ **hilarant, -e** adj hilarious ■ **hilarité** nf hilarity, mirth

**hindou, -e** [ɛ̃du] adj & nmf Hindu

**hip-hop** [ipɔp] adj inv & nm inv hip-hop

**hippie** ['ipi] nmf hippie, hippy

**hippique** [ipik] adj **concours hippique** horse show

**hippodrome** [ipɔdrom] nm Br racecourse, Am racetrack

**hippopotame** [ipɔpɔtam] nm hippopotamus

**hirondelle** [irɔ̃dɛl] nf swallow

**hisser** ['ise] **1.** vt to hoist up **2. se hisser** vpr to heave oneself up

**histoire** [istwar] nf [science, événements] history ; [récit] story

**historien, -enne** [istɔrjɛ̃, -ɛn] nmf historian

**historique** [istɔrik] **1.** adj [concernant l'histoire] historical ; [important] historic **2.** nm historical account

**hiver** [iver] nm winter ■ **hivernal, -e, -aux** adj winter ; [temps] wintry

**HLM** ['aʃɛlɛm] (abr de **habitation à loyer modéré**) nm ou f Br ≃ council flats, Am ≃ low-rent apartment building

**hocher** ['ɔʃe] vt **hocher la tête** [pour dire oui] to nod ; [pour dire non] to shake one's head

**hockey** ['ɔkɛ] nm hockey; **hockey sur glace** ice hockey; **hockey sur gazon** Br hockey, Am field hockey

**hold-up** ['ɔldœp] nm inv hold-up

**Hollande** ['ɔlɑ̃d] nf **la Hollande** Holland ■ **hollandais, -e 1.** adj Dutch **2.** nmf **Hollandais** Dutchman; **Hollandaise** Dutchwoman; **les Hollandais** the Dutch **3.** nm [langue] Dutch

**homard** ['ɔmar] nm lobster

**homéopathie** [ɔmeɔpati] nf homeopathy ■ **homéopathe** adj homeopathic ■ **homéopathique** adj homeopathic

**homicide** [ɔmisid] nm homicide; **homicide involontaire** ou **par imprudence** manslaughter; **homicide volontaire** murder

**hommage** [ɔmaʒ] nm homage (**à** to) ; **rendre hommage à qn** to pay homage to sb; **faire qch en hommage à qn** to do sth as a tribute to sb or in homage to sb

**homme** [ɔm] nm man (pl men) ; **l'homme** [genre humain] man(kind) ; **des vêtements d'homme** men's clothes; **homme d'affaires** businessman; **homme politique** politician ■ **homme-grenouille** (pl **hommes-grenouilles**) nm frogman

**homogène** [ɔmɔʒɛn] adj homogeneous

**homologue** [ɔmɔlɔg] *nmf* counterpart, opposite number

**homologuer** [ɔmɔlɔge] *vt* [décision, accord, record] to ratify

**homonyme** [ɔmɔnim] *nm* [mot] homonym

**homoparental, e, aux** [ɔmɔparɑ̃tal, o] *adj* relating to gay parenting, homoparental

**homophobe** [ɔmɔfɔb] *adj* homophobic

**homosexuel, -elle** [ɔmɔsɛksɥɛl] *adj* & *nmf* homosexual

**Hongrie** ['ɔ̃gri] *nf* **la Hongrie** Hungary ■ **hongrois, -e 1.** *adj* Hungarian **2.** *nmf* **Hongrois, Hongroise** Hungarian **3.** *nm* [langue] Hungarian

**honnête** [ɔnɛt] *adj* [intègre] honest; [vie, gens] decent; [prix] fair ■ **honnêtement** *adv* [avec intégrité] honestly; [raisonnablement] decently ■ **honnêteté** *nf* [intégrité] honesty

**honneur** [ɔnœr] *nm* Br honour, Am honor; **en l'honneur de qn** in Br honour or Am honor of sb; **invité d'honneur** guest of Br honour or Am honor

**honorable** [ɔnɔrabl] *adj* honourable; Fig [résultat, salaire] respectable

**honoraires** [ɔnɔrɛr] *nmpl* fees

**honorer** [ɔnɔre] *vt* to honour (**de** with); **honorer qn** [conduite] to be a credit to sb ■ **honorifique** *adj* honorary

**honte** ['ɔ̃t] *nf* shame; **avoir honte** to be or feel ashamed (**de qch/de faire qch** of sth / to do or of doing sth); **faire honte à qn** to put sb to shame ■ **honteux, -euse** *adj* [personne] ashamed (**de** of); [conduite, acte] shameful

**hooligan, houligan** [uligan] *nm* hooligan

**hôpital, -aux** [ɔpital, -o] *nm* hospital; **à l'hôpital** Br in hospital, Am in the hospital

**hoquet** ['ɔkɛ] *nm* hiccup; **avoir le hoquet** to have the hiccups

**horaire** [ɔrɛr] **1.** *adj* [salaire] hourly; [vitesse] per hour **2.** *nm* timetable, schedule; **horaires de travail** working hours

**horizon** [ɔrizɔ̃] *nm* horizon; [vue, paysage] view; **à l'horizon** on the horizon ■ **horizontal, -e, -aux** *adj* horizontal

**horloge** [ɔrlɔʒ] *nf* clock

**hormone** [ɔrmɔn] *nf* hormone

**horoscope** [ɔrɔskɔp] *nm* horoscope

**horreur** [ɔrœr] *nf* horror; **avoir horreur de qch** to hate or loathe sth; **quelle horreur!** how horrible!

**horrible** [ɔribl] *adj* [effrayant] horrible; [laid] hideous ■ **horriblement** [-əmɑ̃] *adv* [défiguré] horribly; [cher, froid] terribly

**horrifié, -e** [ɔrifje] *adj* horrified

**hors** ['ɔr] *prép* **hors de** [maison, boîte] outside; Fig [danger, haleine] out of; **hors de prix** too or prohibitively expensive; **être hors jeu** [au football] to be offside ■ **hors-bord** *nm inv* speedboat ■ **hors-d'œuvre** *nm inv* [plat] hors-d'oeuvre, starter ■ **hors-jeu** *nm inv* [au football] offside ■ **hors-la-loi** *nm inv* outlaw ■ **hors-piste** *nm inv* SKI off-piste skiing ■ **hors-série 1.** *adj inv* special **2.** *(pl* **hors-séries)** *nm* special issue or edition ■ **hors service** *adj inv* [appareil] out of order ■ **hors taxe** *adj inv* [magasin, objet] duty-free

**horticulteur, -trice** [ɔrtikyltœr, -tris] *nmf* horticulturist ■ **horticulture** *nf* horticulture

**hospice** [ɔspis] *nm* [asile] home

**hospitalier, -ère** [ɔspitalje, -ɛr] *adj* [accueillant] hospitable; **centre hospitalier** hospital (complex); **personnel hospitalier** hospital staff ■ **hospitaliser** *vt* to hospitalize ■ **hospitalité** *nf* hospitality

**hostile** [ɔstil] *adj* hostile (**à** to or towards) ■ **hostilité** *nf* hostility (**envers** to or towards)

**hosto** [ɔsto] *nm* Fam hospital

**hôte** [ot] **1.** *nm* [qui reçoit] host **2.** *nmf* [invité] guest ■ **hôtesse** *nf* hostess; **hôtesse de l'air** air hostess

**hôtel** [otɛl] *nm* hotel; **hôtel particulier** mansion, town house; **hôtel de ville** Br town hall, Am city hall

■ **hôtelier, -ère 1.** *nmf* hotel-keeper, hotelier **2.** *adj* **industrie hôtelière** hotel industry ■ **hôtellerie** *nf* [auberge] inn; [métier] hotel trade

**hotte** ['ɔt] *nf* [panier] basket *(carried on back)*; [de cheminée] hood; **hotte aspirante** extractor hood

**houille** ['uj] *nf* coal; **houille blanche** hydroelectric power ■ **houiller, -ère** *adj* **bassin houiller** coalfield

**houleux, -euse** ['ulø, -øz] *adj* [mer] rough; *Fig* [réunion] stormy

**housse** ['us] *nf* (protective) cover

**houx** ['u] *nm* holly

**HS** *(abr de hors service)* *adj* *Fam* out of order; **je suis HS** I'm completely washed out

**huard, huart** ['ɥar] *nm* *Can* [pièce de un dollar canadien] loonie

**hublot** ['yblo] *nm* [de navire, d'avion] porthole

**huer** ['ɥe] *vt* to boo ■ **huées** *nfpl* boos

**huile** [ɥil] *nf* oil; **huile d'arachide / d'olive** groundnut / olive oil; **huile essentielle** essential oil; **huile solaire** suntan oil ■ **huiler** *vt* to oil ■ **huileux, -euse** *adj* oily

**huis** [ɥi] *nm* **à huis clos** behind closed doors; JUR in camera

**huissier, ère** [ɥisje, ɛr] *nmf* **a)** [appariteur] usher **b)** JUR bailiff

**huit** ['ɥit] (['ɥi] *before consonant*) *adj* & *nm inv* eight; **huit jours** a week ■ **huitième** *adj, nm* & *nmf* eighth; **un huitième** an eighth; SPORT **huitième de finale** last sixteen

**huître** [ɥitr] *nf* oyster

**humain, -e** [ymɛ̃, -ɛn] **1.** *adj* [relatif à l'homme] human; [compatissant] humane **2.** *nmpl* **les humains** humans ■ **humainement** *adv* [relatif à l'homme] humanly; [avec bonté] humanely ■ **humanitaire** *adj* humanitarian ■ **humanité** *nf* [genre humain, sentiment] humanity

**humble** [œ̃bl] *adj* humble

**humecter** [ymɛkte] *vt* to moisten

**humer** ['yme] *vt* [respirer] to breathe in; [sentir] to smell

**humeur** [ymœr] *nf* [disposition] mood; **être de bonne / mauvaise humeur** to be in a good / bad mood

**humide** [ymid] *adj* [linge] damp, wet; [climat, temps] humid ■ **humidifier** *vt* to humidify ■ **humidité** *nf* [de maison] dampness; [de climat] humidity

**humilier** [ymilje] *vt* to humiliate ■ **humiliant, -e** *adj* humiliating ■ **humiliation** *nf* humiliation ■ **humilité** *nf* humility

**humour** [ymur] *nm* *Br* humour, *Am* humor; **avoir le sens de l'humour** to have a sense of *Br* humour or *Am* humor ■ **humoriste** *nmf* humorist ■ **humoristique** *adj* [récit, ton] humorous

**hurler** ['yrle] **1.** *vt* [slogans, injures] to yell **2.** *vi* [loup, vent] to howl; [personne] to scream ■ **hurlement** [-əmɑ̃] *nm* [de loup, de vent] howl; [de personne] scream

**hutte** ['yt] *nf* hut

**hybride** [ibrid] *adj* & *nm* hybrid

**hydrater** [idrate] *vt* [peau] to moisturize

**hydraulique** [idrolik] *adj* hydraulic

**hydravion** [idravjɔ̃] *nm* seaplane

**hydrocarbure** [idrokarbyr] *nm* hydrocarbon

**hydrophile** [idrɔfil] *adj* **coton hydrophile** *Br* cotton wool, *Am* (absorbent) cotton

**hyène** [jɛn] *nf* hyena

**hygiène** [iʒjɛn] *nf* hygiene ■ **hygiénique** *adj* hygienic; [serviette, conditions] sanitary

**hymne** [imn] *nm* hymn; **hymne national** national anthem

**hype** [ajp] *adj inv* [quartier, créateur] trendy

**hyperactif, ive** [iperaktif, iv] *adj* hyperactive

**hypermarché** [ipermarʃe] *nm* hypermarket

**hypermétrope** [ipermetrɔp] *adj* long-sighted

**hypertension** [ipɛʀtɑ̃sjɔ̃] *nf* high blood pressure; **faire de l'hypertension** to have high blood pressure

**hypnose** [ipnoz] *nf* hypnosis ■ **hypnotiser** *vt* to hypnotize

**hypocrisie** [ipɔkʀizi] *nf* hypocrisy ■ **hypocrite 1.** *adj* hypocritical **2.** *nmf* hypocrite

**hypodermique** [ipɔdɛʀmik] *adj* hypodermic

**hypoglycémie** [ipɔglisemi] *nf Br* hypoglycaemia, *Am* hypoglycemia

**hypotension** [ipɔtɑ̃sjɔ̃] *nf* low blood pressure

**hypothèque** [ipɔtɛk] *nf* mortgage

**hypothèse** [ipɔtɛz] *nf* hypothesis; **dans l'hypothèse où…** supposing (that)…

**I, i** [i] *nm inv* I, i

**iceberg** [isbɛrg, ajsbɛrg] *nm* iceberg

**ici** [isi] *adv* here ; **par ici** [passer] this way ; [habiter] around here ; **jusqu'ici** [temps] up to now ; [lieu] as far as this *or* here ; **d'ici à mardi** by Tuesday ; **d'ici peu** before long

**icône** [ikon] *nf* REL & ORDINAT icon

**idéal, -e, -aux** *ou* **-als** [ideal, -o] **1.** *adj* ideal **2.** *nom* ideal ; **l'idéal serait de / que...** the ideal *or* best solution would be to / if... ■ **idéaliser** *vt* to idealize ■ **idéaliste 1.** *adj* idealistic **2.** *nmf* idealist

**idée** [ide] *nf* idea (**de** of ; **que** that) ; **idée fixe** obsession

**identifiant** [idɑ̃tifjɑ̃] *nm* ORDINAT user name, login name

**identifier** [idɑ̃tifje] **1.** *vt* to identify (**à** with) **2. s'identifier** *vpr* to identify (**à** with) ■ **identification** *nf* identification

**identique** [idɑ̃tik] *adj* identical (**à** to)

**identité** [idɑ̃tite] *nf* identity

**idéologie** [ideɔlɔʒi] *nf* ideology

**idiot, -e** [idjo, -ɔt] **1.** *adj* silly, idiotic **2.** *nmf* idiot

**idole** [idɔl] *nf* idol

**idyllique** [idilik] *adj* idyllic

**igloo** [iglu] *nm* igloo

**ignare** [iɲar] **1.** *adj* ignorant **2.** *nmf* ignoramus

**ignifuge** [iɲifyʒ, iɲifyʒ], **ignifugeant, e** [iɲifyʒɑ̃, ɑ̃t, iɲifyʒɑ̃, ɑ̃t] *adj* fire-retardant

**ignoble** [iɲɔbl] *adj* vile

**ignorant, -e** [iɲɔrɑ̃, -ɑ̃t] *adj* ignorant (**de** of) ■ **ignorance** *nf* ignorance

**ignorer** [iɲɔre] *vt* not to know ; **j'ignore si...** I don't know if... ; **je n'ignore pas les difficultés** I am not unaware of the difficulties ; **ignorer qn** [mépriser] to ignore sb ■ **ignoré, -e** *adj* [inconnu] unknown

**il** [il] *pron pers* [personne] he ; [chose, animal, impersonnel] it ; **il est** he / it is ; **il pleut** it's raining ; **il est vrai que...** it's true that... ; **il y a...** there is / are... ; **il y a six ans** six years ago ; **il y a une heure qu'il travaille** he has been working for an hour ; **qu'est-ce qu'il y a ?** what's the matter?, what's wrong? ; **il n'y a pas de quoi !** don't mention it!

**île** [il] *nf* island ; **les îles Anglo-Normandes** the Channel Islands ; **les îles Britanniques** the British Isles

**illégal, -e, -aux** [il(l)egal, -o] *adj* illegal ■ **illégalement** *adv* illegally

**illégitime** [il(l)eʒitim] *adj* [enfant, revendication] illegitimate ; [demande] unwarranted

**illettré, -e** [il(l)etre] *adj* & *nmf* illiterate ■ **illettrisme** *nm* illiteracy

**illicite** [il(l)isit] *adj* unlawful, illicit

**illimité, -e** [il(l)imite] *adj* unlimited

**illisible** [il(l)izibl] *adj* [écriture] illegible ; [livre & ORDINAT] unreadable

**illogique** [il(l)ɔʒik] *adj* illogical

**illuminer** [il(l)ymine] **1.** *vt* to light up, to illuminate **2. s'illuminer** *vpr* [visage, ciel] to light up ■ **illumination** *nf* [action, lumière] illumination ■ **illuminé, -e** *adj* [monument] floodlit

**illusion** [il(l)yzjɔ̃] *nf* illusion (**sur** about) ; **se faire des illusions** to delude oneself (**sur** about) ; **illusion d'optique** optical illusion ■ **illusionniste** *nmf* conjurer ■ **illusoire** *adj* illusory

**illustre** [il(l)ystr] *adj* illustrious

**illustrer** [il(l)ystre] **1.** *vt* [livre, récit] to illustrate (**de** with) **2. s'illustrer** *vpr* to distinguish oneself (**par** by) ■ **illustration** nf illustration ■ **illustré, -e** adj [livre, magazine] illustrated

**îlot** [ilo] nm [île] small island ; [maisons] block

**ils** [il] pron pers m pl they ; **ils sont ici** they are here

**image** [imaʒ] nf picture ; [ressemblance, symbole] image ; [dans une glace] reflection ; ORDINAT **image de synthèse** computer-generated image ■ **imagé, -e** adj [style] Br colourful, Am colorful, full of imagery

**imaginable** [imaʒinabl] adj imaginable ■ **imaginaire** adj imaginary ■ **imaginatif, -ive** adj imaginative

**imagination** [imaʒinɑsjɔ̃] nf imagination

**imaginer** [imaʒine] **1.** vt [se figurer] to imagine ; [inventer] to devise **2. s'imaginer** vpr [se figurer] to imagine (**que** that) ; [se voir] to picture oneself

**imbattable** [ɛ̃batabl] adj unbeatable

**imbécile** [ɛ̃besil] **1.** adj idiotic **2.** nmf idiot, imbecile ■ **imbécillité** nf [état] imbecility ; **une imbécillité** [action, parole] an idiotic thing

**imberbe** [ɛ̃bɛrb] adj beardless

**imbiber** [ɛ̃bibe] vt to soak (**de** with or in)

**imbriquer** [ɛ̃brike] ■ **s'imbriquer** vpr [s'emboîter] to overlap

**imbu, -e** [ɛ̃by] adj **imbu de soi-même** full of oneself

**imbuvable** [ɛ̃byvabl] adj undrinkable

**imiter** [imite] vt to imitate ; [signature] to forge ; **imiter qn** [pour rire] to mimic sb ; [faire comme] to do the same as sb ; [imitateur professionnel] to impersonate sb ■ **imitateur, -trice** nmf imitator ; [professionnel] impersonator ■ **imitation** nf imitation

**immaculé, -e** [imakyle] adj [sans tache, sans péché] immaculate

**immangeable** [ɛ̃mɑ̃ʒabl] adj inedible

**immanquable** [ɛ̃mɑ̃kabl] adj inevitable

**immatriculer** [imatrikyle] vt to register ; **se faire immatriculer** to register ■ **immatriculation** nf registration

**immédiat, -e** [imedja, -jat] **1.** adj immediate **2.** nm **dans l'immédiat** for the time being ■ **immédiatement** adv immediately

**immense** [imɑ̃s] adj immense ■ **immensément** adv immensely ■ **immensité** nf immensity

**immerger** [imɛrʒe] vt to immerse ■ **immersion** nf immersion (**dans** in)

**immeuble** [imœbl] nm building ; [appartements] Br block of flats, Am apartment block

**immigrant, -e** [imigrɑ̃, -ɑ̃t] nmf immigrant ■ **immigration** nf immigration ■ **immigré, -e** adj & nmf immigrant ; **travailleur immigré** immigrant worker

**imminent, -e** [iminɑ̃, -ɑ̃t] adj imminent

**immiscer** [imise] ■ **s'immiscer** vpr to interfere (**dans** in)

**immobile** [imɔbil] adj still, motionless

**immobilier, -ère** [imɔbilje, -ɛr] **1.** adj **marché immobilier** property market **2.** nm **l'immobilier** Br property, Am real estate

**immobiliser** [imɔbilize] **1.** vt [blessé] to immobilize ; [train] to bring to a stop ; [voiture - avec un sabot] to clamp **2. s'immobiliser** vpr to come to a stop

**immonde** [i(m)mɔ̃d] adj [sale] foul ; [ignoble, laid] vile

**immoral, -e, -aux** [i(m)mɔral, -o] adj immoral ■ **immoralité** nf immorality

**immortel, -elle** [i(m)mɔrtɛl] adj immortal ■ **immortaliser** vt to immortalize ■ **immortalité** nf immortality

**immuable** [i(m)mɥabl] adj immutable, unchanging

**immuniser** [i(m)mynize] vt to immunize (**contre** against) ■ **immunitaire** adj MÉD [déficience, système] immune ■ **immunité** nf immunity

**impact** [ɛ̃pakt] *nm* impact (**sur** on)

**impair, -e** [ɛ̃pɛr] **1.** *adj* [nombre] odd, uneven **2.** *nm* [maladresse] blunder

**imparable** [ɛ̃parabl] *adj* [coup] unavoidable

**impardonnable** [ɛ̃pardɔnabl] *adj* unforgivable

**imparfait, -e** [ɛ̃parfɛ, -ɛt] *adj* [connaissance] imperfect

**impartial, -e, -aux** [ɛ̃parsjal, -o] *adj* impartial, unbiased ▪ **impartialité** *nf* impartiality

**impartir** [ɛ̃partir] *vt* **dans le temps qui nous est imparti** within the allotted time

**impasse** [ɛ̃pɑs] *nf* [rue] dead end; *Fig* [situation] impasse; **être dans une impasse** to be deadlocked

**impassible** [ɛ̃pasibl] *adj* impassive

**impatient, -e** [ɛ̃pasjɑ̃, -ɑ̃t] *adj* impatient; **impatient de faire qch** impatient to do sth ▪ **impatience** *nf* impatience ▪ **impatienter 1.** *vt* to annoy **2. s'impatienter** *vpr* to get impatient

**impayé, -e** [ɛ̃peje] *adj* unpaid

**impec** [ɛ̃pɛk] *adj Fam* perfect

**impeccable** [ɛ̃pekabl] *adj* impeccable

**impénétrable** [ɛ̃penetrabl] *adj* [forêt, mystère] impenetrable

**impensable** [ɛ̃pɑ̃sabl] *adj* unthinkable

**impératif, -ive** [ɛ̃peratif, -iv] *adj* [consigne, besoin] imperative; [ton] imperious

**impératrice** [ɛ̃peratris] *nf* empress

**imperceptible** [ɛ̃pɛrsɛptibl] *adj* imperceptible (**à** to)

**imperfection** [ɛ̃pɛrfɛksjɔ̃] *nf* imperfection

**impérial, -e, -aux** [ɛ̃perjal, -o] *adj* imperial ▪ **impérialisme** *nm* imperialism

**impérieux, -euse** [ɛ̃perjø, -øz] *adj* [autoritaire] imperious; [besoin] pressing

**impérissable** [ɛ̃perisabl] *adj* [souvenir] enduring

**imperméable** [ɛ̃pɛrmeabl] **1.** *adj* impervious (**à** to); [tissu, manteau] waterproof **2.** *nm* raincoat

**impersonnel, -elle** [ɛ̃pɛrsɔnɛl] *adj* impersonal

**impertinent, -e** [ɛ̃pɛrtinɑ̃, -ɑ̃t] *adj* impertinent (**envers** to) ▪ **impertinence** *nf* impertinence

**imperturbable** [ɛ̃pɛrtyrbabl] *adj* [personne] imperturbable

**impitoyable** [ɛ̃pitwajabl] *adj* merciless

**implacable** [ɛ̃plakabl] *adj* [personne, vengeance] implacable; [avancée] relentless

**implanter** [ɛ̃plɑ̃te] **1.** *vt* [installer] to establish; [chirurgicalement] to implant **2. s'implanter** *vpr* to become established ▪ **implant** *nm* MÉD implant; **implant capillaire** hair graft ▪ **implantation** *nf* establishment

**implicite** [ɛ̃plisit] *adj* implicit

**impliquer** [ɛ̃plike] **1.** *vt* [entraîner] to imply; **être impliqué dans qch** to be involved in sth; **impliquer que...** to imply that...; **impliquer qn** to implicate sb (**dans** in) **2. s'impliquer** *vpr Fam* **s'impliquer dans** to become involved in ▪ **implication** *nf* [conséquence] implication; [participation] involvement

**implorer** [ɛ̃plɔre] *vt* to implore (**qn de faire** sb to do)

**impoli, -e** [ɛ̃pɔli] *adj* rude, impolite

**impolitesse** [ɛ̃pɔlitɛs] *nf* impoliteness, rudeness

**impopulaire** [ɛ̃pɔpylɛr] *adj* unpopular

**import** [ɛ̃pɔr] *nm* import

**important, -e** [ɛ̃pɔrtɑ̃, -ɑ̃t] **1.** *adj* [personnage, événement] important; [quantité, somme, ville] large; [dégâts, retard] considerable **2.** *nm* **l'important, c'est de...** the important thing is to... ▪ **importance** *nf* importance; [taille] size; [de dégâts] extent; **ça n'a pas d'importance** it doesn't matter

**importer¹** [ɛ̃pɔrte] **1.** *vi* to matter (**à** to) **2.** *v impers* **il importe de faire qch** it's important to do sth; **il importe que vous y soyez** it is important that you're there; **peu importe, n'importe** it doesn't matter; **n'importe qui/quoi/ où/quand/comment** anyone /anything /anywhere /any time /anyhow

**importer²** [ɛ̃pɔʀte] *vt* [marchandises] to import (**de** from) ▪ **importateur, -trice 1.** *adj* importing **2.** *nmf* importer ▪ **importation** *nf* [objet] import; [action] importing, importation

**importun, -e** [ɛ̃pɔʀtœ̃, -yn] **1.** *adj* [personne, question] importunate **2.** *nmf* nuisance

**imposer** [ɛ̃poze] **1.** *vt* [condition] to impose; [taxer] to tax; **imposer qch à qn** to impose sth on sb **2.** *vi* **en imposer à qn** to impress sb **3. s'imposer** *vpr* [faire reconnaître sa valeur] to assert oneself; [gagner] to win; [être nécessaire] to be essential; *Péj* [chez quelqu'un] to impose; **s'imposer de faire qch** to make it a rule to do sth ▪ **imposant, -e** *adj* imposing

**impossible** [ɛ̃pɔsibl] **1.** *adj* impossible (**à faire** to do); **il est impossible que...** (+ *subjunctive*) it is impossible that... **2.** *nm* **tenter l'impossible** to attempt the impossible ▪ **impossibilité** *nf* impossibility

**imposteur** [ɛ̃pɔstœʀ] *nm* impostor ▪ **imposture** *nf* deception

**impôt** [ɛ̃po] *nm* tax; **(service des) impôts** tax authorities; **impôts locaux** local taxes; **impôt sur le revenu** income tax

**impraticable** [ɛ̃pʀatikabl] *adj* [chemin] impassable; [projet] impracticable

**imprécis, -e** [ɛ̃pʀesi, -iz] *adj* imprecise ▪ **imprécision** *nf* imprecision

**imprégner** [ɛ̃pʀeɲe] **1.** *vt* to impregnate (**de** with); *Fig* **être imprégné de qch** to be full of sth **2. s'imprégner** *vpr* to become impregnated (**de** with)

**imprenable** [ɛ̃pʀənabl] *adj* [forteresse] impregnable; [vue] unobstructed

**impression** [ɛ̃pʀesjɔ̃] *nf* **a)** [sensation] impression; **avoir l'impression que...** to have the impression that...; **faire bonne impression à qn** to make a good impression on sb **b)** [de livre] printing

**impressionner** [ɛ̃pʀesjɔne] *vt* [bouleverser] to upset; [frapper] to impress ▪ **impressionnable** *adj* easily upset ▪ **impressionnant, -e** *adj* impressive

**imprévisible** [ɛ̃pʀevizibl] *adj* [temps, réaction, personne] unpredictable; [événement] unforeseeable ▪ **imprévu, -e 1.** *adj* unexpected, unforeseen **2.** *nm* **en cas d'imprévu** in case of anything unexpected

**imprimer** [ɛ̃pʀime] *vt* [livre, tissu] to print; ORDINAT to print (out) ▪ **imprimante** *nf* printer ▪ **imprimé** *nm* [formulaire] printed form ▪ **imprimerie** *nf* [technique] printing; [lieu] *Br* printing works, *Am* print shop ▪ **imprimeur** *nm* printer

**improbable** [ɛ̃pʀɔbabl] *adj* improbable, unlikely

**impropre** [ɛ̃pʀɔpʀ] *adj* inappropriate; **impropre à qch** unfit for sth; **impropre à la consommation** unfit for human consumption

**improviser** [ɛ̃pʀɔvize] *vt* & *vi* to improvise ▪ **improvisation** *nf* improvisation

**improviste** [ɛ̃pʀɔvist] ▪ **à l'improviste** *adv* unexpectedly

**imprudent, -e** [ɛ̃pʀydɑ̃, -ɑ̃t] *adj* [personne, action] rash; **il est imprudent de...** it is unwise to... ▪ **imprudemment** [-amɑ̃] *adv* rashly ▪ **imprudence** *nf* rashness

**impudique** [ɛ̃pydik] *adj* shameless

**impuissant, -e** [ɛ̃pɥisɑ̃, -ɑ̃t] *adj* powerless; MÉD impotent

**impulsif, -ive** [ɛ̃pylsif, -iv] *adj* impulsive ▪ **impulsion** *nf* impulse

**impunément** [ɛ̃pynemɑ̃] *adv* with impunity ▪ **impuni, -e** *adj* unpunished

**impur, -e** [ɛ̃pyʀ] *adj* impure ▪ **impureté** *nf* impurity

**imputer** [ɛ̃pyte] *vt* to attribute (**à** to); [frais] to charge (**à** to)

**inabordable** [inabɔʀdabl] *adj* [prix] prohibitive; [lieu] inaccessible; [personne] unapproachable

**inacceptable** [inakseptabl] adj unacceptable

**inaccessible** [inaksesibl] adj [lieu] inaccessible ; [personne] unapproachable

**inachevé, -e** [inaʃve] adj unfinished

**inactif, -ive** [inaktif, -iv] adj [personne] inactive ; [remède] ineffective ■ **inaction** nf inaction ■ **inactivité** nf inactivity

**inadapté, -e** [inadapte] **1.** adj [socialement] maladjusted ; [physiquement, mentalement] handicapped ; [matériel] unsuitable (**à** for) **2.** nmf [socialement] maladjusted person

**inadmissible** [inadmisibl] adj inadmissible

**inadvertance** [inadvɛrtɑ̃s] ■ **par inadvertance** adv inadvertently

**inamical, -e, -aux** [inamikal, -o] adj unfriendly

**inanimé, -e** [inanime] adj [mort] lifeless ; [évanoui] unconscious ; [matière] inanimate

**inaperçu, -e** [inapɛrsy] adj **passer inaperçu** to go unnoticed

**inappréciable** [inapresjabl] adj invaluable

**inapte** [inapt] adj [intellectuellement] unsuited (**à** for) ; [médicalement] unfit (**à** for) ■ **inaptitude** nf [intellectuelle] inaptitude ; [médicale] unfitness (**à** for)

**inattendu, -e** [inatɑ̃dy] adj unexpected

**inattention** [inatɑ̃sjɔ̃] nf lack of attention

**inaudible** [inodibl] adj inaudible

**inaugurer** [inogyre] vt [édifice] to inaugurate ■ **inaugural, -e, -aux** adj inaugural

**inavouable** [inavwabl] adj shameful

**incalculable** [ɛ̃kalkylabl] adj incalculable

**incapable** [ɛ̃kapabl] adj incapable ; **incapable de faire qch** incapable of doing sth ■ **incapacité** nf [impossibilité] inability (**de faire** to do) ; [invalidité] disability ; **être dans l'incapacité de faire qch** to be unable to do sth

**incarcérer** [ɛ̃karsere] vt to incarcerate ■ **incarcération** nf incarceration

**incarnation** [ɛ̃karnɑsjɔ̃] nf incarnation

**incarné, -e** [ɛ̃karne] adj [ongle] ingrown

**incarner** [ɛ̃karne] vt to embody

**incassable** [ɛ̃kasabl] adj unbreakable

**incendie** [ɛ̃sɑ̃di] nm fire ; **incendie criminel** arson ; **incendie de forêt** forest fire ■ **incendiaire 1.** adj [bombe] incendiary **2.** nmf arsonist ■ **incendier** vt to set on fire

**incertain, -e** [ɛ̃sɛrtɛ̃, -ɛn] adj [résultat] uncertain ; [temps] unsettled ; [personne] indecisive ■ **incertitude** nf uncertainty

**incessamment** [ɛ̃sesamɑ̃] adv very soon

**incessant, -e** [ɛ̃sesɑ̃, -ɑ̃t] adj incessant

**inchangé, -e** [ɛ̃ʃɑ̃ʒe] adj unchanged

**incidence** [ɛ̃sidɑ̃s] nf [influence] impact (**sur** on) ; MÉD incidence

**incident** [ɛ̃sidɑ̃] nm incident ; [accroc] hitch ; **incident de parcours** minor setback

**incinérer** [ɛ̃sinere] vt [ordures] to incinerate ; [cadavre] to cremate ■ **incinération** nf [d'ordures] incineration ; [de cadavre] cremation

**inciser** [ɛ̃size] vt [peau] to make an incision in ; [abcès] to lance ■ **incision** nf [entaille] incision

**incisif, -ive¹** [ɛ̃sizif, -iv] adj incisive

**incisive²** [ɛ̃siziv] nf [dent] incisor (tooth)

**inciter** [ɛ̃site] vt to encourage (**à faire** to do) ■ **incitation** nf incitement (**à** to)

**incivilité** [ɛ̃sivilite] nf **a)** [manque de courtoisie] rudeness, disrespect **b)** [fraude] petty crime ; [insultes, vandalismes] antisocial Br behaviour or Am behavior

**incliner** [ɛ̃kline] **1.** vt [pencher] to tilt ; **incliner la tête** [approuver] to nod ; [saluer] to bow one's head **2. s'incliner** vpr [se pencher] to lean forward ; [pour saluer] to bow ; Fig [se soumettre] to give in (**devant to**) ■ **inclinaison** nf incline, slope ■ **inclination** nf [tendance] inclination

**inclure** [ɛ̃klyr] vt to include ; [dans un courrier] to enclose (**dans** with) ■ **inclus, -e** adj **du 4 au 10 inclus** from the 4th to the 10th inclusive ; **jusqu'à lundi inclus** Br up to and including Monday, Am through Monday ■ **inclusion** nf inclusion

**incognito** [ɛ̃kɔɲito] adv incognito

**incohérent, -e** [ɛ̃kɔerɑ̃, -ɑ̃t] adj [propos] incoherent ; [histoire] inconsistent ■ **incohérence** nf [de propos] incoherence ; [d'histoire] inconsistency

**incolore** [ɛ̃kɔlɔr] adj colourless ; [vernis, verre] clear

**incomber** [ɛ̃kɔ̃be] vi incomber à qn [devoir] to fall to sb ; **il lui incombe de faire qch** it falls to him / her to do sth

**incommoder** [ɛ̃kɔmɔde] vt to bother

**incomparable** [ɛ̃kɔ̃parabl] adj matchless

**incompatible** [ɛ̃kɔ̃patibl] adj incompatible (**avec** with)

**incompétent, -e** [ɛ̃kɔ̃petɑ̃, -ɑ̃t] adj incompetent ■ **incompétence** nf incompetence

**incomplet, -ète** [ɛ̃kɔ̃plɛ, -ɛt] adj incomplete

**incompréhensible** [ɛ̃kɔ̃preɑ̃sibl] adj incomprehensible ■ **incompréhension** nf incomprehension

**incompris, -e** [ɛ̃kɔ̃pri, -iz] **1.** adj misunderstood **2.** nmf **être un incompris** to be misunderstood

**inconcevable** [ɛ̃kɔ̃səvabl] adj inconceivable

**inconciliable** [ɛ̃kɔ̃siljabl] adj [théorie] irreconcilable ; [activité] incompatible

**inconditionnel, -elle** [ɛ̃kɔ̃disjɔnɛl] adj unconditional ; [supporter] staunch

**inconfortable** [ɛ̃kɔ̃fɔrtabl] adj uncomfortable

**inconnu, -e** [ɛ̃kɔny] **1.** adj unknown (**de** to) **2.** nmf [étranger] stranger ; [auteur] unknown **3.** nm **l'inconnu** the unknown **4.** nf MATH **inconnue** unknown (quantity)

**inconscient, -e** [ɛ̃kɔ̃sjɑ̃, -ɑ̃t] **1.** adj [sans connaissance] unconscious ; [imprudent] reckless ; **inconscient de qch** unaware of sth **2.** nm **l'inconscient** the unconscious ■ **inconsciemment** [-amɑ̃] adv [dans l'inconscient] subconsciously ■ **inconscience** nf [perte de connaissance] unconsciousness ; [irréflexion] recklessness

**inconséquence** [ɛ̃kɔ̃sekɑ̃s] nf [manque de prudence] recklessness ; [manque de cohérence] inconsistency

**inconsidéré, -e** [ɛ̃kɔ̃sidere] adj thoughtless

**inconsistant, -e** [ɛ̃kɔ̃sistɑ̃, -ɑ̃t] adj [personne] weak ; [film, roman] flimsy ; [sauce, crème] thin

**inconsolable** [ɛ̃kɔ̃sɔlabl] adj inconsolable

**inconstant, -e** [ɛ̃kɔ̃stɑ̃, -ɑ̃t] adj fickle

**incontestable** [ɛ̃kɔ̃tɛstabl] adj indisputable ■ **incontesté, -e** adj undisputed

**incontournable** [ɛ̃kɔ̃turnabl] adj Fig [film] unmissable ; [auteur] who cannot be ignored

**incontrôlable** adj [invérifiable] unverifiable ; [indomptable] uncontrollable

**incontrôlé, e** [ɛ̃kɔ̃trole] adj [bande, groupe] unrestrained, out of control

**inconvenant, -e** [ɛ̃kɔ̃vnɑ̃, -ɑ̃t] adj improper

**inconvénient** [ɛ̃kɔ̃venjɑ̃] nm [désavantage] drawback ; **l'inconvénient, c'est que...** the annoying thing is that...

**incorporer** [ɛ̃kɔrpɔre] vt [insérer] to insert (**à** in) ; [troupes] to draft ; **incorporer qch à qch** to blend sth into sth ■ **incorporation** nf [mélange] blending (**de qch dans qch** of sth into sth) ; MIL conscription

**incorrect, -e** [ɛ̃kɔrɛkt] adj [inexact] incorrect ; [grossier] impolite ; [inconvenant] improper ■ **incorrection** nf [impolitesse] impoliteness ; [propos] impolite remark ; [faute de grammaire] mistake

**incorrigible** [ɛ̃kɔriʒibl] *adj* incorrigible

**incorruptible** [ɛ̃kɔryptibl] *adj* incorruptible

**incrédule** [ɛ̃kredyl] *adj* incredulous ■ **incrédulité** *nf* incredulity

**incriminer** [ɛ̃krimine] *vt* [personne] to accuse

**incroyable** [ɛ̃krwajabl] *adj* incredible

**incrusté, -e** [ɛ̃kryste] *adj* **incrusté de** [orné] inlaid with

**incubation** [ɛ̃kybɑsjɔ̃] *nf* incubation

**inculper** [ɛ̃kylpe] *vt* [accuser] to charge (**de** with) ■ **inculpation** *nf* charge, indictment ■ **inculpé, -e** *nmf* **l'inculpé** the accused

**inculquer** [ɛ̃kylke] *vt* to instil (**à qn** in sb)

**inculte** [ɛ̃kylt] *adj* [terre, personne] uncultivated

**incurable** [ɛ̃kyrabl] *adj* incurable

**incursion** [ɛ̃kyrsjɔ̃] *nf* [invasion] incursion ; *Fig* [entrée soudaine] intrusion

**Inde** [ɛ̃d] *nf* **l'Inde** India

**indécent, -e** [ɛ̃desɑ̃, -ɑ̃t] *adj* indecent ■ **indécence** *nf* indecency

**indéchiffrable** [ɛ̃deʃifrabl] *adj* [illisible] undecipherable

**indécis, -e** [ɛ̃desi, -iz] *adj* [personne - de caractère] indecisive ; [ponctuellement] undecided ■ **indécision** *nf* [de caractère] indecisiveness ; [ponctuelle] indecision

**indéfendable** [ɛ̃defɑ̃dabl] *adj* indefensible

**indéfini, -e** [ɛ̃defini] *adj* [illimité] indefinite ; [imprécis] undefined ■ **indéfiniment** *adv* indefinitely ■ **indéfinissable** *adj* indefinable

**indélébile** [ɛ̃delebil] *adj* indelible

**indélicat, -e** [ɛ̃delika, -at] *adj* [grossier] insensitive ; [malhonnête] unscrupulous

**indemne** [ɛ̃dɛmn] *adj* unhurt, unscathed

**indemniser** [ɛ̃dɛmnize] *vt* to compensate (**de** for) ■ **indemnisation** *nf* compensation

■ **indemnité** *nf* [dédommagement] compensation ; [allocation] allowance ; **indemnité de chômage** unemployment benefit ; **indemnité de licenciement** redundancy payment

**indéniable** [ɛ̃denjabl] *adj* undeniable

**indépendant, -e** [ɛ̃depɑ̃dɑ̃, -ɑ̃t] *adj* independent (**de** of) ; [chambre] self-contained ; [travailleur] self-employed ■ **indépendamment** [-amɑ̃] *adv* independently ; **indépendamment de** apart from ■ **indépendance** *nf* independence

**indescriptible** [ɛ̃dɛskriptibl] *adj* indescribable

**indésirable** [ɛ̃dezirabl] *adj* & *nmf* undesirable

**indestructible** [ɛ̃dɛstryktibl] *adj* indestructible

**indéterminé, -e** [ɛ̃detɛrmine] *adj* [date, heure] unspecified ; [raison] unknown

**index** [ɛ̃dɛks] *nm* [doigt] forefinger, index finger ; [liste & ORDINAT] index

**indicateur, -trice** [ɛ̃dikatœr, -tris] **1.** *nm* TECH indicator, gauge ; ÉCON indicator ; [espion] informer **2.** *adj* **panneau indicateur** road sign

**indicatif, -ive** [ɛ̃dikatif, -iv] **1.** *adj* indicative (**de** of) **2.** *nm* RADIO theme tune ; **indicatif téléphonique** *Br* dialling code, *Am* area code

**indication** [ɛ̃dikɑsjɔ̃] *nf* indication (**de** of) ; [renseignement] (piece of) information ; [directive] instruction ; **indications...** [de médicament] suitable for...

**indice** [ɛ̃dis] *nm* [signe] sign ; [d'enquête] clue

**indien, -enne** [ɛ̃djɛ̃, -ɛn] **1.** *adj* Indian **2.** *nmf* **Indien, Indienne** Indian

**indifférent, -e** [ɛ̃diferɑ̃, -ɑ̃t] *adj* indifferent (**à** to) ■ **indifférence** *nf* indifference (**à** to)

**indigène** [ɛ̃diʒɛn] *adj* & *nmf* native

**indigent, -e** [ɛ̃diʒɑ̃, -ɑ̃t] *adj* destitute ■ **indigence** *nf* destitution

**indigeste** [ɛ̃diʒɛst] *adj* indigestible ■ **indigestion** *nf* avoir une indigestion to have a stomach upset

**indignation** [ɛ̃diɲasjɔ̃] *nf* indignation

**indigne** [ɛ̃diɲ] *adj* [personne] unworthy ; [conduite] shameful ; **indigne de qn/qch** unworthy of sb/sth ■ **indignité** *nf* [de personne] unworthiness ; [de conduite] shamefulness ; [action] shameful act

**indigner** [ɛ̃diɲe] **1.** *vt* indigner qn to make sb indignant **2. s'indigner** *vpr* to be indignant (**de** at) ■ **indigné, -e** *adj* indignant

**indiquer** [ɛ̃dike] *vt* [sujet : personne] to point out ; [sujet : panneau] to show, to indicate ; [sujet : compteur] to read ; [donner - date, adresse] to give ; **indiquer le chemin à qn** to tell sb the way ■ **indiqué, -e** *adj* [conseillé] advisable ; **à l'heure indiquée** at the appointed time

**indirect, -e** [ɛ̃dirɛkt] *adj* indirect

**indiscipline** [ɛ̃disiplin] *nf* indiscipline ■ **indiscipliné, -e** *adj* unruly

**indiscret, -ète** [ɛ̃diskrɛ, -ɛt] *adj* Péj [curieux] inquisitive ; [qui parle trop] indiscreet ■ **indiscrétion** *nf* indiscretion

**indiscutable** [ɛ̃diskytabl] *adj* indisputable

**indispensable** [ɛ̃dispɑ̃sabl] *adj* essential, indispensable (**à qch** for sth) ; **indispensable à qn** indispensable to sb

**indisponible** [ɛ̃dispɔnibl] *adj* unavailable

**indisposer** [ɛ̃dispoze] *vt* [contrarier] to annoy ; **indisposer qn** [odeur, climat] to make sb feel ill ■ **indisposé, -e** *adj* [malade] indisposed, unwell ■ **indisposition** *nf* indisposition

**indistinct, -e** [ɛ̃distɛ̃(kt), -ɛ̃kt] *adj* indistinct ■ **indistinctement** [-ɛ̃ktəmɑ̃] *adv* [voir, parler] indistinctly ; [également] equally

**individu** [ɛ̃dividy] *nm* individual ; Péj individual, character

**individualiste** [ɛ̃dividɥalist] **1.** *adj* individualistic **2.** *nmf* individualist

**individualité** [ɛ̃dividɥalite] *nf* individuality

**individuel, -elle** [ɛ̃dividɥɛl] *adj* individual ; [maison] detached

**indivisible** [ɛ̃divizibl] *adj* indivisible

**Indochine** [ɛ̃dɔʃin] *nf* l'Indochine Indo-China

**indolent, -e** [ɛ̃dɔlɑ̃, -ɑ̃t] *adj* lazy

**indolore** [ɛ̃dɔlɔr] *adj* painless

**indomptable** [ɛ̃dɔ̃(p)tabl] *adj* [animal] untamable

**Indonésie** [ɛ̃dɔnezi] *nf* l'Indonésie Indonesia

**indue** [ɛ̃dy] *adj f* rentrer à des heures indues to come home at all hours of the night

**induire** [ɛ̃dɥir] *vt* induire qn en erreur to lead sb astray

**indulgent, -e** [ɛ̃dylʒɑ̃, -ɑ̃t] *adj* indulgent ■ **indulgence** *nf* indulgence

**industrie** [ɛ̃dystri] *nf* industry ■ **industrialisé, -e** *adj* industrialized ■ **industriel, -elle 1.** *adj* industrial **2.** *nm* industrialist

**inébranlable** [inebrɑ̃labl] *adj* Fig [certitude, personne] unshakeable

**inédit, -e** [inedi, -it] *adj* [texte] unpublished

**inefficace** [inefikas] *adj* [mesure] ineffective ; [personne] inefficient ■ **inefficacité** *nf* [de mesure] ineffectiveness ; [de personne] inefficiency

**inégal, -e, -aux** [inegal, -o] *adj* [parts, lutte] unequal ; [sol, humeur] uneven ; Fig [travail] inconsistent ■ **inégalable** *adj* incomparable ■ **inégalé, -e** *adj* unequalled ■ **inégalité** *nf* [injustice] inequality ; [physique] disparity (**de** in) ; [de sol] unevenness

**inéluctable** [inelyktabl] *adj* inescapable

**inepte** [inɛpt] *adj* [remarque, histoire] inane ; [personne] inept ■ **ineptie** [inɛpsi] *nf* [de comportement, de film] inanity ; [remarque] stupid remark

**inépuisable** [inepɥizabl] *adj* inexhaustible

**inespéré, -e** [inɛspere] *adj* unhoped-for

**inestimable** [inɛstimabl] *adj* [objet d'art] priceless

**inévitable** [inevitabl] *adj* inevitable, unavoidable

**inexact, -e** [inɛgzakt] *adj* [erroné] inaccurate; [calcul] wrong ■ **inexactitude** *nf* [caractère erroné, erreur] inaccuracy; [manque de ponctualité] unpunctuality

**inexcusable** [inɛkskyzabl] *adj* inexcusable

**inexistant, -e** [inɛgzistɑ̃, -ɑ̃t] *adj* non-existent

**inexpérience** [inɛksperjɑ̃s] *nf* inexperience ■ **inexpérimenté, -e** *adj* inexperienced

**inexplicable** [inɛksplikabl] *adj* inexplicable ■ **inexpliqué, -e** *adj* unexplained

**inexploré, -e** [inɛksplɔre] *adj* unexplored

**inexprimable** [inɛksprimabl] *adj* inexpressible

**inextricable** [inɛkstrikabl] *adj* inextricable

**infaillible** [ɛ̃fajibl] *adj* infallible

**infaisable** [ɛ̃fəzabl] *adj* [travail] impossible

**infâme** [ɛ̃fɑm] *adj* [personne] despicable; [acte] unspeakable; [taudis] squalid; [aliment] revolting

**infantile** [ɛ̃fɑ̃til] *adj* [maladie] childhood; *Péj* [comportement, personne] infantile

**infarctus** [ɛ̃farktys] *nm* MÉD heart attack

**infatigable** [ɛ̃fatigabl] *adj* tireless

**infect, -e** [ɛ̃fɛkt] *adj* foul

**infecter** [ɛ̃fɛkte] **1.** *vt* [atmosphère] to contaminate; MÉD to infect **2. s'infecter** *vpr* to become infected ■ **infection** *nf* MÉD infection; [odeur] stench

**inférieur, -e** [ɛ̃ferjœr] **1.** *adj* [étagère, niveau] bottom; [étage, lèvre, membre] lower; [qualité, marchandises] inferior; **inférieur à la moyenne** below average; **à l'étage inférieur** on the floor below **2.** *nmf* inferior ■ **infériorité** *nf* inferiority

**infernal, -e, -aux** [ɛ̃fɛrnal, -o] *adj* [de l'enfer] & *Fig* [chaleur, bruit] infernal

**infichu, e** [ɛ̃fiʃy] *adj Fam* incapable; **il est infichu de répondre à la moindre question** he's incapable of answering the simplest question

**infidèle** [ɛ̃fidɛl] *adj* unfaithful (**à** to) ■ **infidélité** *nf* unfaithfulness, infidelity

**infiltrer** [ɛ̃filtre] **1.** *vt* [party] to infiltrate **2. s'infiltrer** *vpr* [liquide] to seep (**dans** into); [lumière] to filter in; *Fig* **s'infiltrer dans** [groupe, esprit] to infiltrate ■ **infiltration** *nf* [de liquide, d'espions] infiltration

**infime** [ɛ̃fim] *adj* tiny

**infini, -e** [ɛ̃fini] **1.** *adj* infinite **2.** *nm* MATH & PHOTO infinity; PHIL infinite; **à l'infini** [discuter] ad infinitum; MATH to infinity ■ **infiniment** *adv* infinitely; **je regrette infiniment** I'm very sorry ■ **infinité** *nf* **une infinité de** an infinite number of

**infirme** [ɛ̃firm] **1.** *adj* disabled **2.** *nmf* disabled person ■ **infirmité** *nf* disability

**infirmer** [ɛ̃firme] *vt* to invalidate

**infirmerie** [ɛ̃firməri] *nf* [d'école, de bateau] sick room; [de caserne, de prison] infirmary ■ **infirmier** *nm* male nurse ■ **infirmière** *nf* nurse

**inflammable** [ɛ̃flamabl] *adj* (in)flammable

**inflammation** [ɛ̃flamɑsjɔ̃] *nf* MÉD inflammation

**inflation** [ɛ̃flɑsjɔ̃] *nf* ÉCON inflation

**infléchir** [ɛ̃fleʃir] *vt* [courber] to bend; [politique] to change the direction of ■ **inflexion** *nf* [de courbe, de voix] inflection

**inflexible** [ɛ̃flɛksibl] *adj* inflexible

**infliger** [ɛ̃fliʒe] *vt* to inflict (**à** on) ; [amende] to impose (**à** on)

**influence** [ɛ̃flyɑ̃s] *nf* influence ■ **influençable** *adj* easily influenced ■ **influencer** *vt* to influence ■ **influent, -e** *adj* influential ■ **influer** *vi* **influer sur qch** to influence sth

**info** [ɛ̃fo] *nf Fam* info ; **c'est lui qui m'a donné cette info** I got the info from him ■ **infos** *nfpl Fam* **les infos** the news *sg* ; **regarder/écouter les infos** to watch/listen to the news

**Infographie**® [ɛ̃fɔgrafi] *nf* computer graphics ■ **infographiste** *nmf* computer graphics artist

**informaticien, -enne** [ɛ̃fɔrmatisjɛ̃, -ɛn] *nmf* computer scientist

**information** [ɛ̃fɔrmasjɔ̃] *nf* information ; [nouvelle] piece of news ; ORDINAT data, information ; RADIO & TV **les informations** the news (*sg*)

**informatique** [ɛ̃fɔrmatik] **1.** *nf* [science] computer science ; [technique] data processing ; **un cours d'informatique** a computer course ; **étudier l'informatique** to study computer science ; **travailler dans l'informatique** to work in computers *or* IT **2.** *adj* **programme informatique** computer program ■ **informatisation** *nf* computerization ■ **informatiser** *vt* to computerize

**informe** [ɛ̃fɔrm] *adj* shapeless

**informer** [ɛ̃fɔrme] **1.** *vt* to inform (**de** of *or* about ; **que** that) **2. s'informer** *vpr* [se renseigner] to inquire (**de** about ; **si** if *or* whether)

**inforoute** [ɛ̃fɔrut] *nf* information superhighway

**infortune** [ɛ̃fɔrtyn] *nf* misfortune ■ **infortuné, -e** *adj* unfortunate

**infraction** [ɛ̃fraksjɔ̃] *nf* [à un règlement] infringement ; [délit] *Br* offence, *Am* offense

**infranchissable** [ɛ̃frɑ̃ʃisabl] *adj* [mur, fleuve] impassable ; *Fig* [difficulté] insurmountable

**infrarouge** [ɛ̃fraruʒ] *adj* infrared

**infrastructure** [ɛ̃frastryktyr] *nf* [de bâtiment] substructure ; [équipements] infrastructure

**infructueux, -euse** [ɛ̃fryktɥø, -øz] *adj* fruitless

**infuser** [ɛ̃fyze] *vi* [thé] to brew ; [tisane] to infuse ■ **infusion** *nf* [tisane] herb tea

**ingénier** [ɛ̃ʒenje] ■ **s'ingénier** *vpr* to strive (**à faire** to do)

**ingénieur** [ɛ̃ʒenjœr] *nm* engineer ■ **ingénierie** [-iri] *nf* engineering

**ingénieux, -euse** [ɛ̃ʒenjø, -øz] *adj* ingenious ■ **ingéniosité** *nf* ingenuity

**ingénu, -e** [ɛ̃ʒeny] *adj* ingenuous

**ingérer** [ɛ̃ʒere] ■ **s'ingérer** *vpr* to interfere (**dans** in) ■ **ingérence** *nf* interference (**dans** in)

**ingrat, -e** [ɛ̃gra, -at] *adj* [personne] ungrateful (**envers** to) ; [tâche] thankless ; [sol] barren ; [visage] unattractive ; **l'âge ingrat** the awkward age ■ **ingratitude** *nf* ingratitude

**ingrédient** [ɛ̃gredjɑ̃] *nm* ingredient

**inhabitable** [inabitabl] *adj* uninhabitable ■ **inhabité, -e** *adj* uninhabited

**inhabituel, -elle** [inabitɥɛl] *adj* unusual

**inhérent, -e** [inerɑ̃, -ɑ̃t] *adj* inherent (**à** in)

**inhibé, -e** [inibe] *adj* inhibited ■ **inhibition** *nf* inhibition

**inhospitalier, -ère** [inɔspitalje, -ɛr] *adj* inhospitable

**inhumain, -e** [inymɛ̃, -ɛn] *adj* [cruel, terrible] inhuman

**inhumer** [inyme] *vt* to bury

**inimaginable** [inimaʒinabl] *adj* unimaginable

**inimitable** [inimitabl] *adj* inimitable

**inimitié** [inimitje] *nf* enmity

**ininflammable** [inɛ̃flamabl] *adj* non-flammable

**inintelligible** [inɛ̃teliʒibl] *adj* unintelligible

**ininterrompu, -e** [inɛ̃terɔ̃py] *adj* continuous

**initial, -e, -aux** [inisjal, -o] *adj* initial ■ **initiale** *nf* initial

**initialiser** [inisjalize] *vt* ORDINAT [disque] to initialize ; [ordinateur] to boot

**initiation** [inisjasjɔ̃] *nf* initiation

**initiative** [inisjativ] *nf* initiative ; **de ma propre initiative** on my own initiative

**initier** [inisje] **1.** *vt* [former] to introduce (**à** to) ; [rituellement] to initiate (**à** into) **2. s'initier** *vpr* **s'initier à qch** to start learning sth

**injecter** [ɛ̃ʒɛkte] *vt* to inject (**dans** into) ■ **injection** *nf* injection

**injure** [ɛ̃ʒyr] *nf* insult ■ **injurier** *vt* to insult, to abuse ■ **injurieux, -euse** *adj* abusive, insulting (**pour** to)

**injuste** [ɛ̃ʒyst] *adj* [contraire à la justice] unjust ; [non équitable] unfair ■ **injustice** *nf* injustice

**injustifiable** [ɛ̃ʒystifjabl] *adj* unjustifiable ■ **injustifié, -e** *adj* unjustified

**inlassable** [ɛ̃lɑsabl] *adj* untiring

**inné, -e** [ine] *adj* innate, inborn

**innocent, -e** [inɔsɑ̃, -ɑ̃t] **1.** *adj* innocent (**de** of) **2.** *nmf* [non coupable] innocent person ; [idiot] simpleton ■ **innocence** *nf* innocence ■ **innocenter** *vt* innocenter to clear sb (**de** of)

**innombrable** [inɔ̃brabl] *adj* countless, innumerable ; [foule] huge

**innommable** [inɔmabl] *adj* [conduite, actes] unspeakable ; [nourriture, odeur] vile

**innover** [inɔve] *vi* to innovate ■ **innovant, -e** *adj* innovative ■ **innovateur, -trice** **1.** *adj* innovative **2.** *nmf* innovator ■ **innovation** *nf* innovation

**inoccupé, -e** [inɔkype] *adj* unoccupied

**inoculer** [inɔkyle] *vt* **inoculer qch à qn** to inoculate sb with sth ; **inoculer qn contre qch** to inoculate sb against sth

**inodore** [inɔdɔr] *adj* odourless

**inoffensif, -ive** [inɔfɑ̃sif, -iv] *adj* harmless

**inonder** [inɔ̃de] *vt* [lieu] to flood ; *Fig* [marché] to flood, to inundate (**de** with) ■ **inondation** *nf* flood ; [action] flooding ■ **inondé, e** *adj* **a)** [champ, maison, cave] flooded **b)** *Fig* **être inondé de réclamations / de mauvaises nouvelles** to be inundated with complaints / with bad news ; **inondé de soleil** bathed in sunlight

**inopérable** [inɔperabl] *adj* inoperable

**inopiné, -e** [inɔpine] *adj* unexpected

**inopportun, -e** [inɔpɔrtœ̃, -yn] *adj* inopportune

**inoubliable** [inublijabl] *adj* unforgettable

**inouï, -e** [inwi] *adj* incredible

**Inox®** [inɔks] *nm* stainless steel ; **couteau en Inox®** stainless-steel knife ■ **inoxydable** *adj* [couteau] stainless-steel

**inqualifiable** [ɛ̃kalifjabl] *adj* unspeakable

**inquiet, -ète** [ɛ̃kjɛ, -ɛt] *adj* worried, anxious (**de** about)

**inquiéter** [ɛ̃kjete] **1.** *vt* [préoccuper] to worry **2. s'inquiéter** *vpr* to worry (**de** about) ; **s'inquiéter pour qn** to worry about sb ■ **inquiétant, -e** *adj* worrying

**inquiétude** [ɛ̃kjetyd] *nf* anxiety, worry

**insaisissable** [ɛ̃sezisabl] *adj* elusive

**insalubre** [ɛ̃salybr] *adj* unhealthy

**insatiable** [ɛ̃sasjabl] *adj* insatiable

**insatisfait, -e** [ɛ̃satisfɛ, -ɛt] *adj* [personne] dissatisfied

**insaturé, e** [ɛ̃satyre] *adj* unsaturated

**inscription** [ɛ̃skripsjɔ̃] *nf* [action] entering ; [immatriculation] registration ; [sur écriteau, mur, tombe] inscription

**inscrire** [ɛ̃skrir] **1.** *vt* [renseignements, date] to write down ; [dans un journal, sur un registre] to enter ; [graver] to inscribe ; **inscrire qn à un club** to *Br* enroll or *Am* enroll sb in a club **2. s'inscrire** *vpr* to put one's name down ; [à une activité] *Br* to enrol, *Am* to enroll (**à** at) ; [à l'université] to register (**à** at) ; **s'inscrire à un club** to join a club

**insecte** [ɛ̃sɛkt] *nm* insect

**insécurité** [ɛ̃sekyrite] *nf* insecurity

**insensé, -e** [ɛ̃sɑ̃se] *adj* [projet, idée] crazy; [espoir] wild

**insensible** [ɛ̃sɑ̃sibl] *adj* [indifférent] insensitive (**à** to); [imperceptible] imperceptible

**inséparable** [ɛ̃separabl] *adj* inseparable (**de** from)

**insérer** [ɛ̃sere] *vt* to insert (**dans** in) ■ **insertion** [ɛ̃sɛrsjɔ̃] *nf* insertion

**insidieux, -euse** [ɛ̃sidjø, -øz] *adj* insidious

**insigne** [ɛ̃siɲ] *nm* badge

**insignifiant, -e** [ɛ̃siɲifjɑ̃, -jɑ̃t] *adj* insignificant

**insinuer** [ɛ̃sinɥe] **1.** *vt Péj* to insinuate (**que** that) **2. s'insinuer** *vpr* [froid] to creep (**dans** into); [personne] to worm one's way (**dans** into)

**insipide** [ɛ̃sipid] *adj* insipid

**insister** [ɛ̃siste] *vi* to insist (**pour faire** on doing); **insister sur qch** to stress sth; **insister pour que...** (+ *subjunctive*) to insist that... ■ **insistance** *nf* insistence

**insolation** [ɛ̃sɔlasjɔ̃] *nf* MÉD sunstroke

**insolent, -e** [ɛ̃sɔlɑ̃, -ɑ̃t] *adj* [impoli] insolent; [luxe] unashamed ■ **insolence** *nf* insolence

**insolite** [ɛ̃sɔlit] *adj* unusual, strange

**insoluble** [ɛ̃sɔlybl] *adj* insoluble

**insomnie** [ɛ̃sɔmni] *nf* insomnia ■ **insomniaque** *nmf* insomniac

**insondable** [ɛ̃sɔ̃dabl] *adj* unfathomable

**insonoriser** [ɛ̃sɔnɔrize] *vt* to soundproof

**insouciant, -e** [ɛ̃susjɑ̃, -ɑ̃t] *adj* carefree ■ **insouciance** *nf* carefree attitude

**insoumis, -e** [ɛ̃sumi, -iz] *adj* [personne] rebellious; MIL absentee

**insoupçonnable** [ɛ̃supsɔnabl] *adj* beyond suspicion

**insoutenable** [ɛ̃sutnabl] *adj* [spectacle, odeur] unbearable; [théorie] untenable

**inspecter** [ɛ̃spɛkte] *vt* to inspect ■ **inspecteur, -trice** *nmf* inspector ■ **inspection** *nf* inspection

**inspirer** [ɛ̃spire] **1.** *vt* to inspire; **inspirer qch à qn** to inspire sb with sth **2.** *vi* to breathe in **3. s'inspirer** *vpr* **s'inspirer de qn/qch** to take one's inspiration from sb/sth ■ **inspiration** *nf* [idée] inspiration; [respiration] breathing in ■ **inspiré, -e** *adj* inspired

**instable** [ɛ̃stabl] *adj* unstable; [temps] changeable ■ **instabilité** *nf* instability; [de temps] changeability

**installer** [ɛ̃stale] **1.** *vt* [appareil, meuble] to install, to put in; [étagère] to put up; [cuisine] to fit out; ORDINAT to install; **installer qn** [dans une fonction, dans un logement] to install sb (**dans** in) **2. s'installer** *vpr* [s'asseoir] to settle down; [dans un bureau] to install oneself; [médecin] to set oneself up; **s'installer à la campagne** to settle in the country ■ **installation** *nf* [de machine] installation; [de cuisine] fitting out; [emménagement] move; **installations** [appareils] fittings; [bâtiments] facilities

**instant** [ɛ̃stɑ̃] *nm* moment, instant; **à l'instant** a moment ago; **à l'instant où...** just as...; **pour l'instant** for the moment ■ **instantané, -e 1.** *adj* instantaneous; **café instantané** instant coffee **2.** *nm* [photo] snapshot

**instar** [ɛ̃star] *nm* **à l'instar de qn** after the fashion of sb

**instaurer** [ɛ̃stɔre] *vt* to establish

**instigateur, -trice** [ɛ̃stigatœr, -tris] *nmf* instigator

**instinct** [ɛ̃stɛ̃] *nm* instinct; **d'instinct** by instinct ■ **instinctif, -ive** *adj* instinctive

**instituer** [ɛ̃stitɥe] *vt* to establish

**institut** [ɛ̃stity] *nm* institute; **institut de beauté** beauty salon

**instituteur, -trice** [ɛ̃stitytœr, -tris] *nmf Br* primary *or Am* elementary school teacher

**institution** [ɛ̃stitysjɔ̃] *nf* [création] establishment; [coutume] institution; [école] private school ■ **institutionnel, -elle** *adj* institutional

**instructeur, trice** [ɛ̃stryktœr, tris] *nmf* instructor

**instructif, -ive** [ɛ̃stryktif, -iv] *adj* instructive

**instruction** [ɛ̃stryksjɔ̃] *nf* [éducation] education; MIL training; JUR preliminary investigation; **instructions** [ordres] instructions; **instruction civique** civics (*sg*) ■ **instructeur** *nm* instructor

**instruire** [ɛ̃strɥir] **1.** *vt* to teach, to educate; MIL to train; JUR to investigate; **instruire qn de qch** to inform sb of sth **2. s'instruire** *vpr* to educate oneself ■ **instruit, -e** *adj* educated

**instrument** [ɛ̃strymɑ̃] *nm* instrument; **instrument à vent** wind instrument ■ **instrumental, -e, -aux** *adj* MUS instrumental

**instrumentaliser** [ɛ̃strymɑ̃talize] *vt* to use, to manipulate

**insu** [ɛ̃sy] ■ **à l'insu de** *prép* without the knowledge of; **à mon/son insu** [sans m'en/s'en apercevoir] without my/his/her being aware of it

**insuffisant, -e** [ɛ̃syfizɑ̃, -ɑ̃t] *adj* [en quantité] insufficient; [en qualité] inadequate ■ **insuffisance** *nf* [manque] insufficiency; [de moyens] inadequacy

**insulaire** [ɛ̃syler] **1.** *adj* insular **2.** *nmf* islander

**insulte** [ɛ̃sylt] *nf* insult (**à** to) ■ **insulter** *vt* to insult

**insupportable** [ɛ̃syportabl] *adj* unbearable

**insurger** [ɛ̃syrʒe] ■ **s'insurger** *vpr* to rise up (**contre** against)

**insurmontable** [ɛ̃syrmɔ̃tabl] *adj* insurmountable

**insurrection** [ɛ̃syrɛksjɔ̃] *nf* insurrection, uprising

**intact, -e** [ɛ̃takt] *adj* intact

**intarissable** [ɛ̃tarisabl] *adj* inexhaustible

**intégral, -e, -aux** [ɛ̃tegral, -o] *adj* [paiement] full; [édition] unabridged; **version intégrale** [de film] uncut version ■ **intégralement** *adv* in full, fully ■ **intégralité** *nf* whole (**de** of)

**intègre** [ɛ̃tegr] *adj* upright, honest ■ **intégrité** *nf* integrity

**intégrer** [ɛ̃tegre] **1.** *vt* to integrate (**dans** in); [école] to get into **2. s'intégrer** *vpr* to become integrated ■ **intégrante** *adj f* **faire partie intégrante de qch** to be an integral part of sth ■ **intégration** *nf* [au sein d'un groupe] integration

**intégrisme** [ɛ̃tegrism] *nm* fundamentalism

**intellectuel, -elle** [ɛ̃telɛktɥɛl] *adj & nmf* intellectual

**intelligent, -e** [ɛ̃teliʒɑ̃, -ɑ̃t] *adj* intelligent, clever ■ **intelligence** *nf* [faculté] intelligence; **avoir l'intelligence de faire qch** to have the intelligence to do sth; ORDINAT **intelligence artificielle** artificial intelligence

**intelligible** [ɛ̃teliʒibl] *adj* intelligible

**intello** [ɛ̃telo] *adj inv & nmf Fam & Péj* intellectual

**intempéries** [ɛ̃tɑ̃peri] *nfpl* **les intempéries** the bad weather

**intempestif, -ive** [ɛ̃tɑ̃pestif, -iv] *adj* untimely

**intenable** [ɛ̃tnabl] *adj* [position] untenable

**intendant, -e** [ɛ̃tɑ̃dɑ̃, -ɑ̃t] *nmf* SCOL bursar

**intense** [ɛ̃tɑ̃s] *adj* intense; [circulation] heavy ■ **intensif, -ive** *adj* intensive ■ **intensité** *nf* intensity

**intensifier** [ɛ̃tɑ̃sifje] **1.** *vt* to intensify **2. s'intensifier** *vpr* to intensify

**intenter** [ɛ̃tɑ̃te] *vt* JUR **intenter un procès à qn** to institute proceedings against sb

**intention** [ɛ̃tɑ̃sjɔ̃] *nf* intention; JUR intent; **à l'intention de** for; **avoir l'intention de faire qch** to intend to do sth ■ **intentionné, -e** *adj* **bien**

**intentionné** well-intentioned ; **mal intentionné** ill-intentioned ■ **intentionnel, -elle** adj intentional

**interactif, -ive** [ɛteraktif, -iv] adj ORDINAT interactive

**interaction** [ɛterɑksjɔ̃] nf interaction

**intercaler** [ɛterkale] vt to insert

**intercéder** [ɛtersede] vt to intercede (**auprès de** with ; **en faveur de** on behalf of)

**intercepter** [ɛtersɛpte] vt to intercept

**interchangeable** [ɛterʃɑ̃ʒabl] adj interchangeable

**interclasse** [ɛterklas], **intercours** [ɛterkur] nm Br break, Am recess ; **à l'interclasse** at or during the break

**interdire** [ɛterdir] vt to forbid (**qch à qn** sb sth) ; [film, meeting] to ban ; **interdire à qn de faire qch** [personne] to forbid sb to do sth ■ **interdiction** nf ban (**de** on) ; **'interdiction de fumer'** 'no smoking' ■ **interdit, -e** adj [défendu] forbidden ; [étonné] disconcerted ; **'stationnement interdit'** 'no parking'

**intéresser** [ɛterese] **1.** vt [captiver] to interest ; [concerner] to concern **2. s'intéresser** vpr **s'intéresser à qn/qch** to be interested in sb /sth ■ **intéressant, -e 1.** adj [captivant] interesting ; [prix] attractive **2.** nmf Péj **faire l'intéressant** to show off ■ **intéressé, -e 1.** adj [avide] self-interested ; [motif] selfish ; [concerné] concerned **2.** nmf **l'intéressé** the person concerned

**intérêt** [ɛterɛ] nm interest ; FIN **intérêts** interest ; **tu as intérêt à le faire** you'd do well to do it ; **sans intérêt** [personne, film] uninteresting

**interface** [ɛterfas] nf ORDINAT interface

**intérieur, -eure** [ɛterjœr] **1.** adj [escalier, paroi] interior ; [cour, vie] inner ; [poche] inside ; [partie] internal ; [vol] internal, domestic ; [mer] inland **2.** nm [de boîte, de maison] inside (**de** of) ; [de pays] interior ; [maison] home ; **à l'intérieur (de)** inside ; **d'intérieur** [vêtement, jeux] indoor

**intérim** [ɛterim] nm [travail temporaire] temporary work ; **président par intérim** acting president ■ **intérimaire 1.** adj [fonction, employé] temporary **2.** nmf [travailleur] temporary worker ; [secrétaire] temp

**interlocuteur, -trice** [ɛterlɔkytœr, -tris] nmf [de conversation] speaker ; [de négociation] discussion partner ; **mon interlocuteur** the person I am / was speaking to

**intermède** [ɛtermɛd] nm interlude

**intermédiaire** [ɛtermedjɛr] **1.** adj intermediate **2.** nmf intermediary ; COMM middleman ; **par l'intermédiaire de** through ; **sans intermédiaire** directly

**interminable** [ɛterminabl] adj interminable

**intermittent, e** [ɛtermitɑ̃, ɑ̃t] adj intermittent ; **les intermittents du spectacle** people working in the performing arts ■ **intermittence** nf **par intermittence** intermittently

**internat** [ɛterna] nm [école] boarding school ; [concours de médecine] entrance examination for an internship ■ **interne 1.** adj [douleur] internal ; [oreille] inner **2.** nmf [élève] boarder ; **interne des hôpitaux** Br house doctor, Am intern

**international, -e, -aux** [ɛternasjɔnal, -o] **1.** adj international **2.** nm [footballeur] international ■ **internationalement** adv internationally ; **connu internationalement** world famous

**interner** [ɛterne] vt [prisonnier] to intern ; [aliéné] to commit ■ **internement** [-əmɑ̃] nm [emprisonnement] internment ; [d'aliéné] confinement

**Internet** [ɛternɛt] nm Internet ; **sur (l') Internet** on the Internet ; **avoir accès à Internet** to have access to the Internet, to have Internet access ■ **internaute** nmf Internet surfer

**interpeller** [ɛterpəle] vt [appeler] to call out to ; [dans une réunion] to question ; **interpeller qn** [police] to take sb in for questioning ■ **interpellation** [ɛterpelasjɔ̃] nf [par la police] (arrest for) questioning

**interposer** [ɛ̃tɛrpoze] ■ **s'interposer** *vpr* [intervenir] to intervene (**dans** in)

**interprète** [ɛ̃tɛrprɛt] *nmf* [traducteur] interpreter ; [chanteur] singer ; [musicien, acteur] performer ■ **interprétariat** *nm* interpreting ■ **interprétation** *nf* [de texte, de rôle, de rêve] interpretation ; [traduction] interpreting ■ **interpréter** *vt* [texte, rôle, musique, rêve] to interpret ; [chanter] to sing

**interro** [ɛ̃tɛro] *nf Fam* SCOL test

**interroger** [ɛ̃tɛroʒe] *vt* to question ; [élève] to test ; ORDINAT [banque de données] to query ■ **interrogateur, -trice** *adj* [air] questioning ■ **interrogation** *nf* [question] question ; [de prisonnier] questioning ; SCOL **interrogation écrite/orale** written/oral test ■ **interrogatoire** *nm* interrogation

**interrompre** [ɛ̃tɛrɔ̃pr] **1.** *vt* to interrupt **2. s'interrompre** *vpr* to break off ■ **interrupteur** *nm* switch ■ **interruption** *nf* interruption ; [de négociations] breaking off ; **sans interruption** continuously ; **interruption volontaire de grossesse** termination

**intersection** [ɛ̃tɛrsɛksjɔ̃] *nf* intersection

**intervalle** [ɛ̃tɛrval] *nm* [dans l'espace] gap, space ; [dans le temps] interval ; **dans l'intervalle** [entretemps] in the meantime ; **par intervalles** (every) now and then, at intervals

**intervenir** [ɛ̃tɛrvənir] *vi* [agir, prendre la parole] to intervene ; [survenir] to occur ; **être intervenu** [accord] to be reached ■ **intervention** *nf* intervention ; [discours] speech ; **intervention chirurgicale** operation

**intervertir** [ɛ̃tɛrvɛrtir] *vt* to invert

**interview** [ɛ̃tɛrvju] *nm ou f* interview ■ **interviewer** [-vjuve] *vt* to interview

**intestin** [ɛ̃tɛstɛ̃] *nm* intestine

**intime** [ɛ̃tim] **1.** *adj* intimate ; [ami] close ; [cérémonie] quiet **2.** *nmf* close friend ■ **intimement** [-əmɑ̃] *adv* intimately ; **intimement liés** [problèmes] closely linked ■ **intimité** *nf* [familiarité] intimacy ; [vie privée] privacy ; **dans l'intimité** in private

**intimider** [ɛ̃timide] *vt* to intimidate

**intituler** [ɛ̃tityle] **1.** *vt* to give a title to **2. s'intituler** *vpr* to be entitled

**intolérable** [ɛ̃tolerabl] *adj* intolerable ■ **intolérance** *nf* intolerance ■ **intolérant, -e** *adj* intolerant

**intox** [ɛ̃tɔks] *nf Fam* propaganda, brainwashing ; **tout ça, c'est de l'intox** all that's just propaganda

**intoxiquer** [ɛ̃tɔksike] **1.** *vt* [empoisonner] to poison **2. s'intoxiquer** *vpr* to poison oneself ■ **intoxication** *nf* [empoisonnement] poisoning ; **intoxication alimentaire** food poisoning

**intraitable** [ɛ̃tretabl] *adj* uncompromising

**intransigeant, -e** [ɛ̃trɑ̃ziʒɑ̃, -ɑ̃t] *adj* intransigent

**intrépide** [ɛ̃trepid] *adj* fearless, intrepid

**intrigue** [ɛ̃trig] *nf* intrigue ; [de film, roman] plot ■ **intriguer 1.** *vt* **intriguer qn** to intrigue sb **2.** *vi* to scheme

**introduire** [ɛ̃trɔdɥir] **1.** *vt* [insérer] to insert (**dans** into) ; [marchandises] to bring in ; [réforme, mode] to introduce ; [visiteur] to show in **2. s'introduire** *vpr* **s'introduire dans une maison** to get into a house ■ **introduction** *nf* [texte, action] introduction

**introuvable** [ɛ̃truvabl] *adj* [produit] unobtainable ; [personne] nowhere to be found

**introverti, -e** [ɛ̃troverti] *nmf* introvert

**intrus, -e** [ɛ̃try, -yz] *nmf* intruder ■ **intrusion** *nf* intrusion (**dans** into)

**intuition** [ɛ̃tɥisjɔ̃] *nf* intuition ■ **intuitif, -ive** *adj* intuitive

**inuit** [inɥit] **1.** *adj inv* Inuit **2.** *nmf inv* **Inuit** Inuit

**inusable** [inyzabl] *adj* hard-wearing

**inusité, -e** [inyzite] *adj* [mot, forme] uncommon

**inutile** [inytil] *adj* [qui ne sert à rien] useless ; [précaution, bagage] unnecessary ; **c'est inutile de crier** it's pointless shouting ▪ **inutilement** adv needlessly ▪ **inutilité** nf uselessness

**inutilisable** [inytilizabl] adj unusable ▪ **inutilisé, -e** adj unused

**invaincu, -e** [ɛ̃vɛ̃ky] adj SPORT unbeaten

**invalide** [ɛ̃valid] **1.** adj disabled **2.** nmf disabled person

**invalider** [ɛ̃valide] vt to invalidate

**invariable** [ɛ̃varjabl] adj invariable

**invasion** [ɛ̃vazjɔ̃] nf invasion

**invendable** [ɛ̃vɑ̃dabl] adj unsellable ▪ **invendu, -e 1.** adj unsold **2.** nmpl **invendus** unsold articles ; [journaux] unsold copies

**inventaire** [ɛ̃vɑ̃tɛr] nm COMM [liste] inventory ; **faire l'inventaire** to do the stocktaking (**de** of)

**inventer** [ɛ̃vɑ̃te] vt [créer] to invent ; [concept] to think up ; [histoire, excuse] to make up ▪ **inventeur, -trice** nmf inventor ▪ **inventif, -ive** adj inventive ▪ **invention** nf invention

**inverse** [ɛ̃vɛrs] **1.** adj [sens] opposite ; [ordre] reverse ; MATH inverse **2.** nm **l'inverse** the reverse, the opposite ▪ **inversement** [-əmɑ̃] adv conversely ▪ **inverser** vt [ordre] to reverse ▪ **inversion** nf inversion

**investigation** [ɛ̃vɛstigasjɔ̃] nf investigation

**investir** [ɛ̃vɛstir] **1.** vt [capitaux] to invest (**dans** in) ; [édifice, ville] to besiege **2.** vi to invest (**dans** in) ▪ **investissement** nm FIN investment

**invincible** [ɛ̃vɛ̃sibl] adj invincible

**invisible** [ɛ̃vizibl] adj invisible

**inviter** [ɛ̃vite] vt to invite ; **inviter qn à faire qch** [prier] to request sb to do sth ; [inciter] to urge sb to do sth ; **inviter qn à dîner** to invite sb to dinner ▪ **invitation** nf invitation ▪ **invité, -e** nmf guest

**involontaire** [ɛ̃vɔlɔ̃tɛr] adj [geste] involuntary ; [témoin] unwilling

**invoquer** [ɛ̃vɔke] vt [argument] to put forward ; [loi, texte] to refer to ; [divinité] to invoke ▪ **invocation** nf invocation (**à** to)

**invraisemblable** [ɛ̃vrɛsɑ̃blabl] adj [extraordinaire] incredible ; [alibi] implausible ▪ **invraisemblance** nf [improbabilité] unlikelihood ; [d'alibi] implausibility

**invulnérable** [ɛ̃vylnerabl] adj invulnerable

**ira, irait** [ira, irɛ] voir aller

**Irak, Iraq** [irak] nm **l'Irak** Iraq ▪ **irakien, -enne, iraquien, enne 1.** adj Iraqi **2.** nmf **Irakien, Irakienne** Iraqi

**Iran** [irɑ̃] nm **l'Iran** Iran ▪ **iranien, -enne 1.** adj Iranian **2.** nmf **Iranien, Iranienne** Iranian

**IRC** (abr de **Internet Relay Chat**) nm IRC

**iris** [iris] nm [plante & ANAT] iris

**Irlande** [irlɑ̃d] nf **l'Irlande** Ireland ; **l'Irlande du Nord** Northern Ireland ▪ **irlandais, -e 1.** adj Irish **2.** nmf **Irlandais** Irishman ; **Irlandaise** Irishwoman ; **les Irlandais** the Irish **3.** nm [langue] Irish

**IRM** [iɛrɛm] (abr de **Imagerie par résonance magnétique**) nm MÉD MRI

**iront** [irɔ̃] voir aller

**irrationnel, -elle** [irasjɔnɛl] adj irrational

**irréalisable** [irealizabl] adj [projet] impracticable

**irréaliste** [irealist] adj unrealistic

**irrécupérable** [irekyperabl] adj **a)** [irrécouvrable] irretrievable **b)** [irréparable] beyond repair **c)** [personne] beyond hope

**irrécusable** [irekyzabl] adj [preuve] indisputable ; JUR [témoignage] unimpeachable

**irréductible** [iredyktibl] **1.** adj [ennemi] implacable **2.** nm diehard

**irréel, -elle** [ireɛl] adj unreal

**irréfléchi, -e** [irefleʃi] adj rash

**irréfutable** [irefytabl] adj irrefutable

**irrégulier, -ère** [iregylje, -ɛr] *adj* [rythme, verbe, procédure] irregular; [sol] uneven; [résultats] inconsistent ■ **irrégularité** *nf* irregularity; [de sol] unevenness

**irrémédiable** [iremedjabl] *adj* irreparable

**irremplaçable** [irɑ̃plasabl] *adj* irreplaceable

**irréparable** [ireparabl] *adj* [véhicule] beyond repair; [tort, perte] irreparable

**irrépressible** [irepresibl] *adj* irrepressible

**irréprochable** [ireprɔʃabl] *adj* irreproachable

**irrésistible** [irezistibl] *adj* [personne, charme] irresistible

**irrésolu, -e** [irezɔly] *adj* [personne] indecisive; [problème] unresolved

**irrespirable** [irespirabl] *adj* [air] unbreathable; *Fig* [atmosphère] unbearable

**irresponsable** [irespɔ̃sabl] *adj* [personne] irresponsible

**irréversible** [ireversibl] *adj* irreversible

**irrévocable** [irevɔkabl] *adj* irrevocable

**irrigation** [irigasjɔ̃] *nf* irrigation ■ **irriguer** *vt* to irrigate

**irriter** [irite] **1.** *vt* to irritate **2. s'irriter** *vpr* [s'énerver] to get irritated (**de** with; **contre** at); [s'enflammer] to become irritated ■ **irritable** *adj* irritable ■ **irritation** *nf* [colère & MÉD] irritation

**irruption** [irypsjɔ̃] *nf* **faire irruption dans** to burst into

**Islam** [islam] *nm* **l'Islam** Islam ■ **islamique** *adj* Islamic ■ **islamisme** *nm* Islamism ■ **islamiste** *nmf* islamic fundamentalist

**Islande** [islɑ̃d] *nf* **l'Islande** Iceland ■ **islandais, -e 1.** *adj* Icelandic **2.** *nmf* **Islandais, Islandaise** Icelander

**isolant, -e** [izɔlɑ̃, -ɑ̃t] **1.** *adj* insulating **2.** *nm* insulating material

**isolationniste** [izɔlasjɔnist] *adj* isolationist

**isoler** [izɔle] **1.** *vt* to isolate (**de** from); [du froid & ÉLEC] to insulate **2. s'isoler** *vpr* to isolate oneself ■ **isolation** *nf* insulation ■ **isolé, -e** *adj* [personne, endroit, maison] isolated; [du froid] insulated; **isolé de** cut off *or* isolated from ■ **isolement** *nm* [de personne] isolation ■ **isolément** *adv* [agir] in isolation; [interroger des gens] individually

**isoloir** [izɔlwar] *nm Br* polling *or Am* voting booth

**Israël** [israel] *nm* Israel ■ **israélien, -enne 1.** *adj* Israeli **2.** *nmf* **Israélien, Israélienne** Israeli ■ **israélite 1.** *adj* Jewish **2.** *nmf* Jew

**issu, -e** [isy] *adj* **être issu de** to come from

**issue** [isy] *nf* [sortie] exit; *Fig* [solution] way out; [résultat] outcome; **à l'issue de** at the end of; **issue de secours** emergency exit

**isthme** [ism] *nm* isthmus

**Italie** [itali] *nf* **l'Italie** Italy ■ **italien, -enne 1.** *adj* Italian **2.** *nmf* **Italien, Italienne** Italian **3.** *nm* [langue] Italian

**italique** [italik] **1.** *adj* [lettre] italic **2.** *nm* italics; **en italique** in italics

**itinéraire** [itinerɛr] *nm* route, itinerary

**itinérant, e** [itinerɑ̃, ɑ̃t] **1.** *adj* [spectacle, troupe] itinerant **2.** *nmf Can* homeless

**IUT** [iyte] *(abr de* **institut universitaire de technologie***) nm* vocational higher education college

**IVG** [iveʒe] *(abr de* **interruption volontaire de grossesse***) nf* abortion, termination

**ivoire** [ivwar] *nm* ivory; **statuette en ivoire** *ou* **d'ivoire** ivory statuette

**ivre** [ivr] *adj* drunk (**de** with); *Fig* **ivre de joie** wild with joy ■ **ivresse** *nf* drunkenness; **en état d'ivresse** under the influence of drink ■ **ivrogne** *nmf* drunk(ard)

**J, j** [ʒi] *nm inv* J, j; **le jour J** D-day

**j'** [ʒ] *voir* **je**

**jacasser** [ʒakase] *vi* to chatter, to jabber

**Jacuzzi®** [ʒakuzi] *nm* Jacuzzi®

**jadis** [ʒadis] *adv Litt* in times past

**jaillir** [ʒajir] *vi* [liquide] to gush out; [étincelles] to shoot out

**jalonner** [ʒalɔne] *vt* [marquer] to mark out; [border] to line

**jaloux, -ouse** [ʒalu, -uz] *adj* jealous (**de** of) ■ **jalousie** *nf* [sentiment] jealousy

**Jamaïque** [ʒamaik] *nf* **la Jamaïque** Jamaica

**jamais** [ʒamɛ] *adv* **a)** [négatif] never; **elle ne sort jamais** she never goes out; **sans jamais sortir** without ever going out **b)** [positif] ever; **à tout jamais** for ever; **si jamais** if ever; **le film le plus drôle que j'aie jamais vu** the funniest film I have ever seen ■ **jamais-vu** [ʒamɛvy] *nm inv* **c'est du jamais-vu à Marseille !** it's a first for Marseille!; **c'est du jamais-vu pour la population locale** the locals have never seen anything like it; **c'est du jamais-vu sur Internet** nothing like this has been seen before on the Web

**jambe** [ʒɑ̃b] *nf* leg

**jambette** [ʒɑ̃bɛt] *nf Can* [croc-en-jambe] trip

**jambon** [ʒɑ̃bɔ̃] *nm* ham

**janvier** [ʒɑ̃vje] *nm* January

**Japon** [ʒapɔ̃] *nm* **le Japon** Japan ■ **japonais, -e 1.** *adj* Japanese **2.** *nmf* **Japonais, Japonaise** Japanese *inv*; **les Japonais** the Japanese **3.** *nm* [langue] Japanese

**jardin** [ʒardɛ̃] *nm* garden; **jardin d'enfants** kindergarten; **jardin public** gardens ■ **jardinage** *nm* gardening ■ **jardiner** *vi* to garden ■ **jardinier** *nm* gardener

**jargon** [ʒargɔ̃] *nm* jargon

**jaser** [ʒaze] *vi* **a)** [médire] to gossip **b)** *Can Fam* [bavarder] to chat, to talk

**jasmin** [ʒasmɛ̃] *nm* jasmine; **thé au jasmin** jasmine tea

**JAT** (*abr de* **juste-à-temps**) *adj* JIT (*just-in-time*)

**jaune** [ʒon] **1.** *adj* yellow **2.** *nm* [couleur] yellow; **jaune d'œuf** (egg) yolk

**Javel** [ʒavɛl] ■ **eau de Javel** *nf* bleach

**javelot** [ʒavlo] *nm* javelin

**jazz** [dʒaz] *nm* jazz

**je** [ʒə]

**j'** is used before a word beginning with a vowel or h mute.

*pron pers* I; **je suis ici** I'm here

**jean** [dʒin] *nm* (pair of) jeans; **veste en jean** *Br* denim *or Am* jeans jacket

**je-ne-sais-quoi** [ʒənsɛkwa] *nm inv* **un je-ne-sais-quoi** a certain je ne sais quoi, a certain something; **un je-ne-sais-quoi de qch** a hint of sth

**jérémiades** [ʒeremjad] *nfpl Fam* moaning, whining

**jerrycan, jerrican** [ʒerikan] *nm* jerry can

**Jersey** [ʒɛrzɛ] *nf* Jersey

**jet** [ʒɛ] *nm* [de pierre] throwing; [de vapeur, de liquide] jet; **jet d'eau** fountain

**jetable** [ʒətabl] *adj* disposable

**jetée** [ʒəte] *nf* pier, jetty

**jeter** [ʒəte] **1.** *vt* to throw (**à** to; **dans** into); [à la poubelle] to throw away; [sort] to cast; **jeter un coup d'œil à qn/qch** to have a quick look at sb/sth

**2. se jeter** *vpr* [personne] to throw oneself; **se jeter sur qn** to throw oneself at sb; *Fig* to pounce on sb; **se jeter sur qch** [occasion] to jump at sth; **se jeter contre** [véhicule] to crash into; **se jeter dans** [fleuve] to flow into

**jeton** [ʒətɔ̃] *nm* [pièce] token; [au jeu] chip

**Jet-Ski**® [dʒɛtski] *nm* Jet-Ski

**jeu, -x** [ʒø] *nm* **a)** [amusement] play; [activité, au tennis] game; [d'acteur] acting; **le jeu** [au casino] gambling; **en jeu** [en cause] at stake; [forces] at work; **jeu-concours** competition; **jeu électronique** computer game; **jeu de hasard** game of chance; **jeu de mots** play on words, pun; **jeux de société** board games; **jeu télévisé** television game show; [avec questions] television quiz show; **jeu vidéo** video game **b)** [série complète] set; [de cartes] deck, *Br* pack; [cartes en main] hand; **jeu d'échecs** [boîte, pièces] chess set **c)** TECH [de ressort, de verrou] play

**jeudi** [ʒødi] *nm* Thursday

**jeun** [ʒœ̃] ■ **à jeun 1.** *adv* on an empty stomach **2.** *adj* **être à jeun** to have eaten no food

**jeune** [ʒœn] **1.** *adj* young; [apparence] youthful; **jeunes gens** young people **2.** *nmf* young person; **les jeunes** young people ■ **jeunesse** *nf* youth; [apparence] youthfulness; **la jeunesse** [les jeunes] the young

**jeûner** [ʒøne] *vi* to fast

**joaillier, -ère** [ʒɔaje, -ɛr] *nmf Br* jeweller, *Am* jeweler ■ **joaillerie** *nf* [bijoux] *Br* jewellery, *Am* jewelry; [magasin] *Br* jewellery shop, *Am* jewelry store

**jockey** [ʒɔkɛ] *nm* jockey

**jogging** [dʒɔgiŋ] *nm* SPORT jogging; [survêtement] jogging suit

**joie** [ʒwa] *nf* joy, delight; **avec joie** with pleasure, gladly

**joindre** [ʒwɛ̃dr] **1.** *vt* [réunir] to join; [ajouter] to add (**à** to); [dans une enveloppe] to enclose (**à** with); **joindre qn** [contacter] to get in touch with sb **2. se joindre** *vpr* **se joindre à qn** to join sb

■ **joint, -e 1.** *adj* **à pieds joints** with feet together; **pièces jointes** [de lettre] enclosures **2.** *nm* TECH [articulation] joint; [d'étanchéité] seal; [de robinet] washer; **joint de culasse** gasket

**joker** [ʒɔkɛr] *nm* CARTES joker

**joli, -e** [ʒɔli] *adj* pretty

**jonché** [ʒɔ̃ʃe] *adj* **jonché de** strewn with

**jonction** [ʒɔ̃ksjɔ̃] *nf* junction

**jongler** [ʒɔ̃gle] *vi* to juggle (**avec** with)

**jonquille** [ʒɔ̃kij] *nf* daffodil

**Jordanie** [ʒɔrdani] *nf* **la Jordanie** Jordan

**joue** [ʒu] *nf* [du visage] cheek

**jouer** [ʒwe] **1.** *vt* [musique, carte, rôle] to play; [pièce de théâtre] to perform; [film] to show; [parier] to stake (**sur** on); [cheval] to bet on **2.** *vi* to play; [acteur] to act; [au tiercé] to gamble; [être important] to count; **jouer au tennis / aux cartes** to play tennis / cards; **jouer du piano / du violon** to play the piano / violin; **à toi de jouer!** it's your turn (to play)! **3. se jouer** *vpr* [film, pièce] to be on

**jouet** [ʒwɛ] *nm* toy

**joueur, -euse** [ʒwœr, -øz] *nmf* player; [au tiercé] gambler

**jouir** [ʒwir] *vi* **jouir de qch** to enjoy sth

**jour** [ʒur] *nm* [journée, date] day; [clarté] daylight; [éclairage] light; **il fait jour** it's (day)light; **de jour en jour** day by day; **du jour au lendemain** overnight; **en plein jour, au grand jour** in broad daylight; **de nos jours** nowadays, these days; *Fig* **sous un jour nouveau** in a different light; **mettre qch à jour** to bring sth up to date; **quel jour sommes-nous?** what day is it?; **il y a dix ans jour pour jour** ten years ago to the day; **le jour de l'an** New Year's Day

**journal, -aux** [ʒurnal, -o] *nm* (news) paper; [spécialisé, intime] journal; **journal télévisé** (TV) news ■ **journalisme** *nm* journalism ■ **journaliste** *nmf* journalist

**journalier, -ère** [ʒurnalje, -ɛr] *adj*
daily

**journée** [ʒurne] *nf* day ; **pendant la
journée** during the day(time) ; **toute
la journée** all day (long)

**jovial, -e, -aux** [ʒɔvjal, -o] *adj* jovial,
jolly

**joyau, -x** [ʒwajo] *nm* jewel

**joyeux, -euse** [ʒwajø, -øz] *adj* joyful ;
**joyeux anniversaire !** happy birthday! ; **joyeux Noël !** merry *or Br* happy
Christmas!

**joystick** [dʒɔjstik] *nm* joystick

**JPEG** [ʒipɛg] *(abr de* **joint picture expert
group)** *nm* JPEG ; **fichier JPEG** JPEG
file

**jubiler** [ʒybile] *vi* to be jubilant

**jucher** [ʒyʃe] **1.** *vt* to perch (**sur** on) **2. se
jucher** *vpr* to perch (**sur** on)

**judicieux, -euse** [ʒydisjø, -øz] *adj*
judicious

**judo** [ʒydo] *nm* judo

**juge** [ʒyʒ] *nmf* judge ; **juge d'enfants**
children's judge, *Br* juvenile magistrate ;
**juge de touche** [au football] linesman,
assistant referee ; **juge d'instruction**
examining magistrate

**jugé** [ʒyʒe] ■ **au jugé** *adv* [calculer]
roughly

**jugement** [ʒyʒmɑ̃] *nm* [opinion, dis-
cernement] judgement ; [verdict] sentence ; **porter un jugement sur qch**
to pass judgement on sth ; JUR **passer
en jugement** to stand trial

**juger** [ʒyʒe] **1.** *vt* [personne, question]
to judge ; [au tribunal] to try ; [estimer]
to consider (**que** that) **2.** *vi* **juger de** to
judge ; **jugez de ma surprise !** imagine
my surprise!

**juif, juive** [ʒɥif, ʒɥiv] **1.** *adj* Jewish
**2.** *nmf* **Juif** Jew

**juillet** [ʒɥijɛ] *nm* July

**juin** [ʒɥɛ̃] *nm* June

**jumeau, -elle, -x** [ʒymo, -ɛl] **1.** *adj*
**frère jumeau** twin brother ; **sœur
jumelle** twin sister ; **lits jumeaux**
twin beds **2.** *nmf* twin ■ **jumeler** *vt*
[villes] to twin ■ **jumelles** *nfpl* [pour
regarder] binoculars

**jument** [ʒymɑ̃] *nf* mare

**jungle** [ʒœ̃gl] *nf* jungle

**junior** [ʒynjɔr] *nm & adj inv* SPORT junior

**jupe** [ʒyp] *nf* skirt

**jurer** [ʒyre] **1.** *vt* [promettre] to swear
(**que** that ; **de faire** to do) **2.** *vi* [dire un
gros mot] to swear (**contre** at) ; [contras-
ter] to clash (**avec** with) ; **jurer de qch**
to swear to sth **3. se jurer** *vpr* **se jurer
de faire qch** to swear *or* vow to do sth
■ **juré, -e 1.** *adj* **ennemi juré** sworn
enemy **2.** *nmf* JUR juror

**juridique** [ʒyridik] *adj* legal

**juriste** [ʒyrist] *nmf* legal expert

**juron** [ʒyrɔ̃] *nm* swearword

**jury** [ʒyri] *nm* JUR jury ; [d'examen] board
of examiners

**jus** [ʒy] *nm* [de fruits] juice ; [de viande]
gravy ; **jus d'orange** orange juice

**jusque** [ʒysk] **1.** *prép* **jusqu'à** [espace]
as far as, (right) up to ; [temps] until,
(up) till, to ; [même] even ; **jusque-là**
[lieu] up to there ; [temps] until then ;
**jusqu'en mai** until May ; **jusqu'où ?**
how far ? ; **jusqu'ici** as far as this ;
[temps] up till now ; **jusque chez moi**
as far as my place **2.** *conj* **jusqu'à ce
qu'il vienne** until he comes

**juste** [ʒyst] **1.** *adj* [équitable] fair, just ;
[exact] right, correct ; [étroit] tight ; [rai-
sonnement] sound ; **un peu juste** [quan-
tité, qualité] barely enough **2.** *adv* [devi-
ner, compter] correctly, right ; [chanter]
in tune ; [précisément, à peine] just ; **à
trois heures juste** on the stroke of
three ; **un peu juste** [mesurer, compter]
a bit on the short side ■ **justement**
[-əmɑ̃] *adv* [précisément] exactly ; [avec
justesse, avec justice] justly ; **justement
j'allais t'appeler** I was just going to call
you

**justesse** [ʒystɛs] *nf* [exactitude] accuracy ; **de justesse** [éviter, gagner] just

**justice** [ʒystis] *nf* [équité] justice ; **la justice** [autorité] the law ; **rendre justice
à qn** to do justice to sb

**justificatif, ive** [ʒystifikatif, iv] *adj*
supporting ∎ **justificatif** *nm* written
proof ; **justificatif de domicile** proof
of address

**justifier** [ʒystifje] **1.** *vt* to justify **2. se
justifier** *vpr* to justify oneself (**de** of)
∎ **justification** *nf* [explication] justification ; [preuve] proof

**juteux, -euse** [ʒytø, -øz] *adj* juicy

# K

**K, k** [kɑ] *nm inv* K, k

**kaki** [kaki] *adj inv* khaki

**kamikaze** [kamikaz] **1.** *nm* kamikaze pilot **2.** *nmf Fig* kamikaze

**kangourou** [kɑ̃guru] *nm* kangaroo

**karaoké** [karaɔke] *nm* karaoke

**karaté** [karate] *nm* karate

**karting** [kartiŋ] *nm* karting

**kasher, cascher, cachère** [kaʃɛr] *adj inv* kosher

**kayak** [kajak] *nm* [bateau de sport] canoe

**kel1** (*abr de* **quelqu'un**) SMS SUM1

**Kenya** [kenja] *nm* **le Kenya** Kenya

**kermesse** [kɛrmɛs] *nf* charity fair *or Br* fête ; [en Belgique] village fair

**kérosène** [kerozɛn] *nm* kerosene

**kestudi** SMS *abr écrite de* **qu'est-ce que tu dis?**

**kestufé** SMS *abr écrite de* **qu'est-ce que tu fais?**

**ketchup** [kɛtʃœp] *nm* **a)** ketchup **b)** [kɛtʃɔp] *Can* ketchup

**Kfé** SMS *abr écrite de* **café**

**kidnapper** [kidnape] *vt* to kidnap ▪ **kidnappeur, -euse** *nmf* kidnapper

**kiffer, kifer** [kife] *vt Fam* to love

**kilo** [kilo] *nm* kilo ▪ **kilogramme** *nm* kilogram(me)

**kiloeuro** [kiloørɔ] *nm* one thousand euros

**kilomètre** [kilɔmɛtr] *nm Br* kilometre, *Am* kilometer ▪ **kilométrage** *nm* AUTO ≃ mileage ▪ **kilométrique** *adj* **borne kilométrique** ≃ milestone

**kilo-octet** [kilɔɔktɛ] (*pl* **kilo-octets**) *nm* ORDINAT kilobyte

**kilowatt** [kilɔwat] *nm* kilowatt

**kiné** [kine] *Fam* **1.** *nf* (*abr de* **kinésithérapie**) *Br* physio, *Am* physical therapy ; **5 séances de kiné** 5 sessions of *Br* physio *or Am* physical therapy **2.** *nmf* (*abr de* **kinésithérapeute**) *Br* physio, *Am* physical therapist ; **faire des séances de kiné** to do physiotherapy sessions

**kinésithérapeute** [kineziterapøt] *nmf Br* physiotherapist, *Am* physical therapist

**kiosque** [kjɔsk] *nm* [à fleurs] kiosk, *Br* stall ; **kiosque à journaux** news-stand

**kir** [kir] *nm* kir (*apéritif made with white wine and blackcurrant liqueur*)

**kit** [kit] *nm* (self-assembly) kit ; **en kit** in kit form ; **kit mains libres** [pour mobile] hands-free kit ; **kit auto mains libres** [pour mobile] car kit

**kitesurf** [kajtsœrf], **kite** [kajt] *nm* kitesurfing

**kitsch, kitch** [kitʃ] *adj inv* kitsch

**kiwi** [kiwi] *nm* [oiseau, fruit] kiwi

**Klaxon®** [klaksɔn] *nm* horn ▪ **klaxonner** *vi* to sound one's horn

**km** (*abr de* **kilomètre**) km

**km/h** (*abr de* **kilomètre-heure**) kph, ≃ mph

**koi** (*abr de* **quoi**) SMS WOT

**koi29** SMS *abr écrite de* **quoi de neuf?**

**Kosovo** [kɔsɔvɔ] *nm* **le Kosovo** Kosovo

**Koweït** [kɔwɛjt] *nm* **le Koweït** Kuwait ▪ **koweïtien, -enne 1.** *adj* Kuwaiti **2.** *nmf* **Koweïtien, Koweïtienne** Kuwaiti

**kyrielle** [kirjɛl] *nf* stream ; [d'enfants] horde

**L, l** [ɛl] *nm inv* L, l

**l', la¹** [l, la] *voir* **le**

**la²** [la] *nm inv* [note] A

**là** [la] **1.** *adv* [là-bas] there ; [ici] here ; c'est là que... [lieu] that's where... ; à 5 mètres de là 5 metres away **2.** *excl* oh là là ! oh dear ! **3.** *voir* **ce, celui**

**là-bas** [labɑ] *adv* over there

**labo** [labo] (*abr de* **laboratoire**) *nm* Fam lab (*laboratory*)

**laboratoire** [labɔratwar] *nm* laboratory

**labourer** [labure] *vt* [terre] *Br* to plough, *Am* to plow

**lac** [lak] *nm* lake

**lacet** [lasɛ] *nm* [de chaussure] lace ; faire ses lacets to tie one's laces

**lâche** [lɑʃ] **1.** *adj* [nœud] loose, slack ; *Péj* [personne, acte] cowardly **2.** *nmf* coward ▪ **lâcheté** *nf* cowardice ; une lâcheté [action] a cowardly act

**lâcher** [lɑʃe] **1.** *vt* [ne plus tenir] to let go of ; [bombe] to drop ; [poursuivant] to shake off ; [dans une course] to leave behind ; lâcher prise to let go **2.** *vi* [corde] to break

**là-dedans** [ladədɑ̃] *adv* [lieu] in there, inside

**là-dessous** [ladəsu] *adv* underneath

**là-dessus** [ladəsy] *adv* on there ; [monter] on top

**lagune** [lagyn] *nf* lagoon

**là-haut** [lao] *adv* up there ; [à l'étage] upstairs

**laid, -e** [lɛ, lɛd] *adj* [physiquement] ugly ▪ **laideur** *nf* ugliness

**laine** [lɛn] *nf* wool ; de laine, en laine *Br* woollen, *Am* woolen ; laine polaire (polar) fleece ▪ **lainage** *nm* [vêtement] sweater, *Br* jumper

**laisse** [lɛs] *nf* lead, leash

**laisser** [lese] **1.** *vt* to leave ; laisser qn partir [permettre] to let sb go ; laisser qch à qn [confier, donner] to leave sth with sb **2.** se laisser *vpr* se laisser aller to let oneself go ; se laisser faire to be pushed around

**lait** [lɛ] *nm* milk ; lait entier /demi-écrémé /écrémé whole / part-skim / skim milk ▪ **laitier** *adj m* produit laitier dairy product

**laitue** [lɛty] *nf* lettuce

**lame** [lam] *nf* [de couteau, de rasoir] blade ; [vague] wave

**lamelle** [lamɛl] *nf* thin strip

**lamenter** [lamɑ̃te] ▪ **se lamenter** *vpr* to moan ▪ **lamentable** *adj* [mauvais] terrible, deplorable ; [voix, cri] mournful ; [personne] pathetic

**lampadaire** [lɑ̃padɛr] *nm Br* standard lamp, *Am* floor lamp ; [de rue] street lamp

**lampe** [lɑ̃p] *nf* lamp ; lampe de poche *Br* torch, *Am* flashlight

**lance** [lɑ̃s] *nf* spear

**lancer** [lɑ̃se] **1.** *vt* [jeter] to throw (à to) ; [fusée, produit] to launch ; [appel] to issue ; ORDINAT [programme] to start **2.** se lancer *vpr* [se précipiter] to rush ; se lancer dans [aventure] to launch into **3.** *nm* SPORT lancer du javelot throwing the javelin ; lancer franc [au basket] free throw ▪ **lancement** *nm* [de fusée, de produit] launch(ing) ▪ **lance-pierre** (*pl* **lance-pierres**) *nm Br* catapult, *Am* slingshot ▪ **lance-roquettes** (*pl* **lance-roquettes**) *nm* (hand held) rocket launcher *or* gun

**landau, -s** [lɑ̃do] *nm Br* pram, *Am* baby carriage

**langage** [lɑ̃gaʒ] *nm* language; ORDINAT **langage machine / naturel** computer / natural language

**langer** [lɑ̃ʒe] *vt* [bébé] to change

**langouste** [lɑ̃gust] *nf* crayfish ■ **langoustine** *nf* langoustine

**langue** [lɑ̃g] *nf* ANAT tongue; LING language; **de langue anglaise / française** English- / French-speaking; **langue étrangère** foreign language; **langue maternelle** mother tongue; **langues vivantes** modern languages ■ **languette** *nf* [patte] tongue

**lanière** [lanjɛr] *nf* strap; [d'étoffe] strip

**lapin** [lapɛ̃] *nm* rabbit

**laque** [lak] *nf* [pour cheveux] hair spray

**laquelle** [lakɛl] *voir* **lequel**

**lard** [lar] *nm* [viande] bacon ■ **lardon** *nm* CULIN strip of bacon

**large** [larʒ] **1.** *adj* [route, porte, chaussure] wide; [considérable] **large de 6 mètres** 6 metres wide **2.** *nm* **avoir 6 mètres de large** to be 6 *Br* metres or *Am* meters wide; **au large de Cherbourg** off Cherbourg ■ **largement** [-əmɑ̃] *adv* [répandu, critiqué] widely; [payer, servir] generously; [dépasser] by a long way; **avoir largement le temps** to have plenty of time ■ **largeur** *nf* [dimension] width, breadth; **en largeur, dans la largeur** widthwise

**larguer** [large] *vt* [bombe] to drop; NAUT **larguer les amarres** to cast off

**larme** [larm] *nf* tear; **en larmes** in tears; **rire aux larmes** to laugh till one cries

**las, lasse** [lɑ, lɑs] *adj* weary (**de** of) ■ **lassant, -e** *adj* tiresome ■ **lasser 1.** *vt* to tire **2. se lasser** *vpr* **se lasser de qch / de faire qch** to get tired of sth / of doing sth

**laser** [lazɛr] *nm* laser

**latéral, -e, -aux** [lateral, -o] *adj* side

**latin, -e** [latɛ̃, -in] **1.** *adj* Latin **2.** *nmf* **Latin, Latine** Latin **3.** *nm* [langue] Latin

**latino** [latino] *adj & nmf* Latino

**latino-américain, e** [latinoamerikɛ̃, ɛn] *(mpl* **latino-américains,** *fpl* **latino-américaines)** *adj* Latin-American, Hispanic

**lavabo** [lavabo] *nm* washbasin; **lavabos** [toilettes] *Br* toilet(s), *Am* washroom

**lavande** [lavɑ̃d] *nf* lavender

**lave** [lav] *nf* lava

**laver** [lave] **1.** *vt* to wash; **laver qch à l'eau froide** to wash sth in cold water **2. se laver** *vpr* to wash (oneself), *Am* to wash up; **se laver les mains** to wash one's hands ■ **lavable** *adj* washable ■ **lavage** *nm* washing ■ **lave-auto** *(pl* **lave-autos)** *nm Can* carwash ■ **lave-linge** *nm inv* washing machine ■ **laverie** *nf* [automatique] *Br* launderette, *Am* Laundromat® ■ **laveur** *nm* **laveur de vitres** window *Br* cleaner or *Am* washer ■ **lave-vaisselle** *nm inv* dishwasher ■ **lave-vitre** *nm* AUTO *Br* windscreen or *Am* windshield washer

**LCD** *(abr de* **liquid cristal display)** *nm* LCD

---

**le, la, les** [lə, la, le]

**l'** is used instead of **le** or **la** before a word beginning with a vowel or h mute.

**1.** *art déf* **a)** [pour définir le nom] the; **le garçon** the boy; **la fille** the girl; **les petits** the little ones
**b)** [avec les notions] **la vie** life; **la France** France; **les Français** the French; **les hommes** men; **aimer le café** to like coffee
**c)** [avec les parties du corps] **il ouvrit la bouche** he opened his mouth; **se blesser au pied** to hurt one's foot; **avoir les cheveux blonds** to have blond hair
**d)** [distributif] **10 euros le kilo** 10 euros a kilo
**e)** [dans les compléments de temps] **elle vient le lundi** she comes on Mondays; **l'an prochain** next year
**2.** *pron* [homme] him; [femme] her; [chose, animal] it; **les** them; **je la vois** I see her / it; **je le vois** I see him / it; **je les vois** I see them

**lécher** [leʃe] *vt* to lick

**lèche-vitrines** [lɛʃvitrin] *nm inv* window-shopping; **faire du lèche-vitrines** to go window-shopping

**leçon** [ləsɔ̃] *nf* lesson

**lecteur, trice** [lɛktœr, tris] *nmf* **a)** [de livres] reader **b)** UNIV foreign language assistant ▪ **lecteur** *nm* [gén] head; ORDINAT reader; **lecteur de CD** CD player; **lecteur de DVD** DVD player

**lecture** *nf* reading

**légal, -e, -aux** [legal, -o] *adj* legal ▪ **légaliser** *vt* to legalize ▪ **légalité** *nf* legality **(de** of)

**légende** [leʒɑ̃d] *nf* [histoire] legend; [de carte] key; [de photo] caption

**léger, -ère** [leʒe, -ɛr] **1.** *adj* light; [blessure, odeur] slight; [café, thé] weak; [bière, tabac] mild; [frivole] frivolous; [irréfléchi] thoughtless **2.** *adv* **manger léger** to have a light meal **3.** *nf* **prendre qch à la légère** to make light of sth ▪ **légèrement** *adv* [inconsidérément] lightly; [un peu] slightly ▪ **légèreté** *nf* [poids] lightness; [de blessure] slightness; [d'attitude] thoughtlessness

**légion** [leʒjɔ̃] *nf* MIL legion ▪ **légionnaire** *nm* [de la Légion étrangère] legionnaire

**légionellose** [leʒjɔnɛloz] *nf* MÉD legionnaires' disease

**législatif, ive** [leʒislatif, iv] *adj* legislative ▪ **législatives** *nfpl* **les législatives** the legislative elections, *Br* ≃ the general election *(sg)*, *Am* ≃ the Congressional election *(sg)*

**légitime** [leʒitim] *adj* [action, enfant] legitimate; [héritier] rightful; [colère] justified; **être en état de légitime défense** to be acting in *Br* self-defence or *Am* self-defense

**léguer** [lege] *vt* to bequeath (**à** to)

**légume** [legym] *nm* vegetable

**lendemain** [lɑ̃dmɛ̃] *nm* **le lendemain** the next day; **le lendemain de** the day after; **le lendemain matin** the next morning

**lent, -e** [lɑ̃, lɑ̃t] *adj* slow

**lentille** [lɑ̃tij] *nf* [plante, graine] lentil; [verre] lens; **lentilles de contact** contact lenses

**lequel, laquelle** [ləkɛl, lakɛl] *(mpl* **lesquels**, *fpl* **lesquelles** [lekɛl]*)*

> **lequel** and **lesquel(le)s** contract with **à** to form **auquel** and **auxquel(le)s**, and with **de** to form **duquel** and **desquel(le)s**.

**1.** *pron rel* [chose, animal] which; [personne] who; [indirect] whom; **dans lequel** in which; **parmi lesquels** [choses, animaux] among which; [personnes] among whom **2.** *pron interr* which (one); **lequel préférez-vous ?** which (one) do you prefer?

**les** [le] *voir* **le**

**lessive** [lesiv] *nf* [produit] washing powder; [liquide] liquid detergent; [linge] washing; **faire la lessive** to do the washing

**Lettonie** [lɛtɔni] *nf* **la Lettonie** Latvia

**lettre** [lɛtr] *nf* [missive, caractère] letter; **envoyer/recevoir une lettre** to send / receive a letter; **lettre commerciale** business letter; **lettre de démission** letter of resignation; **lettre de motivation** covering letter *(sent with job application)* ▪ **lettres** *nfpl* [discipline] arts, humanities

**leur** [lœr] **1.** *adj poss* their; **leur chat** their cat; **leurs voitures** their cars **2.** *pron poss* **le leur, la leur, les leurs** theirs **3.** *pron pers* [indirect] to them; **donne-leur ta carte** give them your card

**lever** [ləve] **1.** *vt* [objet] to lift, to raise; [blocus, immunité] to lift; [séance] to close; [impôts] to levy **2.** *vi* [pâte] to rise **3.** **se lever** *vpr* to get up; [soleil] to rise; [jour] to break; [brouillard] to clear, to lift **4.** *nm* **le lever du soleil** sunrise; THÉÂT **lever de rideau** curtain up ▪ **levé, -e** *adj* **être levé** [debout] to be up ▪ **levée** *nf* [d'interdiction] lifting; [du courrier] collection ▪ **lève-tard** [lɛvtar] *nmf Fam* late riser ▪ **lève-tôt** [lɛvto] *nmf Fam* early riser

**levier** [ləvje] *nm* lever; AUTO **levier de vitesse** *Br* gear lever, *Am* gearshift

**lèvre** [levr] *nf* lip

**lévrier** [levrije] *nm* greyhound

**levure** [ləvyr] *nf* yeast

**lézard** [lezar] *nm* lizard ■ **se lézarder** *vpr* to crack

**liaison** [ljezɔ̃] *nf* [rapport] connection ; [entre mots & MIL] liaison ; **liaison aérienne/ferroviaire** air / rail link ; **liaison amoureuse** love affair

**Liban** [libɑ̃] *nm* **le Liban** (the) Lebanon ■ **libanais, -e 1.** *adj* Lebanese **2.** *nmf* **Libanais, Libanaise** Lebanese

**libeller** [libele] *vt* [chèque] to make out

**libéral, -e, -aux** [liberal, -o] *adj & nmf* liberal

**libérer** [libere] **1.** *vt* [prisonnier] to free, to release ; [pays] to liberate (**de** from) ; [chambre] to vacate **2. se libérer** *vpr* to free oneself (**de** from) ; **je n'ai pas pu me libérer** I couldn't get away ■ **libération** *nf* [de prisonnier] release ; [de pays] liberation

**liberté** [liberte] *nf* freedom, liberty ; **mettre qn en liberté** to set sb free

**libraire** [librer] *nmf* bookseller ■ **librairie** *nf* [magasin] bookshop

**libre** [libr] *adj* [personne, siège] free (**de qch** from sth ; **de faire** to do) ; [voie] clear ; **radio libre** independent radio ■ **libre-échange** *nm* ÉCON free trade ■ **libre-service** (*pl* **libres-services**) *nm* [système, magasin] self-service

**Libye** [libi] *nf* **la Libye** Libya ■ **libyen, -enne 1.** *adj* Libyan **2.** *nmf* **Libyen, Libyenne** Libyan

**licence** [lisɑ̃s] *nf* SPORT permit ; COMM *Br* licence, *Am* license ; UNIV (bachelor's) degree ; **licence ès lettres/sciences** arts / science degree ■ **licence-master-doctorat** [lisɑ̃smasterdɔktɔra] (*pl* **licences-masters-doctorats**), **LMD, lmd** [ɛlɛmde] *nm* ≃ Bachelor Master Doctorate, ≃ BMD

**licencier** [lisɑ̃sje] *vt* [pour faute] to dismiss, to fire ; [pour raison économique] to lay off, *Br* to make redundant ; **se faire licencier** to be laid off, *Br* to be made redundant ■ **licenciement** *nm* lay-off, *Br* redundancy

**lien** [ljɛ̃] *nm* [rapport] link, connection ; [attache] bond ; ORDINAT link ; **lien de parenté** family relationship ; ORDINAT **lien hypertexte** hypertext link

**lier** [lje] **1.** *vt* [attacher] to tie up ; [contrat] to be binding on ; [personnes] to bind together ; [paragraphes] to connect, to link ; **lier qn** [unir, engager] to bind sb ; **être très lié avec qn** to be great friends with sb **2. se lier** *vpr* **se lier d'amitié** to become friends

**lierre** [ljer] *nm* ivy

**lieu¹, -x** [ljø] *nm* place ; **les lieux** [locaux] the premises ; **être sur les lieux** to be on the spot ; **avoir lieu** to take place ; **au lieu de qch** instead of sth ; **au lieu de faire qch** instead of doing sth ; **en dernier lieu** lastly ; **lieu de naissance** place of birth ; **lieu public** public place ; **lieu de travail** workplace ; **lieu de vacances** *Br* holiday *or Am* vacation destination

**lieu², -s** [ljø] *nm* [poisson] **lieu noir** coalfish

**lieutenant** [ljøtnɑ̃] *nmf* lieutenant

**lièvre** [ljevr] *nm* hare

**ligne** [liɲ] *nf* [trait] line ; [silhouette] figure ; [rangée] row, line ; **les grandes lignes** [de train] the main lines ; *Fig* [idées principales] the broad outline ; **aller à la ligne** to begin a new paragraph ; *Fig* **sur toute la ligne** completely ; **ligne d'autobus** bus service ; [parcours] bus route ; **ligne de chemin de fer** *Br* railway *or Am* railroad line ; SPORT **ligne de touche** touchline ; **en ligne** [personnes] in a line ; ORDINAT on line

**ligoter** [ligote] *vt* to tie up

**liguer** [lige] ■ **se liguer** *vpr* [États] to form a league (**contre** against) ; [personnes] to gang up (**contre** against)

**lilas** [lila] *nm & adj inv* lilac

**limace** [limas] *nf* slug

**limande** [limɑ̃d] *nf* dab

**lime** [lim] *nf* [outil] file ; **lime à ongles** nail file

**limitation** [limitasjɔ̃] *nf* limitation ; **limitation de vitesse** speed limit

**limite** [limit] **1.** *nf* limit (**à** to) ; [de propriété] boundary ; **sans limite**

unlimited, limitless; **dans la limite des stocks disponibles** while stocks last **2.** adj [vitesse, âge] maximum

**limiter** [limite] **1.** vt [restreindre] to limit, to restrict (**à** to); [territoire] to bound **2. se limiter** vpr **se limiter à qch / à faire qch** to limit or restrict oneself to sth / to doing sth

**limitrophe** [limitʀɔf] adj **a)** [frontalier] border **b)** [voisin] adjacent; **être limitrophe de** to border on

**limoger** [limɔʒe] vt to dismiss

**limonade** [limɔnad] nf [boisson] lemonade

**limpide** [lɛ̃pid] adj [eau, explication] clear, crystal-clear

**lin** [lɛ̃] nm [tissu] linen

**linge** [lɛ̃ʒ] nm [vêtements] linen; [à laver] washing; **linge de corps** underwear ■ **lingerie** nf [de femmes] underwear

**lingette** [lɛ̃ʒɛt] nf wipe; **lingette antibactérienne** anti-bacterial wipe; **lingette démaquillante** eye makeup remover pad

**lingot** [lɛ̃go] nm **lingot d'or** gold bar

**lino** [lino], **linoléum** [linɔleɔm] nm lino, linoleum

**lion** [ljɔ̃] nm lion; **le Lion** [signe] Leo

**lipide** [lipid] nm [d'aliment] fat

**liqueur** [likœʀ] nf liqueur

**liquide** [likid] **1.** adj liquid **2.** nm liquid; [argent] cash; **payer en liquide** to pay cash

**liquider** [likide] vt [stock] to clear ■ **liquidation** nf [de stock] clearing; COMM **liquidation totale** stock clearance

**lire¹** [liʀ] **1.** vt to read; **lire qch à qn** to read sth to sb **2.** vi to read

**lire²** [liʀ] nf [monnaie] lira

**lis, lisant, lise(nt)** [li, lizɑ̃, liz] voir **lire**

**lisible** [lizibl] adj [écriture] legible

**lisière** [lizjɛʀ] nf edge

**lisse** [lis] adj smooth

**liste** [list] nf list; **liste d'attente** waiting list; **liste électorale** electoral roll;

**liste noire** blacklist; **être sur la liste rouge** [du téléphone] to be Br ex-directory or Am unlisted

**listériose** [listeʀjoz] nf MÉD listeriosis

**lit¹** [li] nm bed; **se mettre au lit** to go to bed; **faire son lit** to make one's bed; **lit de camp** Br camp bed, Am cot; **lit d'enfant** Br cot, Am crib; **lits superposés** bunk beds

**lit²** [li] voir **lire**

**litchi** [litʃi], **letchi** [letʃi] nm **a)** [arbre] litchi, lychee **b)** [fruit] litchi, lychee, lichee

**litière** [litjɛʀ] nf [d'animal] litter

**litige** [litiʒ] nm [conflit] dispute

**litre** [litʀ] nm Br litre, Am liter

**littéraire** [liteʀɛʀ] adj literary ■ **littérature** nf literature

**littoral, -e, -aux** [litɔʀal, -o] **1.** adj coastal **2.** nm coast(line)

**Lituanie** [lituani] nf **la Lituanie** Lithuania

**livraison** [livʀɛzɔ̃] nf delivery

**livre** [livʀ] **1.** nm book; NAUT **livre de bord** logbook; **livre de poche** paperback (book) **2.** nf [monnaie, poids] pound

**livrer** [livʀe] **1.** vt [marchandises] to deliver (**à** to); **livrer qn à la police** to hand sb over to the police **2. se livrer** vpr [se rendre] to give oneself up (**à** to) ■ **livreur, -euse** nmf delivery man, f delivery woman

**livret** [livʀɛ] nm [livre] booklet; **livret d'épargne** bankbook, Br passbook; **livret scolaire** school report book

**LMD, lmd** [ɛlɛmde] nm = **licence-master-doctorat**

**local, -e, -aux** [lɔkal, -o] **1.** adj local **2.** nm [pièce] room; **locaux** [bâtiment] premises

**localité** [lɔkalite] nf locality

**locataire** [lɔkatɛʀ] nmf tenant; [chez le propriétaire] lodger, Am roomer

**location** [lɔkasjɔ̃] nf [de maison - par le locataire] renting; [par le propriétaire] renting out, Br letting; [de voiture] renting, Br hiring; [logement] rented Br accommodation or Am accommodations;

[loyer] rent ; [pour spectacle] booking ; **bureau de location** booking office ; **en location** on hire ; **voiture de location** rented *or Br* hired car

**locomotion** [lɔkɔmosjɔ̃] *nf* moyen de locomotion means of transport

**locomotive** [lɔkɔmotiv] *nf* [de train] engine

**loge** [lɔʒ] *nf* [de concierge] lodge ; [d'acteur] dressing-room ; THÉÂT [de spectateur] box

**loger** [lɔʒe] **1.** *vt* [recevoir, mettre] to accommodate ; [héberger] to put up ; **être logé et nourri** to have board and lodging **2.** *vi* [temporairement] to stay ; [en permanence] to live **3. se loger** *vpr* **trouver à se loger** to find somewhere to live ; [temporairement] to find somewhere to stay ▪ **logement** *nm* [habitation] lodging, *Br* accommodation, *Am* accommodations ; **le logement** housing ; **logements sociaux** social housing

**logiciel** [lɔʒisjɛl] *nm* ORDINAT software *inv* ; **logiciel espion** spyware

**logique** [lɔʒik] **1.** *adj* logical **2.** *nf* logic

**loi** [lwa] *nf* law ; **faire la loi** to lay down the law (**à** to)

**loin** [lwɛ̃] *adv* far (away or off) (**de** from) ; **Nice est loin de Paris** Nice is a long way away from Paris ; **plus loin** further, farther ; **au loin** in the distance, far away ; **de loin** from a distance ▪ **lointain, -e** *adj* distant, far-off ; [rapport] remote

**loisirs** [lwazir] *nmpl* [temps libre] spare time, leisure (time) ; [distractions] leisure *or* spare-time activities

**LOL** *(abr de* laughing out loud) SMS LOL

**Londres** [lɔ̃dr] *nm ou f* London ▪ **londonien, -enne 1.** *adj* London, of London **2.** *nmf* **Londonien, Londonienne** Londoner

**long, longue** [lɔ̃, lɔ̃g] **1.** *adj* long ; **long de 2 mètres** 2 metres long **2.** *nm* avoir **2 mètres de long** to be 2 metres long ; **le long de qch** along sth ; **de long en large** [marcher] up and down **3.** *adv* **en savoir long sur qch** to know a lot about sth ▪ **long-courrier** *(pl* **long-**

**courriers)** **1.** *adj* [navire] ocean-going ; [vol] long-haul **2.** *nm* [avion] long-haul aircraft

**longer** [lɔ̃ʒe] *vt* [sujet : personne, voiture] to go along ; [mur, côte] to hug ; [sujet : sentier, canal] to run alongside

**longtemps** [lɔ̃tɑ̃] *adv* (for) a long time ; **trop longtemps** too long ; **aussi longtemps que** as long as

**longue** [lɔ̃g] *voir* **long** ; **à la longue** in the end ▪ **longuement** *adv* [expliquer] at length ; [réfléchir] for a long time ▪ **longueur** *nf* length ; RADIO **longueur d'onde** wavelength ▪ **longueurs** *nfpl* [de film, de livre] boring parts ▪ **longue-vue** *(pl* **longues-vues)** *nf* telescope

**look** [luk] *nm* *Fam* look ; **avoir un look** to have a style

**lopin** [lɔpɛ̃] *nm* **lopin de terre** plot *or* patch of land

**loquet** [lɔkɛ] *nm* latch

**lorgner** [lɔrɲe] *vt* [regarder] to eye ; [convoiter] to have one's eye on

**lors** [lɔr] *adv* **lors de** at the time of ; **dès lors** from then on ; **dès lors que** [puisque] since

**lorsque** [lɔrsk(ə)] *conj* when

**losange** [lɔzɑ̃ʒ] *nm* [forme] diamond

**lot** [lo] *nm* [de marchandises] batch ; [de loterie] prize ; **gros lot** jackpot

**loterie** [lɔtri] *nf* lottery

**lotion** [lɔsjɔ̃] *nf* lotion

**lotissement** [lɔtismɑ̃] *nm* [terrain] building plot ; [habitations] housing *Br* estate *or Am* development

**loto** [lɔto] *nm* [jeu] lotto ; [jeu national] national lottery ; *Can* lottery

**louange** [lwɑ̃ʒ] *nf* praise

**louche**[1] [luʃ] *nf* [cuillère] ladle

**louche**[2] [luʃ] *adj* [suspect] dodgy

**loucher** [luʃe] *vi* to squint

**louer**[1] [lwe] *vt* [prendre en location - maison, appartement] to rent ; [voiture] to rent, *Br* to hire ; [donner en location - logement] to rent out, *Br* to let ; [voiture] to rent out, *Br* to hire out; [réserver] to book; **maison / chambre à louer** house / room to rent or Br to let

**louer²** [lwe] **1.** vt [exalter] to praise (**de** for) **2. se louer** vpr **se louer de qch** to be highly satisfied with sth

**loup** [lu] nm wolf

**loupe** [lup] nf magnifying glass

**lourd, -e** [lur, lurd] **1.** adj heavy (**de** with); [temps] sticky; **il fait lourd** [temps] it's very sticky **2.** adv **peser lourd** [personne, objet] to be heavy ■ **lourdement** [-əmā] adv heavily ■ **lourdeur** nf heaviness; **avoir des lourdeurs d'estomac** to feel bloated

**lousse** [lus] adj Can Fam loose

**loyal, -e, -aux** [lwajal, -o] adj [honnête] fair (**envers** to); [dévoué] loyal (**envers** to) ■ **loyauté** nf [honnêteté] fairness; [dévouement] loyalty (**envers** to)

**loyer** [lwaje] nm rent

**lu** [ly] pp de **lire**

**lubrifier** [lybrifje] vt to lubricate

**lucarne** [lykarn] nf [fenêtre] dormer window; [de toit] skylight

**lucide** [lysid] adj lucid ■ **lucidité** nf lucidity

**lucratif, -ive** [lykratif, -iv] adj lucrative

**lueur** [lɥœr] nf [lumière] & Fig glimmer

**luge** [lyʒ] nf Br sledge, Am sled, toboggan

**lui** [lɥi] pron pers **a)** [objet indirect] (to) him; [femme] (to) her; [chose, animal] (to) it; **je le lui ai montré** I showed it to him / her
**b)** [complément direct] him; **elle n'aime que lui** she only loves him
**c)** [après une préposition] him; **pour / avec lui** for / with him; **elle pense à lui** she thinks of him; **ce livre est à lui** this book is his
**d)** [dans les comparaisons] **elle est plus grande que lui** she's taller than he is or than him

**e)** [sujet] **lui, il ne viendra pas** [emphatique] HE won't come; **c'est lui qui me l'a dit** he is the one who told me
■ **lui-même** pron himself; [chose, animal] itself

**luire** [lɥir] vi to shine ■ **luisant, -e** adj [métal] shiny

**lumière** [lymjɛr] nf light; **à la lumière de** by the light of

**lumineux, -euse** [lyminø, -øz] adj [idée, ciel] bright, brilliant; [cadran] luminous

**lunaire** [lynɛr] adj lunar

**lundi** [lœdi] nm Monday

**lune** [lyn] nf moon; **lune de miel** honeymoon

**lunette** [lynɛt] nf [astronomique] telescope; **lunettes** [de vue] glasses, spectacles; [de protection, de plongée] goggles; **lunette arrière** [de voiture] rear window; **lunettes de soleil** sunglasses

**lurette** [lyrɛt] nf Fam **il y a belle lurette que…** it's been ages since…

**lustre** [lystr] nm [lampe] chandelier; [éclat] lustre

**lutte** [lyt] nf fight, struggle; SPORT wrestling ■ **lutter** vi to fight, to struggle; SPORT to wrestle

**luxation** [lyksasjɔ̃] nf MÉD dislocation

**luxe** [lyks] nm luxury; **modèle de luxe** de luxe model ■ **luxueux, -euse** adj luxurious

**Luxembourg** [lyksābur] nm **le Luxembourg** Luxembourg

**lycée** [lise] nm Br ≃ secondary school, Am ≃ high school; **lycée technique** ou **professionnel** vocational or technical school ■ **lycéen, -enne** nmf pupil (at a lycée)

# M

**M¹, m¹** [ɛm] *nm inv* M, m

**M²** *(abr de* **Monsieur***)* Mr

**m²** *(abr de* **mètre(s)***)* m

**m'** [m] *voir* me

**ma** [ma] *voir* mon

**Mac** [mak] *nm* ORDINAT Mac

**macérer** [masere] *vt & vi* to steep

**mâcher** [maʃe] *vt* to chew

**machine** [maʃin] *nf* [appareil] machine; **machine à calculer** calculator; **machine à coudre** sewing machine; **machine à écrire** typewriter; **machine à laver** washing machine; **machine à laver la vaisselle** dishwasher; **machine à** *ou* **de traitement de texte** word processor ■ **machiniste** *nm* [conducteur] driver

**mâchoire** [maʃwar] *nf* jaw

**mâchonner** [maʃɔne] *vt* to chew

**maçon** [masɔ̃] *nm* [de briques] bricklayer; [de pierres] mason ■ **maçonnerie** *nf* [travaux] building work; [ouvrage de briques] brickwork; [de pierres] masonry, stonework

**macro** [makro] *nf* ORDINAT macro

**Madagascar** [madagaskar] *nf* Madagascar

**madame** [madam] *(pl* **mesdames***) nf* [en apostrophe] madam; **bonjour mesdames** good morning(, ladies); **Madame Legras** Mrs Legras; **Madame** [dans une lettre] Dear Madam

**madeleine** *nf* (small) sponge cake

**mademoiselle** [madmwazɛl] *(pl* **mesdemoiselles***) nf* [avant nom] Miss; **Mademoiselle Legras** Miss Legras; **Mademoiselle** [dans une lettre] Dear Madam

**magasin** [magazɛ̃] *nm Br* shop, *Am* store; [entrepôt] warehouse; [d'arme & PHOTO] magazine; **grand magasin** department store; **en magasin** in stock; **faire les magasins** to go shopping ■ **magasinage** *nm Can* shopping ■ **magasiner** *vi Can* to shop ■ **magasinier, ère** *nmf* warehouseman, storeman

**magazine** [magazin] *nm* [revue] magazine

**magie** [maʒi] *nf* magic ■ **magicien, -enne** *nmf* magician ■ **magique** *adj* [surnaturel] magic; [enchanteur] magical

**magistrat** [maʒistra] *nm* magistrate

**magnanime** [maɲanim] *adj* magnanimous

**magnat** [magna] *nm* tycoon, magnate

**magnésium** [maɲezjɔm] *nm* magnesium

**magnet** [maɲɛt, magnɛt] *nm* fridge magnet

**magnétique** [maɲetik] *adj* magnetic

**magnétophone** [maɲetɔfɔn] *nm* tape recorder; **magnétophone à cassettes** cassette recorder

**magnétoscope** [maɲetɔskɔp] *nm Br* video (recorder), *Am* VCR

**magnifique** [maɲifik] *adj* magnificent

**mai** [mɛ] *nm* May

**maigre** [mɛgr] *adj* [personne, corps] thin; [viande] lean; [fromage] low-fat; [salaire] *Br* meagre, *Am* meager ■ **maigrir** *vi* to get thinner

**mail** [mɛl] *nm* ORDINAT email (message), mail ■ **mailing** [mɛliŋ] *nm* mailing, *Br* mailshot

**maillot** [majo] *nm* [de sportif] jersey, shirt; **maillot de bain** [de femme] swimsuit; [d'homme] (swimming) trunks; **maillot jaune** [du Tour de France] yellow jersey

**main** [mɛ̃] **1.** nf hand; **à la main** [faire, écrire] by hand; **tenir qch à la main** to hold sth in one's hand; **à main droite** on the right-hand side; **à main gauche** on the left-hand side; **de la main** with one's hand; **de la main, elle me fit signe d'approcher** she waved me over; **saluer qn de la main** [pour dire bonjour] to wave (hello) to sb; [pour dire au revoir] to wave (goodbye) to sb, to wave sb goodbye; **de la main à la main** directly, without any middleman; **j'ai payé le plombier de la main à la main** I paid the plumber cash in hand; **de main en main** from hand to hand, from one person to the next; **d'une main** [ouvrir, faire] with one hand; [prendre] with or in one hand; **donner qch d'une main et le reprendre de l'autre** to give sth with one hand and take it back with the other; **en mains propres** in person; **donner la main à qn** to hold sb's hand; **haut les mains !** hands up!; **la main dans la main** [en se tenant par la main] hand in hand; Fig together; Péj hand in glove **2.** adj **fait main** hand-made ▪ **main-d'œuvre** (pl **mains-d'œuvre**) nf Br labour, Am labor ▪ **main-forte** [mɛ̃fɔrt] nf sg **prêter main-forte à qn** to come to sb's assistance

**maintenant** [mɛ̃tənɑ̃] adv now; [de nos jours] nowadays; **maintenant que…** now that…; **dès maintenant** from now on

**maintenir** [mɛ̃tənir] **1.** vt [conserver] to keep, to maintain; [retenir] to hold in position; [affirmer] to maintain (**que** that) **2. se maintenir** vpr [durer] to remain ▪ **maintien** nm [action] maintenance (**de** of); [allure] bearing

**maire** [mɛr] nm mayor ▪ **mairie** nf Br town hall, Am city hall; [administration] Br town council, Am city hall

**mais** [mɛ] conj but; **mais oui, mais si** of course; **mais non** definitely not

**maïs** [mais] nm Br maize, Am corn

**maison** [mɛzɔ̃] **1.** nf [bâtiment, famille] house; [foyer] home; [entreprise] company; **à la maison** at home; **rentrer à la maison** to go /come (back) home; **mai-** son de la culture arts centre; **maison d'édition** publishing house; **maison de repos** rest home; **maison de retraite** old people's home; **maison de santé** nursing home; **maison secondaire** second home **2.** adj inv [artisanal] home-made

**maître** [mɛtr] nm master; **être maître de la situation** to be in control of the situation; **maître d'hôtel** [de restaurant] head waiter; **maître de maison** host; **maître chanteur** blackmailer; **maître nageur (sauveteur)** swimming instructor (and lifeguard) ▪ **maître-chien** [mɛtrəʃjɛ̃] (pl **maîtres-chiens**) nm dog trainer or handler

**maîtresse** [mɛtrɛs] **1.** nf mistress; **être maîtresse de la situation** to be in control of the situation; **maîtresse d'école** teacher; **maîtresse de maison** hostess **2.** adj f [idée, poutre] main; [carte] master

**maîtrise** [mɛtriz] nf [contrôle, connaissance] mastery (**de** of); [diplôme] ≃ master's degree (**de** in); **maîtrise de soi** self-control ▪ **maîtriser 1.** vt [incendie, passion] to control; [peur] to overcome; [sujet] to master; [véhicule] to have under control; **maîtriser qn** to overpower sb **2. se maîtriser** vpr to control oneself

**majesté** [maʒɛste] nf majesty; **Votre Majesté** [titre] Your Majesty

**majeur, -e** [maʒœr] **1.** adj [important & MUS] major; JUR **être majeur** to be of age; **la majeure partie de** most of **2.** nm [doigt] middle finger

**majorer** [maʒɔre] vt to increase

**majorette** [maʒɔrɛt] nf (drum) majorette

**majoritaire** [maʒɔriter] adj majority; **être majoritaire** to be in the majority

**majorité** [maʒɔrite] nf majority (**de** of); [gouvernement] government, party in office; **en majorité** [pour la plupart] in the main

**Majorque** [maʒɔrk] nf Majorca

**majuscule** [maʒyskyl] **1.** adj capital **2.** nf capital letter

**mal**, **maux** [mal, mo] **1.** *adj inv* **être au plus mal** to be extremely ill **2.** *nm* [douleur] pain ; [préjudice] harm ; [maladie] illness ; [malheur] misfortune ; PHIL **le mal** evil ; **avoir mal à la tête / à la gorge** to have a headache /sore throat ; **ça me fait mal, j'ai mal** it hurts (me) ; **avoir le mal de l'air /de mer** to be airsick / seasick ; **avoir le mal des transports** to be travel sick ; **faire du mal à qn** to harm sb ; **avoir du mal à faire qch** to have trouble doing sth ; **avoir le mal du pays** to be homesick ; **mal de gorge** sore throat ; **mal de tête** headache **3.** *adv* [avec médiocrité] badly ; [incorrectement] wrongly ; **aller mal** [personne] to be ill ; **mal comprendre** to misunderstand ; **se trouver mal** to faint ; *Fam* **pas mal** [beaucoup] quite a lot (**de** of)

**malade** [malad] **1.** *adj* ill, sick ; [arbre, dent] diseased ; **être malade du cœur** to have a bad heart **2.** *nmf* sick person ; [de médecin] patient ; **les malades** the sick ■ **maladie** *nf* illness, disease ; **maladie infantile** childhood illness ; **maladie sexuellement transmissible** sexually transmitted disease

**maladroit, -e** [maladrwa, -at] *adj* [malhabile] clumsy, awkward ; [indélicat] tactless ■ **maladresse** *nf* [manque d'habileté] clumsiness, awkwardness ; [indélicatesse] tactlessness ; [bévue] blunder

**malaise** [malɛz] *nm* [angoisse] uneasiness, malaise ; [indisposition] feeling of sickness ; [étourdissement] dizzy spell ; **avoir un malaise** to feel faint

**Malaisie** [malɛzi] *nf* **la Malaisie** Malaysia

**malbouffe** [malbuf] *nf Fam* junk food

**malchance** [malʃɑ̃s] *nf* bad luck ; **jouer de malchance** to have no luck at all ■ **malchanceux, -euse** *adj* unlucky

**mâle** [mal] **1.** *adj* [du sexe masculin] male ; [viril] manly **2.** *nm* male

**malédiction** [malediksjɔ̃] *nf* curse

**maléfique** [malefik] *adj* evil

**malencontreux, -euse** [malɑ̃kɔ̃trø, -øz] *adj* unfortunate

**malentendant, -e** [malɑ̃tɑ̃dɑ̃, -ɑ̃t] *nmf* person who is hard of hearing

**malentendu** [malɑ̃tɑ̃dy] *nm* misunderstanding

**malfaçon** [malfasɔ̃] *nf* defect

**malfaisant, -e** [malfəzɑ̃, -ɑ̃t] *adj* harmful

**malfaiteur** [malfɛtœr] *nm* criminal

**malgré** [malgre] *prép* in spite of ; **malgré tout** for all that, after all

**malhabile** [malabil] *adj* clumsy

**malheur** [malœr] *nm* [drame] misfortune ; [malchance] bad luck ; **par malheur** unfortunately ; **porter malheur à qn** to bring sb bad luck ■ **malheureusement** *adv* unfortunately ■ **malheureux, -euse 1.** *adj* [triste] unhappy, miserable ; [malchanceux] unlucky **2.** *nmf* [infortuné] poor wretch ; [indigent] needy person

**malhonnête** [malɔnɛt] *adj* dishonest ■ **malhonnêteté** *nf* dishonesty

**malice** [malis] *nf* mischievousness ■ **malicieux, -euse** *adj* mischievous

**malin, -igne** [malɛ̃, -iɲ] *adj* [astucieux] clever, smart ; MÉD [tumeur] malignant

**malintentionné, -e** [malɛ̃tɑ̃sjɔne] *adj* ill-intentioned (**à l'égard de** towards)

**malle** [mal] *nf* [coffre] trunk ; [de véhicule] *Br* boot, *Am* trunk

**mallette** [malɛt] *nf* briefcase

**malmener** [malməne] *vt* to manhandle, to treat badly

**malnutrition** [malnytrisjɔ̃] *nf* malnutrition

**malpoli, -e** [malpɔli] *adj Fam* rude

**malsain, -e** [malsɛ̃, -ɛn] *adj* unhealthy

**Malte** [malt] *nf* Malta ■ **maltais, -e 1.** *adj* Maltese **2.** *nmf* **Maltais, Maltaise** Maltese

**maltraitance** [maltrɛtɑ̃s] *nf* (physical) abuse

**maltraiter** [maltrɛte] *vt* to ill-treat

**malveillant, -e** [malvejɑ̃, -ɑ̃t] *adj* malevolent

**maman** [mamɑ̃] nf Br mum, Am mom

**mamie** [mami] nf grandma, granny

**mammifère** [mamifɛr] nm mammal

**manche**[1] [mɑ̃ʃ] nf [de vêtement] sleeve; SPORT & CARTES round ■ **manchette** nf [de chemise] cuff; [de journal] headline

**manche**[2] [mɑ̃ʃ] nm [d'outil] handle; **manche à balai** broomstick; [d'avion, d'ordinateur] joystick

**Manche** [mɑ̃ʃ] nf **la Manche** the Channel

**manchot, -e** [mɑ̃ʃo, -ɔt] **1.** adj one-armed **2.** nmf one-armed person

**mandarine** [mɑ̃darin] nf [fruit] mandarin (orange)

**mandat** [mɑ̃da] nm [de député] mandate; [de président] term of office; **mandat postal** Br postal order, Am money order

**manège** [manɛʒ] nm [de foire] merry-go-round, Br roundabout; ÉQUIT riding school

**manette** [manɛt] nf lever

**manga** [mɑ̃ga] nm manga (comic)

**manger** [mɑ̃ʒe] **1.** vt to eat; [corroder] to eat into **2.** vi to eat; **donner à manger à qn** to give sb sth to eat; **faire à manger** to make something to eat; **manger équilibré** to make a balanced diet **3.** nm [nourriture] food ■ **mangeable** adj edible

**mangue** [mɑ̃g] nf mango

**maniaque** [manjak] adj fussy

**manie** [mani] nf [habitude] odd habit; [idée fixe] mania (**de** for)

**manier** [manje] vt to handle ■ **maniable** adj [outil] handy; [véhicule] easy to handle

**manière** [manjɛr] nf way, manner; **la manière dont elle parle** the way (in which) she talks; **manières** [politesse] manners; **de telle manière que** in such a way that; **de toute manière** anyway, anyhow; **de cette manière** (in) this way; **à la manière de** in the style of; **d'une manière générale** generally speaking ■ **maniéré, -e** adj affected

**manifeste** [manifɛst] **1.** adj manifest, obvious **2.** nm POL manifesto

**manifester** [manifɛste] **1.** vt [exprimer] to show **2.** vi [protester] to demonstrate **3.** se manifester vpr [maladie] to show or manifest itself; [personne] to make oneself known ■ **manifestant, -e** nmf demonstrator ■ **manifestation** nf [défilé] demonstration; [réunion, fête] event

**manipuler** [manipyle] vt [appareils, produits] to handle ■ **manipulation** nf [d'appareils, de produits] handling; **manipulations génétiques** genetic engineering

**manivelle** [manivɛl] nf crank

**mannequin** [mankɛ̃] nm [personne] model; [statue] dummy

**manœuvre** [manœvr] **1.** nm [ouvrier] unskilled worker **2.** nf [opération & MIL] Br manoeuvre, Am maneuver ■ **manœuvrer 1.** vt [véhicule, personne] Br to manoeuvre, Am to maneuver; [machine] to operate **2.** vi Br to manoeuvre, Am to maneuver

**manoir** [manwar] nm manor house

**manque** [mɑ̃k] nm [insuffisance] lack (**de** of); [lacune] gap; **par manque de qch** through lack of sth; **être en manque** [drogué] to have withdrawal symptoms

**manquer** [mɑ̃ke] **1.** vt [cible, train, chance] to miss; [échouer] to fail **2.** vi [faire défaut] to be lacking; [être absent] to be missing; [échouer] to fail; **manquer de** [pain, argent] to be short of; [attention, cohérence] to lack; **tu me manques** I miss you; **ne manquer de rien** to have all one needs **3.** v impers **il manque/il nous manque dix tasses** there are /we are ten cups short; **il manque quelques pages** there are a few pages missing ■ **manquant, -e** adj missing ■ **manqué, -e** adj [occasion] missed; [tentative] unsuccessful

**mansarde** [mɑ̃sard] nf attic

**manteau, -x** [mɑ̃to] nm coat

**manucure** [manykyr] nmf [personne] manicurist

**manuel, -elle** [manɥɛl] **1.** *adj* [travail] manual **2.** *nm* [livre] handbook, manual; **manuel scolaire** textbook

**manufacture** [manyfaktyr] *nf* factory ■ **manufacturé, -e** *adj* [produit] manufactured

**manuscrit** [manyskri] *nm* manuscript; [tapé à la machine] typescript

**maquereau, -x** [makro] *nm* [poisson] mackerel

**maquiller** [makije] **1.** *vt* [personne, visage] to make up **2. se maquiller** *vpr* to put one's make-up on ■ **maquillage** *nm* [fard] make-up

**maraîcher, -ère** [maʀeʃe, -ɛʀ] **1.** *nmf* *Br* market gardener, *Am* truck farmer **2.** *adj* **culture maraîchère** *Br* market gardening, *Am* truck farming

**marais** [maʀɛ] *nm* marsh

**marathon** [maʀatɔ̃] *nm* marathon

**marbre** [maʀbʀ] *nm* marble ■ **marbré, -e** *adj* [surface] marbled; **gâteau marbré** marble cake

**marc** [maʀ] *nm* **marc de café** coffee grounds

**marchand, -e** [maʀʃɑ̃, -ɑ̃d] **1.** *nmf* *Br* shopkeeper, *Am* storekeeper; [de vins] merchant; [de voitures, de meubles] dealer; **marchand de journaux** [dans la rue] newsvendor; [dans un magasin] *Br* newsagent, *Am* newsdealer **2.** *adj* **valeur marchande** market value

**marchander** [maʀʃɑ̃de] **1.** *vt* [objet, prix] to haggle over **2.** *vi* to haggle

**marchandises** [maʀʃɑ̃diz] *nfpl* goods, merchandise

**marche** [maʀʃ] *nf* **a)** [d'escalier] step, stair **b)** [action] walking; [promenade] walk; MUS march; **un train en marche** a moving train; **la bonne marche de** [opération] the smooth running of; **mettre qch en marche** to start sth (up); **faire marche arrière** [en voiture] *Br* to reverse, *Am* to back up; *Fig* to backtrack; **fermer la marche** to bring up the rear; **marche à suivre** procedure

**marché** [maʀʃe] **1.** *nm* [lieu & ÉCON] market; [contrat] deal; **faire son** *ou* **le marché** to go shopping; **vendre qch au marché noir** to sell sth on the black market; **le marché du travail** the labour market; **le Marché commun** the Common Market; **le Marché unique européen** the Single European Market; **marché des changes** foreign exchange market **2.** *adj inv* **être bon marché** to be cheap; **c'est meilleur marché** it's cheaper

**marcher** [maʀʃe] *vi* [personne] to walk; [machine] to run; [plans] to work; **faire marcher qch** to operate sth ■ **marcheur, -euse** *nmf* walker

**mardi** [maʀdi] *nm* Tuesday; **Mardi gras** Shrove Tuesday

**mare** [maʀ] *nf* [étang] pond

**marécage** [maʀekaʒ] *nm* marsh ■ **marécageux, euse** *adj* marshy, boggy

**maréchal, -aux** [maʀeʃal, -o] *nm* **maréchal de France** field marshal ■ **maréchal-ferrant** (*pl* **maréchaux-ferrants**) *nm* blacksmith

**marée** [maʀe] *nf* tide; [poissons] fresh seafood; **marée haute / basse** high / low tide; **marée noire** oil slick

**margarine** [maʀgaʀin] *nf* margarine

**marge** [maʀʒ] *nf* [de page] margin; **en marge de** [en dehors de] on the fringes of; **avoir de la marge** to have some leeway; **marge de manœuvre** room for *Br* manoeuvre *or Am* maneuver ■ **marginal, -e, -aux 1.** *adj* [secondaire] marginal; [personne] on the fringes of society **2.** *nmf* dropout

**marguerite** [maʀgəʀit] *nf* [fleur] daisy

**mari** [maʀi] *nm* husband

**mariage** [maʀjaʒ] *nm* [union] marriage; [cérémonie] wedding; *Fig* [de couleurs] blend

**marier** [maʀje] **1.** *vt* [couleurs] to blend; **marier qn** [sujet : prêtre, maire] to marry sb; [sujet : père] to marry sb off **2. se marier** *vpr* to get married; **se marier avec qn** to get married to sb, to marry sb ■ **marié, -e 1.** *adj* married **2.** *nm* (bride)groom; **les mariés** the bride and groom ■ **mariée** *nf* bride

**marin, -e** [maʀɛ̃, -in] **1.** *adj* [flore] marine; [mille] nautical; **air marin** sea air **2.** *nm* sailor, seaman; **marin pêcheur**

(deep-sea) fisherman ■ **marine**
**1.** *nf* **marine de guerre** navy ; **marine**
**marchande** merchant navy **2.** *adj* &
*nm inv* **bleu marine** [couleur] navy
(blue) ■ **marinier, ère** [marinje, εr]
*nmf* Br bargee, Am bargeman

**mariner** [marine] *vt* & *vi* CULIN to
marinate

**maringouin** [marɛ̃gwɛ̃] *nm* Can ZOOL
mosquito

**marionnette** [marjɔnεt] *nf* puppet ; [à
fils] marionette

**maritalement** [maritalmɑ̃] *adv* **vivre**
**maritalement** to cohabit

**maritime** [maritim] *adj* [droit, climat]
maritime ; **port maritime** seaport ;
**gare maritime** Br harbour or Am harbor
station ; Can **les Provinces maritimes**
the Maritime Provinces

**marmelade** [marməlad] *nf* Br stewed
fruit, Am fruit compote

**marmite** [marmit] *nf* (cooking) pot

**Maroc** [marɔk] *nm* **le Maroc** Morocco
■ **marocain, -e 1.** *adj* Moroccan
**2.** *nmf* **Marocain, Marocaine**
Moroccan

**maroquinerie** [marɔkinri] *nf* [maga-
sin] leather goods shop

**marotte** [marɔt] *nf* Fam [dada] craze

**marque** [mark] *nf* [trace, signe]
mark ; [de confiance] sign ; [de pro-
duit] brand ; [de voiture] make ;
SPORT [points] score ; **de marque**
[hôte, visiteur] distinguished ; [pro-
duit] of quality ; **marque déposée**
(registered) trademark ■ **marque-**
**page** [markpaʒ] *(pl* **marque-**
**pages)** *nm* bookmark

**marquer** [marke] **1.** *vt* [par une marque]
to mark ; [écrire] to note down ; [indi-
quer] to show ; SPORT [point, but] to
score ; **marquer les points** to keep (the)
score **2.** *vi* [laisser une trace] to leave
a mark ; [date, événement] to stand
out ; SPORT to score ■ **marquant, -e**
*adj* [remarquable] outstanding ; [épi-
sode] significant ■ **marqué, -e** *adj*
[différence, accent] marked ; [visage]
lined ■ **marqueur** *nm* [stylo] marker

**marquis** [marki] *nm* marquis ■ **mar-**
**quise** *nm* **a)** [personne] marchioness
**b)** [auvent] canopy

**marraine** [marεn] *nf* godmother

**marre** [mar] *adv* Fam **en avoir marre** to
be fed up (**de** with)

**marron** [marɔ̃] **1.** *nm* [fruit] chestnut ;
[couleur] (chestnut) brown **2.** *adj inv*
[couleur] (chestnut) brown ■ **marron-**
**nier** *nm* (horse) chestnut tree

**mars** [mars] *nm* March

**marteau, -x** [marto] *nm* hammer ;
**marteau piqueur** pneumatic drill
■ **marteler** *vt* to hammer

**martial, -e, -aux** [marsjal, -o] *adj* martial ; **cour martiale** court martial

**Martinique** [martinik] *nf* **la Mar-**
**tinique** Martinique ■ **martini-**
**quais, -e 1.** *adj* Martinican **2.** *nmf*
**Martiniquais, Martiniquaise** Martinican

**martyriser** [martirize] *vt* to torture ;
[enfant] to batter

**masculin, -e** [maskylɛ̃, -in] **1.** *adj* [sexe,
mode] male ; [caractère, femme, nom]
masculine **2.** *nm* [en grammaire] masculine

**masochiste** [mazɔʃist] **1.** *adj* maso-
chistic **2.** *nmf* masochist

**masque** [mask] *nm* mask ; **masque à**
**gaz** gas mask ■ **masquer** *vt* [dissimu-
ler] to mask (**à** from) ; [cacher à la vue]
to block off

**massacre** [masakr] *nm* [tuerie] massacre ■ **massacrer** *vt* to massacre

**massage** [masaʒ] *nm* massage

**masse** [mas] *nf* **a)** [volume] mass ;
[gros morceau, majorité] bulk (**de** of) ;
**de masse** [culture, communication]
mass ; **en masse** en masse **b)** ÉLEC Br
earth, Am ground

**masser** [mase] **1.** *vt* [rassembler] to
assemble ; [pétrir] to massage **2. se**
**masser** *vpr* [foule] to form ■ **mas-**
**seur** *nm* masseur ■ **masseuse** *nf*
masseuse

**massif, -ive** [masif, -iv] **1.** *adj* massive ; [or, chêne] solid **2.** *nm* [d'arbres,
de fleurs] clump ; GÉOG massif

**mauvais**

**master, mastère** [mastɛr] *nm* UNIV master's degree

**mastic** [mastik] *nm* [pour vitres] putty; [pour bois] filler ■ **mastiquer** *vt* [mâcher] to chew

**mat¹, mate** [mat] *adj* [papier, couleur] matt

**mat²** [mat] *adjectif; m inv & nm* ÉCHECS (check-)mate; **faire mat** to (check)mate

**mât** [mɑ] *nm* [de navire] mast; [poteau] pole

**mat'** [mat] *Fam* **1.** *nm (abr de matin)* **trois heures du mat'** three in the morning **2.** *nf (abr de matinée)* **faire la grasse mat'** to have a lie-in

**match** [matʃ] *nm* SPORT *Br* match, *Am* game; **match nul** draw; **faire match nul** to draw; **match aller** first leg; **match retour** return leg

**matelas** [matla] *nm* mattress; **matelas pneumatique** air bed

**matelot** [matlo] *nm* sailor

**mater** [mate] *vt* [dominer] to bring to heel

**matérialiser** [materjalize] **1.** *vt* to materialize **2. se matérialiser** *vpr* to materialize

**matérialiste** [materjalist] **1.** *adj* materialistic **2.** *nmf* materialist

**matériau, -x** [materjo] *nm* material; **matériaux** [de construction] building material(s)

**matériel, -elle** [materjɛl] **1.** *adj* [confort, dégâts, besoins] material; [problème] practical **2.** *nm* [de camping] equipment; ORDINAT **matériel informatique** computer hardware ■ **matériellement** *adv* materially; **matériellement impossible** physically impossible

**maternel, -elle** [matɛrnɛl] **1.** *adj* [amour, femme] maternal; [langue] native **2.** *adj & nf* **(école) maternelle** *Br* nursery school, *Am* kindergarten ■ **maternité** *nf* [hôpital] maternity hospital

**mathématiques** [matematik] *nfpl* mathematics *(sg)* ■ **maths** *nfpl Fam Br* maths, *Am* math

**matière** [matjɛr] *nf* [à l'école] subject; [de livre] subject matter; [substance] material; PHYS **la matière** matter; **en matière de qch** as regards sth; **matière première** raw material; **matières grasses** fat

**Matignon** [matiɲɔ̃] *nm* **(l'hôtel) Matignon** *the French Prime Minister's offices*

**matin** [matɛ̃] *nm* morning; **le matin** [chaque matin] in the morning(s); **le mardi matin** every Tuesday morning; **tous les matins** every morning; **le 8 au matin** on the morning of the 8th; **à sept heures du matin** at seven in the morning; **au petit matin** very early (in the morning) ■ **matinal, -e, -aux** *adj* [heure] early; **être matinal** to be an early riser

**matinée** [matine] *nf* morning; THÉÂT & CINÉ matinée; **dans la matinée** in the course of the morning; **faire la grasse matinée** to sleep late, *Br* to have a lie-in

**matos** [matos] *nm Fam* gear; **ils ont un sacré matos** they've got loads of gear

**matraque** [matrak] *nf* bludgeon; [de policier] *Br* truncheon, *Am* nightstick ■ **matraquage** *nm* **matraquage publicitaire** hype

**matrimonial, -e, -aux** [matrimɔnjal, -o] *adj* matrimonial

**maturité** [matyrite] *nf* maturity; **arriver à maturité** [fromage, vin] to mature; [fruit] to ripen

**maudire** [modir] *vt* to curse ■ **maudit, -e** *adj* [damné] cursed

**Maurice** [mɔris] *nf* **l'île Maurice** Mauritius

**maussade** [mosad] *adj* [personne] sullen; [temps] gloomy

**mauvais, -e** [move, -ɛz] **1.** *adj* bad; [santé, vue] poor; [méchant] nasty; [mal choisi] wrong; [mer] rough; **plus mauvais que...** worse than...; **le plus mauvais** the worst; **être mauvais en anglais** to be bad at English; **être en mauvaise santé** to be in bad *or* ill *or* poor health **2.** *adv* **il fait mauvais**

the weather's bad; **ça sent mauvais** it smells bad **3.** *nm* **le bon et le mauvais** the good and the bad

**mauve** [mov] *adj & nm* [couleur] mauve

**maux** [mo] *pl de* **mal**

**maximal, -e, -aux** [maksimal, -o] *adj* maximum; **les températures maximales** top temperatures

**maximum** [maksimɔm] (*pl* **maxima** [-a] *ou* **maximums**) **1.** *nm* maximum; **faire le maximum** to do one's very best; **au maximum** at the most **2.** *adj* maximum

**mayonnaise** [majɔnɛz] *nf* mayonnaise

**mazout** [mazut] *nm* (fuel) oil

**me** [mə]

**m'** is used before a vowel or mute h.

*pron pers* **a)** [complément direct] me; **il me voit** he sees me **b)** [complément indirect] (to) me; **elle me parle** she speaks to me; **tu me l'as dit** you told me **c)** [réfléchi] myself; **je me lave** I wash myself **d)** [avec les pronominaux] **je me suis trompé** I made a mistake

**mec** [mɛk] *nm Fam* guy, *Br* bloke

**mécanicien** [mekanisjɛ̃] *nm* mechanic; [de train] *Br* train driver, *Am* engineer

**mécanique** [mekanik] **1.** *adj* mechanical **2.** *nf* [science] mechanics (*sg*); [mécanisme] mechanism ■ **mécanisme** *nm* mechanism

**mécène** [mesɛn] *nm* patron (of the arts)

**méchant, -e** [meʃɑ̃, -ɑ̃t] *adj* [personne, remarque] nasty; [enfant] naughty; [chien] vicious; **'attention ! chien méchant'** 'beware of the dog' ■ **méchanceté** *nf* nastiness; **une méchanceté** [parole] a nasty remark; [acte] a nasty action

**mèche** [mɛʃ] *nf* **a)** [de cheveux] lock **b)** [de bougie] wick; [de pétard] *Br* fuse, *Am* fuze; [de perceuse] bit

**méconnaître** [mekɔnɛtr] *vt* [fait] to fail to take into account; [talent] to fail to recognize ■ **méconnaissable** *adj* unrecognizable ■ **méconnu, -e** *adj* unrecognized

**mécontent, -e** [mekɔ̃tɑ̃, -ɑ̃t] *adj* [insatisfait] displeased (**de** with); [contrarié] annoyed ■ **mécontenter** *vt* [ne pas satisfaire] to displease; [contrarier] to annoy

**Mecque** [mɛk] *nf* **La Mecque** Mecca

**médaille** [medaj] *nf* [décoration, bijou & SPORT] medal; [portant le nom] pendant (*with name engraved on it*); [de chien] name tag; SPORT **médaille olympique** Olympic medal; **être médaille d'or/d'argent** to be a gold/silver medallist ■ **médaillé, -e** *nmf* medal holder ■ **médaillon** *nm* [bijou] locket; [de viande] medallion

**médecin** [medsɛ̃] *nm* doctor, physician; **médecin généraliste** general practitioner; **médecin référent** *doctor officially designated by the patient as his or her usual doctor*; **médecin traitant** consulting physician ■ **médecine** *nf* medicine; **médecines douces** alternative medicine; **médecine traditionnelle** traditional medicine; **étudiant en médecine** medical student ■ **médical, -e, -aux** *adj* medical ■ **médicament** *nm* medicine ■ **médicinal, -e, -aux** *adj* medicinal

**média** [medja] *nm* medium; **les médias** the media ■ **médiatique** *adj* **campagne médiatique** media campaign ■ **médiatisation** *nf* media coverage ■ **médiatiser** *vt* to give media coverage to

**médiateur, -trice** [medjatœr, -tris] *nmf* mediator

**médicalisé, e** [medikalize] *adj* **établissement médicalisé** nursing home; **lit/hélicoptère médicalisé** hospital bed/helicopter

**médiéval, -e, -aux** [medjeval, -o] *adj* medieval

**médiocre** [medjɔkr] *adj* mediocre ■ **médiocrité** *nf* mediocrity

**médire** [medir] *vi* **médire de qn** to speak ill of sb ■ **médisance** *nf* [action] gossiping; **médisances** [propos] gossip

**méditer** [medite] **1.** *vt* [réfléchir à] to contemplate **2.** *vi* to meditate (**sur** on) ■ **méditation** *nf* meditation

**Méditerranée** [mediterane] *nf* **la Méditerranée** the Mediterranean ■ **méditerranéen, -enne** *adj* Mediterranean

**médium** [medjɔm] *nmf* [voyant] medium

**méduse** [medyz] *nf* jellyfish

**méfiance** [mefjɑ̃s] *nf* distrust, mistrust

**méfier** [mefje] ■ **se méfier** *vpr* to be careful; **se méfier de qn** not to trust sb; **se méfier de qch** to watch out for sth; **méfie-toi!** watch out!, beware! ■ **méfiant, -e** *adj* suspicious, distrustful

**mégabit** [megabit] *nm* ORDINAT megabit

**mégaoctet** [megaɔktɛ] *nm* ORDINAT megabyte

**mégarde** [megard] ■ **par mégarde** *adv* inadvertently

**mégot** [mego] *nm* cigarette butt or end

**meilleur, -e** [mejœr] **1.** *adj* better (**que** than); **le meilleur résultat/moment** the best result /moment **2.** *nmf* **le meilleur, la meilleure** the best (one) **3.** *adv* **il fait meilleur** it's warmer

**mél** [mel] *nm* [courrier] e-mail

**mélancolie** [melɑ̃kɔli] *nf* melancholy ■ **mélancolique** *adj* melancholy

**mélange** [melɑ̃ʒ] *nm* [résultat] mixture; [opération] mixing ■ **mélanger 1.** *vt* [mêler] to mix; [brouiller] to mix up **2. se mélanger** *vpr* [s'incorporer] to mix; [idées] to get mixed up

**mêlant, e** [mɛlɑ̃, ɑ̃t] *adj* Can [embrouillé, confus] confusing

**mêler** [mele] **1.** *vt* to mix (**à** with); [odeurs, thèmes] to combine; Can [troubler quelqu'un] to mix up; **mêler qn à qch** [affaire, conversation] to involve sb in sth **2. se mêler** *vpr* to combine (**à** with); Can [se tromper] to tangle up in; **se mêler à qch** [foule] to mingle with sth; [conversation] to join in sth; **se mêler de qch** to get involved in sth; **mêle-toi de tes affaires!** mind your own business! ■ **mêlé, -e** *adj* mixed (**de** with) ■ **mêlée** *nf* [au rugby] scrum(mage)

**mélodie** [melɔdi] *nf* melody

**mélodramatique** [melɔdramatik] *adj* melodramatic

**melon** [məlɔ̃] *nm* [fruit] melon; **(chapeau) melon** Br bowler (hat), Am derby

**membre** [mɑ̃br] *nm* [bras, jambe] limb; [de groupe] member

**même** [mɛm] **1.** *adj* [identique] same; **en même temps** at the same time (**que** as); **le même jour** the same day; **le jour même** [exact] the very day; **lui-même/vous-même** himself /yourself **2.** *pron* **le /la même** the same (one); **j'ai les mêmes** I have the same (ones); **cela revient au même** it amounts to the same thing **3.** *adv* [y compris, aussi] even; **même si...** even if...; **ici même** in this very place; **tout de même, Fam quand même** all the same; **de même** likewise; **de même que...** just as...; **être à même de faire qch** to be in a position to do sth

**mémoire** [memwar] **1.** *nf* [gén & ORDINAT] memory; **de mémoire** [citer] from memory; **à la mémoire de** in memory of; ORDINAT **mémoire morte /vive** read-only /random access memory; ORDINAT **mémoire tampon** buffer **2.** *nm* [rapport] report; UNIV dissertation; **Mémoires** [chronique] memoirs ■ **mémorable** *adj* memorable

**mémorial, -aux** [memɔrjal, -o] *nm* [monument] memorial

**menaçant, -e** [mənasɑ̃, -ɑ̃t] *adj* threatening

**menace** [mənas] *nf* threat ■ **menacer** *vt* to threaten (**de faire** to do) ■ **menacé, e** *adj* threatened, under threat, endangered

**ménage** [menaʒ] *nm* [entretien] housekeeping; [couple] couple, household; **faire le ménage** to do the housework

**ménager¹, -ère** [menaʒe, -ɛr] **1.** *adj* [équipement] household **2.** *nf* **ménagère** [femme] housewife

**ménager²** [menaʒe] **1.** *vt* [argent] to use sparingly; [forces] to save; [sortie] to provide; **ménager qn** to treat sb carefully ; **ne pas ménager sa peine** to put in a lot of effort **2. se ménager** *vpr* [prendre soin de soi] to look after oneself ; [se réserver] to set aside

**ménagerie** [menaʒri] *nf* menagerie

**mendier** [mɑ̃dje] **1.** *vt* to beg for **2.** *vi* to beg ■ **mendiant, -e** *nmf* beggar

**mener** [məne] **1.** *vt* [personne] to take (**à** to) ; [course, vie] to lead ; [enquête] to carry out ; **mener une vie saine** to lead a healthy life ; *Fig* **mener qch à bien** to carry sth through **2.** *vi* SPORT to lead ; **mener à un lieu** to lead to a place ■ **meneur, -euse** *nmf* [de révolte] ringleader

**méningite** [menɛ̃ʒit] *nf* meningitis

**menotter** [mənɔte] *vt* to handcuff ■ **menottes** *nfpl* handcuffs

**mensonge** [mɑ̃sɔ̃ʒ] *nm* [propos] lie ; [action] lying ■ **mensonger, -ère** *adj* [propos] untrue ; [publicité] misleading

**mensuel, -elle** [mɑ̃sɥɛl] **1.** *adj* monthly **2.** *nm* [revue] monthly ■ **mensualité** *nf* monthly payment

**mensurations** [mɑ̃syrasjɔ̃] *nfpl* measurements

**mental, -e, -aux** [mɑ̃tal, -o] **1.** *adj* mental **2.** *nm* **le mental** the mind ; **avoir un mental d'acier** to be a tower of strength ■ **mentalité** *nf* mentality

**menterie** [mɑ̃tri] *nf* Can lie

**menthe** [mɑ̃t] *nf* mint

**mention** [mɑ̃sjɔ̃] *nf* [fait de citer] mention ; [à un examen] ≃ distinction ; SCOL **mention passable /assez bien /bien / très bien** ≃ C / B / A ; **faire mention de qch** to mention sth ; **'rayez les mentions inutiles'** 'delete as appropriate' ■ **mentionner** *vt* to mention

**mentir** [mɑ̃tir] *vi* to lie (**à** to) ■ **menteur, -euse 1.** *adj* lying **2.** *nmf* liar

**menton** [mɑ̃tɔ̃] *nm* chin

**menu**[1] [məny] *nm* [de restaurant] set menu ; ORDINAT menu ; **par le menu** in detail

**menu**[2], **-e** [məny] **1.** *adj* [petit] tiny ; [mince] slim **2.** *adv* [hacher] small, finely

**menuisier** [mənɥizje] *nm* carpenter, joiner ■ **menuiserie** *nf* [atelier] joiner's workshop ; [boiseries] woodwork

**mépris** [mepri] *nm* contempt (**pour** for), **scorn** (**pour** for) ; **au mépris de qch** without regard to sth ■ **méprisable** *adj* despicable ■ **méprisant, -e** *adj* contemptuous, scornful ■ **mépriser** *vt* to despise

**méprise** [mepriz] *nf* mistake

**mer** [mɛr] *nf* sea ; [marée] tide ; **en (haute) mer** at sea ; **par mer** by sea ; **aller à la mer** to go to the seaside ; **prendre la mer** to set sail

**mercenaire** [mɛrsənɛr] *nm* mercenary

**mercerie** [mɛrsəri] *nf* [magasin] Br haberdasher's, Am notions store

**merci** [mɛrsi] **1.** *excl* thank you, thanks (**de** *ou* **pour** for) ; **non merci** no thank you ; **merci bien** thanks very much **2.** *nf* **à la merci de qn /qch** at the mercy of sb /sth ; **sans merci** merciless

**mercredi** [mɛrkrədi] *nm* Wednesday

**mercure** [mɛrkyr] *nm* mercury

**mère** [mɛr] *nf* mother ; ORDINAT **carte mère** motherboard ; COMM **maison mère** parent company ; MÉD & BIOL **mère biologique** biological *or* natural mother ; **mère porteuse** surrogate mother

**méridional, -e, -aux** [meridjɔnal, -o] **1.** *adj* southern **2.** *nmf* southerner

**mérite** [merit] *nm* merit ; [honneur] credit ; **avoir du mérite à faire qch** to deserve credit for doing sth ■ **mériter** *vt* [être digne de] to deserve ; [demander] to be worth ; **mériter réflexion** to be worth thinking about ; **ce livre mérite d'être lu** this book is worth reading

**merle** [mɛrl] *nm* blackbird

**merlu** [mɛrly] *nm* hake

**merveille** [mɛrvɛj] *nf* wonder, marvel ; **à merveille** wonderfully (well)

**merveilleux, -euse** [mɛrvejø, -øz] *adj* wonderful, Br marvellous, Am marvelous

**mes** [me] *voir* **mon**

**mésaventure** [mezavɑ̃tyr] *nf* misadventure

**mesdames** [medam] *pl de* **madame**

**mesdemoiselles** [medmwazɛl] *pl de* **mademoiselle**

**mésestimer** [mezɛstime] *vt* to underestimate

**mesquin, -e** [meskɛ̃, -in] *adj* mean, petty ■ **mesquinerie** *nf* meanness, pettiness; **une mesquinerie** an act of meanness

**mess** [mes] *nm inv* MIL [salle] mess

**message** [mesaʒ] *nm* message; **laisser un message** to leave a message; **message publicitaire** advertisement ■ **messager, -ère** *nmf* messenger ■ **messagerie** *nf* courier company; **messagerie électronique** electronic mail service; **messagerie vocale** voice mail

**messe** [mes] *nf* [office, musique] mass; **aller à la messe** to go to mass

**messeigneurs** [mesɛɲœr] *pl de* **monseigneur**

**messieurs** [mesjø] *pl de* **monsieur**

**mesure** [məzyr] *nf* [dimension] measurement; [moyen] measure; [retenue] moderation; MUS [temps] time; MUS [division] bar; **sur mesure** [vêtement] made to measure; **être en mesure de faire qch** to be in a position to do sth; **prendre des mesures** to take measures; **à mesure que... as...; dans la mesure où... in so far as...; dans la mesure du possible** as far as possible

**mesurer** [məzyre] **1.** *vt* [dimension, taille] to measure; [déterminer] to assess **2.** *vi* **mesurer 1 mètre 83** [personne] ≃ to be 6 feet tall; [objet] ≃ to measure 6 feet **3. se mesurer** *vpr Fig* **se mesurer à** *ou* **avec qn** to pit oneself against sb

**met** [me] *voir* **mettre**

**métal, -aux** [metal, -o] *nm* metal ■ **métallique** *adj* [éclat, reflet] metallic ■ **métallisé, -e** *adj* **bleu métallisé** metallic blue

**métallurgie** [metalyrʒi] *nf* [industrie] steel industry; [science] metallurgy ■ **métallurgiste** *nm* metalworker

**métamorphoser** [metamɔrfoze] **1.** *vt* to transform (**en** into) **2. se métamorphoser** *vpr* to transform (**en** into)

**météo** [meteo] *nf Fam* [bulletin] weather forecast; **météo marine** shipping forecast

**météorologie** [meteɔrɔlɔʒi] *nf* [science] meteorology; [service] weather bureau ■ **météorologique** *adj* meteorological; **bulletin météorologique** weather report

**méthode** [metɔd] *nf* [manière, soin] method; [livre] course ■ **méthodique** *adj* methodical

**méticuleux, -euse** [metikylø, -øz] *adj* meticulous

**métier** [metje] *nm* [manuel, commercial] trade; [intellectuel] profession; [savoir-faire] experience; **homme de métier** specialist; **tailleur de son métier** tailor by trade; **être du métier** to be in the business; **métier à tisser** loom

**métrage** [metraʒ] *nm* [action] measuring; [tissu] length; **long métrage** feature film; **court métrage** short film

**mètre** [metr] *nm* [mesure] *Br* metre, *Am* meter; **mètre carré / cube** square / cubic *Br* metre *or Am* meter ■ **métrique** *adj* [système] metric

**métro** [metro] *nm Br* underground, *Am* subway

**métropole** [metrɔpɔl] *nf* [ville] metropolis; [pays] mother country ■ **métropolitain, -e** *adj* metropolitan

**mets** [me] *nm* [aliment] dish

**metteur, euse** [metœr, øz] *nmf* THÉÂT **metteur en scène** producer; CINÉ director

**mettre** [metr] **1.** *vt* to put; [vêtement, lunettes] to put on; [chauffage, radio] to switch on; [réveil] to set (**à** for); **j'ai mis une heure** it took me an hour; **mettre qn en colère** to make sb angry; **mettre qn à l'aise** to put sb at ease; **mettre qch plus fort** to turn sth up; **mettre de la**

**musique** to put some music on; **mettons que...** (+ *subjunctive*) let's suppose that...

**2. se mettre** *vpr* [se placer] to put oneself; [debout] to stand; [assis] to sit; [objet] to go; **se mettre en pyjama** to get into one's pyjamas; **se mettre à table** to sit (down) at the table; **se mettre à l'aise** to make oneself comfortable; **se mettre au salon** to go into the dining room; **se mettre au travail** to start work; **se mettre à faire qch** to start doing sth; **le temps s'est mis au beau** the weather has turned fine

**meuble** [mœbl] *nm* piece of furniture; **meubles** furniture ■ **meublé** *nm* furnished *Br* flat *or Am* apartment ■ **meubler** *vt* to furnish

**meule** [møl] *nf* [d'herbe] stack; [de moulin] millstone; **meule de foin** haystack

**meunier, -ère** [mønje, -ɛr] *nmf* miller

**meurt** [mœr] *voir* **mourir**

**meurtre** [mœrtr] *nm* murder ■ **meurtrier, -ère 1.** *nmf* murderer **2.** *adj* murderous; [épidémie] deadly

**meurtrir** [mœrtrir] *vt* to bruise

**meute** [møt] *nf* pack

**Mexique** [mɛksik] *nm* **le Mexique** Mexico ■ **mexicain, -e 1.** *adj* Mexican **2.** *nmf* **Mexicain, Mexicaine** Mexican

**mi** [mi] *nm inv* [note] E

**mi-** [mi] *préf* **la mi-mars** mid March; **à mi-distance** midway; **cheveux mi-longs** shoulder-length hair

**miauler** [mjole] *vi* [chat] to miaow

**mi-chemin** [miʃmɛ̃] ■ **à mi-chemin** *adv* halfway

**mi-clos, -e** [miklo, -oz] (*mpl* **mi-clos**, *fpl* **mi-closes**) *adj* half-closed

**micro** [mikro] *nm* [microphone] mike ■ **microphone** *nm* microphone

**microbe** [mikrɔb] *nm* germ, microbe

**microcrédit** [mikrokredi] (*pl* **microcrédits**) *nm* microcredit

**microfilm** [mikrɔfilm] *nm* microfilm

**micro-informatique** [mikroɛ̃fɔrmatik] *nf* microcomputing

**micro-ondes** [mikrɔɔ̃d] *nm inv* microwave; **four à micro-ondes** microwave oven

**micro-ordinateur** [mikroɔrdinatœr] (*pl* **micro-ordinateurs**) *nm* microcomputer

**microprocesseur** [mikroprɔsɛsœr] *nm* ORDINAT microprocessor

**microscope** [mikrɔskɔp] *nm* microscope ■ **microscopique** *adj* microscopic

**midi** [midi] *nm* **a)** [heure] twelve o'clock, midday; [heure du déjeuner] lunchtime; **entre midi et deux heures** at lunchtime **b)** [sud] south; **le Midi** the South of France

**mie** [mi] *nf* [de pain] soft part

**miel** [mjɛl] *nm* honey

**mien, mienne** [mjɛ̃, mjɛn] **1.** *pron poss* **le mien, la mienne** mine, *Br* my one; **les miens, les miennes** mine, *Br* my ones; **les deux miens** my two **2.** *nmpl* **les miens** [ma famille] my family

**miette** [mjɛt] *nf* [de pain] crumb

**mieux** [mjø] **1.** *adv* better (**que** than); **aller mieux** to be (feeling) better; **de mieux en mieux** better and better; **le / la /les mieux** [de plusieurs] the best; [de deux] the better; **le mieux serait de...** the best thing would be to...; **le plus tôt sera le mieux** the sooner the better; **pour le mieux** for the best **2.** *adj inv* better; [plus beau] better-looking; **si tu n'as rien de mieux à faire** if you've got nothing better to do **3.** *nm* [amélioration] improvement; **faire de son mieux** to do one's best; **faites au mieux** do the best you can

**mignon, -onne** [miɲɔ̃, -ɔn] *adj* [charmant] cute

**migraine** [migrɛn] *nf* headache; MÉD migraine

**migration** [migrɑsjɔ̃] *nf* migration ■ **migrer** *vi* to migrate

**mijoter** [miʒɔte] **1.** *vt* [avec soin] to cook (lovingly); [lentement] to simmer **2.** *vi* to simmer

**mil** [mil] *adj inv* **l'an deux mil** the year two thousand

**milieu, -x** [miljø] *nm* [centre] middle ; [cadre, groupe social] environment ; [entre extrêmes] middle course ; PHYS medium ; **milieux littéraires** literary circles ; **au milieu de** in the middle of ; **le juste milieu** the happy medium ; **le milieu** [la pègre] the underworld

**militaire** [militɛr] **1.** *adj* military **2.** *nm* serviceman ; [de l'armée de terre] soldier

**militer** [milite] *vi* [personne] to campaign (**pour** for ; **contre** against)

**mille** [mil] **1.** *adj inv* & *nm inv* thousand ; **mille hommes** a *or* one thousand men ; **deux mille** two thousand ; **je vous le donne en mille !** you'll never guess ! **2.** *nm* **a)** [de cible] bull's eye ; **mille (marin)** nautical mile **b)** *Can* [distance] mile ■ **mille-feuille** (*pl* **mille-feuilles**) *nm* *Br* ≃ vanilla slice, *Am* ≃ napoleon ■ **millième** *adj, nm* & *nmf* thousandth ; **un millième** a thousandth ■ **millier** *nm* thousand ; **un millier (de)** a thousand or so ; **par milliers** in their thousands

**millénaire** [milenɛr] **1.** *adj* thousand-year-old **2.** *nm* millennium, thousand years *pl*

**milliard** [miljar] *nm* billion ■ **milliardaire** *adj* & *nmf* billionaire

**milligramme** [miligram] *nm* milligram, *Br* milligramme

**millilitre** [mililitr] *nm* millilitre

**millimètre** [milimɛtr] *nm* millimetre

**million** [miljɔ̃] *nm* million ; **un million de francs** a million francs ; **deux millions** two million ; **par millions** in millions ■ **millionnaire** *nmf* millionaire

**mime** [mim] **1.** *nm* [art] mime **2.** *nmf* [artiste] mime ■ **mimer** *vt* & *vi* [exprimer] to mime

**minable** [minabl] *adj* [lieu, personne] shabby

**mince** [mɛ̃s] *adj* thin ; [élancé] slim ; [insuffisant] slight ■ **minceur** *nf* thinness ; [sveltesse] slimness ■ **mincir** *vi* to get slimmer

**mine** [min] *nf* **a)** [physionomie] look ; **avoir bonne / mauvaise mine** to look

well / ill **b)** [gisement] & *Fig* mine ; **mine de charbon** coalmine **c)** [de crayon] lead **d)** [engin explosif] mine

**miner** [mine] *vt* [terrain] to mine ; *Fig* [saper] to undermine ; **miner qn** [chagrin, maladie] to wear sb down

**minerai** [minrɛ] *nm* ore

**minéral, -e, -aux** [mineral, -o] *adj* & *nm* mineral

**minéralogique** [mineralɔʒik] *adj* **plaque minéralogique** [de véhicule] *Br* number *or Am* license plate

**mineur, -e** [minœr] **1.** *nm* [ouvrier] miner ; **mineur de fond** underground worker **2.** *adj* [secondaire & MUS] minor ; [de moins de 18 ans] underage **3.** *nmf* JUR minor ■ **minière** *adj f* **industrie minière** mining industry

**miniature** [minjatyr] **1.** *nf* miniature **2.** *adj* **train miniature** miniature train

**minibar** [minibar] *nm* minibar

**minibus** [minibys] *nm* minibus

**minigolf** [minigɔlf] *nm* crazy golf

**minijupe** [miniʒyp] *nf* miniskirt

**minimal, -e, -aux** [minimal, -o] *adj* minimal ; **les temperatures minimales** lowest temperatures

**minimum** [minimɔm] (*pl* **minima** [-a] *ou* **minimums**) **1.** *nm* minimum ; **le minimum de** [force] the minimum (amount of) ; **faire le minimum** to do the bare minimum ; **en un minimum de temps** in as short a time as possible ; **au minimum** at the very least ; **le minimum vital** a minimum to live on ; **les minima sociaux** *basic income support* **2.** *adj* minimum

**ministère** [ministɛr] *nm* [département] ministry ; [gouvernement] government, cabinet ; **ministère des Affaires étrangères** *Br* ≃ Foreign Office, *Am* ≃ State Department ; **ministère de l'Intérieur** *Br* ≃ Home Office, *Am* ≃ Department of the Interior ■ **ministériel, -elle** *adj* ministerial

**ministre** [ministr] *nm* POL & REL secretary, *Br* minister ; **ministre des Affaires étrangères** *Br* ≃ Foreign Secretary, *Am* ≃ Secretary of State; **ministre de l'Intérieur** *Br* ≃ Home Secretary, *Am* ≃ Secretary of the Interior

**minorité** [minɔrite] *nf* minority ▪ **minoritaire** *adj* **être minoritaire** to be in the minority

**minuit** [minɥi] *nm* midnight, twelve o'clock

**minuscule** [minyskyl] **1.** *adj* [petit] tiny, minute **2.** *adj & nf* (lettre) **minuscule** small letter

**minute** [minyt] *nf* minute; **à la minute** [tout de suite] this (very) minute; **d'une minute à l'autre** any minute (now) ▪ **minuterie** *nf* [d'éclairage] time switch

**minuter** [minyte] *vt* [chronométrer] to time (precisely)

**minutie** [minysi] *nf* meticulousness ▪ **minutieux, -euse** *adj* meticulous

**mirabelle** [mirabɛl] *nf* mirabelle plum

**miracle** [mirakl] *nm* miracle; **par miracle** miraculously ▪ **miraculeux, -euse** *adj* miraculous

**mirage** [miraʒ] *nm* mirage

**mire** [mir] *nf* **point de mire** [cible & Fig] target

**mirifique** [mirifik] *adj* Fam fabulous

**mirobolant, e** [mirɔbɔlɑ̃, ɑ̃t] *adj* Fam fabulous, fantastic

**miroir** [mirwar] *nm* mirror

**mis, mise**[1] [mi, miz] **1.** *pp de* **mettre** **2.** *adj* **bien mis** [vêtu] well-dressed

**mise**[2] [miz] *nf* **a)** [placement] putting; **mise au point** [de rapport] finalization; PHOTO focusing; [de moteur] tuning; [de technique] perfecting; Fig [clarification] clarification; **mise en garde** warning; **mise en scène** THÉÂT production; CINÉ direction **b)** [argent] stake **c)** **être de mise** to be acceptable

**miser** [mize] *vt* [argent] to stake (**sur** on); **miser sur qn/qch** [parier] to bet on sb/sth; [compter sur] to count on sb/sth

**misère** [mizɛr] *nf* extreme poverty; **être dans la misère** to be poverty-stricken ▪ **misérable 1.** *nf* [pitoyable] miserable; [pauvre] desti-

tute; [existence] wretched; [logement, quartier] seedy, slummy **2.** *nmf* [indigent] poor wretch; [scélérat] scoundrel

**missile** [misil] *nm* missile

**mission** [misjɔ̃] *nf* [tâche, organisation] mission; [d'employé] task; **partir en mission** [cadre] to go away on business; [diplomate] to go off on a mission ▪ **missionnaire** *nmf & adj* missionary

**mistral** [mistral] *nm* **le mistral** the mistral

**mite** [mit] *nf* moth

**mi-temps** [mitɑ̃] **1.** *nf inv* SPORT [pause] half-time; [période] half **2.** *nm inv* part-time job; **travailler à mi-temps** to work part-time

**mitigé, -e** [mitiʒe] *adj* [accueil] lukewarm

**mitoyen, -enne** [mitwajɛ̃, -ɛn] *adj* common, shared

**mitrailler** [mitraje] *vt* **a)** MIL to machinegun **b)** Fam [photographier] to click away at **c)** Fam & Fig [assaillir] **mitrailler qn (de)** to bombard sb (with) ▪ **mitraillette** *nf* submachine gun ▪ **mitrailleur** *adj m* **fusil mitrailleur** machine gun ▪ **mitrailleuse** *nf* machine gun

**mi-voix** [mivwa] ▪ **à mi-voix** *adv* in a low voice

**mix** [miks] *nm inv* **a)** [morceau de musique] mix **b)** [mélange] mixture, combination; **son dernier film est un mix d'action et de violence** his latest film is a mixture or combination of action and violence

**mixer**[1] [mikse] *vt* [à la main] to mix; [au mixer] to blend

**mixer**[2], **mixeur** [miksœr] *nm* [pour mélanger] (food) mixer; [pour rendre liquide] liquidizer

**mixte** [mikst] *adj* mixed; [école] co-educational, *Br* mixed

**mixture** [mikstyr] *nf* mixture

**MJC** [ɛmʒise] (abr de **maison des jeunes et de la culture**) *nf* youth club and arts centre

**MJPEG** [ɛmʒipɛg] (abr de **moving joint photographic experts group**) nm ORDINAT MJPEG

**Mlle** (abr de **Mademoiselle**) Miss

**mm** (abr de **millimètre(s)**) mm

**MM** (abr de **Messieurs**) Messrs

**Mme** (abr de **Madame**) Mrs

**MMS** (abr de **multimedia messaging service**) nm TÉL MMS

**mobile** [mɔbil] **1.** adj [pièce, cible] moving; [panneau] movable; [personne] mobile; [feuillets] loose **2.** nm [décoration] mobile; [motif] motive (**de** for)

**mobilier** [mɔbilje] nm furniture

**mobiliser** [mɔbilize] **1.** vt to mobilize **2. se mobiliser** vpr to mobilize

**mobilité** [mɔbilite] nf mobility; **mobilité sociale** upward mobility

**Mobylette®** [mɔbilɛt] nf moped

**mode¹** [mɔd] nf [tendance] fashion; [industrie] fashion industry; **à la mode** fashionable; **suivre la mode** to follow fashion; **à la mode de** in the manner of

**mode²** [mɔd] nm [manière & ORDINAT] mode; **mode d'emploi** instructions; **mode de transport** mode of transport; **mode de vie** way of life

**modèle** [mɔdɛl] **1.** nm [schéma, exemple, personne] model; [au tricot] pattern; **grand/petit modèle** [de vêtement] large/small size; **modèle déposé** registered design **2.** adj **élève modèle** model pupil ■ **modeler 1.** vt to model (**sur** on) **2. se modeler** vpr **se modeler sur qn** to model oneself on sb

**modem** [mɔdɛm] nm ORDINAT modem

**modérer** [mɔdere] **1.** vt [passions, désirs] to moderate, to restrain; [vitesse] to reduce **2. se modérer** vpr to calm down ■ **modération** nf [retenue] moderation; [réduction] reduction; **avec modération** in moderation ■ **modéré, -e** adj moderate

**moderne** [mɔdɛrn] adj modern ■ **moderniser 1.** vt to modernize **2. se moderniser** vpr to modernize ■ **modernité** nf modernity

**modeste** [mɔdɛst] adj modest ■ **modestie** nf modesty

**modifier** [mɔdifje] **1.** vt to alter, to modify **2. se modifier** vpr to alter ■ **modification** nf alteration, modification; **apporter une modification à qch** to make an alteration to sth

**modulation** [mɔdylɑsjɔ̃] nf [de son, d'amplitude] modulation; RADIO **modulation de fréquence** frequency modulation

**moelle** [mwal] nf [d'os] marrow; **moelle épinière** spinal cord; **moelle osseuse** bone marrow

**moelleux, -euse** [mwalø, -øz] adj [lit, tissu] soft

**mœurs** [mœr(s)] nfpl [morale] morals; [habitudes] customs; **entrer dans les mœurs** to become part of everyday life

**moi** [mwa] **1.** pron pers a) [après une préposition] me; **pour/avec moi** for/with me; Fam **un ami à moi** a friend of mine b) [complément direct] me; **laissez-moi** leave me c) [complément indirect] (to) me; **montrez-le-moi** show it to me, show me it d) [sujet] I; **c'est moi qui vous le dis!** I'm telling you!; **il est plus grand que moi** he's taller than I am or than me **2.** nm inv self, ego ■ **moi-même** pron myself

**moindre** [mwɛ̃dr] adj [comparatif] lesser; [prix] lower; [quantité] smaller; **le/la moindre** [superlatif] the least; **la moindre erreur** the slightest mistake; **dans les moindres détails** in the smallest detail; **c'est la moindre des choses** it's the least I/we/etc can do

**moineau, -x** [mwano] nm sparrow

**moins** [mwɛ̃] ([mwɛ̃z] before vowel) **1.** adv [comparatif] less (**que** than); **moins de** [temps, travail] less (**que** than); [gens, livres] fewer (**que** than); **le/la/les moins** [superlatif] the least; **le moins grand, la moins grande, les moins grand(e)s** the smallest; **au moins, du moins** at least; **de moins en moins** less and less; **qch de moins, qch en moins**

[qui manque] sth missing; **dix ans de moins** ten years less; **en moins** [personne, objet] less; [personnes, objets] fewer; **les moins de vingt ans** those under twenty, the under-twenties; **à moins de battre le record** unless I / you /*etc* beat the record; **à moins que...** (+ *subjunctive*) unless...; **pour le moins** at (the very) least
**2.** *prép* MATH minus; **deux heures moins cinq** five to two; **il fait moins 10 (degrés)** it's minus 10 (degrees)

**mois** [mwa] *nm* month; **au mois de juin** in (the month of) June

**moisir** [mwazir] *vi* to go Br mouldy or Am moldy ■ **moisi, -e 1.** *adj* Br mouldy, Am moldy **2.** *nm* Br mould, Am mold; [sur un mur] mildew; **sentir le moisi** to smell musty ■ **moisissure** *nf* Br mould, Am mold

**moisson** [mwasɔ̃] *nf* harvest; **faire la moisson** to harvest ■ **moissonner** *vt* [céréales] to harvest; [champ] to reap ■ **moissonneuse-batteuse** (*pl* **moissonneuses-batteuses**) *nf* combine harvester

**moite** [mwat] *adj* sticky

**moitié** [mwatje] *nf* half; **la moitié de la pomme** half (of) the apple; **à moitié** [remplir] halfway; **à moitié plein / vide** half-full /-empty; **à moitié prix** (at) half-price

**moit-moit** [mwatmwat] *adv* Fam **faire moit-moit** to go halves

**moka** [mɔka] *nm* [café] mocha; [gâteau] coffee cake

**mol** [mɔl] *voir* **mou**

**molaire** [mɔlɛr] *nf* molar

**molécule** [mɔlekyl] *nf* molecule

**molester** [mɔlɛste] *vt* to manhandle

**molle** [mɔl] *voir* **mou**

**mollet**[1] [mɔlɛ] *nm* [de jambe] calf

**mollet**[2] [mɔlɛ] *adj* **œuf mollet** soft-boiled egg

**mollusque** [mɔlysk] *nm* Br mollusc, Am mollusk

**moment** [mɔmɑ̃] *nm* [instant, durée] moment; **un petit moment** a little

while; **en ce moment** at the moment; **pour le moment** for the moment, for the time being; **sur le moment** at the time; **à ce moment-là** [à ce moment précis] at that (very) moment, at that time; [dans ce cas] then; **à un moment donné** at one point; **le moment venu** [dans le futur] when the time comes; **d'un moment à l'autre** any moment; **dans ces moments-là** at times like that; **par moments** at times; **au moment de partir** when just about to leave; **au moment où...** just as...; **jusqu'au moment où...** until...; **du moment que...** [puisque] seeing that... ■ **momentané, -e** *adj* [temporaire] momentary; [bref] brief ■ **momentanément** *adv* [temporairement] temporarily; [brièvement] briefly

**mon, ma, mes** [mɔ̃, ma, me]

ma becomes **mon** [mɔ̃n] before a vowel or mute h.

*adj poss* my; **mon père** my father; **ma mère** my mother; **mon ami(e)** my friend; **mes parents** my parents

**Monaco** [mɔnako] *nm* Monaco

**monarque** [mɔnark] *nm* monarch ■ **monarchie** *nf* monarchy

**monastère** [mɔnastɛr] *nm* monastery

**mondain, -e** [mɔ̃dɛ̃, -ɛn] *adj* **réunion mondaine** society gathering ■ **mondanités** *nfpl* [événements] social life; [conversations] social chitchat

**monde** [mɔ̃d] *nm* world; [gens] people; **dans le monde entier** worldwide, all over the world; **tout le monde** everybody; **il y a du monde** there are a lot of people; **venir au monde** to come into the world ■ **mondial, -e, -aux** *adj* [crise, renommée] worldwide; **guerre mondiale** world war ■ **mondialement** *adv* throughout or all over the world ■ **mondialisation** *nf* globalization ■ **mondialiste** *adj* pro-globalization

**monégasque** [mɔnegask] **1.** *adj* Monegasque **2.** *nmf* **Monégasque** Monegasque

**monétaire** [mɔnetɛr] *adj* monetary

**mongolien, -enne** [mɔ̃gɔljɛ̃, -ɛn] **1.** *adj* **être mongolien** to have Down's syndrome **2.** *nmf* person with Down's syndrome

**moniteur, -trice** [mɔnitœr, -tris] **1.** *nmf* instructor ; [de colonie] *Br* assistant, *Am* camp counselor **2.** *nm* ORDINAT [écran] monitor

**monnaie** [mɔnɛ] *nf* [argent] money ; [de] currency ; [pièces] change ; **petite monnaie** small change ; **faire de la monnaie** to get change ; **avoir la monnaie de 100 euros** to have change for 100 euros ; **monnaie électronique** plastic money ; **monnaie unique** single currency

**monoparentale** [mɔnoparɑ̃tal] *adj f* **famille monoparentale** one-parent family

**monoplace** [mɔnoplas] *adj & nmf* single-seater

**monopole** [mɔnopɔl] *nm* monopoly ; **avoir le monopole de qch** to have a monopoly on sth ■ **monopoliser** *vt* to monopolize

**monoski** [mɔnoski] *nm* mono-ski ; **faire du monoski** to mono-ski

**monotone** [mɔnɔtɔn] *adj* monotonous ■ **monotonie** *nf* monotony

**monseigneur** [mɔ̃sɛɲœr] *(pl* **messeigneurs)** *nm* [évêque] His / Your Lordship ; [prince] His / Your Highness

**monsieur** [məsjø] *(pl* **messieurs)** *nm* [homme quelconque] gentleman ; **Monsieur Legras** Mr Legras ; **bonsoir, messieurs-dames !** good evening! ; **Monsieur** [dans une lettre] Dear Sir

**monstre** [mɔ̃str] *nm* monster ; **monstre sacré** giant ■ **monstrueux, -euse** *adj* [mal formé, scandaleux] monstrous ; [énorme] huge

**mont** [mɔ̃] *nm* mount

**montage** [mɔ̃taʒ] *nm* TECH assembling ; CINÉ editing ; [image truquée] montage

**montagne** [mɔ̃taɲ] *nf* mountain ; **la montagne** [zone] the mountains ; **à la montagne** in the mountains ; **en haute montagne** high in the mountains ; **montagnes russes** [attraction foraine]

rollercoaster ■ **montagnard, -e** *nmf* mountain dweller ■ **montagneux, -euse** *adj* mountainous

**montant, -e 1.** *adj* [marée] rising ; [col] stand-up **2.** *nm* [somme] amount ; [de barrière] post ; **montants compensatoires** subsidies

**monte-charge** [mɔ̃tʃarʒ] *(pl* **monte-charges)** *nm* service *Br* lift or *Am* elevator

**montée** [mɔ̃te] *nf* [ascension] climb, ascent ; [chemin] slope ; [des prix, du fascisme] rise ; **la montée des eaux** the rise in the water level

**monter** [mɔ̃te] **1.** *(aux avoir) vt* [côte] to climb (up) ; [objet] to bring / take up ; [cheval] to ride ; [son] to turn up ; [tente] to put up ; [machine] to assemble ; [pièce de théâtre] to stage ; **monter l'escalier** to go / come upstairs *or* up the stairs **2.** *(aux être) vi* [personne] to go / come up ; [prix] to rise ; [marée] to come in ; [avion] to climb ; **faire monter qn** to show sb up ; **monter dans un véhicule** to get in(to) a vehicle ; **monter sur qch** to climb onto sth ; **monter sur** *ou* **à une échelle** to climb up a ladder ; **monter en courant** to run up ; SPORT **monter à cheval** to ride (a horse) **3. se monter** *vpr* **se monter à** [s'élever à] to amount to

**monteur, -euse** [mɔ̃tœr, -øz] *nmf* CINÉ editor

**montre** [mɔ̃tr] *nf* [instrument] (wrist) watch ; SPORT & *Fig* **course contre la montre** race against the clock

**Montréal** [mɔ̃real] *nm ou f* Montreal

**montrer** [mɔ̃tre] **1.** *vt* to show (**à** to) ; **montrer qn / qch du doigt** to point at sb / sth ; **montrer le chemin à qn** to show sb the way **2. se montrer** *vpr* to show oneself ; **se montrer courageux** to be courageous

**monture** [mɔ̃tyr] *nf* [de lunettes] frame ; [de bijou] setting

**monument** [mɔnymɑ̃] *nm* monument ; **monument historique** historic building ; **monument aux morts** war memorial ■ **monumental, -e, -aux** *adj* [imposant, énorme] monumental

**moquer** [mɔke] ■ **se moquer** *vpr* se moquer de qn to make fun of sb; se moquer de qch [rire de] to make fun of sth; [ne pas se soucier] not to care about sth ■ **moquerie** *nf* mockery ■ **moqueur, -euse** *adj* mocking

**moquette** [mɔkɛt] *nf Br* fitted carpet, *Am* wall-to-wall carpeting

**moral, -e, -aux** [mɔral, -o] **1.** *adj* moral **2.** *nm* avoir le moral to be in good spirits ■ **morale** *nf* [d'histoire] moral; [principes] morals; [règles] morality; faire la morale à qn to lecture sb ■ **moralité** *nf* [mœurs] morality; [de récit] moral

**morceau, -x** [mɔrso] *nm* piece, bit; [de sucre] lump; [de viande] cut; tomber en morceaux to fall to pieces ■ **morceler** *vt* [terrain] to divide up

**mordiller** [mɔrdije] *vt* to nibble

**mordre** [mɔrdr] **1.** *vt* & *vi* to bite; mordre qn au bras to bite sb's arm **2.** se mordre *vpr Fig* se mordre les doigts d'avoir fait qch to kick oneself for doing sth

**mordu, -e** [mɔrdy] *pp de* mordre

**morgue** [mɔrg] *nf* [d'hôpital] mortuary; [pour corps non identifiés] morgue

**moribond, -e** [mɔribɔ̃, -ɔ̃d] **1.** *adj* dying **2.** *nmf* dying person

**morne** [mɔrn] *adj* [temps] dismal; [silence] gloomy; [personne] glum

**morose** [mɔroz] *adj* morose

**mors** [mɔr] *nm* [de harnais] bit

**morse** [mɔrs] *nm* [code] Morse (code)

**morsure** [mɔrsyr] *nf* bite

**mort**[1] [mɔr] *nf* death; se donner la mort to take one's own life; un silence de mort a deathly silence ■ **mortalité** *nf* death rate, mortality ■ **mortel, -elle 1.** *adj* [hommes, ennemi, danger] mortal; [accident] fatal **2.** *nmf* mortal ■ **mortellement** *adv* [blessé] fatally

**mort**[2]**, morte** [mɔr, mɔrt] **1.** *adj* [personne, plante, ville] dead; mort de fatigue dead tired; mort de froid numb with cold; mort de peur frightened to death; mort ou vif dead or alive **2.** *nmf* dead man, *f* dead woman; les morts

the dead; de nombreux morts [victimes] many deaths; le jour *ou* la fête des Morts All Souls' Day ■ **morte-saison** *(pl* mortes-saisons*) nf* off-season ■ **mort-né, -e** *(mpl* mort-nés, *fpl* mort-nées*) adj* [enfant] stillborn

**morue** [mɔry] *nf* cod

**mosaïque** [mɔzaik] *nf* mosaic

**Moscou** [mɔsku] *nm ou f* Moscow

**mot** [mo] *nm* word; envoyer un mot à qn to drop sb a line; mot à mot word for word; avoir le dernier mot to have the last word; mots croisés crossword (puzzle); mot de passe password ■ **mot-clé** *(pl* mots-clés*),* mot-clef *(pl* mots-clefs*)* [mokle] *nm* keyword

**motel** [mɔtɛl] *nm* motel

**moteur**[1] [mɔtœr] *nm* [de véhicule] engine; [électrique] motor; ORDINAT moteur de recherche search engine

**moteur**[2]**, -trice** [mɔtœr, -tris] **1.** *adj* [nerf, muscle] motor; voiture à quatre roues motrices four-wheel drive (car) **2.** *nf* motrice [de train] engine

**motif** [mɔtif] *nm* [raison] reason (de for); [dessin] pattern

**motiver** [mɔtive] *vt* [inciter, causer] to motivate; [justifier] to justify ■ **motivation** *nf* motivation ■ **motivé, -e** *adj* motivated

**moto** [mɔto] *nf* motorbike ■ **motocycliste** *nmf* motorcyclist

**motoneige** [mɔtɔnɛʒ] *nf Can* snowmobile

**motte** [mɔt] *nf* [de terre] lump, clod; [de beurre] block

**motton** [mɔtɔ̃] *nm Can* a) [petite masse] clump b) [grumeau] lump c) avoir le motton [émotion] to be all choked up; faire le motton [s'enrichir] to make *or* to win a bundle

**mou, molle** [mu, mɔl]

mol is used before masculine singular nouns beginning with a vowel or h mute.

**1.** *adj* soft; [sans énergie] feeble **2.** *nm* [de corde] avoir du mou to be slack ■ **mollesse** *nf* [de matelas] softness; [de personne] lethargy

**mouche** [muʃ] *nf* [insecte] fly; **faire mouche** to hit the bull's-eye ■ **moucheron** *nm* midge

**moucher** [muʃe] **1.** *vt* **moucher qn** to wipe sb's nose **2. se moucher** *vpr* to blow one's nose

**moucheté, -e** [muʃte] *adj* speckled

**mouchoir** [muʃwar] *nm* handkerchief; **mouchoir en papier** tissue

**moudre** [mudr] *vt* to grind

**mouette** [mwɛt] *nf* (sea)gull

**moufle** [mufl] *nf* mitten, mitt

**mouiller** [muje] **1.** *vt* to wet **2.** *vi* NAUT to anchor **3. se mouiller** *vpr* to get wet ■ **mouillé, -e** *adj* wet (**de** with)

**moule¹** [mul] *nm* Br mould, Am mold; **moule à gâteaux** cake tin ■ **moulage** *nm* [objet] cast ■ **moulant, -e** *adj* [vêtement] tight-fitting ■ **mouler** *vt* Br to mould, Am to mold; [statue] to cast

**moule²** [mul] *nf* [mollusque] mussel

**moulin** [mulɛ̃] *nm* mill; **moulin à café** coffee grinder; **moulin à vent** windmill

**moulinet** [mulinɛ] *nm* [de canne à pêche] reel

**moulu, -e** [muly] **1.** *pp de* **moudre 2.** *adj* [café] ground

**mourir** [murir] (*aux* **être**) *vi* to die (**de** of *or* from); **mourir de froid** to die of exposure; *Fig* **mourir de fatigue** to be dead tired; *Fig* **mourir de peur** to be frightened to death; *Fig* **je meurs de faim!** I'm starving! ■ **mourant, -e 1.** *adj* dying; [voix] faint **2.** *nmf* dying person

**mousse** [mus] **1.** *nf* [plante] moss; [écume] foam; [de bière] head; [de savon] lather; **mousse à raser** shaving foam; CULIN **mousse au chocolat** chocolate mousse **2.** *nm* [marin] ship's boy ■ **mousser** *vi* [bière] to froth; [savon] to lather ■ **mousseux, -euse 1.** *adj* [vin] sparkling **2.** *nm* sparkling wine

**mousson** [musɔ̃] *nf* monsoon

**moustache** [mustaʃ] *nf* [d'homme] Br moustache, Am mustache; [de chat] whiskers ■ **moustachu, -e** *adj* with a Br moustache *or* Am mustache

**moustique** [mustik] *nm* mosquito ■ **moustiquaire** *nf* mosquito net; [en métal] screen

**moutarde** [mutard] *nf* mustard

**mouton** [mutɔ̃] *nm* sheep *inv*; [viande] mutton; **moutons** [écume] Br white horses, Am whitecaps; [poussière] fluff; **peau de mouton** sheepskin

**mouvement** [muvmɑ̃] *nm* [geste, groupe, déplacement] movement; [élan] impulse; [de gymnastique] exercise; **en mouvement** in motion; **mouvement de colère** fit of anger; **mouvements sociaux** workers' protest movements ■ **mouvementé, -e** *adj* [vie, voyage] eventful

**mouvoir** [muvwar] **1.** *vi* to move; **mû par** [mécanisme] driven by **2. se mouvoir** *vpr* to move; **mû par** [mécanisme] driven by

**moyen¹, -enne** [mwajɛ̃, -ɛn] **1.** *adj* average; [format, entreprise] medium(-sized) **2.** *nf* **moyenne** average; **en moyenne** on average; **la moyenne d'âge** the average age; **avoir la moyenne** [à un examen] Br to get a pass mark, Am to get a pass; [à un devoir] to get 50 percent, Br to get half marks; **le Moyen Âge** the Middle Ages

**moyen²** [mwajɛ̃] *nm* [procédé, façon] means, way (**de faire** of doing or to do); **moyens** [capacités mentales] ability; [argent, ressources] means; **je n'ai pas les moyens** [argent] I can't afford it; **au moyen de qch** by means of sth

**moyennant** [mwajenɑ̃] *prép* for, in return for

**Moyen-Orient** [mwajenɔrjɑ̃] *nm* **le Moyen-Orient** the Middle East

**Mozambique** [mɔzɑ̃bik] *nm* **le Mozambique** Mozambique

**MP3** *(abr de* **moving picture experts group audio layer 3)** *nm* ORDINAT MP3; **lecteur (de) MP3** MP3 player

**MP4** *(abr de* **moving picture experts group audio layer 4)** *nm* ORDINAT MP4; **lecteur (de) MP4** MP4 player

**MST** [ɛmɛste] *(abr de* **maladie sexuellement transmissible)** *nf* STD

**muer** [mɥe] **1.** *vi* [animal] *Br* to moult,
*Am* to molt ; [voix] to break **2. se muer**
*vpr* **se muer en qch** to change into sth

**muet, muette** [mɥe, mɥɛt] **1.** *adj* [in-
firme] dumb ; [de surprise] speechless ;
[film] silent **2.** *nmf* mute

**muguet** [mɥge] *nm* lily of the valley

**mule** [myl] *nf* [pantoufle, animal] mule
■ **mulet** *nm* [équidé] mule ; [poisson]
mullet

**multicolore** [myltikɔlɔr] *adj Br*
multicoloured, *Am* multicolored

**multilingue** [myltilɛ̃g] *adj* multilin-
gual

**multinationale** [myltinasjɔnal] *nf*
multinational

**multiplateforme** [myltiplatfɔrm] *nf*
ORDINAT [logiciel, jeu] cross-platform

**multiple** [myltipl] *adj* [nombreux]
numerous ; [varié] multiple ■ **multiplication** *nf* [calcul] multiplication ;
[augmentation] increase ■ **multiplier**
**1.** *vt* to multiply **2. se multiplier** *vpr*
to increase ; [se reproduire] to multiply

**multiplexe** [myltiplɛks] *nm* CINÉ multiplex (cinema), multiscreen cinema

**multitude** [myltityd] *nf* multitude

**municipal, -e, -aux** [mynisipal, -o] *adj*
municipal ■ **municipalité** *nf* [maires
et conseillers] local council ; [commune]
municipality

**munir** [mynir] **1.** *vt* **munir de qch** [per-
sonne] to provide with sth **2. se munir**
*vpr* **se munir de qch** to take sth

**munitions** [mynisjɔ̃] *nfpl* ammunition

**mur** [myr] *nm* wall ; *Fig* **au pied du mur**
with one's back to the wall ; **mur du son**
sound barrier ■ **muraille** *nf* (high)
wall ■ **mural, -e, -aux** *adj* **carte murale** wall map ; **peinture murale** mural
(painting) ■ **murer** *vt* [porte] to wall
up

**mûr, mûre¹** [myr] *adj* [fruit] ripe ; [per-
sonne] mature ; **d'âge mûr** middle-
aged ■ **mûrir** *vt* & *vi* [fruit] to ripen ;
[personne] to mature

**mûre²** [myr] *nf* [baie] blackberry

**muret** [myrɛ] *nm* low wall

**murmure** [myrmyr] *nm* murmur
■ **murmurer** *vt* & *vi* to murmur

**musarder** [myzarde] *vi* to dawdle

**muscle** [myskl] *nm* muscle ■ **musclé, -e** *adj* [bras] muscular ■ **mus-
culaire** *adj* [force, douleur] muscular
■ **musculature** *nf* muscles

**muscu** [mysky] *(abr de* **musculation)** *nf*
*Fam* bodybuilding

**museau, -x** [myzo] *nm* [de chien, de
chat] muzzle ■ **museler** *vt* [animal,
presse] to muzzle

**musée** [myze] *nm* museum ; **musée
de peinture** art gallery ■ **muséum**
*nm* natural history museum

**music-hall** [myzikol] *(pl* **music-halls)**
*nm* [genre, salle] music hall

**musique** [myzik] *nf* music ; **écouter de
la musique** to listen to music ■ **musical, -e, -aux** *adj* musical ■ **musicien,
-enne** *nmf* musician **2.** *adj* musical

**musulman, -e** [myzylmɑ̃, -an] *adj* &
*nmf* Muslim, Moslem

**muter** [myte] *vt* to transfer ■ **mutant,
-e** *adj* & *nmf* mutant ■ **mutation** *nf*
[d'employé] transfer ; BIOL mutation

**mutiler** [mytile] *vt* to mutilate, to
maim ; **être mutilé** to be disabled

**mutin** [mytɛ̃] *nm* [rebelle] mutineer
■ **mutinerie** *nf* mutiny

**mutisme** [mytism] *nm* silence

**mutuel, -elle** [mytɥɛl] **1.** *adj* [réci-
proque] mutual **2.** *nf* **mutuelle** mutual
insurance company ■ **mutuellement**
*adv* each other

**mwa** SMS *abr écrite de* **moi**

**myope** [mjɔp] *adj* shortsighted

**myrtille** [mirtij] *nf* [baie] bilberry

**mystère** [mistɛr] *nm* mystery ■ **mys-
térieux, -euse** *adj* mysterious

**mystique** [mistik] **1.** *adj* mystical
**2.** *nmf* [personne] mystic

**mythe** [mit] *nm* myth ■ **mythique** *adj*
mythical ■ **mythologie** *nf* mythology
■ **mythologique** *adj* mythological

**N¹, n** [ɛn] *nm inv* N, n

**N²** *(abr de* **route nationale***)* M

**n'** [n] *voir* **ne**

**nacelle** [nasɛl] *nf* [de ballon] basket

**nacre** [nakr] *nf* mother-of-pearl ■ **nacré, -e** *adj* pearly

**nage** [naʒ] *nf* (swimming) stroke; **traverser une rivière à la nage** to swim across a river; **nage libre** freestyle

**nageoire** [naʒwar] *nf* [de poisson] fin; [de dauphin] flipper

**nager** [naʒe] *vt & vi* to swim ■ **nageur, -euse** *nmf* swimmer

**naïf, naïve** [naif, naiv] *adj* naïve

**nain, naine** [nɛ̃, nɛn] *adj & nmf* dwarf

**naissance** [nɛsɑ̃s] *nf* [de personne, d'animal] birth; **donner naissance à** [enfant] to give birth to; **de naissance** from birth

**naître** [nɛtr] *vi* to be born; [sentiment, difficulté] to arise (**de** from); [idée] to originate

**naïveté** [naivte] *nf* naïvety

**nana** [nana] *nf Fam* girl

**nantir** [nɑ̃tir] *vt* **nantir qn de qch** to provide sb with sth ■ **nanti, -e 1.** *adj* well-to-do **2.** *nmpl Péj* **les nantis** the well-to-do

**nappe** [nap] *nf* [de table] tablecloth; **nappe de brouillard** fogpatch; **nappe d'eau** expanse of water; **nappe de pétrole** layer of oil; [de marée noire] oil slick

**napper** [nape] *vt* to coat (**de** with)

**narcotrafic** [narkotrafik] *nm* narcotrafficking ■ **narcotrafiquant, e** *nmf* drug trafficker

**narguer** [narge] *vt* to taunt

**narine** [narin] *nf* nostril

**narquois, -e** [narkwa, -az] *adj* sneering

**nasal, -e, -aux** [nazal, -o] *adj* nasal

**nasillard, -e** [nazijar, -ard] *adj* [voix] nasal

**natal, -e, -als** [natal] *adj* native

**natalité** [natalite] *nf* birth rate

**natation** [natasjɔ̃] *nf* swimming

**natif, -ive** [natif, -iv] *adj & nmf* native; **être natif de** to be a native of

**nation** [nasjɔ̃] *nf* nation; **les Nations unies** the United Nations ■ **national, -e, -aux** *adj* national ■ **nationale** *nf* [route] *Br* ≃ A road, *Am* ≃ highway ■ **nationaliser** *vt* to nationalize ■ **nationaliste 1.** *adj* nationalistic **2.** *nmf* nationalist ■ **nationalité** *nf* nationality

**natte** [nat] *nf* [de cheveux] *Br* plait, *Am* braid

**naturaliser** [natyralize] *vt* to naturalize ■ **naturalisation** *nf* naturalization

**nature** [natyr] **1.** *nf* [univers, caractère] nature; [campagne] country; **contre nature** unnatural; **en pleine nature** in the middle of the country; **payer en nature** to pay in kind; **nature morte** still life **2.** *adj inv* [omelette, yaourt] plain; [thé] without milk

**naturel, -elle** [natyrɛl] **1.** *adj* natural; **mort naturelle** death from natural causes **2.** *nm* [caractère] nature; [simplicité] naturalness ■ **naturellement** *adv* naturally

**naturopathe** [natyrɔpat] *nmf* naturopath

**naufrage** [nofraʒ] *nm* (ship)wreck; **faire naufrage** [bateau] to be wrecked; [marin] to be shipwrecked

**nausée** [noze] *nf* nausea, sickness; **avoir la nausée** to feel sick

**nautique** [notik] *adj* nautical

**naval, -e, -als** [naval] *adj* naval

**navet** [navɛ] *nm* **a)** BOT turnip **b)** *Can* [rutabaga] turnip **c)** *Fam* [œuvre] trash

**navette** [navɛt] *nf* [véhicule] shuttle; **faire la navette** [véhicule, personne] to shuttle back and forth (**entre** between); **navette spatiale** space shuttle

**navetteur, euse** [navɛtœr, øz] *nmf Belg, Can* commuter

**navigable** [navigabl] *adj* [fleuve] navigable

**navigant, -e** [navigɑ̃, -ɑ̃t] *adj* AVIAT **personnel navigant** flight crew

**navigateur** [navigatœr] *nm* [marin] navigator ■ **navigation** *nf* navigation; ORDINAT browsing

**naviguer** [navige] *vi* [bateau] to sail; **naviguer sur Internet** to surf the Net

**navire** [navir] *nm* ship

**navrer** [navre] *vt* to appal ■ **navrant, -e** *adj* appalling ■ **navré, -e** *adj* [air] distressed; **je suis navré** I'm terribly sorry

**ne** [nə]

> n' before vowel or mute h; used to form negative verb with **pas, jamais, personne, rien** etc.

*adv* **ne... pas** not; **il ne boit pas** he does not *or* doesn't drink; **elle n'ose (pas)** she doesn't dare; **ne... que** only; **je crains qu'il ne parte** I'm afraid he'll leave

**né, -e** [ne] **1.** *pp* (*de* **naître**) born; **il est né en 2001** he was born in 2001; **née Dupont** née Dupont **2.** *adj* born; **c'est un poète-né** he's a born poet

**néanmoins** [neɑ̃mwɛ̃] *adv* nevertheless

**néant** [neɑ̃] *nm* nothingness; [sur formulaire] ≃ none

**nécessaire** [nesesɛr] **1.** *adj* necessary **2.** *nm* **le nécessaire** the necessities; **faire le nécessaire** to do what's necessary; **nécessaire de toilette** toilet bag

**nécessité** [nesesite] *nf* necessity ■ **nécessiter** *vt* to require, to necessitate

**nectarine** [nɛktarin] *nf* nectarine

**néerlandais, -e** [neɛrlɑ̃dɛ, -ɛz] **1.** *adj* Dutch **2.** *nmf* **Néerlandais** Dutchman; **Néerlandaise** Dutchwoman **3.** *nm* [langue] Dutch

**nef** [nɛf] *nf* [d'église] nave

**néfaste** [nefast] *adj* harmful (**à** to)

**négatif, -ive** [negatif, -iv] **1.** *adj* negative **2.** *nm* [de photo] negative

**négligeable** [negliʒabl] *adj* negligible; **non négligeable** [quantité] significant

**négligent, -e** [negliʒɑ̃, -ɑ̃t] *adj* careless, negligent ■ **négligence** *nf* [défaut] carelessness, negligence

**négliger** [negliʒe] **1.** *vt* [personne, travail, conseil] to neglect; **négliger de faire qch** to neglect to do sth **2. se négliger** *vpr* to neglect oneself ■ **négligé, -e** *adj* [tenue] untidy; [travail] careless

**négocier** [negɔsje] *vt & vi* to negotiate ■ **négociable** *adj* negotiable ■ **négociant, -e** *nmf* merchant, dealer ■ **négociateur, -trice** *nmf* negotiator ■ **négociation** *nf* negotiation

**neige** [nɛʒ] *nf* snow; **aller à la neige** to go skiing; **neige fondue** sleet ■ **neiger** *v impers* to snow; **il neige** it's snowing

**nem** [nɛm] *nm* CULIN (Vietnamese) small spring roll

**nénette** [nenɛt] *nf Fam Br* bird, *Am* broad

**néon** [neɔ̃] *nm* [gaz] neon; [enseigne] neon sign; **éclairage au néon** neon lighting

**néo-zélandais, -e** [neozelɑ̃dɛ, -ɛz] (*mpl* **néo-zélandais**, *fpl* **néo-zélandaises**) **1.** *adj* New Zealand **2.** *nmf* **Néo-Zélandais, Néo-Zélandaise** New Zealander

**nerd** [nɛrd] *nm Péj* nerd

**nerf** [nɛr] *nm* nerve ■ **nerveux, -euse** *adj* nervous ■ **nervosité** *nf* nervousness

**n'est-ce pas** [nɛspɑ] *adv* isn't he? / don't you? / won't they? / *etc*; **tu viendras, n'est-ce pas ?** you'll come, won't you?; **il fait beau, n'est-ce pas ?** the weather's nice, isn't it?

**net, nette** [nɛt] **1.** *adj* [propre] clean; [image, refus] clear; [écriture] neat;

[prix, salaire] net; **net d'impôt** net of tax **2.** *adv* [casser, couper] clean; [tuer] outright; [refuser] flatly; **s'arrêter net** to stop dead ■ **nettement** *adv* [avec précision] clearly; [incontestablement] definitely; **il va nettement mieux** he's much better ■ **netteté** *nf* [propreté, précision] cleanness; [de travail] neatness

**Net** [nɛt] *nm* **le Net** the Net ■ **netéconomie** [nɛtekɔnɔmi] *nf* (Inter)net economy ■ **netiquette** [netiket] *nf* ORDINAT netiquette

**nettoyer** [netwaje] **1.** *vt* to clean **2. se nettoyer** *vpr* **se nettoyer les oreilles** to clean one's ears ■ **nettoyage** *nm* cleaning; **nettoyage à sec** dry-cleaning

**neuf¹, neuve** [nœf, nœv] **1.** *adj* new; **quoi de neuf ?** what's new? **2.** *nm* **remettre qch à neuf** to make sth as good as new

**neuf²** [nœf] ([nœv] *before* **heures, ans**) *adj & nm* nine ■ **neuvième** *adj & nmf* ninth

**neurone** [nørɔn] *nm* neuron, neurone

**neutre** [nøtr] **1.** *adj* [pays, personne] neutral **2.** *nm* ÉLEC neutral ■ **neutraliser** *vt* to neutralize ■ **neutralité** *nf* neutrality

**neveu, -x** [nəvø] *nm* nephew

**nez** [ne] *nm* nose; **nez à nez** face to face (**avec** with); **rire au nez de qn** to laugh in sb's face; **parler du nez** to speak through one's nose

**ni** [ni] *conj* **ni... ni...** neither... nor...; **ni Pierre ni Paul ne sont venus** neither Pierre nor Paul came; **il n'a ni faim ni soif** he's neither hungry nor thirsty; **sans manger ni boire** without eating or drinking; **ni l'un(e) ni l'autre** neither (of them)

**niaque** [njak] *nf Fam* determination; **les joueurs ont manqué de niaque** the players lacked drive; **avoir la niaque** to be determined to succeed; **toute l'équipe a la niaque** the whole team is determined to win

**Nicaragua** [nikaragwa] *nm* **le Nicaragua** Nicaragua

**niche** [niʃ] *nf* [de chien] *Br* kennel, *Am* doghouse; [cavité] niche, recess

**nicher** [niʃe] **1.** *vi* [oiseau] to nest **2. se nicher** *vpr* [oiseau] to nest ■ **nichée** *nf* [chiens] litter; [oiseaux] brood

**nickel** [nikɛl] *nm* [métal] nickel

**nicotine** [nikɔtin] *nf* nicotine

**nid** [ni] *nm* nest

**nièce** [njɛs] *nf* niece

**nier** [nje] **1.** *vt* to deny (**que** that) **2.** *vi* [accusé] to deny the charge

**Niger** [niʒɛr] *nm* **le Niger** [pays] Niger

**Nigéria** [niʒerja] *nm* **le Nigéria** Nigeria

**Nil** [nil] *nm* **le Nil** the Nile

**n'importe** [nɛ̃pɔrt] *voir* **importer**

**nippon, -one** *ou* **-onne** [nipɔ̃, -ɔn] *adj* Japanese

**niveau, -x** [nivo] *nm* [hauteur, étage, degré] level; SCOL standard; **au niveau de la mer** at sea level; **niveau de vie** standard of living ■ **niveler** *vt* [surface] to level

**noble** [nɔbl] **1.** *adj* noble **2.** *nmf* nobleman, *f* noblewoman ■ **noblesse** *nf* [caractère, classe] nobility

**noce** [nɔs] *nf* wedding; **noces d'or** golden wedding

**nocif, -ive** [nɔsif, -iv] *adj* harmful ■ **nocivité** *nf* harmfulness

**nocturne** [nɔktyrn] **1.** *adj* [animal] nocturnal **2.** *nf* [de magasin] late-night opening; SPORT **(match en) nocturne** evening match

**Noël** [nɔɛl] *nm* Christmas; **arbre de Noël** Christmas tree; **le père Noël** Father Christmas, Santa Claus

**nœud** [nø] **a)** [entrecroisement] knot; [ruban] bow; **nœud papillon** bow tie **b)** NAUT [vitesse] knot

**noir, -e** [nwar] **1.** *adj* black; [sombre] dark; [idées] gloomy; [misère] dire; **il fait noir** it's dark; **film noir** film noir; *Fig* **noir de monde** heaving with people **2.** *nm* [couleur] black; [obscurité] dark; **Noir** [homme] Black (man) **3.** *nf* **noire** [note] *Br* crotchet, *Am* quarter note; **Noire** [femme] Black (woman) ■ **noirceur** [nwarsœr] *nf* **a)** *Can* [obscurité] darkness **b)** *Fig* [méchanceté] wickedness ■ **noircir 1.** *vt* to blacken **2.** *vi* to turn black

**noise** [nwaz] *nf* chercher noise à qn to pick a quarrel with sb

**noisette** [nwazet] *nf* hazelnut

**noix** [nwa] *nf* [du noyer] walnut; **noix de coco** coconut

**nom** [nɔ̃] *nm* name; GRAM noun; au nom de qn on sb's behalf; **nom de famille** surname; **nom de jeune fille** maiden name; **nom déposé** trade name

**nomade** [nɔmad] **1.** *adj* nomadic **2.** *nmf* nomad

**nombre** [nɔ̃br] *nm* number; être au *ou* du nombre de to be among; ils sont au nombre de dix there are ten of them; le plus grand nombre de the majority of; bon nombre de a good many; MATH nombre premier prime number

**nombreux, -euse** [nɔ̃brø, -øz] *adj* [amis, livres] numerous, many; [famille, collection] large; peu nombreux few; venir nombreux to come in large numbers

**nombril** [nɔ̃bri] *nm* navel

**nominal, -e, -aux** [nɔminal, -o] *adj* nominal

**nomination** [nɔminɑsjɔ̃] *nf* [à un poste] appointment; [pour récompense] nomination

**nommer** [nɔme] **1.** *vt* [appeler] to name; nommer qn [désigner] to appoint sb (à un poste to a post); nommer qn président to appoint sb chairman **2. se nommer** *vpr* [s'appeler] to be called

**non** [nɔ̃] **1.** *adv* no; tu viens ou non ? are you coming or not?; non seulement not only; non (pas) que... (+ *subjunctive*) not that...; non loin not far; je crois que non I don't think so; (ni) moi non plus neither do /am /can /etc I **2.** *nm inv* no

**non-alcoolisé, e** [nɔnalkɔlize] *adj* non-alcoholic

**nonante** [nɔnɑ̃t] *adj & nm* [en Belgique, en Suisse] ninety

**nonchalant, -e** [nɔ̃ʃalɑ̃, -ɑ̃t] *adj* nonchalant

**non-fumeur, -euse** [nɔ̃fymœr, -øz] **1.** *adj* non-smoking **2.** *nmf* non-smoker

**non-retour** [nɔ̃rətur] *nm* point de non-retour point of no return

**non-violence** [nɔ̃vjɔlɑ̃s] *nf* non-violence

**non-voyants** [nɔ̃vwajɑ̃] *nmpl* les non-voyants the unsighted

**nord** [nɔr] **1.** *nm* north; au nord in the north; [direction] (to the) north (de of); du nord [vent, direction] northerly; [ville] northern; [gens] from /in the north; l'Afrique du Nord North Africa; l'Europe du Nord Northern Europe; le grand Nord the Frozen North **2.** *adj inv* [côte] north; [régions] northern ■ **nord-africain, -e** *(mpl* nord-africains, *fpl* nord-africaines) **1.** *adj* North African **2.** *nmf* Nord-Africain, Nord-Africaine North African ■ **nord-américain, -e** *(mpl* nord-américains, *fpl* nord-américaines) **1.** *adj* North American **2.** *nmf* Nord-Américain, Nord-Américaine North American ■ **nord-est** *nm & adj inv* northeast ■ **nord-ouest** *nm & adj inv* northwest

**nordique** [nɔrdik] *adj* Nordic, Scandinavian ■ **Nordique** *nmf* a) [Scandinave] Scandinavian b) *Can* North Canadian

**normal, -e, -aux** [nɔrmal, -o] *adj* normal ■ **normale** *nf* norm; au-dessus /au-dessous de la normale above /below average; *Fam* Normale Sup *university-level college preparing students for senior posts in teaching* ■ **normalement** *adv* normally ■ **normaliser** *vt* [uniformiser] to standardize; [relations] to normalize

**normand, -e** [nɔrmɑ̃, -ɑ̃d] **1.** *adj* Norman **2.** *nmf* Normand, Normande Norman ■ **Normandie** *nf* la Normandie Normandy

**norme** [nɔrm] *nf* norm; normes de sécurité safety standards

**Norvège** [nɔrvɛʒ] *nf* la Norvège Norway ■ **norvégien, -enne 1.** *adj*

Norwegian **2.** *nmf* **Norvégien, Norvégienne** Norwegian **3.** *nm* [langue]
Norwegian

**nos** [no] *voir* **notre**

**nosocomial, e, aux** [nɔzɔkɔmjal, o]
*adj* nosocomial, contracted in hospital

**nostalgie** [nɔstalʒi] *nf* nostalgia
■ **nostalgique** *adj* nostalgic

**notable** [nɔtabl] *adj* & *nm* notable

**notaire** [nɔtɛr] *nmf Br* ≃ solicitor,
≃ lawyer

**notamment** [nɔtamɑ̃] *adv* notably

**note** [nɔt] *nf* [annotation, communication & MUS] note ; SCOL *Br* mark,
*Am* grade ; [facture] *Br* bill, *Am* check ;
**prendre note de qch** to make a note of
sth ; **prendre des notes** to take notes ;
**note de frais** expenses

**noter** [nɔte] *vt* [remarquer] to note ;
[écrire] to note down ; [devoir] *Br* to
mark, *Am* to grade

**notice** [nɔtis] *nf* [mode d'emploi] instructions ; [de médicament] directions

**notifier** [nɔtifje] *vt* **notifier qch à qn** to
notify sb of sth

**notion** [nosjɔ̃] *nf* notion ; **notions** [élé-
ments] rudiments ; **avoir des notions
de qch** to know the basics of sth

**notoriété** [nɔtɔrjete] *nf* [renom] fame ;
**il est de notoriété publique que...** it's
common knowledge that...

**notre, nos** [nɔtr, no] *adj poss* our

**nôtre** [notr] **1.** *pron poss* **le / la nôtre,
les nôtres** ours **2.** *nmpl* **les nôtres**
[parents] our family

**nouer** [nwe] **1.** *vt* [lacets] to tie ; [cravate]
to knot ; *Fig* [relation] to establish **2. se
nouer** *vpr* [intrigue] to take shape

**nougat** [nuga] *nm* nougat

**nouilles** [nuj] *nfpl* noodles

**nounou** [nunu] *nf* nanny

**nounours** [nunurs] *nm Fam* teddy
(bear)

**nourrice** [nuris] *nf* [assistante mater-
nelle] (children's) nurse, *Br* childminder ; [qui allaite] wet nurse

**nourrir** [nurir] **1.** *vt* [alimenter] to feed ;
*Fig* [espoir] to cherish **2. se nourrir** *vpr*
to eat ; **se nourrir de qch** to feed on sth

**nourrisson** [nurisɔ̃] *nm* infant

**nourriture** [nurityr] *nf* food

**nous** [nu] *nm* **a)** [sujet] we ; **nous
sommes ici** we are here
**b)** [complément direct] us ; **il nous
connaît** he knows us
**c)** [complément indirect] (to) us ; **il nous
l'a donné** he gave it to us, he gave us it
**d)** [réfléchi] ourselves ; **nous nous lavons** we wash ourselves ; **nous nous
habillons** we get dressed
**e)** [réciproque] each other ; **nous nous
détestons** we hate each other
■ **nous-mêmes** *pron* ourselves

**nouveau, elle¹, x** [nuvo, -ɛl]

**nouvel** is used before masculine singular
nouns beginning with a vowel or mute h.

**1.** *adj* new ; [mode] latest ; **on craint de
nouvelles inondations** [d'autres] further flooding is feared **2.** *nmf* [à l'école]
new boy, *f* new girl **3.** *nm* **du nouveau**
something new **4.** *adv* **de nouveau, à
nouveau** again ■ **nouveau-né, -e**
*(mpl* **nouveau-nés,** *fpl* **nouveau-nées)**
**1.** *adj* newborn **2.** *nmf* newborn baby

**nouveauté** [nuvote] *nf* novelty ; **nou-
veautés** [livres] new books ; [disques]
new releases

**nouvelle²** [nuvɛl] *nf* **a) une nouvelle**
[annonce] a piece of news ; **la nouvelle
de sa mort** the news of his / her death
**b)** [récit] short story ■ **nouvelles**
*nfpl* news ; **les nouvelles** [média] the
news *sg* ; **il a donné de ses nouvelles**
I / we / *etc* have heard from him ; **avoir
des nouvelles de qn** [directement] to
have heard from sb

**Nouvelle-Calédonie** [nuvɛlkaledɔni]
*nf* **la Nouvelle-Calédonie** New Cale-
donia

**Nouvelle-Zélande** [nuvɛlzelɑ̃d] *nf*
**la Nouvelle-Zélande** New Zealand

**novateur, -trice** [nɔvatœr, -tris] *adj*
innovative

**novembre** [nɔvɑ̃br] *nm* November

**noyade** [nwajad] *nf* drowning

**noyau, -x** [nwajo] *nm* [de fruit] stone, *Am* pit ; [d'atome, de cellule] nucleus ; [groupe] group ; **noyau dur** [de groupe] hard core

**noyauter** [nwajote] *vt* to infiltrate

**noyé, -e** [nwaje] *nmf* drowned person

**noyer¹** [nwaje] **1.** *vt* [personne] to drown ; [terres] to flood **2. se noyer** *vpr* to drown ; **se noyer dans les détails** to get bogged down in details

**noyer²** [nwaje] *nm* [arbre] walnut tree

**NRV** SMS *abr écrite de* **énervé**

**nu, -e** [ny] **1.** *adj* [personne, vérité] naked ; [mains, chambre] bare ; **tout nu** (stark) naked, (in the) nude ; **tête nue, nu-tête** bare-headed ; **aller pieds nus** to go barefoot **2.** *nm* nude ; **mettre qch à nu** to expose sth

**nuage** [nɥaʒ] *nm* cloud ; *Fig* **être dans les nuages** to have one's head in the clouds ■ **nuageux, -euse** *adj* [ciel] cloudy

**nuance** [nɥɑ̃s] *nf* [de couleur] shade ; [de sens] nuance ; [de regret] tinge ■ **nuancé, -e** *adj* [jugement] qualified ■ **nuancer** *vt* [pensée] to qualify

**nucléaire** [nykleɛr] **1.** *adj* nuclear **2.** *nm* nuclear energy

**nudiste** [nydist] *nmf* nudist ■ **nudité** *nf* [de personne] nudity, nakedness

**nuée** [nɥe] *nf* **une nuée de** [foule] a horde of ; [groupe compact] a cloud of

**nuire** [nɥir] *vi* **nuire à qn/qch** to harm sb/sth ■ **nuisible** *adj* harmful (**à** to)

**nuit** [nɥi] *nf* night ; [obscurité] dark, darkness ; **la nuit** [se promener] at night ; **cette nuit** [hier] last night ; [aujourd'hui] tonight ; **avant la nuit** before nightfall ; **il fait nuit** it's dark ; **il fait nuit noire** it's pitch-black ; **bonne nuit !** good night! ■ **nuitée** *nf* overnight stay

**nul, nulle** [nyl] **1.** *adj* [médiocre] hopeless, useless ; [risque] non-existent, nil ; JUR [non valable] null (and void) ; **être nul en qch** to be hopeless at sth **2.** *adj indéf Litt* [aucun] no ; **sans nul doute** without any doubt **3.** *pron indéf m Litt* [aucun] no one ■ **nulle part** *adv* nowhere ; **nulle part ailleurs** nowhere else

**numérique** [nymerik] **1.** *adj* numerical ; [montre, clavier, données] digital **2.** *nm* **le numérique** digital technology

**numéro** [nymero] *nm* [chiffre] number ; [de journal] issue, number ; [au cirque] act ; TÉL **numéro vert** *Br* ≃ Freefone® number, *Am* ≃ toll-free number ; **numéro de téléphone/de fax** telephone/fax number ■ **numéroter** *vt* [pages, sièges] to number

**nunuche** [nynyʃ] *adj Fam* goofy, dumb

**nuptial, -ale, -aux** [nypsjal, -jo] *adj* [chambre] bridal ; **cérémonie nuptiale** wedding ceremony

**nuque** [nyk] *nf* back of the neck

**nutrition** [nytrisjɔ̃] *nf* nutrition ■ **nutritionniste** *nmf* nutritionist, dietician

**Nylon®** [nilɔ̃] *nm* [fibre] nylon ; **chemise en Nylon®** nylon shirt

# O

**O, o** [o] *nm inv* O, o

**obéir** [ɔbeir] *vi* to obey; **obéir à qn / qch** to obey sb /sth ■ **obéissance** *nf* obedience (à to) ■ **obéissant, -e** *adj* obedient

**obèse** [ɔbɛz] *adj* obese ■ **obésité** [ɔbesite] *nf* obesity

**objecter** [ɔbʒɛkte] *vt* **objecter que...** to object that... ■ **objecteur** *nm* **objecteur de conscience** conscientious objector ■ **objection** *nf* objection; **si vous n'y voyez pas d'objection** if you have no objections

**objectif, -ive** [ɔbʒɛktif, -iv] **1.** *adj* objective **2.** *nm* [but] objective; [d'appareil photo] lens ■ **objectivité** *nf* objectivity

**objet** [ɔbʒɛ] *nm* [chose, sujet, but] object; **faire l'objet de** [étude, critiques] to be the subject of; [soins, surveillance] to be given; **objet d'art** object d'art; **objets trouvés** [bureau] *Br* lost property, *Am* lost and found

**obligation** [ɔbligasjɔ̃] *nf* [contrainte] obligation; FIN bond; **se trouver dans l'obligation de faire qch** to be obliged to do sth; **sans obligation d'achat** no purchase necessary ■ **obligatoire** *adj* compulsory, obligatory ■ **obligatoirement** *adv* necessarily; **il doit obligatoirement avoir son diplôme pour s'inscrire** he must have his degree to enrol

**obliger** [ɔbliʒe] **1.** *vt* [contraindre] to force (à faire to do); **être obligé de faire qch** to be obliged to do sth **2. s'obliger** *vpr* **s'obliger à faire qch** to force oneself to do sth ■ **obligé, -e** *adj* [obligatoire] necessary

**oblique** [ɔblik] *adj* oblique

**oblitéré, -e** [ɔblitere] *adj* [timbre] used

**obscène** [ɔpsɛn] *adj* obscene ■ **obscénité** *nf* obscenity

**obscur, -e** [ɔpskyr] *adj* [sombre] dark; [confus, inconnu] obscure ■ **obscurcir 1.** *vt* [rendre sombre] to darken; [rendre confus] to obscure **2. s'obscurcir** *vpr* [ciel] to darken ■ **obscurité** *nf* [noirceur] darkness; **dans l'obscurité** in the dark

**obséder** [ɔpsede] *vt* to obsess ■ **obsédant, -e** *adj* haunting; [pensée] obsessive

**obsèques** [ɔpsɛk] *nfpl* funeral

**observateur, -trice** [ɔpsɛrvatœr, -tris] **1.** *adj* observant **2.** *nmf* observer

**observation** [ɔpsɛrvasjɔ̃] *nf* [étude, remarque] observation; [reproche] remark; [respect] observance

**observatoire** [ɔpsɛrvatwar] *nm* observatory

**observer** [ɔpsɛrve] *vt* [regarder, respecter] to observe; [remarquer] to notice; **faire observer qch à qn** to point sth out to sb

**obsession** [ɔpsesjɔ̃] *nf* obsession ■ **obsessionnel, -elle** *adj* obsessional

**obstacle** [ɔpstakl] *nm* obstacle; **faire obstacle à qch** to stand in the way of sth

**obstétricien, -enne** [ɔpstetrisjɛ̃, -ɛn] *nmf* obstetrician

**obstiner** [ɔpstine] ■ **s'obstiner** *vpr* to persist (à faire in doing) ■ **obstination** *nf* stubbornness, obstinacy ■ **obstiné, -e** *adj* stubborn, obstinate

**obstruction** [ɔpstryksjɔ̃] *nf* obstruction ■ **obstruer** *vt* to obstruct

**obtempérer** [ɔptɑ̃pere] *vi* **obtempérer à qch** to comply with sth

**obtenir** [ɔptənir] *vt* to get, to obtain ■ **obtention** *nf* obtaining

**obus** [ɔby] *nm* [projectile] shell

**occasion** [ɔkazjɔ̃] *nf* **a)** [chance] chance, opportunity (**de faire** to do); [moment] occasion; **à l'occasion** when the occasion arises; **à l'occasion de qch** on the occasion of sth; **pour les grandes occasions** for special occasions **b)** [affaire] bargain; [objet non neuf] second-hand item; **d'occasion** second-hand

**occasionnel, elle** [ɔkazjɔnɛl] *adj* occasional ■ **occasionnellement** [ɔkazjɔnɛlmɑ̃] *adv* occasionally, every now and then, from time to time

**occasionner** [ɔkazjɔne] *vt* to cause; **occasionner qch à qn** to cause sb sth

**occident** [ɔksidɑ̃] *nm* **l'Occident** the West ■ **occidental, -e, -aux 1.** *adj* GÉOG & POL western **2.** *nmpl* POL **les Occidentaux** Westerners

**occulte** [ɔkylt] *adj* occult

**occupant, -e** [ɔkypɑ̃, -ɑ̃t] **1.** *adj* [armée] occupying **2.** *nmf* [habitant] occupant **3.** *nm* MIL **l'occupant** the occupying forces

**occupation** [ɔkypasjɔ̃] *nf* [activité, travail & MIL] occupation

**occupé, -e** [ɔkype] *adj* busy (**à faire** doing); [place, maison] occupied; [ligne téléphonique] *Br* engaged, *Am* busy

**occuper** [ɔkype] **1.** *vt* [bâtiment, pays] to occupy; [place] to take up, to occupy; [poste] to hold; **occuper qn** [jeu, travail] to keep sb busy or occupied **2. s'occuper** *vpr* to keep oneself busy (**à faire** doing); **s'occuper de** [affaire, problème] to deal with; **s'occuper de qn** [malade] to take care of sb; [client] to see to sb

**océan** [ɔseɑ̃] *nm* ocean; **l'océan Atlantique / Pacifique** the Atlantic / Pacific Ocean

**octante** [ɔktɑ̃t] *adj & nm inv* [en Belgique, en Suisse] eighty

**octet** [ɔktɛ] *nm* ORDINAT byte; **milliard d'octets** gigabyte

**octobre** [ɔktɔbr] *nm* October

**octogonal, -e, -aux** [ɔktɔgɔnal, -o] *adj* octagonal

**oculaire** [ɔkylɛr] *adj* **témoin oculaire** eyewitness ■ **oculiste** *nmf* eye specialist

**odeur** [ɔdœr] *nf* smell; [de fleur] scent ■ **odorat** *nm* sense of smell

**odieux, -euse** [ɔdjø, -øz] *adj* odious

**œil** [œj] (*pl* **yeux** [jø]) *nm* eye; **avoir les yeux verts** to have green eyes; **avoir de grands yeux** to have big eyes; **lever / baisser les yeux** to look up / down; **coup d'œil** [regard] look, glance; **jeter un coup d'œil sur qch** to have a look at sth; **à vue d'œil** visibly; **regarder qn dans les yeux** to look sb in the eye; *Fig* **œil au beurre noir** black eye

**œillères** [œjɛr] *nfpl* [de cheval] *Br* blinkers, *Am* blinders

**œillet** [œjɛ] *nm* [fleur] carnation

**œuf** [œf] (*pl* **œufs** [ø]) *nm* egg; **œufs** [de poissons] (hard) roe; **œuf à la coque** boiled egg; **œuf sur le plat** fried egg; **œuf dur** hard-boiled egg; **œufs brouillés** scrambled eggs; **œuf de Pâques** Easter egg

**œuvre** [œvr] *nf* [travail, livre] work; **œuvre d'art** work of art; **œuvre de charité** [organisation] charity

**offense** [ɔfɑ̃s] *nf* insult ■ **offensant, -e** *adj* offensive ■ **offenser 1.** *vt* to offend **2. s'offenser** *vpr* **s'offenser de qch** to take *Br* offence or *Am* offense at sth

**offensif, -ive** [ɔfɑ̃sif, -iv] **1.** *adj* offensive **2.** *nf* **offensive** offensive; **passer à l'offensif** to go on the offensive

**offert, -e** [ɔfɛr, -ɛrt] *pp de* offrir

**office** [ɔfis] *nm* **a)** REL service **b)** [pièce] pantry **c)** [établissement] office, bureau; **office du tourisme** tourist information centre **d)** [charge] office; **d'office** without having any say; **faire office de qch** to serve as sth

**officiel, -elle** [ɔfisjɛl] *adj & nm* official

**officier** [ɔfisje] *nm* [dans l'armée] officer

**officieux, -euse** [ɔfisjø, -øz] *adj* unofficial

**offre** [ɔfr] *nf* offer ; [aux enchères] bid ; ÉCON **l'offre et la demande** supply and demand ; FIN **offre publique d'achat** takeover bid ; **offres d'emploi** [de journal] job vacancies, *Br* situations vacant ▪ **offrande** *nf* offering

**offrir** [ɔfrir] **1.** *vt* [donner] to give ; [proposer] to offer ; **offrir qch à qn** [donner] to give sb sth, to give sth to sb ; [proposer] to offer sb sth, to offer sth to sb ; **offrir de faire qch** to offer to do sth **2. s'offrir** *vpr* [cadeau] to treat oneself to ; [se proposer] to offer oneself (**comme** as) ▪ **offrant** *nm* **au plus offrant** to the highest bidder

**OGM** [ɔʒeɛm] *(abr de* **organisme génétiquement modifié)** *nm* GMO

**oie** [wa] *nf* goose *(pl* geese)

**oignon** [ɔɲɔ̃] *nm* [légume] onion

**oiseau, -x** [wazo] *nm* bird ; **oiseau de proie** bird of prey

**oisif, -ive** [wazif, -iv] *adj* idle ▪ **oisiveté** *nf* idleness

**ola** [ɔla] *nf Br* Mexican wave, *Am* wave

**oléoduc** [ɔleɔdyk] *nm* pipeline

**olive** [ɔliv] **1.** *nf* olive **2.** *adj inv* **vert olive** olive (green) ▪ **olivier** *nm* [arbre] olive tree

**olympique** [ɔlɛ̃pik] *adj* Olympic ; **les jeux Olympiques** the Olympic games

**ombilical, -e, -aux** [ɔ̃bilikal, -o] *adj* umbilical

**ombrage** [ɔ̃braʒ] *nm* [ombre] shade

**ombre** [ɔ̃br] *nf* [forme] shadow ; [zone sombre] shade ; **30° à l'ombre** 30° in the shade ; **sans l'ombre d'un doute** without the shadow of a doubt ; **pas l'ombre d'un reproche / remords** not a trace of blame / remorse

**ombrelle** [ɔ̃brɛl] *nf* sunshade, parasol

**omelette** [ɔmlɛt] *nf* omelette ; **omelette norvégienne** ≃ baked Alaska

**omettre** [ɔmɛtr] *vt* to omit (**de faire** to do) ▪ **omission** *nf* omission

**omnibus** [ɔmnibys] *adj & nm* **(train) omnibus** slow train *(stopping at all stations)*

**omnipotent, -e** [ɔmnipɔtɑ̃, -ɑ̃t] *adj* omnipotent

**omniprésent, -e** [ɔmniprezɑ̃, ɑ̃t] *adj* omnipresent

**omnisports** [ɔmnispɔr] *adj inv* **centre omnisports** sports centre

**omnivore** [ɔmnivɔr] *adj* omnivorous

**on** [ɔ̃] *(sometimes* **l'on** [lɔ̃]*) pron indéf* [les gens] they, people ; [nous] we, one ; [vous] you, one ; **on m'a dit que...** I was told that... ; **on me l'a donné** somebody gave it to me

**oncle** [ɔ̃kl] *nm* uncle

**onctueux, -euse** [ɔ̃ktɥø, -øz] *adj* smooth

**onde** [ɔ̃d] *nf* [à la radio & PHYS] wave ; **grandes ondes** long wave ; **ondes courtes / moyennes** short / medium wave ; **onde de choc** shock wave

**ondée** [ɔ̃de] *nf* sudden downpour

**on-dit** [ɔ̃di] *nm inv* rumour, hearsay

**ondoyer** [ɔ̃dwaje] *vi* to undulate

**ondulé, -e** [ɔ̃dyle] *adj* wavy

**onduler** [ɔ̃dyle] *vi* to undulate ; [cheveux] to be wavy

**onéreux, -euse** [ɔnerø, -øz] *adj* costly

**ONG** [ɔɛnʒe] *(abr de* **organisation non gouvernementale)** *nf* NGO

**ongle** [ɔ̃gl] *nm* (finger)nail

**ont** [ɔ̃] *voir* **avoir**

**ONU** [ɔny] *(abr de* **Organisation des Nations unies)** *nf* UN

**onze** [ɔ̃z] *adj & nm* eleven ▪ **onzième** *adj & nmf* eleventh

**OPA** [ɔpea] *(abr de* **offre publique d'achat)** *nf* FIN takeover bid

**opaque** [ɔpak] *adj* opaque

**opéra** [ɔpera] *nm* [musique] opera ; [édifice] opera house

**opérateur, -trice** [ɔperatœr, -tris] *nmf* [personne] operator ; CINÉ cameraman

**opération** [ɔperasjɔ̃] *nf* [action, MÉD, MIL & MATH] operation ▪ **opérationnel, -elle** *adj* operational

**opérer** [ɔpere] **1.** *vt* [exécuter] to carry out ; [choix] to make ; [patient] to operate on (**de** for) ; **se faire opérer** to have an operation **2.** *vi* [agir] to work; [procéder] to proceed; [chirurgien] to operate

**ophtalmo** [ɔftalmo] *nmf Fam* ophtalmologist, eye specialist

**ophtalmologue** [ɔftalmɔlɔg] *nmf* ophthalmologist

**opiniâtre** [ɔpinjɑtr] *adj* stubborn

**opinion** [ɔpinjɔ̃] *nf* opinion (**sur** about *or* on); **mon opinion est faite** my mind is made up; **opinion publique** public opinion

**opportun, -e** [ɔpɔrtœ̃, -yn] *adj* opportune, timely ■ **opportunité** *nf* timeliness

**opposant, -e** [ɔpozɑ̃, -ɑ̃t] *nmf* opponent (**à** of)

**opposé, -e** [ɔpoze] **1.** *adj* [direction] opposite; [intérêts] conflicting; [armées, équipe] opposing; **être opposé à qch** to be opposed to sth **2.** *nm* **l'opposé** the opposite (**de** of); **à l'opposé** [côté] on the opposite side (**de** to); **à l'opposé de** [contrairement à] contrary to

**opposer** [ɔpoze] **1.** *vt* [résistance, argument] to put up (**à** against); **opposer qn à qn** to set sb against sb; **match qui oppose...** match between... **2. s'opposer** *vpr* [équipes] to confront each other; **s'opposer à qch** to be opposed to sth; **je m'y oppose** I'm opposed to it

**opposition** [ɔpozisjɔ̃] *nf* opposition (**à** to); **faire opposition à** to oppose; [chèque] to stop; **par opposition à** as opposed to

**oppresser** [ɔprese] *vt* [gêner] to oppress ■ **oppressant, -e** *adj* oppressive ■ **oppresseur** *nm* oppressor ■ **oppression** *nf* oppression ■ **opprimer** *vt* [peuple, nation] to oppress ■ **opprimés** *nmpl* **les opprimés** the oppressed

**opter** [ɔpte] *vi* **opter pour qch** to opt for sth

**opticien, -enne** [ɔptisjɛ̃, -ɛn] *nmf* optician

**optimal, -e, -aux** [ɔptimal, -o] *adj* optimal

**optimiser** [ɔptimize] *vt* to optimize

**optimisme** [ɔptimism] *nm* optimism ■ **optimiste 1.** *adj* optimistic **2.** *nmf* optimist

**option** [ɔpsjɔ̃] *nf* [choix] option; [chose] optional extra; SCOL *Br* optional subject, *Am* elective (subject)

**optique** [ɔptik] **1.** *adj* [nerf] optic; [verre, fibres] optical **2.** *nf* optics (*sg*); **d'optique** [instrument, appareil] optical

**opulent, -e** [ɔpylɑ̃, -ɑ̃t] *adj* opulent ■ **opulence** *nf* opulence

**or¹** [ɔr] *nm* gold; **montre en or** gold watch; **règle /âge d'or** golden rule / age; **cœur d'or** heart of gold; **mine d'or** gold mine; **affaire en or** bargain; **or noir** [pétrole] black gold

**or²** [ɔr] *conj* [cependant] now, well

**orage** [ɔraʒ] *nm* (thunder)storm ■ **orageux, -euse** *adj* stormy

**oral, -e, -aux** [ɔral, -o] **1.** *adj* oral **2.** *nm* SCOL & UNIV oral

**orange** [ɔrɑ̃ʒ] **1.** *nf* orange; **orange pressée** (fresh) orange juice **2.** *adj* & *nm inv* [couleur] orange ■ **oranger** *nm* orange tree

**orateur** [ɔratœr] *nm* speaker, orator

**orbite** [ɔrbit] *nf* [d'astre] orbit; [d'œil] socket; **mettre qch sur orbite** [fusée] to put sth into orbit

**orchestre** [ɔrkɛstr] *nm* [classique] orchestra; [de jazz] band; THÉÂT [places] *Br* stalls, *Am* orchestra ■ **orchestrer** *vt* [organiser & MUS] to orchestrate

**ordinaire** [ɔrdinɛr] **1.** *adj* [habituel, normal] ordinary, *Am* regular; [médiocre] ordinary, average; **d'ordinaire, à l'ordinaire** usually; **comme d'ordinaire, comme à l'ordinaire** as usual **2.** *nm* **a)** [moyenne] **l'ordinaire** the ordinary; **sortir de l'ordinaire** to be out of the ordinary **b)** [alimentation] usual diet

**ordinateur** [ɔrdinatœr] *nm* computer; **ordinateur individuel** personal computer; **ordinateur portable** laptop

**ordonnance** [ɔrdɔnɑ̃s] *nf* [de médecin] prescription; [disposition] arrangement

**ordonner** [ɔrdɔne] *vt* **a)** [commander] to order (**que** (+ subjunctive) that) ; **ordonner à qn de faire qch** to order sb to do sth **b)** [ranger] to organize **c)** [prêtre] to ordain ; **il a été ordonné prêtre** he has been ordained (as) a priest ■ **ordonné, -e** *adj* [personne, maison] tidy

**ordre** [ɔrdr] *nm* [organisation, discipline, catégorie, commandement] order ; [absence de désordre] tidiness ; **en ordre** [chambre] tidy ; **mettre de l'ordre dans qch** to tidy sth up ; **rentrer dans l'ordre** to return to normal ; **jusqu'à nouvel ordre** until further notice ; **de l'ordre de** [environ] of the order of ; **du même ordre** of the same order ; **de premier ordre** first-rate ; **par ordre d'âge** in order of age ; **assurer le maintien de l'ordre** to maintain order ; REL **entrer dans les ordres** to take holy orders ; **ordre du jour** agenda ; **l'ordre public** law and order

**ordures** [ɔrdyr] *nfpl* [déchets] *Br* rubbish, *Am* garbage ; **mettre qch aux ordures** to throw sth out (in the *Br* rubbish or *Am* garbage)

**oreille** [ɔrɛj] *nf* ear ; **faire la sourde oreille** to turn a deaf ear

**oreiller** [ɔreje] *nm* pillow

**oreillons** [ɔrɛjɔ̃] *nmpl* [maladie] mumps

**ores et déjà** [ɔrzedeʒa] ■ **d'ores et déjà** *adv* already

**orfèvrerie** [ɔrfɛvrəri] *nf* [magasin] goldsmith's / silversmith's shop ; [objets] gold / silver plate

**organe** [ɔrgan] *nm* ANAT & *Fig* organ ■ **organisme** *nm* [corps] body ; BIOL organism ; [bureaux] organization

**organique** [ɔrganik] *adj* organic

**organisateur, -trice** [ɔrganizatœr, -tris] *nmf* organizer

**organisation** [ɔrganizasjɔ̃] *nf* [arrangement, association] organization

**organiser** [ɔrganize] **1.** *vt* to organize **2. s'organiser** *vpr* to get organized ■ **organisé, -e** *adj* organized

**orge** [ɔrʒ] *nf* barley

**orgue** [ɔrg] **1.** *nm* organ **2.** *nfpl* **orgues** organ

**orgueil** [ɔrgœj] *nm* pride ■ **orgueilleux, -euse** *adj* proud

**orient** [ɔrjɑ̃] *nm* **l'Orient** the Orient, the East ; **en Orient** in the East ■ **oriental, -e, -aux 1.** *adj* [côte, région] eastern ; [langue] oriental **2.** *nmf* **Oriental, Orientale** Oriental

**orientation** [ɔrjɑ̃tasjɔ̃] *nf* [de position] orientation ; [d'antenne] positioning ; [de maison] aspect ; **avoir le sens de l'orientation** to have a good sense of direction ; **orientation professionnelle** careers guidance

**orienter** [ɔrjɑ̃te] **1.** *vt* [bâtiment] to orientate ; [canon, télescope] to point (**vers** at) ; **orienter ses recherches sur** to direct one's research on **2. s'orienter** *vpr* to get one's bearings ; **s'orienter vers** [carrière] to specialize in ■ **orienté, -e** *adj* [peu objectif] slanted ; **orienté à l'ouest** [appartement] facing west

**orifice** [ɔrifis] *nm* opening

**originaire** [ɔriʒinɛr] *adj* **être originaire de** [natif] to be a native of

**original, -e, -aux** [ɔriʒinal, -o] **1.** *adj* [idée, artiste, version] original **2.** *nm* [texte, tableau] original **3.** *nmf* [personne] eccentric ■ **originalité** *nf* originality

**origine** [ɔriʒin] *nf* origin ; **à l'origine** originally ; **être à l'origine de qch** to be at the origin of sth ; **d'origine** [pneu] original ; **être d'origine française** to be of French origin ■ **originel, -elle** *adj* original

**ornement** [ɔrnəmɑ̃] *nm* ornament ■ **ornemental, -e, -aux** *adj* ornamental

**orner** [ɔrne] *vt* to decorate (**de** with)

**orphelin, -e** [ɔrfəlɛ̃, -in] *nmf* orphan ■ **orphelinat** *nm* orphanage

**orteil** [ɔrtɛj] *nm* toe

**orthodoxe** [ɔrtɔdɔks] *adj* orthodox

**orthographe** [ɔrtɔgraf] *nf* spelling ■ **orthographier** *vt* to spell ; **mal orthographier qch** to misspell sth

**orthopédagogie** [ɔrtɔpedagɔʒi] *nf Can* SCOL & MÉD special education, curative education

**ortie** [ɔrti] *nf* nettle

**os** [ɔs] (*pl* [o] *ou* [ɔs]) *nm* bone

**oscar** [ɔskar] *nm* [récompense] Oscar

**osciller** [ɔsile] *vi* TECH to oscillate; [pendule] to swing; [aiguille, flamme] to flicker; *Fig* [varier] to fluctuate (**entre** between)

**oser** [oze] *vt* to dare; **oser faire qch** to dare (to) do sth ■ **osé, -e** *adj* daring

**osier** [ozje] *nm* wicker; **panier d'osier** wicker basket

**ossements** [ɔsmã] *nmpl* bones

**osseux, -euse** [ɔsø, -øz] *adj* [maigre] bony

**otage** [ɔtaʒ] *nm* hostage; **prendre qn en otage** to take sb hostage

**OTAN** [ɔtã] (*abr de* Organisation du traité de l'Atlantique Nord) *nf* NATO

**ôter** [ote] *vt* to take away, to remove (**à qn** from sb); [vêtement] to take off; [déduire] to take (away)

**otite** [ɔtit] *nf* ear infection

**ou** [u] *conj* or; **ou elle ou moi** either her or me

**où** [u] *adv & pron rel* where; **le jour où...** the day when...; **la table où...** the table on which...; **l'état où...** the condition in which...; **par où ?** which way?; **d'où ?** where from?; **le pays d'où je viens** the country from which I come

**ouate** [wat] *nf* [pour pansement] *Br* cotton wool, *Am* absorbent cotton

**oubli** [ubli] *nm* [trou de mémoire] oversight; [lacune] omission; **tomber dans l'oubli** to fall into oblivion

**oublier** [ublije] *vt* to forget (**de faire** to do); [omettre] to leave out

**oubliettes** [ublijɛt] *nfpl* [de château] dungeons

**ouest** [wɛst] **1.** *nm* west; **à l'ouest** in the west; [direction] (to the) west (**de** of); **d'ouest** [vent] west(erly); **de l'ouest** western **2.** *adj inv* [côte] west; [région] western

**ouf** [uf] **1.** *excl* phew **2.** *adj* [fou en verlan] nuts

**Ouganda** [ugãda] *nm* **l'Ouganda** Uganda

**oui** [wi] **1.** *adv* yes; **ah, ça oui !** oh yes (indeed!); **je crois que oui** I think so **2.** *nm inv* **pour un oui pour un non** for the slightest thing

**ouï-dire** [widir] *nm* hearsay; **par ouï-dire** by hearsay

**ouïe** [wi] *nf* hearing

**ouïes** [wi] *nfpl* [de poisson] gills

**ouragan** [uragã] *nm* hurricane

**ourlet** [urlɛ] *nm* hem

**ours** [urs] *nm* bear; **ours blanc** polar bear; **ours en peluche** teddy bear ■ **ourse** *nf* she-bear; **la Grande Ourse** the Great Bear

**oursin** [ursɛ̃] *nm* sea urchin

**outarde** [utard] *nf Can* [bernache du Canada] Canada goose

**outil** [uti] *nm* tool ■ **outillage** *nm* tools; [d'usine] equipment ■ **outiller** *vt* to equip

**outrage** [utraʒ] *nm* insult (**à** to)

**outrance** [utrãs] *nf* [excès] excess; **à outrance** to excess ■ **outrancier, -ère** *adj* excessive

**outre** [utr] **1.** *prép* besides; **outre mesure** unduly **2.** *adv* **en outre** besides; **passer outre** to take no notice (**à** of) ■ **outre-Manche** *adv* across the Channel ■ **outre-mer** *adv* overseas; **d'outre-mer** [marché] overseas; **territoires d'outre-mer** overseas territories

**outré, -e** [utre] *adj* [révolté] outraged; [excessif] exaggerated

**outrepasser** [utrəpase] *vt* to go beyond, to exceed

**ouvert, -e** [uvɛr, -ɛrt] **1.** *pp de* ouvrir **2.** *adj* open; [robinet, gaz] on ■ **ouverture** *nf* opening; [trou] hole

**ouvrable** [uvrabl] *adj* **jour ouvrable** working *or Am* work day

**ouvrage** [uvraʒ] *nm* [travail, livre, objet] work; [couture] (needle)work; **un ouvrage** [travail] a piece of work

**ouvré, e** [uvre] *adj* ADMIN & COMM **jour ouvré** *Br* working day, workday

**ouvreuse** [uvrøz] *nf* usherette

**ouvrier, -ère** [uvrije, -ɛr] **1.** *nmf* worker; **ouvrier qualifié / spécialisé** skilled / semi-skilled worker; **ouvrier agricole** farm worker **2.** *adj* [quartier] working-class

**ouvrir** [uvrir] **1.** *vt* to open; [gaz, radio] to turn on; [hostilités] to begin; [appétit] to whet **2.** *vi* to open **3. s'ouvrir** *vpr* [porte, boîte, fleur] to open ■ **ouvre-boîtes** *nm inv Br* tin opener, *Am* can opener ■ **ouvre-bouteilles** *nm inv* bottle opener

**ovale** [ɔval] *adj & nm* oval

**ovation** [ɔvɑsjɔ̃] *nf* (standing) ovation

**ovni** [ɔvni] *(abr de* objet volant non identifié*) nm* UFO

**oxyder** [ɔkside] **1.** *vt* to oxidize **2. s'oxyder** *vpr* to oxidize

**oxygène** [ɔksiʒɛn] *nm* oxygen; **masque / tente à oxygène** oxygen mask / tent ■ **oxygéné, -e** *adj* **eau oxygénée** (hydrogen) peroxide; **cheveux blonds oxygénés** peroxide blonde hair, bleached hair

**ozone** [ozon] *nm* CHIM ozone

**P, p** [pe] *nm inv* P, p

**pacifique** [pasifik] **1.** *adj* [manifestation] peaceful ; [personne, peuple] peace-loving ; [côte] Pacific **2.** *nm* **le Pacifique** the Pacific

**pacifiste** [pasifist] *adj & nmf* pacifist

**PACS, pacs** [paks] *(abr de* **pacte civil de solidarité)** *nm* civil partnership *(between same-sex or opposite-sex couples)* ■ **pacsé, e** [pakse] **1.** *nmf Fam* person who has signed a PACS agreement, ≃ (life) partner **2. se pacser** *vpr Fam* to enter a civil partnership

**pacte** [pakt] *nm* pact

**pagaie** [page] *nf* paddle

**pagaïe, pagaille** [pagaj] *nf Fam* [désordre] mess ; **semer la pagaïe** to cause chaos

**pagayer** [pageje] *vi* to paddle

**page** [paʒ] *nf* [de livre] page ; **la première page** [d'un journal] the front page ; **être en première page** to be on or to make the front page ; ORDINAT **page d'accueil** home page ; **les Pages Jaunes®** [de l'annuaire] the Yellow Pages® ; RADIO **page de publicité** commercial break

**paie** [pe] *nf* pay, wages

**paiement** [pemã] *nm* payment

**païen, -enne** [pajɛ̃, -ɛn] *adj & nmf* pagan, heathen

**paillasson** [pajasɔ̃] *nm* (door)mat

**paille** [paj] *nf* straw ; [pour boire] (drinking) straw

**paillette** [pajɛt] *nf* [d'habit] sequin ; **paillettes** [de savon, lessive] flakes ; [d'or] gold dust

**paillote** [pajɔt] *nf* straw hut

**pain** [pɛ̃] *nm* bread ; **un pain** a loaf (of bread) ; **petit pain** roll ; **pain au chocolat** *chocolate-filled pastry* ; **pain complet**
wholemeal bread ; **pain d'épices** ≃ gingerbread ; **pain grillé** toast ; **pain de mie** sandwich loaf

**pair, -e** [pɛr] **1.** *adj* [numéro] even **2.** *nm* [personne] peer ; **hors pair** unrivalled ; **aller de pair** to go hand in hand (**avec** with) ; **au pair** [étudiante] au pair ; **travailler au pair** to work as an au pair

**paire** [pɛr] *nf* pair (**de** of)

**paisible** [pezibl] *adj* [vie, endroit] peaceful ; [caractère, personne] quiet

**paître** [pɛtr] *vi* to graze

**paix** [pe] *nf* peace ; **en paix** [vivre, laisser] in peace (**avec** with)

**Pakistan** [pakistã] *nm* **le Pakistan** Pakistan ■ **pakistanais, -e 1.** *adj* Pakistani **2.** *nmf* **Pakistanais, Pakistanaise** Pakistani

**palace** [palas] *nm* luxury hotel

**palais** [palɛ] *nm* [château] palace ; ANAT palate ; **Palais de justice** law courts ; **palais des sports** sports centre

**pâle** [pal] *adj* pale

**Palestine** [palɛstin] *nf* **la Palestine** Palestine ■ **palestinien, -enne 1.** *adj* Palestinian **2.** *nmf* **Palestinien, Palestinienne** Palestinian

**palette** [palɛt] *nf* [de peintre] palette ; [pour marchandises] pallet

**pâleur** [palœr] *nf* [de lumière] paleness ; [de personne] pallor

**palier** [palje] *nm* [niveau] level ; [d'escalier] landing ; [phase] plateau ; **par paliers** in stages

**pâlir** [palir] *vi* to turn pale (**de** with)

**palissade** [palisad] *nf* fence

**pallier** [palje] **1.** *vt* [difficultés] to alleviate **2.** *vi* **pallier à qch** to compensate for sth

**palmarès** [palmarɛs] *nm* prize list ; [de chansons] charts

**palme** [palm] *nf* [de palmier] palm (branch) ; [de nageur] flipper

**palmier** [palmje] *nm* palm (tree)

**palourde** [palurd] *nf* clam

**palper** [palpe] *vt* to feel ■ **palpable** *adj* palpable

**palpiter** [palpite] *vi* [cœur] to flutter ; [plus fort] to throb

**paludisme** [palydism] *nm* malaria

**pamplemousse** [pɑ̃pləmus] *nm* grapefruit

**panaché, -e** [panaʃe] **1.** *adj* Br multicoloured, Am multicolored ; **panaché de blanc** streaked with white **2.** *nm* shandy

**Panama** [panama] *nm* **le Panama** Panama

**pancarte** [pɑ̃kart] *nf* sign, notice ; [de manifestant] placard

**pané, -e** [pane] *adj* [poisson] breaded

**panier** [panje] *nm* [ustensile, contenu] basket ; **panier à linge** Br linen basket, Am (clothes) hamper

**panique** [panik] **1.** *nf* panic ; **pris de panique** panic-stricken **2.** *adj* **peur panique** panic ■ **paniquer** *vt & vi* Fam to panic

**panne** [pan] *nf* breakdown ; **tomber en panne** to break down ; **être en panne** to have broken down ; **tomber en panne sèche** to run out of Br petrol or Am gas ; **panne d'électricité** blackout, Br power cut

**panneau, -x** [pano] *nm* [écriteau] sign, notice, board ; [de porte] panel ; **panneau d'affichage** Br notice board, Am bulletin board ; **panneau de signalisation** road sign ; **panneau indicateur** signpost, road sign ■ **panonceau, -x** *nm* [enseigne] sign

**panoplie** [panɔpli] *nf* [jouet] outfit ; [gamme] set

**panorama** [panɔrama] *nm* panorama ■ **panoramique** *adj* panoramic ; CINÉ **écran panoramique** wide screen

**panser** [pɑ̃se] *vt* [main] to bandage ; [plaie] to dress ; **panser qn** to dress sb's wounds ■ **pansement** *nm* dressing ; **faire un pansement à qn** to put a dressing on sb ; **pansement adhésif** Br sticking plaster, Am Band-aid®

**pantacourt** [pɑ̃takur] *nm* capri pants, capris, clamdiggers

**pantalon** [pɑ̃talɔ̃] *nm* Br trousers, Am pants ; **deux pantalons** two pairs of Br trousers or Am pants

**panthère** [pɑ̃tɛr] *nf* panther

**pantoufle** [pɑ̃tufl] *nf* slipper

**paon** [pɑ̃] *nm* peacock

**papa** [papa] *nm* dad(dy)

**pape** [pap] *nm* pope

**papeterie** [papɛtri] *nf* [magasin] stationer's shop ; [articles] stationery ; [fabrique] paper mill

**papi** [papi] *nm* = **papy**

**papier** [papje] *nm* [matière] paper ; **un papier** [feuille] a piece of paper ; [formulaire] a form ; [de journal] an article ; **papier hygiénique** toilet paper ; **papiers d'identité** identity papers ; **papier à lettres** writing paper ; **papier peint** wallpaper

**papillon** [papijɔ̃] *nm* [insecte] butterfly ; **papillon de nuit** moth

**papy** [papi] *nm* grand(d)ad

**Pâque** [pak] *nf* REL **la Pâque juive, Pâque** Passover

**paquebot** [pakbo] *nm* liner

**pâquerette** [pakrɛt] *nf* daisy

**Pâques** [pak] *nm sg & nfpl* Easter

**paquet** [pakɛ] *nm* [sac] packet ; [de sucre] bag ; [de cigarettes] packet, Am pack ; Br [postal] parcel, package

**par** [par] *prép* **a)** [indique l'agent, la manière, le moyen] by ; **frappé par qn** hit by sb ; **par mer** by sea ; **par le train** by train ; **par la force** by or through force ; **commencer par qch** [récit] to begin with sth ; **par erreur** by mistake ; **par chance** by a stroke of luck
**b)** [à travers] through ; **par la porte** through the door ; **jeter / regarder par la fenêtre** to throw / look out (of) the

window; **par ici / là** [aller] this / that way; [habiter] around here / there; **par les rues** through the streets
c) [à cause de] out of, from; **par pitié** out of pity
d) [pendant] **par ce froid** in this cold; **par le passé** in the past
e) [distributif] **dix fois par an / mois** ten times a *or* per year / month; **50 euros par personne** 50 euros per person; **deux par deux** two by two; **par deux fois** twice f) [avec 'trop'] **par trop aimable** far too kind

**paraben, parabène** [paraben] *nm* paraben; **sans paraben** paraben-free

**parachute** [paraʃyt] *nm* parachute; **parachute ascensionnel** parascending; ÉCON **parachute doré** *ou* **en or** golden parachute ∎ **parachutisme** *nm* parachute jumping ∎ **parachutiste** *nmf* parachutist; [soldat] paratrooper

**parade** [parad] *nf* [défilé] parade; [étalage] show

**paradis** [paradi] *nm* heaven

**paradoxe** [paradɔks] *nm* paradox

**parafer** [parafe] *vt* = **parapher**

**paraffine** [parafin] *nf* paraffin (wax)

**parages** [paraʒ] *nmpl* NAUT waters; **dans les parages de** in the vicinity of

**paragraphe** [paragraf] *nm* paragraph

**Paraguay** [paragwe] *nm* **le Paraguay** Paraguay

**paraître** [parɛtr] **1.** *vi* [sembler] to seem, to appear; [apparaître] to appear; [livre] to come out, to be published **2.** *v impers* **il paraît qu'il va partir** it appears *or* seems (that) he's leaving; **à ce qu'il paraît** apparently

**parallèle** [paralɛl] **1.** *adj* parallel (**à** with *or* to); [police, marché] unofficial **2.** *nf* parallel (line) **3.** *nm* [comparaison & GÉOG] parallel; **mettre qch en parallèle avec qch** to draw a parallel between sth and sth ∎ **parallèlement** *adv* **parallèlement à** parallel to; [simultanément] at the same time as

**paralyser** [paralize] *vt Br* to paralyse, *Am* to paralyze ∎ **paralysé, e** *adj Br*

paralysed, *Am* paralyzed; **être paralysé de peur** to be petrified ∎ **paralysie** *nf* paralysis ∎ **paralytique** *adj* & *nmf* paralytic

**paramédical, -e, -aux** [paramedikal, -o] *adj* paramedical

**paramilitaire** [paramiliter] *adj* paramilitary

**parapente** [parapɑ̃t] *nm* [activité] paragliding; **faire du parapente** to go paragliding

**parapet** [parapɛ] *nm* parapet

**parapher** [parafe] *vt* to initial

**parapluie** [paraplɥi] *nm* umbrella

**parasite** [parazit] **1.** *nm* [organisme, personne] parasite; **parasites** [à la radio] interference **2.** *adj* parasitic

**parasol** [parasɔl] *nm* sunshade, parasol; [de plage] beach umbrella

**paratonnerre** [paratɔner] *nm* lightning *Br* conductor *or Am* rod

**paravent** [paravɑ̃] *nm* screen

**parc** [park] *nm* [jardin] park; [de château] grounds; [de bébé] playpen; **parc d'attractions** amusement park; **parc de stationnement** *Br* car park, *Am* parking lot; **parc naturel** nature reserve

**parcelle** [parsɛl] *nf* small piece; [terrain] plot

**parce que** [parskə] *conj* because

**parchemin** [parʃəmɛ̃] *nm* parchment

**par-ci par-là** *adv* here and there

**parcmètre** [parkmetr] *nm* (parking) meter

**parcourir** [parkurir] *vt* [lieu] to walk round; [pays] to travel through; [mer] to sail; [distance] to cover; [texte] to glance through; **parcourir qch des yeux** *ou* **du regard** to glance at sth; **il reste 2 km à parcourir** there are 2 km to go ∎ **parcours** *nm* [itinéraire] route; **parcours de golf** [terrain] golf course

**par-delà** [pardəla] *prép* & *adv* beyond

**par-derrière** [parderjer] **1.** *prép* behind **2.** *adv* [attaquer] from behind; [se boutonner] at the back; **passer par-derrière** to go in the back door

**par-dessous** [pardəsu] *prép* & *adv* underneath

**pardessus** [pardəsy] *nm* overcoat

**par-dessus** [pardəsy] **1.** *prép* over; **par-dessus tout** above all **2.** *adv* over

**par-devant** [pardəvã] *adv* [attaquer] from the front; [se boutonner] at the front

**pardon** [pardɔ̃] *nm* forgiveness; **pardon !** [excusez-moi] sorry!; **pardon ?** [pour demander] excuse me?, *Am* pardon me?; **demander pardon** to apologize (à to) ▪ **pardonner** *vt* to forgive; **pardonner qch à qn** to forgive sb for sth; **elle m'a pardonné d'avoir oublié** she forgave me for forgetting

**pare-balles** [parbal] *adj inv* **gilet pare-balles** bulletproof *Br* jacket *or Am* vest

**pare-brise** [parbriz] *nm inv Br* windscreen, *Am* windshield

**pare-chocs** [parʃɔk] *nm inv* bumper

**pareil**, **-eille** [parɛj] **1.** *adj* **a)** [identique] the same; **pareil à** the same as **b)** [tel] such; **en pareil cas** in such cases **2.** *adv Fam* the same **3.** *nmf* [personne] equal; **sans pareil** unparalleled, unique **4.** *nf* **rendre la pareille à qn** [se venger] to get one's own back on sb ▪ **pareillement** *adv* [de la même manière] in the same way; [aussi] likewise

**parent**, **-e** [parã, -ãt] **1.** *nmf* [oncle, tante, cousin] relative, relation **2.** *nmpl* **parents** [père et mère] parents **3.** *adj* related (de to) ▪ **parental**, **-e**, **-aux** *adj* parental ▪ **parenté** *nf* relationship; **avoir un lien de parenté** to be related

**parenthèse** [parãtɛz] *nf* [signe] bracket, parenthesis; **entre parenthèses** in brackets

**parer¹** [pare] **1.** *vt* [coup] to parry **2.** *vi* **parer à toute éventualité** to prepare for any contingency

**parer²** [pare] *vt* [orner] to adorn (de with)

**paresseux**, **-euse** [parɛsø, -øz] **1.** *adj* lazy **2.** *nmf* lazy person

**parfaire** [parfɛr] *vt* to finish off ▪ **parfait**, **-e** *adj* perfect ▪ **parfaitement** *adv* [sans fautes, complètement] perfectly; [certainement] certainly

**parfois** [parfwa] *adv* sometimes

**parfum** [parfœ̃] *nm* [essence] perfume; [senteur] fragrance; [de glace] flavour ▪ **parfumer 1.** *vt* [embaumer] to scent; [glace] to flavour (à with) **2. se parfumer** *vpr* to put perfume on ▪ **parfumerie** *nf* [magasin] perfumery

**pari** [pari] *nm* bet; **faire un pari** to make a bet; **Pari Mutuel Urbain®** *Br* ≃ tote, *Am* ≃ pari-mutuel ▪ **parier** *vt* & *vi* to bet (sur on; que that); **il y a fort à parier que...** the odds are that... ▪ **parieur**, **euse** *nmf* punter

**Paris** [pari] *nm ou f* Paris ▪ **parisien**, **-enne 1.** *adj* Parisian **2.** *nmf* **Parisien**, **Parisienne** Parisian

**parking** [parkiŋ] *nm Br* car park, *Am* parking lot; **'parking payant'** *Br* ≃ 'pay-and-display car park'

**parlement** [parləmã] *nm* **le Parlement** Parliament ▪ **parlementaire 1.** *adj* parliamentary **2.** *nmf* member of parliament

**parlementer** [parləmãte] *vi* to negotiate (avec with)

**parler** [parle] **1.** *vi* to talk, to speak (de about *or* of; à to); **sans parler de...** not to mention... **2.** *vt* [langue] to speak; **parler affaires** to talk business **3. se parler** *vpr* [langue] to be spoken; [l'un l'autre] to talk to each other **4.** *nm* speech; [régional] dialect

**parloir** [parlwar] *nm* visiting room

**parmi** [parmi] *prép* among(st)

**paroi** [parwa] *nf* wall; [de rocher] (rock) face

**paroisse** [parwas] *nf* parish

**parole** [parɔl] *nf* [mot, promesse] word; [faculté, langage] speech; **paroles** [de chanson] words, lyrics; **adresser la parole à qn** to speak to sb; **prendre la parole** to speak; **tenir parole** to keep one's word

**parquet** [parkɛ] *nm* [sol] wooden floor

**parrain** [parɛ̃] *nm* REL godfather; [de sportif, de club] sponsor ■ **parrainer** *vt* [sportif, membre] to sponsor

**pars** [par] *voir* **partir**

**parsemer** [parsəme] *vt* to scatter (de with)

**part¹** [par] *voir* **partir**

**part²** [par] *nf* [portion] share, part; [de gâteau] slice; **prendre part à** [activité] to take part in; **faire part de qch à qn** to inform sb of sth; **de toutes parts** on all sides; **de part et d'autre** on both sides; **d'une part d'autre part** on the one hand... on the other hand...; **d'autre part** [d'ailleurs] moreover; **de la part de qn** from sb; **c'est de la part de qui ?** [au téléphone] who's calling?; **pour ma part** as for me; **à part** [mettre] aside; [excepté] apart from; [personne] different; **prendre qn à part** to take sb aside

**partage** [partaʒ] *nm* [action] dividing up; [de gâteau, de responsabilités] sharing out; **faire le partage de qch** to divide sth up

**partager** [partaʒe] **1.** *vt* [avoir en commun] to share (avec with); [répartir] to divide (up); **partager qch en deux** to divide sth in two; **partager l'avis de qn** to share sb's opinion **2. se partager** *vpr* [bénéfices] to share (between themselves); **se partager entre** to divide one's time between ■ **partagé, -e** *adj* [amour] mutual; **les avis sont partagés** opinions are divided

**partance** [partɑ̃s] ■ **en partance** *adv* [train] about to depart; **en partance pour...** for...

**partenaire** [partənɛr] *nmf* partner ■ **partenariat** *nm* partnership

**parterre** [partɛr] *nm* [de fleurs] flower bed; THÉÂT *Br* stalls, *Am* orchestra; *Fam* [sol] floor

**parti¹** [parti] *nm* [camp] side; **tirer parti de qch** to make good use of sth; **parti (politique)** (political) party

**parti², e¹** *adj Fam* [ivre] tipsy

**partial, -e, -aux** [parsjal, -o] *adj* biased ■ **partialité** *nf* bias

**participer** [partisipe] *vi* **participer à** [jeu] to take part in, to participate in; [bénéfices, joie] to share (in); [financièrement] to contribute to ■ **participant, -e** *nmf* participant ■ **participation** *nf* participation; [d'élection] turnout; **participation aux frais** contribution towards costs

**particularité** [partikylarite] *nf* peculiarity

**particule** [partikyl] *nf* particle

**particulier, -ère** [partikylje, -ɛr] **1.** *adj* [propre] characteristic (à of); [remarquable] unusual; [soin, intérêt] particular; [maison, voiture, leçon] private; *Péj* [bizarre] peculiar; **en particulier** [surtout] in particular; [à part] in private; **cas particulier** special case **2.** *nm* private individual; **vente de particulier à particulier** private sale ■ **particulièrement** *adv* particularly; **tout particulièrement** especially

**partie²** [parti] *nf* [morceau] part; [jeu] game; [domaine] field; **en partie** partly, in part; **en grande partie** mainly; **faire partie de** to be a part of; [club] to belong to; [comité] to be on ■ **partiel, -elle** *adj* partial

**partir** [partir] *(aux* être*)* *vi* [s'en aller] to go, to leave; [se mettre en route] to set off; [s'éloigner] to go away; [coup de feu] to go off; [tache] to come out; [peinture] to come off; **partir en voiture** to go by car, to drive; **partir en courant** to run off; **partir de** [lieu] to leave from; [commencer par] to start (off) with; **à partir de** [date, prix] from

**partisan** [partizɑ̃] **1.** *nm* supporter; [combattant] partisan **2.** *adj* [esprit] partisan; **être partisan de qch / de faire qch** to be in favour of sth / of doing sth

**partition** [partisjɔ̃] *nf* MUS score

**partout** [partu] *adv* everywhere; **partout où je vais** everywhere *or* wherever I go; **un peu partout** all over the place

**paru, -e** [pary] *pp de* **paraître**

**parure** [paryr] *nf* [ensemble] set

**parution** *nf* publication

**parvenir** [parvənir] (*aux être*) *vi* **parvenir à** [lieu] to reach ; [objectif] to achieve ; **parvenir à faire qch** to manage to do sth

**pas¹** [pɑ] *adv* [de négation] **(ne...) pas** not ; **je ne sais pas** I do not *or* don't know ; **je n'ai pas compris** I didn't understand ; **je voudrais ne pas sortir** I would like not to go out ; **pas de pain** no bread ; **pas du tout** not at all ; **elle chantera — pas moi !** she'll sing — no I won't !

**pas²** [pɑ] *nm* **a)** [enjambée] step ; [allure] pace ; [bruit] footstep ; [trace] footprint ; **pas à pas** step by step ; **à pas de loup** stealthily ; **à deux pas (de)** close by ; **aller au pas** to go at a walking pace ; **rouler au pas** [véhicule] to crawl along ; **faire un faux pas** [en marchant] to trip ; **revenir sur ses pas** to retrace one's steps ; **marcher à grands pas** to stride along **b)** [de vis] pitch **c) le pas de Calais** the Straits of Dover

**passable** [pɑsabl] *adj* passable, fair

**passage** [pɑsaʒ] *nm* [chemin, extrait] passage ; [ruelle] alley(way) ; [traversée] crossing ; **être de passage dans une ville** to be passing through a town ; **passage clouté** *ou* **pour piétons** *Br* (pedestrian) crossing, *Am* crosswalk ; **passage souterrain** *Br* subway, *Am* underpass ; **passage à niveau** *Br* level crossing, *Am* grade crossing ; **'passage interdit'** 'no through traffic' ; **'cédez le passage'** [au carrefour] *Br* 'give way', *Am* 'yield'

**passager, -ère** [pɑsaʒe, -ɛr] **1.** *adj* momentary **2.** *nmf* passenger ; **passager clandestin** stowaway

**passant, -e** [pɑsɑ̃, -ɑ̃t] **1.** *adj* [rue] busy **2.** *nmf* passer-by **3.** *nm* [de ceinture] loop

**passe** [pɑs] **1.** *nm* *Fam* passkey **2.** *nf* [au football] pass ; *Fig* **une mauvaise passe** a bad patch

**passé, -e** [pɑse] **1.** *adj* [temps] past ; [couleur] faded ; **la semaine passée** last week ; **il est dix heures passées** it's after *or* *Br* gone ten o'clock ; **passé de mode** out of fashion **2.** *nm* [temps,

vie passée] past ; **par le passé** in the past **3.** *prép* after ; **passé huit heures** after eight o'clock

**passe-montagne** [pɑsmɔ̃taɲ] (*pl* **passe-montagnes**) *nm Br* balaclava, *Am* ski mask

**passe-partout** [pɑspartu] *nm inv* master key

**passeport** [pɑspɔr] *nm* passport ; **passeport biométrique** biometric passport

**passer** [pɑse] **1.** (*aux avoir*) *vt* [pont, frontière] to go over ; [porte, douane] to go through ; [ballon] to pass ; [vêtement] to slip on ; [film] to show ; [disque] to play ; [vacances] to spend ; [examen] to take ; [commande] to place ; [visite médicale] to have ; [omettre] to leave out ; **passer qch à qn** [prêter] to pass sth to sb ; *AUTO* **passer la seconde** to change into second ; **passer son temps à faire qch** to spend one's time doing sth ; **passer quelques jours quelque part** to spend a few days somewehere **2.** (*aux être*) *vi* [se déplacer] to go past ; [disparaître] to go ; [facteur] to come ; [temps] to pass (by), to go by ; [film, programme] to be on ; [douleur] to pass ; [courant] to flow ; **laisser passer qn** to let sb through ; **passer de qch à qch** to go from sth to sth ; **passer dans la classe supérieure** to move up a class ; **passer devant qn/qch** to go past sb/sth ; **passer par Paris** to pass through Paris ; **passer chez le boulanger** to go round to the baker's ; **passer à la radio** to be on the radio ; **passer pour** [riche] to be taken for ; **faire passer qn pour** to pass sb off as ; **faire passer qch sous/dans qch** to slide/push sth under/into sth ; **passer sur** [détail] to pass over

**3. se passer** *vpr* **a)** [événement] to happen, to take place ; **comment ça s'est passé ?** how did it go? ; **ça ne se passera pas comme ça !** I'm not putting up with that! ; **l'opération s'est bien/mal passée** the operation went (off) smoothly/badly

b) [crème] to put on c) [s'abstenir] **se passer de qch /de faire qch** to do without sth /doing sth

**passerelle** [pasrɛl] nf [pont] footbridge; **passerelle d'embarquement** [de navire] gangway; [d'avion] steps

**passe-temps** [pɑstɑ̃] nm inv pastime

**passeur, -euse** [pasœr, -øz] nmf [batelier] ferryman, f ferrywoman; [contrebandier] smuggler

**passif, -ive** [pasif, -iv] adj passive

**passion** [pasjɔ̃] nf passion; **avoir la passion des voitures** to have a passion for cars

**passionner** [pasjɔne] 1. vt to fascinate 2. **se passionner** vpr **se passionner pour qch** to have a passion for sth ■ **passionnant, -e** adj fascinating ■ **passionné, -e** adj passionate; **passionné de qch** passionately fond of sth

**passivité** [pasivite] nf passiveness, passivity

**passoire** [paswar] nf [pour liquides] sieve; [à thé] strainer; [à légumes] colander

**pastel** [pastɛl] adj inv & nm pastel

**pastèque** [pastɛk] nf watermelon

**pasteur** [pastœr] nm REL pastor, minister

**pasteurisé, -e** [pastœrize] adj pasteurized

**pastille** [pastij] nf pastille; [médicament] lozenge

**patauger** [patoʒe] vi [s'embourber] to squelch; [barboter] to splash about

**pâte** [pat] nf [pour tarte] pastry; [pour pain] dough; [pour gâteau] mixture; **pâte d'amandes** marzipan; **pâte feuilletée** puff pastry; **pâtes (alimentaires)** pasta

**pâté** [pate] nm [charcuterie] pâté; [tache d'encre] blot; Can **pâté à la viande** meat pie; Can **pâté chinois** shepherd's pie; **pâté de maisons** block of houses; **pâté en croûte** ≃ meat pie

**pâtée** [pate] nf [pour chien] dog food; [pour chat] cat food

**patente** [patɑ̃t] nf Br licence or Am license fee (for traders and professionals)

**paternel, -elle** [patɛrnɛl] adj paternal ■ **paternité** nf [état] paternity, fatherhood; [de livre] authorship

**pathétique** [patetik] adj moving

**pathologique** [patɔlɔʒik] adj pathological

**patibulaire** [patibylɛr] adj sinister

**patience** [pasjɑ̃s] nf patience; **avoir de la patience** to be patient; **perdre patience** to lose patience

**patient, -e** [pasjɑ̃, -ɑ̃t] 1. adj patient 2. nmf [malade] patient ■ **patienter** vi to wait

**patin** [patɛ̃] nm [de patineur] skate; **patin à glace** ice skate; **patin à roulettes** roller skate

**patiner** [patine] vi SPORT to skate; [véhicule] to skid ■ **patinage** nm SPORT skating; **patinage artistique** figure skating ■ **patineur, -euse** nmf skater ■ **patinoire** nf skating rink, ice rink

**pâtir** [patir] vi **pâtir de** to suffer because of

**pâtisserie** [patisri] nf [gâteau] pastry, cake; [magasin] cake shop; [art] pastry-making ■ **pâtissier, -ère** 1. nmf pastry cook; [commerçant] confectioner 2. adj **crème pâtissière** confectioner's custard

**patrie** [patri] nf homeland

**patrimoine** [patrimwan] nm heritage; [biens] property

**patriote** [patrijɔt] 1. adj patriotic 2. nmf patriot ■ **patriotique** adj patriotic ■ **patriotisme** nm patriotism

**patron, -onne** [patrɔ̃, -ɔn] 1. nmf [chef] boss; [propriétaire] owner (**de** of); [gérant] manager, f manageress; [de bar] landlord, f landlady 2. nm COUTURE pattern

**patronat** [patrɔna] nm employers ■ **patronal, -e, -aux** adj employers'

**patrouille** [patruj] nf patrol ■ **patrouiller** vi to patrol

**patte** [pat] *nf* **a)** [membre] leg ; [de chat, de chien] paw **b)** [languette] tab ; [de poche] flap ■ **pattes** *nfpl* [favoris] sideburns

**pâturage** [patyraʒ] *nm* pasture

**paume** [pom] *nf* palm

**paumé, e** [pome] *Fam adj* lost

**paupière** [popjɛr] *nf* eyelid

**paupiette** [popjɛt] *nf* **paupiette de veau** veal olive

**pause** [poz] *nf* [arrêt] break ; [en parlant] pause ■ **pause-café** [pozkafe] *nf* coffee-break

**pauvre** [povr] **1.** *adj* [personne, sol, excuse] poor ; [meubles] shabby ; **pauvre en** [calories] low in ; [ressources] low on **2.** *nmf* poor man, *f* poor woman ; **les pauvres** the poor ■ **pauvreté** [-əte] *nf* poverty

**pavaner** [pavane] ■ **se pavaner** *vpr* to strut about

**paver** [pave] *vt* to pave ■ **pavé** *nm* paving stone ; **pavé numérique** numeric keypad

**pavillon** [pavijɔ̃] *nm* **a)** [maison] detached house ; [d'hôpital] wing ; [d'exposition] pavilion **b)** [drapeau] flag

**payable** [pejabl] *adj* payable

**paye** [pɛj] *nf* pay, wages ■ **payement** *nm* = **paiement**

**payer** [peje] **1.** *vt* [personne, somme] to pay ; [service, objet] to pay for ; [récompenser] to repay ; **se faire payer** to get paid **2.** *vi* to pay ■ **payant, -e** [pejɑ̃, -ɑ̃t] *adj* [hôte, spectateur] paying ■ **payé, e** *adj* **bien / mal payé** well- / low-paid

**pays** [pei] *nm* country ; [région] region ; **un pays étranger** a foreign country ; **aller dans un pays étranger** to go abroad ; **du pays** [vin, gens] local

**paysage** [peizaʒ] *nm* landscape, scenery

**paysan, -anne** [peizɑ̃, -an] **1.** *nmf* farmer **2.** *adj* **coutume paysanne** rural *or* country custom ; **le monde paysan** the farming community

**Pays-Bas** [peiba] *nmpl* **les Pays-Bas** the Netherlands

**PC** [pece] *(abr de* **personal computer)** *nm* ORDINAT PC

**pck** *(abr de* **parce que)** SMS COS, COZ

**PDF®** *nmf* PDF

**P-DG** [pedeʒe] *(abr de* **président-directeur général)** *nm Br* (chairman and) managing director, *Am* chief executive officer

**péage** [peaʒ] *nm* [droit] toll ; [lieu] tollbooth ; **pont à péage** toll bridge ; TV **chaîne à péage** pay channel

**peau, -x** [po] *nf* skin ; [de fruit] peel, skin ; [cuir] hide ■ **Peau-Rouge** *(pl* **Peaux-Rouges)** *nmf* Red Indian

**pêche¹** [pɛʃ] *nf* [activité] fishing ; [poissons] catch ; **pêche à la ligne** angling ; **aller à la pêche** to go fishing ■ **pêcher** [peʃe] **1.** *vt* [attraper] to catch ; [chercher à prendre] to fish for **2.** *vi* to fish ■ **pêcheur** *nm* fisherman ; [à la ligne] angler

**pêche²** [pɛʃ] *nf* [fruit] peach ■ **pêcher** [peʃe] *nm* [arbre] peach tree

**péché** [peʃe] *nm* sin ■ **pécher** *vi* to sin

**pectoraux** [pektɔro] *nmpl* chest muscles

**pédagogie** [pedagɔʒi] *nf* [discipline] pedagogy ■ **pédagogique** *adj* educational ■ **pédagogue** *nmf* teacher

**pédale** [pedal] *nf* [de voiture, de piano] pedal ; **pédale de frein** brake pedal

**Pédalo®** [pedalo] *nm* pedal boat, pedalo

**pédestre** [pedɛstr] *adj* **randonnée pédestre** hike

**pédiatre** [pedjatr] *nmf* paediatrician

**pédicure** [pedikyr] *nmf Br* chiropodist, *Am* podiatrist

**pègre** [pɛgr] *nf* **la pègre** the underworld

**peigne** [pɛɲ] *nm* comb ; **se donner un coup de peigne** to give one's hair a comb ■ **peigner 1.** *vt* [cheveux] to comb ; **peigner qn** to comb sb's hair **2. se peigner** *vpr* to comb one's hair

**peignoir** [pɛɲwar] *nm Br* dressing gown, *Am* bathrobe ; **peignoir de bain** bathrobe

**peindre** [pɛ̃dr] **1.** *vt* to paint **2.** *vi* to paint

**peine** [pɛn] *nf* **a)** [châtiment] punishment; **peine de mort** death penalty; **peine de prison** prison sentence; **'défense d'entrer sous peine d'amende'** 'trespassers will be prosecuted' **b)** [chagrin] sorrow; **avoir de la peine** to be upset; **faire de la peine à qn** to upset sb **c)** [effort] trouble; [difficulté] difficulty; **se donner de la peine** *ou* **beaucoup de peine** to go to a lot of trouble (**pour faire** to do); **avec peine** with difficulty; **ça vaut la peine d'attendre** it's worth waiting; **ce n'est pas** *ou* **ça ne vaut pas la peine** it's not worth it **d)** **à peine** hardly, scarcely; **à peine arrivée, elle...** no sooner had she arrived than she... ■ **peiner 1.** *vt* to upset **2.** *vi* to labour

**peintre** [pɛ̃tr] *nmf* [artiste] painter; **peintre en bâtiment** painter and decorator ■ **peinture** *nf* [tableau, activité] painting; [matière] paint; **peinture à l'huile** oil painting; **'peinture fraîche'** 'wet paint'

**péjoratif, ive** [peʒɔratif, iv] *adj* pejorative

**Pékin** [pekɛ̃] *nm ou f* Peking, Beijing

**pelage** [pəlaʒ] *nm* coat, fur

**pelé, -e** [pəle] *adj* bare

**peler** [pəle] **1.** *vt* to peel **2.** *vi* [personne, peau] to peel

**pelle** [pɛl] *nf* shovel; [d'enfant] spade; **pelle à tarte** cake server

**pellicule** [pelikyl] *nf* [pour photos] film; [couche] thin layer; **pellicules** [de cheveux] dandruff

**pelote** [plɔt] *nf* [de laine] ball; [à épingles] pincushion; SPORT **pelote basque** pelota

**peloton** [p(ə)lɔtɔ̃] *nm* [de ficelle] ball; [de cyclistes] pack; MIL platoon; **peloton d'exécution** firing squad

**pelotonner** [pəlɔtɔne] ■ **se pelotonner** *vpr* to curl up (into a ball)

**pelouse** [pəluz] *nf* lawn

**peluche** [pəlyʃ] *nf* [tissu] plush; **(jouet en) peluche** soft toy; **peluches** [de pull] fluff, lint

**pelure** [pəlyr] *nf* [de légumes] peelings; [de fruits] peel

**pénal, -e, -aux** [penal, -o] *adj* penal ■ **pénaliser** *vt* to penalize ■ **pénalité** *nf* penalty

**penalty** [penalti] *nm* SPORT penalty

**penchant** [pɑ̃ʃɑ̃] *nm* [préférence] penchant (**pour** for); [tendance] propensity (**pour** for)

**penché, -e** [pɑ̃ʃe] *adj* leaning

**pencher** [pɑ̃ʃe] **1.** *vt* [objet] to tilt; [tête] to lean **2.** *vi* [arbre] to lean over **3.** **se pencher** *vpr* to lean over; **se pencher par la fenêtre** to lean out of the window; **se pencher sur qch** [problème] to examine sth

**pendaison** [pɑ̃dɛzɔ̃] *nf* hanging

**pendant¹** [pɑ̃dɑ̃] *prép* [au cours de] during; **pendant deux mois** for two months; **pendant tout le trajet** for the whole journey; **pendant que...** while...

**pendant², -e 1.** *adj* hanging; [langue] hanging out **2.** *nm* **le pendant de** the companion piece to

**pendentif** [pɑ̃dɑ̃tif] *nm* [collier] pendant

**penderie** [pɑ̃dri] *nf Br* wardrobe, *Am* closet

**pendre** [pɑ̃dr] **1.** *vt & vi* to hang (**à** from); **pendre qn** to hang sb **2.** **se pendre** *vpr* [se suicider] to hang oneself; [se suspendre] to hang (**à** from) ■ **pendu, -e** *adj* [objet] hanging (**à** from)

**pendule** [pɑ̃dyl] **1.** *nf* clock **2.** *nm* [balancier] pendulum

**pénétrer** [penetre] **1.** *vi* **pénétrer dans** to enter; [profondément] to penetrate (into) **2.** *vt* [sujet : pluie] to penetrate **3.** **se pénétrer** *vpr* **se pénétrer d'une idée** to become convinced of an idea ■ **pénétration** *nf* penetration

**pénible** [penibl] *adj* [difficile] difficult; [douloureux] painful, distressing; [ennuyeux] tiresome ■ **péniblement** [-əmɑ̃] *adv* with difficulty

**péniche** [peniʃ] *nf* barge

**pénicilline** [penisilin] *nf* penicillin

**péninsule** [penɛ̃syl] *nf* peninsula

**pénitencier** [penitɑ̃sje] *nm* prison, *Am* penitentiary

**pensée** [pɑ̃se] *nf* [idée] thought; **à la pensée de faire qch** at the thought of doing sth

**penser** [pɑ̃se] **1.** *vi* [réfléchir] to think (**à** of or about); **penser à qn/qch** to think of or about sb /sth; **penser à faire qch** [ne pas oublier] to remember to do sth; **penses-tu !** what an idea! **2.** *vt* [estimer] to think (**que** that); [concevoir] to think out; **je pensais rester** I was thinking of staying; **que pensez-vous de… ?** what do you think of or about…?; **penser du bien de qn/qch** to think highly of sb /sth ◼ **pensif, -ive** *adj* thoughtful, pensive

**pension** [pɑ̃sjɔ̃] *nf* **a)** [école] boarding school; **mettre un enfant en pension** to send a child to boarding school **b)** [hôtel] **pension de famille** boarding house; **pension complète** *Br* full board, *Am* American plan **c)** [allocation] pension; **pension alimentaire** maintenance, alimony ◼ **pensionnaire** *nmf* [élève, résident] boarder ◼ **pensionnat** *nm* boarding school

**pente** [pɑ̃t] *nf* slope; **être en pente** to be sloping

**Pentecôte** [pɑ̃tkot] *nf* REL *Br* Whitsun, *Am* Pentecost

**pénurie** [penyri] *nf* shortage (**de** of)

**pépé** [pepe] *nm* grandpa

**pépin** [pepɛ̃] *nm* [de fruit] seed, *Br* pip, *Am* pit

**pépinière** [pepinjer] *nf* [pour plantes] nursery

**pépite** [pepit] *nf* [d'or] nugget; **pépite de chocolat** chocolate chip

**perçant, -e** [persɑ̃, -ɑ̃t] *adj* [cri, froid] piercing; [vue] sharp

**percée** [perse] *nf* [ouverture] opening; MIL, SPORT & TECH breakthrough

**perceptible** [perseptibl] *adj* perceptible (**à** to)

**perception** [persepsjɔ̃] *nf* **a)** [bureau] tax office; [d'impôt] collection **b)** [sensation] perception

**percer** [perse] **1.** *vt* [trouer] to pierce; [avec une perceuse] to drill; [trou, ouverture] to make; [abcès] to lance; [mystère] to solve; **percer une dent** [bébé] to cut a tooth; **percer qch à jour** to see through sth **2.** *vi* [soleil] to break through; [abcès] to burst; [acteur] to make a name for oneself ◼ **perceuse** *nf* drill

**percevoir** [persəvwar] *vt* **a)** [sensation] to perceive; [son] to hear **b)** [impôt] to collect

**perche** [perʃ] *nf* [bâton] pole

**percher** [perʃe] **1.** *vi* [oiseau] to perch **2. se percher** *vpr* [oiseau, personne] to perch

**percuter** [perkyte] **1.** *vt* [véhicule] to crash into **2.** *vi* **percuter contre** to crash into **3. se percuter** *vpr* to crash into each other

**perdant, -e** [perdɑ̃, -ɑ̃t] **1.** *adj* losing **2.** *nmf* loser

**perdre** [perdr] **1.** *vt* to lose; [habitude] to get out of; **perdre qn/qch de vue** to lose sight of sb /sth **2.** *vi* to lose **3. se perdre** *vpr* [s'égarer] to get lost; [disparaître] to die out; **se perdre dans les détails** to get lost in details; **se perdre de vue** to lose sight of each other ◼ **perdu, -e** *adj* [égaré] lost; [gaspillé] wasted; [malade] finished; [lieu] out-of-the-way

**père** [per] *nm* father; **de père en fils** from father to son; REL **mon père** father; **père de famille** father

**péremption** [perɑ̃psjɔ̃] *nf* **date de péremption** use-by date

**perfection** [perfeksjɔ̃] *nf* perfection; **à la perfection** to perfection

**perfectionner** [perfeksjɔne] **1.** *vt* to improve, to perfect **2. se perfectionner** *vpr* **se perfectionner en anglais** to improve one's English ◼ **perfectionné, -e** *adj* advanced ◼ **perfectionnement** *nm* improvement (**de** in; **par rapport à** on); **cours de perfectionnement** proficiency course

**perfectionniste** [pɛrfɛksjɔnist] *nmf*
perfectionist

**perforer** [pɛrfɔre] *vt* [pneu, intestin]
to perforate ; [billet] to punch ; **carte
perforée** punch card

**performance** [pɛrfɔrmɑ̃s] *nf*
performance ■ **performant, e** *adj*
**a)** [personne] efficient **b)** [machine]
high-performance

**perfusion** [pɛrfyzjɔ̃] *nf* drip ; **être sous
perfusion** to be on a drip

**péril** [peril] *nm* danger, peril ; **à tes
risques et périls** at your own risk ;
**mettre qch en péril** to endanger sth
■ **périlleux, -euse** *adj* dangerous,
perilous

**périmé, -e** [perime] *adj* [billet] expired ;
[nourriture] past its sell-by date

**période** [perjɔd] *nf* period ■ **périodique 1.** *adj* periodic **2.** *nm* [revue]
periodical

**périphérie** [periferi] *nf* [limite] periphery ; [banlieue] outskirts

**périphérique** [periferik] **1.** *adj* peripheral ; **radio périphérique** *radio station
broadcasting from outside France* **2.** *nm*
& *adj* **(boulevard) périphérique** *Br* ring
road, *Am* beltway

**périr** [perir] *vi* to perish ■ **périssable**
*adj* [denrée] perishable

**perle** [pɛrl] *nf* [bijou] pearl ; [de bois, de
verre] bead

**permanent, -e** [pɛrmanɑ̃, -ɑ̃t] **1.** *adj*
permanent ; CINÉ [spectacle] continuous ; [comité] standing **2.** *nf* **permanente** perm ■ **permanence** *nf* permanence ; [salle d'étude] study room ;
[service, bureau] duty office ; **être de
permanence** to be on duty ; **en permanence** permanently

**perméable** [pɛrmeabl] *adj* permeable
(**à** to)

**permettre** [pɛrmɛtr] **1.** *vt* to allow, to
permit ; **permettre à qn de faire qch**
to allow sb to do sth ; **vous permettez ?**
may I ? **2. se permettre** *vpr* se permettre de faire qch to take the liberty
of doing sth ; **je ne peux pas me le permettre** I can't afford it

**permis, -e** [pɛrmi, -iz] **1.** *adj* allowed,
permitted **2.** *nm* *Br* licence, *Am* license,
permit ; **permis de conduire** *Br* driving licence, *Am* driver's license ; **passer
son permis de conduire** to take one's
driving test

**permission** [pɛrmisjɔ̃] *nf* permission ;
MIL leave ; MIL **en permission** on leave ;
**demander la permission** to ask permission (**de faire** to do)

**permuter** [pɛrmyte] **1.** *vt* [lettres,
chiffres] to transpose **2.** *vi* to exchange
posts

**Pérou** [peru] *nm* **le Pérou** Peru

**perpendiculaire** [pɛrpɑ̃dikylɛr] *adj*
& *nf* perpendicular (**à** to)

**perpétrer** [pɛrpetre] *vt* to perpetrate

**perpétuel, -elle** [pɛrpetɥɛl] *adj*
perpetual ; [membre] permanent
■ **perpétuer** *vt* to perpetuate ■ **perpétuité** *adv* **à perpétuité** in perpetuity ; **condamnation à perpétuité** life
sentence

**perplexe** [pɛrplɛks] *adj* perplexed,
puzzled

**perquisition** [pɛrkizisjɔ̃] *nf* search
■ **perquisitionner** *vi* to make a
search

**perron** [pɛrɔ̃] *nm* steps (*leading to a
building*)

**perroquet** [pɛrɔkɛ] *nm* parrot

**perruche** [peryʃ] *nf* *Br* budgerigar, *Am*
parakeet

**perruque** [peryk] *nf* wig

**persan, -e** [pɛrsɑ̃, -an] **1.** *adj* Persian
**2.** *nm* [langue] Persian

**persécuter** [pɛrsekyte] *vt* to persecute
■ **persécution** *nf* persecution

**persévérer** [pɛrsevere] *vi* to persevere
(**dans** in) ■ **persévérance** *nf* perseverance ■ **persévérant, -e** *adj* persevering

**persil** [pɛrsi] *nm* parsley

**Persique** [pɛrsik] *adj* **le golfe Persique**
the Persian Gulf

**persister** [pɛrsiste] *vi* to persist (**à faire**
in doing ; **dans qch** in sth) ■ **persistance** *nf* persistence

**perso** [pɛrso] *(abr de* **personnel)** *adj Fam* personal, private

**personnage** [pɛrsɔnaʒ] *nm* [de fiction, individu] character; [personnalité] important person; **personnage célèbre** celebrity; **personnage officiel** VIP

**personnaliser** [pɛrsɔnalize] *vt* to personalize; [voiture] to customize

**personnalité** [pɛrsɔnalite] *nf* [caractère, personnage] personality; **avoir de la personnalité** to have lots of personality

**personne** [pɛrsɔn] **1.** *nf* person; **deux personnes** two people; **personne âgée** elderly person; **en personne** in person **2.** *pron indéf* [de négation] **(ne...) personne** nobody, no one; **je ne vois personne** I don't see anybody *or* anyone; **personne ne saura** nobody *or* no one will know

**personnel, -elle** [pɛrsɔnɛl] **1.** *adj* personal; [joueur, jeu] individualistic **2.** *nm* [de firme, d'école] staff; [d'usine] workforce; **manquer de personnel** to be understaffed; **personnel au sol** ground personnel

**personnifier** [pɛrsɔnifje] *vt* to personify ∎ **personnification** *nf* personification

**perspective** [pɛrspɛktiv] *nf* [de dessin] perspective; [idée] prospect (**de** of); *Fig* [point de vue] viewpoint; **perspectives d'avenir** future prospects

**perspicace** [pɛrspikas] *adj* shrewd ∎ **perspicacité** *nf* shrewdness

**persuader** [pɛrsɥade] *vt* **persuader qn (de qch)** to persuade sb (of sth); **persuader qn de faire qch** to persuade sb to do sth; **être persuadé de qch / que...** to be convinced of sth / that... ∎ **persuasif, -ive** *adj* persuasive ∎ **persuasion** *nf* persuasion

**perte** [pɛrt] *nf* loss; [destruction] ruin; **une perte de temps** a waste of time; **à perte de vue** as far as the eye can see; **vendre qch à perte** to sell sth at a loss

**pertinent, -e** [pɛrtinɑ̃, -ɑ̃t] *adj* relevant, pertinent ∎ **pertinemment** [-amɑ̃] *adv* **savoir qch pertinemment** to know sth for a fact ∎ **pertinence** *nf* relevance, pertinence

**perturber** [pɛrtyrbe] *vt* [trafic, cérémonie] to disrupt; [personne] to disturb ∎ **perturbateur, -trice 1.** *adj* disruptive **2.** *nmf* troublemaker ∎ **perturbation** *nf* disruption

**péruvien, -enne** [peryvjɛ̃, -jɛn] **1.** *adj* Peruvian **2.** *nmf* **Péruvien, Péruvienne** Peruvian

**pervers, -e** [pɛrvɛr, -ɛrs] **1.** *adj* perverse **2.** *nmf* pervert ∎ **perversion** *nf* perversion ∎ **perversité** *nf* perversity ∎ **pervertir** *vt* to pervert

**pesant, -e** [pəzɑ̃, -ɑ̃t] **1.** *adj* heavy, weighty **2.** *nm* **valoir son pesant d'or** to be worth one's weight in gold ∎ **pesanteur** *nf* heaviness; PHYS gravity

**pesée** [pəze] *nf* weighing; [pression] force

**peser** [pəze] **1.** *vt* to weigh **2.** *vi* to weigh; **peser 2 kilos** to weigh 2 kilos; **peser lourd** to be heavy; *Fig* [argument] to carry weight; **peser sur** [appuyer] to press on; [influer] to bear upon; **peser sur qn** [menace] to hang over sb ∎ **pèse-personne** *(pl* **pèse-personnes)** *nm* (bathroom) scales

**pessimisme** [pesimism] *nm* pessimism ∎ **pessimiste 1.** *adj* pessimistic **2.** *nmf* pessimist

**pester** [pɛste] *vi* **pester contre qn / qch** to curse sb / sth

**pétale** [petal] *nm* petal

**pétanque** [petɑ̃k] *nf* [jeu] ≃ bowls

**pétard** [petar] *nm* [feu d'artifice] firecracker, *Br* banger

**pétiller** [petije] *vi* [yeux, vin] to sparkle ∎ **pétillant, -e** *adj* [gazeux] sparkling

**petit, -e** [pəti, -it] **1.** *adj* small, little; [taille, distance] short; [bruit, coup] slight; [somme] small; [accident] minor; [mesquin] petty; **tout petit** tiny; **mon petit frère** my little brother **2.** *nmf* (little) boy, *f* (little) girl; [personne] small person; SCOL junior; **petits** [d'animal] young; [de chien] pups; [de chat] kittens **3.** *adv* **écrire petit** to write small; **petit à petit** little by little ■ **petite-fille** *(pl* **petites-filles)** *nf* granddaughter ■ **petit-fils** *(pl* **petits-fils)** *nm* grandson ■ **petits-enfants** *nmpl* grandchildren

**pétition** [petisjɔ̃] *nf* petition

**pétrifier** [petrifje] *vt* to petrify

**pétrir** [petrir] *vt* to knead

**pétrole** [petrɔl] *nm* oil, petroleum ■ **pétrolier, -ère** **1.** *adj* industrie pétrolière oil industry **2.** *nm* oil tanker ■ **pétrolifère** *adj* gisement pétrolifère oilfield

**peu** [pø] **1.** *adv* [avec un verbe] not much ; [avec un adjectif, un adverbe] not very ; [un petit nombre] few ; **elle mange peu** she doesn't eat much ; **peu intéressant / souvent** not very interesting / often ; **peu ont compris** few understood ; **peu de sel / de temps** not much salt / time, little salt / time ; **peu de gens / de livres** few people / books ; **peu à peu** little by little, gradually ; **à peu près** more or less ; **peu après / avant** shortly after / before ; **sous peu** shortly ; **pour peu que... (**+ *subjunctive)* if by chance... ; **pour un peu** nearly, almost ; **si peu que (**+ *subjunctive)* however little

**2.** *nm* **un peu** a little, a bit ; **un peu grand** a bit big ; **un peu de fromage** a little cheese, a bit of cheese ; **un (tout) petit peu** a (tiny) little bit ; **le peu de fromage que j'ai** the little cheese I have ; **reste encore un peu** stay a little longer

**peuplade** [pœplad] *nf* tribe

**peuple** [pœpl] *nm* [nation, citoyens] people ; **les gens du peuple** ordinary people

**peupler** [pœple] *vt* [habiter] to inhabit ■ **peuplé, -e** *adj* [région] inhabited (**de** by) ; **très / peu peuplé** highly / sparsely populated

**peuplier** [pøplije] *nm* [arbre, bois] poplar

**peur** [pœr] *nf* fear ; **avoir peur** to be afraid *or* frightened (**de qn / qch** of sb / sth ; **de faire qch** to do sth *or* of doing sth) ; **faire peur à qn** to frighten *or* scare sb ; **de peur qu'il ne parte** for fear that he would leave ; **de peur de faire qch** for fear of doing sth ■ **peureux, -euse** *adj* easily fearful

**peut** [pø] *voir* **pouvoir**

**peut-être** [pøtɛtr] *adv* perhaps, maybe ; **peut-être qu'il viendra, peut-être viendra-t-il** perhaps or maybe he'll come ; **peut-être que oui** perhaps ; **peut-être que non** perhaps not

**peuvent, peux** [pœv, pø] *voir* **pouvoir**

**phare** [far] **1.** *nm* [pour bateaux] lighthouse ; [de véhicule] headlight ; **faire un appel de phares** to flash one's lights **2.** *adj* épreuve-phare star event

**pharmacie** [farmasi] *nf* [magasin] *Br* chemist, *Am* drugstore ; [armoire] medicine cabinet ■ **pharmaceutique** *adj* pharmaceutical ■ **pharmacien, -enne** *nmf Br* chemist, pharmacist, *Am* druggist

**phase** [faz] *nf* phase

**phénomène** [fenɔmɛn] *nm* phenomenon

**philharmonique** [filarmɔnik] *adj* philharmonic

**Philippines** [filipin] *nfpl* **les Philippines** the Philippines

**philosophe** [filɔzɔf] **1.** *nmf* philosopher **2.** *adj* philosophical ■ **philosopher** *vi* to philosophize (**sur** about) ■ **philosophie** *nf* philosophy ■ **philosophique** *adj* philosophical

**photo** [fɔto] **1.** *nf* [cliché] photo ; [art] photography ; **prendre une photo de qn / qch, prendre qn / qch en photo** to take a photo of sb / sth ; **photo d'identité** ID photo **2.** *adj inv* appareil photo camera ■ **photogénique** *adj* photogenic ■ **photographe** *nmf* photographer ■ **photographie** *nf* [art] photography ; [cliché] photograph ■ **photographier** *vt* to photograph ; **se faire photographier** to have one's photo taken ■ **photographique** *adj* photographic

**photocopie** [fɔtɔkɔpi] *nf* photocopy ■ **photocopier** *vt* to photocopy

■ **photocopieur** nm = **photoco-pieuse** ■ **photocopieuse** [fotokɔpjøz] nf photocopier

**Photomaton®** [fɔtɔmatɔ̃] nm photo booth

**phrase** [frɑz] nf sentence

**physicien, -enne** [fizisjɛ̃, -ɛn] nmf physicist

**physique** [fizik] **1.** adj physical **2.** nm [de personne] physique **3.** nf [science] physics (sg) ■ **physiquement** adv physically

**piailler** [pjaje] vi a) [oiseaux] to cheep b) Fam [enfant] to squawk

**pianiste** [pjanist] nmf pianist

**piano** [pjano] nm piano; **piano droit / à queue** upright / grand piano ■ **pianoter** vi **pianoter sur qch** [table] to drum one's fingers on sth

**pic** [pik] nm [cime] peak; [outil] pick(axe); [oiseau] woodpecker; **couler à pic** to sink like a stone; **tomber à pic** [falaise] to go straight down; **pic à glace** ice pick

**pichet** [piʃɛ] nm Br jug, Am pitcher

**picorer** [pikɔre] vt to peck

**picoter** [pikɔte] vt j'ai la gorge qui (me) picote I've got a tickle in my throat

**pie** [pi] nf a) [oiseau] magpie b) Fam & Fig [bavard] chatterbox

**pièce** [pjɛs] nf [de maison] room; [morceau, objet] piece; [de pantalon] patch; [de dossier] document; **pièce (de monnaie)** coin; **pièce (de théâtre)** play; **5 euros (la) pièce** 5 euros each; **mettre qch en pièces** to tear sth to pieces; **pièce d'identité** proof of identity; **pièces détachées** ou **de rechange** spare parts

**pied** [pje] nm [de personne] foot (pl feet); [de lit, d'arbre, de colline] foot; [de meuble] leg; [de verre, de lampe] base; **à pied** on foot; **aller à pied** to walk, to go on foot; **au pied de** at the foot or bottom of; **en pied** [portrait] full-length; **sur un pied d'égalité** on an equal footing; **avoir pied** to be within one's depth; **mettre qch sur pied** to set sth up

**piédestal, -aux** [pjedɛstal, -o] nm pedestal

**piège** [pjɛʒ] nm [pour animal] & Fig trap ■ **piéger** vt [animal] to trap; [voiture] to booby-trap; **voiture / lettre piégée** car / letter bomb

**piercing** [pirsiŋ] nm body piercing

**pierre** [pjɛr] nf stone; [de bijou] gem, stone; **pierre précieuse** precious stone, gem ■ **pierreries** nfpl gems, precious stones ■ **pierreux, -euse** adj stony

**piétiner** [pjetine] **1.** vt piétiner qch [en trépignant] to stamp on sth; [en marchant] to trample on sth **2.** vi [ne pas avancer] to stand around; **piétiner d'impatience** to stamp one's feet impatiently

**piéton** [pjetɔ̃] nm pedestrian ■ **piétonne, piétonnière** [pjetɔnjɛr] adj f **rue piétonne** pedestrian(ized) street; **zone piétonne** pedestrian precinct

**pigeon** [piʒɔ̃] nm pigeon

**piger** [piʒe] Fam **1.** vt to understand **2.** vi to get it

**pile** [pil] **1.** nf a) **pile (électrique)** battery; **radio à piles** battery radio b) [tas] pile; **en pile** in a pile c) [de pièce] **pile ou face?** heads or tails?; **jouer à pile ou face** to toss for it **2.** adv Fam **s'arrêter pile** to stop dead; Fam **à deux heures pile** at two on the dot

**piler** [pile] vt [broyer] to crush; [amandes] to grind

**pilier** [pilje] nm pillar

**piller** [pije] vt to loot, to pillage ■ **pillage** nm looting, pillaging

**pilon** [pilɔ̃] nm [de poulet] drumstick

**pilonner** [pilɔne] vt [bombarder] to bombard

**pilote** [pilɔt] **1.** nm [d'avion, de bateau] pilot; [de voiture] driver; **pilote automatique** automatic pilot; **pilote de chasse** fighter pilot; **pilote d'essai** test pilot; **pilote de ligne** airline pilot **2.** adj **usine(-)pilote** pilot factory

■ **pilotage** *nm* piloting ■ **piloter** *vt* [avion] to fly, to pilot ; [bateau] to pilot ; [voiture] to drive

**pilule** [pilyl] *nf* pill ; **prendre la pilule** to be on the pill

**piment** [pimã] *nm* chilli ■ **pimenté, -e** *adj* [épicé] spicy

**pin** [pɛ̃] *nm* [arbre, bois] pine ; **pomme de pin** pine cone ; [de sapin] fir cone

**pince** [pɛ̃s] *nf* [outil] pliers ; [sur vêtement] dart ; [de crustacé] pincer ; **pince à épiler** tweezers ; **pince à linge** (clothes) *Br* peg or *Am* pin

**pincé, -e** [pɛ̃se] *adj* [air] stiff ; [sourire] tight-lipped

**pinceau, -x** [pɛ̃so] *nm* (paint) brush

**pincer** [pɛ̃se] **1.** *vt* to pinch **2. se pincer** *vpr* **se pincer le doigt** to get one's finger caught (**dans** in) ; **se pincer le nez** to hold one's nose ■ **pincée** *nf* pinch (**de** of)

**ping-pong** [piŋpɔ̃g] *nm* table tennis, Ping-Pong®

**pintade** [pɛ̃tad] *nf* guinea fowl

**pioche** [pjɔʃ] *nf* [outil] pick (axe) ; CARTES stock, pile ■ **piocher** *vt* [creuser] to dig *(with a pick)* ; **piocher une carte** to draw a card

**pion** [pjɔ̃] *nm* [au jeu de dames] piece ; ÉCHECS & *Fig* pawn

**pionnier** [pjɔnje] *nm* pioneer

**pipe** [pip] *nf* [de fumeur] pipe

**pipeau, -x** [pipo] *nm* [flûte] pipe

**piquant, -e** [pikã, -ãt] **1.** *adj* [au goût] spicy, hot ; [plante, barbe] prickly ; [détail] spicy **2.** *nm* [de plante] prickle, thorn ; [d'animal] spine

**pique** [pik] **1.** *nm* CARTES [couleur] spades **2.** *nf* [allusion] cutting remark ; [arme] pike

**pique-nique** [piknik] *(pl* **pique-niques)** *nm* picnic ■ **pique-niquer** *vi* to picnic

**piquer** [pike] **1.** *vt* [percer] to prick ; [langue, yeux] to sting ; [sujet : moustique] to bite ; **piquer qch dans** [enfoncer] to stick sth into ; **la fumée me pique les yeux** the smoke is making

my eyes sting **2.** *vi* [moutarde] to be hot **3. se piquer** *vpr* to prick oneself ; **se piquer au doigt** to prick one's finger

**piquet** [pikɛ] *nm* [pieu] stake, post ; [de tente] peg ; **piquet de grève** picket

**piqûre** [pikyr] *nf* [d'abeille] sting ; [de moustique] bite ; [d'épingle] prick ; [de tissu] stitching ; [de rouille] spot ; MÉD injection ; **faire une piqûre à qn** to give sb an injection

**pirate** [pirat] **1.** *nm* [des mers] pirate ; **pirate de l'air** hijacker ; **pirate informatique** hacker **2.** *adj* **radio pirate** pirate radio ; **édition / CD pirate** pirated edition / CD ■ **piratage** *nm* **a)** piracy **b)** ORDINAT hacking ■ **pirater** *vt* [enregistrement] to pirate ; ORDINAT to hack

**pire** [pir] **1.** *adj* worse (**que** than) ; **c'est de pire en pire** it's getting worse and worse **2.** *nmf* **le / la pire** the worst (one) ; **le pire de tout** the worst thing of all ; **au pire** at (the very) worst ; **s'attendre au pire** to expect the (very) worst

**pirogue** [pirɔg] *nf* canoe, dugout

**pis¹** [pi] *nm* [de vache] udder

**pis²** [pi] *adv* **aller de mal en pis** to go from bad to worse

**piscine** [pisin] *nf* swimming pool

**pistache** [pistaʃ] *nf* pistachio

**piste** [pist] *nf* [traces] track, trail ; [indices] lead ; [de magnétophone & SPORT] track ; [de cirque] ring ; [de ski] run, piste ; [pour chevaux] *Br* racecourse, *Am* racetrack ; SPORT tour de piste lap ; **piste d'atterrissage** runway ; **piste cyclable** *Br* cycle path, *Am* bicycle path ; **piste de danse** dance floor

**pistolet** [pistɔlɛ] *nm* gun, pistol ; [de peintre] spray gun ; **pistolet à eau** water pistol

**pistonner** [pistɔne] *vt* to pull strings for ; **se faire pistonner** to get a leg up

**pitié** [pitje] *nf* pity ; **avoir de la pitié pour qn** to pity sb ; **il me fait pitié** I feel sorry for him ; **être sans pitié** to be ruthless ■ **pitoyable** *adj* pitiful ■ **piteux, -euse** *adj* pitiful ; **en piteux état** in a sorry state

**piton** [pitɔ̃] *nm* **a)** [d'alpiniste] piton ; **piton (rocheux)** (rocky) peak **b)** *Can Fam* [touche d'un appareil] button **c)** [dans les jeux de société] peg **d)** *Can Fam* **être sur le piton** to be in good shape, to be in a good mood

**pitonner** [pitɔne] *Can vi Fam* **a)** [sur des touches] to type **b)** [sur un clavier] **pitonner sur l'ordinateur** to work on a computer **c)** [avec une télécommande] to zap ▪ **pitonneux, euse** *nmf Can Fam* zapper

**pittoresque** [pitɔrɛsk] *adj* picturesque

**pivoter** [pivɔte] *vi* to pivot, to swivel ; **faire pivoter qch** to swivel sth round ▪ **pivotant, e** *adj* swivel ; **fauteuil pivotant** swivel chair

**pizza** [pidza] *nf* pizza ▪ **pizzeria** *nf* pizzeria

**PJ** (*abr de* **pièce jointe**) Encl. (*enclosed*)

**placard** [plakar] *nm* [armoire] *Br* cupboard, *Am* closet ; **placard publicitaire** large display advertisement

**place** [plas] *nf* [endroit, rang & SPORT] place ; [lieu public] square ; [espace] room ; [siège] seat ; [emploi] job, post ; **à la place** instead (**de** of) ; **à votre place** in your place ; **se mettre à la place de qn** to put oneself in sb's position ; **sur place** on the spot ; **en place** [objet] in place ; **mettre qch en place** to put sth in place ; **changer de place** to change places ; **faire de la place** to make room (**à** for) ; **faire place à qn/qch** to give way to sb/sth ; **prendre place** to take a seat ; **place de parking** parking space ; **place de train/bus** train/bus fare ; **place assise** seat

**placer** [plase] **1.** *vt* [mettre] to put, to place ; [faire asseoir] to seat ; [trouver un emploi à] to place ; [argent] to invest (**dans** in) **2. se placer** *vpr* [debout] to stand ; [s'asseoir] to sit ▪ **placé, -e** *adj* [objet & SPORT] placed ; **bien/mal placé pour faire qch** well/badly placed to do sth ▪ **placement** *nm* [d'argent] investment

**placotage** [plakotaʒ] *nm Can Fam* gossiping ▪ **placoter** *vi Can Fam* to gab

**plafond** [plafɔ̃] *nm* ceiling ▪ **plafonner** *vi* [prix] to peak ; [salaires] to have reached a ceiling (**à** of) ▪ **plafonnier** *nm* ceiling light

**plage** [plaʒ] *nf* [grève] beach ; [surface] area ; [de disque] track ; **plage de sable** sandy beach ; **plage horaire** time slot

**plaider** [plede] *vt & vi* JUR [défendre] to plead ; **plaider coupable** to plead guilty ▪ **plaidoyer** *nm* JUR speech for the *Br* defence *or Am* defense

**plaie** [plɛ] *nf* [blessure] wound

**plaindre** [plɛ̃dr] **1.** *vt* to feel sorry for, to pity **2. se plaindre** *vpr* [protester] to complain (**de** about ; **que** that) ; **se plaindre de** [douleur] to complain of ▪ **plainte** *nf* complaint ; [gémissement] moan ; **porter plainte contre qn** to lodge a complaint against sb

**plaine** [plɛn] *nf* plain

**plaintif, -ive** [plɛ̃tif, -iv] *adj* plaintive

**plaire** [plɛr] **1.** *vi* **elle me plaît** I like her ; **ça me plaît** I like it **2.** *v impers* **il me plaît de le faire** I like doing it ; **s'il vous/te plaît** please ; **comme il vous plaira** as you like it **3. se plaire** *vpr* [l'un/l'autre] to like each other ; **se plaire à Paris** to like it in Paris

**plaisance** [plɛzɑ̃s] *nf* **navigation de plaisance** yachting

**plaisant, -e** [plɛzɑ̃, -ɑ̃t] **1.** *adj* [drôle] amusing ; [agréable] pleasing **2.** *nm* **mauvais plaisant** joker ▪ **plaisanter** *vi* to joke (**sur** about) ▪ **plaisanterie** *nf* joke ; **par plaisanterie** for a joke ▪ **plaisantin** *nm* joker

**plaisir** [plezir] *nm* pleasure ; **faire plaisir à qn** to please sb ; **pour le plaisir** for the fun of it ; **au plaisir (de vous revoir)** see you again sometime ; **faites-moi le plaisir de...** would you be good enough to...

**plan** [plɑ̃] *nm* [projet, dessin, organisation] plan ; [de ville] map ; MATH plane ; **au premier plan** in the foreground ; PHOTO **au second plan** in the background ; **sur le plan politique, au plan politique** from the political viewpoint ; **sur le même plan** on the same level ; **de premier plan** of importance, major; PHOTO & CINÉ **gros plan** close-up; **plan d'eau** stretch of water; FIN **plan d'épargne** savings plan

**planche** [plɑ̃ʃ] *nf* [en bois] plank; [plus large] board; [illustration] plate; **faire la planche** to float on one's back; **planche à dessin** drawing board; **planche à roulettes** skateboard; **planche à voile** sailboard; **faire de la planche à voile** to go windsurfing; **planche de surf** surfboard

**plancher** [plɑ̃ʃe] *nm* floor

**planer** [plane] *vi* [oiseau, planeur] to glide

**planète** [planɛt] *nf* planet

**planeur** [planœr] *nm* [avion] glider

**planifier** [planifje] *vt* to plan

**plant** [plɑ̃] *nm* [de plante] seedling

**plantation** [plɑ̃tasjɔ̃] *nf* [action] planting; [exploitation agricole] plantation

**plante** [plɑ̃t] *nf* BOT plant; **jardin des plantes** botanical gardens; **plante du pied** sole (of the foot)

**planter** [plɑ̃te] **1.** *vt* a) [arbre, terrain] to plant
**b)** [clou] to hammer in, to drive in; [pieu] to drive in; [couteau, griffes] to stick in
**c)** [tente] to pitch
**d)** *Fam & Fig* [laisser tomber] to dump
**e)** *Fig* [chapeau] to stick; [baiser] to plant; **planter son regard dans celui de qn** to look sb right in the eyes
**2.** *vi Fam* ORDINAT to crash
■ **plantage** *nm Fam* ORDINAT crash

**plaque** [plak] *nf* plate; [de verre, de métal] sheet, plate; [de verglas] sheet; [de marbre] slab; [de chocolat] bar; [commémorative] plaque; [sur la peau] blotch; **plaque chauffante** hotplate; AUTO **plaque minéralogique, plaque d'immatriculation** *Br* number or *Am* license plate

**plaquer** [plake] **1.** *vt* [métal, bijou] to plate; [bois] to veneer; [cheveux] to plaster down; [au rugby] to tackle; [aplatir] to flatten (**contre** against) **2. se plaquer** *vpr* se plaquer contre

to flatten oneself against ■ **plaqué, -e 1.** *adj* [bijou] plated; **plaqué or** gold-plated **2.** *nm* **plaqué or** gold plate

**plasma** [plasma] *nm* BIOL plasma

**plastic** [plastik] *nm* plastic explosive ■ **plastiquer** *vt* to bomb

**plastifier** [plastifje] *vt* to laminate

**plastique** [plastik] *adj & nm* plastic

**plat, -e** [pla, plat] **1.** *adj* flat; [mer] calm, smooth; [ennuyeux] flat, dull; **à plat ventre** flat on one's face; **à plat** [pneu, batterie] flat; **poser qch à plat** to lay sth (down) flat **2.** *nm* **a)** [de la main] flat **b)** [récipient, nourriture] dish; [partie du repas] course; **plat principal** *ou* **de résistance** main course ■ **plate-bande** *(pl* **plates-bandes)** *nf* flower bed ■ **plate-forme** *(pl* **plates-formes)** *nf* platform; **plate-forme pétrolière** oil rig

**plateau, -x** [plato] *nm* tray; [de balance] pan; TV & CINÉ set; GÉOG plateau; **plateau à fromages** cheeseboard

**platine¹** [platin] **1.** *nm* [métal] platinum **2.** *adj inv* platinum; **blond platine** platinum blond

**platine²** [platin] *nf* [d'électrophone, de magnétophone] deck; **platine laser** CD player

**platitude** [platityd] *nf* [propos] platitude

**plâtre** [plɑtr] *nm* [matière] plaster; **un plâtre** [de jambe cassée] a plaster cast; **les plâtres** [de maison] the plasterwork ■ **plâtrer** *vt* [mur] to plaster; [membre] to put in plaster

**plausible** [plozibl] *adj* plausible

**play-back** [plɛbak] *nm inv* **chanter en play-back** to mime

**plein, -e** [plɛ̃, plɛn] **1.** *adj* [rempli, complet] full; [solide] solid; **plein de** full of; **plein à craquer** full to bursting; **en pleine mer** out at sea, on the open sea; **en pleine figure** right in the face; **en pleine nuit** in the middle of the night; **en plein jour** in broad daylight; **en plein hiver** in the depths of winter; **en plein soleil** in the full heat of the sun; **être en plein travail** to be hard at work; **à la pleine lune** at full moon; **un plein**

**temps** a full-time job; **travailler à plein temps** to work full-time; **plein sud** due south; **plein tarif** full price; [de transport] full fare **2.** *adv* **de l'argent plein les poches** pockets full of money; **du chocolat plein la figure** chocolate all over one's face **3.** *nm* AUTO **faire le plein (d'essence)** to fill up (the tank)

**pleurer** [plœre] **1.** *vi* to cry, to weep (**sur** over) **2.** *vt* [personne] to mourn (for) ■ **pleurs** *nmpl* **en pleurs** in tears

**pleuvoir** [pløvwar] **1.** *v impers* to rain; **il pleut** it's raining; *Fig* **il pleut des cordes** it's raining cats and dogs **2.** *vi* [coups] to rain down (**sur** on)

**Plexiglas®** [plɛksiglas] *nm* *Br* Perspex®, *Am* Plexiglas®

**pli** [pli] *nm* **a)** [de papier, de rideau, de la peau] fold; [de jupe, de robe] pleat; [de pantalon, de bouche] crease; **(faux) pli** crease; **mise en plis** set *(hairstyle)* **b)** [enveloppe] envelope; [lettre] letter **c)** CARTES trick

**plier** [plije] **1.** *vt* [draps, vêtements] to fold; [parapluie] to fold up; [courber] to bend; **plier bagages** to pack one's bags (and leave) **2.** *vi* [branche] to bend **3. se plier** *vpr* [lit, chaise] to fold up; **se plier à** to submit to ■ **pliable** *adj* foldable ■ **pliage** *nm* [manière] fold; [action] folding ■ **pliant, -e 1.** *adj* [chaise] folding **2.** *nm* folding stool

**plisser** [plise] *vt* [lèvres] to pucker; [front] to wrinkle; [yeux] to screw up ■ **plissé, -e** *adj* [jupe] pleated

**plomb** [plɔ̃] *nm* [métal] lead; [fusible] *Br* fuse, *Am* fuze; [pour rideau] lead weight; **plombs** [de chasse] lead shot; *Fig* **de plomb** [sommeil] heavy; [soleil] blazing

**plomber** [plɔ̃be] *vt* [dent] to fill; [mettre des plombs à] to weigh with lead ■ **plombage** *nm* [de dent] filling

**plombier** [plɔ̃bje] *nm* plumber ■ **plomberie** *nf* [métier, installations] plumbing

**plonger** [plɔ̃ʒe] **1.** *vi* [personne] to dive (**dans** into); [oiseau, avion] to dive (**sur** onto) **2.** *vt* [enfoncer] to plunge (**dans** into) **3. se plonger** *vpr* **se plonger**

**dans** [lecture] to immerse oneself in; **plongé dans l'obscurité** plunged in darkness ■ **plongée** *nf* diving; [de sous-marin] dive; **plongée sous-marine** skin *or* scuba diving ■ **plongeoir** *nm* diving board ■ **plongeon** *nm* dive; **faire un plongeon** to dive ■ **plongeur, -euse** *nmf* [nageur] diver

**plu** [ply] *pp de* **plaire, pleuvoir**

**pluie** [plɥi] *nf* rain; **sous la pluie** in the rain; **pluies acides** acid rain; **pluies diluviennes** torrential rain; **pluie fine** drizzle

**plume** [plym] *nf* [d'oiseau] feather; [de stylo] nib ■ **plumer** *vt* [volaille] to pluck

**plupart** [plypar] ■ **la plupart** *nf* most; **la plupart du temps** most of the time; **la plupart d'entre eux** most of them; **pour la plupart** mostly

---

**plus¹** [ply] ( [plyz] *before vowel*, [plys] *in end position) adv* **a)** [comparatif] more (**que** than); **plus d'un kilo/de dix** more than a kilo/ten; **plus de thé** more tea; **plus beau/rapidement** more beautiful/quickly (**que** than); **plus tard** later; **plus petit** smaller; **de plus belle** more than ever; **de plus en plus (de)** more and more; **de plus en plus vite** quicker and quicker; **plus ou moins** more or less; **en plus** in addition (**de** to); **au plus** at most; **de plus** more (**que** than); [en outre] moreover; **les enfants de plus de dix ans** children over ten; **j'ai dix ans de plus qu'elle** I'm ten years older than she is; **il est plus de cinq heures** it's after five (o'clock); **plus il crie, plus il s'enroue** the more he shouts, the more hoarse he gets
**b)** [superlatif] **le plus** (the) most; **le plus beau** the most beautiful (**de** in); [de deux] the more beautiful; **le plus grand** the biggest (**de** in); [de deux] the bigger; **j'ai le plus de livres** I have (the) most books; **j'en ai le plus** I have the most

---

**plus²** [ply] *adv* [négation] **(ne...) plus** no more; **ni plus ni moins** no more no less; **il n'a plus de pain** he has no more

bread, he doesn't have any more bread;
**il n'y a plus rien** there's nothing left;
**elle ne le fait plus** she no longer does it,
she doesn't do it any more or any longer;
**je ne la reverrai plus** I won't see her
again; **je ne voyagerai plus jamais**
I'll never travel again

■ **sans plus** *adv* **elle est gentille,
sans plus** she's nice, but no more than
that

---

**plus³** [plys] **1.** *conj* plus; **deux plus deux
font quatre** two plus two are four; **il
fait plus 2 (degrés)** it's 2 degrees above
freezing **2.** *nm* **le signe plus** the plus
sign

**plusieurs** [plyzjœr] *adj & pron* several

**plutôt** [plyto] *adv* rather (**que** than)

**pluvieux, -euse** [plyvjø, -jøz] *adj*
rainy, wet

**PME** *(abr de* **petites et moyennes
entreprises)** *nf* SME

**PMU®** *(abr de* **Pari Mutuel Urbain®)**
*nm* system for betting on horses

**pneu** [pnø] *(pl* **pneus)** *nm* [de roue] *Br*
tyre, *Am* tire ■ **pneumatique** *adj*
[gonflable] inflatable

**poche** [pɔʃ] *nf* [de vêtement] pocket; [de
kangourou] pouch ■ **pochette** *nf* [sac]
bag; [d'allumettes] book; [de disque]
sleeve; [sac à main] (clutch) bag; [mou-
choir] pocket handkerchief

**pocher** [pɔʃe] *vt* [œufs] to poach

**podcast** [pɔdkast] *nm* podcast ■ **pod-
caster** *vt* [une émission] to podcast

**poêle** [pwal] **1.** *nm* [chauffage] stove
**2.** *nf* **poêle (à frire)** frying pan ■ **poêlée** [pwale] *nf* panful; CULIN **poêlée de
champignons** panfried mushrooms

**poème** [pɔɛm] *nm* poem ■ **poésie** *nf*
[art] poetry; [poème] poem ■ **poète**
*nm* poet

**poids** [pwa] *nm* weight; SPORT shot;
**au poids** by weight; **prendre / perdre
du poids** to gain / lose weight; **poids
lourd** [camion] *Br* lorry, *Am* truck; [en
boxe] heavyweight; **poids plume** [en
boxe] featherweight

**poignant, -e** [pwaɲɑ̃, -ɑ̃t] *adj* poignant

**poignard** [pwaɲar] *nm* dagger; **coup
de poignard** stab ■ **poignarder** *vt*
to stab

**poignée** [pwaɲe] *nf* [quantité] handful (**de** of); [de porte, de casserole] handle; [d'épée] hilt; **poignée de main**
handshake

**poignet** [pwaɲɛ] *nm* wrist; [de chemise]
cuff

**poil** [pwal] *nm* hair; [pelage] coat; **poils**
[de brosse] bristles; [de tapis] pile; **poil
à gratter** itching powder ■ **poilu, -e**
*adj* hairy

**poinçonner** [pwɛ̃sɔne] *vt* [billet] to
punch; [bijou] to hallmark

**poing** [pwɛ̃] *nm* fist

**point** [pwɛ̃] *nm* [lieu, score, question]
point; [sur i, à l'horizon] dot; [tache]
spot; [de notation] mark; [de couture]
stitch; **être sur le point de faire qch**
to be about to do sth; **à point** [steak]
medium; **à tel point que** to such an
extent that; **déprimé au point que...**
depressed to such an extent that...;
**mettre au point** [appareil photo] to
focus; [moteur] to tune; [technique]
to perfect; **être au point** to be up to
scratch; **au point où j'en suis...** at the
stage I've reached...; **au plus haut point**
extremely; **point de côté** stitch; **point
de départ** starting point; **point de vue**
[opinion] point of view, viewpoint;
[endroit] viewing point; **point faible /
fort** weak / strong point

**pointage** [pwɛ̃taʒ] *nm* Can SPORT score

**pointe** [pwɛ̃t] *nf* [extrémité] tip, point;
[clou] nail; GÉOG headland; *Fig* [maxi-
mum] peak; **une pointe d'humour** a
touch of humour; **sur la pointe des
pieds** on tiptoe; **en pointe** pointed; **de
pointe** [technologie, industrie] state-of-
the-art; **vitesse de pointe** top speed;
*Fig* **à la pointe de** [progrès] in *or* at the
forefront of; **faire des pointes** [dan-
seuse] to dance on points; **pointe de
vitesse** burst of speed

**pointer** [pwɛ̃te] **1.** *vt* [cocher] *Br* to tick off, *Am* to check (off) ; [braquer] to point (**sur/vers** at) **2.** *vi* [employé - à l'arrivée] to clock in ; [à la sortie] to clock out

**pointillé** [pwɛ̃tije] *nm* dotted line

**pointu, -e** [pwɛ̃ty] *adj* [en pointe] pointed ; [voix] shrill ; *Fig* [spécialisé] specialized

**pointure** [pwɛ̃tyr] *nf* size

**poire** [pwar] *nf* [fruit] pear ▪ **poirier** *nm* pear tree

**poireau, -x** [pwaro] *nm* leek

**pois** [pwa] *nm* [légume] pea ; [dessin] (polka) dot ; **à pois** [vêtement] polka-dot ; **petits pois** *Br* (garden) peas, *Am* peas ; **pois de senteur** sweet pea ; **pois chiche** *Br* chickpea, *Am* garbanzo (bean)

**poison** [pwazɔ̃] *nm* poison

**poisson** [pwasɔ̃] *nm* fish ; **les Poissons** [signe] Pisces ; **poisson d'avril** April fool ; **poisson rouge** goldfish ▪ **poissonnerie** *nf* fish shop ▪ **poissonnier, -ère** *nmf Br* fishmonger, *Am* fish merchant

**poitrine** [pwatrin] *nf* chest ; [seins] bust ; CULIN [de veau] breast

**poivre** [pwavr] *nm* pepper ▪ **poivrer** *vt* to pepper ▪ **poivrière** *nf* pepper pot

**poivron** [pwavrɔ̃] *nm* pepper

**polar** [pɔlar] *nm Fam* thriller, whodunnit

**pôle** [pol] *nm* **a)** GÉOG pole ; **pôle Nord / Sud** North / South Pole **b)** ÉCON **Pôle emploi** *the body that combines the functions of the former ASSEDIC (unemployment benefit office) and ANPE (employment office)* ▪ **polaire** *adj* polar

**polémique** [pɔlemik] **1.** *adj* polemical **2.** *nf* heated debate

**poli, -e** [pɔli] *adj* [courtois] polite (**avec** to *or* with) ; [lisse] polished

**police** [pɔlis] *nf* police ; TYP & ORDINAT **police de caractères** font ; **police secours** emergency services ▪ **policier, -ère 1.** *adj* enquête policière police inquiry ; **roman policier** detective novel **2.** *nmf* policeman, detective

**polichinelle** [pɔliʃinɛl] *nm* [personnage] Punch ; *Fig* **secret de Polichinelle** open secret

**polio** [pɔljo] *nf Fam* polio

**polir** [pɔlir] *vt* to polish

**politesse** [pɔlitɛs] *nf* politeness

**politique** [pɔlitik] **1.** *adj* political **2.** *nf* [activité, science] politics (*sg*) ; [mesure] policy ; **faire de la politique** to be in politics **3.** *nmf* politician ▪ **politicien, -enne** *nmf Péj* politician ▪ **politiquement** *adv* politically ; **politiquement correct** politically correct, PC

**pollen** [pɔlɛn] *nm* pollen

**polluer** [pɔlɥe] *vt* to pollute ▪ **polluant** *nm* pollutant ▪ **pollueur, -euse 1.** *adj* polluting **2.** *nmf* polluter ▪ **pollution** *nf* pollution

**Pologne** [pɔlɔɲ] *nf* **la Pologne** Poland ▪ **polonais, -e 1.** *adj* Polish **2.** *nmf* **Polonais, Polonaise** Pole **3.** *nm* [langue] Polish

**polycopier** [pɔlikɔpje] *vt* to duplicate

**polyester** [pɔliɛstɛr] *nm* polyester

**polygame** [pɔligam] *adj* polygamous

**Polynésie** [pɔlinezi] *nf* **la Polynésie** Polynesia

**polyvalent, -e** [pɔlivalɑ̃, -ɑ̃t] **1.** *adj* [salle] multi-purpose ; [personne] versatile **2.** *adj & nf* **(école) polyvalente** *Br* ≃ secondary school, *Am* ≃ high school

**pommade** [pɔmad] *nf* ointment

**pomme** [pɔm] *nf* **a)** [fruit] apple ; ANAT **pomme d'Adam** Adam's apple ; **pomme de terre** potato ; **pommes chips** *Br* (potato) crisps, *Am* (potato) chips ; **pommes frites** *Br* chips, *Am* (French) fries ; **pommes vapeur** steamed potatoes **b)** [d'arrosoir] rose ▪ **pommier** *nm* apple tree

**pompe¹** [pɔ̃p] **1.** *nf* [machine] pump ; **pompe à essence** *Br* petrol *or Am* gas station ; **pompe à vélo** bicycle pump **2.** *nfpl* **pompes funèbres** undertaker's ; **entrepreneur des pompes funèbres** *Br* undertaker, *Am* mortician

**pompe²** [pɔ̃p] *nf* **en grande pompe** with great ceremony

**pomper** [pɔ̃pe] **1.** vt [eau, air] to pump ; [faire monter] to pump up ; [évacuer] to pump out **2.** vi to pump

**pompeux, -euse** [pɔ̃pø, -øz] adj pompous

**pompier** [pɔ̃pje] nm fireman ; **voiture des pompiers** fire engine

**pompiste** [pɔ̃pist] nmf Br petrol station or Am gas station attendant

**ponce** [pɔ̃s] nf **pierre ponce** pumice stone

**ponctuel, -elle** [pɔ̃ktɥɛl] adj [à l'heure] punctual ; [unique] Br one-off, Am one-of-a-kind ▪ **ponctualité** nf punctuality

**ponctuer** [pɔ̃ktɥe] vt to punctuate (**de** with)

**pondre** [pɔ̃dr] vt [œuf] to lay

**poney** [pɔnɛ] nm pony

**pont** [pɔ̃] nm bridge ; [de bateau] deck ; Fig **faire le pont** to make a long weekend of it ▪ **pont-levis** (pl **ponts-levis**) nm drawbridge

**populaire** [pɔpylɛr] adj [personne, gouvernement] popular ; [quartier, milieu] working-class ; [expression] vernacular ▪ **populariser** vt to popularize ▪ **po-pularité** nf popularity (**auprès de** with)

**population** [pɔpylasjɔ̃] nf population

**porc** [pɔr] nm [animal] pig ; [viande] pork

**porcelaine** [pɔrsəlɛn] nf china, porcelain

**porche** [pɔrʃ] nm porch

**porcherie** [pɔrʃəri] nf Fam, Pr & Fig pigsty

**pornographie** [pɔrnɔgrafi] nf pornography

**port** [pɔr] nm **a)** [pour bateaux] port, harbour ; ORDINAT port **b)** [d'armes] carrying ; [de barbe] wearing ; [prix] carriage, postage ; [attitude] bearing

**portable** [pɔrtabl] **1.** adj [ordinateur] laptop ; [téléphone] Br mobile, Am cellphone **2.** nm [ordinateur] laptop ; [téléphone] Br mobile, Am cellphone

**portail** [pɔrtaj] nm **a)** [de jardin] gate ; [de cathédrale] portal **b)** [gén & ORDINAT] portal

**portant, -e** [pɔrtɑ̃, -ɑ̃t] adj **bien portant** in good health

**portatif, -ive** [pɔrtatif, -iv] adj portable

**porte** [pɔrt] nf door ; [de jardin, de ville, de slalom] gate ; **mettre qn à la porte** [jeter dehors] to throw sb out ; [renvoyer] to fire sb ; **porte d'embarquement** [d'aéroport] (departure) gate ; **porte d'entrée** front door ▪ **porte-fenêtre** (pl **portes-fenêtres**) nf French window

**portée** [pɔrte] nf **a)** [de fusil] range ; Fig scope ; **à la portée de qn** within reach of sb ; **à portée de la main** within reach ; **hors de portée** out of reach **b)** [animaux] litter **c)** [impact] significance **d)** MUS stave

**portefeuille** [pɔrtəfœj] nm Br wallet, Am billfold ; [de ministre, d'actions] portfolio

**portemanteau, -x** [pɔrtmɑ̃to] nm [sur pied] coat stand ; [crochet] coat rack

**porter** [pɔrte] **1.** vt to carry ; [vêtement, lunettes] to wear ; [moustache, barbe] to have ; [trace, responsabilité, fruits] to bear ; [regard] to cast ; [inscrire] to enter ; **porter qch à qn** to take / bring sth to sb ; **porter bonheur/malheur** to bring good / bad luck ; **porter son attention sur qch** to turn one's attention to sth ; **tout (me) porte à croire que...** everything leads me to believe that... ; **se faire porter malade** to report sick **2.** vi [voix] to carry ; [coup] to strike home ; **porter sur** [concerner] to be about **3. se porter** vpr [vêtement] to be worn ; **se porter bien** to be well ; **comment te portes-tu ?** how are you? ; **se porter candidat** Br to stand or Am to run as a candidate ▪ **porté, -e** adj **porté à croire** inclined to believe ; **porté sur qch** fond of sth ▪ **porte-bonheur** nm inv (lucky) charm ▪ **porte-clés, porte-clefs** nm inv key ring ▪ **porte-monnaie** nm inv purse ▪ **porte-parole** nmf inv spokesperson (**de** for) ▪ **porte-savon** (pl **porte-savons**) nm soap dish ▪ **porte-serviettes** nm inv towel rail ▪ **porte-voix** nm inv megaphone

**porteur, -euse** [pɔrtœr, -øz] **1.** *nm* [de bagages] porter **2.** *nmf* [malade] carrier ; [de nouvelles, de chèque] bearer

**portier** [pɔrtje] *nm* doorkeeper, porter ■ **portière** *nf* [de véhicule, de train] door ■ **portillon** *nm* gate

**portion** [pɔrsjɔ̃] *nf* portion

**Porto Rico** [pɔrtoriko] *nm ou f* Puerto Rico

**portrait** [pɔrtrɛ] *nm* [peinture, dessin, photo] portrait ; [description] description ; **faire le portrait de qn** to do sb's portrait ■ **portrait-robot** *(pl* **portraits-robots)** *nm* identikit picture, Photofit®

**Portugal** [pɔrtygal] *nm* **le Portugal** Portugal ■ **portugais, -e 1.** *adj* Portuguese **2.** *nmf* **Portugais, Portugaise** Portuguese *inv* ; **les Portugais** the Portuguese **3.** *nm* [langue] Portuguese

**pose** [poz] *nf* **a)** [de rideau, de papier peint] putting up ; [de moquette] laying **b)** [pour photo, portrait] pose ; PHOTO exposure ; **prendre la pose** to pose

**posé, -e** [poze] *adj* [calme] composed, staid

**poser** [poze] **1.** *vt* to put down ; [papier peint, rideaux] to put up ; [mine, moquette, fondations] to lay ; [bombe] to plant ; [conditions, principe] to lay down ; **poser qch sur qch** to put sth on sth ; **poser une question à qn** to ask sb a question ; **poser sa candidature** [à une élection] to put oneself forward as a candidate ; [à un emploi] to apply **(à** for) **2.** *vi* [modèle] to pose **(pour** for) **3. se poser** *vpr* [oiseau, avion] to land ; [problème, question] to arise ; **se poser sur** [sujet : regard] to rest on ; **se poser des questions** to ask oneself questions

**positif, -ive** [pozitif, -iv] *adj* positive

**position** [pozisjɔ̃] *nf* position ; *Fig* **prendre position** to take a stand **(contre** against)

**posséder** [posede] *vt* [biens, talent] to possess ; [sujet] to have a thorough knowledge of ; [langue] to have mastered ■ **possession** *nf* possession ; **en possession de qch** in possession of sth ; **prendre possession de qch** to take possession of sth

**possibilité** [posibilite] *nf* possibility ; **avoir la possibilité de faire qch** to have the chance *or* opportunity of doing sth

**possible** [posibl] **1.** *adj* possible **(à faire** to do) ; **il (nous) est possible de le faire** it is possible (for us) to do it ; **il est possible que...** (+ *subjunctive*) it is possible that... ; **si possible** if possible ; **le plus tôt possible** as soon as possible ; **autant que possible** as far as possible ; **le plus possible** as much / as many as possible ; **le moins de détails possible** as few details as possible **2.** *nm* **faire (tout) son possible** to do one's utmost **(pour faire** to do)

**postal, -e, -aux** [postal, -o] *adj* postal ; [train] mail

**poste¹** [post] *nf* [service] mail, *Br* post ; [bureau] post office ; **la Poste** the postal services ; **par la poste** by mail, *Br* by post ; **poste aérienne** airmail ; **poste restante** *Br* poste restante, *Am* general delivery

**poste²** [post] *nm* **a)** [lieu, emploi] post ; **être à son poste** to be at one's post ; **poste d'essence** *Br* petrol *or Am* gas station ; **poste d'incendie** fire point ; **poste de police** police station ; **poste de secours** first-aid post **b)** [de radio / télévision] radio / television set **c)** [de standard] extension

**poster¹** [poste] *vt* [lettre] to mail, *Br* to post

**poster²** [poste] **1.** *vt* [sentinelle, troupes] to post, to station **2. se poster** *vpr* to take up a position

**poster³** [postɛr] *nm* poster

**postérieur, -e** [posterjœr] *adj* [dans le temps] later ; [de derrière] back ; **postérieur à** after

**postérité** [posterite] *nf* posterity

**postier, -ère** [postje, -ɛr] *nmf* postal worker

**postillonner** [postijone] *vi* to splutter

**Post-it®** [postit] *nm inv* Post-it®, Post-it® note

**postuler** [pɔstyle] **1.** *vt* MATH to postulate **2.** *vi* **postuler à** *ou* **pour un emploi** to apply for a job ■ **postulant, -e** *nmf* applicant (**à** for)

**posture** [pɔstyr] *nf* posture

**pot** [po] *nm* pot ; [en verre] jar ; [de bébé] potty; **pot d'échappement** *Br* exhaust pipe, *Am* tail pipe

**potable** [pɔtabl] *adj* drinkable; **eau potable** drinking water

**potage** [pɔtaʒ] *nm* soup

**potager, -ère** [pɔtaʒe, -ɛr] **1.** *adj* **jardin potager** vegetable garden; **plante potagère** vegetable **2.** *nm* vegetable garden

**pot-au-feu** [pɔtofø] *nm inv* boiled beef with vegetables

**pot-de-vin** [pɔdvɛ̃] *(pl* **pots-de-vin)** *nm* bribe

**pote** [pɔt] *nm* Fam Br mate, Am buddy

**poteau, -x** [pɔto] *nm* post ; **poteau électrique** electricity pylon; **poteau indicateur** signpost; **poteau télégraphique** telegraph pole

**potelé, -e** [pɔtle] *adj* plump, chubby

**potence** [pɔtɑ̃s] *nf* [gibet] gallows *(sg)*

**potentiel, -elle** [pɔtɑ̃sjɛl] *adj & nm* potential

**poterie** [pɔtri] *nf* [art, objets] pottery ; [objet] piece of pottery ■ **potier, -ère** *nmf* potter

**potimarron** [pɔtimarɔ̃] *nm* variety of small pumpkin

**potion** [posjɔ̃] *nf* potion

**potiron** [pɔtirɔ̃] *nm* pumpkin

**pot-pourri** [popuri] *(pl* **pots-pourris)** *nm* [chansons] medley

**pou, -x** [pu] *nm* louse *(pl* lice)

**poubelle** [pubɛl] *nf Br* dustbin, *Am* garbage can ; ORDINAT recycle bin; **mettre qch à la poubelle** to throw sth out

**pouce** [pus] *nm* [doigt] thumb

**poudre** [pudr] *nf* [poussière, explosif] powder; **en poudre** [lait] powdered; [chocolat] drinking; **poudre à récurer** scouring powder ■ **poudrer 1.** *vt* to powder **2. se poudrer** *vpr* to powder one's face ■ **poudreux, -euse 1.** *adj* powdery **2.** *nf* **poudreuse** [neige] powder snow

**poulain** [pulɛ̃] *nm* foal

**poule¹** [pul] *nf* [animal] hen ; CULIN fowl

**poule²** [pul] *nf* [groupe] group

**poulet** [pulɛ] *nm* [animal] chicken

**poulie** [puli] *nf* pulley

**pouls** [pu] *nm* MÉD pulse; **prendre le pouls de qn** to take sb's pulse

**poumon** [pumɔ̃] *nm* lung; **à pleins poumons** [respirer] deeply

**poupée** [pupe] *nf* doll

**pour** [pur] **1.** *prép* for; **pour toi /moi** for you /me; **faites-le pour lui** do it for him, do it for his sake; **partir pour Paris /l'Italie** to leave for Paris / Italy; **elle part pour cinq ans** she's leaving for five years; **elle est pour** she's all for it, she's in favour of it; **pour faire qch** (in order) to do sth; **pour que tu le voies** so (that) you may see it; **pour quoi faire ?** what for?; **assez grand pour faire qch** big enough to do sth; **pour affaires** on business; **pour cela** for that reason; **pour ma part** as for me; **jour pour jour /heure pour heure** to the day / hour; **dix pour cent** ten percent **2.** *adv* **je suis pour** I'm (all) for it **3.** *nm* **le pour et le contre** the pros and cons

■ **pour que** *conj* (+ *subjunctive*) so that, in order that

**pourboire** [purbwar] *nm* tip

**pourcentage** [pursɑ̃taʒ] *nm* percentage

**pourchasser** [purʃase] *vt* to pursue

**pourparlers** [purparle] *nmpl* negotiations, talks

**pourquoi** [purkwa] **1.** *adv & conj* why; **pourquoi pas ?** why not? **2.** *nm inv* reason (**de** for); **le pourquoi et le comment** the whys and wherefores

**pourra, pourrait** [pura, purɛ] *voir* **pouvoir**

**pourriel** [purjɛl] *nm Can* ORDINAT spam message; **des pourriels** spam

**pourrir** [purir] *vt & vi* to rot ■ **pourri, -e** *adj* [fruit, temps] rotten ■ **pourriture** *nf* rot

**poursuite** [pursɥit] **1.** *nf* [chasse] pursuit ; [continuation] continuation ; **se lancer à la poursuite de qn** to set off in pursuit of sb **2.** *nfpl* JUR **poursuites (judiciaires)** legal proceedings (**contre** against) ; **engager des poursuites contre qn** to start proceedings against sb

**poursuivre** [pursɥivr] **1.** *vt* [chercher à atteindre] to pursue ; [sujet : idée, crainte] to haunt ; [sujet : malchance] to dog ; [harceler] to pester ; [continuer] to continue, to go on with ; JUR **poursuivre qn (en justice)** to bring proceedings against sb ; [au criminel] to prosecute sb **2. se poursuivre** *vpr* to continue, to go on

**pourtant** [purtɑ̃] *adv* yet, nevertheless ; **et pourtant** and yet

**pourtour** [purtur] *nm* perimeter

**pourvoir** [purvwar] **1.** *vt* to provide (**de** with) ; **être pourvu de** to be provided with **2.** *vi* **pourvoir à** [besoins] to provide for **3. se pourvoir** *vpr* JUR **se pourvoir en cassation** to take one's case to the Court of Appeal ■ **pourvoyeur, -euse** *nmf* supplier

**pourvu** [purvy] ■ **pourvu que** *conj* **a)** [condition] provided (that) **b)** [souhait] **pourvu qu'elle soit là !** I just hope (that) she's there!

**pousse** [pus] *nf* [croissance] growth ; [bourgeon] shoot, sprout

**poussée** [puse] *nf* [pression] pressure ; [coup] push ; [d'ennemi] thrust, push ; [de fièvre] outbreak

**pousser** [puse] **1.** *vt* [presser] to push ; [moteur] to drive hard ; **pousser qn à qch** to drive sb to sth ; **pousser qn à faire qch** [sujet : faim] to drive sb to do sth ; [sujet : personne] to urge sb to do sth ; **pousser un cri** to shout ; **pousser un soupir** to sigh **2.** *vi* [presser] to push ; [croître] to grow ; **faire pousser qch** [plante] to grow sth ; **se laisser pousser les cheveux** to let one's hair

grow **3. se pousser** *vpr* [pour faire de la place] to move over ■ **poussé, -e** *adj* [études] thorough

**poussette** [pusɛt] *nf Br* pushchair, *Am* stroller

**poussière** [pusjɛr] *nf* dust ; **une poussière** a speck of dust ■ **poussiéreux, -euse** *adj* dusty

**poussin** [pusɛ̃] *nm* [animal] chick

**poutre** [putr] *nf* [en bois] beam ; [en acier] girder

**pouvoir** [puvwar] **1.** *v aux* [être capable de] can, to be able to ; [avoir la permission] can, may, to be allowed ; **tu peux entrer** you may *or* can come in **2.** *v impers* **il peut neiger** it may snow ; **il se peut qu'elle parte** she might leave **3.** *nm* [puissance, attributions] power ; **au pouvoir** [parti] in power ; **pouvoir d'achat** purchasing power ; **les pouvoirs publics** the authorities

**poux** [pu] *pl de* **pou**

**prairie** [preri] *nf* meadow

**praline** [pralin] *nf* praline

**pratique** [pratik] **1.** *adj* [méthode, personne] practical ; [outil] handy **2.** *nf* [application, procédé, coutume] practice ; [expérience] practical experience ; **la pratique de la natation / du golf** swimming / golfing ; **la pratique d'une langue étrangère** foreign language practice ; **mettre qch en pratique** to put sth into practice ; **dans la pratique** [en réalité] in practice ■ **pratiquement** *adv* [presque] practically ; [en réalité] in practice

**pratiquer** [pratike] **1.** *vt* [religion] *Br* to practise, *Am* to practice ; [activité] to take part in ; [langue] to use ; [sport] to play ; **pratiquer la natation** to go swimming **2.** *vi* [médecin, avocat] *Br* to practise, *Am* to practice ■ **pratiquant, -e 1.** *adj Br* practising, *Am* practicing **2.** *nmf Br* practising *or Am* practicing Christian / Jew / Muslim / *etc*

**pré** [pre] *nm* meadow

**préalable** [prealabl] **1.** *adj* prior, previous ; **préalable à** prior to **2.** *nm* precondition, prerequisite ; **au préalable** beforehand

**préavis** [preavi] *nm* (advance) notice (**de** of) ; **préavis de grève** strike notice ; **préavis de licenciement** notice of dismissal

**précaire** [preker] *adj* precarious ; [santé] delicate ■ **précarité** *nf* precariousness ; **précarité de l'emploi** lack of job security

**précaution** [prekosjɔ̃] *nf* [mesure] precaution ; [prudence] caution ; **par précaution** as a precaution ; **pour plus de précaution** to be on the safe side ; **prendre des précautions** to take precautions

**précédent, -e** [presedɑ̃, -ɑ̃t] **1.** *adj* previous **2.** *nmf* previous one **3.** *nm* precedent ; **sans précédent** unprecedented ■ **précéder** *vt & vi* to precede

**prêcher** [preʃe] *vt & vi* to preach

**précieux, -euse** [presjø, -øz] *adj* precious

**précipice** [presipis] *nm* chasm, abyss ; [de ravin] precipice

**précipiter** [presipite] **1.** *vt* [hâter] to hasten ; [jeter] to hurl down **2. se précipiter** *vpr* [se jeter] to rush (**vers / sur** towards / at) ; [se hâter] to rush ; **les événements se sont précipités** things started happening quickly ■ **précipitamment** [-amɑ̃] *adv* hastily ■ **précipitation** *nf* haste ; **précipitations** [pluie] precipitation ■ **précipité, -e** *adj* hasty

**précis, -e** [presi, -iz] **1.** *adj* precise, exact ; [mécanisme] accurate, precise ; **à deux heures précises** at two o'clock sharp *or* precisely **2.** *nm* [résumé] summary ; [manuel] handbook ■ **précisément** *adv* precisely, exactly ■ **précision** *nf* precision ; [de mécanisme, d'information] accuracy ; [détail] detail ; **donner des précisions sur qch** to give precise details about sth ; **demander des précisions sur qch** to ask for further information about sth

**préciser** [presize] **1.** *vt* to specify (**que** that) **2. se préciser** *vpr* to become clear(er)

**précoce** [prekɔs] *adj* [fruit, été] early ; [enfant] precocious

**préconditionné, e** [prekɔ̃disjɔne] *adj* [produit] pre-packed, pre-packaged

**préconiser** [prekɔnize] *vt* to advocate (**que** that)

**précurseur** [prekyrsœr] **1.** *nm* forerunner, precursor **2.** *adj* **signe précurseur** forewarning

**prédécesseur** [predesesœr] *nm* predecessor

**prédestiné, -e** [predestine] *adj* predestined (**à faire** to do)

**prédilection** [predileksjɔ̃] *nf* predilection ; **de prédilection** favourite

**prédire** [predir] *vt* to predict (**que** that) ■ **prédiction** *nf* prediction

**prédisposer** [predispoze] *vt* to predispose (**à qch** to sth ; **à faire** to do) ■ **prédisposition** *nf* predisposition (**à** to)

**préfabriqué, -e** [prefabrike] *adj* prefabricated

**préface** [prefas] *nf* preface (**de** to)

**préfecture** [prefɛktyr] *nf* prefecture ; **la Préfecture de police** police headquarters

**préférable** [preferabl] *adj* preferable (**à** to)

**préférence** [preferɑ̃s] *nf* preference (**pour** for) ; **de préférence** preferably ; **de préférence à** in preference to ■ **préférentiel, -elle** *adj* preferential

**préférer** [prefere] *vt* to prefer (**à** to) ; **préférer faire qch** to prefer to do sth ; **je préférerais rester** I would rather stay, I would prefer to stay ■ **préféré, -e** *adj & nmf* favourite

**préfet** [prefɛ] *nm* prefect *(chief administrator in a 'département')* ; **préfet de police** *chief commissioner of police*

**préhistorique** [preistɔrik] *adj* prehistoric

**préinstallé, e** [preẽstale] *adj* ORDINAT preinstalled

**préjudice** [preʒydis] *nm* [à une cause] prejudice; [à une personne] harm; **porter préjudice à qn** to do sb harm

**préjugé** [preʒyʒe] *nm* prejudice; **avoir des préjugés** to be prejudiced (**contre** against)

**prélasser** [prelɑse] ■ **se prélasser** *vpr* to lounge

**prélever** [prel(ə)ve] *vt* [échantillon] to take (**sur** from); [somme] to deduct (**sur** from) ■ **prélèvement** *nm* [d'échantillon] taking; [de somme] deduction; **prélèvement automatique** *Br* direct debit, *Am* automatic deduction; **prélèvements obligatoires** *tax and social security contributions*

**préliminaire** [preliminɛr] **1.** *adj* preliminary **2.** *nmpl* **préliminaires** preliminaries

**prélude** [prelyd] *nm* prelude (**à** to)

**prématuré, -e** [prematyre] **1.** *adj* premature **2.** *nmf* premature baby

**préméditer** [premedite] *vt* to premeditate ■ **préméditation** *nf* premeditation; **meurtre avec préméditation** premeditated murder

**premier, -ère** [prəmje, -ɛr] **1.** *adj* first; [enfance] early; [page de journal] front; [qualité] prime; [état] original; [danseuse, rôle] leading; [marche] bottom; **le premier rang** the front row; **les trois premiers mois** the first three months; **à la première occasion** at the earliest opportunity; **en premier** firstly; **en premier lieu** in the first place; **Premier ministre** Prime Minister **2.** *nm* [étage] *Br* first or *Am* second floor; **le premier juin** June the first; **le premier de l'an** New Year's Day **3.** *nmf* first (one); **arriver le premier** *ou* **en premier** to arrive first **4.** *nf* **première** [wagon, billet] first class; [vitesse] first (gear); [événement historique] first; THÉÂT opening night; CINÉ première; SCOL *Br* ≃ lower sixth, *Am* ≃ eleventh grade

**prémonition** [premɔnisjɔ̃] *nf* premonition

**prénatal, -e, -als** [prenatal] *adj Br* antenatal, *Am* prenatal

**prendre** [prɑ̃dr] **1.** *vt* to take (**à qn** from sb); [attraper] to catch; [repas, boisson, douche] to have; [nouvelles] to get; [air] to put on; [bonne] to take on; **prendre qch dans un tiroir** to take sth out of a drawer; **prendre qn pour** to take sb for; **prendre feu** to catch fire; **prendre du temps/une heure** to take time/an hour; **prendre de la place** to take up room; **prendre du poids/de la vitesse** to put on weight/gather speed; **prendre l'eau** [bateau, chaussure] to be leaking

**2.** *vi* [feu] to catch; [ciment, gelée] to set; [greffe, vaccin, plante] to take; [mode] to catch on; **prendre sur soi** to restrain oneself

**3. se prendre** *vpr* **a)** [se considérer] **pour qui se prend-il ?** who does he think he is? **b)** [médicament] to be taken; [s'accrocher] to get caught; **se prendre les pieds dans qch** to get one's feet caught in sth; **s'y prendre bien avec qn** to know how to handle sb; **s'en prendre à qn** to take it out on sb

**prénom** [prenɔ̃] *nm* first name ■ **prénommer** *vt* to name; **il se prénomme Daniel** his first name is Daniel

**préoccuper** [preɔkype] **1.** *vt* [inquiéter] to worry **2. se préoccuper** *vpr* **se préoccuper de qn/qch** to concern oneself with sb/sth ■ **préoccupant, -e** *adj* worrying ■ **préoccupation** *nf* preoccupation, concern ■ **préoccupé, -e** *adj* worried (**par** about)

**préparatifs** [preparatif] *nmpl* preparations (**de** for) ■ **préparation** *nf* preparation ■ **préparatoire** *adj* preparatory

**préparer** [prepare] **1.** *vt* to prepare (**qch pour** sth for); [examen] to study for; **préparer qch à qn** to prepare sth for sb; **plats tout préparés** ready-cooked meals **2. se préparer** *vpr* [être imminent] to be in the offing; [s'apprêter] to prepare oneself (**à** *ou* **pour qch** for sth); **se préparer à faire qch** to prepare to do sth; **se préparer qch** [boisson] to make oneself sth

**prépayer** [prepeje] *vt* to prepay; **'port prépayé'** 'postage paid'

**préposé, -e** [prepoze] *nmf* employee; [facteur] postman, *f* postwoman

**préretraite** [preʀətʀɛt] *nf* early retirement

**près** [pʀɛ] *adv* **près de qn/qch** near sb/sth, close to sb/sth; **près de deux ans** nearly two years; **près de partir** about to leave; **tout près** nearby (**de qn/qch** sb/sth), close by (**de qn/qch** sb/sth); **de près** [suivre, examiner] closely; **à peu de chose près** more or less; **à cela près** except for that; **voici le chiffre à un euro près** here is the figure, give or take a euro; **calculer au euro près** to calculate to the nearest euro

**présage** [pʀezaʒ] *nm* omen, sign ■ **présager** *vt* **ça ne présage rien de bon** it doesn't bode well

**presbyte** [pʀɛsbit] *adj* long-sighted

**presbytère** [pʀɛsbiteʀ] *nm* presbytery

**prescrire** [pʀɛskʀiʀ] *vt* [médicament] to prescribe ■ **prescription** *nf* [ordonnance] prescription

**présence** [pʀezɑ̃s] *nf* presence; [à l'école] attendance (**à** at); **en présence de** in the presence of; **faire acte de présence** to put in an appearance; **présence d'esprit** presence of mind

**présent, -e** [pʀezɑ̃, -ɑ̃t] **1.** *adj* [non absent, actuel] present **2.** *nm* [temps] present; **à présent** at present, now; **dès à présent** as from now

**présenter** [pʀezɑ̃te] **1.** *vt* [montrer] to show, to present; [facture] to submit; [arguments] to present; **présenter qn à qn** to introduce sb to sb **2. se présenter** *vpr* [dire son nom] to introduce oneself (**à** to); [chez qn] to show up; [occasion] to arise; **se présenter à** [examen] to take, *Br* to sit for; [élections] to run in; [emploi] to apply for; [autorités] to report to; **ça se présente bien** it looks promising ■ **présentable** *adj* presentable ■ **présentateur, -trice** *nmf* presenter ■ **présentation** *nf* presentation; [de personnes] introduction; **faire les présentations** to make the introductions; **présentation de mode** fashion show

**préserver** [pʀezɛʀve] *vt* to protect, to preserve (**de** from) ■ **préservation** *nf* protection, preservation

**présidence** [pʀezidɑ̃s] *nf* [de nation] presidency; [de firme] chairmanship ■ **président, -e** *nmf* [de nation] president; [de firme] chairman, *f* chairwoman; **président-directeur général** *Br* (chairman and) managing director, *Am* chief executive officer; **président du jury** [d'examen] chief examiner; [de tribunal] foreman of the jury ■ **présidentiel, -elle** *adj* presidential

**présider** [pʀezide] *vt* [réunion] to chair; [conseil] to preside over

**presque** [pʀɛsk] *adv* almost, nearly; **presque jamais/rien** hardly ever/anything

**presqu'île** [pʀɛskil] *nf* peninsula

**pressant, -e** [pʀɛsɑ̃, -ɑ̃t] *adj* urgent, pressing

**presse** [pʀɛs] *nf* TECH press; TYP (printing) press; **la presse** [journaux] the press; **la presse à sensation** the popular press, *Br* the tabloids

**pressé, -e** [pʀese] *adj* [personne] in a hurry; [air] hurried

**presse-agrumes** [pʀɛsagʀym] *nm inv* electric (orange or lemon) squeezer

**pressentir** [pʀɛsɑ̃tiʀ] *vt* [deviner] to sense (**que** that) ■ **pressentiment** *nm* presentiment; [de malheur] foreboding

**pressing** [pʀɛsiŋ] *nm* dry cleaner's

**pression** [pʀɛsjɔ̃] *nf* TECH pressure; [bouton] snap (fastener); **faire pression sur qn** to put pressure on sb, to pressurize sb

**pressuriser** [pʀesyʀize] *vt* [avion] to pressurize

**prestataire** [pʀɛstatɛʀ] *nmf* [fournisseur] provider; **prestataire de service** service provider

**prestation** [prɛstasjɔ̃] nf a) [allocation] benefit ; **prestations** [services] services ; **prestations sociales** Br social security benefits, Am welfare payments b) [de comédien] performance

**prestidigitateur, -trice** [prɛstidiʒitatœr, -tris] nmf conjurer ■ **prestidigitation** nf tour de prestidigitation conjuring trick

**prestige** [prɛstiʒ] nm prestige ■ **prestigieux, -euse** adj prestigious

**présumer** [prezyme] vt to presume (que that) ; **présumer de qch** to overestimate sth

**prêt¹, -e** [prɛ, prɛt] adj [préparé] ready (à faire to do ; à qch for sth) ; **être fin prêt** to be all set ■ **prêt-à-porter** nm ready-to-wear clothes

**prêt²** [prɛ] nm [somme] loan ; **prêt immobilier** home loan, ≃ mortgage

**prétendre** [pretɑ̃dr] 1. vt [déclarer] to claim (que that) ; [vouloir] to intend (faire to do) ; à ce qu'il prétend according to him 2. vi prétendre à [titre] to lay claim to 3. se prétendre vpr to claim to be ■ **prétendu, -e** adj [progrès] so-called ; [coupable] alleged

**prétentieux, -euse** [pretɑ̃sjø, -øz] adj pretentious ■ **prétention** nf [vanité] pretension ; [revendication, ambition] claim ; **sans prétention** [film, robe] unpretentious

**prêter** [prete] 1. vt [argent, objet] to lend (à to) ; [aide] to give (à to) ; [propos, intention] to attribute (à to) ; **prêter attention** to pay attention (à to) ; **prêter serment** to take an oath ; **prêter main-forte à qn** to lend sb a hand 2. vi prêter à confusion to give rise to confusion 3. se prêter vpr se prêter à [consentir] to agree to ; [convenir] to lend itself to

**prétexte** [pretɛkst] nm excuse, pretext ; **sous prétexte de /que** on the pretext of /that ; **sous aucun prétexte** under no circumstances ■ **prétexter** vt to plead (que that)

**prétimbré, e** [pretɛ̃bre] adj prepaid

**prêtre** [prɛtr] nm priest

**preuve** [prœv] nf piece of evidence ; **preuves** evidence ; **faire preuve de qch** to prove sth ; **faire preuve de courage** to show courage ; **faire ses preuves** [personne] to prove oneself ; [méthode] to be tried and tested

**prévaloir** [prevalwar] vi to prevail (sur over)

**prévenant, -e** [prevnɑ̃, -ɑ̃t] adj considerate

**prévenir** [prevnir] vt a) [mettre en garde] to warn ; [aviser] to inform (de of or about) b) [maladie] to prevent ; [accident] to avert ■ **préventif, -ive** adj preventive ■ **prévention** nf prevention ; **prévention routière** road safety

**prévisible** [previzibl] adj foreseeable

**prévision** [previzjɔ̃] nf forecast ; **en prévision de** in expectation of ; **prévisions météorologiques** weather forecast

**prévoir** [prevwar] vt [météo] to forecast ; [difficultés, retard, réaction] to expect ; [organiser] to plan ; la réunion est prévue pour demain the meeting is scheduled for tomorrow ; comme prévu as planned ; plus tôt que prévu earlier than expected ; prévu pour [véhicule, appareil] designed for

**prévoyant, -e** [prevwajɑ̃, -ɑ̃t] adj farsighted ■ **prévoyance** nf foresight

**prier** [prije] 1. vi REL to pray 2. vt [Dieu] to pray to ; [supplier] to beg ; **prier qn de faire qch** to ask sb to do sth ; je vous en prie [faites-le] please ; [en réponse à 'merci'] don't mention it

**prière** [prijɛr] nf REL prayer ; [demande] request

**primaire** [primɛr] 1. adj primary ; **école primaire** Br primary school, Am elementary school 2. nm SCOL Br primary or Am elementary education ; **entrer en primaire** to be at Br primary or Am elementary school

**prime** [prim] 1. nf [sur salaire] bonus ; [d'État] subsidy ; **en prime** [cadeau] as a free gift ; **prime (d'assurance)** (insurance) premium ; **prime de fin d'année** ≃ Christmas bonus ; **prime de licenciement** severance allowance ;

prime de transport transport allowance **2.** *adj* **de prime abord** at the very first glance

**primé, -e** [prime] *adj* [film, animal] prizewinning

**primer** [prime] *vi* to come first; **primer sur qch** to take precedence over sth

**primitif, -ive** [primitif, -iv] *adj* [société, art] primitive; [état, sens] original

**primordial, -e, -aux** [primɔrdjal, -jo] *adj* vital (**de faire** to do)

**prince** [prɛ̃s] *nm* prince ▪ **princesse** *nf* princess ▪ **princier, -ère** *adj* princely ▪ **principauté** *nf* principality

**principal, -e, -aux** [prɛ̃sipal, -o] **1.** *adj* main, principal; [rôle] leading **2.** *nmf* [de collège] principal, *Br* headmaster, *f* headmistress; **le principal** [l'essentiel] the main thing

**principe** [prɛ̃sip] *nm* principle; **en principe** theoretically, in principle; **par principe** on principle

**printanier, ère** [prɛ̃tanje, ɛr] *adj* **a)** [temps] spring like **b)** [couleur] spring

**printemps** [prɛ̃tɑ̃] *nm* spring; **au printemps** in the spring

**priorité** [priɔrite] *nf* priority (**sur** over); AUTO right of way; AUTO **avoir la priorité** to have (the) right of way; AUTO **priorité à droite** right of way to traffic coming from the right; **'cédez la priorité'** *Br* 'give way', *Am* 'yield'; **en priorité** as a matter of priority ▪ **prioritaire** *adj* **secteur prioritaire** priority sector; **être prioritaire** to have priority; AUTO to have (the) right of way

**pris, -e¹** [pri, priz] **1.** *pp de* **prendre 2.** *adj* [place] taken; **avoir le nez pris** to have a blocked nose; **être pris** [occupé] to be busy; [candidat] to be accepted; **pris de** [peur] seized with; **pris de panique** panic-stricken

**prise²** [priz] *nf* [action] taking; [objet saisi] catch; [manière d'empoigner] grip; [de judo] hold; [de tabac] pinch; **lâcher prise** to lose one's grip; **prise de sang** blood test; ÉLEC **prise (de courant)** [mâle] plug; [femelle] socket; ÉLEC **prise multiple** adaptor; **prise d'otages** hostage-taking

**prison** [prizɔ̃] *nf* prison, jail; [peine] imprisonment; **mettre qn en prison** to put sb in prison, to jail sb ▪ **prisonnier, -ère** *nmf* prisoner; **faire qn prisonnier** to take sb prisoner; **prisonnier de guerre** prisoner of war

**privation** [privɑsjɔ̃] *nf* deprivation (**de** of); **privations** [manque] hardship

**privatiser** [privatize] *vt* to privatize ▪ **privatisation** *nf* privatization

**privé, -e** [prive] **1.** *adj* private **2.** *nm* **le privé** the private sector; SCOL the private education system; **en privé** in private; **dans le privé** privately; [travailler] in the private sector

**priver** [prive] **1.** *vt* to deprive (**de** of) **2. se priver** *vpr* **se priver de** to do without, to deprive oneself of

**privilège** [privilɛʒ] *nm* privilege ▪ **privilégié, -e** *adj* privileged

**prix** [pri] *nm* [coût] price; [récompense] prize; **à tout prix** at all costs; **hors de prix** exorbitant; **attacher du prix à qch** to attach importance to sth

**probable** [prɔbabl] *adj* likely, probable; **peu probable** unlikely ▪ **probabilité** *nf* probability, likelihood; **selon toute probabilité** in all probability

**probant, -e** [prɔbɑ̃, -ɑ̃t] *adj* conclusive

**probité** [prɔbite] *nf* integrity

**problème** [prɔblɛm] *nm* problem; **problème alimentaire** eating disorder; **problème de santé** health problem ▪ **problématique** *adj* problematic

**procédé** [prɔsede] *nm* [technique] process; [méthode] method

**procéder** [prɔsede] *vi* [agir] to proceed; **procéder à** [enquête, arrestation] to carry out; **procéder par élimination** to follow a process of elimination ▪ **procédure** *nf* [méthode] procedure; [règles juridiques] procedure; [procès] proceedings

**procès** [prɔsɛ] *nm* [criminel] trial; [civil] lawsuit; **faire un procès à qn** to take sb to court

**procession** [prɔsesjɔ̃] *nf* procession

**processus** [prɔsesys] *nm* process

**procès-verbal** [prɔsɛverbal] *(pl* **procès-verbaux** [-o]*) nm* [amende] fine

**prochain, -e** [prɔʃɛ̃, -ɛn] *adj* next ; [mort, arrivée] impending ■ **prochainement** *adv* shortly, soon

**proche** [prɔʃ] *adj* [dans l'espace] near, close ; [dans le temps] near, imminent ; [parent, ami] close ; **proche de** near (to), close to ; **de proche en proche** step by step ; **le Proche-Orient** the Middle East ■ **proches** *nmpl* close relations

**proclamer** [prɔklame] *vt* to proclaim (**que** that) ■ **proclamation** *nf* proclamation

**procréer** [prɔkree] *vi* to procreate ■ **procréation** *nf* procreation ; **procréation médicalement assistée** assisted conception

**procuration** [prɔkyrasjɔ̃] *nf* power of attorney ; **par procuration** by proxy

**procurer** [prɔkyre] **1.** *vt* **procurer qch à qn** [sujet : personne] to get sth for sb ; [sujet : chose] to bring sb sth **2. se procurer** *vpr* **se procurer qch** to obtain sth

**prodige** [prɔdiʒ] *nm* [miracle] wonder ; [personne] prodigy ; **tenir du prodige** to be extraordinary ■ **prodigieux, -euse** *adj* prodigious

**prodiguer** [prɔdige] *vt* **prodiguer qch à qn** to lavish sth on sb ; **prodiguer des conseils à qn** to pour out advice to sb

**production** [prɔdyksjɔ̃] *nf* production ; [produit] product ; [d'usine] output ■ **producteur, -trice 1.** *nmf* producer **2.** *adj* producing ; **pays producteur de pétrole** oil-producing country ■ **productif, -ive** *adj* productive ■ **productivité** *nf* productivity

**produire** [prɔdɥir] **1.** *vt* [marchandise, émission, gaz] to produce ; [effet, résultat] to produce, to bring about **2. se produire** *vpr* [événement] to happen, to occur ; [acteur] to perform ■ **produit** *nm* [article] product ; [de vente, de collecte] proceeds ; **produit de beauté**

cosmetic ; **produit chimique** chemical ; **produits frais** fresh produce ; **produits ménagers** cleaning products

**profane** [prɔfan] **1.** *adj* secular **2.** *nmf* lay person

**profaner** [prɔfane] *vt* to desecrate

**proférer** [prɔfere] *vt* to utter

**professer** [prɔfese] *vt* to profess (**que** that)

**professeur, e** [prɔfesœr] *nmf* [gén] teacher ; [dans l'enseignement supérieur] lecturer ; [titulaire] professor ; **professeur principal** *Br* class *or* form teacher, *Am* homeroom teacher

**profession** [prɔfesjɔ̃] *nf* occupation, profession ; [manuelle] trade ; **sans profession** not gainfully employed ; **profession libérale** profession ■ **professionnel, -elle 1.** *adj* professional ; [enseignement] vocational **2.** *nmf* professional

**profil** [prɔfil] *nm* profile ; **de profil** (viewed) from the side ; ORDINAT **profil (utilisateur)** (user) profile ■ **se profiler** *vpr* to be outlined (**sur** against)

**profit** [prɔfi] *nm* profit ; **tirer profit de qch** to benefit from sth ; **mettre qch à profit** to put sth to good use ■ **profitable** *adj* profitable (**à** to) ■ **profiter** *vi* **profiter de** to take advantage of ; **profiter de la vie** to make the most of life ; **profiter à qn** to benefit sb, to be of benefit to sb

**profond, -e** [prɔfɔ̃, -ɔ̃d] **1.** *adj* deep ; [joie, erreur] profound ; [cause] underlying ; **profond de 2 mètres** 2 metres deep **2.** *adv* deep ■ **profondément** *adv* deeply ; [dormir] soundly ; [triste, ému] profoundly ; [creuser] deep ■ **profondeur** *nf* depth ; **faire 6 mètres de profondeur** to be 6 metres deep ; **à 6 mètres de profondeur** at a depth of 6 metres

**profusion** [prɔfyzjɔ̃] *nf* profusion ; **à profusion** in profusion

**programmable** [prɔgramabl] *adj* programmable ■ **programmation** *nf* RADIO & TV programme planning ; ORDINAT programming

**programmateur** [prɔgramatœr] nm
TECH automatic control (device)

**programme** [prɔgram] nm Br
programme, Am program ; [de parti
politique] manifesto ; SCOL curriculum ; [d'un cours] syllabus ; ORDINAT
program ■ **programmer** vt ORDINAT
to program ; RADIO, TV & CINÉ to schedule ■ **programmeur, -euse** nmf
(computer) programmer

**progrès** [prɔgrɛ] nm & nmpl progress ; **faire des progrès** to make
(good) progress ■ **progresser** vi
to progress ■ **progressif, -ive** adj
progressive ■ **progression** nf progression ■ **progressiste** adj & nmf
progressive ■ **progressivement** adv
progressively

**prohiber** [prɔibe] vt to prohibit, to
forbid ■ **prohibitif, -ive** adj prohibitive ■ **prohibition** nf prohibition

**proie** [prwa] nf prey ; **être la proie des
flammes** to be consumed by fire

**projecteur** [prɔʒɛktœr] nm [de monument, de stade] floodlight ; [de prison,
d'armée] searchlight ; THÉÂT spotlight ;
CINÉ projector

**projectile** [prɔʒɛktil] nm missile

**projection** [prɔʒɛksjɔ̃] nf [d'objet, de
film] projection ; [séance] screening

**projet** [prɔʒɛ] nm [intention] plan ;
[étude] project ; **faire des projets
d'avenir** to make plans for the future ;
**projet de loi** bill

**projeter** [prɔʒte] vt [lancer] to project ;
[liquide, boue] to splash ; [lumière] to
flash ; [film] to show ; [ombre] to cast ;
[prévoir] to plan ; **projeter de faire qch**
to plan to do sth

**proliférer** [prɔlifere] vi to proliferate
■ **prolifération** nf proliferation

**prolonger** [prɔlɔ̃ʒe] **1.** vt [vie, débat,
séjour] to prolong ; [mur, route] to extend **2. se prolonger** vpr [séjour]
to be prolonged ; [réunion] to go on ;
[rue] to continue ■ **prolongation**
nf [de séjour] extension ; **prolon-
gations** [au football] extra time

■ **prolongement** nm [de rue] continuation ; [de mur] extension ; **pro-
longements** [d'affaires] repercussions

**promenade** [prɔmnad] nf [à pied]
walk ; [courte] stroll ; [avenue] promenade ; **faire une promenade** to go for a
walk ; **faire une promenade à cheval**
to go for a ride

**promener** [prɔmne] **1.** vt [personne,
chien] to take for a walk ; [visiteur] to
show around ; **promener qch sur qch**
[main, regard] to run sth over sth **2. se
promener** vpr [à pied] to go for a walk
■ **promeneur, -euse** nmf stroller,
walker

**promesse** [prɔmɛs] nf promise ; **tenir
sa promesse** to keep one's promise

**promettre** [prɔmɛtr] **1.** vt to promise
(qch à qn sb sth ; que that) ; **promettre
de faire qch** to promise to do sth ; **c'est
promis** it's a promise **3. vi** Fig to be
promising **3. se promettre** vpr **se
promettre qch** [à soi-même] to promise oneself sth ; [l'un l'autre] to promise
each other sth ■ **prometteur, -euse**
adj promising

**promo** [prɔmo] nf Fam **a)** MIL, SCOL & UNIV
Br year, Am class **b)** COMM special offer

**promoteur** [prɔmɔtœr] nm **promoteur
(immobilier)** property developer

**promotion** [prɔmɔsjɔ̃] nf **a)** [avance-
ment & COMM] promotion ; **en promotion** [produit] on (special) offer ;
**promotion sociale** upward mobility
**b)** [d'une école] Br year, Am class ■ **promouvoir** vt [personne, produit] to
promote ; **être promu** [employé] to be
promoted (à to)

**prompt, -e** [prɔ̃, prɔ̃t] adj prompt ;
**prompt à faire qch** quick to do sth

**promulguer** [prɔmylge] vt to prom-
ulgate

**prononcer** [prɔnɔ̃se] **1.** vt [articuler] to
pronounce ; [dire] to utter ; [discours]
to deliver ; [jugement] to pronounce
**2. se prononcer** vpr [mot] to be
pronounced ; [personne] to give one's
opinion (**sur** about or on) ; **se prononcer pour/contre qch** to come out in fa-

vour of /against sth ■ **prononcé, -e**
*adj* pronounced, marked ■ **prononciation** *nf* pronunciation

**pronostic** [prɔnɔstik] *nm* forecast ;
MÉD prognosis ■ **pronostiquer** *vt*
to forecast

**propagande** [prɔpagɑ̃d] *nf* propaganda

**propager** [prɔpaʒe] **1.** *vt* to spread
**2. se propager** *vpr* to spread ■ **propagation** *nf* spreading

**prophète** [prɔfɛt] *nm* prophet ■ **prophétie** [-fesi] *nf* prophecy ■ **prophétique** *adj* prophetic

**propice** [prɔpis] *adj* favourable (à to) ;
**le moment propice** the right moment

**proportion** [prɔpɔrsjɔ̃] *nf* proportion ;
**en proportion de** in proportion to ;
**hors de proportion** out of proportion
(avec to) ■ **proportionné, -e** *adj* proportionate (à to) ; **bien proportionné**
well-proportioned ■ **proportionnel, -elle 1.** *adj* proportional (à to)
**2.** *nf* **proportionnelle** [scrutin] proportional representation

**propos** [prɔpo] *nm* [sujet] subject ;
[intention] purpose ; **des propos** [paroles] talk, words ; **à propos de qn /qch**
about sb /sth ; **à propos** [arriver] at the
right time ; **à propos** by the way

**proposer** [prɔpoze] **1.** *vt* [suggérer] to
suggest, to propose (**qch à qn** sth to sb ;
**que** (+ subjunctive) that) ; [offrir] to
offer (**qch à qn** sb sth ; **de faire** to do) ;
**je te propose de rester** I suggest (that)
you stay **2. se proposer** *vpr* to offer
one's services ; **se proposer pour faire
qch** to offer to do sth ; **se proposer de
faire qch** to propose to do sth ■ **proposition** *nf* suggestion, proposal ;
[offre] offer ; **faire une proposition à
qn** to make a suggestion to sb

**propre¹** [prɔpr] **1.** *adj* clean ; [soigné]
neat ; **propre comme un sou neuf**
spick and span **2.** *nm* **mettre qch
au propre** to make a fair copy of sth
■ **proprement** [-əmɑ̃] *adv* [avec
propreté] cleanly ; [avec soin] neatly ■ **propreté** [-əte] *nf* cleanliness ;
[soin] neatness

**propre²** [prɔpr] **1.** *adj* [à soi] own ; **mon
propre argent** my own money ; **être
propre à qn /qch** [particulier] to be
characteristic of sb /sth ; **au sens
propre** literally **2.** *nm* **le propre de**
[qualité] the distinctive quality of ;
**au propre** [au sens propre] literally
■ **proprement** [-əmɑ̃] *adv* [strictement] strictly ; **à proprement parler**
strictly speaking ; **le village proprement dit** the village proper

**propriétaire** [prɔprijetɛr] *nmf* owner ;
[de location] landlord, *f* landlady ; **propriétaire foncier** landowner

**propriété** [prɔprijete] *nf* [fait de posséder] ownership ; [chose possédée]
property ; [caractéristique] property ;
**propriété privée** private property

**propulser** [prɔpylse] *vt* to propel

**proscrire** [prɔskrir] *vt* to proscribe,
to ban

**prospecter** [prɔspɛkte] *vt* [sol] to prospect ; [clients] to canvass

**prospectus** [prɔspɛktys] *nm* leaflet

**prospère** [prɔspɛr] *adj* prosperous ;
[santé] glowing ■ **prospérer** *vi* to
prosper ■ **prospérité** *nf* prosperity

**prosterner** [prɔstɛrne] ■ **se prosterner** *vpr* to prostrate oneself (**devant**
before)

**prostituée** [prɔstitɥe] *nf* prostitute
■ **prostitution** *nf* prostitution

**protecteur, -trice** [prɔtɛktœr, -tris]
**1.** *nmf* protector ; [mécène] patron
**2.** *adj* [geste, crème] protective
■ **protection** *nf* protection ; **de protection** [écran] protective ; **assurer la
protection de qn** to ensure sb's safety
■ **protectionnisme** *nm* ÉCON protectionism

**protéger** [prɔteʒe] **1.** *vt* to protect (**de**
from ; **contre** against) **2. se protéger** *vpr* to protect oneself ■ **protégé**
*nm* protégé ■ **protégée** *nf* protégée
■ **protège-poignets** [prɔtɛʒpwaɲe]
*nm inv* wrist guard, wrist protector

**protéine** [prɔtein] *nf* protein

**protestant, -e** [prɔtɛstɑ̃, -ɑ̃t] *adj* & *nmf*
Protestant

**protester** [prɔtɛste] *vi* to protest (**contre** against); **protester de son innocence** to protest one's innocence ■ **protestataire** *nmf* protester ■ **protestation** *nf* protest (**contre** against); **en signe de protestation** as a protest

**prothèse** [prɔtɛz] *nf* prosthesis; **prothèse auditive** hearing aid; **prothèse dentaire** false teeth

**protide** [prɔtid] *nm* protein

**protocole** [prɔtɔkɔl] *nm* protocol

**prototype** [prɔtɔtip] *nm* prototype

**prouesse** [pruɛs] *nf* feat

**prouver** [pruve] *vt* to prove (**que** that)

**Provence** [prɔvɑ̃s] *nf* **la Provence** Provence ■ **provençal, -e, -aux 1.** *adj* Provençal **2.** *nmf* **Provençal, Provençale** Provençal

**provenir** [prɔvənir] *vi* **provenir de** to come from ■ **provenance** *nf* origin; **en provenance de** from

**proverbe** [prɔvɛrb] *nm* proverb

**providence** [prɔvidɑ̃s] *nf* providence ■ **providentiel, -elle** *adj* providential

**province** [prɔvɛ̃s] *nf* province; **la province** the provinces; **en province** in the provinces; **de province** [ville] provincial ■ **provincial, -e, -aux** *adj & nmf* provincial

**proviseur** [prɔvizœr] *nm Br* headmaster, *f* headmistress, *Am* principal

**provision** [prɔvizjɔ̃] *nf* **a)** [réserve] supply, stock; **provisions** [nourriture] shopping; **sac à provisions** shopping bag; **faire des provisions de qch** to stock up on sth **b)** [somme] credit; [acompte] deposit

**provisoire** [prɔvizwar] *adj* temporary; **à titre provisoire** temporarily

**provoquer** [prɔvɔke] *vt* [incendie, mort] to cause; [réaction] to provoke; [colère, désir] to arouse ■ **provocant, -e** *adj* provocative ■ **provocateur** *nm* troublemaker ■ **provocation** *nf* provocation

**proximité** [prɔksimite] *nf* closeness, proximity; **à proximité** close by; **à proximité de** close to; **de proximité** local

**pr tjr** *(abr de* **pour toujours***)* SMS 4eva, 4E

**prude** [pryd] **1.** *adj* prudish **2.** *nf* prude

**prudent, -e** [prydɑ̃, -ɑ̃t] *adj* [personne] cautious, careful; [décision] sensible ■ **prudence** *nf* caution, care; **par prudence** as a precaution

**prune** [pryn] *nf* [fruit] plum ■ **prunier** *nm* plum tree

**pruneau, -x** [pryno] *nm* prune

**pseudonyme** [psødɔnim] *nm* pseudonym

**psychanalyse** [psikanaliz] *nf* psychoanalysis ■ **psychanalyste** *nmf* psychoanalyst

**psychiatre** [psikjatr] *nmf* psychiatrist ■ **psychiatrie** *nf* psychiatry ■ **psychiatrique** *adj* psychiatric

**psychique** [psiʃik] *adj* psychic

**psychologie** [psikɔlɔʒi] *nf* psychology ■ **psychologique** *adj* psychological ■ **psychologue** *nmf* psychologist

**psychose** [psikoz] *nf* psychosis

**PTDR** *Fam* SMS *abr écrite de* **pété de rire**

**PTOM** [ptɔm] *(abr de* **Pays et territoires d'outre-mer***) nm* Overseas Countries and Territories (OCT) of the European Union

**pu** [py] *pp de* **pouvoir**

**puant, -e** [pɥɑ̃, pɥɑ̃t] *adj* stinking ■ **puanteur** *nf* stink, stench

**pub** [pyb] *nf Fam* [secteur] advertising; [annonce] ad

**public, -ique** [pyblik] **1.** *adj* public; **dette publique** national debt **2.** *nm* [de spectacle] audience; **le grand public** the general public; **film grand public** film suitable for the general public; **en public** in public; [émission] before a live audience

**publication** [pyblikasjɔ̃] *nf* [action, livre] publication ■ **publier** *vt* to publish

**publicité** [pyblisite] *nf* [secteur] advertising; [annonce] advertisement, advert ; RADIO & TV commercial ; **agence de publicité** advertising agency ; **faire de la publicité pour qch** to advertise sth ▪ **publicitaire 1.** *adj* **film publicitaire** promotional film **2.** *nmf* advertising executive

**puce** [pys] *nf* [insecte] flea ; ORDINAT (micro-)chip ; **le marché aux puces, les puces** the flea market

**pudeur** [pydœr] *nf* modesty ; **par pudeur** out of a sense of decency ▪ **pudibond, -e** *adj* prudish ▪ **pudique** *adj* modest

**puer** [pɥe] **1.** *vt* to stink of **2.** *vi* to stink

**puériculture** [pɥerikyltyr] *nf* child care ▪ **puéricultrice** *nf* nursery nurse

**puéril, -e** [pɥeril] *adj* puerile ▪ **puérilité** *nf* puerility

**puis** [pɥi] *adv* then ; **et puis** [ensuite] and then ; [en plus] and besides

**puiser** [pɥize] **1.** *vt* to draw (**à** /**dans** from) **2.** *vi* **puiser dans qch** to dip into sth

**puisque** [pɥisk(ə)] *conj* since, as

**puissant, -e** [pɥisɑ̃, -ɑ̃t] *adj* powerful ▪ **puissance** *nf* [force, nation & MATH] power ; **en puissance** [meurtrier] potential ; MATH **dix puissance quatre** ten to the power of four

**puisse(s), puissent** [pɥis] *voir* **pouvoir**

**puits** [pɥi] *nm* well ; [de mine] shaft ; **puits de pétrole** oil well

**pull-over** [pylɔver] *(pl* **pull-overs)**, **pull** [pyl] *nm* sweater, *Br* jumper

**pulluler** [pylyle] *vi* [abonder] to swarm

**pulmonaire** [pylmɔner] *adj* pulmonary

**pulpe** [pylp] *nf* [de fruits] pulp

**pulvériser** [pylverize] *vt* [vaporiser] to spray ; [broyer] to pulverize ▪ **pulvérisateur** *nm* spray

**punaise** [pynɛz] *nf* [insecte] bug ; [clou] *Br* drawing pin, *Am* thumbtack

**punir** [pynir] *vt* to punish ; **punir qn de qch** [bêtise, crime] to punish sb for sth ▪ **punition** *nf* punishment

**pupille** [pypij] **1.** *nf* [de l'œil] pupil **2.** *nmf* [enfant] ward

**pupitre** [pypitr] *nm* [d'écolier] desk ; [d'orateur] lectern

**pur, -e** [pyr] *adj* pure ; [alcool] neat, straight ▪ **pureté** *nf* purity

**purée** [pyre] *nf* purée ; **purée (de pommes de terre)** mashed potatoes, *Br* mash

**purge** [pyrʒ] *nf* [à des fins médicales, politiques] purge

**purger** [pyrʒe] *vt* [patient] to purge ; [radiateur] to bleed ; [peine de prison] to serve

**purifier** [pyrifje] *vt* to purify ▪ **purification** *nf* purification ; **purification ethnique** ethnic cleansing

**puriste** [pyrist] *nmf* purist

**puritain, -e** [pyritɛ̃, -ɛn] *adj* & *nmf* puritan

**pur-sang** [pyrsɑ̃] *nm inv* thoroughbred

**pus¹** [py] *nm* [liquide] pus, matter

**pus², put** [py] *voir* **pouvoir**

**putréfier** [pytrefje] **1.** *vt* to putrefy **2.** **se putréfier** *vpr* to putrefy

**puzzle** [pœzl] *nm* (jigsaw) puzzle

**pyjama** [piʒama] *nm Br* pyjamas, *Am* pajamas ; **un pyjama** a pair of *Br* pyjamas or *Am* pajamas

**pyramide** [piramid] *nf* pyramid

**Pyrénées** [pirene] *nfpl* **les Pyrénées** the Pyrenees

**Pyrex®** [pireks] *nm* Pyrex® ; **plat en Pyrex®** Pyrex® dish

**pyromane** [pirɔman] *nmf* arsonist

# Q

**Q, q** [ky] *nm inv* Q, q

**Qatar** [katar] *nm* **le Qatar** Qatar, Katar

**qch** SMS *abr écrite de* **quelque chose**

**qd** SMS *abr écrite de* **quand**

**qu'** [k] *voir* **que**

**quad** [kwad] *nm* [moto] four-wheel motorbike, quad bike ; [rollers] roller skate

**quadrillage** [kadrijaʒ] *nm* [de carte] grid

**quadriller** [kadrije] *vt* [quartier, ville] to put under tight surveillance ; [papier] to mark into squares ■ **quadrillé, -e** *adj* [papier] squared

**quadrupède** [k(w)adrypɛd] *adj & nm* quadruped

**quadruple** [k(w)adrypl] **1.** *adj* fourfold **2.** *nm* **le quadruple (de)** [quantité] four times as much (as) ; [nombre] four times as many (as) ■ **quadrupler** *vt & vi* to quadruple ■ **quadruplés, -es** *nmf pl* quadruplets

**quai** [kɛ] *nm* [de port] quay ; [de fleuve] embankment ; [de gare, de métro] platform

**qualification** [kalifikasjɔ̃] *nf* [action, d'équipe, de sportif] qualification ; [désignation] description

**qualifier** [kalifje] **1.** *vt* [équipe] to qualify (**pour qch** for sth ; **pour faire** to do) ; [décrire] to describe (**de** as) **2. se qualifier** *vpr* [équipe] to qualify (**pour** for) ■ **qualifié, -e** *adj* [équipe] that has qualified ; **qualifié pour faire qch** qualified to do sth

**qualité** [kalite] *nf* [de personne, de produit] quality ; [occupation] occupation ; **produit de qualité** quality product ; **de bonne qualité** of good quality ; **en qualité de** in his / her /*etc* capacity as

**quand** [kɑ̃] *conj & adv* when ; **quand je viendrai** when I come ■ **quand même 1.** *adv* all the same ; **je pense qu'il ne viendra pas, mais je l'inviterai quand même** I don't think he'll come but I'll invite him all the same ; **tu pourrais faire attention quand même !** you might at least be careful! **2.** *excl* **quand même, à son âge !** really, at his / her age !

**quant** [kɑ̃] ■ **quant à** *prép* as for

**quantité** [kɑ̃tite] *nf* quantity ; **une quantité, des quantités** [beaucoup] a lot (**de** of)

**quarante** [karɑ̃t] *adj & nm inv* forty ; **un quarante-cinq tours** [disque] a single ■ **quarantaine** *nf* a) **une quarantaine (de)** [nombre] (about) forty ; **avoir la quarantaine** [âge] to be about forty b) MÉD quarantine ; **mettre qn en quarantaine** to quarantine sb ■ **quarantième** *adj & nmf* fortieth

**quart** [kar] *nm* a) [fraction] quarter ; **quart de litre** quarter litre, quarter of a litre ; **quart d'heure** quarter of an hour ; **une heure et quart** an hour and a quarter ; **il est une heure et quart** it's a quarter *Br* past *or Am* after one ; **une heure moins le quart** quarter to one ; SPORT **quarts de finale** quarter finals b) NAUT **être de quart** to be on watch ■ **quart-monde** [karmɔ̃d] (*pl* **quarts-mondes**) *nm* **le quart-monde** the Fourth World

**quartier** [kartje] *nm* a) [de ville] district ; **de quartier** local ; **quartier général** headquarters b) [de lune] quarter ; [de pomme] piece ; [d'orange] segment c) [expression] **avoir quartier libre** to be free

**quartz** [kwarts] *nm* quartz ; **montre à quartz** quartz watch

**quasi** [kazi] *adv* almost

**quasiment** [kazimɑ̃] *adv* almost

**quatorze** [katɔrz] *adj & nm inv* fourteen ▪ **quatorzième** *adj & nmf* fourteenth

**quatre** [katr] *adj & nm inv* four ▪ **quatrième** *adj & nmf* fourth ▪ **quatre-heures, quatre heures** [katrœr] *nm inv Fam* afternoon snack ▪ **quatre-quatre** [katkatr] **1.** *adj inv* four-wheel drive **2.** *nm ou f inv* four-wheel drive (vehicle)

**quatre-vingts** [katrəvɛ̃] *adj & nm* eighty ; **quatre-vingts ans** eighty years; **quatre-vingts-un** eighty-one; **page quatre-vingts** page eighty ▪ **quatre-vingt-dix** *adj & nm inv* ninety

**que** [kə]

que becomes **qu'** before a vowel or mute h.

**1.** *conj* **a)** [complétif] that; **je pense qu'elle restera** I think (that) she'll stay; **qu'elle vienne ou non** whether she comes or not; **qu'il s'en aille !** let him leave!; **ça fait un an que je suis là** I've been here for a year **b)** [de comparaison] than ; [avec 'aussi', 'même', 'tel', 'autant'] as ; **plus / moins âgé que lui** older / younger than him; **aussi sage / fatigué que toi** as wise / tired as you; **le même que Pauline** the same as Pauline **c)** (ne...) **que** only; **tu n'as qu'un stylo** you only have one pen **2.** *adv* (ce) **qu'il est bête !** [comme] he's really stupid! **3.** *pron rel* [chose] that, which ; [personne] that, whom ; [temps] when ; **le livre que j'ai** the book (that or which) I have; **l'ami que j'ai** the friend (that or whom) I have **4.** *pron interr* what ; **que fait-il ?, qu'est-ce qu'il fait ?** what is he doing?; **que préférez-vous ?** which do you prefer?

**Québec** [kebɛk] *nm* **le Québec** Quebec ▪ **québécisme** [kebesism] *nm* Quebec French (turn of) phrase

**quel, quelle** [kɛl] **1.** *adj interr* [chose] what, which ; [personne] which; **quel livre préférez-vous ?** which or what book do you prefer?; **quel est cet homme ?** who is that man?; **je sais quel est ton but** I know what your aim is; **je ne sais à quel employé m'adresser** I don't know which clerk to ask **2.** *pron interr* which (one) ; **quel est le meilleur ?** which (one) is the best? **3.** *adj excl* **quel idiot !** what a fool! **4.** *adj rel* **quel qu'il soit** [chose] whatever it may be ; [personne] whoever it or he may be

**quelconque** [kɛlkɔ̃k] **1.** *adj indéf* any; **donne-moi un livre quelconque** give me any book **2.** *adj* [insignifiant] ordinary

**quelque** [kɛlk] **1.** *adj indéf* some ; **quelques** some, a few; **les quelques amies qu'elle a** the few friends she has **2.** *adv* [environ] about, some; **quelque peu** somewhat ; *Fam* **100 euros et quelque** 100 euros and a bit

**quelque chose** [kɛlkəʃoz] *pron indéf* something; **quelque chose d'autre** something else ; **quelque chose de grand** something big; **quelque chose de plus pratique / de moins lourd** something more practical / less heavy

**quelquefois** [kɛlkəfwa] *adv* sometimes

**quelque part** [kɛlkəpar] *adv* somewhere, *Am* someplace ; [dans les questions] anywhere

**quelques-uns, -unes** [kɛlkəzœ̃, -yn] *pron* some

**quelqu'un** [kɛlkœ̃] *pron indéf* someone, somebody ; [dans les questions] anyone, anybody; **quelqu'un d'intelligent** someone clever

**querelle** [kərɛl] *nf* quarrel; **chercher querelle à qn** to try to pick a fight with sb ▪ **se quereller** *vpr* to quarrel

**question** [kɛstjɔ̃] *nf* [interrogation] question ; [affaire] matter, question ; **il n'en est pas question** it's out of the question ; **en question** in question ▪ **questionnaire** *nm* questionnaire ▪ **questionner** *vt* to question (**sur** about)

**quétaine** [keten] *adj Can Fam* camp, corny, coarse, daft, foolish

**quétainerie** [ketɛnri] *nf Can Fam* silliness, corn, foolishness

**quête** [kɛt] *nf* a) [collecte] collection; **faire la quête** to collect money b) [recherche] quest (**de** for); **en quête de** in quest *or* search of ■ **quêter** [kete] **1.** *vt* to seek **2.** *vi* to collect money

**queue** [kø] *nf* a) [d'animal] tail; [de fleur, de fruit] stalk; [de train] rear; **à la queue leu leu** in single file; **queue de cheval** [coiffure] ponytail b) [file] *Br* queue, *Am* line; **faire la queue** *Br* to queue up, *Am* to stand in line

**qui** [ki] **1.** *pron interr* [personne] who; [en complément] whom; **qui (est-ce qui) est là ?** who's there?; **qui désirez-vous voir ?, qui est-ce que vous désirez voir ?** who(m) do you want to see?; **à qui est ce livre ?** whose book is this?; **je demande qui a téléphoné** I'm asking who phoned
**2.** *pron rel* a) [sujet - personne] who, that; [chose] which, that; **l'homme qui est là** the man who's here *or* that's here; **la maison qui se trouve en face** the house which is *or* that's opposite b) [sans antécédent] **qui que vous soyez** whoever you are c) [après une préposition] **la femme de qui je parle** the woman I'm talking about

**quiconque** [kikɔ̃k] *pron* [sujet] whoever; [complément] anyone

**quille** [kij] *nf* [de navire] keel; [de jeu] (bowling) pin, *Br* skittle; **jouer aux quilles** to bowl, *Br* to play skittles

**quincaillerie** [kɛ̃kajri] *nf* [magasin] hardware shop; [objets] hardware

**quinoa** [kinɔa] *nm* quinoa

**quinquennal, -e, -aux** [kɛ̃kenal, -o] *adj* **plan quinquennal** five-year plan ■ **quinquennat** *nm* POL five-year term (of office)

**quintuple** [kɛ̃typl] **1.** *adj* **quintuple de** fivefold **2.** *nm* **le quintuple (de)** [quantité] five times as much (as); [nombre] five times as many (as) ■ **quintupler** *vt & vi* to increase fivefold

**quinze** [kɛ̃z] *adj & nm inv* fifteen; **quinze jours** two weeks, *Br* a fortnight ■ **quinzaine** *nf* **une quinzaine (de)** (about) fifteen; **une quinzaine (de jours)** two weeks, *Br* a fortnight ■ **quinzième** *adj & nmf* fifteenth

**quittance** [kitɑ̃s] *nf* [reçu] receipt

**quitte** [kit] *adj* quits (**envers** with); **quitte à faire qch** even if it means doing sth; **en être quitte pour qch** to get off with sth

**quitter** [kite] **1.** *vt* a) [personne, lieu, poste] to leave; **ne pas quitter qn des yeux** to keep one's eyes on sb b) ORDINAT to exit **2.** *vi* **ne quittez pas !** [au téléphone] hold the line! **3. se quitter** *vpr* to part; **ils ne se quittent plus** they are inseparable

**quoi** [kwa] *pron* what; [après une préposition] which; **à quoi penses-tu ?** what are you thinking about?; **après quoi** after which; **de quoi manger** something to eat; [assez] enough to eat; **de quoi écrire** something to write with; **quoi que je dise** whatever I say; **quoi qu'il en soit** be that as it may; **il n'y a pas de quoi !** [en réponse à 'merci'] don't mention it!; **quoi ?** what?

**quoique** [kwak] *conj* (al)though; **quoiqu'il soit pauvre** (al)though he's poor

**quota** [kwɔta] *nm* quota

**quotidien, -enne** [kɔtidjɛ̃, -ɛn] **1.** *adj* daily **2.** *nm* daily (paper)

# R

**R, r** [ɛr] *nm inv* R, r

**rabâcher** [rabɑʃe] **1.** *vt* to repeat end-lessly **2.** *vi* to say the same thing over and over again

**rabais** [rabɛ] *nm* reduction, discount ■ **rabaisser 1.** *vt* [dénigrer] to belittle **2. se rabaisser** *vpr* to belittle oneself

**rabattre** [rabatr] **1.** *vt* [col] to turn down ; [couvercle] to close **2. se ra-battre** *vpr* [se refermer] to close ; [véhi-cule] to pull back in ; *Fig* **se rabattre sur qch** to fall back on sth

**rabbin** [rabɛ̃] *nm* rabbi

**rabougri, -e** [rabugri] *adj* [personne, plante] stunted

**raccommoder** [rakɔmɔde] *vt* [linge] to mend ; [chaussette] to darn

**raccompagner** [rakɔ̃paɲe] *vt* to take back ■ **raccompagnateur, trice** [rakɔ̃paɲatœr, tris] *nmf Can* [personne qui raccompagne] escort ■ **raccom-pagnement** [rakɔ̃paɲmɑ̃] *nm Can* [action de reconduire] ride

**raccord** [rakɔr] *nm* [dispositif] connec-tion ; [de papier peint] join ; [de peinture] touch-up ■ **raccordement** [-əmɑ̃] *nm* [action, lien] connection ■ **raccorder 1.** *vt* to link up (**à** to) **2. se raccorder** *vpr* to link up (**à** to)

**raccourcir** [rakursir] **1.** *vt* to shorten **2.** *vi* to get shorter ■ **raccourci** *nm* short cut ; **en raccourci** in brief

**raccrocher** [rakrɔʃe] **1.** *vt* [objet tom-bé] to hang back up ; [téléphone] to put down **2.** *vi* [au téléphone] to hang up **3. se raccrocher** *vpr* **se raccrocher à qch** to catch hold of sth ; *Fig* to cling to sth

**race** [ras] *nf* [ethnie] race ; [animale] breed ; **chien de race** pedigree dog

■ **racial, -e, -aux** *adj* racial ■ **ra-cisme** *nm* racism ■ **raciste** *adj* & *nmf* racist

**rachat** [raʃa] *nm* [de voiture, d'apparte-ment] repurchase ; [de firme] buy-out ■ **racheter 1.** *vt* [acheter davantage] to buy some more ; [remplacer] to buy another ; [firme] to buy out ; [faute] to make up for **2. se racheter** *vpr* to make amends, to redeem oneself

**racine** [rasin] *nf* [de plante, de per-sonne & MATH] root

**racler** [rɑkle] **1.** *vt* to scrape ; [peinture, boue] to scrape off **2. se racler** *vpr* **se racler la gorge** to clear one's throat ■ **raclette** *nf* [outil] scraper ; [plat] ra-clette (*Swiss dish consisting of potatoes and melted cheese*)

**racoleur, euse** [rakɔlœr, øz] *adj* *Fam* & *Péj* [air, sourire] come-hither ; [publicité] strident

**racontar** [rakɔ̃tar] *nm* *Fam* piece of gossip

**raconter** [rakɔ̃te] *vt* [histoire, men-songe] to tell ; [événement] to tell about ; **raconter qch à qn** [histoire] to tell sb sth ; [événement] to tell sb about sth ; **raconter à qn que...** to tell sb that... ■ **racontars** *nmpl* gossip

**radar** [radar] *nm* radar ; **contrôle radar** radar speed check

**rade** [rad] *nf* harbour

**radeau, -x** [rado] *nm* raft

**radiateur** [radjatœr] *nm* radiator ; **radiateur électrique** electric heater

**radiation** [radjasjɔ̃] *nf* PHYS radiation ; [suppression] removal (**de** from) ■ **ra-dier** *vt* to strike off (**de** from)

**radical, -e, -aux** [radikal, -o] *adj* rad-ical

**radieux, -euse** [radjø, -øz] *adj* [personne, visage, soleil] radiant ; [temps] glorious

**radio** [radjo] **1.** *nf* **a)** [poste] radio ; [station] radio station ; **à la radio** on the radio ; **écouter la radio / qch à la radio** to listen to the radio / sth on the radio **b)** MÉD X-ray ; **passer une radio** to have an X-ray **2.** *nm* [opérateur] radio operator ▪ **radio-réveil** *(pl* **radios-réveils)** *nm* radio alarm, clock radio

**radioactif, -ive** [radjoaktif, -iv] *adj* radioactive ▪ **radioactivité** *nf* radioactivity

**radiodiffuser** [radjodifyse] *vt* to broadcast ▪ **radiodiffusion** *nf* broadcasting

**radiographie** [radjografi] *nf* [photo] X-ray ; [technique] radiography ▪ **radiographier** *vt* to X-ray ▪ **radiologie** *nf* MÉD radiology ▪ **radiologue** *nmf* [technicien] radiographer ; [médecin] radiologist

**radiophonique** [radjofonik] *adj* **émission radiophonique** radio broadcast

**radis** [radi] *nm* radish

**radoucir** [radusir] ▪ **se radoucir** *vpr* [personne] to calm down ; [temps] to become milder

**rafale** [rafal] *nf* [vent] gust ; [de mitrailleuse] burst

**raffermir** [rafermir] **1.** *vt* [autorité] to strengthen ; [muscles] to tone up **2.** **se raffermir** *vpr* [muscle] to become stronger

**raffiné, -e** [rafine] *adj* refined ▪ **raffinement** *nm* refinement

**raffiner** [rafine] *vt* to refine ▪ **raffinage** *nm* refining

**raffinerie** [rafinri] *nf* refinery

**rafle** [rafl] *nf* raid

**rafraîchir** [rafreʃir] **1.** *vt* **a)** [rendre frais] to chill ; [pièce] to air ; [raviver] to freshen up **b)** ORDINAT to refresh ; [navigateur] to reload **2.** *vi* to cool down **3.** **se rafraîchir** *vpr* [temps] to get cooler ; [se laver] to freshen up

▪ **rafraîchissant, -e** *adj* refreshing
▪ **rafraîchissement** *nm* [boisson] cold drink

**rafting** [raftiŋ] *nm* whitewater rafting

**rage** [raʒ] *nf* [colère] rage ; [maladie] rabies ; **faire rage** [incendie, tempête] to rage ; **Can rage au volant** road rage ; **rage de dents** (raging) toothache

**ragoût** [ragu] *nm* CULIN stew

**raid** [rɛd] *nm* raid

**raide** [rɛd] **1.** *adj* [rigide, guindé] stiff ; [côte] steep ; [cheveux] straight **2.** *adv* [grimper] steeply ; **tomber raide** to fall to the ground ▪ **raideur** *nf* [rigidité] stiffness ; [de côte] steepness ▪ **raidir** **1.** *vt* [bras, jambe] to brace ; [corde] to tauten **2.** **se raidir** *vpr* [membres] to stiffen ; [corde] to tauten ; [personne] to tense up

**raie** [rɛ] *nf* [motif] stripe ; [de cheveux] *Br* parting, *Am* part

**rail** [raj] *nm* rail ; **le rail** [chemins de fer] rail ; **rail de sécurité** crash barrier ▪ **rails** [raj] *nmpl* tracks

**raisin** [rɛzɛ̃] *nm* **raisin(s)** grapes ; **raisin sec** raisin

**raison** [rɛzɔ̃] *nf* **a)** [faculté, motif] reason ; **la raison de mon absence** the reason for my absence ; **la raison pour laquelle...** the reason (why)... ; **en raison de** [cause] on account of ; **à raison de** [proportion] at the rate of ; **à plus forte raison** all the more so **b)** **avoir raison** to be right **(de faire** to do *or* in doing) ; **donner raison à qn** to agree with sb

**raisonnable** [rɛzɔnabl] *adj* reasonable

**raisonner** [rɛzɔne] *vi* [penser] to reason ▪ **raisonnement** *nm* [faculté, activité] reasoning ; [argumentation] argument

**rajeunir** [raʒœnir] **1.** *vt* [moderniser] to modernize ; **rajeunir qn** [faire paraître plus jeune] to make sb look younger ; [donner moins que son âge à] to underestimate how old sb is **2.** *vi* to look younger ▪ **rajeunissement** *nm* [après traitement] rejuvenation ; [de population] decrease in age

**rajouter** [raʒute] *vt* to add (**à** to)

**rajuster** [raʒyste] *vt* [vêtements, lunettes] to straighten, to adjust

**ralentir** [ralɑ̃tir] *vt & vi* to slow down ■ **ralenti** *nm* CINÉ & TV slow motion; **au ralenti** in slow motion; [travailler] at a slower pace; **tourner au ralenti** [moteur, usine] *Br* to tick over, *Am* to turn over ■ **ralentissement** *nm* slowing down; [embouteillage] hold-up

**rallier** [ralje] **1.** *vt* [réunir] to rally; [regagner] to return to; **rallier qn à qch** [convertir] to win sb over to sth **2. se rallier** *vpr* **se rallier à** [avis] to come round to; [cause] to rally to

**rallonge** [ralɔ̃ʒ] *nf* [de table] extension; [fil électrique] extension (lead) ■ **rallonger** *vt & vi* to lengthen

**rallumer** [ralyme] **1.** *vt* [feu, pipe] to light again; [lampe] to switch on again **2. se rallumer** *vpr* [lumière] to come back on; [incendie] to flare up again

**ramasser** [ramɑse] **1.** *vt* [prendre, réunir] to pick up; [ordures, copies] to collect; [fruits, coquillages] to gather **2. se ramasser** *vpr* [se pelotonner] to curl up; [se relever] to pick oneself up ■ **ramassage** *nm* [d'ordures] collection; **ramassage scolaire** school bus service

**rame** [ram] *nf* [aviron] oar; [de métro] train ■ **ramer** *vi* to row ■ **rameur, -euse** *nmf* rower

**ramener** [ramne] *vt* [amener] to bring back; [raccompagner] to take back; [ordre, calme] to restore; **ramener qch à qch** to reduce sth to sth; **ramener qn à la vie** to bring sb back to life

**ramollir** [ramɔlir] **1.** *vt* to soften **2. se ramollir** *vpr* to soften

**ramoner** [ramɔne] *vt* [cheminée] to sweep

**rampe** [rɑ̃p] *nf* [d'escalier] banister; [pente] slope; **rampe d'accès** [de pont] access ramp

**ramper** [rɑ̃pe] *vi* to crawl

**rancœur** [rɑ̃kœr] *nf* rancour, resentment

**rançon** [rɑ̃sɔ̃] *nf* ransom ■ **rançonner** *vt* to hold to ransom

**rancune** [rɑ̃kyn] *nf* spite; **garder rancune à qn** to bear sb a grudge ■ **rancunier, -ère** *adj* spiteful

**randonnée** [rɑ̃dɔne] *nf* [à pied] hike; [en vélo] ride

**rang** [rɑ̃] *nm* **a)** [rangée] row; [classement, grade] rank; **par rang de taille** in order of size; **de haut rang** high-ranking; **se mettre en rang** to line up (**par trois** in threes) **b)** *Can* [peuplement rural] rural district **c)** *Can* [chemin] country road ■ **rangée** *nf* row

**ranger** [rɑ̃ʒe] **1.** *vt* [papiers, vaisselle] to put away; [chambre] to tidy (up); [classer] to rank (**parmi** among) **2. se ranger** *vpr* [se disposer] to line up; [s'écarter] to stand aside ■ **rangé, -e** *adj* [chambre] tidy; [personne] steady ■ **rangement** *nm* putting away; [de chambre] tidying (up); **rangements** [placards] storage space

**ranimer** [ranime] *vt* [personne - après évanouissement] to bring round; [après arrêt cardiaque] to resuscitate; [feu] to rekindle; [souvenir] to reawaken; [débat] to revive

**rapace** [rapas] **1.** *nm* [oiseau] bird of prey **2.** *adj* [personne] grasping

**rapatrier** [rapatrije] *vt* to repatriate

**râpé, -e** [rɑpe] *adj* [fromage, carottes] grated ■ **râper** *vt* [fromage] to grate; [bois] to rasp

**rapetisser** [raptise] **1.** *vt* [rendre plus petit] to make smaller; [faire paraître plus petit] to make look smaller **2.** *vi* [vêtement, personne] to shrink

**rapide** [rapid] **1.** *adj* fast; [progrès] rapid; [esprit, lecture] quick **2.** *nm* [train] express (train); [de fleuve] rapid ■ **rapidité** *nf* speed

**rappel** [rapɛl] *nm* [de diplomate] recall; [d'événement, de promesse] reminder; [au théâtre] curtain call; [vaccin] booster; **descendre en rappel** [en alpinisme] to abseil down

**rappeler** [raple] **1.** *vt* [pour faire revenir, au téléphone] to call back; [souvenir, diplomate] to recall; **rappeler qch à qn** to remind sb of sth **2.** *vi* [au téléphone] to call back **3. se rappeler** *vpr* se rappeler **qn /qch** to remember sb /sth; **se rappeler que...** to remember that...

**rapper** [rape] *vi* to rap ■ **rappeur, euse** *nmf* rapper

**rapport** [rapɔr] *nm* a) [lien] connection, link; **par rapport à** compared with; **rapports** [entre personnes] relations; **rapports (sexuels)** (sexual) intercourse b) [profit] return, yield c) [compte rendu] report

**rapporter** [rapɔrte] **1.** *vt* [rendre] to bring back; [remporter] to take back; [raconter] to report; [profit] to yield; **rapporter de l'argent** to be profitable; [moralement] to bring sb sth; **on rapporte que...** it is reported that... **2.** *vi* [chien] to retrieve **3. se rapporter** *vpr* **se rapporter à qch** to relate to sth; **s'en rapporter à qn /qch** to rely on sb /sth

**rapporteur** *nm* GÉOM protractor

**rapprocher** [raprɔʃe] **1.** *vt* [objet] to move closer (**de** to); [réconcilier] to bring together; [comparer] to compare (**de** to or with) **2. se rapprocher** *vpr* to get closer (**de** to); [se réconcilier] to be reconciled; [ressembler] to be similar (**de** to) ■ **rapproché, -e** *adj* close; [yeux] close-set ■ **rapprochement** *nm* [réconciliation] reconciliation; [rapport] connection

**rapt** [rapt] *nm* abduction

**raquette** [raket] *nf* [de tennis] racket; [de ping-pong] bat; [de neige] snowshoe

**rare** [rar] *adj* rare; [argent, main-d'œuvre] scarce; [barbe, végétation] sparse; **c'est rare qu'il pleuve ici** it rarely rains here ■ **rarement** *adv* rarely, seldom ■ **rareté** *nf* [objet rare] rarity; [de main-d'œuvre] scarcity; [de phénomène] rareness

**ras, -e** [ra, raz] **1.** *adj* [cheveux] close-cropped; [herbe, barbe] short; [mesure] full; **à ras bord** to the brim; **pull (au) ras du cou** crew-neck sweater **2.** *nm* au ras de, à ras de level with; **voler au ras du sol** to fly close to the ground **3.** *adv* [coupé] short

**raser** [raze] **1.** *vt* [menton, personne] to shave; [barbe, moustache] to shave off; [démolir] to raze to the ground; [frôler] to skim **2. se raser** *vpr* to shave ■ **rasé, -e** *adj* **être bien rasé** to be clean-shaven

**rasoir** [razwar] *nm* razor; [électrique] shaver

**rassasier** [rasazje] *vt* [faim, curiosité] to satisfy

**rassembler** [rasɑ̃ble] **1.** *vt* [gens, objets] to gather (together) **2. se rassembler** *vpr* to gather, to assemble ■ **rassemblement** [-əmɑ̃] *nm* [action, groupe] gathering

**rasseoir** [raswar] ■ **se rasseoir** *vpr* to sit down again

**rassis, -e** [rasi, -iz] *adj* [pain] stale

**rassurer** [rasyre] **1.** *vt* to reassure **2. se rassurer** *vpr* **rassure-toi** don't worry ■ **rassurant, -e** *adj* reassuring

**rat** [ra] *nm* rat

**ratatiner** [ratatine] ■ **se ratatiner** *vpr* to shrivel up

**ratatouille** [ratatuj] *nf* CULIN **ratatouille (niçoise)** ratatouille

**râteau, -x** [rato] *nm* rake

**râtelier** [ratəlje] *nm* [pour outils, pour armes] rack

**rater** [rate] *vt* [bus, cible, occasion] to miss; [travail, gâteau] to ruin; [examen] to fail; [vie] to waste ■ **raté, -e** *nmf* loser

**ratifier** [ratifje] *vt* to ratify

**ration** [rasjɔ̃] *nf* ration ■ **rationnement** *nm* rationing

**rationaliser** [rasjonalize] *vt* to rationalize

**rationnel, -elle** [rasjonɛl] *adj* rational

**ratisser** [ratise] *vt* [allée] to rake; [feuilles] to rake up

**rattacher** [rataʃe] **1.** *vt* [lacets] to tie up again; [région] to unite (**à** with) **2. se rattacher** *vpr* **se rattacher à** to be linked to

**rattraper** [ratrape] **1.** *vt* to catch; [prisonnier] to recapture; **rattraper qn** [rejoindre] to catch up with sb; **rat-**

**traper le temps perdu** to make up for lost time **2. se rattraper** *vpr* [se retenir] to catch oneself in time ; [après une faute] to make up for it ; **se rattraper à qch** to catch hold of sth ■ **rattrapage** *nm* SCOL **cours de rattrapage** remedial class

**raturer** [ratyre] *vt* to cross out, to delete

**rauque** [rok] *adj* [voix] hoarse

**ravages** [ravaʒ] *nmpl* devastation ; [du temps, de maladie] ravages ; **faire des ravages** to wreak havoc ; [femme] to break hearts ■ **ravager** *vt* to devastate

**ravaler** [ravale] *vt* [façade] to clean

**rave** [rɛv], **rave-party** [rɛvparti] *nf* rave (party)

**ravi, -e** [ravi] *adj* delighted (**de** with ; **de faire** to do ; **que** that)

**ravin** [ravɛ̃] *nm* ravine

**ravir** [ravir] *vt* [emporter] to snatch (**à** from) ; [plaire à] to delight ; **chanter à ravir** to sing delightfully ■ **ravissement** *nm* [extase] ecstasy ■ **ravisseur, -euse** *nmf* kidnapper

**raviser** [ravize] ■ **se raviser** *vpr* to change one's mind

**ravitailler** [ravitaje] **1.** *vt* [personnes] to supply ; [avion] to refuel **2. se ravitailler** *vpr* to get in supplies ■ **ravitaillement** *nm* [action] supplying ; [d'avion] refuelling ; [denrées] supplies

**raviver** [ravive] *vt* [feu, sentiment] to rekindle ; [douleur] to revive ; [couleur] to brighten up

**rayer** [rɛje] *vt* [érafler] to scratch ; [mot] to cross out ■ **rayé, -e** *adj* [verre, disque] scratched ; [tissu, pantalon] striped ■ **rayure** *nf* [éraflure] scratch ; [motif] stripe ; **à rayures** striped

**rayon** [rɛjɔ̃] *nm* **a)** [de lumière] ray ; [de cercle] radius ; [de roue] spoke ; **dans un rayon de** within a radius of ; **rayon X** X-ray ; **rayon de soleil** sunbeam **b)** [d'étagère] shelf ; [de magasin] department ; [de ruche] honeycomb ■ **rayonnage** *nm* shelving, shelves

**rayonner** [rɛjɔne] *vi* [avenue, douleur] to radiate ; [dans une région] to travel around (*from a central base*) ; [soleil] to beam ; *Fig* **rayonner de joie** to beam with joy ■ **rayonnant, -e** *adj* [soleil] radiant ; *Fig* [visage] beaming (**de** with) ■ **rayonnement** *nm* [du soleil] radiance ; [influence] influence

**raz de marée** [rɑdmare] *nm inv* tidal wave ; **raz de marée électoral** landslide

**rdv** SMS *abr* écrite de **rendez-vous**

**ré** [re] *nm inv* [note] D

**réacheminer** [reaʃmine] *vt* to forward

**réacteur** [reaktœr] *nm* [d'avion] jet engine ; [nucléaire] reactor

**réaction** [reaksjɔ̃] *nf* reaction ; **moteur à réaction** jet engine

**réagir** [reaʒir] *vi* to react (**contre** against ; **à** to) ; *Fig* [se secouer] to shake oneself out of it

**réaliser** [realize] **1.** *vt* [projet] to realize ; [rêve, ambition] *Br* to fulfil, *Am* to fulfill ; [bénéfices] to make ; [film] to direct ; [comprendre] to realize (**que** that) **2. se réaliser** *vpr* [vœu] to come true ; [personne] *Br* to fulfil *or Am* fulfill oneself ■ **réalisable** *adj* [plan] workable ; [rêve] attainable ■ **réalisateur, -trice** *nmf* [de film] director ■ **réalisation** *nf* [de projet] realization ; [de rêve] fulfilment ; [de film] direction

**réalité** [realite] *nf* reality ; **en réalité** in reality ; ORDINAT **réalité virtuelle** virtual reality, VR

**réanimation** [reanimasjɔ̃] *nf* resuscitation ; **(service de) réanimation** intensive care unit ■ **réanimer** *vt* to resuscitate

**rebattu, -e** [rəbaty] *adj* [sujet] hackneyed

**rebelle** [rəbɛl] **1.** *adj* [personne] rebellious ; [mèche] unruly **2.** *nmf* rebel ■ **se rebeller** *vpr* to rebel (**contre** against) ■ **rébellion** *nf* rebellion

**rebondir** [rəbɔ̃dir] *vi* to bounce ; [par ricochet] to rebound

**rebondissement** [rəbɔ̃dismɑ̃] *nm* new development (**de** in)

**rebord** [rəbɔr] *nm* edge ; [de plat] rim ; [de vêtement] hem ; **rebord de fenêtre** windowsill

**reboucher** [rəbuʃe] *vt* [flacon] to put the top back on ; [trou] to fill in again

**rebours** [rəbur] ■ **à rebours** *adv* the wrong way

**rébus** [rebys] *nm* rebus

**rebut** [rəby] *nm* **mettre qch au rebut** to throw sth out

**rebuter** [rəbyte] *vt* [décourager] to put off

**récapituler** [rekapityle] *vt & vi* to recapitulate

**recel** [rəsɛl] *nm* receiving stolen goods ■ **receler, recéler** *vt* [mystère, secret] to conceal ; [objet volé] to receive ; [criminel] to harbour

**recenser** [rəsɑ̃se] *vt* [population] to take a census of ■ **recensement** *nm* [de population] census

**récent, -e** [resɑ̃, -ɑ̃t] *adj* recent

**récepteur** [reseptœr] *nm* [téléphone] receiver ■ **réceptif, -ive** *adj* receptive (**à** to) ■ **réception** *nf* [accueil, soirée & RADIO] reception ; [de lettre] receipt ; [d'hôtel] reception (desk) ; **dès réception de** on receipt of ; **avec accusé de réception** with acknowledgement of receipt ■ **réceptionniste** *nmf* receptionist

**récession** [resesjɔ̃] *nf* ÉCON recession

**recette** [rəsɛt] *nf* CULIN & *Fig* recipe (**de** for) ; [argent, bénéfice] takings ; **recettes** [gains] takings

**recevoir** [rəsəvwar] **1.** *vt* [amis, lettre, proposition, coup de téléphone] to receive ; [gifle, coup] to get ; [client] to see ; [candidat] to admit ; [station de radio] to pick up ; **recevoir la visite de qn** to have a visit from sb ; **être reçu à un examen** to pass an exam ; **être reçu premier** to come first **2.** *vi* [faire une fête] to have guests ■ **receveur, -euse** *nmf* [de bus] (bus) conductor ; **receveur des Postes** postmaster, *f* postmistress

**rechange** [rəʃɑ̃ʒ] ■ **de rechange** *adj* [pièce] spare

**recharge** [rəʃarʒ] *nf* [de stylo] refill ■ **rechargeable** *adj* [briquet] refillable ; [pile] rechargeable ■ **recharger** *vt* [fusil, appareil photo, camion] to reload ; [briquet, stylo] to refill ; [pile] to recharge

**réchaud** [reʃo] *nm* (portable) stove

**réchauffer** [reʃofe] **1.** *vt* [personne, aliment] to warm up **2. se réchauffer** *vpr* [personne] to get warm ■ **réchauffement** *nm* [de température] rise (**de** in) ; **le réchauffement de la planète** global warming

**rêche** [rɛʃ] *adj* rough

**recherche** [rəʃɛrʃ] *nf* **a)** [quête & ORDINAT] search (**de** for) ; **à la recherche de** in search of ; **la recherche d'emploi** job-hunting ; **recherche sur Internet** Internet search ; **faire une recherche sur Internet** to search the Internet **b)** [scientifique] research (**sur** into) ; **faire de la recherche** to do research **c)** **recherches** [de police] search, hunt ; **faire des recherches** to make inquiries **d)** [raffinement] elegance

**rechercher** [rəʃɛrʃe] *vt* [personne, objet] to search for ; [emploi] to look for ; [honneurs] to seek ■ **recherché, -e** *adj* **a)** [très demandé] in demand ; [rare] sought-after ; **recherché pour meurtre** wanted for murder **b)** [élégant] elegant

**rechute** [rəʃyt] *nf* relapse ■ **rechuter** *vi* to have a relapse

**récidive** [residiv] *nf* [de malfaiteur] repeat *Br* offence *or Am* offense ; [de maladie] recurrence (**de** of) ■ **récidiver** *vi* [malfaiteur] to reoffend ■ **récidiviste** *nmf* [malfaiteur] repeat offender

**récif** [resif] *nm* reef

**récipient** [resipjɑ̃] *nm* container

**réciproque** [resiprɔk] *adj* [sentiments] mutual ; [concessions] reciprocal

**récit** [resi] *nm* [histoire] story ; [compte rendu] account ; **faire le récit de qch** to give an account of sth

**récital, -als** [resital] *nm* recital

**réciter** [resite] *vt* to recite

**réclame** [reklam] *nf* [publicité] advertising; [annonce] advertisement; **en réclame** on special offer

**réclamer** [reklame] **1.** *vt* [demander] to ask for; [exiger] to demand; [nécessiter] to require **2.** *vi* to complain ■ **réclamation** *nf* complaint; **(bureau des) réclamations** complaints department; **faire une réclamation** to make a claim

**réclusion** [reklyzjɔ̃] *nf* **réclusion (criminelle) à perpétuité** life imprisonment

**recoin** [rəkwɛ̃] *nm* [de lieu] nook

**recoller** [rəkɔle] *vt* [objet cassé] to stick back together

**récolte** [rekɔlt] *nf* [action] harvesting; [produits] harvest; **faire la récolte** to harvest the crops ■ **récolter** *vt* to harvest

**recommandable** [rəkɔmɑ̃dabl] *adj* **peu recommandable** disreputable

**recommandation** [rəkɔmɑ̃dɑsjɔ̃] *nf* [appui, conseil] recommendation

**recommander** [rəkɔmɑ̃de] *vt* [appuyer] to recommend (**à** to; **pour** for); **recommander à qn de faire qch** to advise sb to do sth ■ **recommandé, -e 1.** *adj* [lettre] registered **2.** *nm* **en recommandé** registered

**recommencer** [rəkɔmɑ̃se] *vt & vi* to start *or* begin again ■ **recommencement** *nm* renewal (**de** of)

**récompense** [rekɔ̃pɑ̃s] *nf* reward (**pour** *ou* **de** for); [prix] award ■ **récompenser** *vt* to reward (**de** *ou* **pour** for)

**recomposé, e** [rəkɔ̃poze] *adj* [famille] blended

**réconcilier** [rekɔ̃silje] **1.** *vt* to reconcile (**avec** with) **2. se réconcilier** *vpr* to become reconciled, *Br* to make it up (**avec** with) ■ **réconciliation** *nf* reconciliation

**reconduire** [rəkɔ̃dɥir] *vt* [contrat] to renew; **reconduire qn (à la porte)** to show sb out ■ **reconduction** *nf* [de contrat] renewal

**réconfort** [rekɔ̃fɔr] *nm* comfort ■ **réconfortant, -e** *adj* comforting ■ **réconforter** *vt* to comfort

**reconnaissable** [rəkɔnɛsabl] *adj* recognizable (**à qch** by sth)

**reconnaissant, -e** [rəkɔnɛsɑ̃, -ɑ̃t] *adj* grateful (**à qn de qch** to sb for sth) ■ **reconnaissance** *nf* [gratitude] gratitude (**pour** for); [de droit, de gouvernement] recognition; MIL reconnaissance; **reconnaissance de dette** IOU

**reconnaître** [rəkɔnɛtr] **1.** *vt* [identifier, admettre] to recognize (**à qch** by sth); [enfant, erreur] to acknowledge; MIL [terrain] to reconnoitre; **être reconnu coupable** to be found guilty **2. se reconnaître** *vpr* [soi-même] to recognize oneself; [l'un l'autre] to recognize each other ■ **reconnu, -e** *adj* recognized

**reconnecter** [rəkɔnɛkte] **1.** *vt* to reconnect **2. se reconnecter** *vpr* ORDINAT to reconnect, to get back on line

**reconquérir** [rəkɔ̃kerir] *vt* [territoire] to reconquer

**reconsidérer** [rəkɔ̃sidere] *vt* to reconsider

**reconstituer** [rəkɔ̃stitɥe] *vt* [armée, parti] to reconstitute; [crime] to reconstruct ■ **reconstitution** *nf* [de crime] reconstruction; **reconstitution historique** historical reconstruction

**reconstruire** [rəkɔ̃strɥir] *vt* to rebuild ■ **reconstruction** *nf* rebuilding

**reconvertir** [rəkɔ̃vertir] **1.** *vt* [entreprise] to convert; [personne] to retrain **2. se reconvertir** *vpr* [personne] to retrain ■ **reconversion** *nf* [d'usine] conversion; [de personne] retraining

**recopier** [rəkɔpje] *vt* [mettre au propre] to copy out; [faire un double de] to recopy

**record** [rəkɔr] *nm & adj inv* record; **record olympique** Olympic record ■ **recordman** [rəkɔrdman] (*pl* **recordmans** *ou* **recordmen** [-mɛn]) *nm* (men's)

record holder ■ **recordwoman**
[rəkɔrdwuman] *(pl* **recordwomans** *ou*
**recordwomen** [-mɛn]*) nf* record holder

**recoucher** [rəkuʃe] ■ **se recoucher**
*vpr* to go back to bed

**recoudre** [rəkudr] *vt* [bouton] to sew
back on ; [vêtement, plaie] to stitch up

**recouper** [rəkupe] **1.** *vt* [couper de nou-
veau] to recut ; [confirmer] to confirm
**2. se recouper** *vpr* [témoignages] to
tally ■ **recoupement** *nm* crosscheck;
**par recoupement** by crosschecking

**recourber** [rəkurbe] **1.** *vt* to bend **2. se
recourber** *vpr* to bend ■ **recourbé,
-e** *adj* [bec] curved

**recours** [rəkur] *nm* recourse ; **avoir
recours à** [chose] to resort to ; [per-
sonne] to turn to ; **en dernier recours**
as a last resort ■ **recourir** *vi* recourir
**à** [moyen, violence] to resort to ; [per-
sonne] to turn to

**recouvrer** [rəkuvre] *vt* [santé, bien] to
recover ; [vue] to regain

**recouvrir** [rəkuvrir] *vt* [revêtir, inclure]
to cover (**de** with) ; [couvrir de nouveau]
to re-cover

**récréation** [rekreasjɔ̃] *nf* SCOL *Br*
break, *Am* recess ; [pour les plus jeunes]
playtime

**recroqueviller** [rəkrɔkvije] ■ **se
recroqueviller** *vpr* [personne] to
huddle up

**recrue** [rəkry] *nf* recruit ■ **recrute-
ment** *nm* recruitment ■ **recruter**
*vt* to recruit

**rectangle** [rɛktɑ̃gl] *nm* rectangle
■ **rectangulaire** *adj* rectangular

**rectifier** [rɛktifje] *vt* [calcul, erreur] to
correct ; [compte] to adjust ■ **rectifi-
catif** *nm* correction ■ **rectification**
*nf* [de calcul, d'erreur] correction

**recto** [rɛkto] *nm* front ; **recto verso** on
both sides

**rectorat** [rɛktɔra] *nm Br* ≃ local education authority, *Am* ≃ board of education

**reçu, -e** [rəsy] **1.** *pp de* **recevoir 2.** *adj*
[idée] received ; [candidat] successful
**3.** *nm* [récépissé] receipt

**recueil** [rəkœj] *nm* [de poèmes, de chan-
sons] collection (**de** of)

**recueillir** [rəkœjir] **1.** *vt* [argent, ren-
seignements] to collect ; [personne,
animal] to take in **2. se recueillir** *vpr*
to meditate ; [devant un monument]
to stand in silence ■ **recueillement**
*nm* meditation

**recul** [rəkyl] *nm* [d'armée, de négociateur, de maladie] retreat ; [de canon]
recoil ; [déclin] decline ; **avoir un mouvement de recul** to recoil

**reculer** [rəkyle] **1.** *vi* [personne] to
move back ; [automobiliste] to reverse,
*Am* to back up ; [armée] to retreat ; [épi-
démie] to lose ground ; [renoncer] to
back down, to retreat ; [diminuer] to
decline ; **faire reculer la foule** to move
the crowd back **2.** *vt* [meuble] to move
back ; [paiement, décision] to postpone
■ **reculé, -e** *adj* [endroit] remote

**reculons** [rəkylɔ̃] ■ **à reculons** *adv*
backwards

**récup** [rekyp] *(abr de* **récupération**)
*Fam nf* **a)** [jour de congé] *compensatory
time off work due to previous overtime*
**b)** [chiffons, papier, ferraille, etc]
*second-hand object*

**récupérer** [rekypere] **1.** *vt* [objet prêté]
to get back, to recover ; [bagages] to retrieve ; [forces] to recover ; [recycler] to
salvage ; *Péj* [détourner à son profit] to
exploit **2.** *vi* [reprendre des forces] to
recover ■ **récupération** *nf* [d'objet]
recovery ; [de déchets] salvage

**recycler** [rəsikle] **1.** *vt* [matériaux] to
recycle **2. se recycler** *vpr* [personne]
to retrain ■ **recyclable** *adj* recyclable
■ **recyclage** *nm* [de matériaux] recycling ; [de personne] retraining

**rédacteur, -trice** [redaktœr, -tris]
*nmf* writer ; [de journal] editor ;
**rédacteur en chef** editor-in-chief
■ **rédaction** *nf* [action] writing ; [de
contrat] drawing up ; [journalistes]
editorial staff ; [bureaux] editorial
offices

**redemander** [rədəmɑ̃de] *vt* to ask for
more ; **il faut que je le lui redemande**
[que je pose la question à nouveau] I'll
have to ask him / her again

**redémarrer** [rədemare] *vi* [voiture] to start again ; ORDINAT to reboot

**redescendre** [rədesɑ̃dr] **1.** (*aux avoir*) *vt* [objet] to bring / take back down **2.** (*aux être*) *vi* to come / go back down

**redevance** [rədəvɑ̃s] *nf* [de télévision] licence fee

**redevenir** [rədəvənir] (*aux être*) *vi* to become again

**rediffusion** [rədifyzjɔ̃] *nf* [de film] repeat

**rédiger** [rediʒe] *vt* to write ; [contrat] to draw up

**redire** [rədir] **1.** *vt* to repeat **2.** *vi* **avoir** *ou* **trouver à redire à qch** to find fault with sth

**redoublant, -e** [rədublɑ̃, -ɑ̃t] *nmf* pupil repeating a year *or* Am a grade

**redoubler** [rəduble] **1.** *vt* to increase ; SCOL **redoubler une classe** to repeat a year *or* Am a grade **2.** *vi* SCOL to repeat a year *or* Am a grade ▪ **redoublement** *nm* increase (**de** in)

**redouter** [rədute] *vt* to dread (**de faire** doing) ▪ **redoutable** *adj* [adversaire, arme] formidable ; [maladie] dreadful

**redresser** [rədrese] **1.** *vt* [objet tordu] to straighten (out) ; [économie, situation] to put right ; **redresser la tête** to hold up one's head **2. se redresser** *vpr* [personne] to straighten up ; [pays, économie] to recover ▪ **redressement** [-ɛsmɑ̃] *nm* **redressement fiscal** tax adjustment

**réduction** [redyksjɔ̃] *nf* reduction (**de** in) ; [rabais] discount

**réduire** [reduir] **1.** *vt* **a)** to reduce (**à** to ; **de** by) ; **réduire qch en cendres** to reduce sth to ashes ; **réduire qn à qch** [misère, désespoir] to reduce sb to sth **b)** ORDINAT to minimize **2.** *vi* [sauce] to reduce **3. se réduire** *vpr* **se réduire à** [se ramener à] to come down to ▪ **réduit, -e 1.** *adj* [prix, vitesse] reduced **2.** *nm* [pièce] small room

**réécrire** [reekrir] *vt* to rewrite

**rééduquer** [reedyke] *vt* [personne] to rehabilitate ▪ **rééducation** *nf* [de personne] rehabilitation ; **faire de la rééducation** to have physiotherapy

**réel, -elle** [reɛl] *adj* real

**réélire** [reelir] *vt* to re-elect

**réévaluer** [reevalɥe] *vt* [monnaie] to revalue ; [salaires] to reassess

**réexpédier** [reɛkspedje] *vt* [faire suivre] to forward ; [à l'envoyeur] to return

**refaire** [rəfɛr] *vt* [exercice, travail] to do again, to redo ; [chambre] to do up ; [erreur, voyage] to make again ; **refaire sa vie** to make a new life for oneself ; **refaire du riz** to make some more rice

**réfectoire** [refɛktwar] *nm* dining hall, refectory

**référence** [referɑ̃s] *nf* reference ; **faire référence à qch** to refer to sth

**référencer** [referɑ̃se] *vt* [sur Internet] to reference

**référer** [refere] ▪ **se référer** *vpr* **se référer à** to refer to

**refermer** [rəfɛrme] **1.** *vt* to close *or* shut again **2. se refermer** *vpr* to close *or* shut again

**réfléchir** [refleʃir] **1.** *vt* [image, lumière] to reflect ; **réfléchir que...** to realize that... **2.** *vi* to think (**à** *ou* **sur** about) **3. se réfléchir** *vpr* to be reflected ▪ **réfléchi, -e** *adj* [personne] thoughtful ; [action, décision] carefully thought-out ; **tout bien réfléchi** all things considered

**reflet** [rəflɛ] *nm* [image] & Fig reflection ; [lumière] glint ; **reflets** [de cheveux] highlights ▪ **refléter 1.** *vt* to reflect **2. se refléter** *vpr* to be reflected

**réflexe** [reflɛks] *nm* & *adj* reflex

**réflexion** [reflɛksjɔ̃] *nf* [d'image, de lumière] reflection ; [pensée] thought, reflection ; [remarque] remark ; **faire une réflexion à qn** to make a remark to sb ; **réflexion faite, à la réflexion** on second Br thoughts *or* Am thought

**reflux** [rəfly] *nm* [de marée] ebb ; [de foule] backward surge

**réforme** [refɔrm] *nf* reform ■ **réformer** *vt* [loi] to reform ; [soldat] to discharge as unfit

**refouler** [rəfule] *vt* [personnes] to force or drive back ; [étrangers] to turn away ; [sentiment] to repress ; [larmes] to hold back

**refrain** [rəfrɛ̃] *nm* [de chanson] chorus, refrain

**réfrigérateur** [refriʒeratœr] *nm* refrigerator

**refroidir** [rəfrwadir] **1.** *vt* to cool (down) **2.** *vi* [devenir froid] to get cold ; [devenir moins chaud] to cool down **3. se refroidir** *vpr* [temps] to get colder ■ **refroidissement** *nm* [de température] drop in temperature ; [de l'eau] cooling

**refuge** [rəfyʒ] *nm* refuge ; [de montagne] (mountain) hut

**réfugier** [refyʒje] ■ **se réfugier** *vpr* to take refuge ■ **réfugié, -e** *nmf* refugee

**refus** [rəfy] *nm* refusal ■ **refuser 1.** *vt* to refuse (**qch à qn** sb sth ; **de faire** to do) ; [offre, invitation] to turn down ; [proposition] to reject ; [candidat] to fail ; [client] to turn away **2. se refuser** *vpr* [plaisir] to deny oneself ; **se refuser à faire qch** to refuse to do sth

**regagner** [rəgaɲe] *vt* [récupérer] to regain, to get back ; [revenir à] to get back to

**régaler** [regale] ■ **se régaler** *vpr* **je me régale** [nourriture] I'm thoroughly enjoying it ; [activité] I'm having the time of my life

**regard** [rəgar] *nm* [coup d'œil, expression] look ; **jeter un regard sur** to glance at

**regardant, e** [rəgardɑ̃, ɑ̃t] *adj Fam* **a)** [économe] mean **b)** [minutieux] **être très / peu regardant sur qch** to be very / not very particular about sth

**regarder** [rəgarde] **1.** *vt* to look at ; [émission, film] to watch ; [considérer] to consider, to regard (**comme** as) ; [concerner] to concern ; **regarder qn fixement** to stare at sb **2.** *vi* [observer] to look ; **regarder par la fenêtre** [du dedans] to look out of the window

**3. se regarder** *vpr* [soi-même] to look at oneself ; [l'un l'autre] to look at each other

**régénérer** [reʒenere] *vt* to regenerate

**régenter** [reʒɑ̃te] *vt* **vouloir tout régenter** to want to be the boss

**régie** [reʒi] *nf* [entreprise] state-owned company ; TV [organisation] production management ; [lieu] control room

**régime** [reʒim] *nm* [politique] (form of) government ; [de bananes] bunch ; **régime (alimentaire)** diet ; **régime amaigrissant** slimming diet ; **être au** *ou* **suivre un régime** to be on a diet

**régiment** [reʒimɑ̃] *nm* [de soldats] regiment

**région** [reʒjɔ̃] *nf* region, area ■ **régional, -e, -aux** *adj* regional

**registre** [rəʒistr] *nm* register

**réglable** [reglabl] *adj* adjustable ■ **réglage** *nm* [de siège, de machine] adjustment ; [de moteur, de télévision] tuning

**règle** [regl] *nf* **a)** [principe] rule ; **en règle** [papiers d'identité] in order ; **en règle générale** as a (general) rule **b)** [instrument] ruler

**règlement** [regləmɑ̃] *nm* **a)** [règles] regulations **b)** [de conflit] settling ; [paiement] payment ; *Fig* **règlement de comptes** settling of scores ■ **réglementaire** *adj* in accordance with the regulations ; MIL **tenue réglementaire** regulation uniform ■ **réglementation** *nf* [règles] regulations ■ **réglementer** *vt* to regulate

**régler** [regle] **1.** *vt* [problème, conflit] to settle ; [mécanisme] to adjust ; [moteur, télévision] to tune ; [payer] to pay ; **régler qn** to settle up with sb **2.** *vi* to pay **3. se régler** *vpr* **se régler sur qn** to model oneself on sb

**réglisse** [reglis] *nf* Br liquorice, Am licorice

**règne** [rɛɲ] *nm* [de souverain] reign ; [animal, minéral, végétal] kingdom ■ **régner** *vi* [roi, silence] to reign (**sur** over) ; [prédominer] to prevail ; **faire régner l'ordre** to maintain law and order

**regorger** [rəgɔrʒe] *vi* **regorger de** to be overflowing with

**régresser** [regrese] *vi* **a)** [personne] to regress **b)** [épidémie] to recede **c)** [ventes] to drop

**regret** [rəgrɛ] *nm* regret; **à regret** with regret; **avoir le regret** *ou* **être au regret de faire qch** to be sorry to do sth ▪ **regrettable** *adj* regrettable ▪ **regretter** [rəgrɛte] *vt* to regret; **regretter qn** to miss sb; **je regrette, je le regrette** I'm sorry; **regretter que...** (+ *subjunctive*) to be sorry that...

**regrouper** [rəgrupe] **1.** *vt* to gather together **2. se regrouper** *vpr* to gather together

**régulariser** [regylarize] *vt* [situation] to regularize

**régulier, -ère** [regylje, -ɛr] *adj* [intervalles, visage] regular; [constant] steady; [légal] legal ▪ **régularité** *nf* [exactitude] regularity; [constance] steadiness

**réhabituer** [reabitɥe] ▪ **se réhabituer** *vpr* **se réhabituer à qch/à faire qch** to get used to sth /to doing sth again

**rein** [rɛ̃] *nm* kidney; **les reins** [dos] the lower back

**réincarner** ▪ **se réincarner** *vpr* to be reincarnated

**reine** [rɛn] *nf* queen; **la reine Élisabeth** Queen Elizabeth

**réinitialiser** [reinisjalize] *vt* ORDINAT to reinitialize

**réinscriptible** [reɛ̃skriptibl] *adj* ORDINAT (re-)recordable; [cédérom] rewritable

**réinsertion** [reɛ̃sɛrsjɔ̃] *nf* reintegration; **réinsertion sociale** rehabilitation

**réintégrer** [reɛ̃tegre] *vt* [fonctionnaire] to reinstate; [lieu] to return to

**rejaillir** [rəʒajir] *vi* to spurt out

**rejet** [rəʒɛ] *nm* [refus & MÉD] rejection ▪ **rejeter** *vt* [relancer] to throw back; [offre, candidature, greffe, personne] to reject; [blâme] to shift (**on** to)

**rejoindre** [rəʒwɛ̃dr] **1.** *vt* [personne] to meet; [rue, rivière] to join; [lieu] to reach; [concorder avec] to coincide with **2. se rejoindre** *vpr* [personnes] to meet up; [rues, rivières] to join up

**réjouir** [reʒwir] **1.** *vt* to delight **2. se réjouir** *vpr* to be delighted (**de** at; **de faire** to do) ▪ **réjoui, -e** *adj* joyful ▪ **réjouissance** *nf* rejoicing; **réjouissances** festivities

**relâche** [rəlɑʃ] *nf* **a) faire relâche** THÉÂT & CINÉ to be closed; NAUT to put in (**dans un port** at a port); **sans relâche** without a break **b)** *Can* SCOL school break

**relâcher** [rəlɑʃe] **1.** *vt* [corde, étreinte] to loosen; [discipline] to relax; [prisonnier] to release **2.** *vi* NAUT to put into port **3. se relâcher** *vpr* [corde] to slacken; [discipline] to become lax; [employé] to slack off

**relais** [rəlɛ] *nm* [dispositif émetteur] relay; SPORT **(course de) relais** relay (race); **passer le relais à qn** to hand over to sb; **prendre le relais** to take over (**de** from); **relais routier** *Br* transport café, *Am* truck stop (café)

**relancer** [rəlɑ̃se] *vt* [lancer à nouveau] to throw again; [rendre] to throw back; [production] to boost; [moteur] to restart; ORDINAT to restart

**relatif, -ive** [rəlatif, -iv] *adj* relative (**à** to)

**relation** [rəlasjɔ̃] *nf* [rapport] relationship; [ami] acquaintance; **être en relation avec qn** to be in touch with sb; **avoir des relations** [amis] to have contacts; **relation (amoureuse)** (love) affair; **relations extérieures** foreign affairs; **relations familiales** family relationships; **relations internationales** international relations

**relayer** [rəleje] **1.** *vt* [personne] to take over from; [émission] to relay **2. se relayer** *vpr* to take turns (**pour faire** doing); SPORT to take over from one another

**relève** [rəlɛv] *nf* relief; **prendre la relève** to take over (**de** from)

**relevé** [rəlve] *nm* list ; [de compteur] reading ; **relevé de compte** bank statement ; SCOL **relevé de notes** list of *Br* marks or *Am* grades

**relèvement** [rəlɛvmɑ̃] *nm* [d'économie, de pays] recovery ; [de salaires] raising

**relever** [rəlve] **1.** *vt* [ramasser] to pick up ; [personne] to help back up ; [pays] to revive ; [copies] to collect ; [faute] to pick out ; [empreinte] to find ; [défi] to accept ; [sauce] to spice up ; [copier] to note down ; [compteur] to read ; [relayer] to relieve ; [augmenter] to raise ; **relever la tête** to look up ; **relever qn de ses fonctions** to relieve sb of his / her duties **2.** *vi* **relever de** [dépendre de] to come under ; [maladie] to be recovering from **3. se relever** *vpr* [après une chute] to get up

**relief** [rəljɛf] *nm* [de paysage] relief ; **en relief** in relief ; *Fig* **mettre qch en relief** to highlight sth

**relier** [rəlje] *vt* to connect, to link (**à** to) ; [idées, faits] to link together ; [livre] to bind

**religion** [rəliʒjɔ̃] *nf* religion ■ **religieuse** *nf* [femme] nun ; [gâteau] cream puff ■ **religieux, -euse 1.** *adj* religious ; **mariage religieux** church wedding **2.** *nm* [moine] monk

**relire** [rəlir] *vt* to reread

**reliure** [rəljyr] *nf* [couverture] binding ; [art] bookbinding

**relooker** [rəluke] *vt* [personne] to give a makeover to ; [produit, journal, site Web] to give a new look to ; **se faire relooker** [personne] to have a makeover

**reluire** [rəlɥir] *vi* to shine, to gleam ; **faire reluire qch** to polish sth up

**remanier** [rəmanje] *vt* [texte] to revise ; [ministère] to reshuffle ■ **remaniement** *nm* [de texte] revision ; **remaniement ministériel** cabinet reshuffle

**remarier** [rəmarje] ■ **se remarier** *vpr* to remarry ■ **remariage** *nm* remarriage

**remarquable** [rəmarkabl] *adj* remarkable (**par** for)

**remarque** [rəmark] *nf* remark ; **faire une remarque** to make a remark

**remarquer** [rəmarke] *vt* [apercevoir] to notice (**que** that) ; [dire] to remark (**que** that) ; **faire remarquer qch** to point sth out (**à** to) ; **se faire remarquer** to attract attention

**rembobiner** [rɑ̃bɔbine] **1.** *vt* to rewind **2. se rembobiner** *vpr* to rewind

**rembourser** [rɑ̃burse] *vt* [personne] to pay back ; [billet, frais] to refund ■ **remboursement** [-əmɑ̃] *nm* repayment ; [de billet] refund

**remède** [rəmɛd] *nm* cure, remedy (**contre** for) ■ **remédier** *vi* **remédier à qch** to remedy sth

**remémorer** [rəmemɔre] ■ **se remémorer** *vpr* to remember

**remercier** [rəmɛrsje] *vt* [dire merci à] to thank (**de** ou **pour qch** for sth) ; **je vous remercie d'être venu** thank you for coming ■ **remerciements** *nmpl* thanks

**remettre** [rəmɛtr] **1.** *vt* [replacer] to put back ; [vêtement] to put back on ; [disque] to put on again ; [différer] to postpone (**à** until) ; [ajouter] to add (**dans** to) ; **remettre qch à qn** [lettre] to deliver sth to sb ; [rapport] to submit sth to sb ; [démission] to hand sth in to sb ; **remettre qn en liberté** to set sb free ; **remettre qch en question** to call sth into question ; **remettre qch en état** to repair sth ; **remettre qch à jour** to bring sth up to date **2. se remettre** *vpr* **se remettre à qch** to start sth again ; **se remettre à faire qch** to start to do sth again ; **se remettre de qch** to recover from sth

**remise** [rəmiz] *nf* **a)** [de lettre] delivery ; **remise à neuf** [de machine] reconditioning ; **remise en question** questioning ; **remise en état** [de maison] restoration **b)** [rabais] discount **c)** JUR **remise de peine** reduction of sentence **d)** [local] shed

**remontée** [rəmɔ̃te] *nf* **remontée mécanique** ski lift

**remonter** [rəmɔ̃te] **1.** (*aux* **être**) *vi* to come / go back up ; [niveau, prix] to rise again, to go back up ; [dans le temps] to go back (**à** to) ; **remonter dans** [voiture] to get back in(to) ; [bus, train] to get back on(to) ; **remonter à dix ans** to go back ten years **2.** (*aux* **avoir**) *vt* [escalier, pente] to come / go back up ; [porter] to bring / take back up ; [montre] to wind up ; [relever] to raise ; [objet démonté] to put back together, to reassemble ; **remonter le moral à qn** to cheer sb up ■ **remonte-pente** *(pl* **remonte-pentes)** *nm* ski lift

**remords** [rəmɔr] *nm* remorse ; **avoir des remords** to feel remorse

**remorque** [rəmɔrk] *nf* [de voiture] trailer ■ **remorquer** *vt* [voiture, bateau] to tow ■ **remorqueur** *nm* tug (boat)

**rempart** [rɑ̃par] *nm* rampart ; **remparts** walls

**remplacer** [rɑ̃plase] *vt* to replace (**par** with) ; [professionnellement] to stand in for ■ **remplaçant, -e** *nmf* [personne] replacement ; [enseignant] substitute teacher, *Br* supply teacher ; [joueur] substitute ■ **remplacement** *nm* replacement ; **en remplacement de** in place of

**remplir** [rɑ̃plir] **1.** *vt* to fill (up) (**de** with) ; [formulaire] to fill out, *Br* to fill in ; [promesse] to fulfil **2. se remplir** *vpr* to fill (up) (**de** with)

**remporter** [rɑ̃pɔrte] *vt* [objet] to take back ; [prix, victoire] to win

**remuer** [rəmɥe] **1.** *vt* [bouger] to move ; [terre] to turn over **2.** *vi* to move ; [gigoter] to fidget

**rémunérer** [remynere] *vt* [personne] to pay ; [travail] to pay for ■ **rémunération** *nf* payment (**de** for)

**renaître** [rənɛtr] *vi* [personne] to be born again ; [espoir, industrie] to revive ■ **renaissance** *nf* rebirth ; [des arts] renaissance

**renard** [rənar] *nm* fox

**renchérir** [rɑ̃ʃerir] *vi* [dire plus] to go one better (**sur** than)

**rencontre** [rɑ̃kɔ̃tr] *nf* [de personnes] meeting ; [match] *Br* match, *Am* game ; **aller à la rencontre de qn** to go to meet sb ■ **rencontrer 1.** *vt* [personne] to

meet ; [difficulté] to come up against, to encounter ; [trouver] to come across **2. se rencontrer** *vpr* to meet

**rendement** [rɑ̃dmɑ̃] *nm* [de champ] yield ; [d'investissement] return, yield ; [de personne, de machine] output

**rendez-vous** [rɑ̃devu] *nm inv* [rencontre] appointment ; [amoureux] date ; [lieu] meeting place ; **donner rendez-vous à qn** to arrange to meet sb ; **prendre rendez-vous avec qn** to make an appointment with sb ; **recevoir sur rendez-vous** [médecin] to see patients by appointment

**rendormir** [rɑ̃dɔrmir] ■ **se rendormir** *vpr* to go back to sleep

**rendre** [rɑ̃dr] **1.** *vt* [restituer] to give back, to return (**à** to) ; [jugement] to deliver ; [armes] to surrender ; [invitation] to return ; [santé] to restore ; [exprimer] to render ; [vomir] to bring up ; **rendre célèbre** to make famous ; **rendre la monnaie à qn** to give sb his / her change ; **rendre l'âme** to pass away ; **rendre les armes** to surrender **2.** *vi* [vomir] to vomit **3. se rendre** *vpr* [criminel] to give oneself up (**à** to) ; [soldats] to surrender (**à** to) ; [aller] to go (**à** to) ; **se rendre à l'évidence** [être lucide] to face facts ; **se rendre malade** to make oneself ill

**renfermer** [rɑ̃fɛrme] *vt* to contain ■ **renfermé, -e 1.** *adj* [personne] withdrawn **2.** *nm* **sentir le renfermé** to smell musty

**renforcer** [rɑ̃fɔrse] *vt* to strengthen, to reinforce

**renfort** [rɑ̃fɔr] *nm* **des renforts** [troupes] reinforcements ; *Fig* **à grand renfort de** with (the help of) a great deal of

**renfrogner** [rɑ̃frɔɲe] ■ **se renfrogner** *vpr* to scowl

**rengaine** [rɑ̃gɛn] *nf* **a)** *Fam* [formule répétée] (old) story **b)** [chanson] (old) song

**renier** [rənje] *vt* [ami, pays] to disown ; [foi] to deny

**renifler** [rənifle] *vt & vi* to sniff ■ **reniflement** [-əmɑ̃] *nm* [bruit] sniff

**renne** [rɛn] *nm* reindeer

**renom** [rənɔ̃] *nm* renown; **de renom** [ouvrage, artiste] famous, renowned ■ **renommé, -e** *adj* famous, renowned (**pour** for) ■ **renommée** *nf* fame, renown

**renoncer** [rənɔ̃se] *vi* **renoncer à qch** to give sth up, to abandon sth; **renoncer à faire qch** to give up doing sth

**renouer** [rənwe] **1.** *vt* [lacet] to tie again **2.** *vi* **renouer avec qch** [tradition] to revive sth; **renouer avec qn** to take up with sb again

**renouveau, -x** [rənuvo] *nm* revival

**renouveler** [rənuvəle] **1.** *vt* to renew; [expérience] to repeat **2. se renouveler** *vpr* [incident] to happen again, to recur; [cellules, sang] to be renewed ■ **renouvelable** *adj* renewable ■ **renouvellement** [-ɛlmɑ̃] *nm* renewal

**rénover** [renɔve] *vt* [édifice, meuble] to renovate ■ **rénovation** *nf* [d'édifice, de meuble] renovation

**renseigner** [rɑ̃seɲe] **1.** *vt* to give some information to (**sur** about) **2. se renseigner** *vpr* to make inquiries (**sur** about) ■ **renseignement** [-əmɑ̃] *nm* piece of information; **renseignements** information; **les renseignements (téléphoniques)** *Br* directory inquiries, *Am* information; **demander des renseignements** to make inquiries

**rentable** [rɑ̃tabl] *adj* profitable ■ **rentabilité** *nf* profitability

**rente** [rɑ̃t] *nf* (private) income; [pension] pension

**rentrée** [rɑ̃tre] *nf* **rentrée des classes** start of the new school year

**rentrer** [rɑ̃tre] **1.** (*aux* **être**) *vi* [entrer] to go / come in; [entrer de nouveau] to go / come back in; [chez soi] to go / come (back) home; **rentrer en France** to return to France; **en rentrant de l'école** on my / his / her / *etc* way home from school; **rentrer dans qch** [pénétrer] to get into sth; [sujet : voiture] to crash into sth; **rentrer dans une catégorie** to fall into a category **2.** (*aux*

**avoir**) *vt* [linge, troupeau] to bring / take in; [chemise] to tuck in; [griffes] to retract

**renverse** [rɑ̃vɛrs] ■ **à la renverse** *adv* [tomber] backwards

**renverser** [rɑ̃vɛrse] **1.** *vt* [faire tomber] to knock over; [liquide] to spill; [piéton] to run over; [tendance, situation] to reverse; [gouvernement] to overthrow **2. se renverser** *vpr* [récipient] to fall over; [véhicule] to overturn

**renvoi** [rɑ̃vwa] *nm* [de marchandise, de lettre] return; [d'employé] dismissal; [d'élève] expulsion; [rot] belch, burp ■ **renvoyer** *vt* [lettre, cadeau] to send back, to return; [employé] to dismiss; [élève] to expel; [balle] to throw back; [lumière, image] to reflect

**réorganiser** [reɔrganize] *vt* to reorganize ■ **réorganisation** *nf* reorganization

**repaître** [rəpɛtr] ■ **se repaître** *vpr Fig* **se repaître de qch** to revel in sth

**répandre** [repɑ̃dr] **1.** *vt* [liquide] to spill; [odeur] to give off; [chargement] to shed; [bienfaits] to lavish **2. se répandre** *vpr* [nouvelle, peur] to spread; [liquide] to spill; **se répandre dans** [fumée, odeur] to spread through ■ **répandu, -e** *adj* [opinion, usage] widespread

**reparaître** [rəparɛtr] *vi* to reappear

**réparer** [repare] *vt* [objet, machine] to repair, to mend; [faute] to make amends for; **faire réparer qch** to get sth repaired ■ **réparable** *adj* [machine] repairable ■ **réparateur, -trice 1.** *nmf* repairer **2.** *adj* [sommeil] refreshing ■ **réparation** *nf* [action] repairing; [résultat] repair; [dédommagement] reparation; **en réparation** under repair

**repartir** [rəpartir] (*aux* **être**) *vi* [continuer] to set off again; [s'en retourner] to go back; [machine] to start again

**répartir** [repartir] *vt* [poids, charge] to distribute; [tâches, vivres] to share (out); [classer] to divide (up); [étaler dans le temps] to spread (out) (**sur** over)

■ **répartition** *nf* [de poids] distribution ; [de tâches] sharing ; [classement] division

**repas** [rəpɑ] *nm* meal

**repasser** [rəpɑse] **1.** *vi* to come /go back ; **repasser chez qn** to drop in on sb again **2.** *vt* [montagne, frontière] to go across again ; [examen] to take again, *Br* to resit ; [film] to show again ; [disque, cassette] to play again ; [linge] to iron ■ **repassage** *nm* ironing

**repêcher** [rəpeʃe] *vt* [objet] to fish out

**repeindre** [rəpɛ̃dr] *vt* to repaint

**répercuter** [repɛrkyte] **1.** *vt* [son] to reflect ; [augmentation] to pass **2. se répercuter** *vpr* [son, lumière] to be reflected ; *Fig* **se répercuter sur** to have repercussions on

**repère** [rəpɛr] *nm* mark ; **point de repère** [espace, temps] reference point ■ **repérer 1.** *vt* [endroit] to locate **2. se repérer** *vpr* to get one's bearings

**répertoire** [repɛrtwar] *nm* [liste] index ; [carnet] (indexed) notebook ; ORDINAT directory ; THÉÂT repertoire

**répéter** [repete] **1.** *vt* to repeat ; [pièce de théâtre, rôle] to rehearse ; **répéter à qn que** to tell sb again that… **2.** *vi* [redire] to repeat ; [acteur] to rehearse **3. se répéter** *vpr* [radoter] to repeat oneself ; [événement] to happen again ■ **répétition** *nf* [redite] repetition ; THÉÂT rehearsal ; **répétition générale** dress rehearsal

**répit** [repi] *nm* rest, respite ; **sans répit** ceaselessly

**replacer** [rəplase] *vt* to replace, to put back

**replanter** [rəplɑ̃te] *vt* to replant

**repli** [rəpli] *nm* [de vêtement, de terrain] fold ; [d'armée] withdrawal ; [de monnaie] fall

**replier** [rəplije] **1.** *vt* [objet] to fold up ; [couteau] to fold away ; [ailes] to fold ; [jambes] to tuck up **2. se replier** *vpr* [objet] to fold up ; [armée] to withdraw

**réplique** [replik] *nf* [réponse] retort ; [d'acteur] lines ; [copie] replica ; **sans réplique** [argument] unanswerable

■ **répliquer 1.** *vt* **répliquer que…** to reply that… **2.** *vi* to reply ; [avec impertinence] to answer back

**répondre** [repɔ̃dr] **1.** *vi* to answer, to reply ; [avec impertinence] to answer back ; [réagir] to respond (**à** to) ; **répondre à qn** to answer sb, to reply to sb ; [avec impertinence] to answer sb back ; **répondre à** [lettre, question, objection] to answer, to reply to ; [besoin] to meet ; **répondre au téléphone** to answer the phone ; **répondre de qn /qch** to answer for sb /sth **2.** *vt* [remarque] to answer or reply with ; **répondre que…** to answer or reply that… ■ **répondeur** *nm* **répondeur (téléphonique)** answering machine

**réponse** [repɔ̃s] *nf* answer, reply ; [réaction] response (**à** to)

**reportage** [rəpɔrtaʒ] *nm* [article, émission] report ; [métier] reporting

**reporter**¹ [rəpɔrte] **1.** *vt* [objet] to take back ; [réunion] to put off, to postpone (**à** until) ; [transcrire] to transfer (**sur** to) **2. se reporter** *vpr* **se reporter à** [texte] to refer to

**reporter**² [rəpɔrtɛr] *nmf* reporter ; **grand reporter** international reporter

**repos** [rəpo] *nm* [détente] rest ; [tranquillité] peace

**reposer** [rəpoze] **1.** *vt* [objet] to put back down ; [problème, question] to raise again ; [délasser] to rest, to relax ; **reposer sa tête sur** [appuyer] to lean one's head on **2.** *vi* [être enterré] to lie ; **reposer sur** [bâtiment] to be built on ; [théorie] to be based on ; **laisser reposer** [liquide] to allow to settle **3. se reposer** *vpr* to rest ; **se reposer sur qn** to rely on sb ■ **reposant, -e** *adj* restful, relaxing ■ **reposé, -e** *adj* rested

**repousser** [rəpuse] **1.** *vt* [en arrière] to push back ; [sur le côté] to push away ; [attaque, ennemi] to beat off ; [offre] to reject ; [dégoûter] to repel **2.** *vi* [cheveux, feuilles] to grow again

**reprendre** [rəprɑ̃dr] **1.** *vt* [objet] to take back ; [évadé, ville] to recapture ; [activité] to take up again ; [vêtement] to alter ; [corriger] to correct ;

**reprendre de la viande** to take some more meat **2.** *vi* [recommencer] to start again; [affaires] to pick up; [continuer de parler] to go on, to continue **3. se reprendre** *vpr* [se ressaisir] to get a grip on oneself; [se corriger] to correct oneself; **s'y reprendre à deux fois** to have another go (at it)

**représenter** [rəprezɑ̃te] **1.** *vt* to represent; [pièce de théâtre] to perform **2. se représenter** *vpr* [s'imaginer] to imagine ■ **représentant, -e** *nmf* representative ■ **représentatif, -ive** *adj* representative (**de** of) ■ **représentation** *nf* representation; [Théât] performance

**répression** [represjɔ̃] *nf* [d'émeute] suppression; [mesures de contrôle] repression ■ **répressif, -ive** *adj* repressive ■ **réprimer** *vt* [sentiment, révolte] to suppress

**réprimander** [reprimɑ̃de] *vt* to reprimand

**reprise** [rəpriz] *nf* [recommencement] resumption; [de l'économie] recovery; [de locataire] *money for fixtures and fittings (paid by outgoing tenant)*; [de marchandise] taking back; [pour nouvel achat] part exchange, trade-in; **faire une reprise à qch** to darn sth; **à plusieurs reprises** on several occasions ■ **repriser** *vt* [chaussette] to darn

**réprobateur, -trice** [reprobatœr, -tris] *adj* disapproving

**reproche** [rəprɔʃ] *nm* reproach; **sans reproche** beyond reproach ■ **reprocher** *vt* **reprocher qch à qn** to blame or reproach sb for sth

**reproduire** [rəprɔdɥir] **1.** *vt* [modèle, son] to reproduce **2. se reproduire** *vpr* [animaux] to reproduce; [incident] to happen again ■ **reproduction** *nf* [d'animaux, de son] reproduction; [copie] copy

**reptile** [reptil] *nm* reptile

**repu, -e** [rəpy] *adj* [rassasié] satiated

**république** [repyblik] *nf* republic ■ **républicain, -e** *adj & nmf* republican

**répugnant, -e** [repyɲɑ̃, -ɑ̃t] *adj* repulsive ■ **répugner** *vi* **répugner à qn** to be repugnant to sb; **répugner à faire qch** to be loath to do sth

**réputation** [repytɑsjɔ̃] *nf* reputation; **avoir la réputation d'être franc** to have a reputation for being frank or for frankness ■ **réputé, -e** *adj* [célèbre] renowned (**pour** for)

**requête** [rəkɛt] *nf* request

**requin** [rəkɛ̃] *nm* [animal] shark

**réquisitionner** [rekizisjone] *vt* to requisition, to commandeer

**RER** *(abr de réseau express régional)* *nm* train service linking central Paris with its suburbs and airports

**rescapé, -e** [reskape] **1.** *adj* surviving **2.** *nmf* survivor

**réseau, -x** [rezo] *nm* network; **réseau ferroviaire /routier** rail /road network; **réseau social** social network ■ **réseauter** *vi Fam* to network

**réservation** [rezervasjɔ̃] *nf* reservation, booking

**réserve** [rezerv] *nf* [provision, discrétion] reserve; [entrepôt] storeroom; [de bibliothèque] stacks; [de chasse, de pêche] preserve; [restriction] reservation; MIL **la réserve** the reserve; **en réserve** in reserve; **sans réserve** [admiration] unqualified; **sous réserve de** subject to; **sous toutes réserves** without guarantee; *Can* **réserve faunique** wildlife reserve; **réserve naturelle** nature reserve

**réserver** [rezerve] **1.** *vt* to reserve; [garder] to save, to keep (**à** for); [marchandises] to put aside (**à** for); [sort, surprise] to hold in store (**à** for) **2. se réserver** *vpr* **se réserver pour qch** to save oneself for sth ■ **réservé, -e** *adj* [personne, place, chambre] reserved

**réservoir** [rezervwar] *nm* [lac] reservoir; [cuve] tank; **réservoir d'essence** *Br* petrol or *Am* gas tank

**résidant, e** [rezidɑ̃, ɑ̃t] *Can* **1.** *adj* resident **2.** *nmf* = **résident**

**résidence** [rezidɑ̃s] *nf* residence; **résidence secondaire** second home; **résidence universitaire** *Br* hall of resi-

dence, *Am* dormitory ■ **résident, -e**
*nmf* resident ■ **résidentiel, -elle**
*adj* [quartier] residential ■ **résider**
*vi* to reside ; **résider dans** [consister
en] to lie in

**résidu** [rezidy] *nm* residue

**résigner** [reziɲe] ■ **se résigner** *vpr* to
resign oneself (**à qch** to sth ; **à faire** to
doing) ■ **résignation** *nf* resignation

**résilier** [rezilje] *vt* to cancel, to terminate

**résistance** [rezistɑ̃s] *nf* resistance (**à**
to) ; HIST **la Résistance** the Resistance

**résister** [reziste] *vi* **résister à** [attaque,
agresseur, tentation] to resist ; [chaleur,
fatigue, souffrance] to withstand ;
[mauvais traitement] to stand up to
■ **résistant, -e 1.** *adj* tough ; **résistant
à la chaleur** heat-resistant **2.** *nmf* HIST
Resistance fighter

**résolu, -e** [rezɔly] **1.** *pp de* **résoudre**
**2.** *adj* determined, resolute ; **résolu à
faire qch** determined to do sth ■ **résolution** *nf* [décision] resolution ; [fer-
meté] determination

**résonance** [rezɔnɑ̃s] *nf* resonance

**résonner** [rezɔne] *vi* [cri] to resound ;
[salle, voix] to echo (**de** with)

**résoudre** [rezudr] **1.** *vt* [problème] to
solve ; [difficulté] to resolve ; **résoudre
de faire qch** to resolve to do sth **2. se
résoudre** *vpr* **se résoudre à faire
qch** to resolve to do sth

**respect** [respe] *nm* respect (**pour/de**
for) ■ **respectable** *adj* [honorable,
important] respectable ■ **respec-
ter** *vt* to respect ; **respecter la loi** to
abide by the law ; **faire respecter la loi**
to enforce the law ■ **respectueux,
-euse** *adj* respectful (**envers** to ; **de** of)

**respirer** [respire] **1.** *vi* to breathe **2.** *vt*
to breathe (in) ■ **respiration** *nf*
breathing ; [haleine] breath

**responsable** [respɔ̃sabl] **1.** *adj* responsible (**de qch** for sth ; **devant qn** to sb)
**2.** *nmf* [chef] person in charge ; [d'orga-
nisation] official ; [coupable] person responsible (**de** for) ■ **responsabilité**
*nf* responsibility ; [légale] liability

**resquille** [reskij] *nf Fam* **a)** [au théâtre,
etc] sneaking in without paying
**b)** [dans autobus, etc] fare-dodging
■ **resquiller** *vi Fam* **a)** [au théâtre, etc]
to sneak in without paying **b)** [dans
autobus, etc] to dodge paying the fare
■ **resquilleur, euse** *nmf Fam* **a)** [au
théâtre, etc] person who sneaks in
without paying **b)** [dans autobus, etc]
fare-dodger

**ressaisir** [rəsezir] ■ **se ressaisir** *vpr*
to pull oneself together

**ressemblance** [rəsɑ̃blɑ̃s] *nf* likeness,
resemblance (**avec** to) ■ **ressembler**
**1.** *vi* **ressembler à** to look like, to resemble **2. se ressembler** *vpr* to
look alike

**ressentir** [rəsɑ̃tir] *vt* to feel

**resserrer** [rəsere] **1.** *vt* [nœud, boulon]
to tighten ; *Fig* [liens] to strengthen
**2. se resserrer** *vpr* [nœud] to tighten

**resservir** [rəservir] **1.** *vi* [outil] to
come in useful (again) **2. se resservir** *vpr* **se resservir de** [plat] to have
another helping of

**ressort** [rəsɔr] *nm* [objet] spring ; **du
ressort de** within the competence
of ; **en dernier ressort** [décider] as a
last resort

**ressortir** [rəsɔrtir] **1.** (*aux* **être**) *vi* [per-
sonne] to go /come back out ; [film] to
be shown again ; [se voir] to stand out ;
**faire ressortir qch** to bring sth out ;
**il ressort de...** [résulte] it emerges
from... **2.** (*aux* **avoir**) *vi* [vêtement] to
get out again

**ressortissant, -e** [rəsɔrtisɑ̃, -ɑ̃t] *nmf*
national

**ressource** [rəsurs] **1.** *nfpl* **ressources**
[moyens, argent] resources ; **être sans
ressources** to be without means
**2.** *nf* [possibilité] possibility (**de faire**
of doing) ; **avoir de la ressource** to be
resourceful ; **en dernière ressource**
as a last resort

**ressusciter** [resysite] *vi* to rise from
the dead

**restant, -e** [rɛstɑ̃, -ɑ̃t] **1.** adj remaining **2.** nm **le restant** the rest, the remainder; **un restant de viande** some leftover meat

**restaurant** [rɛstɔrɑ̃] nm restaurant; **manger au restaurant** to eat out

**restaurateur, -trice** [rɛstɔratœr, -tris] nmf [hôtelier, hôtelière] restaurant owner; [de tableaux] restorer

**restaurer** [rɛstɔre] **1.** vt [réparer, rétablir] to restore **2. se restaurer** vpr to have something to eat ■ **restauration** nf [hôtellerie] catering; [de tableau] restoration

**reste** [rɛst] nm rest, remainder (**de** of); **restes** remains (**de** of); [de repas] leftovers; **au reste, du reste** moreover, besides

**rester** [rɛste] (aux **être**) vi to stay, to remain; [calme, jeune] to keep, to stay, to remain; [subsister] to be left, to remain; **il reste du pain** there's some bread left (over); **il me reste une pomme** I have one apple left; **l'argent qui lui reste** the money he /she has left; **il me reste deux choses à faire** I still have two things to do

**restituer** [rɛstitɥe] vt [rendre] to return (**à** to); [argent] to repay ■ **restitution** nf [d'objet] return

**resto** [rɛsto] nm Fam restaurant; **les Restos du cœur** charity food distribution centres; UNIV **resto-U** university refectory, cafeteria ■ **Restoroute®** [rɛstorut] nm Br motorway cafe, Am highway restaurant

**restriction** [rɛstriksjɔ̃] nf restriction; **sans restriction** [approuver] unreservedly

**résultat** [rezylta] nm result; **avoir qch pour résultat** to result in sth ■ **résulter 1.** vi **résulter de** to result from **2.** v impers **il en résulte que…** the result of this is that…

**résumer** [rezyme] **1.** vt [abréger] to summarize; [récapituler] to sum up **2. se résumer** vpr [orateur] to sum up; **se résumer à qch** [se réduire à] to boil down to sth ■ **résumé** nm summary; **en résumé** in short

**rétablir** [retablir] **1.** vt [communications, ordre] to restore; [vérité] to re-establish; [employé] to reinstate **2. se rétablir** vpr [malade] to recover ■ **rétablissement** nm [d'ordre, de dynastie] restoration; [de vérité] reestablishment; [de malade] recovery

**retard** [rətar] nm [de personne] lateness; [sur horaire] delay; **en retard** late; **en retard sur qn /qch** behind sb /sth; **rattraper** ou **combler son retard** to catch up; **avoir du retard** to be late; [sur un programme] to be behind (schedule); [montre] to be slow; **avoir une heure de retard** to be an hour late; **prendre du retard** [personne] to fall behind

**retarder** [rətarde] **1.** vt [faire arriver en retard] to delay; [date, montre, départ] to put back; **retarder qn** [dans une activité] to put sb behind **2.** vi [montre] to be slow; **retarder de cinq minutes** to be five minutes slow

**retenir** [rətnir] **1.** vt [personne] to keep; [eau, chaleur] to retain; [cotisation] to deduct (**sur** from); [suggestion] to adopt; [larmes, foule] to hold back; MATH [chiffre] to carry; [se souvenir de] to remember; [réserver] to reserve; **retenir qn prisonnier** to keep sb prisoner; **retenir l'attention de qn** to catch sb's attention; **retenir qn de faire qch** to stop sb (from) doing sth **2. se retenir** vpr [se contenir] to restrain oneself; **se retenir de faire qch** to stop oneself (from) doing sth; **se retenir à qn /qch** to cling to sb /sth

**retentir** [rətɑ̃tir] vi to ring (out)

**retenue** [rətəny] nf [modération] restraint; [de salaire] deduction; SCOL [punition] detention

**retiré, e** [rətire] adj [lieu] remote, isolated

**retirer** [rətire] **1.** vt to withdraw; [faire sortir] to take out; [ôter] to take off; [éloigner] to take away; [aller chercher] to pick up; **retirer qch à qn** [permis] to take sth away from sb; **retirer qch de qch** [gagner] to derive sth from sth **2. se retirer** vpr to withdraw (**de** from); [mer] to ebb

**retomber** [rətɔ̃be] *vi* to fall again ; [après un saut] to land ; [intérêt] to slacken ; **retomber dans** [l'oubli] to sink back into

**retouche** [rətuʃ] *nf* [de vêtement] alteration ■ **retoucher** *vt* [vêtement, texte] to alter ; [photo, tableau] to touch up

**retour** [rətur] *nm* return ; [trajet] return journey ; **être de retour** to be back (**de** from) ; **à mon retour** when I get /got back (**de** from) ; **retour à l'envoyeur** return to sender ; **match retour** return *Br* match *or Am* game

**retourner** [rəturne] **1.** (*aux* **avoir**) *vt* [matelas, steak] to turn over ; [terre] to turn ; [vêtement, sac] to turn inside out ; [compliment] to return ; **retourner qch contre qn** [argument] to turn sth against sb ; [arme] to turn sth on sb **2.** (*aux* **être**) *vi* to go back, to return **3. se retourner** *vpr* [pour regarder] to turn round ; [sur le dos] to turn over ; [dans son lit] to toss and turn ; [voiture] to overturn ; *Fig* **se retourner contre** to turn against

**retrait** [rətrɛ] *nm* withdrawal ; [de bagages, de billets] collection ; [des eaux] receding ; **en retrait** [maison] set back ; **rester en retrait** to stay in the background

**retraite** [rətrɛt] *nf* [d'employé] retirement ; [pension] (retirement) pension ; [refuge] retreat, refuge ; [d'armée] retreat ; **prendre sa retraite** to retire ; **être à la retraite** to be retired ; **retraite anticipée** early retirement ■ **retraité, -e 1.** *adj* retired **2.** *nmf* senior citizen, *Br* (old age) pensioner

**retraitement** [rətrɛtmɑ̃] *nm* reprocessing

**retrancher** [rətrɑ̃ʃe] **1.** *vt* [passage, nom] to remove (**de** from) ; [argent, quantité] to deduct (**de** from) **2. se retrancher** *vpr* [soldats] to dig in ; *Fig* **se retrancher dans /derrière qch** to hide in / behind sth

**retransmettre** [rətrɑ̃smɛtr] *vt* to broadcast ■ **retransmission** *nf* broadcast

**rétrécir** [retresir] **1.** *vt* [vêtement] to take in **2.** *vi* [au lavage] to shrink **3. se rétrécir** *vpr* [rue] to narrow

**rétro** [retro] *Fam* **1.** *nm* **a)** [style] old style or fashion **b)** [rétroviseur] rearview mirror **2.** *adj inv* old-style

**rétroactif, -ive** [retrɔaktif, -iv] *adj* retroactive

**rétrograder** [retrɔgrade] **1.** *vt* [fonctionnaire, officier] to demote **2.** *vi* [automobiliste] to change down

**rétroprojecteur** [retrɔprɔʒɛktœr] *nm* overhead projector

**rétrospectif, -ive** [retrɔspɛktif, -iv] **1.** *adj* retrospective **2.** *nf* **rétrospective** retrospective

**retrouver** [rətruve] **1.** *vt* [objet] to find again ; [personne] to meet again ; [forces, santé] to regain ; [se rappeler] to recall ; [découvrir] to rediscover **2. se retrouver** *vpr* [être] to find oneself ; [trouver son chemin] to find one's way (**dans** round) ; [se rencontrer] to meet ; **se retrouver à la rue** to find oneself homeless

**rétroviseur** [retrɔvizœr] *nm* rear-view mirror

**réunion** [reynjɔ̃] *nf* [séance] meeting ; [d'objets] collection, gathering ; [jonction] joining ; **être en réunion** to be in a meeting ; **réunion de famille** family gathering

**Réunion** [reynjɔ̃] *nf* **La Réunion** Réunion

**réunir** [reynir] **1.** *vt* [objets] to put together ; [documents] to gather together ; [fonds] to raise ; [amis, famille] to get together ; [après une rupture] to reunite ; [avantages, qualités] to combine ; **réunir qch à qch** to join sth to sth **2. se réunir** *vpr* [personnes] to meet ; **se réunir autour de qn /qch** to gather round sb /sth

**réussir** [reysir] **1.** *vt* [bien faire] to make a success of ; [examen] to pass **2.** *vi* to succeed, to be successful (**à faire** in doing) ; **réussir à un examen** to pass an exam ■ **réussi, -e** *adj* successful

■ **réussite** *nf* success; CARTES **faire des réussites** to play *Br* patience or *Am* solitaire

**revaloriser** [rəvalɔrize] *vt* [monnaie] to revalue; [salaires, profession] to upgrade

**revanche** [rəvɑ̃ʃ] *nf* revenge; [de match] return game; **prendre sa revanche** to get one's revenge (**sur** on); **en revanche** on the other hand

**rêve** [rɛv] *nm* dream; **faire un rêve** to have a dream

**réveil** [revɛj] *nm* [de personnes] waking; [pendule] alarm (clock); **à son réveil** on waking

**réveiller** [revɛje] **1.** *vt* [personne] to wake (up); *Fig* [douleur] to revive; *Fig* [sentiment, souvenir] to revive **2. se réveiller** *vpr* [personne] to wake (up); [nature] to reawaken; *Fig* [douleur] to come back ■ **réveillé, -e** *adj* awake ■ **réveille-matin** *nm inv* alarm clock

**réveillon** [revɛjɔ̃] *nm* [repas] midnight supper; [soirée] midnight party (*on Christmas Eve or New Year's Eve*) ■ **réveillonner** *vi* to see in Christmas / the New Year

**révéler** [revele] **1.** *vt* to reveal (**que** that) **2. se révéler** *vpr* [personne] to reveal oneself; [talent] to be revealed; **se révéler facile** to turn out to be easy ■ **révélateur, -trice** *adj* revealing; **révélateur de qch** indicative of sth ■ **révélation** *nf* [action, découverte] revelation; [personne] discovery; **faire des révélations** to disclose important information

**revenant** [rəvnɑ̃] *nm* **a)** [fantôme] spirit, ghost **b)** *Fam* [personne] **tiens, un revenant!** hello, stranger!

**revendiquer** [rəvɑ̃dike] *vt* to claim; [attentat] to claim responsibility for ■ **revendication** *nf* claim

**revendre** [rəvɑ̃dr] *vt* to resell

**revenir** [rəvnir] (*aux* **être**) *vi* [personne] to come back, to return; [date] to come round again; **le dîner nous est revenu à 50 euros** the dinner cost us 50 euros; **revenir cher** to work out expensive; **revenir à** [activité, sujet] to go back to,

to return to; [se résumer à] to boil down to; **revenir à qn** [forces, mémoire] to come back to sb; [honneur] to fall to sb; **revenir de** [surprise] to get over; **revenir sur** [décision, promesse] to go back on; [passé, question] to go back over; **revenir sur ses pas** to retrace one's steps

**revenu** [rəvny] *nm* income (**de** from); [d'un État] revenue (**de** from)

**rêver** [reve] **1.** *vt* to dream (**que** that) **2.** *vi* to dream (**de** of; **de faire** of doing)

**réverbère** [reverber] *nm* street lamp

**révérence** [reverɑ̃s] *nf* [respect] reverence; [salut] curtsey

**rêverie** [revri] *nf* daydream

**revers** [rəver] *nm* [de veste] lapel; [de pantalon] *Br* turn-up, *Am* cuff; [d'étoffe] wrong side; [de pièce] reverse; [coup du sort] setback; [au tennis] backhand; **d'un revers de la main** with the back of one's hand; *Fig* **le revers de la médaille** the other side of the coin

**reverser** [rəverse] *vt* [café, vin] to pour more; *Fig* [argent] to transfer (**sur un compte** into an account)

**réversible** [reversibl] *adj* reversible

**revêtir** [rəvetir] *vt* to cover (**de** with); [habit] to don; [caractère, forme] to assume; **revêtir qn** [habiller] to dress sb (**de** in) ■ **revêtement** *nm* [surface] covering; [de route] surface

**rêveur, -euse** [revœr, -øz] **1.** *adj* dreamy **2.** *nmf* dreamer

**revient** [rəvjɛ̃] *nm* **prix de revient** *Br* cost price, *Am* wholesale price

**revirement** [rəvirmɑ̃] *nm* [changement] *Br* about-turn, *Am* about-face; [de situation, d'opinion, de politique] reversal

**réviser** [revize] *vt* [leçon] to revise; [machine, voiture] to service; [jugement, règlement] to review ■ **révision** *nf* [leçon] revision; [de machine] service; [de jugement] review

**revivre** [rəvivr] **1.** *vt* [incident] to relive **2.** *vi* to live again; **faire revivre qch** to revive sth

**revoici** [rəvwasi] *prép* **me revoici** here I am again

**revoilà** [rəvwala] *prép* **la revoilà** there she is again

**revoir** [rəvwar] *vt* to see (again); [texte, leçon] to revise; **au revoir** goodbye

**révolte** [revɔlt] *nf* revolt ■ **révolter 1.** *vt* to appal **2. se révolter** *vpr* to rebel, to revolt (**contre** against)

**révolu, -e** [revɔly] *adj* [époque] past; **avoir trente ans révolus** to be over thirty

**révolution** [revɔlysjɔ̃] *nf* [changement, rotation] revolution ■ **révolutionner** *vt* [transformer] to revolutionize

**revolver** [revɔlvɛr] *nm* revolver

**revue** [rəvy] *nf* [magazine] magazine; [spécialisée] journal; [spectacle] revue; MIL review; **passer qch en revue** to review sth

**rez-de-chaussée** [redʃose] *nm inv* Br ground floor, Am first floor

**Rhin** [rɛ̃] *nm* **le Rhin** the Rhine

**rhinocéros** [rinɔserɔs] *nm* rhinoceros

**Rhône** [ron] *nm* **le Rhône** the Rhône

**rhumatisme** [rymatism] *nm* rheumatism; **avoir des rhumatismes** to have rheumatism

**rhume** [rym] *nm* cold; **rhume des foins** hay fever

**ri** [ri] *pp de* **rire**

**ricaner** [rikane] *vi* [sarcastiquement] Br to snigger, Am to snicker; [bêtement] to giggle

**riche** [riʃ] **1.** *adj* [personne, pays, aliment] rich; **riche en** [vitamines, minérai] rich in **2.** *nmf* rich person; **les riches** the rich ■ **richesse** *nf* [de personne, de pays] wealth; [d'étoffe, de sol] richness; **richesses** [trésor] riches; [ressources] wealth

**ricocher** [rikɔʃe] *vi* to rebound, to ricochet ■ **ricochet** *nm* rebound, ricochet; *Fig* **par ricochet** indirectly

**ride** [rid] *nf* [de visage] wrinkle ■ **ridé, -e** *adj* wrinkled ■ **rider 1.** *vt* [visage, peau] to wrinkle; [eau] to ripple **2. se rider** *vpr* [visage, peau] to wrinkle

**rideau, -x** [rido] *nm* curtain; [métallique] shutter; *Fig* [écran] screen (**de** of)

**ridicule** [ridikyl] **1.** *adj* ridiculous, ludicrous **2.** *nm* [moquerie] ridicule; [absurdité] ridiculousness; **tourner qn/qch en ridicule** to ridicule sb/sth ■ **ridiculiser 1.** *vt* to ridicule **2. se ridiculiser** *vpr* to make a fool of oneself

**rien** [rjɛ̃] **1.** *pron* nothing; **il ne sait rien** he knows nothing, he doesn't know anything; **rien du tout** nothing at all; **rien d'autre/de bon** nothing else/good; **rien de tel** nothing like it; **de rien !** [je vous en prie] don't mention it!; **ça ne fait rien** it doesn't matter; **pour rien au monde** never in a thousand years; **comme si de rien n'était** as if nothing had happened **2.** *nm* (mere) nothing, trifle; **un rien de** a little; **en un rien de temps** in no time

**rieur, -euse** [rijœr, -øz] *adj* cheerful

**rigide** [riʒid] *adj* rigid; [carton] stiff; [éducation] strict

**rigole** [rigɔl] *nf* [conduit] channel; [filet d'eau] rivulet

**rigueur** [rigœr] *nf* [d'analyse] rigour; [de climat] harshness; [de personne] strictness; **être de rigueur** to be the rule; **à la rigueur** if need be ■ **rigoureux, -euse** *adj* [analyse] rigorous; [climat, punition] harsh; [personne, morale, neutralité] strict

**rillettes** [rijɛt] *nfpl* potted minced pork

**rimer** [rime] *vi* to rhyme (**avec** with)

**rincer** [rɛ̃se] *vt* to rinse; [verre] to rinse (out) ■ **rince-bouche** [rɛ̃sbuʃ] *nm inv* Can mouthwash

**ring** [riŋ] *nm* (boxing) ring

**riposte** [ripɔst] *nf* [réponse] retort; [attaque] counterattack ■ **riposter 1.** *vt* **riposter que...** to retort that... **2.** *vi* to counterattack; **riposter à** [attaque] to counter; [insulte] to reply to

**rire** [rir] **1.** *nm* laugh; **rires** laughter; **le fou rire** the giggles **2.** *vi* to laugh (**de** at); [s'amuser] to have a good time; [plaisanter] to joke; **rire aux éclats** to roar with laughter; **faire qch pour rire** to do sth for a joke or laugh

**risible** [rizibl] *adj* laughable

**risque** [risk] *nm* risk; **au risque de faire qch** at the risk of doing sth; **à vos risques et périls** at your own risk; **assurance tous risques** comprehensive insurance

**risquer** [riske] **1.** *vt* to risk; [question] to venture; **risquer de faire qch** to stand a good chance of doing sth **2. se risquer** *vpr* **se risquer à faire qch** to dare to do sth ■ **risqué, -e** *adj* [dangereux] risky; [osé] risqué

**ristourne** [risturn] *nf* discount; **faire une ristourne à qn** to give sb a discount

**rivage** [rivaʒ] *nm* shore

**rival, -e, -aux** [rival, -o] *adj & nmf* rival ■ **rivaliser** *vi* to compete (**avec** with; **de** in) ■ **rivalité** *nf* rivalry

**rive** [riv] *nf* [de fleuve] bank; [de lac] shore

**riverain, -e** [rivərɛ̃, -ɛn] **1.** *adj* [de rivière] riverside; [de lac] lakeside **2.** *nmf* [près d'une rivière] riverside resident; [près d'un lac] lakeside resident; [de rue] resident

**rivière** [rivjɛr] *nf* river

**riz** [ri] *nm* rice; **riz blanc / complet** white / brown rice; **riz au lait** rice pudding ■ **rizière** *nf* paddy (field), rice-field

**RN** *(abr de* route nationale) *nf Br* main road, A-road, *Am* (state) highway

**robe** [rɔb] *nf* [de femme] dress; [d'ecclésiastique, de juge] robe; [pelage] coat; **robe du soir** evening dress; **robe de chambre** *Br* dressing gown, *Am* bathrobe; **pomme de terre en robe des champs** jacket potato, baked potato

**robinet** [rɔbinɛ] *nm Br* tap, *Am* faucet

**robot** [rɔbo] *nm* robot; **robot ménager** food processor

**robuste** [rɔbyst] *adj* robust

**roc** [rɔk] *nm* rock

**rocaille** [rɔkaj] *nf* [terrain] rocky ground; [de jardin] rockery ■ **rocailleux, -euse** *adj* rocky, stony; [voix] harsh

**roche** [rɔʃ] *nf* rock ■ **rocher** *nm* [bloc, substance] rock ■ **rocheux, -euse** *adj* rocky

**Rocheuses** *nfpl* **les Rocheuses** the Rockies

**rock** [rɔk] **1.** *nm* [musique] rock **2.** *adj inv* **chanteur / opéra rock** rock singer / opera ■ **rockeur, -euse** *nmf* [musicien] rock musician

**roder** [rɔde] *vt* [moteur, voiture] *Br* to run in, *Am* to break in

**rôder** [rode] *vi* to be on the prowl ■ **rôdeur, -euse** *nmf* prowler

**rognon** [rɔɲɔ̃] *nm* kidney

**roi** [rwa] *nm* king; **fête des Rois** Twelfth Night

**rôle** [rol] *nm* role, part; [de père] job; **à tour de rôle** in turn

**rolleur, euse** [rɔllœr, øz] *nmf* roller skater

**romain, -e** [rɔmɛ̃, -ɛn] **1.** *adj* Roman **2.** *nmf* **Romain, Romaine** Roman **3.** *nf* **romaine** [laitue] *Br* cos (lettuce), *Am* romaine

**roman** [rɔmɑ̃] *nm* novel; *Fig* [histoire] story ■ **romancier, -ère** *nmf* novelist

**romanesque** [rɔmanɛsk] *adj* romantic; [incroyable] fantastic

**romantique** [rɔmɑ̃tik] *adj* romantic

**romarin** [rɔmarɛ̃] *nm* rosemary

**rompre** [rɔ̃pr] **1.** *vt* to break; [pourparlers, relations] to break off **2.** *vi* [casser] to break; [digue] to burst; [fiancés] to break it off **3. se rompre** *vpr* [corde] to break; [digue] to burst

**ronces** [rɔ̃s] *nfpl* [branches] brambles

**rond, -e**[1] [rɔ̃, -ɔ̃d] **1.** *adj* round; [gras] plump; **chiffre rond** whole number **2.** *adv* **10 euros tout rond** 10 euros exactly **3.** *nm* [cercle] circle; **en rond** [s'asseoir] in a circle ■ **rondement** *adv* briskly ■ **rond-point** (*pl* **rondspoints**) *nm Br* roundabout, *Am* traffic circle

**ronde**[2] [rɔ̃d] *nf* [de soldat] round; [de policier] beat; [danse] round (dance); MUS *Br* semibreve, *Am* whole note; **faire sa ronde** [gardien] to do one's rounds

**rondelle** [rɔ̃dɛl] *nf* [tranche] slice

**ronfler** [rɔ̃fle] *vi* [personne] to snore

**ronger** [rɔ̃ʒe] **1.** *vt* to gnaw (at) ; [ver, mer, rouille] to eat into ; **ronger qn** [maladie, chagrin] to consume sb **2. se ronger** *vpr* **se ronger les ongles** to bite one's nails ■ **rongeur** *nm* rodent

**ronronner** [rɔ̃rɔne] *vi* to purr

**roquet** [rɔkɛ] *nm* **a)** [chien] nasty little dog **b)** *Fam & Péj* [personne] nasty little squirt

**roquette** [rɔkɛt] *nf* MIL rocket

**ROR** [ɛroɛr, rɔr] *(abr de* **rougeole oreillons rubéole***) nm* MMR (vaccine)

**rosace** [rozas] *nf* rosette ; [d'église] rose window

**rosbif** [rɔzbif] *nm* **du rosbif** [rôti] roast beef ; [à rôtir] roasting beef ; **un rosbif** a joint of roast / roasting beef

**rose** [roz] **1.** *adj* [couleur] pink ; [situation, teint] rosy **2.** *nm* [couleur] pink **3.** *nf* [fleur] rose ■ **rosé, -e 1.** *adj* pinkish **2.** *adj & nm* [vin] rosé

**roseau, -x** [rozo] *nm* reed

**rosée** [roze] *nf* dew

**rossignol** [rɔsiɲɔl] *nm* [oiseau] nightingale

**rot** [ro] *nm Fam* burp

**rôti** [roti] *nm* **du rôti** roasting meat ; [cuit] roast meat ; **un rôti** a joint ; **rôti de bœuf** (joint of) roast beef

**rotin** [rɔtɛ̃] *nm* rattan

**rôtir** [rotir] *vt & vi* to roast ; **faire rôtir qch** to roast sth

**roue** [ru] *nf* wheel ; **roue dentée** cogwheel ; **être en roue libre** to freewheel ; **les deux roues** two-wheeled vehicles

**rouer** [rwe] *vt* **rouer qn de coups** to thrash sb, to give sb a beating

**rouge** [ruʒ] **1.** *adj* red ; [fer] red-hot **2.** *nm* [couleur] red ; **le feu est au rouge** the (traffic) lights are at red ; **rouge à lèvres** lipstick

**rougeur** [ruʒœr] *nf* redness ; [due à la honte] blush ; [due à l'émotion] flush ; **rougeurs** [irritation] rash, red blotches

**rougir** [ruʒir] **1.** *vt* [visage] to redden **2.** *vi* [de honte] to blush (**de** with) ; [d'émotion] to flush (**de** with)

**rouille** [ruj] **1.** *nf* rust **2.** *adj inv* [couleur] rust(-coloured) ■ **rouillé, -e** *adj* rusty ■ **rouiller 1.** *vi* to rust **2. se rouiller** *vpr* to rust

**rouleau, -x** [rulo] *nm* [outil, vague] roller ; [de papier, de pellicule] roll ; **rouleau à pâtisserie** rolling pin ; **rouleau compresseur** steamroller

**roulement** [rulmɑ̃] *nm* [bruit] rumbling, rumble ; [de tambour, de tonnerre] roll ; [ordre] rotation ; **par roulement** in rotation ; TECH **roulement à billes** ball bearing

**rouler** [rule] **1.** *vt* to roll ; [crêpe, ficelle, manches] to roll up **2.** *vi* [balle] to roll ; [train, voiture] to go, to travel **3. se rouler** *vpr* to roll ; **se rouler dans** [couverture] to roll oneself (up) in ■ **roulant, -e** *adj* [escalier] moving

**roulette** [rulɛt] *nf* [de meuble] castor ; [de dentiste] drill ; [jeu] roulette

**rouli-roulant** [rulirulɑ̃] *nm Can* skateboard

**roulotte** [rulɔt] *nf* [de gitan] caravan

**Roumanie** [rumani] *nf* **la Roumanie** Romania ■ **roumain, -e 1.** *adj* Romanian **2.** *nmf* **Roumain, Roumaine** Romanian **3.** *nm* [langue] Romanian

**rousse** [rus] *voir* **roux**

**rousseur** [rusœr] *nf* **tache de rousseur** freckle ■ **rousselé, e** [rusle] *adj & nmf Can* freckled ■ **roussi** *nm* **ça sent le roussi** there's a smell of burning ■ **roussir 1.** *vt* [brûler] to scorch, to singe **2.** *vi* [feuilles] to turn brown

**route** [rut] *nf* road (**de** to) ; [itinéraire] way, route ; *Fig* [chemin] path ; **grand-route, grande route** main road ; **code de la route** *Br* Highway Code, *Am* traffic regulations ; **en route** on the way, en route ; **par la route** by road ; *Fig* **faire fausse route** to be on the wrong track ; **mettre qch en route** [voiture] to start sth (up) ; **se mettre en route** to set out (**pour** for) ; **une heure de route** [en voiture] an hour's drive ; **faire route vers Paris** to head for Paris ; **route dépar-**

**tementale** secondary road, *Br* B road; **route nationale** *Br* main road, A-road, *Am* (state) highway

**routier, -ère** [rutje, -ɛr] **1.** *adj* **carte / sécurité routière** road map / safety; **réseau routier** road network **2.** *nmf* [camionneur] (long-distance) *Br* lorry or *Am* truck driver **3.** *nm* [restaurant] *Br* ≃ transport cafe, *Am* ≃ truck stop

**routine** [rutin] *nf* routine; **contrôle de routine** routine check ∎ **routinier, -ère** *adj* **travail routinier** routine work; **être routinier** [personne] to be set in one's ways

**rouvrir** [ruvrir] **1.** *vt & vi* to reopen **2. se rouvrir** *vpr* to reopen

**roux, rousse** [ru, rus] **1.** *adj* [cheveux] red, ginger; [personne] red-haired **2.** *nmf* redhead

**royal, -e, -aux** [rwajal, -jo] *adj* [famille, palais] royal; [cadeau, festin] fit for a king; [salaire] princely

**royaume** [rwajom] *nm* kingdom ∎ **Royaume-Uni** *nm* **le Royaume-Uni** the United Kingdom

**royauté** [rwajote] *nf* [monarchie] monarchy

**RSA** *nm* = **revenu de solidarité active**

**RTT** [ɛrtete] *(abr de* **réduction du temps de travail)** *nf* **a)** (statutory) reduction in working hours **b)** (extra) day off *(as a result of shorter working hours)*; **poser / prendre une RTT** to book or claim a day's holiday, *Am* to take a day off

**ruban** [rybɑ̃] *nm* ribbon; [de chapeau] band; **ruban adhésif** sticky or adhesive tape

**rubis** [rybi] *nm* [pierre] ruby; [de montre] jewel

**rubrique** [rybrik] *nf* [article de journal] column; [catégorie, titre] heading

**ruche** [ryʃ] *nf* beehive

**rude** [ryd] *adj* [pénible] tough; [hiver, voix] harsh; [rêche] rough

**rue** [ry] *nf* street; **être à la rue** [sans domicile] to be on the streets ∎ **ruelle** *nf* alley(way)

**ruer** [rɥe] **1.** *vi* [cheval] to kick (out) **2. se ruer** *vpr* [foncer] to rush (**sur** at) ∎ **ruée** *nf* rush; **la ruée vers l'or** the gold rush

**rugby** [rygbi] *nm* rugby ∎ **rugbyman** [rygbiman] *(pl* **-men** [-men]*) nm* rugby player

**rugir** [ryʒir] *vi* to roar ∎ **rugissement** *nm* roar

**rugueux, -euse** [rygø, -øz] *adj* rough

**ruine** [rɥin] *nf* [décombres, destruction, faillite] ruin; **en ruine** [bâtiment] in ruins; **tomber en ruine** [bâtiment] to become a ruin ∎ **ruiner 1.** *vt* [personne, santé, pays] to ruin **2. se ruiner** *vpr* [perdre tout son argent] to ruin oneself; [dépenser beaucoup d'argent] to spend a fortune ∎ **ruineux, -euse** *adj* [goûts, projet] ruinously expensive; [dépense] ruinous; **ce n'est pas ruineux** it won't ruin me / you / *etc*

**ruisseau, -x** [rɥiso] *nm* stream; [caniveau] gutter ∎ **ruisseler** *vi* to stream (**de** with)

**rumeur** [rymœr] *nf* [murmure] murmur; [nouvelle] rumour

**ruminer** [rymine] **1.** *vt* [herbe] to chew **2.** *vi* [vache] to chew the cud

**r1** *(abr de* **rien)** *SMS* nu fn

**rupture** [ryptyr] *nf* breaking; [de fiançailles, de relations] breaking off; [de pourparlers] breakdown (**de** in); [dispute] break-up; **être en rupture de stock** to be out of stock

**rural, -e, -aux** [ryral, -o] *adj* [population] rural; **vie rurale** country life

**ruse** [ryz] *nf* [subterfuge] trick; **la ruse** [habileté] cunning; [fourberie] trickery ∎ **rusé, -e** *adj* cunning, crafty

**Russie** [rysi] *nf* **la Russie** Russia ∎ **russe 1.** *adj* Russian **2.** *nmf* **Russe** Russian **3.** *nm* [langue] Russian

**Rustine®** [rystin] *nf* small rubber patch for repairing bicycle tyres

**rythme** [ritm] *nm* rhythm; [de travail] rate; [allure] pace; **les rythmes scolaires** *the way in which the school year is organized* ∎ **rythmé, -e** *adj* rhythmic(al)

**S, s** [ɛs] *nm inv* S, s

**s'** [s] *voir* **se, si**

**sa** [sa] *voir* **son**

**sable** [sabl] *nm* sand; **sables mouvants** quicksands

**sablé** [sable] *nm* shortbread *Br* biscuit *or Am* cookie ▪ **sablée** *adj f* **pâte sablée** shortcrust pastry

**sablier** [sablije] *nm* hourglass ; *CULIN* egg timer

**saborder** [saborde] *vt* [navire] to scuttle

**sabot** [sabo] *nm* [de cheval] hoof ; [chaussure] clog; **sabot de Denver** wheel clamp

**saboter** [sabote] *vt* [machine, projet] to sabotage ▪ **sabotage** *nm* sabotage ▪ **saboteur, -euse** *nmf* saboteur

**sabre** [sabr] *nm* sabre

**sac** [sak] *nm* bag ; [grand, en toile] sack; **sac à main** handbag; **sac à dos** rucksack; **sac de voyage** travelling bag

**saccade** [sakad] *nf* jerk, jolt; **par saccades** in fits and starts ▪ **saccadé, -e** *adj* jerky

**saccager** [sakaʒe] *vt* [détruire] to wreak havoc in

**sachant, sache(s), sachent** [saʃɑ̃, saʃ] *voir* **savoir**

**sachet** [saʃɛ] *nm* (small) bag; **sachet de thé** teabag

**sacre** [sakr] *nm* a) [de roi] coronation b) *Can* swearword ▪ **sacrer** *vt* a) [roi] to crown b) *Can* to swear

**sacré, -e** [sakre] *adj* [saint] sacred ▪ **sacrement 1.** *nm REL* sacrament **2.** *adv Fam* dashed

**sacrifice** [sakrifis] *nm* sacrifice ▪ **sacrifier 1.** *vt* to sacrifice (**à** to)

**2.** *vi* **sacrifier à la mode** to be a slave to fashion **3. se sacrifier** *vpr* to sacrifice oneself (**pour** for)

**sacrilège** [sakrilɛʒ] **1.** *adj* sacrilegious **2.** *nm* sacrilege

**sadique** [sadik] **1.** *adj* sadistic **2.** *nmf* sadist

**safari** [safari] *nm* safari; **faire un safari** to go on safari

**safran** [safrɑ̃] *nm* saffron

**sage** [saʒ] **1.** *adj* [avisé] wise ; [tranquille] good **2.** *nm* wise man ▪ **sage-femme** (*pl* **sages-femmes**) *nf* midwife ▪ **sagesse** *nf* [philosophie] wisdom ; [calme] good behaviour

**Sagittaire** [saʒitɛr] *nm* **le Sagittaire** [signe] Sagittarius

**saigner** [seɲe] *vi* to bleed; **saigner du nez** to have a nosebleed ▪ **saignant, -e** *adj* [viande] rare

**saillant, -e** [sajɑ̃, -ɑ̃t] *adj* projecting ▪ **saillie** *nf* [partie avant] projection

**sain, -e** [sɛ̃, sɛn] *adj* healthy ; [nourriture] wholesome, healthy; **sain et sauf** safe and sound

**saint, -e** [sɛ̃, sɛ̃t] **1.** *adj* [lieu] holy ; [personne] saintly; **saint Jean** Saint John; **la Sainte Vierge** the Blessed Virgin **2.** *nmf* saint ▪ **Saint-Esprit** *nm* **le Saint-Esprit** the Holy Spirit ▪ **Saint-Sylvestre** *nf* **la Saint-Sylvestre** New Year's Eve

**sainteté** [sɛ̃təte] *nf* [de lieu] holiness ; [de personne] saintliness

**sais** [sɛ] *voir* **savoir**

**saisie** [sezi] *nf* [de biens] seizure ; *ORDINAT* **saisie de données** data capture, keyboarding

**saisir** [sezir] **1.** *vt* to take hold of ; [brusquement] to grab ; [occasion] to seize, to grasp ; [comprendre] to grasp ; *JUR* to seize ; ORDINAT [données] to enter, to key ; [viande] to seal ; **saisir un texte** to type a text **2. se saisir** *vpr* **se saisir de qn /qch** to take hold of sb / sth ; [brusquement] to grab sb /sth ■ **saisissant, -e** *adj* [film] gripping ; [contraste, ressemblance] striking

**saison** [sɛzɔ̃] *nf* season ; **en /hors saison** in /out of season ; **en haute /basse saison** in the high / low season ; **la saison des pluies** the rainy season ■ **saisonnier, -ère** *adj* seasonal

**sait** [sɛ] *voir* **savoir**

**salade** [salad] *nf* [laitue] lettuce ; **salade verte** green salad ; **salade de fruits** fruit salad ; **salade niçoise** salade niçoise ■ **saladerie** [saladri] *nf* salad bar

**salaire** [salɛr] *nm* [mensuel] salary

**salarié, -e** [salarje] **1.** *adj* [payé mensuellement] salaried **2.** *nmf* [payé mensuellement] salaried employee ; **salariés** [de société] employees

**sale** [sal] *adj* dirty ; [dégoûtant] filthy ■ **salement** *adv* [se conduire, manger] disgustingly ■ **saleté** *nf* [manque de soin] dirtiness ; [crasse] dirt ; **saletés** [détritus] *Br* rubbish, *Am* garbage ; **faire des saletés** to make a mess

**saler** [sale] *vt* to salt ■ **salé, -e** *adj* [goût, plat] salty ; [aliment] salted

**salir** [salir] **1.** *vt* to (make) dirty **2. se salir** *vpr* to get dirty ■ **salissant, -e** *adj* [travail] dirty, messy ; [étoffe] that shows the dirt

**salle** [sal] *nf* room ; [très grande, publique] hall ; [de cinéma] *Br* cinema, *Am* movie theater ; [d'hôpital] ward ; **salle à manger** dining room ; **salle de bain(s)** bathroom ; **salle de classe** classroom ; **salle de concert** concert hall ; **salle de jeux** [pour enfants] games room ; [de casino] gaming room ; **salle de spectacle** auditorium ; **salle d'embarquement** [d'aéroport] departure lounge ; **salle d'opération** [d'hôpital] operating *Br* theatre or *Am* room ; **salle des professeurs** *Br* staff room, *Am* teachers' lounge ; **salle de sport** sports hall

**salon** [salɔ̃] *nm* living room ; [exposition] show ; **salon de coiffure** hairdressing salon ; **salon de thé** tea room

**salopette** [salɔpɛt] *nf Br* dungarees, *Am* overalls

**salubre** [salybr] *adj* healthy ■ **salubrité** *nf* healthiness ; **salubrité publique** public health

**saluer** [salɥe] *vt* to greet ; [en partant] to take one's leave of ; [de la main] to wave to ; [de la tête] to nod to ; MIL to salute

**salut** [saly] **1.** *nm* greeting ; [de la main] wave ; [de la tête] nod ; MIL salute ; [sauvegarde] rescue ; REL salvation **2.** *excl Fam* hi! ; [au revoir] bye!

**salutaire** [salytɛr] *adj* salutary

**samedi** [samdi] *nm* Saturday

**SAMU** [samy] *(abr de service d'aide médicale d'urgence)nm* emergency medical service

**sanctifier** [sɑ̃ktifje] *vt* to sanctify

**sanction** [sɑ̃ksjɔ̃] *nf* [approbation, peine] sanction ■ **sanctionner** *vt* [approuver] to sanction ; [punir] to punish

**sanctuaire** [sɑ̃ktɥɛr] *nm* sanctuary

**sandale** [sɑ̃dal] *nf* sandal

**sandwich** [sɑ̃dwitʃ] *nm* sandwich ■ **sandwicherie** [sɑ̃dwitʃri] *nf* sandwich shop ; [avec possibilité de manger sur place] sandwich bar

**sang** [sɑ̃] *nm* blood ■ **sang-froid** *nm* self-control ; **garder son sang-froid** to keep calm ; **tuer qn de sang-froid** to kill sb in cold blood ■ **sanglant, -e** *adj* bloody

**sangle** [sɑ̃gl] *nf* strap

**sanglier** [sɑ̃glije] *nm* wild boar

**sanglot** [sɑ̃glo] *nm* sob ■ **sangloter** *vi* to sob

**sanguin, -e** [sɑ̃gɛ̃, -in] *adj* [tempérament] full-blooded ; **vaisseau sanguin** blood vessel

**sanguinaire** [sɑ̃ginɛr] *adj* bloodthirsty

**sanitaire** [sanitɛr] *adj* [conditions] sanitary; [personnel] medical; **règlement sanitaire** health regulations

**sans** [sɑ̃] ( [sɑ̃z] *before vowel and mute h*) *prép* without; **sans faire qch** without doing sth; **sans qu'il le sache** without him *or* his knowing; **sans cela, sans quoi** otherwise; **sans importance / travail** unimportant / unemployed; **sans argent / manches** penniless / sleeveless ■ **sans-abri** *nmf inv* homeless person; **les sans-abri** the homeless ■ **sans-emploi** *nmf inv* unemployed person ■ **sans-faute** *nm inv Fig* **faire un sans-faute** not to put a foot wrong ■ **sans faute** *adv* without fail ■ **sans-gêne 1.** *adj inv* ill-mannered **2.** *nm inv* lack of manners ■ **sans-papiers** *nmf inv* illegal immigrant ■ **sans-plomb** *nm inv* unleaded, unleaded *Br* petrol *or Am* gas, lead-free *Br* petrol *or Am* gas

**santé** [sɑ̃te] *nf* health; **en bonne / mauvaise santé** in good / bad health; **santé mentale / physique** mental / physical health; **la santé publique** public health; **(à votre) santé !** [en trinquant] cheers!

**saoul** [su] *adj & nm* = **soûl**

**saper** [sape] *vt* to undermine; **saper le moral à qn** to sap sb's morale

**sapeur-pompier** [sapœrpɔ̃pje] *(pl sapeurs-pompiers)* *nm* fireman, firefighter

**saphir** [safir] *nm* sapphire

**sapin** [sapɛ̃] *nm* [arbre, bois] fir; **sapin de Noël** Christmas tree

**Sardaigne** [sardɛɲ] *nf* **la Sardaigne** Sardinia ■ **sarde 1.** *adj* Sardinian **2.** *nmf* **Sarde** Sardinian

**sardine** [sardin] *nf* sardine

**sarrasin** [sarazɛ̃] *nm* [plante] buckwheat

**Satan** [satɑ̃] *nm* Satan

**satellite** [satelit] *nm* satellite; **télévision par satellite** satellite television

**satiété** [sasjete] *nf* **boire / manger à satiété** to eat / drink one's fill

**satin** [satɛ̃] *nm* satin

**satire** [satir] *nf* satire (**contre** on) ■ **satirique** *adj* satirical

**satisfaction** [satisfaksjɔ̃] *nf* satisfaction; **donner satisfaction à qn** to give sb (complete) satisfaction ■ **satisfaire 1.** *vt* to satisfy **2.** *vi* **satisfaire à qch** [conditions] to satisfy sth; [obligation] to fulfil sth, *Am* to fulfill sth ■ **satisfaisant, -e** *adj* [acceptable] satisfactory ■ **satisfait, -e** *adj* satisfied (**de** with)

**saturer** [satyre] *vt* to saturate (**de** with) ■ **saturation** *nf* saturation; **arriver à saturation** to reach saturation point

**Saturne** [satyrn] *nom* ASTRON Saturn

**sauce** [sos] *nf* sauce

**saucisse** [sosis] *nf* sausage; **saucisse de Francfort** frankfurter ■ **saucisson** *nm* (cold) sausage

**sauf¹** [sof] *prép* except; **sauf erreur** if I'm not mistaken

**sauf², sauve** [sof, sov] *adj* **avoir la vie sauve** to be unharmed

**saumon** [somɔ̃] **1.** *nm* salmon **2.** *adj inv* [couleur] salmon (pink)

**sauna** [sona] *nm* sauna

**saupoudrer** [sopudre] *vt* to sprinkle (**de** with)

**saur** [sɔr] *adj m* **hareng saur** smoked herring

**saura, saurait** [sora, sorɛ] *voir* **savoir**

**saut** [so] *nm* jump, leap; **faire un saut** to jump, to leap; **saut à la corde** *Br* skipping, *Am* jumping rope; **saut à l'élastique** bungee jumping; **saut en hauteur** high jump; **saut en longueur** long jump; **saut en parachute** parachute jump; [activité] parachute jumping; ORDINAT **(insérer un) saut de page** (insert) page break

**sauter** [sote] **1.** *vt* [franchir] to jump (over); [mot, repas, classe, ligne] to skip **2.** *vi* [personne, animal] to jump, to leap; [bombe] to go off, to explode; [fusible] to blow; **faire sauter qch** [pont, mine] to blow sth up; [serrure] to force sth; **sauter à la corde** *Br* to skip, *Am* to jump rope; **sauter en parachute** to do a parachute jump

**sauterelle** [sotʀɛl] *nf* grasshopper

**sautes** [sot] *nfpl* [d'humeur, de température] sudden changes (**de** in)

**sauvage** [sovaʒ] *adj* [animal, plante] wild ; [tribu, homme] primitive ; [cruel] savage ; [farouche] unsociable ; [illégal] unauthorized ■ **sauvagerie** *nf* [insociabilité] unsociability ; [cruauté] savagery

**sauve** [sov] *adj voir* **sauf**

**sauvegarde** [sovgaʀd] *nf* safeguard (**contre** against) ; ORDINAT backup ■ **sauvegarder** *vt* to safeguard ; ORDINAT to save

**sauver** [sove] **1.** *vt* [personne] to save, to rescue (**de** from) ; [matériel] to salvage **2. se sauver** *vpr* [s'enfuir] to run away ; [s'échapper] to escape ■ **sauvetage** *nm* [de personne] rescue ■ **sauveteur** *nm* rescuer

**sauvette** [sovɛt] ■ **à la sauvette** *adv* [pour ne pas être vu] on the sly ; **vendre qch à la sauvette** to peddle sth illegally on the streets

**sauveur** [sovœʀ] *nm* saviour

**sava** SMS *abr écrite de* **ça va**

**savant, -e** [savɑ̃, -ɑ̃t] **1.** *adj* [érudit] learned ; [habile] clever **2.** *nm* [scientifique] scientist

**saveur** [savœʀ] *nf* [goût] flavour

**Savoie** [savwa] *nf* **la Savoie** Savoy

**savoir** [savwaʀ] **1.** *vt* to know ; [nouvelle] to have heard ; **savoir lire /nager** to know how to read /swim ; **faire savoir à qn que...** to inform sb that... ; **à savoir** [c'est-à-dire] that is, namely ; **pas que je sache** not that I know of ; **je n'en sais rien** I have no idea, I don't know ; **en savoir long sur qn /qch** to know a lot about sb /sth **2.** *nm* [culture] learning, knowledge ■ **savoir-faire** *nm inv* know-how

**savon** [savɔ̃] *nm* soap ■ **savonnette** *nf* bar of soap ■ **savonneux, -euse** *adj* soapy

**savourer** [savuʀe] *vt* to savour ■ **savoureux, -euse** *adj* tasty

**savoyard, -e** [savwajaʀ, -aʀd] **1.** *adj* Savoyard **2.** *nmf* **Savoyard, Savoyarde** Savoyard

**saxo** [sakso] *nm Fam* [instrument] sax

**saxophone** [saksɔfɔn] *nm* saxophone

**scalpel** [skalpɛl] *nm* scalpel

**scandale** [skɑ̃dal] *nm* scandal ■ **scandaleux, -euse** *adj* scandalous ■ **scandaliser 1.** *vt* to scandalize, to shock **2. se scandaliser** *vpr* to be shocked *or* scandalized (**de** by)

**Scandinavie** [skɑ̃dinavi] *nf* **la Scandinavie** Scandinavia ■ **scandinave 1.** *adj* Scandinavian **2.** *nmf* **Scandinave** Scandinavian

**scanner 1.** [skanɛʀ] *nm* scanner **2.** [skane] *vt* to scan

**scanneur** [skanœʀ] *nm* scanner

**scaphandrier** [skafɑ̃drije] *nm* diver

**sceau, -x** [so] *nm* seal ■ **sceller** *vt* [document] to seal

**scénario** [senarjo] *nm* script, screenplay ■ **scénariste** *nmf* scriptwriter

**scène** [sɛn] *nf* **a)** [de théâtre] scene ; [plateau] stage ; [action] action ; **mettre qch en scène** [pièce] to stage sth ; [film] to direct sth ; *Fig* **sur la scène internationale** on the international scene **b)** [dispute] scene ; **faire une scène** to make a scene ; **scène de ménage** domestic quarrel

**sceptique** [sɛptik] **1.** *adj Br* sceptical, *Am* skeptical **2.** *nmf Br* sceptic, *Am* skeptic

**schéma** [ʃema] *nm* diagram ■ **schématique** *adj* schematic

**schizophrène** [skizɔfrɛn] *adj & nmf* schizophrenic

**scie** [si] *nf* [outil] saw ■ **scier** *vt* to saw

**sciemment** [sjamɑ̃] *adv* knowingly

**science** [sjɑ̃s] *nf* science ; [savoir] knowledge ; **sciences humaines** social sciences ; **sciences naturelles** biology ■ **science-fiction** *nf* science fiction ■ **scientifique 1.** *adj* scientific **2.** *nmf* scientist

**scinder** [sɛ̃de] ■ **se scinder** *vpr* to split up (**en** into)

**scintiller** [sɛ̃tije] *vi* to sparkle; [étoile] to twinkle ■ **scintillement** *nm* sparkling; [d'étoile] twinkling

**scission** [sisjɔ̃] *nf* [de parti] split (**de** in); **scission de l'atome** splitting of the atom

**sclérose** [skleroz] *nf* MÉD sclerosis; *Fig* ossification; **sclérose en plaques** multiple sclerosis

**scolaire** [skɔlɛr] *adj* **année scolaire** school year; **enfant d'âge scolaire** child of school age ■ **scolariser** *vt* [enfant] to send to school ■ **scolarité** *nf* schooling; **pendant ma scolarité** during my school years

**scooter** [skuter] *nm* (motor) scooter; **scooter des mers** jet ski

**score** [skɔr] *nm* score

**scorpion** [skɔrpjɔ̃] *nm* scorpion; **le Scorpion** [signe] Scorpio

**Scotch®** [skɔtʃ] *nm* [ruban adhésif] *Br* sellotape®, *Am* scotch tape® ■ **scotcher** *vt Br* to sellotape, *Am* to tape ■ **scotché, e** *adj* **être scotché devant la télévision** to be glued to the television

**scout, -e** [skut] *adj & nm* scout

**script** [skript] *nm* [écriture] printing; CINÉ script

**scrupule** [skrypyl] *nm* scruple; **sans scrupules** [être] unscrupulous; [agir] unscrupulously ■ **scrupuleux, -euse** *adj* scrupulous

**scruter** [skryte] *vt* to scrutinize

**scrutin** [skrytɛ̃] *nm* [vote] ballot; [élection] poll; [système] voting system; **premier tour de scrutin** first ballot *or* round; **scrutin majoritaire** first-past-the-post voting system

**sculpter** [skylte] *vt* [statue, pierre] to sculpt; [bois] to carve; **sculpter qch dans qch** to sculpt /carve sth out of sth ■ **sculpteur** *nm* sculptor ■ **sculpture** *nf* [art, œuvre] sculpture

**SDF** [ɛsdeɛf] *(abr de* **sans domicile fixe***) nm* person of no fixed abode

---

**se** [sə]

**se** becomes **s'** before vowel or mute h.

*pron pers* **a)** [complément direct] himself; [féminin] herself; [non humain] itself; [indéfini] oneself, *(pl)* themselves; **il se lave** he washes himself; **ils** *ou* **elles se lavent** they wash themselves **b)** [indirect] to himself / herself / itself /oneself; **il se lave les mains** he washes his hands; **elle se lave les mains** she washes her hands **c)** [réciproque] each other; [indirect] to each other; **ils s'aiment** they love each other; **ils** *ou* **elles se parlent** they speak to each other **d)** [passif] **ça se fait** that is done; **ça se vend bien** it sells well

**séance** [seɑ̃s] *nf* [de cinéma] showing, performance; [d'assemblée, de travail] session

**seau, -x** [so] *nm* bucket

**sec, sèche** [sɛk, sɛʃ] **1.** *adj* dry; [fruits, légumes] dried; [ton] curt; **frapper un coup sec** to knock sharply **2.** *adv* [boire] *Br* neat, *Am* straight; [frapper, pleuvoir] hard **3.** *nm* **à sec** dry; **au sec** in a dry place

**sécession** [sesesjɔ̃] *nf* secession; **faire sécession** to secede

**sèche** [sɛʃ] *voir* **sec**

**sécher** [seʃe] **1.** *vt & vi* to dry **2. se sécher** *vpr* to dry oneself ■ **séchage** *nm* drying ■ **sèche-cheveux** *nm inv* hair dryer ■ **sèche-linge** *nm inv Br* tumble dryer, *Am* (clothes) dryer

**sécheresse** [seʃrɛs] *nf* [d'air, de sol, de peau] dryness; [de ton] curtness; [manque de pluie] drought

**séchoir** [seʃwar] *nm* [appareil] dryer; **séchoir à linge** clothes horse

**second, -e¹** [səgɔ̃, -ɔ̃d] **1.** *adj & nmf* second **2.** *nm* [adjoint] second in command; [étage] *Br* second floor, *Am* third floor **3.** *nf* **seconde** RAIL second class; SCOL *Br* ≈ fifth form, *Am* ≈ tenth grade; AUTO [vitesse] second (gear) ■ **secondaire** *adj* secondary; **école secondaire** *Br* secondary school, *Am* high school

**seconde²** [səgɔ̃d] *nf* [instant] second

**seconder** [sgɔ̃de] *vt* to assist

**secouer** [səkwe] *vt* to shake ; [poussière] to shake off ; **secouer qch de qch** [enlever] to shake sth out of sth ; **secouer la tête** [réponse affirmative] to nod (one's head) ; [réponse négative] to shake one's head

**secourir** [səkurir] *vt* to assist, to help ■ **secourable** *adj* helpful ■ **secourisme** *nm* first aid ■ **secouriste** *nmf* first-aid worker

**secours** [səkur] *nm* help ; [financier, matériel] aid ; MIL **les secours** [renforts] relief ; **au secours !** help! ; **porter secours à qn** to give sb help ; **roue de secours** spare wheel

**secousse** [səkus] *nf* jolt, jerk ; [de tremblement de terre] tremor

**secret, -ète** [səkrɛ, -ɛt] **1.** *adj* secret ; [cachottier] secretive **2.** *nm* secret ; **en secret** in secret, secretly

**secrétaire** [səkretɛr] *nmf* secretary ; **secrétaire d'État** Secretary of State ■ **secrétariat** *nm* [bureau] secretary's office ; [d'organisation internationale] secretariat ; [métier] secretarial work

**sectaire** [sɛktɛr] *adj* & *nmf* Péj sectarian

**secte** [sɛkt] *nf* sect

**secteur** [sɛktœr] *nm* [zone] area ; ÉCON sector ; ÉLEC mains ; **le secteur privé/public** the private/public sector ; **secteur primaire/secondaire/tertiaire** primary/secondary/tertiary sector

**section** [sɛksjɔ̃] *nf* section ; [de ligne d'autobus] stage ; MIL platoon ■ **sectionner** *vt* [couper] to sever

**séculaire** [sekylɛr] *adj* [tradition] age-old

**sécurisé, e** [sekyrize] *adj* ORDINAT [transaction, paiement] secure

**sécurité** [sekyrite] *nf* [absence de danger] safety ; [tranquillité] security ; **Sécurité sociale** *Br* Social Security, *Am* Welfare ; **en sécurité** [hors de danger] safe

**sédentaire** [sedɑ̃tɛr] *adj* [personne, métier] sedentary

**séduire** [seduir] *vt* to charm ; [plaire à] to appeal to ; [abuser de] to seduce ■ **séduisant, -e** *adj* attractive ■ **séducteur, -trice** *nmf* seducer, *f* seductress ■ **séduction** *nf* attraction

**ségrégation** [segregasjɔ̃] *nf* segregation

**seigle** [sɛgl] *nm* rye ; **pain de seigle** rye bread

**seigneur** [sɛɲœr] *nm* HIST [noble, maître] lord ; REL **le Seigneur** the Lord

**sein** [sɛ̃] *nm* breast ; **donner le sein à** [enfant] to breastfeed ; **au sein de** within

**Seine** [sɛn] *nf* **la Seine** the Seine

**séisme** [seism] *nm* earthquake

**seize** [sɛz] *adj* & *nm inv* sixteen ■ **seizième** *adj* & *nmf* sixteenth

**séjour** [seʒur] *nm* stay ; **un séjour court/long** a short/long stay ; **séjour linguistique** language-learning trip ; **(salle de) séjour** living room ■ **séjourner** *vi* to stay

**sel** [sɛl] *nm* salt ; *Fig* [piquant] spice ; **sel de mer** sea salt ; **sels de bain** bath salts

**sélectif, -ive** [selɛktif, -iv] *adj* selective ■ **sélection** *nf* selection ■ **sélectionner** *vt* to select ■ **sélectionneur** *nm* selector

**self** [sɛlf] *nm* self-service restaurant

**selle** [sɛl] *nf* [de cheval, de vélo] saddle

**selon** [səlɔ̃] *prép* according to ; **selon que...** depending on whether...

**semaine** [səmɛn] *nf* week ; **en semaine** in the week

**semblable** [sɑ̃blabl] *adj* similar (**à** to) ; **de semblables propos** such remarks

**semblant** [sɑ̃blɑ̃] *nm* **faire semblant** to pretend (**de faire** to do)

**sembler** [sɑ̃ble] **1.** *vi* to seem (**à** to) ; **il (me) semble vieux** he seems or looks old (to me) ; **sembler faire qch** to seem to do sth **2.** *v impers* **il semble que...** it seems that... ; **il me semble que...** it seems to me that...

**semelle** [səmɛl] *nf* [de chaussure] sole ; [intérieure] insole

**semer** [səme] *vt* [graines] to sow ; *Fig* [poursuivant] to shake off ; *Fig* **semé de** strewn with ■ **semence** *nf* seed

**semestre** [səmɛstr] *nm* half-year ; UNIV semester

**séminaire** [seminɛr] *nm* [colloque] seminar

**semi-précieux, euse** [səmipresjø, øz] *(mpl* **semi-précieux,** *fpl* **semi-précieuses)** *adj* semi-precious

**semi-remorque** [səmirəmɔrk] *(pl* **semi-remorques)** *nm* [camion] *Br* articulated lorry, *Am* semi(trailer), trailer truck

**semoule** [səmul] *nf* semolina

**sénat** [sena] *nm* senate ■ **sénateur** *nm* senator

**sénile** [senil] *adj* senile

**senior** [senjɔr] *adj* & *nmf* **a)** SPORT senior **b)** [personnes de plus de 50 ans] over-50

**sens** [sɑ̃s] *nm* **a)** [faculté, raison, instinct] sense ; **avoir le sens de l'humour** to have a sense of humour ; **avoir du bon sens** to be sensible ; **bon sens** common sense **b)** [signification] meaning, sense ; **ça n'a pas de sens** that doesn't make sense **c)** [direction] direction ; AUTO **sens giratoire** *Br* roundabout, *Am* traffic circle, *Am* rotary ; **sens interdit ou unique** [rue] one-way street ; **'sens interdit'** 'no entry' ; **à sens unique** [rue] one-way ; **dans le sens des aiguilles d'une montre** clockwise ; **dans le sens inverse des aiguilles d'une montre** *Br* anticlockwise, *Am* counterclockwise

**sensation** [sɑ̃sasjɔ̃] *nf* feeling, sensation ; **faire sensation** to create a sensation

**sensé, -e** [sɑ̃se] *adj* sensible

**sensible** [sɑ̃sibl] *adj* sensitive (**à** to) ; [douloureux] tender, sore ; [perceptible] perceptible ; [progrès] noticeable ■ **sensibiliser** *vt* **sensibiliser qn à qch** [problème] to make sb aware of sth ■ **sensibilité** *nf* sensitivity

**sensuel, -elle** [sɑ̃sɥɛl] *adj* sensual ■ **sensualité** *nf* sensuality

**sentence** [sɑ̃tɑ̃s] *nf* JUR [jugement] sentence

**sentier** [sɑ̃tje] *nm* path

**sentiment** [sɑ̃timɑ̃] *nm* feeling ; **avoir le sentiment que...** to have a feeling that... ■ **sentimental, -e, -aux** *adj* sentimental ; **vie sentimentale** love life

**sentinelle** [sɑ̃tinɛl] *nf* sentry

**sentir** [sɑ̃tir] **1.** *vt* [douleur] to feel ; [odeur] to smell ; **sentir le moisi** to smell musty ; **sentir le poisson** to smell of fish **2.** *vi* to smell ; **sentir bon/mauvais** to smell good/bad **3. se sentir** *vpr* **se sentir humilié** to feel humiliated

**séparation** [separasjɔ̃] *nf* separation ; [départ] parting

**séparer** [separe] **1.** *vt* to separate (**de** from) **2. se séparer** *vpr* [couple] to separate ; [cortège] to disperse, to break up ; **se séparer de qn/qch** [donner, jeter] to part with sb/sth ■ **séparé, -e** *adj* [distinct] separate ; [époux] separated (**de** from)

**sept** [sɛt] *adj* & *nm inv* seven

**septante** [sɛptɑ̃t] *adj* [en Belgique, en Suisse] seventy

**septembre** [sɛptɑ̃br] *nm* September

**septième** [sɛtjɛm] *adj* & *nmf* seventh ; **un septième** a seventh

**sépulture** [sepyltyr] *nf* burial ; [lieu] burial place

**séquelles** [sekɛl] *nfpl* [de maladie] after-effects

**séquence** [sekɑ̃s] *nf* sequence

**séquestrer** [sekɛstre] *vt* **séquestrer qn** to keep sb locked up

**sera, serait** [səra, sərɛ] *voir* **être**

**Serbie** [sɛrbi] *nf* **la Serbie** Serbia ■ **serbe 1.** *adj* Serbian **2.** *nmf* **Serbe** Serbian

**serein, -e** [sərɛ̃, -ɛn] *adj* serene

**sérénade** [serenad] *nf* serenade

**sérénité** [serenite] *nf* serenity

**sergent, e** [sɛrʒɑ̃, ɑ̃t] *nmf* sergeant

**série** [seri] *nf* series ; [ensemble] set ; **de série** [article, voiture] standard ;

fin de série discontinued line; **fabrication en série** mass production; **numéro hors série** special issue

**sérieux, -euse** [serjø, -jøz] **1.** *adj* [personne, doute] serious; [de bonne foi] genuine, serious; [fiable] reliable; **de sérieuses chances de...** a good chance of... **2.** *nm* [application] seriousness; [fiabilité] reliability; **prendre qn/qch au sérieux** to take sb/sth seriously

**seringue** [sərɛ̃g] *nf* syringe

**serment** [sɛrmɑ̃] *nm* [affirmation solennelle] oath; [promesse] pledge; **prêter serment** to take an oath; **faire le serment de faire qch** to swear to do sth; JUR **sous serment** on or under oath

**sermon** [sɛrmɔ̃] *nm* [de prêtre] sermon ■ **sermonner** *vt* [faire la morale à] to lecture

**séropositif, -ive** [seropozitif, -iv] *adj* MÉD HIV positive ■ **séronégatif, -ive** *adj* MÉD HIV negative

**serpent** [sɛrpɑ̃] *nm* snake

**serpenter** [sɛrpɑ̃te] *vi* [sentier] to meander

**serpillière** [sɛrpijɛr] *nf* floorcloth; **passer la serpillière dans la cuisine** to clean the kitchen floor

**serre** [sɛr] *nf* greenhouse

**serrer** [sere] **1.** *vt* [tenir] to grip; [nœud, vis] to tighten; [poing] to clench; *Can* [ranger] to put away; *Can* [enfermer, mettre en lieu sûr] to keep in a safe place; **serrer la main à qn** to shake hands with sb; **serrer qn** [sujet: vêtement] to be too tight for sb **2.** *vi* **serrer à droite** to keep (to the) right **3. se serrer** *vpr* [se rapprocher] to squeeze up; **se serrer contre** to squeeze up against ■ **serré, -e** *adj* [nœud, vêtement] tight; [gens] packed (together); [lutte] close ■ **serre-tête** *nm inv* headband

**serrure** [seryr] *nf* lock

**serveur, -euse** [sɛrvœr, -øz] **1.** *nmf* waiter, *f* waitress; [de bar] barman, *f* barmaid **2.** *nm* ORDINAT server

**serviable** [sɛrvjabl] *adj* helpful, obliging

**service** [sɛrvis] *nm* service; [travail] duty; [pourboire] service (charge); [d'entreprise] department; [au tennis] serve, service; **un service** [aide] a favour; **rendre service** to be of service (**à qn** to sb); **être de service** to be on duty; **faire son service (militaire)** to do one's military service; **les services sociaux** the social services; **service à café** coffee set; **service (non) compris** service (not) included; **service après-vente** after sales service

**serviette** [sɛrvjɛt] *nf* [pour s'essuyer] towel; [sac] briefcase; **serviette de bain/de toilette** bath/hand towel; **serviette de table** napkin, *Br* serviette ■ **serviette-éponge** *(pl* **serviettes-éponges)** *nf* terry towel

**servir** [sɛrvir] **1.** *vt* to serve (**qch à qn** sb with sth, **sth** to sb); [convive] to wait on **2.** *vi* to serve; **servir à qch/à faire qch** to be used for sth/to do or for doing sth; **ça ne sert à rien** it's useless, it's no good or use (**de faire** doing); **servir de qch** to be used for sth, to serve as sth **3. se servir** *vpr* [à table] to help oneself (**de** to); **se servir de qch** [utiliser] to use sth

**serviteur** [sɛrvitœr] *nm* servant

**ses** [se] *voir* **son**

**session** [sesjɔ̃] *nf* session; *Can* SCOL & UNIV academic session; ORDINAT **ouvrir une session** to log in or on; ORDINAT **fermer** *ou* **clore une session** to log out or off

**set** [sɛt] *nm* [au tennis] set; **set de table** place mat

**seuil** [sœj] *nm* [entrée] doorway; *Fig* [limite] threshold; *Fig* **au seuil de** on the threshold of

**seul, -e** [sœl] **1.** *adj* [sans compagnie] alone; [unique] only; **tout seul** by oneself, on one's own, all alone; **se sentir seul** to feel lonely or alone; **la seule femme** the only woman; **un seul chat** only one cat; **une seule fois** only once; **pas un seul livre** not a single book; **seuls les garçons...** only the boys... **2.** *adv* **(tout) seul** [rentrer, vivre] by oneself, alone, on one's own; [parler]

to oneself **3.** *nmf* **le seul, la seule** the only one; **un seul, une seule** only one, one only; **pas un seul** not (a single) one

**seulement** [sœlmɑ̃] *adv* only; **non seulement... mais encore...** not only... but (also)...

**sève** [sɛv] *nf* [de plante] sap

**sévère** [sevɛr] *adj* severe; [parents, professeur] strict ▪ **sévérité** *nf* severity; [de parents] strictness

**sévices** [sevis] *nmpl* ill-treatment; **sévices à enfant** child abuse

**sexe** [sɛks] *nm* [catégorie, sexualité] sex; [organes] genitals ▪ **sexiste** *adj* & *nmf* sexist ▪ **sexualité** *nf* sexuality ▪ **sexuel, -elle** *adj* sexual

**SF** *(abr de* **science-fiction***) nf* sci-fi; **film de SF** sci-fi movie

**shampooing** [ʃɑ̃pwɛ̃] *nm* shampoo; **shampooing colorant** rinse; **faire un shampooing à qn** to shampoo sb's hair ▪ **shampouiner** [ʃɑ̃pwine] *vt* to shampoo

**shooter** [ʃute] *vt* & *vi* [au football] to shoot

**shopping** [ʃɔpiŋ] *nm* shopping; **faire du shopping** to go (out) shopping

**short** [ʃɔrt] *nm* (pair of) shorts

**si¹** [si]

si becomes **s'** [s] before **il, ils.**

**1.** *conj* if; **si je pouvais** if I could; **s'il vient** if he comes; **si j'étais roi** if I were *or* was king; **je me demande si...** I wonder whether *or* if...; **si on restait ?** [suggestion] what if we stayed?; **si oui** if so; **si non** if not; **si seulement** if only **2.** *adv* **a)** [tellement] so; **pas si riche que tu crois** not as rich as you think; **un si bon dîner** such a good dinner; **si bien que...** so much so that... **b)** [après négative] yes; **tu ne viens pas ? — si !** you're not coming? — yes (I am)!

**si²** [si] *nm inv* [note] B

**siamois, -e** [sjamwa, -waz] *adj* Siamese; **frères siamois, sœurs siamoises** Siamese twins

**Sicile** [sisil] *nf* **la Sicile** Sicily

**SIDA** [sida] *(abr de* **syndrome immunodéficitaire acquis***) nm* AIDS; **virus du SIDA** AIDS virus

**sidérurgie** [sideryrʒi] *nf* iron and steel industry

**siècle** [sjɛkl] *nm* century

**siège** [sjɛʒ] *nm* **a)** [meuble, centre & POL] seat; [d'autorité, de parti] headquarters; **siège social** head office **b)** MIL siege; **faire le siège de** to lay siege to

**siéger** [sjeʒe] *vi* [assemblée] to sit

**sien, sienne** [sjɛ̃, sjɛn] **1.** *pron poss* **le sien, la sienne, les sien(ne)s** [d'homme] his; [de femme] hers; [de chose] its; **les deux siens** his / her two **2.** *nmpl* **les siens** [sa famille] one's family **3.** *nfpl* **faire des siennes** to be up to one's tricks again

**sieste** [sjɛst] *nf* siesta; **faire la sieste** to have a nap

**siffler** [sifle] **1.** *vi* to whistle; [avec un sifflet] to blow one's whistle; [gaz, serpent] to hiss **2.** *vt* [chanson] to whistle; [chien] to whistle at; SPORT [faute, fin de match] to blow one's whistle for; [acteur, pièce] to boo; **se faire siffler** [acteur] to be booed ▪ **sifflement** [-əmɑ̃] *nm* whistling; [de serpent, de gaz] hissing

**sifflet** [siflɛ] *nm* [instrument] whistle; **sifflets** [de spectateurs] booing ▪ **siffloter** *vt* & *vi* to whistle

**sigle** [sigl] *nm* [initiales] abbreviation; [acronyme] acronym

**signal, -aux** [siɲal, -o] *nm* signal; **signal d'alarme** alarm signal; **signal d'alerte** warning signal; **signal lumineux** warning light; **signal sonore** warning sound

**signalement** [siɲalmɑ̃] *nm* description, particulars

**signaler** [siɲale] **1.** *vt* [faire remarquer] to point out (**à qn** to sb; **que** that); [par panneau] to signpost; [dire à la police] to report (**à** to) **2. se signaler** *vpr* **se signaler par qch** to distinguish oneself by sth

**signalisation** [siɲalizasjɔ̃] *nf* [sur les routes] signposting; **signalisation routière** [signaux] road signs

**signature** [siɲatyr] *nf* signature ; [action] signing

**signe** [siɲ] *nm* [indice] sign, indication ; **en signe de protestation** as a sign of protest ; **faire signe à qn** [geste] to motion (to) sb (**de faire** to do) ; [contacter] to get in touch with sb ; **faire signe que oui** to nod (one's head) ; **faire signe que non** to shake one's head ; **signe particulier** distinguishing mark ; **signe astrologique** astrological sign

**signer** [siɲe] **1.** *vt* to sign **2. se signer** *vpr* to cross oneself

**signet** [siɲe] *nm* [d'un livre & INTERNET] bookmark

**signification** [siɲifikɑsjɔ̃] *nf* meaning ■ **significatif, -ive** *adj* significant, meaningful

**signifier** [siɲifje] *vt* to mean (**que** that)

**silence** [silɑ̃s] *nm* silence ; MUS rest ; **en silence** in silence ; **garder le silence** to keep quiet *or* silent (**sur** about) ■ **silencieux, -euse 1.** *adj* silent **2.** *nm* [de voiture] *Br* silencer, *Am* muffler ; [d'arme] silencer

**silhouette** [silwɛt] *nf* outline ; [en noir] silhouette ; [du corps] figure

**sillonner** [sijɔne] *vt* [parcourir] to criss-cross

**SIM** [sim] *(abr de subscriber identity module)* *nm* **carte SIM** SIM card

**simagrées** [simagre] *nfpl* **faire des simagrées** to make a fuss

**similaire** [similɛr] *adj* similar ■ **similitude** *nf* similarity

**simple** [sɛ̃pl] *adj* [facile, crédule, sans prétention] simple ; [fait d'un élément] single ; [employé, particulier] ordinary ■ **simplicité** *nf* simplicity

**simplifier** [sɛ̃plifje] *vt* to simplify ■ **simplification** *nf* simplification

**simpliste** [sɛ̃plist] *adj* simplistic

**simuler** [simyle] *vt* [reproduire] to simulate ; [feindre] to feign

**simultané, -e** [simyltane] *adj* simultaneous

**sincère** [sɛ̃sɛr] *adj* sincere ■ **sincèrement** [sɛ̃sɛrmɑ̃] *adv* **a)** [franchement]

honestly, sincerely **b)** [vraiment] really, truly ■ **sincérité** *nf* sincerity ; **en toute sincérité** quite sincerely

**sine qua non** [sinekwanɔn] *adj inv* **condition sine qua non** prerequisite

**Singapour** [sɛ̃gapur] *nm* Singapore

**singe** [sɛ̃ʒ] *nm* monkey ; **grand singe** ape

**singulariser** [sɛ̃gylarize] ■ **se singulariser** *vpr* to draw attention to oneself

**singulier, -ère** [sɛ̃gylje, -ɛr] *adj* [peu ordinaire] peculiar, odd ■ **singularité** *nf* peculiarity

**sinistre** [sinistr] **1.** *adj* [effrayant] sinister ; [triste] grim **2.** *nm* disaster ; [incendie] fire ; JUR [dommage] damage ■ **sinistré, -e 1.** *adj* [population, région] disaster-stricken **2.** *nmf* disaster victim

**sinon** [sinɔ̃] *conj* [autrement] otherwise, or else ; [sauf] except (**que** that) ; [si ce n'est] if not

**sinueux, -euse** [sinɥø, -øz] *adj* winding

**sinusite** [sinyzit] *nf* sinusitis ; **avoir une sinusite** to have sinusitis

**siphon** [sifɔ̃] *nm* siphon ; [d'évier] trap, *Br* U-bend

**sirène** [sirɛn] *nf* [d'usine] siren ; [femme] mermaid

**sirop** [siro] *nm* syrup ; [à diluer] (fruit) cordial ; **sirop contre la toux** cough mixture

**sismique** [sismik], **séismique** [seismik] *adj* seismic ; **secousse sismique** earth tremor

**site** [sit] *nm* [endroit] site ; [pittoresque] beauty spot ; **site touristique** place of interest ; **site classé** conservation area ; ORDINAT **site Internet** Internet site ; **site Web** website ; **visiter un site Web** to visit a website

**sitôt** [sito] *adv* **sitôt que...** as soon as... ; **sitôt levée, elle partit** as soon as she was up, she left ; **pas de sitôt** not for some time

**situation** [sitɥɑsjɔ̃] *nf* situation, position ; [emploi] position ; **situation de**

**famille** marital status ■ **situé, -e** *adj* [maison] situated (**à** in) ■ **situer 1.** *vt* [placer] to situate ; [trouver] to locate ; [dans le temps] to set **2. se situer** *vpr* [se trouver] to be situated

**six** [sis] ( [si] *before consonant,* [siz] *before vowel*) *adj* & *nm inv* six ■ **sixième** [sizjɛm] **1.** *adj* & *nmf* sixth ; **un sixième** a sixth **2.** *nf* SCOL *Br* ≃ first form, *Am* ≃ sixth grade

**skate** [skɛt], **skateboard** [skɛtbɔrd] *nm* skateboard ; **faire du skate** to skateboard

**sketch** [skɛtʃ] ( *pl* **sketches**) *nm* sketch

**ski** [ski] *nm* [objet] ski ; [sport] skiing ; **faire du ski** to ski ; **ski alpin** downhill skiing ; **ski de fond** cross-country skiing ; **ski nautique** water skiing ■ **skiable** *adj* [piste] skiable, fit for skiing ■ **skicross** [skikrɔs] *nm* ski cross ■ **skier** *vi* to ski ■ **skieur, -euse** *nmf* skier ■ **sky-surfing** [skajsœrfiŋ] *(pl* **sky-surfings**), **sky-surf** *(pl* **sky-surfs**) *nm* SPORT sky-surfing

**slalom** [slalɔm] *nm* SPORT slalom

**slam** [slam] *nm* [poésie] slam ■ **slameur, euse** *nmf* slammer

**slave** [slav] **1.** *adj* Slav ; [langue] Slavonic **2.** *nmf* **Slave** Slav

**slip** [slip] *nm* [d'homme] briefs, underpants ; [de femme] panties, *Br* knickers

**sloche, slush** [slɔʃ] *nf Can* slush

**slogan** [slɔgɑ̃] *nm* slogan

**Slovaquie** [slɔvaki] *nf* **la Slovaquie** Slovakia

**Slovénie** [slɔveni] *nf* **la Slovénie** Slovenia

**slt** SMS *abr écrite de* **salut**

**slush** [slɔʃ] *Can nf* = **sloche**

**SMIC** [smik] *(abr de* **salaire minimum interprofessionnel de croissance)** *nm* guaranteed minimum wage

**smoking** [smɔkiŋ] *nm* [veston, costume] dinner jacket, *Am* tuxedo

**SNCF** [ɛsɛnseɛf] *(abr de* **Société nationale des chemins de fer français)** *nf* French national railway company

**snob** [snɔb] **1.** *adj* snobbish **2.** *nmf* snob ■ **snobisme** *nm* snobbery

**snowboard** [snobɔrd] *nm* [planche] snowboard ; [sport] snowboarding ; **faire du snowboard** to snowboard

**sobre** [sɔbr] *adj* sober ■ **sobriété** *nf* sobriety

**sociable** [sɔsjabl] *adj* sociable ■ **sociabilité** *nf* sociability

**social, -e, -aux** [sɔsjal, -o] *adj* social ■ **socialisme** *nm* socialism ■ **socialiste** *adj* & *nmf* socialist

**société** [sɔsjete] *nf* [communauté] society ; [compagnie] company ; **société anonyme** *Br* (public) limited company, *Am* corporation ■ **sociétaire** *nmf* [membre] member

**sociologie** [sɔsjɔlɔʒi] *nf* sociology ■ **sociologique** *adj* sociological ■ **sociologue** *nmf* sociologist

**sœur** [sœr] *nf* sister ; [religieuse] sister, nun

**sofa** [sɔfa] *nm* sofa, settee

**soi** [swa] *pron pers* oneself ; **chacun pour soi** every man for himself ; **chez soi** at home ; **cela va de soi** it's self-evident (**que** that) ■ **soi-même** *pron* oneself

**soi-disant** [swadizɑ̃] **1.** *adj inv* socalled **2.** *adv* supposedly

**soie** [swa] *nf* [tissu] silk

**soient** [swa] *voir* **être**

**soif** [swaf] *nf* thirst (**de** for) ; **avoir soif** to be thirsty

**soigner** [swaɲe] **1.** *vt* to look after, to take care of ; [sujet : médecin - malade, maladie] to treat ; [présentation, travail] to take care over ; **se faire soigner** to have (medical) treatment **2. se soigner** *vpr* to take care of oneself, to look after oneself ■ **soigné, -e** *adj* [personne, vêtement] neat, tidy ; [travail] careful

**soigneux, -euse** [swaɲø, -øz] *adj* [attentif] careful (**de** with) ; [propre] neat, tidy

**soin** [swɛ̃] *nm* [attention] care ; MÉD **soins** treatment, care ;

avoir *ou* **prendre soin de qch/de faire
qch** to take care of sth/to do sth; **avec
soin** carefully, with care

**soir** [swar] *nm* evening; **le soir** [chaque
soir] in the evening(s); **à neuf heures
du soir** at nine in the evening; **repas
du soir** evening meal

**soirée** [sware] *nf* evening; [réunion]
party

**sois, soit**[1] [swa] *voir* **être**

**soit**[2] **1.** [swa] *conj* [à savoir] that is (to
say); **soit... soit...** either... or... **2.** [swat]
*adv* [oui] very well

**soixante** [swasɑ̃t] *adj & nm inv* sixty
■ **soixantaine** *nf* **une soixantaine
(de)** [nombre] (about) sixty; **avoir la
soixantaine** [âge] to be about sixty

**soixante-dix** [swasɑ̃tdis] *adj & nm inv*
seventy ■ **soixante-dixième** *adj &
nmf* seventieth

**soixantième** [swasɑ̃tjɛm] *adj & nmf*
sixtieth

**soja** [sɔʒa] *nm* [plante] soya; **germes** *ou*
**pousses de soja** beansprouts

**sol**[1] [sɔl] *nm* ground; [plancher] floor;
[territoire, terrain] soil

**sol**[2] [sɔl] *nm inv* [note] G

**solaire** [sɔlɛr] *adj* solar; **huile solaire**
sun-tan oil

**soldat** [sɔlda] *nm* soldier

**solde** [sɔld] **1.** *nm* [de compte, à payer]
balance; **en solde** [acheter] in the sales,
*Am* on sale; **soldes** [marchandises] sale
goods; [vente] (clearance) sale(s) **2.** *nf*
[de soldat] pay

**solder** [sɔlde] **1.** *vt* [articles] to clear,
to sell off; [compte] to pay the balance
of **2. se solder** *vpr* **se solder par un
échec** to end in failure ■ **soldé, -e** *adj*
[article] reduced

**sole** [sɔl] *nf* [poisson] sole

**soleil** [sɔlɛj] *nm* sun; [chaleur, lumière]
sunshine; **au soleil** in the sun; **il fait
soleil** it's sunny

**solennel, -elle** [sɔlanɛl] *adj* solemn

**solidaire** [sɔlidɛr] *adj* **être solidaire**
[ouvriers] to show solidarity (**de** with)
■ **solidarité** *nf* [entre personnes] solidarity

**solide** [sɔlid] **1.** *adj* [objet, état] solid;
[amitié] strong; [nerfs] sound; [per-
sonne] sturdy **2.** *nm* [corps] solid
■ **solidité** *nf* [d'objet] solidity

**soliste** [sɔlist] *nmf* MUS soloist

**solitaire** [sɔlitɛr] **1.** *adj* [par choix] solitary; [involontairement] lonely **2.** *nmf*
loner; **en solitaire** on one's own ■ **solitude** *nf* solitude; **aimer la solitude** to
like being alone

**solliciter** [sɔlisite] *vt* [audience] to request; [emploi] to apply for; **solliciter
qn** [faire appel à] to appeal to sb (**de
faire** to do) ■ **sollicitation** *nf* request

**sollicitude** [sɔlisityd] *nf* solicitude,
concern

**soluble** [sɔlybl] *adj* [substance, pro-
blème] soluble

**solution** [sɔlysjɔ̃] *nf* [de problème]
solution (**de** to); [mélange chimique]
solution

**sombre** [sɔ̃br] *adj* dark; [triste] sombre,
gloomy; **il fait sombre** it's dark

**sombrer** [sɔ̃bre] *vi* [bateau] to sink;
*Fig* **sombrer dans** [folie, sommeil] to
sink into

**sommaire** [sɔmɛr] **1.** *adj* summary;
[repas] basic **2.** *nm* [table des matières]
contents

**somme** [sɔm] **1.** *nf* sum; **faire la somme
de** to add up; **en somme, somme toute**
in short **2.** *nm* [sommeil] nap; **faire un
somme** to have a nap

**sommeil** [sɔmɛj] *nm* sleep; **avoir sommeil** to feel sleepy; **être en plein sommeil** to be fast asleep ■ **sommeiller**
*vi* to doze

**sommelier** [sɔməlje] *nm* wine waiter

**sommer** [sɔme] *vt* **sommer qn de faire
qch** to summon sb to do sth

**sommes** [sɔm] *voir* **être**

**sommet** [sɔme] *nm* top; [de montagne]
summit, top

**sommier** [sɔmje] *nm* [de lit] base

**sommité** [sɔmite] nf leading light (**de** in)

**somnambule** [sɔmnɑ̃byl] nmf sleep-walker; **être somnambule** to sleep-walk

**somnifère** [sɔmnifɛr] nm sleeping pill

**somnoler** [sɔmnɔle] vi to doze

**somptueux, -euse** [sɔ̃ptɥø, -øz] adj sumptuous

**son¹** [sɔ̃] nm [bruit] sound

**son²** [sɔ̃] nm [de grains] bran

**son³, sa, ses** [sɔ̃, sa, se]

> sa becomes son [sɔ̃n] before a vowel or mute h.

adj poss [d'homme] his; [de femme] her; [de chose] its; [indéfini] one's; **son père / sa mère** his / her / one's father / mother; **son ami(e)** his / her / one's friend

**sondage** [sɔ̃daʒ] nm [de terrain] drilling; **sondage (d'opinion)** opinion poll

**sonder** [sɔ̃de] vt [rivière] to sound; [terrain] to drill; Fig [personne, l'opinion] to sound out

**songe** [sɔ̃ʒ] nm dream

**songer** [sɔ̃ʒe] **1.** vi **songer à qch / à faire qch** to think of sth / of doing sth **2.** vt **songer que...** to think that... ■ **songeur, -euse** adj thoughtful, pensive

**sonné, e** [sɔne] adj a) [passé] **il est trois heures sonnées** it's gone three o'clock; Fam & Fig **il a quarante ans bien sonnés** he's the wrong side of forty b) Fam & Fig [étourdi] groggy

**sonner** [sɔne] **1.** vi to ring; [cor, cloches] to sound; **on a sonné (à la porte)** there's someone at the door **2.** vt [cloche] to ring; [domestique] to ring for; [cor] to sound; [l'heure] to strike

**sonnerie** [sɔnri] nf [son] ring(ing); [de cor] sound; [appareil] bell; [de téléphone] Br ringing tone, Am ring

**sonnette** [sɔnɛt] nf bell; **coup de sonnette** ring; **sonnette d'alarme** alarm (bell)

**sonore** [sɔnɔr] adj [rire] loud; [voix] resonant; **effet sonore** sound effect ■ **sonorité** nf [de salle] acoustics; [de violon] tone

**sont** [sɔ̃] voir être

**sophistiqué, -e** [sɔfistike] adj sophisticated

**soporifique** [sɔpɔrifik] adj [médicament, discours] soporific

**sorbet** [sɔrbɛ] nm sorbet

**sorcellerie** [sɔrsɛlri] nf witchcraft, sorcery ■ **sorcier** nm sorcerer ■ **sorcière** nf witch

**sordide** [sɔrdid] adj [acte, affaire] sordid; [maison] squalid

**sort** [sɔr] nm [destin] fate; [condition] lot; [maléfice] spell

**sortant, -e** [sɔrtɑ̃, -ɑ̃t] adj [numéro] winning; [député] outgoing

**sorte** [sɔrt] nf sort, kind (**de** of); **toutes sortes de** all sorts or kinds of; **en quelque sorte** in a way, as it were; **de (telle) sorte que tu apprennes** so that or in such a way that you may learn; **faire en sorte que...** (+ subjunctive) to see to it that...

**sortie** [sɔrti] nf [porte] exit, way out; [action de sortir] leaving, exit, departure; [promenade] walk; [de film, de disque] release; [de livre] appearance; **être de sortie** to be out; **sortie de bain** bathrobe; **sortie de secours** emergency exit; ORDINAT **sortie imprimante** printout

**sortir** [sɔrtir] **1.** (aux être) vi to go out, to leave; [pour s'amuser] to go out; [film] to come out; [numéro gagnant] to come up; **sortir de** [endroit] to leave; [université] to be a graduate of; [famille, milieu] to come from; [rails] to come off; **sortir de l'ordinaire** to be out of the ordinary **2.** (aux avoir) vt to take out (**de** of); [film, livre] to bring out **3.** se **sortir** vpr a) Fig [de pétrin] to get out; **s'en sortir** [en réchapper] to come out of it b) [y arriver] to get through it

**SOS** [ɛsoɛs] nm SOS; **lancer un SOS** to send (out) an SOS

**sosie** [sozi] nm double

**sottise** [sɔtiz] *nf* foolishness ; [action, parole] foolish thing

**souche** [suʃ] *nf* [d'arbre] stump ; [de carnet] stub, counterfoil ; [de virus] strain

**souci** [susi] *nm* [inquiétude] worry, concern ; [préoccupation] concern (**de** for) ; **se faire du souci** to worry, to be worried ■ **se soucier** *vpr* **se soucier de** to be worried *or* concerned about ■ **soucieux, -euse** *adj* worried, concerned (**de qch** about sth)

**soucoupe** [sukup] *nf* saucer

**soudain, -e** [sudɛ̃, -ɛn] **1.** *adj* sudden **2.** *adv* suddenly ■ **soudaineté** *nf* suddenness

**Soudan** [sudɑ̃] *nm* **le Soudan** Sudan ; **le Soudan du Sud** South Sudan

**souder** [sude] **1.** *vt* [par alliage] to solder ; [par soudure autogène] to weld ; **lampe à souder** blowlamp **2. se souder** *vpr* [os] to knit (together) ■ **soudure** *nf* [par alliage] soldering ; [autogène] welding

**souffle** [sufl] *nm* [d'air, de vent] breath, puff ; [respiration] breathing ; [de bombe] blast ; **reprendre son souffle** to get one's breath back ■ **souffler 1.** *vi* to blow ; [haleter] to puff ; **laisser souffler qn** [se reposer] to give sb time to catch his / her breath **2.** *vt* [bougie] to blow out ; [fumée, verre] to blow ; [faire exploser] to blast ; [chuchoter] to whisper

**souffrance** [sufrɑ̃s] *nf* suffering ; **en souffrance** [colis] unclaimed

**souffrir** [sufrir] *vi* to suffer ; **souffrir de** to suffer from ; **faire souffrir qn** [physiquement] to hurt sb ; [moralement] to make sb suffer ■ **souffrant, -e** *adj* unwell

**souhait** [swɛ] *nm* wish ; **à vos souhaits !** [après un éternuement] bless you ! ■ **souhaitable** *adj* desirable ■ **souhaiter** *vt* [bonheur] to wish for ; **souhaiter qch à qn** to wish sb sth ; **souhaiter faire qch** to hope to do sth ; **souhaiter que...** (+ *subjunctive*) to hope that...

**soûl, -e** [su, sul] **1.** *adj* drunk **2.** *nm* **tout son soûl** [boire] to one's heart's content ■ **soûler, saouler** [sule] **1.** *vt* **a)** *Fam* [enivrer] **soûler qn** to get sb drunk ; *Fig* to intoxicate sb **b)** *Fig* [de plaintes, d'éloges] **soûler qn à** to bore sb silly **2. se soûler** *vpr Fam* to get drunk

**soulager** [sulaʒe] *vt* to relieve (**de** of) ■ **soulagement** *nm* relief

**soulever** [suləve] **1.** *vt* to lift (up) ; [question] to raise **2. se soulever** *vpr* [personne] to lift oneself (up) ; [se révolter] to rise up ■ **soulèvement** [-ɛvmɑ̃] *nm* [révolte] uprising

**soulier** [sulje] *nm* shoe

**souligner** [suliɲe] *vt* [d'un trait] to underline ; [faire remarquer] to emphasize

**soumettre** [sumɛtr] **1.** *vt* [pays, rebelles] to subdue ; [rapport, demande] to submit (**à** to) ; **soumettre qn à** [assujettir] to subject sb to **2. se soumettre** *vpr* to submit (**à** to) ■ **soumis, -e** *adj* [docile] submissive ; **soumis à** subject to ■ **soumission** *nf* [à une autorité] submission ; [docilité] submissiveness

**soupçon** [supsɔ̃] *nm* suspicion ; **au-dessus de tout soupçon** above suspicion ■ **soupçonner** *vt* to suspect (**de** of ; **d'avoir fait** of doing) ■ **soupçonneux, -euse** *adj* suspicious

**soupe** [sup] *nf* soup ; **soupe populaire** soup kitchen ■ **soupière** *nf* (soup) tureen

**souper** [supe] **1.** *nm* supper **2.** *vi* to have supper

**soupir** [supir] *nm* sigh ■ **soupirer** *vi* to sigh

**souple** [supl] *adj* [corps, personne] supple ; [branche] flexible ■ **souplesse** *nf* [de corps] suppleness ; [de branche] flexibility

**source** [surs] *nf* **a)** [point d'eau] spring ; **prendre sa source** [rivière] to rise (**à** at) **b)** [origine] source

**sourcil** [sursi] *nm* eyebrow ■ **sourciller** *vi Fig* **ne pas sourciller** not to bat an eyelid

**sourd, -e** [sur, surd] **1.** *adj* [personne] deaf (**à** to) ; [douleur] dull ; **bruit sourd** thump **2.** *nmf* deaf person ■ **sourd-**

**muet, sourde-muette** *(mpl* **sourds-muets,** *fpl* **sourdes-muettes) 1.** *adj* deaf-and-dumb **2.** *nmf* deaf mute

**sourire** [surir] **1.** *nm* smile ; **faire un sourire à qn** to give sb a smile **2.** *vi* to smile (**à** at)

**souris** [suri] *nf* [animal & ORDINAT] mouse *(pl* mice)

**sournois, -e** [surnwa, -waz] *adj* sly, underhand

**sous** [su] *prép* [position] under, underneath, beneath ; [rang] under ; **sous la pluie** in the rain ; **nager sous l'eau** to swim underwater ; **sous le nom de** under the name of ; **sous Charles X** under Charles X ; **sous peu** [bientôt] shortly

**sous-activité** [suzaktivite] *nf* **être en sous-activité** to be operating below capacity

**sous-alimenté, e** [suzalimãte] *(mpl* **sous-alimentés,** *fpl* **-es)** *adj* malnourished, underfed

**sous-bois** [subwa] *nm* undergrowth

**sous-chef** [suʃɛf] *(pl* **sous-chefs)** *nmf* second-in-command ; [dans un restaurant] sous-chef

**souscrire** [suskrir] *vi* **souscrire à** [payer, approuver] to subscribe to ■ **souscription** *nf* subscription

**sous-développé, -e** [sudevlɔpe] *(mpl* **sous-développés,** *fpl* **sous-développées)** *adj* [pays] underdeveloped

**sous-directeur, -trice** [sudirɛktœr, -tris] *(pl* **sous-directeurs)** *nmf* assistant manager

**sous-effectif** [suzefɛktif] *(pl* **sous-effectifs)** *nm* understaffing ; **en sous-effectif** [entreprise, usine] understaffed

**sous-entendre** [suzãtãdr] *vt* to imply

**sous-entendu** [suzãtãdy] *(pl* **sous-entendus)** *nm* insinuation

**sous-estimer** [suzɛstime] *vt* to underestimate

**sous-jacent, -e** [suʒasã, -ãt] *(mpl* **sous-jacents,** *fpl* **sous-jacentes)** *adj* underlying

**sous-louer** [sulwe] *vt* [sujet : locataire] to sublet

**sous-marin, -e** [sumarɛ̃, -in] *(mpl* **sous-marins,** *fpl* **sous-marines) 1.** *adj* underwater **2.** *nm* submarine ; *Can* CULIN submarine sandwich

**sous-préfet** [suprefɛ] *(pl* **sous-préfets)** *nm* subprefect ■ **sous-préfecture** *nf* subprefecture

**sous-répertoire** [surepɛrtwar] *(pl* **sous-répertoires)** *nm* ORDINAT subdirectory

**soussigné, -e** [susiɲe] *adj &* *nmf* undersigned ; **je soussigné** I the undersigned

**sous-sol** [susɔl] *(pl* **sous-sols)** *nm* [d'immeuble] basement ; GÉOL subsoil

**sous-titre** [sutitr] *(pl* **sous-titres)** *nm* subtitle ■ **sous-titré, -e** *adj* subtitled ; **un film sous-titré (en anglais)** a film with (English) subtitles

**sous-total** [sutɔtal] *(pl* **sous-totaux)** *nm* subtotal

**soustraire** [sustrɛr] **1.** *vt* to remove ; MATH to take away, to subtract (**de** from) ; **soustraire qn à** [danger] to shield *or* protect sb from **2. se soustraire** *vpr* **se soustraire à** to escape from ; [devoir, obligation] to avoid ■ **soustraction** *nf* MATH subtraction

**sous-traitant, e** [sutrɛtã, ãt] *(mpl* **sous-traitants,** *fpl* **-es)** *adj* subcontracting ■ **sous-traitant** *nm* subcontractor

**sous-vêtement** [suvɛtmã] *nm* undergarment ; **sous-vêtements** underwear

**soutenir** [sutnir] *vt* to support, to hold up ; [candidat] to back ; [thèse] to defend ; [regard] to hold ; **soutenir que...** to maintain that... ■ **soutenu, -e** *adj* [attention, effort] sustained

**souterrain, -e** [sutɛrɛ̃, -ɛn] **1.** *adj* underground **2.** *nm* underground passage

**soutien** [sutjɛ̃] *nm* support ; [personne] supporter ■ **soutien-gorge** *(pl* **soutiens-gorge)** *nm* bra

**soutirer** [sutire] *vt* soutirer qch à qn to extract sth from sb

**souvenir**[1] [suvnir] *nm* memory, recollection; [objet] memento; [cadeau] keepsake; [pour touristes] souvenir; **en souvenir de** in memory of

**souvenir**[2] [suvnir] ■ **se souvenir** *vpr* se souvenir de qn /qch to remember sb /sth; **se souvenir que...** to remember that...

**souvent** [suvɑ̃] *adv* often; **peu souvent** seldom; **le plus souvent** usually, more often than not

**souverain, -e** [suvərɛ̃, -ɛn] *nmf* sovereign ■ **souveraineté** *nf* sovereignty

**soviétique** [sɔvjetik] *Anc* **1.** *adj* Soviet; **l'Union soviétique** the Soviet Union **2.** *nmf* Soviet citizen

**soyeux, -euse** [swajø, -øz] *adj* silky

**soyons, soyez** [swajɔ̃, swaje] *voir* être

**spacieux, -euse** [spasjø, -øz] *adj* spacious, roomy

**spaghettis** [spageti] *nmpl* spaghetti

**spam** [spam] *nm* ORDINAT spam

**sparadrap** [sparadra] *nm* [pour pansement] *Br* sticking plaster, *Am* adhesive tape

**spatial, -e, -aux** [spasjal, -o] *adj* **station spatiale** space station; **engin spatial** spaceship, spacecraft

**spécial, -e, -aux** [spesjal, -o] *adj* special; [bizarre] peculiar ■ **spécialement** *adv* [exprès] specially; [en particulier] especially, particularly

**spécialiser** [spesjalize] ■ **se spécialiser** *vpr* to specialize (**dans** in) ■ **spécialisation** *nf* specialization ■ **spécialiste** *nmf* specialist ■ **spécialité** *nf Br* speciality, *Am* specialty

**spécifier** [spesifje] *vt* to specify (**que** that)

**spécifique** [spesifik] *adj* specific

**spécimen** [spesimɛn] *nm* specimen; [livre] specimen copy

**spectacle** [spɛktakl] *nm* **a)** [vue] sight, spectacle **b)** [représentation] show; **spectacle de danse** dance show; **spectacle de variétés** variety show;

**le spectacle** [industrie] show business ■ **spectateur, -trice** *nmf* spectator; [au théâtre, au cinéma] member of the audience; **spectateurs** [au théâtre, au cinéma] audience

**spectaculaire** [spɛktakylɛr] *adj* spectacular

**spéculer** [spekyle] *vi* to speculate ■ **spéculateur, -trice** *nmf* speculator ■ **spéculation** *nf* speculation

**spéléologie** [speleɔlɔʒi] *nf* [activité] *Br* potholing, caving, *Am* spelunking

**sphère** [sfɛr] *nf* [boule, domaine] sphere

**spirituel, -elle** [spiritɥɛl] *adj* [amusant] witty; [pouvoir, vie] spiritual

**spiritueux** [spiritɥø] *nmpl* [boissons] spirits

**splendide** [splɑ̃did] *adj* splendid ■ **splendeur** *nf* splendour

**spontané, -e** [spɔ̃tane] *adj* spontaneous ■ **spontanéité** *nf* spontaneity

**sport** [spɔr] *nm* sport; **faire du sport** to play *Br* sport *or Am* sports; **voiture / terrain de sport** sports car /ground; **sports de combat** combat sports; **sports de glisse** board sports; **sports d'équipe** team sports; **sports d'hiver** winter sports; **aller aux sports d'hiver** to go skiing; **sports individuels** individual sports; **sports mécaniques** motor sports *(on land, in the air, on water)*; **sports de plein-air** outdoor sports ■ **sportif, -ive 1.** *adj* [personne] fond of *Br* sport *or Am* sports; [esprit] sporting; [association, journal, résultats] sports, sporting; [allure] athletic **2.** *nmf* sportsman, *f* sportswoman

**spot** [spɔt] *nm* [lampe] spotlight; **spot publicitaire** commercial

**spray** [sprɛ] *nm* spray

**square** [skwar] *nm* public garden

**squash** [skwaʃ] *nm* [jeu] squash

**squatter 1.** [skwate] *vi* to squat **2.** [skwatœr] *nm* squatter ■ **squatteur, -euse** *nmf* squatter

**squelette** [skəlɛt] *nm* skeleton

**stable** [stabl] *adj* stable ■ **stabiliser 1.** *vt* to stabilize **2. se stabiliser** *vpr* to stabilize ■ **stabilité** *nf* stability

**stade** [stad] *nm* SPORT stadium; [phase] stage

**stage** [staʒ] *nm* [période] training period; [cours] (training) course; **faire un stage** to undergo training; **être en stage** to be on a training course ■ **stagiaire** *adj* & *nmf* trainee

**stagner** [stagne] *vi* to stagnate

**stand** [stɑ̃d] *nm* [d'exposition] stand, stall; **stand de tir** [de foire] shooting range

**standard** [stɑ̃dar] **1.** *nm* [téléphonique] switchboard **2.** *adj inv* [modèle] standard ■ **standardiste** *nmf* (switchboard) operator

**standing** [stɑ̃diŋ] *nm* standing, status; **immeuble de (grand) standing** *Br* luxury block of flats, *Am* luxury apartment building

**station** [stasjɔ̃] *nf* [de métro, d'observation, de radio] station; [de ski] resort; [d'autobus] stop; **station de taxis** *Br* taxi rank, *Am* taxi stand; ORDINAT **station de travail** work station ■ **station-service** (*pl* **stations-service**) *nf* service station, *Br* petrol *or Am* gas station

**stationnaire** [stasjɔnɛr] *adj* stationary

**stationner** [stasjɔne] *vi* [être garé] to be parked ■ **stationnement** *nm* parking

**statistique** [statistik] **1.** *adj* statistical **2.** *nf* [donnée] statistic; **la statistique** [science] statistics (*sg*)

**statue** [staty] *nf* statue

**statut** [staty] *nm* [position] status; **statuts** [règles] statutes

**steak** [stɛk] *nm* steak

**sténographie** [stenɔgrafi] *nf* shorthand, stenography

**stéréo** [stereo] *nf* stereo; **en stéréo** in stereo ■ **stéréophonique** *adj* stereophonic

**stéréotype** [stereɔtip] *nm* stereotype ■ **stéréotypé, -e** *adj* stereotyped

**stérile** [steril] *adj* sterile; [terre] barren ■ **stérilisation** *nf* sterilization ■ **stériliser** *vt* to sterilize ■ **stérilité** *nf* sterility; [de terre] barrenness

**stéthoscope** [stetɔskɔp] *nm* stethoscope

**steward** [stiwart] *nm* [d'avion, de bateau] steward

**sticker** [stikœr] *nm* sticker

**stigmatiser** [stigmatize] *vt* [dénoncer] to stigmatize

**stimuler** [stimyle] *vt* to stimulate ■ **stimulation** *nf* stimulation

**stimulus** [stimylys] (*pl* **stimuli** [-li]) *nm* [physiologique] stimulus

**stipuler** [stipyle] *vt* to stipulate (**que** that)

**stock** [stɔk] *nm* stock (**de** of); **en stock** in stock ■ **stockage** *nm* stocking; ORDINAT storage ■ **stocker** *vt* [provisions] to stock; ORDINAT to store

**stop** [stɔp] **1.** *excl* stop **2.** *nm* AUTO [panneau] stop sign; [feu arrière] brake light, *Br* stoplight; *Fam* [auto-stop] hitching, hitch-hiking; **faire du stop** to hitch, to hitch-hike ■ **stopper** *vt* & *vi* to stop

**stratagème** [strataʒɛm] *nm* stratagem, ploy

**stratège** [stratɛʒ] *nm* strategist ■ **stratégie** *nf* strategy ■ **stratégique** *adj* strategic

**stress** [strɛs] *nm inv* stress ■ **stressant, -e** *adj* stressful ■ **stressé, -e** *adj* under stress ■ **stresser 1.** *vt* **stresser qn** to cause sb stress, to put sb under stress **2.** *vi* to be stressed

**strict, -e** [strikt] *adj* [principes, professeur] strict; [tenue] plain; **le strict minimum** the bare minimum ■ **strictement** [-əmɑ̃] *adv* strictly; [vêtu] plainly

**strident, -e** [stridɑ̃, -ɑ̃t] *adj* shrill, strident

**structure** [stryktyr] *nf* structure ■ **structural, -e, -aux** *adj* structural ■ **structurer** *vt* to structure

**studieux, -euse** [stydjø, -øz] *adj* studious; [vacances] devoted to study

**studio** [stydjo] *nm* [de cinéma, de télévision, de peintre] studio; [logement] *Br* studio flat, *Am* studio apartment

**stupéfait, -e** [stypefɛ, -ɛt] *adj* amazed, astounded (**de** at *or* by) ■ **stupéfaction** *nf* amazement

**stupéfier** [stypefje] vt to amaze, to astound ∎ **stupéfiant, -e 1.** adj amazing, astounding **2.** nm drug, narcotic

**stupeur** [stypœr] nf [étonnement] amazement; [inertie] stupor

**stupide** [stypid] adj stupid ∎ **stupidité** nf stupidity; [action, parole] stupid thing

**style** [stil] nm style; **meubles de style** period furniture ∎ **stylé, -e** adj well-trained ∎ **styliste** nmf [de mode] designer ∎ **stylistique** adj stylistic

**stylo** [stilo] nm pen; **stylo à bille** ballpoint (pen), Br biro®; **stylo à encre, stylo-plume** fountain pen

**su, -e** [sy] pp de **savoir**

**subdiviser** [sybdivize] vt to subdivide (en into) ∎ **subdivision** nf subdivision

**subir** [sybir] vt to undergo; [conséquences, défaite, perte, tortures] to suffer; [influence] to be under; **faire subir qch à qn** to subject sb to sth

**subit, -e** [sybi, -it] adj sudden ∎ **subitement** adv suddenly

**subjectif, -ive** [sybʒɛktif, -iv] adj subjective ∎ **subjectivité** nf subjectivity

**subjuguer** [sybʒyge] vt to subjugate, to subdue; [envoûter] to captivate

**sublime** [syblim] adj & nm sublime

**submerger** [sybmɛrʒe] vt to submerge; Fig [envahir] to overwhelm; Fig **submergé de travail** snowed under with work

**submersible** [sybmɛrsibl] nm submarine

**subside** [sypsid] nm grant, subsidy

**subsistance** [sybzistãs] nf subsistence

**subsister** [sybziste] **1.** vi [chose] to remain; [personne] to subsist **2.** v impers to remain; **il subsiste un doute** there remains some doubt

**substance** [sypstãs] nf substance; Fig **en substance** in essence ∎ **substantiel, -elle** adj substantial

**substituer** [sypstitɥe] **1.** vt to substitute (à for) **2.** se **substituer** vpr se **substituer à qn** to take the place of sb, to substitute for sb ∎ **substitution** nf substitution; **produit de substitution** substitute (product)

**substitut** [sypstity] nm [produit] substitute (de for); [magistrat] deputy public prosecutor

**subtil, -e** [syptil] adj subtle ∎ **subtilité** nf subtlety

**subvenir** [sybvənir] vi **subvenir à** [besoins, frais] to meet

**subvention** [sybvãsjɔ̃] nf subsidy ∎ **subventionner** vt to subsidize

**subversif, -ive** [sybvɛrsif, -iv] adj subversive ∎ **subversion** nf subversion

**suc** [syk] nm [gastrique, de fruit] juice; [de plante] sap

**succéder** [syksede] **1.** vi **succéder à qn** to succeed sb; **succéder à qch** to follow sth, to come after sth **2.** se **succéder** vpr [choses, personnes] to follow one another

**succès** [syksɛ] nm success; **succès de librairie** [livre] best-seller; **avoir du succès** to be successful; **à succès** [auteur, film] successful

**successeur** [syksesœr] nm successor ∎ **successif, -ive** adj successive ∎ **succession** nf succession (de of; à to); [série] sequence (de of); [patrimoine] inheritance, estate; **prendre la succession de qn** to succeed sb

**succinct, -e** [syksɛ̃, -ɛ̃t] adj succinct, brief

**succomber** [sykɔ̃be] vi [mourir] to die; **succomber à** [céder à] to succumb to

**succulent, -e** [sykylã, -ãt] adj succulent

**succursale** [sykyrsal] nf [de magasin] branch; **magasin à succursales multiples** chain store

**sucer** [syse] vt to suck ∎ **sucette** nf lollipop; [tétine] Br dummy, Am pacifier

**sucre** [sykr] nm sugar; [morceau] sugar lump; **sucre en poudre, sucre semoule** Br castor or caster sugar, Am finely ground sugar; Can **sucre (d'érable)** maple sugar; **sucre d'orge** barley sugar

**sucrer** [sykre] *vt* to sugar, to sweeten
■ **sucré, -e** *adj* sweet, sugary; [artificiellement] sweetened; *Fig* [doucereux] sugary, syrupy

**sucrerie** [sykrəri] *nf* **a)** [usine] sugar refinery; **sucreries** [bonbons] *Br* sweets, *Am* candy **b)** *Can* [forêt d'érables] maple forest, sugar bush

**sucrier** [sykrije] *nm* [récipient] sugar bowl

**sud** [syd] **1.** *nm* south; **au sud** in the south; [direction] (to the) south (**de** of); **du sud** [vent, direction] southerly; [ville] southern; [gens] from *or* in the south; **l'Afrique du Sud** South Africa **2.** *adj inv* [côte] south(ern) ■ **sud-africain, -e** *(mpl* **sud-africains,** *fpl* **sud-africaines) 1.** *adj* South African **2.** *nmf* Sud-Africain, Sud-Africaine South African ■ **sud-américain, -e** *(mpl* **sud-américains,** *fpl* **sud-américaines) 1.** *adj* South American **2.** *nmf* Sud-Américain, Sud-Américaine South American ■ **sud-est** *nm & adj inv* south-east ■ **sud-ouest** *nm & adj inv* south-west

**Sudoku®** [sydoky] *nm* Sudoku

**Suède** [sɥɛd] *nf* **la Suède** Sweden ■ **suédois, -e 1.** *adj* Swedish **2.** *nmf* Suédois, Suédoise Swede **3.** *nm* [langue] Swedish

**suer** [sɥe] *vi* [personne, mur] to sweat ■ **sueur** *nf* sweat; **(tout) en sueur** sweating

**suffire** [syfir] **1.** *vi* to be enough (**à** for); **ça suffit !** that's enough! **2.** *v impers* **il suffit de faire qch** one only has to do sth; **il suffit d'une goutte /d'une heure pour faire qch** a drop /an hour is enough to do sth **3. se suffire** *vpr* **se suffire à soi-même** to be self-sufficient

**suffisance** [syfizɑ̃s] *nf* [vanité] conceit

**suffisant, -e** [syfizɑ̃, -ɑ̃t] *adj* [satisfaisant] sufficient, adequate; [vaniteux] conceited ■ **suffisamment** [-amɑ̃] *adv* sufficiently; **suffisamment de** enough, sufficient

**suffoquer** [syfɔke] *vt & vi* to choke, to suffocate

**suffrage** [syfraʒ] *nm* POL [voix] vote; **suffrage universel** universal suffrage

**suggérer** [sygʒere] *vt* [proposer] to suggest (**à** to ; **de faire** doing ; **que** (+ subjunctive) that) ■ **suggestif, -ive** *adj* suggestive ■ **suggestion** *nf* suggestion

**suicide** [sɥisid] *nm* suicide ■ **se suicider** *vpr* to commit suicide

**suie** [sɥi] *nf* soot

**suinter** [sɥɛ̃te] *vi* to ooze ■ **suintement** *nm* oozing

**suis** [sɥi] *voir* **être, suivre**

**Suisse** [sɥis] *nf* **la Suisse** Switzerland; **Suisse allemande /romande** German-speaking /French-speaking Switzerland ■ **suisse 1.** *adj* Swiss **2.** *nmf* Suisse Swiss; **les Suisses** the Swiss ■ **Suissesse** *nf* Swiss *inv*

**suite** [sɥit] *nf* [reste] rest; [continuation] continuation; [de film, de roman] sequel; [série] series, sequence; [appartement, escorte] suite; [cohérence] order; **suites** [séquelles] effects; [résultats] consequences; **faire suite (à)** to follow; **donner suite à** [demande] to follow up; **par la suite** afterwards; **par suite de** as a result of; **à la suite** one after another; **à la suite de** [derrière] behind; [événement, maladie] as a result of; **de suite** [deux jours] in a row

**suivant, -e** [sɥivɑ̃, -ɑ̃t] **1.** *adj* next, following; [ci-après] following **2.** *nmf* next (one); **au suivant !** next!, next person! ■ **suivant** *prép* [selon] according to

**suivi, -e** [sɥivi] *adj* [régulier] regular, steady; [cohérent] coherent; **peu/très suivi** [cours] poorly /well attended

**suivre** [sɥivr] **1.** *vt* to follow; [accompagner] to go with, to accompany; [cours] to attend, to go to; **suivre qn/qch des yeux** *ou* **du regard** to watch sb /sth; **suivre l'exemple de qn** to follow sb's example; **suivre l'actualité** to follow events *or* the news **2.** *vi* to follow; **faire suivre** [courrier, lettre] to forward; **'à suivre'** 'to be continued' **3. se suivre** *vpr* to follow one another

**sujet¹, -ette** [syʒɛ, -ɛt] **1.** *adj* **sujet à** [maladie] subject to; **sujet à caution** [information, nouvelle] unconfirmed **2.** *nmf* [personne] subject

**sujet²** [syʒɛ] *nm* **a)** [question] subject; [d'examen] question; **au sujet de** about; **à quel sujet ?** about what? **b)** [raison] cause; **sujet(s) de dispute** grounds for dispute **c)** [individu] subject; **un brillant sujet** a brilliant student

**super** [sypɛr] *nm* [supercarburant] *Br* four-star (petrol), *Am* premium *or* high-test gas

**superbe** [sypɛrb] *adj* superb

**supercherie** [sypɛrʃəri] *nf* deception

**supérette** [sypɛrɛt] *nf* convenience store

**superficie** [sypɛrfisi] *nf* surface; [dimensions] area ■ **superficiel, -elle** *adj* superficial

**superflu, -e** [sypɛrfly] *adj* superfluous

**supérieur, -e** [sypɛrjœr] **1.** *adj* [étages, partie] upper; [qualité, air, ton] superior; **à l'étage supérieur** on the floor above; **supérieur à** [meilleur que] superior to, better than; [plus grand que] above, greater than; **supérieur à la moyenne** above average; **études supérieures** higher *or* university studies **2.** *nmf* superior ■ **supériorité** *nf* superiority

**supermarché** [sypɛrmarʃe] *nm* supermarket

**superposer** [sypɛrpoze] *vt* [objets] to put on top of each other; [images] to superimpose

**superproduction** [sypɛrprɔdyksjɔ̃] *nf* [film] blockbuster

**superpuissance** [sypɛrpɥisɑ̃s] *nf* POL superpower

**supersonique** [sypɛrsɔnik] *adj* supersonic

**superstar** [sypɛrstar] *nf* superstar

**superstitieux, -euse** [sypɛrstisjø, -øz] *adj* superstitious ■ **superstition** *nf* superstition

**superviser** [sypɛrvize] *vt* to supervise

**supplanter** [syplɑ̃te] *vt* to take the place of

**suppléer** [syplee] *vi* **suppléer à** [compenser] to make up for ■ **suppléant, -e** *adj* & *nmf* [personne] substitute, replacement; **(professeur) suppléant** substitute *or Br* supply teacher

**supplément** [syplemɑ̃] *nm* [argent] extra charge, supplement; [de revue, de livre] supplement; **en supplément** extra; **un supplément de** [information, de travail] extra, additional ■ **supplémentaire** *adj* extra, additional

**supplice** [syplis] *nm* torture ■ **supplier** *vt* **supplier qn de faire qch** to beg *or* implore sb to do sth; **je vous en supplie !** I beg *or* implore you!

**support** [sypɔr] *nm* support; [d'instrument] stand

**supporter¹** [sypɔrte] *vt* [malheur, conséquences] to bear, to endure; [chaleur] to withstand; **je ne peux pas la supporter** I can't bear her ■ **supportable** *adj* bearable; [excusable, passable] tolerable

**supporter²** [sypɔrtɛr] *nm* [de football] supporter

**supposer** [sypoze] *vt* to suppose, to assume (**que** that); [impliquer] to imply (**que** that); **à supposer** *ou* **en supposant que...** (+ *subjunctive*) supposing (that)... ■ **supposition** *nf* assumption, supposition

**supprimer** [syprime] **1.** *vt* to get rid of, to remove; [mot, passage] to cut out, to delete; [train] to cancel; [tuer] to do away with; ORDINAT to delete; **supprimer des emplois** to axe jobs; **supprimer qch à qn** to take sth away from sb **2. se supprimer** *vpr* [se suicider] to do away with oneself ■ **suppression** *nf* removal; [de mot] deletion; [de train] cancellation; [d'emplois] axing

**suprématie** [sypremasi] *nf* supremacy

**suprême** [syprɛm] *adj* supreme

**sur** [syr] *prép* on, upon; [par-dessus] over; [au sujet de] on, about; **six sur dix** six out of ten; **un jour sur deux** every other day; **six mètres sur dix**

six metres by ten; **sur votre gauche** to *or* on your left; **mettre /monter sur qch** to put /climb on (to) sth

**sûr, -e** [syr] *adj* sure, certain (**de** of; **que** that); [digne de confiance] reliable; [lieu] safe; [goût] discerning; [main] steady; **sûr de soi** self-assured; **bien sûr !** of course!

**surbooké, e** [syrbuke] *adj* overbooked

**surbrillance** [syrbrijɑ̃s] *nf* ORDINAT **mettre qch en surbrillance** to highlight sth

**surcharge** [syrʃarʒ] *nf* **a)** [poids] excess weight; **surcharge de travail** extra work; **en surcharge** [passagers] extra **b)** [correction] alteration; [à payer] surcharge ■ **surcharger** *vt* [voiture, personne] to overload (**de** with)

**surchauffer** [syrʃofe] *vt* to overheat

**surcroît** [syrkrwa] *nm* increase (**de** in); **de surcroît, par surcroît** in addition

**surdité** [syrdite] *nf* deafness

**surdose** [syrdoz] *nf* [de drogue] overdose

**surdoué, e** [syrdwe] *adj* exceptionally *or* highly gifted

**sureffectif** [syrefɛktif] *nm* overmanning, overstaffing

**surélever** [syrelve] *vt* to raise

**surendetté, e** [syrɑ̃dete] *adj* overindebted ■ **surendettement** *nm* **a)** [gén] overindebtedness, debt burden **b)** [d'une entreprise] overborrowing

**surestimer** [syrɛstime] *vt* to overestimate; [tableau] to overvalue

**sûreté** [syrte] *nf* safety; [de l'État] security; [garantie] surety; [de geste] sureness; **être en sûreté** to be safe; **mettre qn /qch en sûreté** to put sb / sth in a safe place; **pour plus de sûreté** to be on the safe side

**surévaluer** [syrevalɥe] *vt* to overvalue, to overestimate

**surexcité, -e** [syrɛksite] *adj* overexcited

**surf** [sœrf] *nm* SPORT surfing; **faire du surf** to surf, to go surfing ■ **surfer** *vi* **surfer sur le Net** to surf the Net

**surface** [syrfas] *nf* surface; [étendue] (surface) area; **faire surface** [sous-marin] to surface; **(magasin à) grande surface** hypermarket; **de surface** [politesse] superficial

**surfait, -e** [syrfɛ, -ɛt] *adj* overrated

**surgelé, -e** [syrʒəle] *adj* frozen ■ **surgelés** *nmpl* frozen foods

**surgir** [syrʒir] *vi* to appear suddenly (**de** from)

**surhomme** [syrɔm] *nm* superman ■ **surhumain, -e** *adj* superhuman

**surinformer** [syrɛ̃fɔrme] *vt* to overinform

**sur-le-champ** [syrləʃɑ̃] *adv* immediately

**surlendemain** [syrlɑ̃dəmɛ̃] *nm* **le surlendemain** two days later; **le surlendemain de** two days after

**surligner** [syrliɲe] *vt* to highlight ■ **surligneur** *nm* highlighter (pen)

**surmener** [syrməne] **1.** *vt* to overwork **2. se surmener** *vpr* to overwork ■ **surmenage** *nm* overwork

**sur-mesure** [syrməzyr] *nm inv* **c'est du sur-mesure** it's custom made

**surmonter** [syrmɔ̃te] *vt* [être placé sur] to surmount; *Fig* [obstacle, peur] to overcome

**surnaturel, -elle** [syrnatyrɛl] *adj* & *nm* supernatural

**surnom** [syrnɔ̃] *nm* nickname

**surpasser** [syrpase] **1.** *vt* to surpass (**en** in) **2. se surpasser** *vpr* to surpass oneself

**surpeuplé, -e** [syrpœple] *adj* overpopulated

**surplomb** [syrplɔ̃] *nm* **en surplomb** overhanging ■ **surplomber** *vt* & *vi* to overhang

**surplus** [syrply] *nm* surplus

**surpoids** [syrpwa] *nm* excess weight

**surprendre** [syrprɑ̃dr] *vt* [étonner] to surprise; [prendre sur le fait] to catch ■ **surprenant, -e** *adj* surprising ■ **surpris, -e** *adj* surprised (**de** at; **que** (+ subjunctive) that); **je suis**

**surpris de te voir** I'm surprised to see you ■ **surprise** *nf* surprise; **prendre qn par surprise** to catch sb unawares

**surqualifié, e** [syrkalifje] *adj* over-qualified

**surréaliste** [syrrealist] *adj* [poète, peintre] surrealist

**sursaut** [syrso] *nm* (sudden) start *or* jump; **se réveiller en sursaut** to wake up with a start ■ **sursauter** *vi* to jump, to start

**sursis** [syrsi] *nm* [à l'armée] deferment; *Fig* [répit] reprieve; **un an (de prison) avec sursis** a one-year suspended sentence

**surtout** [syrtu] *adv* especially; [avant tout] above all; **surtout pas** certainly not

**surveiller** [syrveje] *vt* [garder] to watch, to keep an eye on; [contrôler] to supervise; [épier] to watch ■ **surveillance** *nf* watch (**sur** over); [de travaux, d'ouvriers] supervision; [de police] surveillance ■ **surveillant, -e** *nmf* [de lycée] supervisor (*in charge of discipline*); [de prison] (prison) guard, *Br* warder

**survenir** [syrvənir] *vi* to occur; [personne] to turn up

**survêtement** [syrvɛtmɑ̃] *nm* tracksuit

**survie** [syrvi] *nf* survival ■ **survivre** *vi* to survive (**à qch** sth); **survivre à qn** to outlive sb ■ **survivant, -e** *nmf* survivor

**survitaminé, e** [syrvitamine] *adj Fam* [animateur, film] supercharged

**survoler** [syrvɔle] *vt* to fly over; *Fig* [question] to skim over

**susceptible** [syseptibl] *adj* [ombrageux] touchy, sensitive; **susceptible de** [interprétations] open to; **susceptible de faire qch** likely *or* liable to do sth; [capable] able to do sth ■ **susceptibilité** *nf* touchiness, sensitivity

**susciter** [sysite] *vt* [sentiment] to arouse; [ennuis, obstacles] to create

**suspect, -e** [syspɛ, -ɛkt] **1.** *adj* suspicious, suspect; **suspect de qch** sus-

pected of sth **2.** *nmf* suspect ■ **suspecter** *vt* [personne] to suspect (**de qch** of sth; **de faire** of doing)

**suspendre** [syspɑ̃dr] **1.** *vt* [accrocher] to hang (up) (**à** on); [destituer, interrompre] to suspend **2. se suspendre** *vpr* **se suspendre à** to hang from ■ **suspendu, -e** *adj* **suspendu à** hanging from; **pont suspendu** suspension bridge

**suspens** [syspɑ̃] ■ **en suspens** *adv* [affaire, travail] in abeyance; [en l'air] suspended

**suspense** [syspɛns] *nm* suspense

**suspension** [syspɑ̃sjɔ̃] *nf* [d'hostilités, d'employé, de véhicule] suspension

**suspicion** [syspisjɔ̃] *nf* suspicion

**suture** [sytyr] *nf* MÉD **point de suture** stitch

**SVP** [ɛsvepe] (*abr de* **s'il vous plaît**) please

**SVT** (*abr de* **sciences de la vie et de la Terre**) *nfpl* ENS biology

**sweat** [swit] *nm* sweatshirt

**symbole** [sɛ̃bɔl] *nm* symbol ■ **symbolique** *adj* symbolic; [salaire, cotisation, loyer] nominal; **geste symbolique** symbolic *or* token gesture ■ **symboliser** *vt* to symbolize

**sympathie** [sɛ̃pati] *nf* [affinité] liking; [condoléances] sympathy; **avoir de la sympathie pour qn** to be fond of sb ■ **sympathique** *adj* nice; [accueil] friendly ■ **sympathiser** *vi* to get along well, *Br* to get on well (**avec** with)

**symphonie** [sɛ̃fɔni] *nf* symphony

**symptôme** [sɛ̃ptom] *nm* MÉD & *Fig* symptom

**synagogue** [sinagɔg] *nf* synagogue

**synchroniser** [sɛ̃krɔnize] *vt* to synchronize

**syndicat** [sɛ̃dika] *nm* [d'ouvriers] (*Br* trade *or* Am labor) union; [de patrons] association; **syndicat d'initiative** tourist (information) office ■ **syndicaliste** *nmf Br* trade *or* Am labor unionist

**syndiquer** [sɛ̃dike] **1.** *vt* to unionize **2. se syndiquer** *vpr* [adhérer] to join a ( *Br* trade *or Am* labor) union ■ **syndiqué, -e** *nmf* ( *Br* trade *or Am* labor) union member

**syndrome** [sɛ̃drom] *nm* MÉD & *Fig* syndrome; **syndrome immunodéficitaire acquis** acquired immune deficiency syndrome

**synthèse** [sɛ̃tɛz] *nf* synthesis ■ **synthétique** *adj* synthetic

**synthétiseur** [sɛ̃tetizœr] *nm* synthesizer

**Syrie** [siri] *nf* la Syrie Syria ■ **syrien, -enne 1.** *adj* Syrian **2.** *nmf* Syrien, Syrienne Syrian

**système** [sistɛm] *nm* [structure, réseau & ANAT] system; ORDINAT **système d'exploitation** operating system ■ **systématique** *adj* systematic ■ **systématiquement** *adv* systematically

**T**

**T, t** [te] *nm inv* T, t

**t'** [t] *voir* te

**ta** [ta] *voir* ton

**tabac** [taba] *nm* tobacco ; [magasin] *Br* tobacconist's (shop), *Am* tobacco store

**tabagie** [tabaʒi] *nf Can* [bureau de tabac] tobacco shop, corner shop, *Br* tobacconist's

**table** [tabl] *nf* **a)** [meuble] table ; [d'école] desk ; **mettre / débarrasser la table** to set *or Br* lay / clear the table ; **être à table** to be sitting at the table ; **à table !** food's ready! ; **table à repasser** ironing board ; **table de nuit / d'opération** bedside / operating table **b)** [liste] table ; **table des matières** table of contents

**tableau, -x** [tablo] *nm* **a)** [peinture] picture, painting ; [image, description] picture ; **tableau de maître** [peinture] old master **b)** [panneau] board ; [liste] list ; [graphique] chart ; **tableau (noir)** (black)board ; **tableau d'affichage** *Br* notice board, *Am* bulletin board

**tabler** [table] *vi* **tabler sur qch** to count *or* rely on sth

**tablette** [tablɛt] *nf* [de chocolat] bar, slab ; [de lavabo] shelf ; [de cheminée] mantelpiece ; **tablette (tactile)** (tactile) tablet computer *or* tablet

**tableur** [tablœr] *nm* ORDINAT spreadsheet

**tablier** [tablije] *nm* [vêtement] apron ; [d'écolier] smock

**tabouret** [taburɛ] *nm* stool

**tache** [taʃ] *nf* mark ; [salissure] stain ■ **tacher 1.** *vt* [tissu] to stain **2. se tacher** *vpr* [tissu] to stain

**tâche** [taʃ] *nf* task, job ; **tâches ménagères** housework ; **participer aux tâches ménagères** to help with the housework

**tâcher** [taʃe] *vi* **tâcher de faire qch** to try *or* endeavour to do sth

**tacheté, -e** [taʃte] *adj* speckled (**de** with)

**tact** [takt] *nm* tact ; **avoir du tact** to be tactful

**tactile** [taktil] *adj* tactile

**tactique** [taktik] **1.** *adj* tactical **2.** *nf* tactics (*sg*) ; **une tactique** a tactic

**Tahiti** [taiti] *nm* Tahiti ■ **tahitien, -enne** [taisjɛ̃, -ɛn] **1.** *adj* Tahitian **2.** *nmf* **Tahitien, Tahitienne** Tahitian

**taillader** [tajade] *vt* to gash

**taille¹** [taj] *nf* **a)** [hauteur] height ; [dimension, mesure] size ; **de haute taille** [personne] tall ; **de petite taille** short ; **de taille moyenne** medium-sized **b)** [ceinture] waist ; **tour de taille** waist measurement

**taille²** [taj] *nf* cutting ; [de haie] trimming ; [d'arbre] pruning ■ **tailler** *vt* to cut ; [haie, barbe] to trim ; [arbre] to prune ; [crayon] to sharpen

**taille-crayon** [tajkrɛjɔ̃] *nm inv* pencil sharpener

**tailleur** [tajœr] *nm* [personne] tailor ; [costume] suit

**taire** [tɛr] **1.** *vt* to say nothing about **2.** *vi* **faire taire qn** to silence sb **3. se taire** *vpr* [ne rien dire] to keep quiet (**sur qch** about sth) ; [cesser de parler] to stop talking, to fall silent ; **tais-toi !** be quiet!

**Taiwan** [tajwan] *nm ou f* Taiwan

**talc** [talk] *nm* talcum powder

**taquin**

**talent** [talɑ̃] *nm* talent; **avoir du talent** to be talented ■ **talentueux, -euse** *adj* talented

**talkie-walkie** [talkiwalki] *(pl* **talkies-walkies)** *nm* walkie-talkie

**talon** [talɔ̃] *nm* **a)** [de chaussure] heel; **(chaussures à) talons hauts** high heels, high-heeled shoes; **talons aiguilles** stiletto heels **b)** [de chèque] stub, counterfoil

**tambour** [tɑ̃bur] *nm* [de machine, instrument de musique] drum ■ **tambourin** *nm* tambourine

**Tamise** [tamiz] *nf* **la Tamise** the Thames

**tamiser** [tamize] *vt* [farine] to sift; [lumière] to filter

**tampon** [tɑ̃pɔ̃] *nm* **a)** [marque, instrument] stamp; **tampon encreur** ink pad **b)** [bouchon] plug, stopper; [de coton] wad, pad; [pour pansement] swab; **tampon hygiénique** tampon **c)** [de train] & *Fig* buffer; **état tampon** buffer state

**tamponner** [tɑ̃pɔne] **1.** *vt* [lettre, document] to stamp; [visage] to dab; [plaie] to swab; [train, voiture] to crash into **2. se tamponner** *vpr* to crash into each other ■ **tamponneuses** *adj f pl* **autos tamponneuses** Dodgems®

**tandem** [tɑ̃dɛm] *nm* [bicyclette] tandem; *Fig* [duo] duo

**tandis** [tɑ̃di] ■ **tandis que** *conj* [simultanéité] while; [contraste] whereas, while

**tangent, e** [tɑ̃ʒɑ̃, ɑ̃t] *adj Fam & Fig* **c'était tangent** it was close, it was touch and go

**tanière** [tanjɛr] *nf* den, lair

**tank** [tɑ̃k] *nm* tank

**tanker** [tɑ̃kɛr] *nm* [navire] tanker

**tanner** [tane] *vt* [cuir] to tan ■ **tanné, -e** *adj* [visage] weather-beaten

**tant** [tɑ̃] *adv* [travailler] so much **(que** that); **tant de** [pain, temps] so much **(que** that); [gens, choses] so many **(que** that); **tant de fois** so often, so many times; **tant que** [autant que] as much as; [aussi fort que] as hard as; [aussi longtemps que] as long as; **en tant que** [considéré comme] as; **tant mieux !** so much the better!; **tant pis !** too bad!, pity!; **tant mieux pour toi !** good for you!; **tant soit peu** (even) remotely *or* slightly; **un tant soit peu** somewhat; **tant s'en faut** far from it

**tante** [tɑ̃t] *nf* aunt

**tantinet** [tɑ̃tinɛ] *nm Fam* tiny bit ■ **un tantinet** *adv Fam* a tiny (little) bit (**de** of); **un tantinet exagéré / trop long** a bit exaggerated / too long; **un tantinet stupide** a tiny bit stupid

**tantôt** [tɑ̃to] *adv* **a) tantôt... tantôt** sometimes... sometimes... **b)** [cet après-midi] this afternoon

**taon** [tɑ̃] *nm* horsefly, gadfly

**tapage** [tapaʒ] *nm* din, uproar ■ **tapageur, -euse** *adj* [bruyant] rowdy; [criard] flashy

**tape** [tap] *nf* slap

**taper** [tape] **1.** *vt* [frapper] to hit; [marteler] to bang; **taper qch à la machine** to type sth **2.** *vi* [soleil] to beat down; **taper du pied** to stamp one's foot; **taper à la machine** to type; **taper sur qch** to bang on sth ■ **tapant, -e** *adj* **à huit heures tapantes** at eight sharp

**tapis** [tapi] *nm* carpet; **envoyer qn au tapis** [abattre] to floor sb; **mettre qch sur le tapis** [sujet] to bring sth up for discussion; **tapis de bain** bath mat; **tapis roulant** [pour marchandises] conveyor belt; [pour personnes] moving walkway

**tapisser** [tapise] *vt* [mur] to (wall) paper ■ **tapisserie** *nf* [papier peint] wallpaper; [broderie] tapestry

**taponner** [tapɔne] **1.** *vt Can* [tâter, manipuler] to handle **2.** *vi* **a)** [tâtonner] to fiddle **b)** [tergiverser, hésiter] to hesitate, to waver

**tapoter** [tapɔte] **1.** *vt* to tap; [joue] to pat **2.** *vi* **tapoter sur** to tap (on)

**taquin, -e** [takɛ̃, -in] *adj* teasing ■ **taquiner** *vt* to tease ■ **taquineries** *nfpl* teasing

**tard** [tar] *adv* late; **plus tard** later (on); **au plus tard** at the latest; **sur le tard** late in life

**tarder** [tarde] **1.** *vi* [lettre, saison] to be a long time coming; **sans tarder** without delay; **tarder à faire qch** to take one's time doing sth; **elle ne va pas tarder** she won't be long **2.** *v impers* **il me tarde de le faire** I long to do it

**tardif, -ive** [tardif, -iv] *adj* late; [regrets] belated **■ tardivement** *adv* late

**tare** [tar] *nf* [poids] tare; *Fig* [défaut] defect

**targuer** [targe] **■ se targuer** *vpr* **se targuer de faire qch** to pride oneself on doing sth

**tarif** [tarif] *nm* [prix] rate; [de train] fare; [tableau] price list, *Br* tariff; **plein tarif** full price; [de train, bus] full fare **■ tarification** *nf* pricing

**tartare** [tartar] *adj* **sauce tartare** tartar sauce

**tarte** [tart] *nf* (open) pie, tart **■ tartelette** [-ɔlɛt] *nf* (small) tart, tartlet

**tartiflette** [tartiflɛt] *nf* cheese and potato gratin from the Savoy region

**tartine** [tartin] *nf* slice of bread; **tartine de confiture** slice of bread and jam **■ tartiner** *vt* [beurre] to spread; **fromage à tartiner** cheese spread

**tas** [tɑ] *nm* pile, heap

**tasse** [tas] *nf* cup; **tasse à café** coffee cup; **tasse à thé** teacup

**tasser** [tɑse] **1.** *vt* to pack (**dans** into) **2. se tasser** *vpr* [se serrer] to squeeze up; [sol] to sink, to collapse; [se voûter] to become bowed

**tâter** [tɑte] *vt* to feel

**tâtonner** [tɑtɔne] *vi* to grope about **■ tâtons** *adv* **avancer à tâtons** to feel one's way (along); **chercher qch à tâtons** to grope for sth

**tatouer** [tatwe] *vt* [corps, dessin] to tattoo; **se faire tatouer** to get a tattoo **■ tatouage** *nm* [dessin] tattoo; [action] tattooing

**taudis** [todi] *nm* slum

**taupe** [top] *nf* [animal, espion] mole

**taureau, -x** [tɔro] *nm* bull; **le Taureau** [signe] Taurus **■ tauromachie** *nf* bull-fighting

**taux** [to] *nm* rate; **taux de cholestérol** cholesterol level; **taux d'intérêt** interest rate; **taux de natalité** birth rate

**taxe** [taks] *nf* [impôt] tax; **taxe à la valeur ajoutée** value-added tax **■ taxation** *nf* taxation

**taxer** [takse] *vt* [produit, personne, firme] to tax; **taxer qn de qch** to accuse sb of sth **■ taxé, -e** *adj* [produit] taxed

**taxi** [taksi] *nm* taxi

**Taxiphone®** [taksifɔn] *nm* [téléboutique] call shop

**tchat** [tʃat] *nm* = **chat**

**Tchécoslovaquie** [tʃekɔslɔvaki] *nf Anc* **la Tchécoslovaquie** Czechoslovakia **■ tchèque 1.** *adj* Czech; **la République tchèque** the Czech Republic **2.** *nmf* **Tchèque** Czech **3.** *nm* [langue] Czech

**Tchétchénie** [tʃetʃeni] *nf* **la Tchétchénie** Chechnya **■ tchétchène** [tʃetʃɛn] **1.** *adj* Chechen **2.** *nmf* Chechen

**tchin-tchin** [tʃintʃin] *excl Fam* cheers

**te** [tə]

**t'** is used before a word beginning with a vowel or h mute.

*pron pers* **a)** [complément direct] you; **je te vois** I see you **b)** [indirect] (to) you; **il te parle** he speaks to you; **elle te l'a dit** she told you **c)** [réfléchi] yourself; **tu te laves** you wash yourself

**technicien, -enne** [tɛknisjɛ̃, -ɛn] *nmf* technician **■ technique 1.** *adj* technical **2.** *nf* technique **■ technologie** *nf* technology **■ technologique** *adj* technological

**teckel** [tekɛl] *nm* dachshund

**tee-shirt** [tiʃœrt] *nm* tee-shirt

**teindre** [tɛ̃dr] **1.** *vt* to dye; **teindre qch en rouge** to dye sth red **2. se teindre** *vpr* **se teindre (les cheveux)** to dye one's hair

**teint** [tɛ̃] *nm* [de visage] complexion; **bon** *ou* **grand teint** [tissu] colourfast

**teinte** [tɛ̃t] *nf* shade, tint ■ **teinter** *vt* to tint ; [bois] to stain

**teinture** [tɛ̃tyr] *nf* dyeing ; [produit] dye ■ **teinturerie** [-rri] *nf* [boutique] (dry) cleaner's

**tel, telle** [tɛl] *adj* such ; **un tel livre / homme** such a book / man ; **de tels mots** such words ; **tel que** such as, like ; **tel que je l'ai laissé** just as I left it ; **laissez-le tel quel** leave it just as it is ; **en tant que tel, comme tel** as such ; **tel ou tel** such and such ; **rien de tel que…** (there's) nothing like… ; **tel père tel fils** like father like son

**télé** [tele] *nf Fam* TV, *Br* telly ; **à la télé** on TV, *Br* on the telly

**Télécarte®** [telekart] *nf* phone card

**télécharger** [teleʃarʒe] *vt* ORDINAT to download ■ **téléchargeable** *adj* downloadable ■ **téléchargement** *nm* ORDINAT downloading

**télécommande** [telekɔmɑ̃d] *nf* remote control ■ **télécommandé, -e** *adj* remote-controlled

**télécommunications** [telekɔmynikasjɔ̃] *nfpl* telecommunications

**téléconseiller, ère** [telekɔ̃seje, ɛr] *nmf* call centre person

**télécopie** [telekɔpi] *nf* fax ■ **télécopieur** *nm* fax (machine)

**téléfilm** [telefilm] *nm* TV movie

**télégramme** [telegram] *nm* telegram

**télégraphe** [telegraf] *nm* telegraph ■ **télégraphique** *adj* **poteau / fil télégraphique** telegraph pole / wire

**téléguider** [telegide] *vt* to operate by remote control

**téléjournal** [teleʒurnal] *nm Can* television news

**téléopérateur, trice** [teleɔperatœr, tris] *nmf* call centre agent

**télépathie** [telepati] *nf* telepathy

**téléphérique** [teleferik] *nm* cable car

**téléphone** [telefɔn] *nm* (tele)phone ; **coup de téléphone** (phone) call ; **passer un coup de téléphone à qn** to give sb a ring or a call ; **au téléphone** on the (tele)phone ; **avoir le téléphone** to be on the (tele)phone ; **téléphone portable** mobile phone ; **téléphone sans fil** cordless phone ■ **téléphoner 1.** *vt* [nouvelle] to (tele)phone (**à** to) **2.** *vi* to (tele)phone ; **téléphoner à qn** to (tele)phone sb, to call sb (up) ■ **téléphonique** *adj* **appel téléphonique** telephone call

**télé-réalité** [telerealite] *(pl* **télé-réalités)** *nf* TV reality TV, fly-on-the-wall television ; **une émission de télé-réalité** fly-on-the-wall documentary ; [de style feuilleton] docusoap

**télescope** [teleskɔp] *nm* telescope ■ **télescopique** *adj* telescopic

**télescoper** [teleskɔpe] **1.** *vt* [voiture, train] to smash into **2. se télescoper** *vpr* [voiture, train] to concertina

**télésiège** [telesjɛʒ] *nm* chair lift

**téléski** [teleski] *nm* ski tow

**téléspectateur, -trice** [telespɛktatœr, -tris] *nmf* (television) viewer

**télétravail** [teletravaj] *nm* teleworking

**téléuniversité** [teleyniversite] *nf Can* distance university

**téléviser** [televize] *vt* to televise ■ **téléviseur** *nm* television (set) ■ **télévision** *nf* television ; **à la télévision** on (the) television ; **regarder la télévision / qch à la télévision** to watch (the) television / sth on (the) television ; **programme de télévision** television programme

**télex** [telɛks] *nm* [service, message] telex

**telle** [tɛl] *voir* **tel**

**tellement** *adv* [si] so ; [tant] so much ; **tellement grand que…** so big that… ; **crier tellement que…** to shout so much that… ; **tellement de travail** so much work ; **tellement de soucis** so many worries ; **tu aimes ça ? — pas tellement !** [pas beaucoup] do you like it? — not much or a lot! ; **personne ne peut le supporter, tellement il est bavard** nobody can stand him, he's so talkative

**tellurique** [telyrik] *adj* **secousse tellurique** earth tremor

**téméraire** [temerɛr] *adj* reckless
■ **témérité** *nf* recklessness

**témoigner** [temwaɲe] **1.** *vt* [gratitude] to show (**à qn** (to) sb); **témoigner que...** [attester] to testify that... **2.** *vi* JUR to give evidence, to testify (**contre** against); **témoigner de qch** [personne, attitude] to testify to sth ■ **témoignage** *nm* JUR evidence, testimony; [récit] account; **faux témoignage** [délit] perjury; **en témoignage de qch** as a token of sth

**témoin** [temwɛ̃] **1.** *nm* **a)** JUR witness; **être témoin de qch** to witness sth **b)** [de relais] baton **2.** *adj* **appartement témoin** *Br* show flat, *Am* model apartment

**tempérament** [tɑ̃peramɑ̃] *nm* [caractère] temperament; **acheter qch à tempérament** to buy sth on *Br* hire purchase *or Am* on the installment plan

**température** [tɑ̃peratyr] *nf* temperature; **avoir de la température** to have a temperature

**tempérer** [tɑ̃pere] *vt* [ardeurs] to moderate ■ **tempéré, -e** *adj* [climat, zone] temperate

**tempête** [tɑ̃pɛt] *nf* storm

**tempêter** [tɑ̃pete] *vi* [crier] to storm, to rage (**contre** against)

**temple** [tɑ̃pl] *nm* [romain, grec] temple; [protestant] church

**temporaire** [tɑ̃pɔrɛr] *adj* temporary

**temporel, -elle** [tɑ̃pɔrɛl] *adj* temporal; [terrestre] wordly

**temps**[1] [tɑ̃] *nm* [durée, période, moment] time; [étape] stage; **en temps de guerre** in wartime, in time of war; **avoir le temps** to have (the) time (**de faire** to do); **il est temps** it is time (**de faire** to do); **il était temps !** it was about time (too)!; **il est (grand) temps que vous partiez** it's (high) time you left; **ces derniers temps** lately; **de temps en temps** [dətɑ̃zɑ̃tɑ̃], **de temps à autre** [dətɑ̃zaotr] from time to time, now and again; **en temps utile** [ɑ̃tɑ̃zytil] in due course; **en temps voulu** in due course; **en même temps** at the same time (**que** as); **à temps** [arriver] in time; **à plein temps** [travailler] full-time; **à temps partiel** [travailler] part-time; **dans le temps** [autrefois] in the old days; **avec le temps** [à la longue] in time; **tout le temps** all the time; **de mon temps** in my time; **temps d'arrêt** pause, break; **temps libre** free time

**temps**[2] [tɑ̃] *nm* [climat] weather; **il fait beau/mauvais temps** the weather's fine/bad; **quel temps fait-il ?** what's the weather like?

**tenace** [tənas] *adj* stubborn, tenacious ■ **ténacité** *nf* stubbornness, tenacity

**tenailles** [tənaj] *nfpl* [outil] pincers

**tenant, -e** [tənɑ̃, -ɑ̃t] **1.** *nmf* **le tenant du titre** [champion] the title holder **2.** *nm* [partisan] supporter (**de** of)

**tendance** [tɑ̃dɑ̃s] *nf* [penchant] tendency; [évolution] trend (**à** towards); **avoir tendance à faire qch** to tend to do sth, to have a tendency to do sth

**tendre**[1] [tɑ̃dr] **1.** *vt* to stretch; [main] to hold out (**à qn** to sb); [bras, jambe] to stretch out; [cou] to strain, to crane; [muscle] to tense; [arc] to bend; [piège] to set, to lay; [filet] to spread; **tendre qch à qn** to hold out sth to sb; *Fig* **tendre l'oreille** to prick up one's ears **2.** *vi* **tendre à qch/à faire qch** to tend towards sth/to do sth **3. se tendre** *vpr* [rapports] to become strained ■ **tendu, -e** *adj* [corde] tight, taut; [personne, situation, muscle] tense; [rapports] strained

**tendre**[2] [tɑ̃dr] *adj* [personne] affectionate (**avec** to); [parole, regard] tender, loving; [viande] tender; [bois, couleur] soft; **depuis ma plus tendre enfance** since I was a young child ■ **tendresse** *nf* [affection] affection, tenderness

**ténébreux, euse** [tenebrø, øz] *adj* *Litt* **a)** *Fig* [dessein, affaire] mysterious **b)** [personne] serious, solemn

**teneur** [tənœr] *nf* [de lettre] content; **teneur en alcool** alcohol content (**de** of)

**tenir** [tənir] **1.** *vt* [à la main] to hold ; [promesse, comptes, hôtel] to keep ; [rôle] to play

**2.** *vi* [nœud] to hold ; [neige, coiffure] to last, to hold ; [résister] to hold out ; **tenir à qn/qch** to be attached to sb / sth ; **tenir à faire qch** to be anxious to do sth ; **tenir dans qch** [être contenu] to fit into sth ; **tenir de qn** to take after sb ; **tenez !** [prenez] here (you are)! ; **tiens !** [surprise] well!, hey!

**3.** *v impers* **il ne tient qu'à vous de le faire** it's up to you to do it

**4. se tenir** *vpr* **a)** [réunion] to be held **b)** [personnes] to hold one another ; **se tenir par la main** to hold hands **c)** [être présent] to be **d)** [être cohérent] to make sense **e)** [se conduire] to behave (o.s.) **f)** [se retenir] **se tenir (à)** to hold on (to) **g)** [se borner] **s'en tenir à** to stick to ; **se tenir debout** to stand (up) ; **se tenir droit** to stand up / sit up straight ; **se tenir bien** to behave oneself

**tennis** [tenis] **1.** *nm* tennis ; [terrain] (tennis) court ; **tennis de table** table tennis **2.** *nmpl* [chaussures] *Br* tennis shoes

**tension** [tɑ̃sjɔ̃] *nf* tension ; **tension artérielle** blood pressure ; **avoir de la tension** to have high blood pressure

**tente** [tɑ̃t] *nf* tent

**tenter¹** [tɑ̃te] *vt* [essayer] to try ; **tenter de faire qch** to try or attempt to do sth ■ **tentative** *nf* attempt

**tenter²** [tɑ̃te] *vt* [faire envie à] to tempt ; **tenté de faire qch** tempted to do sth ■ **tentant, -e** *adj* tempting ■ **tentation** *nf* temptation

**tente-roulotte** [tɑ̃trulɔt] *(pl* **tentes-roulottes)** *nf Can* tent trailer, camping trailer

**tenture** [tɑ̃tyr] *nf* (wall) hanging ; [de porte] drape, curtain

**tenu, -e** [tǝny] **1.** *pp de* **tenir 2.** *adj* **tenu de faire qch** obliged to do sth ; **bien / mal tenu** [maison] well / badly kept

**ténu, -e** [teny] *adj* [fil] fine ; [différence] tenuous ; [voix] thin

**tenue** [tǝny] *nf* **a)** [vêtements] clothes, outfit ; **tenue de soirée** evening dress **b)** [conduite] (good) behaviour ; [maintien] posture **c)** [de maison, d'hôtel] running ; [de comptes] keeping **d)** **tenue de route** [de véhicule] road-holding

**ter** [tɛr] *adj* **4 ter** ≃ 4B

**TER** [teǝɛr] *(abr de* **train express régional)** *nm* fast intercity train

**terme** [tɛrm] *nm* **a)** [mot] term **b)** [date limite] time (limit) ; [fin] end ; **mettre un terme à qch** to put an end to sth ; **à court / long terme** [conséquences, projet] short- / long-term **c)** **moyen terme** [solution] middle course **d)** **en bons / mauvais termes** on good / bad terms **(avec qn** with sb) **e)** [loyer] rent ; [jour] rent day ; [période] rental period

**terminal, -e, -aux** [tɛrminal, -o] **1.** *adj* final ; [phase de maladie] terminal **2.** *adj & nf* SCOL **(classe) terminale** *Br* ≃ sixth form, *Am* ≃ twelfth grade **3.** *nm* [d'ordinateur, pétrolier] terminal

**terminer** [tɛrmine] **1.** *vt* to end ; [achever] to finish, to complete **2. se terminer** *vpr* to end **(par** with ; **en** in) ■ **terminaison** *nf* [de mot] ending

**terminologie** [tɛrminɔlɔʒi] *nf* terminology

**terminus** [tɛrminys] *nm* terminus

**terne** [tɛrn] *adj* [couleur, journée] dull, drab ; [personne] dull ■ **ternir 1.** *vt* [métal, réputation] to tarnish ; [meuble, miroir] to dull **2. se ternir** *vpr* [métal] to tarnish

**terrain** [terɛ̃] *nm* [sol] & *Fig* ground ; [étendue] land ; [à bâtir] plot, site ; [pour opérations militaires & GÉOL] terrain ; [stade] *Br* playing field, *Am* athletic field ; **un terrain** a piece of land ; **gagner / perdre du terrain** [armée & *Fig*] to give / gain / lose ground ; **terrain de camping** campsite ; **terrain de football / rugby** football / rugby pitch ; **terrain de golf** golf course ; **terrain de jeu(x)** [pour enfants] playground ; **terrain de sport** *Br* sports ground, *Am* athletic field

**terrasse** [teras] *nf* [balcon, plate-forme] terrace ; [toit] terrace (roof) ; [de café] *Br* pavement *or Am* sidewalk area ; **à la terrasse** outside

**terrassement** [terasmɑ̃] *nm* [travail] excavation

**terrasser** [terase] *vt* [adversaire] to floor ; *Fig* [accabler] to overcome

**terre** [tɛr] *nf* [matière, monde] earth ; [sol] ground ; [opposé à mer, étendue] land ; **terres** [domaine] land, estate ; ÉLEC *Br* earth, *Am* ground ; **la terre** [le monde] the earth ; **la Terre** [planète] Earth ; **à** *ou* **par terre** [tomber] to the ground ; [poser] on the ground ; **par terre** [assis, couché] on the ground ; **sous terre** underground ; **terre cuite** (baked) clay, earthenware ; **terre battue** [de court de tennis] clay ■ **terre-à-terre** *adj inv* down-to-earth ■ **terre-plein** *(pl* **terres-pleins)** *nm* (earth) platform ; [de route] *Br* central reservation, *Am* median strip

**terrer** [tere] ■ **se terrer** *vpr* [fugitif, animal] to go to earth

**terrestre** [terɛstr] *adj* [vie, joies] earthly ; **transport terrestre** land transportation

**terreur** [terœr] *nf* terror ■ **terrible** *adj* awful, terrible

**terrien, -enne** [terjɛ̃, -ɛn] **1.** *adj* land-owning ; **propriétaire terrien** landowner **2.** *nmf* [habitant de la terre] earthling

**terrier** [terje] *nm* [de lapin] burrow ; [chien] terrier

**terrifier** [terifje] *vt* to terrify ■ **terrifiant, -e** *adj* terrifying

**terrine** [terin] *nf* [récipient] terrine ; [pâté] pâté

**territoire** [teritwar] *nm* territory ■ **territorial, -e, -aux** *adj* territorial

**terroir** [terwar] *nm* [sol] soil ; [région] region

**terroriser** [terɔrize] *vt* to terrorize ■ **terrorisme** *nm* terrorism ■ **terroriste** *adj* & *nmf* terrorist

**tertiaire** [tersjɛr] *adj* tertiary

**tes** [te] *voir* **ton**

**test** [tɛst] *nm* test ■ **tester** *vt* [élève, produit] to test

**testament** [tɛstamɑ̃] *nm* [document] will ; REL **Ancien / Nouveau Testament** Old / New Testament

**testicule** [tɛstikyl] *nm* ANAT testicle

**tête** [tɛt] *nf* head ; [visage] face ; [cerveau] brain ; [de lit, de clou, de cortège] head ; [de page, de liste] top, head ; [au football] header ; **à la tête de** [entreprise, parti] at the head of ; [classe] at the top of ; **de la tête aux pieds** from head *or* top to toe ; **tête nue** bare-headed ; **en tête** [d'une course] in the lead ; *Fig* **perdre la tête** to lose one's head ■ **tête-à-tête** *nm inv* tête-à-tête ; **en tête-à-tête** in private

**téter** [tete] *vt* [lait, biberon] to suck ; **donner à téter à qn** to feed sb ■ **tétée** *nf* [de bébé] feed ■ **tétine** *nf* [de biberon] *Br* teat, *Am* nipple ; [sucette] *Br* dummy, *Am* pacifier

**têtu, -e** [tety] *adj* stubborn, obstinate

**teuf** [tœf] *nf Fam* party, rave

**texte** [tɛkst] *nm* text ; [de théâtre] lines ■ **textuellement** *adv* word for word

**textile** [tɛkstil] *adj* & *nm* textile

**texto** [tɛksto] **1.** *adv Fam* word for word, verbatim ; **il a dit ça, texto** those were his very *or* exact words **2.** *nm* TÉL text (message)

**texture** [tɛkstyr] *nf* texture

**TGV** [teʒeve] *(abr de* **train à grande vitesse)** *nm* high-speed train

**Thaïlande** [tailɑ̃d] *nf* **la Thaïlande** Thailand ■ **thaïlandais, -e 1.** *adj* Thai **2.** *nmf* **Thaïlandais, Thaïlandaise** Thai

**thé** [te] *nm* [boisson, réunion] tea ■ **théière** *nf* teapot

**théâtre** [teatr] *nm* [art, lieu] theatre ; [œuvres] drama ; **faire du théâtre** to act ■ **théâtral, -e, -aux** *adj* theatrical

**thème** [tɛm] *nm* theme

**théologie** [teɔlɔʒi] *nf* theology

**théorie** [teɔri] *nf* theory ; **en théorie** in theory

**théorique** [teɔrik] *adj* theoretical

**thérapeutique** [terapøtik] **1.** *adj* therapeutic **2.** *nf* [traitement] therapy ∎ **thérapie** *nf* therapy

**thermal, -e, -aux** [tɛrmal, -o] *adj* station thermale spa

**thermique** [tɛrmik] *adj* [énergie, unité] thermal

**thermomètre** [tɛrmɔmɛtr] *nm* thermometer

**Thermos®** [tɛrmɔs] *nm ou f* Thermos® ( *Br* flask *or Am* bottle)

**thermostat** [tɛrmɔsta] *nm* thermostat

**thèse** [tɛz] *nf* [proposition, ouvrage] thesis

**thon** [tɔ̃] *nm* tuna (fish)

**thym** [tɛ̃] *nm* [plante, aromate] thyme

**Tibet** [tibe] *nm* le Tibet Tibet

**tic** [tik] *nm* [contraction] twitch, tic; *Fig* [manie] mannerism

**ticket** [tikɛ] *nm* ticket

**tiède** [tjɛd] *adj* lukewarm, tepid; [vent, climat] mild ∎ **tiédir** *vt & vi* [refroidir] to cool down; [réchauffer] to warm up

**tien, tienne** [tjɛ̃, tjɛn] **1.** *pron poss* le tien, la tienne, les tien(ne)s yours; les deux tiens your two **2.** *nmpl* les tiens [ta famille] your family

**tiens, tient** [tjɛ̃] *voir* tenir

**tiercé** [tjɛrse] *nm* [pari] place betting (*on the horses*); jouer/gagner au tiercé to bet / win on the horses

**tiers, tierce** [tjɛr, tjɛrs] **1.** *adj* third **2.** *nm* [fraction] third; [personne] third party ∎ **Tiers-Monde** *nm* le Tiers-Monde the Third World

**tige** [tiʒ] *nf* [de plante] stem, stalk; [barre] rod

**tigre** [tigr] *nm* tiger ∎ **tigresse** *nf* tigress

**tilleul** [tijœl] *nm* [arbre] lime tree; [infusion] lime blossom tea

**timbre** [tɛ̃br] *nm* a) [vignette] stamp; [pour traitement médicale] patch b) [sonnette] bell c) [d'instrument, de voix] tone (quality) ∎ **timbré, e** *adj* a) [enveloppe] stamped b) *Fam* [fou] *Br* barmy, *Br* doolally ∎ **timbre-poste**

(*pl* **timbres-poste**) *nm* postage stamp ∎ **timbrer** *vt* [lettre] to put a stamp on; [document] to stamp

**timide** [timid] *adj* [gêné] shy; [protestations] timid ∎ **timidité** *nf* shyness

**tinter** [tɛ̃te] *vi* [cloche] to tinkle; [clefs, monnaie] to jingle; [verres] to chink

**tique** [tik] *nf* tick

**tir** [tir] *nm* [sport] shooting; [action] firing, shooting; [au football] shot; **tir (forain)** shooting *or* rifle range; **tir à l'arc** archery

**tirade** [tirad] *nf* [au théâtre] & *Fig Br* monologue, *Am* monolog

**tirage** [tiraʒ] *nm* a) [de journal] circulation; [de livre] print run; TYP & PHOTO [impression] printing b) [de loterie] draw; **tirage au sort** drawing lots

**tirailler** [tiraje] **1.** *vt* to pull at; *Fig* tiraillé entre [possibilités] torn between **2.** *vi* j'ai la peau qui tiraille my skin feels tight

**tire¹** [tir] *nf* vol à la tire pickpocketing

**tire²** [tir] *nf Can* tire d'érable maple taffy

**tirelire** [tirlir] *nf Br* moneybox, *Am* coin bank

**tirer** [tire] **1.** *vt* to pull; [langue] to stick out; [trait, rideaux, conclusion] to draw; [balle] to fire; [gibier] to shoot; [journal, épreuves de livre, photo] to print; **tirer qch de qch** to pull sth out of sth; [nom, origine] to derive sth from sth; [produit] to extract sth from sth; **tirer qn de qch** [danger, lit] to get sb out of sth **2.** *vi* to pull (**sur** on /at); [faire feu] to shoot, to fire (**sur** at); [cheminée] to draw; **tirer au sort** to draw lots; **tirer à sa fin** to draw to a close **3.** se **tirer** *vpr* se tirer de qch [travail, problème] to cope with sth; [danger, situation] to get out of sth ∎ **tiré, -e** *adj* [traits, visage] drawn ∎ **tire-bouchon** (*pl* **tire-bouchons**) *nm* corkscrew

**tireur** [tirœr] *nm* gunman; **tireur d'élite** marksman

**tiroir** [tirwar] *nm* [de commode] drawer

**tisane** [tizan] *nf* herbal tea

**tisser** [tise] *vt* to weave ∎ **tissage** *nm* [action] weaving

**tissu** [tisy] *nm* material, cloth ; BIOL tissue

**titre** [titr] *nm* [nom, qualité] title ; FIN security ; [diplôme] qualification ; **(gros) titre** [de journal] headline ; **faire les gros titres** to hit the headlines ; **à titre d'exemple** as an example ; **à titre exceptionnel** exceptionally ; **à titre indicatif** for general information ; **à juste titre** rightly ; **titre de transport** ticket

**titrer** [titre] *vt* [film] to title ; [journal] to run as a headline ■ **titré, -e** *adj* [personne] titled

**tituber** [titybe] *vi* to stagger

**titulaire** [titylɛr] **1.** *adj* [enseignant] tenured ; **être titulaire de** [permis] to be the holder of ; [poste] to hold **2.** *nmf* [de permis, de poste] holder (**de** of) ■ **titulariser** *vt* [fonctionnaire] to give tenure to

**tjr, tjrs** *(abr de* **toujours)** SMS Alwz

**TNT** *(abr de* **télévision numérique terrestre)** *nf* DTTV

**toast** [tost] *nm* [pain grillé] piece or slice of toast ; [allocution] toast ; **porter un toast à** to drink (a toast) to

**toboggan** [tobɔgɑ̃] *nm* [d'enfant] slide ; *Can* [traîneau] toboggan ; [voie de circulation] *Br* flyover, *Am* overpass

**toc** [tɔk] *nm* **du toc** [camelote] trash ; **bijou en toc** imitation jewel

**TOC** [tɔk] *(abr de* **troubles obsessionnels compulsifs)** *nmpl* MÉD OCD

**toi** [twa] *pron pers* **a)** [après une préposition] you ; **avec toi** with you **b)** [sujet] you ; **toi, tu peux** you may ; **c'est toi qui...** it's you who... **c)** [réfléchi] **assieds-toi** sit (yourself) down ; **dépêche-toi** hurry up ■ **toi-même** *pron* yourself

**toile** [twal] *nf* **a)** [étoffe] cloth ; [à voile, sac] canvas ; **une toile** a piece of cloth or canvas ; THÉÂT & *Fig* **toile de fond** backdrop ; **toile cirée** oil cloth **b)** [tableau] painting, canvas **c)** **toile d'araignée** (spider's) web, cobweb **d)** ORDINAT **la Toile** the Web, the web

**toilette** [twalɛt] *nf* [action] wash(ing) ; [vêtements] clothes, outfit ; **faire sa toi-**

**lette** to wash (and dress) ; **les toilettes** [W-C] *Br* the toilet(s), *Am* the men's / ladies' room

**toit** [twa] *nm* roof ■ **toiture** *nf* roof(ing)

**TOK?** SMS *abr écrite de* **tu es d'accord?**

**tôle¹, taule** [tol] *nf* t *Fam* [prison] *Br* nick, clink

**tôle²** [tol] *nf* sheet metal ; **tôle ondulée** corrugated iron

**tolérer** [tɔlere] *vt* [permettre] to tolerate ■ **tolérable** *adj* tolerable ■ **tolérance** *nf* tolerance ■ **tolérant, -e** *adj* tolerant (**à l'égard de** of)

**TOM** [tɔm] *(abr de* **territoire d'outre-mer)** *nm Anc French overseas territory*

**tomate** [tɔmat] *nf* tomato

**tombe** [tɔ̃b] *nf* grave ; [avec monument] tomb ■ **tombale** *adj f* **pierre tombale** gravestone, tombstone ■ **tombeau, -x** *nm* tomb

**tomber** [tɔ̃be] *(aux* **être)** *vi* to fall ; [température] to drop, to fall ; [vent] to drop (off) ; **tomber malade** to fall ill ; **tomber par terre** to fall (down) ; **faire tomber** [personne] to knock over ; [gouvernement, prix] to bring down ; **laisser tomber** [objet] to drop ; *Fig* **laisser tomber qn** to let sb down ; **tomber un lundi** to fall on a Monday ; **tomber sur qch** [trouver] to come across sth ■ **tombée** *nf* **la tombée de la nuit** nightfall

**tome** [tɔm] *nm* [livre] volume

**ton¹, ta, tes** [tɔ̃, ta, te]

> **ta** becomes **ton** [tɔ̃n] before a vowel or mute h.

*adj poss* your ; **ton père** your father ; **ta mère** your mother ; **ton ami(e)** your friend

**ton²** [tɔ̃] *nm* [de voix] tone ; [de couleur] shade, tone ; MUS [gamme] key ; [hauteur de son] pitch ■ **tonalité** *nf* [timbre, impression] tone ; [de téléphone] *Br* dialling tone, *Am* dial tone

**tondre** [tɔ̃dr] *vt* [mouton] to shear ; [gazon] to mow ■ **tondeuse** *nf* shears ; [à cheveux] clippers ; **tondeuse (à gazon)** (lawn) mower

**tongs** [tɔ̃g] *nfpl Br* flip-flops, *Am* thongs

**tonifier** [tɔnifje] *vt* [muscles, peau] to tone up ; [personne] to invigorate

**tonique** [tɔnik] **1.** *adj* [froid, effet] tonic, invigorating **2.** *nm* [médicament] tonic ; [cosmétique] tonic lotion

**tonnage** [tɔnaʒ] *nm* [de navire] tonnage

**tonne** [tɔn] *nf* [poids] metric ton, tonne

**tonneau, -x** [tɔno] *nm* **a)** [récipient] barrel, cask **b)** [acrobatie] roll ; **faire un tonneau** to roll over

**tonner** [tɔne] **1.** *vi* [canons] to thunder ; *Fig* [crier] to thunder, to rage (**contre** against) **2.** *v impers* **il tonne** it's thundering ■ **tonnerre** *nm* thunder

**tonus** [tɔnys] *nm* [énergie] energy, vitality

**top** [tɔp] *nm* [signal sonore] beep

**topographie** [tɔpɔgrafi] *nf* topography

**toquade, tocade** [tɔkad] *nf Fam* **toquade (pour)** [personne] crush (on) ; [style, mode] craze (for)

**toque** [tɔk] *nf* [de fourrure] fur hat ; [de jockey] cap ; [de cuisinier] hat

**torche** [tɔrʃ] *nf* [flamme] torch ; **torche électrique** *Br* torch, *Am* flashlight

**torchon** [tɔrʃɔ̃] *nm* [à vaisselle] dish towel, *Br* tea towel

**tordre** [tɔrdr] **1.** *vt* to twist ; [linge, cou] to wring ; [barre] to bend **2. se tordre** *vpr* to twist ; [barre] to bend ; **se tordre de douleur** to be doubled up with pain ; **se tordre (de rire)** to split one's sides (laughing) ; **se tordre la cheville** to twist *or* sprain one's ankle ■ **tordu, -e** *adj* twisted ; [esprit] warped

**tornade** [tɔrnad] *nf* tornado

**torpille** [tɔrpij] *nf* torpedo ■ **torpiller** *vt* [navire, projet] to torpedo

**torrent** [tɔrɑ̃] *nm* torrent ; *Fig* **un torrent de larmes** a flood of tears ; **il pleut à torrents** it's pouring (down) ■ **torrentiel, -elle** *adj* [pluie] torrential

**torride** [tɔrid] *adj* [chaleur] torrid

**torse** [tɔrs] *nm* ANAT chest ; **torse nu** stripped to the waist

**tort** [tɔr] *nm* [dommage] wrong ; [défaut] fault ; **avoir tort** to be wrong (**de faire** to do, in doing) ; **être dans son tort** *ou* **en tort** to be in the wrong ; **faire du tort à qn** to harm sb ; **à tort** wrongly ; **à tort ou à raison** rightly or wrongly

**torticolis** [tɔrtikɔli] *nm* **avoir le torticolis** to have a stiff neck

**tortiller** [tɔrtije] **1.** *vt* to twist ; [moustache] to twirl **2. se tortiller** *vpr* [ver, personne] to wriggle

**tortionnaire** [tɔrsjɔnɛr] *nm* torturer

**tortue** [tɔrty] *nf Br* tortoise, *Am* turtle ; [de mer] turtle

**torture** [tɔrtyr] *nf* torture ■ **torturer** *vt* to torture

**tôt** [to] *adv* early ; **au plus tôt** at the earliest ; **le plus tôt possible** as soon as possible ; **tôt ou tard** sooner or later ; **je n'étais pas plus tôt sorti que…** no sooner had I gone out than…

**total, -e, -aux** [tɔtal, -o] *adj & nm* total ; **au total** all in all, in total ; [somme toute] all in all ■ **totaliser** *vt* to total ■ **totalité** *nf* entirety ; **la totalité de** all of ; **en totalité** [détruit] entirely ; [payé] fully

**totalitaire** [tɔtalitɛr] *adj* [État, régime] totalitarian

**touche** [tuʃ] *nf* [de clavier] key ; [de téléphone] (push-)button ; [au football & au rugby] throw-in ; **téléphone à touches** push-button phone ; **une touche de** [un peu de] a touch *or* hint of

**touche-à-tout** [tuʃatu] *nmf inv Fam* [adulte] dabbler ; [enfant] **c'est un petit touche-à-tout** he's into everything

**toucher** [tuʃe] **1.** *nm* [sens] touch ; **au toucher** to the touch **2.** *vt* to touch ; [paie] to draw ; [chèque] to cash ; [émouvoir] to touch, to move ; [concerner] to affect **3.** *vi* **toucher à** to touch ; [sujet] to touch on ; [but, fin] to approach **4. se toucher** *vpr* [lignes, mains] to touch ■ **touchant, -e** *adj* [émouvant] moving, touching

**touffe** [tuf] *nf* [de cheveux, d'herbe] tuft ■ **touffu, -e** *adj* [barbe, haie] thick, bushy

**toujours** [tuʒur] *adv* [exprime la continuité, la répétition] always ; [encore] still ; **pour toujours** for ever

**tour¹** [tur] *nf* [bâtiment & ORDINAT] tower; [immeuble] tower block, high-rise; ÉCHECS castle, rook

**tour²** [tur] *nm* **a)** [mouvement, ordre, tournure] turn; [de magie] trick; [excursion] trip, outing; [à pied] stroll, walk; [en voiture] drive; **tour (de piste)** [de course] lap; **de dix mètres de tour** ten metres round; **faire le tour de** to go round; **faire le tour du monde** to go round the world; **faire un tour** [à pied] to go for a stroll *or* walk; [en voiture] to go for a drive; **à tour de rôle** in turn; **tour à tour** in turn, by turns **b)** TECH lathe; [de potier] wheel

**tourbillon** [turbijɔ̃] *nm* [de vent] whirlwind; [d'eau] whirlpool; [de sable] swirl ▪ **tourbillonner** *vi* to whirl

**tourisme** [turism] *nm* tourism; **faire du tourisme** to do some touring; **agence de tourisme** tourist agency; **industrie du tourisme** tourist industry ▪ **touriste** *nmf* tourist ▪ **touristique** *adj* guide/menu **touristique** tourist guide/menu; **route touristique, circuit touristique** scenic route

**tourmenter** [turmɑ̃te] **1.** *vt* to torment **2. se tourmenter** *vpr* to worry

**tournage** [turnaʒ] *nm* [de film] shooting, filming

**tournant** [turnɑ̃] *nm* [de route] bend; *Fig* [moment] turning point (**de** in)

**tourne-disque** [turnədisk] (*pl* **tourne-disques**) *nm* record player

**tournée** [turne] *nf* [de facteur, de boissons] round; [spectacle] tour; **faire sa tournée** to do one's rounds; **faire la tournée de** [magasins, musées] to go to

**tourner** [turne] **1.** *vt* to turn; [film] to shoot, to make; [difficulté] to get round; **tourner qn/qch en ridicule** to ridicule sb/sth **2.** *vi* to turn; [tête, toupie] to spin; [Terre] to revolve, to turn; [moteur, usine] to run; [lait] to go off; **tourner autour de** [objet] to go round; [maison, personne] to hang around; [question] to centre on; **tourner bien/mal** [évoluer] to turn out well/badly; **tourner au froid** [temps] to turn cold

**3. se tourner** *vpr* to turn (right) *Br* round *or Am* around; **se tourner vers** to turn towards *or Br* toward *or Am* around

**tournesol** [turnəsɔl] *nm* sunflower

**tournevis** [turnəvis] *nm* screwdriver

**tourniquet** [turnikɛ] *nm* [barrière] turnstile; [pour arroser] sprinkler

**tournoi** [turnwa] *nm* [de tennis & HIST] tournament; **participer à un tournoi** to play in a tournament

**tournoyer** [turnwaje] *vi* to swirl (round)

**tournure** [turnyr] *nf* [expression] turn of phrase; **tournure d'esprit** way of thinking; **tournure des événements** turn of events

**Toussaint** [tusɛ̃] *nf* **la Toussaint** All Saints' Day

**tousser** [tuse] *vi* to cough

**tout, toute, tous** [tu, tut, tu, tut] **1.** *adj* all; **tous les livres** all the books; **tout l'argent/le temps/le village** all the money/time/village; **toute la nuit** all night, the whole (of the) night; **tous (les) deux** both; **tous (les) trois** all three

**2.** *adj indéf* [chaque] every, each; [n'importe quel] any; **tous les ans/jours** every *or* each year/day; **tous les deux mois** every two months, every second month; **tous les cinq mètres** every five metres; **tout homme** [tutɔm] every *or* any man

**3.** *pron pl* **tous** [tus] all; **ils sont tous là, tous sont là** they're all there

**4.** *pron m sg* **tout** everything; **dépenser tout** to spend everything, to spend it all; **tout ce qui est là** everything that's here; **tout ce que je sais** everything that *or* all that I know; **en tout** [au total] in all

**5.** *adv* [tout à fait] quite; [très] very; **tout simplement** quite simply; **tout petit** very small; **tout neuf** brand new; **tout seul** all alone; **tout droit** straight ahead; **tout autour** all around, right round; **tout au début** right at the beginning; **le tout premier** the very first; **tout au plus/moins** at the very most/least; **tout en chantant** while singing; **tout rusé qu'il est** ou **soit** however sly he may be; **tout à coup** suddenly, all of a sudden; **tout à fait** completely, quite; **tout de suite** at once **6.** nm **le tout** everything, the lot; **un tout** a whole; **le tout est que...** [l'important] the main thing is that...; **pas du tout** not at all; **rien du tout** nothing at all; **du tout au tout** [changer] entirely, completely

**toutefois** [tutfwa] adv nevertheless, however ■ **tout-puissant, toute-puissante** (mpl **tout-puissants**, fpl **toutes-puissantes**) adj all-powerful ■ **tout-terrain 1.** (pl **tout-terrains**) adj **véhicule tout-terrain** off-road or all terrain vehicle; **vélo tout-terrain** mountain bike **2.** nm **faire du tout-terrain** to do off-road racing

**toutou** [tutu] nm a) Fam [chien] doggie b) Can [peluche] plush toy

**toux** [tu] nf cough

**toxicomane** [tɔksikɔman] nmf drug addict ■ **toxicomanie** nf drug addiction

**toxique** [tɔksik] adj poisonous, toxic

**TP** [tepe] (abr de **travaux pratiques**) nmpl [à l'école] practical work

**TPE** [tepeø] **1.** nmpl (abr de **travaux personnels encadrés**) GIS **2.** nf (abr de **très petite entreprise**) VSB

**trac** [trak] nm **le trac** [peur] the jitters; [de candidat] exam nerves; [d'acteur] stage fright; **avoir le trac** to be nervous

**traçabilité** [trasabilite] nf traceability

**trace** [tras] nf [quantité, tache, vestige] trace; [marque] mark; [de fugitif] trail; **traces** [de bête, de pneus] tracks; **traces de pas** footprints; **disparaître sans laisser de traces** to disappear without trace

**tracer** [trase] vt [dessiner] to draw; [écrire] to trace; **tracer une route** to mark out a route; [frayer] to open up a route ■ **tracé** nm [plan] layout; [ligne] line

**tract** [trakt] nm leaflet

**tractations** [traktɑsjɔ̃] nfpl dealings

**tracter** [trakte] vt to tow

**tracteur** [traktœr] nm tractor

**trader** nm = **tradeur**

**tradeur, euse** [tredœr, øz] nmf trader

**tradition** [tradisjɔ̃] nf tradition ■ **traditionnel, -elle** adj traditional

**traduire** [traduir] vt to translate (**de** from; **en** into) ■ **traducteur, -trice** nmf translator ■ **traduction** nf translation

**trafic** [trafik] nm [automobile, ferroviaire] traffic; [de marchandises] traffic, trade ■ **trafiquant, -e** nmf trafficker, dealer

**trafiquer** [trafike] **1.** vt Fam a) [falsifier] to tamper with b) [manigancer] **qu'est-ce que tu trafiques?** what are you up to? **2.** vi to be involved in trafficking

**tragédie** [traʒedi] nf [pièce de théâtre, événement] tragedy ■ **tragique** adj tragic; **prendre qch au tragique** [remarque] to take sth too much to heart

**trahir** [trair] **1.** vt to betray; [secret] to give away, to betray; [sujet : forces] to fail **2. se trahir** vpr to give oneself away ■ **trahison** nf betrayal; [crime] treason

**train** [trɛ̃] nm a) [de voyageurs, de marchandises] train; **prendre le train** to catch or take the train; **voyager en train** to travel by train; **train à grande vitesse** high-speed train; **train corail** express train; **train couchettes** sleeper b) **en train** [en forme] on form; **être en train de faire qch** to be (busy) doing sth c) [allure] pace; **train de vie** life style d) [de pneus] set; [de péniches, de véhicules] string e) **train d'atterrissage** [d'avion] undercarriage

**traînard, -e** [trɛnar, -ard] nmf Br slowcoach, Am slowpoke

**traîne** [trɛn] nf a) [de robe] train b) **être à la traîne** to lag behind c) Can [traîneau] **traîne sauvage** toboggan

**traîneau, -x** [trɛno] nm sleigh, Br sledge, Am sled

**traînée** [trɛne] nf [de peinture, dans le ciel] streak

**traîner** [trɛne] **1.** *vt* to drag; [wagon] to pull **2.** *vi* [jouets, papiers] to lie around; [s'attarder] to lag behind, to dawdle; [errer] to hang around; [subsister] to linger on; **traîner par terre** [robe] to trail (on the ground); **traîner en longueur** to drag on **3. se traîner** *vpr* [avancer] to drag oneself (along); [par terre] to crawl; [durer] to drag on ▪ **traînant, -e** *adj* [voix] drawling

**traire** [trɛr] *vt* [vache] to milk

**trait** [trɛ] *nm* line; [en dessinant] stroke; [caractéristique] feature, trait; **traits** [du visage] features; **d'un trait** [boire] in one gulp, in one go; **avoir trait à qch** to relate to sth

**traite** [trɛt] *nf* [de vache] milking; [lettre de change] bill, draft; **d'une (seule) traite** [sans interruption] in one go; **traite des Noirs** slave trade

**traité** [trete] *nm* [accord] treaty; [ouvrage] treatise (**sur** on); **traité de paix** peace treaty

**traiter** [trete] **1.** *vt* [se comporter envers, soigner] to treat; [problème, sujet] to deal with; [marché] to negotiate; [matériau, produit] to treat, to process; **traiter qn de tous les noms** to call sb all the names under the sun **2.** *vi* to negotiate, to deal (**avec** with); **traiter de** [sujet] to deal with ▪ **traitement** [tretmɑ̃] *nm* [de personne, de maladie] treatment; [de matériau] processing; [gains] salary; **traitement de données / de texte** data / word processing; **machine à traitement de texte** word processor

**traiteur** [tretœr] *nm* [fournisseur] caterer; **chez le traiteur** at the delicatessen

**traître** [tretr] **1.** *nm* traitor; **en traître** treacherously **2.** *adj* [dangereux] treacherous; **être traître à une cause** to be a traitor to a cause ▪ **traîtrise** *nf* treachery

**trajectoire** [traʒɛktwar] *nf* path, trajectory

**trajet** [traʒɛ] *nm* journey; [distance] distance; [itinéraire] route

**tram** [tram] *nm Fam Br* tram, *Am* streetcar

**tramer** [trame] ▪ **se tramer** *vpr* **il se trame quelque chose** something's afoot

**trampoline** [trɑ̃polin] *nm* trampoline

**tramway** [tramwɛ] *nm Br* tram, *Am* streetcar

**tranche** [trɑ̃ʃ] *nf* [morceau] slice; [bord] edge; [partie] portion; [de salaire, d'impôts] bracket; **tranche d'âge** age bracket

**tranchée** [trɑ̃ʃe] *nf* trench

**trancher** [trɑ̃ʃe] **1.** *vt* to cut; [difficulté, question] to settle **2.** *vi* [décider] to decide; [contraster] to contrast (**sur** with) ▪ **tranchant, -e 1.** *adj* [couteau] sharp; [ton] curt **2.** *nm* (cutting) edge; *Fig* **à double tranchant** double-edged ▪ **tranché, -e** *adj* [couleurs] distinct; [opinion] clear-cut

**tranquille** [trɑ̃kil] *adj* quiet; [mer] calm, still; [esprit] easy; **avoir la conscience tranquille** to have a clear conscience; **soyez tranquille** don't worry; **laisser qn / qch tranquille** to leave sb / sth alone

**tranquilliser** [trɑ̃kilize] *vt* to reassure ▪ **tranquillisant** *nm* tranquillizer

**tranquillité** [trɑ̃kilite] *nf* (peace and) quiet; [d'esprit] peace of mind

**transaction** [trɑ̃zaksjɔ̃] *nf* [opération] transaction; *JUR* compromise

**transatlantique** [trɑ̃zatlɑ̃tik] **1.** *adj* transatlantic **2.** *nm* [paquebot] transatlantic liner; [chaise] deckchair ▪ **transat** *nm* [chaise] deckchair

**transcrire** [trɑ̃skrir] *vt* to transcribe ▪ **transcription** *nf* transcription; [document] transcript

**transe** [trɑ̃s] *nf* **en transe** [mystique] in a trance; [excité] very excited; **entrer en transe** to go into a trance

**transférer** [trɑ̃sfere] *vt* to transfer (**à** to) ▪ **transfert** *nm* transfer

**transformer** [trɑ̃sfɔrme] **1.** *vt* to transform; [maison, au rugby] to convert; [matière première] to process; **transformer qch en qch** to turn sth into sth **2. se transformer** *vpr* to change, to be transformed (**en**

**treillis**

into) ■ **transformateur** *nm* ÉLEC transformer ■ **transformation** *nf* change, transformation ; [de maison] alteration

**transfuge** [trãsfyʒ] *nmf* defector

**transfusion** [trãsfyzjɔ̃] *nf* **transfusion (sanguine)** (blood) transfusion

**transgresser** [trãsgrese] *vt* [ordres] to disobey ; [loi] to infringe

**transi, -e** [trãzi] *adj* [personne] numb with cold

**transiger** [trãziʒe] *vi* to compromise

**transistor** [trãzistɔr] *nm* transistor

**transit** [trãzit] *nm* transit ; **en transit** in transit

**transition** [trãzisjɔ̃] *nf* transition ■ **transitoire** *adj* [qui passe] transient ; [provisoire] transitional

**transmettre** [trãsmɛtr] **1.** *vt* [message, héritage] to pass on (**à** to) ; RADIO & TV [informations] to transmit ; [émission] to broadcast **2. se transmettre** *vpr* [maladie, tradition] to be passed on ■ **transmetteur** *nm* [appareil] transmitter ■ **transmission** *nf* transmission

**transparaître** [trãsparɛtr] *vi* to show (through)

**transparent, -e** [trãsparã, -ãt] *adj* clear, transparent ■ **transparence** *nf* transparency ; **voir qch par transparence** to see sth showing through

**transpercer** [trãspɛrse] *vt* to pierce

**transpirer** [trãspire] *vi* [suer] to sweat, to perspire ■ **transpiration** *nf* perspiration

**transplanter** [trãsplãte] *vt* [organe, plante] to transplant

**transport** [trãspɔr] *nm* [action] transport, transportation (**de** of) ; **transports** [moyens] transport ; **transports en commun** public transport ; **moyen de transport** means of transport

**transporter** [trãspɔrte] *vt* [passagers, troupes, marchandises] to transport, to carry ■ **transporteur** *nm* transporteur (routier) *Br* haulier, *Am* trucker

**transposer** [trãspoze] *vt* to transpose ■ **transposition** *nf* transposition

**trapèze** [trapɛz] *nm* [de cirque] trapeze

**trappe** [trap] *nf* [de plancher] trap door

**trappeur** [trapœr] *nm* trapper

**trapu, -e** [trapy] *adj* [personne] stocky, thickset

**traquer** [trake] *vt* to hunt (down)

**traumatiser** [tromatize] *vt* to traumatize ■ **traumatisant, -e** *adj* traumatic ■ **traumatisme** *nm* [choc] trauma

**travail, -aux** [travaj, -o] *nm* [activité, lieu] work ; [à effectuer] job, task ; [emploi] job ; [façonnage] working (**de** of) ; [ouvrage, étude] work, publication ; ÉCON & MÉD labour ; **travaux** work ; [dans la rue] *Br* roadworks, *Am* roadwork ; [aménagement] alterations ; SCOL & UNIV **travaux pratiques** practical work ; SCOL & UNIV **travaux dirigés** tutorial ; SCOL **travaux manuels** handicrafts ; **travaux ménagers** housework

**travailler** [travaje] **1.** *vi* [personne] to work (**à qch** on sth) ; [bois] to warp **2.** *vt* [discipline, rôle, style] to work on ; [façonner] to work ■ **travailleur, -euse** **1.** *adj* hard-working **2.** *nmf* worker

**travailliste** [travajist] **1.** *adj* POL Labour **2.** *nmf* POL member of the Labour party

**travers** [travɛr] **1.** *prép* & *adv* **à travers** through ; **en travers (de)** across **2.** *adv* **de travers** [chapeau, nez] crooked ; **j'ai avalé de travers** it went down the wrong way

**traverser** [travɛrse] *vt* to cross ; [foule, période, mur] to go through ■ **traversée** *nf* [voyage] crossing

**travesti** [travɛsti] *nm* [acteur] female impersonator ; [homosexuel] transvestite

**travestir** [travɛstir] *vt* to disguise

**trébucher** [trebyʃe] *vi* to stumble (**sur** over) ; **faire trébucher qn** to trip sb (up)

**trèfle** [trɛfl] *nm* [plante] clover ; CARTES [couleur] clubs

**treillis** [treji] *nm* **a)** [treillage] lattice(work) ; [en métal] wire mesh **b)** [tenue militaire] combat uniform

**treize** [trɛz] *adj* & *nm inv* thirteen
■ **treizième** *adj* & *nmf* thirteenth

**trek** [trɛk], **trekking** [trɛkiŋ] *nm* trek,
trekking; **faire un trek** to go on a
trek; **faire du trekking** to go trekking
■ **trekkeur, euse** *nmf* trekker

**tréma** [trema] *nm* di(a)eresis

**trembler** [trɑ̃ble] *vi* to shake, to tremble; [de froid, peur] to tremble (**de**
with); [flamme, lumière] to flicker;
[voix] to tremble, to quaver; [avoir
peur] to be afraid (**que** (+ subjunctive)
that); **trembler pour qn** to fear for sb
■ **tremblement** [-əmɑ̃] *nm* [action,
frisson] shaking, trembling; **tremblement de terre** earthquake ■ **tremblo-
ter** *vi* to quiver

**tremper** [trɑ̃pe] **1.** *vt* to soak, to
drench; [plonger] to dip (**dans** in);
[acier] to temper **2.** *vi* to soak; **faire
tremper qch** to soak sth; *Péj* **tremper
dans** [participer] to be mixed up in

**tremplin** [trɑ̃plɛ̃] *nm* springboard

**trente** [trɑ̃t] *adj* & *nm inv* thirty; **un
trente-trois tours** [disque] an LP; **se
mettre sur son trente et un** to get all
dressed up ■ **trentaine** *nf* **une trentaine (de)** [nombre] (about) thirty;
**avoir la trentaine** [âge] to be about
thirty ■ **trentième** *adj* & *nmf* thirtieth

**trente-six** (*en fin de phrase* [trɑ̃tsis] ,
*devant consonne ou 'h' aspiré* [trɑ̃tsi] ,
*devant voyelle ou 'h' muet* [trɑ̃tsiz]) **1.** *adj*
*Fam* [pour exprimer la multitude] ump-
teen, dozens of; **il n'y a pas trente-six
solutions!** there aren't all that many
solutions!; **j'ai trente-six mille choses
à faire** I've a hundred and one things to
do **2.** *nm inv Fam* **tous les trente-six du
mois** once in a blue moon

**très** [trɛ] ( [trɛz] *before vowel or mute h*)
*adv* very; **très aimé / critiqué** [with
past participle] much *or* greatly liked /
criticized

**trésor** [trezɔr] *nm* treasure; **le Trésor (public)** [service] public revenue
(department); [finances] public funds;
**des trésors de patience** boundless
patience ■ **trésorerie** [-rri] *nf* [bureaux

d'un club] accounts department; [ges-
tion] accounting; [capitaux] funds
■ **trésorier, -ère** *nmf* treasurer

**tressaillir** [tresajir] *vi* [frémir] to shake,
to quiver; [de joie, de peur] to tremble
(**de** with); [sursauter] to jump, to start

**tresse** [trɛs] *nf* [cordon] braid; [cheveux]
*Br* plait, *Am* braid ■ **tresser** [trese] *vt* to
braid; *Br* [cheveux] to plait, *Am* to braid

**trêve** [trɛv] *nf* [de combat] truce

**tri** [tri] *nm* sorting (out); **faire le tri de** to
sort (out); **(centre de) tri** [des postes]
sorting office ■ **triage** *nm* sorting
(out)

**triangle** [trijɑ̃gl] *nm* triangle ■ **triangulaire** *adj* triangular

**tribord** [tribɔr] *nm* [de bateau, d'avion]
starboard

**tribu** [triby] *nf* tribe ■ **tribal, -e, -aux**
*adj* tribal

**tribunal, -aux** [tribynal, -o] *nm* JUR
court; [militaire] tribunal

**tribune** [tribyn] *nf* [de salle publique]
gallery; [de stade] (grand)stand; [d'ora-
teur] rostrum

**tribut** [triby] *nm* tribute (**à** to)

**tricher** [triʃe] *vi* to cheat ■ **tricherie** *nf*
cheating, trickery ■ **tricheur, -euse**
*nmf* cheat, *Am* cheater

**tricolore** [trikɔlɔr] *adj* [cocarde] red,
white and blue; **le drapeau / l'équipe
tricolore** the French flag / team

**tricot** [triko] *nm* [activité, ouvrage]
knitting; [chandail] sweater, *Br* jumper; [ouvrage] piece of knitting; **en tricot** knitted; **tricot de corps** *Br* vest, *Am*
undershirt ■ **tricoter** *vt* & *vi* to knit

**trier** [trije] *vt* [lettres] to sort; [vête-
ments] to sort through

**trilingue** [trilɛ̃g] *adj* trilingual

**trimestre** [trimɛstr] *nm* quarter; SCOL
term; SCOL **premier / second / troisième trimestre** *Br* autumn *or Am* fall /
winter / summer term ■ **trimestriel,
-elle** *adj* [revue] quarterly; **bulletin
trimestriel** end-of-term *Br* report *or
Am* report card

**Trinité** [trinite] *nf* **la Trinité** [fête] Trinity; [dogme] the Trinity

**trinquer** [trɛ̃ke] *vi* to chink glasses; **trinquer à la santé de qn** to drink to sb's health

**trio** [trijo] *nm* [groupe & MUS] trio

**triomphe** [trijɔ̃f] *nm* triumph (**sur** over) ■ **triomphal, -e, -aux** *adj* triumphal ■ **triomphant, -e** *adj* triumphant ■ **triompher** *vi* to triumph (**de** over); (jubiler) to be jubilant

**triple** [tripl] **1.** *adj* treble, triple; SPORT **triple saut** triple jump **2.** *nm* **le triple** three times as much (**de** as) ■ **tripler** *vt* & *vi* to treble, to triple ■ **triplés**, *nmf pl* triplets

**trisomique** [trizɔmik] **1.** *adj* **enfant trisomique** Down's syndrome child **2.** *nmf* Down's syndrome child

**triste** [trist] *adj* sad; (sinistre) dreary; (lamentable) unfortunate■ **tristesse** *nf* sadness; (du temps) dreariness

**triturer** [trityre] **1.** *vt* (mouchoir) to knead **2. se triturer** *vpr Fam* **se triturer l'esprit** *ou* **les méninges** to rack one's brains

**trivial, -e, -aux** [trivjal, -o] *adj* coarse, vulgar

**troc** [trɔk] *nm* exchange; (système économique) barter

**trois** [trwa] *adj* & *nm inv* three; **les trois quarts (de)** three-quarters (of) ■ **troisième 1.** *adj* & *nmf* third; **le troisième âge** (vieillesse) the retirement years; **personne du troisième âge** senior citizen **2.** *nf* **la troisième** SCOL *Br* ≃ fourth year, *Am* ≃ eighth grade; AUTO (vitesse) third gear ■ **troisièmement** *adv* thirdly

**trombe** [trɔ̃b] *nf* **trombe(s) d'eau** (pluie) rainstorm, downpour

**trombone** [trɔ̃bɔn] *nm* (instrument) trombone; (agrafe) paper clip

**trompe** [trɔ̃p] *nf* (d'éléphant) trunk; (d'insecte) proboscis; (instrument de musique) horn

**tromper** [trɔ̃pe] **1.** *vt* (abuser) to fool (**sur** about); (être infidèle à) to be unfaithful to; (échapper à) to elude **2. se tromper** *vpr* to be mistaken; **se tromper de route** to take the wrong road; **se tromper de jour** to get the day

wrong ■ **tromperie** [-pri] *nf* deceit, deception ■ **trompeur, -euse** *adj* (apparences) deceptive, misleading; (personne) deceitful

**trompette** [trɔ̃pɛt] *nf* trumpet ■ **trompettiste** *nmf* trumpet player

**tronc** [trɔ̃] *nm* (d'arbre & ANAT) trunk; (boîte) collection box

**tronçon** [trɔ̃sɔ̃] *nm* section ■ **tronçonner** *vt* to cut into sections

**trône** [tron] *nm* throne ■ **trôner** *vi* *Fig* (vase, personne) to occupy the place of *Br* honour *or* *Am* honor

**trop** [tro] *adv* (avec adjectif, adverbe) too; (avec verbe) too much; **en trop, de trop** too much / many; **2 euros de** *ou* **en trop** 2 euros too much; **une personne de** *ou* **en trop** one person too many; **être de trop** (personne) to be in the way, to be unwelcome; **trop dur /loin** too hard / far; **trop fatigué pour jouer** too tired to play; **lire trop** to read too much; **trop de sel** too much salt; **trop de gens** too many people; **du fromage en trop** too much cheese; **un verre en trop** one glass too many; **trop souvent** too often; **trop peu** not enough ■ **trop-plein** (*pl* **trop-pleins**) *nm* (excédent) overflow; (dispositif) overflow pipe

**trophée** [trɔfe] *nm* trophy

**tropique** [trɔpik] *nm* tropic; **sous les tropiques** in the tropics ■ **tropical, -e, -aux** *adj* tropical

**troquer** [trɔke] *vt* to exchange (**contre** for)

**trot** [tro] *nm* trot; **aller au trot** to trot ■ **trotter** *vi* (cheval) to trot

**trottoir** [trɔtwar] *nm* *Br* pavement, *Am* sidewalk

**trou** [tru] *nm* hole; (d'aiguille) eye; *Fig* **trou de mémoire** memory lapse

**trouble** [trubl] **1.** *adj* (liquide) cloudy; (image) blurred; (affaire) shady **2.** *adv* **voir trouble** to see things blurred **3.** *nm* (désarroi) distress; (désordre) confusion; **troubles** (de santé) trouble; (révolte) disturbances, troubles

**trouble-fête** [trubləfɛt] *(pl* **trouble-fêtes)** *nmf* spoilsport

**troubler** [truble] **1.** *vt* to disturb ; [vue] to blur ; [liquide] to make cloudy ; [esprit] to unsettle ; [projet] to upset ; [inquiéter] to trouble **2. se troubler** *vpr* [liquide] to become cloudy ; [personne] to become flustered ▪ **troublant, -e** *adj* [détail] disturbing, disquieting

**trouer** [true] *vt* to make a hole / holes in ▪ **troué, e** *adj* **un vieux châle troué** a *Br* tatty *or Am* raggedy old shawl ; **des chaussettes toutes trouées** socks full of holes

**troupe** [trup] *nf* [de soldats] troop ; [de théâtre] company, troupe

**troupeau, -x** [trupo] *nm* [de vaches] herd ; [de moutons] flock

**trousse** [trus] *nf* [étui] case, kit ; [d'écolier] pencil case ; **trousse à pharmacie** first-aid kit ; **trousse de toilette** toilet bag

**trousseau, -x** [truso] *nm* [de mariée] trousseau ; **trousseau de clefs** bunch of keys

**trouvaille** [truvaj] *nf* (lucky) find

**trouver** [truve] **1.** *vt* to find ; **aller trouver qn** to go and see sb ; **je trouve que...** I think that... ; **comment la trouvez-vous ?** what do you think of her ? **2. se trouver** *vpr* to be ; [être situé] to be situated ; **se trouver dans une situation difficile** to find oneself in a difficult situation ; **se trouver mal** [s'évanouir] to faint ; **se trouver petit** to consider oneself small **3.** *v impers* **il se trouve que...** it happens that...

**truander** [tryɑ̃de] *vt Fam* to rip off

**truc** [tryk] *nm Fam* **a)** [combine] trick **b)** [chose] thing, thingamajig ; **ce n'est pas son truc** it's not his thing

**trucage** [trykaʒ] *nm* = **truquage**

**truffe** [tryf] *nf* [champignon, confiserie] truffle ; [de chien] nose

**truffer** [tryfe] *vt* [remplir] to stuff (**de** with)

**truite** [trɥit] *nf* trout

**truquer** [tryke] *vt* [photo] to fake ; [élections, match] to rig ▪ **truquage** *nm*

[de cinéma] (special) effect ; [action] faking ; [d'élections] rigging ▪ **truqué, -e** *adj* [élections, match] rigged ; **photo truquée** fake photo

**trust** [trœst] *nm* COMM [cartel] trust

**tsar** [dzar] *nm* tsar, czar

**tsigane, tzigane** [tsigan] *adj* Gypsyish ▪ **Tsigane, Tzigane** *nmf* (Hungarian) Gypsy

**tu¹** [ty] *pron pers* you *(familiar form of address)*

**tu²** [ty] *pp de* **taire**

**tuant, e** [tɥɑ̃, ɑ̃t] *adj Fam* **a)** [épuisant] exhausting **b)** [énervant] tiresome

**tuba** [tyba] *nm* [instrument de musique] tuba ; [de plongée] snorkel

**tube** [tyb] *nm* tube ; **tube à essai** test tube

**tuer** [tɥe] **1.** *vt* to kill **2. se tuer** *vpr* to kill oneself ; [dans un accident] to be killed ▪ **tuerie** *nf* slaughter ▪ **tueur, -euse** *nmf* killer

**tuféköi** SMS *abr écrite de* **tu fais quoi ?**

**tulipe** [tylip] *nf* tulip

**tumeur** [tymœr] *nf* tumour

**tuning** [tyniŋ] *nm* AUTO tuning

**tunique** [tynik] *nf* tunic

**Tunisie** [tynizi] *nf* **la Tunisie** Tunisia ▪ **tunisien, -enne 1.** *adj* Tunisian **2.** *nmf* **Tunisien, Tunisienne** Tunisian

**tunnel** [tynɛl] *nm* tunnel ; **le tunnel sous la Manche** the Channel Tunnel

**tuque** [tyk] *nf Can* wool hat, tuque

**turban** [tyrbɑ̃] *nm* turban

**turbulent, -e** [tyrbylɑ̃, -ɑ̃t] *adj* [enfant] boisterous

**Turquie** [tyrki] *nf* **la Turquie** Turkey ▪ **turc, turque 1.** *adj* Turkish **2.** *nmf* **Turc, Turque** Turk **3.** *nm* [langue] Turkish

**turquoise** [tyrkwaz] *adj inv* turquoise

**tuteur, -trice** [tytœr, -tris] **1.** *nmf* [de mineur] guardian **2.** *nm* [bâton] stake, prop

**tutoyer** [tytwaje] *vt* **tutoyer qn** to address sb using the familiar 'tu' form ■ **tutoiement** *nm* use of the familiar 'tu' instead of the more formal 'vous'

**tutu** [tyty] *nm* tutu

**tuyau, -x** [tɥijo] *nm* pipe; **tuyau d'arrosage** hose(pipe); **tuyau d'échappement** [de véhicule] exhaust (pipe)

**TVA** [teva] *(abr de* **taxe à la valeur ajoutée***) nf* VAT

**twa** SMS *abr écrite de* **toi**

**type** [tip] **1.** *nm* [genre] type; *Fig* **le type même de** the very model of **2.** *adj inv* typical; **lettre type** standard letter ■ **typique** *adj* typical (**de** of)

**typographie** [typɔgrafi] *nf* typography, printing

**tyran** [tirɑ̃] *nm* tyrant ■ **tyrannie** *nf* tyranny ■ **tyranniser** *vt* to tyrannize

**tzigane** [tzigan] *adj & nmf* = **tsigane**

# U

**U, u** [y] *nm inv* U, u

**UE** [yø] *(abr de* **Union européenne)** *nf* EU

**Ukraine** [ykrɛn] *nf* l'**Ukraine** the Ukraine

**ulcère** [ylsɛr] *nm* ulcer

**ULM** [yɛlɛm] *(abr de* **ultraléger motorisé)** *nm inv* AVIAT microlight

**ultérieur, -e** [ylterjœr] *adj* later, subsequent (**à** to) ■ **ultérieurement** *adv* later (on), subsequently

**ultimatum** [yltimatɔm] *nm* ultimatum; **lancer un ultimatum à qn** to give sb or issue sb with an ultimatum

**ultime** [yltim] *adj* last; [préparatifs] final

**ultramoderne** [yltramɔdɛrn] *adj* high-tech

**ultrarésistant, e** [yltrarezistɑ̃, ɑ̃t] *adj* [matériau] ultra-resistant; [virus] resistant

**ultrason** [yltrasɔ̃] *nm* ultrasound

**ultraviolet, -ette** [yltravjɔlɛ, -ɛt] *adj & nm* ultraviolet

**un, une** [œ̃, yn] **1.** *art indéf* a; [devant voyelle] an; **une page** a page; **un ange** [œ̃nɑ̃ʒ] an angel **2.** *adj* one; **la page un** page one; **un kilo** one kilo; **un par un** one by one **3.** *pron & nmf* one; **l'un** one; **les uns** some; **le numéro un** number one; **j'en ai un** I have one; **l'un d'eux, l'une d'elles** one of them; JOURN **la une** the front page, page one

**unanime** [ynanim] *adj* unanimous ■ **unanimité** *nf* unanimity; **à l'unanimité** unanimously

**uni, -e** [yni] *adj* [famille, couple] close; [couleur, étoffe] plain

**unième** [ynjɛm] *adj* first; **trente et unième** thirty-first; **cent unième** hundred and first

**unifier** [ynifje] *vt* to unify ■ **unification** *nf* unification

**uniforme** [yniform] **1.** *adj* [expression] uniform; [sol] even; [mouvement] regular **2.** *nm* uniform ■ **uniformément** *adv* uniformly ■ **uniformiser** *vt* to standardize ■ **uniformité** *nf* [de couleurs] uniformity; [monotonie] monotony

**unilatéral, -e, -aux** [ynilateral, -o] *adj* [décision] unilateral; [contrat] one-sided; [stationnement] on one side of the road/street only

**union** [ynjɔ̃] *nf* [de partis, de consommateurs] union, association; [entente] unity; [mariage] marriage; l'**Union européenne** the European Union; **union monétaire** monetary union; **union libre** cohabitation

**unique** [ynik] *adj* a) [fille, fils] only; [espoir, souci] only, sole; [prix, parti, salaire, marché] single b) [exceptionnel] unique; **unique en son genre** completely unique ■ **uniquement** *adv* only, just

**unir** [ynir] **1.** *vt* [personnes, territoires] to unite; [marier] to join in marriage; [efforts, qualités] to combine (**à** with) **2. s'unir** *vpr* [s'associer] to unite; [se marier] to be joined in marriage; **s'unir à qn** to join forces with sb

**unitaire** [yniter] *adj* [prix] per unit

**unité** [ynite] *nf* [de mesure, élément, régiment] unit; [cohésion] unity; ORDINAT **unité centrale** central processing unit; **unité de longueur** unit of measurement

**univers** [yniver] *nm* universe; *Fig* world ■ **universel, -elle** *adj* universal

**université** [yniversite] *nf* university ; **à l'université** *Br* at university, *Am* in college ■ **universitaire 1.** *adj* ville / restaurant universitaire university town / refectory **2.** *nmf* academic

**uranium** [yranjɔm] *nm* uranium

**urbain, -e** [yrbɛ̃, -ɛn] *adj* urban ■ **urbaniser** *vt* to urbanize ■ **urbanisme** *nm Br* town planning, *Am* city planning

**urgent, -e** [yrʒɑ̃, -ɑ̃t] *adj* urgent ■ **urgence** *nf* [de décision, de tâche] urgency ; [cas d'hôpital] emergency ; **d'urgence** urgently ; POL **état d'urgence** state of emergency ; **(service des) urgences** [d'hôpital] *Br* casualty (department), *Am* emergency room ■ **urgentissime** [yrʒɑ̃tisim] *adj Fam* super urgent ; **elle a un travail urgentissime à finir** she has a massively urgent job to finish ■ **urgentiste** [yrʒɑ̃tist] *nmf* MÉD A&E doctor ■ **urger** [yrʒe] *vi Fam* **ça urge ?** is it urgent?, how urgent is it? ; **j'ai du travail, mais ça n'urge pas** I do have some work to do, but it's not urgent *or* but there's no rush

**URL** *(abr de* **uniform resource locator***) nf* URL

**urne** [yrn] *nf* [vase] urn ; [pour voter] ballot box ; **aller aux urnes** to go to the polls

**Uruguay** [yrygwe] *nm* **l'Uruguay** Uruguay

**usage** [yzaʒ] *nm* [utilisation] use ; [coutume] custom ; [de mot] usage ; **faire usage de qch** to make use of sth ; **d'usage** [habituel] customary ; **à l'usage de** for (the use of) ; **hors d'usage** out of order ■ **usagé, -e** *adj* [vêtement] worn ; [billet] used ■ **usager** *nm* user

**USB** *(abr de* **universal serial bus***) nm* ORDINAT USB ; **clé USB** USB key, *Br* USB stick ; **port USB** USB port

**user** [yze] **1.** *vt* [vêtement] to wear out ; [personne] to wear down ; [consommer] to use (up) **2.** *vi* **user de qch** to use sth **3. s'user** *vpr* [tissu, machine] to wear out ; [talons, personne] to wear down ■ **usé, -e** *adj* [tissu] worn out ; [sujet] stale ; [personne] worn out ; **eaux usées** dirty *or* waste water

**usine** [yzin] *nf* factory ; **usine à gaz** gasworks ; **usine métallurgique** ironworks

**ustensile** [ystɑ̃sil] *nm* implement, tool ; **ustensile de cuisine** kitchen utensil

**usuel, -elle** [yzɥɛl] *adj* everyday

**usure** [yzyr] *nf* [de pneu] wear

**usurper** [yzyrpe] *vt* to usurp

**utile** [ytil] *adj* useful (**à** to)

**utiliser** [ytilize] *vt* to use ■ **utilisateur, -trice** *nmf* user ■ **utilisation** *nf* use ■ **utilité** *nf* usefulness ; **d'une grande utilité** very useful

**utilitaire** [ytiliter] **1.** *adj* utilitarian **2.** *nm* ORDINAT utility (program)

**utopie** [ytɔpi] *nf* [idéal] utopia ; [projet, idée] utopian plan / idea ■ **utopique** *adj* utopian

**UV** [yve] *(abr de* **ultraviolet***) nm inv* UV

**V, v** [ve] *nm inv* V, v

**va** [va] **1.** *voir* **aller 2.** *excl* **courage, va !**
come on, cheer up!; *Fam* **va donc !** come
on!; *Fam* **va pour 10 euros /demain** OK,
let's say 10 euros /tomorrow

**vacances** [vakɑ̃s] *nfpl Br* holiday(s), *Am*
vacation; **être en v** to be on *Br* holiday or
*Am* vacation; **partir en vacances** to go
on *Br* holiday or *Am* vacation; **vacances
actives /culturelles /reposantes** active /cultural /relaxing *Br* holiday(s) or
*Am* vacation; **les vacances scolaires**
the school *Br* holidays or *Am* vacation;
**les grandes vacances** the summer *Br*
holidays or *Am* vacation ▪ **vacancier,
-ère** *nf Br* holidaymaker, *Am* vacationer

**vacant, -e** [vakɑ̃, -ɑ̃t] *adj* vacant

**vacarme** [vakarm] *nm* din, uproar

**vaccin** [vaksɛ̃] *nm* vaccine; **faire un
vaccin à qn** to vaccinate sb ▪ **vaccination** *nf* vaccination ▪ **vacciner** *vt*
to vaccinate; **se faire vacciner** to get
vaccinated (**contre** against)

**vache** [vaʃ] *nf* cow; **maladie de la vache
folle** mad cow disease

**vaciller** [vasije] *vi* to sway; [flamme,
lumière] to flicker

**vadrouille** [vadruj] *nf* a) *Fam* [prome-
nade, voyage] **être /partir en vadrouille**
to be /to go off gallivanting b) *Can* [pour
laver les sols] mop, sweeper

**vagabond, -e** [vagabɔ̃, -ɔ̃d] *nmf* [clo-
chard] vagrant, tramp ▪ **vagabonder**
*vi* to roam, to wander

**vague¹** [vag] *adj* vague; [regard] vacant;
[souvenir] dim, vague

**vague²** [vag] *nf* [de mer] & *Fig* wave;
**vague de chaleur** heat wave; **vague
de froid** cold spell or snap

**vaille, vailles** *voir* **valoir**

**vain, -e** [vɛ̃, vɛn] *adj* [sans résultat]
futile; [vaniteux] vain; **en vain** in vain
▪ **vainement** *adv* in vain

**vaincre** [vɛ̃kr] *vt* [adversaire] to defeat;
*Fig* [maladie, difficulté] to overcome
▪ **vaincu, -e** *nmf* defeated man /
woman; [de match] loser ▪ **vainqueur**
*nm* victor; [de match] winner

**vais** [ve] *voir* **aller**

**vaisseau, -x** [veso] *nm* ANAT vessel;
[bateau] ship, vessel; **vaisseau spatial**
spaceship

**vaisselle** [vesɛl] *nf* crockery; **faire la
vaisselle** to do the washing up, to do
the dishes

**valable** [valabl] *adj* [billet, motif] valid

**valet** [valɛ] *nm* CARTES jack; **valet de
chambre** valet

**valeur** [valœr] *nf* [prix, qualité] value;
[mérite] worth; **avoir de la valeur** to be
valuable; **mettre qch en valeur** [faire
ressortir] to highlight sth; **objets de
valeur** valuables

**valide** [valid] *adj* [personne] fit, able-
bodied; [billet] valid ▪ **valider** *vt* to
validate; [titre de transport] to stamp;
ORDINAT [commande] to confirm; [case]
to select ▪ **validité** *nf* validity

**valise** [valiz] *nf* suitcase; **faire ses
valises** to pack (one's bags)

**vallée** [vale] *nf* valley

**valoir** [valwar] **1.** *vi* [avoir pour valeur]
to be worth; [s'appliquer] to apply
(**pour** to); **valoir mille euros /cher** to
be worth a thousand euros /a lot; **il
vaut mieux rester** it's better to stay;
**il vaut mieux que j'attende** I'd better
wait; **faire valoir qch** [faire ressortir]
to highlight sth; [droit] to assert sth
**2.** *vt* **valoir qch à qn** [ennuis] to bring sb
sth **3. se valoir** *vpr* [objets, personnes]
to be as good as each other

**valse** [vals] *nf* waltz

**valve** [valv] *nf* valve

**vampire** [vɑ̃pir] *nm* vampire

**vandale** [vɑ̃dal] *nmf* vandal ■ **vandalisme** *nm* vandalism

**vanille** [vanij] *nf* vanilla

**vanité** [vanite] *nf* [orgueil] vanity ■ **vaniteux, -euse** *adj* vain, conceited

**vanter** [vɑ̃te] **1.** *vt* to praise **2. se vanter** *vpr* to boast, to brag (**de** about, of)

**vapeur** [vapœr] *nf* vapeur (**d'eau**) steam; **cuire qch à la vapeur** to steam sth

**vaporiser** [vapɔrize] *vt* to spray ■ **vaporisateur** *nm* [appareil] spray

**vaquer** [vake] *vi* **vaquer à qch** to attend to sth; **vaquer à ses occupations** to go about one's business

**varappe** [varap] *nf* rock-climbing

**variable** [varjabl] **1.** *adj* variable; [humeur, temps] changeable **2.** *nf* variable ■ **variation** *nf* variation

**varicelle** [varisɛl] *nf* chickenpox

**varier** [varje] *vt* & *vi* to vary (**de** from) ■ **varié, -e** *adj* [diversifié] varied

**variété** [varjete] *nf* variety

**variole** [varjɔl] *nf* smallpox

**vas** [va] *voir* **aller**

**vase**[1] [vaz] *nm* [récipient] vase

**vase**[2] [vaz] *nf* [boue] mud, silt

**vaste** [vast] *adj* vast, huge

**Vatican** [vatikɑ̃] *nm* **le Vatican** the Vatican

**vaut** [vo] *voir* **valoir**

**veau, -x** [vo] *nm* [animal] calf; [viande] veal

**vécu, -e** [veky] **1.** *pp de* **vivre 2.** *adj* [histoire] real-life **3.** *nm* real-life experience

**vedette** [vədɛt] *nf* a) [acteur] star; **être en vedette** [dans un spectacle] to top the bill b) [bateau] launch

**végétal, -e, -aux** [veʒetal, -o] **1.** *adj* **huile végétale** vegetable oil **2.** *nm* plant ■ **végétalien, -enne** *nmf*

vegan ■ **végétarien, -enne** *adj* & *nmf* vegetarian ■ **végétation** *nf* vegetation

**véhément, -e** [veemɑ̃, -ɑ̃t] *adj* vehement ■ **véhémence** *nf* vehemence

**véhicule** [veikyl] *nm* vehicle; **véhicule tout-terrain** off-road *or* all-terrain vehicle

**veille** [vɛj] *nf* a) [jour précédent] **la veille** the day before (**de qch** sth); **la veille de Noël** Christmas Eve; **à la veille de qch** [événement] on the eve of sth b) [état] wakefulness; ORDINAT standby; **mettre un appareil en veille** to put a machine on standby

**veillée** [veje] *nf* [soirée] evening

**veiller** [veje] **1.** *vi* to stay up *or* awake; **veiller à qch** to see to sth; **veiller à ce que... (**+ *subjunctive***)** to make sure that...; **veiller sur qn** to watch over sb **2.** *vt* [malade] to sit up with

**veine** [vɛn] *nf* ANAT, BOT & GÉOL vein

**véliplanchiste** [veliplɑ̃ʃist] *nmf* windsurfer

**vélo** [velo] *nm* bike, bicycle; [activité] cycling; **faire du vélo** to cycle, to go cycling; **vélo tout-terrain** mountain bike ■ **vélomoteur** *nm* moped

**velours** [vəlur] *nm* velvet; **velours côtelé** corduroy ■ **velouté, -e 1.** *adj* velvety **2.** *nm* **velouté d'asperges** cream of asparagus soup

**velu, -e** [vəly] *adj* hairy

**venaison** [vənɛzɔ̃] *nf* venison

**vendange** [vɑ̃dɑ̃ʒ] *nf* [récolte] grape harvest; [raisin récolté] grapes (harvested); **vendanges** [période] grape-harvesting time; **faire les vendanges** to harvest *or* pick the grapes ■ **vendanger** *vi* to pick the grapes ■ **vendangeur, -euse** *nmf* grape picker

**vendre** [vɑ̃dr] **1.** *vt* to sell; **vendre qch à qn** to sell sb sth, to sell sth to sb; **vendre qch 10 euros** to sell sth for 10 euros; **'à vendre'** 'for sale' **2. se vendre** *vpr* to be sold; **ça se vend bien** it sells well ■ **vendeur, -euse** *nmf* [de magasin] *Br* sales *or* shop assistant, *Am* sales clerk; [non professionnel] seller

**vendredi** [vɑ̃drədi] *nm* Friday; **Vendredi saint** Good Friday

**vénéneux, -euse** [venenø, -øz] *adj* poisonous

**vénérable** [venerabl] *adj* venerable

**Venezuela** [venezɥela] *nm* **le Venezuela** Venezuela

**venger** [vɑ̃ʒe] **1.** *vt* to avenge **2. se venger** *vpr* to get one's revenge (**de qn** on sb; **de qch** for sth) ■ **vengeance** *nf* revenge, vengeance

**venin** [vənɛ̃] *nm* poison, venom ■ **venimeux, -euse** *adj* poisonous, venomous

**venir** [vənir] **1.** (*aux* **être**) *vi* to come (**de** from); **venir faire qch** to come to do sth; **viens me voir** come and see me; **je viens / venais d'arriver** I've / I'd just arrived; **les jours qui viennent** the coming days; **faire venir qn** to send for sb **2.** *v impers* **s'il venait à pleuvoir** if it happened to rain

**vent** [vɑ̃] *nm* wind; **il y a** *ou* **il fait du vent** it's windy

**vente** [vɑ̃t] *nf* sale; **en vente** [en magasin] on sale; **mettre qch en vente** to put sth up for sale; **vente aux enchères** auction (sale); **vente par correspondance** mail order

**ventilateur** [vɑ̃tilatœr] *nm* [électrique] fan ■ **ventilation** *nf* ventilation ■ **ventiler** *vt* to ventilate

**ventre** [vɑ̃tr] *nm* stomach, belly; **à plat ventre** flat on one's face; **avoir du ventre** to have a paunch; **avoir mal au ventre** to have a sore stomach

**ventriloque** [vɑ̃trilɔk] *nmf* ventriloquist

**venu, -e** [vəny] **1.** *pp de* **venir 2.** *adj* **bien venu** [à propos] timely; **mal venu** untimely **3.** *nmf* **nouveau venu, nouvelle venue** newcomer; **le premier venu** anyone **4.** *nf* **venue** [de personne, de printemps] coming

**ver** [vɛr] *nm* worm; [larve] grub; [de fruits, de fromage] maggot; **ver de terre** (earth)worm; **ver à soie** silkworm

**véranda** [verɑ̃da] *nf* veranda(h); [en verre] conservatory

**verbe** [vɛrb] *nm* verb

**verdict** [vɛrdikt] *nm* verdict

**verdir** [vɛrdir] *vt* & *vi* to turn green ■ **verdure** *nf* [végétation] greenery

**verger** [vɛrʒe] *nm* orchard

**verglas** [vɛrgla] *nm* *Br* (black) ice, *Am* glaze; **une plaque de verglas** a sheet of ice ■ **verglacé, -e** *adj* [route] icy

**véridique** [veridik] *adj* truthful

**vérifier** [verifje] **1.** *vt* to check, to verify; [comptes] to audit **2. se vérifier** *vpr* to prove correct ■ **vérifiable** *adj* verifiable ■ **vérification** *nf* checking, verification; [de comptes] audit(ing)

**véritable** [veritabl] *adj* [histoire, ami] true, real; [cuir, or, nom] real, genuine; [en intensif] real

**vérité** [verite] *nf* [de déclaration] truth; [sincérité] sincerity; **en vérité** in fact; **dire la vérité** to tell the truth

**verni, -e** [vɛrni] *adj* [meuble, parquet] varnished

**vernir** [vɛrnir] *vt* [bois] to varnish; [céramique] to glaze ■ **vernis** *nm* varnish; [pour céramique] glaze; **vernis à ongles** nail polish *or Br* varnish ■ **vernissage** *nm* [d'exposition] opening

**verra, verrait** [vera, verɛ] *voir* **voir**

**verre** [vɛr] *nm* [substance, récipient] glass; **prendre un verre** to have a drink; **verre de bière** glass of beer; **verre à bière / à vin** beer / wine glass; **verre de contact** contact lens ■ **verrière** *nf* [toit] glass roof

**verrine** [verin] *nf* appetizer or dessert served in a small glass

**verrou** [veru] *nm* bolt; **fermer qch au verrou** to bolt sth; **sous les verrous** behind bars

**verrouillage** [verujaʒ] *nm* AUTO **verrouillage centralisé** central locking

**verrouiller** [veruje] *vt* [porte] to bolt; [quartier] to seal off

**verrue** [very] *nf* wart; **verrue plantaire** verruca

**vers¹** [vɛr] *prép* [direction] toward(s) ; [approximation] around, about

**vers²** [vɛr] *nm* [de poème] line ; **des vers** [poésie] verse

**versant** [vɛrsɑ̃] *nm* slope, side

**verse** [vɛrs] ▪ **à verse** *adv* **la pluie tombait à verse** the rain was coming down in torrents

**Verseau** [vɛrso] *nm* [signe] Aquarius

**verser** [vɛrse] *vt* to pour (out) ; [larmes, sang] to shed ; [argent] to pay (**sur un compte** into an account) ▪ **versement** *nm* payment

**version** [vɛrsjɔ̃] *nf* [de film, d'incident] version ; CINÉ **en version originale** in the original language ; **en version française** dubbed *(into French)*

**verso** [vɛrso] *nm* back (of the page) ; **'voir au verso'** 'see overleaf'

**vert, verte** [vɛr, vɛrt] **1.** *adj* green ; [pas mûr] unripe ; **aller en classe verte** to go on a school trip to the countryside **2.** *nm* green ; POL **les Verts** the Greens

**vertical, -e, -aux** [vɛrtikal, -o] *adj & nf* vertical ; **à la verticale** vertically

**vertige** [vɛrtiʒ] *nm* [étourdissement] (feeling of) dizziness *or* giddiness ; [peur du vide] vertigo ; **vertiges** dizzy spells ; **avoir le vertige** to be *or* feel dizzy *or* giddy ▪ **vertigineux, -euse** *adj* [hauteur] giddy, dizzy

**vertu** [vɛrty] *nf* virtue ; **en vertu de** in accordance with ▪ **vertueux, -euse** *adj* virtuous

**verveine** [vɛrvɛn] *nf* [plante] verbena ; [tisane] verbena tea

**vessie** [vesi] *nf* bladder

**veste** [vɛst] *nf* jacket, coat

**vestiaire** [vɛstjɛr] *nm* [de théâtre] cloakroom ; [de piscine, de stade] changing room, *Am* locker room

**vestibule** [vɛstibyl] *nm* (entrance) hall

**vestiges** [vɛstiʒ] *nmpl* [ruines] remains ; [traces] relics

**veston** [vɛstɔ̃] *nm* (suit) jacket

**vétéciste** [vetesist] *nmf* hybrid bike rider

**vêtement** [vɛtmɑ̃] *nm* garment, article of clothing ; **vêtements** clothes ; **vêtements de sport** sportswear

**vétéran** [veterɑ̃] *nm* veteran

**vétérinaire** [veterinɛr] **1.** *adj* veterinary **2.** *nmf* vet, *Br* veterinary surgeon, *Am* veterinarian

**vététiste** [vetetist] *nmf* mountain biker

**vêtir** [vetir] **1.** *vt* to dress **2.** **se vêtir** *vpr* to dress

**veto** [veto] *nm inv* veto ; **opposer son veto à qch** to veto sth

**vêtu, -e** [vety] *adj* dressed (**de** in)

**vétuste** [vetyst] *adj* dilapidated

**veuf, veuve** [vœf, vœv] **1.** *adj* widowed **2.** *nm* widower **3.** *nf* widow

**veuille(s), veuillent** [vœj] *voir* **vouloir**

**veut, veux** [vø] *voir* **vouloir**

**vexer** [vɛkse] **1.** *vt* to upset, to hurt **2.** **se vexer** *vpr* to get upset (**de** at)

**VF** [veɛf] *(abr de version française)* *nf* **film en VF** film dubbed into French

**viable** [vjabl] *adj* [entreprise, enfant] viable

**viaduc** [vjadyk] *nm* viaduct

**viande** [vjɑ̃d] *nf* meat

**vibrer** [vibre] *vi* to vibrate ; [être ému] to be stirred (**de** with) ; **faire vibrer qn** to stir sb ▪ **vibrant, -e** *adj* [hommage] stirring ▪ **vibration** *nf* vibration ▪ **vibreur** *nm* TÉL VibraCall® (alert *or* feature)

**vice** [vis] *nm* [perversité] vice ; [défectuosité] defect

**vice versa** [vis(e)versa] *adv* vice versa

**vicié, -e** [visje] *adj* [air, atmosphère] polluted

**vicieux, -euse** [visjø, -øz] *adj* [pervers] depraved ; [perfide] underhand

**victime** [viktim] *nf* victim ; [d'accident] casualty ; **être victime de** [accident, attentat] to be the victim of

**victoire** [viktwar] *nf* victory ; [en sport] win ▪ **victorieux, -euse** *adj* victorious ; [équipe] winning

**vidange** [vidɑ̃ʒ] *nf* emptying, draining; [de véhicule] oil change ■ **vidanger** *vt* to empty, to drain

**vide** [vid] **1.** *adj* empty **2.** *nm* [espace] empty space; [d'emploi du temps] gap; PHYS vacuum; **regarder dans le vide** to stare into space; **emballé sous vide** vacuum-packed; **à vide** empty

**vide-grenier** [vidgrənje] *nm inv* second-hand goods sale, *Br* car-boot sale, *Am* yard sale

**vidéo** [video] *adj inv & nf* video ■ **vidéocassette** *nf* video (cassette) ■ **vidéoclip** *nm* video ■ **vidéoprojecteur** *nm* video projector

**vider** [vide] **1.** *vt* to empty **2. se vider** *vpr* to empty ■ **vide-ordures** *nm inv Br* rubbish or *Am* garbage chute ■ **videur** *nm* [de boîte de nuit] bouncer

**vie** [vi] *nf* life; [durée] lifetime; **en vie** living; **à vie, pour la vie** for life

**vieil, vieille** [vjɛj] *voir* **vieux**

**vieillard** [vjejar] *nm* old man; **les vieillards** old people ■ **vieillerie** *nf* [objet] old thing ■ **vieillesse** *nf* old age

**vieillir** [vjejir] **1.** *vi* to grow old; [changer] to age; [théorie, mot] to become old-fashioned **2.** *vt* **vieillir qn** [vêtement] to make sb look old(er) ■ **vieilli, -e** *adj* [démodé] old-fashioned ■ **vieillissant, -e** *adj* ageing ■ **vieillissement** *nm* ageing

**vieillot, -otte** [vjejo, -ɔt] *adj* old-fashioned

**Vienne** [vjɛn] *nm ou f* Vienna

**viennoiserie** [vjɛnwazri] *nf* pastry made with sweetened dough like croissant, brioche, etc

**viens, vient** [vjɛ̃] *voir* **venir**

**vierge** [vjɛrʒ] **1.** *adj* [femme, neige] virgin; [feuille de papier, film] blank; **être vierge** [femme, homme] to be a virgin **2.** *nf* virgin; **la Vierge** [signe] Virgo

**Viêt-Nam** [vjetnam] *nm* **le Viêt-Nam** Vietnam ■ **vietnamien, -enne 1.** *adj* Vietnamese **2.** *nmf* **Vietnamien, Vietnamienne** Vietnamese

**vieux, vieille, vieux** [vjø, vjɛj]

vieil is used before masculine singular nouns beginning with a vowel or mute h.

**1.** *adj* old; **être vieux jeu** (*adj inv*) to be old-fashioned; **se faire vieux** to get old **2.** *nm* old man; **les vieux** old people **3.** *nf* **vieille** old woman

**vif, vive** [vif, viv] **1.** *adj* [personne] lively; [imagination] vivid; [intelligence, vent, douleur] sharp; [intérêt, satisfaction] great; [couleur, lumière] bright; [froid] biting; [pas, mouvement] quick; **brûler qn vif** to burn sb alive **2.** *nm* **entrer dans le vif du sujet** to get to the heart of the matter; **à vif** [plaie] open

**vigilant, -e** [viʒilɑ̃, -ɑ̃t] *adj* vigilant ■ **vigilance** *nf* vigilance

**vigile** [viʒil] *nm* watchman

**Vigipirate** [viʒipirat] *nom* **le plan Vigipirate** measures to protect the public from terrorist attacks

**vigne** [viɲ] *nf* [plante] vine; [plantation] vineyard ■ **vigneron, -onne** [-ərɔ̃, -ɔn] *nmf* wine grower ■ **vignoble** *nm* vineyard; [région] vineyards

**vignette** [viɲɛt] *nf* [de véhicule] road tax sticker; [de médicament] label (for reimbursement by Social Security)

**vigueur** [vigœr] *nf* vigour; **entrer en vigueur** [loi] to come into force ■ **vigoureux, -euse** *adj* [personne] vigorous

**VIH, V.I.H.** (abr de virus d'immunodéficience humaine) *nm* HIV (human immunodeficiency virus)

**vilain, -e** [vilɛ̃, -ɛn] *adj* [laid] ugly; [peu sage] naughty

**villa** [vila] *nf* villa

**village** [vilaʒ] *nm* village ■ **villageois, -e** *nmf* villager

**ville** [vil] *nf* town; [grande] city; **aller/être en ville** to go (in) to / be in town; **ville d'eaux** spa (town)

**vin** [vɛ̃] *nm* wine ■ **vinicole** *adj* [région] wine-growing

**vinaigre** [vinɛgr] *nm* vinegar ■ **vinaigrette** *nf* [sauce] vinaigrette, *Br* French dressing, *Am* Italian dressing

**vingt** [vɛ̃] ([vɛ̃t] before vowel or mute h and in numbers 22-29) *adj & nm inv* twenty;

**vingt et un** twenty-one ∎ **vingtaine** *nf* **une vingtaine (de)** [nombre] about twenty ∎ **vingtième** *adj* & *nmf* twentieth

**viol** [vjɔl] *nm* rape; [de lieu] violation ∎ **violation** *nf* violation ∎ **violer** *vt* [femme] to rape ∎ **violeur** *nm* rapist

**violent, -e** [vjɔlɑ̃, -ɑ̃t] *adj* violent; [effort] strenuous ∎ **violence** *nf* violence; **acte de violence** act of violence

**violet, -ette** [vjɔlɛ, -ɛt] **1.** *adj* & *nm* [couleur] purple **2.** *nf* **violette** [fleur] violet

**violon** [vjɔlɔ̃] *nm* violin ∎ **violoncelle** *nm* cello ∎ **violoncelliste** *nmf* cellist ∎ **violoniste** *nmf* violinist

**vipère** [vipɛr] *nf* adder, viper

**virage** [viraʒ] *nm* [de route] bend

**virer** [vire] **1.** *vi* to turn; **virer au bleu** to turn blue **2.** *vt* FIN [somme] to transfer (à to) ∎ **virement** *nm* FIN transfer

**virgule** [virgyl] *nf* [ponctuation] comma; MATH (decimal) point; **2 virgule 5** 2 point 5

**viril, -e** [viril] *adj* virile; [force] male ∎ **virilité** *nf* virility

**virtuel, -elle** [virtɥɛl] *adj* potential; [image] virtual; **réalité virtuelle** virtual reality

**virtuose** [virtɥoz] *nmf* virtuoso

**virulent, -e** [virylɑ̃, -ɑ̃t] *adj* virulent

**virus** [virys] *nm* MÉD & ORDINAT virus

**vis¹** [vi] *voir* **vivre, voir**

**vis²** [vis] *nf* screw

**visa** [viza] *nm* [de passeport] visa

**visage** [vizaʒ] *nm* face

**vis-à-vis** [vizavi] **1.** *prép* **vis-à-vis de** [en face de] opposite; [envers] towards **2.** *nm inv* [personne] person opposite

**viser** [vize] **1.** *vt* [cible] to aim at; [concerner] to be aimed at **2.** *vi* to aim (à at); **viser à faire qch** to aim to do sth

**visible** [vizibl] *adj* visible ∎ **visibilité** *nf* visibility

**visière** [vizjɛr] *nf* [de casquette] peak; [en plastique] eyeshade; [de casque] visor

**vision** [vizjɔ̃] *nf* [conception, image] vision; [sens] sight ∎ **visionnaire** *adj* & *nmf* visionary ∎ **visionner** *vt* [film] to view

**visiophone** [vizjɔfɔn] *nm* videophone, viewphone

**visite** [vizit] *nf* visit; [personne] visitor; [examen] inspection; **rendre visite à qn** to visit sb; **avoir de la visite** to have a visitor / visitors; **visite aller** [d'un échange] visit; **visite retour** [d'un échange] return visit; **visite médicale** medical examination; **visite guidée** guided tour; **visite guidée audio** audio tour ∎ **visiter** *vt* [lieu touristique, patient] to visit ∎ **visiteur, -euse** *nmf* visitor

**vison** [vizɔ̃] *nm* mink

**visqueux, -euse** [viskø, -øz] *adj* viscous; [surface] sticky

**visser** [vise] *vt* to screw on

**visuel, -elle** [vizɥɛl] *adj* visual ∎ **visualiser** *vt* to visualize; ORDINAT to display

**vit** [vi] *voir* **vivre, voir**

**vital, -e, -aux** [vital, -o] *adj* vital ∎ **vitalité** *nf* vitality

**vitamine** [vitamin] *nf* vitamin

**vite** [vit] *adv* [rapidement] quickly, fast; [sous peu] soon; **vite !** quick(ly)!

**vitesse** [vitɛs] *nf* speed; [de moteur] gear; **à toute vitesse** at top full speed

**viticole** [vitikɔl] *adj* [région] wine-growing ∎ **viticulteur** *nm* wine grower ∎ **viticulture** *nf* wine growing

**vitre** [vitr] *nf* (window)pane; [de véhicule, de train] window ∎ **vitrage** *nm* [vitres] windows ∎ **vitrail, -aux** *nm* stained-glass window ∎ **vitré, -e** *adj* **porte vitrée** glass door ∎ **vitrier** *nm* glazier

**vitrine** [vitrin] *nf* [de magasin] (shop) window; [meuble] display cabinet

**vivable** [vivabl] *adj* [appartement] livable-in; [situation] bearable, tolerable

**vivace** [vivas] *adj* [plante] perennial ∎ **vivacité** *nf* liveliness; [d'imagination] vividness; [d'intelligence] sharpness; [de couleur] brightness; [emportement] petulance; **vivacité d'esprit** quick-wittedness

**vivant, -e** [vivɑ̃, -ɑ̃t] **1.** *adj* [en vie] alive, living; [récit, rue, enfant] lively; [être, matière] living **2.** *nm* **de son vivant** in one's lifetime; **les vivants** the living

**vive¹** [viv] *voir* **vif**

**vive²** [viv] *excl* **vive le roi !** long live the king!

**vivement** [vivmɑ̃] *adv* quickly; [répliquer] sharply; [regretter] deeply

**vivier** [vivje] *nm* fish pond

**vivifier** [vivifje] *vt* to invigorate

**vivisection** [viviseksjɔ̃] *nf* vivisection

**vivre** [vivr] **1.** *vi* to live; **elle vit encore** she's still alive *or* living; **faire vivre qn** [famille] to support sb; **vivre vieux** to live to be old; **vivre de** [fruits] to live on; [travail] to live by **2.** *vt* [vie] to live; [aventure, époque] to live through; [éprouver] to experience ▪ **vivres** *nmpl* food, supplies

**VO** [veo] *(abr de* **version originale)** *nf* **film en VO** film in the original language

**vocal, -e, -aux** [vɔkal, -o] *adj* vocal

**vocation** [vɔkasjɔ̃] *nf* vocation, calling

**vociférer** [vɔsifere] *vt & vi* to shout angrily

**vœu, -x** [vø] *nm* [souhait] wish; [promesse] vow; **faire un vœu** to make a wish; **tous mes vœux !** best wishes!

**vogue** [vɔg] *nf* fashion, vogue; **en vogue** in vogue

**voici** [vwasi] *prép* here is /are; **me voici** here I am; **voici dix ans** ten years ago; **voici dix ans que...** it's ten years since...

**voie** [vwa] *nf* [route] road; [rails] track, line; [partie de route] lane; [chemin] way; [de gare] platform; [de communication] line; [moyen] means, way; **pays en voie de développement** developing country; **voie sans issue** dead end ▪ **Voie lactée** *nf* **la Voie lactée** the Milky Way

**voilà** [vwala] *prép* there is /are; **les voilà** there they are; **le voilà parti** he has left now; **voilà dix ans** ten years ago; **voilà dix ans que...** it's ten years since...

**voile¹** [vwal] *nm* [étoffe, coiffure] veil ▪ **voilé, -e** *adj* [femme, allusion] veiled; [photo, lumière] hazy ▪ **voiler** [vwale] **1.** *vt* [visage, vérité] to veil **2. se voiler** *vpr* [personne] to wear a veil; [ciel] to cloud over

**voile²** [vwal] *nf* [de bateau] sail; [sport] sailing; **faire de la voile** to sail ▪ **voilier** *nm* sailing boat; [de plaisance] yacht

**voiler** [vwale] **1.** *vt* [roue] to buckle **2. se voiler** *vpr* [roue] to buckle

**voir** [vwar] **1.** *vt* to see; **faire voir qch** to show sth; **voir qn faire qch** to see sb do /doing sth **2.** *vi* to see; **fais voir** let me see, show me; **ça n'a rien à voir avec ça** that's got nothing to do with that **3. se voir** *vpr* a) [se regarder] to see o.s., to watch o.s. b) [s'imaginer] to see *or* to imagine *or* to picture o.s. c) [se rencontrer] to see one another *or* each other d) [se remarquer] to be obvious, to show; **ça se voit !** you can tell!

**voisin, -e** [vwazɛ̃, -in] **1.** *adj* [pays, village] *Br* neighbouring, *Am* neighboring; [maison, pièce] next (**de** to); [état] similar (**de** to) **2.** *nmf Br* neighbour, *Am* neighbor ▪ **voisinage** *nm* [quartier, voisins] *Br* neighbourhood, *Am* neighborhood; [proximité] closeness, proximity ▪ **voisiner** *vi* **voisiner avec** to be side by side with

**voiture** [vwatyr] *nf* car; [de train] carriage, *Br* coach, *Am* car; **en voiture !** [dans le train] all aboard!; **voiture de course** racing /private car

**voix** [vwa] *nf* voice; [d'électeur] vote; **à voix basse** in a whisper; **à haute voix** aloud

**vol** [vɔl] *nm* a) [d'avion, d'oiseau] flight; [groupe d'oiseaux] flock, flight; **attraper qch au vol** to catch sth in the air b) [délit] theft; **vol à main armée** armed robbery

**volaille** [vɔlaj] *nf* **la volaille** poultry;
une volaille a fowl

**volatiliser** [vɔlatilize] ■ **se volatiliser**
*vpr* to vanish into thin air

**volcan** [vɔlkɑ̃] *nm* volcano ■ **volca-
nique** *adj* volcanic

**voler¹** [vɔle] *vi* [oiseau, avion] to fly
■ **volant** *nm* [de véhicule] (steering)
wheel; [de badminton] shuttlecock;
[de jupe] flounce ■ **volée** *nf* [de flèches]
flight; [de coups] thrashing

**voler²** [vɔle] **1.** *vt* [prendre] to steal (à
from); **voler qn** to rob sb **2.** *vi* [prendre]
to steal

**volet** [vɔle] *nm* [de fenêtre] shutter; [de
programme] section, part

**voleur, -euse** [vɔlœr, -øz] *nmf* thief;
**au voleur !** stop thief!

**volière** [vɔljɛr] *nf* aviary

**volley-ball** [vɔlebol] *nm* volleyball
■ **volleyeur, -euse** *nmf* volleyball
player

**volontaire** [vɔlɔ̃tɛr] **1.** *adj* [geste, omis-
sion] deliberate; [travail] voluntary;
[opiniâtre] *Br* wilful, *Am* willful **2.** *nmf*
volunteer ■ **volontairement** *adv*
[spontanément] voluntarily; [exprès]
deliberately

**volontariat** [vɔlɔ̃tarja] *nm* voluntary
work

**volonté** [vɔlɔ̃te] *nf* [faculté, intention]
will; [détermination] willpower; [sou-
hait] wish; **bonne volonté** willingness;
**mauvaise volonté** unwillingness; **à
volonté** [quantité] as much as desired

**volontiers** [vɔlɔ̃tje] *adv* gladly, willingly; **volontiers !** [oui] I'd love to!

**volte-face** [vɔltəfas] *nf inv* **faire volte-
face** to turn round; *Fig* to do a U-turn

**voltige** [vɔltiʒ] *nf* **a)** [au trapèze] trapeze work; **haute voltige** flying trapeze
act; *Fig* mental gymnastics **b)** [à cheval]
circus riding **c)** [en avion] aerobatics

**voltiger** [vɔltiʒe] *vi* [feuilles] to flutter

**volume** [vɔlym] *nm* [de boîte, de son,
livre & ORDINAT] volume ■ **volumineux, -euse** *adj* bulky, voluminous

**volupté** [vɔlypte] *nf* sensual pleasure
■ **voluptueux, -euse** *adj* voluptuous

**vomir** [vɔmir] **1.** *vt* to bring up, to vomit
**2.** *vi* to vomit, *Br* to be sick ■ **vomis-
sements** *nmpl* avoir des vomisse-
ments to vomit

**vont** [vɔ̃] *voir* **aller**

**vorace** [vɔras] *adj* voracious

**vos** [vo] *voir* **votre**

**vote** [vɔt] *nm* [action] vote, voting; [suf-
frage] vote; [de loi] passing; **bureau de
vote** *Br* polling station, *Am* polling place
■ **votant, -e** *nmf* voter ■ **voter 1.** *vt*
[loi] to pass; [crédits] to vote **2.** *vi* to
vote

**votre, vos** [vɔtr, vo] *adj poss* your
■ **vôtre 1.** *pron poss* **le** *ou* **la vôtre,
les vôtres** yours; **à la vôtre !** cheers!
**2.** *nmpl* **les vôtres** [votre famille] your
family

**voudra, voudrait** [vudra, vudrɛ] *voir*
**vouloir**

**vouer** [vwe] **1.** *vt* [promettre] to vow (à
to); [consacrer] to dedicate (à to) **2.** **se
vouer** *vpr* **se vouer à** to dedicate
oneself to

**vouloir** [vulwar] *vt* to want (**faire** to
do); **je veux qu'il parte** I want him to
go; **vouloir dire** to mean (**que** that); **je
voudrais un pain** I'd like a loaf of bread;
**je voudrais rester** I'd like to stay; **je
veux bien attendre** I don't mind waiting; **voulez-vous me suivre** will you
follow me; **si tu veux** if you like *or* wish;
**en vouloir à qn d'avoir fait qch** to be
angry with sb for doing sth; **vouloir
du bien à qn** to wish sb well; **sans le
vouloir** unintentionally; **s'en vouloir
de faire qch** to be cross with o.s. for
doing sth

**voulu, -e** [vuly] *adj* [requis] required;
[délibéré] deliberate, intentional

**vous** [vu] *pron pers* **a)** [sujet, complément direct] you; **vous êtes ici** you
are here; **il vous connaît** he knows
you **b)** [complément indirect] (to) you;
**il vous l'a donné** he gave it to you, he
gave you it **c)** [réfléchi] yourself, (*pl*)
yourselves; **vous vous lavez** you wash
yourself / yourselves **d)** [réciproque]
each other; **vous vous aimez** you

love each other ■ **vous-même** *pron* yourself ■ **vous-mêmes** *pron pl* yourselves

**voûte** [vut] *nf* [arch] vault ■ **voûté, -e** *adj* [personne] bent, stooped

**vouvoyer** [vuvwaje] *vt* **vouvoyer qn** to address sb as 'vous' ■ **vouvoiement** *nm* use of the formal 'vous' instead of the more familiar 'tu'

**voyage** [vwajaʒ] *nm* trip, journey; [par mer] voyage; **aimer les voyages** to like *Br* travelling *or Am* traveling; **faire un voyage, partir en voyage** to go on a trip; **être en voyage** to be (away) *Br* travelling *or Am* traveling; **bon voyage !** have a pleasant trip!; **voyage de noces** honeymoon; **voyage organisé** (package) tour ■ **voyager** *vi* to travel; **voyager à l'étranger** to travel abroad; **voyager sac au dos** to go backpacking ■ **voyageur, -euse** *nmf Br* traveller, *Am* traveler; [passager] passenger; **voyageur de commerce** *Br* travelling *or Am* traveling salesman, *Br* commercial traveller ■ **voyagiste** *nm* tour operator

**voyant¹, -e** [vwajɑ̃, -ɑ̃t] **1.** *adj* [couleur] gaudy, loud **2.** *nm* [signal] (warning) light; [d'appareil électrique] pilot light

**voyant², -e** [vwajɑ̃, -ɑ̃t] *nmf* clairvoyant

**voyou** [vwaju] *nm* hooligan

**vrac** [vrak] ■ **en vrac** *adv* [en désordre] in a muddle; [au poids] loose

**vrai** [vrɛ] *adj* true; [réel] real; [authentique] genuine ■ **vraiment** *adv* really

**vraisemblable** [vrɛsɑ̃blabl] *adj* [probable] likely, probable; [crédible] credible ■ **vraisemblablement** *adv* probably ■ **vraisemblance** *nf* likelihood; [crédibilité] credibility

**vrombir** [vrɔ̃bir] *vi* to hum ■ **vrombissement** *nm* hum(ming)

**VTC** [vetese] (abr de **vélo tout chemin**) *nf* SPORT hybrid bike

**VTT** [vetete] *nm* **a)** (abr de **vélo tout-terrain**) mountain bike **b)** *Can* (abr de **véhicule tout-terrain**) ATV

**vu, -e¹** [vy] **1.** *pp de* **voir 2.** *adj* **bien vu** well thought of; **mal vu** frowned upon **3.** *prép* in view of; **vu que...** seeing that...

**vue²** [vy] *nf* [sens] (eye) sight; [panorama, photo] view; **en vue** [proche] in sight; [en évidence] on view; *Fig* [personne] in the public eye; **avoir qn/qch en vue** to have sb/sth in mind; **à vue** [tirer] on sight; [payable] at sight; **à première vue** at first sight; **à vue d'œil** [grandir] visibly; **de vue** [connaître] by sight; **vue d'ensemble** overall view

**vulgaire** [vylgɛr] *adj* [grossier] vulgar; [ordinaire] common ■ **vulgariser** *vt* to popularize ■ **vulgarité** *nf* vulgarity

**vulnérable** [vylnerabl] *adj* vulnerable ■ **vulnérabilité** *nf* vulnerability

**W, w** [dubləve] *nm inv* W, w

**wagon** [vagɔ̃] *nm* [de voyageurs] carriage, *Br* coach, *Am* car; [de marchandises] *Br* wagon, *Am* freight car ■ **wagon-lit** *(pl* **wagons-lits***) nm* sleeping car, sleeper ■ **wagon-restaurant** *(pl* **wagons-restaurants***) nm* dining or restaurant car

**Walkman**® [wɔkman] *nm* Walkman®, personal stereo

**wallon, -onne** [walɔ̃, -ɔn] **1.** *adj* Walloon **2.** *nmf* Wallon, Wallonne Walloon

**warning** [warniŋ] *nm* AUTO *Br* hazard warning lights, *Am* hazard lights

**watt** [wat] *nm* ÉLEC watt

**w-c** [(dublə)vese] *nm ou nmpl Br* toilet, *Am* bathroom

**Web** [wɛb] *nm* **le Web** the Web, the web ■ **webcam** [wɛbkam] *nf* webcam ■ **webtélé** [wɛbtele] *nf* web TV station

**week-end** [wikɛnd] *(pl* **week-ends***) nm* weekend; **partir en week-end** to go away for the weekend

**whisky** [wiski] *(pl* **-ies** *ou* **-ys***) nm Br* whisky, *Am* whiskey

**Wi-Fi, wi-fi** [wifi] *(abr de* **wireless fidelity***) nm inv* Wi-Fi

**wysiwyg** [wiziwig] *adj & nm* ORDINAT WYSIWYG

**X**, **x** [iks] *nm inv* [lettre, personne ou nombre inconnus] X, x; **Monsieur X** Mr X; **x fois** umpteen times; **dans x années** in x number of years

**xénophobe** [gsenɔfɔb] *adj* xenophobic ▪ **xénophobie** *nf* xenophobia

**xérès** [gzerɛs, kserɛs] *nm* [vin] sherry

**XXL** *(abr de* **extra extra large)** *adj* XXL; **un tee-shirt XXL** an XXL tee-shirt *or* T-shirt

**xylophone** [gsilɔfɔn] *nm* xylophone

# Y

**Y, y¹** [igrɛk] *nm inv* Y, y

**y²** [i] **1.** *adv* there ; [dedans] in it /them ; [dessus] on it /them ; **elle y vivra** she'll live there ; **j'y entrai** I entered (it) ; **allons-y** let's go **2.** *pron* **j'y pense** I'm thinking about it ; **je m'y attendais** I was expecting it ; **ça y est !** that's it !

**ya** SMS *abr écrite de* **il y a**

**yacht** [jɔt] *nm* yacht

**yaourt** [jaurt], **yog(h)ourt** [jɔgurt] *nm* yoghurt

**Yémen** [jemɛn] *nm* **le Yémen** Yemen

**yen** [jɛn] *nm* yen

**yeux** [jø] *voir* **œil**

**yoga** [jɔga] *nm* yoga ; **faire du yoga** to do yoga

**yog(h)ourt** [jɔgurt] *nm* = **yaourt**

**Yougoslavie** [jugɔslavi] *nf* **la Yougoslavie** Yugoslavia ; **l'ex-Yougoslavie** the former Yugoslavia ■ **yougoslave** [jugɔslav] **1.** *adj* Yugoslav, Yugoslavian **2.** *nmf* Yugoslav, Yugoslavian

**Yo-Yo®** [jojo] *nm inv* yo-yo

**yoyo** [jojo] *nm Fam* MÉD grommet

**Z, z** [zɛd] *nm inv* Z, z

**Zaïre** [zair] *nm* le **Zaïre** Zaïre

**zèbre** [zɛbr] *nm* zebra

**zèle** [zɛl] *nm* zeal; **faire du zèle** to overdo it ■ **zélé, -e** *adj* zealous

**zen** [zɛn] *adj inv* Zen; **rester zen** to keep cool

**zéro** [zero] *nm* [chiffre] zero, *Br* nought; [de numéro de téléphone] *Br* 0 [əʊ], *Am* zero; [température] zero; *Fig* [personne] nonentity; **deux buts à zéro** [au football] *Br* two nil, *Am* two zero

**zeste** [zɛst] *nm* **un zeste de citron** a piece of lemon peel

**zigzag** [zigzag] *nm* zigzag; **en zigzag** [route] zigzag(ging) ■ **zigzaguer** *vi* to zigzag

**Zimbabwe** [zimbabwe] *nm* le **Zimbabwe** Zimbabwe

**zinc** [zɛ̃g] *nm* [métal] zinc

**zipper** [zipe] *vt* ORDINAT to zip

**zodiaque** [zɔdjak] *nm* zodiac; **signe du zodiaque** sign of the zodiac

**zone** [zon] *nf* zone; **de seconde zone** second-rate; **zone industrielle** industrial *Br* estate *or Am* park; **zone fumeurs /non-fumeurs** smoking / no-smoking area

**zoo** [zo(o)] *nm* zoo ■ **zoologie** *nf* zoology ■ **zoologique** *adj* zoological; **parc zoologique** zoo

**zoom** [zum] *nm* [objectif] zoom lens